CONWAY'S

ALL THE WORLD'S FIGHTING SHIPS

1860-1905

HMS *Minotaur*, one of the largest of the first generation broadside ironclads.
CPL

CONWAY'S

ALL THE WORLD'S FIGHTING SHIPS 1860-1905

CONWAY MARITIME PRESS

Editorial Director
ROBERT GARDINER
Editors
ROGER CHESNEAU
EUGENE M KOLESNIK
Contributors
N J M CAMPBELL (USA, Russia, France, Sweden, Denmark, Norway, Netherlands, Portugal, Greece, Bulgaria, Roumania)
ALDO FRACCAROLI (Italy)
DAVID LYON (British Torpedo Craft, Germany)
HUGH LYON (Spain, Turkey, China, Argentina, Brazil, Chile, and all the Minor Navies except Bulgaria and Roumania)
JOHN ROBERTS (Great Britain, except Masted Cruisers and Torpedo Craft)
ERWIN SIECHE (Austria-Hungary – in association with Franz Ferdinand Bilzer)
H C TIMEWELL (British Masted Cruisers)
A J WATTS (Japan)
Line drawings by JOHN ROBERTS
Designed by GEOFF HUNT

First published in 1979 by Conway Maritime Press Ltd,
2 Nelson Road, Greenwich, London, SE10 9JB.
ISBN 0 85177 133 5

Typeset by Sunset Phototype, Barnet
Artwork by Letterspace, Barnet
Printed in the UK by Page Bros (Norwich) Ltd
Bound by Newdigate Press Ltd, Dorking

Contents

Foreword

The period 1860-1905 witnessed an unprecedented advance in warship design, but the interest in this development has always been hampered by the lack of a reliable single source. In fact there is very little information in print, and not even an accessible class list before the advent of the famous yearbooks towards the end of the period. Even these are often inaccurate and, of course, cannot benefit from hindsight in their evaluation of ship designs.

All the World's Fighting Ships was originally designed to fill this need for a very basic list of classes and their particulars, but it soon became obvious that far more information could be uncovered. With the documentary material now available it has been possible to give accurate assessments of many ship designs for the first time and to put the rapidly-changing technology into a proper historical context. Unlike the contemporary naval annuals, the treatment of each class in this book is related to the size of ship and the importance of the navy, rather than taking the form of a similar and sketchy reference for every vessel. The result, we feel, is a substantial reference work.

SCOPE

All the World's Fighting Ships 1860-1905 is an ambitious frame of reference, but we feel that the title is fully justified. It would be impossible to include every *naval* vessel of this period in a single volume but, as its title implies, this book is concerned only with *fighting ships*. The editors decided that to qualify for inclusion, vessels should be:

1. Sea-going. Countries with patrol craft on inland waterways are not really naval powers, and by extension most of the river and lake vessels of the maritime states have been omitted.

2. Ships not boats. We have aimed to include all vessels down to about 400 tons and many smaller where information is available. However, at this time torpedo boats assumed an importance out of all proportion to their size, and accordingly they have been given suitable coverage. The omission of submarines may strike the reader as odd, but there were few designs before 1905 that could be described as effective fighting ships. Their development really belongs to a later period, and all early submarines will be covered in the 1906-1921 volume planned for this series.

3. Genuine warships. This rules out not only auxiliaries and mercantile conversions, but also the vessels of other government agencies such as the army, coastguard, fishery protection, police, customs, and revenue services, even if some ships were armed. These exclusions are not as substantial as they might appear, since nearly all of these craft would not meet the size qualification, and were in any case of little fighting value.

Naturally there are exceptions to all these rules – usually because the historical significance of the ships concerned demands their inclusion.

PERIOD

This book covers the era of the ironclad and the pre-dreadnought battleship. Although the wooden-built French *Gloire* was first, it was the launch in 1860 of HMS *Warrior*, the first iron sea-going armoured ship, that rendered the world's wooden battlefleets obsolete. For cruising ships the date is less significant, and therefore a few pre-1860 classes have been included where it seemed logical. The construction of the all-big-gun *Dreadnought* in 1905-6 was the next major turning point in warship design and forms a convenient closing date to this work. Of course, many pre-dreadnought battleships and armoured cruisers were not completed until much later, and if a particular design belongs to the earlier period, it has been included.

ORGANISATION

In the order and division of countries, the editors must admit to indulging in conscious antiquarianism. The categories 'Great Powers', 'Coast Defence Navies', and 'Minor Navies' were often adopted in nineteenth century naval annuals, and this time-honoured practice seemed appropriate for this volume. The Great Powers were those with sea-going battlefleets, and for a strictly traditional approach these countries should have been in order of size, but for technical reasons this proved impossible. Coast Defence Navies (organised geographically from Northern Europe, through the Mediterranean to the Far East, and South America) usually possessed some armoured vessels but these were rarely first class ships. Minor Navies (listed alphabetically) were those with very few ships, and these were unlikely to be larger than small cruisers.

Colonial and Dominion forces of the British Empire are to be found under 'Great Britain', usually in the British classes to which most colonial ships belonged. Many vessels, such as those of Canada and most of the Royal Indian Marine, are excluded on the grounds outlined in the previous section.

Since many navies present special problems, not all are treated in precisely the same way. The US Navy, for example, has always been divided into an 'Old' and a 'New' era, but for most countries (except the Minor Navies) there is a single general introduction on the historical background to naval development. For many of the Great Powers there is further information on important aspects of naval technology, introducing the principal ship types.

Although the book is concerned with ships built after 1860, each national introduction includes a statement of the strength of the navy at about that time. This allows the reader to put the new construction into its proper context and to see the relative growth of each navy.

For each national section, the classes run in chronological order within very basic type-divisions – Armoured Ships or Capital Ships, Cruising Ships, Gunboats, and Torpedo Craft. There are further subdivisions, but the problem of classification in this period is acute – particularly for cruising ships – and it has not been possible always to find a suitable subheading. In many cases a subheading such as 'Masted Cruisers' or 'Unprotected Cruisers' includes ships classified as frigates, corvettes and sloops, and these further divisions are apparent from the descriptions after the name of each class. Occasionally ships have been grouped according to tonnage – the US Navy, for example, never used the term 'corvette' so the sloops are divided into those above and below 1500 tons, and this approach has been adopted in a few other places.

The class lists are largely self-explanatory, but a few points should be made. In many places where the subheading does not precisely designate all of the ships within that sub-division the class name is followed by a short description of the type, but this is not necessarily an official classification. Some of the small craft adopt concise forms of the tables to save space: for torpedo craft this can take the form of a heading giving the names or numbers, builder and launch date of the boats.

SOURCES

It is not possible to list all the sources used, but generally the book has been compiled from primary sources, with some recourse to reliable secondary material. Most of the earlier ships have never been covered in print before, but even for many later ones accurate data is published for the first time and so may disagree with the standard yearbooks of the time.

ILLUSTRATIONS

Ideally, we have tried to use a photo or a drawing for every major class. Where we have both, we have aimed to make them complementary – either different sister-ships, or the same ship at different periods. The emphasis on appearance changes is carried into the captions for the illustrations, which we have dated wherever and as accurately as possible. The principal credits for photos can be found at the ends of sections, with any exceptions credited directly after the relevant caption.

ACKNOWLEDGEMENTS

For the supply of photos we are indebted to Arrigo Barilli for selections from his specialist collection of old and rare ship portraits; to Aldo Fraccaroli for the liberal use of his own magnificent photo library; to W Pym Trotter for access to the Naval Photographic Club archives; and to Norman Polmar for the US Navy official views.

A special vote of thanks is due to John Campbell, who not only wrote the largest proportion of the book, but also put his considerable knowledge and enthusiasm at the disposal of the editors. Indeed, his willingness to step into the breach at times of apparent crisis, saved the book from a number of potential disasters.

In a work of this size and originality, it would be unrealistic to expect no errors or omissions. Where information was not available, we have been obliged to leave gaps or else the book would never have been published, but we welcome supplementary material or corrections from readers. All information sent to Conway Maritime Press will be considered for inclusion in a revised second edition, and all such assistance will be fully acknowledged. However, as it stands *Conway's All the World's Fighting Ships 1860-1905* is a pioneering work and a necessary first step towards a deeper understanding of the ironclad era.

ROBERT GARDINER

Abbreviations

A, Argentina
AA, anti-aircraft
A-H, Austria-Hungary
approx, approximately
aw, above-water

Be, Belgium
BL, breech-loader; breech-loading
BLR, breech-loading rifle
Br, Brazil
BU, broken up
Bul, Bulgaria

c, circa
C, compound
Ca, China
cal, calibre (usually expressed as an oblique stroke after the bore diameter, eg '12in/45(cal)' or in the Continental form '15cm L/35')
Cam, Cambodia
Ce, Chile
CE, compound expansion
Ch, Chantiers
cm, centimetre(s)
Co, Company
COB, compound overhead beam
Col, Columbia
comm, commissioned
comp, completed
conv, converted
CoR, Costa Rica
CR, compound reciprocating
CRCR, compound return connecting rod
CT, conning tower
CT, compound trunk
Cu, Cuba
cyl, cylindrical (of boilers); cylinder(s) (of engines)

DA, direct action
DE, double expansion
DF, double flue
Dk, Denmark
DNC, Director of Naval Construction
DYd, Dockyard

Ec, Ecuador
Eg, Egypt
EOC, Elswick Ordnance Company (gun patterns were designated by letters, eg AA or DD)

F, France
fps, fs, feet per second
ft, feet; foot

G, Germany
GB, Great Britain (including Empire Forces)
Gr, Greece

H, horizontal
Hai, Haiti
Haw, Hawaii
HC, horizontal compound
HCDA, horizontal compound direct acting
HCE, horizontal compound expansion
HCR, horizontal compound reciprocating
HCRCR, horizontal compound return connecting rod
HDA, horizontal direct acting
HDAC, horizontal direct acting compound
HDAG, horizontal direct acting geared
HDAR, horizontal direct acting reciprocating
HF, horizontal flue
HMS, Her/His Majesty's Ship
HN, Harvey nickel
HNC, horizontal non-condensing
hp, horsepower
HP, high pressure
HR, horizontal reciprocating
HRCR, horizontal return connecting rod
HS(E), horizontal single (expansion)
HSET, horizontal single expansion trunk
HT, horizontal trunk
HTE, horizontal triple expansion

I, Italy
IC, inverted compound
IDA, inverted direct acting
ihp, indicated horsepower
in, inch(es)

J, Japan

KC, Krupp cemented
KNC, Krupp non-cemented
kt(s), knot(s)

lb, pound(s)
Lib, Liberia
loco, locomotive
LP, low pressure
lwl, load waterline

m, metre(s)
M, Model (for French guns)
max, maximum
Mex, Mexico
MG, machine gun(s)
min, minute(s)
Mk, Mark
ML, muzzle-loader; muzzle-loading
MLR, muzzle-loading rifle
mm, millimetre(s)
Mor, Morocco

NC, non-condensing
Ne, The Netherlands
nhp, nominal horsepower
nm, nautical miles
No, Norway
No, number
NS, nickel steel
N Yd, Navy Yard

oa, overall

Par, Paraguay
pdr, pounder(s)
Pe, Persia
Po, Portugal
pp, between perpendiculars
psi, pounds per square inch
Pu, Peru

QF, quick-firing
QFC, quick-firer converted (from breech-loading)

R, Russia
RCR, return connecting rod
rec, rectangular
rev, revolver; revolving
RIM, Royal Indian Marine
RML, rifled muzzle-loading; rifled muzzle-loader
Ro, Roumania
rpg, rounds per gun

Sa, Sarawak
SB, smoothbore
SD, San Domingo
SE, single expansion
SET, single expansion trunk
SG, steeple-geared
SH, simple horizontal
shp, shaft horsepower
Si, Siam
Sp, Spain
SPR, simple pressure reciprocating
sq, square
STT, Stabilimento Tecnico Triestino
sub, submerged
Sw, Sweden

t, ton(s). Long tons are used throughout
T, trunk (engine)
TB, torpedo boat
TBD, torpedo boat destroyer
TC, torpedo carriage(s)
TE, triple expansion
TER, triple expansion reciprocating
TGB, torpedo gunboat
TL, torpedo launcher(s)
TLC, torpedo launching carriage(s)
TS, training ship
TT, torpedo tube(s)
Tu, Turkey

Ur, Uruguay
US, United States
USA, United States of America
USS, United States Ship

V, vertical
VC, vertical compound
VCE, vertical compound expansion
VDE, vertical double expansion
Ve, Venezuela
VIC, vertical inverted compound
VL, vibrating lever
VQE, vertical quadruple expansion
VR, vertical reciprocating
VSE, vertical single expansion
VTE, vertical triple expansion

Wks, Works
wl, waterline

x, as for example in (3x2) – the disposition of armament is expressed as number of mountings times number of barrels (three twin mountings, in this example)

Zan, Zanzibar

Great Britain
AND EMPIRE FORCES

In 1860 Great Britain was the world's most powerful industrial nation, and the navy which had won overwhelming superiority in the Napoleonic wars was still without equal in numbers or confidence. Despite the Anglo-French alliance in the Crimean War, France was still seen as the most likely enemy, and at various times in the next half century a war against France – and/or Russia – seemed to present the most serious threat to the Royal Navy. The idea of maintaining a British fleet larger than both these navies was allowed to lapse during the 1870s and 1880s with only the occasional 'war scare' giving temporary impetus to construction. In fact, before 1900 the Admiralty showed little interest in formulating detailed war plans and hardly any consideration was given to strategy, although a good deal of attention was paid to tactics, particularly by senior sea officers. In the event of war, it was assumed, the old system of close blockade would still apply, despite the changes in technology. For example, the lack of endurance in steam vessels compared with their sailing predecessors seems to have escaped notice, although steam power was held to have increased the danger of invasion since the operation could now be carried out far more quickly. This introduced into British defence thinking a new emphasis on coastal fortifications and the coast defence ship, and although in general this 'coastal theory' did little to improve the Navy's lot, the coast defence ships nominally made up some of the deficiency in ocean-going ships and could be used in the secondary role of attacking the enemy main fleet close inshore where the deep-draught battlefleet could not penetrate.

CAPITAL SHIP DEVELOPMENT 1860-1885

The appearance of the French wooden-hulled ironclad *Gloire* in 1859 caused more consternation in the British Press than in the Admiralty, and the construction of the much more powerful iron-built broadside ironclads proceeded smoothly. After some initial fears about the size and speed of French ironclad construction, and the consequent alteration during building of some of the wooden ships-of-the-line to armoured ships, it soon became clear that French shipbuilding capacity was not equal to its ambitious programmes, and that there was no danger of France outbuilding Britain. The period 1865 to 1885 was one of unprecedented experiment, so that the Navy was equipped with a multitude of different types, few of which were suited to working together. This was not simply a matter of rapidly improving technology but it also reflected changing requirements, and on the whole development followed a logical course. After the setback caused by the loss of the *Captain,* the turret slowly gained favour, and no broadside ships were laid down after *Alexandra* and *Temeraire* in 1873, at which time the first true turret ship, *Devastation,* had only just been completed. Thereafter, only turret ships were ordered but the existence of both types under construction simultaneously gives the appearance that the Admiralty did not know what it really wanted.

THE DARK AGES OF THE NAVY

In the 1870s the combination of a strong, economy-minded government and a weak Admiralty kept naval construction to a bare minimum, and this decade is often referred to in Dr Oscar Parkes' evocative but not entirely accurate phrase as the 'Dark Ages of the Victorian Navy'. However, in 1878 the threat of war with Russia led the Admiralty to purchase *Orion, Belleisle, Superb* and *Neptune,* none of which was a great asset, but this action emphasised that the Navy's strength was only adequate for peacetime duties and was not up to the level required for a major war. Furthermore the formation of a Particular Service Squadron revealed the lack of a proper organisation to rapidly mobilise and man a fleet.

In 1879 the Carnarvon Committee set up to investigate the state of the Navy and its ability to defend Britain and the Empire reported that the Navy was too small to fulfil its many duties. However, such a conclusion was politically undesirable in the extreme, and the report was not published. The Navy considered a new construction programme essential but the government refused to sanction an increase in naval expenditure and the programme was deferred.

THE NORTHBROOK PROGRAMME

In 1884 a journalist called Stead began a series of articles entitled 'The Truth about the Navy'. These were based on officially leaked information, and the public outcry they caused suited the Navy's purpose. However, the resulting Northbrook Programme of 1884 authorised only £3,100,000 to be spent over 5 years on 2 battleships, 5 armoured cruisers, 6 torpedo cruisers, and 14 TBs. During 1880-84 Britain had laid down 6 *Admiral* class battleships which equalled the numbers of French orders, but France had later cancelled 2 vessels, and Britain had also built the coast defence ship *Hero* and the armoured cruisers *Warspite* and *Imperieuse.* This moderate level of construction in the early 1880s continued, despite growing pressure from the Press and public opinion, into the second half of the decade. As far as armoured ships were concerned, this was partly an effect of the introduction of the torpedo boat, which cast doubts on the role and indeed the value of battleships.

For an Admiralty trying to decide on the best types of ships to build, the 1880s were particularly difficult. Construction times were protracted and there were great delays before ships entered service, so the evaluation of new designs was a lengthy business. However in February 1887 the design procedure was tightened up, and formulated in detail. Design calculations were to be more accurate and once a design was approved by the Admiralty Board no further alterations or additions were allowed unless sanctioned by the Board. The 'Board Margin' was also introduced to allow for additional equipment and changes during construction, and the new system proved so successful that many ships built during the 1890s were completed below displacement.

The Royal Navy at the height of its power: the Channel Fleet (above) is seen in Mounts Bay; and the Mediterranean Fleet (left) is dressed overall in Grand Harbour, Valetta, for a visit of the Royal Yacht *Victoria and Albert* about 1905

THE RUSSIAN WAR SCARE 1884

In 1884 a threat of war with Russia once again produced a flurry of naval activity, and another Particular Service Squadron (the Baltic Expeditionary Force) was formed in 1885. This squadron was very late in assembling and some ships were still not completely fitted out when the crisis subsided. However, the squadron presented the motley spectacle of 8 broadside ironclads, 4 turret ironclads, 1 armoured cruiser, the merchant cruiser *Oregon,* 3 other cruisers, the torpedo ram *Polyphemus,* the TB carrier *Hecla,* 1 sloop, 2 gunboats, and 4 'flatiron' gunboats. This heterogeneous squadron was useful, however, not only in testing a variety of ships and their equipment, but also in working out some early torpedo boat tactics for both attack and defence. The great value of larger TBs was realised and a number of methods of Fleet defence from TB attack were practiced.

Two years later in 1887, a Colonial Conference resulted in plans to improve the defence of colonial ports and coaling stations, the most tangible feature of which was the construction of cruisers for the Australian station. However the Conference published sections of the suppressed Carnarvon Report which revealed that the Navy was incapable of carrying out all its duties in defence of seaborne trade and the colonies. Public opinion was hardly mollified by the results of the 1888 Annual Manoeuvres (the first of a series of exercises that continued until 1913) which showed that the ships were inadequate in number, and in some cases quality, and that their personnel were lacking in training for modern warfare. The report of a committee on these manoeuvres urged the modernisation of older ships which although obsolescent had sound hulls and could be used in secondary roles, such as port-guard or coast defence duties, until the Navy could be built up to a required strength. The committee also concluded that there was no justification in the belief that the day of the battleship was over, and urged that a return be made to a true 'Two-Power Standard' (that the Royal Navy should be larger than the next two largest navies combined).

THE NAVAL DEFENCE ACT 1889

Both the First Lord of the Admiralty and the First Sea Lord played down many of the criticisms in the report, but ever since the 'Truth about the Navy' articles public opinion in favour of a stronger navy had been increasing. The Russian 'war scare', the belated revelations of the Carnarvon Committee, and controversy surrounding the 1888 manoeuvres all contributed to the agitation which resulted in the passing of the crucially important Naval Defence Act of 1889. This finally established the 'Two-Power Standard', and introduced a continuous and regular construction programme which rapidly altered the character of the Navy. The Act provided for 70 ships at a cost of £21,500,000 and since it coincided with a stabilisation in ship design large classes were built rather than small groups or single types. This provided a fleet with conplementary characteristics capable of operating as a homogeneous unit. The Naval Act was augmented by the Spencer Programme of 1893 which provided for 7 battleships, 30 cruisers, 7 torpedo gunboats, 30 torpedo boats, 1 torpedo boat depot ship, and 82 destroyers. Although the number of cruisers was later reduced, the introduction in large numbers of the destroyer supplied the last element required for a balanced fleet as understood in the twentieth century.

THE 1890s

Despite improvements in ship design and fleet strength during the 1890s, the development of both training and Admiralty organisation was slow. It was not until the Fisher era that real advances were made in fleet organisation and in the training of personnel. A Naval Intelligence Department was formed in the late 1880s, but a much-needed war staff to formulate mobilisation and strategic war plans was not set up until 1912. Traditional thinking might have been satisfactory for confrontations with traditional enemies, but in 1898 Germany passed the first Naval Act, which was the sign of a growing challenge. This was replaced by a new act in 1900 which as an instrument of Tirpitz's 'Risk' theory, was a direct threat to British seapower. Thereafter the overall concept of British naval planning changed irrevocably.

THE BRITISH BATTLEFLEET in 1860

SCREW SHIPS-OF-THE-LINE

Name	Launched	Tons*	Guns	Fate
ABOUKIR[1]	1848	3091	90	Sold 1878
AGAMEMNON	1852	3102	91	Sold 1870
ALGIERS	1854	3099	90	Sold 1870
ANSON	1860	3336	91	BU 1904
ATLAS[2]	1860	3318	91	BU 1904
BRUNSWICK[3]	1855	2492	80	Sold 1867
BULWARK[4]	Building	3716	91	BU 1873
CAESAR	1853	2767	90	Sold 1870
CENTURION[5]	1844	2590	80	Sold 1870
COLOSSUS[3]	1848	2590	80	Sold 1867
CONQUEROR	1855	3225	101	Wrecked 1861
CRESSY	1853	2539	80	Sold 1867
DEFIANCE[6]	Building	3745	81	Sold 1931
DONEGAL	1858	3245	101	Sold 1925
DUKE OF WELLINGTON[7]	1852	3771	131	Sold 1904
DUNCAN	1859	3727	101	Sold 1910
EDGAR	1858	3094	91	Sold 1904
EXMOUTH	1854	3100	90	Sold 1905
FREDERICK WILLIAM[8]	1860	3241	110	BU 1953
GIBRALTAR	1860	3716	101	Sold 1899
GOLIATH[9]	1842	2596	80	Burnt 1875
HANNIBAL	1854	3136	91	Sold 1904
HERO	1858	3148	91	Sold 1871
HOOD[10]	1859	3308	91	Sold 1888
HOWE	1860	4245	110	Sold 1921
IRRESISTIBLE	1859	2589	80	Sold 1894
JAMES WATT[11]	1853	3083	80	Sold 1875
LION[12]	1847	2611	80	Sold 1905
LONDON[13]	1840	2687	72	Sold 1884
MAJESTIC	1853	2589	80	BU 1868
MARLBOROUGH	1855	4000	131	Foundered 1924
MARS[14]	1848	2576	80	Sold 1929
MEEANEE[15]	1848	2591	60	BU 1906
NELSON[16]	1814	2736	90	BU 1928
NEPTUNE[17]	1832	2830	72	Sold 1875
NILE[18]	1839	2622	92	Burnt 1956
ORION	1854	3281	91	BU 1867
PRINCE OF WALES	1860	3994	121	BU 1916
PRINCESS ROYAL[19]	1853	3129	91	Sold 1872
QUEEN[20]	1839	3249	86	BU 1871
RENOWN	1857	3319	91	Sold 1870
REVENGE	1859	3322	91	BU 1923
RODNEY[21]	1833	2770	70	BU 1882
ROYAL ALBERT	1854	3726	121	Sold 1883
ROYAL GEORGE[22]	1827	2616	102	Sold 1875
ROYAL SOVEREIGN	1857	3765	121	Sold 1885
ROYAL WILLIAM[17]	1833	2694	72	Burnt 1899
ST JEAN D'ACRE	1853	3199	101	Sold 1875
ST GEORGE[18]	1840	2864	91	Sold 1883
SANS PAREIL	1851	2339	81	Sold 1867
TRAFALGAR[23]	1841	2900	91	Sold 1906
VICTOR EMANUEL[24]	1855	3087	91	Sold 1899
VICTORIA	1859	4127	121	Sold 1892
WATERLOO[18]	1833	2694	120	Burnt 1918
WINDSOR CASTLE[25]	1858	3101	100	Sold 1908

* Builders' measurement

(1) Undocked as screw ship 1858.
(2) Never completed.
(3) Laid down as sailing 3rd Rate.
(4) Never launched. Work suspended 1861.
(5) Laid down as sailing 3rd Rate. Undocked as screw ship 1855.
(6) Completed 1861.
(7) Ex-*Windsor Castle*.
(8) Ex-*Royal Frederick*.
(9) Laid down as sailing 2nd Rate. Undocked as screw ship 1857.
(10) Originally *Edgar*, 80 guns. Renamed *Hood* 1848 and launched as screw ship.
(11) Ex-*Audacious*.
(12) Laid down as sailing 2nd Rate. Undocked as screw ship 1859.
(13) Laid down as sailing 2nd Rate, 92 guns. Undocked as screw ship 1860.
(14) Laid down as sailing 2nd Rate. Undocked as screw ship 1855.
(15) Laid down as sailing 2nd Rate, 80 guns. Undocked as screw ship 1857. Ex-*Madras*.
(16) Laid down as sailing 1st Rate, 120 guns. Undocked as screw ship 1860.
(17) Laid down as sailing 1st Rate, 120 guns. Undocked as screw ship 1859.
(18) Undocked as screw ship 1854.
(19) Ex-*Prince Albert*.
(20) Laid down as sailing 1st Rate, 110 guns. Undocked as screw ship 1859. Ex-*Royal Frederick*.
(21) Laid down as sailing 2nd Rate, 92 guns. Undocked as screw ship 1860.
(22) Undocked as screw ship 1853. Ex-*Neptune*.
(23) Laid down as sailing 1st Rate, 106 guns. Undocked as screw ship 1859.
(24) Ex-*Repulse*.
(25) Converted to screw while on stocks.

SCREW GUARD SHIPS AND BLOCK SHIPS

Name	Launched	Tons*	Guns	Fate
AJAX[1]	1809	1761	60	BU 1864
BLENHEIM[2]	1813	1822	60	BU 1865
CORNWALLIS[3]	1813	1809	60	BU 1957
EDINBURGH[4]	1811	1772	60	Sold 1866
HASTINGS[5]	1819	1763	60	Sold 1886
HAWKE[6]	1820	1754	60	BU 1865
HOGUE[7]	1811	1846	60	BU 1865
PEMBROKE[3]	1812	1758	60	Sold 1905
RUSSELL[3]	1822	1751	60	BU 1865

*Builders' measurement

(1) Laid down as sailing 3rd Rate, 74 guns. Undocked as screw ship 1846.
(2) Laid down as sailing 3rd Rate, 74 guns. Converted to screw ship 1837.
(3) Laid down as sailing 3rd Rate, 74 guns. Undocked as screw ship 1855.
(4) Laid down as sailing 3rd Rate, 74 guns. Undocked as screw ship 1846.
(5) Ex-Indiaman, ex-3rd Rate, 74 guns. Undocked as screw ship 1855.
(6) Laid down as sailing 3rd Rate, 74 guns. Completed as screw ship 1855.
(7) Laid down as sailing 3rd Rate, 74 guns. Completed as screw ship 1850.

SAILING SHIPS-OF-THE-LINE

Name	Rate	Launched	Tons*	Guns	Fate
On the effective list					
ASIA	2nd	1834	2289	84	Sold 1908
BOSCAWEN	3rd	1844	2212	70	Burnt and BU 1914
CALCUTTA	2nd	1831	2299	84	Sold 1908
CLARENCE	2nd	1827	2288	84	Burnt 1884
CUMBERLAND	3rd	1842	2214	70	Burnt and BU 1889
FORMIDABLE	2nd	1825	2289	84	Sold 1906
GANGES	2nd	1821	2284	84	Sold 1929
MONARCH	2nd	1832	2255	84	BU 1862-66
THUNDERER	2nd	1831	2279	84	Sold 1901
VANGUARD	3rd	1835	2609	78	BU 1875

*Builders' measurement

Not on the effective list

These vessels did not constitute a fighting force in 1860. Some were in the process of being converted to screw ships-of-the-line, but most were being reduced to harbour service, converted into coal hulks, convict ships, training or drill ships, being on the sale list, etc, and would have had most of their guns removed.

Name	Rate	Launched	Tons*	Guns	Fate
ACHILLE[1]	3rd	1798	1981	74	Sold 1865
AGINCOURT	3rd	1817	1747	74	Sold 1884
ALBION[2]	2nd	1842	3111	90	BU 1884
BOMBAY[2]	2nd	1828	2279	84	Burnt 1864
BRITANNIA	1st	1820	2616	120	BU 1869
CANOPUS	3rd		2257	80	Sold 1887
CARNATIC[4]	3rd	1823	1790	72	Sold 1914
COLLINGWOOD[2]	3rd	1841	2589	80	Sold 1867
EGMONT	3rd	1810	1760	74	Sold 1875
EXCELLENT[5]	1st	1810	2289	104	Sold 1892
FOUDROYANT	2nd	1798	2062	80	Wrecked 1897
HIBERNIA	1st	1804	2530	110	Sold 1902
HINDOSTAN	2nd	1841	2029	80	Sold 1921
IMPLACABLE[6]	3rd		1882	74	Scuttled 1949
IMPREGNABLE	2nd	1810	2406	98	Sold 1906
INDUS	2nd	1839	2098	80	Sold 1898
POWERFUL	2nd	1826	2296	84	BU 1860-64
PRINCE REGENT[2]	1st	1823	2613	120	BU 1873
PRINCESS CHARLOTTE	1st	1825	2443	104	Sold 1875
ROYAL ADELAIDE[7]	1st	1828	2446	104	Sold 1905
ST VINCENT	1st	1815	2601	120	Sold 1906
SULTAN	3rd	1807	1751	74	BU 1864
SUPERB	2nd	1842	2583	80	BU 1869
VENGEANCE	2nd	1824	2284	84	Sold 1897
VICTORY	1st	1765	2164	100	Still in commission
WELLESLEY	3rd	1815	1746	74	Sunk by air attack
WELLINGTON[8]	3rd	1816	1756	74	Sold 1908

*Builders' measurement

(1) Rebuilt 1823.
(2) Being converted to screw.
(3) Ex-French *Franklin*, captured 1798.
(4) Never commissioned.
(5) Ex-*Queen Charlotte*.
(6) Ex-French *Duguay-Trouin*, captured 1805.
(7) Ex-*London*.
(8) Ex-*Hero*.

SHIPS-OF-THE-LINE, 1860

Effective list	
Screw ships-of-the-line	53 (+ 2 building)
Screw guard ships and block ships	9
	62 (+ 2)
Sailing ships-of-the-line	10
	72 (+ 2)
Non-effective list	
Sailing ships-of-the-line	21 (+4 being converted to screw)
	21 (+4)

CAPITAL SHIPS

Right: The coast defence turret ship *Hydra* during her 1878-88 period of service as tender to the *Duncan*, seen here in the background

During the Crimean War both Britain and France had constructed armoured floating batteries but only the latter country continued to develop the ironclad idea seriously, seeing in this a means of gaining ascendancy over her old enemy. In Britain various proposals for ironclads were placed before the Admiralty between 1855 and 1859 and experiments, which produced useful data, were carried out with armour plates at Woolwich during 1856–58. It was Admiralty policy, however, not to innovate, it being regarded as better to leave other navies to initiate revolutionary ideas and then use Britain's greater shipbuilding and industrial capacity to regain the Royal Navy's position of supremacy. Nevertheless, after it became known in 1858 that France had laid down the first sea-going ironclad, the arguments against such vessels resulted in the Admiralty delaying the provision of two replies until the Estimates of 1859. These were the *Warrior* and *Black Prince*, designed by the Admiralty's chief constructor Isaac Watts with the assistance of the engineer John Scott Russell. Unlike the French ship (*La Gloire*) they were constructed of iron which allowed for a substantial increase in dimensions. However, this also resulted in increased cost and as the Admiralty were still unconvinced as to their value and were concerned about the relative strength in 'wooden walls' between Britain and France, a large programme of wooden shipbuilding was instituted during 1859-60. At the same time the ironclad programme was only slightly expanded by the addition of two more ships, the *Resistance* and *Defence*, but these vessels were smaller than their predecessors largely due to the reaction against the *Warrior's* size and cost. This placing of financial consideration before military requirements was to continue to occur throughout the Victorian period (and after) with monotonous regularity.

In 1860 the French announced their intention to construct 30 seagoing ironclads which ended the Admiralty's indecision regarding the British programme. All construction work on wooden capital ships was cancelled and plans were made to expand the ironclad fleet. During 1861 two repeats of the *Defence* (*Hector* and *Valiant*) and four larger vessels (the *Achilles, Minotaur, Agincourt* and *Northumberland*) were laid down and approval was given to convert to ironclads eight of the 90-gun two-deckers laid down during 1859–60. In 1862 three small wooden ships still on the stocks (*Research, Enterprise* and *Favorite*) and one completed three-decker (*Royal Sovereign*) were added to the conversion programme. These conversions were undertaken in order to expand the ironclad programme more quickly, Britain's capacity for iron shipbuilding being temporarily limited, and to keep the dockyards employed while the change from wooden to iron construction took place. Six more wooden ironclads, this time purpose-built, were ordered in 1863 to utilise the available stocks of timber but only three (*Lord Clyde, Lord Warden* and *Pallas*) were laid down, the others being cancelled. In the long run the wooden ships were only partially successful: compared with the iron vessels they deteriorated much more quickly, their unarmoured areas were extremely vulnerable to gunfire and their hulls were weaker and had a much lower carrying capacity. Whether or not the wooden ironclads were needed is a debatable point. Britain easily outbuilt the French whose large building programme rapidly fell behind due to lack of finance and their smaller shipbuilding and iron manufacturing facilities.

NAVAL ORDNANCE

The introduction of the ironclad coincided with a revolution in naval ordnance during which rifled guns replaced smooth bores and metal carriages replaced wooden truck mountings. In Britain a series of tests resulted in the adoption of the Armstrong RBL (Rifled Breech Loader) and by 1862 the Fleet was almost completely re-armed with these weapons. Unfortunately the guns proved very dangerous because of the weaknesses in the breech mechanism and manufacturing flaws in the steel barrels. After a long chapter of accidents it was decided to withdraw them from service but it took some time to find a replacement. Various rifled and smooth bore guns were tested during 1863–65 which initially resulted in the adoption of large smooth bores but these proved to be inferior to rifled weapons and were soon abandoned. The problem was finally solved in 1865 with the introduction of the Woolwich MLR (Muzzle Loading Rifle) which was chosen after a series of competitive trials against Lancaster (oval bore), Whitworth (hexagonal bore), Scott and a number of other rifled guns.

The return to muzzle loading represented the usual Admiralty preference for reliable and well tried equipment and in 1865 this was certainly sound policy with regard to guns. However, the muzzle loader was retained in British service well beyond the period required by prudence and it was not until 1879 (when breech loading was well established in many foreign ships) that the Admiralty decided on a return to the breech loader. By this time, however, there was little choice as the introduction of slow burning propellant charges required guns of great length which could not, practically, be loaded at the muzzle.

THE REED ERA – CENTRAL BATTERIES AND TURRETS

The development of guns was the greatest single factor influencing the design of the battleship in the late Victorian period, which is not surprising as the carrying of these weapons was reason for their existence. The main factor in this development was the gradual increase in the size and power of guns between 1865 and 1890. The first change in design characteristics as a result of this coincided with the appointment of E J Reed as the Admiralty's chief constructor in 1863. Reed's influence and ability were exceptional and his ideas regarding the future of ironclad development proved uncannily accurate. His reputation was however marred by his activities after leaving the Admiralty in 1870, when his criticisms of official construction policy, while sometimes correct, were overstated and often erroneous. Reed was responsible for the design of the small wooden ironclads, *Enterprise, Research* and *Favorite* which introduced the central or box battery. This was based on the premise that, with the introduction of larger heavier guns, fewer could be mounted on a given displacement and it was therefore better to place them in a central armoured position which, because of its smaller size, could be given the thicker armour required to give protection from these same guns. In the case of the small ironclads this meant mounting a few heavy (battleship) type guns instead of standard small ship weapons but the growth of heavy guns from the 6.3in 64cwt RML of 1864 to the 12in 25 ton RML of 1870 resulted in the same system being applied to larger ships. The first major vessel of this type was Reed's *Bellerophon*, which set the pattern for Britain's subsequent broadside types until their development ended with the *Alexandra* and *Temeraire* of 1873. With these vessels the only major improvements made on the *Bellerophon*, apart from those resulting from the development of improved ordnance, machinery, etc, were a provision for end-on fire and the adoption of two-storey batteries.

Reed's period in office also coincided with the introduction of the sea-going turret ship and it was in this that Reed made his greatest contribution to the development of the modern battleship. The design of the British turret was largely the result of the work of Captain Cowper Coles, who had developed a practical scheme between the Crimean War and 1860. Initially he had little success in persuading the Admiralty to adopt his ideas but after enlisting the help of the Press and the Prince Consort an experimental turret was mounted in the floating battery *Trusty* in 1861. The installation, tested at Shoeburyness, proved successful and Britain's first turret ship, the *Prince Albert*, was ordered in January 1862. Shortly afterwards, the wooden 3-decker *Royal Sovereign* was taken in hand for conversion to a turret ship and actually entered service before the *Prince Albert*. Both of these vessels were intended for coast defence, neither having a sailing rig, and even before they were completed Coles was engaged in another battle with the Admiralty with the prime object of constructing a sea-going turret ship. The Board however, held its ground until the *Royal Sovereign* had proved successful and, after further pressure from Coles, appointed a Committee to study his

proposals. The Committee's recommendations resulted in the construction of *Monarch* but Coles did not care for this ship because her rig seriously restricted the capabilities of the turrets. With the assistance of Press and Parliament, Coles eventually exerted sufficient pressure to gain permission to construct a ship of his own design with public money. Although wishing to build a ship without sailing rig he was eventually convinced that such a vessel was not practical for sea-going purposes and his new vessel, the *Captain*, was given a full ship rig. However, by employing tripod masts and a flying deck, the turrets did not suffer interference from the rig although the superstructure prevented ahead and astern fire which had been one of Coles' arguments against the *Monarch*. The loss of *Captain* did much to lower Coles' prestige but, although his judgement in matters of naval architecture was limited, his development of the turret for the Royal Navy was of considerable value.

While Coles saw clearly the value of turrets, Reed, one of his greatest opponents, saw clearly their ideal application to ships. He realised that for such a ship to be successful she must be built without the encumberance of top hamper to give clear all round arcs of fire, and in 1867 he produced a virtually silent revolution with the design of the colonial coast defence vessels *Cerberus* and *Magdala*. In general layout these were ideal turret vessels without masts or yards and provided the pattern for the world's first sea-going mastless turret ship, *Devastation*, designed by Reed in 1868. With this ship one of the main arguments against such vessels – that in the event of a machinery breakdown they might find themselves at sea without motive power – was virtually eliminated by the provision of two sets of machinery on the principle that the likelihood of a breakdown in both engines was extremely remote. Unfortunately the loss of the *Captain* had seriously damaged the reputation of the turret ship and this, combined with a reluctance to abandon sails, prevented the general acceptance of Reed's design which, only ten years after the introduction of the ironclad, contained the basic qualities of the battleships of the 1890s.

Also in 1868 the first ironclad ram, the *Hotspur*, was laid down as a result of the realisation that the manoeuvrability made possible by steam propulsion would allow for the use of ramming in action. Although this form of attack might well have had some value in the early 1860s, when guns were comparatively light and battle ranges short, the subsequent development of heavy ordnance rendered such tactics of improbable success. Nevertheless, the principle was highly regarded, and ironclad rams – usually short (for manoeuvrability) with a comparatively high speed and guns concentrated in a single turret forward – continued to be built for some years. While these vessels were mostly coast defence or second class ships the general layout eventually found application in first class battleships (*Victoria* and *Sans Pariel*) before dying out.

THE BARNABY ERA – CENTRAL CITADELS AND BARBETTES

In 1870 Reed was replaced as chief constructor by Nathaniel Barnaby who, initially, continued the development of Reed's turret and central battery types. However, the introduction of very large muzzle loading guns, with sufficient power to penetrate any armour afloat, soon necessitated a substantial change in capital ship design. Basically this involved the provision of much thicker armour which, because of the limited weight available for protection, within the acceptable limits of size, meant an abandonment of the full length belt in favour of a central citadel. The first British example of this type, the *Inflexible* of 1874, constructed in answer to the Italian *Dandolo* and *Duilio*, showed the system in its extreme by having the largest muzzle loading guns (16in RML) and the thickest armour (24in wrought iron) ever carried in a British ship. *Inflexible* was also the last British capital ship to carry a sailing rig.

The *Inflexible* was followed by four generally similar but smaller central citadel ships, the *Agamemnon* and *Ajax* of 1876 and the *Colossus* and *Edinburgh* of 1879. The latter pair, although almost identical in appearance to the first, represent a landmark in British battleship development as they incorporated several new developments of greater importance than the ships themselves. They were the first British battleships to be constructed of steel and to carry compound armour (steel face on a wrought iron back) both of which allowed for savings in weight without loss of strength. In addition they were fitted with the first of a new generation of breech loading guns, the increased power of which was offset by the greater resistance of compound armour. Thus most of the basic materials for future development were introduced in a single class which was otherwise far from being exceptional. It is worth noting that the designation battleship came into more general use with the commencement of steel construction and 'ironclad' gradually fell into disuse (except in reference to the older ships of the fleet).

In the 1880s Barnaby produced his most successful design in the 'Admiral' class. With these ships, the first homogeneous group to be built for some time, a return was made to the sensible armament dispostion of the *Devastation* and *Dreadnought* but in this case the guns were mounted in barbettes instead of turrets. This latter gave considerable advantage in weight saving, the amount of armour required for the citadel being substantially reduced as it was no longer required to protect the turret bases and turret machinery. In addition the barbettes allowed the guns to be placed higher where they had a better command and were less affected by heavy seas, this being a major problem in low freeboard ships. The construction of the 'Admirals' coincided with the period in which the torpedo boat became a major threat to the existence of the battleship and they were among the first ships to carry a substantial secondary armament, as well as several small QF (quick firing) guns, as defence against such vessels. It was soon realised that these same guns could be used to great effect against the unarmoured portions of a battleship, a situation which was strengthened by the introduction of medium calibre QF guns towards the end of the decade. Unfortunately the 'Admirals' had a large area of unprotected hull and their design, which was much criticised for this reason, soon fell into disfavour despite the fact that they were better protected than they appeared to be. Their real fault, if it can be called such, was limited size. Ever since the introduction of the ironclad the Admiralty, under the influence of Parliament, had been reluctant to sanction any increase in the displacement and therefore cost of capital ships. Thus the 'Admirals' displaced little more than the *Warrior* of 1860 despite the need to provide weight for many new features including machinery of greater power for higher speeds. It was hardly surprising therefore to find that they had a low freeboard and a large area of unarmoured hull as the weights available had already been fully utilised.

The 'Admirals' were followed by a reversion to turret ships which, above all else, meant losing the weatherly advantages of the barbette arrangement. The first of these vessels (*Victoria* and *Sans Pareil*) were retrograde in character but the second pair (*Nile* and *Trafalgar*) had the twin advantage of being based on the *Dreadnought* and of breaking the displacement limit by a substantial margin. They were 2000t heavier than the 'Admirals' and were exceptionally well protected but they could still not operate their guns efficiently in a seaway.

THE WHITE ERA – STANDARDISED BATTLESHIPS

To William White, who became chief constructor in 1886, it was clear that the barbette offered the best means of improving on existing designs and in 1888 he was given the chance of putting his ideas to the test. In this year he was requested to prepare an improved *Trafalgar* design with increased displacement to allow for a slighly higher freeboard, more secondary guns and a higher speed and endurance. Using these requirements he prepared outline designs for both turret and barbette ships and in presenting them to the Board pointed out the great advantages of the higher guns and freeboard in the latter type. Despite the opposition of the First Sea Lord, Admiral Hood, he won the support of the Board as a whole and was allowed to proceed with his design which became the *Royal Sovereign* class. These were true ocean-going ships and, although in essence they were only enlarged 'Admirals' with a high freeboard, were one of the best designs for their time ever produced.

The *Royal Sovereign* design was refined in latter battleships classes but the essential features remained the same for the following twelve years, the longest period of stability to be seen since the ironclad was introduced. These refinements included the provisions of hard faced steel armour, which, having a much greater resistance to penetration than wrought iron, allowed for a reduction in thickness in order to give protection over larger areas. To this could be added a steady improvement in the quality of ordnance, machinery and the disposition of armour, but despite these changes the last of White's designs, the *King Edward VII*, was still an obvious derivative of the *Royal Sovereign*. White was succeeded by Phillip Watts in 1902 at which point the true period of Victorian battleship design ended. Watts was however to produce one more class, the *Lord Nelson* and *Agamemnon*, before his *Dreadnought* design rendered White's powerful fleet of fifty battleships obsolete.

BRITISH NAVAL SERVICE MLR GUNS 1864–1878

Date	Calibre/length (in/cal)	Designation	Weight (tons)	Weight of Shell (lbs)	Muzzle Velocity (fps)	Penetration of Wrought Iron at Muzzle (in)*
1864	6.3/15.5	Mk I	3.2	64	1125	–
1865	7/15.9	Mk III	6.5	112	–	7.7
1866	8/14.8	Mk III	9	175	1410	9.6
1865	9/13.9	Mk IV	12	254	1420	11.3
1868	10/14.5	Mk II	18	407	1365	12.9
1867	11/12	Mk II	25	544	1315	14.3
1870	12/12	Mk II	25	609	1300	13.5
1871	12/13.5	Mk I	35	707	1300	15.9
1875	12.5/15.8	Mk I	38	809	1575	18.4
1878	16/18	Mk I	80	1684	1590	24.7

* These figures should not be taken literally – they are intended to give a comparison of the relative powers of the guns.

BRITISH BATTLESHIP MAIN ARMAMENT BL GUNS 1880–1905

Date (Approx)	Calibre/length (in/cal)	Designation	Weight (tons)	Weight of Shell (lbs)	Muzzle Velocity (fps)	Penetration of Wrought iron at Muzzle (in)*
1880	12/25.5	Mk III	45	714	1914	24
1882	13.5/30	Mk II	67	1250	2099	33
1885	16.25/30	Mk I	110	1800	2087	38
1890	10/32	Mk II	29	500	2046	25
1893	12/35†	Mk VIII	46	850	2417	37
1898	12/40†	Mk IX	50	850	2610	40
1905	12/45†	Mk X	58	850	2725	51

† Wire wound guns.
* These figures should not be taken literally – they are intended to give a comparison of the relative powers of the guns.

The Mk VIII 12in was mounted in the *Majestic* and *Canopus* classes, the Mk IX in the *Formidable, Duncan* and *King Edward VII* classes and the Mk X in the *Lord Nelson* class.

Warrior after the reduction of her bowsprit but prior to being rearmed in 1867

Warrior as completed 1861

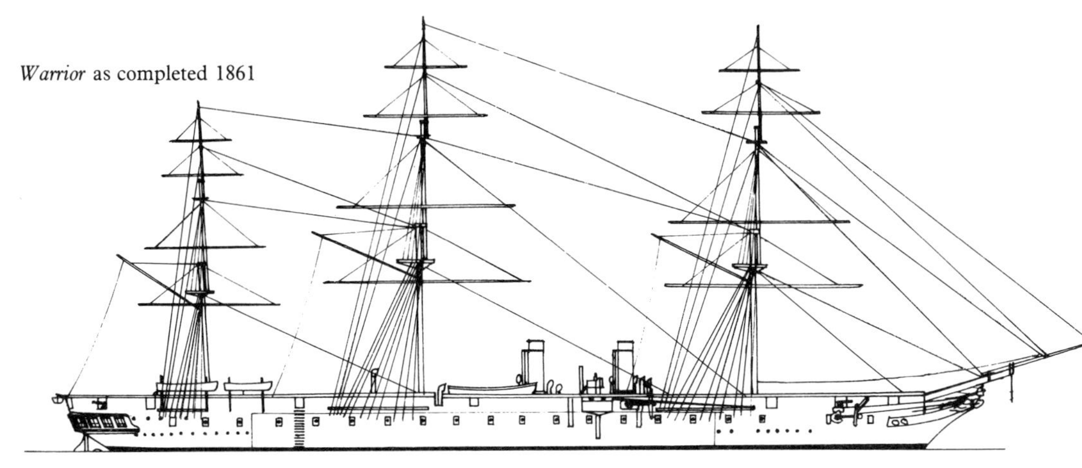

These were the world's first ocean-going iron armoured ships. Provided under the 1859 Programme, *Warrior* was ordered in June and *Black Prince* in October of that year. They were classified as frigates because of their single gun deck, but at the time of completion these were the most powerful warships in existence, having an impregnable battery and a higher speed than the French *Gloire*.

They were given a high length-to-beam ratio (6.5:1) and fine lines forward and aft to secure high speed but this also resulted in poor handling and manoeuvrability. The armour belt over the midships section, 213ft long by 22ft deep, consisted of iron plates 15ft by 3ft weighing four tons each. The plates were tongued and grooved to give mutual support if struck by a shell, but the process was expensive and was not repeated in later ironclads. The unarmoured ends could be bilged without loss of stability but the lack of protection to the steering was a serious fault of the design. The hull was constructed with a partial double bottom, 240ft long, below the machinery and the midships magazine, and was subdivided into 92 water-tight compartments, 57 of which were in the double bottom.

Both vessels were ship-rigged, with a sail area of 48,400 sq ft including stunsails. *Warrior* recorded 13kts under full sail and on one occasion made over 17kts with combined steam and sail. *Black Prince* recorded 11kts under full sail. The funnels were raised by 6ft in 1863 to improve draught to the boilers and with this alteration *Warrior* made 14.35kts at 5469ihp. Endurance was 2100 miles at 11kts. *Warrior* had a lifting screw but *Black Prince* had a fixed screw.

The designed armament was 40-68pdr SB but this was modified to 10-110pdr BL, 26-68pdr SB and 4-70pdr BL while the ships were under construction. Both were rearmed in 1867/8. During refits in 1872/75 they were fitted with a poop and a steam capstan.

The ships were re-classified as armoured cruisers about 1880 when in reserve. *Black Prince* became a training ship in 1899, and was renamed *Emerald* in 1903 and *Impregnable III* in 1910. *Warrior* was converted to a depot ship in 1902, renamed *Vernon III* in 1904, hulked in 1923, used as oil pipeline pier at Pembroke Dock (where she still lies) and renamed *C77* in 1945.

WARRIOR class *broadside ironclads*

Displacement: 9137t, *Black Prince* 9250t
Dimensions: 380ft 2in pp, 420ft oa x 58ft 4in x 26ft (*115.87pp, 128 oa x 17.78 x 7.92m*)
Machinery: 1-shaft, Penn HSET, 10 rectangular boilers, 5267ihp = 14.08kts (*Black Prince* 5770ihp = 13.6kts). Coal 850t
Armour: Belt 4½in with 18in wood backing, bulkheads 4½in
Armament: (1867) 4-8in MLR, 28-7in MLR (*Black Prince* 24-7in MLR), 4-20pdr BL
Complement: 707

Name	Builder	Laid down	Launced	Comp	Fate
WARRIOR	Ditchburn & Mare, Blackwall	25.5.1859	29.12.60	24.10.61	Still afloat 1978
BLACK PRINCE (ex-INVINCIBLE 1859)	Napier Glasgow	12.10.1859	27.2.61	12.9.62	Sold for BU 21.3.1923

These vessels were provided under the 1859 Programme, and were classified as frigates, being smaller editions of *Warrior*, but inferior in almost all respects except manoeuvrability. The belt armour was 140ft long, and arranged as in *Warrior*, with the ends of the ship and the steering gear being unprotected. They had a frigate stern, as in *Warrior*, but a ram bow was adopted in place of the clipper bow. Both ships exceeded the designed speed of 10.75kts.

Armament as designed was 18-68pdr SB and 4-40pdr BL, but *Defence* was completed with 8-7in BL, 10-68pdr SB and 4-5in BL, and *Resistance* with 6-7in BL, 10-68pdr SB and 2-32pdr SB. *Defence* was rearmed 1866/68 and *Resistance* 1867/69. As completed, 10-68pdr and four 7in guns were behind armour, and as rearmed eight 7in and the two 8in guns were behind armour, the endmost ports of the battery being left vacant.

These were barque-rigged vessels with a sail area of 24,500 sq ft; *Defence* was modified to ship rig in 1864 and then reverted to barque during the 1866/68 refit. They could make 10.5kts under sail and handled well, except in a beam sea. Both were fitted with lifting screws.

The sea-going service of *Defence* ended in 1885; she was renamed *Indus* (TS) in 1898, and hulked in 1922. The sea-going service of *Resistance* ended in 1880. She was used as a target for gunnery and torpedo experiments in 1885.

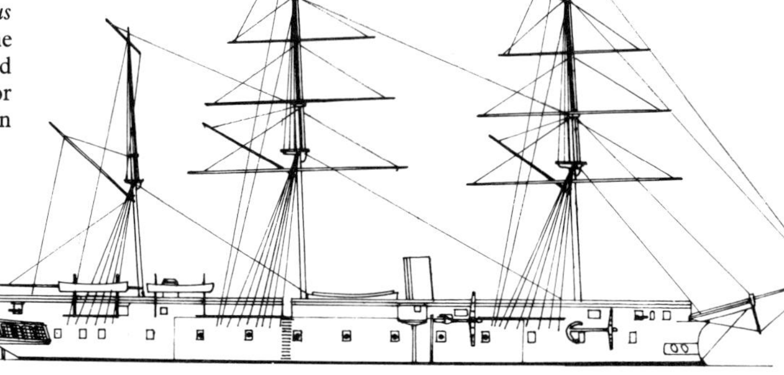

Resistance as completed 1862

DEFENCE class *broadside ironclads*

Displacement: 6150t, (*Resistance* 6070t) load
Dimensions: 280ft pp, 302ft oa x 54ft 2in x 25ft (*85.3 pp, 92.04 oa x 16.51 x 7.62m*)
Machinery: 1-shaft, Penn HSET, 4 rectangular boilers, 2540ihp = 11.62kts (*Resistance* 2430ihp = 11.83kts). Coal 460t
Armour: Belt 4½in with 18in wood backing, bulkheads 4½in
Armament: (1867) 2-8in MLR, 14-7in MLR
Complement: 460

Name	Builder	Laid down	Launched	Comp	Fate
DEFENCE	Palmers, Jarrow	Dec 1859	24.4.61	2.12.61	BU 1935
RESISTANCE	Westwood & Baillie, Millwall	Dec 1859	11.4.61	2.7.62	Sold 1898, foundered Holyhead Bay 1899, raised and BU

Defence shown in her final rig after 1866

Achilles in the late 1860s with her foremast moved forward and bowsprit replaced

Hector and *Valiant* were armoured frigates similar to *Defence* but with increased protection, speed and armament, the beam being increased to compensate for the added top weight. The battery armour extended the full length of the ship, 4½in for 216ft amidships and 2½in at the ends, providing partial protection to the steering gear. Armour bulkheads were fitted across the end of the waterline belt only, the waterline at the bow and stern still being unprotected. They had straight stems with no ram, and a rounded stern unpierced except by gunports. The hull was divided into 92 watertight compartments, 52 being in the partial double bottom and the wings.

As completed *Hector* was seriously overweight and the coal capacity and the armament of both ships was reduced to compensate for this. *Valiant's* original builders, Westwood & Baillie of Millwall, became bankrupt and her construction was taken over in 1861 by the Thames Iron Wks. This and the decision to rearm her with MLR guns resulted in extensive delay to her completion. *Hector's* machinery was manufactured by her builder, and *Valiant's* by Maudslay. The coal capacity of 450 tons gave an endurance of 1600 miles. Both vessels had lifting screws, but lifting tackle was not fitted.

The designed armament was 24-68pdr SB. *Hector* was completed with 4-7in BL on the upper deck and 20-68pdr SB on the battery deck. *Hector* was rearmed in 1867/8 and *Valiant* was completed with the armament shown above, twelve 7in being mounted on the battery deck and the remainder on the upper deck.

These vessels were barque-rigged, and had a sail area of 24,500 sq ft. They rolled badly but manouvered well. Their sea-going service ended in 1885/6. *Hector* became part of the Vernon torpedo school in 1900 and was the first ship fitted with a wireless transmitter. *Valiant* was employed on harbour service, being renamed *Indus* in 1898, *Valiant (Old)* in 1916, and *Valiant III* in 1919. In 1924 she was converted into a floating oil tank.

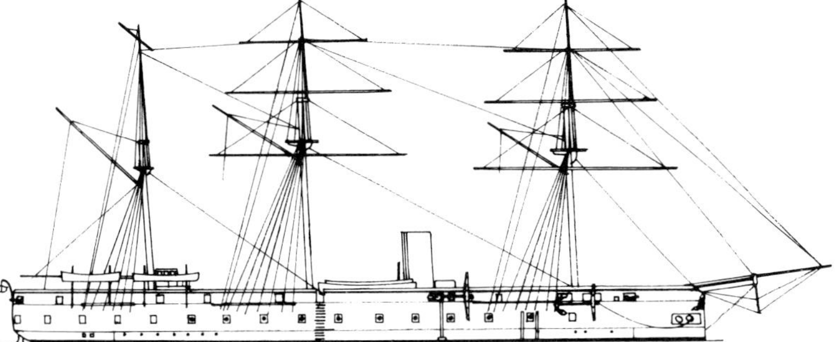

Hector as completed 1864

HECTOR class *broadside ironclads*

Displacement: 6710t load
Dimensions: 280ft 2in pp x 56ft 3in x 25ft (*85.39 pp x 17.14 x 7.62m*)
Machinery: 1-shaft, Maudslay HRCR, 6 boilers, 3260ihp = 12.65kts (*Valiant* 3560ihp = 12.36kts). Coal 450t
Armour: Belt 4½in, battery 4½in, bulkheads 2½in
Armament: 2-8in MLR, 16-7in MLR
Complement: 530

Name	Builder	Laid down	Launched	Comp	Fate
HECTOR	Napier, Glasgow	Mar 1861	26.9.62	22.2.64	Sold for BU 1905
VALIANT	Westwood & Baillie and Thames Iron Wks	Feb 1861	14.10.63	15.9.68	BU 1957

A modified version of *Warrior* with the same basic design and machinery and improved protection, *Achilles* had a 13ft deep waterline belt over her full length, 2½in beyond the battery. The battery armour was 212ft long, enclosed at the ends by 4½in bulkheads to the full depth of the side armour. The steering gear was fully protected, the rounded stern being designed to suit this purpose. The stem was of blunt ram form. She was one of the best early ironclads constructed. The hull was divided into 106 watertight compartments, 66 being in the wings and the double bottom. The boiler pressure was 25psi, compared with 20psi in earlier ironclads.

Armament as completed was 4-110pdr BL on the upper deck and 16-100pdr 'Somerset' SB at the middle ports of the battery; 6-68pdr SB were added at the end ports of the main battery in 1865. The ship was rearmed as shown in 1868, 4-7in being on the main deck and the remainder in the battery, and rearmed again in 1874 with 12-9in MLR in battery and 2-7in and 2-9in MLR on the upperdeck. During the refit of 1889 two 6in BL, eight 3pdr QF and 16MGs were added, the 7in MLR being removed.

Completed with a four-masted rig (bow, fore, main and mizzen masts) and 44,000 sq ft of canvas including stunsails, *Achilles* had the largest sail area ever provided in a British warship, and was the only British warship to have four masts. She had an unsatisfactory sail arrangement and the bow mast and bowsprit were removed in 1865, head sails being rigged to the stem. In 1866 the foremast was moved forward 25ft and the bowsprit was replaced. With this ship rig the sail area was 30,133 sq ft. The vessel was reduced to a barque rig in 1877.

Although difficult to handle because of her great length, she manoeuvred better than *Warrior* and steamed and sailed well under most conditions. Her sea-going service ended in 1885. She was renamed *Hibernia* (base ship) in 1902, *Egmont* in 1904, *Egremont* in 1918, and finally *Pembroke* in 1919.

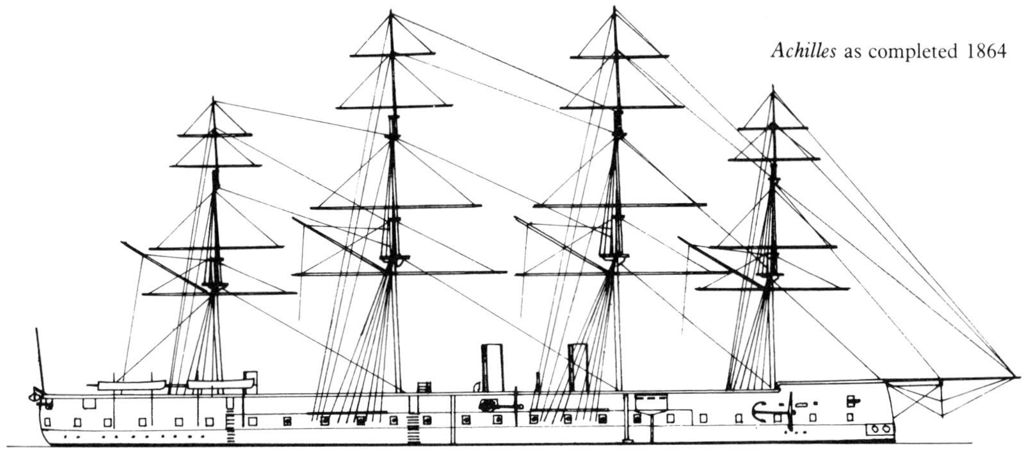

Achilles as completed 1864

ACHILLES *broadside ironclads*

Displacement: 9829t load
Dimensions: 380ft pp x 58ft 3¼in x 27ft 3in (*115.82 pp x 17.77 x 8.31m*)
Machinery: 1-shaft, Penn HSET, 10 rectangular boilers, 5720ihp = 14.32kts. Coal 1000t
Armour: Battery 4½in, belt 4½in with 18in wood backing, bulkheads 4½in
Armament: (1868) 22-7in MLR, 4-8in MLR
Complement: 709

Name	Builder	Laid down	Floated out	Comp	Fate
ACHILLES	Chatham DYd	1.8.1861	23.12.63	26.11.64	Sold for BU 1925

GREAT BRITAIN

These ships were designed as 50-gun armoured frigates with full length protection to the battery to avoid unprotected gun positions on the main deck. Basically, they were enlarged versions of *Achilles* with a ram-shaped bow, heavier armour and armament, and increased engine power to maintain high speed. These were the largest warships to be propelled by single screw.

In *Minotaur* and *Agincourt* the armour covered the entire side from the upper deck to 5ft 9in below the load line, except for the extreme forward end between the main and upper decks. A single 5½in bulkhead closed the forward end of the battery and extended to the top of the bulwarks to give protection to the chase guns on the forecastle.

Northumberland was modified for a heavier armament but fewer guns, enabling the battery to be shorter. The side armour between the main and upper deck was reduced to the length of the battery (184ft 6in) to compensate for the increased armament weight, and the ends were enclosed by 5½in bulkheads extending the full depth of the side armour. *Northumberland* was also provided with an armoured conning tower protected by 4½in thick plates.

Minotaur was actually completed in 1865 but spent 18 months testing experimental armaments and rigs before being commissioned. She originally carried a square rig on her first four masts and a spanker only on her fifth mast; however, this proved unsatisfactory and the yards were removed from the fourth mast. The other vessels were completed with this rig. *Northumberland* had a gaff on all five masts, but the others had no gaff on the second mast. The sail area was 32,377 sq ft. These were unhandy vessels and poor sailers, their best speed being 9-10kts, but they were good seaboats, being very steady, and they steamed well. Handling improved after the fitting of steam steering gear during the 1870s. *Northumberland* was completed with steam steering gear and was the first ship so fitted.

Minotaur was extensively refitted in 1873/75, when her armament was altered to 17-9in MLR and 2-20pdr BL. She was reboilered, a new propeller and steam steering were fitted and she became the first ship in the Royal Navy to carry a searchlight. On post-refit trials she made 14.07kts with 6288ihp. *Agincourt* was similarly refitted in 1875/77. *Northumberland* was rearmed in 1875/79 with 7-9in MLR, 20-8in MLR, 2-20pdr BL and 4 Whitehead torpedo launchers; she also had her second and fourth masts removed and she was re-rigged as a barque. *Minotaur* and *Agincourt* had two 9in MLR replaced by two 6in BL in the early 1880s, and four 4.7in BL, eight 3pdr QF, eight MGs and two torpedo tubes were added in 1891/2. *Northumberland* had two 8in ML replaced by one 5in BL and one 6in BL during her 1885/87 refit; later six 4.7in BL, ten 3pdr QF and six MGs were added.

Minotaur was converted to TS and renamed *Boscawen* in 1904, *Ganges* in 1906 and *Ganges II* in 1908. *Agincourt* was converted to TS, renamed *Boscawen III* in 1904 and *Ganges II* in 1906, and was converted to coal hulk *C109* in 1908. *Northumberland* became TS *Acheron* in 1904 and was converted to coal hulk 'C' in 1909, being re-named *C68* in 1926.

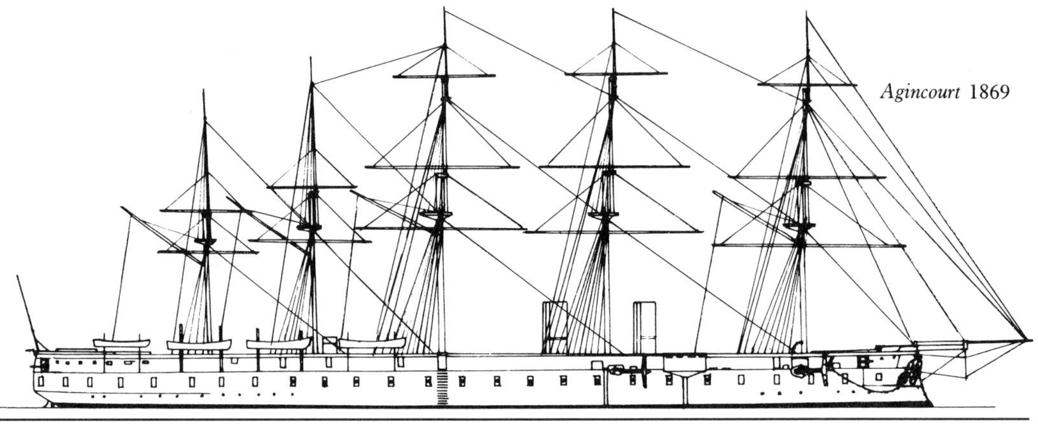

Agincourt 1869

MINOTAUR class *broadside ironclads*

Displacement: 10,600t (*Agincourt*); 10,690t (*Minotaur*); 10,784t (*Northumberland*), load
Dimensions: 400ft 3in pp, 407ft oa x 59ft 6in x 27ft 9in, (*122.0 pp, 124.0 oa x 18.14 x 8.46m*)
Machinery: 1-shaft, Penn 2 cyl HT (*Agincourt* Maudslay return connecting rod engine), 10 rectangular boilers, 6700ihp = 14.32kts *Minotaur*; 6867ihp = 14.8kts *Agincourt*; 6545ihp = 14.13kts *Northumberland*
Armour: Belt and battery 5½in amidships and 4½in at ends with 10in wood backing, bulkhead 5½in
Armament: 4-9in MLR, 24-7in MLR, 8-24pdr SB (*Northumberland* 4-9in MLR, 22-8in MLR, 2-7in MLR)
Complement: 800

Name	Builder	Laid down	Launched	Comp	Fate
MINOTAUR (ex-ELEPHANT, 1861)	Thames Iron Wks Blackwall	12.9.1861	12.12.63	19.12.68	Sold for 1922
AGINCOURT (ex CAPTAIN, 1861)	Lairds, Birkenhead	30.10.1861	27.3.65	1.6.67	Sold for BU 1960
NORTHUMBERLAND	Millwall Iron Wks, Millwall	10.10.1861	17.4.66	8.10.68	Sold 1927. Became hulk *Stedmound*

These vessels were laid down as 91-gun Second Rates, their conversion to ironclad frigates being approved in 1861. They were half sisters to *Royal Oak* and had a similar conversion except for the provision of increased machinery power to secure greater speed. They were unsuccessful because the extra weight of the machinery cancelled the advantages of the extra hp; they were in fact slower than *Royal Oak*. The completion of *Caledonia* was delayed by the late arrival of her armament.

Prince Consort was completed with 7-7in BLR, 8-100pdr SB, and 16-68pdr SB. *Caledonia* was completed with 10-7in BLR, 8-100pdr SB, and 12-68pdr SB. *Ocean* was completed with 24-7in MLR. In 1867 *Ocean* had four 8in MLR fitted in place of four of her 7in MLR, and her two sisters were rearmed to the same standard. *Prince Consort* was again rearmed in 1871 with 7-9in MLR and 8-8in MLR.

These vessels were barque-rigged on completion and were converted to ship rig in 1866. They did not sail well compared with *Royal Oak* but could make 10-12kts. They rolled excessively because of their high level of stability but handled well under sail and steam.

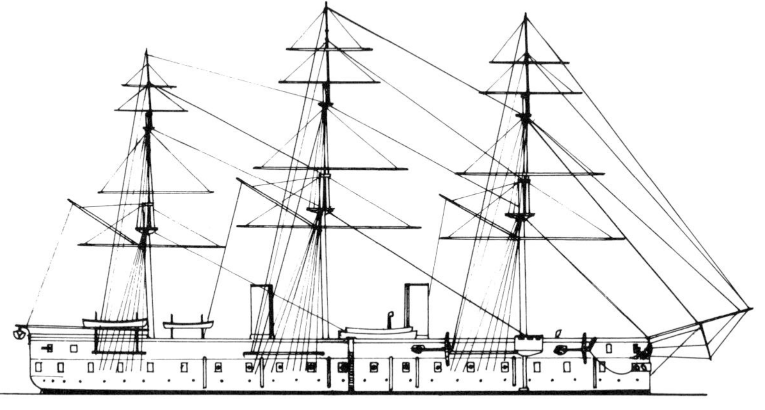

Ocean 1868

PRINCE CONSORT class *wooden broadside ironclads*

Displacement: 6832t (Navy List)
Dimensions: 273ft pp x 58ft 6in x 24ft (*83.21 pp x 17.83 x 7.31m*)
Machinery: 1-shaft, Maudslay HRCR, 8 rectangular boilers, 1000nhp = 12.5kts (*Caledonia* 12.9kts, *Ocean* 12.5kts)
Armour: Belt and battery 4½in amidships, 3in forward and aft
Armament: (1867) 4-8in MLR, 20-7in MLR
Complement: 605

Name	Builder	Laid down	Launched	Comp	Fate
PRINCE CONSORT (ex-TRIUMPH, 1862)	Pembroke DYd	1860	26.6.62	April 1864	Sold for BU 1882
CALEDONIA	Woolwich DYd	1860	24.10.62	July 1865	Sold for BU 1886
OCEAN	Devonport DYd	23.8.1860	19.3.62	July 1865	Sold for BU 1882

Above: *Minotaur* in the 1890s

Right: The *Royal Oak* prior to the addition of yards on the mizzen in 1866. Her funnel is lowered and she has windsails rigged for ventilation

ROYAL OAK *wooden broadside ironclad*

Displacement: 6366t load
Dimensions: 273ft pp x 58ft 3in x 24ft (*83.21 pp x 17.75 x 7.31m*)
Machinery: 1-shaft Maudslay HRCR, 6 rectangular boilers, 3000ihp = 12.5kts. Coal 550t
Armour: 4½in battery, 4½in belt
Armament: (1867) 4-8in MLR, 20-7in MLR
Complement: 585

Name	Builder	Laid down	Launched	Comp	Fate
ROYAL OAK	Chatham DYd	1860	10.9.62	April 1863	Laid up 1871, sold 1885

This vessel was the first British wooden-hulled ironclad, and was laid down as a 91-gun ship of the line. Her conversion to a 36-gun ironclad frigate was approved in 1861. She was razed by one deck and lengthened on the stocks by 21ft to accommodate new armament on one deck, the original bow and stern being modified to ironclad form with a straight stem and a rounded stern. The side armour was extended to the full length of the ship, being 4½in amidships and 2½in at the ends. The hull behind the armour was of 28in thick oak.

Designed for 36-68pdr SB, she completed with eight 7in BLR and 24 68pdr SB on the main deck and three 7in BLR on the upper deck. She was rearmed in 1867, four 7in MLR being on the upper deck with the remainder in the battery.

As completed she was barque-rigged with a sail area of 25,000 sq ft. She was converted to ship rig in 1866. In 1864 she made 13.5kts under sail, which is a record for an ironclad. She rolled heavily but otherwise sailed and handled well. A topgallant forecastle was added during her 1867 refit.

ROYAL ALFRED *wooden central battery ironclad*

Displacement: 6707t load
Dimensions: 273ft pp x 58ft 6in x 25ft 5in (*283.21 pp x 17.83 x 7.75m*)
Machinery: 1-shaft, Maudslay HRCR, 6 rectangular boilers, 3230ihp = 12.36kts
Armour: Belt and battery 6in, bulkheads 4½in
Armament: 10-9in MLR, 8-7in MLR
Complement: 605

Name	Builder	Laid down	Launched	Comp	Fate
ROYAL ALFRED	Portsmouth DYd	1.12.1859	15.10.64	23.3.67	Sold for BU 1885

Royal Alfred was laid down as a 90-gun two-decker and approved for conversion to an ironclad frigate in June 1861. She was lengthened on the stocks prior to the decision to hold up her conversion pending the results obtained from *Royal Oak* and the *Prince Consort* class. Finally, it was decided to adopt a box battery and heavy guns and armour as provided for *Bellerophon*. The full length belt was 6in amidships and 4in at the ends and extended from the main deck to 5ft 6in below the waterline. Between the main and upper deck 6in armour was provided over the length of the central battery (115ft), with 4½in at the extreme bow and stern to protect the main deck chase guns.

9in guns were mounted in the battery and two 7in guns were mounted at each end of the main deck behind armour, and on the upper deck unprotected.

She was ship-rigged, with a sail area of 29,200 sq ft. She was equally as fast under sail or steam, and handled well, being a good seaboat apart from a heavy roll. Her sea-going service ended in 1874.

This was Britain's first small ironclad and first box battery ship. *Research* was laid down as a 17-gun wooden screw sloop of the *Perseus* class, and her conversion to an ironclad sloop was approved in 1862. She was lengthened by 10ft, had her beam increased by 5½ft, and was given a ram bow and a rounded stern. Her displacement was increased by 500t, of which 352t was armour. She had a full length waterline belt 10ft deep with a central armoured box battery 34ft long extending from the belt to the top of the bulwarks. The guns were provided with limited fore and aft fire through ports cut in the armoured bulkheads, embrasures being provided in the wooded sides fore and aft of the battery.

RESEARCH *wooden central battery ironclad sloop*

Displacement: 1743t load, 1900t full load
Dimensions: 195ft pp x 38ft 7in x 14ft 6in (*59.44 pp x 11.76 x 4.42m*)
Machinery: 1-shaft, Watt 2 cyl HDA, 2 tubular boilers, 1040ihp = 10.3kts
Armour: Belt, battery and bulkheads 4½in, backing 19½in wood
Armament: 4-100pdr 'Somerset' SB
Complement: 150

Name	Builder	Laid down	Launched	Comp	Fate
RESEARCH (ex-TRENT, 1862)	Pembroke DYd	3.9.1861	15.8.63	6.4.64	Reserve 1878. Sold for BU 1884

She had a barque rig with a sail area of 18,250 sq ft. Her best speed under sail was 6kts, but she once made 11.5kts with combined steam and sail. She handled well except in heavy weather, being a poor seaboat and a heavy roller.

Research was refitted in 1869/70, the 100pdr SBs being replaced by four 7in MLRs. A spar deck was also fitted, and her funnel was moved forward so as to rise outside instead of inside the box battery, in order to provide more space in the latter which was cramped.

This vessel was laid down as a wooden screw sloop and redesigned as an ironclad sloop before much progress had been made on her construction. The conversion was of the same general type as that applied to *Research*, but with a narrower waterline belt and the guns mounted at upper instead of main deck level. Much effort was directed towards weight saving, and the upper part of the hull was constructed of iron, making her the first vessel of composite construction. The bulwarks fore and aft of the box battery could be hinged back when the guns were in position for end on fire. Her rig was identical to *Research's*. The funnel was moved from the centre of the battery to forward of it in 1864. She was rearmed with 4-7in MLR in 1868.

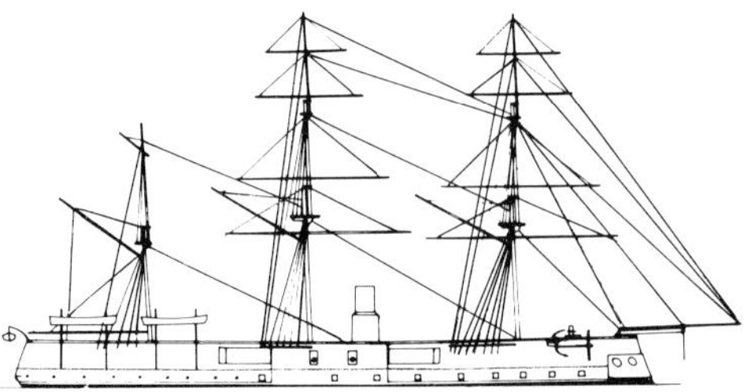

Enterprise as completed 1864

ENTERPRISE *composite central battery ironclad sloop*

Displacement: 1350t load
Dimensions: 180ft pp x 36ft x 13ft 9in (*54.86 pp x 10.97 x 4.19m*)
Machinery: 1-shaft, Ravenhill 2 cyl HDA, 2 tubular boilers, 690ihp=9.9kts
Armour: Belt, battery and bulkheads 4½in, backing 19½in wood
Armament: 2-100pdr SB, 2-110pdr BL
Complement: 130

Name	Builder	Laid down	Launched	Comp	Fate
ENTERPRISE (ex-CIRCASSIAN, 1862)	Deptford DYd	5.5.1862	9.2.64	3.6.64	Reserve 1871. Sold for BU 1886

Favorite as completed 1866

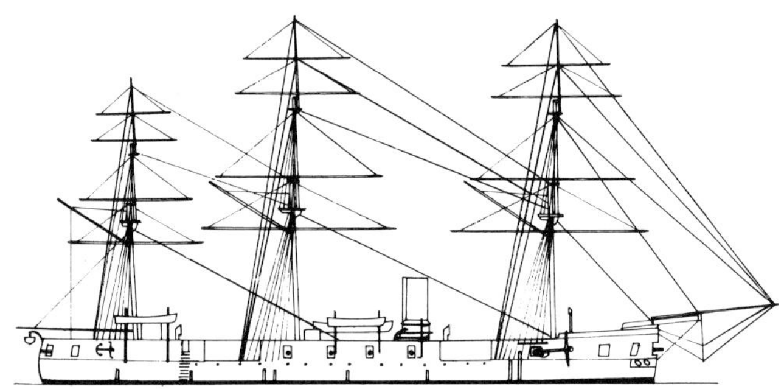

Favorite in 1869

Laid down as a wooden screw corvette, *Favorite's* construction was well advanced when she was approved for conversion to an ironclad corvette. She was modified to have a straight stem, a rounded stern and a full length waterline belt from the upper deck to 3 ft below the waterline. The box battery was 66ft long on the upper deck, with hinged bulwarks fore and aft to give ahead and astern fire as in *Enterprise*. The ship was rearmed in 1869 with 8-7in MLR in the battery and a 64pdr at the forward and after ends of the upper deck as chase guns.

Favorite was ship-rigged, with a sail area of 18,250 sq ft. She could make 10½kts under sail, and was a good seaboat but rolled heavily.

FAVORITE *wooden central battery ironclad corvette*

Displacement: 3232t load
Dimensions: 225ft pp x 46ft 11in x 21ft 6in (*68.58 pp x 14.3 x 6.55m*)
Machinery: 1-shaft, Humphreys & Tennant 2 cyl DA, 4 boilers, 1770ihp = 11.8kts
Armour: Belt 4½in with 26in wood backing, 4½in battery with 19in wood backing, bulkheads 4½in
Armament: 8-100pdr SB
Complement: 250

Name	Builder	Laid down	Launched	Comp	Fate
FAVORITE	Deptford DYd	23.8.1860	5.7.64	17.3.66	Reserve 1876. Sold for BU 1886

Right:
The *Zealous* with funnel lowered. She remained virtually unaltered throughout her career

Zealous was laid down as a 90-gun two-decker and approved for conversion to an ironclad in 1861. The conversion was held up pending results with *Royal Oak* and the *Prince Consort* class. She was not lengthened because it was discovered that earlier vessels were lacking in longitudinal strength. She had a full length waterline belt 4½in amidships and 2½in at the ends, from the main deck to 6ft below waterline. The central battery between the main and upper decks was 103ft long, containing 16-7in MLR. The remaining guns were equally distributed at the fore and aft ends of the upper deck. The areas beyond the armour were unprotected wood.

She was ship-rigged, and had a sail area of 29,200 sq ft. She was handy under both sail and steam and was a good seaboat. During her short seagoing career in the Pacific she operated almost entirely under sail. She returned home to become a guardship at Southampton in 1873.

ZEALOUS *wooden central battery ironclad*

Displacement: 6096t load
Dimensions: 252ft pp x 58ft 6in x 25ft 5in (*76.81 pp x 17.83 x 7.75m*)
Machinery: 1-shaft, Maudslay HRCR, 6 rectangular boilers, 3623ihp = 11.7kts
Armour: Belt and battery 4½in, bulkheads 3in
Armament: 20-7in MLR
Complement: 510

Name	Builder	Laid down	Launched	Comp	Fate
ZEALOUS	Pembroke DYd	24.10.1859	7.3.64	4.10.66	Laid up 1875. Sold for BU 1886

This was the last wooden capital ship constructed for the Royal Navy. She was laid down as a 90-gun two decker and approved for ironclad conversion in 1861 but was held up until 1866 pending the results from earlier conversions. She was similar to *Zealous* but with a shorter (70ft) box battery and heavier guns and armour. The belt was 6in amidships and 4½in at the ends. Eight 8in MLRs were placed in the battery, and the remainder were equaly disposed at the forward and aft ends of the upper deck. She had a straight stem with a light knee head. Woolwich DYd closed shortly after her launch and she was towed to Sheerness for completion.

REPULSE *wooden central battery ironclad*

Displacement: 6190t load
Dimensions: 252ft pp x 59ft x 24ft (*76.81 pp x 17.98 x 7.31m*)
Machinery: 1-shaft, Penn HT, 6 rectangular boilers, 3350ihp = 12.5kts
Armour: Belt and battery 6in, bulkheads 4½in
Armament: 12-8in MLR
Complement: 515

Name	Builder	Laid down	Launched	Comp	Fate
REPULSE	Woolwich & Sheerness DYd	29.4.1859	25.4.68	31.1.70	Reserve 1885. Sold for BU 1889

She was ship-rigged, and the sail area was 29,200 sq ft. Being a good, steady and handy seaboat she handled well under both sail and steam.

Repulse was refitted in 1877/80 with 4-16in torpedo carriages (12 torpedoes), and a net defence. She became a guardship in 1881.

The *Lord Clyde* class were purpose-built, wooden-hulled, ironclad frigates, and the last of the broadside ships. Construction was approved in 1863. *Lord Warden* was the heaviest wooden ship ever built. The ships were based on the design of *Bellerophon* with dimensions modified to suit a wooden hull and the battery armour extended the full length of the ship. The wooden hull had a 1½in iron skin and a waterline belt sheathed with 4in oak, and it was divided by iron bulkheads and strengthened by iron in some sections. *Lord Warden*, like *Bellerophon*, had a clipper/ram bow, whilst *Lord Clyde* had a standard ram bow.

Lord Clyde completed with 24-7in MLR, 23 being on the main deck (20 amidships, 2 forward and 1 aft) and one at the forward end of the upper deck protected by a 4½in semi-circular bulwark. This vessel rearmed in 1869/70 with 10-8in MLRs on the main deck in alternate ports, 1-8in MLR on each side on the upper deck, 2-7in MLRs at the forward end of the main deck, 1-9in MLR at the aft end of the main deck and 1-9in MLR behind the armoured bulwark at the forward end of the upper deck. *Lord Warden* was completed with this armament.

These vessels were ship rigged, the sail area being 31,000 sq ft. They were handy under sail but rolled heavily. They were also good steam vessels but *Lord Clyde's* engines deteriorated quickly and she was re-engined in 1869/70. In 1872 *Lord Clyde* was found to have rotten hull timbers; attempts to correct this were lengthy and unsuccessful and she was sold out of service early.

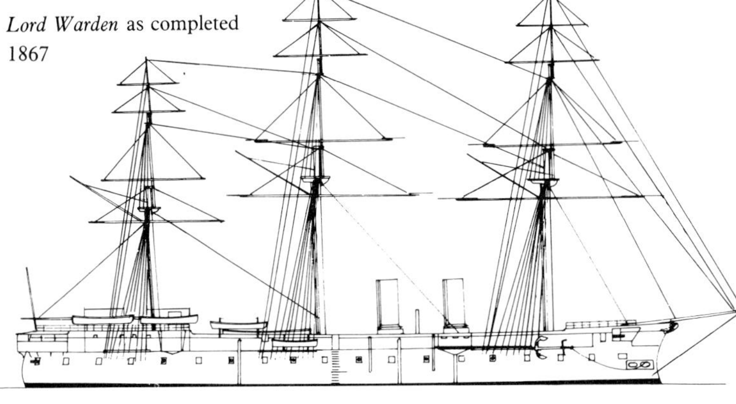
Lord Warden as completed 1867

LORD CLYDE class *wooden broadside ironclad*

Displacement: 7750t load *Lord Clyde*; 7842 load *Lord Warden*
Dimensions: 280ft pp x 59ft x 26ft (*85.34 pp x 17.98 x 7.92m*)
Machinery: 1-shaft, Ravenhill 2 cyl HT (*Lord Warden* Maudslay 3 cyl RCR), 9 rectangular boilers, 6064ihp = 13.4kts (*Lord Warden* 6700ihp = 13.5kts)
Armour: Belt and battery 5½in amidships, 4½in ends with 6in wood backing, CT 4½in
Armament: 2-9in MLR, 14-8in MLR, 2-7in MLR, 2-20pdr BL
Complement: 605

Name	Builder	Laid down	Launched	Comp	Fate
LORD CLYDE	Pembroke DYd	29.9.1863	13.10.64	2.6.66	Sold for BU 1875
LORD WARDEN	Chatham DYd	24.12.1863	27.3.65	30.8.67	BU 1889

A purpose built wooden-hulled ironclad corvette designed as a private venture by Reed and accepted by the Admiralty in 1863, *Pallas* was originally intended as an iron vessel but was modified to have a wooden hull in order to use existing stocks of timber and because Woolwich DYd was not equipped to construct iron hulls. The arrangement of the box battery and belt with embrasures for fore and aft fire was similar to *Research*. The belt from 4½ft below the waterline to the main deck extended at the extreme forward end to the upper deck level to protect the bow guns.

She was intended to serve as a ram, having an extended and strengthened stem below water, a high designed speed of 14kts and a low length to beam ratio (4.5:1) for manoeuvrability. This was the first warship fitted with compound steam engines (2 x hp, 2 x lp, cyl) but she was a successful steamer. She made 12.5kts on trials and 13kts after modifications to her bow and trim.

Pallas was ship-rigged, and had a sail area of 16,716 sq ft. She was a stiff ship with a deep roll, and handled well.

All guns were on the main deck, the 7in MLRs in the box battery and the 7in BLs at the forward and aft ends as chase guns. The 7in MLRs were replaced by 8in MLRs and two 5in BLs were added on the upper deck in 1866. The BL guns were replaced by four 6in MLRs during the 1870/72 refit. A CT was added during the same refit.

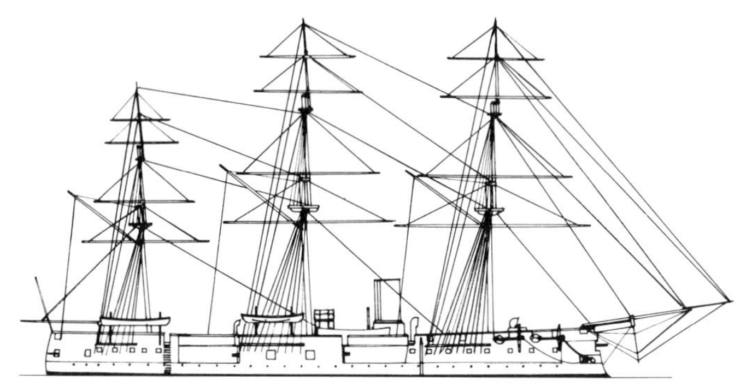

Pallas 1867

PALLAS *wooden central battery ironclad corvette*

Displacement: 3661t laod, 3794t full load
Dimensions: 225ft pp x 50ft x 21 ft 8in (*68.58 pp x 15.24 x 6.6m*)
Machinery: 1-shaft, Humphreys & Tennant HC, 4 rectangular boilers, 3580ihp = 12.5kts
Armour: Belt, battery and bulkheads 4½in with 22in wood backing
Armament: 4-7in MLR, 2-7in BL
Complement: 253

Name	Builder	Laid down	Launched	Comp	Fate
PALLAS	Woolwich DYd	19.10.1863	14.3.65	6.3.66	Sold for BU 1886

Bellerophon represented a major step forward in ironclad design, having increased engine power, protection and armament together with improved hull design, manoeuvrability and seaworthiness. The full length belt from the main deck to 6ft below the waterline was 6in amidships, reducing to 5in before and abaft the battery, 3in at the extreme bow and 4½in at extreme stern. The box battery on the main deck had 6in sides and 5in bulkheads. Chase guns at the forward end of the main deck were protected by 4½in armour around the bow. The hull was constructed on the 'bracket frame' system with a complete double bottom for the first time, resulting in a substantial saving in weight. Some 200-300t of steel was also employed in the hull structure to save weight. The hull form was fuller than in earlier ships, with greater buoyancy forward and aft. She was completed with an ordinary ram bow, but was very wet forward and a knee head was added to give a clipper/ram form.

High power machinery was provided to secure 14kts with a short hull of full form. She handled well under steam, partly because she was the first ship in the Royal Navy equipped with a balanced rudder. She was ship-rigged, her sail area being 23,800 sq ft. She did not handle well under sail.

The 9in MLRs were fitted in the central battery with two 7in MLRs at the forward and after ends of the main deck and one 7in on the aft end of the upper deck.

Bellerophon was refitted and rearmed in 1881-84, the original guns being removed and 10-8in BLs fitted in the central battery, four 6in BLs added on the upper deck, two forward and two aft, and six 4in BLs 4-6pdr QF and 12 MGs mounted on the upperworks. Two launching carriages for 16in Whitehead torpedoes were also fitted on the main deck. She was re-boilered, had steam steering gear fitted and was converted to barque rig. The conversion to new armament was not successful and no other early ironclad was similarly rearmed.

Her sea-going service ended in 1892, when she became a port guardship until 1903. She was converted to TS in 1904 and renamed *Indus III*.

Bellerophon as completed 1866

BELLEROPHON *central battery ironclad*

Displacement: 7551t load
Dimensions: 300ft pp x 56ft 1in x 24ft 8in (*91.44 pp x 17.09 x 7.52m*)
Machinery: 1-shaft, Penn 2 cyl HT, 8 rectangular boilers, 6521ihp = 14.17kts
Armour: Belt and battery 6in with 10in wood backing, bulkheads 5in, CT 8in
Armament: 10-9in MLR, 5-7in MLR
Complement: 650

Name	Builder	Laid down	Launched	Comp	Fate
BELLEROPHON	Chatham DYd	23.12.1863	26.5.65	11.4.66	Sold for BU 1922

Bellerophon as built

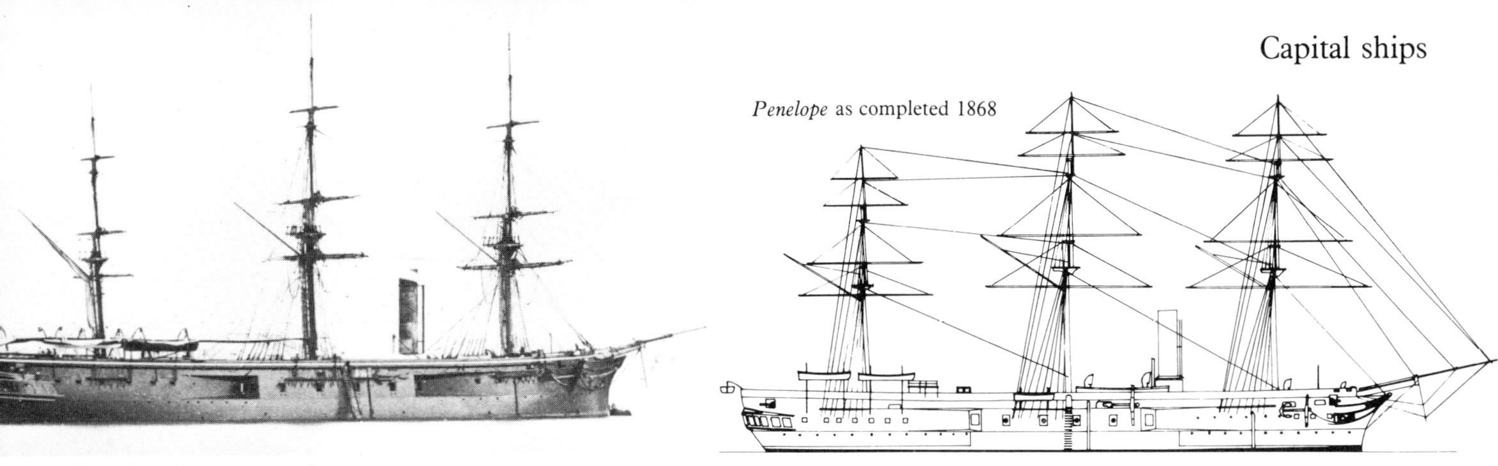

Penelope prior to her 1887-88 refit

PENELOPE *central battery armoured corvette*

Displacement: 4470t load
Dimensions: 260ft pp x 50ft x 16ft 9in (*79.25 pp x 15.24 x 5.10m*)
Machinery: 2-shaft, Maudslay 3 cyl HRCR, 4 boilers, 4763ihp = 12.76kts
Armour: Belt 6in with 10in-11in wood backing, battery 6in, bulkheads 4½in
Armament: 8-8in MLR, 3-5in BLR, 2-20pdr BLR
Complement: 350

Name	Builder	Laid down	Launched	Comp	Fate
PENELOPE	Pembroke DYd	4.9.1865	18.6.67	27.6.68	Sold for BU 1912

Penelope, the last of the small ironclads, was classified as an armoured corvette. She was a shallow draught vessel, this effect being obtained by providing a very square and full hull form. This necessitated twin screws as a single screw would have had insufficient immersion. The space between the shafts was cut away to give two sections of 'deadwood', both screws were of the lifting type, and twin rudders were also provided.

She had limited protection, with a narrow (5ft 6in) waterline belt 6in amidships and 5in at the ends from the lower deck to 4ft below the waterline. The central battery was at main deck level, being 68ft long with 6in sides and 4½in bulkheads. Between the belt and battery a strake of 6in armour, 96ft long, was placed, which was also closed by 4½in bulkheads.

The 8in MLRs were mounted in the central battery, and the corners of the battery were angled and the ship's sides embrasured to provide for fire before and abaft the beam. Two of the 5in guns were mounted forward and one was mounted aft on the upper deck. *Penelope* was refitted in 1887/8, when the 5in guns were removed and four QF and 11 MGs added.

She was ship-rigged, and had a sail area of 18,250 sq ft. She did not sail well as she tended to drift to leeward because of the shallow draught. She was, however, a steady ship and a good gun platform. Her best speed was 8.5kts.

She took part in the bombardment of Alexandria, and fired 231 projectiles, receiving only slight damage. She became a prison hulk at the Cape in 1897.

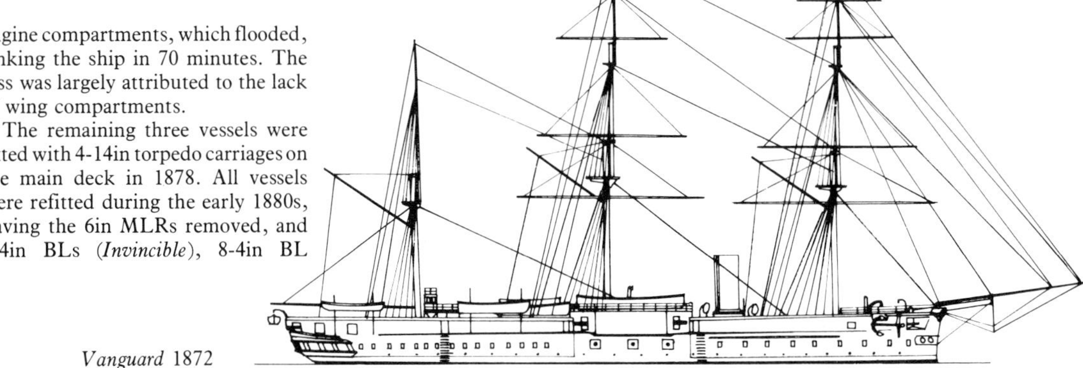
Vanguard 1872

AUDACIOUS class *central battery ironclads*

Displacement: 5909t light, 6010t load
Dimensions: 280ft pp x 54ft x 22ft 7in (*85.34 pp x 16.46 x 6.88m*)
Machinery: 2-shaft, 2-2 cyl HRCR, 6 rectangualr boilers, 4020ihp =13.2kts (*Audacious*); 4830ihp = 14.09kts (*Invincible*); 4270ihp = 13.64kts (*Iron Duke*); –ihp = 14.5kts (*Vanguard*)
Armour: Belt 8-6in with 10in-8in wood backing, battery 6in bulkheads 5in
Armament: 10-9in MLR, 4-6in MLR, 6-20pdr BL saluting
Complement: 450

Name	Builder	Laid down	Launched	Comp	Fate
AUDACIOUS	Napier, Glasgow	26.6.1867	27.2.69	10.9.70	Sold for BU 1922
INVINCIBLE	Napier, Glasgow	28.6.1867	29.5.69	1.10.70	Foundered in tow off Portland 17.9.14
IRON DUKE	Pembroke DYd	23.8.1868	1.3.70	21.1.71	Sold for BU 1906
VANGUARD	Laird, Birkenhead	21.10.1867	3.1.70	28.9.70	Sunk in collision with *Iron Duke* 1.9.75

Provided under the 1867 estimates, these second class ironclads were designed for service on foreign stations. Construction was based on the design of *Defence* but with a more modern layout and shallow draught. The two-storey box battery was adopted and reductions were made in hull weight to secure a lower level of stability for a steady gun platform. They were rather too successful as ballast – about 350t – had to be added to improve stability – but they did prove exceptionally steady ships with almost no roll.

They had a narrow 8ft waterline belt 8in amidships and 6in at the ends. The central battery on the main deck was 59ft long with 6in sides, 5in forward and 4in aft bulkheads. The upper battery on the upper deck had 6in armoured sides and corners only. The main battery carried 6-9in MLRs firing through broadside ports, and the upper battery 4-9in MLRs which gave ahead and astern fire through corner ports. The 6in MLRs were mounted at the extreme forward and aft ends of the upper deck.

These vessels were ship-rigged on completion but were converted to barque-rig in about 1871, with a sail area of 23,700 sq ft. They were very steady and good seaboats but slow under sail. The machinery of *Invincible* and *Vanguard* was made by the builders, and the machinery in the other ships by Ravenhill. *Vanguard* was equipped with half ordinary boilers and half water tube boilers. All except *Iron Duke* were fitted with balanced rudders.

Vanguard sank in 1875 after being accidentally rammed by *Iron Duke* during fog in Dublin Bay. She was rammed between the boiler and engine compartments, which flooded, sinking the ship in 70 minutes. The loss was largely attributed to the lack of wing compartments.

The remaining three vessels were fitted with 4-14in torpedo carriages on the main deck in 1878. All vessels were refitted during the early 1880s, having the 6in MLRs removed, and 6-4in BLs (*Invincible*), 8-4in BL (*Audacious*), 4-5in BL (*Iron Duke*), 4-6pdr QF and 6-3pdr (*Audacious* only) added on the upper deck and upper works generally. *Audacious* was also given a military rig, having most of her yards removed, light topmasts fitted and fighting tops fitted on the fore and main masts. *Iron Duke* was re-engined and re-boilered.

Invincible took part in the bombardment of Alexandria in 1882. During her harbour service she was renamed *Erebus* in 1904, and *Fisgard II* in 1906. *Audacious* was relegated to harbour service in 1902, and renamed *Fisgard* in 1904 and *Imperieuse* in 1914. *Iron Duke* became a coal hulk in 1900.

GREAT BRITAIN

This ship was an improved *Hercules* with the addition of a second armoured battery on the upper deck and the omission of the after embrasure for the main battery. The belt was 9in amidships reducing to 8in and 6in fore and aft. The main battery sides were 9in closed by 6in forward and 5in aft bulkheads. The upper battery had 8in sides with 4½in bulkheads. All the 8in MLRs were mounted in the main battery, and one 9in MLR was on each side upper battery with alternative broadside or astern firing ports. The remaining pair of 9in MLRs were mounted at the forward end of the upper deck and were protected by an athwartships armour bulkhead.

As in *Audacious*, steadiness was one of the requirements aimed at but stability was too low and 600t of ballast was added.

Sultan was ship-rigged, and the sail area of 34,100 sq ft was exclusive of the 15,300 sq ft of stunsails. She was re-rigged as a barque in 1876. She was slow under sail but was a good gun platform with a slow roll.

The ship was refitted in 1879, 7-4in BLs and 4-6pdr QFs being added and 4-14in torpedo carriages fitted on the main deck. She was also equipped to carry two torpedo boats. Two searchlights were fitted, her ventilation was improved and she was reboilered. On post-refit trials she made 15kts at 7736ihp.

She took part in the bombardment of Alexandria in 1882. She grounded and sank on an uncharted rock in South Comino channel, Malta, on 6.3.89, but was salvaged, repaired in Malta and returned to England, where she was reconstructed at Portsmouth during 1893/96. The 4in guns were removed and four 4.7in QFs were added. At the same time she was re-engined and re-boilered, new funnels and two military masts were added, an enlarged bridge structure was placed forward of the funnels, a torpedo net defence was fitted, and 9in thick wood girdling was added around the waterline to increase stability. On post-refit trials she made 14.6kts at 6531ihp.

She was relegated to harbour service and renamed *Fisgard IV* from 1906 until 1931 when her name reverted to *Sultan*.

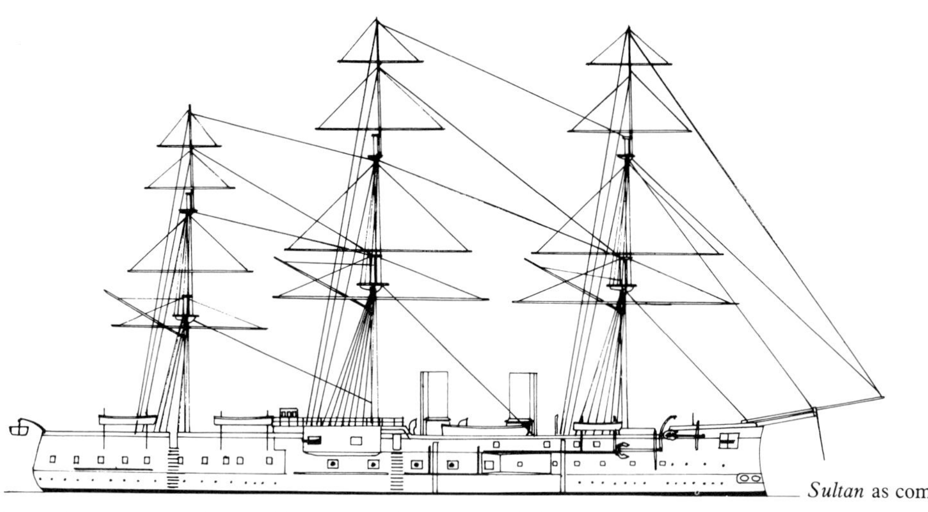

Sultan as completed 1871

SULTAN *central battery ironclad*

Displacement: 9290t load, 9540t full load
Dimensions: 325ft pp x 59ft x 26ft 5in (*99.06 pp x 17.98 x 8.05m*)
Machinery: 1-shaft, Penn 2 cyl HT, 7720ihp = 14.13kts
Armour: Belt 9in-6in with 10on-12in wood backing, main battery 9in, upper battery 8in, bulkheads 6in-4½in
Armament: 8-10in MLR, 4-9in MLR, 7-20pdr BL saluting
Complement: 633

Name	Builder	Laid down	Launched	Comp	Fate
SULTAN	Chatham DYd	29.2.1868	31.5.70	10.10.71	Sold for BU 1946

Sultan after her 1893-96 reconstruction

Swiftsure after conversion to barque rig

This was a modified *Audacious* class with a deeper draught, a single screw and a higher level of stability, designed for service in the Pacific where good sailing and steaming qualities were required. The armour, guns and general layout were identical to *Audacious*. These were the first British capital ships to be sheathed in wood and copper following the discovery that iron hulls fouled more quickly than wood.

The vessels were ship-rigged, with a sail area of 32,900 sq ft, excluding the 9000 sq ft stunsails. They were good, fast, handy and steady sailers, and were the last ships fitted with lifting screws.

Swiftsure was refitted in 1879/81 at Devonport, and was re-rigged as a barque with 22,750 sq ft of sail. Four torpedo launching carriages were added on the main deck, the 6in MLRs were removed, and 8-4in BLs, 4-6pdr QFs and 4-3pdr QFs were added. She was reboilered in 1886. *Triumph* refitted in 1882/84 at Portsmouth, as *Swiftsure* except that 4-5in BL, 8-6pdr QF and 8-3pdr QF guns were added.

Swiftsure was hulked in 1901, and renamed *Orontes* in 1904. *Triumph* was relegated to harbour service in 1900 and renamed *Tenedos* in 1904, *Indus IV* in 1912, and *Algiers* in 1914.

SWIFTSURE class *central battery ironclads*

Displacement: 6910t load *Swiftsure*; 6640t load *Triumph*
Dimensions: 280ft pp x 55ft x 25ft (*85.34 pp x 16.76 x 7.62m*)
Machinery: 1-shaft, Maudslay 2 cyl HRCR, 6 rectangular boilers, 4910ihp = 13.75kts (*Triumph* 4890ihp = 14.07kts)
Armour: Belt 8in-6in with 8in-10in wood backing, battery 6in, bulkheads 5in-4in
Armament: 10-9in MLR, 4-6in MLR, 6-20pdr BL saluting
Complement: 450

Name	Builder	Laid down	Launched	Comp	Fate
SWIFTSURE	Palmers, Jarrow	31.8.1868	15.6.70	27.6.72	Sold for BU 1908
TRIUMPH	Palmers, Jarrow	31.8.1868	27.9.70	8.4.73	Sold for BU 1921

Hercules as completed

HERCULES *central battery ironclad*

Displacement: 8677t load; 8830t full load
Dimensions: 325ft pp x 59ft 0½in x 25ft 4in (*99.06 pp x 18.00 x 7.72m*)
Machinery: 1-shaft, Penn 2 cyl, HT, 9 rectangular boilers, 7178ihp = 14.69kts
Armour: Belt 9in-6in with 10in-20in wood backing, bulkheads 6in-5in, battery 8in-6in
Armament: 8-10in MLR, 2-9in MLR, 4-7in MLR
Complement: 638

Name	Builder	Laid down	Launched	Comp	Fate
HERCULES	Chatham DYd	1.2.1866	10.2.68	21.11.68	Sold for BU 1932

An enlarged version of *Bellerophon*, with heavier guns and armour, improved hull form and embrasures fore and aft of the battery for end on fire, *Hercules* was provided with a narrow waterline strake of 9in armour, 73ft 9in long, reducing to 6in forward and aft. The upper and lower sections of the belt had a uniform 6in thickness from bow to stern. The box battery sides had an 8in lower strake and 6in upper strakes closed at the ends by a 6in bulkhead forward and a 5in bulkhead aft. The 10in MLRs were mounted in the battery, the 9in at each end of the main deck, protected by 6in armour, and the 7in at each end of the upper deck.

The machinery was designed for a speed of 14kts with 6750ihp and a boiler pressure of 30psi. She was ship rigged with a large sail area of 49,400 sq ft, including stunsails, but she was not a good sailer, the best recorded speed being 11kts. She was a good seaboat and a steady gun platform, but was difficult to handle in heavy weather.

Steam steering gear was added in 1874/5, 2-14in torpedo carriages were added in 1878, and a net defence was fitted in 1886. She was reconstructed in 1892/3, and re-engined with an inverted TE and eight cyl boilers of 140psi pressure. Three 4.7in QF guns were added on each side of the upper deck, the bow 7in MLR was replaced by 2-6in QF, and 9-6pdr QF and 13-3pdr QF were fitted in upper works. The rig was reduced to two military masts. On post-refit trials she made 15.91kts with 8530ihp. After trials she was placed in reserve and reclassified as a third class battleship. She was converted to an accommodation ship in 1905, and was renamed *Calcutta* in 1909 and *Fisgard II* in 1915.

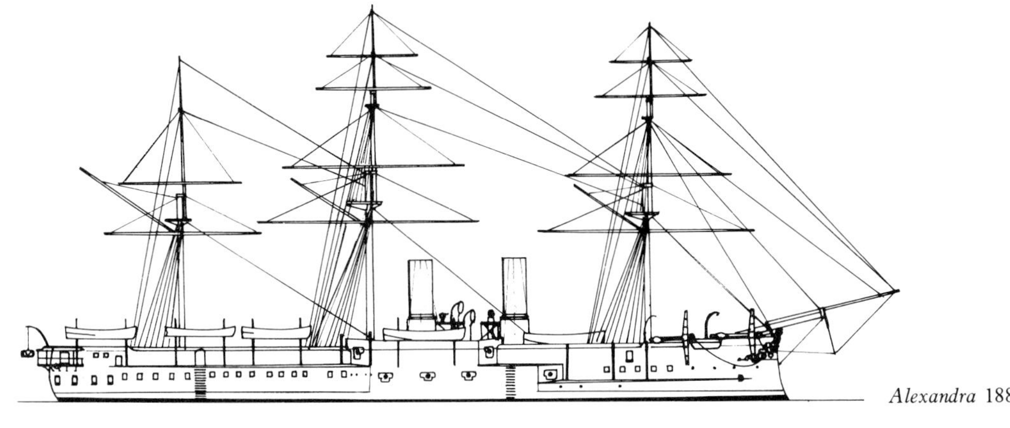

Alexandra 1886

ALEXANDRA *central battery ironclad*

Displacement: 9492t load
Dimensions: 325ft pp, 344ft oa x 63ft 10in x 26ft 3in (*99.06 pp, 104.85 oa x 19.46 x 8m*)
Machinery: 2-shaft, Humphreys 2 cyl VIC, 12 cylindrical boilers, 8498ihp = 15.09kts
Armour: Belt 12in-6in with 10in-12in wood backing, main battery 12in, upper battery 8in, bulkheads 8in-5in, deck 1in-1½in
Armament: 2-11in MLR, 10-10in MLR, 6-20pdr BL saluting, 4 TC
Complement: 674

Name	Builder	Laid down	Launched	Comp	Fate
ALEXANDRA (ex-SUPERB, 1874)	Chatham DYd	5.3.1873	7.4.75	31.1.77	Sold for BU 1908

An improved *Sultan* with heavier armour and armament and 5ft greater beam, *Alexandra* was one of the most successful of the central battery ships although virtually obsolete at the time of her completion. The waterline belt was 10½ft deep, and 12in amidships, reducing to 10in and 6in forward and aft. The lower battery (12in sides, 8in bulkheads) was divided into two sections, the main section containing three 10in MLRs on each broadside and the forward section mounting 10in MLRs in the forward corners. The upper battery (8in sides, 6in bulkheads) was of the same area as the main section of the lower battery and had two 11in MLRs mounted in the forward corners and two 10in MLRs mounted in the aft corners. The ship's side forward of both batteries and abaft the upper battery was set back to give clear ahead and astern fire to the corner ports, but this resulted in possible blast damage to the structure, a narrow, cramped upper deck and a very wet ship in heavy weather. The magazine was protected from raking fire from aft by a 5in bulkhead between the lower and platform decks. She was divided into 115 watertight compartments with the middle line longitudinal bulkhead to within 40ft of stem and stern; there were 74 compartments in the wings and a double bottom. She had four boiler rooms and two engine rooms.

She was the first Royal Navy ship fitted with vertical compound engines. The boiler pressure of 60psi was double that of the earlier rectangular boiler. When completed she was the fastest steaming battleship afloat. She was fitted with auxiliary engines of low power (600ihp) to turn her screws while under sail.

She was barque-rigged, with a sail area of 27,000 sq ft, was a handy but slow sailer and was a good seaboat, apart from the wetness caused by the recessing of the sides.

Six 4in BLs were fitted on the roof upper battery and the 20pdr BLs removed in 1884. She was reconstructed in 1889/91, when 4-9.2in BLs replaced the guns in the upper battery and 6-6pdr QFs, 12-3pdr QFs and 4-16in TCs were added. The rig was cut down to the lower masts, with light topmasts on three masts and fighting tops on the fore and mizzen. She was also re-boilered, had her superstructure enlarged, her ventilation improved and a 12in CT added. The 16in torpedoes were later replaced by 14in. In 1897 the 4in guns were replaced by 4.7in QFs, and in 1898 the funnels were raised to improve draught to the boilers.

Alexandra served as a flagship for 23 years despite her obsolescence. She took part in the bombardment of Alexandria in 1882 and was hit 24 times but suffered no serious damage. Her sea-going service ended in 1889, and she was relegated to harbour service in 1903.

TEMERAIRE *central battery/barbette ship*

Temeraire was a hybrid, being a central battery ship but with two 11in guns carried in barbettes on the upper deck, one forward and one aft. The guns were mounted on Moncrieff disappearing mountings of the type originally designed for land fortifications. The gun was loaded behind armour then raised to fire over the lip of the barbette, the recoil returning it to the loading position. This had the advantage of giving improved protection to the gun and crew, compared with the standard barbette in which the gun was always visible. The system was successful but expensive in weight and space and was not repeated. *Temeraire* was the first British barbette ship.

The belt was 11in amidships at the waterline, 10in above and 9in below, reducing to 6in forward and aft, 5in at the extreme bow and 5½in at the extreme stern. The battery on the main deck had 8in sides and bulkheads, and was divided into two sections by an athwartships 5in bulkhead. The after section contained the four 10in MLRs with broadside ports, and the forward section two 11in MLRs with corner ports for ahead fire. The forward barbette was 10in, the after barbette 8in, and they were 9ft 6in deep with 3ft 6in diameter armoured tubes protecting the hoists between the main and upper decks. The after magazine was protected from raking fire by a 5in bulkhead between the hold and the lower edge of the belt.

Temeraire was brig-rigged, with a sail area of 25,000 sq ft. She was the largest brig ever built and carried the largest sails (foresail 5100 sq ft, main trysail 3200 sq ft) and longest lower yards, lower masts and gaffs ever employed in a Royal Navy ship. She was slow under sail but handy, and a very steady and good seaboat. The machinery was of a similar type and layout to *Alexandra's*. She carried 30 auxiliary steam engines.

In 1884 the 20pdr guns were replaced by 6-4in BLs; 4-6pdr QFs and 10-3pdr QFs were also added. The rig was reduced to the lower masts, with light topmasts and yards, in 1889. At the bombardment of Alexandria in 1882 she took a leading part. Relegated to harbour service in 1902, *Temeraire* was renamed *Indus II* in 1904 and *Akbar* in 1915.

Temeraire 1878

Displacement: 8540t load
Dimensions: 285ft pp x 62ft x 27ft (*86.87 pp x 18.9 x 8.23m*)
Machinery: 2-shaft, Humphreys & Tennant 2 cyl VIC, 12 cylindrical boilers, 7697ihp = 14.65kts
Armour: Belt 11in-5½in with 10in-12in wood backing, battery 8in, bulkheads 8in-5in, barbettes 10in-8in, deck 1½in-1in
Armament: 4-11in MLR, 4-10in MLR, 4-20pdr BL, 2TL
Complement: 580

Name	Builder	Laid down	Launched	Comp	Fate
TEMERAIRE	Chatham DYd	18.8.1873	9.5.76	31.8.77	Sold for BU 1921

BELLEISLE class *armoured rams*

These ships were designed by Ahmed Pasha for Turkey and purchased by the Admiralty on 13.2.78, during the Russian war scare. The vessels were armoured rams intended for service in the Eastern Mediterranean, but with their limited endurance and seagoing qualities were of little use in the British Fleet. *Belleisle* was originally classified as an armoured ram, and *Orion* as an armoured corvette, but both were reclassified as second class battleships and eventually, and more realistically, coast defence ships.

The belt was 10ft deep and 12in amidships, 7in forward, and 6in aft. The ram consisted of 8ft of solid forging projecting 10ft from the bow and was supported by the side armour. The two-storey central battery had an upper section (with 10½in sides and 9½in corners) containing a 12in gun at each corner, and a lower section (with 9in sides and 8in corners) containing coal bunkers at the sides and a ready use ammunition lobby amidships. Unlike earlier central battery ships the magazines were amidships between the engine and the boiler rooms, greatly simplifying ammunition supply.

These were regarded as handy vessels, but they rolled heavily and were very wet in rough weather. *Belleisle* was completed with a short funnel and square rig on the foremast. The funnel was raised by 16ft in 1879 and the square rig discontinued in 1880. *Orion* was completed with a raised funnel and without the rig. In the mid 1880s 6-3pdr QFs, two searchlights and a torpedo net defence were added.

Belleisle was employed as a target from 1900 to 1903. *Orion* was relegated to harbour service in 1902 and renamed *Orontes* in 1909.

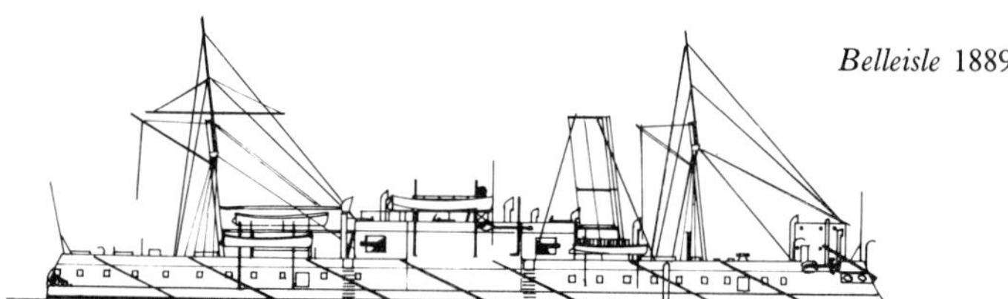
Belleisle 1889

Displacement: 4870t load
Dimensions: 245ft pp x 52ft x 21ft (*74.68 pp x 15.85 x 6.4m*)
Machinery: 2-shaft, Maudslay 2 cyl HDA, 4 boilers, 4040ihp = 12.99kts *Belleisle*
Armour: Belt 12in-6in with 10in-16in backing, battery 10½in-8in, CT 9in, bulkheads 9in-5in, main deck 3in-2in
Armament: 4-12in MLR, 4-20pdr, 2-14in TL
Complement: 250

Name	Builder	Laid down	Launched	Comp	Fate
BELLEISLE (ex-PEKI-SHEREEF)	Samuda, Poplar	1874	12.2.76	19.7.78	Sold for BU 1904
ORION (ex-BOORDHI-ZAFFER)	Samuda, Poplar	–	23.1.79	3.7.82	Sold for BU 1913

SUPERB *central battery ironclad*

Designed by Reed for Turkey, *Superb* was completed in 1877 but detained and purchased on 20.2.78 during the Russian war scare, being modified to Admiralty requirements and commissioned in the Royal Navy in 1880. She was an enlarged *Hercules* with a heavier armament and armour than any other British broadside ironclad.

The belt was 12in (7in lower edge) amidships reducing to 10in and 6in forward, and 10in and 4in aft. The battery on the main deck was 111ft long with 12in sides and 10in bulkheads containing four guns on each broadside and one in each corner firing through embrasures in the ship's sides. The remaining guns were at the forward and aft ends of the upper deck. CTs were positioned on the upper deck at the fore and aft ends of the battery.

She was barque-rigged but almost impossible to handle under sail, although in contrast she was very handy under steam.

In the early 1880s 6-4in BLs were

Displacement: 9710t load
Dimensions: 332ft 4in pp x 59ft x 25ft 6in (*101.3pp x 17.98 x 7.77m*)
Machinery: 1-shaft, Maudslay 2 cyl HDA, 9 rectangular boilers, 6580ihp = 13.2kts
Armour: Belt 12in-7in with 8in-12in backing, battery 12in, bulkheads 10in, CT 8in, decks 1½in
Armament: 16-10in MLR, 4-14in TL
Complement: 654

Name	Builder	Laid down	Launched	Comp	Fate
SUPERB (ex-HAMIDIEH	Thames Iron Wks, Blackwall	1873	16.11.75	15.11.80	Sold for BU 1906

added on the upper deck amidships. She was modernised in 1887/91, being re-engined with TE machinery and new cylindrical boilers and funnels. All upper deck guns were removed and replaced by 12-6in QFs, 6-6pdr QFs and 10-3pdr QFs. The rig was reduced to the lower masts, with light topmasts and yards and fighting tops on the fore and mizzen, and a torpedo net defence was fitted. On post-refit trials she made 13.78kts with 7431ihp.

Superb took part in the bombardment of Alexandria in 1882, and suffered minor damage. She was relegated to harbour service in 1904.

Above: *Prince Albert* as completed

Right: *Royal Sovereign* as completed

Royal Sovereign was the first Royal Navy turret ship to see service. Originally a 121-gun, three decker of 3765t bm and 12.25kts, she was approved for conversion to a turret ship as an experiment at the time of her completion in 1862. The conversion was begun in April 1862, when she was cut down to the lower deck (reclassified as the upper deck), giving 7ft-8ft freeboard. The hull and decks were strengthened with additional wood and iron to accommodate the heavy turrets and the shock of firing the guns. The turrets were mounted on the main deck with the armoured section projecting through the upper deck. The twin turret was mounted abaft the foremast and the singles abaft the funnel and between the main and mizzen masts. The twin weighed 163t, the singles 151t each, and all were hand-worked. The 10.5in SB guns, firing 150lb round shot, were replaced by 9in MLRs in 1867.

She had full length belt armour from the upper deck to 3ft below waterline, 5½in amidships reducing to 4½in fore and aft, the hull behind the armour being 36in oak. The turrets had 5½in walls reinforced with additional 4½in plates in way of gun ports. An armoured CT was fitted abaft the fore turret. For seaworthiness 3½ft iron bulwarks were fitted around the upper deck edge and these hinged down to give clear arcs of fire.

Although *Royal Sovereign* was a coast defence ship, her draught was rather excessive for this task. She was a good seaboat but had a quick roll.

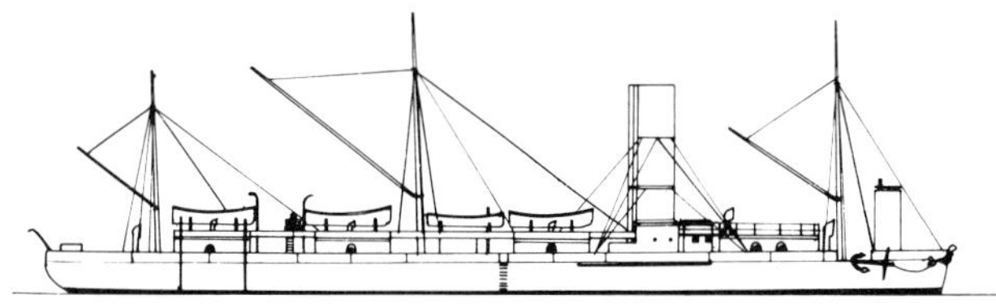

Royal Sovereign as completed 1864

ROYAL SOVEREIGN *coast defence turret ship*

Displacement: 5080t load
Dimensions: 240ft 6in pp x 62ft x 23ft 3in (*73.3 pp x 18.9 x 7.09m*)
Machinery: 1-shaft, Maudslay 2 cyl HRCR, 2460ihp = 11kts
Armour: Belt 5½in-4½in, turrets 10in-5½in, CT 5½in, upper deck 1in
Armament: 5-10.5in (3x1, 1x2) SB
Complement: 300

Name	Builder	Laid down	Launched	Comp	Fate
ROYAL SOVEREIGN	Portsmouth DYd	17.12.1849	25.4.57	20.8.64	Sold for BU 1885

Prince Albert was the first British iron turret ship. She was designed before *Royal Sovereign* but her construction was delayed by a shortage of material and modifications to the armament. Originally she was to have had six turrets but these were reduced to four with the adoption of heavier guns.

This was a simple design with a 7ft freeboard. The hull and turret armour was arranged as in *Royal Sovereign*, except that the belt of 4½in armour reduced to 3½in at the extreme ends. All the turrets were on the centreline, two being abaft the mainmast and one forward and one abaft the foremast. Each weighed 111t but was hand worked. An unarmoured CT was fitted abaft the foremast, and hinged iron bulwarks 5ft high around the upper deck edge.

A hurricane deck was added over the two forward turrets during 1866/67 and the ship was re-boilered in 1878. Six MGs were added on the hurricane deck during the 1880s. To meet the wishes of Queen Victoria, *Prince Albert* remained on the effective list for 33 years.

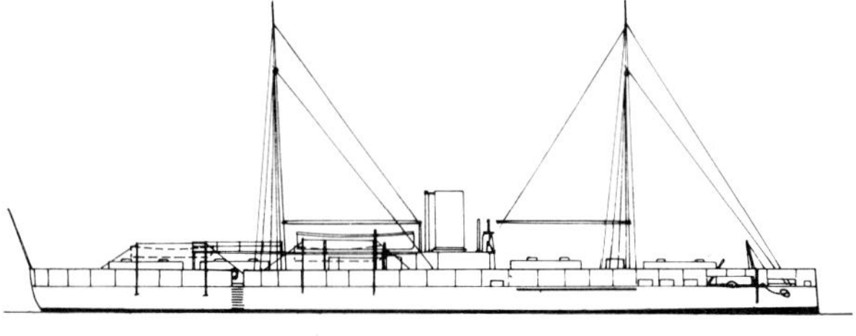

Prince Albert as completed 1866

PRINCE ALBERT *coast defence turret ship*

Displacement: 3687t load
Dimensions: 240ft pp x 48ft 1in x 19ft 8in (*73.15 pp x 14.66 x 5.99m*)
Machinery: 1-shaft, Humphreys & Tennant horizontal 2 cyl DA, 4 rectangular boilers, 2128ihp = 11.26kts
Armour: Belt 4½in with 18in wood backing, turrets 10½in-5½in with 14in wood backing, upper deck 1 1/8in
Armament: 4-9in MLR
Complement: 201

Name	Builder	Laid down	Launched	Comp	Fate
PRINCE ALBERT	Samuda, Poplar	29.4.1862	23.5.64	23.2.66	Sold for BU 1899

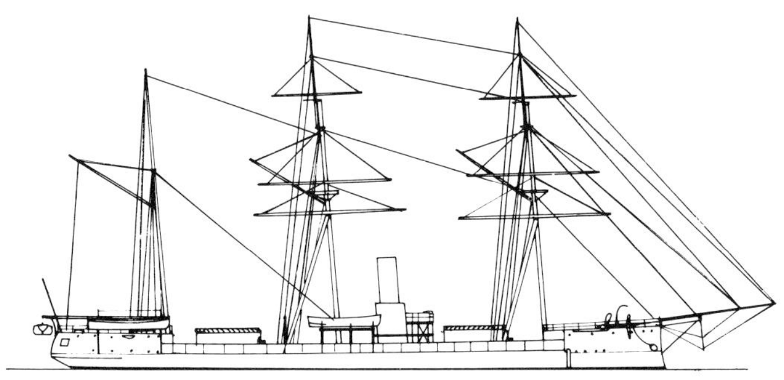

Wivern as completed 1865

These ships were ordered in 1862 by an agent of the Confederate States of America but the Foreign Secretary pointed out that British neutrality could not allow their delivery to a belligerent. The agent arranged for their sale to Egypt but with the real intention of transferring them to the Confederate flag at sea. This plan also came to the attention of the Foreign Secretary and in October 1863 both ships were seized by the British Government, being purchased for the Royal Navy in 1864.

They had a forecastle, poop and barque rig for service as ocean-going ships. They were good seaboats but with a deep roll and low freeboard their fighting efficiency in a seaway was doubtful, and they were soon relegated to coast defence.

The full-length belt extended from the upper deck to 3¼ft below the waterline, it was 3½in amidships, reducing to 3in forward and 2in aft. The turrets were octagonal with 10in faces and 5in sides, and an armoured CT was fitted forward of the funnel. The freeboard amidships was 6ft with

SCORPION class *masted turret ships*

Displacement: 2751t load
Dimensions: 224ft 6in pp x 42ft 4in x 16ft 3in (*68.43 pp x 12.9 x 4.95m*)
Machinery: 1-shaft, Lairds, 2 cyl HDA, 4 boilers, 1450ihp = 10.5kts
Armour: Belt 4½in-2in with 8in-10in wood backing, turrets 10in-5in
Armament: 4-9in MLR (2x2)
Complement: 153

Name	Builder	Laid down	Launched	Comp	Fate
SCORPION	Lairds, Birkenhead	Apr 1862	July 1863	10.10.65	Sold for BU 1903. Foundered on passage to Boston 17.6.1903
WIVERN	Lairds, Birkenhead	Apr 1862	29.8.63	10.10.65	Sold for BU 1922

5ft hinged bulwarks between forecastle and poop.

Wivern was fitted with struts to her fore- and mainmasts to reduce interference of the standing rig with the turrets, and she was the first ship to have tripod masts. During 1866/68 the rig was reduced to fore and aft sails and a flying bridge was added between forecastle and poop.

Scorpion served as guardship at Bermuda from 1869 to 1899, and was sunk as a target in 1901 and then raised for sale in 1902. *Wivern* also served as a guardship, initially in home ports and later at Hong Kong, where she was reduced to harbour service in 1898.

Monarch after her 1872 conversion to barque rig

Monarch was the first sea-going turret ship and the first British warship to carry 12in guns. She originated from an Admiralty design produced as a result of agitation by Coles and the recommendations of a committee appointed in 1865. For ocean service a full rig and forecastle were considered essential, although this resulted in serious restrictions to the turrets' arcs of fire. To compensate for the loss of end-on fire, two 7in guns were mounted forward on the upper deck and one 7in aft on the main deck, protected by 5in armour.

The turrets, fitted forward and aft of the funnel, had 8in sides and 10in faces; the turret bases were protected by a box citadel between the upper and main decks, with 7in sides and 4in-4½in bulkheads. The belt extended from the main deck to 5ft below the waterline and was 7in below the citadel reducing to 6in fore and aft and 4½in at the ends. Hinged bulwarks were provided on the edge of the upper deck. There was an armoured CT positoned forward of the funnel on the hurricane deck.

Monarch was a good steamer and the fastest battleship afloat at the time of her completion. Equipped with auxiliary machinery for steering, capstan and turret training, she was ship-rigged with a sail area of 27,700 sq ft. She proved to be a fast sailer but was difficult to handle, although modifications to the balanced rudder slightly improved matters. She was a steady gun platform and a good seaboat, being very dry in heavy weather.

She was altered to barque-rig in 1872, and two torpedo launchers were added in 1878. Modernised between 1890 and 1897, she was re-engined

MONARCH *masted turret ship*

Displacement: 8322t load
Dimensions: 330ft pp x 57ft 6in x 24ft 3in (*100.58 pp x 17.53 x 7.39m*)
Machinery: 1-shaft, Humphreys & Tennant 2 cyl HRCR, 9 boilers, 7842ihp = 14.94kts
Armour: Belt 7in-4½in with 10in-12in backing, bulkheads 4½in-4in, turrets 10in-8in, CT 8in
Armament: 4-12in MLR, 3-7in MLR
Complement: 575

Name	Builder	Laid down	Launched	Comp	Fate
MONARCH	Chatham DYd	1.6.1866	25.5.68	12.6.69	Sold for BU 1905

Monarch as completed 1869

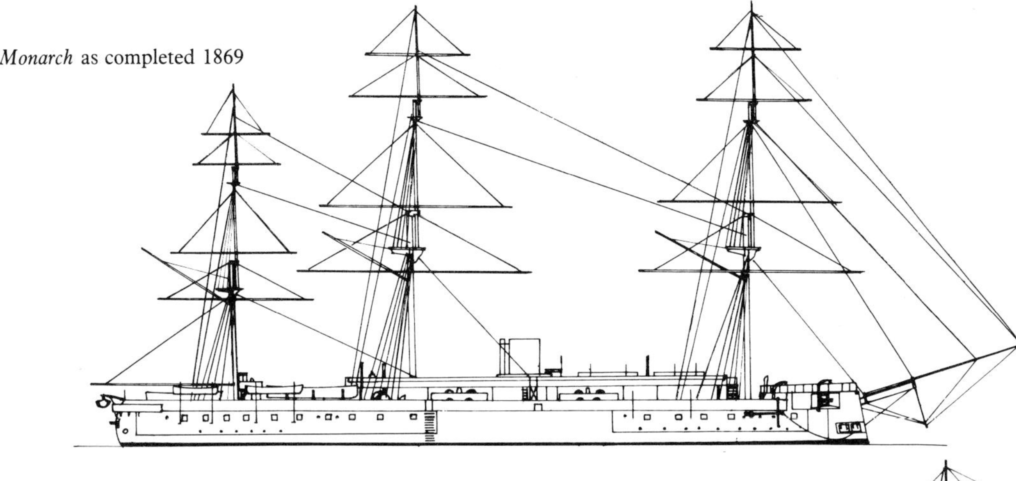

with TE machinery, cyl boilers and a new funnel. The rig was cut down to lower masts, with light topmasts and yards. A new bridge was fitted forward of the funnel, and 4-12pdr QFs and 10-3pdr QFs were added on the structure. On post-refit trials she made 15.75kts with 8216ihp.

Monarch took part in the bombardment of Alexandria in 1882, and became a guardship in 1897 and a depot ship in 1904, when she was renamed *Simoom*.

Coles was very critical of *Monarch* and with the assistance of public opinion gained Admiralty consent to construct a turret ship to his own specification. The design was entrusted to Lairds, with Coles providing outline requirements and technical advice. The ship was similar to *Monarch* but with turrets one deck lower and further apart. She had a large forecastle and poop – reluctantly accepted by Coles as required in a seagoing ship – connected by a flying deck. The rigging was kept clear of the turrets by employing the flying deck to work the sails and adopting tripod masts to dispose of most of the standing rigging.

The belt armour was 7in amidships, increasing to 8in abreast the turrets and reducing to 4in forward and aft. The turrets had 9in walls and 10in faces. The two 7in MLRs were mounted in unprotected positions on the forecastle and poop.

Twin screws gave her good manoeuvrability, this being almost the only respect in which she was superior to *Monarch*. She was ship-rigged, with a sail area 26,322 sq ft (37,990 sq ft max).

Captain was designed as a 6960t vessel with an 8½ft freeboard, but because of additions and lack of attention to material weights during construction she was 800t overweight with her freeboard reduced to 6½ft. Some concern was expressed by both the builders and the Admiralty about her level of stability, and calculations and an inclining experiment, showed she would be unsafe beyond an angle of heel of 21°) However, this did not create any great concern for the ship's safety.

Trials were very successful and appeared to confound her detractors, the most important of whom was Reed. On the night of 6/7 December 1870 she was at sea with the Channel Fleet, in a severe gale, carrying double-reefed topsails and a fore topmast staysail. At 12.15 the wind suddenly increased in strength causing her to heel beyond her safe limit and capsize. Only 17 of her crew survived, 472, including Captain Coles, being lost with the ship. Her loss was subsequently attributed to her low level of stability.

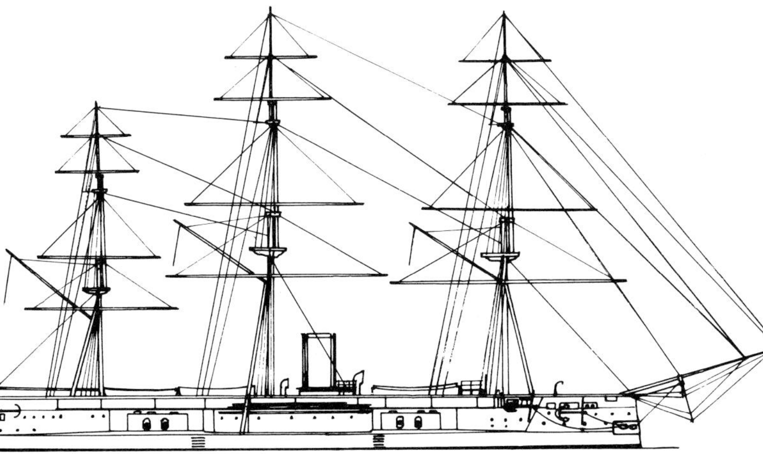

Captain as completed 1869

CAPTAIN *masted turret ship*

Displacement: 7767t load
Dimensions: 320ft pp x 53ft 3in x 24ft 10in (*97.54 pp x 16.23 x 7.57m*)
Machinery: 2-shaft, 4 cyl HT, 8 rectangular boilers, 5400ihp = 15.25kts
Armour: Belt 8in-4in, turrets 10in-9in, CT 7in
Armament: 4-12in MLR (2x2), 2-7in MLR
Complement: 500

Name	Builder	Laid down	Launched	Comp	Fate
CAPTAIN	Lairds, Birkenhead	30.1.1867	27.3.69	Jan 1870	Capsized off Cape Finisterre 7.9.70

CERBERUS class *coast defence monitors*

Displacement: 3344t load
Dimensions: 225ft pp x 45ft x 15ft 4in (*68.58 pp x 13.72 x 4.67m*)
Machinery: 2-shaft Maudslay (*Magdala* Ravenhill), 1369ihp=9.75kts, (*Magdala* 1436ihp = 10.6kts)
Armour: Belt 8in-6in with 11in-9in wood backing, breastwork 9in-8in, turrets 10in-9in, decks 1in-1½in
Armament: 4-10in MLR (2x2)
Complement: 155

Name	Builder	Laid down	Launched	Comp	Fate
CERBERUS	Palmers, Jarrow	1.9.1867	2.12.68	Sept 1870	Sunk as breakwater, Melbourne, 1926, still visible 1978
MAGDALA	Thames Iron Wks, Blackwall	6.10.1868	2.3.70	Nov 1870	Sold for BU 1904

These vessels were low freeboard breastwork monitors intended for service as colonial coast defence ships. Designed by Reed for service at Melbourne (*Cerberus*) and Bombay (*Magdala*), they represent the beginnings of practical turret ship design in Britain, having no sail power and being fitted with fore and aft turrets with almost uninterrupted arcs of fire.

The low freeboard hull was protected by an 8in belt reducing to 6in at the ends, and the turrets were raised on a central armoured breastwork 9in at the ends and 8in amidships. The breastwork served to keep the turrets, hatchways, vents and funnels, comparatively clear of the water, making the ships more practical in a seaway than the low freeboard vessles of the US type which were only suitable for enclosed harbour and river work. The turrets, which were hand worked, had 10in faces and 9in walls. The ships had twin screws and balanced rudders and manoeuvred well. In 1892 *Magdala's* turrets were rearmed with four 8in BL guns.

Both ships were given a three-masted sailing rig for passage to their respective colonial ports which was removed on arrival. *Cerberus* had a pole mast abaft and *Magdala* a pole mast before the funnel. The flying deck originally overlapped the turrets but in *Magdala* it was cut back to the length of the superstructure.

Cerberus was reduced to harbour service 1900, converted to a depot ship in 1918 and renamed *Platypus II*.

Cerberus off Williamstown where she spent the later years of her career as a depot ship

This vessel was a smaller and cheaper edition of *Cerberus*, intended to serve as a coast defence ship at Bombay with *Magdala*. Compared with the previous class she had less freeboard and speed, and a 1in reduction in armour thickness on the belt amidships, breastwork and turret walls. A CT was fitted forward of the funnel.

She made the passage to Bombay under her own power where she remained until sold. In 1892 she was rearmed with four 8in BL guns.

ABYSSINIA *coast defence monitor*

Displacement: 2901t load
Dimensions: 225ft pp x 42ft x 14ft 7in (*68.58 pp x 12.8 x 4.45m*)
Machinery: 2-shaft Dudgeon, 1200ihp= 9.59kts
Armour: Belt 7in-6in with 11in-9in wood backing, breastwork 8in-7in, turrets 10in-8in
Armament: 4-10in MLR (2x2)
Complement: 100

Name	Builder	Laid down	Launched	Comp	Fate
ABYSSINIA	Dudgeon, Poplar	23.7.1868	19.2.70	Oct 1870	Sold for BU 1903

A single turret breastwork monitor of somewhat obscure purpose, *Glatton* was intended to serve in the dual role of coast defence and attack on enemy coast defences. For the latter she was given a deep draught, for sea keeping purposes, as she would be required to accompany the fleet to sea, although this detracted somewhat from her abilities in coast defence. Conversely, her low freeboard of 3ft restricted her ability to operate in the open sea.

She was heavily armoured for her size with a 6½ft deep belt, 12in amidships reducing to 10in at the lower edge and ends and covered by a 3in deck. The breastwork had uniform 12in walls with a 1½in deck and the turret 12in sides and a 14in face. The magazines were protected from raking fire by a 12in bulkhead forward, below the waterline.

The designed speed of 9.75kts was considerably exceeded. She handled well but was difficult to keep on a straight course. During the 1880s she was fitted with 3-6pdr QFs, 4 MGs and launchers for 14in torpedoes. Based at Portsmouth throughout her active life, she was reduced to reserve in 1889.

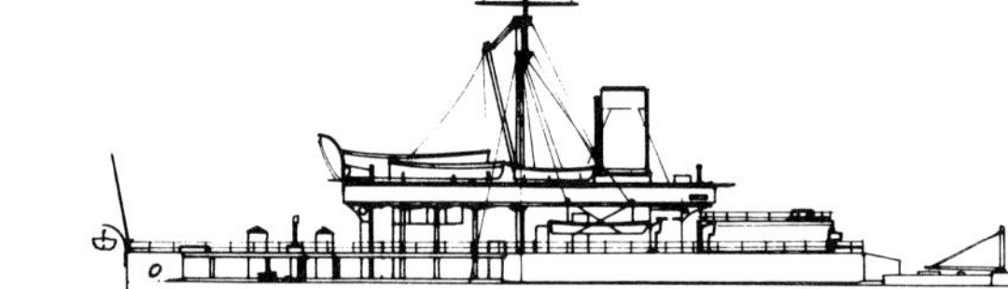

Glatton as completed 1872

GLATTON *breastwork monitor*

Displacement: 4912t load
Dimensions: 245ft pp x 54ft x 19ft (*74.68 pp x 16.46 x 5.79m*)
Machinery: 2-shaft, Lairds, 2870ihp = 12.11kts
Armour: Belt 12in-10in with 21in-15in wood backing, breastwork 12in, turret 14in-12in, CT 9in-6in, decks 3in-1½in, bulkhead 12in
Complement: 185

Name	Builder	Laid down	Launched	Comp	Fate
GLATTON	Chatham DYd	10.8.1868	8.3.71	24.2.72	Sold for BU 1903

Hotspur was an ironclad ram constructed to match French vessels of similar type. The general layout was similar to *Glatton* but the freeboard was increased to the height of the breastwork by the addition of an unarmoured hull structure above the belt. In place of the turret she carried a fixed, armoured gun house with four gun ports, it being considered that the turret would not stand up to the shock of ramming. The 12in MLR was mounted on both traversing arcs and a turntable, allowing for positioning and training at each port. The two 64pdr guns were mounted aft behind bulwarks and were unprotected. The principal weapon was the ram, projecting 10ft from the bow and supported by a downward extension of the side armour.

Her belt was 11in amidships and 8in at ends, with a 2in-2¾in deck, the

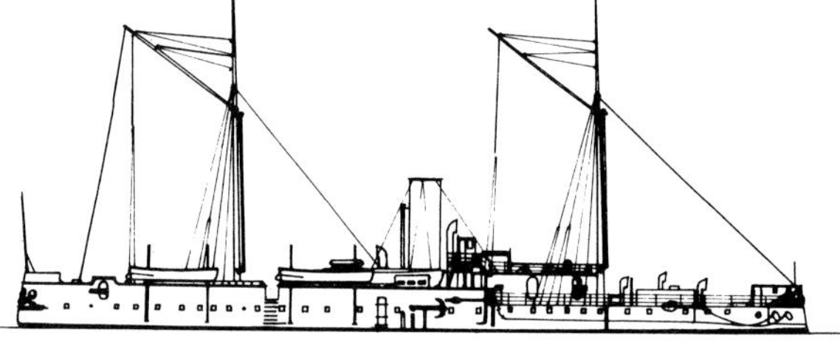

Hotspur as completed 1871

HOTSPUR *ironclad ram*

Displacement: 4331t load
Dimensions: 235ft pp x 50ft x 10ft 10in (*71.63 pp x 15.24 x 6.05m*)
Machinery: 2-shaft, Napier, 3500ihp = 12.65kts
Armour: Belt 11in-8in, breastwork 8in, gun house 10in-8½in, CT 10in-6in, decks 2¾in-1in
Armament: 1-12in MLR, 2-64pdr MLR
Complement: 209

Name	Builder	Laid down	Launched	Comp	Fate
HOTSPUR	Napier, Govan	2.10.1868	19.3.70	17.11.71	Sold for BU 1904

breastwork being of uniform 8in with a 1½in deck. The gun house had 10in walls with an 8½in back, the CT being mounted on its roof.

She was a good gun platform, very steady and manoeuvrable, but was unable to make headway in heavy seas. Virtually useless in her intended role because of her lack of fire power on forward bearings and lack of speed and seakeeping qualities, she was relegated to the role of coast defence ship.

Hotspur was reconstructed at Lairds in 1881-83. The gun house was replaced by a compound armour turret, 2¾in steel on 5¾in iron, containing two 12in MLR guns, and the 64pdrs were replaced by two 6in BLs. The breastwork was removed and replaced by a full-width box citadel with 8in sides and bulkheads. The superstructure was remodelled, and the ship was re-boilered, had steam steering gear added, was fitted with torpedo launching gear and had a torpedo boat added to her boat complement.

Left: The *Hotspur* as completed with fixed gunhouse between the bridge and foremast

Below: *Thunderer* in April 1891 on completion of her major refit when she was rearmed and fitted with new machinery

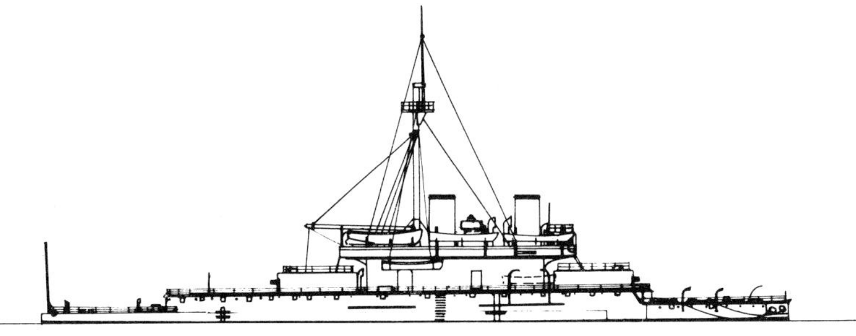

Devastation 1874

DEVASTATION class *turret ships*

Displacement: 9330t load
Dimensions: 285ft pp, 307ft oa x 62ft 3in x 26ft 8in *(86.87 pp, 93.57 oa x 18.97 x 8.03m)*
Machinery: 2 cyl Penn T (*Thunderer* 2 cyl Humphreys & Tennant HDA), 8 rectangular boilers, 6640ihp = 13.84kts (*Thunderer* 6270ihp = 13.4kts)
Armour: Belt 12in-8½in with 18in-16in wood backing, breastwork 12in-10in, turrets 14in-10in, CT 9in-6in, decks 3in-2in, bulkheads 6in-5in
Armament: 4-12in MLR (2x2)
Complement: 358

Name	Builder	Laid down	Launched	Comp	Fate
DEVASTATION	Portsmouth DYd	12.11.1869	12.7.71	19.4.73	Sold for BU 1908
THUNDERER	Pembroke DYd	26.6.1869	25.3.72	26.5.77	Sold for BU 1909

Designed by Edward J Reed in 1868, these were revolutionary vessels that provided the basic pattern for future battleships, being the first mastless, sea-going turret ships. Basically they were enlarged versions of the breastwork monitors of the *Cerberus* type but with armour, armament, speed and endurance increased to that required in an ocean-going ship. They aroused much controversy and, particularly after the loss of *Captain*, were the subject of strong public distrust. As a result of the deliberations of the Committee on Designs, some alterations were made which included raising the freeboard amidships by adding an unarmoured structure to the same height as the central breastwork. This was intended to improve stability, but Reed, who had by this time left the Admiralty, disliked the addition as it was vulnerable to gunfire, although it did provide additional, and much needed, accommodation. So strong was the public dislike of the design that construction of *Thunderer* was held up pending the results of *Devastation's* trials.

The belt was in two strakes of 9½ft total depth and extended from the main deck to 5½ft below the waterline. The upper strake, from fore turret to stern, was 12in amidships and 9in aft, and the lower strake, over the full length, 10in amidships and 8½in at the ends. The breastwork was 12in in way of the turrets and 10in amidships; the turret faces were 14in and their 10in walls were made up in two thicknesses, both with wood backing. A 3in deck was provided over the belt and a 2in deck over the breastwork. The CT was positioned between the funnels on the flying deck. The magazines were protected from raking fire by a 6in bulkhead forward and a 5in bulkhead aft. The upper section of the forecastle was unarmoured to restrict any tendency to pitch by reducing weight on bows. Freeboard was 10¾ft amidships, 8½ft forward and 4ft aft. A large coal capacity of 1600t gave an endurance of 5500 miles at 10kts. There was substantial watertight sub-division, with 68 compartments in the hold and 36 in the double bottom and wings.

Devastation proved successful on trials, being a steady gun platform and a good steamer. Although her forecastle was subject to being washed down in a seaway, she was a good seaboat and rolled and pitched less than many broadside ironclads. She generally remained dry amidships and heavy weather did not affect her fighting ability except for her low freeboard forward limiting her speed.

Thunderer was completed to the same design as *Devastation* but mounted 38t 12in guns in her forward turret instead of 35t weapons. The 38t gun was normally of 12.5in cal and *Thunderer* was the only vessel fitted with 12in type. Her forward turret was also the first to have hydraulic loading gear. A boiler explosion in July 1876, caused by faulty safety valves, resulted in a further delay in her completion. She suffered a second accident in 1879 when one of her 38t guns burst after being double-loaded.

Devastation was refitted in 1879, 2-14in TL, 8-MG, two searchlights and a fighting top being added, ventilation improved and machinery overhauled. *Thunderer* was similarly refitted in 1881. Both ships were modernised during 1890-92, the turrets were rearmed with 10in BLs, and 6-6pdr QF and 8-3pdr QF guns were also added. At the same time, the ships were re-engined with TE machinery and cyl boilers, giving 7000ihp = 14kts.

This vessel was an enlarged version of the *Hotspur* with a *Glatton* type turret in place of the fixed gun house, heavier armour on the decks, breastwork and belt ends, and a larger superstructure with a flying deck. *Rupert* showed some improvement on *Hotspur* but her machinery installation was unsatisfactory, and she could not reach the design speed of 14kts, in fact after some years of service she could make no more than 10kts.

In 1887 2-6in BLs replaced the 64pdrs aft and four TTs and four QF guns were added to the armament. During 1891-93 she was reconstructed and given new TE engines and new boilers, which enabled her to reach her designed speed of 14kts. In addition the turret guns were replaced by 9.2in BLs, and 4-6pdr QFs and 6-3pdr QFs were mounted on the superstructure. The foremast was removed and a fighting top was added to the mainmast. A considerable amount of additional weight was involved in this reconstruction, which increased the draught by 2½ft; the coal capacity was reduced from 550t to 390t as part compensation.

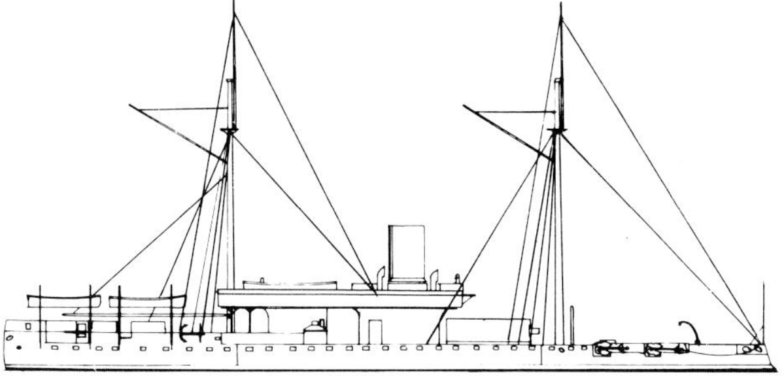

Rupert as completed 1874

RUPERT *ironclad ram*

Displacement: 5440t load
Dimensions: 250ft pp x 53ft x 22ft 6in (*80.48 pp x 16.15 x 6.86m*)
Machinery: 2-shaft, Napier, 4630ihp=13.59kts
Armour: Belt 11in-9in with 10in-14in wood backing, breastwork 10in, turrets 14in-12in, CT 12in, decks 3in-2in
Armament: 2-10in MLR (1x2), 2-64pdr MLR
Complement: 217

Name	Builder	Laid down	Launched	Comp	Fate
RUPERT	Chatham DYd	6.6.1870	12.3.72	1.7.74	Sold for BU 1907

Dreadnought at Malta during her first full commission, 1884-94

Laid down under the 1870 Estimates as an enlarged version of *Devastation* with more powerful machinery and fully armoured bow, *Dreadnought* had her construction suspended in 1871 pending the deliberations of the Committee on Designs and as a result of its recommendations was redesigned to incorporate improved protection, armament and stability. Alterations included replacing the armoured breastwork with a 184ft central citadel extending the full width of the ship, with 11in-14in armour on the sides, 13in curved bulkheads and a 3in deck over. Below this the 8½ft deep belt was increased in thickness to 14in amidships, tapering to 8in at the lower edge and reducing to 8in at the ends, with a 2½in deck over beyond the citadel. The fore end of the belt was extended downwards to support the ram, obviating the need for a forward magazine bulkhead. The after bulkhead was retained. The upper deck was continued fore and aft of the citadel as an unarmoured structure to raise freeboard and improve sea-keeping and speed in heavy weather. The turrets remained as in the original design, with 14in armour, in two thicknesses of 7in each with wood backing, but the guns were increased from 12 to 12.5in cal and power training, elevation and loading were provided. Compound engines (similar to those in *Alexandra*) replaced the horizontal machinery specified in the original design, providing a ½kt increase in speed. She was the first vessel to have a longitudinal middle-line bulkhead which extended for the majority of her length. The coal supply of 1800t provided an endurance of 5700 miles at 10kts.

She was a very successful ship and, unlike her half sisters, was a popular vessel. A steady ship, she rolled little and was more capable of maintaining speed in a seaway than *Devastation* but was wetter and pitched more heavily.

In 1884 10 MGs were added to the superstructure, these being replaced in 1894 by 6-6pdr QFs and 10-3pdr QFs. The ship was re-boilered and had her funnels raised in 1898. Front line service continued until 1894, after which she served as a coastguard vessel. Re-classified as a second class battleship in 1900, *Dreadnought* was reduced to harbour service in 1902 and to reserve in 1905.

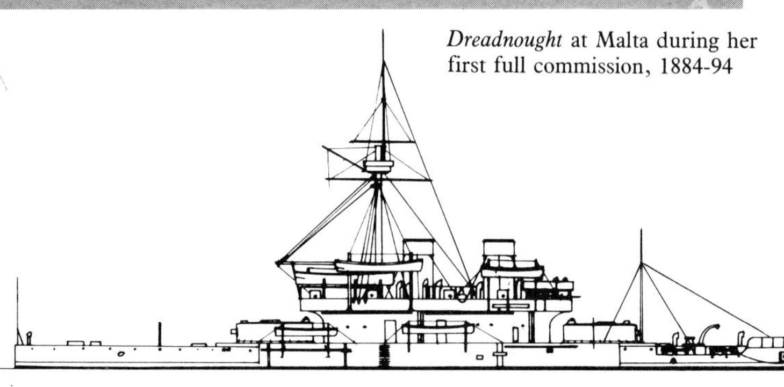

Dreadnought 1885

DREADNOUGHT *turret ship*

Displacement: 10,886t load
Dimensions: 320ft pp, 343ft oa x 63ft 10in x 26ft 6in (*97.54 pp, 104.55 oa x 19.46 x 8.08m*)
Machinery: 2-shaft 2 cyl Humphreys & Tennant VCE, 12 cyl boilers, 8206ihp = 14.52kts. Coal 1800t
Armour: Belt 14in-8in with 15in-18in wood backing, citadel 14in-11in, CT 14in-6in, decks 3in-2½in
Armament: 4-12.5in MLR (2x2)
Complement: 369

Name	Builder	Laid down	Launched	Comp	Fate
DREADNOUGHT	Pembroke DYd	10.9.1870	8.3.75	15.2.79	Sold for BU 1908

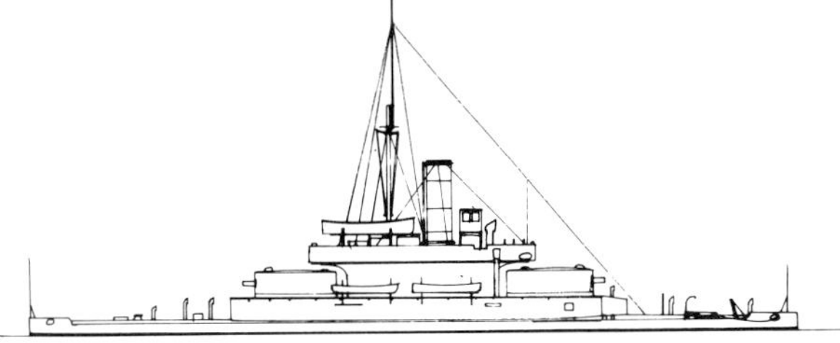
Hydra as completed 1876

Repeats of *Cerberus* class coast defence vessels with minor modificiations, these vessels were ordered during the war scare of 1870. They were delivered from the builders to the Royal dockyards in 1872 for final fitting out and, as the war scare had subsided, were completed at a leisurely pace. The ships were modified during 1885-89 when the breastwork was extended to the sides with light plating (as in *Devastation*) to improve stability and seakeeping. At the same time 4-3pdr QF guns, 5 MGs and 2 searchlights were fitted on the flying deck, bringing their displacement to 3560t.

CYCLOPS class *coast defence monitors*

Displacement: 3480t load
Dimensions: 225ft pp x 45ft x 16ft 3in (*68.58 pp x 13.72 x 4.95m*)
Machinery: 2-shaft, 2 cyl Ravenhill HDA (*Hecate* and *Gorgon*), John Elder 2 cyl compound engines (*Cyclops* and *Hydra*), 1670ihp = 11.14kts (*Gorgon*), 1755ihp = 10.9kts (*Hecate*), 1660ihp = 11kts (*Cyclops*), 1472ihp = 11.2kts (*Hydra*)
Armour: Belt 8in-6in (11in-9in backing) breastwork 9in-8in turrets 10in-9in, CT 9in-8in, decks 1½in
Armament: 4-10in MLR (2x2)
Complement: 150

Name	Builder	Laid down	Launched	Comp	Fate
CYCLOPS	Thames Iron Wks, Blackwall	10.9.1870	18.7.71	4.5.77	Sold for BU 1903
GORGON	Palmers, Jarrow	5.9.1870	14.10.71	19.3.74	Sold for BU 1903
HECATE	Dudgeon, Poplar	5.9.1870	30.9.71	24.5.77	Sold for BU 1903
HYDRA	Napiers, Govan	5.9.1870	28.12.71	31.5.76	Sold for BU 1903

An improved version of *Monarch*, designed by Reed for Brazil in 1872. *Neptune* was an obsolete type with obsolete machinery when compared with the latest Royal Navy vessels. She failed to move on the first attempt at launching on 16.7.74, and on the second attempt, on 30.7.74, she stopped on the slipway with about one third of the length beyond the slipway, causing extensive damage to the outer bottom plating. She was lightened and successfully launched on 10.9.74, and was taken to Samudas, Poplar, and docked for repairs. The ship was completed for trials in December 1877 and made 14.64kts with 8832ihp. Purchased in March 1878 by the British Government during the Russian war scare she was taken to Portsmouth for alterations for Royal Navy service. The modifications included replacing the Whitworth 12in and 8in guns with standard British weapons, altering the rig, adding electric light and firing gear and adding TCs on the main deck.

She was well protected, with a full length waterline belt 8½ft deep (3ft being below load line) which was 12in amidships reducing to 10in fore and aft and 9in at the ends. A citadel between the belt and upper deck protected the hatchways, funnel uptakes and trunks to her machinery and magazine compartments, and her turret bases. Two 9in MLRs were mounted under the forecastle, protected by 6in armour. She was sheathed in wood and copper for tropical service.

Neptune had a barque-rig but the sails on the mainmast were subject to rapid deterioration, being too close to the funnels, and the yards were eventually removed, reducing sails carried to the fore and mizzen only. The sailing rig was virtually useless except in combination with her engines. The mainmast was removed in 1886 and the fore and mizzen converted to military masts with large fighting tops, torpedo net defence being added at the same time. She was a bad seaboat, having a heavy roll and being wet and difficult to manoeuvre. After a short period in the Channel she was sent to the gentler climate of the Mediterranean. She was reduced to coastguard service in 1887 and to reserve in 1893.

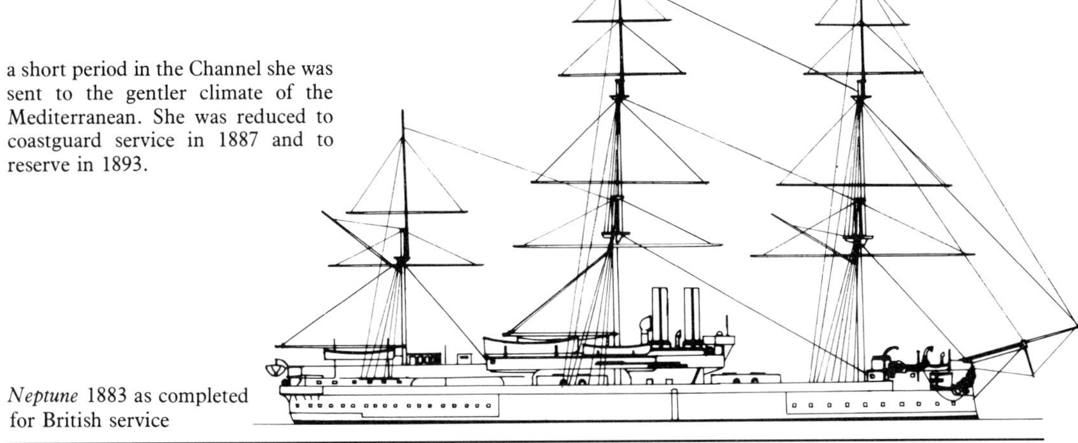
Neptune 1883 as completed for British service

NEPTUNE *masted turret ship*

Displacement: 9130t load
Dimensions: 300ft pp x 63ft x 25ft (*91.44 pp x 19.2 x 7.62m*)
Machinery: 1-shaft, 2 cyl, Penn HT, 8 rectangular boilers, 7993ihp = 14.22kts
Armour: Belt 12in-9in, citadel 10in sides, 8in bulkheads, turrets 13in-11in, decks 3in-2in, CT 8in-6in
Armament: 4-12in MLR (2x2), 2-9in MLR, 6-20pdr BL, 2-14in TC
Complement: 541

Name	Builder	Laid down	Launched	Comp	Fate
NEPTUNE (ex-INDEPENDENCIA)	Dudgeon Millwall	1873	10.9.74	3.9.81	Sold for BU 1903

Neptune as completed prior to the removal of the yards on the mainmast

Built in answer to the Italian battleship *Duilio*, the *Inflexible* was a ship of extremes with the heaviest ML guns in the Royal Navy and the thickest armour ever put afloat. In order to provide for the latter, 'all or nothing' protection was adopted with no armour beyond the central citadel. This citadel was 110ft long, extending 9½ft above and 6½ft below the load line; the sides were in two thicknesses of iron each with wood backing, the outer thickness a uniform 12in and the inner thickness 12in at waterline, 8in above and 4in below, giving a total thickness (armour and backing) of 41in. The bulkheads at the ends of the citadel were of similar construction. The upper deck over the citadel and the lower deck fore and aft of it were of 3in thickness. The citadel and the area below the protective deck required sufficient buoyancy to keep the ship afloat when the 'soft' ends were riddled. This necessitated a high level of stability and to avoid problems with rapid rolling *Inflexible* was fitted with anti-rolling tanks: athwartship chambers partly filled with water which tended to dampen roll. These were to prove successful in some weather conditions but not all. Extra protection to buoyancy was provided by extensive sub-division and cork filled and coal compartments fore and aft of the citadel on the lower and main decks.

The 16in 80t guns fired a 1684lb shell at the rate of one rpg/min. The guns were too long to be loaded from inside the turret so the job was tackled from beneath the armoured deck with the guns depressed into fixed armoured glacis. The 750t hydraulically operated twin turrets were disposed *en échelon* at the corners of the citadel to provide fore and aft fire, but this arrangement restricted broadside fire. The turrets were protected by sandwich armour, like the citadel, the outer layer being of compound armour with a 3½in steel face and a 4½in iron back, the inner layer of 7in iron with an 18in teak backing. She was the first ship to carry compound armour and also the first to have submerged TT. In 1885 her 20pdr guns were replaced by 4in BLs, and in 1897 these were in turn replaced by 4.7in QFs.

Inflexible was a good seaboat and manoeuvred well. Provided with a brig-rig, she carried 18,500 sq ft of sail, for peacetime service only, which was intended for economy and training. She proved to be virtually useless so far as sail propulsion was concerned and in 1885 was converted to a military rig with light yards and topmasts and fighting tops on the lower masts.

She was present at Alexandria, firing 88 rounds of 16in shell, and was the most heavily damaged of the British ships, being hit by several shells including one 10in. Some damage was also caused by her own gun blast.

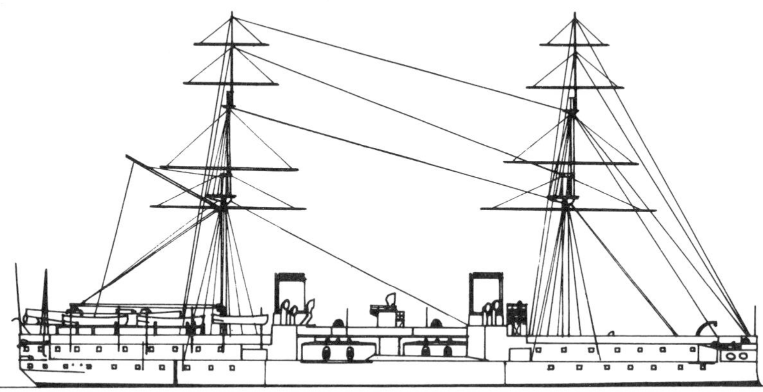

Inflexible as completed 1881

INFLEXIBLE *masted turret ship*

Displacement: 11,880t load, 10,300 light
Dimensions: 320ft pp, 344ft oa x 75ft x 25ft 6in *(97.54pp, 104.85 oa x 22.86 x 7.77m)*
Machinery: 2-shaft, 3 cyl Elder CE, 12 cyl boilers, 8407ihp = 14.75kts
Armour: Citadel 24in-16in sides, 22in-14in bulkheads, turrets 17in-16in, decks 3in, CT 12in
Armament: 4-16in MLR (2x2), 6-20pdr BL, 2-14in TT sub, 2-14in TC
Complement: 440

Name	Builder	Laid down	Launched	Comp	Fate
INFLEXIBLE	Portsmouth DYd	24.2.1874	27.4.76	18.10.81	Sold for BU 1903

Inflexible after her 1885 conversion to military rig

AGAMEMNON class *turret ships*

Displacement: 8510t load
Dimensions: 280ft pp, 300ft 9in oa x 66ft x 23ft 6in *(85.34 pp, 91.67 oa x 20.12 x 7.16m)*
Machinery: 2-shaft, 3 cyl, Penn IC, 10 tubular boilers, 6000ihp = 13kts
Armour: Citadel 18in-15in sides, 16½in-13½in bulkheads, turrets 16in-14in, decks 3in, CT 12in
Armament: 4-12.5in MLR (2x2), 2-6in BL (2x1), 6-6pdr QF, 2 TC
Complement: 345

Name	Builder	Laid down	Launched	Comp	Fate
AGAMEMNON	Chatham DYd	9.5.1876	17.9.79	29.3.83	BU 1903
AJAX	Pembroke DYd	21.3.1876	10.3.80	30.3.83	Sold for BU 1904

Small editions of *Inflexible* with a shallow draught for possible employment against Russia in the Baltic and Black Sea, these were unsatisfactory vessels, whose construction was based on economic rather than military considerations. Unlike *Inflexible*, the central citadel was of insufficient buoyancy to protect the ships' stability in the event of extensive damage to the unarmoured ends. The citadel was 104ft long with sandwich protection on the sides and bulkheads, the sides being 18in at the waterline and 15in above and below, giving a total thickness of

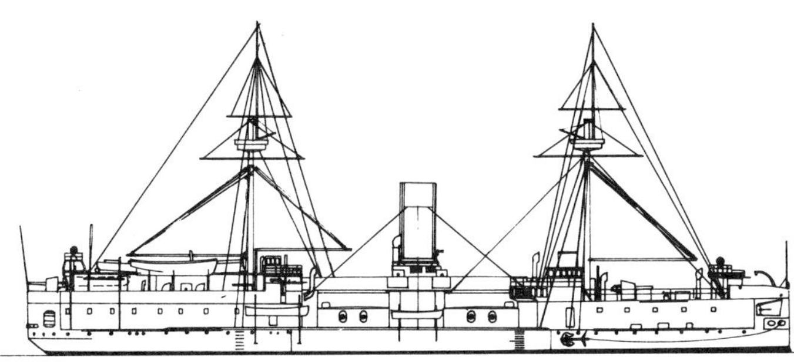

Agamemnon 1884

armour and backing of 37in. The deck over the citadel and lower deck fore and aft of it was 3in. Sandwich protection was provided on the turrets, with 14in walls and 16in faces, the outer thickness being of compound armour.

Agamemnon and *Ajax* were the last British capital ships to carry MLs and the first to have a secondary armament, these being 2-6in BLs mounted on the superstructure, one at the extreme aft end and one forward of the foremast, intended for use against unarmoured structures. Also carried was an anti-torpedo boat armament of 6pdr Nordenfelds and MGs. The 6in BLs were replaced by 6in QFs in 1897.

Unlike *Inflexible*, these ships were designed without a sailing rig. They required a large amount of helm to stay on course and were erratic and dangerous, particularly at high speeds. In 1886 the lower section of stern was extended to provide more deadwood aft, which improved things but did not solve the problem. They were bad seaboats, being very lively, uncomfortable and wet in heavy weather.

Edinburgh as completed

COLOSSUS class *turret ships*

Displacement:	9420t load
Dimensions:	325ft pp x 68ft x 25ft 9in (*99.06 pp x 20.73 x 7.85m*)
Machinery:	2-shaft, Maudslay (*Edinburgh* Humphreys) 3 cyl IC, 7488ihp = 16.5kts (*Edinburgh* 6808ihp = 16kts)
Armour:	Citadel 18in-14in sides, 16in-13in bulkheads, turrets 16in-14in, CT 14in, decks 3in-2½in
Armament:	4-12in BL (2x2), 5-6in BL (5x1), 4-6pdr QF (4x1), 2-14in TT
Complement:	396

Name	Builder	Laid down	Launched	Comp	Fate
COLOSSUS	Portsmouth DYd	6.6.1879	21.3.82	31.10.86	Sold for BU 1908
EDINBURGH (ex-MAJESTIC, 1882)	Pembroke DYd	20.3.1879	18.3.82	8.7.87	Sold for BU 1910

Constructed under the 1878-79 Estimates, *Colossus* and *Edinburgh* were basically enlarged versions of the *Ajax* class with a slightly higher speed, a heavier secondary armament, increased endurance and improved handling and sea-keeping qualities. However, they incorporated several innovations which marked them as a major advance over the earlier design – the substitution of BL guns for ML guns, the use of compound armour for the hull as well as for the turrets and the use of steel instead of iron for the majority of the hull structure.

The citadel was similar to that in *Ajax* but was larger and of oval shape with semi-circular end bulkheads to deflect projectiles. It was 123ft long and 16ft deep, the outer thickness of armour being compound. The area fore and aft of the citadel, above the protective deck, was extensively sub-divided, the compartments at the ships' sides being cork-filled and bounded by cofferdams, while the inner compartments were employed as coal bunkers. The CT gave good all-round vision, being placed forward of the mainmast with the chart-house on its roof. The stability level was even higher than in the earlier citadel ships and anti-rolling tanks and deep bilge keels were provided, but they had a long, fast roll making them bad gun platforms in a seaway. They were difficult to handle and manoeuvre but were better in this respect than the *Ajax* class.

The ships were originally designed to carry the same main armament as the *Ajax* but this was altered to 12in BLs while they were under construction. They were the first ships to have a secondary armament of any significance, with one 6in on each side of the forward superstructure and one 6in on each side and one at the extreme aft end of the after superstructure. These weapons were replaced by 6in QF guns in 1898.

Both ships ran trials during 1883-84, but completion was delayed because of the late delivery of the armament. *Colossus* served in the Mediterranean until 1893 when she became a coastguard ship at Holyhead. She was placed in reserve in 1901, and then became a tender to *Excellent* in 1904. *Edinburgh* served in the Mediterranean from 1887 to 1894, and then as the coastguard ship at Hull and Queensferry from 1894 to 1897. In reserve from 1897 to 1899, she was tender to *Wildfire* at Sheerness from 1899 to 1905, and was to finally employed as a target ship for experiments with shell and armour plate in 1908.

Conqueror as completed 1886

CONQUEROR class *turret rams*

Displacement: 6200t (*Hero* 6440t) load
Dimensions: 270ft pp, 288ft oa x 58ft x 23ft 6in (*82.3 pp, 87.78 oa x 17.68 x 7.16m*)
Machinery: 2-shaft, Humphreys (*Hero* Rennie) 3 cyl IC, 8 cyl boilers, 4500ihp = 14kts
Armour: Belt 12in-8in, citadel 12in-10½in, turret 14in-12in, bulkhead 11in, CT 12in-6in, decks 2½in-1¼in
Armament: 2-12in BL (1x2), 4-6in BL (4x1), 7-6pdr QF (7x1), 5-3pdr QF (5x1), 6-14in TT aw
Complement: 330

Name	Builder	Laid down	Launched	Comp	Fate
CONQUEROR	Chatham DYd	28.4.1879	8.9.81	Mar 1886	Sold for BU 1907
HERO	Chatham DYd	11.4.1884	27.10.85	May 1888	Sunk as gunnery target off Kentish Knock, 18.2.08. Raised and BU

Conqueror, provided under 1878-1879 Estimates, was an enlarged and improved *Rupert* with heavier guns, a steel hull, compound armour and modern machinery. Like *Rupert* it was intended that she serve as a ram, being fast and handy with her main armament concetrated forward. *Hero* was ordered three years after her sister. They were not successful ships as they were too small to serve efficiently as ocean-going vessels and too large for coast defence. Both served for most of their careers as gunnery tenders.

The belt, between lower and main decks, was 12in amidships and 8in at the ends, and stopped 27ft short of the stern where the ends were closed by 11in bulkheads. Beyond this the steering gear was protected by 2½in plating on the lower deck. The citadel between the main and upper decks was 102ft long on the centreline, with 12in sides and 10½in angled bulkheads, covered by a 1¾in deck. The turrets had 12in walls with 14in faces.

The arcs of fire of the turret were seriously restricted by blast effect on the forecastle deck and superstructure. The 6in guns in *Conqueror* were positioned on each side of the upper deck aft, and abreast the mainmast on the superstructure deck. In *Hero* all the 6in were provided with shields and the aftermost pair were moved up to the superstructure deck.

With only 9½ft of freeboard they were very wet forward and could not maintain more than about 10kts in heavy weather. They were bad seaboats and rolled heavily, but they manoeuvred and steamed well in calm weather.

Left: *Conqueror* as completed

Below: *Collingwood* from the port quarter, after the addition of a lower top to the mast but before the fitting of an after bridge

ADMIRAL class (1) *barbette ship*

Displacement:	9500t load
Dimensions:	325ft pp x 68ft x 26ft 4in (*99.06 pp x 20.73 x 8.03m*)
Machinery:	2-shaft, Humphreys 2 cyl IC, 12 cyl boilers, 9600ihp = 16.8kts
Armour:	Belt 18in-8in, bulkheads 16in-7in, barbettes 11½in-10in, CT 12in-2in, decks 3in-2in
Armament:	4-12in BL (2x2), 6-6in BL (6x1), 12-6pdr (12x1), 8-3pdr (8x1), 4-14in TT aw
Complement:	498

Name	Builder	Laid down	Launched	Comp	Fate
COLLINGWOOD	Pembroke DYd	12.7.1880	22.11.82	July 1887	Sold for BU 1909

Collingwood was Britain's first true barbette ship and provided the basic pattern for the majority of subsequent British battleships until the *Dreadnought* of 1906. Her general layout followed that of *Devastation* with the main armament equally disposed fore and aft on the centreline but she carried a larger midships structure, housing secondary and light armaments which, for the first time, were arranged in definite batteries. The model for her design was the French coast defence battleship *Caiman*, initially with the same displacement but as finally designed about 2000t larger. It was required, for economic reasons, that the ship should not exceed 10,000t, which limited the amount of protection and freeboard that could be provided after meeting the requirements of armament, speed and endurance.

Collingwood had fixed, pear-shaped barbettes 50ft long and 45ft wide, each having 11½in sloping sides, a 10in rear and a 3in floor giving protection to the turntable, crew, training and loading gear. The top of the barbette was covered with bullet-proof plating. The guns were loaded in the fixed fore and aft position. A trunk of 12in-10in thickness, between the rear of the barbette and the top of the citadel, protected the ammunition supply. This arrangement allowed for the guns to be carried higher than in turret ships, where they had a better command and were less affected in a seaway. On account of weight considerations, and because the citadel was no longer required to protect the turret bases and training gear, the citadel was reduced to an 18in belt, 140ft long by 7½ft deep, closed at the ends by 16in bulkheads and covered by a 3in deck. The belt extended to 5ft below the waterline and tapered over the lower 3½ft to 8in at the lower edge, bulkheads being 7in at the lower edge. The lower deck was 2½in thick outside the citadel, the area between this and main deck being extensively subdivided and employed for coal bunkers and stores. The coal stowage inside and outside the citadel was arranged to provide additional protection, but cork compartments of the type used in earlier citadel ships were not included, although the ship was fitted with anti-rolling tanks.

The secondary battery was mounted on the upper deck, three weapons on each side, and was unprotected except for splinter plating and 6in armour screens at the ends of the superstructure as a defence against raking fire. The object of the 6in guns was to provide defence against torpedo boats and to attack on enemy ships' unarmoured structures. The 6in BLs were replaced by 6in QF guns in 1896.

Collingwood was the first major warship fitted with forced-draught to her boilers but speed was not much improved because the engines were unable to take the steam generated by the boilers. On six-hour, full-power trials she made 16.6kts with 8369ihp under natural draught, and 16.84kts with 9573ihp under forced draught. She was a good seaboat and manoeuvred well but was very wet and due to her low freeboard could not maintain high speed in heavy weather. She served mainly in the Mediterranean, where weather conditions were comparatively mild. She became a coastguard ship in 1897 and was placed in reserve in 1903.

The *Camperdown* prior to her 1896-97 refit

ADMIRAL class (2) *barbette ships*

Displacement:	10,600t (*Howe* and *Rodney* 10,300t) load
Dimensions:	330ft pp x 68ft 6in x 27ft 10in (*100.58 pp x 20.88 x 8.48m*), (*Howe* and *Rodney* 325ft pp x 68ft x 27ft 10in (*99.06 pp x 20.73 x 8.48m*))
Machinery:	2-shaft, Humphreys (*Camperdown* Maudslay) 3 cyl IC, 12 cyl boilers, 11,500ihp = 17kts
Armour:	Belt 18in-8in, bulkheads 16in-7in, barbettes 11½in-10in (*Anson* and *Camperdown* 14in-12in), CT 12in-2in, decks 3in-2½in
Armament:	4-13.5in BL (2x2), 6-6in BL (6x1), 12-6pdr (12x1), 10-3pdr (10x1), 5-14in TT aw (1 bow, 4 broadside) (*Rodney* 4-14in TT aw, all broadside)
Complement:	530

Name	Builder	Laid down	Launched	Comp	Fate
ANSON	Pembroke DYd	24.4.1883	17.2.86	May 1889	Sold for BU 1909
CAMPERDOWN	Portsmouth DYd	18.12.1882	24.11.85	July 1889	Hulk 1908 Sold for BU 1911
HOWE	Pembroke DYd	7.6.1882	28.4.85	July 1889	Sold for BU 1910
RODNEY	Chatham DYd	6.2.1882	8.10.84	June 1888	Sold for BU 1909

These vessels were repeats of *Collingwood* with 13.5in 67t guns in place of the 12in 45t. *Howe* and *Rodney* were 800t heavier than the prototype, drawing 18in more, which increased the immersion of the belt armour. *Anson* and *Camperdown* were further modified to include heavier barbette armour, a 10ft longer belt and increased length and beam to maintain draught and prevent any further immersion of the belt. The machinery power was increased to maintain speed with the extra weight. Natural draught power was 7500ihp for 16kts; trial speeds with forced draught were 16.9kts (*Howe* and *Rodney*), 17.1kts (*Camperdown*), and 17.4kts (*Anson*). During 1896-1897 all had their 6in BL guns replaced by 6in QFs, and all except *Rodney* were fitted with a tall signal mast between the forefunnel and bridge.

Their completion was late because of delays in the production of their big guns. Service was divided between Home Waters and the Mediterranean. On 2.11.92 *Howe* ran aground on Ferrol Rock during a Mediterranean cruise, but she was salvaged in 1893 and repaired. On 22.6.93 *Camperdown* accidentally rammed and sank *Victoria*, and herself came close to capsizing on account of the subsequent flooding of the forward compartments (see *Victoria*).

Benbow, the last vessel of the 'Admiral' class, mounted 16.25in 110t BL guns in place of the 13.5in weapons of the earlier group. Weight considerations meant that only one gun could be mounted in each barbette but the margin of weight thus obtained allowed for an additional four 6in guns in the secondary battery. In other respects she was virtually identical to *Anson* and *Camperdown*.

The 16.25in gun, also mounted in the *Victoria* and *Sans Pareil*, was the largest calibre gun mounted in a British ship with the exception of the 18in weapons mounted in *Furious* and monitors during the First World War. Oddly enough it was not chosen for its power but because of the limited manufacturing capacity for the 13.5in Woolwich gun. The 16.25in was manufactured by Armstrongs to their own design; it was not entirely successful as it was slow-firing, of limited life and tended to 'droop'.

Benbow was delivered from the builders in 1886 but did not commission until 1888. She served in the Mediterranean from 1888 to 1891 and as a coastguard ship at Greenock from 1894 to 1904. She spent the remainder of her career in reserve, except when commissioned for manoeuvres in 1893.

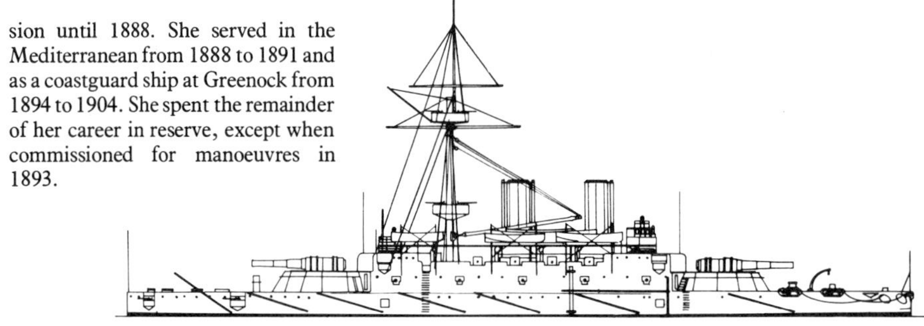

Benbow 1889

ADMIRAL class (3) *barbette ship*

Displacement: 10,600t load
Dimensions: 330ft pp x 68ft 6in x 27ft 10in (*100.58 pp x 20.88 x 8.48m*)
Machinery: 2-shaft, Maudslay 3 cyl IC, 12 cyl boilers, 10,860ihp = 17.5kts, forced draught
Armour: Belt 18in-8in, bulkheads 16in-7in, barbettes 14in-12in, CT 12in-2in, decks 3in-2½in
Armament: 2-16.25in BL (2x1), 10-6in BL (10x1), 12-6pdr QF (12x1), 7-3pdr QF (7x1), 5-14in, TT aw (1 bow, 4 broadside)
Complement: 523

Name	Builder	Laid down	Launched	Comp	Fate
BENBOW	Thames Iron Wks, Blackwall	1.11.1882	15.6.85	June 1888	Sold for BU 1909

The *Benbow* during the 1890s

The 'Admiral' class were severely criticised by sea officers and the public as being insufficiently protected, and therefore, in the *Victoria* class, a reversion was made to the turret ship. The 'Admirals' were in fact comparatively well protected and although the turret system gave better defence to the main armament the hull protection in these later vessels showed no great improvement. The *Victoria* design was basically an improved *Hero*, with size increased to meet the requirements of a first class ship, the concentration of the main armament in a twin turret forward being more economic on weight than single guns mounted fore and aft. As in *Benbow* the adoption of 16.25in Armstrong guns was due mainly to the limited supply of 13.5in guns.

The citadel was similar to that in the 'Admirals' but larger, being 162ft long and 8½in deep. The main deck over the citadel and the lower deck fore and aft of the citadel were 3in thick. The turret base was protected by a pear-shaped redoubt which extended down to the forward end of the citadel. The secondary battery of 6in guns was divided into two groups by an athwartships 3in bulkhead and was protected against raking fire by 6in screen bulkheads at the forward and after ends. An unprotected 10in gun was mounted on the spar deck aft to provide fire astern.

These were the first battleships to have TE engines. The boilers were arranged in four independent compartments, two on each side, and, for the first time in a British ship, two funnels were fitted side by side. Boiler working pressure was 135psi compared with 90psi in the 'Admirals'. *Victoria* completed with short funnels but these were raised 17ft in 1890 to improve natural draught to the boilers. *Sans Pareil* was completed with tall funnels. Both were good steamers and substantially exceeded their designed engine power. The *Victoria* was the first battleship to be built by Armstrongs; both ships were delayed by the late delivery of their main armament. Slightly better seaboats than the 'Admirals', they were steady and better able to maintain speed in a seaway, but their low freeboard made them wet forward which seriously affected the efficiency of the forecastle turret.

On 22 June 1893 *Victoria*, while serving as flagship of the Mediterranean Fleet (Vice-Admiral Sir G Tryon), was lost during manoeuvres off Tripoli as a result of a collision with HMS *Camperdown*.

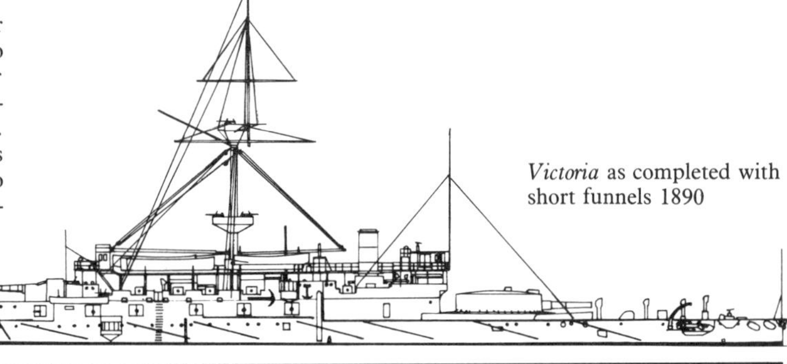

Victoria as completed with short funnels 1890

VICTORIA class *turret ships*

Displacement: 10,470t load
Dimensions: 340ft pp, 363ft oa x 70ft x 26ft 9in (*103.63 pp, 110.64 oa x 21.34 x 8.15m*)
Machinery: 2-shaft, Humphreys 3 cyl TE, 8 boilers, 8000ihp = 16kts natural draught, 14,244ihp = 17.3kts forced draught (*Sans Pareil* 14,482ihp = 17.75kts forced draught)
Armour: Belt 18in, bulkheads 16in, turret 17in, redoubt 18in, battery screens 6in-3in, CT 14in-2in, decks 3in
Armament: 2-16.25in BL (2x1), 1-10in BL, 12-6in BL (12x1), 12-6pdr QF (12x1), 9-3pdr QF (9x1), 4-14in TT, (2 sub on beam, 1 bow, 1 stern aw), 2-14in TLC
Complement: 550

Name	Builder	Laid down	Launched	Comp	Fate
VICTORIA (ex-RENOWN, 1887)	Armstrong, Elswick	23.4.1885	9.4.87	Mar 1890	Sunk 22.6.93
SANS PAREIL	Thames Iron Wks, Blackwall	21.4.1885	9.5.87	8.7.91	Sold for BU 1907

Above: *Sans Pareil* as completed for service

Right: The *Nile* as completed

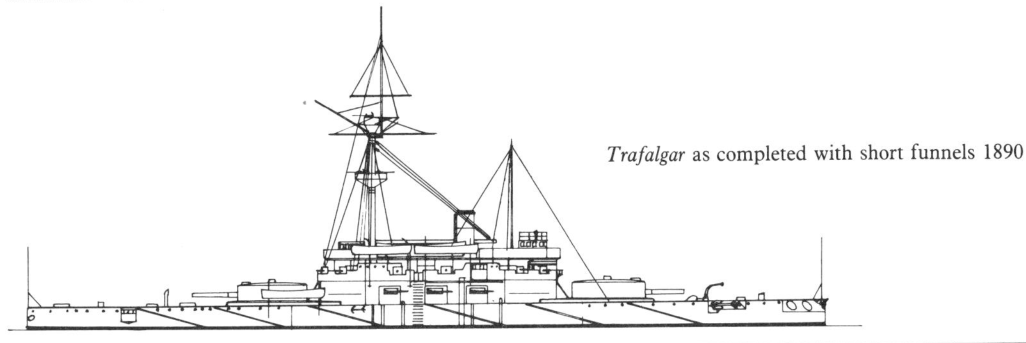

Trafalgar as completed with short funnels 1890

TRAFALGAR class *turret ships*

Displacement: 12,590t load
Dimensions: 345ft pp x 73ft x 28ft 6in (*105.15 pp x 22.25 x 8.69m*)
Machinery: 2-shaft, Humphreys (*Nile* Maudslay) 3 cyl TE, 6 cyl boilers, 7500ihp = 15kts natural draught, 12,000ihp = 16.75kts forced draught
Armour: Belt 20in-14in, bulkheads 16in-14in, citadel 18in-16in, turrets 18in, CT 14in, decks 3in
Armament: 4-13.5in BL (2x2), 6-4.7in QF (6x1), 8-6pdr QF, 9-3pdr QF, 4-14in TT, (2 sub, 1 bow and 1 stern aw)
Complement: 577

Name	Builder	Laid down	Launched	Comp	Fate
TRAFALGAR	Portsmouth DYd	18.1.1886	20.9.87	Mar 1890	Sold for BU 1911
NILE	Pembroke DYd	8.4.1886	27.3.88	10.7.91	Sold for BU 1912

Provided under 1886 Estimates, these vessels were designed to meet the demand for ships with substantially better protection than the *Victoria* and 'Admiral' classes, and were the largest and best protected turret ships to date. They were modelled on *Dreadnought* but lacked a full length belt in favour of heavier armour amidships. The displacement was substantially increased over previous vessels to accommodate a high level of protection.

The belt, between the lower and main decks, was 230ft long by 8ft 6in deep, 3ft being above the waterline, 20in thick amidships reducing to 18in fore and aft, 14in at the ends, and closed by 16in forward and 14in aft bulkheads. The citadel, between the main and upper decks, was 141ft long at the side and 193ft long on the centre-line, and was 16in thick amidships increasing to 18in around turret bases. Decks over the citadel and fore and aft of the belt were 3in. The secondary battery in the superstructure was protected by 4in sides and 5in end bulkheads, as defence against QF guns, the bulkheads being added during construction and accounting for most of the weight increase above the designed displacement of 11,940t.

Designed to carry secondary armament of 8–5in BLs, the vessels were fitted with Armstrong 4.7in QFs shortly before completion. These were in turn replaced by 6in QFs in 1896. *Trafalgar* was completed with short funnels which were raised 17ft in 1891 to improve natural draught to the boilers, and *Nile* was completed with tall funnels. *Trafalgar* was actually completed in 1889 and *Nile* in 1890, both ships being delayed by the late delivery of their armament. As with previous low-freeboard ships, they were very wet and unable to maintain high speeds at sea – the best sea speed was 13-14kts in moderate conditions. Both had active careers in the Mediterranean until 1897-98, when they returned to home waters for service as portguard ships prior to being placed in reserve. *Trafalgar* served as a drillship at Sheerness from 1907 until 1909.

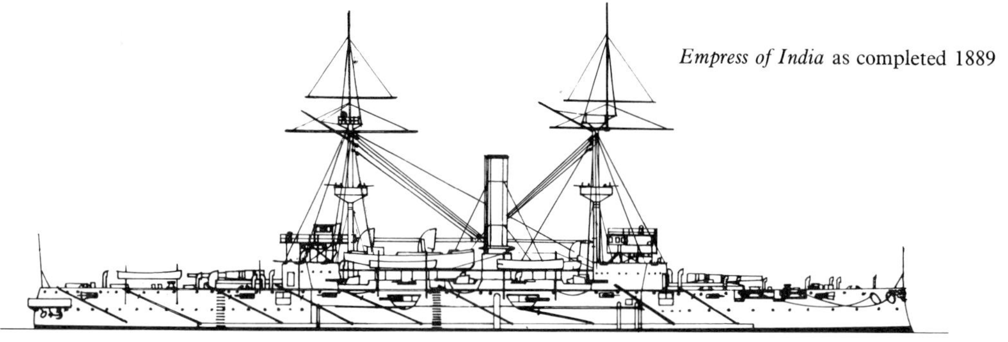

Empress of India as completed 1889

ROYAL SOVEREIGN class *first class battleships*

Displacement: 14,150t load, 15,580t deep
Dimensions: 380ft pp, 410ft 6in oa x 75ft x 27ft 6in (*115.82 pp, 124.97 oa x 22.86 x 8.38m*)
Machinery: 2-shaft, 3 cyl TE, 8 cyl boilers, 9000ihp = 15.5kts natural draught, 11,000ihp = 16.5kts forced draught
Armour: Belt 18in-14in, bulkheads 16in-14in, upper belt 4in-3in, barbettes 17in-11in, casemates 6in, CT 14in, decks 3in-2½in
Armament: 4-13.5in BL (2x2), 10-6in QF (10x1), 16-6pdr QF (16x1), 12-3pdr QF (12x1), 7-18in TT (5 aw, 2 sub)
Complement: 712

Name	Builder	Laid down	Launched	Comp	Fate
EMPRESS OF INDIA (ex-RENOWN, 1890)	Pembroke DYd	9.7.1889	7.5.91	Aug 1893	Sunk as target off Portland 1913
RAMILLIES	Thomson, Clydebank	11.8.1890	1.3.92	Oct 1893	Sold for BU 1913
REPULSE	Pembroke DYd	1.1.1890	27.2.92	Apr 1894	Sold for BU 1911
RESOLUTION	Palmer	14.6.1890	28.5.92	Nov 1893	Sold for BU 1914
REVENGE	Palmer	12.2.1891	3.11.92	Mar 1894	Sold for BU 1919
ROYAL OAK	Laird, Birkenhead	29.5.1890	5.11.92	June 1894	Sold for BU 1914
ROYAL SOVEREIGN	Portsmouth DYd	30.9.1889	26.2.91	May 1892	Sold for BU 1913

Provided under the Naval Defence Act of 1889, the *Royal Sovereigns* represented the beginning of a fifteen year period of stability in British battleship design, and were the first class of what were to become known as the pre-dreadnoughts. Prior to deciding upon the design of the new ships the Admiralty, largely under the influence of the new DNC Sir William White, made a detailed study of various turret and barbette ship designs, and of existing British and foreign ships. One of the main results was the decision that if these ships were to be given adequate seakeeping qualities, a higher freeboard than that of existing designs would be required. Topweight considerations ruled out the turret system in a high freeboard vessel and the design decided upon was virtually an extended and much improved version of the 'Admiral' class barbette ships, whose general layout and distribution of armament was considered to be the best arrangement for the new ships. The main improvements on the 'Admiral' class design were: (1) the raising of the freeboard to 18ft by the addition of another full length deck; (2) barbettes with vertical armour walls extending down to the citadel thus avoiding the danger of shells detonating under the barbette; (3) the addition of an upper belt as protection against QF guns. To these could be added a heavier secondary armament and a higher speed, but in these cases the improvement was largely a result of technical progress. There was of course a penalty in that the *Royal Sovereigns* were 4000t larger than the 'Admirals'.

The belt was 252ft long by 8ft 8in deep, 5ft being below the waterline, and was 18in thick amidships reducing to 16in and 14in forward and aft. It was closed by 16in forward and 14in aft bulkheads and covered by a 3in (middle) deck; the lower deck forward and aft of the belt was 2½in, and the upper belt between the main and middle decks was of 4in NS armour, with 3in NS bulkheads at the ends. These were the first British ships in which this type of armour was used. The barbettes, protecting gun mountings, machinery and loading gear, were pear-shaped, with 17in armour on the major diameter and 16in on the minor one, reducing to 11in behind the upper belt. The areas behind the main and upper belts were employed as coal bunkers for additional protection.

The secondary armament was disposed on two decks to give a wide distribution and to minimise the effect of a single hit. Four of the 6in QFs were mounted on the main deck in casemates, the remainder on the upper deck with splinter shields only. The main faults with this system were that the casemates were too close to the wl, a common fault in the majority of pre-dreadnoughts, and that the shielded mounts were too vulnerable. The latter was corrected during 1902/4 when the upper deck 6in guns were provided with 5in KC armour casemates.

The machinery of the dockyard-built ships was supplied by Humphreys & Tennant, and in the remainder it was provided by the builder. All the vessels exceeded their designed power on trials and made between 17.25 and 18.27kts under forced draught.

The *Royal Sovereigns* were designed for a long, steady roll to provide good gun platforms, but when first completed they were inclined to roll too heavily under certain conditions. This was corrected by the addition of bilge keels, and they subsequently proved to be excellent seaboats quite capable, owing to their high freeboard, of maintaining high speeds in a seaway.

Early service was divided between the Channel and Mediterranean Fleets, but after 1902 they served exclusively in home waters. *Revenge* was rescued from the breakers by the outbreak of the First World War and was employed as bombardment vessel of the Belgian coast 1914-1915. She was renamed *Redoubtable* in 1915 and served as a tender to *Victory* until 1919.

Repulse as completed

The *Hood* in 1893

The eighth battleship of the Naval Defence act, built at the instigation of Admiral Hood as a turret ship. Generally following the design of the *Royal Sovereign* class, with identical compartmentation, armour and armament distribution, *Hood* however lacked these ships' high freeboard, this being rendered impracticable by the topweight involved in the adoption of turrets. *Hood* provided a useful comparison with her half-sisters and vindicated the adoption of the barbette/high freeboard design, as she was a poor seaboat unable to maintain high speeds in a seaway. As with earlier low freeboard turret ships she served mainly in the comparatively calm waters of the Mediterranean. Her four aw TT were removed in 1903. She became a receiving ship at Queenstown in 1910, the 6in guns being removed. She was employed as a target from 1911 to 1914 for underwater protection experiments, and was the first ship to be fitted with a bulge.

HOOD *turret battleship*

Displacement: 14,150t load, 15,590t deep
Dimensions: 380ft pp, 410ft 6in oa x 75ft x 27ft 6in (*115.82 pp, 124.97 oa x 22.86 x 8.33m*)
Machinery: 2-shaft, Humphreys & Tennant 3 cyl, TE, 8 cyl boilers, 9000ihp = 15.7kts natural draught, 11,000ihp = 16.7kts forced draught
Armour: Belt 18in-14in, bulkheads 16in-14in, turrets 17in-11in, casemates 6in, upper belt 4in, CT 14in, decks 3in-2½in
Armament: 4-13.5in BL (2x2), 10-6in QF (10x1), 10-6pdr QF (10x1), 12-3pdr (12x1), 5-18in TT, (2 sub, 4 aw)
Complement: 690

Name	Builder	Laid down	Launched	Comp	Fate
HOOD	Chatham DYd	12.8.1889	30.7.91	May 1893	Sunk as blockship, Portland 1914

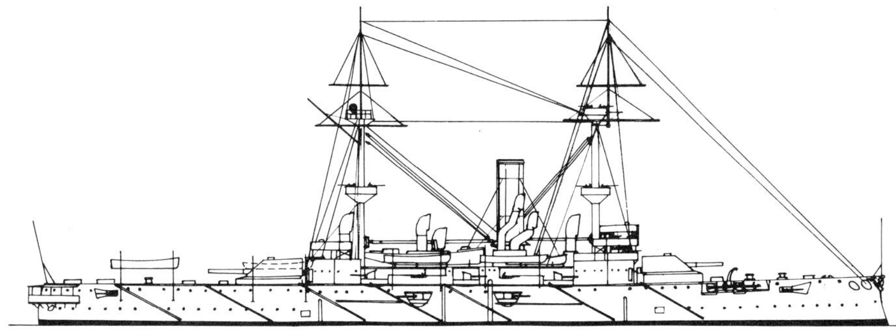

Centurion 1894

These ships were second class battleships constructed for service on the China and Pacific stations. They were virtually small editions of the *Royal Sovereign*; the reduction in size was mainly for economic reasons with regard to both construction and running costs. Designed with a shallow draught, for navigation on Chinese rivers, they shipped a comparatively light armament, had a high speed and a high endurance (6000 nm at 10kts compared with 4700 nm in the *Royal Sovereigns*) and were fitted with wood and copper sheathing for tropical service. Their value was limited as they could not face first class battleships, although they were fast enough to escape from them, but could be employed against slow armoured cruisers in existence at the time of their completion, in particular Russian vessels stationed in the Far East.

CENTURION class *second class battleships*

Displacement: 10,500t load
Dimensions: 360ft pp x 70ft x 25ft 6in (*109.73 pp x 21.34 x 7.77m*)
Machinery: 2-shaft, Greenock Foundry 3 cyl TE, 8 cyl boilers, 9000ihp = 17kts nautral draught, 13,000ihp=18.5kts forced draught
Armour: Main belt 12in-9in, bulkheads 8in, upper belt 4in, barbettes 9in-5in, gun houses 6in, casemates 6in, CT 12in, decks 2½in-2in
Armament: 4-10in BL (2x2), 10-4.7in QF (10x1), 8-6pdr QF (8x1), 12-3pdr QF (12x1), 7-18in TT, (2 sub, 5 aw)
Complement: 620

Name	Builder	Laid down	Launched	Comp	Fate
CENTURION	Portsmouth DYd	30.3.1890	3.8.92	Feb 1894	Sold for BU 1910
BARFLEUR	Chatham DYd	12.10.1890	10.8.92	June 1894	Sold for BU 1910

Armour was disposed as in *Royal Sovereign*. The main belt was 200ft long by 7½ft deep with 5ft below the waterline, 12inch amidships reducing to 10in fore and aft, and 9in at the ends. The main belt was closed by 8in bulkheads, the upper belt by 3in bulkheads. Barbettes were 9in above the upper belt and 8in-5in behind it. Decks were 2in over the belt and 2½in fore and aft of it. The main armament was provided with all round loading, allowing the use of circular barbettes of less weight than the pear shape previously used. The gun mechanism and crew were more exposed than in earlier vessels, and a revolving, armoured hood with an open back, was fitted over the barbette, this being the origin of the armoured gun houses of later ships, which were soon to become generally and incorrectly referred to as turrets. The upper belt, gun houses and casemates were of Harvey NS and the protective deck of NS, the remainder being compound armour.

Both vessels were good steamers and good seaboats. Under natural draught *Centurion* made 17.5kts with 9703ihp and *Barfleur* 17.1kts with 9934ihp. Under forced draught they produced 13,214ihp and 13,163ihp respectively, giving an approximate speed of 18.5kts. Forced draught in these and other ships was subsequently discontinued as it caused damage to boilers, greatly increased maintenance requirements and reduced efficiency.

Centurion was reconstructed in 1901-03 and *Barfleur* in 1902-04, this mainly involving replacing the 4.7in guns with 6in guns, all of which were mounted in 5in armoured casemates. Six 6in guns were fitted on the main deck and four on the upper deck. This modification added considerable extra weight andndrastic weight saving was achieved by replacing the foremast with a light signal mast and removing the after bridge, aw TT and all other unnecessary fittings and structures. As a result the increase in displacement was only 80t. On post–refit trials *Centurion* made 16.8kts with 9270ihp and *Barfleur* 16.75kts with 9137ihp under natural draught.

Centurion saw extensive service on the China station from 1894 to 1901 and from 1903 to 1905, being flagship during the earlier period. *Barfleur* served in the Mediterranean from 1895 to 1898, and on the China station from 1898 to 1902. Both ships spent their later years in home waters.

Constructed under the 1892-1893 Estimates, *Renown* was an enlarged version of the *Centurion* class ships with a heavier secondary armament, all NS armour and increased speed and endurance. She was almost 2000t heavier than the earlier vessels, the length and beam being increased to maintain shallow draught. The use of NS allowed for some thinning of the main belt and barbettes,without any loss of protective value in comparison with compound plates. Protection was also improved by increasing the thickness of the upper belt, which substantially added to the effectiveness of the side armour, and by sloping the outer edge of the protective deck over the citadel to meet the lower edge of the belt. This latter arrangement served to deflect shells which penetrated the belt and reduced the area likely to be flooded by waterline hits.

The main belt was 210ft long, 8in thick amidships and 6in at the ends, and closed by 10in forward and 9in after bulkheads. The upper belt was closed by 6in bulkheads. The deck over the main belt was 2in on the flat and 3in on the slope, the deck fore and aft of the belt being 2in and 3in. The barbettes were 10in above the upper belt and 5in behind it. All the 6in guns were fitted in casemates, six on main deck with 6in armour and four on upper deck with 4in armour. For the first time part of the 12pdr armament was arranged in a definite battery, with four guns on each side of the upper deck between the 6in casemates.

Renown proved to be an excellent steamer, manoeuvring well and being a good seaboat with an easy roll. On trials she made 17.9kts under natural draught with 10,708ihp and 19.75kts under forced draught with 12,901ihp.

Transferred to Devonport DYd in 1896 for final fitting out, she served as flagship to Vice-Admiral Sir John Fisher on the North America and West Indies station from 1897 to 1899, and in the Mediterranean from 1899 to 1902. The main deck 6in guns were removed in 1902 when she was fitted out to carry the Duke and Duchess of Connaught to India. The remaining 6in guns were removed during her 1904/5 refit prior to taking the Prince and Princess of Wales to India. In reserve 1902-04 and 1906-07, *Renown* served as a stokers' TS at Portsmouth from 1909 until 1913.

Renown in 1905

RENOWN *second class battleship*

Displacement:	12,350t load
Dimensions:	380ft pp, 408ft oa x 72ft x 26ft 9in (*115.82 pp, 124.36 oa x 21.95 x 8.15*)
Machinery:	2-shaft, Maudslay 3 cyl TE, 8 cyl boilers, 10,000ihp = 17.5kts natural draught, 12,000ihp = 18kts forced draught
Armour:	Belt 8in-6in, bulkheads 10in-6in, upper belt 6in, barbettes 10in, gun houses 6in, casemates 6in-4in, CT 9in, decks 3in-2in
Armament:	4-10in BL (2x2), 10-6in QF (10x1), 12-12pdr QF (12x1), 12-3pdr QF (12x1), 5-18in TT, (4 sub, 1 aw)
Complement:	674

Name	Builder	Laid down	Launched	Comp	Fate
RENOWN	Pembroke DYd	Feb 1893	8.5.95	Jan 1897	Sold for BU 1914

MAJESTIC class *first class battleships*

Displacement:	14,560t to 14,890t load, 15,730t to 16,060t deep
Dimensions:	390ft pp, 421ft oa x 75ft x 27ft (*118.87 pp, 128.32 oa x 22.86 x 8.23m*)
Machinery:	2-shaft, 3 cyl TE, 8 cyl boilers, 10000ihp = 16kts natural draught, 12000ihp = 17kts forced draught
Armour:	Belt 9in, bulkheads 14in-12in, barbettes 14in, gun houses 10in, casemates 6in, CT 14in, decks 4in-2½in
Armament:	4-12in BL (2x2), 12-6in QF (12x1), 16-12pdr QF (16x1), 12-2pdr QF (12x1), 5-18in TT, (4 sub, 1 aw)
Complement:	672

Name	Builder	Laid down	Launched	Comp	Fate
CAESAR	Portsmouth DYd	25.3.1895	2.9.96	Jan 1898	Sold for BU 1921
HANNIBAL	Pembroke DYd	1.5.1894	28.4.96	Apr 1898	Sold for BU 1920
ILLUSTRIOUS	Chatham DYd	11.3.1895	17.9.96	Apr 1898	Sold for BU 1920
JUPITER	Thomson, Clydebank	26.4.1894	18.11.95	May 1897	Sold for BU 1920
MAJESTIC	Portsmouth DYd	Feb 1894	31.1.95	Dec 1895	Torpedoed and sunk by *U21*, Eastern Mediterranean 27.5.15
MAGNIFICENT	Chatham DYd	18.12.1893	19.12.94	Dec 1895	Sold for BU 1921
MARS	Laird, Birkenhead	2.6.1894	30.3.96	June 1897	Sold for BU 1921
PRINCE GEORGE	Portsmouth DYd	10.9.1894	22.8.95	Nov 1896	Sold for BU 1921 Foundered on passage to Germany 30.12.21
VICTORIOUS	Chatham DYd	28.5.1894	19.10.95	Nov 1896	Sold for BU 1922

The largest class of battleships ever built, the *Majestics* were provided under the Spencer Programme of 1893, and split between the 1893/4 and 1894/5 Estimates. They combined the basic features of the *Royal Sovereign* class with the improvements already adopted in *Renown*. In addition a new 12in wire-wound gun, the Mk VIII, was substituted for the 13.5in gun of the earlier class providing some saving in weight which was employed to enlarge the secondary and light gun batteries. The 12in gun proved superior to the 13.5in except in shell weight, and was to remain the standard British battleship weapon for sixteen years.

All vertical armour was of Harvey NS. Compared with *Renown* the main and upper belts were combined into a single belt 220ft long by 16ft deep, of uniform 9in thickness, and fully enclosed gun houses were provided over the barbettes. The belt was closed by 14in forward and 12in after bulkheads, and the protective decks remained at the same levels as before, being 3in on the flat and 4in on the slope amidships, and 2½in forward and aft. The barbettes reduced to 7in behind the belt. The bridge was fitted around the base of the foremast, with the CT in the clear area forward of it, thus avoiding the danger of damaged bridgework falling across the CT, but in the last three ships, *Hannibal*, *Illustrious* and *Caesar*, the old system of mounting the bridge above the CT was reverted to. Early units had pear-shaped barbettes with fixed loading positions fore and aft, although all-round loading was possible using the limited supply of ready-use ammunition. *Caesar* and *Illustrious* were fitted with new mountings which provided all-round loading, and had circular barbettes. Eight of the 6in guns were mounted on the main deck and four on the upper deck, all being housed in 6in armour casemates. In later years electric hoists were fitted for the 6in ammunition supply.

They proved to be good seaboats, with an easy roll, and manoeuvred well. They were good steamers but had a high fuel consumption. *Mars* was fitted to carry 400t of oil fuel (sacrificing 200t coal) in 1905/6, and the others were similarly fitted by 1908. On trials all exceeded their designed speed, but the trials were run light, and at natural draught they made between 15.8 and 16.9kts and at forced draught 17.6 to 18.7kts.

The vessels served most of their peacetime careers in home waters, mainly with the Channel Fleet (*Majestic*, flagship 1895-1903), the exceptions being *Victorious* (China 1898-1900, Mediterranean 1898 and 1900-1903) and *Caesar* (Mediterranean 1898-1903).

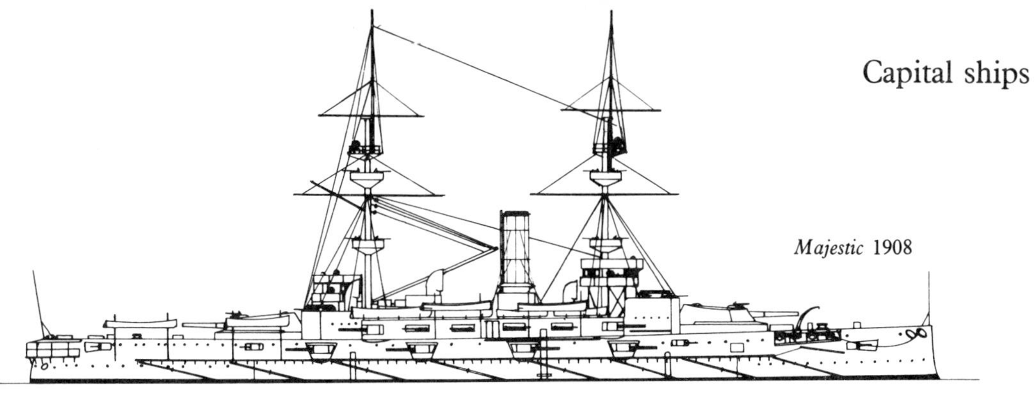

Majestic 1908

Prince George after her 1904 refit. The bridge is positioned around the foremast leaving the CT clear of obstruction

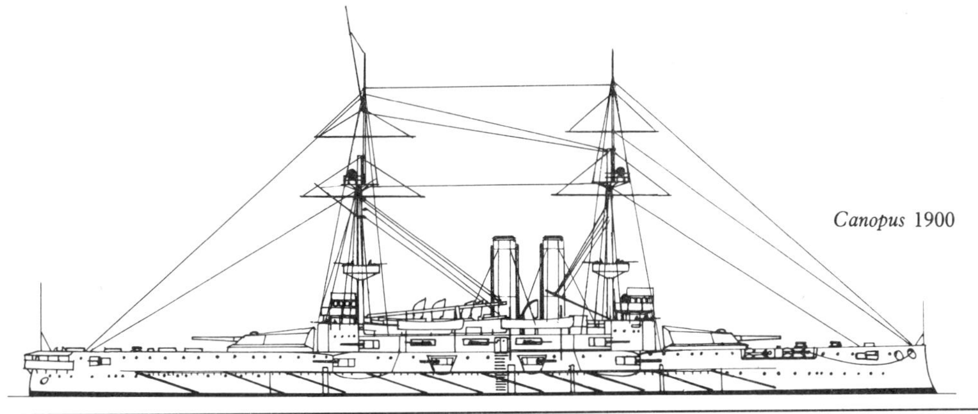

Canopus 1900

CANOPUS class *first class battleships*

Displacement: 13,150t load, 14,300t deep
Dimensions: 390ft pp, 421ft 6in oa x 74ft x 26ft 2in (*118.87 pp, 128.47 oa x 22.56 x 7.98m*)
Machinery: 2-shaft, 3 cyl TE, 20 Belleville boilers, 13,500ihp = 18kts
Armour: Belt 6in, bulkheads 10in-6in, barbettes 12in, gun houses 8in, casemates 6in, CT 12in, decks 2in-1in
Armament: 4-12in BL (2x2), 12-6in QF (12x1), 10-12pdr QF (10x1), 6-3pdr (6x1), 4-18in TT sub
Complement: 682

Name	Builder	Laid down	Launched	Comp	Fate
ALBION	Thames Iron Wks, Blackwall	3.12.1896	21.6.98	June 1901	Sold for BU 1919
CANOPUS	Portsmouth DYd	4.1.1897	12.10.97	Dec 1899	Sold for BU 1920
GLORY	Laird, Birkenhead	1.12.1896	11.3.99	Oct 1900	Sold for BU 1922
GOLIATH	Chatham DYd	4.1.1897	23.3.98	Mar 1900	Torpedoed and sunk by Turkish TB *Mauvenet* in E Mediterranean 15.5.15
OCEAN	Devonport DYd	15.2.1897	5.7.98	Feb 1900	Mined and sunk in Dardenelles 18.3.15
VENGEANCE	Vickers, Barrow	23.8.1898	25.7.99	Apr 1902	Sold for BU 1921

The first five vessels of this class were provided under the 1896/7 Estimates, and *Vengeance* under the 1897/8 Estimates. Smaller and faster editions of the *Majestic*, they were designed partly for the China station, to counter the growing naval power of Japan. A weight saving of 2000t was effected mainly by general reductions of armour thicknesses, but the adoption of Krupp armour for the belt meant that the reduction in the protective value was not as great as the figures suggest (the 6in Krupp belt was approximately as effective as 8in of Harvey steel). They were nevertheless close to being second class ships.

The armour was arranged as in *Majestic* except for an extension of the belt to the stem, with 2in plating and the addition of a second 1in protective deck across the top of the belt. The belt extension was intended to protect buoyancy forward but was ineffective except as splinter protection and against light guns. The 1in deck provided protection against howitzers which, it was reported incorrectly, the French intended to fit in their ships. The rest of the protective decks were a uniform 2in. The belt was 195ft long, excluding the 2in section, by 14ft deep, with the barbettes reduced to 6in behind the belt.

The armament was also arranged as in *Majestic*. The 12in guns were provided with all-round loading and circular barbettes of the same type as in *Caesar* and *Illustrious*. The *Vengeance* was fitted with improved mountings which allowed for loading at any elevation, and her gun houses were constructed of Krupp steel. Because these plates could not be curved easily her gun houses were flat sided.

These were the first British battleships fitted with water-tube boilers, which allowed for higher power without an increase in weight. The Belleville boilers worked at a pressure of 300psi compared with 155psi in the cylindrical boilers of earlier ships. The vessels were good steamers, and on full power trials most achieved about 18.5kts with over 13,500ihp. The side-by-side arrangement of the funnels was abandoned in favour of fore and aft funnels, as this suited the disposition of the Belleville boilers.

All except *Canopus* (Mediterranean 1899-1903) served most of their early careers on the China station (*Glory* flagship 1900-1905), returning to home waters in 1905 (*Goliath* 1903) following the Anglo-Japanese alliance.

The *Goliath* after the addition of fire control gear and wireless rig
By courtesy of John Roberts

Implacable after the addition of fire control platforms on the fore and mainmasts. The first funnel was round and the second oval, but from the beam they presented equal profiles and looked the same size

FORMIDABLE class *first class battleships*

Displacement:	14,500t load, 15,800t deep
Dimensions:	400ft pp, 431ft 9in oa x 75ft x 25ft 11in (*121.92 pp, 131.6oa x 22.86 x 7.9m*)
Machinery:	2-shaft, 3 cyl TE, 20 Belleville boilers, 15,000ihp = 18kts
Armour:	Belt 9in, bulkheads 12in-9in, barbettes 12in, gun houses 10in-8in, casemates 6in, CT 14in, decks 3in-1in
Armament:	4-12in BL (2x2), 12-6in QF (12x1), 16-12pdr QF (16x1), 6-3pdr QF (6x1), 4-18in TT sub
Complement:	780

Name	Builder	Laid down	Launched	Comp	Fate
FORMIDABLE	Portsmouth DYd	21.3.1898	17.11.98	Sept 1901	Torpedoed and sunk by *U24* off Portland 1.1.15
IRRESISTIBLE	Chatham DYd	11.4.1898	15.12.98	Feb 1902	Mined and sunk in Dardanelles 18.3.15
IMPLACABLE	Devonport DYd	13.7.1898	11.3.99	Sept 1901	Sold for BU 1921

Constructed under the 1897/8 Estimates, these ships, although generally referred to as improved *Majestics*, closely resembled an enlarged *Canopus* design, in which the advantages of Krupp armour were used to improve protection rather than reduce size. Their designed load displacement was 15,000t.

The armour layout was similar to *Canopus*', except that the belt continued to the stern as well as to the bow. The belt was 9in Krupp, 218ft long by 15ft deep, and continued to the stem as a 3in belt 12ft deep, and to the stern as a 1½in belt 8ft deep. The barbettes reduced to 6in behind the belt, whilst the gun houses were of Krupp steel with 10in sides and 8in backs. Decks were as *Canopus* except the middle deck, which was increased to 3in on the slope, and the lower deck aft, to 2½in.

The armament disposition followed that of the earlier ships but the main and secondary guns were of increased calibre: 12in/40 in place of 12in/35 and 6in/45 in place 6in/40. The 12in guns could be loaded on any bearing or elevation, and the mounting was provided with a split hoist, with a working chamber beneath the guns to reduce the possibility of cordite fire spreading.

On full power trials they averaged 18.2kts with 15,500ihp. Handier than the *Majestics* due to their improved hull form and the cutting away of deadwood aft, they did not, however, manoeuvre well at slow speeds because of the inward-turning screws, which were adopted because they gave a slight improvement in speed and a reduction in fuel consumption.

The ships served in the Mediterranean from 1901 until 1908, after which they returned to home waters for the remainder of their peacetime service.

The first three ships of the *London* class were constructed under the 1898/9 Estimates and the last two under the 1900/01 Estimates. They were repeats of the *Formidable* class except for some modifications to protection. The forward armour bulkhead was omitted in favour of a stronger forward belt, the main 9in belt being extended 32ft further forward after which thicknesses reduced from 7in, 5in and 3in to 2in at the stem. In addition the main deck was increased to 2in and continued to the stem, reducing to 1½in at the forward end; the middle deck reduced to 1in on the flat and 2in on the slopes; and the lower deck forward reduced to 1in. *Queen* and *Prince of Wales* differed from the others in having open 12pdr gun batteries amidships on the upper deck. *Queen* was fitted with Babcock and Wilcox boilers. The designed displacement was 15,000t. All served in the Mediterranean until 1907-1908, when they returned to home waters.

LONDON class *first class battleships*

Displacement: 14,500t load, 15,700t deep, average (*Queen, Prince of Wales* 14,150t load, 15,400t deep, average)
Dimensions: 400ft pp, 431ft 9in oa x 75ft x 26ft (*121.92 pp, 131.6 oa, x 22.86 x 7.92m*)
Machinery: 2-shaft, 3 cyl TE, 20 Belleville boilers, 15,000ihp = 18kts
Armour: Belt 9in, bulkheads 12in-9in, barbettes 12in, gun houses 10in-8in, casemates 6in, CT 14in, decks 2½in-1in
Armament: 4-12in BL (2x2), 12-6in QF (12x1), 16-12pdr QF (16x1), 6-3pdr QF (6x1), 4-18in TT sub
Complement: 714

Name	Builder	Laid down	Launched	Comp	Fate
BULWARK	Devonport DYd	20.3.1899	18.10.99	Mar 1902	Sank in Medway after magazine explosion 26.11.14
LONDON	Portsmouth DYd	8.12.1898	21.9.99	June 1902	Sold for BU 1920
VENERABLE	Chatham DYd	2.1.1899	2.11.99	Nov 1902	Sold for BU 1920
QUEEN	Devonport DYd	12.3.1901	8.3.02	Mar 1904	Sold fr BU 1920
PRINCE OF WALES	Chatham DYd	20.3.1901	25.3.02	Mar 1904	Sold for BU 1920

Right: *Venerable* after her 1909 refit when she was fitted with high topgallant masts for wireless aerials. Note the enclosed 12 pdr battery on the upper deck amidships

Duncan, Cornwallis, Exmouth and *Russell* were provided under the supplementary estimate of 1898 in answer to large additions to the French and Russian building programmes. The remaining pair were provided under the 1899/1900 Estimates. Smaller editions of *Formidable*, they sacrificed armour for high speed to match the reported fast Russian battleships. The designed load displacement was 14,000t.

The ships were actually designed prior to the *London* class and initiated improvements in protection adopted in those ships, but their construction was delayed and the first two *Londons* were laid down prior to any *Duncans*. The armour distribution was similar to that of *London* but with belt and barbettes of reduced thickness. The main 7in belt was 238ft long by 15ft deep and continued to the bow with 5in, 4in and 3in plates. The barbettes were 10in-11in, reducing to 7in and 4in forward and 4in aft behind the belt. The decks were as in *London* except that the middle deck was 1in on the slope as well as on the flat.

High speed was provided for by increasing the machinery power by 3000ihp and modifying the hull form for a designed maximum speed of 19kts and a sea speed of 18kts. Four-cyl TE engines were adopted for the first time, and these employed windsails instead of cowl ventilators. They were good steamers, the best of the class on trials being *Cornwallis* (19.56kts) and the best in service *Albemarle*.

The vessels operated in the Mediterranean until 1904-05 and then returned to home waters for the remainder of their peacetime service, with the exception of *Duncan, Exmouth* and *Russell* which served a second term in the Mediterranean from 1908 until 1912.

DUNCAN class *first class battleships*

Displacement: 13,270t to 13,745t load, 14,900t to 15,200t deep
Dimensions: 405ft pp, 432ft oa x 75ft 6in x 25ft 9in (*123.44 pp, 131.67 oa x 23.01 x 7.85m*)
Machinery: 2-shaft, 4 cyl TE, 24 Belleville boilers, 18,000ihp = 19kts
Armour: Belt 7in, bulkheads 11in-7in, barbettes 11in-4in gun houses 10in-8in, casemates 6in, CT 12in, decks 2in-1in
Armament: 4-12in BL (2x2), 12-6in QF (12x1), 10-12pdr QF (1;x1), 6-3pdr QF (6x1), 4-18in TT sub
Complement: 720

Name	Builder	Laid down	Launched	Comp	Fate
ALBEMARLE	Chatham DYd	8.1.1900	5.3.1901	Nov 1903	Sold for BU 1919
CORNWALLIS	Thames Iron Wks, Blackwall	19.7.1899	13.7.1901	Feb 1904	Torpedoed & sunk by *U32* E of Malta 9.1.17
DUNCAN	Thames Iron Wks, Blackwall	10.7.1899	21.3.1901	Oct 1903	Sold for BU 1920
EXMOUTH	Laird, Birkenhead	10.8.1899	31.8.1901	May 1903	Sold for BU 1920
MONTAGU	Devonport DYd	23.11.1899	5.3.1901	Oct 1903	Wrecked on Lundy Island 30.5.06
RUSSELL	Palmer, Jarrow	11.3.1899	19.2.1901	Feb 1903	Mined and sunk off Malta 27.4.16

Albemarle as completed. Note the equal size funnels and open 12 pdr battery amidships

King Edward VII, Dominion, Commonwealth were provided under the 1901/02 Estimates, *Hindustan, New Zealand* under the 1902/03 Estimates, and the remainder under the 1903/04 Estimates. The designed load displacement was 16,350t. They were the first class to show any major departure in design from the standard pre-dreadnought type, being over 1,000t larger than previous ships to accommodate an intermediate armament of four 9.2in guns. These were mounted in single turrets on the upper deck abreast the fore and main masts. In addition, casemate protection of the 6in guns was abandoned in favour of central battery with 7in walls and bulkheads, which effectively increased the height of the side armour by one deck. Deck protection was the same as that in *London*, except that the 2in protective plating on the main deck under the battery was omitted, and a 1in upper deck over the battery substituted. The 9.2in turrets had 9in walls and 5in backs and were mounted on shallow barbettes of 4in-2in. The remaining armour was arranged as in *London* but the belt reverted to two thicknesses of 9in at the waterline and 8in above for a length of 285ft. Towards the bow the side armour reduced from 7in, 5in and 4in to 3in at the stem, while aft a uniform 3in strake extended from the main belt to the stern. The barbettes reduced to 8in and 6in behind the side armour; the gun houses had 8in walls and 12in faces. These ships were criticised for not adopting a uniform secondary battery of 9.2in guns, but fire control with 12in and 9.2in proved impracticable because of the difficulty of distinguishing between shell splashes. They were completed with fire control platforms on fore and main masts in place of the fighting tops fitted in earlier vessels.

King Edward VII was fitted with 10 Babcock and Wilcox and 6 cyl boilers, *Dominion* and *Commonwealth* with 16 Babcock and Wilcox, *New Zealand* with 12 Niclausse and 3 cyl, and the remainder with 12 Babcock and Wilcox and 3 cyl. This variation was largely for comparison and represented the last pase of the 'battle of the boilers'. On trials all the ships exceeded their designed power and achieved between 18.1 and 19.3kts. They were the first British battleships fitted with balanced rudders since the 1870s, and proved very handy, with a turning circle of 340 yd at 15kts, but they were difficult to keep on a steady course, which earned them the title of 'the wobbly eight'. They had a higher level of stability than previous ships and had a slightly faster roll but were still good gun platforms. A lower freeboard than usual led to them being wet in heavy weather.

The ships served their peacetime careers in the Atlantic, Channel and Home Fleets.

Dominion 1908

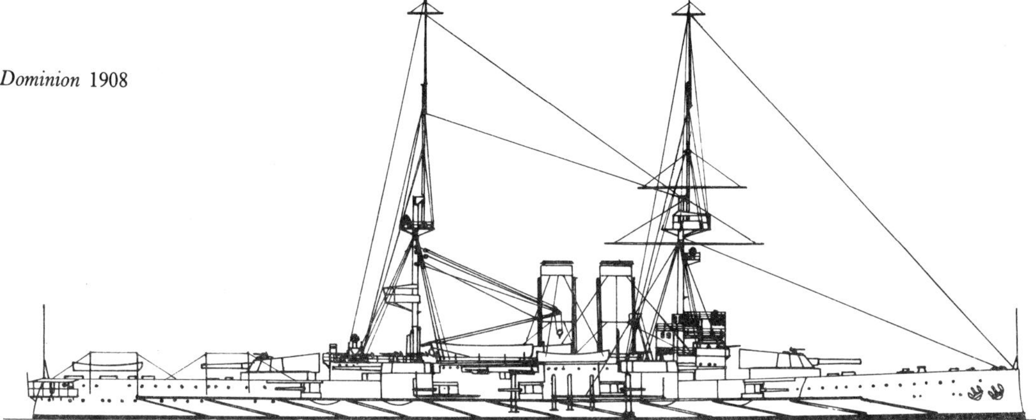

KING EDWARD VII class *first class battleships*

Displacement: 15,585t to 15,885t load, 17,009t to 17,290t deep
Dimensions: 425ft pp, 453ft 9in oa x 78ft x 25ft 8in (*129.54 pp, 138.3 oa x 23.77 x 7.72m*)
Machinery: 2-shaft, 4 cyl TE, (for boilers see notes) 18000ihp = 18.5kts
Armour: Belt 9in-8in, bulkheads, 12in-8in, barbettes 12in, gun houses 12in-8in, 9.2in gun houses 9in-5in, 6in battery 7in, CT 12in, decks 2½in-1in
Armament: 4-12in BL (2x2), 4-9.2in BL (4x1), 10-6in QF (10x1), 14-12pdr QF (14x1), 14-3pdr QF (14x1), 4-18in TT sub
Complement: 777

Name	Builder	Laid down	Launched	Comp	Fate
AFRICA	Chatham DYd	27.1.1904	20.5.05	Nov 1906	Sold for BU 1920
BRITANNIA	Portsmouth DYd	4.2.1904	10.12.04	Sept 1906	Torpedoed and sunk by *UB50* off Cape Trafalgar 9.11.18
COMMONWEALTH	Fairfield, Glasgow	17.6.1902	13.5.03	Mar 1705	Sold for BU 1921
DOMINION	Vickers, Barrow	23.5.1902	25.8.03	July 1905	Sold for BU 1921
HIBERNIA	Devonport DYd	6.1.1904	17.6.05	Jan 1907	Sold for BU 1921
HINDUSTAN	John Brown, Clydebank	25.10.1902	19.12.03	July 1905	Sold for BU 1921
KING EDWARD VII	Devonport DYd	8.3.1902	23.7.03	Feb 1905	Mined and sunk off Cape Wrath 6.1.16
NEW ZEALAND	Portsmouth DYd	9.2.1903	4.2.04	July 1905	Renamed *Zealandia* 1911. Sold for BU 1921

Above: *Hibernia* after the addition of wireless rig. Note the 9.2in gun turrets abreast fore and mainmasts

Right: *Triumph* during her service with the Channel Fleet

SWIFTSURE class *second class battleships*

Displacement: *Swiftsure* 11,800t load, *Triumph* 11,985t load
Dimensions: 436ft pp, 479ft 9in oa x 71ft x 25ft 4in (*132.89pp, 146.23 x 21.64 x 7.72m*)
Machinery: 2-shaft, 3 cyl TE, 12 large-tube Yarrow boilers, 12,500ihp = 19kts
Armour: Belt 7in-3in, bulkheads 6in-2in, barbettes 10in-2in, gun houses 10in-8in, battery 7in, casemates 7in, CT 11in, decks 3in-1in
Armament: 4-10in BL (4x1), 14-7.5in BL (14x1), 14-14pdr QF (14x1), 2-12pdr QF (2x1), 4-6pdr QF (4x1), 2-18in TT sub
Complement: 800

Name	Builder	Laid down	Launched	Comp	Fate
SWIFTSURE (ex-CONSTITUCION)	Armstrong, Elswick	26.2.1902	12.1.03	June 1904	Sold for BU 1920
TRIUMPH (ex-LIBERTAD)	Vickers, Barrow	26.2.1902	15.1.03	June 1904	Torpedoed and sunk by *U21*, Dardenelles 25.5.15

Designed by Reed for Chile and purchased by the British Government on 3.12.03 to prevent their possible purchase by Russia, *Swiftsure* and *Triumph* were comparatively small second class ships intended as a counter to the new armoured cruisers of the Argentine Navy. Compared with British ships, they were lightly constructed, armed and armoured but they had a powerful secondary battery and a high speed. Their uses in the British Fleet were limited as they were insufficiently protected to face the majority of battleships, although their speed would have allowed their use against older cruisers.

Ten of the 7.5in guns were mounted in a central battery on the main deck, with 7in sides and 6in end bulkheads divided into individual gun flats by 1in bulkheads. The remaining 7.5in guns were mounted in casemates abreast the fore and main masts on the upper deck. The belt, 8ft deep, 7in thick amidships reducing to 6in, 3in and 2½in forward and 6in and 3in aft, stopped short of the stern where it was closed by a 3in bulkhead. The redoubt between the belt and battery armour extended from the forward to the aft barbette with 7in sides and 6in-2in bulkheads. The main protective deck over the belt was 1½in amidships and 3in at the ends, and the upper deck over the battery was 1in. The gun houses were 8in with 10in faces and the barbettes reduced to 3in and 2in behind the side armour.

Beam and draught were limited by Chilean docking facilties and, therefore, they were comparatively long vessels, fitted with a balanced rudder, and with the deadwood aft cut away to improve manoeuvring qualities. Both exceeded their designed power and made 20kts with 14,000ihp on six-hour full power trials.

The ships served in the Home, Channel and Mediterranean Fleets until 1913 when *Swiftsure* became flagship of the East Indies station and *Triumph* transferred to the China station.

The *Lord Nelsons* were provided under the 1904/05 Estimates, and had a designed displacement of 16,500t. The progress towards a heavier armament, first seen in *King Edward VII*, was taken a stage further in this design – all 6in guns were abandoned in favour of a complete secondary battery of 9.2in guns. All the 9.2in guns were mounted in turrets, thus disposing of the unsatisfactory main deck batteries which, despite their limitations, had been repeated in every class since the *Royal Sovereigns*. The only other gun armament was 12pdr for TB defence, and these were mounted on a flying deck over a midship structure reminiscent of Reed's turret ships. Owing to the limited space for shrouds, a tripod mainmast was adopted. The vessels were slightly heavier than the *King Edward VIIs* but docking restrictions required that their length be limited, so beam and draught were increased, and a squarer hull form amidships allowed some fining of the lines fore and aft, to give a speed of 18kts. This form was very successful as the speed was achieved easily. They were good sea boats and gun platforms and had exceptional manoeuvrability. On trials *Lord Nelson* made 18.7kts with 17,445ihp and *Agamemnon* 18.5kts with 17,270ihp. In the long term they were not successful ships because of the fire control problems with mixed calibre armament. Their 12in guns were new pattern 45 calibre weapons; the guns and mountings originally ordered for them were employed in the *Dreadnought* and their completion was delayed while new weapons were manufactured.

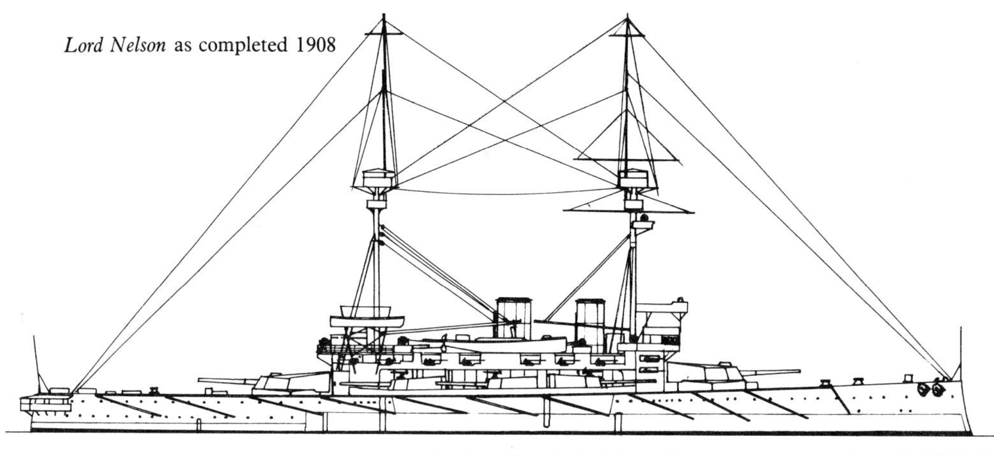
Lord Nelson as completed 1908

LORD NELSON class *first class battleships*

Displacement: 16,090t load, 17,820t deep (*Agamemnon* 15,925t load, 17,683t deep)
Dimensions: 410ft pp, 443ft 6in oa x 79ft 6in x 26ft (*124.97 pp, 135.18 oa x 24.23 x 7.92m*)
Machinery: 2-shaft, 4 cyl TE, 15 Yarrow (*Lord Nelson* Babcock), boilers, 16,750ihp = 18kts
Armour: Belt 12in-8in, bulkheads 8in, citadel 8in, barbettes 12in, gun houses 12in, 9.2in gun houses 8in-7in, CT 12in, decks 4in-1in
Armament: 4-12in BL (2x2), 10-9.2in BL (4x2, 2x1), 24-12pdr QF (24x1), 2-3pdr QF (2x1), 5-18in TT sub
Complement: 800

Name	Builder	Laid down	Launched	Comp	Fate
LORD NELSON	Palmer, Jarrow	18.5.1905	4.9.06	Oct 1908	Sold for BU 1920
AGAMEMNON	Beardmore	15.5.1905	23.6.06	June 1908	Sold for BU 1927

The waterline belt extended over the full length of the hull and was 12in amidships reducing to 9in and 6in forward and 4in aft. The upper belt extended from the stem to the after barbette only, and was 8in amidships reducing to 6in and 4in forward and closed by an 8in bulkhead at the after end. Between the upper belt and upper deck the bases of the 9.2in mountings were protected by a citadel of uniform 8in armour extending from the forward to the aft barbette. There was a main protective deck over the full length, 1in on the flat and 2in on the slope, increasing to 4in over main magazines forward and aft of the barbettes and 2in-3in over the steering gear. The main deck forward of the citadel was 1½in. The barbettes reduced to 3in within the citadel and 3in-8in behind the belt. Main gun houses had 8in walls with a 12in face; the 9.2in gun houses had 7in walls, an 8in face and 6in bases.

Both ships served their peacetime careers with the Home Fleet.

The *Agamemnon* as completed

(All uncredited photos in this section CPL)

MASTED CRUISERS

The unarmoured cruising ships were rated as frigates, corvettes and sloops, fully rigged for sailing and fitted with steam propulsion. Between 1860 and 1904 when the last cruising ship coming within this definition was commissioned, 21 frigates, 53 corvettes and 71 sloops entered service.

The status of the cruising ship in the early years of the Victorian era had changed. Unlike the frigate of Georgian times, when such vessels were the eyes of the battle fleet, the introduction of steam altered the frigate's traditional role. Armoured ships of the battle line were just as fast, frequently faster. Although these cruisers suffered from lack of speed compared with ironclads or some merchant ships, as seaboats they had no equals. In the most adverse weather conditions they remained unscathed, keeping the seas when other much larger ships ran for shelter or were severely mauled.

When in 1858 the United States Government decided to build five powerful frigates and one corvette which would outclass any cruiser in the Royal Navy, the Admiralty's reaction was to build six of the largest wooden-hulled screw-driven frigates ever to enter the navy. In the event, these big frigates proved superior both in speed and in armament to their American counterparts. Furthermore the success achieved by Confederate Navy commerce raiders during the American Civil War had a profound effect on Admiralty thinking. The impressive demonstration of the disruptive effects on trade that could be achieved by a few well-armed fast steam frigates, commanded by resolute men, was a potential threat to the British Empire's expanding trade. In 1863 the *Wampanoag* class of American cruiser commerce raiders was laid down with a designed speed of 16 to 17kts, enhancing the threat. To meet this challenge the *Inconstant* was designed. She proved to be the fastest warship of her day, both under sail and steam, and more than a match for the American ships. It was the last attempt by the United States Navy to build a modern fleet until the late 1880s, but the spectre of fast, well-armed raiders haunted the Admiralty for the rest of the century and, in particular, the ever present threat from the French Navy.

In practice, the big wooden-hulled frigates and iron-hulled frigates of the *Inconstant* class were not economically adaptable to Britain's role of policing the seas. Requiring from 450 to 600 officers and men, their chief function was acting as flagships on overseas stations. The last wooden screw frigate was launched in 1865 and thereafter the corvette took over the frigate's function being smaller, faster and relatively economical in cost and maintenance.

HULL CONSTRUCTION

Cruising ships went through four stages in hull construction, the composition of the 145 vessels mentioned in the text being:

	Wooden	Iron	Composite	Steel
Frigates	18	3	–	–
Corvettes	23	6	13	11
Sloops	21	–	32	18

Wooden frigates were constructed on traditional lines. Hulls were strengthened to carry the weight of machinery and to withstand stresses. Increased stability resulted from this mass of machinery deep down in the hull. The redistribution of weights enabled the designers to place guns higher up in the hull, which was advantageous in gunnery effectiveness. New concepts of hull form, based upon a more scientific approach to a ship's performance, were introduced into corvettes and sloops. The ram bow appeared in the *Eclipse* and *Briton* class corvettes, not for offensive purposes but to obtain additional displacement forward. Iron trusses and riders made for additional strength. Due to the shortage of native timber, teak was widely used. The so-called 'Aberdeen bow' was another departure from traditional construction. Iron hulls in the *Inconstant* class frigates and six corvettes made it possible to build in watertight bulkheads, impracticable in wooden hulls. These iron hulls were sheathed in one or two layers of timber with coppering extending from the waterline to the keel. But iron was a relatively expensive material. The Admiralty decreed that iron hulls could only be used in vessels of more than 3000t. The additional strength of iron was too obvious to be ignored, especially since heavier weapons were entering service. An effective compromise was the composite hull – wrought iron keels, frames, stem and stern posts with wooden planking. The result was a hull almost as strong as iron. In two classes of corvettes, *Emerald* and *Caroline*, a further improvement was to incorporate an internal protected steel deck over the machinery and magazines. The last corvettes to be built until the term was revived in the Second World War received hulls of iron or steel framing and steel plating. They had a protected deck of 1½in steel amidships. The steel plating was clad externally in timber up to the upper deck. Six lateral bulkheads extended to the upper deck, and three more up to the lower deck. Reversing previous Admiralty policy, they were the first cruising ships of less than 3000t to be given metal hulls.

Criticism has been levelled against the Admiralty for adhering to sail so far into the century. However, there were powerful protagonists who claimed that sail was essential to those ships whose service took them to the most remote regions of the earth, where bunkerage facilities were either rare or non-existent. Always present was the possibility of mechanical breakdown which could not be repaired on board or in some distant ill-equipped dockyard. Against such potent arguments was the evidence of greatly increased reliability in machinery while the introduction of multi-stage expansion engines with considerably improved fuel consumption gave a vessel a far greater steaming radius. In 1887 all capital ships were ordered on undocking to replace their sailing rig with pole masts, but sail persisted in cruising ships up to the turn in the century, long after the new breed of mastless cruisers arrived on the scene.

ARMAMENT

Until 1865 guns fitted in cruising ships were smooth bore (SB) muzzle-loaders (ML), except for a brief period from 1860-1865 following the momentous decision by the Admiralty (1859) to abandon SB ordnance in favour of the Armstrong rifled breech-loading (BLR) gun. The deficiencies of this gun, associated with the breech mechanism and to some extent the projectiles, became only too apparent when hostilities, in the Second Opium War, were renewed in 1860, and in the punitive expedition to Kagoshima in Japan in 1863. The policy was completely reversed by a return to ML guns, and it was not until 1880 that BL guns were reintroduced. In this period the ordnance mounted in wooden-hulled frigates comprised 10in or 8in shell guns, 32pdr and 68pdr guns – all SB. The 32pdr guns were supplied in two weights – 56cwt or 58cwt – the lighter ones being positioned on the upper deck and the heavier ones on the main deck. A few corvettes and sloops entering service in the 1860s were issued with the ill-fated Armstrong gun. From 1865 onwards rifled muzzle-loaders (MLR) were supplied, the two calibres generally fitted being the 6in 64pdr and the 7in. Chase guns were 64pdr, 64cwt, or when mounted on the broadside 71cwt. The 8in was either 4½t or 6½t. Guns were mounted on trucks or slide-mounted, traversing over racers let into the deck. From about 1882 BL guns became standard issue as 6in or 5in, central pivot or slide mounted. The Mk I 6in BL gun was an 80pdr made by Armstrong; Mk II was a Woolwich 100pdr, and was withdrawn from service due to failures in the sloop *Cordelia* and other vessels; Mks III, IV and VI were interchangeable, differing only in construction. Mks I and V 5in BL guns were also interchangeable, Mk I usually being kept separate. Mk II was phased out of service. In the last of the sloops 4in QF BL and 3pdr QF BL guns were fitted. To replace the mixed armament in these vessels, the Admiralty standardised on the Mk III 64pdr MLR guns, the 7in MLR – 6½t and 4½t – firing an armour piercing 120lb shell being withdrawn since such weapons were unlikely to be fired offensively by these unarmoured ships against an armoured adversary.

GREAT BRITAIN

Only one frigate and two corvettes received torpedo carriages on completion – a frame-like structure in which the torpedo was placed and pivoted to raise the torpedo to a declining angle towards the sea. At the after end of the frame was a compressed air operated impulse tube containing a piston actuated by a trigger. Machine guns arrived in the 1880s, either Gardner or Nordenfeld or both being supplied to cruising ships. An Admiralty report of 1880 favoured the Nordenfeld following a series of competitive trials.

The old practice of designating ordnance by weight of gun or projectile was replaced by Pattern number in August 1865, to be superseded by Mark number in November 1867. Thereafter the calibre of each gun approved for manufacture carried its relevant Mark number in Roman numerals; a practice which has persisted to this day.

MACHINERY

By 1860 screw propulsion had replaced paddle for all new construction. The last paddle sloop was launched in 1858; and frigate in 1851. In order to protect the ships' machinery from enemy fire, the Admiralty insisted that engines and boilers be positioned below the waterline. This posed a design problem, the solution to which was the horizontal engine. Due to the dimensional limitations of a ship's beam restricting the required length of stroke between the crank and the horizontal cylinder, three basic designs were developed: trunk engine, return connecting rod type, and direct acting. Until the 1870s engines were simple expansion, to be superseded by compound expansion. Triple expansion, first in horizontal form, and then the modern type of vertical or inverted engine, was fitted in the last 25 sloops to be built. Engines supplied to the 145 cruising ships listed in the text were:

	Frigates	Corvettes	Sloops
Simple expansion	20	16	22
Compound expansion	1	37	24
Triple expansion	–	–	25

The advances in engine technology from simple to triple expansion resulted in considerable economies in fuel consumption and, therefore, in radius of action. In wooden screw frigates and earlier sloops and corvettes rectangular or box boilers operated at a pressure of only about 20psi increasing to 30psi in later corvettes with simple engines. With the arrival of compound engines, boilers became cylindrical and working pressures of 60psi were reached, rising to 90psi in the 1880s. Triple expansion engines worked at 130psi to 160psi in the last class of sloop. Forced draught was introduced in 1882 in the *Condor* class sloops. Ships built prior to 1860 and for a brief time afterwards had jet condensers, to be superseded by surface condensers which, when used with box boilers, necessitated strengthening the flat sided boilers with additional stays to contain the increased pressure. With the exception of the last 16 sloops, which were twin-screw driven, all other cruising ships had single-shaft drive.

Hoisting screws and telescopic funnels were general in earlier ships. Alternatives to hoisting screws were feathering screws or, in some cases, disconnecting the screw from the propeller shaft, allowing it to idle when under sail only. In the later classes screws were fixed. A disadvantage of the hoisting screw was that the hoisting well interfered with the mounting and traversing of stern chase guns. Hoisting screws were two-bladed, the diameter varying from 18ft to 20ft in frigates, 15ft to 16ft in corvettes, and 11ft to 15ft in sloops. In the late 1880s dynamos driven by slow running auxiliary stream engines generated electricity for searchlights and for internal illumination. Other auxiliary machinery included circulating pumps, bilge pumps and air pumps.

HABITABILITY

Internal arrangements were of the same general type in all these ships. The open upper deck was the gun deck, being covered only at the extremities. Beneath the topgallant forecastle a chase gun could be mounted, and beneath the poop a stern chase gun. A double wheel stood at the break of the poop. The main or lower deck accommodated ratings. Below this deck the machinery occupied most of the space between the main and foremasts. The rest of that space was taken up with magazines and stores.

Sanitation was primitive, the crew's 'heads' being situated at the bows, and consisting of a wooden plank bored with holes. The officers' 'heads' were at the stern. In the last two decades of the century there was a marked improvement in living quarters: better ventilation and sanitary arrangements, electric lighting, and such hitherto unheard of amenities for the ratings as bathrooms and or ship's library. When the two last sloops were completed in 1904 no more vessels of this rate were built until 1915 when the first mastless sloops were launched.

Rosario, one of the last masted cruisers, was a sloop launched as late as 1898.
NPC by courtesy of W Pym Trotter

BRITISH CRUISING SHIPS in 1860

SCREW FRIGATES

Name	Launched	Tons*	Guns	Fate
AMPHION[1]	1846	2025	34	BU 1864
ARROGANT	1848	2565	46	BU 1867
BACCHANTE	1859	3631	50	BU 1869
CHESAPEAKE	1855	3334	51	BU 1867
CURACOA	1854	2385	31	BU 1869
DAUNTLESS	1847	2520	24	Sold 1885
DIADEM	1856	2483	32	Sold 1875
DORIS	1857	2483	32	Sold 1885
EMERALD	1856	3503	51	Sold 1869
EUROTAS[2]	1856	1293	12	Sold 1865
EURYALUS	1853	3125	51	Sold 1867
FORTE	1858	3456	51	Burnt 1905
FORTH[3]	1856	1792	12	Sold 1883
HORATIO[4]	1850	1175	24	Sold 1865
IMPERIEUSE[5]	1852	3345	51	Sold 1867
LIFFEY	1856	3891	51	Sold 1903
MELPOMENE	1857	2741	51	Sold 1875
MERSEY	1858	3733	40	Sold 1875
NARCISSUS	1859	3548	51	Sold 1883
PHAETON[6]	1859	2840	51	BU 1875
PHOEBE	1859	3677	51	BU 1875
SEAHORSE[7]	1856	1799	12	Sold 1902
SEVERN[8]	1856	3536	51	BU 1876
SHANNON	1855	3636	51	Sold 1871
SUTLEJ[9]	1855	3066	50	BU 1869
TERMAGANT	1847	2403	24	Sold 1867
TOPAZE	1858	3951	51	BU 1884
TRIBUNE	1853	2243	31	BU 1866

(1) Laid down as sailing 5th Rate 1830. Converted to screw while on stocks.
(2) Laid down as sailing 4th Rate 1829. Became screw mortar frigate 1856. Armament is 12 mortars.
(3) Laid down as sailing 5th Rate 1833. Became screw mortar frigate 1856. Armament is 12 mortars.
(4) Laid down as sailing 5th Rate 1807. Start made in 1845 to convert to screw. Became screw mortar frigate 1850. Armament is 24 mortars.
(5) Laid down as sailing 4th Rate. Converted to screw on stocks.
(6) Laid down as sailing Rate 1848. Converted to screw.
(7) Laid down as sailing 5th Rate 1830. Screw frigate 1847. Became screw mortar frigate 1856. Armament is 12 mortars.
(8) Laid down as sailing 4th Rate. Converted to screw.
(9) Laid down as 4th Rate. Undocked as screw frigate 1860.

SCREW CORVETTES

Name	Launched	Tons*	Guns	Fate
ARCHER[1]	1849	973	14	BU 1866
BRISK	1851	1087	14	Sold 1870
CADMUS	1856	2216	21	BU 1879
CHALLENGER	1858	2306	22	Sold 1921
CHARYBDIS	1859	2231	21	BU 1884
CLIO	1858	2350	22	BU 1920
COSSACK	1854	1965	20	Sold 1878
ENCOUNTER[2]	1846	953	14	BU 1866
ESK	1854	1900	21	Sold 1870
HIGHFLYER[3]	1851	1902	21	BU 1871
JASON	1859	2431	21	BU 1877
MIRANDA[4]	1851	1039	14	Sold 1869
NIGER	1846	1013	14	Sold 1869
PEARL	1855	2187	21	BU 1883
PELORUS	1857	2330	21	BU 1868
PYLADES	1854	1991	21	BU 1875
RACOON	1857	2306	22	BU 1877
SATELLITE	1855	2187	21	BU 1879
SCOUT	1856	2187	21	BU 1877
SCYLLA	1856	2187	21	Sold 1883
TARTAR	1854	1350	20	Sold 1866
WASP[5]	1850	1371	13	Deleted 1869

(1) Laid down as screw sloop. Reclassed as corvette 1854.
(2) Laid down as sailing sloop. Converted and reclassed as corvette.
(3) Laid down as screw sloop. Launched as screw frigate. Reclassed as screw corvette 1855.
(4) Launched as screw sloop. Later reclassed as corvette.
(5) Launched as screw sloop. Later reclassed as corvette.

PADDLE FRIGATES

Name	Launched	Tons*	Guns	Fate
CENTAUR	1845	1269	6	BU 1864
CYCLOPS	1839	1195	6	Sold 1864
DRAGON	1845	1269	6	Sold 1864
FIREBRAND	1842	1190	6	Sold 1864
FURIOUS	1850	1287	16	Sold 1884
GLADIATOR	1844	1190	6	BU 1879
LEOPARD	1850	1406	18	Sold 1867
MAGICIENNE	1849	1258	16	BU 1866
ODIN	1846	1326	18	Sold 1865
PENELOPE	1843	1616	16	Sold 1864
RETRIBUTION	1844	1641	10	Sold 1864
SAMPSON	1844	1299	6	Sold 1864
SIDON	1846	1329	8	Sold 1864
TERRIBLE	1845	1858	19	Sold 1879
VALOROUS	1851	1257	16	Sold 1891
VULTURE	1843	1190	6	Sold 1866

*Builders' measurement

SCREW SLOOPS

Name	Launched	Tons*	Guns	Fate
ALERT	1856	1044	17	Sold 1896
ARIEL	1854	548	9	Sold 1865
CONFLICT[1]	1846	1752	17	Sold 1863
CORDELIA	1856	876	11	BU 1870
CRUIZER	1852	1073	17	Sold 1912
CURLEW	1854	486	9	Sold 1865
DESPERATE[2]	1849	1663	8	BU 1865
FALCON	1854	1139	17	BU 1869
FAWN	1856	1108	17	Sold 1884
GANNET	1857	890	11	Sold 1876
GREYHOUND	1859	1268	17	Sold 1906
HARRIER	1854	1047	17	BU 1866
HORNET	1854	937	17	BU 1868
ICARUS	1858	868	11	Sold 1875
LYRA	1857	653	9	BU 1876
MALACCA[3]	1853	1758	17	Sold 1869
MUTINE	1859	1291	17	Sold 1870
PANTALOON	1860	798	11	Sold 1867
PHOENIX[4]	1832	1460	6	Sold 1864
PLUMPER	1848	652	9	BU 1866
RACER	1857	868	11	BU 1876
RATTLER[5]	1843	1112	6	Deleted 1856
REYNARD	1856	850	11	BU 1866
RIFLEMAN	1846	592	9	Sold 1869
SHARPSHOOTER[6]	1846	653	9	Sold 1869
SWALLOW	1854	625	9	Sold 1866

(1) Launched as sailing sloop, converted to screw.
(2) Launched as sailing sloop, converted to screw.
(3) Reclassed as corvette after new engines fitted 1862.
(4) Originally built as paddle sloop. Converted to screw sloop 1846.
(5) Laid down as paddle sloop, converted on stocks to screw sloop.
(6) Iron hull.

PADDLE SLOOPS

Name	Launched	Tons*	Guns	Fate
ALECTO[1]	1839	796	5	BU 1865
ANTELOPE	1846	650	3	Sold 1883
ARDENT	1841	801	5	BU 1865
ARGUS	1849	981	6	BU 1881
BARRACOUTA	1851	1053	6	BU 1882
BASILISK	1848	1031	6	BU 1882
BULLDOG	1845	980	6	Destroyed 1865
BUZZARD	1849	980	6	BU 1883
DEE	1832	704	4	BU 1872
DEVASTATION	1841	1058	6	BU 1866
DRIVER	1840	1058	6	Wrecked 1861
FURY	1845	1124	6	Sold 1864
GEYSER	1841	1054	6	BU 1866
GORGON	1837	1111	6	BU 1864
HECATE	1839	817	6	Sold 1865
HECLA	1839	817	6	Sold 1863
HERMES	1835	830	6	BU 1864
HYDRA	1838	818	6	Sold 1870
INFERNAL[2]	1843	1059	6	BU 1865
INFLEXIBLE	1845	1122	6	Sold 1864
MEDEA	1833	835	4	Sold 1867
OBERON[1]	1847	649	3	Sold 1880
PROMETHEUS	1839	796	5	Sold 1863
RHADAMANTHUS	1832	813	5	BU 1864
SALAMANDER	1832	818	6	BU 1883
SCOURGE	1844	1128	6	BU 1865
SPHYNX	1846	1056	6	BU 1881
SPITEFUL	1842	1054	6	Sold 1883
STROMBOLI	1839	967	6	Sold 1866
STYX	1841	1057	6	BU 1866
TRIDENT[1]	1845	850	6	BU 1866
TRITON[1]	1846	654	3	Sold 1873
VESUVIUS	1839	970	4	Sold 1865
VIRAGO	1842	1059	6	BU 1876
VIXEN	1841	1054	6	Sold 1862
VOLCANO	1836	720	2	BU 1894

*Builders' measurement
(1) Iron hulls
(2) Launched as *Infernal*, name changed to *Rosamond*.

GREAT BRITAIN

SAILING FRIGATES

On the effective list

Name	Rate	Launched	Tons*	Guns	Fate
ACTIVE	5th	1845	1627	36	Sold 1908
CAMBRIAN	5th	1842	1622	36	Sold 1892
CHICHESTER	4th	1843	2468	52	Sold 1889
INDEFATIGABLE	4th	1848	2044	50	Sold 1914
NANKIN	4th	1850	2049	50	BU 1905

Not on the effective list

These vessels no longer constituted a fighting force, being reduced to harbour service, converted into coal hulks, convict ships, training or drill ships, or being on the sale list. By 1860, most would have been demilitarised, or have had most of their guns removed.

Name	Rate	Launched	Tons*	Guns	Fate
AFRICAINE	5th	1828	1173	44	BU 1903
AIGLE	5th	1801	990	36	Sold 1870
AMAZON	5th	1821	1078	46	Sold 1863
AMPHITRITE	5th	1816	1064	46	BU 1875
ANDROMEDA	5th	1829	1215	46	Sold 1863
ARETHUSA	5th	1817	1085	46	BU 1883
BELVIDERA	5th	1809	946	36	Sold 1906
BLANCHE	5th	1819	1074	46	BU 1865
BRILLIANT	5th	1814	954	36	Sold 1908
BRITON	5th	1812	1080	38	BU 1860
CERBERUS	5th	1827	1079	46	BU 1866
CIRCE	5th	1827	1079	46	Sold 1922
CLYDE	5th	1828	1081	46	Sold 1904
DAEDALUS	5th	1826	1083	46	Sold 1911
DIANA	5th	1822	1083	46	BU 1874
ENDYMION	4th	1797	1277	50	BU 1868
FISGARD	5th	1819	1068	46	BU 1879
FLORA	5th	1844	1634	36	Sold 1891
HAMADRYAD	5th	1823	1082	46	Sold 1905
HEBE	5th	1826	1078	46	BU 1873
HOTSPUR	5th	1828	1171	46	Sold 1902
ISIS	4th	1819	1321	60	Sold 1867
JUPITER	4th	1813	1173	50	BU 1870
LANCASTER	4th	1823	1476	58	Sold 1864
LATONA	5th	1821	1071	46	BU 1875
LAVINIA	5th	1806	1172	48	Sunk 1868
LEDA	5th	1828	1171	46	Sold 1906
LEONIDAS	5th	1807	1067	36	Sold 1894
LIVELY	5th	1813	1080	38	Sold 1862
MADAGASCAR	5th	1822	1167	46	Sold 1863
MAEANDER	5th	1840	1221	44	Wrecked 1870
MELAMPUS	5th	1820	1089	46	Sold 1906
MERCURY	5th	1826	1084	46	Sold 1906
MINERVA	5th	1820	1082	46	Sold 1895
NEMESIS	5th	1826	1128	46	BU 1866
PIQUE	5th	1834	1633	36	Sold 1910
PORTLAND	4th	1822	1476	52	Sold 1862
PROSPERINE	5th	1830	1063	46	Sold 1864
SIRIUS	5th	1813	1090	38	BU 1862
SOUTHAMPTON	4th	1820	1476	60	Sold 1912
STAG	5th	1830	1218	46	BU 1866
SYBILLE	5th	1847	1633	36	BU 1866
THALIA	5th	1830	1082	46	BU 1867
THISBE	5th	1824	1083	46	Sold 1892
TRINCOMALEE	5th	1817	1066	46	Still afloat
UNICORN	5th	1824	1084	46	Still afloat
VERNON	4th	1832	2080	50	Sold 1893
WINCHESTER	4th	1822	1487	52	Sold 1921
WORCESTER	4th	1844	1468	52	BU 1885

*Builders' measurement

FULLY RIGGED CRUISERS, 1860

Steam Navy:	
Screw Frigates	28
Screw Corvettes	22
Screw Sloops	26
Paddle Frigates	16
Paddle Sloops	36
	128
Sailing Navy:	
Effective List	
Frigates	5
Sloops	5
	10
Non-effective List	
Frigates	49
Sloops	35
	84

SAILING SLOOPS

6th Rate sloops still in commission by 1860 were referred to as corvettes although corvettes as a distinct class did not appear until the advent of the screw corvette. Brigs and brig-sloops are excluded from this list of ships.

Name	Rate	Launched	Tons*	Guns	Fate
On the effective list					
ACTAEON	6th	1831	620	16	Sold 1889
CAMILLA	Sloop	1847	549	16	Foundered 1861
CALYPSO	6th	1845	731	20	BU 1866
EURYDICE	6th	1843	908	24	Foundered 1878
FROLIC	sloop	1842	511	16	Sold 1864
6th Rate sloops not on the effective list					
ALARM		1845	910	28	Sold 1904
ALLIGATOR		1821	500	18	Sold 1865
AMETHYST		1844	923	26	Sold 1869
ANDROMACHE		1832	709	28	BU 1875
CALLIOPE		1837	717	28	BU 1883
CARYSFORT		1836	911	26	Sold 1861
CLEOPATRA		1835	918	26	BU 1862
CONWAY		1832	652	26	BU 1871
CREOLE		1845	911	26	BU 1875
CROCODILE		1825	500	28	Sold 1861
DAPHNE		1838	726	18	Sold 1864
DIDO		1836	734	18	Sold 1903
DIAMOND		1848	1051	28	Sold 1885
EGERIA		1807	424	26	BU 1865
IRIS		1841	906	26	Sold 1869
JUNO		1843	923	26	Foundered 1880
NIOBE		1849	1051	28	Sold 1862 to Prussian Navy
SAMARANG		1822	500	28	Sold 1883
SAPPHIRE		1827	604	28	Sold 1864
SPARTAN		1841	911	26	Sold 1862
TALBOT		1824	500	28	Sold 1896
VESTAL		1833	913	26	BU 1862
Sloops not on the effective list					
ARACHNE		1847	602	18	BU 1866
CHAMPION		1824	456	18	BU 1867
COLUMBINE		1826	492	18	Sold 1892
COMUS		1828	462	18	BU 1862
ELECTRA		1837	462	18	Sold 1862
ENTERPRISE		1848	471	18	Sold 1903
FAVOURITE		1829	434	18	Sold 1905
HAZARD		1837	431	18	BU 1866
HYACINTH		1829	435	18	BU 1871
LARNE		1829	463	18	BU 1866
MODESTE		1837	562	18	Sold 1866
RACEHORSE		1830	438	18	Sold 1901
TERPISCHORE		1847	602	18	BU 1866

*Builders' measurement

Emerald, a composite corvette launched in 1876, at Plymouth in December 1892.
NPC by courtesy of W Pym Trotter

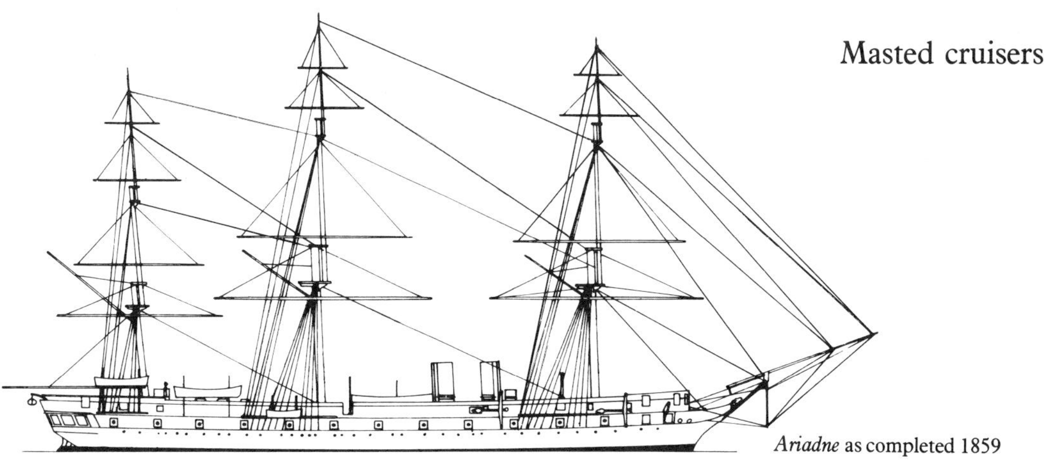
Ariadne as completed 1859

Designed by Sir Baldwin Walker. As there was no class name for these three pairs, they were generally known as 'Walker's Big Frigates.'

These ships played an important role in the development of the masted steam cruiser, for it could be said that they anticipated the battlecruiser of the Fisher era as their speed, with weight of armament, enabled them to act as a fast division with the battle fleet. The decision to build these ships was precipitated by the action of the United States Navy which in 1854 authorised the construction of five powerful steam frigates and one steam corvette. To meet this challenge, Sir Baldwin Walker designed these frigates. The first, *Diadem*, had already been laid down as a sailing frigate and was converted to screw, whilst her sister ship was built as a screw vessel from the laying of her keel. The size of these ships increased in three stages, with the last pair being the longest wooden ships ever built for the Royal Navy. There were two designs, based on experience gained in the Crimean War, to select from. The first was a ship with long range gunfire and sufficient speed to keep outside the range of any adversary, but armed heavily enough to destroy her opponent. The second design was for an armour-protected ship built to fight at short range where weight of armour and gun power would be more essential than speed. The navy opted for speed and heavy armament and the first design was chosen. In the event, these ships proved to be faster and more heavily armed than the American big frigates. It has been said that *Orlando* and *Mersey* were unable to withstand the stresses of their powerful engines, hence the reasons for their comparatively short service life. But it would seem that they really were too large and expensive to maintain in upkeep and manpower for the duties demanded of cruising ships in mid-Victorian times

From the constructional point of view, these vessels incorporated all the features of a sailing frigate, and demonstrated a definite link between ships-of-the-line and the navy's first armoured capital ship, *Warrior*. The lower deck accommodated the ship's complement; the 10in shell guns were mounted on the main deck; and the 32pdr and 68pdr guns were on the upper deck. Not long after commissioning *Ariadne* and *Galatea* received Armstrong 110pdr BL slide-mounted guns in place of their pivoted 68pdrs. They all had the old-fashioned rectangular boilers operating at about 20psi. Their HSE trunk engines were impressive in size, the cylinders being nearly eight feet in diameter.

Walker's large wooden screw frigates

Displacement: *Diadem* 3880t; *Doris* 3677t; *Ariadne* 4426t; *Galatea* 4686t; *Mersey* 5643t; *Orlando* 5643t

Dimensions: *Diadem, Doris* 240ft x 48ft x 20ft 6in (*73.15 x 14.63 x 6.63m*); *Ariadne, Galatea* 280ft x 50ft x 21ft 4in (*85.34 x 15.24 x 6.5m*); *Mersey, Orlando* 336ft x 52ft x 21ft 6in (*102.41 x 15.84 x 6.55m*)

Machinery: 1-shaft HSE; *Diadem* Maudslay, 2979ihp = 12.0kts; *Doris* John Penn, 2588ihp = 11.52kts; *Ariadne* Maudslay, 3350ihp = 13.1kts; *Galatea* John Penn, 3061ihp = 11.8kts; *Mersey* Maudslay, 3691ihp = 12.58kts; *Orlando* John Penn, 3617ihp = 13.0kts

Armament: *Diadem, Doris* 20-10in ML SB, 10-32pdr ML SB, 2-68pdr ML SB; *Ariadne, Galatea* 24-10in ML SB, 2-68pdr ML SB; *Mersey, Orlando* 28-10in ML SB, 12-68pdr ML SB

Complement: *Diadem, Doris* 475; *Ariadne, Galatea* 450; *Mersey, Orlando* 600

Name	Builder	Laid down	Launched	Comp	Fate
DIADEM	Pembroke DYd	June 1855	14.10.56	Aug 1857	Sold 1875
DORIS	Pembroke DYd	June 1856	23.5.57	Mar 1859	Sold 1885
ARIADNE	Deptford DYd	Aug 1856	4.6.59	Nov 1859	Sold 1922
GALATEA	Woolwich DYd	Feb 1857	14.9.59	Feb 1862	BU 1882
MERSEY	Chatham DYd	Dec 1856	13.8.58	Mar 1859	Sold 1875
ORLANDO	Pembroke DYd	Nov 1856	12.6.58	Dec. 1861	Sold 1871

Immortalité with funnel lowered and windsails rigged.

These five frigates were comparable in dimensions and tonnage to the four converted 4th Rates, and were of a design that originated during the *régime* of Sir William Symonds (Surveyor of the Navy 1832-1848). *Immortalité* was laid down in 1849 as a 4th Rate sailing frigate, later to be enlarged and converted to screw propulsion. Sir William Symonds' influence is demonstrated in the structural feature of the quarterdeck joined to the forecastle in a complete spar deck. The adoption of diagonal framing, perfected by Symonds' predecessor, Sir Robert Seppings, gave added rigidity enabling the designer to increase the length of hull. For example, the gun deck in *Undaunted* was almost 70ft longer than the gun deck in Nelson's *Victory*. *Immortalité* was reputed to be the fastest wooden ship under sail, making about 12kts. The armament in these ships was reduced in the course of their service: *Bristol* and *Glasgow* to 31 and then 28 guns; *Immortalité* to 28 guns; *Undaunted* to 39 then 31 guns; and *Newcastle* to 31 guns. All were fitted with telescopic funnels and hoisting screws of 18ft diameter. Standard ship rig throughout. *Undaunted* was the last wooden vessel on active service to be a flagship, and was often described as the finest example of the, then fast disappearing, wooden hulled screw frigate.

IMMORTALITÉ class *wooden screw frigates*

Displacement: *Immortalité* 3984t; *Bristol* 3996t; *Glasgow* 3984t; *Newcastle* 4020t; *Undaunted* 4094t

Dimensions: *Immortalité* 251ft x 52ft 1in x 21ft 8in (*76.5 x 16.09 x 6.73m*); *Bristol* 250ft x 52ft x 22ft 5in (*76.20 x 15.84 x 6.83m*); *Glasgow* 250ft x 52ft 1in x 22ft 5in (*76.20 x 16.09 x 6.83m*); *Newcastle* 250ft x 52ft 21ft (*76.20 x 15.84 x 6.40m*); *Undaunted* 250ft x 52ft 1in x 22ft 9in (*76.20 x 16.09 x 6.93m*)

Machinery: 1-shaft HSE; *Immortalité* Maudslay, 2366ihp = 12.3kts; *Bristol* Robert Napier, 2088ihp = 11.27kts; *Glasgow* Ravenhill & Salkeld, 2020ihp = 11.54kts; *Newcastle* Ravenhill & Salkeld, 2354ihp = 12.41kts; *Undaunted* Ravenhill & Salkeld, 2503ihp = 12.92kts

Armament: 30-8in ML SB, 20-32pdr ML SB, 1-68pdr ML SB

Complement: 550-600

Name	Builder	Laid down	Launched	Comp	Fate
IMMORTALITÉ	Pembroke DYd	Dec 1849	25.10.59	Nov 1860	Sold 1883
BRISTOL	Woolwich DYd	Sept 1859	12.2.61	Oct 1865	Sold 1883
GLASGOW	Woolwich DYd	Sept 1859	28.3.61	1870	Sold 1884
NEWCASTLE	Deptford DYd	Dec 1858	16.10.60	Sept 1874	Sold 1929
UNDAUNTED	Chatham DYd	May 1859	1.1.61	–	Sold 1882

Arethusa saw service as a 4th Rate sailing frigate of 50 guns, and was subsequently lengthened and converted into a screw frigate. Propulsion was provided by Penn trunk engines. *Constance*, designed by John Fincham, was also laid down as a 4th Rate and then converted to screw. It was decided to experiment with a compound engine in this ship, Randolph and Elder building an engine with two high-pressure and four low-pressure cylinders driving a three-throw crankshaft, the cylinders being disposed in V-form. *Octavia* and *Sutlej* received Maudslay's return connecting rod engines. To ascertain the relative efficiency in fuel consumption between compound and simple engines, a trial race was arranged from Plymouth Sound to Madeira, between *Constance*, *Arethusa* and *Octavia*. In September 1865 the three ships set off and the race came to an end seven days later as each ship almost ran out of coal, when *Constance* was about 30nm from Funchal, *Octavia* 160 miles and *Arethusa* 200nm. The fuel consumption in *Constance* was 2.5lb per ihp compared with the highest in *Arethusa* of 3.64lb. Although this was a good practical demonstration of the economy of compound engines, it was conceded that the engine was too complicated, unreliable and beyond the technical capacity of the engine room staff. As originally completed they were 180ft long, being lengthened by about 70ft on conversion to allow space for boilers, engines, and bunkerage. The decision to convert these frigates was brought about by the French naval programme of 1860 which was thought to pose a threat to England's supremacy at sea. In 1861 the order was given to complete four two-deckers as ironclads and to set up in frame only six iron-hulled vessels. Thus the conversion programme saved time in maintaining a lead over France in steam frigates. In general construction and armament they were almost identical with the *Immortalité* class. Armament in *Arethusa*, *Constance* and *Sutlej* was reduced to 35 guns. In *Octavia* the main deck carried eight 8in and twenty-two 32pdr; the upper deck had two 8in, eighteen 32pdr and one pivot-mounted 68pdr.

Converted Fourth Rate sailing frigates

Displacement:	*Arethusa* 3708t; *Constance* 3786t; *Octavia* 3832t; *Sutlej* 3826t
Dimensions:	*Arethusa* 252ft 4in x 52ft 8in x 22ft 4in (*76.91 x 16.26 x 6.80m*); *Constance* 253ft 11in x 53ft x 22ft 4in (*77.39 x 16.15 x 6.80m*); *Octavia* 252ft 5in x 52ft 10in x 22ft 4in (*76.93 x 16.10 x 6.80m*); *Sutlej* 254ft 6in x 51ft 8in x 22ft 4in (*77.57 x 15.74 x 6.80m*)
Machinery:	1-shaft HSE; *Arethusa* John Penn, 3165ihp = 11.7kts; *Octavia* Maudslay, 2415ihp = 11.53kts; *Sutlej* Maudslay, 2270ihp = 11.8kts; *Constance* Randolph & Elder, 1-shaft ECE, 2300ihp = 10.8kts
Armament:	*Arethusa, Constance* 10-8in ML SB, 40-32pdr ML SB; *Octavia, Sutlej* 28-10in ML SB, 22-32pdr ML SB
Complement:	525

Name	Builder	Launched	Undocked	Fate
ARETHUSA	Pembroke DYd	20.6.1849	9.8.61	BU 1934
CONSTANCE	Pembroke DYd	12.3.1846	15.4.62	Sold 1875
OCTAVIA	Pembroke DYd	18.8.1849	11.4.61	BU 1876
SUTLEJ	Pembroke DYd	17.4.1855	26.3.60	BU 1869

Top: *Constance* after being engined, in the mid 1860s.
Right: *Endymion* of 1865, the last wooden screw frigate.

Aurora and Narcissus were sister ships with minor dimensional differences. *Aurora* was built from the frames of a 4th Rate which had been left to season. *Narcissus* was laid down as a 4th Rate named *Arachne*, being converted to screw while on the stocks. Both *Aurora* and *Narcissus* carried their armament, consisting of eight 8in shell guns and twenty-two 32pdr, on the main deck with two 8in and eighteen 32pdr and one pivot-mounted 68pdr on the upper deck. *Aurora* had her armament reduced to 28 guns when she became a training ship. It was intended to build five frigates to *Endymion's* design, and, in fact, names had already been allocated – *Astraea, Blond, Dartmouth* and *Ister* – when this programme was cancelled. *Endymion* became the last wooden screw frigate to be built. Thereafter, the corvette took over.

Wooden screw frigates (not classed)

Displacement:	*Aurora* 3498t; *Narcissus* 3535t; *Endymion* 3200t
Dimensions:	*Aurora* 227ft x 51ft 1in x 22ft (*69.18 x 15.79 x 6.70m*); *Narcissus* 228ft x 51ft 3in x 21ft 10in (*69.49 x 16.30 x 6.65m*); *Endymion* 240ft x 48ft x 17ft 4in (*73.15 x 14.63 x 5.28m*)
Machinery:	1-shaft HSE; *Aurora* Maudslay, 1576ihp = 10.2kts; *Narcissus* Ravenhill & Salkeld, 1731ihp = 10.6kts; *Endymion* Robert Napier, 1620ihp = 11.25kts
Armament:	*Aurora, Narcissus* 10-8in ML SB, 40-32pdr ML SB, 1-68pdr ML SB; *Endymion* 8-6in MLR, 22-32pdr ML SB
Complement:	*Aurora, Narcissus* 540; *Endymion* 450

Name	Builder	Laid down	Launched	Comp	Fate
AURORA	Pembroke DYd	Sept 1854	22.6.61	Nov 1863	BU 1881
NARCISSUS	Devonport DYd	April 1857	26.10.59	Dec 1860	Sold 1883
ENDYMION	Deptford DYd	Oct 1860	18.11.65	Sept 1866	Sold 1885

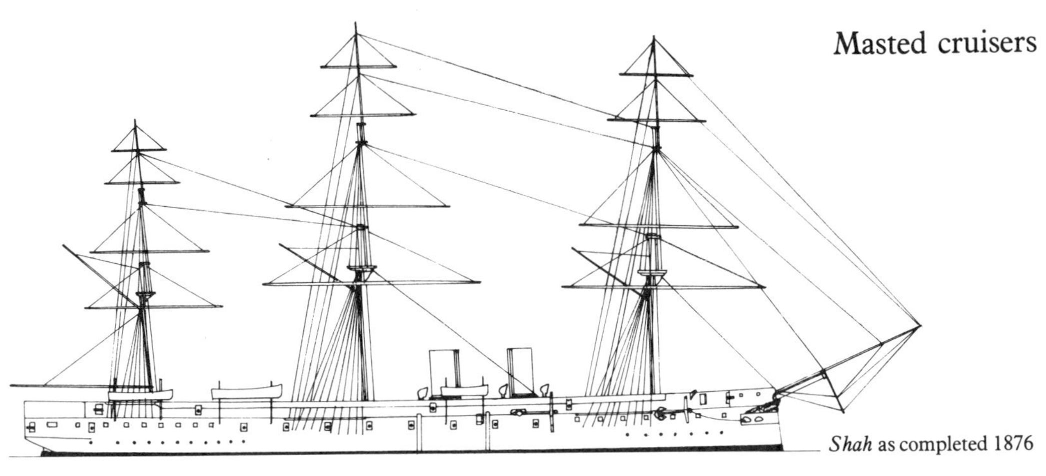
Shah as completed 1876

Designed by Sir Edward Reed. The *Inconstant* was the direct result of the American *Wampanoag* class, and when completed proved to be the fastest warship afloat. After the completion of *Shah* in 1876 the Navy Board's policy was to limit the size of a cruising ship to about half that of a contemporary ironclad's. In all three vessels the iron hulls, from keel to bulwarks, were clad with a double layer of 3in timber. In *Inconstant* and *Raleigh* the first layer was applied vertically and the second layer horizontally. In *Shah* both layers were horizontal. All three were coppered. They were without double bottoms or wing compartments, but had lateral watertight bulkheads extended up to the upper deck. They had three complete decks. Only *Inconstant* was fitted with a balanced rudder, controlled by two treble-hand wheels – one on deck, the other below.

The 9in guns in *Inconstant* formed the main deck broadside battery; the 7in guns were mounted on the upper deck and two of these were chase guns firing through embrasures forward. The two 9in guns in *Raleigh* were chase guns, mounted at the extremities. Four of the 64pdr guns were truck-mounted on the upper deck, on the broadside. The sixteen 7in guns were the main deck broadside battery. Between 1872 and 1880 *Inconstant* received six 20pdr BL guns, four light guns, 10 MGs and two TCs. In 1884 *Raleigh* was partially rearmed, having eight 6in BL, eight 5in BL, four light guns, 12 MGs and two TCs; eight 7in MLR remained, mounted on broadside. *Shah* was due for rearming, but as she was not recommissioned in the mid-1880s she retained her original armament. She was hulked in 1892.

The engines of all three were of greater size and power than any existing cruiser. It was a retrogressive step to retain simple expansion engines but nevertheless they provided a speed which, in the example of *Inconstant*, was unprecedented for the times – she logged 15½ kts for 24 hours. *Inconstant* and *Shah* were fitted with trunk engines and *Raleigh* with the return connecting-rod type. All three had telescopic funnels and hoisting screws. They were ship rigged, with fixed bowsprits, and the sail plan was identical in *Inconstant* and *Shah*, which had 26,655 sq ft of canvas each. *Raleigh's* sail plan had no counterpart in the navy. Her lower and topsail yards were on a second class scale, whilst her topgallants and royals were equal to the largest, and because of this, apart from gaffs and courses, her sails were not interchangeable with any other vessel. Under canvas *Inconstant* and *Shah* were first rate sailing vessels, logging 13.5kts. *Raleigh* was slightly slower. Boilers (11 in *Inconstant*, 10 in *Shah*, 9 in *Raleigh*) in all three ships operated at 30psi. At 6840nm at 10kts *Shah* had the greatest radius of action.

Unarmoured iron frigates

Displacement: *Inconstant* 5780t; *Raleigh* 5200t; *Shah* 6250t

Dimensions: *Inconstant* 337ft 4in x 50ft 3in x 25ft 6in (*102.81 x 15.31 x 7.77m*); *Raleigh* 298ft x 49ft x 24ft 7in (*90.83 x 14.93 x 7.48m*); *Shah* 334ft x 52ft x 25ft 5½in (*101.80 x 15.84 x 8.06m*)

Machinery: 1-shaft HSE; *Inconstant* John Penn, 7360ihp = 16.2kts; *Raleigh* Humphreys & Tennant, 5640ihp = 15.3kts; *Shah* John Penn, 7480ihp = 16.2kts

Armament: *Inconstant* 10-9in MLR, 6-7in MLR; *Raleigh* 2-9in MLR, 14-7in MLR, 6-64pdr MLR; *Shah* 2-9in MLR, 16-7in MLR, 8-64pdr MLR, 4 light guns, 12 MGs, 2 TC

Complement: *Inconstant, Shah* 600; *Raleigh* 530

Name	Builder	Laid down	Launched	Comp	Fate
INCONSTANT	Pembroke DYd	Nov 1866	12.11.68	1869	BU 1956
RALEIGH	Chatham DYd	1871	1.3.73	1874	Sold 1905
SHAH	Portsmouth DYd	1870	9.73	1876	Sold 1919

Above: *Shah* in her early days.
NPC by courtesy of W Pym Trotter
Right: *Raleigh* with her fore funnel lowered.

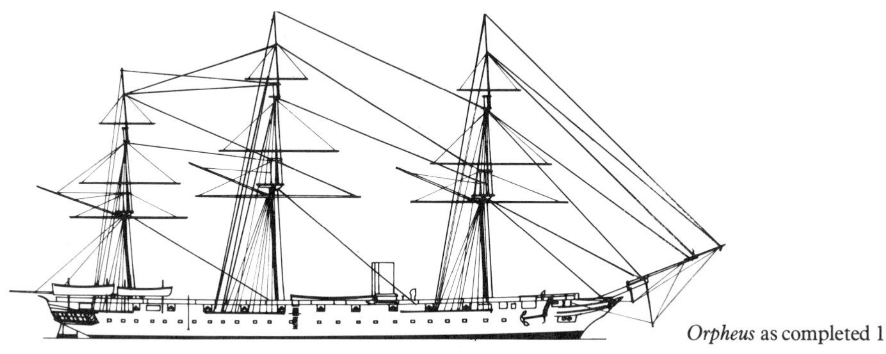
Orpheus as completed 1861

These ships were slightly larger than their immediate predecessors, *Cadmus, Charybdis, Pearl, Scout* etc. All were ship rigged, and fitted with telescopic funnels and hoisting screws. Their Armstrong BL guns were withdrawn in 1864 following a series of accidents. *Wolverine's* double piston-rod engine was never satisfactory, being re-engined by the same maker in 1876 with a return connecting-rod type, and her displacement increased to 2568t. On trials the new engine developed 1493ihp to give 11.31kts. With the demand for increased speed, these ships had a comparatively short service life, the next class to be built (*Eclipse*) being able to average about two to three knots more in performance.

JASON class *wooden screw corvettes*

Displacement: *Jason* 2431t; *Barossa* 2302t; *Orestes* 1720t (on trials, not masted); *Orpheus* 2365t; *Rattlesnake* 2431t; *Wolverine* 2424
Dimensions: 225ft x 40ft 8in x 19ft (*68.58 x 12.39 x 5.79m*)
Machinery: *Jason* Ravenhill & Salkeld, 1516ihp = 12.04kts; *Rattlesnake* Ravenhill & Salkeld, 1628ihp = 11.66kts; *Wolverine* Ravenhill & Salkeld, 1339ihp = 10.21kts; *Barossa* James Watt, 1616ihp = 11.51kts; *Orestes* Robert Napier, 1522ihp = 12.26kts on trials, running light; *Orpheus* Humphreys & Tennant, 1333ihp = 11.15kts
Armament: 20-8in ML SB, 1-110pdr Armstrong pivot-mounted BL
Complement: 240

Name	Builder	Laid down	Launched	Comp	Fate
JASON	Devonport DYd	June 1858	10.11.59	Nov 1860	BU 1877
BAROSSA	Woolwich DYd	Aug 1858	10.3.60	Sept 1862	BU 1877
ORESTES	Sheerness DYd	Aug 1858	18.8.60	Sept 1861	BU 1866
ORPHEUS	Chatham DYd	May 1858	23.6.60	Oct 1861	Wrecked 7.2.1863
RATTLESNAKE	Chatham DYd	Sept 1859	9.7.61	Aug 1862	Sold 1880
WOLVERINE	Woolwich DYd	Apr 1859	29.8.63	Apr 1864	Sold 1905

Designed by Sir Edward Reed, Surveyor to the Navy 1863–70. Both vessels were designed primarily for carrying troops. The soldiers were berthed on the lower deck, and the sailors on the upper deck. In 1876, to comply with Admiralty policy on standardisation of ordnance, *Juno* was rearmed with eight 64pdr MLR and *Thalia* with six 64pdr MLR. In design they resembled the spar-decked corvette *Challenger* (launched 1855), the type of construction consisting of a light deck in the form of a wooden grill supported on stanchions above the upper deck and forecastle deck. Both vessels were fitted with four boilers, working at 23psi in *Juno*, and at 20psi in *Thalia*. The hoisting screws were 16ft and 15ft 9in respectively. They were ship-rigged, and each vessel had a telescopic funnel. *Thalia* was the last ship to be built in the historic Woolwich Royal Dockyard, which was then closed down.

JUNO class *wooden screw corvettes*

Displacement: *Juno* 2083t; *Thalia* 2240t
Dimensions: 200ft x 40ft 4in x 16ft 7in (*60.96 x 12.29 x 5.05m*)
Machinery: 1-shaft HSE; *Juno* Humphreys & Tennant, 1090ihp = 10.53kts; *Thalia* Robert Napier, 1597ihp = 11.13kts
Armament: 2-7in MLR, 4-64pdr MLR
Complement: 200

Name	Builder	Laid down	Launched	Comp	Fate
JUNO	Deptford DYd	1866	28.11.67	May 1868	Sold 1887
THALIA	Woolwich DYd	1866	14.7.69	Mar 1870	Sold 1920

Designed by Sir Edward Reed, this class were laid down as ram-bow sloops, and then they were upgraded to corvettes. They were similar to the six wooden sloops of the *Amazon* class, with the same depth and beam, but built 25ft longer. They were the smallest corvettes to that date in the Victorian Navy. The distinctive feature was the ram bow, which was not for offensive purposes but to obtain additional displacement forward, and as a means of lightening that end of the submerged hull by reversing the angle of slope of the superstructure above it. In all, Reed designed 16 wooden corvettes and sloops with ram bows. Their full lines, extending well towards the extremities, made them tubby little vessels. Except for their iron cross beams they were entirely built of wood, and were copper-sheathed. They had heavy, rounded, battleship-type sterns, decorated with false ports but no quarter galleries. The poop and topgallant forecastle projected slightly above the waist bulwarks. There were no embrasures, the gun ports being pierced along the upper deck level. The two slide-mounted 7in guns were carried amidships, and could be pivoted through curved training races to any of four ports, two on either side. The truck-mounted 64pdrs were divided into two at either end of the waist. When a chase gun was needed, one of these guns could be run to ports beneath the poop or the topgallant forecastle. Two additional 64pdrs were added after their second commissions. Later, to comply with the rearmament policy, the 7in guns were removed and the 64pdr armament increased to 12. *Blanche, Dido, Spartan* and *Tenedos* were ship-rigged; the others were barque-rigged. All had running-in bowsprits.

Sirius, Spartan and *Tenedos* were the first corvettes to receive compound engines. Those in *Spartan* and *Sirius* were troublesome. The engine consisted of two HP and two LP cylinders working on one pair of cranks. There was difficulty in maintaining steam pressure due to the distance the HP steam had to pass from the boilers to the HP cylinders. A contributory factor to the unsatisfactory performance was the stokers' inexperience with compound machinery. *Tenedos* achieved the results sought for, being engined by Elders, the pioneers and foremost builders of marine compound engines. In 1875 *Spartan* was re-engined with the same type, which improved her performance (1988ihp = 13.15kts). Because a hoisting-screw well interfered with

ECLIPSE class *wooden screw corvettes*

Displacement: *Eclipse* 1755t; *Blanche* 1682t; *Danae* 1719t; *Sirius* 1755t; *Spartan* 1755t; *Tenedos* 1755t
Dimensions: 212ft x 36ft x 16ft 4in (*64.61 x 10.97 x 4.97m*)
Machinery: 1-shaft HSE: *Eclipse* John Penn, 1594ihp = 12.24kts; *Blanche* Ravenhill & Hodgson, 2158ihp = 13.63kts; *Danae* Robert Napier, 2089ihp = 13.17kts: *Dido* Humphreys & Tennant, 2518ihp = 13.68kts. 1-shaft HCE: *Sirius* Maudslay, 2302ihp = 13.1kts; *Spartan* G and J Rennie, 1582ihp = 12.3kts; *Tenedos* J Elder, 3028 ihp = 13.0kts
Armament: 2-7in MLR, 4-64pdr MLR
Complement: 180

Name	Builder	Launched	Comp	Fate
ECLIPSE	Sheerness DYd	14.11.1867	June 1868	Sold 1921
BLANCHE	Chatham DYd	17.8.1867	Jan 1868	Sold 1886
DANAE	Portsmouth DYd	21.5.1867	Nov 1868	Sold 1906
DIDO	Portsmouth DYd	23.10.1869	April 1871	Sold 1922
SIRIUS	Portsmouth DYd	24.4.1868	1869	Sold 1885
SPARTAN	Deptford DYd	24.11.1868	Aug 1871	Sold 1882
TENEDOS	Devonport DYd	13.5.1870	July 1872	Sold 1887

1

stern fire, three of these ships were fitted with Mangin fixed-blade propellers, ie four narrow blades which, it was thought, would present less drag under sail. The other ships had removable blades necessitating a diver to remove or replace them, therefore proving quite impractical in any seaway. The performance varied considerably under sail, from 11kts in *Eclipse* to an exceptional 13.5kts in *Blanche*. Later in their careers, the ship-rigged vessels were changed into barque-rigged vessels.

1. *Wolverine,* a wooden screw corvette, as completed 1864.
NPC by courtesy of W Pym Trotter
2. *Juno* in later life reduced to a barque rig.
3. *Sirius,* an *Eclipse* class corvette.

2

3

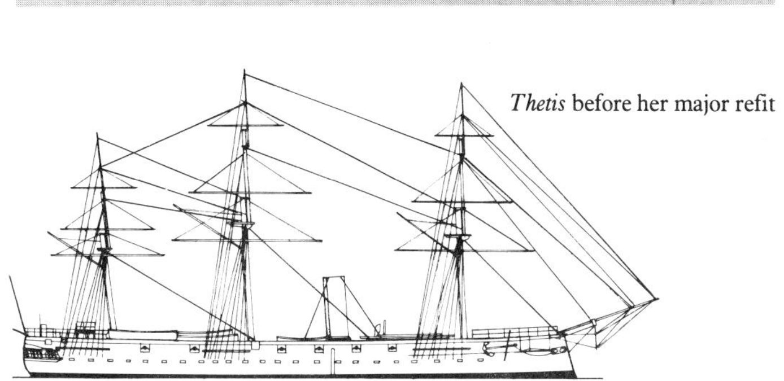

Thetis before her major refit

BRITON class *wooden screw corvettes*

Displacement: *Briton* 1831t; *Druid* 1791t; *Thetis* 1854t
Dimensions: 220ft x 36ft x 17ft 1in (*67.05 x 10.97 x 5.43m*)
Machinery: 1-shaft HSE: *Druid* Maudslay, 2038ihp =12.85kts. 1-shaft HCE: *Briton* J & G Rennie, 2150ihp = 13.13kts; 1-shaft HCE: *Thetis* J & G Rennie, 2270ihp = 13.4kts
Armament: *Briton, Druid* 2-7in MLR, 8-64pdr MLR; *Thetis* 14-64pdr MLR
Complement: 220

Name	Builder	Laid down	Launched	Comp	Fate
BRITON	Sheerness DYd	1868	6.11.69	Nov 1871	Sold 1887
DRUID	Deptford DYd	1868	13.3.69	Feb 1872	Sold 1886
THETIS	Devonport DYd	1870	26.10.71	Jan 1873	Sold 1887

Designed by Sir Edward Reed. These three ram-bowed corvettes were a continuation of the *Eclipse* class, the main difference being that they were eight feet longer and carried a heavier armament. *Thetis*, being the last of the class, received the revised armament of fourteen 64pdr guns. In 1881 the other two vessels were equipped with the same scale of armament. The general construction was similar to the *Eclipse* class, with two complete decks, poop and topgallant forecastle, and a light bridge spanning the bulwarks just forward of the telescopic funnel. A feature of the upper deck was a long hammock-box positioned on the centreline between the funnel and the foremast. All three had Griffiths fixed screws of 15ft diamater (14ft 9in in *Thetis*), with detachable blades and disconnecting tail shafts. The two ships with HCE engines had six boilers working at 60/64psi, and *Druid* had four rectangular boilers working at 30psi.

They were not good under canvas, the steering being sluggish, and their relatively shallow draught made them poor at keeping the seas. None logged more than 11kts under plain sail. All three were ship-rigged, on the same sail plan as similar ships in the previous class, with a total spread of canvas of 15,000 sq ft. In the first pair the heaviest guns were slide-mounted, and were sited beneath the poop and the forecastle, resulting in the heaviest end–on fire in any cruising ship, with the exception of *Inconstant*, and not inferior to contemporary ironclads. When rearmed, *Briton* and *Druid*, in common with *Thetis*, had the 64pdrs slide-mounted on cross skids, the slide centring on a rear pivot bolt-fixed to the midships fore and aft line of the deck. The gun could then be swung round from one side of the ship to the other, a disadvantage being that the arc of swing necessitated a deck clear of cowls, ventilators and other obstructions that might otherwise foul the slide. Between 1876 and 1881 all three went through major refits. The amidship flying bridge was removed, and the compass and engine room telegraph were remounted on the forward end of the poop, the poop serving as the bridge. Bullet-proof sponsons were erected on either beam at the break of the poop. *Druid* was the last ship to be built in the historic Deptford Dockyard.

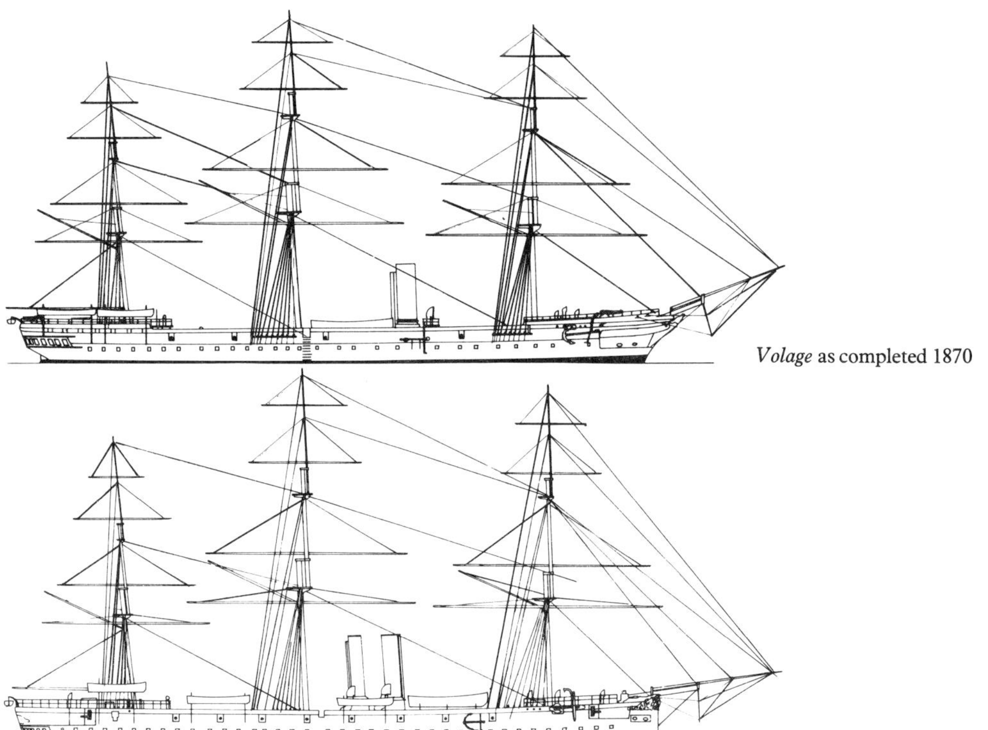

Volage as completed 1870

Rover as completed 1875

VOLAGE class *iron screw corvettes*

Displacement:	*Volage, Active* 3080t; *Rover* 3460t
Dimensions:	*Active, Volage* 270ft x 42ft x 22ft (*82.29 x 12.80 x 6.70m*); *Rover* 280ft x 43ft 6in x 23ft (*85.34 x 13.25 x 7.01m*)
Machinery:	1-shaft HSE: *Active* Humphreys & Tennant, 4130ihp = 15.0kts; *Volage* John Penn, 4530ihp = 15.3kts. 1-shaft HCE: *Rover* Ravenhill & Salkeld, 4960ihp = 14.53kts
Armament:	*Active, Volage* 6-7in MLR, 4-64pdr MLR; *Rover* 2-7in MLR, 16-64pdr MLR
Complement:	*Active, Volage* 340; *Rover* 315

Name	Builder	Laid down	Launched	Comp	Fate
VOLAGE	Thames Sb Co	1867	27.2.69	1870	Sold 1904
ACTIVE	Thames Sb Co	1867	13.3.69	1870	Sold 1906
ROVER	Thames Sb Co	1872	12.8.74	1875	Sold 1893

Volage with funnel lowered.

Designed by Sir Edward Reed. The Admiralty decided to revert to the true concept of a cruising ship, following the big wood and iron frigates, by constructing a ship of half the tonnage, and combining speed with seaworthy qualities. The result was the two handsome corvettes *Active* and *Volage*, which epitomised all the grace of the transitional ship. To obtain speed a hitherto unheard of ratio of length to beam was designed, the hull cut away at below the waterline to give very fine ends, permitting the water to have the maximum action on the rudder and thus meeting the wishes of naval officers for high manoeuvreability. Although handling easily, they were unsteady gun platforms, pitching deep into a head sea, and rolling heavily in a beam sea. The latter fault was subsequently reduced by fitting large bilge keels. They were the first cruisers to steam at over 15kts. The construction of the hull resembled that of the *Inconstant*, lateral watertight bulkheads reaching up to the upper deck. The hull was encased in a single layer of 3in oak. These vessels had rounded sloping sterns with false ports without quarter galleries, and had no embrasures. They both had a large poop and topgallant forecastle rising slightly above the sheer of the 6ft-high waist bulwark. A patent capstan worked the cable which was led in through the upper deck. They had double hand-wheel steering at the break of the poop.

As completed, the slide-mounted 7in guns were carried in the waist on broadside, and two of the truck-mounted 64pdrs were almost amidships. The other two 64pdrs were chase guns on traversing mounts at the poop and topgallant forecastle respecitvely. In 1873, in line with the rearming policy, the 7in guns were removed, the armament then consisting of eighteen 6in 64pdr guns. A further rearming took place in 1880 when all the broadside guns were removed leaving only the chase guns. These two ships then carried ten 6in BL (80pdr) and two 6in MLR chase guns, two light guns, 10 MGs, and two TCs. The 6in BL guns were placed five on either broadside.

Volage received her trunk-type engines from John Penn, whilst *Active's*, by Humphrey & Tennant, were of the return connecting-rod type. Both were fitted with 19ft diameter hoisting screws, single telescopic funnels and five boilers.

They were given full ship-rig, the height of the mainmast from deck to truck being 136ft and the area of sail 16,593 sq ft, or about the same area of canvas for a wooden corvette of 2000t. The best logged speeds under canvas were 12.5kts for *Active*, and 13kts for *Volage*.

Rover incorporated design modifications to remedy some of the deficiencies in the previous ships. She had a different metacentre and a false keel, to reduce rolling, a vertical stem, without a knee, to save weight forward, and a narrower convergence aft at the waterline. These design changes made her a steadier vessel, but she floated with an excessive trim aft, adversely affecting steering and sailing. Through a redistribution of weights later in her career, these faults were reduced and although slower than the previous pair in smooth water, she was faster in heavier seas. Construction and sub-division followed the same design as in the other two ships, the main difference being that she was zinc- instead of copper-sheathed. Her cross section amidships was not so square, and a false keel was fitted. The compound engines, with one HP and two LP cylinders, were fed from 10 boilers working at 70psi. The hoisting screw was 21ft in diameter. Her sail plan was as in the other two ships. She was not a good sailer, never logging more than 11kts, but this was only of secondary importance because of her greatly superior steaming power. The mounting of her guns was a reversal of the system in *Active* and *Volage*. The 7in MLRs became the chase guns and the 64pdrs were truck-mounted on broadside.

Following her first commission, she was completely rearmed with fourteen 6in BLs (80pdr), three light guns, eight MGs and two TCs. Twelve of the 6in were slide-mounted on broadside, the other two were chase guns; displacement was thereby increased to 3494t. A bridge was sited between the forefunnel and the mainmast, and the chart house abaft the mizzen.

Designed by Nathaniel Barnaby who reintroduced the knee-bow and square frigate type of stern. The first three were similar to *Briton*, having heavy, rounded sterns, the last pair having the outward sloping frigate-type stern. They were the first complete class of their size to be fitted with compound engines. All were ship-rigged, except *Encounter* which was barque-rigged. They were excellent seaboats, being the only class of small cruisers able to sail or steam at just over 13kts. In hull form, their lines were rather full towards the extremities, but they did not have the bulbous ram bow. They were deeply embrasured, the use of embrasures aft overcoming the difficulty of combining the hoisting screw with stern fire. They had neither quarter galleries nor bilge keels, nor watertight bulkheads. All except *Encounter* had a heavy knee added to their stems. *Amethyst, Diamond* and *Sapphire* were given two lighter (64 cwt) 64pdrs as chase guns, the 12 broadside 64pdrs (71 cwt) being the heavier pattern. The entire armament of *Encounter* and *Modeste* was of the heavier type. On the second commission the three mentioned previously received a lighter 64pdr, mounted on iron slides to produce a higher rate of fire. Their broadside armament was reduced to ten guns.

All had six cylindrical boilers working at 60psi, giving them a radius of 2000/2500nm at 10kts. With speeds of 13 to 13.6kts they were the fastest, and most economical in fuel, of the wooden cruising ships in the service. All ships in this class logged over 13kts under canvas. The total area of plain sail was 18,000 sq ft. *Sapphire* was the last wooden cruiser built for the Royal Navy, and *Diamond* was the last wooden hull to be built at Sheerness Dockyard.

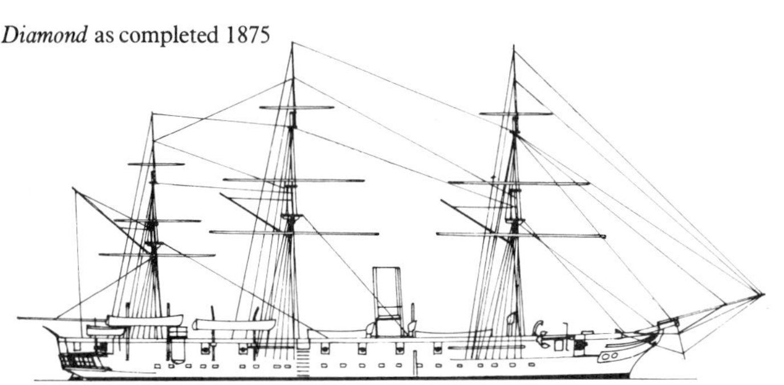
Diamond as completed 1875

AMETHYST class *wooden screw corvettes*

Displacement: 1970t
Dimensions: 220ft x 37ft x 18ft *(67.05 x 11.27 x 5.48m)*
Machinery: 1-shaft HCE; *Amethyst* J & G Rennie, 2144ihp = 13.24kts; *Encounter* J & G Rennie, 2031ihp = 13.0kts; *Diamond* R & W Hawthorn, 2140ihp = 12.5kts; *Sapphire* R & W Hawthorn, 2364ihp = 13.58kts; *Modeste* Robert Napier, 2068ihp = 12.51kts
Armament: 14-64pdr MLR
Complement: 225

Name	Builder	Launched	Comp	Fate
AMETHYST	Devonport DYd	19.4.1873	July 1873	Sold 1887
DIAMOND	Sheerness DYd	26.8.1874	July 1875	Sold 1889
ENCOUNTER	Sheerness DYd	1.1.1873	July 1873	Sold 1888
MODESTE	Devonport DYd	23.5.1873	Jan 1874	Sold 1888
SAPPHIRE	Devonport DYd	24.9.1874	Aug 1875	Sold 1892

Amethyst, a wooden screw corvette launched in 1873.

Designed by Nathaniel Barnaby. The introduction of the steel-hulled despatch vessels *Iris* and *Mercury*, with a speed of 18kts, made all other materials for hull construction obsolete, so the period of composite construction was brief. Care had to be taken in the distribution and support of weights in wooden hulls, to avoid excessive hogging and sagging. In composite hulls, the additional longtitudinal strength gave designers more freedom in hull lines and weight distribution. The theory that a fine entry gave extra speed was influenced by the performance of tea clipper ships with their 'Aberdeen bow', ie extending the stem out to form a cutwater, drawing the waterlines finer at the bow, giving greater buoyancy forward and enabling the ship to divide the water easily. In practice, however, this theory did not work with the *Emerlad* class. To compensate for buoyancy they were given a short but very full midships section. Receiving little help from the ends, they tended to behave like a see-saw in heavy weather. Their faulty underwater lines adversely effected their performance under sail, none exceeding much more than 12kts.

The frames and keels of this class were of wrought iron and the stem and stern post of cast iron. The cladding was a double layer of teak, the inner 3½in, the outer 3in in thickness. The first layer of timber was secured direct to the frames, the second to the first with a waterproof coating between. Watertight bulkheads extended to the upper deck. The compound engines were far from satisfactory due to the Admiralty's decision to invite competitive tenders, resulting in price cutting and inferior workmanship. In fact, the engine in *Tourmaline* was so troublesome that her chief engineer suffered a nervous breakdown, committing suicide. The HCE engines were of two cylinders – one HP and one LP. The six cylindrical boilers worked at 60psi. The radius was from 2000 to 2280nm at 10kts.

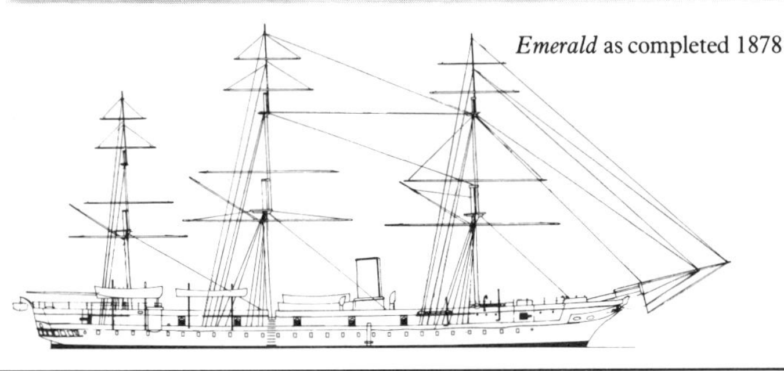
Emerald as completed 1878

EMERALD class *composite screw corvettes*

Displacement: 2120t
Dimensions: 220ft x 40ft x 18ft *(67.05 x 12.19 x 5.48m)*
Machinery: 1-shaft HCE; *Emerald* J & G Thompson, 2170ihp = 13.87kts; *Garnet* R & W Hawthorn, 2000ihp = 13.2kts; *Tourmaline* R & W Hawthorn, 1972ihp = 12.62kts; *Opal* Robert Napier, 2100ihp = 12.53kts; *Ruby* Earle, 2018ihp = 12.28kts; *Turquoise* Earle, 1994ihp = 12.32kts
Armament: 12-64pdr MLR
Complement: 230

Name	Builder	Laid down	Launched	Comp	Fate
EMERALD	Pembroke DYd	–	18.8.76	June 1878	Sold 1906
GARNET	Chatham DYd	Mar 1875	30.6.77	Oct 1878	Sold 1904
OPAL	Wm Doxford, Sunderland	–	9.3.75	Jan 1876	Sold 1892
RUBY	Earle, Hull	July 1874	9.8.76	June 1877	Sold 1921
TOURMALINE	Wm Raylton, Dixon & Co	July 1874	30.10.75	Oct 1876	Sold 1920
TURQUOISE	Earle, Hull	July 1874	22.4.76	Sept 1877	Sold 1892

All guns were slide-mounted, with a broadside fire of five a side and two chase guns firing through embrasures at both ends of the ship. Between 1882 and 1886 all MLR guns in *Emerald* and *Tourmaline* were replaced by four 6in BL and eight 5in BL guns. The 6in were mounted in large sponsons on either beam. The 5in were equally divided between the two sponsons. *Garnet* was rearmed with fourteen 5in BLs ten divided on either broadside, the other four as chase guns between the poop and topgallant forecastle.

As completed they were all ship-rigged, carrying 18,250 sq ft of plain sail. The lower masts were of iron. Between 1880 and 1890 all were altered to barque-rig. MGs were added, varying from seven to nine in each.

GREAT BRITAIN

Designed by Nathaniel Barnaby. The large iron frigates were somewhat of a misfit in the fleet and therefore it was decided to scale down the size of cruising ships. These vessels were the same length as *Rover* but with a slight increase in beam and much fuller lines towards the extremities. At the time of completion, they were the largest ships to receive compound engines. The increased efficiency and steaming reliability gave them a cruising radius of 4000 miles at 10kts. Under sail they were not good performers, but this was acceptable in view of the far greater efficiency of their engines. All were ship-rigged, the total area of canvas being 38,300 sq ft. Their best logged sailing speeds were: *Bacchante* 11½kts; *Boadicea* 11kts; and *Euryalus* 9½kts. The hull construction followed the same pattern as in earlier iron cruisers – without double bottoms or wing compartments. Ten watertight bulkheads rose only up to the main deck level. They were clad in a double layer of teak, *Boadicea* receiving a double layer throughout and being copper sheathed. In *Bacchante* and *Euryalus* the double layer extended to a few feet below the waterline and thereafter a single layer to the keel. *Euryalus* was copper- and *Bacchante* zinc-sheathed. It was this single layer of casing below the waterline that explains why *Bacchante* and *Euryalus* were given 6in extra beam. *Boadicea* had a knee bow, figurehead and fixed bowsprit. All had outward sloping square sterns, rising from the counter. *Bacchante* and *Euryalus* had vertical square bows with a running-in bowsprit. All had poops and topgallant forecastles, embrasured for chase guns. They were the last vessels to have their cables enter on the main deck. The rudder was pintle-hung and like other warships of less than 5000t their capstans and steering were manually handled.

Twelve of the 7in iron slide-mounted guns were on the main deck as a broadside battery, the other two being on the upper deck as chase guns. The two 6in 64pdrs in *Boadicea* and *Euryalus* were truck-mounted to move to any of the six vacant ports on that deck.

Bacchante had four of her 7in removed and replaced by four 6in BL Mk II guns in 1882/5 and she also received eight light guns, eight MGs and two TCs. Between 1885 and 1888 *Boadicea* and *Euryalus* had two of their 7in MLR guns replaced by two 6in BL Mk II guns and at the same time were fitted with 6/7 light guns, 8/11 MGs and two TCs. In her last commission *Boadicea* carried searchlights on the bridge wings. Later in their careers they were given additional ballast which increased their draught by about 6in.

All three had return connecting-rod type engines, with one HP and two LP cylinders, and ten cylindrical boilers working at 70psi, exhausting to two telescopic funnels. Bunkerage at 550/570t gave them a radius of up to 3000nm at 10kts. The hoisting screw was 21ft in diameter, and was raised by means of a triple iron-girder strongback.

This class represented the half way stage between the old and the new, a decisive evolutionary step to the eventual advent of the all-steel cruiser. Although retaining many of the features of a wooden screw frigate, such as rig, steering and conning aft, hoisting screw, and main deck broadsides, the new features were the iron hull and frames, divided into watertight compartments, a protection that set the pattern for ships to follow. They were, in fact, the last ships built of iron for the Royal Navy.

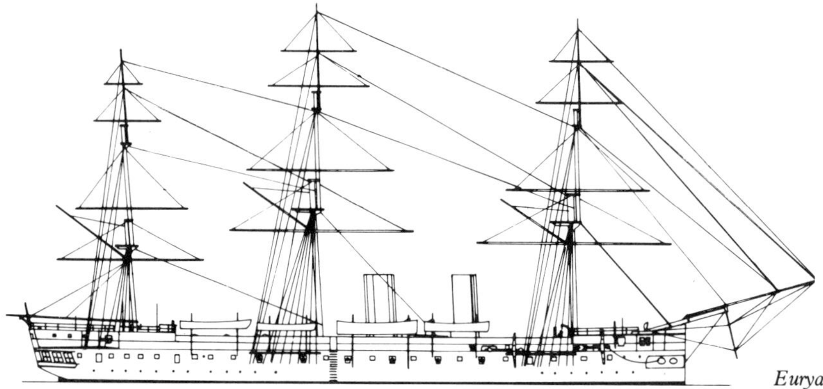

Euryalus as completed 1878

BACCHANTE class *iron screw corvettes*

Displacement: *Bacchante* 4070t; *Boadicea* 3913t; *Euryalus* 3932t

Dimensions: *Bacchante* 280ft x 45ft 6in x 23ft 9in (*85.34 x 13.86 x 7.23m*); *Boadicea* 280ft x 45ft x 23ft 8in (*85.34 x 13.71 x 7.21m*); *Euryalus* 280ft x 45ft 6in x 23ft 3in (*85.34 x 13.86 x 7.08m*)

Machinery: 1-shaft HC; *Bacchante* J & G Rennie, 5420ihp = 15.06kts; *Boadicea* J & G Rennie, 5130ihp = 14.7kts; *Euryalus* Ravenhill & Salkeld, 5110ihp = 14.72kts

Armament: *Bacchante* 14-7in 4½t MLR, 2 TC; *Boadicea, Euryalus* 14-7in 4½t MLR, 2-6in (64pdr) MLR

Complement: 375 (later increased to 420)

Name	Builder	Launched	Comp	Fate
BACCHANTE	Portsmouth DYd	19.10.1876	1878	Sold 1897
BOADICEA	Portsmouth DYd	16.10.1875	1877	Sold 1905
EURYALUS	Chatham DYd	31.1.1877	1878	Sold 1897

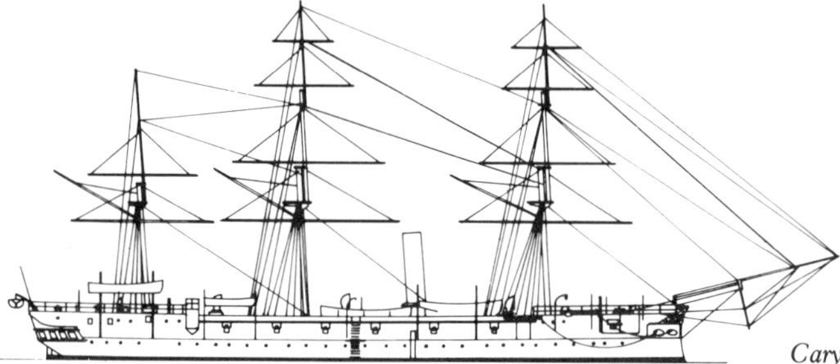

Carysfort as completed 1879.

COMUS class *steel corvettes*

Designed by Nathaniel Barnaby. These were the first cruisers of less than 3000t to be given metal hulls. The hull was constructed of iron or steel framing, a gun metal stem casting leading to a pointed ram, and steel plating. They were all timber-clad up to the upper deck, from the keel upwards to about three feet above the waterline in two layers, the inner of 3in teak. The outer cladding, 2½in thick, was left to the builder's choice as regards the kind of timber used. All the ships were copper-sheathed, and fitted with bilge keels. The internal watertight protection consisted of six lateral bulkheads extending to the upper deck and another three stopped short at the lower deck.

A protective deck of 1½in steel, extending for 100ft amidships, was positioned over the machinery. The lower deck accommodated the ship's company, with the officers' quarters being aft to the after end of the engine

Displacement: 2380t

Dimensions: 225ft x 44ft 6in x 19ft 3in (*68.58 x 13.56 x 5.86m*)

Machinery: 1-shaft HC; *Comus* Elder, 2450ihp = 12.93kts; *Carysfort* Elder, 2403ihp = 12.96kts; *Champion* Elder, 2310ihp = 13.0kts; *Cleopatra* Humphreys & Tennant, 2610ihp = 13.0kts; *Conquest* Humphreys & Tennant, 2670ihp = 13.0kts; *Curacoa* Humphreys & Tennant, 2540ihp = 13.0kts; *Constance* John Penn, 2590ihp = 13.72kts; *Canada* C & G Rennie, 2430ihp = 13.0kts; *Cordelia* C & G Rennie, 2420ihp = 13.0kts

Armament: *Comus* 4-6in BL Mk II, 8-64pdr MLR, 2 light guns, 8 MGs, 2 TCs; *Carysfort, Champion, Cleopatra, Conquest, Curacoa, Constance* 2-7in MLR, 12-64pdr MLR; *Canada, Cordelia* 10-6in BL Mk II, 2 light guns, 6 MGs (*Cordelia* 10 MGs), 2TCs

Complement: 265

Name	Builder	Laid down	Launched	Comp	Fate
COMUS	Elder, Glasgow	1876	3.4.78	1878	Sold 1904
CARYSFORT	Elder, Glasgow	1876	26.9.78	1879	Sold 1899
CHAMPION	Elder, Glasgow	1876	1.7.78	1878	Sold 1931
CLEOPATRA	Elder, Glasgow	1876	1.8.78	1878	Sold 1931
CONQUEST	Elder, Glasgow	1876	28.10.78	1879	Sold 1899
CURACOA	Elder, Glasgow	1876	18.4.78	1878	Sold 1904
CONSTANCE	Chatham DYd	1878	9.6.80	1880	Sold 1899
CANADA	Portsmouth DYd	1879	26.8.81	1881	Sold 1897
CORDELIA	Portsmouth DYd	1879	25.10.81	1881	Sold 1904

room. Warrant and petty officers berthed forward. Decided improvements were the provision of a sick bay, a bathroom for ratings, a ship's library and improved ventilation. The poop was where the commanding officer, first lieutenant and navigating officer lived. A double hand-wheel stood at the break of the poop. On either beam there were small semicircular bullet-proof conning towers containing voice pipes and engine and steering telegraph for use when in action.

All MLR guns were iron slide-mounted. *Carysfort* and *Constance* retained their original armament, but on rearming the other ships had: *Champion* four 6in BL Mk III, eight 5in BL Mk III, four 3pdr BL QF, two light guns, six MGs, and two TCs; *Cleopatra* received the same scale of armament excepting that her 5in BL guns were Mk IV; *Curacoa* differed in having nine MGs, one 3pdr BL QF, and her 6in BL guns were Mk IV; *Conquest* was rearmed with nine 6in BL Mk IV, eight MGs, two light guns, and two TCs. The TCs were located on the lower deck on either beam forward of the boiler room. In the Elder engined ships the compound engine had one HP and two LP cylinders, and in the others, two HP and two LP cylinders arranged as tandem compounds, and all had six boilers. Except for *Carysfort* and *Constance* they were all fitted with hoisting screws, the latter having a feathering screw. The first six built were ship-rigged, the remaining three being rigged as barques. The area of sail plan was from 14,512 sq ft to 15,940 sq ft.

Successful as this class was, with the passing of the Naval Defence Act of 1888 which brought about a flood of new construction, these ships were soon obsolescent.

1

2

1. *Bacchante* between 1879 and 1884.
2. *Satellite* early in her career.
Both NPC by courtesy of W Pym Trotter

SATELLITE class *composite screw sloops upgraded to corvettes*

Displacement:	1420t
Dimensions:	200ft x 38ft x 15ft 9in (*60.96 x 11.58 x 4.80m*)
Machinery:	1-shaft HCE; *Satellite* Humphreys & Tennant, 1400ihp = 13.0kts; *Heroine* Humphreys & Tennant, 1470ihp = 13.1kts; *Hyacinth* Humphreys & Tennant, 1470ihp = 13.1kts; *Caroline* Maudslay, 1400ihp = 13.0kts; *Rapid* Maudslay, 1400ihp = 13.0 kts; *Royalist* Maudslay, 1510ihp = 13.0kts; *Pylades* Laird, 1640ihp = 13.0kts
Armament:	*Satellite, Rapid* 2-6in BL, 10-5in BL, 4 MGs, 1 light gun; *Royalist, Heroine, Hyacinth* 8-6in BL, 4 MGs, 1 light gun; *Caroline, Pylades* 14-5in BL, 8 MGs, 1 light gun
Complement:	170/200

Name	Builder	Laid down	Launched	Comp	Fate
SATELLITE	Sheerness DYd	Oct 1880	13.8.81	Dec 1882	Sold 1904
CAROLINE	Sheerness DYd	Oct 1881	25.11.82	Dec 1885	Sold 1929
HEROINE	Devonport DYd	Aug 1880	3.12.81	June 1883	Sold 1902
HYACINTH	Devonport DYd	Aug 1880	20.12.81	July 1883	Sold 1902
RAPID	Devonport DYd	April 1881	21.3.83	July 1884	Sold 1948
PYLADES	Sheerness DYd	Jan 1883	5.11.84	Aug 1886	Sold 1906
ROYALIST	Devonport DYd	April 1881	7.3.83	Nov 1884	Transferred 1923

Designed by Nathaniel Barnaby. This was the only class of wooden or composite-hulled ships to receive a protective steel deck of 1in to ¾in, extending for 73ft over the vitals. Laid down as sloops, they were upgraded to corvettes in 1884, and as such they were the smallest ships to be rated as corvettes. In construction, they were of the same general principle as in the *Emerald* class. The sailing rig was changed from ship- to barque-rig. *Pylades* was the last corvette built for the navy until this rate was revived in the Second World War. The only change in armament was in *Satellite* when the 5in guns were removed and her armament was increased by six 6in to a total of eight 6in BL. In 1892/3 *Hyacinth, Rapid* and *Royalist* changed their 6in BL Mk II guns for three Mk VI and five Mk IV 6in in *Hyacinth; Rapid* for Mk IV 6in and one Mk I, four Mk III, and five Mk V 5in BL; *Royalist* had two 6in Mk II replaced by two Mk VI, and a year later, one Mk VI was replaced by a Mk IV. Mk I was an 80pdr Armstrong gun. The 6in Mks III, IV and VI were interchangeable, differing only in construction. The 5in Mks I to V were also interchangeable. In contrast to the *Emerald* class, the mechanical improvements and better workmanship of the compound engines gave these ships a radius of action of over 6000nm at 10kts. *Royalist* was transferred to the Irish Government on 19.2.1923.

Designed by Nathaniel Barnaby, they were probably the most successful design of cruising ship built for the Navy. Their construction and internal layout was virtually a repetition of the last vessels in the *Comus* class. The main differences were the protective deck of steel being three feet longer and positioned four feet below the lower deck, a bilge keel 95ft long, and the lower deck two feet above the water line. Both were barque-rigged, the mainmast being 136ft from deck to truck. Both had feathering screws, and at speeds over 5kts under sail the screw was allowed to turn over to reduce drag. The Rennie compound engines had two HP and two LP cylinders fed by six boilers. A small auxiliary steam-driven starting engine was located between the two HP cylinders, and another steam engine drove a dynamo to generate electricity.

The 6in BL guns were carried in sponsons on Vavasseur mountings and the 5in guns were mounted six on either side. The MGs were placed on the topgallant forecastle, poop and forebridge. Searchlights were mounted over the centreline CT. They were able to steam at 15kts, and the radius of action at 10kts was 4000nm. Together with their near sisters of the *Comus* class, with their speed and heavy armament, they were the finest ships of the Victorian era, bringing to a close the role of the steam and sail corvette.

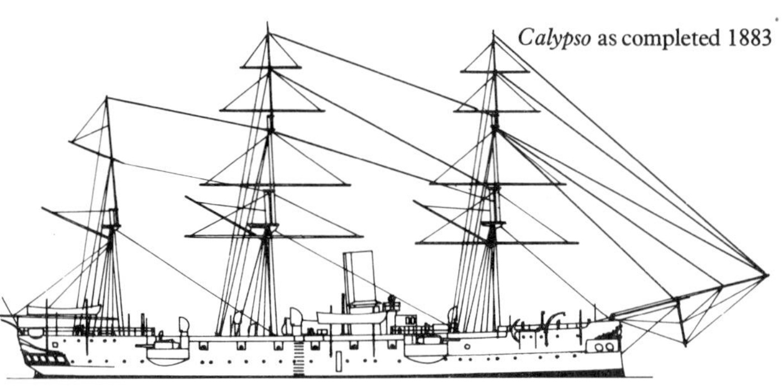

Calypso as completed 1883

CALYPSO class *steel corvettes*

Displacement: 2770t
Dimensions: 235ft x 44ft 6in x 19ft 11in (*71.62 x 13.59 x 6.07m*)
Machinery: 1-shaft J & G Rennie HCE, 3000ihp = 13.75kts
Armament: 4-6in BL Mk IV, 12-5in BL Mk II, 10 MGs, 2 light guns, 2 TCs
Complement: 317

Name	Builder	Laid down	Launched	Comp	Fate
CALYPSO	Chatham DYd	1881	7.6.83	1883	Sold 1922
CALLIOPE	Portsmouth DYd	1881	24.7.84	1884	Sold 1951

CAMELEON class *wooden screw sloops*

Displacement: *Cameleon* 1292t; *Chanticleer* 1419t; *Pelican* 1240t; *Reindeer* 1365t; *Rinaldo* 1365t; *Rattler* 1280t; *Perseus* 1365t; *Zebra* 1336t
Dimensions: 185ft x 33ft 2in x 14ft 8in (*56.38 x 10.55 x 4.47m*)
Machinery: 1-shaft HSE; *Cameleon* Maudslay, 702ihp = 9.36kts; *Chanticleer* A & J Ingles, 694ihp = 10.13kts; *Pelican* Miller, Ravenhill & Salkeld, 671ihp = 10.0kts; *Reindeer* J & J Rennie, 577ihp = 9.1kts; *Rinaldo* Humphreys & Tennant, 745ihp = 9.8kts; *Rattler* Maudslay, 843ihp = 10.0kts; *Perseus* J & J Rennie, 614ihp = 10.15kts; *Zebra* Humphreys & Tennant, 654ihp = 9.63kts
Armament: 5-40pdr ML SB, 12-32pdr ML SB
Complement: 180

Name	Builder	Laid down	Launched	Fate
CAMELEON	Deptford DYd	Nov 1858	23.2.60	Sold 1883
CHANTICLEER	Portsmouth DYd	Feb 1860	9.2.61	Sold 1878
PELICAN	Pembroke DYd	June 1859	9.7.60	Sold 1867
REINDEER	Chatham DYd	May 1860	29.3.66	BU 1876
RINALDO	Portsmouth DYd	Mar 1858	26.3.60	Sold 1884
RATTLER	Deptford DYd	Aug 1860	18.3.62	Wrecked 1868
PERSEUS	Pembroke DYd	–	21.8.1861	Sold 1931
ZEBRA	Deptford DYd	–	13.11.1860	Sold 1873

Designed by Isaac Watts, these sloops were half way between corvettes and gun vessels, and most were barque-rigged. With certain exceptions, there was no poop, quarterdeck or topgallant forecastle. Guns were carried on the open deck exposed to the air above. Some had a complete lower deck, ie the main deck, while in others the main deck was divided by the engine room. Some had their guns mounted on broadside, while in others the guns were positioned on the centre line. They were built for cruising in the open ocean rather than for coastal work. *Cameleon* was originally intended to be a sister ship to *Greyhound* but it was decided to make her the prototype for a new class and she was lengthened by 12ft. *Reindeer* was cancelled while on the stocks, and then restarted in 1865, hence the reasons for her late entry into this class. Two ships in this class were altered while on the stocks to ironclads – *Circassian* became the ironclad *Enterprise*, and *Trent* the *Research*. Six more were cancelled whilst still on the slips. All were fitted with telescopic funnels, and hoisting screws of about 12ft to 13ft in diameter. The boilers worked at 20 to 23psi. *Rattler* was wrecked while on the China station on 24.9.1868.

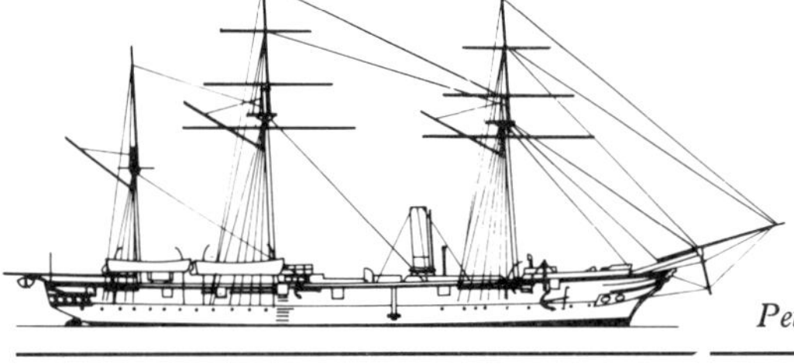

Peterel in 1862

ROSARIO class *wooden screw sloops*

Displacement: *Rosario* 927t; *Rapid* 896t; *Royalist* 918t; *Peterel* 849t; *Shearwater* 811t; *Columbine* 858t; *Africa* 913t
Dimensions: 160ft x 30ft 4in x 13ft 6in (*48.76 x 9.24 x 5.02m*)
Machinery: 1-shaft HSE; *Rosario* Greenock Foundry Co, 464ihp = 7.87kts; *Rapid* Greenock Foundry Co, 460ihp = 9.1kts; *Royalist* Greenock Foundry Co, 627ihp = 9.3kts; *Peterel* Greenock Foundry Co, 478ihp = 8.9kts; *Columbine* Greenock Foundry Co, 521ihp = 9.6kts; *Africa* Greenock Foundry Co, 530ihp = 9.6kts; *Shearwater* R & W Hawthorn, 502ihp = 9.4kts
Armament: 6-32pdr ML SB, 4-20pdr Armstrong BL, 1-40pdr Armstrong BL
Complement: 130

Name	Builder	Laid down	Launched	Fate
ROSARIO	Deptford DYd	June 1859	17.10.60	Sold 1882
RAPID	Deptford DYd	Aug 1859	29.11.60	BU 1881
ROYALIST	Devonport DYd	Oct 1860	14.12.61	BU 1875
PETEREL	Devonport DYd	Dec 1859	10.11.60	Sold 1901
SHEARWATER	Pembroke DYd	April 1860	17.10.61	BU 1877
COLUMBINE	Deptford DYd	May 1860	2.4.62	BU 1875
AFRICA	Devonport DYd	Dec 1860	14.2.62	Sold 1862

Designed during the office of Isaac Watts, these small sloops were only about the same tonnage, and were less in length and beam, than the contemporary class of *Cormorant* gun vessels, and were about two knots slower. But the gun power of these sloops was superior, with 11 guns compared with the four guns originally received by the *Cormorant* class. The 20pdr Armstrong guns were pivot-mounted, the 40pdr slide-mounted, and the 32pdr guns were truck-mounted, carried on broadside. They had two boilers working at about 22psi, a hoisting screw ten feet in diameter, and a telescopic funnel. They were barque-rigged. The reason for *Africa's* short life in the navy was because she was sold to China on 13.8.1862 to become a unit of the Vampire Fleet.

Calypso, a steel corvette and one of the first ships fitted with a protective deck.
IWM

Designed by Sir Edward Reed, this class was the first break through from the traditional sloop. The vessels were the first to be constructed with a poop and a topgallant forecastle, and the first to be fitted with Reed's design of ram bow, hitherto only appearing in armoured ships. They were also the heaviest of this rate ever officially termed sloops in the navy. In design they were the smaller antecedents of the ram-bowed *Eclipse* class corvettes (1867/70). In design, the *Amazon* class had the same beam as the *Eclipse* corvettes, an identical form of timber construction, with iron cross beams, and the same general internal arrangements for berthing, bunkering and stores – on a length of 25ft less than even the smaller corvettes. A five to one ratio of length to beam was adopted as an acceptable proportion for sloops. This class was characterised by the very full beam towards both ends of the ship and their fine-lined extremities. With timber in short supply, the dockyards were forced to use different kinds of timber to build these ships. *Amazon* and *Vestal* were of teak, while *Niobe* and *Nymphe* had frames in English oak, with teak cladding, and *Daphne* had English oak frames and Italian oak planking. *Dryad* was constructed half English and half Italian oak frames, with teak planking, and *Niobe* and *Nymphe* had decks made of fir.

AMAZON class *wooden screw sloops*

Displacement: *Amazon* 1525t; *Daphne* 1640t; *Dryad* 1574t; *Niobe* 1570t; *Nymphe* 1555t; *Vestal* 1597t
Dimensions: 187ft x 36ft x 15ft 5in (*56.99 x 10.97 x 4.69m*)
Machinery: 1-shaft HSE; *Amazon* Ravenhill & Salkeld, 1455ihp = 12.3kts; *Daphne* Ravenhill & Salkeld, 1927ihp = 12.47kts; *Dryad* Robert Napier, 1464ihp = 11.96kts; *Niobe* Ravenhill & Salkeld, 1833ihp = 12.32kts; *Nymphe* Maudslay, 2172ihp = 13.06kts; *Vestal* Maudslay, 2154ihp = 12.8kts
Armament: 2-7in MLR, 2-64pdr MLR
Complement: 150

Name	Builder	Laid down	Launched	Fate
AMAZON	Pembroke DYd	–	23.5.1865	Sunk 1866
DAPHNE	Pembroke DYd	–	23.10.1866	Sold 1882
DRYAD	Devonport DYd	–	25.9.1866	Sold 1885
NIOBE	Deptford DYd	–	31.5.1866	Wrecked 1874
NYMPHE	Deptford DYd	–	24.11.1866	Sold 1882
VESTAL	Pembroke DYd	–	16.11.1865	Sold 1884

The 7in guns were slide-mounted, pivoted to the ship's centreline to enable them to be traversed to fire from either side. The two 64pdrs were truck-mounted, one on each side. In accordance with the Admiralty's ordnance policy between 1870 and 1875, *Drayd, Nymphe* and *Vestal* were rearmed with nine 64pdr MLRs, the 7in guns being removed. These guns were mounted four on each side and one in the bows as a chase gun. *Daphne* received an extra 64pdr which was a chase gun. If stern fire were required, there were ports under the poop to which one of the broadside guns could be moved. Those ships rearming with nine 64pdrs increased their complements from 150 to 170. They were far better steamships than their predecessors. Four boilers working at 30/32psi fed steam to the simple expansion engines. *Amazon, Daphne* and *Niobe* logged 12½kts on trials. The class, rigged as barques, marked the final change in rig, sloops hitherto being a mixture of barque- and ship-rig. The ships had fixed screws of 15ft diameter, and the best that they could do under canvas was 11kts. For the size of ship and their complement, they were generously supplied with ship's boats: a 27ft pinnace stowed on high crutches amidships, between the foremast and the funnel; a 25ft steam cutter over the quarter deck; two 25ft cutters suspended from iron davits abaft the main rigging; and a 16ft jolly boat at the taffrail. They were the last class of all wooden-hulled sloops to be built. *Amazon* was sunk in a collision in the English Channel on 10.7.1866, and *Niobe* was wrecked off Miquelon Island on 21.5.1874.

Nymphe, an *Amazon* class wooden sloop of 1866.

Designed by Nathaniel Barnaby. With his appointment as Surveyor, there was a return to the smaller size of sloop, a policy which was brought about by the declining status of this rate of ship. Reed's ram-bow was not repeated. Although an interesting and somewhat theoretical concept of hull design, its disadvantage was that it made a ship too lively. The *Fantome* class consisted of the first composite-built sloops, the first to be fitted with compound engines, and all guns were pivoted. Simple expansion engines were no longer fitted since compounding had a marked effect on fuel economy. With a bunkerage capacity of around 250t, their radius of action was 1000nm at 10kts. Three cylindrical boilers supplied steam pressure at 60psi.

These sloops were the largest warships in the navy to retain the system of all guns pivoted, in contrast to the larger sloops where both traversing and broadside mountings were fitted. The guns were slide-mounted, pivoted at the after or inboard end, with runners forward, engaging in racers let into the deck, and fired through embrasures. They were fitted with a Griffiths 11ft diameter screw. With the exceptions of *Egeria* and *Flying Fish*, no vessels in this class were rearmed. The two named ships were converted into survey vessels, the former in 1897 when her armament was replaced by four 20pdr Armstrong BL guns, and the latter in 1878. All these vessels had rounded sterns but were not particularly handsome with their tall thin funnels and vertical stems.

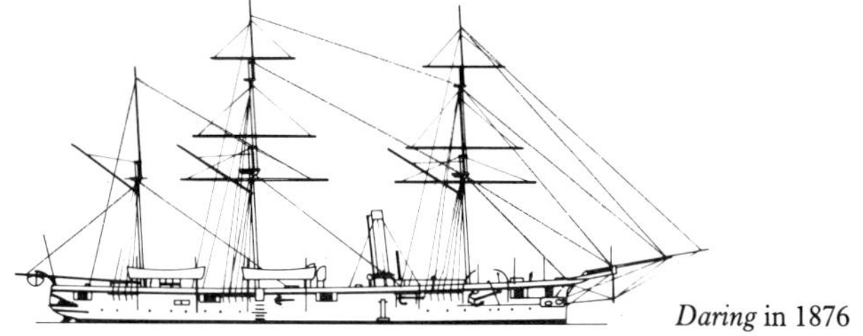

Daring in 1876

FANTOME class *composite screw sloops*

Displacement: 940t
Dimensions: 160ft x 31ft x 12ft 6in (*48.76 x 9.44 x 3.81m*)
Machinery: 1-shaft HCE; *Fantome* Humphreys & Tennant, 975ihp = 11.06kts; *Albatross* Humphreys & Tennant, 929ihp = 11.22kts; *Egeria* Humphreys & Tennant, 1011ihp = 11.30kts; *Flying Fish* Humphreys & Tennant, 836ihp = 10.96kts; *Sappho* Humphreys & Tennant, 936ihp = 11.19kts; *Daring* John Penn, 915ihp = 10.63kts
Armament: 2-7in MLR, 2-64pdr MLR
Complement: 125

Name	Builder	Laid down	Launched	Comp	Fate
FANTOME	Pembroke DYd	–	26.3.1873	1873	Sold 1889
ALBATROSS	Chatham DYd	–	24.7.1873	1874	BU 1889
DARING	Wigram, Blackwall	–	4.2.1874	1874	Sold 1889
EGERIA	Pembroke DYd	–	1.11.1873	1874	Sold 1911
FLYING FISH	Chatham DYd	–	27.11.1873	1874	Sold 1888
SAPPHO	Wigram, Blackwall	–	20.10.1873	1874	Sold 1887

Albatross, a *Fantome* class composite sloop of 1873.

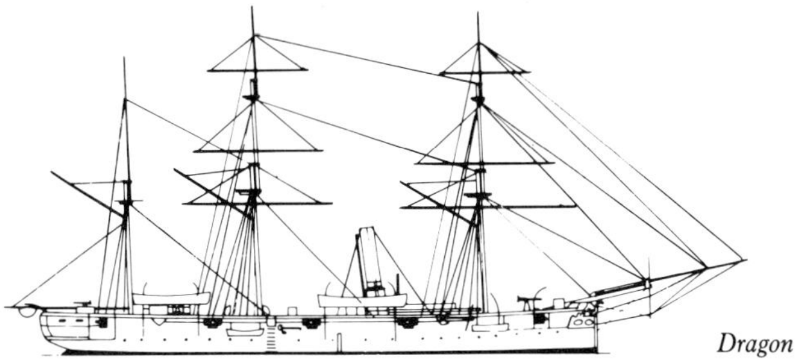

Dragon in 1880

OSPREY and DOTEREL classes *composite screw sloops*

Designed by Nathaniel Barnaby as a follow on from the *Fantome* class, who endeavoured to achieve handiness with increased speed. The speed was never realised, *Wild Swan* and *Penguin* in particular failing to reach the contract speed. After their first commissions, they were re-engined at Devonport DYd with engines built there. The system of mounting the guns was similar to that in the *Amazon* class. In the mid-1880s all ships in this class had received four to six MGs, and one light gun. *Pelican*, *Wild Swan* and *Espeigle* were completely rearmed with BL guns: *Pelican* with two 6in and six 5in; *Wild Swan* with two 6in and six 5in; and *Espeigle* with ten 5in. By 1892 *Mutine* was rearmed with ten 5in BL guns and 10 MGs. *Gannet* exchanged her 64pdrs for two 5in BLs. The remainder continued to carry their original armament. All had three boilers working at 60psi, and Griffiths hoisting screws of 13ft 1in diameter. All were barque-rigged. The two groups were distinguished by the shape of the bows: Group 1 had knee-bows, and Group 2 had vertical stems. *Doterel* exploded and sank off Punta Arenas on 26.4.1881, and *Phoenix* was wrecked off Prince Edward Island on 12.9.1882.

Displacement: 1130t
Dimensions: 170ft x 36ft x 15ft 9in (*58.81 x 10.97 x 4.80m*)
Machinery: 1-shaft HCE; *Osprey* Humphreys & Tennant, 946ihp = 11.38kts; *Cormorant* Humphreys & Tennant, 951ihp = 11.31kts; *Pelican* Humphreys & Tennant, 1056ihp = 12.24kts; *Penguin* R & W Hawthorn, 666ihp = 9.87kts; *Wild Swan* R & W Hawthorn, 797ihp = 10.35kts; *Doterel* Maudslay, 900ihp = 11.0kts; *Espeigle* Maudslay, 1140ihp = 11.5kts; *Dragon* Maudslay, 1056ihp = 11.52kts; *Gannet* Humphreys & Tennant, 1107ihp = 11.53kts; *Kingfisher* Maudslay, 1090ihp = 11.64kts; *Miranda* Robert Napier, 1020ihp = 11.0kts; *Mutine* Maudslay, 1120ihp = 11.64kts; *Pegasus* Laird, 972ihp = 11.47kts; *Phoenix* Humphreys & Tennant, 1128ihp = (not recorded)
Armament: 2-7in MLR, 4-64pdr MLR
Complement: 140/150

Name	Builder	Laid down	Launched	Fate
OSPREY	Sheerness DYd	–	5.8.1876	Sold 1890
CORMORANT	Chatham DYd	–	12.9.1877	BU 1949
PELICAN	Devonport DYd	–	26.4.1877	Sold 1901
WILD SWAN	Napier, Glasgow	–	28.1.1876	Sold 1920
PENGUIN	Napier, Glasgow	–	25.3.1876	Sold 1924
DOTEREL	Chatham DYd	–	2.3.1880	Sunk 1881
DRAGON	Devonport DYd	–	30.5.1878	Sold 1892
ESPEIGLE	Devonport DYd	–	3.8.1880	Sold 1921
GANNET	Sheerness DYd	–	31.8.1878	Still afloat 1978
KINGFISHER	Sheerness DYd	–	16.12.1879	Sold 1919
MIRANDA	Devonport DYd	–	30.9.1879	Sold 1892
MUTINE	Devonport DYd	–	20.7.1880	Sold 1921
PEGASUS	Devonport DYd	–	13.6.1878	Sold 1892
PHOENIX	Devonport DYd	–	16.9.1879	Wrecked 1882

Espeigle, a composite sloop, photographed in 1897.

Dolphin in 1884

DOLPHIN class *composite screw sloops*

Designed by Nathaniel Barnaby. These were the first sloops to benefit by the Admiralty's rearmament policy of replacing ML guns with modern BLs. *Dolphin* only exchanged her original guns for two 6in Mk IV and two 5in Mk V in 1892. The MGs were a mixture of 1in Nordenfelds and 0.45in Gardners. Apart from their up-to-date armament, they were a repeat of the *Wild Swan* class, *Dolphin's* chief distinction being that she gave her name to the submarine base when she became an accommodation hulk for submarines in 1907.

Displacement: 925t
Dimensions: 157ft x 32ft x 14ft (*47.85 x 9.75 x 4.26m*)
Machinery: 1-shaft HCE; *Dolphin* R & W Hawthorn, 720ihp = 11.3kts; *Wanderer* R & W Hawthorn, 750ihp = 11.3kts
Armament: 2-6in BL Mk II, 2-5in BL Mk I, 1 light gun, 3 MGs
Complement: 115

Name	Builder	Laid down	Launched	Fate
DOLPHIN	Raylton Dixon, Middlesbrough	–	9.12.1882	Sold 1925
WANDERER	Raylton Dixon, Middlesbrough	–	8.2.1883	Sold 1907

This class were originally rated as gun vessels but were re-rated as sloops in 1884. They were amongst the last sloops designed under the *régime* of Sir Nathaniel Barnaby. The decision to build *Melita* in the Malta dockyard to alleviate the employment situation, from laying down in 1882 to launching in 1888, cost 20 per cent more than to build a comparable ship in the Royal Dockyards. The only minor change in armament was in *Racer* which exchanged her MK II 5in guns for Mk Vs in 1891. All vessels were barque-rigged with the exception of *Icarus* which was schooner-rigged, with square topsails on the foremast. Two of the 5in guns were mounted behind shields just forward of the foremast, and another two were similarly mounted by the mizzen mast. The other four guns were broadside mounted. The radius of action was 1900/2300nm at 10kts.

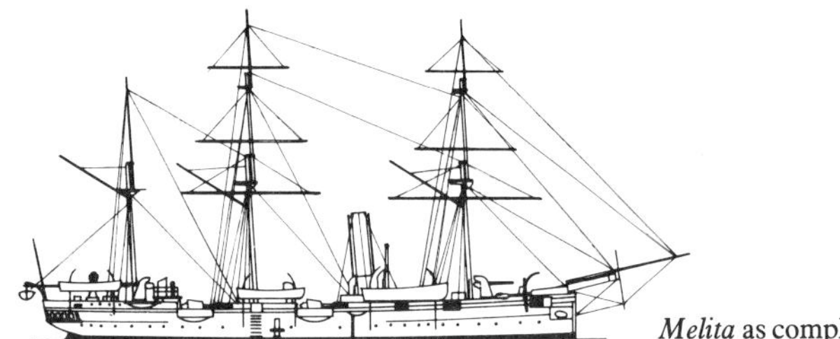

Melita as completed 1889

MARINER class *composite screw sloops*

Displacement: 970t
Dimensions: 167ft x 32ft x 14ft (*50.90 x 9.75 x 4.26m*)
Machinery: 1-shaft HCE; *Mariner* R & W Hawthorn, 970ihp = 11.5kts; *Racer* R & W Hawthorn, 920ihp = 11.5kts; *Reindeer* R & W Hawthorn, 1030ihp = 11.5kts; *Acorn* Maudslay, 1380ihp = 11.5kts; *Icarus* Barrow Sb Co, 1230ihp = 12.5kts; *Melita* Malta DYd, 1200ihp = 12.5kts
Armament: *Mariner, Acorn, Icarus, Racer* 8-5in BL Mk II, 1 light gun, 8 MGs; *Melita*, 8-5in BL Mk IV, 1 light gun, 8 MGs; *Reindeer* 6-5in Mk I, 1 light gun, 8 MGs
Complement: 126

Name	Builder	Laid down	Launched	Fate
MARINER	Devonport DYd	–	23.6.1884	Sold 1929
ACORN	Milford Haven Sb Co	–	6.9.1884	Sold 1889
ICARUS	Devonport DYd	–	27.7.1885	Sold 1903
MELITA	Malta DYd	–	20.3.1888	Sold 1920
RACER	Devonport DYd	–	6.8.1884	Sold 1928
REINDEER	Devonport DYd	–	14.11.1883	Sold 1924

Melita at Malta.

Designed and constructed during the office of Sir William White, Director of Naval Construction between 1885 and 1902. These were the last composite-hull sloops to be built. They were the first to have two-screw propulsion and TE engines. Since they were not armoured vessels, the Admiralty's policy of placing machinery below the waterline persisted to the extent of positioning these engines horizontally. To accomodate the engines within a beam of only 28ft, they were staggered, the port side engine being positioned foremost. Although a length to beam ratio of four to one was the acceptable dimension, in this class the ratio was extended to seven to one. With their superior steaming power the radius of action was 3000nm at 10kts. All vessels were schooner-rigged with square sails on the foremast, and fore and aft sails on the main and mizzen. However, the need for sail-power, as a complement to steam, had by then almost disappeared.

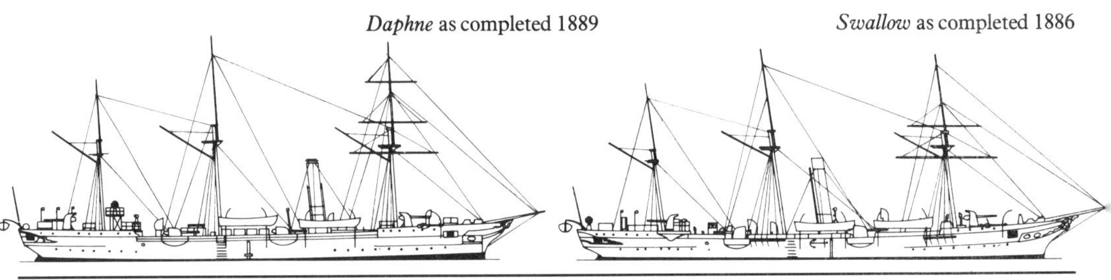

Daphne as completed 1889

Swallow as completed 1886

NYMPHE class *composite screw sloops*

Displacement: 1140t
Dimensions: 195ft x 28ft x 12ft 6in (*59.43 x 8.53 x 3.81m*)
Machinery: 2-shaft HTE; *Nymphe* Greenock Foundry Co, 2000ihp = 14.5kts; *Daphne* Greenock Foundry Co, 1570ihp = 13.5kts; *Buzzard* Barrow Sb Co, 2000ihp = 14.5kts; *Swallow* J & G Rennie, 1570ihp = 13.5kts
Armament: *Nymphe, Buzzard* 8-5in BL Mk III, 8 MGs; *Daphne* 8-5in BL Mk IV, 8 MGs; *Swallow* 8-5in BL Mk II, 8 MGs
Complement: 138

Name	Builder	Laid down	Launched	Comp	Fate
NYMPHE	Portsmouth DYd	5.7.1887	1.5.88	Feb 1889	Sold 1920
BUZZARD	Sheerness DYd	1.5.1886	10.5.87	May 1888	Sold 1921
DAPHNE	Sheerness DYd	20.6.1887	29.5.88	May 1889	Sold 1904
SWALLOW	Sheerness DYd	1.1.1885	27.10.85	Oct 1886	Sold 1904

This class was the first steel-sheathed version of the composite-hulled *Nymphe* class, and with the same dimensions. Both were schooner-rigged. Two guns were mounted forward on either beam, forward of the foremast, and four guns were mounted amidships, two on either side, abaft the funnel and mainmast. Two guns were also mounted on the poop deck. With bunkerage of 180t these ships had a radius of action of 3000 miles at 10kts. Machine guns were two .45in and four 1in Nordenfelds, and two .45in Gardners. The steel hulls were copper-sheathed from the waterline downwards. Standard equipment included one 25ft steam cutter, one whaler, one gig, one skiff and one dinghy. This class, and later classes of steel-hull sloops, had a protective deck of 1in to 1½in steel extending over the machinery and boilers.

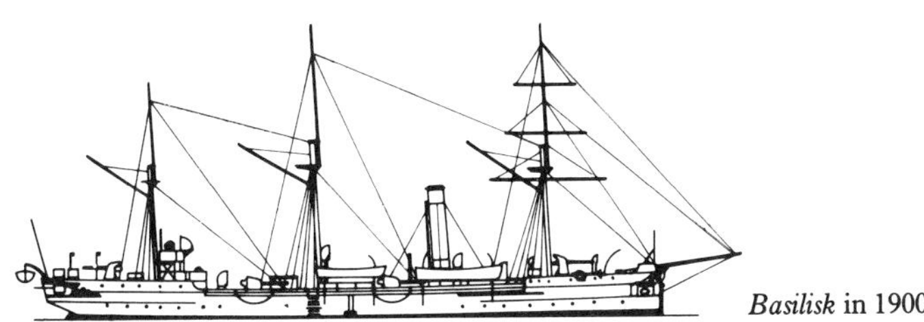

Basilisk in 1900

BEAGLE class *steel screw sloops*

Displacement: 1170t
Dimensions: 195ft x 28ft x 12ft 6in *(59.44. x 8.53 x 3.81m)*
Machinery: 2-shaft, J & G Rennie HTE, 2000ihp =14.5kts
Armament: 8-5in BL Mk IV, 8 MGs
Complement: 138

Name	Builder	Laid down	Launched	Comp	Fate
BEAGLE	Portsmouth DYd	14.5.1888	28.2.89	Sept 1889	Sold 1905
BASILISK	Sheerness DYd	1.5.1888	6.4.89	Dec 1889	Sold 1905

The hulls being of steel frames and steel sheathing were constructed on the same principle as the *Beagle*. These were the first sloops to receive the modern type of vertical engine, and the first to be fitted with QF guns. Originally they were schooner-rigged but later their yards were removed, although they retained their three masts. In appearance they differed from the *Beagle* class with their raised forecastle and poop. Guns were mounted two on the forecastle, two in the waist amidships and two on the quarter deck. The MGs were .45in Maxims. Even at this late date they retained features such as scrolls on the trail boards.

Torch as completed 1895

ALERT class *steel screw sloops*

Displacement: 960t
Dimensions: 180ft x 32ft 6in x 11ft 6in *(54.86 x 9.90 x 3.5m)*
Machinery: 1-shaft, Sheerness DYd VTE, 1400ihp = 13.25kts
Armament: 6-4in QF BL Mk III, 4-3pdr QF BL, 2 MGs
Complement: 106

Name	Builder	Laid down	Launched	Comp	Fate
ALERT	Sheerness DYd	8.12.1893	28.12.94	Sept 1895	Sold 1926
TORCH	Sheerness DYd	8.12.1893	28.12.94	Oct 1895	Sold 1920

These vessels had the same hull construction as the *Alert* class. Gun mountings, protected by gun shields of .22in armour, were positioned two forward, two amidships and two aft. The schooner rig was removed later, both ships retaining their three masts. The MGs were .45in Maxims. *Phoenix* capsized off Hong Kong on 18.9.1906.

PHOENIX class *steel screw sloops*

Displacement: 1050t
Dimensions: 185ft x 32ft 6in x 13ft 1in *(56.38 x 9.90 x 4.21m)*
Machinery: 2-shaft, Devonport DYd, inverted VTE, 1400ihp = 13.0kts
Armament: 6-4in QF BL Mk III, 4-3pdr QF BL, 3 MGs
Complement: 106

Name	Builder	Laid down	Launched	Comp	Fate
PHOENIX	Devonport DYd	26.7.1894	25.4.95	May 1896	Capsized 1906
ALGERINE	Devonport DYd	25.7.1894	6.6.95	April 1896	Sold 1919

Shearwater in her appearance as completed 1902.

The rigging of this class reverted to former practice. On completion they were barque-rigged, but for service on the China and East African stations, the yards were removed and in, for example, *Vestal* left with two pole masts. The foremast was fitted with a large rectangular platform erected at a height of 20ft from the deck, on which MGs were mounted. MGs were not included at the time of completion but added later according to the particular duty and station. The 4in QF guns were 25pdrs – two on the forecastle, two amidships, and two aft, with gun shields of .22in armour. *Vestal's* shields were removed from the forecastle guns when she shipped her unsightly foremast platform. The bridge was located aft on the poop deck. Figureheads and scrolled trail boards helped to make these handsome ships when in their full barque-rig. They had rounded sloping sterns, clipper bows, and a slightly raked funnel gave them a yacht-like appearance. Endurance at 10kts was about 3000nm.

Four of these sloops were launched at the end of Sir William White's term of office, who was succeeded by Sir Philip Watts (1902/12) as Director of Naval Construction. These were the last of the long line of sloops still retaining the elements of sail power. They were schooner-rigged, with square sails on the foremast. All yards and canvas disappeared prior to 1914. *Espiegle* is credited as being the last ship built for the navy with a figurehead. On their official steam trials these ships logged about half a knot better than their designed speed. Radius of action at 10kts was about 4000nm. The 25pdr guns, with their armoured shields, were mounted two on the forecastle forward of the foremast, two amidships almost in line with the funnel, and two on the poop deck under the bridge. A searchlight was positioned between the two bow-mounted guns. The steel hull was sheathed in timber to about three feet above the waterline. *Espiegle* never received sails. Naval opinion was critical towards the construction of these ships, considering that they were worthless for purposes of war. All survived the First World War, several serving in their traditional policing roles in Eastern waters. After this class, no more sloops were built until 1915 when the first 'mastless' sloops appeared.

Shearwater in 1905 with reduced rig

CONDOR class *steel screw sloops*

Displacement: 980t
Dimensions: 180ft x 32ft 6in x 11ft 6in (*54.86 x 9.90 x 3.5m*)
Machinery: 2-shaft VTE; *Condor* Thames Iron Wks, *Mutine, Rinaldo* Laird, *Rosario* Government, *Shearwater* Thames Iron Wks, *Vestal* Devonport DYd, 1400ihp = 13.5kts
Armament: 6-4in QF BL Mk III, 4-3pdr QF BL
Complement: 130

Name	Builder	Laid down	Launched	Fate
CONDOR	Sheerness DYd	–	17.12.1898	Foundered 1901
MUTINE	Laird, Birkenhead	–	1.3.1900	Sold 1932
RINALDO	Laird, Birkenhead	–	25.5.1900	Sold 1921
ROSARIO	Sheerness DYd	–	17.12.1898	Sold 1921
SHEARWATER	Sheerness DYd	–	10.2.1900	Sold 1922
VESTAL	Sheerness DYd	–	10.2.1900	Sold 1921

CADMUS class *steel screw sloops*

Displacement: 1070t
Dimensions: 185ft x 33ft x 11ft 3in (*56.38 x 10.05 x 3.42m*)
Machinery: 2-shaft VTE; *Cadmus, Clio* J and S White, Cowes, *Espeigle* Wallsend Slipway Co, *Fantome, Merlin, Odin* Devonport DYd, 1400ihp = 13.25kts
Armament: 6-4in QF BL Mk III, 4-3pdr, 3 MGs
Complement: 150

Name	Builder	Laid down	Launched	Comp	Fate
CADMUS	Sheerness DYd	–	29.4.1903	1904	Sold 1921
CLIO	Sheerness DYd	–	14.3.1903	1904	Sold 1920
ESPIEGLE	Sheerness DYd	–	8.12.1900	1902	Sold 1923
FANTOME	Sheerness DYd	–	23.3.1901	1902	Sold 1925
MERLIN	Sheerness DYd	–	30.11.1901	1902	Sold 1923
ODIN	Sheerness DYd	–	30.11.1901	1902	Sold 1920

Clio, one of the last class of masted sloops.
NPC by courtesy of W Pym Trotter
(All uncredited photos in this section: CPL)

CRUISERS

Compared with the development of the ironclad, progress in the design of cruising ships during the 1860s and 70s was comparatively slow and conservative. In general the cruisers constructed during this period, mainly corvettes and sloops, represented the continued development of pre-ironclad types with major improvements restricted to the adoption of the latest types of machinery and ordnance. To Britain, with her world-wide empire and trade, these vessels were essential for service on foreign stations where great distances and limited coaling facilities made sail power essential and the lack of docking facilities made wooden hulls a more economic proposition than iron ones. However they were more representative of peacetime ships than wartime ships, providing a relatively inexpensive means of carrying out police work, showing the flag and dealing with minor conflicts in distant waters. In a major war they would have been of little use for they lacked one essential of a cruising ship – speed. Most could make little more than 13kts, which could be exceeded by more and more ironclads as the development of capital ships progressed, and if employed as fleet scouts or even on trade route patrols they stood a very good chance of being run down by a more powerful enemy. There were a few exceptions, all constructed of iron, such as the frigate *Inconstant* and the corvettes *Active* and *Volage* which were capable of 15–16kts, but these were too few to provide the battle fleet with a balanced cruiser force. Apart from these early iron frigates and corvettes the only major cruising ships constructed for the Royal Navy until the 1880s were the armoured cruisers *Shannon*, *Nelson* and *Northampton* of 1873-74 but these vessels were essentially second class ironclads designed to serve on distant stations and again were too slow to be correctly classed as cruising ships. Two more ships of this type, the *Imperieuse* and *Warspite*, were laid down in 1881, and although a considerable improvement on the earlier trio they were of equally limited value. They did however serve to finalise the end of sail propulsion as a serious proposition in British warships. The captain of *Imperieuse*, in his report on her trials, carried out in 1886, stressed the fact that her brig rig served little purpose and that she would be a far better fighting ship without it. Shortly afterwards it was removed and henceforward British cruisers joined their battleship counterparts in being constructed without sailing rig.

THE GENESIS OF THE CRUISING SHIP

It was during the Barnaby era of 1870-86 that the true cruising ship of the British fleet underwent its initial development. The pattern was provided by the despatch vessels *Iris* and *Mercury* built during 1875-79. These were the first British warships to be constructed of steel and, with comparatively fine lines and powerful machinery, were designed for a speed of 17kts. They relied for protection on sub-division and coal bunkers and were of limited endurance but their basic design, with the addition of a protective deck and an increase in coal capacity, was utilised to provide Britain's first modern cruisers, the *Leander* (1880) and *Mersey* (1883) classes, which were designed primarily for trade protection. The eight ships of these two classes were however hardly sufficient to fulfil Britain's needs and the Northbrook Programme of 1884 laid particular emphasis on the provision of cruising ships. The result was the seven armoured, or belted, cruisers of the *Orlando* class and the eight torpedo cruisers of the *Archer* class, none of which was entirely successful. Unlike the earlier armoured cruisers, the *Orlando*s were true cruisers and not second class battleships, and were given a speed and endurance to match their designation, but their system of protection, a narrow waterline belt, was of such insignificant value as to represent no more than so much deadweight. As a result the Admiralty abandoned side protection in cruisers for 13 years (although it continued to be employed in foreign ships) and concentrated on the construction of protected cruisers. The *Archer* class were small fleet cruisers, based on the earlier *Scout* and *Fearless* and designed to carry out torpedo attacks and defend the fleet against torpedo boats, but they were too slow and insufficiently seaworthy to carry out their functions effectively and the type was not repeated.

THE WHITE ERA

The final stabilisation of cruiser types and designs was provided by William White who became chief constructor in 1886. His early designs, the *Medea* class of the 1886-87 Programme and the *Blake*, *Barracouta* and *Barham* classes of the 1887-88 Programme, introduced a number of important features. Two of the *Medea*s were fitted with vertical engines which were more efficient than horizontal engines and occupied a shorter length of the ship as they could be mounted side by side instead of fore and aft. The main objection to this arrangement, that the engine cylinders were above water and vulnerable to gunfire, was overcome by fitting a raised armoured glacis in the protective deck above the engines. The 1887-88 Programme ships were the first to carry QF guns, which rendered the earlier cruisers virtually obsolete. Barnaby's ships were designed to carry only such protection as was necessary to preserve the ships' stability, the majority of the above water hull, including the guns and their crews, being left open to attack. With the slow firing BLR gun this was an acceptable risk, but not with the QF gun. In *Blake* and *Blenheim* the problem was partially solved by providing a wider distribution of the armament and fitting armoured casemates and shields for the guns. The casemate, which was to become a major feature of White's first class cruisers and battleships, proved a mixed blessing. In general the majority of guns so mounted were fitted on the main deck where their close proximity to the waterline made them almost useless in anything but calm weather, but the arrangement continued until White left the Admiralty in 1903. In the smaller cruisers there was insufficient weight available to provide casemates, and gun protection was effected solely by shields and the widest possible distribution. It is worth noting here that White's ships were often criticised for being undergunned compared with their foreign counterparts but in most cases the British vessels were designed for more exacting requirements of seaworthiness and endurance which could not have been combined successfully with a heavier gun battery. However, this is a generalisation, and it is clear from the fact that several of White's cruisers were refitted with heavier or additional weapons that there was room for some improvement, although not on the scale suggested by some critics.

White's early cruiser designs coincided with a considerable enthusiasm for the provision of forced draught in which the power generated by boilers was greatly increased by raising the air pressure in the stokehold to force air through the furnaces. The system had been in use for several years but in the late 1880s was taken to extremes, much to the cost of the Royal Navy. Utilising this feature, White designed the *Medea*s for 20kts, the *Blakes* for 22kts and the *Barham* class for 19.5kts, but in no case did the completed ships achieve these speeds. The heat generated by forcing was so great that the water in contact with the boiler tubes tended to be lifted away completely by the generation of steam leaving the tubes to become overheated, whence they quickly began to break down and leak, causing extensive and costly damage. The worst cases were those of *Barham* and *Bellona*, whose small boilers were designed to accept a forced power 60% above that of their nominal power, and on trials their boiler tubes started to break down long before reaching this extreme limit. Subsequently the difference between natural and forced draught power was considerably reduced and was abandoned completely in the late 1890s when machinery design had improved sufficiently to provide the necessary speed without forcing. It is interesting here to note that throughout White's period of office the speed of all except the first class cruisers remained at around 20kts, which gave only a limited margin of speed over the battle fleet. It seems likely however that this was not so much a matter of policy as technical feasibility, since higher speeds were only possible at this time with greatly increased size.

THE NAVAL DEFENCE ACT

In 1886 the Russian war scare revealed the fact that the Navy was short of cruisers as it was necessary to take merchant vessels into service to fill the gaps, and in the following year the Press began a campaign of agitation about the state of the Navy. The campaign reached its climax in 1888-89 and resulted in the passing of the Naval Defence Act and the introduction of the 'two-power standard'. The Naval Defence Act provided for the construction of no fewer than 70 ships, of which 42 were cruisers, over a five-year period. The cruisers consisted of 17 first class ships (the *Edgar* and *Astraea* classes) 21 second class ships (the *Apollo* class) and only 4 third class ships (the *Pearl* class), which makes an interesting comparison with the 11 first class, 12 second class and 16 third class cruisers laid down between 1880 and 1889. The designations of first, second and third class had been introduced in 1888 and the majority of the older classes were re-rated to the new system, although not always accurately. The rating was largely a matter of size as all were expected to fulfil requirements as fleet and trade cruisers together with the usual peacetime duties although they did not all possess the necessary qualities in equal degrees. In general the cruisers constructed in the 1890s were built mainly to protect trade and were designed to overcome their contemporaries in the French and Russian Navies, in particular the former as it was the declared intention of the French to make war on commerce and avoid fleet actions.

The second class cruisers constructed between the Naval Defence Act and 1901 followed a logical pattern of steadily increasing size which allowed for improvements in seaworthiness and gunpower, but the design of first class ships fluctuated considerably from the very large hybrids *Powerful* and *Terrible* of 14,000t down to the more economic *Monmouth* class of 9800t. These variations were mainly the result of designing vessels to match particular threats from foreign ships–a policy of doubtful value as there is no guarantee that the vessel in question will necessarily meet and engage her opposite number even if operating in the correct area. The first class ships were also subject to a major design change with the return of side armour in the *Cressy* class of 1897. This change in policy resulted from the development of hard-faced steel armour which allowed for the provision of armour of sufficient strength to withstand medium calibre shells over an adequate area of the side without necessitating a reduction in speed or armament. The *Cressy* class were designed in part to counter the French *Montcalm* and her contemporaries, but much of the influence for the design came from the Italian *Carlo Alberto* and *Garibaldi* which were intended to operate in conjunction with the battle fleet and to fight in the line as a fast wing. This dangerous concept was also adopted for the *Cressys*, although they were still intended to fulfil the standard functions as fleet and trade cruisers, and subsequently became a requirement for all British armoured cruisers except the 'County' classes. In the late 1890s both France and Russia increased their construction programmes, which included a number of fast cruisers largely intended for attack on commerce. The British followed by raising the speed requirement for first class ships to 23kts, achieved in the *Drake* class by increased size and in the *Monmouth* class by reductions in protection and armament. The latter ships were not however intended to operate with the fleet, their armament, speed and protection all being scaled to deal with the latest types of French cruisers in defence of the trade routes. The 'Counties' were however the last true trade cruisers to be built for Britain for many years. The new century brought with it a new potential enemy in the shape of the rising German Navy and the basis of British cruiser construction rapidly shifted from trade requirements to fleet requirements. The last of the armoured cruisers, the *Duke of Edinburgh*, *Warrior* and *Minotaur* classes, were intended primarily to provide the fleet with a fast wing and differed substantially from earlier ships. They were generally a much better proposition, with their guns mounted in turrets, more extensive protection and uncluttered superstructures, but the whole concept of cruisers engaged with the battle fleet was incorrect. The type disappeared with the introduction of the even more disastrous concept of the big-gun armoured cruiser in the *Invincible* class of 1906.

At the turn of the century the design of second class cruisers also ceased, although in this case temporarily, with the laying down of the *Challenger* class, and only the third class ships remained to continue the line of development of the true cruising ship. However, even in this case the type became restricted in being designed specifically to serve as leaders to destroyers flotillas and as fleet scouts. Thus White's period ended as it began, with the large armoured ship and the small torpedo craft being given preference over the construction of the medium-sized cruisers which were so essential for the defence of the British Empire.

Royal Arthur in the late 1890s

CRUISERS 1st class

Shannon after her 1881 refit
NMM

Shannon, 1881

Britain's first armoured cruiser and of somewhat obscure origin. She was intended for service on foreign stations and it appears that she combined the requirements of a ship which was both economical to build and operate with the need for an armoured vessel of sufficient size to engage any ironclad likely to be encountered in distant waters. The result was a ship too weakly armed and protected to be classed as a battleship and too slow to adequately fulfil the war functions of a cruiser. She would however have made a reasonable peacetime flagship in distant waters and was suitable for 'showing the flag', but apart from a couple of months on the China station and 2 years in the Pacific she spent most of her service in home waters where her value was negligible.

All her guns were mounted on the upper deck with the heaviest, 2-10in 18t MLRs, mounted at the rear of the forecastle which was deeply embrasured to allow ahead as well as broadside fire. The ports for these guns were cut in the angled corners of a 9in armour screen which extended across the full width of the ship and for a short distance down each side. The remaining armament of 7-9in 12t MLRs was unprotected; 3 were carried on each side and 1 aft, the latter with alternate embrasured ports to port and starboard which allowed astern or broadside fire.

The 9ft deep waterline belt, positioned between the main and lower decks, was 8in-9in thick amidships and 6in aft. The side armour terminated in a 9in bulkhead about 70ft short of the stem. This bulkhead was extended upwards by an 8in bulkhead between the main and upper decks to join the armour screen of the two forward guns, thus forming a barrier against raking fire which extended from the lower deck to the forecastle. Forward of this bulkhead the lower deck was constructed of 3in plating while the area above it, in the region of the waterline, was subdivided into coal bunkers, cofferdams and store rooms whose contents would serve to restrict the flooding resulting from damage on the waterline. This, the first use of a protective deck and watertight subdivision in place of full length side armour, was the most important feature of the design and one which was to be employed extensively in future vessels. The remaining protection consisted of a 1½in main deck over the area of the belt.

For economy and because there were few facilities for coaling in foreign stations, sailing qualities were regarded as paramount. Her design therefore provided for a full ship rig, of 24,000sq ft sail area, a lifting screw and a coal stowage of only 280t. Shortly after completion she was changed to barque rig with 21,500sq ft of sail and her foremast and bowsprit were cut down slightly, while the coal capacity was doubled. Other modifications at this time included the fitting of a 9in armoured CT abaft the foremast, 6-20pdr BL guns and Whitehead torpedo launchers, which resulted in the ship being overweight with 1ft more draught than designed. She proved poor under sail but was a good seaboat, being steady and handy. During 1881 four TT and a number of machine guns were added to the armament. Her sea-going service ended only 4 years after completion; in 1883 she was relegated to coastguard duty and in 1893 she was placed in reserve.

SHANNON *armoured cruiser*

Displacement: 5670t load
Dimensions: 260ft pp x 54ft x 22ft 3in *(79.25 pp x 16.46 x 6.78m)*
Machinery: 1-shaft, Laird compound HRCR, 8 cyl boilers, 3370ihp = 12.25kts. Coal 560t
Armour: Belt 6in-9in with 10in-13in wood backing, bulkhead 8in-9in, decks 3in-1½in, CT 9in
Armament: 2-10in MLR, 7-9in MLR, 6-20pdr BL
Complement: 452

Name	Builder	Laid down	Launched	Comp	Fate
SHANNON	Pembroke DYd	29.8.1873	11.11.75	17.9.77	Sold Dec 1899

Enlarged versions of the *Shannon* and of similarly limited value despite an increase in displacement of almost 2000t. The increased size resulted from the adoption of more powerful machinery, for a 1¾kt increase in speed, improved protection and heavier armament. The general distribution of armour and armament was similar to that in *Shannon* except that the arrangement forward, with a protective deck, deep bulkhead and upper deck armour screen with corner ports for two 10in guns, was repeated aft. The addition of a protective deck aft was made possible by the adoption of twin screws which allowed the steering gear to be placed below the waterline and under the 3in lower deck whereas that in *Shannon*, being above the waterline, required the protection of side armour. The lower strake of the belt, which was 181ft long, was reduced to 6in in thickness while the main deck over the length of the belt was 2in. In place of the forecastle and poop of *Shannon* they carried a full length deck which covered the unprotected battery of 6-9in guns. The main deck guns were divided into four groups by 1in steel bulkheads which gave some measure of splinter protection and reduced the risk of several guns being knocked out by one hit. The side plating, abreast the midships guns, was also constructed of 1in steel.

Northampton's engines had three equal size cylinders with adjustable volumes allowing their use as all high pressure, all low pressure or compound. Despite several trials and modifications to the propellers and engines she never achieved her designed speed of 14kts. Both completed with a barque rig of 24,766sq ft sail area but unlike *Shannon* they were intended mainly for steam cruising and were given sufficient coal stowage to provide an endurance of 5000nm at 10kts, or 7500nm at 7kts. This was fortunate for although reasonable sea boats they proved to be poor sailers.

Nelson served on the Australia station 1881/89 and then underwent a 2-year refit during which she was converted to a military rig with fighting tops on fore and mizzen and fitted with 4-4.7in QF guns, 6-6pdr QFs, 14-3pdr QFs and two torpedo tubes and torpedo net gear. Her 20pdr guns were removed. She served as a guardship at Portsmouth 1891/94 and was then placed in reserve until 1901 when she was converted to a stokers' training ship.

Northampton was flagship on the NAWI station until 1886 when she also was refitted but on a lesser scale. The military rig had a top on the mizzen only and while the 20pdr guns were removed only 6-6pdr QFs, 8-3pdr QFs and 2 TT were added. After refit she was placed in reserve but commissioned regularly to take part in manoeuvres until 1894 when she became a boys' training ship.

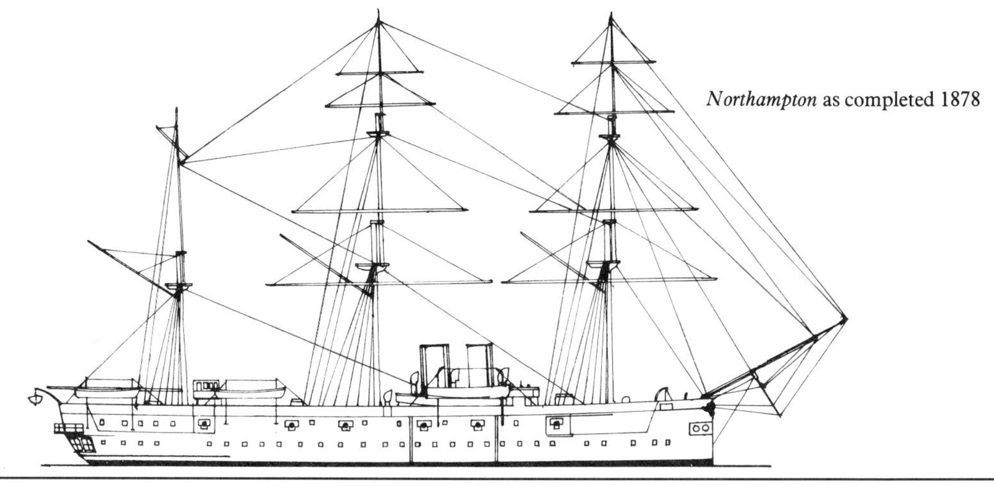

Northampton as completed 1878

NELSON class *armoured cruisers*

Displacement: 7473t, *Northampton* 7630t, load
Dimensions: 280ft pp x 60ft x 24ft 10in (*85.34pp x 18.29 x 7.57m*)
Machinery: 2-shaft, Elder (*Northampton* Penn) 3 cyl IC, 10 oval boilers, 6624ihp = 14kts (*Northamptom* 6073ihp = 13.17kts). Coal 1150t
Armour: Belt 6in-9in with 13in-10in wood backing, bulkheads 6in-9in, decks 3in-2in, CT 9in
Armament: 4-10in MLR, 8-9in MLR, 6-20pdr
Complement: 560

Name	Builder	Laid down	Launched	Comp	Fate
NELSON	Elder	2.11.1874	4.11.76	26.7.81	Sold July 1910
NORTHAMPTON	Napier	26.10.1874	18.11.76	7.12.78	Sold April 1905

Northampton with fighting-top added to the mizzen

Warspite as built with military rig

IMPERIEUSE class *armoured cruisers*

Cruiser contemporaries of the *Admiral* class battleships with 'all or nothing' protection, barbette mounted BL guns etc. Despite their modern features they were intended to fulfil the same function as the early armoured cruisers and were equally unsuccessful, largely due to their being seriously overweight as completed partly as a result of additions during construction and partly because of inaccurate design calculations and inefficient control of construction material. Shortly after con-

Displacement: 8500t load
Dimensions: 315ft pp x 62ft x 26ft 9in (*96.01 pp x 18.9 x 8.15m*)
Machinery: 2 shaft, Maudslay (*Warspite* Penn) 3 cyl IC, 12 cyl and oval boilers, 8000ihp = 16kts natural draught, 10,000ihp = 16.75kts forced draught. Coal 1130t
Armour: Belt 10in with 10in wood backing, bulkheads 9in, barbettes 8in, ammunition tubes 3in, decks 4in-2in, gunshields 2in, CT 9in
Armament: 4-9.2in BL, 10-6in BL, 4-6pdr QF, 6-18in TT aw
Complement: 555

Name	Builder	Laid down	Launched	Comp	Fate
IMPERIEUSE	Portsmouth DYd	10.8.1881	18.12.83	Sept 1886	Sold 24.9.1913
WARSPITE	Chatham DYd	25.10.1881	29.1.84	June 1888	Sold 4.4.1905

struction began it was decided to improve stability by increasing the thickness of their sheathing (wood and copper for tropical service) from 4 to 10in, which increased the beam by 1ft and raised the designed displacement by 210t to 7600t. In addition the 9.2in 18t and 6in 4½t guns were replaced by 24t and 5t weapons of the same calibre, the machinery was modified and the nominal coal stowage increased from 400 to 900t (max capacity from 900t to 1130t) which together with other minor additions and the overweight condition of the ships' structure raised the load displacement by 900t and increased the draught by 2ft 1in.

Protection to the machinery consisted of an 8ft by 140ft waterline belt of compound armour closed at the ends by 9in bulkheads and covered by a 2in deck. Fore and aft of this was a 4in protective deck extending, below water, to bow and stern. As designed the top of the belt was 3ft 3in above lwl but as completed this was reduced to 1ft 2in and at deep displacement the belt would have been virtually submerged. However the effectiveness of such a small area of side armour is doubtful and the increased immersion only serves to emphasise the point.

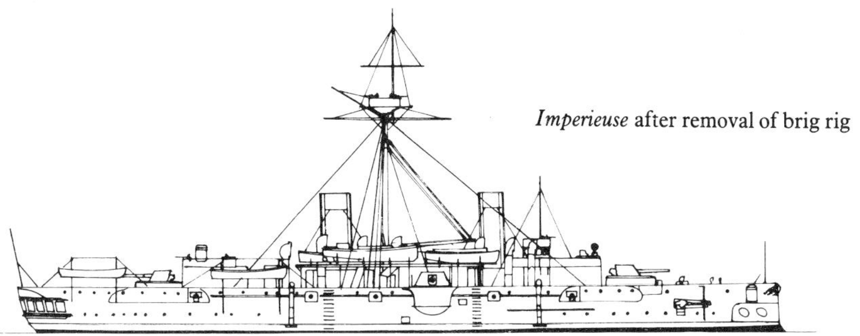
Imperieuse after removal of brig rig

The main armament disposition followed French practice with four 9.2in BL guns mounted in individual barbettes in a diamond arrangement which gave theoretical fire for 3 guns on any bearing but this was not possible in practice due to blast effects. To give the two wing guns arcs of fire clear of the rig and superstructure it was necessary to place the barbettes in sponsons and to give the hull an unusual tumblehome of semi-circular form. The 6in guns were fitted 5 on each side with the endmost parts embrasured for end-on fire. As a result of their overweight condition the number of 6in guns was restricted to 6 but on the reduction of rig this number was increased to 8 with the remaining pair as a 'war only' fitting. Also due to the overweight condition the torpedo ports were raised by 2ft in 1887. During the 1890s the 6in BL guns were replaced by 6in QFs.

As completed *Imperieuse* carried a 'peacetime only' brig rig of 20,575sq ft sail area for economical cruising on distant stations. On trials she proved a very poor and sluggish sailing ship and the rig was subsequently removed from both ships (saving 100t) and replaced by a single mast, with fighting top, amidships. Fortunately they did have a reasonable endurance, about 6500nm at 10kts with full bunkers, and were reasonably good steam vessels and steady gun platforms.

Imperieuse served as flagship on the China station 1889-94, and on the Pacific station 1896-99. *Warspite* also served as flagship of the Pacific station 1890-93 and 1899-1902 and was portguard ship at Queenstown 1893-96. They spent the majority of their remaining time in reserve with occasional breaks for manoeuvres, refits, etc. *Imperieuse* became a destroyer depot ship at Portland in 1905 and was renamed *Sapphire II*, but she reverted to her original name in 1909.

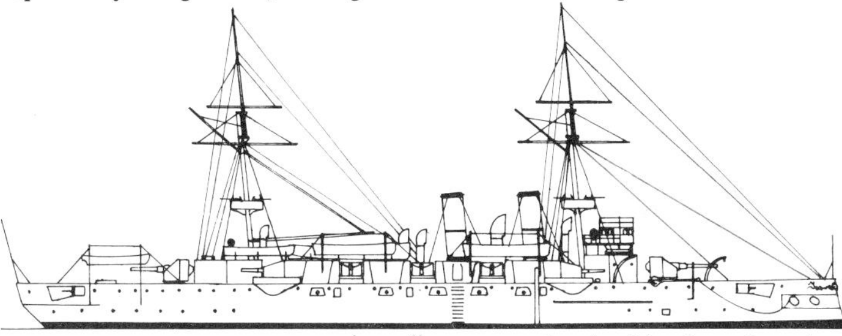
Australia as completed with short funnels

ORLANDO class *armoured cruisers*

Displacement: 5600t load
Dimensions: 300ft pp x 56ft x 22ft 6in (*91.44 pp x 17.07 x 6.86m*)
Machinery: 2-shaft, 3 cyl TE, 4 double-ended boilers, 5500ihp = 17kts natural draught, 8500ihp = 18kts forced draught. Coal 900t
Armour: Belt 10in, bulkheads 16in, CT 12in, decks 2in-3in
Armament: 2-9.2in BL, 10-6in BL, 6-6pdr QF, 10-3pdr QF, 6-18in TT, 4 broadside aw, 1 bow and 1 stern sub
Complement: 484

Name	Builder	Laid down	Launched	Comp	Fate
AURORA	Pembroke DYd	1.2.1886	28.10.87	July 1889	Sold 2.10.1907
AUSTRALIA	Fairfield, Govan	21.4.1885	25.11.86	Oct 1888	Sold 4.4.1905
GALATEA	Napier, Glasgow	21.4.1885	10.3.87	Mar 1889	Sold 4.4.1905
IMMORTALITÉ	Chatham DYd	18.1.1886	7.7.87	July 1889	Sold 1.1.1907
NARCISSUS	Earle, Hull	27.4.1885	15.12.86	July 1889	Sold 11.9.1906
ORLANDO	Palmer, Jarrow	23.4.1885	3.8.86	June 1888	Sold 11.7.1905
UNDAUNTED	Palmer, Jarrow	23.4.1885	25.11.86	July 1889	Sold 9.4.1907

Enlarged versions of the protected cruiser *Mersey* with side armour substituted for the protective deck amidships, these were smaller, cheaper and more successful than the earlier armoured cruisers but their narrow waterline belt was of little value and the weight could have been utilised to better effect in a full length protective deck. Designed as trade protection cruisers for worldwide service, they had an endurance of 8000nm at 10kts with a full coal capacity of 900t. Five were ordered in 1885 and two, *Immortalité* and *Aurora*, in 1886.

The ships were designed with a load displacement of 5040t, a steel hull, 2 cyl IC engines of 7500ihp, 440t nominal coal capacity and 9.2in 18t and 6in 4½t guns. During construction the design was altered to incorporate 3 cyl TE engines of 8500ihp and 9.2in 22t and 6in 5t guns, and the nominal coal capacity was increased to 750t. These together with several additions to equipment and hull weights raised the designed displacement to 5535t and increased the draught by 18in which placed the top of belt at load water line. However, apart from the reduced value of the protection this did not seriously affect the design and they proved reasonably successful in service, being popular ships which were both good sea boats and good steamers. All exceeded their designed power on trials, *Galatea* being the best at 9205ihp, and made between 18.8kts (*Australia*) and 19.4kts (*Undaunted*) on the measured mile, although the trials were run light.

The main armament was fitted in shielded mountings on the upper deck with the 9.2in guns on the centreline fore and aft and 5-6in on each side amidships. Most of the 6pdr and 3pdr QF guns were mounted in broadside positions on the main deck. The entry into service of many of the class was delayed by the late arrival of their armament and some commissioned for the 1887 Review with dummy wooden guns. During 1895/97 they were rearmed with 9.2in 30cal and 6in QF guns and their funnels were increased in height. There was a 10in thick belt of compound armour 200ft by 5ft 6in, closed at the ends by 16in wrought iron bulkheads. Above the belt the lower deck was constructed of 2in plating over the full length of the ship with 3in sloping edges beyond the side armour. Protection was enhanced by extensive sub-division and by the provision of wing coal bunkers both above and below the protective deck.

They commissioned for full service between 1888 and 1893, *Orlando* going to the Australia station, *Australia* and *Undaunted* to the Mediterranean and the remainder joining the Channel Fleet. In 1893 *Aurora, Australia* and *Galatea* joined the Coast Guard Squadron and in 1895 *Immortalité, Narcissus* and *Undaunted* went to China where they were joined by *Aurora* and *Orlando* in 1899. Between 1899 and 1902 they were reduced to subsidiary duties or were placed in reserve.

Australia as completed with short funnels; note the absence of shields to the 9.2in guns

GREAT BRITAIN

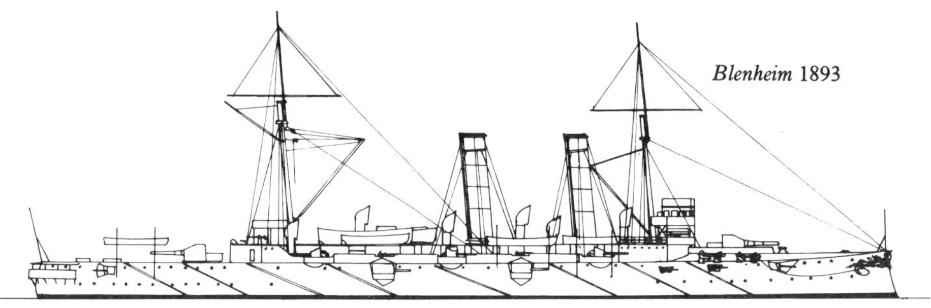
Blenheim 1893

BLAKE class *first class protected cruisers*

Displacement:	9150t load
Dimensions:	375ft pp, 399ft 9in oa x 65ft x 24ft (*114.3 pp, 121.84 oa x 19.81 x 7.32m*)
Machinery:	2-shaft, 3 cyl TE, 6 double-ended cyl boilers, 13,000ihp = 20kts natural draught, 20,000ihp = 22kts forced draught. Coal 1800t
Armour:	Deck 3in-6in, 9.2in gunshields 4½in, casemates 6in, CT 12in
Armament:	2-9.2in BL, 10-6in QF, 16-3pdr QF, 4-14in TT, 2 sub, 2 aw broadside
Complement:	570

Name	Builder	Laid down	Launched	Comp	Fate
BLAKE	Chatham DYd	July 1888	23.11.89	2.2.92	Sold 9.6.1922
BLENHEIM	Thames Iron Wks, Blackwall	Oct 1888	5.7.90	26.5.94	Sold 13.7.1926

Designed by Willian White, these two ships provided the pattern for British first class cruiser construction for the following decade. In general they followed the layout of the *Orlando*, having the same armament and a similar appearance, but they relied for protection on a full length armoured deck, hitherto employed only in smaller cruisers. They were also the largest cruisers built to date, mainly as a result of incorporating exceptionally powerful machinery and a large coal capacity. Thus White provided a true first class cruiser with high speed and endurance combined with adequate seakeeping, armament and protection to meet the Admiralty's requirements for a ship suitable for long range trade protection or work with the fleet. Unfortunately the machinery was not capable of meeting the design specification: neither ship achieved the designed speed while endurance was about 10,000nm at 10kts instead of the designed 15,000nm. However, both exceeded the designed power and proved capable of steaming at 19kts under natural draught for long periods. The best trial speeds at forced draught were 21.4kts (*Blake*) and 21.8kts (*Blenheim*), but forcing caused serious boiler deterioration and could not be employed generally. *Blake's* boilers proved the most troublesome and she was reboilered in 1899.

As designed the guns were disposed as in *Orlando* but the need to provide a wider distribution as defence against the appearance of medium calibre QF guns resulted in two of the 6in on each side being moved down to the main deck. These four guns were provided with armoured casemates, the first appearance of this feature which was to become typical of White's ships. The arched steel protective (lower) deck was 3in on the crown and 6in at the sides, the top being 18in above lwl and the outer edge 6ft 6in below. The engine cylinders projected above this deck and were protected by an 8in glacis around the engine hatch. Each ship had four engines, two for each shaft, arranged in two engine rooms each divided by a centreline bulkhead. At full power all engines were employed but for low speed the forward engines were disconnected and only the after pair used. Besides the main double-ended boilers they carried a single-ended auxiliary boiler.

Both ships completed in 1892 but *Blenheim* did not commission until 1894. *Blake* was flagship on the NAWI station 1892-95 and served in the Channel Fleet 1895-98. *Blenheim* served in the Channel Fleet 1894-98 and on the China station 1901-04. In 1907 both ships were partially disarmed and converted to depot ships.

Crescent 1908

EDGAR class *first class protected cruisers*

Displacement:	7350t load; *Gibraltar, St George, Crescent, Royal Arthur* 7700t load
Dimensions:	360ft pp, 387ft 6in oa x 60ft x 23ft 9in (*109.73 pp, 118.11 oa x 18.29 x 7.24m*)
Machinery:	2-shaft, 2 cyl TE, 4 double-ended cyl boilers, 12,000ihp = 20kts forced draught, 10,000ihp = 18kts natural draught. Coal 1250t
Armour:	Deck 5in-3in, casemates 6in, 9.2in gun shields 3in, ammunition hoists 7in-2in, CT 12in
Armament:	2-9.2in, 10-6in QF (*Crescent, Royal Arthur* 1-9.2in, 12-6in QF), 12-6pdr QF, 5-3pdr QF, 4-18in TT sub
Complement:	544

Name	Builder	Laid down	Launched	Comp	Fate
CRESCENT	Portsmouth DYd	13.10.1890	30.3.92	22.2.94	Sold 1921
EDGAR	Devonport DYd	3.6.1889	24.11.90	2.3.93	Sold 1921
ENDYMION	Earle, Hull	21.11.1889	22.7.91	26.5.94	Sold 1920
GIBRALTAR	Napier, Glasgow	2.12.1889	27.4.92	1.11.94	Sold 1923
GRAFTON	Thames Iron Wks, Blackwall	1.1.1890	30.1.92	18.10.94	Sold 1920
HAWKE	Chatham DYd	17.6.1889	11.3.91	16.5.93	Torpedoed by *U9*, 15.10.1914
ROYAL ARTHUR (ex-CENTAUR)	Portsmouth DYd	20.1.1890	26.2.91	2.3.93	Sold 1921
ST GEORGE	Earle, Hull	23.4.1890	23.6.92	25.10.94	Sold 1920
THESEUS	Thames Iron Wks, Blackwall	16.7.1890	8.9.92	14.1.96	Sold 1921

Provided under the Naval Defence Act of 1889, these ships were reduced editions of the *Blake* class with the same armour and armament arrangement. Displacement was reduced by 1800t by adopting a smaller machinery plant, for a designed speed of 20kts, and a reduced coal stowage giving an endurance of 10,000nm at 10kts. However, the machinery proved very reliable and most exceeded the designed speed on trial. As the *Blake* class had not achieved their designed speed and endurance, the *Edgars* proved equal to their predecessors in everything except the thickness of their armoured deck while representing a substantial saving in size and cost. In service they proved to be very good seaboats and exceptional steamers. The *Royal Arthur* averaged 18kts for 48 hours after serving 18 months as flagship of the Pacific station without entering a dockyard, and her sisters achieved similar performances at various times. Besides the main boiler plant they carried a single-ended cyl boiler for auxiliary use.

The *Gibraltar, Crescent, Royal Arthur* and *St George* were sheathed in wood and copper for tropical service which added 350t to their displacements, reduced speed by ½kt and lowered their endurance. The *Crescent* and *Royal Arthur* were fitted with a forecastle, to increase freeboard forward and improve seaworthiness, and carried two 6in QF guns forward in place of the single 9.2in.

Their early years were spent mainly on foreign stations and ships of the class served in the Mediterranean and Pacific and on the Cape, China and Australia stations, whilst the *Crescent* was flagship of the NAWI station 1895-97 and 1899-1902. Although obsolete by 1914 they saw extensive service in the First World War.

Blake as completed

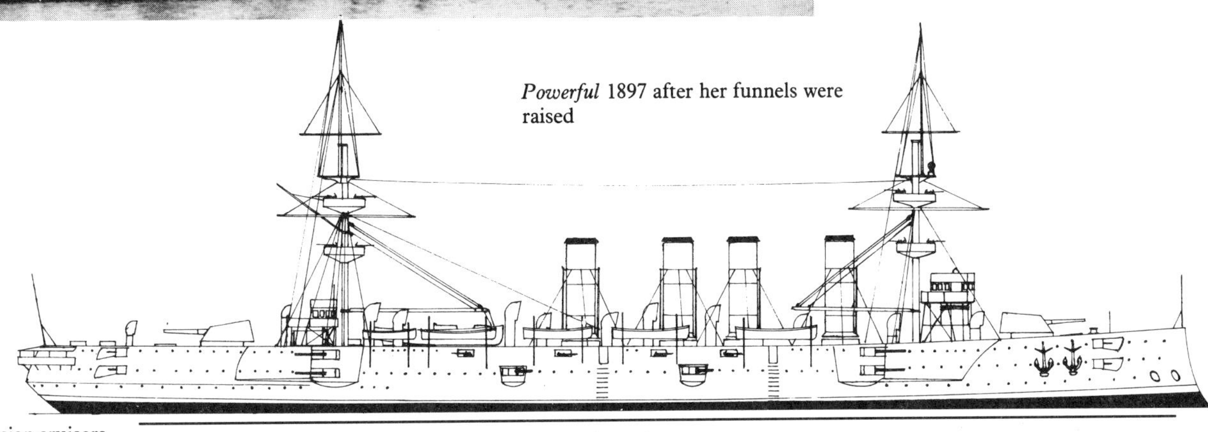

Powerful 1897 after her funnels were raised

POWERFUL class *first class protected cruisers*

Displacement: 14,200t load
Dimensions: 500ft pp, 538ft oa x 71ft x 27ft (*152.4 pp, 163.98 oa x 21.64 x 7.32m*)
Machinery: 2-shaft, 4 cyl TE, 48 Belleville boilers, 25,000ihp = 22kts. Coal 3000t
Armour: Deck 6in-2in, barbettes 6in, turrets 6in, ammunition hoists 2in, casemates 6in-2in, CT 12in
Armament: 2-9.2in, 12-6in QF, 16-12pdr QF, 12-3pdr QF, 4-18in TT sub
Complement: 894

Name	Builder	Laid down	Launched	Comp	Fate
POWERFUL	Vickers, Barrow	1894	24.7.95	8.6.97	Sold 1929
TERRIBLE	Thompson, Clydebank	1894	27.5.95	24.3.98	Sold 1932

Built in answer to the Russian cruisers *Rurik* and *Rossiya,* these vessels were the largest cruisers and longest warships in existence at the time of their completion. They were expensive to build, costing almost twice as much per ship as the *Edgar* class, and proved to be white elephants as they required a very large crew, were costly to operate and did not fulfil any true requirement of the Navy. Most of the increased displacement over earlier ships was necessary to provide for the large machinery plant and coal capacity required for a speed of 22kts and an endurance of 7000nm at 14kts. They were the first large British ships to employ watertube boilers, a bold step which later caused several problems mainly due to inexperience in the operation and construction of the Belleville boiler. Both completed for trials in 1896 but considerable trouble was experienced with the engines and it was some time before they commissioned. On trials *Powerful* achieved 21.8kts with 25,886ihp and *Terrible* 22.4kts with 25,572ihp and, although they continued to have engine problems throughout their careers, they proved to be capable of maintaining high sea speeds for long periods. They were the first four-funnelled cruisers to be built for the Royal Navy, and after their initial trials the funnels were raised to improve the draught to the boilers.

They carried one more deck than earlier first class cruisers although this full-length 'boat deck' had a large well amidships around the funnel uptakes and engine room hatches. The crown of the protective deck was 3ft 6in above and its outer edge 6ft 6in below the lwl, and it was 6in thick over the machinery, thinning to $2\frac{1}{2}$in over a narrow section of the crown and 4in over the magazines and reducing to 2in forward and 3in aft. For the first time in a cruiser all the main guns were given full protection, the 9.2in weapons being mounted in armoured turrets, on the forecastle and quarterdeck, and the 6in guns in casemates. The two foremost and aftermost 6in guns on each side had two-storey casemates, the first time this arrangement was used in a British ship, while the remaining four guns were mounted amidships in single casemates on the main deck. The latter were converted to two-storey configuration 1902/04, when four more 6in guns were added on the upper deck. The 9.2in turrets had shallow armoured barbettes and the 9.2in ammunition hoists for these and the 6in casemates were protected by 2in armoured tubes down to the protective deck.

Their great length gave these cruisers a very large turning circle, but they were very good seaboats mainly because of their high freeboard. Both served their early commissions on the China stations and became famous in 1899 when they landed naval brigades at the Cape to assist in the relief of Ladysmith during the Boer War. After their 1902/04 refits they spent most of their time in reserve. *Terrible* was employed as a troop ship in 1915 and then served as an accommodation ship until 1920 when she became TS *Fisgard III*. *Powerful* was employed as a TS at Devonport from 1915 until the late 1920s and was renamed *Impregnable II* in 1919.

Terrible as completed with short funnels

GREAT BRITAIN

These ships were reduced editions of the *Powerful* class, with a lower speed and a thinner protective deck which saved 3000t displacement and about £100,000 per ship in cost. *Andromeda, Diadem, Europa* and *Niobe* were provided under the 1895/96 Estimates and the others under the 1896/97 Estimates. The second group were provided with machinery of higher power for a ½kt increase in speed and could be distinguished from the earlier group by the addition of a low wall around the quarterdeck 6in guns and a bulwark around the after superstructure. All exceeded their designed power and averaged 20.5kts (1st group) and 21kts (2nd group) on full power trials. The completion of *Spartiate* was delayed by the late arrival of her machinery from the contractors. In general they were good steamers but *Niobe* suffered from several machinery breakdowns in her early years and boiler problems arose in some ships after a couple of years' service.

The guns were disposed as in the *Powerful* except that four single 6in on shielded mountings were substituted for the 9.2in turrets on the forecastle and quarterdeck. They were heavily criticised for their lack of heavy guns and the fact that the guns with the best command were only protected by shields. In other respects they were of similar layout to the *Powerful* class except that the forecastle deck terminated at the after superstructure.

The class served their early careers mainly in home waters with the exception of *Amphitrite* (China 1902-05) *Andromeda* (Mediterranean 1899-1902, China 1904-07) *Argonaut* (China 1900-04) and *Ariadne* (NAWI 1902-05). *Niobe* was transferred to the RCN in 1910.

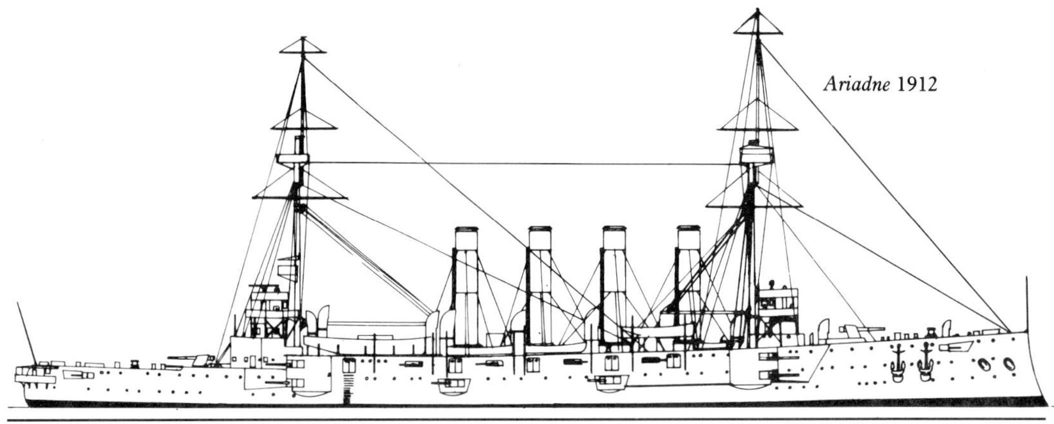
Ariadne 1912

DIADEM class *first class protected cruisers*

Displacement: 11,000t load
Dimensions: 435ft pp, 462ft 6in oa x 69ft x 25ft 6in *(132.59 pp, 140.97 oa x 21.03 x 7.77m)*
Machinery: 2-shaft, 4 cyl TE, 30 Belleville boilers, 16,500ihp = 20.25kts (*Ariadne, Spartiate, Amphitrite* and *Argonaut* 18,000ihp = 20.75kts). Coal 1900t
Armour: Deck 4in-2½in, casemates 4½in-2in, 6in gun shields 4½in-2in, ammunition hoists 2in, CT 12in
Armament: 16-6in QF, 14-12pdr QF, 3-3pdr QF, 3-18in TT, 1 aw stern, 2 sub broadside
Complement: 677

Name	Builder	Laid down	Launched	Comp	Fate
AMPHITRITE	Vickers, Barrow	8.12.1896	5.1.98	17.9.1901	Sold 1920
ANDROMEDA	Pembroke DYd	2.12.1895	30.4.97	5.9.99	Sold 1956
ARGONAUT	Fairfield, Govan	23.11.1896	24.1.98	19.4.1900	Sold 1920
ARIADNE	Thompson, Clydebank	29.10.1896	22.4.98	5.6.1902	Torpedoed by *UC65* 26.7.17
DIADEM	Fairfield, Govan	23.1.1896	21.10.96	19.7.98	Sold 1921
EUROPA	Thompson, Clydebank	10.1.1896	20.3.97	23.11.99	Sold 1920, foundered Jan 1921, raised and BU
NIOBE	Vickers, Barrow	16.12.1895	20.2.97	6.12.98	BU 1922
SPARTIATE	Pembroke DYd	10.5.1897	27.10.98	17.3.1903	Sold 1932

Provided under the 1897/98 Programme, these vessels were armoured cruiser versions of the *Diadems* with more powerful machinery and the same armament as the *Powerful* class. The adoption of side armour was made possible by the development of hard faced steel armour which allowed for a comparatively large area of the side to be protected without an excessive increase in displacement. The main 6in Krupp steel belt was 231ft long by 11ft 6in deep extending from the main deck to 5ft below the waterline. It was closed at the ends by 5in bulkheads and extended to the bow by 2in armour. The protective deck was correspondingly reduced in thickness to 1½in but increased to 2½in abaft the belt and to 3in over the steering gear, the main deck from the after bulkhead to the stem being 1in thick. Armoured tubes were provided to protect the ammunition hoists to the 9.2in guns but these were not fitted for the casemate guns as the hoists were behind the side armour. The 9.2in turrets were hydraulically powered and the guns could be loaded at any angle of training or elevation; the hoists were electrically powered.

The class was 1000t larger than the *Diadems* and had a fuller hull form which improved stability, but the ships had finer lines forward which increased their pitching motion. On trials all exceeded the designed speed except *Cressy* (20.7kts), the best being

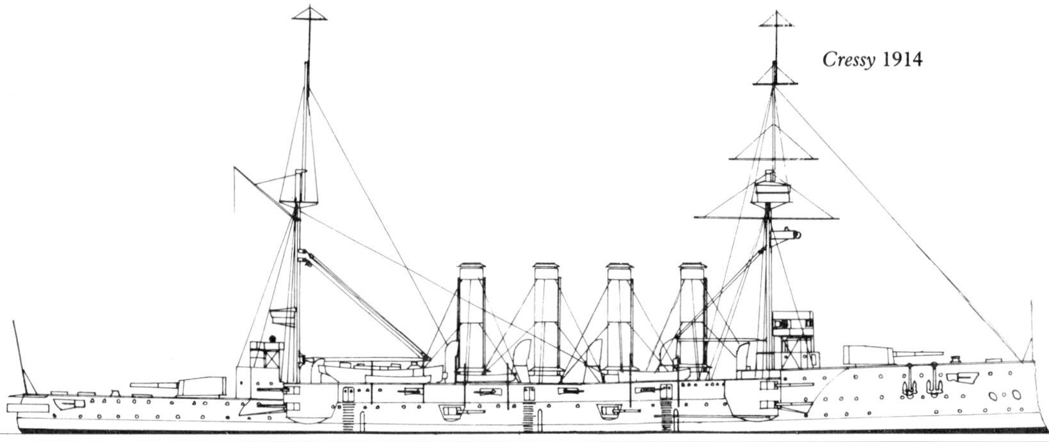
Cressy 1914

CRESSY class *first class armoured cruisers*

Displacement: 12,000t load
Dimensions: 440ft pp, 472ft oa x 69ft 6in x 26ft *(134.11 pp, 143.87 oa x 21.18 x 7.92m)*
Machinery: 2-shaft, 4 cyl TE, 30 Belleville boilers, 21,000ihp = 21kts. Coal 1600t
Armour: Belt 6in-2in, bulkheads 5in, decks 3in-1in, casemates 5in, turrets 6in, barbettes 6in, ammunition tubes 3in, CT 12in
Armament: 2-9.2in, 12-6in QF, 12-12pdr QF, 3-3pdr QF, 2-18in TT sub
Complement: 760

Name	Builder	Laid down	Launched	Comp	Fate
ABOUKIR	Fairfield, Govan	9.11.1898	16.5.1900	3.4.02	Torpedoed by *U9*, 22.9.14
BACCHANTE	J Brown, Clydebank	15.2.1899	21.2.1901	25.11.02	Sold 1920
CRESSY	Fairfield, Govan	12.10.1898	4.12.99	28.5.1901	Torpedoed by *U9*, 22.9.14
EURYALUS	Vickers, Barrow	18.7.1899	20.5.1901	5.1.04	Sold 1920
HOGUE	Vickers, Barrow	14.7.1898	13.8.1900	19.11.02	Torpedoed by *U9*, 11.9.14
SUTLEJ	J Brown, Clydebank	15.8.1898	18.11.99	6.5.1902	Sold 1921

Hogue which made 22.06kts with 21,432ihp. The completion of *Euryalus* was delayed by a series of accidents and she was two years late in entering service. On completion *Hogue* and *Sutlej* joined the Channel Fleet and *Aboukir* and *Bacchante* the Mediterranean Fleet, *Cressy* went to the China station and *Euryalus* to Australia. During 1906-07 the latter four joined the NAWI station and during 1908-12 all returned to home waters where they remained for the rest of their peacetime careers.

Euryalus in about 1911

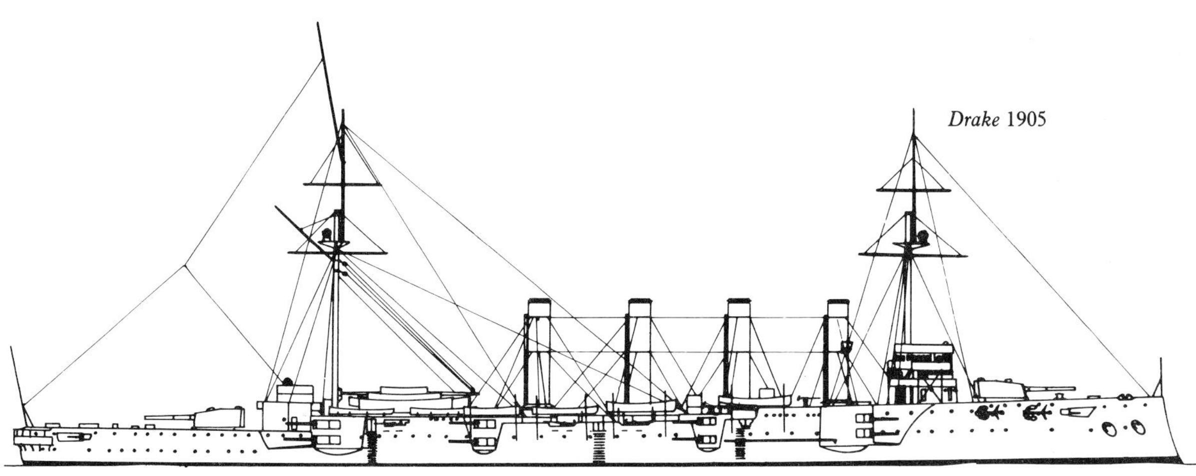

Drake 1905

DRAKE class *first class armoured cruisers*

Displacement:	14,150t load
Dimensions:	500ft pp, 533ft 6in oa x 71ft 4in x 26ft *(152.4 pp, 162.61 oa x 21.74 x 7.92m)*
Machinery:	2-shaft, 4 cyl TE, 43 Belleville boilers, 30,000ihp = 23kts. Coal 2500t
Armour:	Belt 6in-2in, decks 2½in-1in, bulkhead 5in, turrets 6in, barbettes 6in, casemates 5in-2in, ammunition tubes 3in, CT 12in
Armament:	2-9.2in, 16-6in QF, 14-12pdr QF, 3-3pdr QF, 2-18in TT sub
Complement:	900

Name	Builder	Laid down	Launched	Comp	Fate
DRAKE	Pembroke DYd	24.4.1899	5.3.1901	13.1.03	Torpedoed by *U79*, 2.10.17
GOOD HOPE (ex-AFRICA)	Fairfield, Govan	11.9.1899	21.2.1901	8.11.02	Sunk 1.11.14
KING ALFRED	Vickers, Barrow	11.8.1899	28.10.1901	22.12.03	Sold 1920
LEVIATHAN	J Brown, Clydebank	30.11.1899	3.7.1901	16.6.03	Sold 1920

Provided under the 1898/99 Programme, these ships were enlarged versions of the *Cressy* class and were armoured cruiser equivalents of the *Powerful* class. Compared with the *Cressys* displacement was increased by 3000t to provide more powerful machinery (giving a 2kt increase in designed speed), four more 6in guns and some minor improvements in protection. The side armour was 6in for a length of 257ft amidships and then reduced through 4in to 2in at the bow, the thicker armour here being adopted in place of the forward armour bulkhead of the *Cressy* class. The protective deck was 2½in thick between the stern and after bulkhead and 1in thick from the after bulkhead to the stem. The remaining protection was the same as that in the *Cressy* class. The four additional guns were accommodated by providing double-storey casemates amidships as well as at the ends. To reduce the amount of vulnerable target to a minimum, most of the midship structure, which formed the boat deck in earlier vessels, was omitted, cowl ventilators were replaced by windsails and all other fittings and structures above the upper deck were kept to a minimum.

At the time of completion they were among the fastest ships in the world and proved to be good seaboats and exceptional steamers. On trials they exceeded their designed power by over 1000ihp but only *Drake* exceeded the designed speed by a substantial margin in making 24.11kts. They often exceeded their trial performance in service and for many years were capable both of running for long periods at high power and of achieving high speeds.

During their peacetime service they were employed extensively as cruiser squadron flagships which perhaps helped to give some justification to their great size. The *King Alfred* was flagship of the CinC China station from 1906 to 1910 and *Leviathan* served on the China station during 1903-04 and in the Mediterranean during 1905-06. They spent the remaining periods up to 1914 in home waters. The *Drake* and *Good Hope* served almost exclusively in home waters from completion until 1914.

Good Hope in her early years with original rig

The *Monmouth* class was built in answer to a general increase in armoured cruiser construction in foreign navies, *Kent* and *Essex* being provided under a supplementary estimate to the 1898/99 Programme, *Bedford* and *Monmouth* under the 1899/1900 Programme and the remainder under the 1900/01 Programme. The ships represented an attempt to provide first class cruisers of equal speed to the *Drake* class but of smaller size so that they would be cheaper to build and operate, more economic on manpower and could be built in larger numbers. This object was achieved by substantial reductions in both armour and armament, enabling the displacement to be bought down to 9800t. However they were heavily criticised for these reductions in fighting power and were regarded by many as second rate ships which could not adequately fulfil the functions for which they had been designed.

The arrangement of armour was the same as that in *Cressy* but of generally reduced thickness. The main 4in belt was 242ft long by 11ft 6in deep amidships and was continued to the stem by 2in thick side armour. The protective deck was 2½in thick abaft the armoured bulkhead and ¾in for the length of the belt, while the main deck was 1¼in for the length of the belt. Four of the 6in guns were mounted in twin turrets on the forecastle and quarterdeck while the remainder were mounted in two-storey casemates abreast the fore- and mainmasts and in single casemates on each side amidships. The turrets were electrically operated and promised to be one of the best features of the design but the electrical gear proved to be unreliable, the gunhouses too cramped for efficient operation and the guns difficult to align due to their being fitted in a single cradle.

All exceeded the designed power on trials, but three, *Essex*, *Monmouth* and *Kent* were accepted at slightly less than the design speed. *Lancaster* and *Suffolk*, however, made 24 and 24.7kts respectively at full power, while the remainder averaged 23.6kts. In general they were good steamers and seaboats but they had very fine lines fore and aft which, combined with the weight of the turrets, tended to cause heavy pitching in rough weather.

Most served their early years in home waters except *Lancaster* and *Monmouth* which went to the Mediterranean. From 1906 onwards the majority of the class were dispersed on distant foreign stations.

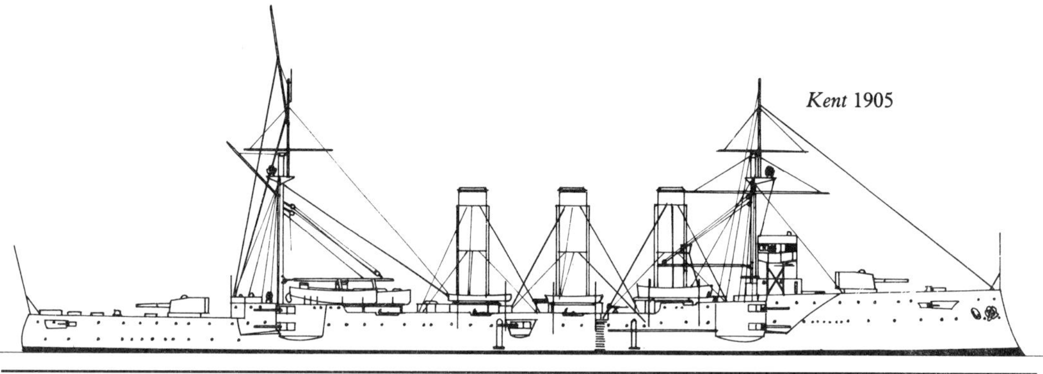

Kent 1905

MONMOUTH class *first class armoured cruisers*

Displacement: 9800t
Dimensions: 440ft pp, 463ft 6in oa x 66ft x 25ft (*134.11 pp, 141.27 oa x 20.12 x 7.62m*)
Machinery: 2-shaft, 4 cyl TE, 31 Belleville boilers (*Berwick* and *Suffolk* Niclausse boilers, *Cornwall* Babcock boilers), 22,000ihp = 23kts. Coal 1600t
Armour: Belt 4in-2in, bulkhead 5in, barbettes 5in, turrets 5in, casemates 4in-2in, ammunition hoists 2in, decks ¾in-2in, CT 10in
Armament: 14-6in QF (2x2, 10x1) 10-12pdr QF, 3-3pdr QF, 2-18in TT sub
Complement: 678

Name	Builder	Laid down	Launched	Comp	Fate
BEDFORD	Fairfield, Govan	19.2.1900	31.8.01	11.11.03	Wrecked 21.1.10
BERWICK	Beardmore, Dalmuir	19.4.1901	20.9.02	9.12.03	Sold 1920
CORNWALL	Pembroke DYd	11.3.1901	29.10.02	1.12.04	Sold 1920
CUMBERLAND	London & Glasgow, Glasgow	19.2.1901	16.12.02	1.12.04	Sold 1921
DONEGAL	Fairfield, Govan	14.2.1901	4.9.02	5.11.03	Sold 1920
ESSEX	Pembroke DYd	1.1.1900	29.8.01	22.3.04	Sold 1921
KENT	Portsmouth DYd	12.2.1900	6.3.01	1.10.03	Sold 1920
LANCASTER	Armstrong, Elswick	4.3.1901	22.3.02	5.4.04	Sold 1920
MONMOUTH	London & Glasgow, Glasgow	29.8.1899	13.11.01	2.12.03	Sunk 1.11.14
SUFFOLK	Portsmouth DYd	25.3.1901	15.1.03	21.5.04	Sold 1920

Cumberland as built

Antrim as completed without roofs to her fighting tops

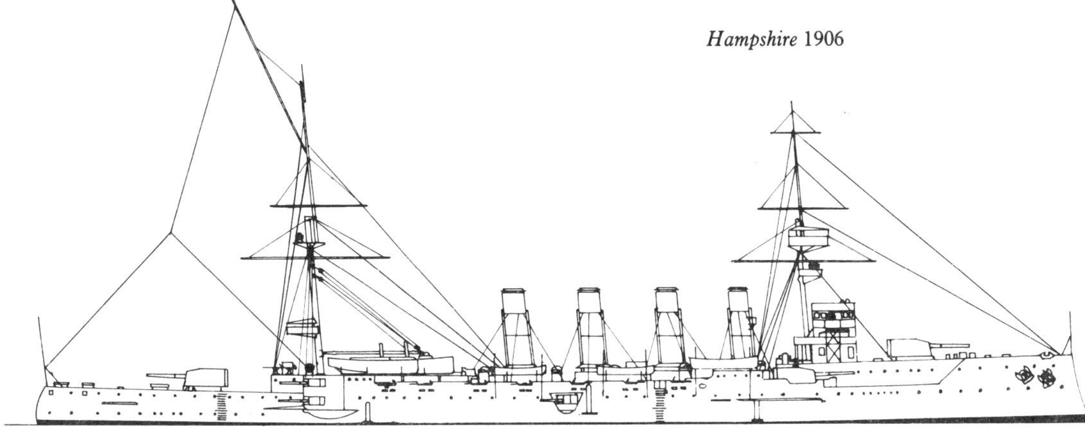

Hampshire 1906

Provided under the 1901/02 Programme, these ships were an attempt to improve on the *Monmouth* design without an excessive increase in size. Both armour and armament were improved but the increase in displacement was restricted to 1000t by retaining the machinery power of the *Monmouth* and accepting a ¾kt loss in speed. As designed they carried the same armament as the previous class except that single 7.5in turrets were mounted in place of the twin 6in, but while under construction two more 7.5in turrets, mounted abreast the foremast on the upper deck, were substituted for the four forward 6in and their double-storey casemates. The main belt was increased to 6in thickness and 246ft in length but was reduced in height by 1ft. The casemate armour was also increased to 6in but otherwise protection was similar to that in *Monmouth*, the arrangement and thickness of the decks and forward belt being identical.

The class was contemporary with the *King Edward VII* class battleships and like them carried mixed boiler arrangements in order to give the many watertube boiler designs then available a practical test. The *Antrim* and *Hampshire* carried 17 Yarrow boilers, *Argyll* 16 Babcock, *Roxburgh* 17 Durr, *Devonshire* 15 and *Carnarvon* 17 Niclausse. These boilers were distributed between the three forward boiler rooms while the after boiler room in all six vessels was fitted with 6 cylindrical boilers. On trials all exceeded their designed power and all except *Argyll* exceeded 23 kts but in the long term they did not prove to be good steamers.

All joined the Channel Fleet on completion except the *Carnarvon* which served in the Mediterranean from 1905 to 1907. *Hampshire* went to the Mediterranean in 1911 and then to the China station, 1912-14, while the remainder operated in home waters until 1914.

DEVONSHIRE class *first class armoured cruisers*

Displacement: 10,850t load
Dimensions: 450ft pp, 473ft 6in oa x 68ft 6in x 24ft (*137.16 pp, 144.32 oa x 20.88 x 7.32m*)
Machinery: 2-shaft, 4 cyl TE, 15-17 water tube and 6 cyl boilers (see notes), 21,000ihp = 22kts. Coal 1950t
Armour: Belt 6in-2in, bulkhead 5in, turrets 5in, barbettes 6in, ammunition tubes 3in, casemates 6in-2in, decks ¾-2in, CT 12in
Armament: 4-7.5in, 6-6in QF, 2-12pdr QF, 18-3pdr QF, 2-18in TT sub
Complement: 655

Name	Builder	Laid down	Launched	Comp	Fate
ANTRIM	J Brown, Clydebank	27.8.1902	8.10.03	23.6.05	Sold 1922
ARGYLL	Scott, Greenock	1.9.1902	3.3.04	Dec 1905	Wrecked 28.10.15
CARNARVON	Beardmore, Dalmuir	1.10.1902	7.10.03	29.5.05	Sold 1921
DEVONSHIRE	Chatham DYd	25.3.1902	30.4.04	24.8.05	Sold 1921
HAMPSHIRE	Armstrong, Elswick	1.9.1902	24.9.03	15.7.05	Mined 5.6.16
ROXBURGH	London & Glasgow, Glasgow	13.6.1902	19.1.04	5.9.05	Sold 1921

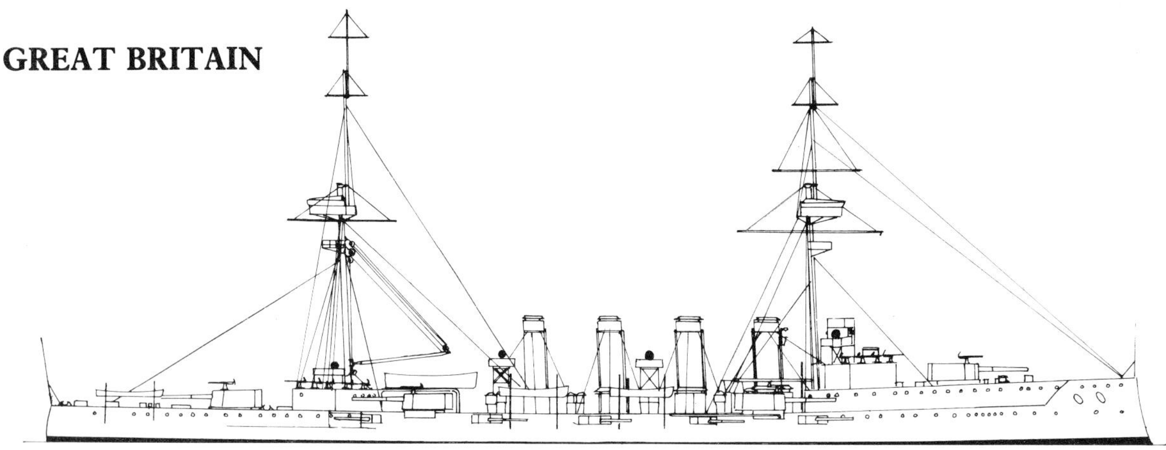

Black Prince 1914

DUKE OF EDINBURGH class *first class armoured cruisers*

Displacement: 13,550t load
Dimensions: 480ft pp, 505ft 6in oa x 73ft 6in x 26ft (*146.3 pp, 154.08 oa x 22.4 x 7.92m*)
Machinery: 2-shaft, 4 cyl TE, 20 Babcock + 6 cyl boilers, 23,000ihp = 23kts. Coal 2150t
Armour: Belt 6in-3in, bulkheads 2in, 6in battery 6in, barbettes 6in, turrets 7½-4½in, ammunition tubes 3in, decks ¾in-1½in, CT 10in
Armament: 6-9.2in, 10-6in QF, 22-3pdr QF, 3-18in TT sub
Complement: 790

Name	Builder	Laid down	Launched	Comp	Fate
BLACK PRINCE	Thames Iron Wks, Blackwall	3.6.1903	8.11.04	17.3.06	Sunk 31.5.16
DUKE OF EDINBURGH	Pembroke DYd	11.2.1903	14.6.04	20.1.06	Sold 1920

Provided under the 1902/03 Programme, these ships were the first RN vessels to be designed under the direction of Phillip Watts and showed a substantial change in style over earlier types. In addition, attempts to restrict the size of first class cruisers was finally abandoned and displacement increased to allow for improvements in armament, protection and machinery power. The 9.2.in gun was re-adopted and fitted in single turrets arranged similarly to those in the *Devonshire* class except that wing positions were provided abreast the mainmast as well as the foremast. As in the *King Edward VII* class battleships the 6in gun casemate protection of earlier ships was abandoned in favour of a central armoured battery on the main deck with ports for five guns on each side; the aftermost ports were embrasured, to allow astern fire, but not those forward, presumably to avoid spray problems. Unfortunately the 6in guns were so close to the waterline that they were unworkable in anything but very calm weather. The reduction of shell-bursting structures reached its final stage in these ships which had clear upper decks without the traditional high bulwarks, but this, combined with a low freeboard, resulted in their being wet amidships although the high forecastle allowed them to maintain a high speed in a seaway.

They had a full length waterline belt which was 6in thick over 260ft amidships reducing to 4in forward and 6in aft. The central battery had 6in sides and bulkheads and effectively increased the height of the side armour amidships to the level of the upper deck. The engine room hatch between the lower and main decks was protected by 2in plating and 2in screens were provided between the 6in guns in the battery. The wing barbettes reduced to 3in behind the battery armour and the turrets had 7½in faces, 5½in sides and 4½in backs. Deck protection was very weak with a ¾in lower deck increasing to 1½in over the steering gear, a 1in main deck reducing to ¾in under the central battery, and a 1in upper deck over the battery.

The 3pdr guns were virtually useless as anti-torpedo weapons and their adoption in this and the following class is inexplicable. Eight were mounted on the forward and after superstructures and one on each 9.2in turret. Despite the apparent improvements over earlier classes the ineffective secondary battery reduced the value of these ships considerably and they did not enjoy a high reputation.

Duke of Edinburgh shortly after completion

WARRIOR class *first class armoured cruisers*

Displacement: 13,550t load
Dimensions: 480ft pp, 505ft 4in oa x 73ft 6in x 25ft (*146.3 pp, 154.03 oa x 22.4 x 7.62m*)
Machinery: 2-shaft, 4 cyl TE, 19 Yarrow and 6 cyl boilers, 23,000ihp = 23kts. Coal 2050t
Armour: Belt 6in-3in, bulkheads 6in-2in, upper belt 6in, barbettes 6in, turrets 7½in-4½in, ammunition tubes 3in, decks ¾in-1½in, CT 10in
Armament: 6-9.2in, 4-7.5in, 26-3pdr QF, 3-18in TT sub
Complement: 712

Name	Builder	Laid down	Launched	Comp	Fate
ACHILLES	Armstrong, Elswick	22.2.1904	17.6.05	22.4.07	Sold 1921
COCHRANE	Fairfield, Govan	24.3.1904	20.5.05	18.2.07	Wrecked 1918
NATAL	Vickers, Barrow	6.1.1904	30.9.05	5.3.07	Sunk by internal explosion 31.12.15
WARRIOR	Pembroke DYd	5.11.1903	25.11.05	12.12.06	Sunk 1.6.16

Constructed under the 1903/04 Programme, these vessels were modified versions of the *Duke of Edinburgh* class in which the broadside 6in guns were omitted in favour of four 7.5in guns mounted in single turrets in the upper deck amidships. The 6in battery armour was retained to protect the turret bases and the 7.5in turrets were provided with the same protection as the 9.2in turrets. The remaining armour was identical to that in the *Duke of Edinburgh* except that the upper deck amidships was reduced to ¾in in thickness. The additional topweight involved in these modifications resulted in a lowering of the level of stability, making them very steady ships, good gun platforms and excellent seaboats. These features, combined with the ability to fight all their guns in almost any weather, gained them, in contrast to their half-sisters, a very high reputation.

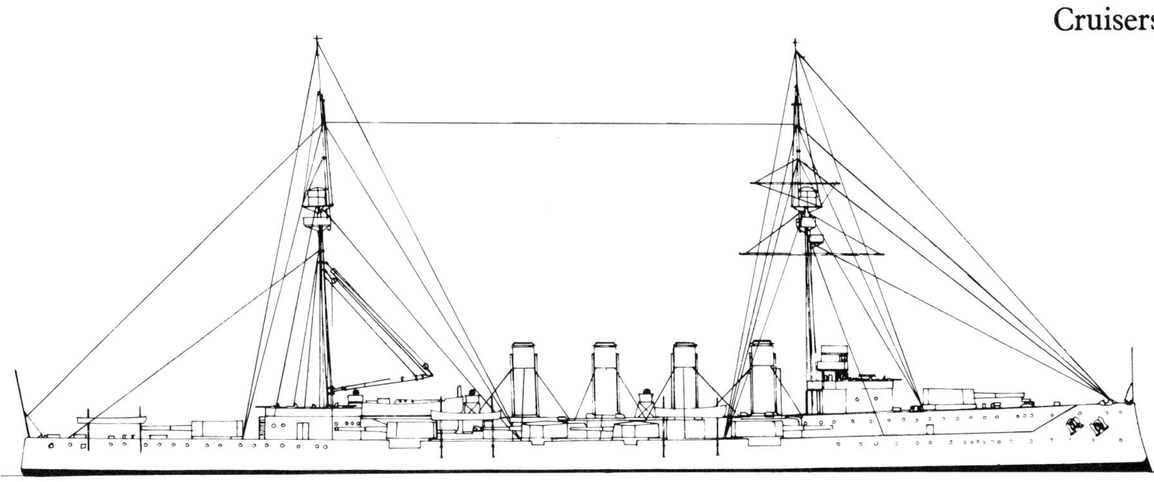

Cochrane 1908

Achilles as completed

Minotaur 1909

MINOTAUR class *first class armoured cruisers*

Displacement: 14,600t load
Dimensions: 490ft pp, 519ft oa x 74ft 6in x 26ft (*149.35 pp, 158.19 oa x 22.71 x 7.92m*)
Machinery: 2-shaft, 4 cyl TE, 24 Yarrow (*Minotaur* Babcock) boilers, 27,000ihp = 23kts. Coal 2060t
Armour: Belt 6in-3in, barbettes 7in-3in, ammunition tubes 3in-2in, turrets 8in-4½in, decks ¾in-1½in, CT 10in
Armament: 4-9.2in (2x2), 10-7.5in, 16-12pdr QF, 5-18in TT sub
Complement: 755

Name	Builder	Laid down	Launched	Comp	Fate
DEFENCE	Pembroke DYd	22.2.1905	24.4.07	9.2.09	Sunk 31.5.16
MINOTAUR	Devonport DYd	2.1.1905	6.6.06	1.4.08	Sold 1920
SHANNON	Chatham DYd	2.1.1905	20.9.06	10.3.08	Sold 1922

These ships, provided under the 1904/05 Programme, were the last and largest British armoured cruisers of the conventional type. They were enlarged *Warriors* with displacement increased by 1000t to allow for a heavier armament, which involved some reductions in the level of protection. The result was outwardly impressive but they were overgunned and under protected and the extra weight might well have been employed to better effect in additional deck protection. The 9.2in guns were carried in twin turrets fore and aft and the 7.5in guns in ten single turrets equally disposed on each side of the upper deck. The anti-torpedo boat armament was considerably improved by the fitting of 12pdr guns, which were disposed on the forward and after superstructures and turret roofs. The main belt was 6in for a length of 272ft amidships reducing to 4in forward and 3in aft. No side armour was provided between the main and upper decks, and the ammunition hoists for the 7.5in turrets were provided with 7in armour tubes between these decks reducing to 2in behind the side armour between the main and lower decks. The 7.5in barbettes were 7in on the outboard side and 3in inboard while the turrets had 8in faces, 6in sides and 4½in rears. The 9.2in turrets had 8in faces and 7in sides and rears, while the barbettes were a uniform 7in with 3in floors. The forward 9.2in ammunition hoist was protected by a 7in tube from the barbette to the main deck and then reduced to 2in, while aft the tube was 4in only, being entirely behind the side armour. Deck protection was very weak with a ¾in protective deck increasing to 1½in over the steering gear and a main deck of ¾in amidships and 1in fore and aft. Besides the forward 10in CT they were fitted with an after CT protected by 3in armour, both positions having a 3in communication tube down to the protective deck.

The *Shannon* had a modified hull form and was 1ft wider than her sisters with slightly less draught, which resulted in some loss of speed, and, despite achieving the highest power on trial, she recorded the lowest speed, making 22.5kts compared with 22.9kts (*Defence*) and 23kts (*Minotaur*).

Shannon as built with short funnels

CRUISERS 2nd class

Britain's first warships to be constructed of steel, these two vessels were designed for high speed at the expense of protection and armament. Although classified as despatch vessels they originated the development of later cruiser designs and in the late 1880s they were reclassified as 2nd class cruisers. *Iris* was the first to run trials and considerably exceeded the designed power at 7086ihp although speed was only 16.6kts. However, after fitting new propellers, she achieved a remarkable 17.89kts with 7330ihp while *Mercury*, benefiting from the experience gained with her sister, made 18.57kts with 7735ihp, making her the fastest warship in existence at the time of her completion. Each ship had two engine rooms with the after engine driving the port shaft and the forward engine the starboard shaft. The boilers were equally disposed in two boiler rooms and each could be operated independently in the event of damage to the other. As no armour was fitted the ships were extensively subdivided with a double bottom over the full length of the machinery compartments (150ft), while some protection was afforded by the coal bunkers which were arranged in wing compartments abreast the machinery extending from the main deck to the hold. The ships completed with a light barque rig but after a few years in commission the yards were removed. The full coal stowage of 780ft provided an endurance of 6000nm at 10kts or about 2000nm at full speed; nominal coal stowage was 500t.

The original armament consisted of 10-64pdr of which 4 were mounted on each side of the main deck and one each on the forecastle and poop. Shortly after completion *Iris* had her main deck guns replaced by 4-6in and 4-5in BLRs and both ships were rearmed during 1886/87 with 13-5in BLRs, ten on the main deck, two on the forecastle and one on the poop.

The two were very similar in appearance except that *Iris* had a clipper bow while *Mercury* had a straight stem. *Mercury* became a submarine depot ship in 1905 and served as a hulk at Chatham 1914-18.

IRIS class *despatch vessels*

Displacement: 3730t load
Dimensions: 300ft pp, 333ft (*Mercury* 315ft) oa x 46ft x 22ft (*91.44 pp, 10.15 (Mercury 96.01) oa x 14.02 x 6.71m*)
Machinery: 2-shaft, Maudslay 2 cyl HDAC, 8 oval and 4 cyl boilers, 6000ihp = 17kts. Coal 780t
Armament: 13-5in BLR, 4-3pdr QF, 4 TC
Complement: 275

Name	Builder	Laid down	Launched	Comp	Fate
IRIS	Pembroke DYd	10.11.1875	12.4.77	April 1879	Sold 1905
MERCURY	Pembroke DYd	16.3.1876	17.4.78	Sept 1879	Sold 1919

Iris as built; note clipper bow

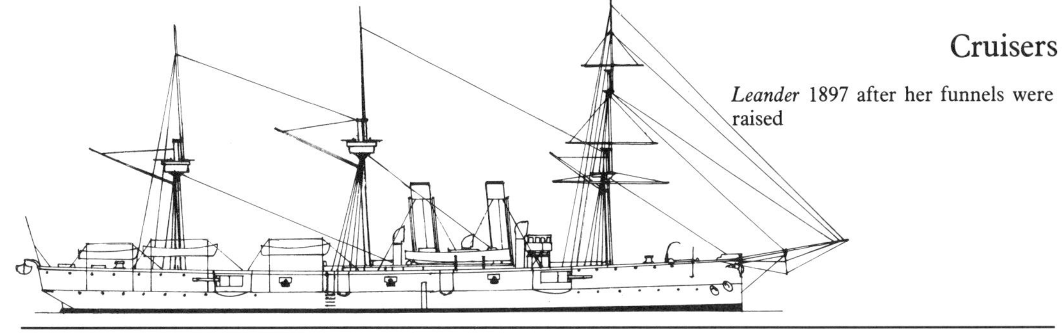
Leander 1897 after her funnels were raised

Repeats of *Mercury* but modified to include a protective deck and improved machinery and armament. Originally classified as despatch vessels, they were redesignated second class cruisers prior to completion. The arrangement of the hull and subdivision was as in the previous class except that the lower deck over the length of the machinery compartments (165ft) was constructed of 1½in thick plating with sloped sides to deflect shells entering at the waterline. The 6in guns were mounted on each side of the main deck with those furthest forward and aft fitted on central pivot mounts and the remainder on broadside mounts. The end guns were positioned in sponsons to provide ahead and astern fire and were protected by 1½in shields as defence against machine guns. As built they also carried 2 Gatling, 4 Gardner and 10 Nordenfeld MGs; 4 of these weapons (8 in *Arethusa*) were later replaced by 3pdr QFs.

After trials with the *Phaeton,* the funnels were raised 6ft to improve the draught to the boilers and subsequently all exceeded the designed speed, averaging 17-18kts on trial. The improved economy of the TE engine and an increase in the maximum coal stowage gave an endurance of 11,000nm at 10kts, a substantial improvement on the *Mercury* which had been criticised in this respect. They were good steam vessels but poor sea boats with a heavy roll in certain conditions of sea. They carried a barque rig identical to that in *Mercury* and retained their yards until the late 1890s. *Leander* became a depot ship in 1904. *Phaeton* was sold in 1913 and became the TS *Indefatigable*; she was repurchased in 1941 and renamed *Carrick II,* serving as a Royal Navy TS throughout the Second Word War.

LEANDER class *second class cruisers*

Displacement: 4300t load
Dimensions: 300ft pp, 315ft oa x 46ft x 20ft 6in (*91.44 pp, 96.01 oa x 14.02 x 6.25m*)
Machinery: 2-shaft, 2 cyl HDAC, 12 cyl boilers, 5500ihp = 16.5kts. Coal 1016t
Armour: Deck 1½in, gunshields 1½in
Armament: 10-6in BLR, 16 MGs, 4 TT aw
Complement: 278

Name	Builder	Laid down	Launched	Comp	Fate
AMPHION	Pembroke DYd	25.4.1881	13.10.83	1887	Sold 1906
ARETHUSA	Napier, Glasgow	14.6.1880	23.12.82	1886	Sold 1905
LEANDER	Napier, Glasgow	14.6.1880	28.10.82	29.5.85	Sold 1920
PHAETON	Napier, Glasgow	14.6.1880	27.2.83	20.4.86	Sold 1947

Leander prior to the raising of her funnels

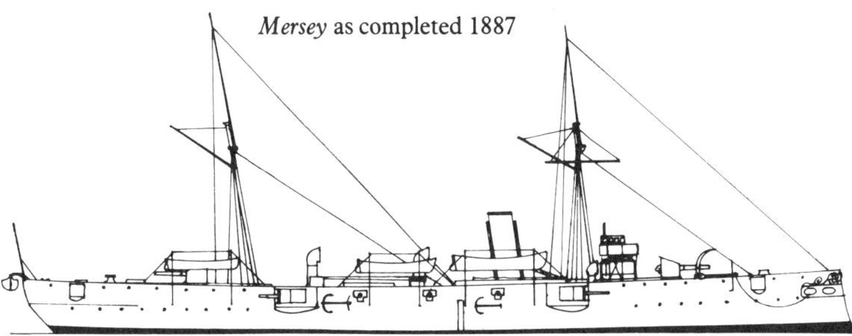
Mersey as completed 1887

These ships completed the stabilisation of the designs begun with the *Iris* and *Mercury* and established the pattern for future British second class cruisers. They followed closely the design of the *Leander* class but incorporated, for the first time, a full length protective deck. They were also the first vessels of the type to abandon any form of sailing rig and to be fitted with an armoured conning tower, which was positioned on the forecastle just forward of the mainmast. The 6in guns were arranged as in *Leander,* except that all were mounted in sponsons on central pivot mountings in the *Thames* and *Forth,* while the two 8in were mounted on the centreline on the forecastle and poop. They had much higher bulwarks than the *Leanders* and carried a spar deck amidships on which were mounted some of their MGs. The armoured deck was 2in on the flat and 3in on the slope and at the forward end curved down to provide support behind the ram bow. The remaining internal arrangements were similar to those of the earlier types but they were the only major British cruisers of the late Victorian period with single funnels.

On trials both *Thames* and *Severn* exceeded 18kts, but *Forth* ran her trials in bad weather and only made 17.3kts while *Mersey,* which developed the highest power at 6628ihp, did not have her speed recorded. During 1893/96 all four had their funnels raised to improve the draught to the boilers. Endurance was 8750nm at 10kts. They were handy ships, steady gun platforms and good sea boats.

Thames and *Forth* were converted to depot ships 1903/4. *Thames* was sold in 1920 and became the TS *General Botha* based at the Cape; in 1942 she reverted to her old name and was employed as an accommodation ship until 1945.

MERSEY class *second class cruisers*

Displacement: 4050t load
Dimensions: 300ft pp, 315ft oa x 46ft x 19ft 6in (*91.44 pp, 96.01 oa x 14.02 x 5.94m*)
Machinery: 2-shaft, 2 cyl HDAC, 12 boilers, 4500ihp = 17kts natural draught, 6000ihp = 18kts forced draught. Coal 900t
Armour: Deck 2in-3in, CT 9in, gunshields 2in
Armament: 2-8in BLR, 10-6in BLR, 3-6pdr QF, 3-3pdr QF, 9 MGs, 2 TT sub, 2 TC
Complement: 300

Name	Builder	Laid down	Launched	Comp	Fate
MERSEY	Chatham DYd	9.7.1883	31.3.85	1887	Sold 1905
SEVERN	Chatham DYd	1.1.1884	29.9.85	1888	Sold 1905
THAMES	Pembroke DYd	14.4.1884	3.12.85	1888	Scuttled 1947
FORTH	Pembroke DYd	1.12.1884	23.10.86	1889	Sold 1921

GREAT BRITAIN

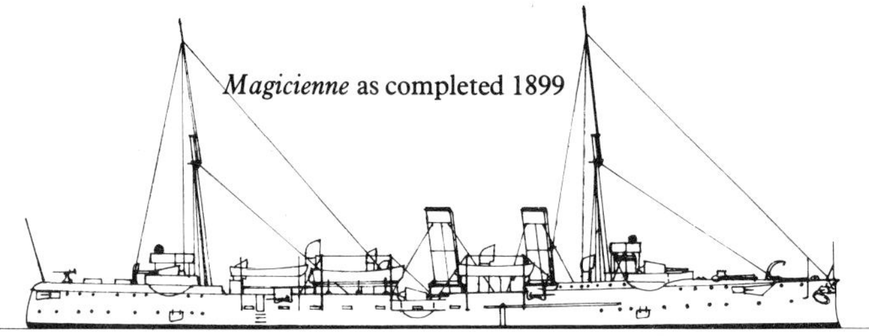
Magicienne as completed 1899

MEDEA class *second class cruisers*

Displacement:	2800t load, sheathed vessels 2950t
Dimensions:	265ft pp x 41ft (sheathed vessels 42ft) x 16ft 6in *(80.77 pp x 12.54 (12.80) x 5.03m)*
Machinery:	2-shaft, VC (sheathed vessels HDAC), 6 cyl boilers, 9000ihp = 20kts, (sheathed vessels 19.75kts). Coal 400t
Armour:	Deck 1in-2in, CT 3in, gunshields 4½in
Armament:	6-6in BLR, 9-6pdr QF, 1-3pdr QF, 3 MGs, 2 TT, 2 TC
Complement:	218

Name	Builder	Laid down	Launched	Comp	Fate
MARATHON	Fairfield, Govan	10.8.1887	23.8.88	1889	Sold 1905
MAGICIENNE	Fairfield, Govan	10.8.1887	12.5.88	1889	Sold 1905
MEDEA	Chatham DYd	25.4.1887	9.6.88	1889	Sold 1914
MEDUSA	Chatham DYd	25.8.1887	11.8.88	1889	Sold 1920
MELPOMENE	Portsmouth DYd	10.10.1887	20.9.88	1890	Sold 1905

Provided under the 1887/88 Programme, these ships were reduced editions of the *Mersey* class and were inferior to those ships in all respects. They were reclassified third class cruisers shortly after completion. Three of the class, *Melpomene, Magicienne* and *Marathon,* were sheathed in wood and copper for tropical service which increased the beam by 1ft, added 150t to the displacement and reduced the designed speed by ¼kt. They also differed from the unsheathed pair in having horizontal engines. The protective deck was 1in on the flat and 2in on the slope, the flat being 1ft above the load line and the outer edge of the slope 5ft below. Three 6in guns, mounted on sponsons, were fitted on each side, one on the forecastle, one amidships on the upper deck and one on the poop. Eight of the 6pdr QF guns were mounted on the upper deck, 4 amidships, 2 forward and 2 aft and the ninth on the centreline at the after end of the poop. During the 1890s they were rearmed with 6in QF guns. They did not achieve their designed speeds on trials, averaging 19kts, and proved poor steamers in service particularly in a seaway. An open upper deck amidships with low bulwarks made them very wet and they proved to be bad sea boats. They were fitted with a turtle back forecastle and the forward 6in guns were provided with a low breakwater indicating that the designers expected them to be wet ships. They also suffered from cramped accommodation and insufficient space in the boiler rooms for efficient stoking, and it was generally concluded that all their troubles resulted from their small size. Endurance as designed was 8000nm at 10kts.

APOLLO class *second class cruisers*

Displacement:	3400t load (sheathed vessels 3600t)
Dimensions:	300ft pp, 314ft oa x 43ft (sheathed vessels 43ft 8in) x 17ft 6in (sheathed vessels 18ft 6in) *(91.44 pp, 95.7 oa x 13.11 (13.31) x 5.33 (5.64) m)*
Machinery:	2-shaft, 2 cyl TE, 3 double-ended and 2 single-ended cyl boilers, 7000ihp = 18.5kts natural draught, 9000ihp = 20kts forced draught (sheathed vessels 19.75kts). Coal 535t
Armour:	Deck 1¼in-2in, CT 3in, gunshields 4½in, engine hatch 5in
Armament:	2-6in QF, 6-4.7in QF, 8-6pdr QF, 1-3pdr QF, 4 MGs, 4-14in TT aw
Complement:	273

Name	Builder	Laid down	Launched	Comp	Fate
AEOLUS	Devonport DYd	1890	13.11.91	6.1.94	Sold 1914
ANDROMACHE	Chatham DYd	April 1889	14.8.90	1892	Sold 1920
APOLLO	Chatham DYd	April 1889	10.2.91	1892	Sold 1920
BRILLIANT	Sheerness DYd	1890	24.6.91	1893	Sunk as blockship 23.4.1918
INDEFATIGABLE	London & Glasgow, Glasgow	1890	12.3.91	1892	Sold 1913
INTREPID	London & Glasgow, Glasgow	1890	20.6.91	1894	Sunk as blockship 23.4.1918
IPHIGENIA	London & Glasgow, Glasgow	1890	19.11.91	1892	Sunk as blockship 23.4.1918
LATONA	Naval Construction & Armaments Co, Barrow	1889	22.5.90	1893	Sold 1920
MELAMPUS	Naval Construction & Armaments Co, Barrow	1889	2.8.90	–	Sold 1910
NAIAD	Naval Construction & Armaments Co, Barrow	1889	29.11.90	1893	Sold 1922
PIQUE	Palmer, Jarrow	1889	13.12.90	–	Sold 1911
RAINBOW	Palmer, Jarrow	1890	25.3.91	1892	Sold 1920
RETRIBUTION	Palmer, Jarrow	1890	6.8.91	–	Sold 1911
SAPPHO	Samuda, Poplar	1890	9.5.91	1893	Sold 1921
SCYLLA	Samuda, Poplar	1890	17.10.91	1892	Sold 1914
SIRIUS	Armstrong, Elswick	Sept 1889	27.10.90	1891	Sunk as blockship 23.4.1918
SPARTAN	Armstrong, Elswick	Dec 1889	25.2.91	1892	Sold 1931
SYBILLE	Stephenson Newcastle	1889	27.12.90	–	Wrecked 16.1.1901
TERPISCHORE	Thompson, Glasgow	1889	30.10.90	–	Sold 1914
THETIS	Thompson, Glasgow	1889	13.12.90	1892	Sunk as blockship 23.4.1918
TRIBUNE	Thompson, Glasgow	1889	24.2.91	–	Sold 1911

The 21 ships of this class were provided under the Naval Defence Act of 1889. In design they were enlarged versions of the *Medea* class with the main armament modified to mixed calibre QF guns only. The two 6in guns were placed on the centreline of the forecastle and poop and the 4.7in were mounted 3 on each side of the upper deck amidships. The 6pdr guns were all on the upper deck, 4 being amidships, between the 4.7in, and 2 forward and 2 aft firing through embrasured ports for ahead and astern fire. The 4.7in guns were not fitted on sponsons and the class were severely criticised for their lack of ahead and astern fire and for lack of gunpower generally in comparison to foreign cruisers of similar type. Two TT were fitted broadside abreast the mainmast on the upper deck and could be trained through an arc of 90°; one was carried in the bow, also on the upper deck; and a stern tube was fitted at main deck level.

The protective deck was 1¼in thick on the flat and 2in on the slope, and the engine cylinders, where they projected above this deck, were protected by a 5in armoured glacis around the engine room hatch. The engines, being vertical instead of horizontal, were mounted side by side and separated from each other by a centreline bulkhead. The after boiler room contained two double-ended boilers while the forward room contained one double-ended and two single-ended boilers. Endurance with maximum coal capacity was 8000nm at 10kts. Most of the class achieved the designed speed on trial and they were generally regarded as good steamers, and while several suffered early deterioration of their machinery and consequent loss of speed many others proved capable of achieving their designed speed until late in their careers. Ten of the class, *Aeolus,Brilliant, Indefatigable, Intrepid, Iphigenia, Pique, Rainbow, Retribution, Sirius* and *Spartan* were sheathed in wood and copper for tropical service which added 200t to the displacement and resulted in a ¼kt loss in designed speed.

Although larger than the *Medea* class, the *Apollos* had the same layout with a turtle back forecastle and a low freeboard, and although slightly better than their predecessors, they were wet ships and poor sea boats which would have found great difficulty in fighting their waist guns in a seaway. During 1907-10 *Andromache, Apollo, Intrepid, Iphigenia, Latona, Naiad* and *Thetis* were converted to minelayers.

In 1910 *Rainbow* was transferred to the RCN and *Indefatigable* was renamed *Melpomene*. *Brilliant* and *Sirius* were sunk as blockships at Ostend and *Intrepid, Ihphigenia* and *Thetis* at Zeebrugge. *Spartan* was renamed *Defiance* in 1921.

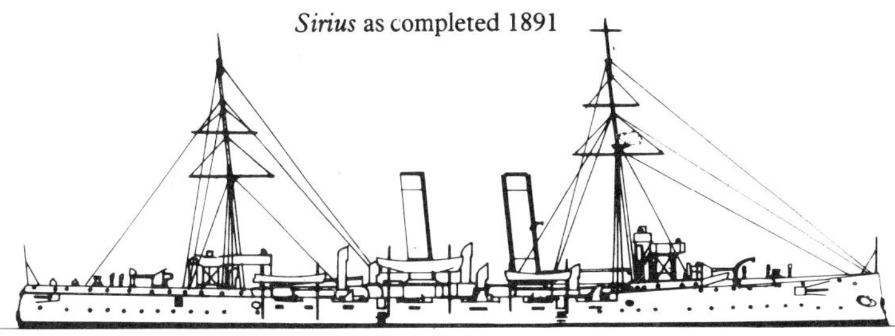

Sirius as completed 1891

1. *Medea* prior to being rearmed with QF guns
2. *Rainbow* as built
3. *Bonaventure* during the 1890s

Provided under the Naval Defence Act of 1889, these vessels were improved *Apollos* in which an increase of 1000t in displacement was employed to provide a hull of improved seaworthiness and a slightly heavier and better placed armament. The general arrangement of the hull, protection, armament and machinery was similar to that in the *Apollo* but the broadside guns were increased to 4-4.7in and 3-6pdr on each side and fitted on a new full length deck provided in place of the separate forecastle and poop. This greatly increased the freeboard amidships, making the ships drier and giving the guns a higher command. The end 4.7in guns on each side were fitted in sponsons to supplement the 6in weapons in ahead and astern fire. The class was heavily criticised for showing little or no improvement on the *Apollos* in armament, speed and endurance despite being larger and more costly, but the fact that the increased weight was largely absorbed in improving seaworthiness was ignored by many of these critics. Whatever the faults of the design they were certainly improvements on the *Apollo* class and with a further increase in size formed the basis for future second class cruiser designs. On trials the ships of the class averaged 9250ihp and speeds varied between 19.5 and 20.5kts. Endurance was 7000nm at 10kts. All the ships of the class were sheathed in wood and copper.

Bonaventure became a depot ship in 1910; *Flora* became TS *Indus II* in 1915; *Cambrian* was reduced to harbour service in 1916; and *Hermione* was sold in 1922, becoming TS *Warspite* until 1939.

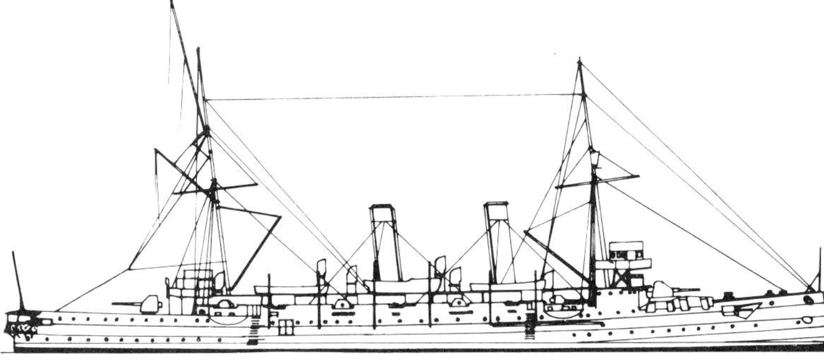

Astraea 1904

ASTRAEA class *second class cruisers*

Displacement: 4360t load
Dimensions: 320ft pp, 339ft 6in oa x 49ft 6in x 19ft (*97.54 pp, 103.48 oa x 15.09 x 5.79m*)
Machinery: 2-shaft, 3 cyl TE, 8 cyl boilers, 7500ihp = 18kts natural draught, 9500ihp = 19.5kts forced draught. Coal 1000t
Armour: Deck 2in, CT 3in, 6in gunshields 4½in, engine hatch 5in
Armament: 2-6in QF, 8-4.7in QF, 10-6pdr QF, 1-3pdr QF, 4-18in TT aw
Complement: 318

Name	Builder	Laid down	Launched	Comp	Fate
ASTRAEA	Devonport DYd	–	17.3.1893	5.11.95	Sold 1920
BONAVENTURE	Devonport DYd	–	2.12.1892	5.7.94	Sold 1920
CAMBRIAN	Pembroke DYd	–	30.1.1893	–	Sold 1923
CHARYBDIS	Sheerness DYd	1891	15.6.93	14.1.96	Sold 1922
FLORA	Pembroke DYd	–	21.11.1893	–	Sold 1922
FORTE	Chatham DYd	–	9.12.1893	–	Sold 1914
FOX	Portsmouth DYd	–	15.6.1893	14.4.96	Sold 1920
HERMIONE	Devonport DYd	–	7.11.1893	14.1.96	Sold 1940

GREAT BRITAIN

Following the criticisms of earlier second class cruisers the *Eclipse* class, provided under the Spencer Programme of 1893/94, were designed with a heavier armament but as this was combined with another major increase in size they were subject to as much abuse as their predecessors. The arrangement of hull and protection was the same as that of the *Astraea* class except that seaworthiness was further improved by the addition of a turtleback forecastle extending as far aft as the foremast. The armament was also arranged like that in *Astraea* except that the two foremost 4.7in guns were replaced by two 6in, the single 6in on the quarterdeck was replaced by two sided 6in and the 6pdr guns were replaced by 12pdrs. This arrangement was chosen to secure the maximum improvement in ahead and astern fire and resulted in broadside fire being a little better than that of *Astraea* — 3-4.7in and 3-6in compared with 4-4.7in and 2-6in. It was eventually accepted that they were under-gunned for their size and during 1903-05 all except *Eclipse* were rearmed, the old 6in and 4.7in guns being replaced by a uniform armament of 11-6in guns. Apart from a slight increase in power the machinery was similar to that in *Astraea* and designed speed and endurance were the same. On trials the ships achieved between 9760 and 9875ihp and speeds of 20 to 21.2kts. With the exception of *Talbot* they were the first British second class cruisers to be fitted with fighting tops which were positioned low on both masts. *Dido* and *Iris* had single pole masts while the remainder of the class had fidded topmasts.

Dido and *Eclipse* became depot ships in 1913 and 1916 respectively.

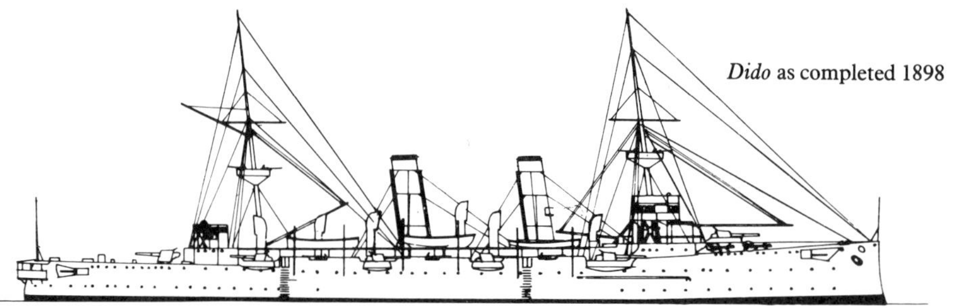

Dido as completed 1898

ECLIPSE class *second class cruisers*

Displacement: 5600t load
Dimensions: 350ft pp, 373ft oa x 53ft 6in x 20ft 6in (*106.68 pp, 113.69 oa x 16.31 x 6.25m*)
Machinery: 2-shaft, 3 cyl TE, 8 cyl boilers, 8000ihp = 18.5kts natural draught, 9600ihp = 19.5kts forced draught. Coal 1075t
Armour: Deck 1½in-3in, CT 6in, gunshields 3in, engine hatch 6in
Armament: 5-6in QF, 6-4.7in QF, 8-12pdr QF, 6-3pdr QF, 2 MGs, 3-18in TT, 1 stern aw, 2 broadside sub
Complement: 450

Name	Builder	Laid down	Launched	Comp	Fate
DIANA	Fairfield	13.8.1894	5.12.95	15.6.97	Sold 1920
DIDO	London & Glasgow, Glasgow	30.8.1894	20.3.96	10.5.98	Sold 1926
DORIS	Naval Construction & Armaments Co, Barrow	29.8.1894	3.3.96	18.11.97	Sold 1919
ECLIPSE	Portsmouth DYd	11.12.1893	19.7.94	23.3.97	Sold 1921
ISIS	London & Glasgow, Glasgow	30.1.1895	27.6.96	10.5.98	Sold 1920
JUNO	Naval Construction & Armaments Co, Barrow	22.6.1894	16.11.95	16.6.97	Sold 1920
MINERVA	Chatham DYd	4.12.1893	23.9.95	4.2.97	Sold 1920
TALBOT	Devonport DYd	5.3.1894	25.4.95	15.9.96	Sold 1921
VENUS	Fairfield	28.6.1894	5.9.95	9.11.97	Sold 1921

Venus in 1904

Provided under the 1895/96 Programme the *Arrogant* class were intended for use with the fleet rather than on the trade routes and were designed to employ ramming tactics in action. For the latter they required good manoeuvrability and this was secured by reducing the length-to-beam ratio to 5.6:1 (compared with 6.5:1 in the *Eclipse* class), providing a second auxiliary rudder forward of the main rudder and reducing the deadwood aft. The ram was heavier and of more pronounced form than usual, and was well supported by the bow structure which included the forward end of the protective deck and 2in side plating which extended aft for 40ft. In addition the CT was given much thicker armour than was usual in a second class cruiser in order to provide protection at close range. They certainly proved successful in manoeuvrability, the tactical diameter being 380yds compared with 650yds for one of the *Astraea* class but the idea of designing a ram at this late date is rather strange and the best that can be assumed is that they were intended for attack on an already crippled enemy.

They were the first British second class cruisers to be fitted with water tube boilers, six Bellevilles being mounted in each of three boiler rooms. This provided a substantial increase in power but the designed speed was less than in preceding ships owing to the altered form although they proved good for 20kts on forced draught and 18kts natural draught on trial. The armament was identical to that in the *Eclipse* class except that only one 6in gun was fitted on the quarterdeck instead of two. They were rearmed during 1903/04 when the existing 6in and 4.7in guns were replaced by a uniform armament of 10-6in. They were flush-decked except for a slightly raised forecastle and tops were only fitted on the foremasts.

Arrogant became a depot ship in 1911, *Furious* was hulked and renamed *Forte* in 1915, and *Vindictive* was sunk as a blockship at Ostend.

ARROGANT class *second class cruisers*

Displacement: 5750t load
Dimensions: 320ft pp, 342ft oa x 57ft 6in x 20ft (*97.54 pp, 104.24 oa x 17.53 x 6.1m*)
Machinery: 2-shaft, 3 cyl TE, 18 Belleville boilers, 10,000ihp = 19kts forced draught. Coal 1175t
Armour: Deck 1½in-3in, sides (forward) 2in, CT 9in, gunshields 4½in, engine hatch 4in
Armament: 4-6in QF, 6-4.7in QF, 8-12pdr, 3-3pdr QF, 5 MGs, 3-18in TT
Complement: 480

Name	Builder	Laid down	Launched	Comp	Fate
ARROGANT	Devonport DYd	1895	26.5.96	1898	Sold 1923
FURIOUS	Devonport DYd	10.6.1895	3.12.96	1.7.98	Sold 1923
GLADIATOR	Portsmouth DYd	Jan 1896	18.12.96	Apr 1899	Sunk 25.4.1908, raised and sold 1909
VINDICTIVE	Chatham DYd	27.1.1896	9.12.97	4.7.1900	Sunk as blockship 10.5.1918

Arrogant as built with mixed calibre main armament

Hermes as completed

Hermes as completed 1899

Challenger as completed 1904

Repeats of *Eclipse* class except for the provision of uniform 6in gun armament and installation of watertube boilers. The first three were provided under the 1896/97 Programme, the last pair under the 1900/01 Programme. The *Highflyer* class employed the same machinery as the *Arrogant* which gave a ½kt improvement in designed speed and a 100t saving in weight compared with the *Eclipse*. On trials *Hermes* achieved 20.5kts with 10,224ihp, and the *Highflyer* 20.1kts with 10,344ihp, but *Hyacinth* was some time out of dock and only made 19.4kts with 10,536ihp. Subsequently some trouble was experienced with the boilers particularly in *Hermes* which was refitted with Babcock boilers during 1901-03.

The *Challenger* and *Encounter* differed from the earlier group in adopting more powerful machinery and wind sails in place of cowls. On trials *Challenger* made 21.09kts with 12,806ihp and the *Encounter* 21.3kts with 13,000ihp. The latter ship was transferred to the RAN in 1912, becoming a depot ship and being renamed *Penguin* in 1923.

HIGHFLYER and CHALLENGER classes *second class cruisers*

Displacement: 5650t *Highflyer* class, 5880t *Challenger* class
Dimensions: 350ft pp, 372ft oa x 54ft x 20ft 6in (*106.68 pp, 113.39 oa x 16.46 x 6.25m*)
Machinery: 2-shaft, 4 cyl TE, 18 Belleville boilers (*Challenger* Babcock boilers and *Encounter* Durr boilers), 10,000ihp = 20kts *Highflyer* class, 12,500ihp = 21kts *Challenger* class. Coal 1100t
Armour: Deck 1½in-3in, CT 6in, gunshields 3in, engine hatches 5in
Armament: 11-6in QF, 9-12pdr QF, 6-3pdr QF, 2-18in TT sub
Complement: 450

Name	Builder	Laid down	Launched	Comp	Fate
HERMES	Fairfield	30.4.1897	7.4.98	5.10.99	Sunk by *U27* 31.10.1914
HIGHFLYER	Fairfield	7.6.1897	4.6.98	7.12.99	Sold 1921
HYACINTH	London & Glasgow Glasgow	27.1.1897	27.10.98	3.9.1900	Sold 1923
CHALLENGER	Chatham DYd	1.12.1900	27.5.02	3.5.04	Sold 1920
ENCOUNTER	Devonport DYd	28.1.1901	18.6.02	21.11.05	Scuttled 1932

CRUISERS 3rd class

Surprise and *Alacrity* were laid down as unarmed despatch vessels but in 1885 it was decided to provide them with guns so they could be employed as fleet scouts in wartime. They were similar in design to the contemporary *Scout* class torpedo cruisers, with the same arrangement of machinery, protection and sub-divisions, but were of finer form and had elaborate passenger accommodation (for diplomats, high ranking officers, etc). On trials *Alacrity* made 18kts with 3180ihp and *Surprise* 17.85kts with 3018ihp. Both had lengthy careers and were always classed as despatch vessels. In the late 1890s *Alacrity* had her original gun armament replaced with 10-6pdr QFs. *Surprise* was renamed *Alacrity* when her sister was sold in 1913.

SURPRISE class *despatch vessels*

Displacement: 1650t load, *Alacrity* 1700t
Dimensions: 250ft pp x 32ft 6in x 13ft (*76.2 pp x 9.91 x 3.96m*)
Machinery: 2-shaft, 2 cyl HDAC, 4 cyl boilers, 2000ihp = 16kts natural draught, 3000ihp = 17kts forced draught. Coal 400t
Armour: Deck 3/8in
Armament: 4-5in BLR, 4-6pdr QF, 2 MGs
Complement: 93

Name	Builder	Laid down	Launched	Comp	Fate
ALACRITY	Palmer, Jarrow	14.2.1884	28.2.85	22.6.86	Sold 1913
SURPRISE	Palmer, Jarrow	14.2.1884	17.1.85	20.7.86	Sold 1919

Scout after rearming with 4.7in guns
By courtesy of John Roberts

Scout and *Fearless* were an attempt to produce small sea-going vessels of high speed and endurance capable of providing the fleet with defence against torpedo boat attacks and carrying out torpedo attacks on an enemy fleet. They had therefore to be larger than torpedo boats, which were not sufficiently seaworthy, but not so large as to be too expensive to build and operate in reasonable numbers. Unfortunately they proved to be poor seaboats and were too slow to operate effectively as fleet torpedo craft and they were therefore employed as small cruisers for commerce protection, scouting and independent duties. They were reclassified third class cruisers a few years after completion.

SCOUT class *torpedo cruisers*

Displacement: 1580t load
Dimensions: 220ft pp, 225ft wl x 34ft 3in x 14ft 6in (*67.06 pp, 68.58 wl x 10.44 x 4.42m*)
Machinery: 2-shaft, 2 cyl HDAC, 4 boilers, 2000ihp = 16kts natural draught, 3200ihp = 17kts forced draught. Coal 450t
Armour: Deck 3/8in, shields to guns and torpedoes 1in, CT 3in
Armament: 4-5in BLR, 8-3pdr QF, 2 MGs, 1 TT aw, 2 TC
Complement: 147

Name	Builder	Laid down	Launched	Comp	Fate
FEARLESS	Naval Construction & Armaments Co	22.9.1884	20.3.86	July 1887	Sold 1905
SCOUT	Thompson, Glasgow	8.1.1884	30.7.85	20.8.85	Sold 1904

They carried one 5in BLR gun on each side of the poop and forecastle, abreast the fore- and mizzenmasts, and eight 3pdr QFs on the upper deck, two each side amidships and one each side forward and aft. There was a fixed TT in the bow and two upper deck traversing TC, one under the forecastle and one under the poop, which could be moved across the ship to fire through ports on either side. During the 1890s the 5in guns were replaced by 4.7in QF weapons. A 3/8in steel deck, just below water level, provided splinter protection to the machinery compartments, and 1in plating was fitted around the torpedo ports, but the main forms of protection were extensive watertight subdivision and the provision of wing coal bunkers abreast the boiler rooms and above the protective deck over the length of the machinery compartments. They had two boiler rooms, with two boilers in each room, and a single engine room containing two engines fore and aft of each other. On trials *Fearless* made 17.27kts with 3302ihp and *Scout* 17.6kts with 3370ihp. Endurance was 6900nm at 10kts or 2500nm at full speed.

These vessels were modified versions of the *Scout* class with dimensions increased to accommodate a main armament of six 6in guns. Four of these weapons were disposed as in the earlier class while the extra pair were mounted one each side on the upper deck amidships. The remaining weapons and the system of protection was arranged as in the *Scout*. Machinery power was increased but the wider beam and increased displacement resulted in a ½kt drop in design speed except in the two ships built in the Royal Dockyard, *Serpent* and *Racoon*, in which the engine power was raised to 4500ihp for a designed speed of 17.5kts. All exceeded their designed power on trials (which were run light) and most exceeded 17kts while the Royal Dockyard pair exceeded 18kts. The machinery was arranged as in the *Scout* except that the two engines were fitted in separate engine rooms, that forward driving the port shaft and that aft the starboard shaft. The machinery power was comparatively high for the size of ship and the engine and boiler rooms were very cramped but the plant proved reliable and most of the ships of the class enjoyed long careers. They were the last British cruisers to be fitted with horizontal engines. In appearance they differed from the *Scout* class in having three masts instead of two, and a clipper stem. They were reasonable sea boats but were overgunned for their size which caused them to roll abnormally at times and made them very wet in heavy weather. Like the *Scout* class they were too small and too slow to serve as effective torpedo vessels and were reclassified third class cruisers shortly after completion.

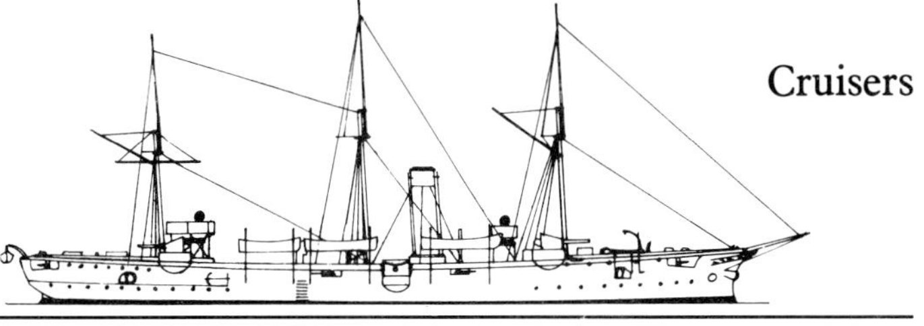
Archer as completed 1888

ARCHER class *torpedo cruisers*

Displacement: 1770t load, 1950t full load
Dimensions: 225ft pp, 240ft oa x 36ft x 14ft 6in (*68.58 pp, 73.15 oa x 10.97 x 4.42m*)
Machinery: 2-shaft, 2 cyl HDAC, 4 boilers, 2500ihp = 15kts natural draught, 3500ihp = 16.5kts forced draught. Coal 475t
Armour: Deck 3/8in, shields to guns and torpedoes 1in, CT 3in
Armament: 6-6in BLR, 8-3pdr QF, 2 MGs, 3-14in TT aw
Complement: 176

Name	Builder	Laid down	Launched	Comp	Fate
ARCHER	Thompson, Glasgow	2.3.1885	23.12.85	11.12.88	Sold 1905
BRISK	Thompson, Glasgow	2.3.1885	8.4.86	20.3.88	Sold 1906
COSSACK	Thompson, Glasgow	2.3.1885	3.6.86	1.1.89	Sold 1905
MOHAWK	Thompson, Glasgow	2.3.1885	6.2.86	16.12.90	Sold 1905
PORPOISE	Thompson, Glasgow	2.3.1885	7.5.86	12.2.88	Sold 1905
RACOON	Devonport DYd	1.2.1886	6.5.87	Mar 1888	Sold 1905
SERPENT	Devonport DYd	9.11.1885	10.3.87	Mar 1888	Wrecked 10.11.90
TARTAR	Thompson, Glasgow	2.3.1885	28.10.86	30.6.91	Sold 1906

Brisk as built

The *Barracouta* class were small cruisers designed for service on distant stations where docking facilities were limited, and all four vessels were sheathed in wood and copper. Although of similar size and general arrangement to the earlier torpedo cruisers they had the advantage of the latest advances in technology and were the first British cruisers to be fitted with TE machinery and a main armament of QF guns. They were also the first British vessels of this size to be given a true protective deck, an essential feature with the introduction of the medium calibre QF gun. This deck was similar to that of the *Medea* class and extended to the full length of the ships, being 1in on the flat and 2in on the slope amidships and uniform 1in at the ends. The fitting of this protection in a vessel no larger than the *Scout* class was made possible mainly by the savings in weight and space resulting from the adoption of TE engines and lighter boilers of higher pressure. The ships had twin funnels fitted side by side which from many angles looked like a single funnel. The machinery was reasonably reliable but the boilers gave some trouble after a few years' service, and in 1900/2 *Blonde* and *Blanche* were reboilered with Laird boilers; the twin funnels of *Blonde* were converted into a single uptake prior to her being reboilered. The 4.7in QF guns were arranged in the same manner as the 6in guns in the *Archer* class and the 3pdrs were fitted at the forward and after ends of the upper deck firing through embrassured ports on each side of the bow and quarters. The superstructure arrangement was similar to that of the *Archer* class but there were lower bulwarks amidships, making the poop and forecastle more obvious, and a lower freeboard generally which gave the appearance of sleeker ships with some similarities to contemporary torpedo gunboats. The ships were steadier than their predecessors but were poor sea boats which were wet in heavy weather particularly amidships. Despite their intended purpose they served mainly in home waters and in the Mediterranean.

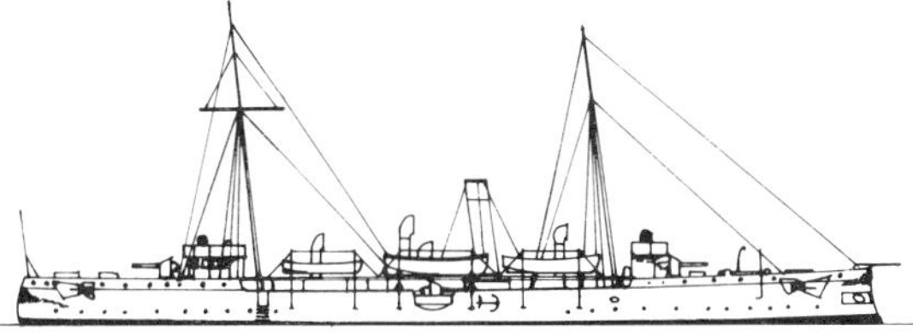
Blonde 1897

BARRACOUTA class *third class cruisers*

Displacement: 1580t load
Dimensions: 220ft pp, 233ft oa x 35ft x 15ft (*67.06 pp, 71.02 oa x 10.67 x 4.6m*)
Machinery: 2-shaft, 3 cyl TE, 4 double-ended cyl boilers, 1750ihp = 15kts natural draught, 3000ihp = 16.5kts forced draught. Coal 160t
Armour: Deck 2in-1in, gunshields 2in
Armament: 6-4.7in QF, 4-3pdr QF, 2 MGs, 2-14in TT aw
Complement: 160

Name	Builder	Laid down	Launched	Comp	Fate
BARRACOUTA	Sheerness DYd	1888	16.5.89	1890	Sold 1905
BARROSA	Portsmouth DYd	May 1888	16.4.89	1890	Sold 1905
BLANCHE	Pembroke DYd	May 1888	6.9.89	1890	Sold 1905
BLONDE	Pembroke DYd	May 1888	22.10.89	1890	Sold 1905

GREAT BRITAIN

Barrosa as completed

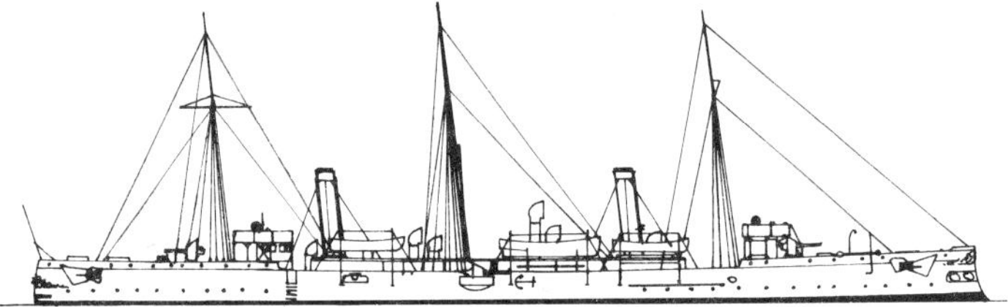

Bellona 1895

BARHAM class *third class cruisers*

Displacement: 1830t load
Dimensions: 280ft pp x 35ft x 13ft 3in (*85.34 pp x 10.67 x 4.04m*)
Machinery: 2-shaft, 3 cyl TE, 6 locomotive boilers, 3600ihp = 16.5kts natural draught, 6000ihp = 19.5kts forced draught. Coal 140t
Armour: Deck 2in-1in, gunshields 2in
Armament: 6-4.7in QF, 4-3pdr QF, 2 MGs, 2-14in TT aw
Complement: 170

Name	Builder	Laid down	Launched	Comp	Fate
BARHAM	Portsmouth DYd	22.10.1888	11.9.89	1890	Sold 1914
BELLONA	Hawthorn, Hebburn	1889	29.8.90	1891	Sold 1906

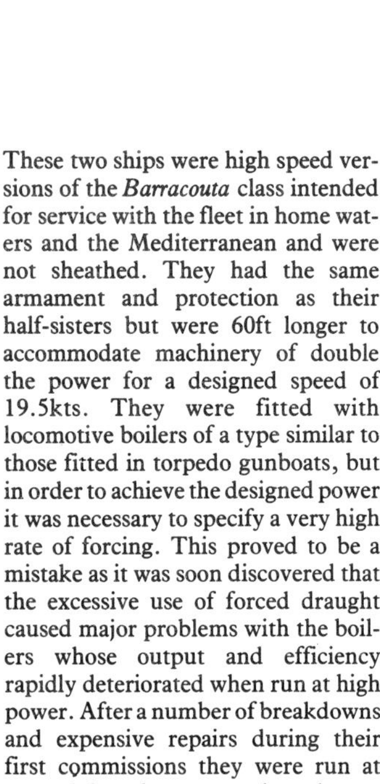

These two ships were high speed versions of the *Barracouta* class intended for service with the fleet in home waters and the Mediterranean and were not sheathed. They had the same armament and protection as their half-sisters but were 60ft longer to accommodate machinery of double the power for a designed speed of 19.5kts. They were fitted with locomotive boilers of a type similar to those fitted in torpedo gunboats, but in order to achieve the designed power it was necessary to specify a very high rate of forcing. This proved to be a mistake as it was soon discovered that the excessive use of forced draught caused major problems with the boilers whose output and efficiency rapidly deteriorated when run at high power. After a number of breakdowns and expensive repairs during their first commissions they were run at natural draught power only and employed mainly as 16kt despatch vessels. During 1898-1899 both vessels were refitted with Thornycroft water tube boilers which gave them a designed power of 4700ihp for a speed of 18kts.

The engine room was placed amidships between the two boiler rooms, which necessitated widely spaced funnels and gave them an ungainly profile. Apart from this, and the fitting of three masts, the upperworks were arranged similarly to those of the *Barracouta* class. When they were reboilered the rig was reduced to two masts.

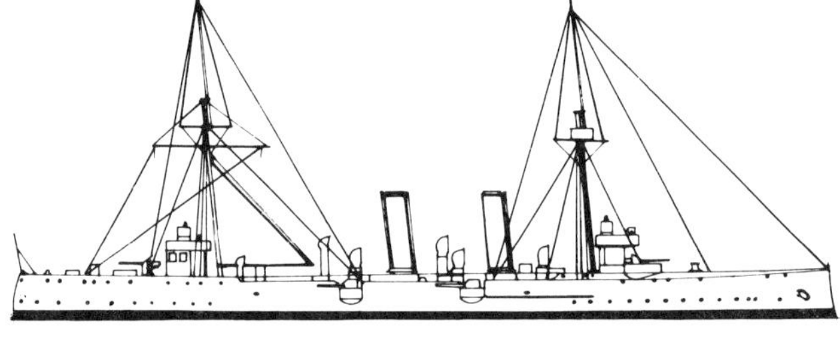

Philomel as completed 1891

PEARL class *third class cruisers*

Displacement: 2575t
Dimensions: 265ft pp, 278ft oa x 41ft x 15ft 6in (*80.77 pp, 84.73 oa x 12.5 x 4.72m*)
Machinery: 2-shaft, 3 cyl TE, 4 double-ended cyl boilers, 4000ihp = 17kts natural draught, 7500ihp = 19kts forced draught
Armour: Deck 1in-2in, gunshields 2in, CT 3in
Armament: 8-4.7in QF, 8-3pdr QF, 4 MGs, 2-14in TT, 2 TC
Complement: 217

Name	Builder	Laid down	Launched	Comp	Fate
KATOOMBA (ex-PANDORA)	Armstrong, Elswick	15.8.1888	27.8.89	24.3.91	Sold 1906
MILDURA (ex-PELORUS)	Armstrong, Elswick	15.8.1888	25.11.89	18.3.91	Sold 1906
PALLAS	Portsmouth DYd	1.7.1889	30.6.90	30.6.91	Sold 1906
PEARL	Pembroke DYd	1.4.1889	28.7.90	Oct 1892	Sold 1906
PHOEBE	Devonport DYd	23.4.1889	1.7.90	1.12.92	Sold 1906
PHILOMEL	Devonport DYd	8.5.1889	28.8.90	10.11.91	Scuttled 1949
RINGAROOMA (ex-PSYCHE)	Thompson, Glasgow	6.12.1888	10.12.89	3.2.91	Sold 1906
TAURANGA (ex-PHOENIX)	Thompson, Glasgow	1.12.1888	28.10.89	27.1.91	Sold 1906
WALLAROO (ex-PERSIAN)	Armstrong, Elswick	16.8.1888	5.2.90	31.3.91	Sold 1920

Five of this class were provided under the terms of the Imperial Defence Act of 1887 and were paid for by Australia on the understanding that they were to be stationed in Australian waters. They were, however, manned by the Royal Navy and remained under Admiralty control. They were all originally given 'P' names but were allotted new names of Australian origin in 1890. In design they were modified versions of the *Medea* with the same dimensions and protection but reduced engine power and a main armament of eight 4.7in QF instead of six 6in BL guns. A further four were ordered by the Admiralty under the Naval Defence Act of 1889 but these differed from the Australian group in having the nominal power of the machinery raised from 4000 to 4500ihp for a ½kt improvement in speed although forced draught power was retained at 7500ihp in an attempt to avoid boiler troubles. Their machinery power and speed dropped off after a few years' service although this was of course more marked in the Australian ships.

The main guns were disposed as in the *Medea* except that two were mounted on each side of the upper deck instead of one. All the 3pdr QF guns were mounted on the upper deck with four in the waist and two each at bow and stern firing through embrasured ports. They had a fixed

TT at the stem and stern and two TCs abreast the mainmast, all being carried at upper deck level. The Australian ships had fidded topmasts while the remainder had single pole masts. They were originally classified as second class cruisers but were rerated prior to completion.

Philomel was transferred to the New Zealand Government in 1914, became a base ship in 1921, was sold in 1947 and was scuttled off New Zealand in 1949. *Wallaroo* was reduced to harbour service in 1906 and was renamed *Wallington* in 1949.

Katoomba in the 1890s

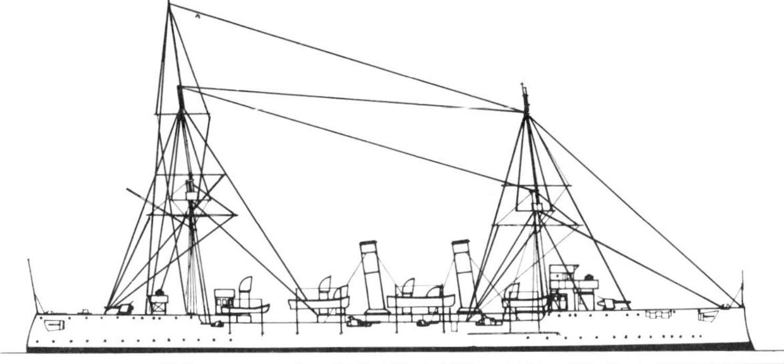

Pioneer 1906

PELORUS class *third class cruisers*

Displacement: 2135t load
Dimensions: 300ft pp, 313ft 6in oa x 36ft 6in x 16ft (*91.44 pp, 95.55 oa x 11.13 x 4.88m*)
Machinery: 2-shaft, 3 cyl TE, 16 Thornycroft watertube boilers (see notes), 5000ihp = 18.5kts natural draught, 7000ihp = 20kts forced draught. Coal 500t
Armour: Deck 1½in-2in, gunshields ¼in, CT 3in
Armament: 8-4in QF, 8-3pdr QF, 3 MGs, 2-18in TT aw
Complement: 224

Name	Builder	Laid down	Launched	Comp	Fate
PANDORA	Portsmouth DYd	–	17.1.1900	1901	Sold 1913
PELORUS	Sheerness DYd	May 1895	15.12.96	1897	Sold 1920
PEGASUS	Palmer, Jarrow	May 1896	4.3.97	1899	Sunk by *Konigsburg* 20.9.1914
PERSEUS	Earle, Hull	May 1896	15.7.97	1901	Sold 1914
PACTOLUS	Armstrong, Elswick	May 1896	21.12.96	Sept 1898	Sold 1921
PIONEER	Chatham DYd	Dec 1897	28.6.99	1900	Scuttled 1931
POMONE	Sheerness DYd	21.12.1896	25.11.97	May 1899	Sold 1922
PROMETHEUS	Earle, Hull	–	20.10.98	–	Sold 1914
PROSERPINE	Sheerness DYd	Mar 1896	5.12.96	1899	Sold 1919
PSYCHE	Devonport DYd	Nov 1897	19.7.1898	1900	Sold 1922
PYRAMUS	Palmer, Jarrow	May 1896	15.5.97	1900	Sold 1920

The *Pelorus* class were very similar in appearance and general arrangement to the earlier *Pearl* class but were slightly smaller, with a lighter armament, and demonstrated a different approach to the problem of obtaining high speed. They had more powerful machinery that the the earlier class with a natural draught power of 5000ihp compared with 4000ihp, but forced draught power was restricted to a realistic 7000ihp which was 500ihp less than that in *Pearl* and her sisters. In order, therefore, to provide for the high designed speed of 20kts they were made longer and narrower than the *Pearls*, with a length to beam ratio of 8.2:1 compared with 6.5:1. The narrower beam also meant a reduction in the level of stability and although their lighter armament compensated for this to some extent, they proved to be poor sea boats, having a heavy roll and being very wet in heavy weather.

The protective deck was 1½in-1¾in on the flat and 1¾in-2in on the slope with the thicker sections over the machinery. Apart from the substitution of 4in QFs for 4.7in QFs, the gun armament was identical to that in the *Pearl* class and was disposed in the same manner.

They were fitted with a variety of boilers to test the qualities of some of the many water tube types available: *Pomone* and *Pactolus* were fitted with Blechynden boilers, *Pelorus* with Normand, *Pegasus* and *Pyramus* with Reed and the remainder with Thornycroft. The results were varied and, while most of the class exceeded their designed power, making between 20 and 21kts on trial, they all suffered from a certain amount of boiler trouble and after a few years' service average maximum speeds were around 16-17kts. The least successful were *Pomone* and *Pactolus*, whose Blechynden boilers were so troublesome that the ships were removed from the effective list after only a few years' service.

Pioneer and *Psyche* were transferred to the RAN in 1912 and 1915 respectively, *Pactolus* became a depot ship in 1912, and *Pomone* became a TS in 1910.

Pyramus about the turn of the century

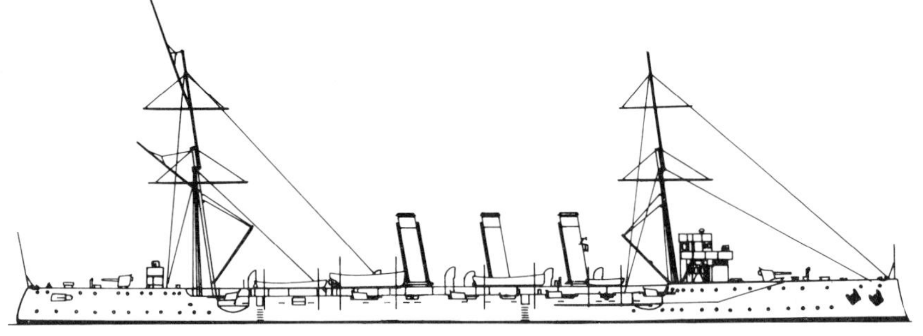

Amethyst 1904

The *Gem* class were the last and largest of Britain's 3rd class cruisers. *Topaze* and *Amethyst* were ordered under the 1902/03 Programme and the other pair under the 1903/04 Programme, while a further four projected vessels were cancelled. In general they followed the style of earlier ships but were faster, carried more guns, were better protected and had improved seakeeping qualities. Two of the 4in guns were fitted on the centreline of the forecastle and poop while the remainder were equally disposed along each side of the upper deck. The 3pdr guns were mounted 4 on each side with 1 on the forecastle, 2 in the waist and 1 on the poop. The protective deck was 1in on the flat and 2in on the slope amidships, reducing to ¾in flat and 1in slope at the ends.

The *Amethyst* was the first warship larger than a destroyer to be fitted with turbines, a modification decided upon so that she could be used for comparative trials with her TE-engined sisters. Turbines were more economic on fuel at high powers but less economic at low powers, and to compensate for this she was also fitted with cruising turbines which gave her an endurance of 5500nm at 10kts compared with 7000nm in her sisters; however, at 20kts her endurance was 3000nm compared with 2000nm in the others. On trials she achieved 23.4kts with 14,200shp and subsequently proved the most reliable ship of the class. All the remaining ships exceeded 22kts on trials, averaging 10,000ihp. *Amethyst* was fitted with Yarrow boilers, *Sapphire* with Reed and the remaining pair with Laird-Normand.

GEM class *third class cruisers*

Displacement: 3000t load
Dimensions: 360ft pp, 373ft 9in x 40ft x 14ft 6in (*109.73 pp, 113.92 x 12.19 x 4.42m*)
Machinery: 2-shaft, 4cyl TE (*Amethyst* 3-shaft Parsons turbines), 10 boilers (see notes), 9800ihp = 21.75kts forced draught (*Amethyst* 12,000shp = 22.5kts.) Coal 750t
Armour: Deck 2in-¾in, gunshields 1in, CT 3in
Armament: 12-4in QF, 8-3pdr QF, 4 MGs, 2-18in TT aw
Complement: 296

Name	Builder	Laid down	Launched	Comp	Fate
AMETHYST	Armstrong, Elswick	7.1.1903	5.11.03	17.3.05	Sold 1920
DIAMOND	Laird, Birkenhead	24.3.1903	6.1.04	Jan 1905	Sold 1921
SAPPHIRE	Palmer, Jarrow	30.3.1903	17.3.04	7.2.05	Sold 1921
TOPAZE	Laird, Birkenhead	14.8.1902	23.7.03	Nov 1904	Sold 1921

Sapphire as completed

ADVENTURE class *scout cruisers*

Displacement: 2640t load
Dimensions: 374ft pp, 395ft oa x 38ft 3in x 12ft 3in (*114.00 pp, 120.4 oa x 11.66 x 3.73m*)
Machinery: 2-shaft, 3 cyl TE, 12 Yarrow boilers, 16,000ihp = 25kts. Coal 450t
Armour: Deck 2in-¾in, CT 3in
Armament: 10-12pdr QF, 8-3pdr QF, 2-18in TT aw
Complement: 268

Name	Builder	Laid down	Launched	Comp	Fate
ADVENTURE (ex-EDDYSTONE)	Armstrong, Elswick	7.1.1904	8.9.04	Oct 1905	Sold 1920
ATTENTIVE	Armstrong, Elswick	8.1.1904	24.11.04	Oct 1905	Sold 1920

These eight cruisers were intended to work in company with destroyers as scouts, to lead torpedo attacks and to back up their flotillas when attacked by enemy destroyers. The Admiralty provided a broad specification for the ships and left the detailed design to the builders, a common practice when ordering torpedo craft but unusual with cruisers. The Admiralty requirement was for a 25kt ship, with a 1½in protective deck or equivalent side armour, shallow draught for operating in inshore waters, and an armament of 10-12pdr, 8-3pdr and 2TT. They were ordered in four pairs which, as might be expected, resulted in four sub-classes that varied substantially in form, machinery and structure. Only one builder, Fairfield, followed traditional small cruiser style in providing a poop as well as a forecastle, but all abandoned the bulwarks amidships which had become a common feature of Victorian cruisers. The Armstrong pair differed from all the others in having

Forward during the First World War

four instead of three funnels and a clipper bow, while the Vickers ships had shorter funnels than the other ships. The Fairfield pair employed side armour abreast the machinery compartments with a protective deck at the ends, while Cammell provided side armour abreast the engine rooms only with a protective deck over the remainder of the ship, an expedient intended to protect the engine cylinders. The remaining ships were fitted in the usual manner with a full length protective deck. The 12pdr QF guns were mounted 3 abreast on the forecastle and aft and two on each side amidships, but this armament was heavily criticised for being too light. Shortly after completion an additional 12pdr QF was added on each side amidships and the 3pdr guns were replaced by 6-6pdr QFs. During 1911/12 they were rearmed with 9-4in guns.

FORWARD class *scout cruisers*

Displacement: 2860t load
Dimensions: 365ft pp, 379ft oa x 39ft 3in x 14ft 3in (*111.25 pp, 115.52 oa x 11.96 x 4.34m*)
Machinery: 2-shaft, 3 cyl TE, 12 Thornycroft boilers, 16,500ihp = 25kts. Coal 500t
Armour: Belt 2in, deck 5/8in-1 1/8in, CT 3in
Armament: 10-12pdr QF, 8-3pdr QF 2-18in TT aw
Complement: 268

Name	Builder	Laid down	Launched	Comp	Fate
FORESIGHT	Fairfield	24.10.1903	8.10.04	8.9.05	Sold 1920
FORWARD	Fairfield	22.10.1903	27.8.04	22.8.05	Sold 1921

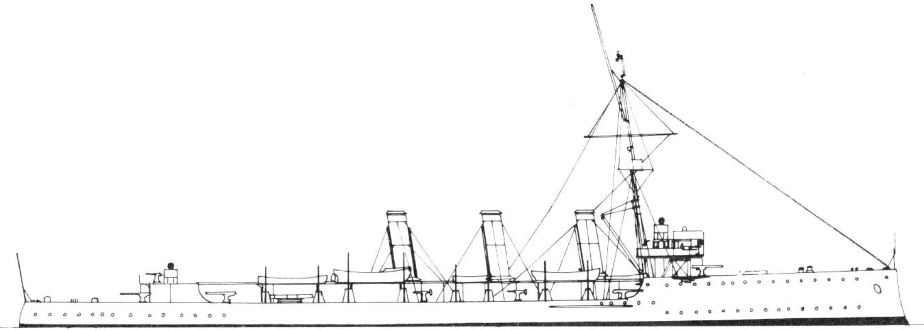

Patrol 1906

PATHFINDER class *scout cruisers*

Displacement: 2900t load
Dimensions: 370ft pp, 379ft oa x 38ft 6in x 13ft (*112.78 pp, 115.52 oa x 11.77 x 3.96m*)
Machinery: 2-shaft, 4 cyl TE, 12 Laird-Normand boilers, 16,500ihp = 25kts. Coal 600t
Armour: Belt 2in, deck 5/8in-1½in, CT 3in
Armament: 10-12pdr QF, 8-3pdr QF, 2-18in TT aw
Complement: 268

Name	Builder	Laid down	Launched	Comp	Fate
PATHFINDER (ex-FASTNET)	Cammell Laird, Birkenhead	15.8.1903	16.7.04	18.7.05	Sunk by *U21* 5.9.14
PATROL	Cammell Laird, Birkenhead	31.10.1903	13.10.04	26.9.05	Sold 1920

SENTINEL class *scout cruisers*

Displacement: 2880t load
Dimensions: 360ft pp, 381ft oa x 40ft x 14ft (*109.73 pp, 116.13 oa x 12.19 x 4.27m*)
Machinery: 2-shaft, 4 cyl TE, 12 Vickers-Express boilers, 17,000ihp = 25kts. Coal 410t
Armour: Deck 5/8in-1½in, CT 3in
Armament: 10-12pdr QF, 8-3pdr QF, 2-18in TT aw
Complement: 268

Name	Builder	Laid down	Launched	Comp	Fate
SENTINEL (ex-INCHKEITH)	Vickers, Barrow	8.6.1903	19.4.04	Apr 1905	Sold 1923
SKIRMISHER	Vickers, Barrow	29.7.1903	7.2.05	July 1905	Sold 1920

(*All uncredited photos in this section CPL*)

Sentinel as completed

TORPEDO CRAFT

A close-up of the destroyer *Bittern*, a Vickers-built 30-knotter of 1897

The 1860s saw the beginnings of torpedo warfare. During the War between the States both Federals and Confederates used spar torpedoes with success. A Liverpool firm even began building spar torpedo boats similar to the 'Davids' for the South, though these were never, apparently, completed. An English naval officer, Harvey, began developing his towing torpedo which would briefly equip a number of Royal Navy vessels in the 1870s. Most importantly the English engineer Robert Whitehead, working at Fiume in Austria (now Rijeka in Yugoslavia) was developing Luppis' original crude concept of a clockwork remote controlled explosive boat into the first practicable 'fish' or 'locomotive' torpedo. For the first time in naval history weapons were appearing which would enable a much smaller vessel to sink a larger ship.

In 1868 the Admiralty received its first notification of Whitehead's experiments. A year later a team of officers from the Mediterranean Fleet visisted Fiume and were impressed by what they saw. In 1870 Whitehead gave a successful demonstration of his device in Britain, and the next year the Royal Navy purchased the 'secret' (the hydrostatic device which was the invention which permitted the torpedo to keep a constant depth), and also manufacturing rights. Though some torpedoes were bought from Whitehead, and later in an emergency from the German Schwartzkopff works, most British torpedoes were to be built at the 'Royal Laboratory', part of the Royal Arsenal at Woolwich.

The question of how the new weapon was to be used was answered in four ways by the Committee set up in 1873. Firstly ordinary ships' boats could be adapted to carry it and soon the steam boats beginning to be carried on board larger warships at this time (and some of the larger rowing and sailing boats as well) were fitted with 'dropping gear' for Whiteheads, and also spar torpedoes.

Secondly, torpedoes could be fitted as part of the armament of conventional types of warship and by the end of the decade most ironclads and large cruising vessels carried several of the new weapons. In 1877 the large frigate *Shah* was the first vessel to use a torpedo in action, though without obtaining a hit, against the piratical Peruvian ironclad *Huascar*. At first above water launching carriages were used (legend has it that the *Shah* found the upended wardroom table more effective for tipping the torpedo over the side) but soon tubes both above and below the waterline became a regular feature of major warships, and remained such well beyond the end of our period.

Thirdly specialised ships could be built for torpedo warfare – comparatively large, fast and probably armoured. Finally small and very fast steam launches specially built for carrying torpedoes could be used. This prescient document outlined the development of the specialised torpedo vessel for the rest of the century.

THE FIRST BRITISH TORPEDO VESSELS

Vesuvius and *Polyphemus* represent two quite different attempts to produce a seagoing vessel designed round the submerged torpedo tube. Though in many ways *Polyphemus* was an enlarged and much more powerful version of the earlier ship, her mode of attack would have been very different, as *Vesuvius* would have relied on stealth and the larger vessel on speed and protection. Both represent interesting and promising approaches to the problem of using the new weapon, and neither deserve the somewhat contemptuous dismissal that has been their lot from subsequent commentators. The concept of the seagoing torpedo ship was carried on into the 'torpedo cruisers', but these in the event proved to be more cruisers than torpedo vessels, and they have been dealt with as such.

TORPEDO BOATS

Already by the time the Torpedo Committee report appeared two new specialist firms, Thornycroft and Yarrow, which had successfully built very light and fast steel launches for commercial and pleasure use, had modified their designs to take spar (and in at least one case, towing) torpedoes for foreign navies. By 1874 Thornycroft were pestering the Royal Navy to order a torpedo boat, and two years later were building *Lightning, TB No 1*. This was the first 'First Class' TB intended for coastal defence use. Thornycroft also built the first group of 'Second Class' TBs, light and small enough to be carried in the davits of a large ship. These boats were intended for offensive use, attacking enemy harbours or taking part in fleet actions after being lowered from their mother ship. A merchantman, *Hecla*, was converted to operate them, and later the specially built and cruiser-like *Vulcan* was ordered for this purpose. Both were also fitted as depot ships for larger TBs and for all forms of mine and torpedo stores.

The Second Class boats proved to be rather fragile, and eventually, by way of experience with the wooden boats built by Whites as Second Class *TBs 1-12*, it became obvious that it was better to rely on the sturdier, if slower, steam pinnaces and other craft built primarily as ships' boats. For a while, however, most battleships had carried a couple of the small steel boats. The numbering system of Second Class boats in somewhat confusing, as the earliest boats were numbered from 51 on, presumably with the idea that the numbering of First Class boats would never rise above 50. Later a series of wooden boats were numbered 1 to 12, whilst the final series of Yarrow boats started working backwards from 50! The majority were sold around 1905.

There was a steady increase in the size, speed and power of the larger torpedo boats, as it became evident that earlier boats were insufficiently seaworthy for most purposes, and advances in marine engineering and torpedo technology produced improved machinery and weapons. Most were built by specialist firms, who were able to tackle the skilled and expensive task of producing very lightly but strongly built craft. The most successful were Thornycroft and Yarrow, both Thames firms at this time, whilst White in the Isle of Wight were particularly successful in building wooden Second Class boats. It is worth noting that, whilst for nearly all other types of vessel it was the Admiralty that produced the design, in this specialised case it was the firms that drew up the designs and also did much experimental work on hull construction, lines and machinery.

From the first torpedo boat until nearly the end of our period the most important demand was for speed, more and more speed. Builders, Admiralties and the general public were mesmerised by unrealistically high trial speeds obtained in smooth water and the most favourable conditions. The Royal Navy showed rather more realisation than most of the need for improving seakeeping ability, and the fact that trial speed was a poor indication of what would be possible in action. Even the Royal Navy, however, did not abandon the 'trial speed' mentality in a major way until right at the end of our period when the 'River' class destroyers were built. There was, of course, very little in the way of active service experience to show that seakeeping ability, the exploitation of surprise in attacks, adequate torpedo and gun armaments and reliability were all far more important than smooth-water speed.

TORPEDO GUNBOATS

In a sense the story of the development of the seagoing torpedo vessel is continued by both the torpedo gunboat and the destroyer; however, the primary purpose of both types was defensive. By the time of the Russian scare of 1885 the Admiralty was very well aware of the great threat posed by the numerous torpedo boats of both France and Russia, particularly to a British fleet attempting to fulfil its traditional rôle of blockading enemy bases.

One answer to this threat was to produce smaller and faster variants of contemporary cruiser designs as 'torpedo gunboats,' sometimes known as 'catchers,' powerfully armed for their size with guns, and also carrying torpedoes so that they could take over the job of torpedo attack from the boats that it was hoped they would have the speed to catch and destroy. They were not a great success, one reason being that they had very bad boiler trouble and could not make their intended speed. The second reason was linked with this: the fact that the contemporary obsession with speed, and with hunting down enemy boats, meant that their failure to keep up with the boats they were supposed to catch, even in the good weather conditions usual on summer manoeuvres, ensured that they were condemned out of hand. The fact that they could probably still have accomplished an adequate job by escorting the fleet and preventing torpedo attacks, and that rough weather conditions might have made a difference to the relative performance of TB and TGB, tended to be ignored. In the event the survivors gave useful service as minesweepers during the 1914–18 war, by which time most had been reboilered.

DESTROYERS

It was the Royal Navy which introduced the new type of warship known as the torpedo boat destroyer, or destroyer for short, in the mid-1890s. However the normally accepted version of the story behind that introduction, which attributes it to the joint inspiration of 'Jackie' Fisher and Yarrow, is only a half truth. The destroyer was basically an enlarged, slightly faster torpedo boat, given a more powerful gun armament. The 1880s had seen several attempts to produce an effective counter to the torpedo boat by enlarging it and giving it more guns, the '125-footers' and *Swift* (*TB 81*) being cases in point, and the term 'torpedo boat destroyer' had already been used for some of these types. The Germans had been building their 'Division Boats', though admittedly not for anti-torpedo boat work and without a strengthened gun armament. Leading torpedo boat firms (with both Thornycroft and Yarrow to the fore) had been producing designs for destroyer-type vessels for some years before the first destroyers were ordered.

The catalysts which produced the first order for the new type were the combination of the fear of the increasing number of new, large and fast torpedo boats being built by the French, the continuing insufficiency of the torpedo gunboat designs, and the presence of a dynamic Controller in Fisher, backed by an equally active and powerful Board of Admiralty. Fisher consulted with *both* the leading torpedo boat specialists (it is worth noting that Thornycroft actually obtained their order for destroyers a couple of days before Yarrow) and several other builders were given an opportunity to tender for vessels of 200 or 300 tons, capable of 27kts. (Thornycroft actually offered 28kts for their larger design.) Eventually the Board decided on the smaller design, but with the armament of the larger one, which resulted in some increase in dimensions and tonnage in the designs which were built.

From the start, though the primary purpose was to sink torpedo boats, the possibility of using the new vessels to replace TBs for torpedo attack was borne in mind. The earliest destroyers had alternative armaments for one purpose or the other, but their immediate successors had a single outfit which combined the two. As the faster, more powerful and more seaworthy destroyer rendered the torpedo boat virtually obsolescent, it took over the rôle of the smaller vessel. Inevitably the destroyers themselves increased in size as time went on, and the need for, in the first instance, more speed, and, later, greater seaworthiness, influenced new designs. By the end of our period, with the 'River' class, the torpedo boat destroyer, which was only a slightly larger torpedo boat, had changed into the true destroyer, a very different sort of vessel and one which fitted the 1870s conception of a purpose-designed seagoing torpedo vessel.

Most reference works split early British destroyers into 'A', 'B', 'C' and 'D' classes. This was a classification adopted for ease of recognition in September 1913, and is of little use in giving a historical account of the development of the destroyer. The 'A' class were the '27-knotters', the 'B', 'C' and 'D' classes being the '30-knotters' with, respectively, four (or more), three or two funnels. The diversity is in fact far greater, as each builder produced his own design, within certain broad outlines set by the Admiralty, and then usually built slightly modified versions of it for each subsequent order. Of course the change from 27kts to 30 kts as a requirement meant a change in basic designs, as did the ordering of the 'River' class, and the '33-knotters' and turbine boats were different again.

CONCLUSIONS

The Royal Navy's initial response to the torpedo was to build up a force of largely experimental vessels, *Vesuvius*, *Polyphemus*, the *Lightnings* and the early Second Class boats. There was then a comparative lull until the Russian war scare of 1885/6 produced a mild panic at the thought of the growing Russian and French torpedo flotillas, and the mass production of the '125-footer' torpedo boats. With the 1889 Naval Defence Act the 'Dark Ages' of the Victorian Navy came to a final end, and steady accretions of TBs, TGBs and finally TBDs built up the British torpedo force.

In the 1870s and 1880s there had been a steady increase in the range, speed, reliability and explosive power of the torpedo; the 14in replaced the original crude 16in, then the 18in began to enter service in the early 1890s. However by this time the great improvement in range, accuracy and rate of fire of guns, made possible by improvements in metallurgy, explosives and hydraulics, were making the torpedo seem a much less dangerous weapon. This advantage of gun over torpedo was only temporary; the end of the century saw the adoption of gyroscopic guidance and of internal combustion (so called 'heated air') in torpedoes with an enormous increase in both range and accuracy. These developments, together with the emergence of the submarine as a viable weapon, bring our period to an end with appropriate indications of future developments.

VESUVIUS *torpedo vessel*

Displacement: 245t
Dimensions: 90ft pp x 22ft x 8½ft (*27.43pp x 6.71 x 2.59m*)
Machinery: 2-shaft compound, 350ihp = 9.7kts
Armament: 1 bow 16in TT sub
Complement: 15

Name	Builder	Laid down	Launched	Comp	Fate
VESUVIUS	Pembroke DYd	16.3.1873	24.3.74	11.9.74	BU 1924

Commenced soon after the Royal Navy adopted the Whitehead torpedo, *Vesuvius* has a better claim to the title of that services' first torpedo boat than the celebrated *Lightning*. She had a fairly deep hull, a very low freeboard, and engines as near to noiseless as could be made. To make her as inconspicuous as possible she was built without a funnel, smoke being released through vents along her sides, and she burnt coke so not much smoke was produced in the first place. She carried a battery of reload torpedoes in the compartment from which her submerged bow tube was operated. With her low silhouette, and quiet engines she would have stood a fair chance of making successful surprise night attacks on enemy harbours, but contemporary opinion was obsessed by speed and she was overshadowed by the somewhat impractical early torpedo boats. She was soon relegated to experimental and instructional work for the naval torpedo school, HMS *Vernon*.

When she was fitting out at Portsmouth after being towed from Pembroke she was given a tall funnel, to make it easier to raise steam, and never seems to have used her smoke ducts.

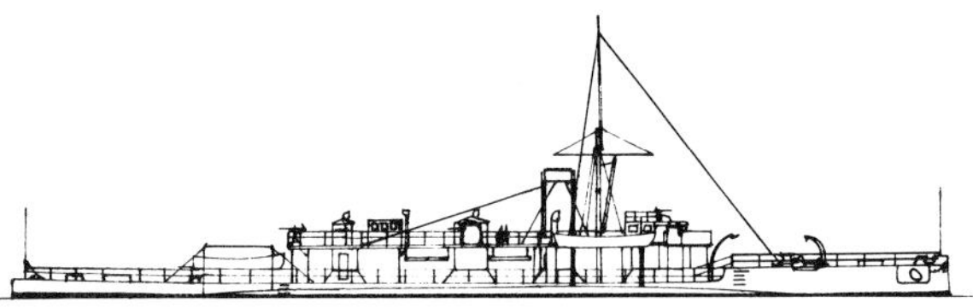
Polyphemus as completed 1882

POLYPHEMUS *torpedo ram*

Displacement: 2640t
Dimensions: 240ft pp x 40ft x 20½ft (*73.15 pp x 12.19 x 6.25m*)
Machinery: 2-shaft compound, 7000ihp = 18kts (forced draught)
Armament: 5 14in TT sub, 18 torpedoes, 6-1in Nordenfeld twin-barrelled MGs
Complement: 146

Name	Builder	Laid down	Launched	Comp	Fate
POLYPHEMUS	Chatham DYd	21.9.1878	15.6.81	Sept 1882	BU1903

This unusual vessel is one of the best known Victorian warships, but for all the wrong reasons. Regarded as a freak designed mainly for ramming, she was in fact a well thought out and combat-worthy design intended chiefly for torpedo attack. Her story can be said to start when Nathaniel Barnaby, the Director of Naval Construction, produced a design for a much larger and faster version of *Vesuvius* in 1872, before that vessel was even commenced. However when Barnaby finally came to produce the definitive design for *Polyphemus* the concept had become both larger and more complex. Four broadside submerged tubes were added to the bow tube, and a truly impressive number of reloads were carried. In case the broadside tubes – a new concept at the time – were not the success they proved to be, *Polyphemus* was given a spur ram so that she could also use ramming as a method of attack. The design documents show quite conclusively that ramming was very much a secondary function, and the old story that she was inspired by Admiral Sartorius' ideas on steam rams is completely false.

To enable *Polyphemus* to bring her powerful torpedo battery to bear she was not only given the phenomenal speed for her day of 18kts but also was protected by an armoured curved deck of 3in steel. The basic form of the protected part of the hull was like a cigar, or a submarine, the hull being built up on top of this to give a more conventional, if low-lying appearance.

It took some time to eliminate the teething troubles of both broadside tubes and boilers, but thereafter *Polyphemus* was an eminently battle-worthy vessel. However, there were few obvious functions for her in a peacetime navy, her main achievement apart from proving the validity of broadside tubes being the famous episode of charging the boom at Berehaven (Ireland) at full speed and spectacularly demolishing it. Gradually the increasing size and range of QF guns made it less likely that she would be able to survive to bring her torpedoes into action (it should be remembered that when she was designed guns heavy enough to pierce her armour were too slow-firing and difficult to train to stand much chance of hitting so fast a ship). She herself was rearmed with 6pdr guns in place of the Nordenfelds.

TORPEDO GUNBOATS

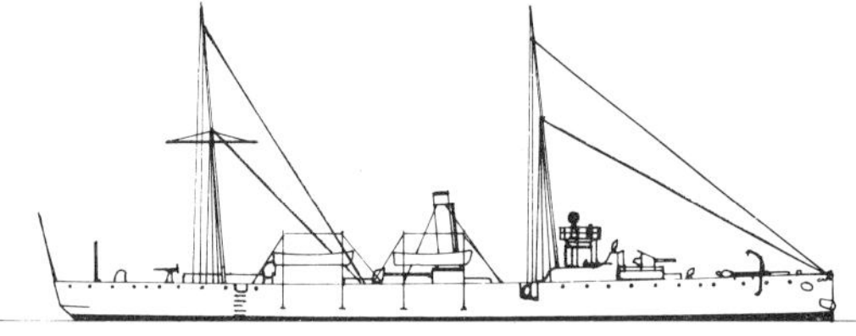
Rattlesnake as completed 1887

RATTLESNAKE *torpedo gunboat*

Displacement: 550t
Dimensions: 200ft pp x 23ft x 10ft 4in (*60.96 pp x 7.01 x 3.15m*)
Machinery: 2-shaft TE, 2700ihp = 19¼kts (forced draught)
Armament: 4-14in TT, 4 reloads, 1-5in, 6-3pdr
Complement: 66

Name	Builder	Laid down	Launched	Comp	Fate
RATTLESNAKE	Laird	16.11.1885	11.9.86	May 1887	Sold 1910

Unlike later TGBs *Rattlesnake* had a protective deck of ¾in steel. She had bow and stern fixed tubes and one training tube on either beam. The 4in gun was mounted forward, and she was the same length as contemporary small cruisers but much narrower and shallower, the latter feature being intended to make torpedoes pass harmlessly under her. Ordered as a result of the Russian war scare, she proved a successful vessel, being kept in service, and still able to make her original speed, when her near-sisters of the *Grasshopper* class had all been removed from the effective list.

GRASSHOPPER class *torpedo gunboats*

Name	Builder	Laid down	Launched	Comp	Fate
GRASSHOPPER	Sheerness DYd	27.4.1886	30.8.87	1888	Sold 1905
SANDFLY	Devonport DYd	19.4.1886	20.9.87	July 1888	Sold 1905
SPIDER	Devonport DYd	9.6.1886	17.10.87	Dec 1888	Sold 1903

Very similar to *Rattlesnake*, but 526t, these vessels were engined by Maudslay. Their performance was not as good as their near-sister however.

This numerically large class showed a considerable increase in size over the *Grasshoppers*, and was sometimes known as the *Assaye* or *Gossamer* class. One of the torpedo tubes was fixed in the bow, the others in paired mounts on either side amidships. The resemblance to contemporary small cruisers was marked. Whilst the vessels built in the Royal Dockyards were allocated to the Royal Navy, the four built by Armstrong were allocated to colonial stations, two to the Royal Indian Marine, and two, originally named *Whiting* and *Wizard* (the names were changed in 1890) to the Australian station. *Gossamer, Seagull, Skipjack* and *Spanker* were converted to minesweepers in 1908/9. *Sharpshooter* was renamed *Northampton* in 1904 and relegated to instructional duties. She was broken up in 1922. The original intention had been to fit a similar gun armament to the *Grasshoppers* (1-4in, 6-3pdr) but trials at Elswick had shown that the 4.7in QF gun could fire 10 times per minute as against 2 times for the old 4in BL so the new gun was adopted instead. Initially the class suffered from hull weakness.

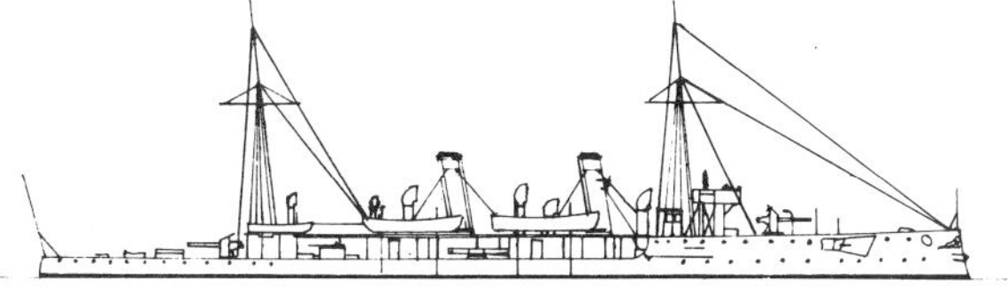

Gossamer after reboilering 1905

SHARPSHOOTER class *torpedo gunboats*

Displacement: 735t
Dimensions: 230ft pp x 27ft x 10½ft (*70.10 pp x 8.23 x 3.20m*)
Machinery: 2-shaft TE, 3500ihp = 19kts (forced draught)
Armament: 5-14in TT, 3 reloads, 2-4.7in, 4-3pdr
Complement: 91

Name	Builder	Laid down	Launched	Comp	Fate
ASSAYE (RIM)	Armstrong	19.11.1888	11.2.90	Feb 1892	Sold 1904
GLEANER	Sheerness DYd	21.1.1889	9.1.90	21.12.91	Sold 1905
GOSSAMER	Sheerness DYd	21.1.1889	9.1.90	16.9.91	Sold 1920
PLASSEY (RIM)	Armstrong	19.11.1888	5.7.90	Feb 1892	Sold 1904
SALAMANDER	Chatham DYd	23.4.1888	31.5.89	July 1891	Sold 1906
SEAGULL	Chatham DYd	23.4.1888	31.5.89	Jan 1891	Lost in collision 1918
SHARPSHOOTER	Devonport DYd	13.1.1888	30.11.88	Aug 1889	Harbour service 1904
SHELDRAKE	Chatham DYd	4.7.1888	30.3.89	18.3.90	BU 1907
SKIPJACK	Chatham DYd	4.7.1888	30.4.89	July 1891	BU 1920
SPANKER	Devonport DYd	12.4.1888	27.2.89	17.10.90	BU 1920
SPEEDWELL	Devonport DYd	18.4.1888	15.3.89	1.7.90	BU 1920
BOOMERANG (Australia)	Armstrong	17.8.1899	24.7.89	14.2.91	Sold 1905
KARAKATTA (Australia)	Armstrong	17.8.1888	27.8.89	Feb 1891	Sold 1905

Gleaner, a *Sharpshooter* class torpedo gunboat, as built

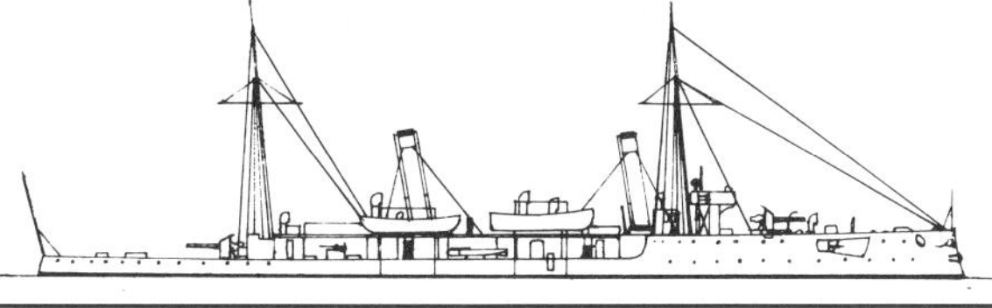

Circe 1897

ALARM class *torpedo gunboats*

The *Alarms* were basically slightly enlarged versions of the *Sharpshooters*, differing little in appearance except for *Speedy* which was the only TGB to have three funnels. She was also the most successful of her type, as instead of having the unreliable and troublesome locomotive boilers of her sisters (these boilers worked reasonably well in smaller craft, but were unsuitable for such large vessels as the TGBs) she was fitted with Thornycroft's own design of water-tube boilers. In consequence she was far more reliable and could keep her speed better than the other ships. She was much the largest warship built by that firm up to that date, and they built her to the same high standards as their torpedo boats. In 1908/9 *Speedy, Circe, Jason, Leda, Niger* and *Hebe* were converted to minesweepers, though the latter almost immediately became a submarine depot ship; *Antelope* was similarly converted in 1915. She was broken up in 1919, *Onyx* was renamed *Vulcan II* in the same year and broken up in her turn in 1924, whilst *Hebe* suffered the same fate in 1920.

Displacement: 810t
Dimensions: 230ft pp x 27ft x 12ft (*70.10 pp x 8.23 x 3.66m*)
Machinery: 2-shaft TE, 3500ihp = 18.7kts (forced draught)
Armament: 5-14in TT, 3 reloads, (except 3-18in TT in *Speedy, Jason, Niger, Jaseur, Onyx*), 2-4.7in, 4-3pdr, 1 Gardner MG
Complement: 91

Name	Builder	Laid down	Launched	Comp	Fate
ALARM	Sheerness DYd	25.6.1891	13.9.92	Mar 1894	Sold 1907
ANTELOPE	Devonport DYd	21.10.1889	12.7.93	May 1894	Harbour service 1914
CIRCE	Sheerness DYd	11.1.1890	14.6.92	May 1893	BU 1920
HEBE	Sheerness DYd	11.1.1890	15.6.92	9.10.94	Submarine depot ship 1910
JASEUR	Naval Construction & Armament Co	14.9.1891	24.9.92	July 1893	Sold 1905
JASON	Naval Construction & Armament Co	7.9.1891	14.5.92	June 1893	Mined 1917
LEDA	Sheerness DYd	25.6.1891	13.9.92	Nov 1893	BU 1922
NIGER	Naval Construction & Armament Co	17.9.1891	17.12.92	25.4.93	Torpeoed 1914
ONYX	Laird	8.10.1891	7.9.92	Jan 1894	Submarine depot ship 1907
RENARD	Laird	26.10.1891	6.12.92	Jan 1894	Sold 1905
SPEEDY	Thornycroft	4.1.1892	18.5.93	20.2.94	Mined 1914

1

2

3

These were rather odd-looking ships, with their two funnels very far apart, and, unlike their predecessors, they had a raised poop as well as a raised forecastle. However they were only slightly larger and more powerfully armed versions of the *Alarms*, sharing their predecessors' weaknesses. They were building at the same time as the first destroyers, and were immediately put into the shade by these smaller but faster vessels. In 1914 all except *Halcyon* and *Hazard* were converted to minesweepers, the former vessels becoming, respectively, minesweeper and submarine depot ships. *Hazard* was lost in a collision in 1918, and *Halcyon* was broken up in 1919. In 1918 *Dryad* was briefly relegated to harbour duty under the name of *Hamadryad*.

1. *Jason* in the Thames, 1904, after reboilering
2. *Speedy*, the only TGB with three funnels
3. *Hazard*, a *Dryad* class TGB

DRYAD or HALCYON class *torpedo gunboats*

Displacement: 1070t
Dimensions: 250ft pp x 30½ft x 11½ft (*76.20 pp x 9.30 x 3.51m*)
Machinery: 2-shaft TE, 3500ihp = 18.2kts (forced draught)
Armament: 5-18in TT, 2 reloads, 2-4.7in, 4-6pdr, 1 Nordenfeld 5-barrelled MG
Complement: 120

Name	Builder	Laid down	Launched	Comp	Fate
DRYAD	Chatham DYd	15.4.1893	22.11.93	July 1894	BU 1920
HALCYON	Devonport DYd	2.1.1893	6.4.94	Feb 1895	Depot ship 1915
HARRIER	Devonport DYd	21.1.1893	20.2.94	Feb 1895	BU 1920
HAZARD	Pembroke DYd	1.12.1892	17.2.94	Sept 1894	Depot ship 1915
HUSSAR	Devonport DYd	3.4.1893	3.7.94	Jan 1895	BU 1921

DESTROYERS

The first 5 destroyers were 26-knotters with an armament of 3-18in TT (one fixed bow tube, two single deck tubes), 1-12pdr and 3-6pdr. This was the armament carried, but provision was made for landing the two deck tubes and replacing them by an extra 2-6pdr if they were to be used entirely for anti-torpedo boat work. By 1902 they were only fitted with the bow tube, the 12pdr and 3-6pdr. All these destroyers had twin shafts and triple expansion engines, though the Thornycroft boats had a special four cylinder triple expansion design. *Havock* was the only destroyer with locomotive boilers, and with this well-tried installation she could therefore be completed before the others, the first destroyer. She had only two funnels very close together whilst *Hornet* with water-tube boilers had four.

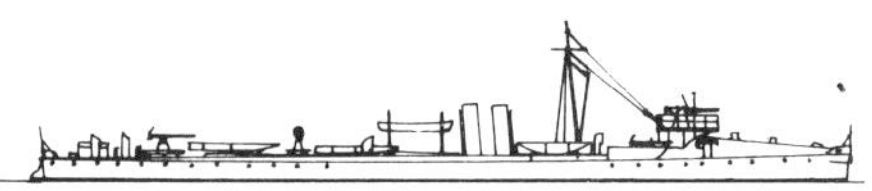

Havock as completed 1894

1892 ORDER: Yarrow *26-knotters*

Displacement: 275ft
Dimensions: 185ft oa, 180ft pp x 18½ft x 7¼ft (*56.38 oa, 54.86 pp x 5.64 x 2.21m*)

Name	Laid down	Launched	Comp	Fate
HAVOCK	July 1892	12.8.93	Jan 1894	BU 1912
HORNET	July 1892	23.12.93	July 1894	BU 1909

1892 ORDER: Thornycroft *26-knotters*

Rather more strongly built than the Yarrow vessels, these two were also faster, though they took longer to build. *Daring* made nearly 28¼kts with 4644ihp on the measured mile. Like most subsequent Thornycroft destroyers they had two funnels (so that they would resemble torpedo boats) and flat sterns.

Displacement: 280t
Dimensions: 185ft oa x 19ft x 7ft (*56.38 oa x 5.79 x 2.13m*)
Machinery: 4000ihp = 27½kts

Name	Laid down	Launched	Comp	Fate
DARING	July 1892	25.11.93	Feb 1895	BU 1912
DECOY	July 1892	2.2.94	June 1895	Collision 1904

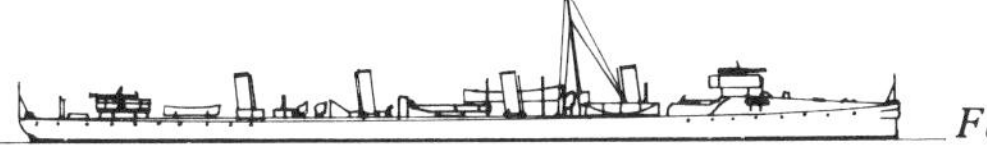

Ferret 1906

1893 ORDER: Laird *26-knotters*

Whilst not specialising in building torpedo boats, Laird had already had some success in building torpedo vessels and were a logical choice to follow Thornycroft and Yarrow in laying down destroyers. They produced a four funnelled design with French-designed (Normand) boilers.

Displacement: 280t
Dimensions: 199ft oa, 195ft pp x 19¼ft x 9ft (*60.66 oa, 59.44 pp x 5.87 x 2.74m*)
Machinery: 4475ihp = 27¼kts

Name	Laid down	Launched	Comp	Fate
FERRET	July 1893	9.12.93	March 1895	Sunk as target 1911
LYNX	July 1893	24.1.94	Aug 1895	BU 1912

1893-4 INITIAL ORDER: Thornycroft *27-knotters*

Before the *Havock* had completed it was decided to order another six destroyers from Thornycroft and Yarrow. Another nine were ordered from other builders making up, a few months later, the 1893/94 Programme. Apart from a slight increase in size the main difference was that the gun armament was increased by 2-6pdr. The first six (the Thornycroft and Yarrow boats) had a bow tube fitted, but it was found to throw up clouds of spray in anything except a flat calm, had a bad effect on seakeeping and was soon removed. Thereafter all had the following armament which was to be standard on all destroyers up to and including the 'River' class: 2-18in TT, 1-12pdr, 5-6pdr.

The *Ardent* class were larger versions of the *Daring*, also with two funnels.

Displacement: 265t (295t full load)
Dimensions: 200½ft oa, 200ft pp x 19ft x 7ft 1in (*61.11 oa, 60.96 pp x 5.79 x 2.16m*)

Name	Laid down	Launched	Comp	Fate
ARDENT	Dec 1893	16.10.94	April 1895	BU 1911
BOXER	March 1894	28.11.94	June 1895	Collision 1918
BRUISER	April 1894	27.2.95	June 1895	BU 1914

Dasher, a Yarrow-built 27-knotter of 1894

1893-4 INITIAL ORDER: Yarrow *27-knotters*

Slightly enlarged versions of the *Hornet* and, like most Yarrow-built vessels, both fast and lightly built. Overall length varied slightly.

Displacement: 255t (295t full load)
Dimensions: 195ft oa, 190ft 8in pp x 18½ft x 7¼ft (*59.44 oa, 58.11 pp x 5.64 x 2.21m*)
Machinery: 3800ihp

Name	Laid down	Launched	Comp	Fate
CHARGER	Nov 1893	15.9.94	Feb 1896	BU 1912
DASHER	Dec 1893	28.11.94	March 1896	BU 1912
HASTY	Dec 1893	16.6.94	May 1896	BU 1912

1893-4 FOLLOW UP ORDER: Doxford *27-knotters*

The Admiralty accepted a slightly lower contract speed from Doxford than from any other builder, and these boats were officially only credited with 26kts, though both made over 27 on trials. They had three funnels.

Displacement: 260t (325t full load)
Dimensions: 200¼ft oa, 196ft pp x 19ft x 7¾ft (*61.04 oa, 59.74 pp x 5.79 x 2.36m*)
Machinery: 4200ihp

Name	Laid down	Launched	Comp	Fate
HARDY	4.6.1894	16.12.95	Aug 1896	BU 1911
HAUGHTY	28.5.1894	18.9.95	Aug 1896	BU 1912

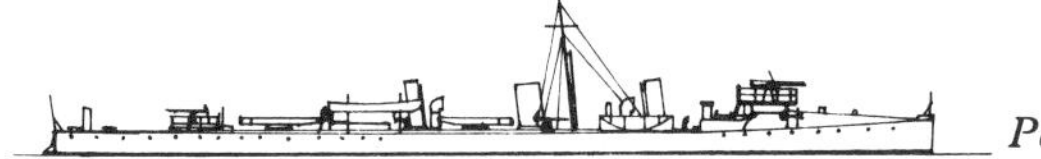

Porcupine as completed 1896

It was with these three funnelled boats that Palmer began to establish their reputation of building the most sea-worthy of all the builders' destroyers.

1893-4 FOLLOW UP ORDER: Palmer *27-knotters*

Displacement: 275t (320t full load)
Dimensions: 204½ft oa, 200ft pp x 19½ft x 8ft *(62.26 oa, 60.96 pp x 5.94 x 2.44m)*
Machinery: 3900ihp

Name	Laid down	Launched	Comp	Fate
JANUS	28.3.1894	12.3.95	Nov 1895	BU 1914
LIGHTNING	28.3.1894	10.4.95	Jan 1896	Mined 1915
PORCUPINE	28.3.1894	19.9.95	March 1896	BU 1920

These vessels had four funnels, the middle pair closely spaced.

1893-4 FOLLOW UP ORDER: Earle *27-knotters*

Displacement: 305t (340t full load)
Dimensions: 204¾ft oa, 200ft pp x 19½ft x 7¾ft *(62.41 oa, 60.96 pp x 5.94 x 2.36m)*
Machinery: 3600ihp

Name	Laid down	Launched	Comp	Fate
SALMON	12.3.1894	15.1.95	Jan 1896	BU 1912
SNAPPER	2.4.1894	30.1.95	Jan 1896	BU 1912

Four funnelled, slightly improved versions of the earlier Laird boats.

1893-4 FOLLOW UP ORDER: Laird *27-knotters*

Displacement: 290t (345t full load)
Dimensions: 213ft oa, 208ft pp x 19¼ft x 9½ft *(64.92 oa, 63.40 pp x 5.87 x 2.90m)*
Machinery: 4400ihp

Name	Laid down	Launched	Comp	Fate
BANSHEE	March 1894	17.11.94	July 1895	BU 1912
CONTEST	March 1894	1.12.94	July 1895	BU 1911
DRAGON	March 1894	15.12.94	June 1895	BU 1912

These three funnelled vessels had some difficulty in reaching their contract speed, which explains both their late entry into service and their builder's failure to win any contracts for 30-knotters.

Wizard was unique in having inward turning propellers, which made her very difficult to handle. As one of her captains put it, 'she was notorious amongst destroyers for her contrary ways'.

1893-4 FOLLOW UP ORDER: White *27-knotters*

Displacement: 320t (360t full load)
Dimensions: 205½ft oa, 200ft pp x 20ft x 8¼ft *(62.64 oa, 60.96 pp x 6.10 x 2.51m)*
Machinery: 4500ihp

Name	Laid down	Launched	Comp	Fate
CONFLICT	3.1.1894	13.12.94	July 1899	BU 1920
TEAZER	3.2.1894	9.2.95	March 1899	BU 1912
WIZARD	3.4.1894	26.2.95	July 1899	BU 1920

Zephyr, a 27-knotter of 1895, after reboilering

These were the only destroyers built with one funnel until the Italians built some in the 1930s. They were also quite the most unsuccessful of the 27-knotters, and their complete failure to meet the contract speed finally drove their builder out of business. They had to be reboilered, and even then could only make 26kts. The reboilering meant that they eventually entered service as four funnelled ships.

1893-4 FOLLOW UP ORDER: Hanna Donald and Wilson *27-knotters*

Displacement: 275t (320t full load)
Dimensions: 204¼ft oa, 200ft pp x 19ft x 7¼ft *(62.26 oa, 60.96 pp x 5.79 x 2.21m)*
Machinery: 4000ihp

Name	Laid down	Launched	Comp	Fate
FERVENT	27.3.1894	20.3.95	June 1900	BU 1920
ZEPHYR	23.4.1894	10.5.95	July 1901	BU 1920

Two funnels.

1893-4 FOLLOW UP ORDER: Fairfield *27-knotters*

Displacement: 275t (310t full load)
Dimensions: 197¼ft oa, 194ft pp x 19ft 5in x 7½ft *(60.12 oa, 59.13 pp x 5.92 x 2.29m)*
Machinery: 4000ihp

Name	Laid down	Launched	Comp	Fate
HANDY	7.6.1894	9.3.95	Oct 1895	BU 1916
HART	7.6.1894	27.3.95	Jan 1896	BU 1912
HUNTER	7.6.1894	28.12.95	May 1896	BU 1912

Ranger, a Hawthorn Leslie-built 27-knotter of 1895

Sturdy vessels with three funnels.

1893-4 FOLLOW UP ORDER: Hawthorn Leslie *27-knotters*

Displacement: 310t (340t full load)
Dimensions: 204ft oa, 200ft pp x 19ft x 8ft 7in (*62.18 oa, 60.96 pp x 5.79 x 2.62m*)
Machinery: 4000ihp

Name	Laid down	Launched	Comp	Fate
OPOSSUM	17.9.1894	9.8.95	March 1896	BU 1920
RANGER	17.9.1894	4.10.95	June 1896	BU 1920
SUNFISH	29.8.1894	28.5.95	Feb 1896	BU 1920

Three funnelled vessels built with great speed by the Clydeside yard.

1893-4 FOLLOW UP ORDER: J & G Thomson *27-knotters*

Displacement: 280t (325t full load)
Dimensions: 203¾ft oa, 200ft pp x 19½ft x 6¾ft (*62.10 oa, 60.96 pp x 5.94 x 2.06m*)
Machinery: 4100ihp

Name	Laid down	Launched	Comp	Fate
ROCKET	14.2.1894	14.8.94	July 1895	BU 1912
SHARK	14.2.1894	22.9.94	July 1895	BU 1911
SURLY	14.2.1894	10.11.94	July 1895	BU 1920

Three funnels.

1893-4 FOLLOW UP ORDER: Naval Construction & Armament Co *27-knotters*

Displacement: 300t (340t full load)
Dimensions: 194½ft oa, 190ft pp x 19ft x 7ft 7in (*59.28 oa, 57.91 pp x 5.79 x 2.31m*)
Machinery: 4000ihp

Name	Laid down	Launched	Comp	Fate
SKATE	20.3.1894	13.3.95	Jan 1896	BU 1907
STARFISH	22.3.1894	26.1.95	Jan 1896	BU 1912
STURGEON	1.3.1894	21.7.94	Jan 1896	BU 1912

Three funnels.

1893-4 FOLLOW UP ORDER: Armstong *27-knotters*

Displacement: 320t (355t full load)
Dimensions: 204¼ft oa, 200ft pp x 19ft x 7¾ft (*62.26 oa, 60.96 pp x 5.79 x 2.36m*)
Machinery: 4500ihp

Name	Laid down	Launched	Comp	Fate
SPITFIRE	4.6.1894	7.6.95	Nov 1896	BU 1912
SWORDFISH	4.6.1894	27.3.95	Dec 1896	BU 1910

Three funnels.

1893-4 FOLLOW UP ORDER Thames Iron Works *27-knotter*

Displacement: 310t (365t full load)
Dimensions: 204½ft oa, 200ft pp x 20ft x 7½ft (*62.33 oa, 60.96 pp x 6.10 x 2.29m*)
Machinery: 4800ihp

Name	Laid down	Launched	Comp	Fate
ZEBRA	July 1894	3.12.95	Jan 1900	BU 1914

1894-5 ORDERS: Thornycroft *30-knotters*

Displacement: 310t light (350t full load)
Dimensions: 210ft oa, 208ft pp x 19½ft x 7ft (*64.01 oa, 63.40 pp x 5.94 x 2.13m*)
Machinery: 5700ihp

Name	Laid down	Launched	Comp	Fate
DESPERATE	1.7.1895	15.2.96	Feb 1897	BU 1920
FAME	4.7.1895	15.4.96	June 1897	BU 1921
FOAM	16.7.1895	8.10.96	July 1897	BU 1914
MALLARD	13.9.1895	19.11.96	Oct 1897	BU 1920

The successful trials of the first destroyers, particularly *Daring,* showed that higher speeds than the Admiralty had at first thought possible could be obtained, and in 1894 Thornycroft, Yarrow and Laird were all asked to submit designs for destroyers capable of 30kts, though at that stage orders could not be placed immediately. The first orders went to Thornycroft and Laird, and later other firms produced their own designs and built to them. Yarrow, however, thanks to conflicts with the Admiralty over their 27 knotter destroyers, did not receive any more destroyer orders from the Admiralty for several years, and concentrated on building for foreign navies instead.

As with the 27-knotters all the firms built to their own designs, the only common feature being the complement of 63 and the standard armament of 1-12pdr and 5-6pdr guns, plus 2-18in TT. All except Thornycroft used triple expansion engines, whilst Thornycroft continued with their four cylinder compounds. Hulls were lengthened and the machinery was more powerful than the 27-knotters, but fundamentally the 30-knotters were only enlarged versions of the earlier destroyers.

As with the 27-knotters the high trial speeds were never achieved in service, or even in subsequent trials. Sea speed was more often around the 25kts mark, if that. The light structure of these destroyers caused some trouble with leakage and fractures, though in fact it stood up remarkably well to the strains of wartime service between 1914 and 1918 when these by then elderly vessels were mainly used for coastal patrol work. Many had their funnels raised in an attempt to minimise smoke and cinders at deck level.

Though quite a few of these vessels were delayed in their entrance into the service by difficulties in reaching the contract speed, more delay was caused with the later groups of vessels by the severe labour troubles in the late 1890s in the shipbuilding trades.

This class, like most Thornycroft boats, kept their speed well and were particularly manoeuvrable thanks to their 'semi-tunnel' sterns, but they tended to be wet forward. They had two funnels.

Virago as completed 1897

1894-5 PROGRAMME: Laird *30-knotters*

Four funnels. *Thrasher* was involved in a serious accident just after completion and had to undergo major repairs, after which she was never as fast as her sisters. *Sparrowhawk* was wrecked in the mouth of the Yangtze river. These Laird boats were strongly built but not very manoeuvrable.

Displacement: 355t light (415 full load)
Dimensions: 218ft oa, 213ft pp x 21½ft x 9½ft (*66.45 oa, 64.92 pp x 6.55 x 2.90m*)
Machinery: 6300ihp

Name	Laid down	Launched	Comp	Fate
QUAIL	28.5.1895	24.9.95	June 1897	BU 1919
SPARROWHAWK	30.5.1895	8.10.95	June 1897	Wrecked 1904
THRASHER	30.5.1895	5.11.95	June 1897	BU 1919
VIRAGO	13.6.1895	19.11.95	June 1897	BU 1919

1895-6 ORDERS: Thornycroft *30-knotters*

Details as *Desperate*. *Ariel* was wrecked by running into the rocks off a breakwater at Malta in a pitch-dark night during a gale.

Name	Laid down	Launched	Comp	Fate
ANGLER	21.2.1896	2.2.97	July 1898	BU 1920
ARIEL	23.4.1896	5.3.97	Oct 1898	Wrecked 1907

1895-6 PROGRAMME: Vickers *30-knotters*

Three funnels. When these vessels were ordered the builder was known as the Naval Construction & Armaments Co but became Vickers before they were completed. *Otter* was ordered slightly later than the first pair.

Displacement: 355t light (405t full load)
Dimensions: 214¼ft oa, 210ft pp x 20ft x 8¼ft (*65.38 oa, 64.01 pp x 6.10 x 2.52m*)
Machinery: 6300ihp

Name	Laid down	Launched	Comp	Fate
AVON	17.2.1896	10.10.96	Feb 1899	BU 1920
BITTERN	18.2.1896	1.2.97	April 1897	Lost in collision 1918
OTTER	9.6.1896	23.11.96	March 1900	BU 1916

1895-6 ORDERS: Laird *30-knotters*

Details as *Quail*, except draught 9¾ft (*2.97m*). *Wolf* was originally to be called *Squirrel*.

Name	Laid down	Launched	Comp	Fate
EARNEST	2.3.1896	7.11.96	Nov 1897	BU 1920
GRIFFON	7.3.1896	21.11.96	Nov 1897	BU 1920
LOCUST	20.4.1896	5.12.96	July 1898	BU 1919
PANTHER	19.5.1896	21.1.97	Jan 1898	BU 1920
SEAL	17.6.1896	6.3.97	May 1898	BU 1921
WOLF	12.11.1896	2.6.97	July 1898	BU 1921

1895-6 ORDERS: Palmer *30-knotters*

The first pair were ordered on 23.12.1895 and the remainder on 9.1.1896. Palmer boats were generally considered as perhaps the best all-round vessels of the 30-knotters. Certainly their machinery seems to have had the best reputation amongst engineers. *Chamois* was lost in a very unusual way: one of her propeller blades came off when she was doing a speed run in the Gulf of Patras (Greece) and cut a big enough gash to sink her.

Displacement: 390t light (440t full load)
Dimensions: 220ft oa, 215ft pp x 20¾ft x 9¾ft (*67.06oa, 65.53 pp x 6.32 x 2.97m*)
Machinery: 6200ihp

Name	Laid down	Launched	Comp	Fate
STAR	23.3.1896	11.8.96	Sept 1898	BU 1919
WHITING	13.4.1896	26.8.96	June 1897	BU 1919
BAT	28.5.1896	7.10.96	Aug 1897	BU 1919
CRANE	2.8.1896	17.12.96	April 1898	BU 1919
CHAMOIS	28.5.1896	9.11.96	Nov 1897	Foundered 1904
FLYING FISH	9.8.1896	4.3.97	June 1898	BU 1919

1895-6 ORDERS: Thomson *30-knotters*

All were three funnelled vessels.

Displacement: 380t light (425t full load) (except *Vulture* 345t light, 385t full load)
Dimensions: 214ft oa, 210ft pp (except *Recruit* 218ft oa, 214ft pp; and *Vulture* 222¼ft oa, 218ft pp) x 20ft x 8¼ft (*65.23 oa, 64.01 pp (Recruit 66.45 oa, 65.23 pp; Vulture 67.74 oa, 66.45pp) x 6.10 x 2.52m*)
Machinery: 5800ihp

Name	Laid down	Launched	Comp	Fate
BRAZEN	18.10.1895	3.7.96	July 1900	BU 1919
ELECTRA	18.10.1895	14.7.96	July 1900	BU 1920
RECRUIT	18.10.1895	22.8.96	Oct 1900	Torpedoed 1915
VULTURE	26.11.1895	22.3.98	May 1900	BU 1919

1896-7 ORDERS: Doxford *30-knotters*

Three funnelled vessels.

Displacement: 350t light (400t full load)
Dimensions: 214¾ft (*Sylvia* 215ft) oa, 210ft pp x 21ft x 9ft 7in (*65:46 (65.53) oa, 64.01pp x 6.40 x 2.92m*)
Machinery: 6300ihp

Name	Laid down	Launched	Comp	Fate
VIOLET	13.7.1896	3.5.97	June 1898	BU 1920
SYLVIA	13.7.1896	3.7.97	Jan 1899	BU 1919

Sylvia, a Doxford-built 30-knotter of 1897

Probably the most seaworthy of all the 30-knotters, these three funnelled destroyers were the first of a long line from this yard which were especially popular with their users.

1896-7 ORDERS: Hawthorn Leslie *30-knotters*

Displacement: 355t light (400t full load)
Dimensions: 215ft oa, 210ft pp x 21ft x 8ft 2in (*65.53 oa, 64.01 pp x 6.40 x 2.49m*)
Machinery: 6100ihp

Name	Laid down	Launched	Comp	Fate
MERMAID	7.9.1896	22.2.98	June 1899	BU 1919
CHEERFUL	7.9.1896	14.7.97	Feb 1900	Mined 1917

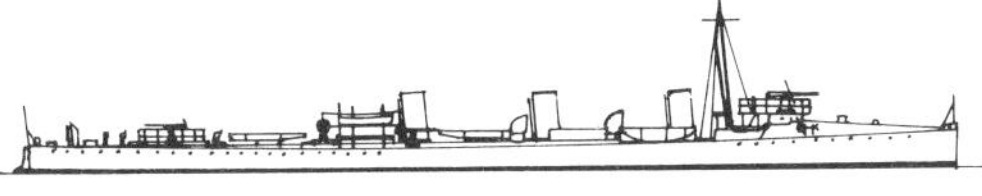

Gipsy as completed 1898

Three funnelled ships. *Fairy* rammed and sank the German submarine *UC 75* which was bigger than herself, and as a result was so badly damaged that she sank shortly afterwards. *Gipsy's* hulk was in use as a floating pontoon at Dartmouth for many years after her disposal.

1896-7 ORDERS: Fairfield *30-knotters*

Displacement: 355t light (400t full load)
Dimensions: 215½ft oa, 209¾ft pp x 21ft x 8ft 2in (*65.68 oa, 63.93 pp x 6.40 x 2.49m*)
Machinery: 6300ihp

Name	Laid down	Launched	Comp	Fate
OSPREY	14.11.1896	7.4.97	July 1898	BU 1919
FAIRY	19.10.1896	29.5.97	Aug 1898	Foundered 1918
GIPSY	1.10.1896	9.3.97	July 1898	Sold 1921

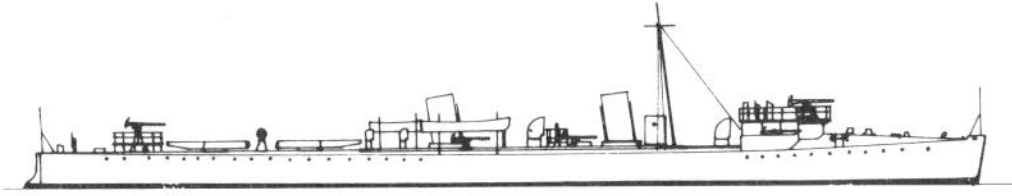

Cygnet as completed 1900

These were a lengthened version of the original Thornycroft 30-knotters, with improved lines but the same machinery and twin funnels as before.

1896-7 ORDERS: Thornycroft *30-knotters*

Displacement: 335t light (375t full load)
Dimensions: 215½ft oa, 208ft pp x 19½ft x 7ft 5in (*65.68 oa, 63.40 pp x 5.94 x 2.26m*)
Machinery: 5700ihp

Name	Laid down	Launched	Comp	Fate
COQUETTE	8.6.1896	25.11.97	Nov 1899	Mined 1916
CYNTHIA	16.7.1896	8.1.98	June 1899	BU 1920
CYGNET	25.9.1896	3.9.98	Feb 1900	BU 1920

This Hull firm went bankrupt before these vessels were delivered, hence the late completion date. Three funnels.

1896-7 ORDERS: Earle *30-knotters*

Displacement: 345t light (390t full load)
Dimensions: 214½ft oa, 210ft pp x 20½ft x 7ft 10in (*65.38 oa, 64.01 pp x 6.25 x 2.39m*)
Machinery: 5800ihp

Name	Laid down	Launched	Comp	Fate
DOVE	17.9.1896	21.3.98	July 1901	BU 1920
BULLFINCH	17.9.1896	10.2.98	June 1901	BU 1919

Generally similar to earlier boats from this firm which was shortly to be renamed John Brown.

1896-7 ORDERS: Thomson *30-knotter*

Displacement: 350t light (395t full load)
Dimensions: 222½ft oa, 218ft pp x 20½ft x 8ft 11in (*67.82 oa, 66.45 pp x 6.25 x 2.72m*)
Machinery: 5800ihp

Name	Laid down	Launched	Comp	Fate
KESTREL	2.9.1896	25.3.98	April 1900	BU 1921

Details as earlier Palmer boats (see *Star*). *Flirt* was sunk by a force of modern German destroyers during a night raid on the British patrol forces in the Dover Straits.

1896-7 ORDERS: Palmer *30-knotters*

Name	Laid down	Launched	Comp	Fate
FAWN	5.9.1896	13.4.97	Dec 1898	BU 1919
FLIRT	5.9.1896	15.5.97	April 1899	Sunk in action 1916

As earlier Barrow-built boats (see *Avon*) except 350t light (400t full load).

1896-7 ORDERS: Vickers *30-knotters*

Name	Laid down	Launched	Comp	Fate
LEOPARD	10.6.1896	20.3.97	July 1899	BU 1919

As earlier Laird boats (see *Quail*) except 216¼ft oa, 9ft 7in draught (*65.91oa, 2.92m*) and 360t light (410t full load).

1897-8 ORDERS: Laird *30-knotter*

Name	Laid down	Launched	Comp	Fate
ORWELL	9.11.1897	29.9.98	Jan 1900	BU 1922

As *Sylvia* except 365t light (410t full load).

1897-8 ORDERS: Doxford *30-knotter*

Name	Laid down	Launched	Comp	Fate
LEE	4.1.1898	27.1.99	March 1901	Wrecked 1909

As *Osprey* except 370t light (420t full load).

1897-8 ORDERS: Fairfield *30-knotter*

Name	Laid down	Launched	Comp	Fate
LEVEN	24.1.1898	28.6.98	July 1899	BU 1920

Peterel details as *Star* except 219½ft oa, 8ft 11in draught (*66.90 oa, 2.72m*), 370t light (420t full load); *Spiteful* similar except 9ft 1in (*2.77m*) draught, 400t light (450t full load).

1897-8 ORDERS: Palmer *30-knotters*

Name	Laid down	Launched	Comp	Fate
PETEREL	29.7.1898	30.3.99	July 1900	BU 1919
SPITEFUL	12.1.1898	11.1.99	Feb 1900	BU 1920

Peterel, a Palmer-built 30-knotter of 1899

A further development of the Thornycroft two funnelled design with altered lines.

1897-8 ORDERS: Thornycroft *30-knotter*

Displacement: 320t light (365t full load)
Dimensions: 215ft oa, 208ft pp x 19¾ft x 7ft 1in (*65.53 oa, 63.40 pp x 6.52 x 2.16m*)
Machinery: 5800ihp

Name	Laid down	Launched	Comp	Fate
STAG	16.4.1898	18.11.99	Sept 1900	BU 1921

Slightly altered development of *Mermaid*.

1899 ORDERS: Hawthorn Leslie *30-knotters*

Displacement: 385t light (430t full load)
Dimensions: 214½ft oa, 210ft 11in pp x 21ft 1in x 13ft (*65.38 oa, 64.29 pp x 6.43 x 3.96m*)
Machinery: 6000ihp

Name	Laid down	Launched	Comp	Fate
GREYHOUND	18.7.1899	6.10.1900	Jan 1902	BU 1919
RACEHORSE	23.10.1899	8.11.1900	March 1902	BU 1920
ROEBUCK	2.10.1899	4.1.1901	March 1902	BU 1919

A three funnelled development of *Violet*.

1899 ORDERS: Doxford *30-knotter*

Displacement: 380t light (425t full load)
Dimensions: 214¾ft oa, 210ft pp x 21ft x 8ft 10in (*65.46 oa, 64.01 pp x 6.40 x 2.69m*)
Machinery: 6000ihp

Name	Laid down	Launched	Comp	Fate
SUCCESS	18.9.1899	21.3.1901	May 1902	Wrecked 1914

Slightly improved versions of earlier Palmer boats (see *Peterel*).

1899 ORDERS: Palmer *30-knotters*

Displacement: 370t light (420t, 440t *Syren,* full load)
Dimensions: 220¼ft, *Syren* 219¾ft oa, 215ft pp x 20¾ft x 8ft 11in, *Syren* 9ft 4in (*67.13, Syren 66.98 oa, 65.53 pp x 6.34 x 2.72, Syren 2.84m*)
Machinery: 6200ihp

Name	Laid down	Launched	Comp	Fate
MYRMIDON	23.10.1899	26.5.1900	May 1901	Collision 1917
SYREN	24.11.1899	20.12.1900	Feb 1902	BU 1920

As earlier Vickers boats (see *Avon*) except 400t light (445t full load), 6000ihp.

1899 ORDERS: Vickers *30-knotter*

Name	Laid down	Launched	Comp	Fate
VIXEN	7.9.1899	29.3.1900	March 1902	BU 1921

As *Osprey* except 214½ft oa, 209ft pp, 8¾ft draught (*65.38, 63.70, 2.67m*), 375t light (420t full load), 6250ihp. *Falcon* similar except 215½ft oa, 207¾ft pp (*65.68, 63.32m*).

1899 ORDERS: Fairfield *30-knotters*

Name	Laid down	Launched	Comp	Fate
OSTRICH	28.6.1899	22.3.1900	Dec 1901	BU 1920
FALCON	26.6.1899	29.12.1899	Dec 1901	Collision 1918

As *Kestrel* except 222ft oa, 9ft draught (*67.67, 2.74m*), 380t light (425t full load), 6400ihp. This and the following two classes were speculative vessels purchased from their builders while under construction. *Tiger* was lost in a collision with the cruiser *Berwick* off St Catherine's.

PURCHASED: Brown 31.3.1900

Name	Laid down	Launched	Comp	Fate
THORN	–	17.3.1900	June 1901	BU 1919
TIGER	–	19.5.1900	June 1901	Collision 1908
VIGILANT	–	16.8.1900	June 1901	BU 1920

As *Myrmidon* except 219¾ft oa (*66.98m*), 390t light (420t full load).

PURCHASED: Palmer 1900

Name	Laid down	Launched	Comp	Fate
KANGAROO	29.12.1899	8.9.1900	July 1901	BU 1920

Altered versions of earlier Laird designs.

PURCHASED: Laird 1901

Displacement: 385t light (435t full load)
Dimensions: 219ft oa, 215ft pp x 21¼ft x 8ft 7in (*66.75 oa, 65.53 pp x 6.48 x 2.62m*)
Machinery: 6250ihp

Name	Laid down	Launched	Comp	Fate
LIVELY	20.6.1899	14.7.1900	April 1902	BU 1920
SPRIGHTLY	20.6.1899	25.9.1900	March 1902	BU 1921

1896-7 ORDERS: Thornycroft *33-knot 'special'*

Displacement: 430t light (490t full load)
Dimensions: 232¾ft oa, 225½ft pp x 21¼ft x 9ft 1in (*70.94 oa, 68.73 pp x 6.48 x 2.77m*)
Machinery: 7500 = 31½kts
Complement 69

Name	Laid down	Launched	Comp	Fate
ALBATROSS	27.11.1896	19.7.98	July 1900	BU 1920

As part of the 1896/7 programme the Admiralty decided to order three vessels with the unprecedented contract speed of 33kts. This was mainly a reaction to the 31kts of the French torpedo boat *Forban* on trial in 1895. In fact that was an exceptional result as none of her immediate sisters reached anything like that speed. In the event, the requirement for 33kts proved too ambitious. The vessels built, with exactly the same armament as the 30-knotters, on longer and more expensive hulls and with more powerful and therefore more expensive machinery, completely failed to make the desired speed. The first two both spent years running acceptance trials testing various propeller shapes and other devices in a vain attempt to reach 33kts, though Thornycroft's *Albatross* came quite close.

After their final acceptance it was realised that all they had proved to be were rather more expensive 30-knotters, and so they were not kept apart as a separate class.

Albatross was the most successful of these specials, but she made a big loss for her builders who spent a considerable time (from October 1898 to July 1900) endeavouring to make her meet her intended speed. She was also delayed by labour troubles, which made her even more expensive. Unlike Thornycroft's other destroyers of the time she had three funnels.

Albatross, a Thornycroft-built 33-knotter, running one of her many speed trials

GREAT BRITAIN

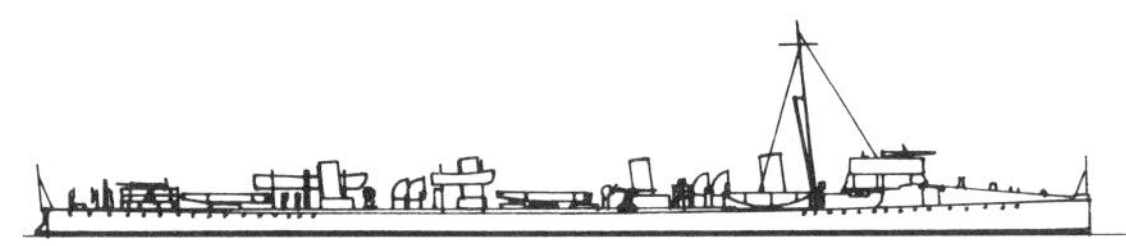
Express as completed 1902

1896-7 ORDERS: Laird *33-knot 'special'*

Displacement: 465t light (540t full load)
Dimensions: 239¼ft oa, 235ft pp x 23½ft x 10¼ft (*72.92 oa, 71.63 pp x 7.16 x 3.12m*)
Machinery: 9250ihp = 31kts

Name	Laid down	Launched	Comp	Fate
EXPRESS	1.12.1896	11.12.97	Feb 1902	BU 1921

This four funnelled destroyer began her trials in 1898, was badly damaged during their course, and tried many different variants of propeller shape without real success. Her appearance was unusual because she had 'reverse sheer' (in other words the upper deck was higher amidships than at the ends). Early in her career she had a very poor reputation for reliability, breaking down when she was called on to do any speed. Her complement was 74.

1896-7 ORDERS: Thomson *33-knot 'special'*

Displacement: 470t light (530t full load)
Dimensions: 232ft oa, 227½ft pp x 22¼ft x 9¾ft (*70.71 oa, 69.34 pp x 6.78 x 2.97m*)
Machinery: 8600ihp = 30¾kts

Name	Laid down	Launched	Comp	Fate
ARAB	5.3.1900	9.2.1900	Jan 1903	BU 1919

Though ordered under the same 1896/7 programme as the other two specials, *Arab* was not commenced until after both had been running trials for some time. It is surprising that the Admiralty bothered to continue with her, particularly as comparatively few attempts were made to 'tune' her up to a higher speed than the very low 30¾kts she actually obtained. Her complement was 69.

Viper as completed 1900

VIPER *turbine destroyer*

Displacement: 344t light
Dimensions: 210ft 3½in pp x 21ft (*64.10 pp x 6.40m*)
Machinery: 4-shaft turbines = 33¾kts

Name	Laid down	Launched	Comp	Fate
VIPER	1898	6.9.99	1900	Stranded Channel Is 1901

The 33-knotters had been failures, but already by the time these were running their trials a new form of machinery had appeared which would prove the answer to higher speed requirements. In 1897 Parsons' *Turbinia* had made her spectacular appearance at the Jubilee Review at Spithead, and shown that the steam turbine was a workable device. In fact Director of Naval Construction had known about Parsons' trials for some time before, and had followed them with interest. It was not therefore surprising that a turbine-powered destroyer should be ordered from Parsons on 4.3.1898. Soon afterwards Armstrong began a turbine destroyer 'on spec' at their Elswick yard which would be taken over by the Admiralty before completion.

Initial results with these vessels were encouraging, but both were lost almost immediately. Fortunately in neither case did the tubines have anything to do with the loss. To fill the need for further testing the *Velox*, building 'on spec', was purchased. All of these three turbine destroyers were 30-knotters in all respects including armament (except their machinery).

The hull of the *Viper* was subcontracted to Hawthorn Leslie by Parsons. Three funnelled. To cope with the problems of absorbing the power from the turbines two propellers were fitted per shaft. The great boon of the turbine, its lack of vibration compared to reciprocating engines, became obvious during trials, as did its much greater ability to sustain high speed.

COBRA *turbine destroyer*

Displacement: 375t light
Dimensions: 213ft 7½in pp x 20½ft x 7ft (*65.11 pp x 6.25 x 2.13m*)
Machinery: 4-shaft turbines = 30kts

Name	Laid down	Launched	Comp	Fate
COBRA	–	28.6.1899	1901	Foundered 1901

This four funnelled destroyer was purchased in 1900 from Armstrong. She had run her first trials as early as July 1899, but had then suffered damage in a collision. Three propellers were fitted to each shaft. Construction was lighter than was normal for Royal Navy destroyers, and may help to explain her loss on her delivery voyage. This loss is still something of a mystery, as *Cobra* suddenly broke in two and sank in heavy weather off the Yorkshire coast. The Court Martial certainly attributed the loss to structural weakness, but the survivors reported feeling an impact before she split, and though no wreckage was subsequently found in the area it still remains a distinct possibility that hitting a mast or spar from a wreck initiated the break.

Her loss caused a Committee to be set up to enquire into the strength of destroyers which cleared the 30-knotters of the suspicion that they might founder from structural weakness.

VELOX *turbine destroyer*

Displacement: 400t light (445t full load)
Dimensions: 215ft oa, 210ft pp x 21ft x 9ft (*65.53 oa, 64.01 pp x 6.00 x 2.74m*)
Machinery: 4-shaft turbines, with TE cruising engines on 2 shafts, ?shp = 27kts

Name	Laid down	Launched	Comp	Fate
VELOX	10.4.1901	11.2.02	Feb 1904	Mined 1915

Parsons began this destroyer, originally to be named *Python*, as a private venture, with the hull constructed by Hawthorn Leslie, to experiment with a mixed power plant. She was purchased in 1901. Turbines intended for high speeds were not economical in fuel at ordinary cruising speeds. Therefore a separate pair of TE engines were coupled to the low pressure turbine shafts. The problem would eventually be solved by fitting separate cruising turbines, as was done to *Velox* in 1906. *Velox* had three funnels, the middle one thicker than the others, and two propellers on each shaft. The complement was 63.

Another turbine boat was ordered a little later, but as she was basically one of the 'River' class she is listed under that class.

A Schichau destroyer built for China, this vessel was captured at Taku 17.6.1900 with the sisters which were allocated to Germany, Russia and France, by Roger Keyes. Though reputed to have done 32kts on trial when first completed her service speed was well below this, and she did not compare very well with contemporary British destroyers. Her accommodation was particularly bad. She had two funnels, and spent her life on the China station.

TAKU *captured destroyer*

Displacement: 305t light (334t full load)
Dimensions: 194ft pp x 21ft x 5ft 10in (mean) (*59.13 x 6.40 x 1.78m*)
Machinery: 6000ihp = under 30kts
Armament: 6.47mm, 2-14in TT
Complement: 58

Name	Laid down	Launched	Comp	Fate
TAKU (?ex-HAI NJU)	–	1898	–	BU 1916

RIVER class: Palmer

Displacement: 550t light (620t full load)
Dimensions: 233½ft oa, 225ft pp x 23½ft x 9¾ft (*71.17 oa, 68.58 x 7.16 x 2.97m*)
Machinery: 7000ihp

Name	Laid down	Launched	Comp	Fate
ERNE	3.7.1902	14.1.1903	Feb 1904	Wrecked 1915
ETTRICK	9.7.1902	28.2.1903	Feb 1904	BU 1919
EXE	14.7.1902	27.4.1903	March 1904	BU 1920

Experience with earlier types of destroyer had shown quite clearly that concentrating on high trial (= smooth water) speed was a snare and delusion. The combination of seaworthiness with the ability to *maintain* a less spectacular speed when it became rough was of far more real value. The early destroyers were too lightly built, too small and too delicate to be fully effective in all conditions as fighting ships. The lesson was underlined by the success of the German *S90* class which had a raised forecastle and proved very seaworthy. The Admiralty decided therefore to ask for more heavily built destroyers with raised forecastles and a contract speed of only 25½kts. The larger size and sturdiness of the new design was correctly held to allow the new destroyers to maintain this speed in most conditions when the earlier destroyers dropped well below it.

The raised forecastle proved a particularly desirable feature as it enabled speed to be kept up when steaming into waves and also allowed the forward guns to be fought in comparatively bad conditions, besides keeping the watchkeepers much drier. The latters' condition was much improved anyway by being given a bridge. The armament of this class was identical to the 30-knotters, the forward 6pdr guns being sponsoned out on either side of the forefunnel in the first group. However this made their positions somewhat wet in a head sea, so in the 1902/3 group and subsequent ships they were moved up to either side of the 12pdr on the forecastle. Experience in the Russo-Japanese war showed that the 6pdr was too light for real effect, and so in 1906 it was decided to replace the 5-6pdr with 3-12pdr, thereby giving a total of 4-12pdr as well as the 2-18in TT.

These vessels marked the real break between the torpedo boat and the true destroyer, and set the pattern for destroyer development both in Britain and in most foreign countries until the 'V & W' class of the latter part of the 1914–18 war. One, the *Eden*, was given turbine propulsion. The class gave good service, being used in the First World War on patrol and escort duties. They had been designated the 'E' class in 1912. They were generally considered less easy to manoeuvre than earlier destroyers, and much more visible thanks to their higher silhouette and therefore less suited to surprise torpedo attacks. Their lower smooth water speed caused them to be the target of much ill-informed public criticism, but experience showed just how ignorant this criticism was, as *effective* speed was so much better. All had a speed of 25½kts (the fastest on trials being *Eden* and *Gala* with 26¼kts) and were armed with 1-12pdr, 5-6pdr and 2-18in TT. The complement was 70.

The Palmer boats had four funnels in two close groups. 1901/2 Programme.

Four funnels in two closely spaced groups. 1901/2 Programme.

RIVER class: Yarrow

Displacement: 590t light (660t full load)
Dimensions: 231¼ft oa, 225ft pp x 23½ft x 10ft (*70.49 oa, 68.58 pp x 7.16 x 3.05m*)
Machinery: 7500ihp

Name	Laid down	Launched	Comp	Fate
RIBBLE	4.7.1902	19.3.1904	June 1904	BU 1920
TEVIOT	10.7.1902	7.11.1903	April 1904	BU 1919
USK	30.7.1902	25.7.1903	March 1904	BU 1920

1901/2 Programme, two funnels. These two sisters were used for a series of comparative trials to test the differences in performance between turbines and reciprocating engines. The former came out of the comparison well and eventually replaced the latter as the standard type of destroyer machinery.

RIVER class: Hawthorn Leslie

Displacement: 550t light (620t full load)
Dimensions: 225½ft oa, 220ft pp x 23½ft x 9ft (*68.73 oa, 67.06 pp x 7.16 x 2.74m*)
Machinery: 7000ihp (*Eden* had 3-shaft Parsons turbines)

Name	Laid down	Launched	Comp	Fate
DERWENT	12.6.1902	14.2.1903	July 1904	Mined 1917
EDEN	12.6.1902	13.3.1903	June 1904	Collision 1916

Two funnels. 1901/2 Programme.

RIVER class: Laird

Displacement: 550t light (625t full load)
Dimensions: 226¾ft oa, 220ft pp x 23¾ft x 9½ft (*69.11 oa, 67.06 x 7.24 x 2.90m*)
Machinery: 7000ihp

Name	Laid down	Launched	Comp	Fate
FOYLE	15.8.1902	25.2.1903	March 1904	Mined 1917
ITCHEN	18.8.1902	17.3.1903	Jan 1904	Torpedoed 1917

Thornycroft based the lines for these vessels on an enlarged version of those of *TB 98*, with a modified stern. Two funnels. 1902/3 Programme.

RIVER class: Thornycroft

Displacement: 550t light (615t full load)
Dimensions: 225ft oa, 220ft pp x 23ft 10½in x 9ft 3½in (*68.58 oa, 67.06 pp x 7.28 x 2.83m*)
Machinery: 7500ihp

Name	Laid down	Launched	Comp	Fate
KENNET	5.2.1902	4.12.1903	Jan 1905	BU 1919
JED	27.2.1903	16.2.1904	Jan 1905	BU 1920

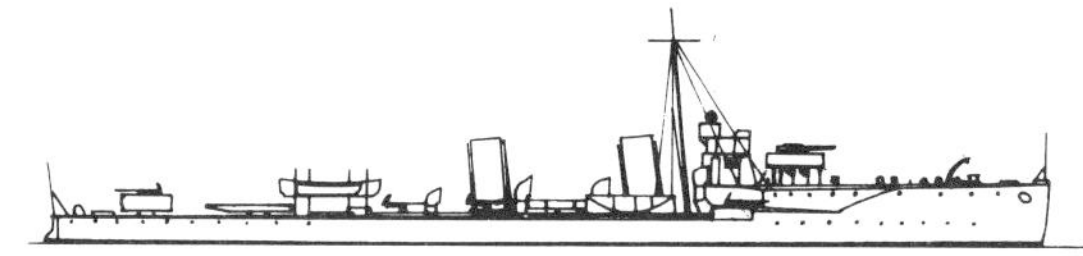

Itchen as completed 1904

RIVER class: Yarrow

As *Ribble*. 1902/3 Programme.

Name	Laid down	Launched	Comp	Fate
WELLAND	1.10.1902	14.4.1904	July 1904	BU 1920

RIVER class: Palmer

As *Erne* except 230ft oa (*70.10m*), 545t light (615t full load); 550t and 620t for *Dee*. 1902/3 Programme.

Name	Laid down	Launched	Comp	Fate
CHERWELL	20.1.1903	23.7.1903	March 1904	BU 1904
DEE	5.3.1903	10.9.1903	May 1904	BU 1904

RIVER class: Laird

As *Foyle*. 1902/3 Programme.

Name	Laid down	Launched	Comp	Fate
ARUN	27.8.1902	29.4.1903	Feb 1904	BU 1920
BLACKWATER	27.8.1902	25.7.1903	March 1904	Collision 1909

RIVER class: Hawthorn Leslie

As *Derwent* 1902/3 Programme.

Name	Laid down	Launched	Comp	Fate
WAVENEY	20.10.1902	16.3.1903	June 1904	BU 1920

RIVER class: Thornycroft

As *Kennet*. 1903/4 Programme.

Name	Laid down	Launched	Comp	Fate
CHELMER	11.12.1904	8.12.1904	June 1905	BU 1920
COLNE	21.3.1904	21.5.1905	July 1905	BU 1919

RIVER class: Yarrow

As *Ribble*. *Garry* was fitted with a new type of flat overhanging stern. She was lost in a collision with the cruiser *Attentive*. 1903/4 Programme.

Name	Laid down	Launched	Comp	Fate
GALA	1.2.1904	7.1.1905	–	Collision 1908
GARRY	25.4.1904	21.3.1905	Sept 1905	BU 1919

RIVER class: White

Two funnels. 1903/4 Programme.

Displacement: 555t light (630t full load)
Dimensions: 229½ft oa, 224½ft pp x 23ft 10in x 9½ft (*69.95 oa, 68.43 pp x 7.26 x 2.90m*)
Machinery: 7000ihp

Name	Laid down	Launched	Comp	Fate
NESS	5.5.1904	5.1.1905	Aug 1905	BU 1919
NITH	5.5.1904	7.3.1905	Oct 1905	BU 1919

RIVER class: Palmer

As *Cherwell* except 23ft 11in breadth, 9ft 4in draught (*7.29, 2.84m*), 550t light (620t full load). 1903/4 Programme.

Name	Laid down	Launched	Comp	Fate
SWALE	23.2.1904	20.4.1905	Sept 1905	BU 1919
URE	1.3.1904	25.10.1904	June 1905	BU 1919
WEAR	7.3.1904	21.1.1905	Aug 1905	BU 1919

RIVER class: Laird

As *Foyle*. 1903/4 Programme.

Name	Laid down	Launched	Comp	Fate
LIFFEY	22.3.1904	23.9.1904	May 1905	BU 1919
MOY	22.3.1904	10.11.1904	June 1905	BU 1919
OUSE	22.3.1904	7.1.1905	Sept 1905	BU 1919

RIVER class: Hawthorn Leslie

As *Derwent* except 23ft 7in breadth (*7.19m*), 545t light (615t full load). 1903/4 Programme.

Name	Laid down	Launched	Comp	Fate
BOYNE	16.2.1904	12.9.1904	May 1905	BU 1919
DOON	16.2.1904	8.11.1904	June 1905	BU 1919
KALE	16.2.1904	8.11.1904	Aug 1905	Mined 1918

RIVER class: Palmer

As *Swale* except 23ft 6in breadth (*7.16m*), 592t light (662t full load). Purchased while building on speculation.

Name	Laid down	Launched	Comp	Fate
ROTHER	23.3.1903	5.1.1904	May 1905	BU 1919

Note: two extra destroyers of the 'River' type (*Stour* and *Test*) built on speculation were purchased as replacements after our period ends, as were two of the 30-knotter type (*Albacore* and *Bonetta*), whilst an improved version of the 'River' design built in Italy was purchased by roundabout means during the First World War as the *Arno*.

Wear as completed 1905

Boyne, a Hawthorn Leslie-built 'River' class destroyer of 1904

TORPEDO BOATS 1st class

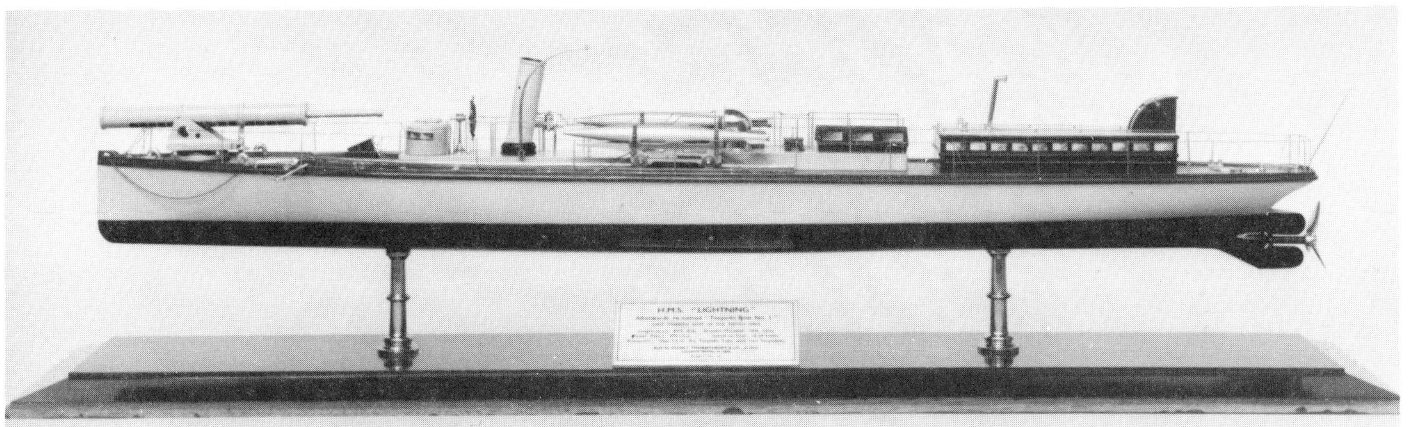

A model of the *Lightning* as she appeared after the mounting of the bow TT in 1879
Science Museum

TB1 (LIGHTNING) Thornycroft 1876-7

Displacement: 32½t
Dimensions: 87ft oa, 84½ft pp x 10¾ft x 5ft 2in (*26.52 oa, 25.76 pp x 3.28 x 1.57m*)
Machinery: Compound, 460ihp = 19kts

From 1874 John Thornycroft, who had had considerable success in building fast steam launches, had been urging the Admiralty to let him build them a torpedo launch, and finally he was given an order for one. He had thought of utilising 'air lubrication' (an early version of the hovercraft principle), but probably wisely built a conventional steam launch hull instead. She was very similar to the yacht *Gitana* built for Lake Geneva a year earlier, shown clearly in *Lightning's* 'coach roof' cabin aft, a feature none of her descendants had. She was originally built with two 'torpedo frames', cages carrying torpedoes which could be lowered into the water on either side of the boat and the torpedo then released. These could not be used at any speed and were replaced in 1879 by a torpedo tube mounted on the bow, with a reload carried on a trolley on either side amidships. The complement, as with all the early boats, was 15.

The first torpedo boat spent her life as a tender to the torpedo school, HMS *Vernon*, at Portsmouth, and was used for many experiments. In 1881 her original propeller (mounted *behind* the divided rudder) was temporarily replaced by Thornycroft's 'guide blade screw', also known as a 'turbine propeller'. This was a form of ducted screw, and worked quite adequately. This boat, referred to indiscriminately by both name and number, was broken up in 1896, though her engine survived for some time driving machinery in Portsmouth Dockyard, a not unusual event with early torpedo boats, whose hulls and boilers wore out before the engines did.

TB 2-12 Thornycroft 1878-9

Displacement: 28t
Dimensions: 87ft oa, 86ft 4in pp (91½ft oa, 90ft 10in pp for *TB10*) x 10¼ft x 5¼ft (*26.52 oa, 26.31 pp (27.89, 27.69 for TB10) x 3.12 x 1.60m*)
Machinery: Compound 460ihp = 20kts

With the success of the *Lightning* a class of improved sisters was ordered from her builder. These differed from her in not having the coach top aft, and they all had her final armament arrangement from the start. *TB10* was the odd man out, having a ram bow and therefore somewhat different lines, but otherwise was the same. For some time they were considered 'very fair seaboats' but were really too small and fragile for successful service in the open sea, and became rapidly obsolete. By 1886 they could make about 16kts at sea. They were later fitted with 2 torpedoes in dropping gear. A couple were used for trials with various forms of spar torpedo. They were all sold for breaking up between 1894 and 1906, *TB6* at the Cape, *TB7* at Gibraltar, *TB8* at Hong Kong and *TB9*, *10* and *11* at Hong Kong where they had been sent early in their careers.

OTHER BUILDER'S 'LIGHTNINGS'

This batch of boats was ordered from builders who had been provided with details of *Lightning*, and all were generally similar.

TB 13 Maudslay 1878/87

Displacement: 28t
Dimensions: 87ft oa, 82ft pp x 10¾ft (*26.52oa, 24.99 pp x 3.28m*)
Machinery: 450ihp = 20kts (less on trial)

Unusual in having a brass hull. She proved a very bad seaboat and slow in the bargain, rolling excessively, though her engines were considered very good. By 1886 she could only make 11kts. Broken up 1896.

TB 14 Yarrow 1878-9

Displacement: 33t
Dimensions: 86ft oa, 84ft pp x 11ft (*26.21 oa, 25.60pp x 3.35m*)
Machinery: 550ihp = 21¾kts

Generally considered the best of the batch, a good seaboat and fast (she made 16kts at sea in 1886), but her accommodation was very bad. Broken up in 1904.

TB 15 Hanna, Donald & Wilson 1879

Displacement: 28t
Dimensions: 87ft oa, x 10¼ft x 5ft 7in (*26.52 oa, x 3.12 x 1.70m*)
Machinery: 450ihp = 21kts

Soon after completion she was sent out to the Cape, where in 1903 her hull was used as a retaining wall. (*TB16* was building by Lewin at Poole, but was cancelled because of delays in construction).

TB 19 White 1878

Displacement: 28t
Dimensions: 93ft oa x 10¾ft (*28.35 oa x 3.28m*)
Machinery: 460ihp = 21kts

By 1886 no longer considered fit for service, but she was not finally broken up until 1899.

TB 20 Rennie 1880

Displacement: 28t
Dimensions: 87ft oa x 10ft x 4ft (*26.52 oa x 3.05 x 1.22m*)
Machinery: 360ihp = 16¾kts

This slow boat spent most of her life at Hong Kong where she was sold for breaking up in 1903. In 1894 she was reported to be unable to keep up her top speed of 11kts for very long, and her turning powers were very bad. All of this batch were originally armed with a similar armament to that adopted by *Lightning* in 1879, though in several cases this was not fitted for some time. Later they were rearmed with two 14in torpedoes in dropping gear. All had a complement of 15. *TB 21*, built by Des Vignes in 1879, was not accepted because of lack of performance.

TB 17-18 Yarrow 1878

Displacement: 33t
Dimensions: 86ft oa, 81ft pp x 11ft x 4½ft (*26.21 oa, 24.6 pp x 3.35 x 1.37m*)
Machinery: 450ihp = 21kts

These two boats were built for Russia when the Russo–Turkish War and the subsequent war scare caused the Admiralty to purchase them. They were described as 'notoriously shaky and weak in construction', and had to be virtually rebuilt. Their propeller shaft projected underneath the rudder, and their conning towers were aft. They had the usual two funnels abreast, typical of Yarrow boats of the time. *TB 17* was used for some spectacular 'boom jumping' trials in 1887 at Malta, where she was finally sold in 1907. Her sister was sent to Gibraltar where she was sold in 1902. Both were rearmed when their single tube and spare torpedo were replaced with dropping gear for two torpedoes. Complement was 15.

113-FOOTERS

All carried 2 TT (two bow, one deck) and 2-3pdr guns, with a complement of 14.

TB 21-22 Thornycroft 1884-5

Displacement: 64t
Dimensions: 113½ft oa x 12½ft x 5ft 10in (*34.59 oa x 3.81 x 1.78m*)
Machinery: 700ihp = 20kts

Slightly modified versions of the *Childers* built by the same firm for the state marine of Victoria, Australia. Both were sent to Malta on completion and were sold there in 1907. Before this they had been reboilered with water-tube boilers, and towards the end lost their deck tubes and could only make about 15kts.

TB 23-24 Yarrow 1884-6

Displacement: 67t
Dimensions: 113½ft oa x 12ft 7in x 6¾ft (*34.59oa x 3.84 x 2.06m*)
Machinery: 600ihp = 18¾kts

Neither were considered worth reboilering. They were finally sold in 1905 and 1904 respectively.

125-FOOTERS

These boats were ordered in numbers because of the 1885/6 war scare with Russia, and because of the realisation that both France and Russia were building up their torpedo boat arms to a much larger extent than Britain. The original intention was to use them as 'torpedo catchers', as escorts for the fleet against Russian TBs, and therefore they were to have an armament of 2-3pdr and 2-twin-barrelled Nordenfeld MGs (later replaced by 5-barrelled 0.45in guns) plus one fixed bow TT (14in). However, they were also intended from the start to double as TBs, and they were all completed with the alternative armament of two pairs of deck TT instead of the 3pdr guns. Their complement was 16 men.

TB 25 Thornycroft 1885-6

Displacement: 60t
Dimensions: 128¼ft oa, 127½ft wl x 12½ft x 6ft (*39.09 oa, 38.86 wl x 3.81 x 1.82m*)
Machinery: 700ihp = 20¾kts

Ordered in February 1885 before the Russian war scare had started, she was the prototype for the class. Unfortunately her 'bull nose' ram bow proved to be totally unseaworthy, and she was rapidly returned to dockyard hands to have the ram bow and the fixed TT removed, and thereafter proved a useful vessel, with only the deck tubes and a conventional straight bow. She steered well, having Thornycroft's own special design of stern with a slight hollow to it and curved rudders on either side of the propeller to give a 'tunnel effect'. She was reboilered in 1901 with water-tube boilers, served as a patrol boat during the First World War, and was broken up soon afterwards.

TB 26-29, TB 41-60 Thornycroft 1885-6

As the danger of war increased firstly four, then another 20 repeats of *TB 25* were ordered from Thornycrofts. They were identical in all respects except that ihp varied from 700 to 750 and speed from 19½ to 21½kts; the last few were not completed by the time that the defect of the 'bull nose' bow was 'universally condemned', and their completion was delayed by having the straight bow without the fixed tube substituted. The earlier boats were soon taken out of service to have this essential modification made. *TB 28* was stranded and then expended as a target at Cape Town in 1898, but most of the others were refitted with water-tube boilers in the early years of the new century. *TB 56* sank in 1906, *TB 47, 48, 51, 53* and *59* were broken up at various times between 1905 and 1913, but all the others survived to be used for local patrol during the 1914–18 war. Some were rearmed with a 3pdr fitted on an AA mounting, and most seem to have been given a depth charge armament. *TB 46* sank in tow in 1915, but was raised and put back into service. All were scrapped in 1919/20.

TB 42, a Thornycroft 125-footer of 1880 with the straight bow
By courtesy of John Roberts

TB 60, another Thornycroft 125-footer, after renumbering as *060*

TB 75, a Yarrow 125-footer of 1887, which was lost in 1892

TB80 before reboilering 1887

TB 30-33, TB 61-78 Yarrow 1885-7

Displacement: 60t
Dimensions: 125¼ft oa x 13ft (*38.18 oa x 3.96m*)
Machinery: 670ihp = 19½kts

Ordered at the same time and to much the same basic concept as the Thornycroft boats, the Yarrow 125ft design differed in having a better-designed ram bow and so did not have to be rebuilt. *TB 75* was lost in collision in 1892; most of the rest were reboilered in the first decade of the twentieth century. *TB 30, 31, 32, 61, 62* were broken up before 1914. The remainder served during the war as patrol boats, and *TB 64* was wrecked in 1915. The rest were broken up between 1919 and 1923.

TB 34-38 White 1885-7

Displacement: 60-66t
Dimensions: 125ft pp x 14½ft x 4ft (*38.10 pp x 4.42 x 1.32m*)
Machinery: 950ihp = 18-19kts

White's version of the 125ft design had the stern 'cut up' in a rounded curve, meant to improve the steering (a feature introduced in their 'turnabout' Second Class boats). These boats were reboilered in the early 1900s by which time the bow TT had been removed. By 1914 all except *TB 34* were based at Hong Kong, and all were broken up in 1919.

TB 79 Yarrow 1886

Displacement: 75t
Dimensions: 128ft 8in oa, 128ft pp x 13ft x 5½ft (*39.22 oa, 39.01 pp x 3.96 x 1.68m*)
Machinery: 1000ihp = 22¼kts

Unlike the earlier Yarrow 125-footers *TB 79* was fitted with a triple expansion engine, and her hull form was altered to improve the rather poor steering of her predecessors. She could be immediately distinguished from them by having two funnels, though some of them acquired this feature when they were reboilered. She was reboilered in 1901, having already had the distinction of being commanded by the officer who later became King George V. After war service as a patrol boat she was broken up in 1919.

LARGER BOATS AND PURCHASES

TB 39-40 Yarrow 1882-5

Displacement: 40t
Dimensions: 100ft pp x 12½ft x 4ft (*30.48 pp x 3.81 x 1.22m*)
Machinery: 500ihp = 20kts
Armament: 1-14in TT, 2-1in twin-barrelled Nordenfeld
Complement: 15

Built for Chile, they had reached that country in a disassembled state when the Russian war scare of 1885 caused them to be hastily purchased to reinforce the Pacific Squadron based at Esquimault in British Columbia. They were assembled in Chile and escorted up to Canada. Here they remained as tenders to the flagship *Swiftsure,* and inevitably were unofficially christened *Swift* and *Sure.* By the beginning of the new century they were rearmed with two 14in torpedoes in dropping gear and 0.45in 5-barrelled Nordenfelds. They were sold for scrap in 1905.

TB 80 Yarrow 1886-7

Displacement: 105t
Dimensions: 135ft pp x 14ft x 6ft (*41.15 pp x 4.27 x 1.83m*)
Machinery: 1500ihp = 23kts
Armament: 1 fixed 14in bow TT, twin deck TT, 3-3pdr
Complement: 21

This was the first British TB to be fitted with the 'turtle back' bow, which made for greater seaworthiness, as did her greater size. She was based on a design produced by Yarrow for Austria, and was often referred to as the *Falke* type. Like the previous boats she was ordered as part of the 1885/6 programme. She was considered rather superior to the slightly later *TB 82* type by the same builder, being better able to keep up her speed, but she had to be reboilered early in her career (1898), when her original single funnel was replaced by two. The original intention appears to have been to carry two pairs of deck TTs, and the alternative armament of 4-3pdr with only the bow tube for anti-TB work was retained as a possibility throughout her early career. After war service as a patrol craft she was broken up in 1921.

TB 81 (SWIFT) White 1884-7

Displacement: 137t
Dimensions: 153ft 8½in oa, 150ft pp x 17½ft x 9½ft (*46.85 oa, 45.72 pp x 5.33 x 2.90m*)
Machinery: 1330ihp = 23¾kts
Armament: 1 fixed bow 14in TT, 2 single 14in deck TT, 4-3pdr
Complement: 25

In 1888 White began building as a private venture, with an eye to Admiralty purchase, a larger version of their 'turnabout' boat equipped with the cut-up stern, a ram bow with a spur ram, and referred to her as a 'torpedo boat destroyer'. In 1885 the Admiralty was glad to buy this formidable vessel just before she ran her first trials. Her original name of *Swift* was changed to the prosaic *TB 81,* but as the Russian war scare died away she spent some time incomplete whilst it was decided whether to complete her as a pure 'catcher' with 6-3pdr and only the bow tube, or with the mixed armament finally adopted. In 1901 she ran aground off Alderney, but was salved. She was reboilered in 1905, and later had her gun armament reduced by one. During the First World War hydrophones and depth charges were added for her patrol duties. She was broken up in 1921.

TB 82-87 Yarrow 1884

Displacement: 85t
Dimensions: 130ft 2in pp x 13ft 7in x 5¾ft (*39.67 pp x 4.14 x 1.75m*)
Machinery: 1800ihp = 23kts
Complement: 19

This 130ft Yarrow design was basically similar to *TB 79*, but with a 'turtle back' forecastle. They were not initially a great success, being so lightly built that they had to be strengthened soon after entering service. All were reboilered in the years around 1900. *TB 84* sank in the Mediterranean after a collision with the destroyer *Ardent* in 1906. The rest survived war service to be broken up between 1919 and 1921.

140-FOOTERS

Ordered at the same time as the first destroyers, these boats had an armament of 3-18in TT (one bow, two deck), though originally 14in were suggested, and 3-3 pdr. All had a complement of 18.

TB 88-89 Yarrow 1892-4

Displacement: 105t
Dimensions: 142ft pp x 14¾ft x 7½ft (*43.28 pp x 4.50 x 2.29m*)
Machinery: 1850ihp = 23½kts

Improved versions of the Yarrow 130-footers, with increased dimensions but little else changed, and therefore more seaworthy craft. Reboilered 1904/5, both survived their wartime patrolling to be broken up in 1919.

TB 90 Yarrow 1892-5

Displacement: 105t
Dimensions: 140¼ft pp x 14ft 4in x 6½ft (*42.75 pp x 4.37 x 1.98m*)
Machinery: 1500ihp = 23kts

Originally ordered as a sister of *TB 88*, but then a four-cylinder engine and water-tube boilers were installed as an experiment. She capsized off Gibraltar in 1918.

TB 91-92 Thornycroft 1892-4

Displacement: 141t
Dimensions: 140½ft (142½ft *TB 91*) oa x 15½ft x 7½ft (*42.82 (43.34 TB 91) oa x 4.72 x 2.29m*)
Machinery: 2350ihp = 24½kts

TB 91 was built slightly longer as an experiment to place the propeller further aft. Four-cylinder TE engines were fitted, as were water-tube boilers. After war service at Gibraltar both were broken up in 1919/20.

TB 93 Thornycroft 1892-4

Displacement: 136t
Dimensions: 140½ft oa x 15½ft x 5ft 1in (*42.82 oa x 47.24 x 1.55m*)
Machinery: 2200ihp = 23½kts

The first twin-screw TB in the Royal Navy, and the only such with reciprocating (four-cylinder TE) engines. Sold for breaking up in 1919.

TB 94 as completed 1893

TB 94-96 White 1892-5

Displacement: 130t
Dimensions: 142¼ft pp x 15¼ft x 8¾ft (*43.43 pp x 4.65 x 2.67m*)
Machinery: 2000ihp = 23kts

Fitted with TE engines built by Maudslay, these White boats had locomotive-type boilers, and therefore were reboilered a decade or so after completion with water-tube ones. War service was in the Mediterranean and off Gibraltar, where *TB 96* was sunk in a collision in 1915. The other pair were scrapped in 1919. These boats, having less metacentric height than the others, were easier in a seaway.

TB 97 Laird 1892-4

Displacement: 130t
Dimensions: 140ft 4in pp x 16ft x 7½ft (*42.77pp x 4.88 x 2.29m*)
Machinery: 2000ihp = 23kts

Fitted with locomotive boilers and reboilered with water-tube boilers in 1909. Sold in 1920 at Gibraltar, where she had spent her career.

1892 TRANSFER OF ROYAL INDIAN MARINE BOATS

In 1887 the India Office ordered seven boats which were to be slightly enlarged versions of the 125-footers. These appear never to have been delivered to India, and in 1892 were taken over by the Royal Navy, though their numbering as *TB 100-106* did not take place until 1901. The standard armament was similar to the 125-footers (5-14in TT, 2-1in twin-barrelled Nordenfeld), with the same option of replacing the deck TT with 3pdr guns. Complement was 18 men.

TB 100, 102-103 Thornycroft 1887-8

Displacement: 96t
Dimensions: 134ft 7½in oa, 133ft 7½in pp x 14¾ft x 7ft (*41.03oa, 40.73 pp x 4.50 x 2.13m*)
Machinery: 1260ihp = 23kts

Unlike the others these boats had water-tube boilers. Reboilered soon after 1900 and broken up 1909. Originally had RIM numbers 1-3 and were named *Baluchi*, *Karen* and *Pathan*.

TB 101 Hanna, Donald & Wilson 1887-8

Displacement: 92t
Dimensions: 135ft oa, 130ft pp x 14ft x 7ft (*41.15 oa, 39.62 pp x 4.27 x 2.13m*)
Machinery: 1000ihp = 21½kts

Generally resembled Yarrow's 125-footers but with a bow more like the White boats. Originally RIM number 7, *Gurkha*. Reboilered 1905, broken up 1920.

TB 104-106 White 1889

Displacement: 95t
Dimensions: 135ft oa, 130ft pp x 14½ft x 7½ft (*41.15 oa, 39.62 pp x 4.42 x 2.29m*)
Machinery: 1000ihp = 22kts

Like the other boats built by White on the 'turnabout' system they were very manoeuvrable. *TB 106* was broken up in 1910, the other two lasted until 1920. Originally RIM numbers 4-6, *Mahratta*, *Sikh* and *Rajput*.

160-FOOTERS

All followed the basic arrangement of the original Thornycroft design with 3-18in TT and 3-3pdr, both guns and torpedoes being disposed in a triangular layout, one on each side forward and one amidships aft. Though bigger and more seaworthy than their predecessors they were quite overshadowed by the destroyers which were in service in considerable numbers whilst the earliest of these TBs were building. Complement was 32 men.

TB 98-99, 107-108 Thornycroft 1900-1901

Displacement: 185t
Dimensions: 164ft oa, 160ft pp x 17ft x 5ft 10in (*49.99 oa, 48.77 pp x 5.18 x 1.78m*)
Machinery: 3000ihp = 25kts

The first pair were ordered under the 1899/1900 programme, the others a year later. They proved to be very short ranged (only capable of 6 hours' steaming at full speed), as indeed were all this group. *TB 99* sank in 1907 but was salved, all four being finally broken up in 1920.

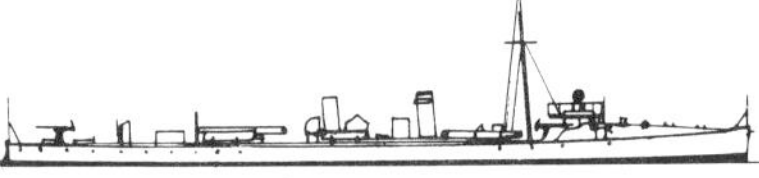
TB 109 as completed 1902

TB 109-113 Thornycroft 1901-1903

Displacement: 200t
Dimensions: 166ft oa, 164¾ft wl x 17¼ft x 5½ft (*50.60 oa, 50.22 pp x 5.26 x 1.68m*)
Machinery: 3050ihp = 25kts

Slightly larger and more powerful than their predecessors. All served in the First World War and were broken up in 1919/1920. *TB 113* was ordered half a month later than the others.

TB 114-117 White 1902-5

Displacement: 219t
Dimensions: 165ft pp x 17½ft (*50.29 pp x 5.33m*)
Machinery: 3050ihp = 25kts

These White boats were slightly larger than their Thornycroft predecessors but very little different. *TB 117* was sunk in a collision in 1917, the others being broken up between 1919 and 1921.

2nd class

The concept of purpose-built small TBs capable of being lifted by the davits of large ships seems to have originated with the Royal Navy; certainly more were built for that service than for any other. One TB carrier, *Vulcan*, was specially built to carry them, and for some years numbers of this type of boat were built. However, in the long run experience showed it was better to use the slower but much sturdier and more seaworthy steam pinnaces for this purpose, rather than the frail specially built Second Class boats.

This view shows the deck layout of a typical Yarrow 1st Class TB

TB 51-62 Thornycroft 1878-9

Displacement: 10¾t
Dimensions: 60½ft x 7½ft *(18.44 x 2.29m)*
Machinery: 120-150ihp = 15-16kts
Armament: 2 torpedoes in lowering cages (later dropping gear)
Complement: 7

Small, lightly built steam launches.

TB 63 Herreschoff 1878

Displacement: 15t
Dimensions: 60ft x 7½ft *(18.29 x 2.29m)*

This most unusual boat was unique in being the only foreign-built warship purchased for the Royal Navy in our period. She was brought over from the USA on speculation, and purchased as an experimental vessel through the intervention of the Director of Naval Construction, Nathaniel Barnaby. Her hull was unusual in having a wooden bottom and steel topsides, and the positioning of the propeller well forward and quite a distance below the hull was eccentric, whilst her most interesting feature of all was the coil boiler, a very temperamental device but very efficient and quick to raise steam when working. Though theoretically she was meant to carry two torpedoes it is doubtful whether she had the stability to carry any torpedo gear. She was only used for experiments and never put into service, unlike the Thornycroft boats against which she was tried, but she had her importance in bringing Thornycroft's attention to the possibility of developing the idea of the water-tube boiler. She had a speed of 16kts and a complement of 7.

TB 64-73 Thornycroft 1880-1

Displacement: 13t
Dimensions: 63ft oa x 7¾ft x 3ft 4in *(19.20 oa x 2.36 x 1.02m)*
Machinery: 110ihp = 16½kts

TB 68 was sent to Newfoundland. Ram bows. 2-14in torpedoes in dropping gear, 7 men.

TB 74-5, 96-7 Yarrow 1881-3

Displacement: 12t
Dimensions: 63ft 7½in oa x 7¾ft x 3½ft *(19.39 oa, x 2.36 x 1.07m)*
Machinery: 220ihp = 16kts

The TTs were fired by steam. 2-14in bow TT, 1 MG.

TB 76-95 Thornycroft 1880-3

Displacement: 12½t
Dimensions: 63ft pp x 7½ft x 3½ft *(19.20 pp x 2.29 x 1.07m)*
Machinery: 170ihp = 16½kts

The first two boats of this order were fitted with Herreschoff coil boilers for comparative purposes, but these were soon replaced by locomotive boilers similar to those in their sisters. 2-14in bow TT, 7 men.

TB 98 Thornycroft 1880-3

Displacement: 14½t
Dimensions: 66ft 4in wl x 7½ft x 2¾ft *(20.22 wl x 2.29 x 0.84m)*
Machinery: 167ihp = 11¾kts

Built as an experiment to test the Ruthven 'turbine' (water jet propulsion by centrifugal pump), in a hull as similar as possible to the other Second Class boats (though the boiler had to be placed aft). Her speed compared badly with her sisters, manoeuvrability was 'disappointing', she had difficulty in going astern, and, worst of all for a TB, the propulsion system made a noise that could be heard 10 miles away on a calm day. 2-14in bow TT, 7 men.

TB 99-100 Thornycroft 1884-6

Displacement: 12t
Dimensions: 65ft oa, 63ft pp x 8ft x 3½ft *(19.81 oa, 19.20 pp x 2.44 x 1.07m*
Machinery: 190ihp = 16½kts

TB 100 was fitted with one of the earliest Thornycroft water-tube boilers, whilst her sister still had a locomotive boiler. It was on these boats that the Thornycroft 'semi-tunnel' stern, with double rudders almost enclosing the propeller, was introduced. This gave them very good turning ability. 2 fixed 14in TT, 7 men.

TB 1-12 White 1883-8

Displacement: 10½-14t
Dimensions: 56ft x 9¼ft x 4¾ft *(17.07 x 2.82 x 1.45m)* but dimensions varied somewhat
Machinery: 140-200ihp = 15½kts

They were armed with 2-14in torpedoes in dropping gear or 1-14in torpedo in tube or spar torpedo and 1 or 2 MGs, and had a complement of 9 men. The first nine boats were ordered together in 1883, the next pair (which were slightly different) some years later, and finally *TB 12* was ordered a year after them. Unlike their predecessors they were wooden-hulled and built on the White 'turnabout' system with a 'cut away' stern for extra manoeuvrability. They were successful boats and were the first of a long lived and successful class, the 56ft picket boats. After these first twelve the design was altered, and the emphasis changed from the primary purpose of torpedo attack to a boat which was capable of many and varied duties including torpedo attack when required. These sturdy and seaworthy boats soon replaced the faster but frailer Second Class TBs as the largest steam boats carried on board British major warships.

TB 49-50 Yarrow 1888

Displacement: 15t (15½t for *TB 50*)
Dimensions: 59½ft pp x 8¼ft x 3ft *(18.14pp x 2.51 x 0.91m)*; 60ft x 8½ft for *TB 50 (18.29 x 2.59m)*
Machinery: 200ihp = 16½kts

Armament was 1-14in TT and 1 Nordenfeld MG, and the complement was 9 men.

TB 39-48 Yarrow 1889

Displacement: 16½t
Dimensions: 60ft x 9¼ft *(18.29 x 2.82m)*
Machinery: 240ihp = 16½kts

Armament comprised 2-14in torpedoes in dropping gear, 1 MG; the complement was 9 men. These two classes were the swan-song of the purpose-built Second Class TB. The last class was built on the lines of the aluminium boat Yarrow had built for the French Navy. Larger than their predecessors, six were intended to be carried on the 'torpedo boat carrier' *Vulcan*.

COLONIAL TORPEDO VESSELS

A few torpedo boats had been purchased by colonial governments for local defence in the later years of the century.

AUSTRALIA: NEW SOUTH WALES

ACHERON, AVERNUS Sydney 1879

Displacement: 16t
Dimensions: 78ft x 10ft *(23.77 x 3.05m)*
Machinery: 300ihp = 16kts

The only TBs not built in Europe or America.

AUSTRALIA: VICTORIA

NEPEAN, LONSDALE Thornycroft 1884

Identical to the early 63ft Second Class boats built for the Royal Navy. Both were broken up about 1906.

CHILDERS Thornycroft 1882-4

Displacement: 65ft
Dimensions: 113ft oa, 111ft 8in wl x 12½ft x 5½ft *(34.44 oa, 34.04 pp x 3.81 x 1.68m)*
Machinery: 670ihp = 19kts
Armament: 2-15in TT, 2-?3pdr

Thornycroft First Class type, she became the prototype for the Royal Navy 125-footers, which were often referred to as the '*Childers* type'. She went out to Australia under her own steam in an epic voyage.

COUNTESS OF HOPETOWN Yarrow 1890

Displacement: 82t
Dimensions: 130ft x 13½ft *(36.62 x 4.11m)*
Machinery: 1150ihp = 23kts
Armament: 3-14in TT, 3-3pdr
Complement: 19

Generally similar to the Royal Navy's *TB 79*. Broken up in 1924.

AUSTRALIA: TASMANIA

– Thornycroft 1884

Dimensions: 63 ft pp x 7½ft *(19.20 pp x 2.29 x 0.96m)*
Machinery: ?ihp = 17kts
Armament: 1 spar torpedo, 1 Nordenfeld MG

No name or number. Sister to the New Zealand boats below and contemporary Royal Navy Second Class TBs. In 1885 she was fitted with torpedo dropping gear in place of the spar. Out of service 1900.

NEW ZEALAND

Four boats (Nos 1-4) were built in 1883 and shipped in 1884. They were Thornycroft Second Class TBs and identical to the Tasmanian boat above. In 1885 three sets of torpedo dropping gear were supplied, to carry two torpedoes on each of three boats. A later proposal to fit torpedo tubes appears to have been vetoed on the grounds of excess weight.

INDIA

Baluchi, Karen, Pathan, Gurkha, Mahratta, Sikh, Rajput: see under First Class *TB 100-106* in the main Royal Navy list.

TORPEDO DEPOT SHIPS

TORPEDO DEPOT SHIPS

HECLA *torpedo depot ship*

Displacement: 6400t
Dimensions: 391½ft pp x 38ft 9½in x 24ft 4in *(119.33pp x 11.82 x 7.42m)*
Machinery: 2-shaft compound, 2400ihp = 13kts
Armament: 5-64pdr, 1-40pdr
Complement: 277

Name	Builder	Laid down	Launched	Fate
HECLA	Harland & Wolff	–	7.3.1878	Sold 13.7.1926

Hecla was the merchant ship *British Crown* purchased whilst building and *Vulcan* (below) was purpose-built, but both ships played a very similar role in the development of the British torpedo force. Each carried a number of Second Class TBs, and were fitted to service other TBs and to see to the torpedo and mining needs of a fleet. Both served, one after the other, with the Mediterranean Fleet, and both were commanded by a succession of distinguished officers who were amongst the leading torpedo specialists. Many of the most important experiments in torpedo tactics were carried out under their control. Had war come no doubt the two ships would have proved useful launching strikes with their small TBs against enemy bases.

Hecla was described as a 'torpedo depot ship and floating factory'. Later one of her 68pdr RML guns was replaced by 1-5in BL gun. In 1912 she was rebuilt, rearmed with 4-12pdr guns, and re-measured as 5600t. By this time she was operating as a destroyer depot ship. In 1916 two 4in guns were added to her armament.

VULCAN *torpedo boat carrier*

Displacement: 6600t
Dimensions: 373ft oa, 350ft pp x 58ft x 22ft *(113.69 oa, 106.68 pp x 17.68 x 6.71m)*
Machinery: 2-shaft TE, 12,000ihp = 20kts
Armament: 8-4.7in, 12-3pdr, ?-14in TT, 6 Second Class TBs
Complement: 432

Name	Builder	Laid down	Launched	Fate
VULCAN	Portsmouth DYd	18.6.1888	13.6.89	BU 1955

Vulcan was a most unusual vessel, built with the general appearance, lines and speed of a cruiser, and a respectable armament of her own. Her main purpose in wartime would have been to launch her TBs against the enemy, though she also had the full equipment of a depot ship. Her appearance was much as that of contemporary cruisers, except for the distinguishing feature of her two large 'goose neck' cranes, used for embarking and disembarking her boats. Like the cruisers of the time she had a protective deck of armour varying in thickness from 5in to 2½in.

Her trials were delayed because of trouble both with other vessels with similar boilers and with her own boilers, and she became one of the victims in the 'battle of the boilers' which raged over the type of boilers to adopt in the early 1890s. In 1902 she was reboilered completely. She suffered from other teething troubles, as some of the hull structure proved somewhat weak and had to be strengthened before completion. However her relatively wide beam in proportion to her length produced a reasonable performance.

In 1915, when she was being used as a submarine depot ship, her 4.7in guns were removed and 4-3pdr were added. In 1931 she became a training hulk and was renamed *Defiance III*.

The torpedo boat carrier *Vulcan*, with *TBs 39, 42, 43* and *44* visible on deck

GUNBOATS

Goldfinch of the *Redbreast* class

Before the advent of steam, the term 'gunboat' had in the Royal Navy been applied to small craft with one or two large guns, usually propelled by oars but often capable of hoisting sail. These were used principally for coastal defence and so were deemed unnecessary after the Napoleonic wars, the Royal Navy preferring more seaworthy sailing brigs. The largest of these were rated as brig-sloops, being in the charge of a Commander, while the smaller gun-brigs were commanded by Lieutenants, a distinction later applied to gunvessels and gunboats. These all-purpose small warships served the Navy well, and it was not until the late 1840s that steam-powered screw-driven replacements were contemplated.

THE CRIMEAN WAR

However, the screw-driven gunboat was essentially the product of the Crimean War. The need for manoeuvrable shallow-draught vessels for bombardment and blockade soon became apparent in both the Black Sea and Baltic inshore operations, the only suitable ships in 1854 being the 6 *Arrow* class gunvessels, armed with 2-68pdr Lancaster MLRs. However, even the *Arrows* were rather large and the Admiralty called for a vessel armed with 2-68pdrs that would draw only 6½ft of water. The resulting design was necessarily radical, with centreline traversing carriages for two of the largest guns then in use, and relatively powerful 60hp engines, with only a light sailing rig (although this was later increased). They were also highly successful, the first 6 being ordered in the middle of 1854 (the *Gleaner* class) rapidly followed by 20 *Dapper* class (ordered in October), and eventually no fewer than 98 *Albacores* – all built to virtually the same design. These classic Crimean gunboats became known, from their engine power, as 'Sixties', and were widely employed, although usually with the armament reduced to 1-68pdr and 1-32pdr. The succeeding *Cheerful* class were an attempt to produce a gunboat with only 4ft draught, stemming from experience in the Baltic campaign of 1855, but their construction proved too frail, and they were followed by the larger and more robust *Clown* class. The last 'Crimean gunboat' class was a considerable improvement, being larger and more seaworthy than previous gunboat types. These 6 *Algerines* were, in effect, the first gunboats capable of making an unaccompanied ocean passage in safety, and as such had more substantial accommodation, while the introduction of a hoisting screw made them handier under sail.

GUNVESSELS

Two further classes of gunvessels were built during the Crimean war, 6 very large *Intrepids*, rated as first class gunvessels, and 14 of the smaller second class *Vigilants*. However the 20 *Philomels* were not derived from the preceding gunvessels but were based on the successful *Algerine* class gunboats although with a larger hull and a heavier barque rig, and consequently improved seaworthiness. Six more of this class were cancelled in 1863.

Designed to match the combined firepower of two gunboats, the *Cormorant* class were enlarged to the dimensions of the *Vigilants*, but the 8ft designed draught was considerably exceeded as completed, which restricted their employment inshore. Four further vessels were cancelled. The slightly smaller *Plover* class adopted twin screws to achieve a shallow-draught hull but this, and the need to mount a traversing stern-chase gun, prevented the fitting of hoisting screws so they were unresponsive and leewardly under sail. They were the last British wooden gunvessels and the smallest ships in the Navy with telescopic funnels. *Philomel*, *Magpie*, *Seagull*, *Swallow*, *Vulture* and *Woodlark* later had topgallant forecastles and poops added for better accommodation on the tropical stations to which they were assigned.

The composite-built *Beacon* class were designed for service in China and as an economy measure were fitted with pairs of 60hp engines removed from laid-up Crimean gunboats. Originally they were intended to mount 2-68pdr SBs as the Armstrong gun controversy was at its height, but they were completed with a 7in 'Woolwich' MLR and a 64pdr instead. Later *Flirt*, *Hornet*, *Lynx* and *Rocket* were rearmed with 2-7in of the lighter 4½t pattern on an iron carriage, and *Avon* and *Elk* received one in lieu of their 6½t 7in. Poops were added to *Beacon*, *Boxer*, *Dwarf*, *Flirt*, *Midge* and *Teazer*. The four *Frolics*, laid down in 1871, were repeats of the *Beacon* class, but the *Arab* class was an improvement with a simplified armament of two rather than three calibres.

Up to this point gunvessel development was dominated by the inshore experience of the Crimean war and the 'coastal theory' of the early 1870s, but the *Condor* and the slightly larger *Linnet* and *Algerine* classes were better suited for deep-sea employment. They were given the barque rig of contemporary sloops and became genuine cruising ships, but they reverted to single-screw propulsion, *Falcon* and *Griffon* having feathering propellers. Those rearmed with 5in Vavasseur BLs in the mid-1880s were re-rated as first class gunvessels after the Naval Defence Act.

FLATIRON GUNBOATS

In contrast to the growing Imperial cruising role of the gunvessels, the invasion scares of the late 1860s and early 1870s produced a renewed emphasis on inshore warfare and these small iron mastless gunboats were built in response to Parliamentary pressure for improved coastal defence. They were very slow and totally unseaworthy but thirty of these 'flatirons' were laid down between 1867 and 1881. They were also known as Rendel gunboats after their originator, Armstrong's naval architect, who produced many similar vessels for overseas navies. The prototypes were followed by 24 of the similar *Ant* and *Gadfly* classes, and two of the larger *Bouncer* class. All were armed with one 10in MLR.

As their nickname implies, these vessels were strange enough to the seaman's eye, but the *Medina* class were bizarre in the extreme, being given a full three-masted rig. One of the 3-64pdrs was mounted on a fixed forward bearing, but with a marked tumblehome and even a small poop and forecastle, the resemblance to genuine 'flatirons' was minimal. However, they had bow rudders and some were used on Chinese rivers with reasonable success.

Like the two later 'flatirons' *Hardy* and *Drudge* built by Armstrong for gun mounting tests, most ended their days as gunnery tenders.

GUNBOATS

Ten improved *Dappers* were ordered from commercial builders in

1859, followed by ten more from Portsmouth DYd in 1861, although only six were completed. The *Britomart* class, as they became, introduced to gunboats the hoisting screw with its consequent improvement in handling under sail, and a barquentine rig (with square sails on the foremast only) that became known as the 'gunboat rig'. Thereafter there was a lull in gunboat building until the *Ariel* class of 1870. Huge numbers of gunboats had survived the Crimean war but many had been skimpily constructed of unseasoned timbers and their hulls became rapidly worn out or rotten. New construction had concentrated on gunvessels, but the composite-built *Ariels* represented a different concept from both the gunvessels and the previous wooden gunboats. There was a move towards greater seakeeping qualities at the expense of coastal and riverine capabilities, and they introduced both watertight bulkheads and compound engines to the Navy's small warships. With 2-68pdr MLRs on the centreline and 2-20pdr Armstrong BLs as chasers they were also an advance in offensive power, and they proved so successful that the general design was repeated in the *Forester* and *Banterer* classes (although these last were distinguished by vertical stems).

The *Albacore* class of 1881 reintroduced BL guns on gunboats, although paradoxically they were the last to use centreline traversing mountings. For the *Bramble* class of 1885 the new light 4in BL was broadside-mounted on the forecastle, amidships and aft. The *Bramble* design served as a model for all the remaining composite gunboats – the *Pygmy* and *Redbreast* classes – down to 1889. In 1889 all gunvessels and gunboats were reclassified as first or second class depending on whether they mounted BL or ML guns, and later in the year the momentous Naval Defence Act was passed. This marked the end of the gunboat navy in favour of large battleships and modern cruisers, and the only gunboats completed after the Act were the four vessels of the second *Bramble* class, designed for service in West Africa and China. They were quite unlike previous classes in appearance with two light masts and a steel hull, but were sheathed to prevent fouling in tropical waters.

THE GUNBOAT FLEET IN 1860

SCREW GUNVESSELS (2-6 GUNS)

Name	Fate
ARROW class, 1854, 477t bm	
Arrow	Sold 1862
Beagle	Sold 1863
Lynx	Sold 1862
Snake	Sold 1865
Viper	Sold 1862
Wrangler	BU 1866
INTREPID class, 1855-56, 868t bm	
Flying Fish	BU 1866
Intrepid	Sold 1864
Nimrod	Sold 1865
Pioneer	Sold 1864
Roebuck	Sold 1864
Victor	Sold 1863
VIGILANT class, 1855-56, 670t bm	
Alacrity	Sold 1864
Assurance	Sold 1970
Coquette	Sold 1868
Foxhound	BU 1866
Lapwing	Sold 1864
Mohawk	Sold 1862
Osprey	Wrecked 1867
Renard	BU 1866
Ringdove	Sold 1865
Sparrowhawk	Sold 1872
Surprise	BU 1866
Vigilant	Sold 1869
Wanderer	BU 1866

Cormorant was sunk in action, China, June 1859

SCREW GUNBOATS (2-4 GUNS)

Name	Fate
GLEANER class, 1854, 216t bm	
Badger	BU 1864
Gleaner	Sold 1868
Pelter	Sold 1864
Pincher	BU 1864
Ruby	BU 1868
Snapper	Hulked 1865, sold 1906
DAPPER class, 1855, 232t bm	
Biter	Hulked 1865
Boxer	BU 1866
Clinker	Sold 1871
Cracker	BU 1864
Dapper	Hulked 1855, sold 1922
Fancy	Hulked 1876, sold 1905
Grinder	BU 1864
Hind	BU 1872
Jackdaw	Hulked 1868, sold 1888
Lark	Sold 1878
Magpie	Wrecked 1864
Redwing	Sold 1878
Skylark	Sold 1906
Snap	Sold 1868
Starling	Sold 1871
Stork	Hulked 1874, sold 1884
Swinger	BU 1864
Thistle	BU 1863
Weazel	Sold 1869

Jasper was wrecked in 1855

Name	Fate
ALBACORE class, 1855-56, 232t average	
Albacore	BU 1885
Amelia	BU 1865
Banterer	Sold 1872
Beacon	Discarded 1864
Blazer	Sold 1877
Bouncer	Sold 1871
Brave	BU 1869
Brazen	BU 1864
Bullfinch	BU 1864
Bullfrog	BU 1878
Bustard	Sold 1869
Camel	BU 1864
Carnation	BU 1863
Caroline	BU 1862
Charger	Sold 1887
Charon	BU 1865
Cherokee	BU 1869
Cochin	BU 1863
Cockchafer	Sold 1872
Confounder	BU 1864
Crocus	BU 1864
Delight	Sold 1867
Dove	Sold 1873
Earnest	Sold 1885
Erne	BU 1874
Escort	BU 1865
Fervent	BU 1879
Firm	Sold 1872
Flamer	Hulked 1867, sold 1874
Fly	BU 1862
Foam	BU 1867
Forester	Lost in typhoon 1871
Forward	Sold 1869
Goldfinch	BU 1869
Goshawk	BU 1869
Grappler	Sold 1868
Grasshopper	Sold 1871
Griper	BU 1869
Growler	BU 1864
Hardy	Sold 1869
Hasty	BU 1866
Haughty	Sold 1867
Havock	Sold 1871
Herring	BU 1865
Highlander	Sold 1884
Hyaena	Sold 1870
Insolent	Sold 1869
Julia	BU 1865
Leveret	BU 1867
Lively	Wrecked 1863
Louisa	Sold 1867
Mackerel	BU 1862
Magnet	BU 1874
Manly	BU 1863
Mastiff	BU 1863
Mayflower	BU 1867
Mistletoe	BU 1864
Nightingale	Sold 1867
Opossum	Hulked 1876, sold 1896
Parthian	BU 1864
Partridge	Sold 1864
Peacock	BU 1869
Pheasant	BU 1877
Pickle	BU 1864
Porpoise	BU 1864
Primrose	BU 1864
Procris	Hulked 1869, sold 1893
Prompt	BU 1864
Quail	BU 1861
Rainbow	Hulked 1873, sold 1888
Raven	BU 1864
Redbreast	BU 1864
Ripple	BU 1866
Rocket	BU 1864
Rose	BU 1868
Sandfly	Sold 1867
Savage	BU 1888
Seagull	Sold 1864
Sepoy	BU 1868
Shamrock	Sold 1867
Sheldrake	Sold 1865
Skipjack	Hulked 1874, BU 1879
Spanker	BU 1874
Spey	BU 1864
Spider	Sold 1870
Staunch	Sold 1866
Surly	Sold 1869
Swan	Hulked 1869, discarded 1906
Thrasher	Sold 1883
Tickler	BU 1863
Tilbury	BU 1865
Traveller	BU 1864
Violet	Sold 1864
Wave	Sold 1890
Whiting	BU 1881
Wolf	BU 1864

Plover was lost in action, China, June 1859. Many of the above were never completed.

Name	Fate
CHEERFUL class, 1855-56, 212t bm	
Angler	BU 1869
Ant	BU 1869
Blossom	BU 1864
Cheerful	BU 1869
Chub	BU 1869
Daisy	BU 1869
Decoy	BU 1869
Dwarf	BU 1863
Fidget	BU 1863
Flirt	BU 1864
Gadfly	BU 1864
Garland	BU 1864
Gnat	BU 1864
Midge	BU 1864
Nettle	BU 1867
Onyx	Sold 1873
Pert	Discarded 1864
Pet	Sold 1904
Rambler	BU 1869
Tiny	Discarded 1863
CLOWN class, 1856, 233t bm	
Clown	Lost 1871
Drake	Sold 1869
Fenella	Bu 1878
Garnet	Discarded 1864
Handy	Sold 1868
Janus	Sold 1871
Kestrel	Sold 1866
Ready	BU 1864
Thrush	BU 1864
Watchful	Sold 1871
Woodcock	Sold 1871

Hunter was never completed

Name	Fate
ALGERINE class, 1857, 301t bm	
Algerine	Sold 1872
Jasper	Sold 1862
Leven	Sold 1873
Slaney	Wrecked 1870

Jaseur was wrecked in 1859 and *Lee* was sunk in action, China, June 1859

PADDLE GUNBOATS

Name	Fate
Avon (NZ)	Sold 1863
Bloodhound	BU 1866
Caradoc	Sold 1870
Coromandel	Sold 1866
Firefly[1]	BU 1866
Harpy	Sold *c*1909
Jackal	Sold 1887
Lizard	Sold 1869
Locust	Tug 1869, sold 1895
Merlin	Sold 1863
Otter	Tug 1865, sold 1893
Pluto	BU 1861
Porcupine	Sold 1883
Recruit	Sold 1869
Spitfire[1]	Tug 1862, BU 1888
Weser	Sold 1873

(1) Survey vessels by 1860.

The Navy also operated the paddle packets *Adder* (sold 1870), *Dover* (sold 1866), *Dasher* (sold 1885), *Cuckoo* (sold 1864), *Medina* (sold 1865), *Medusa* (sold 1865) and *Princess Alice* (BU 1878).

SAILING BRIGS

The sailing navy's equivalents of steam gunboats were the brig-sloops and gun-brigs, of which the following were still in service in 1860:

16 GUNS

Name	Fate
Arab	BU 1879
Atalanta	BU 1868
Childers	Sold 1865
Elk	Coast Guard 1863
Fantome	Sold 1864
Grecian	BU 1865
Helena	Hulked 1861, BU 1921
Jumna	Sold 1862
Mariner	Sold 1865
Musquito	Sold 1862
Persian	BU 1866
Pilot	Sold 1862
Rover	Sold 1862
Siren	BU 1868

12 GUNS

Name	Fate
Acorn	Hulked 1861, sold 1869
Contest	BU 1868
Daring	Sold 1864
Despatch	Coast Guard 1863
Espiegle	Sold 1861
Kangaroo	Coast Guard 1863
Kingfisher	Sold 1890
Squirrel	BU 1879

There were also the training brigs *Liberty* (sold 1905), *Martin* (sold 1907) and *Sealark* (sold 1898) and the smaller gun-brigs *Waterwitch* (sold 1861) and *Ferret* (wrecked 1869). The Navy also operated 5 packet brigs and 8 smaller brigantines, schooners and cutters.

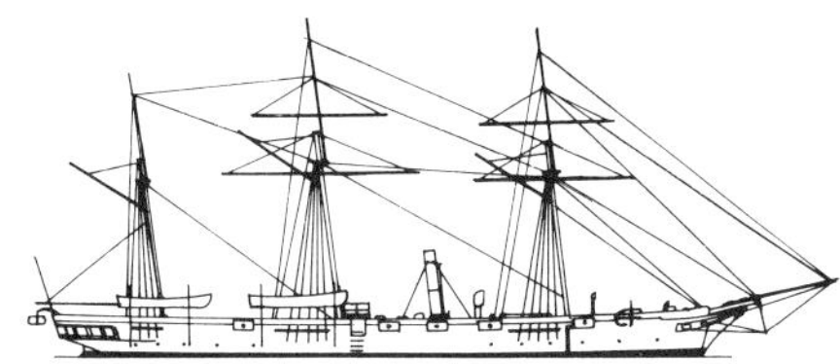
Nimble (*Philomel* class) 1875

PHILOMEL class *wooden gunvessels* (launched 1859-62, *Newport* 1867)

Displacement:	570t
Dimensions:	145ft x 25ft 4in x 11ft-12ft (*44.20 x 7.72 x 3.35-3.65m*)
Machinery:	1-shaft, reciprocating, 276-382ihp = 8-11kts
Armament:	1-68pdr SB, later 1-110pdr BL, 2-24pdr howitzers, 2-20pdr BL
Complement:	60

Class (builder, fate): *Cygnet* (Wigram, BU 1868), *Dart* (Mare, sold 1884), *Espoir* (Pembroke DYd, converted to dredger *YC19* 1869), *Griffon* (Pitcher, stranded 1866), *Jaseur* (Deptford DYd, sold 1874), *Landrail* (Deptford DYd, sold 1869), *Lee* (Wigram, BU 1875), *Mullet* (Lungley, sold 1872), *Newport* (Pembroke DYd, completed as survey vessel 1868 and sold 1881), *Nimble* (Pembroke DYd, sold 1906), *Pandora* (Pembroke DYd, sold 1875), *Penguin* (Miller, sold 1870), *Philomel* (White, sold 1865), *Plover* (Green, sold 1865), *Ranger* (Deptford DYd, sold 1869), *Snipe* (Scott Russell, sold 1869), *Sparrow* (Scott Russell, BU 1868), *Speedwell* (Deptford DYd, BU 1867), *Steady* (Miller, sold 1870), *Torch* (Green, BU 1881)

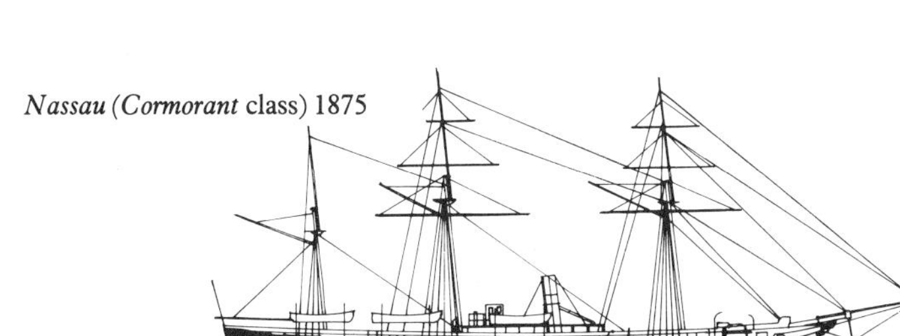
Nassau (*Cormorant* class) 1875

CORMORANT class *wooden gunvessels* (launched 1860-67)

Displacement:	877t
Dimensions:	185ft x 28ft 2in x 11ft-12ft (*56.39 x 8.59 x 3.35-3.65m*)
Machinery:	1-shaft, reciprocating, 690-774ihp = 10kts
Armament:	1-110pdr BL, 1-68pdr SB, 2-20pdr; later 1-7in MLR, 2-64pdr
Complement:	90

Class (builder, fate): *Cormorant* (Wigram, sold 1870), *Eclipse* (Scott Russell, BU 1867), *Lily* (Scott Russell, BU 1867), *Myrmidon* (Chatham DYd, completed as survey vessel 1867 and sold 1889), *Nassau* (Pembroke DYd, completed as survey vessel 1866 and BU 1880), *Racehorse* (Wigram, wrecked 1864), *Serpent* (Mare, sold 1875), *Star* (Mare, BU 1877), *Sylvia* (Woolwich DYd, completed as survey vessel 1866 and sold 1890)

Dwarf of the *Beacon* class

Seagull of the *Plover* class

PLOVER class *wooden gunvessels* (launched 1867-71)

Displacement:	755t
Dimensions:	170ft x 29ft x 9ft 6in-10ft 6in (*51.82 x 8.84 x 2.90-3.20m*)
Machinery:	2-shaft, SPR, 800-970ihp = 10kts average
Armament:	1-7in MLR, 2-40pdr BL; some later 1-7in MLR, 2-64pdr MLR
Complement:	90

Class (builder, fate): *Bittern* (Pemboke DYd, sold 1887), *Bullfinch* (Sheerness DYd, sold 1885), *Curlew* (Deptford DYd, sold 1882), *Lapwing* (Devonport DYd, sold 1885), *Magpie* (Portsmouth DYd, sold 1885), *Philomel* (Deptford DYd, sold 1887), *Plover* (Deptford DYd, sold 1886), *Ringdove* (Portsmouth DYd, sold 1882), *Seagull* (Devonport DYd, sold 1887), *Swallow* (Portsmouth DYd, sold 1882), *Vulture* (Sheerness DYd, sold 1885), *Woodlark* (Chatham DYd, sold 1887)

BEACON class *composite gunvessels* (launched 1867-68)

Displacement:	576t designed, 603t actual
Dimensions:	155ft x 25ft x 8ft-9ft 6in (*47.24 x 7.62 x 2.44-2.90m*)
Machinery:	HDAR, 465-696ihp = 9-10¼kts
Armament:	1-7in MLR, 1-64pdr MLR, 2-20pdr BL
Complement:	80

Class (builder, fate): *Avon* (Portsmouth DYd, sold 1890), *Beacon* (Chatham DYd, sold 1888), *Boxer* (Deptford DYd, sold 1886), *Cracker* (Portsmouth DYd, BU 1889), *Dwarf* (Woolwich DYd, BU 1886), *Elk* (Portsmouth DYd, sold 1905), *Flirt* (Devonport DYd, sold 1888), *Fly* (Devonport DYd, sold 1887), *Gnat* (Pembroke DYd, wrecked 1868), *Growler* (Laurie, sold 1887), *Hart* (Thompson, sold 1888), *Hornet* (Penn, discarded 1889), *Lynx* (Harland & Wolff, sold 1888), *Midge* (Elder, sold 1907), *Pert* (Reid, sold 1888), *Rocket* (London Eng Co, sold 1888), *Teazer* (Laird, BU 1887), *Thistle* (Deptford DYd, sold 1888)

FROLIC class *wooden gunvessels* (launched 1872)

Displacement:	610t
Dimensions:	155ft x 25ft x 7ft 9in-9ft 6in (*47.24 x 7.62 x 2.36-2.90m*)
Machinery:	2-shaft, CT, 130-190ihp = 10½-11kts
Armament:	1-7in MLR, 1-64pdr MLR, 2-20pdr BL
Complement:	80

Class (builder, fate): *Frolic* (Chatham DYd, sold 1908), *Kestrel* (Chatham DYd, sold 1888), *Ready* (Chatham DYd, sold 1920), *Rifleman* (Chatham DYd, sold 1890)

Condor, a composite gunvessel of 1876

ARAB class *composite gunvessels* (launched 1874)

Displacement: 620t
Dimensions: 150ft x 28ft 6in x 10ft 6in-12ft 10in (*45.72 x 8.69 x 3.20-3.91m*)
Machinery: 1-shaft, 2 cyl CR, 570ihp = 10½kts
Armament: 1-7in MLR, 2-64pdr MLR
Complement: 90

Class (builder, fate): *Arab* (Napier, sold 1889), *Lily* (Napier, wrecked 1889 and sold in 1890)

CONDOR class *composite gunvessels* (launched 1876-77)

Displacement: 774ft designed, 780t actual
Dimensions: 157ft x 29ft 6in x 13ft (*47.85 x 8.99 x 3.96m*)
Machinery: 1-shaft, CR, 721-795ihp = 11½kts
Armament: 1-7in MLR, 2-64pdr MLR
Complement: 100

Class (builder, fate): *Condor* (Devonport DYd, sold 1889), *Falcon* (Laird, sold 1920), *Falmingo* (Devonport DYd, sold 1923), *Griffon* (Laird, sold 1891)

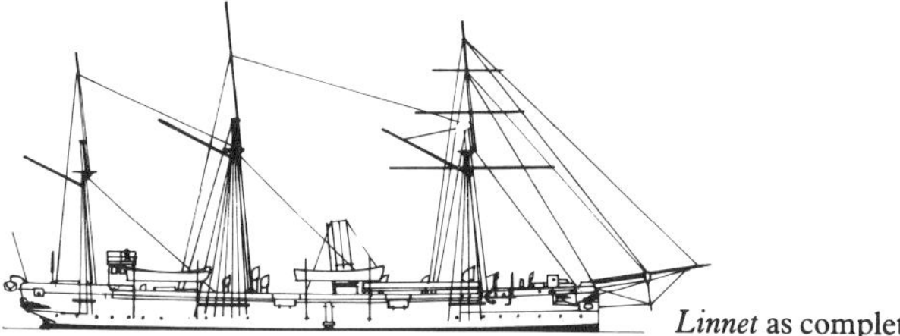

Linnet as completed 1880

LINNET class *composite gunvessels* (launched 1879-80)

Displacement: 756t designed, 788t actual
Dimensions: 165ft x 29ft x 10ft 3in-10ft 10in (*50.29 x 8.84 x 3.12-3.30m*)
Machinery: 1-shaft, reciprocating, 870ihp = 11.8kts
Armament: 2-7in MLR, 3-20pdr BL
Complement: 92

Class (builder, fate): *Linnet* (Thames Sb Co, sold 1904), *Swift* (Thames Sb Co, sold 1902)

Algerine as completed 1881

ALGERINE class *composite gunvessels* (launched 1880)

Displacement: 835t
Dimensions: 157ft x 29ft 6in x 13ft 6in (*47.85 x 8.99 x 4.11m*)
Machinery: 1-shaft, reciprocating, 810ihp = 10½kts
Armament: 1-7in MLR, 2-64pdr MLR; later 2-5in BL, 2-64pdr MLR
Complement: 100

Class (builder, fate): *Algerine* (Harland & Wolff, sold 1892), *Rambler* (Elder, completed as survey ship 1884 and sold 1907), *Ranger* (Elder, sold 1892)

Landrail and her sister represented the final stage in the evolution of the gunvessel, although the addition of a torpedo armament and the absence of the sailing rig made them hybrids without any obvious role

CURLEW class *gun and torpedo vessels*

Displacement: 950t
Dimensions: 195ft pp x 28ft x 10ft 6in (*59.44 pp x 8.53 x 3.20m*)
Machinery: 2-shaft, Penn 2 cyl HDAC engines, 4 cyl boilers, 1500ihp = 14.5kts
Armament: 1-6in BLR, 3-5in BLR, 7 MGs, 1 TT, 2 TC aw
Complement: 46

Name	Builder	Laid down	Launched	Comp	Fate
CURLEW	Devonport DYd	5.1.1885	23.10.85	22.6.86	Sold for BU 1906
LANDRAIL	Devonport DYd	5.1.1885	19.1.86	10.3.87	Sunk as target 4.10.1906

The *Curlew* class were what might be described as an attempt to modernise the gunvessel but as the resultant type fulfilled no real need they were not repeated and soon became obsolete. They were of similar size and general arrangement to a standard composite gunvessel but were constructed of steel with a finer, shallower hull and more powerful, forced draught machinery to provide a higher speed, had no sailing rig and were given a torpedo as well as a gun armament. Unfortunately they were too slow and too small to operate effectively with the fleet and were too sophisticated to take up the duties of their 'old-fashioned' predecessors. They cost about 25% more to construct than a standard gunvessel and the very fact that they had no sails and an unsheathed steel hull made them an uneconomic proposition on distant stations.

They carried a single 6in BLR, on the forecastle, and three 5in BLR, one on the poop and two in the waist on the upper deck. A fixed torpedo tube was mounted at the extreme forward end of the upper deck firing through the stem while the two torpedo carriages, one under the forecastle and one under the poop, were provided with alternate discharge ports to port and starboard. They originally carried two masts but in 1903 *Curlew's* mainmast was removed. *Landrail* served mainly on foreign stations and *Curlew* in home waters, their first commissions being on the Cape station and with the Channel squadron respectively.

These three rather odd vessels represented an attempt to apply ironclad principles to the gunboat/gunvessel class and were largely experimental. They were not successful as they were slow, unhandy and unseaworthy and they spent the majority of their careers in harbour service. *Viper* and *Vixen* were the first ships to be fitted with twin screw machinery and *Vixen* was the first gunboat of composite construction, having a timber hull on iron frames. *Viper* and *Waterwitch* were constructed of iron. *Waterwitch* was fitted with hydraulic reaction machinery, an early form of turbine propulsion, designed by J Ruthven upon principles laid down by James Rumsey in 1787. The engine drove a centrifugal pump which drew in water from openings in the ship's bottom forward and forced it out under high pressure at the stern giving a form of jet propulsion. The whole system was reversible and *Waterwitch* was double-ended with a rudder and ram shape at both bow and stern. Her engine room was positioned amidships with the boiler room abaft it which gave her an unusual profile as the funnel was positioned well aft between the main- and mizzenmasts. She proved almost unmanoeuvrable and was a complete failure, although this was as much the fault of the design of the ship as that of the machinery, and she was withdrawn from service before either of her sisters. *Viper* and *Vixen* were towed to Bermuda, being insufficiently seaworthy to undertake the journey under their own power, where they served as harbour vessels until the end of their careers; *Viper* was converted to a tank vessel in 1901.

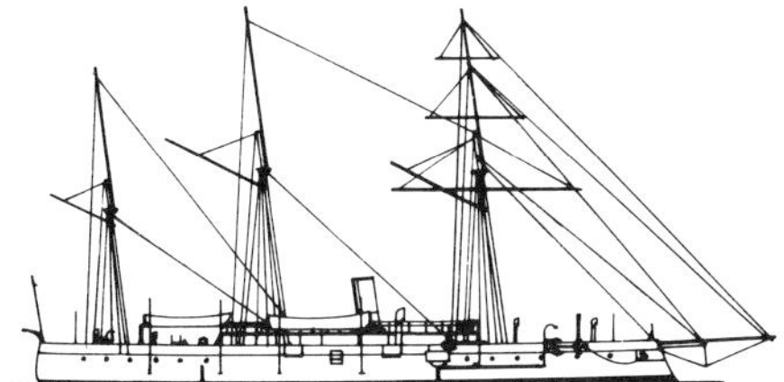

Viper as completed 1867

VIXEN class *armoured gunboats*

Displacement: 1230t load, *Waterwitch* 1280t
Dimensions: 160ft (*Waterwitch* 162ft) pp x 32ft (*Waterwitch* 32ft 1in, *Vixen* 32ft 5in) x 11ft 8in (*Waterwitch* 11ft 11in) *(48.77 (49.38) pp x 9.75 (9.78, 9.88) x 3.55 (3.63)m)*
Machinery: 2-shaft, Maudslay H (*Waterwitch* Ruthven hydraulic turbine) engines, 700ihp = 9.59kts *Viper*, 740ihp = 8.89kts *Vixen*, 780ihp = 8.88kts *Waterwitch*. Coal 110t (*Waterwitch* 100t)
Armour: 4½in sides, 4½in bulkheads, 10in wood backing
Armament: 2-7in MLR, 2-20pdr BL
Complement: 80

Name	Builder	Laid down	Launched	Comp	Fate
VIPER	Dudgeon, Limehouse	1864	21.12.65	1867	Sold 1908
VIXEN	Lungley, Deptford	1864	18.11.65	1866	BU 1896
WATERWITCH	Thames Iron Wks, Blackwall	1864	28.6.66	1867	Sold 1890

BRITOMART class *wooden gunboats* (launched 1860-67)

Displacement: 330t
Dimensions: 120ft x 22ft x 8ft *(37.19 x 6.71 x 2.44m)*
Machinery: 1 cyl reciprocating, 260ihp = 9kts
Armament: 2-68pdr, later 2-64pdr MLR
Complement: 36-40

Class (builder, fate): *Bramble* (Portsmouth DYd, cancelled), *Britomart* (Smith, BU 1946), *Bruizer* (Portsmouth DYd, BU 1886), *Cherub* (Portsmouth DYd, sold 1890), *Cockatrice* (Smith, sold 1885), *Cromer* (Portsmouth DYd, sold 1886), *Crown* (Portsmouth DYd, cancelled), *Danube* (Portsmouth DYd, cancelled), *Doterel* (Miller, sold 1871), *Heron* (Miller, BU 1879), *Linnet* (Briggs, BU 1872), *Minstrel* (Portsmouth DYd, discarded 1907), *Netley* (Portsmouth DYd, sold 1885), *Orwell* (Portsmouth DYd, discarded 1890), *Pigeon* (Briggs, BU 1876), *Protector* (Portsmouth DYd, cancelled), *Speedy* (Lamport, discarded 1889), *Trinculo* (Banks, wrecked 1870), *Tyrian* (Courtenay, BU 1891), *Wizard* (Smith, BU 1878)

Goshawk of the *Ariel* class

ARIEL class *composite gunboats* (launched 1871-73)

Displacement: 430t, *Ariel* and *Zephyr* 438t
Dimensions: 125ft x 22ft 6in (*Ariel* and *Zephyr* 23ft) x 8ft 6in-10ft 6in *(38.1 x 6.86 (7.01) x 2.59-3.20m)*
Machinery: 1-shaft, HCR, 400-540ihp = 9½-10½kts
Armament: 2-64pdr MLR, 2-20pdr BL
Complement: 60

Class (builder, fate): *Ariel* (Chatham DYd, sold 1889), *Coquette* (Pembroke DYd, sold 1889), *Decoy* (Pembroke DYd, sold 1885), *Foam* (Pembroke DYd, BU 1887), *Goshawk* (Pembroke DYd, sold 1906), *Merlin* (Pembroke DYd, sold 1891), *Mosquito* (Pembroke DYd, sold 1888), *Swinger* (Pembroke DYd, sold 1924), *Zephyr* (Chatham DYd, sold 1889)

PLUCKY *flatiron gunboat* (launched July 1870)

Displacement: 212t
Dimensions: 80ft x 25ft 1½in x 6ft 1½in *(24.38 x 7.66 x 1.87m)*
Machinery: 2-shaft, 2 cyl, 224ihp = 7½kts
Armament: 1-9in MLR
Complement: 31

Prototype. Sold 1928

STAUNCH *flatiron gunboat* (launched Dec 1867)

Displacement: 200t
Dimensions: 75ft x 25ft x 6ft 6in *(22.86 x 7.62 x 1.98m)*
Machinery: 2-shaft, 2 cyl, 134ihp = 7½kts
Armament: 1-9in MLR
Complement: 31

Prototype. Sold 1904.

Arrow (*Ant* class) as completed 1872

ANT class *flatiron gunboats* (launched 1870-74)

Displacement: 254t
Dimensions: 85ft x 26ft 1½in x 6ft-6ft 6in *(25.91 x 7.96 x 1.83-1.98m)*
Machinery: 2 cyl reciprocating, 260ihp = 8½kts
Armament: 1-10in MLR
Complement: 30

Class (builder, fate): *Ant* (Laird, sold 1926), *Arrow* (Rennie, sold 1922), *Badger* (Chatham DYd, sold 1908), *Blazer* (Portsmouth DYd, sold 1919), *Bloodhound* (Armstrong, sold 1921), *Bonetta* (Rennie, sold 1909), *Bulldog* (Campbell Johnston, sold 1906), *Bustard* (Napier, sold 1923), *Comet* (Portsmouth DYd, sold 1908), *Cuckoo* (Laird, sold 1959), *Fidget* (Chatham DYd, sold 1905), *Hyaena* (Laird, sold 1906), *Kite* (Napier, sold 1920), *Mastiff* (Armstrong, sold 1931), *Pickle* (Campbell Johnston, sold 1906), *Pike* (Campbell Johnston, sold 1920), *Scourge* (Chatham DYd, tank vessel *C79* 1903), *Snake* (Chatham DYd, cable lighter *YC15* 1907), *Snap* (Campbell Johnston, sold 1909), *Weazel* (Laird, oil lighter *C118* 1904)

GADFLY class *flatiron gunboats* (launched 1879)

Displacement: 254t
Dimensions: 85ft x 26ft 1½in x 6ft-6ft 6in *(25.91 x 7.96 x 1.83-1.98m)*
Machinery: 2 cyl reciprocating, 260ihp = 8½kts
Armament: 1-10in MLR
Complement: 30

Class (builder, fate): *Gadfly* (Pembroke DYd, sold 1918), *Griper* Pembroke DYd, BU ?1951), *Pincher* (Pembroke DYd, sold 1905), *Tickler* (Pembroke DYd, BU 1937)

Bouncer (IWM)

Medina in 1882

Cockchafer of the *Banterer* class

Watchful of the *Albacore* class

Bramble, a composite gunboat of 1886

BOUNCER *flatiron gunboats* (launched 1881)

Displacement: 265t
Dimensions: 87ft 4in x 26ft 1⅛in x 6ft-6ft 6in (*26.63 x 7.96 x 1.83-1.98m*)
Machinery: 2 cyl reciprocating, 268ihp = 8½kts
Armament: 1-10in MLR
Complement: 30

Class (builder, fate): *Bouncer* (Pembroke DYd, sold 1905), *Insolent* (Pembroke DYd, wrecked 1922 and sold 1925)

MEDINA class *flatiron gunboats* (launched 1876-77)

Displacement: 386t designed
Dimensions: 110ft x 34ft x 5ft 7in-5ft 9in (*33.53 x 10.36 x 1.70-1.75m*)
Machinery: 2 cyl reciprocating, 310ihp = 9½kts designed
Armament: 3-64pdr MLR
Complement: 51

Class (builder, fate): *Dee* (Palmer, sold 1902), *Don* (Palmer, sold 1914), *Esk* (Palmer, sold 1903), *Medina* (Palmer, sold 1904), *Sabrina* (Palmer, sold 1922), *Slaney* (Palmer, sold 1919), *Spey* (Palmer, sold 1923), *Tay* (Palmer, sold 1920), *Tees* (Palmer, sold 1907), *Trent* (Palmer, sold 1923), *Tweed* (Palmer, sold 1905)

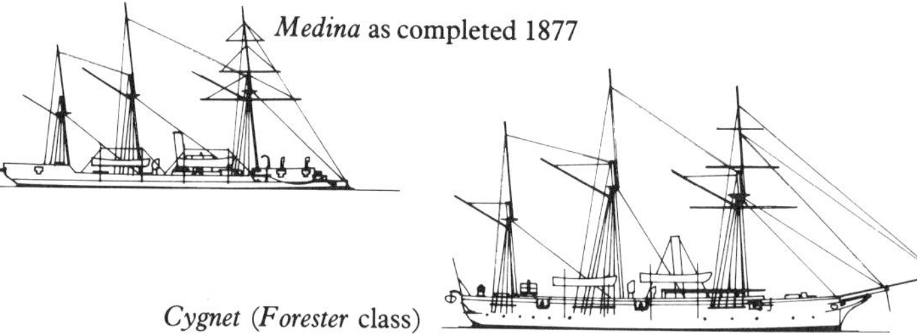
Medina as completed 1877

Cygnet (*Forester* class)

FORESTER class *composite gunboats* (launched 1874-77)

Displacement: 455t
Dimensions: 125ft x 23ft 6in x 8ft 6in-10ft 6in (*38.10 x 7.16 x 2.59-3.20m*)
Machinery: 1-shaft, CR (*Moorhen* and *Sheldrake* reciprocating), 387-515ihp = 10kts
Armament: 2-64pdr MLR, 2-20pdr BL
Complement: 60

Class (builder, fate): *Contest* (Doxford, BU 1889), *Cygnet* (Doxford, BU 1889), *Express* (Doxford, sold 1889), *Firebrand* (Thompson, sold 1905), *Firefly* (Thompson, sold 1931), *Firm* (Earle, sold 1907), *Forester* (Earle, sold 1904), *Forward* (Barrow, sold 1903), *Foxhound* (Barrow, sold 1920), *Mallard* (Earle, sold 1889), *Moorhen* (Napier, sold 1888), *Sheldrake* (Napier, sold 1906)

BANTERER class *composite gunboats* (launched 1880-82)

Displacement: 465t
Dimensions: 125ft x 23ft 6in x 10ft mean (*38.10 x 7.16 x 3.05m*)
Machinery: 1-shaft, reciprocating, 440ihp = 9½kts
Armament: 2-64pdr MLR, 2-20pdr BL
Complement: 60

Class (builder, fate): *Banterer* (Barrow, sold 1907), *Bullfrog* (Pembroke DYd, sold 1933), *Cockchafer* (Pembroke DYd, sold 1905), *Espoir* (Barrow, deleted 1904), *Grappler* (Barrow, sold 1907), *Raven* (Samuda, sold 1925), *Redwing*, ex-*Espoir* (Pembroke DYd, sold 1905), *Starling* (Samuda, sold 1905), *Stork* (Samuda, sold 1950), *Wrangler* (Barrow, sold 1919), *Wasp* (Barrow, wrecked 1884)

ALBACORE class *composite gunboats* (launched 1883)

Displacement: 560t
Dimensions: 135ft x 26ft x 7ft-10ft 3in (*41.15 x 7.92 x 2.13-3.12m*)
Machinery: 1-shaft, reciprocating, 650ihp = 10.7kts
Armament: 2-5in BL, 2-4in BL
Complement: 60

Class (builder, fate): *Albacore* (Laird, sold 1906), *Mistletoe* (Laird, sold 1907), *Watchful* (Laird, sold 1907)

BRAMBLE class *composite gunboats* (launched 1886)

Displacement: 715t, 810t full load
Dimensions: 165ft x 29ft x 11ft (*50.29 x 8.84 x 3.35m*)
Machinery: 1-shaft, TE, 1000ihp = 13kts designed
Armament: 6-4in QF
Complement: 76

Class (builder, fate): *Bramble* (Harland & Wolff, sold 1906), *Lizard* (Harland & Wolff, sold 1905), *Rattler* (Elswick, sold 1924), *Wasp* (Elswick, foundered 1887)

Plover of the *Pygmy* class

(All uncredited photos: CPL)

REDBREAST class *composite gunboats* (launched 1889)

Displacement:	805t
Dimensions:	165ft x 31ft x 11ft-13ft 9in *(50.29 x 9.45 x 3.35-4.19m)*
Machinery:	1-shaft, TE, 1200hp = 13kts max
Armament:	6-4in QF, 2-3pdr
Complement:	76

Class (builder, fate): *Goldfinch* (Sheerness DYd, sold 1907), *Lapwing* (Devonport DYd, sold 1910), *Magpie* (Pembroke DYd, sold 1921), *Redbreast* (Pembroke DYd, sold 1910), *Redpoll* (Pembroke DYd, sold 1906), *Ringdove* (Devonport DYd, sold 1920), *Sparrow* (Scott, sold 1922), *Thrush* (Scott, wrecked 1917), *Widgeon* (Pembroke DYd, sold 1906)

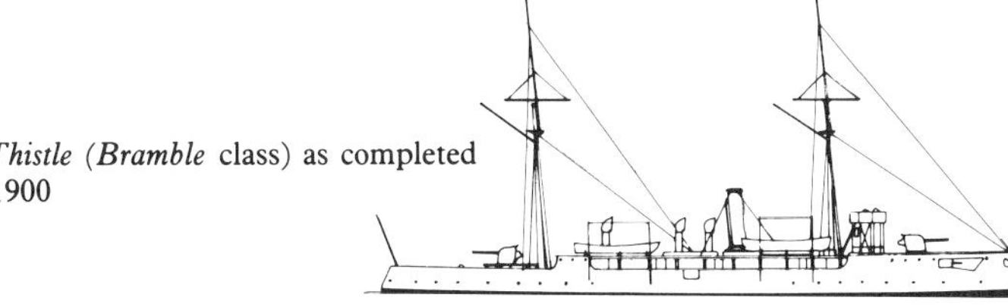

Thistle (Bramble class) as completed 1900

PIGMY class *composite gunboats* (launched 1888)

Displacement:	755t
Dimensions:	165ft x 30ft x 11ft 3in *(50.29 x 9.14 x 3.43m)*
Machinery:	1-shaft, TE, 1200hp = 13.2kts
Armament:	6-4in QF
Complement:	76

Class (builder, fate): *Partridge* (Devonport DYd, sold 1912), *Peacock* (Pembroke DYd, sold 1906), *Pheasant* (Devonport DYd, sold 1906), *Pigeon* (Pembroke DYd, sold 1906), *Pigmy* (Sheerness DYd, sold 1905), *Plover* (Pembroke DYd, sold 1927)

BRAMBLE class *steel gunboats* (launched 1898-99)

Displacement:	710t
Dimensions:	180ft x 33ft x 8ft *(54.86 x 10.06 x 2.44m)*
Machinery:	2-shaft, TE, 1300hp = 13kts
Armament:	2-4in QF, 4-12pdr
Complement:	85

Class (builder, fate): *Bramble* (London & Glasgow Co, sold 1926), *Britomart* (Potter, sold 1920), *Dwarf* (London & Glasgow Co, sold 1926), *Thistle* (London & Glasgow Co, sold 1926)

COLONIAL GUNBOATS

A number of gunboats were built for the naval forces of the individual Australian colonies from about 1883 onwards, and the most important are listed below. Surviving vessels were turned over to the new Australian Navy on the foundation of the Commonwealth of Australia in 1901.

SOUTH AUSTRALIA

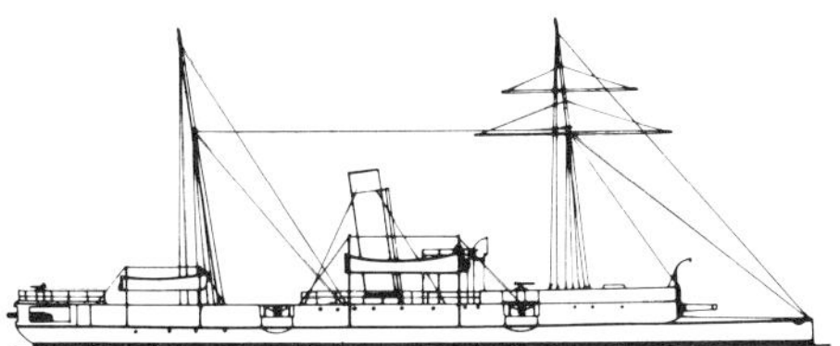

Protector as completed 1885

PROTECTOR *steel cruiser* (launched 1884)

Displacement:	920t
Dimensions:	188ft oa, 180½ft wl x 30ft x 12½ *(57.30, 55.02 x 9.14 x 3.81m)*
Machinery:	2-shaft, 1500ihp = 14kts
Armament:	(As built) 1-8in BL, 4-3pdr, 5 MGs
Complement:	90

Although referred to as a cruiser this Armstrong-built vessel resembled a very large flatiron gunboat. She had an active career including participation in the suppression of the Boxer uprising in China, and was not sold until 1924. Her hulk was still visible off Heron Island, Queensland in 1978.

QUEENSLAND

GAYUNDAH class *steel gunvessels* (launched 1884)

Displacement:	360t
Dimensions:	120ft oa x 26ft x 9½ft *(36.58 x 1.83 x 2.90m)*
Machinery:	2-shaft compound, 400ihp = 10½kts. Coal 60t
Armament:	(As built) 1-8in BL, 2-1½in, 2 MGs

Gayundah and *Paluma* were large flatiron gunboats. The first vessels ordered for Queensland's navy, both were launched in May 1884 by Armstrongs. The 8in BL was never mounted in *Paluma*. *Gayundah* was sold in 1921 and *Paluma* in 1913 although the latter was not scrapped until 1955.

OTTER *gunboat*

220t, 1-5in BL (later 1-64pdr added), 12kts. Launched by Ramage and Ferguson on 19.7.1884, and scrapped in 1946. Designed as a tug but purchased and converted during building.

There were also the gunboats *Bonito, Bream, Dolphin, Pumba* and *Stingaree*, converted from government hopper barges while building in 1874 and each armed with 1-5in BL.

VICTORIA

ALBERT *steel gunvessel* (launched 1883)

Very similar to Queensland's *Gayundah* and *Paluma* (except 350t) and also built by Armstrongs. She was sold in 1897.

VICTORIA *steel gunvessel* (launched 1884)

Displacement:	530t
Dimensions:	145ft oa, 140ft wl, 27ft x 11ft *(44.20, 42.67 x 8.23 x 3.35m)*
Machinery:	2-shaft compound, 800ihp = 12kts. Coal 90t
Armament:	1-10in BL, 2-12pdr, 2 MGs

An enlarged version of the *Albert* also built by Armstrongs. She was sold in 1896.

Victoria also operated the following converted merchantmen as gunboats: *Batman* and *Fawkner*, 387t, ex-hopper barges purchased in 1883/4; *Gannet*, 346t, built in 1884 and paid off in 1893; and *Lady Loch*, 336t, built in 1886 by Campbell at Melbourne, and sold in 1927. They were all armed with 1-6in BL and 2 smaller QFs or MGs.

United States of America

'THE OLD NAVY' 1860-1882

For a nation of over 31 million inhabitants with 5,350,000 net tons of merchant shipping of which over 47 per cent was classed as ocean going, the US Navy in 1860 was a small, and bearing in mind the considerable industrial resources of the United States, by no means an up to date force. There were none of the screw-propelled wooden two-decker battleships favoured in the 1850s by Britain and France, and of the five large frigates and one outsize corvette that were the most formidable ships, only the latter could reach 10½kts under steam, while the five frigates could barely achieve 9kts. At the beginning of 1860 only two, and later in the year, one of the six were in commission due to the near bankruptcy of President Buchanan's government. In spite of this small squadrons were maintained round the world as shown in the list for 1.1.1860.

The great naval issue of the day was the use of iron armour and at the above date France had six and Great Britain four ocean-going armoured battleships in various stages of construction, while the United States had the suspended second version of the 'Stevens Battery', a project which to a dispassionate eye was not likely to be completed or to be satisfactory if it were.

Thus when the Civil War broke out and President Lincoln proclaimed the blockade of the Southern States on 19 April 1861, an enormous effort had to be made by the North to increase their naval strength, as at that period, to be legal under International Law, a blockade must be seen to be effective. The North had far the larger part of the country's industry but the population of 19 million was about 60 per cent of the total. The 1861 programme of unarmoured ships comprised 14 wooden-hulled screw corvettes or cruisers as they are perhaps better called, 23 screw gunboats and 12 side-wheel gunboats, although such a means of propulsion was already obsolescent for warships other than river craft. The cruisers and nine of the side-wheelers were built in the navy yards, and the rest of the gunboats were contract. The coastal waters of the South were often shallow and the mean draught of the screw gunboats was 10ft4in, while that of the side-wheel ones did not exceed 9ft 11in, and that of the cruisers 16ft6in. The latter, comprising the *Kearsarge*, *Ossipee*, *Sacramento* and *Ticonderoga* classes, were of modest size, 1457 to 2526t displacement, and nine of the fourteen as well as all the gunboats were completed by the end of 1862. Eight further screw gunboats built in the navy yards, and 27 side-wheelers of which 18 were built by contract, with respective mean draughts of 11ft6in and 8ft6in, were completed in 1863-1864. Neither cruisers nor gunboats were particularly powerful ships, and the fastest of them, the *Kearsarge* class, had a speed under steam of 11–12kts. Their numbers were reinforced by a considerable number of purchased merchant ships, many of them side-wheelers, and in some cases carrying a relatively powerful armament. However useful all these ships and those built prior to the Civil War proved to be in many varied operations and in the blockade, they are surpassed in interest by the armoured vessels, the great majority of which were of the type to be known as monitors.

A serious difficulty was that there was little capacity in the USA for making heavy wrought iron plates or large forgings, and it was considered dangerous to rely on manufacture in Britain, where in any event the firms capable of such work were fully engaged on home and European orders. As a result most of the US monitors had their armour built up from 1in plates rivetted or bolted together, very much a second best alternative to having the whole thickness in one plate. For armament the principal weapon was the 15in smooth-bore gun, a very fine example of iron casting but an inferior armour piercing weapon for its weight of 18½–19t. The 15in solid shot weighed 440lb, the cored shot 400lb and the shell 350lb. The other important guns in the armoured ships were the cast iron 11in smooth bore of seven tons firing projectiles of 170–136lb and the 8in Parrott rifled muzzle-loader of cast iron with a wrought iron hoop shrunk over the chamber. This gun weighed 7.4t and fired projectiles of about 150lb.

The US Navy Department suffered much from resignations by Confederate sympathisers at the outbreak of the war and it is not surprising that there was some delay in undertaking the construction of armoured ships. However in October 1861 contracts were placed for the broadside ship *New Ironsides*, the *Monitor* which gave her name to the type, and the gunboat *Galena*. All were commissioned in 1862, in August, February and April respectively. The ironclad programme for 1862 was far larger, as in that year, neglecting river craft, contracts were placed for ten improved monitors of the *Passaic* class and nine of the *Canonicus* class, as well as for the much larger *Dictator* and *Puritan*. Contracts were also placed for the *Onondaga*, a monitor of a different type, for the conversion of the frigate *Roanoke*, for the large casemate ship *Dunderberg* and for the gunboat *Keokuk*, while four large monitors of the *Miantonomoh* class were laid down in the navy yards. Of these 29 ships, three were commissioned in 1862, eight in 1863, eight in 1864, four in 1865 and six never or long after the war.

The low freeboard monitors were well protected in general against gunfire, but reserve buoyancy was very low and they were highly vulnerable to mines. They were also exceedingly uncomfortable for their crews in anything but calm weather, and for most of them with only one turret the rate of fire was extremely low. This was improved in the two-turret *Onondaga* and *Miantonomoh* class, but the three-turret *Roanoke* was structurally weak and a failure. The *Monitor* and the *Passaic* class had the advantage of a mean draught of 10½ft. In the *Onondaga* and the *Canonicus* and *Miantonomoh* classes, it did not exceed 13ft, but it was 20ft or more in the *Dictator*, *Puritan* and *Roanoke*. Of

A deck view of the famous *Kearsarge* after her engagement with the *Alabama* CPL

the other ships the *Dunderberg* was never commissioned and the *Galena* and *Keokuk* were failures, but the *New Ironsides* was a success as her 16-gun battery gave her a higher rate of fire and her mean draught of 15ft and speed of only 7kts did not inhibit operations against Confederate coast defences.

The last of the war programmes for armoured ships, that of 1863, comprised contracts for the 20 light draught monitors of the *Casco* class which were a failure though one was commissioned as a monitor and three as spar torpedo vessels during the war, and also the four large sea-going monitors of the *Kalamazoo* class, laid down in the navy yards and never launched. Of unarmoured ships contracts were placed for seven iron-hulled, side-wheel gunboats of the *Mohongo* class, and a large number of wooden-hulled screw ships were to be laid down in 1863-1864 comprising 36 cruisers of approximately 2400–4500t and six sloops. This programme clearly looked beyond the Civil War, and sought to re-establish a worldwide US naval presence. In the event 20 of the cruisers and four of the sloops were laid down, all except two of the cruisers in navy yards. As was not unusual in other navies the stocks of seasoned timber were overestimated.

The four sloops commissioned between the end of 1865 and 1869, and 13 of the cruisers advanced at least as far as trials from 1866 to 1870 including three of the 15–17kt *Wampanoag* class, but of all the unarmoured ships only one of the side-wheel gunboats completed in time to serve in the war which came to an end in April to May 1865.

The cost of the four years of the Civil War had been great. About 300,000 men had been killed on each side, the economy of the South was in ruins, and that of the North severely strained. Contemporary estimates give a rise in prices of 90 per cent between 1861 and 1866 in the North while wages rose by 60 per cent. The ordinary revenue which had grossed about 197 million dollars for the fiscal years 1858 to 1861 rose to 729 million for 1862 to 1865 in the North, while the national debt of 65 million dollars in 1860 rose to a maximum for the North of nearly 2846 million in August 1865. In these circumstances a lack of new naval construction apart from the completion of some of the wartime ships was to be expected, but neglect of the US Navy continued until the 1880s, although the population had risen to 38½million in 1870 and to over 50 million in 1880. There were several reasons for this neglect. Attention was centred on the development of the great area between the line of the Mississippi and California, and the associated construction of railways. Then in 1873 there was a financial panic, precipitated by the failure in September of Jay Cooke, the financier of the Northern Pacific railway. For over five years railway building almost ceased, the iron industry was badly affected and as late as 1877 over 18 per cent of the railway mileage was in the hands of the receivers, while business failures amounted to 775 million dollars in four years.

Besides these economic reasons the great part that the US Navy had played in the defeat of the South was not recognised and it was held to have had a secondary role to that of the army. The losses and damage of the struggle had led to a general abhorrence of everything to do with war, and there was also the belief that a fleet could be quickly improvised in an emergency, which if partly true in 1861, was becoming continually less valid. There also seems to have been a wish among certain senior officers to return to the days of sail plus auxiliary steam, and such money as was voted was not spent on the construction of powerful and up-to-date ships. Great progress in naval guns had been made in Europe between 1865 and 1882, but all that had been done in the United States was the conversion of 11in smooth bores to 8in rifled muzzle loaders and of 6.4in and smaller Parrott guns to breech loaders.

The actual new construction and conversion was as follows; ships are listed under the year that work began:

- 1867 – Three *Alaska* class, cruisers, navy yards, 2394t.
- 1869 – Addition of spar-decks to cruisers *Tennessee* (ex-*Madawaska*), and *Guerriere* of 1863 programme.
- 1872 – Five *Galena* class, cruisers, navy yards, 1900t. *Vandalia* the same but of 2033t.
- 1873 – *Trenton*, cruiser, navy yard, 3900t. Three *Alert* class, iron-hulled sloops, contract, 1020t. *Alarm*, iron-hulled spar-torpedo ram, navy yard, 800t. *Intrepid*, iron-hulled spar-torpedo ram, navy yard, 1150t.
- 1874 – Five *Enterprise* class, sloops, three navy yards, two contract, 1375t.

Except where noted all were wooden-hulled. *Alarm* differed from the rest in having Fowler wheel propulsion instead of screw. None exceeded 13kts under steam. The most powerful of the above was the *Trenton* with a battery of 10-8in RML, but the majority were weak ships of obsolescent types.

An attempt was made in 1874-1875 by Secretary of the Navy GM Robeson to build five powerful new monitors under the guise of repairing the four *Miantoñomohs*, whose wooden hulls were rotten, and the iron-hulled but unfinished *Puritan*. Congress approved funds for the repairs on 23 June 1874, but a major scandal arose when it was discovered that entirely new ships were being built under the disguise of repairs, and it was not until 1891 that the first of the five was completed.

Thus at the end of 1882 the only armoured ships apart from the spar-torpedo ship *Intrepid*, which was under conversion, were the eight surviving *Passaics* and six *Canonicus* class, plus the *Dictator* sold in 1883. Squadrons were still maintained round the world, and it may be noted that some of the most powerful ships so deployed were the *Brooklyn*, *Hartford*, *Lancaster*, *Richmond* and *Pensacola* launched in 1858–1860 and of 2550–3290t displacement.

UNITED STATES NAVY in 1860

SCREW FRIGATES

Name	Launched	Displacement	Original armament	Speed	Service 1.1.1860	Fate
FRANKLIN	1864	5170t	4-6.4in RML, 1-11in SB, 34-9in SB	9 kts	On stocks Portsmouth N Yd	Sold 1915
MERRIMACK	1855	4636t	2-10in SB, 24-9in SB, 14-8in SB	8¾ kts	Passage. Pacific to Norfolk	CSS *Virginia* 1862
WABASH	1855	4774t	2-10in SB, 28-9in SB, 14-8in SB	9 kts	Ordinary. New York	Sold 1912
MINNESOTA	1855	4833t	2-10in SB, 28-9in SB, 14-8in SB	9¼ kts	Ordinary. Boston	Sold 1901
ROANOKE	1855	4772t	2-10in SB, 28-9in SB, 14-8in SB	9 lts	Aspinawall. awaiting Japanese delegation	Converted to monitor 1862
COLORADO	1856	4772t	2-10in SB, 28-9in SB, 14-8in SB	9 kts	Ordinary. Boston	Sold 1885
NIAGARA	1855	5540t	12-11in SB	10½ kts	Refit, New York	Sold 1885

Franklin, laid down in 1854, was not commissioned till 1867. *Niagara* was technically a corvette (sloop), but on account of her size, usually classed as a frigate.

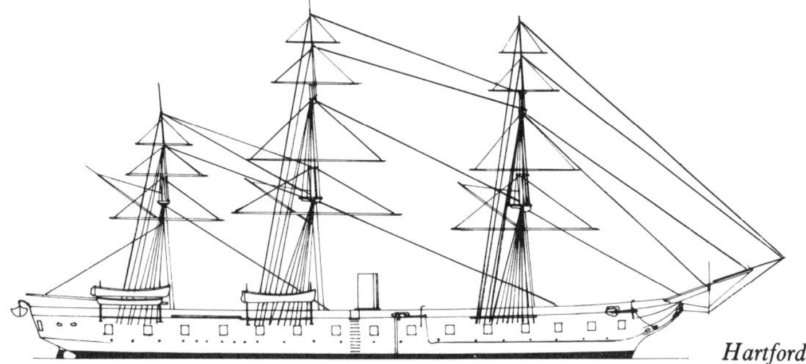

Hartford

SCREW CORVETTES (SLOOPS) (2200 tons and over)

Name	Launched	Displacement	Original armament	Speed	Service 1.1.1860	Fate
SAN JACINTO	1850	2200t	12-8in SB, 4-32pdr SB	8kts	Africa Sqdn	Wrecked 1865
BROOKLYN	1858	2686t	1-10in SB, 20-9in SB	9¼kts	Home Sqdn	Sold 1891
HARTFORD	1858	2550t	20-9in SB	9½kts	Flag East India Sqdn	Sank at berth 1956
LANCASTER	1858	3290t	24-9in SB	10kts	Flag Pacific Sqdn	Broken up 1933
RICHMOND	1860	2604t	1-6.4in RML, 20-9in SB	9kts	On stocks Norfolk N Yd	Sold 1919
PENSACOLA	1859	3000t	1-11in SB, 16-9in SB	8¾kts	Completing Washington N Yd	Sunk 1912

SMALLER SCREW SHIPS

Name	Launched	Displacement	Original armament	Speed	Service 1.1.1860	Fate
ALLEGHANY	Rebuilt 1851-52	1020t	4-8in SB	6kts	Receiving ship Baltimore	Sold 1869
PRINCETON	1851	1370t	4-8in SB, 6-32pdr Carr	8kts	Receiving ship Philadelphia	Sold 1866
MOHICAN	1859	1461t	2-11in SB, 4-32pdr SB	10½kts	Preparing to join Africa Sqdn	Sunk at mooring 1872
IROQUOIS	1859	1488t	1-5.1in RML, 4-32pdr SB	11kts	Preparing for Mediterranean	Stricken 1910
WYOMING	1859	1457t	2-11in SB, 4-32pdr SB	9¾kts	Pacific coast USA	Sold 1892
DACOTAH	1859	1369t	1-6.4in RML, 1-10in SB, 4-32pdr SB	11kts	Completing Norfolk N Yd	Sold 1873
NARRAGANSETT	1859	1235t	1-11in SB, 4-32pdr SB	9½kts	E Coast USA	Sold 1883
SEMINOLE	1859	1230t	1-4.2in RML, 1-11in SB, 6-32pdr SB	–	Completing Pensacola N Yd	Sold 1870
PAWNEE	1859	1533t	8-9in SB	10kts	Completing Philadelphia N Yd	Sold 1884
POCAHONTAS	Rebuilt 1859-60	694t om	1-3.7in RML, 4-32pdr SB	–	Completing Norfolk N Yd	Sold 1865

Alleghany was iron-hulled. *Pocahontas* was the rebuilt *Despatch* and renamed 27.1.60.

Six smaller screw steamers (217-549t om), chartered for the Paraguay expedition of 1858-59, were purchased by the USN in 1859 and named *Anacostia, Crusader, Mohawk, Mystic, Sumpter* and *Wyandotte*.

'STEVENS BATTERY'

The 'Stevens Battery' first authorised in 1842, was as partially built to a new design in 1854-46 to be of 4683t, iron-hulled with 6¾in vertical armour, and a hoped for speed of 17kts. The design was again altered in 1861, but the USN would not authorise further work, though some was done to a further modification of the design in 1869-70 after the ship had been bequeathed to the State of New Jersey. She was never launched and was broken up in 1881.

SIDE-WHEEL FRIGATES AND SLOOPS

Name	Launched	Displacement	Original armament	Speed	Service 1.1.1860	Fate
MISSISSIPPI	1842	3220t	2-10in SB, 8-8in SB	8kts	Chinese waters	Sunk at Port Hudson 1863
SUSQUEHANNA	1850	3824t	2-64pdr SB, 12-8in SB	10kts	Ordinary. New York	Sold 1883
POWHATAN	1850	3765t	2-64pdr SB, 12-8in SB	10½kts	Japan, awaiting delegation	Sold 1886
SARANAC	1848	2200t	1-64pdr SB, 8-8in SB	9kts	West coast USA	Wrecked 1875

1. The corvette *Brooklyn* during the Naval Review 29 April 1889
2. The corvette *Hartford* at the Mare Island Navy Yard
   CPL
3. *Pensacola* at Alexandria in 1886.
4. The side-wheel steamer *Wolverine* (ex *Michigan*) at a Great Lakes port in the early 1900s

1

2

3

4

SMALLER SIDE-WHEEL SHIPS

Name	Launched	Displacement	Original armament	Speed	Service 1.1.1860	Fate
FULTON	1837	1200t	4-32pdr SB	10kts	Laid up at Pensacola	Burned 1862
MICHIGAN	1843	685t	1-18pdr SB	8kts	On Great Lakes	Cut up for scrap 1949

Michigan, renamed *Wolverine* 17.6.1905, was iron-hulled.

Three small side-wheel steamers of 378t-453t om were *Water Witch, Saginaw* and *Pulaski*. The last named was chartered for the Paraguay expedition and purchased in 1859.

SAILING SHIPS OF THE LINE

Name	Launched	Tonnage om	Number of guns	Service 1.1.1860	Fate
COLUMBUS	1819	2480t	92	Ordinary. Norfolk	Burned 1861
DELAWARE	1820	2633t	90	Ordinary. Norfolk	Burned 1861
NEW HAMPSHIRE	1864	2633t	90	On stocks. Portsmouth N Yd	Sunk at pier 1921
NEW ORLEANS	Never	2805t	90	On stocks. Sacketts Harbor	Sold 1883
NEW YORK	Never	2633t	90	On stocks. Norfolk N Yd	Burned 1861
NORTH CAROLINA	1820	2633t	90	Receiving ship. New York	Sold 1867
OHIO	1820	2757t	90	Receiving ship. Boston	Sold 1883
PENNSYLVANIA	1837	3105t	120	Receiving ship. Norfolk	Burned 1861
VERMONT	1848	2633t	90	Incomplete at Boston	Sold 1902
VIRGINIA	Never	2633t	90	On stocks. Boston N Yd	Broken up 1884

New Hampshire, originally named *Alabama* until 28.10.63 and later *Granite State* from 30.11.04, was completed as a store ship, as was *Vermont*.

SAILING FRIGATES AND LARGE CORVETTES (SLOOPS)

Name	Launched	Tonnage om	Number of guns	Service 1.1.1860	Fate
BRANDYWINE	1825	1726t	44	Ordinary. New York	Burned 1864
COLUMBIA	1836	1726t	54	Ordinary. Norfolk	Burned 1861
CONGRESS	1841	1867t	50	Flag. Brazil Sqdn	Destroyed by *Virginia* 1862
CONSTELLATION	1855	1265t	24	Flag. Africa Sqdn	Stricken 1955. Preserved
CONSTITUTION	1797	1576t	38	Ordinary. Portsmouth	Still in commission
CUMBERLAND	Razeed 1856	1726t	24	Home Sqdn	Sunk by *Virginia* 1862
INDEPENDENCE	Razeed 1836	2243t	54	Receiving ship. Mare Is	Sold 1914
MACEDONIAN	Razeed 1852	1341t	22	Home Sqdn	Sold 1875
POTOMAC	1822	1726t	50	Ordinary. New York	Sold 1877
RARITAN	1843	1726t	50	Ordinary. Norfolk	Burned 1861
SABINE	1855	1726t	50	Home Sqdn	Sold 1883
ST LAWRENCE	1848	1726t	50	Ordinary. Philadelphia	Sold 1875
SANTEE	1855	1726t	50	Completing. Portsmouth N Yd	Sank at moorings 1912
SAVANNAH	1842	1726t	54	Flag. Home Sqdn	Sold 1883
UNITED STATES	1798	1576t	44	Ordinary. Norfolk	Sunk as block-ship 1862

Constellation, Cumberland Macedonian were corvettes.

The following sloops were in existence in 1860 and mostly in commission: *Cyane, Dale, Decatur, Germantown, Jamestown, John Adams, Levant, Marion, Plymouth, Portsmouth, Preble, St Louis, St Mary's, Saratoga, Vandalia, Vincennes.* The brigs *Bainbridge, Dolphin* and *Perry* were also in commission.

BROADSIDE IRONCLADS

NEW IRONSIDES *broadside ironclad*

Displacement: 4120t
Dimensions: 232ft oa x 57ft 6in x 15ft mean (*70.71 x 17.53 x 4.57m*)
Machinery: 4 Martin boilers, 1-shaft HDA, 700ihp = 7kts. Coal 350t
Armour: Iron. Belt 4½in-3in, battery 4½in, deck 1in
Armament: 2-8in Parrott RML, 2-5.1in Dahlgren RML, 14-11in SB, 1-3.4in RML, 1-12pdr SB
Complement: 449

Name	Builder	Laid down	Launched	Comm	Fate
NEW IRONSIDES	Cramp	Contract 15.10.1861	10.5.62	21.8.62	Burnt 16.12.1866

Wooden-hulled and barque-rigged (without royals) on passage, *New Ironsides* was flat-bottomed and of shallow draught by European standards, though found inconveniently deep in the attacks on Charleston. The contract speed of 9½kts could not be approached. The 4½in side armour was rolled in one thickness and was reduced to 3in at the lower edge 4ft below wl. The sides were inclined at 17° inwards and although often credited with a complete belt, operational reports indicate that the ends were unarmoured. The 8in RML and 11in SB were in a broadside battery 170ft long, closed by bulkheads and with the 1in upper deck above. These guns had no axial fire as the ports only allowed 4-4½° training and elevation. The 5.1in RML, replaced in 1864 by 2-5.3in Parrotts, were on the upper deck, and there was a 4½in pilot house, later thickened by 4 x 1in plates, abaft the mainmast. In spite of the above obvious defects, *New Ironsides* took part in many bombardments without serious damage, and successfully withstood a 70lb spar torpedo abreast the engine room which sprung in the wooden sides 4-5in for 40ft. She was destroyed by fire at Philadelphia Navy Yard.

Build largely of green wood with weak framing and very heavy longitudinal timbers, the sides being 7½ft thick at the knuckle, this ship had a low hull with pronounced ram bow and an amidships casemate on the lines of the better known *Virginia* (*Merrimack*). The hull armour sloped outwards and the casemate inwards, both at 35°. There were 22 gun ports, six on each broadside, two at each corner and two axial, four of the 11in being arranged to traverse at these end ports, while the 15in were at the foremost broadside ones. The port sill height was only 4ft 8in. There was a light brigantine rig, and though US trials in June 1867 gave only 11.7 kts at 3778 ihp, a maximum of 15.07 kts at 4535 ihp and designed draught was claimed in France a year later. Named the *Rochambeau* by the French she was armed with 4-10.8in and 10-9.4in BL guns of M1864 or 1864/66, but was only commissioned for some weeks in 1870 and was stricken in 1872.

DUNDERBERG *broadside ironclad*

Displacement: 7800t
Dimensions: 377ft 4in oa x 72ft 10in x 21ft 5in mean (*115.01 x 22.19 x 6.52m*)
Machinery: 6 'return flame' boilers, 1-shaft RCR, 4500ihp = 15kts (contract). Coal 540/1000t
Armour: Iron. Belt 3½in-2½in, casemate 4½in with 3ft timber backing
Armament: 4-15in SB, 12-11in SB
Complement: –

Name	Builder	Laid down	Launched	Comm	Fate
DUNDERBERG	W H Webb	Contract 3.7.1862	22.7.65	Not by US Navy	Sold to France 1867

MONITORS

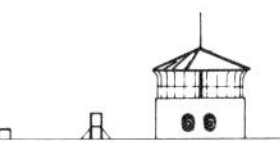

Monitor as completed 1862

Before discussing this famous prototype designed by Ericsson, it should be noted that the USN's Bureau of Construction and Rèpair favoured a more conventional type of low freeboard ironclad with two single 11in turrets on the Coles principle, turning on a roller race near the periphery of the turret, and not on a centre spindle as in the Ericsson turret, which, unless stated to the contrary, was used for all monitors in the US 'Old Navy'. The *Monitor's* hull consisted of an armoured wood and iron 'raft' of the length and beam given above and about 5ft deep, with a slab sided iron lower hull 126ft x 34ft maximum, with a width of 18ft at the bottom. The overhang of the upper part was 14ft forward, 32ft aft and 3ft 9in a side amidships, and served to protect the lower hull, screw and rudder from ramming, while the anchor was located below the 'raft' deck with the hawse pipe dangerously sited just above water in the hull proper. The contract called for 8 kts, but the *Monitor's* best speed was 1-2 kts down on this, the long overhang aft being detrimental. Freeboard was only 14in when fully laden, and waves washing over the low hull served to limit rolling. Ventilation was by means of a blower drawing from two pipes 4½ft above deck, which was too low, and hatches could only be opened in calm conditions. Even with the blowers running and hatches open, 178°F in the engine room and 120°F in the berth deck were recorded in the summer of 1862. The two square funnels rose only 6ft above deck. Ericsson's original sketch designs had a 6in side and 2in deck the weights of which would have sunk the ship and as given above the armour, made up of 1in or thinner plates bolted or rivetted together, was much reduced. The side was thinned below water to 3in and finally 2in, while the turret was only 9 x 1in round the ports and 8 x 1in elsewhere. The turret was 20ft internal diameter and 9ft high with a grating roof of railway rails through which the ventilation system exhausted, and the lower edge of the turret skirt which was faced with bronze, rested on a bronze ring let into the deck. The turret was steam trained, and control was not precise, while the pendulum port-stoppers were difficult to work. There was a small pilot house forward constructed from 9in thick iron blocks, and later a 3in glacis was added round it.

The *Monitor* fought her famous action with the *Virginia* in Hampton Roads on 9.3.1862, a contest in which neither ship could seriously damage the other, but a renewal of the fight in April 1862 with the *Virginia* improved by extra plating and solid shot for her guns, was declined. The *Monitor* foundered in tow in Force 7 winds and it was thought that the main leakage was due to the upper part of the hull pulling away from the lower.

MONITOR

Displacement: 987t
Dimensions: 172ft oa x 41ft 6in x 10ft 6in mean (*52.42 x 12.64 x 3.20m*)
Machinery: 2 Martin boilers, 1-shaft Ericsson VL, 320ihp = 6kts. Coal 100t
Armour: Iron. Side 4½in-2in, turret 9in-8in, deck 1in
Armament: 2-11inSB (1 x 2)
Complement: 49

Name	Builder	Laid down	Launched	Comm	Fate
MONITOR	Continental Iron Wks	25.10.1861	30.1.62	25.2.62	Foundered 31.12.62

The monitor *Catskill* in Charleston Harbour, 1865

Camanche 1898

The *Passaic* class, which bore the brunt of the attacks on Charleston, were enlarged and improved *Monitors*. *Catskill*, *Nahant*, and *Nantucket* were briefly renamed *Goliath*, *Atlas* and *Medusa* from 15.6.1869 to 10.8.1869, but *Sangamon* retained the name *Jason* given at the same time. There was a less pronounced overhang than in *Monitor*, and the shape of the lower hull and its junction with the 'raft' were improved. Ventilation was better, and an 18ft high funnel was fitted, protected by 8 x 1in armour to a height of 6ft. The pilot house was located on top of the turret but did not rotate with it, and had 8 x 1in sides and a 2 x 1in roof. As in *Monitor* all the armour was built up from 1in plates (deck ½in) and the side was reduced to 4in-3in below water. The 15in gun muzzle did not project from the turret which was 21ft internal diameter, and a smoke box was fitted to keep smoke and fumes out. As a result the 15in gunners could not see the target and had to aim via the 11in or 8in. The pendulum portstoppers were replaced by crank-shaped forgings needing a 90° turn. As originally completed *Lehigh* had an 11in SB but in all her actions mounted an 8in Parrot instead. *Passaic* also had an 8in Parrott in lieu of the 11in by late July 1863, and eventually all the survivors had 2-15in SB. Extra protection was added to some of the class as a result of experience at Charleston. Rings were fitted round the bases of turrets and pilot houses, the roofs of the latter were increased to 3 x 1in and an extra 50 tons of 1in deck plating added over magazines and machinery spaces. Two light guns were also added, the most favoured being a 12pdr SB howitzer on field carriage. *Weehawken* foundered from shipping too much water through open hatches and the hawse pipe before proper measures were taken, and it may be noted that *Lehigh* survived a Force 10 gale off Cape Hatteras when the water was more than 4ft over her deck. These monitors were very vulnerable to mines and *Patapsco* sank in about 15 seconds after striking a mine with 60-65lb cannon powder charge which exploded 35ft from the stem.

Camanche was built in Jersey City, taken to pieces and sent to California on board *Aquila* which sank at San Francisco in November 1863. The sections were salvaged and reassembled, and *Camanche* launched as given above. None of them except *Passaic* was much employed after 1878, until a brief period of coastal duty in the Spanish-American War.

PASSAIC class *monitors*

Displacement: 1875t
Dimensions: 200ft oa x 46ft x 10ft 6in mean (*60.96 x 14.01 x 3.20m*)
Machinery: 2 Martin boilers, 1-shaft Ericsson VL, 320ihp = 7kts. Coal 150t
Armour: Iron. Side 5in-3in, turret 11in, deck 1in
Armament: 1-15in SB, 1-11in SB. *Lehigh*, *Patapsco* 1-15in SB, 1-8in Parrott RML. *Camanche* 2-15in SB
Complement: 75

Name	Builder	Launched	Comm	Fate
CAMANCHE	Donohue, Ryan & Secor	14.11.1864	24.5.65	Sold 1899
CATSKILL	Continental Iron Wks	16.12.1862	24.2.63	Sold 1901
LEHIGH	Reaney, Son & Archbold	17.1.1863	15.4.63	Sold 1904
MONTAUK	Continental Iron Wks	9.10.1862	17.12.62	Sold 1904
NAHANT	Harrison Loring	7.10.1862	29.12.62	Sold 1904
NANTUCKET	Atlantic Iron Wks	6.12.1862	26.2.63	Sold 1900
PASSAIC	Continental Iron Wks	30.8.1862	25.11.62	Sold 1899
PATAPSCO	Harlan & Hollingsworth	27.9.1862	2.1.63	Mined 15.1.65
SANGAMON	Reaney, Son & Archbold	27.10.1862	9.2.63	Sold 1905
WEEHAWKEN	Secor	5.11.1862	18.1.63	Foundered 6.12.63

Catskill photographed in 1898
Aldo Fraccaroli Collection

The first ship to be commissioned with more than two turrets, *Roanoke* was the former wooden frigate of that name, razed to the battery deck. The side armour was in one thickness with 3½in lower edge, but the turret armour was 11 x 1in as in *Passaic*. Pilot houses were located on top of the first two turrets, and there was a single tall funnel abaft the fore turret with a hurricane deck between the two after ones. The fore turret had 1-15in SB and 1-8in RML, the middle one 1-15in SB and 1-11in SB and the after 1-11in SB and 1-8in RML. 3-12pdr SB howitzers on field carriages were listed in January 1865. The *Roanoke* had never been satisfactory, the after part having broken when launched, the hull was too weak for the weight of the turrets and as converted she rolled excessively. In consequence she served as harbour defence ship at Hampton Roads and was not in action during the Civil War.

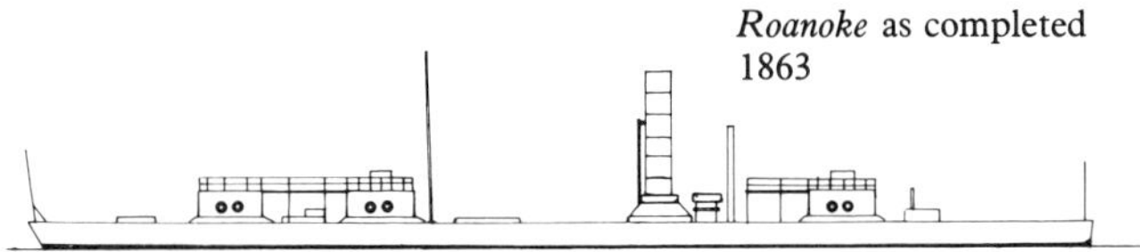
Roanoke as completed 1863

ROANOKE *monitor*

Displacment: 4395t
Dimensions: 265ft oa x 53ft x 22ft mean (*80.77 x 16.15 x 6.70m*)
Machinery: 4 Martin boilers, 1-shaft Penn trunk, ?ihp (440 nominal) = 6kts. Coal 550t
Armour: Iron. Side 4½in-3½in, turrets 11in, deck 1½in
Armament: 2-15in SB, 2-11in SB, 2-8in Parrott RML
Complement: 350

Name	Converted by	Date of Conversion	Comm	Fate
ROANOKE	Novelty Iron Wks	May 1862-April 1863	29.6.1863	Sold 1883

Onondago probably on the James River, 1865

Designed by Quintard, the *Onondaga* differed from the Ericsson monitors in having a normal iron hull though of only 14in freeboard. There were two *Passaic* type turrets each with 1-15in SB and 1-8in RML, and a large funnel between them. There was a pilot house on the fore turret, the funnel base was armoured, and as in the Ericsson monitors the armour was built up from 1in or thinner plates. *Onondaga's* service in the Civil War was confined to the James River. She retained her name when sold to France, was rearmed with 4-9.4in BL M1864 or M1864/66, later replaced by M1870, and was not stricken until 1904.

ONONDAGA *monitor*

Displacement: 2551t
Dimensions: 228ft 7in oa x 51ft 2in x 12ft 10in mean *(69.67 x 15.60 x 3.91m)*
Machinery: 4 Martin boilers, 2-shaft HRC, 610ihp = 7kts. Coal 160t
Armour: Iron. Side 5½in maximum, turrets 11in, deck 1in
Armament: 2-15in SB, 2-8in Parrott RML
Complement: 150

Name	Builder	Contracted	Launched	Comm	Fate
ONONDAGA	Continental Iron Wks	26.5.1862	29.7.1863	24.3.1864	Sold to France 1867

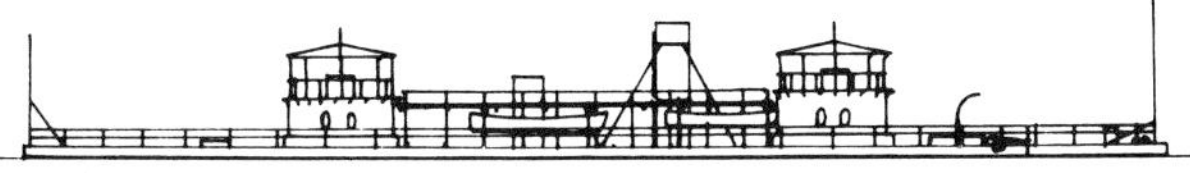

Miantonomah as completed 1865

This class was designed by the Bureau of Construction and Repair, and although unfortunately they were wooden-hulled, *Monadnock*, the only one to take part in the Civil War, was usually considered the best of the US monitors. In 1865/6 she went to San Francisco via the Straits of Magellan, and although three ships were in company, she was not towed. *Miantonomoh* crossed the Atlantic in 1866, though she was towed for 1100 miles by the side-wheel steamer *Augusta*. She returned in 1867 after a cruise of 17,767 miles. *Agamenticus* and *Tonawanda* were renamed *Terror* and *Amphitrite* respectively, 15 June 1869. The hull was of normal form without the Ericsson overhang, and freeboard is given as 2ft 7in. The armour was made up of 1in plates and there were pilot houses on both turrets, with armoured bases to the funnel and large ventilation shaft abaft it. The turrets were 23ft internal diameter and thus 2ft larger than in the *Passaic* class, and a light hurricane deck was rigged between them.

The wooden hulls decayed and their supposed rebuilding into the iron-hulled 'New Navy' monitors of the same names, was a fiction to get round Congressional refusal to allocate any funds for new construction.

MIANTONOMOH class *monitors*

Displacement: 3400t
Dimensions: 258ft 6in oa x 52ft 9in x 12ft 8in mean *(78.80 x 16.07 x 3.86m)*
Machinery: 4 Martin boilers, 2 shafts: in *Agamenticus, Monadnock, Ericsson* VL: in *Miantonomoh, Tonawanda* HRCR, 1400ihp = 9-10kts. Coal. 300t
Armour: Iron. Side 5in, turrets 10in, deck 1½in
Armament: 4-15in SB (2 x 2)
Complement: 150

Name	Builder	Laid down	Launched	Comm	Fate
AGAMENTICUS	Portsmouth N Yd	1862	19.3.63	5.5.65	Broken up 1874/5
MIANTONOMOH	New York N Yd	1862	15.8.63	18.9.65	Broken up 1874/5
MONADNOCK	Boston N Yd	1862	23.3.64	4.10.64	Broken up 1874/5
TONAWANDA	Philadelphia N Yd	1862	6.5.64	12.10.65	Broken up 1874/5

The iron-hulled *Dictator* was Ericsson's idea of a sea-going monitor. The overhang of the 'raft' which was given better lines, was removed at the bows and reduced elsewhere. Draught was greater than intended reducing the freeboard to 16in, and she never approached her designed speed of 15 kts. The 6 x 1in side armour was backed by 3-5in square iron stringers over a depth of 25in near the wl, but was reduced to 2 x 1in and then 1in at the lower edge. The turret, of 24ft internal diameter, had 10 x 1in plates with 5in thick segments of 12in broad iron hoops in the middle, and the pilot house above was protected by 12 x 1in plates. The funnel and ventiliation shaft bases were also armoured. It is thought that a light hurricane deck was provided amidships. The main shaft bearings were too short, and excessive wear forced *Dictator* to turn back on her way to take part in the attack on Fort Fisher.

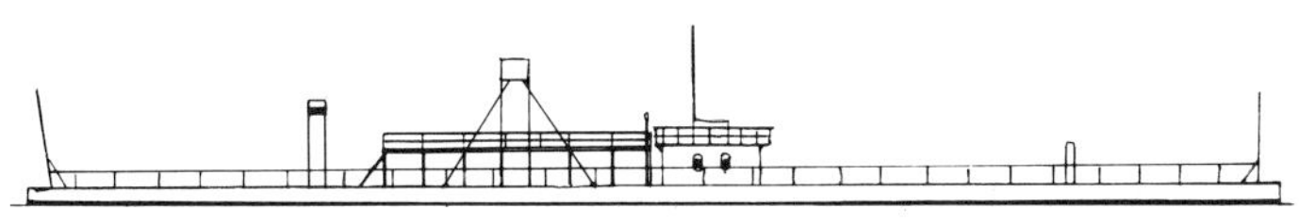

Dictator as completed 1864

DICTATOR *monitor*

Displacement: 4438t
Dimensions: 312ft oa x 50ft x 20ft 6in mean *(95.10 x 15.24 x 6.25m)*
Machinery: 6 Martin boilers, 1-shaft Ericsson VL, 3500ihp = 11kts. Coal 300/1000t
Armour: Iron. Side 6in-1in, turret 15in, deck 2in
Armament: 2-15in SB (1 x 2)
Complement: 175

Name	Builder	Laid down	Launched	Comm	Fate
DICTATOR	Delameter Iron Wks	16.8.1862	26.12.63	11.11.64	Sold 1883

PURITAN monitor

Displacement: 4912t
Dimensions: 340ft oa x 50ft x 20ft mean (*103.62 x 15.24 x 6.10m*)
Machinery: 6 Martin boilers, 2-shaft Ericsson VL, ihp and speed probably as *Dictator*. Coal 1000t maximum
Armour: Iron. Side 6in-2in, turret 15in, deck 2in
Armament: 2-20in SB (1 x 2)
Complement: –

Name	Builder	Contracted	Launched	Comm	Fate
PURITAN	Continental Iron Wks	28.7.1862	2.7.1864	Never completed	Broken up 1874/5

The *Puritan* would have been a slightly larger *Dictator* with a 26ft internal diameter turret and 20in SB guns. The US Navy wanted two turrets but Ericsson, who objected strongly to this, got his way though he had to yield over the matter of two shafts. Designed speed was 15 kts but it is extremely unlikely that this would have been reached. Construction of this iron-hulled monitor was suspended in 1865 and her subsequent rebuilding into the 'New Navy' *Puritan* was as fictional as that of the *Miantonomoh* class.

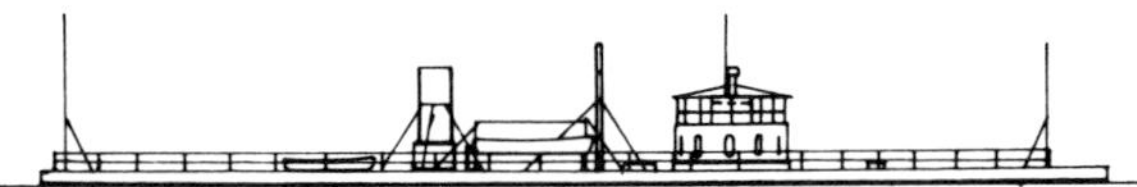
Saugus as completed 1864

CANONICUS class monitors

Displacement: 2100t
Dimensions: 223ft-225ft oa x 43ft-43ft 4in x 12ft 5in-13ft mean (*67.97-68.58 x 13.10-13.20 x 3.78-3.96m*)
Machinery: 2 Stimers or Martin boilers, 1-shaft Ericsson VL, 320ihp = 8kts. Coal 140-150t
Armour: Iron. Side 5in-3in, turret 10in, deck 1½in
Armament: 2-15in SB (1 x 2)
Complement: 100

Name	Builder	Contracted	Launched	Comm	Fate
CANONICUS	Harrison Loring	15.9.1862	1.8.63	16.4.64	Sold 1908
CATAWBA	Alex Swift & Niles Wks	10.9.1862	13.4.64	Never (completion 10.6.65)	Sold to Peru 1868
MAHOPAC	Secor	15.9.1862	17.5.64	22.9.64	Sold 1902
MANAYUNK	Snowden & Mason	15.9.1862	18.12.64	1.1.71 (completion 27.9.65)	Sold 1899
MANHATTAN	Perine, Secor	15.9.1862	14.10.63	6.6.64	Sold 1902
ONEOTA	Alex Swift & Niles Wks	10.9.1862	21.5.64	Never (completion 10.6.65)	Sold to Peru 1868
SAUGUS	Harlan & Hollingsworth	13.10.1862	16.12.63	7.4.64	Sold 1891
TECUMSEH	Secor	15.9.1862	12.9.63	19.4.64	Mined 5.8.64
TIPPECANOE	Miles Greenwood	15.9.1862	22.12.64	? (completion December 1865)	Sold 1899

This class were improved *Passaics*, with wood and iron upper and iron lower hulls, modified in accordance with war experience. *Catawba* and *Oneota* were named *Atahuallpa* and *Manco Capac* by the Peruvians, and the six other survivors were renamed on 15 June 1869 *Scylla, Castor, Ajax, Neptune, Centaur* and *Vesuvius*. They reverted to their original names on 10 August 1869 except that *Ajax* was retained and *Vesuvius* became *Wyandotte*. The four ships not commissioned during the war, were built on the Ohio river, three at Cincinnati and *Manayunk* as far up as South Pittsburgh. The hull lines were improved and designed speed is given as 13 kts but there was no hope of getting near this. The 5 x 1in side armour was backed by two iron stringers 6½in deep and 6in thick for 70ft from the bows, but 4in elsewhere, and the armour lower edge was 3 x 1in. The turret, of 21ft internal diameter, had 10 x 1in plates as did the pilot house above, and the funnel base was also armoured. The turret skirt was protected by a 5in thick 15in high ring fixed to the deck, and as in other later monitors the 15in guns were longer than in the *Passaic* class and fired with their muzzles outside the turret. *Tecumseh* was sunk in Mobile Bay by a mine that exploded under her turret and went down in 25-30 seconds. *Canonicus*, the last survivor, was finally decommissioned 31 years before being sold.

KALAMAZOO class monitors

Displacement: 5660t
Dimensions: 345ft oa x 56ft 8in x 17ft 6in mean (*105.15 x 17.27 x 5.33m*)
Machinery: 8 Martin Boilers, 2 shaft HDA, *about* 2000ihp = 10kts. Coal 500t
Armour: Iron. Side 6in-3in, turrets 15in, deck 3in
Armament: 4-15in SB (2 x 2)
Complement: –

Name	Builder	Laid down	Fate
KALAMAZOO	New York N Yd	Dec 1863	Never launched, broken up on stocks 1884
PASSACONAWAY	Portsmouth N Yd	November 1863	Never launched, broken up on stocks 1884
QUINSIGAMOND	Boston N Yd	Early 1864	Never launched, broken up on stocks 1884
SHACKAMAXON	Philadelphia N Yd	November or December 1863	Never launched, broken up on stocks 1874

This class of wooden-hulled ships, the largest monitors laid down during the Civil War, were an official design and generally resembled enlarged, deeper draught *Miantonomohs* with finer lines. Freeboard was to be 3ft 9in. Iron truss girders were to take the turret weights, but unseasoned timber was used in the hulls. The side armour was 2 x 3in reduced to 1 x 3in at the lower edge, and the wl part was reinforced by 3-8in square iron stringers. The turrets were apparently as in *Dictator* with pilot houses on top, and there would have been two funnels and a high ventiliation shaft, and probably an amidships hurricane deck. Although never launched they had their share of renaming, being respectively named *Colossus, Thunderer, Hercules* and *Hecla* on 15.6.1869. *Colossus* was retained, but on 10.8.1869 the others became *Massachusetts, Oregon* and *Nebraska*.

Although designed by J B Eads for river service, these iron-hulled turtle-deck monitors were also employed in the coastal waters of the Gulf of Mexico. They are believed to be the only Civil War monitors that ever made their designed speed. The side armour of 3 x 1in plates, except in *Winnebago* where it was in one 3in thickness, only extended to 4in below the deep load wl at the bows, and amidships does not seem to have been more than 2ft below. Additional 1in plating was later added to the deck over ammunition spaces and possibly over the machinery. There was a pilot house abaft the forward turret and there was some protection to the funnel base, as it was recommended this be increased to 6in for a height of 6ft. The turrets of 21ft internal diameter, had 8 x 1in plating and while the after one was of the usual Ericsson type, the fore turret was designed by Eads with the guns on a steam operated platform

MILWAUKEE class *shallow draught monitors*

Displacement: 1300t
Dimensions: 229ft oa x 56ft x 6ft mean (*69.80 x 17.07 x 1.83m*)
Machinery: 7 H tubular boilers, 4-shaft HNC ?ihp = 9kts. Coal 156t
Armour: Iron. Side 3in, turrets 8in, deck ½in
Armament: 4-11in SB (2 x 2)
Complement: 120

Name	Builder*	Contracted	Launched	Comm	Fate
CHICKASAW	Union Iron Wks	26.5.1862	10.2.64	10.5.64	Sold 1874
KICKAPOO	Union Iron Wks	27.5.1862	12.3.64	8.7.64	Sold 1874
MILWAUKEE	Union Iron Wks	27.5.1862	4.2.64	27.8.64	Mined 28.3.65
WINNEBAGO	Union Iron Wks	27.5.1862	4.7.63	27.4.64	Sold 1874

lowered into the hold for loading and raised for firing. Elevation was 20° in this turret compared to 10° in the other.

Milwaukee was sunk in the Blakely River, Mobile Bay, by a mine which exploded on the port side abaft the after turret and about 40ft from the stern. This sank in about three minutes but the forward compartments did not fill for nearly an hour, indicating better subdivision than usual in monitors at that time. The three surviving ships were renamed *Samson*, *Cyclops* and *Tornado* from 15.6.1869 to 10.8.1869 when they reverted to their former names, except for *Kickapoo* which became *Kewaydin*.

**The Union Iron Works at Carondelet on the Mississippi must be distinguished from the San Francisco yard that built many 'New Navy' ships.*

Details given here are for the vessels as originally designed. Gross miscalculations of available displacement were made in this design (for which Ericsson was not responsible) as was shown when *Chimo*, as launched and without turret or stores, had a freeboard of 3in. It is ironical that the intended freeboard, as completed, of 15in was to be reduced by water ballast in action. *Casco, Chimo, Modoc, Napa, Naubuc* were completed as spar torpedo vessels with Wood-Lay gear, a thinner deck, no turrets but 1-11in SB (*Chimo* 1-8in Parrott RML) on an unprotected pivot mounting, and an 8in pilot house, while coal was reduced to about 60 tons. *Casco* was used to clear the James River of mines but her speed of 5kts made her useless for spar torpedo attack. *Tunxis* which appears to have been lighter than most, was commissioned till 21.9.1864 as a monitor with 1-11in SB and 1-8in Parrott RML, but she and the other 14 then had their hulls deepened by 22in to enable them to carry the intended weights. The displacement of these iron-hulled, turtle-deck monitors varied, *Squando* reaching 1618t at 8ft 3in (*2.52m*) mean. The armour was built up from 1in plates and the turret, of 20ft internal diameter, had a 10in pilot house on top. There was some overhang of the deck aft and slots were cut through it for the upper part of the screws.

**Most resumed their former names 10.8.1869, but 'Casco', 'Shiloh', 'Waxsaw' retained their new ones, while 'Chimo', 'Naubuc', 'Squando', 'Tunxis' became respectively 'Piscataqua', 'Minnetonka', 'Algoma', 'Otsego'.*

CASCO class *shallow draught monitors*

Displacement: 1175t
Dimensions: 225ft oa x 45ft x 6ft 4½in mean (*68.58 x 13.72 x 1.94m*)
Machinery: 2 Stimers boilers, 2-shaft Stimers IDA, 600ihp = 9kts (actually about 5kts). Coal 130t
Armour: Iron. Side 3in, turret 8in, deck ½in
Armament: 2-11in SB (1 x 2)
Complement: 60

Name*	New Name 15.6.1869	Builder	Contracted	Launched	Comm	Fate
CASCO	HERO	Atlantic Iron Wks	14.3.1863	7.5.64	4.12.64	Broken up 1875
CHIMO	ORION	Aquilla Adams	17.3.1863	5.5.64	20.1.65	Sold 1874
COHOES	CHARYBDIS	Continental Iron Wks	17.4.1863	31.5.1865	Never (delivered 19.1.66)	Sold 1874
ETLAH	HECATE	Charles W McCord	24.6.1863	3.7.65	Never (delivered 12.3.66)	Sold 1874
KLAMATH	HARPY	Alex Swift	26.3.1863	20.4.65	Never (delivered 6.5.66)	Sold 1874
KOKA	ARGOS	Wilcox & Whiting	24.4.1863	18.5.65	Never (delivered 28.11.65)	Sold 1874
MODOC	ACHILLES	J S Underhill	4.6.1863	21.3.65	Never (completed 23.6.65)	Sold 1875
NAPA	NEMESIS	Harlan & Hollingsworth	2.3.1863	26.11.64	Never (completed 4.5.65)	Sold 1875
NAUBUC	GORGON	W Perine	2.4.1863	19.10.64	27.3.65	Sold 1875
NAUSETT	AETNA	Donald McKay	10.6.1863	26.4.65	10.8.65	Sold 1875
SHAWNEE	EOLUS	Curtis & Tilden	2.4.1863	13.3.65	18.8.65	Sold 1875
SHILOH	IRIS	Charles W McCord	24.6.1863	14.7.65	17.9.74 (delivered 12.3.66)	Sold 1874
SQUANDO	EREBUS	Donald McKay	4.5.1863	31.12.64	6.6.65	Broken up 1874
SUNCOOK	SPITFIRE	Globe Wks	17.3.1863	1.2.65	27.7.65	Sold 1874
TUNXIS	HYDRA	Reaney, Son & Archbold	9.3.1863	4.6.64	12.7.64	Sold 1875
UMPQUA	FURY	Snowden & Mason	9.3.1863	21.12.65	Never (completed 7.5.66)	Sold 1874
WASSUC	STROMBOLI	G W Lawrence	2.6.1863	25.7.65	Never (completed 28.10.65)	Sold 1875
WAXSAW	NIOBE	A & W Denmead	13.3.1863	4.5.65	Never (completed 21.10.65)	Sold 1874
YAZOO	TARTAR	Cramp	2.3.1863	8.5.65	Never (completed 15.12.65)	Sold 1874
YUMA	TEMPEST	Alex Swift	26.3.1863	30.5.65	Never (delivered 6.5.66)	Sold 1874

OTHER ARMOURED SHIPS

(Also see under Torpedo Vessels)

A schooner-rigged, wooden-hulled steamer with a broadside battery and considerable tumble home. Originally she was to have had 2½in iron (plates and rails) backed by 1½in rubber but the latter was dispensed with. Her protection failed to keep out shot from the batteries at Drewry's Bluff on 15.5.1862, and in May 1863 – February 1864 her armour was removed and she became a wooden ship with an armament of 1-6.4in Parrott RML, 1-4.2in Parrott RML and 8-9in SB.

GALENA *armoured ship*

Displacement: 738t old measurement
Dimensions: 210ft oa x 36ft x 11ft mean *(64.01 x 10.97 x 3.35m)*
Machinery: 2 H tubular boilers, 1-shaft Ericsson VL 320ihp = 8 kts. Coal ?
Armour: Iron. Side 3in max.
Armament: 2-6.4in Parrott RML, 4-9in SB.
Complement: 164

Name	Builders	Laid down	Launched	Comm	Fate
GALENA	Maxon-Fish	*Circa* Oct 1861	14.2.1862	21.4.1862	Broken up 1872

Originally named *Moodna, Keokuk* was iron-hulled with armoured sides inclined sharply inwards above water, and fore and aft fixed gunhouses each with three ports. There was a spur ram, and her armour consisted of horizontal iron bars alternating with strips of oak and covered wih thin iron plates. In the attack on Charleston, on 7.4.1863, she was severely hit by 7in RML and 10in SB shot and sank next day.

KEOKUK *armoured ship*

Displacement: 677t old measurement
Dimensions: 159ft 6in oa x 36ft x 8ft 6in mean *(48.61 x 10.97 x 2.59m)*
Machinery: 2 H boilers, 2-shaft HDA, *about* 500ihp = 9kts. Coal ?
Armour: Iron. 3in
Armament: 2-11in SB (2 x 1)
Complement: 92

Name	Builder	Laid down	Launched	Comm	Fate
KEOKUK	J S Underhill	13.4.1862	6.12.62	March 1863	Sunk 8.4.1863

CRUISERS

This class were renamed on 15.5.1869 *Iowa, Tennessee, Arizona, Connecticut, Florida* respectively and *Arizona* was named *Nevada* 10.8.1869. A sixth ship to be named *Bon Homme Richard* was never built. Designed as commerce destroyers if USA and Britain were at war, which appeared not unlikely in 1863, this class were not a success. The machinery accounted for nearly 30 per cent of the displacement, there was little space for crew and stores, the lines too fine forward for bow guns, and the wooden hulls, although heavily strapped, were longitudinally weak. They had a light barque rig with a short bowsprit and straight stem, and four tall funnels in two groups, the engines being between the groups of boilers. There was apparently no water-tight subdivision and the balanced rudders were exposed. *Ammonoosuc* was laid up after her trials, and *Wampanoag,* which reported 17.75kts on trials, was condemned for naval purposes in 1869 as excessively engined and laid up till 1874 when she became receiving ship at New London with the addition of 2-6.4in Parrott RML. *Madawaska,* now named *Tennessee,* was taken in hand 1869-1871 and timbered up to a sufficient height to allow a spar deck to be installed. The boilers were changed and new engines provided which, like the original, were not very successful. Now described as a gun deck frigate, she was ship rigged with a clipper stem and 2 funnels located fore and aft of the mainmast. Her details were: Displacement: 4840t; Dimensions: 335ft wl x 45ft 2in x 21ft 8in *(102.10 x 13.76 x 6.60m)*; Machinery: 10 cyl boilers, 1-shaft H CRC, 3200ihp = 13 kts. Coal 380t; Armament: 2-8in Parrott RML, 2-6.4in Parrott RML, 1-5.3in Parrott RML, 18-9in SB; Complement: 480.

An official British report of 1.9.1886, the year *Tennessee* was sold, gives her an armament of 2-8in RML (converted 11in SB) 4-6.4in BL (converted Parrott RML), 16-9in SB, and notes that she had no heavy bow fire. An ihp of 1900 was given = about 10 kts.

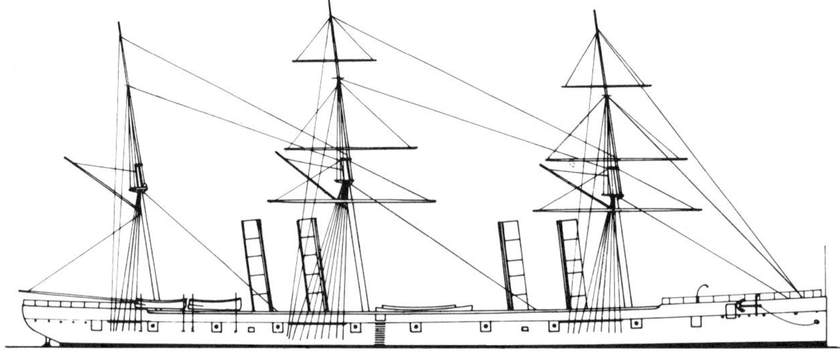

Wampanoag as completed 1868 with barque rig

WAMPANOAG class *wooden screw frigates*

Displacement: *Ammonoosuc, Neshaminy,* 3850t, *Madawaska* 4105t, *Pompanoosuc* 4446t, *Wampanoag* 4215t
Dimensions: 335ft wl x 44ft 4in *Ammonoosuc, Neshaminy,* 45ft 2in *Madawaska, Wampanoag,* 48ft *Pompanoosuc* x 18ft 2in *Madawaska,* 18ft 6in *Wampanoag* mean *(102.10 x 13.51, 13.76, 14.63 x 5.54, 5.64m)*
Machinery: 8 Martin boilers (4 superheaters), 1-shaft HDAG, *Madawaska* Ericsson VL, 4100ihp = 17kts, *Madawaska* 15kts. Coal 700t
Armament: 3-5.3in Parrott RML, 10-9in SB, 2-24pdr SB howitzers
Complement: 330

Name	Builder	Laid down	Launched	Comm	Fate
AMMONOOSUC	Boston N Yd	1863	21.7.64	Trials 15.6.68	Sold 1883
MADAWASKA	New York N Yd	1863	8.7.65	Trials 14.1.67	Sold 1886
NESHAMINY	Philadelphia N Yd	1863	5.10.65	Never completed	Sold 1874
POMPANOOSUC	Boston N Yd	1863	Never launched		Broken up 1883
WAMPANOAG	New York N Yd	3.8.1863	15.12.64	Trials 7.2.68	Sold 1885

An alternative to the *Wampanoag* class, *Chattanooga* was intended to maintain 15kts for 24 hours, and an unsuitable propeller may have accounted in part for her poor performance. Ship-rigged with straight stem, bowsprit and two funnels, she was laid up after trials, and was holed and sunk by drifting ice at League Island, Philadelphia.

CHATTANOOGA *wooden screw frigate*

Displacement: 3043t
Dimensions: 315ft wl x 46ft x 14ft 11½in mean (*96.01 x 14.01 x 4.56m*)
Machinery: 8 H tubular (superheaters) boilers, 1-shaft RCR, 1737ihp = 13.37kts on trials. Coal ?
Armament: 17 guns
Complement: –

Name	Builder	Laid down	Launched	Comm	Fate
CHATTANOOGA	Cramp	1863	13.10.64	Trials 17.8.66	Sunk by ice December 1871

Intended to maintain 15kts for 24 hours *Idaho* was a complete failure in steaming. Her machinery was removed and she was converted to a full-rigged sailing ship, one of the fastest ever known. Recommissioned 3.10.1867, she went out to Nagasaki as store and hospital ship for the Asiatic Squadron. On her return voyage in September 1869 she was dismasted in a typhoon and remained at Yokohama until sold.

IDAHO *wooden screw frigate*

Displacement: 3241t
Dimensions: 298ft wl x 44ft 6in x 17ft 1in mean (*90.83 x 13.56 x 5.20m*)
Machinery: Dickerson boilers, 2-shaft Dickerson, 645ihp = 8.27kts on trials. Coal ?
Armament: 8 guns
Complement: –

Name	Builder	Laid down	Launched	Comm	Fate
IDAHO	George Steers	May 1863 Contract	8.10.64	Trials 15.5.66	Sold 1874

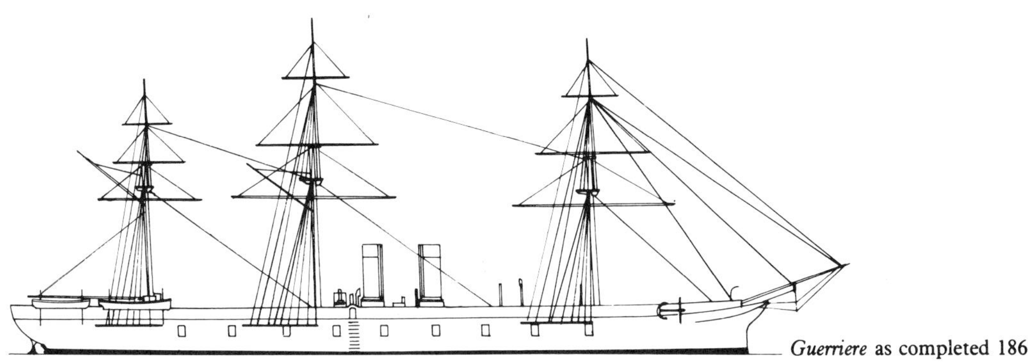

Guerriere as completed 1867

The last four were renamed on 15.5.1869 respectively *Pennsylvania, California, New York, Delaware*. Ship-rigged vessels with two funnels, intended for general cruising. The hulls had diagonal iron bracing but much green wood was used and life was very short. *Delaware (Piscataqua)* sank at New York Navy Yard, having been decommissioned as early as 5.12.1870. This ship and *California (Minnetonka)* completed as frigates with a spar deck, while *Guerriere* completed as a corvette (USN sloop) and a spar deck was added in 1869-1870.

Two somewhat larger ships *Hassalo* and *Wautaga* were never built.

JAVA class *wooden screw frigates*

Displacement: 3953t
Dimensions: 312ft 6in wl, *Minnetonka* 316ft 6in x 46ft, *Ontario* 47ft x 17ft 3in mean (*95.25, 96.47 x 14.01, 14.32 x 5.26m*)
Machinery: 4 Martin boilers (2 superheaters) 1-shaft, RCR, ?ihp =12-13kts. Coal 480t
Armament: *Guerriere, Minnetonka* 2-6.4in Parrott RML, 1-5.3in Parrott RML, 18-9in SB, (*Guerriere* had 6), 2 to 4-4in RML boat guns; *Piscataqua* had 20-9in SB
Complement: 325

Name	Builder	Laid down	Launched	Comm	Fate
ANTIETAM	Philadelphia N Yd	1863	13.11.75	Completed as sailing store ship 1876	Sold 1888
GUERRIERE	Boston N Yd	1863	9.9.65	21.5.67	Sold 1872
ILLINOIS	Portsmouth N Yd	1864	Never	–	Broken up 1872
JAVA	New York N Yd	1863	Never	–	Broken up 1884
KEWAYDIN	Boston N Yd	1864	Never	–	Broken up 1884
MINNETONKA	Portsmouth N Yd	1863	3.7.67	12.12.70	Sold 1875
ONTARIO	New York N Yd	1863	Never	–	Broken up 1888
PISCATAQUA	Portsmouth N Yd	1863	11.6.66	21.10.67	Sank 1876

Renamed on 15.5.1869 *Albany, Worcester, Severn, Cambridge* respectively, and the last again renamed *Congress* 10.8.1869. Six further ships – *Arapahoe, Keosauqua, Mondamin, Tahgayuta, Wanalosett, Willamette* – were cancelled. Ship-rigged with one funnel, this class were of long, shallow form with small beam. *Albany (Contoocook)* was completed as a corvette (USN sloop) and decommissioned in January 1870 to become a quarantine ship at New York. The other three had spar decks added before completion and thus became frigates, while a 14in false keel, was also added.

CONTOOCOOK class *wooden screw frigates*

Displacement: 3003t
Dimensions: 290ft wl x 41ft x 15½ft mean (*88.40 x 12.49 x 4.72m*)
Machinery: 4 Martin boilers (2 superheaters), 1-shaft HRCR, ?ihp = 12½kts
Armament: 1-5.3in Parrott RML, 14-9in SB, 3-12pdr
Complement: 350

Name	Builder	Laid down	Launched	Comm	Fate
CONTOOCOOK	Portsmouth N Yd	1863	3.12.64	14.3.68	Sold 1872
MANITOU	Boston N Yd	November 1863	–	1870	Sold 1883
MOSHOLU	New York N Yd	October 1864	22.12.67	27.8.69	Sold 1877
PUSHMATAHA	Philadelphia N Yd	1864	17.7.68	4.3.70	Sold 1883

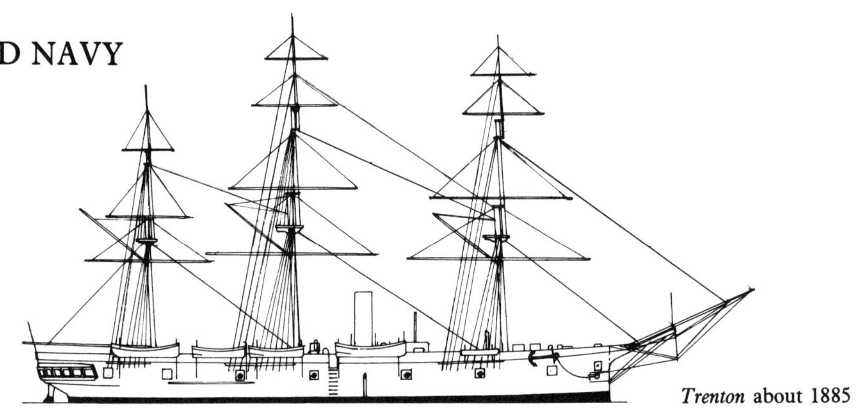

Trenton about 1885

Built of live oak with a heavy cast iron ram, the point 8ft forward of the straight stem and 9ft below water, *Trenton* was ship-rigged with a single funnel, and was of shorter and fuller form than her immediate predecessors. The all rifled main battery is to be noted, and four of the guns could be used for ahead fire. She was wrecked in Apia harbour, Samoa, during the *Calliope* typhoon when she drifted on to the *Vandalia* already on the reef.

TRENTON *wooden screw frigate*

Displacement: 3900t
Dimensions: 253ft pp x 48ft x 20ft 6in mean (*77.11 x 14.63 x 6.25m*)
Machinery: 8 cyl boilers, 1-shaft CRCR, 3100ihp = 12.8kts (USN 1887 gives 2414ihp = 12.6kts), Coal 337t
Armament: 10-8in RML (converted 11in SB), 5 smaller
Complement: 416

Name	Builder	Laid down	Launched	Comm	Fate
TRENTON	New York N Yd	Dec 1873	1.1.76	1877	Wrecked 16.3.89

Trenton
Aldo Fraccaroli Collection

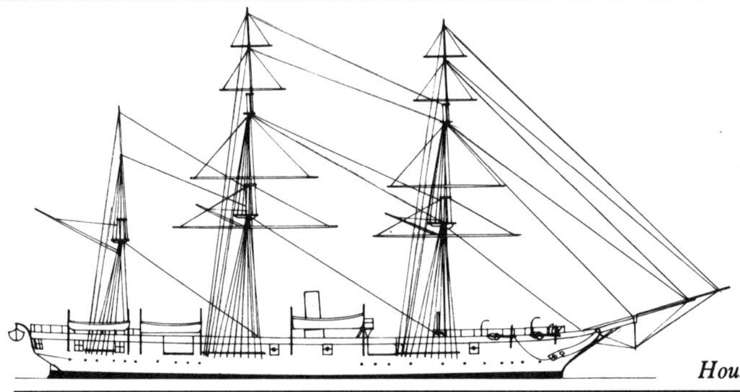

Housatonic as completed 1862

Barque-rigged, single funnel 'sloops'. *Adirondack* was wrecked on the Little Bahama Bank, while *Housatonic* was the first of all the many ships that have since been sunk by an enemy submarine. *Juniata* had a long active career as did *Ossipee* which had taken part in the Battle of Mobile Bay. By 1887 the armament of these two survivors was 1-8in RML (converted 11in SB), 1-5.3in BL (converted Parrott RML), 6-9in SB and three or four smaller guns.

OSSIPEE class *wooden screw sloops*

Displacement: 1934t
Dimensions: 205ft pp x 38ft x 16ft 6in mean (*62.48 x 11.58 x 5.02m*)
Machinery: 2 Martin boilers, 1-shaft HRCR, about 700ihp = 9-10kts. Coal 220-235t
Armament: *Adirondack* 2-11in SB, 4-32pdr SB, *Housatonic* 1-6.4in Parrott RML, 3-4.2in Parrott RML, 1-11in SB, 2-32pdr SB, *Juniata* as *Housatonic* but 4-4.2in and no 32pdr, *Ossipee* as *Housatonic* but 6-32pdr, all in addition 2 to 5 smaller guns. In 1865 *Juniata* 1-6.4in Parrott RML, 2-4.2in Parrott RML, 2-9in SB, 10-8in SB
Complement: 200-214

Name	Builder	Laid down	Launched	Comm	Fate
ADIRONDACK	New York N Yd	1861	22.2.1862	June 1862	Wrecked 23.8.62
HOUSATONIC	Boston N Yd	1861	20.11.1861	29.8.62	Sunk, spar torpedo by *HL Hunley* 17.2.1864
JUNIATA	Philadelphia N Yd	June 1861	20.3.1862	4.12.62	Sold 1891
OSSIPEE	Portsmouth N Yd	June 1861	16.11.1861	6.11.62	Sold 1891

SACRAMENTO class *wooden screw sloops*

Displacement: 2030-2100t
Dimensions: 225ft-229ft wl x 37ft 9in-38ft 4in x 16ft 6in mean (*68.58-69.80 x 11.50-11.68 x 5.02m*)
Machinery: 2 Martin boilers, 1-shaft HRCR, about 720ihp = 8-10kts
Armament: 1-8in Parrott RML, 1-4.2in Parrott RML (not in *Monongahela* and *Canandaigua* 3-3.7in Parrott RML instead), 2-11in SB, also up to 6 smaller guns. In 1864 *Sacramento* 3-6.4in Parrott RML, 1-4.2in Parrott RML, 6-8in SB
Complement: 240

Name	Builder	Laid down	Launched	Comm	Fate
CANANDAIGUA	Boston N Yd	1861	28.3.62	1.8.62	Broken up 1884
MONONGAHELA	Philadelphia N Yd	1861	10.7.62	15.1.63	Burnt 17.3.1908
SACRAMENTO	Portsmouth N Yd	1861	28.4.62	7.1.63	Wrecked 19.6.67
SHENANDOAH	Philadelphia N Yd	1861	8.12.62	20.6.63	Sold 1887

Canandaigua was named *Detroit* 15.5.1869-10.8.1869. Barque-rigged with one funnel, this type was a lengthened version of the *Ossipee* class. *Sacramento* was wrecked on reefs at the mouth of the Godavari River in India. *Monongahela* which took part in the attempt to pass Port Hudson and in the Battle of Mobile Bay, was thrown ashore by a tidal wave at St. Croix 18.11.1867, but was refloated six months later. Her machinery was removed in 1883 and she served as a sailing supply, training and finally store ship until she was destroyed by fire at Guantanamo Bay. *Shenandoah* is listed in 1886 with 2-8in RML (converted 11in SB), 1-5.3in BL (converted Parrott RML), and 6-9in SB.

TICONDEROGA class *wooden screw sloops*

Displacement: 2526t
Dimensions: 234ft 4in wl x 38ft 2in x 16ft 3in mean (*71.43 x 11.63 x 4.95m*)
Machinery: 2 Martin boilers, 1-shaft HRCR, 820ihp = 9-10.5kts
Armament: 1-8in Parrott RML, 1-5.1in Dahlgren RML, 2-11in SB, 4-9in SB, 2-6 smaller guns. *Ticonderoga* 1-4.2in Parrott RML, 12-9in SB, 2 smaller; in 1864 1-6.4in Parrott RML
Complement: 270

Name	Builder	Laid down	Launched	Comm	Fate
LACKAWANNA	New York N Yd	1861	9.8.62	8.1.63	Sold 1887
TICONDEROGA	New York N Yd	1861	16.10.62	12.5.63	Sold 1887

Barque-rigged, single funnel ships, sometimes considered as part of the *Sacramento* class of which they were longer versions. *Lackawanna* was present at the Battle of Mobile Bay. 1886 data give the armament for both as 2-8in RML (converted 11in SB), 1-5.3in BL (converted Parrott RML), and 6-9in SB.

ALASKA class *wooden screw sloops*

Displacement: 2394t
Dimesnions: 250ft 6in pp x 38ft x 16ft 6in mean (*76.35 x 11.58 x 5.02m*)
Machinery: H tubular boilers, 1-shaft HRCR, about 950ihp = 11.5 – 12kts, Coal 150t
Armament: 1-5.3in Parrott RML, 2-3.7in Parrott RML, 1-11in SB, 10-9in SB, *Alaska* had no 3.7in RML or 9in SB, but 6-8in SB
Complement: 273-291

Name	Builder	Laid down	Launched	Comm	Fate
ALASKA	Boston N Yd	1867	31.10.68	8.12.69	Sold 1883
ALGOMA	Portsmouth N Yd	1864	18.8.68	1.12.69	Sold 1884
ASTORIA	Philadelphia N Yd	1867	10.6.69	12.9.72	Sold 1915
KENOSHA	New York N Yd	1867	1868	20.1.69	Broken up 1884

Algoma renamed *Benicia*, and *Kenosha* renamed *Plymouth* on 15.5.1869. *Astoria* renamed *Omaha* on 10.8.1869. Seven ships, *Confiance, Detroit, Meredosia, Peacock, Serapis, Taghkanic, Talledaga*, of the first eight were cancelled, and three more later built. Barque-rigged ships with two funnels, and considered by the British Naval Attache in 1869 to be an excellent design. *Benicia* (*Algoma*) was finally decommissioned in 1875 and *Omaha* (*Astoria*) in 1891, the latter then serving as a quarantine ship at San Francisco. *Omaha's* armament in 1887 comprised 1-8in RML (converted 11in SB), 1-5.3in BL (converted Parrott RML), 10-9in SB, and seven smaller guns.

GALENA class and VANDALIA *wooden screw sloops*

Displacement: 1900t, *Vandalia* 2033t
Dimensions: 216ft pp x 37ft, *Vandalia* 39ft x 16ft 6in mean, *Vandalia* 17ft 3in, (*65.84 x 11.27, 11.88, x 5.02m, 5.25*
Machinery: 10 cyl boilers (*Vandalia* 8), 1-shaft HCRCR, about 800 ihp = 10-11kts, (*Vandalia* 1150ihp = 12kts), Coal 160-185t
Armament: 1-8in RML (*Marion* 1-11in SB,) 1-5.3in RML, (*Galena* had BL, *Swatara* 1-4.2in RML instead), 6-9in SB, *Mohican* 8
Complement: 212-230

Name	Builder	Laid down	Launched	Comm	Fate
GALENA (2nd)	Norfolk N Yd	1872	1879	26.8.80	Sold 1892
MARION (2nd)	Portsmouth N Yd	1872	1873	12.1.76	Sold 1907
MOHICAN (2nd)	Mare Island N Yd	4.9.1872	27.12.83	25.5.85	Sold 1922
QUINNEBAUG (2nd)	Philadelphia N Yd	1872	28.9.75	2.10.78	Sold 1891
SWATARA (2nd)	New York N Yd	1872	17.9.73	11.5.74	Sold 1896
VANDALIA	Boston N Yd	1872	23.10.74	1876	Wrecked 16.3.89

Ship- or barque-rigged vessels, *Marion* being usually considered a rebuild of the first *Marion*. Except for *Galena* and *Mohican*, the engines were conversions of those built for the cancelled ships of the *Serapis* (*Alaska*) class. *Vandalia* was driven on the reef in Apia harbour, Samoa, in the *Calliope* typhoon and further wrecked by *Trenton* drifting on to her. The long careers of some of this class are misleading as *Swatara* was laid up disarmed in 1891, *Marion* became a naval militia training ship in 1898, while *Mohican* was a training ship 1898-1904, then station ship at Olongapo and from 1910 to 1921 receiving ship at Cavite, serving also as a stationary submarine tender to the end of 1915. The armament of all the class in 1887 was 1-8in RML (converted 11in SB), 1-5.3in BL (converted Parrott RML), and 6-9in SB, three to four smaller guns.

Kearsarge
Aldo Fraccaroli Collection

KEARSARGE class *wooden screw sloops*

Ship- or barque-rigged vessels authorised in February 1861, the first three named being virtual replicas of the *Mohican, Iroquois* and *Wyoming* of 1858. *Kearsarge* sank the famous Confederate raider *Alabama* on 19.6.64 and after a long active career was wrecked on Roncador Reef. *Oneida* was present at the Battle of Mobile Bay, and in 1870 was sunk off Yokohama in a collision with the iron hulled P & O steamer *City of Bombay* which, disgracefully, did not stop. *Wachusett* attacked and captured the Confederate raider *Florida* in Bahia harbour 7.10.1864. *Kearsarge* in 1887 mounted 2-8in RML (converted 11in SB), 1-5.3in BL (converted Parrott RML), 4-9in SB, and one smaller gun.

Displacement: 1457-1488t, later 1550-1575t
Dimensions: 198ft 6in-198ft 11in pp x 33ft 2in-33ft 10in x 15ft 6in mean *(60.50-60.63 x 10.10-10.30 x 4.72m)*
Machinery: 2 Martin boilers, 1-shaft HRCR, about 840ihp = 11-12kts. Coal 165t
Armament: *Kearsarge* 1-4.2in Parrott RML, 2-11in SB, 4- to 6-32pdr SB; *Oneida* 3-4.2in Parrott RML, 2-9in SB, 4-32pdr SB; *Wachusett* as *Kearsarge* but 2-4.2in, 1-3.7in Parrott RML, in 1864 3-6.4in Parrott RML, 2-4.2in Parrott RML, 4-32pdr SB; *Tuscarora* originally as *Kearsarge* but 6-32pdr SB, in 1864 1-6.4in Parrott RML, 2-4.2in Parrott RML, 1-11in SB, 6-8in SB
Complement: 163-212

Name	Builder	Laid down	Launched	Comm	Fate
KEARSARGE	Portsmouth N Yd	1861	11.9.61	24.1.62	Wrecked 2.2.94
ONEIDA	New York N Yd	1861	20.11.61	28.2.62	Collision 24.1.70
TUSCARORA	Philadelphia N Yd	June 1861	24.8.61	5.12.61	Sold 1883
WACHUSETT	Boston N Yd	June 1861	10.10.1861	3.3.62	Sold 1887

SWATARA class *wooden screw sloops*

Two of the class, *Alert* at Washington Navy Yard and *Epervier* at Portsmouth, were never built. Barque-rigged ships of short life as *Nantasket* was stricken in 1875. *Quinnebaug's* engines were obtained from England, but were not satisfactory as shown by her low speed. It was originally intended to mount an 11in SB pivot instead of the 5.3in RML, but it proved too heavy.

Displacement: 1113-1129t
Dimensions: 216ft wl x 30ft-31ft x 12ft mean *(65.84 x 9.14-9.45 x 3.66m)*
Machinery: *Quinnebaug* 2-shaft HDA, 7kts; rest 1-shaft HRCR, 11kts
Armament: *Nantasket, Quinnebaug, Swatara*, 1-5.3in Parrott RML, 6-32pdr SB *Quinnebaug* 4, *Resaca* as *Swatara* but 1-8in Parrott RML instead of 5.3in, all 1-3 smaller guns
Complement: 164

Name	Builder	Laid down	Launched	Comm	Fate
NANTASKET	Boston N Yd	1864	15.8.67	22.10.69	Sold 1883
QUINNEBAUG	New York N Yd	1864	31.3.66	19.7.67	Broken up 1871
RESACA	Portsmouth N Yd	1864	18.11.65	1866	Sold 1873
SWATARA	Philadelphia N Yd	1864	23.5.65	15.11.65	Broken up 1872

ENTERPRISE class *wooden screw sloops*

Alliance was launched as *Huron*. Barque-rigged steamers, whose long life is somewhat deceptive. Thus *Adams* was a training and station ship from 1907, *Alliance* had her engines removed as a store ship in 1904, *Enterprise* was a training ship from 1892, and *Essex* also for most of her career from 1893. *Nipsic* was thrown on the beach in the Calliope typhoon in Apia Harbour 16.3.1889 and was repaired, but from 1892 she was receiving and prison ship at Puget Sound. The armament of the class in 1887 comprised 1-8in RML (Parrott in *Adams*, converted 11in SB in others), 1-5.3in BL (converted Parrott RML), 4-9in SB, and 2-4 smaller guns.

Displacement: 1375t
Dimensions: 185ft pp x 35ft x 14ft 3in mean *(56.38 x 10.66 x 4.35m)*
Machinery: 8 cyl boilers, 1-shaft HCRCR, 700-800ihp = 10-11kts. Coal 130-150t
Armament: 1-5.3in Parrott RML, 1-11in SB, 4-9in SB
Complement: 178-193

Name	Builder	Laid down	Launched	Comm	Fate
ADAMS	Boston N Yd	1874	1876	21.7.76	Sold 1920
ALLIANCE	Norfolk N Yd	1874	3.3.75	18.1.77	Sold 1911
ENTERPRISE	J W Griffiths	1874	13.6.74	16.3.77	Sold 1909
NIPSIC (2nd)	Rebuilt Washington N Yd	1874	1878	11.10.79	Sold 1913
ESSEX	D McKay	1874		3.10.76	Sold 1930

Ranger was renamed *Rockport* 30.10.1917 and *Nantucket* 20.2.1918. Classed as iron gunboats in the USN. *Huron* and *Ranger* were originally fore and aft rigged, but after the loss of *Huron* on the North Carolina coast, *Ranger* was given a barque-rig as *Alert*. The last named was converted to a submarine tender in 1911–12, while *Ranger* was a surveying ship 1880 to 1891 and from 1909 was mostly employed as a training ship for the State of Massachusetts. In 1887 *Alert* mounted 1-5.3in BL (converted Parrott RML), 1-11in SB, 2-9in SB and four smaller guns, while *Ranger* had only 1-5.3in Parrott RML as survey ship.

ALERT class *wooden screw sloops*

Displacement: 1020t
Dimensions: 175ft pp x 32ft x 12ft 9in mean (*53.34 x 9.75 x 3.89m*)
Machinery: 5 cyl boilers, 1-shaft HCRCR, 380ihp = 10kts. Coal 130t
Armament: 1-5.3in Parrott RML, 1-11in SB, 2-9in SB
Complement: 148

Name	Builder	Laid down	Launched	Comm	Fate
ALERT	Roach	Sept 1873	9.1874	1875	Sold 1922
HURON (2nd)	Roach	1873	1874	15.11.75	Wrecked 24.11.1877
RANGER	Harlan & Hollingsworth	1873	1876	27.11.76	Stricken 1940

Ranger at Algiers, 6 July 1913

The famous '90-day' schooner-rigged gunboats. Contracts were placed in July 1861 prior to Congressional approval, and the first four were commissioned by mid-October. They were much used in coastal and river operations, and *Itasca* and *Kennebec* took part in the Battle of Mobile Bay, while *Sciota* later struck a mine in these waters.

UNADILLA class *gunboats*

Displacement: 691t
Dimensions: 158ft 4in wl x 28ft x 10ft 4in mean (*48.26 x 8.53 x 3.15m*)
Machinery: 2 Martin boilers, 1-shaft RCR, 400ihp = 10-11kts
Armament: typically 1-3.7in Parrott RML, 1-11in SB, 2-24pdr SB howitzers, but considerable variation in smaller guns. *Itasca* and *Tahoma* originally had 1-10in instead of 1-11in SB and *Ottawa*, *Tahoma* and *Wissahickon* later had 1-8in Parrott RML replacing the large SB
Complement: 78-90

Name	Builder	Laid down	Launched	Comm	Fate
AROOSTOOK	N W Thompson	1861	1861	20.2.62	Sold 1869
CAYUGA	Gildersleeve	1861	21.10.61	21.2.62	Sold 1865
CHIPPEWA	Webb & Bell	1861	14.9.61	13.12.61	Sold 1865
CHOCURA	Curtis & Tilden	1861	5.10.61	15.2.62	Sold 1867
HURON	Paul Curtis	1861	21.9.61	8.1.62	Sold 1869
ITASCA	Hillman & Streaker	1861	1.10.61	28.11.61	Sold 1865
KANAWHA	Goodspeed	1861	21.10.61	21.1.62	Sold 1866
KATAHDIN	Larrabee & Allen	1861	12.10.61	17.2.62	Sold 1865
KENNEBEC	G W Lawrence	1861	5.10.61	8.2.62	Sold 1865
KINEO	J W Dyer	1861	9.10.61	8.2.62	Sold 1866
MARBLEHEAD	G W Jackman	1861	16.10.61	8.3.62	Sold 1868
OTTAWA	Westervelt	1861	1861	7.10.61	Sold 65
OWASCO	C Mallory	1861	5.10.61	23.1.62	Sold 1865
PEMBINA	Thomas Stack	1861	1861	16.10.61	Sold 1865
PENOBSCOT	C P Carter	1861	19.11.61	Delivered 16.1.62	Sold 1869
PINOLA	Abrahams	1861	1861	29.1.1862	Sold 1865
SAGAMORE	A & G T Sampson	1861	1.9.61	7.12.1861	Sold 1865
SCIOTA	Jacob Birley	1861	15.10.61	15.12.1861	Mined 14.4.65
SENECA	Simonson	1861	27.8.61	14.10.1861	Sold 1868
TAHOMA	Thatcher	1861	2.10.61	20.12.61	Sold 1867
UNADILLA	John English	1861	17.8.61	30.9.61	Sold 1869
WINONA	C & R Poillon	1861	14.9.61	11.12.61	Sold 1865
WISSAHICKON	John Lynn	1861	2.10.61	25.11.61	Sold 1865

Ship- or barque-rigged with one funnel, these gunboats differed considerably in machinery: *Nipsic*, *Nyack* and *Shawmut* had two Martin boilers with horizontal return connecting-rod engines, while *Saco* had 14 small return fire-tube boilers and Corliss vibrating lever engines, later replaced by return connecting-rod. *Maumee* had Ericsson vibrating lever engines, and *Yantic* horizontal direct-acting, while *Pequot* had Wright segmental engines in each case with 2 Martin boilers. *Kansas* had two straight fire-tube boilers with horizontal direct-acting engines taken from the cargo of the blockade runner *Princess Royal*. It would seem that return connecting-rod engines gave the best results. *Pequot* was sold to Haiti, and *Nipsic* was 'rebuilt' at Washington Navy Yard, and became one of the *Enterprise* class. *Yantic's* armament in 1887 comprised 1-8in RML (converted 11in SB), 1-5.3in BL (converted Parrott RML), 2-9in SB, and two smaller guns.

KANSAS class *gunboats*

Displacement: 836t
Dimensions: 179ft 6in pp x 30ft x 11ft 6in mean *(54.71 x 9.14 x 3.50m)*
Machinery: See text. All 1-shaft, 225-670ihp =8-11kts. Coal 120t
Armament: 1-8in Parrott RML or 6.4in in *Maumee, Nyack, Saco, Shawmut*, 1-4.2in Parrott RML, and 2-3.7in Dahlgren RML in *Kansas*, 2-9in SB or 6-32pdr SB in *Pequot, Saco*, 2-32pdr in *Maumee*, 2-5 smaller guns. In 1865 *Kansas* 1-4.2in. Parrott RML, 2-11in SB, 2-9in SB, 5 smaller
Complement: 96-130

Name	Builder	Laid down	Launched	Comm	Fate
KANSAS	Philadelphia N Yd	1863	29.9.63	21.12.63	Sold 1883
MAUMEE	New York N Yd	1863	2.7.63	29.9.64	Sold 1869
NIPSIC	Portsmouth N Yd	24.12.1862	15.6.63	2.9.63	'Rebuilt' 1874-79
NYACK	New York N Yd	1863	6.10.63	28.9.64	Sold 1883
PEQUOT	Boston N Yd	1863	4.6.63	15.1.64	Sold 1869
SACO	Boston N Yd	1863	28.8.63	11.7.64	Sold 1883
SHAWMUT	Portsmouth N Yd	2.2.1863	17.4.63	1.11.64	Sold 1877
YANTIC	Philadelphia N Yd	1863	19.3.1864	1864	Sticken 1930

Shawmut of the *Kansas* class in the Potomac River

The first group of 'double-enders', schooner-rigged paddle gunboats of very full section, were laid down in the summer and autumn of 1861. With bow and stern rudders they were well suited to river and coastal waters, but much less satisfactory for sea service. Among the many activities of their class in the Civil War, *Octorara* and *Port Royal* took part in the Battle of Mobile Bay, *Miami* engaged the ironclad *Albemarle* on 19.4.1864 and *Genesee* was one of the ships that attempted to pass Port Hudson on 14.3.1863.

The armament of some of this class was altered during the war. The 6.4in Parrott was retained except that for a time in 1864 *Cimarron* had 1-8in Parrott. The 6in Dahlgren RML in *Miami, Octorara* were replaced by 6.4in Parrotts and the 5.1in Dahlgren RML in *Paul Jones* removed, though 2 were added to *Port Royal*. Heavy SBs were usually increased and in 1864 *Conemaugh* mounted 1-11in and 6-9in.

OCTORARA class *side-wheel gunboats*

Displacement: 981-1210t no figures for *Maratanza, Miami*
Dimensions: 205ft-232ft wl x 33ft-35ft 4in x 8ft-9ft 11in mean *(62.48-70.71 x 10.06-10.76 x 2.44-3.02m)*
Machinery: 2 Bartol boilers, Martin in *Paul Jones*, IDA, about 590ihp = 8-11 kts
Armament: 1-6.4in Parrott RML *Miami* and *Octorara* 1-6in Dahlgren RML, 1-9in SB *Conemaugh* and *Sonoma* 1-11in SB, *Paul Jones* 2-11in SB, *Genesse, Port Royal, Tioga* 1-10in SB, 4 to 8 smaller guns mostly 24pdr SB howitzers, *Paul Jones* included 2-5.1in Dahlgren RML
Complement: 125-156

Name*	Builder	Laid down	Launched	Comm	Fate
CIMARRON	D S Merschon	1861	16.3.62	5.7.62	Sold 1865
CONEMAUGH	Portsmouth N Yd	1861	1.5.62	16.7.62	Sold 1867
GENESEE	Boston N Yd	1861	2.4.62	3.7.62	Sold 1867
MAHASKA	Portsmouth N Yd	1861	10.12.61	5.5.62	Sold 1868
MARATANZA	Boston N Yd	1861	26.11.61	12.4.62	Sold 1868
MIAMI	Philadelphia N Yd	1861	16.11.61	29.1.62	Sold 1865
OCTORARA	New York N Yd	1861	7.12.61	28.2.62	Sold 1866
PAUL JONES	J J Abrahams	1861	30.1.62	9.6.62	Sold 1867
PORT ROYAL	Thomas Stack	1861	17.1.62	26.4.62	Sold 1866
SEBAGO	Portsmouth N Yd	1861	30.11.61	26.3.62	Sold 1867
SONOMA	Portsmouth N Yd	1861	15.4.62	8.7.62	Sold 1867
TIOGA	Boston Y Nd	1861	18.4.62	30.6.62	Sold 1867

**The above ships were not a homogeneous class and can be split into nine different groups, but for convenience they are treated together. 'Cimarron' was originally spelt 'Cimerone', and 'Conemaugh' as 'Cinemaugh'.*

Schooner-rigged 'double-enders' of very full section and light draught, this class were mainly used in coastal and river waters during the Civil War, and were not very satisfactory at sea though several were so employed. The contracts were placed in the autumn of 1862. *Sassacus* rammed the ironclad *Albemarle* in the action of 5.5.1864, and survived though badly damaged, while *Metacomet* took apart in the Battle of Mobile Bay where she forced the gunboat *Selma* to strike. *Otsego* was lost in the Roanoke after striking two mines in quick succession, and *Wateree* was carried 400 yards inland by a tidal wave at Arica, though little damaged. The long stroke Dickerson engine in *Algonquin* proved a failure, and though it was intended to sell her to Haiti in 1869, her condition was so bad that the screw gunboat *Pequot* was substituted. *Tallapoosa*, sunk in a collision in August 1884, was salved and recommissioned January 1886. USN 1887 figures give 1-8in RML (converted 11in SB), 5-5.3in Parrott RML and six smaller guns, with 872ihp = 12.1kts, and 201t coal capacity.

**Only 'Wateree' was iron-hulled*

SASSACUS class *side-wheel gunboats*

Displacement: 1173t
Dimensions: 240ft wl x 35ft x 8ft 6in mean (*73.15 x 10.66 x 2.59m*)
Machinery: 2 Martin boilers, 2 Dickerson in *Algonquin*, IDA Dickerson in *Algonquin* 515-545ihp = 8.5-11kts
Armament: 2-6.4in Parrott RML, 4-9in SB, 4 to 8 smaller guns typically 2-3.7in Parrott RML, 2-24pdr SB howitzers.1-6.4in RML was later replaced by 1-11in SB in *Iosco, Pontoosuc, Sassacus* and both 6.4in by 2-11in SB in *Tacony* and by 1-11in and 2-9in SB in *Mackinaw*
Complement: 135-173

Name	Builder	Laid down	Launched	Comm	Fate
AGAWAM	G W Lawrence	1862	21.4.63	9.3.64	Sold 1867
ALGONQUIN	New York N Yd	March 1863	21.12.63	Never (failed trials)	Sold 1869
ASCUTNEY	G W Jackson	1862	4.4.63	28.7.64	Sold 1868
CHENANGO	Simonson	1862	19.3.63	29.2.64	Sold 1868
CHICOPEE	Paul Curtis	1862	4.3.63	7.5.64	Sold 1867
EUTAW	Abrahams	1862	2.63	2.7.63	Sold 1867
IOSCO	Larrabee & Allen	1862	20.3.63	26.4.64	Coal hulk 1868
LENAPEE	E Lupton	1862	28.5.63	30.12.64	Sold 1868
MACKINAW	New York N Yd	1862	22.4.63	23.4.64	Sold 1867
MASSASOIT	Curtis & Tilden	1862	8.3.63	8.3.64	Sold 1867
MATTABESETT	A & G Sampson	1862	1863	7.4.64	Sold 1865
MENDOTA	F Z Tucker	1862	13.1.63	2.5.64	Sold 1867
METACOMET	Thomas Stack	1862	7.3.63	4.1.64	Sold 1865
MINGOE	D S Merschon	1862	6.8.63	29.7.64	Sold 1867
OSCEOLA	Curtis & Tilden	1862	29.5.63	10.2.64	Sold 1867
OTSEGO	Westervelt	1862	31.3.63	April 1864	Mined 9.12.64
PAWTUXET	Portsmouth N Yd	1862	19.3.63	26.8.64	Sold 1867
PEORIA	New York N Yd	1862	29.10.63	26.12.66	Sold 1868
PONTIAC	Hillman & Streaker	1862	1863	7.7.64	Sold 1867
PONTOOSUC	G W Lawrence	1862	1863	10.5.64	Sold 1866
SASSACUS	Portsmouth N Yd	1862	23.12.62	5.10.63	Sold 1868
SHAMROCK	New York N Yd	1862	17.3.63	13.6.64	Sold 1868
TACONY	Philadelphia N Yd	1862	2.5.63	13.2.64	Sold 1868
TALLAHOMA	New York N Yd	1862	28.11.63	–	Sold 1868
TALLAPOOSA	Boston N Yd	1862	17.2.63	13.9.64	Sold 1892
*WATEREE	Reany, Son & Archbold	1862	12.8.63	8.4.64	Wrecked 13.8.68
WINOOSKI	Boston N Yd	1862	30.7.63	–	Sold 1868
WYALUSING	C H & W H Cramp	1862	12.5.63	8.2.64	Sold 1867

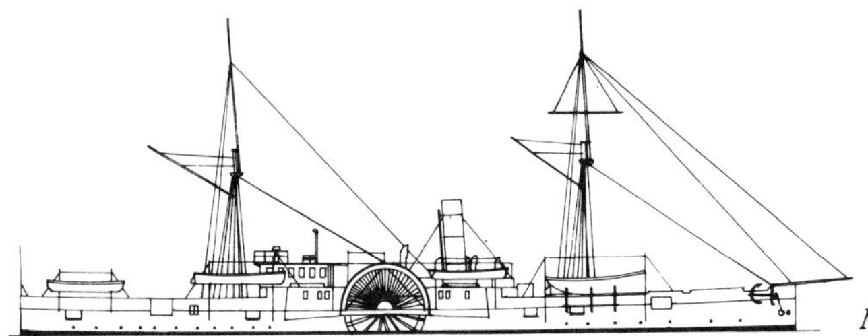

Monocacy late in her career

'Double-enders' contracted for in June-July 1863. As with the wooden-hulled gunboats of this type, the *Mohongo* class were schooner-rigged, of very full section and were reported unsatisfactory at sea, though *Ashuelot* accompanied *Miantonomoh* to Europe and then proceeded to the Far East, and *Mohongo* navigated the Straits of Magellan in a severe gale. *Ashuelot* was lost on the Lamock rocks near Swatow, and *Suwanee* in Shadwell Passage, Queen Charlotte Sound, British Columbia. *Monocacy*, the last survivor of a class already obsolescent as paddle warships when laid down, took part in the Korean troubles of 1871 and the Chinese 'Yi Ho Tuan' rebellion of 1900. According to 1887 lists her armament was then 2-5.3in Parrott RML, 4-8in SB and eight smaller guns.

**'Wateree' listed under 'Sassacus' class*

MOHONGO class *side-wheel gunboats*

Displacement: 1370t
Dimensions: 255ft wl x 35ft x 9ft mean (*77.72 x 10.66 x 2.74m*)
Machinery: 2 H tubular boilers, DA, about 850ihp = 11-12kts. Coal 224t
Armament: 2-6.4in Parrott RML, 4-9in SB, 2-4in RML howitzer, 2-24pdr SB howitzers
Complement: 159-190

Name*	Builder	Laid down	Launched	Comm	Fate
ASHUELOT	Donald McKay	1863	12.7.65	4.4.66	Wrecked 18.2.83
MOHONGO	Secor	1863	9.7.64	23.5.65	Sold 1870
MONOCACY	Denmead	1863	14.12.64	1866	Sold 1903
MUSCOOTA	Continental Iron Wks	1863	1864	5.1.65	Sold 1869
SHAMOKIN	Reany, Son & Archbold	1863	1864	17.10.65	Sold 1869
SUWANEE	Reany, Son & Archbold	1863	13.3.64	23.1.65	Wrecked 9.7.68
WINNEPEC	Harrison Loring	1863	20.8.64	1865	Sold 1869

SPAR-TORPEDO VESSELS

The converted shallow draught monitors 'Casco', 'Chimo', 'Modoc', 'Napa' and 'Naubuc' are listed under their original class of ship. Apart from picket boats such as sank the 'Albemarle' a number of small tugs — 'Alpha', 'Belle', 'Delta', 'Gamma', 'Hoyt', 'Martin' — were fitted with spar torpedoes during the Civil War, and the much larger 420t tug 'Nina' was used for experimental torpedo work from 1870 to 1884. There were also three specially built torpedo vessels in the 'Old Navy'.

SPUYTEN DUYVIL *spar-torpedo vessel*

Displacement: 207t
Dimensions: 84ft 2in x 20ft 8in x 7ft 5in (*25.66 x 6.30 x 2.26m*)
Machinery: ? HP=8kts
Armament: 1 spar torpedo, power worked
Complement: 22

Name	Builder	Laid down	Launched	Comm	Fate
SPUYTEN DUYVIL	S M Pook	1864 Contracted 1.6.64	1864	Probably Nov 1864	Stricken 1880

Named *Stromboli* until 19.11.1864. *Spuyten Duyvil* was designed by William Wood, Chief Engineer of the USN. The torpedo bar was run out through a water-tight box in the bows, the charge detached and fired automatically at the extreme reach of the bar, and at the same time the return motion of the bar began. The water-tight box was pumped out in a few seconds and another charge then attached. 12 torpedo charges could be stowed. The torpedo handling machinery weighed 10t and the ship's engine only two and a half. The wooden hull was partially iron armoured with 5in on sides and pilot-house and 3in on deck, and draught was increased to about 9ft in action. Two torpedoes were successfully fired on 25.11.1864 and *Spuyten Duyvil* was later used to blow up obstructions on the James River, though she was not able to attack the Confederate ships on 24.1.1865. She was subsequently employed on experimental work.

ALARM *torpedo ram*

Displacement: 800t
Dimensions: 173ft oa x 28ft x 10ft 6in mean (52.73 x 8.53 x 3.20m)
Machinery: 4 cyl boilers, Fowler wheel, 1-shaft, 2 sets C, 600ihp = 10kts. Coal 40½t
Armament: 1-15in SB, bow and side spar torpedoes
Complement: 40

Name	Builder	Laid down	Launched	Comm	Fate
ALARM	New York N Yd	1873	13.11.73	1874	Sold 1898

Iron-hulled experimental torpedo ram built for the Bureau of Ordnance. A one-funnel, mastless vessel with a 15ft long 'snout' bow, propelled by a horizontal feathering paddle wheel, later replaced by a steering propeller. The 30ft bow torpedo boom was controlled by steam winch and tackles, and there were also 2-18ft long side spars. Although she had no rudder *Alarm* was said to manoeuvre well, but was much too slow for her role. There was 1½in bow protection, and the skeg framework for the Fowler wheel gave her a draught of 15ft 9in aft, as it projected 3ft 6in below the keel. She was laid up in 1885 and fitted out as a gunnery training ship in 1890-91 but seems to have been little used.

INTREPID *torpedo ram*

Displacement: 1150t
Dimensions: 170ft pp x 35ft 3½in x 11ft mean (*51.82 x 10.75 x 3.35m*)
Machinery: 6 cyl boilers, 2-shaft C, 1800ihp = 11 kts. Coal 180t
Armament: Bow and side spar torpedoes
Complement: –

Name	Builder	Laid down	Launched	Comm	Fate
INTREPID	Boston N Yd	1873	5.3.74	31.7.74	Sold 1892

Iron-hulled experimental torpedo ram. Little used and apparently not very handy, as well as being slow, *Intrepid* was to have been converted to a light draught gunboat in 1882-23, but work progressed slowly and was suspended in 1889. As originally completed she had one bow and four side spars for torpedoes, and was protected by a 5in-4in belt and 9in on the lower part of the funnel, both being built up from 1in plates. There was also a 1½in deck.

ARMED MERCHANT CRUISERS

A large number of armed merchant ships were acquired during the Civil War. Neglecting purely river craft, the total of these auxiliary warships was somewhere between 100 and 200, depending on where the boundaries between supply ships and auxiliary cruisers, tugs and gunboats and river and coastal water vessels are drawn. On the whole there were more side-wheel than screw steamers. Armaments were usually light compared with those of similar sized warships, and although 1-6.4in Parrott RML was not uncommon as part of the armament of the larger ships, only a single 11in SB has been found and the old 32pdr was much in evidence. Some of the side-wheelers attained 15 or 16kts, but only in the *Rhode Island*, given below, was this accompanied by a relatively heavy armament. No screw steamer faster than 14 kts has been found.

Of the larger ships, the four most heavily armed are listed below.

Name	In USN	Tonnage	Dimensions	Speed	Armament
VANDERBILT	1862-1873	3360	250ft x 38½ft x 21½ft *(76.19 x 11.73 x 6.56m)*	14kts	2-6.4 in RML, 2-4.2in RML 12-9in SB
FORT JACKSON	1863-1865	1770	250ft x 38½ft x 18ft *(76.19 x 11.73 x 5.49m)*	14kts	1-6.4in RML, 2-4.2in RML, 8-9in SB
RHODE ISLAND	1864-1867(*)	1517	236½ft x 36²/₃ft x 15ft *(72.09 x 11.17 x 4.57m)*	16kts	1-4.2in RML, 1-11in SB 8-8in SB, 1-12pdr RML
GLAUCUS	1864-1865	1244	209ft x 35½ft x 13ft 9in *(63.70 x 10.81 x 4.19m)*	10kts	1-6.4in RML, 2-4.2in RML, 8-8in SB

* *As auxiliary cruiser.*

The first three were side-wheelers, and *Glaucus* screw-driven, and all were wooden-hulled. *Vanderbilt*, a strongly built ship launched in 1855, was by far the most formidable of the above, but her vertical beam engine seriously limited her value as a warship. She was sold in 1873, and later with her engines removed, became a fast sailing ship under the name of *Three Brothers*.

Of smaller ships suitable for coastal waters, some of the most heavily armed were former New York side-wheel ferries. Details of two with higher speeds than most are given below.

Name	In USN	Tonnage	Dimensions	Speed	Armament
COMMODORE JONES	1863-1864*	542	154ft x 32ft 6in x 9ft *(46.93 x 9.90 x 2.74m)*	12kts	1-5.1in RML, 2-4.2in RML 4-9in SB, 4-24pdr SB
HUNCHBACK	1861-1865	517	179ft x 29ft x 8ft 6in *(54.56 x 8.84 x 2.59m)*	12kts	1-6.4in RML, 3-9in SB

* *Mined*

Confederate States

The construction policy of the Confederate Navy in its short existence from 1861 to 1865 was to concentrate on armoured ships and unarmoured commerce raiders. Confederate resources in ironworks and particularly in marine engines, were however so poor that great efforts had to be made to obtain sea-going ships from Britain and France. These were largely prevented by representations made by the USA to the two European governments. Of armoured ships the Danish broadside ironclad *Danmark*, the British turret ships *Scorpion* and *Wivern* and the Prussian fixed-turret ram *Prinz Adalbert* all began as Confederate-ordered ships. The *Stonewall*, sister to the *Prinz Adalbert*, was, however, eventually commissioned in the Confederate Navy.

ARMOURED SHIPS

The composite-hulled *Stonewall* had a long ram bow, was rigged as a brig with a bowsprit that could be run in, and had a single funnel. The fixed 'turret' for the 10in gun was right forward with a bow port and one on either beam, while the 6.4in were abaft the mainmast, each gun having a stern and a broadside port. The French government forbade her original sale to the Confederacy, and she was sold to Denmark for use in the war with Prussia and Austria, via a Swedish intermediary. As the war was over the Danes would not accept her, and the ship, under the name of *Sphinx*, was now the property of her builders who sold her to the Confederacy. She was named *Stonewall* in December 1864, and left Copenhagen in January, using the names *Staerkodder* and *Olinde* to disguise ownership.

STONEWALL *armoured ram*

Displacement: 1400t, 1535 deep load
Dimensions: 171ft 10in pp, 187ft oa x 32 ft 8in x 14ft 4in mean *(52.38, 56.99 x 9.95 x 4.37m)*
Machinery: 2 tubular boilers, 2-shaft RCR, 1200ihp = 10kts. Coal 200/280t
Armour: Iron. Side 4¾in-3½in, turret 4½in, after guns 4in
Armament: 1-10in/300pdr Armstrong RML, 2-6.4in/70pdr Armstrong RML
Complement: 130

Name	Builder	Contracted	Launched	Comm	Fate
STONEWALL	Arman, Bordeaux	16.7.1863	21.6.1864	Jan 1865	See below

On 24 March 1865 she offered battle off Ferrol to the unarmoured *Niagara* and *Sacramento* (7640t combined displacement) but this was declined. On arrival at Havana in May 1865 it was learnt that the war was over, and she was surrendered to the Spanish authorities and by them to the USA. Sold to Japan in 1867 she was known as the *Kotetsu* and later *Azuma*, and was eventually sold to a fishing company in 1891.

The armoured vessels built in the Confederacy were in no sense sea-going ships and the waters of Hampton Roads, Mobile Bay or off Charleston bar in calm weather, were their limit. The most important and/or interesting were the first and second *Virginia*, the second *Tennessee* and the *Nashville*, and these are described below. All four were wood-hulled.

The first *Virginia* set the pattern for Confederate armoured ships, with the forward and after parts of the hull awash except for a low coaming at the bows, and a casemate with inclined sides rising amidships. The lower edge of the casemate was only 6in below water, a foot less than intended, and after the fight with the *Monitor* the hull below was increased to 3in for 160ft from the bows for a depth of 3½ft. The 7in guns were fore and aft in the casemate, each with three ports, the other guns at the sides and the howitzers fore and aft on the casemate roof, where the 3in or 4in pilot-house was also located forward. The famous drawn battle with the *Monitor* was fought on 9.3.1862 but when the *Virginia* reappeared on 11.4.1862 the *Monitor* declined to engage her. On the abandonment of Norfolk, the Confederates burnt *Virginia* as her draught was too deep to ascend the James River.

Virginia as completed 1862

VIRGINIA *ironclad*

Displacement: –
Dimensions: 275ft oa x 38ft 6in x 22ft (*83.81 x 11.73 x 6.70m*)
Machinery: 4 Martin boilers, 1-shaft RCR, ihp = 7½kts.
Armour: Iron. Casemate 4in (2 x 2in), side below 1in, later 3in-1in
Armament: 2-7in Brooke RML, 2-6.4in Brooke RML, 6-9in SB, 2-12pdr SB howitzers
Complement: 320

Name	Converted	Comm	Fate
VIRGINIA	From partly burned USS *Merrimack* at Norfolk N Yd 1861-62	17.2.1862	Burned 11.5.1862

The best of the Confederate James River ships. The casemate was 6in on the forward face and elsewhere 5in. The 7in or 8in Brooke RML was forward, the heavy SB aft and the 6.4in on the beam. The 2-12pdr howitzers were on the casemate roof. At one period the 2-6.4in appear to have been exchanged for 2-7in. *Virginia* was scuttled on the evacuation of Richmond.

VIRGINIA (2nd) *ironclad*

Displacement: –
Dimensions: 197ft oa x 47ft 6in x 14ft (*60.04 x 14.47 x 4.26m*)
Machinery: 1-shaft, 10kts
Armour: Iron. Casemate 6in-5in
Armament: 1-7in Brooke RML (later 1-8in), 2-6.4in Brooke RML, 1-10in Brooke SB (later 1-11in), 2-12pdr SB howitzers
Complement: 150

Name	Builder	Laid down	Launched	Comm	Fate
VIRGINIA	Richmond N Yd	1863	1864	1864	Scuttled 3.4.1865

More details have survived of *Tennessee* than of most Confederate ships. The casemate was 3 x 2in forward and elsewhere 2 x 2in + 1in, while the 2 x 2in side plating extended to about 6ft below water. The casemate roof consisted of wrought iron grating bars 2in thick and 6in wide, laid flat on 12in square wood beams about 5ft apart. The hull deck fore and aft was 2in iron. The 7in guns were fore and aft, each with three ports, and the 6.4in on the broadside. *Tennessee* surrendered at the battle of Mobile Bay 5.8.1864 and was subsequently commissioned in the USN.

TENNESSEE (*2nd) *ironclad*

Displacement: –
Dimensions: 209ft oa x 48ft x 14ft mean (*63.69 x 14.62 x 4.26m*)
Machinery: 4 HF boilers, 1-shaft NC, ex-side-wheel *Alonzo Child*, 5kts
Armour: Iron. Casemate 6in-5in, side below 4in
Armament: 2-7in Brooke RML, 4-6.4in Brooke RML
Complement: 133

Name	Builder	Laid down	Launched	Comm	Fate
TENNESSEE	H D Bassett. Selma, Alabama	October 1862	February 1863	16.2.1864	Sold 1867

Other Confederate ironclads that entered service, of generally similar type to the three foregoing, were: *Atlanta* 204ft pp, (ex-blockade runner *Fingal*); *Charleston* 180ft pp; *Fredericksburg* 170ft pp; *Arkansas* 165ft pp; *Richmond* 150ft pp; *Raleigh; North Carolina; Chicora; Palmetto State; Savannah; Albemarle* 139ft pp; *Neuse, Huntsville, Tuscaloosa*. All were wood-hulled, except *Atlanta*.

**The first 'Tennessee' was never launched.*

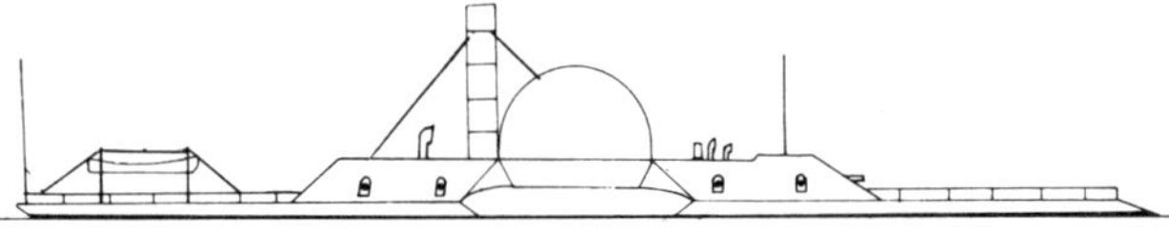

Nashville as designed

Surrendered to USA 10.5.1865. The only armoured side-wheel ship designed and built as such. The casemate was 142ft long with a very low wood hull which, according to USN officers who examined the *Nashville*, was hogged and not strong enough for the full weight of armour. An unnamed sister ship building at Selma was badly damaged in lauching and sold for scrap in April 1864.

NASHVILLE *side-wheel ironclad*

Displacement: –
Dimensions: 271ft oa x 62ft 6in, 95ft 6in over wheels x 10ft 9in (*82.60 x 19.05, 29.10 x 3.27*)
Machinery: 7 DF boilers, side wheels
Armour: Iron. Casemate 6in, (3 x 2in) maximum
Armament: ? intended. Had 3-7in Brooke RML, 1-24pdr SB howitzer
Complement: –

Name	Builder	Laid down	Launched	Comm	Fate
NASHVILLE	Montgomery, Alabama	1863	1864	Never completed	Sold 1867

The screw ironclad *Mississippi* of 260ft pp, 20 guns, 3¾in maximum armour at 30° to the horizontal, and the screw and centre wheel *Louisiana* of 264ft pp, 20 guns, armoured with two courses of 'T' railroad iron, were both launched but incomplete in April 1862, and were burned by their commanders after the US ships passed the New Orleans forts.

The ram *Manassas*, sunk in the New Orleans fighting on 24.4.1862, was converted from the *Enoch Train*, and was 143ft pp with a freeboard of 2½ft; she was protected with 1½in iron on the hull and turtle deck and had 1-32pdr carronade only.

COMMERCE RAIDERS

Of the Confederate commerce raiders, the French government stopped the sale of four which became the Prussian *Victoria* and *Augusta*, and the Peruvian *Union* and *America*. Several of the ships contracted in Britain never got into service. Thus the *Alexandra* built by William C Miller, the *Texas* (*Pampero*) by J and G Thompson, the *Rappahannock* (*ex*-HMS *Victor* sold out of the Royal Navy in 1863) and the *Georgiana* wrecked off Charleston, had no career as raiders. Near the end of the war the Confederates relinquished interest in the *Enterprise* and *Adventure* building at Denny's, and intended to convert to cruisers after running the blockade. Of the seven raiders that caused considerable havoc, five were rigged steamships and four of these, and the two not heavily rigged, were built in Britain.

A barque-rigged steamer, formerly the *Habana* of the McConnell line. Took 18 prizes before laying up at Gibraltar in January 1862. When sold became the blockade runner *Gibraltar*.

SUMTER

Tonnage: 437t
Dimensions: 184ft x 30ft x 12ft depth (*56.07 x 9.14 x 3.66m*)
Machinery: 1-shaft, 10 kts. Coal, 8 days supply
Armament: 1-8in SB, 4-32pdr SB
Complement: –

Name	Builder	Purchased	Comm	Fate
SUMTER	(At Philadelphia 1859)	April 1861	3.6.1861	Sold 1862

A full-rigged steamer with two funnels and a lifting screw, the *Florida* was originally known as *Oreto* and then as *Manassas*. She took 37 prizes and her sailing tenders *Clarence* and *Tacony* 23 more. Captured at Bahia with half her crew ashore, she was ordered to be returned to Brazil, but sank in Hampton Roads apparently from a collision.

FLORIDA

Tonnage: –
Dimensions: 191ft pp x 27ft 2in x 13ft (*58.20 x 8.28 x 3.96m*)
Machinery: 1-shaft, 9.5 kts
Armament: 2-7in Blakely RML, 4-6.4in Blakely RML, 1-12pdr SB
Complement: 146

Name	Builder	Left Britain	Comm	Fate
FLORIDA	W C Miller 1861	22.3.1862	17.8.1862	Captured by *Wachusett* 17.10.1864

The famous Laird 'Hull No 290' launched as the *Enrica*, was a barque-rigged steamer with one funnel and a lifting screw. It will be seen that her armament was very weak compared with the *Florida's*, but she was the most successful of Confederate raiders, taking 69 prizes and sinking the side-wheel converted gunboat *Hatteras*.

ALABAMA

Tonnage: 1050t
Dimensions: 220ft x 31ft 8in x 14ft (*67.05 x 9.65 x 4.26m*)
Machinery: 1-shaft, 13kts
Armament: 1-6.4in Blakely RML, 1-68pdr SB, 6-32pdr SB
Complement: 145

Name	Builder	Left Britain	Comm	Fate
ALABAMA	Laird 1862	29.7.1862	24.8.1862	Sunk by *Kearsarge* 19.6.1864

The brig-rigged, iron-hulled merchant ship *Japan* purchased in March 1863. Too little sail power and fouling troubles, not at that date solved for iron hulls, limited her usefulness and she did not operate after 28.10.1863. She took nine prizes.

GEORGIA

Tonnage: 751t, displacement 1150t
Dimensions: 210ft pp x 27ft x 12ft depth (*64.01 x 8.23 x 3.66m*)
Machinery: 2 tubular boilers, 1-shaft SG, 830ihp = 13kts. Coal 228t
Armament: 2-100pdr, 1-32pdr, 2-24pdr, all Whitworth RML
Complement: –

Name	Builder	Left Britain	Comm	Fate
GEORGIA	Denny 1862	1.4.1863	9.4.1863	Sold 1.6.1864

Stephen 'Hull No 42' originally named *Sea King,* was designed as an Indian troop transport and purchased in 1864. She was full-rigged, composite-hulled and had a lifting screw. *Shenandoah* took 38 prizes, mostly whalers, and two thirds after the war ended.

The other two raiders relied on steam power only, or almost so. Little is known of the *Chickamauga*, formerly the blockade runner *Edith*, a two funnelled steamer with light schooner-rig, purchased at Wilmington, North Carolina in 1864. Of 585t, she had a complement of 120 and was armed with three rifled guns. *Chickamauga* made one cruise from 28.10.64 to 19.11.64 and took several prizes. She was scuttled after Wilmington was evacuated.

SHENANDOAH

Tonnage: 1160t
Dimensions: 230ft x 32ft x 20ft 6in depth (*70.11 x 9.75 x 6.25m*)
Machinery: 1-shaft, 9kts
Armament: 2-32pdr Whitworth RML, 2-12pdr RML, 4-8in SB
Complement: 109

Name	Builder	Left Britain	Comm	Fate
SHENANDOAH	Stephen, 1863	8.10.1864	19.10.1864	Surrendered to Britain 6.11.1865

The blockade runner *Atalanta*, formerly a London, Chatham and Dover Railway Co cross-channel steamer, was purchased at Wilmington in 1864. She was two-funnelled and apparently not rigged for sail. In a short cruise from 6-26.8.1864 she took 33 prizes, and six more in a second cruise under the name of *Olustee*. She then returned to blockade running and was renamed *Chameleon.*

TALLAHASSEE

Tonnage: 500 dw
Dimensions: 220ft x 24ft x 14ft depth (*67.05 x 7.32 x 4.26m*)
Machinery: 2-shafts, 200 nominal hp =17kts
Armament: 3 guns, size not known
Complement: 120

Name	Builder	Comm	Fate
TALLAHASSEE	J & W Dudgeon	July 1864	Handed over to USA 1866

GUNBOATS

A number of unarmoured side-wheel ships were used as gunboats, notably the *Morgan* and *Gaines*, built at Mobile, which had partial 2in protection and the *Governor Moore, Jamestown, Patrick Henry* and *Selma* adapted from merchant ships. Of much greater interest are the ones listed below.

Strongly built iron-hulled ships intended to run the blockade at Wilmington, and to be converted to gunboats there for local use.

AJAX class *iron gunboats*

Tonnage: 515t, displacement 600t
Dimensions: 176ft pp x 25ft x 8ft 6in aft (*53.65 x 7.62 x 2.59m*)
Machinery: 2 tubular boilers, 2-shaft HRCR, 525ihp = 12kts. Coal 70t
Amament: Intended 1-9in RML, 1-8in RML
Complement: –

Name	Builder	Contracted	Left Britain	Fate
AJAX (to be OLUSTEE)	Denny	16.9.1864	12.1.1865	
HERCULES (to be VICKSBURG)	Denny	16.9.1864	Expected to be six weeks behind *Ajax*	

SPAR-TORPEDO VESSELS

Of the various spar torpedo launches and small craft, the most remarkable was the *David*, a cigar-shaped vessel 50ft x 6ft x 5ft (*15.24 x 1.83 x 1.52m*) with a tall funnel and a crew of four. The spar torpedo had a charge of 60-70lb. Although resembling a submarine in appearance, she was a very low freeboard surface craft, and quite distinct from the submarine *H L Hunley*. Built at Charleston in 1863, *David* attacked and damaged *New Ironsides* on 5.10.63. Other attacks were made without success, but her later history is obscure as the name *David* was applied to other boats of the same type.

United States of America

'THE NEW NAVY'

THE UNITED STATES NAVY: 1883-1905

In this period the United States became the major industrial power in the world. The population which was over 50 million in 1880 rose to nearly 63 million in 1890, to 76 million in 1900 and to about 84 million in 1905, and this was accompanied by a huge increase in the production of raw materials and manufactured goods of all kinds. In the 1880s there was a new burst of railway construction in the centre and west of the country, and the development of a very large frozen meat industry. In the 1890s traffic on the Great Lakes showed a remarkable increase in which the Lake Superior iron ore deposits, particularly the Mesabi range opened in 1892, were an important factor. For this period the production of iron and steel is perhaps the best indication of a nation's industrial power, and the following table shows the pig iron production in millions of long tons for 1880, 1890, 1900 and 1907, for the USA, Great Britain and Germany plus Luxemburg. Steel production figures tell much the same story.

Year	USA	Great Britain	Germany and Luxemburg
1880	3.84	7.75	2.69
1890	9.20	7.90	4.58
1900	13.79	8.96	8.39
1907	25.78	9.92	12.67

This progress was not achieved without setbacks to the country's economy. In 1886 drought and plagues of grasshoppers seriously affected the agriculture of the mid-west, so that prosperity did not return to the region for a decade, and the financial panic of 1893 in which iron production fell by a quarter and 22,000 miles of railway line were under the receiver, inaugurated a four year depression. It must be remembered too that the Federal Government ordinary revenue, obtained mainly from customs and excise, was very small in proportion to the country's output and for the decade 1900-1909 averaged 587 million dollars a year, or 7.11 dollars a head.

Although internal expansion of the United States was still the main issue, greater attention was paid to overseas interests particularly in the Pacific and in relations with Latin America. The Samoan islands had been placed under the joint control of the United States, England and Germany in 1889, and after the disturbances of ten years later, the United States were in possession of Tutuila with the harbour of Pago-Pago. The Hawaiian islands were annexed in July 1898 and meanwhile war broke out with Spain on 21 April 1898. The immediate cause was the *Maine* blowing up in Havana harbour for which Spain was held responsible, but the USA had long been sensitive to events in Cuba, and the Spanish failure to subdue the Cuban rebels would probably have brought United States intervention eventually. The 'new' US navy was not at that date a very large fleet, comprising four battleships, seven small battleships and monitors, 19 cruisers and 13 torpedo boats as its principal units. It proved perfectly capable of dealing with the Spanish squadrons, annihilating them at trifling cost in the Battles of Santiago and Manila. As a result of this war, which was ended by the Treaty of Paris, signed on 10 December 1898, the United States obtained Puerto Rico, the Philippine Islands and Guam while Cuba was to become independent but under strong US influence and protection. The 'new navy' building programmes listed below, show the important boost to naval construction given by the Spanish-American War, and also how small some of the earlier programmes were.

Authorising Act	Battleships	Monitors	Armoured Cruisers	Cruisers	Destroyers	Torpedo Boats	Patrol Gunboats	Other
3.3.1883	—	—	—	3	—	—	1	—
3.3.1885	—	—	—	2	—	—	2	—
3.8.1886	2	4	—	1	—	1	—	1
3.3.1887	—	2	—	2	—	1	2	—
7.9.1888	—	—	1	6	—	—	1	—
2.3.1889	—	—	—	—	—	—	2	2
30.6.1890	3	—	—	1	—	1	—	—
2.3.1891	—	—	—	1	—	—	—	—
19.7.1892	1	—	1	—	—	—	—	—
3.3.1893	—	—	—	—	—	—	3	—
26.7.1894	—	—	—	—	—	3	—	—
2.3.1895	2	—	—	—	—	3	6	—
10.6.1896	3	—	—	—	1	9	—	—
3.3.1897	—	—	—	—	3	—	—	—
4.5.1898	3	4	—	—	16	12	1	—
3.3.1899	3	—	3	6	—	—	—	—
7.6.1900	2	—	6	—	—	—	—	—
1.7.1902	2	—	2	—	—	—	2	—
3.3.1903	5	—	—	—	—	—	—	—
27.4.1904	1	—	2	3	—	—	—	—

The classification 'Other' includes an armoured ram of 1889, and dynamite gun cruisers of 1886 and 1889, of which the last was never built, nor was the one patrol gunboat of 1898. Two cruisers, one torpedo boat and one patrol gunboat purchased in Europe in 1898 are not included. Ex-Spanish prizes are also omitted. The authorisations for five of the six monitors in 1886 and 1887 were for their completion, as they had been begun as noted in the introduction to the 'Old Navy', and had been launched in 1876 to 1883.

The great majority of the ships in the above table were built by contract, navy yards only laying down the two battleships of 1886, one of 1902 and two of the cruisers of 1888, though the four monitors of 1886, one of 1887 and two of the cruisers of 1883 were completed in navy yards. Building times were generally long in the earlier programmes, improved latterly though they were usually some months longer than the British average times for ships of similar size.

The production of armour plates seems to have given no special difficulties. Heat treated nickel steel plates were made in 1887 and the first use of the Harvey carburising process, which was an American invention, dates from 1890. Harveyed plates were much improved, and in view of its home origins, it is perhaps not surprising that the replacement of this process by that of Krupp was a little delayed. Nickel-chromium plates carburised and face-hardened by the Krupp process and known as KC, were introduced in 1900.

The production of heavy guns was more difficult and serious troubles occurred initially with some designs, particularly the 12in/40 as mounted in the *Maine, Arkansas* and *Virginia* classes and the 8in/40 Mark 5 originally in the *Pennsylvania* class. The US Navy was by no means alone in this, as most if not all European navies experienced many and varied difficulties with their heavy guns during the 1883-1905 period. According to Bureau of Ordnance figures dated 1.10.1900, the reserve of heavy guns was then extremely small with only 2-13in for 32 afloat, 2-12in for 12 afloat, 4-10in for 18 afloat and 4-8in/35 and 40 cal for 70 afloat.

The United States were the last of the major naval powers to adopt the self-propelled torpedo, and it was not until 1890 that torpedo tubes began to appear in US ships. Unfortunately the Howell inertia flywheel torpedo was adopted at first, with the result that as late as October 1906 only 176 effective torpedoes (all 18in) were available with a further 100-18in and 300-21in on order. These figures must be borne in mind when the torpedo tube armament of US ships is considered.

As will be seen from the table 27 battleships and ten monitors were authorised between 1886 and 1904. Of the monitors, four of them authorised in 1886-1887, the *Amphitrite* class, were obsolescent when completed, and though the *Monterey* was better, the main virtue of the five was that they provided armoured ships with a mean draught of under 15ft. The *Puritan* which was a more powerful ship, drew 18ft. Similarly the only justification for the *Arkansas* class of 1898 was their mean draught of 12ft 6in. The two battleships of 1886, the *Texas* and *Maine,* were small second class ships, and US battleship construction can be said to have begun with the *Indiana* class of the 1890 programme. Even then this class were considerably smaller than their British contemporaries at only 10,288t, and it was not until the *Maine* class of the 1898 programme that 12,000t was exceeded. The *Virginia* class of 1899-1900 attained 14,948t normal displacement, and their successors of the *Connecticut* and *Vermont* classes 16,000t, with an unfortunate attempt to revert to 13,000t in the *Mississippi* class. It was not possible to give these ships as shallow a draught as was desired but in no case did the mean draught at normal displacement fall outside the range of 23ft 6in to 24ft 8in. All the classes were characterised by a heavy armament, and by thick armour particularly prior to the introduction of KC, a limitation of speed to 15-16kts being accepted previous to 1898, as was in some instances a low freeboard and indifferent seaworthiness. The 13in/35 gun used in the *Indiana* class, the *Kearsarge* class of 1895 and the *Illinois* class of 1896, was roughly comparable to the British 13.5in mounted in the *Royal Sovereign* class and other earlier ships. The 12in/35 in the *Iowa* of 1892 resembled the 13in while the 12in/40 in the *Maine* and *Virginia,* and the 12in/45 in later ships resembled the British 12in Mark IX and X respectively in performance.

A curious feature of US battleships was the mounting of 8in twin turrets as secondary armament which were only omitted in the *Illinois* and *Maine* classes. The rate of fire from these was never high, 1909 practices giving a maximum of under three rounds per gun per minute with an average of two. Other guns, 4in, 5in or 6in were carried as well up to the *Virginia* class, but later ships had 7in – a remarkable mixing of calibres–on pedestal mountings. In spite of the 165lb shell being much too heavy for one man, 1909 practices gave a maximum of over six rounds per minute with an average of four and a half.

The 15 US armoured cruisers fall into three groups, the first comprising the *New York* of the 1888 programme and the *Brooklyn* of 1892. These were of 8200t and 9215t, with main armaments of 6 and 8-8in/35 and little belt armour, reliance being largely placed on the heavy deck, 6in on the slopes and 3in flat amidships. The *St Louis* class of 1900 formed the second group, and were 9700t with 6in main armament and poor protection, while the third group comprised the six *Pennsylvania* class of 1899 and 1900 and the four *Tennessees* of 1902 and 1904. These were much larger, 13,680t and 14,500t, with good protection for armoured cruisers and in the *Tennessee* class a main armament of 4-10in guns, though that of the *Pennsylvanias* was only 4-8in, very weak for a ship of their size.

There was much variation among the 25 smaller cruisers, and for convenience they can be classed as follows:

(1) Fore and aft 8in guns with 6in and 5in amidships — the two *Atlanta* class of 1883 (only 13kts), the *Charleston* of 1885 and the *Olympia* of 1888. The last was larger and faster than the others at 5865t and 20kts, and had 4-8in in armoured twin turrets.

(2) Half the guns on each broadside— the *Chicago* of 1883, *Newark* of 1885, *Baltimore* of 1886, *Philadelphia* and *San Francisco* of 1887. All in the 4000-4500t range and principally armed with 6in guns though the *Chicago* and *Baltimore* had 4-8in also.

(3) As 2, but smaller and with 5in guns plus one axial 6in — two *Cincinnati* class of 1888.

(4) Light 16½–17kt cruisers with 5in guns intended for a similar role to that of British sloops—the three *Montgomery* class of 1888, and the six *Denvers* of 1899.

(5) Commerce raiders of 7375t and 21kts but lightly armed with 1-8in, 2-6in, 8-4in.—Two *Columbia* class of 1890-1891.

(6) Fast scout cruisers of 24-25kts.—The three *Chester* class of 1904.

It may be noted that no more cruisers were authorised until the first of the *Omaha* class in 1916.

As would be expected from the delay in introducing self-propelled torpedoes, the USA lagged behind with torpedo boats and destroyers, and it was not until the programmes of 1896 and 1898 that considerable numbers were authorised, while the 16 destroyers of the latter programme were the first that could be compared to the British '30-knot' type launched from late 1895 onwards. The most unusual feature of the US destroyers, and of several of the torpedo boats, was the large bunker capacity.

CAPITAL SHIPS

Authorised under the Act of 3.8.1886. A second class battleship designed by John of the Barrow Shipbuilding Co. Although selected from 13 designs the *Texas* was not originally very successful and was thought rather weak for her 12in guns. The short 12in belt extended from 2ft above to 4ft 6in below lwl and tapered to 6in at the lower edge ending in 6in bulkheads. The armour deck was flat over the belt and 2in with 3in-2in at the ends, but the side between the belt and the diagonal redoubt on the main deck was unarmoured. The two 12in turrets were echeloned amidships on the upper deck and four of the 6in were in main deck sponsons and the other two fore and aft on the upper deck. The 12in mountings were hydraulic and originally had fixed loading positions but this was changed to all round loading. *Texas* was engaged at the Battle of Santiago but her protection was not tested on that occasion. Renamed *San Marcos* 16.2.1911, she was used as the target in important firing trials which determined the uselessness of all but heavy armour against large calibre AP shell.

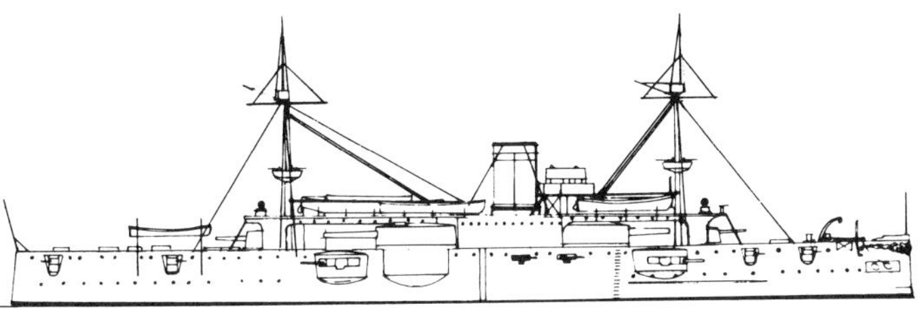

Texas as completed 1895

TEXAS

Displacement: 6135t (6665 full load)
Dimensions: 308ft 10in oa x 64ft 1in x 22ft 6in mean *(94.13 oa x 19.53 x 6.86m)*
Machinery: 4 cyl boilers, 2-shaft VTE, 8600ihp = 17kts. Coal 500/850t
Armour: Harvey and NS. Belt 12in-6in, redoubt 12in, turrets 12in, hoists 6in, CT 12in
Armament: 2-12in/35 cal (2 x 1), 6-6in/35, 12-6pdr, 6-1pdr, 4-14in TT aw
Complement: 392/508

Name	Number	Builder	Laid down	Launched	Comm	Fate
TEXAS	—	Norfolk N Yd	1.6.1889	28.6.92	15.8.95	Target 1911-12

Texas in 1898

Authorised under the Act of 3.8.1886. A second class battleship, originally rated an armoured cruiser, and designed by the Navy Department though considered by some to be a copy of the *Riachuelo* built by Samuda for Brazil. The armour belt was 180ft long and 3ft above to 4ft below lwl. The top 4ft was 12in tapering to 6in at the lower edge and the armour deck 2in flat over the belt, 2in forward and 3in-2in aft. There was no after belt bulkhead and the forward one was 6in. The 10in turrets were echeloned but more widely spaced than in *Texas*, and with individual barbettes, while the 6in guns were in the superstructure, two forward, two amidships and two aft.

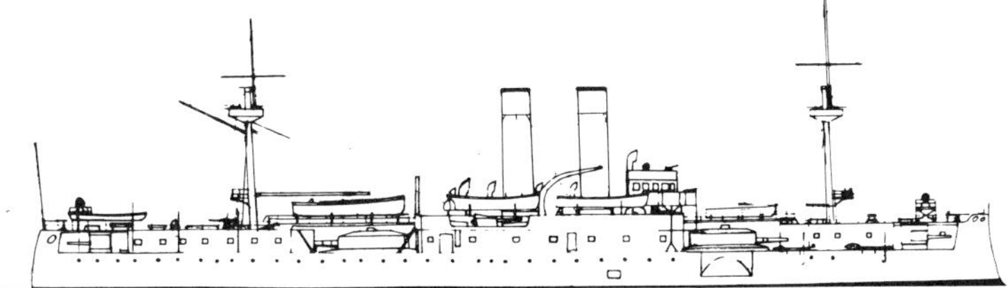

Maine 1897

MAINE

Displacement: 6682t (7180 full load)
Dimensions: 319ft oa x 57ft x 21ft 6in mean *(97.23 oa x 17.37 x 6.55m)*
Machinery: 4 cyl boilers, 2-shaft VTE, 9000ihp = 17kts. Coal 400/896t
Armour: Harvey and NS. Belt 12in-6in, barbettes 12in, turrets 8in, CT 10in
Armament: 4-10in/30 (2 x 2), 6-6in/30, 7-6pdr, 8-1pdr, 4-14in TT aw
Complement: 374

Name	Number	Builder	Laid down	Launched	Comm	Fate
MAINE	originally ACRI	New York N Yd	17.10.1888	18.11.89	17.9.95	Blew up 15.2.98

The *Maine*'s forward magazines blew up after she had been anchored three weeks in Havana harbour, and as the Court of Inquiry found that a mine had been exploded under the ship, the USA declared war on Spain 21.4.1898. The wreck was raised in 1911/12 and a second inquiry found that a small external explosion had been responsible. These verdicts were not generally accepted outside the USA, and there seems little doubt that the explosion was internal and caused by decomposing propellant, though the spontaneous combustion of bituminous coal has also been considered the initial cause.

Maine in Bar Harbor.

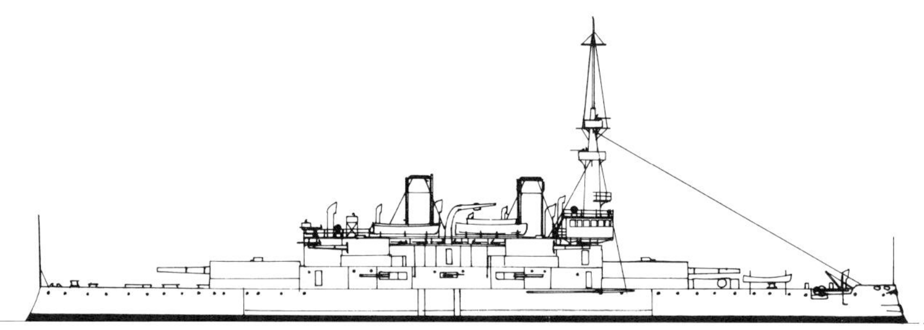

Indiana as completed 1895

INDIANA class

Displacement:	10,288t (11,688 full load)
Dimensions:	350ft 11in oa (*Oregon* 351ft 2in) x 69ft 3in x 24ft mean *(106.95 oa (107.03) x 21.10 x 7.32m)*
Machinery:	6 cyl boilers, 2-shaft VTE, 9000ihp = 15kts. Coal 400/1640t
Armour:	Harvey and NS. Belt 18in-4in, barbettes 17in, turrets 15in, secondary guns 8in-5in, CT 9in
Armament:	4-13in/35 (2 x 2), 8-8in/35 (4 x 2), 4-6in/40, 20-6pdr, 6-1pdr, 6-18in TT aw
Complement:	473/586-636

Name	Number	Builder	Laid down	Launched	Comm	Fate
INDIANA	BB1	Cramp	7. 5.1891	28. 2.93	20.11.95	Sunk as target 1920
MASSACHUSETTS	BB2	Cramp	25. 6.1891	10. 6.93	10. 6.96	Scuttled as target 1921
OREGON	BB3	Union Iron Wks	19.11.1891	26.10.93	15. 7.96	Sold 1956

Authorised under the Act of 30.6.1890. The prototype first class battleships of the 'New Navy', and not very successful as too much was attempted on a very limited displacement. Freeboard was only 11ft 4in forward at legend draught, and the belt extended for 150ft with angled 14in bulkheads to the barbettes, and from 3ft above to 4ft 6in below lwl. It was 18in to 1ft below lwl, 8½in at the lower edge but the upper belt was only 4in. The armour deck was flat on top of the 18in belt and 2¾in, increased to 3in at the ends where it sloped downwards. The main turret crowns were 3in and the turrets were originally unbalanced with hydraulic training in *Oregon* and steam in the other two. The 13in axis height above lwl was 17ft 9in but the 8in turrets, two on either beam, were carried high (gun axis 25ft), and the 6in guns were amidships in sponsoned upper deck casemates.

In 1905–1908 some needed alterations were made, the 13in turrets being partially balanced, the 6in guns, most of the 6pdrs and the TT removed, and 12-3in/50 added amidships and on the turret crowns, while the boilers were replaced by eight Babcock & Wilcox. Originally there was a military foremast and no mainmast, but a cage one was added in 1907–1908. *Indiana* and *Oregon* took part in the Battle of Santiago in 1898 but neither were seriously tested. On 29.3.1919 *Indiana* and *Massachusetts* were renamed Coast Battleship No 1 and No 2. *Oregon* was moored at Portland as a floating monument from 1925 to 1942 but was sold for scrap in December 1942. The work was halted when the upper deck was reached and the interior cleared out, and in July 1944 she was loaded as an ammunition hulk for the reconquest of Guam and towed there where she remained, apart from breaking adrift in a typhoon, until finally sold.

Massachusetts about 1900.

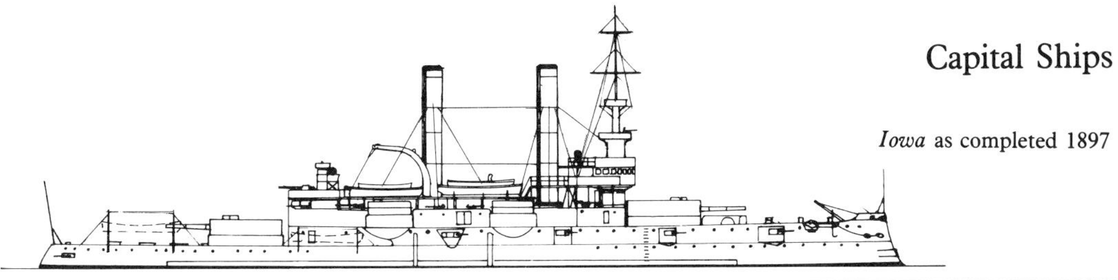

Iowa as completed 1897

IOWA

Displacement:	11,410t (12,647 full load)
Dimensions:	362ft 5in oa x 72ft 3in x 24ft mean (*110.47 oa x 22.03 x 7.32m*)
Machinery:	5 cyl boilers, 2-shaft VTE, 11,000ihp = 16kts. Coal 625/1795t
Armour:	Harvey. Belt 14in-4in, barbettes 15in-12½in, turrets 17in-15in, secondary guns 8in-4in, CT 10in
Armament:	4-12in/35 (2 x 2), 8-8in/35 (4 x 2), 6-4in/40, 20-6pdr, 4-1pdr, 4-14in TT aw
Complement:	486/654

Name	Number	Builder	Laid down	Launched	Comm	Fate
IOWA	BB4	Cramp	5.8.1893	28.3.96	16.6.97	Sunk as target 1923

Authorised under the Act of 19.7.1892. A distinct improvement on the *Indiana* class apart from the 12in main armament. There was a forecastle deck to just forward of the after turret and the belt was 186ft long though its depth was unaltered. The lower edge was 7in, there were angled 12in bulkheads to the barbettes, and the upper belt was still only 4in. The armour deck was flat at the upper edge of the 14in belt and 2¾in but lowered at the ends where it was 3in. The 12in turrets were balanced and hydraulically trained with axis heights of 25ft 6in fore and 18ft 3in aft, above lwl, while the 8in turrets, at the same height as the fore 12in, were closer together and further outboard than in *Indiana*. Of the 4in guns four were in sponsons below the forecastle deck and two aft on the superstructure. *Iowa* was faster than the *Indianas* and made 17.09kts with 12,105ihp and 0.98in forced draught. She was engaged at Santiago but not seriously tested.

Originally *Iowa* had only a military foremast but a cage mainmast was added in 1909 when the 12in mountings were modified, most of the 6pdrs removed and 4-4in added (TT previously removed). She was renamed Coast Battleship No 4 on 29.3.1919 and was the first radio controlled target ship to be used in a fleet exercise. She was finally sunk by a salvo of 14in shells.

1

2

1. *Iowa* at Plymouth, Devon in June 1910.
2. *Kearsage* in the early years of this century.
Both CPL

Authorised under the Act of 2.3.1895. Flush deck ships with freeboard of 14ft 6in forward at legend draught. The thick belt extended from 3ft 6in above to 4ft below lwl and from the centre line of the after barbette to the forward end of the boiler rooms, it was 16½in at the top, tapering to 13¼in at lwl and 9½in at the lower edge. It was gradually reduced to 10½in maximum at the centre line of the fore barbette, and in the next 30ft to a uniform 4in. The bulkheads were 10in fore and 12in aft and the upper belt 5in. The armour deck was 2¾in on the flat, at the top of the heavy belt and curved down at the ends, being locally increased to 3in forward and 5in aft. The 8in turrets were fixed on the roofs of the 13in and trained with them as one unit, a most unfortunate arrangement. Training was electric and the 13in turret crowns were 3½in while the 8in ones were 2in. The 5in guns were in an upper deck battery with 6in armour. These were the first US battleships to make extensive use of electrical auxiliary machinery, the total output of the dynamos being 350kw. They were reputed very bad gun platforms. In 1909–1911 the turrets were modified, most of the 6pdrs removed and replaced by four more 5in on the superstructure – the TT had already been removed – cage fore and mainmasts fitted, and the boilers replaced by eight Mosher. By 1919 the 5in had been reduced to eight and 2-3in AA added. *Kearsarge* was converted to a crane ship in 1920, stability being increased by bulges and a very large 250t revolving crane fitted. She was renamed Crane Ship No 1 in November 1941.

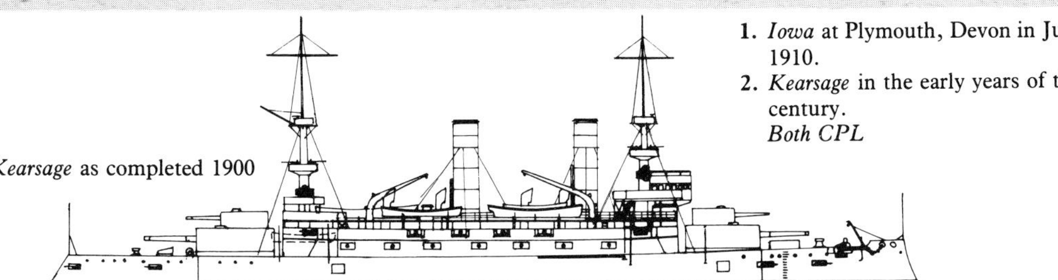

Kearsage as completed 1900

KEARSARGE class

Displacement:	11,540t (12,850 full load)
Dimensions:	375ft 4in oa x 72ft 3in x 23ft 6in mean (*114.40 oa x 22.03 x 7.16m*)
Machinery:	5 cyl boilers, 2-shaft VTE, 10,000ihp = 16kts. Coal 410/1591t
Armour:	Harvey. Belt 16½in-5in, forward 4in, barbettes 15in-12½in, turrets 17in-15in, secondary guns 11in-6in, CT 10in
Armament:	4-13in/35 (2 x 2), 4-8in/35 (2 x 2), 14-5in/40, 20-6pdrs, 8-1pdrs, 4-18in TT aw
Complement:	553 *Kearsarge*; 554 *Kentucky*/686-690

Name	Number	Builder	Laid down	Launched	Comm	Fate
KEARSARGE	BB5	Newport News	30.6.1896	24.3.98	20.2.1900	Sold 1955
KENTUCKY	BB6	Newport News	30.6.1896	24.3.98	15.5.1900	Sold 1923

Authorised under the Act of 10.6.1896. Although of the same dimensions as the previous class, these ships were quite dissimilar. There was a forecastle deck as far as the mainmast giving a freeboard of 19ft 7in forward, and for the only time in US battleships the two funnels were abreast. The heavy belt was as in the *Kearsarge*, while the fore bulkhead was increased to 12in and the upper belt to 5½in. The armour deck was also as in *Kearsarge* except that it was 4in maximum aft. British type barbette turrets were introduced for the 13in, and of the 6in guns eight were in an upper deck battery amidships, two in sponsoned casemates forward and four in casemates amidship on the forecastle deck. It will be noted that 8in guns were not mounted for the first time since the *Indiana* class. On trials *Illinois* was the fastest with 12,899ihp = 17.45kts at 0.7in forced draught.

In 1909–1912 the turrets were modified, 4-3in/50 replaced 12-6pdr, cage fore and mainmasts were fitted and *Illinois* was reboilered with eight Mosher boilers. TT had already been removed. By 1919 the 6in were reduced to eight and 2-3in AA fitted. *Illinois* was used as an armoury and later as an accommodation ship from 1924 to 1955. She was renamed *Prairie State*, IX-15, in January 1941.

Illinois as completed 1901

ILLINOIS class

Displacement: 11,565t (*Wisconsin* 11,653t), (12,250 full load)
Dimensions: 375ft 4in *Illinois*; 374ft *Alabama*; 373ft 10in *Wisconsin* oa x 72ft 3in x 23ft 6in (23ft 8in *Wisconsin*) *(114.40; 114.0; 113.95 oa x 22.03 x 7.16; 7.21; m)*
Machinery: 8 cyl boilers, 2-shaft VTE, 10,000ihp = 16kts. Coal 800/1400t *Illinois*/1355 *Alabama*/1310 *Wisconsin*
Armour: Harvey. Belt 16½in-5½in, forward 4in, barbettes 15in-10in, turrets 14in, secondary guns 6in-5½in, CT 10in
Armament: 4-13in/35 (2 x 2), 14-6in/40, 16-6pdr, 6-1pdr, 4-18in TT aw
Complement: 536 (*Wisconsin* 531) /690-713

Name	Number	Builder	Laid down	Launched	Comm	Fate
ILLINOIS	BB7	Newport News	10. 2.1897	4.10.98	16. 9.1901	Sold 1956
ALABAMA	BB8	Cramp	2.12.1896	18. 5.98	16.10.1900	Sunk as target 1921
WISCONSIN	BB9	Union Iron Wks	9. 2.1897	26.11.98	4. 2.1901	Sold 1922

An unidentified *Illinois* class battleship
CPL

Authorised under the Act of 4.5.1898. This class broke away from previous designs, with the introduction of higher velocity 12in guns and of KC armour which allowed thickness to be reduced. There was a forecastle deck to the mainmast, and freeboard forward was 19ft 5in-20ft. The main belt was 3ft 3in above lwl to 4ft 3in below, and between the barbettes it was 11in for the top 4ft 3in tapered to 7½in at the lower edge. There were 9in angled bulkheads to the barbettes. The upper belt was 5½in and the armour deck 2½in on the flat, over the main belt, with 2¾in slopes at the ends and 4in maximum aft. The turrets were electrically powered and of the 6in guns ten were in an upper deck battery, two in upper deck casemates forward, and four in a forecastle deck battery. The 12in gun axis heights above lwl were 26ft 10in forward and 18ft 10in aft and 6in from 23ft 4in to 15ft 2in. The 12in guns gave considerable trouble originally and had to be chase-hooped, while on 13.4.1904 there was a serious accident in *Missouri*'s after turret when back-flame from the left gun caused three charges to ignite, the flame going straight down to the handing room. As a result modifications were made to US turrets which were tested in action in January 1918 when the British monitor *Raglan*, which had US turrets, was sunk by *Sultan Selim* (ex-*Goeben*). An explosion occurred in her turret but did not get below the gun-well floor, and *Raglan* sank with her magazines intact.

These were the first 18kt US battleships, though *Ohio* only reached 17.82kts on trials, and had the reputation of being wet in bad weather. They were refitted 1909–1911, cage masts being stepped and *Maine* reboilered with 12 Babcock & Wilcox boilers. In 1919 eight of the 6in and all the 3in guns had been removed and 2-3in AA added.

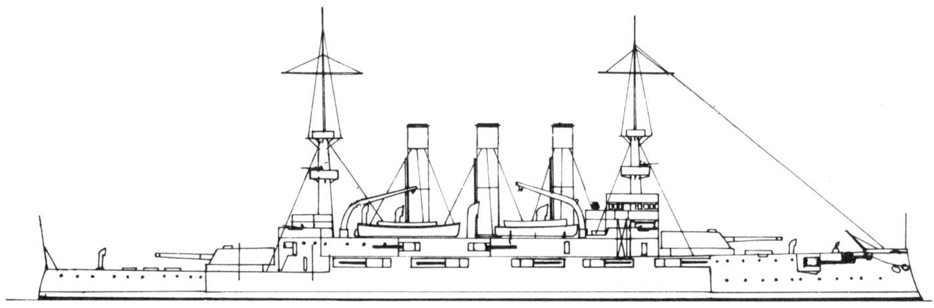

Missouri 1908

MAINE class

Displacement: *Maine* 12,846t; *Missouri* 12,362t; *Ohio* 12,723t (*c* 13,700 full load)
Dimensions: 393ft 11in oa x 72ft 3in x 24ft 4in mean *Maine*; 23ft 9in *Missouri*; 23ft 10in *Ohio* *(120.06 oa x 22.03 x 7.42; 7.24; 7.26m)*
Machinery: 12 Thornycroft boilers (*Maine* 24 Niclausse), 2-shaft VTE, 16,000ihp = 18kts. Coal 1000/1867t *Maine*; /1837 *Missouri*;/2150 *Ohio*
Armour: KC, Harvey. Belt 11in-5½in, forward 8in-4in, barbettes 12in-8in, turrets 12in-11in, secondary guns 6in-5½in, CT 10in
Armament: 4-12in/40 (2 x 2), 16-6in/50 Mk 6, 6-3in/50, 8-3pdr, 6-1pdr, 2-18in TT sub
Complement: 561 /779-813

Name	Number	Builder	Laid down	Launched	Comm	Fate
MAINE	BB10	Cramp	15.2.1899	27. 7.1901	29.12.02	Sold 1922
MISSOURI	BB11	Newport News	7.2.1900	28.12.1901	1.12.03	Sold 1922
OHIO	BB12	Union Iron Wks	22.4.1899	18. 5.1901	4.10.04	Sold 1923

Maine

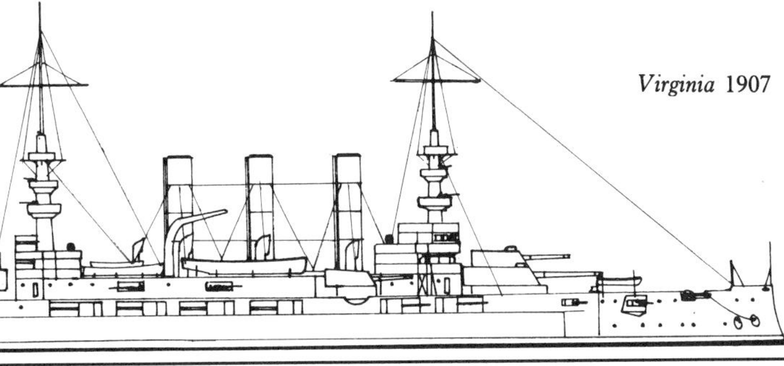

Virginia 1907

VIRGINIA class

Displacement: 14,948t (16,094 full load)
Dimensions: 441ft 3in oa x 76ft 3in x 23ft 9in mean *(134.50 oa x 23.25 x 7.24m)*
Machinery: 12 Babcock & Wilcox boilers (*Virginia, Georgia* 24 Niclausse), 2-shaft VTE, 19,000ihp = 19kts. Coal 900/1900t *Virginia*;/1700 *Nebraska, Rhode Island*;/1925 *Georgia*;/1955 *New Jersey*
Armour: KC, Harvey. Belt 11in-6in, ends 6in-4in, barbettes 10in-6in, turrets 12in-6in, secondary guns 12in-4in, CT 9in
Armament: 4-12in/40 (2 x 2), 8-8in/45 (4 x 2), 12-6in/50 Mk 8, 12-3in/50, 12-3pdr, 4-21in TT sub (*New Jersey, Rhode Island* also 2-1pdr)
Complement: 812

Name	Number	Builder	Laid down	Launched	Comm	Fate
VIRGINIA	BB13	Newport News	21.5.1902	5. 4.04	7.5.06	Sunk as target 1923
NEBRASKA	BB14	Moran	4.7.1902	7.10.04	1.7.07	Sold 1923
GEORGIA	BB15	Bath Iron Wks	31.8.1901	11.10.04	24.9.06	Sold 1923
NEW JERSEY	BB16	Fore River	3.4.1902	10.11.04	12.5.06	Sunk as target 1923
RHODE ISLAND	BB17	Fore River	1.5.1902	17. 5.04	19.2.06	Sold 1923

Authorised under the Acts of 3.3.1899 (first three) and 7.6.1900 (last two). Flush-deck ships with freeboard of 19ft 6in forward at legend draught, and considerably larger than previous designs. The main belt was from 3ft above to 5ft below lwl, and for 192ft amidships it was 11in for the upper 5ft, tapering to 8in at the lower edge. For the next 60ft forward and 32ft aft it was 9in at the upper edge with a uniform taper to 6in, and was then reduced to 6in-4½in, 5in-4in, and finally 4in. The bulkheads and upper belt were 6in and the armour deck 1½in on the flat with 3in slopes to the belt lower edge and 3in ends. Two of the 8in turrets were fixed to the roofs of the 12in and trained with them, in spite of the unsatisfactory experience of this arrangement in the *Kearsarge* class. These 8in turrets were armoured as the 12in except that the crowns were 1½in instead of 3½in. The other two 8in turrets were on the upper deck beam and had 6½in-4in armour. The 6in guns were in a maindeck battery with 6in armour. The turrets were electrically powered and the total output of the ships' dynamos was 500kW. They all made 19-19¼kts on trials with 1.56in to 1.9in forced draught.

Cage masts were fitted in 1909–1910, as well as a 9ft RF and the 3pdrs removed while safety modifications were made to the turrets. By 1919 the Niclausse boilers in *Virginia* and *Georgia* had been replaced by 12 Babcock & Wilcox, and the 6in guns had been removed from all, the 3in reduced to eight and 2-3in AA added.

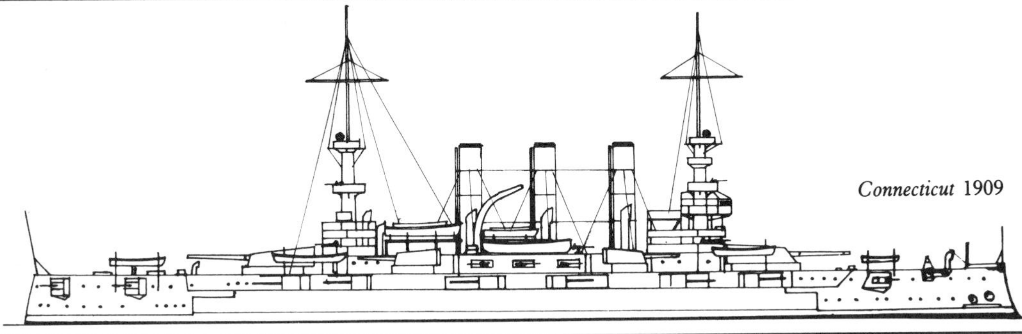

Connecticut 1909

CONNECTICUT class

Displacement: 16,000t (17,666 full load)
Dimensions: 456ft 4in oa x 76ft 10in x 24ft 6in mean *(139.09 oa x 23.42 x 7.47m)*
Machinery: 12 Babcock & Wilcox boilers, 2-shaft VTE, 16,500ihp = 18kts. Coal 900/2249t *Connecticut*;/2376 *Louisiana*
Armour: KC, Harvey. Belt 11in-6in, ends 7in-4in, barbettes 10in-6in, turrets 12in-8in, secondary guns 7in-3¾in, CT 9in
Armament: 4-12in/45 (2 x 2), 8-8in/45 (4 x 2), 12-7in/45, 20-3in/50, 12-3pdr, 4-1pdr *Connecticut*, 2-1pdr *Louisiana*, 4-21in TT sub
Complement: 827/881-896

Name	Number	Builder	Laid down	Launched	Comm	Fate
CONNECTICUT	BB18	New York N Yd	10.3.1903	29.9.04	29.9.06	Sold 1923
LOUISIANA	BB19	Newport News	7.2.1903	27.8.04	2.6.06	Sold 1923

Authorised under the Act of 1.7.1902. An improvement on previous designs, larger and good sea boats, which many of the preceding ships were not. The stability range was 68° and freeboard 20ft 6in forward at lwl. The weak point was the inclusion of both 8in and 7in guns, hits and splashes from which would be indistinguishable. The main belt ran from 4ft 3in above to 5ft below lwl and for the midships 192ft it was 11in for the top 5ft 3in and tapering to 9in at the lower edge. For the next 49ft fore and aft, it was 9in and 7in, tapering similarly, and was then reduced to 3ft above lwl and to 7in-5in, 5in and finally 4in. The upper belt and the bulkheads were 6in and the armour deck 1½in flat, and 3in slopes amidships, and 3in at the ends. The main turrets had 12in faces, 8in sides and rear and 2½in crowns, while the 8in turrets fore and aft on either beam had respectively 6½in, 6in, 2in and the 7in guns, in the main deck battery 7in. The gun axis height for the latter was 15ft 1in above lwl compared to 26ft 8in for the 8in. Both 12in and 8in turrets were electrically powered and the total output of the ships' dynamos was 800kW, the highest yet in any US warship.

On trials *Connecticut* made 18.78kts at 16,220t with 1.36in forced draught, and *Louisiana* 18.82kts at 16,000t with 1.98in. Cage masts were fitted in 1909 and the 3pdrs removed, a 9ft RF mounted and work done to improve the safety of the turrets. By 1919 all the 7in and 8-3in had been removed and 2-3in AA mounted.

Connecticut off the US East Coast in 1909

VERMONT class

Displacement:	16,000t (17,666 full load)
Dimensions:	456ft 4in oa x 76ft 10in x 24ft 6in mean (*139.09 oa x 23.42 x 7.47m*)
Machinery:	12 Babcock & Wilcox boilers, 2-shaft VTE, 16,500ihp = 18kts. Coal 900/2405t *Vermont*;/2310 *Kansas*;/2387 *Minnesota*;/2287 *New Hampshire*
Armour:	KC, Harvey. Belt 9in-7in, ends 7in-4in, barbettes 10in-6in (*New Hampshire* 11in-6in), turrets 12in-8in, secondary guns 7in-3¾in, CT 9in
Armament:	4-12in/45 (2 x 2), 8-8in/45 (4 x 2), 12-7in/45, 20-3in/50, 12-3pdr (*Vermont* 10, *New Hampshire* nil), 2-1pdr, 4-21in TT sub
Complement:	880 (*New Hampshire* 850)

Name	Number	Builder	Laid down	Launched	Comm	Fate
VERMONT	BB20	Fore River	21. 5.1904	31.8.05	4.3.07	Sold 1923
KANSAS	BB21	New York SB	10. 2.1904	12.8.05	18.4.07	Sold 1923
MINNESOTA	BB22	Newport News	27.10.1903	8.4.05	9.3.07	Sold 1924
NEW HAMPSHIRE	BB25	New York SB	1. 5.1905	30.6.06	19.3.08	Sold 1923

Authorised under the Acts of 3.3.1903 (first three) and 27.4.1904 (last one). The first three ships of this class were very similar to the *Connecticut*, from which they differed in details of armouring. The main belt amidships extended for 290ft at a uniform 9in, and where reduced in height its thicknesses were as in the previous class, but it ran from 4ft 3in above to 3ft 9in below lwl. The upper belt and bulkheads were 7in but otherwise the armouring was unchanged. In *New Hampshire* the 12in mountings allowed loading at any angle of elevation, the arrangement of the 7in upper belt and bulkheads was slightly altered. The faces of the main barbettes were 11in instead of 10in, and of the 8in barbettes 6½in instead of 6in. The main belt was, however, as in the other three ships of the class, and the rest of the armour as in *Connecticut*. On trials *Minnesota* was fastest with 18.85kts at 16,000t and 0.94in forced draught. Alterations in 1909–1910, and armament in 1919, were as in *Connecticut*, though a photograph of *Vermont* taken in 1918, shows a 20ft RF on a somewhat precarious looking mounting over the bridge. *Minnesota* struck a mine laid by *U117* on 29.9.1918 which seriously damaged her to starboard, but there were no casualties, though repairs took five months.

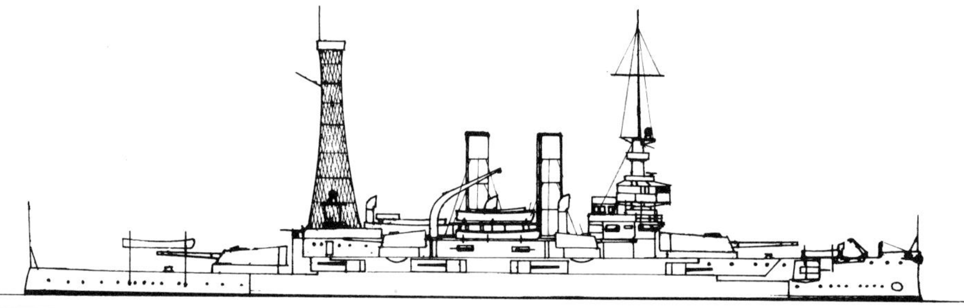

Idaho 1910

MISSISSIPPI class

Displacement:	13,000t (14,465 full load)
Dimensions:	382ft oa x 77ft x 24ft 8in mean (*116.43 oa x 23.47 x 7.52m*)
Machinery:	8 Babcock & Wilcox boilers, 2-shaft VTE, 10,000ihp = 17kts. Coal 600/1800t
Armour:	KC, Harvey. Belt 9in-7in, ends 7in-4in, barbettes 10in-6in, turrets 12in-8in, secondary guns 7in-3¾in, CT 9in
Armament:	4-12in/45 (2 x 2), 8-8in/45 (4 x 2), 8-7in/45, 12-3in/50, 6-3pdr, 2-1pdr, 2-21in TT sub
Complement:	744

Name	Number	Builder	Laid down	Launched	Comm	Fate
MISSISSIPPI	BB23	Cramp	12.5.1904	30. 9.05	1.2.08	Sold to Greece 30.7.14
IDAHO	BB24	Cramp	12.5.1904	9.12.05	1.4.08	Sold to Greece 30.7.14

Authorised under the Act of 3.3.1903. An attempt to reproduce the main features of the *Vermont* class on a displacement of 3,000t less, and like most such attempts only a qualified success, the reduction in speed being particularly unfortunate. Except that the 9in part of the belt extended for 244ft, their armour details were as in *Vermont*. On four hours trial *Idaho* was slightly the faster, attaining 17.14 kts at 13,093t and 0.93in forced draught. Originally there was no mainmast, but cage fore and mainmasts were fitted from 1909. In this year *Mississippi* went up the river of that name calling at Natchez and other river ports, and in early 1914 served as a seaplane base ship establishing the base at Pensacola and operating off Vera Cruz during the Mexican fighting. She was named *Lemnos* and *Idaho* named *Kilkis* by Greece, and both were sunk by German aircraft at Salamis in April 1941.

1. *Kansas* in 1911
2. *Mississippi* as the Greek *Kilkis* at Malta
Both CPL

1

MONITORS

The largest of the 'New Navy' monitors, *Puritan* had no resemblance to the uncompleted Civil War ship of which she was nominally a repair. Her completion to the above design was authorised under the Act of 3.8.1886 and ordered 26.6.1889. She was heavily gunned and armoured and a powerful ship for her size, but except for coast defence her very low freeboard was a serious disadvantage. *Puritan* was iron-hulled and the steel deck over the belt was 2in. She served in the Caribbean during the Spanish-American war, but was otherwise seldom in full commission and was finally decommissioned in April 1910, and stricken in February 1918.

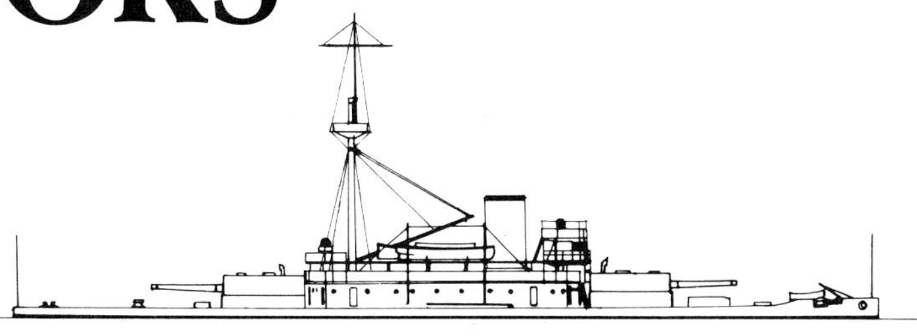

Puritan as completed 1896

PURITAN

Displacement: 6060t
Dimensions: 296ft 3in oa x 60ft 1½in x 18ft mean (*90.30 oa x 18.33 x 5.49m*)
Machinery: 8 cyl boilers, 2-shaft HC, 3700ihp = 12.4kts. Coal 410t
Armour: Harvey and NS. Belt 14in-6in, barbettes 14in, turrets 8in, CT 10in
Armament: 4-12in/35 (2 x 2), 6-4in/40, 6-6pdr, no TT
Complement: 200/270

Name	Number	Builder	Laid down	Launched	Comm	Fate
PURITAN	Later BM1	John Roach and New York N Yd	May 1876	6.12.82	10.12.96	Sold 1922

Puritan in the early years of her career

Amphitrite, date unknown

AMPHITRITE class

Displacement: 3990t

Dimensions: 262ft 9in oa *Amphitrite*; 263ft 1in *Miantonomoh*, *Terror*; 262ft 3in *Monadnock* x 55ft 4in *Amphitrite*, *Miantonomoh*; 55ft 6in *Terror*; 55ft 5in *Monadnock* x 14ft 6in (14ft 8in *Terror*) mean (*80.08 oa; 80.18; 79.93 x 16.86; 16.91; 16.89 x 4.42; 4.47m*)

Machinery: 4 Babcock & Wilcox boilers *Amphitrite*, 4 cyl *Monadnock*, 6 cyl *Miantonomoh*, *Terror*, 2-shaft HC (HTE *Monadnock*), 1600ihp = 12kts (3000ihp = 14.5kts *Monadnock*). Coal 250/270t (386 *Monadnock*)

Armour: Steel and wrought iron. *Amphitrite* and *Monadnock*: belt 9in, barbettes 11½in, turrets 7½in, CT 7½in; *Terror* and *Miantonomoh*: belt 7in, turrets 11½in, CT 7½in (*Miantonomoh* 9in)

Armament: 4-10in/30 (2 x 2) but *Miantonomoh* 2-10in/35, 2-10in/30, 2-4in/40 in *Amphitrite* and *Monadnock* only, 2-6pdr, 2-3pdr, no TT

Complement: 150/163-191

Name	Number	Builder	Laid down	Launched	Comm	Fate
AMPHITRITE	Later BM2	Harlan & Hollingsworth and Norfolk N Yd	1874	7. 6.83	23. 4.95	Sold 1920
MONADNOCK	Later BM3	Continental Iron Wks and Mare Is N Yd	1875	19. 9.83	20. 2.96	Sold 1923
TERROR	Later BM4	Cramp and New York N Yd	1874	24. 3.83	15. 4.96	Sold 1923
MIANTONOMOH	Later BM5	John Roach and New York N Yd	1874	5.12.76	27.10.91	Sold 1922

As with *Puritan* this class bore little resemblance to the Civil War ships of which they were 'repairs'. *Miantonomoh* was commissioned when quite incomplete from October 1882 to March 1883, but the completion of the ships as above was not authorised till the Act of 3.8.1886 – *Miantonomoh* 3.3.1887 – and ordered 1887–1890. They were iron-hulled with a 1¾in steel deck over the belt, and *Amphitrite* and *Monadnock* differed from the other two in having barbettes to their turrets, while *Terror* had pneumatically powered mountings. *Monadnock* never made her intended 14.5kts, trial speed being 11.63kts. She crossed the Pacific from 23.6.1898 to 16.8.1898 and served in the Philippines and in Chinese waters for the rest of her career. The other three were rarely in full commission except during the Spanish-American war. *Miantonomoh* was stricken at the end of 1915 for use as a target but not sold till 1922, and *Terror* was also stricken at the same time.

MONTEREY

Displacement: 4084t

Dimensions: 260ft 11in oa x 59ft 0½in x 14ft 10in mean (*79.52 oa x 18.0 x 4.52m*)

Machinery: 4 Babcock & Wilcox, 2-shaft VTE, 5250ihp = 13.6kts. Coal 230t

Armour: Harvey and NS. Belt 13in-5in, barbettes 13in-11½in, turrets 8in-7½in, CT 10in

Armament: 2-12in/35 (1 x 2), 2-10in/30 (1 x 2), 6-6-pdr, No TT

Complement: 190/218

Name	Number	Builder	Laid down	Launched	Comm	Fate
MONTEREY	Later BM6	Union Iron Wks	20.12.1889	28.4.91	13.2.93	Sold 1921

Authorised under the Act of 3.3.1887. The belt tapered from 13in at the edge of the 3in deck over it, to 6in-5in at the lower edge, and it was possible to reduce the low freeboard on going into action by means of water ballast tanks. The 12in guns were in the fore turret and the 10in in the after one. *Monterey* crossed the Pacific from 11.6.1898 to 13.8.1898 in company with the collier *Brutus* (which towed her for nearly half the 8000 miles) and served in the Philippines and Chinese waters until late 1917 when she became station ship at Pearl Harbor. Her original design included an armament of 1-16in and 1-12in, together with a 15in pneumatic Zalinsky gun.

Arkansas (later *Ozark*)

ARKANSAS class

Displacement: 3225t
Dimensions: 255ft 1in oa x 50ft x 12ft 6in mean (*77.75 oa x 15.24 x 3.81m*)
Machinery: 4 boilers: *Arkansas* Thornycroft; *Nevada* Niclausse; *Florida* Mosher; *Wyoming* Babcock & Wilcox; 2-shaft VTE, 2400ihp = 12.5kts. Coal 350t
Armour: Harvey. Belt 11in-5in, barbettes 11in-9in, turrets 10in-9in, CT 7½in
Armament: 2-12in/40 (1 x 2), 4-4in/50 Mk 7, 3-6pdr, no TT
Complement: 220

Name	Number (given later)	Builder	Laid down	Launched	Comm	Fate
ARKANSAS	BM7	Newport News	14.11.1899	10.11.1900	28.10.02	Sold 1922
NEVADA	BM8	Bath Iron Wks	17. 4.1899	24.11.1900	5. 3.03	Sold 1922
FLORIDA	BM9	Lewis Nixon	23. 1.1899	30.11.1901	18. 6.03	Sold 1922
WYOMING	BM10	Union Iron Wks	11. 4.1899	8. 9.1900	8.12.02	Sold 1939

Authorised under the Act of 4.5.1898. The above class are better known as renamed in order from BM7 to BM10: *Ozark*, 2.3.1909; *Tonopah* 2.3.1909; *Tallahassee*, 1.7.1908; *Cheyenne*, 1.1.1909. It should be noted that *Nevada* was launched as *Connecticut* and renamed for the first time in January 1901. The belt was 11in at the 1½in flat deck edge only, tapering to 8in at lwl and to 5in at the lower edge and at the ends. The funnel uptakes were 6in for the height of one deck. They were intended for harbour defence but not a worthwhile expenditure. *Tallahasee* was used in the firing trials against the *Katahdin* in 1909, and in other experiments including tests for the suitability of cage masts, while in the same period *Cheyenne* was employed in oil fuel trials. Latterly they were all employed as submarine tenders for some part of their career. *Cheyenne* was finally decommissioned in June 1926 but not sold till 1939.

Arkansas

ARMOURED CRUISERS

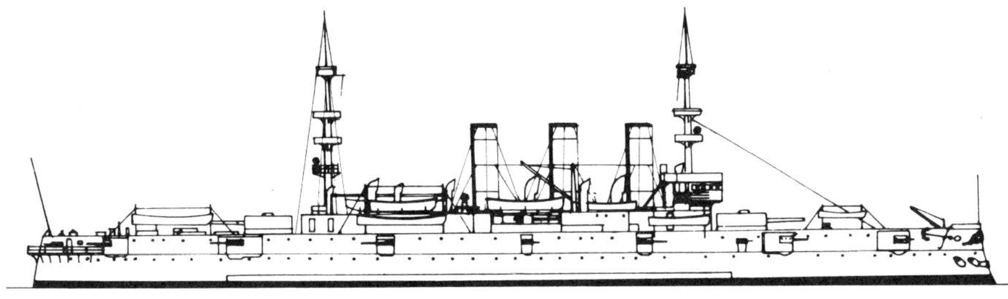
New York 1895

NEW YORK

Displacement: 8200t (9021 full load)
Dimensions: 384ft oa x 64ft 10in x 23ft 10in mean (*117.04 oa x 19.76 x 7.26m*)
Machinery: 8 cyl boilers, 2-shaft VTE, (2 per shaft) 16,000ihp = 20kts. Coal 750/1290t
Armour: NS. Belt 4in, barbettes 10in-5in, turrets 5½in, secondary guns 4in, CT 7½in
Armament: 6-8in/35 (2 x 2, 2 x 1), 12-4in/40, 8-6pdr, 4-1pdr, 3-14in TT aw
Complement: 566

Name	Number	Builder	Laid down	Launched	Comm	Fate
NEW YORK	ACR2	Cramp	30.9.1890	2.12.91	1.8.93	Scuttled Dec 1941

Authorised under the Act of 7.9.1888. The first US armoured cruiser as the *Maine*, originally ACR1, was better classified as a small battleship. The *New York* was a handsome flush-decked ship with the 4in belt covering the machinery spaces only, and the armour deck 3in on the flat amidships with 6in slopes and 2½in at the ends. The fore and aft twin 8in had shallow 10in barbettes with 5in ammunition tubes, and the other two were to port and starboard amidships in shields with 2in base rings. The 4in guns were on the main deck, the four forward and four after guns being in sponsons, and had 4in local protection. On the mile *New York* made 17,401ihp = 21.0kts at 8480t. She was the flagship of Rear-Admiral Sampson in the Spanish-American War and was modernised in 1905–1909. The armament was changed to 4-8in/45 in fore and aft twin turrets, with 10-5in/50 and 8-3in/50 on the main deck, the latter at the ends, and TT were removed. The new turrets had 6½in KC armour with 6in-4in on the barbettes, and the old boilers were replaced by 12 Babcock & Wilcox with higher funnels. By 1919 the 5in were reduced to eight, the 3in removed and 2-3in AA added.

New York was renamed *Saratoga* 16.2.1911 and *Rochester* 1.12.1917, and after an active and varied career did not finally decommission until 29.4.1933, although she was reduced to four boilers and two funnels in 1927. She remained at Olongapo in the Philippines, being stricken 28.10.1938, and was scuttled to avoid capture by the Japanese.

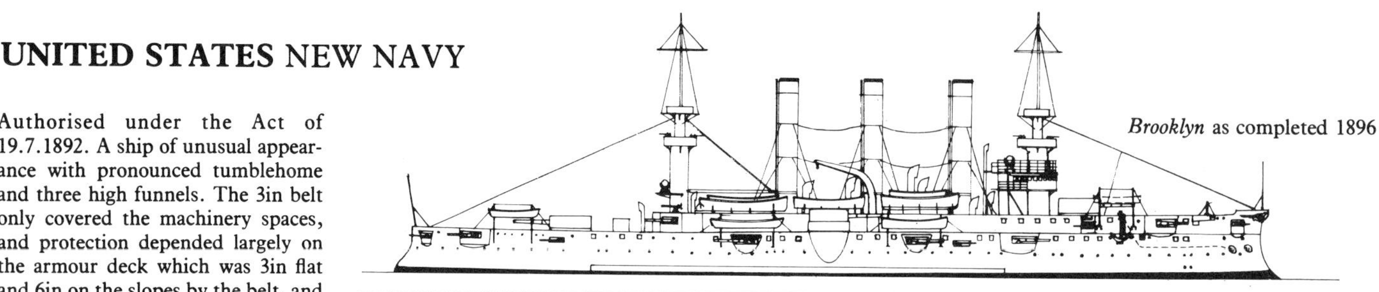
Brooklyn as completed 1896

BROOKLYN

Displacement: 9215t (10,068 full load)
Dimensions: 402ft 7in oa x 64ft 8in x 24ft mean (*122.70 oa x 19.71 x 7.32m*)
Machinery: 7 cyl boilers, 2-shaft VTE, (2 per shaft) 16,000ihp = 20kts. Coal 900/1753t
Armour: Harvey and NS. Belt 3in, barbettes 8in-3in, turrets 5½in, secondary guns 4in, CT 8½in
Armament: 8-8in/35 (4 x 2), 12-5in/40, 12-6pdr, 4-1pdr, 5-18in TT aw
Complement: 561/581

Name	Number	Builder	Laid down	Launched	Comm	Fate
BROOKLYN	ACR3	Cramp	2.8.1893	2.10.95	1.12.96	Sold 1921

Authorised under the Act of 19.7.1892. A ship of unusual appearance with pronounced tumblehome and three high funnels. The 3in belt only covered the machinery spaces, and protection depended largely on the armour deck which was 3in flat and 6in on the slopes by the belt, and 2½in fore and aft. The barbettes were shallow 8in-4in rings with 3in ammunition tubes. The fore 8in turret was at forecastle deck and the others at upper deck level with the supports for the wing turrets rising from the inward sloping side. Originally the forward and starboard wing turrets were electrically trained and the other two steam. Eight of the 5in guns were in main deck sponsons and four at upper deck level with the foremost pair sponsoned under the forecastle. On trials *Brooklyn* attained 18,770ihp = 21.91kts but she was very light at only 8150t.

Brooklyn was flagship of Commodore Schley at the Battle of Santiago, but her obvious weaknesses in protection were not tested in that action. She was out of commission from 1908 to 1914, and during this time the turret hoists were improved, fire-control fitted and the TT removed. By 1919 the 5in guns had been reduced to eight and 2-3in AA fitted. Her last year's commission from January 1920 was as flag of the Pacific Fleet destroyers.

Brooklyn after the Spanish American war
CPL

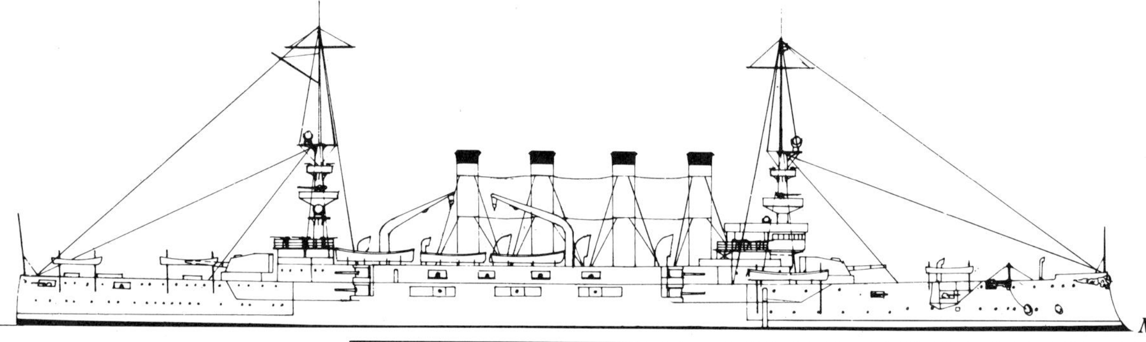
Maryland as completed 1905

PENNSYLVANIA class

Displacement: 13,680t (15,138 full load)
Dimensions: 503ft 11in oa x 69ft 7in x 24ft 1in mean (*153.58 oa x 21.20 x 7.34m*)
Machinery: 16 Babcock & Wilcox boilers, (32 Niclausse *Pennsylvania, Colorado*). 2-shaft VTE, 23,000ihp = 22kts. Coal 900/1825t *Pennsylvania, Colorado*;/1950 *West Virginia, Maryland*;/2075 *California, South Dakota*
Armour: KC, Harvey. Belt 6in-5in, ends 3½in, barbettes 6in-3in, turrets 6½in-6in, secondary guns 5in, CT 9in
Armament: 4-8in/40 Mk 5 (2 x 2), 14-6in/50 Mk 6, 18-3in/50, 12-3pdr, 2-1pdr, 2-18in TT sub
Complement: 829/891-928

Name	Number	Builder	Laid down	Launched	Comm	Fate
PENNSYLVANIA	ACR4	Cramp	7. 8.1901	22.8.03	9.3.05	Sold 1931
WEST VIRGINIA	ACR5	Newport News	16. 9.1901	18.4.03	23.2.05	Sold 1930
CALIFORNIA	ACR6	Union Iron Wks	7. 5.1902	28.4.04	1.8.07	Mined or Torpedoed 19.7.18
COLORADO	ACR7	Cramp	25. 4.1901	25.4.03	19.1.05	Sold 1930
MARYLAND	ACR8	Newport News	29.10.1901	12.9.03	18.4.05	Sold 1930
SOUTH DAKOTA	ACR9	Union Iron Wks	30. 9.1902	21.7.04	27.1.08	Sold 1930

Authorised under the Acts of 3.3.1899 (first three) and 7.6.1900 (second three). These ships are perhaps better known as renamed, the new names and dates being in order from ACR4 to ACR9: *Pittsburgh* 27.8.1912; *Huntington* 11.11.1916; *San Diego* 1.9.1914; *Pueblo* 9.11.1916; *Frederick* 9.11.1916; *Huron* 7.6.1920. Much larger than the two previous US armoured cruisers, they were distinctly undergunned for their size. The belt was 5in except on the waterline, and the barbette bases and ammunition tubes 3in. Turret crowns were 1½in as was the armour deck on the flat behind the belt, but the slopes were 4in as were the deck ends. The 8in guns were replaced by 8in/45s in *Colorado* in 1909, and later in the rest of the class, while the 6in guns of which ten were in a main deck battery, were temporarily reduced to as few as four in some of the class during and after the First World War. The 3in were also reduced to ten and 2-3in AA mounted. The Niclausse boilers in *Pennsylvania* and *Colorado* were replaced by 16 Babcock & Wilcox and the former was reduced to three funnels and 12 boilers in 1922. Cage foremasts were fitted from 1911.

The first landing by an aeroplane on a ship was made by Eugene Ely, in a Curtiss pusher, on a platform erected over the quarter deck and after turret of *Pennsylvania*, at anchor in San Francisco Bay on 18 January 1911, and for a time in 1917 *Huntington* was equipped with a catapult and four planes, and also operated a balloon. She was finally decommissioned in 1920, *Frederick* in 1922, *Huron* and *Pueblo* in 1927, the latter after six years as a receiving ship at New York, and *Pittsburg* in 1931. *San Diego* was either mined or torpedoed by *U156* and capsized and sank in about 20 minutes. The explosion was abreast of the fore part of the port engine room, and this and several nearby compartments flooded, and water also entered the port after boiler room, and as the ship heeled, came in through the main deck gun ports.

Pittsburg (ex *Pennsylvania*) in 1919
CPL

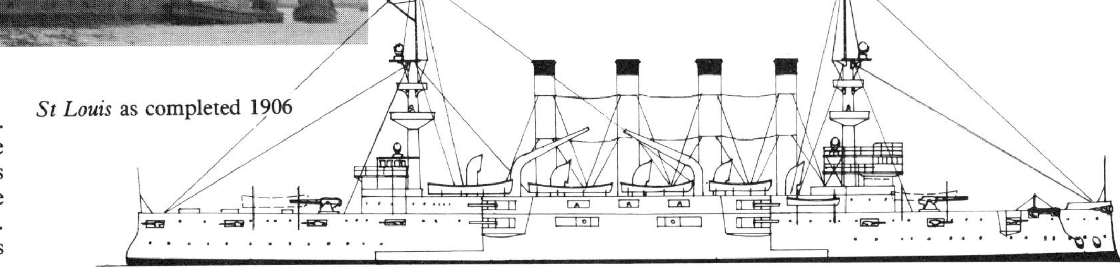

St Louis as completed 1906

Authorised under the Act of 7.6.1900. Not considered a good design. The 4in belt covered the machinery spaces only, and the upper 4in side only the length of the amidships 6in battery. The armour deck was 2in amidships with 3in slopes and 3in at the ends. The 6in guns were disposed with one forward and one aft in shields, four in upper deck casemates, and eight in the main deck battery, while 12 of the 3in were also on the main deck. The armament was later reduced to 12-6in, the after main deck pair being removed, 4-3in and 2-3in AA. *St Louis* was finally decommissioned in March 1922 and *Charleston* in December 1923, while *Milwaukee* was stranded off Eureka, California, when attempting to salve the submarine *H3*, and then broke in two in a storm in November 1918.

ST LOUIS class

Displacement: 9700t (10,839 full load)
Dimensions: 426ft 6in oa x 66ft x 22ft 6in mean (*129.91 oa x 20.12 x 6.86m*)
Machinery: 16 Babcock & Wilcox boilers, 2-shaft VTE 21,000ihp = 22kts. Coal 650/1650t; /1700 *Charleston*
Armour: Harvey. Belt 4in, main armament 4in, CT 5in
Armament: 14-6in/50 Mk 6 (*Milwaukee* Mk 8), 18-3in/50, 12-3pdr, 8-1pdr, no TT
Complement: 673/767

Name	Number	Builder	Laid down	Launched	Comm	Fate
ST. LOUIS	C20	Neafie & Levy	31.7.1902	6.5.05	18. 8.06	Sold 1930
MILWAUKEE	C21	Union Iron Wks	30.7.1902	10.9.04	11. 5.06	Wrecked 13.1.17
CHARLESTON	C22	Newport News	30.1.1902	23.1.04	17.10.05	Sold 1930

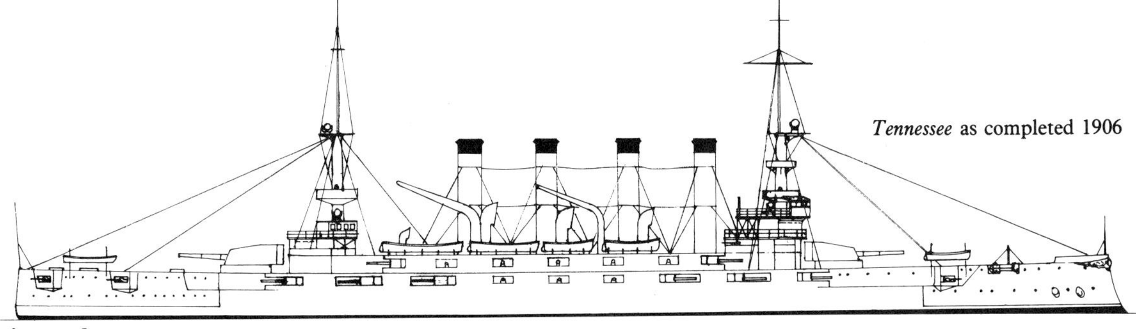

Tennessee as completed 1906

TENNESSEE class

Displacement: 14,500t (15,715 full load *Tennessee, Washington*; 15,981 *North Carolina, Montana*)
Dimensions: 504ft 6in oa x 72ft 11in x 25ft mean (*153.76 oa x 22.23 x 7.62m*)
Machinery: 16 Babcock & Wilcox boilers, 2-shaft VTE, 23,000ihp = 22kts. Coal 900/1975t *Tennessee*;/1939 *Washington*;/1950 *North Carolina, Montana*
Armour: KC, Harvey. Belt 5in ends 3in, barbettes 7in-4in (8in-4in *North Carolina, Montana*) turrets 9in-5in, secondary guns 5in, CT 9in
Armament: 4-10in/40, 16-6in/50 Mk 8, 22-3in/50, 12-3pdr, 2-1pdr (4-1pdr *North Carolina, Montana*) 4-21in TT sub
Complement: 856 *Tennessee, Washington*, 859 *North Carolina, Montana*/914

Name	Number	Builder	Laid down	Launched	Comm	Fate
TENNESSEE	ACR10	Cramp	20.6.1903	3.12.04	17.7.06	Wrecked 29.8.16
WASHINGTON	ACR11	New York SB	23.9.1903	18. 3.05	7.8.06	Sold 1946
NORTH CAROLINA	ACR12	Newport News	21.3.1905	6.10.06	7.5.08	Sold 1930
MONTANA	ACR13	Newport News	29.4.1905	15.12.06	21.7.08	Sold 1930

Authorised under the Acts of 1.7.1902 (first two) and 27.4.1904 (second two). Probably better known as renamed, the new names and dates in order ACR10 to ACR13 being: *Memphis* 25.5.1916; *Seattle* 9.11.1916; *Charlotte* 7.6.1920; *Missoula* 7.6.1920. This class was a considerable improvement on previous US armoured cruisers. The armour deck was 1½in on the flat behind the belt with 4in slopes, and 3in fore and aft, and the barbettes were only reduced to 4in when behind the belt, and were taken down to the armour deck. The turrets had 9in faces, 7in sides, 5in rears and 2½in roofs, while the 10in guns though only 40 cal, were more powerful than the 10in/45s in the British *Swiftsure* and *Triumph*. Of the 6in guns 12 were on the main deck in two six-gun batteries separated by 6-3in, and four in upper deck casemates, while of the 22-3in, 12 were on the main deck and ten on the upper. During and after the First World War the 6in guns were temporarily reduced to four in some of the class, while the 3in were reduced to 12 and 2-3in AA added. Four-hour trials gave 21.92 to 22.27kts but with 27,274 to 28,280ihp. Cage foremasts were fitted from 1911. Considerable use was made of electrical auxiliary machinery, the output of the dynamos being 600kW, 100kW more than in the *Pennsylvania* class. The first aircraft launching from a ship by catapult was made from *North Carolina* on 5 November 1915, and at one period in the First World War *Seattle* was also equipped with a catapult and four aeroplanes. *Missoula* and *Charlotte* were both finally decommissioned in 1921, while *Seattle* was administrative flagship of the US fleet 1923–1927 and then receiving ship at New York until 1941 when she was numbered IX39 as a miscellaneous auxiliary. *Memphis* was struck by a 100-foot high tsunami (a tidal wave of seismic origin) a fate not known to have happened to any other ship of her size, in the roadstead of Santo Domingo and was driven ashore, a total wreck.

CRUISERS

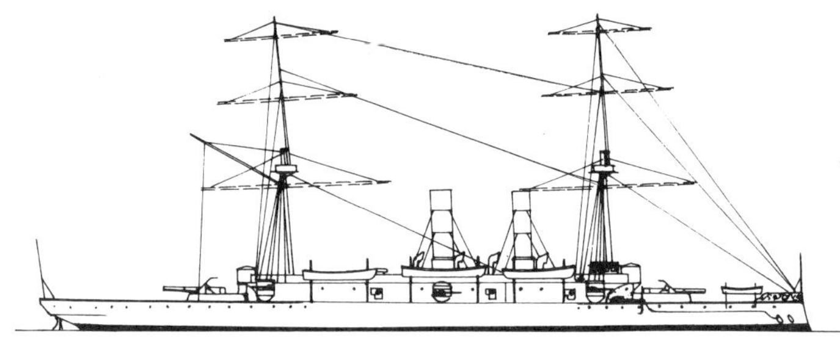
Atlanta as completed 1886

Authorised under the Act of 3.3.1883. From November 1905 *Atlanta* served as an accommodation ship for torpedo boat crews, while *Boston* acted as a training ship for the Oregon Naval Militia from June 1911 to September 1916, and was receiving ship at Yerba Buena from 1918 to 1946, and renamed *Despatch* in August 1940. The 8in guns in 2in barbettes were echeloned to port forward and starboard aft, with the end 6in in the central superstructure counter-echeloned, to permit axial fire of 1-8in and 1-6in fore and aft. A 1½in deck extended for 100ft over the machinery spaces, and the 8in guns were later in shielded mountings. They were much too slow to be effective cruisers, and the partial deck gave very inadequate protection. Sail, in the form of a brig rig without royals or head gear, was later removed.

ATLANTA class

Displacement: 3189t
Dimensions: 283ft oa x 42ft x 17ft mean (*86.26 oa x 12.80 x 5.18m*)
Machinery: 8 cyl boilers, 1-shaft HC, 3500ihp = 13kts. Coal 380/490t
Armament: 2-8in/30, 6-6in/30, 2-6pdr, 2-3pdr, 2-1pdr, no TT
Complement: 284

Name	Number	Builder	Laid down	Launched	Comm	Fate
ATLANTA	—	John Roach	8.11.1883	9.10.84	19.7.86	Sold 1912
BOSTON	—	John Roach (Both completed at New York N Yd)	15.11.1883	4.12.84	2.5.87	Scuttled 8.4.1946

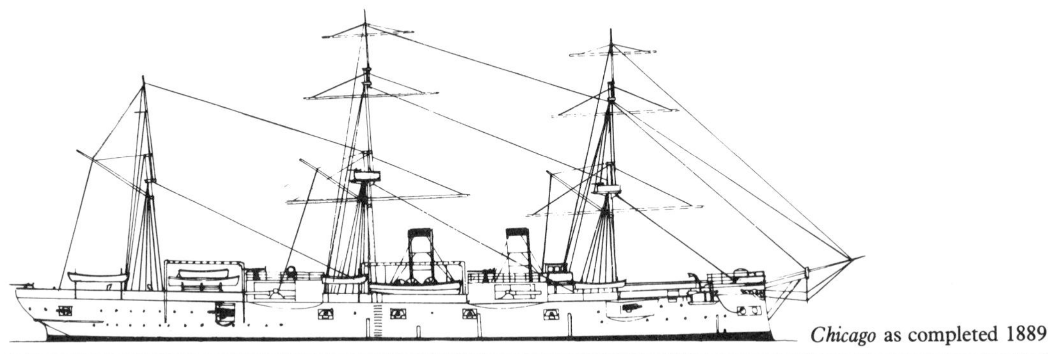
Chicago as completed 1889

Authorised under the Act of 3.3.1883. *Chicago* was poorly protected with a 1½in deck extending for 136ft over the machinery spaces but only ¾in over the magazines. The 8in guns were in four upper deck sponsons with the 6in and 5in on the main deck, the 5in being aft. The boilers were unusual in being externally fired and trials gave 5084ihp = 15.4kts, while sail was provided, *Chicago* being rigged as a barque without royals. She was reconstructed 1895–1898, the nominal displacement rising to 5000t, 1½in deck plating was added over the steering gear, a strip of 1in side to protect the gun crews and 70ft of 1⅛in at the bows for ramming, the CT having 3in. The 8in/30s were replaced by 8in/35s, and the 6in and 5in by 14-5in/40. New machinery comprising six Babcock & Wilcox and four cylindrical boilers with 2-shaft HTE gave 9000ihp = 18kts, and the sails were removed. From 1910 to 1917 she was with the Massachusetts and then Pennsylvania Naval Militia, and from 1917 to 1923 mostly served with submarines, her guns being reduced to 4-5in/51. Classified as CA14 in July 1920, *Chicago* was an accommodation ship at Pearl Harbor 1923–1935 (renamed *Alton* July 1928) and foundered after sale when in tow to San Francisco.

CHICAGO

Displacement: 4500t (4864 full load)
Dimensions: 342ft 2in oa x 48ft 3in x 19ft mean (*104.29 oa x 14.70 x 5.79m*)
Machinery: 5 cyl boilers, 2-shaft COB, 5000ihp = 14kts. Coal 593/831t
Armament: 4-8in/30, 8-6in/30, 2-5in/30, 2-6pdr, 2-1pdr, no TT
Complement: 409/471

Name	Number	Builder	Laid down	Launched	Comm	Fate
CHICAGO	—	John Roach (Completed at Delaware River, successors to John Roach)	29.12.1883	5.12.85	17.4.89	Foundered 8.7.1936

Chicago as built with barque rig and short funnels
CPL

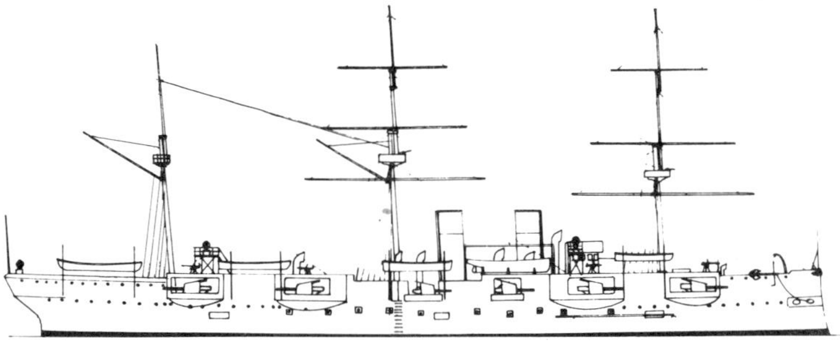

Authorised under the Act of 3.3.1885. A considerable improvement on *Chicago* with a complete protective deck, 2in amidship with 3in slopes, 2in forward and 3in aft. The CT had 3in. The 6in guns were all in sponsons and *Newark* was re-armed with 12-6in/40 in 1901–1902. She was stricken from the Navy in June 1913 but served as a quarantine hulk at Providence RI and temporarily as a naval hospital annex, until 1926. As originally commissioned *Newark* was rigged as a barque without royals or head gear, but sails were later removed, and as in other three-masted US cruisers laid down in the 1880s the original mainmast was unstepped as well.

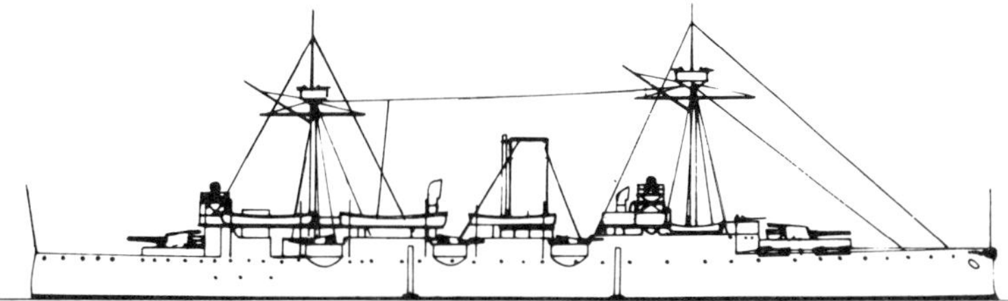

Newark 1897

NEWARK

Displacement: 4083t (4592 full load)
Dimensions: 328ft oa x 49ft 2in x 18ft 10in mean (*99.97 oa x 14.98 x 5.74m*)
Machinery: 4 cyl boilers, 2-shaft HTE, 8500ihp = 18kts. Coal 400/800t
Armament: 12in-6in/30, 4-6pdr, 4-3pdr, 2-1pdr, no TT
Complement: 384

Name	Number	Builder	Laid down	Launched	Comm	Fate
NEWARK	C1	Cramp	12.6.1888	19.3.90	2.2.91	Sold 1926

Authorised under the Act of 3.3.1885. Virtually a copy of the Elswick cruiser *Naniwa* built for Japan, with the 2-8in guns in fore and aft low barbettes. These had 2in plating, the CT 2in also, and the protective deck was 2in with 3in slopes. *Charleston* ran aground on an uncharted reef off Camiguin Island in the Philippines, and was damaged beyond salvage.

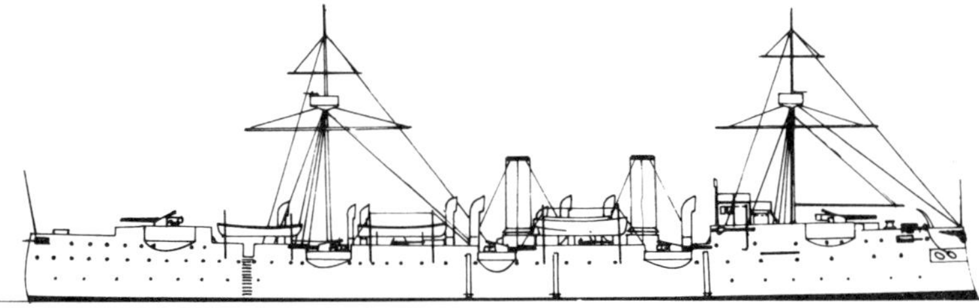

Charleston 1897

CHARLESTON

Displacement: 3730t (*c* 4200 full load)
Dimensions: 320ft oa x 46ft x 18ft 6in mean (*97.54 oa x 14.01 x 5.64m*)
Machinery: 6 cyl boilers, 2-shaft HC, 7650ihp = 18.9kts. Coal 328/758t
Armament: 2-8in/35, 6-6in/30, 4-6pdr, 2-3pdr, 2-1pdr, no TT
Complement: 300

Name	Number	Builder	Laid down	Launched	Comm	Fate
CHARLESTON	C2	Union Iron Wks	20.1.1887	19.7.88	26.12.89	Wrecked 2.11.99

Authorised under the Act of 3.8.1886. Based on an Elswick design which was unsuccessful in the competition for the ill-fated Spanish cruiser *Reina Regente*. The 4-8in were in sponsons from forecastle and poop and the 6in in sponsons from the upper deck amidships. The protective deck was 2½in with 4in slopes amidships and the CT 3in. In 1900–1903 she was re-armed with 12-6in/40 Mk 7 guns, two on the forecastle, two on the poop, eight amidships on the upper deck, none being in sponsons. She was also reboilered with eight Babcock & Wilcox boilers. The *Baltimore* served as a receiving ship at Charleston in 1911–1912, and was converted to a minelayer at that yard in 1913–1914. During the First World War *Baltimore* took part in laying the Northern Mine Barrage, and her armament in 1919 is given as 4-5in/51 and 2-3in AA. Decommissioned at Pearl Harbor in 1922, *Baltimore* was not sold for 20 years. She was perhaps the best of the US cruisers laid down in the 1880s.

Baltimore as completed 1890

BALTIMORE

Displacement: 4413t (5436 full load)
Dimensions: 335ft oa x 48ft 6in x 19ft 6in mean (*102.11 oa x 14.78 x 5.94m*)
Machinery: 4 cyl boilers, 2-shaft HTE, 10,750ihp = 19kts. Coal 400/1144t
Armament: 4-8in/35, 6-6in/30, 4-6pdr, 2-3pdr, 2-1pdr, no TT
Complement: 386

Name	Number	Builder	Laid down	Launched	Comm	Fate
BALTIMORE	C3	Cramp	5.5.1887	6.10.88	7.1.90	Sold 1942

Baltimore in New York Harbour

PHILADELPHIA

Authorised under the Act of 3.3.1887. Originally rigged as a three-masted schooner without head gear and similar to *Baltimore* in protection. *Philadelphia*'s 12-6in guns were mounted as in the re-armed *Baltimore* except that the eight midships guns were in sponsons. Sent to Puget Sound Navy Yard for extensive repairs in August 1902, *Philadelphia* was housed over as a receiving ship at the above yard in 1904 and so remained, apart from a period as a prison ship, until stricken in 1926.

Displacement: 4324t (5305 full load)
Dimensions: 335ft oa x 48ft 6in x 19ft 2in mean (*102.11 oa x 14.78 x 5.84m*)
Machinery: 4 cyl boilers, 2-shaft HTE, 9000ihp = 19kts. Coal 400/1031t
Armament: 12-6in/30, 4-6pdr, 4-3pdr, 2-1pdr, no TT
Complement: 384

Name	Number	Builder	Laid down	Launched	Comm	Fate
PHILADELPHIA	C4	Cramp	22.3.1888	7.9.89	28.7.90	Sold 1927

San Francisco with her original light schooner rig
CPL

SAN FRANCISCO

Authorised under the Act of 3.3.1887. Originally rigged as a three-masted schooner without head gear, *San Francisco* generally resembled *Newark* except that the two forward and two after 6in were carried a deck higher and were not in sponsons. The protective deck was 2in with 3in slopes amidships and the CT 3in. *San Francisco* was re-armed with 6in/40 guns in 1902, and in 1908–1911 was converted to a minelayer at Norfolk Navy Yard, her gun armament being 8-5in/40, while eight Babcock & Wilcox boilers were fitted. During the First World War she took part in laying the Northern Mine Barrage, and in 1918 her armament was 4-5in/51. *San Francisco* was decommissioned at Philadelphia in 1921, and remained in reserve until stricken in 1937. She was renamed *Tahoe* and then *Yosemite* in 1930–1931.

Displacement: 4088t (4583 full load)
Dimensions: 324ft 6in oa x 49ft 2in x 18ft 10in mean (*98.91 oa x 14.98 x 5.74m*)
Machinery: 4 cyl boilers, 2-shaft HTE, 10,500ihp = 19kts. Coal 350/627t
Armament: 12-6in/30, 4-6pdr, 4-3pdr, 2-1pdr, no TT
Complement: 384

Name	Number	Builder	Laid down	Launched	Comm	Fate
SAN FRANCISCO	C5	Union Iron Wks	14.8.1888	26.10.89	15.11.90	Sold 1939

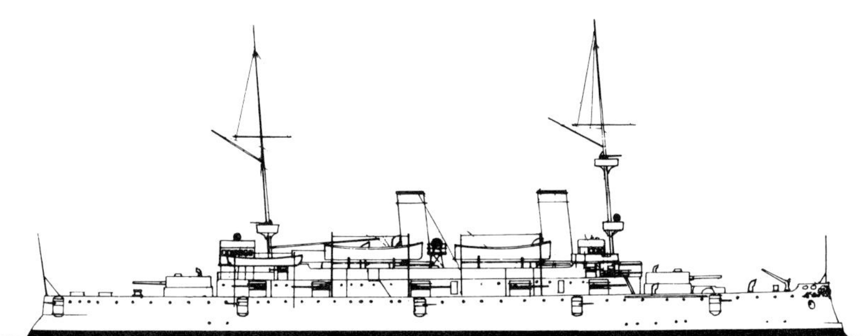

Olympia 1898

OLYMPIA

Authorised under the Act of 7.9.1888. In this ship the 4-8in guns were in fore and aft twin turrets protected by 3½in Harvey with 4½in nickel steel barbettes and 3in ammunition tubes. The 5in guns to port and starboard amidships in the superstructure had 4in shields, the CT 5in and the protective deck was 2in on the flat with the slopes 4¾in amidships and 3in at the ends. The engine cylinders were protected by a 4in glacis. On trials *Olympia* reached 17,313ihp = 21.68kts on the mile but she was 300t below her normal displacement. Flagship of Commodore Dewey at the Battle of Manilla, *Olympia* was not seriously tested in this action. Her TT were removed in 1900.

She was an accommodation ship at Charleston from 1912–1916, but was on active service during the First World War with an armament of 10-5in/51, and finally decommissioned 9.12.1922, being reclassified as IX-40 in 1931.

Displacement: 5865t (6558 full load)
Dimensions: 344ft 1in oa x 53ft x 21ft 6in mean (*104.87 oa x 16.15 x 6.55m*)
Machinery: 6 cyl boilers, 2-shaft VTE, 13,500ihp = 20kts. Coal 400/1093t
Armament: 4-8in/35 (2 x 2), 10-5in/40, 14-6pdr, 6-1pdr, 6-18in TT aw
Complement: 411/447

Name	Number	Builder	Laid down	Launched	Comm	Fate
OLYMPIA	C6	Union Iron Wks	17.6.1891	5.11.92	5.2.95	Still preserved

Olympia lying off Gravesend in 1904
CPL

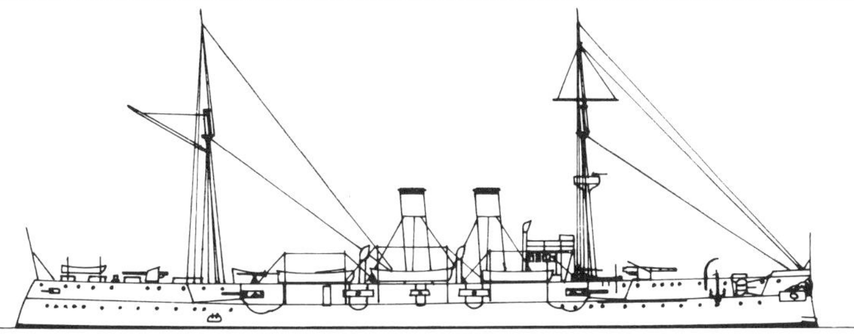

Raleigh 1895

Authorised under the Act of 7.9.1888. In these ships the 6in was on the upper deck forward, two of the 5in abreast on the upper deck aft and the remainder in main deck sponsons amidships with local 4in protection. The CT was 2in and the protective deck 1in on the flat with slopes 2½in amidships and 2in fore and aft. Both were altered, *Cincinnati* in 1899–1901 and *Raleigh* in 1899–1903. The 6in gun was replaced by a 5in, TT were removed and eight Babcock & Wilcox boilers with new VTE engines installed, while the mainmast was removed from *Cincinnati*. The 5in guns were reduced to nine during the First World War. As originally completed they had fore and aft sails but these were removed in or before 1899.

CINCINNATI class

Displacement: 3183t (3339 full load)
Dimensions: 305ft 9in oa x 42ft x 18ft mean *(93.19 oa x 12.80 x 5.49m)*
Machinery: 6 cyl boilers, 2-shaft VTE, 10,000ihp = 19kts. Coal 350/460t
Armament: 1-6in/40, 10-5in/40, 8-6pdr, 2-1pdr (*Raleigh* 4-1pdr), 4-18in TT aw
Complement: 312/322

Name	Number	Builder	Laid down	Launched	Comm	Fate
CINCINNATI	C7	New York N Yd	29. 1.1890	10.11.92	16.6.94	Sold 1921
RALEIGH	C8	Norfolk N Yd	19.12.1889	31. 3.92	17.4.94	Sold 1921

Marblehead, date unknown
CPL

Authorised under the Act of 7.9.1888. Slow and weak ships with no effective deck protection (½in maximum). One 5in gun was on the upper deck forward and the rest in main deck sponsons. TT were removed in 1899. 1919 figures credit the two survivors with 8-4in, and *Montgomery,* which had served as a torpedo experimental ship 1908–1914, was renamed *Anniston* March 1918, with six Almy boilers.

MONTGOMERY class

Displacement: 2094t (2235 full load)
Dimensions: 269ft 6in oa x 37ft x 14ft 7in mean *(82.14 oa x 11.27 x 4.44m)*
Machinery: 6 cyl boilers, 2-shaft VTE, 5400ihp = 17kts. Coal 200/340t
Armament: 9-5in/40, 6-6pdr, 2-1pdr, 3-18in TT aw
Complement: 274

Name	Number	Builder	Laid down	Launched	Comm	Fate
MONTGOMERY	C9	Columbian Iron Wks	Feb 1890	5.12.91	21.6.94	Sold 1919
DETROIT	C10	Columbian Iron Wks	Feb 1890	28.10.91	20.7.93	Sold 1910
MARBLEHEAD	C11	City Point Iron Wks	Oct 1890	11. 8.92	2.4.94	Sold 1921

Columbia authorised under the Act of 30.6.1890, and *Minneapolis* under that of 2.3.1891. Designed as commerce raiders, these ships differed much in appearance, *Columbia* having four funnels and *Minneapolis* two. They were very lightly gunned for their size. The 8in was in a shield on the quarterdeck and the 2-6in abreast forward, while the 4in were in main deck sponsons, protected by 4in steel. The CT had 5in, and the protective deck was 2½in with 4in slopes amidships. The 8in gun was later replaced by a third 6in, and in 1919 their armament also included 4-4in/40 and 2-3in AA. TT had been removed. *Columbia* was out of commission from May 1907 to June 1915 and *Minneapolis* from November 1906 to July 1917, presumably because of their high coal consumption, though they were good steamers, *Columbia* taking six days 23 hours 49 minutes from Southampton to Sandy Hook in 1895, when the best trip was the *Fürst Bismarck*'s six days ten hours 32 minutes.

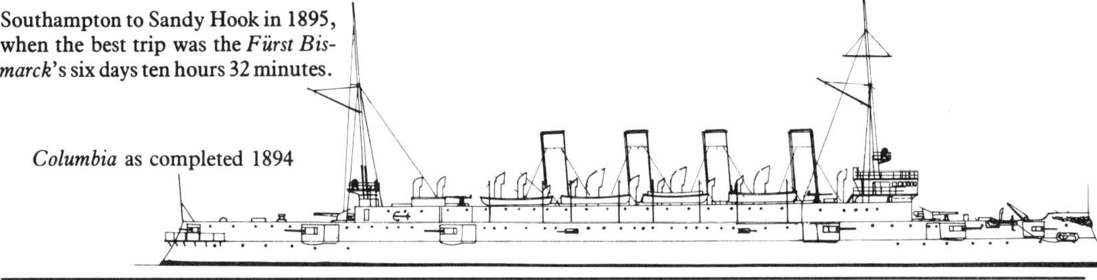

Columbia as completed 1894

COLUMBIA class

Displacement: 7375t (8270 full load)
Dimensions: 413ft 1in oa x 58ft 2in x 22ft 7in mean (*125.90 oa x 17.72 x 6.88m*)
Machinery: 8 cyl boilers, 3-shaft VTE, 21,000ihp = 21kts. Coal 730/1670t
Armament: 1-8in/40 Mk 3, 2-6in/40, 8-4in/40, 12-6pdr, 4-1pdr, 4-14in TT aw *Columbia*; 4-18in TT aw *Minneapolis*
Complement: 477

Name	Number	Builder	Laid down	Launched	Comm	Fate
COLUMBIA	C12	Cramp	30.12.1890	26.7.92	23. 4.94	Sold 1922
MINNEAPOLIS	C13	Cramp	16.12.1891	12.8.93	13.12.94	Sold 1921

Minneapolis in 1904
CPL

Albany in her early years
CPL

Purchased from Brazil under the Act of 9.3.1898, *New Orleans* being ex-*Amazonas* and *Albany* ex-*Almirante Abreu*. They were sisters of the *Barroso*. The 6in guns were on the forecastle and poop, and in sponsons to port and starboard located just abaft the fore and main-masts. The 4.7in were between the latter 4-6in. The protective deck was 1¼in with 3½in slopes amidships, and there was 4in on the boiler room glacis and CT. They were rearmed in 1907 with 10-5in/50 in place of the 6in and 4.7in – TT previously removed – the number of 5in being finally reduced to eight. Both were ultimately decommissioned in late 1922 after long and varied service, and it would appear that the USA made a good buy with these two ships.

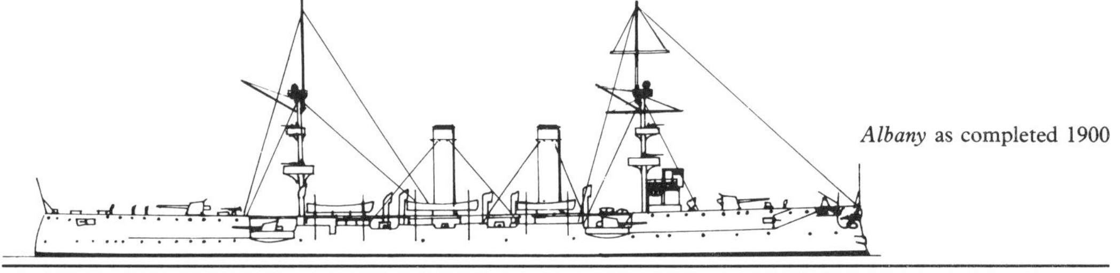

Albany as completed 1900

NEW ORLEANS class

Displacement: 3769t (4011 full load)
Dimensions: 354ft 5in oa x 43ft 9in x 18ft mean (*108.03 oa x 13.33 x 5.49m*)
Machinery: 4 cyl boilers, 2-shaft VTE, 7500ihp = 20kts. Coal 512/747t *New Orleans*;/767 *Albany*
Armament: 6-6in/50 US Mk 5 EOC DD, 4-4.7in/50 EOC AA, 10-6pdr, 8-1pdr, 3-18in TT aw
Complement: 366

Name	Number	Builder	Laid down	Launched	Comm	Fate
NEW ORLEANS	—	Armstrong	1895	4.12.96	18.3.1898	Sold 1930
ALBANY	—	Armstrong	1897	14. 1.99	25.5.1900	Sold 1930

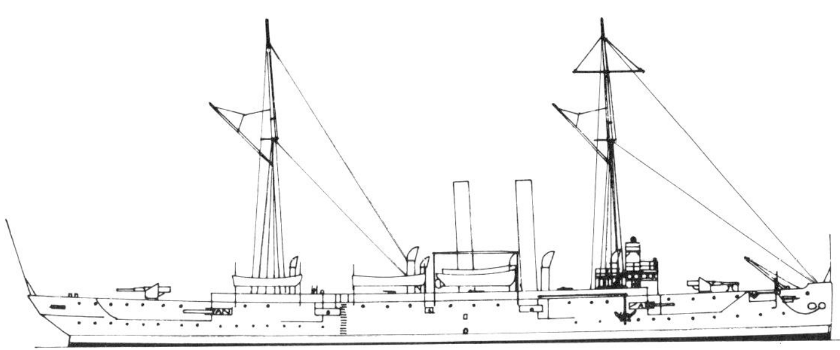

Denver as designed 1900

Authorised under the Act of 3.3.1899. Slow and weak ships on the lines of a larger *Montgomery*. The 5in guns were mounted with one fore and aft on the upper deck, and eight on the main deck in casemates (1¾in) the hull being recessed to give better axial fire. Later the foremost main deck pair were removed. The protective deck was 1in at the ends and 2½in on the amidships slopes but only 5/16in on the flat. *Tacoma* was wrecked on Blanquilla Reef near Vera Cruz.

DENVER class

Displacement: 3200t (3514 full load)
Dimensions: 308ft 10in oa x 44ft x 15ft 9in mean (*94.13 oa x 13.41 x 4.80m*)
Machinery: 6 Babcock & Wilcox boilers, 2-shaft VTE, 4500ihp = 16.5kts. Coal 467/675t(/700 *Des Moines, Galveston*)
Armament: 10-5in/50 Mk 5, 8-6pdr, 2-1pdr, no TT
Complement: 339

Name	Number	Builder	Laid down	Launched	Comm	Fate
DENVER	C14	Neafie & Levy	28.6.1900	21.6.02	17. 5.04	Sold 1933
DES MOINES	C15	Fore River	28.8.1900	20.9.03	5. 3.04	Sold 1930
CHATTANOOGA	C16	Crescent	29.3.1900	7.3.03	11.10.04	Sold 1930
GALVESTON	C17	WR Trigg	19.1.1901	23.7.03	15. 2.05	Sold 1933
TACOMA	C18	Union Iron Wks	27.9.1900	2.6.03	30. 1.04	Wrecked 16.1.24
CLEVELAND	C19	Bath Iron Wks	1.6.1900	28.9.01	2.11.03	Sold 1930

Cleveland off Gravesend 1904.
CPL

Authorised under the Act of 27.4.1904. 'Scout-cruisers' with high freeboard forward. *Chester* and *Salem* were the first turbine-engined ships in the USN. There was an area of 2in side protection in wake of the machinery spaces, and 1½in by the steering gear, but the deck was 1in maximum. The armament was very light, the 5in guns being on the forecastle deck forward and upper deck aft, and the 3in to port and starboard on the upper deck, the foremost being in sponsons under the forecastle. In 1917–1918 the armament was changed to 4-5in/51, 2-3in/50, 1-3in AA and 2-21in TT aw. *Salem* was the worst of the three with the highest coal consumption, and in April 1917–March 1918 she was re-engined with GE geared turbines of 20,000shp.

The first take-off by an aeroplane from a ship was made from a wooden platform built on the bow of *Birmingham*, anchored in Hampton Roads, on 14 November 1910, by Eugene Ely piloting a 50hp Curtiss. Final decommissioning dates were *Chester* 10.6.1921 (renamed *York* 10.7.1928), *Birmingham* 1.12.1923, *Salem* 16.8.1921.

Chester as completed 1908

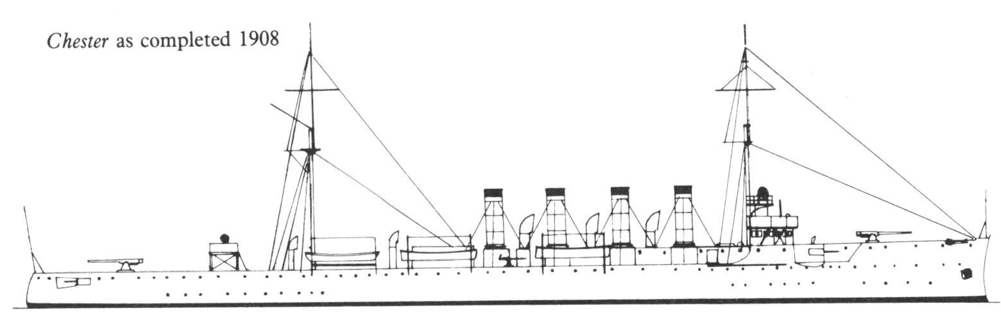

CHESTER class

Displacement: 3750t (4687 full load)
Dimensions: 423ft 2in oa x 47ft 1in x 16ft 9in mean (*128.98 oa x 14.34 x 5.10m*)
Machinery: *Chester* 12 Normand boilers, 4-shaft Parsons turbines; *Birmingham* 12 Fore River boilers, 2-shaft VTE; *Salem* 12 Fore River boilers, 2-shaft Curtis turbines, 16,000hp = 24kts. Coal 475/1400t, /1375 *Birmingham*
Armament: 2-5in/50 Mk 6, 6-3in/50, 2-21in TT sub
Complement: 359

Name	Number	Builder	Laid down	Launched	Comm	Fate
CHESTER	CS1	Bath Iron Wks	25.9.1905	26.6.07	25.4.08	Sold 1930
BIRMINGHAM	CS2	Fore River	14.8.1905	29.5.07	11.4.08	Sold 1930
SALEM	CS3	Fore River	28.8.1905	27.7.07	1.8.08	Sold 1930

Chester, date unknown
CPL

Katahdin as completed 1898

KATAHDIN *armoured ram*

Authorised under the Act of 2.3.1889. Intended as a harbour defence ram, she differed from the British *Polyphemus* in having no torpedo armament. The 6in side armour, 3in at lower edge, was inclined outwards and joined the turtle deck which was 6in at the edge, then 5½in and 2½in-2in at the centre line. The knuckle was backed by 45in of timber, and the hull normally 5ft-6ft maximum above water, was lowered 6in for action by water ballast. *Katahdin* was only commissioned up to April 1897 and again from March to October 1898. Stricken 9.7.1909, she was used as 'Ballistic Experimental Target A' in important firing trials which determined the need for 13½in armour in future battleship designs.

Displacement: 2155t (2383 full load)
Dimensions: 250ft 9in wl x 43ft 5in x 15ft 1in mean (*76.42 oa x 13.23 x 4.60m*)
Machinery: 3 cyl boilers, 2-shaft HTE, 5068ihp = 16kts. Coal 175/202t
Armour: Harvey and NS, side 6in-3in, uptakes 6in, deck 6in-2in CT 18in
Armament: 4-6pdr, no TT
Complement: 97

Name	Number	Builder	Laid down	Launched	Comm	Fate
KATAHDIN	—	Bath Iron Wks	July 1891	4.2.93	20.2.96	Sunk as Target 1909

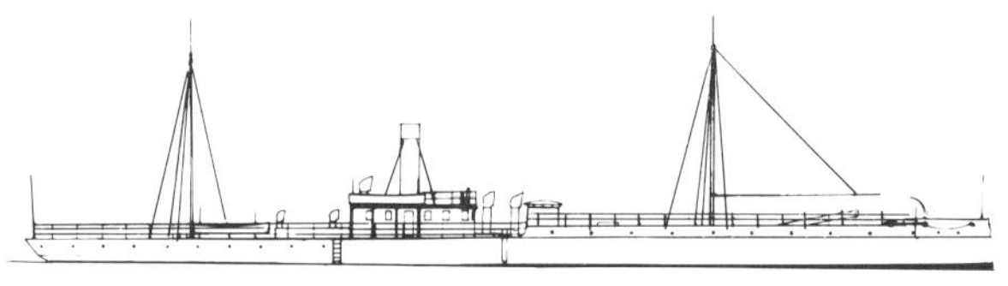

Vesuvius as completed 1890

VESUVIUS *dynamite-gun cruiser*

Authorised under the Act of 3.8.1886 as a 'dynamite-gun cruiser'; a second such ship authorised under the Act of 2.3.1889 was never built. *Vesuvius* had a CT protected by 1in plating, and recorded a maximum of 4295ihp = 21.65kts on trials. The 15in Zalinsky pneumatic gun was 55ft long and the full calibre shell weighed 980lb with a 500lb dynamite warhead. The range was 1700–1750 yards, but three times this could be reached with sub-calibre shells. In *Vesuvius* the guns were fixed at 18° elevation and trained by moving ship. A total of 30 shells was carried. She bombarded Santiago in 1898 but accuracy was very poor, and the pneumatic guns were later removed, and *Vesuvius* used as an experimental torpedo vessel.

Displacement: 929t
Dimensions: 252ft 4in oa x 26ft 5in x 9ft mean (*76.91 oa x 8.06 x 2.74m*)
Machinery: 4 cyl boilers, 2-shaft VTE, 3200ihp = 20kts. Coal 152t
Armament: 3-15in pneumatic guns, 3-3pdr, no TT
Complement: 70

Name	Number	Builder	Laid down	Launched	Comm	Fate
VESUVIUS	—	Cramp	Sept 1887	28.4.88	7.6.90	Sold 1921

Vesuvius when new

DESTROYERS

Authorised under the Act of 10.6.1896. Classed as a torpedo boat, but her displacement indicates that she was the first US destroyer. Attained 30.13kts on trials. There were two funnels and two single TT abaft the second funnel and far aft. Renamed Coast Torpedo Boat No 5 in August 1918.

FARRAGUT

Displacement: 279t
Dimensions: 214ft oa x 20ft 8in x 6ft mean (*65.22 oa x 6.30 x 1.83m*)
Machinery: 3 Thornycroft boilers, 2-shaft VTE, 5878ihp = 30kts. Coal 95t
Armament: 4-6pdr, 2-18in TT
Complement: 66

Name	Number	Builder	Laid down	Launched	Comm	Fate
FARRAGUT	TB11	Union Iron Wks	26.7.1897	16.7.98	22.3.99	Sold 1919

Authorised under the Act of 3.3.1897. Never made her designed speed, the trials figure being given as 25.33kts, which accounts for the delay in commissioning. Turtle deck forward, three equally spaced funnels and two single TT aft. Stricken from navy 26.11.1913, but not sold until 1923.

STRINGHAM

Displacement: 340t
Dimensions: 228ft 3in oa x 22ft x 6ft 6in mean (*69.57 oa x 6.70 x 1.98m*)
Machinery: 4 Thornycroft boilers, 2-shaft VTE, 7200ihp = 30kts. Coal 95t
Armament: 4-6pdr, 2-18in TT
Complement: 59

Name	Number	Builder	Laid down	Launched	Comm	Fate
STRINGHAM	TB19	Harlan & Hollingsworth	21.3.1898	10.6.99	7.11.1905	Sold 1923

Authorised under the Act of 3.3.1897. Much trouble on trials and had to be re-engined before commissioning. General layout as in *Farragut*. Renamed Coast Torpedo Boat No 7 in August 1918.

GOLDSBOROUGH

Displacement: 255t
Dimensions: 198ft oa x 20ft 7in x 6ft 10in mean (*60.35 oa x 6.27 x 2.08m*)
Machinery: 3 Thornycroft boilers, 2-shaft VTE, 6000ihp = 27kts. Coal 89t
Armament: 4-6pdr, 2-18in TT
Complement: 59

Name	Number	Builder	Laid down	Launched	Comm	Fate
GOLDSBOROUGH	TB20	Wolf & Zwicker	14.7.1898	29.7.99	9.4.1908	Sold 1919

Authorised under the Act of 3.3.1897. Made 30.2kts on trials. Three funnels, one forward and two aft with two single TT between the first and second. Renamed Coast Torpedo Boat No 8 in August 1918.

BAILEY

Displacement: 235t
Dimensions: 205ft oa x 19ft 2in x 6ft mean (*62.48 oa x 5.84 x 1.83m*)
Machinery: 4 Seabury boilers, 2-shaft VTE, 5600ihp = 30kts. Coal 99t
Armament: 4-6pdr, 2-18in TT
Complement: 56

Name	Number	Builder	Laid down	Launched	Comm	Fate
BAILEY	TB21	Gas Engine & Power and CL Seabury	30.4.1898	5.12.99	20.7.1901	Sold 1920

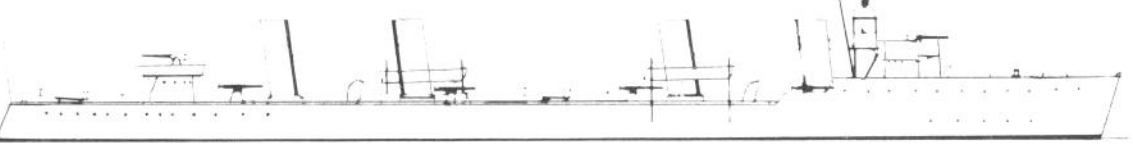

Bainbridge as completed 1902

Authorised under the Act of 4.5.1898. Trial speeds 28.0kts to 28.64kts. Forecastle deck, not turtle, forward. Four funnels in two groups, with one TT between the groups and one far aft. For most of their life, the destroyers of this class were based at Cavite in the Philippine Islands.

BAINBRIDGE class

Displacement: 420t
Dimensions: 250ft oa x 23ft 7in x 6ft 6in mean (*76.19 oa x 7.18 x 1.98m*)
Machinery: 4 Thornycroft boilers, 2-shaft VTE, 8000ihp = 29kts. Coal 213t (203t *Dale, Decatur*)
Armament: 2-3in/25, 5-6pdr, 2-18in TT
Complement: 73

Name	Number	Builder	Laid down	Launched	Comm	Fate
BAINBRIDGE	1	Neafie & Levy	15. 8.1899	27. 8.1901	24.11.02	Sold 1920
BARRY	2	Neafie & Levy	2. 9.1899	22. 3.1902	24.11.02	Sold 1920
CHAUNCEY	3	Neafie & Levy	2.12.1899	26.10.1901	20.11.02	Rammed by SS *Rose* 19.11.1917
DALE	4	WR Trigg	12. 7.1899	24. 7.1900	24.10.1902	Sold 1920
DECATUR	5	WR Trigg	26. 7.1899	26. 9.1900	19. 5.02	Sold 1920

HOPKINS class

Authorised under the Act of 4.5.1898. Resembled *Bainbridge* class in general layout but had turtle deck forward, and also differed in having 3in/50 guns, and eventually 4-18in TT in two twin mountings.

Displacement: 408t
Dimensions: 248ft 8in oa x 24ft 6in x 6ft mean (*75.79 oa x 7.47 x 1.83m*)
Machinery: 4 Thornycroft boilers, 2-shaft VTE, 7200ihp = 29kts. Coal 153t
Armament: 2-3in/50, 5-6pdr, 2-18in TT
Complement: 73

Name	Number	Builder	Laid down	Launched	Comm	Fate
HOPKINS	6	Harlan & Hollingsworth	2.2.1899	24.4.1902	23.9.03	Sold 1920
HULL	7	Harlan & Hollingsworth	22.2.1899	21.6.1902	20.5.03	Sold 1921

LAWRENCE class

Authorised under the Act of 4.5.1898. Turtle deck forward and four funnels in one group with two single TTs aft and far aft. Apparently the least satisfactory sea-boats of the '400-tonners' as the gun armament was reduced to 7-6pdr. Designed speed of 30kts was not made on trials by at least a knot.

Displacement: 430t
Dimensions: 246ft 3in oa x 22ft 3in x 6ft 8in mean (*75.05 oa x 6.78 x 2.03m*)
Machinery: 4 Fore River boilers, 2-shaft VTE, 8400ihp = 30kts. Coal 123t *Lawrence*; 110t *MacDonough*
Armament: 2-3in/25, 5-6pdr, 2-18in TT
Complement: 72

Name	Number	Builder	Laid down	Launched	Comm	Fate
LAWRENCE	8	Fore River	10.4.1899	7.11.1900	14.4.03	Sold 1920
MACDONOUGH	9	Fore River	21.4.1899	24.12.1900	5.9.03	Sold 1920

Preble of the *Paul Jones* class

Paul Jones on her speed trials, 8 July 1902, when she reached 28.9kts

PAUL JONES class

Authorised under the Act of 4.5.1898. Trial speeds were 28.03kts to 28.91kts. Similar to *Bainbridge* class, but latterly two single TT replaced by one twin mounting.

Displacement: 480t
Dimensions: 250ft 7in oa x 23ft 6in x 7ft 3in mean (*76.37 oa x 7.16 x 2.21m*)
Machinery: 4 Thornycroft boilers, 2-shaft VTE, 8000ihp = 29kts. Coal 202t
Armament: 2-3in/25, 5-6pdr, 2-18in TT
Complement: 73

Name	Number	Builder	Laid down	Launched	Comm	Fate
PAUL JONES	10	Union Iron Wks	20.4.1899	14. 6.1902	14.12.03	Sold 1920
PERRY	11	Union Iron Wks	19.4.1899	27.10.1900	4. 9.02	Sold 1920
PREBLE	12	Union Iron Wks	21.4.1899	2. 3.1901	14.12.03	Sold 1920

STEWART

Authorised under the Act of 4.5.1898. The fastest of the '400-tonners' with a trial speed of 29.7kts. Similar to the *Bainbridge* class.

Displacement: 420t
Dimensions: 250ft 6in oa x 23ft 8in x 6ft 6in mean (*76.34 oa x 7.21 x 1.98m*)
Machinery: 4 Seabury boilers, 2-shaft VTE, 8000ihp = 29kts. Coal 172t
Armament: 2-3in/25, 5-6pdr, 2-18in TT
Complement: 71

Name	Number	Builder	Laid down	Launched	Comm	Fate
STEWART	13	Gas Engine & Power and CL Seabury	24.1.1900	10.5.02	17.12.02	Sold 1920

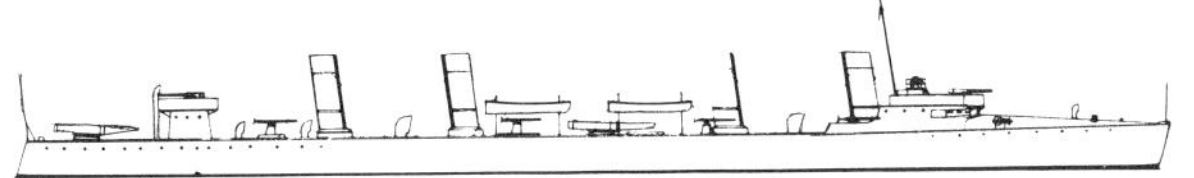

Truxton as completed 1902

TRUXTON class

Authorised under the Act of 4.5.1898. Resembled *Hopkins* class but funnels were lower. Subsequently *Truxton* and *Worden* had 4-18in TT in two twin mountings, and *Whipple* two in one twin. None made 30kts, *Truxton* being the fastest on trials with 29.58 kts.

Displacement: 433t
Dimensions: 259ft 6in oa x 23ft 3in x 6ft mean (*79.10 oa x 7.08 x 1.83m*)
Machinery: 4 Thornycroft boilers, 2-shaft VTE, 8300ihp = 30kts. Coal 171t
Armament: 2-3in/50, 6-6pdr, 2-18in TT
Complement: 73

Name	Number	Builder	Laid down	Launched	Comm	Fate
TRUXTON	14	Maryland Steel	13.11.1899	15.8.1901	11. 9.02	Sold 1920
WHIPPLE	15	Maryland Steel	13.11.1899	15.8.1901	21.10.02	Sold 1920
WORDEN	16	Maryland Steel	13.11.1899	15.8.1901	31.12.02	Sold 1920

TORPEDO BOATS

Stilleto laid up in 1889 after a collision with a steam launch

STILETTO

Built by Herreshoff as a private speculation and purchased under the Act of 3.3.1887. A single funnel, wood-hulled boat used for experimental work. Oil fuel trials in 1897 were unsatisfactory.

Displacement: 31t
Dimensions: 94ft oa x 11ft 6in x 3ft mean (*28.64 oa x 3.50 x 0.91m*)
Machinery: 1 Almy boiler, 1-shaft VC, 359ihp = 18.2kts. Coal 4t
Armament: None originally. Had 2 Howell torpedoes in 1898
Complement: 6

Name	Number	Builder	Laid down	Launched	Comm	Fate
STILETTO	WTB1	Herreshoff	1885	1886	July 1887	Sold 1911

Cushing as completed 1890

CUSHING

Authorised under the Act of 3.8.1886, and used initially for experimental work. Two funnels far apart, and ram bow, with turtle deck forward. Two broadside training TT and one fixed forward.

Displacement: 116t
Dimensions: 140ft oa x 15ft 1in x 4ft 10in (*42.68 oa x 4.60 x 1.47m*)
Machinery: 2 Thornycroft boilers, 2-shaft VQE, 1600ihp = 23kts. Coal 35.4t
Armament: 3-6pdr, 3-18in TT
Complement: 22

Name	Number	Builder	Laid down	Launched	Comm	Fate
CUSHING	TB1	Herreshoff	April 1888	23.1.90	22.4.90	Target sunk 1920

ERICSSON

Authorised under the Act of 30.6.1890. Two funnels far apart. One TT fixed forward and two training mounted well aft.

Displacement: 120t
Dimensions: 149ft 7in oa x 15ft 6in x 4ft 9in mean (*45.59 oa x 4.73 x 1.45m*)
Machinery: 2 Thornycroft boilers, 2-shaft VQE, 1800ihp = 24kts. Coal 35.4t
Armament: 4-1pdr, 3-18in TT
Complement: 22

Name	Number	Builder	Laid down	Launched	Comm	Fate
ERICSSON	TB2	Iowa Iron Wks	21.7.1892	12.5.94	18.2.97	Target sunk 1912

FOOTE class

Authorised under the Act of 26.7.1894. Two funnels far apart. Three single TT, to port and starboard of fore funnel and far aft. *Foote* renamed Coast Torpedo Boat No 1 and *Rodgers* No 2, August 1918.

Displacement: 142t
Dimensions: 160ft oa x 16ft 1in x 5ft mean (*48.76 oa x 4.91 x 1.52m*)
Machinery: 2 Thornycroft boilers *Foote*; 2 Mosher *Rodgers*, *Winslow*, 2-shaft VTE, 2000ihp = 25kts. Coal 44t
Armament: 3-1pdr, 3-18in TT
Complement: 20

Name	Number	Builder	Laid down	Launched	Comm	Fate
FOOTE	TB3	Columbian Iron Wks	1.5.1896	1.10.96	7. 8.97	Sold 1920
RODGERS	TB4	Columbian Iron Wks	6.5.1896	10.11.96	2. 4.98	Sold 1920
WINSLOW	TB5	Columbian Iron Wks	8.5.1896	6. 1.97	29.12.97	Sold 1911

PORTER class

Authorised under the Act of 2.3.1895. Three funnels, the second and third far apart. Three single TT, to port and starboard of forward funnels and far aft. *Du Pont* renamed Coast Torpedo Boat No 3 in August 1918.

Displacement: 165t
Dimensions: 175ft 6in oa x 17ft 9in x 4ft 8in mean (*53.50 oa x 5.41 x 1.42m*)
Machinery: 3 Normand boilers, 2-shaft VQE, 3200ihp = 27.5kts. Coal 76t
Armament: 4-1pdr, 3-18in TT
Complement: 24

Name	Number	Builder	Laid down	Launched	Comm	Fate
PORTER	TB6	Herreshoff	Feb 1896	9.9.96	20.2.97	Sold 1912
DU PONT	TB7	Herreshoff	Feb 1896	30.3.97	23.9.97	Sold 1920

ROWAN

Authorised under the Act of 2.3.1895. Funnels and TT arranged as in *Porter* class, but had raised forecastle. Stricken from navy 29.10.1912 but not sold until 1918.

Displacement: 182t
Dimensions: 170ft oa x 17ft x 6ft mean (*51.82 oa x 5.18 x 1.83m*)
Machinery: 3 Mosher boilers, 2-shaft VQE, 3200ihp = 26kts. Coal 62t
Armament: 4-1pdr, 3-18in TT
Complement: 24

Name	Number	Builder	Laid down	Launched	Comm	Fate
ROWAN	TB8	Moran	22.6.1896	8.4.98	1.4.99	Sold 1918

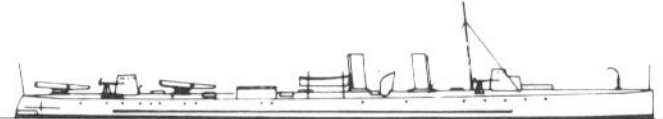
Dahlgren as completed 1900

DAHLGREN class

Authorised under the Act of 10.6.1896. Two funnels not far apart. Two single TT, aft and far aft. *Dahlgren* renamed Coast Torpedo Boat No 4, August 1918.

Displacement: 146t
Dimensions: 151ft 4in oa x 16ft 5in x 4ft 8in mean (*46.13 oa x 5.01 x 1.42m*)
Machinery: 2 Normand boilers, 2-shaft VTE, 4200ihp = 31kts. Coal 32t
Armament: 4-1pdr, 2-18in TT
Complement: 29

Name	Number	Builder	Laid down	Launched	Comm	Fate
DAHLGREN	TB9	Bath Iron Wks	11.12.1897	29.5.99	16.6.1900	Sold 1920
CRAVEN	TB10	Bath Iron Wks	6.12.1897	25.9.99	9.6.1900	Target 1913

DAVIS class

Authorised under the Act of 10.6.1896. Two funnels far apart, three single TT to port and starboard, and far aft. *Davis* finally decommissioned 28.3.1913, but not sold till 1920.

Displacement: 155t
Dimensions: 148ft oa x 15ft 4in x 5ft 10in mean (*45.11 oa x 4.68 x 1.78m*)
Machinery: 2 Thornycroft boilers, 2-shaft VTE, 1750ihp = 23kts. Coal 40t
Armament: 3-1pdr, 3-18in TT
Complement: 24

Name	Number	Builder	Laid down	Launched	Comm	Fate
DAVIS	TB12	Wolff & Zwicker	2.3.1897	4.6.98	10.5.99	Sold 1920
FOX	TB13	Wolff & Zwicker	4.3.1897	4.7.98	8.7.99	Sold 1916

Authorised under the Act of 10.6.1896. Served mostly as torpedo range tender. Two funnels not far apart. Three single TT to port and starboard, and far aft. Renamed Coast Torpedo Boat No 6, August 1918.

MORRIS

Displacement: 105t
Dimensions: 139ft 6in oa x 15ft 6in x 4ft 1in mean *(42.53 oa x 4.73 x 1.24m)*
Machinery: 2 Normand boilers, 2-shaft VTE, 1750ihp = 23kts. Coal 26t
Armament: 3-1pdr, 3-18in TT
Complement: 26

Name	Number	Builder	Laid down	Launched	Comm	Fate
MORRIS	TB14	Herreshoff	19.11.1897	13.4.98	11.5.98	Sold 1924

Authorised under the Act of 10.6.1896. Single funnel, two single TT forward of funnel and far aft. *Gwin* decommissioned and used as ferry April 1914, later under name *Cyane. Talbot* was used for oil fuel trials in 1900.

TALBOT class

Displacement: 46t
Dimensions: 100ft oa x 12ft 6in x 3ft 3in mean *(30.48 oa x 3.81 x 0.99m)*
Machinery: 1 Normand boiler, 1-shaft VTE, 850ihp = 20kts. Coal 9t
Armament: 1-1pdr, 2-18in TT
Complement: 12

Name	Number	Builder	Laid down	Launched	Comm	Fate
TALBOT	TB15	Herreshoff	8.4.1897	14.11.97	4.4.98	Ferry 1912
GWIN	TB16	Herreshoff	14.4.1897	15.11.97	4.4.98	Sold 1925

Authorised under the Act of 10.6.1896. Two funnels not far apart. Two single TT forward of funnels and far aft.

MACKENZIE class

Displacement: 65t
Dimensions: 101ft 6in oa x 12ft 9in x 4ft 3in mean *(30.94 oa x 3.89 x 1.29m)*
Machinery: 2 Thornycroft boilers, 1-shaft VTE, 850ihp = 20kts. Coal 15t
Armament: 1-1pdr *Mackenzie*; 2-1pdr *McKee*, 2-18in TT
Complement: 12

Name	Number	Builder	Laid down	Launched	Comm	Fate
MACKENZIE	TB17	Charles Hillman	15.4.1897	19.2.98	1.5.99	Target 1916
MCKEE	TB18	Columbian Iron Wks	11.9.1897	5.3.98	16.5.98	Target 1912–20

Built by Schichau as a private speculation and purchased 25.3.1898. Single funnel and three masts. Two training deck TT and one submerged bow TT. Crossed the Atlantic on board SS *Manhattan*. In August 1918 renamed Coast Torpedo Boat No 9.

SOMERS

Displacement: 143t
Dimensions: 156ft oa x 17ft 6in x 5ft 10in mean *(47.55 oa x 5.33 x 1.78m)*
Machinery: 1 Loco boiler, 1-shaft VQE, 1700ihp = 23kts. Coal 37t
Armament: 4-1pdr, 3-18in TT
Complement: 24

Name	Number	Builder	Laid down	Launched	Comm	Fate
SOMERS	TB22	Schichau	—	1897	26.3.98	Sold 1920

Authorised under the Act of 4.5.1898. Two funnels far apart. Three single TT to port and starboard, between funnels and far aft. Renamed Coast Torpedo Boat No 10, No 11, No 12 respectively in August 1918.

BAGLEY class

Displacement: 168t
Dimensions: 157ft oa x 17ft x 5ft mean *(47.85 oa x 5.18 x 1.52m)*
Machinery: 2 Normand boilers, 2-shaft VTE, 4200ihp = 28kts. Coal 47t
Armament: 3-1pdr, 3-18in TT
Complement: 29

Name	Number	Builder	Laid down	Launched	Comm	Fate
BAGLEY	TB24	Bath Iron Wks	4.1.1900	25.9.00	18.10.01	Sold 1919
BARNEY	TB25	Bath Iron Wks	3.1.1900	28.7.00	21.10.01	Sold 1920
BIDDLE	TB26	Bath Iron Wks	21.2.1900	18.5.01	26.10.01	Sold 1920

Barney at Camden, NJ in 1908

BLAKELY class

Authorised under the Act of 4.5.1898. Three funnels with the second and third far apart. Three single TT to port and starboard between second and third funnels and far aft. *Blakely* renamed Coast Torpedo Boat No 13 and *De Long* No 14, August 1918.

Note. *Manley*, TB23, a 30-ton 17-kt Yarrow boat, purchased 13.4.1898, does not appear to have had any armament.

Displacement: 196t
Dimensions: 175ft oa x 17ft x 5ft 11in mean (*53.35 oa x 5.18 x 1.80m*)
Machinery: 3 Normand boilers, 2-shaft VTE, 3000ihp = 26kts. Coal 72t
Armament: 3-1pdr, 3-18in TT
Complement: 28 *Blakely*; 29 *De Long*

Name	Number	Builder	Laid down	Launched	Comm	Fate
BLAKELY	TB27	George Lawley	12.1.1899	22.11.1900	27.12.04	Sold 1920
DE LONG	TB28	George Lawley	24.1.1899	23.11.1900	27.10.02	Sold 1920

NICHOLSON class

Authorised under the Act of 4.5.1898. Funnels and TT arranged as in *Blakely* class.

Displacement: 218t *Nicholson*; 220t *O'Brien*
Dimensions: 175ft oa x 17ft x 6ft 5in *Nicholson*; 6ft 6in *O'Brien* mean (*53.35 oa x 5.18 x 1.96; 1.98m*)
Machinery: 3 Mosher boilers, 2-shaft VTE, 3000ihp = 25kts. Coal 80t
Armament: 3-1pdr, 3-18in TT
Complement: 28

Name	Number	Builder	Laid down	Launched	Comm	Fate
NICHOLSON	TB29	Lewis Nixon	6.12.1898	23.9.1901	10.1.05	Target 1909
O'BRIEN	TB30	Lewis Nixon	29.12.1898	24.9.1900	15.7.05	Target 1909

SHUBRICK class

Authorised under the Act of 4.5.1898. Funnels and TT arranged as in *Blakely* class. *Shubrick* renamed Coast Torpedo Boat No 15, August 1918, and *Thornton* Coast Torpedo Boat No 16. *Stockton* stricken from the navy 15.11.1913.

Displacement: 200t
Dimensions: 175ft oa x 17ft 8in x 6ft 2in (*53.35 oa x 5.38 x 1.88m*)
Machinery: 3 Thornycroft boilers, 2-shaft VTE, 3375ihp = 25kts (26kts *Shubrick*). Coal 82t *Shubrick*; 80t *Stockton*; 96t *Thornton*
Armament: 3-3pdr (3-1pdr *Shubrick*), 3-18in TT
Complement: 29 (28 *Shubrick*)

Name	Number	Builder	Laid down	Launched	Comm	Fate
SHUBRICK	TB31	WR Trigg	11.3.1899	31.10.99	1901	Sold 1920
STOCKTON	TB32	WR Trigg	18.3.1899	27.12.99	14.3.1901	Target 1914–16
THORNTON	TB33	WR Trigg	16.3.1899	15. 5.1900	9.6.02	Sold 1920

TINGEY

Authorised under the Act of 4.5.1898. Funnels and TT arranged as in *Blakely* class.

Displacement: 165t
Dimensions: 175ft oa x 17ft 8in x 4ft 8in mean (*53.35 oa x 5.38 x 1.42m*)
Machinery: 3 Thornycroft boilers, 2-shaft VTE, 3000ihp = 25kts. Coal 70t
Armament: 3-1pdr, 3-18in TT
Complement: 29

Name	Number	Builder	Laid down	Launched	Comm	Fate
TINGEY	TB34	Columbian Iron Wks	29.3.1899	25.3.1901	7.1.04	Sold 1920

WILKES

Authorised under the Act of 4.5.1898. Funnels and TT arranged as in *Blakely* class.

Displacement: 175t
Dimensions: 175ft oa x 17ft 8in x 4ft 8in mean (*53.35 oa x 5.38 x 1.42m*)
Machinery: 3 Seabury boilers, 2-shaft VTE, 3000ihp = 27kts. Coal 66t
Armament: 3-1pdr, 3-18in TT
Complement: 29

Name	Number	Builder	Laid down	Launched	Comm	Fate
WILKES	TB35	Gas Engine & Power and CL Seabury	3.6.1899	28.9.1901	18.9.02	Sold 1914

PATROL GUNBOATS and other minor warships

Dolphin with rig reduced to two light pole masts

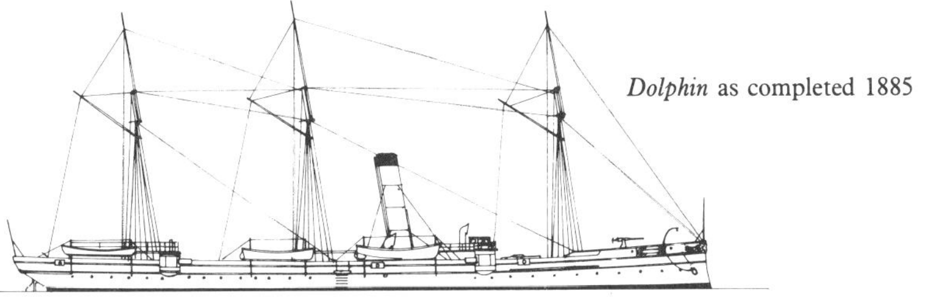

Dolphin as completed 1885

Authorised under the Act of 3.3.1883. The first ship of the 'New Navy' and usually classified as a despatch boat, *Dolphin* was originally given a light barque rig with no head gear, and was later rigged as a three-masted schooner, before reducing to two masts. For much of her career from 1899 *Dolphin* served as a despatch vessel for the secretary of the navy. Her 6in was on an upper deck traversing mounting just abaft the foremast, and was later replaced by 2-4in/40, one on each side, the smaller guns being 1-6pdr, 6-3pdr.

DOLPHIN *despatch vessel*

Displacement: 1486t
Dimensions: 256ft 6in oa x 32ft x 14ft 3in mean *(78.18 oa x 9.75 x 4.35m)*
Machinery: 4 cyl boilers, 1-shaft VC, 2255ihp = 16kts. Coal 265t
Armament: 1-6in/30, 2-6pdr, 4-47mm revolvers
Complement: 152

Name	Number	Builder	Laid down	Launched	Comm	Fate
DOLPHIN	—	John Roach	1883	12.4.84	8.12.85	Sold 1922

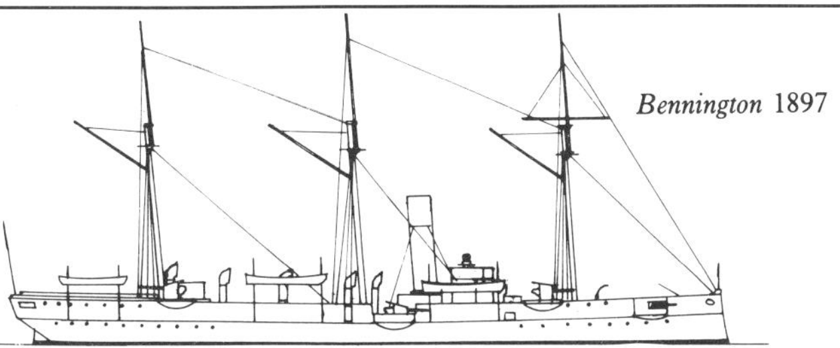

Bennington 1897

Authorised under the Act of 3.3.85 *Yorktown* and the other two under that of 3.3.87. These ships were originally rigged as three-masted schooners with no head gear, and were classed as cruisers in official British lists resembling the *Archer* class in some ways. The 6in guns were in small sponsons, fore and aft on the upper and amidships on the main deck. There was a 2in CT. The armament was eventually reduced and *Yorktown*, in 1919, had 6-5in/40. *Bennington* had a disastrous burst of two boilers in 1905 and was not recommissioned, while *Concord* served as an accommodation ship from 1909 to 1914 and then as a quarantine station vessel under the Treasury until 1929.

YORKTOWN class *patrol gunboats*

Displacement: 1710t (1921 full load)
Dimensions: 244ft 6in oa x 36ft x 14ft mean *(74.52 oa x 10.97 x 4.27m)*
Machinery: 4 cyl boilers, 2-shaft HTE, 3400ihp = 16kts. Coal 200/370t
Armament: 6-6in/30, 2 to 4-6pdr, nil to 2-3pdr, nil to 4-1pdr
Complement: 187–201

Name	Number	Builder	Laid down	Launched	Comm	Fate
YORKTOWN	PG1	Cramp	14.5.1887	28.4.88	23.4.89	Sold 1921
CONCORD	PG3	NF Palmer	May 1888	8.3.90	14.2.91	Sold 1929
BENNINGTON	PG4	Delaware River Iron Wks	May 1888	3.6.90	20.6.91	Sold 1910

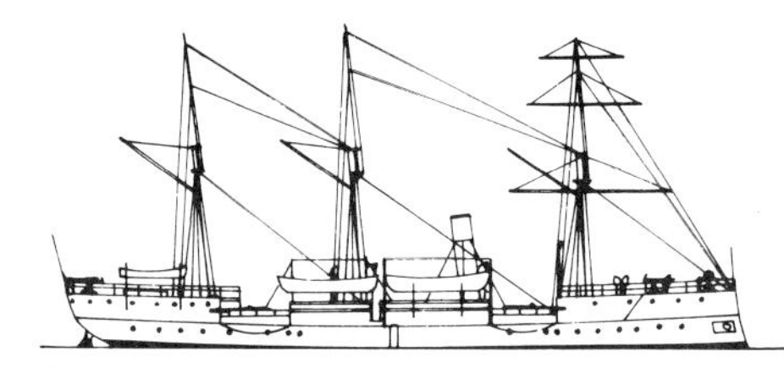

Petrel 1890

PETREL *patrol gunboat*

Authorised under the Act of 3.3.1885. Originally rigged as a barquentine with no head gear, the mainmast was later removed, and the 6in replaced by 4-4in/40. These guns were mounted in sponsons between the forecastle and poop.

Displacement: 867t
Dimensions: 188ft oa x 31ft x 11ft 6in mean (*57.30 oa x 9.44 x 3.50m*)
Machinery: 4 cyl boilers, 1-shaft HC, 1000ihp = 11.4kts. Coal 125/200t
Armament: 4-6in/30, 2-3pdr, 2-1pdr
Complement: 138

Name	Number	Builder	Laid down	Launched	Comm	Fate
PETREL	PG2	Columbia Iron Wks	27.8.1887	13.10.88	10.12.89	Sold 1920

BANCROFT *patrol gunboat*

Authorised under the Act of 7.9.1888. Originally barquentine-rigged; the 4in guns were mounted to port and starboard between forecastle and poop. Became the Revenue Cutter *Itasca*. TT were removed in 1899.

Displacement: 839t
Dimensions: 189ft oa x 32ft x 12ft 2in mean (*57.61 oa x 9.75 x 3.71m*)
Machinery: 2 cyl boilers, 2-shaft VTE, 1200ihp = 14.5kts. Coal 100/139t
Armament: 4-4in/40, 8-3pdr, 1-1pdr, 2-18in TT aw
Complement: 123/148

Name	Number	Builder	Laid down	Launched	Comm	Fate
BANCROFT	—	SL Moore	Feb 1891	30.4.92	3.3.93	To Revenue Cutter Service 1906

MACHIAS class *patrol gunboats*

Authorised under the Act of 2.3.1889. Cut in half and lengthened by 14ft to correct instability, this class consisted of single-funnelled, two-masted ships, usually rated as sloops outside the USA. Two of the 4in guns were fore and aft, while six were in main deck sponsons with 2in protection. *Castine* served as a submarine tender 1908-1913, and the 4in guns were eventually reduced to two or four in both, and they were reboilered with Normand boilers. *Machias* was named *Agua Prieta* by the Mexicans and disposed of in 1935.

Displacement: 1177t (1318 full load)
Dimensions: 204ft oa x 32ft 1in x 12ft mean (*62.18 oa x 9.77 x 3.66m*)
Machinery: 2 loco boilers, 2-shaft VTE, 1900ihp = 15.5kts. Coal 125/250-290t
Armament: 8-4in/40, 4-6pdr, 2-1pdr
Complement: 154

Name	Number	Builder	Laid down	Launched	Comm	Fate
MACHIAS	PG5	Bath Iron Wks	Feb 1891	8.12.91	20. 7.93	Sold to Mexico 29.10.1920
CASTINE	PG6	Bath Iron Wks	Feb 1891	11. 5.92	22.10.94	Sold 1921

Castine, date unknown

NASHVILLE *patrol gunboat*

Authorised under the Act of 3.3.1893. Distinguished by two tall funnels and two masts. *Nashville* had 2-4in forward and two aft on the upper deck, and four in main deck sponsons with 2¼in protection. Except in the USA she was usually classed as a sloop.

Displacement: 1371t (1719 full load)
Dimensions: 233ft 8in oa x 38ft 1in x 11ft mean (*71.22 oa x 11.60 x 3.35m*)
Machinery: 4 Yarrow 2-cyl boilers, 2-shaft VQE, 2530ihp = 16.3kts. Coal 150/395t
Armament: 8-4in/40, 4-6pdr, 2-1pdr
Complement: 180

Name	Number	Builder	Laid down	Launched	Comm	Fate
NASHVILLE	PG7	Newport News	9.8.1894	19.10.95	19.8.97	Sold 1921

Nashville CPL

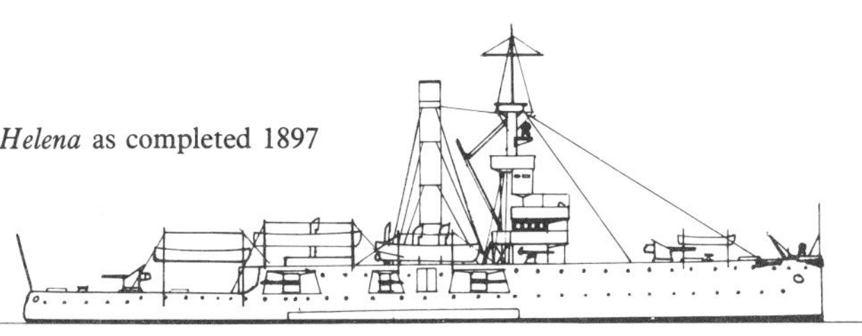
Helena as completed 1897

Wilmington CPL

WILMINGTON class *patrol gunboats*

Displacement: 1397t (1689 full load)
Dimensions: 250ft 9in oa x 40ft 11in x 9ft mean (*76.42 oa x 12.47 x 2.74m*)
Machinery: 6 cyl boilers, 2-shaft VTE, 1900ihp = 15kts. Coal 100/277t
Armament: 8-4in/40, 4-6pdr, 4-1pdr
Complement: 183/199

Name	Number	Builder	Laid down	Launched	Comm	Fate
WILMINGTON	PG8	Newport News	8.10.1894	19.10.95	13.5.97	Sold 1946
HELENA	PG9	Newport News	11.10.1894	30. 1.96	8.7.97	Sold 1932

Authorised under the Act of 2.3.1893. Single-masted ships, rated as sloops in British lists, with one tall funnel, and were cut down to the main deck aft. Two of the 4in guns were on the upper deck forward with two aft and four amidships on the main deck. The latter had 1½in protection and there was a strip of 1in amidships on the wl. Their draught was shallower than in other US gunboats of their size. *Wilmington* was latterly a training ship, and in the Second World War was renamed *Dover* and numbered IX-30.

ANNAPOLIS class *patrol gunboats*

Displacement: 1000–1153t
Dimensions: 204ft 5in oa, 168ft wl x 36ft x 12ft–12ft 9in mean (*62.31 oa, 51.21 wl x 10.97 x 3.66-3.89m*)
Machinery: 2 cyl boilers (2 Babcock & Wilcox *Annapolis*) 1-shaft VTE, 1000ihp = 11–13kts. Coal 100/235t (/324 *Annapolis*)
Armament: 6-4in/40, 4-6pdr, 2-1pdr
Complement: 135/156

Name	Number	Builder	Laid down	Launched	Comm	Fate
ANNAPOLIS	PG10	Lewis Nixon	April 1896	23.12.96	20. 7.97	To Maritime Commission 1940
VICKSBURG	PG11	Bath Iron Wks	Mar 1896	5.12.96	23.10.97	To Coast Guard 1921
NEWPORT	PG12	Bath Iron Wks	Mar 1896	5.12.96	5.10.97	Disposed of 1934
PRINCETON	PG13	JH Dialogue	May 1896	3. 6.97	27. 5.98	Sold 1919

Authorised under the Act of 2.3.95. Originally barquentine-rigged with a clipper bow and long bowsprit, this class consisted of composite-built vessels, rated as sloops in British lists. The 4in guns were mounted fore and aft on the upper deck with four amidships on the main deck; reductions were later made though *Annapolis* and *Vicksburg* are listed with 6-4in in 1919. *Annapolis* served as a training ship from 1920 onwards, as did *Newport* from 1907 to 1931. *Vicksburg* was renamed *Alexander Hamilton* by the Coast Guard.

Authorised under the Act of 2.3.1895. These vessels were single-funnelled, two-masted, composite-built, and were rated as sloops in British lists. The 4in guns were mounted one forward and one aft on the upper deck with four amidships on the main deck. The armament was later reduced to four 4in. *Wheeling* was latterly employed as a training ship and numbered IX-28 in the Second World War.

WHEELING class *patrol gunboats*

Displacement: 1000t (1170 full load)
Dimensions: 189ft 7in oa x 34ft x 12ft mean *(57.79 oa x 10.36 x 3.66m)*
Machinery: 2 Babcock & Wilcox boilers *Marietta*; 2 cyl *Wheeling*, 2-shaft VTE, 1050ihp = 13kts. Coal 120/231t
Armament: 6-4in/40, 4-6pdr, 2-1pdr
Complement: 140

Name	Number	Builder	Laid down	Launched	Comm	Fate
WHEELING	PG14	Union Iron Wks	11.4.1896	18.3.97	10.8.97	Sold 1946
MARIETTA	PG15	Union Iron Wks	13.4.1896	18.3.97	1.9.97	Sold 1920

Purchased 2.4.1898 as the *Diogenes* from Thames Iron Works, *Topeka* was a two-funnel, iron-hulled steamer, which in British lists was classed as an unarmoured cruiser, presumably because of her displacement. Her 4in guns were later reduced to six.

Note. Gunboat No 16 authorised under the Act of 4.5. 1898 was never built.

TOPEKA *patrol gunboat*

Displacement: 2372t
Dimensions: 250ft wl x 35ft x 17ft 9in mean *(76.19 oa x 10.66 x 5.41m)*
Machinery: 4 cyl boilers, 2-shaft HC 2200ihp = 16kts. Coal 273/394t
Armament: 8-4in/40, 2-6pdr, 4-3pdr, 2-1pdr
Complement: 152

Name	Number	Builder	Launched	Comm	Fate
TOPEKA	—	Howaldt, Kiel	1881	June 1898	Prison Ship 1907

Scuttled by the Spaniards at the Battle of Manila and salved, this ship had the 4in guns on forecastle and poop and a 2½in-1in deck. Reboilered with Babcock & Wilcox boilers in 1911, she served with the Louisiana and Illinois Naval Militia 1903–1918, and finally with the Naval Torpedo Station as a yard craft.

ISLA DE LUZON *gunboat*

Displacement: 1020t
Dimensions: 195ft oa x 30ft x 11ft 4¾in mean *(59.43 oa x 9.14 x 3.47m)*
Machinery: 2 cyl boilers, 2-shaft HTE, 535ihp = 11.2kts. Coal 160t
Armament: 4-4in/40, 4-6pdr, 3-14in TT aw
Complement: 137

Name	Number	Builder	Launched	Comm	Fate
ISLA DE LUZON	—	Armstrong	1887	31.1.1900	Sold 1920

Scuttled by the Spaniards at the Battle of Manila and salved, this ship was generally similar to the *Isla de Luzon*. She was renamed *Mariscal Sucre* by Venezuela and survived until 1940.

ISLA DE CUBA *gunboat*

Displacement: 950t
Dimensions: 197ft oa x 30ft x 10ft 7in mean *(60.04 oa x 9.14 x 3.22m)*
Machinery: 2 cyl boilers, 2-shaft HTE, 800ihp = 13kts. Coal 160t
Armament: 4-4in/40, 4-6pdr, 3-14in TT aw
Complement: 137

Name	Number	Builder	Launched	Comm	Fate
ISLA DE CUBA	—	Armstrong	1886	11.4.1900	Sold to Venezuela 2.4.12

Sunk at the Battle of Manila and salved, *Don Juan de Austria* had her 5in guns in main deck sponsons. Her armament was changed and eventually 4-4in were mounted. She served with the Michigan Naval Militia from 1907 until 1917.

DON JUAN DE AUSTRIA *gunboat*

Displacement: 1015t
Dimensions: 215ft 6in oa x 32ft x 12ft 6in mean *(65.68 oa x 9.75 x 3.81m)*
Machinery: 4 cyl boilers, 1-shaft HC, 1200ihp = 12kts. Coal 225t
Armament: 4-5in/40, 4-6pdr
Complement: 153

Name	Number	Builder	Launched	Comm	Fate
DON JUAN DE AUSTRIA	—	Cartagena	1887	11.4.1900	Sold 1919

Paducah, date unknown

Authorised under the Act of 1.7.1902, these vessels were two-funnelled, two-masted, composite-built, with a bowsprit, rated as sloops in British lists. The 4in guns were mounted to port and starboard on the upper deck. Both served on the Great Lakes with a reduced armament from 1922 to 1940–1941, training Naval Reservists, and during the Second World War they were employed training armed guards for merchant ships, and were numbered respectively IX-9 and IX-23.

DUBUQUE class *patrol gunboats*

Displacement: 1084t
Dimensions: 200ft 5in oa, 174ft wl x 35ft x 13ft 4in mean (*61.09 oa, 53.04 wl x 10.66 x 4.07m*)
Machinery: 2 Babcock & Wilcox boilers, 2-shaft VTE, 1250ihp = 13kts. Coal 200t
Armament: 6-4in/50 Mk 7, 4-6pdr, 2-1pdr
Complement: 184–198

Name	Number	Builder	Laid down	Launched	Comm	Fate
DUBUQUE	PG17	Gas Engine & Power	22.9.1903	15. 8.04	3.6.05	Sold 1946
PADUCAH	PG18	and CL Seabury	22.9.1903	11.10.04	2.9.05	Sold 1946

SMALL GUNBOATS

A number of small ex-Spanish gunboats were taken over in the Philippine Islands, and two, *Alvarado* and *Sandoval* in Cuba, as a result of the Spanish-American war. Those of 100t displacement or more, are listed in alphabetical order:

Name	Builder	Launched	Comm	Fate	Displacement (tons)	Speed (kts)	Armament
ALBAY	Hong Kong & Whampoa	1886	21.5.1899	Sold 1906	173	8	1-6pdr, 2-1pdr
ALVARADO	Clydebank	1895	4. 8.1898	Sold 1912	106	19	1-6pdr, 1-1pdr
ARAYAT	Manila Ship Co	1888	10. 8.1900	Sold 1910	243	9	1-6pdr, 1-3pdr
CALAMIANES	Cavite DYd	1888	25. 7.1899	Sold 1907	173	8	1-3pdr, 2-1pdr
CALLAO	Manila Ship Co	1888	2. 7.1898	Sold 1923	243	10	4-3pdr, 2-1pdr
ELCANO	Carraca	1885	20.11.1902	Target 1928	620	11	4-4in/40
LEYTE	Hong Kong & Whampoa	1887	22. 3.1900	Sold 1907	151	8	1-6pdr, 2-1pdr
MANILENO	Hong Kong & Whampoa	1885	25. 5.1899	Sold 1906	142	6.5	1-6pdr, 2-1pdr
MARIVELES	Hong Kong & Whampoa	1886	17. 6.1899	Sold 1909	170	7	1-3pdr, 2-1pdr
MINDORO	Hong Kong & Whampoa	1886	12. 6.1899	Sold 1912	142	7	1-3pdr, 1-1pdr
PAMPANGA	Manila Ship Co	1888	9.11.1899	Target 1928	243	10	1-6pdr, 3-3pdr
PANAY	Cavite DYd	1885	3. 6.1899	Sold 1920	162	8	1-6pdr, 2-1pdr
PARAGUA	Manila Ship Co	1888	29. 5.1899	Sold 1911	243	10	1-6pdr, 3-3pdr, 2-1pdr
QUIROS	Hong Kong & Whampoa	1895	14. 3.1900	Target 1923	350	11	2-6pdr, 2-3pdr
SAMAR	Manila Ship Co	1887	26. 5.1899	Sold 1921	243	10.5	1-6pdr, 1-3pdr, 2-1pdr
SANDOVAL	Clydebank	1895	2. 9.1898	Sold 1919	106	19	2-3pdr
VILLALOBOS	Hong Kong & Whampoa	1895	5. 3.1900	Target 1933	370	11	2-6pdr, 2-3pdr, 2-1pdr

Although these gunboats were useful for maintaining order in the Philippines, only *Elcano* had any fighting value:

	Dimensions	Shafts	ihp	Coal	Complement
ELCANO	165ft 6in x 26ft x 10ft (50.44 x 7.93 x 3.05m)	2	c 600	98t	103

Was based at Shanghai for most of her career, and took part in the fighting at Nanking in 1927.

ARMED MERCHANT CRUISERS

A number of merchant ships and yachts were taken up during the Spanish-American war and some were purchased by the navy. The most important were four fast liners belonging to the International Navigation Company:

ST LOUIS and ST PAUL

Displacement: 14,910t
Dimensions: 554ft x 63ft x 25ft (*168.86 x 19.20 x 7.62m*)
Machinery: cyl boilers, 2-shaft VQE, 20,000ihp = 22kts. Coal 2677t
Armament: 4-5in/40, 8-6pdr *St Louis*; 6-5in/40, 6-6pdr, 6-3pdr *St Paul*
Complement: 377 *St Louis*; 381 *St Paul*

Name	Builder	Launched	Comm in Navy	Fate
ST LOUIS	Cramp	12.11.1894	24.4.98	Returned to owners 2.9.98
ST PAUL	Cramp	10. 4.1895	20.4.98	Returned to owners 2.9.98

These were of the two-funnelled, two-masted, straight stem and counter stern type, popular at the time. *St Louis* was equipped with heavy drag lines for cutting cables, while *St Paul* engaged and drove off the Spanish destroyer *Terror* at San Juan 22.6.1898, and was later used as a transport. She rammed and sank the British cruiser *Gladiator* in a collision in the Solent 25.4.1908. Subsequently *St Louis* was used as a transport under the name of *Louisville* at the end of the First World War, and was burnt out while reconditioning in 1920, and eventually sold in 1925. *St Paul* was also used as a transport during the First World War, and capsized in the North River, New York, when being towed from dry dock on 28 April 1918. She was raised and reconditioned but was sold in 1923.

These vessels were three-, then later two-funnelled and three-masted, with clipper bows, and were built as *City of New York* and *City of Paris* for the Inman Line, transferring to American registry in 1893, 'City of' being dropped from their names which were again changed while commissioned. Used as scouts and then as transports during the Spanish-American war. *Paris* ran aground on the Manacles in 1899 and on refit was named *Philadelphia*. They were again used as transports in the First World War, named respectively *Plattsburg* and *Harrisburg*, and returned to their owners in 1919, and were sold and eventually scrapped in 1923.

HARVARD and YALE

Displacement: 13,000t
Dimensions: 585ft x 63ft 3in x 23ft (*178.31 x 19.28 x 7.0m*)
Machinery: cyl boilers, 2-shaft VTE, 20,600ihp = 21.8kts. Coal 2656t
Armament: 8-5in/40, 8-6pdr *Harvard*; 8-5in/40, 4-6pdr, 4-3pdr *Yale*
Complement: 407

Name	Builder	Launched	Comm in Navy	Fate
HARVARD	J & G Thompson	1888	26.4.98	Returned to owners 2.9.98
YALE	J & G Thompson	1888	2.5.98	Returned to owners 2.9.98

The remaining armed merchant ships were all slower, and their particulars were as follows:

Name	Former Name	Builder	Launched	Comm	Fate	Displacement (tons)
BADGER	YUMURI	John Roach	1889	25.4.98	To War Dept 1900	4784
BUFFALO	EL CID then NICTHEROY	Newport News	1892	22.9.98	Training Ship 1900	6888
DIXIE	EL RIO	Newport News	1893	19.4.98	Training Ship 1900	6114
PANTHER	AUSTIN	Cramp	1889	22.4.98	Training Ship 1902	4260
PRAIRIE	EL SOL	Cramp	1890	8.4.98	Training Ship 1901	6872
YANKEE	EL NORTE	Newport News	1892	14.4.98	Sank in tow 4.12.1908	6888
YOSEMITE	EL SUD	Newport News	1892	13.4.98	Foundered 13.11.1900	6179

Name	Dimensions	Shafts	ihp	Speed (kts)	Coal (tons)	Armament	Complement
BADGER	329ft 7in x 42ft x 18ft 6in (*100.45 x 12.80 x 5.64m*)	1	3200	16	836	6-5in/40, 6-3pdr	235
BUFFALO	406ft 1in x 48ft 3in x 22ft (*123.76 x 14.70 x 6.70m*)	1	3600	14.5	1000	2-5in/40, 4-4in/40, 6-6pdr	297
DIXIE	391ft 6in x 48ft 3in x 19ft 11in (*119.33 x 14.70 x 6.07m*)	1	3800	16	1371	10-6in/30, 6-6pdr	181
PANTHER	324ft 4in x 40ft 6in x 18ft 3in (*98.86 x 12.34 x 5.56m*)	1	3200	13	475	6-5in/40, 2-4in/40, 6-3pdr	198
PRAIRIE	404ft 9in x 48ft 3in x 22ft (*123.36 x 14.70 x 6.70m*)	1	3800	14.5	1000	10-6in/30, 6-6pdr	285
YANKEE	406ft 1in x 48ft 3in x 22ft (*123.76 x 14.70 x 6.70m*)	1	3800	14.5	1000	10-5in/40, 6-6pdr	282
YOSEMITE	391ft 6in x 48ft 3in x 20ft 1in (*119.33 x 14.70 x 6.12m*)	1	3800	16	1371	10-5in/40, 6-6pdr	285

Badger, renamed *Lawton* by War Department was returned to the navy in 1902 as a supply ship, and to mercantile service in 1907, became a barge in 1930. *Buffalo*, as *Nictheroy* took part in the Brazilian Civil War of 1893–1894 when she mounted a 15in Zalinsky gun, she was a transport 1906–1917, destroyer tender (AD-8) 1918–1922, then a barracks ship until sold in 1927. *Dixie* mainly as transport 1903–1907, then destroyer tender (AD-1) 1909–1922, until sold in 1922. *Panther* was a repair ship 1907–1917, then destroyer tender (AD-6) 1917–1922, until sold in 1923. *Prairie* served as a transport 1906–1907, then destroyer tender (AD-5) 1917–1922, until sold in 1923. *Yankee* training ship, transport, supply ship 1903–1908. Sank in Buzzards Bay after stranding. *Yosemite* foundered in a typhoon off Guam. *Panther, Prairie, Yankee* and *Yosemite* were iron-hulled, the others were steel-hulled.

ARMED YACHTS

Of the armed yachts, the most famous was the *Gloucester*, formerly Pierpont Morgan's *Corsair*, which took part in the Battle of Santiago, where her 6pdr guns were used with effect particularly against the destroyer *Pluton*. *Mayflower* served as Presidential Yacht from 1905 to 1929. Details of the eight most powerful yachts are given below:

Name	Builder	Launched	Comm	Fate
DOROTHEA	Cramp	1897	1.6.98	Sold 1919
EAGLE	Harlan & Hollingsworth	1890	5.4.98	Sold 1920
GLOUCESTER	Neafie & Levy	1891	23.4.98	Sold 1919
HORNET	Harlan & Hollingsworth	1890	12.4.98	Sold 1910
MAYFLOWER	J & G Thompson	1896	24.3.98	Sold 1931
SCORPION	JN Robins	1896	11.4.98	Sold 1929
VIXEN	Lewis Nixon	1896	11.4.98	Sold 1923
WASP	Cramp	1898	11.4.98	Sold 1920

Name	Dimensions	Displacement (tons)	ihp	Speed (kts)	Coal (tons)	Armament	Complement
DOROTHEA	182ft 4in x 23ft 5in x 11ft 6in *(55.57 x 7.14 x 3.51m)*	594	1558	15	90	4-6pdr, 2-3pdr, 4-1pdr	69
EAGLE	155ft 6in x 24ft x 11ft 6in *(47.39 x 7.32 x 3.51m)*	434	850 nominal	15.5	85	4-6pdr	64
GLOUCESTER	240ft 8in x 27ft 2in x 12ft *(73.35 x 8.28 x 3.66m)*	786	2000	17	120	4-6pdr, 4-3pdr	94
HORNET	180ft x 24ft x 11ft *(54.86 x 7.32 x 3.35m)*	425	800 nominal	15	65	3-6pdr, 2-1pdr, 2-37mm revolver	55
MAYFLOWER	273ft x 36ft x 17ft 3in *(83.21 x 10.97 x 5.26m)*	2690	4700	16.8	584	2-5in/40, 12-6pdr	171
SCORPION	212ft 10in x 28ft 1in x 11ft *(64.87 x 8.56 x 3.35m)*	850	2800	17.85	200	6-6pdr	111
VIXEN	200ft 3in x 28ft x 12ft 8in *(61 x 8.53 x 3.86m)*	806	1250	16	190	4-6pdr, 4-1pdr	82
WASP	180ft x 23ft x 12ft *(54.86 x 7.02 x 3.66m)*	630	1800	16.5	108	4-6pdr	55

All had VTE engines with one shaft except *Mayflower* and *Scorpion* which had two.

President Theodore Roosevelt addressing the officers and men of USS *Connecticut* after the cruise around the world by the Great White Fleet, 1908. This voyage finally established the USA as a Great Power of the first rank.

(All uncredited photos: USN official by courtesy of Norman Polmar)

Russia

RUSSIA AND THE RUSSIAN NAVY, 1860–1905

At first sight the power of Russia from 1860 to 1905 was not that to be expected from an empire with estimated populations of 74 million in 1859 and 146 million in 1905, and which extended from the Polish salient in 17°E to the Bering Strait 174° further east, with a total area in 1905 of 8,660,000 square miles, or one sixth of the earth's land surface. Considering the difficulties to be overcome it is remarkable, however, that so much was achieved. The population was very far from uniform, the 1897 census recording over 50 different races based on linguistic differences, the precise figure depending on how the various inhabitants of the Caucasus were classified. The great majority of the population was in European Russia, including Poland, Finland and Caucasia and only 10.5 per cent in the huge areas of Siberia and Central Asia. Russians, divided into Great, Little and White on linguistic grounds, totalled 65.5 per cent of the whole in the 1897 census. The urban population was less than 10 per cent in 1860, rising to 13 per cent for the whole empire in 1897, and at that time only 20 cities had more than 100,000 inhabitants.

This diverse population was governed by what can best be described as an inefficient autocracy headed by the Czar and his appointed ministers, and the post of prime minister was first created under the law of 1 November 1905. Whether under the relatively liberal rule of Alexander II in the 1860s, or under the stricter conditions of the later part of his reign and of his successors, Alexander III and Nicholas II, the system remained much the same, until the unrest arising from the disasters of the war with Japan forced the first steps towards a more constitutional regime in the autumn of 1905. Perhaps the worst failing of the system was the shortage of able and honest civil servants in the lower and middle grades, for though government employers proliferated, far too many were ignorant and bribable. This is not to say that Russia did not produce many able men, including noted scientists, and the universities had in general a high standard of learning, but the average educational level was low with illiteracy rates in 1897 of 45 to 89 per cent in the rural districts and 37 to 63 per cent in the towns.

With such a large country transport was a major problem and Russia was late in building railways. In 1860 the mileage was less than 1000, by 1885 16,155, by 1895 22,600 and in 1905 40,550 of which 6400 miles were in Asia, the total being less than a fifth of that in the USA. Among important strategic lines were those connecting the Trans-Caucasian line with the main Russian system, the Trans-Caspian line joining Krasnovodsk on the Caspian with Bokhara, Samarkand, Andijan and Tashkent, built in 1880 to 1888, and the line from Orenburg to Tashkent completed in 1905. The most important was however the Trans-Siberian. It was completed to Stryetensk at the head of the Amur basin navigation in 1901, except for the section round Lake Baikal which was not finished until 1905, but the 1400-mile section to Khabarovsk on the Amur which was linked to Vladivostock in 1898 was likely to be so expensive that in 1896 an agreement was made with China to build a line straight across Manchuria to Vladivostock, and this, together with an extension to Port Arthur and Dalny (Dairen) in the Liao Tung peninsula, leased from China in 1898, was completed by 1903. Initially the Tran-Siberian track was not well laid and travel was somewhat hazardous, but it was improved and served better than expected in the Russo-Japanese War.

The rivers and canals were an important means of transport, and traffic in 1904 amounted to nearly 39 million tons, an increase of over 66 per cent since 1894. Unfortunately this traffic was seriously interrupted by the rivers freezing, when they were used as sledge ways. The Volga froze for 150 days in its northern parts and for 90 days at Astrakhan, the Don froze for 100 to 110 days and the Dnieper for 83 to 122. Even the Vistula at Warsaw froze for 77 days. The great Siberian river systems, based on the Ob, Yenisei and Lena were more severely affected, the more southerly parts being iced up for five to seven months, and the lower Lena being open only for 70 days. The Amur which was confined to south-eastern Siberia was open to traffic for about seven months.

In these circumstances transport by sea was of great importance, particularly before the growth of the railway system, and it is interesting to read in the official report of the Russian dockyards for 1862, that by far the cheapest way to send stores from St Petersburg to the Black Sea was to ship them to London and tranship them there for the Black Sea. Russia had, however, only limited access to the open sea. The Baltic and Black Sea were almost landlocked, particularly the latter, and conditions on the long Arctic coast were so bad that only the White Sea at the western end was available for sea traffic, and Archangel, the chief port, was usually open only from May to October. The eastern Siberian coast bordered on the fog-bound Bering Sea and Sea of Okhotsk in its more northerly parts, and the principal port Vladivostock was well to the south.

Neglecting river craft the Russian mercantile marine was small and in 1904 totalled about 700,000 tons, of which 70 per cent was divided fairly equally between the giant lake of the Caspian Sea and the Black Sea. Only 8.3 per cent of the vessels that traded with Russian ports were Russian owned.

The main Russian industry was agriculture which since the liberation of the serfs in 1861 had largely been based on peasant farmers. The standards were not high but thanks to the wonderfully fertile soils of the black earth districts in European Russia and the more advanced methods of Poland, there was usually a large surplus of cereals for export principally to Germany and Great Britain. This gave the Russian Empire a favourable trade balance averaging about £37 million for the years 1902 to 1905. The mineral resources were very great but little developed. The chief fuel was wood, of which an estimated 170 million tons was used every year, and although Europe's largest coal field was located in the Donets basin, the total output of coal was less than 300,000 tons in 1860, 3,280,000 tons in 1880 and 18,620,000 tons in 1904 which was about one twelfth of the British figures at the time. The Baku oilfields had begun producing in the 1870s, and Russia was soon the world's second largest source of oil with an output of 10 to 11 million tons a year.

About two thirds of Russia's iron ore requirements were mined in the empire in 1904 when the output of pig iron was 2,900,000 tons and that

Slava coaling during a visit to Portsmouth

of wrought iron and steel 2,200,000 tons, most of the latter being used by the railways and the shipyards and armament industry. Growth had been fairly rapid as the 1891 output of pig iron was just under a million tons.

The ordinary revenue of the Russian empire amounted to £132,750,000 in 1895 and £214,360,000 in 1905 and was obtained from the state monopoly on the sale of spirits, and state railways, customs duties, trade licences, and various taxes and duties. There was usually a balance on ordinary revenue, but extraordinary expenditure on such matters as the Siberian railways and the Russo-Japanese War was mostly financed by loans. The national debt stood at £145,500,000 in 1862 and in 1892 at £526,109,000 rising to £812,040,000 in 1906 and was for the most part funded at 4 per cent.

The internal state of the Russian Empire was not always peaceful and apart from terrorist activities such as the assassination of Czar Alexander II in 1881, there was the Polish uprising of 1863–1864, caused by Russian repression, and the insurrection in the Caucasus in 1904–1905, during which many of the Baku oil wells were burnt. Some territorial adjustments were made. The whole of Alaska including the Aleutian Islands was sold to the USA in 1867 for $7,200,000, one of the most remarkable transactions in history, and in 1875 a convention was made with Japan under which the Russians withdrew from the Kurile Islands and the Japanese from Sakhalin.

Intermittent campaigns in the 1860s and 1870s led to the conquest of West Turkestan, though Khiva and Bokhara were nominally protectorates, but Britain made it clear in 1885 that an attempt to take over Afghan territory would mean war, though to the east Russian penetration in the Pamirs continued until the Anglo-Russian convention of 1895. The Russo-Turkish War of 1877–1878 was less successful, for although Russia was victorious, the presence of a British fleet in the Sea of Marmora and the fear of Austrian action on land forced a revision of the Treaty of San Stefano and all that Russia gained in territory was the recovery of Bessarabia from her ally Rumania, and the districts of Batum, Ardahan and Kars on the eastward side of the Black Sea.

The Russo-Japanese War of 1904–1905 was totally disastrous as some of the more farsighted Russians, including Kuropatkin, the minister of war, had foreseen. Russia, aided by France and Germany, had put great diplomatic pressure on Japan in 1895 to modify the Treaty of Shimonoseki which concluded the 1894–1895 war between China and Japan, and the latter had given up the Liao Tung Peninsula ceded by China. Russia then proceeded to obtain the railway concession from China as related above and also the lease of the Liao Tung Peninsula, with the obvious intention of making Manchuria virtually a Russian province. Japan might perhaps have acquiesced if given similar opportunities in Korea, but Russia would not agree and the Japanese attacked. The Russians were defeated on land and two fleets were destroyed by the Japanese, while internal disorder threatened in European Russia, and the war ended with the Treaty of Portsmouth (USA) under which Russia ceded southern Sakhalin, transferred the lease of the Liao Tung Peninsula to Japan, recognized Japan's sphere of influence in Korea, and evacuated Manchuria, though retaining control of the railway line to Vladivostock.

With the western frontier adjoining Germany and Austria, the army was the more important service, with a peace-time strength of over a million in 1905, but the navy was also vital as much of the Baltic coast was vulnerable, and a strong navy was essential to Russia's Far Eastern schemes. The 1905 naval estimates totalled about £12,000,000, a third of those for the army. The navy was manned by conscription and as far as possible from the maritime and river districts, though the Finns, who were the best Russian seamen, were exempted under the Finnish constitution, this part of the Russian Empire being ruled by the Czar as

The principal Baltic shipbuilding yards were at St Petersburg, the three most important now being the New Admiralty, Galernii Island and the Baltic Works. St Petersburg was linked by a dredged channel, difficult for large ships, to the dockyard and naval base at Kronstadt. An ice-free base at Libau was being developed in 1905, while Sevastopol and the building yards at Nicolaiev served the Black Sea fleet. Vladivostock and latterly Port Arthur were the bases in the Far East, but neither was adequate for difficult repairs. A number of ships were built for Russia by companies in France, Germany, Britain and the USA and a few in Belgium, Sweden and Denmark. Guns were made at Obuchov and until about 1890 mostly to Krupp designs, this firm also supplying many guns. Thereafter they were made to Schneider-Canet designs, though the *Rurik*, laid down in 1905, obtained her guns from Vickers. The length of Russian guns in calibres always indicates the overall length, as in Germany and Austria, and not the bore length as was usual in Britain, France and the USA. Whitehead's at Fiume supplied torpedoes originally, but they were later made at Obuchov.

In 1860 the Russian navy followed those of Britain and France in strength, and consisted principally of screw-propelled wooden ships: battleships, frigates, corvettes and sloops with many gunboats and smaller craft. Sailing ships were being gradually phased out. In 1862 the major screw vessels comprised three three-deck and six two-deck battleships, seven frigates, of which one was very large, with two more building and two completing, 18 corvettes plus two completing and one building, and nine sloops with three more completing. Practically all the remaining sailing ships were stricken in 1862. The battleships were in the Baltic, the remainder also in the Far East or Mediterranean where they depended on the bases of well-disposed countries. The

Russian fleet in the Black Sea had been limited by the Treaty of Paris in 1856, which ended the Crimean War, to six steamers of 164ft (50m) waterline length and 800 tons max, included in the 18 corvettes above, and to four smaller ships of 200 tons max.

The actions at Hampton Roads in 1862 made a great impression in Russia and it was decided to convert the two frigates building, *Petropavlovsk* and *Sevastopol*, to broadside armoured ships, and to order the smaller broadside ironclad *Pervenetz* from Britain. From 1863 to 1867, one turret ship, the *Minin*, later converted to an armoured cruiser, three broadside ironclads and 17 coast defence monitors were begun for Russia. The emphasis was clearly on the defence of the Russian Baltic coast. Nothing was laid down in 1869 and from 1869 to 1881 the total of ships begun amounted to a large turret ship, *Petr Veliki*, four armoured cruisers, eight sloops, nine gunboats and 116 torpedo boats, all but one being small. The naval limitation clauses of the Treaty of Paris were denounced by Russia in 1871, but the only ships built for the Black Sea up to 1881 were the two circular ships, *Novgorod* and *Popov*, a cruiser, a gunboat and a torpedo boat, not included in the totals above. It should be noted that most of the smaller torpedo boats could be sent to the Black Sea by rail, and 12 to 15 were usually stationed there. In the Russo-Turkish War of 1877–1878, torpedo launches were used in the Black Sea, either carried on the davits of purchased merchant steamers or towed astern. A small Turkish monitor, the *Seife* was sunk by spar torpedoes in the Danube, but of the four Whiteheads expended at Batum, two were found on the beach unexploded and no warship was hit, though the customs vessel *Intibakh* may have been sunk.

Nothing was begun in 1882 but from 1883 to 1889 a total of nine battleships were laid down, mostly of rather mediocre designs, with two armoured cruisers, three other cruisers, eleven gunvessels, three torpedo gunboats and 26 torpedo boats. Of these, five battleships, six gunvessels, two torpedo gunboats and 12 torpedo boats were for the Black Sea. From 1890 to 1897 the totals were eight battleships, three coast defence battleships, two large armoured cruisers, three cruisers, three gunvessels, six torpedo gunboats, three destroyers and 37 torpedo boats. The Black Sea fleet's share was smaller, amounting to two battleships, one torpedo gunboat and ten torpedo boats.

The increase of the Russian fleet continued in the period 1897 to 1903 with 12 battleships laid down, two armoured cruisers, 11 other cruisers, 56 destroyers and 24 torpedo boats. One destroyer was also acquired. Although a very limited passage of Russian warships into and out of the Black Sea was occasionally allowed, any major movement was not, and yet of the above totals, three battleships, two cruisers and 13 destroyers were for the Black Sea fleet.

During the war years of 1904 and 1905 one battleship, four armoured cruisers, five gunvessels, 24 large and 34 smaller destroyers were laid down and a turbine-driven torpedo boat acquired, of which only four of the large destroyers were for the Black Sea.

In conclusion the total Russian warship losses in the 1904–1905 war with Japan were 14 battleships, three coast defence battleships, five armoured cruisers, six cruisers, two old sloops, five gunvessels, two torpedo gunboats, two minelayers, 21 destroyers, and three torpedo boats. This left the Russian Navy at the end of 1905 exceedingly short of effective large warships since there were only two battleships and two armoured cruisers of any fighting value, apart from the Black Sea fleet.

RUSSIAN NAVY in 1860

Only ships laid down prior to 1860 are included in this list. Of those laid down in 1860, or later, and described in detail, only the *Almaz* and *Jemtchug* were completed in 1862, leaving for US and Chinese waters respectively in November.

SCREW THREE-DECKERS

Name	Launched	Displacement	Guns	NHP	Service 1862
IMPERATOR NICOLAI I	1860	5426t	111	600	Baltic
SINOP	1860	5585t	131	800	Baltic Built Nicolaiev
TSESSAREVITCH	1860	5850t	135	800	Baltic Built Nicolaiev

SCREW TWO-DECKERS

Name	Launched	Displacement	Guns	NHP	Service 1862
CONSTANTIN	Conv 1856	3697t	74	450	Baltic
GANGUT	Conv 1859	3814t	81	500	Baltic, Gunnery School ship
OREL	Conv 1856	3713t	74	450	Baltic
RETVISAN**	Conv 1857	3823t	84	500	Baltic
VIBORG	Conv 1855	3505t	74	450	Baltic
VOLA	Conv 1858 (?)	3814t	84	500	Baltic

SCREW FRIGATES

Name	Launched	Displacement	Guns	NHP	Service 1862
ALEXANDER NEVSKI	1861	4500t	51	800	Trials spring 1863
DMITRI DONSKOI	1861	4500t	51	800	To Mediterranean 1.11.1862
GENERAL ADMIRAL	1858	6000t	68	800	Mediterranean. Built Webb, New York
GROMOBOI	1855 (?)	3200t	53	360	Baltic, from Mediterranean
ILIA MUROMETZ	1854 (?)	c 2900t	45	360	Baltic
OLEG	1857 (?)	(?) 4500t	57	800	Baltic, from Mediterranean
OSLIABIA*	1855 (?)	2976t	45	360	Mediterranean
PERESVIET*	1860	3837t	53	450	Trials spring 1863
SVIETLANA**	1858	3200t	40	450	Baltic, from Far East

Few of these ships lasted for very long. An 1874 list includes only those marked with an asterisk, a further asterisk being added for those still listed in 1882.

The Russian Navy in 1862 also included seven paddle 'frigates' of 1200t to 1900t displacement stationed in the Baltic, 80 screw gunboats, not including the *Opyt* described elsewhere, mostly in the Baltic, 25 steam schooners and 54 small steamers which included tugs. Sailing warships had nearly vanished. The last nine ships of the line, *Ezekiel*, *Imperator Petr I*, *Imperatritsa Alexandra*, *Krasnoi*, *Netron Menya*, *Pamiat Azova*, *Prokhor*, *Veliki Kniaz Mikhail* and *Vladimir*, were all stricken in 1862, as were the frigates *Borodino*, *Narva*, *Sissoi Veliki*, *Vilagosh*, and the corvettes *Kniaz Varshavski*, *Olivutsa and Smolensk*. The only sailing warships left were the frigate *Castor*, the corvette *Buivol*, which had been converted from screw, and ten schooners.

SCREW CORVETTES

Name	Launched	Displacement	Guns	NHP	Service 1862
BAYAN**	1857	2000t	17	300	Baltic. Built Arman, Bordeaux. Composite
BOGATYR**	1860	2215t	17	360	Far East
BOYARIN*	1856 (?)	903t	11	160	Baltic
GRIDEN**	1856	870t	11	160	Baltic, from Far East
KALEVALA	1857 (?)	(?) 1500t	15	250	Far East
KINDA	1856 (?)	(?) 900t	11	200	Baltic from Far East
KRECHET	1860	800t	9	220	Mediterranean. Built Nicolaiev
NOVIK	1856 (?)	(?) 900t	11	200	Baltic, from Far East
POSADNIK	1856 (?)	(?) 900t	11	200	Far East
RHYS	1856 (?)	800t	11	(?) 200	Black Sea
SOKOL**	1859	1060t	11	220	Baltic. Built Nicolaiev
UDAV	1856 (?)	800t	11	200	Black Sea
VEPR	1856 (?)	800t	11	(?) 200	Black Sea
VOIEVODA**	1856	940t	11	160	Baltic
VOL	1856 (?)	(?) 900t	11	200	Baltic
VOLK	1856 (?)	800t	11	(?) 200	Black Sea
YASTREB*	1860	800t	9	220	Black Sea
ZUBR	1856 (?)	800t	11	(?) 200	Black Sea

SCREW SLOOPS (CLIPPERS)

Name	Launched	Displacement	Guns	NHP	Service 1862
ABREK**	1860	1070t	5	300	Far East
DJIGIT	1856 (?)	–	6	150	Baltic
GAIDAMAK**	1860	1215t	7	250	Baltic from Far East. Built in England
NAJEZDNIK	1856 (?)	–	6	90	Far East
OPRITCHNIK	1856 (?)	–	6	150	Far East
RAZBOINIK	1856 (?)	–	6	150	Far East
STRYELOK	1856 (?)	–	6	150	Baltic from Far East
VSADNIK**	1860	1225t	5	(?) 300	Failed trials, being re-engined

CAPITAL SHIPS

Laid down in 1860 as a wooden unarmoured frigate of 5212t and converted to an ironclad with complete side armour to 5ft 2in below lwl, except for 50ft at either end of the battery deck. British official reports credit her with a uniform 4½in but some descriptions say it was reduced to 4in–3in at the ends and to 2in below water after. Of the 8in guns 14 were in the armoured battery. The *Sevastopol* had a blunt ram bow and was lightly rigged as a three-masted schooner.

SEVASTOPOL *broadside ironclad*

Displacement: 6130t
Dimensions: 295ft wl x 52ft x 26ft max (*89.9 x 15.85 x 7.92m*)
Machinery: Rectangular boilers, 1-shaft HRCR, 3090ihp = 12kts
Armour: Wrought iron. Side 4½in, battery 4½in
Armament: Originally intended 28-60pdr SB, later 16-8in/22, 1-6in/23, 8-3.4in
Complement: 607

Name	Builder	Conv begun	Floated out	Comp	Fate
SEVASTOPOL	Kronstadt	1862	Aug 1864	1865	Stricken *c*1887

Laid down in 1861 as a sister of the *Sevastopol* and converted to an ironclad. Her armouring was the same with identical discrepancies in the various accounts. Of the 8in guns 20 were in the armoured battery. The *Petropavlovsk's* ram projected over 8ft and she was rigged as a ship without topgallants. A report of 1878 states that her timbers were unsound.

PETROPAVLOVSK *broadside ironclad*

Displacement: 6040t
Dimensions: 293ft 3in wl x 56ft x 24ft 6in max (*89.38 x 17.07 x 7.47m*)
Machinery: Rectangular boilers, 1-shaft HRCR, 2800ihp = 11.9kts
Armour: Wrought iron. Side 4½in, battery 4½in
Armament: 24-8in/22, 4-6in/23, 10-3.4in, spar and Harvey torpedoes
Complement: 680

Name	Builder	Conv begun	Launched	Comp	Fate
PETROPAVLOVSK	New Admiralty	1862	1864	1865	Stricken *c*1885

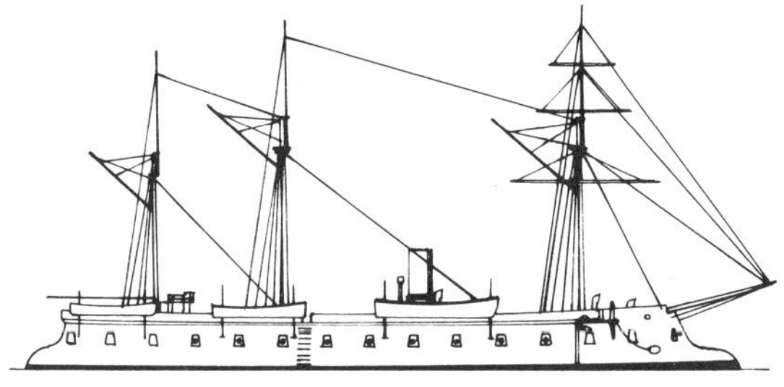

Pervenetz as completed 1864

Broadside iron-hulled coast defence ships with projecting bows and pronounced tumblehome, particularly in *Pervenetz*. The hull was completely armoured above water except in *Kreml* where the battery armour was not taken to the bow and stern. The 8in and 6in guns were in the battery except for three 6in on the upper deck in *Pervenetz*, two 6in in *Kreml* and two 8in in *Netron Menya*. The engines of the two latter came from Russian wooden screw ships, and all three were rigged as three-masted schooners.

PERVENETZ class *coast defence ironclads*

Displacement: *Pervenetz* 3277t; *Netron Menya* 3340t; *Kreml* 4000t (3412t designed)
Dimensions: 221ft 9in–225ft 1in wl x 53ft 9in x 16ft 3in–19ft 6in max (*67.59–68.60 x 16.15–16.38 x 4.95–5.94m*)
Machinery: Rectangular boilers, 1-shaft HDA, 1067–1630ihp = 9-10kts. Coal 250/500t
Armour: Wrought iron. Side 4½in, battery 4½in (*Kreml* 5½in), CT 4½in
Armament: *Pervenetz* originally 34 SB, later 6-8in/22, 9-6in/23, 4-4.2in, 4-3.4in, 5-1pdr revolvers; *Kreml* 8-8in/22, 6-6in/23, 8-3.4in, 2-1pdr revolvers; *Netron Menya* 14-8in/22, 4-3.4in, 2-2½pdr
Complement: Originally 395, later 170-190

Name	Builder	Laid down	Launched	Comp	Fate
PERVENETZ	Thames Iron Wks	1862	1863	1864	Stricken 1905
KREML	Baltic Wks	1864	1865	1866	Stricken 1905
NETRON MENYA	Mitchell, St Petersburg	1863	1864	1865	Stricken 1905

Pervenetz in the 1890s
Aldo Fraccaroli Collection

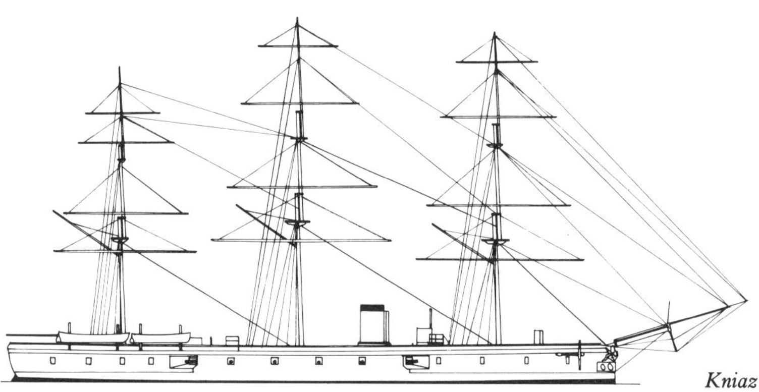

Kniaz Pojarski as completed 1870

An iron-hulled, wood-sheathed, central battery ship, the hull being recessed fore and aft of the battery to allow some axial fire. The 8in guns were in a short battery with the 6in fore and aft on the upper deck. The belt was complete on the waterline, and the ram projected 8ft. The *Kniaz Pojarski* was fully rigged and was said to be a bad seaboat.

KNIAZ POJARSKI *central battery ship*

Displacement: 4506t designed, 5138t actual
Dimensions: 272ft 8in wl x 49ft x 24ft 6in max (*83.10 x 14.94 x 7.47m*)
Machinery: 8 cyl boilers, 1-shaft HDA, 2835ihp = 11.7kts. Coal 350/600t
Armour: Wrought iron. Belt 4½in, battery 4½in
Armament: 8-8in/22, 2-6in/23, 4-3.4in. Also 3 spar and 3 towing torpedoes. Later 4-3pdr revolvers, 6-1pdr revolvers, 2-15in TT sub added
Complement: 455

Name	Builder	Laid down	Launched	Comp	Fate
KNIAZ POJARSKI	Mitchell, St Petersburg	1864	1867	1870	Stricken 1907

The *Minin* was originally launched as a low freeboard turret ship, intended to be similar to the *Captain* with full rig, 4-11in guns in twin turrets and 4-6in, 2 on the forecastle and 2 on the poop. After the disaster to the *Captain* in 1871 her completion was stopped and she was reconstructed as an armoured cruiser. There was a complete waterline belt from 2ft above to 5ft below lwl with a 1in steel deck at the belt upper edge, but the guns were unprotected on the upper deck with the 8in in sponsons. The *Minin* was sheathed and coppered and heavily ship-rigged. Her details were altered several times, a report of 1893 indicating 30 cal 8in and 28 cal 6in guns with the addition of 8-3pdr revolvers. Later, as a training ship the 8in and 6in were replaced by 10-6in/45. She was also reboilered with 18 Bellevilles and her rig reduced to that of a barque. In 1909 she became the minelayer *Ladoga* with a capacity of 900 mines, and was sunk in the Baltic on a mine laid by *UC4*.

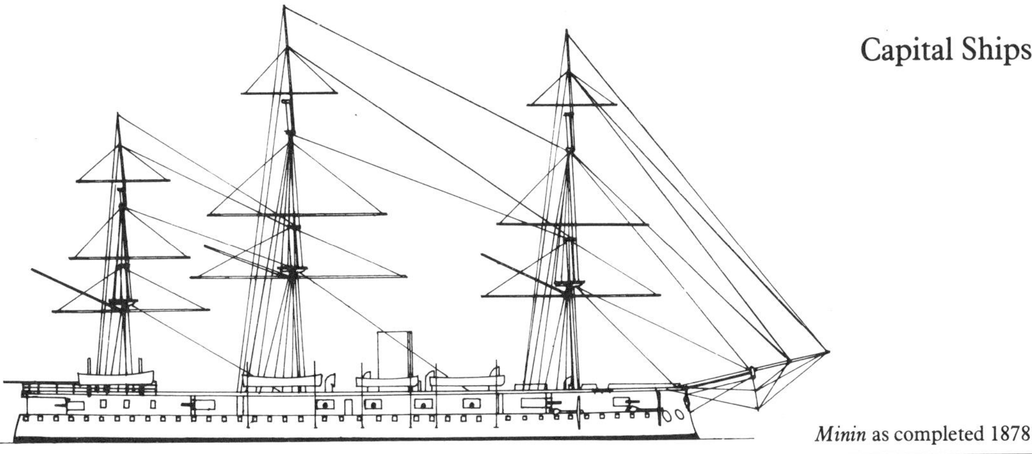

Minin as completed 1878

MININ *turret ship/armoured cruiser*

Displacement: 6136t
Dimensions: 295ft wl x 49ft 6in x 25ft 5in max (*89.91 x 15.09 x 7.75m*)
Machinery: 12 cyl, 1-shaft VC, 5290ihp = 14kts. Coal 1000t max
Armour: Compound. Belt 7in-6in
Armament: 4-8in/22, 12-6in/23, 4-3.4in, 8-1pdr revolvers, 2-15in TT aw, spar torpedoes and 150 mines
Complement: 545

Name	Builder	Laid down	Launched	Comp	Fate
MININ	Baltic Wks	1866	1869	1878	Sunk 15.8.1915

Minin with full ship rig

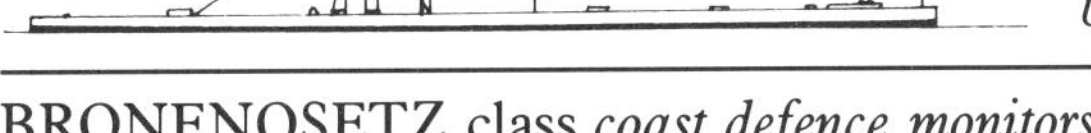

Uragan as completed 1866

Low freeboard, single turret monitors of United States type. The two built at Seraing were sent to Russia in sections and assembled. The side armour extended to 3ft 6in below water and was 5in increased to 9in forward and reduced to 3in at the lower edge. The funnel base had 8in, and there was a protecting ring 15in high and 5in thick round the base of the turret. There was no double bottom and only *Perun* had a 1in armour deck, the absence of which was a serious weakness in the others. The hull form seems to have been very similar to that of the US *Passaic* class and the above displacement is in this case much too low and should be about 2000t.

BRONENOSETZ class *coast defence monitors*

Displacement: 1565t (see below)
Dimensions: 201ft wl x 46ft x 11ft 5in-12ft 7in max (*61.26 x 14.02 x 3.48-3.84m*)
Machinery: 2 rectangular boilers, 1-shaft HDA, 340-530ihp = 6.5-8kts. Coal 100 tons.
Armour: Wrought iron (built up from 1in plates). Side 9in-3in, turret 10in, pilot house 8in
Armament: Originally 2-9in SB, then 2-9in/20(1x2) (later *Latnik*, *Lava* 2-9in/22), 4-2½pdr
Complement: 111

Name	Builder	Laid down	Launched	Comp	Fate
BRONENOSETZ	Carr & Macpherson, St Petersburg	1863	1864	1865-1866	Stricken *c*1900
EDINOROG	Galernii Is	1863	1864	1865-1866	Stricken *c*1900
KOLDUN	Cockerill, Seraing	1863	1864	1865-1866	Stricken *c*1900
LATNIK	Carr & Macpherson, St Petersburg	1863	1864	1865-1866	Stricken *c*1900
LAVA	Baltic Wks	1863	1864	1865-1866	Stricken *c*1900
PERUN	Baltic Wks	1863	1864	1865-1866	Stricken *c*1900
STRYELETZ	Galernii Is	1863	1864	1865-1866	Stricken *c*1900
TIFON	New Admiralty	1863	1864	1865-1866	Stricken *c*1900
URAGAN	New Admiralty	1863	1864	1865-1866	Stricken *c*1900
VYESHTCHUN	Cockerill, Seraing	1863	1864	1865-1866	Stricken *c*1900

A low freeboard turret ship very similar to the Danish *Rolf Krake*, but differing in having a partial double bottom. The hull above water was completely armoured and there was a 1in deck. The *Smerch* was rigged with three pole signal masts.

SMERCH *coast defence turret ship*

Displacement: 1460t
Dimensions: 188ft 2in wl x 38ft 2in x 12ft max (*57.35 x 11.63 x 3.66m*)
Machinery: 2 rectangular boilers, 2-shaft HDA, 700ihp=8kts. Coal 100/250t
Armour: Wrought iron. Side 4½in, turrets 6in-4½in
Armament: 4-60pdr SB (2x2) originally, later 2-9in/20 (2x1), 4-1pdr revolvers added
Complement: 155

Name	Builder	Laid down	Lauched	Comp	Fate
SMERCH	Mitchell, St Petersburg	1863	1864	1865	Stricken *c*1900

Low freeboard turret ships with the hull completely armoured above water. They were rigged with two pole masts. According to some accounts there was a 1in deck but this is not mentioned in official British reports.

CHARODEIKA class *coast defence turret ship*

Displacement: 2100t
Dimensions: 206ft 6in wl x 42ft x 12ft 7in max (*62.94 x 12.80 x 3.84m*)
Machinery: 2 rectangular boilers, 2-shaft HDA, 875ihp = 8.5kts. Coal 250t max
Armour: Wrought iron. Side 4½in, turrets 6in
Armament: 4-9in/20(2x2), 4-3.4in, later 2-9in replaced with 22 cal, and 2-3pdr, 2-1pdr revolvers added
Complement: 178

Name	Builder	Laid down	Launched	Comp	Fate
CHARODEIKA	Mitchell, St Petersburg	1866	1867	1868	Stricken 1907
RUSSALKA	Mitchell, St Petersburg	1866	1867	1868	Lost 19.9.93

Admiral Lazarev with original schooner rig

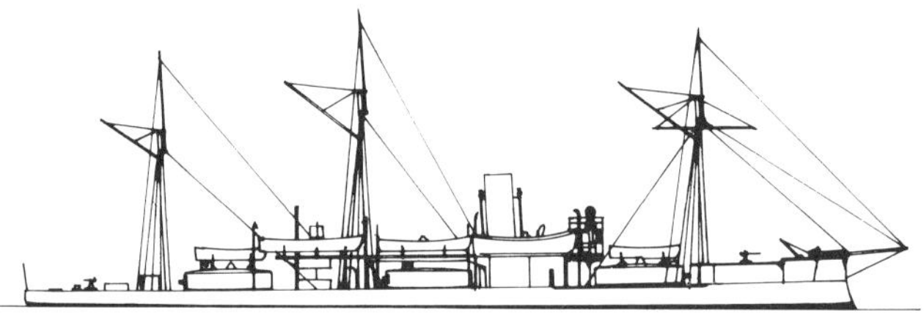

Admiral Lazarev in 1895

Turret ships generally resembling the *Prince Albert* except in the number of turrets. The side armour was complete, and at designed draught extended from 5ft 6in above wl to 6ft below. There was no armour deck. The CT was small and located on the bridge with no tube to the deck. There were three masts and originally a fore and aft rig was provided. They were twice reboilered, the second time in 1900-1903 with cylindrical boilers.

ADMIRAL LAZAREV class *coast defence turret ships*

Displacement: *Lazarev* 3820t, *Greig* 3768t (both 3462t designed)
Dimensions: 254ft 10in wl x 43ft x 20ft 2in-20ft 6in max (*77.67 x 13.11 x 6.15-6.25m*)
Machinery: 4 rectangular boilers, 1-shaft HDA, 2020ihp = 10.5/11kts. Coal 300t max
Armour: Wrought iron. Side 4½in, turrets 4½in, CT 5in
Armament: Originally 6-9in/20(3x2), next 3-11in/20(3x1) and later 3-11in/22; also 2/4-3.4in and later 1-3pdr, 2-1pdr revolvers
Complement: 269-274

Name	Builder	Laid down	Launched	Comp	Fate
ADMIRAL LAZAREV	Carr & Macpherson, St Petersburg	1866	1867	1869	Stricken 1907
ADMIRAL GREIG	Carr & Macpherson, St Petersburg	1867	1868	1870	Stricken 1907

Similar to the *Lazarev* class but with two turrets and heavier armour. *Chichagov* was reboilered with cylindrical boilers in 1887 and *Spiridov* in 1904.

ADMIRAL CHICHAGOV class *coast defence turret ships*

Displacement: *Chichagov* 3925t, *Spiridov* 3851t (3492t as designed)
Dimensions: 254ft 5in wl x 43ft x 19ft 6in-20ft 5in max (*77.5 x 13.11 x 5.94-6.22m*)
Machinery: 4 rectangular boilers, 1-shaft HDA, 2030ihp = 10.5kts. Coal 300t max
Armour: Wrought iron. Side 6in, turrets *Chichagov* 6in, *Spiridov* 7in
Armament: Originally 4-9in/20(2x2), later 2-11in/20(2x1), finally in *Chichagov* 2-11in/22; also 4-3.4in and later 1-3pdr, 4-1pdr revolvers
Complement: 260

Name	Builder	Laid down	Launched	Comp	Fate
ADMIRAL CHICHAGOV	Baltic Wks	1867	1868	1870	Stricken 1907
ADMIRAL SPIRIDOV	Baltic Wks	1867	1868	1870	Stricken 1907

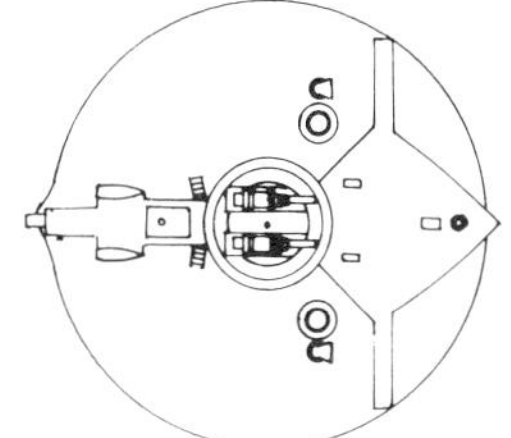

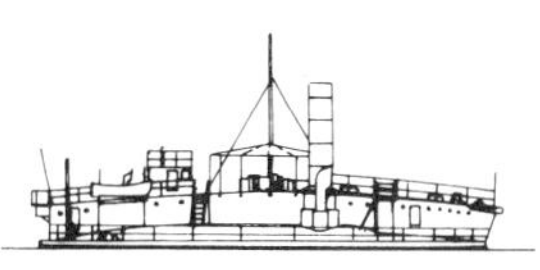

Novgorod as completed 1874

Black Sea Fleet. The first of the two famous circular ships intended for the defence of Nicolaiev and the Dnieper estuary, the *Novgorod* was built in sections at St Petersburg and assembled at Nicolaiev. The side armour extended from the deck edge 1½ft above wl to 4½ft below, and was 9in for the upper 3ft and then 7in. Hughes backing with heavy iron stringers was used. The deck rose to 5ft 3in aw and was 2¾in thick, while the 9in barbette extended 7ft above the deck, and the funnels had 4½in for a height of 3ft. The hull was heavily wood sheathed with 27in outside the armour, and was coppered. The two outer propellers and engines were later removed, reducing ihp to 2000 = 5½kts.

NOVGOROD *coast defence ship*

Displacement: 2491t
Dimensions: 101ft x 101ft x 13ft 6in max (*30.78 x 30.78 x 4.11m*)
Machinery: 8 cylindrical boilers, 6-shaft HC, 3000ihp = 6-7kts. Coal 160t
Armour: Wrought iron. Sides 9in-7in, barbette 9in
Armament: 2-11in/20(1x2), 2-3.4in, 2-2½pdr, spar torpedoes
Complement: 149

Name	Builder	Laid down	Launched	Comp	Fate
NOVGOROD	Nicolaiev	1872	1873	1874	Stricken *c*1900

Black Sea Fleet. Originally named *Kiev*, the *Popov* was an enlarged *Novgorod*. The side and barbette armour was as in the earlier ship with additional 7in plates outside separated from the inner plates by 4in wood. The lower part of the funnels had 7in and the deck was increased to 3in. The 12in guns were in a hydraulic disappearing mounting, and as in *Novgorod* the two outer propellers and engines were subsequently removed, ihp becoming 3066 = 6kts.

VICE-ADMIRAL POPOV *coast defence ship*

Displacement: 3550t
Dimensions: 120ft x 120ft x 13ft 6in max (*36.58 x 36.58 x 4.11m*)
Machinery: 8 cylindrical boilers, 6-shaft HC, *c*4500ihp = 8kts. Coal 170t
Armour: Wrought iron. Sides 16in-14in, barbette 16in
Armament: 2-12in/20(1x2), 8-3.4in (later 6) and 2-1pdr revolvers, spar torpedoes
Complement: 203

Name	Builder	Laid down	Launched	Comp	Fate
VICE-ADMIRAL POPOV	Nicolaiev	1874	1875	1877	Stricken *c*1900

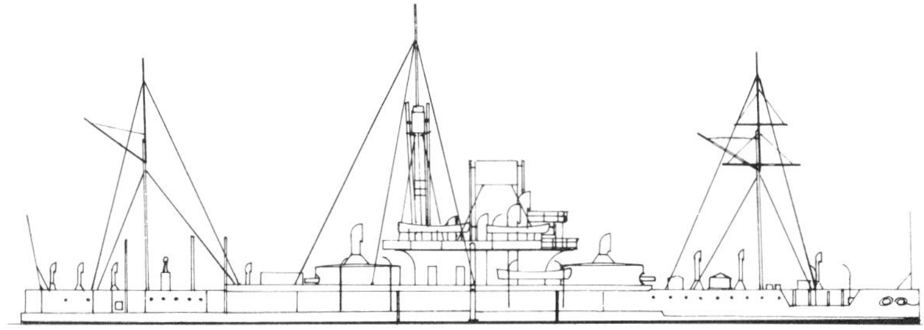

Petr Veliki as completed 1878

A turret ship of about 8ft max freeboard and cut down aft except along the centre line. The belt was complete but nearly submerged at actual load displacement; and the citadel was only 160ft long. The side armour had Hughes backing of 22in of wood between the two 7in plates. The armour deck was 3in over the belt outside the citadel and 1½in over the latter. The firing of her heavy guns caused low temperature damage to hull and machinery in the winter of 1876–1877, and her original engines, which had never been satisfactory, were replaced by Messrs Elder during an extensive refit at Glasgow in 1881. Metacentric height is given as 8.64ft – it is not known at what loading – and not surprisingly she was a bad roller. The *Petr Veliki* was reconstructed in 1905-1906 and became a two-funnel high freeboard ship with 4-8in/50 in sponsons at upper deck level and 12-6in/45 below on the original upper deck. She now had cylindrical boilers and displaced 9790t and was renamed *Respublikanets* in 1917.

PETR VELIKI *turret ship*

Displacement: 10,406t (designed 9665t)
Dimensions: 339ft 8in oa x 62ft 3in x 27ft 2in max (*103.53 x 18.97 x 8.28m*)
Machinery: Originally 12 rectangular boilers, 2-shaft HRCR; in 1881-1882 2-shaft VC; oval boilers 8250ihp = 14kts. Coal 960/1200t
Armour: Wrought iron. Belt 14in-11½in, belt ends 10in-8in, citadel 14in, turrets 14in (7in + 7in), CT none
Armament: 4-12in/20(2x2), 6-3.4in (later reduced to 4 and 6-3pdr added), 2-15in TT sub
Complement: 432

Name	Builder	Laid down	Launched	Comp	Fate
PETR VELIKI	Galernii Is	1.6.1869	27.8.72	14.10.76	Scrapped 1922

Petr Veliki in the 1890s

Black Sea Fleet. As can be seen above there were differences among the four ships. The design was unique with the 12in mountings at the corners of an amidships triangular redoubt, one forward on either beam and one on the centre line aft. In *Ekaterina* the 12in were in hydraulic disappearing mountings made by Easton and Anderson, and all had 3-2in shields of varying shape. The 6in guns were in unarmoured positions on the main deck. The lower strake of the belt was complete and 16in amidships with 8in lower edge, but at actual normal draught only reached about one foot above lwl. The 12in upper belt was 102ft long ending in 10-9in bulkheads. The armour deck was 2¼in over the lower belt and 2in over the upper belt and redoubt except in *Ekaterina* where it was 1½in over the upper belt and absent over the redoubt. *Tchesma*, the heaviest of the four, was reported to be somewhat deficient in stability. The *Sinop* was fitted with a kind of bulge in 1914 for service as a barrage-breaker or 'mine-bumper', her armament being 4-8in and 8-6in, while the *Georgi Pobiedonosets* finally became a port guardship, armed with 8-6in, both having a few 3pdr AA also. *Tchesma* and *Georgi Pobiedonosets* were both built at the yard of the Russian Steam Navigation Co.

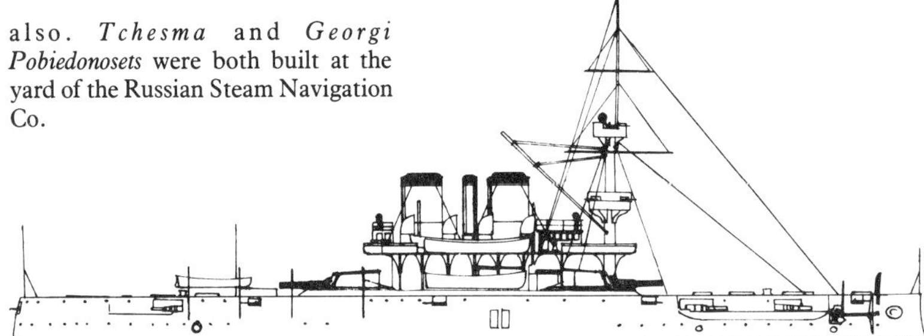

Georgi Pobiedonosets in 1895

EKATERINA II class *barbette ships*

Displacement: 11,032t-11,396t (as designed 10,100t to 10,280t)
Dimensions: 339ft 6in oa x 69ft x 27ft 10in-28ft 9in max (*103.48 x 21.03 x 8.48-8.76m*)
Machinery: *Ekaterina, Tchesma* 14 cyl boilers, 2-shaft, VC, 9100ihp = 15kts; *Georgi, Sinop* 16 cyl boilers, 2-shaft, VTE, 13000ihp = 16/16.5kts. Coal in all 700/870t
Armour: Compound, but steel in *Georgi*. Belt 16in-8in, belt ends 8in-6in, redoubt 12in, CT 9in-8in but *Georgi* 12in
Armament: 6-12in (3x2) (30 cal in *Ekaterina, Sinop*, 35 cal in *Tchesma, Georgi*), 7-6in/35, 8-3pdr (revolvers except in *Georgi*), 4-1pdr revolvers (*Georgi* 10-1pdr), 7-15in TT aw, 100 mines
Complement: 650-674

Name	Builder	Laid down	Launched	Comp	Fate
EKATERINA II	Nicolaiev	1883	May 1886	1889	Stricken 1907
TCHESMA	Sevastopol	1883	May 1886	1889	Stricken 1907
SINOP	Sevastopol	1883	June 1887	1890	Scrapped 1922
GEORGI POBIEDONOSETS	Sevastopol	July 1889	9.3.92	1894	To Bizerta 1920

Ekaterina II
Aldo Fraccaroli Collection

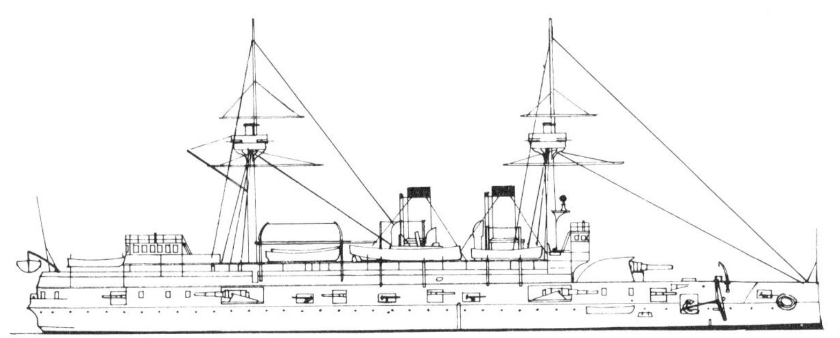

Imperator Alexander II as completed 1891

IMPERATOR ALEXANDER II class *barbette/turret ships*

Displacement: 9500t (as designed 8440t), *Nikolai* 9672t in 1905
Dimensions: 333ft 6in wl x 67ft x 25ft 10in max (*101.65 x 20.42 x 7.87m*)
Machinery: 12 cyl boilers: *Alexander* 2-shaft VC, *Nikolai* 2-shaft HTE, 8500ihp = 15.3kts. Coal 1000-1200t max
Armour: Compound. Belt 14in-6in, barbette/turret 10in, secondary guns 6in-3in, CT 10in *Alexander* (8in *Nikolai*)
Armament: 2-12in/30(1x2), 4-9in/35, 8-6in/35, 10-3pdr revolvers, 8-1pdr revolvers 5-15in TT aw (6 in *Nikolai*)
Complement: 611

Name	Builder	Laid down	Launched	Comp	Fate
IMPERATOR ALEXANDER II	New Admiralty	Nov 1885	July 1887	June 1891	Stricken 1925
IMPERATOR NIKOLAI I	Galernii Is	1885	June 1889	July 1891	Stricken 1918

The 12in guns were in a barbette with 3in shield in *Alexander* and in a turret in *Nikolai*. In both, the 9in and 6in were on the main deck, only the 9in having any protection. The belt was complete and about 8ft wide with a 2½in deck over it. *Nikolai* was reboilered with 16 Bellevilles in 1898-1900 while 16-3pdrs replaced the revolvers. She took part in the Battle of Tsushima and surrendered next day, being repaired and renamed *Iki* by the Japanese. *Alexander* was reconstructed at La Seyne in 1902-1904, and her old 9in and 6in replaced by 5-8in/45 (the extra gun in a shield aft) and 8-6in/45, the revolvers being replaced by 10-3pdr and the TT removed. She was renamed *Saria Svobodi* in 1917.

Dvienadsat Apostolov about 1905

DVIENADSAT APOSTOLOV *barbette ship*

Black Sea Fleet. The 12in guns were in barbettes with 3in cupola shields, and the 6in in a main deck battery. The lower strake of the belt was 220ft long, and the upper strake 212ft. It was 14in-12in with 7in-6in lower edge, and ended in 12in-9in bulkheads. The armour deck was 2in over the belt and 2½in at the ends. She was a considerably better fighting ship than the *Imperator Alexander II*.

Displacement: 8709t (as designed 8076t)
Dimensions: 342ft oa x 60ft x 27ft 6in max (*104.24 x 18.29 x 8.38m*)
Machinery: 8 cyl boilers, 2-shaft VTE, 8750ihp = 15.7kts. Coal 800t max
Armour: Compound. Belt 14in-6in, barbettes 12in-10in, battery 5in (steel), CT 8in (steel)
Armament: 4-12in/30 (2x2), 4-6in/35, 12-3pdr, 10-1pdr, 4-1pdr revolvers, 6-15in TT aw
Complement: 599

Name	Builder	Laid down	Launched	Comp	Fate
DVIENADSAT APOSTOLOV	Nicolaiev	Feb 1888	Sept 1890	Dec 1892	Stricken 1911

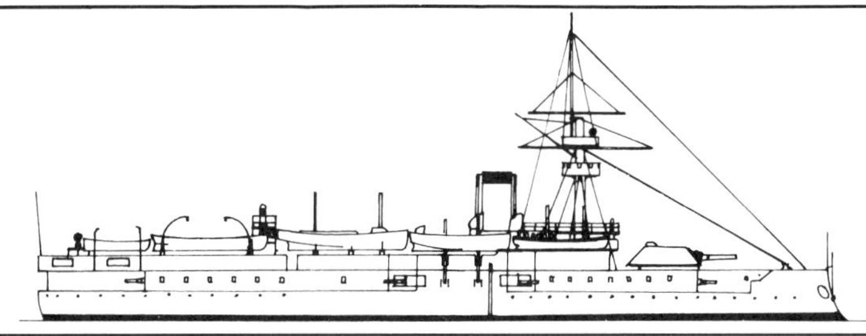

Gangut as completed 1894

GANGUT *barbette ship*

A smaller, shallower draught version of the *Imperator Alexander II*. The single 12in gun was in a barbette with a 4in shield, and the 9in protected by the main deck battery armour but not the 6in. The belt extended for 193ft ending in 9in bulkheads, and was 8ft wide with a 2in armour deck over it, increased to 3in at the ends. The *Gangut* was lost on an uncharted rock.

Displacement: 6590t
Dimensions: 289ft 9in wl x 62ft x 21ft max (*88.32 x 18.90 x 6.40m*)
Machinery: 8 cyl boilers, 2-shaft VTE, 6000ihp = 14.7kts. Coal 500/650t
Armour: Compound. Belt 16in-10in, barbette 9in-7in, battery 5in, CT 10in
Armament: 1-12in/30, 4-9in/35, 4-6in/35, 4-3pdr, 10-1pdr, 6-1pdr revolvers, 6-15in TT aw
Complement: 521

Name	Builder	Laid down	Launched	Comp	Fate
GANGUT	New Admiralty	1889	Oct 1890	1894	Lost 1897

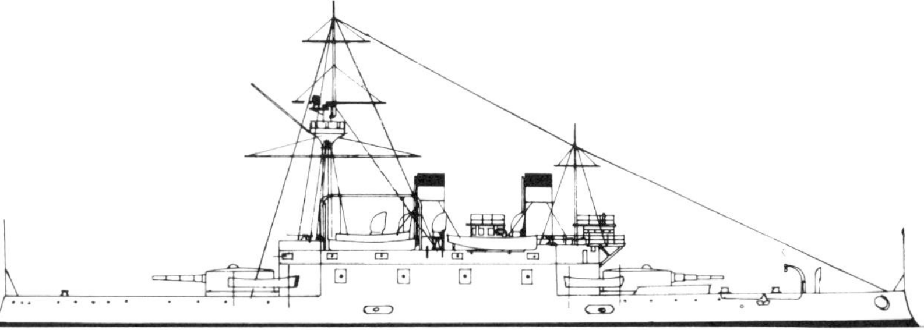

Navarin as completed 1896

NAVARIN *turret ship*

A turret ship of 10ft freeboard as completed. The turret bases were not individually armoured, and the 6in guns were in an upper deck battery. The belt was 220ft long, the lower strake being 16in-14in with an 8in lower edge and reaching from 5ft below to 2ft above lwl, while the upper strake was 150ft long, 8ft wide and a uniform 12in. The bulkheads were 12in and the armour deck 2½in-2in over the belt and 3in at the ends. The *Navarin* suffered from insufficient boiler power, but for her date was well protected. A most unusual feature was the location of the four funnels in two pairs abreast. At Tsushima she withstood shell damage and a torpedo hit aft before being sunk by one or perhaps two mines of 24 laid across her bows.

Displacement: 10,206t (as designed 9476t)
Dimensions: 357ft 8in oa x 67ft x 27ft 6in max (*109.0 x 20.42 x 8.38m*)
Machinery: 12 cyl boilers, 2-shaft VTE, 9140ihp = 15.5kts. Coal 400/700t
Armour: Compound. Belt 16in-8in, turrets 12in (nickel steel), battery 5in, CT 10in (nickel steel)
Armament: 4-12in/35 (2x2), 8-6in/35, 8-3pdr, 15-1pdr, 6-15in TT aw
Complement: 622

Name	Builder	Laid down	Launched	Comp	Fate
NAVARIN	Galernii Is	1889	20.10.91	1896	Sunk 28.5.1905

Navarin about 1900

Black Sea Fleet. In general conception very similar to the *Nile* and *Trafalgar*, the turrets not having individual armoured bases. The 6in guns were in a cramped upper deck battery, and the 4.7in with 6 of the 3pdrs in an unarmoured battery above. The lower strake of the belt ran for 246ft and from 1ft 6in above to 6ft 6in below lwl. It was 18in max reduced to 9in at the lower edge and to 16in fore and aft, ending in 16in-14in bulkheads. The upper strake ran for 218ft and was 8ft wide and 16in thick, ending in curved 16in bulkheads. The 3in-2in armour deck was only present outside the area covered by the belt upper strake. The *Tri Svititelia* was reconstructed to some extent in 1912, the superstructure being reduced and the 4-4.7in and smaller guns being replaced by 4 more 6in in shields above the battery. The TT were also removed and later 4-6pdr AA added on the turret crowns. In spite of her obsolete design she was a useful member of the Black Sea Fleet in the First World War and took part in several operations with the other predreadnoughts.

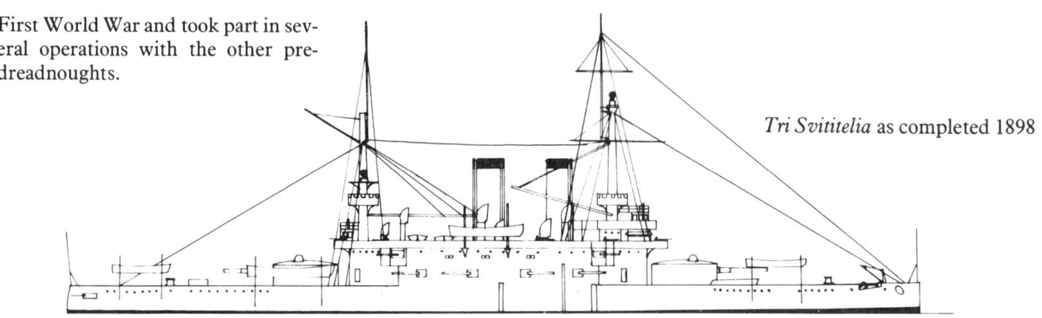

Tri Svititelia as completed 1898

TRI SVITITELIA *turret ship*

Displacement: 13,318t (as designed 12,480t)
Dimensions: 377ft 9in oa x 73ft x 28ft 5in max (*115.14 x 22.25 x 8.66m*)
Machinery: 14 cyl boilers, 2-shaft VTE, 11,300ihp = 17kts. Coal 750/1000t
Armour: Harvey and nickel steel. Belt 18in-9in, turrets 16in secondary guns 5in, CT 12 in
Armament: 4-12in/40(2x2), 8-6in/45, 4-4.7in/45, 10-3pdr, 30-1pdr, 10-1pdr revolvers; later 34-1pdr, 4-1pdr pompoms, 6-18in TT 4 aw, 2 sub
Complement: 753

Name	Builder	Laid down	Launched	Comp	Fate
TRI SVITITELIA	Nicolaiev	14.8.1891	12.11.93	1898	Scrapped 1922

A small battleship for her armament, with a moderately high freeboard, the 12in axis height being 23ft. The 12in turrets were of the French centre-pivot type with the 6in guns in a main deck battery. The lower belt was 16in-12in with 4in lower edge and 9in bulkheads, and the upper belt 5in. The armour deck was $1\frac{3}{4}$in over the lower belt and 3in at the ends, where there was no side armour. There was a serious accident in the *Sissoi* in 1897 when a 12in gun was fired before the breech was properly closed. At Tsushima she was considerably damaged by gunfire and was hit by a torpedo right aft, but would have remained afloat if flooding valves had not been opened on her surrender to the Japanese.

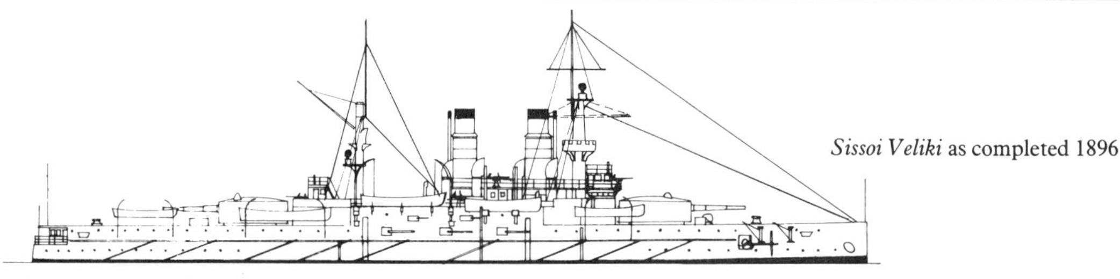

Sissoi Veliki as completed 1896

SISSOI VELIKI *battleship*

Displacement: 10,400t
Dimensions: 351ft 10in oa x 68ft x 25ft 6in (*107.23 x 20.73 x 7.77m*)
Machinery: 12 Belleville boilers, 2-shaft VTE, 8500ihp = 15.7kts. Coal 500/800t
Armour: Nickel steel. Belt 16in-4in, turrets 12in, secondary guns 5in, CT 8in
Armament: 4-12in/40 (2x2), 6-6in/45, 12-3pdr, 18-1pdr, 6-18in TT aw
Complement: 586

Name	Builder	Laid down	Launched	Comp	Fate
SISSOI VELIKI	New Admiralty	May 1892	June 1894	1896	Scuttled after Tsushima 28.5.1905

Sissoi Veliki about 1900

Intended to match Swedish ships, and unsuited for the voyage half way round the world which ended at Tsushima, where *Ushakov* was sunk and *Seniavin* and *Apraksin* surrendered, becoming the Japanese *Mishima* and *Okinoshima*. The 10in guns were a lighter, lower velocity pattern than in the *Peresviet* class, and *Apraksin* differed from the other two in having a one-gun after turret. The belt was 170ft by 7ft ending in 8in-6in bulkheads, and the armour deck 2in with 3in ends.

ADMIRAL USHAKOV class *coast defence battleships*

Displacement: *Seniavin* on trials 4971t (as designed 4126t)
Dimensions: 286ft 6in oa x 52ft x 19ft 6in max (*87.32 x 15.85 x 5.94m*)
Machinery: 8 cyl boilers (*Ushakov* 4), 2-shaft VTE, 5750ihp = 16kts. Coal 300/450t
Armour: Harvey. Belt 10in-4in, turrets 8in, CT 8in
Armament: 4-10in/45 (2x2) (*Apraksin* 3), 4-4.7in/45, 6-3pdr, 10-1pdr, 6-1pdr revolvers, 4-15in TT aw
Complement: 404

Name	Builder	Laid down	Launched	Comp	Fate
ADMIRAL USHAKOV	New Admiralty	1892	Nov 1893	1895	Sunk 28.5.1905
ADMIRAL SENIAVIN	Baltic Wks	1892	Aug 1894	1896	Scrapped 1928
GENERAL ADMIRAL GRAF APRAKSIN	New Admiralty	Oct 1894	May 1896	1899	Scrapped 1926

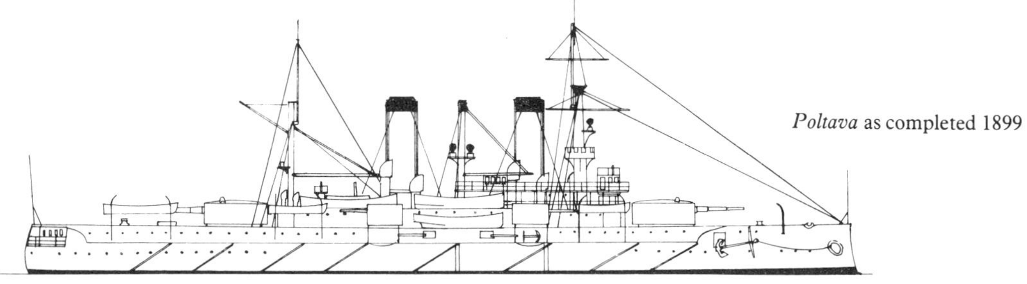

Poltava as completed 1899

Flush deck ships with appreciable tumblehome, *Sevastopol* having shorter funnels than the other two. The 12in guns were in French-type turrets (gun axis height 21½ft) and the four 6in turrets were amidships on either beam with the other 6in between them but on the main deck. The main belt ran for 240ft and was 7½ft wide, being reduced to 14in fore and aft and to 8in, *Sevastopol* 6in, at the lower edge, and ending in 9in-8in bulkheads. Above this was a shorter length of 5in armour for a height of 7½ft but there was no side armour above the main deck. The armour deck was 2¾in over the main belt and 3in at the unarmoured bow and stern. All three ships were at Port Arthur on the outbreak of the Russo-Japanese War. The *Petropavlovsk* was blown up by the explosion of her magazines after striking a mine, while the *Poltava* was hit by 14-12in to 8in shells at the Yellow Sea battle on 10.8.1904 and considerably damaged. During the seige of Port Arthur she was hit by 6-11in howitzer shells, one of which caused a serious magazine fire. She was raised by the Japanese, and served in their navy as the *Tango* until 1916 when she was sold to Russia, renamed *Tchesma*, and stationed in the White Sea. The *Sevastopol* was mined on 23.6.1904 and again on 23.8.1904 but was not very seriously damaged. She had the same number of hits as *Poltava* at the Yellow Sea, and at the siege of Port Arthur was taken outside the harbour after 5-11in hits, and, protected by nets and booms, survived 3 torpedo explosions close to her hull in the nets and a hit right aft. At the surrender she was towed to deep water and scuttled.

PETROPAVLOVSK class *battleships*

Displacement: *Petropavlovsk* 11,354t, *Sevastopol* 11,842t (as designed 10,960t)
Dimensions: 369ft wl x 70ft x 25ft 6in designed mean (*112.47 x 21.34 x 7.77m*)
Machinery: 12-16 cyl boilers, 2-shaft VTE, 11,250ihp = 16.5kts. Coal 700/1500t
Armour: Harvey-nickel. Belt 16in-5in (*Sevastopol* 14½in-5in), turrets 14in-10in, secondary turrets 5in, CT 8in
Armament: 4-12in/40(2x2), 12-6in/45(4x2, 4x1), 12-3pdr, 28-1pdr, 6-18in TT 2 aw, 4 sub, 60 mines
Complement: 632

Name	Builder	Laid down	Launched	Comp	Fate
PETROPAVLOVSK	Galernii Is	May 1892	9.11.94	1899	Sunk 13.4.1904
POLTAVA	New Admiralty	May 1892	6.11.94	1899	Scrapped 1923
SEVASTOPOL	Galernii Is	May 1892	1.6.95	1899	Scuttled 2.1.1905

Sevastopol shortly before the outbreak of the Russo-Japanese war

ROSTISLAV *battleship*

Displacement: 8880t designed
Dimensions: 351ft 10in oa x 68ft x 22ft max (*107.23 x 20.73 x 6.71m*)
Machinery: 12 cyl boilers, 2-shaft VTE, 8700ihp = 15.6kts. Coal 500/800t
Armour: Harvey. Belt 14in-5in, turrets 10in-5in, secondary turrets 5in, CT 6in
Armament: 4-10in/45(2x2), 8-6in/45(4x2), 20 then 12-3pdr, 16-1pdr, 6-18in TT 4 aw 2 sub
Complement: 650

Name	Builder	Laid down	Launched	Comp	Fate
ROSTISLAV	Nicolaiev	1895	Sept 1896	1898	Sunk Nov 1920

Black Sea Fleet. Originally intended as a sister ship to the *Sissoi Veliki*, the *Rostislav* had her 10in guns in French-type turrets, and the 6in turrets were amidships on either beam. The main belt was 227ft long and 7ft wide, 14in-10in on the waterline with an 8in-6in lower edge. The bulkheads were compound not Harvey, and 9in-5in while the 5in upper belt was 150ft by 7½ft. The armour deck was 2in over the main belt and 3in at the ends, and the turret crowns 2½in. Although a slow and weak ship, the *Rostislav* took part in several of the early First World War Black Sea operations. At some time 4-11pdr AA guns were added to her armament. When little more than a hulk she was sunk in shallow water at Kertch.

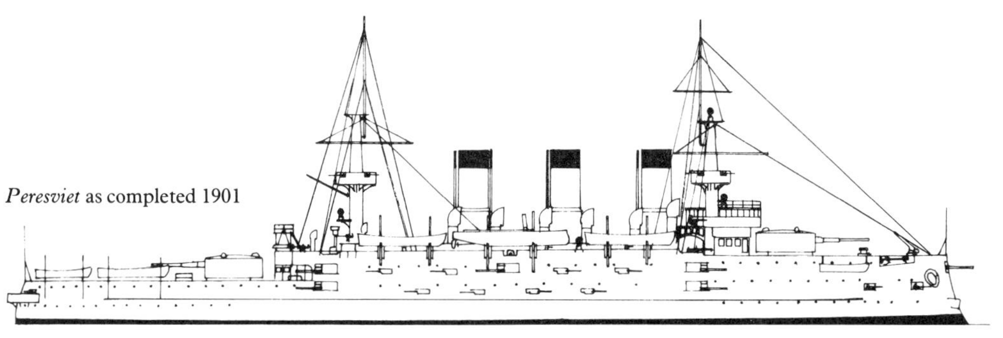
Peresviet as completed 1901

PERESVIET class *battleships*

Displacement: 12,683t
Dimensions: 434ft 6in oa x 71ft 6in x 26ft max (*Pobieda* 26ft 3in) (*132.43 x 21.79 x 7.92 (8.00)m*)
Machinery: 32 Belleville boilers (*Pobieda* 30), 3-shaft VTE, 15,000ihp = 18-18.5kts. Coal 1500/2100t, later 250t oil
Armour: KC and Harvey (*Pobieda* KC). Belt 9in-5in, turrets 9in-5in (*Pobieda* 10in-5in), casemates 5in, CT 6in (*Pobieda* 8¼in)
Armament: 4-10in/45 (2x2), 11-6in/45, 20-11pdr, 20-3pdr, 8-1pdr, 5-15in TT 3 aw 2 sub, also mines
Complement: 752

Name	Builder	Laid down	Launched	Comp	Fate
PERESVIET	New Admiralty	21.11.1895	May 1898	July 1901	Sunk 4.1.1917
OSLIABIA	New Admiralty	21.11.1895	Nov 1898	1901	Sunk Tsushima 27.5.1905
POBIEDA	Baltic Wks	1.8.1898	May 1900	June 1902	Scrapped 1922

Three-funnelled ships with a high forecastle deck extending to the mainmast and considerable tumblehome. A thoroughly unsatisfactory design, both armament and protection being poor and speed not exceptional. The 10in guns were in French-type turrets and of the 6in 6 were in upper deck and 4 in main deck casemates, with 1 unprotected in the bows. Most of the 11pdrs were in unarmoured upper and main deck batteries. The main belt was 312ft long and 7ft 10in wide, 9in-7in thick with a 5in lower edge, and the 5in upper belt, reaching the main deck, was only 188ft long. Both belts ended in 4in bulkheads, and there were similar bulkheads between the end casemates. The armour deck was 2½in-2in amidships and 3in at the ends, and in *Pobieda* alloy steel was used. *Osliabia* was sunk by gunfire at Tsushima, mainly from the effect of shells near the wl forward. The other two were at Port Arthur in February 1904. *Peresviet* was seriously damaged by gunfire at the Yellow Sea battle, and in the seige of Port Arthur was scuttled on 7.12.1904 after a total of at least 23 11in howitzer shells had hit her. She was raised and repaired by the Japanese and served as the *Sagami*. Sold back to Russia in 1916, she ran aground off Vladivostock 26.5.1916 and remained so until July. She was finally sunk by a mine laid by *U73* about 10 miles from Port Said. *Pobieda* struck a mine on 13.4.1904 which exploded under a main coal bunker, and was repaired by mid June. She was not so badly damaged at the Yellow Sea as *Peresviet* but sank at Port Arthur on 7.12.1904 from the effects of 21 11in shells. Raised and repaired by the Japanese, she served as the *Suwo* until scrapped.

Peresviet about 1903

PANTELIMON *battleship*

Displacement: 12,582t
Dimensions: 378ft 6in oa x 73ft x 27ft max (*115.36 x 22.25 x 8.23m*)
Machinery: 22 Belleville boilers, 2-shaft VTE, 10,600ihp = 16.6kts. Coal 870t max
Armour: KC. Belt 9in-5in, turrets 10in-5in, battery 5in, casemates 6in, CT 9in
Armament: 4-12in/40(2x2), 16-6in/45, 14-11pdr, 6-3pdr, 5-15in TT sub
Complement: 750

Name	Builder	Laid down	Launched	Comp	Fate
PANTELIMON	Nicolaiev	Feb 1898	Oct 1900	Nov 1903	Scrapped 1922

Black Sea Fleet. Formerly the *Kniaz Potemkin Tavritcheski,* but renamed after the notorious mutiny. She was again named *Potemkin* in April 1917 and *Boretz za Svobodu* a month later. A three-funnelled ship cut down to a high main deck aft. The 12in guns were in French-type turrets, 4 of the 6in in upper deck casemates and 12 in a main deck battery. The main belt ran for 237ft and was 7ft 6in wide and 9in-8in thick with a 5in lower edge. The 6in upper belt was taken to the main deck for 156ft, which was 14ft less than the extent of the battery armour. The bulkheads were 7in-5in and the alloy steel armour deck 2in on the flat with 2½in slopes outside the area of the battery, increased to 3in at the ends. The battery roof was 1½in and the turret crowns 3in. The *Pantelimon* took part in many of the Black Sea operations in the First World War, during which two 11pdr AA were added.

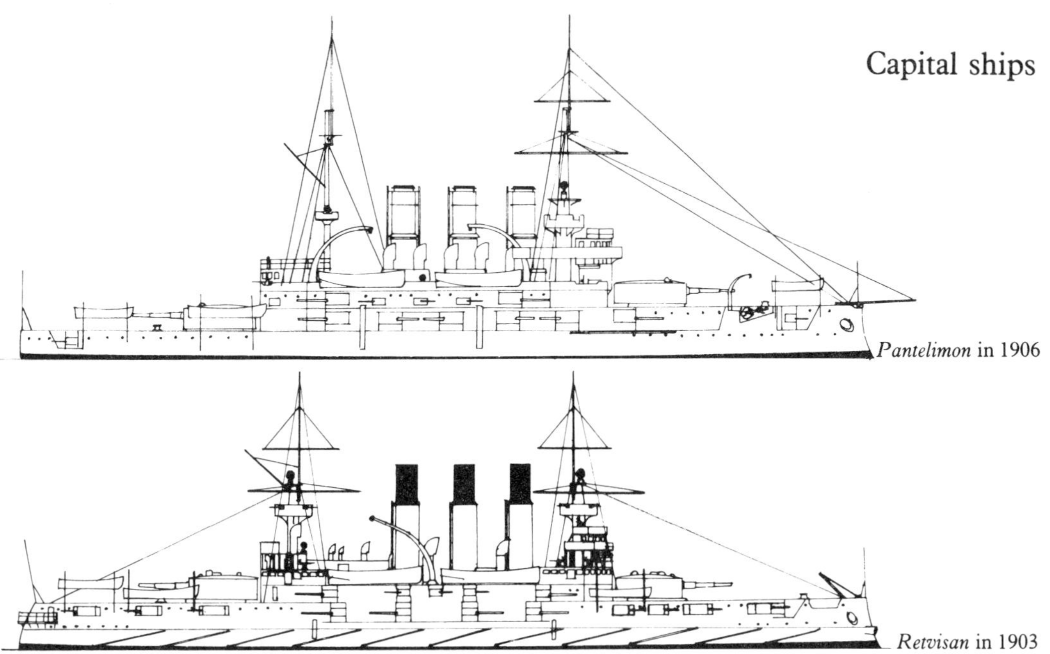
Pantelimon in 1906

Retvisan in 1903

A three-funnelled, flush-deck ship, and the best Russian battleship so far described. The 12in guns were in French-type turrets, 4 of the 6in in upper deck casemates and 8 in a main deck battery. The belt was complete, the lower strake from 4ft below lwl to 3½ft above, being 9in with a 5in lower edge for 256ft, and the upper strake to the main deck was 6in between turrets, 7in bulkheads closing these parts of the belt which tapered beyond to 2in at bow and stern. The alloy steel armour deck was 2in with 3in slopes. The *Retvisan* was torpedoed in the Japanese attack at Port Arthur on 9.2.1904 when she took on 2100t water, and was damaged in the Yellow Sea battle where she was apparently hit by 18-12in to 8in shells. During the siege of Port Arthur she was hit by 13-11in howitzer shells and sank on 6.12.1904. Three shells, one of which burst in a boiler room, were very damaging. She was raised and repaired by the Japanese and served as the *Hizen*.

RETVISAN *battleship*

Displacement: 12,900t
Dimensions: 386ft 8in oa x 72ft 2in x 26ft max (*117.85 x 22.00 x 7.92m*)
Machinery: 24 Niclausse boilers, 2-shaft VTE, 17,000ihp = 18kts. Coal 1000/2000t
Armour: KC. Belt 9in-5in, belt ends 2in, turrets 9in-8in, battery and casemates 5in, CT 10in
Armament: 4-12in/40(2x2), 12-6in/45, 20-11pdr, 24-2pdr, 8-1pdr, 6-15in TT 4 aw 2 sub, 45 mines
Complement: 738

Name	Builder	Laid down	Launched	Comp	Fate
RETVISAN	Cramp	May 1898	Oct 1900	Dec 1901	Sunk as target July 1924

Retvisan about 1903

Renamed *Grashdanin* in 1917. Of obvious French design with the forecastle deck extending to the main mast and very pronounced tumblehome. The 6in turrets were on either beam, the forward and after at forecastle deck level and the middle ones rising from the sloping sides to upper deck level. The belt was complete from 5ft below lwl to 7ft above. The lower strake was 10in amidships with a 7in lower edge, and the upper strake 8in. Forward and aft the lower strake was reduced to 6in and 6¾in respectively and the upper to 5¾in and 4¾in. The turret and CT crowns were 2½in, and there were two armour decks, the main deck being 2½in over the belt and the lower deck 1¼in. The latter was curved down near the sides to form a 1½in torpedo bulkhead which extended from forward of 'A' turret to just abaft 'Y'. This protection was based on the Toulon tests of 1890 but the bulkhead's maximum distance of 6ft 8in inboard was inadequate. The *Tsessarevitch* was torpedoed in the attack at Port Arthur on 9.2.1904, but too far aft to test the torpedo bulkhead. In the Yellow Sea battle on 10.8.1904 she was hit by a 12in shell on the foremast, which killed Rear Admiral Vitgeft, and by another which hit the sighting slit of the CT and jammed the helm, putting the ship out of control. She was interned at Kiao-Chau after the battle, but apart from the above two shells, no very great damage had been caused by the total of 13-12in hits. In the First World War the *Tsessarevitch* was stationed in the Baltic. She was engaged by the powerful dreadnought *Kronprinz* in the action off Moon Sound on 17.10.1917 but escaped with only two damaging hits.

Tsessarevitch as completed 1903

TSESSAREVITCH *battleship*

Displacement: 12,915t
Dimensions: 388ft 9in oa x 76ft 1in x 26ft max (*118.50 x 23.20 x 7.92m*)
Machinery: 20 Belleville boilers, 2-shaft VTE, 16,500ihp = 18.5kts. Coal 1350t max
Armour: KC. Belt 10in-7in, belt ends 6¾in-4¾in, turrets 10in, secondary turrets 6in, CT 10in
Armament: 4-12in/40(2x2), 12-6in/45(6x2), 20-11pdr, 20-3pdr, 4-15in TT 2 aw, 2 sub, later 2 sub only, 45 mines
Complement: 782

Name	Builder	Laid down	Launched	Comp	Fate
TSESSAREVITCH	La Seyne	June 1899	23.2.1901	Aug 1903	Scrapped 1922

Tsessarevitch as completed

This ill-fated class generally resembled the *Tsessarevitch*, with the armouring altered, but not for the better. The belt was thinned and was also a foot narrower, while the 3in side armour between the main and upper decks, covering the 11pdr battery, was of little value. The upper deck was 2½in-1½in over this battery, while the main deck was 2in, the lower deck 1½in-1in and the torpedo bulkhead 1¼in. The latter was no longer formed by a continuation of the lower deck slope, but was joined to it by a narrow flat. The first four ships were present at Tsuṣhima where the *Borodino* blew up from a magazine explosion caused by shell hits, the *Alexander* was sunk probably as a result of flooding from a very large shell hole near the wl forward, and the *Suvarov*, badly battered by shells, sank from hits by one 18in and two to four 14in torpedoes. The *Orel* escaped large shell holes near the wl but, considerably damaged elsewhere, surrendered to the Japanese next day. She was partially reconstructed and served as the *Iwami*. In the First World War the *Slava* was frequently employed in the Gulf of Riga, and was badly damaged by the dreadnought *König* off Moon Sound on 17.10.1917 and, too deep in the water to escape, was scuttled by a torpedo. The elevation of her 12in guns had been increased to 30°, and they outranged the *König's* powerful 12in/50 which were limited to 16°.

On 9.3.1905 during the voyage which ended at Tsushima, the *Orel's* displacement with 2450t coal aboard, was 16,800t at 32ft 6in forward and 30ft 6in aft.

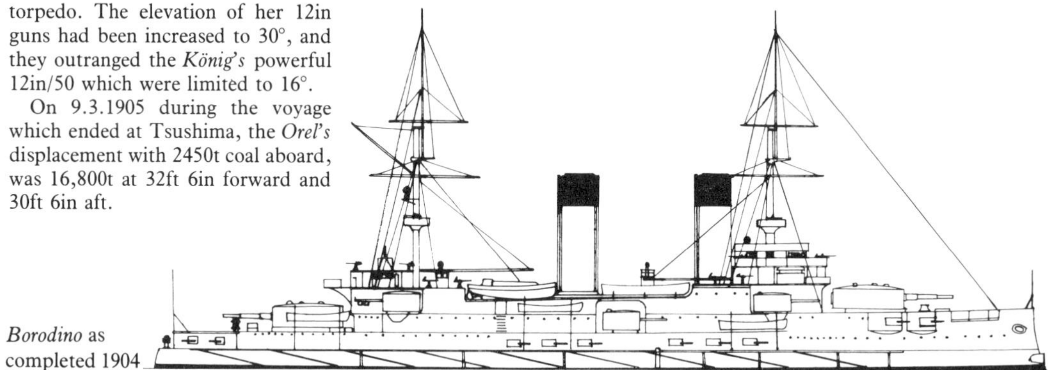

Borodino as completed 1904

BORODINO class *battleships*

Displacement: 13,516t designed (see below)
Dimensions: 397ft oa x 76ft 2in x 26ft 2in max (*121.00 x 23.22 x 7.97m*) see below
Machinery: 20 Belleville boilers, 2-shaft VTE, 16,300ihp = 17.5-17.8kts. Coal 800/1520t
Armour: KC. Belt 7½in-6in, belt ends 5¾in-4in, turrets 10in-4in, secondary turrets 6in, 11pdr battery 3in, CT 8in
Armament: 4-12in/40(2x2), 12-6in/45(6x2), 20-11pdr, 20-3pdr, 4-15in TT 2 aw, 2 sub
Complement: 835

Name	Builder	Laid down	Launched	Comp	Fate
BORODINO	New Admiralty	July 1899	8.9.1901	Aug 1904	Sunk 27.5.1905
IMPERATOR ALEXANDER III	Baltic Wks	July 1899	3.8.1901	Nov 1903	Sunk 27.5.1905
OREL	Galernii Is	Mar 1900	19.7.1902	Oct 1904	Scrapped 1922
KNIAZ SUVAROV	Baltic Wks	July 1901	25.9.1902	Sept 1904	Sunk 27.5.1905
SLAVA	Baltic Wks	Oct 1902	29.8.1903	June 1905	Sunk 17.10.1917

Slava in 1909

Black Sea Fleet. Similar to the *Pantelimon* but with some alterations made in the light of Russo-Japanese war experience. The 4 upper deck 6in were replaced by 8in and 3in armour added at the ends of the main belt and to the 11pdrs between the 8in guns. The armour deck was increased to 2¾in, with 3in slopes over the area between the main and upper belts. Both ships took part in many of the Balck Sea operations in the First World War and *Evstafi* was for some time flagship. During the war 2-11pdr AA guns were added to each ship. It may be noted that the two *Evstafis* with the *Pantelimon* and *Tri Svititelia* twice encountered the powerful battlecruiser *Goeben,* each side getting the better of one of the two actions.

EVSTAFI class *battleships*

Displacement:	12,840t
Dimensions:	387ft 3in oa x 74ft x 27ft max (*118.03 x 22.55 x 8.23m*)
Machinery:	22 Belleville boilers, 2-shaft VTE, 10,800ihp = 16.5kts. Coal 800t max
Armour:	KC. Belt 9in-5in, belt ends 3in, turrets 10in-4in, battery and casemates 5in, 11pdr battery 3in, CT 9in
Armament:	4-12in/40(2x2), 4-8in/50, 12-6in/45, 14-11pdr, 6-3pdr, 3-18in TT sub
Complement:	879

Name	Builder	Laid down	Launched	Comp	Fate
EVSTAFI	Nicolaiev	Dec 1903	3.11.1906	5.8.1910	Scrapped 1922
IOANN ZLATOUST	Sevastopol	Nov 1903	13.5.1906	11.8.1910	Scrapped 1922

Ioann Zlatoust under German control in 1918
Aldo Fraccaroli Collection

Andrei Pervoswanni as completed in 1910
Aldo Fraccaroli Collection

The design of this class was much altered as a result of Russo-Japanese war experience. They were flush deck ships with completely armoured hulls and no scuttles. The 12in guns were in French-type turrets allowing 35° elevation, and the after turret was sited as near the stern as possible. The 8in turrets were on either beam amidships and the other 8in guns in an upper deck battery with the 4.7in in a battery above with 3½in armour. The belt was 8½in-6½in to 6½ft above lwl, but only 5in above this. The main deck was 2¼-1½in and the lower deck 1½in with 3in slopes. There was no thick torpedo bulkhead. Originally they had cage masts, but these were cut down to funnel top height in *Pavel* and further in *Andrei,* and the pole masts stepped. They took little part in the Baltic fighting in the First World War. *Pavel* was renamed *Respublika* in 1917, and *Andrei* was torpedoed in the CMB attack on Kronstadt 18.8.1919. The two ships could be distinguished by *Pavel* having goose-neck boat cranes and *Andrei* derricks. Both had 2-11pdr AA guns added during the war.

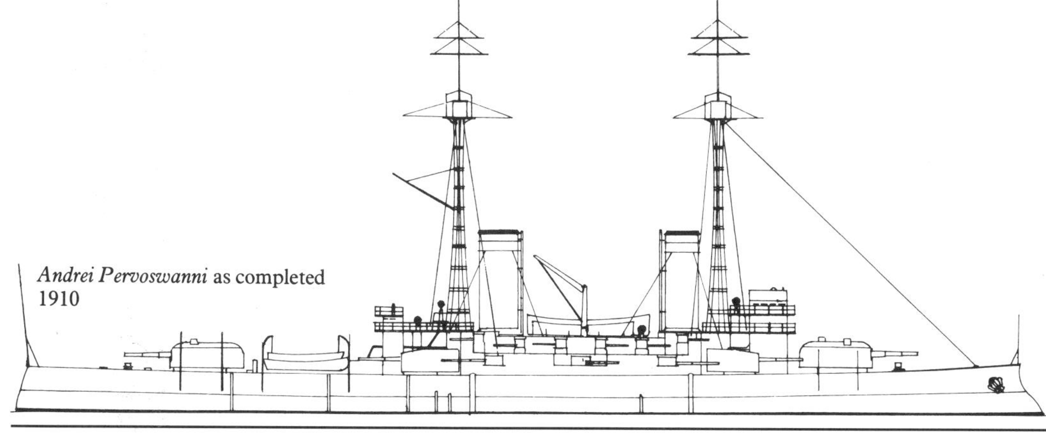

Andrei Pervoswanni as completed 1910

IMPERATOR PAVEL class *battleships*

Displacement:	17,400t
Dimensions:	460ft oa x 80ft x 27ft mean (*140.20 x 24.38 x 8.23m*)
Machinery:	22 Belleville boilers, 2-shaft VTE, 18,000ihp = 17.5kts. Coal 1325t-1500t max
Armour:	KC. Belt 8½in-5in, belt ends 5in-3½in, turrets 8in-4in, secondary turrets 6in-4in, battery 6½in-5in, CT 8in
Armament:	4-12in/40(2x2), 14-8in/50(4x2, 6x1), 12-4.7in/45, 4-3pdr, 3-18in TT sub
Complement:	933

Name	Builder	Laid down	Launched	Comp	Fate
IMPERATOR PAVEL	Baltic Wks	Apr 1904	7.9.1907	7.9.1910	Scrapped 1923
ANDREI PERVOSWANNI	Galernii Is	Apr 1903	20.10.1906	27.7.1910	Scrapped 1925

ARMOURED CRUISERS

General Admiral with full rig but topgallants struck
Aldo Fraccaroli Collection

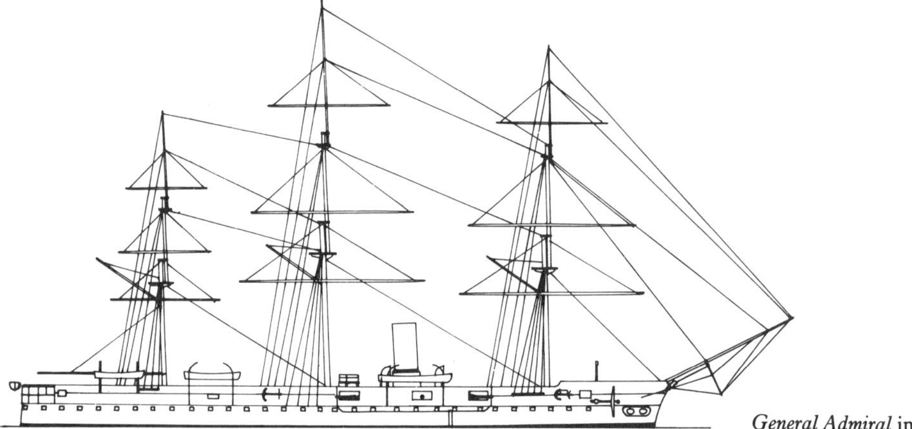

General Admiral in 1880

Iron-hulled ships without a ram, sheathed and coppered and fully rigged. When built they had a considerable reputation as the first armoured cruisers. The belt was complete and extended from 2ft above to 5ft below lwl. There was a 1in deck over the belt and a 6in coaming 4½ft high round the engine room hatch, but no other armour. The 8in guns were amidships on the upper deck and the 6in below the forecastle and poop. The gun armament was altered during their long careers and *Gerzog Edinburgski* had 4-8in/30, 5-6in/28, 6-4in/20 and 10-1pdr revolvers in 1889. They were re-engined in 1892 and 1896 respectively, and then had 4 cylindrical boilers. Latterly used as training ships, they were converted to minelayers in 1909, *General Admiral* becoming the *Narova* and later *25 Oktiabrya* and *Gerzog Edinburgski* the *Onega*, each with 600 mines.

GENERAL ADMIRAL class

Displacement: *General Admiral* 5031t, *Gerzog Edinburgski* 4838t (as designed 4602t)
Dimensions: 285ft 10in wl x 48ft x 24ft – 24ft 5in max (*87.12 x 14.63 x 7.32-7.44m*)
Machinery: 12 rectangular boilers, 1-shaft VC, *General Admiral* 4470ihp = 12.3kts, *Gerzog Edinburgski* 5222ihp = 13.2kts. Coal 500/1000t
Armour: Wrought iron. Belt 6in-5in
Armament: 6-8in/22, 2-6in/23, 4-3.4in, 8-1pdr revolvers, 2-15 TT aw added
Complement: 480/490

Name	Builder	Laid down	Launched	Comp	Fate
GENERAL ADMIRAL	Nevski	1870	1873	1875	Stricken 1938
GERZOG EDINBURGSKI	Baltic Wks	1870	1875	1877	Hulked 1915

Originally, with a heavy full rig, the *Monomakh* had a complete 6in belt, with a 4½in lower edge from 2½ft above to 5½ft below lwl. There were 4-3in bulkheads between the main and upper deck protecting 8 of the 6in guns from raking fire and also the 4 sponsoned 8in, but otherwise the guns were unprotected. The armour deck was 3in-2in. The *Monomakh* was modernised in 1897-1898 and rearmed with 5-6in/45, 8-4.7in/45, and 8-3pdr, retaining the 1pdrs and TTs. She was torpedoed during the night at Tsushima and surrendered next day but could not be kept afloat.

VLADIMIR MONOMAKH

Displacement: (1905) 5593t (as designed 6000t)
Dimensions: 296ft 3in wl x 52ft x 26ft 3in max (*90.30 x 15.85 x 8.00m*)
Machinery: 6 cyl boilers, 2-shaft VC, 7000ihp = 15.2kts. Coal 900/1100t
Armour: Compound. Belt 6in-4½in, battery 4in-3in bulkheads only
Armament: 4-8in/30(4x1), 12-6in/28, 4-3.4in, 4-3pdr revolvers, 8-1pdr revolvers, 3-15in TT aw
Complement: 566, later 495

Name	Builder	Laid down	Launched	Comp	Fate
VLADIMIR MONOMAKH	Baltic Wks	1880	1882	1885	Sunk 28.5.1905

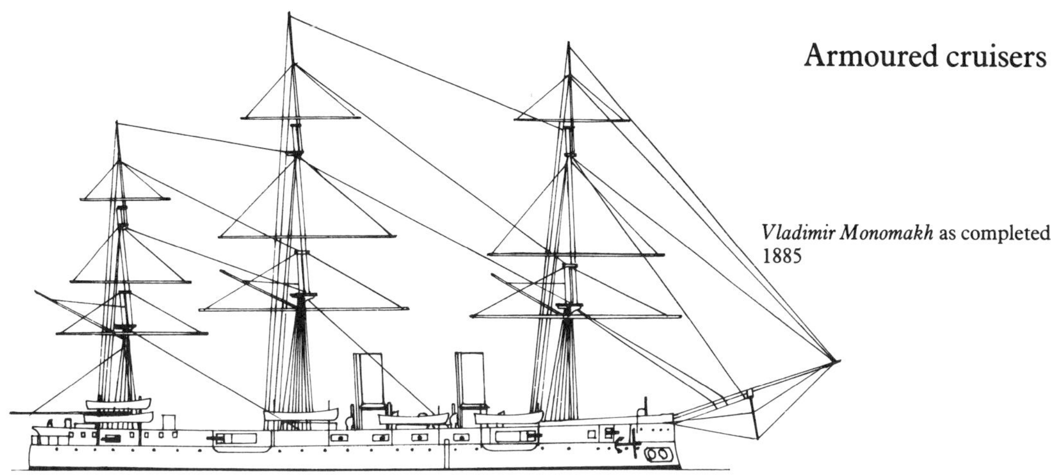

Vladimir Monomakh as completed 1885

Above: *Vladimir Monomakh* with *Dimitri Donskoi* in the background. Both have been modernised and have light pole masts substituted for the original full rig

Right: *Dmitri Donskoi* with a heavy barque rig before modernisation
Both Aldo Fraccaroli Collection

According to official British reports the *Donskoi,* which originally had a heavy full rig, was not well subdivided and if the very large engine room had flooded she would have sunk. The belt was as in the *Monomakh* and there was a 2in deck, but the 14 6in guns on the main deck had no protection and the two 8in in upper deck sponsons only small 2in shields. She was modernised in 1895 and rearmed with six 6in/45, ten 4.7in/45, six 3pdr, and ten 1pdr, retaining the revolvers and TT. The *Donskoi* survived Tsushima and a destroyer attack on the night of the 28th but was scuttled next morning.

DMITRI DONSKOI

Displacement: (1905) 6200t (as designed 5796t)
Dimensions: 296ft 8in wl x 52ft x 25ft 9in max (*90.43 x 15.85 x 7.85m*)
Machinery: 6 cyl boilers, 1-shaft VC (2 engines), 7000ihp = 16.5kts. Coal 800t max
Armour: Compound. Belt 6in-4½in
Armament: 2-8in/30(2x1), 14-6in/28, 4-3.4in, 14-1pdr revolvers, 5-15in TT aw
Complement: 571, later 507

Name	Builder	Laid down	Launched	Comp	Fate
DMITRI DONSKOI	New Admiralty	1881	1883	1885	Scuttled 29.5.1905

The *Nakhimov* was in many ways a close copy of the *Imperieuse* and *Warspite*, of which the Russians had managed to obtain drawings, though they contrived, by alteration of bunkers and hatches, to impair the protection of the machinery. She was sheathed and coppered and originally rigged as a brig. The belt was 147ft long with a 6in lower edge and extended from about 3ft above to 5ft below lwl, ending in 10in-6in bulkheads. The barbettes were 8in – wing 8in-7in – to the main deck with 3in ammunition tubes below, and 2½in-2in shields, but the 6in guns on the main deck were unprotected. The armour deck was 3in over the belt and at the level of the belt lower edge fore and aft. The *Nakhimov* was reboilered in 1899, the 3.4in removed and the lighter guns altered to twelve 3pdr and four 1pdr revolvers. She appears to have escaped serious shell damage at Tsushima but was torpedoed during the night and her crew opened the sea-valves on surrendering to the Japanese.

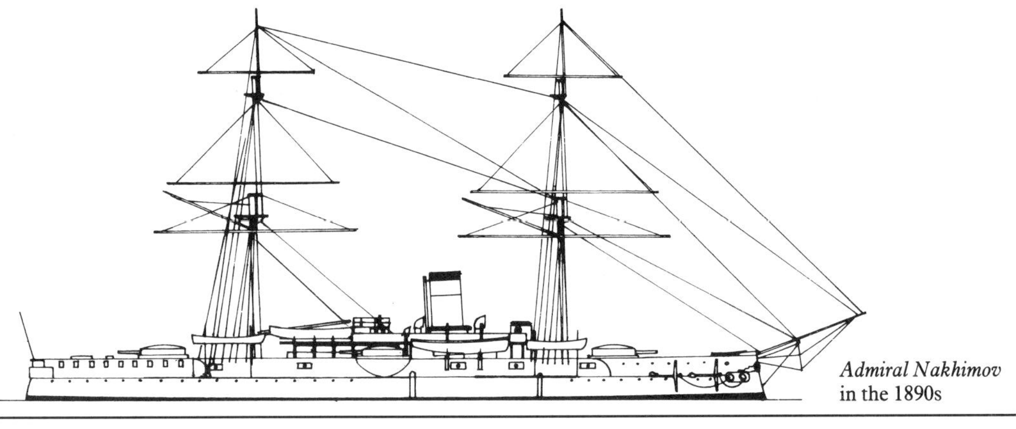
Admiral Nakhimov in the 1890s

ADMIRAL NAKHIMOV

Displacement: 8524t
Dimensions: 333ft wl x 61ft x 27ft 6in max (*101.50 x 18.59 x 8.38m*)
Machinery: 12 cyl boilers, 2-shaft VC, 9000ihp = 17kts. Coal 1200t max
Armour: Compound. Belt 10in-6in, barbettes 8in-3in, CT 6in
Armament: 8-8in/35(4x2), 10-6in/35, 4-3.4in, 6-3pdr revolver, 4-1pdr revolver, 3-15in TT aw, 40 mines
Complement: 570

Name	Builder	Laid down	Launched	Comp	Fate
ADMIRAL NAKHIMOV	Baltic Wks	1884	Nov 1885	1888	Scuttled 28.5.1905

Admiral Nakhimov with reduced rig about 1900
Aldo Fraccaroli Collection

Pamiat Azova with full barque rig

A three-funnelled ship, sheathed and coppered and originally barque-rigged without royals. The belt stopped 45ft from the stem and 35ft from the stern and extended from 2½ft above to 5ft below lwl. It was 6in amidships, reduced to 4in fore and aft and at the lower edge, and ending in 4in bulkheads. The 8in guns in sponsons had small 2in shields while the main deck 6in were unprotected. The armour deck was 2½in reduced to 1½in at the ends. The *Pamiat Azova* was reconstructed in 1904 and reboilered with 18 Bellevilles. Russian official figures, of uncertain date, give only 5664ihp = 16kts. She became the torpedo school ship *Dvina* in 1909 and was torpedoed by *CMB79* in the attack on Kronstadt.

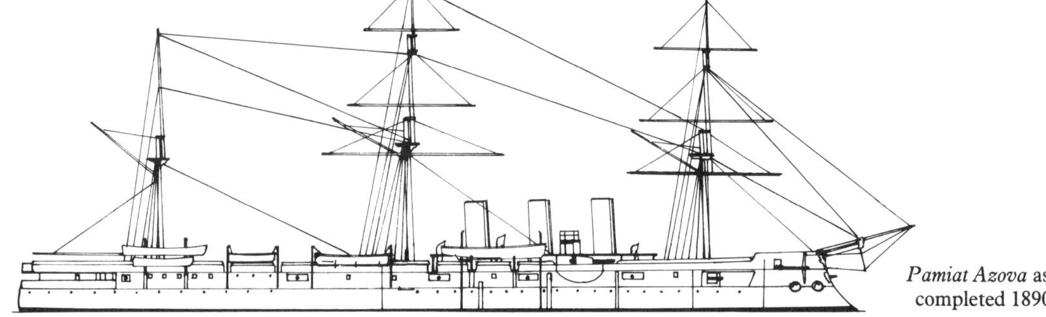
Pamiat Azova as completed 1890

PAMIAT AZOVA

Displacement: 6674t (as designed 6000t)
Dimensions: 384ft 6in oa x 56ft 6in x 26ft 10in max (*117.19 x 17.22 x 8.18m*)
Machinery: 6 cyl boilers, 2-shaft VTE, 8500ihp = 17kts. Coal 1200t max
Armour: Compound. Belt 6in-4in, CT 1½in
Armament: 2-8in/35(2x1), 13-6in/35, 7-3pdr, 8-1pdr revolver. 3-15in TT aw
Complement: 640

Name	Builder	Laid down	Launched	Comp	Fate
PAMIAT AZOVA	Baltic Wks	1886	June 1888	1890	Sunk 18.8.1919

Although the *Rurik* caused a considerable stir when first built, she was a thoroughly unsatisfactory design with only half her armament available on the broadside, inadequate protection and poor compartmentation. The belt was 320ft long, 6ft 9in wide and 10in-8in reduced to 5in at the lower edge and ending in 10in-9in bulkheads which were taken to the upper deck. The 8in guns in sponsons, the 6in on the main deck and the 4.7in on the upper deck were protected by shields while the heavy bulkheads gave some protection to 14 of the 6in. The armour deck was 2½in over the belt, increased to 3½in forward and 3in aft. *Rurik* was barque-rigged and sheathed and coppered. She was sunk at Ulsan by 8in and 6in shells from the Japanese cruisers.

Rurik as completed 1895

RURIK

Displacement: 11,690t (as designed 10,933t)
Dimensions: 435ft oa x 67ft x 27ft 3in max (*132.58 x 20.42 x 8.30m*)
Machinery: 8 cyl boilers, 2-shaft VTE (4 engines), 13,250ihp = 18.7kts light. Coal 2000t max
Armour: Steel. Belt 10in-5in, battery 10in-9in bulkheads only, CT 8in
Armament: 4-8in/35(4x1), 16-6in/45, 6-4.7in/45, 6-3pdr, 10-1pdr, 4-15in TT aw
Complement: 683 (817 at Ulsan)

Name	Builder	Laid down	Launched	Comp	Fate
RURIK	Baltic Wks	1890	Nov 1892	1895	Sunk 14.8.1904

Rurik in her early days

Rossia in October 1910

Rossia as completed 1897

An unfortunate design, though an improvement on the *Rurik*. The armour belt ran from the stern to 80ft short of the bows, and from 4ft 6in above to 4ft below lwl. It was 8in-6in with a 4in lower edge and a 7in fore bulkhead. A patch of 5in side armour above the belt, with a 5in bulkhead forward, protected the engine rooms, with, in addition, a 3in glacis between lower and main decks. Apart from the battery bulkheads the guns had only thin shields, 1in traverses and lightly armoured hoists for the 8in. The mild steel armour deck was 3¾in over the belt and 2in forward. The 8in guns were in sponsons on the upper deck with 3-6in forward under the forecastle, 6 on each side of the main deck and 1 aft. At full power only the 2 wing shafts were used, giving the ihp quoted above, as there was insufficient boiler powe to use the 2500ihp centre engine in addition, and this was kept for cruising with the wing screws disconnected. The *Rossia*, which was sheathed and coppered, was rearmed to some extent in 1906, 6-6in being added in sponsons on the upper deck while the foremost 6in was remounted on the forecastle and the lighter guns reduced to 15-11pdr and 2-3pdr, with 2 TT. In 1916–1917 the 6in were reduced to 14 and 2-8in added at bow and stern to give a total of 6. She was considerably damaged by the Japanese armoured cruisers at Ulsan in 1904 and had heavy casualties but could still steam well. In the First World War she was employed in the Baltic, at times as a minelayer with 100 mines.

ROSSIA

Displacement: 13,675t (as designed 12,195t)
Dimensions: 480ft 6in oa x 68ft 6in x 26ft max (*146.45 x 20.88 x 7.92m*)
Machinery: 32 Belleville boilers, 3-shaft VTE (see below), 15,500ihp = 20.2kts. Coal 2500t max
Armour: Harvey-nickel. Belt 8in-4in, battery 5in bulkheads only, CT 12in
Armament: 4-8in/45(4x1), 16-6in/45, 12-11pdr, 20-3pdr, 16-1pdr, 5-15in TT aw
Complement: 842

Name	Builder	Laid down	Launched	Comp	Fate
ROSSIA	Baltic Wks	1894	May 1896	1897	Scrapped 1922

RUSSIA

Generally similar to the *Rossia* but with some important changes including normal 3-shaft machinery. The belt was 300ft long and ran from 2ft 9in above to 5ft below lwl, ending in 6in bulkheads. The 8in and 6in guns were disposed as in the *Rossia*, but the 2 forward 8in and the 12 midships 6in were in 5in casemates. These for 10 of the 6in had 2½in rear walls and 1½in ammunition tubes, but the 2-8in and the 2 foremost of the 12-6in were in a two-deck casemate which extended across the ship with 2in bulkheads. The nickel steel armour deck was 2in amidships with 3in slopes, and 2in fore and aft. The *Gromoboi* was partially rearmed in 1906, 6-6in being added on the upper deck and the foremost 6in remounted on the forecastle, the lighter guns now comprising 19-11 pdr and 6-3pdr. In 1916–1917 the bow and stern 6in were replaced by 2-8in/45 and 4-11pdr AA added. *Gromoboi* could steam well after Ulsan, where she was considerably damaged and had heavier casualties than *Rossia*. She was mined on 23.5.1905 off Vladivostock but was repaired and served in the Baltic during the First World War.

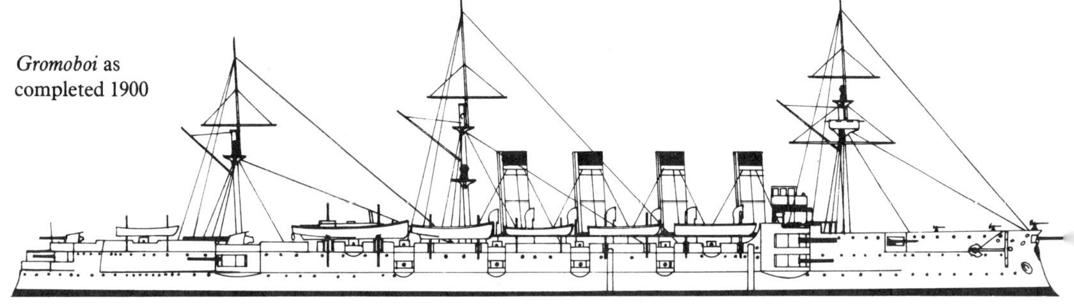

Gromoboi as completed 1900

GROMOBOI

Displacement: 13,220t (as designed 12,960t)
Dimensions: 481ft oa x 68ft 6in x 27ft 10in max (*146.60 x 20.88 x 8.48m*)
Machinery: 32 Belleville boilers, 3-shaft VTE, 15,500ihp = 20kts. Coal 1720t max
Armour: KC. Belt 6in, casemates 5in-2in, CT 12in
Armament: 4-8in/45(4x1), 16-6in/45, 24-11pdr, 4-3pdr, 4-1pdr, 4-15in TT sub
Complement: 877

Name	Builder	Laid down	Launched	Completed	Fate
GROMOBOI	Baltic Wks	1897	May 1899	1900	Scrapped 1922

Gromoboi before rearming in 1906

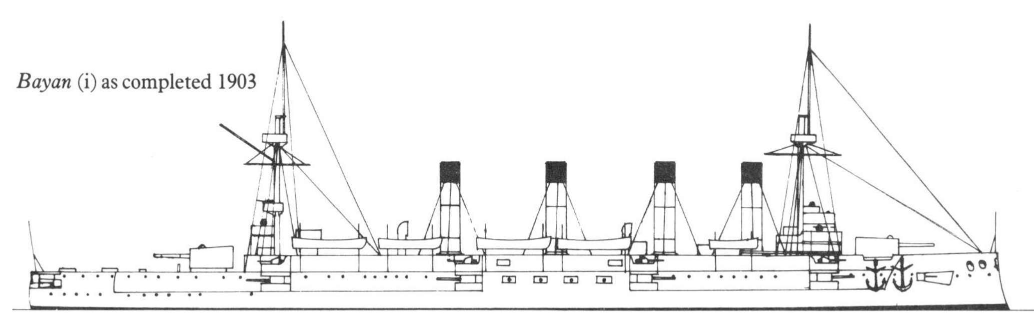

Bayan (i) as completed 1903

Medium-size armoured cruisers of better design than such ships as the *Rossia*. The main belt ran from the stem to the after turret and from 2ft above to 4ft below lwl, ending in a 7in-8in bulkhead. The belt was reduced to 4in at the lower edge and ends. The upper belt was 2½in to the main deck as were the casemates for the 6in guns and the midships battery for 8 of the 11pdrs. The armour deck was a uniform 2in. The first *Bayan* took part in the Russo-Japanese war, being mined on 27.7.1904, and was sunk at Port Arthur by 11in howitzers on 8.12.1904. She was raised and served in the Japanese Navy as the *Aso*. In the First World War *Pallada* was blown up by a torpedo from *U26*. The remaining two ships had two 11pdr or two 3pdr AA added and when used as minelayers could carry up to 150 mines. *Bayan* (ii) took part in the action off Moon Sound on 17.10.1917 when one 12in hit from the *König* caused a serious fire.

BAYAN class

Displacement: 7775t (*Bayan* (i) 7725t)
Dimensions: 449ft 7in oa x 57ft 6in x 21ft 3in-22ft max (*137.03 x 17.52 x 6.48-6.71m*)
Machinery: 26 Belleville boilers, 2-shaft VTE, 16,500ihp = 21kts (*Markarov* on trials 19,000ihp = 22.5). Coal 950-1100t max
Armour: KC (*Bayan* (i) HN). Belt 7in-2½in, turrets 6in-5¼in, CT 5½in (*Bayan* (i) belt 8in-2½in, turrets 6¾in-6in, CT 6¾in)
Armament: 2-8in/45(2x1), 8-6in/45,20-11pdr, 4-6pdr, 2-18in TT sub (*Bayan* (i) 16-11pdr, 8-3pdr, 2-15in TT)
Complement: 568-593

Name	Builder	Laid down	Launched	Comp	Fate
BAYAN (i)	La Seyne	Feb 1899	June 1900	Apr 1903	Sunk as target 8.8.1932
ADMIRAL MAKAROV	La Seyne	Apr 1905	May 1906	Apr 1908	Scrapped 1922
BAYAN (ii)	New Admiralty	Aug 1905	Aug 1907	Dec 1911	Scrapped 1922
PALLADA	New Admiralty	Aug 1905	Nov 1906	Feb 1911	Sunk 11.10.1914

Admiral Makarov shortly after completion in 1909

Rurik in 1912
By courtesy of John Roberts

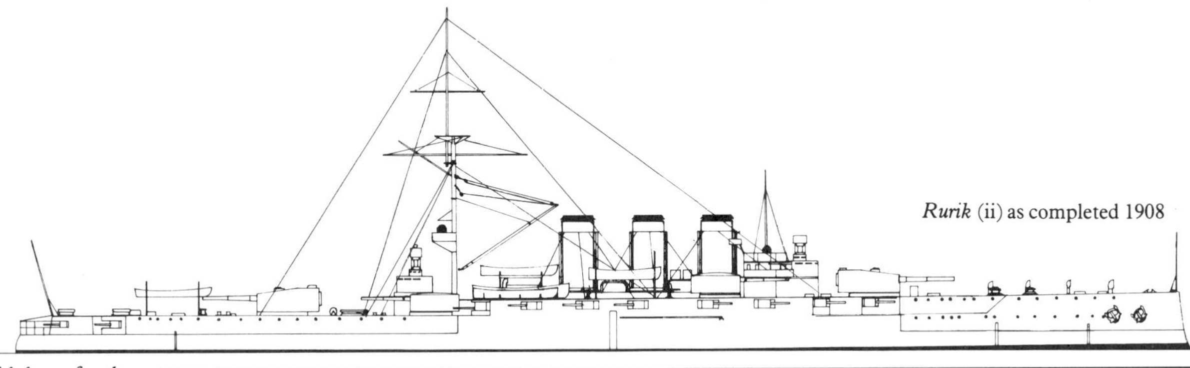

Rurik (ii) as completed 1908

The best large ship laid down for the Russian Navy up to 1905, and one of the best armoured cruisers ever built. The 10in mountings allowed 35° elevation, and the magazine flooding arrangements with drenching sprays were far ahead of British practice. The armour belt extended from 7ft 9in above to 5ft below lwl and between the 10in barbettes was 6in with a 4in lower and a 5in upper edge. It was continued to the bows at 4in-3in and aft at 3in, ending in a 3in bulkhead. The 3in armour of the upper deck battery was continued down to the belt upper edge. The main turrets were 8in with 2½in crowns and 7¼in barbettes reduced to 4¼in-2in behind the side armour, while the secondary turrets were 7in with 2in crowns and 6in barbettes reduced to 3in-1½in.

RURIK

Dislacement: 15,190t
Dimensions: 529ft oa x 75ft x 26ft max *(161.23 x 22.86 x 7.92m)*
Machinery: 28 Belleville boilers, 2-shaft VTE, 19,700ihp = 21kts. Coal 1920t max
Armour: KC. Belt 6in-4in, belt ends 4in-3in, turrets 8in-7¼in, secondary turrets 7in-6in, battery 3in, CT 8in
Armament: 4-10in/50(2x2), 8-8in/50(4x2), 20-4.7in/50, 4-3pdr, 2-18in TT sub
Complement: 899

Name	Builder	Laid down	Launched	Comp	Fate
RURIK	Vickers	Aug 1905	17.11.1906	Sept 1908	Scrapped 1923

There were two armour decks, the main deck at 1½in and the lower at 1in, with 1½in slopes amidships, while the battery roof was 1in. There was a 1½in torpedo bulkhead about 11ft from the side between end barbettes. During the First World War the *Rurik* was much employed in the Baltic and was usually flagship of the cruiser squadron. She was at times used for minelaying and is said to have been able to carry 400 mines. Two 3pdr AA guns were added during the war. The *Rurik* was twice badly damaged forward, on 13.2.1915 by grounding and on 19.11.1916 by a mine. As completed she had a mainmast only, but a foremast was later added and in 1917 this became a tripod.

CRUISERS

Wooden-hulled screw corvettes with full rig, *Vitiaz* being very slow under sail. *Vitiaz* was later renamed *Skobeleff*. *Variag* had the engines of the older screw frigate *Balkan*. After the actions in Hampton Roads there was considerable doubt whether to proceed with the *Askold*, and she was the last unarmoured warship of over 2000t laid down in Russia for 20 years. The armament was frequently changed and in 1884 was: *Variag* 1-6in/23, 10-4.2in/20; *Vitiaz* 8-6in/23, 4-4.2in/20; *Askold* as *Vitiaz*, with one 3.4in and spar torpedoes.

The *Azia* and *Afrika* of 2500-2590t and the *Europe* of 3160t were iron-hulled, barque-rigged, screw merchant ships launched in the USA in 1874–1878 and acquired by the Russian Navy, and then equipped as cruisers. The engines were in part exposed above the waterline and they cannot be considered as true warships.

VARIAG class *wooden screw corvettes*

Displacement: *Variag* 2155t; *Vitiaz* 2350t; *Askold* 2200t
Dimensions: 217ft 6in wl x 39ft 8in x 19ft 3in-20ft 1in max (*66.29 x 12.09 x 5.87-6.12m*)
Machinery: Rectangular boilers, 1-shaft, 910-1018ihp = *c*10kts
Armament: 17 SB (later see below)
Complement: 324

Name	Builder	Laid down	Launched	Comp	Fate
ASKOLD	Okhta	1862	1863	1864	Stricken *c*1890
VARIAG	Uleaborg	1861	1862	1863	Stricken *c*1887
VITIAZ	Berneborg	1861	1862	1863	Stricken *c*1894

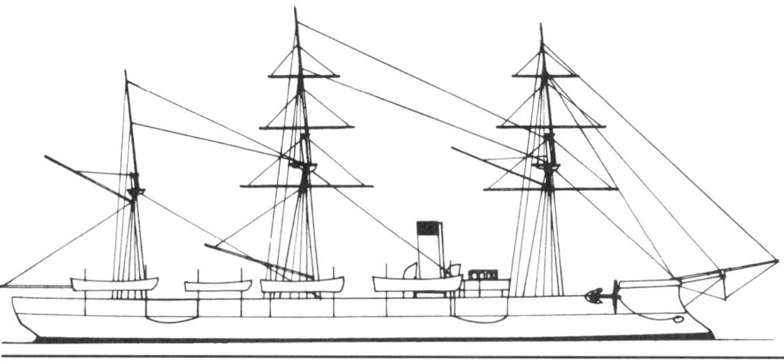

Pamiat Merkuria about 1890

Black Sea Fleet. Originally named *Yaroslav*, the *Pamiat Merkuria* was a barque-rigged, unprotected steel and iron cruiser with a projecting ram bow. She was reckoned to be a good sea-boat. The 6in guns were without shields, and were located at bow and stern with four in upper deck sponsons. The smaller guns eventually comprised 4-3pdr, 2-1pdr and 2-1pdr revolvers, with 2 TT.

PAMIAT MERKURIA *unprotected cruiser*

Displacement: 2997t
Dimensions: 295ft 3in wl x 40ft 8in x 19ft 7in max (*90.00 x 12.40 x 5.97m*)
Machinery: 6 cyl boilers, 1-shaft HC, 3000ihp = 14kts. Coal 300t max
Armament: 6-6in/28, 4-4.2in/20, 5-2½pdr, 4-1pdr revolvers, 4-15in TT aw
Complement: 341

Name	Builder	Laid down	Launched	Comp	Fate
PAMIAT MERKURIA	Le Havre	1878	1879	1881	Stricken 1906

Pamiat Merkuria with her original barque rig

Steel and iron-hulled partly protected cruisers with clipper bows and barque-rig. They were sheathed and coppered. *Rynda* at least is believed to have shown signs of weakness and to have been strengthened. Protection was limited to a 1½in deck over boiler and engine rooms. The 6in guns were on the upper deck with four in sponsons and three on each side. *Rynda* was latterly a training ship, and 1901 reports give her armament as 4-6in/28, 2-3.4in, 2-11pdr, 10-1pdr revolvers and 4-15in TT. She was reported to have had diesel engines fitted as an experimental ship in 1911.

VITIAZ class *protected cruiser*

Displacement: *Rynda* 3537t (as designed 2950t)
Dimensions: 260ft 6in wl x 45ft x 19ft 11in max (*79.40 x 13.72 x 6.07m*)
Machinery: 10 cyl boilers, 1-shaft HC, 3000ihp = 14.4kts. Coal 500t max
Armament: 10-6in/28, 4-3.4in, 8-1pdr revolvers, 3-15in TT aw
Complement: 330

Name	Builder	Laid down	Launched	Comp	Fate
VITIAZ	Galernii Is	1883	1884	1886	Wrecked May 1893
RYNDA	Galernii Is	1883	1885	1887	Stricken 1914

Rynda probably during the 1890s

Admiral Kornilov, photographed about 1902 with a reduced rig
Aldo Fraccaroli Collection

A steel protected cruiser, sheathed and coppered, with a pronounced ram bow and originally rigged as a barque. There was a 2½in-1in deck with 3in CT and 4½in-3in engine room hatch glacis, but the 6in guns had shields only. These were on each side of the upper deck with the end guns in slightly projecting sponsons. For most of the waterline there was a cofferdam filled with coconut fibre. The *Kornilov* was rearmed in 1904/1905, 10-6in/45 replacing the 14 older guns, and from 1908 onwards was a torpedo school ship.

ADMIRAL KORNILOV *protected cruiser*

Displacement: 5863t (as designed 4950t)
Dimensions: 368ft oa x 48ft 8in x 25ft 6in max (*112.16 x 14.83 x 7.77m*)
Machinery: 8 cyl boilers, 2-shaft HTE, 5977ihp = 17.6kts. Coal 1000t max
Armament: 14-6in/35, 6-3pdr, 10-1pdr revolvers, 6-15in TT aw
Complement: 479

Name	Builder	Laid down	Launched	Comp	Fate
ADMIRAL KORNILOV	St Nazaire	1886	1887	1888	Stricken 1911

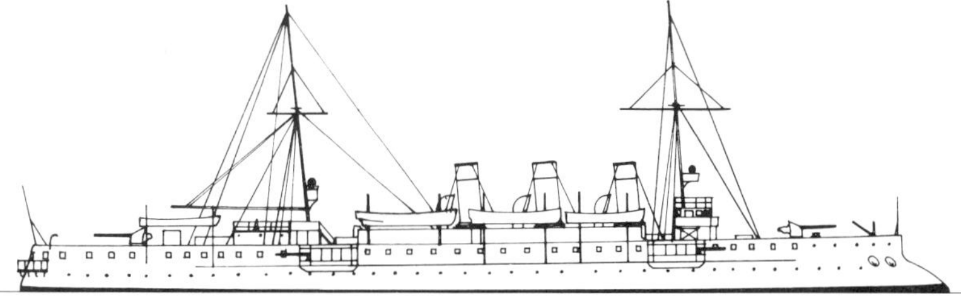

Svietlana as completed 1897

A three-funnelled cruiser with a pronounced ram bow, and sheathed and coppered, the *Svietlana* was in peacetime fitted out as a yacht for the Grand Duke commanding the Russian Navy, and had a considerable amount of woodwork installed. There was a 1in deck with 2in slopes, a 2in hood over the engine room and 5in glacis to the hatches. The CT was 4in and the ammunition tube to the forecastle 6in gun and the broadside patches protecting the TT were 2in. Four of the 6in guns were in main deck sponsons and two fore and aft on the upper deck. *Svietlana* was sunk on the day after Tsushima by the *Otowa* and *Niitaka*.

SVIETLANA *protected cruiser*

Displacement: 3862t (1905, 3727t)
Dimensions: 331ft 4in wl x 42ft 8in x 18ft 8in max (*101.00 x 13.00 x 5.69m*)
Machinery: 18 Belleville boilers, 2-shaft VTE, 8500ihp = 21.6kts. Coal 400t max
Armament: 6-6in/45, 10-3pdr, 2-15in TT aw, 20 mines
Complement: 401

Name	Builder	Laid down	Launched	Comp	Fate
SVIETLANA	Le Havre	Dec 1895	Dec 1896	1897	Sunk 28.5.1905

Svietlana during the 1890s

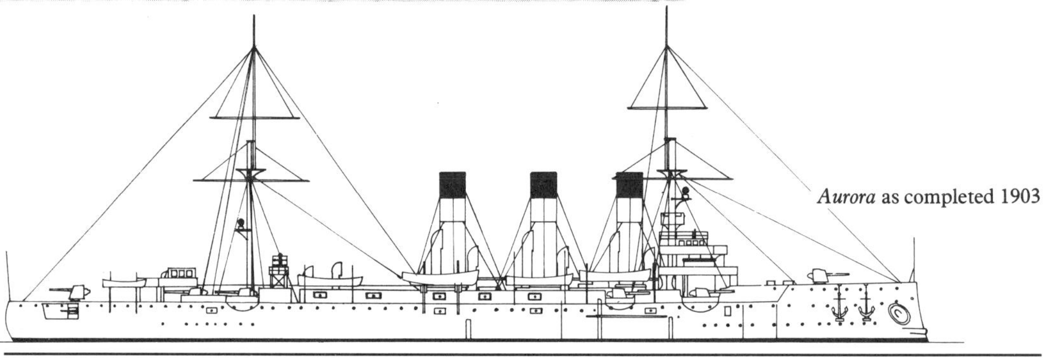
Aurora as completed 1903

PALLADA class *protected cruisers*

Displacement: *Pallada* 6823t; *Diana* 6657t (as designed 6731t)
Dimensions: 415ft 8in oa x 55ft x 20ft 10in-21ft 6in max (*126.69 x 16.76 x 6.35-6.55m*)
Machinery: 24 Belleville boilers, 3-shaft VTE, 12,000-13,000ihp = 19-19.3kts. Coal 1430t max
Armament: 8-6in/45, 24-11pdr, 8-1pdr, 3-15in TT 2 sub
Complement: 571-581

Name	Builder	Laid down	Launched	Comp	Fate
PALLADA	Galernii Is	Dec 1895	Aug 1899	1902	Scrapped 1923
DIANA	Galernii Is	Dec 1895	Oct 1899	1902	Scrapped 1922
AURORA	New Admiralty	June 1897	May 1900	1903	Preserved

Three-funnelled cruisers with a forecastle deck as far as the mainmast. The protective deck was 2in with 3in slopes, the CT 6in, the funnel uptakes 2½in for one deck and the hoists to the 6in guns 1½in. All three ships were sheathed and coppered. There was one 6in gun forward on the forecastle deck, four in sponsons at upper deck level near the bridge and fore funnel, and three aft. The 11pdrs were on the main and upper decks. Two more 6in were later added by the mainmast, and in the First World War *Aurora's* armament was increased to 14-6in, while *Diana* had the 6in replaced by 10-5.1in/55. One and two 11pdr AA guns were also added respectively. The *Pallada* was torpedoed but not badly damaged in the Japanese attack on 8/9.2.1904, and was sunk by 11in howitzers in the siege of Port Arthur on 8.12.1904. She was raised by the Japanese and served in their navy as the *Tsugaru*. *Aurora* is still preserved as a relic of the Russian Revolution.

Aurora in 1910
By courtesy of John Roberts

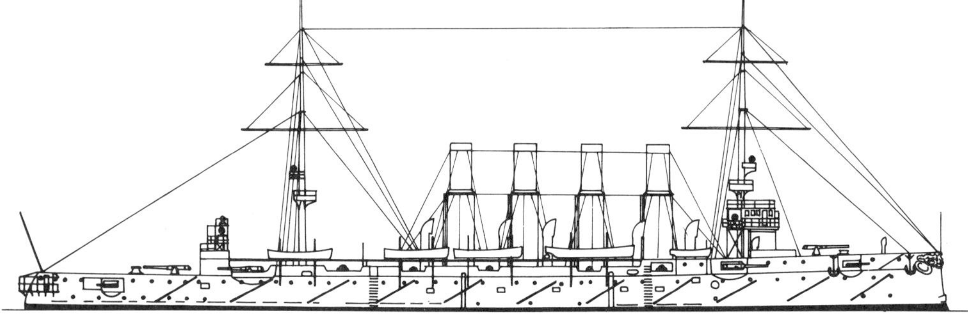
Variag as completed 1900

A four-funnelled cruiser with a forecastle deck extending to between the first two funnels. The 6in guns had no shields and were mounted two abreast forward and aft, and the other eight in sponsons from the upper deck, four abaft the foremast and four by the mainmast. Except for two right aft, the 11pdr were at upper deck level. The protective deck was 1½in with 3in slopes, the CT 6in, ammunition hoists 1½in and there was a patch of 3in protection for the bow and stern TT. The *Variag* was badly damaged by the *Asama* at Chemulpo 9.2.1904 and was scuttled after the action. She was raised and served in the Japanese Navy as the *Soya*. Sold to Russia in 1916, she was sent to the White Sea and in February 1917 arrived at Liverpool for repairs that were never carried out, the *Variag* remaining as a hulk in British waters until scrapped.

VARIAG *protected cruiser*

Displacement: 6500t
Dimensions: 425ft oa x 52ft x 20ft 8in max *(129.54 x 15.85 x 6.30m)*
Machinery: 30 Niclausse boilers, 2-shaft VTE, 21,000ihp = 23.2kts. Coal 1300t max
Armament: 12-6in/45, 12-11pdr, 8-3pdr, 2-1pdr, 6-15in TT aw, 22 mines
Complement: 580

Name	Builder	Laid down	Launched	Comp	Fate
VARIAG	Cramp	1898	Oct 1899	1900	Scrapped 1921

Variag about 1903

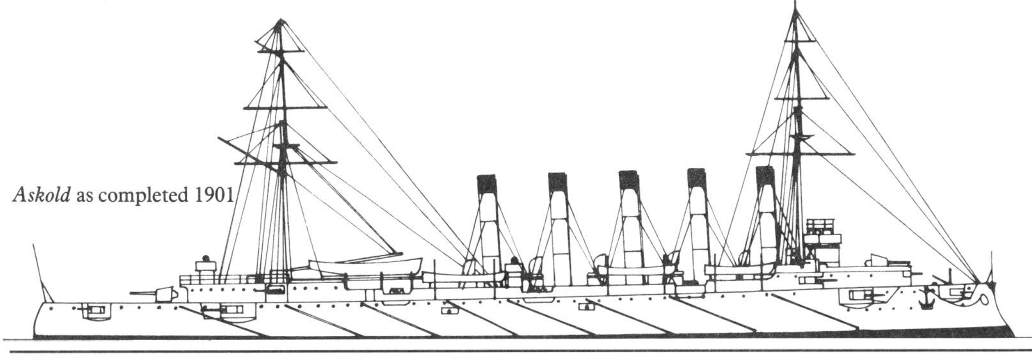

Askold as completed 1901

Of unique appearance with five tall funnels, the *Askold* was flush-decked with a short forward superstructure which did not reach the bows. One of the 6in was mounted on this, and the rest at upper deck level, 1 aft and 5 on either broadside. The 11pdrs were at main deck level. The protective deck was 2in with 3in slopes and 4in on the engine room hatch glacis. The CT had 6in, the ammunition tubes 1½in and the bow and stern TT 2½in-1½in. *Askold* was usually reckoned the fastest of the larger Russian cruisers. In the First World War she served in the Mediterranean and subsequently in the White Sea, where she was later seized by the British and commissioned in August 1918 as *Glory IV*.

ASKOLD *protected cruiser*

Displacement: 5905t
Dimensions: 437ft oa x 49ft 2½in x 20ft 4in max *(133.20 x 15.00 x 6.20m)*
Machinery: 9 Schulz-Thornycroft boilers, 3-shaft VTE, 20,420ihp = 23.8kts (1in wg). Coal 720/1100t
Armament: 12-6in/45, 12-11pdr, 8-3pdr, 2-1pdr pompom, 6-15in TT 2 sub
Complement: 576

Name	Builder	Laid down	Launched	Comp	Fate
ASKOLD	Krupp, Germania	Aug 1898	Mar 1900	1901	Scrapped 1921

Askold during her first commission

BOGATYR class *protected cruisers*

Displacement:	6645t
Dimensions:	439ft 8in oa x 54ft $5\frac{1}{2}$in x 20ft $7\frac{1}{2}$in max (*134.00 x 16.60 x 6.29m*)
Machinery:	16 Normand boilers, 2-shaft VTE, 23,000ihp = 23kts. Coal 720/1100t
Armament:	12-6in/45 (2x2, 8x1), 12-11pdr, 8-3pdr, 2-1pdr, 2-15in TT sub
Complement:	576-589

Name	Builder	Laid down	Launched	Comp	Fate
BOGATYR	Vulkan, Stettin	1898	Jan 1901	1902	Scrapped 1922
OLEG	New Admiralty	1901	Aug 1903	1904	Sunk 17.6.1919
KAGUL	Sevastopol	1900	Oct 1902	1905	To Bizerta 1920
PAMIAT MERKURIA	Nicolaiev	1900	June 1903	1907	Sunk 17.7.1942

Kagul, ex-*Ochakov*, later renamed *Ochakov* for a time and finally *General Kornilov*, and *Pamiat Merkuria*, ex-*Kagul* and finally *Komintern*, were in the Black Sea Fleet.

Three-funnelled cruisers with a short forecastle and poop. The 6in guns were in twin turrets fore and aft, with four in upper deck casemates by the fore and mainmasts and four in upper deck sponsons amidships. Eight of the 11pdrs were at upper deck level with four over the casemates. The protective deck was 1.3in on the flat with 2.1in slopes increased to 2.7in in wake of the engine and boiler rooms, with a 3.3in-1.3in dome over the engines. The turrets had 5in-$3\frac{1}{2}$in with 1in roofs, and the casemates $3\frac{1}{4}$in-$\frac{3}{4}$in. The ammunition tubes were 3in-$2\frac{1}{2}$in, the CT $5\frac{1}{2}$in with a 1in roof, and funnel uptakes $1\frac{1}{2}$in for one deck. In all they were better protected than previous Russian cruisers of their type. During the First World War *Bogatyr* and *Oleg* were rearmed with 16-5.1in/55 and also had 4-11pdr AA added and could take 100 mines. *Kagul* was rearmed with 12-5.1in/55, but *Pamiat Merkuria* appears to have mounted 16-6in/45, both having 2-11pdr AA. *Bogatyr* was very badly damaged by running aground near Vladivostock on 15.5.1904. *Oleg* was torpedoed and sunk by *CMB4*, and *Komintern* was latterly a training ship, the after funnel being removed, and when sunk she was a disarmed base ship.

Bogatyr shortly after completion

Novik as completed 1901

NOVIK *protected cruiser*

Displacement:	3080t
Dimensions:	360ft 5in wl x 40ft x 16ft 5in max (*109.86 x 12.20 x 5.00m*)
Machinery:	12 Schulz-Thornycroft boilers, 3-shaft VTE, 17,000ihp = 25kts. Coal 500t max
Armament:	6-4.7in/45, 6-3pdr, 5-15in TT aw
Complement:	337

Name	Builder	Laid down	Launched	Comp	Fate
NOVIK	Schichau	1898	Aug 1900	1901	Stricken 1913

A three-funnelled cruiser with a single mast between the second and third funnels, and a ram bow. The *Novik* was lightly built as a much enlarged destroyer, but there was a $1\frac{1}{4}$in deck increased to 2in on the slopes and to 3in over the top of the engines. The 4.7in guns were mounted fore and aft with two on either beam. For her day the *Novik* was a very fast ship and attained 19,000ihp = 25.6kts on trials. She was scuttled at Korsa Kovsk in Sakhalin after an action with the light cruiser *Tsushima* on 20.8.1904 and was later salved by the Japanese and served in their navy as the *Suzuya*.

Novik as completed

BOYARIN *protected cruiser*

Displacement: 3200t
Dimensions: 345ft wl x 41ft x 16ft max (*105.16 x 12.50 x 4.88m*)
Machinery: 16 Belleville boilers, 2-shaft VTE, 11,500ihp = 22kts. Coal 600t max
Armament: 6-4.7in/45, 8-3pdr, 4-1pdr, 5-15in TT aw
Complement: 266

Name	Builder	Laid down	Launched	Comp	Fate
BOYARIN	Burmeister and Wain	1899	June 1901	1902	Sunk 12.2.1904

Very different from the *Novik* in appearance, the *Boyarin* resembled a lighter version of the *Bogatyr* class with a short forecastle and poop, three funnels and two masts. There was a 1¼in deck with 2in slopes amidships and 3in on the CT. One 4.7in gun was mounted far forward, one aft and the others in upper deck sponsons by the fore and mainmasts. *Boyarin* struck a Russian mine off Dairen near Port Arthur and was abandoned by her crew. Towing appeared possible, but the *Boyarin* broke loose during the night and drifted on to another mine and sank.

Boyarin about 1903

Jemtchug as completed 1904

IZUMRUD class *protected cruisers*

Displacement: 3103t
Dimensions: 364ft oa x 40ft x 16ft 5in max (*110.95 x 12.20 x 5.00m*)
Machinery: 16 Yarrow boilers, 3-shaft VTE, 17,000ihp = 24kts. Coal 510t max
Armament: 6-4.7in/45, 6-3pdr, 2-1pdr, 3-18in TT aw
Complement: 350

Name	Builder	Laid down	Launched	Comp	Fate
IZUMRUD	Nevski	1901	Oct 1903	1904	Wrecked 29.5.1905
JEMTCHUG	Nevski	1901	Aug 1903	1904	Sunk 28.10.1914

Three-funnelled cruisers resembling the *Novik* but with three masts. The protective deck was 1.2in with 2in slopes and 3in hoods over the engines, and the CT 1¼in. The 4.7in guns were arranged as in *Novik*, but *Jemtchug* later had another two added to give a total of eight 4.7in. *Izumrud* was wrecked NE of Vladivostock after Tsushima and *Jemtchug* was surprised and sunk at Penang by the *Emden* with torpedoes and gunfire.

SLOOPS ('clippers' in most Russian lists)

Barque-rigged, wooden-hulled ships with a single funnel between the fore and mainmasts, and principally intended for maintaining a Russian presence in distant waters. *Jemtchug* attained 11.96kts on trials but was only drawing 12ft forward and 15ft 3in aft at the time. The guns were all on the upper deck.

The Black Sea *Lvitza* and *Pamiat Merkuria,* launched at Nicolaiev in 1865, are sometimes included. These wooden hulled ships of 994t and 1028t displacement had engines of only 411ihp and 382ihp respectively and were too slow to qualify as steam sloops.

ALMAZ class

Displacement: 1530t; in 1884 *Almaz* 1820t, *Jemtchug* 1725t
Dimensions: 240ft wl x 30ft 9in x 16ft-17ft 2in max (*73.15 x 9.37 x 4.88-5.23m*)
Machinery: ? rectangular boilers, 1-shaft HDA ?, 1250-1450ihp = 11kts
Armament: 7 guns, later 3-6in/23, 4-4.2in/20
Complement: 169

Name	Builder	Laid down	Launched	Comp	Fate
ALMAZ	?Mitchell, St Petersburg	1860	1861	Nov 1862	Stricken 1884
IZUMRUD	?New Admiralty	1861	Sept 1862	1863	Stricken *c*1887
JEMTCHUG	?Mitchell, St Petersburg	1860	Oct 1861	Nov 1862	Stricken *c*1887
YAKHONT	?Galernii Is	1861	Oct 1862	1863	Stricken *c*1880

Djigit photographed off Gravesend

Mostly iron-hulled ships but *Vyestnik* part steel and *Nayezdnik, Plastun, Opritchnik* composite, with a heavy barque-rig and double topsail yards. The iron-hulled vessels were sheathed with wood and Muntz metal. There were other differences between the ships, but they are best treated as one class. The 6in guns were on the upper deck and could fire on either broadside. They were later changed in some, *Kreiser* and *Djigit* having 2-6in/28, *Nayezdnik* and *Stryelok* 1-6in/28 and 2-6in/23 and *Razboinik* 2-6in/23. The last named and *Djigit* were scuttled at Port Arthur.

The *Zabiaka* was adapted from a merchant ship built in the USA and was not a true warship.

KREISER class

Displacement: *Kreiser* up to 1653t (as designed 1335t)
Dimensions: 207ft 6in wl x 33ft x 14ft 6in-16ft 8in max (*63.24 x 10.06 x 4.42-5.08m*)
Machinery: Cyl boilers, 1-shaft HC, 1200-1780ihp = 11.4-13.5kts. Coal 200-250t max
Armament: 3-6in/23, 4-4.2in/20, 4 to 6-1pdr revolvers, 1-15in TT aw but 2 in *Nayezdnik*, none in *Djigit*
Complement: 185

Name	Builder	Laid down	Launched	Comp	Fate
KREISER	Galernii Is	1873	1875	1876	Sticken 1908
DJIGIT	Galernii Is	1874	1876	1877	Scuttled 2.1.1905
NAYEZDNIK	Galernii Is	1876	1878	1879	Stricken 1902
RAZBOINIK	Nevski	1877	1878	1880	Scuttled 2.1.1905
PLASTUN	Baltic Wks	1877	1879	1880	Stricken 1906
STRYELOK	Baltic Wks	1878	1879	1880	Stricken 1906
OPRITCHNIK	Baltic Wks	1879	1880	1881	Hulked 1898
VYESTNIK	Nevski	1878	1880	1881	Stricken 1905

ARMOURED GUN VESSELS

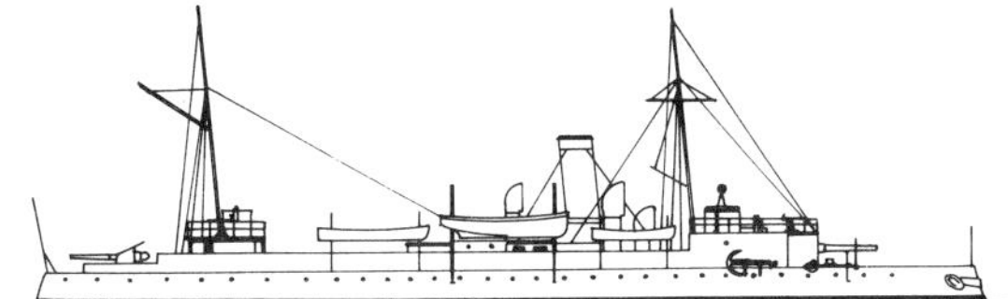
Grozyashchi as completed 1891

This class comprised an unusual type of small armoured ship. The 9in gun was forward and covered in all round, with a large port allowing about 100° training, and the 6in aft in a shield. The belt ran from the stern to about 30ft from the ram, ending in a 3½in bulkhead, and from 2ft above to 3ft below wl. The protective deck was 1in increased to 1½in forward. During the First World War *Grozyashchi* was rearmed with 4-6in/45 of which one was forward and three on the centreline aft, and also had 2-11pdr AA. *Gremyashchi* was sunk by a mine near Port Arthur, and *Otvajni* scuttled there.

GROZYASHCHI class

Displacement: 1627t *Grozyashchi*; 1700t *Gremyashchi*; 1854t *Otvajni* (as designed 1492t)
Dimensions: 237ft 1in oa x 41ft 7in x 12ft 2in max (*72.26 x 12.67 x 3.71m*)
Machinery: 6 Belleville boilers, 2-shaft VTE, 2050-2500ihp = 13-14kts. Coal 160-200t max
Armour: Steel. Belt 5in-2½in, CT 1in
Armament: 1-9in/35, 1-6in/35, 4 to 6-3pdr, 4-1pdr revolver, 2-15in TT aw, 20 mines
Complement: 178-188

Name	Builder	Laid down	Launched	Comp	Fate
GROZYASHCHI	New Admiralty	1889	May 1890	1891	Scrapped 1922
GREMYASHCHI	New Admiralty	1890	May 1892	1893	Sunk 18.8.1904
OTVAJNI	Baltic Wks	1890	May 1892	1894	Scuttled 2.1.1905

Groszyashchi about 1900

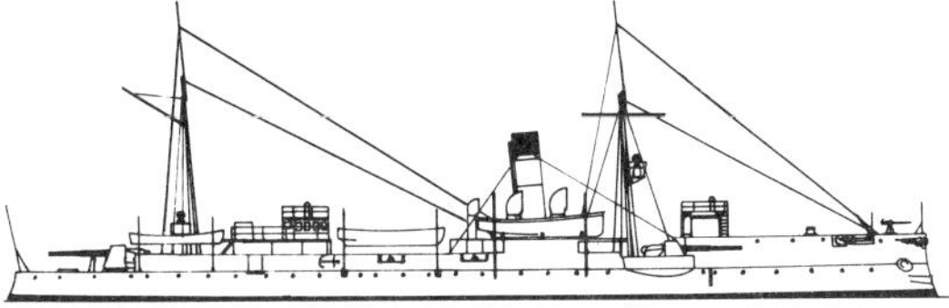
Khrabri as completed 1897

Named *Krasnoye Znamya* after the Revolution. The 8in guns were in sponsons by the foremast and the 6in aft, all in 1½in shields, and the armour was otherwise arranged as in the *Grozyashchi* class. The *Khrabri* was originally even more overweight than indicated above, and in 1899-1900 the armour backing was lightened at Toulon to reduce her draught. She was rearmed in the First World War with 5-5.1in/55, one in each sponson, one forward and two aft on the centreline, and in addition 2-3pdr and 1-2pdr AA. After a career as a gunnery tender between the wars, the *Krasnoye Znamya* was torpedoed by a Finnish MTB in the autumn of 1942, but was raised and reconstructed.

KHRABRI

Displacement: 1735t (as designed 1492t)
Dimensions: 237ft 1in oa x 41ft 7in x 12ft 6in max (*72.26 x 12.67 x 3.81m*)
Machinery: 8 Niclausse boilers, 2-shaft VTE, 2100ihp = 14kts. Coal 200t max
Armour: Harvey. Belt 5in-3½in
Armament: 2-8in/45, 1-6in/45, 5-3pdr, 4-1pdr, 1-15in TT aw, 20 mines
Complement: 199

Name	Builder	Laid down	Launched	Comp	Fate
KHRABRI	New Admiralty	1894	Nov 1895	1897	Scrapped *c* 1962

Khrabri at Toulon, possibly for the modifications of 1899-1900

GUN VESSELS

Sivuch with original brig rig

Flat-bottomed ships with fine bow lines and originally brig-rigged. The 9in was mounted as a bow chaser with 36° training on either side and the 6in right aft with a total arc of 270°. They were later given three masts. *Bobr* was sunk in the siege of Port Arthur and *Sivuch* blown up by her crew in the Liao river.

SIVUCH class

Displacement: *Sivuch* 1134t; *Bobr* 1230t (as designed 950t)
Dimensions: 187ft 6in wl x 35ft x 9ft 6in max (*57.14 x 10.67 x 2.90m*)
Machinery: 6 cyl boilers, 2-shaft HC, 1130ihp = 11.5kts. Coal 250t max
Armament: 1-9in/30, 1-6in/28, 6-4.2in/20, 4-1pdr revolvers
Complement: 170

Name	Builder	Laid down	Launched	Comp	Fate
SIVUCH	Bergsund, Stockholm	1883	1884	1885	Scuttled 2.8.1904
BOBR	Crichton, Abo	1883	1885	1885	Sunk 26.12.1904

Korietz on a visit to a French port about 1900

Barquentine-rigged ships, *Korietz* having a much more pronounced ram bow than *Mandjur*. Both were reckoned poor performers under sail. The 8in guns were in forward sponsons with ¾in shields, and the 6in aft. The 4.2in were on the broadside and were sponsoned in *Korietz*. The latter was scuttled after the action at Chemulpo in which she took virtually no part.

KORIETZ class

Displacement: 1270t *Korietz;* 1437t *Mandjur*
Dimensions: 206ft wl *Korietz*, 219ft oa *Mandjur* x 35ft x 10ft 6in-12ft 4in max (*62.79, 66.75 x 10.67 x 3.20—3.76m*)
Machinery: 6 cyl boilers, 2-shaft HC, 1560-1960ihp = 13.3kts. Coal 250t max
Armament: 2-8in/35, 1-6in/35, 4-4.2in/20, 2-3pdr revolvers, 4-1pdr revolvers, 1-15in TT aw
Complement: 179

Name	Builder	Laid down	Launched	Comp	Fate
KORIETZ	Bergsund, Stockholm	1885	Aug 1886	1887	Scuttled 9.2.1904
MANDJUR	Burmeister and Wain	1886	Dec 1886	1888	Scrapped 1923

All Black Sea Fleet. The Sevastopol ships were built at the yard of the Russian Steam Navigation Company. *Teretz* was renamed *Znamya Sozialisma* after the Revolution. The general construction was considered weak and the workmanship in the Nicolaiev ships indifferent. The 8in guns were in forward sponsons and the 6in aft. They were shielded in the Nicolaiev ships but not in the others. All except *Zaporozhetz* and *Chernomoretz* were later rearmed with 2-6in/45, 1-4.7in/45 and 2-11pdr, and also reboilered with 4 Bellevilles, while the fore and mizzen masts were removed from the survivors during the First World War. *Donetz* was torpedoed and sunk by the Turkish destroyer *Gairet* at Odessa 29.10 1914 but was raised and repaired. *Znamya Sozialisma* was latterly a diving school base ship, and *Kubanetz* was serving as an oiler under the name of *Krasni Kuban* when lost.

Gilyak, launched in 1896, was built as a large river gunboat and therefore is not included.

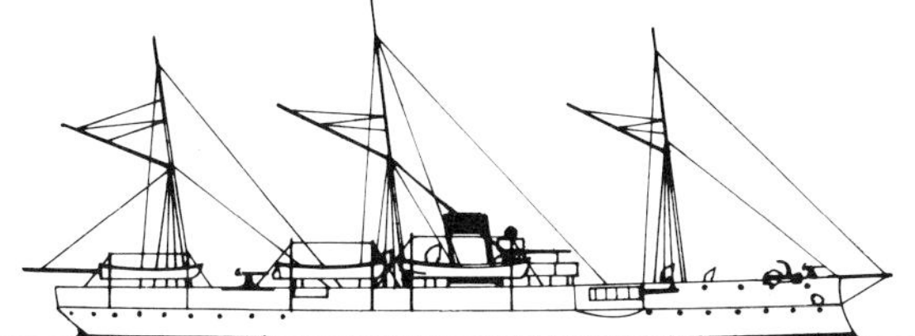

Kubanetz as completed 1888

KUBANETZ class

Displacement: 1224-1393t
Dimensions: 220ft 6in oa x 35ft x 11ft 10in-12ft 8in max (*67.21 x 10.67 x 3.61-3.86m*)
Machinery: 6 cyl boilers, 2-shaft HC in Sevastopol ships, HTE in Nicolaiev ships, 1500ihp = 12-14kts. Coal 250t max
Armament: 2-8in/35,1-6in/35, 6-3pdr revolvers, 2-15in TT aw
Complement: 180

Name	Builder	Laid down	Launched	Comp	Fate
KUBANETZ	Sevastopol	1886	April 1887	1888	Sunk 1941-1945
TERETZ	Sevastopol	1886	Aug 1887	1889	Scrapped *c*1946
URALETZ	Sevastopol	1886	Dec 1887	1889	Stricken 1914
ZAPOROZHETZ	Nicolaiev	1886	June 1887	1890	Stricken 1911
CHERNOMORETZ	Nicolaiev	1886	Sept 1887	1890	Stricken 1911
DONETZ	Nicolaiev	1886	Nov 1887	1890	Sunk May 1919

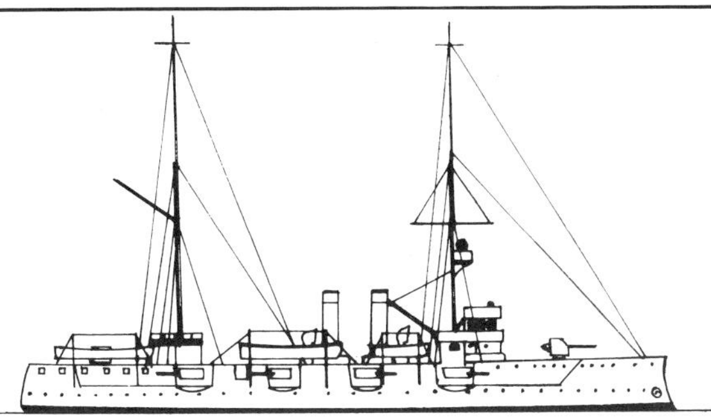

Khivinetz as completed 1906

KHIVINETZ

Named *Krasnaya Zviezda* after the Revolution. A two-funnelled ship with, originally, a foremast only, *Khivinetz* was of relatively high freeboard. The 4.7in guns were mounted fore and aft on the upper deck and the 11pdrs in unarmoured main deck casemates, though the CT had 1.8in steel. She was rearmed during the First World War with four 4.7in and two 3pdr AA, and was finally used as a gunnery tender.

Displacement: 1340t
Dimensions: 231ft 2in oa x 37ft x 11ft 4in max (*70.46 x 11.28 x 3.45m*)
Machinery: 8 Belleville boilers, 2-shaft VTE, 1400ihp = 13.5kts. Coal 250t max
Armament: 2-4.7in/45, 8-11pdr
Complement: 161

Name	Builder	Laid down	Launched	Comp	Fate
KHIVINETZ	New Admiralty	1904	May 1905	1906	Scrapped *c*1946

Gilyak before the First World War

GILYAK class

Generally resembling a smaller *Khivinetz* but cut down aft and with a military foremast and pole mainmast. Only the two forward 11pdrs were in casemates. *Korietz* had four additional 11pdrs added in 1915. *Sivuch* was sunk by the dreadnought *Posen* in the Gulf of Riga; *Korietz* escaped but ran aground and was blown up by her crew. *Bobr* was taken over by the Germans as *Bieber* in April 1918 and in 1919 became the Esthonian *Lembit*, while *Gilyak* was taken over by Finland in 1918.

Displacement: 875t
Dimensions: 218ft 2in oa x 36ft x 7ft 11in max (*66.50 x 10.97 x 2.41m*)
Machinery: 4 Belleville boilers, 2-shaft VTE, 900ihp = 12kts. Coal 130t max
Armament: 2-4.7in/45, 4-11pdr, 40 mines
Complement: 140

Name	Builder	Laid down	Launched	Comp	Fate
GILYAK	New Admiralty	1905	Oct 1906	1908	Scrapped 1922
BOBR	Nevski	1905	Aug 1907	1908	Scrapped 1927
SIVUCH	Nevski	1905	Aug 1907	1908	Sunk 19.8.1915
KORIETZ	Putilov	1905	May 1907	1908	Scuttled 20.8.1915

RUSSIA

TORPEDO GUNBOATS

A two-funnelled, two-masted ship with a ram bow and the fore funnel and mast well forward. There was some protection from a ¾in-½in deck. There were five fixed TT, two right ahead, one on each bow and one in the stern, and in addition two trainable broadside TT. 16 torpedoes, 15ft long, were stowed in racks on the lower deck with suitable gear for bringing them under a tramway which ran the whole length of the ship to the rear of each tube. The armament was later changed to 5-3pdr, 10-1pdr and 5 TT, the trainable tubes being removed.

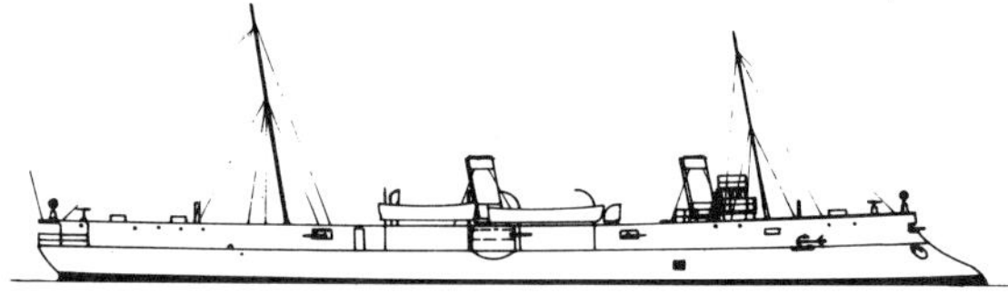

Leitenant Ilin as completed 1887

LEITENANT ILIN

Displacement: 714t
Dimensions: 237ft 3in oa x 24ft 4in x 10ft 7in max (*72.31 x 7.42 x 3.23m*)
Machinery: 6 loco boilers, 2-shaft VTE, 3500ihp = 20.8kts. Coal 97t max
Armament: 7-3pdr, 6-3pdr revolvers, 6-1pdr revolvers, 7-15in TT aw
Complement: 132

Name	Builders	Laid down	Launched	Comp	Fate
LEITENANT ILIN	Baltic Wks	1885	July 1886	1887	Stricken 1911

Leitenant Ilin before rearming

Black Sea Fleet. Similar to the *Leitenant Ilin* with the differences indicated above. No fewer than 19 torpedoes were carried. The *Kapitan Saken* was reboilered with 6 Bellevilles in 1898 and had four TT later removed. According to some reports she had 18in TT fitted at this time.

KAPITAN SAKEN

Displacement: 742t
Dimensions: 235ft oa x 24ft 4in x 10ft 3in max (*71.63 x 7.42 x 3.12m*)
Machinery: 6 loco boilers, 2-shaft VTE, 3000ihp = 18.3kts. Coal 97t max
Armament: 6-3pdr, 4-1pdr revolvers, 7-15in TT aw
Complement: 125

Name	Builder	Laid down	Launched	Comp	Fate
KAPITAN SAKEN	Nicolaiev	1886	May 1889	1890	Stricken 1907

Kazarski in 1896

Kazarski and *Griden* Black Sea Fleet. Small single-funnelled torpedo gunboats with two masts. One TT was fixed in the bows and one training on deck. The three Schichau-built units were used as despatch vessels in the First World War and were armed with 2 or 3-11pdrs. *Vsadnik* and *Gaidamak* were respectively sunk on 15.12.1904 and scuttled on 2.1.1905 in the siege of Port Arthur, and later raised by the Japanese and became the *Makikumo* and *Shikinami*. *Voevoda* and *Posadnik* were taken over by Finland in 1918 and renamed *Klas Horn* and *Matti Kurki*. *Kazarski* was disarmed for at least seven years before scrapping.

KAZARSKI class

Displacement: 394-432t
Dimensions: 197ft 6in oa x 24ft 4in x 10ft 8in-11ft 6in max (*60.20 x 7.42 x 3.25-3.50m*)
Machinery: 2 loco boilers, 1-shaft VTE, 3500ihp = 21-22.5kts. Coal 90t max
Armament: 6-3pdr, 3-1pdr, 2-15in TT aw
Complement: 65

Name	Builder	Laid down	Launched	Comp	Fate
KAZARSKI	Schichau	1889	1889	1890	Scrapped 1927
VOEVODA	Schichau	1891	1892	1892	Scrapped 1938
POSADNIK	Schichau	1891	1892	1892	Scrapped 1938
VSADNIK	Crichton, Abo	1892	July 1893	1894	Scrapped 1914
GAIDAMAK	Crichton, Abo	1892	July 1893	1894	Scrapped 1914
GRIDEN	Nicolaiev	1892	Nov 1893	1895	Stricken 1911

Voevoda in the late 1890s

ABREK

A single-funnelled, two-masted ship intended as an improved *Leitenant Ilin*, and a better seaboat than the latter. The 11pdrs had 1in shields, and 8 torpedoes, 21ft long, were carried for the two TT, one fixed in the bow and one training aft. The *Abrek* was a despatch vessel in the First World War and had previously served as a yacht for the Revenue Service.

Displacement: 675t
Dimensions: 215ft oa x 25ft 5in x 10ft 6in max (*65.53 x 7.75 x 3.20m*)
Machinery: 4 Normand-Du Temple boilers, 2-shaft VTE, 4500ihp = 21.2kts. Coal 120t max
Armament: 2-11pdr, 4-3pdr, 2-16in TT aw
Complement: 88

Name	Builder	Laid down	Launched	Comp	Fate
ABREK	Crichton, Abo	June 1895	1896	Sept 1897	Scrapped *c* 1920

OPYT

Iron-hulled and originally armoured, the *Opyt* was later named *Mina*. The 3.4in were subsequently replaced by 2½pdrs and the 11in eventually removed. A report of 1901 states that she then had the engines formerly in *TB75* and *TB81*. She was finally employed as a torpedo school tender.

Displacement: 270t
Dimensions: 123ft 7in x 22ft 3in x 6ft max (*37.67 x 6.78 x 1.83m*)
Machinery: 1 boiler, 2-shaft HP, 195ihp = 9kts
Armament: 3 SB, later 1-11in/20, 2-3.4in/20
Complement: 43

Name	Builder	Laid down	Launched	Comp	Fate
OPYT	Carr & Macpherson St Petersburg	1861	Oct 1861	1862	Stricken 1906

SOBOL class

Barque-rigged, wooden-hulled ships, similar to some of the gunboats built prior to 1860. The 64pdrs and later the 6in were fore and aft pivot guns. Both ships spent much of their time under the orders of the Russian minister in Peking.

Displacement: 455t
Dimensions: 148ft 9in x 22ft 11in x 8ft 4in max (*45.34 x 6.98 x 2.54m*)
Machinery: 80nhp
Armament: 2-64pdr SB, 4-9pdr SB, later 2-6in/23, 4-3.4in/20
Complement: 90

Name	Builder	Laid down	Launched	Comp	Fate
SOBOL	Berneborg	Sept 1862	May 1863	1864	Harbour service 1888
GORNOSTAI	Berneborg	Sept 1862	May 1863	1864	Harbour service 1888

PISHTCHAL class

Iron-hulled gunboats for service in the Caspian Sea where oil fuel was available. They were re-eingined by Sormof in 1872. It is not clear whether there was any connection between these two ships and the previous gunboats of the same names, sent from the Baltic to the Caspian in 1862.

Displacement: 328t
Dimensions: 121ft 3in x 25ft 2in x 7ft 2in max (*36.96 x 7.67 x 2.18m*)
Machinery: 120-170ihp (burnt oil residue)
Armament: 1-6in/23, 2-3.4in/20
Complement: –

Name	Builder	Laid down	Launched	Comp	Fate
PISHTCHAL	Watkins	–	1866	–	Stricken *c* 1898
SYEKIRA	Watkins	–	1866	–	Stricken *c* 1898

Composite-hulled, with the 11in mounted as a pivot gun on a descending platform and training 12° each side of the keel line by means of a steam capstan. The 11in was eventually removed.

ERSH

Displacement: 321t
Dimensions: 97ft wl x 28ft x 7ft 4in max *(29.57 x 8.53 x 2.23m)*
Machinery: 2 cyl boilers, 2-shaft HC, 240ihp = 8kts
Armament: 1-11in/20, later also 1-3pdr revolver, 1-1pdr revolver
Complement: 53

Name	Builder	Laid down	Launched	Comp	Fate
ERSH	New Admiralty	1873	1874	1874	Stricken 1906

Wooden-hulled. Although built at Nicolaiev, *Nerpa* served mainly in the Far East and for much of the time under the orders of the Russian minister in Peking. Her engines were apparently made in New York in 1860. A sister ship to be named *Sivuch* was never begun.

NERPA

Displacement: 380t
Dimensions: 124ft 8in x 24ft 6in x 8ft max *(37.99 x 7.47 x 2.44m)*
Machinery: 60nhp
Armament: 1-6in/23, 2-4.2in/20, 2-3.4in/20
Complement: 90

Name	Builder	Laid down	Launched	Comp	Fate
NERPA	Nicolaiev	? 1876	1877	? 1877/8	Harbour service 1888

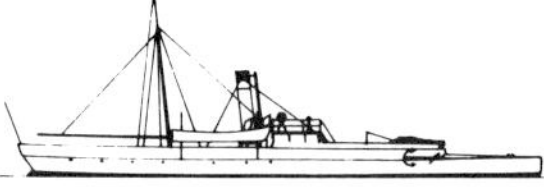

Burya as completed 1882

Composite-hulled, with the 11in mounted as a pivot gun on a descending platform. In most of the class 2-2½pdr later replaced the 3.4in, while *Burun*, *Tutcha* and *Dojd* also had 1-3pdr and 2-1pdr revolvers. *Tutcha* was sent to the Caspian on canal barges in 1899. She was adapted for oil fuel and a 1901 list shows her and *Burun* with 4-3.4in/20 and 3-3pdr revolvers only. *Vikhr* also went to the Caspian in 1902, and it appears that only *Burya* had her 11in at the end.

BURUN class

Displacement: 383-400t
Dimensions: *Burun, Tutcha, Burya, Groza* 119ft 4in wl x 29ft x 7ft 9in-8ft max *(36.37 x 8.84 x 2.36-2.44m)*; *Dojd, Snyeg, Grad* 110ft wl x 35ft 5in x 8ft-8ft 6in max *(33.53 x 10.80 x 2.44-2.59m)*; *Vikhr* 110ft wl x 38ft x 7ft max *(33.53 x 11.58 x 2.13m)*
Machinery: 2 cyl boilers, 2-shaft HC, *Burun, Tutcha, Burya, Groza* 250ihp = 8-9kts; *Dojd, Snyeg, Grad, Vikhr* 440ihp = 8-9kts
Armament: 1-11in/20, (*Burya* 1-11in/22), all also 2-3.4in/20
Complement: 54-57

Name	Builder	Laid down	Launched	Comp	Fate
BURUN	New Admiralty	1878	1879	1880	Stricken 1906
TUTCHA	New Admiralty	1878	1879	1880	–
BURYA	New Admiralty	1880	1881	1881/2	Stricken 1906
GROZA	New Admiralty	1880	1881	1881/2	Stricken 1906
DOJD	New Admiralty	1878	1879	1880	Stricken 1906
VIKHR	New Admiralty	1878	1879	1880	–
SNYEG	Crichton, Abo	1880	1881	1881/2	Stricken 1902
GRAD	Crichton, Abo	1880	1881	1881/2	Stricken 1906

Yenisei (i) about 1900

Mining or torpedo transports with the general appearance of small cruisers that served as minelayers in the Russo-Japanese War. One of the most successful of all mining operations was carried out by *Amur* on 14 May 1904 when she laid a field of 50 mines which sank the Japanese battleships *Hatsuse* and *Yashima*. The *Yenisei* was sunk by one of her own mines and the *Amur* by the Japanese 11in howitzers at Port Arthur.

AMUR class (first) *minelayers*

Displacement: 3010t
Dimensions: 300ft wl x 41ft x 18ft max *(91.44 x 12.50 x 5.49m)*
Machinery: 12 Belleville boilers, 2-shaft VTE, 4700ihp = 18kts. Coal 400t
Armament: 5-11pdr, 7-3pdr, 1-15in TT aw, 500 mines
Complement: 317

Name	Builder	Laid dwon	Launched	Comp	Fate
AMUR	Baltic Wks	1898	Nov 1898	1899	Sunk 18.12.1904
YENISEI	Baltic Wks	1898	Feb 1899	1899	Sunk 11.2.1904

Two-funnelled ships with ram bows and counter sterns. *Amur's* armament was increased to 9-4.7in and 1-11pdr AA during the First World War, during which *Yenissei* was torpedoed and sunk by *U26*. *Amur* was latterly used as a training ship.

AMUR class (second) *minelayers*

Displacement: 2926t
Dimensions: 300ft oa x 46ft x 14ft 6in mean (*91.44 x 14.02 x 4.42m*)
Machinery: 12 Belleville boilers, 2-shaft VTE, 4700ihp = 17kts. Coal 670t max
Armament: 1-4.7in/45, 11-11pdr, 320 mines
Complement: 318

Name	Builder	Laid down	Launched	Comp	Fate
AMUR	Baltic Wks	May 1905	June 1907	1909	Scrapped *c*1950
YENISEI	Baltic Wks	May 1905	July 1906	1910	Sunk 4.6.1915

ARMED YACHT

An armed yacht with two funnels, three masts, clipper bows and bowsprit, the *Almaz* would not qualify for inclusion as a true warship except for her interesting career. Apart from two destroyers she was the only ship to reach Vladivostock after the disaster of Tsushima, and transferred to the Black Sea in 1911, serving as a seaplane carrier in the First World War. The *Almaz* was at that time armed with 7-4.7in/45, 4-11pdr AA and carried up to four seaplanes.

ALMAZ

Displacement: 3285t
Dimensions: 365ft 8in oa x 43ft 6in x 17ft 6in max (*111.45 x 13.26 x 5.33m*)
Machinery: Belleville boilers, 2-shaft VTE, 7500ihp = 19kts. Coal 560t
Armament: 4-11pdr, 8-3pdr
Complement: 336

Name	Builder	Laid down	Launched	Comp	Fate
ALMAZ	Baltic Wks	April 1902	June 1903	Dec 1903	To Bizerta 1920

Almaz as completed 1903

DESTROYERS

A four-funnel destroyer with one mast, later two, and a ram bow. The 11pdr was mounted on the roof of the 'conning tower' with two 3pdrs forward and one aft. There were two single deck TT on the centreline aft, for which six torpedoes were carried, and the second 11pdr was mounted near the stern. Nickel steel was largely employed in the construction of the hull and there was some use of aluminium for fittings. The *Pruitki* was one of the fastest of the early destroyers, and famous under her original name of *Sokol*. She was used as a minesweeper in the First World War.

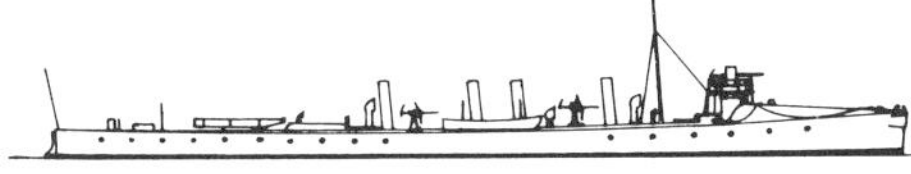

Sokol as completed 1895

PRUITKI

Displacement: 220t
Dimensions: 190ft oa x 18ft 6in x 7ft 6in mean (*57.91 x 5.64 x 2.29m*)
Machinery: 8 Yarrow boilers, 2-shaft VTE, 3800ihp = 29kts (trials 4500 = 30.2). Coal 60t
Armament: 1-11pdr, 3-3pdr (later 2-11pdr only), 2-15in TT aw, later also 10 mines
Complement: 54

Name (name until 1902)	Builder	Laid down	Launched	Comp	Fate
PRUITKI (SOKOL)	Yarrow	1894	1895	1895	Scrapped 1922

Rastoropni just before scuttling, 1904

The four Crichton, Okhta, boats went to the Black Sea on completion. *Ryeshitelni*, *Razyashchi*, *Rastoropni* and the nine 'S' Nevski boats were sent to the Pacific in sections and assembled at Port Arthur. In general this class resembled *Pruitki* though all 13 Nevski boats had straight stems. *Puilki*, *Poslushni*, *Prochni*, *Porazhayushchi*, *Pronzitelni*, *Ryeshitelni* and ? *Podvizhni* had 8 boilers and the others 4 larger ones. None was as fast as *Pruitki* though *Podvizhni* is credited with 29kts. The vessels assembled at Port Arthur all took part in the Russo-Japanese War. *Silni* was scuttled there on 2.1.1905, and was raised by the Japanese and served as the *Fumizuki*, while *Ryeshitelni*, captured at Chefoo on 12.8.1904, became the *Yamabiko*. The four surviving destroyers *Serditi*, *Smyeli*, *Skori* and *Statni* were based at Vladivostock in the First World War. Of the Black Sea units *Strogi* and *Sviryepi* were named *Badina* and *Leitenant Schmidt* after the Revolution. *Puilki* and *Pronzitelni* were transferred to the Caspian in 1907, and the remaining eight served as minesweepers in the Baltic during the First World War. *Ryani*, *Prozorlivi*, *Ryezvi*, *Poslushni*, and *Podvizhni* were taken over by the Finnish in 1918 and became *S1* to *S5*.

PUILKI class

Displacement: 220-240t
Dimensions: 190ft oa x 18ft 6in x 7ft 6in mean (*57.91 x 5.64 x 2.29m*)
Machinery: 4 or 8 Yarrow boilers, 2-shaft VTE, 3800ihp = 26.5-27.5kts. Coal 60t
Armament: 1-11pdr, 3-3pdr (later 2-11pdr only), 2-15in TT aw, later also 10-12 mines in some
Complement: 51-58

Name (name until 1902)	Builder	Laid down	Launched	Comp	Fate
PUILKI (KRETCHET)	Crichton, Abo	1896	1898	1898	Scrapped 1911
POSLUSHNI (KORSHUN)	Crichton, Abo	1896	1898	1898	Scrapped 1921
PROCHNI (YASTREB)	Izhora	1897	1898	1900	Scrapped 1922
PORAZHAYUSHCHI (NYROK)	Izhora	1897	1898	1900	Scrapped 1922
PRONZITELNI (BERKUT)	Izhora	1897	1899	1900	Scrapped 1911
RYESHITELNI (KONDOR)	Izhora	1897	Assembled	1902	Scrapped 1918
PROZORLIVI (GAGARA)	Nevski	1898	1899	1901	Foundered Oct 1925
RYEZVI (VORON)	Nevski	1898	1899	1901	Scrapped 1921
RETIVI (FILIN)	Nevski	1898	1900	1901	Scrapped 1922
RYANI (SOVA)	Nevski	1898	1900	1901	Stricken 1930
PODVIZHNI (ALBATROSS)	Izhora	1898	1900	1901	Stricken 1930
RAZYASHCHI (DROZD)	Izhora	1899	Assembled	1902	Scuttled 2.1.1905
RASTOROPNI (DYATEL)	Izhora	1899	Assembled	1902	Scuttled 16.11.1904
STROGI (LEBED)	Crichton, Okhta	1899	1901	1902	Stricken 1939 (?)
SMYETLIVI (PELIKAN)	Crichton, Okhta	1899	1901	1902	Scuttled 18.6.1918
SVIRYEPI (PAVLIN)	Crichton, Okhta	1899	1901	1902	Stricken 1939 (?)
STREMITELNI (FAZAN)	Crichton, Okhta	1899	1901	1902	Scuttled 18.6.1918
SERDITI (BEKAS)	Nevski	1899	Assembled	1902	Scrapped 1922
SMYELI (GORLITZA)	Nevski	1899	Assembled	1902	Scrapped 1922
SKORI (PEREPEL)	Nevski	1900	Assembled	1903	Scrapped 1922
STATNI (SHTCHEGOL)	Nevski	1900	Assembled	1903	Scrapped 1922
SILNI (BAKLAN)	Nevski	1899	Assembled	1902	Scrapped 1913
STEREGUSHCHI (KULIK)	Nevski	1900	Assembled	1903	Sunk 10.3.1904
STOROZHEVOI (GRATCH)	Nevski	1899	Assembled	1902	Scuttled 2.1.1905
STRASHNI (SKVORETZ)	Nevski	1900	Assembled	1903	Sunk 13.4.1904
STROINI (STRIJ)	Nevski	1900	Assembled	1903	Sunk 13.11.1904

A four-funnel destroyer of the usual Laird type, with the 11pdr forward and two single deck TT abaft the second and fourth funnel. *Boevoi* was torpedoed by a Japanese picket boat on 24.7.1904 but managed to make Port Arthur.

BOEVOI

Displacement: 350t
Dimensions: 213ft wl x 21ft 6in x 9ft 7in max (*64.92 x 6.55 x 2.92m*)
Machinery: 4 Laird boilers, 2-shaft VTE, 6000ihp = 27.5kts. Coal 80t
Armament: 1-11pdr, 5-3pdr, 2-15in TT aw
Complement: 62

Name (name until 1902)	Builder	Laid down	Launched	Comp	Fate
BOEVOI (SOM)	Laird	1898	1899	1900	Scuttled 2.1.1905

Two-funnel, two-masted destroyers with the 11pdr forward and three deck TT for which 6 torpedoes were carried. The TT were on the centreline with two between the funnels and one abaft them. In the Russo-Japanese war, *Bditelni* was scuttled at Port Arthur and the other three interned at Kiao Chau after the battle of 10.8.1904. In the First World War they were employed at Vladivostock and in the White Sea.

BEZSTRASHNI class

Displacement: 346t
Dimensions: 202ft 7in oa x 22ft x 9ft 6in max (*61.75 x 6.70 x 2.90m*)
Machinery: 4 Schichau boilers, 2-shaft VTE, 6000 = 27kts. Coal 80t
Armament: 1-11pdr, 5-3pdr (later 2-11pdr only), 3-15in TT aw
Complement: 64

Name (name until 1902)	Builder	Laid down	Launched	Comp	Fate
BEZSTRASHNI (DELFIN)	Schichau	1898	1899	1900	Scrapped 1922
BDITELNI (KIT)	Schichau	1898	1900	1900	Scuttled 2.1.1905
BEZPOSHTCHADNI (SKAT)	Schichau	1898	1900	1900	Scrapped 1923
BEZSHUMNI (KASATKA)	Schichau	1898	1900	1900	Scrapped 1922

LEITENANT BURAKOV

Originally the Chinese *Hai Hoha* captured by the British destroyers *Fame* and *Whiting* in the attack on the Taku forts, and assigned to Russia. She had two large funnels and two deck TT and was easily the fastest of the Russian flotilla in the war with Japan. She was torpedoed by the picket boats of the *Mikasa* and *Fuji* in Ta Ho Bay to the east of Port Arthur.

Displacement: 280t
Dimensions: 193ft 7in oa x 21ft x 8ft 6in max (*59.00 x 6.40 x 2.60m*)
Machinery: 4 Thornycroft boilers, 2-shaft VTE, 6000ihp = 33.6kts. Coal 67t
Armament: 6-3pdr, 2-14in TT aw, TT possibly changed to 15in
Complement: 56

Name	Builder	Launched	Acquired by Russia	Fate
LEITENANT BURAKOV	Schichau	1898	1900	Sunk 24.7.1904

VNIMATELNI class

Resembled the French *Durandal* class but with two groups of two funnels. The 11pdr was on the 'conning tower' roof forward with a deck TT abaft each funnel group. In the Russo-Japanese War *Vnushitelni* was sunk by the Japanese fleet and *Vuinoslivi* mined. *Grozovoi*, interned at Shanghai after the battle of 10.8.1904, and *Vlastni*, at Chefoo after the fall of Port Arthur, served at Vladivostock and then in the White Sea during the First World War, and then were taken over by Britain in 1918.

Displacement: 312t
Dimensions: 185ft 8in oa x 19ft 4in x 9ft 11in max (*56.60 x 5.90 x 3.02m*)
Machinery: 4 Normand boilers, 2-shaft VTE, 5200ihp = 26.5kts. Coal 60-70t
Armament: 1-11pdr, 5-3pdr (later 2-11pdr only), 2-15in TT aw
Complement: 57-59

Name (name until 1902)	Builder	Laid down	Launched	Comp	Fate
VNIMATELNI (FOREL)	Normand	1898	1900	1901	Wrecked 26.5.1904
VUINOSLIVI (STERLYAD)	Normand	1898	1901	1902	Sunk 24.8.1904
VNUSHITELNI (OSETR)	F & C, Le Havre	1898	1900	1902	Sunk 25.2.1904
VLASTNI (KEFAL)	F & C, Le Havre	1899	1901	1902	Scrapped 1921
GROZOVOI (LOSOS)	F & C, Le Havre	1899	1902	1902	Scrapped 1921

BOIKI class

Zadorni later named *Leitenant Pushchin*. The five Belgian Works' destroyers (at Nicolaiev) and the four Nicolaiev were Black Sea Fleet boats. Yarrow-type, four-funnel destroyers resembling an enlarged *Pruitki*. There were two single deck TT and one in the stem which was later removed, and 6 torpedoes were carried. Only the 5 built by Belgian Works had Normand boilers. In the Russo-Japanese War *Boiki* and *Burni* were at Port Arthur, the former escaping at the surrender while *Buini*, *Bravi*, *Blestyashtchi*, *Buistri*, *Bodri*, *Byedovi*, *Bezuprechni*, *Gromki* and *Grozni* were at Tsushima. *Byedovi* with the seriously wounded Admiral Rozhestvenski on board, was captured by the Japanese and served as the *Satsuki*. *Boiki*, *Bravi*, *Bodri* and *Grozni* were at Vladivostock during the First World War and *Vidni* and *Gromyaschi* in the Baltic. *Zhivoi* was lost in the Sea of Azov, when part of Wrangel's fleet. *Bravi*, *Zavidni* and *Grozni* were renamed *Anisimov*, *Marti* and *Balyank* after the Revolution.

Displacement: 350t
Dimensions: 210ft oa x 21ft x 8ft 6in max (*64.00 x 6.40 x 2.59m*)
Machinery: 4 Yarrow or Normand boilers, 2-shaft VTE, 5700ihp = 26kts. Coal 80t
Armament: 1-11pdr, 5-3pdr (later 2-11pdr only), 3-15in TT aw, later 2TT, possibly 18in in some, 12-18 mines
Complement: 62-69

Name (name until 1902)	Builder	Laid down	Launched	Comp	Fate
BOIKI (AKUVLA)	Nevski	1900	1901	1902	Stricken 1923
BUINI (BYCHOK)	Nevski	1900	1901	1902	Scuttled 28.5.1905
BURNI (MAKREL)	Nevski	1900	1901	1902	Driven ashore 11.8.1904
BRAVI (NALIM)	Nevski	1900	1901	1902	Stricken 1931 (?)
BLESTYASHTCHI (OKUN)	Nevski	1900	1901	1902	Scuttled 28.5.1905
BUISTRI (PLOTVA)	Nevski	1900	1901	1902	Driven ashore 28.5.1905
BODRI (PESKAR)	Nevski	1900	1902	1903	Scrapped 1922
BYEDOVI (KETA)	Nevski	1900	1902	1903	Scrapped 1922
BEZUPRECHNI (PALTUS)	Nevski	1900	1902	1903	Sunk 28.5.1905
VIDNI (SIG)	Nevski	1900	1902	1905	Scrapped 1922
ZAVIDNI (KARP)	Belgian Wks	1902	1902	1903	Stricken 1938
ZAVEYTNI (BELUGA)	Belgian Wks	1902	1902	1903	Scrapped 1922
ZADORNI	Belgian Wks	1903	1904	1905	Sunk 9.3.1916
ZORKI	Belgian Wks	1903	1905	1905	To Bizerta 1920
ZVONKI	Belgian Wks	1903	1905	1905	To Bizerta 1920
ZHIVOI	Nicolaiev	1902	1904	1905	Sunk 16.11.1920
ZHIVUCHI	Nicolaiev	1902	1904	1906	Sunk 25.4.1916
ZHUTKI	Nicolaiev	1902	1904	1906	Scrapped 1922
ZHARKI	Nicolaiev	1902	1904	1906	To Bizerta 1920
GROMKI	Nevski	1903	1904	1904	Sunk 28.5.1905
GROZNI	Nevski	1903	1904	1904	Stricken 1923
GROMYASCHI	Nevski	1903	1904	1905	Scrapped 1922

TVERDI class

Virtually repeats of the *Puilki* class but with 18in TT. Sent out to Vladivostock in sections and assembled there. *Tverdi* and *Tochni* were renamed *Lazo* and *Potapenko* after the Revolution.

Displacement: 240t
Dimensions: 190ft oa x 18ft 6in x 7ft 6in mean (*57.91 x 5.64 x 2.29m*)
Machinery: 4 Yarrow boilers, 2-shaft VTE, 3800ihp = 26kts. Coal 60t
Armament: 1-11pdr, 3-3pdr (later 2-11pdr only), 2-18in TT aw
Complement: 60

Name	Builder	Laid down	Assembled	Fate
TVERDI	Nevski	1904	1906	Stricken 1931 (?)
TOCHNI	Nevski	1904	1906	Stricken 1931 (?)
TREVOZHNI	Nevski	1904	1906	Scrapped 1923
LEITENANT MALYEEV	Crichton, Okhta	1905	1908	Scrapped 1922
ING MECH ANASTASOV	Crichton, Okhta	1905	1908	Scrapped 1922

RUSSIA

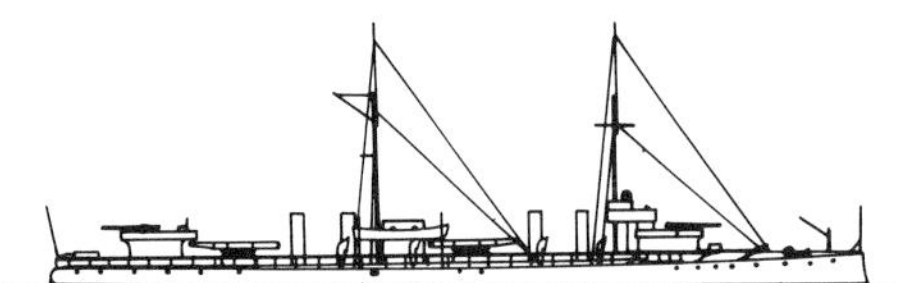

Lovki class as completed 1906

French-type destroyers with four funnels in two groups abaft the fore and mainmasts. The 11pdrs were on the roof of the forward and after 'conning towers' and the two single deck TT abaft the groups of funnels. All served in the Baltic during the First World War in which *Ispolnitelni* was lost by the explosion of one of her own mines on the same occasion as *Letuchi* capsized in a violent snow storm. *Burakov* was mined when acting as a despatch vessel.

LOVKI class

Displacement: 335t
Dimensions: 185ft 8in oa x 21ft x 11ft 2in max (*56.60 x 6.40 x 3.40m*)
Machinery: 4 Normand boilers, 2-shaft VTE, 5700ihp = 27kts. Coal 100-110t
Armament: 2-11pdr, 2-18in TT aw, later also 10 mines
Complement: 67

Name	Builder	Laid down	Launched	Comp	Fate
LOVKI	Normand	1904	1905	1906	Scrapped 1922
LETUCHI	Normand	1904	1905	1906	Capsized 12.12.1914
LIKHOI	Normand	1904	1905	1906	Scrapped 1922
ISKUSNI	La Seyne	1904	1905	1906	Scrapped 1922
ISPOLNITELNI	La Seyne	1904	1905	1906	Sunk 12.12.1914
KRYEPKI	La Seyne	1904	1905	1906	Scrapped 1925
LEGKI	La Seyne	1904	1905	1906	Scrapped 1922
LEITENANT BURAKOV	F & C, Le Havre	1904	1905	1906	Sunk 12.8.1917
MOSHCHNI	F & C, Le Havre	1904	1905	1906	Scrapped 1923
MOLODETZKI	F & C, Le Havre	1904	1905	1906	Scrapped 1922
MYETKI	F & C, Le Havre	1904	1905	1906	Scrapped 1922

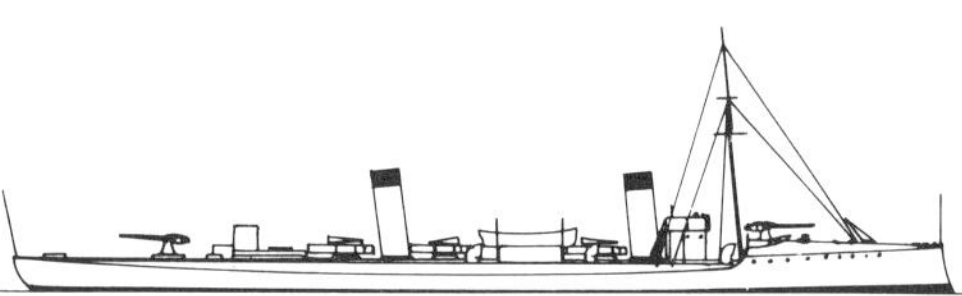

Bditelni class as completed 1906

Ram-bowed destroyers with a short forecastle and two widely spaced funnels. The 11pdrs were on the forecastle-deck forward and upper deck aft and the three single deck TT on the centreline, two being between the funnels and one between the after funnel and mainmast. *Vuinoslivi* appears to have been the fastest of the class with 28.72kts on trials. During the First World War *Yurasovski* and *Sergyeev* served at Vladivostock and later in the White Sea, while the rest were in the Baltic where *Bditelni* was lost on a mine. After the Revolution *Dmitriev, Zvyerev, Vnushitelni* and *Vuinoslivi* were named *Roshal II, Zhemchuzhny, Martinov,* and *Artemev*, being latterly employed as training ships, as according to some accounts was *Vnimatelni* under the name of *Osoaviakhim*.

BDITELNI class

Displacement: 380t
Dimensions: 208ft 6in oa x 23ft x 8ft 6in max (*63.55 x 7.00 x 2.60m*)
Machinery: 4 Schulz-Thornycroft boilers, 2-shaft VTE, 6000ihp = 27kts. Coal 125t
Armament: 2-11pdr, 3-18in TT aw, later also 16 mines
Complement: 65

Name	Builder	Laid down	Launched	Comp	Fate
BDITELNI	Schichau	1904	1905	1906	Sunk 27.11.1917
BOEVOI	Schichau	1904	1905	1906	Scrapped 1922
BURNI	Schichau	1904	1906	1906	Scrapped 1922
ING MECH DMITRIEV	Schichau	1904	1905	1906	Stricken 1946(?)
ING MECH ZVYEREV	Schichau	1904	1905	1906	Stricken 1946(?)
KAPITAN YURASOVSKI	Schichau	1904	1905	1906	Scrapped 1923
LEITENANT SERGYEEV	Schichau	1904	1905	1906	Scrapped 1923
VNIMATELNI	Schichau	1904	1906	1906	Scrapped 1922(?)
VNUSHITELNI	Schichau	1904	1906	1906	Stricken 1948 (?)
VUINOSLIVI	Schichau	1904	1906	1906	Stricken 1948 (?)

Similar to the *Boiki* class and of Yarrow-type with four funnels. The 11pdrs were mounted on the roof of the fore 'conning tower' and right aft, with the two single deck TT fore and aft of the after 'conning tower'. All served in the Baltic in the First World War, when *Stroini* grounded in the Gulf of Riga and was so badly damaged by a 130lb bomb from a large German seaplane that salvage was abandoned. Some were transferred to the Volga or Caspian during the Civil War.

STOROZHEVOI class

Displacement: 350t
Dimensions: 210ft oa x 21ft x 8ft 6in max (*64.00 x 6.40 x 2.60m*)
Machinery: 4 Normand boilers, 2-shaft VTE, 5800ihp = 27kts. Coal 100t
Armament: 2-11pdr, 2-18in TT aw, later also 12 mines
Complement: 67

Name	Builder	Laid down	Launched	Comp	Fate
STOROZHEVOI	Nevski	1904	1906	1906	Scrapped 1925
SILNI	Nevski	1904	1905	1906	Scrapped 1922
STROINI	Nevski	1904	1906	1907	Lost 21.8.1917
RAZYASHCHI	Nevski	1904	1906	1907	Scrapped 1922
RASTOROPNI	Nevski	1905	1907	1907	Scrapped 1922
DOSTOINI	Nevski	1905	1907	1907	Scrapped 1922
DYELNI	Nevski	1905	1907	1907	Scrapped 1922
DYEYATELNI	Nevski	1905	1907	1907	Scrapped 1923

This class comprised the first of the larger Russian destroyers and the ships were of distinctive appearance with a ram bow, high forecastle, rounded stern and three funnels. The 11pdrs were forward and aft with the 6pdr on each beam, a single deck TT between the second and third funnel, and a twin deck TT mounting abaft the mainmast. Originally they were reported as lacking in stability. The armament was altered to 2-4in/60 mounted fore and aft and 2 single deck TT fore and aft of the third funnel, the mainmast being restepped further aft. During the First World War, in which they served in the Baltic, *Kazanetz* being lost on a mine, the gun armament was again altered to 3-4in/60 all aft, with a 40mm AA on the forecastle. After the Revolution *Ukraina*, *Voiskovoi* and *Turkhmenetz* were renamed *Bakinski Rabochi*, *Markin* and *Altvater* and were stationed in the Caspian, latterly as gunboats.

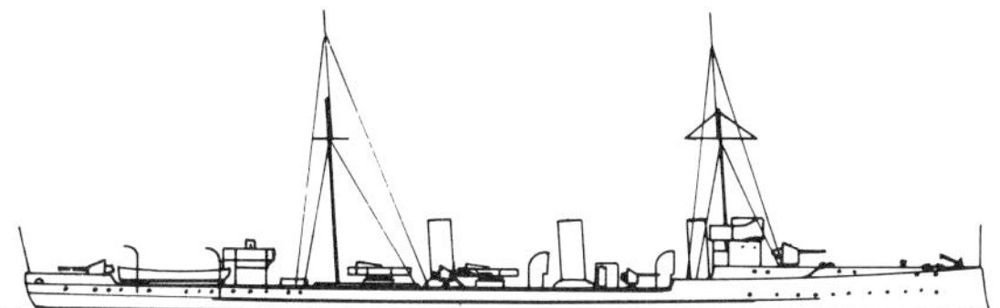

Ukraina class: early ships as completed 1905

UKRAINA class

Displacement: 580t
Dimensions: 240ft oa x 23ft 6in x 7ft 6in mean *(73.15 x 7.16 x 2.30m)*
Machinery: 4 Normand boilers, 2-shaft VTE, 7000ihp = 26kts. Coal 134t
Armament: 2-11pdr, 4-6pdr, 3-18in TT aw
Complement: 90

Name	Builder	Laid down	Launched	Comp	Fate
UKRAINA	Lange & Sohn	1904	1904	1905	Stricken 1958 (?)
VOISKOVOI	Lange & Sohn	1904	1904	1905	Stricken 1958 (?)
TURKHMENETZ-STAVROPOLSKI	Lange & Sohn	1904	1905	1905	Stricken 1958 (?)
KAZANETZ	Lange & Sohn	1904	1905	1905	Sunk 28.10.1916
STEREGUSHCHI	Lange & Sohn	1904	1905	1906	Scrapped 1922
STRASHNI	Lange & Sohn	1905	1906	1906	Scrapped 1922
DONSKOI-KAZAK	Lange & Sohn	1905	1906	1906	Scrapped 1922
ZAIBAIKALETZ	Lange & Sohn	1904	1906	1906	Scrapped 1922

Built to drawings prepared by Schichau, who also supplied the machinery, these ships resembled an enlarged *Bditelni* class. The 11pdrs were fore and aft with the 6pdr on either beam and three single centreline deck TT, two between the funnels and one abaft the after funnel. Shortly before the First World War these guns were replaced by 2-4in/60, and during the war, in which they served in the Baltic, 1-37mm AA was added. There was also provision for 20 mines. *Dobrovoletz* was lost on a Russian mine and *Moskvityanin* was sunk by the 6in and 4in gunfire of the improvised British Caspian squadron in the action at Alexandrovsk. *Emir Bukharski* and *Finn* were renamed *Yacob Sverdlov* and *Karl Liebknecht* after the Revolution and were employed in the Caspian.

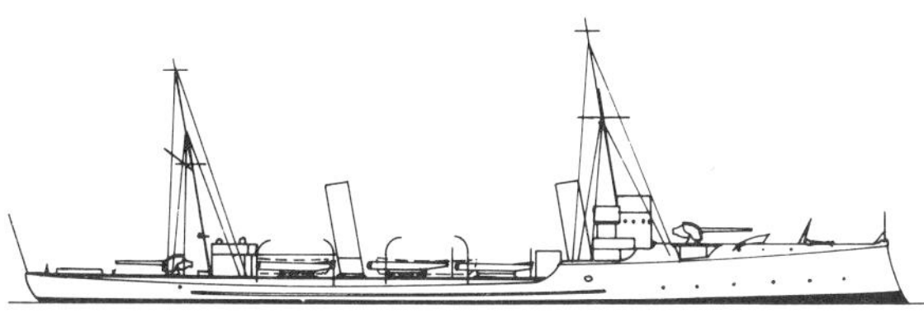

Dobrovoletz as completed 1906

EMIR BUKHARSKI class

Displacement: 570t
Dimensions: 235ft 9in oa x 23ft 6in x 7ft 10in mean *(71.86 x 7.16 x 2.40m)*
Machinery: 4 Schulz-Thornycroft boilers, 2-shaft VTE, 6500ihp = 25kts. Coal 150t max
Armament: 2-11pdr, 6-6pdr, 3-18in TT
Complement: 99

Name	Builder	Laid down	Launched	Comp	Fate
EMIR BUKHARSKI	Skeppsdocka, Helsingfors	1904	1905	1905	Stricken 1938 (?)
FINN	Skeppsdocka, Helsingfors	1904	1905	1905	Stricken 1937 (?)
MOSKVITYANIN	Putilov	1904	1905	1905	Sunk 21.5.1919
DOBROVOLETZ	Putilov	1904	1905	1906	Sunk 21.8.1916

Two-funnel destroyers with a high forecastle and straight stem. Material for *Amuretz* and *Ussurietz* was supplied by Krupp, Germania. The 11pdrs were fore and aft, with four of the 6pdrs on either beam and two in sponsons below the bridge, the forecastle being recessed to allow ahead fire. The TT were in single deck mountings on the centreline, between the funnels, abaft the second funnel and abaft the mainmast. Shortly before the First World War they were rearmed with 2-4in/60 and the sponsons and forecastle recess removed. All were in the Baltic during the war and had 1-37mm AA added, while 25 mines could be carried. After the Revolution *Vsadnik*, *Amuretz* and *Ussurietz* were renamed *Sladkov*, *Zhelesniakov* and *Roshal*, being latterly employed as gunboats or training ships.

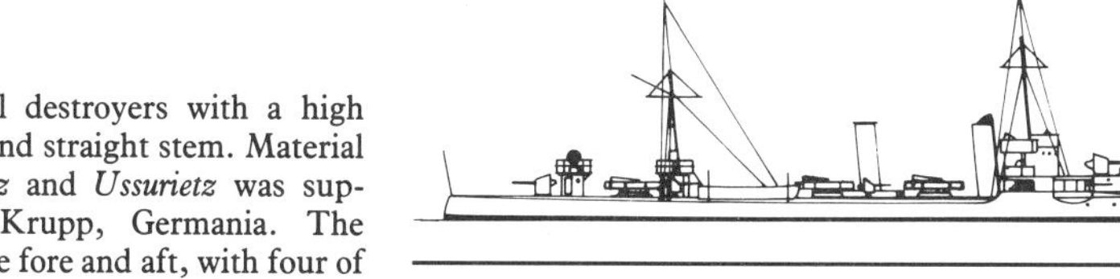

Ussurietz as completed 1907

GAIDAMAK class

Displacement: 570t
Dimensions: 235ft 9in oa x 23ft 6in x 7ft 10in mean *(71.86 x 7.16 x 2.40m)*
Machinery: 4 Schulz-Thornycroft boilers, 2-shaft VTE, 6500ihp = 25kts. Coal 205t max
Armament: 2-11pdr, 6-6pdr, 3-18in TT aw
Complement: 99

Name	Builder	Laid down	Launched	Comp	Fate
GAIDAMAK	Krupp, Germania	1904	1905	1906	Scrapped 1926
VSADNIK	Krupp, Germania	1904	1905	1906	Stricken 1942 (?)
AMURETZ	Broberg, Helsingfors	1905	1905	1906	Stricken 1945 (?)
USSURIETZ	Broberg, Helsingfors	1905	1905	1907	Stricken 1939 (?)

Resembled a two funnel version of the *Ukraina* class in appearance. The 11pdrs were fore and aft, the 6pdrs on either beam and the three single deck TT between the funnels, abaft the second funnel and abaft the mainmast, all on the centreline. It should be noted that photographs distinctly show the above armament, though some accounts credit them with 2-4.7in/30 instead of 11pdrs. The original guns were replaced by 2-4in/60 mounted fore and aft, and during the First World War, in which they served in the Baltic, this was increased to 3-4in/60 by adding another gun aft. There were also two 3pdr AA, and 40 mines were carried when used as minelayers, the four destroyers forming a special half-flotilla. *Okhotnik* was sunk by a German mine. *Sibirski Stryelok* was renamed *Konstruktor* after the Revolution and was later used as leader of minesweepers, and finally as a gunboat.

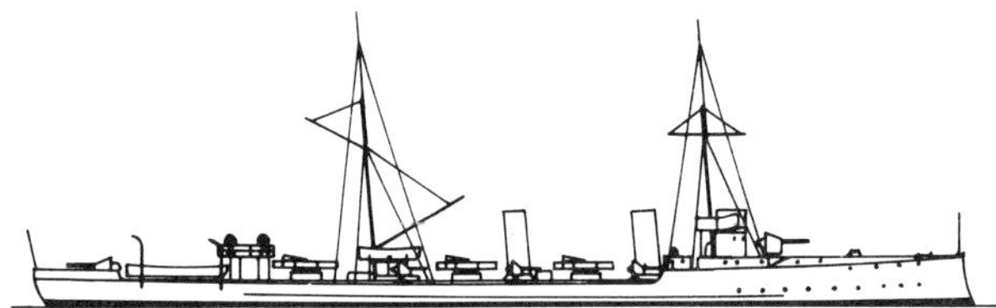

Okhotnik as completed 1906

OKHOTNIK class

Displacement: 615t
Dimensions: 246ft 8in oa x 26ft 10in x 8ft mean *(75.18 x 8.18 x 2.44m)*
Machinery: 4 Normand boilers, 2-shaft VTE, 7300ihp = 25.5kts. Coal 215t max
Armament: 2-11pdr, 6-6pdr, 3-18in TT
Complement: 102

Name	Builder	Laid down	Launched	Comp	Fate
OKHOTNIK	Crichton, Abo	1905	1905	1906	Sunk 26.9.1917
POGRANICHNIK	Crichton, Abo	1905	1905	1906	Scrapped 1925
GENERAL KONDRATENKO	Skeppsdocka, Helsingfors	1905	1905	1906	Scrapped 1922
SIBIRSKI STRYELOK	Skeppsdocka, Helsingfors	1905	1905	1906	Stricken 1957 (?)

Black Sea Fleet boats, the Belgian Works being at Nicolaiev. *Kapitan Saken* was originally to be named *Leitenant Pushchin*. Resembled the *Gaidamak* class in appearance but differed in gun armament with the 4.7in forward, one 11pdr aft, one on each beam and one in each sponson below the bridge. These guns were later changed to 2-4.7in/30 mounted fore and aft, with 2-3pdr AA and provision for 40 mines. *Leitenant Zatzarenni* was sunk by a mine. This class is seldom mentioned in accounts of First World War Black Sea fighting, possibly because of their lack of speed as *Saken* the fastest, only did 24.8kts wth 7130ihp on trials.

LEITENANT SHESTAKOV class

Displacement: 640t
Dimensions: 243ft 3in oa x 27ft 2in x 9ft max *(74.14 x 8.28 x 2.74m)*
Machinery: 4 Normand boilers, 2-shaft VTE, 6500ihp = 25kts. Coal 200t max
Armament: 1-4.7in/30, 5-11pdr, 3-18in TT aw
Complement:91

Name	Builder	Laid down	Launched	Comp	Fate
LEITENANT SHESTAKOV	Belgian Wks	1905	28.7.1907	1908	Scuttled 18.6.1918
KAPT LEITENANT BARANOV	Belgian Wks	1905	5.11.1907	1908	Scuttled 18.6.1918
LEITENANT ZATZARENNI	Belgian Wks	1905	29.10.1907	1908	Sunk 30.6.1917
KAPITAN SAKEN	Belgian Wks	1905	14.9.1907	1908	To Bizerta 1920

TORPEDO BOATS

The larger Russian boats are described individually below, but except for the first one they were preceded by a large number of small boats. In the Russo-Turkish War of 1877/1878 most of the boats used spar or towing torpedoes, and only *Tchesma,* which had a tube rigged under the keel, and the *Sinop,* which discharged her torpedo from a raft secured alongside, employed Whiteheads. None of the boats used in this war appears to have been longer than 68ft and most were considerably smaller, but in 1877 the construction of 100 Yarrow-designed boats was begun by the Russian yards in the Baltic. These boats were 75ft oa by 10ft 6in and displaced 24.5t, with a speed of 17kts and engines of 200-220ihp. They could be transferred between the Baltic and Black Sea by rail. Some had a single 15in TT but most were originally armed with spar torpedoes and/or the 'fired' torpedo, a 9in diameter weapon propelled to about 200ft by a gunpowder launching charge. None was actually built by Yarrow though four sets of machinery were supplied by them, and of the Russian yards the Baltic Works and Baird were the principal builders. All the above 100 boats seem to have been launched in 1877 or 1878, and another 15 boats of different designs but of similar size had been acquired by the end of 1880, mostly from Schichau. Very few small boats were added subsequently, except for ten 90ft, 37t boats from Nixon of New Jersey in 1905. These were powered by two 300hp petrol engines to give 20kts, and had a 12in training TT, but were found to be unsuitable for the Russian Navy.

A list of 1896 shows 98 small torpedo boats still in use, of which 55 apparently had 1-15in TT and the rest spars, and in 1906, discounting the above petrol-engined boats, these figures had fallen to 74 and 44.

The above small torpedo boats were originally named, but in about 1887 they were given numbers from 51, actually 46, to 100 for boats with Whiteheads and 101 upwards for spar torpedo boats. In April 1895 these numbers were changed to 1 to 100, apparently without relevance to the former number. At the same time the larger boats, except the first, *Vzruiv,* were allocated numbers from 101 if in the Baltic, and from 251 if in the Black Sea. The Vladivostock boats retained their names for a time, but were then numbered 201 to 211, while 212-223 were given to the Baltic boats launched in 1901/1902. The last of all, the *Lastochka,* was not numbered.

VZRUIV

The first large Russian torpedo boat, resembling a steam yacht in appearance. The TT were on either beam just forward of midships, and pointed nearly ahead. Latterly used as a torpedo school tender. There is some doubt about the above speed as later figures give 800ihp = 12.3kts.

Displacement: 160t
Dimensions: 119ft 8in oa x 16ft 2in x 11ft 1in max *(36.47 x 4.93 x 3.38m)*
Machinery: 1 loco boiler, 1-shaft VC, 1000ihp = 17kts. Coal 16t max
Armament: 2-1pdr revolvers, 2-15in TT
Complement: 33

Name	Later No	Builder	Launched	Fate
VZRUIV	None	Baltic Wks (?)	1877	Stricken 1908

Batum as completed

BATUM

Yarrow number 472. Black Sea Fleet. Ram-bowed with turtle deck forward, two funnels abreast, an after rudder showing above water and a drop rudder in the bow. The two bow TT were fixed under the turtle deck and two spare torpedoes were carried on deck. The first torpedo boat to steam from London to the Mediterranean.

Displacment: 43t
Dimensions: 96ft 6in oa x 11ft 1¼in x 6ft 3in max *(29.41 x 3.39 x 1.9m)*
Machinery: 1 loco boiler, 1-shaft VC, 500ihp = 22.5kts light. Coal 10t max
Armament: 2- later 1-1pdr revolver, finally 1-1pdr QF, 2-15in TT
Complement: 15

Name	Later No	Builder	Launched	Fate
BATUM	251	Yarrow	1880	Stricken 1908

SUKHUM

Thornycroft number 167. Black Sea Fleet. Ram-bowed with turtle deck forward, two funnels abreast and three masts on which fore and aft sails could be set. There was ¼in steel on the sides and deck near the machinery. The two TT were fixed in the bows.

Displacement: 64t
Dimensions: 112ft 11in oa x 12ft 6in x 6ft 6in max *(34.42 x 3.81 x 1.98m)*
Machinery: 1 loco boiler, 1-shaft VC, 704ihp = 17.9kts. Coal 10t max
Armament: 2-1pdr, 2-15in TT
Complement: 18

Name	Later No	Builder	Launched	Fate
SUKHUM	257	Thornycroft	1883	Stricken 1908

POTI

Black Sea Fleet. A very successful boat of the usual early Normand type with two funnels abreast. The two TT were fixed in the bows. The boiler was fitted for oil fuel *c*1902.

Displacement: 63t
Dimensions: 124ft 7in oa x 10ft x 6ft 8in max *(37.97 x 3.05 x 2.03m)*
Machinery: 1 loco boiler, 1-shaft VC, 575ihp = 18.5kts. Coal 11t max
Armament: 2-1pdr, 2-15in TT
Complement: 18

Name	Later No	Builder	Launched	Fate
POTI	258	Normand	1883	Stricken 1908

GHELENDJIK

Black Sea Fleet. Three small masts and two funnels abreast. The TT were fixed in the bows.

Displacement: 70.5t
Dimensions: 122ft 8in oa x 12ft 5in x 7ft max *(37.40 x 3.78 x 2.13m)*
Machinery: 1 loco boiler, 1-shaft VC, 520ihp = 18kts. Coal 11t max
Armament: 1-1pdr, 1-1pdr revolver, 2-15in TT
Complement: 18

Name	Later No	Builder	Launched	Fate
GHELENDJIK	255	La Seyne	1884	Stricken 1908

GAGRI

Black Sea Fleet. Two fixed bow TT. The boiler was fitted for oil fuel *c*1902

Displacement: 80t
Dimensions: 120ft 7in oa x 13ft 4in x 6ft 6in max *(36.75 x 4.06 x 1.98m)*
Machinery: 1 loco boiler, 1 shaft VC, 574ihp = 17.8kts. Coal 12t max
Armament: 1-1pdr, 1-1pdr revolver, 2-15in TT
Complement: 18

Name	Later No	Builder	Launched	Fate
GAGRI	254	Claparède, Rouen	1884	Stricken 1908

KOTLIN

Bow rounded at top with a spur, deck curved with fore part raised to form a cover for two fixed bow TT. Two funnels abreast. TT difficult to reload, and not a success as 18kts intended.

Displacement: 67t
Dimensions: 124ft 6in oa x 12ft 11in x 4ft 6in max *(37.95 x 3.94 x 1.37m)*
Machinery: 1 loco boiler, 2-shaft VC, 472ihp = 16.5kts. Coal 14t max
Armament: 2-1pdr revolvers, 2-15in TT
Complement: 21

Name	Later No	Builder	Launched	Fate
KOTLIN	101	Baltic Wks	1885	Stricken 1907

RUSSIA

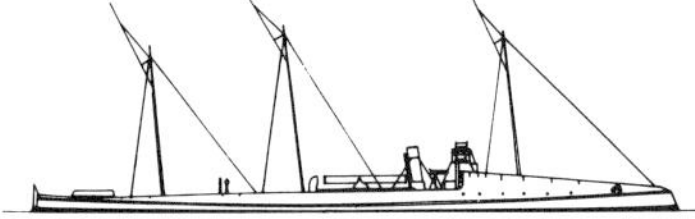

Viborg as completed

VIBORG

Rounded ram bow, turtle deck forward, three masts and two funnels abreast. Balanced rudder fitted. Two fixed bow TT and one revolving abaft funnels. A total of six torpedoes carried. Converted to oil fuel *c*1893, the tanks holding 9t.

Displacement: 166t
Dimensions: 142ft 6in oa x 17ft x 7ft max *(43.43 x 5.18 x 2.13m)*
Machinery: 2 loco boilers, 2-shaft VC, 1300ihp = 20kts. Coal 40t max
Armament: 2-1pdr revolvers, 3-15in TT
Complement: 24

Name	Later No	Builder	Launched	Fate
VIBORG	102	Clydebank	1886	Stricken 1910

ABO class

Single funnel boats with three signal masts, fore and aft 'conning towers' and two rudders. The stem was straight and the stern rounded. Two fixed bow TT and four spare torpedoes could be stowed.

Displacement: 76t
Dimensions: 126ft 4in oa x 14ft 10in x 6ft 3in max *(38.50 x 4.52 x 1.90m)*
Machinery: 1 loco boiler, 1-shaft VC, 640ihp = 19.3-20kts. Coal 18t max
Armament: 4-1pdr revolvers, 2-15in TT
Complement: 21

Name	Later No	Builder	Launched	Fate
ABO	108	Schichau	1886	Stricken 1910
VINDAVA	109	Schichau	1886	Stricken 1910
LIBAVA	110	Schichau	1886	Stricken 1910

YALTA class

Black Sea Fleet. Improved *Abo* class, differing mainly in TE engines. At one period four 1pdr revolvers were mounted. All except *No 263* were fitted for oil fuel *c*1899/1902.

Displacement: 85-90t
Dimensions: 126ft 6in oa, *Reni* 128ft 6in x 15ft x 6ft 2in-6ft 9in max *(38.55; 39.15 x 4.57 x 1.88-2.06m)*
Machinery: 1 loco boiler, 1-shaft VTE, 900ihp = 20-20.8kts. Coal 21t max
Armament: 2-1pdr revolvers, 2-15in TT
Complement: 18

Name	Later No	Builder	Launched	Fate
YALTA	266	Schichau	1886	Stricken 1911
NOVOROSSISK	263	Schichau	1886	Stricken 1913
TCHARDAK	265	Schichau	1886	Stricken 1911
KODOR	261	Schichau	1886	Stricken 1911
KILIA	262	Schichau	1886	Stricken 1911
RENI	264	Schichau	1886	Stricken 1911

IZMAIL class

Izmail Black Sea Fleet. Russian copies of the *Poti*, and not very successful. The three New Admiralty boats were reboilered with Yarrow boilers fitted for oil fuel in 1899, and *Izmail* was also fitted for oil fuel *c*1902.

Displacement: 73-76t
Dimensions: 127ft 7in oa x 11ft 7in x 7ft 2in-7ft 6in max (38.89 x 3.53 x 2.18-2.28m)
Machinery: 1 loco boiler, 1-shaft VC, 296ihp = 15.8kts (*Izmail* 520ihp = 17.5kts). Coal 17t max
Armament: 4-1pdr revolvers, *Izmail* 2, 2-15in TT
Complement: 21

Name	Later No	Builder	Launched	Fate
IZMAIL	267	Nicolaiev	1886	Stricken 1908
LAKHTA	105	New Admiralty	1886	Stricken 1907
LUGA	106	New Admiralty	1887	Stricken 1909
NARVA	107	New Admiralty	1888	Stricken 1910

SVEABORG class

Very satisfactory boats with two fixed bow and one training TT. They were later shipped to Vladivostock in sections.

Displacement: *Sveaborg* 96t; *Revel* 107.5t
Dimensions: 153ft 6in oa x 11ft 3in x 8ft 8in max *Sveaborg*, 12ft 3in x 8ft 3in max *Revel (46.80 x 3.43 x 2.64, 3.73 x 2.51m)*
Machinery: 1 Normand boiler, 1-shaft VTE, 737ihp = 19.2kts *Sveaborg*, 837ihp = 19.7kts *Revel*. Coal 29t max
Armament: 2-1pdr revolvers, 3-15in TT
Complement: 21

Name	Later No	Builder	Launched	Fate
SVEABORG	205	Normand	1886	Stricken 1911
REVEL	206	Normand	1886	Stricken 1911

SUTCHENA class

Single funnel boats with straight stem and stern and three masts, resembling the Schichau-built *Abo* class. Two fixed bow TT. Both later shipped to Vladivostock in sections.

Displacement: 76t
Dimensions: 127ft 11in oa x 14ft 10in x 6ft 1in max *(39.00 x 4.52 x 1.85m)*
Machinery: 1 loco boiler, 1-shaft VC, 970ihp = 16.8-17.2kts. Coal 29t max
Armament: 2-1pdr revolvers, 2-15in TT
Complement: 21

Name	Later No	Builder	Launched	Fate
SUTCHENA	202	Nevski	1887	Stricken 1911
YANTCHIKHE	201	Nevski	1887	Wrecked 21.8.1904

ANAKRIA

Black Sea Fleet. In appearance of the usual single funnel, three-masted Schichau type. One TT was fixed in the bows and one training on deck. Fitted for oil fuel in 1900.

Displacement: 100t
Dimensions: 126ft 6in oa x 15ft 8in x 6ft 10in max (*38.55 x 4.78 x 2.08m*)
Machinery: 1 loco boiler, 1-shaft VTE, 1100ihp = 21kts. Coal 18t max
Armament: 2-1pdr revolvers, 2-15in TT
Complement: 16

Name	Later No	Builder	Launched	Fate
ANAKRIA	260	Schichau	1889	Stricken 1917

SUNGARI class

Later shipped to Vladivostock in sections. A 1901 report that they had two fixed stern TT appears to have been a misprint for two stem TT. *No 204* was blown up by her crew after running ashore off Gensan.

Displacement: 175t
Dimensions: 135ft 2in oa x 16ft 5in x 8ft 8in max (*41.20 x 5.00 x 2.64m*)
Machinery: (?) 2 loco boilers, 2-shaft VTE, 1956ihp = 20.3kts *Sungari*; 2039ihp = 19.5kts *Ussuri*. Coal 30t max
Armament: 3-1pdr revolvers, 3-15in TT
Complement: 21

Name	Later No	Builder	Launched	Fate
SUNGARI	203	Crichton, Abo	1889	Stricken 1911
USSURI	204	Crichton, Abo	1889	Scuttled 30.6.1904

ADLER

Black Sea Fleet. A larger boat of the one-funnel Schichau type. One TT was fixed in the bows and two were in single training mountings on deck. Fitted for oil fuel *c*1900.

Displacement: 164t
Dimensions: 153ft 10in oa x 16ft 7in x 6ft 8in max (*46.90 x 5.05 x 2.03m*)
Machinery: 1 loco boiler, 1-shaft VTE, 2000ihp = 26.7kts. Coal 20t max
Armament: 2-1pdr revolvers, 3-15in TT
Complement: 22

Name	Later No	Builder	Launched	Fate
ADLER	259	Schichau	1890	Stricken 1917

EKENES class

Borgo was shipped to Vladivostock in sections.

Displacement: 106t
Dimensions: 136ft 8in oa x 14ft 8in x 8ft 5in max (*41.66 x 4.47 x 2.57m*)
Machinery: 1 loco boiler, 1-shaft VTE, 1245ihp = 20kts
Armament: 2-1pdr revolvers, 2-15in TT
Complement: 21

Name	Later No	Builder	Launched	Fate
EKENES	117	Crichton, Abo	1890	Stricken 1910
BORGO	207	Crichton, Abo	1890	Lost 1900

BIERKE class

Boats with ram bows and two masts on which fore and aft sails could be set. The two TT trained 35° on each bow. *No 112* was reboilered with a Yarrow boiler fitted for oil fuel in 1899, and *No 114* was also fitted for oil fuel.

Displacement: 81t
Dimensions: 126ft oa x 14ft 8in x 8ft 5in max (*38.40 x 4.47 x 2.57m*)
Machinery: 1 loco boiler, 1-shaft VTE, 1000-1100ihp = 17.8-19kts. Coal 17t max
Armament: 2-1pdr revolvers, 2-15in TT
Complement: 21

Name	Later No	Builder	Launched	Fate
BIERKE	111	Putilov	1890	Stricken 1910
ROTCHENSALM	112	Putilov	1890	Stricken 1910
GAPSAL	113	Putilov	1891	Stricken 1910
MOONZUND	114	Putilov	1891	Stricken 1910

DAGO class

Kotka Black Sea Fleet. One fixed bow TT and one training aft. *No 256* is believed to have been the boat that later became the seaplane tender *Lietchik* and served until 1937.

Displacement: 100-104t
Dimensions: 152ft 6in-153ft 6in oa x 12ft 10in x 7ft 8in-8ft max (*46.50-46.80 x 3.91 x 2.34-2.44m*)
Machinery: 1 loco boiler, 1-shaft VTE, 1000-1030ihp = 16.2-19kts. Coal 15t max
Armament: 2-1pdr revolvers (2-3pdr revolvers in *Dago*), 2-15in TT
Complement: 21

Name	Later No	Builder	Launched	Fate
DAGO	118	Crichton, Abo	1891	Stricken 1910
KOTKA	256	Crichton, Abo	1891	Stricken 1917 as TB
KRONSHLOT	123	Izhora	1891	Stricken 1910
SESKAR	124	Izhora	1891	Stricken 1910

Bierke about 1900
(All uncredited photos in this section CPL)

Black Sea Fleet.

ANAPA class

Displacement: 91.5-96t
Dimensions: 126ft oa x 14ft 8in x 4ft 9in-5ft max – probably not over screw *(38.40 x 4.47 x 1.45-1.52m)*
Machinery: 1 loco boiler, 1-shaft VTE, 1000-1100ihp = 17.2-19kts
Armament: 2-1pdr, 2-15in TT
Complement: 18

Name	Later No	Builder	Launched	Fate
ANAPA	252	Bellino-Fendrich, Odessa	1891	Stricken 1917
AITODOR	253	Bellino-Fendrich, Odessa	1892	Stricken 1917

Two-funnel boat similar to the French *Dragon* class. One TT was fixed in the bows, and two were in single training mountings located between the funnels and aft. She was reboilered with Yarrow boilers in 1899. The above speed may be optimistic as trial figures were 1800ihp = 25.46kts at 116.5t.

PERNOV

Displacement: 120t
Dimensions: 137ft 10in oa x 14ft 9in x 6ft 9in max *(42.00 x 4.50 x 2.06m)*
Machinery: 2 Du Temple boilers, 2-shaft VTE, 2000ihp = 26kts. Coal 16t max
Armament: 2-1pdr revolvers, 3-15in TT
Complement: 21

Name	Later No	Builder	Launched	Fate
PERNOV	103	Normand	1892	Stricken 1910

A smaller boat than *Pernov* with one fixed bow and one training deck TT. Trials gave 1350ihp = 24.5kts at 76.5t.

SESTRORETSK

Displacement: 80t
Dimensions: 118ft oa x 13ft x 8ft max *(36.00 x 3.96 x 2.44m)*
Machinery: 1 Du Temple–Normand boiler, 1-shaft VTE, 1300ihp = 23kts. Coal 17t max
Armament: 2-1pdr revolvers, 2-15in TT
Complement: 21

Name	Later No	Builder	Launched	Fate
SESTRORETSK	104	Normand	1893	Stricken 1910

Russian versions of the Schichau boat *Anakria*. The four Putilov boats were reboilered from 1899 with Yarrow boilers fitted to burn oil fuel.

TOSNA class

Displacement: 85-99t
Dimensions: 127ft 5in-128ft 2in oa x 15ft 3in-15ft 6in x 6ft 3in-6ft 10in max *(38.84-39.07 x 4.65-4.72 x 1.90-2.08m)*
Machinery: 1 Du Temple boiler, 1-shaft VTE, 1000ihp = 20kts. Coal 17t max
Armament: 2-1pdr revolvers (2-3pdr in *Tosna* and *Domesnes*), 2-15in TT
Complement: 21

Name	Later No	Builder	Launched	Fate
TOSNA	115	Putilov	1893	Stricken 1910
DOMESNES	116	Putilov	1893	Stricken 1910
ASPE	125	Putilov	1893	Stricken 1910
TRANZUND	126	Putilov	1893	Stricken 1910
NARGEN	121	Izhora	1894	Stricken 1910
GOGLAND	122	Izhora	1894	Stricken 1910

Nos 270 to *273* Black Sea Fleet. Russian versions of the Normand boat *Pernov*, the Nicolaiev boats differing in having three masts. *Nos 119* and *120* were reboilered with Yarrow boilers in 1899 and they, as well as *Nos 127-130, 138* and *139* were fitted for oil fuel, as were the Black Sea boats.

POLANGEN class

Displacement: 120t
Dimensions: 137ft 10in oa x 14ft 9in x 6ft 9in max *(42.00 x 4.50 x 2.06m)*
Machinery: 2 Du Temple boilers, 2-shaft VTE, 2000ihp = 19.5-23.2kts. Coal 10-20t max
Armament: 2-1pdr revolvers, 3-15in TT
Complement: 21

Name	Later No	Builder	Launched	Fate
POLANGEN	119	Crichton, Abo	1894	Stricken 1913 as TB
PAKERORT	120	Crichton, Abo	1894	Stricken 1913 as TB
–	127	Izhora	1896	Stricken 1911
–	128	Izhora	1896	Stricken 1921
–	129	Izhora	1897	Stricken 1921
–	130	Izhora	1897	Stricken 1911
–	133	Nevski	1896	Stricken 1911
–	134	Nevski	1896	Stricken 1914
–	135	Nevski	1896	Stricken 1911
–	136	Nevski	1896	Stricken 1913
–	137	Izhora	1897	Stricken 1911
–	138	Izhora	1897	Stricken 1911
–	139	Izhora	1897	Stricken 1911
–	140	Izhora	1897	Stricken 1914
–	141	Nevski	1897	Stricken 1911
–	142	Nevski	1897	Stricken 1921
–	270	Nicolaiev	1895	Stricken 1917
–	271	Nicolaiev	1895	Stricken 1917
–	272	Nicolaiev	1896	Collision 28.8.1914
–	273	Nicolaiev	1896	Stricken 1917

Smaller versions of the *Polangen* class, with one fixed bow and one training deck TT.

NUMBERS 131, 132, 268, 269

Displacement: 100t
Dimensions: 126ft 6in oa x 15ft 8in x 6ft 10in max *(38.55 x 4.77 x 2.08m)*
Machinery: 2 Du Temple boilers, 2-shaft VTE, 1000ihp = 21kts. Coal 20t max
Armament: 2-1pdr revolvers, 2-15in TT
Complement: 18

Number	Builder	Launched	Fate
131	Izhora	1895	Stricken 1910
132	Izhora	1895	Stricken 1910 as TB
268	Nicolaiev	1895	Stricken 1911
269	Nicolaiev	1895	Collision 1896

Similar to the *Polangen* class but slower and with larger bunkers. They were shipped to Vladivostock in sections. *No 208* was sunk by a mine.

NUMBERS 208-211

Displacement: 120t
Dimensions: 137ft 10in oa x 14ft 9in x 6ft 9in max *(42.00 x 4.50 x 2.06m)*
Machinery: (?) 2 Du Temple boilers, 2 shaft VTE, 1460ihp = 18.5kts. Coal 40t max
Armament: 2-1pdr, 3-15in TT
Complement: 21

Number	Builder	Assembled Vladivostock	Fate
208	New Admiralty	1899	Sunk 17.7.1904
209	New Admiralty	1899	Stricken 1911
210	New Admiralty	1899	Stricken 1911
211	New Admiralty	1899	Stricken 1915

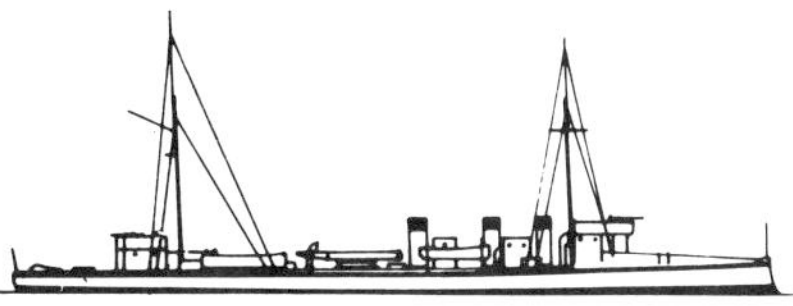
TB 213 as completed

Three-funnel Yarrow-type boats, larger than most TBs and with fore and aft 'conning towers'. They were employed as minesweepers in the Baltic during the First World War.

NUMBERS 212,213

Displacement: 186t
Dimensions: 171ft 9in oa x 17ft 3in x 4ft 10in mean *(52.35 x 5.25 x 1.47m)*
Machinery: (?) 4 Yarrow boilers, 2-shaft VTE, 3800ihp = 24kts. Coal 60t max
Armament: 3-1pdr, later 2-3pdr, 3 later 2-15in TT
Complement: 26

Number	Builder	Launched	Fate
212	Crichton, Abo	1901	Stricken 1921
213	Crichton, Abo	1901	Scrapped 1925

Russian copies of the French *Cyclone* class, with the TT in a twin training deck mounting. The survivors served in the Baltic as minesweepers during the First World War.

NUMBERS 214-223

Displacement: 150t
Dimensions: 147ft 8in oa x 15ft 3in x 8ft 9in max *(45.00 x 4.65 x 2.67m)*
Machinery: 2 Normand or Yarrow boilers, 2-shaft VTE, 3700ihp = 29kts. Coal 30t max
Armament: 2-3pdr, 2-15in TT
Complement: 28

Number	Builder	Launched	Fate
214	Nevski	1902	Stricken 1930 (?)
215	Nevski	1902	Stricken 1921
216	Nevski	1902	Stricken 1921
217	Nevski	1902	Stricken 1930 (?)
218	Nevski	1902	Stricken 1921
219	Crichton, Abo	1903	Stricken 1930 (?)
220	Crichton, Abo	1902	Stricken 1930 (?)
221	Crichton, Abo	1902	Foundered 1904
222	Crichton, Abo	1902	Stricken 1921 (?)
223	Crichton, Abo	1902	Stricken 1912

Built by Yarrow as an experiment and originally named *Caroline*. The hull form was the same as that of the Vanderbilt's yacht *Tarantula,* built by Yarrow in 1902. The HP turbine was on the port shaft and the LP on the starboard, with the VTE engine on the centre shaft. The TT were to port and starboard forward of the fore-funnel and aft on the centreline. *Lastochka* was the first turbine-engined vessel in the Russian Navy.

LASTOCHKA

Displacement: 140t
Dimensions: 152ft 6in oa x 15ft 3in x (?) 5ft mean *(46.50 x 4.65 x 1.52m)*
Machinery: 2 Yarrow boilers, 3-shaft, 2 Rateau turbines, 1 VTE, 2000shp + 250ihp = 26.39kts
Armament: 2-3pdr, 3-15in TT
Complement: 23

Name	Builder	Launched	Acquired by Russia	Fate
LASTOCHKA	Yarrow	1903	1905	Stricken 1914

Japan

INTRODUCTION

When Commodore Perry appeared off Uraga on 8 July 1853 Japan was still a feudal state completely lacking any form of industrialisation. At the head was the Emperor, the spiritual leader of the country, who had no political power. Under the Emperor was the Shogun who wielded absolute political power controlling the Lords (or heads) of some 240 clans throughout the country. Each Lord had the right to strike his own coinage, administer law and order within his clan, and to retain his own army recruited from within the clan.

To maintain the feudal *status quo* all contact with, and travel to, foreign lands and people was expressly forbidden and no ships larger than 50 registered tons were allowed to be built. The arrival of Commodore Perry and subsequent foreign expeditions to Japan, together with a Shogun ready and willing to treat with foreigners spelt the end of the old feudal system. The intransigence of nationalistic clans, with the tacit support of the traditionally minded Emperor, led to a civil war which ended with the abolition of the Shogunate, the formation of a proper Government and the restoration of governing power to the Emperor.

FORMATION OF THE IMPERIAL NAVY

By the end of the civil war in June 1869 the nucleus of an Imperial Navy had been formed which incorporated the finest units captured from the Shogunate forces, and units loaned to the Emperor by loyal clans. The Imperial fleet comprised the armoured ram *Kotetsu* – later renamed *Adzuma*, gunboat *Chiyodogata*, corvette *Yoshun* and the paddle ships *Fujiyama*, *Kanko*, *Choyo* and *Shokaku* and four old sailing vessels.

Many of these vessels lacked any armament, however, and were sadly in need of repair and refit, and their crews lacked any form of training. A British mission was invited to Japan to organise and train a new navy. At that time all the Imperial forces came under the control of the Ministry of War, but in February 1872 the Navy Department was formed as an autonomous unit with complete control over administration and deployment of its allocated finances. Little, however, could be done at that time to build up Japan's naval strength. There had to be a long period of retrenchment while the ravages of the civil war were repaired, industrial techniques learnt, the last remnants of the old feudal system obliterated and minor insurrections following the civil war put down.

Japan's internal problems and political reforms meant that little money was available for defence and an ambitious naval programme of 70 warships asked for in 1873 had to be dropped. The generally weak state of the country enabled pirates on the island of Formosa to become increasingly more active until 1874 when a Japanese expedition had to be sent to the area to quell them. Although the expedition encountered severe difficulties the operation did, nevertheless, focus national interest on the need for a strong navy. The poor state of the navy, coupled with deteriorating relations with Korea, finally convinced the Japanese Government of the necessity for a modern navy. Authorisation for a new construction programme was given in 1875 and as Japanese shipyards and industry were not then sufficiently advanced to embark on the construction of sophisticated warships the order for three armoured units, *Fuso*, *Hiei* and *Kongo*, was placed with British shipyards. The Yokosuka shipyard under French direction undertook to complete the smaller, less sophisticated vessels. These ships were of fairly basic design with wooden hulls, simple reciprocating machinery of the horizontal compound type and iron-type locomotive boilers developing very low pressures; armament was generally supplied by the German firm of Krupps. In addition to these ships four small torpedo boats were ordered from Yarrow in 1879.

THE FIRST NAVAL CONSTRUCTION PROGRAMMES

With the internal situation rapidly stabilising, Japan made great advances in the technological and economic fields. In 1882 the First Navy Expansion Bill, providing for an expenditure of some 26,670,000 Yen, was passed. Under the provisions of the Bill the Imperial Navy would receive 48 vessels built over a period of eight years, but two of the ships were subsequently dropped. Apart from the construction of warships the Bill also provided funds for the development of shipyards and industries associated with warship construction, and for the training of officers and technicians. Under the scheme naval officers were to be trained in Britain while France was to provide the necessary technical training and background.

The Japanese were strongly influenced by the *Jeune École* school of naval thought developing in France. This advocated the formation of fleets based around the cruisers, supported by torpedo craft, which, the theoreticians argued, had made the battleship concept obsolete, and as such, battleships might well disappear from the fleet lists. Of the 46 vessels finally built under the First Expansion Bill 14, including two cruisers, were constructed in Japanese yards while the remaining vessels, mainly cruisers, were built in British and French yards. Included in the order for the 46 ships, provision was also made for ordering 22 torpedo boats from overseas yards. These were to be built complete and then broken down for shipment to Japan where they would be re-erected.

The eight years covered by the First Expansion Bill witnessed great advances in the Japanese shipbuilding industry. In 1882 the first Japanese composite-hulled vessel, the *Katsuragi*, was laid down with British assistance and was followed three years later by the first iron-hulled ship, the *Maya*. The French constructor, Émile Bertin, took over the management of the Yokosuka yard in 1886 and Japan laid down her first steel-hulled ships, the *Atago* and *Takao*. Rapid developments were also made in the field of machinery. Up to 1882 the standard machinery in Japanese built ships was the relatively simple horizontal compound type with steam supplied from low pressure boilers. Gradually cylindrical steel boilers with increasing pressures were introduced. The *Yaeyama*, a small despatch vessel, introduced the HTE engine in 1892 while the first VTE engines were constructed in Japan in 1890 for the gunboat *Oshima*. The specialised field of naval ordnance was still beyond the capabilities of Japanese industry, however, and armaments were usually purchased from either Armstrong, Canet or Krupp.

Asahi in 1900. The line passing across the turret front plate is a crack in the original negative *(Author's collection)*

As planned the First Navy Expansion Bill had provided Japan with a well balanced fleet of cruisers, gunboats and torpedo boats. Deteriorating relations with China over Korea dictated that Japan should somehow acquire new armoured vessels to match the Chinese ships. The old *Fuso*, *Hiei* and *Kongo* were obsolete and no match for the Chinese battleships. A plan to construct two battleships, to be ordered in Britain, and a cruiser was authorised in 1893. However, none of the ships was completed when the Sino-Japanese war broke out. With war imminent and the distinct possibility that the three recently ordered units would not be ready in time extra funds were voted for the immediate purchase of a foreign cruiser – the Chilean *Esmeralda*. In addition, construction of another cruiser, the *Akashi*, in a Japanese yard, was authorised. The *Esmeralda* was not finally acquired until November 1894 and did not enter service until after the war had ended.

THE SINO-JAPANESE WAR

War broke out in July 1894 with the bulk of the fighting at first borne by the Japanese Army supported by the Navy. The one major naval action occurred on 17 September 1894, when a Japanese force of seven cruisers and three gunboats, plus two other smaller units, joined action with the Chinese Fleet, of four armoured ships and six cruisers, at the Battle of the Yalu – Battle of the Yellow Sea. During the ensuing action five Chinese ships, one armoured ship and four cruisers, were sunk and three armoured ships and one cruiser heavily damaged. The damaged and surviving units retired to Port Arthur for temporary repairs before returning to the main Chinese base at Wei-Hai-Wei for more permanent repairs. Four Japanese ships suffered slight damage in the action. Only the *Matsushima* was severely hit and she was almost lost. A 9.8in shell struck the main barbette while an 11.8in shell destroyed two 4.7in guns in the battery and set fire to powder charges stored nearby. This hit resulted in a serious fire and killed or wounded over 120 men. It was not long before the remnants of the Chinese Fleet were blockaded in the port of Wei-Hai-Wei. Japanese torpedo boats carried out a number of raids on the port causing the stranding of the battleship *Ting Yuen*, and sinking the *Wei Yuen* and *Lai Yuen*. A number of Chinese torpedo boats which attempted to break out were either sunk or damaged by the cruiser *Yoshino*. Once the Japanese Army had invested the port on the land side the end was near. Wei-Hai-Wei finally fell on 12 February 1895 and the surviving Chinese ships were captured and incorporated into the Imperial Navy.

THE 1896 TEN YEAR NAVY EXPANSION PROGRAMME

Although she had won the war Japan was soon left in a humiliating position. Under pressure from Russia, supported by France and Germany, Japan was forced to relinquish her claims to Port Arthur and the Liao Tung peninsula. Feeling cut off and threatened, Japan at once began efforts to strengthen her economy and build up her military forces in preparation for an anticipated confrontation with Russia. The Sino-Japanese War and the Battle of the Yalu had given Japanese naval officers ample opportunity to assess the Fleet's needs and to develop a satisfactory naval strategy and tactics. The foremost requirement was obviously for modern well armed and heavily protected battleships. The Battle of the Yalu had shown that Japan's armoured ships were of obsolete design and poorly armed. In spite of being modern vessels the *Matsushima* class had not played the important part in the battle expected of them. The damage suffered by the *Matsushima* had highlighted deficiencies in protection, and the main armament, although of large calibre, had such a slow rate of fire that to all intents and purposes it was useless. It was essential, therefore, to order a number of heavily armoured, faster, battleships armed with guns with a much higher rate of fire, able to deliver a heavier broadside. The two ships ordered before the war, *Fuji* and *Yashima*, although meeting some of these requirements, were still not enough to provide Japan with a powerful navy capable of countering the Russian Far East Fleet. The other important lesson learnt from the Sino-Japanese war was the value of fast cruisers embodying a certain amount of protection and armed with QF guns. The torpedo boat had also proved itself as an ideal cutting out weapon, capable of inflicting great fear in the mind of a demoralised enemy.

On the basis of these lessons the Ten Year Naval Expansion Programme, finally passed in 1896, provided for the construction of four battleships, six armoured cruisers, six other cruisers, 23 torpedo boat destroyers and 63 torpedo boats, as well as four other minor warships. In addition base facilities, shipyards and training establishments were to be expanded.

Japanese shipyards would clearly be unable to cope with such a vast programme of construction so the bulk of the orders were placed with foreign yards. Most of the orders went to British yards, with only a few units being ordered from French and German yards, these being mostly torpedo boats.

Technological developments within Japan enabled the country to set up her own steel industry and by the turn of the century armour plate and heavy ordnance of the Vickers type was being turned out in Japanese factories. The design of Japanese built machinery continued to improve during the period and the power of the VTE engine was continually being increased. Boilers continued to improve, water-tube models being fitted in many of the foreign-built ships. At home Japanese engineers brought out their own designs for a simply constructed large tube, Miyabara, boiler, which began to enter service in May 1903 along with the Kanpon small tube three-drum type which was first fitted in the *Otowa*.

The rapidly deteriorating situation between Russia and Japan at the turn of the century led to a supplementary construction programme being approved. Passed in 1903, this programme provided for the construction of three battleships, three armoured cruisers and two smaller cruisers. However, these units were not completed before the outbreak of war with Russia. As a stop-gap measure two armoured cruisers, *Kasuga* and *Nisshin*, built in Italy for Argentina, were purchased by the Japanese Government. When war finally broke out the Imperial Fleet consisted of seven battleships, eight armoured cruisers, 16 other cruisers, 13 gunboat-type vessels, 11 old ships rated as coast defence vessels, 19 torpedo boat destroyers and 80 torpedo boats.

CAPITAL SHIPS

The first capital ship in the Imperial Navy, or vessel which can be considered to have exhibited capital ship qualities, was the armoured ram *Adzuma*. Originally purchased from America in 1867 for the Shogunate Fleet, she was commandeered by the Emperor's forces on her arrival in Japan. Her armament was obsolete and the composite-hulled vessel, powered by HC machinery, was sorely in need of refit and repair. The Japanese at that time were unable to maintain and operate such a complex vessel and she was soon placed in reserve. It was to be some time before the new navy was capable of operating and maintaining such a large unit – many new techniques had to be learnt by a nation just emerging from a state of medieval feudalism.

The 1874 expedition to Formosa, to quell pirates, focused attention on the need for a stronger navy. Relations with Korea were deteriorating and in view of the political situation three armoured ships, *Fuso*, *Kongo* and *Hiei*, were ordered from British yards under the 1875 Programme. The *Fuso* was a central battery, barque-rigged ironclad fitted with Krupp armament. The other two vessels were barque-rigged armoured corvettes. All three vessels were designed by Sir Edward Reed and were the most powerful units in the Japanese Navy when completed. With them the Japanese gained first class experience in the handling of steam warships, and their naval constructors were able to observe, at close hand, construction techniques, methods and type of protection, and the various types of armament available. Although the vessels had almost identical dimensions, *Fuso* was more heavily armed than the other two ships. She was also more strongly protected, which was partly responsible for her higher displacement. Being a more powerful vessel with heavier armament the *Fuso* was equipped with two sets of HC engines, compared to the single units in the *Kongo* and *Hiei*, although the latter developed a higher ihp than *Fuso*.

Apart from the two captured Chinese battleships *Chen Yuan* and *Ping Yuen*, which were incorporated into the Japanese Navy, the first true battleships to be ordered were the *Fuji* and *Yashima*. Although not completed in time for the Sino-Japanese war these two ships formed a valuable addition to the Japanese fleet when they entered service in 1897. They were the only really modern vessels in the navy and showed the great advances made in warship design and construction over the previous 20 years.

The major noticeable difference between the *Fuso*, *Kongo* and *Fuji* was that steam had completely eclipsed sail. They were the largest warships Japan had ever possessed and displacement had risen from the 3717t of the *Fuso* to 12,320t. The design was an improvement of the British *Royal Sovereign* class which had introduced a much improved scheme of armour protection based on the compound armour plate developed in 1877.

The most important difference between the two designs lay in the armament. The *Fuji* mounted a much more powerful, lighter, weapon with a much higher rate of fire than the *Royal Sovereign*. These were features which were shown to be of vital necessity during the Battle of the Yalu. The weight saved by adopting the new Armstrong gun enabled the 12in guns of the *Fuji* to be mounted in totally enclosed armoured turrets, whereas the 13.5in guns of the *Royal Sovereign* were in open barbettes. The siting and number of secondary 6in QF guns was the same in both classes. The hp developed by the *Fuji* class was greater than in the *Royal Sovereign* and the speed rose from 15½kts to 18kts. To supply the engines with steam the eight boilers in the *Royal Sovereign* were increased to ten in the *Fuji* and 14 in the *Yashima*. The pressure in all cases remained identical.

The inadequate strength of the Japanese fleet led the Government to authorise funds for the construction of four more battleships. These were to be built in Britain to a design similar to the *Majestic* class. *Shikashima*, *Hatsuse*, *Asahi* and *Mikasa* were all very similar, the design gradually being improved upon with each successive vessel. In 1891 Harvey NS armour plate had been tested and this was adopted for the *Majestic* class and the Japanese battleships. By the time *Mikasa*, the last unit, was due to be laid down Krupp Cemented armour (KC) had been developed in Germany and was incorporated into the ship. The greatly increased strength of the armour allowed the designers to devise a different scheme of protection for the new battleships which resulted in a great saving in weight. As a result the thickness of the main armoured belt was halved, from 18in in the *Fuji* to 9in in the *Shikashima*, and it maintained a constant thickness for a much greater proportion of its length over the vital machinery and magazine spaces, only being thinned out at the very ends. In addition the upper belt extended for the whole length of the citadel and its thickness was increased from the 4in of the *Fuji* to 6in in the *Shikashima*. A new arrangement for the armoured deck was also incorporated, based on the features introduced in the British *Renown*.

One of the most important features of the last six battleships was their complete compatibility which, when necessary, enabled them all to operate together as a homogeneous unit. All the armament consisted of Armstrong QF guns and calibres were standardised, simplifying ammunition supply and storage, and greatly easing the problems of gunnery officers when in action.

Ryujo as the *Jhosho Maru* as completed, 1869 *(CPL)*

The ironclad ram *Adzuma* was originally ordered for the Confederate States as the CSS *Sphinx*, subsequently renamed CSS *Stonewall*. While crossing the Atlantic, however, the American Civil War ended and the vessel was taken over by the Federal Government on her arrival and put up for sale. She was purchased by the Shogun in 1867 but was taken over by the Emperor's forces on her arrival in Japan. She was renamed *Kotetsu* (iron-covered ship) and commissioned as the flagship of the first Imperial Naval Squadron, which sailed on 20 April 1869 to attack the Shogunate forces at Hakodate. She was renamed *Adzuma* in December 1871.

The original armament consisted of a 300pdr Armstrong SB gun in a bow casemate and two rifled 70pdr Armstrong guns in a fixed mounting amidships. The composite-built hull consisted of 3½in wrought iron plates bolted to 3in teak planks, which in turn were backed by a further iron plate of 1¼in, the whole being designed to withstand the impact of a 15in shell. The ram extended 20ft in front of the stem, but the design restrictions imposed by the Confederates, including a draught limitation of 14ft for use on the Mississippi, gave rise to a large displacement on a small hull, which resulted in a poor seaboat; she tended to plough through the waves rather than ride them.

She was re-armed with a 9in Armstrong MLR gun in December 1871 and four Parrot 6.5in MLR guns were also added. Two months later she was placed in reserve, being removed from the effective fleet in 1888 to lie as a rusting hulk for twenty years.

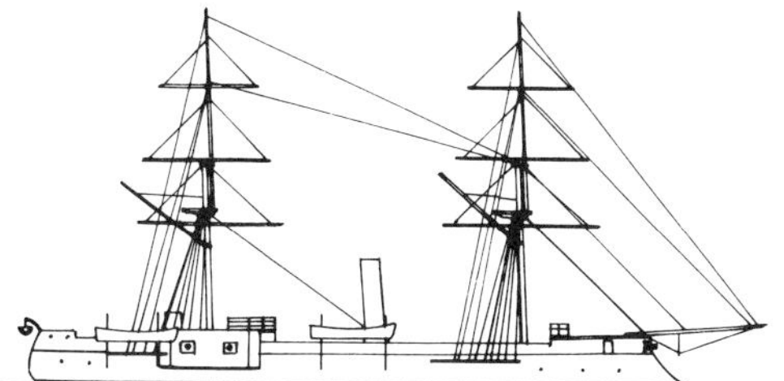

As completed

ADZUMA *ironclad ram*

Displacement: 1358t normal
Dimensions: 183ft wl, 194ft oa x 31ft 6in x 15ft 3in (*55.7 wl, 59 oa x 9.6 x 4.6m*)
Machinery: 2-shaft reciprocating HDA, 1200ihp = 9kts. Coal 95t
Armour: Main belt 3½in-4½in, main battery 4½in
Armament: 1-300pdr, 2-70pdr
Complement: 135

Name	Builder	Laid down	Launched	Comp	Fate
ADZUMA	Arman Bros, Bordeaux	1863	21.6.64	25.10.64	Discarded 28.1.88

The broadside armoured corvette *Ryujo* was built speculatively by a firm in Scotland, probably with the idea of selling the vessel to the Confederate States. When the Confederates failed to purchase the ship she was placed on the open market and bought by Prince Hizen in 1869. The Prince loaned the composite-hulled vessel to the Emperor for the war against the Shogun. After the civil war she was returned to the Prince who presented the ship to the Emperor in 1870. She was commissioned into the Imperial Navy and shortly afterwards underwent a refit, being re-armed with two 6.7in Krupp guns. She was reduced to a gunnery training ship in 1894, all guns being removed and a 6in Krupp and five 6.3in being added. She was finally discarded four years later in 1898.

RYUJO *armoured corvette*

Displacement: 1429t normal
Dimensions: 213ft 3in pp x 34ft 6in x 17ft 6in (*65 pp x 10.5 x 5.3m*)
Machinery: 1-shaft compound reciprocating, 800ihp = 9kts. Coal 350t
Armour: Main belt 4½in, battery 4in
Armament: 2-6.5in, 10-5.5in
Complement: 275

Name	Builder	Laid down	Launched	Comp	Fate
RYUJO	Aberdeen	—	1864	27.4.69	Scrapped 1904

The central battery ironclad *Fuso* was laid down in September 1875 as part of the 1875 Programme, which provided for a stronger navy in anticipation of war between Japan and Korea. The *Fuso* was built to a design prepared by Sir Edward Reed, and was a smaller edition of the British *Iron Duke*. The barque-rigged vessel was equipped with machinery supplied by Penn and Sons of Greenwich. She had two pairs of CHSCT engines, and a radius of 4500 nm was achieved at a steaming rate of 10 kts. The Krupp armament was disposed in a layout very similar to the French *Redoutable*.

Just before the war with China, in 1894, the *Fuso* was refitted, the mainmast being removed and military tops added to the fore and mizzen masts. Two 6in/50 QF guns replaced the 6.7in and two more 6in/50 guns in shields were added, one on the foc's'le and one on the poop. Eleven 3pdr QF guns were added and two above water 18in TT.

Fuso was damaged at the Battle of the Yalu. Three years later she collided with the *Matsushima* and ran aground on Shikoku Island. She underwent repairs at Kure Naval Dockyard 1898–1899, during which the 9.4in BL guns were replaced with 6in QFs, and an extra 3pdr QF added. The *Fuso* was re-classified as a coast defence ship in 1903, with a reduced armament of two 6in QF in the central battery and four 4.7in/40 QF on the upper deck. She was discarded in 1908 and subsequently scrapped.

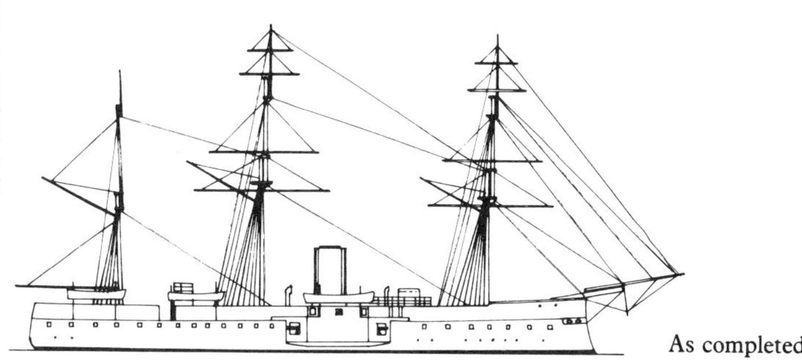

As completed

FUSO *central battery ironclad*

Displacement: 3717t normal
Dimensions: 220ft pp x 48ft x 18ft 4in mean (*67 pp x 14.6 x 5.5m*)
Machinery: 2-shaft reciprocating HC, 3932ihp = 13kts. Coal 360t
Armour: Main belt 4in-9in, battery 8in, bulkheads 7in
Armament: 4-9.4in, 2-6.7in, 6-3in, 1 four-barrelled Nordenfeld MG
Complement: 250

Name	Builder	Laid down	Launched	Comp	Fate
FUSO	Samuda Bros, Poplar	Sept 1875	14.4.77	Jan 1878	Scrapped 1910

Kongo as completed *(CPL)*

KONGO class *armoured corvettes*

The design of these armoured corvettes was prepared by Sir Edward Reed, and was based on the Russian *General Admiral* and the British *Gem* class cruisers. The composite-hulled *Kongo* and iron-hulled *Hiei* were ordered under the 1875 Programme. They were barque-rigged but the topmasts were subsequently removed during a refit in 1895. The radius of action was 3100 nm at 10kts. During the 1895 refit an extra 1pdr gun was added and by 1903 two 3in, two 2½pdr and six MGs had been added.

Hiei was present at the Battle of the Yalu and was severely damaged by the Chinese battleships. The *Kongo* was involved in the Hawaiian Revolution in 1898, after which both ships were removed from the operational fleet and used as survey vessels.

Displacement: 2200t normal
Dimensions: 220ft pp, 230ft wl x 40ft 9in x 17ft 4in *(67 pp, 70 wl x 12.4 x 5.3m)*
Machinery: 1-shaft reciprocating HC, 2500ihp = 14kts. Coal 280t
Armour: Main belt 3½in-4½in
Armament: 3-6.7in (3 x 1), 6-5.9in (6 x 1), 4-1pdr (4 x 1), 2-14in TT in *Hiei*
Complement: 308

Name	Builder	Laid down	Launched	Comp	Fate
KONGO	Earle's Sb Co, Hull	Sept 1875	April 1877	Jan 1878	Scrapped 1909
HIEI	Milford Haven Sb Co, Pembroke	Sept 1875	12.6.77	Mar 1878	Discarded 1.4.11

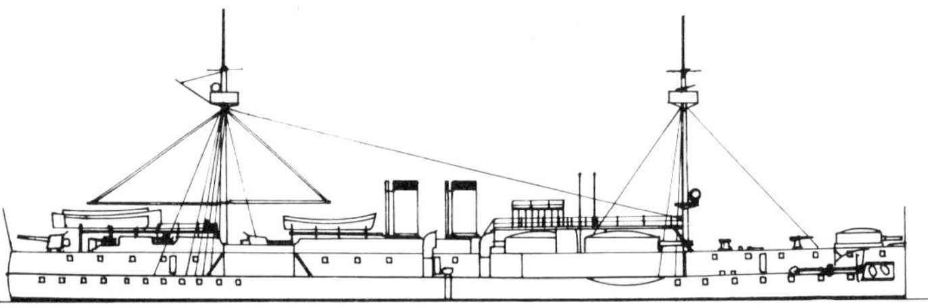

As re-armed

CHIN YEN (as re-armed by the Japanese)

The Chinese central citadel battleship *Chen Yuan* was captured by Japanese forces during the Sino-Japanese war when the port of Wei-Hai-Wei surrendered on 12 February 1895. She was refitted and re-armed, commissioning into the Imperial Navy as the *Chin Yen* to become the Japanese Navy's first battleship. She remained in service during the Russo-Japanese war and although present at the bombardment of Port Arthur and the Battle of the Yellow Sea she did not actually go into action. She was removed from the effective fleet in 1910 to become a training ship for pilots.

Displacement: 7220t normal
Dimensions: 298ft 6in wl, 308ft oa x 59ft x 20ft mean *(91 wl, 93.8 oa x 17.9 x 6m)*
Machinery: 2-shaft reciprocating HC, 6200ihp = 14½kts. Coal 1000t
Armour: Main belt 10in-14in, turret 12in, bow turret 2in, deck 3in, CT 8in
Armament: 4-12in (2 x 2), 4-6in QF (4 x 1), 2-6pdr QF (2 x 1), 8-3pdr QF (8 x 1)
Complement: 250

Name	Number	Builder	Laid down	Launched	Comp	Fate
CHIN YEN		Vulcan, Stettin	1880	28.11.82	1885	Scrapped 1914

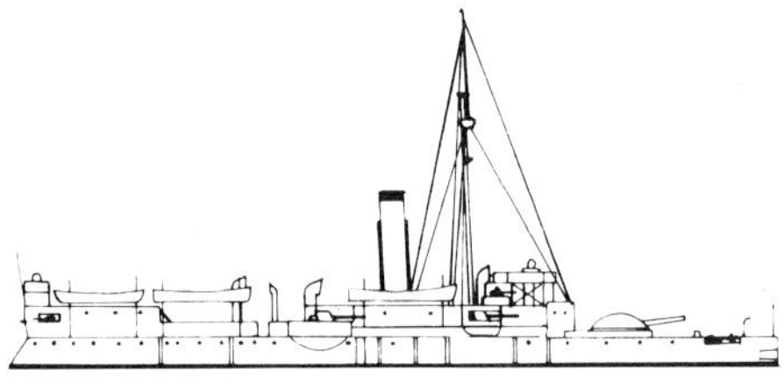

As re-armed

HEI YEN *coastal defence ironclad*

The *Hei Yen* (ex-Chinese *Ping Yuen*) was captured at Wei-Hai-Wei on 12 February 1895. She was refitted and armed with British guns in place of the former Krupp pieces and commissioned into the Imperial Navy as a gunnery training ship. During the Russo-Japanese war she served as a coastal bombardment ship and was mined and sunk off Pigeon Bay, Port Arthur in 1904.

Displacement: 2150t normal
Dimensions: 200ft wl x 40ft x 13ft 6in *(60.95 wl x 12.2 x 4.15m)*
Machinery: 2-shaft reciprocating VTE, 2400ihp = 10kts. Coal 350t
Armour: Main belt 8in, turret 5in, deck 2in, CT 5in
Armament: 1-10.2in, 2-6in QF, 8-3pdr QF (8 x 1), 4-18in TT
Complement: 250

Name	Builder	Laid down	Launched	Comp	Fate
HEI YEN	Foo Chou	1883	1890	1890	Lost 18.9.1904

Fuji and *Yashima* were ordered under the 1893 Programme, which planned to build up the strength of the Japanese Fleet as a counter to the Chinese Fleet, which had two modern German-built capital ships. The two Japanese ships were built to a design of G C Macrow and were an improved type of British *Royal Sovereign*, but with more powerful guns of smaller calibre. Being lighter weapons the weight saved was used to increase the armour on the turrets. Only four of the secondary guns were in casemates amidships, the remaining guns being in shields on the upper deck. *Yashima* had a much smaller turning circle than the *Fuji* on account of her builders having cut away the keel aft towards the rudder. This modification turned out to be a qualified success, however, the smaller turning circle straining the hull. The engines were fed by 14, ten in *Fuji*, single-ended cylindrical boilers with a water pressure of 155lb/in². The radius was 4000 nm at 10 kts.

The ships were refitted during 1901 when all the 3pdr guns, except four in the fighting tops, were replaced by sixteen 12pdr. Both ships took part in actions against Russian warships during the Russo-Japanese war and *Fuji* fired the last shell at the Battle of Tsushima on 27 May 1905, to sink the *Borodino*. The *Yashima* struck a mine off Port Arthur on 15 May 1904 and was taken in tow, but capsized later in the day. *Fuji* was re-boilered and refitted, the 12in Armstrong guns being replaced by a Japanese model, in 1910 and reclassed as a coast defence ship. She was disarmed and immobilised under the terms of the Washington Treaty in 1922–1923 and used as a training ship. Her propellers were removed and tonnage was reduced to 9179t with a draught of 21ft 9in. She capsized in 1945 and her hulk was scrapped after the war.

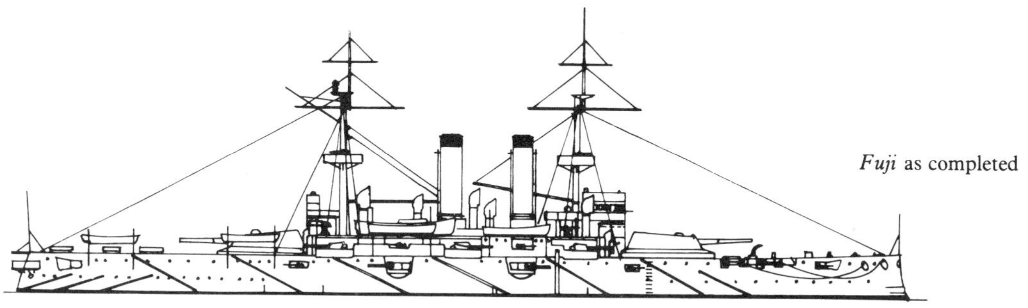

Fuji as completed

FUJI class *battleships*

Displacement: 12,320t normal, *Fuji* 12,533t normal
Dimensions: 390ft wl, 412ft oa x 73ft 9in; *Fuji* 73ft, x 26ft 3in; *Fuji* 26ft 6in *(118.8 wl, 125.5 oa x 22.4; 22.2, x 8m; 8.07)*
Machinery: 2-shaft reciprocating VTE, 14,000 ihp = 18 kts. Coal 700/1200t
Armour: Main belt 14in-18in, barbettes 9in-14in, casemates 2in-6in, deck 2½in, CT 14in
Armament: 4-12in (2 x 2), 10-6in (10 x 1), 20-3pdr (20 x 1), 4-2½pdr (4 x 1), 5-18in TT
Complement: 637

Name	Builder	Laid down	Launched	Comp	Fate
YASHIMA	Armstrong Whitworth, Elswick	28.12.1894	28.2.96	9.9.97	Capsized 15.5.1904
FUJI	Thames Iron Wks, Poplar	1. 8.1894	31.3.96	17.8.97	Scrapped 1948

Fuji (Author's collection)

These two ships, ordered under the 1896 Ten Year Naval Expansion Programme, were built to a design by G C Macrow and were an improved type of British *Majestic*. The armament was identical to that of the *Fuji* class and the machinery was similar, enabling the classes to act together as a homogeneous unit. The ships were built on the bracket frame system, the wing passages being used for extra bunkerage. Amidships there was a double bottom and the ships had a total of 261 watertight compartments. The Harvey NS armour was also improved, a new type of armoured deck, first introduced in the British *Renown*, being fitted. This deck, instead of resting flat on top of the armoured belt, sloped up from the bottom of the belt, thereby increasing vertical protection, any shell penetrating the main belt having also to pass through the slope of the deck before reaching the machinery spaces. By providing, in effect, two belts spaced apart, the thickness of the main belt could be reduced, saving weight, which was used to extend the belt and also to provide a thinner belt of armour above the main belt amidships, slightly longer in the *Hatsuse* than in the *Shikishima*.

Twenty-five Belleville boilers supplied steam for the engines; and the radius was 5000nm at 10kts.

On completion the *Hatsuse* represented the Emperor of Japan at Queen Victoria's funeral before sailing to join the Japanese Fleet. Both ships were present at the bombardment of Port Arthur on 9 February 1904, and the subsequent blockade, the *Hatsuse* striking a Russian mine there on 15 May 1904. She was taken in tow by *Asahi* but struck a second mine and sank almost immediately when her magazine exploded. *Shikishima* was present at both the Battle of the Yellow Sea and the Battle of Tsushima. She was classed as a coast defence ship in September 1921 and then disarmed and immobilised under the terms of the Washington Treaty. From 1923 she served as a seamen's training ship and was scrapped at Sasebo in 1947.

Hatsuse in 1901 *(Author's collection)*

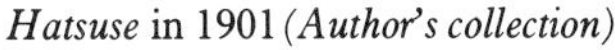

SHIKISHIMA class *battleships*

Displacement: 14,850t normal, 15,453t full load; *Hatsuse* 15,000t normal, 15,255t full load
Dimensions: 415ft wl 438ft oa; *Hatsuse* 439ft 9in, x 75ft 6in; *Hatsuse* 76ft 9in, x 27ft 6in *(126.5 wl, 133.5 oa; 134, x 23; 23.4, x 8.29m)*
Machinery: 2-shaft reciprocating VTE, 14,500 ihp = 18 kts. Coal 700/1722t, *Hatsuse* 1900t
Armour: Main belt 4in-9in, upper belt 6in, deck 2½in-4in, barbettes 8in-14in, casemates 2in-6in, CT 3in-14in
Armament: 4-12in (2 x 2), 14-6in (14 x 1), 20-12pdr QF (20 x 1), 6 (*Hatsuse* 8)-3pdr (6 x 1), 6 (*Hatsuse* 4)-2½pdr (6 x 1), 5 (*Hatsuse* 4)-18in TT
Complement: 836, *Hatsuse* 741

Name	Builder	Laid down	Launched	Comp	Fate
SHIKISHIMA	Thames Iron Wks, Blackwall	29.3.1897	1.11.98	26.1.1900	Scrapped 1947
HATSUSE	Armstrong Whitworth, Elswick	10.1.1898	27. 6.99	18.1.1901	Lost 15.5.1904

Ordered under the same programme as the previous class, the *Asahi* was a virtual repeat of that design, the major visual difference being that she only carried two funnels instead of the three in the previous class. This resulted from a re-arrangement of the boiler rooms, which still encompassed 25 Belleville boilers delivering steam at a pressure of 300lb/in^2; the radius was 4000 nm at 10 kts. At first the machinery suffered from a number of minor faults and *Asahi* gained a reputation as a coal eater, but this was subsequently improved and the designed figures achieved. Internally the layout differed from the previous class, the watertight subdivision being improved with a total of 288 watertight compartments.

Asahi saw action throughout the Russo-Japanese War and was severely damaged on 26 October 1904 when she struck a floating mine. She was repaired in time to take part in the Battle of Tsushima where she received a number of hits and suffered eight killed and 23 wounded.

At the start of the First World War the *Asahi* was relegated to a minor role as a gunnery training ship and was disarmed under the terms of the Washington Treaty in April 1923. In 1926–1927 she was converted at Kure Naval Dockyard to a submarine salvage vessel. She was placed in reserve until 1938 when she was re-activated for service as a repair ship. She was torpedoed and sunk by the American submarine *Salmon* southwest of Cape Paderas, French Indo-China, on 25 May 1942.

ASAHI *battleship*

Displacement: 15,200t normal, 15,374t full load
Dimensions: 415ft wl, 425ft 6in oa x 75ft 3in x 27ft 3in (*126.5 wl, 129.6 oa x 22.92 x 8.3m*)
Machinery: 2-shaft reciprocating VTE, 15,000 ihp = 18 kts. Coal 700/1549t
Armour: Main belt 4in-9in, upper belt 6in, deck 1in-4in, barbettes 8in-14in, casemates 2in-6in, CT 3in-14in
Armament: 4-12in (2 x 2), 14-6in (14 x 1), 20-12pdr QF (20 x 1), 6-3pdr (6 x 1), 6-2½pdr (6 x 1), 4-18in TT
Complement: 836

Name	Builder	Laid down	Launched	Comp	Fate
ASAHI	J Brown, Clydebank	1.8.1898	13.3.99	31.7.1900	Lost 25.5.1942

Asahi in 1900 (*Author's collection*)

Mikasa was the last of the four battleships to be ordered under the 1896 Ten Year Programme. The design was very similar to the preceding classes, exhibiting only minor differences, mainly to the protection scheme. The main armament was given alternative systems of handling in case of breakdown – electric, hydraulic or manual, and like the previous ships the guns could be loaded at any angle of elevation, irrespective of the training angle. The 12in guns could fire at the rate of three shells every two minutes while magazine storage was provided for 240 shells.

The number of 6in guns carried was the same as in the previous vessels but they had greater protection. Ten of the 6in were sited in a box battery on the main deck, rather than in lightly protected casemates on the upper deck. This meant that any shells approaching from behind the gun had first to penetrate the armour on the far side before reaching the gun. Previously it had been possible for a shell to penetrate between two casemates, and then only to be faced by the thin 2in armour at the rear of the casemate on the opposite side. This box battery was given extra protection fore and aft by extending the armoured bulkheads to the upper deck. The eight 3in guns sited broadside on the upper deck were also afforded some protection by the resiting of the 1in splinter deck on the upper deck.

Mikasa was the flagship of Admiral Togo at the Battle of Tsushima during the Russo-Japanese war. In 1905 she sank in shallow water following a magazine explosion, but was raised and subsequently repaired, being armed with new 12in and 6in guns. She was disarmed in 1922 but was still in existence at the end of the Second World War and has since been refurbished and is retained as a national monument.

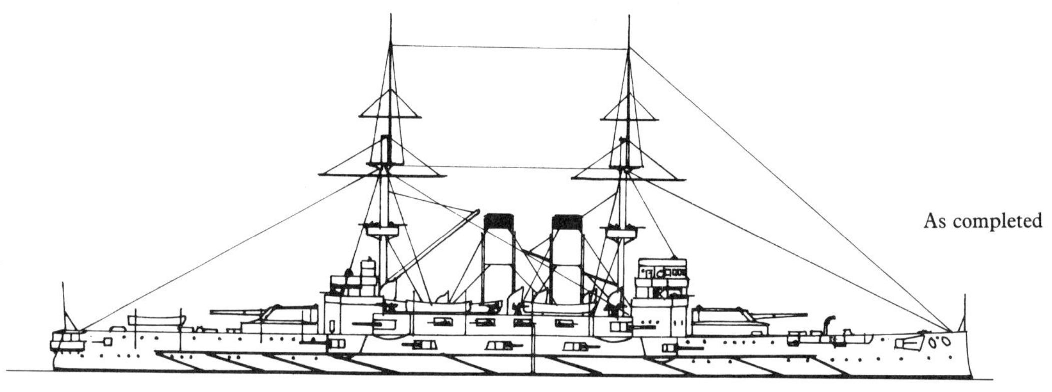
As completed

MIKASA *battleship*

Displacement: 15,140t normal, 15,179t full load
Dimensions: 415ft wl, 432ft oa x 76ft x 27ft (*126.5 wl, 131.7 oa x 23.23 x 8.28m*)
Machinery: 2-shaft reciprocating VTE, 15,000 ihp = 18 kts. Coal 700/1521t
Armour: KC. Main belt 4in-9in, upper belt 6in, deck 2in-3in, barbettes 8in-14in, casemates 2in-6in
Armament: 4-12in (2 x 2), 14-6in (14 x 1), 20-12pdr (20 x 1), 8-3pdr (8 x 1), 4-2½pdr (4 x 1), 4-18in TT
Complement: 830

Name	Builder	Laid down	Launched	Comp	Fate
MIKASA	Armstrong, Elswick	24.1.1899	8.11.1900	1.3.1902	Lost 12.9.1905. Salvaged, retained as museum

Mikasa as completed, 1902 (*Author's collection*)

CRUISERS

The first cruising type ships to be acquired by the Imperial Japanese Navy were a hotchpotch of vessels captured from the Shogunate forces after the civil war, vessels lent by loyal clans, or vessels purchased from foreign countries.

The first cruisers to be completed for the Imperial Navy were the Elswick-designed *Naniwa* and *Takachiho*, completed in 1885 and 1886. Their design was developed from Chilean *Esmeralda* but with increased protection and Krupp armament instead of Armstrong guns. At that time the finest cruisers in the world were being built at Elswick and, therefore, it is somewhat surprising that the Japanese approached a French yard for their second protected cruiser. On reflection this was understandable, for Japanese naval officers were being strongly influenced by the French *Jeune École* school of thought and many French technicians were supervising the setting up of the Japanese shipbuilding industry. The cruiser *Unebi* did not, however, come up to the usual standard of French construction and she was lost in peculiar circumstances very soon after completion. When she was completed she was the first ship in the Japanese Navy to have HTE engines, but her untimely loss prevented the Japanese from gaining valuable experience with this type of machinery. It was to be another four years before a Japanese warship was equipped with TE machinery.

The small unprotected cruiser *Takao*, the next to be completed, was the first Japanese-built ship to have a steel hull. Being designed by the French constructor Emile Bertin, her armament layout closely followed French practice, with the broadside guns in sponsons. The armament, however, was much lighter than that of the earlier cruisers.

The protected cruisers *Hashidate*, *Itsukushima* and *Matsushima* were also French-designed, but the Battle of the Yalu showed the design and armament to be obsolete and no more ships of this type were built. From then on the majority of Japanese cruisers were built either at home or in Britain.

The first armoured cruiser to be built for the Japanese Navy was the *Chiyoda*. Built in Britain, she was not a large ship, and for an armoured cruiser carried only a light armament of 4.7in guns. She was the first Japanese cruiser to have TE machinery.

The protected cruisers *Suma* and *Akashi* were the first to be built to an entirely Japanese design. Being their first attempt at building a large vessel, the design was kept fairly basic, the Elswick QF armament being in a standard disposition. The design was not a success, however, and the vessels were found to lack stability. As a result no more large vessels were built in a Japanese yard until 1901 when the *Tsushima* was laid down. In the meantime Japan continued to expand her cruiser force, ordering lightly protected and heavily armoured cruisers from Britain. These were all constructed to fairly standard designs, taking into account any technological advances in armour, machinery and armament. The protected cruisers, *Takasago*, *Kasagi* and *Chitose*, followed the standard Elswick pattern for this type of vessel, while the armoured cruisers, *Asama*, *Tokiwa*, *Idzumo* and *Iwate*, were also built to an almost standard design. Advances in the design and strength of armour plate allowed these ships to be given sufficient protection against all but the most modern and heaviest of shells permitting them to form part of the main battle line. With the new armour and lighter but more powerful QF guns, they were superior to many of the older battleships then afloat. Two other armoured cruisers, *Yakumo* and *Adzuma*, were ordered from Germany and France respectively, mainly for comparison purposes. The general design was not as successful as that of the Elswick cruisers, although in some respects they were superior.

The protected cruisers *Tsushima*, *Niitaka* and *Otowa* were the last cruisers to be laid down for the Japanese Navy before the outbreak of the Russo-Japanese war. They were built to a Japanese design based on British ideas, but with a much heavier armament than comparable British cruisers. The *Otowa* design was developed from the *Tsushima* but was a slightly smaller vessel with lighter armament. The three cruisers were the first to be fitted with completely Japanese-designed and built TE machinery, and the *Otowa* was the first Japanese ship to have the Kanpon three-drum boiler, similar in design to the Yarrow boiler.

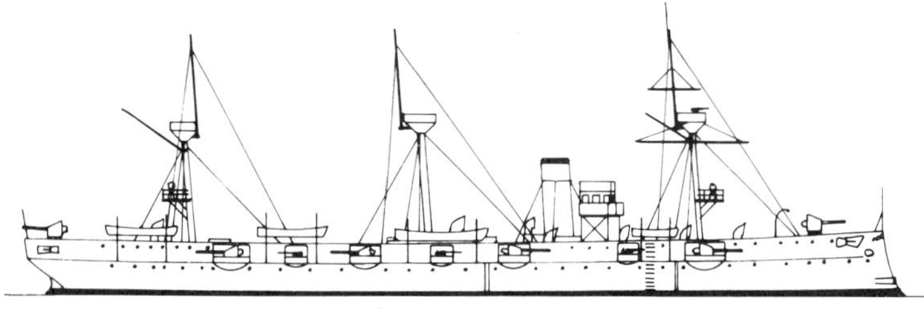

As completed

CHIYODA *armoured cruiser*

Displacement: 2400t normal
Dimensions: 310ft wl x 42ft x 14ft (*94.49 wl x 12.98 x 4.27m*)
Machinery: 2-shaft reciprocating VTE, 5600 ihp = 19kts. Coal 240/420t
Armour: Main belt 4½in, deck 1in-1½in
Armament: 10-4.7in QF (10 x 1), 14-3pdr QF (14 x 1), 3 Gatling MGs, 3-14in TT
Complement: 350

Name	Builder	Laid down	Launched	Comp	Fate
CHIYODA	J Brown, Clydebank	Nov 1888	3.6.90	Dec 1890	Scrapped 1927

The *Chiyoda* was a replacement for the protected cruiser *Unebi*. The order was placed with a British yard, for several unfortunate mishaps had caused the Japanese to lose faith in French designs. The *Chiyoda* was the first armoured cruiser to be completed for the Japanese Navy, and one of the first to carry an armament of shielded Elswick 4.7in guns, well sited in sponsons on the broadside and as bow and stern chasers. The QF guns gave the *Chiyoda* a great advantage over contemporary armoured cruisers; the brass cartridges, used instead of the previous silk-cased charges, dispensed with the need for sponging out the breech after each firing. This resulted in an increase in the rate of fire of nearly six times over older guns.

The original design had planned for the ship to carry two 12.6in Canet guns, but this would have resulted in excessive top weight, so 4.7in QF guns were substituted.

The armoured belt of chrome steel was narrow, but extended for 200ft along the waterline. A total of 84 watertight compartments was incorporated in the design. The original six locomotive boilers caused much trouble, and were replaced in 1898 with 12 Belleville boilers. At the same time the fighting tops on the three raked masts were removed to improve stability.

Chiyoda saw action in the Sino-Japanese and Russo-Japanese wars. On 27 July 1904, she struck a Russian mine off Takhe Bay, but was towed to Dalny where repairs were carried out in time to enable her to take part in the Battle of Tsushima. After 1920 she was used as a submarine depot ship and removed from the operational fleet. She was disarmed in April 1922 and discarded, being scrapped a few years later.

Ordered under the 1896 Second Naval Expansion Programme and built to a design prepared by Sir Philip Watts. The design was an improved version of the Chilean *O'Higgins*, with increased protection and a more powerful armament in better sited positions. The main belt of Harvey NS extended for 284ft and was 7ft deep. Above the main belt a secondary belt, also 7ft deep, extended for a length of 214ft. A total of 163 watertight compartments were provided, 32 of them in the double bottom.

Twelve single-ended boilers fed the engines with steam and the radius of action was 4600 nm at 11½ kts. On trials both ships exceeded their designed speed by about 1½ kts and proved to be economical steamers. Performance deteriorated, mainly because of poor maintenance, and by 1904 the speed of the *Asama* had dropped to 19 kts. The *Tokiwa* was re-boilered in 1910, and the *Asama* in 1915–1917, with 16 Miyabara boilers. *Tokiwa* was again re-boilered in 1937-1938 with eight Kanpon boilers.

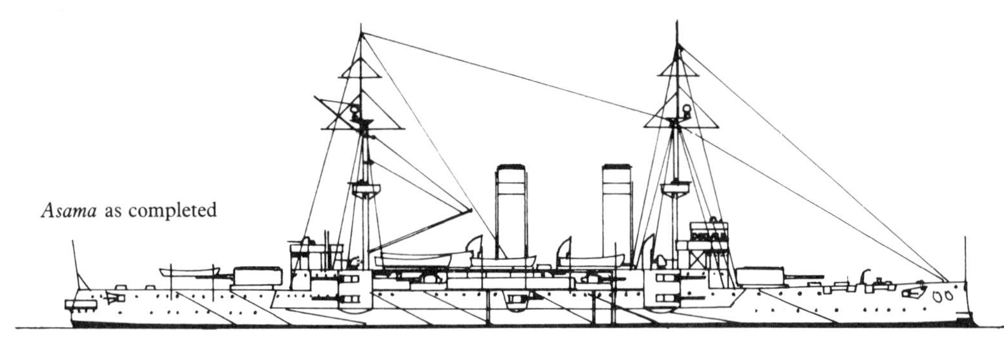

Asama as completed

ASAMA class *armoured cruisers*

Displacement: 9700t normal
Dimensions: 408ft pp, 442ft oa x 67ft 3in x 24ft 6in *(124.36 pp, 134.72 oa x 20.45 x 7.43m)*
Machinery: 2-shaft reciprocating VTE, 18,000 ihp = 21½ kts. Coal 600/1406t
Armour: Main belt 3½in-7in, upper belt 5in, deck 2in, barbettes, turrets and casemates 6in, CT 3in-14in
Armament: 4-8in (2 x 2), 14-6in QF (14 x 1), 12-12pdr QF (12 x 1), 7-2½pdr QF (7 x 1), 5-18in TT
Complement: 726

Name	Builder	Laid down	Launched	Comp	Fate
ASAMA	Armstrong, Elswick	Nov 1896	22.3.98	18.3.99	Scrapped 1947
TOKIWA	Armstrong, Elswick	Jan 1898	6.7.98	18.5.99	Lost 9.8.1945

At the Battle of Tsushima both ships were damaged, the *Asama* having her steering gear disabled. Following service in the First World War the *Asama* was relegated to a training ship.

The *Tokiwa* was refitted for use as a minelayer, a total of 300 mines being carried. An accidental mine explosion caused severe damage in August 1927 and *Tokiwa* was placed in reserve. With the outbreak of the Sino-Japanese war in 1937 she was refitted and recommissioned for use as a minelayer, mine capacity being increased to 500 mines. Various minor alterations were made to her light AA during the war and by 1945 she carried four 6in, one 3in, two 40mm and 30-25mm. Storage for 80 depth charges was also provided. *Tokiwa* was mined in April 1945 and repaired, only to be sunk in shallow water in an air raid in August, the wreck being scrapped after the war.

Asama running trials, 1899 *(Author's collection)*

Yakumo after 1912 *(CPL)*

Ordered under the Second Naval Expansion Programme of 1896–1897, when Japan turned to a German yard for assistance. (Previously Germany had been closely involved in constructing warships for China, Japan's recent enemy.)

The protection of the *Yakumo* was well designed, the main belt of Krupp armour 7ft deep extending 224½ft along the waterline. The upper belt, also 7ft deep, was slightly shorter, being only 202ft long. A total of 247 watertight compartments were provided, 38 of them being in the double bottom.

Although the ship was built in a German yard, the Japanese stipulated that she be armed with British manufactured Elswick guns to ensure ammunition compatibility with all her other major warships. Magazine storage comprised 80 8in per gun, and 150 6in per gun.

Yakumo served throughout the Russo-Japanese war and at the Battle of Tsushima played a major part in the sinking of *Admiral Ushakov*. After 1920 she was used as a training ship, and her armament was gradually reduced. During the 1920s the Belleville boilers were replaced by six Yarrow boilers taken from the battleship *Haruna* when she was refitted.

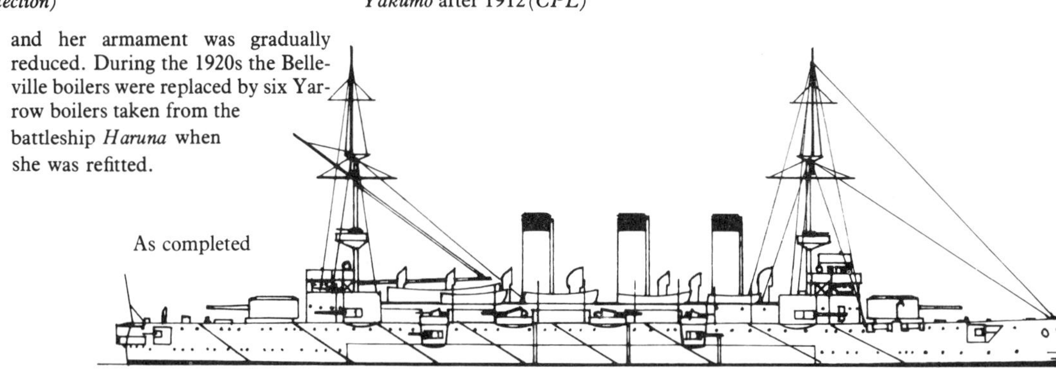

As completed

YAKUMO *armoured cruiser*

Displacement: 9646t normal
Dimensions: 409ft pp, 434ft oa x 64ft 3in x 23ft 9in *(124.64 pp, 132.3 oa x 19.57 x 7.24m)*
Machinery: 2-shaft reciprocating VTE, 15,500 ihp = 20½ kts. Coal 600/1242t
Armour: Main belt 3½in-7in, upper belt 5in, deck 2½in, barbettes and turrets 6in, casemates 2in-6in, CT 3in-14in, TT compartment 6in
Armament: 4-8in (2 x 2), 12-6in QF (12 x 1), 12-12pdr QF (12 x 1), 7-2½pdr QF (7 x 1), 5-18in TT
Complement: 700

Name	Builder	Laid down	Launched	Comp	Fate
YAKUMO	Vulcan, Stettin	Mar 1898	8.7.99	20.6.1900	Scrapped 1947

Although the length was slightly increased in the *Adzuma*, her displacement was slightly less than the previous cruisers. This was partly because, unlike the British-built armoured cruisers, she lacked an after armoured bulkhead, as did the *Yakumo*. In spite of an average decrease of about 400t in displacement the *Adzuma* was no faster than the earlier cruisers, and developed 1500 hp more than *Yakumo*. The armoured belts extended for a length of 210ft and were 7ft deep. Bunkerage and radius of action, 3900 nm at 10½ kts, were very similar to the other cruisers.

Adzuma was in action throughout the Russo-Japanese war and after 1914 was employed on training duties. She was partially disarmed in 1921 to carry four 8in, eight 6in, four 12pdr, one 12pdr AA and four 18in TT. She was completely disarmed in 1941 and in July 1945 suffered severe damage in an air raid, the hulk being scrapped after the war.

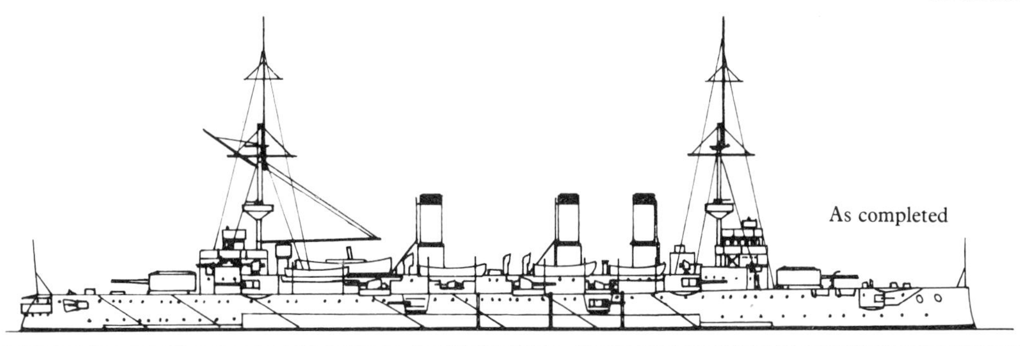
As completed

ADZUMA *armoured cruiser*

Displacement: 9307t normal
Dimensions: 431ft 6in pp, 452ft 6in oa x 68ft 9in x 23ft 9in *(131.5 pp, 137.9 oa x 20.94 x 7.21m)*
Machinery: 2-shaft reciprocating VTE, 17,000 ihp = 20 kts. Coal 600/1275t
Armour: Main belt 3½in-7in, upper belt 5in, deck 2½in, barbettes and turrets 6in, casemates 2in-6in, TT compartment 6in, CT 3in-14in
Armament: 4-8in (2 x 2), 12-6in QF (12 x 1), 12-12pdr QF (12 x 1), 12-3pdr QF (12 x 1), 5-18in TT
Complement: 650

Name	Builder	Laid down	Launched	Comp	Fate
ADZUMA	Ateliers et Ch de La Loire, St Nazaire	Mar 1898	24.6.99	28.7.1900	Scrapped 1946

Idzumo, 6 September 1900 *(Author's collection)*

Adzuma (Author's collection)

The design, by Sir Philip Watts, was practically the same as the earlier *Asama*, but improvements made in machinery design enabled the builders to equip the new class with 24 of the much lighter and more efficient Belleville boilers instead of the 12 single-ended cylindrical boilers of the *Asama*. Altogether the new machinery led to a saving in weight of some 300t. Armament and protection were also very similar, except that the armour in the new class was of Krupp CS in place of the Harvey NS used in the *Asama*. The length of the armoured belt was reduced in the *Idzumo*, the main belt being 275ft compared to 284ft in the *Asama* while the upper belt was reduced from 214ft to 175ft (168ft in *Iwate*). The total number of watertight compartments was 166, 30 of which were in the double bottom.

Like all the other pre-First World War warships these armoured cruisers were re-rated and partially disarmed under the terms of the Washington Treaty, being used as training ships. They were refitted with six boilers, Yarrow in *Iwate* and Kanpon in *Idzumo*, developing 7000 ihp to give them a speed of 16 kts. In July 1945 both ships sank in shallow water from air raid damage.

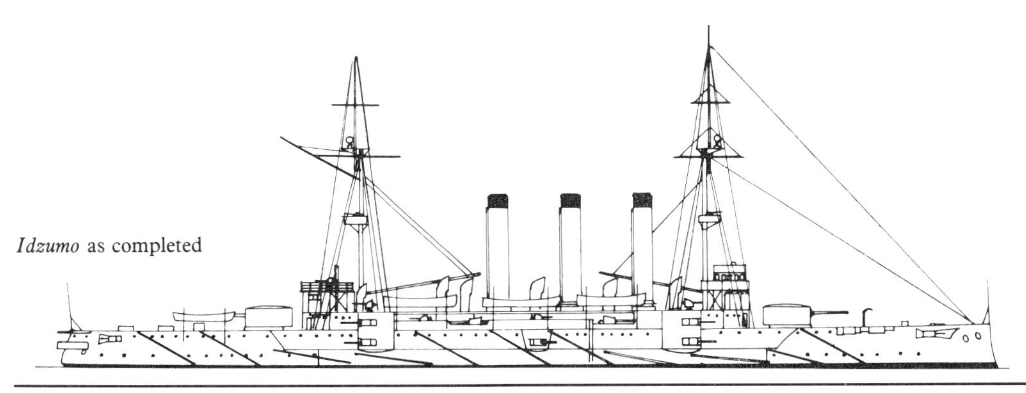
Idzumo as completed

IDZUMO class *armoured cruisers*

Displacement: 9750t normal
Dimensions: 400ft pp, 434ft oa x 68ft 9in x 24ft 6in *(121.9 pp, 132.28 oa x 20.94 x 7.37m)*
Machinery: 2-shaft reciprocating VTE, 14,500 ihp = 20¾ kts. Coal 600/1402, 1412t
Armour: Main belt 3½in-7in, upper belt 5in, deck 2½in, barbettes 4in-6in, turrets 6in, casemates 6in, CT 3in-14in
Armament: 4-8in (2 x 2), 14-6in QF (14 x 1), 12-12pdr QF (12 x 1), 8-2½pdr QF (8 x 1), 4-18in TT
Complement: 672

Name	Builder	Laid down	Launched	Comm.	Fate
IDZUMO	Armstrong, Elswick	May 1898	19.9.1899	25.9.1900	Scrapped 1947
IWATE	Armstrong, Elswick	Nov 1898	29.3.1900	18.3.1901	Scrapped 1947

Originally laid down for the Italian Navy, but bought by Argentina for the war against Chile after they were launched. The war had ended by the time they were completed and Argentina, having no further use for such large ships, sold them to Japan who wished to match the Russian Far East Fleet. The *Kasuga*, laid down as the *Mitra*, was renamed *Rivadavia* by Argentina, and the *Nisshin*, laid down as the *Roca*, was renamed *Mariano Moreno* by Argentina.

They were the final development of the Italian *Giuseppe Garibaldi* and were exceedingly powerful ships. Although the main belt was only 6in thick compared to the 7in belt on Japan's other armoured cruisers, it extended over a greater proportion of the hull. The belt also extended for a greater depth at its maximum thickness, there being no upper belt of thinner armour. This single armour belt extended from the waterline to the upper deck, encasing ten of the 6in guns in the midships battery.

After serving in the Russo-Japanese war, where the *Nisshin* suffered considerable damage at the Battle of the Yellow Sea and Tsushima, the ships were partially disarmed during the 1920s and used as training ships. The number of 6in and 3in guns were reduced to four of each calibre.

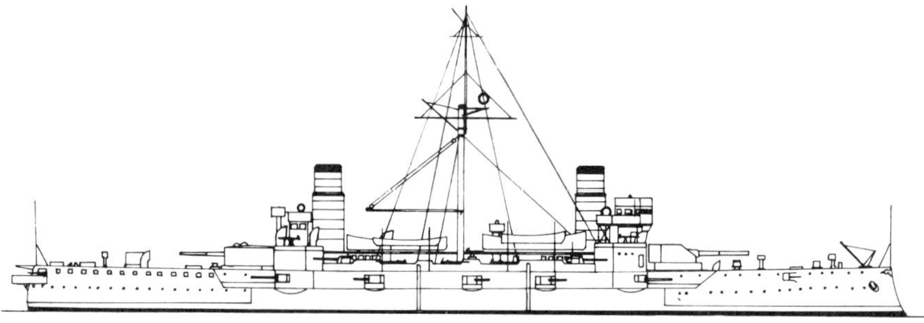

Kasuga, 1904

KASUGA class *armoured cruisers*

Displacement: 7628t normal, *Nisshin* 7698t
Dimensions: 357ft wl, 366ft 6in oa x 61ft 6in x 24ft (*108.8 wl, 111.73 oa x 18.9 x 7.32 m*)
Machinery: 2-shaft reciprocating VTE, 13,500ihp = 20kts. Coal 581/1565, 1316t
Armour: Main belt 2¾in-6in, deck 1in-1½in, barbettes 4in-6in, battery 6in, CT 6in
Armament: 1-10in (not in *Nisshin*), 2-8in (*Nisshin* 4), 14-6in (14 x 1), 10-3in (10 x 1), 6-3pdr, 2 Maxim MGs, 4-18in TT
Complement: 600

Name	Builder	Laid down	Launched	Comp	Fate
KASUGA	Ansaldo, Genoa	10.3.1902	22.10.02	7.1.04	Scrapped 1948
NISSHIN	Ansaldo, Genoa	May 1902	9. 2.03	7.1.04	Used as target 1936

Nisshin at Port Said, October 1917
(Author's collection)

PROTECTED CRUISERS

The first protected cruisers built for the Japanese Navy, they were to an improved *Esmeralda* design prepared by Sir William White. They were completed with a cellular double bottom as an added protection against underwater damage from mine or grounding. The space could be flooded to adjust trim for the operation of the guns. Armour protection was much stronger than in *Esmeralda* and increased freeboard enabled the designer to arrange for the armoured deck to be placed above the waterline. Further protection was afforded by using the wing passages above and below the armoured deck abreast the machinery spaces as coal bunkers.

The armament was similar to *Esmeralda*'s with the 25t 10.3in Krupp guns having a 240° arc of fire forward and aft about the keel line. Three 5.9in/35 Krupp guns were mounted to port and starboard amidships, each commanding a field of fire

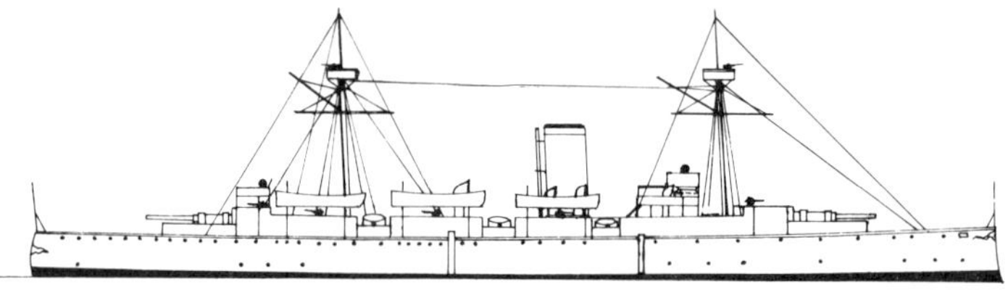

Naniwa, 1886

NANIWA class *protected cruisers*

Displacement: 3650t normal
Dimensions: 300ft pp x 46ft x 20ft 3in full load (*91.4 pp x 14 x 6.1m*)
Machinery: 3-shaft reciprocating HC, 7000ihp = 18½kts. Coal 350/800t
Armour: Deck 2in-3in, gun shields 1½in, CT 1½in
Armament: 2-10.3in (2 x 1), 6-5.9in (6 x 1), 2-6pdr (2 x 1), 10 four-barrelled Nordenfeld guns, 4 Gatling MGs, 4-14in TT
Complement: 325

Name	Builder	Laid down	Launched	Comp	Fate
NANIWA	Armstrong, Walker	27.3.1884	18.3.85	1.12.85	Wrecked 26.7.1912
TAKACHIHO	Armstrong, Walker	10.4.1884	16.5.85	26. 3.86	Lost 17.10.1914

of 130°. Ammunition storage consisted of 200 10.3in shells and 450 rounds of 5.9in ammunition. By 1895 the 5.9in guns had been converted to QF guns, and were replaced in 1900 by Elswick 6in QFs. In 1903 the ships were re-armed throughout with 6in QFs, the 10.3in guns being removed. The fighting tops were removed in 1898.

Both ships served with distinction at the Battle of the Yalu and during the Russo-Japanese war. They were relegated to minor duties in 1907. *Naniwa* was wrecked off Uruppa Island, in the Kuriles, in 1912. *Takachiho* was used as a minelayer and was torpedoed and sunk by the German TB *S90* while taking part in the attack on Tsing Tao.

Takachiho (CPL)

For this ship the Japanese turned to their other popular supplier of warships, the French. This time, however, the usually competent French designers fell into disrepute. In an endeavour to mount heavier armament than in *Naniwa*, the French sited four 18t 9.4in/30 Krupp guns in two sponsons on each beam amidships. Three 5.9in were also mounted along each beam with an extra 5.9in bow chaser.

The Japanese accepted *Unebi* in December 1886 after she had run her preliminary trials. There has been speculation that she lacked stability, and it is possible that her metacentric height was too small. With the heavy broadside armament and a heavy spread of canvas the righting moment would have been insufficient to overcome any roll experienced. Whatever the cause, and this is the most probable, the ship disappeared at sea somewhere between Singapore and Japan in October 1887.

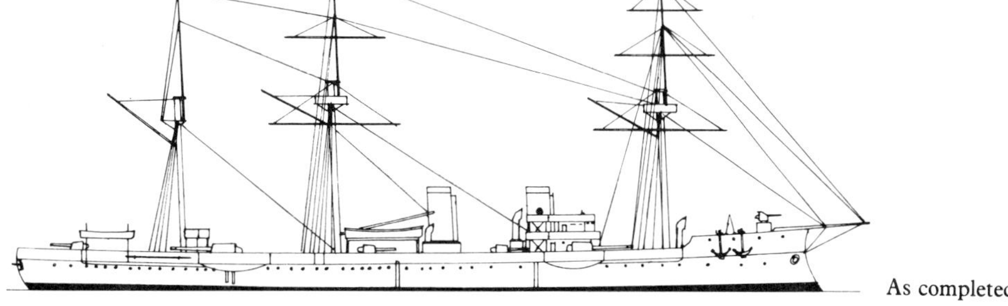
As completed

UNEBI *protected cruiser*

Displacement: 3615t normal
Dimensions: 321ft 6in pp x 43ft x 18ft 9in *(98 pp x 13.1 x 5.72m)*
Machinery: 2-shaft reciprocating HTE, 6000 ihp = 17½ kts.
Armour: Deck 2⅓in
Armament: 4-9.4in (4 x 1), 7-5.9in (7 x 1), 2-6pdr (2 x 1), 10-1pdr 4-barrelled Nordenfeld guns, 4 Gatling, 4-17.7in TT
Complement: 280

Name	Builder	Laid down	Launched	Comp	Fate
UNEBI	Forges et Ch, Le Havre	May 1884	6.4.86	Oct 1886	Lost Oct 1887

The deteriorating situation between Japan and China made it essential for Japan to acquire ships capable of matching the Chinese fleet. Japan had not, at that time, sufficient expertise or training to build and man large battleships and so turned to the French constructor, Émile Bertin, for assistance. The request was for protected cruisers armed with a large gun capable of penetrating the armour on the Chinese battleships. One of the most powerful guns available at the time was the Canet 12.6in, and this was duly fitted in the ships. The guns had a slow rate of fire of one round every five minutes, and at the Battle of the Yalu proved all but useless.

The design was not a success, the stipulated displacement being too low to mount such heavy armament. Consequently protection was to a large extent sacrificed, except around the heavy gun, and the ships were extremely vulnerable to any shells larger than 4.7in. In addition seaworthiness was poor and the designed speed was never achieved.

Matsushima carried her gun aft with the secondary armament forward, while *Itsukushima* carried the 12.6in gun forward and the secondary armament aft. *Hashidate* was identical to *Itsukushima*, except that her 6pdr guns were in unarmoured sponsons to give an increased arc of fire.

The ships were re-boilered in 1901–1902, *Hashidate* being the first Japanese warship to have the large Miyabara watertube boilers – a total of eight. *Matsushima* and *Itsukushima* were both refitted with eight Belleville boilers with increased steam pressure.

All three were at the Battle of the Yalu where *Matsushima* was hit by 10in and 12in shells which damaged the barbette and caused 100 casualties. The three vessels were also present at the Battle of Tsushima. They were relegated to a training role in 1906. *Matsushima* was lost in Mako Harbour in 1908 as a result of a magazine explosion.

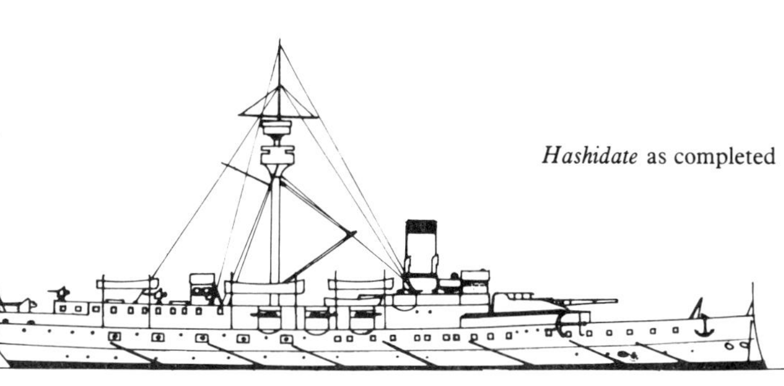
Hashidate as completed

MATSUSHIMA class *protected cruisers*

Displacement: 4217t normal
Dimensions: 301ft wl x 51ft 3in x 20ft *(91.81 wl x 15.59 x 6.05m)*
Machinery: 2-shaft reciprocating HTE, 5400ihp = 16½kts. Coal 405/680t
Armour: Deck 2in, turret 12in, gun shield 4in
Armament: 1-12.6in, 11 (*Matsushima* 12)-4.7in (11 x 1), 5 (*Matsushima* 16)-6 pdr QF (5 x 1), 11 (*Matsushima* none)-3pdr QF (11 x 1), 6-1pdr QF (*Matsushima* only), 4-14in TT
Complement: 360

Name	Builder	Laid down	Launched	Comp	Fate
HASHIDATE	Yokosuka N Yd	Sept 1888	24.3.91	June 1894	Scrapped 1927
ITSUKUSHIMA	Forges et Ch, La Seyne	Jan 1888	11.7.89	Aug 1891	Scrapped 1922
MATSUSHIMA	Forges et Ch, La Seyne	Feb 1888	22.1.90	Mar 1891	Lost 30.4.1908

Akitsushima was erected at the Yokosuka N Yd from imported materials, the design being a reduced version of the American cruiser *Baltimore*. Both designs were prepared by Sir William White of Armstrong's. She was not a success, proving a bad sea boat, suffering from excessive rolling, and being a poor steamer. The 6in armament was mounted on sponsons on either beam towards the foc's'le and aft towards the poop. Between the sponsoned 6in on either broadside were two other sponsons carrying 4.7in, while the remaining 4.7in were sited one on the foc's'le and one on the poop.

After taking part in the Battle of the Yalu, *Akitsushima* assisted the cruiser *Naniwa* to sink the Chinese cruiser *Kuang Chi*. She also took part in the Russo-Japanese war and was finally removed from the operational fleet in 1921.

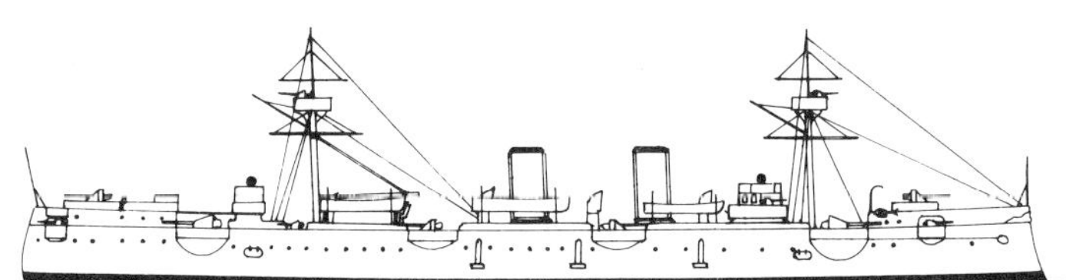

As in 1895

AKITSUSHIMA *protected cruiser*

Displacement: 3100t normal
Dimensions: 301ft pp x 43ft x 17ft 6in (*91.7 pp x 13.14 x 5.32m*)
Machinery: 2-shaft reciprocating HTE, 8400 ihp = 19 kts. Coal 500/800t
Armour: Deck 3in, gun shields 4½in
Armament: 4-6in QF (4 x 1), 6-4.7in QF (6 x 1), 8-3pdr QF (8 x 1), 4-14in TT
Complement: 330

Name	Builder	Laid down	Launched	Comp	Fate
AKITSUSHIMA	Yokosuka N Yd	Mar 1890	6.7.92	Feb 1894	Scrapped 1923

Yoshino (NMM)

The *Yoshino* was built to an improved design of the Argentinian *25 de Mayo* prepared by Sir Philip Watts. When completed she was the fastest cruiser afloat, and with her powerful armament of well-sited QF guns was unmatched for her size. Two of the 6in were sited on the keel line fore and aft, while the other two were on beam sponsons on the upper deck, just aft of the bridge. The 4.7in were sited in beam sponsons on the upper deck.

The *Yoshino*, with her QF guns, played a significant part in the Japanese victory at the Battle of the Yalu, the new Elswick QF guns, although lighter, proving far superior to heavier pieces with a slow rate of fire and poor ammunition. *Yoshino* was rammed and sunk by the armoured cruiser *Kasuga* on 15 May 1904 after taking part in the bombardment of Port Arthur.

YOSHINO *protected cruiser*

Displacement: 4150t normal
Dimensions: 360ft pp x 46ft 6in x 17ft (*109.73 pp x 14.17 x 5.18m*)
Machinery: 2-shaft reciprocating compound, 15,000 ihp = 23 kts. Coal 400/1000t
Armour: Deck 4½in (slope), 1¾in (flat), gun shields 4½in
Armament: 4-6in QF (4 x 1), 8-4.7in QF (8 x 1), 22-3 pdr QF (22 x 1), 5-14in TT
Complement: 360

Name	Builder	Laid down	Launched	Comp	Fate
YOSHINO	Armstrong, Elswick	Feb 1892	20.12.92	Sept 1893	Lost 15.5.1904

Idzumi, the ex-*Esmeralda*, was purchased from Chile in November 1894 in time for the Sino-Japanese war. Although she arrived in Japan within a very short time of her purchase she was not finally ready for service until after the war had ended. She had been designed to operate in the relatively calm waters near the South American coast and proved unsuitable for duties in the rough waters around Japan. Stability was improved in 1899 by replacing the 6in guns with 4.7in models. Finally in 1901 the 10in guns were replaced by 6in QF, and 18in TT replaced the 15in. She was also reboilered with Niclausse boilers. After the Russo-Japanese war she was relegated to a subsidiary role.

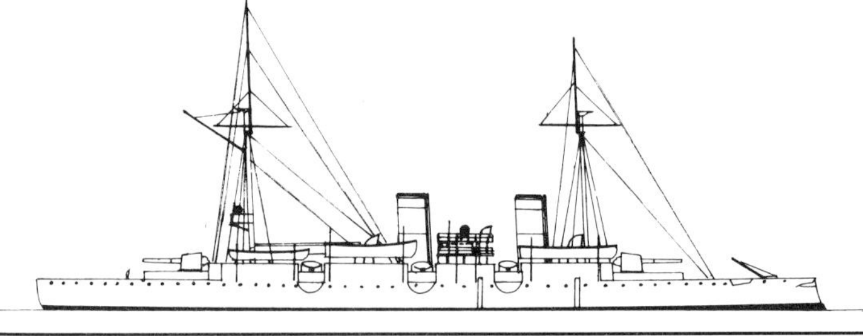

After re-arming, 1899

IDZUMI *protected cruiser*

Displacement: 2920t normal
Dimensions: 270ft pp x 42ft x 18ft 3in (*82.29 pp x 12.8 x 5.64m*)
Machinery: 2-shaft reciprocating HC, 6083 ihp = 18¼ kts. Coal 400/600t
Armour: Deck 1in (slope), ½in (flat)
Armament: 2-10in (2 x 1), 6-6in (6 x 1), 2-6pdr QF (2 x 1), 5-2pdr QF, 2 Gardner MGs, 3-15in TT
Complement: 300

Name	Builder	Laid down	Launched	Comp	Fate
IDZUMI	Armstrong, Elswick	5.4.1881	6.6.83	15.7.84	Discarded 1912

The *Sai Yen*, ex-Chinese *Chi Yuan*, was captured at Wei-Hai-Wei on 12 February 1895. She was refitted during the late 1890s, eight 3pdr QF replacing the 6pdr and 2pdr guns. She was mined during the Russo-Japanese war.

SAI YEN *protected cruiser*

Displacement: 2440t normal
Dimensions: 236ft pp x 35ft x 15ft 3in *(72 pp x 10.7 x 4.67m)*
Machinery: 2-shaft reciprocating compound, 2800 ihp = 15 kts. Coal 230t
Armour: Deck 3in, turret 2in
Armament: 2-8.2in (1 x 2), 1-5.9in, 4-6pdr QF, 6-2pdr QF, 4-15in TT
Complement: 230

Name	Builder	Laid down	Launched	Comp	Fate
SAI YEN	Vulcan, Stettin	—	1883	1885	Lost 30.11.1904

These were the first cruisers to be built entirely to Japanese designs and with Japanese materials, except for the guns which were imported from Britain. The design and disposition of the armament were similar in many ways to the *Akitsushima*, and dimensions were practically the same. Machinery, however, was VTE, instead of the HTE of the *Akitsushima*. Power developed at forced draught was almost the same as in the *Akitsushima*, giving an extra knot at maximum speed. The boilers, on the other hand, were not so efficient, comprising eight locomotive boilers in the *Suma* and nine single-ended in the *Akashi*.

The *Suma* was found to lack stability when completed and proved to be a very wet ship. The *Akashi* was still on the stocks when these faults came to light and so she was altered and completed with greater freeboard amidships, making her flush-decked, and she lacked fighting tops to her masts. Subsequently both ships had their mainmasts removed and the *Suma* had her fighting top removed from the foremast. In addition both ships were re-boilered, *Suma* having four Miyabara watertube boilers in 1908, and *Akashi* having nine Niclausse in 1912. Both ships were in action during the Russo-Japanese war, the *Akashi* being mined, but subsequently repaired. They were disarmed in 1922.

Akashi as completed

SUMA class *protected cruisers*

Displacement: 2657t normal, *Akashi* 2756t
Dimensions: 306ft 9in pp; *Akashi* 295ft 3in x 40ft; *Akashi* 41ft 9in x 15ft 3in; *Akashi* 15ft 9in *(93.5pp; Akashi 90 x 12.24; Akashi 12.7 x 4.63; Akashi 4.8m)*
Machinery: 2-shaft reciprocating VTE, 8500 ihp = 20 kts. Coal 200/600t
Armour: Deck 2in (slope), 1in (flat), gun shields 4½in
Armament: 2-6in QF (2 x 1), 6-4.7in QF (6 x 1), 10-3pdr QF (10 x 1), 4-2½pdr QF (2 x 1), 4 Maxim MGs, 2-15in TT
Complement: 310

Name	Builder	Laid down	Launched	Comp	Fate
SUMA	Yokosuka N Yd	Aug 1892	9. 3.95	Dec 1896	Scrapped 1928
AKASHI	Yokosuka N Yd	Aug 1894	18.12.97	Mar 1899	Sunk as target Aug 1930

Suma (Marius Bar)

Takasago as completed *(Author's collection)*

The *Takasago* was designed by Sir Philip Watts and was a typical Elswick cruiser of the period. With a high freeboard at the foc's'le and poop, where the 8in guns were sited high up, she suffered from instability and was prone to roll heavily in any kind of sea. Nevertheless she was a fast steamer. The four single-ended and four double-ended boilers feeding the engines gave her a radius of 5500 nm at a cruising speed of 10 kts.

The Harvey steel armour protection was designed to withstand the impact of 8in AP shells, and watertight integrity was ensured with a total of 109 watertight compartments, including 18 in the double bottom.

The real value of the *Takasago* lay in her armament of all QF guns of the Elswick pattern, the 8in guns having a rate of fire of four rounds per minute. The fore and aft shielded 4.7-in guns were sited to port and starboard in open casemates abreast the bridge and near the after emergency steering position. The remainder of the 4.7in guns were sited in shields behind the low bulwark in the waist of the ship.

Previous Japanese protected cruisers, including those built by Armstrong's, suffered from stability problems, and to reduce these in the *Takasago* the fighting tops, which each carried two 2½pdr guns, were carried lower down the masts than in earlier cruisers.

The *Takasago* was mined off Port Arthur on 12 December 1904 and sank the following day with the loss of 204 lives.

TAKASAGO *protected cruiser*

Displacement: 4160t normal
Dimensions: 360ft pp, 387ft 6in oa x 46ft 6in x 17ft *(109.73 pp, 118.2 oa x 14.78 x 5.18m)*
Machinery: 2-shaft reciprocating VTE, 15,500 ihp = 23½ kts. Coal 350/1000t
Armour: Deck 4½in (slope), 2½in (flat), 8in gun shields 4½in (face), 2½in (side), 4.7in gun shields 2½in
Armament: 2-8in QF (2 x 1), 10-4.7in QF (10 x 1), 12-12pdr QF (12 x 1), 6-2½pdr QF (6 x 1), 5-18in TT
Complement: 425

Name	Builder	Laid down	Launched	Comp	Fate
TAKASAGO	Armstrong, Elswick	April 1896	18.5.97	6.4.98	Lost 13.12.1904

These two cruisers were almost identical externally to the *Takasago*, but were slightly longer and had greater displacement. Armament was identical to the *Takasago*, except that the bow TT was omitted, and disposed in a similar fashion. Internally the ships differed, watertight compartments being increased to 130 in *Chitose* and 142 in *Kasagi*, compared to the 109 in the *Takasago*. However, the number of watertight compartments in the double bottom were reduced to 16 in the *Chitose* and 15 in the *Kasagi*.

The machinery also differed from the *Takasago's*, twelve single-ended cylindrical boilers being mounted and the engines having slightly larger cylinders, although the stroke remained the same.

Both ships were present at the Battle of the Yellow Sea and the Battle of Tsushima, where both were damaged. The *Kasagi* was used as a training ship from 1910 and was wrecked in the Tsugaru Strait in 1916. The *Chitose* was disarmed in 1922 and served as a coast defence vessel until 1928 when she was discarded, being finally expended as a target in July 1931.

Chitose in 1907 *(Author's collection)*

CHITOSE class *protected cruisers*

Displacement: 4760t normal, *Kasagi* 4900t
Dimensions: *Chitose* 376ft 6in pp, 396ft oa x 49ft 3in x 17ft 6in; *Kasagi* 374ft 6in pp, 402ft oa x 48ft 9in x 17ft 9in *(Chitose 114.9 pp, 120.4 oa x 15 x 5.37m; Kasagi 114.1 pp, 121.47 oa x 14.9 x 5.41m)*
Machinery: 2-shaft reciprocating VTE, 15,000 ihp = 22½ kts. Coal 350/1000t
Armour: Deck 4½in (slope), 2½in (flat), 8in gun shield 4½in (face), 2½in (side), 4.7in gun shield 2½in, CT 4½in
Armament: 2-8in QF (2 x 1), 10-4.7in QF (10 x 1), 12-12pdr QF (12 x 1), 6-2½pdr QF (6 x 1), 4-18in TT
Complement: 434, *Kasagi* 405

Name	Builder	Laid down	Launched	Comp	Fate
CHITOSE	Union Iron Wks, San Francisco	16.5.1897	23.1.98	1.3.99	Sunk as target 19.7.1931
KASAGI	Cramp, Philadelphia	Mar 1897	20.1.98	Dec 1898	Lost 13.8.1916

This was the second cruiser class built to a completely Japanese design. There was little difference between these ships and the earlier Japanese designed *Suma* class. They were somewhat larger and the increased displacement helped the designers to overcome certain of the faults experienced with the *Suma*. As before freeboard was high, but the 6in guns, which replaced the 4.7in of the *Suma*, in broadside sponsons were sited slightly lower down on the hull. No fighting tops were fitted to the masts. The combination of a much heavier armament sited lower down resulted in a more seaworthy and powerful vessel, which outclassed many other contemporary protected cruisers. The ships were fitted with 16 Niclausse boilers, a great improvement on the locomotive boilers of the *Suma*. They developed a pressure of $213lb/in^2$.

Both ships saw action in the Russo-Japanese war. The *Niitaka* was lost in a typhoon off the Kamchatka coast in August 1922. The *Tsushima* was re-armed in 1922 to carry six 6in QF and eight 12pdr guns, but later an extra 12pdr was added. She was partially disarmed in 1930 and discarded in 1936 to serve as a training ship, being completely disarmed in 1939, the hulk sinking during an air raid in 1944.

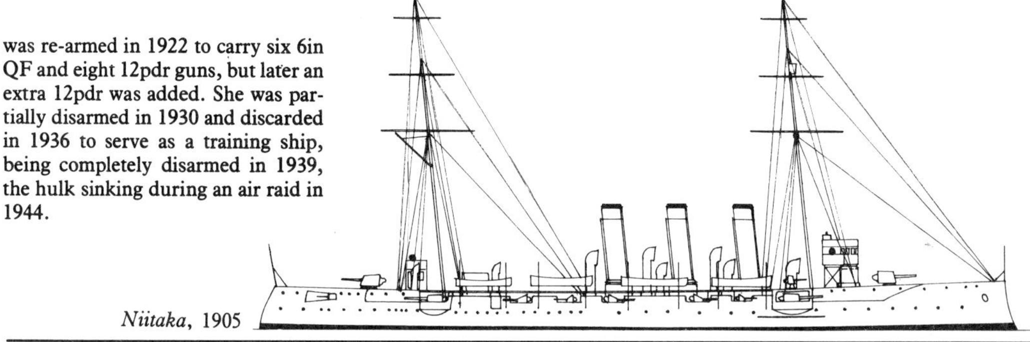

Niitaka, 1905

TSUSHIMA class *protected cruisers*

Displacement: 3366t normal
Dimensions: 334ft 6in pp x 44ft x 16ft 3in *(102 pp x 13.44 x 4.92m)*
Machinery: 2-shaft reciprocating compound, 9500 ihp = 20 kts. Coal 250/600t
Armour: Deck 2½in, CT 4in
Armament: 6-6in QF (6 x 1), 10-12pdr QF (10 x 1), 4-2½pdr QF (4 x 1)
Complement: 320

Name	Builder	Laid down	Launched	Comp	Fate
TSUSHIMA	Kure N Yd	1.10.1901	15.12.02	14.2.04	Lost 1944
NIITAKA	Yokosuka N Yd	7. 1.1902	15.11.02	27.1.04	Lost 26.8.1922

The *Otowa*, ordered under the 1896-1897 Programme, was a smaller, faster version of the *Tsushima* class, but with a lighter armament. The design reverted to the sponsoned 4.7in as in the earlier *Suma;* instead of beam-mounted 6in guns, the fore and aft 6in were retained. The *Otowa* was the first ship to be equipped with the Japanese-designed Kanpon water-tube boiler which developed $227lb/in^2$ compared to the $213lb/in^2$ pressure of the Niclausse boilers in the *Tsushima*. The engines were identical to those in the *Tsushima* with a slight increase in hp. The boilers were of the three-drum pattern and apart from having curved tubes, were very similar to the Yarrow boiler.

The armoured deck was ½in thicker than in the *Tsushima*, but still not as strong as that fitted to the Elswick designed cruisers. The *Otowa* was present at the Battle of Tsushima and was lost when she ran aground on the Japanese coast in August 1917.

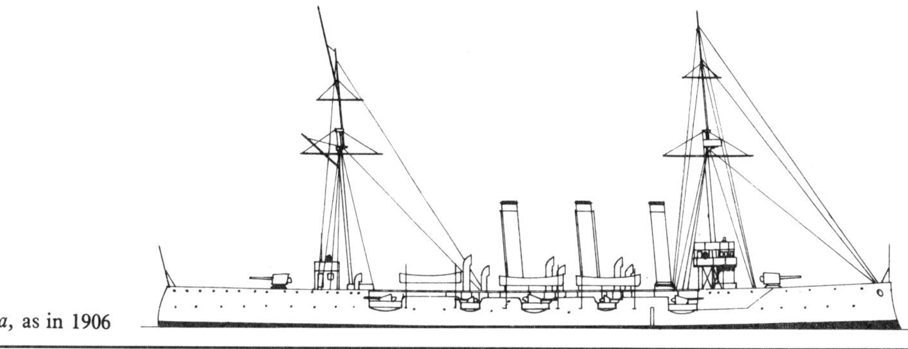

Otowa, as in 1906

OTOWA *protected cruiser*

Displacement: 3000t normal
Dimensions: 321ft 6in pp, 341ft oa x 41ft 6in x 15ft 9in *(98 pp, 103.88 oa x 12.62 x 4.8m)*
Machinery: 2-shaft reciprocating VTE, 10,000 ihp = 21 kts. Coal 270/575t
Armour: Deck 3in (amidships), 2in (ends), gun shields 1½in, CT 4in
Armament: 2-6in QF (2 x 1), 6-4.7in QF (6 x 1), 4-12pdr QF (2 x 1)
Complement: 312

Name	Builder	Laid down	Launched	Comp	Fate
OTOWA	Yokosuka N Yd	3.1.1903	2.11.03	6.9.04	Lost 1.8.1917

FRIGATES, CORVETTES, UNPROTECTED CRUISERS

The full rigged wooden-hulled frigate *Fujijama* was acquired by the Shogun from the United States in 1866. She was commissioned into the Imperial Navy in 1869 and was subsequently re-armed with one 6.5in and two 6in guns. She served as a training ship from 1880.

FUJIJAMA *screw frigate*

Displacement: 1000t normal
Dimensions: 207ft wl x 33ft 9in x 10ft 9in *(63 wl x 10.3 x 3.27m)*
Machinery: 1-shaft reciprocating, 350 ihp = 13 kts
Armament: 1-6.3in ML, 2-5.9in, 10 small guns
Complement: 134

Name	Builder	Laid down	Launched	Comm.	Fate
FUJIJAMA	New York	—	1864	1866	Sold 1896

The *Kasuga* (ex-*Chiangtzu*) was a full rigged, wooden-hulled vessel purchased from China in 1867 by the Satsuma clan. After serving as the personal yacht of the Shogun she was commissioned into the Imperial Navy in 1869 where she served as a despatch vessel.

KASUGA *paddle frigate*

Displacement: 1289t normal
Dimensions: 248ft 6in wl x 29ft x 13ft *(75.7 wl x 8.8 x 3.96m)*
Machinery: 1 HR, 1217 ihp = 9 kts
Armament: 1-7in, 4-4.5in, 2-30pdr
Complement: 138

Name	Builder	Laid down	Launched	Comp	Fate
KASUGA	J S White, Cowes	—	1863	1863 ?	Scrapped 1896

This wooden, screw corvette was the ex-British *Malacca* acquired in 1870. She was re-armed in 1892 with four 6in QF guns.

TSUKUBA *screw corvette*

Displacement: 1947t normal
Dimensions: 192ft 6in wl, 198ft oa x 34ft 9in x 18ft *(58.6 wl, 60.3 oa x 10.6 x 5.48m)*
Machinery: 1-shaft reciprocating, 526 ihp = 10 kts
Armament: 6-4.5in (6 x 1), 2-30pdr (2 x 1), 2-24pdr (2 x 1)
Complement: 301

Name	Builder	Laid down	Launched	Comp	Fate
TSUKUBA	Moulmein, Burma	—	9.4.1853	1854	Scrapped 1906

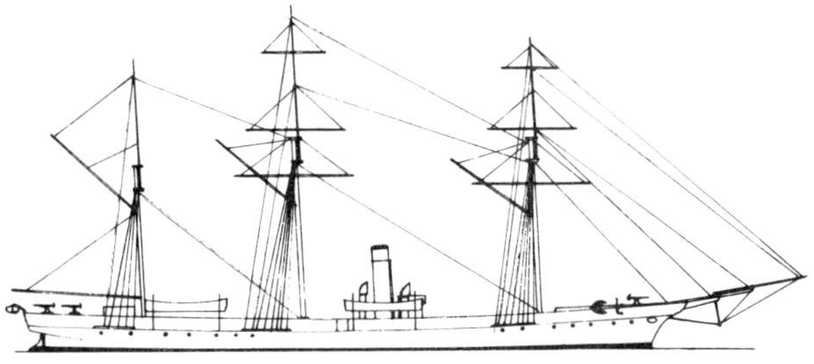

As completed

The barque-rigged, wooden-hulled *Nisshin* was originally built for the Shogun, but was not completed until after the Shogunate forces were defeated during the civil war, when she was acquired by the Hizen clan. She was commissioned into the Imperial Navy in May 1870. The Armstrong 7in ML and the 30pdrs were replaced in 1885 by six Krupp 4.7in BL guns, and the vessel was removed from the active fleet on 30 May 1892.

NISSHIN *screw corvette*

Displacement: 1490t normal
Dimensions: 203ft pp x 28ft 9in x 14ft *(61.8 pp x 8.76 x 4.2m)*
Machinery: 1-shaft reciprocating, 710 ihp = 11 kts
Armament: 1-7in, 6-30pdr (6 x 1)
Complement: 145

Name	Builder	Laid down	Launched	Comp	Fate
NISSHIN	Gips & Son, Dordrecht	—	1869	—	Scrapped 1893

JAPAN

The composite-hulled *Asama* was purchased from France in 1874 and was relegated to the role of training ship in 1887. She was removed from the fleet list in 1891 and served as a torpedo school at Yokosuka.

ASAMA *composite corvette*

Displacement: 1422t normal
Dimensions: 228ft 9in pp x 28ft 9in x 14ft *(69.72 pp x 8.76 x 4.26m)*
Machinery: 1-shaft reciprocating HC, 300ihp = 11 kts
Armament: 8-6.7in, 4-4.5in
Complement: —

Name	Builder	Laid down	Launched	Comp	Fate
ASAMA	—	—	1869	July 1874	Sold Dec 1896

The barque-rigged, wooden-hulled *Seiki* was the first ship to be built at Yokosuka N Yd. The shipyard was managed for the Japanese by French engineers and the *Seiki* was designed and built under the direction of Mr Verny and his staff, as were the machinery and the two cylindrical boilers. The main armament was manufactured by Krupps while the 6pdr gun was an Armstrong model. The *Seiki* was the first Japanese warship to visit the British Isles. She grounded in the Fuji river, Suruya Wan in 1888 and became a constructive total loss.

SEIKI *screw sloop*

Displacement: 897t normal
Dimensions: 203ft 9in wl x 30ft 6in x 13ft *(60.96 wl x 9.14 x 3.96m)*
Machinery: 1-shaft reciprocating HCRA, 443ihp = 9½ kts
Armament: 1-5.9in, 1-4.7in, 1-6pdr, 3 four-barrelled Nordenfeld MGs
Complement: 167

Name	Builder	Laid down	Launched	Comp	Fate
SEIKI	Yokosuka N Yd	20.6.1873	5.5.75	June 1876	Wrecked 7.12.88

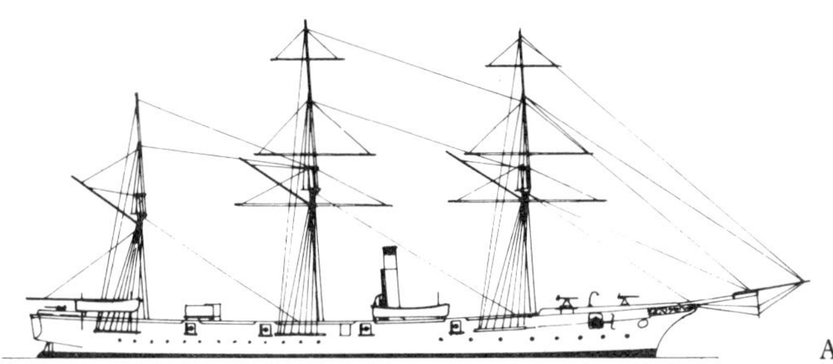

As in 1880

The wooden-hulled *Amagi* was a slightly larger and more heavily armed version of the *Seiki*, both vessels being built at the same yard. The *Amagi* mounted identical machinery to the *Seiki* but the hp was almost doubled from 443 to 720 to give an extra 2 kts. Like the *Seiki* the armament was supplied by Krupps. *Amagi* was reclassified as a gunboat in 1898 and sold for scrap just before the Russo-Japanese war.

AMAGI *screw sloop*

Displacement: 911t normal
Dimensions: 204ft pp x 35ft 9in x 14ft 4in *(62.17 pp x 10.89 x 4.36m)*
Machinery: 1-shaft reciprocating HC, 720ihp = 11kts. Coal 150t
Armament: 1-6.7in, 4-4.7in, 3-12pdr, 3-four-barrelled Nordenfeld MGs
Complement: 159

Name	Builder	Laid down	Launched	Comp	Fate
AMAGI	Yokosuka N Yd	Sept 1875	Mar 1877	April 1878	Sold 1903

The wooden-hulled paddle corvette *Jingei* took nearly nine years to complete, mainly as a result of problems arising with the installation of the machinery. She served as the Imperial yacht before being relegated to the role of training ship in 1894.

JINGEI *paddle corvette*

Displacement: 1465t normal
Dimensions: 249ft wl x 32ft x 14ft 6in *(76 wl x 9.75 x 4.42m)*
Machinery: 2 paddles, 1 reciprocating diagonal DA, 1450ihp = 14kts
Armament: 2-4.7in
Complement: —

Name	Builder	Laid down	Launched	Comp	Fate
JINGEI	Yokosuka N Yd	Sept 1873	1876	1881	Discarded 1894

These barque-rigged corvettes were the most effective of the smaller types of warship in service in the Japanese Navy towards the end of the 19th century. They were built under French supervision and completed with Krupp armament. Both vessels were refitted, a new bow replacing the original graceful knee stem, and military masts replacing the fore and main masts. The ships carried out a number of operations during the Russo-Japanese war, the *Kaimon* being lost off Talien Wan Bay in July 1904 when she struck a mine. *Tenryu* survived the war and was finally removed from active service in 1906.

KAIMON class *screw corvettes*

Displacement: 1358t, *Tenryu* 1525t normal
Dimensions: 210ft 9in; *Tenryu* 212ft 3in pp x 32ft 6in; *Tenryu* 35ft 3in x 16ft 6in; *Tenryu* 17ft *(64.26, 64.68 pp x 9.9; 10.8 x 5; 5.2m)*
Machinery: 1-shaft reciprocating HCRA, 1267ihp = 12kts. Coal 256t
Armament: 1-6.7, (*Tenryu* 5.9in), 6 (*Tenryu* 4)-4.7in, 1-3in, 4-four-barrelled Nordenfeld MGs, 1 four-barrelled 11.5mm Nordenfeld MG (*Kaimon* only)
Complement: 210

Name	Builder	Laid down	Launched	Comp	Fate
KAIMON	Yokosuka N Yd	Aug 1877	Sept 1882	13.8.84	Lost 5.7.1904
TENRYU	Yokosuka N Yd	Jan 1878	Sept 1883	Mar 1885	Discarded 1906

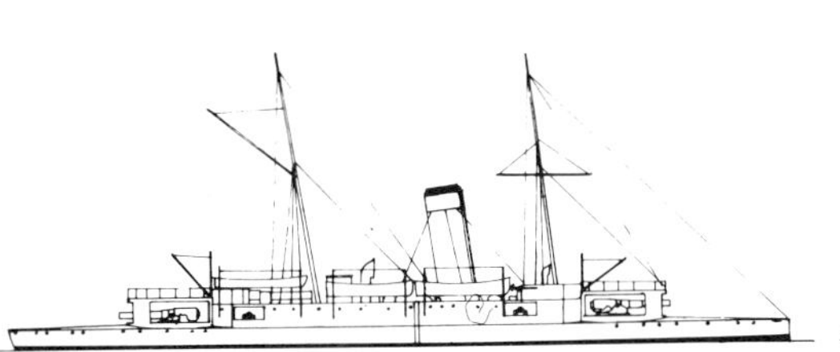
As in 1886

Tsukushi in 1885 built up forward for her delivery voyage from Armstrongs (*CPL*)

Similar in design to the Chinese *Tchao Yung* cruisers, *Tsukushi* was originally laid down for the Chilean Government as the *Arturo Prat*. The design was drawn up by Sir Edward Reed as an intermediate design between the *Rendel* gunboats and the *Esmeralda*. At the time of her completion her main armament was unmatched – except for the British *Inflexible* and Italian *Caio Duilio*; but the guns took about 2½ minutes to load and fire. The reciprocating machinery and five cylindrical boilers propelled the vessels at an exceptionally high speed. At eight knots the ship had a radius of action of 5380 nm.

Soon after her completion the war between Chile and Peru ended and the *Arturo Prat* was put up for sale and purchased in 1885 by the Japanese under the 1882 Programme. She was re-armed in 1898, the 9pdr and 1pdr guns being replaced by a 12pdr QF and two 3pdr QF. She was removed from the fleet list in 1907 and served as a training ship until about 1910 when she was broken up.

TSUKUSHI *unprotected cruiser*

Displacement: 1350t normal
Dimensions: 210ft pp x 31ft 9in x 14ft (*64 pp x 9.7 x 4.4m*)
Machinery: 2-shaft reciprocating HC, 2887 ihp = 16½kts. Coal 300t
Armament: 2-10in (2 x 1), 4-4.7in, 2-9pdr, 4-1pdr Hotchkiss, 2-18in TT
Complement: 186

Name	Builder	Laid down	Launched	Comp	Fate
TSUKUSHI	Armstrong, Elswick	2.10.1879	11.8.80	June 1883	Scrapped 1910 ?

The three composite-built vessels of the *Katsuragi* class were ordered under the 1882 Programme and were a much more modern design than the previous *Kaimon*. They were completed with straight bows and recessed gunports which allowed the two forward guns to fire on a forward arc instead of only on the broadside, as in previous designs.

They were refitted in 1900 when the barque-rig was removed and the vessels re-armed with eight 2½pdr QF and six MGs. The 15in TT were replaced by 18in tubes. They were re-armed yet again in 1907 with four 3in and four 50mm, and finally only mounted two 3in. The *Musashi* ran aground near Nemoro on 30 April 1902 but was later refloated and repaired. The ships were all reclassified as survey vessels in 1907 and served for a number of years before finally being scrapped. The *Yamato* was used as a drillship after 1935 and sank in Kobe harbour during a storm in September 1935, the wreck being broken up during 1950.

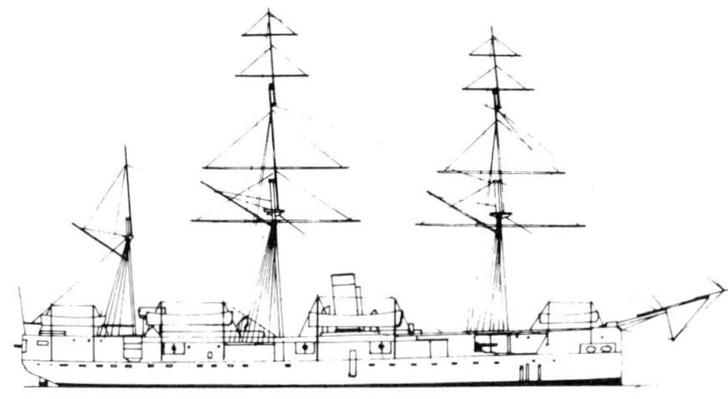
Yamato, 1888

KATSURAGI class *screw corvettes*

Displacement: 1476t normal
Dimensions: 201ft pp, 206ft wl x 35ft x 15ft 3in (*61.26 pp, 62.78 wl x 10.7 x 4.6m*)
Machinery: 1 (*Katsuragi* 2)-shaft reciprocating HCRA, 1622 ihp = 13 kts. Coal 145t
Armament: 2-6.7in (2 x 1), 5-4.7in (5 x 1), 1-3in, 4 four-barrelled Nordenfeld MGs, 2-15in TT
Complement: 231

Name	Builder	Laid down	Launched	Comp	Fate
KATSURAGI	Yokosuka N Yd	Dec 1882	31.3.85	Oct 1887	Sold for scrap 1913
MUSASHI	Yokosuka N Yd	Oct 1884	30.3.86	Feb 1888	Scrapped 1931
YAMATO	Onohama, Kobe N Yd	Feb 1883	April 1885	Oct 1887	Lost 18.9.1945

The *Takao*, ordered under the 1882 Programme to a design prepared by Émile Bertin, was the first steel-hulled warship to be laid down in Japan. Laid down in October 1886, the *Takao* was completed on 16 November 1889. The main armament of Krupp guns was sited in sponsons amidships – similar to many French cruisers of the period – with a Krupp 4.7in gun at the stern. She was re-armed in 1907 with two 6in and two 4.7in and was removed from front line service in 1911. She then served as a survey ship until 1918 when she was sold out of naval service.

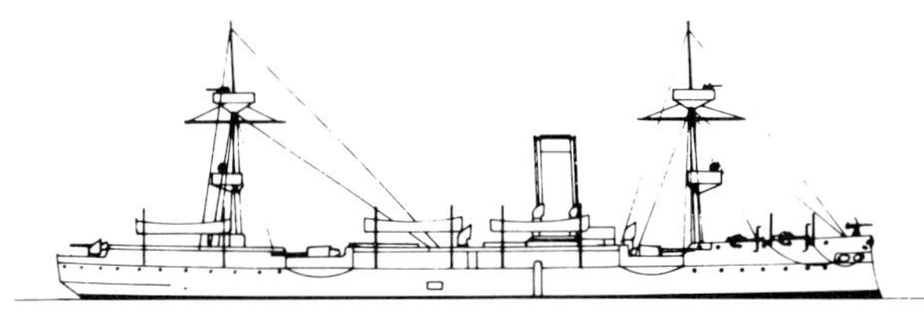
As in 1895

TAKAO *unprotected cruiser*

Displacement: 1750t normal
Dimensions: 232ft wl x 34ft 6in x 13ft (*70.4 wl x 10.5 x 4m*)
Machinery: 2-shaft reciprocating HC, 2330 ihp = 15 kts
Armament: 4-5.9in (4 x 1), 1-4.7in, 1-6pdr, 2-four-barrelled Nordenfeld MGs, 2-15in TT
Complement: 220

Name	Builder	Laid down	Launched	Comp	Fate
TAKAO	Yokosuka N Yd	Oct 1886	15.10.88	16.11.89	Sold? 1918

JAPAN

Yaeyama was built to a design prepared by the French engineer, M Bertin. The machinery was imported from Britain and was TE instead of the compound-type previously installed in Japanese warships. The *Yaeyama* was re-boilered in 1902, eight Niclausse boilers replacing the original six cylindrical boilers; an extra funnel was also added. She was again refitted after the Russo-Japanese war and between 1906–1908 was used as a test-bed for experiments with oil-fired boilers.

YAEYAMA *steel unprotected cruiser*

Displacement: 1584t normal
Dimensions: 318ft pp x 34ft 6in x 13ft 3in mean (*96.9 pp x 10.5 x 4m*)
Machinery: 2-shaft reciprocating HDA, 5630ihp = 20¾kts. Coal 350t
Armament: 3-4.7in, 8-3pdr QF, 2-18in TT
Complement: 200

Name	Builder	Laid down	Launched	Comp	Fate
YAEYAMA	Yokosuka N Yd	June 1887	Mar 1889	Mar 1892	Scrapped 1911

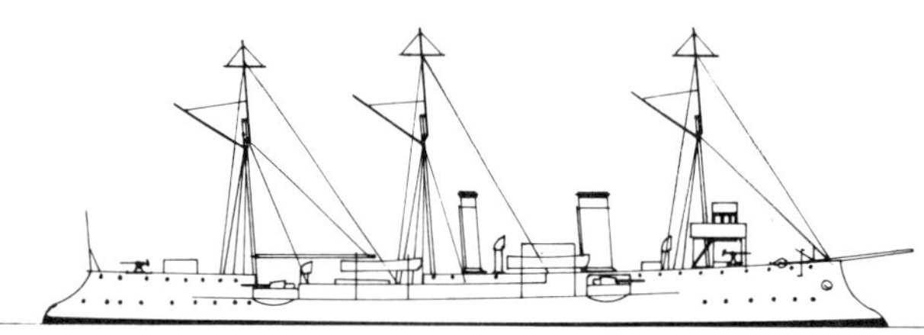
As completed

Chishima was ordered under the 1882 Programme and was delivered on 24 November 1892. The 3in guns were mounted in sponsons on the beam, with the fifth gun in the bows. The 1pdr guns were sited two on the bridge, two on the poop and one on each beam amidships. The TT were all above water, one in the bow and two on the upper deck. The *Chishima* was sunk in collision with the British steamer *Ravenna* in the Inland Sea in November 1892.

CHISHIMA *unprotected cruiser*

Displacement: 741t normal
Dimensions: 233ft pp x 25ft 3in x 9ft 9in mean (*71 pp x 7.7 x 2.97m*)
Machinery: 2-shaft reciprocating VTE, 5000ihp = 22kts
Armament: 5-3in QF (5 x 1), 6-1pdr QF (6 x 1), 3-15in TT
Complement: —

Name	Builder	Laid down	Launched	Comp	Fate
CHISHIMA	Ch de La Loire, St Nazaire	Jan 1890	Nov 1890	April 1892	Lost 30.11.1892

Tatsuta was ordered from Britain as a replacement for the *Chishima*. She was hurriedly built to be ready for the expected war with China, but was on her way to the Far East, refuelling at Aden when war broke out. She was at once interned as war contraband and did not finally reach Japan until December 1896, when the war was over.

She was re-rated as a despatch vessel in 1898, and in 1903 was refitted with four Kanpon small tube boilers in place of the original cylindrical boilers, three tall thin funnels replacing the single squat fat funnel. She was also re-armed, 12pdr guns replacing the 3pdrs. The *Tatsuta* ran aground on the Elliot Islands on 15 May 1904, but was refloated and repaired. In 1918 she was renamed *Nagaura Maru* to allow the name *Tatsuta* to be used for a new light cruiser. She then served as a submarine depot and repair ship until 1926 when she was scrapped.

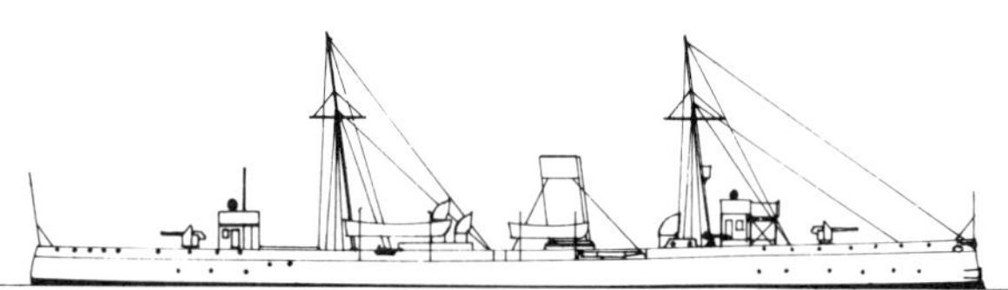
As completed

TATSUTA *unprotected cruiser*

Displacement: 850t normal
Dimensions: 240ft pp x 27ft 6in x 9ft 6in mean (*73.1 pp x 8.38 x 2.89m*)
Machinery: 2-shaft reciprocating VTE, 5500ihp = 21kts. Coal 188/200t
Armament: 2-4.7in QF, 4-3pdr QF, 5-2½pdr QF, 5-18in TT (2 x 2, 1 x 1)
Complement: 100

Name	Builder	Laid down	Launched	Comp	Fate
TATSUTA	Armstrong, Elswick	April 1893	6.4.94	31.7.94	Scrapped 1926

Miyako, built under the 1892 Programme, but was not completed in time for the Sino-Japanese war, not entering service until September 1899. The engines were fed with steam from eight locomotive boilers. She struck a mine off Port Arthur in May 1904 and the wreck was subsequently raised and scrapped.

MIYAKO *unprotected cruiser*

Displacement: 1772t normal
Dimensions: 314ft 9in pp x 34ft 6in x 14ft mean (*96 pp x 10.5 x 4.28m*)
Machinery: 2-shaft reciprocating VTE, 6130ihp = 20kts. Coal 400t
Armament: 2-4.7in QF (2 x 1), 8-3pdr QF (8 x 1), 2-18in TT
Complement: 200

Name	Builder	Laid down	Launched	Comp	Fate
MIYAKO	Kure N Yd	Mar 1894	Oct 1898	Mar 1899	Lost 14.5.1904

Chihaya was laid down under the 1896 Programme, being completed with a bow TT which was subsequently removed. Four Normand boilers developed 210lb/in².

She was stricken in 1927, and used at the Etajima Naval College as a training ship until 1939. The hulk was still afloat at Kure at the end of the Second World War.

CHIHAYA *unprotected cruiser*

Displacement: 1238t normal
Dimensions: 273ft pp, 288ft oa x 31ft 6in x 9ft mean *(83.19 pp, 87.7 oa x 9.6 x 2.76m)*
Machinery: 2-shaft reciprocating VTE, 6000 ihp = 21 kts. Coal 123/344t
Armament: 2-4.7in QF (2 x 1), 4-12pdr QF (4 x 1), 3-18in TT
Complement: 125

Name	Builder	Laid down	Launched	Comp	Fate
CHIHAYA	Yokosuka N Yd	May 1898	26.5.1900	Sep 1901	Discarded 1939

GUNBOATS

When the bulk of the Imperial Navy was formed, as a distinct unit of the Army, in February 1872, it took over a number of old steam vessels which had formerly belonged to the Shogun and various clans. Included in this grouping were the first corvettes and sloops of war built for the Imperial Navy between 1873 and 1887 as well as ships designed from the outset as gunboats. The category also included units classified as despatch vessels, third class cruisers and torpedo gunboats. By 1898 most of these obsolete units had been re-rated as coast defence vessels.

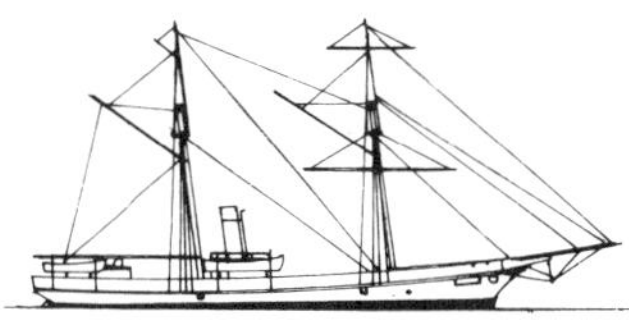

As completed

This brig-rigged, third class, wooden gunboat was the first warship to be built in Japan. She was taken over, from the Shogun, by the Imperial Navy in May 1868, and was captured by the Shogunate forces during the civil war on 4 October 1868. She was recaptured at Hakodate by the Imperial Navy after grounding. *Chiyodogata* was removed from the effective fleet in June 1869 and sold to a whaling company in January 1888. She was finally broken up in 1911.

CHIYODOGATA

Displacement: 140t normal
Dimensions: 97ft 3in pp, 103ft wl x 16ft x 6ft 9in mean *(29.7pp, 31.3 wl x 4.8 x 2m)*
Machinery: 1-shaft reciprocating HDA, 60 ihp = 5 kts
Armament: 1-5.5in, 2 small guns
Complement: 35

Name	Builder	Laid down	Launched	Comp	Fate
CHIYODOGATA	Ishikawajima N Yd	7.5.1861	2.7.63	May 1866	Sold 28.1.1888

These two third class, barque-rigged, wooden gunboats were originally built for mercantile purposes. *Dai Ichi Teibo* had been completed in 1867 as the SS *Hinda* and *Dai Ni Teibo*, also completed in 1867, as the SS *Assunta*. They were purchased by the Choshu clan in 1868 when they were renamed *Teibo Maru No 1* and *Teibo Maru No 2* respectively. *Teibo Maru No 1* was lent to the Imperial Navy early in 1868 and armed for use in the civil war. In July she was returned to her owners but both vessels were given to the Imperial Navy as gifts in 1870, and renamed *Dai Ichi Teibo* and *Dai Ni Teibo*. *Dai Ichi Teibo* was used as a survey vessel from 1873 until she was wrecked in the Kurile Islands in 1875. *Dai Ni Teibo* was removed from the operational fleet in 1885 and wrecked at Anori Point, Shimane Ken, on 2 April 1885.

TEIBO

Displacement: 236t normal
Dimensions: 120ft wl, 125ft 3in oa x 21ft x 7ft 6in mean *(36.5 wl, 38 oa x 6.4 x 2.28m)*
Machinery: 1-shaft reciprocating DA, 60 ihp = 10 kts
Armament: *Dai Ichi Teibo* 1-5.9in, 1-5.5in BLR; *Dai Ni Teibo* 2-6.5in BLR, 2 small guns
Complement: 87

Name	Builder	Laid down	Launched	Comp	Fate
DAI ICHI TEIBO	London	—	1867	1867	Lost 1875
DAI NI TEIBO	London	—	1866	1867	Lost 2.4.85

The third class, composite, schooner-rigged gunboat *Moshun* was originally completed in 1867 as the steamer *Eugénie*. She was sold to the Hizen clan in February 1868 and taken over by the Imperial Navy in July 1869 for service in the civil war. She was presented to the navy by the clan in 1870, and hulked in 1887.

MOSHUN

Displacement: 305t normal
Dimensions: 143ft wl, 150ft oa x 22ft x 7ft 9in mean *(43.5 wl, 45.7 oa x 6.7 x 2.36m)*
Machinery: 1-shaft reciprocating HDA, 120 ihp = 10 kts
Armament: 1-7in, 1-5.5in, 2 small guns
Complement: 88

Name	Builder	Laid down	Launched	Comp	Fate
MOSHUN	London	—	1865	1867	Scrapped

JAPAN

The composite-built, full-rigged, *Hosho* was purchased in 1872.

HOSHO

Displacement: 316t normal
Dimensions: 144ft pp x 22ft x 6ft 9in (*43.9 pp x 6.7 x 2.05m*)
Machinery: 1-shaft reciprocating HDA, 240ihp = 11kts. Coal 810t
Armament: 1-7in, 1-5.5in
Complement: 65

Name	Builder	Laid down	Launched	Comp	Fate
HOSHO	A Hall & Co, Aberdeen	—	1868	1869	Scrapped 1899

Banjo was the smallest of the wooden-hulled vessels, and could be distinguished from the others by her prominent poop.

BANJO

Displacement: 656t normal
Dimensions: 154ft x 25ft 9in x 12ft 9in (*46.9 x 7.88 x 3.9m*)
Machinery: 1-shaft reciprocating HC, 590ihp = 10½kts. Coal 107t
Armament: 1-5.9in, 1-4.7in, 2-12pdr, 3 4-barrelled Nordenfeld MGs
Complement: 112

Name	Builder	Laid down	Launched	Comp	Fate
BANJO	Yokosuka N Yd	Feb 1877	July 1878	Aug 1880	Sold ? 1913

The armed paddle yacht *Raiden* was the ex-British iron-hulled HMS *Emperor*, built for and presented to the Shogun by Queen Victoria in 1856. The brigantine-rigged vessel was renamed *Banryu* but was acquired by the Imperial forces in March 1868. In April she deserted to the Shogunate forces and after the war was sold to an American commercial concern. She was re-purchased by the Emperor in 1873 and commissioned into the Imperial Navy as the *Raiden* in 1877.

RAIDEN

Displacement: 400t normal
Dimensions: 135ft pp x 22ft x 8ft 6in (*41.15 pp x 6.7 x 2.6m*)
Machinery: 1-shaft reciprocating HDA, 600 ihp = 9 kts
Armament: 4 ML
Complement: —

Name	Builder	Laid down	Launched	Comp	Fate
RAIDEN	Blackwall	—	1856	—	Sold 1888

These four schooner-rigged vessels were ordered under the 1882 Programme, the first two having iron hulls, the third a combination of iron and steel and the fourth an all steel hull. The *Akagi* was distinguished from the other ships by having a raised foc'sle. The ships were later re-armed, the *Chokai* and *Maya* having two 5.9in, which on the *Maya* were again altered to four 4.7in in 1906. The other two vessels were both given four 4.7in QF.

MAYA class

Displacement: 612t normal
Dimensions: 154ft 3in pp x 27ft x 9ft 9in (*47 pp x 8.2 x 2.95m*)
Machinery: 2-shaft reciprocating HCDA, 960ihp = 12kts. Coal 60t
Armament: 1-8.2in, 1-4.7in
Complement: 104

Name	Builder	Laid down	Launched	Comp	Fate
MAYA	Onohama, Kobe	May 1885	18.8.86	Dec 1887	Scrapped 1913
CHOKAI	Ishikawajima, Tokyo	Dec 1885	20.9.87	Oct 1888	Scrapped 1914
ATAGO	Yokosuka N Yd	July 1886	June 1887	Mar 1889	Lost 6.11.1904
AKAGI	Onohama, Kobe	June 1886	Aug 1888	July 1890	Sold 1912

The *Oshima* was notable for being the first ship to be equipped with Japanese built VTE machinery. The steel-hulled vessel showed strong French influence in her design, with pronounced ram, and the guns being sited on the foc'sle and poop and on sponsons amidships.

OSHIMA

Displacement: 630t normal
Dimensions: 175ft 6in pp x 26ft 3in x 9ft (*53.5 pp x 8 x 2.75m*)
Machinery: 2-shaft reciprocating VTE, 1200ihp = 16kts. Coal 140t
Armament: 4-4.7in QF, 5-3pdr QF
Complement: 130

Name	Builder	Laid down	Launched	Comp	Fate
OSHIMA	Onohama, Kobe	August 1889	Sept 1891	March 1892	Lost 17.5.1904

Uji was a shallow-draught vessel for use in coastal waters.

UJI

Displacement: 620t normal
Dimensions: 189ft 6in oa x 27ft 3in x 7ft (*57.8 oa x 8.4 x 2.1m*)
Machinery: 2-shaft reciprocating VTE, 1000ihp = 13kts. Coal 150t
Armament: 4-12pdr QF
Complement: 86

Name	Builder	Laid down	Launched	Comp	Fate
UJI	Kure N Yd	Sept 1902	14.3.03	Aug 1904	Scrapped 1932

TORPEDO BOATS, DESTROYERS

The contract for the first torpedo boats to be ordered on behalf of the Imperial Japanese Navy was awarded in 1879. Japan was then just recovering from a series of minor uprisings and there was little national interest in naval matters. Consequently the funds allocated for naval construction were small. Furthermore, the Imperial Navy lacked experience in maintaining and operating a large fleet. Consequently only small numbers of various types of warship were ordered so that sufficient experience would be gained in their operation. The initial order, for only four torpedo boats, was placed with the British firm of Yarrow, then the most experienced in the construction of torpedo boats. These vessels, *Nos 1–4*, were initially built at the Poplar yard and then dismantled for shipment to Japan, arriving during July 1880. The sections were then re-erected at the Yokosuka Navy Yard under the supervision of British engineers. The design of the boats closely resembled the Russian *Batoum*, Yarrow's most successful 100ft design produced in large numbers for various countries. The boats originally carried the TT on two spar mountings on the foredeck and one amidships. These were replaced in 1885 with rotating mounts with Schwarzkopf torpedoes. The gun was a twin Hotchkiss mounting carried on the after superstructure. The torpedo boats were removed from the fleet list in May 1899.

During the early 1880s the principles advanced by the French *Jeune École* theoreticians advocated fleets of fast, lightly armoured cruisers developed for commerce raiding, supported by small high speed torpedo craft for coastal defence. With the advent of the torpedo boat the *Jeune École* theorised that the day of the battleship was over and therefore smaller ships should be developed. This was the classic formulation of the weaker naval power unable to afford, build and operate large heavily armed warships. As a recently developed naval power, with limited funds available and with a large overseas Empire to manage, and possibly having to face much stronger naval adversaries, Japan was strongly influenced by these new French ideas. As a result a fleet concept was developed, based on a main body of cruisers supported by torpedo boats and gunboats. The 1885 Programme proposed that Japan build three fleets, each composed of six cruisers and six gunboats supported by a torpedo boat flotilla consisting of a transport carrying eight small torpedo boats and a second flotilla of six armoured torpedo boats. The last was an entirely new development, and Japan placed an order for such an experimental boat, the *Kotaka*, with Yarrow. The *Kotaka* was designed to Japanese requirements and was built in sections which were shipped to Japan for rebuilding. The *Kotaka* was laid down in Japan on 7 September 1886 and launched on 21 January 1887, commissioning on 10 October 1888. To meet the request for an armoured torpedo boat the deck and hull sides of the *Kotaka* around the machinery spaces were provided with 1in thick armour. The design did not prove a success and the concept of flotillas of armoured torpedo boats was not developed. The *Kotaka* was removed from the operational Fleet in April 1908 and the hulk scrapped during 1927.

Apart from the experimental *Kotaka* a total of 44 torpedo boats – 12 50t first class and 32 25t second class – were ordered under the 1885 Programme. Financial restrictions led to a modification of this programme, which in fact increased the number of 50t torpedo boats to 16 and reduced the number of small boats to 12. Having gained experience with the Yarrow designs the Japanese next turned to France, the other country with great experience in torpedo boat design and construction. Fourteen of the new torpedo boats, *Nos 5–14, 16–19*, were ordered to the standard French 35m design and two, *Nos 15, 20*, to a modified Normand 34m design. The *No 5* class differed from the French boats in having the bow TT sited as a spar mount rather than as an internally mounted tube. The other tube was sited amidships on a trainable mounting. The *No 15* class was similar to the French *No 130* but had a single funnel and TT sited as in the *No 5* class. The boats were all completed between 1892 and 1894 and were discarded about 1910.

In February 1888 the Navy Minister put forward plans to increase the fleet with 46 warships, including 30 torpedo boats. Financial restrictions again severely curtailed the plans and only three torpedo boats were sanctioned. These were *No 21*, a Normand design similar to the French *No 126*, and *Nos 22* and *23* built to a standard design by the German yard of Schichau. Another programme providing for the construction of 53 warships, including 20 100t torpedo boats and six 30t torpedo boats, was requested in September 1890, but this too was curtailed, only two torpedo boats, *No 24* from Normand and *No 25* from Schichau, being sanctioned.

With the conclusion of the Sino-Japanese war four Chinese torpedo boats were incorporated into the Imperial Japanese Navy (*Fukuriu* ex-*Foolung*, *Nos 26* and *27* ex-Yu Tui *Nos 1* and *3*), and a small 16t vedette. The success of the torpedo boats during the war led to a decision, in the post-war programme, to concentrate on the building up of a large force of torpedo boats. Under the Ten Year Naval Extension Programme, put forward in 1896, funds were requested for the construction of 16 120t, 37 80t and ten 54t torpedo boats. The 120t units consisted of the 15 vessels of the *Aotaka* class assembled in Japan from a design and materials supplied by Normand, and based on the French *Cyclone* and the *Shirataka* built in Germany to a Schichau design. The ships were completed between 1900 and 1904 and were scrapped after the First World War. The 80t units were *Nos 29–30* assembled from material supplied by Normand and based on the French Navy's *No 201*, and the *No 31* class, *Nos 31–38, 44–49, 60–61*, built to a modified Schichau 39m design. These latter boats were developed from the *No 22* class, with the funnel amidships and the midships TT sited in front of the funnel rather than abaft it as in *No 22*. The boats were all completed between 1900–1901 and surviving units scrapped 1913–1916. A further ten units, *Nos 39–43, 62–66*, were ordered from Yarrow to an improved Austrian *Viper* design. The last nine 80t torpedo boats to be ordered, *Nos 67–75*, were built to a Japanese design developed from the Schichau 39m design. The boats were built in Japanese yards and were completed just in time to take part in the Russo-Japanese war, being discarded in 1922–1923. The first Japanese designed and built torpedo boats were the ten 54t units of the *No 50* class, *Nos 50–59*. These boats were developed from the Normand 34m design with increased firepower and more modern machinery.

In addition to the torpedo boats ordered under the Ten Year Programme, 23 destroyers were also ordered. These comprised six Yarrow built *Ikazuchi* class vessels, six Thornycroft *Murakumo* type, two Yarrow *Akatsuki*, two Thornycroft *Shirakumo* and seven *Harusame* class built in Japan to a design developed from the *Shirakumo*. The *Ikazuchi* class were the first destroyers to be ordered for the Japanese Navy and were developed from the *Corrientes* class built for Argentina by Yarrow. The *Murakumo* vessels were developed from the British *Angler*. In both these designs the 12pdr gun was sited aft, and later in their careers they had the forward 6pdr gun replaced by a 12pdr. The *Akatsuki* and *Shirakumo* classes were enlarged editions of the *Ikazuchi* and *Murakumo*, equipped with more powerful machinery. The *Akatsuki* class were fitted with boilers developing higher steam pressure while the *Shirakumo* was equipped with an extra boiler.

The first all Japanese designed and built destroyers were the *Harusame* class. These were slightly larger than the *Shirakumo* and the Japanese designed machinery was very similar to the Thornycroft-built model on which it was based. The surviving units were all scrapped during the mid-1920s.

DESTROYERS

Sazanami (Author's collection)

IKAZUCHI class

Displacement, normal: 305t
Dimensions: 220ft 9in x 20ft 6in x 5ft 3in *(67.26 x 6.27 x 1.58m)*
Machinery, shaft/type: 2/VTE
hp/speed: 6000/31 kts
Armament: 1-12pdr, 5-6pdr, 2-18in TT
Complement: 55

MURAKUMO class

Displacement, normal: 275t
Dimensions: 208ft 6in x 19ft 6in x 5ft 6in *(63.5 x 5.96 x 1.7m)*
Machinery, shaft/type: 2/VTE
hp/speed: 5800/30 kts
Armament: 1-12pdr, 5-6pdr, 2-18in TT
Complement: 54

Kasumi in 1903 *(Author's collection)*

AKATSUKI class

Displacement, normal: 363t
Dimensions: 220ft 6in x 20ft 6in x 5ft 6in *(67.26 x 6.26 x 1.73m)*
Machinery, shaft/type: 2/VTE
hp/speed: 6500/31 kts
Armament: 2-12pdr, 4-6pdr, 2-18in TT
Complement: 59

The *Ikazuchi* class, all launched in 1899, were completed from 1899–1900, and comprised the following vessels: *Akebono*, *Ikazuchi*, *Inazuma*, *Niji*, *Oboro* and *Sazanami*. The *Murakomu* class, launched and completed from 1898–1900, comprised *Kagero*, *Murakumo*, *Shinonome*, *Shiranu*, *Usugumo*, and *Yugiri*. The *Akatsuki* class, comprising *Akatsuki* and *Kasumi*, was laid down in 1901 and launched and completed from 1901–1902.

Asashio in 1902 *(Author's collection)*

SHIRAKUMO class

Displacement, normal: 342t
Dimensions: 216ft x 20ft 9in x 6ft *(65.89 x 6.34 x 1.83m)*
Machinery, shaft/type: 2/VTE
hp/speed: 7000/31 kts
Armament: 2-12pdr, 4-6pdr, 2-18in TT
Complement: 59

HARUSAME class

Displacement, normal: 375t
Dimensions: 227ft x 21ft 6in x 6ft *(69.2 x 6.57 x 1.83m)*
Machinery, shaft/type: 2/VTE
hp/speed: 6000/29 kts
Armament: 2-12pdr, 4-6pdr, 2-18in TT
Complement: 55

Asashio and *Shirakumo* of the *Shirakumo* class were laid down, launched and completed from 1901–1902. The *Harusame* class, laid down *circa* 1902–1903, launched from 1902–1905, and completed from 1903–1905, comprised *Arare*, *Ariake*, *Asagiri*, *Fubuki*, *Harusame*, *Hayatori*, and *Murasame*.

TORPEDO BOATS 1st class

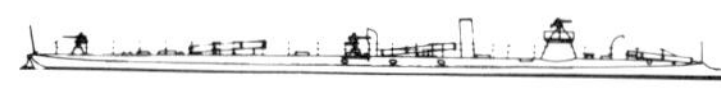

Kotaka, 1886

KOTAKA class

Displacement, normal: 203t
Dimensions: 165ft x 19ft x 5ft 6in *(50.3 x 5.8 x 1.7m)*
Machinery, shaft/type: 1/HC
hp/speed: 1217/19 kts
Armament: 4-1pdr, 6-14in TT
Complement: —

HAYABUSA class

Displacement, normal: 150t
Dimensions: 147ft 6in x 16ft x 4ft 9in *(45 x 4.9 x 1.5m)*
Machinery, shaft/type: 2/VTE
hp/speed: 4200/29 kts
Armament: 1-6pdr, 2-2½pdr, 3-14in TT
Complement: 30

SHIRATAKA class

Displacement, normal:	126t
Dimensions:	152ft 6in x 16ft 9in x 4ft 3in (*46.5 x 5.1 x 1.26m*)
Machinery, shaft/type:	2/VTE
hp/speed:	2600/28 kts
Armament:	3-2½pdr, 4-14in TT
Complement:	26

Kotaka was laid down on 7.9.1886, launched on 21.1.1887, and completed on 10.10.1888. The *Hayabusa* class, laid down from 1899–1903, launched from 1899–1904, and completed from 1900–1904, comprised the following vessels: *Aotaka*, *Azura*, *Chidori*, *Hashitaki*, *Hato*, *Hayabusa*, *Hibari*, *Kamome*, *Kari*, *Kasasagi*, *Kiji*, *Manazuru*, *Ootori*, *Sagi*, and *Tsubame*. *Shirataka* was laid down on 24.1.1899, launched on 10.6.1899, and completed on 27.4.1900.

2nd class

21, 24 class

Displacement, normal:	79t
Dimensions:	118ft x 12ft 6in x 5ft 3in (*36 x 3.9 x 1.6m*)
Machinery, shaft/type:	1/VTE
hp/speed:	1121/20¾ kts
Armament:	2-1pdr, 3-14in TT
Complement:	—

22, 23, 25 class

Displacement, normal:	85t
Dimensions:	128ft x 15ft 9in x 3ft 6in (*39 x 4.8 x 1.8m*)
Machinery, shaft/type:	1/VTE
hp/speed:	990/22½ kts
Armament:	2-1pdr, 3-14in TT
Complement:	20

29, 30 class

Displacement, normal:	88t
Dimensions:	121ft 6in x 13ft 6in x 4ft (*37 x 4.1 x 1.2m*)
Machinery, shaft/type:	1/VTE
hp/speed:	2000/22½ kts
Armament:	1-3pdr, 3-14in TT
Complement:	20

31–61 class

Displacement, normal:	89t
Dimensions:	128ft x 15ft 9in x 3ft 6in (*39 x 4.8 x 1.6m*)
Machinery, shaft/type:	1/VTE
hp/speed:	1260/24 kts
Armament:	2-2½pdr, 3-14in TT
Complement:	20

These classes were laid down from *circa* 1893–1900, launched from 1894–1901 and completed from 1894–1901.

39 class

Displacement, normal:	110t
Dimensions:	152ft 6in x 15ft 3in x 5ft 3in (*46.48 x 4.6 x 1.5m*)
Machinery, shaft/type:	1/VTE
hp/speed:	1920/26 kts
Armament:	2-3pdr
Complement:	20

67 class

Displacement, normal:	89t
Dimensions:	131ft 6in x 16ft x 3ft 3in (*40.1 x 4.9 x 1.3m*)
Machinery, shaft/type:	1/VTE
hp/speed:	1200/23½ kts
Armament:	2-3pdr, 3-14in TT
Complement:	24

The laying down dates for the *No 39* class are not known; however, they were launched from 1900–1901, and completed from 1901–1902. The *No 67* class was laid down from 1901–1902, launched from 1902–1903 and completed from 1903–1904.

3rd class

1–4 class

Displacement, normal:	40t
Dimensions:	100ft x 12ft 6in x 3ft 3in (*30.5 x 3.7 x 1m*)
Machinery, shaft/type:	1/HC
hp/speed:	430/22 kts
Armament:	2-1pdr, 3-14in TT
Complement:	–

Torpedo boat *No 8* (*Author's collection*)

5–19 class

Displacement, normal:	54t
Dimensions:	114ft 9in x 10ft 6in x 3ft (*35 x 3.5 x 0.9m*)
Machinery, shaft/type:	1/HC
hp/speed:	525/20 kts
Armament:	2-1pdr, 2-14in TT
Complement:	16

15, 20 class

Displacement, normal:	52t
Dimensions:	111ft 6in x 11ft 6in x 3ft (*34 x 3.5 x 0.9m*)
Machinery, shaft/type:	1/HC
hp/speed:	657/21 kts
Armament:	2-1pdr, 2-14in TT
Complement:	20

50–59 class

Displacement, normal:	52t
Dimensions:	111ft 6in x 11ft 6in x 3ft 3in (*34 x 3.5 x 0.9m*)
Machinery, shaft/type:	1/VTE
hp/speed:	660/20 kts
Armament:	1-2½pdr, 2-14in TT
Complement:	16

Germany

The German fleet in review at Kiel in 1895 for the visit of an Anglo-French squadron

The German State and the German Navy were creations of the second half of the 19th century. In 1860 Germany was still a patchwork of independent states. Only Prussia, the most powerful of these, had a navy, and even that was being created from virtually nothing. In 1864 Prussia, allied with Hapsburg Austria, the power that still dominated Germany, defeated Denmark in Schleswig-Holstein. In this war the Prussian Navy played a small part in the Battle of Heligoland between Danish and Austrian steam frigates. Two years later Prussia defeated Austria at Sadowa in a 'six weeks war' in which her fleet was not engaged. The removal of Austrian influence left Prussia free to found the North German Federation, to which her fleet was officially transferred in 1867.

THE CREATION OF THE IMPERIAL NAVY

In 1870 Bismarck successfully provoked France into declaring war, and the army of the German Federation broke the forces of Napoleon III. The overwhelming superiority of the French fleet had meant that the German ships, blockaded in thier ports, played little part in the struggle which enabled the King of Prussia to be proclaimed Kaiser of the German Reich at Versailles in 1871.

With Germany united it was inevitable that the new Imperial Navy should grow, more particularly as Germany was becoming the most powerful industrial nation in Europe. Germany soon had a naval force which was the equal of those of the traditional naval powers of Northern Europe, Denmark, Holland and Sweden. It was not until the 1890s that Kaiser Wilhelm II and Admiral Tirpitz, combined with the ever-growing industrial strength of Germany, created a situation in which the Imperial Navy attempted to equal the largest navies in existence. By 1905 the German Navy had surpassed the French in size and was rivalling the American Navy as the second largest in the world, while its ambitious plans for expansion made it a potent threat to even the Royal Navy.

THE 'RISK' THEORY

This was a deliberate threat, as Tirpitz and his allies were quite plainly aiming to challenge Britain, even before the Navy Law of 1898 set out the blueprint for expansion. This would have seemed a ridiculous challenge, even ten years before, when the German Navy, though well-trained and efficient, was still very definitely of the second rank. It was the phenomenal industrial growth of Germany, allied to the fact that the navy was one of the few genuinely national forces in a newly united country, that created the economic, financial and political support to make the challenge possible. A love-hate relationship with England, with the element of hate gradually increasing, provided an atmosphere in which Tirpitz could win general support for his 'Risk' theory. That is, the German Navy, it it could never actually achieve the strength of the Royal Navy, would be able to do enough damage in wartime to destroy the Royal Navy's superiority over its traditional rivals, particularly France and Russia. England could never risk this, and would therefore be blackmailed into supporting Germany on the Continent, and giving her concessions overseas.

However, this ploy recoiled on the blackmailer: by 1906 England, rather than give in to the threat, had reached an informal understanding with her old enemy France, and was about to do the same with Russia. In any case the British shipbuilding industry was far stronger and in most respects more efficient than the German, and provided the British people felt the threat was large enough to warrant the necessary expenditure, could easily outbuild Germany, or any other rival. The true measure of Tirpitz's policy would be seen in 1914, when Britain joined France and Russia against Germany, leaving it supported only by the weakened Austrian Empire.

THE ORIGINS OF THE IMPERIAL NAVY

An attempt had been made to set up a Federal German Navy in the first flush of enthusiasm for the 1848 revolutions. It was not a success, most of the men had to be recruited from abroad, and the ships purchased for it were sold by auction in 1853. Prussia had had a handful of rowing gunboats and schooners for coastal defence since the 1820s, but it was not until the early 1850s that it was decided to set up a navy, under Prince Heinrich of Prussia, large enough to make a real contribution to the defence of German waters. From the start the emphasis was on training: the new navy rapidly acquired a reputation for professionalism and seamanship which the German Navy never lost, and this was the real reason why it so quickly became a threat. Known as the Prussian Navy until 1866, and the Navy of the North German Federation before 1871, it is more convenient to use the blanket term German Navy from now on.

THE FIRST MODERN WARSHIPS

In 1859 the new navy began to receive its first steam corvettes and steam gunboats and it is from this point that the list below begins, rather than 1860. It was not until the mid 1860s that the fleet began to purchase armoured vessels, at first from foreign yards, the first German-built battleships being laid down in 1868. The last foreign-built ironclads were ordered in 1872, and the last major warship built abroad was the *Zieten* of 1876. After that, apart from a few torpedo

vessels, Germany relied entirely on her own shipbuilding resources. New naval dockyards were set up at Wilhelmshaven and Kiel, and considerable use was also made of private shipyards. A shaky start was made with the *Hansa*, and for a while building speeds were slow. Foreign industry (mainly British) had to be relied on for heavy castings and the best engines, but German yards soon proved to be competent builders of all types or warships. Before the 19th century was over, one yard, Schichau at Stettin, had scored a great export success with its torpedo boat and destroyer designs, proving itself the equal of the British builders Thornycroft and Yarrow and the French Le Normand yard. By the mid 1870s the then head of the German Navy, General von Stosch, could feel he was succeeding in his aim to produce a good navy of the second rank, adequate for coast defence and covering Germany's overseas commitments, with sufficient numbers of ironclads, curising ships and gunboats.

During the late 1870s and 1880s the emphasis began to shift. The new head of the navy, General von Caprivi, was particularly keen on the new underwater weapons, the mine and torpedo, and it is from this time that Germany began to build up formidable and well-trained torpedo flotillas and also began building mines which in 1914 proved to be the best in the world. Out of the interest in torpedo craft came the world's first genuine light cruisers, but the construction of larger vessels was neglected, and only a few small coastal defence battelships were completed.

THE TIRPITZ ERA

The 1890s saw a new phase, with Kaiser Wilhelm II coming to the throne, and an increasing public interest in naval expansion. This culminated in Tirpitz's appointment as Secretary of State for the Navy, in 1897. A year later the First Naval Law provided for a navy of 19 battleships, 8 coastal defence ships, and 12 heavy and 30 light cruisers by 1903. Two years later a new programme was laid down, to build a navy of 38 battleships, 14 heavy cruisers, 34 light cruisers and 96 destroyers by 1920. British reactions heightened the atmosphere of tension and then came the blow which temporarily halted the German construction programme of major ships. The *Dreadnought* and *Invincible* presented completely new ideas regarding the design of capital ships, so that more new designs had to be produced to rival them.

By any standards the growth of the German Navy from nothing to the second in the world in under 50 years was an impressive achievement. The development spanned less than one lifetime, indeed there was one young German who wished to become a naval officer in the middle of the last century, could not do so in his own country, and so joined the Royal Navy. In 1914, ironically, Prince Louis of Battenburg was First Sea Lord when the First World War broke out.

THE GROWTH OF THE GERMAN NAVY

	1860	1865	1870	1875	1880	1885	1890	1895	1900	1905
Battleships	—	—	5	5	9	12	12	21	24	29
Heavy cruisers	2	3	5	5	11	9	6	2	6	9
Light cruisers	1	3	4	6	7	12	20	25	26	34
Torpedo craft	—	—	—	6	7	28	77	99	92	124

In the above table battleships include coast defence battleships and ironclads of all kinds, heavy cruisers include all the larger cruising ships, and light cruisers the smaller ones. Gunboats and other light vessels are not included.

ARMAMENT

Although some of the first vessels had SB or RML gùns, the German Navy adopted Krupp BL guns at an early date, and the vast majority of the ships listed below had BL guns of one kind or another. The standard German QF anti-torpedo boat gun in the 1880s and 1890s was the five-barrelled revolving Hotchkiss 37mm. The approximate Imperial measure equivalents of the calibres of guns and torpedo tubes in general use with the German Navy are as follows: 280mm = 11in; 260mm = 10in; 240mm = 9.4in; 210mm = 8.2in; 170mm = 6.7in; 150mm = 5.9in; 125mm = 5in; 120 mm = 4.7in; 105mm = 4.1in; 88mm = 3.5in; 87mm = 3.5in; 50mm = 2in; 37mm = 1.5in. *Torpedo tubes:* 350mm = 14in; 450mm = 18in.

STRENGTH OF THE PRUSSIAN FLEET 1860

Steam corvettes: *Arcona, Gazelle*
Steam paddle frigates: *Barbarossa* (ex-Cunarder *Britannia*. Hulked 1865, torpedoed in experiments 1880); *Danzig* (launched 1851 at Danzig, burnt out 1869); *Loreley* (launched 1859 at Danzig, sold 1896)
Sailing frigates: *Gefion* (ex-*Eckernförde*, ex-*Gefion*, captured from the Danes when she grounded in 1848, broken up 1891); *Thetis* (built for the Royal Navy in 1846, exchanged with another vessel for two steam gunboats at the time of the Crimean War, broken up 1895)
Sailing corvettes: *Amazone* (built 1843 and lost in a storm 1861)
Armed steam yacht: *Grille* (built in France 1857, later rebuilt, broken up 1920)
Transport: *Mercur* (built 1847, broken up 1861)
Schooners: *Hela, Frauenlob* (built 1853/5, scrapped in 1871, lost in 1860)
Steam gunboats: The first of the *Jäger* and *Chamäleon* class were coming into service
Rowing and sailing gunboats: 42
Unarmed steamer: *Royal Viktoria*
TOTAL: Approximately 55 vessels mounting about 270 guns in all.

CAPITAL SHIPS

German battleship development up to 1906 can best be seen as a four-stage process. Initially in the mid 1860s a number of vessels already begun for other customers and designed by the yards concerned were purchased from British and French builders as the quickest way of building up a naval force. By these means two mediocre turret ships, *Prinz Adalbert* and *Arminius,* and a powerful central battery vessel, *Konig Wilhelm,* were acquired. Two other central battery ships were ordered, *Kronprinz* and *Friedrich Karl,* from Britain and France respectively, to German requirements.

The period of 'job lots' obtained from abroad was followed by one in which Germany attempted to build up a reasonably uniform ironclad fleet of adequate power. Four vessels were ordered from German yards between 1868 and 1870. One was the small and unsatisfactory *Hansa,* but the remaining three were an adequate class of central battery ships, the *Grosser Kurfürsts.* As these were the first ships of their kind built in Germany, and since most of the yards were new foundations, it is hardly surprising that they all took a long time to complete. Meanwhile another pair of British designed and built central battery ships, the *Kaisers,* were ordered.

Thus by the mid-1870s Germany had built, or was building, a force consisting mainly of central battery ironclads, whose designs were either foreign or very derivative, and all of which were fairly conventional by the standards of the time. Having acquired a fleet capable of acting on the high seas, the German Navy concentrated, for the next 15 years, on building coastal defence battleships. The first of these were the four *Sachsens,* an original and interesting design. The *Oldenburg,* which followed, was an anachronism of little fighting value, only ordered because political conflicts meant financial restraints too fierce to allow the purchase of anything better. This vessel was the only battleship laid down between 1876 and 1888, when the *Siegfried,* the first of a large class of coastal defence ships, was laid down. These bore more resemblance in size and fighting power to the ships of Germany's neighbours in Scandinavia and Holland than they did to the much larger battleships of the major powers. Their chief distinction was an unusual, but also unnecessarily complicated, arrangement of the forward guns.

While these small vessels were still being laid down, the four much larger *Brandenburgs* were begun, and with these ships the German Navy entered the pre-dreadnought era. The third turret amidships in these vessels was a daring innovation but was not justified by success. The remaining pre-dreadnought classes, the *Kaisers, Wittelsbachs, Braunschweigs* and *Deutschlands* were much more conventional designs, showing a steady but not spectacular development. Their most notable features were lighter main guns and heavier secondary guns than the majority of their contemporaries. Several of the secondary guns were, unusually for the time, in turrets instead of casemates. Though in most respects workmanlike designs, there were a number of weaknesses, such as the arrangement of the magazines for the secondary armament, almost certainly the cause of the *Pommern's* destruction by a single torpedo. None of the classes compares well with their British contemporaries. It was not until after Germany began building dreadnoughts that her naval architects were to enter their brief but brilliant period of success, producing world-beating capital ship designs.

PRINZ ADALBERT *ironclad ram*

Displacement: 1535t
Dimensions: 186ft 8in oa, 165ft 7in wl x 32ft 6in x 16ft 6in (*56.9 oa, 50.48 wl x 9.92 x 5.02m*)
Machinery: 2-shaft HSE, 1200ihp = 10kts
Armour: Wrought iron. Belt 5in, tower 4½in
Armament: 1-210mm, 2-170mm
Complement: 130

Name	Builder	Laid down	Launched	Delivered	Fate
PRINZ ADALBERT	Arman Bros	1863	1864	10.7.65	BU 1878

This ironclad ram, originally known as the *Cheops,* was under construction at Bordeaux for the Confederacy, to her builders' design, together with a sister ship, *Stonewall Jackson,* later the Japanese *Adzuma.* She was purchased for the Prussian Navy in June 1865, but not put into service until a year later. She was not a particularly good bargain, being a bad seaboat, and the timbers of her composite hull rapidly fell prey to rot. Though the Prussians replaced her original intended armament of three 32pdrs with bigger guns in the five-ported bow position and in the two-gun octagonal citadel abaft the funnel, she could not be considered a particularly powerful ship. She was schooner-rigged. She was placed in reserve because of wood rot as early as October 1871, and disarmed in 1875/6.

Prinz Adalbert as completed 1865

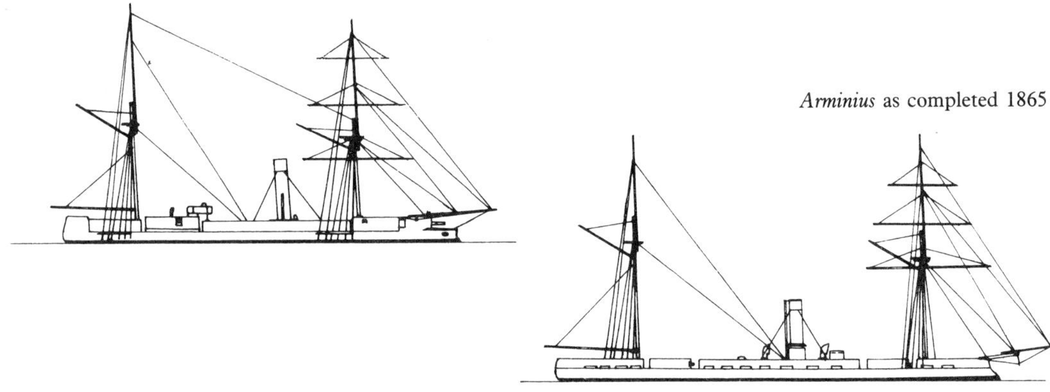

Arminius as completed 1865

ARMINIUS *turret ship*

Displacement: 1800t
Dimensions: 207ft 4½in oa, 202ft 1in wl x 35ft 9in x 14ft 11in (*63.21 oa, 61.6 wl x 10.9 x 4.55m*)
Machinery: 1-shaft HSE, 1440ihp = 11kts
Armour: Wrought iron. Belt 4½in, turrets 4½in
Armament: 4-210mm
Complement: 132

Name	Builder	Laid down	Launched	Purchased	Fate
ARMINIUS	Samuda Bros	1863	20.8.64	22.4.65	BU 1902

Arminius was a twin-turret monitor of the Coles type constructed as a speculation by her London builders. Her original armament was to have consisted of bronze 72pdr guns. Her waterline was protected by a belt of wrought iron armour 4½in thick amidships, on a teak backing, while similar thicknesses protected the turrets. In 1870 her schooner rig was removed, and later she was given a flying deck over the turrets. Four 37mm revolver cannon and a 350mm torpedo tube were added to her armament in 1881. By this time, after some service as a guard ship, she was being used as an engineers' instruction vessel. After 1892 her main use was as an ice-breaker at Kiel, though she was not taken out of service until 1901.

Friedrich Carl in 1888 with barque rig

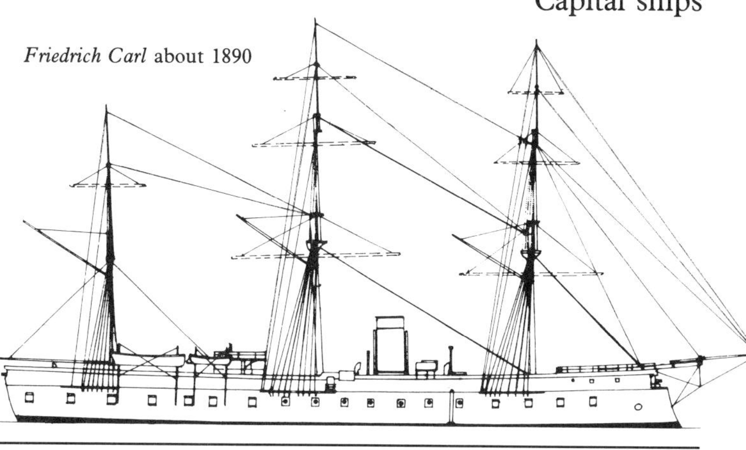

Friedrich Carl about 1890

FRIEDRICH CARL *central battery ironclad*

Designed and built at Toulon, this ship-rigged central-battery ship was originally intended to carry twenty-six 72pdrs. The wrought iron armour was backed, as usual, by thick teak planks. She was considered an excellent seaboat, and later had six revolving cannon and five 350mm torpedo tubes added. In 1892 she was relegated to a torpedo school ship. In 1902 she was renamed *Neptun*, but was sold three years later.

Displacement: 6822t
Dimensions: 308ft 10in oa, 299ft wl x 54ft 6in x 26ft 5in (*94.14 oa, 91.13 wl x 16.6 x 8.05m*)
Machinery: 1-shaft HSE, 3550ihp = 13½kts
Armour: Wrought iron. Belt 5in-4½in, battery 4½in
Armament: 16-210mm
Complement: 531

Name	Builder	Laid down	Launched	Comp	Fate
FRIEDRICH CARL	Cie des Forges et Ch	1866	16.1.67	3.10.67	BU 1906

Kronprinz about 1890

Kronprinz before the open bow was closed in

KRONPRINZ *central battery ironclad*

Though she was built on the Thames to a design by Edward Reed, *Kronprinz* was broadly similar to her French-built contemporary *Friedrich Carl*. The main points of difference were the British design's less prominent ram and two funnels. Armour and armament were similar, though *Kronprinz* was originally intended for thirty-two 72pdrs, only some of which would have been inside her central protected battery. QF guns and torpedoes were added in the same numbers as in *Friedrich Carl*. She was used as a machinery hulk at Kiel until sold in 1921.

Displacement: 6197t
Dimensions: 293ft 5in oa, 289ft 4in wl x 50ft x 25ft 9in (*89.44 oa, 88.2 wl x 15.2 x 7.85m*)
Machinery: 1-shaft HSE, 4870ihp = 14½kts
Armament: 16-210mm
Complement: 541

Name	Builder	Laid down	Launched	Comp	Fate
KRONPRINZ	Samuda Bros	1866	6.5.67	17.9.67	Hulked 1901

KÖNIG WILHELM *central battery ironclad*

Displacement: 10,591t
Dimensions: 368ft 1in oa, 356ft 3½in wl x 60ft x 28ft (*112.2 oa, 108.6 wl x 18.3 x 8.56m*)
Machinery: 1-shaft HSE, 8440ihp = 14¼kts
Armour: Wrought iron. Belt 6in-12in, battery 8in-6in, deck 2in
Armament: 18-240mm, 5-210mm
Complement: 730

Name	Builder	Laid down	Launched	Comp	Fate
KÖNIG WILHELM	Thames Iron Wks	1865	25.4.68	20.6.69	Sold 1921

Reed-designed central battery ship, begun as the Turkish *Fatikh*. While still on the stocks she was purchased for the German Navy, originally under the name *Wilhelm*, as an armoured frigate. She was for some time the largest and most powerful ship in the German Navy, and served as flagship.

She was reboilered by Wilhelmshaven Dockyard between 1878 and 1882, as part of a thorough repair after the collision with *Grosser Kurfürst*, and was also given a stronger ram. By the 1890s she was carrying one less 210mm but had added seven 150mm, four 80mm guns, six 37mm automatic cannon and five 350mm torpedo tubes. In 1895/6 a major rebuild by Blohm & Voss converted her to a heavy cruiser, in the same way as several of her British contemporaries. She retained her main battery of 240mm guns, and also the torpedo tubes, but the rest of her armament now consisted of one 150mm and sixteen 88mm. Her ship rig was reduced to two military masts with fighting tops, and a small mizzen mast was soon removed. The refit could not prevent her from being obsolete, but there was still much life left in the strong old hull, and in 1907, after three years as a harbour ship, she became the school ship of the Naval Academy, with only the sixteen 88mm guns left, reduced by 1915 to only four guns.

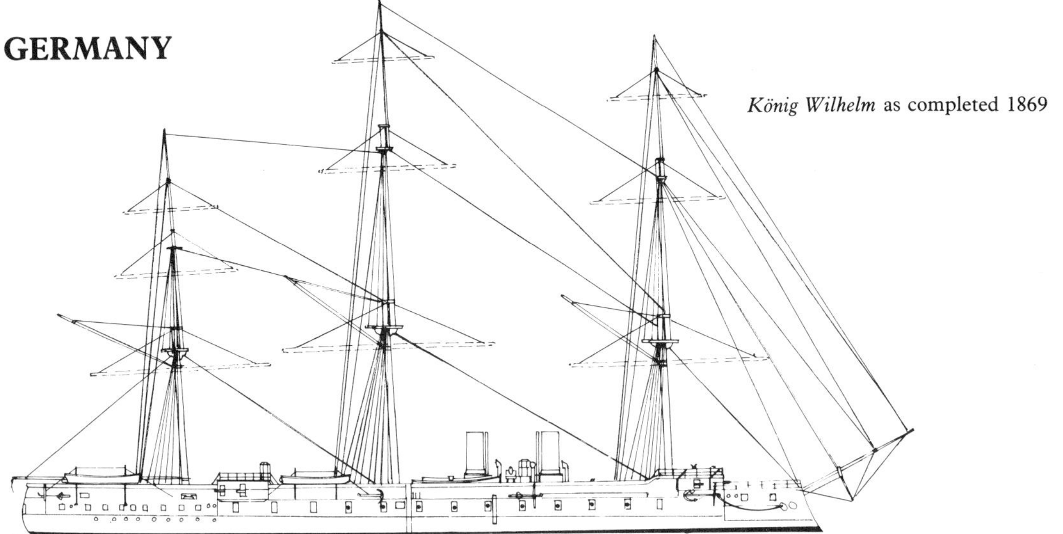

König Wilhelm as completed 1869

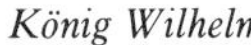

König Wilhelm

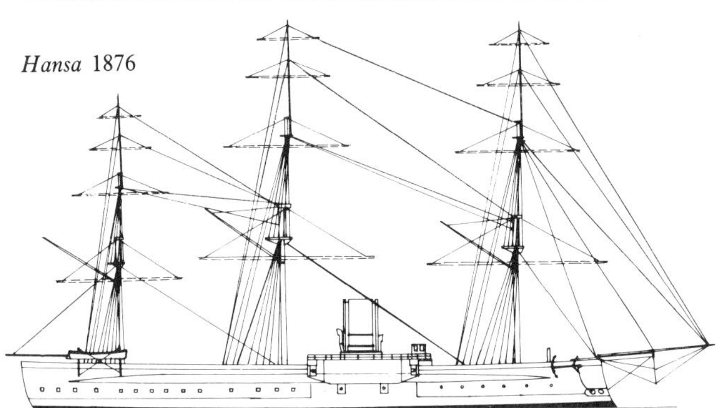

Hansa 1876

Hansa was the first armoured ship designed and built in Germany. She was not a great success, principally because the iron of her hull was corroding badly even before her long building period was over. She was not particularly handy, but as a first effort this small central battery ship, classed as an armoured corvette, was not a negligible vessel. The casemate contained all the guns, four firing on the broadside on the lower level, four, with angled ports and cut away sides to give some degree of end-on fire, on the upper deck.

After a short period of overseas service she became a guard ship. As a hulk she was used for training stokers till broken up in 1906.

HANSA *central battery ironclad*

Displacement: 4334t
Dimensions: 241ft 1in oa, 235ft 4in wl x 46ft 3in x 22ft 3in (*73.5 oa, 71.73 wl x 14.1 x 6.8m*)
Machinery: 1-shaft HSE, 3275ihp = $12\frac{1}{2}$kts
Armour: Belt $4\frac{1}{2}$in-6in, battery $4\frac{1}{2}$in
Armament: 8-210mm
Complement: 399

Name	Builder	Laid down	Launched	Comp	Fate
HANSA	Danzig DYd	1868	26.10.72	19.5.75	Hulked 1888

The original 1868 design for this class showed them as central battery ships, and *Grosser Kurfürst* was laid down as such. However, the design was reworked in the next year, with two turrets replacing the central casemate. *Grosser Kurfürst* was altered on the stocks, which was one reason why she was so long building. Another was that the Royal, later Imperial, Dockyards which built her and *Friedrich der Grosse* were still being established. It is not, perhaps, surprising that a longer established commercial yard should begin last and finish first with their sister, even though all three yards were new to the building of ironclads.

In this period of constant change it was most unusual for any navy to build as many as three major warships to the same design. Unfortunately, the advantages the Germans should have gained from a group of ships with the same characteristics were tragically short lived, as an error in helm orders caused the *Grosser Kurfürst* to be rammed and sunk by the *Konig Wilhelm*, with heavy loss of life, on her maiden voyage. Her two sisters served with the fleet until the 1890s. From 1903 both served as harbour ships, with *Preussen*, which had been heavily refitted in 1892, renamed *Saturn* so that her original name could be used for a new battleship. Both ended their days as coal hulks for torpedo boats.

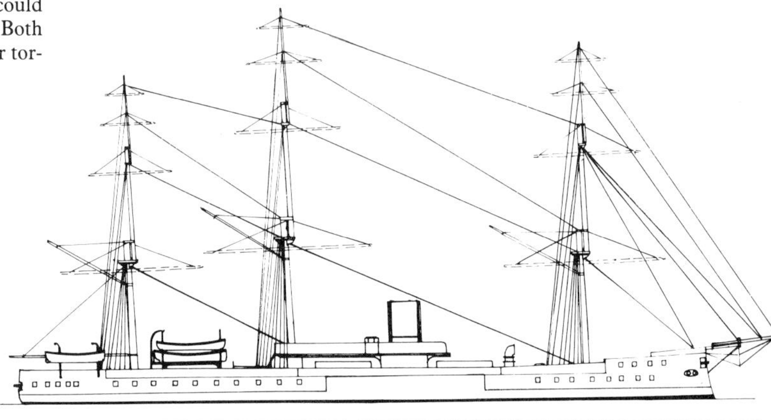

Preussen as completed 1876

GROSSER KURFÜRST class *central citadel ironclads*

Displacement: 7596t
Dimensions: 316ft 10in oa, 310ft wl x 53ft $0\frac{3}{4}$in x 23ft 6in (*96.59 oa, 94.5 wl x 16.3 x 7.18m*)
Machinery: 1-shaft HSE, 5000ihp = 14kts
Armour: Belt 4in-9in, Citadel 8in, turrets 8in
Armament: 4-260mm, 2-170mm
Complement: 500

Name	Builder	Laid down	Launched	Comp	Fate
GROSSER KURFÜRST	Wilhelmshaven DYd	1868	17.9.75	6.5.78	Collision 31.5.78
FRIEDRICH DER GROSSE	Kiel DYd	1869	20.9.74	22.11.77	Hulked 1906
PREUSSEN (ex-BORUSSIA)	Vulcan	1870	22.11.73	4.7.76	Hulked 1906

Friedrich der Grosse after refit, in the mid-1890s

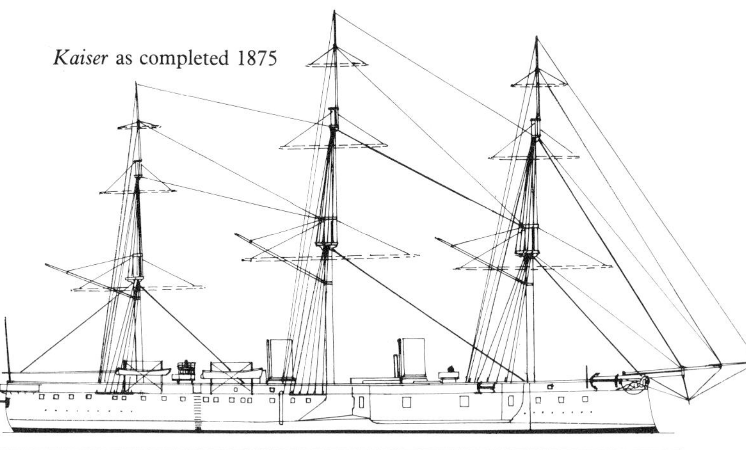

Kaiser as completed 1875

KAISER class *central battery ironclads*

The *Kaiser* class were Germany's last foreign-built capital ships. They were built on the Thames to an 1869 design by Sir Edward Reed, and their engines were built by Penn. These two central battery ships were classed as armoured frigates. All the side armour was mounted on a teak backing.

In 1882 both ships had seven 150mm added in place of the single 210mm. Four 80mm and six 37mm were also added. Both were considered good seaboats, and in the early 1890s they were given a new lease of life by being rebuilt as heavy cruisers at Wilhelmshaven. Their heavy ship-rig was removed and two military masts were fitted, and their heaviest guns were left, but while *Kaiser* was given one 150mm, six 105mm and nine 85mm, her sister, emerging from her refit two years later in 1897, had eight 150mm and eight 88mm. Both ships were given five torpedo tubes. After the rebuilds both served for a while abroad. *Kaiser*, made a harbour ship in 1904, was renamed *Uranus* a year later, while her sister, also as a harbour ship, was renamed *Jupiter* in 1904. *Deutschland* was taken out of service two years later, and used briefly as a target ship before her sale in 1908.

Displacement: 8799t
Dimensions: 293ft 1in oa, 290ft 4in wl x 62ft 8in x 26ft (*89.34 oa, 88.5 wl x 19.1 x 7.93m*)
Machinery: 1-shaft HSE, 5700ihp = 14½kts
Armour: Belt 10in-5in, casemate 8in-7in, deck 2in iron
Armament: 8-260mm, 1-210mm
Complement: 656

Name	Builder	Laid down	Launched	Comp	Fate
KAISER	Samuda Bros	1872	19.3.74	13.2.75	BU 1920
DEUTSCHLAND	Samuda Bros	1872	12.9.74	20.7.75	BU 1909

Kaiser about 1880

Baden in 1889

The *Sachsens*, classed as armoured corvettes, had a somewhat unusual main armament layout. Two guns were mounted side by side on the forecastle, in a pear-shaped barbette, and the others were mounted in the corners of a square barbette occupying the space just behind the four funnels, also arranged in a square. The patent sandwich wrought iron armour of the citadel and barbettes varied from 10in, though one source suggests it was 16in, to 8in thick.

All four ships were rebuilt in the second half of the 1890s with Krupp armour replacing the original, the funnels being reduced to one, compound engines fitted to increase the speed by at least a knot and the secondary armament changed to eight 88mm. From 1886 onwards they all carried three 350mm torpedo tubes. In 1906 *Würtemberg* became an experimental and instructional ship for torpedo warfare, with only four 88mm guns but seven 450mm torpedo tubes. *Sachsen* and *Bayern* became target ships in 1911 and were broken up in 1919, while *Baden* was used as a hulk for boom defence from 1912, relegated to a target ship in 1920, but not scrapped until 1939. *Würtemberg* was broken up in 1920.

Sachsen as completed 1878

SACHSEN class *central citadel ironclads*

Displacement: 7677t
Dimensions: 322ft 2in oa, 305ft 1in wl x 60ft 4in x 21ft 5in (*98.2 oa, 93.0 wl x 18.4 x 6.53m*)
Machinery: 2-shaft HSE, 5000ihp = 13½kts
Armour: Wrought iron. Citadel 10in-8in, deck 2in-2½in
Armament: 6-260mm, 6-87mm, 8-37mm revolving cannon
Complement: 317

Name	Builder	Laid down	Launched	Comp	Fate
SACHSEN	Vulcan	1875	21.7.77	20.10.78	Discarded 1910
BAYERN	Kiel DYd	1874	13.5.78	1.4.82	Discarded 1910
WÜRTEMBERG	Vulcan	1876	9.11.78	9.5.81	Discarded 1920
BADEN	Kiel DYd	1876	28.7.80	13.10.83	Discarded 1910

OLDENBURG *central battery ironclad*

Displacement: 5652t
Dimensions: 261ft 2in oa, 257ft 2in wl x 59ft x 20ft 8in (*79.8 oa, 78.4 wl x 18.0 x 6.3m*)
Machinery: 2-shaft HC, 3942ihp = 13½kts
Armour: Belt 8in-11¾in, battery 8in, bulkheads 6in
Armament: 8-240mm, 4-150mm, 2-87mm, 4-350mm TT
Complement: 389

Name	Builder	Laid down	Launched	Comp	Fate
OLDENBURG	Vulcan	1883	20.12.84	8.4.86	Discarded 1912

The *Oldenburg*, designed between 1879 and 1881, was considered to be of little fighting value by the time she was completed. She had originally been intended as a ship of the *Sachsen* class, but funds for this proved insufficient. Her main armament was mounted in a central battery, six guns on the main deck, two firing on the broadside, and the others set in embrasures to give an approach to end-on fire fore and aft. The remaining two 240mm guns were placed above the battery on the upper deck, firing on the broadside. Later the number of 87mm guns was increased to eight. Nicknamed the 'Flatiron', she became a harbour guard ship in 1900. After 1912 she continued to be used as a target ship. She was broken up in 1919.

Oldenburg in Aug 1887

Hagen, appearance as completed

SIEGFRIED class *coast defence battleships*

Displacement: 3691t
Dimensions: 259ft 2in oa, 250ft 8in wl x 49ft x 19ft (*79.0 oa, 76.4 wl x 14.9 x 5.74m*)
Machinery: 2-shaft TE, 5000ihp = 14½kts
Armour: Belt 7in-9½in (*Odin, Ägir* 7in-9in), deck 1¼in (*Odin, Ägir* 2¾in-2in), barbettes and turrets 8in
Armament: 3-240mm, 8-88mm (*Odin, Ägir* 10-88mm), 4-350mm TT (*Siegfried* 6-350mm, *Odin, Ägir* 3-450mm TT)
Complement: 276

Name	Builder	Laid down	Launched	Comp	Fate
SIEGFRIED	Germaniawerft	1888	10.8.89	19.4.90	Sold 1919
BEOWULF	Weser	1890	8.11.90	1.4.92	Sold 1919
FRITHJOF	Weser	1890	21.7.91	23.2.93	Sold 1919
HEIMDALL	Wilhelmshaven DYd	1891	27.7.92	7.4.94	Sold 1919
HILDEBRAND	Kiel DYd	1890	6.8.92	28.10.93	Sold 1919
HAGEN	Kiel DYd	1891	21.10.93	2.10.94	BU 1919
ODIN	Danzig DYd	1893	3.11.94	7.7.96	Sold 1919
ÄGIR	Kiel DYd	1892	3.4.95	15.1.96	Sold 1919

These small armoured ships, intended for the defence of the approaches to German harbours, had an unusual distribution of their main armament, the two forward turrets being mounted side by side. The last two ships, besides the different armament and *Ägir's* two funnels, differed from the others in their armour protection and also in having fighting tops. The earlier ships were later given ten 88mm, and all were rebuilt between 1900 and 1904 except *Hagen*, whose rebuild was from 1898 to 1900. The rebuild included reboilering, and all ships emerged with two funnels instead of the original one. They were lengthened to 282ft 6in oa and to 275ft 6in wl and the tonnage was increased to 4158t.

In 1915 this class were reclassified as coastal defence ships after a brief attachment to the fleet, but a year later all were disarmed. Their histories, after being removed from service and sold in 1919, are more than usually interesting. It was planned to convert *Siegfried* to a salvage ship, but this fell through and she was broken up in 1920. *Beowulf* had briefly been used as an icebreaker before being sold, but was broken up in 1921. *Frithjof* was rebuilt in 1923 as a motor cargo ship, and not broken up till 1930. A conversion of *Heimdall* into a slavage ship never materialised and she was broken up in 1921. *Hildebrand* was towed away to Holland for breaking up, but was wrecked on the Dutch coast, her remains being finally broken up in 1933. *Hagen* was broken up after her sale, but *Odin* was converted into a motor cargo ship in 1922, and served until broken up in 1935. *Ägir* underwent the same conversion, only to be wrecked in 1929.

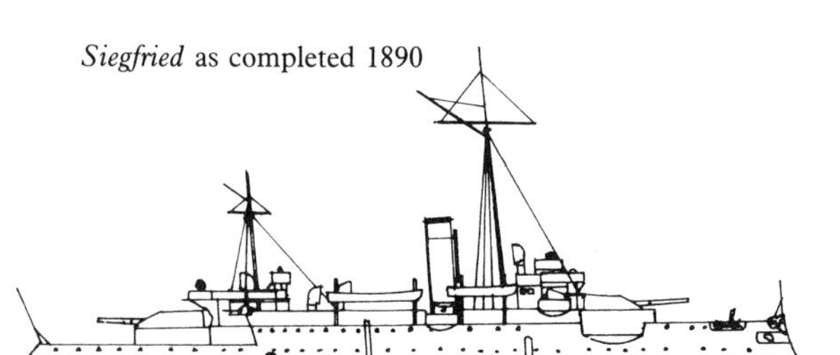
Siegfried as completed 1890

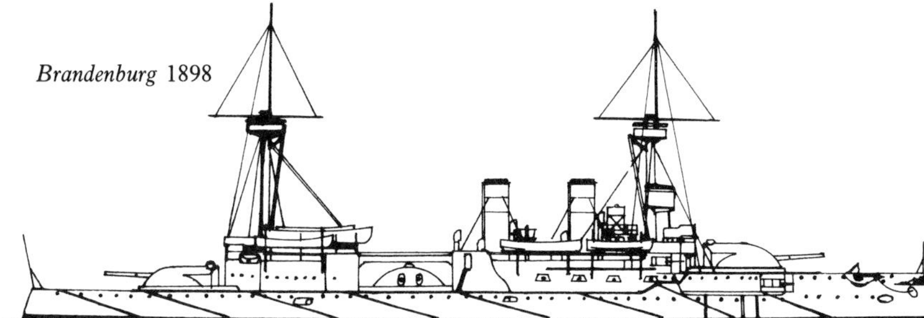
Brandenburg 1898

Wörth in her early years

The *Brandenburg* class were unusual amongst the pre-dreadnoughts of their era in having two different lengths of gun in their main armament. While the fore and aft turrets were 40 cal, the midship turret had 35 cal guns, to make them short enough to be trained round from one side to the other. This midships mounting proved unsatisfactory—the guns were too near the deck and caused blast damage when fired — and the secondary armament was weak by the standards of the time. However, the Germans were at last building sea-going battleships with a powerful main armament. An extra pair of 105mm guns were added later, and one torpedo tube was removed. These were the first German warships to be fitted with radio. In 1910 two of the class went to Turkey as the *Heireddin Barbarossa*, (ex-*Kurfürst Friedrich Wilhelm)*, torpedoed by a British submarine in 1915, and as the *Torgud Reis*, (ex-*Weissenburg*), which the Turks hulked as a school ship in 1924 and broke up in 1938. The remaining pair were transferred to coastal defence in 1915, disarmed and used as accommodation ships in 1916, and discarded in 1919. A conversion of *Brandenburg* to a target ship was never completed.

BRANDENBURG class *battleships*

Displacement: 10,501t
Dimensions: 379ft 7in oa, 373ft 8in wl x 64ft x 26ft (*115.7 oa, 113.9 wl x 19.5 x 7.9m*)
Machinery: 2-shaft TE, 10,200ihp = 16½kts
Armour: Belt 12in-16in, barbettes 12in, gun house 5in
Armament: 6-280mm, 6-105mm, 8-88mm, 12 MGs, 6-450mm TT
Complement: 568

Name	Builder	Laid down	Launched	Comp	Fate
BRANDENBURG	Vulcan	1890	21.9.91	19.11.93	BU 1920
KURFÜRST FRIEDRICH WILHELM	Wilhelmshaven DYd	1890	30.6.91	19.11.93	Sold to Turkey 1910
WEISSENBURG	Vulcan	1890	14.12.91	5.6.94	Sold to Turkey 1910
WÖRTH	Germaniawerft	1890	6.8.92	31.10.93	BU 1919

This class of ships, all named after German Emperors, set the pattern for German pre-dreadnoughts with their comparatively light main armament, and their triple-screw installation. With these ships Germany was becoming a major naval power, but the design still compares unfavourably with that of British contemporaries. The secondary armament was heavy, with six of the forecastle deck guns being mounted in turrets instead of casemates.

Between 1907 and 1910 these ships were reconstructed, with taller funnels, much of the superstructure cut down, and four of the 150mm guns and one of the torpedo tubes removed. The tertiary armament of 88mm guns was repositioned, several being placed on the upper deck, from which the 150mm had been taken, instead of their original much higher position, while their number was increased by two. *Kaiser Wilhelm II*, with a complement increased by 63, had been the fleet flagship until 1906. All were disarmed and used as hulks in 1916, being quite useless for war by that time.

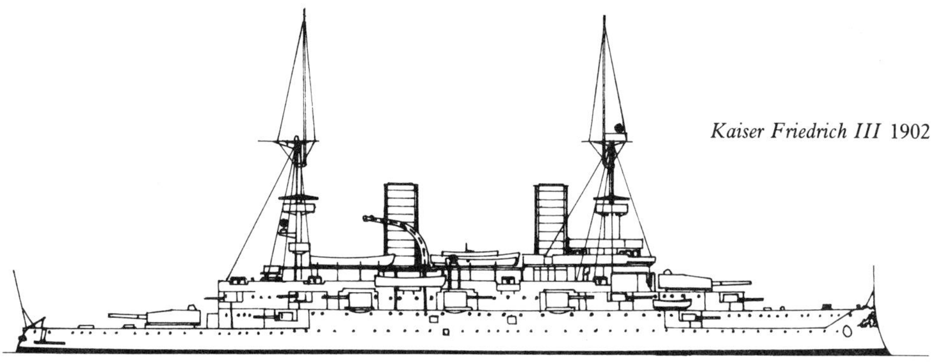

Kaiser Friedrich III 1902

KAISER class *battleships*

Displacement: 11,599t
Dimensions: 411ft oa, 396ft 9in wl x 67ft x 27ft (*125.3 oa, 120.9 wl x 20.4 x 8.25m*)
Machinery: 3-shaft TE, 14,000ihp = 17kts
Armour: Belt 12in, deck 2½in, ammunition hoists 10in
Armament: 4-240mm, 18-150mm, 12-88m, 12 MGs, 6-450mm TT
Complement: 651

Name	Builder	Laid down	Launched	Comp	Fate
KAISER FREIDRICH III	Wilhelmshaven	1895	31.7.96	7.10.98	BU 1920
KAISER WILHELM II	Wilhelmshaven	1896	14.9.97	7.10.98	BU 1921
KAISER WILHELM DER GROSSE	Germaniawerft	1898	18.10.99	4.2.1902	BU 1920
KAISER BARBAROSSA	Schichau	1898	21.4.1900	10.6.1901	BU 1920

Kaiser Wilhelm der Grosse about 1900

GERMANY

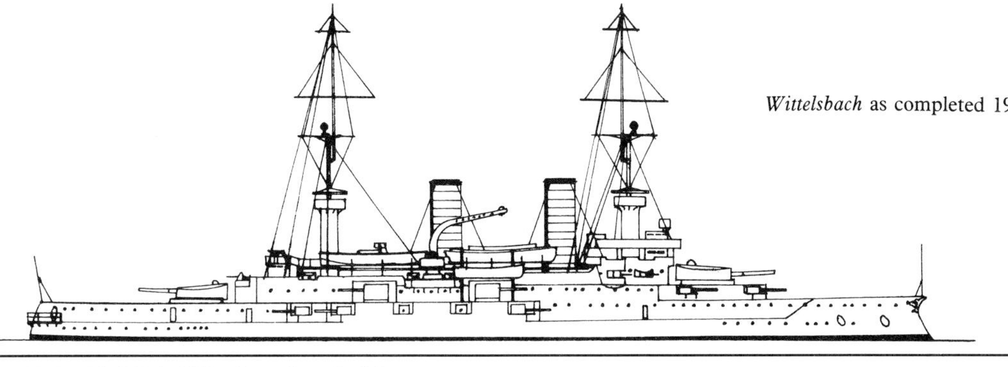

Wittelsbach as completed 1902

The *Wittelsbach* class were the first battleships to be ordered under Tirpitz's Navy Law of 1898 but marked no great step forward in German design as they resembled their predecessors in most respects, although the armour belt was rather more extensive. By 1916 they were considered useless as fighting ships and disarmed. *Zähringen* was used as a target ship in 1917. After the end of the war she was hulked, but in 1926 she was converted to a radio controlled target ship, with only a two-shaft machinery installation. She was bombed and sunk at Gdynia (Gotenhafen) in 1944 and broken up where she lay. *Wittelsbach* and *Schwaben* were converted to depot ships for minesweeping motor launches, carrying 12 each, but they did not last long in this role.

WITTELSBACH class *battleships*

Displacement: 12,596t
Dimensions: 416ft oa, 410ft 9in wl x 74ft 9in x 26ft 4in (*126.8 oa, 125.2 wl x 22.8 x 8.04m*)
Machinery: 3-shaft TE, 15000ihp = 17½kts
Armament: 4-240mm, 18-150mm, 12-88mm, 12 MGs, 6-450mm TT
Complement: 683

Name	Builder	Laid down	Launched	Comp	Fate
WITTELSBACH	Wilhelmshaven	1899	3.7.1900	15.10.02	BU 1921
WETTIN	Schichau	1899	6.6.1901	1.10.02	BU 1922
ZÄHRINGEN	Germaniawerft	1899	12.6.1901	25.10.02	Discarded 1920
SCHWABEN	Wilhelmshaven	1900	19.8.1901	13.4.04	BU 1921
MECKLENBURG	Vulcan	1900	9.11.1901	25.6.03	BU 1921

Schwaben about 1906
Aldo Fraccaroli Collection

Hessen after the First World War

Besides being bigger and faster than the previous class the *Braunschweigs* also carried heavier guns as both main and secondary armament, though still, in the former case, lighter than the 12in guns carried by the British battleships of the time. Visually they differed in carrying the forward main turret on the forecastle deck instead of mounted above it, and also they had three funnels. Their armour was the same thickness as the previous class, except for an increase of 10mm for the main armament.

Between 1916 and 1917 all were disarmed, except for *Lothringen* which retained ten 170mm for another year. In 1919 *Preussen* and *Lothringen* were converted to depot ships for minesweeping motor boats. Both were broken up in 1931. However, a section of the midships part of the hull of the *Preussen* was retained as a test bed for torpedoes, and named *Vierkant*. This part of the old ship was sunk by bombing in 1944, raised and not finally broken up till 1954. The remaining three ships of the class were rebuilt as coastal defence ships for the Reichsmarine in the 1920s, re-equipped with 280mm and 170mm guns (14 in *Hessen*, 12 in *Braunschweig* and 10 in *Elsass*), with four 88mm AA guns and four 500mm (20in) torpedo tubes. *Braunschweig* and *Elsass* were both hulked in 1931, the former being broken up shortly afterwards and the latter being sold to North German Lloyd in 1935. *Hessen* in her new guise as a target ship survived the war and was taken over by the Soviet Navy as the *Tsel* in 1946.

BRAUNSCHWEIG class *battleships*

Displacement: 14,167t
Dimensions: 419ft oa, 413ft 4in wl x 84ft x 26ft 7in (*127.7 oa, 126 wl x 25.6 x 8.1m*)
Machinery: 3-shaft TE, 17,000ihp = 18¼kts
Armament: 4-280mm, 14-170mm, 18-88mm, 4 MGs, 6-450mm TT
Complement: 743

Name	Builder	Laid down	Launched	Comp	Fate
BRAUNSCHWEIG	Germaniawerft	1901	20.12.02	15.10.04	BU 1931
ELSASS	Schichau	1901	26.5.03	29.11.04	Discarded 1931
HESSEN	Germaniawerft	1902	18.9.03	19.9.05	Converted to radio-controlled target ship 1935/6
PREUSSEN	Vulcan	1902	30.10.03	12.7.05	Discarded 1929
LOTHRINGEN	Schichau	1902	27.5.04	18.5.06	BU 1931

Except for different shaped funnels, a larger tertiary armament of 88mm guns, and a slightly thicker 9½in belt, with about 1in more armour on the main armament, Germany's last pre-dreadnoughts were very similar to the previous class. The weakness in the protection and magazine arrangements of the secondary armament was almost certainly the cause of the loss of the *Pommern* to one torpedo fired by a British destroyer at the Battle of Jutland, where these ships were the only pre-dreadnoughts present. Soon afterwards the class was re-allocated to secondary duties, *Deutschland* being disarmed, then discarded in 1920. The three survivors were rebuilt after the war, and then *Schlesien* and *Schleswig-Holstein* rebuilt again about 1930. The latter rebuild involved the trunking of the forefunnel into the midships one. Already the two ships concerned had replaced their 170mm with 150mm guns; 105mm AA guns later replaced the 88mm, while during the Second World War numbers of 40mm and 20mm light AA guns were added. Before the war both ships had served for a while as cadet schoolships, and both of their hulks were broken up after the war as they had been bombed in harbour.

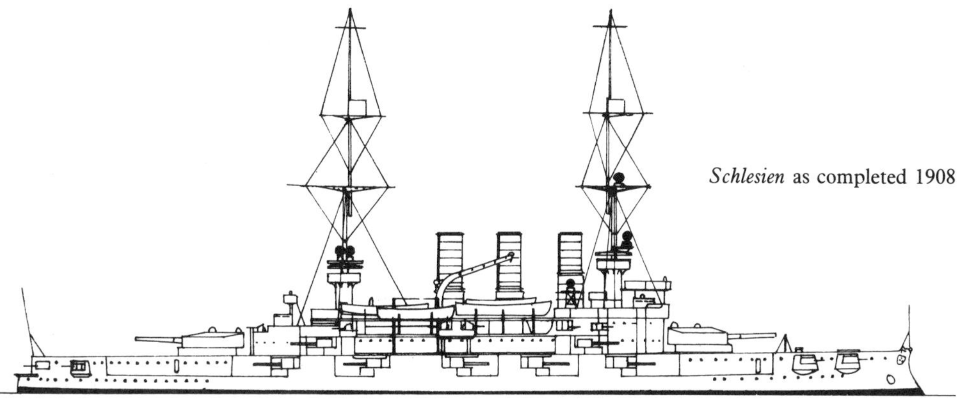

Schlesien as completed 1908

DEUTSCHLAND class *battleships*

Displacement: 13,993t
Dimensions: 418ft 8in oa, 413ft wl x 73ft x 27ft (*127.6 oa, 125.9 wl x 22.2 x 8.25m*)
Machinery: 3-shaft TE, 19,000ihp = 18½kts
Armament: 4-280mm, 14-170mm, 20-88mm, 4 MGs, 6-450mm TT
Complement: 743

Name	Builder	Laid down	Launched	Comp	Fate
DEUTSCHLAND	Germaniawerft	1903	19.11.04	3.8.06	BU 1920-22
HANNOVER	Wilhelmshaven	1904	29.9.05	1.10.07	Discarded 1935
POMMERN	Vulcan	1904	2.12.05	6.8.07	Torpedoed 1.6.16
SCHLESIEN	Schichau	1904	28.5.06	5.5.08	Mined and bombed 4.5.45
SCHLESWIG-HOLSTEIN	Germaniawerft	1905	7.12.06	6.7.08	Bombed 18.12.44

CRUISERS

Cruiser development in this period covers a wide variety of types, from frigates to *avisos*, a French word meaning despatch vessels, and from armoured cruisers to light cruisers. The category of cruisers merges at its lower end into colonial sloops and torpedo vessels. However, it may be useful to draw a broad distinction between two fundamentally different categories in the German Navy of this period. The first is those vessels intended for distant cruising, for acting as school ships and for service on foreign stations, the second is those ships, developing from torpedo vessels, which were meant for use in home waters, and were primarily intended for fighting rather than training or showing the flag. It is the second category which is of much greater interest, for it was here that German designs were most original and were responsible for developing an entirely new type of ship, the light cruiser.

The first category, cruising ships, can be subdivided into masted ships and true cruisers. Though this is basically a chronological division, masted ships for training and colonial use continued to be built well after the turn of the century. The original masted cruising vessels built for the German Navy were wooden-hulled ships classed as either frigates or corvettes, mainly built at Danzig Dockyard where good supplies of Baltic timber were available, though two half completed vessels were also purchased from a French yard. Basically similar iron-hulled vessels followed these classes, all with timber-sheathed hulls to enable the vessels to be coppered as a measure against fouling during long commissions in foreign seas. The earlier vessels were classed as corvettes, the later ones as cruisers, and there was a considerable variety in size and power, but all were intended as much for sailing as for a steaming. None showed any marked originality in design, but they were useful workhorses for the training of men and the policing of distant seas.

When the Germans started building protected cruisers and then armoured cruisers, classed as heavy cruisers, they were again content to follow foreign developments. The armoured cruisers, however, as cruiser equivalents of contemporary battleship designs, differed in much the same ways from their foreign contemporaries as did German battleships, which had a lighter main armament and a heavier secondary armament. When compared with their British contemporaries they do not show up particuarly well, in fact, with the possible exception of the last pair, *Scharnhorst* and *Gneisenau*, it is probably true to say that the armoured cruisers were Germany's worst designed and least battleworthy ships in service in 1905.

The German light cruiser evolved from what the Royal Navy would have called torpedo cruisers or torpedo gunboats. Germany had been interested in the potential of the Whitehead torpedo from very early on, and ordered a comparatively large torpedo vessel, the *Zieten*, from a British yard in 1875. Six years later two vessels, classed by the Germans as *avisos* but in fact the first true light cruisers, were laid down. They were the first cruiser-type vessels in which purely military factors were paramount, as against ones that contributed to cruising ability, and the first without sails. They were not unlike the later torpedo gunboats, but considerably larger. In the next 12 years comparatively few vessels of this type were built, but between them they provided experience of various permutations of size and armament, culminating in the *Hela*. Her contemporary, *Gefion*, although looking like the later light cruisers, was basically a smaller version of contemporary heavy cruisers, and does not fit into the development which produced the *Gazelle* class, the first of which were completing at the end of the century. This large class set the pattern for the next few years: comparatively small, sturdy ships, well armed and well fitted for their primary purpose of scouting in the North Sea or the Baltic, but also quite capable of overseas service. From this point on each new class of light cruisers added a few improvements to the initial excellent and well-balanced design. The one major difference was that all subsequent classes were named after cities.

Vineta about 1870

Arcona as completed 1859

The original design of these wooden, copper-sheathed, fully rigged frigates dated from 1854 and differed little from other ships of the same period and type. They spent most of their service overseas, *Arcona* serving as a school ship. In 1870 the first pair were rearmed with 17, later 8, 150mm guns, while a year earlier the later three had been given either 19 or 17 150mm and 2 125mm guns. The hulks of the last four ships were in existence until 1906, 1897, 1902 and 1904 respectively, when they were sold for breaking up.

ARCONA class *wooden screw frigates*

Displacement: 2353t; *Vineta, Hertha* 2464t; *Elisabeth* 2866t
Dimensions: 236ft oa, 208ft 6in wl x 42ft 8in x 21ft (*71.95 oa, 63.55 wl x 13.0 x 6.35m*); *Vineta, Hertha* 240ft 6in oa, 215ft wl x 42ft 4in x 21ft 5in (*73.32 oa, 65.5 wl x 12.9 x 6.53m*); *Elisabeth* 260ft oa, 234ft 6in wl x 43ft 3in x 21ft (*79.3 oa, 71.5 wl x 13.2 x 6.4m*)
Machinery: 1-shaft, hoisting screw, HSE, 1350ihp = 12kts
Armament: 6-68pdr, 20-36pdr; *Vineta, Hertha, Elisabeth* 28-68pdr only
Complement: 380

Name	Builder	Laid down	Launched	Comp	Fate
ARCONA	Danzig DYd	1855	19.5.58	15.4.59	Target ship, then BU 1884
GAZELLE	Danzig DYd	1856	19.12.59	22.4.61	Hulked 1884
VINETA	Danzig DYd	1860	4.6.63	3.3.64	Hulked 1884
HERTHA	Danzig DYd	1860	1.10.64	1.11.65	Hulked 1884
ELISABETH	Danzig DYd	1866	18.10.68	29.9.69	Hulked 1887

Copper-sheathed, ship-rigged vessels intended for overseas service, in which they spent most of their active lives. Both hulks were sold in 1891. The machinery was built in England. They were reboilered during their careers, and rearmed in 1869 with 17, later reduced to nine, 120mm guns.

NYMPHE class *wooden flush-decked screw corvettes*

Displacement: 1183t
Dimensions: 213ft oa, 192ft wl x 33ft 5in x 14ft 8in (*64.9 oa, 58.54 wl x 10.2 x 4.47m*)
Machinery: 1-shaft HSE, 800ihp = 12kts
Armament: 10-36pdr, 6-12pdr
Complement: 190

Name	Builder	Laid down	Launched	Comp	Fate
NYMPHE	Danzig DYd	1862	15.4.63	25.11.63	Hulked 1887
MEDUSA	Danzig DYd	1862	20.10.64	10.4.67	Hulked 1881

These ships were originally begun by their French builders for the Confederacy, then sold to Japan as the *Jeddo* and *Osaka*. On 13.5.1864 they were sold again to Prussia, as the Japanese had not been able to pay. They were full-rigged ships but performed much better under steam than under sail. After 1879 *Victoria* was rigged as a barque. Both were rearmed in 1872 with four 150mm, six 120mm and one 80mm. Later six Hotchkiss revolving 37mm cannon were also added. *Augusta* was lost with all hands in the Gulf of Aden. *Victoria* was scrapped a year after being hulked. Both spent their service lives mostly overseas.

AUGUSTA class *wooden flush-decked screw corvettes*

Displacement: 2236t
Dimensions: 267ft 4in oa, 246ft 8in wl x 36ft 5in x 18ft 5in (*81.5 oa, 75.2 wl x 11.1 x 5.62m*)
Machinery: 1-shaft HSE, 1300ihp = 13½kts
Armament: 8-24pdr, 6-12pdr
Complement: 230

Name	Builder	Laid down	Launched	Comp	Fate
AUGUSTA	Arman Bros	1863	1864	3.7.64	Lost in hurricane 2.6.85
VICTORIA	Arman Bros	1863	1864	14.9.64	BU 1892

Nymphe during the 1870s

Augusta about 1870

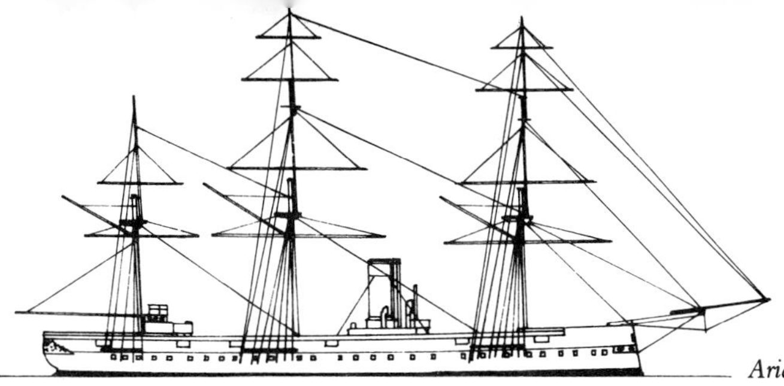

Ariadne as completed 1872

Freya was a longer version of the other two. These ram-bowed ship-rigged vessels were poor seaboats and sailed very badly, and in manoeuvring *Freya* was even worse than the other two. In 1882, four 37mm Hotchkiss revolving cannon were added to the armament. *Freya* was reduced to seven 150mm, and also to barque rig. All served abroad for most of their careers.

ARIADNE class *wooden flush-decked screw corvettes*

Displacement: 2039t; *Freya* 2368t
Dimensions: 223ft 7in oa, 216ft wl (*Freya* 280ft oa, 274ft 3in wl) x 35ft 5in x 18ft 8in (*68.16 oa, 65.8 wl (85.35 oa, 83.6 wl) x 10.8 x 5.7m)*
Machinery: 1-shaft CE, 2300ihp = 14kts (*Freya* 2800ihp = 15kts)
Armament: 6-150mm, 2-120mm; *Freya* 8-150mm only
Complement: 233; *Freya* 248

Name	Builder	Laid down	Launched	Comp	Fate
ARIADNE	Danzig DYd	1870	21.7.71	23.11.72	BU 1891
LUISE	Danzig DYd	1871	16.12.72	4.6.74	BU 1897
FREYA	Danzig DYd	1872	29.12.74	21.8.76	BU 1896

1. *Nixe* in Aug 1887

2. *Leipzig* with two funnels after her 1880 reboilering

1

2

These corvettes were sheathed, a layer of wooden planks over the hull below the waterline being covered by copper plating. The wood prevented electrolytic action between the copper and the iron of the hull. In 1878 the *Sedan*'s name was changed to *Prinz Adalbert* presumably to be tactful to the French, whose defeat at Sedan was less than a decade old. *Leipzig* was originally named *Thusnelda*, but this was changed before her launch. The vessels were ship-rigged with a straight bow. They were later fitted with four revolving cannon and two 350mm torpedo tubes each. In 1890 *Leipzig* was given two funnels as part of her reboilering. Both served mainly overseas. Their hulks were sold in 1921 and 1907 respectively.

LEIPZIG class *iron flush-decked corvettes*

Displacement: 4553t
Dimensions: 287ft oa, 285ft 5in x 46ft x 22ft 7in (*87.5 oa, 87.0 wl x 14.0 x 6.9m*)
Machinery: 1-shaft, lifting screw, HSE, 6050ihp = 15½kts
Armament: 12-170mm
Complement: 425

Name	Builder	Laid down	Launched	Comp	Fate
LEIPZIG	Vulcan	1874	13.9.75	1.6.77	Hulked 1894
SEDAN	Vulcan	1875	17.6.76	28.8.77	Hulked 1890

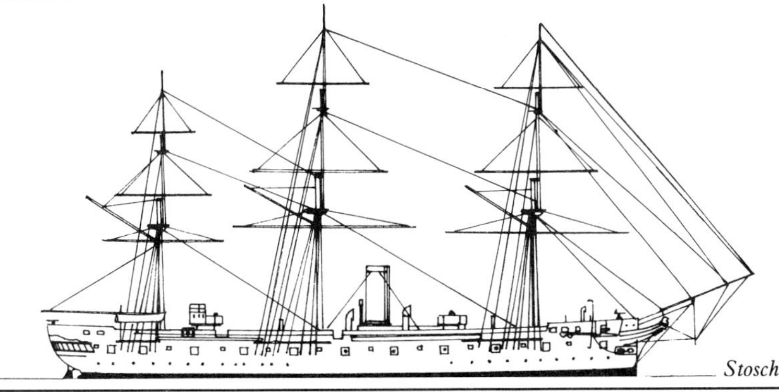

Stosch 1902

Similar to the *Leipzigs* but somewhat smaller. Later the last four carried rather fewer 150mm (numbers varied according to ship), two 88mm and six revolving cannon. *Bismarck* later had two 350mm TT fitted, whilst *Blücher*, acting as a torpedo research and school ship, had four, then seven, TT. All her guns were removed except for 13 revolving cannon and a couple of boat guns. Apart from her the rest of the class spent most of their service in foreign waters. All of the last four served as school ships. *Gneisenau* was still serving as such when wrecked on the mole at Malaga in a storm. *Blücher* was sold to be a coal hulk at Vigo; *Moltke* was broken up in 1920, as were *Bismarck* and *Stein*.

BISMARCK class *iron flush-decked corvettes*

Displacement: 2947t; *Bismarck, Blücher* 3332t
Dimensions: 269ft (*Bismarck, Blücher* 270ft 8in) oa, 236ft 10in wl x 45ft x 20ft 8in (*Bismarck, Blücher* 20ft 3in) (*82.0 (82.5) oa, 72.18 wl x 13.7 x 6.3 (6.18) m*)
Machinery: 1-shaft, lifting screw, HSE, 2500ihp = 12½kts
Armament: 16-150mm
Complement: 404

Name	Builder	Laid down	Launched	Comp	Fate
BISMARCK	Norddeutsche	1875	25.7.77	1878	Hulked 1891
BLÜCHER	Norddeutsche	1876	20.9.77	21.12.79	Sold as hulk 1908
STOSCH	Vulcan	1876	8.10.77	Mar 1878	BU 1907
MOLTKE	Danzig DYd	1875	18.10.77	16.4.78	Hulked 1910
GNEISENAU	Danzig DYd	1877	4.9.79	3.10.80	Wrecked 16.12.1900
STEIN	Vulcan	1878	14.9.79	3.10.80	Hulked 1908

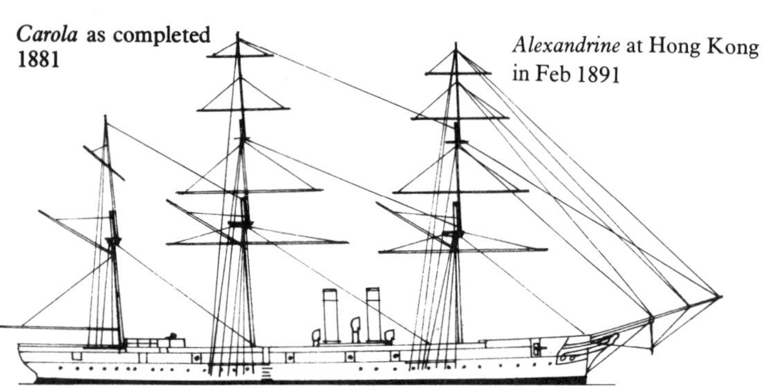
Carola as completed 1881

Alexandrine at Hong Kong in Feb 1891

The basic design of this class dated from 1875, so they were obsolescent even when they were laid down. *Marie* and *Sophie* had single funnels, the rest two each, while the last pair were rigged as ships, unlike their barque-rigged sisters. With their wood and copper sheathing they spent the early years of their service lives overseas. In 1893 *Carola* became an artillery training ship, and in 1889 *Olga* was converted to a school ship. Both had their rigging removed and were given two military masts with fighting tops instead. *Carola* was rearmed with six 150mm, two 105mm, eight 88mm and two 50mm. *Olga* had only two 88mm and ten MGs. *Marie* and *Sophie* later had minor armament changes, and both served for a while as school ships. *Sophie* was not broken up till 1921. In 1902 *Arcona*'s name was changed to *Mercur* to free her original name for a new cruiser.

CAROLA class *iron flush-decked corvettes*

Displacement: 2387t
Dimensions: 250ft 6in oa, 231ft 7in wl x 41ft x 20ft (*76.35 oa, 70.6 wl x 12.5 x 6.08m*)
Machinery: 1-shaft HC, 2200ihp = 13½kts
Armament: 10-150mm, 2-87mm, 6 rev 37mm cannon
Complement: 269

Name	Builder	Laid down	Launched	Comp	Fate
CAROLA	Vulcan	1879	27.11.80	1.9.81	BU 1906
OLGA	Vulcan	1879	11.12.80	10.9.81	Sold 1906, BU 1908
MARIE	Reiherstieg	1880	20.8.81	12.9.82	Discarded 1904, BU 1909
SOPHIE	Danzig DYd	1879	10.11.81	10.8.82	Hulked 1908

Displacement: 2620t
Dimensions: 266ft 5in oa, 235ft 7in wl x 41ft 4in x 20ft 6in (*81.2 oa, 71.8 wl x 12.6 x 6.25m*)
Machinery: 1-shaft HC, 2300ihp = 14kts
Armament: 10-150mm, 4-105mm, 6 rev 37mm cannon
Complement: 269

Name	Builder	Laid down	Launched	Comp	Fate
ALEXANDRINE	Kiel DYd	1882	7.2.85	6.10.86	BU 1907
ARCONA	Danzig DYd	1882	7.5.85	1.12.86	BU 1906

Though a hopeless anachronism as a fighting ship the *Nixe*, with her full rig and wood and copper-sheathed bottom was useful as a school ship, though she was a bad seaboat and awkward under sail. Her armament was later changed by the removal of first one gun, then a second, and the addition of two 88mm. In 1900 she was relegated to being a workshop ship, and from 1901 to 1906 she was used as an office at Kiel. She was broken up in 1916.

NIXE *corvette*

Displacement: 1951t
Dimension: 207ft 8in oa, 178ft 4in wl x 43ft 3in x 20ft 10in (*63.3 oa, 54.35 wl x 13.2 x 6.36m*)
Machinery: 1-shaft, hoisting screw, HC, 733ihp = 10kts
Armament: 8-125mm
Complement: 358

Name	Builder	Laid down	Launched	Comp	Fate
NIXE	Danzig DYd	1883	23.7.85	1.4.86	Hulked 1911

The *Charlotte* was in many respects a repeat of the *Bismarck* class. A fully-rigged ship, she was sheathed in wood. She was later cut down to a barque, and had the coupled engines replaced by a single one and the main armament reduced to twelve 150mm. From 1899 she carried two 105mm, sixteen 88mm and four revolving cannon. She had been used as a training ship since 1897, and from 1903 to 1905 was given a rebuild at Kiel. In 1921 she was sold, allegedly as a store ship.

CHARLOTTE *flush-decked corvette*

Displacement: 3703t
Dimensions: 275ft oa, 252ft wl x 47ft 11in x 22ft 6in (*83.85 oa, 76.85 wl x 14.6 x 6.86m*)
Machinery: 1-shaft, lifting screw, 2 coupled HC, 3100ihp = 13½kts
Armament: 18-150mm, 16-88mm, 6 rev 37 mm cannon
Complement: 430

Name	Builder	Laid down	Launched	Comp	Fate
CHARLOTTE	Wilhelmshaven DYd	1883	5.8.85	1.11.86	Hulked 1910

Though classed as light cruisers, these slow, composite-built (steel and wood with copper sheathing), ram-bowed, barquentine-rigged vessels fall more readily into the sloop or colonial gunboat class, and spent their early careers overseas. Both were used as hulks during the First World War, and broken up in 1922. *Schwalbe* had a rebuild between 1903 and 1905 and had her rig cut down to steadying sails.

SCHWALBE class *light cruisers*

Displacement: 1337t
Dimensions: 219ft 5in oa, 205ft 4in wl x 30ft 8in x 15ft 5in (*66.9 oa, 62.59 wl x 9.36 x 4.72m*)
Machinery: 2-shaft HC, 1600ihp = 14kts
Armament: 8-105mm, 5 rev 37mm cannon
Complement: 117

Name	Builder	Laid down	Launched	Comp	Fate
SCHWALBE	Wilhelmshaven DYd	1887	16.8.87	4.5.88	Harbour ship 1911
SPERBER	Danzig DYd	1888	23.8.89	2.4.89	Hulked 1912

Schwalbe as completed 1882

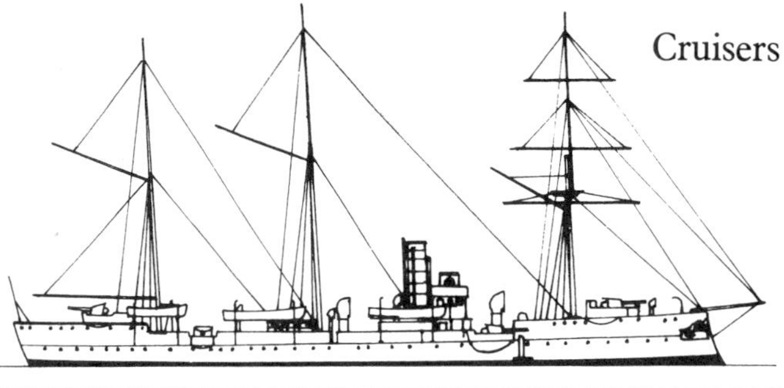

Seeadler 1898

The particulars for the vessels in this class are the same for each ship, unless shown otherwise in the table. The *Bussard* class were intended for colonial work, with their barquentine rig, ram bows and wooden sheathing. All except *Falke* and *Condor* were rebuilt at various times between 1898 and 1909, and re-rigged as topsail schooners. The bridges were also enlarged. *Seeadler* was in use as a mine hulk in the Jade when she blew up in 1917. *Condor* was also used for the same purpose but survived to be broken up in 1921. *Seeadler* was launched as the *Kaiseradler*, her name being changed just afterwards.

BUSSARD class *light cruisers (IV class)*

Displacement: 1838t
Dimensions: 271ft oa, 261ft 2in wl x 41ft x 14ft 7in (*82.6 oa, 79.62 wl x 12.5 x 4.45m*)
Machinery: 2-shaft HTE, 2800ihp = 15½kts
Armament: 8-105mm (also 5 rev cannon, 2-350mm TT in *Falke*)
Complement: 161

Name	Builder	Laid down	Launched	Comp	Fate
BUSSARD	Danzig DYd	1888	23.1.90	7.10.90	BU 1913
FALKE	Kiel DYd	1890	4.4.91	14.9.91	BU 1913

Displacement: 1834t
Dimensions: 271ft oa, 261ft wl x 41ft 8in x 17ft 6in (*82.6 oa, 79.6 wl x 12.7 x 5.35m*)
Armament: As in *Falke*

Name	Builder	Laid down	Launched	Comp	Fate
SEEADLER	Danzig DYd	1890	2.2.92	17.8.92	Hulked 1914
CONDOR	Blohm & Voss	1891	23.2.92	9.12.92	Hulked 1914
CORMORAN	Danzig DYd	1890	17.5.92	25.7.93	Scuttled at Tsingtao 28.9.1914

Displacement: 1888t
Dimensions: 275ft 3in oa, 261ft 3in wl x 34ft 9in x 17ft (*83.9 oa, 79.62 wl x 10.6 x 5.22m*)
Armament: 2-450mm TT

Name	Builder	Laid down	Launched	Comp	Fate
GEIER	Wilhelmshaven DYd	1893	18.10.94	24.10.95	Taken over by USN 1917

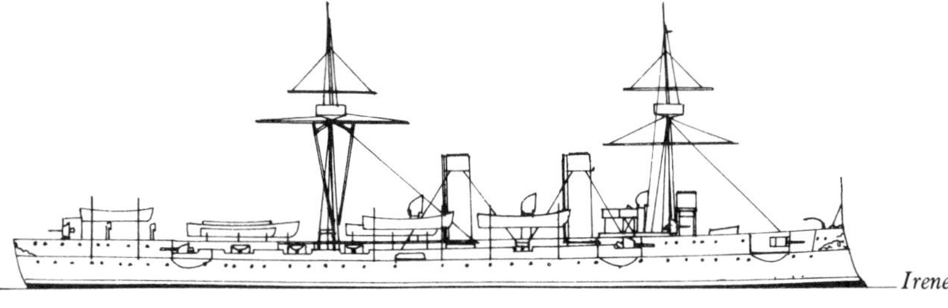

Irene 1896

The *Irene* and her sister were the first German protected cruisers. They had a compound steel armoured deck 3in thick amidships and were also wood-sheathed. In 1893 their gun armament was changed to four 150mm, eight 105mm and six 50mm. Both were refitted at Wilhelmshaven, *Irene* from 1903 to 1907, her sister from 1899 to 1902. The were broken up in 1921 and 1922 respectively.

IRENE II class *protected cruiser-corvettes (II class)*

Displacement: 4947t
Dimensions: 340ft 2in oa, 324ft 5in wl x 46ft 7in x 25ft (*103.7 oa, 98.9 wl x 14.2 x 7.63m*)
Machinery: 2-shaft HC, 8000ihp = 18kts
Armament: 14-150mm, 6 rev 37mm cannon, 3-350mm TT
Complement: 365

Name	Builder	Laid down	Launched	Comp	Fate
IRENE	Vulcan	1886	23.7.87	25.5.88	U-boat depot ship 1914
PRINZESS WILHELM	Germaniawerft	1886	22.9.87	13.11.89	Minehulk 1914

Kaiserin Augusta in the late 1890s

GERMANY

KAISERIN AUGUSTA *cruiser-corvette (II class)*

The design of this wood-sheathed protected cruiser was begun in 1887. Because of the power needed to obtain the design speed, which would be difficult to obtain at the time on only two screws, it was decided to try a triple shaft installation, the first time a German vessel had the machinery arrangement for heavy ships that was typical later. Her protective deck was 2¾in thick amidships. Her initial armament, given above, was a temporary one, and rather light. In 1898 it was improved by being altered to twelve 150mm, eight 88mm. Between 1903 and 1907 she was rebuilt with a bigger bridge, but was only left with the bow TT. In 1914 she became a gunnery school ship, and from 1916 had an armament of one 150mm, four 105mm, and fourteen 88mm of four different types.

Displacement: 6218t
Dimensions: 404ft oa, 401ft wl x 51ft x 24ft 3in (*123.2 oa, 122.2 wl x 15.6 x 7.4m*)
Machinery: 3-shaft TE, 15,650ihp = 21½kts
Armament: 4-150mm, 8-105mm, 8-88mm, 4 rev cannon, 5-350mm TT
Complement: 430

Name	Builder	Laid down	Launched	Comp	Fate
KAISERIN AUGUSTA	Germaniawerft	1890	15.1.92	29.8.92	BU 1920

Hansa with two funnels after reboilering

VICTORIA LOUISE class *heavy cruisers (II class)*

These protected cruisers show distinct affinities with contemporary German battleship designs, with fewer guns, more speed, and only a 100mm (4in) protective deck amidships, and the same protection for the turrets. They also introduced the rather massive appearance and the combined clipper and ram bow which were to mark the classes of German heavy cruiser up to the 1907 *Scharnhorst*. These ships, and their immediate successors, were rather top-heavy. All ships of the class were rebuilt between 1905 and 1911 (*Freya* was rebuilt again between 1911 and 1913), and were reboilered, with two funnels replacing the original three. The original tower foremast and fighting top were replaced by an ordinary pole mast. Two of the 150mm guns were removed, and an extra 88mm added, whilst all the MGs were landed. In 1916 all the ships were disarmed and used for accommodation, except for *Freya*, employed as a schoolship, which retained 1-150mm, 4-105mm and 14-88mm. *Victoria Louise* underwent the unusual transformation in 1920 of conversion to the cargo ship *Flora Sommerfeld* for a Danzig Firm. She did not last long in her new guise, being broken up in 1923.

Displacement: 6389t (*Vineta, Hansa* 6599t)
Dimensions: 363ft 2in oa, 358ft 3in wl x 57ft 2in x 22ft 9in (*110.6 oa, 109.1 wl x 17.4 x 6.94m*); *Vineta, Hansa* 362ft 10in oa, 360ft 6in wl x 57ft 9in x 24ft 1in (*110.5 oa, 109.8 wl x 17.6 x 7.34m*)
Machinery: 3-shaft TE, 10,500ihp = 18½kts
Armament: 2-210mm, 8-150mm, 10-88mm, 10 MGs, 3-450mm TT
Complement: 477

Name	Builder	Laid down	Launched	Comp	Fate
VICTORIA LOUISE	Weser	1896	29.3.97	20.2.98	Sold 1919
HERTHA	Vulcan	1896	14.4.97	23.7.98	BU 1920
FREYA	Danzig DYd	1896	27.4.97	Oct 1898	BU 1921
VINETA	Danzig DYd	1896	14.4.97	13.9.99	BU 1920
HANSA	Vulcan	1896	12.3.98	20.4.99	BU 1920

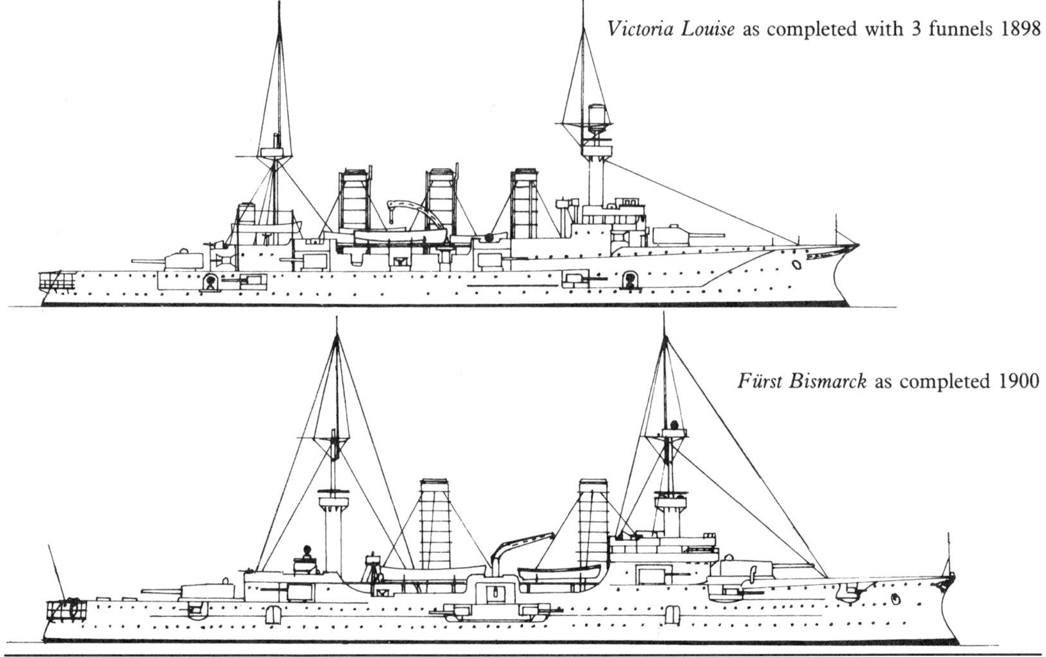

Victoria Louise as completed with 3 funnels 1898

Fürst Bismarck as completed 1900

FÜRST BISMARCK *heavy cruiser (I class)*

Fürst Bismarck was Germany's first armoured cruiser, though apart from her narrow but thick (200mm (8in) amidships) belt and more and heavier big guns she was very much an enlarged version of the *Victoria Louise* class. She still had a protective deck of 50mm (2in). The main armament had 200mm and the secondary armament 100mm armour (8in and 4in). Her 150mm guns were later reduced by two. She was wood-sheathed and spent her first decade in overseas service. She was rebuilt between 1910 and 1915, only to spend a short time in coast defence and then be disarmed and relegated to training stokers in 1916.

Displacement: 11,281t
Dimensions: 417ft oa, 412ft 9in wl x 67ft x 27ft 9in (*127 oa, 125.7 wl x 20.4 x 8.46m*)
Machinery: 2-shaft TE, 13,800ihp = 18¾kts
Armament: 4-240mm, 12-150mm, 10-88mm, 4 MGs, 6-450mm TT
Complement: 621

Name	Builder	Laid down	Launched	Comp	Fate
FÜRST BISMARCK	Kiel DYd	1896	25.9.97	1.4.1900	BU 1919-20

The *Prinz Heinrich*, specially intended for overseas service, was a more lightly armed but faster version of the *Fürst Bismarck*. She had thinner armour – only 100mm (4in) in the belt amidships – but it was spread wider to cover the central citadel in which all ten of the 150mm guns were concentrated amidships on two decks. This concentration of the secondary armament was to be a feature of all the German armoured cruisers from here on. The main turrets, each with only a single gun, were protected by 150mm (6in) armour, and the deck was 50mm (2in) at its thickest. She was rebuilding in 1914, but there was little place for her in the struggle in the North Sea, so she was disarmed to become a depot ship in 1916.

PRINZ HEINRICH *heavy cruiser*

Displacement: 9652t
Dimensions: 415ft 4in oa, 410ft 1in wl x 64ft 4in x 26ft 6in *(126.5 oa, 124.9 wl x 19.6 x 8.07m)*
Machinery: 3-shaft TE, 15,700ihp = 20¼kts
Armament: 2-240mm, 10-150mm, 10-88mm, 4MGs, 4-450mm TT
Complement: 567

Name	Builder	Laid down	Launched	Comp	Fate
PRINZ HEINRICH	Kiel DYd	1898	22.3.1900	11.3.02	BU 1920

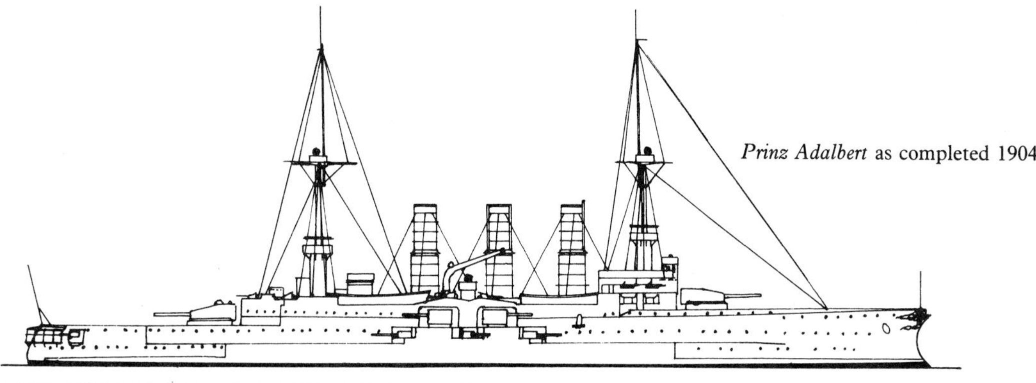
Prinz Adalbert as completed 1904

These vessels were very similar to the *Prinz Heinrich* apart from their three funnels instead of two and four instead of two big guns. Like her they were wood-sheathed, and the armour protection, apart from there being a rather more extensive belt, was virtually the same. The lower part of the central casemate was a weak point, as it flooded easily even in a moderate sea: though a common feature in secondary batteries of the time, and not just in the German Navy, it happened particularly easily in this class, which greatly reduced the ships' fighting ability. *Prinz Adalbert* spent most of her career as a gunnery schoolship, her sister in a similar role for torpedo warfare. Both were sunk in the Baltic, though *Prinz Adalbert*, torpedoed by the British submarine *E8*, sank with very heavy loss of life, unlike her sister.

PRINZ ADALBERT class *heavy cruisers*

Displacement: 9719t
Dimensions: 415ft 4in oa, 410ft 1in wl x 64ft 4in x 25ft 7in *(126.5 oa, 124.9 wl x 19.6 x 7.8m)*
Machinery: 3-shaft TE, 18,500ihp = 20½kts
Armament: 4-210mm, 10-150mm, 12-88mm, 4 MGs, 4-450mm TT
Complement: 586

Name	Builder	Laid down	Launched	Comp	Fate
PRINZ ADALBERT	Kiel DYd	1900	22.6.01	12.1.04	Torpedoed 23.10.15
FRIEDRICH CARL	Blohm & Voss	1901	21.6.02	12.12.03	Mined 17.11.14

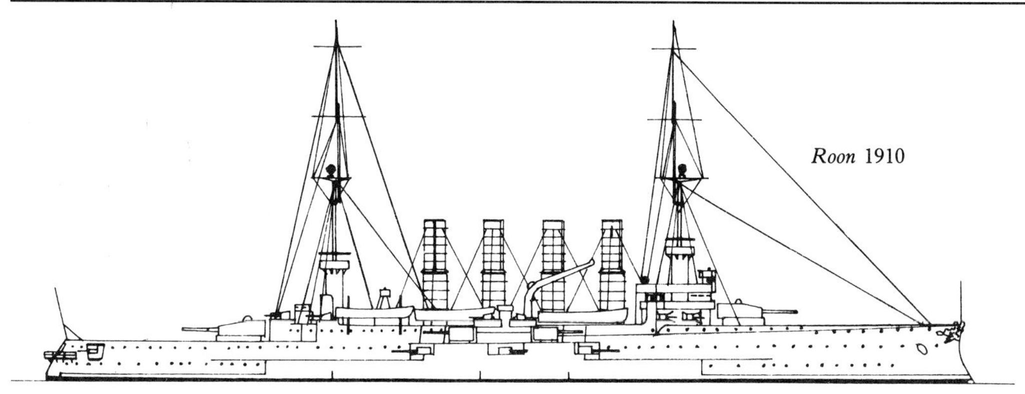
Roon 1910

Apart from their four funnels this class were little more than repeats of the previous design, though with minor adjustments to the armour. Like previous classes they were not very well protected, and were not considered particularly successful in service. After her sister was lost on German mines in the Jade, *Roon* soon followed the earlier armoured cruisers into retirement as a disarmed accommodation ship in 1916. A project to convert her into a seaplane carrier with 4 seaplanes, carried in a hangar aft, and 6-150mm and 6-88mm AA guns never materialised.

ROON class *heavy cruisers*

Displacement: 10,104t
Dimensions: 419ft 7in oa, 418ft wl x 66ft 4in x 25ft 6in *(127.8 oa, 127.3 wl x 20.2 x 7.76m)*
Machinery: 3-shaft TE, 20,000ihp = 21kts
Armament: 4-210mm, 10-150mm, 14-88mm, 4 MGs, 4-450mm TT
Complement: 633

Name	Builder	Laid down	Launched	Comp	Fate
ROON	Kiel DYd	1902	27.6.03	5.4.06	BU 1921
YORCK	Blohm & Voss	1903	14.5.04	21.11.05	Mined 4.11.14

Scharnhorst as completed 1907

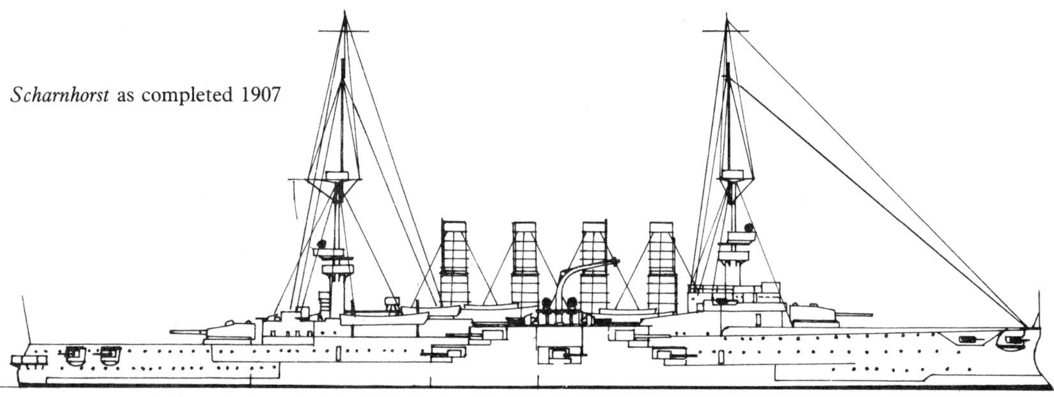

GERMANY

Germany's last and best armoured cruisers were still basically bigger and faster *Roons*. With an almost identical armour scheme they carried twice the number of heavy guns (the extra weapons were disposed in casemates at the corners of the midships citadel at upper deck level) though with fewer secondary guns. However, they compare less well with their British contemporaries on the China Station in 1914: *Minotaur* and *Defence* which admittedly were slightly bigger, carried an armament of 4-9.2in (larger, though fewer than the German guns), and 8-7.5in, far better distributed than the German armament, in hulls with much the same protection and speed.

SCHARNHORST class *heavy cruisers*

Displacement: 12,781t
Dimensions: 474ft 9in oa, 472ft 2in wl x 71ft x 27ft 6in (*144.6 oa, 143.8 wl x 21.6 x 8.37m*)
Machinery: 3-shaft TE, 30,000ihp = 23½kts
Armament: 8-210mm, 6-150mm, 18-88mm, 4 MGs, 4-450mm TT
Complement: 764

Name	Builder	Laid down	Launched	Comp	Fate
SCHARNHORST	Blohm & Voss	1905	22.3.06	4.10.07	Sunk 8.12.14
GNEISENAU	Weser	1904	14.6.06	6.3.08	Sunk 8.12.14

This torpedo vessel, designed in Britain, initially only had bow and stern TTs, both submerged, but was later armed with 6 (later 4) 50mm guns. She was primarily used as a tender for torpedo development, but could be said to fall into the later category of torpedo gunboat, or torpedo cruiser. An elegant ship with a clipper bow, looking very much like a steam yacht, she had a good speed for her day. Before the general adoption of the QF guns, her powerful reserve of torpedo reloads and her good qualities as a seaboat could have proved useful in action, despite her lack of guns or protection. From 1899 she was used as a fishery protection vessel, and from 1914 as a coastal patrol ship.

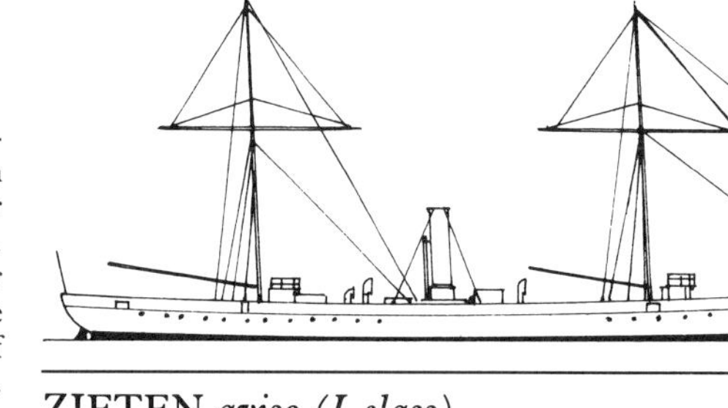

Zieten as completed 1876

ZIETEN *aviso (I class)*

Displacement: 1152t
Dimensions: 260ft 8in oa, 228ft 2in wl x 28ft 1in x 15ft 2in (*79.4 oa, 69.5 wl x 8.56 x 4.63m*)
Machinery: 2-shaft HC, 2000ihp = 16kts
Armament: 2-381mm TT (10 torpedoes)
Complement: 94

Name	Builder	Laid down	Launched	Comp	Fate
ZIETEN	Thames Iron Wks	1875	9.3.76	15.7.76	BU 1921

The design of these vessels dates from 1879, and they were the first true torpedo cruisers, having a respectable gun armament (unlike the *Zieten*), and so were the ancestors of the light cruiser. Their main purpose in war would be scouting. They were built of steel, and had ram bows. Both were rebuilt in the early 1890s and rearmed with 8-88mm and 3-350mm TT, their original schooner rig being removed. *Blitz* was used as a flotilla leader for TBs until 1900; *Pfeil* was used briefly for fishery protection. Both continued in service as tenders, with their TTs long gone, until the end of the 1914-18 war.

BLITZ class *avisos (I class)*

Displacement: 1463t
Dimensions: 257ft 6in oa, 247ft 3in wl x 32ft 6in x 14ft 5in (*78.43 oa, 75.3 wl x 9.9 x 4.4m*)
Machinery: 2-shaft HC, 2,800ihp = 16kts
Armament: 1-125mm, 4-87mm, 1-350mm TT bow (3 torpedoes)
Complement: 134

Name	Builder	Laid down	Launched	Comp	Fate
BLITZ	Norddeutsche	1881	26.8.82	28.3.83	BU 1921
PFEIL	Wilhelmshaven DYd	1881	16.9.82	25.11.84	BU 1922

Blitz about1890

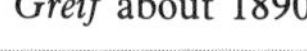

Greif about 1890

The *Greif*, a larger version of the *Blitz* design but without the torpedo armament, represents a further step in the evolution of the light cruiser. With her ram bow, three funnels and low silhouette she bears a distinct resemblance to much later vessels. However she does not seem to have been successful in service as she was given little employment. In 1891 she was rearmed with 8 (later 6) 88mm, and the number of revolvers was reduced first to 6 then to 4. After service as a mine hulk she was scrapped in 1921.

GREIF *aviso*

Displacement: 2230t
Dimensions: 336ft 10in oa, 326ft 8in wl 30ft x 14ft 3in (*102.6 oa, 99.5 wl x 9.75 x 4.34m*)
Machinery: 2-shaft HC, 5795ihp = 19kts
Armament: 2-105mm, 10-37mm revolvers
Complement: 170

Name	Builder	Laid down	Launched	Comp	Fate
GREIF	Germaniawerft	1885	29.7.86	9.7.87	Hulked 1912

These single-funnelled vessels were poor seaboats, and had poor manoeuvrability. However, with their TTs and guns they were a better answer to the problem of producing a small fighting vessel for the North Sea or Baltic than any of their contemporaries. Shortly after completion they were rearmed with 4-88mm guns. *Wacht* was lost in the Baltic in a collision with the *Sachsen*. *Jagd* was broken up in 1920.

WACHT class *avisos*

Displacement: 1475t
Dimensions: 280ft 9in oa, 275ft 10in wl 31ft 6in x 15ft 4in (*85.5 oa, 84.0 wl x 9.6 x 4.67m*)
Machinery: 2-shaft DTE, 3450ihp = 18½kts
Armament: 3-105mm, 3-350mm TT
Complement: 141

Name	Builder	Laid down	Launched	Comp	Fate
WACHT	Weser	1886	27.8.87	9.8.88	Lost 4.9.1901
JAGD	Weser	1887	7.7.88	25.6.89	Hulked 1910

Wacht about 1890

The *Meteor* and her slightly faster near-sister were smaller than their predecessors, and very similar to the British torpedo gunboats. They had a protected deck, 25mm (1in) at its thickest. They proved to be very poor seaboats, and vibrated considerably at high speeds, so it is not surprising that they saw little service. They were broken up in 1919 and 1921 respectively.

METEOR class *avisos*

Displacement: 1055t, *Comet* 1093t
Dimensions: 262ft 2in oa, 259ft 5in wl x 31ft 5in (*Comet* 31ft 5in) x 14ft 9in (*Comet* 12ft 2in) (*79.86 oa, 79.0 wl x 9.56 (9.58) x 4.5 (3.7)m*)
Machinery: 2-shaft TE, 4500ihp = 19kts (*Comet* 5000ihp = 19½kts)
Armament: 4-88mm, 3-350mm TT
Complement: 115

Name	Builder	Laid down	Launched	Comp	Fate
METEOR	Germaniawerft	1888	20.1.90	19.5.91	Hulked 1911
COMET	Vulcan	1890	15.1.92	29.4.93	Hulked 1911

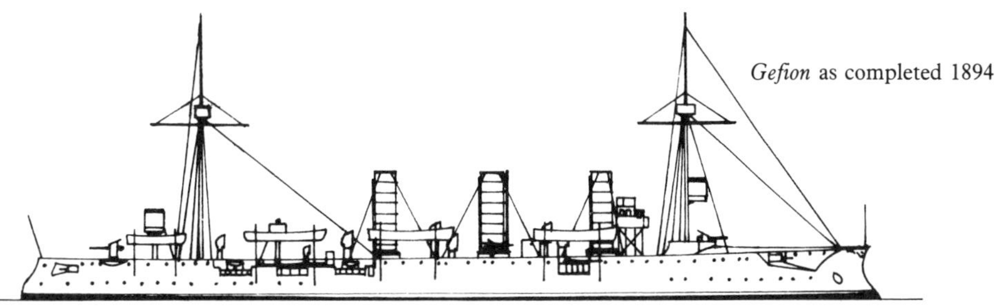

Gefion as completed 1894

Though she resembles later German light cruisers, this three funnelled cruiser stands rather by herself as a separate development. She was originally designed for 150mm guns, but the smaller 105mm weapons were fitted instead. She was lightly built, though she did have a protective deck varying from 25mm (1in) to 40mm (1¾in) in thickness. She was wood-sheathed, and served for a while abroad. She was rebuilt in 1901-04. In 1916 she was reduced to an accommodation ship, but after the war was rebuilt as the merchantman *Adolf Sommerfeld*. She was however broken up in 1923, so the conversion was hardly a success, and can be explained only by the shortage of shipping immediately after the war.

GEFION *cruiser-corvette (III class)*

Displacement: 4208t
Dimensions: 362ft 6in oa, 358ft 6in wl x 43ft 4in x 21ft 3in (*110.4 oa, 109.2 wl x 13.2 x 6.47m*)
Machinery: 2-shaft TE, 9000ihp = 19kts
Armament: 10-105mm, 6-50mm, 2-450mm TT
Complement: 302

Name	Builder	Laid down	Launched	Comp	Fate
GEFION	Schichau	1892	31.5.93	27.6.94	Mercantile 1920

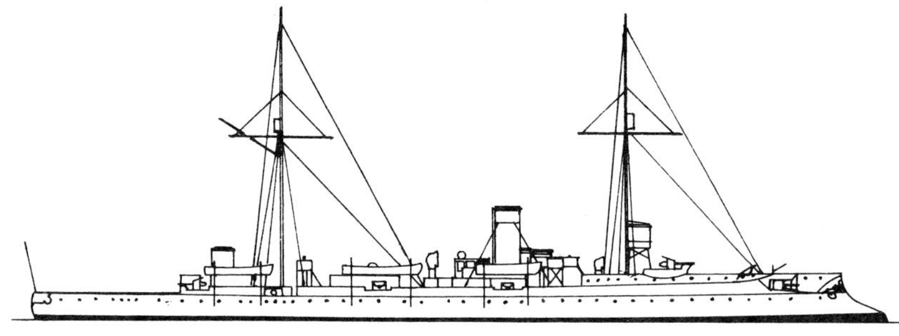

Hela as completed 1896

With this enlarged version of the *Jagd*, the *aviso* was developing into a light cruiser. This 1893 design had a 25mm (1in) armoured deck and a very pronounced ram bow. She was considered a good seaboat, and served for two years abroad, as well as with the home fleet. She was rebuilt between 1903 and 1906, her superstructure being altered and her two after 88mm guns removed. From 1910 she was used as a fleet tender. In 1914 she was used for patrol duty, and was torpedoed by the British submarine *E 9* in the North Sea.

HELA *aviso*

Displacement: 2049t
Dimensions: 344ft 9in oa, 343ft 5in wl x 36ft 1in x 15ft 3in (*105.0 oa, 104.6 wl x 11.0 x 4.64m*)
Machinery: 2-shaft TE, 6000ihp = 20kts
Armament: 4-88mm, 6-50mm, 3-450mm TT
Complement: 178

Name	Builder	Laid down	Launched	Comp	Fate
HELA	Weser	1893	28.3.95	3.5.96	Torpedoed 13.9.1914

The *Gazelle* class were the first modern light cruisers. They were well armed with the 105mm guns the German Navy believed best for dealing with destroyers and TBs (this preference for the lighter gun with the greater rate of fire as compared to the heavier 6in remained a constant feature of German light cruisers up to 1914). They inherited the pronounced ram of the *Hela*, though only the *Gazelle* had a bow TT. Another difference from her sisters was that the two broadside TTs of the lead ship of the class were above water, whilst in all the other ships they were submerged. *Gazelle* also differed in having her charthouse placed between her two funnels, whilst all the others had it in the normal position in front of the forefunnel. The main protection was a 50mm (2in) deck amidships.

Gazelle was rebuilt between 1905 and 1907, as was *Arcona* between 1911 and 1912, but with few major changes. The earlier ships of the class were allocated to coastal defence in 1914, and by the end of 1916 the survivors had been reduced to second line duties and most had been disarmed. *Arcona* was used as a minelayer with a capacity of 200 mines. *Ariadne* was sunk by the fire of the British battlecruisers during the Heligoland Bight raid, *Undine* was torpedoed by the British submarine *E 19* in the Baltic, whilst *Frauenlob* was torpedoed by the British cruiser *Southampton* during the battle of Jutland.

Gazelle was scrapped in 1920, but the remaining members of the class were amongst the few ships left in service with the German Navy in the 1920s. *Niobe*, *Nymphe* and *Amazone* were soon rebuilt with clipper bows and with 500mm TTs. The last two were struck off in 1931, though *Amazone* survived as an accommodation hulk to be broken up in 1954. In 1942 *Medusa* and *Arcona* became fighting ships again, as floating AA batteries with 5-105mm, 2-37mm and 4-20mm guns. Both were broken up in 1948-9.

However the most interesting career of all of these vessels was that of the *Niobe*, purchased in 1925 as a schoolship for the Yugoslav Navy and renamed *Dalmacija*. In 1941 she was seized by the Italians who renamed her *Cattaro*. By this time she was armed with 6-8.5in Skoda guns and 6-20mm. In 1943 she was taken back by her original owners and given her original German name. Though she also served for a short time as part of the puppet Croatian Navy she was under German control when she was sunk by the torpedoes of the British MTBs *276* and *298* in the Adriatic on 22.12.1943.

GAZELLE class *light cruisers (IV class)*

Displacement: 3033t (*Gazelle, Niobe* 2916t, *Frauenlob, Arcona, Undine* 3130t)
Dimensions: 345ft 1in oa, 341ft 10in wl x 40ft 1in x 17ft 9in (*105.1 oa, 104.1 wl x 12.2 x 5.4m*); *Gazelle, Niobe* 344ft 9in oa, 342ft 9in wl x 40ft 1in x 18ft 2in (*105.0 oa, 104.4 wl x 12.2 x 5.53m*); *Frauenlob, Arcona, Undine* 344ft 9in oa, 342ft 9in wl x 40ft 9in x 18ft 5in (*105.0 oa, 104.4 wl x 12.4 x 5.62m*)
Machinery: 2-shaft TE, 8500-9000ihp = 20¾-21½kts (*Gazelle* 6000ihp = 20kts, *Niobe* 8000ihp = 22kts)
Armament: 10-105mm, 10 MGs, 3-(*Niobe* 2-)450mm TT
Complement: 249 (*Frauenlob, Arcona, Undine* 259)

Name	Builder	Laid down	Launched	Comp	Fate
GAZELLE	Germaniawerft	1897	31.3.98	6.10.1900	Hulked 1916
NIOBE	Weser	1898	18.7.99	25.6.1900	Sold to Yugoslavia 1925
NYMPHE	Germaniawerft	1898	21.11.99	20.9.1900	BU 1932
THETIS	Danzig DYd	1899	3.7.1900	14.9.01	BU 1930
ARIADNE	Weser	1899	10.8.1900	18.5.01	Sunk 28.8.14
AMAZONE	Germaniawerft	1899	6.10.1900	15.11.01	Hulked 1931
MEDUSA	Weser	1900	5.12.1900	26.7.01	Hulked 1929
FRAUENLOB	Weser	1901	22.3.02	17.2.03	Torpedoed 31.5.16
ARCONA	Weser	1901	22.10.02	12.5.03	Hulked 1930
UNDINE	Howaldtswerke	1901	11.12.02	5.1.04	Torpedoed 7.11.15

Nymphe after the First World War

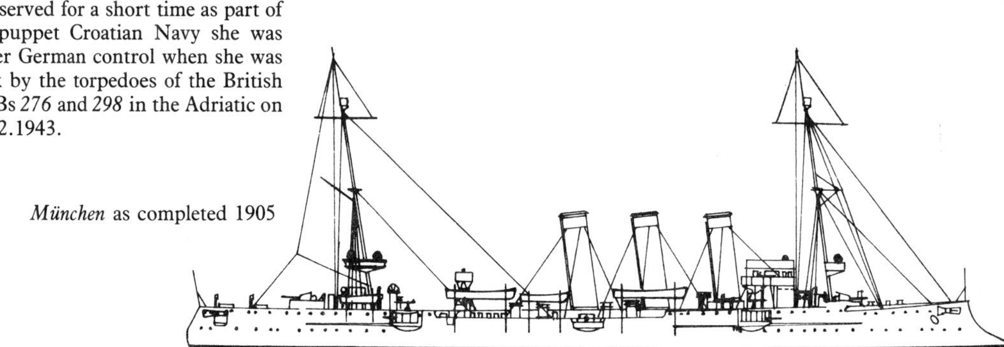

München as completed 1905

Having hit on a very satisfactory light cruiser design with the *Gazelles* the German Navy merely enlarged it and gave it more power and speed to produce the *Bremens*, the first class to adopt the city names which were henceforward to be standard. The main appearance difference was that the new class had three instead of two funnels. They also had a thicker deck, 80mm (3¼in) at its maximum and with 100mm (4in) slopes. As a very sensible experimental move, *Lübeck*, otherwise identical to her sisters, was given the first turbine plant used by the German Navy, thus enabling successful comparative trials to be run. In an attempt to convert the high speed of rotation of the turbines to power, the *Lübeck* was originally fitted with four separate propellers on each shaft, though this number was later cut down to two.

Bremen was rebuilt between 1914 and 1915 and given 2-150mm guns in place of the 4-105mm paired on forecastle and poop, indicating a belated realisation of the need to 'beef up' the armament with something heavier than 105mm, which had already been foreseen by the British. *Lübeck* was refitted in 1916 with a similar rearmament, but she was also given a raked bow in place of the ram, 500mm TTs instead of 450mm, and accommodation for 50 mines. *Berlin* was also briefly used as a minelayer in 1915-16 carrying 80 mines. *Leipzig* was sunk in the battle of the Falkland Islands by the British cruisers *Cornwall* and *Glasgow*; *Bremen* was mined in the Baltic; *München* and *Berlin* were disarmed in 1916; and *Lübeck*, *München* and *Danzig* were all surrendered to Britain as war reparations and scrapped immediately afterwards. *Hamburg*, having been reduced to 6-105mm guns in 1916, was rearmed after the war, as was *Berlin*, with 8-105mm and 2-500mm TT. *Berlin* was also rebuilt in 1921-3 with a raked bow; she was scuttled in 1947 with a cargo of poison gas. *Hamburg*, sunk by bombing in 1944, was salvaged and broken up after the end of the war.

BREMEN class *light cruisers*

Displacement: 3756t
Dimensions: 364ft 9in oa, 363ft 2in wl x 43ft 8in x 18ft 5in *(111.1 oa, 110.6 wl x 13.3 x 5.61m)*
Machinery: 2-shaft TE (*Lübeck* 2-shaft Parsons turbines), 11,750ihp = 23kts (*Lübeck* 14,400shp = 23kts)
Armament: 10-105mm, 10 MGs, 2-450mm TT
Complement: 288

Name	Builder	Laid down	Launched	Comp	Fate
BREMEN	Weser	1902	9.7.03	19.5.04	Mined 17.2.15
HAMBURG	Vulcan	1902	25.7.03	8.3.04	Hulked 1931
BERLIN	Danzig DYd	1902	22.9.03	4.4.05	Hulked 1935
LÜBECK	Vulcan	1903	26.3.04	26.4.05	BU 1922
MÜNCHEN	Weser	1903	30.4.04	10.1.05	BU 1919
LEIPZIG	Weser	1904	21.3.05	20.4.06	Sunk 8.12.1914
DANZIG	Danzig DYd	1904	23.9.05	1.2.07	BU 1921-3

GUNBOATS

The word 'gunboat' can cover almost as many diverse types as does 'cruiser'. In this category are grouped the small wooden vessels, very similar to the British 'Crimean gunboats', building at the beginning of the period and intended primarily for coastal defence; and the sloop-type vessels used for colonial policing and ranging from the masted *Albatross* class of the 1870s to the *Iltis* class at the end of the century which resembled smaller versions of the contemporary light cruisers. None of these was fundamentally very different from foreign contemporaries. The *Wespe* class were rather more unusual, though basically just larger versions of the British 'Rendel gunboat' design. (One could also consider them as the logical decendents of the old one-gun rowing gunboats of the previous era.) The *Brummer* class were the most unusual, not unlike a mating of a torpedo gunboat with the *Wespe* class, and an interesting answer to the problem of getting a big gun into action, though not one with much future in view of increasing ranges.

Comet, a *Chamäleon* class gunboat

JÄGER class *gunboats (II class)* (launched 1860)

Displacement: 279t
Dimensions: 135ft 3in oa, 124ft 9in wl x 22ft x 7ft 3in *(41.2 oa, 38 wl x 6.69 x 2.2m)*
Machinery: 1-shaft HS, 220ihp = 9kts
Armament: 1-24pdr, 2-12pdr
Complement: 40

Class (builder): *Jäger, Crocodill* (Mitzlaff), *Fuchs, Hay* (Klawitter), *Scorpion, Sperber* (Domcke), *Hyäne, Habicht* (Keier & Devrient), *Pfeil* ex-*Donner, Natter* ex-*Blitz* (Lübcke), *Schwalbe, Salamander* (Nüscke & Co), *Wespe, Tiger* (Zieske), *Wolf* (Liegnitz).

These small wooden gunboats were very similar to the British 'Crimean Gunboats' of the time, being small, shallow draught vessels designed to carry a small number of heavy guns close inshore. They had a three-masted schooner rig, and should have been useful coastal defence vessels. They were , however, very poor seaboats, and spent most of their time stored on slips. From 1872 they were rearmed with a single 150mm, whilst *Fuchs* from 1878 had an 87mm instead. They were taken out of service at various dates between 1867 and 1880, though some continued to serve for a time as mine barges after that.

CHAMÄLEON class *gunboats (I class)* (launched 1860-65)

Displacement: 415t
Dimensions: 142ft 1in oa, 134ft 8in wl x 22ft 10in x 8ft 9in *(43.28 oa, 41.02 wl x 6.96 x 2.67m)*
Machinery: 1-shaft HS, 250-320ihp = 9-9¼kts
Armament: 1-24pdr, 2-12pdr
Complement: 71

Class (builder): *Chamäleon, Comet, Cyclop, Delphine* (Danzig DYd), *Blitz, Basilisk, Meteor, Drache* (Lübcke).

Again, very similar to British prototypes, these wooden gunboats were barquentine rigged. The Danzig-built vessels were laid down in 1859 and the remainder in 1861. The second quartette had more powerful engines provided by the English firm of Penn. Of the first group only *Delphin* saw much service. *Drache* briefly carried a 68pdr gun, whilst *Basilisk* was fitted with a TT in 1873 for experimental work. They were taken out of service at various times from 1872 to 1887, though some were used as barges thereafter.

GERMANY

ALBATROSS class *gunboats* (launched 1871)

Displacement:	774t
Dimensions:	196ft 10in oa, 168ft 2in wl x 27ft 4in x 12ft 4in *(59.95 oa, 51.21 wl x 8.32 x 3.75m)*
Machinery:	1-shaft HS, hoisting screw, 500ihp = 10½kts
Armament:	2-150mm, 2-120mm
Complement:	103

Class (builder, fate): *Albatross* (Danzig DYd, sold 1899), *Nautilus* (Danzig DYd, hulked 1896).

These wooden gunboats with their three-masted schooner rig were rated as *avisos*; they were intended for colonial use, and spent most of their lives overseas. They were later given 3-37mm revolving cannon, but ended their days disarmed. After service as a coal hulk *Nautilus* was broken up in 1905.

CYCLOP *gunboat (I class)* (launched 1874)

Displacement:	523t
Dimensions:	142ft 2in oa, 138ft 7in wl x 23ft x 9ft 10in *(43.3 oa, 42.22 wl x 7.0 x 3.0m)*
Machinery:	Engine of previous *Cyclop* = 9kts
Armament:	2-120mm, 2 'balloon cannon'
Complement:	69

Class (builder, fate): *Cyclop* (Danzig DYd, hulked 1888).

Officially a 'rebuild' of the 1860 *Cyclop*, this vessel was actually built of iron, though to much the same lines and using the same machinery. She was no more successful as a seaboat than her predecessor. The 'balloon cannon' fitted briefly at the start of her career were probably the first seagoing AA guns, designed by the Germans for use against the balloons the French had used at the siege of Paris. They were soon replaced by 2-87mm guns, and 3-37mm revolvers were fitted later. *Cyclop* spent her life overseas, and was scrapped after serving as a hulk in the Cameroons in 1900.

OTTER *gunboat* (launched 1877)

Displacement:	161t
Dimensions:	101ft 9in oa, 95ft 7in wl x 20ft 2in x 5ft 4in *(31.0 oa, 29.1 wl x 6.15 x 1.63m)*
Machinery:	Simple, 140ihp = 8kts
Armament:	1-120mm (in bow, designed but never fitted)
Complement:	43

Class (builder, fate): *Otter* (Schichau, hulked 1907).

This curious little schooner-rigged, iron-hulled gunboat was intended to be an anti-pirate vessel for China, but, perhaps because she was a bad seaboat, never left German waters. She was used as a mining instruction ship. She was sold as a coal barge in 1913, and broken up in 1926.

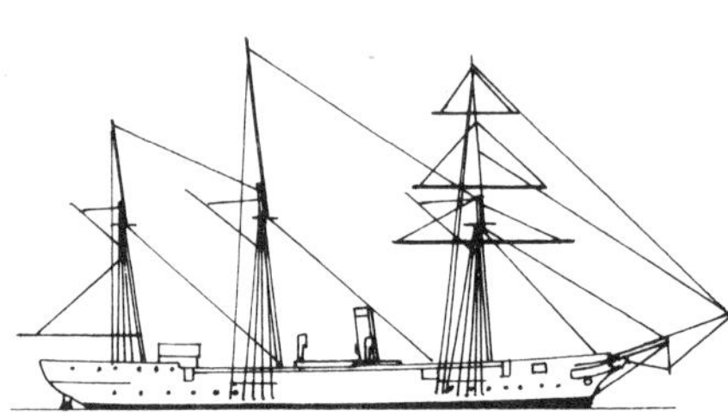

Wolf as completed 1879

WOLF class *gunboats (I class)* (launched 1878)

Displacement:	561t
Dimensions:	155ft oa, 146ft 1in wl x 25ft 2in x 11ft 2in *(47.2 oa, 44.5 wl x 7.66 x 3.4m)*
Machinery:	Engines ex-*Blitz*, *Basilisk* and *Delphin*, hoisting screw, 142ihp = 8kts
Armament:	2-125mm, 2-87mm, 2-37mm revolvers
Complement:	85

Class (builder, fate): *Wolf* (Wilhelmshaven DYd, hulked 1906), *Hyäne* (Wilhelmshaven DYd, sold 1920), *Iltis* (Danzig DYd, foundered in typhoon 23.7.1896).

These iron-built colonial gunboats were an improved version of the *Cyclop* (1873) design. They sailed well with their barquentine rig, and were considered good seaboats. *Wolf* later had her armament reduced to 1-87mm and 1-50mm, plus 2 revolving cannon. *Hyäne* was disarmed in 1897 and her rig reduced to steadying sails in 1905, by which time she was used as an accommodation ship. However, in 1914 she was used as a watch ship. Sold in 1920, she served as the three-masted schooner *Seewolf* (fitted with an auxiliary motor) until sunk in 1924. *Iltis* was lost in the China Sea. *Wolf* after use as a depot ship was broken up in 1919.

Möwe, a *Habicht* class gunboat, in 1895

HABICHT class *gunboats (I class)* (launched 1879)

Displacement:	989t (*Adler* 1024t)
Dimensions:	187ft 10in oa, 176ft 8in wl x 29ft 3in x 13ft 9in *(57.2 oa, 53.8 wl x 8.9 x 4.18m)*; *Adler* 202ft 11in oa, 190ft 9in wl x 28ft 11in x 13ft 2in *(61.4 oa, 58.1 wl x 8.8 x 4.02m)*
Machinery:	1-shaft compound, hoisting screw, 800ihp = 11½kts (*Adler* 950ihp = 11¼kts)
Armament:	1-150mm, 4-120mm
Complement:	127

Class (builder, fate): *Habicht* (Schichau, BU 1906), *Möwe* (Schichau, hulked 1905), *Adler* (Kiel DYd, lost 16.3.1889).

Iron-hulled, barquentine-rigged colonial gunboats, considered very good under sail and as seaboats. From 1882 they carried 5-125mm and 5-37mm revolving cannon. *Möwe* from 1890 had three of the 125mm removed, and later all of them. She remained as a hulk at Tsingtau until sold in 1910. *Adler* was lost in Apia harbour during the *Calliope* typhoon of 1889.

HAY *gunboat* (launched 1881)

Displacement:	243t
Dimensions:	111ft 8in 0a, 102ft 5in wl x 21ft x 9ft 3in *(34.0 oa, 31.2 wl x 6.4 x 2.81m)*
Machinery:	1-shaft compound, 202ihp = 9.3kts
Armament:	4-87mm, 4-37mm revolvers
Complement:	40

Class (builder, fate): *Hay* (Danzig DYd, hulked 1906).

Wooden, copper-sheathed gunboat which spent her life as the tender to the gunnery school ship *Mars*. Rearmed in 1891 with 2-88mm. Broken up in 1919.

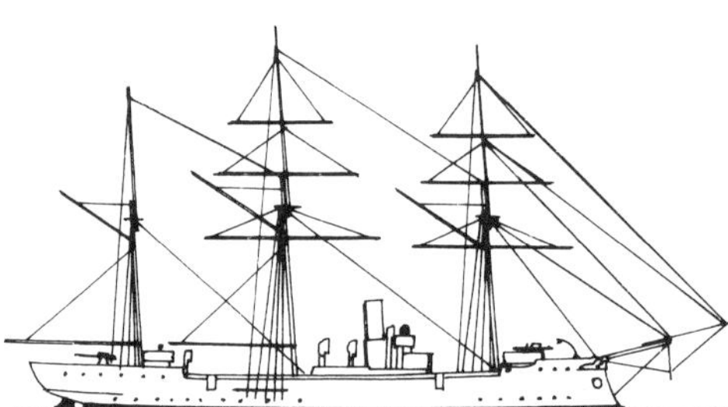

Eber as completed 1887

EBER *gunboat* (launched 1887)

Displacement:	723t
Dimensions:	169ft 9in oa, 159ft 3in wl x 26ft 3in x 12ft 6in *(51.7 oa, 48.5 wl x 8.0 x 3.8m)*
Machinery:	1-shaft compound, hoisting screw, 760ihp = 11kts
Armament:	3-105mm, 4-37mm revolvers
Complement:	81

Class (builder, fate): *Eber* (Kiel DYd, lost 16.3.1889).

This barque-rigged colonial gunboat differed from her predecessors in having a ram bow. She was lost in the *Calliope* typhoon with *Adler* in 1889.

ILTIS class *gunboats* (launched 1898-1901)

Displacement:	1031t (*Tiger, Luchs* 1090t, *Panther, Eber* 1193t)
Dimensions:	214ft 1in oa, 209ft 10in wl x 29ft 11in x 11ft 11in *(65.2 oa, 63.9 wl x 9.1 x 3.63)*; *Panther, Eber* 219ft 6in oa, 210ft 3in wl x 31ft 10in x 10ft 3in *(66.9 oa, 64.1 wl x 9.7 x 3.12m)*
Machinery:	2-shaft TE (*Iltis, Jaguar* HTE), 1400ihp (*Panther, Eber* 1300ihp) = 14kts (*Iltis, Jaguar* 14½kts)
Armament:	2-105mm (*Iltis, Jaguar* 4-88mm), 6 MGs
Complement:	130

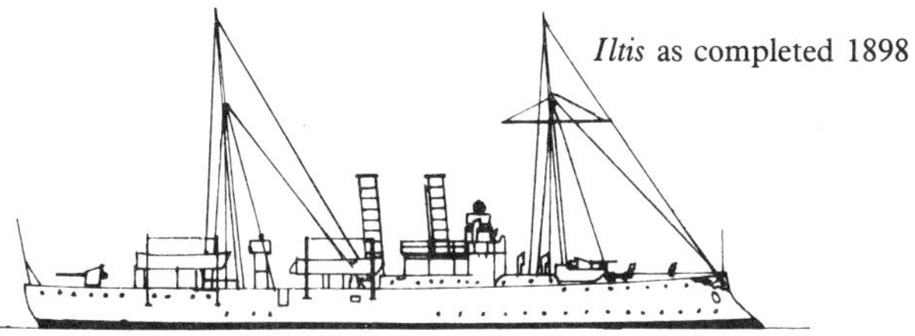

Class (builder, fate): *Iltis* (Schichau, sunk 28.9.1914), *Jaguar* (Schichau, sunk 7.11.1914), *Luchs* (Danzig DYd, sunk 28.9.1914), *Tiger* (Danzig DYd, sunk 29.10.1914), *Panther* (Danzig DYd, BU 1931), *Eber* (Vulcan, blown up 16.10.1917).

This group of vessels, which another navy might have classed as colonial sloops, or even cruisers, were handsome, two-funnelled ships resembling small cruisers. The first two had ram bows, the others straight ones. *Panther* became one of the most famous vessels of her day, and her name is still recorded in the history books, when she was sent to Agadir by the Kaiser as an anti-French gesture in 1908. This was one of the steps which finally led to war, and it is perhaps ironical that *Panther* should be the only one of these ships to survive that war, as a disarmed accommodation ship. *Eber* met the liner *Cap Trafalgar* in the middle of the Atlantic on the outbreak of war, and transferred her guns and some of her crew, so that the liner could become a raider (she was sunk by the armed merchant cruiser *Carmania* in an epic battle). The now disarmed gunboat was interned in Brazil until that country joined the Allies, when her crew blew her up. All the other vessels were lost in the course of the Japanese siege and capture of Tsingtao.

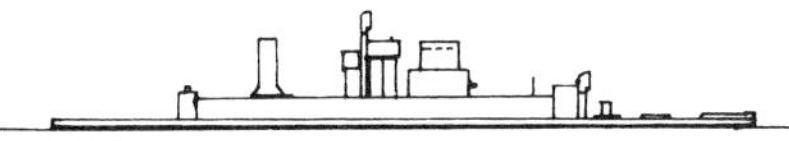

Mosel as completed 1874

RHEIN class *river monitors* (built 1872-4)

Displacement:	279t
Dimensions:	162ft 10in oa, 157ft 1in wl x 25ft 9in x 3ft 6in *(49.6 oa, 47.85 wl x 7.85 x 1.07m)*
Machinery:	2-shaft SH, 320ihp = 8¼kts
Armament:	2-120mm RML
Complement:	22

Class (builder, fate): *Rhein* (Weser, sold 1884), *Mosel* (Weser, sold 1884).

These vessels were the only monitor-type ships to serve in the German Navy, and were specifically intended for use on the Rhine, being attached to the Coblenz fortifications. As the immediate prospect of a French war of revenge for 1870 receded there was less use for them and they did not remain in service for long.

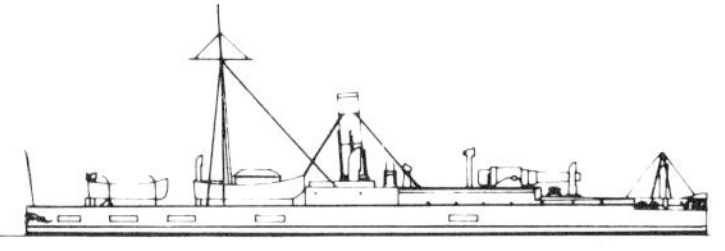

Wespe as completed 1876

WESPE class *armoured steamers* (launched 1876-81)

Displacement:	1139t
Dimensions:	152ft 4in oa, 149ft 5in wl x 34ft 10in x 10ft 10in *(46.4 oa, 45.5 wl x 10.6 x 3.3m)*
Machinery:	2-shaft compound
Armament:	1-305mm
Complement:	76

Class (builder, fate): *Wespe, Viper, Biene, Mücke, Scorpion, Basilisk, Camäleon, Crocodill, Salamander, Natter, Hummel.* (All Weser, out of service 1909-11).

These shallow draught, coastal defence gunboats were like larger versions of the British 'Rendel gunboats' and were intended to be capable of grounding themselves on the sandbanks off the German coast to act as fixed batteries. The big gun forward had only a limited traverse and was aimed by pointing the boat in the direction of the enemy. The gun was protected by an armoured breastwork 203mm (8in) thick, and the waterline belt was the same at its thickest. They were very poor seaboats, and were laid up for most of their lives, though no doubt they would have been useful vessels in any war off Germany's coast, in their earlier years. Later a shield was provided over the gun and 2-87mm and 2-37mm revolving cannon were added. Later still two submerged 350mm bow TT were fitted. Most of the class were used as barges after being struck off, *Salamander* being lost in 1910. *Viper* was still in use as a barge in the 1960s.

Viper, a Wespe class armoured gunboat

BRUMMER class *armoured steamers* (launched 1884)

Displacement:	914t
Dimensions:	212ft 9in oa, 205ft 6in wl 27ft 11in x 15ft 8in *(64.8 oa, 62.6 wl x 8.5 x 4.77m)*
Machinery:	1-shaft compound, 1650-2000ihp = 14-15kts
Armament:	1-210mm, 1-87mm, 2-37mm revolvers, 1-350mm TT bow
Complement:	78

Class (builder, fate): *Brummer* (Weser, hulked 1907), *Bremse* (Weser, hulked 1903).

Another approach to the one-gun gunboat idea, longer, lighter and less well armoured than the *Wespe* class, but also intended for coastal defence. Their main protection was a 160mm (6¼in) bulkhead to shelter them from end-on fire. They were good seaboats, and *Brummer* started life as the flagship of the torpedo forces, later being allocated to fishery protection, and later still being used as a weapons and machinery school. She was not broken up until 1922. Her sister was converted to an oil barge, and sold in this role in 1910.

Brummer in 1888

TORPEDO CRAFT

It was in the field of torpedo warfare that the young German Navy showed the most originality, and from this developed, as we have already seen, the light cruiser. It is for this reason that the *Zieten* and her successors, though fundamentally torpedo vessels, have been listed under cruisers. At the time the *Zieten* was ordered experiments had already been made with small launches and bigger tug-type vessels using spar torpedoes. Later a few boats armed with 'fish' torpedoes were built, but it was not until 1884 that Germany started building up a large force of torpedo boats. Orders were placed with a number of German builders, and two boats were purchased from the best British builders for comparison. The result of this sensible procedure was to establish the primacy of the firm of Schichau who then built nearly all the subsequent classes of German torpedo boats. They also successfully exported their boats and designs to many foreign navies. Schichau's foreign sales were Germany's one export success with warships in this period, but a very noteworthy one. The typical Schichau boat had a distinctive, almost pear-shaped hull, with its greatest breadth well aft, and two funnels side by side well forward.

The German Navy very sensibly insisted on sturdiness and seaworthiness as being more important than a high trial speed in their boats, and equally sensibly built rather larger versions of each class as leaders for each flotilla (Division Boats or 'D' boats). Though in a way a prefiguration of the torpedo boat destroyer their basic purpose was different; they were scaled-up torpedo boat designs, it is true, but their extra size was for carrying the extra complement of a flotilla leader, and for extra seaworthiness, not to carry the heavier gun armament to deal with their smaller sisters. They were also considerably slower than the first British destroyers, so it was a sensible move to order a modified version of one of these (*D10*) to investigate the new type.

Afterwards Germany continued to pursue her own course by continuing to give more importance than other navies to torpedoes than to guns in her designs, which, though similar to foreign destroyers, she continued to class as 'large torpedo boats'. Another peculiarly German feature was the short raised trawler-type forecastle, which was adopted in her first destroyers and as part of the search for seaworthiness which continued to be a distinctive feature of German ships of this type until after 1914. Because of the continuing emphasis on the primacy of torpedo attack, German vessels remained lower in silhouette, and less well armed with guns than their British contemporaries. The First World War was to prove that the heavier guns of British destroyers were, paradoxically, the better answer for successful torpedo attacks, as British destroyers were more successful in breaking through escort screens of their own type of ship than their German equivalents. However the German torpedo craft were excellent, seaworthy designs, and not to be despised as fighting ships.

Although examples of foreign designs were purchased, Germany did not otherwise build any second class torpedo boats designed to be carried and launched by larger ships. Instead she concentrated on the more sensible course of adapting ordinary ships' boats to carry torpedoes when necessary.

EARLY TORPEDO CRAFT

I-III Devrient 1871-2 *spar torpedo boats*

Displacement: 33t
Dimensions: 66ft 8in x 10ft 10in x 6ft 3in (*20.3 x 3.3 x 1.9m*)
Machinery: 1-shaft simple, 250ihp = 8kts
Armament: 1 spar torpedo
Complement: 8

Small steam launches. Reclassified in 1875 as minelayers *Nos 4-6*. In 1881 fitted with a 381mm bow TT and reclassed as harbour defence torpedo boats *Nos I-III*. Discarded 1885.

I-III Waltjen 1871 *spar torpedo boats*

Displacement: 24t
Dimensions: 47ft 11in x 10ft 7in x 5ft 11in (*14.6 x 3.22 x 1.8m*)
Machinery: 1-shaft simple, 60ihp = 7½kts
Armament: 1 spar torpedo
Complement: 8

Smaller versions of the Devrient boats. Reclassed as minelayers *Nos 1-3* in 1875 and discarded in 1881.

I-III Vulcan 1872-4 *spar torpedo vessels*

Notus (ex-*No I*), *Zephir* (ex-*No II*), *Rival* (ex- *No III*). *Notus* was bigger (303t as against 129t) than the other two, but all were of the paddle tug type and fitted with a spar torpedo. *Rival* was originally fitted with hydraulic (water jet) propulsion. The first two were re-allocated as tugs almost immediately. *Rival* spent some time as a torpedo research vessel, then in 1881 became minelayer *No 4*, but in 1884 reverted to being a tug.

ULAN Möller e Holberg 1875-6 *spar torpedo vessel*

Displacement: 431t
Dimensions: 119ft 5in oa, 115ft 1in wl x 26ft 9in x 15ft 5in (*36.38 oa, 35.05 wl x 8.0 x 4.7m*)
Machinery: 1-shaft simple, 782ihp = 12kts
Armament: 1 spar torpedo
Complement: 41

Ex-torpedo steamer *No IV*, the *Ulan* was like a large two-funnelled tug, and was rebuilt almost as soon as completed to take a 381mm bow TT and 3 revolving 37mm cannon. She was used for research, then as a torpedo school tender until converted to a barge in 1909. She was sold as such in 1919, and broken up in 1926.

V-XI Weser 1882-3 *first class torpedo boats*

Displacement: 55t
Dimensions: 103ft 5in x 12ft 11in x 6ft 9in (*31.5 x 3.93 x 2.05m*)
Machinery: 1-shaft compound, 590ihp = 19¾kts
Armament: 2-350mm TT bow, 2 spare torpedoes, 1 Hotchkiss gun
Complement: 13

Schutze (*No V*), *Flink* (*No VI*), *Scharf* (*No VII*), *Tapfer* (*No VIII*), *Kühn* (*No IX*), *Wörwarts* (*No X*) and *Sicher* (*No XI*), Germany's first class of torpedo boats, were not particularly satisfactory. In 1891 they were all taken out of service and put to subsidiary duties.

JÄGER Weser 1883 *torpedo gunboat*

Displacement: 138t
Dimensions: 114ft 3in oa, 109ft 11in wl x 18ft 4in x 8ft 6in (*34.8 oa, 33.5 wl x 5.58 x 2.6m*)
Machinery: 1-shaft compound, 550ihp = 15kts
Armament: 2-350mm TT, 1 Hotchkiss gun
Complement: 22

Originally intended to carry fixed 87mm guns forward and aft, but bow TT were substituted. The idea of a small fast boat using guns instead of torpedoes as its main weapons presumably did not seem too sensible by the time she was completing. *Jäger* was used for research but discarded in 1889 as being of no great operational value. She was broken up in 1900.

Thornycroft/White *second class torpedo boats*

The German Navy ordered one of Thornycroft's standard 63ft second class boats as *Th 2* (or *No IV*) in 1883 and also three of White's wooden second class boats (I-III), but apart from these British-built vessels made no further attempt to acquire specially-designed torpedo boats for carrying by larger ships. Like all other navies they equipped the standard steam boats of their larger warships with torpedoes, however.

FIRST CLASS TORPEDO BOATS

W1-W6 Weser 1884 *first class torpedo boats*

Displacement: 90t
Dimensions: 114ft 7in x 12ft 10in x 7ft 10in (*34.91 x 3.92 x 2.38m*)
Machinery: 1-shaft TE, 910ihp = 19¾kts

Ex-*XII-XVII*. 2-350mm TT bow, 2 spare torpedoes, 2-37mm Hotchkiss guns. Complement 15.

V1-V10 Vulcan 1884 *first class torpedo boats*

Displacement: 68t
Dimensions: 107ft 5in x 12ft 4in x 6ft (*32.75 x 3.76 x 1.84m*)
Machinery: 1-shaft TE, 590ihp = 17¾kts

Ex-*XVII-XXVII*. 2-350mm TT bow, 2 spare torpedoes, 2-37mm Hotchkiss guns. *V3* was damaged in an accident in 1885 and scrapped but her machinery was used in a later boat (*A*). Complement 14.

S1-S6 Schichau 1884-5 *first class torpedo boats*

Displacement: 97t
Dimensions: 123ft 10in x 16ft 2in x 7ft 4in (*37.72 x 4.92 x 2.23m*)
Machinery: 1-shaft TE, 870ihp = 19¼kts

Ex- *XXVIII-XXXIII*. 2-350mm TT bow, 2 spare torpedoes, 2-37mm Hotchkiss guns. Complement 15. The most seaworthy of the 1884-5 TBs. Later re-equipped with swivelling deck tubes. *S1* was sent to the Deutsches Museum at Munich in 1905; *S2* was used as a torpedo recovery boat, was redesignated *T2* in 1910 and was not broken up until 1915.

TH1 Thornycroft 1884 *first class torpedo boat*

Displacement: 80t
Dimensions: 122ft 2in x 12ft 7in x 6ft 10in (*37.22 x 3.82 x 2.07m*)
Machinery: 1-shaft compound, 650ihp = 17¾kts

2-350mm TT bow, 2 spare torpedoes, 2-37mm Hotchkiss guns. Complement 14.

Y Yarrow 1884-5 *first class torpedo boat*

Displacement: 82t
Dimensions: 119ft 4in x 13ft 2in x 6ft 6in (*36.35 x 4.02 x 2.3m*)
Machinery: 1-shaft compound, 600ihp = 18¼kts

2-350mm TT bow, 2 spare torpedoes, 2-37mm Hotchkiss guns. Complement 14.

G Germaniawerft 1884-5 *first class torpedo boat*

Displacement: 85t
Dimensions: 120ft 6in x 13ft 2in x 7ft 7in (*36.7 x 4.00 x 2.3m*)
Machinery: 1-shaft TE, 722ihp = 18¾kts

2-350mm TT bow, 2 spare torpedoes, 2-37mm Hotchkiss guns. Complement 14.

A Wilhelmshaven DYd 1887-9 *first class torpedo boat*

Displacement: 104t
Dimensions: 124ft 6in x 15ft 10in x 7ft 5in (*37.92 x 4.82 x 2.25m*)
Machinery: 1-shaft TE, 950ihp = 19kts

3-350mm TT (1 bow, 2 swivelling deck tubes), 2 spare torpedoes, 2 Hotchkiss guns. Complement 17. Experimentally built of diagonal mahogany planking on steel frames. This was not particularly satisfactory; the vessel was little used and was broken up in 1894.

K Kiel DYd 1887-9 *first class torpedo boat*

Displacement: 100t
Dimensions: 123ft 5in x 15ft 8in x 8ft 8in (*37.58 x 4.77 x 2.63m*)
Machinery: 1-shaft TE, 996ihp = 18¾kts

2-350mm TT bow, 2 spare torpedoes, 2 Hotchkiss guns. Complement 17. This experimental vessel was fitted with the Thornycroft 'guide blade screw', a form of ducted propeller. She was broken up in 1899.

A Danzig DYd 1888-9 *first class torpedo boat*

Displacement: 87t
Dimensions: 113ft 8in x 13ft 7in x 7ft 1in (*34.63 x 4.14 x 2.15m*)
Machinery: 1-shaft TE, 590ihp = 16½kts

2-350mm TT (1 deck, 1 bow), 2 spare torpedoes, 2 Hotchkiss guns. Complement 14. Built to use the machinery of the sunken *V3*. Disarmed from 1895, and in 1899 converted at Danzig to become the Baltic Station yacht, with a cabin built on deck aft, and given the name *Schneewittchen*. Broken up 1921.

S7-S23 Schichau 1885 *first class torpedo boats*

Displacement: 96t
Dimensions: 123ft 11in x 16ft 2in x 7ft 3in (*37.74 x 4.92 x 2.2m*)
Machinery: 1-shaft TE, 830ihp = 20¼kts

S24-S31 Schichau 1886-7 *first class torpedo boats*

Displacement: 101t
Dimensions: 123ft 11in x 15ft 9in x 7ft 8in (*37.74 x 4.8 x 2.34m*)
Machinery: 1-shaft TE, 840ihp = 19kts

S32 Schichau 1886 *first class torpedo boat*

Displacement: 117t
Dimensions: 128ft 5in x 17ft 5in x 8ft 3in (*39.12 x 5.3 x 2.52m*)
Machinery: 1-shaft TE, 900ihp =19¾kts

S33-S41 Schichau 1887 *first class torpedo boats*

Displacement: 111t
Dimensions: 130ft 11in x 15ft 9in x 7ft 8in (*39.88 x 4.8 x 2.33m*)
Machinery: 1-shaft TE, 1100ihp = 20kts

S42 Schichau 1889 *first class torpedo boat*

Displacement: 151t
Dimensions: 145ft 1in x 16ft 5in x 8ft 6in (*44.2 x 5.0 x 2.6m*)
Machinery: 1-shaft TE, 1420ihp = 22kts

S43-S57 Schichau 1889-90 *first class torpedo boats*

Displacement: 150t
Dimensions: 145t 1in x 16ft 5in x 8ft 10in (*44.2 x 5.0 x 2.7m*)
Machinery: 1-shaft TE, 1570ihp = 21½kts

S58-S65 Schichau 1891-2 *first class torpedo boats*

Displacement: 150t
Dimensions: 145ft 6in x 16ft 5in x 8ft 6in (*44.31 x 5.0 x 2.59m*)
Machinery: 1-shaft TE, 1232ihp = 20kts

All the boats in the *S7-S65* group were armed with 3-350mm TT (1 spare torpedo) and 2 Hotchkiss guns. The complement was 16 (*S7-S31*) or 20 (*S32-S65*). All adhered to Schichau's standard torpedo boat form, with the maximum breadth of hull well aft, producing a plan that resembled a pear shape. From 1893 a single 50mm gun replaced the Hotchkiss guns. Some of the earliest boats were discarded 1900-1910, becoming target boats or tenders, or just being broken up, but the majority were rebuilt and reboilered. In 1910 the survivors had their designations changed from *S* to *T*, to clear the *S* numbers for new destroyers. During the war they were used as minesweepers. Pre-war losses were *S12*, in a collision at the mouth of the Elbe on 13.3.1908; *T21*, in a collision with her sister *T38* on 16.8.1911; *S26*, which foundered in a storm at the mouth of the Elbe; *S32*, which was lost on 17.8.1910 in a collision with *S76* in the Baltic; *S41*, which sank in a storm on 28.8.1895; *S42*, sunk in a collision in 1902 but raised and put back into service; and *S48*, lost in a collision in the Jade on 11.4.1896. The following boats were lost during the war from various causes: *T25*, *T43*, *T46*, *T47*, *T50*, *T51*, *T52*, *T54*, *T56*, *T57*, *T58*, *T64* and *T65*. This loss rate indicates the use the German Navy was still getting out of these sturdy boats. The survivors were all disposed of in the years immediately following the war.

S66 Schichau 1892 *first class torpedo boat*

Displacement: 169t
Dimensions: 157ft 5in x 17ft 10in x 8ft 11in *(47.94 x 5.42 x 2.74m)*
Machinery: 1-shaft TE, 1610ihp = 22kts

S67-S73 Schichau 1892-4 *first class torpedo boats*

Displacement: 163t
Dimensions: 157ft 5in x 17ft 10in 8ft 6in *(47.94 x 5.42 x 2.58m)*
Machinery: 1-shaft TE, 1600ihp = 21¾kts

S74 Schichau 1894-5 *first class torpedo boat*

Displacement: 183t
Dimensions: 163ft 10in x 18ft 7in x 9ft 2in *(49.9 x 5.5 x 2.79m)*
Machinery: 1-shaft TE, 2500ihp = 23½kts

S75-S81 Schichau 1894-6 *first class torpedo boats*

Displacement: 177t
Dimensions: 160ft 11in x 17ft 5in x 9ft 4in *(49.0 x 5.3 x 2.85m)*
Machinery: 1-shaft TE, 1744ihp = 22½kts

S82-S87 Schichau 1897-8 *first class torpedo boats*

Displacement: 167t
Dimensions: 158ft 3in x 16ft 9in x 8ft 5in *(48.2 x 5.1 x 2.57m)*
Machinery: 1-shaft TE, 2140ihp = 25½kts

The *S66-S87* series boats were all armed with 3-450mm TT (1 spare torpedo) and 1-50mm gun. Complements varied from 22 to 29. These vessels continued the same process of steady improvement of the basic design begun by their predecessors. Most were rebuilt and reboilered in the opening years of the new century. *S76* was lost in a collision in 1910, and *S85* was stranded in 1898, but both were salved and returned to service. In September 1914 all were redesignated with the letter *T* beginning their numbers, and were used during the war as minesweepers and as tenders to instructional vessels. *S66, S67, S68* and *S78* were lost during the course of the war, the survivors being sold for breaking up between 1920 and 1921.

G88-G89 Germaniawerft 1897-8 *first class torpedo boats*

Displacement: 174t
Dimensions: 159ft 11in x 16ft 7in x 7ft 2in *(48.7 x 5.04 x 2.81m)*
Machinery: 1-shaft TE, 2468ihp = 26kts

Very similar to *S82-S87* and with an identical armament.

DIVISION BOATS

D1-D2 Schichau 1886-7 *division boats*

Displacement: 295t
Dimensions: 184ft x 21ft 8in x 11ft 2in *(56.05 x 6.6 x 3.4m)*
Machinery: 1-shaft TE, 2020ihp = 20½kts

D3-D4 Schichau 1887-8 *division boats*

Displacement: 295t
Dimensions: 189ft 3in x 22ft 4in x 10ft 7in *(57.64 x 6.8 x 3.23m)*
Machinery: 1-shaft TE, 2200ihp = 20¼kts

D5-D6 Schichau 1888-9 *division boats*

Displacement: 400t
Dimensions: 195ft 7in x 24ft 4in x 11ft 6in *(59.58 x 7.4 x 3.5m)*
Machinery: 1-shaft TE, 3200ihp = 22½kts

D7-D8 Schichau 1890-1 *division boats*

Displacement: 404t
Dimensions: 196ft 1in x 24ft 4in x 11ft 2in *(59.72 x 7.4 x 3.4m)*
Machinery: 1-shaft TE, 3600ihp = 22½kts

D9 Schichau 1894 *division boat*

Displacement: 451t
Dimensions: 206ft 10in x 25ft 3in x 12ft 3in *(63.0 x 7.7 x 3.73m)*
Machinery: 1-shaft TE, 4200ihp = 23½kts

These 'division boats', or flotilla leaders, were basically larger versions of the torpedo boats they were intended to lead, with a similar armament and speed, but of a larger size in order to accommodate the extra staff needed. The most interesting design was the last, *D9*, which had the beginnings of the 'trawler bow', a raised forecastle which did not extend back as far as the bridge. *D1-D6* were armed with 3-350mm TT (1 spare torpedo) and 6 Hotchkiss guns; *D7-D8* had 3-450mm TT (1 spare torpedo) and 6 Hotchkiss guns; and *D9* was fitted with 3-450mm TT and 3-50mm Hotchkiss. Complement was 46, except *D9* 52. All were rebuilt and reboilered in the first decade of the new century. By 1893, 3-50mm guns had replaced the Hotchkiss revolving cannon. *D1* and *D2* were converted to yachts for the Baltic and North Sea stations respectively, being named *Carmen* (1905) and *Alice Roosevelt* (1902). They were converted back for more warlike duties in 1914, and with the others were used for coastal defence patrols or training tasks, being finally discarded in 1920-21.

S84 and *S86* in June 1913

DESTROYERS

D10 Thornycroft 1896-8 *torpedo boat destroyer*

Displacement: 365t
Dimensions: 217ft x 19ft 6in x 7ft 9in *(66.1 x 5.95 x 2.35m)*
Machinery: 2-shaft TE, 5780ihp = 27¼kts

In most respects *D10* was very similar to the Royal Navy's '30-knotters' built by Thornycroft, but with 5-50mm guns and 3-450mm TT was more lightly armed. She later lost one of her TT, the fixed bow tube which was an unseaworthy feature. *D10* served during the 1914-18 war in coastal defence and training duties, and was broken up in 1922. Complement 47.

S90-S101 Schichau 1898-1901 *torpedo boat destroyers*

Displacement: 388t
Dimensions: 206ft 10in x 22ft 11in x 9ft 4in *(63.0 x 7.0 x 2.23m)*
Machinery: 2-shaft TE, 3900ihp = 26½kts

S102-S107 Schichau 1900-2 *torpedo boat destroyers*

Displacement: 400t
Dimensions: 207ft 6in x 22ft 11in x 8ft 10in *(63.2 x 7.0 x 2.68m)*
Machinery: 2-shaft TE, 5900ihp = 27½kts

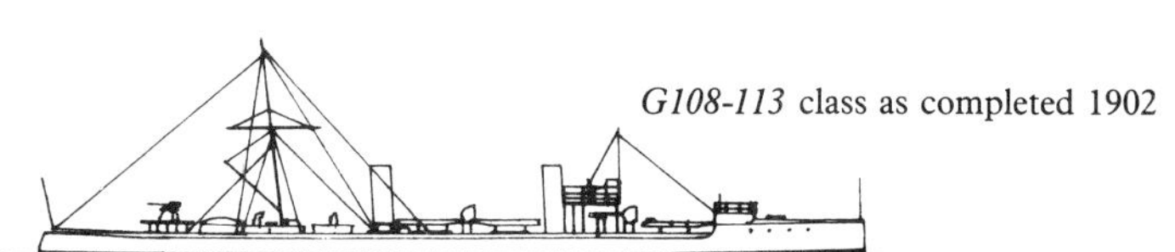

G108-113 class as completed 1902

G108-G113 Germaniawerft 1900-2 *torpedo boat destroyers*

Displacement: 433t
Dimensions: 216ft 1in x 21ft 11in x 9ft 5in *(65.8 x 6.7 x 2.87m)*
Machinery: 2-shaft TE, 6000ihp = 29kts

S114-S119 Schichau 1902-3 *torpedo boat destroyers*

Displacement: 408t
Dimensions: 207ft 6in x 22ft 11in x 8ft 10in (*63.2 x 7.0 x 2.69m*)
Machinery: 2-shaft TE, 5900ihp = 28kts

S120-S124 Schichau 1903-4 *torpedo boat destroyers*

Displacement: 461t
Dimensions: 212ft 5in x 22ft 11in x 8ft 8in (*64.7 x 7.0 x 2.63m*)
Machinery: 2-shaft TE, 6400ihp = 27½kts

S126-S131 Schichau 1904-5 *torpedo boat destroyers*

Displacement: 474t
Dimensions: 212ft 5in x 22ft 11in x 9ft 1in (*64.7 x 7.0 x 2.76m*)
Machinery: 2-shaft TE, 6490ihp = 28kts

S125 Schichau 1903-4 *torpedo boat destroyer*

Displacement: 447t
Dimensions: 212ft 5in x 22ft 11in x 10ft 5in (*64.7 x 7.0 x 3.17m*)
Machinery: 2-shaft Parsons turbines, 6600shp = 27¾kts

S90-S107, *G108-G113* and *S114-S131* were all armed with 3-450mm TT and 3-50mm guns. The complement varied from 57 to 61. Apart from the experimental turbine vessel (another was building at the end of the period), these units, classed as large torpedo boats but, despite their lighter guns, really the equivalent of contemporary foreign destroyers, show a large degree of homogeneity. They all shared the 'trade mark' of the torpedo tube placed before the bridge in a well deck between the raised forecastle and the charthouse. All had two funnels. In fact this design was a combination of the best features of the *D9* and the *D10*, of the German torpedo boat traditional design, and of the British destroyer. The result was a sturdy and seaworthy vessel, not as fast as foreign boats, but probably more useful than most. *S97* was converted before entering service to be the tender to the Imperial yacht *Hohenzollern* and was renamed *Sleipnir*. She was reconverted to a fighting ship when war broke out, and with all her sisters was reclassed as a *T*-boat in September 1914. Several of these boats were rearmed, wholly or partly, with 88mm guns. *S90* was deliberately run ashore during the siege of Tsingtao in 1914. *T116* was torpedoed and sunk by the British submarine *E9* on 6.10.1914. On 17.10.1914 British destroyers and the cruiser *Undaunted* sank *T115*, *T117*, *T118* and *T119*. *T100* was lost in a collision in 1915, *T122* was mined in 1918 and *T123* in 1916, *T124* sank in 1914 in a collision, and *T129* was lost in 1915. *T126* had been lost in 1905 but was raised, and with her surviving sisters was disposed of in the early 1920s.

TAKU 1898-9 *captured destroyer*

Displacement: 280t
Dimensions: 193ft 9in x 21ft x 8ft 4in (*59.0 x 6.4 x 2.55m*)
Machinery: 2-shaft TE, 6000ihp = 32kts

Ex-Chinese, built by Schichau, and armed with 6-47mm guns and 2-450mm TT. Complement 57. Captured by Roger Keyes' boarding party in 1900, during the allied operations against the Taku forts, with her three sisters, one each of which went to the Royal Navy, France and Russia. The German Navy rearmed its vessel with 2-50mm guns. She was lost during the Japanese siege of Tsingtao in 1914, having spent her career on the China station. See also under China.

(All uncredited photos in this section: CPL)

MISCELLANEOUS SHIPS

PELIKAN *minelayer*

Displacement: 2384t
Dimensions: 276ft 5in oa, 265ft 7in wl x 38ft 5in x 16ft 11in (*84.2 oa, 80.9 wl x 11.7 x 5.14m*)
Machinery: 2-shaft TE, 3150ihp = 15¼kts
Armament: 4-88mm, 400 mines
Complement: 195

Name	Builder	Launched	Fate
PELIKAN	Wilhelmshaven DYd	29.7.90	BU 1921

Though basically a mercantile hull, this vessel is interesting as one of the first specialised minelayers built and the first example of a German ship of this type. Laid down in 1889 and completed in October 1891, she was principally intended to transport mines and not lay them, but the mines were carried on deck rails, and could be lowered over the side if required. She was rebuilt in 1908.

There was also a smaller vessel, the *Rhein*, built in 1867 and used as a mine transporter and school ship until hulked in 1911.

TRAINING SHIPS

As part of the programme of setting up a really effective training organisation, the old Royal Navy wooden screw ship-of-the-line *Renown* was purchased for use as a gunnery school ship in 1870. She was broken up in 1892, but had already been replaced by a purpose-built vessel. This unusual ship was the *Mars*, built 1877-1881. Though she carried an impressive outfit of examples of all types of guns in service with the German Navy at the time, and resembled a contemporary broadside ironclad, she was not intended as a fighting ship. She did not carry anything except practice ammunition, was unarmored and very slow. Her nickname of 'the rubber battleship' sums her up. However she was a sensible investment, and gave good service in a task most navies allocated to out-of-date fighting ships until broken up in 1921.

Two ex-British big-sloops *Musquito* and *Rover* were purchased for sail training in 1862 and 1861; they were hulked in 1891-2. A similar vessel, *Undine*, was built at Danzig in 1869-71; she was wrecked in 1884.

The ex-British training brig *Rover*

Austria-Hungary

Although the history of the Austrian Navy can be traced back to 1382 when Trieste came under Austrian protection, it was not until the eighteenth century that a small naval force was established. This was expanded in the 1830s, but was always dominated by northern Italian elements in the Navy. However, after the events of 1848, Venice became an independent Republic and three corvettes and many small vessels of the Austrian Navy in Venice fell into rebel hands, as did the arsenal and its stores. Losses of Italian territory and crews deprived the Austrian Navy of its Italian character. All the nationalities of the monarchy were now represented and traditions began to follow northern European patterns rather than Italian ones. Some Italian republics and cities declared war on Austria but were defeated in 1849, and when the Austrians reconquered Venice they took over all naval vessels there.

In 1848 Franz Joseph I became Emperor of Austria. In order to strengthen the northern influence in his navy, he appointed a Dane, Rear-Admiral Hans Birch von Dahlerup as C in C. British naval practice was followed and naval vessels were designated SMS (*Seiner Majestät Schiff*). After only two and a half years of reorganisation, he resigned. Two years later Archduke Ferdinand Max, brother of the Emperor, became C in C and developed his country into an important seapower. In 1856 the steam frigate *Radetzky* was ordered from England and used as a model for Austrian shipbuilding, marking the beginning of the industry in Austria. From then on most of the country's naval vessels were built in Austrian yards.

At that time, the torpedo, had been designed and constructed in Austria. In 1859 the Austrian Commander Johann Luppis had been trying to develop a self-propelled weapon to be directed from the coast, which he called a 'coast saver'. Later, he took his idea to the British engineer Robert Whitehead, director of a machine factory at Fiume (Rijeka). Whitehead developed the first really automotive torpedo leaving little of Luppis' original plan except the basic concept. Another Austrian designer, Ludwig Obry, then made one of the first major improvements in the Whitehead torpedo, adding a gyroscope to keep the missile on course.

In 1863 the King of Denmark tried once more to incorporate the Duchy of Schleswig into Denmark and in the following year Austria joined Prussia in an alliance against Denmark. As the German forces consisted only of some Prussian gunboats, the Danish islands were safe from invasion, but the Danish fleet inflicted heavy losses on German commerce. The Austrian Government then gave in to the urgent pleas of the Germans and agreed to send a squadron of steamships to the North Sea.

On 2 March 1866 the screw frigate *Schwarzenberg* (51 guns) and the gunboat *Seehund* (4 guns) under the command of Commodore Tegetthoff received orders to go north via Lisbon. He was to be joined *en route* by the screw frigate *Radetzky* (37 guns). At Lisbon they were to wait for the rest of the promised Austrian squadron under the command of Rear-Admiral von Wüllerstorff but as this reinforcement did not arrive, Tegetthoff steamed to the Downs for coaling. Arriving in Germany his force was joined by three small Prussian gunboats. At sea on 9 May Tegetthoff sighted the Danish squadron near Heligoland. The Danish squadron consisted of the steam frigates *Niels Juel* (42 guns), *Jylland* (44 guns) and the steam corvette *Heimdal* (16 guns). The fighting went on for an hour and a half, before the superiority of the Danish guns began to tell. Tegetthoff's flagship, *Schwarzenberg*, caught fire and burned so fiercely that he had to withdraw his little force to Heligoland. As soon as the fire was under control, he returned to continue the battle, but Suenson had left, having received news of the armistice.

In spite of the damage they had sustained, the Austrians had won a strategic victory: the blockade of the German North Sea had been lifted and German merchantmen could sail unhindered. Tegetthoff went on to Hamburg, where he and his men were enthusiastically welcomed. Austria as well as Germany was overjoyed by the result of the action and the bravery of the sailors. Tegetthoff was promoted to Rear-Admiral. However, the battle near Heligoland was of no great significance, except perhaps in that it was the last fight between squadrons of wooden vessels.

Two years after the German-Danish War the former allies, Austria and Prussia, faced each other in the Seven Weeks War, from June to August 1866. In preparation for the coming conflict, Prussia took advantage of the fact that Italy, having proclaimed herself a kingdom in 1861, was trying to acquire Italian-speaking provinces still under Austrian rule, and concluded an alliance with Italy. War was fought on three separate fronts but the Austrian Navy only took part in the engagements with the Italians. The Italian Navy consisted of 11 ironclads, and a twelfth vessel, the ram *Affondatore*, was nearing completion in England and was soon to be delivered. The builders of the *Affondatore* had based her construction on lessons learned from the American Civil War. According to a correspondent of *The Times*, she looked formidable enough to sink the entire Austrian fleet single handed. The Italian fleet was commanded by the 61-year-old Admiral Count Carlo Pellion di Persano.

A different picture was presented by the Austrian fleet. Though five ironclads were afloat and two more nearing completion at Trieste, not one was in service. Most of the ships were either disarmed or undergoing repairs. All the newer ships had been built in Austria, along simple lines and armoured with excellent Styrian iron. However, Austria lagged behind the leading industrial nations in manufacturing modern rifled guns and even her newer ships had old muzzle-loaders. Modern weapons were on order from Krupp's for the two new ships under construction, but when war broke out the Prussians prevented their delivery. When Rear-Admiral Tegetthoff was appointed C in C he ordered all ships to be refitted, regardless of their condition.

On 24 June the Italian army was defeated at the second battle of Custozza and in the hope of regaining some prestige, the Italian authorities began to press for naval action. After some half-hearted sorties di Persano finally left Ancona on 15 July to invade the island of Lissa (now Vis). Its fortifications dated from Napoleonic times, when the British had occupied it, but the Italian landing was carried out so slowly that a nearby signal station could keep Tegetthoff informed. When the Austrian commander heard that Lissa was being attacked, he first thought that it was a feint to lure him away from Pola and Trieste, but when it became clear that the assault was genuine, his fleet put to sea.

The next day at 10.45 a fierce battle began between the opposing fleets. There is no doubt about the superiority of the Italian fleet over the Austrian fleet at Lissa: 37 Italian fighting vessels with 645 guns faced 27 Austrian vessels with 532 guns. But through his gallant leadership, Tegetthoff defeated the enemy, using his ships to ram the Italians. Lissa was the first naval action on the high seas since Trafalgar and also the first battle between armoured squadrons. Despite the close gunnery ranges and the numerous hits the artillery proved largely ineffective and the ram acquired a largely spurious credibility for decades.

The battle was followed by the Peace of Vienna with Italy, and the Peace of Prague with Prussia, the North German Confederation being replaced by the German Confederation to which Austria did not belong.

The successful C in C, Tegetthoff, was also an able administrator and introduced reforms still in force some 50 years later but his recommendation to build a fleet of 15 armoured vessels could not be carried out because of small naval budgets. When Tegetthoff died in 1871, Austria had only acquired three new armoured ships.

In 1867, following Prussia's defeat of Austria at Königgrätz in 1866, the Austrian Emperor had to accept Hungarian demands for far-reaching autonomy. The Compromise (*Ausgleich*) concluded in 1867 split the Hapsburg monarchy in two almost independent parts: the Empire of Austria and the Kingdom of Hungary. Each part of the new dual state, henceforth called the Austro-Hungarian Monarchy, had its own parliament and government. This led to severe setbacks in naval development, because a Hungarian veto on naval budget estimates could block the whole budget.

In 1889 the dual character of the monarchy was also expressed in the different designations for the various services. The joint army and the joint navy were designated as KuK (*Kaiserlich und Königlich*, meaning Imperial and Royal).

The development and construction of warships for the Austro-Hungarian Navy depended, as in other navies, on two factors: shipyard facilities and armour/gun production. The main Austrian yard, Stabilimento Tecnico Triestino (STT) was privately founded in 1857 and most Austrian merchant vessels and warships were built there. The second important yard was the Pola Navy Yard (Pola N Yd). At the same time the Skoda Ironworks at Witkowize (now Czechoslovakia) started production, but before the full development of these key industries, ships and guns had to be ordered abroad.

The official government view of naval power in general and capital ships in particular was heavily influenced by the continental situation of the Hapsburg Empire. The access to the Adriatic Sea did not affect continental thinking, so naval budget estimates were drastically cut down every year.

Shortage of money and dockyard facilities meant that Austro-Hungarian capital ships were always smaller than their contemporaries in other navies and to acquire the necessary gunpower Austrian constructors were forced to build very compact ships. The main concern of Austrian design was to match their most probable opponent, the rapidly growing Italian Navy. Apart from the first ships of some types ordered in England, Austrian constructors developed solutions of their own, and in the last decades of the century a fully developed indigenous armament industry supplied all modern weaponry.

Not until 1895, under the impact of Mahan's naval doctrines, was a modern Austro-Hungarian Navy to be established. Austria's navy needed this 15-year peace period as it was unprepared for hostilities. However, in 1900 an Austrian cruiser squadron and a landing detachment took part in the actions against the Boxer rebels in China. It is not widely known that Austria's percentage losses were higher than those of any other nation involved. In 1905 an Austrian admiral was C in C of a combined Western fleet cruising off the Turkish island of Mytilene (Lesbos) to watch the armistice between Turkish and Greek civilians.

STRENGTH OF THE AUSTRO-HUNGARIAN FLEET 1860

Ship of the line: *Kaiser*, 91 guns – see tables below

Screw frigates: *Radetzky*, *Adria* and *Donau*, 50 guns – see tables below

Screw corvettes: *Dandolo*, *Erzherzog Friedrich*, 22 guns – see tables below

Sailing frigates: *Bellona*, 34 guns, 1240t, launched 1842 (stricken 1868, BU 1903); *Venus*, 12 guns, 1552t, launched 1832 (cadet training ship, sold 1872)

Sailing sloops: *Minerva*, 14 guns, 590t, launched 1833 (cadet training ship, BU 1893); *Carolina*, 20 guns, 800t, launched 1844 (BU 1870); *Diana*, 20 guns, 710t, launched 1834 (BU 1870)

Sailing brigs: *Hussar*, *Montecuccoli*, *Pola*, *Pylades*, 12-16 guns, 390-480t, launched 1831-49 (BU 1870-72)

Paddle steamers: *Kaiserin Elisabeth*, *Prinz Eugen*, *Volta*, *Santa Lucia*, *Curtatone*, *Custoza*, *Vulkan*, *Taurus*, *Achilles*, *Messagiere*, *Gorzkowski*, *Jupiter*, *Roma*, 2-6 guns, 42-1560t, launched 1843-54

Gunboats: *Möve*, *Kerka*, *Narenta*, *Pelikan*, *Auslugger*, *Deutschmeister*, 2-6 guns, 230-520t, launched 1858-60 (BU 1906-7); there were also 6 new paddle gunboats for the defence of Venice numbered *I-VI*; and the floating batteries *Feuerspeier*, *Vesuvio*, *Mongibello* and *Fermo*

Schooners: *Camäleon*, *Fido*, *Bravo*, *Dromedar*, *Saida*, *Arethusa*, *Arthemisia*

ARMOURED SHIPS

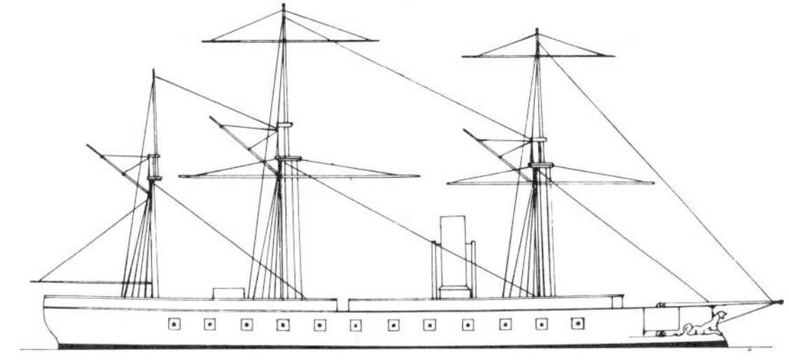

Salamander as completed 1862

Rated as 3rd Class armoured frigates, these ship belong to the earliest period of armoured ship design and were the first built as such for the Austro-Hungarian fleet. They were designed by Joseph von Romako, Director of Austrian Naval Construction. Both vessels had wooden hulls with iron armour plates, and both took part in the Battle of Lissa. *Drache* was refitted and rearmed between 1869 and 1872, and the sail area was also increased to 11,733 sq ft (1090m²). She was stricken 13.6.1875 and scrapped in 1883/4. *Salamander* was refitted and rearmed 1869-70, the sail area being similarly increased. She was stricken on 18.3.1883, then served as a mine store ship, and was finally scrapped in 1895/6.

DRACHE class *broadside ironclads*

Displacement: 2750t
Dimensions: 206ft pp x 45ft 8in x 20ft 7in (*62.78 pp x 13.94 x 6.30m*)
Machinery: 1 shaft, 2 cyl horizontal LP engine, 1842ihp=11kts
Armour: Belt 115mm
Armament: As built: 18-24pdr MLR, 10-48pdr ML (also 1-8pdr ML, 1-4pdr ML landing guns); as rearmed Nov 1867: 10-7in Armstrong ML, 2-2in bronze MLR
Complement: 346

Name	Builder	Laid down	Launched	Comp	Fate
DRACHE	STT	Feb 1861	9.9.61	Nov 62	Scrapped 1883/4
SALAMANDER	STT	Feb 1861	22.8.61	May 62	Scrapped 1895/6

AUSTRIA-HUNGARY

These three 2nd Class armoured frigates were enlarged versions of the *Drache* class armoured frigates, but had more powerful engines, the same rigging and more guns. They all had a sternchase casemate. These three units had extremely bad seakeeping capabilities, pitched considerably and were very wet. During a minor rebuilding in 1867 the figureheads were removed, and the open bow sections plated in to improve seakeeping qualities. All three units took part at the Battle of Lissa. *Kaiser Max* and *Juan de Austria* were handed over to Stabilimento Tecnico Triestino for 'rebuilding' in December 1873. In 1873 the hulk of *Prinz Eugen* was handed over to Pola Navy Yard for 'rebuilding'. For further details see under centre battery ships of the same name.

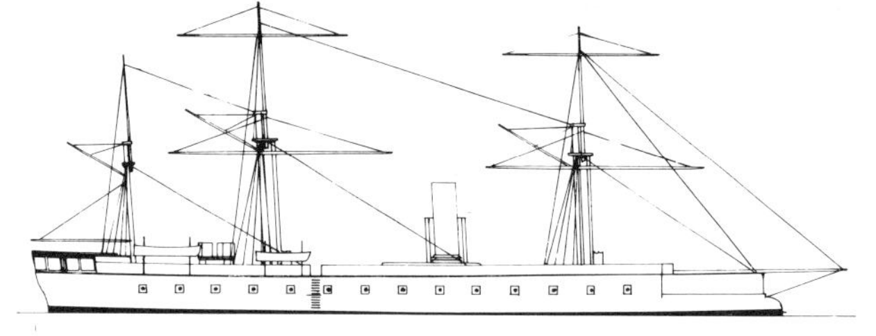

Kaiser Max as completed 1863

KAISER MAX class *broadside ironclads*

Displacement: 3588t
Dimensions: 232ft 2in pp x 45ft 11in x 20ft 9in *(70.78 pp x 14.00 x 6.32m)*
Machinery: 1-shaft, 2 cyl horizontal engine, 1900ihp = 11kts; *Kaiser Max* 1926ihp = 11.4kts
Armour: Belt 110mm
Armament: 1863: 15-24pdr (15cm) MLR, 16-48pdr, 1-12pdr, 1-6pdr; as rearmed 1867: 12-7in Armstrong ML, 2-3in (4pdr) boat guns
Complement: 386

Name	Builder	Laid down	Launched	Comp	Fate
KAISER MAX	STT	Oct 1861	14.3.62	1863	Rebuilt Dec 1873
PRINZ EUGEN	STT	Oct 1861	14.6.62	Mar 1863	Rebuilt Nov 1873
JUAN DE AUSTRIA	STT	Oct 1861	26.7.62	1863	Scrapped 1886

1

2

3

1. *Salamander* after 1869-70 refit
2. *Juan de Austria* after 1867 refit with plated-up bow section
3. *Erzherzog Ferdinand Max* during her last commission

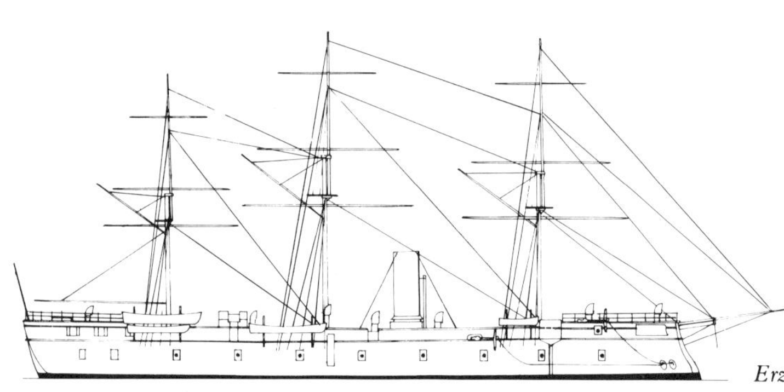

Erzherzog Ferdinand Max 1867

These two wooden broadside battery ships were built to the design of the Director of Naval Construction, Jospeh von Romako. They superficially resembled the French *Gloire*, and originally were to be armed with 32 unrifled 48pdrs. They were armoured for the whole length of their hull. *Erzherzog Ferdinand Max* was Tegetthoff's flagship at Lissa. In 1867 she had her bow repaired at the Royal Navy dockyard at Malta. She was stricken on 19.5.1886, but between 1889 and 1908 she was a tender to the gunnery training ship. She was scrapped in 1916. *Habsburg* saw active service from 1867 to 1886 and between 1886 and 1898 was accommodation and guard ship at Pola. She was stricken on 22.10.1898 and scrapped in 1900.

ERZHERZOG FERDINAND MAX class *broadside ironclads*

Displacement: 5130t
Dimensions: 274ft 9in oa, 262ft 4in pp x 52ft 4in x 23ft 5in *(83.75oa, 79.97 pp x 15.96 x 7.14m)*
Machinery: 1-shaft, 2 cyl H engine, 2925ihp = 12.54kts
Armour: Belt (battery) 123mm, fore and aft 87mm
Armament: 1866: 16-48pdr, 4-8pdr, 2-3pdr; 1869: 14-8in Krupp BL; 1874: 14-7in Armstrong ML, 4 light guns; 1882: 14-7in Armstrong ML, 4-9cm BL, 2-7cm BL, 2-47mm QF (rev), 3-25mm MGs; 1886:8-10cm; 1887: 1-24cm, 1-26cm
Complement: 511

Name	Builder	Laid down	Launched	Comp	Fate
ERZHERZOG FERDINAND MAX	STT	6.5.1863	24.5.65	–	Scrapped 1916
HABSBURG	STT	June 1863	24.6.65	–	Scrapped 1899-1900

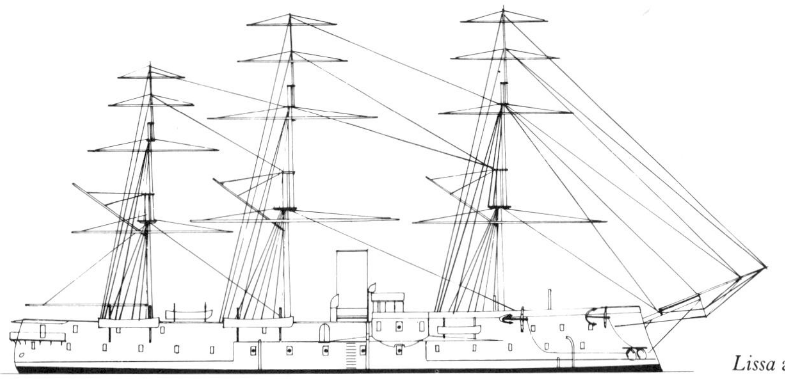

Lissa as completed 1871

Lissa was the first centre battery or casemate ship of the Austro-Hungarian fleet. The hull and the casemates were built of wood and armoured with iron plates. The parts fore and aft of the casemates were built of iron. The gunports were situated only 1.96m above the waterline. She was originally fully-rigged with 33,497sq ft (3112m²) of sail, which was reduced to 15,113sq ft (1404m²) in 1886. She was stricken 13.11.1892 and scrapped between 1893 and 1895.

LISSA *centre battery ship*

Displacement: 7086t
Dimensions: 293ft 3in oa, 284ft 8in wl x 56ft 10in x 27ft 10in (*89.38 oa, 86.76 wl x 17.32 x 8.5m*)
Machinery: 1-shaft, 2 cyl H engine, 3619ihp = 12.83kts
Armour: Belt 152mm on 770mm wood, battery 127mm on 724mm wood, bulkheads 114mm
Armament: As built: 12-9in Krupp BL, 4-8pdr MLR, 2-3pdr MLR; 1881: 12-9in Krupp BL, 4-9cm/24 BL, 2-7cm/15 BL, 3-47mm MGs, 2-25mm MGs
Complement: 620

Name	Builder	Laid down	Launched	Comp	Fate
LISSA	STT	27.6.1867	25.2.69	May 1871	Scrapped 1893-95

Lissa after 1886 reduction to barquentine rig

Erzherzog Albrecht

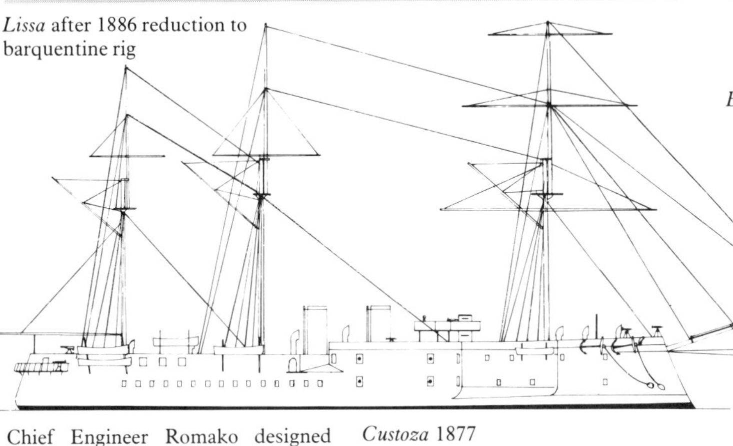

Custoza 1877

Erzherzog Albrecht as completed 1874

Chief Engineer Romako designed these two casemate ships – the first iron ships of the Austro-Hungarian Navy – after studying the results of the Battle of Lissa. He arranged the guns at two levels, so that they could bear forward while the ship was speeding up to ram the enemy. His designs emphasised less speed and fewer guns, in favour of high defensive capability. *Erzherzog Albrecht* saw active service from 1874 to 1908. In 1908 she was renamed *Feuerspeier* and became the tender of the gunnery training ship, and from October 1915 she served as accommodation ship for German naval personnel. In 1920 she was ceded to Italy as war reparation and renamed *Buttafuoco*. *Custoza* was named after the Battle of Custozza in northern Italy, but due to a spelling error in the official papers she was christened *Custoza*. Originally she was fully-rigged, but the spars were reduced in 1877 to schooner rig with three square sails on the foremast. From 1914 she served as a workers' accommodation ship and in 1920 she was ceded to Italy as a war reparation.

The exact fate and date of scrapping of both vessels are unknown.

CUSTOZA *centre battery ship*

Displacement: 7609t
Dimensions: 311ft 9in oa, 302ft 3in pp x 58ft x 26ft (*95.03 oa, 92.14 pp x 17.70 x 7.90m*)
Machinery: 1-shaft, 2 cyl H engine, 4158ihp = 13.75kts
Armour: Belt 229mm, casemate 178-152mm
Armament: As built: 8-26cm L/22 Krupp BL, 6-9cm L/24, 2-7cm L/15; from 1882 additionally: 4-47mm QF guns, 5-47mm MGs (rev), 2-25mm MGs, 4-35cm TT
Complement: 548

Name	Builder	Laid down	Launched	Comp	Fate
CUSTOZA	STT	17.11.1869	20.8.72	Feb 1875	Scrapped?

ERZHERZOG ALBRECHT *centre battery ship*

Displacement: 5980t
Dimensions: 294ft 3in oa, 288ft 3in wl x 56ft 3in x 22ft (*89.69 oa, 87.87 wl x 17.15 x 6.72m*)
Machinery: 1-shaft, 2 cyl H engine, 3969ihp = 12.84kts
Armour: Belt 203mm, casemates 177mm
Armament: 8-24cm L/22 Krupp BL, 6-9cm L/24 Krupp BL, 2-7cm L/15 Krupp BL, 5-47mm MGs (rev), 4-47mm L/35 QF guns, 2-25mm MGs, 4-35cm TT (1 bow, 1 stern, 2 beam)
Complement: 540

Name	Builder	Laid down	Launched	Comp	Fate
ERZHERZOG ALBRECHT	STT	1.6.1870	24.4.72	June 1874	Scrapped?

In 1869 an inspection of the old 91-gun ship of the line *Kaiser* showed that the framing was in good condition. She was docked on 2.2.1869 and wooden planks were renewed, she was given a new bow and stern, and the hull above water was rebuilt in iron. She emerged as a casemate ship similar to *Lissa*. She retained her old machinery but had superheaters to obtain more power. In 1902 the engines were removed, she was renamed *Bellona* and became an accommodation hulk. She remained at Pola until the end of the First World War, but her fate is unknown.

KAISER *centre battery ship*

Displacement: 5720t
Dimensions: 255ft wl x 58ft 3in x 24ft 2in (*77.75 wl x 17.76 x 7.37m*)
Machinery: 1-shaft, 2 cyl H engine, 2786ihp = 11.55kts
Armour: Wl belt amidships 152mm, fore and aft 102mm, casemates 127mm
Armament: As built: 10-23pdr (9in) Armstrong ML, 6-8pdr RML; rearmed 1882: 10-23pdr (9in) Armstrong ML, 6-9cm/24 BL, 2-7cm/15 BL, 4-47mm L/33 QF guns, 3-47mm MGs (rev), 4-25mm MGs; added 1885: 3-35cm TT (1 bow, 2 beam)
Complement: 471

Name	Builder	Laid down	Launched	Comp	Fate
KAISER	Pola N Yd	25.3.1855	1871	Dec 1873	Scrapped?

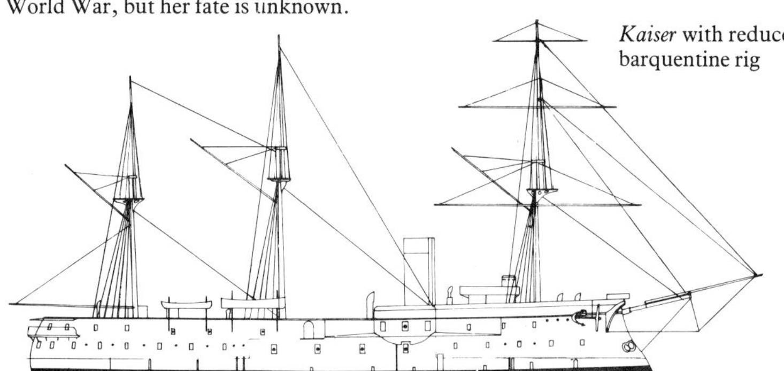
Kaiser with reduced barquentine rig

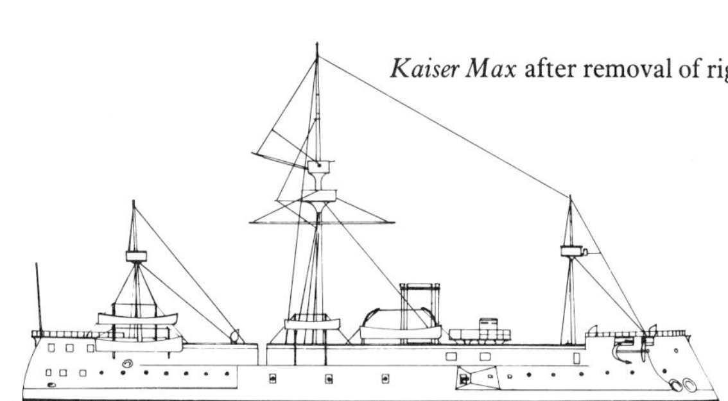
Kaiser Max after removal of rig

For political reasons new ships were at times not approved in the budget, but the rebuilding of existing ships was generally passed without opposition. Therefore the three obsolete armoured frigates of the *Kaiser Max* class were 'officially rebuilt'. In fact the rotten wooden hulls were scrapped, only the machinery without boilers, parts of the armour and serviceable parts of the equipment being used on completely new iron casemate ships with the same names. This often leads to confusion between old and 'rebuilt' ships. However, one conversion was three times as expensive as the building of a new warship, so the policy was ill advised. The original sail area of 1633.15m² was reduced to 1158.60m² in 1880.

Kaiser Max was stricken on 30.12.1904, and from 1909 she was an accommodation ship at Cattaro Bay; in 1920 she was ceded to Yugoslavia and renamed *Tivat*; her fate is unknown.

KAISER MAX class *centre battery ships*

Displacement: 3548t
Dimensions: 249ft oa, 240ft 3in wl x 50ft x 20ft 2in (*75.87 oa, 73.23 wl x 15.25 x 6.15m*)
Machinery: 1-shaft, 2 cyl H LP engine, 2755ihp = 13.28kts
Armour: Wl belt 203mm, armoured bulkheads 115mm, casemate 125mm (2 rows of new armour plates, all others came from the old armoured frigates)
Armament: 8-21cm L/20 Krupp BL, 4-9cm L/24 Uchatius BL, 2-7cm L/15 (landing gun), 6-47mm L/33 QF guns, 3-47mm MGs (rev), 2-25mm MGs, 4-35cm TT (1 bow, 1 stern, 2 beam)
Complement: 400

Name	Builder	Laid down	Launched	Comp	Fate
KAISER MAX	STT	14.2.1874	28.12.75	26.10.76	To Yugoslavia in 1920
DON JUAN D'AUSTRIA	STT	14.2.1874	25.10.75	26.6.76	Sank in 1919
PRINZ EUGEN	Pola N Yd	Oct 1874	7.9.77	Nov 1878	Confiscated by Italy in 1919

Prinz Eugen was stricken on 30.12.1904; she was converted to a repair ship and renamed *Vulkan*; later her name was needed for one of the new *Tegetthoff* class dreadnoughts. In 1919 she was confiscated by Italy and towed away. In 1920 she was allocated to Yugoslavia but was never handed over to her new owners; her fate is unknown.

Don Juan d'Austria (the different spelling serves to distinguish her from her predecessor, *Juan de Austria*) was stricken on 29.6.1904, and in 1905 she became an accommodation ship for torpedo boat staff. She sank in 1919 in circumstances which are not clear.

One of the most interesting ships of her time. Von Romako's intention was to design a 'bow-battery' ship that could use its guns during pursuit and ramming. The ship's design shows a good balance between low displacement and six fully protected heavy guns. These were sited in a citadel and had overlapping arcs of fire. The heavily armoured battery was designed without overhanging sponsons to give a flush surface without projections, so the ship's artillery was in no danger of being put out of action in case of a close fight or after being rammed. The ammunition was stored directly under the guns. Another innovation was the shape of the hull about the waterline so that the armour plates had to be bent in only one direction.

During a major refit she was converted to twin screws with new Schichau-built engines. The masts were removed, two heavy military masts with fighting tops were erected, and she was given modern guns. From 1897 she served as harbour guard ship at Pola; in 1912 she was renamed *Mars* when her name was needed for one of the new *Tegetthoff* class dreadnoughts. She was ceded to Italy and scrapped there in 1920.

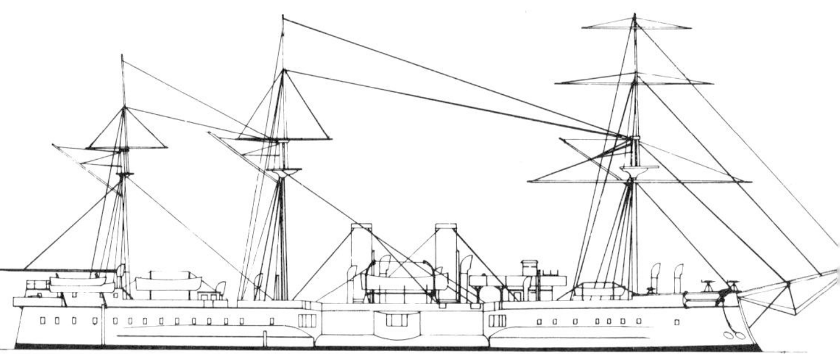
Tegetthoff as completed 1881

TEGETTHOFF *centre battery ship*

Displacement: 7431t
Dimensions: 303ft 4in oa, 293ft 3in wl x 71ft 5in x 24ft 10in (*92.46 oa, 89.39 wl x 21.78 x 7.57m*)
Machinery: As built: 1-shaft, 2 cyl horizontal LP engine, 6706ihp = 13.97kts; 1891/2 after reconstruction: 2-shaft, 2-3 cyl TE, 8160ihp = 15.32kts
Armour: Belt and casemates 356mm, bulkheads 254-305mm, CT 127-178mm
Armament: As built: 6-28cm L/18 Krupp BL, 6-9cm L/24 BL, 2-7cm L/15 BL, 4-47mm QF guns, 5-47mm MGs, 2-25mm MGs; after reconstruction: 6-24cm L/35 Krupp C 86, 5-15cm L/35 QF guns, 2-7cm L/15, 9-47mm L/44 QF guns, 6-47mm L/33 MGs, 2-8mm MGs, 2-35cm TT (1 bow, 1 stern)
Complement: As built 525, after reconstruction 568/575

Name	Builder	Laid down	Launched	Comp	Fate
TEGETTHOFF	STT	1.4.1876	15.10.78	Oct 1881	Scrapped 1920

1. *Kaiser* as completed 1873
2. *Prinz Eugen* after 1880 reduction of rig
3. *Kronprinzessin Erzherzogin Stefanie* at Pola about 1895

Kronprinzessin Erzherzogin Stefanie as completed 1889

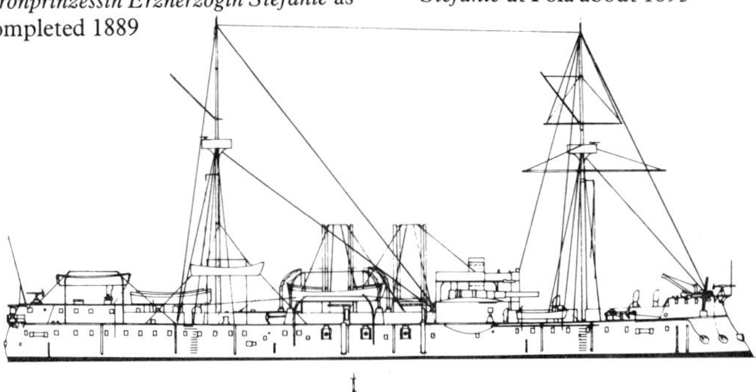

Kronprinz Erzherzog Rudolph as completed 1889

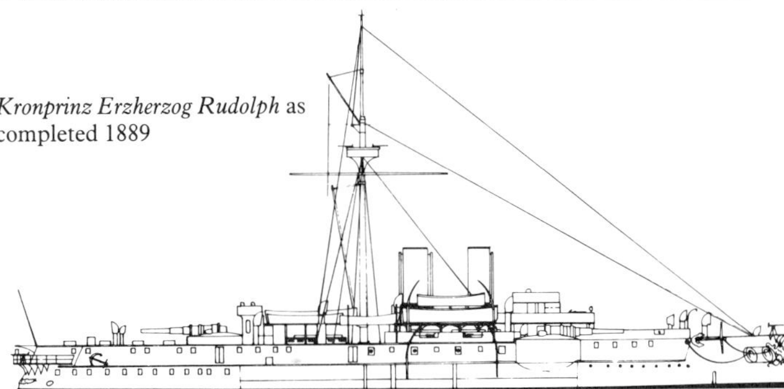

These barbette ships were designed by the new Austrian Director of Naval Construction, Josef Kuchinka. The hull was constructed from transverse and longitudinal frames, and was highly subdivided, although the armour enclosed only the vital parts of the ship. Externally, the ships were characterised by main battery guns mounted side by side facing forward (plus one firing stern on *Kronprinz Erzherzog Rudolf*). The origin of this arrangement seems to have been the French custom of placing guns in open barbettes, so that their arc of fire was greater – as in the old citadel arrangements. However, open barbettes were no longer effective after 1890, due to the introduction of rapid loading heavy guns so that these ships quickly became obsolete. The remarkable number of 37 additional auxiliary steam engines were installed. *Kronprinzessin Erzherzogin Stefanie* became a hulk in 1910 and in 1914 she became an accommodation ship for the mine warfare school. In 1920 she was ceded to Italy as war reparation and scrapped there in 1926. *Kronprinz Erzherzog Rudolf* was ceded to Yugoslavia in 1919 and renamed *Kumbor*. She was sold for scrap in 1922.

KRONPRINZESSIN ERZHERZOGIN STEFANI *barbette ship*

Displacement: 5075t
Dimensions: 286ft 2in wl, 280ft pp x 55ft 11in x 21ft 8in *(87.24 wl 85.36 pp x 17.06 x 6.60m)*
Machinery: 2-shaft, CE, 8000ihp = 17kts
Armour: Belt 229mm, turrets 283mm, CT 50mm
Armament: 2-30.5cm L/35 (2x1) (guns by Krupp, carriage by Armstrong Mitchell & Co), 6-15cm L/35 Krupp (6x1), 7-47mm L/44 Hotchkiss QF guns, 2-47mm L/33 Hotchkiss QF guns, 2-37mm L/44 QF guns, 2-7cm L/15 Uchatius landing guns, 4-40cm TT (1 bow, 1 stern, 2 beam)
Complement: 430

Name	Builder	Laid down	Launched	Comp	Fate
KRONPRINZESSIN ERZHERZOGIN STEFANIE	STT	12.11.1884	14.4.87	July 1889	Scrapped 1926

KRONZPRINZ ERZHERZOG RUDOLF *barbette ship*

Displacement: 6829t
Dimensions: 320ft 2in oa, 296ft pp x 63ft 2in x 24ft 3in *(97.6 oa, 90.26 pp x 19.27 x 7.39m)*
Machinery: 2-shaft, 2 cyl VTE engines, 6000ihp = 15.5kts
Armour: Belt 62-305mm, bulkheads 242-203mm, turrets 254mm
Armament: 3-30.5cm L/35 (1x2, 1x1) (guns by Krupp, carriages by Armstrong Mitchell & Co), 6-12cm L/35 Krupp, 5-47mm L/44 Hotchkiss QF guns, 2-47mm L/33 Hotchkiss QF guns, 2-37mm L/44 QF guns, 2-7cm L/15 Uchatius landing guns, 4-40cm TT, (1 bow, 1 stern, 2 beam)
Complement: 447/450

Name	Builder	Laid down	Launched	Comp	Fate
KRONPRINZ ERZHERZOG RUDOLF	Pola N Yd	25.1.1884	6.7.87	Sept 1889	Sold for scrap in 1922

AUSTRIA-HUNGARY

With the construction of the *Monarch* class, Austria embarked on a new path with Siegrfried Popper, the new Director of Naval Construction. For the first time genuine turrets were used, but like all Austrian warships, because of the budget limitations, they were too small to be efficient, well-balanced battleships, and were officially designed as Coast Defence Ships.

Monarch had a mutiny on board in February 1918 while in Cattaro harbour. From April 1918 she was accommodation ship of the submarine base, and she was allocated to Great Britain as war reparation, and scrapped in Italy.

Wien was sunk during the night of 9/10 December 1917 off Trieste by the Italian MTB *MAS 15* under the command of Luigi Rizzo.

Budapest was decommissioned in March 1918 to serve as accommodation ship for the Pola submarine base. In May/June 1918 a 38cm/17cal howitzer was installed instead of No 1 turret for a planned coastal bombardment which never took place. In 1920 she was allocated to Great Britain and scrapped in Italy.

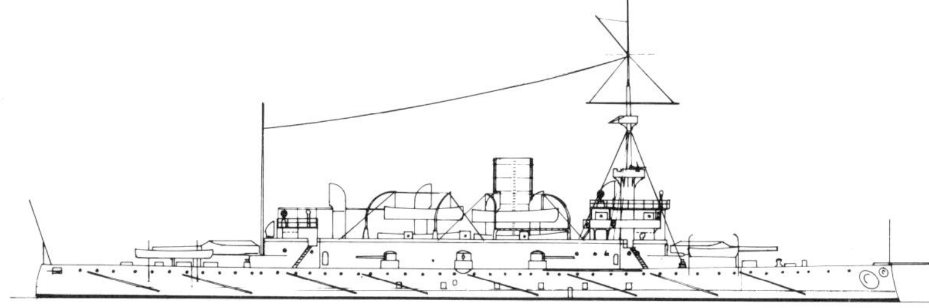

Wien as completed 1898

MONARCH class *coast defence ships*

Displacement: 5547t
Dimensions: 325ft 6in oa, 320ft 6in wl x 55ft 9in x 21ft (*99.22 oa, 97.70 wl x 17.00 x 6.40m*)
Machinery: 2-shaft, 3 cyl VTE engines, 8500ihp = 17.5kts
Armour: Belt 220-270mm, turrets 250mm, casemates 80mm, deck 40mm
Armament: 4-24cm L/40 Krupp C 94 (2x2), 6-15cm L/40 Skoda (6x1), 10-47mm L/44 Skoda QF guns, 4-47mm L/33 Hotchkiss QF guns, 1-8mm MG, 2-7cm L/15 Uchatius landing guns, 2-45cm TT (beam); *Wien, Budapest* 1-7cm AA added in 1917
Complement: 426

Name	Builder	Laid down	Launched	Comp	Fate
MONARCH	Pola N Yd	31.7.1893	9.5.95	11.5.98	To Great Britain in 1920
WIEN	STT	16.2.1893	6.7.95	13.5.98	Torpedoed at Trieste 10.12.1917
BUDAPEST	STT	16.2.1893	27.4.96	12.5.98	To Great Britain in 1920

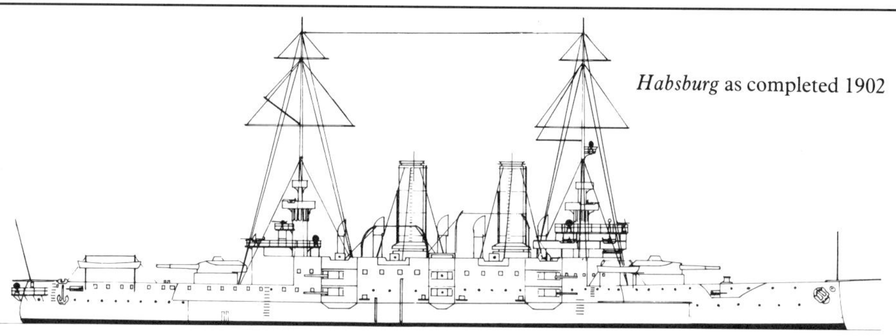

Habsburg as completed 1902

With this class the Austrian Navy acquired its first seagoing battleships since the *Tegetthoff*, even though they were the smallest in existence. If Popper had been allowed a few more tons, these ships would have been equal to if not better than their contemporaries. In 1910/11 *Habsburg* and *Árpád* had one superstructure deck removed to save topweight. During the war the ships formed the IV Division; later in the war they were decommissioned and served as harbour guard ships. All were ceded to Great Britain in 1920 and scrapped in Italy in 1921.

HABSBURG class *battleships*

Displacement: 8232t as designed, 8823t full load (*Arpad* 8748t full load)
Dimensions: 375ft 10in oa, 371ft wl x 65ft x 24ft 6in (*114.57 oa, 113.11 x 19.86 x 7.46m*)
Machinery: 2-shaft, 4 cyl VTE engines, 16 Belleville boilers, *Habsburg* 15,063ihp = 19.62 kts; *Árpád* 14,307ihp = 19.65kts; *Babenberg* 16,000ihp = 19.85kts
Armour: Belt 180-220mm, turrets and casemates 210-280mm, CT 200mm, deck 40mm
Armament: 3-24cm L/40 Krupp C 97 (1x2, 1x1), (bow: twin turret, stern: single turret), 12-15cm L/40 Krupp C 96, 10-7cm L/45 Skoda, 6-47mm L/44 Skoda QF guns, 2-47mm L/33 Skoda QF guns, 2-45cm TT (beam)
Complement: 638

Name	Builder	Laid down	Launched	Comp	Fate
HABSBURG	STT	13.3.1899	9.9.1900	31.12.02	Scrapped 1921
ÁRPÁD	STT	10.6.1899	11.9.1901	15.6.03	Scrapped 1921
BABENBERG	STT	19.1.1901	4.10.1902	15.4.04	Scrapped 1921

Monarch

Erzherzog Ferdinand Max

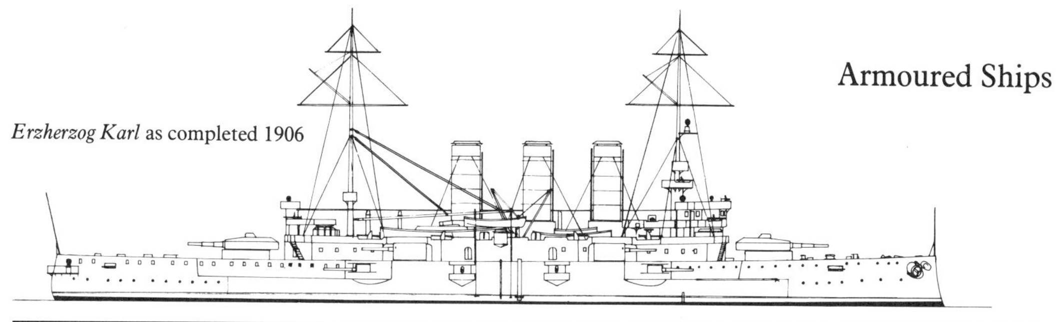
Erzherzog Karl as completed 1906

Because of the limits of docks and tight naval budgets, the three pre-dreadnoughts of the *Erzherzog Karl* class were very compact, well-protected battleships, although they were inferior to their contemporaries in other navies. For the first time the secondary armament was concentrated in fully electric powered turrets. At the outbreak of the First World War they formed the III Division. All were taken over by Yugoslavia in 1919, but *Erzherzog Karl* and *Erzherzog Friedrich* were ceded as war reparation to France in 1920 and *Erzherzog Ferdinand Max* to Great Britain.

ERZHERZOG KARL class *battleships*

Displacement: 10,472t
Dimensions: 414ft 2in oa, 408ft wl x 71ft 5in x 24ft 7in (*126.24 oa, 124.35 wl x 21.78 x 7.51m*)
Machinery: 2-shaft, 4 cyl VTE engines, 18,000ihp = 20.5kts
Armour: Belt 210mm, turrets 240mm, casemates 150mm, CT 220mm, bulkheads 200mm, deck 55mm
Armament: 4-24cm L/40 (2x2), 12-19cm L/42 (12x1), 12-7cm L/45, 4-47mm L/44 QF guns, 2-47mm L/33 QF guns (all Skoda), 4-37mm Vickers MGs, 4-8mm Skoda MGs, 2-45cm TT (2 beam); added 1916: 1-7cm L/45 Skoda AA
Complement: 700

Name	Builder	Laid down	Launched	Comp	Fate
ERZHERZOG KARL	STT	24.7.1902	4.10.03	17.6.06	Scrapped 1920
ERZHERZOG FRIEDRICH	STT	4.10.1902	30.4.04	31.1.07	Scrapped 1920
ERZHERZOG FERDINAND MAX	STT	9.3.1904	21.5.05	21.12.07	Scrapped 1920

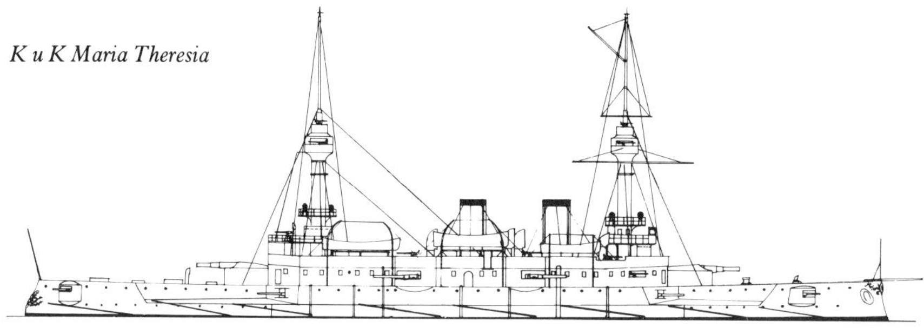
K u K Maria Theresia

The executive committee of the Austro-Hungarian Navy, the *Marinesektion*, agreed with foreign navies in their estimate of the high value of a modern type armoured cruiser which could perform some of a battleship's duties. In addition the success of the two light cruisers of the *Kaiserin Elisabeth* class persuaded the authorities to build an improved successor with more displacement, heavier armament and heavier armour. Five British yards were asked to tender designs: Cammell Laird, Vickers-Armstrong, Fairfield, Napier (Glasgow) and Thomson. However, eventually the first ship, officially designated as 'torpedo-ram-cruiser C' was ordered at STT to give work to the Austrian yard personnel.

Kaiserin und Königin Maria Theresia was originally planned with six 15cm and fourteen 47mm, but the number of guns was increased during construction. From August 1914 to 1916 she was stationed at Sebenico (now Sibenik); she was disarmed 31.1.1917, decommissioned 7.2.1917 and served as an accommodation ship for German submarine crews. Her guns were transferred to the Italian front.

Kaiser Karl IV and *Sankt Georg* were improved versions. All three ships saw active service during the First World War and took part in some cruiser actions as backing units. All were ceded as war reparation to Great Britain in 1920, then sold to Italy and scrapped there.

KAISERIN UND KÖNIGIN MARIA THERESIA *armoured cruiser*

Displacement: 5330t as designed, 6026t full load
Dimensions: 373ft oa, 366ft 4in wl x 53ft 4in x 22ft 5in (*113.7 oa, 111.67 wl x 16.25 x 6.81m*)
Machinery: 2-shaft, 3 cyl horizontal TE engines, 9755ihp = 19.35kts
Armour: Belt and turrets 100mm, casemates 80mm, CT 50mm, deck 57-38mm
Armament: As built: 2-24cm L/35 (2x1) Krupp, 8-15cm L/35 Krupp QF guns, 12-47mm L/44 Skoda QF guns, 6-47mm L/33 Hotchkiss QF guns, 2-7cm L/15 landing guns, 4-45cm TT (1 bow, 1 stern, 2 beam); after rebuilding in 1909/10: 2-19cm L/42 (2x1) Skoda, 8-15cm L/35 Krupp QF guns, 12-47mm L/44 Skoda QF guns, 2-47mm L/33 Hotchkiss QF guns, 4-37mm Vickers MGs, 2-7cm L/15 landing guns, 4-45cm TT (1 bow, 1 stern, 2 beam)
Complement: 475

Name	Builder	Laid down	Launched	Comp	Fate
KAISERIN UND KÖNIGIN MARIA THERESIA	STT	6.10.1891	29.4.93	Nov 1894	Scrapped *c*1920

KAISER KARL IV *armoured cruiser*

Displacement: 6166t as designed, 6864t full load
Dimensions: 390ft 3in oa, 386ft 10in wl x 56ft 10in x 22ft 2in (*118.96 oa, 117.9 wl x 17.27 x 6.75m*)
Machinery: 2-shaft, 2-4 cyl VTE engines, 12,000ihp = 20.83kts
Armour: Belt 170-220mm, turrets 200mm, CT 200-100mm, casemates 80mm, deck 60-40mm
Armament: 2-24cm L/40 (2x1) Krupp C 94, 8-15cm L/40 (8x1) Skoda, 16-47mm L/44 Skoda QF guns, 2-47mm L/33 Hotchkiss QF guns, 2-8mm Skoda MGs, 2-7cm L/15 landing guns, 2-45cm TT (2 beam)
Complement: 535

Name	Builder	Laid down	Launched	Comp	Fate
KAISER KARL IV	STT	1.6.1896	4.10.98	23.5.1900	Scrapped *c*1920

SANKT GEORG *armoured cruiser*

Displacement: 7289t as designed, 8070t full load
Dimensions: 407ft 9in oa, 404ft 3in wl x 62ft 5in x 22ft 5in (*124.30 oa, 123.23 wl x 19.01 x 6.83m*)
Machinery: 2-shaft, 2-4 cyl VTE engines, 15,000ihp = 22kts
Armour: Belt 165-210mm, bulkheads 190mm, turrets 210mm, CT 200mm, deck 36-50mm
Armament: 2-24cm L/40 (1x2), 5-19cm L/42 (5x1), 4-15cm L/40, 9-7cm L/45, 2-7cm L/15 landing guns, 6-47mm L/44 Skoda QF guns, 2-37mm L/33 QF guns, 2-8mm MGs (all Skoda), 2-45cm TT (2 beam); 1-7cm L/50 AA added 1916
Complement: 630

Name	Builder	Laid down	Launched	Comp	Fate
SANKT GEORG	Pola N Yd	11.3.1901	8.12.03	21.7.05	Scrapped *c*1920

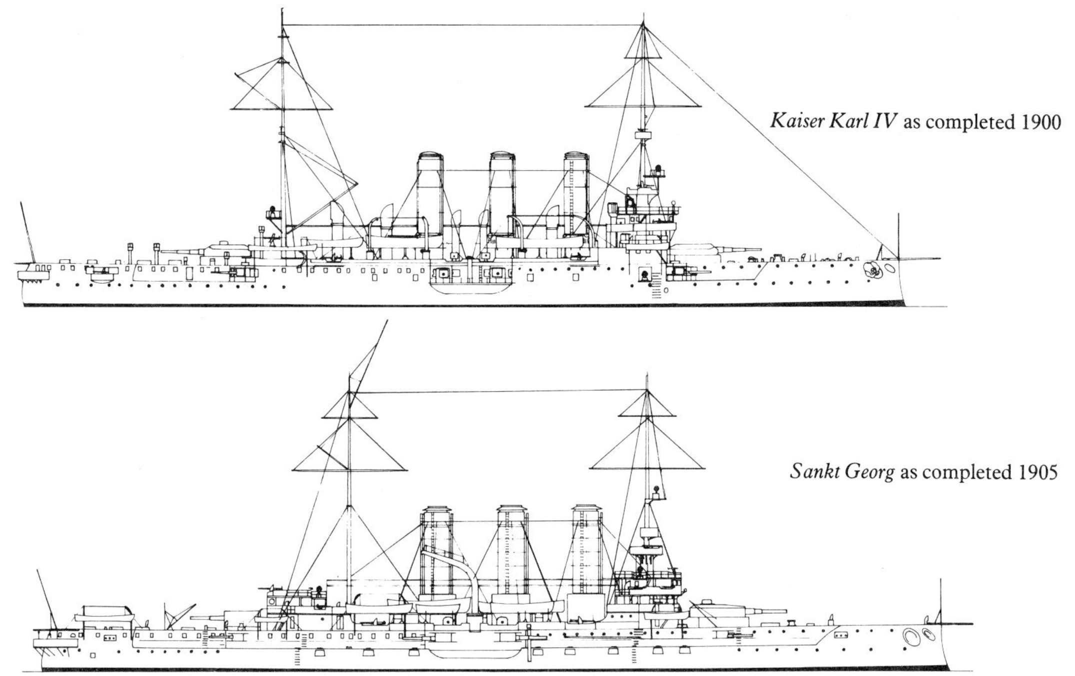

Kaiser Karl IV as completed 1900

Sankt Georg as completed 1905

Left: *Kaiser Karl IV*

Below: *Kaiserin und Königin Maria Theresia*

CRUISERS

Unlike other European nations the Austrian Monarchy had no colonies and had no wish to acquire any. The cruising ships of the Austro-Hungarian Navy did not serve as station ships in the colonies but were used extensively as training ships for young officers and cadets. They also undertook large and successful world cruises returning with an overwhelming amount of ethnological, geographical, meteorological and hydrographical material – today still partially unevaluated in Austrian museums.

At the end of the century all these early steam vessels were obsolete. Most of them had their engines removed, and some were renamed when their names were needed for new ships and they served in ancillary roles.

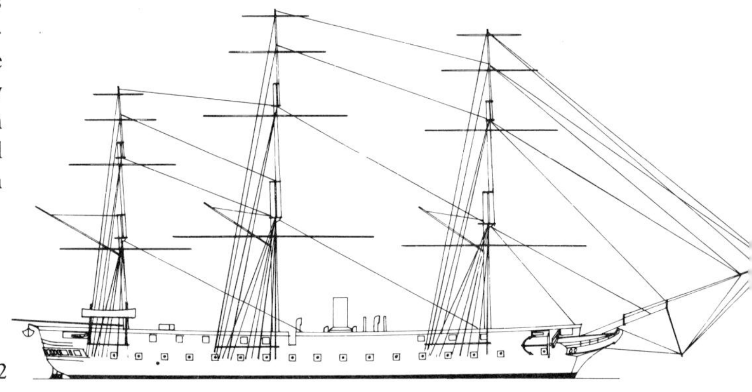

Novara as converted 1862

NOVARA *screw frigate*

Displacement: 2615t, 2865t full load
Dimensions: 252ft oa, 221ft 10in pp x 47ft x 19ft (*76.79 oa, 67.62 pp x 14.32 x 5.80m*)
Machinery: 1-shaft 2 cyl H engine, 1200ihp = 12kts
Armament: 1863: 2-24pdr BL, 4-60pdr Paixhans shell guns, 28-30pdr Novara guns, 1-12pdr landing gun, 1-6pdr landing gun; 1868: 13-24pdr Wahrendorf BL, 32-30pdr ML, 2-4pdr ML; 1872: 20-24pdr BL, 10-24pdr BL on deck, 2-24pdr BL on pivots, 2-3pdr landing guns
Complement: 550 (1872: 447)

Name	Builder	Laid down	Launched	Comp	Fate
NOVARA	Arsenal, Venice	20.9.1843	4.11.50	10.7.62 (conversion)	Scrapped 1899

Originally completed as the sailing frigate *Minerva* in June 1851, the ship was rebuilt at San Rocco's at Trieste as a steam screw frigate. The hull was lengthened and she was fitted with an engine built by STT.

She became a hulk on 22.8.1876. The engines were removed in 1881, and she became a gunnery training ship on 22.6.1881. She was stricken on 22.10.1898 and scrapped in 1899.

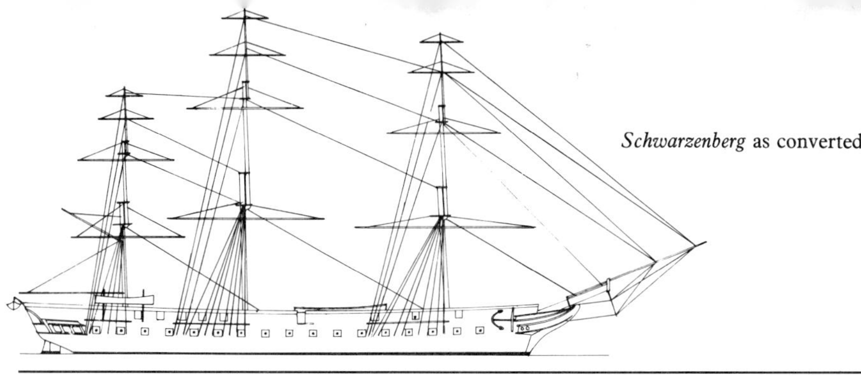

Schwarzenberg as converted 1862

Originally built as a sailing frigate, she was converted into a screw steamship in 1861/2, and in 1864 she took part in the battle off Heligoland. From 1870 to 1890 she served as a cadet training ship and was stricken on 20.11.1890.

SCHWARZENBERG *screw frigate*

Displacement: 2614t
Dimensions: 242ft 9in oa, 211ft 3in pp x 48ft 10in x 21ft 4in *(74.00 oa, 64.40 pp x 14.88 x 6.50m)*
Machinery: 1-shaft, 2 cyl H engine, 1700ihp = 11kts
Armament: 1864: 6-60pdr Paixhans shell guns, 40-30pdr ML, 4-24pdr BLR; in 1866 after the Heligoland battle 4-30pdrs were removed
Complement: 547

Name	Builder	Laid down	Launched	Comp	Fate
SCHWARZENBERG	Arsenal, Venice	1851	23.4.53	1854	Stricken 20.11.1890

In 1852 the high command of the Austro-Hungarian Navy proposed the construction of a modern steam frigate. The first ship was ordered in Britain, but further ships were built from the same plans in Austria. All three ships took part at the Battle of Lissa.

Radetzky was sunk on 2.2.1869 10 miles NNW of Lissa after a powder explosion; 344 men were killed, and only 24 survived. *Adria* became a gunnery training ship in 1868 and was stricken and scrapped in 1888. *Donau* was stricken and scrapped in 1872.

RADETZKY class *screw frigates*

Displacement: *Radetzky* 2234t full load; *Adria, Donau* 2165t
Dimensions: 231ft 8in oa x 42ft 10in x 18ft *(70.62 oa x 13.06 x 5.46m)*
Machinery: 1-shaft, 2 cyl H engine, 1200ihp = 9kts
Armament: 1863: 6-60pdr Paixhans shell guns, 26-30pdr 2nd class ML, 14-30pdr 4th class ML, 4-24pdr BLR; 1867: 32-30pdr ML, 14-24pdr BLR, 4-4pdr
Complement: 1859: 354; 1866: 398

Name	Builder	Laid down	Launched	Comp	Fate
RADETZKY	Wigram, London	1852	13.4.54	Sept 1854	Sunk by internal explosion 20.2.69
ADRIA	STT	1.8.1855	26.1.56	1857	Scrapped 1888
DONAU	STT	May 1855	20.11.56	1857	Stricken 1.5.1872

The *Donau (ii)*, officially rated as a *gedeckte Korvette*, was designed for cruising service and cadet training in the Adriatic. In 1884 she circumnavigated Africa, and in 1885 she visited the West Indies. She was scrapped in 1888.

DONAU (ii) *corvette*

Displacement: 2490t, 2642t full load
Dimensions: 244ft oa, 232ft 10in pp x 41ft 6in x 19ft 6in *(74.36 oa, 70.96 pp x 12.66 x 5.95m)*
Machinery: 1-shaft, 2 cyl vertical engine, 1300hp = 10.8kts
Armament: 11-15cm/35 Krupp, 2-7cm/15, 2-25mm MGs
Complement: 334

Name	Builder	Laid down	Launched	Comp	Fate
DONAU (ii)	Navale Adriatico, Trieste	18.6.1873	15.10.74	14.8.75	Scrapped 1888

This conversion is a typical example of an 'official reconstruction' as understood in the Austro-Hungarian Navy. In fact the hull of the frigate *Donau (ii)* was scrapped and only the machinery and some equipment from the old ship were used in the new one. Like her forerunner she was designed for long cruises and cadet training. In 1894/5 she visited North and South America, in 1900 she visited South America and East Asia and in 1901 she visited Central America and Japan. In 1906 the obsolete ship was disarmed and used as an accommodation and training ship for cadets. After the First World War she went to Yugoslavia as war reparation and was renamed *Sibenik*. Her fate is unknown.

DONAU (iii) *corvette*

Displacement: 2306t
Dimensions: 229ft 8in wl x 42ft x 18ft 3in *(70.00 wl x 12.84 x 5.56m)*
Machinery: 1-shaft, 2 cyl vertical engine
Armament: 10-12cm/35, 1-7cm/15, 4-25mm MGs
Complement: 333

Name	Builder	Laid down	Launched	Comp	Fate
DONAU (iii)	Pola N Yd	Oct 1888	28.6.93	Aug 1894	Yugoslavian *Sibenik*, 1920

Left: *Donau* (iii) in 1894

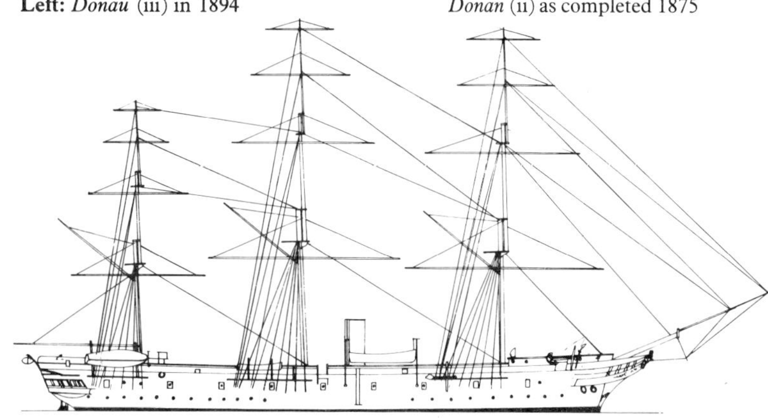

Donan (ii) as completed 1875

AUSTRIA-HUNGARY

Both ships took part at the battle off Lissa in 1866. *Erzherzog Friedrich* made visits to America, India, China and Japan. Between 1877 and 1880 she was completely overhauled. To her original flush deck a topgallant forecastle and poop was added to give more accommodation for cadets. In August 1897 she was stricken and used for shipping boilers from Pola to Trieste. *Dandolo* saw active service as a cruising ship off the south Dalmatian and Albanian coast in her first years. In 1865/6 she was the station ship in Mexico, where the brother of the Austrian Emperor became the short-lived Emperor of Mexico. In the following years she made many oceanic voyages. In 1879 she became a gunnery training ship. In 1881/2 the boilers and engines were removed and she became an accommodation ship. From 1886 she served as an accommodation ship for boy seamen. In 1890 she was renamed *Schwarzenberg* and served as a training ship at Sebenico (now Sibenik).

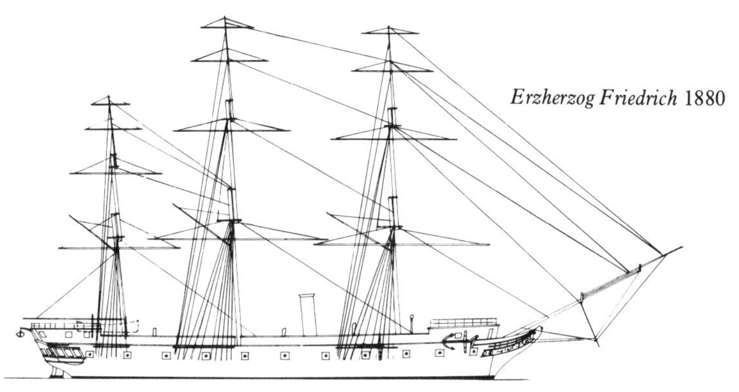
Erzherzog Friedrich 1880

ERZHERZOG FRIEDRICH class *corvettes*

Displacement: 1697t
Dimensions: 222ft 5in oa, 183ft 9in pp x 39ft 11in x 16ft 8in (*67.80 oa, 56.00 pp x 12.16 x 5.08m*)
Machinery: 1-shaft, 2 cyl H engine, 920ihp = 8-9kts
Armament: As built: 17-30pdr Type No 3, 4-60pdr Paixhans shell guns, 1-48pdr Type No 2; 1866: 16-30pdr, 4-60pdr, 2-24pdr, rifled; 1871: 14-24pdr, 1-3pdr; 1877: 12-15cm/?cal Wahrendorf BL, 2-7cm/?cal
Complement: 294

Name	Builder	Laid down	Launched	Comp	Fate
ERZHERZOG FRIEDRICH	Arsenal, Venice	14.2.1854	11.4.57	1858	Scrapped 1899
DANDOLO	Arsenal, Venice	26.9.1854	7.8.58	Feb 1859	Scrapped 1900/01

Radetzky (ii) was converted into a gunnery training ship in 1897, and in 1908 she was renamed *Adria* when her name was needed for a new dreadnought. From 1915 she served as an accommodation ship for German naval personnel at Pola where she stayed until the end of the First World War: her fate is unknown. In 1900 *Laudon's* engines were removed and she became a stationary cadet training ship, and was renamed *Schwarzenberg*. In 1919 she was allocated to Yugoslavia and renamed *Prvi*, and in the same year she was confiscated by Italy, and towed away to be scrapped in 1923.

RADETZKY (ii) class *frigates*

Displacement: 3394t, 3956t full load
Dimensions: 259ft 6in oa, 253ft pp x 47ft x 23ft (*79.10m oa, 77.10 pp x 14.33 x 7.00m*)
Machinery: 1-shaft, 2 cyl horizontal LP engine, *Radetzky* 3385ihp = 13.37kts; *Laudon* 2500ihp = 13.2 kts
Armament: 15-15cm L/26 Krupp BL, 2-7cm L/15, 4-47mm L/? QF guns, 3-47mm MGs, 3-35cm TT (1 stern, 2 beam)
Complement: 450

Name	Builder	Laid down	Launched	Comp	Fate
RADETZKY (ii)	STT	Sept 1870	20.6.72	10.8.73	Unknown
LAUDON	STT	Aug 1871	20.9.73	22.7.74	Scrapped 1923

Saida was stricken on 26.2.1906. In 1908 her engines were removed and she served as a mine storage ship. In 1912 she was renamed *Minerva* when her name was needed for a new light cruiser, and in 1920 she was ceded as war reparation to Italy and scrapped there.

SAIDA *corvette*

Displacement: 2662t
Dimensions: 260ft 7in oa x 43ft x 19ft; 20ft full load (*79.44 oa x 13.14 x 5.83m; 6.11m full load*)
Machinery: 1-shaft, 2 cyl H engine, 1790ihp = 12.01kts
Armament: As completed: 11-15cm L/25 BL, 1-7cm L/15 landing gun, 2-25mm MGs (after 1892); 1904: 8-15cm L/25, 1-7cm L/15 landing gun, 2-47mm L/33 QF guns
Complement: 333-359

Name	Builder	Laid down	Launched	Comp	Fate
SAIDA	Pola N Yd	Sept 1876	2.7.78	14.8.79	Scrapped 1920

Fasana was stricken on 7.8.1897 and became a hulk. In 7.8.1902 she was renamed *Gamma* and served as a mine storage ship until the end of the First World War. She was probably scrapped in Italy in 1920.

HELGOLAND *sloop*

Displacement: 1798t
Dimensions: 243ft 7in oa x 37ft 4in x 17ft 4in (*74.26 oa x 11.38 x 5.30m*)
Machinery: 1-shaft, 2 cyl H engine, 1127ihp = 10.5kts
Armament: 2-7in Armstrong ML, 4-8pdr rifled, 1-3pdr rifled
Complement: 235

Name	Builder	Laid down	Launched	Comp	Fate
HELGOLAND	Pola N Yd	17.9.1866	23.12.67	3.4.69	Scrapped 1897

FASANA *sloop*

Displacement: 2382t
Dimensions: 223ft 11in oa x 38ft 4in x 19ft (*68.26 oa x 11.69 x 5.78m*)
Machinery: 1-shaft, 2 cyl H engine, 1590ihp = 11.58kts
Armament: As built: 2-21cm/20 Krupp, 4-8pdr rifled; 1880: 4-15cm/26 Krupp, 3-7cm/15 Uchatius guns
Complement: 257

Name	Builder	Laid down	Launched	Comp	Fate
FASANA	Navale Adriatico, Trieste	9.10.1869	1.9.70	5.5.71	Scrapped 1920?

1

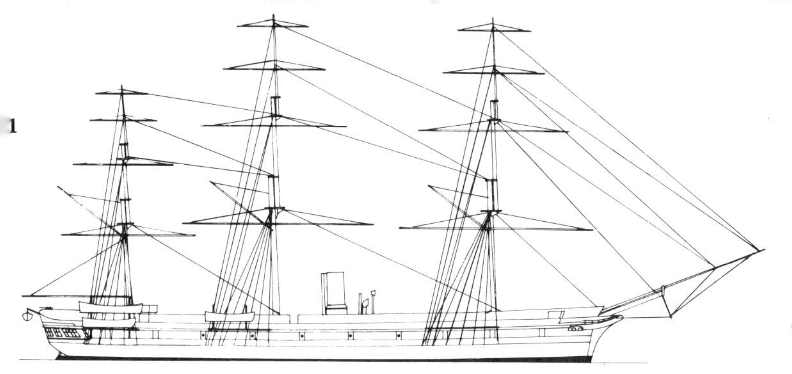

2

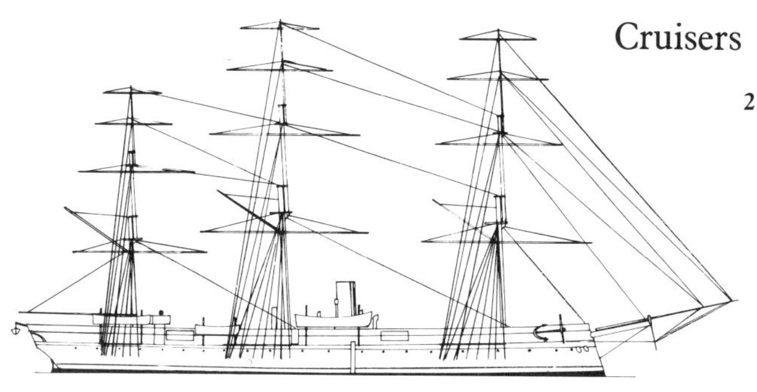

1. *Saida* as completed 1879

2. *Fasana* as completed 1871

3. *Radetsky* (ii)

4. *Helgoland*

3

4

Aurora went to Yugoslavia in 1920, and was renamed *Skradin*; her fate is unknown. *Frundsberg* became a hulk in 1905, served as mine storage ship at Sibenik during the First World War, and was ceded to Yugoslavia in 1920, renamed *Zlarin*; her fate is unknown. *Zrinyi* became a hulk in 1905, and in 1908 she was renamed *Delta* when her name was needed for a new dreadnought. During the First World War she served as a mine storage ship at Pola; her post-war fate is unknown.

AURORA class *sloops*

Displacement: 1353t
Dimensions: 226ft 7in oa, 193ft 10in pp x 34ft 3in x 16ft 4in *(69.08 oa, 59.10 pp x 10.45 x 5.00m)*
Machinery: 1-shaft, 2-cyl HTE, 1000ihp = 11kts; *Aurora* 1165ihp = 11.2kts
Armament: As built: 4-15cm/21 Wahrendorf BL, 2-7cm L/15, 2-25mm MGs; 1891: 2-15cm/21 Wahrendorf BL, 4-9cm/24 BL, 1-7cm/15 BL, 2-47mm QF guns (rev)
Complement: 210

Name	Builder	Laid down	Launched	Comp	Fate
AURORA	STT	11.11.1871	20.11.73	1.7.74	Ceded to Yugoslavia
FRUNDSBERG	STT	19.6.1871	11.2.73	Oct 1873	Ceded to Yugoslavia
ZRINYI	STT	17.1.1870	10.12.70	26.8.71	Unknown

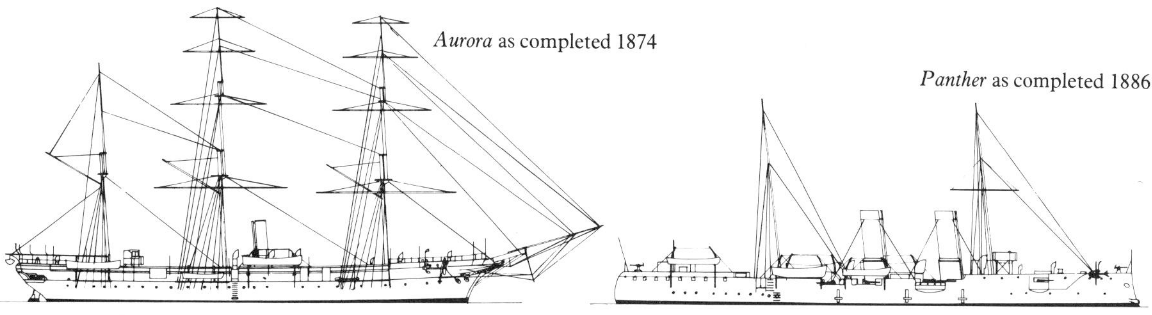

Aurora as completed 1874

Panther as completed 1886

These two small cruisers (officially called torpedo ram cruisers) were ordered in England to gain experience in modern shipbuilding techniques. They, and their enlarged successor *Tiger*, were obsolete by the beginning of the First World War and their main armament was removed in 1909/10.

Panther was attached in 1917 to the submarine commanders' school at Cattaro as a seagoing training ship.

Leopard was decommissioned 15.5.1914 and used as harbour defence ship at Pola. Both were allocated as war reparation to Great Britain, but sold to Italy and scrapped there in 1920.

PANTHER class *protected cruisers*

Displacement: 1557t
Dimensions: 240ft oa, 234ft 2in wl x 34ft x 14ft *(73.19 oa, 71.38 wl x 10.39 x 4.28m)*
Machinery: 2-shaft, 2 cyl VCE, *Panther* 5940ihp = 18.4kts; *Leopard* 6380ihp = 18.7kts
Armour: Deck 12mm
Armament: 2-12cm/35 Krupp, 4-47mm/44 QF guns, 6-47mm/44 QF guns (rev), 4-35cm TT (1 bow, 1 stern, 2 beam). *Panther* (from June 1909) 4-7cm/45, *Leopard* (from Oct 1910) 10-47mm/44 QF guns
Complement: 186

Name	Builder	Laid down	Launched	Comp	Fate
LEOPARD	Armstrong, Elswick	Jan 1885	10.9.85	31.3.86	Scrapped 1920
PANTHER	Armstrong, Elswick	29.10.1884	13.6.85	31.12.85	Scrapped 1920

AUSTRIA-HUNGARY

Leopard

Tiger was an enlarged and improved version of the British-built *Panther* class. In 1905/6 she was converted into an admiralty yacht, her main armament was removed and she was renamed *Lacroma*. In 1915 she was completely disarmed; 1918 she became Yugoslavian, and in 1920 she was ceded to Italy and scrapped there.

TIGER *light cruiser*

Displacement: 1657t
Dimensions: 249ft 5in oa, 243ft 3in wl, x 34ft 7in x 14ft (*76.02 oa, 74.16 wl x 10.55 x 4.30m*)
Machinery: 2-shafts, 2-2 cyl CE, 5700ihp = 18.56kts
Armament: 4-12cm/35 Krupp, 6-47mm/44 QF, 4-47mm/?cal QF guns (rev), 4-35cm TT (1 bow, 1 stern, 2 beam); 1906: after conversion to admiralty yacht, armament reduced to 6-47mm/44 QF
Complement: 188 (after conversion 177)

Name	Builder	Laid down	Launched	Comp	Fate
TIGER	STT	5.10.1886	28.6.87	Mar 1888	Scrapped 1920

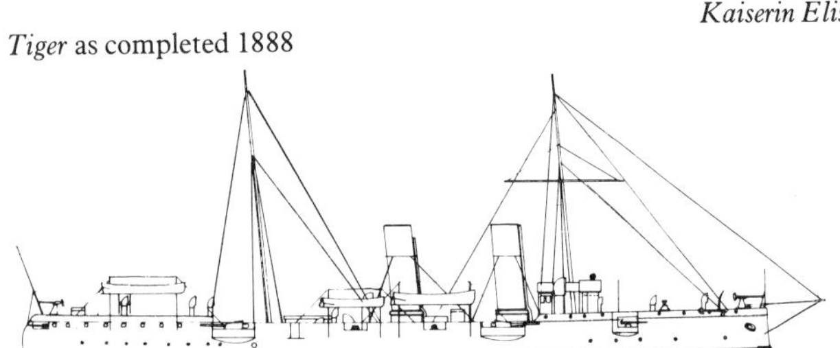

Tiger as completed 1888

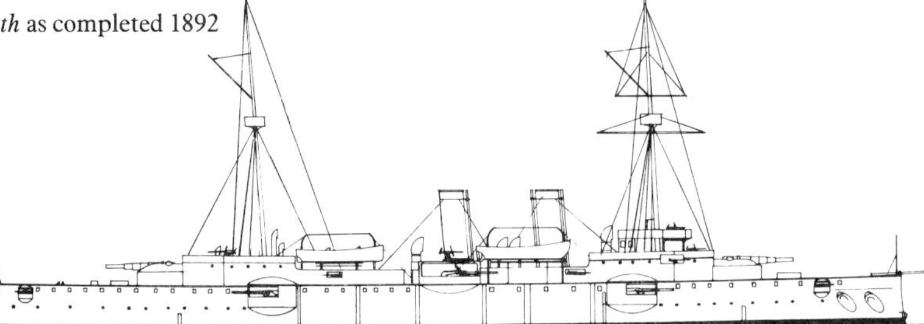

Kaiserin Elisabeth as completed 1892

These two light cruisers were officially designed as 'torpedo ram cruisers'; during a refit in 1905/6 the 24cm guns were removed and the light armament changed. At the outbreak of the First World War both ships were obsolete.

Kaiser Franz Joseph I was used as a harbour defence ship at Cattaro. In 1917 she was completely disarmed and became a floating headquarters. She was ceded to France as war reparation and foundered off Kumbor in the Bay of Cattaro in 1919.

Kaiserin Elisabeth was stationed in China in 1914 and took part in the defence of the German naval base at Tsingtao. Her 15cm and 47mm guns were removed and mounted ashore in the 'Elisabeth' battery. She was scuttled on 2 November 1914, two days before the base surrendered to the Japanese.

KAISER FRANZ JOSEPH I class *protected cruisers*

Displacement: 3967t as designed, 4494t full load
Dimensions: 340ft 3in oa, 321ft 22in pp x 48ft 4in x 18ft 8in (*103.70 oa, 97.90 pp x 14.75 x 5.70m*)
Machinery: 2-shaft, 3 cyl HTE engines, 8450ihp = 19kts
Armour: Turrets 90mm, CT 50mm, deck 38mm, hull 57mm
Armament: As built: 2-24cm/35, 6-15cm/35, 2-7cm/15, 5-47mm/44 QF, 4-47mm/33 QF, 3-37mm MGs, 4-40cm TT (1 bow, 1 stern, 2 beam); from 1905/6: 2-15cm/40 in barbettes, 6-15cm/35 C 86, 12-47mm/44 QF guns, 2-47cm/33 QF guns, 2-7cm/15 landing guns, 4-40cm TT
Complement: 367

Name	Builder	Laid down	Launched	Comp	Fate
KAISER FRANZ JOSEPH I	STT	3.1.1888	18.5.89	2.7.90	Sunk Oct 1919
KAISERIN ELISABETH	Pola N Yd	July 1888	25.9.90	24.1.92	Scuttled by crew at Tsingtao 2.11.1914

Although obsolete these three light cruisers saw active service at the beginning of the First World War. During the war the remaining two units were de-activated.

Zenta was the leader of six torpedo boats blockading the Montenegrian coast. During a one hour sea battle she was sunk by French battleships on 16.8.1914. The torpedo boat *Ulan*, accompanying her, escaped. *Aspern* was disarmed in 1918 and served as an accommodation ship at Pola. *Szigetvár* was disarmed in 1918 and served the Torpedo Warfare School as an accommodation and target ship. Both were ceded to Great Britain as war reparation, but were sold to Italy and scrapped there in 1920.

ZENTA class *protected cruisers*

Displacement: 2313t normal, full load: *Zenta* 2503t; *Aspern* 2625t; *Szigetvár* 2562t
Dimensions: 317ft 10in oa, 315ft wl x 34ft 6in x 13ft 11in (*96.88 oa, 96.00 wl x 11.73 x 4.24m*)
Machinery: 2-shaft, 4 cyl VTE engines (built by STT), 8160ihp = 20.8kts
Armour: Belt 2 x 25mm, casemates 35mm, CT 2 x 25mm
Armament: 8-12cm/40 Skoda QF guns on single pivots, 8-47mm/44 Skoda QF guns, 2-47mm/33 Hotchkiss QF guns, 2-8mm MGs, 2-45cm TT, beam aw
Complement: 308

Name	Builder	Laid down	Launched	Comp	Fate
ZENTA	Pola N Yd	8.8.1896	18.8.97	28.5.99	Sunk 16.8.1914
ASPERN	Pola N Yd	4.10.1897	3.5.99	29.5.1900	Scrapped 1920
SZIGETVÁR	Pola N Yd	25.5.1899	29.10.1900	30.9.01	Scrapped 1920

Kaiserin Elisabeth in her early years
CPL

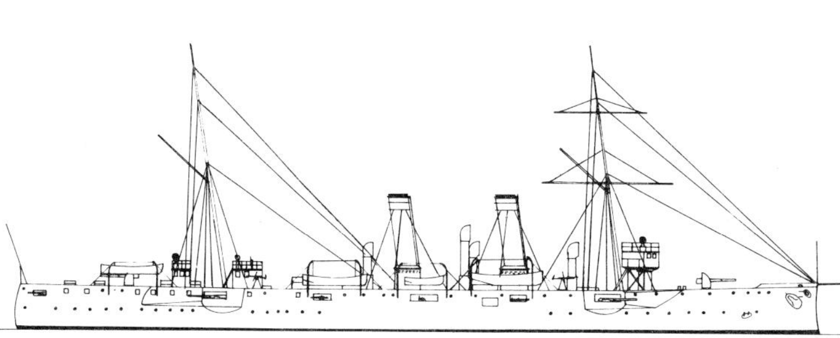

Zenta as completed 1899

TORPEDO BOATS

Name	Builder	Launched	Disp (t)	Dimensions (m)	HP	Kts	Armament	Crew	Fate
Design Studies I	Thornycroft, London	19.6.1875	7.5/10	20.7 x 2.61 x 1.23	184	18		9	1893 transferred to Danube River as patrol boat, sold 1907
II	Thornycroft, London	21.5.1878	28.4	26.5 x 3.5 x 1.55	300	18.2	2 TT bow	10	Sold 1905
Type leader III, IV	Yarrow, London	Sept 1879	27	26.4 x 3.3 x 1.5	430	17.5	2 TT bow	10	Sold 1905
III class									
V		4.12.1880							
VI	Navy Yard Pola	21.12.1880	27.7/30	27.7 x 3.3 x 1.35	430	18.3	2 TT bow	10	All sold 1905 for scrapping
VII		8.1.1881							
VIII		14.2.1881							
II class, A-type *Type leader*									
IX	Yarrow, London	9.9.1881	37/47	31.2 x 3.69 x 1.60	500	18	2 TT bow, 1-37mm QF gun	15	Sold 1905 for scrapping
X		29.8.1881							
II class, B-type									
XI		4.7.1885							Sold 1907
XII		10.9.1885							Sold 1907
XIII		30.8.1883							Sold 1904
XIV		18.9.1883							Sold 1904
XV		12.5.1884							Sold 1909
XVI		31.5.1884							Sold 1909
XVII		8.11.1884							From 1907 gunnery target
XVIII	Navy Yard, Pola	6.12.1884	47/55	34.3 x 3.8 x 1.7	600	18/19	2 TT bow, 1-37mm QF gun	16	Sold 1907
XIX		19.6.1885							Sold 1904
XX		8.7.1885							Sold 1909
XXI		14.12.1885							From 1909 gunnery target
XXII		7.1.1886							Sold 1909
XXIII		27.12.1885							1909 converted to a transport
XXIV		18.1.1886							Sold 1909
XXV		9.11.1885							Sold 1904
XXVI		5.12.1885							Sold 1909

TB *VI*

B-type Second Class TB *XXII*

AUSTRIA-HUNGARY

Name (Number from 1910)	Builder	Launched	Disp (t)	Dimensions (m)	HP	Kts	Armament	Crew	Fate
I class									
ADLER (41)	Yarrow, London	Dec 1884	95/100	41.2 x 4.2 x 1.7	1300	22	2 TT bow, 2-37mm QF guns	16	Straight stern from 1899
FALKE (42)		Dec 1884							Stricken 1911
SPERBER (31)	Schichau, Elbing	7.5.1884	78/93	39.9 x 4.8 x 1.9	970	18.5	2 TT bow, 2-37mm QF guns	16	From 1905 oil burners, Yarrow boilers. 1920 to Italy
HABICHT (32)									
KUKUK (20)	Schichau, Elbing	Dec 1888							1920 to Italy, scrapped
STAR (21)		Nov 1888							1920 to Jugoslavia, as *D1*
KRRÄHE (22)		19.10.1888							1920 to Italy, scrapped
RABE (23)		May 1888							1896 watertube boilers, 2 funnels. 1920 to Italy
ELSTER (24)		19.9.1888							
BUSSARD (33)	Navy Yard, Pola	1886							1920 to Italy, scrapped
CONDOR (34)		1886							
GEIER (35)		1886							
UHU (36)		1886	78/88	39.9 x 4.8 x 1.9	1000	19	2 TT (1 bow, 1 deck), 2-37mm QF guns	16	1920 to Jugoslavia as *D2*
WÜRGER (37)		1887							1920 to Italy, scrapped
KRANICH (38)		1887							1920 to Jugolsavia as *D3*
REIHER (39)		1887							1920 to Italy, scrapped
IBIS (40)		1887							1920 to Italy, scrapped
KIBITZ (19)		1890							1920 to Jugoslavia as *D4*
GAUKLER (25)	Stabilimento Tecnico Triestino (STT)	1889							1920 to Italy, scrapped
FLAMINGO (26)		1889							1920 to Italy, scrapped
SEKRETÄR (27)		1889							1920 to Italy, scrapped
WEIHE (28)		1889							Stricken 18.9.1911, scrapped
MARABU (29)		1889							1920 to Italy, scrapped
HARPIE (30)		1889							1920 to Italy, scrapped
II Class, C-type									
XXVII	Navy Yard, Pola	19.6.1886							Scrapped 1909
XXVIII		23.6.1886							Sold 1905
XXIX		26.1.1887	47/55	34.3 x 3.8 x 1.7	600	18/19	2 TT bow, 1-37mm QF gun	16	Sold 1905
XXX		1.2.1887							Sold 1905 to Danubius
XXXI		23.12.1887							Sold 1904
XXXII		7.1.1888							Gunnery target in 1910
XXXIII (43)	Navy Yard, Pola	29.9.1887	66/70	36.8 x 4.5 x 1.9	700	17	2 TT bow, 2-37mm QF guns	16	Scrapped 1911
II class, D-type									
XXXIV (44)	Schichau, Elbing	March 1889							Sold 1912
XXXV (45)	Navy Yard, Pola	Jan 1891							Sold 1915
XXXVI (46)		Jan 1891							Sold 1911
XXXVII (47)		Jan 1891	64	36.9 x 4.8 x 1.9	750	20.3	2 TT (1 bow 1 deck), 2-37mm QF guns	16	Sold 1911
XXXVIII (48)		Jan 1891							Sold 1912
XXXIX (49)		Jan 1891							Sold 1912

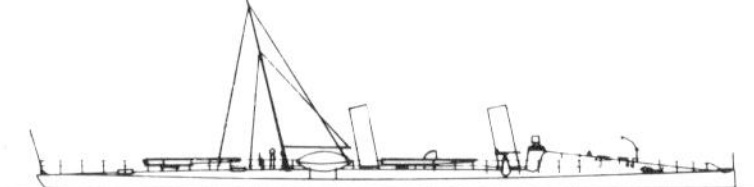

Natter as completed 1896

Name (Number from 1910)	Builder	Launched	Disp (t)	Dimensions (m)	HP	Kts	Armament	Crew	Fate
NATTER (18)	Schichau, Elbing	Feb 1896	166	47.3 x 5.3 x 2.8	2200	24	3 TT 45cm on deck, 2 QF guns 47mm 1911 reduced to 2 TT	21	After 1910 mobile T-battery at Pola harbour; 1920 as war reparation to GB, scrapped in Italy
VIPER (17)	Yarrow, London	Jan 1896	124	44.96 x 4.5 x 2.3	1900	25	3 TT 45cm, deck 2 QF guns 47mm	21	1920 to France
PYTHON (13)	Yarrow, London	11.4.1899							1920 to France
KIGYO (14)		11.4.1899					3 TT 45cm, deck	21	1920 to Britain
BOA (15)		Aug 1898	132	46.5 x 4.7 x 2.3	2000	24.5	2 QF guns 47mm		1920 to France
COBRA (16)		Sept 1898							1920 to France
KAIMAN (50E)	Yarrow, London	3.6.1905	203.3	56 x 5.4 x 1.5	3000	26.2	3 TT 45cm, deck 4 QF guns 47mm	31	1920 to GB, sold to Italy and scrapped

Kaiman was the British-built prototype of a very efficient and successful class of ocean-going torpedo boats and was followed by 23 units built in Austria from the original plans. At first these boats had the names *Anaconda*, *Alligator* etc, but in 1913 this was changed to a number/letter code similar to the German practice, the letter indicating the builder. *Kaiman* became torpedo boat *50E* (England); *Anaconda* became torpedo boat *51T* (Trieste, STT) and so on.

3

4

1. *Sperber*, First Class TB, 1884

2. *Rabe*, First Class TB, 1888

3. *XXXI*, C-type Second Class TB, 1887

4. *Planet*, torpedo boat destroyer, 1889

5. *Huszár*, torpedo boat destroyer, 1905
Aldo Fraccaroli Collection

(All uncredited photos in this section: Kriegsarchiv, Vienna)

5

DESTROYERS

Name (Number from 1910)	Builder	Launched	Disp (t)	Dimensions (m)	HP	Kts	Armament	Crew	Fate
METEOR	Schichau,	16.6.1887	435	57 x 6.7 x 2.6	2242	17.5	2-45cm TT, 9-47mm QF guns	60	1920 to Italy, scrapped
BLITZ KOMET	Elbing	7.7.1888	425	58.4 x 7.4 x 3.2	2360	21	2-45cm TT, 8-47mm QF guns	60	*Komet* after 1914 had two funnels. Both 1920 to Italy, scrapped
PLANET	Palmer, Newcastle	25.6.1889	525	64 x 7.1 x 2.8	3000	19	2-40cm TT, 2-7cm guns, 8-47mm QF guns	84	1915 adapted as a minesweeper. 1920 to Italy, scrapped
TRABANT	STT	21.5.1890	540	67.2 x 8.2 x 2.5	3500	20.4	2-45cm TT, 2-7cm guns, 8-47mm QF guns	84	1915 adapted as a minesweeper. 1920 to Italy, scrapped
SATELLIT	Schichau, Elbing	21.9.1892	616	68.9 x 8.1 x 2.7	4500	21.9	2-45cm TT, 1-7cm gun, 8-47mm QF guns	85	1912/13 new Yarrow boilers, three funnels instead of one; 1920 to France, scrapped
MAGNET	Schichau, Elbing	21.3.1896	544	67 x 8.2 x 3.3	5652	24	2-45cm TT, 6-47mm QF guns; after refit: 3-45cm TT, 2-7cm (45cal) guns, 4-47mm QF guns	80	2.8.1916 stern destroyed by enemy submarine torpedo; after refit new 'Yarrow' stern. 1920 to Italy, scrapped
HUSZÁR (i)	Yarrow, London	31.5.1905	390/428	68.4 x 6.3 x 1.9	6000	28.16	2-45cm TT, 7-47mm QF guns (as built); later 7cm/cal 30 guns, 1-7cm/cal 45 gun	65	Ran aground near Traste (South Adriatic) 3.12.1908; sank 12.12.1908

All destroyers were built by various yards to different designs – except the *Blitz* and *Komet* – to evaluate a standard design suitable for Austria. *Huszár* was the last of these boats built abroad, and thereafter all destroyers were built in Austrian yards.

France

A visit of a French battle squadron (ships of the *Liberté* class) to Malta about 1912

THE FRENCH NAVY 1860–1905

For all but the last few years of the above period France was unquestionably the second naval power to Britain and there were times in the 1860s and again in the late 1870s and early 1880s when it seemed that the French Navy might be the first. Although the contrary opinion was often expressed at the time, it is difficult to believe that Napoleon III ever had any serious intention of war with Britain, and after the disasters of the Franco-Prussian War in 1870, the German danger on the eastern frontier prevented any such action by the Third Republic. In fact the rise in French relative strength in the late 1870s was due more to British parsimony and inertia than to any French action. In spite of this it was desirable for France to have a navy sufficiently powerful always to be reckoned a serious factor in British calculations, and essential to have one that could command the Mediterranean and ensure communications with Algeria against any combination of continental states.

In more distant waters Napoleon III's attempt to establish an empire in Mexico which would be under French influence needed considerable naval forces, though its abandonment in 1867 as a result of United States pressure was due to the menace of the war-experienced American army and not to that of their navy which though highly formidable in the coastal operations of the Confederate War was far less so in more distant areas. French overseas possessions were second only to those of Britain, and in 1905 amounted to 4,224,000 square miles with a population of perhaps 43,000,000. Although much of this great area was taken up by the Sahara desert, there were, apart from Algeria and Tunis, important possessions in West and Equatorial Africa as well as French Somaliland in Africa, Indo-China in Asia and French Guiana in South America. Of island territories Madagascar was by far the largest, the others including Réunion, Martinique, Guadeloupe, New Caledonia and Tahiti among the more important.

THE FRENCH ECONOMY

Although the United Kingdom and France had comparable populations, the latter with a much smaller rate of growth being overtaken at a figure of about 38,500,000 in 1893, their economic structures were different. France was nearly self-sufficient while food was the United Kingdom's main import, and foreign trade far more valuable than that of France particularly in the latter part of the period. Average figures for 1901 to 1905 show French imports at £233 million and exports at £228 million compared with British 1905 figures of £565 million and £408 million respectively, and in the 1901 to 1905 period 74 per cent of the tonnage engaged in French overseas trade belonged to other nationalities. Coal production in France averaged 11.6 million tons for theyears 1861 to 1870 and attained nearly 36 million in 1905, in which year United Kingdom production stood at 236 million tons. French production of wrought iron and steel averaged 830,000 tons in 1861 to 1870 and rose to 1,865,000 tons in 1903 while United Kingdom figures for 1890 were 5,573,000 tons. In spite of this the French Navy was the first to introduce wrought iron armour, largely due to the support given by Napoleon III to this development, though it must be noted that the difficulties of building iron hulls were such that of the 34 seagoing armoured ships laid down from 1858 to 1870, 31 had wooden hulls. The French firm of Schneider were the first to make satisfactory steel heavy armour plates, and the chromium steel projectiles made by Holtzer in the early 1880s and soon after by Firminy and other companies were the first to be suitable for the attack of compound and early steel armour, and were in fact supplied in considerable quantities to Britain. The French Navy was also the first to adopt smokeless propellant though failure to realise the dangers from spontaneous ignition of impure nitrocellulose caused the loss of the battleships *Iéna* and *Liberté* long after the first adoption of this propellant in 1886.

HEAVY GUN DEVELOPMENT

Like other navies the French had considerable trouble over the construction of heavy guns, the British remedy of wire winding being only used experimentally. It was usual for guns to be delivered by the contractors such as Schneider-Canet or St Chamond when about 90 per cent complete and the final work was done by the naval gun factory at Ruelle. Certain troublesome forgings such as the bodies for the M1881 guns were on occasion obtained from Firth in England. The original M1858 6.4in guns were cast iron and it was soon found necessary to reinforce them by a layer of steel hoops. This construction of a cast iron body with one, or in the larger calibres two layers of steel hoops was retained up the M1870 guns which had in addition a steel 'A' tube. M1875 and 1875-1879 guns were all-steel with an 'A' tube, a body in one or two pieces and up to three layers of hoops. Building was found to be difficult particularly for the M1875-79 14.6in which were 28 calibres long as against the previous heavy gun maximum of 22. As a result the M1881 guns were much simpler with a one piece heat-treated steel body and hoops over the breech end. It was found difficult to harden the heavy steel bodies satisfactorily, and an 'A' tube and additional hoops were later added, while with the M1884 guns a return was made to a similar construction to that of 1875-79. The 40/45 calibre guns of M1887 and later patterns differed considerably in detail, but comprised a heavy 'A' tube over which hoops were shrunk for part of its length, a jacket or breech piece and various external tubes and/or hoops.

WARSHIP CONSTRUCTION

French warships were built at the five dockyards Cherbourg, Brest, Lorient, Rochefort and Toulon and by various private yards. Of the latter Arman at Bordeaux was the best known in the earlier part of the

period, and latterly F C de la Méditerranée at La Seyne and Le Havre, Soc de la Loire and Penhoët at St Nazaire and Soc de la Gironde at Bordeaux were contractors for the larger ships while Normand at Le Havre specialised in torpedo craft. Of the 97 ships of 5000 tons displacement or over built in the period under consideration 71 were laid down in the dockyards, the first by a private yard being the large cruiser *Tourville* at La Seyne in 1873. Construction was at times excessively slow.

Manning of the French Navy was partly voluntary, partly from a small proportion of each year's army conscripts but mainly from the '*inscription maritime*', a system devised in Louis XIV's reign by Colbert and introduced in 1681. In theory this included every French seaman who had to be enrolled from the ages of 18 to 50, and if required usually served 5 to 7 years from the age of 20.

The French ships of 1860 to 1905 were not seriously tested in war until 1914-1918 when some of the more recent of them proved at least as vulnerable as their contemporaries in other navies. The operations against Sfax in 1881 and in 1884-85 against China had very weak opposition to contend with, and only one indecisive action between minor warships occurred in the Franco-Prussian War of 1870-71. The original French intention had been to land 30,000 men in Schleswig to join with 40,000 Danes, but Denmark declined to take part in the war, and the German advance on land was so rapid that any idea of landing on the German coast had to be abandoned. Even so the threat was sufficient to detain over 80,000 first line German troops for 4 to 8 weeks on the Baltic and Schleswig coasts. The French Navy was far from ready for immediate operations, though much larger than the German, but with some difficulty the German North Sea coast was blockaded and for a time the Baltic coast also. Altogether the French captured 80 German merchant ships during the war.

Interest in French construction largely concentrates on the extremes of battleships and torpedo craft.

The construction of battleships between 1860 and 1905 may be summarised as follows (laying down dates):

1858-1861 – 3 *Gloire* class, *Couronne*, 2 *Magenta* class, 10 *Provence* (all broadside ironclads).
1865-1870 – 3 *Océan* class, *Friedland*, *Richelieu*, 2 *Colbert* class (all central battery ships).
1873-1876 – *Redoubtable*, 2 *Courbet* class (all central battery ships).
1877-1879 – *Amiral Duperré*, 4 *Terrible* class, 2 *Amiral Baudin* class (all barbette ships).
1881-1883 – *Hoche* (turret and barbette ship). 3 *Marceau* class (barbette ships).
From here on all ships had centre pivot turrets.
1889 – *Brennus*.
1891-1893 – *Charles Martel*, *Carnot*, *Jauréguiberry*, *Masséna*, *Bouvet*.
1894-1899 – 3 *Charlemagne* class, *Iéna*, *Suffren*. Also experimental *Henri IV*.
1901-1903 – 2 *République* class, 4 *Liberté* class.

Although there was considerable variation in French designs, some features tended to be constant. All the broadside ironclads were completely armoured above water except the *Magenta* class which were two-deckers. The central battery ships had complete waterline belts except the *Courbet* class in which the belt stopped 28ft from the stern, and except in the last three axial fire was not possible from the battery guns, but was provided in all by guns on the upper deck. It was normal to allow 20° to 25° elevation for the upper deck guns, a provision likely to be more useful for engaging high sited coastal batteries than ships at long range.

The 1877-1883 ships all had complete waterline belts, the *Terrible* class being of fairly low freeboard, as was the *Hoche* apart from a very high superstructure, while the rest had high freeboard. Heavy gun distribution varied, that adopted in the *Marceau* being one forward, one aft and one on either beam, while the *Hoche* had a more complicated version with 13.4in in the axial turrets and 10.8in in the beam barbettes.

Neglecting the experimental *Henri IV*, the ships from 1889 to 1899 were all of high freeboard forward though some were cut down aft and all had complete waterline belts except the *Masséna* where it ended 30ft from the stern. A thin upper belt of varied width was present in all to burst projectiles other than AP. The *Brennus* had powerful 13.4in guns and could only accommodate a twin turret forward and a single aft. The next five reverted to a mixed calibre main armament with single 12in fore and aft and 10.8in on either beam, while *Charlemagne*, *Iéna* and *Suffren* had twin 12in fore and aft. All this group were of inadequate displacement, and this was remedied in the *République* and *Liberté* classes where the heavy belt could be taken up to the main deck.

It should be noted that a large sea-going monitor was seriously considered in the first half of 1870, and two ships to be named *Brennus* and *Charles Martel* with partial waterline belts were proposed in 1882 but cancelled after some delay.

FRANCE

The armoured coast defence ships were laid down as follows:

1859-1862 – 4 *Palestro* class, 3 *Arrogante* class, 4 *Embuscade* class (all floating batteries).

1863-1865 – *Taureau*, 4 *Cerbère* class (all rams).

1873-1878 – 2 *Tonnere* class, 2 *Tempête* class (monitors). *Tonnant*, *Furieux* (barbette ships).

1882-1889 – 4 *Fusée* class, 4 *Achéron* class (all armoured gunboats).

1890 – 2 *Jemmapes* class, 2 *Bouvines* class (all turret ships).

The most interesting of these were the last four which were heavily gunned and probably built with operations against the German coast in mind.

For the purpose of this summary cruisers are divided into over and under 2500 tons displacement. The early smaller seagoing ironclads are included. Unless indicated, cruisers are without side armour and in these, protective decks were introduced in the *Sfax* and *Condor* class.

Those over 2500 tons were laid down or converted as follows:

1858-1861 – 11 converted frigates, 2 *Vénus* class.

1863-1865 – *Belliqueuse* (broadside ironclad). 7 *Alma* class (armoured central battery ships).

1868-1873 – 3 *La Galissonnière* class (armoured central battery ships). *Duquesne*, *Tourville*, *Duguay-Trouin*.

1876-1880 – 2 *Bayard* class, 2 *Vauban* class (armoured barbette ships). *Iphigénie*, *Naïade*, *Aréthuse*, *Dubordieu*.

1882-1886 – *Sfax*, *Tage*, *Amiral Cécille*.

1888-1891 – *Dupuy de Lôme*, 4 *Amiral Charner* class (armoured cruisers). *Davout*, *Suchet*, 3 *Alger* class, 3 *Friant* class.

1892-1896 – *Pothuau*, *Jeanne d'Arc* (armoured cruisers). *D'Entrecasteaux*, 3 *D'Assas* class, 2 *Catinat* class.

1897-1903 – 3 *Gueydon* class, 3 *Dupleix* class, 5 *Gloire* class, 3 *Léon Gambetta* class (armoured cruisers). *Jurien de la Gravière*.

1904-1906 – *Jules Michelet*, *Ernest Renant*, 2 *Edgar Quinet* class (armoured cruisers).

Those under 2500 tons were laid down or converted as follows:

1856-1862 – 2 *Cosmao* class, *Résolue*, *Desaix*, *Decrès*, *Talisman*.

1864-1868 – *Châteaurenault*, 4 *Infernet* class, 3 *Sané* class, 5 *Limier* class, *Linois*, 10 *Bourayne* class.

1873-1877 – 2 *Rigault de Genouilly* class, 4 *Lapérousse* class, 4 *Villars* class. *Hirondelle*.

1882-1884 – *Milan*, 4 *Condor* class.

1886-1891 – 3 *Forbin* class, 3 *Troude* class, 2 *Wattignies* class.

1892-1897 – 3 *Linois* class, 2 *D'Estrées* class.

It will be noted that the small unarmoured cruiser featured largely in the early years of the period, but towards the end armoured ships virtually monopolised the cruiser programme. Very few French cruisers were of outstanding design though the *Duquesne*, *Tourville*, *Sfax*, *Tage* and *Amiral Cécille* aroused much contemporary interest as did the *Milan* among the smaller ships. The *Dupuy de Lôme* was a remarkable conception with complete 4in side armour to the upper deck but the design was spoilt by the distribution of the turrets. None of the larger French armoured cruisers had a satisfactory armament until the *Edgar Quinet* class which were the last and obsolescent by their completion, and even in this class four of the 7.6in guns were still in casemates of which two were on the main deck.

THE FRENCH NAVY in 1860

SCREW THREE-DECKERS

Name	Launched	Displacement	Guns	Fate
BRETAGNE	1855	6770t	130	School ship 1866
FRIEDLAND	1856*	5170t	114	Hulked 1865
LOUIS XIV	1857*	5170t	114	Stricken 1880
SOUVERAIN	1854*	5170t	114	Stricken 1882
VILLE DE PARIS	1858*	5170t	114	Stricken 1882
MONTEBELLO	1852*	4920t	114	Stricken 1867

SCREW TWO-DECKERS

Name	Launched	Displacement	Guns	Fate
NAPOLEON	1850	5040t	90	Stricken 1876
ALGÉSIRAS	1855	5040t	90	Transport 1869
ARCOLE	1855	5040t	90	Stricken 1870
IMPÉRIAL	1856	5040t	90	Hulked 1869
REDOUTABLE	1855	5040t	90	Stricken 1869
VILLE DE BORDEAUX	1860	5070t	90	Stricken 1879
VILLE DE LYON	1861	5070t	90	Stricken 1883
VILLE DE NANTES	1858	5070t	90	Stricken 1872
ALEXANDRE	1857	4920t	90	Stricken 1877
CASTIGLIONE	1860	4920t	90	Stricken 1881
EYLAU	1856	4920t	90	Stricken 1877
MASSÉNA	1860	4920t	90	Stricken 1879
NAVARIN	1854	4560t	90	Transport 1873
ULM	1854	4560t	90	Coal hulk 1867
WAGRAM	1854	4560t	90	Stricken 1867
FLEURUS	1853	4490t	90	Stricken 1869
PRINCE JÉRÔME	1853	4490t	90	Transport 1872
AUSTERLITZ	1852	4430t	86	Stricken 1872
DUGUAY-TROUIN	1858*	4530t	82	Stricken 1872
TAGE	1858*	4530t	82	Transport 1875
TURENNE	1859*	4530t	82	Stricken 1867
BRESLAW	1857*	4530t	80	Stricken 1872
BAYARD	1860*	4430t	80	Stricken 1872
DONAWERTH	1858*	4330t	80	Stricken 1880
TILSITT	1856*	4330t	80	Stricken 1872
DUQUESNE	1853	4330t	80	Hulked 1867
TOURVILLE	1853	4330t	80	Stricken 1872
ST LOUIS	1858*	4160t	80	School ship 1881
CHARLEMAGNE	1851	4060t	80	Transport 1867
FONTENOY	1858*	4000t	80	Transport 1881
JEAN BART	1852	4010t	76	Stricken 1869

SCREW FRIGATES

Name	Launched	Displacement	Guns	Fate
ARDENTE	1857	3765t	56	Stricken 1869
AUDACIEUSE	1856	3765t	56	Stricken 1870
FOUDRE	1856	3765t	56	Stricken 1872
IMPÉRATRICE EUGÉNIE	1856	3765t	56	Stricken 1870
IMPÉTUEUSE	1856	3765t	56	Hulked 1869
SOUVERAINE	1856	3765t	56	Stricken 1872
ISLY	1849	2690t	40	Stricken 1872
RENOMMÉE	1857*	2600t	40	Stricken 1878
BELLONE	1853	2350t	36	Stricken 1877
DANAÉ	1857*	2350t	36	Stricken 1878
PANDORE	1857*	2350t	36	Coal hulk 1877
ZÉNOBIE	1857*	2350t	36	Stricken 1868
POMONE	1845	1900t	36	Stricken 1877
CLORINDE	1857*	1780t	36	Stricken 1888
ASTRÉE	1859	3000t	28	Stricken 1877

*Date of conversion from sail.

SCREW CORVETTES

Name	Launched	Displacement	Guns	Fate
D'ASSAS	1854	*c*2000t	16	Stricken 1878
DU CHAYLA	1855	*c*2000t	16	Stricken 1875
LAPLACE	1852	*c*1900t	10	Stricken 1879
PHLEGETON	1853	*c*1900t	10	Stricken 1868
PRIMAUGUET	1852	*c*1900t	10	Stricken 1877
ROLAND	1850	1970t	8	Stricken 1870
REINE HORTENSE*	1846	1100t	4	Stricken 1882
FORBIN	1859	1300t	6	Stricken 1884
FORFAIT	1859	1300t	6	Collision 1875
JÉRÔME NAPOLÉON	1859	1300t	6	Stricken 1879
MONGE	1859	1300t	6	Stricken 1868
CATON*	1847	890t	4	Stricken 1874
CHAPTAL*	1845	940t	2	Wrecked 1862

*Iron-hulled

SCREW FLOATING BATTERIES

Name	Launched	Displacement	Guns	Fate
CONGRÈVE	1855	1600t	18	Stricken 1867
DÉVASTATION	1855	1600t	18	Stricken 1871
FOUDROYANTE	1855	1600t	18	Stricken 1871
LAVE	1855	1600t	18	Stricken 1871
TONNANTE	1855	1600t	18	Stricken 1871

These vessels had 4in wrought iron armour.

PADDLE FRIGATES

Name	Launched	Displacement	Guns	Fate
ALBATROS	1844	2460t	14	Stricken 1879
ASMODÉE	1841	2700t	16	Stricken 1865
CACIQUE	1843	2680t	14	Stricken 1869
CAFFARELLI	1847	2700t	12	Stricken 1867
CANADA	1843	2470t	14	Stricken 1871
CHRISTOPHE COLOMB	1843	2480t	16	Stricken 1868
DARIEN	1842	2470	14	Stricken 1869
DESCARTES	1844	2980t	20	Stricken 1867
ELDORADO	1843	2560t	14	Stricken 1871
GOMER	1841	2700t	20	Stricken 1868
LABRADOR	1842	2460t	14	Stricken 1871
MAGELLAN	1843	2460t	14	Stricken 1879
MOGADOR	1848	2700t	8	Stricken 1878
MONTEZUMA	1843	2460t	14	Wrecked and burnt 1863
ORÉNOQUE	1843	2460t	14	Stricken 1878
PANAMA	1843	2460t	14	Stricken 1871
ULLOA	1842	2460t	14	Stricken 1865
VAUBAN	1845	2820t	20	Mining trials 1866

PADDLE CORVETTES

Name	Launched	Displacement	Guns	Fate
BERTHOLLET	1850	1600t	10	Stricken 1866
CATINAT	1851	1600t	10	Stricken 1880
COLBERT	1848	1270t	6	Stricken 1867
PRONY	1847	1350t	5	Wrecked 1861
COLIGNY*	1850	900t	4	Stricken 1888
EUMÉNIDE	1848	900t	4	Hulked 1887
GORGONE*	1848	900t	4	Wrecked 1869
TANGER	1849	900t	4	Stricken 1874
TISIPHONE	1851	900t	4	Stricken 1872
CASSINI	1845	1080t	6	Hulked 1863
TITAN	1844	940t	6	Stricken 1868
GASSENDI	1840	1260t	6	Stricken 1865
LAVOISIER	1838	1260t	6	Stricken 1865
VÉLOCE	1838	1260t	6	Stricken 1860

*Iron-hulled.

SCREW SLOOPS (400-900t, 2-6 guns)

Name	Launched	nhp	Fate
BICHE*	1848	200	Stricken 1868
BOUGAINVILLE	1859	150	Stricken 1889
COËTLOGON	1859	150	Stricken 1877
CORSE	1850**	120	Stricken 1890
D'ENTRECASTEAUX	1858	150	Stricken 1876
D'ESTAING	1859	150	Stricken 1876
LAMOTTE PICQUET	1859	150	Stricken 1881
LATOUCHE TREVILLE	1860	150	Stricken 1886
LUCIFER	1853	200	Stricken 1874
LUTIN	1861	–	Stricken 1868
LYNX	1861	–	Stricken 1866
MARCEAU	1852	120	Stricken 1871
MÉGÈRE	1853	200	Stricken 1875
PREGENT	1857	150	Stricken 1874
RENAUDIN	1857	150	Stricken 1873
SENTINELLE*	1848	120	Stricken 1869
SURCOUF	1858	150	Stricken 1878
TANCRÈDE	1861	–	Stricken 1866

*Iron-Hulled.
**Date of acquisition.

PADDLE SLOOPS (400-900t, 2-6 guns)

Name	Launched	nhp	Fate
ACHÉRON	1836	160	Stricken 1869
AJACCIO	1850**	120	Stricken 1871
ARDENT	1830	160	Stricken 1860
AUSTRALIE*	1844	160	Hulked 1867
BISSON	1850	120	Stricken 1871
BRANDON	1846	160	Stricken 1867
CASABIANCA	1859	160	Stricken 1877
CERBÈRE	1836	160	Stricken 1864
CHAMOIS*	1855**	150	Stricken 1878
CHIMÈRE	1833	160	Stricken 1861
COCYTE	1837	160	Stricken 1867
DAIM	1849	120	Stricken 1877
DAUPHIN*	1847	180	Stricken 1868
ECLAIREUR*	1847	200	To Peru 1868
EUPHRATE	1839	160	Stricken 1862
FLAMBEAU	1837	120	Stricken 1861
FULTON	1833	160	Stricken 1867
GALILÉE	1851	120	Stricken 1868
GOËLAND*	1848	200	Stricken 1872
GREGÉOIS	1839	160	Stricken 1865
GRONDEUR	1839	160	Stricken 1860
HÉRON*	1847	200	Stricken 1871
MÉTEORE	1833	160	Stricken 1867
MILAN	1849	200	Stricken 1865
MOUETTE*	1847	200	Stricken 1867
NARVAL*	1844	160	Stricken 1875
PHARE	1835	160	Stricken 1865
PHENIX*	1848	200	Stricken 1871
PROMÉTHÉE*	1848	200	Stricken 1868
REQUIN*	1847	180	Stricken 1862
SÉSOSTRIS	1851**	160	Stricken 1861
SOLON*	1846	160	Stricken 1867
SOUFFLEUR*	1849	200	Stricken 1887
STYX	1834	160	Stricken 1867
TARTARE	1836	160	Stricken 1867
TÉNARE	1840	220	Stricken 1861
VAUTOUR	1834	160	Stricken 1863

*Iron-hulled.
**Date of acquisition.

SCREW GUNBOATS

These comprised *Comète* (4 guns, 120nhp); *Alarme*, *Avalanche*, *Eclair*, *Etincelle*, *Flamme*, *Flèche*, *Fulminante*, *Fusée*, *Grenade* and *Mitraille* (4 guns, 110nhp); *Alerte*, *Bourrasque*, *Couleuvrine*, *Meurtrière*, *Mutine*, *Rafale* and *Tirailleuse* (3 guns, 25nhp); and *Arquebuse*, *Lance*, *Poudre*, *Redoute*, *Sainte-Barbe*, *Salve*, *Tempête* and *Tourmente* (2 guns, 90nhp). There were also *canonnières* nos *1-5* and *11* (1 gun, sectional, 4in wrought iron shield) and nos *12-31* (1 gun, sectional, iron-hulled, unarmoured, 12nhp).

SAILING SHIPS-OF-THE-LINE

Still in service in 1860 were *Valmy* (114 guns), *Hercule* and *Jemmapes* (90), *Iéna*, *Inflexible* and *Suffren* (82), *Jupiter* (80) and *Duperré* (70).

SAILING FRIGATES

The 56-gun frigates *Andromaque*, *Belle Poule*, *Didon*, *Forte*, *Indépendante*, *Iphigénie*, *Persévérante*, *Uranie* and *Vengeance* were effective in 1860, as were *Alceste*, *Andromède*, *Némésis*, *Néréide*, *Poursuivante*, *Sibylle*, *Sirène* and *Virginie* (52 guns), *Africaine*, *Algérie*, *Constitution*, *Erigone*, *Héliopolis*, *Isis*, *Jeanne d'Arc*, *Pénélope* and *Psyché* (42), and *Cléopâtre* (38).

SAILING CORVETTES

These consisted of *Artémise*, *Bayonnaise*, *Capricieuse*, *Constantine*, *Cordelière*, *Cornélie*, *Embuscade*, *Eurydice*, *Galatée*, *Sérieuse* and *Thisbé* (22 guns), and *Triomphante* (16 guns).

SAILING BRIGS

Effective in 1860 were *Génie* (14 guns), *Alcibiade*, *Beaumanoir*, *Chasseur*, *Chevert*, *Entreprenant*, *Euryale*, *Faune*, *Hussard*, *Janus*, *Lapérouse*, *Mercure*, *Nisus*, *Obligado*, *Olivier*, *Victor* and *Zèbre* (12 guns), *Agile*, *Dupetit-Thouars*, *Léger* and *Railleur* (8 guns) and *Palinure* (2 mortars).

CAPITAL SHIPS

Although the *Gloire* will always be famous as the first armoured battleship, this class were not very successful ships. Designed by Dupuy de Lôme, the two Toulon ships were ordered 4.3.1858 and the *Normandie* 6 months later. They were wooden hulled and as vulnerable to damage below the armour as one of the screw 2-deckers. The belt extended from stem to stern and from 6½ft below water to the upper deck, being backed by the 26in-24in wooden hull. The CT was 12ft high and unroofed, and there was 0.4in iron under the wooden upper deck. The 6.4in RMLs had a very poor performance against armour, and were soon replaced by 6.4in BLs (M1860) which were no more powerful. There were two guns on the upper deck and the rest on the broadside behind armour only 6ft 2in above water. According to reliable British information the battery guns were changed by 1865 to 12/16-6.4in M1864 which were a little more powerful, and 12-55pdr SB, with 4-8.8in RML howitzers, converted from Paixhans shell guns, on the upper deck. In 1868 *Invincible* and *Normandie* were completely rearmed with 8-9.4in and 6-7.6in of M1864 or 1866. These were BLs as were all French guns from then on, but they compared very badly with the British 9in RML. The *Gloire* appears to have had 6-9.4in and 2-6.4in.

Originally a light barquentine rig of 11,800 sq ft was provided but the economics of peacetime cruising caused this to be changed for a full rig of 27,000 sq ft which was later much reduced. They were not good seaboats and as to be expected from a metacentric height of about 7ft rolled badly. The *Normandie* was the first armoured ship to cross the Atlantic, being sent to Mexico in July 1862 and returning in 1863 after a bad yellow fever outbreak. Both she and *Invincible* were built of unsound timber and were completely rotted after less than ten years' service. *Normandie*'s engines were later installed in the monitor *Tonnerre*.

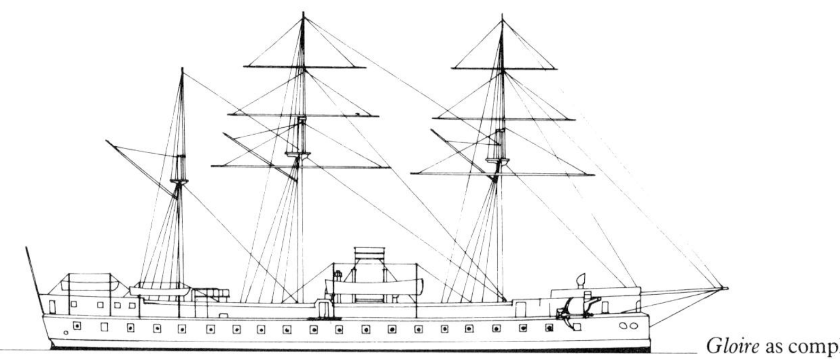

Gloire as completed 1860

GLOIRE class *broadside ironclads*

Displacement: 5630t
Dimensions: 255ft 6in wl x 55ft 9in x 27ft 10in max *(77.88 x 16.99 x 8.48m)*
Machinery: 1-shaft HRCR, 8 oval boilers, 2500ihp = 12.5-13kts. Coal 665t
Armour: Wrought iron. Belt 4.7-4.3in, CT 4in
Armament: 36-6.4in RML (M1858/60)
Complement: 570

Name	Builder	Laid down	Launched	Comp	Fate
GLOIRE	Toulon	March 1858	24.11.59	Aug 1860	Stricken 1879
INVINCIBLE	Toulon	May 1858	4.4.61	March 1862	Stricken 1872
NORMANDIE	Cherbourg	14.9.1858	10.3.60	13.5.62	Stricken 1871

Ordered the same day as the *Gloire*, the iron-hulled *Couronne* was delayed during construction by alterations to the plans of her designer Audenet. She was however the first iron-hulled armoured battleship to be laid down, though launched and completed after the *Warrior*. The *Couronne* was similar in general layout to the *Gloire* but was a better ship. The armour backing was unusual, comprising 4in teak, 1.3in of iron lattice work, 11in teak and then the 0.8in hull plating. As in the *Gloire* the sides were completely armoured above water, and the upper deck comprised 4in oak and ½in iron with the main beams also iron but did not cover the machinery spaces. There was no effective compartmentation. Of the guns, 36 were in the broadside battery behind armour 7ft above water and 4-6.4in were on the upper deck, the latter being replaced in 1864 by 4-8.8in RML howitzers. The battery 6.4in were then replaced by M1864 guns, and this was followed by rearmament with 16-7.6in M1864 or 1866 in the battery and 4-6.4in on the upper deck. The final armament comprised 8-9.4in/19cal M1870 and 4-7.6in M1870 in the battery with 2-4.7in and 12-1pdr revolvers on the upper deck, the 9.4in being between the 9in and 10in RML in performance.

The *Couronne* was converted to a gunnery training ship in 1881-85, the armour being removed and a light iron spar deck and poop added, so that she resembled a screw 2-decker in appearance. An illustration of 1865 shows a full rig similar to that of the *Gloire*, and she was a better sea boat than the latter with a metacentric height of about 6ft. Her iron hull seems to have lasted well and she reamined afloat until 1932.

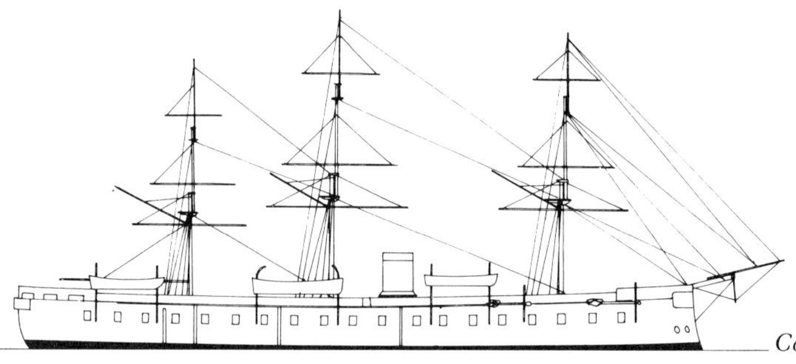

Couronne as completed 1862

COURONNE *broadside ironclad*

Displacement: 5983t
Dimensions: 262ft 5in wl x 54ft 9in x 26ft 11in max *(79.98 x 16.69 x 8.20m)*
Machinery: 1-shaft HRCR, 8 oval boilers, 2900ihp = 12.5-13kts. Coal 650/1000t
Armour: Wrought iron. Belt 4in-3.2in
Armament: 10-55pdr SB, 30-6.4in BL M1860
Complement: 570

Name	Builder	Laid down	Launched	Comp	Fate
COURONNE	Lorient	14.2.1859	28.3.61	2.2.62	Hulked 1910

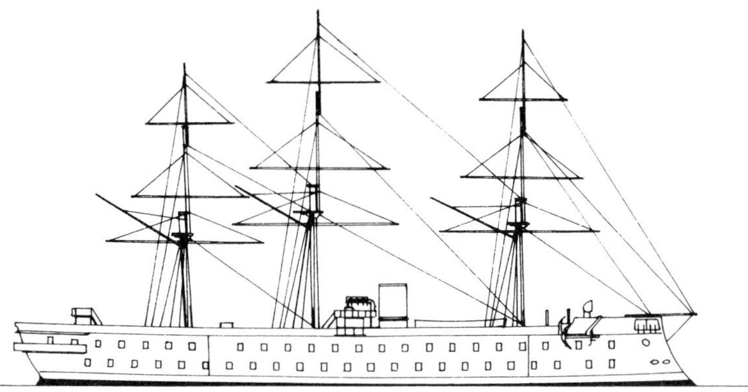
Solferino in 1864

MAGENTA class *broadside ironclads*

These wooden-hulled ships designed by Dupuy de Lôme were the only broadside ironclads with two gun decks and were also the first with a spur ram. The latter projected 6½ft and was covered by a 14t steel cone supported by some of the heaviest longitudinal timbers, but as the tactical diameter was 870yds the ships were not very suited to ramming. The belt was complete but the armour on the gun decks ended in thin bulkheads and did not reach bow or stern where the sides were unprotected wood. The lower gun deck had 16-55pdr and 10-6.4in and the main deck 24-6.4in with respective heights above water of 6ft 3in and 14ft. The two howitzers were on the upper deck. The first alteration was to replace the 6.4in M1860 by M1864, and then in *Magenta* the main deck guns were replaced by 4-9.4in and 4-7.6in with 4 more 7.6in on the upper deck, all being M1864. Finally in 1867/8 the lower deck guns were removed, and the main deck rearmed with 10-9.4in M1864 or 1866, the upper deck guns being unchanged. *Solferino* was rearmed in 1868/9 with no lower deck guns, 10-9.4in M1864 or 1866 on the main deck and four more in half-barbettes on the upper deck.

Metacentric height was about 5¼ft and the class were considered good seaboats. They were originally rigged as barquentines with 18,400 sq ft of sail but were altered to barques with 21,000 sq ft in 1864. The loss of *Magenta* was due to a fire that began at night in the wardroom galley and got out of control. The forward magazines were flooded but the after ones could not be reached and after 175 minutes the ship blew up.

Displacement: 6715t
Dimensions: 282ft 1in wl x 56ft 8in x 27ft 8in max (*Solferino* 28ft 6in) (*85.98 x 17.27 x 8.43 (8.69)m*)
Machinery: 1-shaft HRCR, 9 oval boilers, 3450ihp = 13kts. Coal 740t
Armour: Wrought iron. Belt 4.7in, battery 4.7in-4.3in
Armament: 16-55pdr SB, 34-6.4in BL M1860, 2-8.8in RML howitzers
Complement: 674

Name	Builder	Laid down	Launched	Comp	Fate
MAGENTA	Brest	22.6.1859	22.6.61	2.1.62	Sunk by internal explosion 31.10.75
SOLFERINO	Lorient	24.6.1859	24.6.61	25.8.62	Stricken 1882

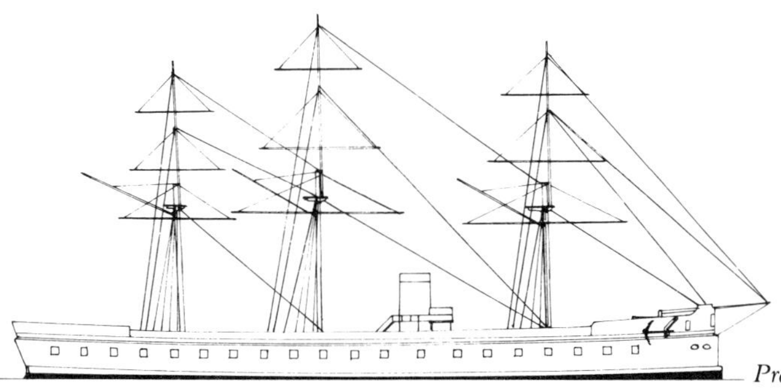
Provence as completed 1865

PROVENCE class *broadside ironclads*

These ships, the most numerous class of French battleships, were ordered as improved *Gloires* on 16.11.1860. All were wooden hulled except *Héroïne*, and she had no effective compartmentation. The sides were completely armoured above water with 6in on wl and 4.3in above. The CT was apparently roofed. In *Flandre*, *Provence* and *Héroïne* the two howitzers and two 6.4in guns were on the upper deck, as were four 7.6in in the rest of the class. The battery guns were 7¼ft above water in the lighter ships and at least a foot less in the heaviest. The individual changes of armament are not fully known. In 1865 11-7.6in, one of which fired ahead from a port under the forecastle, may have been mounted in some and in 1868 the armament seems to have been standardised at 8-9.4in M1864 or 1866 in the battery and 4-7.6in on the upper deck. 9.4in/19cal M1870 are recorded for *Surveillante* in 1873 and *Flandre* and *Valeureuse* in 1875. There was little point in fitting compound engines with 26lb boiler pressure and jet condensers, and single expansion engines worked better. Metacentric height was about 4½ft, and the class were generally barque-rigged with about 21,000 sq ft of sail. The breech blew off a 9.4in in *Valeureuse* in 1870, and a bad boiler explosion occurred in *Revanche* in 1877. *Héroïne* was scuttled at Dakar in 1901 after an outbreak of yellow fever.

Displacement: 5700t-6122t
Dimensions: 262ft 5in wl x 55ft 9in x 26ft 10in-28ft max (*79.98 x 16.99 x 8.18-8.53m*)
Machinery: 1-shaft HRCR (compound in most of class), 9 oval boilers, 3050/3600ihp = 13-14kts. Coal 590/640t
Armour: Wrought iron. Belt 6in-4.3in, CT 4in
Armament: 4-9.4in M1864 or 1866, 10-7.6in M1864 (*Flandre, Provence, Héroïne* 10-55pdr SB, 22-6.4in M1864, 2-8.8in RML howitzers)
Complement: 579/594

Name	Builder	Laid down	Launched	Comp	Fate
FLANDRE	Cherbourg	21.1.1861	12.6.64	May 1865	Stricken 1886
GAULOISE	Brest	21.1.1861	26.4.65	12.4.67	Stricken 1883
GUYENNE	Rochefort	March 1861	6.9.65	15.4.66	Stricken 1882
MAGNANIME	Brest	27.2.1861	19.8.64	1.11.65	Stricken 1882
PROVENCE	Toulon	March 1861	29.10.63	1.2.65	Stricken 1884
REVANCHE	Toulon	March 1861	28.12.65	1.5.67	Scrapped 1893
SAVOIE	Toulon	March 1861	29.9.63	25.3.65	Stricken 1888
SURVEILLANTE	Lorient	28.1.1861	18.8.64	21.10.67	Stricken 1890
VALEUREUSE	Brest	23.5.1861	18.8.64	Feb 1867	Stricken 1886
HÉROÏNE	Lorient	10.6.1861	10.12.63	July 1865	Hulked 1894

ROCHAMBEAU

This ship, formerly the USS *Dunderberg*, is described in the United States section. She was bought by France in 1867, but was only commissioned for some weeks in the late summer of 1870 and was stricken in 1872. In French service her armament comprised 4-10.8in and 10-9.4in M1864 or 1864/66.

OCÉAN class *central battery ships*

Displacement: 7580/7775t
Dimensions: 287ft 10in wl x 57ft 6in x 29ft 6in-29ft 9in max (*87.73 x 17.52 x 8.99-9.07m*)
Machinery: 1-shaft HRCR compound, 8 oval boilers, 3780/4180ihp = 13/14kts. Coal 650t
Armour: Wrought iron. Belt 8in-7in, battery 6.3in, barbettes 6in
Armament: 4-10.8in, 4-9.4in (originally M1864 or 1866, later M1870 of 18 and 19cal) 6-5.5in M1870, 12-1pdr revolvers, 4-14in TT aw eventually added
Complement: 750/778

Name	Builder	Laid down	Launched	Comp	Fate
OCÉAN	Brest	July 1865	15.10.68	21.7.70	Stricken 1894
MARENGO	Toulon	July 1865	4.12.69	1872	Sold 1896
SUFFREN	Cherbourg	July 1866	26.12.70	1875	Stricken 1897

Wooden-hulled central battery ships, altered and much delayed in construction. The original design envisaged a displacement of 7200t with 4-7.6in and 4-6.4in in the battery instead of 4-10.8in. The waterline belt was complete and the unarmoured wooden areas above were plated with 0.6in iron. For the first time in a French battleship iron watertight bulkheads were fitted, though as there were only three their efficacy in a wooden hull was dubious. The barbette armour was later removed to reduce topweight as metacentric height was only 1.7/2.2ft. The 10.8in guns in the battery were about 11½ft above water and the hull was not recessed to give axial fire, which was provided by the 9.4in in upper deck half-barbettes over the corners of the battery. The ram projected nearly 9ft and was tipped by a 20t bronze casting. A full rig seems to have been originally intended, but the vessels were later rigged as barquentines or barques. Sail area is given as 21,000/22,000 sq ft. Except for the greater power of the 10.8in/18cal M1870 compared with that of the 10in RML, this class were much inferior to HMS *Hercules*.

Marengo with reduced barquentine rig

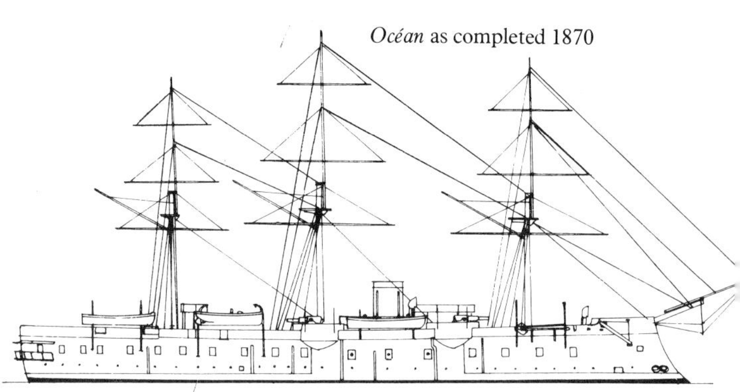

Océan as completed 1870

FRIEDLAND *central battery ship*

Displacement: 8850t
Dimensions: 317ft 2in wl x 58ft x 29ft 6in max (*96.67 x 17.68 x 8.99m*)
Machinery: 1-shaft HRCR compound, 8 oval boilers, 4400ihp = 13.3kts. Coal 630t
Armour: Wrought iron. Belt 8in-7in, battery 6.3in
Armament: 8-10.8in/18cal M1870, 8-5.5in M1870, 8- later 22-1pdr revolvers, 2- later 4-14in TT aw added
Complement: 700

Name	Builder	Laid down	Launched	Comp	Fate
FRIEDLAND	Lorient	July 1865	25.10.73	1876	Stricken 1902

Originally designed as an iron-hulled unit of the *Océan* class, the *Friedland* was much altered during eight years on the stocks. There was a complete waterline belt and six of the 10.8in were in the battery with ports 34ft apart and sills 10ft 8in above water. The hull was not recessed for axial fire from the battery and the remaining two 10.8in were in upper deck unarmoured half-barbettes projecting 4½ft from the side. The 5.5in were originally on the upper deck but were remounted on the battery deck forward of the armour. The hull was compartmented by five watertight bulkheads but there was no double bottom though the sides were double from the turn of the bilge. The spur ram was replaced by the continuation of the inclined stem below water. Metacentric height was a little over 3ft and the *Friedland* was originally rigged as a ship, then as a barque and eventually with fore and aft sails on two masts only, the mainmast being removed.

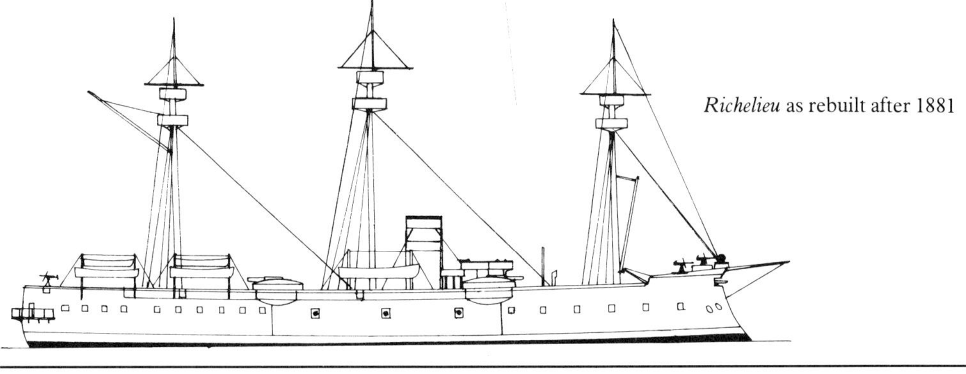

Richelieu as rebuilt after 1881

RICHELIEU *central battery ship*

Displacement: 8984t
Dimensions: 322ft wl x 57ft 3in x 28ft 6in max (*98.15 x 17.45 x 8.69m*)
Machinery: 2-shaft HRCR compound, 8 oval boilers, 4200ihp = 13kts. Coal 640t
Armour: Wrought iron. Belt 8.7in-7in, over ram 4½in, battery 6.3in, barbettes 6.3in
Armament: 6-10.8in/18cal M1870, 5-9.4in/19cal M1870, 10-4.7in (later replaced by 6-5.5in) M1870, 8 then 18-1pdr revolvers, 4-14in TT aw added
Complement: 750

Name	Builder	Laid down	Launched	Comp	Fate
RICHELIEU	Toulon	1869	3.12.73	1876	Sold 1901

A wooden-hulled central battery ship originally intended to be of 7400t with only 9.4in guns. The belt was complete and the unarmoured wooden sides above were plated as in the *Océan* class. The 10.8in guns were in a similar battery to that in *Friedland* with 4-9.4in in barbettes above the corners of the battery and the fifth gun firing forward under the forecastle. There were more compartments than in *Friedland* and the spur ram projected 10ft, while twin screws were intended to give greater handiness in ramming. Metacentric height was only about 1½ft and although originally full rigged, *Richelieu* later had fore and aft sails only. She capsized following a fire on 29.12.80 at Toulon but was raised and repaired. In September 1885 she was used for trials of torpedo nets at up to 4kts. She sank in the Bay of Biscay after sale.

Colbert as completed 1877

COLBERT class *central battery ship*

This class were the last French wooden hulled sea-going battleships. The complete belt extended for 5ft 10in above and below wl and there was iron plating on the unarmoured wooden sides above, and in addition 0.6in on the main deck. The battery was shorter than in the *Richelieu* and accommodated 6-10.8in which had no axial fire, the other two being in unarmoured barbettes with the upperworks much recessed to give a wide arc of training. One 9.4in was forward under the forecastle and the second was added shortly after completion in place of two 5.5in. It was mounted at the stern on a centre pivot mounting with light protection. Metacentric height was 2-2¾ft and as completed they were full rigged with 23,000 sq ft of sail. A British report notes that the *Colbert* had steam steering and was said to be very handy.

Displacement: 8750t
Dimensions: 317ft 9in wl x 57 ft 3in x 28-29ft max (*96.85 x 17.45 x 8.53-8.84m*)
Machinery: 1-shaft HRCR compound, 8 oval boilers, 4600ihp = 14kts. Coal 540/620t
Armour: Wrought iron. Belt 8.7in-7in, battery 6.3in with 4.7in bulkheads
Armament: 8-10.8in/18cal M1870, 1- later 2-9.4in/19cal M1870, 8- later 6-5.5in/M1870, 14/18-1pdr revolvers added, 4/6-14in TT aw
Complement: 774

Name	Builder	Laid down	Launched	Comp	Fate
COLBERT	Brest	1870	16.9.75	1877	Stricken 1900
TRIDENT	Toulon	1870	9.11.76	1878	Hulked 1904

2

1. *Trident* with reduced barquentine rig
2. *Redoutable* with barquentine rig

Redoutable as completed 1878

REDOUTABLE *central battery ship*

This ship was of quite different design to previous central battery ships. Beam was increased, draught reduced and the central battery shortened with only four guns mounted at the corners. With very marked tumblehome and the battery taken out to the full beam of the hull, all-round fire was obtained at the price of very limited broadside arcs, so that in most directions only one of the battery guns would bear. For the first time steel was used in large amounts for the hull though the armour was still wrought iron. The belt was complete and ran from 5ft below to 4ft 10in above wl. It was 14in amidships thinning to 8.7in forward and to 9in aft and at the lower edge. The battery armour upper edge was 19ft above wl, and there was a 2.4in deck at the belt upper edge outside the battery but no armoured roof to the latter. There was a double bottom but there were no watertight longitudinal bulkheads, and the steam steering engine was above water. The four battery guns were of a lighter, lower velocity pattern than the four unarmoured upper deck ones, which were mounted under the forecastle, at the stern and on either beam in half-barbettes. The 5.5in, later replaced by 3.9in, were on the upper deck. Magazines for the battery guns were liable to be overheated by the machinery spaces. As first rearmed the bow gun (which had a cracked tube) was replaced by a 10.8in/28cal M1881 and the battery guns by 4-10.8in/18cal M1870. The second rearmament involved the replacement of the battery guns by 4-9.4in/28cal M1881, which in the final rearmament were changed for 30cal M1884s, and the 3-10.8in M1875 still on the upper deck were finally replaced by 3-10.8in/40cal M1893/96, the 10.8in M1881 being left. It seems likely that the 10.8in/40cal would have somewhat overstrained the old ship if ever fired with full charges. The final light guns comprised 5-9pdr, 14-3pdr, 5-1pdr and 5-1pdr revolvers.

Metacentric height is given as 2.8ft and originally she was full rigged with 24,000 sq ft, but later rigged as a barquentine. Ultimately the *Redoutable* had two military masts which, with the large funnel, gave her an imposing appearance. She was reboilered with 8 cyl boilers in 1894 and had a new VTE engine.

Displacement: 9224t
Dimensions: 318ft 8in wl x 64ft 6in x 25ft 7in max (*97.13 x 19.66 x 7.80m*)
Machinery: 1-shaft HRCR compound, 8 oval boilers, 6200ihp = 14.7kts. Coal 620t
Armour: Wrought iron. Belt 14in-8.7in, battery 9.5in
Armament: 8-10.8in/20cal M1875, 6-5.5in M1870, 12-1pdr revolvers, 2-14in TT aw
Complement: 705

Name	Builder	Laid down	Launched	Comp	Fate
REDOUTABLE	Lorient	Aug 1873	Sept 1876	Dec 1878	Stricken 1910

FRANCE

Courbet was originally to be named *Foudroyant*. These ships resembled the *Redoubtable* in general layout and were the largest central battery ships ever built. The belt was 9¼ft wide, 2¼ft being above water, and extended from the bows to 28ft from the stern, ending in a 12in bulkhead. It was 15in amidships, 10.3in forward and 12in aft with the lower edge 10in amidships and 7in at the ends. The top of the battery armour was 19½ft above water, and according to reliable British reports, the backing round the gunports in *Courbet* was replaced by 12in steel. The 2.4in armour deck outside the battery was at the belt upper edge except abaft the stern bulkhead where it was at lower edge level. Compartmentation was better than in *Redoubtable*. The 13.4in guns in the battery were worked by hydraulic power but were cramped and slow-firing. They were the largest mounted in a central battery ship. In *Courbet* the 13.4in guns were later replaced by 21cal M1875s, and the 4-10.8in by 3-9.4in/40cal M1893s. In *Dévastation* the 13.4in guns were removed after the failure of a weapon of this pattern in the *Amiral Duperré*, and were replaced by 12.6in/25cal M1870-81s which were converted coast defence guns. These were later replaced by 4-10.8in/20cal M1875 and the 4 original 10.8in by 2-9.4in/40cal M1893/96, while the 5.5in were replaced by 3.9in. The number of small guns was much increased and an 1895 list credits *Courbet* with 4-9pdr, 14-3pdr, 7-1pdr and 19-1pdr revolvers. Metacentric height was a little over 3ft and the ships were only lightly rigged. They could be distinguished from *Redoubtable* by having two funnels close abreast. *Dévastation* was reboilered in 1901 with 12 Bellevilles and had new VTE engines.

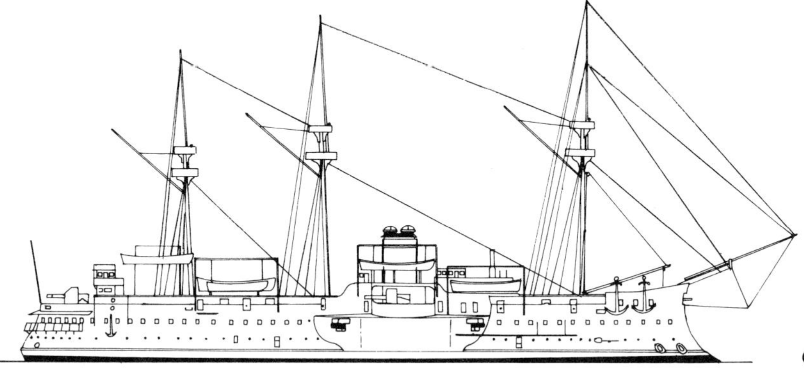

Courbet as completed 1886

COURBET class *central battery ships*

Displacement: 10,450t
Dimensions: 311ft 6in wl x 69ft 9in x 26ft 6in/27ft max (*94.95 x 21.26 x 8.08*/8.23m)
Machinery: 2-shaft VC, 12 cyl boilers, 8300ihp = 15/15.5kts. Coal 600/1100t max
Armour: Wrought iron. Belt 15in-7in, battery 9.5in
Armament: *Courbet* 4-13.4in/21cal M1881, 4-10.8in/20cal M1875, 6-5.5in M1881, 12-1pdr revolvers, 5-14in TT aw; *Dévastation* 4-13.4in/18cal M1875, 4-10.8in/18 cal M1870M, 6-5.5in M1870, 8-1pdr revolvers, 5-14in TT aw
Complement: 689

Name	Builder	Laid down	Launched	Comp	Fate
COURBET	Toulon	July 1875	April 1882	1886	Stricken 1910
DÉVASTATION	Lorient	Jan 1876	April 1879	Oct 1882	Scrapped 1922

1

2

A break with previous designs, the *Amiral Duperré* was a high freeboard barbette ship. The complete belt was 22in amidships with 16in at the lower edge and a uniform 10in fore and aft with 6in over the spur ram. It only extended from 6ft 7in below water to 1ft 6in above and the sides above were unarmoured, while the barbettes, with a gun axis height of 29ft, were shallow rings of armour only. The armour deck was at the top of the belt and of 2.4in steel on 0.7in plating, while there were 16 transverse watertight bulkheads and also longitudinals to 49ft from bow and stern. The 13.4in barbettes were disposed two abreast forward, one on the centreline amidships and one aft, while the 6.4in was in the bows and the 5.5in in an unarmoured main deck battery. One of the 13.4in failed, probably due to overheated brown powder as the magazines were extremely hot, and she was rearmed with 3-13.4in/21cal M1881, retaining one of the former guns. The small guns were later increased in number, an 1895 list giving 2-9pdr and 40 other guns from 3pdr to 1pdr revolver. Metacentric height is believed to have been about 2ft, and originally a full rig was intended. The two funnels were abreast, and she eventually had two masts each with two armed tops. Although the waterline was well protected, she was very vulnerable above and would not have stood much chance against HMS *Inflexible*.

1. *Courbet* with fore and main gaffs removed

2. *Amiral Duperré* 1889

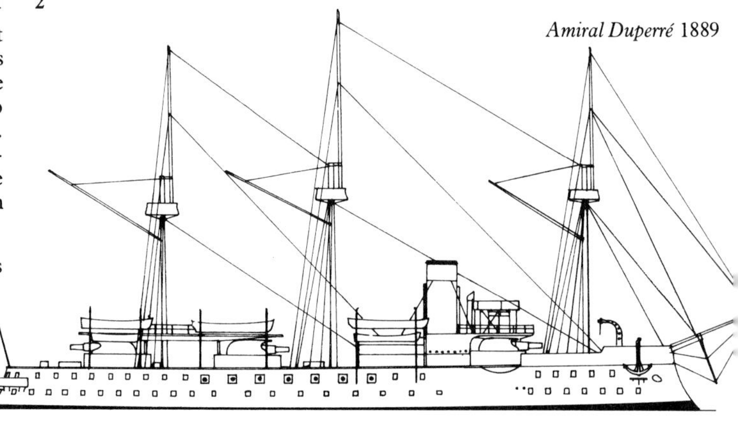

Amiral Duperré 1889

AMIRAL DUPERRÉ *barbette ship*

Displacement: 11,030t
Dimensions: 319ft 10in wl x 66ft 11in x 27ft 8in max (*97.48 x 20.40 x 8.43m*)
Machinery: 2-shaft VC, 12 cyl boilers, 7300ihp = 14kts. Coal 787t max
Armour: Wrought iron. Belt 22in-10in, barbettes 12in with 4in tubes, shields 2in max (steel), CT 1.5in (steel)
Armament: 4-13.4in/18cal M1875 (4x1), 1-6.4in/28cal M1881, 14-5.5in M1870, 18-1pdr revolvers, 4-14in TT aw
Complement: 660

Name	Builder	Laid down	Launched	Comp	Fate
AMIRAL DUPERRÉ	La Seyne	Jan 1877	Sept 1879	1883	Stricken 1909

This class bore little resemblance to the *Admiral Duperré*, their ancestor being the coast defence battleship *Tonnant*, and were of moderately low freeboard. The complete belt was almost entirely submerged at normal load and was 20in amidships with a 16in lower edge reduced to 12in-10in forward and 12in-8in aft. The barbette bases were unarmoured except for the tube which was taken to the armour deck. This was at the belt upper edge and of 3.2in max iron or steel over 1in steel. There were 10 or 11 transverse watertight bulkheads. The 16.5in guns were slow-firing and far less powerful than the British 16.25in. The guns in *Terrible* had to be cut back because of proving ground failures near the muzzle. In 1898 she was briefly rearmed with 2-13.4in/35cal M1893, the other three ships being reconstructed at about this time and armed with 2-10.8in/40cal M1893/96 in centre pivot turrets, while the lighter guns were changed to 6-3.9in QF M1893 and 14-3pdr. The TT were removed from *Requin* and reduced to two in the others. *Requin* was reboilered with 12 Niclausse boilers and the original four funnels in close pairs abreast were replaced by two on the centreline. She also had new VTE engines and served in the eastern Mediterranean and Suez Canal during the First World War.

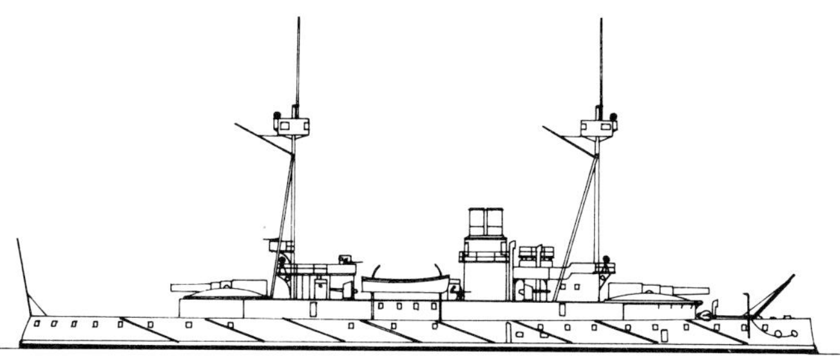

Requin as completed 1888

TERRIBLE class *barbette ships*

Displacement: 7530t
Dimensions: 271ft 6in pp x 59ft x 26ft 2in max (*82.75 x 17.98 x 7.98m*)
Machinery: 2-shaft VC, 12 (*Requin* 10) cyl boilers, 6500ihp = 14.5/15kts. Coal 500t
Armour: Compound (*Terrible* steel). Belt 20in-8in, barbettes 18in, tubes 8in, shields and CT 1.2in (steel)
Armament: 2-16.5in/22cal (*Terrible* 19.3cal) M1875 (2x1), 4-3.9in M1881 (later QFC), 2/4-3pdr, 16-1pdr revolvers, 4-14in TT
Complement: 373 (332 as reconstructed)

Name	Builder	Laid down	Launched	Comp	Fate
CAÏMAN	Toulon	Dec 1878	May 1885	1888	Scrapped 1927
INDOMPTABLE	Lorient	June 1878	Sept 1883	Feb 1887	Scrapped 1927
REQUIN	Ch de la Gironde	Dec 1878	June 1885	Dec 1888	Stricken 1920
TERRIBLE	Brest	Dec 1877	1881	Jan 1887	Stricken 1911

1

2

3

1. *Requin* in 1891

2. *Requin* as reconstructed, seen during the First World War

3. *Amiral Baudin* in 1893

With this class there was a return to the high-freeboard barbette ship with pronounced ram bow and considerable tumblehome. The steel belt was complete and 7ft 2in wide but only about 1ft above water; amidships it was 22in tapering to 20in at the upper edge and 16in at the lower, while forward it was 15½in-14in and aft 14in. The shallow barbettes were compound with steel ammunition tubes. The armour deck was at the belt upper edge slightly crowned on the centreline and was 4in-3in steel. The 14.6in guns had about the same performance as the early British 13.5in weapons. They were 71.4t Creusot in *Baudin* and 75.1t St Chamond in *Formidable* and were in 3 single barbettes on the centreline, forward, midships and aft. The 6.4in were in fore and aft main deck sponsons and the 5.5in on the main deck. In 1896-98 the midships barbette was removed and replaced by a light armoured redoubt with the 4-6.4in from the sponsons, and in *Baudin* the 5.5in were replaced by 45cal M1887 QF guns. The light guns were also altered in this ship to 2-9pdr, 20-3pdr, 6-1pdr and 6-1pdr revolvers. Both ships had military foremasts but differed in *Formidable* having a larger funnel. Their chief fault was the large area of unprotected side from just above the waterline.

AMIRAL BAUDIN class *barbette ships*

Displacement: 11,720t
Dimensions: 331ft 6in wl x 70ft x 27ft 9in max (*101.04 x 21.34 x 8.46m*)
Machinery: 2-shaft VC, 12 cyl boilers, 8400ihp = 15kts (*Formidable* 9700 = 16kts). Coal 790t
Armour: Steel and compound. Belt 22in-14in, barbettes and tubes 16in, shields 1.2in, CT 4.7in-3.1in
Armament: 3-14.6in/28cal M1875-9 (3x1), 4-6.4in/30cal M1884 (later QFC), 8/10-5.5in M1881 (later QFC), 4-3pdr, 1-3pdr revolver, 14-1pdr revolvers (*Formidable* 1-3pdr, 12-3pdr revolvers, 18-1pdr revolvers), 6- later 4-15in TT aw
Complement: 625/650

Name	Builder	Laid down	Launched	Comp	Fate
AMIRAL BAUDIN	Brest	Oct 1879	June 1883	Dec 1888	Hulked 1909
FORMIDABLE	Lorient	Sept 1879	April 1885	Feb 1889	Stricken 1911

The *Hoche* was a solitary example of a combined turret and barbette ship though the *Magenta* of the next class was originally designed as a sister ship. The hull was of relatively low freeboard and there was a towering superstructure amidships which gained her the name of 'Grand Hotel'. The belt was complete, and amidships tapered from 18in at the upper edge 2ft above water to 14in at the lower edge 5½ft below. It was 12in aft and 10in forward where there was a 6-4ft wide thin upper belt and cellulose cofferdam as far as the fore turret. The armour deck of 3.1in max iron on 0.8in steel was slightly below the top of the belt. The 13.4in guns were in fore and aft turrets with their muzzles well above the deck, and the 10.8in were in shallow barbettes on the beam with gun axes 27¼ft above water. Of the 5.5in, 14 (later 8) were in a broadside battery at the base of the superstructure and 4 located two decks higher. The two funnels were abreast and there was a military foremast. The *Hoche* suffered from inadequate stability and in 1898 she was taken in hand for the superstructure to be reduced, and at the same time 16 Belleville boilers and VTE engines were installed and displacement apparently reduced to 10,580 tons full load.

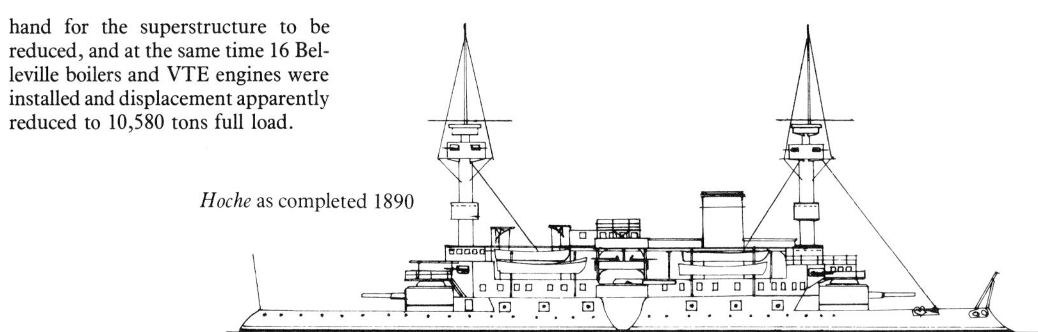
Hoche as completed 1890

HOCHE *turret/barbette ship*

Displacement: 10,820t
Dimensions: 336ft 7in wl x 66ft 4in x 27ft 3in max (*102.59 x 20.22 x 8.31m*)
Machinery: 2-shaft VC (4 engines), 8 cyl boilers, 12,000ihp = 16.5kts. Coal 590/740t
Armour: Compound. Belt 18in-10in, upper belt 3.2in (steel), turrets and barbettes 16in, tubes 9in (iron), CT 2.5in
Armament: 2-13.4in/28cal M1881 (2x1), 2-10.8in/28cal M1881 (2x1), 18-5.5in M1881 (later 12 QFC), 10-3pdr, 10-1pdr revolvers, 4-9pdr later added, 5- later 3-15in TT aw
Complement: 611

Name	Builder	Laid down	Launched	Comp	Fate
HOCHE	Lorient	June 1881	Sept 1886	1890	Target 25.11.1913

The ships of this class were not identical, but can be treated as one. They were high freeboard barbette ships with the usual marked tumblehome and except in *Marceau* high superstructures. The belt was complete and about 7½ft wide of which 2-2½ft was above water. Amidships it was 18in at the upper edge tapering to 14in at the lower and was reduced to 10in-9in forward and 12in-10in aft. There was a cofferdam above the belt filled with cellulose forward, and the armour deck was 3.2in max iron on 0.4in steel located at the belt upper edge. In *Magenta* belt and barbettes were steel, and in *Marceau* compound, while *Neptune* had a compound belt and steel barbettes. The 13.4in were M1881 in *Magenta*, M1884 in *Neptune* and two of each in *Marceau*, and they were far less powerful than the British 13.5in of the period. The barbettes were located forward and aft and on either beam, and the 5.5in were mostly in an unprotected main deck battery. These ships were so long in building that they were quite obsolescent when completed. There was a single funnel and *Neptune* had two heavy military masts, *Magenta* one and *Marceau* two lighter ones. A reliable British report on *Magenta* notes that there were a great number of unlined magazines scattered about the ship below the armour deck. *Marceau* was reboilered with 16 Niclausse boilers in 1901.

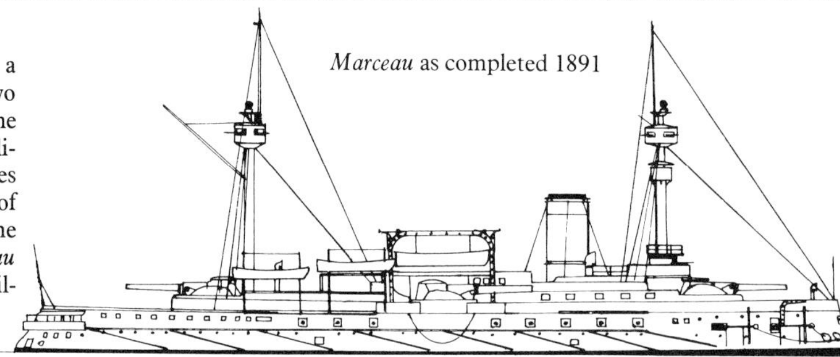
Marceau as completed 1891

MARCEAU class *barbette ships*

Displacement: 10,558t *Marceau*, 10,680t *Magenta*, 10,810t *Neptune*
Dimensions: 323ft 6in pp x 65ft 10in-66ft 3in x 27ft-27ft 8in max (*98.60 x 20.06-20.19 x 8.23-8.43m*)
Machinery: 2-shaft VC (*Magenta*, *Neptune* 4 engines), 8 (*Neptune* 12) cyl boilers, 11,000ihp = 16kts. Coal 600/740t
Armour: Compound or steel. Belt 18in-9in, barbettes 16in, tubes 9in-8in, shields 2.5in, CT 6in-4.7in
Armament: 4-13.4in/28cal M1881 or 1884 (4x1), 16/17-5.5in M1884 QFC, 3/6-9pdr, 9/18-3pdr, 8/12-1pdr revolvers, 3/5-15in TT aw
Complement: 643-651

Name	Builder	Laid down	Launched	Comp	Fate
MAGENTA	Toulon	Jan 1883	April 1890	Feb 1893	Stricken 1910
MARCEAU	La Seyne	1881	May 1887	Feb 1891	Scrapped 1922
NEPTUNE	Brest	Feb 1882	May 1887	July 1892	Stricken 1913

This ship had several important new features but was spoilt for lack of adequate displacement. As first completed in 1893 she was 15in over designed draught without her ammunition on board, and was seriously deficient in initial stability, so that the superstructure had to be reduced and the military mainmast removed. The belt was complete and 7ft 3in wide of which 2ft or less was above water. Amidships it was 18in with a 12in lower edge and fore and aft 12in with a 10in lower edge. The upper belt was also complete and extended almost to the main deck, while the battery armour was taken to the upper deck. The armour deck was at the level of the main belt upper edge and was 2.4in-2in on double 0.4in plates. The 13.4in were very powerful guns for their day and were in centre pivot turrets with the twin forward and single aft. Of the 6.4in, six were in the main deck battery amidships and four in single turrets above the battery. There was no ram, a most unusual feature at this time, and

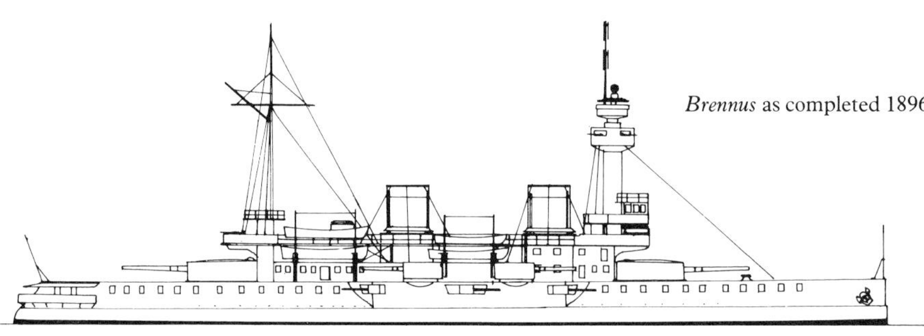
Brennus as completed 1896

BRENNUS *turret battleship*

Displacement: 11,190t
Dimensions: 361ft 10in pp x 66ft 11in x 27ft 2in max (*110.29 x 20.40 x 8.28m*)
Machinery: 2-shaft VTE, 32 Belleville boilers, 13,900ihp = 17.5-18kts. Coal 600/980t
Armour: Steel and compound. Belt 18in-10in, upper belt and battery 4in, turrets 18in max, secondary turrets 4in, CT 6in
Armament: 3-13.4in/42cal M1887 (1x2, 1x1), 10-6.4in/45cal QF M1893, 4-9pdr, 14-3pdr, 8-1pdr, 6-1pdr revolvers (later removed), 4-18in TT aw (removed)
Complement: 673

Name	Builder	Laid down	Launched	Comp	Fate
BRENNUS	Lorient	Jan 1889	Oct 1891	1896	Scrapped 1922

Brennus was the first battleship with Belleville boilers, though of an elementary type without economisers, and was also the first to have long, high-velocity main armament guns. Her displacement and dimensions, particularly her beam, were however quite inadequate.

Brennus early in her career

CHARLES MARTEL *battleship*

Displacement: 11,693t
Dimensions: 378ft 11in pp x 71ft x 27ft 6in max (*115.49 x 21.64 x 8.38m*)
Machinery: 2-shaft VTE, 24 Lagrafel d'Allest boilers, 14,900ihp = 18kts. Coal 650/980t
Armour: NS. Belt 18in-10in, upper belt 4in, turrets 15in, bases 6in, secondary turrets 4in, CT 9in
Armament: 2-12in/45cal M1887 (2x1), 2-10.8in/45cal M1887 (2x1), 8-5.5in/45cal QF M1888-91, 4-9pdr, 12- later 16-3pdr, 8-1pdr revolvers, 2-18in TT sub (2 aw removed)
Complement: 644

Name	Builder	Laid down	Launched	Comp	Fate
CHARLES MARTEL	Brest	April 1891	Aug 1893	June 1897	Stricken 1922

The first to be laid down of five similar ships but with sufficient differences to prevent them being considered as one class. The *Charles Martel* had a forecastle deck giving a high freeboard forward but was cut down to the main deck at the stern and could be distinguished by a flying deck between the two military masts. The armour belt was complete and 7ft 7in wide, of which 1ft 8in was above water. Amidships it was 18in at the upper edge tapering to 10in at the lower and was 12in to 10in forward and aft. The upper belt was also complete and 4ft wide, increased to 10ft forward and 6ft 6in aft. The armour deck was somewhat arched from the main belt upper edge and sloped down at the bows. It is usually given as 2.7in steel on two layers of 0.4in plating, but this is probably a maximum figure. A second deck of 1in or less 2ft 8in below was formed by a continuation of the inner bottom, the space between being divided into small compartments, as was much of the space amidships on the armour deck. These small compartments, which could be filled with coal or stores, formed the *tranche cellulaire* or cellular layer much favoured by advocates of French designs. The 12in centre pivot turrets were fore and aft at forecastle and upper deck level, with the 10.8in on either beam rising fromthe tumblehome to upper deck level. The 5.5in were in single turrets, two by the foremast at upper deck level, and the rest at main deck level, four being by the 10.8in and two by the after 12in. Metacentric height is given as 4ft but British reports state that stability was inadequate.

Charles Martel about 1900

Carnot about 1900

CARNOT *battleship*

In essentials a sister ship of *Charles Martel* but differing in hull form and ihp. She was also dissimilar in appearance, with no flying deck, and to save weight the bridges were cut down and the military mainmast removed. The funnels were more widely spaced and the forefunnel larger than the after one.

Displacement: 11,954t
Dimensions: 374ft pp x 70ft 6in x 27ft 5in max (*114.00 x 21.4 x 8.36m*)
Machinery: As *Charles Martel* but 16,300ihp = 17.8kts. Coal 680/980t
Armour: As *Charles Martel*
Armament: As *Charles Martel*
Complement: 647

Name	Builder	Laid down	Launched	Comp	Fate
CARNOT	Toulon	July 1891	July 1894	July 1897	Stricken 1922

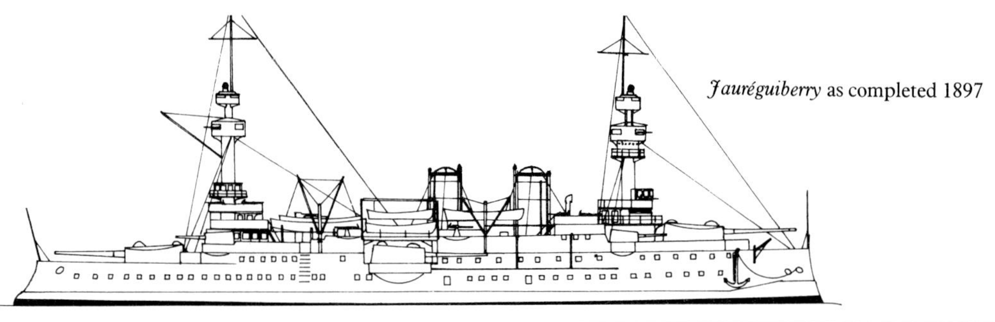
Jauréguiberry as completed 1897

The third ship of the *Charles Martel* type with a shorter hull which brought the 12in turrets near the ends of the deck. The hull was not cut down to the main deck at the stern. Although there were two large military masts, there was no flying deck and the superstructure was not great by French standards. The 5.5in guns were in twin turrets at forecastle deck level abreast the fore and mainmasts, and an improvement was made by increasing the boiler rooms from the four to six. Although in a bad condition *Jauréguiberry* served in the earlier part of the First World War.

JAURÉGUIBERRY *battleship*

Displacement: 11,637t
Dimensions: 356ft pp x 72ft 8in x 27ft 8in max (*108.51 x 22.15 x 8.43m*)
Machinery: As *Charles Martel* but 14,400ihp = 17.7kts. Coal 680/980t
Armour: As *Charles Martel*
Armament: As *Charles Martel* but later 18-3pdr
Complement: 631

Name	Builder	Laid down	Launched	Comp	Fate
JAURÉGUIBERRY	La Seyne	Nov 1891	Nov 1893	Feb 1897	Scrapped 1934

Jauréguiberry when new

Masséna about 1900

The *Masséna* was not a very successful ship and as seen above was 900t overweight. As in *Charles Martel* the hull was cut down to the main deck at the stern and to increase buoyancy forward there was a pronounced snout bow. The two funnels were far apart, there was little superstructure and although there were two military masts, the mainmast was short. The belt ended 30ft from the stern in a 10in bulkhead and is described in a British report as 'unduly immersed'. It was 18in amidships with a 10in lower edge and 10in forward and aft. The upper belt was raised at the bow, and the armour decks were as in *Charles Martel* except that they appear to have been further apart with the cellular layer between them. The main and secondary armament was arranged as in *Charles Martel* with the 3.9in in shields at forecastle deck level. The hulk of *Masséna* was towed from Toulon to Cape Helles to form a breakwater for the January 1916 evacuation.

MASSÉNA *battleship*

Displacement: 11,735t (10,835t designed)
Dimensions: 369ft 7in pp x 66ft 6in x 29ft max (approx) (*112.65 x 20.27 x 8.84m*)
Machinery: 3-shaft VTE, 24 Lagrafel d'Allest boilers, 14,200ihp = 17kts. Coal 620/980t
Armour: NS. Belt 18in-10in, upper belt 4in, turrets 14in, bases 6in, secondary turrets 4in, CT 14in
Armament: 2-12in/40cal M1893 (2x1), 2-10.8in/45cal M1893 (2x1), 8-5.5in/45cal M1888-91, 8-3.9in, 12-3pdr, 5-1pdr, 3-1pdr revolvers, 2-18in TT sub, 2 TT aw removed
Complement: 667

Name	Builder	Laid down	Launched	Comp	Fate
MASSÉNA	Ch de la Loire	Sept 1892	July 1895	June 1898	Hulked 1915

The last ship of the *Charles Martel* type, *Bouvet* differed in the hull not being cut down to the main deck at the stern and in having a moderate superstructure with two relatively small military masts. The armour belt was complete from 2ft above water to 5ft below and was 16in amidships with a 10in lower edge and reduced to 12in forward and aft and to 8in at the stem. The upper belt was also complete and 4ft wide, increased to 8ft forward and 6ft aft. The upper armour deck is given as 1¾in located at the top of the main belt, and the lower as nearly flat at the belt lower edge and 1in thick. There was the usual cellular layer with a cofferdam inboard of the upper belt. The main and secondary guns were disposed as in *Charles Martel*, with the 3.9in on the superstructure. Owing to her face-hardened armour the *Bouvet* was the best of the five ships of her type. She took part in the Dardanelles operations in 1915 and on 18 March was hit about 8 times above the waterline by the forts and had her fore turret put out of action from failure of the propellant gas extraction apparatus. She then struck a mine with a 176lb TNT charge which exploded deep below the starboard 10.8in turret, and the *Bouvet* capsized and sank in under two minutes. About 660 of her complement were lost. The *Bouvet* is known to have been in poor condition at the time and it does not appear necessary to postulate a magazine explosion to account for her rapid sinking.

BOUVET *battleship*

Displacement: 12,007t
Dimensions: 386ft 6in pp x 70ft 2in x 27ft 6in max (*117.81x 21.39 x 8.38m*)
Machinery: 3-shaft VTE, 32 Belleville boilers, 15,000ihp = 18kts. Coal 610/980t
Armour: Harvey nickel. Belt 16in-8in, upper belt 4in, turrets 15in, bases 8in, secondary turrets 4.7in, CT 12in
Armament: 2-12in/45cal M1893 (2x1), 2-10.8in/45cal M1893 (2x1), 8-5.5in/45cal QF M1893, 8-3.9in, 12-3pdr, 5-1pdr, 2-1pdr pompom, 2-18in TT sub, 2 TT aw removed
Complement: 666 (about 710 in wartime)

Name	Builder	Laid down	Launched	Comp	Fate
BOUVET	Lorient	16.1.1893	27.4.96	June 1898	Sunk 18.3.1915

Bouvet about 1905

St Louis as completed 1900

CHARLEMAGNE class *battleships*

Dsiplacement: 11,100t
Dimensions: 374ft pp x 66ft 5in x 27ft 6in max *(114.00 x 20.24 x 8.38m)*
Machinery: 3-shaft VTE, 20 Belleville boilers, 15,000ihp = 18kts. Coal 1080t max
Armour: Harvey nickel. Belt 14.5in-8in, upper belt 4in, battery 3in, turrets 15in, bases 8in, CT 13in
Armament: 4-12in/40cal M1893-96 (2x2), 10-5.5in/45cal QF M1893, 8-3.9in, 20-3pdr (later reduced), 4-1pdr, 2-18in TT sub, 2 TT aw removed
Complement: 694

Name	Builder	Laid down	Launched	Comp	Fate
CHARLEMAGNE	Brest	14.7.1894	17.10.95	Dec 1899	Stricken 1920
ST LOUIS	Lorient	March 1895	9.9.96	Sept 1900	Scrapped 1933
GAULOIS	Brest	Jan 1896	8.10.96	Dec 1899	Sunk 27.12.1916

The first French battleships with two twin mountings for the heavy guns as was usual in most other navies. They were spoilt by the low displacement and in particular the small beam, and like previous French ships were exceedingly vulnerable to damage above the waterline. The belt was complete and extended from 1ft 6in above to 5ft below water. Amidships it was 14.5in for the upper 2ft 4in, tapering to 8in at the lower edge and to 12in-10in at the ends. The upper belt was taken to the main deck forward but elsewhere only to a height of 3ft 4in. There was a cofferdam inboard of this and the usual cellular layer between the armour decks. Of the latter, the deck at the belt upper edge had a max total thickness of 3.3in and that at the lower edge 1.5in to 0.8in. The 12in guns were in centre pivot turrets at forecastle and upper deck level, whilst 8 of the 5.5in were at upper deck level in the battery, the amidships part of which was sponsoned out over the tumblehome. The two other 5.5in were in shields at forecastle deck level with the 3.9in on the superstructure, and there were two relatively light military masts. All three ships took part in the First World War and *Gaulois* was seriously damaged and had to be beached in the Dardanelles attack on 18.3.1915. The damage was caused by a large shell which burst below water close to the port bow and tore the hull plating below the armour shelf for 25ft. The flood water spread via faulty ventilation trunks and *Gaulois* was lucky to survive. She was sunk the following year by a torpedo from *UB47* about 80 miles from Milo, remaining afloat for 25 minutes.

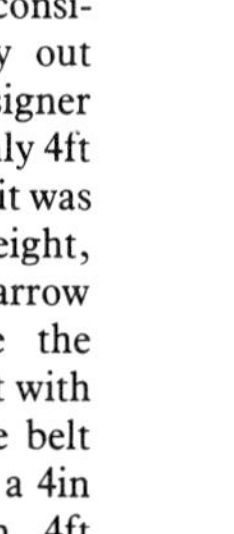

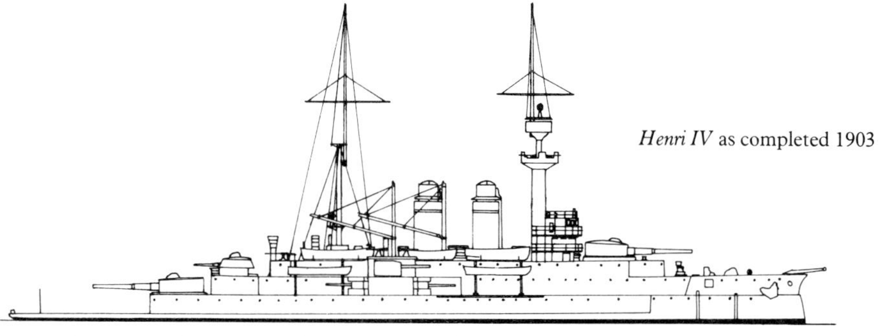

Henri IV as completed 1903

HENRI IV *battleship*

Dsiplacement: 8807t
Dimensions: 354ft 4in wl x 72ft 10in x 22ft 11in max *(108.00 x 22.20 x 6.98m)*
Machinery: 3-shaft VTE, 12 Niclausse boilers, 11,000ihp = 17kts. Coal 725/1080t
Armour: Harvey nickel. Belt 11in-3in, upper belt 4in-3in, turrets 12in, bases 9.5in, secondary guns 6.4in-3in, CT 9.5in
Armament: 2-10.8in/40cal M1893-96 (2x1), 7-5.5in/45cal QF M1893, 12-3pdr, 2-1pdr, 2-18in TT sub
Complement: 464

Name	Builder	Laid down	Launched	Comp	Fate
HENRI IV	Cherbourg	15.7.1897	23.8.99	Sept 1903	Stricken 1921

This remarkable ship is best considered as an experiment to try out some of the ideas of her designer Émile Bertin. The hull was of only 4ft freeboard except forward where it was built up to normal upper deck height, and this was continued in a narrow superstructure recessed above the main deck to abaft the mainmast with an amidships shelter deck. The belt ended just short of the stern in a 4in bulkhead and extended from 4ft above to 4ft 3in below water. It was 11in amidships with a 7in lower edge reduced at the ends to 7in with a 3in lower edge. The upper belt was mostly 4in and ran from the bows to 30ft aft of the mid section along the superstructure side. It was 6½ft wide, increased to 13ft forward, and ended in a 3in bulkhead. The armour deck at main belt upper edge level was 2.4in reduced to 1.2in at the ends; the deck below this was 0.8in on the centreline increased to 1.3in near the sides and curved down about 3ft inboard to form a torpedo bulkhead before joining the inner bottom. There was the usual cellular layer between the armour decks and a large number of small compartments inboard of the torpedo bulkhead. This system was based on experiments at Lorient in 1894 and was of a later design than that in the *Tsessarevitch*. It was never tested in war but the torpedo bulkhead was clearly much too near the side. The fore 10.8in turret had a gun axis height of 29ft 6in and that aft one of 13ft 8in, while of the 5.5in guns four were in 4.5in-3in main deck casemates with 6.4in ammunition tubes, two in shields on the upper deck and one in a 4.5in turret superfiring over the after 10.8in. This was the first time that superfiring turrets had been fitted in a ship, and in this case blast effects were said to be bad since the 5.5in was too short to clear the sighting hood of the 10.8in turret. Metacentric height was 5ft 10in and there was a military foremast and pole mainmast. *Henri IV* served in the First World War and supported the army in the Gallipoli campaign.

In general design *Iéna* was an enlarged *Charlemagne*. The belt was complete and extended from 3ft above water to 4ft 11in below. For 275ft amidships it was 12.8in and was gradually reduced to 9in at the ends, the lower edge being a uniform 4.7in. The upper belt was in two strakes, the lower 4.7in and the upper 3.2in, with a combined width of 6ft 7in increased at the bows and reduced at the stern. There was the usual cellular layer with the armour deck at the main belt upper edge 2.5in max hardened steel on 0.7in plating and the deck at the belt lower edge 1.3in max. The 12in guns were arranged as in *Charlemagne* with the 6.4in in casemates on the main deck, the four amidships weapons being sponsoned out over the tumblehome. The casemates had 3.5in armour with 8in on the ammunition tubes. The 3.9in guns were on the forecastle deck and superstructure. Though fitted with large bilge keels *Iéna* was reported to roll considerably and to pitch heavily. She blew up in dry dock at Toulon, the whole after section and much of the midships part being wrecked, though she was afterwards patched up as a target. The explosion was due to spontaneous ignition of decomposing nitrocellulose propellant in an after 3.9in magazine, and the after 12in magazines and shell rooms were later involved. It may be noted that most of the 3.9in ammunition contained propellant that was known to be dangerous, and that the magazine cooling gear had been removed when the ship was in dock.

IÉNA

Displacement:	11,860t
Dimensions:	400ft 9in wl x 68ft 3in x 27ft 6in max (*122.15 x 20.80 x 8.38m*)
Machinery:	3-shaft VTE, 20 Belleville boilers, 16,500ihp = 18kts. Coal 1080t max
Armour:	Harvey nickel. Belt 12.8in-4.7in, upper belt 4.7in-3.2in, turrets 11.5in, bases 8in, secondary guns 8in-3.5in, CT 12in
Armament:	4-12in/40cal M1893-96 (2x2), 8-6.4in/45cal QF M1893-96, 8-3.9in, 20-3pdr, 4-1pdr, 2-18in TT sub, 2 TT aw removed
Complement:	682

Name	Builder	Laid down	Launched	Comp	Fate
IÉNA	Brest	15.1.1898	1.9.98	4.4.1902	Sunk by internal explosion 12.3.07

Iéna

This ship was a further development of *Charlemagne* and *Iéna* and was marked by the reintroduction of turrets for some of the secondary armament. The belt was complete, extending from 3ft 7in above to 4ft 7in below water, and was 12in amidships with a 4.8in lower edge reduced to 9in and 4in at the ends. The upper belt ended in a 4.3in bulkhead near the stern and was 6ft 7in wide. The armour deck at belt upper edge level was 2.7in reduced to 2in forward and aft, and the deck at the belt lower edge was 1.6in max. There was cellular layer and cofferdams, while in addition there were four longitudinal semi-bulkheads 2ft 3in high on the armour deck to try and localise flooding. The 12in guns were disposed as in *Charlemagne* and four of the 6.4in were in main deck amidships casemates sponsoned out as previously. Two of the single turrets were above these casemates, two by the foremast and two abaft the after funnel, all being at upper deck level. The casemates had 5in armour with 6in ammunition tubes and the secondary turrets 5in with 4in bases.

Suffren took part in the Dardanelles attack on 18 March 1915 and was hit about 14 times. A large shell burst below water close to the hull forward and flooded some compartments, causing an appreciable list, and a 9.4in pierced the roof of a port casemate and burst, putting three 6.4in guns out of action and starting a dangerous ammunition fire which might have been disastrous if the charges had not been in metal QF cases. *Suffren* was later torpedoed and sunk by *U52* off the Portuguese coast. She was on her way to refit at Lorient and was unescorted. It is thought that magazines exploded, and she sank at once with no survivors.

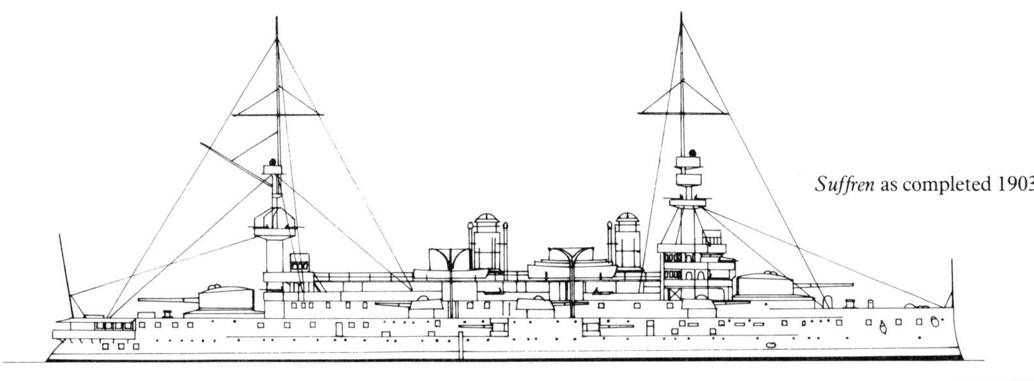

Suffren as completed 1903

SUFFREN

Displacement:	12,527t
Dimensions:	411ft 9in wl x 70ft 2in x 27ft 6in max (*125.50 x 21.39 x 8.38m*)
Machinery:	3-shaft VTE, 24 Niclausse boilers, 16,700ihp = 17.9kts. Coal 1120t max
Armour:	Harvey nickel. Belt 12in-4in, upper belt 5.1in-4.3in, turrets 12.8in, bases 11in, secondary guns 6in-4in, CT 12in-10in
Armament:	4-12in/40cal M1893-96 (2x2), 10-6.4in/45cal QF M1893-96, 8-3.9in, 22-3pdr, 2-1pdr, 2-18in TT sub, 2 TT aw removed
Complement:	714

Name	Builder	Laid down	Launched	Comp	Fate
SUFFREN	Brest	5.1.1899	25.7.99	Oct 1903	Sunk 26.11.16

The defects of previous ships were well known to French designers, and it was not until this class that they were able to increase displacement and beam, but the ships took too long to build so that their general design was outdated when they entered service. Their appearance was distinctive, with a high forecastle deck reaching to the mainmast, much reduced tumblehome and three funnels, two forward and one well aft. A relatively small military foremast was retained. The belt extended from the bows to near the stern and from the main deck 7ft 7in above water to 4ft 11in below. Amidships it was 11in at the waterline tapering to 9.5in at the top and 3.2in at the lower edge, while forward and aft it was 7in at the waterline, 5.5in at the upper edge and 3.2in at the lower. In addition there was 3.2in armour to a height of 16ft 5in above water from the bows to the foremast. Amidships the main deck was 2.1in comprising one alloy steel and two mild steel layers, whilst the lower deck was 2.0in made up in the same way and thickened to 2.75in on the slopes to the belt lower edge. The cellular layer between the armour decks is believed to have comprised a 2ft 3in cofferdam, a 3ft passage, three coal bunkers totalling 18ft 7in and then a central passage. The gun axis heights for the 12in centre pivot turrets were 33ft 7in and 25ft 7in, and there were 6 twin 6.4in turrets at forecastle deck level with 2 guns in upper deck casemates forward and 4 in main deck casemates aft of amidships. The casemates had 5.5in armour and the 6.4in turrets 6in with 11in rear plates (presumably for balancing) and 3.5in bases. Metacentric height is given as 3.6ft. The 12in and 6.4in M1893-96M guns were powerful weapons roughly equivalent to the British 12in/45 and 6in/50cal, and the 3pdr was of a new higher velocity pattern. Compared with British ships of similar displacement, weight was saved in the hull and in the 12in turrets, but the latter still had hand loading and, according to some French reports, the scantlings were too light. Both vessels served in the Mediterranean during the First World War. It is believed that four of the 3pdrs were transferred to AA mountings and in *Patrie* the six 6.4in in casemates were removed and mounted at Salonica.

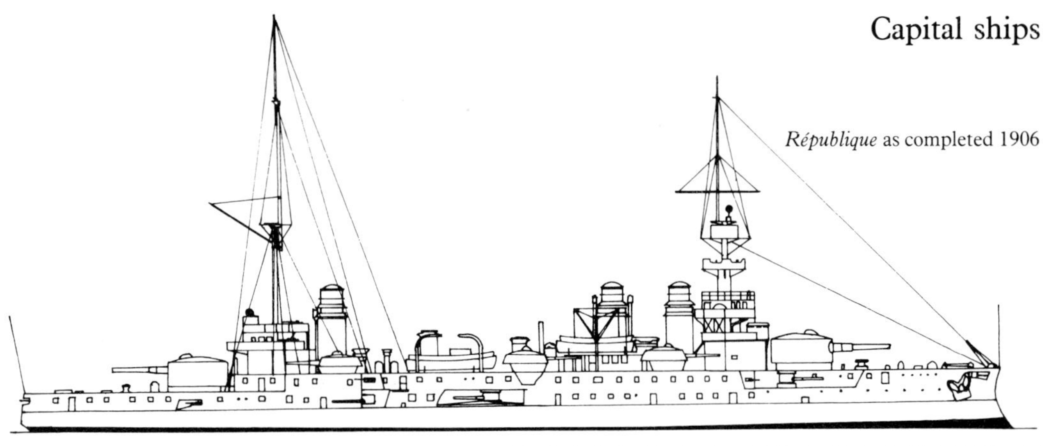
République as completed 1906

RÉPUBLIQUE class

Displacement: 14,605t, *Patrie* 14,900t
Dimensions: 439ft pp x 79ft 7in x 27ft 7in max (*133.81 x 24.26 x 8.41m*)
Machinery: 3-shaft VTE, 24 Niclausse boilers, 18,000ihp = 19kts. Coal 1800t max
Armour: KC. Belt 11in-3.2in, turrets 14in-11in, bases 10in, secondary guns 6in-3.5in, CT 12in
Armament: 4-12in/40cal M1893-96M (2x2), 18-6.4in/45cal M1893-96M, 25-3pdr, 2-18in TT sub
Complement: 766/825

Name	Builder	Laid down	Launched	Comp	Fate
RÉPUBLIQUE	Brest	Dec 1901	4.9.02	Dec 1906	Stricken 1921
PATRIE	La Seyne	1.4.1902	17.12.03	Dec 1906	Stricken 1928

In most respects this class was the same as the *République*, the main difference being in the secondary armament of 10-7.6in guns. These were very powerful guns for their size and were arranged in six single turrets at forecastle deck level with two guns in upper deck casemates below the foremast and two in main deck casemates below the after funnel. Armour on the secondary guns was not altered except that the turret bases were 5.5in-3.5in. The *Liberté* class also differed in having a mixed anti-torpedo craft armament of 9pdrs of a new high velocity pattern and 3pdrs of the same type as in the *République*. *Liberté* blew up in Toulon harbour, the cause being spontaneous ignition of decomposing nitrocellulose propellant in one of the forward 7.6in magazines. Flooding arrangements were inadequate and most of the magazines and shells in the forward part of the ship exploded. The wreck was eventually raised in 1925. The other three ships served in the Mediterranean during the First World War, and the 3pdrs were reduced to eight of which four were AA.

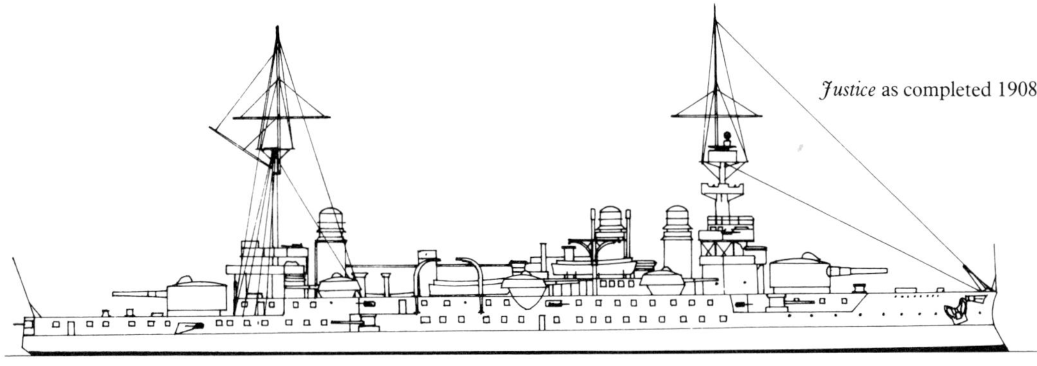
Justice as completed 1908

LIBERTÉ class

Displacement: 14,489t (*Verité*) to 14,860t (*Justice*)
Dimensions: 439ft pp x 79ft 7in x 27ft 5in-27ft 7in max (*133.81 x 24.26 x 8.36-8.41m*)
Machinery: 3-shaft VTE, 22 Belleville boilers, (*Justice* 24 Niclausse), 18,500ihp = 19kts. Coal 1800t max
Armour: KC. Belt 11in-3.2in, turrets 14in-11in, bases 10in, secondary guns 6in-3.5in, CT 12in
Armament: 4-12in/40cal M1893-96M (2x2), 10-7.6in/50cal M1902, 13-9pdr, 10-3pdr, 2-18in TT sub
Complement: 739/769

Name	Builder	Laid down	Launched	Comp	Fate
DÉMOCRATIE	Brest	1.5.1903	30.4.04	Jan 1908	Stricken 1921
JUSTICE	La Seyne	April 1903	27.10.04	Feb 1908	Stricken 1922
LIBERTÉ	Ch de la Loire	Nov 1902	19.4.05	March 1908	Sunk by internal explosion 25.9.11
VERITÉ	Ch de la Gironde	April 1903	28.5.07	June 1908	Stricken 1922

Démocratie on trials

FRANCE

COAST DEFENCE SHIPS

Wooden-hulled floating batteries which were somewhat smaller but faster than the five built at the time of the Crimean War. The sides were vertical with a battery height of 4ft, and there were two funnels abreast with a light fore and aft rig on two masts. *Paixhans*, *Palestro* and *Saigon* were commissioned for a few months in 1870 but otherwise they were laid up in ordinary. *Saigon's* hull served as a landing stage at Rochefort until 1884.

PALESTRO class *floating batteries*

Displacement: 1508-1539t
Dimensions: 152ft 3in-155ft 10in pp x 46ft 1in x 8ft 8in mean (*46.41-47.50 x 14.04 x 2.65m*)
Machinery: 2-shaft HP, 150nhp = 7kts
Armour: Wrought iron. Side 4.7in-4.3in
Armament: 12-6.4in M1860
Complement: 200

Name	Builder	Laid down	Launched	Comp	Fate
PAIXHANS	Arman	24.5.1859	Sept 1862	Jan 1863	Stricken 1871
PALESTRO	Arman	20.7.1859	Aug 1862	Sept 1862	Stricken 1871
PEIHO	Arman	20.7.1859	Sept 1862	Oct 1862	Stricken 1869
SAIGON	Arman	20.7.1859	Sept 1862	Oct 1862	Stricken 1871

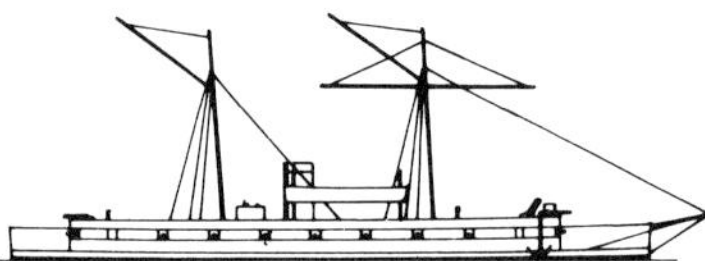

Arrogante as completed 1865

Iron-hulled floating batteries differing from previous classes in having a central casemate with 9 gunports a side and 3 at each end. The battery height was 4ft 9in and there was a single funnel with a light fore and aft rig on two masts. A 9.4in gun was tried in *Arrogante* in 1867; in March 1879 this ship went ashore but was refloated seven weeks later.

ARROGANTE class *floating batteries*

Displacement: 1412t (*Arrogante* 1490t)
Dimensions: 131ft 3in pp (*Arrogante* 144ft 4in) x 48ft 5in x 8ft 10in mean (*40.00 (44.00) x 14.76 x 2.70m*)
Machinery: 2-shaft HP, 470ihp = 6.7/7kts. Coal 40t
Armour: Wrought iron. Belt 4.7in, battery 4.3in
Armament: 9-6.4in M1864, later 4-7.6in, 2-6.4in
Complement: 190

Name	Builder	Laid down	Launched	Comp	Fate
ARROGANTE	Gouin	1861	June 1864	Jan 1865	Stricken 1881
IMPLACABLE	Gouin	1861	21.1.64	July 1864	Stricken 1884
OPINIÂTRE	Gouin	1861	23.3.64	Jan 1865	Stricken 1885

This class of iron-hulled floating batteries were shorter and had more beam than the *Arrogante*, and differed also in that the battery was continued to the ends. There were 2 gunports at both bow and stern and 6 on either beam with a battery height of only 3ft. *Embuscade* was a hulk at Rochefort until 1922, while *Imprenable* was used for torpedo firing on the Cherbourg range up to 1939.

EMBUSCADE class *floating batteries*

Displacement: 1555t (*Imprenable* 1589t, *Refuge* 1426t)
Dimensions: 129ft 7in pp x 51ft 10in x 10ft 9in-13ft 1in max (*39.50 x 15.80 x 3.27-4.00m*)
Machinery: 2-shaft HP, 440ihp = 7.5kts. Coal 78t
Armour: Wrought iron. Belt 5½in, battery 4.3in
Armament: 4-7.6in M1864 or 1866
Complement: 190

Name	Builder	Laid down	Launched	Comp	Fate
EMBUSCADE	Arman	1862	18.11.65	Jan 1866	Stricken 1885
IMPRENABLE	Arman	1862	17.12.67	1868	Stricken 1882
PROTECTRICE	Arman	1862	8.12.66	Jan 1867	Stricken 1889
REFUGE	Arman	1862	1.6.66	Oct 1866	Stricken 1884

This ship was wooden-hulled and, specially designed by Dupuy de Lôme for ramming, was said to have had a tactical diameter of 230yds. There was a long spur ram with the point 8ft 3in below water and the complete belt reached to 2ft 4in above water at which height there was a 2in armour deck. Above this was a thin iron turtledeck covering the crew space and supporting the upper deck. It was originally intended to fit a fixed turret forward with two or more ports but this was changed to a barbette. There was a single funnel, and she was reported to be a very bad sea boat.

TAUREAU *armoured ram*

Displacement: 2433t
Dimensions: 196ft 10in wl x 48ft 6in x 17ft 9in max (*60.00 x 14.78 x 5.40m*)
Machinery: 2-shaft HRCR, ?6 oval boilers, 1790ihp = 12.5kts. Coal 170t
Armour: Wrought iron. Belt 6in, barbette 4.7in
Armament: 1-9.4in M1864 or 1866
Complement: 135

Name	Builder	Laid down	Launched	Comp	Fate
TAUREAU	Toulon	Nov 1863	10.6.65	1866	Stricken 1890

The general conception of this class was of an enlarged *Taureau*: the vessels were wooden-hulled and had a spur ram projecting 10ft. The belt was complete with a 7in lower edge and extended from 2ft 5in above to 4ft 10in below water, but the displacement was insufficient for an armour deck, and there was only a 0.6in deck at the belt upper edge, with a turtledeck above as in the *Taureau*. The 9.4in guns were in a turret designed by Dupuy de Lôme. This resembled the British Coles turret but the roller path was on top of an armoured tower which protected the turret steam turning gear. Metacentric height is given as 7.6ft and tactical disameter as 310-370yds. The class could be distinguished from *Taureau* by having two funnels close abreast. The hull timbers in *Tigre* were reported as being rotten as early as 1878.

The twin-turret monitor *Onondaga* was acquired from the United States in 1867, but is described in the section dealing with that navy. In French service she mounted 4-9.4in M1864 or 1866 guns, later replaced by 19cal M1870s, and was retained until 1904.

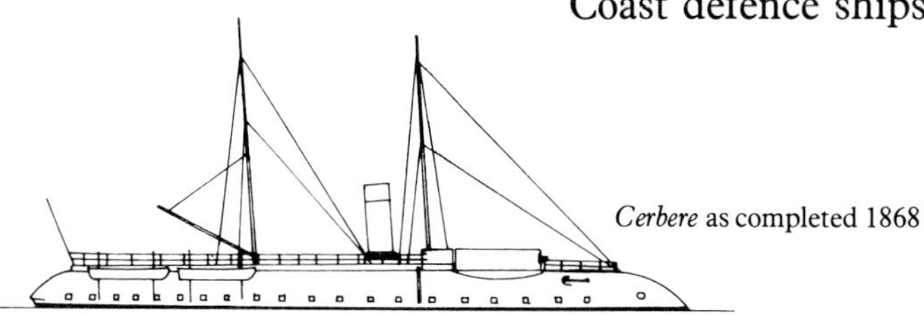
Cerbere as completed 1868

CERBÈRE class *armoured rams*

Displacement: 3532t
Dimensions: 215ft 1in pp x 53ft 10in x 18ft 7in max *(65.56 x 16.40 x 5.66m)*
Machinery: 2-shaft HRCR, 6 oval boilers, 1800ihp = 12-12.5kts. Coal 180t
Armour: Wrought iron. Belt 8.7in-7in, turret 7in
Armament: 2-9.4in M1864 or 1866 (1x2), later 19cal M1870, 4-1pdr revolvers added
Complement: 159

Name	Builder	Laid down	Launched	Comp	Fate
BELIER	Cherbourg	1.4.1865	29.8.70	June 1872	Stricken 1896
BOULEDOGUE	Lorient	5.12.1865	26.3.72	1873	Stricken 1897
CERBÈRE	Brest	14.9.1865	23.4.68	Oct 1868	Stricken 1887
TIGRE	Rochefort	1865	9.3.71	Aug 1874	Stricken 1892

Single-turret vessels with the hull mostly steel though retaining wrought iron armour. The belt was 13in amidships with 10in forward and 12in aft and there was a 2in deck over the belt outside the breastwork. The turret was 34ft 6in in diameter with a central fixed 4ft 8in diameter shaft which supported a conning tower protected by an armoured collar on the turret. The superstructure was only 8ft wide and it was theoretically possible to fire right astern, though it was reported that an attempt by *Tonnerre* to do so in 1884 blew away the fore part of the superstructure. *Tonnerre* is also said to have come near to capsizing when turning hard a port under the combined action of screw and rudder. She had the reconstructed engine of the *Normandie* and during the 1890s both monitors were employed as torpedo depot ships.

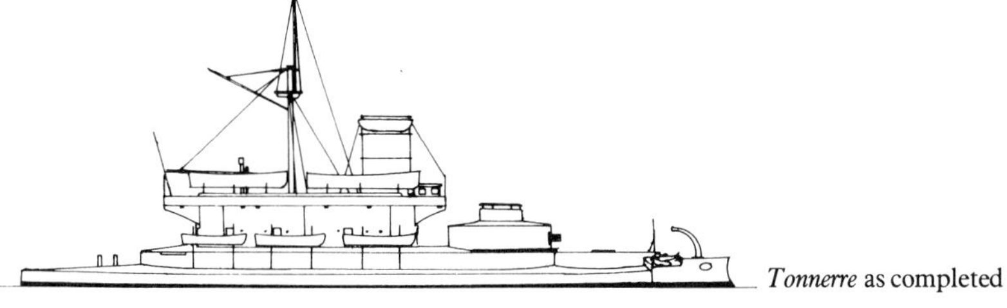
Tonnerre as completed 1879

TONNERRE class *breastwork monitors*

Displacement: 5765t (*Fulminant* 5871t)
Dimensions: 241ft 6in pp x 57ft 9in x 21ft 4in-23ft 7in max *(73.60 x 17.60 x 6.50-7.19m)*
Machinery: 1-shaft HC, 8 cyl boilers, 4200-4500ihp = 13.7kts. Coal 280/390t
Armour: Wrought iron. Belt 13in-10in, breastwork 13in, turret 13in-12in
Armament: 2-10.8in/20cal M1875 (1x2), later 4-3pdr, 4/6-1pdr revolvers
Complement: 220

Name	Builder	Laid down	Launched	Comp	Fate
TONNERRE	Lorient	Oct 1873	Sept 1875	1879	Stricken 1905
FULMINANT	Cherbourg	Jan 1875	Aug 1877	1882	Stricken 1908

Left: *Tonnerre* about 1885
Above: *Tempête* early in her career

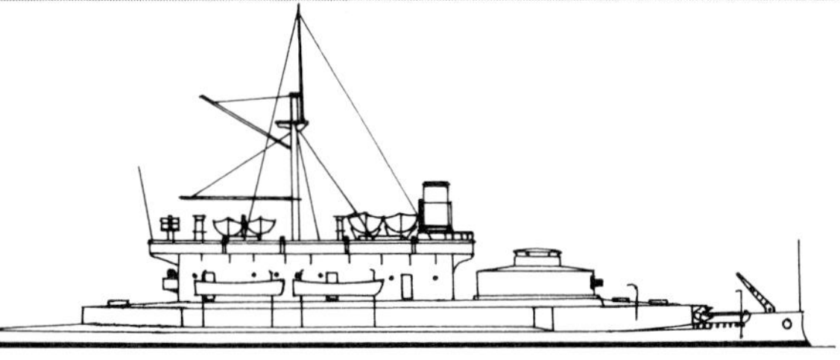
Tempête as completed 1879

Similar to the *Tonnerre* class but of shallower draught and reduced speed and bunker capacity. They could be distinguished by the smaller funnel which, as in the preceding class, was forward of the single mast.

TEMPÊTE class *breastwork monitors*

Displacement: 4793t (*Vengeur* 4635t)
Dimensions: 241ft 6in pp x 57ft 9in x 19ft max *(73.60 x 17.60 x 5.79m)*
Machinery: 1-shaft (*Vengeur* 2-shaft) HC, 4 cyl boilers, 2000ihp = 11.7kts (*Vengeur* 10.7kts). Coal 118t
Armour: Wrought iron. Belt 13in-10in, breastwork 13in, turret 14in-12in
Armament: 2-10.8in/20cal M1875 (1x2), (*Vengeur* 2-13.4in/18cal M1875), later 4/6-1pdr revolvers (*Vengeur* also 2-3pdr, 2-14in TT aw)
Complement: 174

Name	Builder	Laid down	Launched	Comp	Fate
TEMPÊTE	Brest	1873	Aug 1876	1879	Stricken 1907
VENGEUR	Brest	1875	May 1878	1882	Stricken 1905

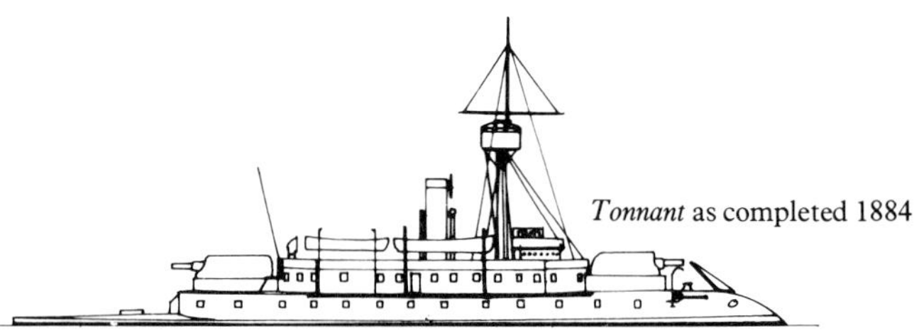
Tonnant as completed 1884

Tonnant about 1890

A ship with a low freeboard hull built up by a superstructure which was turtle-backed forward. The belt was 18in at the waterline amidships reducing to 13½in at the ends with a 2in deck at the belt upper edge. The barbettes were shallow rings with armoured ammunition tubes and thin tunnel-shaped shields to the guns. They were located fore and aft on the lower superstructure one deck above the hull proper. There was a military foremast and single funnel.

TONNANT *barbette ship*

Displacement: 5010t
Dimensions: 242ft pp x 58ft 5in x 17ft 3in max *(73.76 x 17.80 x 5.26m)*
Machinery: 1-shaft HC, 4 cyl boilers, 2000ihp = 11.6kts. Coal 118t
Armour: Wrought iron. Belt 18in-13½in, barbettes 14½in max
Armament: 2-13.4/18cal M1875 (2x1), 8-1pdr revolvers
Complement: 175

Name	Builder	Laid down	Launched	Comp	Fate
TONNANT	Rochefort	Jan 1875	1880	1884	Stricken 1903

Somewhat similar to the *Tonnant* but with the hull extending one deck above the armour belt. This was 18in at the waterline amidships, reducing to 13in forward and 14in aft, whilst the armour deck at the belt upper edge is given as 3.6in max. The barbettes, located fore and aft, were shallow, with ammunition tubes and 0.6in tunnel shields. The stem curved upwards and inwards and the hull forward was described as whale-backed. The one military mast was located abaft the funnel. The *Furieux* was reconstructed in 1902/4 and rearmed with 2-9.4in/40cal M1893-96 in single centre pivot turrets, and 16-3pdrs or 1pdrs. She was reboilered with 8 Bellevilles and had her engines converted to VTE giving 5145ihp = 14.3kts, while her appearance was altered with two funnels, a light pole foremast and a heavier mainmast. The *Furieux* was eventually used as a submarine depot ship.

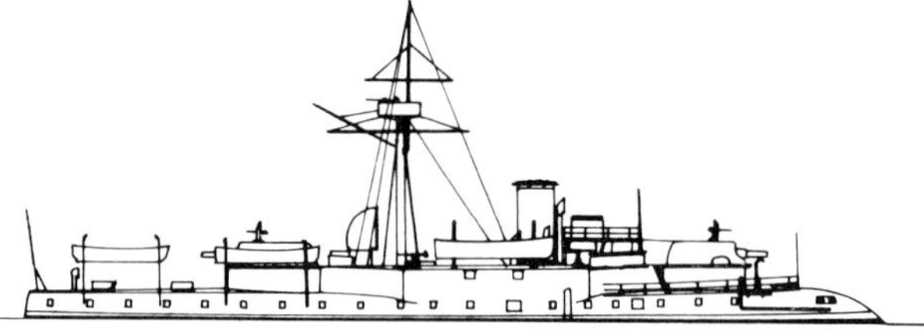
Furieux as completed 1887

FURIEUX *barbette ship*

Displacement: 5925t, 5683t as reconstructed
Dimensions: 238ft pp x 58ft 6in x 23ft 3in max (22ft 9in max as reconstructed) *(72.54 x 17.83 x 7.09 (6.94)m)*
Machinery: 2-shaft VC, 8 cyl boilers, 4600ihp = 13kts. Coal 285t. For alterations see below
Armour: Steel. Belt 18in-13in, barbettes 18in, tubes 12in (turrets 8in, bases 6½in, CT 3in as reconstructed)
Armament: 2-13.4in/21cal M1875 (2x1), 4-3pdr, 10-1pdr revolvers, 2-14in TT aw. For alterations see below
Complement: 235

Name	Builder	Laid down	Launched	Comp	Fate
FURIEUX	Cherbourg	April 1878	July 1883	Feb 1887	Stricken 1913

These vessels had a complete belt 2ft 9in wide increased to 4ft 1in at the ram. The upper edge was 9½in forward, 8in amidships and 4.7in aft, and the lower edge 7in, 4.7in and 4in. There was a 2in deck at the belt upper edge, but the barbette for the 9.4in gun had no shield.

FUSÉE class *armoured gunboats*

Displacement: 1073-1124t
Dimensions: 165ft wl x 32ft 6in x 10ft 4in max *(50.30 x 9.90 x 3.15m)*
Machinery: 2-shaft VC, 3 loco boilers, 1500ihp = 12.5kts. Coal 118t
Armour: Steel (*Flamme, Mitraille* compound). Belt 9½in-4in, barbette 8in-4.7in
Armament: 1-9.4in/28cal M1881, 1-3.5in, 4-1pdr revolvers
Complement: 89

Name	Builder	Laid down	Launched	Comp	Fate
FLAMME	Cherbourg	June 1883	Aug 1885	Apr 1887	Stricken 1906
FUSÉE	Lorient	Oct 1882	May 1884	Dec 1885	Stricken 1910
GRENADE	Lorient	1884	Oct 1888	1889	Stricken 1906
MITRAILLE	Rochefort	1883	July 1886	Feb 1888	Stricken 1910

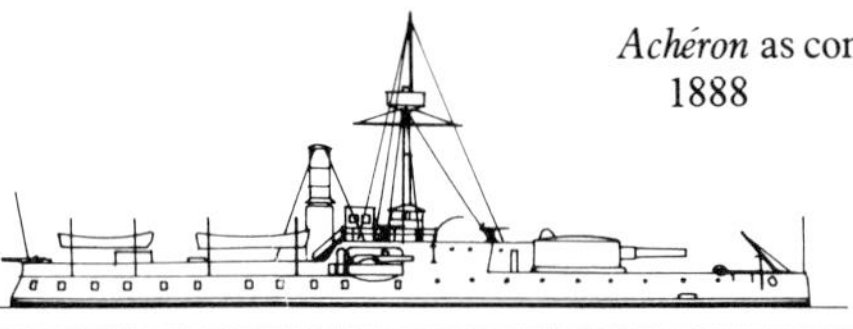
Achéron as completed 1888

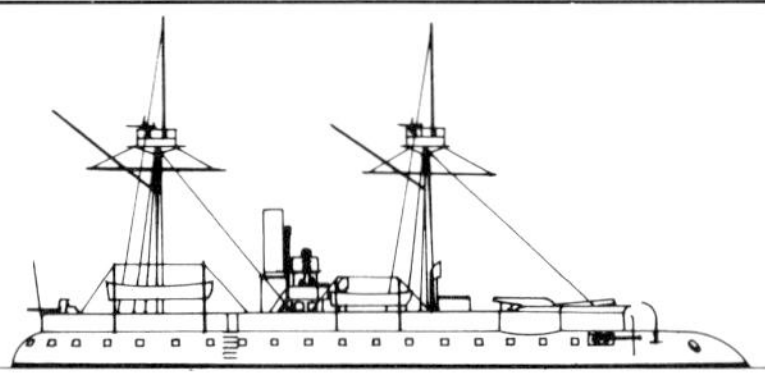
Fusée as completed 1885

These vessels had a complete belt from 1ft 6in above to 3ft 3in below water, and a 2in mild steel deck at the belt upper edge. The 10.8in gun was in a conical turret.

ACHÉRON class *armoured gunboats*

Displacement: 1690t (*Phlegeton, Styx* 1767t)
Dimensions: 181ft 1in (*Phlegeton, Styx* 192ft 7in) wl x 40ft 5in x 11ft 8in max *(55.20 (58.70) x 12.32 x 3.56m)*
Machinery: 2-shaft HC, 4 loco boilers, 1600ihp = 11.6-13kts. Coal 98t (*Phlegeton, Styx* 71t)
Armour: Compound. Belt 8in, turret 8in
Armament: 1-10.8in/28cal M1881, 2/3-3.9in (*Phlegeton, Styx* 1-5.5in), 2-3pdr, 4/7-1pdr revolvers
Complement: 110

Name	Builder	Laid down	Launched	Comp	Fate
ACHÉRON	Cherbourg	Nov 1883	Apr 1885	Feb 1888	Stricken 1913
COCYTE	Cherbourg	Dec 1883	Jan 1887	Feb 1890	Stricken 1911
PHLEGETON	Cherbourg	July 1885	Dec 1890	1892	Stricken 1910
STYX	Cherbourg	Sept 1889	Aug 1891	Oct 1892	Stricken 1919

Turret vessels of about 11ft freeboard with an appreciable tumblehome. The 13.4in guns were fore and aft with the 3.9in in the superstructure, and the quarterdeck was much strengthened to stand the firing of the after 13.4in. The waterline belt was 18in amidships, 12in forward and 17in aft, the lower edge being a uniform 10in. The turret crowns were 2.7in and there was a very heavy curved armour deck apparently consisting of double 0.4in plates covered by 4in-2.8in steel amidships, 3½in forward and 2.8in aft. There were two funnels and a military foremast. The 13.4in were very powerful guns for their day and of the same type as in the *Brennus*. The armour of the *Jemmapes* class was thick but the ships would have been vulnerable to hits above the armour deck, and it would seem that a single 13,000t vessel would have been a better proposition.

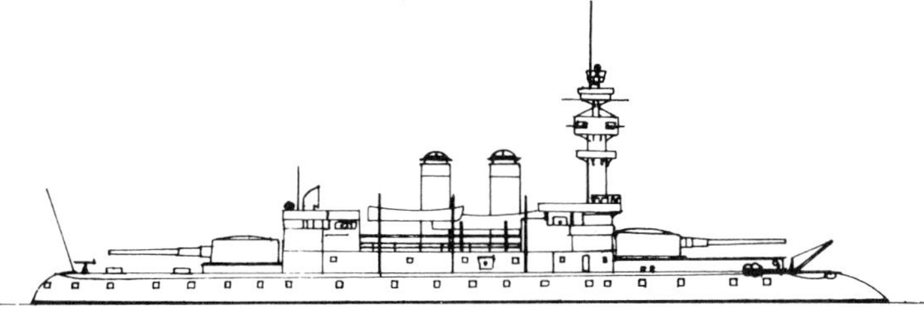

Valmy as completed 1894

JEMMAPES class *coast defence ships*

Displacement: 6476t
Dimensions: 283ft 9in pp x 57ft 4in x 23ft 2in max (*86.50 x 17.47 x 7.06m*)
Machinery: 2-shaft HTE, 16 Lagrafel d'Allest boilers, 9000ihp = 16.7kts. Coal 443t max
Armour: NS and steel. Belt 18in-10in, turrets 18in, bases 16in, CT 4in
Armament: 2-13.4in/42cal M1887 (2x1),4-3.9in/45cal QF, 4-3pdr, 10-1pdr revolvers, 2-18in TT aw
Complement: 313

Name	Builder	Laid down	Launched	Comp	Fate
JEMMAPES	Soc de la Loire	1890	Apr 1892	1894	Hulked 1911
VALMY	Soc de la Loire	1890	Oct 1892	1894	Stricken 1911

Amiral Tréhouart about 1898

Bouvines as completed 1894

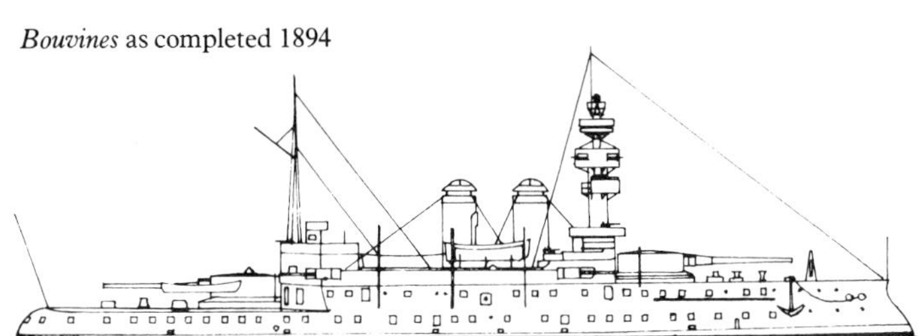

These ships were of the same general type as the *Jemmapes* class but differed in having a forecastle deck extending to the mainmast. The armour details were the same except that the belt was 16in aft instead of 17in. The 3.9in guns were divided equally between the upper deck and superstructure and both ships had a military foremast. They differed in *Tréhouart* having a single funnel and *Bouvines* two. Both vessels were eventually used as submarine depot ships.

BOUVINES class *coast defence ships*

Displacement: 6681t
Dimensions: 283ft 9in pp x 58ft 4in x 23ft 5in max (*86.50 x 17.78 x 7.14m*)
Machinery: 2-shaft VTE, 16 Lagrafel d'Allest boilers (*Tréhouart* 16 Belleville), 8500ihp = 16.5-17kts. Coal 511t max
Armour: NS and steel. Belt 18in-10in, turrets 18in, bases 16in, CT 4in.
Armament: 2-12in/45cal M1887 (2x1), 8-3.9in/50cal QF, 4-3pdr, 10-1pdr revolvers (*Tréhouart* 4-1pdr, 8 revolvers), 2-18in TT aw
Complement: 343 (*Tréhouart* 362)

Name	Builder	Laid down	Launched	Comp	Fate
AMIRAL TRÉHOUART	Lorient	Oct 1890	May 1893	May 1896	Stricken 1922
BOUVINES	La Seyne	Sept 1890	Mar 1892	Dec 1894	Stricken 1920

ARMOURED CRUISING SHIPS

A wooden-hulled ship with no plating outside the armour. There was a complete belt from the battery deck to 4ft 11in below water, but the battery bulkheads were only thin plating. The 7.6in and 4-6.4in were in the battery 6ft above water and 2-6.4in, later the 5.5in, on the upper deck. There was a bronze pointed ram 10ft below water, and the *Bellinqueuse* was rigged as a barque with 15,600 sq ft, later increased to 19,000 sq ft of sail. She was the first French armoured ship to double Cape Horn.

BELLIQUEUSE *broadside ironclad*

Displacement: 3717t
Dimensions: 229ft 8in wl x 46ft x 22ft 10in max (*70.00 x 14.01 x 6.97m*)
Machinery: 1-shaft HRCR, 4 oval boilers, 1200ihp = 11kts. Coal 250t
Armour: Wrought iron. Belt 6in, battery 4.7in
Armament: 4-7.6in M1864, 6-6.4in M1864, later 7.6in M1870, 5-5.5in, 4-1pdr revolvers added and 2-6.4in removed
Complement: 300

Name	Builder	Laid down	Launched	Comp	Fate
BELLIQUEUSE	Toulon	Sept 1863	6.9.65	1866	Target 1886

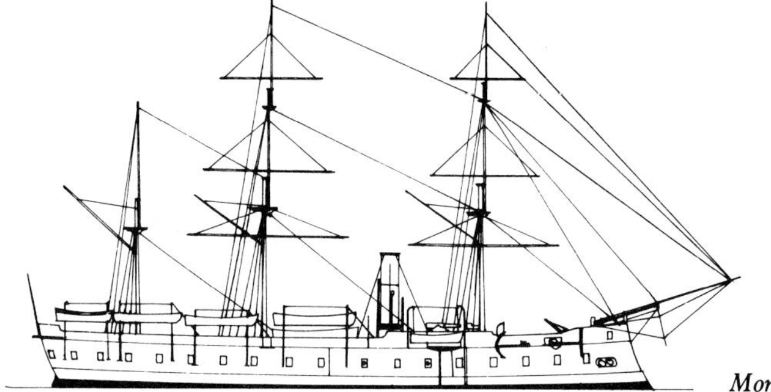

Montcalm as completed 1869

Wooden-hulled central battery ships with 0.6in iron plating above water where not armoured and 4.7in closing bulkheads for the battery. The waterline belt was complete and about 8ft wide, and it was originally intended to have an upper battery with 4-6.4in at the corners, but this was given up in favour of four barbettes reduced to two for reasons of topweight. The battery height varied from 5ft 7in to 6ft 10in and 4-7.6in were mounted here with two in the barbettes. The metal reinforced ram projected 9ft and *Alma* is credited with a tactical diameter of only 360yds. They were rigged as barques with about 15,500 sq ft of sail and had single funnels except *Jeanne d'Arc* and *Thetis* which had two abreast. *Reine Blanche* was rammed by *Thetis* in July 1877 but both ships survived. *Thetis* was commissioned at the end of 1885 for the Pacific but had to return as unseaworthy and eventually went to Noumea as a stationary hulk.

ALMA class *central battery ironclads*

Displacement: 3513t (*Thetis*) to 3828t (*Montcalm*)
Dimensions: 226ft pp x 45ft 9in-46ft 7in x 20ft 6in-21ft 10in mean (*68.88 x 13.94-14.20 x 6.26-6.66m*)
Machinery: 1-shaft HCRCR, 4 oval boilers, 1580-1890ihp = 11-11.9kts. Coal 250t
Armour: Wrought iron. Belt 6in, battery 4.7in, barbettes 4in
Armament: 6-7.6in M1864 or 1866, later M1870, in some 4-4.7in or 5.5in and 8-1pdr revolvers added
Complement: 316

Name	Builder	Laid down	Launched	Comp	Fate
ALMA	Lorient	1.10.1865	26.11.67	1869	Hulked 1886
ARMIDE	Rochefort	1865	12.4.67	1867	Stricken 1887
ATALANTE	Cherbourg	June 1865	9.4.68	1869	Stricken 1887
JEANNE D'ARC	Cherbourg	1865	28.9.67	1868	Stricken 1883
MONTCALM (ex-INDIENNE)	Rochefort	26.10.1865	16.10.68	1869	Stricken 1891
REINE BLANCHE	Lorient	1865	10.3.68	1869	Stricken 1886
THETIS	Toulon	1865	22.8.67	1868	Stricken 1895

Reine Blanche with original barque rig

Victorieuse about 1890

This class were wooden-hulled ships with iron plating above water where not armoured. There was a complete belt extending to about 4ft 10in below water, and a central battery with 4-9.4in guns in broadside ports. The remaining 2-9.4in were in barbettes over the forward corners of the battery, with the 7.6in firing ahead from under the forecastle, and the smaller guns on the upper deck. There was no armour deck. They were rigged as ships or barques with 16,500 sq ft of sail and had one funnel, though by 1892 *Triomphante* had pole topmasts with no yards.

LA GALISSONNIÈRE class *central battery ironclads*

Displacement: 4585t (*La Galissonnière* 4645t)
Dimensions: 258ft (*La Galissonnière* 256ft) wl x 48ft 9in (*La Galissonnière* 49ft) x 24ft 2in max (*78.64 (78.03) x 14.86 (14.94) x 7.37m*)
Machinery: 1-shaft (*La Galissonnière* 2-shaft) VC, 4 oval boilers, 2200-2400ihp = 12.7kts. Coal 330t (*La Galissonniere* 500t)
Armour: Wrought iron. Belt 6in, battery 4.7in, barbettes 4.7in
Armament: 6-9.4in/19cal M1870, 1-7.6in M1870, 6-5.5in (*La Galissonnière* 6-9.4in-4-4.7in. later 6-3.9in) 4/8-1pdr revolvers added, (*Triomphante* also 4-14in TT aw)
Complement: 352/382

Name	Builder	Laid down	Launched	Comp	Fate
LA GALISSONNIÈRE	Brest	22.6.1868	7.5.72	1874	Stricken 1894
TRIOMPHANTE	Rochefort	5.8.1869	28.3.77	1879	Sold 1903
VICTORIEUSE	Toulon	5.8.1869	18.11.75	1877	Hulked 1900

Wooden-hulled ships with steel upperworks and ram bows. The belt was complete and extended from 4ft 3in above water to 5ft 3in below. It was 10in amidships reducing to 6in at the lower edge and ends. The barbettes had unarmoured ammunition tubes and were sponsoned on either beam forward of the funnel and on the centreline amidships and aft, the arrangement being similar to that in the *Amiral Duperré*. There was a 2in armour deck at the belt upper edge. The 7.6in were forward and aft under the forecastle and poop and the 5.5in in an unarmoured main deck battery. Both vessels were ship rigged and had one funnel.

BAYARD class *barbette ships*

Displacement: 5915t (*Turenne* 6260t)
Dimensions: 265ft 9in wl x 57ft 3in x 25ft-25ft 2in max (*81.00 x 17.45 x 7.62-7.67m*)
Machinery: 2-shaft VC, 8 cyl boilers, 4400ihp = 14-14.5kts. Coal 400/450t
Armour: Wrought iron. Belt 10in-6in, barbettes 8in
Armament: 4-9.4in/19cal M1870 (4x1), 2-7.6in, 6-5.5in, 4-3pdr, 12-1pdr revolvers, (*Turenne* also 2-14in TT aw)
Complement: 451

Name	Builder	Laid down	Launched	Comp	Fate
BAYARD	Brest	Oct 1876	Mar 1880	1882	Hulked 1899
TURENNE	Lorient	1876	Oct 1879	1882	Stricken 1901

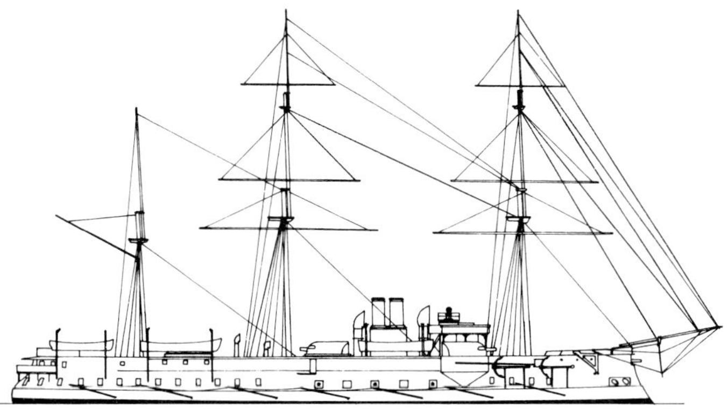
Bayard as completed 1882

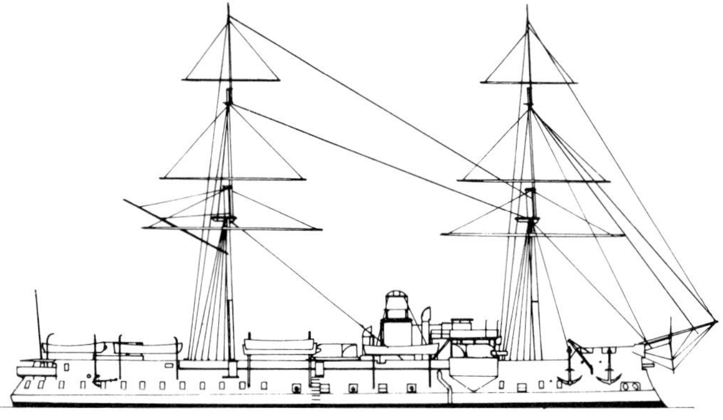
Vauban as completed 1885

Very similar to the *Bayard* class but differing in having steel hulls which were wood sheathed and coppered. The belt extended from 5ft above water to 5ft below, the barbettes had compound armour and there was no stern 7.6in. The ships were originally rigged as brigs with royals and 23,200 sq ft of canvas, but latterly did not carry sail and had two masts with military tops. The steel hulls allowed better compartmentation, but otherwise details were as in the *Bayard* class. *Duguesclin* could be distinguished by her peculiar sloping stern rising from the waterline in a convex curve.

VAUBAN class *barbette ship*

Displacement: 6112t
Dimensions: 265ft 9in wl x 57ft 3in x 25ft-25ft 3in max *(81.00 x 17.45 x 7.62-7.70m)*
Machinery: 2-shaft VC, 8 cyl boilers, 4400ihp = 14-14.5kts. Coal 400/450t
Armour: Wrought iron. Belt 10in-6in, barbettes 8in compound
Armament: 4-9.4in/19cal M1870 (4x1), 1-7.6in, 6-5.5in, 12-1pdr revolvers (*Vauban* also 4-3pdr), 2-14in TT aw
Complement: 440

Name	Builder	Laid down	Launched	Comp	Fate
DUGUESCLIN	Rochefort	Dec 1878	1883	Aug 1886	Stricken 1904
VAUBAN	Cherbourg	Feb 1879	July 1882	1885	Stricken 1905

1

2

1. *Duguesclin* with military rig

2. *Dupuy de Lôme* in First World War camouflage

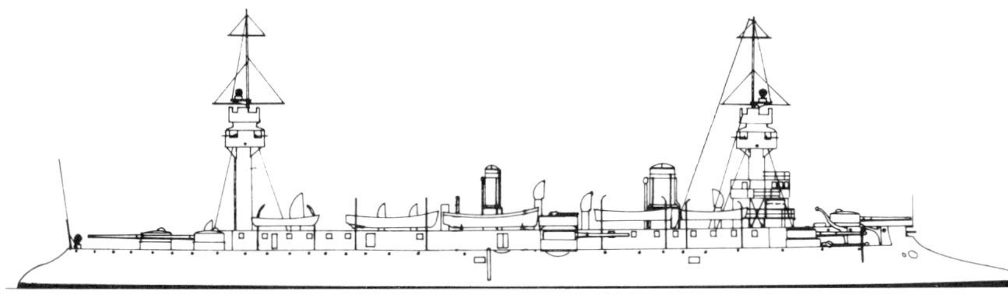
Dupuy de Lôme 1896

DUPUY DE LÔME *armoured cruiser*

Displacement: 6676t
Dimensions: 364ft 2in pp x 51ft 6in x 24ft 7in max *(111.00 x 15.70 x 7.49m)*
Machinery: 1-shaft VTE, 2-shaft HTE, 13 cyl boilers, 13,000ihp = 19.7kts. Coal 1080t max
Armour: Steel. Side 4in, turrets 4in, CT 5in
Armament: 2-7.6in/45cal M1887 (2x1), 6-6.4in/45cal QF M1887, 4-9pdr, 8-3pdr, 8-1pdr revolvers, 2-18in TT aw
Complement: 526

Name	Builder	Laid down	Launched	Comp	Fate
DUPUY DE LÔME	Brest	July 1888	Oct 1890	1895	Sold 1920

This ship was entirely different from previous French cruisers. The side was completely armoured from 4ft 6in below water to the upper deck and there was a 0.8in curved protective deck rising from the belt lower edge to the waterline. Below this was a splinter deck and over the engines and boilers the space between these decks, which was about 5ft high on the centreline, was filled with coal. Above the protective deck there was a cellulose-filled cofferdam 2ft 8in wide to a height of 3ft 3in above water. The 7.6in guns were in turrets on either beam rising from the tumblehome, and the 6.4in turrets were in close groups of three forward and aft, one turret in each group being on the centreline. The after group were all on the upper deck but the centre forward turret was on the forecastle deck which was much recessed to make space for the other two turrets. The ammunition tubes were not armoured. In appearance the *Dupuy de Lôme* was remarkable with a very marked snout or plough bow and a sloping stern. There were two funnels and two heavy military masts. Her completion was delayed by an accident to her boilers, which had to be changed, and in 1905 she was reconstructed to some extent, having 20 Normand boilers with three funnels installed and the military mainmast removed. The *Dupuy de Lôme* was sold to Peru in 1912 as the *Commandant Elias Aguirre* but was never delivered; she was resold to Belgium in 1920 and converted to a cargo ship under the name *Peruvier*.

Bruix with pole masts about 1914

A class of small armoured cruisers with a complete belt of 3 x 1.2in plates on 2 x 0.4in skin plating. The belt extended from 4ft below water to about 8ft 6in above and there was a curved armour deck rising to 1ft 4in above water. This was 1.8in on the slopes and 1.6in on the flat, with a light splinter deck over the machinery spaces. There was a cofferdam to 4ft above water, and the turrets had 4.3in tubes where above the side armour. The 7.6in turrets were fore and aft on the upper deck and the 5.5in in single turrets on the beam at main deck level, the sides being recessed above. There was a plough bow, and two heavy military masts and two funnels were shipped. The military masts were later replaced by poles and most of the smaller guns except the 9pdr were eventually removed. *Chanzy* was wrecked in Chinese waters, but the others gave useful service in the First World War. *Amiral Charner* was torpedoed by *U21* and sank in 4 minutes.

AMIRAL CHARNER class *armoured cruisers*

Displacement: 4681-4736t
Dimensions: 347ft 9in pp x 45ft 10in x 19ft 8in max (*106.00 x 13.97 x 6.00m*)
Machinery: 2-shaft HTE (*Bruix* VTE), 16 Belleville boilers, 8000ihp (*Bruix* 8700ihp) = 18.2-19kts. Coal 600t max
Armour: Steel. Belt 3.6in, turrets 4.3in, CT 4.3in
Armament: 2-7.6in/45cal M1887 (2x1), 6-5.5in/45cal QF M1887 or M1891, 4-9pdr, 4-3pdr, 6-1pdr revolvers, 4-18in TT aw
Complement: 393

Name	Builder	Laid down	Launched	Comp	Fate
AMIRAL CHARNER	Rochefort	July 1889	Mar 1893	1894	Sunk 8.2.1916
BRUIX	Rochefort	Oct 1890	Aug 1894	May 1896	Stricken 1920
CHANZY	Soc de la Gironde	1890	Jan 1894	1894	Wrecked 30.5.1907
LATOUCHE TRÉVILLE	Brest	1890	Oct 1892	1894	Stricken 1926

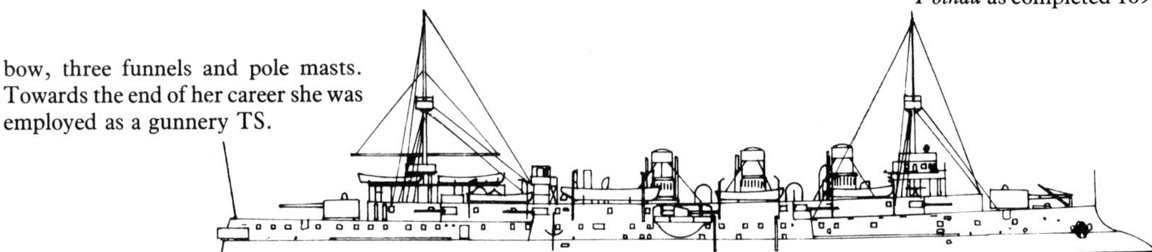
Pothau as completed 1897

This ship is sometimes classed as a protected cruiser on account of the thin belt, which was complete from 4ft 11in below to 8ft 2in above water and was reinforced by a curved armour deck 3.3in on the slopes and 1.7in on the flat with a thin splinter deck over the machinery. The 7.6in guns were in fore and aft turrets at upper deck level and the 5.5in were at the same level on either beam, with the 4 forward and 4 after guns in casemates protected only by port shields and the 2 amidships guns sponsoned out with open back shields. The *Pothuau* had a plough bow, three funnels and pole masts. Towards the end of her career she was employed as a gunnery TS.

POTHUAU *armoured cruiser*

Displacement: 5374t
Dimensions: 360ft 10in pp x 50ft 2in x 21ft 3in max (*110.00 x 15.30 x 6.48m*)
Machinery: 2-shaft VTE, 18 Belleville boilers, 10,000ihp = 19kts. Coal 640t max
Armour: NS. Belt 2.3in, turrets 7in-5½in, CT 9in
Armament: 2-7.6in/40cal M1893 (2x1), 10-5.5in/45cal QF M1891 and 1893, 10-3pdr, 8-1pdr, 4-18in TT aw
Complement: 459

Name	Builder	Laid down	Launched	Comp	Fate
POTHUAU	F C de la Méditerranée	Jan 1893	Sept 1895	Jan 1897	Stricken 1929

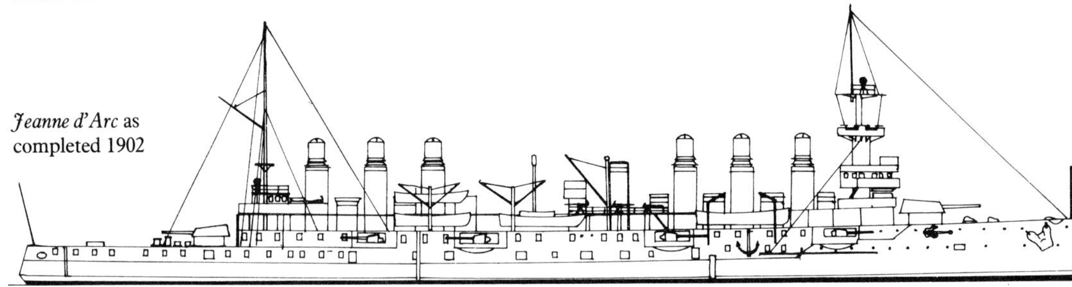
Jeanne d'Arc as completed 1902

Jeanne d'Arc was the first large French armoured cruiser but she had a light armament for her size and was of novel appearance with a slightly projecting ram at the waterline, a high forecastle deck extending as far as the mainmast and six funnels in two widely separated groups of three. There was a light military foremast and a pole mainmast. The belt was complete and 14ft 2in wide, of which the 8ft 2in lower strake was 6in reducing to 2in at the lower edge and ending past the rudder-head in a 4in bulkhead. The upper strake was 4in reducing to 1.6in at the ends and taken to the forecastle deck forward. The curved lower armour deck was 2.6in on the flat with 1.4in slopes, and there was a flat 0.7in deck at the belt upper edge, the space between the two decks being subdivided to form a cellular layer as was later developed in the *République* class battleships. The 7.6in turrets were fore and aft, and, presumably for balancing purposes, the 6.3in armour was at the rear of the turret. The 5.5in guns had 3in shields and were distributed on the beam with 6 at forecastle deck level and 8 in upper deck sponsons with 1.6in plating. Ammunition passages for the 5.5in guns ran inboard of the cofferdam which formed the outer part of the cellular layer. Each funnel served one boiler room with six boilers, and the engine rooms were located between the groups of boilers.

Jeanne d'Arc does not seem to have been very successful as 23kts was hoped for, and she was extremely unhandy with a tactical diameter of 2200yds. She was employed as a TS for midshipmen before the First World War, when she took part in the Gallipoli operations. She reverted to her former role after the war.

JEANNE D'ARC *armoured cruiser*

Displacement: 11,092t
Dimensions: 477ft oa x 63ft 8in x 26ft 7in max (*145.38 x 19.40 x 8.10m*)
Machinery: 3-shaft VTE, 36 Guyot du Temple boilers, 33,000ihp = 21.8kts. Coal 1970t max
Armour: Harvey nickel. Belt 6in-1.6in, turrets 6.3in-4.7in, bases 5½in-2in, CT 6in
Armament: 2-7.6in/40cal M1893-96 (2x1), 14-5.5in/45cal QF M1893, 16-2pdr, 6-1pdr, 2-18in TT sub
Complement: 651

Name	Builder	Laid down	Launched	Comp	Fate
JEANNE D'ARC	Toulon	Oct 1896	June 1899	1902	Stricken 1934

In general layout this class resembled smaller versions of the *Jeanne d'Arc* but the forecastle extended to beyond the after turret and there were four boiler rooms, with four funnels in groups of two. The belt reached from 4ft 5in below water to the main deck and to the upper deck for 141ft from the bows. It ended 13ft from the stern in a 3.3in-1.6in bulkhead. The lower strake was 6in decreasing to 3.6in forward, 3.2in aft and 2in at the lower edge, while the upper strake was 3.8in-3in and 2.3in-1.6in between the main and upper decks. The curved lower armour deck was 2.2in-2in with a 0.8in deck at the belt upper edge. There was a cellular layer between these decks. The 7.6in guns were in fore and aft turrets and the 6.4in guns in upper deck casemates on the beam. These had 1.2in rears, 0.9in roofs and 2in ammunition tubes, and the 3.9in guns were in shields on the forecastle deck. The casemate area had a 4.7in forward bulkhead between forecastle and upper decks and a 4in after one taken down to the lower armour deck. Tactical diameter was about 1000yds. *Dupetit-Thouars* was torpedoed by *U62* off Brest when escorting a convoy and sank with small loss of life. *Gueydon* became a gunnery and then a boys TS after the First World War.

Gueydon as completed 1903

GUEYDON class *armoured cruisers*

Displacement: 9367t (*Gueydon* 9548t, *Montcalm* 9177t)
Dimensions: 452ft 8in oa x 63ft 7in x 25ft 2in max (*137.97 x 19.38 x 7.67m*)
Machinery: 3-shaft VTE, 28 Niclausse (*Thouars* 28 Belleville, *Montcalm* 20 Normand Sigaudy) boilers, 19,600ihp = 21kts (*Thouars* 22,000ihp = 22kts). Coal 1575t max
Armour: Harvey nickel. Belt 6in-1.6in, turrets 8in, bases 8in-2in, casemates 4.7in, CT 6.3in
Armament: 2-7.6in/40cal M1893-96 (2x1), 8-6.4in/45cal QF M1893-96, 4-3.9in, 16-3pdr, 4-1pdr, 2-18in TT sub
Complement: 566

Name	Builder	Laid down	Launched	Comp	Fate
DUPETIT-THOUARS	Toulon	Apr 1899	July 1901	1905	Sunk 7.8.1918
GUEYDON	Lorient	Aug 1898	Sept 1899	1903	Stricken 1942
MONTCALM	La Seyne	Apr 1898	Mar 1900	1902	Hulked 1933

A class of smaller, weakly armed ships with the forecastle deck taken beyond the after turret, four funnels in groups of two and pole masts. There was a small ram at the waterline. The belt ran from the bows to 62ft from the stern and from 4ft below to 6ft 10in above water rising to 8ft at the bows; it was 4in reduced to 3.3in forward and to 1½in at the lower edge with a 3.6in after bulkhead. The armour deck had high slopes with a total thickness of 2.8in amidships and the crown at the level of the belt upper edge was 1.6in. Forward and aft the deck totalled 2in. The cellular layer was mostly unprotected by the side armour. The 6.4in turrets were fore and aft on the forecastle deck with one on each beam at upper deck level. The 6.3in armour was at the rear of the turrets, presumably for balancing purposes, and the 3.9in guns were in unprotected ports on the upper deck. *Kléber* was sunk by a mine at the entrance to Brest and 38 men were lost with her.

Kléber as completed 1904

DUPLEIX class *armoured cruisers*

Displacement: 7578t designed; *Desaix* 7547t, *Dupleix* 7432t, *Kléber* 7602t actual
Dimensions: 426ft 6in wl x 58ft 6in x 24ft 4in max (*130.00 x 17.83 x 7.42m*)
Machinery: 3-shaft VTE, 24 Belleville boilers (*Kléber* 20 Niclausse), 17,500ihp = 20.7-21kts. Coal 1180t max
Armour: Harvey nickel. Belt 4in-1½in, turrets 6.3in-4.7in, bases 4.7in-1½in, CT 3.2in
Armament: 8-6.4in/45cal QF M1893-96 (4x2), 4-3.9in, 10-3pdr, 4-1pdr, 2-18in TT aw
Complement: 531

Name	Builder	Laid down	Launched	Comp	Fate
DESAIX	Ch de la Loire	Nov 1897	Mar 1901	1904	Stricken 1927
DUPLEIX	Rochefort	Feb 1898	Apr 1900	1903	Stricken 1922
KLÉBER	Ch de la Gironde	Apr 1898	Sept 1902	1904	Sunk 27.6.17

Later versions of the *Gueydon* class with a different distribution of the 6.4in guns. The belt extended from the stem to near the stern and from 4ft below to 7ft 6in above water and was raised to the upper deck for 129ft from the bows. The lower strake was 6in reduced to 3.2in at the ends and to 2.8in at the lower edge, with the upper strake 4.7in-3.2in, and 2.3in above the main deck forward. The stern bulkhead was 3.2in and there were two armour decks, the lower 1.6in with 1.8in amidships slopes and that at the belt upper edge 1.4in reduced to 0.8in at the ends. There was the usual cellular layer between the armour decks. The fore and aft 7.6in turrets were at forecastle deck level as were the four midships 6.4in

GLOIRE class *armoured cruisers*

Displacement: 9856t designed; *Aube* 9534t, *Condé* 10,233t, *Marseillaise* 9458t, *Gloire* 10,212t actual
Dimensions: 458ft 7in wl x 66ft 3in x 24ft 6in-25ft 2in max (*139.78 x 20.19 x 7.47-7.67m*)
Machinery: 3-shaft VTE, 28 Niclausse (*Aube, Marseillaise, Sully* 24 Belleville) boilers, 21,800ihp = 21.5kts. Coal 1565t max
Armour: Harvey nickel. Belt 6in-2.3in, turrets 6.8in, bases 5½in-4in, secondary turrets 4in, casemates 3.3in, CT 6in
Armament: 2-7.6in/40cal M1893-96 (2x1), 8-6.4in/45cal QF M1893-96, 6-3.9in, 18-3pdr, 2-18in TT sub
Complement: 615

Name	Builder	Laid down	Launched	Comp	Fate
AMIRAL AUBE	Penhoët	Oct 1899	May 1902	1904	Stricken 1922
CONDÉ	Lorient	Mar 1901	Mar 1902	1904	Stricken 1933
GLOIRE	Lorient	Sept 1899	June 1900	1904	Stricken 1922
MARSEILLAISE	Brest	Jan 1900	July 1900	1903	Stricken 1929
SULLY	La Seyne	June 1899	June 1901	1903	Wrecked 30.9.05

turrets, but two 6.4in were in upper deck casemates forward and two in main deck ones aft. These casemates had 1.6in rear walls, and the 3.9in guns were unprotected, two being at forecastle deck and four at upper deck level. Provision was made for burning oil fuel in conjunction with coal and 80t could be carried. *Sully* was wrecked in Along Bay in Indo-China, and salvage attempts failed. *Marseillaise* was employed as a gunnery TS after the First World War.

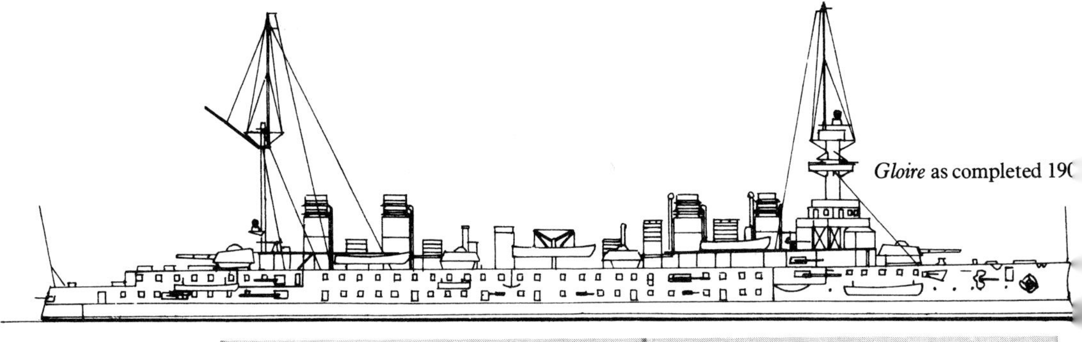

Gloire as completed 190[illegible]

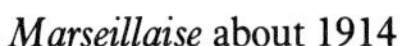

Marseillaise about 1914

This class were larger than previous French armoured cruisers, with double the armament of the *Gloire* class, but were deficient in heavy guns. The forecastle deck extended to the mainmast and there were again four funnels in widely spaced groups of two. The stem was almost straight and there was a short military foremast and pole mainmast. The belt ran from the bows to just short of the stern and from 3ft 3in below to 8ft 3in above water rising to the upper deck from stem to foremast. It was 6in reducing to 4.7in at the upper edge and to 4in at the ends with 2.8in where raised forward. There was a 4in stern bulkhead and the usual two armour decks, the lower being 2.6in max on the slopes and 1.8in flat and the upper 1.4in, with a cellular layer between. The twin 7.6in turrets were fore and aft with three twin 6.4in turrets on each beam at forecastle deck level, two 6.4in in forward upper deck casemates and two in after main deck ones. The casemates had 2.5in rear walls and there was a 4.7in bulkhead joining the two forward ones. The main turret crowns were 2in and the secondary 1.2in. In *Victor Hugo* the 3pdr guns were of a new higher velocity pattern; in *Ferry* and *Hugo* the number of 3pdrs was later reduced and 4 were given AA mountings.

Victor Hugo as completed 1907

LÉON GAMBETTA class *armoured cruisers*

Displacement: 12,351t designed; *Gambetta* 11,959t, *Ferry* 12,379t, *Hugo* 13,108t actual
Dimensions: 480ft 6in wl x 70ft 3in x 26ft 5in-27ft 7in max *(146.45 x 21.41 x 8.05-8.41m)*
Machinery: 3-shaft VTE, 28 Niclausse (*Hugo* 28 Belleville, *Ferry* 20 Guyot du Temple) boilers, 28,500ihp = 22.5kts. Coal 2065t max
Armour: KC. Belt 6in-2.8in, turrets 8in, bases 7.2in-4in, secondary turrets 6½in-5.2in, bases 5.2-2½in, casemates 5½in, CT 8in
Armament: 4-7.6in/40cal M1893-96 (2x2), 16-6.4in/45cal QF M1893-96, 24-3pdr, 2-1pdr, 2-18in TT sub
Complement: 728,821 war as flagship

Name	Builder	Laid down	Launched	Comp	Fate
LÉON GAMBETTA	Brest	Jan 1901	Nov 1901	July 1905	Sunk 27.4.15
JULES FERRY	Cherbourg	Aug 1901	Aug 1903	Sept 1905	Stricken 1927
VICTOR HUGO	Lorient	Mar 1903	Mar 1904	1907	Stricken 1930

Gambetta was delayed in completion by running aground in fog early in her trials in December 1903, and these were not resumed until August 1904. In 1915, she sank in ten minutes after two 18in torpedo hits from the Austrian *U5*. 137 of the crew survived, all the officers following Rear Admiral Sénès in going down with the ship. Like most armoured cruisers the *Gambetta* showed little resistance to underwater attack.

This ship was generally similar to the *Léon Gambetta* class, but differed in having more boiler power, more powerful marks of gun and in having four fewer 6.4in with single instead of twin turrets. There were four of these on each beam at forecastle deck level, the remaining 6.4in being in casemates as in the previous class. Armour details were similar to those of the *Gambetta*. The 3pdrs, which were of the same type as in *Victor Hugo*, appear to have been reduced to 16 (4 AA) in the First World War. *Jules Michelet* was eventually employed as an artificers TS.

JULES MICHELET *armoured cruiser*

Displacement: 13,105t
Dimensions: 489ft oa x 70ft 3in x 27ft 7in max *(146.53 x 21.41 x 8.41m)*
Machinery: 3-shaft VTE, 28 Guyot du Temple boilers, 30,000ihp = 22.5kts. Coal 2070t (later 1870t) max
Armour: KC. Belt 6in-2.8in, turrets 8in, bases 7.2in-4in, secondary turrets 6.5in-5.2in, bases 5.2in-2½in, casemates 5½in, CT 8in
Armament: 4-7.6in/50cal M1902 (2x2), 12-6.4in/45cal M1893-96M, 24-3pdr, 2-18in TT sub
Complement: 770

Name	Builder	Laid down	Launched	Comp	Fate
JULES MICHELET	Lorient	June 1904	Aug 1905	Nov 1908	Stricken 1937

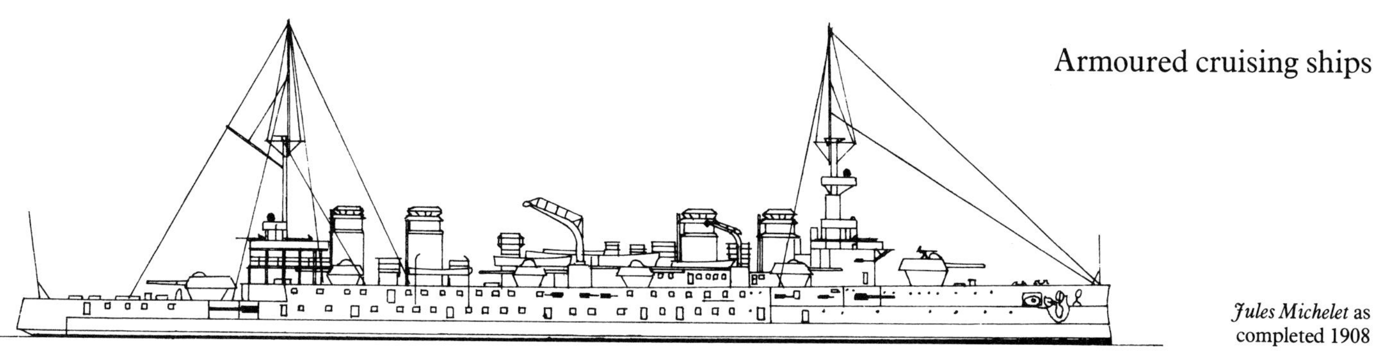

Jules Michelet as completed 1908

ERNEST RENAN *armoured cruiser*

Displacement: 13,504t
Dimensions: 521ft 7in oa x 70ft x 27ft 5in max (*158.97 x 21.34 x 8.36m*)
Machinery: 3-shaft VTE, 42 Niclausse boilers, 36,000ihp = 23kts. Coal 2260t (later 1870t) max
Armour: KC. Belt 6in-2.3in, turrets 8in, bases 7.2in-4in, secondary turrets 6½in-5.2in, bases 5.2-2½in, casemates 5½in, CT 8in
Armament: 4-7.6in/50cal M1902 (2x2), 12-6.4in/45cal M1893-96M, 16-9pdr, 8-3pdr, 2-1pdr, 2-18in TT sub
Complement: 824

Name	Builder	Laid down	Launched	Comp	Fate
ERNEST RENAN	Penhoët	July 1904	Apr 1906	Feb 1909	Stricken 1931

Originally intended to be of the *Léon Gambetta* type, the plans of the *Ernest Renan* were continually altered and it was eventually decided to increase the length of the hull in order to obtain a higher speed. There were six funnels in two widely separated groups of three, the forecastle deck extended to the mainmast and the stem was almost straight. A light military foremast was provided, together with a pole mainmast which was removed in 1918/22. The armour belt ran from the bows to near the stern, and from 4ft 5in below to 7ft 7in above water, rising to the upper deck from the stem to the after end of the forward 6.4in casemates. It was 6in from just forward of the foremast to just abaft the mainmast and reduced to 4in forward, 3.3in aft and 2.3in to the upper deck forward. The stern bulkhead was 3.5in, the lower armour deck 2.6in on the slopes and 1.8in on the flat amidships increasing to 2.8in over the rudder, and the upper armour deck at main deck level was 1.4in with the usual cellular layer between the armour decks. The twin 7.6in turrets were located fore and aft and the 6.4in guns were in four single turrets at forecastle deck level on each beam, with two guns in forward upper deck and two in after main deck casemates. The 7.6in turret crowns were 2in, the 6.4in crowns 1.2in and the casemate rear walls 2½in with a 4.7in bulkhead joining the forward casemates. On trials the *Ernest Renan* was the fastest of the French armoured cruisers, attaining 37,685ihp = 24.4kts, but her designer Émile Bertin stated that she would easily have made 25kts at 42,000ihp if the intended small tube boilers had not been changed for what he described as reasons other than military. During and after the First-World War some AA guns were added, 14pdrs, 9pdrs and 3pdrs being reported at various times, and a sea-plane is listed as being carried in 1927. The ship was finally employed as a gunnery TS.

Ernest Renan about 1912

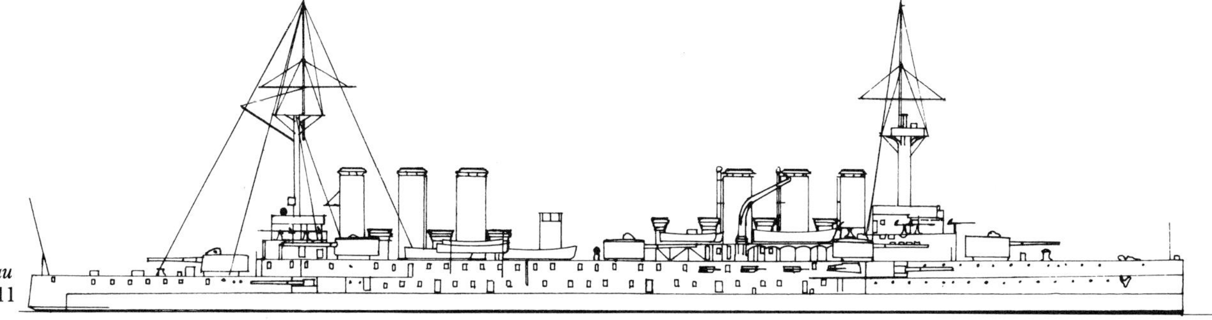

Waldeck-Rousseau as completed 1911

EDGAR QUINET class *armoured cruisers*

Displacement: 13,847t (*Waldeck-Rousseau* 13,995t)
Dimensions: 521ft 4in oa x 70ft 7in x 27ft 7in max (*158.90 x 21.51 x 8.41m*)
Machinery: 3-shaft VTE, 40 Belleville (*Waldeck-Rousseau* 42 Niclausse) boilers, 36,000ihp = 23kts. Coal 2260t max (later 1870/2000t)
Armour: KC. Belt 6in-1⅗in, turrets 8in, bases 8in max, casemates 7.6in, CT 8in, tube 6in
Armament: 14-7.6in/50cal M1902 (2x2, 10x1), 20-9pdr, 2-18in TT sub
Complement: 859/892

Name	Builder	Laid down	Launched	Comp	Fate
EDGAR QUINET	Brest	Nov 1905	Sept 1907	Jan 1911	Wrecked 9.1.30
WALDECK-ROUSSEAU	Lorient	June 1906	4.3.08	Aug 1911	Hulked 1936

This class were the most powerful French armoured cruisers, having a much improved uniform main armament, but their type was virtually obsolete by their completion. As with the *Renan* the plans were much altered, and as built they resembled the former ship in general appearance. The 7.6in guns were in two twin turrets fore and aft and six single turrets at forecastle deck level of which three were on each side, and there were two casemates forward on the upper deck and two aft on the main deck. The twin and single turrets were of a new type with loading at any angle of elevation and a reported rate of fire of 4 rounds per gun per minute. It was however unfortunate that four of the powerful 7.6in were still mounted in casemates. The armouring generally resembled that of the *Renan* but thicknesses were altered in detail: the belt was reduced to 2.8in forward with 3½in-1⅗in between the main and upper decks; the lower armour deck was increased to 2½in forward; and the upper armour deck was slightly reduced to 1.3in. The two forward casemates were linked by a 7.6in forward and 4.7in after bulkhead, and the two after ones by a 4.7in forward and 7.6in after bulkhead, enabling the casemate rear walls to be reduced to 0.8in. *Edgar Quinet* achieved 40,294ihp = 23.9kts on trials, but *Waldeck-Rousseau* was not taken beyond 35,286ihp = 23.1kts. A number of 14pdr and 9pdr AA guns were later added at the expense of the 9pdr battery, and *Waldeck-Rousseau* is listed as carrying a seaplane in 1930. *Edgar Quinet* became a midshipmans TS in 1928 and the 4 casemate 7.6in and the first and sixth funnels were removed; she was wrecked on the Algerian coast in early 1930.

CRUISERS
PROTECTED CRUISERS

The first French protected cruiser, the *Sfax* was a two-funnelled ship with a ram bow and an overhanging stern. There was a forecastle and poop and she was rigged as a barque with 21,400 sq ft of sail. The 6.4in guns were at upper deck level with two in embrasured ports forward and the others in sponsons amidships and aft, while the 5.5in were on the main deck amidships between the sponsons. The armour deck was 2-3ft below water and was 2.4in thick in four layers of steel. There was a cofferdam and early form of cellular layer between the armour and main decks, and there was 1in on the CT located on the bridge abaft the forefunnel. The hull plating was wrought iron with steel frames and the *Sfax* was sheathed and coppered. The mainmast and all sails were later removed, and the 6.4in and 5.5in guns were replaced by QFC with 6-3pdr, 6-1pdr, 4-1pdr revolvers and only 2 TT.

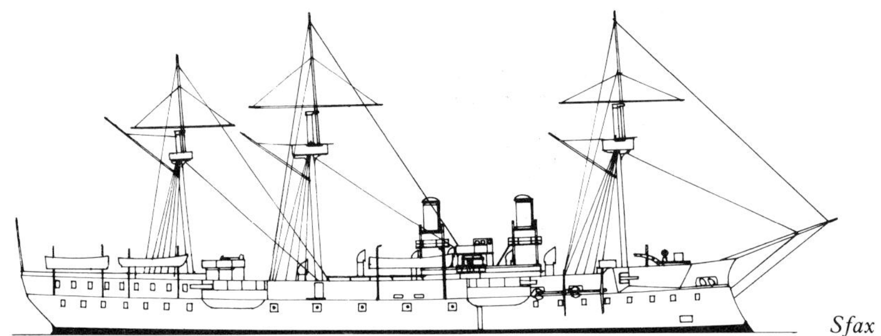

Sfax 1895

SFAX *protected cruiser*

Displacement: 4561t
Dimensions: 300ft 5in wl x 49ft 4in x 25ft 2in max *(91.57 x 15.04 x 7.67m)*
Machinery: 2-shaft HC, 12 cyl boilers, 6500ihp = 16.7kts. Coal 590/980t
Armament: 6-6.4in/28cal, 10-5.5in/30cal, 2-3pdr, 10-1pdr revolvers, 5-14in TT aw
Complement: 486

Name	Builder	Laid down	Launched	Comp	Fate
SFAX	Brest	Mar 1882	May 1884	June 1887	Stricken 1906

Tage with original barque rig

A three-funnelled protected cruiser with marked tumblehome, a pronounced plough bow and an overhanging stern. There was a forecastle and poop and she was originally rigged as a barque. The 6.4in guns were on the upper deck with two in embrasure ports forward and the rest in sponsons, while the 5.5in were on the main deck broadside. The protective deck was complete and of 2in total thickness, with 2.2in on the slopes which ran to 4ft 3in below water. There was a 3ft 3in wide cofferdam above the protective deck, and 3.5in bulkheads from this deck to the upper deck enclosed the main deck battery. There was a CT with 3.5in-3in. The *Tage* was given Belleville boilers in 1900, and other alterations in her career included the removal of the mainmast, 2-5.5in guns and 3 TT. The lighter guns were altered to 6-3pdr and 16-1pdr and coal reduced to 980t max.

TAGE *protected cruiser*

Displacement: 7469t
Dimensions: 390ft wl x 53ft 6in x 25ft 2in max *(118.87 x 16.30 x 7.67m)*
Machinery: 2-shaft HTE, 12 cyl boilers, 12,500ihp = 19.2kts. Coal 915/1500t
Armament: 8-6.4in/30cal (later QFC), 10-5.5in/30cal (later QFC), 5-3pdr, 1-3pdr revolver, 14-1pdr revolvers, 7-15in TT aw
Complement: 538

Name	Builder	Laid down	Launched	Comp	Fate
TAGE	Soc de la Loire	July 1885	Oct 1886	Dec 1890	Stricken 1910

More usually known as the *Cécille*, this ship generally resembled the *Tage* and was originally rigged as a barque without royals. Seven of the 6.4in were on the upper deck, six being in sponsons and one firing right ahead, while the eighth gun was right aft on the poop. The 5.5in were on the main deck broadside. The protective deck was 2.2in total on the flat and 4in on the slopes which ended 4ft 3in below water. There was a cofferdam above

AMIRAL CÉCILLE *protected cruiser*

Displacement: 5839t
Dimensions: 379ft oa x 49ft 2in x 22ft 4in max *(115.50 x 15.00 x 6.81m)*
Machinery: 2-shaft VC (4 engines), 12 cyl boilers, 10,200ihp = 19.4kts. Coal 925t max
Armament: 8-6.4in/30cal (later QFC), 10-5.5in/30cal (later QFC), 6-3pdr, 14-1pdr revolvers, 4- later 3-15in TT aw
Complement: 517

Name	Builder	Laid down	Launched	Comp	Fate
AMIRAL CÉCILLE	La Seyne	Aug 1886	May 1888	Sept 1890	BU 1919

the protective deck, and the battery was closed by 3.1in bulkheads between the main and upper deck, with 3.5in on the CT. She appears to have had better underwater compartmentation than the *Tage*.

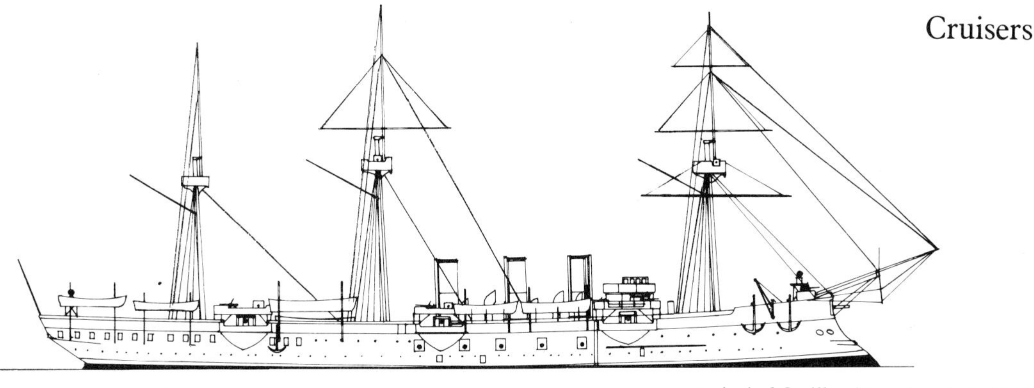

Amiral Cécille with reduced rig 1897

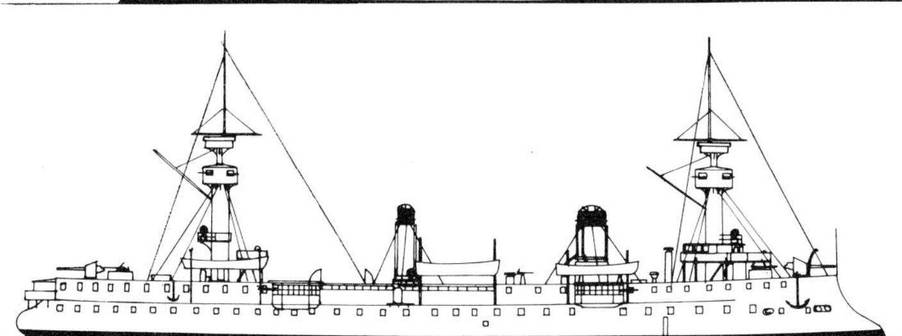

Davout as completed 1891

DAVOUT *protected cruiser*

Displacement:	3031t
Dimensions:	288ft 9in oa x 39ft 4in x 21ft 7in max (*88.00 x 12.00 x 6.58m*)
Machinery:	2-shaft ITE, 8 cyl boilers, 9000ihp = 20.7kts. Coal 840t max
Armament:	6-6.4in/30cal (later QFC), 4-9pdr, 4-3pdr, 2-1pdr, 6-14in TT aw
Complement:	329

Name	Builder	Laid down	Launched	Comp	Fate
DAVOUT	Toulon	Sept 1887	Oct 1889	1891	Stricken 1910

A two-funnelled cruiser with a pronounced plough bow, overhanging stern and considerable tumblehome. There were originally two large military masts. There was a 6.4in gun on forecastle and poop with four in upper deck sponsons. The armour deck was curved from 1ft 8in above water to 3ft 7in below amidships with a max total thickness of 2in increased to 4in at the sides. There was a cofferdam about 4ft wide above the armour deck, and the small CT had 2.8in armour. The boilers were replaced by 10 Niclausse in 1901. The TT were later reduced to 4 and finally 2.

SUCHET *protected cruiser*

Displacement:	3362t
Dimensions:	318ft 3in oa x 39ft 4in x 20ft mean (*97.00 x 12.00 x 6.10m*)
Machinery:	2-shaft HTE, 24 Belleville boilers, 9500ihp = 20.4kts. Coal 836t max
Armament:	6-6.4in/30cal (later QFC), 4-3.9in, 8-3pdr, 8-1pdr, 7-14in TT, 6 aw 1 sub
Complement:	335

Name	Builder	Laid down	Launched	Comp	Fate
SUCHET	Toulon	Oct 1887	Aug 1893	1894	Stricken 1906

Suchet was originally intended as a sister of the *Davout*, and was similar to this vessel but had a longer hull. The 3.9in guns were located abaft and before the forecastle and poop 6.4in, and the armour deck is given as 3.2in total. There was a cellular layer above with a height of about 18in at the armour deck crown, and a light debris deck over the machinery spaces. The original military masts were replaced by light poles.

Suchet with light pole masts

Forbin with later two-masted rig

FORBIN class *protected cruisers*

Displacement:	1935t, *Surcouf* 2012t, *Coëtlogon* 1901t
Dimensions:	311ft 8in wl x 29ft 6in x 17ft 2in max (*95.00 x 9.00 x 5.23m*)
Machinery:	2-shaft HC, 6 cyl boilers, 5800ihp = 20/20.5kts. Coal 300t max
Armament:	4-5.5in/30cal (later QFC), 3-3pdr, 4-1pdr revolvers (later QF), 4-14in TT aw, 150 mines max
Complement:	199

Name	Builder	Laid down	Launched	Comp	Fate
COËTLOGON	Penhöet	1887	Dec 1888	Aug 1894	Stricken 1906
FORBIN	Rochefort	May 1886	Jan 1888	Feb 1889	Collier 1913
SURCOUF	Cherbourg	May 1886	Oct 1888	1890	Stricken 1921

This class were of very fine lines with plough bows, forecastle and poop, two funnels and three light masts, later two except in *Surcouf*. There was considerable tumblehome. The 5.5in, of which only two were originally carried by *Forbin*, were in upper deck sponsons, and there was a curved 1.6in armour deck with a cofferdam above and a thin splinter deck over the machinery spaces. A CT was added to *Surcouf* in 1893, and she and *Forbin* were later fitted to burn oil with coal, while the TT were removed from *Fourbin* and *Surcouf* and the 3pdrs increased to eight. *Coëtlogon* failed on trials and her engines were replaced, resulting in a three year delay in completion.

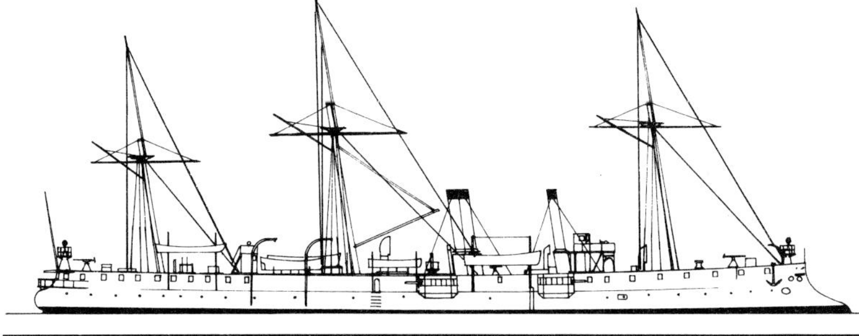

Cosmao as completed 1891

Of similar type to the *Forbin* class but distinguished by raked funnels with the mainmast abaft instead of between them. The 5.5in sponsons were also closer together. *Troude* and *Lalande* had CTs with 1in plating, and in all the TT were removed and the 3pdrs increased to 10. Protection was as for the *Forbin* class. It was reported that neither hull nor engines were strong enough to withstand the vibrations set up at over 20kts.

TROUDE class *protected cruisers*

Displacement: 1994t, *Cosmao* 1923t, *Lalande* 1968t
Dimensions: 311ft 8in wl x 29ft 6in x 17ft max (*95.00 x 9.00 x 5.18m*)
Machinery: 2-shaft HC, 5 cyl boilers, 5800ihp = 20.5kts. Coal 300t max
Armament: 4-5.5in/30cal (later QFC), 4-3pdr, 4-1pdr revolvers (later QF), 4-14in TT aw, 150 mines max
Complement: 201

Name	Builder	Laid down	Launched	Comp	Fate
COSMAO	Soc de la Gironde	1887	Aug 1889	1891	Stricken 1922
LALANDE	Soc de la Gironde	1887	Mar 1889	Oct 1890	Stricken 1912
TROUDE	Soc de la Gironde	Nov 1886	Oct 1888	Jan 1891	Stricken 1908

Lavoisier in her early years

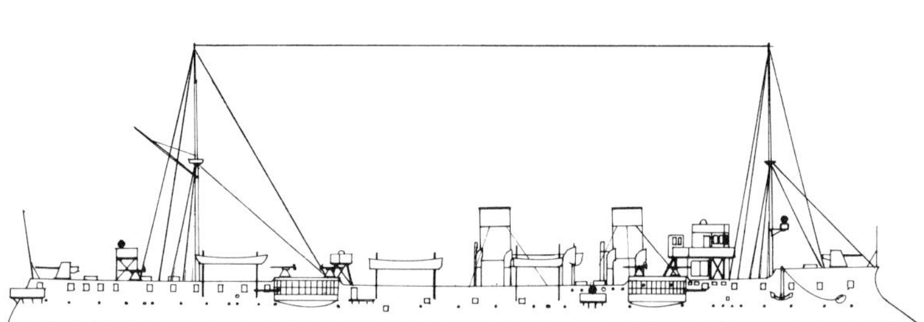

Lavoisier as completed 1898

Of higher freeboard than the *Forbin* and *Troude* classes with a forecastle deck nearly to the stern, two funnels and two widely spaced masts. The 5.5in guns were in upper deck sponsons with 3in shields, and the 3.9in were at bow and stern with 2in shields. There was a small CT with 5in armour and the curved armour deck was 1.6in with a cofferdam above and a light debris deck over the engines. *Lavoisier* was fitted to burn oil fuel with coal.

LINOIS class *protected cruisers*

Displacement: 2285/2318t
Dimensions: 330ft 2in oa (*Linois* 321ft 6in) x 34ft 10in (*Galilée* 36ft) x 17ft 10in max (*100.63 (98.00) x 10.62 (10.97) x 5.44m*)
Machinery: 2-shaft VTE, 16 Belleville (*Linois* 6 cyl) boilers, 6800ihp = 20.5kts. Coal 339t (*Linois* 400t) max
Armament: 4-5.5in/45cal QF, 2-3.9in, 8-3pdr, 2-1pdr, 4-1pdr revolvers, 2-, *Linois* 4-18in TT aw, 120 mines max (not *Lavoisier*)
Complement: 250/269

Name	Builder	Laid down	Launched	Comp	Fate
GALILÉE	Rochefort	1893	Apr 1896	1897	Stricken 1911
LAVOISIER	Rochefort	Jan 1895	Apr 1897	Apr 1898	Stricken 1920
LINOIS	La Seyne	Aug 1892	Jan 1894	1895	Stricken 1910

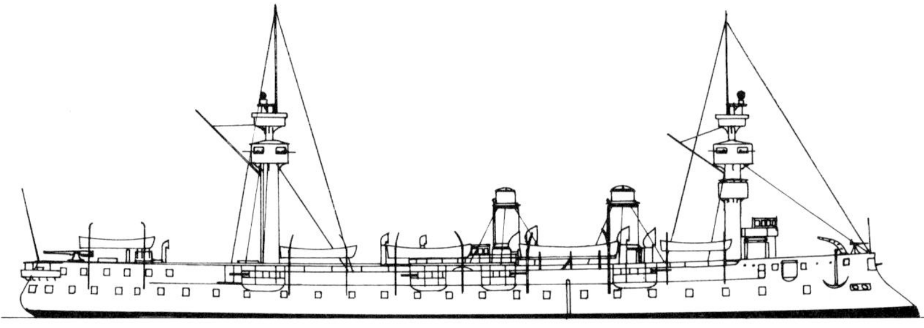

Isly as completed 1893

Two-funnelled cruisers with plough bows, tumblehome and in *Alger* an overhanging stern. There were originally two large military masts. The 6.4in were in fore and aft upper deck sponsons with four 5.5in in midships ones, one 5.5in under the forecastle and one on the poop. In *Isly* and later in *Jean Bart* these guns had 2in shields. The CT had 3in/2in and the curved armour deck was 2in total on the flat amidships with 4in max on the slopes. There was a cofferdam 2ft 7in wide above the armour deck and an early type of cellular layer. The TT in all three ships were later reduced to 2 or 3. The class were reckoned to be good steamers, and the early use of Belleville boilers in *Alger* should be noted. *Jean Bart* was reboilered with 8 Niclausse in 1903, and attained 10,000ihp = 20kts, but was lost on the Sahara coast four years later.

ALGER class *protected cruisers*

Displacement: 4313t, *Jean Bart* 4044t, *Isly* 4406t
Dimensions: 344ft 6in pp x 42ft 7in x 20ft-21ft 2in max (*105.00 x 12.98 x 6.10-6.45m*)
Machinery: 2-shaft VTE (*Jean Bart, Isly* HTE), 24 Belleville (*Jean Bart, Isly* 8 cyl) boilers, 8000ihp = 19/19.5kts. Coal 860t max
Armament: 4-6.4in/28cal (later QFC), 6-5.5in/30cal (later QFC), 2-9pdr, 8/12-3pdr, 8/10-1pdr revolvers, 5-14in TT aw
Complement: 387/405

Name	Builder	Laid down	Launched	Comp	Fate
ALGER	Cherbourg	Nov 1887	Nov 1889	1891	Hulked 1911
ISLY	Brest	Aug 1887	June 1891	1893	Stricken 1914
JEAN BART	Rochefort	Sept 1887	Nov 1889	1891	Wrecked 11.2.1907

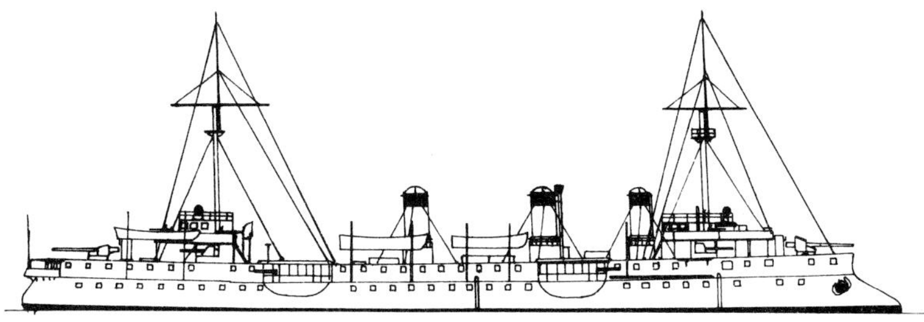

Bugeaud as completed 1896

A class of three-funnelled cruisers with tumblehome and a pronounced plough bow. The 6.4in guns were forward and aft at forecastle deck level and in upper deck sponsons located abreast of the middle funnel and forward of the mainmast. The 3.9in guns were just abaft the foremast and mainmast at forecastle deck level. All had 2in shields and there was 3in on the CT. The curved armour deck was 1.2in on the flat with 3.2in slopes and there was the usual cofferdam and cellular layer above and also a debris deck below over the machinery spaces. *Friant* was used as a repair ship in the First World War.

FRIANT class *protected cruiser*

Displacement: 3982t, *Chasseloup-Laubat* 3824t, *Bugeaud* 3809t
Dimensions: 308ft 4in pp x 42ft 7in x 20ft 8in max (*94.00 x 12.98 x 6.30m*)
Machinery: 2-shaft VTE, 20 Niclausse (*Chasseloup-Laubat* 20 Lagrafel d'Allest, *Bugeaud* 24 Belleville) boilers, 9500ihp = 18.7kts. Coal 577t max
Armament: 6-6.4in/45cal QF M1891 or 1893, 4-3.9in, 4-3pdr, 11-1pdr, 2-14in TT aw
Complement: 339

Name	Builder	Laid down	Launched	Comp	Fate
BUGEAUD	Cherbourg	June 1891	Aug 1893	May 1896	Stricken 1907
CHASSELOUP-LAUBAT	Cherbourg	June 1891	Apr 1893	1895	Hulked 1911
FRIANT	Brest	1891	Apr 1893	Apr 1895	Stricken 1920

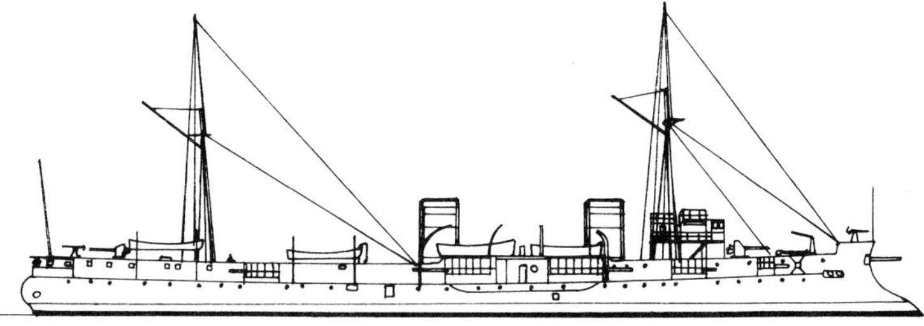

Descartes as completed 1896

Two-funnelled cruisers with plough bows and tumblehome. They were wood-sheathed and coppered. The 6.4in guns were in midships sponsons on the upper deck, while of the 3.9in two were abreast forward and aft on the forecastle deck and four forward and two aft on the upper deck, the sides being recessed for axial fire. The 3.9in guns had 2in shields with 2.8in on the CT, and the armour deck was 1.8in total on the flat amidships with 2.4in slopes. There was a cellular layer above the armour deck and a light debris deck below over the machinery spaces. *Descartes* was reported as attaining 21.8kts on trials, but both had to be ballasted to improve stability and in *Descartes*, at least, the magazines were excessively hot.

DESCARTES class *protected cruisers*

Displacement: 3960t
Dimensions: 316ft pp x 42ft 7in x 21ft 4in max (*96.32 x 12.98 x 6.50m*)
Machinery: 2-shaft VTE, 16 Belleville boilers, 8500ihp = 19.5kts. Coal 543t max
Armament: 4-6.4in/45cal QF M1891 or M1893, 10-3.9in, 8-3pdr, 4-1pdr (*Pascal* 14-3pdr, 8-1pdr), 2-18in TT aw
Complement: 383/401

Name	Builder	Laid down	Launched	Comp	Fate
DESCARTES	Soc de la Loire	Aug 1892	Sept 1894	July 1896	Stricken 1920
PASCAL	Toulon	Dec 1893	Sept 1895	1897	Stricken 1911

Du Chayla, probably as completed

Similar to the *Friant* class, differing as indicated above and also in having 4in on the CT and an armour deck 2.8in max on the flat with 3.2in to 4in slopes. *D'Assas* was reported to be distinctly deep in the water and of doubtful stability.

D'ASSAS class *protected cruisers*

Displacement: 3962t, *Du Chayla, Cassard* 3890t
Dimensions: 315ft 5in pp x 44ft 10in x 20ft 6in max (*96.14 x 13.67 x 6.25m*)
Machinery: 2-shaft VTE, 20 Lagrafel d'Allest boilers, 10,000ihp = 20kts. Coal 600t max
Armament: 6-6.4in/45cal QF M1893, 4-3.9in, 10-3pdr, 5/9-1pdr, 2-18in TT aw
Complement: 370/392

Name	Builder	Laid down	Launched	Comp	Fate
CASSARD	Cherbourg	1894	May 1896	Feb 1898	Stricken 1924
D'ASSAS	Soc de la Loire	1894	Mar 1896	Mar 1898	Stricken 1914
DU CHAYLA	Cherbourg	Mar 1894	Sept 1895	Feb 1898	Stricken 1921

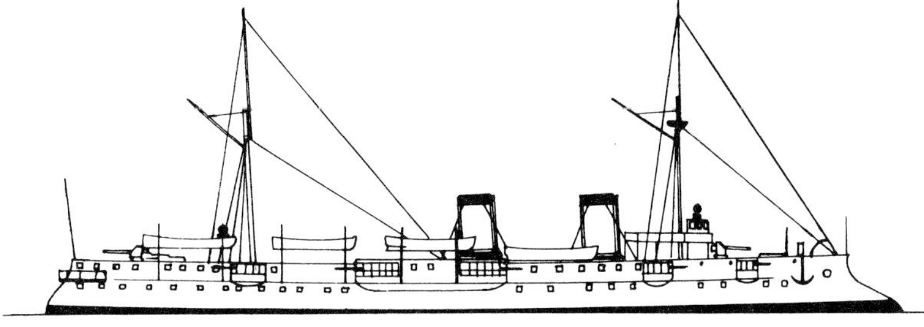

Catinat as completed 1898

CATINAT class *protected cruisers*

Similar to the *Descartes* class, differing as indicated above and also in having the 6.4in guns and the second upper deck pair of 3.9in mounted further aft. The armour deck was reduced to 1in at the ends. When carried, the mines were stowed in the steering engine compartment with a rail fitted through the captain's cabin for dropping them from a stern port. The stability of *Protet* was reported as doubtful and ballast had to be added.

Displacement: 4048t, *Protet* 4001t
Dimensions: 321ft 10in pp x 44ft 7in x 21ft 1in max (*98.09 x 13.59 x 6.43m*)
Machinery: 2-shaft VTE, 16 Belleville boilers, 9500ihp = 19.5/20kts. Coal 560t max
Armament: 4-6.4in/45cal QF M1893, 10-3.9in, 10-3pdr, 4-1pdr, 2-14in TT aw, 50 mines
Complement: 400

Name	Builder	Laid down	Launched	Comp	Fate
CATINAT	F C de la Méditerranée	Feb 1894	Oct 1896	1898	Stricken 1911
PROTET	Soc de la Gironde	Mar 1896	July 1898	Feb 1899	Stricken 1910

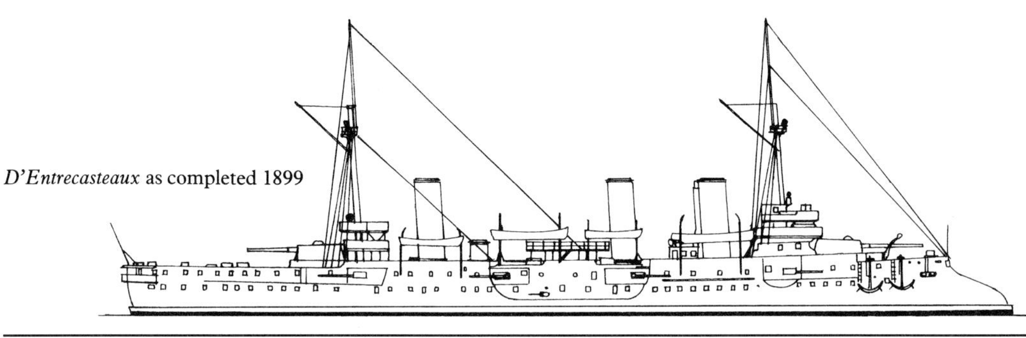

D'Entrecasteaux as completed 1899

D'ENTRECASTEAUX *protected cruiser*

A flush-decked cruiser with a plough bow and three funnels, a forward group of two serving four boilers and an after one serving a single boiler. All boilers were double ended. The 9.4in guns were in fore and aft turrets protected by 10in max nickel steel; the 5.5in guns were in 8 main deck casemates with 4 guns in shields on the upper deck. All had 2.2in protection, and there was 10in on the small CT. The armour deck was 2.2in max on the flat with 4in slopes, and there was a 0.8in deck above this with a cofferdam at the sides between. *D'Entrecasteaux* was sheathed with wood and coppered below water, and the sides were recessed fore and aft above the main deck to improve axial fire from the 5.5in. She was reported to be extremely hot, particularly in the magazines which were, however, provided with cooling equipment. *D'Entrecasteaux* was the only French cruiser of any type to have 9.4in guns since the *Duguesclin* completed 13 years previously.

Displacement: 7995t
Dimensions: 383ft 10in pp x 58ft 6in x 24ft 7in max (*117.00 x 17.83 x 7.50 m*)
Machinery: 2-shaft VTE, 5 cyl boilers, 14,500ihp = 19.2kts. Coal 980t max
Armament: 2-9.4in/40cal M1893 (2x1), 12-5.5in/30cal QFC, 12-3pdr, 6-1pdr, 2-18in TT sub, 4 TT aw removed
Complement: 559

Name	Builder	Laid down	Launched	Comp	Fate
D'ENTRECASTEAUX	La Seyne	Sept 1894	June 1896	1899	Presented to Belgium 1922

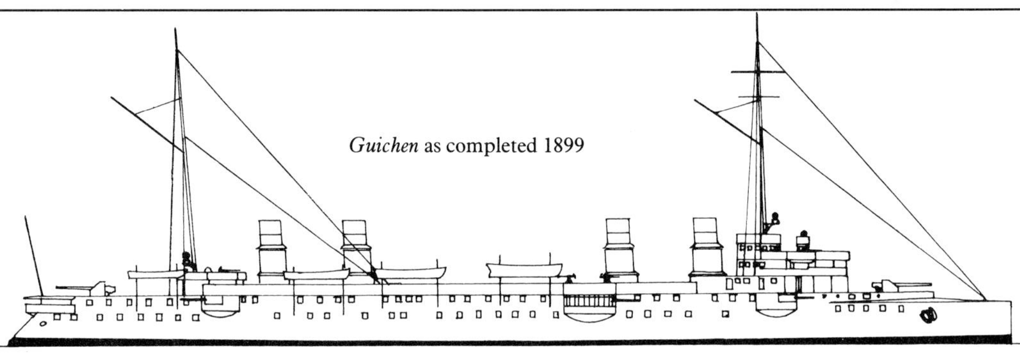

Guichen as completed 1899

GUICHEN *protected cruiser*

A cruiser of a different type, intended for commerce raiding, and very lightly armed for her size. There was a spar deck from just short of the straight stem to the stern, four funnels in widely spaced groups of two and two masts, though a third mast was added between the funnel groups for a time. Early plans show the 6.4in guns in upper deck sponsons on either beam with four 5.5in in upper deck casemates and the other two forward and aft on the spar deck, but photographs indicate that the 6.4in were fore and aft on the spar deck and the 5.5in guns in the sponsons. The guns had 2.2in protection and there was 6.2in Harvey nickel on the CT with a 6in tube. The armour deck rose from 4ft 6in below the water to 2ft 7in above amidships, and was here 2.2in on the flat and 4in on the slopes reduced to 1.6in at the ends. There was a splinter deck 4ft above the armour deck crown with a cofferdam between them at the sides. The boilers were fitted to burn oil with coal.

Displacement: 8151t
Dimensions: 436ft 4in pp x 54ft 9in x 24ft 7in max (*133.00 x 16.96 x 7.49m*)
Machinery: 3-shaft VTE, 36 Lagrafel d'Allest boilers, 25,000ihp = 23.5kts. Coal 1960t max
Armament: 2-6.4in/45cal QF M1893, 6-5.5in/45cal QF M1893, 10-3pdr, 5-1pdr, 2-18in TT aw later removed
Complement: 604

Name	Builder	Laid down	Launched	Comp	Fate
GUICHEN	Soc de la Loire	Oct 1895	Oct 1897	1899	Stricken 1922

Guichen with third mast added

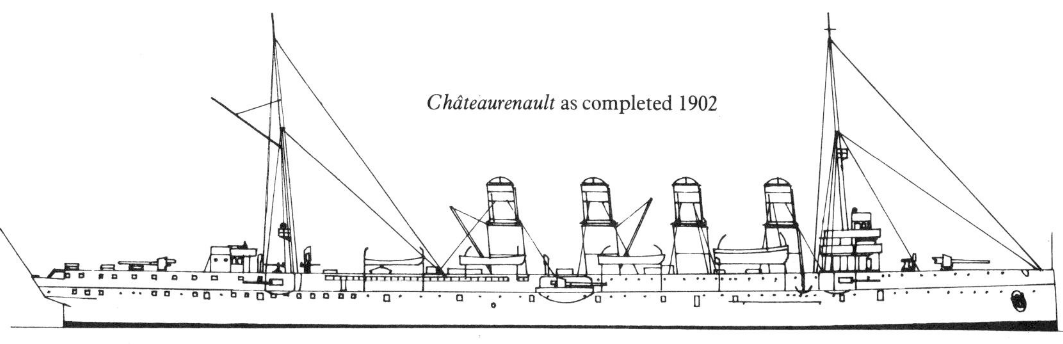
Châteaurenault as completed 1902

In essentials similar to the *Guichen* and with identical protection but of very different appearance. There were four equally spaced funnels, two masts, and a forecastle deck running from the slightly sloped stem to just short of the overhanging stern, the intention being to make disguise as an unknown liner relatively easy. The 6.4in were fore and aft with the 5.5in in upper deck casemates or sponsons. The *Châteaurenault* was considered a better steamer than *Guichen*. She was torpedoed and sunk by *UC38* between Taranto and Corfu, but the loss of life was small.

CHÂTEAURENAULT *protected cruiser*

Displacement: 7898t
Dimensions: 442ft 11in wl x 55ft 9in x 24ft 3in max *(135.00 x 17.00 x 7.39m)*
Machinery: 3-shaft VTE, 14 Normand Sigaudy boilers, 23,000ihp = 24kts. Coal 1960t max
Armament: 2-6.4in/45cal QF M1893, 6-5.5in/45cal QF M1893, 10-3pdr, 5-1pdr
Complement: 604

Name	Builder	Laid down	Launched	Comp	Fate
CHÂTEAURENAULT	La Seyne	May 1896	May 1898	1902	Sunk 14.12.17

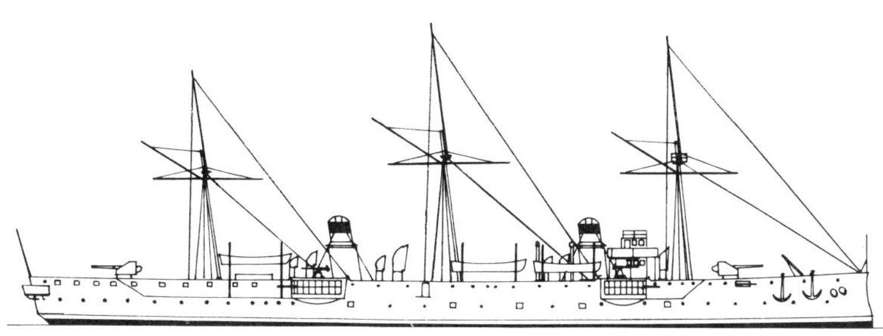
D'Estrées as completed 1899

Foreign service cruisers with a ram bow, overhanging stern, two widely spaced funnels and three (later two) masts. The 5.5in were on the forecastle and poop and the 3.9in in upper deck sponsons, all having shields. There was a small CT, and the curved armour deck was 1.7in-1.5in amidships and 0.8in at the ends. There was a cofferdam and cellular layer but no double bottom or longitudinal bulkhead, and the ships were wood-sheathed and coppered.

D'ESTRÉES class *protected cruisers*

Displacement: 2428t
Dimensions: 311ft 8in oa x 39ft 4in x 17ft 8in max *(95.00 x 12.00 x 5.39m)*
Machinery: 2-shaft VTE, 8 Normand boilers, 8500ihp = 20-20.5kts. Coal 470t
Armament: 2-5.5in/45cal QF, 4-3.9in, 8-3pdr, 2-1pdr
Complement: 235

Name	Builder	Laid down	Launched	Comp	Fate
D'ESTRÉES	Rochefort	Mar 1897	Oct 1897	1899	Stricken 1922
INFERNET	Soc de la Gironde	Dec 1896	Sept 1899	1900	Stranded 1910

Jurien de la Gravière as completed 1903

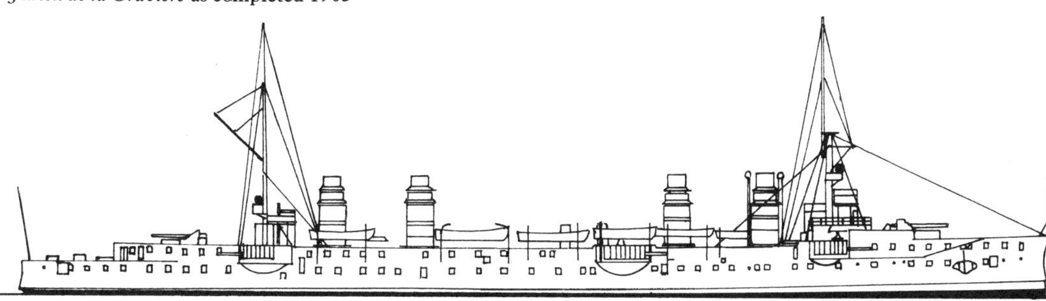

Of finer lines than most of the larger French cruisers, this ship had four funnels in widely spaced groups of two, a slightly overhanging stem and cruiser stern and a forecastle deck extending beyond the mainmast. The 6.4in were fore and aft on the forecastle deck with two guns on the upper deck in embrasures forward, two in midships sponsons and two in after ones. The guns had 2.8in shields and bases, the ammunition tubes 1in, and the CT 4in. The armour deck was 2.2in with 2.6in slopes amidships reduced to 2.2in-1.4in at the ends, and the deck above had 1in with a 15in wide cofferdam and cellular layer above the lower armour deck. The *Jurien de la Gravière* was wood sheathed and coppered and was very lightly built, vibrating greatly at speed. The engine rooms were very cramped and she was extremely unhandy with a reported tactical diameter of 2200yds. She was the last cruiser without side armour to be built for the French Navy until the *Duguay-Trouin* class laid down in 1922/1923.

JURIEN DE LA GRAVIÈRE *protected cruiser*

Displacement: 5595t
Dimensions: 449ft 5in oa x 49ft 3in x 20ft 8in max *(137.00 x 15.00 x 6.30m)*
Machinery: 3-shaft VTE, 24 Guyot du Temple boilers, 17,400ihp = 22.9kts. Coal 886t max
Armament: 8-6.4in/45cal QF M1893, 10-3pdr, 6-1pdr, 2-18in TT sub
Complement: 463

Name	Builder	Laid down	Launched	Comp	Fate
JURIEN DE LA GRAVIÈRE	Lorient	Nov 1897	June 1899	1903	Stricken 1922

UNPROTECTED CRUISERS

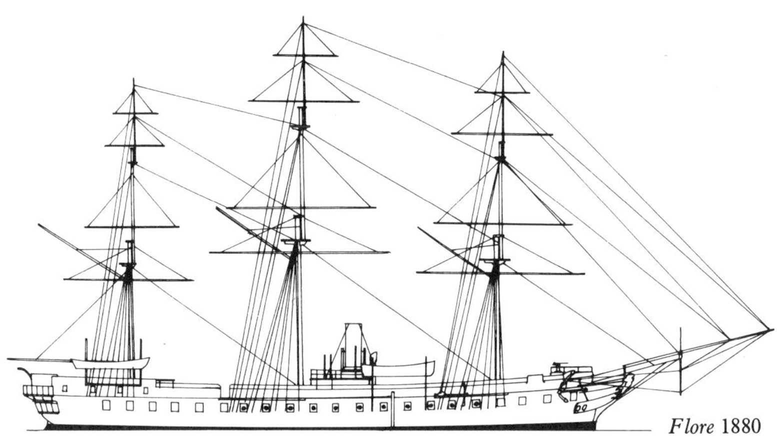

Flore 1880

Displacement, dimensions and machinery data are given for a selection only. Laid down as sailing frigates, *Guerrière*, *Pallas*, *Sémiramis* and *Victoire* being 56-gun, *Armorique* 42 and the rest 46. They were cut in half and lengthened amidships on the stocks and converted to screw under the programme of 1858. *Guerrière* later became a transport. *Flore* was nearly ready for launching in 1862 but this was delayed for seven years. Her final armament was 22-5.5in M1879M, of which 18 were on the main deck and 4 on the upper deck, and 3-3.9in on the upper deck and forecastle.

Converted sailing frigates

Displacement: *Armorique* 2740t, *Flore* 3430t, *Guerrière* 3935t, *Magicienne* 3355t
Dimensions: *Armorique* 249ft 3in pp x 44ft 7in x 19ft 4in max (*75.97 x 13.59 x 5.89m*); *Flore* 244ft 8in pp x 45ft 6in x 23ft 6in max (*74.57 x 13.87 x 7.16m*); *Guerrière* 245ft wl x 47ft 10in x 24ft 7in max (*74.67 x 14.58 x 7.49m*); *Magicienne* 246ft wl x 47ft 3in x 23ft max (*74.98 x 14.40 x 7.01m*)
Machinery: 1 shaft; *Armorique* 1175ihp = 10.4kts, coal 335t; *Flore* 1465ihp = 12.5kts, coal 350t; *Guerrière* 1736ihp = 11.2kts, coal 410t; *Magicienne* 1402ihp = 10.3kts, coal 430t
Armament: 24 to 36 guns, principally 6.4in M1860 and 5.5in RML
Complement: 344/399

Name	Builder	Laid down	Launched	Comp	Fate
ARMORIQUE	Lorient	Apr 1850	Mar 1862	1863	Hulked 1884
CIRCÉ	Rochefort	Apr 1847	1860	1862	Stricken 1875
FLORE	Rochefort	July 1847	Feb 1869	1870	Stricken 1886
GUERRIÈRE	Brest	June 1848	May 1860	1862	Stricken 1888
HERMIONE	Brest	May 1847	1860	1862	TS 1877
JUNON	Brest	Apr 1847	1861	1863	Stricken 1876
MAGICIENNE	Toulon	July 1845	Dec 1861	1863	Stricken 1886
PALLAS	Lorient	June 1848	1860	1862	Hulked 1883
SÉMIRAMIS	Rochefort	July 1829	1861	Jan 1863	Stricken 1877
THÉMIS	Toulon	Apr 1847	1862	1863	Stricken 1882
VICTOIRE	Lorient	June 1830	1861	Nov 1863	Stricken 1880

Wooden-hulled screw corvettes. The armament was later changed to 12-5.5in M1870 or 1870M.

COSMAO class

Displacement: 1795t
Dimensions: 220ft 8in wl x 37ft 4in x 18ft 8in max (*67.26 x 11.38 x 5.69m*)
Machinery: 1 shaft, oval boilers, 1215ihp = 11.4kts
Armament: 12-6.4in M1860
Complement: 203

Name	Builder	Laid down	Launched	Comp	Fate
COSMAO	Lorient	1856	1861	1862	Stricken 1881
DUPLEIX	Cherbourg	1856	1861	Jan 1863	Stricken 1887

A wooden-hulled, barque-rigged ship with clipper bows and a rounded and overhanging stern. She was later rearmed with 4-5.5in M1870 on the upper deck broadside, 2-3.9in mounted fore and aft and 4-1pdr revolvers.

TALISMAN

Displacement: 1387t
Dimensions: 224ft 3in wl x 33ft 7in x 16ft 1in max (*68.36 x 10.24 x 4.90m*)
Machinery: 1-shaft HC, 2 oval boilers, 690ihp = 11.3kts. Coal 265t
Armament: 2-6.4in, 4-4.7in
Complement: 148

Name	Builder	Laid down	Launched	Comp	Fate
TALISMAN	Normand	1860	1862	1863	Depot ship 1896

A 42 gun sailing frigate converted on the stocks to screw. Her engines were later removed and she served for many years as a sail training ship, surviving until 1913.

RÉSOLUE

Displacement 1795t
Dimensions: 167ft 3in pp x 43ft 9in x 21ft 3in max *(50.98 x 13.34 x 6.48m)*
Machinery: 1 shaft, oval boilers, 400nhp = 10kts
Armament: 13-6.4in or 5.5in
Complement: 299

Name	Builder	Laid down	Launched	Comp	Fate
RÉSOLUE	Cherbourg	Oct 1846	1863	1864	Stricken as warship 1890

Wooden-hulled screw frigates of traditional type. They were later rearmed with 14- or 16-5.5in/21cal M1870 of which 12 were on the gun deck. *Minerve* was accidentally destroyed by fire in 1897.

VÉNUS class

Displacement: 2745t
Dimensions: 246ft 1in pp x 42ft 5in x 21ft 6in max *(75.00 x 12.93 x 6.55m)*
Machinery: 1-shaft V, 6 oval boilers, 1200-1300ihp = 10.7kts. Coal 320t
Armament: 14-6.4in M1864, 8-33pdr SB
Complement: 344

Name	Builder	Laid down	Launched	Comp	Fate
MINERVE	Brest	1861	July 1865	1866	Hospital hulk 1888
VÉNUS	Brest	1861	Dec 1864	1866	Hulked 1887

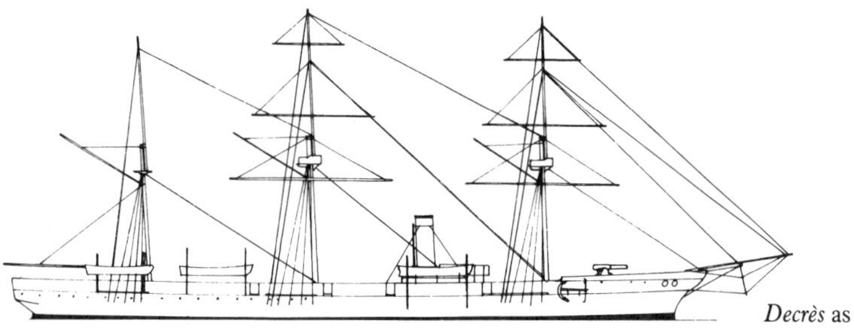
Decrès as completed 1869

A wooden-hulled cruiser. Her guns were altered to 1-6.4in/21cal M1870 and 9-5.5in/21cal M1870M on the upper deck, and a list of 1888 gives a sail area of 14,770 sq ft.

DECRÈS

Displacement: 1870t
Dimensions: 244ft 6in wl x 38ft 9in x 18ft 9in max *(74.52 x 11.81 x 5.72m)*
Machinery: 1-shaft HC, 4 oval boilers, 1470ihp = 12kts
Armament: 2-6.4in M1864 or 1866, 4-5.5in M1864 or 1867
Complement: 199

Name	Builder	Laid down	Launched	Comp	Fate
DECRÈS	Lorient	1861	Sept 1866	1868	Stricken 1890

This ship, named *Cassard* until 1866 and then *Jérôme Napoléon* to 1870, was wooden-hulled with clipper bow, forecastle and overhanging stern, and was originally used as an imperial yacht. She was schooner-rigged with a raking funnel between the masts and was later armed with 4-3.9in, 4-1pdr revolvers and 2-14in TT aw.

DESAIX

Displacement: 1722t
Dimensions: 259ft x 34ft 5in x 17ft 7in max *(78.94 x 10.49 x 5.36m)*
Machinery: 1-shaft VC, 4 oval boilers, 1440ihp = 14.2kts
Armament: 5-4.7in
Complement: 155

Name	Builder	Laid down	Launched	Comp	Fate
DESAIX	Normand	1861	1866	1868	Stricken 1894

Wooden-hulled ships mostly rigged as barques. The armament was later changed to 1-6.4in M1870 on the forecastle, 5-5.5in M1870 of which four were on the broadside and one on the poop, and 2-1pdr revolvers in *D'Estrées* and *Hamelin*, while *Limier* and *Volta* had another 5.5in instead of the 6.4in.

LIMIER class

Displacement: 1323t
Dimensions: 208ft wl x 34ft x 14ft 8in-15ft 11in max *(63.40 x 10.36 x 4.47-4.85m)*
Machinery: 1-shaft HC, 2 oval boilers, 1000-1100ihp = 12-12.5kts. Coal 200/235t
Armament: 1-6.4in M1864 or 1866, 4-5.5in M1864 or 1867
Complement: 154

Name	Builder	Laid down	Launched	Comp	Fate
D'ESTRÉES	Cherbourg	1864	1867	1869	Stricken 1891
HAMELIN	Lorient	1864	1866	1868	Hulked 1889
L'HERMITTE	Brest	1864	1867	1869	Wrecked 1874
LIMIER	Brest	1864	1866	1868	Stricken 1887
VOLTA	Cherbourg	1864	1867	1869	Stricken 1892

A wooden-hulled, barque-rigged cruiser, faster than most previous French ships of her size. She was later rearmed with 7-5.5in M1870 and 4-1pdr revolvers. Sail area is given as 14,100 sq ft.

CHÂTEAURENAULT

Displacement: 1820t
Dimensions: 256ft 6in pp x 35ft 3in x 18ft 10in max (*78.18 x 10.74 x 5.74m*)
Machinery: 1-shaft HC, 4 oval boilers, 1700ihp = 14.3kts
Armament: 1-6.4in M1864 or 1866, 6-5.5in M1864-67
Complement: 202

Name	Builder	Laid down	Launched	Comp	Fate
CHÂTEAURENAULT	Normand	1865	1868	1869	Hulked 1895

A wooden-hulled, barque-rigged small cruiser. The armament was later changed to 6-5.5in M1870, 2-1pdr revolvers and, it is thought, 2-14in TT aw. The machinery was rebuilt from that of the iron corvette *Chaptal* wrecked off Vera Cruz in 1862.

LINOIS

Displacement: 1191t
Dimensions: 203ft 4in wl x 32ft 1in x 15ft 11in max (*61.97 x 9.78 x 4.85m*)
Machinery: 1-shaft HC, 2 oval boilers, 720ihp = 11.5kts. Coal 215t
Armament: 4-5.5in M1864-67
Complement: 145

Name	Builder	Laid down	Launched	Comp	Fate
LINOIS	Toulon	1866	1867	1868	Stricken 1891

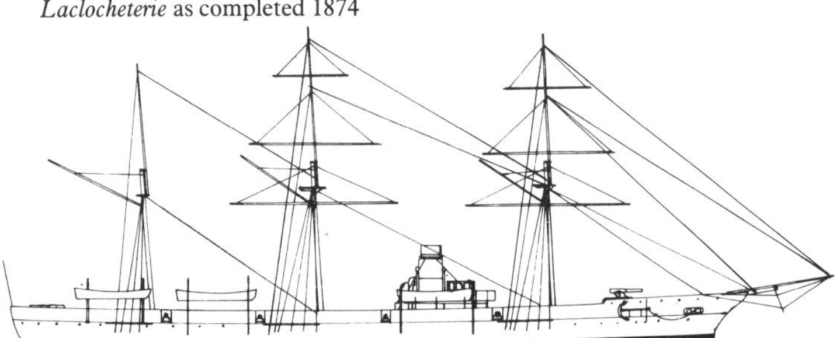

Laclocheterie as completed 1874

Laclocheterie at Hong Kong, 31 May 1886

Wooden-hulled ships rigged as barques without royals. There was a short forecastle and *Champlain*, *Dupetit-Thouars* and *Infernet* had straight stems whilst *Laclocheterie* had clipper bows. The 5.5in guns were on the upper deck broadside with a bow and stern chase gun. Tripod masts were tried in *Infernet*, and originally this ship had 3-7.6in guns, forward, midships and aft on the centreline, but they were removed after storm damage in January 1871.

INFERNET class

Displacement: 2042t average
Dimensions: 262ft wl x 35ft 9in x 18ft 9in max (*79.86 x 10.89 x 5.71m*)
Machinery: 1-shaft VC (*Laclocheterie* HC), 4 oval boilers, 1800-2000ihp = 13.7-15kts. Coal 300/330t
Armament: 8/10-5.5in M1870 or 1870M, later 4/8-1pdr revolvers and in *Champlain*, *Infernet* 2-14in TT aw added
Complement: 205

Name	Builder	Laid down	Launched	Comp	Fate
CHAMPLAIN	Brest	1867	1872	1874	Stricken 1893
DUPETIT-THOUARS	Brest	1867	1874	1876	Hulked 1897
INFERNET	Brest	1866	1869	1871	Stricken 1891
LACLOCHETERIE	Cherbourg	1867	1872	1874	Stricken 1901

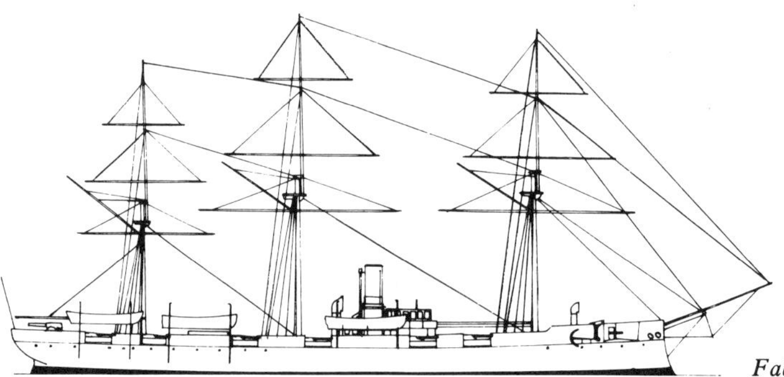

Fabert as completed 1876

Wooden-hulled, straight-stemmed ships rigged as barques without royals. There was a short forecastle and *Sané* had a tripod foremast. The 5.5in guns included a bow and a stern chaser with the rest on the upper deck broadside, the four in *Sané* being two to a sponson amidships.

SANÉ class

Displacement: 2017t average
Dimensions: 260ft 5in wl x 36ft 1in x 18ft 4in-19ft 3in max (*79.38 x 11.00 x 5.59-5.87m*)
Machinery: 1-shaft VC (*Fabert* HC), 4 oval (*Seignelay* 6 cyl) boilers, 1800-2000ihp = 14.9-15kts. Coal 330/350t
Armament: 8-, *Sané* 6-5.5in M1870 or 1870M, later 6/8-1pdr revolvers added
Complement: 203

Name	Builder	Laid down	Launched	Comp	Fate
FABERT	Rochefort	1868	1874	1876	Stricken 1899
SANÉ	Toulon	1867	1869	1872	Stricken 1892
SEIGNELAY	Toulon	1866	1874	1876	Wrecked 1892

A group of wooden-hulled ships, mostly barque-rigged without royals and differing in detail. The 6.4in or one of the 5.5in was mounted on the forecastle with a 5.5in on a raised platform aft and the others on the broadside. *Beautemps-Beaupré* and *Bourayne* had tripod foremasts, and *Bourayne* and *Dayot* originally had 1-7.6in and 6-5.5in. *Dayot* was lost in a cyclone at Tamatave.

BOURAYNE class

Displacement: 1330t
Dimensions: 207ft 6in wl x 34ft 2in x 16ft 4in max (*63.24 x 10.41 x 4.98m*)
Machinery: 1-shaft HC, 2 oval boilers, 900-1200ihp = 11.3-12.8kts. Coal 175/295t
Armament: 1-6.4in M1870, 5-5.5in M1870 or 6-5.5in only, 2/8-1pdr revolvers later added
Complement: 154

Name	Builder	Laid down	Launched	Comp	Fate
BEAUTEMPS-BEAUPRÉ	Brest	1867	1872	1874	Stricken 1896
BOURAYNE	Nantes	1867	1869	1870	Coal-hulk 1890
DAYOT	Nantes	1867	1869	1870	Foundered 28.2.88
DUCHAFFAULT	Cherbourg	1867	1872	1874	Stricken 1896
DUCOUËDIC	Brest	1867	1869	1872	Stricken 1889
HUGON	Brest	1867	1872	1874	Stricken 1896
KERGUELEN	Cherbourg	1867	1872	1874	Stricken 1894
KERSAINT	Lorient	1868	1869	1872	Stricken 1886
SEGOND	Nantes	1867	1869	1872	Stricken 1896
VAUDREUIL	Nantes	1867	1870	1873	Stricken 1889

Originally an Imperial yacht, the *Hirondelle* was wooden-hulled and ship-rigged. She was later reboilered with Bellevilles.

HIRONDELLE

Displacement: 1181t
Dimensions: 249ft 4in wl x 30ft 4in x 13ft 3in max (*76.00 x 9.25 x 4.04m*)
Machinery: 2-shaft VC, 4 oval boilers, 1900ihp = 15.6kts. Coal 160t
Armament: 4-3.9in, later 8-1pdr revolvers, 2-14in TT aw added
Complement: 135

Name	Builder	Laid down	Launched	Comp	Fate
HIRONDELLE	Le Havre	1869	1869	Converted 1873	Stricken 1896

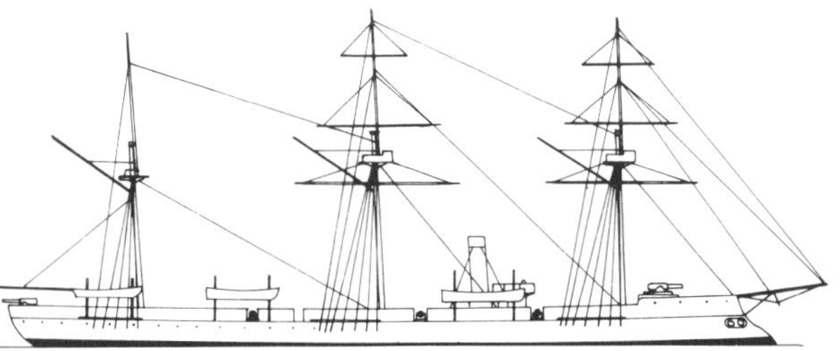

Éclaireur as completed 1879

Wooden-hulled ships but with iron beams and longitudinals. There was a very pronounced curved ram bow and a short forecastle and overhanging stern. *Rigualt de Genouilly* was rigged as a barque without royals and *Éclaireur* as a ship. The former was reboilered with Bellevilles in 1889/90, and in both the 5.5in were on the upper deck broadside with a bow and a stern chaser.

RIGAULT DE GENOUILLY class

Displacement: 1722t, *Éclaireur* 1800t
Dimensions: 242ft 6in wl x 35ft 5in x 17ft 7in-18ft max (*73.91 x 10.80 x 5.36-5.49m*)
Machinery: 1-shaft HC, 6 cyl boilers, 2400ihp = 15kts. Coal 205t
Armament: 8-5.5in M1870, 6/8-1pdr revolvers
Complement: 194

Name	Builder	Laid down	Launched	Comp	Fate
RIGAULT DE GENOUILLY	Brest	1873	1876	1878	Coal hulk 1899
ÉCLAIREUR	Toulon	1874	1877	1879	Stricken 1902

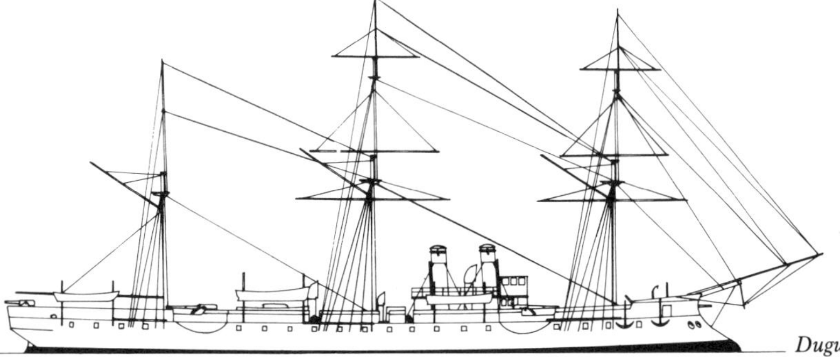

Duguay-Trouin as completed 1879

An iron-hulled cruiser, sheathed and coppered, with a pronounced curved ram bow and overhanging stern. She was rigged as a ship, later as a barque, with two funnels between the fore- and mainmasts, and had a short forecastle. There was a double bottom with 8 watertight transverse bulkheads and a collision bulkhead. The height between decks was small. The guns were on the upper deck with one 7.6in under the forecastle and four in sponsons, while there was one stern 5.5in and the rest on the broadside. The 7.6in were later replaced by 6.4in M1881 and the 10 revolvers reduced to 5 with 4-3pdr added. The *Duguay-Trouin* was renamed *Vétéran* when hulked, and the transport *Tonquin* took her name as a TS.

DUGUAY-TROUIN

Displacement: 3479t
Dimensions: 294ft 6in wl x 43ft 3in x 20ft 6in max (*89.76 x 13.18 x 6.25m*)
Machinery: 1-shaft HC, 8 oval boilers, 4800ihp = 15.5kts. Coal 490t max
Armament: 5-7.6in M1870, 5-5.5in M1870, 10-1pdr revolvers, 2-14in TT aw added
Complement: 322

Name	Builder	Laid down	Launched	Comp	Fate
DUGUAY-TROUIN	Cherbourg	1873	1877	1879	Hulked 1900

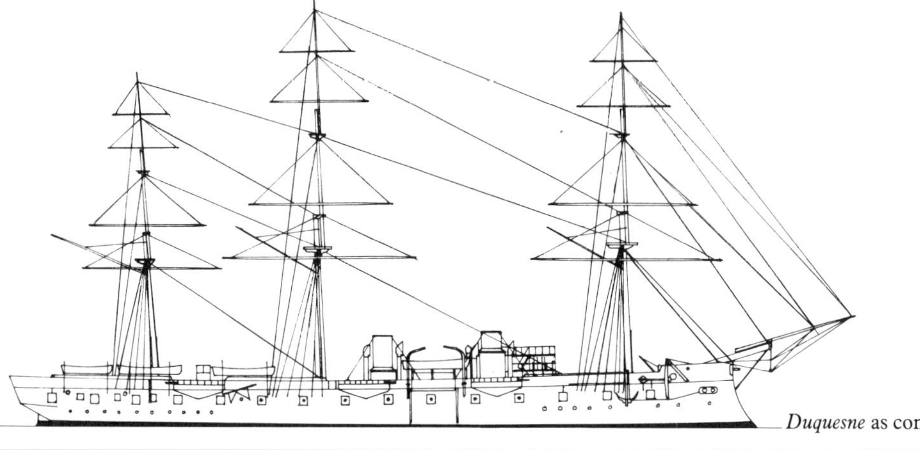
Duquesne as completed 1878

An iron-hulled cruiser, wood-sheathed and coppered, with a ram bow, overhanging stern and short forecastle. She was ship-rigged with two funnels between the fore- and mainmasts. There was a double bottom with eight watertight transverse bulkheads carried up to the main deck and a collision bulkhead in addition. The 7.6in were on the upper deck with one under the forecastle and the rest in sponsons, while the 5.5in were on the maindeck amidships. There were two boiler rooms and the engines appear to have given a good deal of trouble. *Duquesne* was reboilered with cylindrical boilers and had new HC engines in 1894, and a year later her guns were changed to 7-6.4in QFC, 14-5.5in QFC, 1-3.5in and 19-3pdr and 1pdr.

DUQUESNE

Displacement: 5905t
Dimensions: 329ft 4in wl x 50ft x 26ft 2in max (*100.37 x 15.24 x 7.98m*)
Machinery: 1-shaft HC, 12 oval boilers, 8000ihp = 16.8kts. Coal 900t max
Armament: 7-7.6in M1870, 14-5.5in M1870, 1-3.5in, 8-1pdr revolvers
Complement: 551

Name	Builder	Laid down	Launched	Comp	Fate
DUQUESNE	Rochefort	1873	1876	June 1878	Stricken 1901

Very similar to the *Duquesne*, but with engines on the Wolfe System which also appear to have given considerable trouble. Tactical diameter was said to be 680yds. The 7.6in guns were replaced by 6.4in M1881s, and in 1892 she was overhauled but did not receive new machinery, though her guns were later changed to QFC as in the *Duquesne*, with 1-3.5in and 18-3pdr and 1pdr.

TOURVILLE

Displacement: 5698t
Dimensions: 323ft 6in wl x 50ft 6in x 25ft 9in max (*98.60 x 15.39 x 7.85m*)
Machinery: 1-shaft HC, 12 oval boilers, 7460ihp = 16.9kts. Coal 650/1080t
Armament: 7-7.6in M1870, 14-5in M1870, 1-3.5in, 8-1pdr revolvers
Complement: 540

Name	Builder	Laid down	Launched	Comp	Fate
TOURVILLE	La Seyne	Aug 1873	1876	Nov 1877	Stricken 1901

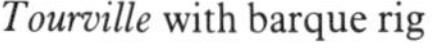
Tourville with barque rig

Lapérouse about 1890

Primauguet was laid down as the *Monge* and renamed in 1882. Wooden-hulled ships with iron beams and longitudinals and two strakes of iron and angle iron in the bottom. There was a plough bow with a forecastle, and they had a light barque or ship rig without royals. *Primauguet* differed in having two funnels close together on the centreline instead of one. Two of the 5.5in were on the forecastle with one on a raised platform aft and the rest on the upper deck broadside in slightly sponsoned ports with thin iron shields. In *Primauguet* the 5.5in were later replaced by QFC.

LAPÉROUSE class

Displacement: 2363t
Dimensions: 268ft 9in wl x 37ft 4in x 18ft 7in-19ft 3in max (*81.92 x 11.38 x 5.66-5.87m*)
Machinery: 1-shaft HC, 6 cyl boilers, 2750ihp = 15kts. Coal 300t
Armament: 15-5.5in M1870M, 8/10-1pdr revolvers
Complement: 264

Name	Builder	Laid down	Launched	Comp	Fate
D'ESTAING	Brest	1877	1879	1881	Stricken 1901
LAPÉROUSE	Brest	1875	1877	Feb 1880	Wrecked 1898
NIELLY	Brest	1876	1880	1882	Stricken 1902
PRIMAUGUET	Rochefort	1876	1882	Mar 1884	Stricken 1901

VILLARS class

Wooden-hulled ships with iron beams and longitudinals and a partial double bottom. There was a ram bow and forecastle and they were lightly rigged as barques or ships without royals. The 5.5in were arranged as in the *Lapérouse* class except that in *Magon* and *Roland* the two forward guns were below and not on the forecastle.

Displacement: 2382t average
Dimensions: 249ft 3in wl x 38ft x 17ft 2in-18ft max (*75.97 x 11.58 x 5.23-5.49m*)
Machinery: 1-shaft HC, 6 cyl boilers, 2750ihp = 14.5kts. Coal 400t
Armament: 15-5.5in M1870 or 1870M, 6/8-1pdr revolvers
Complement: 264

Name	Builder	Laid down	Launched	Comp	Fate
FORFAIT	Toulon	1876	1879	1880	Stricken 1897
MAGON	Cherbourg	1877	1880	1882	Stricken 1896
ROLAND	Cherbourg	1877	1882	1885	Stricken 1898
VILLARS	Cherbourg	1875	1879	1881	Stricken 1896

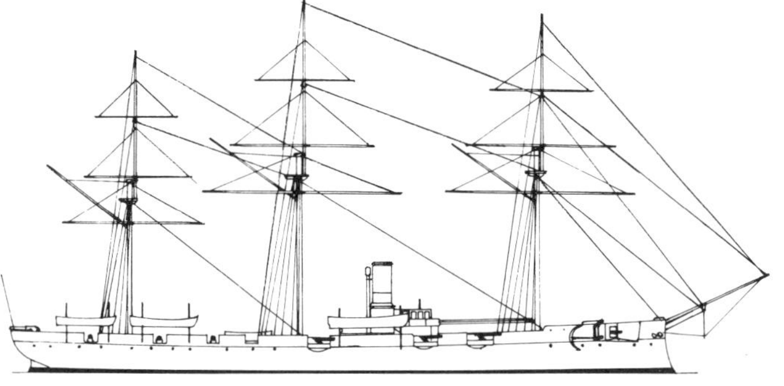
Villars as completed 1881

Iphigénie with full ship rig

IPHIGÉNIE

A wooden-hulled cruiser with ship rig, overhanging bow and stern, and short forecastle and poop. The funnel was abaft the mainmast. The 6.4in were in embrasure ports under the forecastle with 2-5.5in similarly under the poop, 4 on the upper deck and 12 on the main deck broadside. She later served, with a reduced armament, as a seagoing TS for midshipmen.

Displacement: 3346t
Dimensions: 240ft wl x 46ft 7in x 22ft 4in max (*73.15 x 14.20 x 6.81m*)
Machinery: 1-shaft HC, 6 cyl boilers, 2780ihp = 14kts. Coal 400t max
Armament: 2-6.4in M1870, 18-5.5in M1870M, 2-3.9in, 8-1pdr revolvers, 1-14in TT aw
Complement: 435

Name	Builder	Laid down	Launched	Comp	Fate
IPHIGÉNIE	Brest	Apr 1877	1881	Oct 1883	Stricken 1905

NAÏADE

A wooden-hulled cruiser with clipper bows, forecastle and poop. She was ship-rigged and the funnel was abaft the foremast. The guns were arranged as in the *Iphigénie*, but the 6.4in were later changed to M1881, and the TT removed. Her engines gave considerable trouble on trials.

Displacement: 3637t
Dimensions: 244ft wl x 46ft 9in x 23ft 6in max (*74.37 x 14.25 x 7.16m*)
Machinery: 1-shaft HC, 8 cyl boilers, 2800ihp = 14.7kts. Coal 450t
Armament: 2-6.4in M1870, 18-5.5in M1870M, 2-3.9in, 8-1pdr revolvers, 1-14in TT aw
Complement: 439

Name	Builder	Laid down	Launched	Comp	Fate
NAÏADE	Brest	1878	1881	Feb 1882	Stricken 1900

Naïade in the mid-1880s
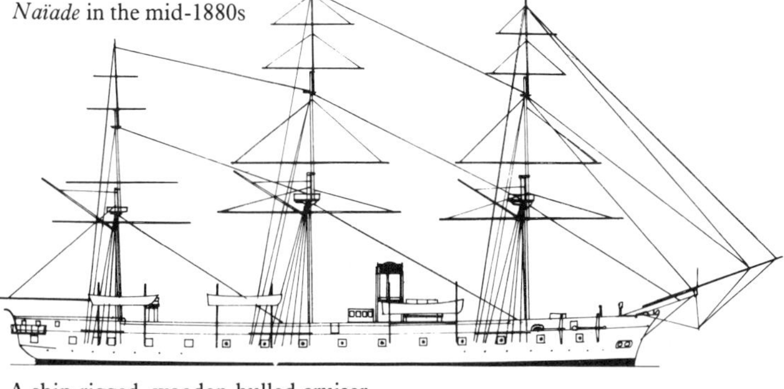

Aréthuse in the late-1880s

ARÉTHUSE

A ship-rigged, wooden-hulled cruiser with a ram bow and overhanging stern. There was a forecastle and poop with the funnel abaft the foremast. The 6.4in were in upper deck sponsons with 20-5.5in on the maindeck broadside and the other 2 on forecastle and poop. *Aréthuse* was reboilered in 1891 and had her engines repaired, and on trials in January 1892 attained 17kts with about 4000ihp. The 5.5in were reduced to 16, all on the main deck, and the 1pdr revolvers increased to 12.

Displacement: 3487t
Dimensions: 244ft wl x 46ft 9in x 22ft 8in max (*74.37 x 14.25 x 6.91m*)
Machinery: 1-shaft HC, 8 cyl boilers, 3200ihp = 15.5kts. Coal 500t
Armament: 4-6.4in/28cal M1881, 22-5.5in/30cal M1881, 8-1pdr revolvers
Complement: 467

Name	Builder	Laid down	Launched	Comp	Fate
ARÉTHUSE	Toulon	Feb 1879	1882	July 1885	Hulked 1899

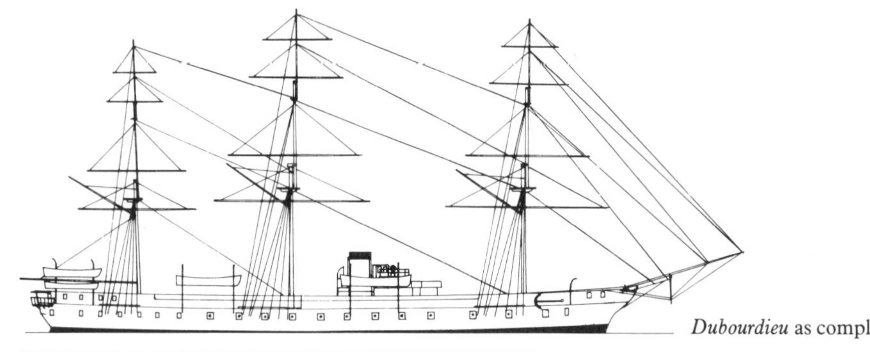
Dubourdieu as completed 1886

A ship-rigged, wooden-hulled cruiser with clipper bow, overhanging stern, forecastle and poop. The funnel was abaft the foremast. The 6.4in were in upper deck sponsons with the 5.5in on the main deck, two being right aft and the rest on the broadside. As in several other French ships of this type, touble was experienced with the engines.

DUBOURDIEU

Displacement: 3700t
Dimensions: 253ft 6in wl x 46ft x 21ft 8in max (*77.26 x 14.02 x 6.60m*)
Machinery: 1-shaft HC, 12 cyl boilers, 3000ihp = 13.9kts. Coal 600t
Armament: 4-6.4in/28cal M1881, 12-5.5in/30cal M1881, 1-3pdr revolver 10-1pdr revolvers, 2-14in TT aw
Complement: 412

Name	Builder	Laid down	Launched	Comp	Fate
DUBOURDIEU	Cherbourg	1880	1884	Sept 1886	Stricken 1899

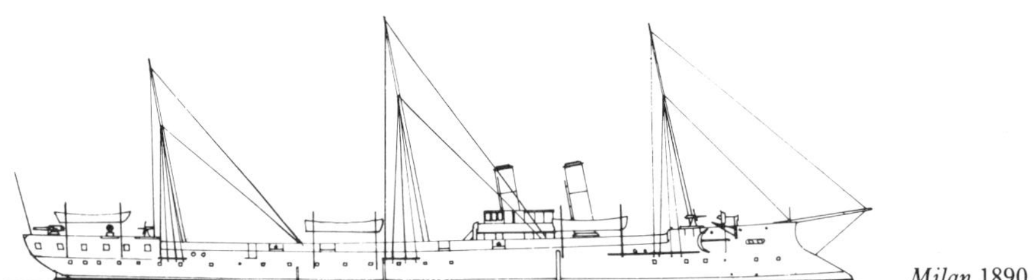
Milan 1890

A complete break with previous cruisers in this size range and the forerunner of the protected cruisers of the *Forbin* and *Troude* classes. The *Milan* was steel-hulled with a pronounced plough bow, overhanging stern, forecastle and poop. There were three light raking masts with a fore and aft rig, and two raking funnels abaft the foremast. The ship was lightly gunned and it had at one time been proposed to build her as an unarmed scout. The 3.9in guns were on the forecastle and poop with originally one on either beam in addition. Her engines were complicated and bulky but appear to have worked well after some alterations. Propeller vibration was excessive at high speed.

MILAN

Displacement: 1705t
Dimensions: 302ft oa x 32ft 9in x 15ft 7in max (*92.05 x 10.00 x 4.75m*)
Machinery: 2-shaft HC, 12 Belleville boilers, 4000ihp = 18.4kts. Coal 330t max
Armament: 4-3.9in, 8-1pdr revolvers, later 2-3.9in QFC, 12-3pdr, 2-14in TT aw
Complement: 194

Name	Builder	Laid down	Launched	Comp	Fate
MILAN	Soc de la Loire	1882	May 1884	1885	Stricken 1908

SLOOPS AND GUNBOATS

CURIEUX class

Displacement: 856t
Dimensions: 184ft 4in wl x 31ft 9in x 13ft mean (*56.18 x 9.68 x 3.96m*)
Machinery: 1 shaft, oval boilers, 560ihp = 10kts
Armament: 6-4.7in
Complement: 87

Name	Builder	Launched	Fate
CURIEUX	Honfleur	1860	Stricken 1879
DIAMANT	Bordeaux	1861	Stricken 1878

Wooden-hulled sloops laid down in 1860. The above dimensions are those of the *Bougainville*, laid down in 1858, which this class is believed to have resembled closely. *Curieux* was completed in 1861 and *Diamant* the following year.

ADONIS class

Displacement: 750t
Dimensions: 178ft wl x 28ft x 12ft mean (*54.25 x 8.53 x 3.66m*)
Machinery: 1 shaft, oval boilers, 550ihp = 10kts
Armament: 4-4.7in
Complement: 88

Name	Builder	Launched	Fate
ADONIS	Ajaccio	1863	Hulked 1883
AMPHION	Ajaccio	1863	Wrecked 21.4.66

Wooden-hulled sloops laid down in 1860 and completed in 1864. *Amphion* was lost off Vera Cruz.

GUICHEN class

Displacement: 748/787t
Dimensions: 182ft 6in wl x 28ft 1in x 12ft 11in max (*55.63 x 8.56 x 3.94m*)
Machinery: 1-shaft HC, 2 oval boilers, 575ihp = 10.7kts. Coal 90/100t
Armament: 1-6.4in, 4-4.7in
Complement: 85/99

Name	Builder	Launched	Fate
BOUVET	Rochefort	May 1865	Wrecked 17.9.71
BRUAT	Rochefort	Oct 1867	Hulked 1886
GUICHEN	Rochefort	1865	Stricken 1888

Barque-rigged wooden hulled sloops with clipper bows and raked masts and funnel. *Bruat* was laid down in 1866 and completed in 1868; the other pair were laid down in 1863 and completed in 1866. *Guichen* was later rearmed with 1-6.4in M1870 and 2-5.5in M1870, while *Bruat* finally had 3-5.5in, 1-3.9in and 3-1pdr revolvers. *Bouvet*, often confused with the next sloop of that name, was wrecked near Haiti. She was the only French warship to fight a sea action in the Franco-Prussian War, when she and the gunboat *Meteor* engaged indecisively off Havana on 9 November 1870.

RENARD

Displacement: 800t
Dimensions: 224ft 8in wl x 27ft 6in x 14ft 8in max (*68.48 x 8.38 x 4.47m*)
Machinery: 1-shaft HC, oval boilers, 550ihp = 11.5kts
Armament: 3 small guns
Complement: 88

Name	Builder	Launched	Fate
RENARD	Bordeaux	Jan 1866	Wrecked June 1885

Of finer lines than other French sloops, the *Renard* was wooden-hulled with a long plough bow. Laid down in 1864 and completed in 1867, she was rigged as a barquentine and her funnel and masts were raked. She was wrecked off Aden.

BRUIX class

Displacement: 767t
Dimensions: 200ft 10in wl x 28ft x 12ft 9in max (*61.20 x 8.53 x 3.89m*)
Machinery: 1-shaft HC, 2 cyl boilers, 680ihp = 11.5kts. Coal 100t max
Armament: 1-6.4in, 4-4.7in
Complement: 94

Name	Builder	Launched	Fate
BOURSAINT	Rochefort	1872	Stricken 1892
BRUIX	Bordeaux	1867	Stricken 1882

Ram-bowed, wooden-hulled sloops with iron beams and braces and rigged as barques without royals. *Bruix* was laid down in 1865 and completed in 1868, the respective dates for *Boursaint* being 1868 and 1873. *Boursaint* later mounted 1-5.5in M1870, 2-3.9in and 4-1pdr revolvers.

PARSEVAL class

Displacement: 856t
Dimensions: 199ft 4in wl x 28ft 1in x 13ft max (*60.75 x 8.56 x 3.96m*)
Machinery: 1-shaft HC, 2 cyl boilers, 800ihp = 11.4kts. Coal 150t
Armament: 4-5.5in M1870 (*Bouvet* 3-5.5in, 1-3.9in) 5/6-1pdr revolvers
Complement: 119

Name	Builder	Launched	Fate
BOUVET	Rochefort	May 1876	Stricken 1891
PARSEVAL	Rochefort	1879	Stricken 1900

Wooden-hulled ships with iron beams and braces and rigged as barques without royals, laid down in 1872. There was a short forecastle with ram bow and overhanging stern and one funnel which was raked, as were the masts. In *Parseval*, completed in 1880, the 5.5in were on the centreline, forward and aft with two amidships, while *Bouvet*, completed three years earlier, had one on the centreline between main and mizzenmasts with two on the broadside before the funnel and the 3.9in on the forecastle. *Bouvet* went ashore on Zanzibar in December 1889 and, though refloated, was never fully repaired. *Parseval* was renamed *Amiral Parseval* in 1895.

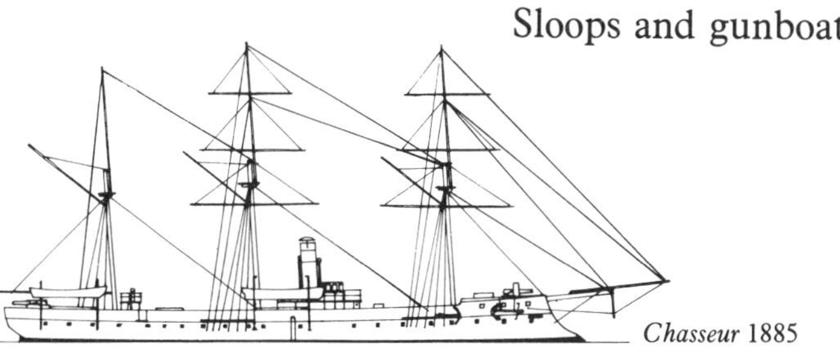
Chasseur 1885

BISSON class

Displacement: 846/935t
Dimensions: 201ft-201ft 10in wl x 28ft 6in x 12ft 8in-14ft 1in max (*61.26-61.51 x 8.69 x 3.86-4.29m*)
Machinery: 1-shaft VC (*Chasseur, Voltigeur* HC), 2 cyl boilers, 800ihp = 11.5-12kts. Coal 110/200t
Armament: 4-5.5in M1870 or 1870M, (*Bisson, Dumont d'Urville* 3-5.5in, 1-3.9in), 4/6-1pdr revolvers
Complement: 116

Name	Builder	Launched	Fate
BISSON	Normand	1874	Stricken 1892
CHASSEUR	Brest	1878	Stricken 1894
DUMONT D'URVILLE	Normand	1878	Stricken 1897
HUSSARD	Normand	1877	School ship 1897
LABOURDONNAIS	Normand	1875	Wrecked 21.2.93
VOLTIGEUR	Brest	1878	Stricken 1899

Laid down 1873-76 and completed 1875-79, this class generally resembled the *Parseval*, but the masts and funnel were not raked. The 5.5in were mounted fore and aft with two amidships on the centreline, the 3.9in replacing the forward 5.5in in the two ships with it. *Voltigeur* was later reboilered with Bellevilles. *Labourdonnais* was wrecked off Madagascar on Sainte-Marie.

INCONSTANT class

Displacement: 877/898t
Dimensions: 201ft oa x 26ft 3in x 13ft 8in max (*61.26 x 8.00 x 4.16m*)
Machinery: 1-shaft HC, 6 (*Papin* 4) cyl boilers, 1100ihp = 12kts (*Fulton* 13.8kts). Coal 160t max
Armament: 3-5.5in/30 M1881 or 1884, 1-3.9in, 5-1pdr revolvers
Complement: 116

Name	Builder	Launched	Fate
FULTON	Lorient	Jan 1887	Hulked 1910
INCONSTANT	Toulon	Aug 1886	Guard vessel 1900
PAPIN	Toulon	Nov 1886	Stricken 1900

Wooden-hulled sloops with iron beams, rigged as barques or barquentines and laid down in 1882. There was a short high forecastle, a pronounced ram bow, overhanging stern and a single tall funnel. One 5.5in was on the forecastle and two were amidships on the centreline with the 3.9in aft on a raised platform. *Inconstant* and *Papin* were completed in 1887 and were sold to Ecuador in 1901; *Fulton* was completed in 1888.

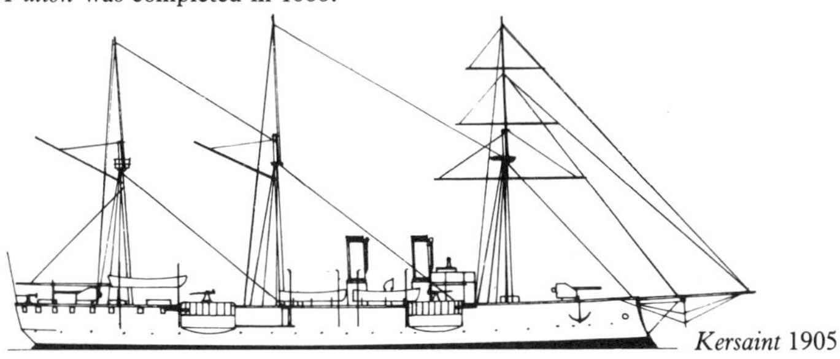
Kersaint 1905

KERSAINT

Displacement: 1276t
Dimensions: 225ft 2in oa x 34ft 5in x 15ft max (*68.63 x 10.49 x 4.57m*)
Machinery: 1-shaft VTE, 4 Lagrafel d'Allest boilers, 2400ihp = 16kts. Coal 196t max
Armament: 1-5.5in/45 QF M1893, 5-3.9in, 7-1pdr
Complement: 146

Name	Builder	Launched	Fate
KERSAINT	Rochefort	Aug 1897	Wrecked 5.3.1919

A steel-hulled sloop, sheathed and coppered with a ram bow and overhanging stern, laid down in 1896 and completed in October 1898. She was rigged as a barquentine, with two funnels between the fore and mainmast. The 5.5in was on the forecastle with one 3.9in on the poop and the others in upper deck sponsons. She was lost by stranding on a reef at Tahiti.

GUNBOATS

PIQUE class *wooden gunboats* (launched 1862-64)

Displacement: 360/405t
Dimensions: 127ft 4in wl x 22ft x 8ft 7in-9ft 10in max (*38.80 x 6.71 x 2.62-3.00m*)
Machinery: 1 shaft (*Pique* 2 shafts), oval boilers, 175/205ihp = 7.3/9.2kts. Coal 25/35t
Armament: 2-4.7in
Complement: 62

Class (builder, fate): *Décidée* (Toulon, stricken 1884), *Diligente* (Lorient, stricken 1878), *Pique* (Toulon, stricken 1886), *Surprise* (Toulon, hulked 1885) *Tactique* (Toulon, stricken 1886).

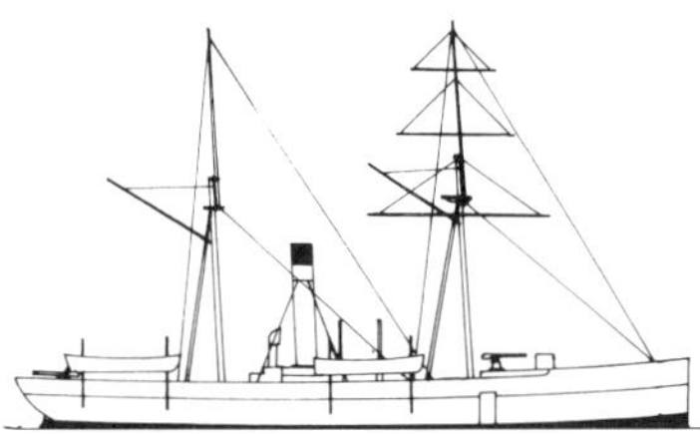

Étendard as completed 1869

ÉTENDARD class *wooden gunboats* (launched 1868)

Displacement: 445/500t
Dimensions: 142ft 6in wl x 24ft 3in x 8ft 3in-9ft max (*43.43 x 7.39 x 2.51-2.74m*)
Machinery: 2-shaft VC, 1 or 2 cyl boilers, 220/275ihp = 8.4/9.6kts. Coal 35/55t
Armament: 1-5.5in M1864-67, 1-4.7in
Complement: 69

Class (builder, fate): *Chacal* (La Seyne, stricken 1888), *Étendard* (Bordeaux, stricken 1892), *Fanfare* (Bordeaux, stricken 1891), *Gladiateur* (Bordeaux, stricken 1890), *Hyène, Jaguar, Léopard* (La Seyne, stricken 1889), *Oriflamme* (Bordeaux, stricken 1884).

CROCODILE class *composite gunboats* (launched 1874-82)

Displacement: 465/492t
Dimensions: 144ft 7in wl x 23ft 11in x 9ft 6in-10ft 10in max (*44.07 x 7.29 x 2.90-3.30m*)
Machinery: 1-shaft HC, 2 cyl boilers, 440ihp = 10/11kts. Coal 50t
Armament: 2-5.5in M1870 or 1870M, 2-3.9in, 2/4-1pdr revolvers
Complement: 76

Class (builder, fate): *Crocodile* (Cherbourg, hulked 1899), *Lionne* (Bordeaux, stricken 1888), *Lutin* (Cherbourg, transferred to Cambodia 1897), *Lynx* (Cherbourg, stricken 1899), *Aspic* (Rochefort, stricken 1906), *Capricorne* (Normand, stricken 1907), *Sagittaire* (Normand, stricken 1896), *Vipère* (Rochefort, stricken 1905).

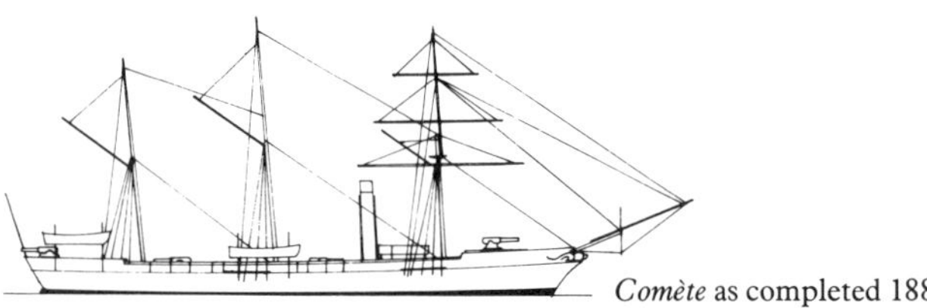

Comète as completed 1885

COMÈTE class *composite gunboats* (launched 1884-85)

Displacement: 492t
Dimensions: 151ft 6in pp x 24ft 9in x 10ft 6in max (*46.18 x 7.54 x 3.20m*)
Machinery: 1-shaft HC, 2 cyl boilers, 500ihp = 11-12kts. Coal 60/70t
Armament: 2-5.5in M1870M, 2-3.9in, 3-1pdr revolvers
Complement: 76

Class (builder, fate): *Comète* (Cherbourg, stricken 1909), *Gabès* (Rochefort, hulked 1902), *Lion* (Normand, stricken 1904), *Météore* (Cherbourg, stricken 1900), *Scorpion* (F C de la Méditerranée, stricken 1904).

ÉTOILE *river gunboat* (launched 1885)

Displacement: 442t
Dimensions: 149ft 2in pp x 24ft 7in x 8ft 4in max (*45.46 x 7.50 x 2.54m*)
Machinery 2-shaft VC, 2 cyl boilers, 400ihp = 11kts. Coal 45t
Armament: 6-3.9in, 2-1pdr revolvers
Complement: 78

Built at Lorient and stricken in 1898.

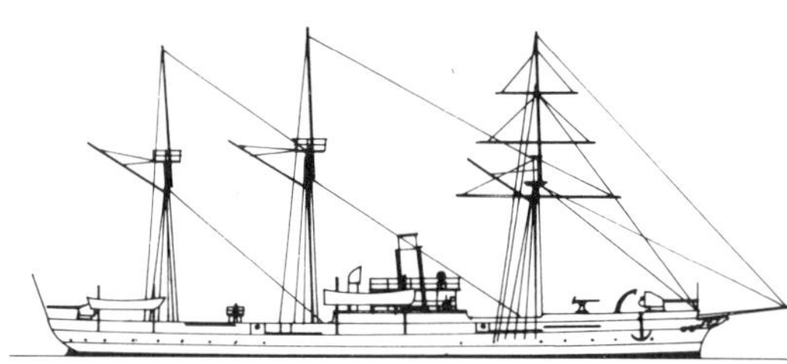

Surprise 1905

SURPRISE class *steel gunboats* (launched 1895-99)

Displacement: 617-637t
Dimensions: 183ft 9in-184ft 8in pp x 26ft-26ft 3in x 12ft 2in max (*56.00-56.28 x 7.92-8.00 x 3.71m*)
Machinery: 1-shaft HTE, 2 cyl boilers (*Décidée*, *Zélée* Niclausse), 900ihp = 13kts. Coal 74t
Armament: 2-3.9in, 4-9pdr, 4-1pdr
Complement: 99

Class (builder, fate): *Surprise* (Normand, sunk 3.12.1916), *Décidée* (Lorient, stricken 1922), *Zélée* (Rochefort, scuttled 29.9.1914).

UNDER 250 TONS

HACHE class *iron gunboats*

Displacement: 93t
Dimensions: 86ft 4in x 16ft 2in x 4ft 7in mean (*26.31 x 4.93 x 1.40m*)
Machinery: 60ihp = 5-6kts
Armament: 1-6.4in or 5.5in
Complement: 30

This class were originally numbered *Canonnière 32* to *40* but in 1866 were named *Hache*, *Hallebarde*, *Harpon*, *Javeline*, *Massue*, *Mousqueton*, *Sagaie*, *Yatagan* and *Caïman*. Where known, the builder was La Seyne. All were launched in1862 except *Caïman* 1864. The last survivor, *Sagaie*, was scrapped in 1898.

ARBALÈTE class *iron gunboats* (launched 1866-69)

Displacement: 100t
Dimensions: 81ft 9in x 15ft 7in x 4ft 6in mean (*24.92 x 4.75 x 1.37m*)
Machinery: 50ihp = 5/5.5kts. Coal 6.5t
Armament: 1-6.4in or 5.5in
Complement: 27

The 24 iron-hulled gunboats of this class resembled the *Hache* class and were named *Arbalte*, *Aspic*, *Baionnette*, *Biscaïen*, *Boutefeu*, *Caronade*, *Claymore*, *Couleuvre*, *Dard*, *Epieu*, *Escopette*, *Estoc*, *Flambant*, *Frelon*, *Fronde*, *Javelot*, *Lance*, *Mousquet*, *Obus*, *Pertuisane*, *Pierrier*, *Rapière*, *Sabre* and *Scorpion*. Where known the builder was usually La Seyne, but *Claymore* was built by Claparède and *Aspic*, *Couleuvre*, *Frelon* and *Scorpion* at Lorient.

REVOLVER class *iron gunboats* (launched 1869)

Displacement: 48t
Dimensions: 52ft pp x 15ft x 3ft 7in max (*15.85 x 4.57 x 1.09m*)
Machinery: 35ihp = 6.5kts. Coal 3t
Armament: 1-5.5in
Complement: 16

Iron-hulled gunboats of peculiar shape, resembling a slipper with an arched hollow on each side of the keel. They originally mounted a 9.4in and then a 7.6in, both of which were much too heavy. The class comprised *Revolver* and *Matrailleuse*, both built by Claparède, launched in 1869 and scrapped in 1889.

EPÉE *steel gunboat* (launched 1873)

Displacement: 185t
Dimensions: 78ft 9in x 23ft x 6ft max *(24.00 x 7.00 x 1.83m)*
Machinery: 2-shaft, 180ihp = 8.6kts. Coal 25t
Armament: 1-9.4in/19 M1870, 1-3.9in
Complement: 25

Built at Lorient and stricken in 1896.

TROMBLON *steel gunboat* (launched 1875)

Displacement: 202t
Dimensions: 82ft x 20ft 5in x 7ft 6in max *(25.00 x 6.22 x 2.29m)*
Machinery: 2-shaft, 200ihp = 9kts. Coal 25t
Armament: 1-9.4in/19 M1870, 1-3.9in
Complement: 25

Built at Toulon and stricken in 1898.

GABRIEL CHARMES *gunboat* (launched 1886)

Displacement: 73t
Dimensions: 137ft 4in oa x 12ft 6in x 6ft 7in max *(41.85 x 3.80 x 2.00m)*
Machinery: 1-shaft VC, 1 loco boiler, 580ihp = 19kts. Coal 11t
Armament: 1-5.5in/30 M1881
Complement: 23

Built at Toulon and stricken in 1907.

TORPEDO CRAFT

Because of the British war-time policy of close blockade, France had always shown an interest in mines and torpedoes for the defence of her coast. France experimented with the early spar- and towing-torpedoes and naturally the *'Commission des défenses sous-marines'* (reformed in 1872 after the Prussian War) took an active interest in Whitehead's experiments. Trials were carried out with various craft, to test launching systems, and in 1875 it was concluded that specially-built fast craft were the best launching vehicles, and that these should be of two types – a sea-going vessel for use in the North Sea, and a port-defence craft. Seven trials boats were ordered including one from Yarrow and two from Thornycroft in England, varying in type from No *1*, which was the attempt at a sea-going design, to No 7 which was little more than an enlarged steam picket boat. No *1* was an interesting vessel with two centreline submerged TT, one forward and one aft, which fired the torpedo by means of a steam-powered ram. However, this craft was a great disappointment and the construction of sea-going boats was abandoned for 10 years; the Thornycroft TBs were a corresponding success, a dozen more being ordered. Meanwhile three French builders were invited to submit designs, and this *27-metre* type became the first successful French-designed TB.

Between 1878 and 1884, three types of TB were built: a series of standard and improved *27-metre* boats; a small group of *'torpilleurs-vedettes'* designed to be carried into action by a special transport; and three larger experimental craft. During this period Normand established his reputation as the finest TB builder in France and of the larger craft the Normand design became the model for the successful *33-metre* type, the first French TBs with a reasonable radius of action. However, the French Navy was very much under the spell of the *'Jeune École'* who stressed the value of large numbers of small craft, and this influential lobby resisted the natural growth in TB size.

However, in 1884 a new type of sea-going TB was planned, but at much the same time Admiral Aube (the leading light of the *'Jeune École'*) became Minister of Marine and re-affirmed the need for small TBs. The resulting class of *35-metres* must be ranked among the worst TBs ever built, but although heavily criticised, political pressure caused a total of 50 to be constructed. In the ensuing controversy Aube was forced to resign but not before he had organised local port defence flotillas (1886), and henceforth all the small TBs were known as *'Torpilleurs de défense mobile'*.

After the disastrous *35-metres*, Normand produced the classic *126* design, which became the model for virtually all the succeeding TBs, of the *'défense mobile'*, which continued to be built down to 1908.

SEA-GOING TORPEDO BOATS

Despite the coast defence emphasis of the *'Jeune École'*, TBs for fleet duties were planned and in 1884 a Normand design was accepted. The *Balny* class were reasonable TBs but showed the baleful influence of the *'Jeune École'* in their small size and were rapidly relegated to the *'défense mobile'*. The succeeding *Ouragan* class, although larger, were dismal failures, and in 1887 a series of prototypes was ordered from Thornycroft *(Coureur)*, Normand *(Avant-Garde)* and la Seyne *(Agile)*, followed in each case by other boats to the same design. From 1890 these larger TBs were known as *'Torpilleurs de haute mer'*. This was a period of major developments in boiler design and in the 1890s the French TB force became involved in a series of lengthy, difficult and in some cases disastrous experiments with various forms of watertube boiler. They offered power advantages but very few were robust or reliable enough for torpedo craft.

In 1891 a further series of prototypes was ordered, intended to test the feasibility of a 27kt TB. As usual the Normand boat, *Chevalier*, was the most successful, although three different groups were ordered in 1892. Normand further improved upon *Chevalier* with the famous *Forban*, the first vessel to make more than 30kts, and the succeeding *Cyclone* and *Mistral* (1898) classes were based on this design. However, even with the splinter-armour fitted to the *Mistrals*, the *'torpilleurs de haute mer'* were outclassed by the new destroyers and no more were ordered after 1898.

DESTROYERS

France, like Britain, had built a number of unsuccessful 'torpedo-catchers' (*aviso-torpilleurs*) and when the first British torpedo boat destroyers appeared in 1893-94 the French were already working on the same lines. Various plans were considered in 1895-96, and these resulted in Normand designing the *Durandal* in 1896. The hull of this vessel was an enlarged version of that of the *'torpilleur de haute mer' Filibustier*, but the scantlings were increased to make the hull stronger. All the *300 tonnes* were given a well-rounded hull form, with a flying deck amidships and aft, and except for the four-funnelled *Framée* class they resembled each other closely. They had good initial stability and a high command for the guns (though these were not as powerful as those on the British TBDs), and their two single tubes each had a reload torpedo. Their boilers and machinery were relatively reliable and their screws were well submerged, lessening the danger of cavitation. They were however top-heavy, particularly the *Claymores* and the *Branlebases* which had a less rounded upper hull and extra superstructure; apart from this, they were good sea boats although the speed fell off in heavy seas.

When the first *300 tonnes* were built they were equal to any foreign equivalent, but they were developed too slowly and by 1903 they had been outclassed by the larger and more heavily armed British TBDs. Unfortunately, only detail improvements were made to the design, owing to the remaining influence of the *Jeune École* which still stressed the advantages of relatively small craft. Even the fitting of splinter armour to the *Branlebas* class and the ordering of the first *450-tonne contre-torpilleur* in 1906 were not enough to catch up with foreign designs.

After the Russo-Japanese War had been evaluated four *300 tonnes*, *Flamberge*, *Baliste*, *Hache* and *Massue*, were fitted for minelaying between 1909 and 1912, and a number of others were fitted with light sweeps. Wartime experience showed the need for anti-aircraft and anti-submarine armament, and in 1915 the two aft 47mm guns in each ship were modified to give AA fire. In 1917-18 some received 8mm MGs as well. Many *300 tonnes* had the 65mm gun replaced by an Army 75mm, and in the autumn of 1917 some were fitted with a Thornycroft AS mortar in place of the aft torpedo tube. However, this was landed in 1918 and the torpedo tube replaced. After the war, some *300 tonnes* were used for instruction and were disarmed. They were employed either in squadrons of six or as leaders to the torpedo boat squadrons.

FRANCE

TORPEDO CRUISERS

Small, one-funnelled cruisers with plough bows, forecastle and poop and originally three masts, later reduced to two. They were usually classed as torpedo cruisers, that is, as large torpedo gunboats. The 3.9in guns were distributed two forward on the upper deck in embrasure ports, two in upper deck sponsons and one on the poop. The TT were later removed. The curved armour deck was 1.6in and there was a cofferdam above and splinter deck below over the machinery spaces. *Vautour* was later fitted to burn oil with coal.

CONDOR class *torpedo cruisers*

Displacement: 1229t (1268t *Épervier*, 1311t *Faucon*, 1266t *Vautour*)
Dimensions: 223ft 1in pp x 29ft 6in x 15ft 5in max (*68.00 x 9.00 x 4.70m*)
Machinery: 2-shaft IC (*Vautour* HC), 4 cyl (*Vautour* 4 loco) boilers, 3000ihp = 17/17.5kts. Coal 160t max
Armament: 5-3.9in, 4-3pdr, 6-1pdr revolvers, 4-14in TT aw
Complement: 156

Name	Builder	Laid down	Launched	Comp	Fate
CONDOR	Rochefort	Apr 1883	May 1885	Nov 1886	Stricken 1907
ÉPERVIER	Rochefort	May 1884	1886	1887	Stricken 1911
FAUCON	Toulon	Feb 1884	1887	Nov 1887	Stricken 1920
VAUTOUR	Toulon	Apr 1884	Apr 1889	Dec 1889	Stricken 1908

Vautour about 1890

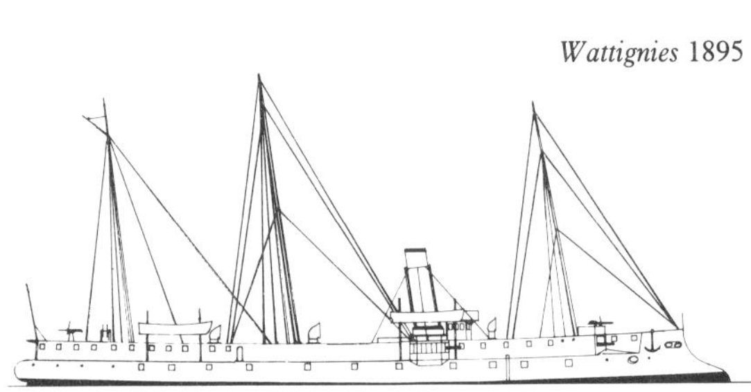
Wattignies 1895

Similar to the earlier *Condor* class except where indicated above. *Fleurus* should have been completed in 1894 but was delayed by defective boilers. The TT were later removed.

WATTIGNIES class *torpedo cruisers*

Displacement: 1280t
Dimensions: 223ft 1in pp x 29ft 3in x 15ft 9in max (*68.00 x 8.92 x 4.80m*)
Machinery: 2-shaft HTE, 4 loco (*Fleurus* 8 Niclausse) boilers, 4000ihp = 18/18.5kts. Coal 160t max
Armament: 5-3.9in, 6-3pdr, 4-1pdr, 4-14in TT aw
Complement: 162/173

Name	Builder	Laid down	Launched	Comp	Fate
FLEURUS	Cherbourg	Mar 1891	Mar 1893	Oct 1898	Stricken 1910
WATTIGNIES	Rochefort	Oct 1889	Apr 1891	May 1892	Stricken 1908

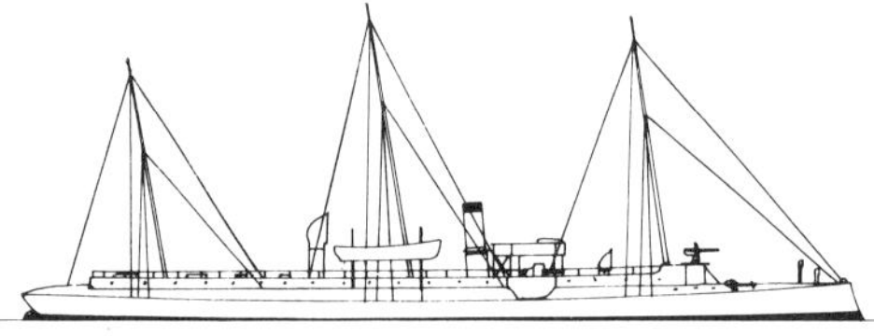
Bombe as completed 1887

These vessels had three light raking masts, originally with a fore and aft rig, and a single raking funnel abaft the foremast. The bow was slightly ram-shaped with an overhanging stern and the sides curved in to a narrow upper deck. The CT had 0.5in plating and the 3pdrs were mounted forward and aft and in sponsons on either beam, with the TT in sponsons further aft. *Dragonne* was fitted for experiments with howitzers in 1896. The boilers in this class gave great trouble and led to delay in completion. Eventually *Bombe, Dague, Lance, Saint-Barbe* and *Salve* had 4 Guyot du Temple, *Flèche* 4 Lagrafel d'Allest boilers, although *Couleuvrine* and *Dragonne* retained 4 locomotive boilers.

BOMBE class *torpedo gunboats*

Displacement: 369t (*Couleuvrine*) to 430t (*Sainte-Barbe*)
Dimensions: 194ft 3in pp x 19ft 7in x 10ft 5in max (*59.20 x 5.97 x 3.17m*)
Machinery: 2-shaft VC, 4 loco boilers, 1800ihp = 18-19kts. Coal 108t max
Armament: 2-3pdr, 5-1pdr revolvers (soon changed to 4-3pdr, 3-1pdr revolvers), 2-14in TT aw
Complement: 70

Name	Builder	Laid down	Launched	Comp	Fate
BOMBE	F C de la Méditerranée	Nov 1883	Apr 1885	Oct 1887	Stricken 1911
COULEUVRINE	F C de la Méditerranée	1883	June 1885	1887	Stricken 1911
DAGUE	F C de la Méditerranée	June 1884	June 1885	1888	Stricken 1905
DRAGONNE	F C de la Méditerranée	Oct 1884	Aug 1885	1888	Stricken 1910
FLÈCHE	F C de la Méditerranée	Oct 1884	Nov 1885	1888	Stricken 1912
LANCE	F C de la Méditerranée	Dec 1884	Apr 1886	1890	Stricken 1914
SAINTE-BARBE	Claparède	1884	Oct 1885	1890	Stricken 1911
SALVE	Claparède	1884	Feb 1886	1890	Stricken 1906

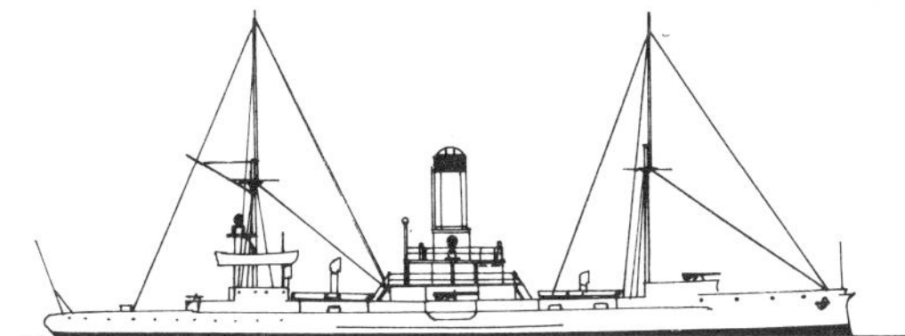
Léger 1896

This class had a single large funnel and two masts. The stem was straight and there was a forecastle continued by the upperworks to 30ft from the stern, with the hull sides curved as in the previous class. The 9pdr was forward, the 3pdrs aft and sponsoned on either beam, and the TT were forward and aft of the funnel. The bow TT was removed.

LÉVRIER class *torpedo gunboats*

Displacement: 503t
Dimensions: 206ft 7in oa x 22ft 10in x 10ft 6in max *(62.97 x 6.96 x 3.20m)*
Machinery: 2-shaft VTE, 6 Belleville boilers, 2400ihp = 18.7kts. Coal 127t max
Armament: 1-9pdr, 3-3pdr, 2-1pdr, 3- later 2-18in TT aw
Complement: 89

Name	Builder	Laid down	Launched	Comp	Fate
LÉGER	Lorient	Feb 1890	Aug 1891	Dec 1891	Stricken 1910
LÉVRIER	Lorient	Feb 1890	Apr 1891	Dec 1891	Stricken 1910

Sainte Barbe, an *'aviso-torpilleur'*

Cassini in August 1906

Two-funnelled ships with a forecastle and poop, a ram bow and two masts. The 3.9in was forward and the 9pdrs aft and on either beam. *D'Iberville* had a 0.8in deck thickened to 1.6in on the slopes in wake of the machinery spaces, and 1.6in on the CT, while the other two had 0.8in on the deck over the machinery spaces and 0.8in on the side in wake. They were reported to roll very heavily in a seaway. The TT were removed from *d'Iberville* by 1899 and reduced to 2 in *Casabianca* and *Cassini*. The two latter were converted to minelayers in 1913; *Casabianca* blew up on a mine off Smyrna, whilst *Cassini* was sunk by a submarine in the Strait of Bonifacio.

D'IBERVILLE class *torpedo gunboats*

Displacement: 952t, *Casabianca, Cassini* 970t
Dimensions: 262ft 6in pp x 26ft 6in-26ft 11in x 11ft 4in max *(80.00 x 8.08-8.20 x 3.45m)*
Machinery: 2-shaft VQE (*Casabianca* VTE), 8 Lagrafel d'Allest boilers, 5000ihp = 21.5-22kts. Coal 115t max
Armament: 1-3.9in, 3-9pdr, 6/7-3pdr, 6-, *Cassini, Casabianca* 3-18in TT aw
Complement: 140/143

Name	Builder	Laid down	Launched	Comp	Fate
CASABIANCA	Soc de la Gironde	Jan 1894	Sept 1895	1896	Sunk 3.6.1915
CASSINI	F C de la Méditerranée	Nov 1892	June 1894	1895	Sunk 20.2.1917
D'IBERVILLE	Soc de la Loire	Aug 1891	aug 1893	1894	Stricken 1922

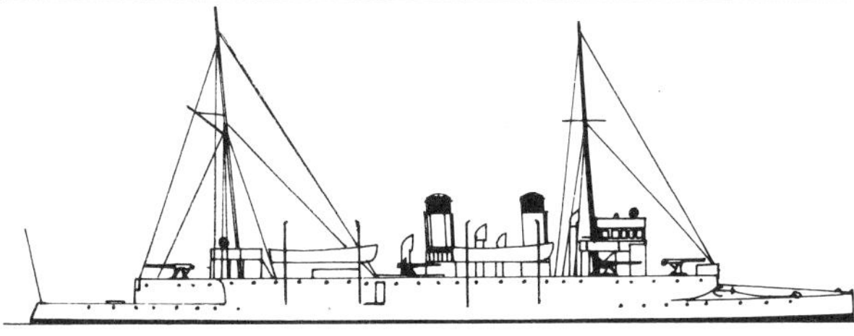
Dunois as completed 1898

Two-funnelled, two-masted ships with a straight stem, turtledeck forward and a spar deck amidships on which the 9pdr guns were mounted with one forward and aft and two on each side. There were no TT in this class. The lower deck was 0.4in thick and there was 2in on the CT. The French classed these ships as *contre-torpilleurs*, ie destroyers, but they were much too slow to be so rated.

DUNOIS class *torpedo gunboats*

Displacement: 889t
Dimensions: 255ft 11in oa x 27ft 10in x 12ft 8in max *(78.00 x 8.48 x 3.86m)*
Machinery: 2-shaft VTE, 8 Normand Sigaudy boilers, 7500ihp = 21.7-22kts. Coal 135t max
Armament: 6-9pdr, 6-3pdr
Complement: 137

Name	Builder	Laid down	Launched	Comp	Fate
DUNOIS	Cherbourg	Sept 1896	Oct 1897	Dec 1898	Stricken 1920
LAHIRE	Cherbourg	Nov 1897	Nov 1898	1899	Stricken 1922

A ship of cruiser type with three funnels close together and overhead gear for handling her TBs forward and aft of the funnels. The 3.9in were at bow and stern with six in upper deck sponsons. The armour deck was 2.3in total on the flat and 4.6in max on the slopes, and there was the usual cofferdam and cellular layer above, with 4.7in on the CT. The 60ft TBs for the *Foudre* were known by letters *A* to *I*. Of these, eight were built by Le

FOUDRE *torpedo depot ship*

Displacement: 5994t
Dimensions: 380ft 7in oa x 51ft 2in x 23ft 5in max *(116.00 x 15.60 x 7.14m)*
Machinery: 2-shaft VTE, 24 Lagrafel d'Allest boilers, 11,500ihp = 19kts. Coal 1260t max
Armament: 8-3.9in, 4-9pdr, 4-1pdr, 8- max 10-60ft TBs
Complement: 410

Name	Builder	Laid down	Launched	Comp	Fate
FOUDRE	Soc de la Gironde	June 1892	Oct 1895	Sept 1897	Stricken 1921

Creusot at Chalons-sur-Saône, and one, *C*, by Yarrow. The *Foudre* was converted to a minelayer and then in 1912 to a seaplane carrier with a hangar abaft the funnels, and operated two aircraft in the 1913 manoeuvres, one being hoisted out and the other launched from a runway.

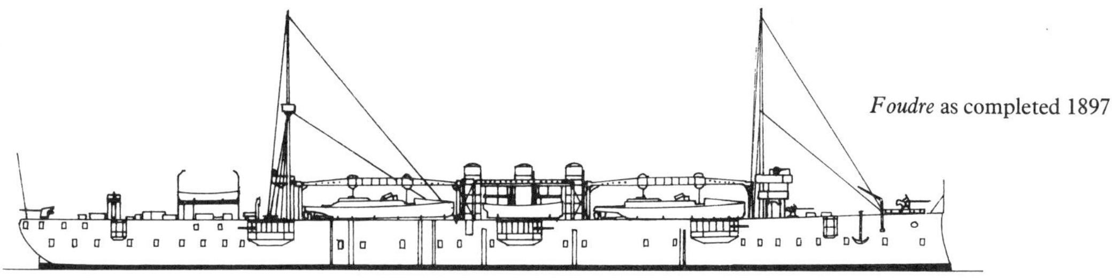

Foudre as completed 1897

DESTROYERS

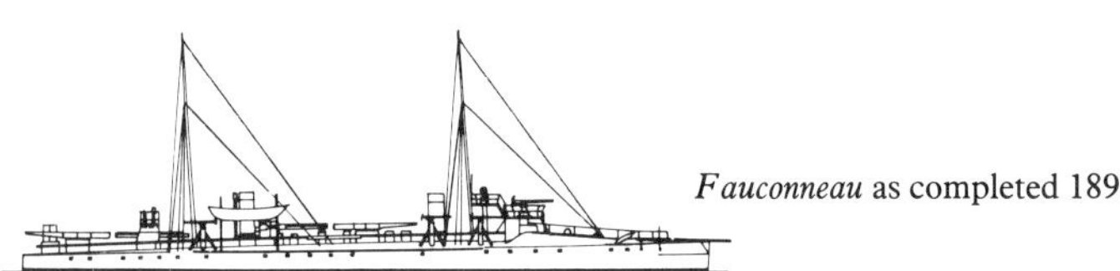

Fauconneau as completed 1897

DURANDAL class

Displacement: 296t, *Fauconneau* and *Espingole* 306t
Dimensions: 188ft 8in oa x 20ft 8in x 10ft 5in (*57.50 x 6.30 x 3.17m*)
Machinery: 2-shaft TE, 2 Normand wt boilers, 4800ihp = 26kts. Coal 38.2/?t
Armament: 1-65mm, 6-47mm (6x1), 2-15in TT (2x1)
Complement: 52

Name	Builder	Launched	Fate
DURANDAL	Normand	11.2.1899	Stricken 7.4.1919
HALLEBARDE	Normand	8.6.1899	Stricken 4.3.1920
FAUCONNEAU	Normand	2.4.1900	Stricken 15.1.21
ESPINGOLE	Normand	28.6.1900	Sunk 4.2.03

Durandal and *Hallebarde* were designed by Normand and ordered on 25.8.1896 as prototypes of the *300 tonne contre-torpilleur*. They had a turtledeck forecastle and a flying deck aft, with two masts and two funnels separated by the machinery. *Fauconneau* and *Espingole* differed by having a stronger hull and a slightly raised bow. The boilers in this class were long and difficult to fire. Laid down 1896/7, trials 1899/1900.

ROCHEFORTAIS class

Displacement: 306t
Dimensions: 188ft 8in oa x 20ft 8in x 10ft 5in (*57.50 x 6.30 x 3.17m*)
Machinery: 2-shaft TE, 2 boilers, 4800ihp = 26kts. Coal 38.2/?t
Armament: 1-65mm, 6-47mm (6x1), 2-15in TT (2x1)
Complement: 52

Name	Builder	Launched	Fate
PERTUISANE	Rochefort	5.12.1900	Stricken 16.3.23
ESCOPETTE	Rochefort	20.12.1900	Stricken 4.4.21
FLAMBERGE	Rochefort	28.10.1901	Stricken 1.10.20
RAPIÈRE	Rochefort	16.7.1901	Stricken 27.10.21

Also known as the *Pertuisane* class, these vessels were ordered 8.6.1899 to Normand plans and were laid down between June 1899 and January 1900. They were very similar to *Fauconneau* and *Espingole* except that their funnels were slightly raked. Trials 1902/3.

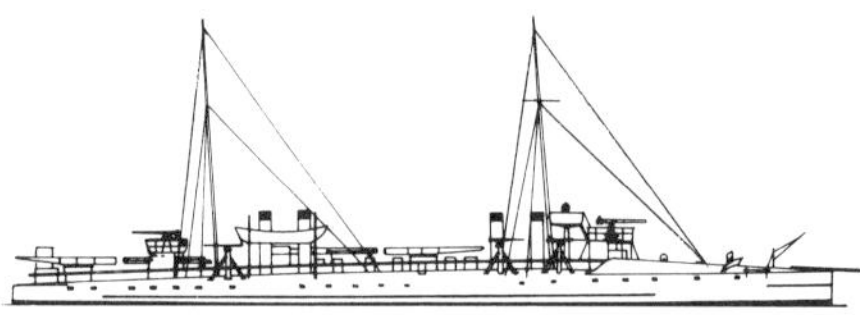

Pique as completed 1901

FRAMÉE class

Displacement: 314t
Dimensions: 190ft 7in oa x 20ft 8in x 9ft 10in (*58.09 x 6.30 x 3.00m*)
Machinery: 2-shaft TE, 4 boilers, 4800-5200ihp = 26kts. Coal 38.2/79.1t
Armament: 1-65mm, 6-47mm (6x1), 2-15in TT (2x1)
Complement: 48

Name	Builder	Launched	Fate
FRAMÉE	St Nazaire	21.10.1899	Sunk 11.8.1900
YATAGAN	St Nazaire,	20.7.1900	Sunk 3.11.1916
PIQUE	La Seyne	31.3.1900	Stricken 28.1.21
EPÉE	La Seyne	27.7.1900	Stricken 1.10.20

Laid down in 1897, these differed from the *Durandals* mainly in having four boilers and four funnels. The weights were also redistributed to give a higher centre of gravity, but this led to instability. *Pique* especially had too much topweight, and the mainmasts and aft control positions were removed from each ship. They had problems reacing their designed speed on trials.

ARQUEBUSE class

Displacement: 298t
Dimensions: 190ft 11in oa x 21ft x 10ft 5in (*58.19 x 6.40 x 3.17m*)
Machinery: 2-shaft TE, 2 Normand or Du Temple boilers, 6300ihp = 28kts. Coal 26.4/46.6t
Armament: 1-65mm, 6-47mm (6x1), 2-15in TT (2x1)
Complement: 60

Name	Builder	Launched	Fate
CARABINE	Rochefort	21.7.1902	Stricken 8.1.19
SARBACANE	Rochefort	12.3.1903	Stricken 1.10.20
ARQUEBUSE	Normand	15.11.1902	Stricken 10.5.20
ARBALÈTE	Normand	28.4.1903	Stricken 21.6.20
MOUSQUET	St Nazaire	7.8.1902	Sunk 28.10.14
JAVELINE	St Nazaire	15.10.1902	Stricken 12.1.20
SAGAIE	La Seyne	15.11.1902	Stricken 1.10.20
EPIEU	La Seyne	17.1.1903	Stricken 28.2.21
HARPON	Bordeaux	20.10.1902	Stricken 5.3.21
FRONDE	Bordeaux	17.12.1902	Stricken 30.10.19
FRANCISQUE	Rochefort	2.3.1904	Stricken 4.4.21
SABRE	Rochefort	15.4.1904	Stricken 5.1.21
DARD	Penhoët, St Nazaire	10.9.1903	Stricken 3.4.19
BALISTE	Penhoët, St Nazaire	22.10.1903	Stricken 30.10.19
MOUSQUETON	Schneider	4.11.1902	Stricken 10.5.20
ARC	Schneider	24.12.1903	Stricken 1.10.20
PISTOLET	St Nazaire	29.5.1903	Stricken 19.9.19
BÉLIER	St Nazaire	29.5.1903	Stricken 25.1.21
CATAPULTE	La Seyne	1.4.1903	Sunk 18.5.18
BOMBARDE	La Seyne	26.6.1903	Stricken 10.5.20

The first ten vessels of this class were ordered under the 1900 Programme and laid down 1900/1, the second ten under the 1901 Programme and laid down 1901/2. Trials took place 1902/4. They had a higher boiler pressure and more superstructure than the preceding *300 tonnes*. The increased boiler pressure enabled most to exceed the designed speed, and the removal of the mainmast improved stability. *Arbalète* and *Mousqueton* were used for the French Navy's first experiments with wireless. The class trimmed down by the bow.

Rapière about 1905

1. *Arbalète* of the *Arquebuse* class
2. *Fleuret* of the *Claymore* class
3. *Fanion* of the *Branlebas* class
4. *Capitaine Cuny*, a *Balny* class *'torpilleur de Haute Mer'*

1

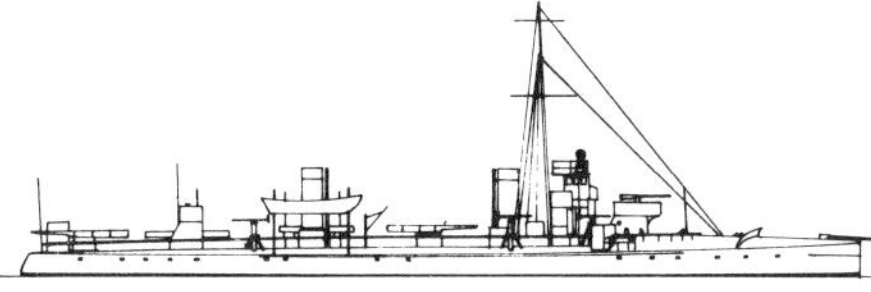

Massue as completed 1909

2

3

4

CLAYMORE class

Displacement: 350t
Dimensions: 190ft wl x 21ft 3in x 9ft 10in (*58.52 x 6.48 x 3.00m*)
Machinery: 2-shaft TE, 2 Normand or Du Temple boilers, 6800ihp = 28kts. Coal 29.5/?t
Armament: 1-67mm, 6-47mm (6x1), 2-17.7in TT (2x1)
Complement: 60

Name	Builder	Launched	Fate
STYLET	Rochefort	18.5.1905	Stricken 14.5.21
TROMBLON	Rochefort	17.6.1905	Stricken 14.5.21
PIERRIER	Rochefort	28.2.1907	Stricken 27.7.21
OBUSIER	Rochefort	9.3.1906	Stricken 27.5.21
MORTIER	Rochefort	23.3.1906	Stricken 30.3.27
CLAYMORE	Normand	14.3.1906	Stricken 19.3.26
CARQUOIS	Rochefort	26.6.1907	Stricken 29.11.30
TRIDENT	Rochefort	5.12.1907	Stricken 13.11.31
FLEURET	Rochefort	14.12.1906	Stricken 12.1.20,
COUTELAS	Rochefort	12.1.1907	Stricken 28.1.21
COGNÉE	Toulon	26.11.1907	Stricken 27.7.21
HACHE	Toulon	15.2.1908	Stricken 27.2.21
MASSUE	Toulon	19.9.1908	Stricken 30.3.27

The prototype, *Claymore*, was ordered 2.9.1903, and orders for five *Arquebuse* class to be built at Rochefort DYd were converted into orders for *Claymores* at the same time, the vessels being laid down 1904/6. The new hull form and extra weight of torpedoes made them top-heavy, so the upperworks were reduced and the closed bridge was replaced by an open position. The Dockyard-built *Claymores* did not prove very satisfactory. *Pierrier* was initially fitted with a Delaunay-Belleville 4 cyl experimental TE engine – it arrived two years late and was not a success – and as a result the ship did not enter service until November 1910. She reverted to a 3 cyl engine in 1911.

BRANLEBAS class

Displacement: 339t
Dimensions: 190ft wl x 21ft 7in x 7ft 10in (*57.91 x 6.58 x 2.39m*)
Machinery: 2-shaft TE, 2 Normand or Du Temple boilers, 6800ihp = 27.5kts. Coal 29.5/78.7t
Armour: Belt ⅝in (over machinery and boilers)
Armament: 1-67mm, 6-47mm (6x1), 2-17.7in TT (2x1)
Complement: 60

Name	Builder	Launched	Fate
SLAIVE	Rochefort	10.9.1908	Stricken 13.2.32
POIGNARD	Rochefort	3.7.1909	Stricken 3.5.26
SABRETACHE	Brasse et Fouché	5.2.1908	Stricken 10.5.20
ORIFLAMME	Brasse et Fouché	4.4.1908	Stricken 27.5.21
ÉTENDARD	Dyle et Bacalan	20.3.1908	Sunk 25.4.17
FANION	Dyle et Bacalan	4.5.1908	Stricken 27.5.21
SAPE	Penhoët, St Nazaire	23.9.1907	Stricken 3.5.26
GABION	Penho4t, St Nazaire	21.12.1907	Stricken 14.5.21
BRANLEBAS	Normand	8.10.1907	Sunk 30.9.15
FANFARE	Normand	19.12.1907	Stricken 28.9.25

This was a slightly improved version of the preceding *Claymore* class. Because of the weight and a desire to limit the boiler pressure, the official speed was reduced by ½kt. The vessels had splinter protection over their boilers and machinery, and a large navigating bridge. They were the last development of the *300 tonnes contre-torpilleur*, and were laid down 1905/6.

SEA-GOING TORPEDO BOATS

BALNY class *sea-going torpedo boats*

Displacement: 58t normal, 65t full load
Dimensions: 133ft 10in wl x 10ft 11in x 3ft 9in (*40.74 x 3.33 x 1.15m*)
Machinery: 1-shaft CR, 1 loco boiler, 580ihp = 19kts. Coal 12t
Armament: 2-14in TT (bow), 2-37mm revolvers
Complement: 22

Name	Builder	Launched	Fate
BALNY	Normand	Jan 1886	Sold 1913
DÉROULÈDE	Normand	19.4.1886	Sold 1907
DOUDART DE LA GRÉE	Normand	5.7.1886	Sold 1906
EDMOND FONTAINE	Claparède	23.1.1886	Sold 1903
BOUET WILLAUMEZ	Claparède	12.2.1886	Wrecked 1.9.1900
DEHORTER	Claparède	9.3.1886	Sold 1904
CAPITAINE CUNY	Loire, St Nazaire	3.6.1886	Sold 1912
CAPITAINE MEHL	Loire, St Nazaire	3.6.1886	Sold 1910
CHALLIER	Loire, St Nazaire	3.7.1886	Sold 1906

The Normand boats were ordered on 9.8.1884, the Claparède and Loire vessels on 23.2.1885. Designed by Normand on the basis of the TB *Poti* they had built for Russia, the plans were reluctantly released to the other builders on the orders of the Ministry of the Marine. At service displacement the Normand boats could reach 19kts and the Loire boats about 18.7kts, but the Claparède vessels could only manage 18.25kts. Experience proved that they were too small for fleet duties and in January 1890 they were assigned to the *'défense mobile'*.

OURAGAN class *sea-going torpedo boats*

Displacement: 104/112t as designed, 177t full load after modifications
Demensions: 153ft 5in wl x 15ft 10in x 5ft 11in *(46.72 x 4.82 x 1.79m)*
Machinery: 1-shaft QE, 2 loco boilers, 1400ihp = 16kts
Armament: 4-14in TT (4x1), 2-47mm guns
Complement: 29/32

Name	Builder	Launched	Fate
OURAGAN	Loire, Nantes	12.3.1887	Sold 1903
ALARME	Loire, Nantes	1.6.1889	Sold 1906
TÉMÉRAIRE	Loire, Nantes	1.5.1889	Sold 1911
AVENTURIER	Loire, Nantes	13.4.1889	Sold 1910
DÉFI	Loire, Nantes	29.6.1889	Sold 1911

Ouragan was laid down as a private speculation and bought on 6.9.1886, the remainder being ordered on 19.12.1888 in response to a petition from the builders. The novel quadruple expansion engine was designed for 1600ihp (1700ihp in *Ouragan*), and a speed of 25kts was promised. This speed was never approached, 19.21kts being the best on trials, although the later four did slightly better. The trials period was extended over nearly 2 years during which the original boilers were replaced and the hulls were strengthened. They were completed with a light 3-masted schooner rig (the mainmast was removed by order of June 1899) and the last 3 were again reboilered in 1897-9.

Ouragan originally had 2-37mm revolvers; the TT were mounted singly on each side abreast the CT and aft. Since they were unstable and poor seaboats their armament and radius of 2000nm at 10kts were their best features.

Véloce of the *Coureur* class

COUREUR class *sea-going torpedo boats*

Displacement: 117t normal, 131t full load (*Coureur* 101/125t)
Dimensions: 148ft wl x 14ft 6in x 4ft 7in (*Coureur* 147ft 7in x 14ft 3in x 4ft 5in) *(45.07 x 4.42 x 1.39m; 44.94 x 4.34 x 1.35m)*
Machinery: 2-shaft TE (*Coureur* CR), 2 Thornycroft boilers, 1750ihp (*Coureur* 1500ihp) = 23.5kts. Coal 14t (*Coureur* 8t)
Armament: 2-14in TT (bow), 2-47mm

Name	Builder	Launched	Fate
COUREUR	Thornycroft	13.6.1888	Sold 1912
VÉLOCE	Méditerranée, Graville	4.11.1891	Sold 1910
GRONDEUR	Méditerranée, Graville	13.2.1892	Sold 1926

Coureur, ordered on 16.8.1887, was designed to test the Thornycroft watertube boiler, which had a very high power/weight ratio. This boat was virtually a copy of the *Ariete* and *El Rayo* built for Spain, and the fine-lined lightweight hull was constructed of steel, which proved too fragile in service. She had two rudders, one ahead and the other aft of the propellers, and achieved 23.62kts on trials, although she never again came near to this figure. The first French TB with reasonable accommodation, she was designed with a 3-masted schooner rig, but retained only the mainmast between the two funnels. The other pair were ordered on 16.4.1890 and were basically of the same design but with heavier scantlings, and were poorer seaboats in consequence.

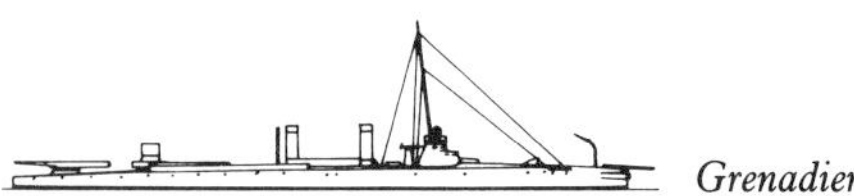

Grenadier as designed

AVANT-GARDE class *sea-going torpedo boats*

Displacement: 116t normal, 128t full load (first pair), 127t full load (second pair), 129t full load (remainder)
Dimensions: 137ft 8in pp (138ft first pair) x 14ft 10in x 4ft 3in *(41.93 (42.02) x 4.51 x 1.30m)*
Machinery: 2-shaft TE (CR first pair), 2 du Temple (2 loco, first pair, 2 Oriolle, second pair) boilers, 1750ihp (1250ihp, first pair) = 21kts (20.5kts, first pair). Coal 22t (15t, first pair)
Armament: 2-15in TT (1 bow, 1 trainable) 4 torpedoes (1 spar-torpedo, 2-14in TT, *Avant-Garde*), 2-47mm
Complement: 27

Name	Builder	Launched	Fate
AVANT-GARDE	Normand	11.10.1889	Wrecked 25.2.1890
ARCHER	Normand	30.5.1893	Sold 1908
TURCO	Loire, Nantes	20.11.1891	Sold 1911
ZOUAVE	Loire, Nantes	Jan 1892	Sold 1908
DRAGON	Normand	29.4.1892	Stricken Aug 1910
GRENADIER	Normand	20.8.1892	Sold 1919
LANCIER	Normand	19.12.1892	Sold 1911

Ordered on 7.11.1887, *Avant-Garde* was Normand's contribution to the series of design studies for a suitable *'torpilleur de haute mer'*. An enlarged version of the highly successful TBs of the *126* series, this boat proved to be robust and seaworthy, and also reasonably fast – 20.97kts on trials. She had twin funnels abreast and originally a light 3-masted rig. When this vessel's career was prematurely curtailed, a replacement was ordered (10.11.1889) to use her undamaged machinery and this boat became the *Archer*. The only differences were the single funnel and the same armament as the later boats. This design was considered so successful that in April 1890 two modified boats were ordered from Loire,and three more from Normand. The Normand boats were highly satisfactory, being the first French TBs to exceed 25kts on trials, although only designed for 21kts. The Loire boats, however, had machinery originally designed by the builders for the 34-metre type TBs, although the hull was to the Normand design, and neither reached 21kts on trials.

AGILE class *sea-going torpedo boats*

Displacement: 102t, 119t full load (102t, 129t full load, last pair)
Dimensions: 143ft wl (145ft last pair) x 14ft 11in x 3ft 7in *(43.55 (44.15) x 4.55 x 1.10m)*
Machinery: 1-shaft TE, 1 loco boiler (first pair); 2 Thornycroft boilers (next 3); 2 Babillot boilers (last pair), 1100ihp = 20kts. Coal 14½t/35t
Armament: 3-14in TT (3x1); 2-15in TT (1 bow) in last 3, 3-37mm revolvers

Name	Builder	Launched	Fate
AGILE	La Seyne	4.7.1889	Sold 1912
AUDACIEUX	La Seyne	8.5.1889	Sunk in collision 10.7.96
ECLAIRE	La Seyne	29.8.1891	Sold 1911
KABYLE	La Seyne	Nov 1891	Sold 1911
ORAGE	La Seyne	15.10.1891	Sold 1921
SARRAZIN.	Gironde, Bordeaux	25.6.1892	Sold 1908
TOURBILLON	Gironde, Bordeaux	10.10.1892	Sold 1911

The prototype pair were ordered on 3.8.1888 to the design of the director of the La Seyne yard. They were not as fast as the *Avant-Garde* at between 20 and 21kts, but were robust and economical, with a high level of stability, and an unrivalled radius of 3000nm at 10.5kts. The major disadvantages were the single boiler and propeller. They originally had one funnel and two masts. The repeat order for three boats was placed on 2.5.1890, but these were constructed with heavier scantlings and two watertube boilers (hence two funnels). The boilers were highly successful and all three made 21½kts on trials.

Two further boats had been ordered on 9.4.1890 to a design modified by the Gironde yard, but a series of boiler accidents culminating in the explosion aboard *Sarrazin* on 13.1.1894 delayed their entry into service for nearly two years while du Temple boilers were substituted. They never achieved 21kts, and their Cail-built engines gave frequent trouble. As early as 1896 they could do not more than 18kts.

CORSAIRE *sea-going torpedo boat*

Displacement: 148t trials, 168t full load
Dimensions: 165ft 10in wl x 14ft 8in x 5ft 5in *(50.50 x 4.46 x 1.66m)*
Machinery: 2-shaft TE, 2 du Temple boilers, 2500ihp = 25.5kts. Coal 16/21t
Armament: 2-15in TT, 4 torpedoes, 2-37mm revolvers

Name	Builder	Launched	Fate
CORSAIRE	Loire, St Denis	5.10.1892	Sold 1913

One of three designs for very fast TBs authorised in April 1891. The last TB built in the Paris area (at the old Claparède yard) was an unmitigated failure – her maximum trial speed was only 24.23kts, her manoeuvring and seakeeping abilities were very poor, and the enormous consumption of fuel made nonsense of her *'haute mer'* designation. She was reclassified as a *'torpilleur de défense mobile'* in 1897.

MOUSQUETAIRE *sea-going torpedo boat*

Displacement: 123t
Dimensions: 157ft 7in wl x 15ft 5in x 4ft 2in *(48.00 x 4.70 x 1.26m)*
Machinery: 2-shaft TE, 2 du Temple boilers, 2100ihp = 24.5kts. Coal 22t
Armament: 2-18in TT, 2-37mm revolvers

Name	Builder	Launched	Fate
MOUSQUETAIRE	Méditerranée, Graville	8.8.1892	Sold 1911

The second high-speed design of 1891. After mediocre initial trials (23.85kts and excessive fuel consumption) Normand-designed modifications to the boilers produced better results (25.44kts maximum, and a radius of 800nm at 11kts). She was a good seaboat, solidly-built and with comfortable accommodation, but of poor manoeuvrability.

CHEVALIER *sea-going torpedo boat*

Displacement: 118t designed, 135t full load
Dimensions: 143ft 9in wl x 14ft 9in x 4ft 9in *(43.78 x 4.50 x 1.45m)*
Machinery: 2-shaft TE, 2 du Temple boilers, 2200ihp = 24.5kts. Coal 16t
Armament: 2-18in TT, 4 torpedoes, 2-37mm revolvers

Name	Builder	Launched	Fate
CHEVALIER	Normand	15.6.1893	Sold 1920

The undoubted 'star' of the three high-speed designs, *Chevalier* made 27.6kts on trials (at that time the world record) with remarkably little vibration. Furthermore, she was a good seaboat and well-built, and retained her speed longer than most of her contemporaries. After reboilering in 1902-4, she served actively as a patrol craft throughout World War I.

LANSQUENET *sea-going torpedo boat*

Displacement: 136t designed, 197t actual
Dimensions: 171ft 5in wl x 17ft 6in x 5ft 7in *(52.22 x 5.33 x 1.70m)*
Machinery: 2-shaft TE, 4 Oriolle boilers, 2500/4250ihp = 20/25kts
Armament: 2-18in TT, 2137mm revolvers

Name	Builder	Launched	Fate
LANSQUENET	Oriolle, Nantes	18.5.1893	Stricken 1900

Ordered some months after the high-speed designs, this experimental vessel was built by the boiler-designer Oriolle who had no experience of TB construction. This bizarre-looking vessel had three heavily-raked funnels, a ram bow surmounted by the TT mounting, and superstructure in the form of an armoured carapace; the hull and superstructure were built of steel. She made only 24kts on trials instead of the 26 promised by the builder, and the boilers were so disappointing that they had to be replaced after a few months' trials. *Lansquenet* was only accepted in 1898 (and for only 22kts) but trials continued and she was not put into service until 1900 – after 7 years of trials. She was involved in a collision almost immediately and laid up, but not sold until 1905.

AVERNE class *sea-going torpedo boats*

Displacement: 113t designed, 131t full load
Dimensions: 144ft wl x 15ft 1in x 4ft 2in *(43.85 x 4.60 x 1.28m)*
Machinery: 2-shaft TE, 2 du Temple boilers, 1750ihp = 23.5kts
Armament: 2-15in TT (1 bow), 2-47mm

Name	Builder	Launched	Fate
AVERNE	Méditerranée, Graville	23.12.1893	Sold 1920
DAUPHIN	Méditerranée, Graville	23.2.1894	Sold 1913

Ordered on 31.8.1892. Although this pair were the product of the same designer as *Mousquetaire*, they were inspired by Normand's *Dragon* of the modified *Avant-Garde* type. On trials they made 25.4kts, and generally were regarded as good steamers and seaboats but were plagued by their obsolescent and temperamental boilers. They kept their speed throughout their careers and in 1900 *Averne* was reboilered. They had 2 funnels.

ARGONAUTE class *sea-going torpedo boats*

Displacement: 113t, 129t full load
Dimensions: 141ft wl x 14ft 10in x 5ft 8in max *(42.94 x 4.51 x 1.72m)*
Machinery: 2-shaft TE, 2 du Temple boilers, 2000ihp = 23.5kts
Armament: 2-15in TT (1 bow), 2-47mm
Complement: 27

Name	Builder	Launched	Fate
ARGONAUTE	Loire, Nantes	11.10.1893	Sold 1911
TOURMENTE	Loire, Nantes	12.9.1893	Sold 1910

Ordered on 31.8.1892, these boats were based on Normand's *Avant-Garde* and not Loire's unsuccessful *Corsaire* design. They had a better hull-form than the latter but suffered from delicate boilers (which were replaced in 1896/8), and generally were judged less successful than the *Averne* class. With two rudders they handled well, and were reasonable seaboats although prone to sharp and uncomfortable rolling. They made around 24kts on trials.

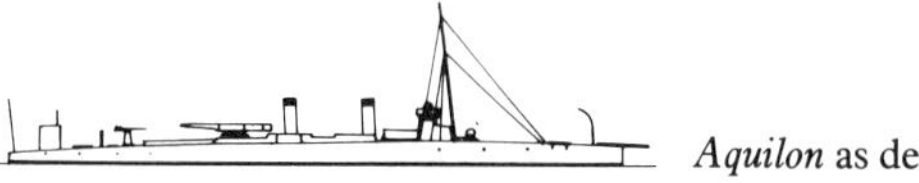
Aquilon as designed

FILIBUSTIER class *sea-going torpedo boats*

Displacement: 123t normal
Dimensions: 137ft 9in wl x 14ft 9in x 5ft 6in *(41.96 x 4.50 x 1.67m)*
Machinery: 2-shaft TE, 2 du Temple (*Aquilon* 2 Normand) boilers, 2000ihp = 23.5kts. Coal 20t
Armament: 2-15in TT, 2-47mm

Name	Builder	Launched	Fate
FILIBUSTIER	Normand	27.12.1894	Sunk 29.3.98
ARIEL	Normand	9.5.1895	Sold 1923
AQUILON	Normand	2.12.1895	Sold 1919

As usual, the Normand design was the best of the three groups ordered in August 1892. The first pair achieved 25½kts on trials, and possessed superb seakeeping qualities. *Ariel* was rammed and sunk by the *Friant* during night exercises. *Filibustier* was reboilered in 1906-7. *Aquilon* was ordered later (12.7.1893) to test the new Normand boilers on an established design, and achieved 26.16kts on trials; this speed was remarkably consistent, and as late as 1905 she could still make over 26kts.

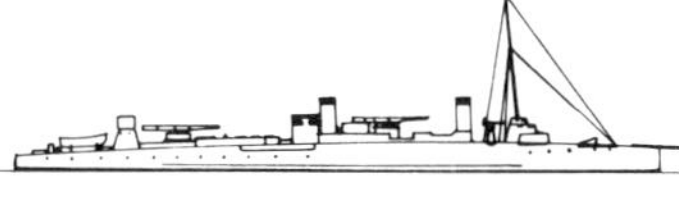
Forban as completed 1896

FORBAN *sea-going torpedo boat*

Displacement: 121t normal, 150t full load
Dimensions: 144ft 6in wl x 15ft 3in x 4ft 5in *(44.00 x 4.64 x 1.35m)*
Machinery: 2-shaft TE, 2 Normand boilers, 3260ihp = 29kts. Coal 18t
Armament: 2-14in TT, 2-37mm

Name	Builder	Launched	Fate
FORBAN	Normand	25.7.1895	Sold 1920

Ordered on 23.2.1893, *Forban* was an improved *Filibustier* with similar but more powerful engines. She made the spectacular speed of 31.03kts on trials, the first vessel in the world to pass 30kts. *Forban* was also a good seaboat and an economical steamer, and naturally caused great interest at the time. The 14in TT were replaced by 18in TT in 1907.

MANGINI *sea-going torpedo boat*

Displacement: 127t normal, 140t full load
Dimensions: 147ft 9in pp x 15ft 3in x 4ft 9in *(45.00 x 4.65 x 1.45m)*
Machinery: 2-shaft TE, 2 du Temple boilers, ?ihp = 24kts. Coal 25t
Armament: 2-15in TT (1 bow), 2-47mm
Complement: 27

Name	Builder	Launched	Fate
MANGINI	Loire, Nantes	13.6.1896	Sold 1911

Ordered on 31.1.1895, to a design by the builders (an improved *Tourmente*). Named after the engineer who died in the *Sarrazin* accident, *Mangini* was one of the better TBs of this period and enjoyed a long and active service. Maximum trials speed was 26.62kts, but she remained capable of 24kts for most of her career and in 1900 averaged 18kts for 24 hours.

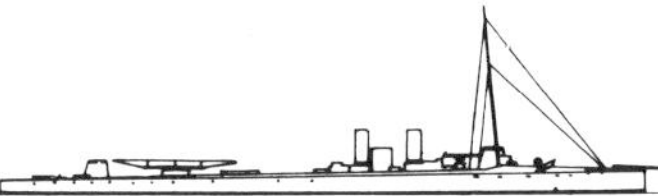

Bourrasque as designed

TORPEDO BOATS

CYCLONE class *sea-going torpedo boats*

Displacement: 119t (*Cyclone* 113t) normal, 165t (*Cyclone* 150t) full load
Dimensions: 147ft 9in wl x 16ft 7in (*Cyclone* 16ft 1in) x 4ft 11in (*45.00 x 5.06 (4.90) x 1.50m*)
Machinery: 2-shaft TE, 2 Normand boilers, 3800ihp (*Cyclone* 4200ihp) = 29kts. Coal 18/33t
Armament: 2.5in TT, 4 torpedoes, 2-47mm

Name	Builder	Launched	Fate
CYCLONE	Normand	21.5.1898	Stricken 1920
BOURRASQUE	Normand	31.8.1901	Sold 1923
RAFALE	Normand	27.11.1901	Sold 1922
BORÉE	Gironde	23.3.1901	Sold 1921
TRAMONTANE	Gironde	21.5.1901	Sold 1923

The prototype *Cyclone* was ordered on 17.8.1896 and the other Normand boats on 21.6.1899 and the last pair on 26.7.1899. This class was an improved version of the highly successful *Forban*, and *Cyclone* made 30.38kts on trials. The hull was constructed of nickel-steel of lighter scantlings because of reduced vibration from the engines, and had twice the radius of action of *Forban* (2000nm at 10kts). On trials *Bourrasque* was the fastest at 31.54kts, but neither of the Gironde boats made 30kts. From completion they were assigned to the *'défense mobile'* of Mediterranean ports, indicating that they were already outmoded, and their role was taken over by the first French destroyers.

MISTRAL class *sea-going torpedo boats*

Displacement: 113t normal, 183t full load
Dimensions: 147ft 9in wl x 16ft 11in x 5ft 2in (*45.00 x 5.15 x 1.60m*)
Machinery: 2-shaft TE, 2 Normand boilers, 4200ihp = 26kts. Coal 25t
Armament: 3-15in TT, 2-47mm
Complement: 30

Name	Builder	Launched	Fate
MISTRAL	Normand	4.5.1901	Sold 1928
SIROCCO	Normand	20.2.1901	Sold 1925
SIMOUN	Méditerranée, Graville	23.3.1901	Sold 1924
TYPHON	Méditerranée, Graville	15.6.1901	Sold 1928
TROMBE	Loire, Nantes	30.7.1900	Sold 1928
AUDACIEUX	Loire, Nantes	29.8.1900	Sold 1926

Ordered 10.8.1898 to a Normand design. Essentially a *Cyclone* modified with splinter-armour, these were the last *'torpilleurs de haute mer'*. For 10 years Normand had advocated armoured TBs, but this was the only class so built. The boilers and engines were protected by a 24mm nickel-steel box (side and bulkheads) with a 9mm deck, which Normand considered invulnerable to the 6pdrs and 12pdrs of British TBDs. The extra 18t was expected to reduce the speed to 26kts, but the Normand boats reached 28½kts on trials, and only the Loire boats made no more than their designed speed. One of the TTs was originally mounted on a pivot on the forecastle, but this was soon removed. Otherwise, they were successful and popular boats, retaining their good qualities for the whole of their service. All were actively employed during World War I; *Mistral* was renamed *Borée* in 1925.

Note: There was also the captured Chinese destroyer *Takou* (ex-*Hai Ching*). For details see p99. *Takou* was rearmed with 4-47mm, 2-37mm and 2-15in TT. She spent her French service on the Saigon station and was wrecked on 22.2.1911.

Simoun of the *Mistral* class (*All photos in this section: CPL*)

An early TB *'de défense mobile'*

NO 1 Claparède 1876

Displacement: 102t
Dimensions: 126ft 8in oa x 13ft 9in x 8ft 6in (*38.61 x 4.19 x 2.59m*)
Machinery: 2-shaft VC, 2 loco boilers, 800ihp = 17kts. Coal 9.5/?t
Armament: 2-14in TT (2x1)
Complement: 9

Ordered 12.7.1875, laid down 25.9.75 and commisioned 17.5.76, *No 1* had two funnels side by side and a fixed bow and stern sub TT. After trials it was intended to discard her on 30.5.83, but she was renamed *Isard* and reclassified as a 3rd class *aviso de flottille* and used for the defence of Cherbourg. She was rearmed with 2-47mm (2x1) and a spar torpedo forward. Stricken 1889.

NO 2 Rochefort 1876

Displacement: 31½t
Dimensions: 70ft 9in wl x 11ft 6in x 8ft 6in (*21.56 x 3.51 x 2.59m*)
Machinery: 1-shaft CR, 1 loco boiler, 100ihp = 13kts
Armament: 1 spar torpedo
Complement: 8

Ordered 12.7.1875, laid down 21.9.75 and completed in July 1878, *No 2* proved to have insufficient stability and made only 11kts. Renamed *Vergeroux* in December 1880, she was used as a workboat for the coastal artillery at Rochefort. Stricken 1899.

NO 3 Claparède 1876

Displacement: 27½t
Dimensions: 67ft 6in oa x 9ft 10in x 7ft 6in (*20.57 x 3.00 x 2.29m*)
Machinery: 1-shaft CR, 1 boiler, 280ihp = 14kts
Armament: 1 spar torpedo
Complement: 8

Ordered 12.7.1875 and laid down later that year, *No 3* was a good sea boat but could only make 12.4kts. She made the first trials of compressed air launched torpedoes. Reclassified in March 1883 as an *aviso de flottille* and renamed *Chevrette*, she was used in trials with petrol. Stricken 1885.

NO 4 Yarrow 1875

Displacement: 17½t
Dimensions: 72ft pp x 9ft 10in x 6ft (*21.95 x 3.00 x 1.83m*)
Machinery: 1-shaft CR, 1 loco boiler, ?ihp = 13kts
Armament: 1 spar torpedo
Complement: 8

Ordered 10.5.1875. Both stability and speed were insufficient and she made too much smoke. She was judged unusable as a torpedo boat and it was proposed to sell her in December 1874. In 1883 she was transformed into an *aviso de flottille*, renamed *Djoné* and transported to the Congo. Discarded 1895.

NOS 5, 6 Thornycroft 1875-76

Displacement: 12t
Dimensions: 66ft 10in oa x 8ft 6in x 3ft 4in (*20.37 x 2.59 x 1.02m*)
Machinery: 1-shaft CR, 1 loco boiler, 220ihp = 18kts
Armament: 2 spar torpedoes (2x1)
Complement: 8

Ordered 9.5.1875, laid down that year and completed July/August 1876, these were the most successful of the French trial boats, and were typical Thornycroft products. By the 1880s they were being used for instruction. *No 6* was stricken in May 1888 but was renamed *Lupin* and employed on Rochefort's underwater defences until 1890. Stricken 1887-90.

NO 7 Brest 1875

Displacement: 22t
Dimensions: 48ft 6in oa x 9ft 2in x 3ft 3in (*14.78 x 2.79 x 0.99m*)
Machinery: 1-shaft CR, 1 Belleville boiler, 105ihp = 14kts
Armament: 1 bow TT
Complement: 10

Ordered 9.5.1875, laid down that year and completed the next, *No 7* was unable to make her designed speed, the best on trials being 10.17kts. The TT was not satisfactory and was replaced by a spar torpedo. Condemned as a TB in 1887, she was renamed *Compagnon* and used as a utility craft. Finally discarded 1910.

NOS 8-19 Thornycroft 1877-78

Displacement: 26t
Dimensions: 87ft 2in oa x 10ft 10in x 4ft 11in (*26.57 x 3.30 x 1.50m*)
Machinery: 1-shaft CR, 1 loco boiler, 300ihp = 18kts
Armament: 1 spar torpedo
Complement: 10

The first six were ordered 13.3.1877 and the remaining six 9.7.77. All were laid down in 1877 and completed the following year. They performed very well and were excellent sea boats for their size. All remained in service for over 15 years. *No 14* was used for trials on a Du Temple boiler and after being stricken as a TB in 1894 was reclassified as a *remorquer* and renamed *Économe*. Both No *10* and No *16* were rearmed with 2 Maupóu TT. Most had a small funnel so that the spar torpedo would clear it, but No *19* was fitted with 2 funnels on trials and with a Trépardoux boiler, and also received TTs. All were stricken between 1894-99.

THE 27-METRE TYPE

Having ordered the Thornycroft boats in March 1877, the French Navy approached builders to produce a series of French-designed craft closely based on the Thornycroft model. The builders were Normand at Le Havre, Claparède on the Seine, and Forges et Chantiers de la Méditerranée at La Seyne near Toulon. Results from the first trials were encouraging and repeat orders were placed in November 1878.

NOS 20, 21, 41, 42, 47-49, 54, 55 Normand 1877-80

Displacement: 30t designed, 32-35t trials
Dimensions: 85ft 4in wl x 10ft 1in x 3ft (*26.00 x 3.28 x 0.91m*)
Machinery: 1-shaft VCR, 1 loco boiler, 320ihp = 18kts
Armament: 1 spar torpedo (*54, 55* 2 TT bow)

Ordered in four groups, the first pair on 16.7.1877, the second pair on 18.11.1878, the next three on 10.2.1879 and the remaining two on 6.12.1880. They made between 18.59kts (*47*) and 19.84kts (*55*) on trials, and they were considered excellent boats with good seakeeping qualities. From *47* onwards the hull form was altered slightly and the last pair had one funnel instead of two. They were designated second class TBs in 1883, and were sold between 1896 and 1900.

NOS 22, 23, 37-40, 51-53 Claparède 1878-82

Displacement: 30t, 33t trials
Dimensions: 88ft 8in wl x 11ft 7in x 2ft 9in (*27.00 x 3.55 x 0.85m*)
Machinery: 1-shaft 3 cyl CR, 1 loco boiler, 320/500ihp = 18kts
Armament: 2 TT bow (*22, 23* 1 spar torpedo)

Ordered in groups on 16.7.1876, 18.11.1878 and 10.2.1879. *22* and *23* had two funnels, the rest one. They made between 18.32kts (*22*) and 20.79kts (*39*) on trials. Designated second class TBs in 1883 they were sold or stricken between 1897 and 1903.

NOS 24, 25, 33-36, 43-46, 50 La Seyne 1878-80

Displacement: 31t, 32-35t trials
Dimensions: 85ft 4in pp x 11ft 9in x 2ft 8in (*26.00 x 3.60 x 0.80m*)
Machinery: 1-shaft 3 cyl CR, 1 loco boiler, 320/500ihp = 18kts
Armament: 1 spar torpedo (*33-36, 50* 2 TT bow)

Ordered 16.7.1877, 18.11.1878 and 10.2.1879. Nos *24* and *25* were the first 27-metre boats completed, and on trials were considered particularly successful, making 18.03kts and 18.27kts respectively. No *45* was lost in a storm in Mar 1885 and *46* foundered while under tow a month later. Designated second class TBs in 1883, the surviving boats were stricken between 1903 and 1908.

'TORPILLEURS-VEDETTES'

The 1877 Commission on Underwater Defence examined a Thornycroft proposal for 4-6t torpedo craft that could be carried aboard large warships, but decided that such vessels would be too small for effective high seas employment. However, they concluded that it would be worth building special torpedo launches and a transport to carry them into action. Eventually a pair of small torpedo boats were ordered from Thornycroft (1.4.1878) as prototypes for the '*torpilleurs-vedettes*' which could be embarked aboard armoured ships. However, this idea proved impractical and finally the transport *Japon* was fitted as a TB carrier. In the years following 1881 *Japon* carried out almost continuous trials and exercises – normally carrying 4 of the 6 boats – and after the ship was laid up, a new 18½kt purpose-built ship, *La Foudre*, was ordered in her place. *La Foudre* was launched on 20.10.1895 by which time the *torpilleurs-vedettes* were obsolete. A number of spar-torpedo carrying picket boats had been built between 1884 and 1890, which were designed to be carried aboard battleships but these 9-13t craft had speeds of between 10 and 12kts and an inadequate radius of action. Therefore a new group of *torpilleurs-vedettes* were designed in 1893 and instead of numbers were designated by the first 8 letters of the alphabet.

An experimental aluminium craft was also ordered from Yarrow in Britain. This 14t vessel measured 19 x 2.85 x 1.45m and made 20.5kts on trials. She became *C* of the alphabetical series.

NOS 29, 30, 56-59 Thornycroft type 1879-81

Displacement: 8t, 9t trials (*56, 57* 11t)
Dimensions: 60ft 1in wl x 7ft 5in x 1ft 11in (*18.30 x 2.28 x 0.58m*)
Machinery: 1-shaft CR, 1 loco boiler, ?ihp = 12kts
Complement: 12

The first pair were ordered 1.4.1878, *58* and *59* on 16.8.1880 and the remainder on 15.2.1881. *56* and *57* were built to a modified design at La Seyne, and had a ram bow; they proved to be a full 2kts slower on trials than the straight-stemmed Thornycroft boats (14.6kts as opposed to 16.2-16.9kts). The French-built boats were fitted with two 'impulse-tubes' which fired the torpedo using an explosive charge whereas the others had the usual torpedo 'frame' dropping gear. They spent most of their careers aboard the TB transport *Japon* and later aboard the cruiser-like *La Foudre* until replaced by the specially-built 'alphabetical' TBs. They were stricken or sold between 1897 and 1904, although *56* survived until 1910.

NOS 31, 32 Yarrow 1879

Displacement: 27t light
Dimensions: 88ft 8in oa x 10ft 10in x 2ft 9in (*27.00 x 3.30 x 0.84m*)
Machinery: 1-shaft CR, 1 loco boiler, 500ihp = 19kts
Armament: 2 TC as delivered; 2 Maupeou TT fitted in 1885

Generally very similar to the '27-metre' boats and although classed as '*torpilleurs-vedettes*' they could not be embarked. With a bow and stern rudder they proved highly manoeuvrable. They were ordered 17.6.1878; both were sold in 1901.

A, B, D-I Schneider 1894-8

Displacement: 14t load
Demensions: 60ft 9in oa x 9ft 10in x 4ft 8in (*18.50 x 3.00 x 1.43m*)
Machinery: 1-shaft CR, 1 du Temple boiler, 250ihp = 17kts
Armament: 1-14in TT bow

The first pair were ordered in 1893 and the remainder in 1897. They proved to be reasonable seaboats and highly manoeuvrable, with a radius of about 100nm and a maximum trials speed of 17.5kts. They finished their careers in 1909 in the '*défense mobile*' at Saigon. Note that *C* was the Yarrow-built aluminium boat.

LARGER TORPEDO BOATS

At the same time as the first French '27-metre' boats were ordered, one larger craft was ordered from each builder. The most successful of these experimental craft, No *27*, was the forerunner of TBs with a larger radius of action, capable of offshore deployment.

NO 26 La Seyne 1878

Displacement: 44t
Dimensions: 112ft 3in wl x 11ft 11in x 2ft 6in *(34.20 x 3.64 x 0.77m)*
Machinery: 1-shaft 3 cyl VCR, 1 loco boiler, 320/500ihp = 18kts
Armament: 1-15in TT sub, 2-37mm revolvers
Complement: 11

Ordered on 12.11.1877. The first French TB with a gun armament; originally fitted with a Claparède submerged tube that launched the torpedo by means of a steam-powered ram but this was replaced by a straight stem with a tube on each side fired by compressed air. Stricken in 1901 and sold in 1914.

NO 27 Normand 1879

Displacement: 43t
Dimensions: 104ft 5in wl x 10ft 10in x 2ft 11in *(31.80 x 3.30 x 0.90m)*
Machinery: 1-shaft 2 cyl VCR, 1 loco boiler, 320/500ihp =18kts
Complement: 12

Ordered 12.11.1877. The original bow TT was converted to compressed air in 1880 after it was found that steam obscured the helmsman's view on launching the torpedo. This was replaced during 1887-9 by a spar torpedo and a twin trainable TT mounting aft, but stability was adversely affected and the spar was removed and the superstructure cut down. This vessel was particularly successful and served as a prototype for the '33-metre' type. No *27* was stricken in 1903 and sold in 1904.

NO 28 Claparède 1879

Displacement: 43t
Dimensions: 113ft 3in wl x 12ft x 2ft 8in *(34.50 x 3.66 x 0.82m)*
Machinery: 1-shaft 3 cyl VCR, 1 loco boiler, 320/500ihp = 18kts
Complement: 11

Ordered 20.9.1877. Originally fitted with a Claparède submerged TT, which was replaced by twin 14in TT forward, then by 2 fixed bow TT, and finally by a trainable twin mounting aft. After several boiler changes and trials with smoke-making equipment, No *28* served as a tender to the torpedo TS *L'Algesiras*, was stricken in 1908 and sold in 1911.

NOS 60-74 Normand *33-metre type* 1882-5

Displacement: 45t
Dimensions: 108ft 4in wl x 10ft 9in x 3ft 7in *(33.00 x 3.28 x 1.10m)*
Machinery: 1-shaft 2 cyl VCR, 1 loco boiler, 500ihp = 20kts
Armament: 2-15in TT bow (*65-74* 2-14in TT bow), 6 torpedoes
Complement: 11

Ordered 5.11.1880 (*60*), 31.10.1881 (*61-64*), 29.1.1883 (*65-68*), 14.4.1883 (*69-74*). Following the success of No *27* Normand was approached to produce a class of TBs based on this craft. There were actually two series, the later boats (from *65*) having a ram bow, which was subsequently considered a mistake since it produced a very visible bow wave and required shorter, smaller calibre TTs, which were also difficult to use. Designed for a larger radius of action than previous boats, they were considered economical steamers and could reach 800-850nm at 10kts; they all made over 20kts on trials and *71* was the first French TB to make 21kts. In 1886, because of the problem of the ram bow it was planned to convert the *65* series into torpedo boat destroyers with 4-37mm Hotchkiss revolvers, but in the event only *68* was converted. They were stricken around 1900 and sold in the early years of this century.

NOS 75-125 *35-metre type* 1887-9

Displacement: 53t
Dimensions: 114ft 11in pp x 10ft 11in x 2ft 11in *(35.00 x 3.35 x 0.89m)*
Machinery: 1-shaft CR, 1 loco boiler, 525ihp = 20kts
Armament: 2-15in TT bow, 4 torpedoes; later 2-37mm revolvers added
Complement: 16

The first series (Nos *75-104*) were ordered on 22.6.1885 and although the design was already under heavy criticism Nos *105-125* were ordered on 15.2.1886. Builders were: Chantiers de la Loire, Nantes (Nos *75-80*, *85*, *86*); Chantiers de la Loire, St Denis, who took over the Claparède yard (Nos *81-84*); Cail, Paris (Nos *87-92*); Schneider (Nos *93-98*, *121-125*); La Seyne (Nos *99-104*); Graville-Le Havre (Nos *105-114*); Gironde (Nos *115-120*). Although based on the preceding Normand boats, they had a raised turtleback bow section and a second stern rudder in tandem, but proved to be highly unsatisfactory. They were unstable and slow and their entry into service was considerably delayed by a decision to replace their boilers. In February 1887 it was decided that 2 torpedoes would have to be landed, but even so their modifications had made them heavier and they never again reached their trial speeds – below the designed 20kts in most cases. The surviving boats were stricken or scrapped in the first decade of this century.

NOS 126-129 Normand 1889-90

Displacement: 71t, 78t full load
Dimensions: 118ft wl x 12ft 10in x 3ft 9in *(35.95 x 3.92 x 1.15m)*
Machinery: 1-shaft CR, 1 loco boiler, 900ihp = 21kts
Armament: 2-15in TT, 2-37mm revolvers
Complement: 21

Ordered 12.9.1887 (*126*, *127*) and 23.5.1888. Normand was highly critical of the 35-metre design, and their dismal history vindicated his decision not to become involved in the building programme. Instead he proposed his own design, which was in every way superior. With two trainable TT in single mountings and 2 QF guns, this class was still more stable – and faster – than the 35-metre type. They were originally given a light schooner rig and were used for extensive trials and manoeuvres. In many ways they were the forerunners of all the small TBs of the French *'défense mobile'* down to 1908. They were stricken between 1908 and 1914.

NOS 130-144 Normand *34-metre type* 1890-92

Displacement: 52t
Dimensions: 111ft 8in pp x 11ft 6in x 2ft 11in *(34.00 x 3.50 x 0.90m)*
Machinery: 1-shaft TE, 1 du Temple watertube boiler, 720ihp = 20kts
Armament: 1 spar torpedo, 1-15in TT, 2-37mm
Complement: 18

Ordered on 23.1.1889 (Nos *130-135*) from Normand, and on 13.2.1889 (Nos *136-138*) from Chantiers de la Loire, (Nos *139-141*) from Schneider, and (Nos *142-144*) from Chantiers de la Gironde. These Normand-designed boats were the first French TBs with watertube boilers and also adopted triple expansion machinery. They were economical steamers and good seaboats, but the accommodation was cramped. Furthermore, the boilers gave some trouble in the early stages, and they were not considered an advance on the *126* type. The TT was on a pivot mounting aft, and the spar torpedo was replaced in 1900 with a second trainable TT forward.

They were reduced to auxiliary roles and disposed of around 1910, except *133* (lost November 1897), and *135* (tender to torpedo school until 1921).

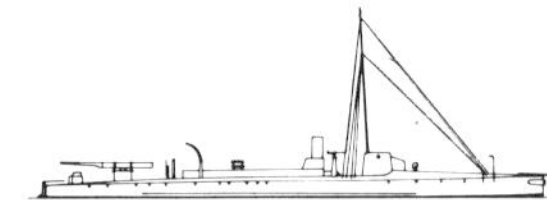

145 as completed

NOS 145-9, 152-171 *modified '126' type* 1891-3

Displacement: 78t
Dimensions: 118ft pp x 12ft 10in x 3ft 9in *(35.94 x 3.90 x 1.15m)*
Machinery: 1-shaft TE, various types of boilers (see notes), 1000ihp = 21kts
Armament: 2-15in TT, 2-37mm revolvers
Complement: 22/23

Normand submitted the design in the autumn of 1889 and they were ordered on 2.9.1890 (Nos *145-149*, *152-154*) from Normand; 9.4.1890 (Nos *155-160*) from Gironde, engined by Cail, and (Nos *164-166*) from the Graville-Le Havre yard of F & C de la Méditerranée; 16.4.1890 (Nos *161-163*) from Loire; April 1890 (Nos *167-169*) from Schneider; and 26.11.1890 (Nos *170*, *171*) from Normand. An experimental group for comparative trials of machinery and boilers, each builder constructing their own version of the TE engines. Nos *148*, *149*, *152*, *153* had one Normand boiler; Nos *145-147*, *154-160* and *170* and *171* had one du Temple boiler; Nos *161-163* were fitted with two Oriolle boilers; Nos *164-166* had two Thornycroft type; and Nos *167-169* two of the Dion-Bouton-Trépardoux type. As would be expected, trials results varied widely, from 20.28kts (No *163*) to 24.51kts (No *149*). One of the TT was fixed in the bow, and the other on a trainable mount right aft. All were stricken just before World War I, except *158* which survived until 1920.

NOS 172-200 *modified '126' type* 1892-5

A further series of modified *126* type TBs with the same specification, except that Nos *192-200* were a metre longer to accommodate larger boilers. The machinery, constructed by the builders, was also more powerful – 1350ihp, although Nos *182-187* achieved 1700ihp on trials – for a designed speed of 22kts (23kts in Nos *195-200*). The only difference in the armament was that the training TT was mounted amidships. The boilers varied as in the previous series, although Nos *186-187* had du Temple-Normand type, and Nos *195-200* a du Temple return-tube boiler. Builders (and order dates) were as follows: Loire Nos *172-176* (4.11.1891); Graville-Le Havre *177-179* (11.11.1891) and *188-191* (22.10. 1892); Schneider *180*, *181* (26.11.1891); Normand *182-187* (27.7.1892); Gironde *192-194* (12.10.1892); Cail *195-198* (23.11.1892) and *199*, *200* (14.6.1893). Their trials were protracted, especially for the last six which never reached the designed 23kts, but all except *175*, *181*, *196* and *200* made 22kts. On average the Normand boats were the fastest with 24kts or over, although *191* made 25.38kts. Most were stricken just before World War I.

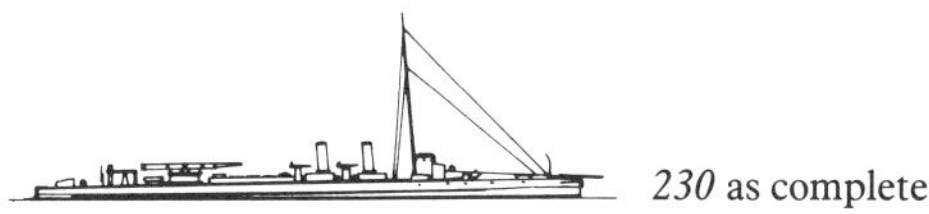
230 as completed

NOS 201-292, 9S *37-metre type* 1897-1904

Displacement: 83t-90t
Dimensions: 121ft 6in wl x 13ft 9in x 4ft *(37.00 x 4.20 x 1.22m)* (varied slightly between builders)
Machinery: 1-shaft TE, 2 boilers (various types), 1500ihp (except *212-222*, *227-229*, *233-235*, *243*, *245-250*, *253-257*, *260-277* 1800ihp, and *278-292* 1900ihp) = 24kts (except *278-292* 26kts)
Armament: 2-15in TT, 2-37mm revolvers
Complement: 23

A large class with many variations in details. The Normand-built *201-205* were the prototypes, and during the construction of the class Normand-inspired modifications continually uprated the engines, reaching an actual figure of 2000ihp in *278-279*. They were the first class designed with two boilers (and consequently had two funnels) and were considered economical steamers. *243* was completed with two experimental Rateau turbines, the first in the French Navy. *9S* was shipped to Saigon for assembly and *242*, *244-249*, *254*, *255*, *277*, *284-286*, *291* and *292* went to Saigon; *261*, *262*, *270*, *272*, *287* and *290* went to the Indian Ocean flotilla based at Diego Suarez.

Builders (and order dates) were as follows: Normand *201-205* (4.6.1895), *212-215* (3.2.1897), *278-280* (16.10.1901); Gironde *206*, *207* (24.2.1896), *208-211* (16.3.1896), *230-232* (23.8.1897), *239-241* (1.9.1897), *258-260* (20.6.1900), *275*, *276* (8.5.1901); Schneider *216-220* (17.2.1897), *233-235* (23.8.1897), *242* (23.3.1898), *244* (19.12.1898), *245-250* (29.3.1899), *261-263* (20.6.1900), *271*, *272* (8.5.1901), *277* (25.2.1901), *9S* (14.8.1902), *287-289* (1903); Loire *221*, *222*, *236-238* (18.3.1897), *251-252* (29.3.1899), *266-268* (8.5.1901); Cherbourg *223*, *224* (28.4.1897); Toulon *225*, *226* (28.4.1897); Graville *227-229* (1.9.1897), *243* (7.9.1898), *253-255* (2.8.1899), *256*, *257* (20.6.1900), *284-286* (7.1.1903); Dyle et Bacalan *264*, *265* (20.6.1900), *273*, *274* (8.5.1901); La Seyne *269*, *270* (8.5.1901); St Nazaire-Penhoët *290-292* (1903).

Those not stricken shortly before World War I were sold between 1919 and 1923.

NO 293 *experimental turbine type* 1904

Displacement: 94t
Dimensions: 129ft 8in wl x 13ft 6in x 4ft 1in *(39.50 x 4.12 x 1.25m)*
Machinery: 3-shaft Parsons turbines, 2 Normand boilers, 2000ihp = 26kts
Armament: 2-15in TT (1 bow), 2-37mm revolvers

Ordered on 29.10.1902 from Normand, the design was essentially a lengthened *278* with modified hull lines, intended to test Parsons turbines. Considerably more successful than the Rateau-engined *243*, making a maximum of 27.3kts on trials, nevertheless *293* suffered from the high fuel consumption which was the major drawback of early turbine installations. She was stricken in 1910 but survived until 1916 as a tender to the engineering school at Brest.

NO 294 *experimental turbine type* 1904

Displacement: 96t designed, 100t actual
Dimensions: 126ft 3in wl x 13ft x 4ft 7in *(38.45 x 3.95 x 1.40m)*
Machinery: 2-shaft Bréguet-Laval turbines, 2 du Temple boilers, 1800ihp = 24kts
Armament: 2-15in TT (1 bow), 2-37mm revolvers

Ordered 11.3.1903 from Bréguet (hull subcontracted to Chantiers de la Gironde), to test the only other French turbine design available. No *294* proved to be not only slower than *293* (achieving a trial speed of 25.14kts) but without a cruising turbine was also less economical. She was also stricken in 1910, but survived at the engineering school at Brest until 1914.

LIBELLULE *experimental turbine type* 1905

Displacement: 39t
Dimensions: 119ft 6in pp x 11ft 2in x 6ft 3in *(36.40 x 3.40 x 1.90m)*
Machinery: 1-shaft Rateau turbine, 1 Renard boiler, 1000shp = 13kts
Armament: 1-15in TT

Ordered on the initiative of Emile Bertin on 10.3.1898, this vessel was a *'torpilleur-vedette'* although the hull form was based on the Normand 34-metre type. Built by Forges et Chantiers de la Méditerranée, *Libellule* was designed as a test-bed for the revolutionary Renard steam generator. This device, although theoretically offering high power almost instantly, was immensely complex and capricious in the extreme, and the prototype took 6 years to construct. On trials it was very disappointing, 15.2kts being *Libellule*'s best speed, and the boat was decommissioned as soon as the trials were over and never again employed. She was stricken in 1911.

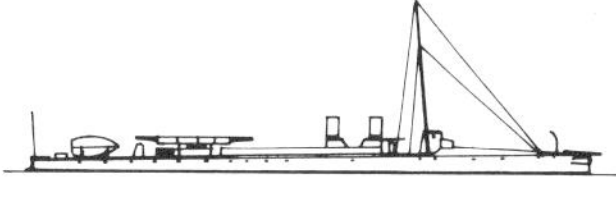
295 as completed

NOS 295-369 *38-metre type* 1905-8

Displacement: 96t designed, 99t-101t actual
Dimensions: 124ft 9in wl x 14ft 5in x 6ft 2in *(38.00 x 4.40 x 1.88m)*
Machinery: 1-shaft TE, 2 Normand or du Temple boilers, 2000ihp = 26kts (designed), 23kts best sea speed
Armament: 3-18in TT (1 bow, 2 trainable), 2-37mm revolvers
Complement: 23

Builders (and order dates) were as follows: Normand *295*, *296* (11.11.1903), *318-321* (20.7.1904); Gironde *297-299* (23.12.1903), *325-331* (3.8.1904); Dyle et Bacalan *300-302* (23.10.1903), *332-337* (17.8.1904); Loire *303-305* (23.12.1903), *347-352* (3.8.1904); Graville *306-308* (6.2.1904), *341-346* (3.8.1904); Schneider *309-311* (12.12.1903), *353-358* (3.8.1904); St Nazaire-Penhoët *312-314* (23.12.1903), *359-367* (3.8.1904); Dubigeon *315-317* (23.12.1903), *322-324* (20.7.1904); de la Brosse et Fouché *338-340* (17.8.1904); Toulon *368*, *369* (23.7.1904).

This last series of TBs for the *'défense mobile'* formed a particularly homogeneous class. They were based on the previous 37-metre type – most of the extra tonnage being attributable to the greater torpedo armament – but with a number of Normand modifications. Not only was the TT calibre increased but the two trainable tubes were mounted end-to-end on a single pivot aft. An increase in gun calibre was considered but rejected on the grounds of weight and the impossibility of matching contemporary destroyer armament, so this class retained the 37mm/20cal Hotchkiss 1885 model despite criticism of its low muzzle velocity.

All except 3 boats were fitted with the Normand-designed engines that were so successful in the preceding *278* and *279*, and although they achieved less speed they were economical, giving 600nm at 18kts or 2000nm at 10kts. Nos *366*, *368* and *369* had experimental machinery, *366*'s Lentz engine being so disappointing that her entry into service was delayed for 2 years while she was re-engined at the builder's expense; *368* and *369* had Delauncey-Belleville engines (with forced lubrication) of reduced power (1800ihp) and lower speed but increased economy.

Although generally satisfactory, this class was received into service with no great enthusiasm. Small TBs were considered obsolescent, and the concept of the *'défense mobile'* no longer seemed practical. All served during World War I, when *300*, *317*, *319* and *325* were mined, and most of the survivors were sold around 1920 although a few continued to serve in auxiliary capacities.

Italy

An historic moment for the Italian Navy – King Victor Emmanuel's arrival in Naples, 7 Nov 1860. The ships dressed overall are *Garibaldi* (ex-Neapolitan) on the far left and the Piedmont-Sardinian ships *Carlo Alberto* (next right), *Constituzione* (foreground) and *Governolo* (beyond *Constituzione's* bow). The line of battle ship in the right background is HMS *Hannibal,* flagship of Sir George Mundy: she is not dressed overall because at that time Great Britain still recognised Francis II as King of Naples. However the US frigate *Iroquois* (not visible in this photo) was dressed overall.

The National Italian Navy was created on 17 November 1860, when the regional navies – Sardinian, Bourbon, Garibaldi's Sicilian, Tuscan and Papal – combined. Four months later, on 17 March 1861, it became the *Regia Marina Italiana,* following the proclamation of the Kingdom of Italy.

The traditions of the various navies stretched back many years. Without going back to Republican or Imperial Rome, or exploring the Italian republican navies in the Middle Ages (Venice, Amalfi, Pisa, Genoa), it is sufficient to mention the strong Italian presence at the Battle of Lepanto in 1571.

THE SARDINIAN NAVY

In 1713 the Duke of Savoy's own navy was instituted when he became King of Sicily. But in 1720, when Sicily was exchanged for Sardinia, the Savoy Navy became Sardinian. It was a small but courageous force which distinguished itself in action against the Turks, the Barbary States and later against the Republican French. After the fall of Napoleon in 1815, Victor Emmanuel I re-formed his navy, which was increased after an assignment of land belonging to the Republic of Genoa. Under the strict control of Admiral Giorgio des Geneys, the Sardinian fleet was considerably enlarged with ships built at Genoa, Leghorn and in Great Britain. Following the success of the Sardinian attack on Tripoli in 1825 the King, Carlo Felice, was encouraged to add to his fleet, and the following vessels were ordered from La Foce yard: the frigates *Bereldo* and *Haute Combe* (50 guns) and the corvette *Aurora* (20 guns), all launched in 1827; the frigate *Euridice* (44 guns), launched in 1828; the frigate *Carlo Felice* and *Regina* (60 guns), launched in 1829. The Sardinian fleet had excellent officers and crews, and after 1834 Sardinian warships were regularly sent into South American waters to protect Italian interests. In that same year the first steam warship of the Sardinian Navy was launched, the paddle sloop *Gulnara,* ordered from a British yard. Three years later the sloop *Ichnusa* was launched in Genoa, built on the same lines as *Gulnara,* although her engine was made in Britain. The yards at La Foce, near the naval base of Genoa, produced a number of good ships until after 1870. In 1838 the corvette *Aquila* (24 guns) was launched, the paddle corvette *Tripoli* in 1840, the fine frigate *San Michele* in 1841, masterpiece of Filippo Delève, the chief constructor. Her displacement was 2386 metric tonnes, her original armament being eight 80pdr Paixhans shell-guns and 56 36pdr guns. The brig *Eridano* was also launched (16 guns).

THE BOURBON NAVY

The Bourbon Navy, called 'the Navy of the Two Sicilies' was created in 1734 but its development was due to the efforts of an Englishman, J F E Acton, who had distinguished himself against the Algerians in 1775 when in command of the Tuscan frigate *Etruria.* He was made Minister of the Neapolitan Navy in 1778, and in the space of a few years the shipyards of Castellammare di Stabia opened, naval schools expanded, good Swedish guns were bought and the fleet increased to five ships of the line, eight frigates and six corvettes. With the Bourbon Restoration of 1815, the Neapolitan Navy improved. It was technically superior to the Sardinian Navy and its organisation was better, but it had little opportunity to show its true potential. Naples was the first Mediterranean navy to possess a steam ship, *Ferdinando II,* built in 1817-1818 near Naples, the machinery and engines being British. The Neapolitan Navy was technically and scientifically extremely advanced, and one of the first navies in the world to have Paixhans guns, about 12 years before the Royal Navy.

The Mechanical Engineering School of the Fabbrica di Pietrarsa was founded in 1840. It produced capable naval engineers as well as steam engines, capstans, chains and other apparatus used on board ships.

THE CAMPAIGN OF 1848

In 1848, when half of Europe was in the throes of revolution, two Sardinian divisions left for the Northern Adriatic to support Venice in its revolt against the Austrians. Venice had been the Austrian Navy's base for a few decades, housing its arsenal and the Naval School called the Marine Collegium. Tegetthoff, Sterneck, Petz and nearly all the senior Austrian naval officers who distinguished themselves at Lissa in 1866, were educated there. In the Hapsburg fleet the sailors were Italian and the language used on board was Italian (Venetian dialect). A Neapolitan squadron also came to the aid of Venice, comprising two sailing frigates, five steam corvettes (officially steam frigates) and one brig.

Therefore, in the Adriatic in 1848 there were nine Sardinian warships under Rear-Admiral Guiseppe Albini and eight Neapolitan ones under Commodore Raffaele de Cosa, with five major ships of the new Republic of Venice – the corvettes *Lombardia,* ex-*Carolina,* launched in 1844, 810 tonnes, 24 18pdr guns; *Civiva,* ex-*Clemenza,* launched in 1838, 485 tonnes, 16 36pdr carronades and four 18pdr guns; *Indipendenza,* ex-*Lipsia,* launched in 1826, 482 tonnes, 16 24pdr carronades and four 18pdr guns; and the brigs *Crociato,* ex-*Ussaro,* launched in 1847, 168 tonnes, 12 24pdr carronades, four 12pdr guns and *San Marco,* ex-*Tritone,* launched 1836, 450 tonnes, 12 24pdr carronades, four 9pdr guns. They were all ex-Austrian warships, built in the naval yard of Venice, but they were unsuccessful in overcoming the Austrian squadron, which included three sail frigates, three brigs, one steam corvette and four steamers of the Austrian Lloyd shipping line, and the defeats sustained on land by the Piedmontese in 1848-1849 forced the Sardinian naval forces to retreat. The Neapolitans had already been recalled by their king.

CAVOUR

The Sardinian Navy benefited a great deal from the activity of Cavour, appointed Minister in 1850. Not only did this great statesman enlarge and improve the fleet, but he was also able to restore discipline after the disorder and insubordination evident on board Sardinian ships in the Adriatic in 1848. As regards equipment Cavour ordered a 'screw frigate, first class', *Carlo Alberto,* from a British yard, the first of the kind in the Sardinian fleet, being commissioned in 1854. Again Navy Minister in 1860, Cavour ordered the first Italian ironclads, *Terribile* and *Formidabile* from French yards. It was thanks to Cavour that Piedmon-

tese armed forces took part in the Crimean War, and that an alliance was made with the French. His skill brought about Austria's declaration of war against Sardinia in 1859 and France's intervention. The French and Sardinian fleets operated in the Adriatic at the same time as the forces on land. Meanwhile General Alfonso Ferrero della Marmora became Navy Minister and ordered frigates to be laid down in Genoa, *Vittoria Emanuele* in 1854, *Maria Adelaide* in 1857, and *Duca di Genova* on 1858. They were all designed by Felice Mattei, director of naval construction. *Maria Adelaide,* one of the fastest and most powerful frigates of the time, was considered the best in the Mediterranean.

From 1859-1861, with another war of independence, the expedition of Garibaldi's 'Thousand' and the annexing of central Italy, almost the whole peninsula was freed from most of its foreign and absolutist domination, the exceptions being the areas of Venice, Trento, Trieste and Istria, still in Austrian hands, and Rome, Civitavecchia and part of the Lazio area, still under the Pope. Victor Emmanuel II was elected King of Italy. The new Italian fleet included ships from the Sardinian-Piedmontese and from the Kingdom of Two Sicilies, from Tuscany and the Papal States. The Sicilian Navy had deteriorated in the previous decade, in particular because of the conduct of officers with liberal ideas who supported unification, some of whom would not resign from the service whether or not they were loyal to the King. When the man-of-war *Monarca* was launched on 5 June 1850, a Neapolitan officer is reported to have whispered in the ear of one of his colleagues, 'Who knows what flag this ship will fly?' This incident was typical of the time. On 17 December 1856, a magazine exploded, causing many casualties, and the steam corvette *Carlo III* was blown up at Naples on 4 January 1857, and 39 officers and men were killed. It was rumoured that arson had been the cause, even though the incidents were supposed to have been accidents.

THE ITALIAN NAVY

The constitution of the new Italian fleet created on 17 March 1861 is given in the table below. It can be seen that the fleet consisted mostly of the Sardinian and Neapolitan navies, while one screw corvette (under construction), one sloop and four gunboats came from the Grand Duchy of Tuscany and two tugs from the Papal Navy. It is interesting to note that the Sicilian Navy, rebelling against the government at Naples, had already bought some ships in 1848-1849 from overseas, in particular from Great Britain. However, even before the revolution was quelled, the Bourbon or loyalist ships had prevented the ships from reaching the insurgents.

During the Piedmontese army's invasion of the Marches and Umbria, the Papal forces had been kept back at Ancona, after their defeat at the Battle of Castelfidardo. The capture of Ancona depended on a sea attack, so a division was sent under Rear-Admiral Persano, with the steam frigates *Maria Adelaide* (flag), *Carlo Alberto, Vittorio Emanuele*, the sail frigate *San Michele* and the paddle corvettes *Governolo, Constituzione* and *Monzambano. Carlo Alberto* opened well-directed and continuous fire against La Lanterna, the naval base, and caused a good deal of damage. Captain Battista Albini ordered the *Vittorio Emanuele* to head for the battery and discharged a full broadside against it: the battery exploded and Ancona surrendered on 29 September 1860. The fortress of Gaeta in the Kingdom of Two Sicilies remained loyal to Francis I. Besieged by the Piedmontese army, and blockaded by Persano's squadron on 19 January 1861, the fortress surrendered less than a month later.

THE AUSTRIAN WAR, 1866

In the years that followed, Italy prepared for another war against Austria. The quarrel was over Venice, which would have united with the Kingdom of Sardinia in 1859 after the Piedmontese and French victories, if Napoleon III had not drawn up an armistice with the Austrians at Villafranca. In the course of General L F Menabrea's ministry from 12.6.1861 to 3.3.1862, three ironclad steam frigates were laid down. Two first class frigates were ordered from Webb's Yard, New York, *Re d'Italia* and *Don Luigi Re di Portogallo,* and one second class frigate, *Messina,* was laid down at Castellammare. Italian industry could not yet build iron ships, and Italian shipyards could not cope with preparing the kind of fleet required for a peninsula with over 5000 kilometres of coastline, or for the war against Austria which now seemed imminent. Therefore, the *Re d'Italia* and the *Re di Portogallo* were wooden-hulled. The former was sunk at the Battle of Lissa and the other had a life almost as short, since some serious faults, above all the poor quality of the timber used for her hull, meant that she had to be relegated to harbour duties in 1870, only six years after being commissioned. The *Messina* took no fewer than 65 months to complete.

With Vice-Admiral Persano as Navy Minister from 3.3.1862 to 8.12.1862, four ironclad second class frigates were laid down in three French yards. These were the *Regina Maria Pia, San Martino, Castelfidardo* and *Ancona.* They were called 'the French ships' and fought at Lissa. From Wigram's Yard in London the fast sloops *Esploratore* and *Messaggiere* were ordered, which were then amongst the fastest ships in the world. During the four and a half months office of three other Navy Ministers, the first class ironclad frigates *Roma* and *Venezia* were laid down at La Foce Yard, Genoa, and in the San Rocca Yard, Leghorn, the ironclad second class frigate *Conte Verde*, a sister ship to *Messina,* already named, but fitted with timber armour. The most interesting vessel was the ironclad turret ram *Affondatore*, conceived by the Italian Commander Simone Pacoret de Saint Bon, who had designed a very strong ram as the ship's only armament. In fact the plans were altered by an engineer called Harrison, who added two Armstrong 300pdr guns (228mm cal) in two training turrets. Fearing that the British authorities would seize the unit, as the Italo-Austrian war was about to begin, the Italian Government ordered the Commander, Frederico Martini, to leave British waters and finish fitting out at Cherbourg. *Affondatore* sailed from there on 20 June 1866 to the Adriatic, where she arrived just in time to take part in the Battle of Lissa. Admiral Persano relied on the new ship to the extent of transferring his flag from the *Re d'Italia* shortly before action started. However, since she had not been able to exercise with the squadron, she did not achieve the success Persano had expected of her.

Two ironclad gunboats, *Palestro* and *Varese*, and two transport steamers *(Città di Napoli* and *Città di Genova)* were laid down during Cugia's 17 months of ministry (22.4.1863 to 24.9.1864). The two ironclads were ordered from the French Forges et Chantiers de la Méditerranée. Two ironclads floating batteries (*Guerriera* and *Voragine*) were laid down in Italian yards late in 1864.

While the *Palestro* and *Varese* fought at Lissa (*Palestro* exploded at the end of the action), none of the following warships was ready in time for the war of 1866: the first class ironclad frigates *Palestro,* so named after the sinking of the first *Palestro,* and *Principe Amedeo;* three ironclad second class gunboats, *Temeraria,* after Lissa renamed *Alfredo Cappellini,* after *Palestro's* captain who died in action; *Impavida,* renamed *Faà di Bruno,* (without the Christian name Emilio, this was the noble family name of the *Re d'Italia's* dead captain) and *Audace*.

At the time of the Battle of Lissa, in which there was less than one hour's firing, the Italian Navy consisted of 12 ironclads, plus four in the process of completion and seven still building, 20 screw fighting ships, plus one building, 49 steam warships, either fighting or auxiliary and 13 sailing ships, fighting or auxiliary. Only about 52 per cent of these vessels were actually in the Adriatic during the naval operations of 1866, and less actually fought in the battle against Tegetthoff's fleet. None of Vice-Admiral G B Albini's wooden squadron took part.

The unfortunate outcome of Lissa for the Italian fleet is well known. They fought against small numbers and inferior vessels, but Rear-Admiral Wilhelm von Tegetthoff's vigorous command united his ships and inspired his officers and men to win. The excuse that the Italian Navy consisted of men from many different origins is not sufficient. It is true that they came from Piedmont, Liguria, Naples, Sicily, Tuscany, Venice and so on, and that unification of Italy was very recent, but Austria also consisted of many different races. Indeed, the Venetians aboard the ships of the Imperial Navy might well have felt some hostility towards Austria, but they fought extremely well, demonstrating once more the truth of Nelson's words, 'Men fight, not ships'.

RETRENCHMENT AND REVIVAL

The first move after Lissa was to reduce the Navy's budget. The largest amount in previous years had been 78.2 million lire in 1862, and now it was cut from 61.9 million in 1866 to 45.6 million in 1867, and to 25.1 million in 1870. With such small appropriations, work progressed very slowly, and ships became old before they left the slips. The Navy had to wait until 1883 for a budget that exceeded 60 million lire. These were dark, sad years for the Navy, relegated to a position of minor importance after Lissa. Financial restrictions were such that in September 1870 it had great difficulty in arming a small squadron, ten ironclads, three minor vessels, three auxiliaries, to attack Civitavecchia which still belonged to the Papal States. In fact, the ships were disarmed and the last group of conscripts had been discharged. It was even debated in Parliament whether it was appropriate for Italy to have a fleet, or whether she should rely on coastal batteries for sea defence.

The revival began with Rear Admiral Augusto Riboty's second ministry (31.8.1871 to 11.7.1873). He drew up a plan to sell out-of-date ships and began building a few very powerful ones. He opened the way for that fine sailor, Rear-Admiral Saint Bon, who held office until 25.3.1876. It was thanks to them and to the engineer Benedetto Brin, that the Italian fleet reached third place amongst the navies of the world in less than 20 years. Italy had fewer ships than Britain and France, but the quality of their vessels was about equal to the Royal Navy. The answer to the Italian Navy's difficulty had been to build up first rate ships while economic conditions would not permit a large fleet. The first examples of the new fleet were the turret ships *Duilio* and *Dandolo,* both laid down in 1873, armed with the largest guns then in existence, and faster than any other battleships. They elicited the admiration of Captain 'Jacky' Fisher among others, when he was commanding officer of the largest ship in the Royal Navy, HMS *Inflexible*, and he communicated his approval to Admiral Sir Beauchamp Seymour on 12 September 1882.

Brin was also responsible for building the large fast battleships *Italia* and *Lepanto*, forerunners of the battlecruisers, and other excellent ships, which stood comparison with any of their type. Amongst these were the *Piemonte*, built in Great Britain in 1887 to 1889, the first ship to be provided with the new 6in and 4.7in QF guns. The first all-big-gun battleships were conceived in Italy. In 1899 Rear-Admiral Giovanni Bettòlo ordered the chief constructor Vittorio Cuniberti, to plan an armoured ship with 12 8in guns, 6in armour and a speed of 22 knots. This only remained in the planning stage, but the *Regina Elena* class did resemble it. Cuniberti managed to place two 12in and 12 8in guns on a ship of a little more than 12,000 tons. He had also produced a design for a large and powerful battleship, armed entirely with 12in guns, but the Italian Navy judged it too ambitious a project, although he was authorised to publish it. In the 1903 edition of *Jane's Fighting Ships*, he revealed 'An Ideal Battleship for the British Fleet', a study of a large, 17,000-ton ship armed with 12 12in guns in single and double turrets, with 12in armour and a high speed of 24kts. We know the design contributed, along with the Board of Admiralty's plans, (the First Sea Lord being Vice-Admiral Sir John Fisher), and the results of Tsushima, to the construction of the all-big-gun battleship, the *Dreadnought.*

THE ITALIAN NAVY in 1861

SCREW SHIPS OF THE LINE

Name	Launched	Tons	Guns	Fate
RE GALANTUOMO[1]	1850	3611	82	Laid up 1875

(1) Ex-*Monarca*. From Neapolitan Navy

SCREW FRIGATES

Name	Launched	Tons	Guns	Fate
CARLO ALBERTO[1]	1853	3231	57	Laid up 1869
VITTORIO EMANUELE[1]	1856	3201	47	Laid up 1900
MARIA ADELAIDE[1]	1859	3429	51	Laid up 1900
GARIBALDI[2]	1860	3390	46	Laid up 1894
DUCA DI GENOVA[1]	1860	3459	50	Laid up 1875
ITALIA[3]	Building	3622	54	Laid up 1875
PRINCIPE UMBERTO[1]	Building	3446	54	Laid up 1875
GAETA[4]	Building	3917	54	Laid up 1875
PRINCIPE DI CARIGNANO	Building	4021	22	Laid up 1875

(1) From Sardinian Navy.
(2) Ex-*Borbone*. From Neapolitan Navy.
(3) Ex-*Farnese*. From Neapolitan Navy.
(4) From Neapolitan Navy.

SCREW CORVETTES

Name	Launched	Tons	Guns	Fate
SAN GIOVANNI[1]	Building	1752	32	Laid up 1875
MAGENTA[2]	Building	2669	20	Laid up 1875
ETNA[3]	Building	1538	12	Laid up 1875
PRINCIPESSA CLOTILDE[1]	Building	2184	24	Laid up 1875

(1) From Sardinian Navy.
(2) From Tuscan Navy.
(3) From Neapolitan Navy.

SAILING FRIGATES

Name	Launched	Tons	Guns	Fate
PARTENOPE[1]	1834	2542	36	Laid up 1868
REGINA[1]	1840	2867	50	Laid up 1870
SAN MICHELE[2]	1841	2348	66	Laid up 1875

(1) From Neapolitan Navy. Machinery fitted 1862.
(2) From Sardinian Navy.

SAILING CORVETTES

Name	Launched	Tons	Guns	Fate
CARACCIOLO[1]	1811	1616	46	Laid up 1865
CRISTINA[2]	1812	750	22	Laid up 1866
EURIDICE[3]	1828	1419	20	Laid up 1869
IRIDE[4]	1838	740	12	Laid up 1869

(1) Ex-*Amalia*, ex-*Maria Carolina*. From Neapolitan Navy.
(2) Ex-Murat's *Letizia*. From Neapolitan Navy.
(3) From Sardinian Navy.
(4) Ex-*Aquila*. From Sardinian Navy.

PADDLE CORVETTES

Name	Launched	Tons	Guns	Fate
STABIA[1]	1833	571	3	Laid up 1863
TRIPOLI[2]	1840	651	4	Laid up 1876
MONZAMBANO[3]	1841	886	4	Laid up 1875
RUGGIERO[4]	1843	1342	6	Laid up 1877
GUISCARDO[4]	1843	1343	6	Laid up 1862
TANCREDI[4]	1843	1342	6	Laid up 1868
ROBERTO[4]	1843	1339	6	Laid up 1863
ERCOLE[5]	1843	1285	6	Laid up 1875
ARCHIMEDE[4]	1844	1285	10	Laid up 1882
MALFATANO[2]	1844	671	4	Laid up 1870
PALINURO[4]	1844	571	3	Laid up 1863
MISENO[4]	1844	587	3	Laid up 1870
STROMBOLI[4]	1844	571	8	Laid up 1865
TUKERY[6]	1848	947	10	Laid up 1870
FULMINANTE[7]	1848	1389	10	Laid up 1872
CONSTITUZIONE[2]	1849	2135	10	Laid up 1875
GOVERNOLO[2]	1849	2243	12	Laid up 1882
ETTORE FIERAMOSCA[4]	1850	1388	6	Laid up 1883

(1) Ex-*Ferdinando II*. From Sardinian, then Neapolitan Navy.
(2) From Sardinian Navy.
(3) Ex-merchant ship *Mongibello*. From Neapolitan Navy.
(4) From Neapolitan Navy.
(5) Ex-*Gaeta*. From Neapolitan Navy.
(6) Ex-British *Vectis*. From Neapolitan and Sicilian Navies (frequent changes of ownership and of name).
(7) Ex-British *SS Bombay*. From Neapolitan and Sicilian Navies (frequent changes of ownership and of name).

GUNBOATS

Name	Launched	Tons	Guns	Fate
ARDITA[1]	1859	285	2	Laid up 1880
VELOCE[1]	1859	285	2	Laid up 1880
VINZAGLIO[2]	1860	258	4	Laid up 1869
CONFIENZA[2]	1860	258	4	Laid up 1880
CURTATONE[1]	1860	258	4	Laid up 1875
MONTEBELLO	1860	258	4	Laid up 1872
PALESTRO[1]	1860	288	4	Laid up 1890
VARESE[2]	1860	288	4	Laid up 1888

(1) From Tuscan Navy.
(2) From Sardinian Navy.

SLOOPS ('AVVISI')

Name	Launched	Tons	Guns	Fate
GULNARA[1]	1834	443	4	Laid up 1875
ICHNUSA[1]	1837	443	4	Laid up 1867
AQUILA[2]	1840	567	5	Laid up 1875
PELORO[3]	1842	287	4	Laid up 1875
GIGLIO[4]	1846	246	2	Laid up 1879
AUTHION[1]	1847	492	3	Laid up 1882
GARIGLIANO[5]	1854	325	4	Laid up 1883
SIRENA[6]	1859	348	3	Laid up 1884
BALENO[7]	1860	192	2	Laid up 1907

(1) From Sardinian Navy.
(2) Ex-British steamer. Ex-Sicilian Revolutionary Government and Neapolitan Navies (frequent changes of name). Re-launched 1854.
(3) From Neapolitan Navy. Rebuilt in Naples DYd 1857 and re-launched 1861.
(4) From Tuscan Navy.
(5) From Neapolitan, then Sardinian Navy.
(6) From Neapolitan Navy.
(7) Ex-British *SS Fairy Queen*. From Sicilian Navy.

BRIGS

Name	Launched	Tons	Guns	Fate
AURORA[1]	1827	632	10	Laid up 1866
GENEROSO[2]	1828	467	18	Laid up 1863
ZEFFIRO[3]	1832	585	20	Laid up 1869
VALOROSO[3]	1837	902	20	Laid up 1869
INTREPIDO[3]	1839	630	18	Laid up 1863
ERIDANO[1]	1841	443	16	Laid up 1868
COLOMBO[1]	1843	472	16	Laid up 1867 or 1869
DAINO[1]	1844	472	8	Laid up 1869

(1) From Sardinian Navy.
(2) Ex-*Principe Carlo*. From Neapolitan Navy.
(3) From Neapolitan Navy.

In addition to the vessels listed above there were 6 screw transports and 7 paddle transports totalling 26 guns, 6 unarmed paddle tugs, and 8 sailing transports totalling 2 guns. There were also 6 lake gunboats. The Navy in 1861, therefore, consisted of 90 vessels mounting about 870 guns. In addition, 8 vessels, carrying 272 guns, were under construction.

CAPITAL SHIPS

Ordered during Cavour's ministry from French yards and designed as armoured floating batteries for coastal actions these vessels, the first Italian ironclads, were modified before completion into ironclad corvettes, able to fight also in open water, and their projected armament was reduced from 30 to 20 guns. Their sides were entirely protected by 4.3in thick iron plates. They were rigged as three-masted schooners. In 1872-3 they were reboilered and in 1878 their armament was altered to 8-8in guns. After 1885 *Terribile* was used as a TS, for experiments and for other duties, her armament having been modified in 2-6in, 2-5.9in and 2-4.7in guns, plus 2 TT. After 1887 *Formidabile* served as a TS for gunners, with 6-4.7in guns.

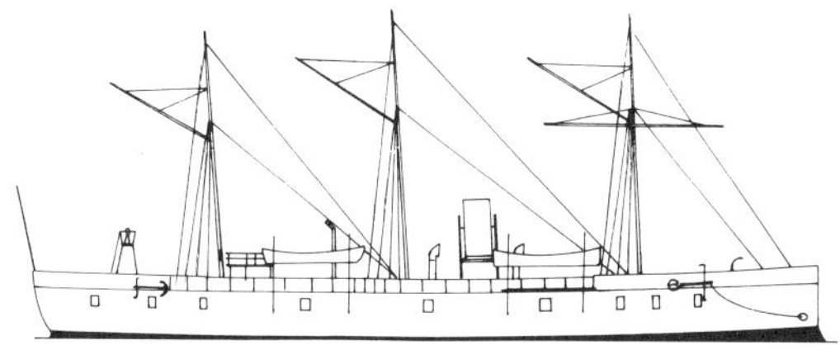

Formidabile as completed 1862

FORMIDABILE class *broadside ironclads*

Displacement: 2682t normal; *Terribile* 2807t, *Formidabile* 2618t full load
Dimensions: 206ft 10in pp, 215ft 10in oa x 47ft 3in x 17ft 10½in (*63.05, 65.80 x 14.44 x 5.45m*)
Machinery: 1-shaft SE, 6 rec boilers, 1100ihp (*Formidabile* 1080ihp) = 10kts. Endurance about 1300nm (10kts)
Armour: Iron. Belt 4.3in, citadel 4in
Armament: 16-164mm, 4-203mm
Complement: 371

Name	Builder	Laid down	Launched	Comp	Fate
TERRIBILE	La Seyne	June 1860	16.2.61	Sept 1861	Stricken 1904
FORMIDABILE	La Seyne	Dec 1860	1.10.61	May 1862	Stricken 1903

ITALY

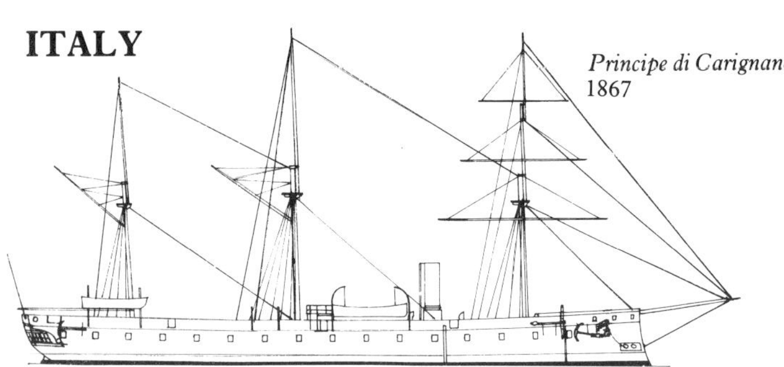
Principe di Carignano 1867

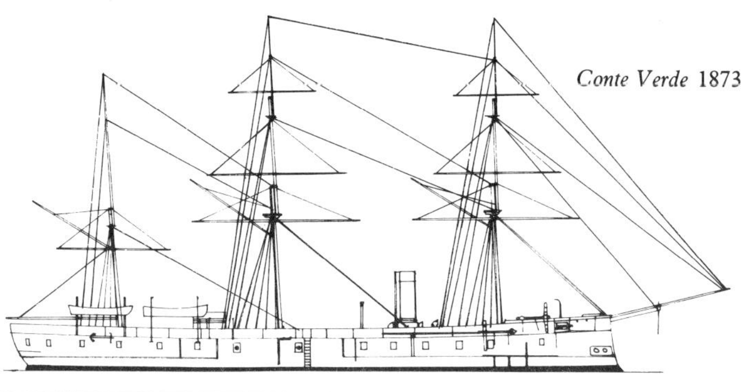
Conte Verde 1873

Although in many respects similar, these ships belonged to two different types. Originally, the *Principe di Carignano* was a sister-ship to the screw frigate *Principe Umberto* and the *Messina* was practically identical to them, all having been designed by Insp Eng Felice Mattei. While on slip, *Principe di Carignano* and *Messina* were converted into ironclads, with armour plates 4¾in thick. The *Conte Verde*, on the other hand, was designed as an ironclad frigate by Insp Eng Giuseppe De Luca, but, strangely enough, she was not a true ironclad as she had timber armour and only parts of her bows and stern protected by iron plates. *Principe di Carignano* was rigged as a barquentine, the other two ships as barques. In about 1870 the armament was modified as follows: *Principe di Carignano* 4-8in, 16-164mm; *Messina* 2-10in, 4-8in, 8-164mm; *Conte Verde* 6-10in, 1-8in. The last, removed from the Naval list in 1880, was scrapped eighteen years later.

PRINCIPE DI CARIGNANO class *broadside ironclads*

Displacement: *Principe di Carignano* 3446t normal, 3912t full load; *Messina* 3868t normal, 4245t full load; *Conte Verde* 3514t normal, 3866t full load
Dimensions: *Principe di Carignano* 239ft 5in pp x 49ft 6½in x 23ft 6½in (*72.98 x 15.10 x 7.18m*); *Messina* 238ft 10in x 49ft 6½in x 23ft 10in (*72.8 x 15.10 x 7.27m*); *Conte Verde* 241ft 9½in x 50ft 2in x 21ft 4in (*73.7 x 15.3 x 6.50m*)
Machinery: 1-shaft SE, 6 cyl (*Principe di Carignano* 4 rec) boilers, 1968ihp max (*Conte Verde*) = 10.2kts (*Principe di Carignano*), 10.4kts (*Messina*), 11.4kts (*Conte Verde*). Endurance about 1200nm (10kts)
Armour: Iron. Side 4¾in. See notes
Armament: 4-72pdr (8in) (*Principe di Carignano* 10-8in), 18-164mm (*Principe di Carignano* 12-164mm)
Complement: 572

Name	Builder	Laid down	Launched	Comp	Fate
PRINCIPE DI CARIGNANO	La Foce, Genoa	Jan 1861	15.9.63	11.6.65	Discarded 1875
MESSINA	Castellammare N Yd	28.9.1861	20.12.64	Feb 1867	Discarded 1880
CONTE VERDE	San Rocco, Leghorn	2.3.1863	29.7.67	Dec 1871	Discarded 1880

Messina off Naples, winter 1867

The heaviest Italian warships for some time, these vessels were ordered from an American shipyard during the Civil War of 1861-5. Their hulls were wooden and therefore without watertight compartments, and as their rudders and propellers were not protected, the *Re d'Italia* had her rudder easily disabled and she was rammed and sunk in a very short time by the *Ferdinand Max* at the Battle of Lissa. The *Re di Portogallo* (more correctly named *Don Luigi Re di Portogallo*), also had a rather short life, her timber being unseasoned and the ship herself revealing several faults. Both were barque-rigged, with 21,317 sq ft of sail. *Re di Portogallo*'s armament was altered in 1870 to 2-10in, 6-8in and 12-164mm; after 1871, as an artillery TS, she carried 20-8in, 2-4.7in and 8-80mm guns.

RE D'ITALIA class *broadside ironclads*

Displacement: 5610t normal; *Re d'Italia* 5869t, *Re di Portogallo* 6082t full load
Dimensions: 275ft pp, 326ft 9½in oa x 55ft x 20ft 3in (*Re di Portogallo* 23ft 6½in) (*83.82, 99.61 x 16.76 x 6.17 (7.18)m*)
Machinery: 1-shaft SE, 4 rec boilers, 1845-1812ihp = 10.8-10.6kts. Endurance about 1800nm (10½kts)
Armour: Iron. Side 4¾in max
Armament: 6-72pdr (8in) (*Re di Portogallo* 2-10in), 32-164mm (*Re di Portogallo* 26-164mm)
Complement: 565, *Re di Portogallo* 552

Name	Builder	Laid down	Launched	Comp	Fate
RE D'ITALIA	Webb, New York	21.11.1861	18.4.63	14.9.64	Sunk 20.7.66
RE DI PORTOGALLO	Webb, New York	Dec 1861	29.8.63	23.8.64	Stricken 31.3.75

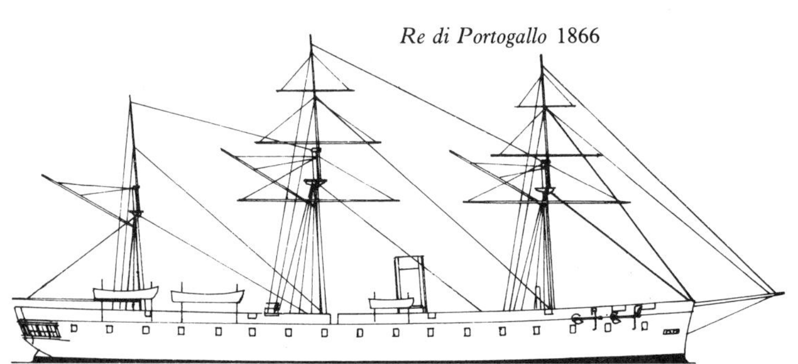
Re di Portogallo 1866

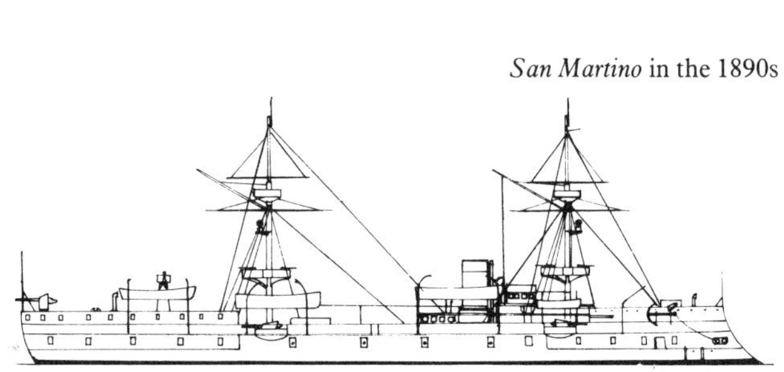
San Martino in the 1890s

Ordered by the Italian Government from French yards (who also drew up the designs), these ships varied slightly, one group consisting of *Regina Maria Pia* and *San Martino*, and the other of *Castefidardo* and *Ancona*. All were iron-hulled with complete iron belts and sides. After 1866, the armament and armour system were modified so that the ships, provided with a central armoured casemate, could fire ahead and astern (two guns forward, one astern). The armour for the end guns was removed. They were rigged at first as three-masted schooners, but during their long life, the rig was altered, first to barque and finally, about 1888-90, to two military masts with fighting tops. *Regina Maria Pia* and *San Martino*'s armament was changed to 2-220mm and 9-8in and later 8-6in, 5-4.7in, 4-57mm QF, 8-37mm revolvers and 3 TT. *Castelfidardo* and *Ancona* received, in about 1871, 2-10in, 8-8in and in about 1880, 2-220mm, 9-8in. *Castelfidardo*, from 1884, carried 8-6in, 6-4.7in, 4-57mm QF and 8-37mm revolvers, and in 1900 was converted to a torpedo TS with 1-3in QF, 1-75mm, 4-57mm QF, 1-47mm QF, 2-37mm revolvers and 2 TT. *Ancona*'s final armament was 8-6in, 6-4.7in, 4-57mm QF, 2-37mm revolvers and 3 TT.

Castelfidardo as completed, at Naples in 1866

REGINA MARIA PIA class *broadside ironclads*

Displacement: 4201t normal, 4527t full load; (*Castelfidardo* 4192t normal, 4527t full load; *Ancona* 4157t normal, 4619t full load)

Dimensions: 247ft $7\frac{1}{2}$in pp, 265ft $9\frac{1}{2}$in oa x 50ft x 20ft 10in (*75.48, 81.2 x 15.24 x 6.35m*); *Castlefidardo* and *Ancona* 249ft 4in pp, 268ft 4in oa x 49ft 9in x 20ft 10in (*76.0, 81.8 x 15.16 x 6.35m*)

Machinery: Reciprocating, 6 (*Castelfidardo*, *Ancona* 8) rec boilers, 2924ihp = 12.96kts (*San Martino* 2620ihp = 12.6kts, *Castelfidardo* 2125ihp = 12.1kts, *Ancona* 2548ihp = 13.74kts). Endurance 2600nm (10kts)

Armour: Iron. Belt $4\frac{3}{4}$in (*Castelfidardo* and *Ancona* 4.3in), battery 4.3in

Armament: 4-8in, 22-164mm

Complement: 480-485

Name	Builder	Laid down	Launched	Comp	Fate
REGINA MARIA PIA	La Seyne	22.7.1862	28.4.63	17.4.64	Stricken 1904
SAN MARTINO	La Seyne	22.7.1862	21.9.63	9.11.64	Stricken 1903
CASTELFIDARDO	Gouin et Guibert, St Nazaire	27.7.1862	1.8.63	May 1864	Stricken 1910
ANCONA	Arman, Bordeaux	11.8.1862	17.10.64	Apr 1866	Stricken 1903

Designed by Insp Eng Giuseppe De Luca, these two ships had a very protracted building period. The *Venezia* emerged as a more modern vessel than *Roma* – in fact the latter had the traditional broadside arrangement, while the *Venezia* had a central battery, from which two guns could fire ahead and two others astern. Both hulls were wooden, but some unarmoured parts were of iron, and both were rigged as barques, with 31,833 sq ft of sail. From 1874-5 the armament was modified: *Roma* had 11-10in and *Venezia* 8-10in and 1-220mm. After 1886 *Roma* carried 11-220mm and from 1890, serving as the principal ship for the defence of La Spezia, she had 5-8in guns. In 1881 *Venezia* began conversion into a torpedo TS, had her rig reduced and was fitted with 4-75mm and 4-57mm QF guns and no TT, and had a complement of 302. She served at La Spezia until 23.8.1895 and was scrapped in 1895-6. *Roma*, removed from the Navy list on 5.5.1895, was employed as a floating ammunition depot ship at La Spezia; on 28.7.1896 she was set on fire by lightning and was scuttled to prevent her total destruction. She was refloated in August 1896 but was immediately broken up.

ROMA class *broadside/central battery ironclads*

Displacement: 5698t (*Venezia* 5722t) normal, 6151t full load

Dimensions: 261ft $4\frac{1}{2}$in pp x 57ft x 24ft 10in (*79.67 x 17.33 x 7.57m*); *Venezia* 261ft 4in pp x 57ft 4in x 24ft 11in (*79.65 x 17.48 x 7.60m*)

Machinery: 1-shaft SE, 6 cyl boilers, 3670ihp = 13kts. Endurance 1940nm (10kts)

Armour: Iron. Battery $4\frac{3}{4}$in (not *Roma*), side 5.9in

Armament: *Roma* 5-10in, 12-8in; *Venezia* 18-10in

Complement: 549-551

Name	Builder	Laid down	Launched	Comp	Fate
ROMA	La Foce, Genoa	Feb 1863	18.12.65	May 1869	Stricken 1895
VENEZIA	La Foce, Genoa	Feb 1863	21.1.69	1.4.73	Stricken 1895

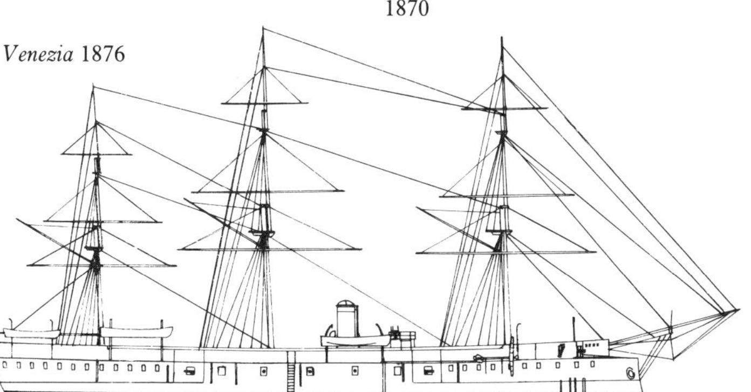

Venezia 1876

Right: *Roma* as completed, in Sept 1870

The building of this ship was originally contracted with Mare of Millwall on 11.10.1862, but because of the yard's financial difficulties the Italian Government signed a new contract with Harrison, who recast the plans. However, financial problems arose once more; the planned 18 months for the delivery of the ship expired, and the ship eventually sailed from London, uncompleted, on 20 June 1866, the day the Italo-Austrian war broke out, since the Italian Government

AFFONDATORE *turret ram*

Displacement: 4006t normal, 4307t full load

Dimensions: 293ft 10in pp, 307ft 9in oa x 40ft x 20ft 10in (*89.56, 93.8 x 12.20 x 6.35m*)

Machinery: 1-shaft SE, 8 rec boilers, 2717ihp = 12kts. Endurance 1647nm (10kts)

Armour: Iron. Side 5in max, turrets 5in, deck 2in

Armament: 2-228mm

Complement: 309/356

Name	Builder	Laid down	Launched	Comp	Fate
AFFONDATORE	Harrison, Millwall	11.4.1863	3.11.65	See notes	Stricken 1907

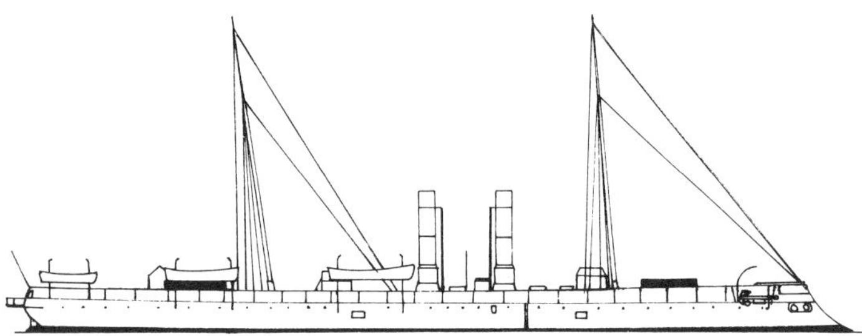

Affondatore as completed 1866

feared a possible sequestration of the ship by the British authorities. The *Affondatore* joined the Italian fleet off Lissa a few hours before the action.

She had an iron hull, a complete iron belt 5in thick, two single turrets with 228mm Armstrong guns, and was schooner-rigged. She was sunk in a storm off Ancona harbour on 6.8.1866. Refloated, she was rebuilt in 1867-70. During a second rebuilding (1883-5) the ship was re-engined (3240ihp) and was fitted with one military mast and a CT. Her armament was changed during a third rebuilding (1888-9) to 2-10in, 6-4.7in, 1-75mm QF, 8-57mm QF and 4-37mm revolvers. In 1891 2 TT were added and *Affondatore* served as a torpedo TS and, in 1904-7, as the principal ship for the defence of Venice. Removed from the Navy list on 11.10.1907, she served her final years as a floating ammunition depot at Taranto.

PRINCIPE AMEDEO class *central battery ironclads*

Displacement: 5761t normal, 6318t (*Principe Amedeo* 6020t) full load
Dimensions: *Palestro* 258ft 7in pp x 56ft 9in x 26ft 3in (*78.82 x 17.30 x 8.00m*); *Principe Amedeo* 261ft 7in pp x 57ft 0¼in x 25ft 11in (*79.73 x 17.40 x 7.90m*)
Machinery: 1-shaft SE, 6 cyl boilers, 6117ihp = 12.85kts (*Principe Amedeo* 12.2kts). Endurance 1780nm (10kts)
Armour: Iron. Belt 8.7in, battery 5½in, CT 2.4in
Armament: 1-11in, 6-10in
Complement: 548

Name	Builder	Laid down	Launched	Comp	Fate
PALESTRO	La Spezia N Yd	Aug 1865	30.9. or 2.10.71	11.7.75	Stricken 1900
PRINCIPE AMEDEO	Castellammare N Yd	Aug 1865	15.1.72	15.12.74	Stricken 1895

These two vessels were the first ironclads built and fitted out entirely by Italian yards, but 9-10 years passed from the time they were laid down to completion. They were designed by Insp Eng Giuseppe De Luca and, although projected as wooden-hulled ships, they actually had composite wood and iron hulls, protected by a complete belt and with iron sides amidships. The *Palestro* had three armoured casemates (5½in thick plates), one beginning some 20ft from the bows, protecting the 11in 'chaser' gun and two 10in guns, another beginning 33ft from the stern and containing the two starboard and two port 10in guns, and the third protecting the stern. The *Principe Amedeo* had one central casemate, containing all six 10in guns, it too protected with 5½in plates. A primitive conning tower was protected by 2.4in plates. Rigged as barques, and with sail areas of 37,361 sq ft (*Palestro*) and 36,738 sq ft (*Principe Amedeo*), they were the last Italian wooden ironclads, and the last to be provided with sails. The *Palestro* served from 1889 to 1894 as the headquaters ship of the defence of La Maddalena, and subsequently at La Spezia as a TS for coxswains and boys; removed from the naval list on 14.4.1900, she was scrapped in 1902-4. The *Principe Amedeo* served as the headquarters ship for the defence of Taranto in 1888-9, and after she was stricken on 28.3.1895 her hull was employed as a floating ammunition depot at Buffoluto (Taranto) until 1910, when she was sold for scrapping.

Palestro about 1886-7

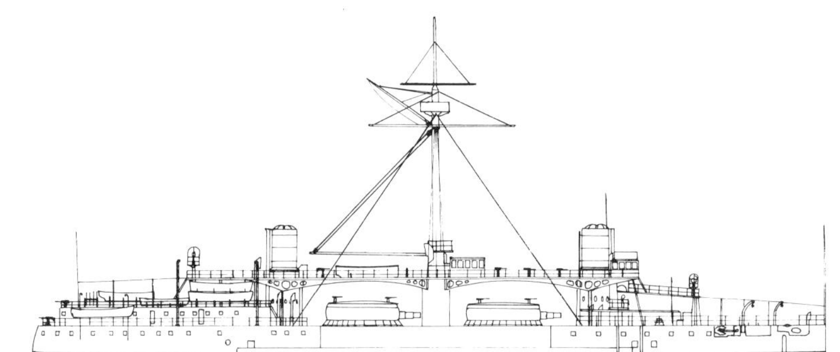

Duilio 1895

DUILIO class *turret ships*

Displacement: *Duilio* 10,962t normal, 12,071t full load; *Dandolo* 11,025t normal, 12,037t full load
Dimensions: 339ft 7in pp, 358ft 1½in oa x 64ft 9in (*Dandolo* 64ft 5½in) x 27ft 3in (*Dandolo* 27ft 5in) (*103.50, 109.16 x 19.74 (19.65) x 8.31 (8.36)m*)
Machinery: *Duilio* 2-shaft vertical, 8 rec boilers, 7711ihp = 15.04kts; *Dandolo* 2-shaft VC, 8 rec boilers, 8045ihp = 15.6kts. Endurance 3760nm (10kts), 2875nm (13kts)
Armour: Steel. Side 21½in max, deck 1.2in-2in, turrets 17in, citadel 17in, transverse frames 15¾in max
Armament: 4-17.7in/20, 3-14in TT
Complement: 420, later 515

Name	Builder	Laid down	Launched	Comp	Fate
DUILIO	Castellammare N Yd	6.1.1873	8.5.76	6.1.80	Stricken 1909
DANDOLO	La Spezia N Yd	6.1.1873	10.7.78	11.4.82	Stricken 1920

These two vessels were the first battleships in the world rigged only with a military mast and armed with giant guns, and were the first Italian 2-shaft capital ships. They were designed by Director Eng Benedetto Brin. The original plan was for four 35t guns, then for 60t guns, but 100t weapons were actually fitted. Armstrong-built MLs, these fired one 1905lb projectile every 15 minutes, with a muzzle velocity of 1490-1670fs. The belt was of Creusot steel plates; the armoured central citadel, redoubt and turrets were NS, the turrets being mounted *en echelon* close together amidships. There was a cellular raft at the bows and stern between an underwater deck and that next above, subdivided into 83 watertight compartments. Aboard *Duilio*, at the stern, was a compartment for a small TB (*Clio*, 26½t). To *Duilio*, in 1890, 3-4.7in/40 guns were added, and in 1900 2-75mm, 8-57mm/40 QF and 4-37mm/20 revolvers. *Duilio* was disarmed on 27.6.1909, hulked and, renumbered *GM40*, used as a floating coal and oil tank. *Dandolo* was rebuilt in 1895/8 to Insp Eng Giacinto Pullino's design. Her armament was altered to 4-10in/40, 7-6in/40, 5-4.7in/40, 16-57mm/43, 8-37mm/20 revolvers, 4 MGs and 4-17.7in TT. The displacement was reduced to 10,679t (11,264t full load); the turret armour was reduced to 8.8.in; the original engine was replaced by a 2-shaft VC, 7500-8045ihp = 15.6kts (as originally); and the complement rose to 495. During World War I 6-37mm were removed and she served as a local defence ship, first at Brindisi and later at Valona. She was removed from the Navy list on 23.1.1920.

Dandolo after rebuilding, on 6 Dec 1898

Italia at La Spezia in 1897

Lepanto as completed 1887

ITALIA class *battleships*

Displacement: *Italia* 13,678t normal, 15,407t full load; *Lepanto* 13,336t normal, 15,649t full load

Dimensions: 400ft 3in pp, 409ft 1in oa x 73ft 11in (*Lepanto* 73ft 4in) x 28ft 8$\frac{1}{2}$in (*Lepanto* 30ft 9$\frac{1}{2}$in) *(122.00, 124.70 x 22.54 (22.34) x 8.75 (9.39)m)*

Machinery: 4-shaft VC, 8 oval and 16 cyl boilers, 11,986ihp = 17.8kts (*Lepanto* 15,797ihp = 18.4kts). Endurance about 5000nm (10kts)

Armour: Steel. Deck 4in, citadel 19in, funnel base 16in, CT 4in

Armament: *Italia* 3-17in/26, 1-17in/27, 7-5.9in/26, 4-4.7in/23, 4-14in TT; *Lepanto* 4-17in/27, 8-6in/32, 4-4.7in/32, 4-14in TT

Complement: 669, later 701

Name	Builder	Laid down	Launched	Comp	Fate
ITALIA (ex-STELLA D'ITALIA)	Castellammare N Yd	3.1.1876	29.9.80	16.10.85	Stricken 16.11.1921
LEPANTO	Orlando, Leghorn	4.11.1876	17.3.83	16.8.87	Stricken 15.1.1914

Forerunners of the battlecruisers, these two vessels were for several years the largest and fastest warships in the world. Their designer, Insp Eng Benedetto Brin, rejected side armour, the fitting of which would have added an unbearable increase in weight to an already huge vessel; on the grounds that, at that time, the gun was superior to any armour that could be put into a belt, he adopted the pure cellular raft type. The hull of *Italia* was of iron and steel, and was covered with wood and zinc-sheathed; *Lepanto's* hull was of steel and was not covered. The 17in guns in *Italia* were of two slightly different types: three of them were Model 431C (26cal) but the fourth was Model 431B (27cal). The weight of the 431C was 102$\frac{1}{2}$t, while that of 431B was 103$\frac{1}{2}$t. Both fired a 2000lb projectile with a muzzle velocity of 1755fs. *Italia* originally had six funnels and *Lepanto* four.

The *Italia* class were in reality large, fast, strategic cruisers, with the capability of carrying, on board each ship, an entire infantry division (10,000 men). To their original armament were subsequently added 2-75mm, 6/12-57mm/40 QF, 10/12-37mm/25 revolvers and 2 MGs. *Italia* received two more TT, but those of *Lepanto* were removed in 1910. In 1905/08 *Italia*'s six funnels were reduced to four, and the single central mast was replaced by two masts; 1-5.9in, 6-57mm and 8-37mm revolvers were removed. In 1909-10 she served as a torpedo TS, in 1912 as a TS for petty officers and later (1914) she became the central ship for the defence of Taranto. On 1.6.14 she was laid up and on 4.6.14 removed from the Navy list. On 20.4.15 she was towed to Brindisi, where she served as a floating battery in the outer harbour of that base until 16.12.17. Reinstated in the Navy list on 23.5.15 and recommissioned on 1.6.15 as a 'first class auxiliary', she was moved to La Spezia for conversion to a cereal carrier, armed with 2-4.7in guns. She was transferred on 27.7.19 to the State Railways, but returned yet again to the Navy on 13.1.1921 and was finally stricken on 16.11.1921. *Lepanto* served as a TS for gunners from 1902, and in her two last years (1910-12) she was a depot ship at La Spezia, being removed from the list on 26.5.1912. She was, however, reinstated as a 'first class auxiliary' on 13.1.1913 but was stricken twelve months later and sold for scrap on 27.3.1915.

This class was a considerable compromise, because the minister of the Navy, Vice-Admiral Ferdinando Acton, opposed the building of large vessels such as the *Italia* class. He favoured ships of not more than 8000-10,000t with a maximum speed of 15kts, and was critical of huge guns – on 8 March 1880, a large muzzle-loader aboard *Duilio* blew up, having been double-loaded, and this incident roused public opinion against such large ships and guns. Acton gave the job of designing the new ships to Eng Insp Giuseppe Micheli. This naval architect, after having produced some original projects, elected to design an improved *Duilio*, and, indeed, the *Ruggiero di Lauria* class was essentially a repetition of the *Duilios*. Some improvements were incorporated – a high forecastle, breech-loading 17in guns in barbettes, a better quality and distribution of armour – but in fact the design was already obsolete when the ships entered service.

Authorised under the 1880 Naval programme, the three ships were unremarkable and had rather short lives. After being struck off, *Ruggiero di Lauria* was used as a floating oil depot at La Spezia until 1943, her hulk, sunk in shallow waters by bombing, being finally broken up in 1946-7. *Andrea Doria* was used as a floating battery (*GR104*) and served at Brindisi until after World War I, when she became an oil depot until broken up in 1929.

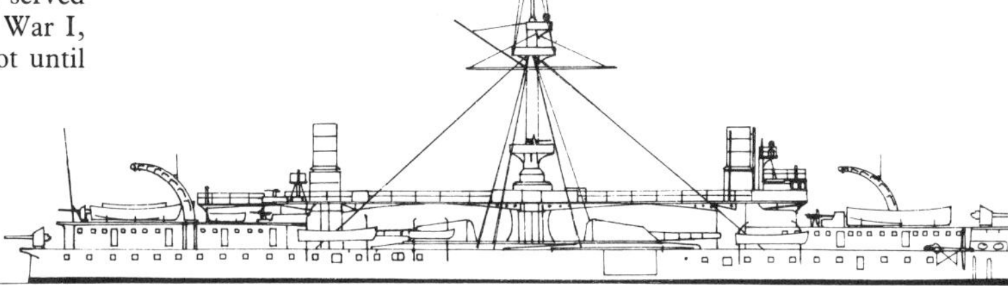

Ruggiero di Lauria, 1905

RUGGIERO DI LAURIA class *battleships*

Displacement: 9886t normal; *Ruggiero di Lauria* 10,997t, *Morosini* 11,145t, *Andrea Doria* 11,027 full load

Dimensions: 328ft 1in pp, 347ft 5in oa x 65ft 1in x 27ft 2in (*Morosini* 27ft 6in, *Andrea Doria* 27ft 3½in) (*100.00, 105.9 x 19.84 x 8.29 (8.37, 8.32)m*)

Machinery: 2-shaft compound, 8 cyl (*Morosini* 8 oval) boilers, 10,591ihp = 17kts (*Morosini* 10,000ihp = 16kts, *Andrea Doria* 10,500ihp = 16.1kts). Endurance 2800nm (10kts)

Armour: Steel. Side 17¾in, citadel and barbettes 14.2in, CT 9.8in, deck 3in

Armament: Originally 4-17in/27 (2x2), 2-6in/32, 4-4.7in/32, 2-14in TT sub; from 1900 also 2-75mm, 10-57mm/40 QF, 12-37mm, 5-37mm/20 revolvers, 2 MGs

Complement: 507, later 509

Name	Builder	Laid down	Launched	Comp	Fate
RUGGIERO DI LAURIA	Castellammare N Yd	3.8.1881	9.8.84	1.2.88	Stricken 11.11.1909
FRANCESCO MOROSINI	Venice N Yd	4.12.1881	30.7.85	21.8.89	Sunk as target 15.9.1909
ANDREA DORIA	La Spezia N Yd	7.1.1882	21.11.85	16.5.91	Stricken 1911

1

2

1. *Andrea Doria*, 18 Apr 1899

2. *Sicilia* at full speed, 11 Sept 1895

The first pair were authorised under the 1883 Naval programme but Eng Insp General Benedetto Brin, who as the president of the Committee for Naval projects had designed the ships, again become minister of the Navy, and proposed in 1885 the building a third ship, so giving Italy a modern and powerful squadron. The third ship (*Sardegna*) was slightly different in some particulars, especially with regard to machinery – she was in fact the first Italian warship fitted with 3 cyl TE machinery. As with some battleships of other navies the *Re Umbertos* had three funnels, the first pair being abreast. The *Sardegna* was also one of the first warships fitted with the new Marconi wireless telegraph.

Re Umberto was laid up at Genoa in Oct 1912 and used as a depot ship. Removed from the Navy list on 10.5.1914, she was towed to La Spezia in June 1915 and employed as a depot ship for the dreadnought *Andrea Doria*. She was reinstated on 9.12.1915 and became a floating battery, first at Brindisi and then at Valona (Albany). In 1918, when the Italian Navy were planning to force the main enemy base of Pola, the *Re Umberto* was modified as an assault ship, having all her former armament removed and mounting eight shielded 3in guns and a number of trench mortars, and a special saw and cutters were installed for use against boom and net defences. About 40 MAS-boats would have followed her, but the war ended before the operation could be carried out. She was finally removed from the Navy list on 4.7.1920. *Sicilia* was stricken on 9.7.14, but re-entered service as a depot ship at Taranto, and was later used as a repair ship before being finally deleted.

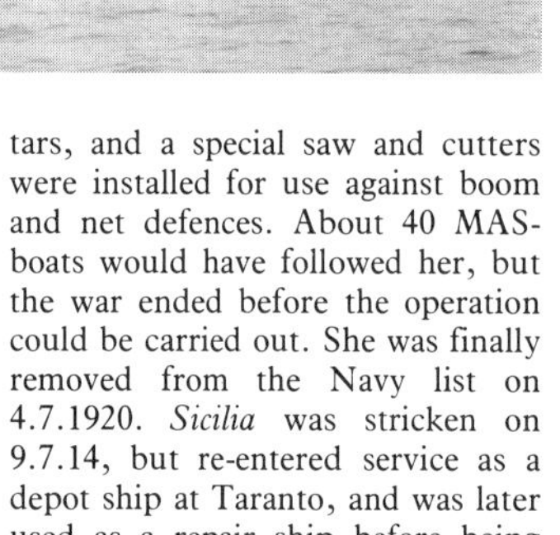

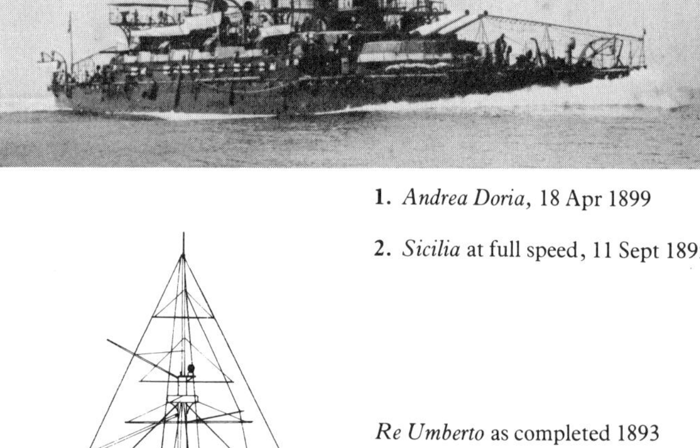

Re Umberto as completed 1893

RE UMBERTO class *battleships*

Displacement: *Re Umberto* 13,673t normal, 15,454t full load; *Sicilia* 13,058t normal, 14,842t full load; *Sardegna* 13,641t normal, 15,426t full load

Dimensions: 400ft 3in (*Sardegna* 411ft 9in) pp, 418ft 7½in (*Sardegna* 428ft 10½in) oa x 76ft 10½in x 30ft 6in (*Sicilia* 28ft 11½in, *Sardegna* 29ft) (*122.00 (125.50), 127.60 (130.73) x 23.44 x 9.29 (8.83, 8.84)m*)

Machinery: 2-shaft VC (*Sardegna* TE), 18 cyl boilers, 19,500ihp = 18½kts (*Sicilia* 19,131ihp = 20.1kts, *Sardegna* 22,800ihp = 20.3kts). Endurance 4000-6000nm (10kts)

Armour: Schneider steel. Side 4in, deck 3in, CT 11.8in, turrets 4in, barbettes 13¾in, battery 4in, 6in gunshields 2in

Armament: 4-13.5in/30 (2x2), 8-6in/40, 16-4.7in/40, 16-6pdr (57mm/43) (*Sicilia* and *Sardegna* 20-6pdr), 10-37mm/30, 5-17.7in TT aw

Complement: 733 (*Sicilia* 736, *Sardegna* 794)

Name	Builder	Laid down	Launched	Comp	Fate
RE UMBERTO	Castellammare N Yd	10.7.1884	17.10.88	16.2.93	Stricken 1920
SICILIA	Venice N Yd	3.11.1884	6.7.91	4.5.95	Stricken 1923
SARDEGNA	La Spezia N Yd	24.10.1885	20.9.90	16.2.95	Stricken 4.1.1923

Vice-Admiral Saint Bon, then minister of the Navy, proposed a medium-sized battleship, as a more convenient type for the Italian Navy and also as a reaction to the huge and expensive battleships of the previous classes. On his death (November 1892), the temporary minister Brin and the new one, Vice-Admiral Racchia, ordered some modifications to the original project. So modified, the *Saint Bons* were laid down in 1893. They had a low freeboard (only 9ft 10in from the upper deck to the waterline) and heavy guns of reduced calibre (even though the model fitted was a remarkable design), and were not powerful ships; even if one considers them as a half-measure between a battleship and a cruiser, it must be admitted that the speed of 18kts was low for a cruiser. Had it not been for the outbreak of the First World War, the *Saint Bons* would have been broken up in about 1914-15. The two vessels were commissioned before completion, *Saint Bon* on 1.2.1901 and *Filiberto* on 6.9.1901.

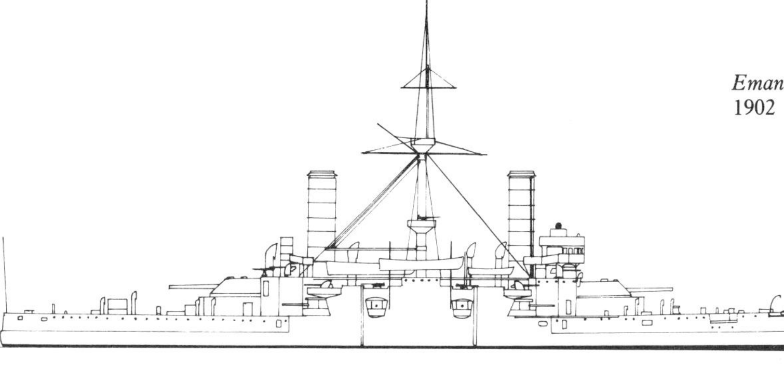

Emanuele Filiberto as completed 1902

AMMIRAGLIO DI SAINT BON class *battleships*

Displacement: 10,082 normal, 10,531t full load (*Emanuele Filiberto* 9645t normal, about 9940t full load)
Dimensions: 344ft 6in pp, 366ft 9½in oa x 69ft 3½in x 25ft 2½in (*Emanuele Filiberto* 23ft 10in) (*105.00, 111.80 x 21.12 x 7.69 (7.27)m*)
Machinery: 2-shaft TE, 12 cyl boilers, 14,296ihp = 18.3kts (*Emanuele Filiberto* 13,552ihp = 18.1kts). Endurance 3400-5500nm (10kts)
Armour: Harvey. Side 9.8in, deck 2¾in, CT 9.8in, turrets 9.8in, battery 5.9in, 4.7in gunshields 2in
Armament: 4-10in/40 (2x2), 8-6in/40, 8-4.7in/40, 8-57mm/43 (*Emanuele Filiberto* 6-3in/40, 8-47mm/40), 2-37mm/20 (not in *Emanuele Filiberto*), 4-17.7in TT aw
Complement: 557, *Emanuele Filiberto* 565

Name	Builder	Laid down	Launched	Comp	Fate
AMMIRAGLIO DI SAINT BON	Venice N Yd	18.7.1893	29.4.97	24.5.1901	Stricken 18.6.20
EMANUELE FILIBERTO	Castellammare N Yd	5.10.1893	29.9.97	16.4.1902	Stricken 29.3.20

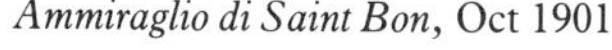

Ammiraglio di Saint Bon, Oct 1901

Regina Margherita (with *Giuseppe Garibaldi* in the background) about 1908

Designed under the 1898 Naval programme by Eng Admiral Benedetto Brin, then minister of the Navy, who required a modern, well-armed and fast ship even if this meant some sacrifice in respect of protection (a feature too often neglected in Italian warships). The armament originally comprised 2-12in and 12-8in guns (identical to that of the four *Regina Elenas* laid down in 1901-03), but after Brin's death the design was modified by Eng Admiral Ruggero Alfredo Micheli. As with other large vessels of the Italian fleet, these ships emerged as hybrids between the powerful but slow battleship and the fast cruiser type, and had only moderate protection. Actually, the two *Regina Margheritas*, though neither as large as the major contemporary foreign battleships nor as fast as cruisers, proved to be good warships, and very seaworthy. One peculiar aspect was the 'double-symmetrical' bridge/conning tower, one forward the other aft. While the *Morosini* and the two *Saint Bons* could burn not only coal but also oil, the two *Regina Margheritas* represented a backward step, since they burnt only coal. *Regina Margherita* was sunk in 1916 off Valona by two mines laid by the German submarine *UC14*; *Benedetto Brin* was lost as a result of Austrian sabotage at Brindisi.

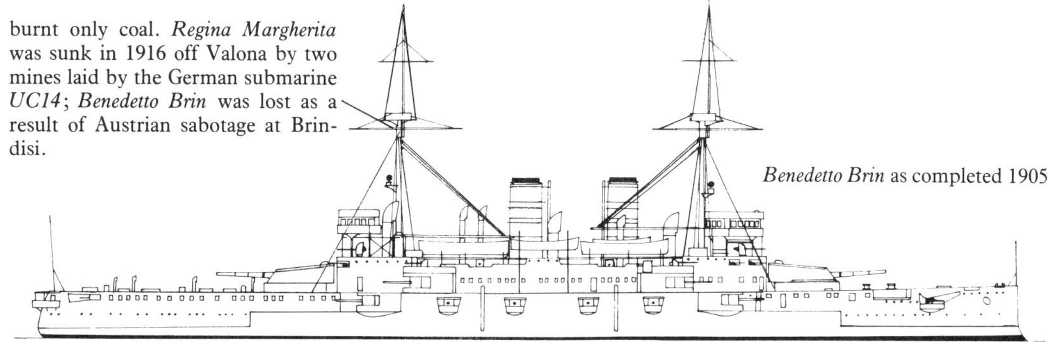

Benedetto Brin as completed 1905

REGINA MARGHERITA class *battleships*

Displacement: 13,215t normal, 14,093t (*Brin* 14,737t) full load
Dimensions: 426ft 6in pp, 454ft 10½in oa x 78ft 2½in x 28ft 11in (*Brin* 29ft 6in) (*130.00, 138.65 x 23.84 x 8.81 (9.00)m*)
Machinery: 2-shaft TE, 28 Niclausse (*Brin* 28 Belleville) watertube boilers, 21,790ihp = 20.3kts (*Brin* 20,475ihp = 20kts). Endurance 5000-10,000nm (10kts)
Armour: Terni Harvey steel. Side 6in, deck 3.1in, CT 6in, turrets 8in, battery 6in
Armament: 4-12in/40 (2x2), 4-8in/40, 12-6in/40, 20-3in/40, 2-47mm/40, 2-37mm/20, 2-10mm Maxim MGs, 4-17.7in TT sub
Complement: 812/900

Name	Builder	Laid down	Launched	Comp	Fate
REGINA MARGHERITA	La Spezia N Yd	20.11.1898	30.5.1901	14.4.04	Sunk 11.12.16
BENEDETTO BRIN	Castellammare N Yd	30.1.1899	7.11.1901	1.9.05	Blew up 27.9.15

In 1899 the minister of the Italian Navy, Rear-Admiral Giovanni Bettolo, ordered the Chief Engineer, Vittorio Cuniberti, to design a ship armed with twelve 8in guns, protected with 6in armour and provided with a speed of 22kts – all this on a displacement of 8000 tonnes (7874t). This vessel was to be the forerunner of the 'single-calibre' ship, even if the maximum calibre of its guns was inferior to that which armed the battleships (12in). The project was not proceeded with, but Cuniberti was then requested to prepare a project for a fast battleship, which on 13,000 tonnes (12,795t) had to be faster than any British and French capital ship and stronger than the major armoured cruisers of those fleets. The result was successful, and the new ships were praised by all the naval experts. Incidentally, Cuniberti also designed an all-big-gun battleship of 17,000t with 12-12in guns, 12in armour, and a speed of 24kts which was considered too ambitious for the Italian Navy, and he received permission to publish his project in the 1903 edition of *Jane's Fighting Ships*.

Only two battleships of the *Regina Elena* class were initially authorized (under the 1901 Naval programme), but it soon became clear that a squadron of four would be necessary for the Italian fleet, bearing in mind that Italy was then an ally of Austria-Hungary and Germany, and, opposed to Great Britain and France, would have borne the brunt of any sea warfare in the Mediterranean. *Roma* and *Napoli* were therefore authorized under the 1902 programme.

The three funnels in all four ships were very tall, especially so in the second pair where they rose to 108ft above the waterline. The funnels were shortened during sea trials, with some loss of speed resulting. All four vessels were removed from the effective list 1923-27, although *Roma* served as a harbour TS until 1932.

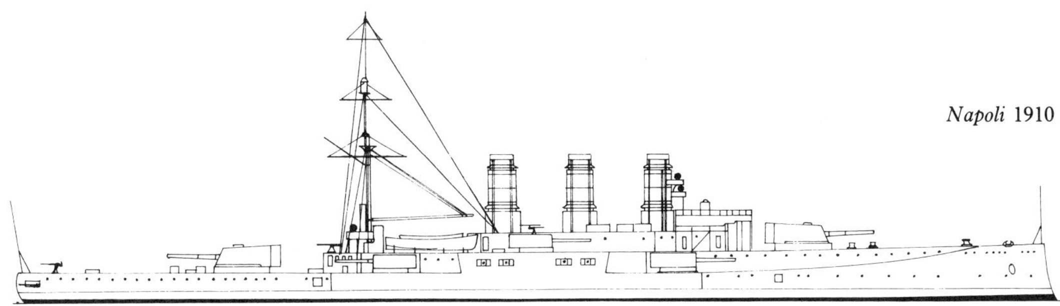

Napoli 1910

REGINA ELENA class *battleships*

Displacement: 12,550t to 12,658t normal, 13,771t to 13,914t full load
Dimensions: 435ft pp, 474ft 5in oa x 73ft 6in x 25ft 11½in-28ft 1½in (*132.60, 144.60 x 22.40 x 7.91-8.58m*)
Machinery: 2-shaft VTE, 28 Belleville (*Roma, Napoli* 28 Babcock & Wilcox) boilers, 19,299ihp = 20.8kts (*Emanuele* 19,424ihp = 21.36kts, *Roma* 21,968ihp = 21.39kts, *Napoli* 19,618ihp = 22.15kts). Endurance 5000-10,000nm (10kts), 1700nm (19kts)
Armour: Terni KC. Side 9.8in, deck 1½in, CT10in, turrets 8in, secondary turrets 6in, battery 3.1in
Armament: 2-12in/40 (2x1), 12-8in/45 (6x2), 16-3in/40 (*Roma, Napoli* 24-3in/40), 2-17.7in TT sub
Complement: 742-764

Name	Builder	Laid down	Launched	Comp	Fate
REGINA ELENA	La Spezia N Yd	27.3.1901	19.6.04	11.9.07	Stricken 16.2.23
VITTORIO EMANUELE	Castellammare N Yd	18.9.1901	12.10.04	1.8.08	Stricken 1.4.23
ROMA	La Spezia N Yd	20.9.1903	21.4.07	17.12.08	Stricken 1.9.27
NAPOLI	Castellammare N Yd	21.10.1903	10.9.05	1.9.08	Stricken 3.9.26

Regina Elena on 17 May 1907 before being commissioned

CRUISERS

This fully-rigged corvette was designed by Eng Insp Giuseppe Micheli and laid down as *Brilliante*, her name being changed to *Caracciolo* in Jan 1869. From 1875 to 1880 she served as a TS for torpedo specialists. In 1893-94 her engine was removed and she served as a sailing ship, but with her sail plan and armament modified.

CARACCIOLO *wooden corvette*

Displacement: 1553t
Dimensions: 210ft 11⅓in pp x 35ft 10½in x 16ft 3½in (*64.30 x 10.94 x 4.97m*)
Machinery: 1-shaft reciprocating, 4 cyl boilers, 973ihp = 9.2kts. Endurance 960nm (8½kts)
Armament: Originally 6-160mm ML; 1893-4: 2-75mm, 4-57mm; 1875-80: also 1-15in TT
Complement: 247

Name	Builder	Laid down	Launched	Comp	Fate
CARACCIOLO (ex-BRILLIANTE)	Castellammare N Yd	Oct 1865	18.1.69	20.7.70	Discarded 10.3.1907

Caracciolo about 1997 as a TS

Cristoforo Colombo about 1880

VETTOR PISANI *wooden corvette*

Designed by Eng Insp Giuseppe Micheli as a fully-rigged corvette, this vessel was laid down as *Briosa*, her name being changed to *Vettor Pisani* in 1868. Her machinery was built by Guppy of Naples. In 1879 she was reconstructed and from 1885 she served as a TS for naval cadets of the Naval Academy of Leghorn.

Displacement: 1676t
Dimensions: 213ft 7in pp x 38ft 10in x 17ft 4in *(65.10 x 11.84 x 5.28m)*
Machinery: 1-shaft reciprocating, 2 cyl boilers, 1004ihp = 9.76kts
Armament: Originally 6-4.7in, 2-75mm, 2-57mm, 2-37mm; 1879-85: 10-4.7in BL; from 1885: 6-4.7in BL
Complement: 226

Name	Builder	Laid down	Launched	Comp	Fate
VETTOR PISANI (ex-BRIOSA)	Venice N Yd	11.5.1867	22.7.69	10.4.71	Discarded 12.2.93

CRISTOFORO COLOMBO *wooden corvette*

A barquentine-rigged vessel designed by Eng Insp Benedetto Brin, with machinery by Penn of London. She was laid down as a sloop-cruiser of 2500t and only 13kts with 1700ihp, but Penn built an engine of nearly 4000ihp weighting only 46.3t and so the plans were modified. *Cristoforo Colombo* was the first true cruiser in the Italian Navy.

Displacement: 2325t
Dimensions: 248ft 5in pp x 37ft 1in x 17ft 2¼in *(75.72 x 11.30 x 5.25m)*
Machinery: 1-shaft reciprocating, 6 boilers, 3782ihp = 16kts
Armament: 8-4.7in BL (probably also 1-14in TT, fitted later)
Complement: 207

Name	Builder	Laid down	Launched	Comp	Fate
CRISTOFORO COLOMBO	Venice N Yd	1.2.1873	17.9.75	16.11.76	Discarded 1891

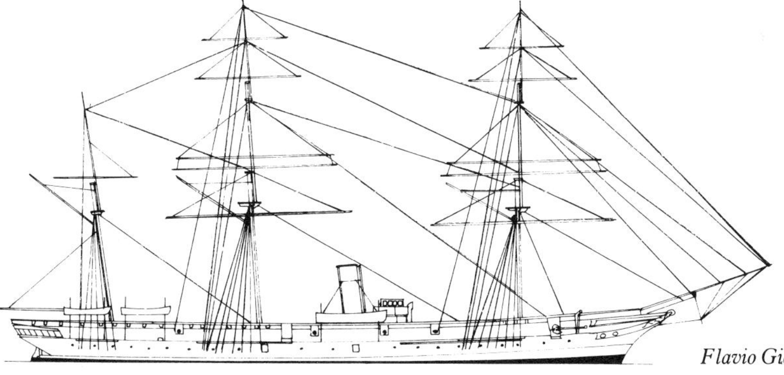

Flavio Gioia as completed 1883

FLAVIO GIOIA *steel corvette*

A barque-rigged steel corvette designed by Eng Insp Carlo Vigna, with machinery built by Penn. There was a sloping protective deck and cellular layer. In 1892 she was converted to a TS. After having been discarded in 1920 she was used as a TS for boys at Naples under the designation *CM181* and unofficial name of *Caracciolo* until 4.3.1923.

Displacement: 2493t
Dimensions: 255ft 11in pp x 41ft 11in x 17ft *(78.00 x 12.78 x 5.19m)*
Machinery: 1-shaft HR, 8 boilers, 4156ihp = 14kts
Armament: Originally 8-149mm/40, 3-75mm/24; after 1892: 4-4.7in/40, 2-14in TT
Complement: 268

Name	Builder	Laid down	Launched	Comp	Fate
FLAVIO GIOIA	Castellammare N Yd	26.6.1879	12.6.81	26.1.83	Discarded 10.9.1920

AMERIGO VESPUCCI *steel corvette*

A barque-rigged steel corvette designed by Eng Insp Carlo Vigna. Her machinery was built by Ansaldo, and there was a sloping protective deck and cellular layer. In 1893 she was converted to a TS and had her armament reduced.

Displacement: 2493t normal, 2751t max
Dimensions: 255ft 11in pp x 41ft 11in x 17ft 11½in *(78.00 x 12.78 x 5.48m)*
Machinery: 1-shaft HR, 8 boilers, 3340ihp = 13.66kts trials
Armament: Originally 8-149mm/26, 3-75mm/21, 4 Maxim MGs; after 1893: 4-4.7in/40, 2-14in TT
Complement: 268, 270 from 1893

Name	Builder	Laid down	Launched	Comp	Fate
AMERIGO VESPUCCI	Venice N Yd	9.12.1879	31.7.82	1.9.84	Discarded 22.1.1928

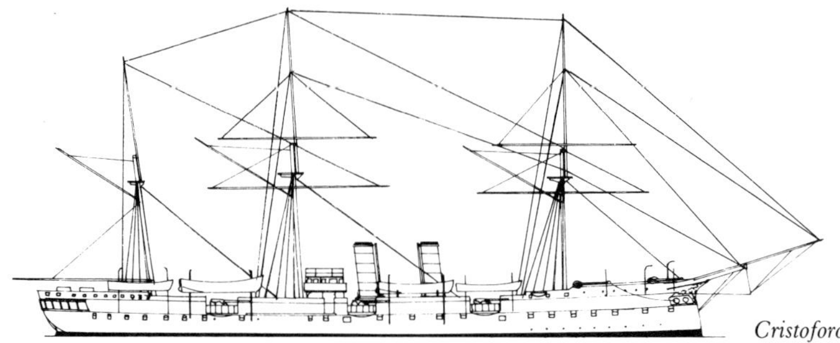

Cristoforo Colombo as completed 1894

This vessel was virtually a repetition, in steel, of the previous *Cristoforo Colombo*, and was designed by Eng Insp Benedetto Brin as a station ship for the Red Sea. Barque-rigged, she had a copper-sheathed hull and used the same machinery as her namesake although developing less power. The original armament was later reduced to 6-4.7in.

CRISTOFORO COLOMBO *steel corvette*

Displacement: 2713t full load
Dimensions: 250ft 8in pp x 37ft 0½in x 18ft 8in (*76.40 x 11.30 x 5.69m*)
Machinery: 1-shaft reciprocating, 6 boilers, 2321ihp = 13kts
Armament: 8-4.7in/40, 2-75mm/24
Complement: 238

Name	Builder	Laid down	Launched	Comp	Fate
CRISTOFORO COLOMBO	Venice N Yd	1.9.1890	24.9.92	16.10.94	Discarded 10.3.1907

TORPEDO CRUISERS

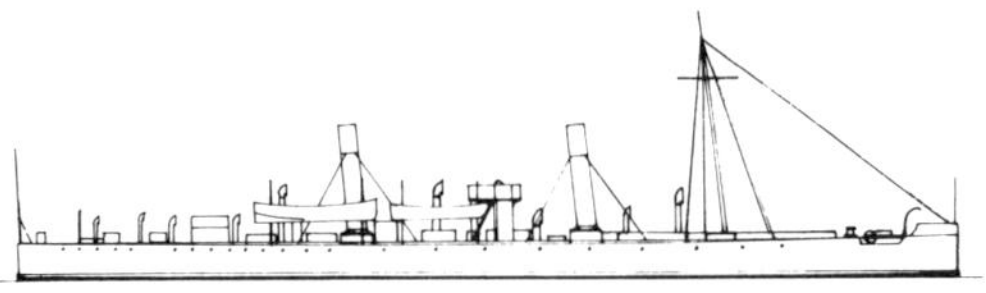

Pietro Micca as completed 1877

Pietro Micca was the experimental forerunner of the large, fast torpedo cruiser, a type conceived by the minister of the Navy, Rear-Admiral Saint Bon, and was designed by Eng Insp Felice Mattei. Her hull shape prevented her from reaching the hoped-for speed of 20kts or even the designed 17kts, and after her trials she was almost immediately placed in reserve. Officially discarded in 1893, her name did not, however, appear in the Navy lists for some years before that. She had an iron hull, and her machinery was built by Ansaldo.

PIETRO MICCA *torpedo cruiser*

Displacement: 526½t, 598t full load
Dimensions: 203ft pp x 19ft 7in x 11ft 10½in (*61.87 x 5.97 x 3.62m*)
Machinery: 1-shaft VSE, 4 boilers, 571ihp = 12.88kts max
Armour: Protective deck ½in-¾in
Armament: 1-16in(?) TT, 2 MGs
Complement: 73

Name	Builder	Laid down	Launched	Comp	Fate
PIETRO MICCA	Venice N Yd	15.2.1875	1.8.76	3.7.77	Discarded 7.11.93

Tripoli as completed
Musée de la Marine

An experimental steel-hulled ship, the first real torpedo cruiser of the Italian Navy and the first Italian warship fitted with 3 propellers. She originally carried two masts with light fore and aft rig. Designed by Eng Insp Benedetto Brin, she was used as a minelayer during World War I, and was officially classed as a minelayer on 1.7.1921. From 1904 she was armed with 1-3in/40, 6-57mm/40, 1-47mm/40 and 3-14in TT; from 1910 she carried 2-3in/40, 4-57mm/40 and 64 mines, her TT having been removed.

TRIPOLI *torpedo cruiser*

Displacement: 835t, 952t full load
Dimensions: 229ft 8in pp, 240ft 9½in oa x 25ft 10in x 11ft 11½in (*70.00, 73.40 x 7.88 x 3.65m*)
Machinery: 2-shaft DE, 6 loco boilers, 2543ihp = 17.5kts. Endurance about 1000nm (10kts)
Armour: Protective deck 1½in
Armament: 1-4.7in/32, 6-57mm/43, 2-37mm/20, 3-37mm revolvers, 5-14in TT
Complement: 105-111

Name	Builder	Laid down	Launched	Comp	Fate
TRIPOLI	Castellammare N Yd	10.6.1885	25.8.86	1.12.86	Discarded 4.3.1923

Designed by Eng General Insp Benedetto Brin (except *Confienza*, designed by Eng Director Giacinto Pullino), these steel-hulled ships may all be considered experimental. There were considerable differences among them (notably in their hull shape, boilers, machinery, armament and general appearance), and several alterations were made to them during their service. *Monzambano* and *Goito* had two funnels, *Montebello* three and *Confienza* one funnel. All were originally rigged with 2 fore and aft sails. The careers of *Monzambano* and *Confienza* were short. *Goito* was fitted with new oil-burning boilers and had her central engine and shaft removed in 1894, giving her 2521ihp = 17.2kts; she was converted to a minelayer in 1897 when her TT were removed and provision was made for carrying 60 mines. *Montebello* was used as a TS for mechanics after 1898; in 1903 she was accordingly modified and reboilered with Pattison, Yarrow and Thornycroft watertube boilers, both coal and oil burners.

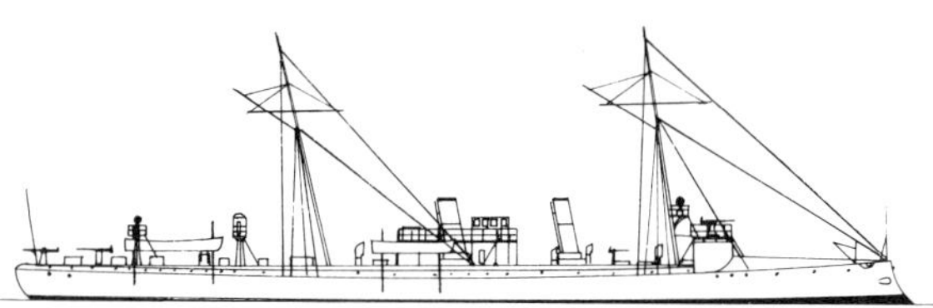

Monzambano as completed 1889

GOITO class *protected cruisers*

Displacement: *Monzambano* 856t; *Goito* 829t normal, 974t full load; *Montebello* 801/955t; *Confienza* 756/969t

Dimensions: 229ft 8in pp, 240ft 9¼in oa x 25ft 10in (*Confienza* 26ft 5in) x 11ft 9in (*Monzambano* 11ft 6in, *Montebello* 10ft 10in, *Confienza* 10ft) (*70.00, 73.40 x 7.88 (8.05) x 3.60 (3.50, 3.31, 3.04)m*)

Machinery: 3-shaft (*Confienza* 2-shaft) DE (*Montebello TE*), 4 loco (*Goito, Montebello* 6 loco) boilers, 2500-3180ihp = about 18kts (*Confienza* 1962ihp = 17kts). Endurance about 1100nm (10kts)

Armour: Protective deck 1½in

Armament: *Monzambano* 6-57mm/40, 5-14in TT; *Goito* 5-57mm/40, 2-37mm/20, 3-37mm revolvers, 5-14in TT; *Montebello* 6-57mm/40, 2-37mm/20, 4-14in TT (from 1898 4-57mm/40, 2-, from 1903 1-37mm/20); *Confienza* 1-4.7in/32, 6-57mm/40, 2-37mm/20, 5-14in TT

Complement: 105-121

Name	Builder	Laid down	Launched	Comp	Fate
MONZAMBANO	La Spezia N Yd	25.8.1885	14.3.88	11.8.89	Discarded 26.8.1901
GOITO	Castellammare N Yd	Sept 1885	6.7.87	16.2.88	Discarded 15.3.1920
MONTEBELLO	La Spezia N Yd	25.9.1885	14.3.88	21.1.89	Discarded 26.1.1920
CONFIENZA	La Spezia N Yd	Sept 1887	28.7.89	11.4.90	Discarded 26.8.1901

Officially described as *torpediniere-avvisos*, these vessels were designed by Gen Insp Benedetto Brin and were steel-hulled, with engines by Hawthorn Leslie and Co. *Folgore* was damaged in a collision with *Bausan* off Capri on 5.7.89 and was consequently put in reserve and, never again reaching her original efficiency, was discarded. *Saetta* was used for experiments with oil fuel in 1892; in 1897-1900 she was a torpedo TS. In 1901 she became a TS for gunners, and in 1902 mounted a number of different light guns.

FOLGORE class *torpedo despatch vessels*

Displacement: 364t, *Saetta* 394t

Dimensions: 186ft x 20ft 8½in x 7ft 0½in (*Saetta* 7ft 5in) (*56.70 x 6.31 x 2.15 (2.27)m*)

Machinery: 2-shaft DE, 4 loco boilers, 2150ihp (*Saetta* 2130ihp) = 17kts

Armament: 3-14in TT, 2-57mm/43.5, 4-37mm/25

Complement: 57-70

Name	Builder	Laid down	Launched	Comp	Fate
FOLGORE	Castellammare N Yd	–	29.9.1886	16.2.87	Discarded 12.4.1900
SAETTA	Castellammare N Yd	–	30.5.1887	16.2.88	Discarded 14.5.1908

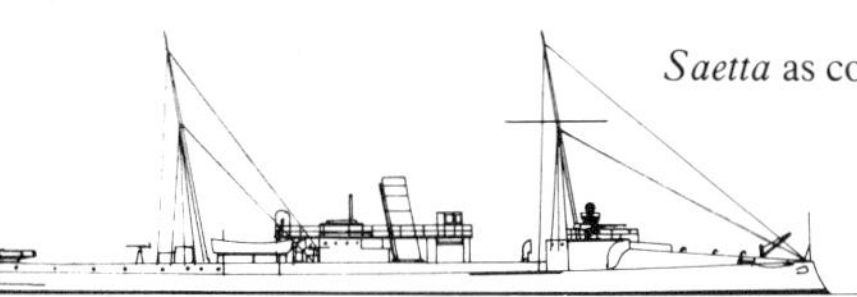

Saetta as completed 1888

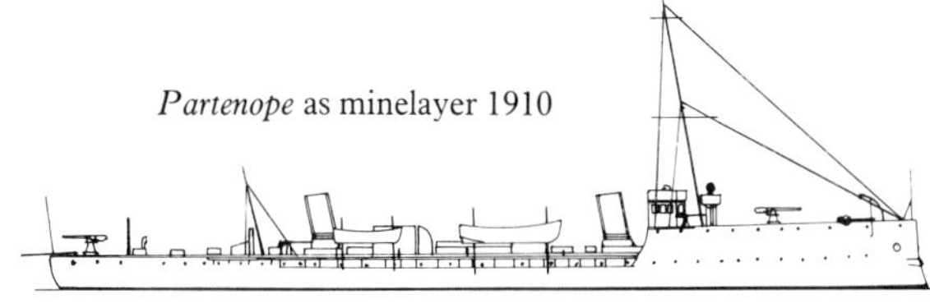

Partenope as minelayer 1910

Designed by Eng Insp Carlo Vigna, this class was an improved version of *Tripoli* and an economical type of small, steel-hulled cruiser. They originally had a fore and aft rig, with 2 masts. *Partenope* in 1906-08, and *Minerva* in 1909-10 were reboilered and converted to minelayers, with armament reduced to 2-3in/40, 4-57mm/43 and 2-37mm/20. They were now oil-fired, gut their speed was reduced (*Partenope* 2481ihp = 17.05kts, *Minerva* 3524ihp = 18.28kts). *Caprera* was laid down as *Clio* but had her name changed on 23.2.1893; *Calatafimi* was originally named *Tersicore* but had her named changed on the same day.

PARTENOPE class *torpedo cruisers*

Displacement: 833t; *Partenope* 821t; *Euridice* 904t; *Calatafimi* 839t; *Urania, Iride* 931t

Dimensions: 229ft 8in pp, 242ft 5¾in oa x 26ft 11½in x about 11ft 5in (*70.0, 73.09 x 8.22 x about 3.48m*)

Machinery: 2-shaft TE, 4 loco boilers, 3884-4422ihp = 18.1-20.8kts. Endurance about 1800nm (10kts)

Armour: Deck 1.6in max, CT 1.6in

Armament: 1-4.7in/40 (*Caprera* 2-4.7in/40), 6-57mm/43 (*Caprera* 4-57mm/43), 3-37mm/20 (*Caprera* 2-37mm/20), 6-17.7in TT (*Partenope, Caprera* 5-17.7in TT)

Complement: 96-121

Name	Builder	Laid down	Launched	Comp	Fate
PARTENOPE	Castellammare N Yd	8.6.1888	23.12.89	11.9.90	Sunk by *UC67* 23.3.1918
MINERVA	Ansaldo	1.2.1889	27.2.92	20.8.92	Discarded 15.5.1921
EURIDICE	Castellammare N Yd	14.2.1889	22.9.90	1.5.91	Discarded 10.3.1907
URANIA	Odero, Genoa	16.2.1889	18.6.91	21.7.93	Discarded 14.1.1912
IRIDE	Castellammare N Yd	21.2.1889	20.7.91	1.11.92	Discarded 16.12.1920
ARETUSA	Orlando, Leghorn	1.6.1889	14.3.91	1.9.92	Discarded 14.11.1912
CAPRERA	Orlando, Leghorn	27.7.1891	6.5.94	12.12.95	Discarded 18.5.1913
CALATAFIMI		15.9.1891	18.3.93	16.1.94	Discarded 10.3.1907

1. *Montebello* about 1906
2. *Partenope* as completed
Richard Perkins

2

Agordat as completed 1900

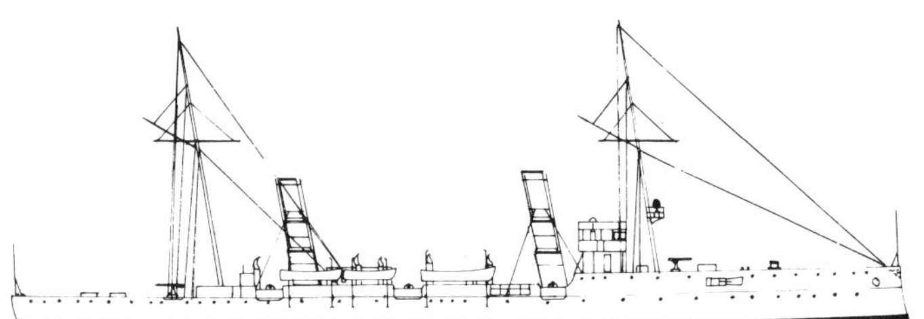

1

Designed by Eng Director Nabor Soliani, these were not successful ships, being too slow for scouting purposes and with too small an endurance at speed. Originally they had two masts, but the mainmast was later removed, and *Agordat* had taller funnels than her sister. From 4.6.1914 they were classed as *esploratori* (scouts). *Coatit* was fitted as a minelayer in 1919, with her armament modified to 2-4.7in/40 and 4-3in/40; *Agordat* had her armament altered to 2-4.7in/40 and 8-3in/40 in 1921, when she was reclassified as a gunboat.

AGORDAT class *protected cruisers*

Displacement: 1340t, *Coatit* 1292t
Dimensions: 287ft 4½in pp, 300 ft 6in oa x 30ft 7in x 11ft 11in (*Coatit* 11ft 7½in) (*87.60, 91.60 x 9.32 x 3.64 (3.54)m*)
Machinery: 2-shaft TE, 8 Blechynden boilers, 8129ihp = 22kts (*Coatit* 8215ihp = 23kts). Endurance about 300nm (10kts).
Armour: Deck ¾in
Armament: 12-3in/40, 2-17.7in TT
Complement: 153-185

Name	Builder	Laid down	Launched	Comp	Fate
AGORDAT	Castellammare N Yd	18.2.1897	11.10.99	26.9.1900	Discarded 4.1.23
COATIT	Castellammare N Yd	8.4.1897	15.11.99	1.10.1900	Discarded 11.6.20

PROTECTED CRUISERS

This vessel, the first torpedo ram of the Italian Navy, was designed by George Rendel and was officially classed as an *ariete-torpediniere*. She was steel-hulled and was originally provided with a 2-masted fore and aft rig. Her 6in/32s were exchanged for 6in/40s in 1899, and in 1905 she was rearmed with 2-10in/40, 1-75mm, 4-57mm/50, 2-37mm/20, 6-37mm revolvers and 2 MGs. After 1913 *Bausan* was employed as a distilling ship at Tobruk, and later also as a headquarters for the Tobruk Naval Commander. In 1915 her 2-10in and 2 of her 6in were removed, and she was later disarmed totally. From 1.7.1916 she was a submarine depot ship at Brindisi. She was sold for scrap in March 1920.

GIOVANNI BAUSAN *protected cruiser*

Displacement: 3079t, 3277t full load
Dimensions: 276ft pp, 293ft oa x 42ft 2in x 19ft 7½in (*84.12, 89.32 x 12.85 x 5.98m*)
Machinery: 2-shaft DE, 4 cyl boilers, 6470ihp = 17.4kts. Endurance 5000nm (10kts)
Armour: Deck 1½in, CT ½in
Armament: 2-10in/20, 6-6in/32, 4-57mm/40, 3-37mm/20, 6-37mm revolvers, 2 MGs, 2-14in TT
Complement: 295, later 256

Name	Builder	Laid down	Launched	Comp	Fate
GIOVANNI BAUSAN.	Armstrong, Walker	21.8.1882	15.12.83	9.5.85	Discarded 15.1.1920

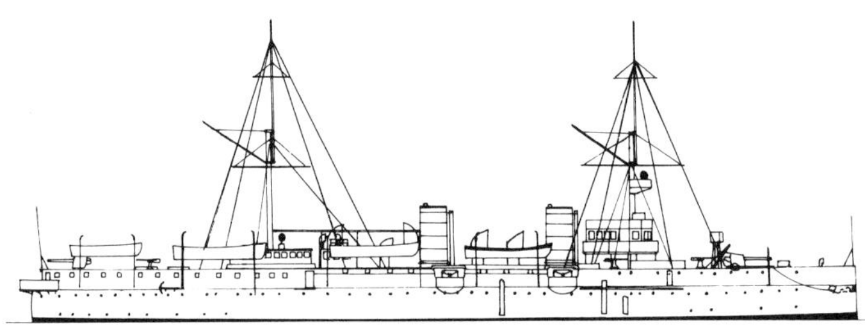

Etna as a TS 1907

These vessels were designed by Eng Director Carlo Vigna and were a repetition of the *Bausan*. In 1900 the armament was modified to 2-10in/30, 6-6in/32, 1-75mm, 5-57mm/40, 5-37mm/20, 1-37mm revolver, 2 MGs and 4-14in TT (with slight variations in *Fieramosca*); it was further altered to 4-6in/40, 2-4.7in/40, 2-47mm/40, 2-37mm/20 and 2-14in TT in 1907. The *Etna* served as a TS from 1907 to Sept 1914; during the First World War she was employed as a harbour headquarters ship, later as a harbour defence ship and lastly as a depot ship and headquarters for the C-in-C Italian Fleet at Taranto.

ETNA class *protected cruisers*

Displacement: 3373t-3538t, 3737t-3888t full load
Dimensions: 283ft 5½in pp, 299ft 10½in oa x 43ft 4½in x about 18ft 8in (*86.40, 91.40 x 13.22 x about 5.83m*)
Machinery: 2-shaft DE, 4 cyl boilers, 6252-7480ihp = 16.6-18kts. Endurance 3500nm (10kts)
Armour: Deck 1½in, CT ½in
Armament: 2-10in/30, 6-6in/32 (*Fieramosca* 6-6in/40), 5-57mm/40 (*Fieramosca* 6-57mm/40), 5-37mm/20 (*Fieramosca* 8-37mm/20), 1-37mm revolver (none in *Fieramosca*), 2 MGs, 2-14in TT (*Fieramosca* 3-14in TT)
Complement: 308, later 320-321

Name	Builder	Laid down	Launched	Comp	Fate
ETNA	Castellammare N Yd	19.1.1883	26.9.85	3.12.87	Discarded 15.5.1921
VESUVIO	Orlando, Leghorn	10.7.1883	21.3.86	16.3.88	Discarded 11.5.1911
STROMBOLI	Venice N Yd	27.9.1883	4.2.86	21.3.88	Discarded 10.3.1907
ETTORE FIERAMOSCA	Orlando, Leghorn	31.12.1885	30.8.88	16.11.89	Discarded 15.7.1909

2

3

4

1. *Coatit* in overall grey

2. *Giovanni Bausan* about 1889
Marius Bar

3. *Piemonte* in Aug 1894

4. *Stromboli* in May 1895

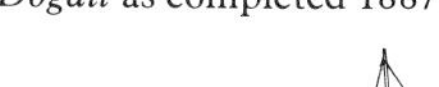

Dogali as completed 1887

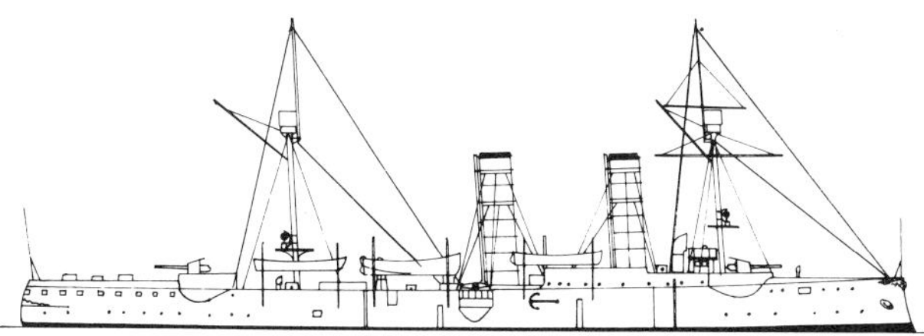

Dogali, originally rigged with 2 masts and fore and aft sails, was the first warship to have TE engines. Laid down as *Salamis* for the Greek Navy to a design by Sir William White, she was bought by the Italian Government and renamed first *Angelo Emo* and later *Dogali*. She ended her life under Italian colours in Montevideo where, in January 1908, she was sold to the Uruguayan Government, and was renamed *24 de Agosto* and in 1910 *Montevideo*. She was discarded in 1914 but not scrapped until about 1930.

DOGALI *protected cruiser*

Displacement: 2050t
Dimensions: 250ft x 37ft x 14ft 6in (*76.20 x 11.28 x 4.42m*)
Machinery: 2-shaft TE, 4 cyl boilers, 5012ihp = 17.68kts (7179ihp = 19.66kts max). Endurance 4000nm (10kts)
Armour: Deck 2in, 6in gunshields 4½in, CT 2in
Armament: 6-6in/40, 9-57mm/40, 6 Gatling MGs, 4-14in TT (from about 1897 also 1-75mm)
Complement: 224, later 247

Name	Builder	Laid down	Launched	Comp	Fate
DOGALI	Armstrong, Elswick	13.2.1885	23.12.85	28.4.87	Sold to Uruguay 16.1.1908

Designed by Philip Watts, *Piemonte* was the first warship in the world armed exclusively with QF guns. Her armament proved too heavy, however, so her 6in guns were first reduced in number and then removed: from 1891-1912 she carried 2-6in/40 and 10-4.7in/40, plus her smaller guns and TT; from 1913 she carried 10-4.7in/40, 6-57mm/40, 2-37mm/20 and 2-14in TT. She was well protected but had no double bottom, and watertight bulkheads were not fitted in the boiler rooms and in the crank-pits.

PIEMONTE *protected cruiser*

Displacement: 2443t, 2597t full load
Dimensions: 304ft 2½in pp, 320ft 11½in oa x 38ft 1½in x 15ft 11in (*92.73, 97.83 x 11.62 x 4.86m*)
Machinery: 2-shaft VTE, 4 cyl boilers, 7100ihp = 20.44kts (12,980ihp = 22.3kts max). Endurance 13,500nm (10-12kts), 1950nm (full speed)
Armour: Deck 3in, gunshields 4½in, CT 3in
Armament: 6-6in/40, 6-4.7in/40, 10-57mm/40, 6-37mm/20, 4-10mm Maxim MGs, 2-14in TT
Complement: 298-310

Name	Builder	Laid down	Launched	Comp	Fate
PIEMONTE	Armstrong, Elswick	1887	23.8.88	8.8.89	Discarded 15.5.1920

These ships, designed by Chief Eng Edoardo Masdea and originally fitted with a 2-masted fore and aft rig, proved unsuccessful, lacking both protection and speed, but they saw considerable service in difficult conditions. Their armament was altered on several occasions: from about 1905 it comprised 2-6in/40, 8-4.7in/40, 8-57mm/40 (*Puglia* 6-57mm/40), 8-37mm/40 (*Puglia* 2-37mm/40), 2 MGs and 2-17.7in TT (not in *Puglia*); from 1915 *Lombardia* and *Etruria* carried 6-4.7in/40, 8-57mm/40 (*Etruria* 6-57mm/40), 2-37mm/20 and 2-17.7in TT; *Liguria* from 1914 carried 8-4.7in/40, 8-57mm/40, 2-37mm/20, 2 MGs and 2-17.7in TT and in 1917 was fitted for minelaying, with only 6-4.7in/40 and 2-37mm/20; *Elba* from 1915 had 6-4.7in/40, 2-37mm/20, 1 MG and 2-17.7in TT;

UMBRIA class *protected cruisers*

Displacement: 2245t-2689t, 2411t-3110t full load
Dimensions: 262ft 5½in pp, 278ft 2½in oa x 39ft 5½in x 15ft 11½in (*Liguria* 15ft 4in, *Umbria* 17ft 6½in) (*84.80, 80.00 x 12.03 x 4.87 (4.67, 5.35)m*); *Elba* 272ft 11½in pp, 289ft 4in oa x 41ft 9in x 15ft 11in (*83.20, 88.20 x 12.72 x 4.86m*); *Puglia* 272ft 11½in pp, 289ft 6in oa x 38ft 11in x 17ft 10½in (*83.20, 88.25 x 12.13 x 5.45m*)
Machinery: HTE (*Puglia* VTE), 4 cyl boilers, 6842-7677ihp = 17.8-19.8kts. Endurance about 2100nm (10kts)
Armour: Deck 2in (*Puglia* 1in), CT 2in
Armament: 4-6in/40, 6-4.7in/40, 8-57mm/40 (*Lombardia* 10-57mm/40, *Umbria* 1-75mm), 7-57mm/40, 2-37mm/20 (*Umbria* 9-37mm/20, *Elba* 6-37mm/20, *Puglia* 8-37mm/20, none in *Lombardia*), 2 MGs, 2-17.7in TT
Complement: 213-278

Name	Builder	Laid down	Launched	Comp	Fate
UMBRIA	Orlando, Leghorn	1.8.1888	23.4.91	16.2.94	Discarded 29.7.1909. See notes
LOMBARDIA	Castellammare N Yd	19.11.1888	12.7.90	16.2.93	Discarded 4.7.1920
ETRURIA	Orlando, Leghorn	1.4.1889	23.4.91	11.7.94	Sunk 13.8.1918
LIGURIA	Ansaldo, Genoa	1.7.1889	8.6.93	1.12.94	Discarded 15.5.1921
ELBA	Castellammare N Yd	22.9.1890	12.8.93	27.2.96	Discarded 5.1.1920
PUGLIA	Taranto N Yd	Oct 1893	22.9.98	26.5.1901	Discarded 22.3.23

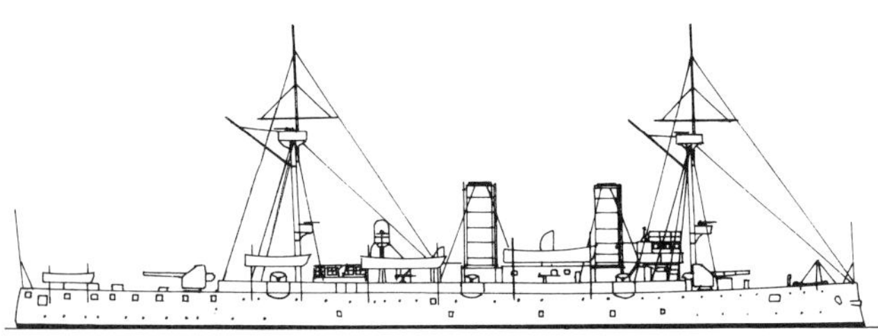
Liguria as completed 1894

and *Puglia*, which carried 6-4.7in/40, 6-57mm/40 and 2-37mm/20 in 1916, was converted for minelaying the following year and then shipped 7-3in/45, 1-37mm/43 and 1-40mm/39 MG.

Umbria, sold to Haiti in 1911 and renamed *Ferrier* under her new colours, sank because of her new crew's inexperience. *Lombardia* was converted in 1906-08 to a depot ship for submarines. *Etruria* fulfilled a similar role from 1916; she was sunk in Leghorn harbour by the explosion of an ammunition barge. *Liguria* was fitted as a balloon-ship from 1908 to 1911. *Elba*, which had a copper-sheathed hull, was fitted as a balloon-ship from 1907-13 and in 4.6.1914 became a depot ship for 3 seaplanes. *Puglia*, the first warship built at the Taranto Naval Yard, was from 1.7.1916 classed as a minelayer.

CALABRIA *protected cruiser*

Designed by Chief Eng Edoardo Masdea, this zinc-sheathed, timber-hulled ship was specially built for long campaigns and colonial service. The armament was changed in 1914 to 6-4.7in/40, 6-57mm/40, 2-37mm/20, 1 MG and 2-17.7in TT, and again in 1921 (when classed as a gunboat) to 1-6in/40, 6-4.7in/40, 8-57mm/40, 2-37mm/20 and 1-40mm/39 MG.

Displacement: 2453t, 2660t full load
Dimensions: 249ft 4in pp, 265ft 9in oa x 41ft 8½in x 16ft 6½in (*76.00, 81.00 x 12.71 x 5.05m*)
Machinery: VTE, 4 cyl boilers, 4260ihp = 16.4kts. Endurance about 2500nm (10kts)
Armour: Deck 2in, CT 2in
Armament: 4-6in/40, 4-4.7in/40, 8-57mm/40, 8-37mm/20, 2 MGs, 2-17.7in TT
Complement: 214-254

Name	Builder	Laid down	Launched	Comp	Fate
CALABRIA	La Spezia N Yd	Feb 1892	20.9.94	12.7.97	Discarded 13.11.1924

1

2

1. *Calabria* in May 1897

2. *Marco Polo* in Jan 1898

MARCO POLO *armoured cruiser*

Marco Polo, the first Italian armoured cruiser, was designed by Eng Insp Carlo Vigna, who modified an earlier, improved *Etna* class cruiser design. She was too lightly armed and protected to be considered successful, and her designed speed of 19kts was never attained. Her armament was reduced in 1911 to 6-6in/40, 4-4.7in/40, 6-57mm/40, 2-37mm/20, 1 MG, 4-17.7in TT and 2-75mm field guns. In 1917-18 she was converted at Venice NYd to a troop-transport, taking the name *Cortellazzo* on 4.4.1918. On 1.10.1920 she was again renamed, this time *Europa*, and discarded 16.1.1921 but almost immediately reinstated in the Navy list with the name *Volta*. She was finally discarded on 5.1.1922 and sold for breaking up.

Displacement: 4511t, about 4820t full load
Dimensions: 326ft 11in pp, 347ft 11in oa x 48ft 1½in x 19ft 3½in (*99.65, 106.05 x 14.67 x 5.88m*)
Machinery: 2-shaft VTE, 4 cyl boilers, 10,663ihp = 17.8kts
Armour: Belt 4in, deck 1in, CT 2in, deck gunshields 2in
Armament: 6-6in/40, 10-4.7in/40, 9-57mm/40, 2-37mm/20, 2 MGs, 5-17.7in TT, 2-75mm field guns
Complement: 315/402

Name	Builder	Laid down	Launched	Comp	Fate
MARCO POLO	Castellammare N Yd	7.1.1890	27.10.92	21.7.94	Discarded 5.1.1922

VETTOR PISANI class *armoured cruisers*

Good ships, but deficient in heavy armament. *Carlo Alberto* which could be distinguished from her sister by the presence of a mainmast, was used from 1902 for Marconi's first long range radio experiments at sea. In 1907-10 she served as a TS for torpedo ratings and gunners, and in 1917 she began conversion, in Venice NYd, to a troop transport, the work being completed in 1917-18 in Taranto NYd. From 4.4.1918 she was renamed *Zenson*, being recommissioned on the same day. She was discarded on 12.6.1920. Both vessels were designed by Eng Insp Edoardo Masdea.

Displacement: 6614t, 7128t full load; *Carlo Alberto* 6397t, 7057t full load
Dimensions: 324ft 9½in pp, 346ft 9½in oa x 59ft 2in x 23ft 7½in (*99.00, 105.70 x 18.04 x 7.20m*)
Machinery: 2-shaft VTE, 8 cyl boilers, 13,259ihp = 18.6kts (*Carlo Alberto* 13,219ihp = 19.1kts). Endurance about 5400nm (10kts)
Armour: Belt 5.9in, deck 1½in, CT 5.9in, deck gunshields 2in
Armament: 12-6in/40, 4-4.7in/40 (*Carlo Alberto* 6-4.7in/40), 14-57mm/40, 8-37mm/20 (*Carlo Alberto* 6-37mm/20), 2 MGs, 4-17.7in TT, 2-75mm field guns
Complement:

Name	Builder	Laid down	Launched	Comp	Fate
CARLO ALBERTO	La Spezia N Yd	1.2.1892	23.9.96	1.5.98	Discarded 12.6.1920
VETTOR PISANI	La Spezia N Yd	7.12.1892	14.8.95	1.4.99	Discarded 2.1.1920

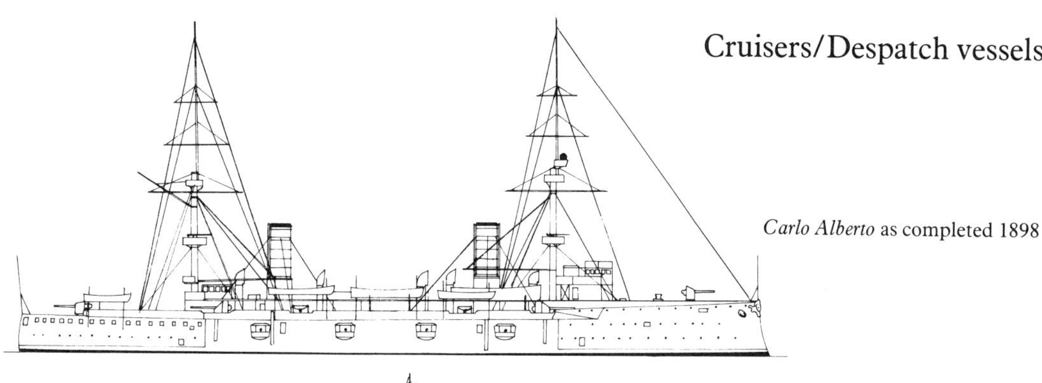

Carlo Alberto as completed 1898

Francesco Ferruccio 1906

A very successful class of ships, designed by Eng Insp Edoardo Masdea, which was intermediate between the battleship and the cruiser types, with the ability to fight in the battle fleet, and provided with sufficient speed to avoid action with superior enemy ships if necessary. On a relatively small displacement they were well armed, well protected and fast cruisers. The original Italian ships of this class were bought by other navies – *Giuseppe Garibaldi (i)*, *Varese (i)*, *Varese (ii)* and *Giuseppe Garibaldi (iii)* going to Argentina and *Giuseppe Garibaldi (ii)* to Spain – and the sixth vessel was the first to enter Italian service. Two other vessels of the class were originally transferred to Argentina but were ultimately purchased by Japan, becoming *Kasuga* and *Nisshin*. *Varese* was converted and employed as a TS from 1920 to 1922; *Francesco Ferruccio* was converted and employed as a TS for the cadets of the Naval Academy of Leghorn from 1924 till 1929. See also under Argentina, Japan and Spain.

GARIBALDI class *armoured cruisers*

Displacement: 7234t, 7972t full load
Dimensions: 344ft pp, 366ft 8in oa x 59ft 10½in x 23ft 3½in (*104.86, 111.76 x 18.25 x 7.10m*)
Machinery: VTE, 24 boilers, 13,655-14,713ihp = 19.3-20.02kts. Endurance 4400nm (10kts)
Armour: Belt 4.8in, deck 1½in, CT 4.8in, turrets 4.8in, deck gunshields 2in
Armament: 1-10in/40, 2-8in/45, 14-6in/40, 10-3in/40, 6-47mm/40, 2 Maxim MGs, 4-17.7in TT
Complement: 510-559

Name	Builder	Laid down	Launched	Comp	Fate
VARESE	Orlando, Leghorn	21.4.1898	6.8.99	5.4.1901	Discarded 4.1.23
GIUSEPPE GARIBALDI	Ansaldo	8.6.1898	29.6.99	1.1.1901	Sunk by *U4* 18.7.15
FRANCESCO FERRUCCIO	Venice N Yd	19.8.1899	23.4.1902	1.9.05	Discarded 1.4.30

Varese on 1 Oct 1904

DESPATCH VESSELS

SESIA *paddle despatch vessel*

Displacement: 455t
Dimensions: 163ft 6½in pp x 22ft 3in x 7ft 8½in (*49.85 x 6.78 x 2.35m*)
Machinery: Reciprocating, 2 boilers, 280ihp = 7½kts
Armament: 2-80mm ML
Complement: 57-66

Name	Builder	Launched	Fate
SESIA	Glasgow	–	Discarded 15.8.1905

This composite, gaff-rigged ketch was laid down in 1830 as Neapolitan merchant ship *Etna*, was bought in 1851 by Florio and was requisitioned in 1860 by the Neapolitan Navy. She was sunk on 22.1.1861 by Sardinian gunfire during the siege of Gaeta but was refloated on 7.7.1862 by the Italian Navy and rebuilt with an iron hull. She was entered in the Navy list on 27.12.1862 and commissioned on 21.1.1863 although the installation of new machinery (340ihp) delayed her service entry until 1865. She served as a station ship at Constantinople and as a surveying ship. She was rearmed with 2-75mm/21 in 1891.

1

2

3

1. *Sesia* after her first rebuilding (1869)

3. *Rapido* about 1880

2. *Messaggiere* about 1869
Melin Collection

ESPLORATORE class *wooden paddle despatch vessels*

Displacement: 981t, 1220t full load
Dimensions: 235ft 5½in pp x 30ft x 11ft 10½in (*71.77 x 9.14 x 3.62m*)
Machinery: Reciprocating, 4 rec boilers, 1681ihp = 17kts (*Messaggiere* 1615ihp = 15¼kts). Endurance about 1840nm (full speed)
Armament: 2-4.7in ML
Complement: 125 (1873), 193 (1891)

Name	Builder	Launched	Fate
ESPLORATORE	Wigram, London	Feb 1863	BU 1907-8
MESSAGGIERE	Wigram, London	May 1863	Discarded 1885

Designed by Wigram with a 3-masted schooner rig, these vessels were laid down on 5.7.1862 and completed in August 1863. *Esploratore* was one of the fastest ships of her time and was used as a scout (together with her sister-ship) in the war of 1866. *Esploratore* was rebuilt, being relaunched on 4.3.1873, and was reboilered in 1877. From 1873 the armament of both vessels was 2-75mm/21 and from 1891 4-57mm/43. *Esploratore* was used as the local defence ship at Venice from 1888; discarded 25.4.95, she was redesignated *GM10* and used as a depot ship. *Messaggiere*'s machinery was used for the new vessel *Messagero* (see below).

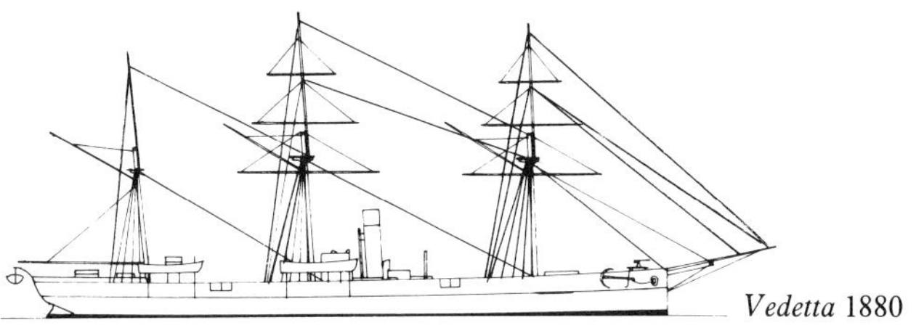
Vedetta 1880

VEDETTA *iron sloop*

Displacement: 814t
Dimensions: 184ft 6½in x 27ft x 11ft 8in (*56.25 x 8.24 x 3.56m*)
Machinery: 1-shaft reciprocating, 2 boilers, 670ihp = 11kts. Endurance 1000nm (9kts)
Armament: 1-75mm/21
Complement: 95, 85 (1878), 46 (1900)

Name	Builder	Launched	Fate
VEDETTA	La Foce, Genoa	24.10.1866	Depot ship 1901

Barque-rigged, and the first iron warship built in Italian yards, *Vedetta* was laid down in 1862 and completed on 16.4.69. From 1896 the armament was 2-37mm/25 and 2-37mm/20 revolvers. Discarded 30.8.1903, she was transferred to the Garaventa Institute, Genoa.

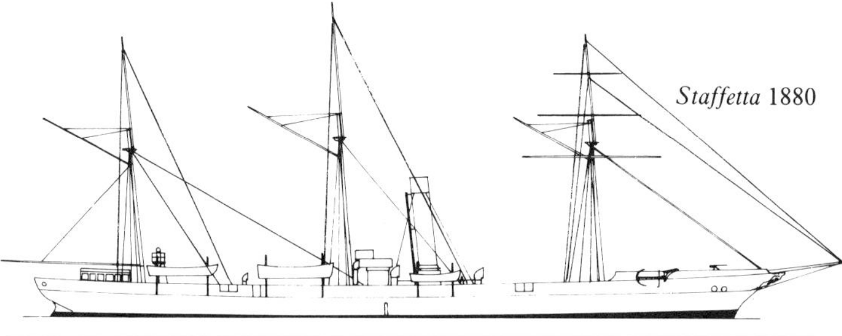
Staffetta 1880

STAFFETTA *iron despatch vessel*

Displacement: 1366t, 1777t full load
Dimensions: 252ft 10½in pp x 30ft 11in x 13ft (*77.08 x 9.43 x 3.97m*)
Machinery: 1-shaft DE, 2 cyl boilers, 1700ihp = 12½kts. Endurance 1800nm (12kts)
Armament: 4-4.7in/20, 1-14in TT
Complement: 144, 137 (1897), 126 (1903)

Name	Builder	Launched	Fate
STAFFETTA	Ansaldo, Sampierdarena	24.6.1876	Discarded 19.7.1914

Laid down in August 1873 and completed on 1.12.77, this iron-hulled, barquentine-rigged vessel was designed by Eng Director Guglielmo Pucci. Her machinery was that previously built for the *Cristoforo Colombo*. 4-57mm/43 were added in 1897, and in 1900-03 she was converted to a surveying ship, with 4-57mm/43 only.

RAPIDO *iron despatch vessel*

Displacement: 1433t
Dimensions: 256ft 5in pp x 30ft 5in x 12ft 6in (*78.16 x 9.27 x 3.81m*)
Machinery: 1-shaft VDE, 4 cyl boilers, 1920ihp = 13½kts
Armament: 2-75mm/21, 1-14in TT
Complement: 144, 128 (1891), 137 (1897), 124 (1905)

Name	Builder	Launched	Fate
RAPIDO	Orlando, Leghorn	16.11.1876	Discarded 8.9.1907

Designed by Chief Eng Luigi Borghi and rigged as a 4-masted topsail schooner, *Rapido* was laid down in October 1873 and completed on 1.5.77. In 1890 the armament was modified to 5-57mm/43 and 2 MGs. After 1907 she served as a harbour hulk at Genoa until 1912, when she was scrapped.

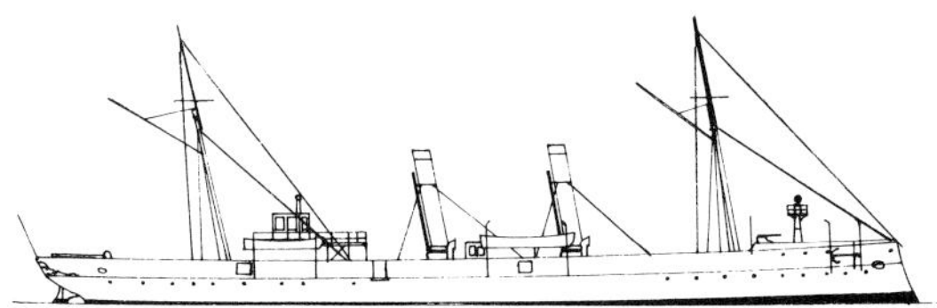
Barbarigo 1885

BARBARIGO class *steel despatch vessels*

Displacement: 614t, 805t full load (*Colonna* 646t, 770t full load)
Dimensions: 216ft 6½in pp x 24ft 1½in x 11ft 3in (*Colonna* 10ft 11½in) (*66.00 x 7.35 x 3.43 (3.34)m*)
Machinery: 1-shaft VTE, 4 cyl boilers, 1760-1827ihp (*Colonna* 1704ihp) = about 15kts. Endurance about 2500nm (8kts)
Armament: 5-75mm/21, 1-14in TT
Complement: 104, later 95-99

Name	Builder	Launched	Fate
AGOSTINO BARBARIGO	Venice N Yd	23.1.1879	Discarded 5.1.1913
MARCANTONIO COLONNA	Venice N Yd	6.8.1879	Discarded 5.1.1913

Gaff schooner rigged vessels designed by Eng Insp Benedetto Brin, laid down in 1876-77 and completed some three years later. The armament was changed in 1889-90 to 5-57mm/43 and 2-25mm/41 MGs, and both vessels were rebuilt and reboilered in 1895-8. In 1912 *Barbarigo* became a gunnery TS; from 1913 she served as a depot ship at Genoa until sold for scrapping in 1916.

MESSAGGERO *steel paddle despatch vessel*

Displacement: 1005t
Dimensions: 236ft 2¼in x 30ft x 10ft 4½in (*72.00 x 9.14 x 3.16m*)
Machinery: Reciprocating, 4 rec boilers, 1797ihp = about 14kts
Armament: 4-75mm/21
Complement: 104-107

Name	Builder	Launched	Fate
MESSAGGERO	Odero, Sestri Ponente	13.7.1885	Discarded 11.3.1907

Laid down in 1883 and completed on 11.10.88, this vessel was built on the plans of the *Messaggiere* with a light gaff rig but modified by Chief Eng Edoard Masdea in order to re-use this ship's very good machinery. The armament was later changed to 4-57mm/43 and, from 1889, 4-37mm/20 revolvers were added. After 1907 she served for some time as a depot ship at Panigaglia.

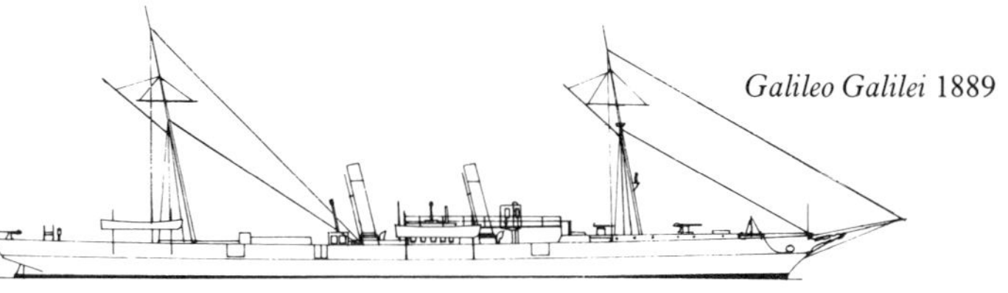

Galileo Galilei 1889

ARCHIMEDE class *steel despatch vessels*

Displacement: 772t, 950t full load (*Galileo Galilei* 776t, 886t full load)
Dimensions: 229ft 7¾in pp x 26ft 4in x about 12ft 4in (*70.00 x 8.03 x about 3.75m*)
Machinery: 1-shaft VTE, 4 cyl boilers, 1411ihp (*Galileo Galilei* 1384ihp) = about 12kts (15.9kts max on trials)
Armament: 4-4.7in/24
Complement: 73, 104 from 1904

Name	Builder	Launched	Fate
GALILEO GALILEI	Venice N Yd	3.5.1887	Discarded 14.12.1913
ARCHIMEDE	Venice N Yd	8.3.1887	Discarded 19.9.1907

Designed by Eng Director Carlo Vigna, and carrying a light gaff rig, these vessels were laid down in 1885-86 and completed in 1888. 2-57mm/43 and 2-37mm revolvers were added in about 1895-7. From 1906, *Galileo Galilei* carried 4-57mm/43 and 1 MG only, and in 1910 her complement was reduced to 76. She was sold for scrapping on 22.2.1915. *Archimede* was used as a powder hulk at La Spezia for some years after she was discarded.

COAST DEFENCE SHIPS

Above: *Varese* about 1867

Left: *Messaggero*

PALESTRO class *coast defence ships*

Displacement: 2165t normal, 2559t full load (*Varese* 1968t normal, 2362t full load)
Dimensions: 202ft 9in wl x 42ft 8in x 14ft 1in (*Varese* 13ft 1½in) (*61.80 x 13.00 x 4.30 (4.00)m*)
Machinery: Reciprocating, 2 boilers, 930ihp = 8kts. Endurance 800nm (8kts)
Armour: Side 4¾in (*Varese* 4½in), citadel 4¾in (*Varese* 4½in)
Armament: 4-200mm, 1-165mm
Complement: 216-252

Name	Builder	Launched	Fate
PALESTRO	La Seyne	5.9.1865	Sunk 20.7.66
VARESE	La Seyne	23.12.1865	Discarded 29.5.91

Iron-hulled, barque-rigged vessels designed by Eng Insp Giuseppe De Luca, laid down in 1864 and completed in 1866. Both fought at Lissa in the battle line, and *Palestro* was sunk by a magazine explosion. In 1870 *Varese* was rearmed with 4-8in, 1-6.5in and 2-80mm landing guns. She was used as a hospital ship from 1886 until 1891; thereafter she was a TS and depot ship.

GUERRIERA class *armoured floating batteries*

Displacement: 1821t, 2352t full load
Dimensions: 183ft 9in x 47ft 4in x 14ft (*56.00 x 14.43 x 4.27m*)
Machinery: 1-shaft SE, 4 tub boilers, 454-588ihp = 6.3kts, 6.9kts max
Armour: Side 5½in
Armament: 12 guns
Complement: –

Name	Builder	Launched	Fate
GUERRIERA	Castellammare NYd	12.5.1866	Discarded 1875
VORAGINE	La Foce, Genoa	13.6.1866	Discarded 31.3.75

Wooden-hulled vessels laid down in 1864 and completed in 1868-69.

ALFREDO CAPPELLINI class *armoured gunboats*

Displacement: 631t
Dimensions: 137ft 9½in pp x 32ft 9½in x 6ft 6½in *(42.00 x 10.00 x 2.00m)*
Machinery: 2 SE, 2 boilers, 210ihp = 12kts
Armour: 4¾in max
Armament: 1 gun (see notes)
Complement: –

Name	Builder	Launched	Fate
ALFREDO CAPPELLINI (ex-TEMERARIA)	Orlando, Leghorn	24.12.1868	Discarded 1875
RISOLUTA	Naples N Yd	Dec 1868	Discarded 1870
FAÀ DI BRUNO (ex-IMPAVIDA)	Orlando, Leghorn	19.9.1869	Discarded 1875
AUDACE	Castellammare N Yd	12.8.1871	Discarded 31.2.75

Iron-hulled, gaff ketch rigged vessels designed by Eng F Fiasella, laid down in 1866 and commissioned in 1869-71. Two of the class were renamed after the Battle of Lissa (20.7.1866), where Commander Alfredo Cappellini (commanding officer of the *Palestro*) and Captain Emilio Faà di Bruno (*Re d'Italia*) lost their lives in action. They were built for the attack on Venice, but with the transfer of that city to Italy after the war of 1866 they were practically redundant and were disposed of shortly afterwards. *Audace* was probably never armed, and the armament of the other three ships is uncertain – they were each designed to carry 2 guns but probably only mounted one. *Audace*, after being discarded, was used as a powder hulk at Panigaglia (La Spezia).

1. *Voragine*

2. Left to right: *Affondatore*, armoured gunboats *Faà di Bruno*, *Alfredo Cappellini* in the summer of 1871
Franco Bargoni Collection

3. *Sebastiano Veniero*
Musée de la Marine

GUNBOATS

GUARDIANO class *iron gunboats*

Displacement: 261t
Dimensions: 100ft 0½in x 27ft 3in x 6ft 6in *(30.50 x 8.31 x 1.98m)*
Machinery: 2-shaft H, 1 boiler, 231ihp (*Sentinella* 260ihp) = 8.7kts (*Guardiano* 9.05kts max)
Armament: 1-9in ML
Complement: 48, later 35-39

Name	Builder	Launched	Fate
GUARDIANO	La Spezia N Yd	1.5.1874	Discarded 4.3.1923
SENTINELLA	La Spezia N Yd	31.12.1874	Discarded 22.5.1904

Laid down in 1871-72 and completed in October-December 1874. *Guardiano* was reclassed as a harbour duty ship from 1895. The armament of both vessels was altered in 1900 to 1-5.9in and 1 MG, and later to 1-4.7in and 1 MG.

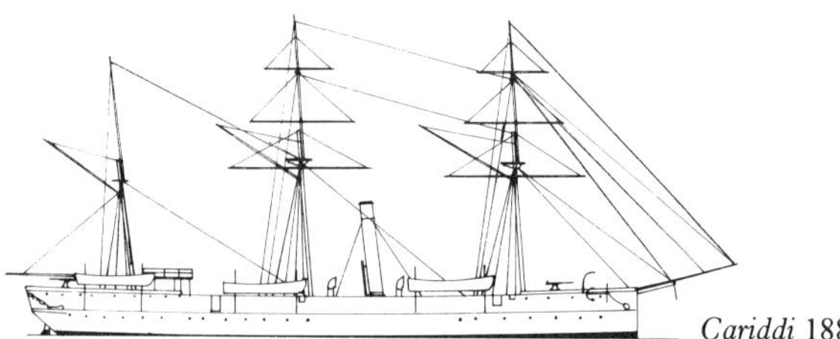

Cariddi 1880

SCILLA class *wooden gunboats*

Displacement: 1059t, *Cariddi* 1084t
Dimensions: 178ft 5in pp, 189ft 1½in wl x 28ft 7in-28ft 8½in x 13ft 11in *(54.39, 57.65 x 8.72-8.76 x 4.25m)*
Machinery: 1 shaft, 826ihp (*Cariddi* 956ihp) = 10.5kts, 10.9kts max
Armament: 1-165mm ML, 2-4.7in BL, 2-75mm, 2 MGs
Complement: 136-139, 111 from 1883

Name	Builder	Launched	Fate
SCILLA	Castellammare N Yd	10.10.1874	Discarded 22.5.1904
CARIDDI	Castellammare N Yd	22.3.1875	Wrecked 1900

Completed in 1876, these two vessels underwent several changes during their careers. Originally barque-rigged and later barquentines, they had their armament altered so that *Scilla* carried 1-165mm ML and 3-4.7in BL in 1879, 2-57mm/43 and 2-37mm/25 from 1883 and 4.57mm/43 only 1900; and *Cariddi* mounted 2-4.7in/20 and 1-165mm ML from 1883 and 2-4.7in/20; 4-57mm/42 and 4-37mm/25 from 1900. *Cariddi* was stranded 70nm N of *Massawa* (Red Sea) on 23.12.1900 and her wreck was sold.

PROVANA class *steel gunboats*

Displacement: 632t, *Veniero* 619t
Dimensions: 168ft 11½in x 26ft 3in x 11ft 2in *(51.50 x 8.01 x 3.40m)*
Machinery: 1 shaft, 1087ihp = 13.6kts (*Veniero* 1160ihp = 13.4kts)
Armament: 6-4.7in/21, 4 MGs
Complement: 95-107

Name	Builder	Launched	Fate
ANDREA PROVANA	Orlando, Leghorn	25.5.1884	Discarded 26.8.1901
SEBASTIANO VENIERO	Orlando, Leghorn	25.5.1884	Discarded 30.8.1903

Barque-rigged vessels designed by Insp Eng Giuseppe Micheli for operations on the rivers of the Plata basin. They were completed in 1885. 2-4.7in were removed in 1883, and from 1900 *Provana* carried 4-3in only and *Veniero* 4-4.7in and 3-37mm/25.

Curtatone
Marius Bar

Governolo

CURTATONE class *steel gunboats*

Displacement: 1155t, *Curtatone* 1039t normal, 1272t full load
Dimensions: 177ft 5in pp x 32ft 5in-32ft 7½in x 14ft 10½in (*54.08 x 9.89-9.95 x 4.53m*)
Machinery: 1-shaft compound, 3 cyl boilers, 1110ihp = 11.45kts (*Curtatone* 1043ihp = 10.71kts)
Armament: 4-4.7in/32, 4-57mm/43, 2-37mm/25, 2 MGs, 1-14in TT
Complement: 121-144

Name	Builder	Launched	Fate
VOLTURNO	Venice N Yd	23.12.1887	Discarded 1.3.1914
CURTATONE	Venice N Yd	14.8.1888	Discarded 8.6.1913

Barque-rigged vessels designed by Eng Insp Antenore Bozzoni, laid down in 1885-86 and commissioned in 1889-90. The 37mm and MGs were removed in 1900 but replaced in *Volturno* in 1905. The armament of *Curtatone* in that year was altered to 4-57mm/43, 2 MGs and 1-14in TT.

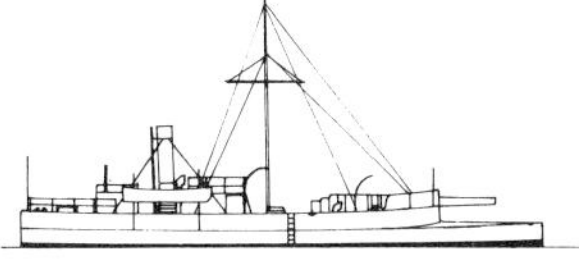
Polluce 1890

CASTORE class *gunboats*

Displacement: 640t
Dimensions: 115ft 0½in x 37ft x 8ft (*35.07 x 11.28 x 2.45m*)
Machinery: 1 shaft, 364ihp = 8kts
Armament: 1-400mm/32, 2 TT
Complement: 40-49

Name	Builder	Launched	Fate
CASTORE	Armstrong, Pozzuoli	1888	Discarded 8.10.1925
POLLUCE	Armstrong, Pozzuoli	1888	Discarded 6.8.1911

Built originally for the Ministry of War laid down in about 1888 and completed 1889-91, these interesting vessels were transferred to the Navy in 1891-92 for experiments with the Krupp 400mm/32 gun. This weapon weighed 117t, had a maximum elevation of 13° and fired a 1980lb shell with a muzzle velocity 1837fs. *Castore*'s gun was landed in 1889, reducing the displacement to 522t, and she was rearmed with 1-4.7in and 1 MG, the TT also being removed. In 1899 *Polluce*'s gun and TT were landed and she was similarly rearmed. Both vessels were disarmed and converted to barges later that year.

GOVERNOLO *steel gunboat*

Displacement: 1203t
Dimensions: 185ft pp x 33ft 9in x 15ft 1½in (*56.40 x 10.28 x 4.61m*)
Machinery: 1 shaft, 1100ihp = 14kts
Armament: 4-4.7in/32, 4-57mm/43, 2-37mm/25, 2 MGs, 1-17.7in TT
Complement: 137

Name	Builder	Launched	Fate
GOVERNOLO	Venice N Yd	1.5.1894	Discarded 28.11.1912

Barque-rigged, copper-sheathed gunboat designed by Eng Insp Ernesto Martinez. Laid down on 12.4.1892 and completed on 1.5.1896.

TORPEDO CRAFT

FULMINE *destroyer*

Displacement: 293t, 337t full load
Dimensions: 200ft 1¼in pp, 203ft 11¼in oa x 21ft x 7ft 6½in (*61.00, 62.17 x 6.41 x 2.30m*)
Machinery: 2-shaft TE, 4 Blechynden boilers, 4729ihp = 24kts. Endurance 800nm (15kts)
Armament: 5-57mm/43, 3-14in TT
Complement: 47-48

Name	Builder	Launched	Fate
FULMINE	Odero, Sestri Ponente	4.12.1898	Discarded 15.5.1921

Designed by Eng Insp Ernesto Martinez, laid down on 14.7.1897 and commissioned on 26.10.1900, this was the first destroyer projected and built entirely in Italy. She was an experimental ship, and not successful, her designed speed of 26½kts never being reached. She was rearmed in 1901 with 1-3in/40, 3-57mm/43 and 2-14in TT.

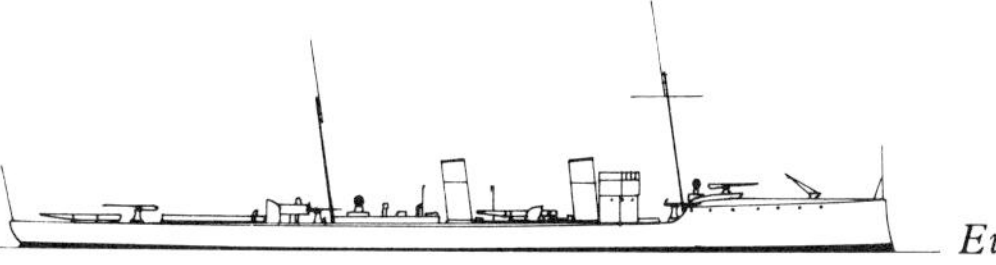
Euro 1908

LAMPO class *destroyers*

Displacement: 315t, 348t full load
Dimensions: 196ft 10in pp, 203ft 7in oa x 21ft 4in x 8ft 6½in (*60.00, 62.05 x 6.50 x 2.60m*)
Machinery: 2-shaft TE, 4 Thornycroft boilers, 5230-5998ihp = over 31kts. Endurance 2000nm (12kts), 290nm (26kts)
Armament: 1-3in/40 (not in *Strale* and *Ostro*), 5-57mm/43 (*Strale, Ostro* 6-57mm/43), 2-14in TT
Complement: 53-61

Name	Builder	Launched	Fate
LAMPO	Schichau, Elbing	7.10.1899	Discarded 18.3.1920
FRECCIA	Schichau, Elbing	23.11.1899	Beached 12.10. 1911
DARDO	Schichau, Elbing	7.2.1900	Discarded 18.3.20
STRALE	Schichau, Elbing	19.5.1900	Discarded 13.1.24
EURO	Schicahu, Elbing	27.8.1900	Discarded 13.11.24
OSTRO	Schichau, Elbing	9.2.1901	Discarded 30.9.20

Designed by Schichau, laid down in 1899-1900 and commissioned in 1900-1902, these were strong, fast boats, but they were lacking in seaworthiness. In 1915-18 they were fitted for minelaying (12+ mines). *Freccia* was beached during the Italo-Turkish war at the entrance to Tripoli harbour. *Euro* was reclassified as a TB on 1.7.1921 and renamed *Strale* on 9.9.24, having been used since 1923 as a target.

Fulmine, the first Italian destroyer

Nembo as completed 1902

NEMBO class *destroyers*

Displacement: 325t, 380t full load
Dimensions: 207ft 11½in pp, 210ft oa x 19ft 6in x 7ft 6in *(63.39, 64.00 x 5.94 x 2.29m)*
Machinery: 2-shaft TE, 3 Thornycroft watertube boilers, 5200-5350ihp = 30.2kts trials
Armament: 5-57mm/43, 4-14in TT; *Nembo, Turbine* 1-3in/40, 5-57mm/43, 2-14in TT
Complement: 51-58

Name	Builder	Launched	Fate
NEMBO	Pattison, Naples	18.5.1901	Sunk 17.10.16
TURBINE	Pattison, Naples	21.11.1901	Sunk 24.5.15
AQUILONE	Pattison, Naples	16.10.1902	Discarded 4.3.23
BOREA	Pattison, Naples	12.12.1902	Sunk 14/15.5.17
ZEFFIRO	Pattison, Naples	14.5.1904	Discarded 13.3.24
ESPERO	Pattison, Naples	9.7.1904	Discarded 5.4.23

Designed by Eng Luigi Scaglia in association with Thornycroft. *Nembo* and *Turbine* had their armament modified in 1905 to that carried by the other ships of the class. From 1908 to 1912 all were reboilered (fuel oil) and from 1909 their armament was altered to 4-3in/40 and 2-17.7in TT. Minelaying gear (10-16 mines) was added in 1915-18. After the 1914-18 war, the forward boiler and its funnel were removed, together with a 3in gun, and 1 MG was added. *Nembo* was torpedoed in the Southern Adriatic by the Austrian submarine *U16*, which was herself sunk, probably by the explosion of *Nembo*'s depth charges. *Turbine* was sunk in the Southern Adriatic in an action with the Austrian vessels *Helgoland*, *Csepel*, *Tatra* and *Lika*. *Borea* was sunk off the Albanian coast in action with the Austrian destroyers *Csepel* and *Balaton*. The surviving vessels were reclassified as TBs on 1.7.1921.

TORPEDO BOATS

NIBBIO Thornycroft 1878

Displacement: 25½t
Dimensions: 79ft 8in x 10ft x 3ft 5½in *(24.38 x 3.05 x 1.06m)*
Machinery: 1-shaft TER, 1 loco boiler, 250ihp = 18kts
Armament: 2-14in TT
Complement: 10

First Italian TB, classed as fourth class. Commissioned 1881, redesignated *1T* (T = Thornycroft) from 1886, discarded 1904. Later converted to steam boat *PE44*.

The Yarrow-built *Avvoltoio*, being embarked aboard the Greek steamer *Ellen* for passage to Italy, 1879

AVVOLTOIO Yarrow 1879

Displacement: 25r
Dimensions: 86ft x 10ft 10in x 3ft 2in *(26.21 x 3.30 x 0.95m)*
Machinery: 1-shaft VTE, 1 loco boiler, 420ihp = 21.3kts
Armament: 2-14in TT
Complement: 10

Fourth class TB, commissioned 1881 and discarded 1904. From 1886 redesignated *2Y* (Y = Yarrow).

SPARVIERO class Yarrow 1881

Displacement: 39½t
Dimensions: 99ft 10in x 12ft 6in x 4ft 10½in *(30.43 x 3.81 x 1.49m)*
Machinery: 1-shaft VR, 1 loco boiler, 620ihp = 22½kts
Armament: 1-25mm twin-barrelled MG, 2-14in TT
Complement: 11

Classed as third class TBs, *Sparviero* and *Falco* were commissioned in 1881, redesignated *22Y* and *25Y* respectively in 1886, and discarded in 1904.

Cabbiano, renamed *24T* in 1886

AQUILA class Thornycroft 1881

Displacement: 34½t
Dimensions: 95ft 9in x 10ft 9in x 4ft 9½in *(29.18 x 3.28 x 1.47m)*
Machinery: 1-shaft VDE, 1 loco boiler, 470-475ihp = 20kts
Armament: 1-25mm twin-barrelled MG, 2-14in TT
Complement: 11

Classed as third class TBs, *Aquila* and *Gabbiano* were commissioned in 1882, redesignated *23T* and *24T* respectively in 1886, and discarded in 1907.

CLIO Orlando 1882

Displacement: 30½t
Dimensions: 76ft 6in x 9ft 10in x 5ft *(23.35 x 3.00 x 1.53m)*
Machinery: 1-shaft TER, 1 loco boiler, 250ihp = 18kts
Armament: 2-14in TT
Complement: 10

The first Italian-built TB. Designed by Eng Director Luigi Borghi and classed as a fourth class TB, *Clio* was carried aboard the capital ship *Duilio* in total fighting trim. She was commissioned in 1885, redesignated *11T* in 1886 and discarded in 1904.

ALDEBARAN class (1st group) Thornycroft 1882-4

Displacement: 38½t
Dimensions: 100ft 4in x 11ft 9in x 5ft 6in *(30.58 x 3.58 x 1.67m)*
Machinery: 1-shaft VDE, 1 loco boiler, 430-455ihp = 21kts
Armament: 1-25mm twin-barrelled MG, 1-14in TT
Complement: 11

This class comprised *Aldebaran* (redesignated *26T* in 1886), *Antares* (*27T*), *Andromeda* (*28T*), *Centauro* (*29T*), *Dragone* (*30T*), *Pegaso* (*32T*), *Sagittario* (*33T*), *Sirio* (*34T*), *Orione* (*35T*) and *Canopo* (*40T*). Classed as third class TBs and discarded 1904-11.

One of the eight *Euterpe* class (1st group) built by Thornycroft

EUTERPE class (1st group) Thornycroft 1883

Displacement: 13½t
Dimensions: 63ft x 7ft 6in x 3ft 9in *(19.20 x 2.29 x 1.14m)*
Machinery: 1-shaft VTE, 1 loco boiler, 170ihp = 17.3kts
Armament: 1-25mm revolver, 2-14in TT
Complement: 10

This class comprised *Euterpe* (redesignated *3T* in 1886), *Talia* (*4T*), *Erato* (*5T*), *Melpomene* (*6T*), *Tersicore* (*7T*), *Polimnia* (*8T*), *Urania* (*9T*) and *Calliope* (*10T*). They were fourth class TBs and all were discarded 1896-99, *Talia* and *Tersicore* being transferred to Customs service in 1898.

MOSCA class Thornycroft 1883

Displacement: 16t
Dimensions: 66ft x 8ft x 4ft 5in *(20.12 x 2.44 x 1.34m)*
Machinery: 1-shaft VR, 1 loco boiler, 250ihp = 20kts
Armament: 2-14in TT
Complement: 10

The class consisted of *Mosca* (redesignated *12T* in 1886), *Ape* (*13T*), *Vespa* (*14T*) and *Farfalla* (*15T*). All were discarded in 1898, *Mosca* being transferred to Customs service. Fourth class TBs.

EUTERPE class (2nd group) Thornycroft 1883

Displacement: 13½t
Dimensions: 63ft x 7ft 6in x 3ft 9in *(19.20 x 2.29 x 1.14m)*
Machinery: 1-shaft VTE, 170ihp = 17.3kts
Armament: 1-25mm revolver, 2-14in TT
Complement: 10

Fourth class TBs. The class comprised *Lucciola* (redesignated *16T* in 1886), *Formica* (*17T*), *Cicala* (*18T*), *Locusta* (*19T*), *Grillo* (*20T*) and *Zanzara* (*21T*). *Cicala* and *Locusta* were carried on board *Duilio* and were discarded in 1904 and 1896 respectively, *Locusta* being transferred to Customs service. The remaining vessels were all discarded in 1898, *Grillo* and *Lucciola* also being taken over for Customs duties.

ALDEBARAN class (2nd group) Odero 1883-6

Displacement: 38½t
Dimensions: 100ft 4in x 11ft 9in x 5ft 6in *(30.58 x 3.58 x 1.67m)*
Machinery: 1-shaft VDE, 1 loco boiler, 430ihp = 21kts
Armament: 1-25mm twin-barrelled MG, 2-14in TT
Complement: 11

Third class TBs comprising *Arturo* (redesignated *38T* from 1886 and discarded 1911), *Spica* (*46T*, discarded 1913), *Cigno* (*47T*, discarded 1904, *50T* (discarded 1907) and *51T* (discarded 1910).

ALDEBARAN class (3rd group) Orlando 1883-7

Displacement: 38½t
Dimensions: 100ft 4in x 11ft 9in x 5ft 6in *(30.58 x 3.58 x 1.67m)*
Machinery: 1-shaft VDE, 1 loco boiler, 430ihp = 21kts
Armament: 1-25mm twin-barrelled MG, 2-14in TT
Complement: 11

Further third class TBs comprising *Vega* (redesignated *36T* in 1886), *Rigel* (*41T*), *Castore* (*44T*), *Polluce* (*45T*), *52T* and *53T*. All were discarded 1907-13.

ALDEBARAN class (4th group) Pattison 1884-6

Displacement: 38½t
Dimensions: 100ft 4in x 11ft 9in x 5ft 6in *(30.58 x 3.58 x 1.67m)*
Machinery: 1-shaft VDE, 1 loco boiler, 390-430ihp = 21kts
Armament: 1-1in twin-barrelled MG, 2-14in TT
Complement: 11

The fourth *Aldebaran* group of third class TBs comprised *Procione* (redesignated *37T* in 1886), *Lira* (*39T*), *Idra* (*48T*), *Regolo* (*49T*), *54T* and *55T*. *Lira* was sunk in a collision with TBs *153S* and *68S* on 22.6.1904; the remaining vessels were discarded 1907-14.

ALDEBARAN class (5th group) Guppy 1885

Displacement: 38½t
Dimensions: 100ft 4in x 11ft 9in x 5ft 6in *(30.58 x 3.58 x 1.67m)*
Machinery: 1-shaft VDE, 1 loco boiler, 387-430ihp = 21kts
Armament: 1-1in twin-barrelled MG, 2-14in TT
Complement: 11

Further third class *Aldebaran* TBs – *Acquario* (*42T* from 1886, discarded 1904) and *Cassiopea* (*43T*, discarded 1914).

77YA, as completed. Eleven years later her original boilers were replaced by watertube boilers

YA class Yarrow 1886-7/Venice N Yd 1894-5

Displacement: 108½t
Dimensions: 135ft 1in x 14ft x 5ft 1in (*41.18 x 4.27 x 1.54m*)
Machinery: 2-shaft VDE, 2 loco boilers, 1600-1640ihp = 26kts (*78YA*, *79YA* 22kts)
Armament: 1-37mm/25 revolver, 1-37mm/20 revolver, 4-(*78YA*, *79YA* 3-)14in TT
Complement: 20

Second class TBs. *78YA* and *79YA* were Italian-built and suffered protracted building periods owing to lack of funds. *76YA* and *77YA* were British-built. Although there was a 4kt difference in speed between the two pairs, all were considered to be very successful vessels. In 1898 *77YA* was fitted with watertube boilers. All four boats were discarded 1907-10.

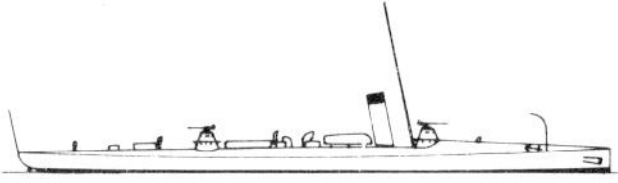
99S as completed

SCHICHAU type Schichau 1886-7

Displacement: 78t
Dimensions: 128ft pp, 130ft 8in oa x 15ft 9in x 6ft 7in (*39.00, 39.84 x 4.80 x 2.01m*)
Machinery: 1-shaft VDE, 1 loco boiler, 902-1080ihp = 21-22kts
Armament: 2-37mm/25, 2-14in TT
Complement: 17

This group of Schichau boats comprised *56S*, *57S* (later renumbered *81S*), *58S* (*82S*), *58S* (*83S*), *84S*, *85S* and *99S-111S* (19 vessels in all). In boats *56S-106S* the TT were fixed in the bows, whilst *107S-111S* had one fixed bow TT and one trainable tube aft. In 1890, *104S* was used in experiments with oil fuel, under the direction of Eng Vittorio Cuniberti, and other boats of the class were adapted subsequently. The replacement of the former Schichau boiler with two watertube boilers, in *82S*, involved the addition of a second funnel. *106S* was used for wireless telegraphy experiments in 1902. *56S* was sunk in the Bay of Biscay after colliding with *57S* on 27.11.1886, and *105S* foundered in a gale in the Piombino Channel 17.10.1890; the rest of the class were discarded 1907-14 with the exception of *102S*, which served in World War I as a pilot boat and was not stricken until 1923.

75S, Schichau type, Odero-built, with a second funnel added because of the two new watertube boilers fitted about 1898

SCHICHAU type Odero 1887-95

Particulars as for the Schichau-built boats except 662-1100ihp. This group comprised 26 vessels, *72S-75S*, *93S-98S*, *105S* (second boat so numbered), *102S-123S*, *128S-131S*, *136S-138S* and *147S-150S*. *93S*, *97S* and *120S* were later converted for oil fuel, whilst in about 1898 *75S* and *95S* received two watertube boilers and a second funnel. *137S* was wrecked on 29.11.1906 off Favignana; the rest of the class were discarded 1904-14 except *128S* (discarded 1920), *129S* (target) and *105S* (converted to minesweeper).

SCHICHAU type Cravero 1887-94

Particulars as for the Schichau-built boats except 723-1046ihp. 12 boats, comprising *68S-71S*, *116S-199S*, *145S*, *146S*, *153S* and *154S*. *68S* served as a pilot boat 1915-19 and was discarded in 1919; *117S* was lost 17.12.1894 near Brindisi, whereupon *154S* was renumbered *117S*. The remaining boats were discarded 1905-14.

SCHICHAU type Guppy 1888

Two boats, *66S* and *67S*, built at Naples. *67S* was used for experiments with new types of training TT and both vessels were removed from active service in 1905. Details as for previous group.

67S, Schichau type, Guppy-built, while experimenting with a new type of training TT about 1898

SCHICHAU type Pattison 1888-94

Details as for Schichau-built boats except 683-1082ihp. The class comprised *60S-65S*, *112S-115S*, *132S-135S*, *151S* and *152S* (16 boats), of which *60S*, *63S* and *113S* were later converted for oil fuel. All were deleted 1907-15 except: *113S*, which was fitted with the experimental Belluzo turbine engine in 1914 and finally discarded in 1921; *114S*, which was used for wireless telegraphy experiments 1899-1901 and discarded in 1920; *115S*, which was disarmed in 1913 and fitted with a MAN diesel engine (850bhp = about 19kts), finally being deleted in 1922; and *134S*, fitted in 1898 with 2 Normand watertube boilers and remaining in service until 1920.

The last Ansaldo-built Schichau type TB, *144S*, as completed 1893

SCHICHAU type Ansaldo 1888-93

Particulars as for Schichau-built boats except 728-1079ihp. 18 boats, comprising *56S* (second boat so numbered and renumbered *80S* on 31.1.1894), *86S-92S*, *124S-127S* and *139S-144S*. *91S*, *124S*, *125S* and *139S* were converted for oil fuel in 1896-7. All were discarded 1907-15; *87S* sank following a collision with *Terribile* in La Spezia Bay 11.6.1894 but was refloated the next day.

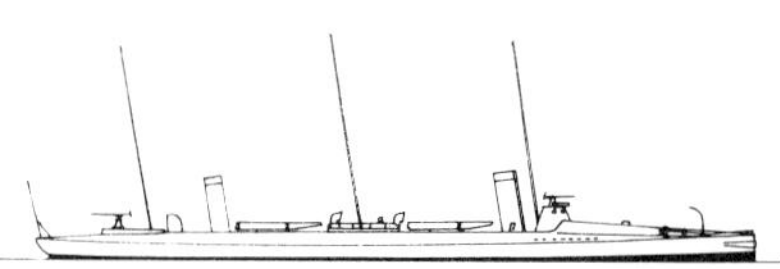
Aquila as completed 1889

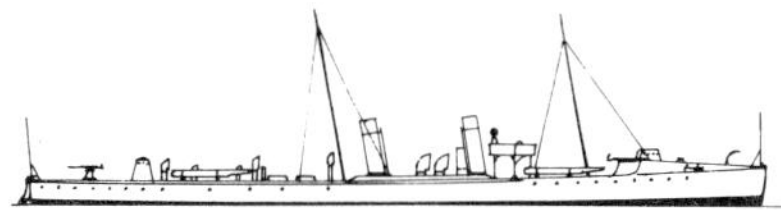
Pegaso as completed 1906

AQUILA class Schichau 1888

Displacement: 137t
Dimensions: 152ft 7in pp, 156ft 2in oa x 16ft 9in x 7ft 2in (*46.50, 47.61 x 5.10 x 2.20m*)
Machinery: 2-shaft VDE, 2 loco boilers, 2180ihp = about 24kts
Armament: 1-37mm/25, 1-37mm/20 revolver, 3-14in TT
Complement: 24

This class comprised *Falco*, *Sparviero*, *Aquila*, *Nibbio* and *Avvoltoio* and were originally rigged as three-masted schooners. From about 1897 the armament was 2-37mm/25 and 3-14in TT. First class TBs, they were discarded 1912-14.

CONDORE Ansaldo 1898

Displacement: 138t
Dimensions: 154ft 2in pp, 157ft 6in oa x 18ft 2in x 4ft 6in (*47.00, 48.00 x 5.55 x 1.36m*)
Machinery: 2-shaft VTE, 3 Yarrow boilers, 2370ihp = 26kts
Armament: 2-37mm/25, 2-14in TT
Complement: 31

The first TB designed and built entirely in Italy and a successful boat if somewhat lightly armed. A first class TB, she was launched in 1898 and commissioned in 1900. Her original coal-burning boilers were replaced by two oil-burning Normands later in service. Discarded 1920.

PELLICANO Odero 1899

Displacement: 148½t, 181t full load
Dimensions: 156ft 4in pp, 159ft 10in x 18ft 10in x 5ft (*47.65, 48.72 x 5.74 x 1.53m*)
Machinery: 2-shaft VTE, 3 Blechynden boilers, 2740ihp = about 21kts
Armament: 2-37mm/25, 2-14in TT
Complement: 30

A first class TB commissioned in 1900. *Pellicano* was a good sea-boat but her machinery was unsuccessful and her designed speed of 25.7kts was never attained. Her armament was also considered to be inadequate. Discarded 1920.

SIRIO class Schichau 1905

Displacement: 206½t
Dimensions: 164ft pp, 167ft 6in oa x 19ft 8in x 5ft 3in (*50.00, 51.07 x 6.00 x 1.60m*)
Machinery: 2-shaft VTE, 2 Schultz-Thornycroft watertube boilers, 3000-3100ihp = about 25½kts
Armament: 3-47mm/40, 3-17.7in TT
Complement: 38

Classed as High Seas Torpedo Boats, these successful vessels comprised *Sirio*, *Sagittario*, *Spica*, *Scorpione* and *Saffo*. *Scorpione* was rammed and sunk by the French gunboat *Surveillante* off Pantelleria on 15.5.1917. The other boats had their gun armament modified to 2-3in/30 AA in 1917-19. *Saffo* sank after running aground near Scalanova Bay, Turkey, on 2.4.1920; the three surviving boats were discarded in 1923.

PEGASO class (*Perseo* group) Pattison 1905-6

Displacement: 206½t
Dimensions: 164ft 3in pp, 165ft 2in oa x 17ft 5in x 5ft 8in (*50.06, 50.35 x 5.30 x 1.72m*)
Machinery: 2-shaft VTE, 2 Thornycroft watertube boilers, 2900-3279ihp = 25-26.6kts
Armament: 2-57mm/43, 1-47mm/43, 3-17.7in TT
Complement: 35-42

These four vessels, *Perseo*, *Pegaso*, *Procione* and *Pallade*, were further High Seas Torpedo Boats and proved very strong and seaworthy. During World War I their armament was altered to 2-17.7in TT, 2-3in/40 and 1-13.2mm MG. *Perseo* sank on 6.2.1917 after a collision with *Astore* off Stromboli; the other boats, which were converted for oil fuel 1908-11, were discarded in 1923-4.

1

2

3

1. *Condore*, the first totally Italian designed and built TB

2. *Sirio*, the name-ship of a class of five TBs built by Schichau

3. *Pegaso*, built by Pattison of Naples, one of the 27 'high seas' TBs built between 1905 and 1909
(All uncredited photos in this section: Aldo Fraccaroli Collection)

Sweden

The Swedish Navy in 1860 was still for the most part one of sailing ships, the principal steam vessels being 2 slow two-deckers and 2 corvettes, and until the 1880s little was done to raise it beyond the level of a small coast defence navy of ships suitable for sheltered waters. Construction between 1860 and 1880 was limited to 4 monitors of the American type, 7 armoured and 8 unarmoured gunboats of over 200t and 2 wooden-hulled screw cruisers of moderate size; but in the next 25 years much more was done. This increase was certainly linked to the revival of Russian naval strength in the same period. Altogether the ships launched between 1880 and 1905 amounted to 12 coast defence battleships of approximately 3050t to 4600t, a powerful small armoured cruiser of 4734t, 5 torpedo gunboats, 1 gunboat, 2 destroyers and 32 torpedo boats. Of these all except the 2 destroyers and 4 of the torpedo boats were built in Sweden, though many of the latter were of overseas design. Except for 3 coast defence battleships, 15 torpedo boats and the gunboat, all were launched between 1896 and 1905.

This force could not have stood up to the full strength of the Russian Baltic fleet in open waters, but in the channels among the many islands off the Swedish coast it would have been a dangerous opponent. Although the area of Sweden was approximately 173,000 square miles or nearly twice that of Britain, the population in 1905 was only about 5,300,000, and as with most European countries the army was much the larger service. One great asset that Sweden possessed was the high purity iron ore of world-famous quality which was available in large deposits, so that the Swedish iron and steel industry was well placed in spite of the lack of native coal. High quality guns of medium and light calibres were made by Bofors and in the earlier part of the period by Finspong, but there was reluctance to acquire the expensive specialised plant needed for long steel heavy gun construction as the likely market would be small. Thus the 10in guns for the coast defence battleships of the *Svea* class were made by Armstrong, those for the *Oden* and *Thor* by Canet, and only those of *Niord* by Bofors. The short 10.8in and 9.4in made by Finspong were cast iron with steel hoops, but the steel 10.8in/24 was made by Armstrong.

THE SWEDISH NAVY in 1860

SCREW BATTLESHIPS

Name	Launched	Displacement	Guns	Speed
KARL XIV JOHAN	1824, converted 1852-1854	2608t	4-8.9in shell 24-36pdr, 40-24pdr	6.5kts
STOCKHOLM	1856	2846t	6-8.9in shell, 60-30pdr	6.5kts

SCREW CORVETTES

Name	Launched	Displacement	Guns	Speed
GEFLE	1848	1260t	8	9 kts
ORÄDD	1853	810t	10	10kts

There were also 2 screw gunboats, the side-wheel corvette *Thor* (6 guns), and 3 smaller side-wheel steamers. The principal sailing ships were: *Skandinavien*, launched 1860, 62 guns; *Karl XIII*, 74 guns; *Försiktigheten*, 72 guns; *Gustaf Den Store*, 68 guns; *Prins Oskar*, 66 guns; *Fäderneslandet*, *Manligheten*, 62 guns each; *Desirée*, 50 guns; *Göteborg*, 44guns; *Josephine*, *Eugenie*, 36 guns each; *Nörrköping*, 32 guns; *Af Chapman*, 24 guns; *Lagerbjelke*, *Najaden*, *Karlskrona*, 18 guns each; *Jaramas*, 20 guns.

MONITORS AND COAST DEFENCE BATTLESHIPS

JOHN ERICSSON class *monitors*

Displacement: 1476t
Dimensions: 199ft 10in wl x 45ft 3in x 12ft max (*60.90 x 13.80 x 3.66m*)
ihp/speed: 380 = 7kts. Coal 115-120t max
Armour: Laminated iron. Hull 4¾in, turret 10¼in
Armament: 2-9.4in/17 (*John Ericsson* 2-15in SB)
Complement: 80

Name	Builder	Launched
JOHN ERICSSON	Nörköping	1865
THORDON	Nörköping	1866
TIRFING	Nörköping	1867

Monitors of the United States Ericsson-type. The heavy guns were later replaced by 2-6in or 2-4.7in and 2 to 8-6pdr, or 3pdr, added.

Tirfing

LOKE *monitor*

Displacement:	1574t
Dimensions:	204ft 9in wl x 45ft x 11ft 10in max (*62.40 x 13.72 x 3.61m*)
ihp/speed:	430 = 8.5kts. Coal 134t max
Armour:	Laminated iron. Hull 5in, turret 17½-15in
Armament:	2-9.4in/17, later /19
Complement:	80

Name	Builder	Launched
LOKE	Nörköping	1871

Generally similar to the *John Ericsson* class.

SVEA class *coast defence ships*

Displacement:	*Svea* 3051t, *Göta* 3238t, *Thule* 3248t
Dimensions:	*Svea* 248ft 5in wl x 48ft 6in x 17ft max (*75.70 x 14.78 x 5.18m*); *Göta, Thule* 258ft 6in-260ft 10in wl x 47ft 10in x 16ft 9in max (*78.80-79.50 x 14.60 x 5.11m*)
ihp/speed:	4700 = 16kts (*Svea* 3640 = 14.7kts). Coal 288-300t max
Armour:	Creusot steel (*Svea* compound). Belt 11½-8in turret 11½-9½in
Armament:	2-10in/32, 4-6in/34 (*Svea* 6in/28), 5 to 6-6pdr, 1 to 3-15in TT
Complement:	252

Name	Builder	Launched
SVEA	Lindholmen	1886
GÖTA	Lindholmen	1891
THULE	Bergsund	1893

Coast defence ships with an amidships belt and the 10in guns in a twin turret. They were reconstructed in 1901-1904 and the armament changed to 1-8.3in/44 in a 7½in max KNC turret, 7-6in/44 also in single turrets, and 11-6pdr. Although the stem projected forward, only *Thule* had an actual ram.

ODEN class *coast defence ships*

Displacement:	3445t
Dimensions:	278ft 3in wl x 48ft 6in x 17ft 4in max (*84.80 x 14.78 x 5.28m*)
ihp/speed:	5350 = 16.5kts. Coal 300t max
Armour:	HN (*Oden* Creusot steel). Belt 9½in, turrets 8in (*Oden* 10-8in)
Armament:	2-10in/42, 6-4.7in/45, 10-6pdr (*Oden* originally 4-6pdr, 8-3pdr), 1-18in TT
Complement:	254

Name	Builder	Launched
ODEN	Bergsund	1897
THOR	Bergsund	1899
NIORD	Lindholmen	1899

Belt amidships, 10in guns in fore and aft single turrets and 4.7in guns in an upper deck battery.

Dristigheten 1906

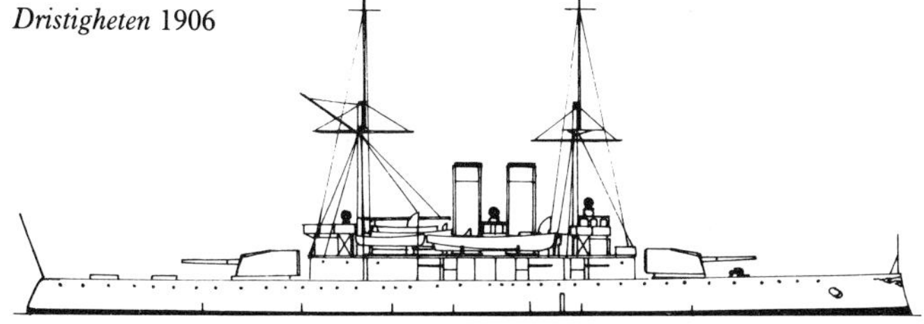

DRISTIGHETEN *coast defence ship*

Displacement:	3445t
Dimensions:	285ft wl x 48ft 6in x 16ft max (*86.87 x 14.78 x 4.88m*)
ihp/speed:	5400 = 16.5kts. Coal 300t max
Armour:	HN. Belt 8in, turrets 8in-6in
Armament:	2-8.3in/44, 6-6in/44, 10-6pdr, 2-18in TT
Complement:	262

Name	Builder	Launched
DRISTIGHETEN	Lindholmen	1900

Amidships belt, 8.3in guns in single fore and aft turrets and 6in guns in upper deck battery.

1

2

3

1. *Thule*
2. *Oden*
3. *Oscar II,* August 1907 *CPL*

ÄRAN class *coast defence ships*

Displacement:	3592t
Dimensions:	287ft wl x 49ft 3in x 16ft 5in max (*87.48 x 15.00 x 5.00m*)
ihp/speed:	6500 = 17kts (*Tapperheten* 5500 = 16.5kts). Coal 300t max
Armour:	KC, KNC. Belt 7in, turrets 7½-5in
Armament:	2-8.3in/44, 6-6in/44, 10-6pdr, 2-18in TT
Complement:	285

Name	Builder	Launched
ÄRAN	Lindholmen	1902
WASA	Bergsund	1902
TAPPERHETEN	Kockum	1904
MANLIGHETEN	Kockum	1904

Differed from *Dristigheten* in having the 6in guns in single turrets amidships.

OSCAR II *coast defence ship*

Displacement:	4584t
Dimensions:	313ft 8in wl x 50ft 6in x 18ft max (*95.60 x 15.40 x 5.49m*)
ihp/speed:	9000 = 18kts. Coal 350/500t
Armour:	KC, KNC. Belt 6-4in, turrets 7½-5in
Armament:	2-8.3in/44, 8-6in/50, 10-6pdr, 2-18in TT
Complement:	331

Name	Builder	Launched
OSCAR II	Lindholmen	1905

Differed from previous ships in having the side armour taken to the upper deck for a short distance amidships. 8.3in guns in single and 6in guns in twin turrets. The only Swedish coast defence battleship with three funnels.

ARMOURED GUNBOATS

The *Garmer, Sköld* and *Fenris* can only be classed as suitable for service on lakes, but the later *Berserk* class might be considered coast defence vessels.

BERSERK class

Displacement: 453t
Dimensions: 130ft 3in wl x 26ft 3in x 8ft 6in max (*39.70 x 8.00 x 2.59m*)
ihp/speed: 133/155 = 8kts. Coal 22-25t
Armour: Laminated iron. Hull $3\frac{3}{4}$-3in max, fixed turret $16\frac{1}{2}$-3in
Armament: 1-9.4in/17
Complement: 45

Name	Builder	Launched
BERSERK	Nörköping	1874
BJÖRN	Nörköping	1874
FOLKE	Nörköping	1875
GERDA	Stockholm	1873
HILDUR	Stockholm	1872
SÖLVE	Nörköping	1875
ULF	Nörköping	1873

Berserk, Sölve and *Ulf* were rearmed in 1896-1901 with 1-4.7in and 2-6pdr.

ARMOURED CRUISER

FYLGIA

Displacement: 4734t
Dimensions: 377ft 8in wl x 48ft 6in x 20ft 8in max (*115.10 x 14.78 x 6.30m*)
ihp/speed: 12,000 = 22kts. Coal 350/900t
Armour: KC, KNC. Belt 4in, turrets 5in-2in
Armament: 8-6in/50, 14-6pdr, 2-18in TT
Complement: 320

Name	Builder	Launched
FYLGIA	Bergsund	Dec 1905

A three-funnelled ship with amidships waterline belt and the 6in guns in twin turrets, fore and aft and on either beam.

CRUISERS

VANADIS *screw frigate*

Displacement: 2140t
Dimensions: 210ft pp x 42ft x 20ft max (*64.00 x 12.80 x 6.10m*)
ihp/speed: 1400 = 11.5kts. Coal 250t
Armament: 8-6.6in BL, 8-7.5in SB shell guns
Complement: 316

Name	Builder	Launched
VANADIS	Karlskrona	1862

Wooden-hulled, fully-rigged.

BALDER *wooden screw corvette.*

Displacement: 1850t
Dimensions: 202ft 9in wl x 36ft 5in x 18ft 4in max (*61.80 x 11.10 x 5.59m*)
ihp/speed: 1380 = 12kts. Coal 270t
Armament: 4-6.6in BL, 2-30pdr
Complement: 218

Name	Builder	Launched
BALDER	Karlskrona	1870

Later used as a training ship

The *Saga*, of 1590t displacement, launched at Karlskrona in 1878, and the *Freja* of 2000t, built by Kockum and launched in 1885, were primarily training ships.

1

2

1. *Fylgia*, as completed in 1907
Aldo Fraccaroli Collection
2. *Vanadis*
CPL

TORPEDO GUNBOATS

ÖRNEN class

Displacement: 801-833t
Dimensions: 222ft 2in oa x 26ft 11in x 10ft 1in max (*67.72 x 8.20 x 3.07m*); *Psilander* and *Clas Uggla* 232ft oa x 27ft 3in x 9ft 10in max (*70.71 x 8.30 x 3.00m*)
ihp/speed: 4000/4500 = 20kts. Coal 100t max
Armament: 2-4.7in/45, 4-6pdr, 1-15in TT
Complement: 99

Name	Builder	Launched
ÖRNEN	Lindholmen	1896
JAKOB BAGGE	Kockum	1898
CLAS HORN	Bergsund	1898
PSILANDER	Bergsund	1899
CLAS UGGLA	Bergsund	1899

Thin protective deck $\frac{3}{4}$-$\frac{1}{2}$in. One bow submerged TT.

Örnen, August 1907
CPL

DESTROYERS

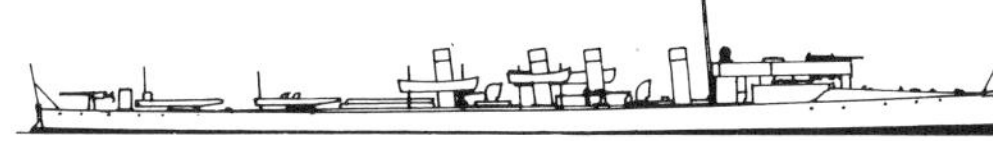
Magne as completed

MODE

Displacement: 394t
Dimensions: 220ft 1in oa x 20ft 4in x 8ft 9in max (*67.08 x 6.20 x 2.67m*)
ihp/speed: 5800 = 30kts. Coal 86t max
Armament: 6-6pdr, 2-18in TT
Complement: 62

Name	Builder	Launched
MODE	Yarrow	1902

Four-funnelled destroyer with 2 single TT aft. On trials made over 32kts, with 6800ihp, apparently using oil fuel sprays.

MAGNE

Displacement: 423t
Dimensions: 215ft 10in wl x 20ft 8in x 8ft 2in max (*65.78 x 6.30 x 2.49m*)
ihp/speed: 7200 = 30kts. Coal 80t max
Armament: 6-6pdr, 2-18in TT
Complement: 67

Name	Builder	Launched
MAGNE	Thornycroft	1905

Four-funnelled destroyer with 2 single TT aft. Trials figures were 7700ihp = 30.7kts.

FIRST CLASS TORPEDO BOATS

Name/Number	Builder	Launched	Displacement	Length	ihp/speed	Armament
No 1	Thornycroft	1884	64t	113ft 2in wl (*34.49m*)	620 = 18.5kts	1 MG, 2-15in TT (bow)
No 2, 3, 4	Bergsund	1887	66t	114ft 2in wl (*34.80m*)	620 = 18.5kts	1 MG, 2-15in TT (bow)
GONDUL, GUNDUR	Karlskrona	1894	85t	126ft 7in wl (*38.58m*)	850 = 19.5kts	2 MG, 2-15in TT (1 bow)
KOMET class	See text	See text	90t	128ft wl (*39.00m*)	1050/1350 = 22¼/24kts	2-1pdr, 2-15in TT (1 bow)
PLEJAD	Normand	1905	98t	124ft 8in wl (*38.00m*)	2000 = 26.2kts	2-1pdr, 2-18in TT (1 bow)

No *1* originally named *Hugin*. Nos *2, 3, 4* originally were Nos *3, 5, 7* and named *Munin, Freke, Gere*. *Gondul, Gundur* were also numbered *9* and *11*. The *Komet* class were built and launched as follows: Schichau: *Komet* 1896; Karlskrona: *Blixt* 1898, *Meteor, Stjerna* 1899, *Orkan, Bris, Vind* 1900, *Virgo, Mira* 1902; Bergsund: *Sirius, Orion* 1903. Lindholmen: *Kapella* 1904. *Mira* differed from the rest in having both TT trainable.

SECOND CLASS TORPEDO BOATS

Name/Number	Builder	Launched	Displacement	Length	ihp/speed	Armament
No 61	Stockholm	1882	38t	91ft 6in oa (*27.89m*)	350 = 16kts	1 MG, 1-14in TT (bow)
No 63, 65	Thornycroft/ Stockholm	1883/1885	43t	100ft oa (*30.48m*)	420 = 19kts	1 MG, 2-14in TT (bow)
No 67, 69	Stockholm	1886	45t	100ft 9in oa (*30.70m*)	440 = 19.5kts	1 MG, 2-14in TT (bow)
No 71, 73	Stockholm	1887	57t	103ft 4in oa (*31.50m*)	460 = 18.5kts	1 MG, 2-15in TT (bow)
No 75, 77	Stockholm/ Karlskrona	1892/1891	55t	100ft 4in oa (*30.58m*)	460 = 18.9kts	1 MG, 2-15in TT (1 bow)
No 79, 81	Stockholm	1903	55t	104ft oa (*31.70m*)	700 = 20.5kts	1-1pdr, 2-15in TT (1 bow)
No 83, 85	Motala	1903	56t	106ft 4in oa (*32.40m*)	635 = 20.8kts	1-1pdr, 2-15in TT (1 bow)

This series began at No *61* and only odd numbers were used. Original names were: *61, Blink; 63, Blixt; 65, Galdr; 67, Narf; 69, Nörve; 71, Bygve; 73, Bylgia; 75, Agne; 77, Agda*. The original Nos *1-7* (odd and even numbers) were spar-torpedo launches 50-55½ft long. No *1* was later numbered *101* and named *Glimt*.

GUNBOATS (OVER 200 TONS)

Name	Builder	Launched	Displacement	Length pp	ihp/speed	Armament
BLENDA class	See text	See text	492t	167ft 4in (*51.00m*)	590 = 11.5kts	1-10.8in/18, 1-4.7in RML
URD class	See text	1877/1879	527t	171ft 7in (*52.30m*)	780 = 13kts	1-10.8in/18, 1-4.7in RML
EDDA	Karlskrona	1885	630t	183ft 9in (*56.00m*)	960 = 13.6kts	1-10.8in/24, 1-6in/26, 2-1½pdr

Blenda class comprised *Blenda* built at Gothenburg, launched 1874, and *Disa* built at Karlskrona, launched 1877. *Urd* class comprised *Urd* built at Malmo, *Skagul, Skäggald* and *Rota* built at Stockholm. *Skuld* and *Verdande* were built at Karlskrona. In the *Blenda* and *Urd* classes the 4.7in RML was replaced by a 4.7in/24 or /28 BL, and the 10.8in later removed or replaced by a 6in/26 or /32 in *Disa, Urd* and *Skagul*. These three also differed in having a 1.7-2in CT. *Edda* was later armed with 4-6pdr only as a minelayer.

Skagul
CPL
(all uncredited photos in this section Arrigo Barilli)

Denmark

The Danish Navy in 1860 consisted mainly of sailing ships, the principal screw vessels being one 64-gun battleship, two frigates and two corvettes. It was clear however that sooner or later war would occur with the German Confederation over Schleswig-Holstein, which amounted to a third of the total area of Denmark though Holstein was predominantly German. Thus by the end of 1863 the Danes had converted their best sail battleship, the *Dannebrog,* to a broadside ironclad, their best frigate, the *Tordenskjold,* to screw, acquired the small turret ship *Rolf Krake* and two lightly armoured gunboats as well as completing a screw wooden cruiser (frigate), a screw sloop and two 550t gunboats. In 1864 when Austria and Prussia invaded, the Danes, though hopelessly outnumbered on land, were able with some difficulty to blockade the Prussian coast. The Elbe and Weser blockades were broken after an action off Heligoland on 9 May in which the *Niels Juel, Jylland* and *Heimdal* had the better of the fighting against 2 Austrian frigates and 3 small Prussian gunboats. The *Rolf Krake* was driven off by the Prussian batteries when she attempted to prevent the crossing of the channel between Schleswig and Alsen on 29 June, and the war ended on 1 August, with the cession of Schleswig-Holstein.

In the period from 1864 to 1872 the Danes built or acquired 2 more broadside ironclads, 2 small turret ships and a low freeboard central battery ship, as well as a small wooden-hulled cruiser, while 5 gunboats were launched in 1873-1875. Subsequently in the ten years from 1878 to 1888, 2 coast defence battleships, a torpedo ram, 2 cruisers of which one was intended for the Danish West Indies, 2 gunboats and 17 torpedo boats were launched, but construction then slackened and from 1889 to 1895 the only ships launched were 3 small cruisers and 5 torpedo boats. The next 10 years saw the launching of 3 low freeboard coast defence battleships and 3 torpedo boats.

After the loss of Schleswig-Holstein the area of Denmark was only 14,830 square miles with a population in 1905 of about 2,500,000, and any attempt to maintain a large navy was clearly impossible. Greenland, Iceland and the Faeröe islands, the latter an integral part of the Kingdom, belonged to Denmark but their occupation by a major power would not have been tolerated by Britain. The three Danish West Indian islands of St Thomas, St John and St Croix were relatively unimportant except for the fine harbour in St Thomas, so that the Danish fleet was essentially a coast defence one.

The majority of Danish ships were built at Copenhagen dockyard. The torpedo boats were mainly Thornycroft though the last 6 were built at Copenhagen. Heavy guns were at first Armstrong RML, but then Krupp BL, followed by Canet and then Bofors.

THE DANISH NAVY in 1860

SCREW BATTLESHIPS

Name	Launched	Displacement	Guns	Speed
SKJOLD	1833, converted 1858-1860	2550t	64-30pdr	8kts

SCREW FRIGATES AND CORVETTES

Name	Launched	Displacement	Guns	Speed
NIELS JUEL	1855	2320t	42-30pdr	10kts
SJAELLAND	1858	2320t	42-30pdr	10kts
THOR	1851	1000t	12-30pdr	9kts
HEIMDAL	1856	1170t	16-30pdr	9kts

There was also one screw mortar vessel and six side-wheel steamers with 2 to 12 guns each. The principal sailing ships were: *Waldemar* and *Frederik VI,* 30-30pdr, and 54-18pdr in each; *Dannebrog,* 72-30pdr; *Thetis,* 48-18pdr; *Rota, Havfruen and Bellona,* 46-18pdr in each; *Tordenskjold,* 44-30pdr; *Galathea,* 26-18pdr; *Valkyrien,* 20-18pdr; *Najaden,* 14-30pdr; *Saga,* 12-18pdr. *Dannebrog* and *Tordenskjold* were later converted to screw.

BROADSIDE IRONCLADS

DANNEBROG

Displacement: 3057t
Dimensions: 185ft 4in pp x 53ft 6in x 22ft 2in max (*56.50 x 16.30 x 6.76m*)
ihp/speed: 1150 = 9kts
Armour: Iron. 4½in
Armament: 16-60pdr
Complement:

Name	Converted
DANNEBROG	Copenhagen 1863

Built in 1850 as a 72-gun, sail, two-decker and converted to an armoured frigate.

PEDER SKRAM

Displacement: 3330t
Dimensions: 228ft pp x 49ft 9in x 20ft 7in max (*67.26 x 15.16 x 6.27m*)
ihp/speed: 1680 = 11.5kts
Armour: Iron 4½in
Armament: 6-8in RML, 12-rifled 26pdr/49cwt
Complement: 435

Name	Builder	Launched
PEDER SKRAM	Copenhagen	1864

A wooden-hulled broadside ironclad.

DANMARK

Displacement: 4670t
Dimensions: 270ft pp x 50ft x 19ft 6in max (*82.29 x 15.24 x 5.94m*)
ihp/speed: 1000 = 8.5kts. Coal 625t
Armour: Iron. 4½in
Armament: 12-8in RML, 12-rifled 26pdr/49cwt
Complement: 530

Name	Builder	Launched
DANMARK	Thompson	1864

An iron-hulled broadside ship with the hull completely armoured above the waterline. Originally intended for the Confederate States and built under the names of *Santa Maria* or *Glasgow*.

MONITORS AND COAST DEFENCE BATTLESHIPS

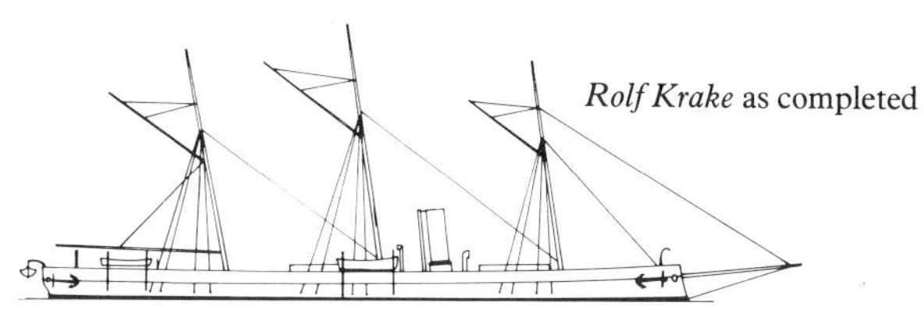

Rolf Krake as completed

ROLF KRAKE

Displacement: 1320t
Dimensions: 183ft 9in pp x 38ft 2in x 10ft 6in max (*56.00 x 11.63 x 3.20m*)
ihp/speed: 750 = 9.5kts. Coal 135t
Armour: Iron. Side $4\frac{1}{2}$in, turret $4\frac{1}{2}$in
Armament: 4-68pdr SB
Complement: 150

Name	Builder	Launched
ROLF KRAKE	Napier	1863

A twin-turret ship with lowering bulwarks and schooner-rigged on three masts. The first ship with Coles turrets. The 4-68pdr SB were later replaced by 2-8in RML and 2-3.4in/24 and 4-1pdr revolvers were added.

LINDORMEN

Displacement: 2048t
Dimensions: 217ft 11in x 39ft 4in x 14ft 7in max (*66.42 x 11.99 x 4.44m*)
ihp/speed: 1500 = 12kts. Coal 125t max
Armour: Iron. Side 5in, turret $5\frac{1}{2}$in
Armament: 2-9in RML
Complement: 150

Name	Builder	Launched
LINDORMEN	Copenhagen	1868

A low freeboard single-turret ship. 4-3in/24 and 4-1pdr revolvers were later added, and the 9in RMLs replaced by 2-5.9in.

GORM

Displacement: 2313t
Dimensions: 233ft 4in pp x 40ft x 14ft 4in max (*71.11 x 12.19 x 4.37m*)
ihp/speed: 1600 = 12.5kts. Coal 113t max
Armour: Iron. Side 7in, turret 8in
Armament: 2-10in RML
Complement: 160

Name	Builder	Launched
GORM	Copenhagen	1870

A low freeboard single-turret ship. The armament was altered, 4-3.4in/24 and 4-1pdr revolvers being added, the 3.4in then being replaced by 6pdrs, and finally the 2-10in RML by 2-5.9in/43.

ODIN

Displacement: 3170t
Dimensions: 240ft 10in pp x 48ft 6in x 16ft 5in max (*73.40 x 14.78 x 5.00m*)
ihp/speed: 2300 = 12kts. Coal 177t max
Armour: Iron. Side and battery 8in
Armament: 4-10in RML
Complement: 206

Name	Builder	Launched
ODIN	Copenhagen	1872

A low freeboard central battery ship, completely armoured above water, and with the unusual feature of a withdrawable spur ram. The 10in RMLs were converted to 16 calibre BLs by Krupp, and the final armament also included 4-3.4in/24, 4-1pdr revolvers and 2-1pdr pompoms.

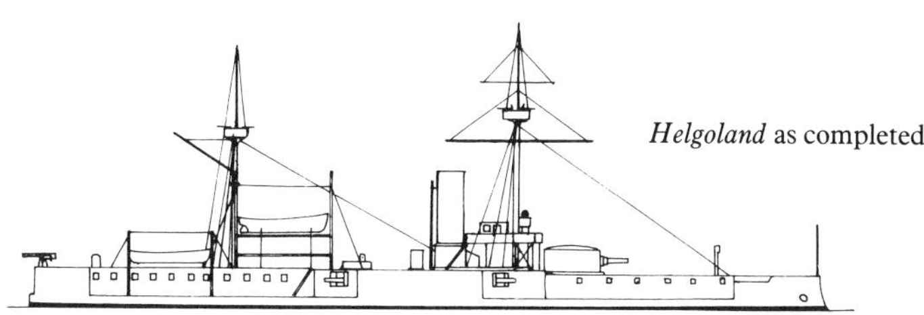

Helgoland as completed

HELGOLAND

Displacement: 5332t
Dimensions: 259ft 7in x 59ft 2in x 19ft 4in max (*79.12 x 18.03 x 5.89m*)
ihp/speed: 4000 = 13.75kts. Coal 224t max
Armour: Iron. Belt 12-8in, barbette and battery 10in
Armament: 1-12in/22, 4-10.2in/22, 5-4.7in/25, 10-1pdr revolvers, 2-15in, 3-14in TT
Complement: 331

Name	Builder	Launched
HELGOLAND	Copenhagen	1878

An unusual design with a complete belt and the 4-10.2in guns in a main deck battery of which the forward part formed a barbette for the 12in guns. The light guns eventually comprised 2-6pdr, 4-1pdr revolvers, 3-1pdr pompoms.

IVER HVITFELDT

Displacement: 3392t
Dimensions: 242ft 10in pp x 49ft 7in x 18ft 4in max (*74.00 x 15.11 x 5.59m*)
ihp/speed: 5100 = 15.25kts. Coal 290t max
Armour: Compound. Belt $11\frac{1}{2}$-7in, barbettes $8\frac{1}{2}$in
Armament: 2-10.2in/35, 4-4.7in/30, 12-1pdr revolvers, 2-15in, 2-14in TT
Complement: 277

Name	Builder	Launched
IVER HVITFELDT	Copenhagen	1886

A coast defence battleship with an amidships belt and the 10.2in guns in fore and aft single barbettes. She was reconstructed in 1904 and her final armament was 2-10.2in, 10-6pdr, 6-1pdr revolvers, 2-15in TT.

Odin

Iver Hvitfeldt

SKJOLD

Displacement: 2160t
Dimensions: 227ft 2in pp x 38ft 1in x 13ft 8in max (*69.24 x 11.60 x 4.16m*)
ihp/speed: 2400 = 14kts. Coal 109t max
Armour: Harvey. Belt 9in-7in, turret 10in
Armament: 1-9.4in/40, 3-4.7in/40, 4-3pdr, 1-1pdr revolver, no TT
Complement: 138

Name	Builder	Launched
SKJOLD	Copenhagen	1896

A low freeboard ship with the 9.4in turret forward and the 3-4.7in guns in single turrets aft. The armour belt was complete.

HERLUF TROLLE class

Displacement: *Trolle* 3494t; *Fischer* 3592t
Dimensions: 271ft 11in pp x 49ft 5in (*Fischer* 50ft 6in) x 16ft 2in (*Fischer* 16ft 5in) max (*82.87 x 15.06 (15.39) x 4.93 (5.00)m*)
ihp/speed: 4200 = 15.5kts. Coal 245-255t max
Armour: *Trolle* Creusot. Belt 8-7in, turrets 7-6in; *Fischer* KC. Belt 7½-6in, turrets 7½-6½in
Armament: 2-9.4in/40 *Trolle* (*Fischer* /43), 4-5.9in/43, 10-6pdr, 3-18in TT; *Trolle* also 3-1pdr revolvers, 8-1pdr pompoms, *Fischer* 6-3pdr, 2-1pdr, 2-1pdr revolvers
Complement: 254

Name	Builder	Launched
HERLUF TROLLE	Copenhagen	1899
OLFERT FISCHER	Copenhagen	1903

Low freeboard coast defence battleships with single 9.4in turrets fore and aft, and 5.9in guns in amidships casemates. The third ship of the type, *Peder Skram*, was not launched until May 1908. The armour belt was complete in *Olfert Fischer* but stopped 20ft from the bows in *Herluf Trolle*.

Skjold

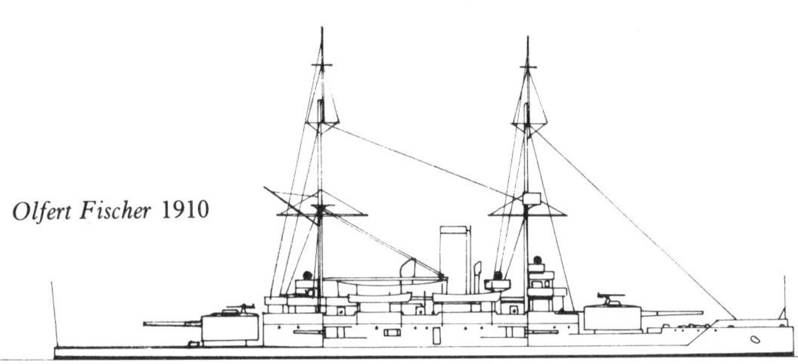

Olfert Fischer 1910

TORPEDO RAM

TORDENSKJOLD

Displacement: 2462t
Dimensions: 222ft 3in x 43ft 5in x 15ft 9in max (*67.75 x 13.23 x 4.80m*)
ihp/speed: 2600 = 12.75kts. Coal 170t max
Armour: Iron. Belt nil, barbette 8in
Armament: 1-14in/25, 4-4.7in/25, 8-1pdr revolvers, 1-15in, 3-14in TT
Complement: 206

Name	Builder	Launched
TORDENSKJOLD	Copenhagen	1880

A ship of unusual type with the 14in barbette forward and the 4.7in guns in shields aft. The light guns were eventually altered to 4 revolvers and 2-1pdr pompoms. The protective deck was 1½in on the flat with 3.8in slopes.

1

2

CRUISERS

JYLLAND *wooden-hulled screw frigate*

Displacement: 2420t
Dimensions: 200ft x 42ft 7in x 19ft 4in mean (*60.96 x 12.98 x 5.89m*)
ihp/speed: 1350 = 11kts
Armament: 44-30pdr SB, later 2-8in RML, 24-6in RML
Complement: 406

Name	Builder	Launched
JYLLAND	Copenhagen	1860

Took part in the action with an Austrian/Prussian squadron off Heligoland in 1864. Preserved.

TORDENSKJOLD *screw frigate*

Displacement: 1718t
Dimensions: 160ft pp x 42ft x 18ft 2in mean (*48.77 x 12.80 x 5.54m*)
ihp/speed: 700 = 9kts
Armament: 34-30pdr SB
Complement: –

Name	Builder	Launched/Converted
TORDENSKJOLD	Copenhagen	1852/1861-1862

ST THOMAS *screw corvette*

Displacement: 1550t
Dimensions: 230ft x 32ft 9in x 17ft mean (*70.10 x 9.98 x 5.18m*)
ihp/speed: 1800 = 13kts. Coal 190t max
Armament: 1-8in RML, 4-6in RML, 1 smaller gun
Complement: 182

Name	Builder	Launched
ST THOMAS	Copenhagen	1871

Wooden-hulled, barque-rigged, screw corvette, later a training ship.

1. The ram *Tordenskjold* in 1907
   CPL
2. *St Thomas*

FYEN *unprotected cruiser*

Displacement: 2663t
Dimensions: 226ft 5in pp x 45ft 4in x 20ft max (*69.00 x 13.82 x 6.10m*)
ihp/speed: 2600 = 12.5kts. Coal 260t max
Armament: 4-5.9in/35, 14-5.9in/22, 8-1pdr revolvers, 2-14in TT
Complement: 300

Name	Builder	Launched
FYEN	Copenhagen	1882

Full-rigged, iron-hulled ship with a strong ram bow, designed for service in the Danish West Indies.

1

VALKYRIEN *protected cruiser*

Displacement: 2972t
Dimensions: 266ft 8in pp x 43ft 5in x 18ft 2in max (*81.28 x 13.23 x 5.54m*)
ihp/speed: 5200 = 17kts. Coal 488t max
Armament: 2-8.2in/35, 6-5.9in/35, 4-6pdr, 8-1pdr revolvers, 5-15in TT
Complement: 282

Name	Builder	Launched
VALKYRIEN	Copenhagen	1888

A protected cruiser with the principal guns in shields, the 8.2in fore and aft and the 5.9in amidships. The deck was 2½in.

2

Hekla as completed

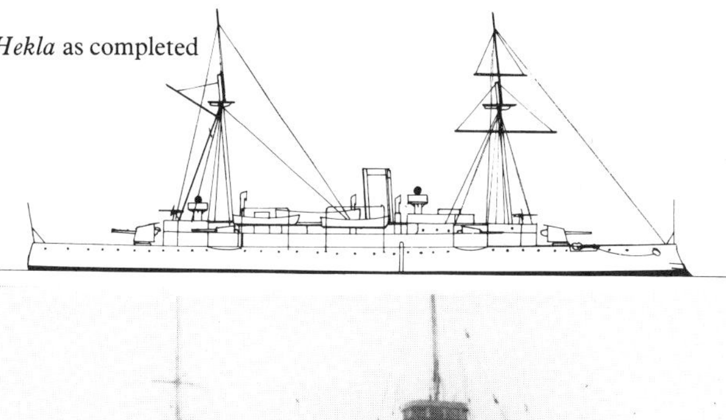

HEKLA *protected cruiser*

Displacement: 1300t
Dimensions: 231ft 7in pp x 34ft x 11ft 4in max (*70.58 x 10.36 x 3.45m*)
ihp/speed: 3000 = 17kts. Coal 113t max
Armament: 2-5.9in/35, 4-6pdr, 6-1pdr revolvers, 4-15in TT
Complement: 156

Name	Builder	Launched
HEKLA	Copenhagen	1890

A small cruiser with 1.7-1in deck. Two of the revolvers were later replaced by 1pdr pompoms.

3

GEJSER class *protected cruisers*

Displacement: *Gejser* 1262t; *Heimdal* 1320t
Dimensions: 231ft 7in x 34ft x 11ft 4in-11ft 9in max (*70.58 x 10.36 x 3.45-3.58m*)
ihp/speed: 3000 = 17kts. Coal 117t max
Armament: 2-4.7in/40, 4-3.4in/40, 6-1pdr revolvers, 1-18in, 4-15in TT
Complement: 156

Name	Builder	Launched
GEJSER	Burmeister and Wain	1892
HEIMDAL	Copenhagen	1894

Similar to *Hekla* but different armament. Two of the 1pdr revolvers were later replaced by 2-1pdr pompoms. The protective deck was 1.7in-1in in *Heimdal* but 1.9in-1.2in in *Gejser*.

1. *Fyen*
2. *Valkyrien* *CPL*
3. *Gejser*

FIRST CLASS TORPEDO BOATS

Name	Builder	Launched	Displacement	Length oa	ihp/speed	Armament
SVAERDFISKIN	Thornycroft	1881	58t	110ft (*33.53m*)	600 = 17kts	1-1pdr revolver, 2-15in TT (bow)
DELFINEN	Thornycroft	1883	66t	110ft 2in (*33.58m*)	670 = 17kts	1-1pdr revolver, 2-15in TT (bow)
HVALROSSEN	Thornycroft	1884	73t	110ft 1in (*33.55m*)	660 = 17kts	1-1pdr revolver, 2-15in TT (bow)
STÖREN, SÖLÖVEN	Thornycroft	1887	107t	130ft (*39.62m*)	1200 = 18.5kts	2-1pdr revolver, 4-15in TT (2 bow)
NARHVALEN, HAVNESTEN	Thornycroft	1888	111t	134ft 11in (*41.12m*)	1200 = 18.5kts	2-1pdr revolver, 4-15in TT (2 bow)
SPRINGEREN	Copenhagen	1891	87t	119ft (*36.27m*)	800 = 17.5kts	2-1pdr revolver, 2-18in TT (bow)
NORDKAPEREN, MAKRELEN	Copenhagen	1893	127t	140ft (*42.67m*)	1300 = 19kts	2-1pdr revolver, 2-18in TT (bow) 2-15in TT
HAJEN	Copenhagen	1896	139t	144ft (*42.89m*)	2000 = 22kts	1-3pdr, 1-1pdr revolver, 2-18in TT (bow), 2-15in TT
HAVÖRNEN, SÖBJÖRNEN	Copenhagen	1897/1898	140t	145ft 6in (*44.35m*)	2000 = 22kts	1-3pdr, 1-1pdr revolver, 4-18in TT (2 bow)

SECOND AND THIRD CLASS TORPEDO BOATS

Name	Builder	Launched	Displacement	Length oa	ihp/speed	Armament
No 2 (HAIEN)	Thornycroft	1879	32t	91ft 3in (*27.81m*)	350 = 15.5kts	1-1pdr, 1-14in TT (bow)
No 3 (SØULVEN)	Le Havre	1880	37t	95ft 1in (*28.98m*)	450 = 15kts	1-1pdr, 2-14in TT (bow)
Nos 4, 5	Thornycroft	1882	15t	61ft 8in (*18.80m*)	150 = 13kts	1-1pdr, 2-14in TT (bow)
Nos 6, 7	Thornycroft	1884	15t	66ft (*20.12m*)	150 = 13kts	1-1pdr, 2-14in TT (bow)
Nos 8, 9	Thornycroft	1886	15t	67ft 6in (*20.57m*)	170 = 13 kts	1-1pdr, 2-14in TT (bow)
Nos 10, 11	Thornycroft	1888	16t	69ft (*21.03m*)	180 = 13.5kts	1-1pdr, 2-14in TT (bow)
Nos 12,13	Thornycroft	1889	25t	78ft (*23.77m*)	350 = 15kts	1-1pdr, 2-14in TT (bow)

The original Nos 1, 2, 3 were spar-torpedo boats.

The TB *Delfinen*
CPL

The sloop *Dagmar*
CPL
(all uncredited photos in this section Arrigo Barilli)

SLOOPS

Name	Builder	Launched	Displacement	Length pp	ihp/speed	Armament
DAGMAR	Copenhagen	1861	1175t	173ft 10in (*53.00m*)	800 = 9kts	14-6in RML

Wooden-hulled, later rearmed with 8-4.7in and 2-1pdr revolvers. *Ingolf*, 996t, launched 1876, was primarily a training ship.

GUNBOATS (OVER 200 TONS)

Name	Builder	Launched	Displacement	Length pp	ihp/speed	Armament
ABSALON class	Thames Iron Wks	1862	516t	150ft 10in (*46.00m*)	? = 11kts	3-6in RML
FYLLA, DIANA	Copenhagen	1862/1863	550t	154ft 2in (*47.00m*)	? = 9/10kts	3-6in RML
FALSTER	Copenhagen	1873	383t	112ft 6in (*34.30m*)	500 = 10.5kts	1-10in RML, 2-10pdr RML, 2-1pdr revolvers
ÖRESUND class	Copenhagen	1874/1875	240t	85ft 8in (*26.10m*)	200 = 7.5kts	1-10in RML, 4-1pdr revolvers
MÖEN	Copenhagen	1875	410t	109ft (*33.22m*)	500 = 9kts	1-10in RML, 2-10pdr RML, 2-1pdr revolvers
GRÖNSUND class	Copenhagen	1883/1884	243/264t	119ft (*36.27m*)	300/400 =10/10.5kts	2-4.7in/25, 2-1pdr revolvers

Absalon class also comprised *Esbern Snare*, later a torpedo ship. These had a 2.4in-2in iron belt. *Öresund* class also comprised *Store Belt and Lille Belt*, and *Grönsund* class *Guldborgsund*. *Fylla* and *Diana* were wooden-hulled. The 10pdr RMLs in *Falster* and *Möen* were later replaced by 2-3.4in/24, and eventually these two ships and the *Öresund* class had only 1-6pdr and 6-1pdr revolvers, while the *Grönsund* class had 2-3 pdr and 2-1pdr revolvers.

Norway

For the whole of the 1860-1905 period, except for the last part of 1905, the King of Sweden was also King of Norway, though the two countries were separate Kingdoms and relations between them were sometimes difficult. Norway was a much poorer country than Sweden, without appreciable mineral resources, and had a population in 1905 of about 2,350,000. The Norwegian mercantile marine was however the fourth largest in the world, surpassed only by those of Britain, Germany and the USA so that some naval force was needed, though it developed into one of a purely coast defence type. In 1860 the principal ships were 3 frigates of which one was screw, and 2 screw corvettes, and up to 1880 additions comprised 4 American type monitors, 2 wooden-hulled cruisers and 7 gunboats of over 200t. The navy was increased between 1880 and 1905 by 4 coast defence battleships, 2 small cruisers, a destroyer, 32 torpedo boats and 4 gunboats. Of these the coast defence battleships were built by Armstrong, the destroyer and 3 torpedo boats by Schichau, and the other ships in Norway. The heavier guns of the fleet were initially Armstrong RML, and then Krupp or Armstrong BL.

THE NORWEGIAN NAVY in 1860

SCREW FRIGATE AND CORVETTES

Name	Launched	Displacement	Guns	Speed
ST OLAF	1856	2180t	34	10.5kts
NORNEN	1855	960t	14	7kts
ELLIDA	1856	950t	6	7kts

There were also 4 smaller screw warships, 2 to 20 guns each, and 2 side-wheel steamers, 2 guns in each. The principal sailing ships were a 44-gun and a 40-gun frigate, and a 16-gun and a 10-gun corvette.

MONITORS AND COAST DEFENCE BATTLESHIPS

Skorpionen as completed

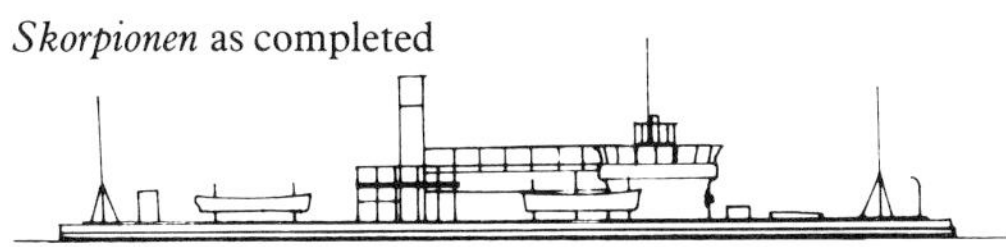

SKORPIONEN class

Displacement: 1490t, *Skorpionen* 1425t
Dimensions: 204ft 6in oa (*Skorpionen* 200ft) x 45ft 6in x 11ft-11ft 6in max (*62.33 (60.96) x 13.87 x 3.35-3.50m*)
ihp/speed: 450 = 8kts (*Skorpionen* 330 = 6kts). Coal 130-140t max
Armour: Laminated iron. Hull 5in, turret 12in
Armament: 2-10.5in RML
Complement: 85

Name	Builder	Launched
SKORPIONEN	Horten	1866
MJÖLNER	Nörköping	1868
THRUDVANG	Horten	1869

United States Ericsson-type monitors. The heavy guns were later removed, and 2-4.7in, 2-9pdr and 2-1pdr added.

THOR

Displacement: 1975t
Dimensions: 204ft 6in oa x 47ft 6in x 12ft 6in max (*62.33 x 14.48 x 3.81m*)
ihp/speed: 600 = 8kts. Coal 200t max
Armour: Laminated iron. Hull 7in, turret 14in
Armament: 2-10.5in RML
Complement: 95

Name	Builder	Launched
THOR	Horten	1872

A larger version of the *Skorpionen* class, and later rearmed in the same way.

Skorpionen

Tordenskjold about 1912

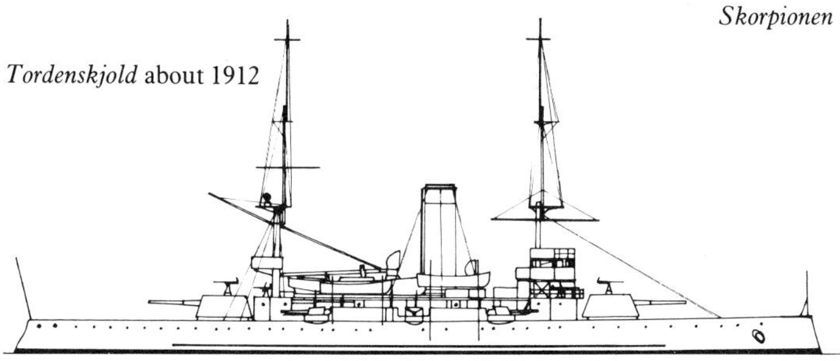

HARALD HAARFAGRE class

Displacement: 3858t
Dimensions: 304ft oa x 48ft 6in x 17ft 8in max (*92.66 x 14.78 x 5.38m*)
ihp/speed: 4500 = 16.9kts. Coal 550t max
Armour: Belt 7-4in Harvey, turrets 8-5in NS
Armament: 2-8.2in/44, 6-4.7in/44, 6-12pdr, 6-1pdr, 2-18in TT
Complement: 245

Name	Builder	Launched
HARALD HAARFAGRE	Armstrong	Jan 1897
TORDENSKJOLD	Armstrong	Mar 1897

Coast defence ships with amidships waterline belt. The 8.2in guns were in fore and aft single turrets and the 4.7in guns in shields amidships. In the Second World War they became the German floating AA batteries *Thetis* and *Nymphe*.

NORGE class

Displacement: 4165t
Dimensions: 310ft 3in oa x 50ft 6in x 17ft 8in max (*94.57 x 15.39 x 5.38m*)
ihp/speed: 4500 = 16.5kts. Coal 440/550t
Armour: Belt 6in KC, turrets 9-5in NS
Armament: 2-8.2in/44, 6-5.9in/46, 8-12pdr, 4-3pdr, 2-18in TT
Complement: 266

Name	Builder	Launched
NORGE	Armstrong	March 1900
EIDSVOLD	Armstrong	June 1900

Belt amidships only, with 4 of the 5.9in guns in upper deck casemates, and 2 in shields. Both ships were torpedoed and sunk by German destroyers at Narvik in April 1940.

Eidsvold

CRUISERS

KONG SVERRE *wooden-hulled screw frigate*

Displacement: 3485t
Dimensions: 218ft 2in pp x 50ft 10in x 22ft 4in max (*66.50 x 15.49 x 6.81m*)
ihp/speed: 1800 = 11.5kts
Armament: Originally 52 guns; finally 2-8in RML, 4-6.6in RML, 6-6.1in RML, 22-8in SB
Complement: 550

Name	Builder	Launched
KONG SVERRE	Horten	1860

NORDSTJERNA *wooden-hulled corvette*

Displacement: 1610t
Dimensions: 185ft 4in pp x 38ft 8in x 17ft 10in max (*56.48 x 11.78 x 5.43m*)
ihp/speed: 800 = 10kts
Armament: Finally 6-6.1in RML, 10-8in SB
Complement: 220

Name	Builder	Launched
NORDSTJERNA	Horten	1862

VIKING *small protected cruiser*

Displacement: 1181t
Dimensions: 208ft 3in oa x 30ft 6in x 12ft max (*63.48 x 9.30 x 3.66m*)
ihp/speed 2000 = 15kts. Coal 140t
Armament: 2-5.9in/40, 4-6pdr, 4-1pdr, 3-14in TT
Complement: 125

Name	Builder	Launched
VIKING	Horten	1891

On the borderline between cruiser and gunboat, but the 1.4in deck places this ship as a cruiser. Reconstructed in 1903, and the armament changed to 2-4.7in/44, 4-12pdr, 6-3pdr and 1-16in TT.

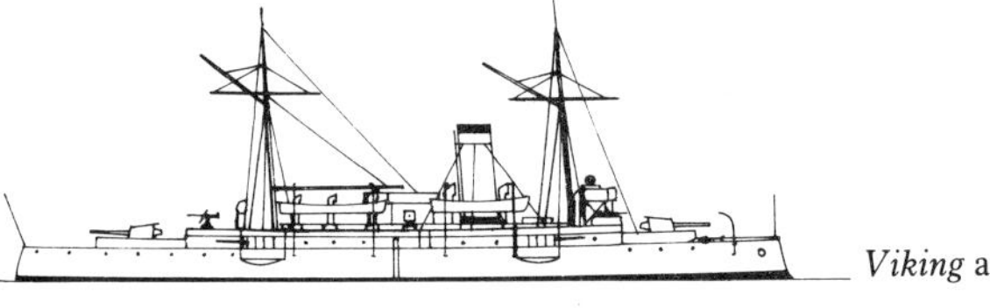

Viking as completed

FRITHJOF *small protected cruiser*

Displacement: 1360t
Dimensions: 223ft 8in oa x 32ft 9in x 13ft 2in max (*68.17 x 9.98 x 4.01m*)
ihp/speed: 2800 = 15kts. Coal 160t
Armament: 2-4.7in/44, 4-12pdr, 4-1pdr, 1-18in TT
Complement: 154

Name	Builder	Launched
FRITHJOF	Horten	1896

Classified as *Viking* on grounds of 1¼in deck.

DESTROYERS

VALKYRJEN

Displacement: 375t
Dimensions: 190ft 3in oa x 24ft 4in x 8ft 6in max (*57.98 x 7.42 x 2.59m*)
ihp/speed: 3300 = 23kts. Coal 88t
Armament: 2-12pdr, 4-1pdr, 2-18in TT
Complement: 59

Name	Builder	Launched
VALKYRJEN	Schichau	1896

Slower than other destroyers, this ship resembled the German divisional torpedo-boats of the 'D' series.

GUNBOATS (OVER 200 TONS)

Name	Builder	Launched	Displacement	Length oa	ihp/speed	Armament
GLOMMEN, LOUGEN	Horten	1863	280t	134ft 10in (?oa) (*41.10m*)	180 = 9kts	1-6.6in RML, 1-6.1in RML, 4 smaller guns
ULLER, VALE	Horten	1874/1876	229t	89ft 6in (*27.28m*)	200 = 8kts	1-10.6in RML, 1-1pdr, 2-1pdr revolvers
SLEIPNER	Horten	1877	571t	174ft 9in (*53.26m*)	650 = 10kts	1-10.2in/22, 1-5.9in/25
BRAGE, NOR	Horten	1878	264t	94ft 9in (*28.88m*)	220 = 8.5kts	1-10.6in RML, 1-1pdr, 2-1pdr revolvers
VIDAR	Horten	1881	262t	94ft 9in (*28.88m*)	330 = 9.5kts	1-10.6in RML, 1-1pdr, 2-1pdr revolvers
GOR, TYR	Horten	1885/1887	273t	102ft 7in (*31.27m*)	420 = 10.5kts	1-10.2in/30, 1-1pdr, 2-1pdr revolvers
AEGIR	Horten	1903	413t	109ft (*33.22m*)	350 = 9kts	1-8.2in/35, 1-10pdr, 2-4pdr

Glommen and *Lougen* were wooden-hulled. *Sleipner* was later rearmed with 1-5.9in/40, 2-12pdr, 2-9pdr and 2-1pdr revolvers. *Sleipner*, *Nor*, *Gor* and *Tyr* also had 1-14in TT. In *Tyr* the 1pdr was replaced by a 6pdr. *Aegir* differed from the others in having a 1½in deck.

FIRST CLASS TORPEDO BOATS

The gunboat *Sleipner*
(All photos in this section: Arrigo Barilli)

Name	Builder	Launched	Displacement	Length oa	ihp/speed	Armament
HVAL class	Schichau	1896	100t	130ft 11in *(39.90m)*	1100 = 21kts	2-1pdr, 2-18in TT
STORM class	Horten	1898	100t	130ft 11in *(39.90m)*	1100 = 21kts	2-1pdr, 2-18in TT
LAKS class	Horten	1900/1901	100t	126ft 4in *(38.50m)*	1150 = 21kts	2-1pdr, 2-18in TT

Hval class also comprised *Delfin* and *Hai*; *Storm* class *Brand* and *Trods*; *Laks* class *Sild, Sael* and *Skrei*.

SECOND CLASS TORPEDO BOATS

Name	Builder	Launched	Displacement	Length oa	ihp/speed	Armament
OD	Horten	1882	41t	95ft 1in *(28.98m)*	420 = 18kts	1-1pdr revolver, 1-14in TT (bow)
SPRINGER	Horten	1883	44t	98ft 5in *(30.00m)*	420 = 18kts	1-1pdr revolver, 2-14in TT (bow)
RASK, PIL	Horten	1885/1886	44t	100ft *(30.48)*	500 = 19kts	1-1pdr revolder, 2-14in TT (bow)
SNAR	Horten	1887	49t	105ft *(32.00m)*	600 = 19kts	1-1pdr revolver, 2-14in TT (bow)
ORM, OTER	Horten	1888	54t	108ft 3in *(33.00m)*	600 = 19kts	1-1pdr revolver, 2-16in TT (bow)
VARG, RAKET	Horten	1894	64t	113ft 2in *(34.50m)*	650 = 19kts	1-1pdr, revolver, 2-18in TT (bow)
LYN class	see text	1896	64t	113ft 2in *(34.50m)*	650 = 19kts	1-1pdr, 2-18in TT (1 bow)
DJERV class	see text	1897/1898	66t	113ft 2in *(34.50m)*	650 = 19kts	2-1pdr, 2-18in TT (1 bow)
HVAS, KJOEK	Frederikstad	1901	63t	111ft 10in *(34.08m)*	650 = 19kts	2-1pdr, 2-18in TT (1 bow)
HAUK, FALK	Horten	1903	62t	114ft 5in *(34.87m)*	750 = 20kts	2-1pdr, 2-18in TT (1 bow)
ÖRN, RAVN	Horten	1904	68t	113ft 2in *(34.50m)*	850 = 23kts	2-1pdr, 2-18in TT (1 bow)

Lyn class comprised *Lyn* and *Blink* built at Trondhjem, and *Glimt* built at Horten. *Djerv* class comprised *Djerv*, built at Horten, and *Kvik* and *Dristig*, built at Frederikstad.

THIRD CLASS TORPEDO BOATS

Name	Builder	Launched	Displacement	Length oa	ihp/speed	Armament
MYG	Horten	1900	26t	82ft *(25.00m)*	285 = 17.7kts	1-1pdr, 1-14in TT

The original Nos *1*, *2* and *3*, also named *Lyn, Rasp* and *Ulven,* were spar-torpedo boats.

SLOOPS

The wooden-hulled *Ellida* of 1028t displacement, launched in 1880, was primarily a training ship and is not included.

The Netherlands

The problems of the Dutch Navy were difficult to solve considering that Holland, though a highly successful commercial nation, had a population of only 5,400,000 in 1905. On the one hand was the defence of Holland in the event of a serious invasion, and on the other the protection of the Dutch East and West Indies. The first of these covered about 600,000 square miles of islands with a population of perhaps 23 million, and the second, which included the South American colony of Surinam, about 60,000 square miles and 90,000 inhabitants. In 1860 the Dutch had gone some way towards the reinforcement of sail by steam, the principal screw ships being 3 frigates, 5 corvettes and 5 sloops with 2 more building. These were more suited to the protection of the colonies that to that of Holland itself, and from 1860 to 1865 this pattern continued, the ships launched comprising 7 cruisers of the frigate or corvette type, 1 sloop and 12 650t gunboats.

There was a marked change in the period from 1866 to 1880 when a sailing frigate was converted to a central battery ironclad, and 2 turret ships and 17 monitors or small turret rams were launched. In addition 7 rigged cruisers, 2 sloops and 17 gunboats of over 500t were added, together with 30 local defence gunboats of 200-300t. This was followed by a pause between 1880 and 1889 when only 2 rigged cruisers, 2 sloops and 2 gunboats were launched with the important addition of 15 torpedo boats. From 1890 to 1894, 3 coast defence battleships, a monitor, 2 short range cruisers, 6 torpedo boats and 3 gunboats were launched, but in the last ten years of the period under review the 5 coast defence battleships and 6 cruisers that were added were given increased bunker capacity to make them more suitable for service in the East Indies. Other additions in this period comprised 18 torpedo boats and 7 gunboats of about 800t.

The majority of the above ships were built in Holland, the important exceptions being 7 of the early ironclads from Laird, Napier or La Seyne and 9 of the torpedo boats from Yarrow. Heavy guns were originally Armstrong RML, but later Krupp BL.

THE DUTCH NAVY in 1860

Wassenaer

SCREW FRIGATES

Name	Launched	Displacement	Guns	Speed
ADMIRAAL VAN WASSENAER	1856	2795t	45	7kts
EVERTSEN	1857	3300t	51	10kts
ZEELAND	1859	3400t	51	10kts

SCREW CORVETTES

Name	Launched	Displacement	Guns	Speed
PRINSES AMALIA class	1855/1856	1700t	19	6kts
GRONINGEN class	1856/1858	1700t	14	9kts

The first of these classes also comprised *Medusa* and the second *Citadel Van Antwerpen* and *Vice Admiraal Koopman*.

SCREW SLOOPS

Name	Launched	Displacement	Guns	Speed
VESUVIUS class	1859/1862	760t	10	7kts

Also comprised *Cornelis Dirks*, *Het Loo*, *Reinier Claeszen*, *Reteh*, and in addition *Prinses Marie* and *Soembing* building. There were ten smaller screw ships and 14 side-wheelers.

The principal effective sailing ships were two 74-gun, three 52-gun, four 32-gun and seven of 20-28 guns.

IRONCLADS AND COAST DEFENCE BATTLESHIPS

1\. *Prins Hendrik der Nederlanden* as completed

2\. *Guinea*

1 

2 

DE RUYTER *broadside ironclad*

Displacement: 2828t
Dimensions: 211ft 8in x 47ft 5in x 22ft 4in max (*64.52 x 14.46 x 6.80m*)
ihp/speed: 400 nominal, 1750 = ?kts
Armour: Iron. 6in max
Armament: 14-long 60pdr SB, later 4-9in RML
Complement: 250

Name	Converted
DE RUYTER	1863

Laid down at Flushing in 1831 as a 74 gun ship, converted to a 54 gun frigate in 1850 and launched in 1853. Converted to screw (45 guns) in 1860 and three years later to an ironclad. She was not very successful and was scrapped in 1874.

PRINS HENDRIK DER NEDERLANDEN *turret ship*

Displacement: 3320t
Dimensions: 240ft oa x 44ft x 18ft max (*73.15 x 13.41 x 5.49m*)
ihp/speed: 2000 = 11.4kts. Coal 467t max
Armour: Iron. Belt 4½in, turrets 11in-5½in
Armament: 4-9in RML, 4-4.7in/16
Complement: 267

Name	Builder	Launched
PRINS HENDRIK DER NEDERLANDEN	Laird	1866

A rigged turret ship resembling a small *Monarch*. The belt was taken to the upper deck amidships at 8ft 9in above water. Later 4-1pdr and 6-1pdr revolvers were added.

BUFFEL class *turret rams*

Displacement: *Buffel* 2284t, *Guinea* 2402t
Dimensions: 195ft 10in pp x 40ft x 16ft 3in max (*Guineau* 16ft 9in) (*59.69 x 12.19 x 4.95 (5.10) m)*
ihp/speed: 2000 = 11.2/11.5kts. Coal 150t max
Armour: Iron. Belt 6in, turret 8in
Armament: 2-9in RML, 4-4.7in/16
Complement: 159

Name	Builder	Launched
BUFFEL	Napier	1868
GUINEA	Amsterdam	1870

Small turret rams originally rigged with two masts. There was a waterline belt with 8in on the turret base. The guns were finally altered to 1-11in/22, 4-1pdr, 2-1pdr revolvers.

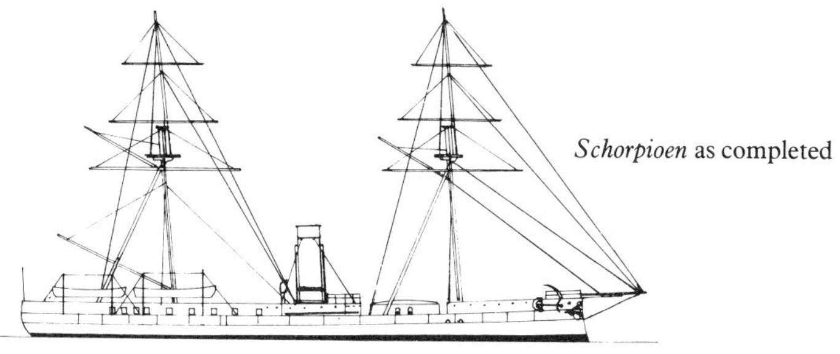
Schorpioen as completed

1. *Stier*
2. *Krokodil*
3. *Bloedhond*
4. *Luipaard*

SCHORPIOEN class *turret rams*

Displacement: *Schorpioen* 2140t, *Stier* 2078t
Dimensions: 205ft oa x 39ft x 15ft 10in max (*Stier* 16ft 9in) *(62.48 x 11.89 x 4.82 (5.10)m)*
ihp/speed: 2225 = 13kts *Schorpioen*, 2260 = 12.5kts *Stier*. Coal 246t *Schorpioen*, 197t *Stier* (both max)
Armour: Iron. Side 6in, turret 11-8in
Armament: 2-9in RML
Complement: 136

Name	Builder	Launched
SCHORPIOEN	La Seyne	1868
STIER	Laird	1868

Small turret rams originally rigged with two masts. The upper deck was 3ft 6in above water with fore and aft superstructures. The guns were finally altered to 1-11in/22, 5-1pdr and 2-1pdr revolvers.

HEILIGERLEE class *monitors*

Displacement: 1520t (*Tijger* 1427t)
Dimensions: 187ft oa x 44ft 2in x 10ft max (*Tijger* 9ft 2in max) *(57.00 x 13.46 x 3.05 (2.79)m)*
ihp/speed: 630-680 = 8¼-9kts. Coal 131t max (*Tijger* 80t max)
Armour: Iron. Side 5½in, turret 11in-8in
Armament: 2-9in RML
Complement: 117

Name	Builder	Launched
HEILIGERLEE	Laird	1868
KROKODIL	Laird	1868
TIJGER	Napier	1868

Low freeboard monitors without ram bows, and with narrow fore and aft superstructures. The armament finally became 1-11in/22, 2-1pdr, 2-1pdr revolvers.

BLOEDHOND class *monitors*

Displacement: *Bloedhond* 1656t, *Cerberus* 1559t
Dimensions: *Bloedhond* 182ft 9in oa x 46ft 5in x 10ft 4in max *(55.70 x 14.15 x 3.15m)*; *Cerberus* 185ft 6in oa x 43ft 10in x 9ft 10in max *(56.53 x 13.36 x 3.00m)*
ihp/speed: *Bloedhond* 680 = 7.7kts. Coal 128t max; *Cerberus* 534 = 7kts. Coal 98t max
Armour: Iron. Side 5½in, turret 11-8in
Armament: 2-9in RML
Complement: 117

Name	Builder	Launched
BLOEDHOND	Amsterdam	1869
CERBERUS	Amsterdam	1869

Similar to *Heiligerlee* class and later rearmed in same way.

ADDER class *monitors*

Displacement: 1555t (*Luipaard* 1585t)
Dimensions: 192ft 3in-195ft 5in oa x 44ft x 9ft 9in max *(58.60-59.56 x 13.41 x 2.97m)*
ihp/speed: 560-740 = 7-8kts. Coal 93t max
Armour: Iron. Side 5½in, turret 11-8in
Armament: 2-9in RML (*Luipaard* 1-11in/22)
Complement: 117

Name	Builder	Launched
ADDER	Fijenoord	1871
HAAI	Fijenoord	1871
HYENA	Amsterdam	1870
LUIPAARD	Fijenoord	1876
PANTER	Amsterdam	1870
WESP	Amsterdam	1871

Low freeboard monitors with ram bows and a small after superstructure. All except *Adder,* which was lost, eventually had 1-11in/22, 2-1pdr, 2-1pdr revolvers.

1

2

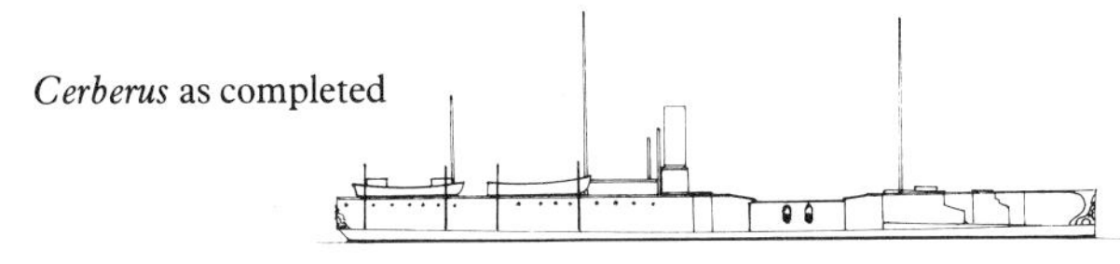
Cerberus as completed

3

4

KONING DER NEDERLANDEN *rigged turret ship*

Displacement:	5315t
Dimensions:	279ft oa x 49ft 8in x 19ft 6in max *(85.03 x 15.14 x 5.94m)*
ihp/speed:	4400 = 12kts. Coal 650t max
Armour:	Iron. Belt 8in, turrets 11$\frac{1}{2}$in
Armament:	4-11in RML, 4-4.7in/16; 4-1pdr, 6-1pdr revolvers later added
Complement:	256

Name	Builder	Launched
KONING DER NEDERLANDEN	Amsterdam	1874

A three-funnelled, barquentine-rigged, turret ship with a complete waterline belt and high armoured bases to the two turrets.

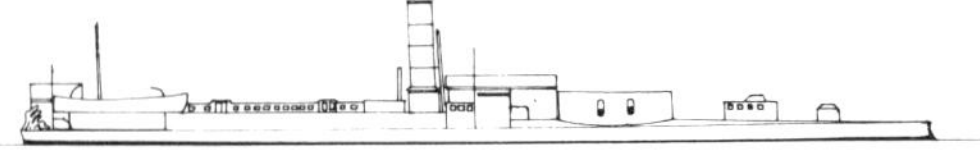

Draak as completed

DRAAK *monitor*

Displacement:	2198t
Dimensions:	213ft 7in oa x 49ft 3in x 11ft 11in max *(65.10 x 15.01 x 3.63m)*
ihp/speed:	807 = 8.4kts. Coal 109t max
Armour:	Iron. Side 8-5$\frac{1}{2}$in, turret 12-9in
Armament:	2-11in/22; 2-1pdr, 2-1pdr revolvers later added
Complement:	131

Name	Builder	Launched
DRAAK	Amsterdam	1877

Low freeboard monitor with ram bow. The twin turret was forward with superstructure aft.

MATADOR *monitor*

Displacement:	1968t
Dimensions:	209ft 8in oa x 47ft 5in x 10ft 6in max *(63.90 x 14.45 x 3.20m)*
ihp/speed:	690 = 7.5kts. Coal 109t max
Armour:	Iron. Side 5$\frac{1}{2}$-4$\frac{1}{2}$in, turret 12-9in
Armament:	2-11in/22; 2-1pdr, 2-1pdr revolvers later added
Complement:	131

Name	Builder	Launched
MATADOR	Fijenoord	1878

Similar to *Draak*.

REINIER CLAESZEN *monitor*

Displacement:	2440t
Dimensions:	229ft 8in oa x 44ft 3in x 14ft 11in max *(70.00 x 13.49 x 4.55m)*
ihp/speed:	2315 = 12.5kts. Coal 96t max
Armour:	Compound. Belt 4$\frac{3}{4}$in, turret 11in
Armament:	1-8.2in/35, 1-6.7in/35, 4-4pdr, 2-14in TT
Complement:	161

Name	Builder	Launched
REINIER CLAESZEN	Amsterdam	1891

A low freeboard monitor with an amidships superstructure, the 8.2in gun in a turret forward and the 6.7in aft in a shield.

EVERTSEN class *coast defence ships*

Displacement:	3464t
Dimensions:	282ft 10in oa x 47ft x 17ft 2in max *(86.20 x 14.33 x 5.23m)*
ihp/speed:	4700 = 16kts. Coal 289t max
Armour:	Steel. Belt 6-4in, barbette 9$\frac{1}{2}$in
Armament:	3-8.2in/35, 2-5.9in/35, 6-13pdr, 8-1pdr, 3-18in TT
Complement:	263

Name	Builder	Launched
EVERTSEN	Fijenoord	1894
PIET HEIN	Amsterdam	1894
KORTENAER	Schelde	1894

Coast defence battleships with a complete waterline belt. Two of the 8.2in were in a barbette forward and one in a shield aft, with the 5.9in guns in shields amidships.

1

2

3

4

KONINGIN REGENTES class *coast defence ships*

Displacement:	5002t
Dimensions:	317ft oa x 49ft 10in x 19ft 1in max *(96.62 x 15.19 x 5.82m)*
ihp/speed:	6500 = 16.5kts. Coal 722-736t max
Armour:	KC. Belt 6in-4in, barbettes and turrets 10in-5in
Armament:	2-9.4in/40, 4-5.9in/40, 8-13pdr, 4-1pdr, 3-18in TT
Complement:	340

Name	Builder	Launched
KONINGIN REGENTES	Amsterdam	1900
DE RUYTER	Fijenoord	1901
HERTOG HENDRIK	Amsterdam	1902

Coast defence battleships with a complete waterline belt. The 9.4in guns were mounted singly fore and aft and the 5.9in on either beam in shields. *Hertog Hendrik* became the German floating AA battery *Ariadne* in the Second World War.

1. *Koning der Nederlanden CPL*

2. *Reinier Claeszen*

3. *Piet Hein CPL*

4. *Koningin Regentes*

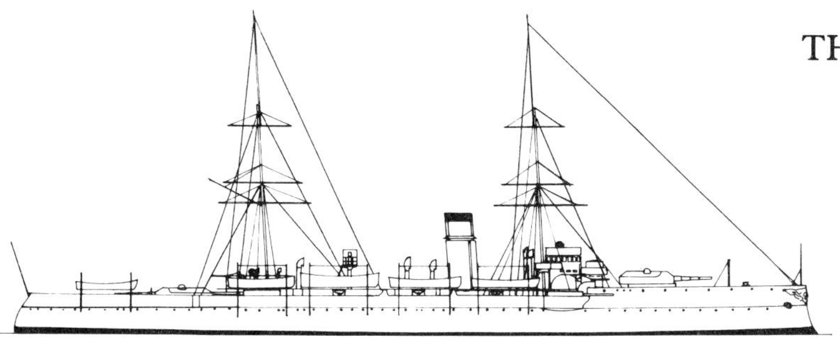

Tromp as completed

MARTEN HARPERTZOON TROMP *coast defence ship*

Displacement: 5210t
Dimensions: 330ft 8in oa x 49ft 10in x 18ft 8in max (*100.78 x 15.19 x 5.69m*)
ihp/speed: 6400 = 16.5kts. Coal 722t max
Armour: KC. Belt 6-4in, barbettes and turrets 8-5in
Armament: 2-9.4in/40, 4-5.9in/40, 8-13pdr, 4-1pdr, 3-18in TT
Complement: 340

Name	Builder	Launched
MARTEN HARPERTZOON TROMP	Amsterdam	1904

Generally similar to the *Koningin Regentes* class, but with the 5.9in guns in single turrets.

JACOB VAN HEEMSKERCK *coast defence ship*

Displacement: 4920t
Dimensions: 321ft 6in oa x 49ft 10in x 18ft 8in max (*98.00 x 15.19 x 5.69m*)
ihp/speed: 6400 = 16.5kts. Coal 680t max
Armour: KC. Belt 6-4in, barbettes and turrets 8-5in
Armament: 2-9.4in/40, 6-5.9in/40, 6-13pdr, 4-1pdr, 2-18in TT
Complement: 340

Name	Builder	Launched
JACOB VAN HEEMSKERCK	Amsterdam	1906

Similar to the *Tromp* with the two additional 5.9in guns in shields amidships. Became the German floating AA battery *Undine* in the Second World War.

CRUISERS

ADOLF HERTOG VAN NASSAU *wooden-hulled screw frigate*

Displacement: 3690t
Dimensions: 239ft x 51ft 7in x 22ft 4in max (*72.86 x 15.72 x 6.80m*)
ihp/speed: 400 nominal = ?kts
Armament: 51 guns, believed to comprise 8-6.3in, 1-60pdr SB, 42-30pdr SB
Complement: 500

Name	Builder	Launched
ADOLF HERTOG VAN NASSAU	Flushing	1861

ANNA PAULOWNA *wooden-hulled screw frigate*

Displacement: 3345t
Dimensions: 301ft 4in x 43ft 8in x 20ft 4in max (*91.85 x 13.30 x 6.20m*)
ihp/speed: 600 nominal = ?kts
Armament: 10-6.3in, 10-30pdr SB
Complement: 325

Name	Builder	Launched
ANNA PAULOWNA	Amsterdam	1867

Rebuilt as a training ship in 1877.

DJAMBI class *wooden-hulled screw corvettes*

Displacement: 2030-2180t
Dimensions: 206ft 2in x 40ft 2in x 18ft-18ft 4in max (*62.84 x 12.25 x 5.50-5.60m*)
ihp/speed: About 830 = 8½-10kts. Coal 340-400t max
Armament: 16 guns (8-6.3in RML, 8-30pdr SB); later 14-6.3in RML, but two last ships 4-7in RML, 8-6.3in RML
Complement: 225-250

Name	Builder	Launched
DJAMBI	Amsterdam	1860
WILLEM	Amsterdam	1863
ZOUTMAN	Amsterdam	1861
LEEUWARDEN	Amsterdam	1861
METALLEN KRUIS	Amsterdam	1862
CURACAO	Flushing	1863
ZILVEREN KRUIS	Amsterdam	1869
VAN GALEN	Amsterdam	1872

Some authorities credit *Van Galen* with 1480ihp = 10.5kts.

ATJEH class *unprotected cruisers*

Displacement: 3425-3669t
Dimensions: 301ft 2in-302ft 2in oa x 41ft x 21ft-22ft 10in max (*91.80-92.10 x 12.50 x 6.40-6.96m*)
ihp/speed: 2700-3300 = 13.5-14.8kts. Coal 440-580t max
Armament: 6-6.7in/25, 8-4.7in/16 (later 8-1pdr, 6-1pdr revolvers added)
Complement: 277-306

Name	Builder	Launched
ATJEH	Amsterdam	1876
TROMP	Amsterdam	1877
KONINGIN EMMA DER NEDERLANDEN	Amsterdam	1879
DE RUYTER	Amsterdam	1880
VAN SPEYK	Amsterdam	1882
JOHAN WILLEM FRISO	Amsterdam	1886

Ship-rigged unprotected cruisers with sheathed iron hulls.

Sumatra

SUMATRA *protected cruiser*

Displacement: 1693t
Dimensions: 229ft 7in oa x 37ft 1in x 15ft 4in max (*69.97 x 11.30 x 4.67m*)
ihp/speed: 2350 = 17kts. Coal 207/276t
Armament: 1-8.2in/35, 1-5.9in/35, 2-4.7in/35, 4-1pdr, 2-1pdr revolvers, 2-14in TT
Complement: 181

Name	Builder	Launched
SUMATRA	Amsterdam	1890

Protected cruiser with 1½in deck. The 8.2in gun was forward and the 5.9in aft, both in shields, with the 4.7in sponsoned abreast the foremast.

1

2

1. *Koningin Wilhelmina* as completed

2. *Utrecht* about 1901
Aldo Fraccaroli collection
(All uncredited photos in this section: Arrigo Barilli)

KONINGIN WILHELMINA DER NEDERLANDEN *protected cruiser*

Displacement: 4530t
Dimensions: 327ft 5in oa x 48ft 11in x 19ft 11in max (*99.80 x 14.91 x 6.07m*)
ihp/speed: 4600 = 15.8kts. Coal 411t max
Armour: Compound. Belt nil, barbette and turret 11in
Armament: 1-11in/30, 1-8.2in/35, 2-6.7in/35, 4-13pdr, 6-1pdr, 4-1pdr revolvers, 4-14in TT
Complement: 296

Name	Builder	Launched
KONINGIN WILHELMINA DER NEDERLANDEN	Amsterdam	1892

A ship of unusual design with the 11in turret forward, the 8.2in gun in a shield aft and the 6.7in also in shields on either beam. The protective deck was 2in flat with 3in slopes, the engine room glacis 5in and the boiler room glacis 11in.

HOLLAND class *protected cruisers*

Displacement: 3840t first three; 3970t second three
Dimensions: 306ft 1in-310ft 8in oa x 48ft 7in x 17ft 9in max (*93.30-94.70 x 14.80 x 5.41m*)
ihp/speed: 10,000 = 19.5-20kts. Coal 814-875t max
Armament: 2-5.9in/40, 6-4.7in/40, 4-13pdr, 4-1pdr, 2-18in TT
Complement: 324/371

Name	Builder	Launched
HOLLAND	Amsterdam	1896
ZEELAND	De Schelde	1897
FRIESLAND	Fijenoord	1896
GELDERLAND	Fijenoord	1898
NOORDBRABANT	De Schelde	1899
UTRECHT	Amsterdam	1898

Protected cruisers of normal type with the guns in shields, the 5.9in fore and aft and the 4.7in on either beam. The protective deck was 2in with 5in on the engine room glacis. *Gelderland* became the German floating AA battery *Niobe* in the Second World War.

FIRST CLASS TORPEDO BOATS

Name	Builder	Launched	Displacement	Length oa	ihp/speed	Armament
ARDJOENO	Yarrow	1886	82t	125ft 10in (*38.35m*)	800 = 21kts	2-1pdr, 2-18in TT
BATOK	Amsterdam	1887	84t	126ft 1in (*38.43m*)	725 = 20.7kts	2-1pdr, 2-18in TT
DEMPO	Fijenoord	1887	82t	125ft 10in (*38.35m*)	760 = 20.5kts	2-1pdr, 2-18in TT
CYCLOOP	Amsterdam	1887	84t	126ft 8in (*38.60m*)	680 = 19.8kts	2-1pdr, 2-18in TT
HABANG	Amsterdam	1888	79t	128ft 8in (*39.22m*)	928 = 21.7kts	2-1pdr, 2-18in TT
GOENTOER	Amsterdam	1888	85t	126ft 8in (*38.60m*)	728 = 20kts	2-1pdr, 2-18in TT
EMPONG	Yarrow	1888	85t	126ft 8in (*38.60m*)	1089 = 22.8kts	2-1pdr, 2-18in TT
FOKA	Amsterdam	1888	85t	126ft 8in (*38.60m*)	962 = 22.1kts	2-1pdr, 2-18in TT
KRAKATAU	Amsterdam	1888	86t	128ft 8in (*39.22m*)	746 = 19.1kts	2-1pdr, 2-18in TT
IDJEN	Amsterdam	1889	90t	128ft 8in (*39.22m*)	836 = 20.6kts	2-1pdr, 2-18in TT
CERBERUS	Schelde	1888	82t	125ft 4in (*38.20m*)	912 = 21.2kts	2-1pdr, 3-18in TT (1 bow)
LAMONGAN class	Amsterdam	1890/1891	59t	108ft (*32.92m*)	780 = 20.4kts	2-1pdr, 2-18in TT
HYDRA class	See text	See text	101t	130ft (*39.62m*)	1320 = 24.6kts	2-1pdr, 3-18in TT
OPHIR class	See text	See text	140t	153ft (*46.63m*)	1900 = 25kts	2-4pdr, 2-18in TT
G1, G2, G3, G4	See text	1904	140t	153ft (*46.63m*)	2000 = 25kts	2-4pdr, 2-18in TT

The first ten boats named above are sometimes called the *Ardjoeno* class. *Lamongan* class also comprised *Makjan and Nobo*. *Hydra* class comprised *Hydra* and *Scylla*, built by Yarrow and launched in 1900, and *Minotaurus*, *Python* and *Sphinx*, built at Schelde and launched in 1902/1903. *Ophir* class comprised *Ophir, Pangrango* and *Rindjani*, built by Yarrow and launched in 1901, and *Smeroe*, *Tangka* and *Wajang*, built at Fijenoord and launched in 1903. *G1* and *G2*, also named *Johan Van Brakel* and *Jan Danielzoon van de Rijn*, were built at Schelde and *G3* and *G4*, named *Meijndert Jentjes* and *Willem Willemsze*, were built at Fijenoord.

SECOND CLASS TORPEDO BOATS

Name	Builder	Launched	Displacement	Length oa	ihp/speed	Armament
XV, XVI	Fijenoord	1881	30t	80ft 9in (*24.60m*)	250 = 17kts	1-1pdr, 2-14in TT (bow)
ETNA, HEKLA	Yarrow	1882	45t	101ft 8in (*31.00m*)	550 = 21.4kts	2-1pdr, 2-14in TT (bow)
III, XXI, XXII	Amsterdam	1890/1891	37t	84ft (*25.60m*)	440 = 17.5kts	1-1pdr, 2-14in TT
K1, K2, K3	Fijenoord	1904/1905	47t	98ft 5in (*30.00m*)	560 = 18.7kts	2-1pdr, 2-14in TT

I-XIV, *XVII-XX*, including original *III*, had spar-torpedoes only. *III*, *XXI* and *XXII* were named *Jan Haring*, *Jasper Leynssen* and *Jacob Hobein*. *K1*, *K2 and K3* were named *Michiel Gardeyn*, *Christiaan Cornelis* and *Willem Warmont*.

SLOOPS

Name	Builder	Launched	Displacement	Length oa	ihp/speed	Armament
WATERGEUS	Amsterdam	1864	1405t	190ft 4in (*58.00m*)	720 = 10kts	6-6.3in RML
MARNIX	Amsterdam	1867	1488t	198ft 10in (*60.60m*)	770 = 10kts	6-6.3in RML
ALKMAAR	Amsterdam	1874	1051t	178ft 8in (*54.46m*)	686 = 10.3kts	1-5.9in/25, 6-4.7in/18
SOMMELSDIJK	Amsterdam	1882	997t	178ft 9in (*54.50m*)	759 = 11.4kts	1-5.9in/25, 3-4.7in/18, 2-1pdr, 2-1pdr revolvers
JAVA	Rotterdam	1885	1280t	205ft 3in (*62.56m*)	1017 = 12.6kts	1-5.9in/25, 3-4.7in/18, 2-1pdr

The wooden-hulled *Watergeus* was similar to *Marnix*. *Alkmaar* was composite-hulled, and 2-1pdr and 2-1pdr revolvers were later added.

GUNBOATS (OVER 500 TONS)

Name	Builder	Launched	Displacement	Length oa	ihp/speed	Armament
AMSTEL class	–	1860/1863	650t	–	280 = 7kts	7-30pdr SB
BANDA, RIOUW	Fijenoord	1872	689t	160ft 8in (*48.97m*)	200 = 7kts	1-6.3in RML, 2-4.7in/18
PONTIANAK class	See text	1873/1874	718t	163ft 7in (*49.86m*)	370 = 9kts	1-7in RML, 2-4.7in/18
ARUBA	Amsterdam	1873	786t	164ft (*50.00m*)	413 = 9.5kts	1-5.9in/25, 2-4.7in/18
BATAVIA class	See text	See text	837t	175ft 10in (*53.60m*)	400/500-8.4/ 9.3kts	1-5.9in/25, 3-4.7in/18, 2-1pdr
SURINAME class	See text	1877/1878	870t	177ft 2in (*54.00m*)	450 = 9.5kts	1-5.9in/25, 3-4.7in/18 2-1pdr
CERAM class	See text	1887	541t	173ft 4in (*52.83m*)	800 = 12.8kts	3-4.7in/18, 2-1pdr
LOMBOK class	See text	1891	590t	172ft (*52.43m*)	960 = 12.3kts	3-4.7in/18, 2-1pdr
BORNEO	Thompson	1892	787t	176ft 7in (*53.83m*)	1040 = 13.2kts	6-4.1in/35, 2-1pdr, 2-1pdr revolvers
NIAS class	–	1895/1897	797/808t	176ft 10in (*53.90m*)	1300 = 12.9kts	2-4.1in/35, 4-1pdr, 2-1pdr revolvers
KOETEI class	Amsterdam	1898/1900	778/788t	176ft 2in (*53.70m*)	1380 = 13.7kts	2-4.1in/35, 4-1pdr, 2-1pdr revolvers

The wooden-hulled *Amstel* class also comprised *Aart van Nes, Bommelerwaard, Coehoorn, Den Briel, Dommel, Haarlemmermeer, Kijkduin, Maas en Waal, Schouwen, Soestdijk* and *Stavoren*.

Banda, Riouw and the *Pontianak* class were composite-hulled. The latter comprised *Pontianak* and *Bandjermasin* built at Amsterdam, and *Palembang* and *Sambas* built at Fijenoord. *Pontianak* had 1-6.3in RML instead of 7in. The *Batavia* class were built as follows: Amsterdam: *Batavia* 1876, *Macassar* 1877 and *Madura* 1880; Fijenoord: *Samarang* 1876, *Bonaire* 1877, *Bali* 1878, *Padang* 1878, *Benkoelen* 1879. *Batavia, Samarang, Macassar* had 1-7in RML (6.3in *Macassar*), 2-4.7in/18. The *Suriname* was built at Amsterdam, her sister, *St Eustat*, at Fijenoord, the *Ceram* at Flushing and her sister *Flores* at Amsterdam, the *Lombok* at Amsterdam, and her sister *Sumbawa* at Flushing. *Borneo* was composite-hulled and resembled the British *Goldfinch* type. Of the *Nias* class, *Nias* and *Mataram* were built at Amsterdam and *Edi* and *Serdang* at Flushing. *Nias* was originally listed with 3-4.7in/18, 2-1pdr. The *Koetei* class also comprised *Siboga* and *Assahan*.

GUNBOATS (200-500 TONS)

Name	Builder	Launched	Displacement	Length oa	ihp/speed	Armament
HYDRA class	See text	1873/1876	218t	84ft 11in (*25.88m*)	124/146 = 7.5/8kts	1-9in RML
WODAN class	See text	1877/1879	264/280t	91ft 4in (*27.80m*)	101/171 = 7/8.3kts	1-11in/22, 2-1pdr, 1-1pdr revolver

The *Hydra* class were built as follows: Armstrong: *Hydra* and *Ever*; Amsterdam: *Das, Dog, Fret, Geep, Gier, Havik* and *Raaf*; Fijenoord: *Brak, Lynx* and *Vos*; Delfshaven: *Bever* and *Sperwer*. All were later rearmed with 1-8.2in/35, 2-1pdr, and 1-1pdr revolver.

The *Wodan* class were built as follows: Delfshaven: *Wodan, Balder, Braga, Freyr, Heimdall, Njord, Thor* and *Tyr*; Fijenoord: *Hefring, Vali* and *Vidar*; Amsterdam: *Bulgia, Dufa, Hadda, Udur* and *Ulfr*. Except in *Bulgia, Dufa, Hadda, Hefring* and *Udur* the 11in/22 was replaced by an 11in/30, and in 1908 *Wodan* is listed with 1-4.7in/40 instead.

Portugal

Owing to financial difficulties and mismanagement, and to the failure or inability to develop her large overseas possessions, which amounted to fully 800,000 square miles, nearly all in Africa, Portugal was unable to afford the kind of navy to be expected from a country with 5,500,000 inhabitants in 1905. In 1860 the Portuguese Navy had 3 screw frigates or corvettes and the total additions to 1905 amounted to a small coast defence battleship, 5 cruisers of which 4 were small, a destroyer, 4 torpedo boats, 5 sloops and 15 gunboats of 450t or more. Of these the cruisers and the destroyer were launched from 1896 to 1901. Although some ships were built at Lisbon, the majority were built in Britain with two small cruisers in France and one in Italy.

THE PORTUGUESE NAVY in 1860

SCREW FRIGATES AND CORVETTES

Name	Launched	Displacement	Guns	Speed
BARTHOLOMEU DIAS	1858	2339t	28	10kts
ESTEPHANIA	1859	2331t	28	10kts
SAGRIS	1858	1360t	14	12kts

There were also 6 side-wheel steamers totalling 26 guns. The principal sailing ships were: *Vasco da Gama* of 74 guns, *Dom Fernando II e Gloria* of 50 then later 24 guns, and *Dom Joao I, Goa* and *Damao*, of 14 guns each.

COAST DEFENCE BATTLESHIP

VASCO DA GAMA

Displacement:	2384t
Dimensions:	200ft pp x 40ft (46ft 6in over battery) x 19ft max (*60.96 x 12.19 (14.17) x 5.79m*)
ihp/speed:	3000 = 10.3kts. Coal 300t max
Armour:	Iron. Belt 9-4in, battery 10-6in
Armament:	2-10.2in/20, 1-5.9in/25, 4-9pdr
Complement:	232

Name	Builder	Launched
VASCO DA GAMA	Thames Iron Wks	1876

Barquentine-rigged ship with complete belt, designed for the defence of Lisbon and the Tagus. The 2-10.2in guns were in a raised battery and the 5.9in aft. She was drastically reconstructed by Orlando in 1901-1903, the hull being cut in half and 32ft 6in added. The details were then: Displacement: 2972t; Dimensions: 232ft 6in pp x 40ft x 20ft 7in max (*70.86 x 12.19 x 6.27m*); ihp/speed: 6000 = 15.5kts. Coal 300t max; Armour: Steel. Belt 10-4in; Armament: 2-8in/40, 1-5.9in/45, 1-12pdr, 4-9pdr, 6-3pdr; Complement: 260. The complete belt was renewed and the battery removed, the 8in guns being in sponsons and the 5.9in aft.

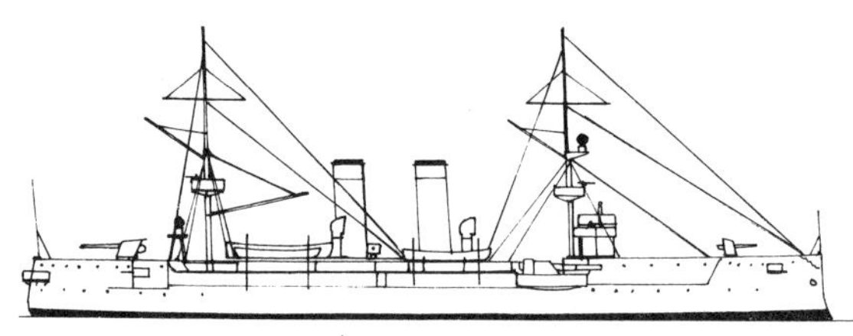

Vasco da Gama as reconstructed 1903

1

CRUISERS

1. *Vasco da Gama* before her reconstruction *CPL*
2. *Adamastor* about 1898 *Aldo Fraccaroli collection*
3. *Sao Gabriel* *CPL*
4. *Dom Carlos I*

2

ADAMASTOR *unprotected cruiser*

Displacement:	1729t
Dimensions:	242ft 2in pp x 35ft 2in x 15ft 3in max (*74.00 x 10.72 x 4.65m*)
ihp/speed:	4000 = 18kts. Coal 420t max
Armament:	2-5.9in/30, 4-4.1in/40, 4-9pdr, 2-1pdr, 3-14in TT
Complement:	237

Name	Builder	Launched
ADAMASTOR	Orlando	1896

Small unprotected cruiser with 5.9in guns fore and aft.

3

SÃO GABRIEL class *protected cruisers*

Displacement:	1771t
Dimensions:	242ft 1in pp x 35ft 6in x 14ft 3in max (*73.78 x 10.82 x 4.34m*)
ihp/speed:	4000 = 17.5kts. Coal 300t max
Armament:	2-5.9in/45, 4-4.7in/45, 8-3pdr, 2-1pdr, 1-14in TT
Complement:	242

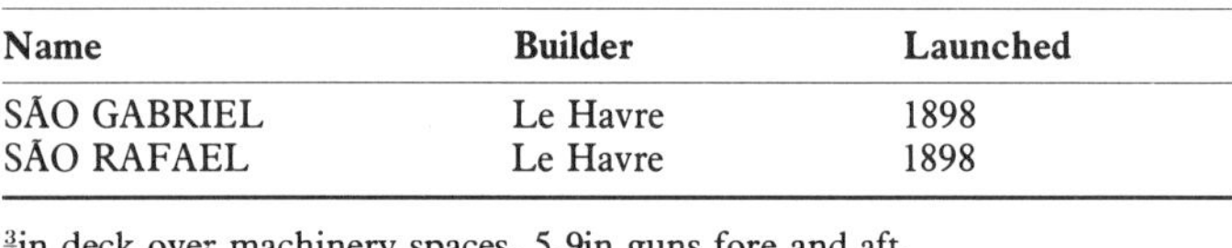

Name	Builder	Launched
SÃO GABRIEL	Le Havre	1898
SÃO RAFAEL	Le Havre	1898

¾in deck over machinery spaces. 5.9in guns fore and aft.

DOM CARLOS I *protected cruiser*

Displacement:	4186t
Dimensions:	360ft 10in pp x 47ft 3in x 17ft 6in max (*109.98 x 14.40 x 5.33m*)
ihp/speed:	12,500 = 22kts. Coal 700/1000t
Armament:	4-5.9in/45, 8-4.7in/44, 16-3pdr, 2-1pdr, 5-14in TT
Complement:	473

Name	Builder	Launched
DOM CARLOS I	Armstrong	1898

One of the usual designs of Armstrong (Elswick) cruisers with a protective deck 1½in flat and 4.3in on slopes. Later renamed *Almirante Reis*. The 5.9in guns were fore and aft and on either beam abreast the foremast.

4

RAINHA DONA AMELIA *protected cruiser*

Displacement: 1630t
Dimensions: 246ft pp x 38ft 8in x 14ft 7in max (*74.98 x 11.78 x 4.45m*)
ihp/speed: 5000 = 20kts. Coal 322t max
Armament: 4-5.9in/45, 2-3.9in/45, 2-3pdr, 2-1pdr, 2-14in TT
Complement: 273

Name	Builder	Launched.
RAINHA DONA AMELIA	Lisbon	1899

Small cruiser with 1.2in max deck, 5.9in guns in sponsons and 3.9in fore and aft. Later renamed *Republica*.

DESTROYER

TEJO

Displacement: 522t
Dimensions: 229ft 8in x 22ft 10in x 8ft 3in max (*70.00 x 6.96 x 2.51m*)
ihp/speed: 7000 = 25kts. Coal 155t max
Armament: 1-3.9in/45, 1-9pdr, 4-3pdr, 2-14in TT
Complement: 85

Name	Builder	Launched
TEJO	Lisbon DYd	1901

A four-funnelled destroyer with the 9pdr gun forward and the 3.9in aft.

1

2

1. *Rainha Dona Amelia*

2. The sloop *Mindello*
CPL
(All uncredited photos in this section: Arrigo Barilli)

TORPEDO BOATS

Name/Number	Builder	Launched	Displacement	Length pp	ihp/speed	Armament
No 1 (ESPADATE)	Yarrow	1880	53t	86ft (*26.21m*)	450 = 19.7kts	2-14in TT (bow)
Nos 2, 3, 4	Yarrow	1886	65t	119ft 7in (*36.45m*)	700 = 19kts	2-1pdr revolvers, 2-14in TT (bow)

SLOOPS

Name	Builder	Launched	Displacement	Length pp	ihp/speed	Armament
SÁ DA BANDEIRA	Lisbon	1862	about 1300t	180ft (*54.86m*)	about 600 = 9kts	13 guns
DUQUE DE TERCEIRA	Lisbon	1864	1406t	180ft (*54.86m*)	660 = 9kts	13 guns, later 8-6in RML
MINDELLO class	Thames Iron Wks	1875	1106t	170ft (*51.82m*)	900 = 11.5kts	2-7in RML, 6-4.7in RML
ALFONSO D'ALBUQUERQUE	Thames Iron Wks	1884	1092t	203ft 6in (*62.00m*)	1360 = 13.3kts	2-6in/26, 5-5in/25, 2-3pdr

Bandeira and *Terceira* were wooden-hulled. The *Mindello* class, which also comprised *Rainha De Portugal*, were composite.

GUNBOATS (OVER 200 TONS)

Name	Builder	Launched	Displacement	Length pp	ihp/speed	Armament
TEJO, DOURO, QUANZA	Lisbon	1869/1877	578t	143ft (*43.58m*)	400 = 10kts	1-6.3in RML, 2-4.7in RML
RIO LIMA	Laird	1875	628t	142ft 2in (*43.33m*)	500 = 11kts	1-7in RML, 4-4.7in RML
TAMEGA, SADO	Laird	1875	635t	148ft 9in (*45.34m*)	500 = 11kts	1-7in RML, 4-4.7in RML
BENGO, MANDOVI	Laird	1879	455t	125ft 4in (*38.20m*)	400 = 10.5kts	1-6in/26, 2-3.4in/24
ZAMBEZI	Lisbon	1880	631t	143ft (*43.58m*)	460 = 10kts	1-6in/26, 2-3.9in/27
VOUGA	Lisbon	1882	710t	161ft (*49.08m*)	600 = 10kts	1-6in/26, 4-3.9in/27
LIBERAL, ZAIRE	Laird	1884	549t	139ft 5in (*42.50m*)	500 = 10kts	1-6in/26, 2-3.9in/27, 1-1pdr
DIU	Lisbon	1889	717t	147ft 8in (*45.00m*)	700 = 11.5kts	1-5.9in/30, 2-4.1in/35
DOM LUIZ	Lisbon	1895	789t	150ft 6in (*45.87m*)	500 = 10kts	4-4.1in/35, 2-3pdr
PATRIA	Lisbon	1903	626t	196ft 9in (*60.00m*)	1800 = 16.7kts	4-3.9in/45, 6-3pdr

The *Tejo* class, *Vouga*, *Diu* and *Dom Luiz* were wooden-hulled, and the *Tamega* class and *Zambezi* composite. In *Tejo* the 6.3in RML was replaced by a 3.9in/27, while the armament of *Rio Lima* was changed to 1-6in/26, 2-3.9in/27, and the armament of the *Tamega* class to 2-4.1in/35, 2-9pdr, 1-1pdr. *Zambezi* was also rearmed with 3-3.9in/27, 1-1pdr and *Vouga* with 2-3.9in/27, 2-3pdr.

Spain

Despite the loss of her South American empire in the first half of the nineteenth century, Spain still possessed large territories overseas, and kept a reasonably-sized navy. In 1860 the most modern ships were 3 screw frigates (*Asturias*, *Berenguela* and *Blanca*), 5 screw sloops or gunboats, 3 paddle frigates and 26 paddle gunboats. The sailing navy consisted of 2 86-gun ships-of-the-line, 4 frigates, 4 corvettes and 25 smaller craft. Under construction were 2 screw frigates (*Concepcion*, 2300t and *Lealtad*, 3075t) and six smaller steam vessels. Spain was one of the few naval powers of the second rank to build broadside ironclads, most being converted from wooden frigates at various stages of design and construction, although the two largest (acquired from Britain and France) were constructed of iron. Thus by the early 1870s Spain possessed – on paper at least – an impressive squadron of 7 ironclads. Spain also manufactured her own Hontoria guns, but these weapons were mainly licensed versions of Pallisers at first and Schneider-Canet designs later. Parrot, Armstrong and Krupp guns were also purchased and Spain used Schwartzkopf torpedoes.

The Spanish Navy was involved, without any great glory, in the 1864-66 war against Peru and Chile, and the Cadiz mutiny of 1868 played a significant part in ending Isabella II's long and despotic rule. There followed a period of political unrest which eventually erupted into open civil war between three factions, during which Cartagena and its squadron were seized by radical republicans. The civil war was settled in 1874 by the restoration of the monarchy, at which time Spain was faced with the prospect of war with the USA over the *Virginius* affair. Mercenaries aboard this steamer were thought to be en route to aid the Cuban rebels (the guerrilla war had been going on since 1868), the steamer was seized by the *Tornado* and many of the American and British crew were shot. The incident was smoothed over and a Cuban settlement was reached in 1879 but it left a legacy of resentment against Spanish policy in the New World.

In 1898 the USS *Maine* blew up in Havana harbour – but certainly not by Spanish agency – and the USA had a perfect cause for declaring war. During this short war Spain lost not only most of her fleet in the Battles of Manila Bay and Santiago but ultimately also Cuba, the Philippines and most of her remaining colonies. After this blow, there was no real attempt to rebuild the Spanish Navy and even vessels under construction such as the *Asturias* class armoured cruisers took many years to complete.

ARMOURED SHIPS

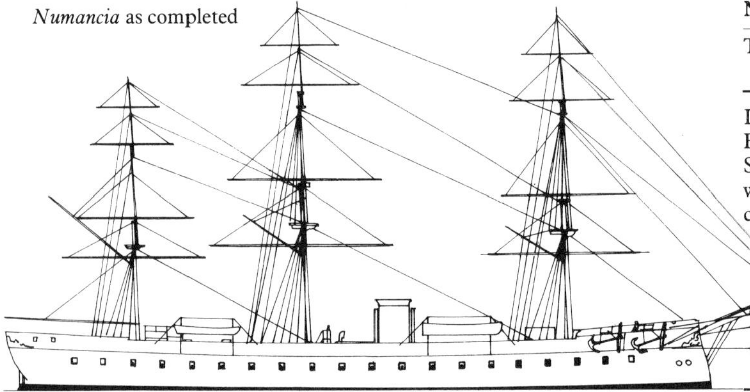
Numancia as completed

NUMANCIA *broadside ironclad*

Displacement: 7189t
Dimensions: 315ft pp x 57ft x 27ft max (*96.01 x 17.37 x 8.22m*)
Machinery: 1 shaft, 3700ihp = 10kts. Coal 1100t
Armour: Iron. 5½in belt, 4¾in battery
Armament: 8-10in RML, 7-8in RML, 1-7.9in BL, 8 MGs, 2-14in TT
Complement: 500

Name	Builder	Launched	Fate
NUMANCIA	La Seyne	19.11.1863	–

An iron-hulled ship-rigged vessel with one funnel and a ram bow. As built she was armed with 40-68pdr SB but by 1890 the armament was as above. The 10in guns were 18t Armstrong weapons mounted on the main deck; 4 of the 9t 8in Armstrongs were also mounted on the main deck, with the other 3 on the upper deck and the 7.8in Hontoria gun on the forecastle. *Numancia* was completely rebuilt at La Seyne in 1897-98 and rearmed with 4-6.4in QF, 6-5.5in QF, 3-4.7in QF, 12 MGs and 2 TT. She was also re-engined, and could then reach 13kts.

TETUAN *wooden broadside ironclad*

Displacement: 6200t
Dimensions: 279ft 1in wl (*85.00m*)
Machinery: 1-shaft HT, 5000nhp = 10kts. Coal 1200t
Armour: Iron. Belt and battery 5in
Armament: 30-68pdr and 32pdr SB
Complement: 500

Name	Builder	Launched	Fate
TETUAN	Ferrol	1863	Blown up 30.12.73

Laid down in 1861 and originally intended to carry 41 guns. She resembled the French *Normandie* in overall appearance, but with noticeably small gunports. Seized by Red mutineers during the civil war, she was badly damaged in action with the loyalist *Vitoria* and eventually blown up in Cartagena harbour to avoid capture.

VITORIA *centre battery ironclad*

Displacement: 7135t
Dimensions: 316ft 2in pp x 57ft x 26ft 5in max (*96.37 x 17.37 x 8.07m*)
Machinery: 1 shaft, 4500ihp = 12kts. Coal 875t
Armour: Iron. Belt 5½in, battery 5⅛in
Armament: 8-9in RML, 2-8in RML, 1-7.9in BL, 8 MGs, 2-14in TT
Complement: 500

Name	Builder	Launched	Fate
VITORIA	Thames Iron Wks	4.11.1865	–

Iron-hulled, ship-rigged vessel with two funnels and a ram bow, originally armed with 30-68pdr SB. In 1890 the 9in Armstrongs were mounted on the broadside with the 8in Armstrongs in an upper deck redoubt on the broadside and the single Hontoria 7.9in under the topgallant forecastle. The armour belt extended from 13ft above wl to 7ft below. There was a CT in the redoubt. *Vitoria* was reconstructed at La Seyne in 1897-8, reduced to military rig and rearmed with 6-6.4in, 6-5.5in QF, 6-6pdr, 6 MGs and 2 TT. She was used as a TS after 1900.

Vitoria about 1888

SAGUNTO *wooden centre battery ironclad*

Displacement: 7352t
Dimensions: 294ft wl x 57ft x 29ft mean, 31ft max (*89.61 x 17.37 x 8.83, 9.44m*)
Machinery: 1-shaft HT, 3700ihp = 8kts. Coal 900t
Armour: Belt 6in (considerably reduced fore and aft), battery 5½in, bulkheads 4in, barbettes 5in
Armament: 6-9in RML, 2-8in RML, 3-7.1in, 8 QFs, 2 MGs

Name	Builder	Launched	Fate
SAGUNTO	Ferrol	1869	–

Originally laid down as the ship-of-the-line *Principe Alfonso*, reportedly intended for 100 guns, but altered during building to a 30-gun armoured frigate. As completed she could make 11kts. The armament in 1885 was as above, with the 7.1in modified Pallisers in barbettes and one under the forecastle. There was no CT. By 1885 the hull was completely rotten.

Arapiles as completed
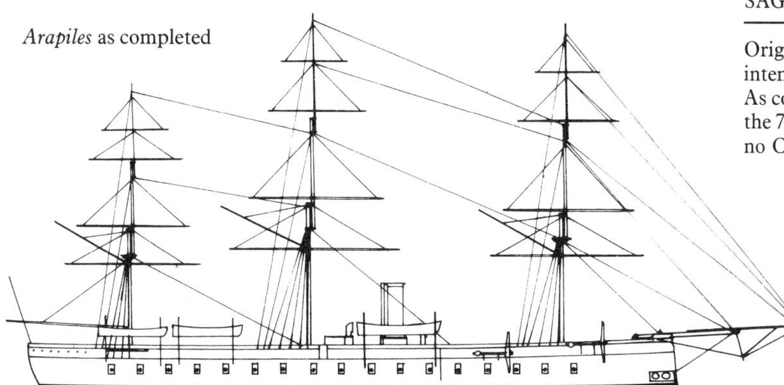

ARAPILES *wooden broadside ironclad*

Displacement: 5500t designed, 5700t as completed
Dimensions: 280ft 11in x 54ft as completed (*85.37 x 16.45m*)
Machinery: 100nhp = 12kts designed
Armour: Iron. Belt 4¾-4¼in
Armament: 2-10in RML, 5-8in RML, 10-7.9in BL

Name	Builder	Launched	Fate
ARAPILES	Green, Blackwall	1864	Condemned *c*1873

Originally designed as a wooden screw frigate, but altered during building to carry a midships belt, thus increasing the beam by 2ft and the displacement by 200t. A ship-rigged vessel, with a single funnel. The above armament of Armstrong guns was as carried in 1870 but by 1878 all the 7.9in and 3 of the 8in had been replaced by 12-6.3in Hontoria BL. The hull was too weak for the armour and the ship had a relatively short career.

MENDEZ NUNEZ *wooden centre battery ironclad*

Displacement: 3382t
Dimensions: 236ft 3in x 49ft 4in x 21ft 11in mean (*72.02 x 15.05 x 6.43m*)
Machinery: 1 shaft, 500nhp = 8kts. Coal 400t
Armour: Iron. Belt 5in, battery 5in
Armament: 4-9in RML, 2-8in RML

Name	Builder	Launched	Fate
MENDEZ NUNEZ	–	1869	–

Originally the 38-gun wooden screw frigate *Resolucion* launched in 1861. She was badly damaged in the 1864-66 war with Peru and Chile, and during redocking was rebuilt as an armoured corvette. The 1880 armament above comprised entirely of Armstrong guns.

Note: There were also two other armoured ships:
Puigcerda, a 553t low freeboard 2-turret monitor built by La Seyne in 1874 for service on the Bilbao during the Carlist war, armed with 2-6.2in and 2-4.7in. Used as a torpedo TS in 1890s.
Duque de Tetuan a 700t floating battery built at Ferrol in 1874, armed with 1-6.2in and 4-4.7in.

Zaragosa about 1880
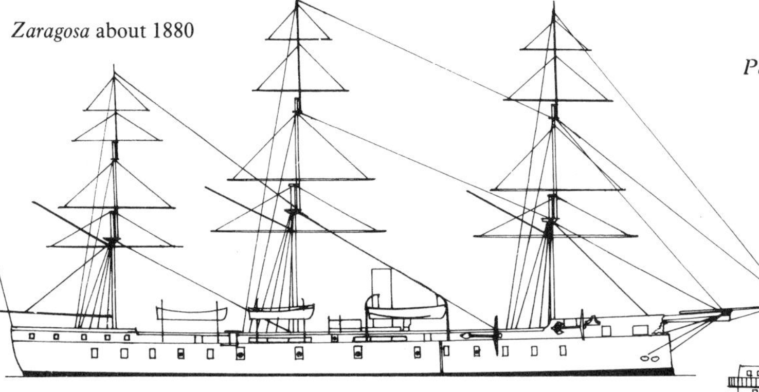

ZARAGOSA *wooden centre battery ironclad*

Displacement: 5530t
Dimensions: 280ft wl x 54ft 6in x 26ft 6in max (*85.34 x 16.64 x 8.10m*)
Machinery: 1 shaft, 1900ihp = 8kts. Coal 690t
Armour: Iron. Belt 5¼-4in, battery 5¼in, sponsons 5in
Armament: 4-9in RML, 3-7.1in, 8-6.4in, 1-4.7in, 6-12pdr
Complement: 500

Name	Builder	Launched	Fate
ZARAGOSA	Cartagena	1867	Stricken *c*1899

A wooden-hulled, belted centre battery ironclad, originally armed with 21-68pdr SBs. By 1885 the above armament was broadside-mounted on the main deck for the 9in Armstrongs, with one Hontoria 7.1in (modified Palliser) under the forecastle, and two on broadside sponsons, with the Hontoria 6.4in on the main deck broadside. The ship was refitted in 1889 but became a torpedo TS in the mid-1890s.

Pelayo as completed 1888
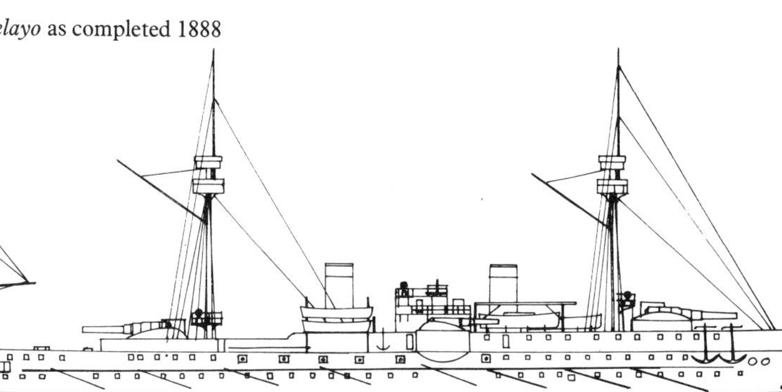

PELAYO *barbette ship*

Displacement: 9745t
Dimensions: 334t 8in pp x 66ft 3in x 24ft 9in max (*102.04 x 20.20 x 7.58m*)
Machinery: 2-shaft VC, 12 boilers, 9600ihp = 16.7kts (forced draught). Coal 800t
Armour: Creusot steel. Belt 17¾-11¾in, barbettes 15¾-11¾in, shields 3¹/₈in, CT 6¹/₈in, deck 2¾-2in
Armament: 2-12.5in, 2-11in, 1-6.4in, 12-4.7in, 5-6pdr QF, 14 MGs, 7 TT
Complement: 520

Name	Builder	Launched	Fate
PELAYO	La Seyne	5.2.1887	–

Ordered in Nov 1884, laid down Apr 1885 and completed in the summer of 1888, *Pelayo* was based on the design of the contemporary French *Marceau* but with reduced draught to allow passage through the Suez Canal fully loaded. She originally had 4000 sq ft of sail but was soon reduced to military masts. The main armament of Hontoria guns was mounted in barbettes on the Canet system which allowed loading in any position, with the 6.4in as a bow chaser. The armour belt was 6ft 11in wide amidships and 2ft above wl, and the hull had a double bottom and 13 complete transverse bulkheads. During trials she reached 8000ihp = 16.2kts with natural draught.

She was reconstructed at La Seyne in 1897 when 16 Niclausse boilers replaced the original 12 return-tube type; she made 16kts after reboilering. The 6.4in and 4.7in were replaced by 9-5.5in (1 forward and the remainder on the broadside) and 3in plate was added to the previously unarmoured midships battery.

CRISTÓBAL COLÓN *armoured cruiser*

Ex-Italian *Giuseppe Garibaldi* (ii) purchased in May 1896. (See under Italy for details.) She was delivered to the Spaniards at Genoa on 16.5.1897 but without her single 10in guns, and was lost in this condition at the Battle of Santiago, 3.7.1898. A second ship of the class proposed in 1896 was never purchased.

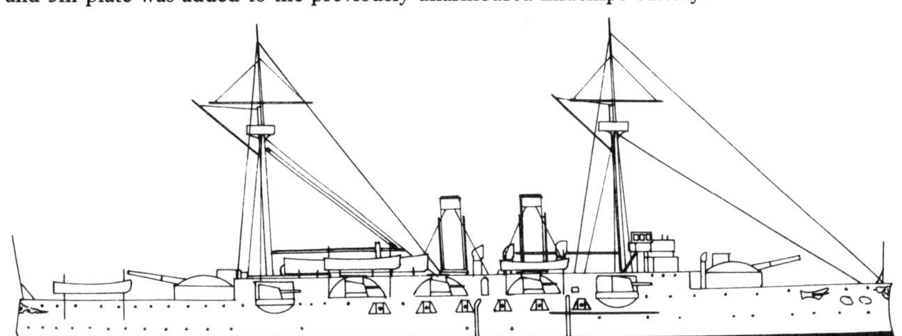

Infanta Maria Teresa as completed

INFANTA MARIA TERESA class *armoured cruisers*

Displacement: 6890t
Dimensions: 364ft oa, 340ft pp x 65ft 2in x 21ft 6in max (*110.94, 103.63 x 19.87 x 6.58m*)
Machinery: 2-shaft VTE, 13,700ihp = 20.2kts (forced draught). Coal 1050t
Armour: Belt 12-10in, barbettes 9in, CT 12in, deck 2-3in
Armament: 2-11in, 10-5.5in, 8-12pdr QF, 10-3pdr Hotchkiss revolvers, 8 Nordenfeld and 2 Maxim MGs, 8 TT (2 sub)
Complement: 484

Name	Builder	Launched	Fate
INFANTA MARIA TERESA	Bilbao	30.8.1890	Sunk 3.7.98
VIZCAYA	Bilbao	8.7.1891	Sunk 3.7.98
ALMIRANTE OQUENDO	Bilbao	4.10.1891	Sunk 3.7.98

Ordered June 1889. Heavily armed but poorly protected. The 11in guns were mounted fore and aft in single barbettes with lightly armoured hoods and the 5.5in guns were mounted on the open upper deck. The narrow armour belt extended for two-thirds of the hull length, with a protective deck flat over the belt and curved at the extremities. The high unprotected freeboard suffered badly during the Battle of Santiago, where all three were sunk.

PRINCESA DE ASTURIAS class *armoured cruisers*

Displacement: 6888t
Dimensions: 364ft 1in oa, 347ft 9in pp x 61ft x 21ft 7in mean (*110.97, 106.03 x 18.59 x 6.61m*)
Machinery: 2-shaft HTE, 14,800ihp = 20kts (forced draught). Coal 935/1180t
Armour: Harvey. Belt 11⁷/₈in amidships, barbettes 7⁷/₈in, turrets 3⁷/₈in, CT 7⁷/₈in, deck 2½in
Armament: 2-9.4in/40, 8-5.5in/35, 8-6pdr, 10-1pdr, 5 TT
Complement: 542

Name	Builder	Launched	Fate
PRINCESA DE ASTURIAS	Caracca	17.10.1896	–
CARDENAL CISNEROS	Ferrol	19.3.1897	Wrecked 1905
CATALUÑA	Cartagena	24.9.1900	–

Begun in 1890, *Asturias* was not completed until 1902, *Cataluña* 1903 and *Cisneros* a year later. They were virtually repeats of the *Infanta Maria Teresa* class but with a more modern and better balanced armament. On trials they averaged 10,000ihp = 18kts with natural draught.

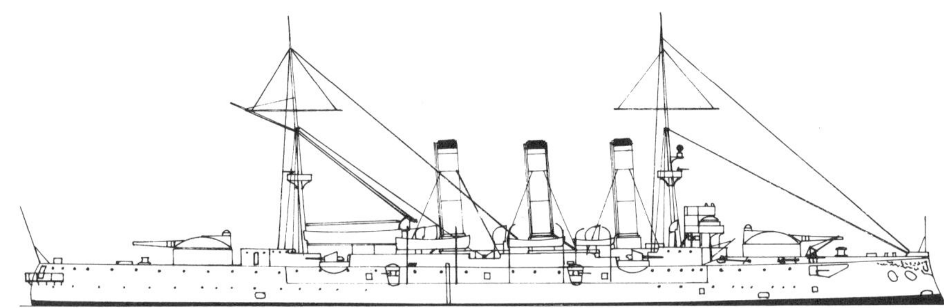

Emperador Carlos V 1906

EMPERADOR CARLOS V *armoured cruiser*

Displacement: 9090t
Dimensions: 380ft oa x 67ft x 25ft mean (*115.82 x 20.42 x 7.62m*)
Machinery: 2-shaft, 4 cyl VTE, 18,500ihp = 20kts (forced draught). Coal 1200/1800t
Armour: Belt and battery 2in, deck 6½in, CT 12in, barbettes 9¾in, hoods 3⁷/₈in
Armament: 2-11in, 8-5.5in QF, 4-3.9in QF, 2-12pdr QF, 4-6pdr QF, 4-1pdr QF, 2 MGs, 6 TT
Complement: 600

Name	Builder	Launched	Fate
EMPERADOR CARLOS V	Cadiz	13.3.1895	–

A three-funnelled vessel completed in 1898. The belt and battery protection was scanty and made up of two laminated plates, 1in of Siemens and 1in of chrome steel, the principal protection being the armoured deck. On trials with natural draught she made 15,000ihp = 19kts.

CRUISERS

CARMEN *wooden screw frigate*

Displacement: 3116t
Dimensions: 242ft 8in x 46ft x 20ft 10in mean (*74.00 x 14.02 x 6.12m*)
Machinery: 1 shaft, 2400ihp = 9kts
Armament: 16-8in, 4-6.4in, 4 smaller guns

Name	Builder	Launched	Fate
CARMEN	Cartagena	1861	–

Armament as in 1885, comprising Palliser or Parrot guns. Used as TS at Cadiz in 1890s.

VILLA DE MADRID *wooden screw frigate*

A 4878t frigate launched in 1862. Still in service in 1873.

ALMANSA *wooden screw frigate*

Displacement: 3900t
Dimensions: 275ft x 50ft x 21ft mean (*83.82 x 15.24 x 6.40m*)
Machinery: 1 shaft, 2400ihp = 7kts. Coal 650t
Armament: 17-6.4in modified Palliser, 6-6.4in Parrot, 8 smaller guns, 3 MGs

Name	Builder	Launched	Fate
ALMANSA	Ferrol	1864	–

A ship-rigged wooden frigate. Above armament as in 1896. Used as a TS for seamen at Ferrol in the 1890s.

GERONA *wooden screw frigate*

Displacement: 3917t
Dimensions: 265ft oa, 228ft 2in pp x 50ft 6in x 20ft 8in max (*80.77, 69.55 x 15.42 x 6.33m*)
Machinery: 1 shaft, 2400ihp = 9kts. Coal 675t
Armament: 19-6.4in BL, 4-5.9in BL, 3 MGs
Complement: 600

Name	Builder	Launched	Fate
GERONA	Cartagena	1864	–

Ship-rigged. Originally carried 21 SB guns; above armament as carried in 1885. Gunnery school from 1890s.

NAVAS DE TOLOSA *wooden screw frigate*

Displacement: 4460t
Dimensions: 265ft 9in x 49ft 3in x 22ft 4in mean (*81.04 x 15.02 x 6.82m*)
Machinery: 1 shaft, 600nhp = 7kts. Coal 620t
Armament: 22-6.4in RML Palliser, 4-6.4in SB, 4 smaller guns

Launched in 1865. Above armament as in 1885. She was taken out of active service before 1890.

TORNADO *composite screw corvette*

Displacement: 2090t
Dimensions: 220ft 8in x 33ft 2in x 19ft 8in (*67.20 x 10.10 x 6.00m*)
Machinery: 1 shaft, 330nhp = 13kts
Armour: Belt 4in wl
Armament: 1-7.8in RML, 2-6.4in BL, 2-4.7in RML
Complement: 202

Name	Builder	Launched	Fate
TORNADO	Denny, Glasgow	1865	Stricken 1896

Built as a commerce-raider for the Confederate States of America, she was originally named *Pampero*. She was acquired by Chile, and captured by the Spanish *Gerona* during the 1864-66 war while on passage from the builders. A single-funnelled barque-rigged vessel with an iron-framed hull and a partial armour belt around the boilers and engines. The armament was of Hontoria models (modified Pallisers). She became a torpedo TS at Ferrol in the 1880s.

MARIA DE MOLINA *wooden screw corvette*

Displacement: 1677t
Dimensions: 203ft 5in x 36ft x 16ft 9in mean (*62.02 x 10.97 x 5.15m*)
Machinery: 1 shaft, 435nhp = 7kts. Coal 330t
Armament: 10-6.4in RML, 4 smaller guns

Launched in 1868. The above armament of Palliser guns was as mounted in 1885.

1

2

1. *Navarra* about 1887 2. *Velasco* about 1890

ARAGON class *unprotected cruisers*

Displacement: 3289t
Dimensions: 236ft wl x 44ft x 23ft 6in max (*71.93 x 13.41 x 7.19m*)
Machinery: 1-shaft, 3 cyl HC, 4400ihp = 14kts. Coal 460t
Armament: 4-5.9in BL, 2-4.7in BL (*Aragon* 6-6.4in), 2-87mm, 4-75mm, 10 MGs (*Castilla* only), 2-14in TT
Complement: 389 (*Castilla* 392)

Name	Builder	Launched	Fate
ARAGON	Cartagena	1879	Stricken *c*1905
NAVARRA	Ferrol	1881	Cadet TS 1900
CASTILLA	Cadiz	1881	Sunk 1.5.98

Wooden-hulled barque-rigged vessels with two funnels and a ram bow; heavily and clumsily built having been designed as ironclads. As completed they were armed with 8-180pdr (Armstrong 8in RML) guns and were already obsolescent. The 5.9in BLs of the above armament, as in 1885, were mounted in sponsons; all except the small guns were of Krupp manufacture in the last pair, but *Aragon* had Hontoria 6.4in BLs instead of the 5.9in and 4.7in guns. *Castilla* was sunk at the Battle of Manila Bay.

VELASCO class *unprotected cruisers*

Displacement: 1152t
Dimensions: 210ft pp x 32ft x 13ft 8in max (*64.00 x 9.75 x 4.20m*)
Machinery: 1-shaft HC, 4 cyl boilers, 1500ihp = 13kts. Coal 220t
Armament: 4-4.7in, 4-6pdr, 1 MG, 2-14in TT (*Velasco*, *Gravina* 2-6in, 2-3in, 2 MGs)
Complement: 173

Name	Builder	Launched	Fate
VELASCO	Blackwall	1881	Sunk 1.5.98
GRAVINA	Blackwall	1881	Lost 1885
INFANTA ISABEL	Cadiz	1885	Stricken *c*1910
ISABEL II	Ferrol	May 1886	Stricken *c*1905
CRISTÓBAL COLÓN	Carraca	1887	Lost off Cuba Oct 1895
DON JUAN DE AUSTRIA	Cartagena	23.1.1887	Sunk 1.5.98
DON ANTONIO ULOA	Carraca	23.1.1887	Sunk 1.5.98
CONDE DEL VENADITO	Cartagena	15.8.1888	Stricken *c*1905

Iron-hulled barque-rigged cruisers with one funnel. The first pair were slightly faster and armed differently from the rest, although *Cristóbal Colón* made 15kts on trials. The Spanish-built vessels were laid down in 1883 but not completed until 1888-9. Of this ill-fated class two were lost at sea and three were sunk during the Spanish-American War, although *Don Juan de Austria* was raised and repaired by the Americans (see page 166).

SPAIN

ISLA DE LUZON class *protected cruisers*

Displacement: 1030t
Dimensions: 184ft 10in pp x 29ft 11in x 12ft 6in max (*56.11 x 8.87 x 3.84m*)
Machinery: 2-shaft HTE, 2 cyl boilers, 1897/2627ihp = 14.2/15.9kts (natural/forced draught). Coal 160t
Armour: Deck 2½-1in, CT 2in
Armament: 6-4.7in, 4-6pdr QF, 4 MGs, 3-14in TT
Complement: 164

Name	Builder	Launched	Fate
ISLA DE LUZON	Elswick	Nov 1886	Scuttled 1.5.98
ISLA DE CUBA	Elswick	Dec 1886	Scuttled 1.5.98
MARQUES DE LA ENSENADA	Carraca	Feb 1890	–

Steel-hulled, single-funnelled, small protected cruisers laid down in 1886 and 1887 (*Ensenada*) and completed 1887 and 1892 (*Ensenada*). The Elswick-built vessels were scuttled during the Battle of Manila Bay but raised and repaired by the US Navy (see page 166).

Alfonso XII as completed

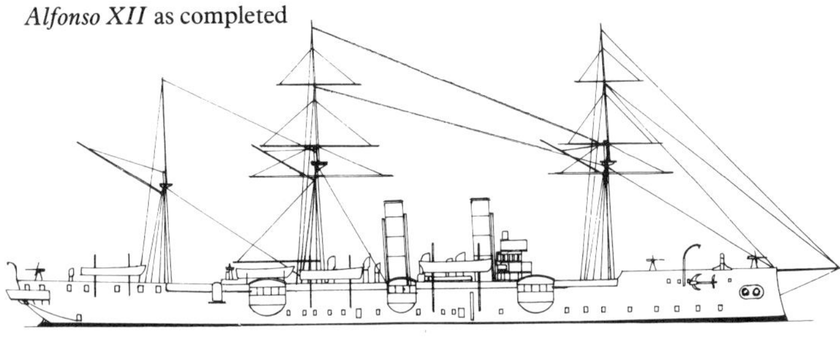

ALFONSO XII class *unprotected cruisers*

Displacement: 3042t
Dimensions: 278ft 3in x 43ft 4in x 20ft max (*84.82 x 13.22 x 6.09m*)
Machinery: 1-shaft compound, 4400ihp = 17kts (forced draught). Coal 500t
Armament: 6-6.4in, 8-6pdr Hotchkiss QF, 6-3pdr Hotchkiss revolvers, 5-14in TT
Complement: 370

Name	Builder	Launched	Fate
ALFONSO XII	Ferrol	21.9.1887	–
REINA CRISTINA	Ferrol	2.5.1887	Sunk 1.5.98
REINA MERCEDES	Cartagena	9.9.1887	–

Alsonso XII was laid down in August 1881 but delayed for 5 years by shortages of materials. Two-funnelled unprotected cruisers, but built on the cellular system with 12 watertight compartments. The Hontoria main armament was mounted in sponsons, and all the TT were fixed – 2 forward, 1 aft and 1 on each beam.

REINA REGENTE class *protected cruisers*

Displacement: 4725t
Dimensions: 317ft pp x 50ft x 20ft 4in mean (*96.62 x 15.24 x 6.21m*)
Machinery: 2-shaft HTE, 11,500ihp = 20.4kts (forced draught). Coal 1200t
Armour: Deck 4¾-3⅛in amidships, 1in fore and aft, gunshields 3in
Armament: 4-7.9in, 6-4.7in, 6-6pdr QF, 6 Nordenfeld MGs, 5 TT
Complement: 440

Name	Builder	Launched	Fate
REINA REGENTE	Thomson, Glasgow	1887	Foundered Mar 1895
ALFONSO XIII	Ferrol	31.8.1891	–
LEPANTO	Cartagena	1892	–

The construction of this class spanned 10 years from the laying down of *Reina Regente* in June 1886 to the completion of the *Lepanto* in 1895. The main Hontoria guns were mounted singly on the broadside forward and aft with the 4.7in in a battery amidships. The TT were fixed (aw), 2 forward, 1 aft and 1 on each broadside. On trials a mean speed of 18.6kts was obtained with natural draught by *Reina Regente*.

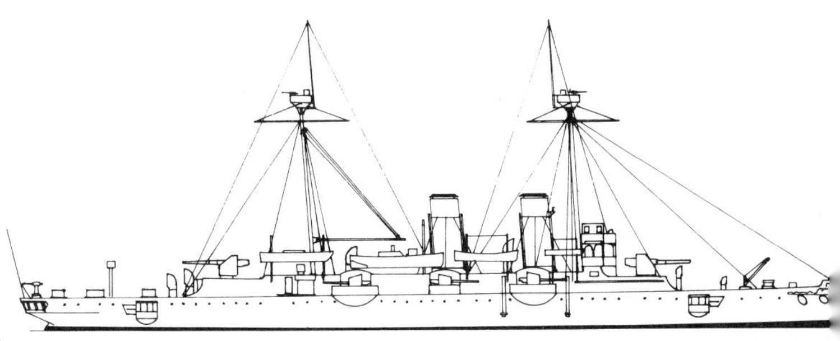

Reina Regente as completed

Rio de la Plata about 1910

RIO DE LA PLATA *protected cruiser*

Displacement: 1875t
Dimensions: 246ft x 35ft 5in x 14ft 3in max (*74.98 x 10.82 x 4.35m*)
Machinery: 2-shaft VTE, Normand Sigaudy boilers, 7100ihp = 20kts (forced draught). Coal 270t
Armour: Steel. Deck ½-¾in
Armament: 2-5.9in, 4-4.7in QF, 6-6pdr QF, 2-37mm revolvers, 4 MGs, 2 TT

Name	Builder	Launched	Fate
RIO DE LA PLATA	Le Havre	17.9.1898	–

A steel protected cruiser with two funnels; sheathed and coppered for overseas service. Presented to Spain by the Spaniards of Argentina and Uruguay. Still in service in 1913.

ESTRAMADURA *protected cruiser*

Displacement: 2030t
Dimensions: 290ft x 36ft x 14ft mean (*88.39 x 10.97 x 4.26m*)
Machinery: 2-shaft TE, 7000ihp = 20kts (trials). Coal 430t
Armour: Deck 2in
Armament: 8-4in, 4-6pdr, 2-3pdr, 1 MG
Complement: 246

Name	Builder	Launched	Fate
ESTRAMADURA	Cadiz	1900	–

Small two-funnelled cruiser with protective deck, first reported as the *Isabel la Catolica* and laid down in April 1899. Originally designed for Hontoria 5.5in and Krupp 4in, she was actually fitted with Vickers weapons. She had no TT.

REINA REGENTE *protected cruiser*

Displacement: 5287t
Dimensions: 337ft x 52ft 9in x 19ft 9in mean (*102.71 x 16.12 x 6.06m*)
Machinery: 2-shaft TE, 15,000ihp = 20kts. Coal 1200t
Armour: Deck 3½in, CT 3½in, shields 3in
Armament: 10-5.5in, 12-6pdr, 2-1pdr, 8 MGs, 3 TT
Complement: 497

Name	Builder	Launched	Fate
REINA REGENTE	Ferrol	1906	–

A three-funnelled vessel, originally proposed in 1896, laid down in 1899 but not completed until 1908.

Reina Regente about 1914
(All photos in this section: CPL)

TORPEDO CRAFT

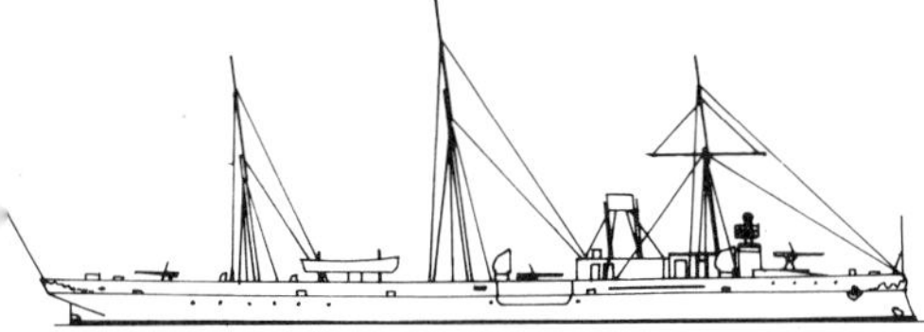

Destructor as completed

DESTRUCTOR *torpedo gunboat*

Displacement:	348t
Dimensions:	192ft 6in oa x 25ft x 7ft max *(58.70 x 7.62 x 2.13m)*
Machinery:	2-shaft TE, 4 loco boilers, 3784ihp = 23kts. Coal 37/93t
Armament:	1-3.5in, 4-6pdr, 2-3pdr revolvers, 5-15in TT
Complement:	45

Built by Thomson (Clyde) and launched 29.7.1886, *Destructor* had two raked funnels abreast, three hinged masts and light ⅜in splinter plating abreast the machinery and on the CT. Of the TT 2 bow and 1 stern were fixed, with a pair on a trainable mounting on deck. She was one of the very first ships to have TE machinery. Service speed was nearer 20kts, and at full bunker capacity the radius was 4000nm at 10kts.

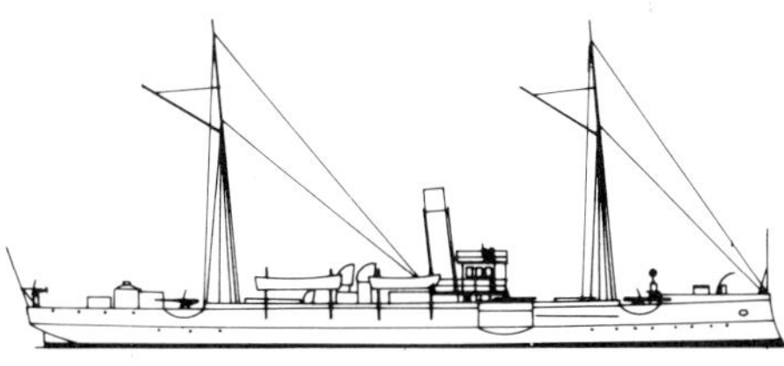

Nueva España as completed

TEMERARIO class *torpedo gunboats*

Displacement:	562t
Dimensions:	190ft 3in x 22ft 10in x 10ft 4in max *(58.00 x 6.73 x 3.16m)*
Machinery:	2-shaft VTE, 4 boilers, 2600ihp = 19kts (forced draught). Coal 106/130t
Armour:	Steel. Deck ½in over machinery and boilers
Armament:	2-4.7in, 4-6pdr QF, 1-25mm MG, 2 TT
Complement:	91

Class (builder, launched): *Temerario* (Cartagena, 1889), *Nueva España* (Carraca, 1889), *Galicia* (la Graña, 1891), *Marques de Molins* (La Graña, 1891), *Martin Alonzo Pinzon*, ex-*Audaz* (La Graña, 1889), *Rapido* (Carraca, 1891), *Vincente Yanez Pinzon* (La Graña, 1891). Steel TGBs with a single funnel and a light two-masted rig.

FILIPINAS *torpedo gunboat*

Displacement:	747t
Dimensions:	232ft 10in x 27ft x 8ft max *(70.74 x 8.22 x 2.43m)*
Machinery:	2 shafts, 4500ihp = 20kts. Coal 100/130t
Armament:	2-4.7in QF, 4-3pdr QF, 4 MGs, 4 TT
Complement:	110

One-funnelled steel TGB, built at Cadiz and launched in 1892. Stricken by 1906.

DOÑA MARIA DE MOLINA class *torpedo gunboats*

Displacement:	830t
Dimensions:	235ft x 26ft 2in x 10ft max *(71.62 x 7.98 x 3.04m)*
Machinery:	2-shaft VTE, loco boiler, 3500ihp = 19.5kts (forced draught). Coal 120t
Armour:	CT 6in
Armament:	2-4.7in QF, 4-3pdr QF, 2 MGs, 3 TT (1 sub)
Complement:	89

Class (builder, launched): *Doña Maria de Molina* (Ferrol, 9.10.1896), *Marques de la Vitoria* (Ferrol, 4.2.1897), *Don Alvaro de Bazan* (Ferrol, 14.9.1897). Two-funnelled TGBs laid down in 1894. All were still in service in 1913.

FUROR class Clydebank 1896

Displacement:	370t
Dimensions:	220ft x 22ft x 5ft 6in *(67.05 x 6.70 x 1.70m)*
Machinery:	2-shaft, 4-cyl TE, 4 Normand boilers, 6000ihp = 28kts. Coal 100t max
Armament:	2-14pdr QF, 2-6pdr QF, 2-1pdr Maxim, 2-14in TT
Complement:	67

Class: *Furor*, *Terror*. Three-funnelled destroyers. *Furor* was sunk at the Battle of Santiago.

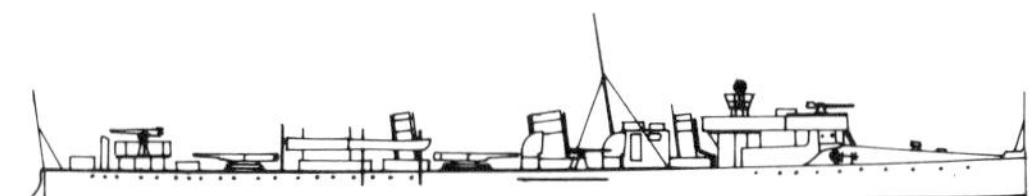

Audaz about 1910

AUDAZ class Clydebank 1897

Displacement:	400t
Dimensions:	225ft x 22ft 6in x 5ft 9in *(66.58 x 6.88 x 1.79m)*
Machinery:	2-shaft TE, 4 Normand boilers, 7500ihp = 30kts

Class: *Audaz*, *Osado*, *Pluton*, *Proserpine*. Improved version of the *Furor* class which they resembled (except *Proserpine* which had two funnels). Armament and complement were the same. *Pluton* was sunk at Santiago.

CASTOR La Seyne 1878

An iron second class TB of 23t, 76ft 2in x 9ft 7in x 2ft 3in max *(23.22 x 2.95 x 0.70m)*; 265ihp = 19kts; spar torpedo and 1-3pdr Hotchkiss revolver.

POLLUX Yarrow 1879

An iron second class TB of 33t, 85ft 5in x 10ft 7in x 4ft 6in max *(25.75 x 3.26 x 1.40m)*; 15kts; spar torpedo.

RIGEL Bremen 1883

A wooden second class TB of 29t, 105ft oa *(32.00m)*; 700ihp = 14kts; 2 TT (bow), 4 torpedoes, 1-3pdr Hotchkiss revolver.

ACEVEDO, JULIÁN ORDÓÑEZ Thornycroft 1885

Single-funnelled first class TBs with a turtleback forecastle. 66t, 117ft 8 in x 12ft 6in x 5ft 5in max *(35.90 x 3.84 x 1.67m)*; compound engines, 660ihp = 20kts; 2-14in TT bow), 2 MGs.

RETAMOSA Yarrow 1885

First class TB. 70t, 117ft x 12ft 6in x 5ft 1in max *(35.66 x 3.84 x 1.55m)*; TE, 700ihp = 20kts; 2 TT, 4 torpedoes, 2 MGs.

ORION Germaniawerft 1885

First class TB. 88t, 124ft 8in x 15ft 7in x 6ft 7in max *(38.00 x 4.78 x 2.04m)*; 3-cyl VCR, 1000ihp = 21kts; 2 TT, 4 torpedoes, 2 MGs.

BARCEZÓ, BUSTAMENTE Normand 1886-7

First class TBs. 65t, 124ft 8in x 10ft 10in x 7ft 3in max (*38.00 x 3.07 x 2.22m*); compound engines, 800ihp = 20kts; 2 TT (bow), 2 MGs (*Bustamente* 2-3pdr).

HABANA Thornycroft 1886

First class TB. 67t, 127ft 6in x 12ft 6in x 5ft 11in max (*38.89 x 3.84 x 1.55m*); 24.5kts; 2 TT (bow), 1 MG.

AZOR, HALCÓN Yarrow 1887

First class TBs. 100t, 135ft pp x 13ft 9in x 7ft max (*41.14 x 4.23 x 2.13m*); compound engines, 1300ihp = 24kts; 2 TT (bow), 4 torpedoes, 3-3pdr QF.

ARIETE, RAYO Thornycroft 1887

First class TBs. 120t, 147ft 6in oa x 14ft 6in x 4ft 8in max (*44.98 x 4.45 x 1.46m*); 2-shaft compound, 2 Thornycroft boilers, 1300ihp = 26.2kts; 2 TT, 4 torpedoes, 4-3pdr QF. Both were destroyed by fire at Cadiz 10.12.1905.

EJÉRCITO Germaniawerft 1887

First class TB. 60t, 111ft 5in x 13ft x 3ft 3in (*33.98 x 3.96 x 1.00m*), 1000ihp = 25kts.

There were also 3 third class 'vedette' boats built by White in 1892, and the 25t *Aire* built for the defence of Port Mahon.

SLOOPS AND GUNBOATS

VENCEDORA *wooden screw sloop*

Displacement: 778t
Dimensions: 177ft 2in x 26ft 3in x 12ft 5in mean (*54.01 x 8.01 x 3.81m*)
Machinery: 1 shaft, 200ihp = 8kts. Coal 210t
Armament: 2-6.4in SB, 1-4.7in SB, 2 smaller guns

Launched in 1861.

AFRICA *wooden screw sloop*

Displacement: 629t
Dimensions: 157ft 5in x 23ft 3in x 15ft 3in mean (*48.00 x 7.10 x 4.66m*)
Machinery: 1 shaft, 280ihp = 7kts. Coal 120t
Armament: 2-6.4in SB

Launched in 1862. The above armament was carried in 1885.

BAZAN *iron screw sloop*

Displacement: 757t
Dimensions: 164ft x 24ft 7in x 10ft 10in mean (*49.98 x 7.52 x 3.07m*)
Machinery: 2 shafts, 739ihp = 10kts
Armament: 1-4.9in Parrot RML, 1-4.7in SB

Launched in 1873. Out of active service by 1890.

JORGE JUAN class *composite screw sloops*

Displacement: 920t
Dimensions: 209ft 10in oa x 29ft 7in x 15ft 5in (*63.73 x 9.05 x 4.72m*)
Machinery: 1 shaft, 1100ihp = 13kts. Coal 128t
Armament: 3-6.2in, 2-75mm, 2 MGs
Complement: 146

Class (builder, launched): *Jorge Juan* (La Seyne, 1876), *Sánchez Barcáiztegui* (La Seyne, 1876). Barque-rigged composite screw sloops with one funnel. *Sánchez Barcáiztegui* was lost off Cuba in Sept 1895.

SIRENA class *wooden screw gunboats*

Displacement: 445t
Dimensions: 147ft 7in x 23ft 7in x 8ft 10in mean (*45.01 x 7.22 x 2.46m*)
Machinery: 1 shaft, 393ihp = 7kts. Coal 180t
Armament: 2-6.4in Parrot RML, 1-4.7in SB

Class (launched): *Sirena* (1863), *Ligera* (1864). Out of service by 1890.

PROSPERIDAD *gunboat*

Displacement: 420t
Dimensions: 141ft x 22ft 7in x 10ft 9in max (*42.97 x 6.91 x 3.32m*)
Machinery: 1 shaft, 135ihp = 6kts. Coal 80t
Armament: 2-4.7in, 1-3in, 1MG

Wooden screw schooner-rigged gunboat built at Cartegena in 1865.

FERNANDO EL CATOLICO class *gunboats*

Displacement: 492t
Dimensions: 157ft 5in x 23ft 6in x 10ft 10in max (*48.00 x 7.19 x 3.07m*)
Machinery: 2 shafts, 550ihp = 10kts. Coal 89t
Armament: 1-6.4in RML, 2-4.7in SB, 1 MG
Complement: 98

Class (builder, launched): *Fernando el Catolico* (La Seyne, 1875), *Marques del Duero* (La Seyne, 1875). Iron-hulled schooner-rigged gunboats with one funnel and a very prominent ram bow. *Fernando el Catolico* was rammed and sunk by the ironclad *Numancia* in 1873, and *Marques del Duero* was lost at the Battle of Manila Bay, 1.5.1898.

GENERAL CONCHA class *gunboats*

Displacement: 515t
Dimensions: 160ft x 26ft x 11ft 2in (*48.76 x 7.92 x 3.41*)
Machinery: 2-shaft CR, 600ihp = 11kts. Coal 80t
Armament: 3-4.7in (2-4.7in and 1-3.5in in *Lezo* and *El Cano*), 2 or 3 MGs (more in *El Cano*), 1 TT in *Lezo* and 2 TT in *El Cano*
Complement: 98

Class (builder, launched): *General Concha* (Ferrol, 1883), *Mallaganes* (Carraca, 1885), *El Cano* (Carraca, 1885), *General Lezo* (Cartagena, 1885). Iron-hulled gunboats with a single funnel and light schooner rig.

Note: Spain also maintained up to 30 smaller gunboats at various times. These were mainly designed for colonial duties and most were less than 100t.

Greece

For much of the period between 1860 and 1905 the political and financial state of Greece approached the chaotic, and as the country was poor with a population of about 2,500,000 in 1905, naval development would clearly be limited. In 1860 there were 6 screw gunboats to which 2 small ironclads and a sloop had been added up to 1870. Nothing was then launched until 1879, but additions from that date to 1890 comprised 3 4800t battleships, a small cruiser, 17 torpedo boats and 6 gunboats. In the disastrous war with Turkey in 1897 the Greek Navy was used most ineffectually though the Turkish warships remained inactive.

None of the above ships was built in Greece. They were obtained from Britain, France – including the three battleships – Germany and Austria.

THE GREEK NAVY IN 1860

Six iron-hulled screw gunboats, *Aphroësa, Nauplion, Plixavra, Paralos, Salaminia, Syros,* launched 1856-1858, 300t-374t, 4-6 guns, 10kts. Also one six-gun side-wheel steamer. The principal sailing ships were one 26-gun and one 22-gun corvette.

ARMOURED SHIPS

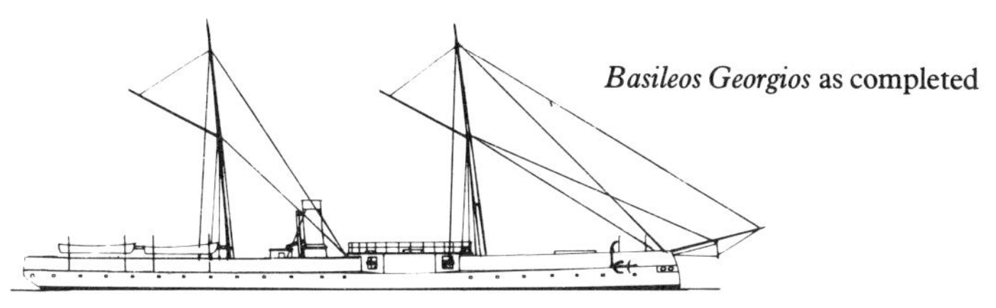

Basileos Georgios as completed

BASILEOS GEORGIOS

Displacement: 1774t
Dimensions: 200ft pp x 33ft x 16ft max (*60.96 x 10.06 x 4.88m*)
ihp/speed: 2100 = 12.2kts. Coal 210t max
Armour: Iron. Belt 7-6in, battery 6in
Armament: 2-9in RML, 2-20pdr
Complement: 152

Name	Builder	Launched
BASILEOS GEORGIOS	Thames Iron Wks	1867

Small central battery ship with a complete belt. The 9in RML were later replaced by 2-8.2in BL.

BASILISSA OLGA

Displacement: 2030t
Dimensions: 249ft 4in pp x 39ft x 19ft mean (*76.00 x 11.89 x 5.79m*)
ihp/speed: 1950 = 10kts. Coal 240t max
Armour: Iron. Belt 6in, battery 4¾in
Armament: 2-9in RML, 10-70pdr
Complement: 258

Name	Builder	Launched
BASILISSA OLGA	STT	1869

A wooden-hulled broadside battery ship later rearmed with 4-6.7in/25, 2-6.7in/20, 4-1pdr.

Basilissa Olga date unknown
Arrigo Barilli Collection

SPETSAI class

Displacement: 4808t
Dimensions: 334ft 8in pp x 51ft 10in x 18ft mean (*102.00 x 15.80 x 5.49m*)
ihp/speed: 6700 = 17kts. Coal 500/690t
Armour: Creusot and compound. Belt 12in-4in, battery 14-12in, barbette 12in
Armament: 2-10.8in/34, 1-10.8in/28, 5-5.9in/36, 4-3.4in/22, 4-3pdr, 4-1pdr, 6-1pdr revolvers, 3-14in TT
Complement: 440

Name	Builder	Launched
SPETSAI	Graville	1889
PSARA	Graville	1890
HYDRA	St Nazaire	1889

Ships of unusual design with a two-storey battery forward accommodating 4-5.9in on the lower floor and the 2 longer 10.8in and 1-5.9in firing over the top from the upper floor. The shorter 10.8in was in a barbette aft. The complete belt was submerged at full load when waterline protection depended on an area of 3in armour amidships above the belt. The lighter guns were changed to 1-3.9in/50 forward, 8-9pdr, 4-3pdr, 10-1pdr revolvers in 1897-1900 and the TT to 1-15in and 2-14in.

Psara about 1895
CPL

CRUISER

NAUARCHOS MIAOULIS

Displacement: 1820t
Dimensions: 246ft 1in pp x 36ft 1in x 14ft 5in mean (*75.00 x 11.00 x 4.40m*)
ihp/speed: 2400 = 13.5kts. Coal 220t max
Armament: 3-6.7in/25, 1-6.7in/20, 6-1pdr, 3-14in TT
Complement: 180

Name	Builder	Launched
NAUARCHOS MIAOULIS	La Seyne	1879

Iron-hulled, barque-rigged cruiser, sheathed and coppered.

1 2

1. *Nauarchos Miaoulis*
2. *Akteon*
Arrigo Barilli Collection

TORPEDO BOATS

Name	Builder	Launched	Displacement	Length oa	ihp/speed	Armament
CHIOS class	Yarrow	1881	40t	100ft (*30.48m*)	450 = 19.5kts	2-1pdr revolvers, 2-14in TT (bow)
KALITHEA class	La Seyne	1881	42t	100ft (*30.48m*)	320 = 16kts	2-14in TT (bow) and spar
V11-V16	Vulcan	1885	85t	123ft (*37.50m*)	1000 = 18kts	1-1pdr, 1 Nord, 3-14in TT (2 bow)

Chios class also comprised *Cyprus, Kos, Mytelene, Rhodes, Samos*. *Kalithea* class also comprised *Pherinika, Persephone, Terpsichore, Terpsithea*. Other boats had spar-torpedoes only, except that *Delos, Sappho, Sphinx, Ionia* had dropping gear as well, and *Alpha, Beta, Gamma, Delta* only the latter.

SLOOPS

Name	Builder	Launched	Displacement	Length pp	ihp/speed	Armament
HELLAS	Northfleet	1861	1628t	200 ft 2in (*61.00m*)	700 = c8kts	Later 12-5.9in/26, 4 smaller guns

Note: Wooden-hulled.

GUNBOATS (OVER 200 TONS)

Name	Builder	Launched	Displacement	Length pp	ihp/speed	Armament
AMBRAKIA, AKTEON	Thames Iron Wks	1881	433t	128ft (*39.00m*)	380 = 10kts	1-10.2in/30, 1-5.9in/30, 2-1pdr
ACHELAOS class	see below	1884	404t	131ft 3in (*40.00m*)	400 = 10.5kts	2-3.8in/26, 3-1pdr

Ambrakia and *Akteon* originally named *Hydra* and *Spetsai*. *Ambrakia* later had 1-10.2in only and *Akteon* 1-10.2in and 4-3pdr. The *Achelaos* class comprised *Achelaos* and *Alpheos* built by Thames Iron Works, and *Eurotas* and *Peneos* by Denny.

Turkey

In 1860 the Ottoman Empire still controlled large areas of Europe in the Balkans, all of Asia Minor, and much of the Middle East, but in economic and military terms Turkey was known among the Great Powers as 'The Sick Man of Europe'. The Empire encompassed a vast number of races and creeds, and the frequent troubles among the more reluctant of the Sultan's subjects gave many opportunities for intervention to those Powers with predatory ambitions. Throughout the century Russia, posing as the champion of oppressed peoples, attempted to expand her influence into Turkish territory, and was invariably opposed by Britain (with more or less support from other Western nations). Most of Turkey's wars were predominantly land campaigns, and since the Sultan could usually rely on the support of the British Mediterranean Fleet, there was little incentive to maintain a powerful navy.

Turkish seapower had been eroded by the Greek War of Independence and the virtual secession of Egypt after 1841, both of which had taken large numbers of trained seamen out of the Empire's service. The complete destruction of a Turkish squadron at Sinope in 1853 was not in material terms the 'catastrophe' often claimed, but it marked the end of any attempt to keep a first class navy.

In 1860 the Turkish fleet consisted of 7 line-of-battle-ships, 6 frigates, 4 corvettes and 9 smaller vessels, but under Sultan Abdul Aziz (1861-76) a modest programme of ironclad construction was started with the help of Britain and France. Even this limited rebuilding of the

Navy was too much for Turkey's chronic finances, and after Abdul Hamid came to power in 1876 no major ships were ordered for over a decade. The new Sultan was suspicious of the Navy, which had played a significant part in deposing his predecessor, and the fleet was reduced to the lowest level of efficiency.

In the 1890s growing German influence at Constantinople led to the purchase of torpedo craft from Schichau and Germania but these rapidly became unserviceable also. Training among the largely conscript seamen was very poor and it was not until after 1905 that any real effort was made to improve and modernise the Turkish Navy.

CAPITAL SHIPS

Osmanieh as completed

OSMANIEH class *broadside ironclads*

Displacement:	6400t normal
Dimensions:	293ft pp x 55ft 9in x 25ft 7in max (*89.31 x 16.99 x 7.80m*)
Machinery:	1-shaft HC, 6 boilers, 3735ihp = 12kts. Coal 546/750t
Armour:	Iron. Belt 5½in, ends 3in, battery 5in, ends 4½in
Armament:	1-9in, 14-8in (14 x 1), 10-36pdr (10 x 1)
Complement:	340

Name	Builder	Launched	Fate
OSMANIEH	Napier	2.9.1864	Discarded 1911
MAHMUDIEH	Thames Iron Wks	13.12.1864	Discarded 1911
ABDUL AZIZ	Napier	Jan 1865	Discarded 1911
ORKANIEH	Napier	26.6.1865	Discarded 1911

Iron-hulled broadside ironclads laid down in 1863 and completed in 1865-66. They were rigged as three-masted barques and had a single telescopic funnel. The rig was removed in the 1880s. They had a ram bow with a 4in iron breastwork on the upper deck forward protecting the 9in 12.5t Armstrong ML gun. The 8in 9t Armstrong MLRs were on the upper and main deck broadsides, as were the 36pdr smoothbores. The belt extended 2ft 6in above lwl and 6ft below amidships, but only 4ft 6in below at the ends. By 1890 the forward 9in had been replaced by two 5.9m (2 x 1) and a 9.2in was mounted aft. *Abdul Aziz* was renamed *Azizieh* in about 1870, and was modernised with *Osmanieh* by Ansaldo at Genoa in 1890-91. *Orkanieh* and *Mahmudieh* were modernised by the same firm between 1892 and 1895. They were converted to central battery ships, and were rearmed with 2-9.2in/35 Krupp BL (2 x 1), 8-5.9in/25 Krupp BL (8 x 1), 6-4.1in Krupp QF (6 x 1), 4-47mm (4 x 1) and 2-14in TT (2 x 1). The 9.2in were mounted fore and aft in 10in wooden barbettes plated with ½in steel and had 1in shields. The 5.9in and 4.1in were on the broadside amidships. They were cut down fore and aft and fitted with a CT and two military masts. The original machinery was retained but they were fitted with cyl boilers. Their normal displacement was reduced to 6299t. In 1904 it was proposed to reconstruct them, but they were in such poor condition that this was not carried out. They were to have been re-engined, reboilered, and rearmed with 1-8in/45 QF and 9-5.9in QF. New steel armour was to have been fitted, with a 10in belt, 5in barbettes, 3in turrets and a 1½in protective deck. They served as hulks during World War I and were scrapped after the war.

ASSARI TEWFIK *barbette/battery ironclad*

Displacement:	4687t normal
Dimensions:	272ft 4in pp x 52ft 6in x 21ft 4in max (*83.01 x 16.00 x 6.50m*)
Machinery:	1-shaft compound, 6 boilers, 3560ihp = 13kts. Coal 400/?t
Armour:	Iron. Belt 8in, ends 3in, battery 6in, barbettes 5in
Armament:	8-9in (8 x 1)
Complement:	320

Name	Builder	Launched	Fate
ASSARI TEWFIK	La Seyne	1868	Lost Feb 1913

Completed in 1870, this iron-hulled vessel had a partial double bottom, a ram bow and a single funnel, and was barque-rigged. She was a reduced version of the French *Trident*, and had 6-9in 12.5t Armstrong ML in the battery amidships with two more in single barbettes set side by side on the upper deck above them. The shrouds were fixed inboard to allow the barbette guns to fire directly ahead and astern. The complete wl belt extended 6ft 3in below and 4ft 7in above lwl. By 1891 she had been rearmed with 2-8.3in Krupp BL (2 x 1) in the barbettes and was also fitted with 2-87mm Krupp BL (2 x 1) and 2-63.5mm Krupp BL (2 x 1), though she retained the 6-9in battery guns. She was reboilered in 1894, and was sent to Ansaldo at Genoa to be rebuilt in 1899. However, no work was carried out and she was finally modernised at Kiel by Krupps in 1903-06. She was converted into a central battery ship. The ends were cut down and she was rearmed with 3-5.9in/40 QF (3 x 1), two side by side forward and one each side amidships, 7-4.7in/40 QF (7 x 1), six in the battery and one aft, 6-6pdr (6 x 1) and 3-3pdr (3 x 1). She retained her original armour but was fitted with a 3in protective deck, new engines and Niclausse cyl boilers. She had a 6in CT, one funnel set well forward and a military mast amidships. She hit a rock off Tcherness in the Black Sea in February 1913 and was further damaged by Bulgarian field guns and rough seas, eventually becoming a constructive total loss.

Assari Tewfik as completed
Arrigo Barilli Collection

FATIKH *ironclad*

The 9757t ironclad *Fatikh*, designed by Sir Edward Reed, was ordered by Turkey. However, Turkey could not pay for her so she was offered first to the British Admiralty and then to the Prussian Navy, who purchased her on 6.2.67. She was renamed *Wilhelm I*, and was again renamed *Konig Wilhelm* on 14.12.67. See under Germany for details.

ASSARI SHEVKET class *central battery ironclads*

Displacement:	2047t normal
Dimensions:	203ft 5in pp x 42ft 7in x 16ft 5in max (*62.00 x 12.98 x 5.00m*)
Machinery:	1 shaft, 1750ihp (*Nijmi Shevket* 1900ihp) = 12kts. Coal 300/?t
Armour:	Iron. Belt 6in-4½in, battery 4½in, barbette 4½in
Armament:	1-9in, 4-7in (4 x 1)
Complement:	170

Name	Builder	Launched	Fate
ASSARI SHEVKET	La Seyne	1868	Discarded *c*1900
NIJMI SHEVKET	La Seyne	1868	Discarded *c*1900

Small iron-hulled ironclads, completed in 1869, brig-rigged and with a ram bow and a single funnel. There was a complete wl belt, 6in thick above lwl and 4½in thick below, which extended 4ft 3in above and 6ft below lwl. Amidships there was a central box battery, with 4-7in Armstrong ML, surmounted by a single 9in 12.5t Armstrong ML in a centreline barbette mounted between the mainmast and the funnel and training 100° on each beam. By 1891 the ships had also been fitted with 2-87mm Krupp BL (2 x 1), 2-63.5mm Krupp BL (2 x 1) and 2-37mm (2 x 1). *Nijmi Shevket* was later fitted with 1-14in TT. They were reboilered in 1892. The hull had a double bottom, but was very lightly built. They were originally ordered by Egypt but were delivered to Turkey.

Above: *Assari Shevket* as completed
Arrigo Barilli Collection

Above: Muin-I-Zaffer about 1890
CPL

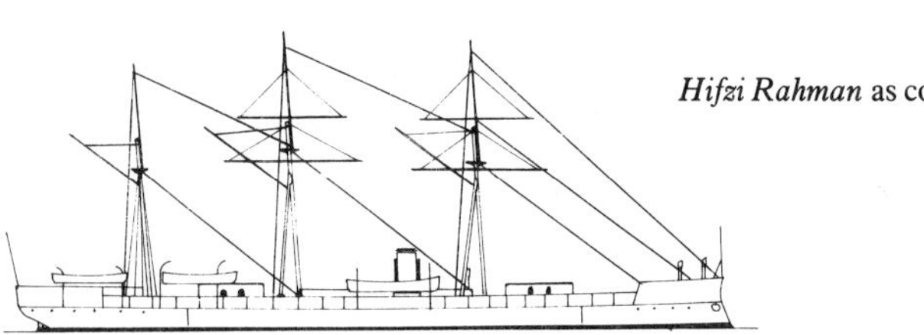

Hifzi Rahman as completed

LUTFI DJELIL class *coast defence turret ships*

Displacement: 2540t normal
Dimensions: 204ft pp x 45ft 11in x 14ft 6in max *(62.18 x 14.00 x 4.42m)*
Machinery: 2 shafts, 2000ihp = 12kts. Coal 300/?t
Armour: Iron. Belt 5½in, ends 4.6in, side 3in, turrets 5½in
Armament: 2-8in (1 x 2), 2-7in (1 x 2)
Complement: 130

Name	Builder	Launched	Fate
LUTFI DJELIL	Bordeaux	1868	Sunk by internal explosion 10.5.77
HIFZI RAHMAN	Bordeaux	1868	Discarded *c*1900

Iron-hulled ships completed in 1869. They had a ram bow and a raised forecastle and poop, with two turrets on the centreline fore and aft of the funnel. There was a light barque rig and one funnel, and there were collapsible bulwarks amidships. They had a complete wl belt 5in amidships, tapering to 4.6in at the ends and extending 2ft 6in above and below the lwl. The magazines, turret bases and machinery amidships were protected by 3in side armour, covered by a 1½in protective deck. They had two 8in Armstrong MLs in the forward turret and two 7in Armstrong MLs in the aft turret. *Lutfi Djelil* blew up when her magazine exploded (probably due to Russian shellfire) when she was off Braila on the Danube during the Russo-Turkish war. *Hifzi Rahman* was later rearmed with 2-5.9in/25 Krupp BLR (1 x 2) in the aft turret, and she was also fitted with 1-4.7in/25 Krupp BLR right forward and 2-37mm (2 x 1). The ships were originally ordered by Egypt but were delivered to Turkey.

AVNI ILLAH class *casemate ironclads*

Displacement: 2362t
Dimensions: 226ft 4in x 36ft x 16ft 5in max *(68.99 x 10.97 x 5.00m)*
Machinery: 1-shaft HC, 2200ihp = 12kts. Coal 220/?t
Armour: Iron. Belt 6in-5in, ends 3in, casemates 5in
Armament: 4-9in (4 x 1)
Complement: 140

Name	Builder	Launched	Fate
AVNI ILLAH	Thames Iron Wks	1869	Lost 1912
MUIN-I-ZAFFER	Samuda	1869	Discarded *c*1922

Small, iron-hulled casemate ironclads with a ram bow, one funnel and two masts, and rigged as brigantines. There was a partial double bottom. The complete wl belt was 6in thick above lwl and 5in thick below. It extended 3ft 9in below and 3ft above lwl. The 4-9in 12.5t Armstrong ML guns were in casemates on the main deck amidships. The sides were cut away so that each gun could fire both ahead and astern on restricted arcs. By 1891 they had also been fitted with 2-87mm Krupp BLR (2 x 1), 2-63.5mm Krupp BLR (2 x 1) and 2-37mm (2 x 1). Both were reconstructed by Ansaldo between 1903 and 1907, when the ends were cut down and they were rearmed with 4-5.9in/40 Krupp QF (4 x 1) in the casemates, 6-3in QF (3 x 1), 10-6pdr (10 x 1) and 2-3pdr (2 x 1). They were reboilered with cyl boilers but retained their existing engines and armour. They received a CT and were fitted with a military mast amidships. The crew was increased to 220. *Avni Illah* was lost in the Turkish-Italian war. *Muin-i-Zaffer* was laid up during World War I and scrapped a few years later.

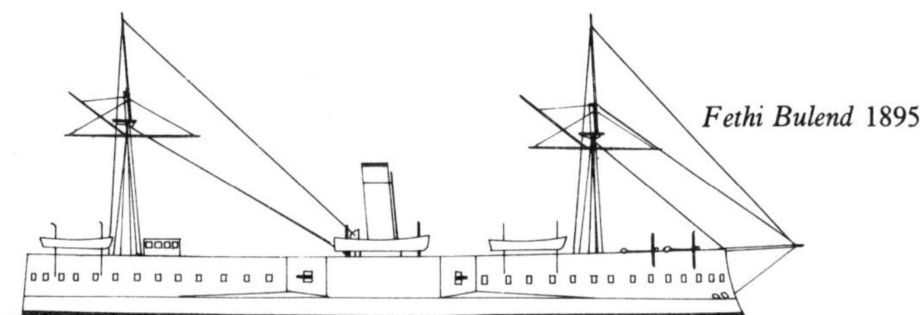

Fethi Bulend 1895

FETHI BULEND class *casemate ironclads*

Displacement: 2761t normal
Dimensions: 236ft 3in pp x 39ft 4in x 18ft 1in max *(72.01 x 11.99 x 5.51m)*
Machinery: 1-shaft HC, 3250ihp = 13kts (*Mukaddami Khair* 3000ihp = 12kts). Coal 300/?t
Armour: Iron. Belt 9in-6in, ends 3in, casemates 9in-6in
Armament: 4-9in (4 x 1)
Complement: 180

Name	Builder	Launched	Fate
FETHI BULEND	Thames Iron Wks	1870	?
MUKADDAMI KHAIR	Constantinople	1873	?

Small, iron-hulled casemate ironclads resembling the *Avni Illah* class except that the casemates were not cut away between the guns, so that the forward guns could only fire on forward bearings and the aft guns on aft bearings. They were very high out of the water. By 1891 they had been fitted with 2-87mm Krupp BL (2 x 1) 2-63.5mm Krupp BL (2 x 1) and 2-37mm (2 x 1). The complete wl belt extended for 4ft below to 2ft above lwl, and was 9in thick above and 6in thick below lwl. The casemates were 9in thick below the port sills and 6in thick above. *Fethi Bulend* was reconstructed by Ansaldo between 1903 and 1907, being rearmed with 4-5.9in/40 Krupp QF (4 x 1) in the casemates, 6-3in QF (6 x 1), 10-6pdr (10 x 1) and 2-3pdr (2 x 1). The crew was increased to 220.

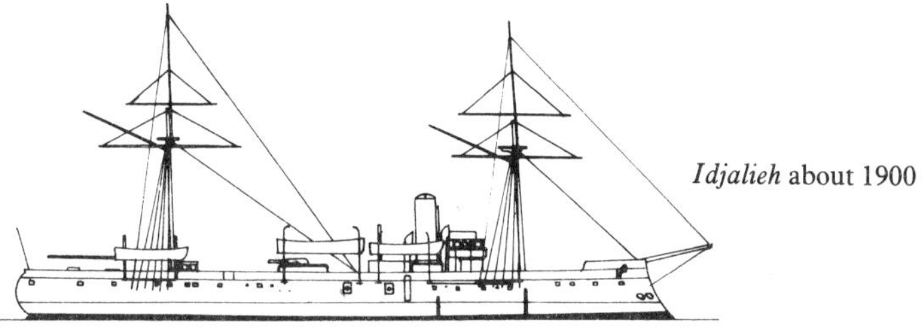

Idjalieh about 1900

IDJALIEH *barbette/battery ironclad*

Displacement: 2266t normal
Dimensions: 213ft 3in pp x 42ft 7in x 17ft 4in max *(65.00 x 12.98 x 5.28m)*
Machinery: 1 shaft, 1800ihp = 12kts. Coal 300/?t
Armour: Iron. Belt 6in-4½in, ends 4in, battery 4½in, barbette 5in
Armament: 2-9in (2 x 1), 3-7in (3 x 1)
Complement: 180

Name	Builder	Launched	Fate
IDJALIEH	Trieste	1870	BU *c*1922

Completed in 1871. Very similar to the slightly smaller *Assari Shevket* class except that she had a raised forecastle. She had one 7in Armstrong ML in the barbette and two in the battery, with the two 9in 12.5t Armstrong MLs. The complete belt was 6in thick above and 4½in thick below lwl, and it extended from 6ft 6in above to 6ft below lwl. By 1891 the barbette 7in had been replaced by a 5.9in Krupp BL, and she had also been fitted with 2-87mm Krupp BL (2 x 1), 2-63.5mm Krupp BL (2 x 1) and 2-37mm (2 x 1). She was hulked in about 1897 and was used first for training and then as an accommodation ship during World War I. She was scrapped after the war.

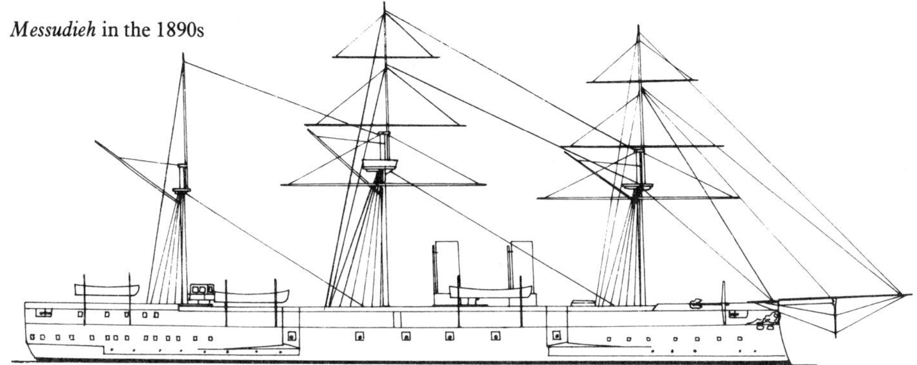
Messudieh in the 1890s

MESSUDIEH class *central battery ironclads*

Displacement: 9120t, 9710t full load
Dimensions: 331ft 5in x 59ft x 25ft 11in max (*101.02 x 17.98 x 7.90m*)
Machinery: 1-shaft HC, 8 rectangular boilers, 7431ihp = 13.7kts. Coal ?/600t
Armour: Iron. Belt 12in-6in, ends 5in-3in, battery 10in-7in, CT 8in
Armament; 12-10in (12 x 1), 3-7in (3 x 1), 6-20pdr (6 x 1)
Complement: 700

Name	Builder	Launched	Fate
MESSUDIEH	Thames Iron Wks	28.10.1874	Sunk 1.12.1914
MEMDOUHIED	Thames Iron Wks	16.11.1875	Purchased by Great Britain 20.2.78

Iron-hulled vessels with a ram bow, a raised forecastle and poop, two funnels and three masts, and rigged as barques. Laid down in 1872 and completed in 1876-7. The complete wl belt extended from 5ft below to 4ft above lwl, and had three strakes amidships. The middle one was 12in thick, the upper 10in and the lower 9in, tapering to 6in at the bottom. The ends tapered from 5in to 3in. The lower battery strake was 10in thick and the upper 7in, and it was 153ft long. The 10in 18t Armstrong MLRs were in the battery, and the 7in 6½t Armstrong MLRs were on the upper deck, two forward and one aft.

Memdouhied was renamed *Hamidieh* in 1876 and was purchased by Great Britain and renamed *Superb* on 20.2.78. *Messudieh* had her 7in replaced by 5.9in Krupp BLs (3 x 1) in about 1891, and was completely rebuilt by Ansaldo at Genoa between 1898 and 1903. She was cut down fore and aft and fitted with a built-up superstructure amidships. She was intended to mount a single 9.2in/40 Vickers BL fore and aft in 9in-6in steel turrets with 3in barbettes, but although the turrets were fitted the guns were never mounted in them even though they were delivered, and she was sunk with wooden dummies in their place. She was fitted with 12-6in/45 Vickers QF (12 x 1) in the battery, with 14-3in QF (14 x 1) in the upper battery and 10-57mm QF (10 x 1) and 2-47mm QF (2 x 1). She was re-engined with inverted TE machinery and 16 Niclausse watertube boilers, giving 16kts on 11,000ihp. She was fitted with two shafts, with the port screw forward of the starboard one because they overlapped. The complement was increased to 600. In 1914 she was moored as a stationary guardship in the Dardanelles off Charnak, and she was torpedoed and sunk there by the British submarine *B11*. The ships were designed by Sir Edward Reed and were based on the British *Hercules*.

PEIKI SHEREEF class *armoured rams*

The two *Peiki Shereef* class 4870t ships, *Peiki Shereef* and *Boordji Zaffer* were ordered by Turkey from Samudas and launched on 12.2.1876 and 23.1.1879 respectively. They were purchased by Great Britain on 13.3.1878. *Peiki Shereef* was renamed *Belleisle* and *Boordji Zaffer* was renamed *Orion*. See under Great Britain for full details.

HAMIDIEH *central battery ironclad*

Displacement: 6594t normal
Dimensions: 292ft pp x 55ft 9in x 24ft 10in max (*89.00 x 16.99 x 7.57m*)
Machinery: 1-shaft SE, 6800ihp = 13kts. Coal 600/?t
Armour: Iron. Belt 9in, ends 5in, battery 7in, CT 7in
Armament: 4-9in (4 x 1), 10-5.9in/35 (10 x 1), 6-37mm (6 x 1), 2-14in TT aw (2 x 1)

Name	Builder	Launched	Fate
HAMIDIEH	Constantinople	1885	Discarded *c*1911

Laid down in 1874 and completed in 1892, this ship was a reduced version of the *Messudieh* class, and had cut-away sides fore and aft. The 9in Armstrong ML guns were mounted on the upper deck, two forward and two aft, and the 5.9in/35 Krupp BLs were carried in the battery. She was fitted with available equipment, including engines originally intended for the frigate *Selimieh*. The armour was very spongy and flaky. The belt extended from 5ft below to 6ft 2in above lwl amidships, and from 4ft below forward and 3ft below aft, where it tapered to 5in. She was considered for rebuilding in 1903 but was in too poor a state.

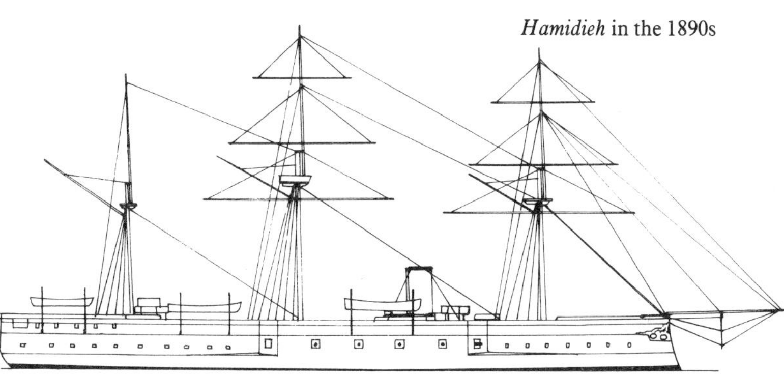
Hamidieh in the 1890s

ABDUL KADIR *battleship*

Displacement: 8100t
Dimensions: 340ft x 65ft x 23ft 6in (*103.63 x 19.81 x 7.16m*)
Machinery: 2 shafts, 12,000ihp = 18kts estimated
Armour: Steel. Belt 9in, ends 4in, barbettes 6in
Armament: 4-11in (4 x 1), 6-5.9in (6 x 1), 8-87mm (8 x 1), 8-37mm (8 x 1), 6-14in TT (6 x 1)

Name	Builder	Launched	Fate
ABDUL KADIR	Constantinople	–	Scrapped on slip *c*1911

Laid down in October 1892, *Abdul Kadir* was in frame and plated near the keel when worked ceased. By 1904 she was to have been armed with 4-8in (4 x 1), 10-5.9in (10 x 1) in casemates, 10-3in (10 x 1), 10-37mm (10 x 1) and 4 trainable TT aw; however, her blocks had moved and the ground had given way beneath her, so she was never completed. The belt was to have been 6ft 6in deep, but there was no side armour above it.

CRUISERS

ERTOGRUL *wooden frigate* (Launched 1863)

Displacement: 2344t
Dimensions: 250ft x 49ft 10in x 23ft 7in (*76.20 x 15.19 x 7.19m*)
Machinery: 1 shaft, 600ihp = 10kts. Coal 120/350t
Armament: 23-9in (23 x 1)

A wooden-hulled, three-masted, fully-rigged frigate. By 1885 she was armed with 9in Armstrong ML guns. She was used as a TS and was lost with all hands off Japan in a storm in 1890.

SELIMIEH *wooden frigate*

Displacement: 4642t
Dimensions: 279ft 10in pp x 59ft x 23ft 7in mean (*85.29 x 17.98 x 7.19m*)
Machinery: 1 shaft, 600ihp = 12kts. Coal 350/?t
Armament: 2-8in (2 x 1), 2-7in (2 x 1), 6-5.9in (6 x 1), 3-37in (3 x 1)
Complement: 580

Name	Builder	Launched	Fate
SELIMIEH	Constantinople	1865	Discarded *c*1900

A wooden-hulled, fully-rigged frigate completed in 1866. She was rebuilt as a gunnery TS in 1879 and armed with 8in Armstrong MLRs, 7in Armstrong MLRs and 5.9in Krupps. Her original machinery, which was never fitted, was later used in the ironclad *Hamidieh*.

REHBERI TEWFIK *wooden frigate* (Launched 1876)

Displacement: 2100t
Dimensions: 225ft pp x 37ft x 19ft max (*68.58 x 11.28 x 5.79m*)
Machinery: 1 shaft, 180ihp = 9kts
Armament: 22 ML (22 x 1)

A wooden-hulled, fully-rigged frigate completed in 1879. She was later used as a torpedo school ship and armed with 4 MLRs (4 x 1). Discarded *c*1900.

MEHEMET SELIM *wooden frigate*

Displacement: 1280t
Dimensions: 196ft 10in pp x 32ft 10in x 21ft mean (*59.99 x 10.01 x 6.40m*)
Machinery: 1 shaft, 450ihp = 9kts. Coal 250/?t
Armament: 10-5.9in (10 x 1), 4-37mm (4 x 1), 1-14in TT aw

Name	Builder	Launched	Fate
MEHEMET SELIM	Ismid	1875	Discarded *c*1900

A wooden-hulled, fully-rigged frigate completed in 1880. She was used as a sea-going cadet TS, and was armed with 5.9in Krupp guns.

HEIBETNUMA *third class cruiser*

Displacement: 1463t normal
Dimensions: 226ft pp x 37ft x 17ft max (*68.88 x 11.28 x 5.18m*)
Machinery: 1-shaft HTE, 6 rectangular boilers, 2785ihp = 14kts. Coal ?/280t
Armament: 3-6.7in/25 (3 x 1), 6-4.7in/25 (6 x 1), 4-47mm (4 x 1), 2-14in TT

Name	Builder	Launched	Fate
HEIBETNUMA	Constantinople	30.1.1890	Discarded *c*1911

A composite-hulled vessel laid down in 1881 and completed in 1893. Sheathed and coppered and fitted with one funnel, she was armed with 6.7in/25 5.6t Krupp BL fore and aft and 4.7in/25 Krupp BL guns in sponsons amidships.

LUTFI HUMAYUN *third class cruiser*

Displacement: 1292t normal
Dimensions: 210ft pp x 30ft x 13ft max (*64.01 x 9.14 x 3.96m*)
Machinery: 1-shaft HC, 2160ihp = 14kts. Coal 200/?t
Armament: 3-6.7in/25 (3 x 1), 6-4.7in/25 (6 x 1), 4-47mm (4 x 1)

Name	Builder	Launched	Fate
LUTFI HUMAYUN	Constantinople	1892	Discarded *c*1911

This composite-hulled cruiser, laid down in 1882 and completed in 1894, was a reduced version of *Heibetnuma*, and was wood-sheathed and had one funnel. She was armed with 6.7in/25 5.6t Krupp BLs fore and aft and 4.7in/25 Krupp BLs in sponsons amidships.

SHADIEH class *third class cruisers*

Displacement: 1600t normal
Dimensions: 225ft pp x 36ft x 13ft 6in (*68.58 x 10.97 x 4.11m*)
Machinery: 2 shafts, 3500ihp = 17kts estimated
Armament: 6-5.9in (6 x 1), 7 TT aw (7 x 1)

Name	Builder	Launched	Fate
SHADIEH	Ismid	–	Scrapped on slip *c*1911
FEIZI BAHRI	Ismid	–	Scrapped on slip *c*1911

Laid down in 1891, these two steel-hulled cruisers were originally to be armed with 5.9in BL guns, but this arrangement was later altered to 6-4.7in QF (6 x 1), 4-47mm (4 x 1), 4-37mm (4 x 1) and 5-18in TT aw (4 x 1), one fixed in the bow and four training on the broadside. By 1904 they were in frame and partly plated but were completely rotten.

HADEVENDIGHIAR *unarmoured cruiser*

Displacement: 4050t
Dimensions: 280ft wl x 50ft x 20ft mean (*85.34 x 15.24 x 6.10m*)
Machinery: 1 shaft
Armament: 2-8.3in (2 x 1), 6-5.9in (6 x 1), 4-4.1in (4 x 1), 5 TT aw

Name	Builder	Launched	Fate
HADEVENDIGHIAR	Constantinople	–	Scrapped on slip *c*1911

A steel-hulled, unarmoured cruiser laid down about 1892; a sister, *Selimieh*, was projected but not laid down. The armament was to have been 8.3in Krupp BLs fore and aft, and 5.9in Krupp BLs and 4.1in Krupp QFs on the broadside amidships. By 1904 *Hadevendighiar* was in frame and partially plated, and the Turkish Navy wished to complete her as a twin-screw 18kt cruiser armed with 2-6in/45 or 5.9in QF (2 x 1), 6-4.7in/50 QF (6 x 1), 4-3in QF (4 x 1), 4-47mm (4 x 1) and 4 TT aw (4 x 1).

Medjidieh as completed

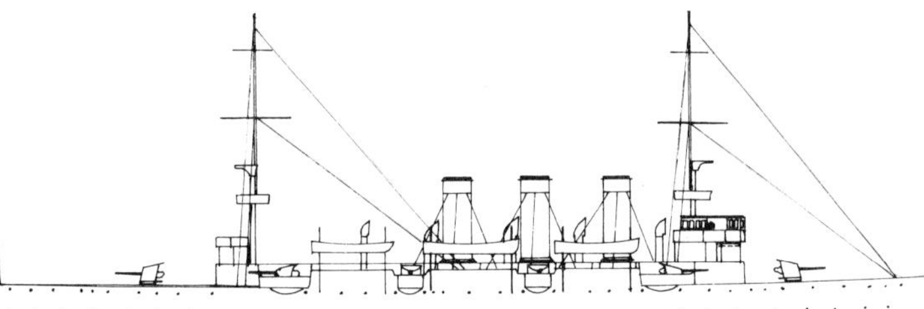

MEDJIDIEH *protected cruiser*

Displacement: 3330t normal
Dimensions: 330ft wl x 42ft x 17ft 6in max (*100.58 x 12.80 x 5.33m*)
Machinery: 2-shaft VTE, 16 Niclausse boilers, 12,500ihp = 22kts. Coal 300/600t
Armour: Krupp. Protective deck 4in slopes, 1½in flats
Armament: 2-6in/45 (2 x 1), 8-4.7in/45 (8 x 1), 6-3pdr (6 x 1), 6-1pdr (6 x 1), 2-18in TT aw
Complement: 312

Name	Builder	Launched	Fate
MEDJIDIEH	Cramp	25.7.1903	Discarded *c*1947

A steel-hulled cruiser with three funnels and prominent ventilator cowls, laid down in November 1901 and completed in 1904. She had a complete protective deck. The 6in/45 Bethlehem QFs were mounted fore and aft, and the 4.7in/45 Bethlehem QFs were on the broadside amidships. She was mined and sunk 15 miles off Odessa in the Black Sea on 3.4.1915, but was salvaged by the Russians in June of that year. After being refitted and rearmed at Nicolaiev with 10-5.1in Vickers (10 x 1) and 4-3in (4 x 1) AA, she was renamed *Prut* and entered Russian service in October 1915. In 1918 she was recaptured by the Germans at Sevastopol and returned to Turkey, reverting to her original name, and rebuilt with Babcock & Wilcox watertube boilers and two funnels. Her armament was reduced to 4-5.1in (4 x 1) and 4-3in/50 (4 x 1), and her complement increased to 365.

ABDUL HAMID *protected cruiser*

Displacement: 3830t normal
Dimensions: 340ft x 47ft 6in x 16ft max (*103.63 x 14.48 x 4.88m*)
Machinery: 2-shaft VTE, cyl boilers, 12,500ihp = 22kts
Armour: Krupp. Protective deck 4in slopes, 1½in flats
Armament: 2-6in/45 (2 x 1), 8-4.7in/50 (8 x 1), 6-3pdr (6 x 1), 6-1pdr (6 x 1), 2-18in TT aw
Complement: 302

Name	Builder	Launched	Fate
ABDUL HAMID	Armstrong	25.9.1903	Discarded *c* 1947

This vessel, laid down in April 1902 and completed 27.4.04, closely resembled *Medjidieh* but had less prominent ventilating cowls. The guns were 6in/45 Armstrong QFs and 4.7in/50 Armstrong QFs. The 18in TT were in trainable mountings beneath the forebridge. She was renamed *Hamidieh* in 1908. On 21.11.12 she was badly damaged by a torpedo off Varna in the Black Sea, but was repaired. After World War I she was rearmed with 2-5.9in/45 Krupp QF and 8-3in/50 Krupp QF; she then became a cadet TS.

Hamidieh (ex-*Abdul Hamid*) about 1914
CPL

SLOOPS AND DESPATCH VESSELS

SED-EL-BAHR class *wooden sloops* (launched 1860-4)

Displacement: 599t normal
Dimensions: 173ft 6in x 26ft 7in x 12ft 10in max (*52.88 x 8.10 x 3.91m*)
Machinery: 1 shaft, rectangular boilers, 160nhp = 10kts (*Merikh* 11kts). Coal 120/?t
Armament: 2-4.7in/25 (2 x 1), 4-1pdr (4 x 1)
Complement: 86, *Merikh* 100

Class: *Sed-el-Bahr, Beirut, Zuhaf, Iskenderieh, Atarid, Merikh.* The first pair were built in England, the next pair in Constantinople, and the last two by Gemlik. This class were wooden-hulled barque-rigged sloops, wood- and copper-sheathed and armed with 4.7in/25 Krupp BL guns. They had two funnels, a straight stem and an overhanging stern. *Merikh* was rebuilt in 1888, *Beirut* in 1889 (when she was given new boilers) and *Iskenderieh* in 1893. *Atarid, Merikh* and *Beirut* were fitted with a 14in TT. Some of their machinery and equipment was used in new gunboats after they were discarded 1894-1905.

SINUB class *wooden sloops* (launched 1860-3)

Displacement: 769-787t
Dimensions: 172ft (*Mansurah, Muzaffer* 174ft 10in) x 30ft 6in x 14ft 2in-15ft 2in (*52.43 (52.68) x 9.30 x 4.32-4.62m*)
Machinery: 1 shaft, rectangular boilers, 150nhp = 11kts (*Sinub* 10kts). Coal 120/?t
Armament: 2-5.9in/22 (2 x 1), 2-4.7in/25 (2 x 1), 3-37mm (3 x 1), 1-14in TT aw
Complement: 153

Class: *Sinub, Edirneh, Brussah, Mansurah, Muzaffer.* The first three were built in England and the remainder by Ismid. Wooden-hulled, ship-rigged sloops, these vessels were sheathed and coppered and featured raked masts and one funnel between the fore- and mainmasts. All were rebuilt and rearmed with 5.9in/22 3.9t Krupp BLs, 4.7in/25 Krupp BLs, 37mm guns and 14in TT between 1886 and 1890. Discarded 1900-1905.

RETIMO *paddle dispatch vessel* (launched 1862)

Displacement: 765t
Dimensions: 229ft x 26ft x 7ft max (*69.80 x 7.92 x 2.13m*)
Machinery: Rectangular boilers, 270nhp = 10kts. Coal 150/?t
Armament: 3 light guns (3 x 1)
Complement: 90

An iron-hulled vessel originally built in England which was rebuilt in 1896. Discarded *c* 1911.

HANIEH *paddle dispatch vessel* (launched 1863)

Displacement: 816t
Dimensions: 230ft x 27ft x 6ft 8in (*70.10 x 8.23 x 1.93m*)
Machinery: 180nhp = 10kts. Coal 120/?t
Armament: 3 light MGs (3 x 1)

Iron-hulled; built in England. Discarded after 1896.

KANDIA *paddle dispatch vessel* (launched 1863)

Displacement: 820t
Dimensions: 239ft 6in x 26ft 3in x 6ft 10in max (*73.00 x 8.00 x 2.08m*)
Machinery: ?nhp = 10.5kts
Armament: 3 light guns (3 x 1)

Discarded after 1896.

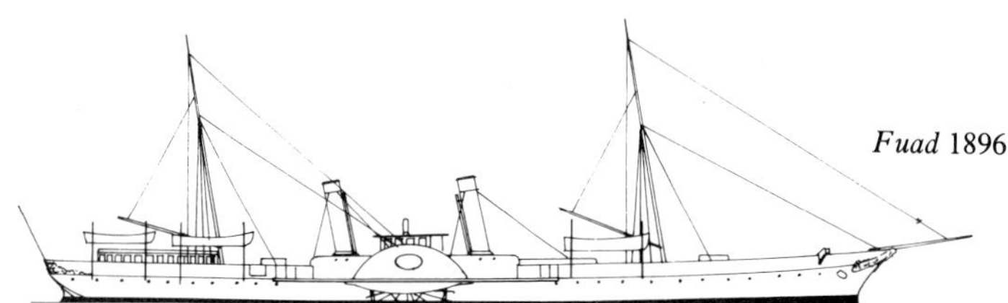

Fuad 1896

IZ-ED-DIN class *paddle dispatch vessels* (launched 1864-5)

Displacement: 1058t
Dimensions: 250ft x 30ft x 12ft (*76.20 x 9.14 x 3.66m*)
Machinery: 300nhp = 12.5kts. Coal 150/?t
Armament: 1-4.7in, 3-3in (3 x 1)
Complement: 135

Class: *Iz-ed-Din, Taliah, Ismail, Faud.* Iron-hulled. All built in England, and discarded after 1896.

SURYA *dispatch vessel* (launched 1865)

Displacement: 500t
Dimensions: 184ft x 28ft x 7ft max (*56.08 x 8.53 x 2.13m*)
Machinery: 120nhp = 10kts. Coal 120/?t
Armament: 1-4.7in

Iron-hulled; built in England. Discarded after 1896.

ARKADI *paddle dispatch vessel* (launched 1896)

Displacement: 755t
Dimensions: 256ft x 26ft 3in x 6ft 10in max (*78.03 x 8.00 x 2.08m*)
Machinery: 250nhp = 10kts. Coal 150/?t
Armament: 3 light guns (3 x 1)

Discarded after 1896.

SED-EL-BAHR class *sloops* (launched 1894)

Displacement: 632t
Dimensions: 190ft x 24ft x 11ft 6in max (*57.91 x 7.32 x 3.51m*)
Machinery: 1 shaft, 600ihp = 12kts
Armament: 4-4.7in (4 x 1), 6-37mm (6 x 1), 2-14in TT; *Zuhaf* 4-87mm (4 x 1), 2-14in TT
Complement: 82

Class (builder, fate): *Sed-el-Bahr, Zuhaf* (both Constantinople, both discarded *c* 1911). Steel-hulled and barque-rigged, these two vessels reused machinery and equipment from earlier vessels. *Sed-el-Bahr* was renamed *Kilid-el-Bahr* prior to 1899.

TORPEDO CRAFT

TIMSAH Des Vignes 1885

Displacement: 30t
Dimensions: 94ft x 12ft x 4ft 8in max (*28.65 x 3.66 x 1.42m*)
Machinery: 1-shaft VC, 400ihp = 17.4kts. Coal ?/5t
Armament: 2-14in TT

A two-funnelled second class TB converted from a steam yacht and with two bow torpedo tubes. She carried two reload Whitehead torpedoes. Discarded after 1900.

SHEMSHIR HUJUM La Seyne 1886

Displacement: 14t
Dimensions: 62ft 4in x 7ft 8in (*19.00 x 2.34m*)
Machinery: 2 shafts, 120ihp = 15kts
Armament: 2-14in TT

Third class TB armed with two 14in Whitehead torpedoes in side frames.

MEDJIDIEH class Constantinople 1885-90

Displacement: 42t
Dimensions: 101ft 8in x 11ft 6in x 5ft 6in (*30.99 x 3.51 x 1.68m*)
Machinery: 1 shaft, 450ihp = 19kts (*Burhan-ed-Din*, *Tewfik* 550ihp = 20.2kts). Coal 2.5/–t
Armament: 2-1in (*Burhan-ed-Din*, *Tewfik* 1-1in), 2-14in TT, 1 spar torpedo

Class: *Medjidieh, Burhan-ed-Din, Tewfik, Assari Teraki, Nimet, Shan Aver. Burhan-ed-Din* and *Tewfik* were built at La Seyne. Steel-hulled second class TBs with two 14in bow TT with a spar torpedo mounted between them, a ram bow, and two slightly raked funnels. All were discarded 1911-14.

MAHABET class Des Vignes 1886

Displacement: 83t
Dimensions: 125ft pp x 15ft x 6ft 10in max (*38.10 x 4.57 x 2.08m*)
Machinery: 2-shaft VC, locomotive boilers, 950ihp = 19kts. Coal 12/22t
Armament: 2-14in TT

Class: *Mahabet, Satvet.* Steel-hulled first class TBs with a ram bow and armed with two 14in bow TT. Four reload torpedoes were carried. They had poor manoeuvrability. Both discarded *c*1914.

GILJOM class Schichau 1886

Displacement: 85t
Dimensions: 121ft 4in x 15ft 8in x 6ft 6in (*36.98 x 4.78 x 1.98m*)
Machinery: 2 shafts, 1000ihp = 20kts. Coal 10/18t
Armament: 2-37mm (2 x 1), 2-14in TT
Complement: 18

Class: *Giljom, Saiki, Tiri Zaffer, Seifi Bahri, Vesirehi Nusret* (numbered S-25 to S-29). Steel-hulled first class TBs fitted with two conning towers, one forward and one aft, and a bow and a stern rudder. There were two 14in bow TT under the turtledeck forecastle, and they carried the reload Schwartzkoff torpedoes. On trials they averaged 22.4kts. All discarded *c*1911.

WASIR class Germania 1887-92

Displacement: 87t
Dimensions: 128ft x 15ft 9in x 8ft 6in (*39.01 x 4.80 x 2.59m*)
Machinery: 2-shaft TE, locmotive boilers, 1300ihp = 23kts. Coal 8/30t
Armament: 2-37mm (2 x 1), 2-14in TT
Complement: 18

Class: *Wasir, Fatih, Nusret, Shehab, Tarik, Pervin, Seham,* (numbered S-3 to S-10). These steel-hulled first class TBs had a straight stem, a turtledeck forecastle over the two 14in bow TT, and one funnel set to one side. They carried two reload torpedoes. *Seham* sank in the outer harbour at Beirut after a boiler explosion on 21.4.1900; 27 lives were lost. The remainder were discarded *c*1911, except *Wasir* which survived to *c*1922.

EDIJDER Germania 1890

Displacement: 150t
Dimensions: 154ft 2in x 18ft 4in x 7ft 3in max (*46.99 x 5.69 x 2.21m*)
Machinery: 2-shaft TE, 2200ihp = 22kts. Coal ?/50t
Armament: 6-47mm (6 x 1), 2-14in TT

Steel-hulled first class TB, with three masts and one 14in bow TT. The other 14in TT was in a trainable mounting aft. Discarded *c*1914.

SHAHANI DERIA *torpedo gunboat* (launched 1892)

Displacement: 443t
Dimensions: 200ft x 23ft x 8ft max (*60.96 x 7.01 x 2.44m*)
Machinery: 2-shaft TE, 4 loco boilers, 3000ihp = 22kts. Coal 101/?t
Armament: 1-4.1in, 6-47mm (6 x 1), 4-14in TT (4 x 1)

Steel-hulled, with a raised poop and forecastle, two masts and one funnel, built at Constantinople. The 4.1in Krupp BL was on the forecastle, and there were two 47mm on the forecastle, in the waist and on the poop. The 14in TT were on trainable mountings amidships.

NAMET class *torpedo gunboats* (launched 1890-1)

Displacement: 900t
Dimensions: 229ft 7in pp x 31ft 2in x 16ft 5in mean (*70.00 x 9.50 x 5.02m*)
Machinery: 2-shaft TE, loco boilers, 4500ihp = 19kts
Armament: 2-4.1in, 6-6pdr, 3 TT (1 bow)
Complement: 111

Class: *Namet, Pelenki-Deria.* Both built at Constantinople. Krupp QF guns.

BERK-EFSHAN class *destroyers* (launched 1894)

Displacement: 270t
Dimensions: 187ft pp x 21ft 7in (*56.99 x 6.61m*)
Machinery: 2-shaft, 3500ihp = 25kts
Armament: 2 TT, 6-1pdr revolvers

Class: *Berk-Efshan, Tajjar.* Both built at Constantinople.

China

During the nineteenth century China was the target of blatant economic imperialism by virtually all of the industrial nations. China was regarded as a large untapped market, and gradually her traditional isolation was eroded by Western commercial intervention, backed where necessary by military force. Britain went to war with China in 1840 and 1857 (with French collaboration) to force trade concessions on the Chinese; Russia occupied all territory north of the Amur in 1860; the USA launched a 'punitive expedition' against Korea in 1871; and Britain again clashed with China over Burma trade in 1871. The Chinese Navy, with its traditional armed junks, was no match for Western forces, although small composite gunboats began to be built at Foochow after 1869. The Navy was divided into the Northern (Peiyang) and the Southern (Nanking) Fleets, the former being far stronger, although there were also smaller fleets at Foochow (*Fukien*) and Canton (*Kwangtung*).

Russia had occupied the north western provinces in 1871 during serious civil disturbances and they were not forced to withdraw until 1879. This taught China the value of Western technology, and from 1880 modern warships were ordered abroad and the Navy reorganised with the aid of a few British officers. A dispute with France over Indo-China in 1882 began the long and unfortunate history of Western involvement in Vietnam, and on 23.8.1884 the Foochow fleet was destroyed by a French squadron.

The Navy was rebuilt with British and German assistance, but after Admiral Lang resigned in 1890, there was a rapid return to the old corruption and inefficiency. The larger Northern fleet that had been slowly built up during this decade was lost in its entirety at the Battle of the Yalu and the surrender of the Wei-Hai-Wei during the war with Japan (1894-5). France and Russia, who had opposed Japan's demands during the peace negotiations, exploited their influence to obtain concessions and by the end of the century China was carved into 'spheres of influence' by the Great Powers. After 1898, when Russia seized Port Arthur (and Britain took Wei-Hai-Wei as 'compensation'), China had no facility for docking ships over 3000t, and little was spent on the remnants of the Navy until the reforms of 1909-10.

CAPITAL SHIPS

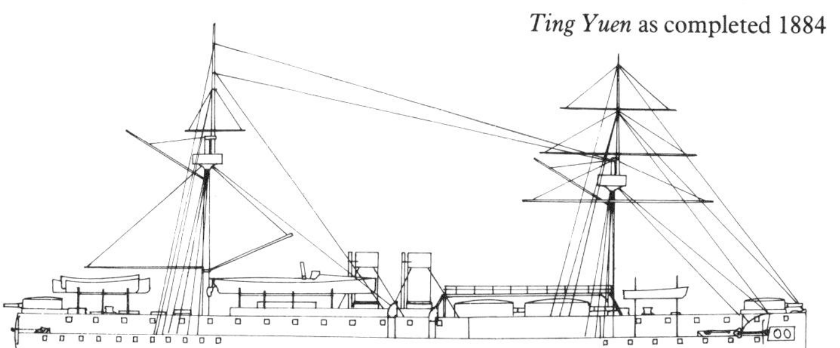

Ting Yuen as completed 1884

TING YUEN class *armoured turret ships*

Displacement: 7220t normal, 7670t full load
Dimensions: 308ft oa x 59ft x 20ft (*93.88 x 17.98 x 6.10m*)
Machinery: 2-shaft HCR, 8 cyl boilers, 7500ihp = 15.7kts. Coal 650/1000t
Armour: Compound. Belt 14in, deck 3in, barbettes 14in-12in, shields 7/8in, casemates 8in, CT 8in
Armament: 4-12in/20 (2x2), 2-5.9in (2x1), 3-14in TT (3x1)
Complement: 350

Name	Builder	Launched	Fate
TING YUEN	Vulcan	28.12.1881	Sunk 6.2.1895
CHEN YUAN	Vulcan	28.11.1882	Captured by Japan

Ting Yuen when new
CPL

Two-masted, steel-hulled, two-funnelled ships built for the Peiyang fleet. The 12in/20 Krupp BL guns were mounted in pairs in two turrets arranged *en échelon* just forward of the funnels. *Ting Yuen* had the forward barbette to port, whilst *Chen Yuan* had it to starboard. The 5.9in/40 Krupp BL guns were mounted at the extreme bow and stern. They had a steel hull and a 144ft long citadel amidships covering the machinery and magazines. The hull was low in the water, but the barbettes were at the same level as the narrow superstructure, which ran from bow to stern. They had a radius of action of 4500nm at 10kts.

Ting Yuen was laid down in 1879 and *Chen Yuan* the following year, both ships completing in 1884. Delivery was delayed by the Franco-Chinese war and they did not arrive in China until November 1885. Both were badly damaged at the Battle of the Yalu on 17.9.94. *Ting Yuen* was torpedoed at Wei-Hai-Wei by the Japanese *TB-23* on 5.2.95 and sank next day in shallow water. *Chen Yuen* was sunk in shallow water at Wei-Hai-Wei by a Japanese Army gun on 9.2.95 but was later raised and refitted by the Japanese and renamed *Chin Yen* – for her subsequent career, see under Japan.

CRUISERS

CHIANGTZU *wooden paddle frigate*

This vessel was built for China in 1863, but the Chinese Government refused delivery and she was sold to the Diamyo of Satsuma and renamed *Kasuga* in 1867. See under Japan.

HAI AN class *screw frigates*

Displacement: 2630t
Dimensions: 300ft oa x 42ft x 21ft (*91.44 x 12.80 x 6.40m*)
Machinery: 1-shaft reciprocating, 1750ihp = 12kts
Armament: 2-9in (2x1), 24-70pdr (24x1)
Complement: 372

Name	Builder	Launched	Fate
HAI AN	Kiangyan	May 1872	–
YU YUEN	Kiangyan	1873	Sunk 15.2.85

Wooden-hulled steam frigates, built for Nanyang fleet. They had one funnel and were ship-rigged. The 9in 12t ML guns were on the upper deck, and the 70pdrs were on the main deck. *Yu Yuen* was sunk by two spar torpedo boats from the French cruiser *Bayard* at Shei-Poo on the night of 14/15.2.85. *Hai An* was later rearmed with 2-8.2in Krupp (2x1) on the upper deck and 4-5.9in (4x1) and 20-4.7in (20x1) Krupp on the main deck. The ships were unseaworthy and were not very successful.

CHINA

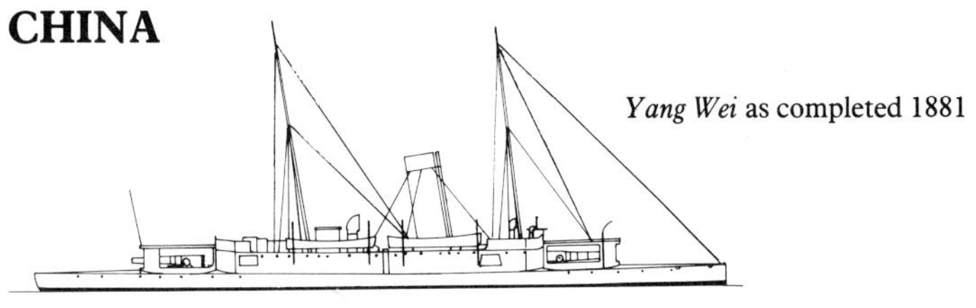

Yang Wei as completed 1881

CHAO YUNG class *protected cruisers*

Displacement: 1380t normal, 1542t full load
Dimensions: 210ft pp x 32ft x 15ft *(64.00 x 9.75 x 4.57m)*
Machinery: 2-shaft HCR, 4 cyl boilers, 2887ihp = 16.5kts. Coal 250/300t
Armour: Steel. Protective deck 0.27in, turrets 1in, CT ½in
Armament: 2-10in (2x1), 4-4.7in (4x1), 2-2.75in (2x1)
Complement: 177

Name	Builder	Launched	Fate
CHAO YUNG	Mitchell	4.11.1880	Sunk 17.9.94
YANG WEI	Mitchell	29.1.1881	Sunk 17.9.94

Steel-hulled, two-masted, single-funnelled, partially protected cruisers, built for the Peiyang fleet, these vessels were laid down on 15.1.1880, *Chao Yung* being completed on 15.7.81, one day after her sistership. The 10in Armstrong 25t BLR guns were mounted on revolving turntables in fixed turrets fore and aft, and the 4.7in 40pdr Armstrong guns were arranged at each corner of the superstructure. The ships were very lightly built. The freeboard forward was only 6ft and they were built up fore and aft for delivery. The protective deck only extended over the boiler and engine rooms and the machinery. They were designed by George Rendel, and had a radius of action of 5000nm at 8kts. Both were sunk by the Japanese at the Battle of the Yalu.

CHI YUAN *protected cruiser*

Displacement: 2300t
Dimensions: 236ft wl x 34ft x 17ft max *(71.93 x 10.36 x 5.18m)*
Machinery: 2-shaft CR, 4 cyl boilers, 2800ihp = 16.5kts. Coal 230/300t
Armour: Compound. Deck 4in, barbette 14in, shields 1½in, CT 1½in
Armament: 2-8.2in/35 (1x2), 1-5.9in/35, 4-3in (4x1), 4-15in TT (4x1)
Complement: 200

Name	Builder	Launched	Fate
CHI YUAN	Vulcan	1883	Captured 12.2.95

This steel-hulled cruiser, built for Peiyang fleet, was laid down in 1880 and completed in 1885. She had a flush deck, three masts and one funnel. There was a complete protective deck, with a 14in barbette forward, but no double bottom. The two 8.2in/35 Krupp BLRs were mounted in a hooded barbette forward of the superstructure with the single 5.9in/35 Krupp BLR aft. The 3in were mounted amidships. There was one fixed Schwarzkopf TT underwater in the stem, two on the lower deck aft, and one in the stern. The ship was temporarily rigged for the delivery voyage, but the fore- and mizzen masts were later removed. She was captured by the Japanese at Wei-Hai-Wei on 12.2.95 and renamed *Sai Yen* – see under Japan.

Chi Yuan after the removal of fore- and mainmast

KAI CHE class *unprotected cruisers*

Displacement: 2110t, *King Ch'ing* 2100t
Dimensions: 250ft wl x 36ft x 20ft *(76.20 x 10.97 x 6.10m)*
Machinery: 1-shaft TE (*Kai Che* compound), 8 cyl boilers, 2400ihp = 14.5kts. Coal ?/360t
Armament: 2-8.2in (2x1) (*King Ch'ing, Huan T'ai* 3-7in (3x1)), 7-4.7in (7x1), 2-14in TT aw (not in *Kai Che*)
Complement: 300

Huan T'ai with later barquentine rig

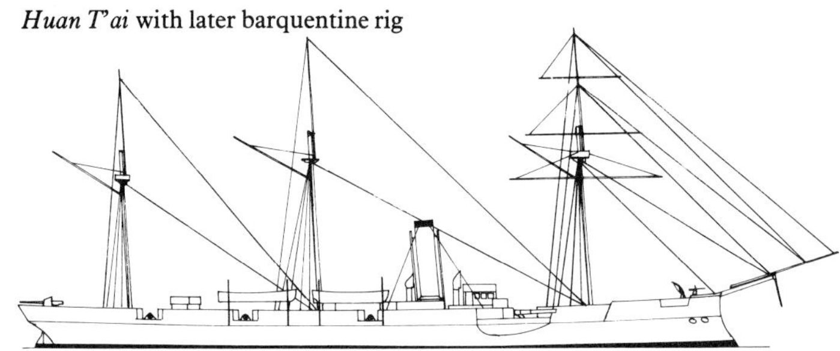

Name	Builder	Launched	Fate
KAI CHE	Foochow	1882	Sunk 22.6.1902
KING CH'ING	Foochow	17.1.1886	–
HUAN T'AI	Foochow	3.11.1886	Lost 17.8.1902

Composite-hulled, barque-rigged unprotected cruisers, built for the Nanyang fleet. They had a ram bow, a raised forecastle and poop, and one funnel. *Kai Che* mounted 8.2in 10t Krupp BL guns in sponsons ahead of the funnel, with four 4.7in Krupp BLs on the broadside amidships, two in sponsons aft and one on the poop. *King Ch'ing* and *Huan T'ai* mounted two 7in Armstrong BL guns in the forward sponsons and one on the poop. Their 4.7in 40pdr Armstrong BL guns were mounted four on the broadside amidships, two in the aft sponsons and one in the bow under the forecastle. They also had two 14in Whitehead TT on the broadside amidships. *Kai Che* was completed in 1883, *King Ch'ing* on 11.8.86 and *Huen T'ai*, laid down in December 1885, in February 1888. *Kai Che* accidentally blew up at Nanking and was a total loss. *Huan T'ai* was lost in a collision with the Canadian Pacific liner *Empress of India* off Hong Kong.

Nan Thin

NAN THIN class *unprotected cruisers*

Displacement: 2200t
Dimensions: 252ft 6in wl x 36ft x 18ft *(76.96 x 10.97 x 5.49m)*
Machinery: 1-shaft reciprocating, 2400ihp = 15kts (*Nan Shuin* 13kts). Coal ?/600t
Armament: 2-8.2in (2x1), 8-4.7in (8x1), 10 MGs, 1 TT (2 TT in *Fu Ch'ing*)
Complement: 250

Name	Builder	Launched	Fate
NAN THIN	Howaldt	12.12.1883	–
NAN SHUIN	Howaldt	8.1.1884	–
FU CH'ING	Foochow	1893	Lost 1898

Steel-hulled, barque-rigged cruisers. The first two were built for the Nanyang fleet but *Fu Ch'ing* was built for the Fukien fleet. They had a ram bow, a raised forecastle and poop, and two funnels. The 8.2m Armstrong BL guns were mounted in sponsons ahead of the funnel, and the 4.7in 40pdr Armstrong BL were mounted on the forecastle and poop, on the broadside amidships, and in sponsons at the break of the poop. *Fu Ch'ing*, which differed in many details (including a single funnel), was lost in a storm in 1898.

CHIH YUAN class *protected cruisers*

Displacement: 2300t
Dimensions: 250ft pp x 38ft x 15ft *(76.20 x 11.58 x 4.57m)*
Machinery: 2-shaft HTE, cyl boilers, 6850ihp = 18kts. Coal 200/520t
Armour: Protective deck 4in slopes, 2in flat, gun shields 2in, CT 3in
Armament: 3-8.2in (1x2, 1x1), 2-6in (2x1), 8-57mm, 4-18in TT (4x1)
Complement: 260

Name	Builder	Launched	Fate
CHIH YUAN	Armstrong	29.9.1886	Sunk 17.9.94
CHING YUAN	Armstrong	14.12.1886	Sunk 9.2.95

Steel-hulled, two-masted, one-funnelled vessels built for the Peiyang fleet. Two of the 8.2in guns were in a twin mounting forward and the other was mounted aft. There was a fixed TT aw at the bow and stern and a trainable tube on either broadside. The ships had a complete protective deck, but the guns were in open shields. *Chih Yuan* made 18.5kts on 6892ihp with forced draught on trials. They were designed by William White; both were laid down on 20.10.1885, *Ching Yuan* being completed on 9.7.87, two weeks ahead of her sister. *Chih Yuan* was sunk at the Battle of the Yalu and *Ching Yuan* was blown up by being sunk in shallow water at Wei-Hai-Wei. She was raised and scrapped in 1896-7.

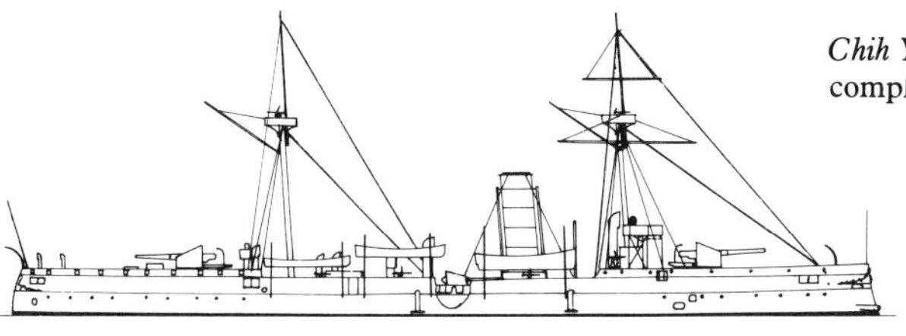

Chih Yuan as completed 1887

King Yuan

KING YUAN class *armoured cruisers*

Displacement: 2900t
Dimensions: 270ft 4in pp x 39ft 4in x 16ft 9in max (*82.40 x 11.99 x 5.11m*)
Machinery: 2-shaft VTE, 4 cyl boilers, 4400ihp = 16kts. Coal 325/350t
Armour: Compound. Belt 9.4in, ends 5.1in, deck 1½in amidships, 3in ends, barbette 8in, shield 1½in, CT 5.9in
Armament: 2-8.2in/35 (1x2), 2-5.9in (2x1), 4-18in TT (4x1)
Complement: 270

Name	Builder	Launched	Fate
KING YUAN	Vulcan	3.1.1887	Sunk 17.9.94
LAI YUAN	Vulcan	25.3.1887	Sunk 5.2.95

Steel-hulled, single-masted, two-funnelled cruisers, built for the Peiyang fleet. They had a flush deck aft of the turret, and a double bottom for 2/3 the length of the ship. The two 8.2in/35 Krupp BL guns were mounted in a twin barbette forward and the two 5.9in Krupp BLs were mounted singly in sponsons amidships. There was a fixed aw Schwarzkopf TT at the bow and stern and a trainable tube on either broadside. The 5ft 11in wide main belt covered the engine and boiler rooms and the magazines, and at full load its top was flush with the waterline. *King Yuan* was sunk at the Battle of the Yalu and *Lai Yuan* was torpedoed and sunk by the Japanese TB *Kotaka* at Wei-Hai-Wei.

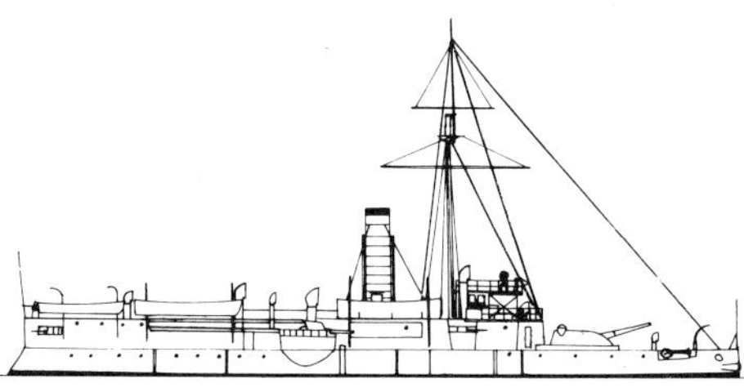

Ping Yuen about 1894

PING YUEN *armoured cruiser*

Displacement: 2150t normal, 2640t full load
Dimensions: 196ft 10in pp x 40ft x 13ft 9in (*59.99 x 12.19 x 4.19m*)
Machinery: 2-shaft VTE, 4 loco boilers, 2400ihp = 10.5kts. Coal ?/350t
Armour: Steel. Belt 9.4in, deck 2in, barbette 5in, shield 1½in, CT 5in
Armament: 1-10.2in, 2-5.9in (2x1), 4-18in TT (4x1)
Complement: 202

Name	Builder	Launched	Fate
PING YUEN (ex-LUNG WEI)	Foochow	June 1888	Captured 12.2.95

Steel-hulled, single-masted, single-funnelled vessel laid down in 1883 and completed in April 1889 for the Peiyang fleet. The 10.2in Krupp BL was mounted forward, with the 5.9in guns in sponsons amidships. There was a fixed bow and stern TT and two trainable broadside tubes. *Ping Yuen* had a complete wl belt. Captured by the Japanese at Wei-Hai-Wei, she was renamed *Ping Yuen Ho* and later *Sai Yen*. See also under Japan.

TUNG CHI class *unprotected cruisers*

Displacement: 1900t
Dimensions: 252ft x 34ft x 16ft (*76.80m x 10.36 x 4.88m*)
Machinery: 1-shaft reciprocating, 1600ihp = 10.5kts. Coal 170t
Armament: (*Tung Chi*) 2-5.9in (2x1), 5-4in (5x1), 3-57mm
Complement: 335, *Fu An* 105

Name	Builder	Launched	Fate
FU AN	Foochow	1894	In existence 1931
TUNG CHI	Foochow	1895	Sunk 11.8.1937

Steel-hulled, two-masted, single-funnelled cruisers. *Fu An* was armed with 2-57mm (2x1) and used as a transport; *Tung Chi* laid down in 1892 and completed in 1896, was used as a training cruiser. The 5.9in guns were mounted on the raised forecastle and poop and the 4in guns were in sponsons amidships.

Hai Chi
(*Uncredited photos: Arrigo Barilli Collection*)

HAI TIEN class *protected cruisers*

Displacement: 4300t
Dimensions: 396ft pp x 46ft 8in x 16ft 9in mean (*120.70 x 14.22 x 5.11m*)
Machinery: 2-shaft TE, 12 cyl boilers, 17,000ihp = 24kts. Coal 300/1000t
Armour: Harvey. Protective deck 3in slopes, 1½in flat, hoists 4in, shields 4½in, CT 6in
Armament: 2-8in (2x1), 10-4.7in (10x1), 16-3pdr (16x1), 5-18in TT (5x1)
Complement: 350

Name	Builder	Launched	Fate
HAI TIEN	Armstrong	25.11.1897	Lost Apr 1904
HAI CHI	Armstrong	24.1.1898	Sunk 1937

Steel-hulled two-masted two-funnelled protected cruisers laid down in 1896 and completed in 1899. The 8in guns were mounted in turrets fore and aft, and the 4.7in guns were on the broadside amidships. There was one fixed bow TT, and four more fixed aw tubes on the broadside. The vessels featured a complete protective deck. The 8in guns could be worked electrically. *Hai Tien* made 24.1kts on 17,000ihp with forced draught.

HAI YUNG class *protected cruisers*

Displacement: 2680t normal
Dimensions: 328ft oa x 40ft 9in x 19ft (*99.97 x 12.42 x 5.79m*)
Machinery: 2-shaft VTE, 8 cyl boilers, 7500ihp = 19.5kts. Coal 200/580t
Armour: Protective deck 2¾in amidships, 1½in ends, shields 2in, CT 1½in
Armament: 3-5.9in (3x1), 8-4.1in (8x1), 3-14in TT (3x1)
Complement: 244

Name	Builder	Launched	Fate
HAI YUNG	Vulcan	1897	Discarded *c*1935
HAI CHOU	Vulcan	1897	Discarded *c*1935
HAI CHEN	Vulcan	1898	Discarded *c*1935

Steel-hulled, two-masted, two-funnelled cruisers completed in 1898. Two 5.9in guns were mounted side by side on the raised forecastle, and the third was mounted on the raised poop. The 4.1in guns were arranged on the broadside in the waist. A submerged bow TT and two aw tubes on the broadside amidships in trainable mountings were fitted, the broadside tubes later being removed. There was a complete deck, 2¾in thick over the engine and boiler rooms and 1½in thick at the ends.

SLOOPS AND GUNBOATS

TIEN TSIW *iron gunboat* (launched 1863)

Displacement: 448t
Dimensions: 150ft x 25ft x 12ft 8in *(45.72 x 7.62 x 3.86m)*
Machinery: 1-shaft reciprocating, 320ihp = 9.5kts
Armament: 1-64pdr, 4-32pdr (4x1)
Complement: 70

A three-masted, schooner-rigged boat with an iron hull. She was later used as a customs cruiser at Canton. Her armament consisted of Whitworth 64pdr and 32pdr ML guns. Built by Laird.

KWANG TUNG class *composite gunboats* (launched 1868)

Displacement: 439t
Dimensions: 140ft oa x 23ft x 9ft *(42.67 x 7.01 x 2.74m)*
Machinry: 1-shaft HR, 3 cyl boilers, 255ihp = 9.3kts. Coal 45/?t
Armament: 1-7in, 2-4in (2x1)
Complement: 60

Class: *Kwang Tung, Shang Tung.*
Composite-hulled, brig-rigged vessels completed by Denny on 13.4.1868 for the Kwangtung fleet. They were originally armed with ML guns, but by 1891 had been rearmed with one 7in MLR and two 4in 20pdr Armstrong BL guns.

WAN NIEN CH'ING *wooden sloop* (launched 1869)

Displacement: 1450t
Dimensions: 223ft 2in x 29ft 6in x 13ft 2in *(68.02 x 8.99 x 4.01m)*
Machinery: 1-shaft reciprocating, 600ihp = 9kts
Armament: 6-5.5in (6x1)
Complement: –

Wooden-hulled fully-rigged sloop, built at Foochow for the Fukien fleet. She was sunk in a collision in 1887.

MEI YUAN class *composite gunboats* (launched 1869)

Displacement: 578t
Dimensions: 169ft 6in x 22ft 9in x 10ft 6in max *(51.66 x 6.93 x 3.20m)*
Machinery: 1-shaft reciprocating, 300ihp = 8kts
Armament: 1-6.3in, 2-4.7in (2x1)
Complement: 100

Class: *Mei Yuan, Fu Hsing.*
Composite-hulled and fully-rigged. *Mei Yuan* was built at Foochow for the Peiyang fleet and *Fu Hsing* for the Fukien fleet. *Fu Hsing* was sunk by the French at Foochow on 23.8.84. By 1891 *Mei Yuan* was armed with 1-64pdr ML and 4-4in 20pdr (4x1).

PENG CHAO HAI *composite gunboat* (launched 1869)

Displacement: 600t
Dimensions: 180ft x 24ft x 10ft max *(54.86 x 7.32 x 3.05m)*
Machinery: ?2-shaft reciprocating, 120nhp = about 12kts
Armament: 2-47in (2x1), 2-4in (2x1)
Complement: 120

Composite-hulled vessel, built at London for the Kwangtung fleet. She was later employed on customs duties and by 1891 was armed with 2-4.7m 40pdr Armstrong BL (2x1) and 2-4in 20pdr Armstrong BL (2x1).

FU PO class *wooden sloops* (launched 1870-76)

Displacement: 1258t
Dimensions: 200ft x 32ft 9in x 11ft 6in *(60.96 x 9.98 x 3.51m)*
Machinery: 1-shaft SR, 600ihp = 10kts
Armament: 1-6.3in, 4-4.7in (4x1)
Complement: 180

Class: *Fu Po, An Lan, Fei Yuan, Chi An, Yuan Kai, Teng Ying Chen, T'ai An.*
Wooden-hulled, fully-rigged sloops, built at Foochow for the Fukien fleet. *Fei Yuan* and *Chi An* were sunk by the French at Foochow on 23.8.84. *Fu Po* was badly damaged but was repaired and returned to service. By 1890 *Fu Po* was armed with 1-5in 2.25t Vavasseur BL and 4-4in 1.5t Vavasseur BL (4x1), and *Yuan Kai, Teng Ying Chen* and *T'ai An* with 6-4in 1.5t Vavasseur BL (6x1).

CHEN HAI class *wooden gunboats* (launched 1871-72)

Displacement: 578t
Dimensions: 160ft x 26ft 3in x 11ft 6in *(48.77 x 8.00 x 3.51m)*
Machinery: 1-shaft reciprocating, 480ihp = 10kts
Armament: 2-6.3in (2x1), 2-4.7in (2x1)
Complement: –

Class: *Chen Hai, Ching Yuan, Chen Wei.* All built at Foochow.
Wooden-hulled, fully-rigged gunboats. *Chen Hai* was built for the Peiyang fleet, *Ching Yuan* for the Nanyang fleet and *Chen Wei* for the Fukien fleet. *Chen Wei* was sunk by the French at Foochow. By 1890 *Chen Hai* was armed with two 64pdr Krupp (2x1), 4-4.7in 40pdr Vavasseur (4x1) and 2-24pdr ML (2x1); *Chang Yuan* was similarly armed except for having only one 64pdr. By that date both vessels were with the Fukien fleet. The fates of the two survivors are not known.

YANG WU *wooden sloop* (launched 1872)

Displacement: 1608t
Dimensions: 190ft 4in x 36ft 2in x 16ft 5in *(58.01 x 11.02 x 5.00m)*
Machinery: Reciprocating, 1250ihp = 13kts
Armament: 1-7.5in, 2-6.3in (2x1)
Complement: –

A wooden-hulled, fully-rigged vessel built at Foochow for the Fukien fleet. She was sunk by the French at Foochow.

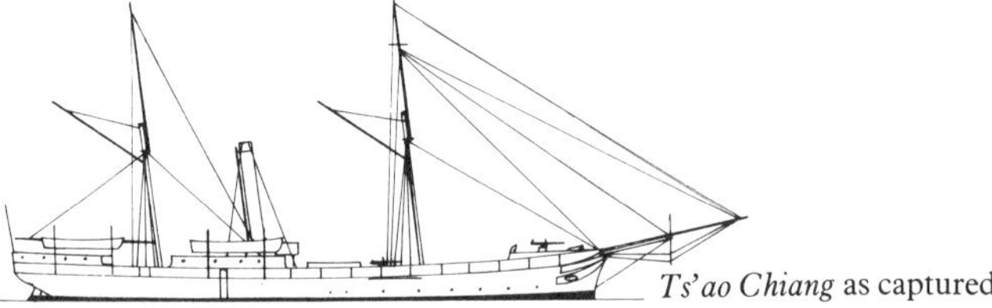
Ts'ao Chiang as captured 1894

TS'AO CHIANG *composite gunboats* (launched *c*1876)

Displacement: 600t
Dimensions: 156ft 8in pp x 28ft 3in x 10ft 4in *(47.75 x 8.61 x 3.25m)*
Machinery: 1-shaft HR, cyl boilers, 400ihp = 9kts
Armament: 4-6.3in
Complement: 79

Composite-hulled fully-rigged gunboat, built at Kiangyan for the Nanyang fleet. She was captured by the Japanese cruiser *Akitsushima* off the west coast of Korea on 25.7.1894, and was renamed *Soko.*

CHIEN SHENG class *flatiron gunboats* (launched 1875)

Displacement: 256t
Dimensions: 87ft x 26ft x 8ft 3in *(26.52m x 7.92 x 2.51m)*
Machinery: ?2-shaft HR, cyl boilers, 180ihp = 8kts
Armament: 1-10in
Complement: –

Class: *Chien Sheng, Fu Sheng.*
Steel-hulled Rendel flatiron gunboats, built by Laird for the Fukien fleet. The 10in 16t Armstrong ML gun was mounted forward and the single funnel was well aft. Both vessels were sunk by the French at Foochow on 23.8.1884.

TIONG SING *armoured gunboat* (launched 1875)

Displacement: 200t
Dimensions: 104ft wl x 20ft 4in x 6ft 9in mean *(31.70 x 6.20 x 2.06m)*
Machinery: 2-shaft ICR, 340ihp = 10kts
Armour: Iron. Belt 2¾in, ends 1⅞in, turret 2⅜in
Armament: 1-6.7in
Complement: 40

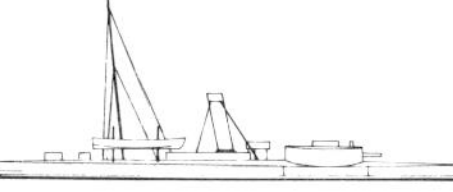
Tiong Sing as completed

An iron-hulled vessel, built at Shanghai for the Nanyang fleet. She was flush decked, and had a complete armour belt up to the upper deck. The 6.7in Krupp ML gun was in a fixed turret forward, and she had a single raked funnel amidships and a raked mast aft. She was captured by the Japanese at Wei-Hai-Wei and renamed *Hei Yuen*.

ALPHA class *flatiron gunboats* (launched 1876)

Displacement: 320t
Dimensions: 118ft pp x 27ft x 7ft 6in (*35.97 x 8.23 x 2.29m*)
Machinery: 2-shaft HCR, 2 cyl boilers, 235ihp = 10kts. Coal 40/50t
Armour: Iron. Sheild ½in, CT ½in
Armament: 1-11in, 2-12pdr (2x1)
Complement: 30

Class: *Alpha, Beta.*

Iron-hulled Rendel flatiron gunboats completed in 1876 for the Nanyang fleet. The 11in 26.5t Armstrong MLR gun was mounted well forward and the two 3in 12pdr Armstrong BLR (2x1) were on the upper deck aft. The boats were designed by George Rendel and ordered in April 1875. They had two tripod masts and one funnel and were rigged as topsail schooners. *Alpha* was later renamed *Lung Hsiang*, and *Beta* became *Hu Wei*. Both were built by Mitchell and discarded *c*1895.

GAMMA class *flatiron gunboats* (launched 1876)

Displacement: 420t
Dimensions: 120ft x 30ft x 8ft (*36.58 x 9.14 x 2.44m*)
Machinery: 2-shaft HCR, 1 cyl boiler, 270ihp = 9.5kts
Armour: Iron. Shield ½in, CT ½in
Armament: 1-12.5in, 2-2.75in (2x1)
Complement: 30

Class: *Gamma, Delta.*

Iron-hulled Rendel flatiron gunboats completed in 1877 for the Nanyang fleet. The 12.5in 38t Armstrong MLR gun was mounted well forward and the two 2.75in Armstrong 9pdr BLR (2x1) were on the upper deck aft. The boats were designed by George Rendel and ordered in April 1875. They had two tripod masts and one funnel and were rigged as topsail schooners. *Gamma* was later renamed *Fei Ting* and *Delta* became *Tse Tien*. Built by Mitchell and discarded *c*1905.

WEI YUEN type *composite sloops* (launched 1877-80)

Displacement: 1100-1258t
Dimensions: 210ft x 29ft 6in x 12ft 6in (*64.00 x 8.99 x 3.81m*)
Machinery: 1-shaft reciprocating, 750ihp = 11kts
Armour: Iron. Shield 1¼in-½in
Armament: 1-7in, 6-4.7in (6x1)
Complement: 180

Class: *Wei Yuen, Chao Wu, Kang Chi, Teng Ch'ing.* All were built at Foochow. *Ching Ch'ing* and *Heng Hai* (launched at Foochow 1884-86) were 7ft longer and 3kts faster.

Composite-hulled, fully-rigged sloops, *Wei Yuen* and *Kang Chi* being built for the Peiyang fleet and *Chao Wu* and *Teng Ch'ing* for the Nanyang fleet. They were armed with a 7in Armstrong MLR and six 4.7in 40pdr guns. *Wei Yuen* was disarmed in July 1885 and became a TS for midshipmen; she was torpedoed and sunk by the Japanese *TB23* at Wei-Hai-Wei. *Chao Wu* was rearmed with two 6in BL in sponsons forward (2x1) and seven 4.7in 40pdr (7x1). *Kang Chi* was disarmed and fitted with two TT for her new role as a torpedo TS, her crew being reduced to 160. *Teng Ch'ing* was sunk by spar TBs from the French cruiser *Bayard* off Shei-Poo on the night of 14/15.21885.

EPSILON class *flatiron gunboats* (launched 1879)

Displacement: 430t
Dimensions: 125ft wl x 29ft x 9ft 6in (*38.10 x 8.84 x 2.90m*)
Machinery: 2-shaft HCR, 2 cyl boilers, 450ihp = 10kts. Coal 60/?t
Armament: 1-11in/23cal, 2-3in (2x1)
Complement: 28

Class: *Epsilon, Zeta, Eta, Theta.* All built by Mitchell.

Steel-hulled Rendel flatiron gunboats built for the Peiyang fleet. The 11in/23 35t Armstrong MLR was mounted well forward, and the two 3in 12pdr Armstrong BLR on the upper deck aft. There was one funnel aft and two tripod masts, and the boats were rigged as topsail schooners. All were captured by the Japanese at Wei-Hai-Wei. *Epsilon* was renamed *Chen Tung* by the Chinese and after capture became *Chinto*; *Zeta* became *Chen Hsi* and then the Japanese *Chin Sei*; *Eta* was later *Chen Nan* and renamed *Chin Nan* by the Japanese; and *Theta* became *Chen Pei* and subsequently *Chin Hoku* in Japanese service.

IOTA class *flatiron gunboats* (launched 1880)

Displacement: 440t
Dimensions: 125ft x 29ft x 9ft 10in (*38.10 x 8.84 x 3.00m*)
Machinery: 2-shaft HCR, 2 cyl boilders, 455ihp = 10.3kts. Coal 60/?t
Armament: 1-11in/23cal, 2-3in (2x1)
Complement: 28

Class: *Iota, Kappa, Lamda.* All built by Mitchell.

Further Rendel flatirons for the Peiyang fleet, broadly similar to the *Epsilon* class but featuring pole masts and rigged as fore-and-aft schooners. *Iota*, later renamed *Chen Chung* by the Chinese, became the Japanese *Chin Chu*; *Kappa*, later *Chen Pien*, became the Japanese *Chim Pien* and both vessels being captured by Japan on 12.2.1895. *Lamda* was renamed *Chen Hai* by the Chinese.

HOI TUNG HUNG *flatiron gunboat* (launched 1880)

Displacement: 430t
Dimension: 125ft x 30ft x 7ft 11in mean (*38.10 x 9.14 x 2.41m*)
Machinery: 2-shaft reciprocating, 70nhp = 7.5kts. Coal 40/?t
Armament: 1-11in, 2-2.75in (2x1)
Complement: –

Composite-hulled Rendel flatiron gunboat built in China for the Kwangtung fleet. Her 11in 25t Armstrong MLR gun was mounted forward and the two 2.75in 9pdr Krupp BLRs were on the upper deck aft. She was too lightly built and was not a success.

PAO MIN *unprotected cruiser*

Displacement: 1480t
Dimensions: 213ft pp x 36ft x 14ft (*64.92 x 10.97 x 4.27m*)
Machinery: 1-shaft reciprocating, 1900ihp = 9kts. Coal ?/300t
Armament: 2-5.9in (2x1), 6-5in (6x1), 2-3pdr (2x1)
Complement: 200

Name	Builder	Launched	Fate
PAO MIN	Kiangyan	1883	Hulked 1903

Schooner-rigged, steel-hulled cruiser built for the Nanyang fleet. She had a ram bow, two masts and one funnel. One 5.9in was mounted in the bow and the other on the quarterdeck. The 5in were mounted on the broadside.

KUANG CHIA *composite dispatch vessel* (launched 1887)

Displacement: 1296t
Dimensions: 221ft x 33ft x 12ft 4½in mean (*67.36 x 10.06 x 3.77m*)
Machinery: 1-shaft reciprocating, 1600ihp = 14.2kts
Armament: 1-5.9in, 4-4.7in (4x1), 6-37mm (2x1)
Complement: About 150

Composite-hulled despatch vessel, laid down at Foochow in December 1885 and completed in May 1888 for the Kwangtung fleet. She was armed with Krupp BLR guns. She was badly damaged by the Japanese at the Battle of the Yalu on 17.9.94 and was beached near Port Arthur, becoming a total loss.

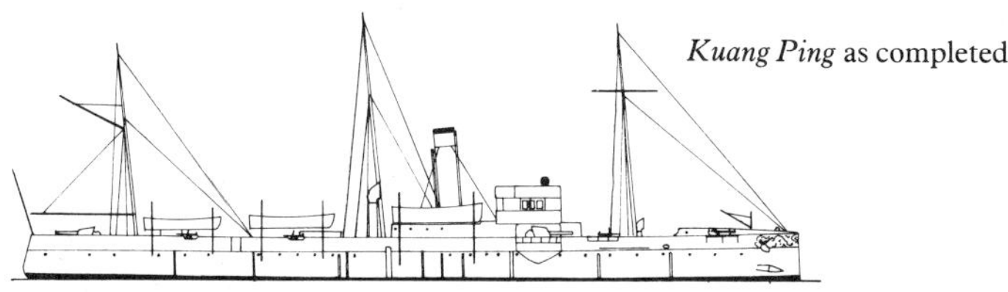
Kuang Ping as completed

KUANG YI class *torpedo gunboats* (launched 1890-91)

Displacement: 1000t
Dimensions: 235ft x 27ft x 13ft (*71.63 x 8.23 x 3.96m*)
Machinery: 2-shaft HTE, cyl boilers, 2400ihp = 16.5kts
Armour: Steel. Protective deck 1in, CT 2in
Armament: 3-4.7in/40 (3x1), 4-3pdr (4x1), 4-14in TT aw
Complement: 120

Class: *Kuang Yi, Kuang P'ing, Kuang Ting.*

Steel-hulled vessels, built at Foochow for the Kwangtung fleet. They had a ram bow, a raised turtledeck forecastle, three masts and one funnel. The three 4.7in/40 Krupp QFs were mounted one each side of the funnel and one aft. Two 14in TT were mounted beneath the turtledeck forcastle and the other two were on the main deck broadside aft. *Kuang Yi* was sunk by the Japanese at the Battle of Asan on 25.7.94 and *Kuang P'ing* was captured by them at Wei-Hai-Wei and renamed *Kohei Go*.

TORPEDO CRAFT

Vulcan *first class torpedo boats* (built 1881)

Displacement: 28t
Dimensions: 88ft x 10ft x 3ft 4in (*26.82 x 3.05 x 1.02m*)
Machinery: 1-shaft reciprocating, 1 boiler, 650ihp = 18.2kts. Coal ?/12t
Armament: 1-37mm, 1-14in TT aw, 4 spar torpedoes (4x1)
Complement: 16

Two steel-hulled boats with three watertight compartments. There was one 14in bow TT, two bow spar torpedoes and two amidships spar torpedoes which could be swung through 150°. The boats had one conning tower. Names and fates not known.

Vulcan *first class torpedo boats* (built 1883-84)

Displacement: 58t, last two 64t
Dimensions: 110ft (last two 114ft 10in) wl x 13ft x 5ft 6in max (*33.53 (35.00) x 3.96 x 1.68m*)
Machinery: 1-shaft VTE, 2 boilers, 900ihp = 18.5kts (last two 700ihp = 19.8kts). Coal 10/?t
Armament: 2-37mm (2x1), 2-14in TT aw (2x1)
Complement: 20

Six steel-hulled boats with a straight stem, one funnel, two conning towers and lifting bow rudders. The first four were badly reassembled at Tokio in 1884 and made only 12kts on trials. Two 14in TT were fitted beneath the forecastle, with one spare torpedo, and two 37mm Hotchkiss revolving cannon were mounted. Names and fates unknown.

Vulcan *second class torpedo boats* (built 1883)

Displacement: 15.7t
Dimensions: 64ft 9in x 8ft 6in x 3ft 6in max (*19.74 x 2.59 x 1.07m*)
Machinery: 1-shaft reciprocating, 200ihp = 15kts
Armament: 1-37mm, 1-14in TT aw
Complement: –

Steel-hulled vessels intended to be carried on the Chinese armoured cruisers. The 14in TT was mounted in the bow. One boat was captured by the Japanese off Wei-Hai-Wei on the night of 7/8.2.95 and was subsequently renamed *TB28*. Her original name and those of her three sisters are unknown.

FU LUNG (S10) *first class torpedo boat* (launched 1885)

Displacement: 120t
Dimensions: 140ft 3in pp x 16ft 5in x 7ft 6½in max (*42.75 x 5.00 x 2.30m*)
Machinery: 1-shaft TE, 1 loco boiler, 1597ihp = 24.2kts. Coal 14½/24t
Armament: 2-37mm (2x1), 2-14in TT aw (2x1)
Complement: 20

Steel-hulled boat, laid down in 1885 and completed the following year for the Peiyang fleet. She had a single funnel and a full length flat-topped turtledeck. The two 14in Schwarzkopf TT were in the bows, with two reload torpedoes. There were two conning towers, one either side of the funnel. *Fu Lung* was captured by the Japanese off Wei-Hai-Wei on the night of 7/8.2.95 and renamed *Fukuryu* by them.

FEI TING *torpedo gunboat* (launched 1887)

Displacement: 401t
Dimensions: 200ft pp x 23ft x 8ft (*60.96 x 7.01 x 2.44m*)
Machinery: 2-shaft TE, 3000ihp = 20kts. Coal 50/90t
Armour: Steel. CT 1¾in
Armament: 2-4in (2x1), 4-3pdr (4x1), 5-18in TT aw (1x1, 2x2)
Complement: 50

Originally named *Sea Serpent* this steel-hulled vessel was laid down in 1887 as a stock boat by J S White and was purchased, rebuilt and strengthened by Armstrong at Elswick between March and September 1894. She was purchased by China but delivery was delayed until June 1895 by the Sino-Japanese war. She had a ram bow, two pole masts and two funnels side by side abaft the foremast. The two 4in 25pdr Armstrong QFs were mounted fore and aft, with the 3pdr QFs amidships. She had one fixed 18in bow TT and two centreline twin training mountings on the upper deck amidships. She carried twelve Schwarzkopf torpedoes. *Fei Ting* was captured by the joint British-French-German-Russian expedition in drydock at Taku on 17.6.1900.

TSO I *first class torpedo boat* (built 1887)

Displacement: 90t
Dimensions: 128ft x 12ft 6in x 6ft 3in (*39.01 x 3.81 x 1.91m*)
Machinery: 1-shaft VTE, 1 loco boiler, 1000ihp = 23.8kts. Coal 12/20t
Armament: 2-3pdr (2x1), 3-14in TT aw (3x1)
Complement: 25

A steel-hulled boat, built by Yarrow for the Peiyang fleet and featuring a turledeck forecastle and one funnel. Two 14in Schwarzkopf TT were fixed in the bows and the other was on a trainable mounting abaft the funnel. There were two spare torpedoes.

Vulcan *third class torpedo boats* (built 1894)

Displacement: 66t, second boat 74t
Dimensions: 110ft 7in x 11ft 6in x 3ft 6in (*33.71 x 3.51 x 1.07m*)
Machinery: Reciprocating, 338ihp = 13.8kts (second boat 442ihp = 15.5kts)
Armament: 2-37mm (2x1), 2-14in TT aw
Complement: –

The second of this pair of steel-hulled boats had different lines and machinery and was faster. Both were captured by the Japanese off Wei-Hai-Wei on the night of 7/8.2.95 and were subsequently renamed *TB26* and *TB27*, but their original names are unknown.

Schichau *torpedo boats* (built 1895-97)

Displacement: 90t
Dimensions: 128ft x 15ft 8in x 5ft (*39.01 x 4.78 x 1.52m*)
Machinery: 1-shaft reciprocating, 1200ihp = 24kts
Armament: 2-37mm (2x1), 3-14in TT aw (3x1)
Complement: 36

Class: *Chang (No 1), Lieh (No 3).*

Steel-hulled boats with a turtledeck forecastle and one raked mast and funnel. Two 14in TT were fixed in the bows and the other was on a trainable mounting aft.

Vulcan *torpedo boats* (built 1895)

Displacement: 120t
Dimensions: 144ft x 17ft x 8ft (*43.89 x 5.18 x 2.44m*)
Machinery: 1-shaft reciprocating, 1250ihp = 24kts
Armament: 2-37mm (2x1), 3-14in TT aw (3x1)
Complement: 38

Class: *Chen (No 2), Su (No 4).*

These steel-hulled vessels had a turtledeck forecastle and two raked masts and funnels. There were two fixed bow TT, and the other was on a trainable mounting aft. The fates of these vessels are unknown.

HAI HOLA class *destroyers* (launched 1898)

Displacement: 280t, 305t full load
Dimensions: 193ft 6in x 20ft x 6ft 6in (*58.98 x 6.10 x 1.98m*)
Machinery: 2-shaft VTE, Schichau-Thornycroft watertube boilers, 6000ihp = 32kts. Coal ?/67t
Armament: 6-3pdr (6x1), 2-18in TT aw (2x1)
Complement: 50

Class: *Hai Hola, Hai Lung, Hai Nju, Hai Ying.*

These steel-hulled destroyers featured a ram bow, a turtledeck forecastle and two raked funnels. The 3pdr QFs were mounted on the broadside abreast the first and second funnels and aft, and the 18in TT were in trainable centreline mountings fore and aft of the second funnel. All four vessels were captured at Taku on 17.6.1900 by the International expedition that was relieving the Peking Legations, and one each went in service with the British, French, German and Russian navies, all being renamed *Taku* (*Takou* in the case of the French boat).

FEI YING *torpedo gunboat* (launched 1895)

Displacement: 837t
Dimensions: 246ft oa x 28ft 4in x 13ft mean *(74.98 x 8.64 x 3.96m)*
Machinery: 2-shaft TE, 8 Yarrow watertube boilers, 5430ihp = 22kts. Coal 75/170t
Armour: Steel. Shields 2in
Armament: 2-4.1in (2x1), 6-6pdr (6x1), 4-1pdr (4x1), 3-14in TT aw (3x1)
Complement: 90

Completed by Vulcan in 1896, this steel-hulled gunboat had a turtledeck forecastle, two masts and four equally-spaced raked funnels. The two 4.1in QFs were mounted fore and aft, and the 6pdr 3.5in QF were mounted on the broadside abreast the forebridge, and on the quarterdeck. Two 14in TT were in trainable mountings on the broadside amidships, and the third was on the main deck at the stern. Three spare torpedoes were carried. *Fei Ying* was later reclassified as a destroyer. Fate not known.

CHIEN AN class *torpedo gunboats* (launched 1900-02)

Displacement: 861t
Dimensions: 255ft x 26ft 8in x 11ft 5in max *(77.72 x 8.13 x 3.48m)*
Machinery: 2-shaft TE, Normand watertube boilers, 6500ihp = 23kts. Coal 180/360t
Armour: Steel. Belt 1in, deck 1in
Armament: 1-4.1in, 3-9pdr (3x1), 6-1pdr (6x1), 2-14in TT aw (2x1)
Complement: 139

Class: *Chien An, Chien Wei*.

These steel-hulled boats were built at Foochow and had a ram bow, a raised forecastle and poop, two masts and two funnels. There was a 1in steel wl belt amidships over the machinery, covered by a 1in steel deck. The 4.1in Schneider-Canet QF gun was mounted on the foecastle and the 9pdr QFs were on sponsons amidships and on the poop. The TT were amidships. Both vessels were completely rebuilt between 1930 and 1931, when *Chien An* was renamed *Ta Tung* and *Chien Wei* was renamed *Tze Chion*. They were designed by M Doyère.

Argentina

Before the foundation of the Argentine State, the coastal province of Buenos Aires played a prominent part in the Spanish colonies' struggle for independence. However, freedom from Spanish rule was followed by a long period of civil wars and border fighting between the victorious provinces. This left Argentina with a legacy of rivalry between the capital and the outlying parts of the country, which frequently manifested itself in rebellion, political coups or open warfare. The almost continual civil disturbances hampered Argentina's economic development, and kept the navy in a decidedly secondary role to that of the army. At the establishment of the republic in 1860 there were no seagoing warships, and although Argentina virtually led the Triple Alliance (with Brazil and Uruguay) in the 1865-70 Paraguayan War, Brazil provided the fleet. (The naval side of the fighting, although intense, was mainly confined to the rivers.) Argentina began to build up a modest coast defence navy in the 1870s, most of the ships being supplied by British yards, but the navy was never a popular service, and only reached a degree of efficiency at the very end of the century. A substantial naval programme was undertaken in the 1890s, in response to a dispute with Chile over the Andean frontier, but the tension was dissolved by a treaty in 1902, two of the armoured cruisers building in Italy were sold to Japan, and other construction was cancelled.

CAPITAL SHIPS

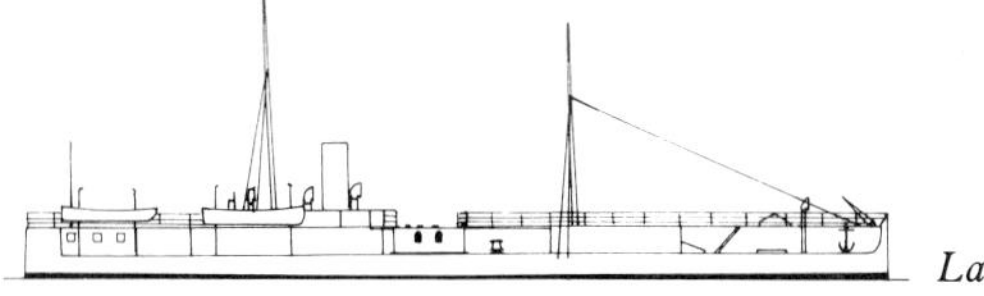

La Plata 1896

LA PLATA class *coast defence battleships*

Displacement: 1500t full load
Dimensions: 186ft 0in wl x 44ft 0in x 10ft 6in max *(56.69 x 13.41 x 3.20m)*
Machinery: 2-shaft compound, 750ihp = 9.5kts. Coal 120/?t
Armour: Iron. Belt 6in, ends 4½in-4in, breastwork 8in, turret 9in-8in
Armament: 2-7.8in (1 x 2), 2-4in (2 x 1), 2-9pdr (2 x 1), 2-3pdr (2 x 1) (*Los Andes* also 4-1in Nordenfeld MG)
Complement: 200

Name	Builder	Launched	Fate
LA PLATA	Laird	29.8.1874	Scrapped *c*1925
LOS ANDES	Laird	29.10.1874	Scrapped *c*1929

Low-freeboard monitors with narrow superstructure fore and aft permitting end-on fire from a single central turret. They had one funnel abaft the turret, and two light pole masts, and a light flying bridge extending fore and aft over the superstructure. The belt over the machinery and magazine was 6in thick and 5ft high (3ft above, 2ft below lwl) reducing to 4in at the ends. The funnel casing was 4½in, and there was an 8in breastwork round the turret. The area round the gunports was 9in, and the rest of the turret 8in. The 12.5t Armstrong BLR 7.8in guns were mounted well apart in the turret to permit end-on fire.

ALMIRANTE BROWN *central battery corvette*

Displacement: 4200t full load
Dimensions: 240ft 0in pp x 50ft 0in x 20ft 6in max *(73.15 x 15.24 x 6.25m)*
Machinery: 2-shaft compound, 8 cyl boilers, 5400ihp = 14kts. Coal 450/650t
Armour: Compound. Belt 9in-6in, ends 7½in-1½in, battery 8in-6in, CT 8in
Armament: 8-8in (8 x 1), 6-4.7in (6 x 1), 2-9pdr (2 x 1), 2-7pdr (2 x 1)
Complement: 520

Name	Builder	Launched	Fate
ALMIRANTE BROWN	Samuda	1880	Scrapped *c*1930

She had a ram bow, a short forecastle and poop, two masts with military tops and a single funnel. The steel hull had a double bottom and was sheathed in wood and zinc. The main belt under the battery was 9in thick above lwl and 6in below, reducing from 7½in to 1½in at the end. It extended from 4ft below lwl to 3ft above. The bulkheads were 7½in to 5½in thick, whilst the battery had a 6in upper strake and an 8in lower strake. The deck above the battery was of ⁵/₈in plating, and there was a 1½in-1¼in armoured lower deck at the ends. Six 8in 11.5t Armstrong BLR guns were in the battery, four firing ahead, two astern, with one at the bow and one at the stern. The central part of the battery overhung the hull. The ship was refitted at La Seyne in 1897/98 when the 8in guns were replaced by 10-5.9in/50cal Canet QF (six in battery, two forward and two aft) and the old 4.7in guns by 6-4.7in/50cal QF. The complement was reduced to 380.

ARGENTINA

Independencia as completed

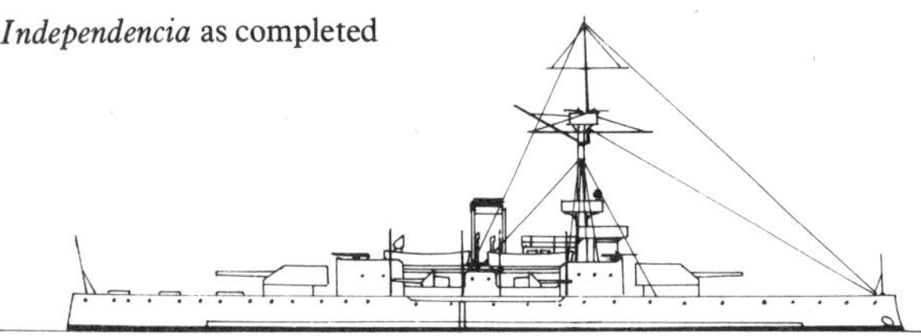

INDEPENDENCIA class *coast defence battleships*

Displacement: 2330t normal
Dimensions: 230ft pp x 43ft x 13ft mean (*70.10 x 13.11 x 3.96m*)
Machinery: 2-shaft VTE, 4 cyl boilers, 2780ihp = 14.2kts. Coal 230/340t
Armour: Steel. Belt 8in, barbettes 8in-6in, hoods 5in, secondary gun-shields 1¼in, CT 4in
Armament: 2-9.4in/35 (2 x 1), 4-4.7in/40 (4 x 1), 4-3pdr, 2-18in TT aw
Complement: 230

Name	Builder	Launched	Fate
LIBERTAD (ex-NUEVE DE JULIO)	Laird	11.12.1890	Scrapped *c*1940
INDEPENDENCIA	Laird	26.2.1891	Scrapped *c*1940

Laid down in 1890, these vessels were flush-decked and had one mast and one funnel. The 8in belt was 5ft deep and 172ft long, with a 1in deck over it and a 2in protective deck at the ends. The forward bulkhead was 8in and the aft one 6in. The 9.4in Krupp guns were mounted in barbettes at each end of the superstructure with the 4.7in Elswick QF guns in shields amidships. The 18in TT were on the main deck abreast the mast. The steel hull had a double bottom the length of the belt and its freeboard was 10ft amidships. *Nueve de Julio*, completed in 1891, was renamed *Libertad* in 1892, the year her sister was completed.

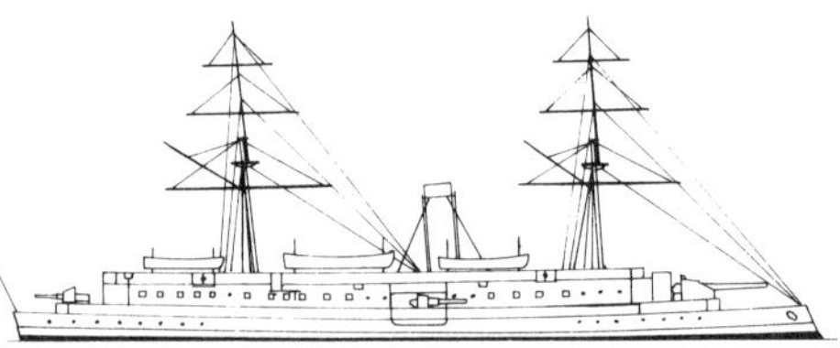

Patagonia as completed

PATAGONIA *protected cruiser*

Displacement: 1450t normal
Dimensions: 213ft 3in pp x 32ft 9in x 12ft 10in mean (*64.92 x 9.98 x 3.91m*)
Machinery: 2-shaft HC, 2730ihp = 14kts. Coal 260/350t
Armour: Steel. Protective deck 1¼in, shield 4in, CT 1½in
Armament: 1-10in (1 x 1), 3-6in (3 x 1), 4-9pdr
Complement: 210

Name	Builder	Launched	Fate
PATAGONIA	Trieste	1885	Discarded *c*1930

A steel-hulled, wood- and copper-sheathed vessel, *Patagonia* had a ram bow, a flush deck and a low freeboard hull. There were two masts and one funnel. The protective deck ran the length of the ship. The 10in 27.5t Armstrong BLR gun was mounted forward, and the 6in Armstrong BLR guns were mounted in sponsons amidships and aft. A long superstructure extended between the 10in and aft 6in guns. Completed in February 1887, she was reconstructed in 1909 as a surveying ship and rearmed with 1-6in forward, 1-4.7in aft and 8-3in (8 x 1) amidships. She was rebuilt as a transport in 1919 and fitted with 500ihp oil-fired machinery. She carried 263t of oil and had a maximum speed of 10kts.

VEINTICINCO DE MAYO *protected cruiser*

Displacement: 3180t normal
Dimensions: 330ft pp x 43ft x 16ft mean (*100.58 x 13.11 x 4.88m*)
Machinery: 2-shaft VTE, 4 cyl boilers, 14,050ihp = 22.4kts. Coal 300/620t
Armour: Steel. Protective deck 4½in-3½in slopes, 3½in-1in flats, glacis 5in, shields 2in, CT 4in
Armament: 2-8.2in (2 x 1), 8-4.7in/40 (8 x 1), 12-3pdr (12 x 1), 3-18in TT aw (3 x 1)

Name	Builder	Launched	Fate
VEINTICINCO DE MAYO (ex-NICOCHEA)	Armstrong	5.5.1890	Discarded *c*1915

Almirante Brown as completed
CPL

Veinticino de Mayo as completed

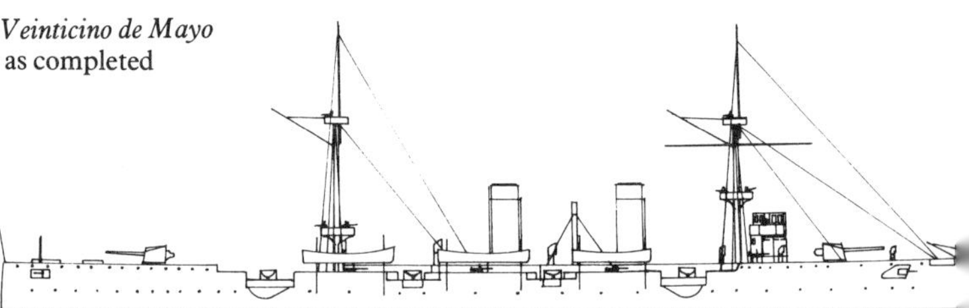

Steel-hulled, with a double bottom except in the boiler and engine rooms. The protective deck ran the length of the ship, 3½in on the lower slopes, 4½in on the upper slopes, and 3½in over the engine room and 1¾in elsewhere on the flat except at the ends where it reduced to 1in. The 8.2in Krupp BLR guns were mounted on the raised forecastle and poop, and the 4.7in BLR guns were mounted in the waist. There was one fixed bow TT, and two on the main deck broadsides on the quarter. There were two masts with military tops and two broad funnels. She was laid down as the stock cruiser *Nicochea* and the name was changed when she was purchased by Argentina. Armstrong proposed fitting a 7ft wide armour belt against QF gunfire but she was completed to the original design. The ship was laid down on 18.6.85 to a design by Philip Watts and was completed in February 1891.

NUEVE DE JULIO *protected cruiser*

Displacement: 3600t normal
Dimensions: 354ft pp x 44ft x 16ft 6in mean (*107.90 x 13.41 x 5.03m*)
Machinery: 2-shaft VTE, 8 cyl boilers, 14,500ihp = 22.25kts. Coal 350/750t
Armour: Steel. Protective deck 4½in-3½in slopes, 3½in-1¾in flats, 5in glacis, shields 2in, CT 4in
Armament: 4-6in/40 (4 x 1), 8-4.7in/40 (8 x 1), 12-3pdr (12 x 1), 5-18in TT aw (5 x 1)
Complement: 327

Name	Builder	Launched	Fate
NUEVE DE JULIO	Armstrong	26.7.1892	Discarded 1930

This vessel was an improved *Veinticinco de Mayo* with QF instead of BLR guns and could be distinguished by her smaller guns on the forecastle and poop and by the raised funnels. She also had a steel hull with a double bottom except in the boiler and engine rooms, where the depth of the hull was insufficient to allow it to be fitted. There was a 6in/40 Armstrong QF gun fore and aft, and the other two were mounted firing forward at the break of the forecastle. At normal draught she made 21.75kts on 9500ihp, 0.5kt faster than *Veinticinco de Mayo* The extra pair of torpedo tubes were on the main deck between the bridge and forefunnel. She was designed by Philip Watts and laid down in February 1891 and completed on 27.1.93. Her construction was slightly delayed by changing the torpedoes from 14in to 18in.

Nueve de Julio as completed
CPL

BUENOS AIRES *protected cruiser*

Displacement: 4788t normal
Dimensions: 396ft pp x 42ft 2in x 18ft 5in mean (*120.70 x 12.85 x 5.61m*)
Machinery: 2-shaft VTE, 8 cyl boilers, 17,000ihp = 24kts. Coal 350/1000t
Armour: Steel. Protective deck 5in-3in slopes, 1½in flats, glacis 5in, shields 4½in, CT 6in
Armament: 2-8in/45 (2 x 1), 4-6in/45 (4 x 1), 6-4.7in/45 (6 x 1), 16-3pdr (16 x 1), 5-18in TT aw (5 x 1)
Complement: 350

Name	Builder	Launched	Fate
BUENOS AIRES	Armstrong	18.5.1895	Discarded 1931

A steel-hulled, wood-sheathed, flush-decked vessel with a complete double bottom, *Buenos Aires* resembled the Chilean *Blanco Encalada* but had a mixed secondary armament and lower fighting tops to reduce topweight. She had two funnels and two masts, with the foremast in front of the bridge. The protective deck ran the length of the ship, and was 5in over the machinery. The 8in/45 Armstrong QF guns were mounted fore and aft, with the 6in/45 Armstrong QF on either side of the fore and aft bridges, the 4.7in/45 QF were mounted amidships and the torpedo tubes were arranged as the *Nueve de Julio*. There were no official forced draught trials, but with normal draught she made 22.92kts on 13,292ihp. She was designed by Philip Watts, laid down in February 1893 and completed in February 1896.

Buenos Aires about 1911
CPL

PARANA class *gunboats* (launched 1873)

Displacement: 515t full load
Dimensions: 152ft pp x 25ft x 10ft max (*46.33 x 7.62 x 3.04m*)
Machinery: 1-shaft compound, 2 cyl boilers, 475ihp = 11.0kts. Coal ?/80t
Armament: 2-6in (2 x 1), 2-4in (2 x 1)
Complement: 100

Class (builder, fate): *Parana* (Laird, discarded *c*1910), *Uruguay* (Laird, discarded *c*1930). Barque-rigged gunboats with one funnel between the masts, a raised forecastle and poop and a clipper bow. They had an iron hull sheathed in wood with five watertight bulkheads, but no double bottom. The 6in 4½t MLR guns were in the waist fore and aft of the funnel, and the 4in were on the broadside at the break of the poop. *Uruguay* received new boilers and was resheathed in teak and zinc in 1889. She was later converted into a surveying ship.

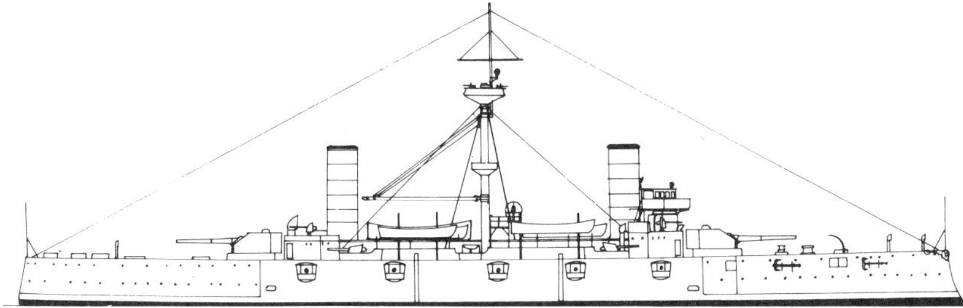

General Garibaldi as completed

GARIBALDI class *armoured cruisers*

Displacement: 6773t normal, *Belgrano* 7069t
Dimensions: 344ft 2in wl x 59ft 8 in x 23ft 4 in mean (*104.90 x 18.19 x 7.11m*)
Machinery: 2-shaft VTE, 8 cyl boilers (*Pueyrredon* Belleville watertube boilers), 13,000ihp = 20kts
Armour: Harvey (*Pueyrredon* Krupp). Belt 5.9in, ends 3.1in, barbettes 5.9in, turrets 5.9in, secondary battery 5.9in, shields 1.9in, CT 5.9in
Armament: 2-10in/40 (2 x 1) (*San Martin* 4-8in/45 (2 x 2)), 10-6in/40 (10 x 1) (*Belgrano*, *Pueyrredon* 14-6in/40 (14 x 1)), 6-4.7in/40 (6 x 1) (*Belgrano*, *Pueyrredon* 2-3in (2 x 1)), 10-6pdr (10 x 1), 4-18in TT aw (4 x 1)
Complement: 500 (*San Martin* 540, *Belgrano* 520)

Name	Builder	Launched	Fate
GENERAL GARIBALDI (ex-GIUSEPPE GARIBALDI)	Ansaldo	27.5.1895	Discarded 1935
GENERAL SAN MARTIN (ex-VARESE)	Orlando	25.5.1896	Discarded 1935
GENERAL BELGRANO (ex-VARESE)	Orlando	25.7.1897	Discarded 1948
GENERAL PUEYRREDON (ex-GIUSEPPE GARIBALDI)	Ansaldo	25.9.1897	Discarded 1954

These flush-decked, steel-hulled cruisers were designed by Eduardo Masdea and were laid down 1895-7. They had a single mast amidships with two funnels set fore and aft. The complete wl belt, 8ft 3in deep, was 3.1in thick at the ends, but 5.9in amidships up to upper deck level over the magazines, machinery and battery. *Garibaldi*, *Belgrano* and *Pueyrredon* had a single 10in/40 Armstrong gun fore and aft, whilst *San Martin* had two twin 8in/45cal Armstrong turrets. All four ships had 10-6in/40 in the battery amidships; *Garibaldi* and *San Martin* had 6-4.7in above this, whilst *Belgrano* and *Pueyrredon* had 4-6in/40 and 2-3in instead. On trials they made 19.8-20.1kts on 13,208-13,885ihp. In the early 1930s *San Martin*, *Belgrano* and *Pueyrredon* were converted to oil firing. *Garibaldi* was used as a TS.

Two improved *Garibaldi*-type cruisers, *Rivadvia* (ex-*Mitra*) and *Moreno* (ex-*Roca*), were ordered from Ansaldo in 1901 and laid down the following year, but the ships were sold to Japan 31.12.03 just before completion, becoming *Kasuga* and *Nisshin* respectively (see under Japan).

PILCOMAYO class *gunboats* (launched 1875)

Displacement: 420t full load
Dimensions: 105ft pp x 30ft x 7ft 9in max (*32.00 x 9.14 x 2.36in*)
Machinery: 2-shaft compound, 2 cyl boilers, 430ihp = 9.7kts. Coal ?/42t
Armament: 1-11in, 2-3.1in (2 x 1), 2-7pdr (2 x 1)
Complement: 60

Class (builder, fate): *Pilcomayo* (Rennie, BU *c*1930), *Burmejo* (Rennie, BU *c*1920), *Republica* (Laird, BU *c*1915), *Constitucion* (Laird, BU *c*1915). Rendel 'flatiron' gunboats which had an iron hull with four watertight compartments but no double bottom. The single 11in 26½t Armstrong MLR gun was mounted on a movable platform forward which could be lowered into a well when at sea. It had no traverse and was aimed by moving the ship. The two 3.1in Krupp BLR guns were on the upper deck. These vessels had one funnel set well aft. *Pilcomayo* had its 11in gun removed and replaced by a 30t sheerleg derrick in 1896 and was used as a salvage vessel; *Burmejo* was later used as a transport.

TORPEDO CRAFT

ESPORA class *torpedo gunboats* (launched 1890)

Displacement: 520t normal
Dimensions: 200ft pp x 25ft x 8ft 3in mean (*60.96 x 7.62 x 2.51m*)
Machinery: 2-shaft TE, 4 loco boilers, 3420ihp = 19.4kts. Coal 100/130t
Armament: 2-3in (2 x 1), 1-8pdr, 2-3pdr (2 x 1), 5-18in TT aw (1 x 1, 2 x 2)
Complement: 47

Class (builder, fate): *Espora* (Laird, discarded *c*1920), *Rosales* (Laird, foundered 1892). *Espora* and *Rosales* were steel-hulled boats with a raised forecastle and poop and two raked masts and funnels. The 3in Nordenfeld 14pdr QF guns were mounted *en échelon* on the forecastle, with the 8pdr and two 3pdr guns on the poop. There was one fixed bow TT, and the others were in pairs on trainable mountings forward and aft of the second funnel. They were both laid down in 1889 and completed in December 1890. *Espora* was reconstructed in 1905, retaining the bow TT and the two 3in guns, but the remaining armament was replaced by 5-3pdr (5 x 1) and the trainable tubes were removed. Her loco boilers were replaced by six Yarrow watertube boilers.

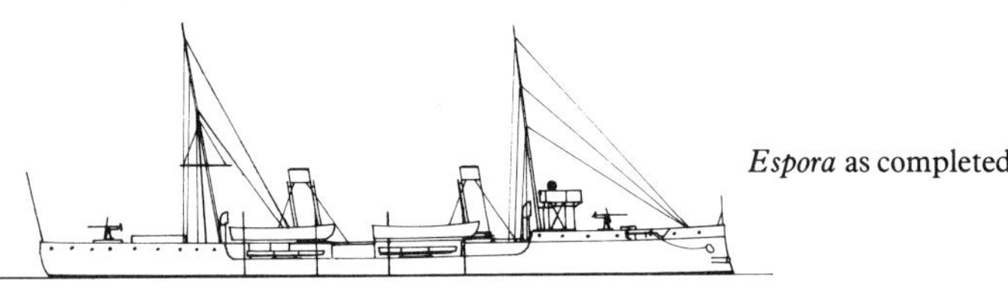

Espora as completed

Class: *Commodoro Py, Muratore.* Steel-hulled first class vessels with three masts and two funnels placed fore and aft. There were twelve watertight compartments. One 3pdr Nordenfeld QF gun was on the conning tower and the other two were on the broadside. There was one fixed bow TT, and the other two were on trainable mountings aft. These boats were almost identical to the Brazilian *Araguary* class.

PATRIA *torpedo gunboat* (launched 1893)

Displacement: 1029t trials
Dimensions: 250ft pp x 31ft 6in x 9ft 8in trials (*76.20 x 9.60 x 2.95m*)
Machinery: 2-shaft VTE, 4 loco boilers, 5000ihp = 20.5kts. Coal 250/288t
Armament: 2-4.7in/40 (2 x 1), 4-8pdr (4 x 1), 2-3pdr (2 x 1), 5-18in TT aw (5 x 1)
Complement: 100

A Laird-built steel-hulled gunboat, *Patria* had a flush deck to improve seaworthiness, and two raking masts and funnels. The 4.7in/40 Armstrong QF guns were mounted fore and aft, with the 8pdrs on the broadside. There was one fixed bow TT and four fixed main deck broadside TT. On trials she made 20.55kts on 5074ihp, exceeding her guaranteed speed by 1kt. She was discarded *c*1930.

Patria
Arrigo Barilli Collection

FERRÉ class Yarrow 1880-2

Displacement: 40t normal
Dimensions: 100ft x 12ft 6in (*30.48 x 3.81m*)
Machinery: 1-shaft compound, loco boiler, 500ihp = 18.5-20kts. Coal 10/?t
Armament: 2 MGs (2 x 1), 2-14in TT aw (2 x 1)
Complement: 11

Class: *Ferré, Enrique Py, Centella, Alerta.* These first class boats had a steel hull, a ram bow, two masts and funnels and a turtleback forecastle. The TTs were fixed in the bow on deck and they carried two reload torpedoes in cradles on deck amidships. All were discarded *c*1910.

NOS 1, 2 Thornycroft 1880

Displacement: 10.9t
Dimensions: 60ft 6in pp x 7ft 6in x 3ft 6in max (*18.44 x 2.29 x 1.07m*)
Machinery: 1shaft, ?ihp = 16kts
Armament: 1 spar torpedo

These third class boats had a steel hull with a ram bow, one funnel and a conning tower abaft the funnel. The single McEvoy spar torpedo was carried in the bow. Both were discarded *c*1910.

COMMODORO PY class Thornycroft 1890

Displacement: 110t normal
Dimensions: 150ft x 14ft 6in x 3ft 6in mean (*45.72 x 4.42 x 1.07m*)
Machinery: 1-shaft TE, 2 Thornycroft watertube boilers, 1800ihp = 25kts. Coal 12/20t
Armament: 3-3pdr (3 x 1), 3-18in TT aw (1 x 1, 1 x 2)
Complement: 27

NOS 1-8 Yarrow 1890

Displacement: 15t full load
Dimensions: 60ft x 9ft 3in x 3ft 6in max (*18.28 x 2.82 x 1.07m*)
Machinery: 1-shaft TE, loco boiler (one had watertube boiler), 230ihp = 17kts. Coal ?/1.25t
Armament: 1-3pdr, 1-14in TT

Steel-hulled second class TBs, almost identical to the British *No 50* type. The boat fitted with a watertube boiler made 18kts on 250ihp. The 3pdr QF was mounted forward and the torpedo tube on deck aft. All were discarded *c*1920.

BUCHARDO class Yarrow 1890

Displacement: 85t full load
Dimensions: 130ft pp x 14ft x 6ft max (*39.62 x 4.27 x 1.83m*)
Machinery: 1-shaft TE (*Bathurst* QE), 2 loco boilers, 1110ihp = 23.5kts (*Bathurst* 1230ihp = 24.4kts). Coal 20/25t
Armament: 3-3pdr (3 x 3), 3-18in TT aw
Complement: 15

Class: *Buchardo, Thorne, Pinedo, King, Jorge, Bathurst.* These first class boats had a steel hull with eleven watertight compartments. There was one 3pdr QF on the conning tower and two *en échelon* amidships. One TT was under the turtledeck forecastle in the bow, the other two on training mountings aft. *Bathurst* was fitted with a quadruple expansion engine which gave an extra 120ihp and 1kt more speed for the same fuel consumption as the other vessels' TE engines. All were discarded 1920-5.

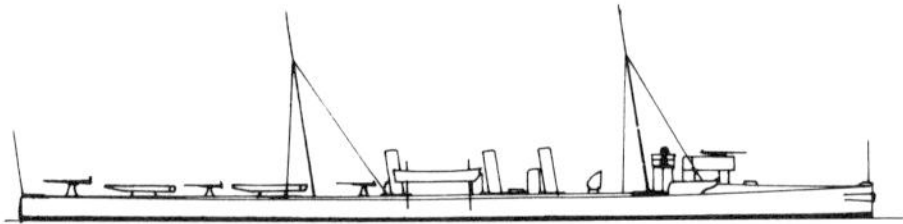

Corrientes as completed

CORRIENTES class Yarrow 1896-8

Displacement: 240t, 280t full load
Dimensions: 190ft x 19ft 6in x 7ft 4in mean (*57.9 x 5.94 x 2.23m*)
Machinery: 2-shaft TE, 6 Yarrow watertube boilers, 4200ihp = 27kts. Coal ?/80t
Armour: Steel. Belt 0.8in-0.5in
Armament: 1-3in, 3-6pdr (3 x 1), 3-18in TT aw (3 x 1)
Complement: 54

Class: *Corrientes, Entre Rios, Misiones, Santa Fé.* Steel-hulled TBDs, with a turtledeck forecastle and three funnels, the forward two set close together. The armour plating extended over the boilers and machinery at the wl. The 3in 14pdr QF gun was mounted forward, with the 6pdr QF on the centreline aft. One TT was fixed in the bow, the others being on training mountings aft. The contract speed of these vessels was 26kts for 3 hours, but they had difficulty achieving this; on the measured mile they made 26.52-27.4kts. *Sanfa Fé* was lost in 1897 and the remainder discarded *c*1925.

Brazil

In marked contrast to most of South America, Brazil's independence from her colonial ruler Portugal was achieved with little bloodshed. In essence it was a dynastic struggle and Brazil continued to be ruled after independence by members of the Portuguese royal family. The Portuguese government – and navy – had taken refuge in Brazil during the Napoleonic invasion, and the new state inherited some of the naval resources and expertise. From the start Brazil supported a navy of frigate-size ships and smaller which in 1860 consisted of 7 screw sloops and 8 paddle vessels, and a sailing fleet of 1 frigate, 5 corvettes and 14 smaller barques, brigs and brigantines; in addition, 1 screw frigate, 3 sailing frigates and 4 corvettes were nearing completion.

During the extremely bloody war with Paraguay (1865-70) Brazil's fleet was greatly expanded and a number of small ironclads suitable for the river fighting were acquired from Britain and France. However, Brazil was relatively little affected by the war, and a long period of peace, prosperity – and little naval construction – under Dom Pedro II only came to an end with the military coup of 1889. Opposition to the military regime gradually increased and culminated in the naval revolt of 1893, in which the fleet in Rio de Janeiro harbour declared against the government, and was supported by rebellions in some of the provinces. After initial successes the insurgents failed to exploit their seapower and the government built up a respectable naval force. In the subsequent fighting, the most notable incident was the sinking of the rebel ironclad *Aquidaban* by the torpedo gunboat *Gustavo Sampaio*.

After the 1893-4 rebellion very few ships were added to the ageing fleet until Brazil embarked on her ambitious 1905 programme of 3 large battleships, 3 armoured cruisers, 6 destroyers, 12 torpedo boats and 3 submarines.

CAPITAL SHIPS

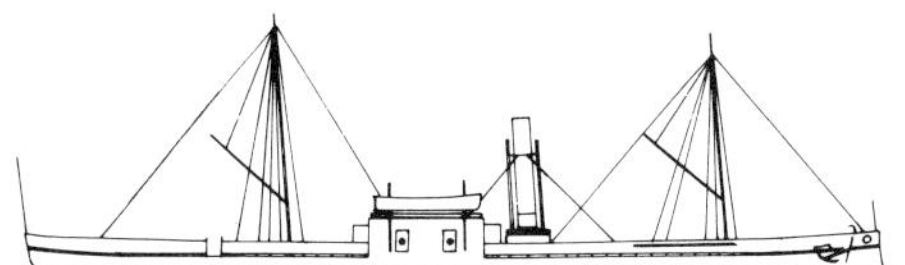
Barrozo as completed

BARROZO *coast defence battleship*

Displacement:	1354t
Dimensions:	186ft x 37ft x 8ft 10in (*56.69 x 11.28 x 2.69m*)
Machinery:	1-shaft SE, 420ihp = 9kts
Armour:	Iron. Belt and battery 3.8in-2.5in
Armament:	2-7in (2 x 1), 3-32pdr (3 x 1), 2-68pdr (2 x 1)

Name	Builder	Built	Fate
BARROZO	–	1864	Discarded *c*1885

Armoured central battery ship with a wooden hull. The armour extended over the guns and machinery amidships. The guns were 7in Whitworth MLRs, 32pdr Whitworth MLRs and 68pdr smoothbores.

The only known illustration of *Brasil*

BRASIL *coast defence battleship*

Displacement:	1518t
Dimensions:	179ft 8in x 35ft x 12ft 5in (*54.76 x 10.67 x 3.77m*)
Machinery:	1-shaft SE, 975ihp = 11.3kts
Armour:	Iron. Belt and battery 4½in-3in
Armament:	4-7in (4 x 1), 4-68pdr (4 x 1)

Name	Builder	Built	Fate
BRASIL	La Seyne	1864	BU *c*1905

Fully rigged armoured central battery ship with an iron hull. The guns were 7in Whitworth MLRs and 68pdr smoothbores and were mounted in the armoured battery. She was hulked as a floating battery in about 1890.

TAMANDARE *coast defence battleship*

Displacement:	980t
Dimensions:	166ft 3in x 36ft x 7ft 10in (*50.70 x 10.97 x 2.39m*)
Machinery:	1-shaft SE, 273ihp = 8.5kts
Armour:	Iron. Belt and battery 3.8in-2.5in
Armament:	2-5.8in (2 x 1), 2-68pdr (2 x 1)

Name	Builder	Built	Fate
TAMANDARE	–	1865	Discarded *c*1885

Wooden-hulled armoured central battery ship, the armour extending over the guns and machinery amidships. The guns were 5.8in 70pdr Whitworth MLRs and 68pdr smoothbores.

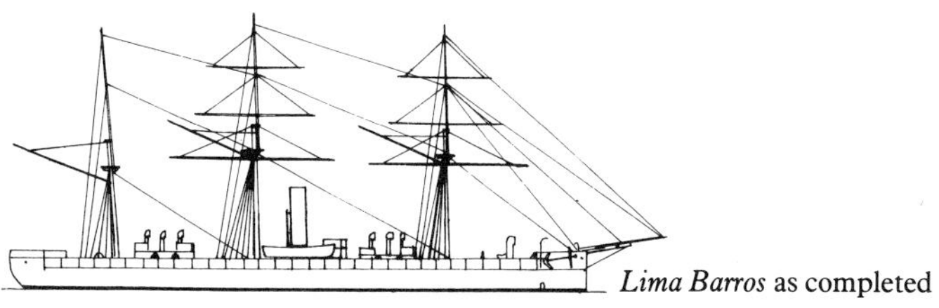
Lima Barros as completed

LIMA BARROS *coast defence battleship*

Displacement:	1330t
Dimensions:	196ft x 38ft x 15ft 7½in (*59.7 x 11.58 x 4.76m*)
Machinery:	2-shaft SE, 2100ihp = 12kts
Armour:	Iron. Belt and turret 4½in-3in
Armament:	4-7in (2 x 2)

Name	Builder	Launched	Fate
LIMA BARROS (ex-BELLONA)	Laird	21.12.1865	BU *c*1905

This iron-hulled armoured turret ship was an enlarged *Bahia* with the turrets and was originally ordered by Paraguay as *Bellona*. She was sold to Brazil and renamed *Lima Barros* in 1865. The guns were 7in Whitworth MLRs. She was hulked as a floating battery in about 1890.

RIO DE JANEIRO *coast defence battleship*

An armoured casemate ship with a 4in iron belt, SE engines and a complement of 115. Sunk by mines 2.9.1866.

BRAZIL

BAHIA *coast defence battleship*

Displacement: 1008t
Dimensions: 175ft 8in x 35ft x 10ft 3in *(53.54 x 10.67 x 3.12m)*
Machinery: 2-shaft SE, 1200ihp = 10kts. Coal 114/?t
Armour: Iron. Belt 4½in, turret 4½in
Armament: 2-7in (1 x 2), 2-2pdr (2 x 1)
Complement: 125

Name	Builder	Launched	Fate
BAHIA (ex-MINERVA)	Laird	6.10.1865	Discarded *c*1895

Iron-hulled armoured turret ship. Ordered by Paraguay as *Minerva*, but sold to Brazil and renamed *Bahia* in 1865. She had a barque rig, a ram bow and a raised forecastle and poop. There was one turret amidships and one funnel. She was fitted with bulwarks which were lowered in action. The guns were 7in Whitworth MLRs and 2pdr MLRs.

SILVADO *coast defence battleship*

Displacement: 1150t
Dimensions: 190ft x 36ft x 10ft 6in *(57.91 x 10.97 x 3.20m)*
Machinery: 2-shaft SE, 947ihp = 10.7kts
Armour: Iron. Belt and turret 4½in-3in
Armament: 4-5.8in (2 x 2)

Name	Builder	Built	Fate
SILVADO (ex-NEMESIS)	Arman	1866	Discarded *c*1885

Iron-hulled, armoured turret ship, fully rigged and with a high freeboard and two turrets. The guns were 5.8in 70pdr Whitworth MLRs. She was ordered as *Nemesis* by Paraguay, sold to Brazil and renamed *Silvado* in 1865.

MARIZ E BARROS class *coast defence battleships*

Displacement: 1196t, *Herval* 1353t
Dimensions: 191ft x 36ft x 8ft 2in (*Herval* 9ft 6in) *(58.22 x 10.97 x 2.49(2.90)m)*
Machinery: 2-shaft SE, 600 ihp = 9kts. Coal 140/?t
Armour: Iron. Belt and battery 4½in-3in
Armament: 2-7in (2 x 1) 2-68pdr (2 x 1) (*Herval* 4-7in (4 x 1)),
Complement: 125

Name	Builder	Built	Fate
MARIZ E BARROS (ex-TRITON)	Rennie	1866	Discarded *c*1890
HERVAL (ex-MEDUZA)	Rennie	1866	Discarded *c*1885

Iron-hulled, fully rigged armoured central battery ships. The guns were 7in Whitworth MLRs and 68pdr smoothbores. *Mariz e Barros* was originally ordered by Paraguay as *Triton* and *Herval* as *Meduza*, but the ships were sold to Brazil and renamed in 1865.

Herval

CABRAL class *coast defence battleships*

Displacement: 1033t
Dimensions: 160ft x 35ft 6in x 11ft 9in (*Colombo* 12ft 1in) *(48.77 x 10.82 x 3.58(3.68)m)*
Machinery: 2-shaft SE, 750ihp = 10.5kts
Armour: Iron. Belt and battery 4½in-3in
Armament: 2-5.8in (2 x 1), 2-68pdr (2 x 1) (*Colombo* 4-7in (4 x 1))

Name	Builder	Built	Fate
CABRAL	Rennie	1866	Discarded *c*1885
COLOMBO	Rennie	1866	Discarded *c*1885

Iron-hulled armoured central battery ships. The guns were 7in and 5.8in (70pdr) Whitworth MLRs and 68pdr smoothbores.

SETE DE SETEMBRO *coast defence battleship*

Displacement: 2172t
Dimensions: 220ft pp x 46ft 6in x 13ft 8in *(67.06 x 14.17 x 4.17m)*
Machinery: 2-shaft SE, 2000ihp = 10.5kts. Coal 177/263t
Armour: Iron. Belt and battery 4½in
Armament: 4-9in (4 x 1), 1-2pdr
Complement: 185

Name	Builder	Built	Fate
SETE DE SETEMBRO	Rio de Janeiro	1874	Discarded *c*1895

Wooden-hulled, armoured central battery ship. The 9in 18t Whitworth MLRs were mounted at the angles of the central battery. She had one funnel and no watertight compartments.

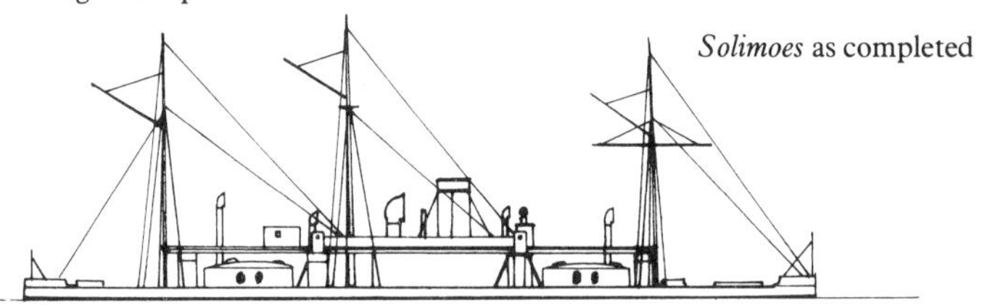
Solimoes as completed

JAVARY class *coast defence battleships*

Displacement: 3543t
Dimensions: 240ft x 57ft x 11ft 5in *(73.15 x 17.37 x 3.48m)*
Machinery: 2-shaft compound, 2200ihp = 10kts (*Solimoes* 2200ihp = 11.2kts). Coal 200/?t
Armour: Iron. Belt 12in, ends 7in, turrets 12in-11in, CT 4in
Armament: 4-10in (2 x 2), 4-1in (4 x 1), (*Solimoes* 2-2pdr (2 x 1))
Complement: 135

Name	Builder	Built	Fate
JAVARY	Le Havre	1874	Sunk 22.11.93
SOLIMOES	La Seyne	1874	?Discarded

Iron-hulled, armoured turret ships with a low freeboard, a single funnel, and two centreline turrets amidships. There was a flying deck over the turrets. The iron belt was 12in thick amidships, tapering to 7in at the ends, and it extended from 2ft 3in below to 3ft 3in above the lwl and was topped by the 3in thick upper deck. There was a complete double bottom extending up to the belt, and three light pole masts were carried. The guns were 10in 25t Whitworth MLRs.

INDEPENDENCIA

A masted turret ship ordered by Brazil but purchased by Great Britain during the Russian war scare and renamed *Neptune*. See under Great Britain for details.

RIACHUELO *battleship*

Displacement: 5610t, 6100t full load
Dimensions: 305ft pp x 52ft x 19ft 8in *(92.96 x 15.85 x 5.99in)*
Machinery: 2-shaft VC, 10 cyl boilers, 7300ihp = 16.7kts. Coal 400/800t
Armour: Compound. Belt 11in-7in, turrets 10in, CT 10in
Armament: 4-9.2in (2 x 2), 6-5.5in (6 x 1), 15-1pdr (15 x 1), 5-14in TT aw (5 x 1)
Complement: 367

Name	Builder	Launched	Fate
RIACHUELO	Samuda	7.6.1883	BU 1910

Riachuelo as originally completed
CPL

A steel-hulled, armoured turret ship completed in February 1883. She was designed with a full rig but went into service with two pole masts. She was fitted with a ram bow and two funnels set close together. The two hydraulically worked turrets were *en échelon*, projecting beyond the ship's side to give end-on fire and having a 50° arc of fire on their inboard side. The guns were 9.2in 20t Armstrong BLRs and 5.5in 70pdr Armstrong BLRs. The belt extended 250ft over the machinery and magazines. It was 7in thick below water, 11in above water over the engines and boilers and 10in elsewhere. There was a 2in steel deck over the belt, a 3in steel deck over the breastwork and a 3in protective deck fore and aft. *Riachuelo* had a complete double bottom and was sheathed in wood and yellow metal. She was rebuilt at La Seyne in 1893/95 when she was rearmed with 4-9.4in/40 BL (4 x 1) in the turrets, 6-4.7in/45 QF (6 x 1) and 6-47mm QF (6 x 1). Two large military masts were fitted but were removed in 1904, when she also received new cyl boilers.

Aquidaban as originally completed
CPL

AQUIDABAN *battleship*

Displacement: 4921t
Dimensions: 280ft x 52ft x 18ft 4in (*85.34 x 15.85 x 5.59m*)
Machinery: 2-shaft IC, 8 cyl boilers, 6500ihp = 15.8kts. Coal 300/800t
Armour: Compound. Belt 11in-7in, turrets 10in, CT 10in
Armament: 4-9.2in (2 x 2), 4 x 5.5in (4 x 1), 13-1pdr (13 x 1), 5-14in TT, 3 aw, 2 sub (5 x 1)
Complement: 277

Name	Builder	Launched	Fate
AQUIDABAN (ex-VINTE QUATRO DE MAYO, ex-AQUIDABAN)	Samuda	17.1.1885	Sunk 22.1.06

This steel-hulled armoured turret ship was laid down on 18.6.1883 and was a shorter and lighter-draught version of *Riachuelo*, with identical main armament and armour. Her appearance was similar except that she only had one funnel. After being torpedoed and sunk on 16.4.94 she was refloated in June 1894 and renamed *Vinte Quatro de Mayo* the following month. Completed in 1887, she was reconstructed by Vulcan in 1897/98 and rearmed. In 1900 she was renamed *Aquidaban*, and in 1904 was refitted, the two heavy military masts added in 1898 being removed.

MARSHAL DEODORO class *coast defence battleships*

Displacement: 3162t
Dimensions: 267ft 6in x 47ft 3in x 13ft 9in (*81.53 x 14.40 x 4.19m*)
Machinery: 2-shaft VTE, 8 Lagrafel d'Allest boilers, 3400ihp = 15kts. Coal ?/232t
Armour: Harvey. Belt 13.7in-5.9in, ends 3.9in, turrets 8.6in, casemates 2.9in, CT 4.9in
Armament: 2-9.4in/45 (2 x 1), 4-4.7in/50 (4 x 1), 6-6pdr (6 x 1), 2-18in TT sub (2 x 1)
Complement: 200

Name	Builder	Launched	Fate
MARSHAL DEODORO (ex-YPIRANGA)	La Seyne	18.6.1898	Sold to Mexico 1924
MARSHAL FLORIANO	La Seyne	6.7.1899	Discarded 1936

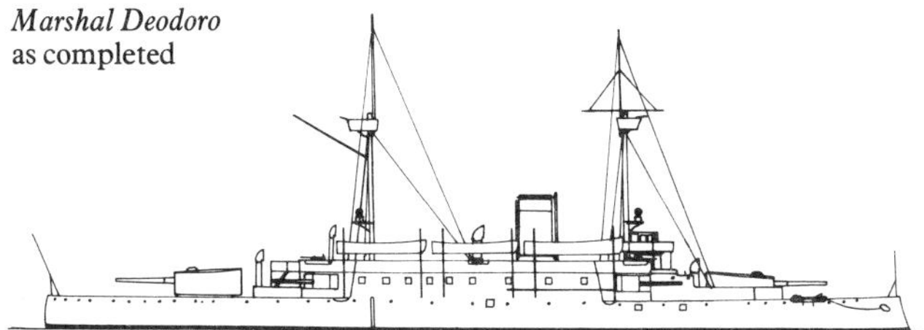

Marshal Deodoro as completed

These steel-hulled vessels had a low freeboard and a long superstructure with a single funnel. The 9.4in/45 Armstrong BLR guns were mounted in turrets at either end of the superstructure, with the 4.7in/50 Armstrong QFs at each corner. The complete 5ft 6in deep belt was 13.7in thick at the top and 5.9in at the bottom amidships, tapering to 3.9in at the ends, and there was a 1.8in sloping protective deck. *Deodoro* was laid down in 1896 and completed in 1900; *Floriano* was laid down in 1897 and completed in 1901. *Deodoro*, when sold to Mexico, was renamed *Anahuac*.

CRUISERS

NICTHEROY *wooden corvette*

Displacement: 1790t
Dimensions: 191ft 6in x 41ft 2in x 17ft 9in (*58.37 x 12.55 x 5.41m*)
Machinery: 1-shaft SET, 1000ihp = 7kts. Coal ?/170t
Armament: 12-5.8in (12x1)
Complement: 271

Name	Builder	Built	Fate
NICTHEROY	Rio de Janeiro DYd	1862	Discarded *c*1900

A wooden-hulled, fully rigged corvette with 5.8in 70pdr Whitworth MLR guns. Became a TS for midshipmen.

VITAL DE OLIVEIRA *wooden corvette*

Displacement: 1402t
Dimensions: 203ft 5in x 34ft 2in x 13ft 9in (*62.00 x 10.41 x 4.19m*)
Machinery: 1-shaft SET
Armament: 4-5.8in (4 x 1), 2-5in (2 x 1), 2 x 68pdr (2 x 1)

Name	Builder	Built	Fate
VITAL DE OLIVEIRA	?Rio de Janeiro DYd	1867	?Discarded *c*1885

Wooden-hulled, fully rigged corvette. The guns were 5.8in 70pdr Whitworth MLRs, 5in 32pdr Whitworth MLRs and 68pdr smoothbores.

Trajano

TRAJANO *wooden sloop* (launched 1873)

Displacement: 1392t
Dimensions: 200ft pp x 34ft 4in x 15ft 5in (*60.96 x 10.46 x 4.70m*)
Machinery: 1-shaft compound, 2400ihp = 11kts. Coal ?/120t
Armament: 6-5in (6 x 1)
Complement: 206

Wooden-hulled, barque-rigged sloop with one funnel built at Rio de Janeiro DYd. The guns were 5in 32pdr Whitworth MLRs. She was later classed as a second class cruiser after reconstruction 1896-6, and renamed *Tonelero*.

GUANABARA *wooden corvette*

Displacement: 1914t
Dimensions: 200ft pp x 41ft 3in x 17ft 9in *(60.96 x 12.57 x 5.41m)*
Machinery: 1-shaft SE, rectangular box boilers, 3000ihp = 13kts. Coal ?/394t
Armament: 9-5.8in (9 x 1), 2-9pdr (2 x 1), 1 spar torpedo
Complement: 287

Name	Builder	Built	Fate
GUANABARA	Rio de Janeiro DYd	1877	?Discarded *c*1905

Wooden-hulled, fully rigged corvette. She had a raised forecastle and poop and one funnel. Her guns were 5.8in 70pdr Whitworth MLRs and 9pdr MLRs. She was later reclassified as a first class cruiser and renamed *Paysandú*.

PARNAHYBA *wooden sloop* (launched 1878)

Displacement: 742t
Dimensions: 172ft 3in pp x 29ft 3in x 11ft 5in *(52.50 x 8.92 x 3.48m)*
Machinery: 1-shaft SE, 900ihp = 11.5kts. Coal ?/130t
Armament: 6-5in (6 x 1)
Complement: 149

A wooden-hulled, barque-rigged sloop with one funnel, built at Rio de Janeiro DYd. The guns were 5in 32pdr Whitworth MLRs. She was later reclassified as a second class cruiser.

PRIMEIRO DE MARCO *sloop* (launched 1881)

Displacement: 750t
Dimensions: 166ft 6in pp x 27ft 8in x 11ft 5in *(50.75 x 8.43 x 3.48m)*
Machinery: 1-shaft compound, 750ihp = 8.5kts. Coal ?/84t
Armament: 7-5in (7 x 1)
Complement: 142

Barque-rigged and with one funnel built at Rio de Janeiro DYd, this vessel was a smaller, composite version of *Trajano*. She was later reclassified as a second class cruiser. Her guns were 5in 32pdr Whitworth MLRs. She was reconstructed in 1904 as a TS and rearmed with 4-6pdr (4 x 1) and 2-1pdr (2 x 1).

Primeiro de Marco

Almirante Barrozo *(Uncredited photos: Arrigo Barilli Collection)*

ALMIRANTE BARROZO *composite corvette*

Displacement: 1928t
Dimensions: 233ft pp x 37ft 3in x 17ft 5in *(71.02 x 11.35 x 5.31m)*
Machinery: 1-shaft SE, 2200ihp = 13kts
Armament: 8-4.7in (8 x 1)
Complement: 285

Name	Builder	Built	Fate
ALMIRANTE BARROZO	Rio de Janeiro DYd	1882	Foundered 1893

A sloop-rigged corvette with one funnel and engines that could be worked either with single or with compound expansion. Six of the 4.7m 40pdr Armstrong BLR guns were mounted in sponsons on each broadside and the other two were mounted forward on the upper deck. *Barrozo* was later reclassified as a first class cruiser, and was lost on a round-the-world voyage with cadets in the Gulf of Suez.

ALMIRANTE TAMANDARE *protected cruiser*

Displacement: 4735t
Dimensions: 294ft 2in lwl x 47ft 4in x 19ft 9in *(89.66 x 14.43 x 6.02m)*
Machinery: 2-shaft HTE, 7 cyl boilers, 7500ihp = 17kts. Coal 400/750t
Armour: Steel. Casemates 3in, protective deck 1.6in, CT 2in
Armament: 10-6in (10 x 1), 2-4.7in (2 x 1), 10-3pdr (10 x 1)
Complement: 400

Name	Builder	Launched	Fate
ALMIRANTE TAMANDARE	Rio de Janeiro DYd	20.3.1890	Discarded *c*1920

Laid down in 1885 and completed in 1893, this flush-decked barque-rigged vessel had two funnels and was wood-sheathed. Four 6in Armstrong QF guns were in casemates on the upper deck and the other six were on the broadside on the main deck, as were the two 4.7in Armstrong QFs.

BENJAMIN CONSTANT *protected cruiser*

Although officially classified as a TS, this ship, with its 4-6in, 8-4.7in, 2-12pdr, 2-1pdr, 2 revolvers and 4 TT aw, had cruiser-like qualities and may be considered as such. Launched in 1892 at La Seyne, *Constant* displaced 2750t and had dimensions of 236ft 6in x 44ft 6in x 18ft 6in max *(72.09 x 13.56 x 5.64m)*. Armour was 2in deck and 3¼in CT. Her 2-shaft engines gave her a speed of around 14-15kts.

REPUBLICA *protected cruiser*

Displacement: 1300t
Dimensions: 210ft pp x 35ft x 12ft 9in mean *(64.01 x 10.67 x 3.89m)*
Machinery: 2 shafts, cyl boilers, 3800ihp = 17.4kts. Coal 100/170t
Armour: Steel. Protective deck 2in slopes, 1in flats
Armament: 6-4.7in (6 x 1), 4-6pdr (4 x 1), 3-14in TT (3 x 1)
Complement: 160

Name	Builder	Launched	Fate
REPUBLICA (ex-QUINZE DE NOVEMBRO, ex-REPUBLICA)	Armstrong	26.5.1892	Discarded *c*1920

A steel-hulled protected cruiser with a raised forecastle and poop and a tall, raked funnel. With normal draught she made 16kts on 2600ihp. She was renamed *Quinze de Novembro*, but reverted to *Republica* in 1894 and was later refitted as a minelayer. Two 4.7in Armstrong QF guns were mounted fore and aft and the other four were at the break of the poop and forecastle. There was one fixed bow TT and the other two were on the main deck amidships.

ALMIRANTE BARROZO *protected cruiser*

Displacement: 3437t
Dimensions: 330ft pp x 43ft 9in x 16ft 10¾in *(100.58 x 13.33 x 5.15m)*
Machinery: 2-shaft VTE, 4 cyl boilers, 7500ihp = 20.25kts. Coal 450/850t
Armour: Steel. Protective deck 3½in slopes, 1¼in flats, CT 4in
Armament: 6-6in (6 x 1), 4-4.7in/50 (4 x 1), 10-6pdr (10 x 1), 4-1pdr (4 x 1), 3-18in TT aw (3 x 1)
Complement: 366

Name	Builder	Launched	Fate
ALMIRANTE BARROZO	Armstrong	25.8.1896	Discarded *c*1948

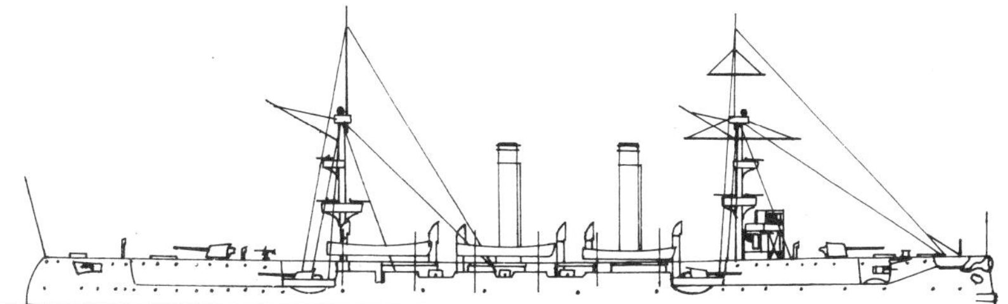

Almirante Barrozo as completed

Laid down in 1895 and completed in April 1897, *Almirante Barrozo* differed from the Chilean *Ministro Zenteno* only in having a mixed armament of 6in and 4.7in Armstrong QFs instead of eight 6in. She had two on the forecastle and poop and the others on the upper deck abreast the fore- and mainmasts, whilst the 4.7in were on the upper deck amidships. A ram bow was featured along with a fixed TT and two funnels.

Two sister ships, *Amazonas* and *Almirante Abreu*, were sold to the USA before they had been delivered to Brazil, being renamed *New Orleans* and *Albany* respectively. For further details see under USA.

TIRADENTES *torpedo gunboat* (launched 1892)

Displacement: 795t
Dimensions: 165ft pp x 30ft x 10ft 9in mean (*50.29 x 9.14 x 3.28m*)
Machinery: 2 shafts, 1646ihp = 14.5kts. Coal 50/110t
Armour: Steel. CT 1in
Armament: 4-4.7in (4 x 1), 3-6pdr (3 x 1), 2-14in TT
Complement: 110

A steel-hulled, wood-sheathed vessel with one funnel and a raised forecastle and poop. The 4.7in Armstrong QF guns were mounted fore and aft. She had a bowsprit and three pole masts. Laid down in 1891 and completed in 1893 by Armstrong; discarded *c*1920.

TORPEDO CRAFT

NOS 1-5 Yarrow 1882

Displacement: 52t, *No 1* 40t
Dimensions: 110ft (*No 1* 100ft) x 12ft 6in x 5ft 6in (*33.53 (30.48) x 3.81 x 1.68m*)
Machinery: 1-shaft compound, 1 boiler, 500ihp = 20.4kts (*No 1* 20kts)
Armament: 1-37in, 2-14in TT aw (2 x 1)

Steel-hulled first class TBs, with two funnels side by side, a ram bow, and a turtle deck forecastle with two fixed TT. Two spare Whitehead torpedoes were carried amidships. *No 1* had a shorter hull and was slower than the rest of the class. All were discarded *c*1910.

?TAMBORIN Yarrow 1884

Displacement: 16t
Dimensions: 63ft x 8ft x 3ft mean (*19.20 x 2.44 x 0.91m*)
Machinery: 1 shaft, 1 boiler, 60ihp = 18kts
Armament: 1 MG, 1 spar torpedo

Steel-hulled second class TB, with a ram bow, a funnel set well forward and a conning tower aft. Discarded *c*1901.

?SABINO VOERA Thornycroft 1884

Displacement: 12.9tons
Dimensions: 63ft pp x 7ft 6in x 3ft 3in (*19.20 x 2.29 x 0.99m*)
Machinery: 1 shaft, ?ihp = 17kts
Armament: 2-14in TT

Steel-hulled second class TB; discarded *c*1901.

ALPHA class Thornycroft 1885-6

Displacement: 3.5t
Dimensions: 45ft pp x 6ft x 1ft 2in (*13.72 x 1.83 x 0.36m*)
Machinery: 1 shaft, 1 Thornycroft locomotive boiler, ?ihp = 12.28kts
Armament: 2 MGs (2 x 1), 1 spar torpedo

Class: *Alpha, Beta, Gamma.* Steel-hulled third class TBs for river patrols. They had a ram bow, one funnel and a single high-pressure cyl engine. The McEvoy Spar torpedo was worked from the starboard side. All were probably discarded *c*1905.

ARAGUARY class Thornycroft 1890

Displacement: 110t normal
Dimensions: 150ft x 14ft 6in x 3ft 6in mean (*45.72 x 4.42 x 1.07m*)
Machinery: 1-shaft TE, 2 Thornycroft watertube boilers, 1800ihp = 25kts. Coal 12/20t
Armament: 2-3pdr (3 x 1), 3-18in TT aw (1 x 1, 1 x 2)
Complement: 27

Class: *Araguary, Bento Gonzalves,* (ex-*Marulio Dias*), *Iguatemi.* These first class TBs had a steel hull, three masts and two funnels placed fore and aft. There were 12 watertight compartments. One 3pdr Nordenfeld QF gun was on the CT forward, the other being mounted aft. There was one fixed bow TT and two trainable tubes aft. The class were almost identical to the Argentinian *Commodoro Py* class. Discarded 1910-15.

PANNE class Schichau 1892-3

Displacement: 130t
Dimensions: 152ft x 17ft 3in x 7ft 9in (*46.33 x 5.26 x 2.36m*)
Machinery: 2 shafts, loco boilers, 2200ihp = 26kts. Coal ?/30t
Armament: 2-1pdr (2 x 1), 3-14in TT aw (3 x 1)
Complement: 24

Class: *Panne, Pedro Affonso, Pedro Ivo, Pernambuco, Silvado.* Steel-hulled first class TBs, with the well-spaced funnels, a turtledeck forecastle, one TT fixed and three masts. These were stock boats purchased by Brazil in 1893. All were discarded 1910-15.

PIRATINY Ericsson *c*1879

Displacement: ?
Dimensions: 130ft x 17ft (*39.62 x 5.18m*)
Machinery: ?ihp = 10kts
Armour: Iron. Breastwork 16in
Armament: 2-1pdr (2 x 1), 1 Howell TT

An armoured coast defence torpedo boat built as a speculation and named *Destroyer*, this vessel was purchased by Brazil and renamed *Piratiny* in October 1891. She had an inclined breastwork across the deck to deflect projectiles, and was intended to have her freeboard reduced by flooding to make her less vulnerable in action. Her main armament was the unsuccessful Howell flywheel torpedo. She was of little practical use, and was discarded *c*1901.

POTY Herreshoff ?date

Displacement: 30t
Dimensions: 126ft x 12ft x 3ft (*38.40 x 3.66 x 0.91m*)
Machinery: ?ihp = 18kts
Armament: 1-1pdr, 1 Howell TT

Built as the yacht *Javelin* and bought by Brazil and renamed *Poty* in 1893. She was fitted with the unsuccessful Howell flywheel torpedo. Discarded *c*1900.

GUSTAVO SAMPAIO *torpedo gunboat* (launched 1893)

Displacement: 480t
Dimensions: 196ft 9in pp x 20ft x 8ft 6in mean (*59.97 x 6.10 x 2.59m*)
Machinery: 2 shafts, 2000ihp = 18kts. Coal ?/150t
Armour: Steel. CT ¾in
Armament: 2-4in (2 x 1), 4-3pdr (4 x 1), 3-14in TT aw
Complement: 60

Completed in October 1893, this steel-hulled vessel had a raised forecastle, one funnel and two masts. The 4in 20pdr QF were mounted fore and aft and there was a fixed bow TT and two trainable tubes, one on each side abaft the break of the forecastle. She was wood-sheathed. Built by Armstrong as the stock ship *Aurora,* she was renamed *Gustavo Sampaio* on purchase by Brazil on 8.10.1893. Discarded *c*1920.

MOXOTO Yarrow 1893

Displacement: 16.5t
Dimensions: 60ft x 9ft 3in x 3ft 8in (*18.29 x 2.82 x 1.2m*)
Machinery: 230ihp = 16kts
Armament: 2-1pdr (2 x 1), 1 Howell TT

A steel-hulled third class TB purchased by Brazil in 1893. She had a Howell flywheel TT.

TUPY class *torpedo gunboats* (launched 1893)

Displacement: 1014t
Dimensions: 249ft 6in x 30ft 9in x 10ft 3in (*76.05 x 9.37 x 3.12m*)
Machinery: 2-shaft TE, cyl boilers, 7000ihp = 22.5kts. Coal 100/250t
Armour: Steel. Deck ½in, shields 4½in, CT 1in
Armament: 2-4.1in (2 x 1), 6-6pdr (6 x 1), 2-1pdr (2 x 1), 3-14in TT aw
Complement: 110

Class: *Tupy*, *Timbria*. Steel-hulled. They had a raised forecastle and a cut-away quarterdeck, and two well-spaced funnels and masts. The 4.1in QF guns were mounted fore and aft and there was a fixed bow TT and two trainable tubes amidships. There was a prominent cowl between the funnels. Both vessels were completed in 1897. They were built by Germania and were discarded *c*1920.

INHANDUAY City Island, New York 1893

Displacement: 17t
Dimensions: 63ft 5in x 9ft 10in x 3ft mean (*19.33 x 3.00 x 0.91in*)
Machinery: ?ihp = 23kts
Armament: 1-1pdr, 1 Howell TT

Originally the yacht *Feiseen*, this vessel was sold to Brazil on 18.11.93 and renamed *Inhanduay*. She had a Howell flywheel TT.

TAMAYO *torpedo gunboat* (launched 1898)

Displacement: 1063t
Dimensions: 269ft x 28ft 9in x 9ft 9in (*81.99 x 8.76 x 2.97m*)
Machinery: 2-shaft TE, cyl boilers, 6500ihp = 23kts. Coal 100/293t
Armour: Steel. Deck ½in, shields 4½in, CT 1in
Armament: 2-4.1in (2 x 1), 6-6pdr (6 x 1), 2-1pdr (2 x 1), 3-14in TT
Complement: 110

A steel-hulled, modified *Tupy* class boat with a different hull form giving ½kt extra speed on 500ihp less power. She could be distinguished from the *Tupys* by the prominent tops on both masts. Built by Germania and completed 1900. Discarded *c*1920.

Chile

It was in the fight for Chilean independence that the brilliant British naval officer Lord Cochrane performed some of his most outstanding feats, so it is singularly fitting that Chile should have developed the best trained and most vigorously employed navy in South America. Nevertheless, following a long period of peace, the fleet consisted of only 1 steamer of 20 guns, an 18-gun corvette, 2 brigs and a schooner in 1860. However, in 1865 Chile supported Peru in an ill-advised war with Spain, and the bombardment of Valparaiso by a Spanish squadron persuaded Chile of the need for a sizable navy to protect her long coastline. Under the firm government of President Errazuriz, the navy was reorganised and expanded and was well prepared in 1879 when war broke out with Peru over disputed northern territories.

This predominantly maritime conflict was closely observed and analysed by the major navies interested in the new technology being used in action for the first time. In her use of blockade and amphibious operations Chile demonstrated the classic virtues of sea-power, but it was a series of small but spectacular ship-to-ship engagements, including the destruction of the *Independencia* and the capture of the *Huascar*, that caught the public imagination. The war ended in total victory for Chile, but was followed by a period of unrest under the dictatorial President Balmaceda which culminated in the 1891 revolution. Most of the navy supported the anti-government party but one vessel which did not was the torpedo gunboat *Almirante Lynch* which sank the *Blanco Encalada* – the first successful use of the self-propelled torpedo against an armoured ship. However, this had no effect on the progress of the rebellion, and the navy leader Admiral Montt eventually became president. Under his government the navy was reorganised but not substantially enlarged until the border dispute with Argentina in the late 1890s. On the amicable settlement of this issue, the two most powerful ships under construction, the battleships *Constitucion* and *Libertad* were sold to the Royal Navy.

CAPITAL SHIPS

ALMIRANTE COCHRANE class *central battery ships*

Displacement: 3370t, 3560t full load
Dimensions: 210ft pp x 45ft 9in x 21ft 10in max (*64.01 x 13.94 x 6.65m*)
Machinery: 2-shaft compound HT, 6 cyl boilers, 2920ihp = 12.75kts. Coal ?/500t
Armour: Iron. Belt 9in, ends 6in-4½in, battery 8in-6in, CT 3in
Armament: 6-9in (6 x 1), 1-4.7in, 1-9pdr, 1-7pdr
Complement: 300

Name	Builder	Launched	Fate
ALMIRANTE COCHRANE	Earle	25.1.1874	Scrapped *c*1935
VALPARAISO	Earle	1875	Sunk 23.4.91

Iron-hulled, barque-rigged ships with fighting tops on the main- and foremasts. They had a ram bow and one funnel. The complete belt was 9in thick at the lwl amidships, with a 6in strake above and below, reducing to 4½in at the ends. The lower strake of the battery armour was 8in-7in thick with a 6in strake above it. There was ½in plating on the upper and main decks. The battery amidships overhung the ships' sides, which were recessed fore and aft. There was a double bottom under the magazines, engine and boiler rooms, and the hull was sheathed in wood and zinc. *Almirante Cochrane* was rebuilt by Earle in 1889 and rearmed with 6-8in 13½ton Armstrong BLRs in place of the 9in 12ton Armstrong MLRs, and 3-6pdr Hotchkiss QF, 6-37mm Hotchkiss and 3-14in TT, one either side of the bow and one at the stern. *Valaparaiso* was rebuilt by Armstrong in 1885-86 and received 6-8in BLR, 4-14pdr BLR, 3-6pdr QF and 2-14in bow TT. *Cochrane* was also given new cyl boilers and horizontal TE engines, giving 13.6kts on 4300ihp. *Valparaiso* was renamed *Blanco Encalada* about 1890 and was torpedoed and sunk in 1891. *Cochrane* was rebuilt as a gunnery TS between

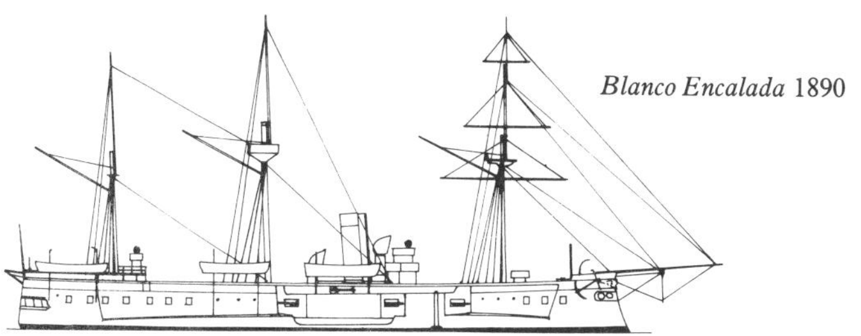
Blanco Encalada 1890

1897 and 1900 when her existing armament was removed as well as her fore- and mizzenmasts. Her subsequent armament varied, but in 1919 she had 4-4.7in, 2-12pdr and 4-3pdr guns. She was hulked by 1908. The ships were designed by Sir Edward Reed; both were laid down in 1873, *Cochrane* completing in December 1874 and *Valparaiso* the following year.

HUASCAR *armoured turret ship*

The Peruvian 2030t *Huascar* was captured by Chile in a badly damaged condition on 8.10.79. She was rebuilt and rearmed with 2-8in Armstrong BLR (1 x 2) in the turret, 2-4.7in 40pdr BLR (2 x 1), 2-6pdr Hotchkiss QF (2 x 1) and 3-37mm Hotchkiss revolving cannon. She was later fitted as a gunnery training ship and was then preserved as a museum. For full details see under Peru.

CAPITAN PRAT *battleship*

Displacement: 6901t
Dimensions: 328ft pp x 60ft 8in x 22ft 10in *(99.97 x 18.49 x 6.96m)*
Machinery: 2-shaft HTE, 5 cyl boilers, 12,000ihp = 18.3kts. Coal 400/1100t
Armour: Creusot steel. Belt 11.8in-7.8in, ends 5.9in-3.9in, citadel 3.1in, barbettes 10.8in-8in, hoods 2in, CT 10½in
Armament: 4-9.4in/35 (4 x 1), 8-4.7in/45 (4 x 2), 6-6pdr (6 x 1), 4-3pdr (4 x 1), 10-1pdr (10 x 1), 4-18in TT aw (4 x 1)
Complement: 480

Name	Builder	Launched	Fate
CAPITAN PRAT	La Seyne	20.12.1890	Discarded *c*1935

Steel-hulled high freeboard battleship. She was wood and copper sheathed and had a ram bow, two masts with military tops and two funnels. The complete belt extended 2ft 4in above lwl and 4ft 7in below. Above lwl amidships it was 11.8in thick, tapering to 4.9in forward and 5.9in aft; below lwl it reduced to 7.8in, tapering to 3.9in at the ends. The citadel amidships protected the engine and boiler rooms and extended to the upper deck, and was closed by 3.1in bulkheads. There was a 2in deck on the belt outside the citadel. The 9.4in electrically-worked turrets were arranged in the French 'lozenge' fashion, with the forward turret very near the bow. The twin 4.7in QF turrets were abreast the masts. There were fixed bow and stern TT; the other two were on the broadside amidships. *Capitan Prat* was reconstructed in 1909/10, when 12 new Babcock watertube boilers were fitted and the funnels raised. The speed was increased to 19.5kts. In 1931 she was being used as a temporary submarine depot ship.

Capitan Prat after the funnels had been raised

CONSTITUCION class *battleships*

The two 11,800t battleships *Constitucion* and *Libertad* were ordered by Chile in late 1901, and were designed by Sir Edward Reed. They were purchased by Great Britain on 3.12.1903 before they had been delivered, *Constitucion* being renamed *Swiftsure* and *Libertad* becoming *Triumph*. For full details see under Great Britain.

CRUISERS

ABTAO *composite corvette*

Displacement: 1600t
Dimensions: 227ft 4in x 29ft 6in x 16ft 10in max *(69.29 x 8.99 x 5.13m)*
Machinery: 1-shaft SE, 800ihp = 10kts. Coal ?/300t
Armament: 1-5.8in, 4-4.7in (4 x 1)
Complement: 130

Name	Builder	Built	Fate
ABTAO	Glasgow	1865	?Discarded *c*1900

Barque-rigged, with a clipper bow and one funnel set well aft. The guns were 5.8in 70pdr and 4.7in 40pdr BLRs.

ARTURO PRAT *unprotected cruiser*

This 1380t cruiser was ordered by Chile but was sold to Japan without having sailed for South America. Renamed *Tsukushi* by the Japanese, she was identical to the Chinese *Chao Yung* class, and was designed by George Rendel. See under Japan.

Esmeralda when new
CPL

ESMERALDA *protected cruiser*

Displacement: 2950t
Dimensions: 270ft pp x 42ft x 18ft 6in mean *(82.30 x 12.80 x 5.64m)*
Machinery: 2-shaft HC, 4 cyl boilers, 6803ihp = 18.3kts. Coal 400/600t
Armour: Steel. Protective deck 2in-½in, shields 2in-1½in, CT 2in
Armament: 2-10in/30 (2 x 1), 6-6in/26 (6 x 1), 2-6pdr (2 x 1), 3-14in TT aw (3 x 1)
Complement: 296

Name	Builder	Launched	Fate
ESMERALDA	Armstrong	6.6.1883	Sold to Japan 15.11.1894

A steel-hulled cruiser with a ram bow, two funnels and two masts, *Esmeralda* was designed by George Rendel. Her freeboard was only about 11ft, and she was flush-decked. There was no double bottom. The full length protective deck was 2in over the magazines, 1in over the engine and boiler rooms and ½in at the ends. The 10in/30 25t Armstrong guns were mounted in barbettes fore and aft, whilst the 6in/26 4t Armstrong BLRs were in sponsons amidships.

Sold to Japan via Ecuador, she was renamed *Idzumi* by the Japanese. See also under Japan.

PRESIDENTE ERRAZURIZ class *protected cruisers*

Displacement: 2047t
Dimensions: 268ft 4in pp x 35ft 9in x 14ft 5in mean *(81.79 x 70.90 x 4.39m)*
Machinery: 2-shaft HTE, 4 cyl boilers, 5400ihp = 18.35kts. Coal 200/400t
Armour: Steel. Protective deck 2.4in-1.4in slopes, 1.4in-1in flats, shields 3½in, CT 2in
Armament: 4-5.9in/36 (4 x 1), 2-4.7in/36 (2 x 1), 4-6pdr (4 x 1), 3-14in TT aw (3 x 1)
Complement: 170

CHILE

Presidente Pinto
CPL

Name	Builder	Launched	Fate
PRESIDENTE ERRAZURIZ	La Seyne	21.6.1890	Discarded *c*1920
PRESIDENTE PINTO	La Seyne	4.9.1890	Discarded *c*1910

Laid down in 1889 and completed in 1892, these steel hulled vessels had a ram bow, one funnel and two masts. The wood- and copper-sheathed hull had a raised forecastle and poop. There was a full length protective deck. The 5.9in/36 Canet QF guns were mounted in sponsors at the break of the forecastle and poop, and the 4.7in/36 Canet QFs were mounted fore and aft. With normal draught they made 17kts on 3550ihp. *Presidente Errazuriz* was refitted in 1908 when Belleville watertube boilers were installed; the fighting tops were removed from the masts and she was rearmed with 4-6in/45 QF (4 x 1) and 2-4.7in/45 QF (2 x 1).

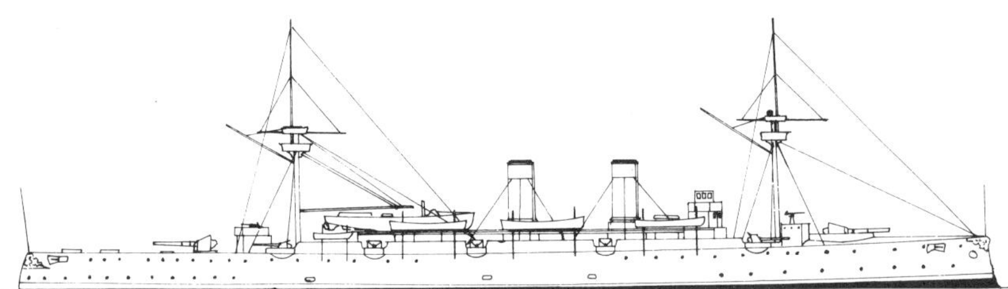

Blanco Encalada as completed

BLANCO ENCALADA *protected cruisers*

Displacement: 4568t
Dimensions: 370ft pp x 46ft 6in x 18ft 6in (*112.78 x 14.17 x 5.64m*)
Machinery: 2-shaft TE, cyl boilers, 14,600ihp = 22.8kts. Coal 350/866t
Armour: Steel. Protective deck 4in-3in slopes, 1¾in flats, shields 6in-2in, CT 6in
Armament: 2-8in/40 (2 x 1), 10-6in/40 (10 x 1), 12-3pdr (12 x 1), 12-1pdr (12 x 1), 5-18in TT aw
Complement: 427

Name	Builder	Launched	Fate
BLANCO ENCALADA	Armstrong	9.9.1893	Discarded 1946

A steel-hulled flush-deck vessel having a ram bow, two funnels and two masts, with the foremast well before the bridge. There was a complete protective deck, 4in thick on the slopes amidships reducing to 3in at the ends. The 8in/40 Armstrong QF guns were mounted fore and aft, and the 6in/40 Armstrong QFs were in sponsons amidships. There was a fixed bow TT and the remaining tubes were on the broadside. With normal draught she made 21.7kts on 9500ihp. She was refitted at Talcahuano in 1920 and became a sea-going TS and was later hulked. She was designed by Philip Watts, laid down in August 1892 and completed in April 1894.

Esmeralda about 1890

Ministro Zenteno as completed

MINISTRO ZENTENO *protected cruiser*

Displacement: 3437t
Dimensions: 330ft pp x 43ft 9in x 16ft 10¼in (*100.58 x 13.33 x 5.14m*)
Machinery: 2-shaft VTE, cyl boilers, 7500ihp = 20.25kts. Coal 400/850t
Armour: Steel. Protective deck 3½in slopes, 1¼in flats, CT 4in
Armament: 8-6in/40 (8 x 1), 10-6pdr (10 x 1), 4-1pdr (4 x 1), 3-18in TT aw
Complement: 317

Name	Builder	Launched	Fate
MINISTRO ZENTENO	Armstrong	1.2.1896	Discarded 1931

This vessel differed from the Brazilian *Almirante Barrozo* class only by having a uniform armament of 6in guns instead of mixed 6in and 4.7in. She had a ram bow, two masts and two funnels. Two 6in/40 Armstrong QF guns were mounted on the forecastle deck fore and aft, and the others were mounted on the upper deck amidships. There was a full length protective deck and a fixed bow TT, the other two TTs being mounted on the broadside aft. She was designed by Philip Watts.

ESMERALDA *armoured cruiser*

Displacement: 7000t
Dimensions: 436ft pp x 53ft 2in x 20ft 3in mean (*132.89 x 16.21 x 6.17m*)
Machinery: 2-shaft VTE, cyl boilers, 16,000ihp = 22.25kts. Coal 550/1300t
Armour: Harvey. Belt 6in, protective deck 2in-1½in slopes, 2in-1½in flats, shields 4½in, CT 8in
Armament: 2-8in/40 (2 x 1), 16-6in (16 x 1), 8-12pdr (8 x 1), 3-18in TT, 1 aw, 2 sub
Complement: 500

Name	Builder	Launched	Fate
ESMERALDA	Armstrong	14.4.1894	Discarded 1929

Steel-hulled, wood- and copper-sheathed armoured cruiser. She had a flush deck hull, with a ram bow, two funnels set well apart and two masts. The foremast was in front of the bridge. The 328ft belt extended 2ft above and 5ft below lwl, and was closed by 6in bulkheads. There was a complete protective deck, 1in behind the belt and 2in at the ends. The 8in/40 Armstrong QF were

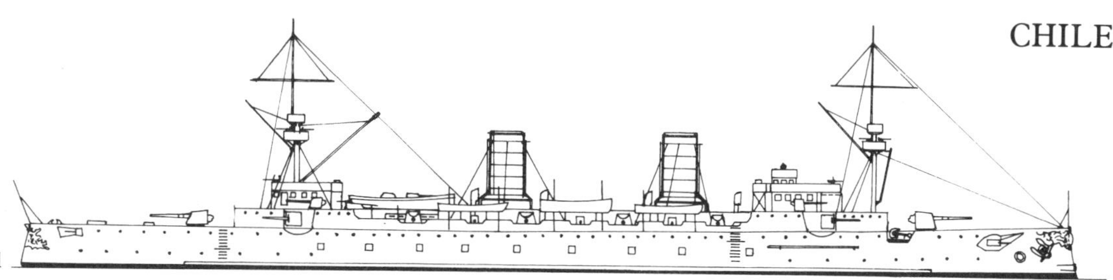

Esmeralda as completed

mounted fore and aft, and ten 6in/40 Armstrong QFs were also mounted on the forecastle deck, the rest being carried on the superstructure. There was one fixed stern TT and two on the broadside. The full power trials were run with normal draught; forced draught gave 18,000ihp. Laid down on 4.7.1895 and completed on 4.9.1896, *Esmeralda* was refitted in 1910, and the four superstructure 6in were removed at about this time. She was designed by Philip Watts.

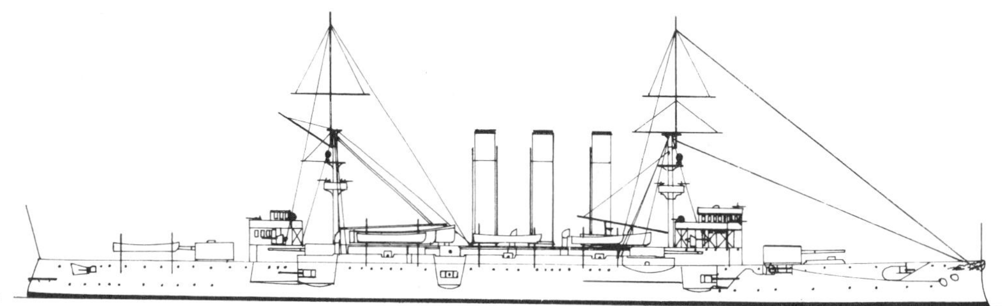

O'Higgins as completed

O'HIGGINS *armoured cruiser*

Displacement: 8500t
Dimensions: 412ft x 62ft 9in x 22ft (*125.5 x 19.1 x 6.7m*)
Machinery: 2-shaft VTE, 30 Belleville watertube boilers, 16,250ihp = 21.6kts. Coal 550/1200t
Armour: Harvey nickel. Belt 7in-5in, protective deck 3in-1½in slopes, 2in-1½in flats, main turrets 7in-5in, secondary turrets and casemates 6in-5in, CT 9in
Armament: 4-8in/45 (4 x 1), 10-6in/40 (10 x 1), 4-4.7in/45 (4 x 1), 10-12pdr (10 x 1), 10-6pdr (10 x 1), 3-18in TT, 1 aw, 2 sub
Complement: 500

Name	Builder	Launched	Fate
O'HIGGINS	Armstrong	17.5.1897	Discarded 1946

A steel-hulled, wood- and copper-sheathed vessel, flush-decked and with a ram bow, three funnels and two masts. The belt was 260ft long and 7ft deep, and was 7in thick over the engine and boiler rooms and 6in fore and aft. There was a complete protective deck, 1½in thick behind the belt and 3in-2in thick at the ends. Two of the 8in/45 Armstrong QF turrets were mounted fore and aft, the other two abreast the forefunnel. The 6in/40 Armstrong QF were in casemates on the main deck alongside the fore and aft bridges and amidships, and in turrets mounted over the midships and aft casemates. There was one fixed stern TT and two on the broadside. *O'Higgins* was designed by Philip Watts, laid down on 4.4.1896 and completed on 2.4.1898.

CHACABUCO *protected cruiser*

Displacement: 4160t
Dimensions: 360ft pp x 46ft 6in x 17ft mean (*109.73 x 14.17 x 5.18m*)
Machinery: 2-shaft VTE, cyl boilers, 15,700ihp = 23kts. Coal 350/1000t
Armour: Harvey nickel. Protective deck 4½in slopes, 1¾in flats, main shields 4½in, secondary shields 2½in, CT 3in
Armament: 2-8in/45 (2 x 1), 10-4.7in/40 (10 x 1), 12-12pdr (12 x 1), 6-3pdr (6 x 1), 3-18in TT aw (3 x 1)
Complement: 400

Name	Builder	Launched	Fate
CHACABUCO	Armstrong	4.7.1898	Discarded 1952

A stock ship purchased by Chile in 1902, the year of her completion, and identical to the Japanese *Takasago*, *Chacabuco* was designed by Watts and laid down on 14.8.1896. She had a ram bow, two masts and two funnels, and a complete protective deck. The 8in/45 Armstrong QF were mounted on the forecastle and poop, and the 4.7in/40 Armstrong QF were on the upper deck amidships. She made 21.5kts on 10,300ihp with natural draught. She was refitted in 1941 and rearmed with 6-6in/50 (6 x 1) and 10-20mm AA (10 x 1). She was given funnel caps and a new, enlarged bridge.

CHACABUCO *wooden screw corvette* (launched 1866)

Displacement: 1101t
Dimensions: 218ft 6in pp x 33ft 4in x 17ft 4in (*66.62 x 10.18 x 5.30m*)
Machinery: 1 shaft, 1200ihp = 10kts. Coal 400t
Armament: 3-8.2in, 2-70pdr, 4-40pdr

The guns were all Armstrong BL. Survived as a coal hulk until after 1900.

Chacabuco shortly after commissioning

MAGALLANES *composite gunboat* (launched 1872)

Displacement: 950t
Dimensions: 196ft 9in x 29ft 10in x 11ft 6in max (*59.89 x 9.09 x 3.51m*)
Machinery: 2 shafts, 1040ihp = 11kts. Coal ?/300t
Armament: 1-7in, 1-64pdr, 2-4in (2 x 1)
Complement: 143

A barque-rigged boat with one funnel, built by Green on the Thames. The guns were a 7in Armstrong MLR, a 64pdr Armstrong MLR and two 4in 20pdr Armstrong MLRs. Completed in 1874. Discarded *c*1900

PILCOMAYO *wooden gunboat* (launched 1874)

Displacement: 800t
Dimensions: 181ft 9in x 24ft 6in x 11ft 6in max (*55.40 x 7.47 x 3.51m*)
Machinery: 1 shaft, 1080ihp = 11kts
Armament: 2-5.8in (2 x 1), 2 x 4in (2 x 1)
Complement: 130

A barque-rigged boat with one funnel built on the Thames, armed with 5.8in 70pdr Armstrong BLRs and 4in Armstrong 20pdr BLRs. By 1890 she was a boys' TS and was discarded *c*1910.

Pilcomayo
CPL

TORPEDO CRAFT

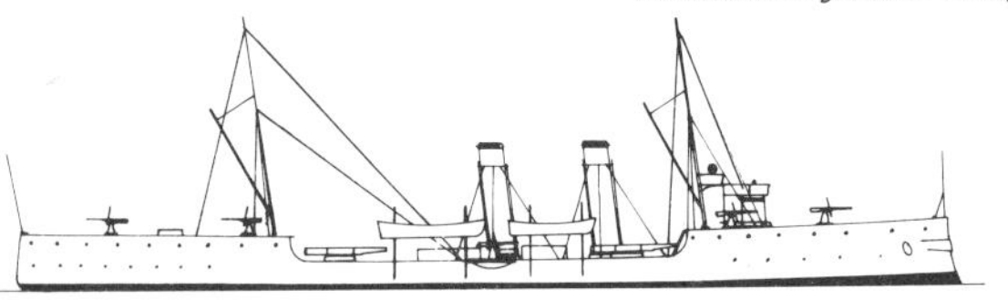
Almirante Lynch as completed

ALMIRANTE LYNCH class *torpedo gunboats* (launched 1890)

Displacement: 713t
Dimensions: 230ft pp x 27ft 6in x 8ft 3¾in (*70.10 x 8.38 x 2.53m*)
Machinery: 2-shaft TE, 4 locomotive boilers, 4532ihp = 20.3kts (*Almirante Condell* 4275ihp = 20.65kts). Coal 100/150t
Armour: Steel. Plating 1in, CT 1in
Armament: 3-3in (3 x 1), 4-3pdr (4 x 1), 5-14in TT aw (5 x 1)
Complement: 87

Class (builder, fate): *Almirante Lynch, Almirante Condell* (both Laird, both discarded *c*1920). Laid down in 1889 and completed the following year, these were steel-hulled boats with a ram bow, raised forecastle and poop, and two raked masts and funnels. There was 1in steel plating over the engine and boiler rooms. Two 3in 14pdr Hotchkiss QFs were mounted *en échelon* on the forecastle and the other one on the poop. They had one fixed bow TT and two trainable tubes on each broadside amidships. Both were reconstructed in 1900 and fitted with Belleville watertube boilers. The 3in and 4pdr guns were replaced by 6-6pdr/50s. *Lynch* was renamed *Tomé* and *Condell* became *Alcahuano* in about 1910.

ALMIRANTE SIMPSON *torpedo gunboat* (launched 1896)

Displacement: 800t
Dimensions: 240ft x 27ft 6in x 14ft max (*73.15 x 8.38 x 4.27m*)
Machinery: 2-shaft TE, 4 Normand watertube boilers, 4500ihp = 21.5kts. Coal 100/?t
Armour: Steel. Plating 1in, CT 1in
Armament: 2-4.7in (2 x 1), 4-3pdr (4 x 1), 3-18in TT aw (3 x 1)

This steel-hulled torpedo gunboat was laid down in 1895 by Laird and completed in 1896. She had a ram bow, a raised forecastle and poop, two masts and two funnels set very close together. There was 1in steel plating over the engine and boiler rooms. The 4.7in Armstrong QF guns were mounted on the forecastle and poop. One 18in TT was fixed in the bow, one was in a trainable mounting ahead of the funnels to starboard, and the third in a trainable mounting abaft the funnels to port. She was sold to Ecuador in 1907 and renamed *Libertador Bolivar*.

COLOCOLO class Yarrow 1880

Displacement: 5t
Dimensions: 48ft x 8ft (*14.63 x 2.44m*)
Machinery: 1 shaft, 60ihp = 12kts
Armament: 2 MGs (2 x 1), 2-14in TT aw (2 x 1)

Steel-hulled third class TBs. The class comprised two vessels, *Colocolo* and *Tucapel*; both were discarded about 1915.

GLAURA class Yarrow 1880-1

Displacement: 35t
Dimensions: 100ft x 12ft 6in x 6ft 9in mean (*30.48 x 3.81 x 2.06m*)
Machinery: 1 shaft, 400ihp = 18-19kts. Coal 9/?t
Armament: 1 MG, 2 spar torpedoes
Complement: 15

Class: *Glaura, Guale, Janequeo, Rucamilla, Teguelda, Janequeo (2)*. Steel-hulled boats with two funnels and one outrigger for the spar torpedoes. *Janequeo* was sunk on 25.5.1880, and the rest were discarded *c*1915. Although the first *Janequeo* was salvaged she was not returned to service but was replaced by an identical vessel of the same name.

FRESIA class Yarrow 1880-1

Displacement: 25t
Dimensions: 86ft x 12ft 6in x 5ft mean (*26.21 x 3.81 x 1.52m*)
Machinery: 1 shaft, 400ihp = 19-20kts
Armament: 1 MG, 2 spar torpedoes
Complement: 15

Steel-hulled second class TBs, with a ram bow and two funnels. The class comprised *Fresia*, *Lauca* and *Quidora*; all served until about 1915.

Third class torpedo boat White

Displacement: –
Dimensions: 50ft x 8ft 8in (*15.24 x 2.64m*)
Machinery: 1 shaft, ?ihp = 15kts
Armament: 1 spar torpedo

Built by J S White about 1880.

GUACOLDA *spar torpedo boat*

This 59ft spar torpedo boat was built as the Peruvian *Republica* class boat *Allay*, and was captured in December 1879 by Chile and renamed. In 1881 she was wrecked on the Chilean coast. See under Peru for details.

SARGENTE ALDEA Yarrow 1886

Displacement: 80t
Dimensions: 125ft x 13ft x 7ft max (*38.10 x 3.96 x 2.13m*)
Machinery: 1 shaft, 700ihp = 20kts. Coal 12/20t
Armament: 2-1in (2 x 1), 2-14in TT aw
Complement: 16

Steel-hulled first class TB, with a turtledeck forecastle and two funnels. The guns were 1in Nordenfeld 2-barrelled MGs. Discarded *c*1905.

NOS 7-9 Thornycroft 1891

Displacement: 110t
Dimensions: 150ft x 14ft 6in x 3ft 6in max (*45.72 x 4.42 x 1.07m*)
Machinery: 1 shaft, Thornycroft watertube boilers, 1800ihp = 25kts
Armament: 2-3pdr, 3-18in TT aw (3 x 1)

Steel-hulled first class TBs, with three masts and two centreline funnels. One 3pdr Nordenfeld QF was mounted on the CT and the other was mounted aft. There was one fixed bow TT and two trainable tubes aft. They were identical (except for the gun armament) with the Argentinian *Commodoro Py* class. They were discarded *c*1905.

Second class torpedo boat White

Displacement: 15t
Dimensions: 60ft x 9ft 6in x 5ft mean (*18.29 x 2.90 x 1.52m*)
Machinery: 1 shaft, 270ihp = 19kts
Armament: 1-3pdr, 1-14in TT aw

This boat, built by J S White about 1890, served until about 1915.

INJENIERO HYATT class Yarrow 1896-8

Displacement: 140t
Dimensions: 152ft 6in x 15ft 3in x 7ft 9in max (*46.48 x 4.65 x 2.36m*)
Machinery: 1 shaft, 2200ihp = 26.5-27.5kts. Coal ?/40t
Armament: 3-3pdr (3 x 1), 3-14in TT aw
Complement: 28

This class of first class TBs was made up of six vessels: *Injeniero Hyatt*, *Cirujano Vidella*, *Injeniero Mutilla*, *Guardia-Marina Contreras*, *Teniente Rodriguez* and *Capitan Thompson*. All were in service until about 1920. They had two funnels. *Injeniero Hyatt* and *Cirujano Vidella* were sailed across the Atlantic but the remaining four were shipped in pieces to Chile and reassembled at Balcachuamo.

Capitan Merino Jarda (Uncredited photos: Arrigo Barilli Collection)

CAPITAN ORELLA class Laird 1896

Displacement: 300t
Dimensions: 213ft pp x 21ft 6in x 5ft 10½in trials (*64.92 x 6.55 x 1.79m*)
Machinery: 2-shaft TE, Normand boilers, 6250ihp = 30kts. Coal ?/90t
Armament: 1-3in, 5-6pdr (5 x 1), 2-18in TT aw (2 x 1)
Complement: 65

Class: *Capitan Orella, Capitan Munez Gamero, Teniente Serrano, Guardia-Marina Riquelme.* Steel-hulled TBDs, with a turtleback forecastle and four equally-spaced raked funnels. The 3in 12pdr QF was mounted forward, and the 18in TT were on trainable centreline mountings amidships and aft. On trials the vessels achieved between 30.1 and 30.42kts on 6313-6398ihp. All were discarded *c*1930.

CAPITAN MERINO JARPA class Laird 1901

Displacement: 321t
Dimensions: 215ft pp x 21ft 3in x 5ft 11in trials (*65.53 x 6.48 x 1.80m*)
Machinery: 2-shaft TE, Normand boilers, 6250ihp = 30kts
Armament: 1-3in, 5-6pdr (5 x 1), 2-18in TT aw (2 x 1)
Complement: 65

Class: *Capitan Merino Jarpa, Capitan O'Brien.* These steel-hulled TBDs were improved versions of the *Capitan Orella* class without the bow TT and with slightly taller funnels. On trials *Capitan Merino Jarpa* made 29.29kts on 6017ihp and *Capitan o'Brien* 30.16kts on 6310ihp. They were discarded *c*1930.

Minor Navies

BELGIUM

During this period Belgium, although possessing a naval organisation, had no sea-going warships. In 1860 the Government owned the 12-gun brig *Duc de Brabant* and the 12-gun schooner *Louise Marie*. However the naval service also operated Government packets (19 mail vessels by 1900) and the fishery protection and training ship *Ville d'Anvers* built at Antwerp in 1865 (684t, 214ft x 30ft, *65.22 x 9.14m*). There were also several river gunboats in the Congo and one on the Nile.

BULGARIA

Bulgaria became independent from Turkey in 1878, though the sultan was a very nominal suzerain for another 30 years. The population was about 4,000,000 in 1905 but the army absorbed nearly all the money available, and only one warship of any importance was launched, in 1898.

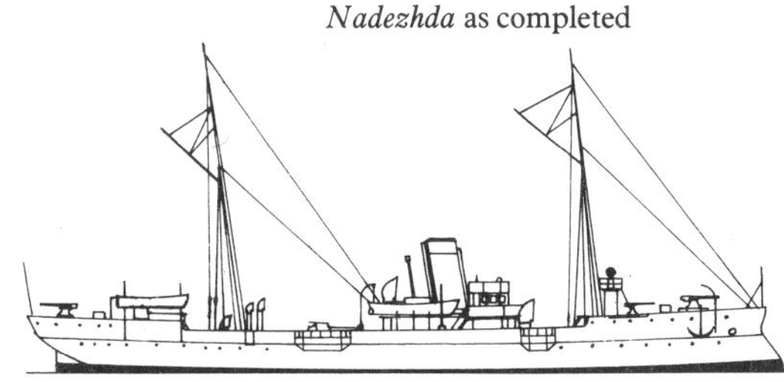

Nadezhda as completed

NADEZHDA *torpedo gunboat*

Displacement: 715t
Dimensions: 219ft 10in oa x 27ft 3in x 10ft 2in max (*67.00 x 8.30 x 3.10m*)
ihp/speed: 2600 = 18kts. Coal 110t
Armament: 2-3.9in, 2-9pdr, 2-3pdr, 2-TT
Complement: 97

Name	Builder	Launched
NADEZHDA	Bordeaux	1898

CAMBODIA

Lutin, a 490t composite-built vessel of 1877, length 141ft (*42.97m*), 373ihp = 10kts. Mainly used as a yacht, but fitted with one small gun.

COLOMBIA

ALMIRANTE LEZO *cruiser*

This 1200t cruiser was built as the Moroccan *El Bashir*. She was sold to Colombia in 1902 and renamed *Almirante Lezo*. She was renamed again in 1904, becoming *Cartagena*. She was out of service by 1924.

COSTA RICA

Second class torpedo boat Yarrow 1890

Displacement: 15t
Dimensions: 60ft x 9ft 3in x 3ft 6in (*18.29 x 2.82 x 1.07m*)
Machinery: 1 shaft TE, 230ihp = 17kts
Armament: 1-3pdr, 1-14in TT aw

Similar to the British *No 50* type, this boat had a turtledeck forecastle and a single funnel amidships. Discarded *c*1920.

CUBA

Baire about 1920
CPL

BAIRE *gunboat* (launched 1906)

Displacement: 500t
Dimensions: 196ft x 23ft x 9ft (*59.74 x 7.01 x 2.74m*)
Machinery: 1 shaft, Babcock boilers, 1200ihp = 14kts. Coal ?/120t
Armament: 2-6pdr (2 x 1), 2-3pdr (2 x 1)

One funnel and two masts. Built by Schichau; discarded *c*1930.

ECUADOR

Ex-PAPIN class *gunvessels*

The French '*avisos*' *Papin* and *Inconstant*, 811t, were purchased by Ecuador in 1900. They were discarded by 1920.

There was also a 65t Yarrow torpedo boat called *Tungurahua*.

EGYPT

NIJMI SHEVKET class *coast defence ironclads*

The 2080t *Nijmi Shevket* and *Assari Shevket* were ordered by Egypt from La Seyne and launched in 1868, but were delivered to Turkey in 1869.

LUTFI DJELIL class *turret ironclads*

Lutfi Djelil and *Hifzi Rahman* were 2540t twin-turretted vessels ordered by Egypt and built in Bordeaux. They were launched in 1868, but were delivered to Turkey in 1869.

MEHEMET ALI *iron frigate*

Displacement: 1760t
Dimensions: 290ft x 36ft x 16ft (*88.39 x 10.97 x 4.88m*)
Machinery: 1 shaft, 800ihp = ?kts
Armament: 20-4.7in (20 x 1), 10-40pdr (10 x 1)

Iron-hulled fully rigged frigate. Her machinery was removed about 1890 and she became a stationary guardship at Alexandria. She was armed with Krupp 4.7in BLRs and Armstrong 4.7in/40pdr BLRs. She was discarded in about 1898.

IBRAHIM *iron frigate*

Displacement: 4700t
Dimensions: 288ft 9in oa x 49ft 3in x 21ft 4in max (*88.01 x 15.01 x 6.50m*)
Machinery: 3560ihp = 13.34kts
Armament: –

An iron-hulled fully rigged frigate, built by La Seyne, launched on 30.11.1868 and scrapped about 1890.

SAKKA *wooden corvette*

Displacement: 970t
Dimensions: 205ft x 37ft 5in (*62.48 x 11.40m*)
Machinery: 300nhp = ?kts
Armament: 10-40pdr (10 x 1)

Name	Builder	Launched	Fate
SAKKA	Alexandria	1869	Scrapped *c*1900

This fully rigged corvette was armed with 4.7in/40pdr Armstrong BLRs. Her machinery was removed in about 1890 and she became a stationary guardship at Port Said.

HAITI

22 DÉCEMBRE *iron gunboat* (launched 1860)

Displacement: 900t
Dimensions: 208ft x 30ft x 16ft mean (*63.40 x 9.14 x 4.88m*)
Machinery: 1 shaft, 360ihp = 9kts
Armament: 4-4.7in (4 x 1)

One funnel and armed with 4.7in 40pdr Armstrong guns. Discarded after 1912.

1804 *iron gunboat* (launched 1875)

Displacement: 600t
Dimensions: 145ft x 29ft x 10ft mean (*44.20 x 8.84 x 3.05m*)
Machinery: 1 shaft, 100nhp = 12kts
Armament: 6-4in (6 x 1)

One funnel and armed with 4in Armstrong BLRs. Originally also had 1-10in MLR. Discarded after 1912.

SAINT MICHAEL *iron gunboat* (launched 1875)

Displacement: 850t
Dimensions: 162ft x 35ft x 11ft mean (*49.38 x 10.67 x 3.35m*)
Machinery: 1 shaft, 120nhp = 12kts
Armament: 1-11in, 8-4in (8 x 1)

One funnel, and armed with an 11in MLR and 4in Armstrong BLR guns. Originally the steamer *Jacmel*. Discarded after 1912.

DESSALINES *iron corvettes* (launched 1883)

Displacement: 1200t
Dimensions: 185ft x 32ft x 14ft 9in mean (*56.39 x 9.75 x 4.50m*)
Machinery: 1 shaft, 760ihp = 16kts
Armament: 3-3.9in (3 x 1), 2-4.7in (2 x 1)

A brig-rigged corvette with one funnel, and built in Philadelphia as the fruit steamer *Ethel*. She was armed with one 3.9in Canet QF, two 3.9in Krupp BLRs, and two 4.7in 30pdr Parrot guns. Discarded after 1912.

TOUSSAINT-LOUVERTURE *gunboat* (launched 1886)

Displacement: 500t
Dimensions: 164ft pp x 24ft 7in x 10ft 8in max (*50.00 x 7.49 x 3.25m*)
Machinery: 1-shaft compound, cyl boilers, 790ihp = 13kts. Coal ?/120t
Armament: 1-6.3in/30, 2-4.7in/30 (2 x 1)

A steel-hulled, brig-rigged gunboat with a flush deck and one funnel built at Le Havre, armed with a 6.3in/30 Canet BLR and two 4.7in/30 Canet QF guns. Discarded after 1912.

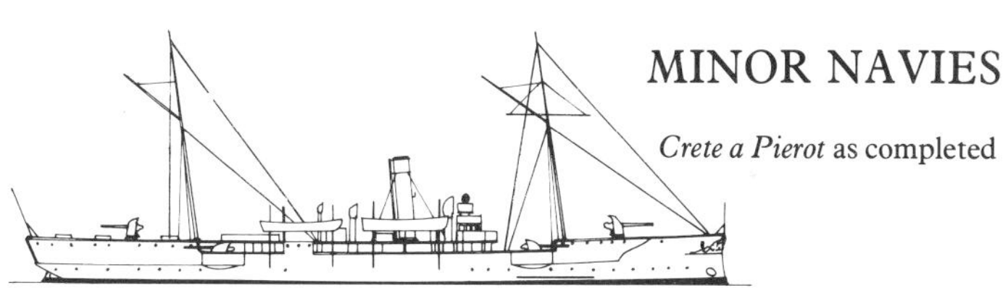

Crete a Pierot as completed

CAPOIS LA MORT class *gunboats* (launched 1893)

Displacement: 256t
Dimensions: 147ft 7in x 20ft 2in x 6ft 9in mean (*44.98 x 6.15 x 2.06m*)
Machinery: 2 shafts, 680ihp = 14kts
Armament: 1-3.9in, 4-1pdr (4 x 1)

Class: *Capois La Mort, Alexander Petion*. Steel-hulled boats with two pole masts, one funnel, a ram bow and a raised forecastle; built by Graville. They were armed with a 3.9in Canet QF and four Hotchkiss 1pdr QFs. Both were discarded after 1920.

CRÈTE À PIEROT *gunvessel* (launched 1895)

Displacement: 950t
Dimensions: –
Machinery: 1-shaft VTE, ?ihp = 16kts
Armament: 1-6.3in, 1-4.7in, 4-3.9in (4 x 1)

A steel-hulled gunvessel built by Earle and armed with Canet QF guns. She was sunk in 1902 by the German gunboat *Panther*.

HAWAII

KAIMILOA *gunvessel* (launched 1871)

Displacement: 291t gross
Dimensions: –
Machinery: 1 shaft, 40hp = 6-8kts
Armament: 4 brass cannon, 2 Gatling MGs

A wooden-hulled, three-masted gunvessel built at Blyth as the steamer *Firebrick*, and later renamed *Explorer*. She was purchased in December 1886 by the King of Hawaii. Sold to the Inter Island Steamship Co in 1887, she was finally broken up in 1910.

LIBERIA

GORRONOMAH *steel gunboat*

Launched at Belfast, December 1892. 150t, length 98ft 6in (*30.05m*). Speed 12kts. Armament 1-6pdr QF, 1-3pdr QF, 2 saluting guns.

ROCKTOWN *steel gunboat*

Launched at Rotterdam in 1894. 100ft x 20ft (*30.48 x 6.09m*). Speed 12kts. Armament 1-6pdr QF, 3MGs. A single-funnelled steamer rigged as schooner.

MEXICO

ZARAGOSA *third class cruiser*

Displacement: 1200t
Dimensions: 223ft 1in x 30ft 6in x 14ft mean (*68.00 x 9.30 x 4.27m*)
Machinery: 1 shaft, cyl boilers, 1300ihp = 15kts
Armament: 4-4.7in/40 (4 x 1), 2-6pdr (2 x 1)
Complement: 270

Name	Builder	Launched	Fate
ZARAGOSA (ex-PORFIRO DIAZ)	Graville	9.4.1891	Discarded *c*1920

Steel-hulled and barque-rigged, this vessel had a ram bow, one funnel and a raised forecastle and poop. The 4.7in/40 Canet QFs were in sponsons at the break of the forecastle and poop. Intended mainly for use as a training cruiser, she was laid down in April 1890 as *Porfiro Diaz* but was renamed *Zaragosa* before she was launched. She was completed in 1892.

INDEPENDENCIA class flatiron gunboats (launched 1874)

Displacement: 480t
Dimensions: 125ft x 24ft x 8ft 9in mean (*38.10 x 7.32 x 2.67m*)
Machinery: 1-shaft HC, Navy type boilers, 425ihp = 10kts. Coal ?/60t
Armament: 1-100pdr, 4-20pdr (4 x 1)
Complement: 63

Class (builder, fate): *Independencia, Libertad* (both Laird, both discarded *c* 1920). Schooner-rigged. The single 100pdr was mounted forward, and aimed by steering the ship. They had one funnel, and were sheathed in wood. Both were hulked in about 1914 after serving as troop transports and customs cruisers.

DEMOCRATA class *gunboats* (launched 1875)

Displacement: 445t
Dimensions: 140ft x 24ft 11in x 11ft 2in (*42.67 x 7.59 x 3.40m*)
Machinery: 1 shaft, 600ihp = 11kts
Armament: 2-100pdr (2 x 1), 2-20pdr (2 x 1)
Complement: 80

Class (builder, fate): *Democrata, Mexico* (both Rennie, both discarded 1910-20). Iron-hulled, schooner-rigged gunboats with one funnel and three masts. They were armed with 100-pdr 6in MLRs and 20pdr 4in Vavasseur BLR guns. By 1890 *Mexico* was a stationary ship at Mazatlon. *Democrata* was reclassified as a TS in 1914.

TAMPICO class *gunboats* (launched 1902)

Displacement:	980t
Dimensions:	200ft x 33ft x 11ft (*60.96 x 10.06 x 3.35m*)
Machinery:	2 shafts, Mosher boilers, 2400ihp = 16kts. Coal ?/170t
Armament:	2-4in (2 x 1), 6-6pdr (6 x 1), 1-14in TT aw
Complement:	98

Class (builder, fate): *Tampico, Vera Cruz* (both Elizabethport NJ, both discarded *c*1925). Steel-hulled gunboats with a ram bow, two masts, one funnel and a raised forecastle and poop. The 4in were mounted fore and aft, two 6pdr were in casemates abreast the bridge and the other four in sponsons amidships. There was a fixed bow TT. They were fitted to carry 200 troops.

NICHOLAS BRAVO class *gunboats* (launched 1903)

Displacement:	1227t
Dimensions:	242ft x 34ft x 9ft 9in (*73.76 x 10.36 x 2.97m*)
Machinery:	2 shafts, Blechynden boilers, 2565ihp = 17kts. Coal ?/200t
Armament:	2-4in (2 x 1), 6-6pdr (6 x 1), 1-14in TT aw
Complement:	116

Class (builder, fate): *Nicholas Bravo, Morales* (both Odero, both discarded *c*1935). Steel-hulled gunboats completed in 1904. They had a ram bow with a fixed TT, two raked masts and funnels and a raised poop and stern. *Morales* was renamed *Blanquet* in about 1920. Both were fitted for oil-firing about 1923-25, and had an oil capacity of 226t.

MOROCCO

EL BASHIR *cruiser*

Displacement:	1200t
Dimensions:	229ft 6in x 32ft 9 in (*69.98 x 10.02m*)
Machinery:	2500ihp = 18kts
Armament:	2-4.7in BL, 4-1pdr QF, 4 TT
Complement:	150

A small cruiser or torpedo gunvessel launched at Leghorn in 1892. In 1902 she was sold to Columbia and renamed *Almirante Lezo*.

There were also two 450t gunboats built at Sampierdarena in 1898, and the 1164t barquentine-rigged steamer *El Massaneh* built at Middlesbrough in 1882.

PARAGUAY

TRITON *central battery ship*

Ordered by Paraguay but sold by builders to Brazil and renamed *Mariz e Barros* in 1865. See under Brazil.

TACUARI *gunvessel*

Purchased as a paddle-driven merchant ship in 1854 and armed with 6 guns in November 1864.

MEDUZA *central battery ship*

Ordered by Paraguay but sold by builders to Brazil and renamed *Herval* in 1865. Sister-ship to *Triton*. See under Brazil.

BELLONA *armoured turret ship*

An iron-hulled vessel ordered by Paraguay but sold by builders to Brazil and renamed *Lima Barros* in 1865. See under Brazil for details.

MINERVA *armoured turret ship*

Ordered by Paraguay but sold by builders to Brazil and renamed *Bahia* in 1865. See under Brazil.

NEMESIS *armoured turret ship*

Ordered by Paraguay but sold by builders to Brazil and renamed *Silvado* in 1865. See under Brazil.

In 1905 the navy of Paraguay comprised one 440t gunboat and two smaller steamers.

PERSIA

PERSEPOLIS *gunvessel* (launched 1885)

Displacement:	1200t
Dimensions:	207ft x 32ft 9in x 19ft 6in mean (*63.09 x 9.98 x 5.94m*)
Machinery:	1 shaft, 450ihp = 10kts
Armament:	4-2.7in (4 x 1)

Iron-hulled vessel with a ram bow, two masts, one funnel and a three-island hull, built at Bremen. Discarded *c* 1925.

PERU

INDEPENDENCIA *central battery ship*

Displacement:	3500t
Dimensions:	215ft x 44ft 9in x 21ft 6in (*65.53 x 13.64 x 6.55m*)
Machinery:	1 shaft, 2200ihp = 12kts
Armour:	Iron. Belt 4½in, battery 4½in
Armament:	2-7in (2 x 1), 12-70pdr (12 x 1), 4-30pdr (4 x 1)
Complement:	250

Name	Builder	Launched	Fate
INDEPENDENCIA	Samuda	8.8.1865	Destroyed 21.5.79

An iron-hulled, barque-rigged ship with a ram bow and one funnel, completed in December 1866. The 7in 150pdr 7.5t Armstrong MLRs were on pivot-mountings on the spar deck, and the remaining MLR guns were in the battery. The 7in were replaced (shortly before she was destroyed) by an 8in 250pdr 9t Vavasseur MLR in the bow and a 7in 150pdr Parrot MLR in the stern. Reboilered in 1878, she was wrecked on 21.5.1879 and blown up.

ATAHUALPA *monitor*

This vessel was built as the US monitor *Catawba* and was purchased by Peru after the American Civil War. She was scuttled at Callao on 16.1.1881, but was raised later that year and hulked. She was finally discarded in about 1910.

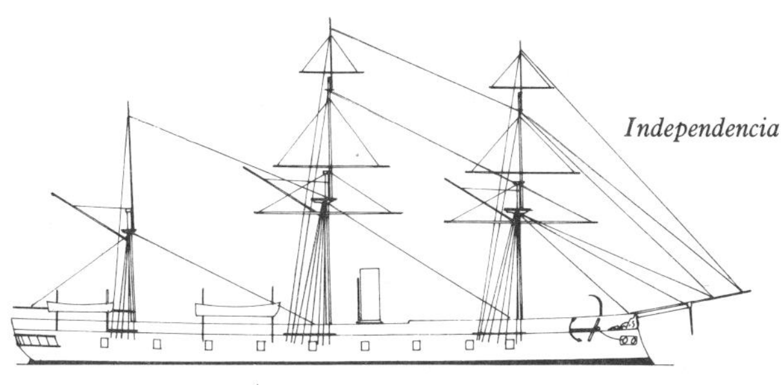
Independencia as completed

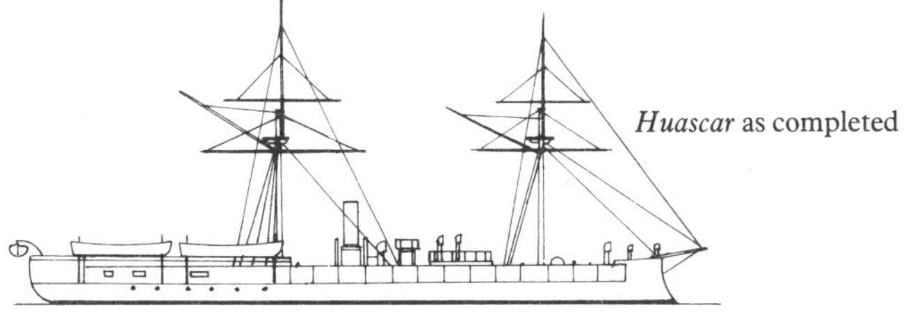
Huascar as completed

HUASCAR *turret ship*

Displacement:	2030t
Dimensions:	190ft pp x 35ft x 18ft 3in max *(57.91 x 10.67 x 5.56m)*
Machinery:	1-shaft SE, 4 boilers, 1650ihp = 12.3kts. Coal 200/300t
Armour:	Iron. Belt 4½in, ends 2in, turret 8in-5½in, CT 3in
Armament:	2-10in (2 x 1), 2-40pdr (2 x 1)
Complement:	170

Name	Builder	Launched	Fate
HUASCAR	Laird	6.10.1865	Captured by Chile 8.10.79

An iron-hulled turret ship with a raised forecastle and poop, a ram bow, two masts, one funnel and a single turret amidships containing two 10in 12.5t Armstrong MLR guns. The ports had 8in armour and the rest of the turret was 5in thick. The belt extended 5ft above and 3ft below lwl, and was 4½in thick amidships, tapering to 2in fore and aft. There was a double bottom beneath the engine and boiler rooms and the magazine, and she had hinged bulwarks amidships that were lowered in action.

LIMA class *cruisers*

Displacement:	1700t
Dimensions:	250ft x 35ft x 15ft max *(76.20 x 10.67 x 4.57m)*
Machinery:	2-shaft HC, 1800ihp = 16.2kts. Coal ?/300t
Armament:	2-6in (2 x 1), 3-3pdr (3 x 1)
Complement:	150

Name	Builder	Launched	Fate
LIMA (ex-SOCRATES)	Howaldt	1880	Discarded *c*1935
DIOGENES	Howaldt	1881	Sold to Japan, then USA 2.4.98

Lima after refit

This class of iron-hulled cruisers had a straight bow, two masts with a light brig rig and two funnels. Both were built as merchant ships for Portugal but were purchased by Peru and converted to cruisers in England in 1881. *Socrates* was renamed *Lima* and armed with two 6in Armstrong BLRs. She was eventually refitted at Panama in 1920, rearmed with 4-4in (4 x 1) and used first as a transport and then as a submarine depot ship. *Diogenes* was never armed or delivered to Peru. She was purchased by Japan in 1895 but not delivered, and was finally taken over by the USA on 2.4.1898 and renamed *Topeka*. See under USA.

APURIMAC *wooden screw frigate*

This fully-rigged single-screw vessel was built around 1850 and served until about 1915. From before 1890 she was a TS. She carried 34 guns.

AMERICA *corvette*

Ordered by the Confederacy from France as *Texas*, but sold by her builders to Peru and renamed *America*. Discarded prior to 1880.

UNION *corvette*

Ordered by the Confederacy from France as *Georgia*, but sold by her builders to Peru and renamed *Union*. Discarded after 1881.

Nos 2, 3 Herreshoff 1879

Displacement:	–
Dimensions:	59ft oa x 7ft x 5ft *(17.98 x 2.13 x 1.52m)*
Machinery:	1-shaft compound, 100ihp = 16kts. Coal ?/3t
Armament	2 spar torpedoes (2 x 1)

Class: *Republica* (No *2*), *Allay* (No *3*). These third class TBs were armed with a spar torpedo fore and aft. The machinery was aft and drove a single screw positioned forward of amidships. They were equally fast ahead or astern. *Allay* was captured on her delivery voyage by Chile and renamed *Guacolda*. No *2* was sunk on 3.1.1881. A sister-vessel, No *4*, was never completed.

ROUMANIA

Independence from Turkey was not obtained until 1878, though Roumania previously possessed considerable autonomy. The population in 1905 was about 6,500,000, but the money available for defence was mostly spent on the army and on land fortifications. Apart from the Danube flotilla, only one small cruiser and 3 torpedo boats were launched, in 1888.

ELISABETA *protected cruiser*

Displacement:	1300t
Dimensions:	239ft 6in oa x 33ft 6in x 12ft mean *(73.00 x 10.21 x 3.66m)*
ihp/speed:	4700 = 17.3kts. Coal 80/300t
Armament:	4-6.7in/35, 4-6pdr, 2-1pdr revolvers, 4-14in TT
Complement:	190

Name	Builder	Launched
ELISABETA	Armstrong	1888

Small cruiser with 2-1in protective deck increased to 3½in on slopes. The 6.7in and 6pdr guns were later replaced by 4-4.7in and 4-12pdr.

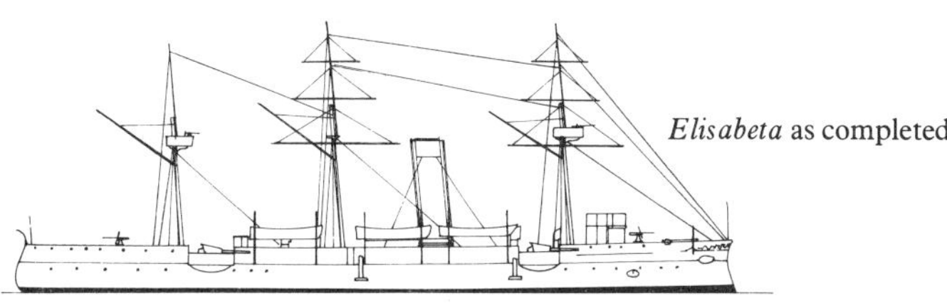
Elisabeta as completed

TORPEDO BOATS

Name	Builder	Launched	Displacement	Length oa	ihp/speed	Armament
NALUCA class	Le Havre	1888	56t	120ft 8in *(36.78m)*	540 = 16kts	2-1pdr revolvers, 2-14in TT (bow) and spar

Naluca class also comprised *Sborul* and *Smeul*. Other boats had spar torpedoes only.

GUNBOATS (OVER 200 TONS)

The well known *Mircea* was an auxiliary-engined brig used for training, and does not qualify for inclusion.

SAN DOMINGO

EL PRESIDENTE *gunboat* (launched 1873)

Displacement: 389t
Dimensions: 209ft x 21ft 6in (*63.70 x 6.55m*)
Machinery: 1 shaft, 105nhp = 15kts
Armament: 1-12pdr, 1-37mm
Complement: 50

Built by Rutherglen and armed with a 12pdr Armstrong gun and a 37mm Hotchkiss revolving cannon. Reconstructed at Grangemouth 1896/97, rearmed with 4-4.7in 40pdr guns, and also re-engined, making 13.8kts on trial. Discarded after 1914.

INDEPENDENCIA *gunboat* (launched 1894)

Displacement: 322t
Dimensions: 170ft x 25ft (*51.82 x 7.62m*)
Machinery: 2-shaft TE, ?ihp = 15kts
Armament: 7 small QF (7 x 1)

A steel-hulled gunboat fitted with Hotchkiss QF guns, laid down and completed in 1894 by Napier. Discarded after 1914.

RESTAURACION *gunboat* (launched 1896)

Displacement: 1000t
Dimensions: 214ft x 30ft (*65.23 x 9.14m*)
Machinery: 2-shaft TE, ?ihp = 14kts
Armament: 4-4.7in (4 x 1), 5 small QF (5 x 1)

A steel-hulled gunboat laid down and launched by Napier in 1896 which made nearly 15kts on trials. Discarded after 1914.

SARAWAK

LORNA DOONE *gunboat*

Displacement: 118t gross
Dimensions: 103ft 4in x 17ft 2in (*31.50 x 5.23m*)
Machinery: 1 shaft, 40nhp
Armament: 2 small guns

Iron-hulled, schooner-rigged and with one funnel and two masts, built at Port Glasgow. Discarded after 1914.

ADEN *paddle gunvessel* (launched 1884)

Displacement: 300t gross
Dimensions: 149ft 9in x 25ft 2in (*45.64 x 7.67m*)
Machinery: 75nhp = ?kts
Armament: 1 small gun

Iron-hulled and schooner-rigged built at Port Glasgow. Discarded after 1914.

ALINE *gunboat* (launched 1875)

Displacement: 175t gross
Dimensions: 142ft 6in x 21ft 3in (*43.43 x 6.48m*)
Machinery: 1 shaft, 35nhp
Armament: 2 small guns (2 x 1)

Iron-hulled and schooner-rigged, with one funnel and two masts, built at Port Glasgow. Discarded after 1914.

SIAM

Maha Chakrkri

MAHA CHAKRKRI *protected cruiser*

Displacement: 2500t
Dimensions: 290ft x 39ft 4in x 13ft 9in (*88.39 x 11.99 x 4.19m*)
Machinery: 2-shaft TE, 5 cyl boilers, 3000ihp = 15kts. Coal 280/?t
Armour: Steel. Protective deck 2in
Armament: 4-4.7in (4 x 1), 10-6pdr (10 x 1)
Complement: 318

Name	Builder	Launched	Fate
MAHA CHAKRKRI	Leith	27.6.1892	BU 1917

A steel-hulled protected cruiser with a ram bow, two masts and two funnels. The 4.7in guns were in upper deck sponsons amidships. Completed in 1893, she was fitted out as the Royal Yacht but was classified as a protected cruiser. Her engines and fittings were taken out when she was scrapped and reused in a ship of the same name built by Kawasaki in 1918.

MAHA PHICHAIATHEP *wooden gunboat* (launched 1867)

Displacement: 580t
Dimensions: 151ft x 25ft x 11ft 6in (*46.02 x 7.62 x 3.51m*)
Machinery: 435ihp = 10kts
Armament: 1-70pdr, 4-12pdr (4 x 1)

Discarded after 1912.

REGENT *gunboat* (launched 1868)

Displacement: 660t
Dimensions: 166ft x 26ft x 10ft 6in (*50.60 x 7.92 x 3.20m*)
Machinery: 2 shafts
Armament: 8 guns (8 x 1)

Iron-hulled and fully-rigged, this vessel was built as a merchant ship and purchased and converted in about 1870. Discarded after 1912.

SIAM MOUGKUT *floating battery* (launched 1870)

Displacement: 950t
Dimensions: Length 210ft (*64.00m*)
Machinery: None
Armour: Iron. Battery 2½in
Armament: 8-4in (8 x 1)

Iron-hulled and by 1899 was armed with 8-4in 32pdr BLR (8 x 1). Discarded after 1912.

RAN RUK *gunboat* (launched 1879)

Displacement: 700t
Dimensions: 126ft x 26ft x 11ft 6in (*38.40 x 7.92 x 3.51m*)
Machinery: 540ihp = 11kts
Armament: 4-4.7in (4 x 1), 1-6pdr, 3 TT (3 x 1)

Iron-hulled. Discarded after 1912.

MURATHA class *gunboats* (launched 1898-1901)

Displacement: 530t, *Bali* and *Sugrib* 580t
Dimensions: 145ft (*Bali* and *Sugrib* 162ft) x 23ft x 10ft (*44.20 (49.38) x 7.01 x 3.05m*)
Machinery: 500ihp = 11.4kts
Armament: 1-4.7in, 5-6pdr (5 x 1), 4-1pdr (4 x 1)
Complement: 83

Class (builder, fate): *Muratha, Bali, Sugrib* (all Hong Kong, all discarded *c* 1930). Steel-hulled boats with a ram bow, two masts, one funnel and a flush deck. The 4.7in BLR was mounted on the forecastle and the 6pdrs were in sponsons amidships.

Siam also had one 45t second class torpedo boat. It was built prior to 1890 and discarded after 1905.

MONGKUT RAJAKUMARN *gunboat* (launched 1887)

Displacement: 700t
Dimensions: 175ft x 23ft 6in x 11ft (*53.34 x 7.16 x 3.35m*)
Machinery: 2 shafts, 800ihp = 14kts. Coal ?/90t
Armament: 2-4.7in (2 x 1), 4-6pdr (4 x 1), 3-1pdr (3 x 1), 1-14in TT aw
Complement: 100

This steel hulled gunboat was schooner-rigged and had two masts with military tops, one funnel and a ram bow. She was built at Whampoa for Spain for service in the Philippines as the *Filipinas* but failed to make her designed speed. She was then sold to Siam in 1891 and renamed *Mongkut Rajakumarn*. By 1905 her speed was 11kts. Discarded after 1930.

URUGUAY

GENERAL SUAREZ *gunboat*

This vessel built by France as the 400t gunboat *Tactique*, and was purchased by Uruguay in 1887 and renamed *General Suarez*. She was refitted with 4-2.9in Krupp BLR guns (4 x 1). She was discarded after 1913.

MALVINAS *gunboat*

Displacement: 400t
Dimensions: 141ft x 22ft 10in x 10ft mean (*42.98 x 6.96 x 3.05m*)
Machinery: 1 shaft, 280ihp = 8kts
Armament: 2 small QF (2 x 1)

Iron-hulled gunboat built at Elbing as a merchant steamer and purchased and armed by Uruguay. Discarded after 1912.

GENERAL ARTIGAS *gunboat* (launched 1883)

Displacement: 270t
Dimensions: 128ft x 20ft 6in x 8ft 6in mean (*39.01 x 6.25 x 2.59m*)
Machinery: 1-shaft compound, 520ihp = 12.5kts
Armament: 2-4.7in/30 (2 x 1)

An iron hulled gunboat armed with 4.7in/30 Krupp BL guns built at Trieste. Discarded after 1913.

GENERAL RIVERA *gunboat* (launched 1884)

Displacement: 300t
Dimensions: 117ft 8in x 20ft 10in (*35.86 x 6.35m*)
Machinery: 1 shaft, 360ihp = 12kts
Armament: 1-5.9in, 1-2.4in
Complement: 75

An iron-hulled gunboat armed with Krupp BLR guns, built at Montevideo. Sunk by internal explosion October 1903.

VENEZUELA

Bolivar

(Uncredited photos: Arrigo Barilli Collection)

BOLIVAR *gunboat*

This 571t vessel was built as the Spanish *Galacia* in 1891 and was sold to Venezuela and renamed *Bolivar* in 1898. She was discarded in about 1920.

MIRANDA *gunboat*

This 200t gunboat was built as the Spanish *Miranda* on Clydebank in 1895. She was sold to Venezuela in 1898 and retained her original name. She was discarded in about 1930.

RESTAURADOR *gunboat* (launched 1884)

Displacement: 750t
Dimensions: 240ft x 26ft x 13ft max (*73.15 x 7.92 x 3.96m*)
Machinery: 1900ihp = 10kts. Coal ?/200t
Armament: 1-12pdr, 4-6pdr (4 x 1)
Complement: 65

A flush-decked gunboat with a clipper bow, two masts and one funnel. She was built in Philadelphia as the US yacht *Atlanta*, and was bought and armed by Venezuela in 1900, when she was renamed *Restaurador*. She was seized by the German Navy on 7.12.1902 and temporarily commissioned by them. She was returned to Venezuela on 24.2.1903, being renamed *General Salom* in about 1920, and discarded after 1930.

JOSE FELIX RIBAS *gunboat* (launched 1894)

Displacement: 300t
Dimensions: 127ft x 23ft x 12ft (*38.71 x 7.01 x 3.66m*)
Machinery: ?hp = 10kts. Coal ?/60t
Armament: 2-6pdr (2 x 1)

Flush-decked and with one funnel. Built as the tug *Zumbador*, and purchased, armed and renamed *Jose Felix Ribas* in 1903. Renamed *Zumbador* in about 1910. Discarded after 1930.

ZANZIBAR

6 small iron single screw steamers. These were: *Swordsman* (North Shields 1880, 1124t gross), *Akola* (Greenock 1875, 578t gross), *Kiha* (Flensburg 1885, 350t gross), *Nyanza* (Blackwall 1864, 2128t gross), *Explorateur* (Thomas 1868, 213t gross), *Barawa* (Flensburg 1885, 330t gross). Some were armed with small QF or old BL guns.

Index

A, Argentina; **A-H**, Austria-Hungary; **Be**, Belgium; **Br**, Brazil; **Bul**, Bulgaria; **Ca**, China; **Cam**, Cambodia; **Ce**, Chile; **Col**, Columbia; **CoR**, Costa Rica; **Cu**, Cuba; **Dk**, Denmark; **Ec**, Ecuador; **Eg**, Egypt; **F**, France; **G**, Germany; **GB**, Great Britain (including Empire forces); **Gr**, Greece; **Hai**, Haiti; **Haw**, Hawaii; **I**, Italy; **J**, Japan; **Lib**, Liberia; **Mex**, Mexico; **Mor**, Morocco; **Ne**, The Netherlands; **No**, Norway; **Par**, Paraguay; **Pe**, Persia; **Po**, Portugal; **Pu**, Peru; **R**, Russia; **Ro**, Roumania; **Sa**, Sarawak; **SD**, San Domingo; **Si**, Siam; **Sp**, Spain; **Sw**, Sweden; **Tu**, Turkey; **Ur**, Uruguay; **USA**, United States of America; **Ve**, Venezuela; **Zan**, Zanzibar.

A

A, Argentina; **A-H**, Austria-Hungary; **Be**, Belgium; **Br**, Brazil; **Bul**, Bulgaria; **Ca**, China; **Cam**, Cambodia; **Ce**, Chile; **Col**, Columbia; **CoR**, Costa Rica; **Cu**, Cuba; **Dk**, Denmark; **Ec**, Ecuador; **Eg**, Egypt; **F**, France; **G**, Germany; **GB**, Great Britain (including Empire forces); **Gr**, Greece; **Hai**, Haiti; **Haw**, Hawaii; **I**, Italy; **J**, Japan; **Lib**, Liberia; **Mex**, Mexico; **Mor**, Morocco; **Ne**, The Netherlands; **No**, Norway; **Par**, Paraguay; **Pe**, Persia; **Po**, Portugal; **Pu**, Peru; **R**, Russia; **Ro**, Roumania; **Sa**, Sarawak; **SD**, San Domingo; **Si**, Siam; **Sp**, Spain; **Sw**, Sweden; **Tu**, Turkey; **Ur**, Uruguay; **USA**, United States of America; **Ve**, Venezuela; **Zan**, Zanzibar.

C

A, Argentina; A-H, Austria-Hungary; Be, Belgium; Br, Brazil; Bul, Bulgaria; Ca, China; Cam, Cambodia; Ce, Chile; Col, Columbia; CoR, Costa Rica; Cu, Cuba; Dk, Denmark; Ec, Ecuador; Eg, Egypt; F, France; G, Germany; GB, Great Britain (including Empire forces); Gr, Greece; Hai, Haiti; Haw, Hawaii; I, Italy; J, Japan; Lib, Liberia; Mex, Mexico; Mor, Morocco; Ne, The Netherlands; No, Norway; Par, Paraguay; Pe, Persia; Po, Portugal; Pu, Peru; R, Russia; Ro, Roumania; Sa, Sarawak; SD, San Domingo; Si, Siam; Sp, Spain; Sw, Sweden; Tu, Turkey; Ur, Uruguay; USA, United States of America; Ve, Venezuela; Zan, Zanzibar.

D

E

F

A, Argentina; **A-H,** Austria-Hungary; **Be,** Belgium; **Br,** Brazil; **Bul,** Bulgaria; **Ca,** China; **Cam,** Cambodia; **Ce,** Chile; **Col,** Columbia; **CoR,** Costa Rica; **Cu,** Cuba; **Dk,** Denmark; **Ec,** Ecuador; **Eg,** Egypt; **F,** France; **G,** Germany; **GB,** Great Britain (including Empire forces); **Gr,** Greece; **Hai,** Haiti; **Haw,** Hawaii; **I,** Italy; **J,** Japan; **Lib,** Liberia; **Mex,** Mexico; **Mor,** Morocco; **Ne,** The Netherlands; **No,** Norway; **Par,** Paraguay; **Pe,** Persia; **Po,** Portugal; **Pu,** Peru; **R,** Russia; **Ro,** Roumania; **Sa,** Sarawak; **SD,** San Domingo; **Si,** Siam; **Sp,** Spain; **Sw,** Sweden; **Tu',** Turkey; **Ur,** Uruguay; **USA,** United States of America; **Ve,** Venezuela; **Zan,** Zanzibar.

G

H

I

A, Argentina; **A-H**, Austria-Hungary; **Be**, Belgium; **Br**, Brazil; **Bul**, Bulgaria; **Ca**, China; **Cam**, Cambodia; **Ce**, Chile; **Col**, Columbia; **CoR**, Costa Rica; **Cu**, Cuba; **Dk**, Denmark; **Ec**, Ecuador; **Eg**, Egypt; **F**, France; **G**, Germany; **GB**, Great Britain (including Empire forces); **Gr**, Greece; **Hai**, Haiti; **Haw**, Hawaii; **I**, Italy; **J**, Japan; **Lib**, Liberia; **Mex**, Mexico; **Mor**, Morocco; **Ne**, The Netherlands; **No**, Norway; **Par**, Paraguay; **Pe**, Persia; **Po**, Portugal; **Pu**, Peru; **R**, Russia; **Ro**, Roumania; **Sa**, Sarawak; **SD**, San Domingo; **Si**, Siam; **Sp**, Spain; **Sw**, Sweden; **Tu**, Turkey; **Ur**, Uruguay; **USA**, United States of America; **Ve**, Venezuela; **Zan**, Zanzibar.

J

K

L

M

A, Argentina; **A-H**, Austria-Hungary; **Be**, Belgium; **Br**, Brazil; **Bul**, Bulgaria; **Ca**, China; **Cam**, Cambodia; **Ce**, Chile; **Col**, Columbia; **CoR**, Costa Rica; **Cu**, Cuba; **Dk**, Denmark; **Ec**, Ecuador; **Eg**, Egypt; **F**, France; **G**, Germany; **GB**, Great Britain (including Empire forces); **Gr**, Greece; **Hai**, Haiti; **Haw**, Hawaii; **I**, Italy; **J**, Japan; **Lib**, Liberia; **Mex**, Mexico; **Mor**, Morocco; **Ne**, The Netherlands; **No**, Norway; **Par**, Paraguay; **Pe**, Persia; **Po**, Portugal; **Pu**, Peru; **R**, Russia; **Ro**, Roumania; **Sa**, Sarawak; **SD**, San Domingo; **Si**, Siam; **Sp**, Spain; **Sw**, Sweden; **Tu**, Turkey; **Ur**, Uruguay; **USA**, United States of America; **Ve**, Venezuela; **Zan**, Zanzibar.

N

O

P

A, Argentina; **A-H,** Austria-Hungary; **Be,** Belgium; **Br,** Brazil; **Bul,** Bulgaria; **Ca,** China; **Cam,** Cambodia; **Ce,** Chile; **Col,** Columbia; **CoR,** Costa Rica; **Cu,** Cuba; **Dk,** Denmark; **Ec,** Ecuador; **Eg,** Egypt; **F,** France; **G,** Germany; **GB,** Great Britain (including Empire forces); **Gr,** Greece; **Hai,** Haiti; **Haw,** Hawaii; **I,** Italy; **J,** Japan; **Lib,** Liberia; **Mex,** Mexico; **Mor,** Morocco; **Ne,** The Netherlands; **No,** Norway; **Par,** Paraguay; **Pe,** Persia; **Po,** Portugal; **Pu,** Peru; **R,** Russia; **Ro,** Roumania; **Sa,** Sarawak; **SD,** San Domingo; **Si,** Siam; **Sp,** Spain; **Sw,** Sweden; **Tu,** Turkey; **Ur,** Uruguay; **USA,** United States of America; **Ve,** Venezuela; **Zan,** Zanzibar.

Q

R

S

A, Argentina; **A-H**, Austria-Hungary; **Be**, Belgium; **Br**, Brazil; **Bul**, Bulgaria; **Ca**, China; **Cam**, Cambodia; **Ce**, Chile; **Col**, Columbia; **CoR**, Costa Rica; **Cu**, Cuba; **Dk**, Denmark; **Ec**, Ecuador; **Eg**, Egypt; **F**, France; **G**, Germany; **GB**, Great Britain (including Empire forces); **Gr**, Greece; **Hai**, Haiti; **Haw**, Hawaii; **I**, Italy; **J**, Japan; **Lib**, Liberia; **Mex**, Mexico; **Mor**, Morocco; **Ne**, The Netherlands; **No**, Norway; **Par**, Paraguay; **Pe**, Persia; **Po**, Portugal; **Pu**, Peru; **R**, Russia; **Ro**, Roumania; **Sa**, Sarawak; **SD**, San Domingo; **Si**, Siam; **Sp**, Spain; **Sw**, Sweden; **Tu**, Turkey; **Ur**, Uruguay; **USA**, United States of America; **Ve**, Venezuela; **Zan**, Zanzibar.

T

A, Argentina; **A-H**, Austria-Hungary; **Be**, Belgium; **Br**, Brazil; **Bul**, Bulgaria; **Ca**, China; **Cam**, Cambodia; **Ce**, Chile; **Col**, Columbia; **CoR**, Costa Rica; **Cu**, Cuba; **Dk**, Denmark; **Ec**, Ecuador; **Eg**, Egypt; **F**, France; **G**, Germany; **GB**, Great Britain (including Empire forces); **Gr**, Greece; **Hai**, Haiti; **Haw**, Hawaii; **I**, Italy; **J**, Japan; **Lib**, Liberia; **Mex**, Mexico; **Mor**, Morocco; **Ne**, The Netherlands; **No**, Norway; **Par**, Paraguay; **Pe**, Persia; **Po**, Portugal; **Pu**, Peru; **R**, Russia; **Ro**, Roumania; **Sa**, Sarawak; **SD**, San Domingo; **Si**, Siam; **Sp**, Spain; **Sw**, Sweden; **Tu**, Turkey; **Ur**, Uruguay; **USA**, United States of America; **Ve**, Venezuela; **Zan**, Zanzibar.

U

V

The Last Sailing Battlefleet

Maintaining Naval Mastery 1815-1850

ANDREW LAMBERT

This book
is dedicated to
Zohra and Tama-Sophie

First published in Great Britain 1991 by
Conway Maritime Press Ltd,
101 Fleet Street,
London EC4Y 1DE

British Library Cataloguing in Publication Data
Lambert, Andrew D. *1956–*
The Last Sailing Battlefleet. Maintaining Naval Mastery
1815–1850.
1. Navies, Military Equipment
I. Title
359.8320941
ISBN 0-85177-591-8

Designed by Tony Hart.
Typeset by Lasertext, Stretford, Manchester
Printed and bound by The Bath Press, Bath.

W

Y

Z

A, Argentina; **A-H,** Austria-Hungary; **Be,** Belgium; **Br,** Brazil; **Bul,** Bulgaria; **Ca,** China; **Cam,** Cambodia; **Ce,** Chile; **Col,** Columbia; **CoR,** Costa Rica; **Cu,** Cuba; **Dk,** Denmark; **Ec,** Ecuador; **Eg,** Egypt; **F,** France; **G,** Germany; **GB,** Great Britain (including Empire forces); **Gr,** Greece; **Hai,** Haiti; **Haw,** Hawaii; **I,** Italy; **J,** Japan; **Lib,** Liberia; **Mex,** Mexico; **Mor,** Morocco; **Ne,** The Netherlands; **No,** Norway; **Par,** Paraguay; **Pe,** Persia; **Po,** Portugal; **Pu,** Peru; **R,** Russia; **Ro,** Roumania; **Sa,** Sarawak; **SD,** San Domingo; **Si,** Siam; **Sp,** Spain; **Sw,** Sweden; **Tu,** Turkey; **Ur,** Uruguay; **USA,** United States of America; **Ve,** Venezuela; **Zan,** Zanzibar.

Contents

Acknowledgements

It is one of the great pleasures of any book to end by recalling the valued and appreciated assistance of so many friends and colleagues. This has been the more important in this case because of the long and somewhat complex development of the theme. It began as a study of the politics of Sir William Symonds's term as Surveyor of the Navy, and developed as my research into the politics, strategy and administration the nineteenth century navy took me along different paths and into new archives. The battlefleet remains at the centre of the work, but I hope that it has become a more rounded and useful study, for the ships and their designers were only the pinnacle of a system designed to sustain British seapower. Those who write about navies and warships are often accused of avoiding the great issues because of an obsession with technical detail. It would perhaps profit those who make such remarks to read the books concerned, rather than make judgements based on the size of the pages or the presence of illustrations. This is not a book just about ships; I hope it places the ships, the fleet of which they were part, and the service which built them, in their true context.

Thanks are due to the staffs of the British Library, both the Department of Manuscripts and of Printed Books; to the Public Record Office; the National Maritime Museum, Greenwich; the Scottish Record Office and National Library of Scotland; the Borthwick Institute, York; the Cambridge University Library; the National Register of Archives; the Manuscript Department of Nottingham University Library; Bedford Record Office; the University of Durham and most recently to Andrew Orgill, the Librarian at Sandhurst, who has proved indefatigable in obtaining on loan those hard-to-find books.

Personal thanks are due to many individuals for their help and support. With particular reference to this book I would like to thank David Lyon, Alan Pearsall ISO, Roger Morriss and David Topliss at, or once of, the National Maritime Museum for assistance, discussion, comment and criticism of the best sort; Basil Greenhill and Anne Giffard for support, advice and invaluable discussions; Professor Bryan Ranft for sound advice, great encouragement and a due sense of proportion, David K Brown RCNC for his unfailing fund of knowledge and willingness to advise even the most ignorant of fellow labourers; Tom Adams for his efforts on behalf of the opposition and Eric Grove, whose abilities and enthusiasm are an example to all. Particular thanks are due to Rob Gardiner and all at Conway for once more trusting their reputation for publishing good books to so uncertain a vessel. To all those of my friends and colleagues who have had to suffer parts, or, the most unfortunate of all, the entire work in one shape or another, my sincere apologies. To Stephen Badsey, who had the misfortune to wrestle with one particularly metaphysical chapter, I can only add the hope that he will still think kindly of the navy. Those named and unnamed will hardly need me to tell them that they bear no responsibility for any errors, omissions or failings in this book; they tried bravely enough, but the ignorant and stubborn author proved impossible to advise.

On a more personal level this book would never have been written without the support of Zohra, of my parents and all our friends. Halfway through its writing Tama-Sophie arrived to teach me the value of time, and the supreme irrelevance of all such endeavours as this.

ANDREW LAMBERT
Norfolk 1991

INTRODUCTION

This book is a study of the British sailing battlefleet at the zenith of its power. It considers the strategy, policy, tactics, technology, design history and construction of this fleet, and the service history of the ships. Many have found this period uninspiring and have been content to talk of a *Pax Britannica* and the gunboat navy. The truth is that between 1815 and 1850 Britain built, maintained and operated a battlefleet of unrivalled power, which sustained a world empire and exercised a profound influence with the other nations of the world. This force was not the product of haphazard, fortuitous decisions. It reflected the conscious efforts of intelligent and rational statesmen and naval administrators. There is an underlying theme to the book, namely the continuous process of maintaining a fleet capable of meeting any threat. Everything else in naval administration was subordinated to this imperative.

Before examining the structure of the fleet it is necessary to understand the politico-strategic environment within which it had to operate. The questions are simply put: what were the objects of British seapower in peace and war, and how far could naval forces meet them? The answers are more complex, and reveal a great deal of ignorance among historians unwilling to question the received wisdom of earlier generations.

Fleets and armies exist to meet national requirements, requirements determined by international situations, national politics and above all by economic strength. Between 1815 and 1850 the battlefleet was transformed, for although the careers of several ships spanned the period, they were better armed and stronger in 1850 than they had been in 1815. Every aspect of the fleet had been affected by an integrated revolution, a revolution that achieved the ultimate object of creating a weapons system better able to carry out its task than it had been before. In every area, from timber seasoning to gun founding, the Navy worked to build a durable fleet capable of meeting all comers. This was the most powerful and effective wooden battlefleet. It allowed the British Empire to maintain her dominant position on the world's oceans at very low cost and cemented by the Treaties of 1815.

The strategy of seapower

Britain, as a maritime economic power, depended on seaborne trade and sea communications for wealth and imperial cohesion. In addition, there were the particular defence requirements of an island nation. These requirements could only be achieved by sea control. With the technology of the period, sea control could only be guaranteed by the acid test of battle. The battlefleet strategy, outlined by Mahan, dictated the size of the fleet and the design of individual units; it underpinned the entire structure of the Empire. As a result, statesmen and politicians of all parties were willing to fund the Navy, and the only questions concerned the details of expenditure. In essence, the Naval Estimates were trimmed to fit the national pocket, and ranged between 8 and 12 per cent of gross expenditure during the period under review. When the House of Commons voted out the Income or War Tax in 1816 they deprived the Liverpool Administration of the central plank of their postwar planning. The Ministers wanted to prepare for another 20 years of war by overhauling the fleet and the infrastructure, while keeping up a reasonable peace-time force. In the event both the dockyards and active ships were sacrificed to continue work on the reserve fleet. In periods of political tension funds were always short and policy-makers had to act within tight constraints. Indeed, the Whig Ministries of the 1830s bought political support with retrenchment. In 1839, realising they had gone too far, they ordered ten battleships, more than had been called for in the past 14 years combined. The restoration of the Income Tax in 1843 placed naval funding on more certain ground, but revealed serious weaknesses in the policy-making machinery created by the Whig Admiralty reform of 1832. As late as 1848 the Board of Admiralty was only able to exercise control over spending and programming after it had reorganised the Surveyor's Office. Within two years the screw steamship reached maturity, throwing all that had been achieved out of gear. After 1850 there could never again be the same certainty about the future, and naval programming became less amenable to long-term decisions.

Battlefleet strategy lay at the heart of British success in the 20-year war with France. It was the strategy for a long war in which reserves, economic strength and manufacturing base would all play an important role. By taking a long-term view the Navy cut back on the construction of small craft, which could be provided more quickly in wartime. The other mobilisation resource, manpower, was subject to prolonged discussion, but the basic policy was unaltered up to 1850. All naval administrators, from Melville and Martin in 1816 to Baring in 1850, were adamant that in the event of a war with France impressment would have to be used to man the fleet. For all the horror expressed by those of liberal persuasion this was the only answer to the problem before the introduction of continuous service and a statutory reserve in 1853. In the event of war the liberties of the individual would have, necessarily, been subsumed within the national interest.

The battlefleet was the contemporary deterrent. In periods of international tension it was used to signal British intentions. Most historians have argued that the Navy was incapable of influencing the major powers, but the fact is that the rulers of France, Russia and the United States all respected and feared the Royal Navy; all were vulnerable to seapower, as they demonstrated by building large coastal fortifications. As a case study in crisis management the Syrian campaign of 1840 could hardly be improved upon. By the skilful use of force against Egypt, Turkey was sustained, France deterred and Russia reconciled. Palmerston's diplomacy was based on seapower, not bluff.

The lessons of war

After 20 years of almost continuous warfare, not all of it as successful or as glorious as Trafalgar, Britain possessed a wealth of experience. This had a significant impact on postwar decision-making. While it tended to confirm the wisdom of the battlefleet strategy it added the requirement to prepare for another war of similar duration. At a more pragmatic level the emphasis was laid on the accurate use of heavy guns, larger ships and better supplies of seasoned timber. By addressing these issues in a rational manner the postwar fleet was better configured for the task of maintaining British pre-eminence. Furthermore, at a time when other nations were improving their fleets, the relative power of the Royal Navy was equally impressive.

The Establishment

The size and composition of the fleet in 1816, the Establishment, was based on the fleet of 1792, the last year of peace, and the number of men that could be raised in the first year of war, about 100,000, rather than any detailed calculation of the fleets of potential rivals. A figure of 100 battleships and 160 frigates was rather more than a two-power standard. Within the global totals the numbers of First, Second and Third Rate ships were determined by utility, relative cost and the availability of ships and timber. Large 84-gun two-deckers were popular as the cheapest vessels for mounting guns, while the three-decker remained the pre-eminent symbol of British strategy. They were irresistible in battle, as the French were the first to testify with their post-Trafalgar programme. For peace service the Navy Board elected to employ small and old ships, enabling them to save the large modern fleet for war and reduce the level of manpower. After 1816 the number of battleships on the list gradually declined as new construction failed to keep pace with the decay of the war-built emergency 74s. By 1850 the measure of a battleship had shifted; the 74 was no longer fit for fleet service, while a fleet of eighty First and Second Rates was far more powerful than the one hundred units of 1816. The desired Establishment was never achieved in practice, although in 1850 there were fifty-seven of the required eighty ships afloat or building, with twenty-seven old 74s as a reserve. This force was far larger than that of any other nation.

The battlefleet of 1815

As might be expected at the end of a long war, the existing battlefleet was large, consisting of over two hundred units. However, it suffered from block obsolescence, war damage and widespread decay. Hardly a dozen ships afloat could be said to meet postwar requirements. Although policy makers realised that an ideal fleet should be all new, they also recognised that they would have to rely on the existing units for many years to come due to the lack of money, slipways, manpower and timber. Furthermore, the ships afloat represented massive investment in timber, one that could not be thrown away without a serious impact on the price of new timber. As a result, the Navy Board adopted a programme of inspecting every ship, reporting on the probable cost of repair, and making recommendations as to whether they should be carried out. The Admiralty would then decide. Rebuilds were costly, but they employed skilled labour rather than timber, and as such kept up the war reserve of labour and preserved the standing timber, the latter further assisted by exploiting foreign sources of supply. Old or decayed ships were generally demolished in a Royal dockyard in order to save serviceable materials, or patched up for use as powder hulks, quarantine vessels, lazarettos or sheer hulks.

Ships already under construction in 1815 were suspended, save those building in merchant yards; allowed to stand over for seasoning; and often modified to fit in with the postwar requirement for larger and more powerfully-armed vessels. The last three 74s were stretched to carry 80 guns, with a heavier calibre on the main deck.

Designs for the new fleet

The first new postwar battleship to be ordered was the *Formidable*, an 84-gun facsimile of the *Canopus* and built from timber captured at Genoa, then a French dockyard. Four sisters were constructed at Bombay and another four in Royal yards. The only other class ordered before 1830 were further, broadened, editions of the 120-gun *Caledonia*. These two classes were the backbone of the battlefleet up to 1850. Both were modified to carry heavier guns, all 32-pounders after 1826. The large force of 74s precluded any work on Third Rates, although one was ordered in 1826, and two actually built in the following decade, albeit to a more powerful design. After 1826 any small 74 in need of a middling to large rebuild was cut down into a razee 50-gun Fourth Rate frigate, which was the only way to make such ships into modern war vessels. The type was employed by other fleets for commerce destruction, but had no role in the Royal Navy and used timber better employed in small two-deckers, which were a more powerful and flexible investment. As a result, only one new ship of that Rate, the experimental *Vernon* of 1831, was built before 1841.

The timber problem and foreign resources

During the war much effort had been given to securing foreign timber, both for hulls and the more traditional area of concern, masts. This reflected the failure of native sources of *seasoned* timber, something that can hardly be considered surprising given the astonishing demands and the extended period. There was always enough timber on the market, even if the price sometimes went beyond that which the Navy Board was prepared to pay (indeed, local competition for other uses often out-bid the Navy). The need was for a substitute that would allow the native woods to recover and produce mature trees in the future.

The East India Company offered to build battleships and frigates at cost plus 20 per cent at Bombay. The Navy accepted the offer, at first in desperation, but later from the high regard in which teak-built ships were held. However, the company, or its servants in India, were not above creative accounting and sharp practice, while the dockyard administration collapsed after the death of Jamsetjee, the last of the great Parsee master builders, in 1822. With the failure of local teak supplies, the inability of the Company to provide the duplicate frames that had always sweetened the bargain, and the serious downturn in shipbuilding in English merchant yards, the Indian connection was severed. The brief resumption of this link in the 1840s produced one battleship. In contrast to the position outlined by R G Albion, the native supply did not fail. Orders for British oak up to 1818 were as high as any in war time. However, the gradual shift to Italian oak and African teak gave British forests a breathing space to repair the ravages of two centuries of neglect and to build up a stock of mature timber for war time. Foreign timber also helped to bring down domestic prices. By 1839 first-class oak could not cover the cost of transport from Bedford to the Thames. British forestry, following Evelyn's *Sylva*, favoured single species plantations which promised to produce more timber per acre than the traditional mixed woodland. The object was to free land for arable farming. However, the advantages were impossible to achieve and the biological complexity of woodlands led to persistent failure. Forty years hard work in the Forest of Dean resulted in stunted, low-crowned trees of limited value. Italian oak provided the frames of the last British battleships, though they were planked with British oak.

War-time experience persuaded the constructors that much greater care had to be taken of the timber if the ships were to last. Seasoning in salt water, building slowly under cover, and improved maintenance in the Ordinary were all adopted. The results were good with more than half the postwar ships remaining afloat for 50 years. Few were ever given a significant repair and only the rush-built *Vernon* developed a major outbreak of dry rot. British ships cost less to build, less to maintain and lasted longer than their foreign contemporaries, with the possible exception of the United States. If British seapower was 'cheap', as many have suggested, the primary reason was the care taken in building the battlefleet.

Structural improvements

The one aspect of the postwar fleet that has been studied in some detail is the series of structural improvements developed by Sir Robert Seppings. However, these have never been accorded their proper place in the integrated naval revolution. There would have been little sense in building ships strong enough to resist the wracking strains of sea service if they were launched in a state of decay, while it would have been impossible to increase their armament unless the decks had been reinforced. Seppings's work allowed ships to be built on larger dimensions and carry heavier weights. Iron diagonals reinforced the frame, and superior timber inhibited the establishment of dry rot in the joint faces.

Guns and gunnery

The main reason for enlarged ships was the pressure to carry heavier weapons. The mixed battery of 1805 was at first improved, and in 1826 replaced by a uniform arming of 32-pounders throughout. Postwar designs were all selected for their ability to carry a heavy arming, and for their superior performance under sail. The former trend, driven by the Admiralty, was resisted by the Navy Board. The Controller, Admiral Byam Martin, steadfastly refused to mount any weapons that the ship could not carry on prolonged blockade service. Despite the trend towards over-arming evident in both the American and French services, Byam Martin wanted a fleet that could carry out a long blockade, not make the occasional fair weather cruise. Consequently, the first modern design for which he drew up the specification, the 90-gun *Nile*, Seppings's masterpiece, was the first battleship in the world to carry a uniform battery of long 32-pounder guns.

The battlefleet strategy forced British commanders to seek a decision, and this could only be guaranteed by close-range action. However, this did not blind them to the need for accuracy at long-range. With the establishment of the *Excellent* gunnery training ship in 1830 scientific gunnery came of age. British ships were now both more powerfully armed, and able to make better use of their weapons. Although new guns of increased range and power were cast, the battlefleet was slow to move from the tried and tested 32-pounder. Only at the very end of the sailing era were significant numbers of shell guns mounted, as a supplement to the concentrated fire of solid shot. The great object was to fight at point-blank range, where no elevation was required, so that every round would tell. For this the ship required a battery of guns with similar performance, not a collection of samples. Heavier guns were seen as a substitute for numbers in steam ships which lacked the space for a proper battery.

The end of the Navy Board

The Whig Administration of 1830 came into office committed to economic retrenchment and political reform; the first, a popular measure, was to earn support for the other about which few were concerned. This, along with Earl Grey's long-standing aversion to the Navy Board ensured that part of the financial saving would be secured by a radical overhaul of naval administration, in particular by abolishing the Navy Board. In 1832 the Controller and Surveyor were replaced by a new Surveyor, Captain William Symonds, an amateur yacht builder with powerful political patrons. The post of Surveyor was to be changed from that of chief designer to policy programmer. Unfortunately, this was never made explicit and Symonds elected to promote his own design ideas, which were radical and not entirely successful, rather than act as a Controller, which was the real object of the new system. In addition, the political nature of the reforms made his ships the subject of bitter political and technical controversy throughout his term of office. Symonds built a series of large, fast and powerful ships that broke the mould of design and allowed his rivals to build on the same generous dimensions. They provided a vital element of the integrated revolution, resolving the age-old tactical dilemma because they had the speed to force a flying enemy to fight. This aspect of his work has never been given due credit, while the bitter attack by the new scientific naval architects, which has been sustained to this day, explains why he has received such a poor press. Symonds was more successful, and more significant, than his detractors were prepared to admit, and the political and professional passions which his tenure in office raised have served to obscure the truth ever since. His battleships were unequalled by any foreign designs. In the brief period before the end of the sailing fleet new ships were drafted, with less beam and flatter floors, but none were completed before they were all converted to steam. Naval policy making was overhauled during the last half of the 1840s, and with the retirement of Symonds this resulted in the effective recreation of a policy-programming department at Somerset House under an officer who would be renamed the Controller of the Navy in 1860.

Infrastructure

No battlefleet can exist in a vacuum, as Russian attempts to operate in the Black Sea without a drydock demonstrated. The construction and repair of wooden warships occupied a major part of their careers. In 1815 Britain possessed an unrivalled combination of bases and construction yards. During the last years of the War some had hoped to form an entirely new arsenal on the Thames at Northfleet. In the event, the postwar Navy never had the funds for such an ambitious project, and instead restricted new work to the old sites. The Sheerness yard was rebuilt by Sir John Rennie in the first decade of peace, but all other major yard improvements before 1850 were concerned with stores and victualling, or the advance of steam.

The shortage of dockyard space, docks and slipways was highlighted by the postwar policy of building ships slowly to allow them to season in frame and plank. Slip time trebled, and then doubled again when it was decided to leave ships out of the water until they were required. Additional slips were rendered more costly by the decision taken to roof over all slips and docks.

The impact of finance on the yards was, if anything, more severe than elsewhere in the fleet. Infrastructure was repeatedly sacrificed to extra ships or men afloat. Economy, for all its political attractions, could not be carried too far. Deptford was closed as a construction yard, but had to be re-opened within a few years.

The British battlefleet sustained the one world empire of the period, deterred her rivals, and defeated those who dared to presume, from Algiers to China. All this was achieved on low estimates and with only a modest active fleet a fitting tribute to the strength of the Navy and basic soundness of strategic and naval thought.

The three-decker St. Vincent, *anchored off Whale Island in Portsmouth Harbour at the turn of the century. Launched in 1815 to a design by the Surveyors of the Navy, the* St. Vincent *was among the most active of all the postwar battleships. In 1849 her poop was removed, leaving her with the unique profile on view here, a flush upper deck with unbroken sheer. This deck was armed with two heavy pivot guns, reflecting the new thinking of the steam era. Her last seagoing service as a Flagship was between 1847 and 1849, when she flew the Flag of Rear Admiral Sir Charles Napier, the most controversial sea officer of his generation. In 1854 she carried French troops to the Baltic, but thereafter was restricted to harbour service. Built before the introduction of Sir Robert Seppings's diagonal frame the* St. Vincent *was extensively repaired, given stronger decks and an increased weight of arming, so that by 1849 she was a far more powerful ship than she had been in 1815. Curiously enough this work also appears to have improved her sailing qualities.* (NMM)

Part One

THE FOUNDATIONS OF SEAPOWER

1 *Strategy*

Between 1815 and 1850 Great Britain was, in comparative terms, at the apogee of its power. The combination of industrial primacy and economic power with the prestige of Trafalgar and Waterloo earned Britain the respect, albeit grudging, of all nations. To maintain that position in a rapidly changing world where political, economic and technical developments constantly shifted the bases of decision-making required the constant supervision of clear-sighted statesmen. To meet the situation they required a close understanding of the interests and abilities of Britain, an informed view of the world and a clear understanding of the need to sustain a national strategy, without bankrupting the exchequer. British strategy was dictated by her position as a maritime empire with an insular base off the coast of Europe. Alone among her contemporaries, Britain depended entirely upon seapower for national security and economic prosperity.[1] This forced her to adopt the battlefleet strategy, a programme which Mahan argued in 1890 was the foundation of British primacy. Securing control of the sea by superior naval force was the foundation of British policy. From it flowed a variety of rewards and options. In order of priority these were: In wartime:

1 The defence of the British Isles from invasion.
2 The defence of the Empire, both the maritime communications that held it together, and the ability to send troop reinforcements in time of war.
3 The defence of oceanic trade.
4 Carrying the war to the enemy, by interdicting trade, launching amphibious operations and supporting hostile coalitions.

In time of peace:

1 Deterrence, preventing war by the possession of overwhelming force.
2 The protection of British commercial interests.
3 Expansion of trade and the safe use of the seas for the benefit of British trade.

After 1815 the roles of war and diplomacy in British foreign policy reflected the new situation, but both remained vital elements in an enhanced world position. Despite the illusion of a 'Pax Britannica', armed force was in almost constant use around the world, to preserve the only world empire of the period from a variety of challenges, both external and internal. Foreign policy attempted to control the external environment, the framework within which military power might have to be employed, and it established the current dangers to British interests. Yet for all the success of diplomatic efforts there remained an underlying requirement for military force in case diplomacy could not resolve international disputes. Decisions on the size and composition of those forces was, in peace time, the major military input into national strategy. The instability of French regimes, with five changes of government between 1815 and 1851, in combination with the overt hostility of all five at some stage in their development, ensured that Britain had to maintain powerful forces to face her closest rival, while giving serious consideration to the strategic challenge posed by Russia and the United States.

Strategy

'War', to use Clausewitz's time-honoured expression, 'is merely the continuation of policy by other means'.[2] Strategy is the political exploitation of war, actual or threatened. During this period, largely spent at peace or in small conflicts, the great bulk of strategic deliberation took place away from the actual conduct of war and was therefore both more reflective and less urgent. The decisions concerned force levels and budgets, rather than campaigns and battles. Furthermore, Britain's world position was such that policy makers were conscious of the very limited freedom of action they possessed short of war. However, once at war the vision of British statesmen was truly global. Three case studies reveal particular aspects of this: the exploitation of opportunities which came about as a result of the collapse of the Napoleonic empire; the rapid overthrow of Egypt in 1840 and the war against Russia.

It has been suggested that naval officers were ignorant of strategy, confined to the tactical dimension by their fleet-bound horizons. While it is true that naval officers compiled tactical doctrine from the early sixteenth century and made no written contribution to the strategic debate until the middle of the nineteenth century this is not a true reflection of their role or intelligence. Senior British Admirals, both at sea and at the Admiralty had displayed considerable skill in the handling of warfare at the strategic level. From the time of Anson there was an accepted programme for a French war, although no-one thought it sufficiently remarkable to warrant publication. Nelson's 1805 campaign, along with his attempt to exploit the battle of the Nile, reveal the sure touch of a great mind. Other British Admirals were capable of coherent and logical argument on strategic issues and were well aware of the national interest.

Their political masters took care that they were kept abreast of the views of the government so that they had a sound framework within which to act. If the Navy was reluctant to write on strategy this was at least in part a reflection on the national character. Only in the nineteenth century did strategic thought become a topic for publication. It is hardly surprising that the works of Mahan, Colomb and Corbett should take so many examples of sound strategy from the history of the Royal Navy; for a Navy to have been successful for so long it must have had a sound appreciation of strategy. By contrast the French, who were rather earlier into the field of strategic analysis, were always seeking tactical or technical solutions for their basic strategic problem, and in consequence were rarely successful.

Conference strategy and the reduction of risk: 1814–15

During the Wars of the French Revolution and Empire, Britain made an unprecedented commitment of her resources in efforts to prevent France sustaining the continental hegemony. For example, the levels of direct taxation were far higher during these wars than during either of the World Wars of the twentieth century. The explanation for this determination can be found in two, connected, areas. First, Britain could not afford to leave France in a position to mobilise the united resources of Europe, for war or commerce. Second, French occupation of the Low Countries posed a specific and vital threat to British insular security. After the war British statesmen sought peace and stability, conditions under which British economic expansion could thrive. These could not be assumed, or left to other countries to guarantee; Britain would have to take a part in maintaining the *status quo*. A major element in the peace strategy was the creation of viable buffer states on the frontiers of France. Prussia was brought onto the Rhine, while the Low Countries and Sardinia were reinforced and linked with British interests.

The Victory *around the turn of the century, with Gosport in the background. Between March 1814 and January 1816 the* Victory*, which had been re-rated as a Second Rate, was rebuilt with a round bow and heavy poop deck bulwarks at a cost of £80,000. After 1817 she was once again classed as a First Rate and fulfilled a variety of duties in Portsmouth Harbour for the rest of the century.* (CMP)

At the end of the Napoleonic Wars Britain was left with a large empire, burgeoning international trade sustained by economic and industrial primacy, and an unprecedented degree of influence in the Councils of the European nations. All these factors were deployed by British statesmen in an effort to sustain British power and the first opportunities arose before the fighting had stopped when British statesmen directed the efforts of their forces, and those in their pay, to secure strategic points that were certain to be contentious at the peace.

The Napoleonic War forced British policy makers to realise that while their means were inadequate to overthrow France national security demanded nothing less. The diplomatic and financial sacrifices accepted in the formation of four major coalitions are clear evidence of an underlying desire to restrict France to her prewar frontiers. The key to sustained British opposition to French hegemony lay in the Austrian Netherlands, modern Belgium. The occupation of this province by France in 1793 had been the *causus belli* for Britain, and Napoleon's intransigence in this area destroyed his last hopes of a negotiated settlement in 1814.

Pitt the Younger had always hoped to return these provinces to their previous rulers, the Austrian Hapsburgs, who had no interest in developing the commercial or strategic power of Antwerp and the Scheldt River. After Austria signed away her claims he shifted his aims to uniting the territory with the Netherlands, a policy that was central to the programme of the Third Coalition against Napoleon. At the same time he expressed a desire to hand over the threatening naval base at Genoa to Sardinia. These aims forced Pitt to consider the overthrow of Napoleon, and to achieve this he required the united strength of the three eastern monarchies, in particular Prussia, hitherto largely content to watch the progress of the struggle. Prussian refusal ensured that only Antwerp and a narrow barrier were to be transferred, but Pitt must have realised that French ambitions, indicated by the new arsenal, would not be given up short of complete defeat.

After Pitt's death the abortive combined operation against Antwerp in 1809 reflected British disquiet at the steady growth of the arsenal and the battlefleet on the Scheldt. Only in 1813, with the European situation turning in their favour, could British policy makers again consider action for the future of Belgium. The Liverpool Cabinet, with disciples of Pitt as Prime Minister and, in Lord Castlereagh, as Foreign Secretary, made this a priority. They were committed to the most favourable solution, Pitt's Netherlands union scheme of 1804–5. A rising broke out in the Netherlands on 15 November 1813 providing the opportunity to promote the claims of the Prince of Orange in Belgium, and possibly to capture the arsenal before the end of hostilities in central Europe, thereby simplifying the process of handing it over to the Netherlands at the peace table. A small, make-shift, army under General Sir Thomas Graham, later Lord Lynedoch, was quickly dispatched to link up with Russian, Prussian and Swedish forces. At the same time Castlereagh opened a diplomatic offensive at allied headquarters, initially through his envoys Lord Cathcart to the Tsar, and Lord Aberdeen at the Austrian Court. They were to explain the strategic imperative to the allied monarchs, and make use of the greatest instrument of coercion left to the British Government:

Victory in 1963, following her extensive reconstruction in No 2 dock at Portsmouth, and the overhaul of her rigging. (CMP)

> I must particularly entreat you to keep your attention upon Antwerp. The destruction of that arsenal is essential to our safety. To leave it in the hands of France is little short of imposing upon Great Britain the charge of a perpetual war establishment. After all we have done for the continent this war, they owe it to us and to themselves to extinguish this fruitful source of danger to both. Press this as a primary object of their operations; and, in order to render the value of the fleet, if taken or destroyed, more available for their present expenses, we shall be ready to pay them immediately in credit bills, which they can now realise as advantageously on the continent as a bill upon the Treasury.[3]

Finally, Britain offered considerable direct, and indirect, financial inducements to her allies, while the Cabinet were willing to return colonial conquests.[4] To avoid difficulties with the allies, Castlereagh had pressed for an early liberation of Belgium. Unfortunately, Graham's campaign in the Netherlands was crippled by the paucity and poor quality of his troops, and the failure of allied co-operation. Lacking the resources to take Antwerp he made a bold assault on Bergen op Zoom in March, but was beaten off with heavy casualties.[5] Napoleon took great interest in Antwerp, sending General Carnot to command the defences, although he did strip the arsenal of workers to reinforce his armies after the disastrous Battle of Leipzig. At the Chatillon negotiations Caulaincourt, the French representative, tried to use Antwerp as a lever to separate the continental allies from Britain, something Castlereagh had anticipated. Napoleon claimed that British intransigence on this point was the only barrier to a settlement. After Napoleon's abdication Castlereagh quickly secured the consent of the new French regime to the union of Belgium with the Netherlands, before negotiating the peace settlement at Paris in May 1814. Having secured the vital British interest he directed his efforts toward a moderate European settlement, one which would help to preserve peace and stability. To this end the French were allowed to remove two-thirds of their fleet in the Scheldt. This, as Castlereagh knew, was no great sacrifice as the ships had been built hurriedly of unseasoned Hainault timber and would soon decay.[6] As the United Netherlands already possessed a number of naval arsenals he expected the Prince of Orange would agree to leave Antwerp as a commercial port, without the facilities and fortifications of a major naval base and the Scheldt would be a free river for commerce for the first time since 1585. Old objections to commercial navigation were replaced by the need to reconcile the Belgians to their new master, for Castlereagh saw in the stability of the United Netherlands a barrier to French expansion, leading to the security of Britain. After 1830 Palmerston had to reconsider

Foudroyant, the second British 80-gun two-decker, was launched in 1798 and served as Flagship to both Lord Nelson and Sir Sidney Smith. She is seen here after her reconstruction by Wheatley Cobb in 1892. (CMP)

this assumption. By the Treaty of London of 1837 he ensured the independence and neutrality of Belgium, achieving the same result by new means. In addition, Belgium took a Coburg King, increasing her links with Britain. He would not allow France to control Belgium, and the only way to prevent this was to undo the 1814 Union.[7] Castlereagh was also cultivating the Prince of Orange, planning a dynastic alliance between Princess Charlotte and the Prince's son.

In a similar vein the capture of Genoa in April 1814 offered an opportunity to improve the strategic situation. The city was handed over to Sardinia. Here also the prime consideration had been strategic. The French dockyard increased the naval resources of the Napoleonic Empire, and the danger to Britain, in a sea where British influence was paramount. Therefore the city had to be linked with a stable barrier nation, to prevent its early return to France.[8] The dockyard at Genoa contained large stocks of first class timber, and a recently launched battleship. The timber was loaded aboard this ship, taken back to Britain, and used to build the first postwar British battleship. The French 74 *Brilliant*, renamed *Genoa*, served the Royal Navy for twenty years, notably at Navarin.

Foudroyant on Blackpool beach. After her reconstruction Wheatley Cobb took the ship around Britain to raise funds, but she was driven ashore during a gale on 16 June 1897 and later broken up in situ. (CMP)

Wellington considered that any money given to the Sardinians should be spent on fortifying Genoa, rather than raising troops. Thirteen years later, in response to a request for assistance in obtaining artillery and powder, he observed that 'the King of Sardinia is the best friend that we have in Europe. He is our natural ally, and the least likely to be burthensome to us.'[9]

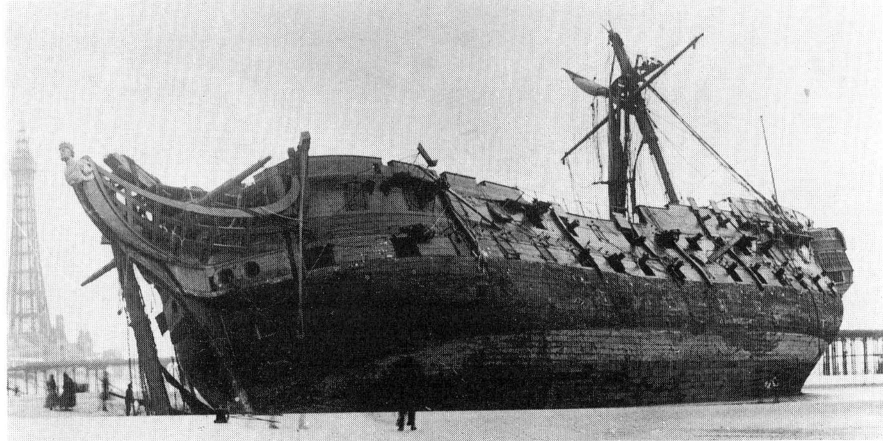

Venice, another important Napoleonic dockyard, was handed over, complete with the ships, to form the base and nucleus of the Austrian Navy. Austria, having no particular interest in seapower, made an ideal custodian for the base. Naples was returned to her unpopular and oppressive rulers, as much to ensure she remained an Austrian client as from any interest in the dockyard. As with Antwerp, Genoa and Venice the object was to place these dangerous arsenals in the hands of nations capable of holding them in the event of another war. That they were also third rate naval powers was an added benefit.

The wartime threat posed by these dockyards, along with those of metropolitan France during the high years of the Napoleonic Empire, from 1809 to 1812, had been immense.[10] However, recent revisionist work exaggerates the danger to Britain posed by the number of French ships, paying little attention to the seamanship of the French and satellite fleets, manned as they were by unwilling conscripts from as far afield as Greece and Albania; the difficulties of linking up widely scattered forces in the face of British blockading squadrons; and to the impact of premature decay on this rush-built armada. In truth, the first ships had decayed beyond effective service before their sisters were complete, as Baron Charles Dupin made clear in his harsh, contemporary French account.[11] Even so, this was the first time the combined naval resources of Europe had been exploited in an attempt to overpower British command of the sea in battle and this posed a far more serious threat to Britain than the gamble of 1805. A superior battlefleet could obtain command of the sea, and cut Britain off from her overseas colonies and trade. This would destroy the base of her prosperity, and with it her ability to challenge French hegemony in Europe. An invasion would merely complete the defeat. British statesmen were very conscious of this danger when they approached the peace settlement. Peace diplomacy in 1814 and 1815 was dominated by the need to preserve maritime superiority. To this end they prohibited discussion on the troubled issue of maritime rights, believing economic warfare had played a significant part in the overthrow of Napoleon. All other interests, therefore, were sacrificed, as far as necessary, to the reduction of the strategic threat from France. A cabinet of statesmen experienced in war placed this danger above all other issues. Castlereagh's diplomacy should be judged by the degree to which he reduced the strategic menace inherent in the French bases outside the 1792 frontiers. His success laid the foundation for half a century of cheap security and created a position unchallenged until the full effect of industrial developments, only dimly perceived in his time, had revolutionised the fabric and capabilities of seapower.

French seapower was not a fundamental concern especially while the French had other security concerns; it had been dealt with before. The danger came when Europe was united by France, and this could be more effectively, and economically, prevented by diplomacy rather than by increased naval spending. The first element of British strategy in the period 1815–50 had been decided before Waterloo. That Napoleon elected to make his gamble for power in 1815 by invading Belgium was no accident; he still believed this was the one area where he could drive a wedge between Britain and the Continental powers. Guided by Castlereagh, Britain accepted a major role in postwar European affairs which was exploited to maintain a favourable strategic situation. The 1814–15 settlement was

Bellerophon of 80 guns. Launched in 1818 as the *Waterloo*, the *Bellerophon* had a distinguished career, which included the bombardment of Sevastopol on 17 October 1854. With her round bow and square stern she is typical of the state of British battleship design at the end of the Napoleonic Wars. (NMM)

used to reduce the strategic danger to British interests, something that in turn allowed a reduction in defence spending. By the same token the capture of French bases during the war had been a major benefit for the defence of trade. For example, without Mauritius, French frigate squadrons and privateers could not operate in the Indian Ocean. In this context positive strategic assets, retained in 1815, particularly Malta and the Cape of Good Hope, were as important as those denied to France. A strategic naval base had a financial value for while bases in potentially hostile hands imposed a requirement for higher levels of naval activity, those in British hands reduced demand. Though the Whigs attacked the retention of so many bases after 1815 as expensive, they represented in essence an economy measure. They allowed the Navy to operate in distant waters, and denied rivals the same advantages. In the late 1840s the Third Earl Grey, as Secretary of State for War and the Colonies, attempted to reduce the colonial garrisons to create a reserve or expeditionary force in Britain. This was not carried through to the extent envisaged, leaving his successor with serious problems in finding an army for the Russian War.[12]

To replace the fear of a united Europe Castlereagh, for one, began to see that Russia, having made tremendous progress, was already a serious rival. In alliance with France she would be almost as dangerous as the Napoleonic Empire. Russian pressure on Turkey, Sweden and Persia gave considerable cause for concern and the decision to retain the Ionian Islands in 1814 was largely conditioned by concern with the Balkan activities of Russia.[13] By the time the great powers assembled at Aix-la-Chapelle in 1818, Castlereagh referred to a Franco-Russian combination as 'the only one that can prove really formidable to the liberties of Europe'.[14] The preceding year he had stressed that a two-power naval standard remained central to British strategy, and it was not difficult to see which two powers he had in mind. By 1820 his policy had become a complex balancing act which attempted to detach France from Russian influence, without, at the same time driving Austria and Russia together. However, France remained the most serious threat to British hegemony in the Mediterranean, limiting the extent to which she could be trusted.

The Greek revolt of 1821 posed a new menace in the Mediterranean, that of a Russian fleet. The Tsar's ambitions in the Ionian Islands had been defeated by Castlereagh in 1814–15; but Canning had to face the renewed danger of a Russian fleet entering the Mediterranean. This threat coloured the official reaction to the Greek cause throughout the War of Independence.[15]

To sum up, the task of Castlereagh and his successors at the Foreign Office was to prevent the repetition of a threat such as that posed by the Napoleonic Empire. This was initially a diplomatic problem, which could, however, lead to war. As Britain was largely a *status quo* power in Europe after 1815, the success of her diplomacy could be measured by the extent to which British interests were upheld without recourse to war. That there was no repeat of the Napoleonic threat was, in part, a reflection of the success of British diplomacy, backed by deterrence. There were many challenges to British interests in

Greece, Belgium, the Ottoman Empire, North America, the Caribbean, Persia, China and Scandinavia but few led to conflict and none reached the scale of the Napoleonic Wars.

'The sheet anchor of Europe': The Navy and the maintenance of supremacy[16]

The great investment of effort and money in the settlement of 1814–15 was rendered necessary by the particular demands of Britain's position in the world. As an insular maritime power, economically dependent on trade, her commitment to the sea was not equalled by any other nation and required her to maintain large naval forces paid for by the prosperity which flowed from the world trading empire they protected.

Throughout the nineteenth century British maritime strategy was necessarily based on sea control. Given the technology of the era this required a superior battlefleet for, in the last resort, the ability to defeat any rivals in battle was the acid test of British power. Consequently, the battlefleet became the principal peace-time concern of the Admiralty and the ability to sustain a fleet equal to that of any two other powers was the key element in British strategic thinking. With a superior battlefleet the navy could guarantee the security of the home islands, restrict the enemy attack on commerce and play a major role in supporting any European alliance. Without it the British position was indefensible. In every major war sea control had been the vital prerequisite for victory and so all other naval issues revolved around, and were subordinate to, the battlefleet.

One of the perennial postwar debates concerned the balance between forces protecting British commercial interests in the wider world, and the battlefleet in home waters and the Mediterranean. Given the importance of a strong economy to long-term funding the issue was by no means as simple as some policy makers appeared to believe. After 1815 the Navy had to meet increasing commitments outside Europe in defence of British commerce and built warships for this role, often at the expense of the battlefleet.

One of the abiding problems for historical commentators on the British strategic position has been their ignorance of contemporary sea control strategy. Given the limitations of contemporary ships, sea control was a reactive concept and British statesmen had to meet whatever strategic programme their rivals might devise, without sacrificing the fighting power of the battlefleet. During the nineteenth century the British response to new technology was clear: understand and develop, but only introduce to meet an obvious need, brought on by the actions of a rival.[17]

Naval decision-making was complicated by the economic limitations facing a Government. These limitations were a vast National Debt and a House of Commons unwilling to retain the Income Tax. As a result, priority decisions had to be made on shrinking budgets. The contrast between the ideal response outlined in 1815 and the repeated constriction of funding after 1817 emphasised the stark contrast between ambition and ability. In practice, manpower was cut in an effort to sustain work on the battlefleet and its infrastructure. By the late 1820s this process had gone so far that the Government was forced to ignore the individual heads of expenditure contained in the estimates and switch money from timber to manpower in an effort to meet a sudden emergency in the eastern Mediterranean without opening its policy to scrutiny by calling for additional funds.

The use of force in diplomacy

The value of naval power, short of war, was based on the perception of what it could achieve. Some historians have argued that this role was small. They suggest that a succession of relatively short European and colonial wars in the eighteenth century demonstrated that in order to have any real influence on the continent Britain required an ally. The limitations of naval power as a factor in European affairs were demonstrated, it is suggested, by the Ochakov crisis of 1790, when Pitt the Younger backed down from threatening Russia because seapower alone was inadequate to coerce the Tsarist state.[18]

This is a superficial analysis. British power could have had a serious impact on Russia in war, but in 1790 the issue at stake, Russian expansion in the Black Sea, was not one for which Britain was prepared to fight alone for a variety of reasons that had nothing to do with the value of naval forces against continental states. In fact, the ability of seapower to influence continental conflicts increased with the duration of a war. After twenty years of conflict Castlereagh realised that the French economy had been broken by the blockade and counter blockade.[19] Furthermore, the increasing efficiency of the sailing ship had made blockades and coastal operations more certain than they had been in the preceding century. The naval history of the war after 1805 is dominated by the small-scale operations against mercantile traffic and minor ports and these could only be carried out under the *aegis* of a successful battlefleet.

To judge from the amounts of money expended by Britain's

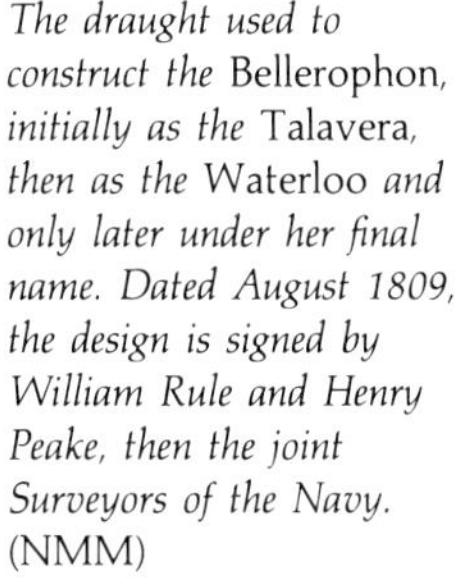

The draught used to construct the Bellerophon, *initially as the* Talavera, *then as the* Waterloo *and only later under her final name. Dated August 1809, the design is signed by William Rule and Henry Peake, then the joint Surveyors of the Navy.* (NMM)

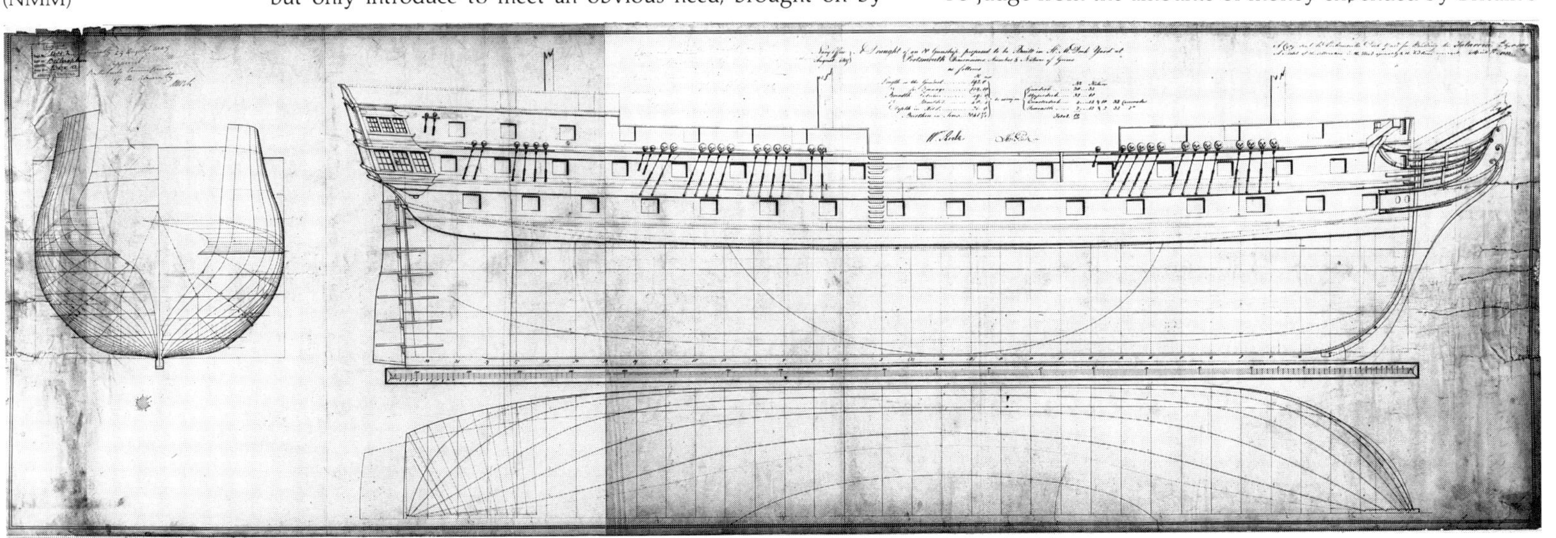

rivals on coastal defences and fleets between 1815 and 1850 it would appear that Russia, France and the United States all maintained a healthy respect for the power of naval forces. This in turn amplified the deterrent value of naval forces in European diplomacy. While it was ever obvious to other powers that they had little or no chance of defeating the Royal Navy, they were also acutely conscious of the threat it posed to their interests. Consequently, naval forces were a vital method of signalling British intentions to rivals. British fleets occupied the entrance to the Dardanelles on four occasions in the nineteenth century, to warn Russia of Britain's abiding interest in the fate of Turkey. On three occasions diplomacy and threat proved adequate and only once was it necessary to go to war. French bluster and newspaper threats of invasion in the late 1840s were met by the careful maintenance in the Western Approaches of a battlefleet equal to the force available at Brest and Cherbourg, a clear warning of the fate awaiting any attempt to cross a contested sea. The one linking factor that connects all uses of force in this period is the perception of the nature of the British interests that were under threat. British statesmen made it perfectly clear that they would commit their forces, if diplomacy failed, to preserve the strategic position. The success of the reserve fleet was of critical importance for deterrence diplomacy and the ability to mobilise a large force at short notice gave Britain her voice. During the Spanish crisis of 1823–24 George Canning, the Foreign Secretary, stressed the role of the reserve fleet to the people of Plymouth.

> But ... let it not be said that we cultivate peace either because we fear, or because we are unprepared for, war ... Our present repose is no more a proof of inability to act, than the state of inertness and inactivity in which I have seen those mighty masses that float in the waters above your town, is a proof they are devoid of strength, and incapable of being fitted out for action. You well know how soon one of those stupendous masses, now reposing in their shadows in perfect stillness – how soon, upon any call of patriotism, or of necessity, it would assume the likeness of an animated thing, instinct with life and motion – how soon it would ruffle, as it were, its swelling plumage – how quickly it would collect all its beauty and its bravery, collect its scattered elements of strength, and awaken its dormant thunder. Such is one of these magnificent machines when springing from inaction into a display of its might – such is England herself: while apparently passive and motionless, she silently concentrates the power to be put forth on an adequate occasion.[20]

Subsequent British statesmen may have lacked Canning's eloquence, but all appreciated the point. The reserve fleet gave Britain the power to act. Those who take the 'Pax Britannica' argument to the extreme, suggesting that the nineteenth-century Royal Navy was nothing more than a collection of gunboats have missed this point. The reserve strength of the Royal Navy was so great that it could safely operate as a gunboat force in time of peace, but it had the ability to mobilise a battlefleet equal or superior to that of any potential rival.[21]

The multiple crises of 1830–34 had revealed the weakness of British deterrence in a more complex situation. The Belgian revolt, leading ultimately to the separation of the Low Countries, was the first and most important issue. The British response, given the sensitive nature of Antwerp and the desire to maintain a viable barrier to French control of the ports of Belgium and the Netherlands, was fraught with danger. The peace-time Army had no disposable reserves with which to mount an operation in Europe, which meant that the only force capable of removing the Dutch garrison from the citadel at Antwerp was the French Army, the last thing any British government wanted to see in Belgium, and in particular at Antwerp. Naval pressure could have no short-term benefit, although the powerful squadron cruising against Dutch trade was at least a signal to France that her word would be judged by performance rather than accepted on trust. The Civil War in Portugal, in which the British played a major, if supposedly unofficial, part also called for the presence of a battle squadron, this time anchored in the Tagus. Once both these forces had been committed, removing or weakening either would have given dangerous signals. Consequently, when Mehemet Ali, Pasha of Egypt, defeated the Ottoman army and threatened Constantinople, Britain had no disposable force with which to respond to the Sultan's request for assistance. This allowed Russia to meet the despairing Turkish plea and secure the dominant place in the Sultan's councils. Although Britain and France sent ships to Besika Bay they were too late. Russia secured her influence with the Treaty of Unkiar Skelessi in 1834. Alarmist opinion in Britain believed this included a secret clause allowing Russian warships to pass through the Dardanelles. Had this been true Britain's strategic position would have been seriously weakened but, in fact, Russia had no such ambition for her anxieties and aims were defensive, fearing Britain would pass through the Bosphorus.[22]

Implacable *of 74 guns, previously the French* Duguay-Trouin, *captured by Sir Richard Strachan in November 1805.* (Tenby)

The recovery of British influence in Turkey during the Syrian campaign of 1840 involved deterrence, crisis management and war. In a complex situation British policy required the maintenance of Turkey against Russia, the defeat of Egyptian efforts to increase their share of the Ottoman Empire, and the removal of French support for Egypt. Palmerston understood that if Mehemet Ali succeeded he would destroy the Ottoman Empire, leaving Russia to occupy Constantinople. The rapid overthrow of Mehemet Ali's hold on Syria, before France could prepare a fleet or muster the political will to fight, ended the pressure on the Turkish Empire that had forced the Sultan to accept Russian 'protection' in 1833–34. This had, in turn, been seen as entirely counter to British interests. Palmerston was determined to reverse this treaty, and in 1840 he took the

The Bombay-built teak 74-gun Wellesley *as the training ship* Cornwall *lying off Gravesend sometime this century. Fate had a curious end in store for this fine old ship for she was sunk in an air attack on 24 September 1940.* (CMP)

opportunity, despite strong opposition within the Cabinet. In addition, the Egyptian fleet, in combination with that of France, posed a second serious challenge to British power in the Mediterranean. The Straits Convention of 1841 replaced the Russo-Turkish treaty of 1834 with a five-power guarantee; restored the *status quo* at Constantinople, so reconciling Britain and Russia; ended the threat from Egypt; and administered to the French a sharp lesson in power politics. While Palmerston provided the diplomacy, he relied on the British battlefleet to back up his policy. Less obvious results were a Mediterranean fleet reduced to its lowest level for a decade and a sharp reduction in Russian naval expenditure. Palmerston saw in the rapid capture of Acre an invaluable lesson for the rest of the world, a reminder that the Royal Navy had the power to take on coastal fortresses.[23]

The great powers were not afraid to use their power to coerce smaller nations and in this Britain was no exception. In most cases such action was too petty to involve the battlefleet but in Portugal, Greece and the Italian states heavy units were deployed in support of diplomacy. In the Far East British commercial pressure on China ended with three battleships clearing away the forts below Canton. Lord Exmouth's attack on Algiers in August 1816, almost repeated in 1824, was a spectacular reassertion of power in support of European ideals.

It would be possible to examine each use of force in the period and extract strategic motives but it would be of little value. Britain was prepared to fight for her interests and to exploit the inability of other states to match her power. Her response to each new challenge was based on a clear understanding of the dangers posed, and the level of force required to ensure a favourable outcome. British battlefleet units were involved in many crises between 1815 and 1860: Algiers 1816, the independence of South America 1815–30, Algiers 1825, Portugal 1825–29, Greece 1827–30, Belgium 1830–34, Portugal 1832–35, the Dardanelles 1833–34, Syria 1840, China 1840–43, Tahiti 1843–45, the Oregon territory 1844–45, Portugal 1846–48, Morocco 1848–50, Sicily and Genoa 1848–49, Dardanelles 1848, Don Pacifico blockade of Athens 1850, Burma 1852, Dardanelles 1853, the Russian War 1854–56, Portugal 1855–56, Serpents' Island 1856 and China 1856–60. The failure of British diplomacy often reflected a weakness in the available fleet combined with the lack of political will to summon up the reserve strength; it was not a reflection on the ultimate power of the battlefleet or on the power of Britain to influence events.

The weak response to the French occupation of Algiers in 1830 provides a particularly clear demonstration. The Wellington Administration, on the verge of collapse in the face of domestic pressures, would not commit forces to the Mediterranean to prevent or supervise the French invasion. Having accepted a transparent French promise to evacuate after 'chastising' the Algerians, members of that Administration had to live with the strategic threat posed by a steadily growing French base on the North African coast for the remainder of their political lives. A more resolute government could have prevented the French move for the Royal Navy was so superior to the French fleet that no sane man would have embarked on the operation while there remained a chance of British intervention.

The Russian War: an attempt to change strategic parameters

While British strategy between 1815 and 1850 has been seen as essentially reactive and defensive, seeking to sustain the 1815 position, it should be understood that once at war British policy makers were always prepared to exploit success to secure further advantages. The late nineteenth-century view that the British Empire had no ambitions, and only went to war to protect her friends, should not be extended back to cover the earlier period. Whatever later apologists might argue, British statesmen in the period under review had a clear conception of Britain's interests, and made certain they were upheld.

In this respect the Russian War of 1854–56 provides the most important example. Hitherto, this conflict has been misunderstood, leading many to ignore the aggressive intent and strategic ambitions of Palmerston. Briefly, although Palmerston did not want to start the war he hoped, from the opening of the crisis in 1853, to use a war between Russia and Turkey to drive the Tsarist Empire out of several important regions where it posed a strategic threat to Britain, direct or otherwise, and use the peace settlement to establish barriers against any future advances. It was no coincidence that the three theatres that attracted his particular interest – the Black Sea, the Baltic and the Northern Ocean – had long been recognised as important areas of conflicting ambition. Palmerston sought to push back Russian frontiers, deprive her of access to open waters, naval command of the Black Sea and Baltic and access to territories bordering on Persia. The programme was similar in ambition, if not in its ultimate success, to that of Pitt and Castlereagh. Even so, Palmerston was able to impose lasting limits on Russian expansion. Her position in the Baltic was compromised and never recovered; on the shores of the Northern Ocean her ambitions were permanently halted; while the demilitarisation of the Black Sea, although abrogated in 1870, deprived her of effective naval power in the war of 1877–79, and in combination with a British fleet in the Marmora was enough to preserve Turkey into the twentieth century.

There are other examples of British strategic ambition being furthered by aggression such as the occupation of Aden in 1839, a small but significant act, which reflected the need for secure steam communications between Suez and Bombay.[24]

Naval rivals and alternative strategies

When Mahan suggested that a battlefleet strategy was the royal road to world power his object was to persuade his countrymen to create a fleet that would provide security for the United States. This message was taken up by contemporaries in states which had little requirement for sea control. Mahan's views have also been applied retrospectively to criticise the programmes of Britain's less successful rivals, without considering how far those powers created their own national strategies to meet requirements that they perceived with the same clarity that Britain applied to the battlefleet. In this period no other power shared Britain's advantages and requirements as a naval power, in particular none depended on sea control for national survival.[25]

Britain's dependence on the sea forced her to react to the alternative strategies adopted by her rivals. Yet it is the measure of her success that after 1815 the Royal Navy was able to meet and counter the strategic and technical programmes of France, the United States and Russia.

The paradox of French naval strategy in the age of sail was in part resolved between 1815 and 1830. Until 1802 she had possessed a widespread overseas empire and an economically significant oceanic trade, both of which required defending, in addition to land frontiers with other major powers. Although the richest European nation in the eighteenth century, France lacked the resources to mount simultaneously a major land war and contest the supremacy of the seas with Britain. Consequently, peace-time preparations for a battlefleet strategy were repeatedly disrupted by the overriding requirements of the war on land, the failure of naval finance and the impact of defeat. The alternative was to shift over to the cheap, private enterprise strategy of the *guerre de course*. Even this, it should be noted, reflected the inability of French merchants to use the sea for more profitable activity in the face of British sea control. Despite high returns in the War of the League of Augsburg, the *guerre de course* was ultimately defeated by the strength of British maritime trade and of the London insurance market, by close co-operation between the Admiralty and merchants, and by the convoy system which could only operate once the British battlefleet had secured a working command of the sea. The convoy system had been developed to a sophisticated level during the eighteenth century, ending up with the Convoy Act of 1798, whereby sailing in convoy was made compulsory for all foreign trade. Privateers were of little value against convoys and this forced the French to seek out the distant waters beyond the Cape where there were no convoys, or send out squadrons of warships. Neither could be decisive, because they could only threaten a small part of British trade.[26]

During the wars of the Revolution and Empire France had once more veered between battlefleet and *guerre de course*, and found both wanting. The disaster of 1805 was followed by the failure of the battle squadrons which were sent to attack British commerce, particularly that of Lessigues, destroyed by Duckworth off San Domingo in 1806. Thereafter, Napoleon accepted that only raw numbers, built through a continental construction programme, would defeat British naval preponderance. His programme included over 100 battleships, with transports for 100,000 men stationed at Boulogne and in the Scheldt.[27] Even so, his conception of naval strategy remained flawed, his object being to secure a passage for an army to invade Britain and create a number of Mediterranean bases, rather than attempt to gain control of the sea. This threat, because of the scale on which it was mounted, was well known in Britain and was countered by a modest expansion of existing active forces. It also offered the possibility of delaying or preventing any such attempt by either destroying the arsenals or cutting the supplies of naval stores. Both strategies had been adopted with success in earlier conflicts. In addition, the cost to the French Empire was ruinous. France relearned a lesson in those years, a lesson made clear in the American War of

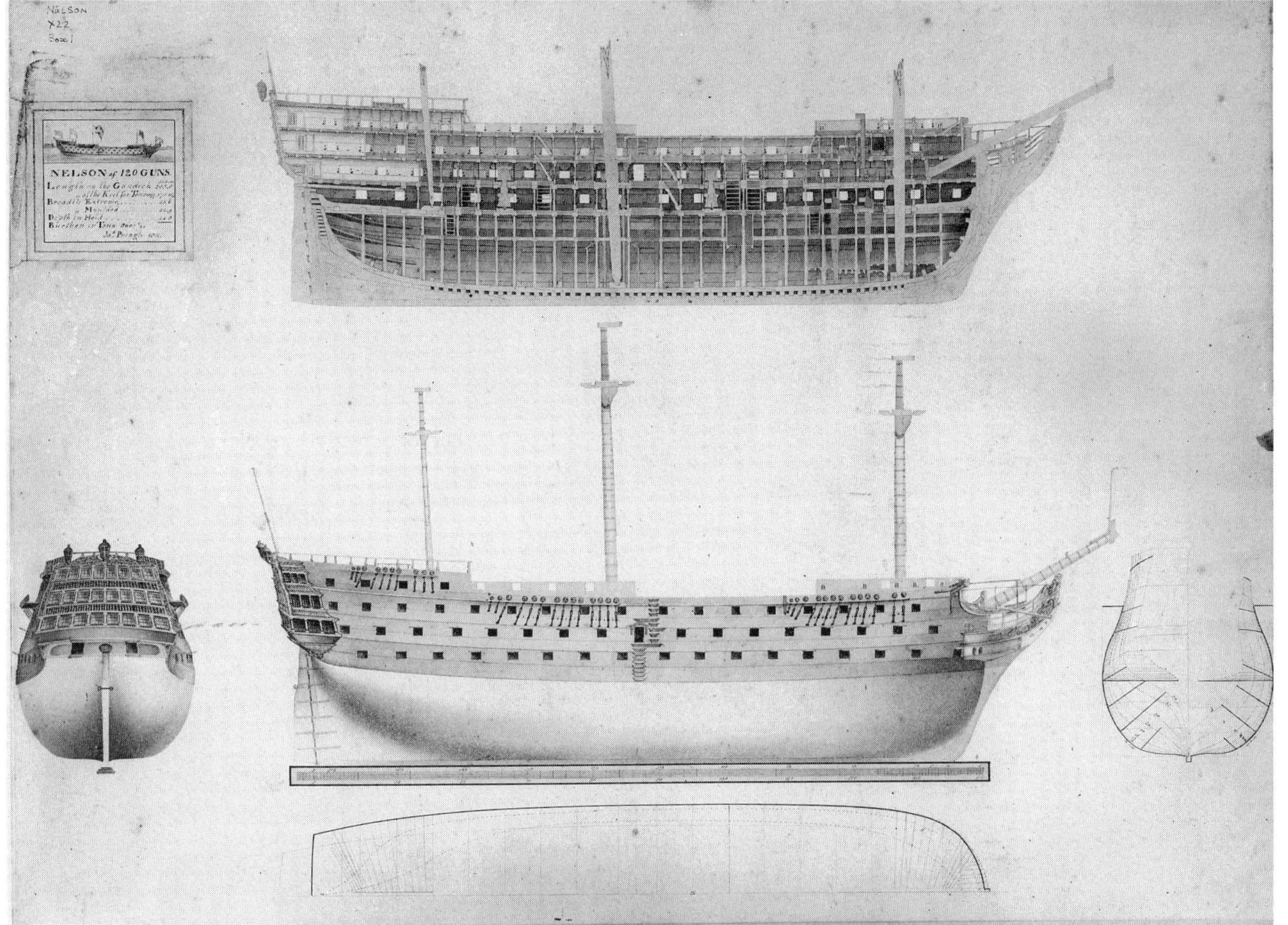

Nelson *of 1814, a 120-gun ship of the Surveyor's-class. Destined never to be commissioned for service as a British battleship, the* Nelson *was built in response to the post-1805 French shift to three-decked ships. Although considered inferior under canvas to the* Caledonia*-class, the three ships of this class were a major element in the early postwar fleet, having been launched in 1814–15.* (NMM)

Royal William *of 1833, serving as harbour Flagship at Plymouth before 1858. The postwar three-deckers were the backbone of the British deterrent policy, and the key to the battlefleet strategy.* (CMP)

Independence, that seapower cannot be extemporised in war-time, it must have solid foundations, a corps of skilled officers and men and enough ships to make an effective challenge at the outbreak, even if the strategic ambition is comparatively limited.[28]

After 1815 the weakness of the French economy rendered her incapable of mounting a serious challenge to the Royal Navy. At the same time the strategic options were examined. The first decision was to accept that France would not be, in the foreseeable future, the equal or superior of Britain at sea. Therefore, she had to develop a strategy suited to a nation in second position. The decision was for a fleet-based *guerre de course*, and the retention of a battlefleet to deal with any other power, and to assist the heavy frigate squadrons that would carry the war at sea to Britain. By 1817 the basic programme of French national strategy was in place, and with the improving economic situation, it was carried into effect during the 1820s. The war against commerce, supplemented by coastal raids and the threat of invasion, were seen as the measures to restrain Britain. This programme was modified in detail, and carried into effect with varying degrees of commitment, but it remained at the heart of French naval strategy until the Second Empire. A large proportion of French ships remained on the slipways, unlaunched until required, which limited their mobilisation and reinforced the block obsolescence of her ships after 1830.[29] The French strategic programme was closely reflected in their ship design, but it should be noted that these were generally inferior to their British equivalents in size, structure and armament, for the first time in 200 years.

Seapower 1815–1850

It has been argued by many, both contemporaries and twentieth-century analysts, that the technological developments of the early nineteenth century gave the French a real opportunity to invade Britain. They suggest that steam power had so far altered the balance between offence and defence at sea that an inferior naval force was able to carry out a large-scale sea-borne invasion across the Channel, so making it necessary to reinforce the land defences of the British Isles. In a recent work Michael Partridge argues that after 1840 the Royal Navy was faced with technical problems that prevented it being as efficient in the defence of the United Kingdom as it had been hitherto, and that this forced policy makers to rely more on land forces. This is simply not true. The Royal Navy handled technology with a sure touch, made better use of new equipment than any of its rivals, and could call upon the world's largest manufacturing base to outbuild any potential enemy. In addition, steam provided new opportunities for offensive action by naval forces against French bases.[30]

In the sailing ship era it had been accepted that invasion remained impossible for the French while they were unable to achieve a working command of the Channel. Napoleon's ambitious 1805 strategy broke down before Villeneuve sailed from Toulon because any local superiority achieved by the combined fleet would have been transitory. As in 1778, the problem was not to secure a fleeting window of opportunity, but to keep open the vital logistics supply line back to France until the army had been successful. It was in an attempt to obtain this working command that Bonaparte switched to the creation of a battlefleet navy after 1807. By maintaining a superior battlefleet in favourable locations Britain could guarantee her security but the idea that an enlarged army would provide additional security to Britain if her fleet was defeated in the Channel is simply untenable. No politically acceptable expansion of the British Army in peace time could do this, but a modest improvement in naval funding would always ensure a working command in home waters, particularly in view of the lower demands of defence at sea. Furthermore, the French Army was far from sanguine about the possibility of crossing the Channel for French officers were unwilling to face the Royal Navy aboard merchant ships crowded with troops and the dangers were unacceptable.[31]

British naval strategy in the sailing ship era was based on powerful fleets operating at both ends of the Channel and out in the Western Approaches. In any state of wind or tide one of these forces would be able to intercept the invasion fleet and make short work of lightly-built merchant vessels and flotilla craft. In peace time these forces were kept in reserve. When required they would be formed from the thirty advanced ships that were kept in a high state of readiness at Sheerness, Portsmouth and Plymouth. These ships, 74s at Sheerness and larger types at the other two bases, would be manned from the Port Guard ships, and the flagships, with seaman gunners, marines and, in a French war, with impressed men, as well as bounty volunteers. They could be ready for sea in a matter of days, and British policy makers would not wait for a declaration of war before they mobilised the fleet. With reliable intelligence available from the consuls at the French ports they could pre-empt any French attempt to use the 'steam bridge'. Once the advanced ships were at sea no invasion force could cross the Channel unmolested, while the effect of battleship gunnery at close quarters on merchant vessels crowded with troops would have been particularly destructive.

Steam, which has been seen as a great leveller ending the advantage possessed by Britain in sailing experience and seamanship, was, in fact, just as much in her favour. France did not have the engineering resources to compete with the world's industrial powerhouse and was quite incapable of altering the old order at sea whatever Paixhan and Joinville might have contended. Britain had more steam warships, more mercantile steamships suitable for auxiliary service, more engine works, better harbours on the Channel coast and a greater commitment to sea control than France. Once the steam warship had become a serious weapon of war, in the early 1840s, British policy makers were careful to build up a superiority in this class to support the battlefleet, and to maintain a superiority in both classes in the Channel in times of tension.

In order to make the invasion scare effective the alarmists argued that steam was better suited to an offensive operation and that it altered the old strategy of war with France. As the

Russian War and the American Civil War demonstrated, steam conferred the greatest benefit to the stronger side and made seapower more effective. Blockade became more certain with steam; the attack of coastal forts became more precise; the logistics of a cruising squadron were now based on steam transports.

Those who argue that the Royal Navy had been technically or doctrinally weakened by steam entirely ignore the offensive power of the Navy, a power that was greatly increased after 1815. By 1845 Wellington noted that Napoleonic coastal fortifications were no longer capable of resisting warships. Weak squadrons of sailing battleships were perfectly capable of taking on forts, as Algiers and Acre demonstrated. The support of specialist flotilla craft made such operations more certain and far less costly. With steam and improved artillery the offensive power of fleets was increased. This gave the Royal Navy the power to strike at French bases rather than wait lamely in the Channel for an invasion.

The Cherbourg strategy

After 1840 the Navy prepared a 'Cherbourg strategy', to assault and destroy the dominant French base; the weapons to be used included poison gas, rockets, mortars, steam gunboats and finally the battlefleet. The development of British grand strategy in 1853–54, culminating in the raid on Sevastopol, can be linked back to the plans of the preceding decade. The fate of Sweaborg, the Russian naval arsenal razed to the ground in early August 1855 by allied flotilla craft, stands as a clear statement of the offensive power of properly configured naval forces. This was the fate held in store for Cherbourg by British defence planners, not the meek and weak blockade operations discussed by the Army school of thought.[32] The object was to gain the initiative, to take the war to the enemy, denying him the luxury of an undisturbed embarkation. As Clausewitz made clear, success in war can only flow from the offensive, from imposing the will of one side upon the other. The strategy of raiding enemy bases can be traced back to 1587, while the last example, in 1809, was familiar to all.

The strategy of the grand raid required the battlefleet to secure a working command of the sea. This would cover the build-up and use of specialist flotilla vessels to assault the fortress in support of, or in place of, the battlefleet. In addition, troops could be landed to complete the work of destruction should they be available.

In the 1840s two strands of technical development worked to provide the equipment for the Cherbourg strategy. Improved long-range guns and rockets, together with the most effective bombardment system – the mortar – provided the firepower, while steam ships offered the tactical mobility to exploit these weapons. At the same time, the 1840s programme of so-called defensive measures was dominated by projects which had a dual purpose. The harbours of refuge could also be used to attack France, as well as to defend Britain, for they were intended to serve as the bases for bombarding flotillas. The screw propeller Royal Yacht, *Fairy*, was a mobilisation prototype steam gunboat, while the harbour defence blockships were also configured for coastal attack.

In essence, the threat of French invasion was not real. The reservations of the French army, the number of troops required, and the inability of the French Navy to contest command of the sea precluded anything more than an annoying raid. Consequently, while the fortification of British bases was a sound policy, the attempt to fortify the country and build up a reserve Army proved to be practically and politically impossible.

Much confusion has resulted from the lack of a major spokesman for the naval case. The Navy had a sound doctrine to defeat an invasion, developed a new strategy to exploit the increased offensive power of naval forces, and maintained a battlefleet capable of keeping command of the sea. Invasion was a chimera employed to talk up Army Estimates, support flagging political careers and provide a platform for alarmists of every hue. It had no foundation.

The United States

The United States conducted a wide-ranging strategic debate following the war of 1812 in which her trade had been destroyed, her coastal cities and capital assaulted and her coast defence flotilla shown up as an ideologically motivated fraud. The wartime programme to construct a number of battleships

The 46-gun frigate Daedalus, *launched in 1826 at Sheerness, as the Royal Naval Reserve training ship at Bristol in the early years of the twentieth century. She was broken up in 1911. This class of frigate was a vital part of the early post-1815 reconstruction of the Navy, replacing many of the worn out decaying and unsatisfactory ships left over from 20 years of conflict.* (CMP)

and frigates provided a fleet for a more adventurous strategy, but this was still confined within the limits of the *guerre de course* by the inability of an American fleet to contest the command of the sea with Britain. In truth, the most powerful threat the United States could muster was one aimed at Canada, a threat that exercised the minds of all British planners from 1815 to 1865. British seapower was seen as a counterweight to the American Army. By conducting amphibious operations in the Southern States, using West Indian troops and attempting to provoke a slave revolt pressure would be taken off Canada. Again, American design philosophy reflected strategic requirements. The battleships were large, over-armed and able to carry a disproportionately large quantity of stores.[33] While these ships caused occasional alarm they were not a major source of danger. After 1826, their growing obsolescence and lack of seagoing service reduced British concern, which became concentrated on the threat of extensive American privateering.

Although this threat could have been very serious, it was not one that concerned the battlefleet, save that the fleet would have to cover all operations on the American coast in the event of war, blockade the ports and in all probability provide the resources for extemporised cruisers. After 1829, American peace-time deployment patterns shifted the United States Navy to a role more intimately connected with the aggressive promotion of American economic expansion.[34] The design of their new ships reflected this trend and consequently the USN became simply a potential ally for France, rather than a serious threat in its own right. The maturity of steam shipping ended the danger of American privateers in the decades after 1850, while the Civil War destroyed what remained of American merchant shipping.

Rather than relying on existing forces, American statesmen saw their maritime and riverine population and resources as the real strength of their defence. The crises of Anglo-American relations in this period were all resolved peacefully, and this may in part be attributed to a feeling of mutual weakness. America could not resist the Royal Navy, and Britain could do little in the short term to secure Canada. Mutual deterrence avoided both war and humiliation.[35]

Russian seapower

The Russian Navy in this period was a curious contrast between the ambition of its rulers and the incompetence displayed at every level of the administration. From the beginning of the nineteenth century Russian policy-makers had been convinced that the Tsarist state was the most powerful in the world. In attempting to translate the tremendous material and human resources of their empire into power, applicable beyond their own frontiers, policy makers encountered a series of problems that have bedevilled Russian ambition to this day.

The active Russian battlefleet was, particularly in the mid to late 1830s, the world's largest. Every summer her Baltic and Black Sea forces were mobilised and sent to sea, often with disastrous consequences. Contemporary commentators and later analysts confused the possession of a battlefleet with offensive ambitions in the world's broad oceans, particularly against Britain.[36] Nicholas I (1825–55) was well aware of the power of the Royal Navy and so his fleet existed to defend the Russian coast and overawe the weak regional Navies of Turkey and Sweden. Following the war scare of 1833–34 the height of his ambition was to have a force adequate to keep the Royal Navy from the approaches of St Petersburg. In 1854 he realised this policy had failed; his ships were tied up as blockships at Kronstadt while the Royal Navy attacked the length and breadth of the Russian coast.

Impregnable, *ex-*Howe, *of 1859 in process of demolition on the Thames in 1921. After many years as a training ship at Devonport, the* Howe *was sold to Garnham and Company, leaving for the Thames on 1 September 1921. At 7,000 tons displacement she was the largest of all wooden battleships, and a testimony to possibilities opened up by the developments in naval architecture in the first half of the nineteenth century.* (CMP)

The defence of trade

The interrelationship between naval power and trade requires no elucidation. In the eighteenth century the economic world was divided into a handful of significant trading empires, with the remaining regions open to exploitation by any small cruiser. Indeed, nothing larger was employed in peace time due to the rapid rise in mortality aboard large ships in the tropics. However, the Revolutionary Wars opened up new regions for trade and, of more significance, increased the number of important trading nations. In 1815–16 Melville had hoped to get by with no battleships outside home waters, but the Mediterranean soon acquired a two-decker.

The independence of Latin America, first threatened by a series of conflicts between Spain and her dependencies, and later by possible attempts by either France or the United States to exploit the opportunities there, required more substantial protection. Thereafter, the demands increased and the presence of powerful Spanish and insurgent warships on the two coasts of South America made a two-decker vital to sustain British influence, not least because the insurgent commander, Lord Cochrane, had little compunction about using the flag of his old service as a *ruse de guerre*. After the 1820s the East Indies was never without a battleship, while the Pacific station ended the era with a Symondite 80, the *Collingwood*, and two heavy 50-gun ships, the razee *America* and the new *Constance*. These forces were necessary to counter American and French squadrons of similar power, during crises over Tahiti and California. The level and disposition of naval forces outside the European theatre before 1850 reflected the pressures of the moment, and were subject to constant calls for reduction. Permanent force levels on the various stations would follow the expansion of the formal Empire in the late Victorian age. By its flexibility the battlefleet became the arbiter of diplomacy and the shield of British trade world wide. This did not require any permanent peace-time detachment of battlefleet units, merely the maintenance of supremacy in home waters. In wartime battlefleet superiority at home would deprive the French of any opportunity to send large forces outside Europe. British policy on the protection of sea borne trade did not receive any more thorough review until the work of the Carnarvon Committee in the 1870s.[37]

2 Economics

Although the direction of naval policy was governed by the perception of national requirements, the level of expenditure had to reflect economic reality and in this area the Royal Navy had a vital advantage over its rivals. British naval power has come to be closely associated with her economic strength. Paul Kennedy put forward a cogent case for treating seapower as a product of economic power and more recent studies have examined the nature of the relationship between finance and seapower, an essential development from Kennedy's position because for much of the eighteenth century France was economically stronger than Britain. The key to the difference between the two countries was that Britain was able to organise long-term borrowing much earlier than France. By creating the Bank of England in 1689, subjecting government expenditure to the control of the Treasury and the review of Parliament, Britain demonstrated a degree of financial probity that encouraged capitalists to lend large sums of money over long periods at reasonable rates of interest. The French state did not achieve a similar credit-worthiness until the 1830s and Imperial Russia was never so favoured.[1]

This secure finance enabled Britain to sustain the heavy cost of long naval wars, something the French state repeatedly failed to do in the eighteenth century. The Royal Navy had, for geostrategic reasons, a more important position in the national strategy than the Army, in contrast to the position in France, and therefore had both first call on resources and a more secure fiscal base. In the eighteenth century the French always entered war with a better Navy than that with which they left it, the Royal Navy was always enlarged and improved by war.[2]

By contrast with the insecure finances of the autocracies, Parliament was always willing to vote the funds required to maintain the Navy, although it often questioned the manner in which such monies were employed. Opposition attacks on details of naval administration between 1815 and 1830, notably Ridley's motion of 1 March 1822 which removed one junior Lord of the Admiralty, were a matter of political pressure on the Tory Government and not a reflection of political philosophy.[3] Whatever the Opposition tried it should be noted that between 1815 and 1850 no government was ever denied the money it requested from Parliament. By contrast, all too many ministries cut the estimates of future naval expenditure in order to meet political needs. The Administrations of Grey, Melbourne and Peel between 1830 and 1841 provide the clearest case, but the impact of long-term pressure on the weak Tory Administrations after 1827 was, if anything, more significant.

These three elements – the political will to pay for naval power, the economic strength to fund it, and the financial probity to borrow money in times of crisis – provided the Royal Navy with a base as strong as Sir Robert Seppings' new frames. Furthermore, it could not be so easily emulated abroad as could the technical developments. Throughout the period under review this position, the foundation of seapower, remained unrivalled. Financial power was a key element in British preparations for a long war. Always confident of a large cash inflow the Admiralty could expect to pay a bounty to raise seamen, contract out the construction of all the support craft required, make bulk purchases of crucial naval stores, such as hemp and masts, and even lay down new battleships.

In 1815 policymakers were faced with a dilemma common at the end of a long war: they had to decide on the level of postwar defence spending. In this they were faced with two extremes, between which a balance had to be struck. They could sustain wartime levels of spending, preserving British power in the most obvious manner, or they could cut back to the bare essentials leaving little more than a nucleus for some future mobilisation. Initially, the Liverpool Ministry favoured a high level of overall spending of £15m in contrast to only £6m in 1791. The extra cost was partly explained by new commitments, but in private Liverpool admitted the real fear was for the stability of France after Waterloo. He realised the difficulty would lie in persuading Parliament to allow the Government adequate overall funding to support such levels of expenditure.[4]

Within these figures the impact of reduction was far less marked for the Navy than the Army, partly to allow for the higher costs of running down the fleet. Decisions on the postwar establishment were also taken within this framework.[5] These plans, however, were thrown into confusion by the opposition. The Income Tax, the main prop of postwar economic planning and the guarantor of sound finance, was removed by a combination of opposition and defectors from the government on 18 March 1816. With almost half the remaining revenue committed to servicing the National Debt, a vital symbol of government credit-worthiness, service expenditure had to be reduced. Following this success the Opposition mounted a major assault on the Navy Estimates on 25 March. They failed, having ignored the cost of paying off the wartime fleet, but the Government had been warned that close scrutiny of the estimates could be expected, and this encouraged small concessions. Yet it should be remembered that the Navy, in contrast to the Army, had the support of all political factions.[6]

There were three options for the Government if it was determined to prepare for another long war. It could reduce spending to the bare essentials in order to build up public credit; promote the creation of private wealth by reducing taxation, leaving a reserve to be tapped in time of crisis; or hoard a surplus of revenue against the crisis. The second course was adopted in preference to making any further cuts in defence spending because this would have defeated the diplomatic object of the policy. Unfortunately, this was of little use in the short term as poor tax returns for 1817 forced further reductions.[7] The Select Committee on Finance urged additional retrenchment to restore the economy, but there was no real opportunity for significant reductions and the estimates constantly crept over the base level of £6m suggested by the Committee and adopted by Liverpool.[8]

In January 1817, the Controller of the Navy, Admiral Sir Thomas Byam Martin told Melville, Hope and Croker that the estimates would only cover the necessary expenses if no stores were purchased and so called for an extra half a million. A Cabinet Committee of Melville, Vansittart who was the Chancellor of the Exchequer, and Huskisson, the Government's leading economist, considered the problem. The reduction of wages would not solve the shortfall and they agreed to an additional £1,200,000 to cover naval debts. To emphasise the severity of the problem the supplies were initially only voted for six months, a practice entirely inconsistent with the maintenance of government credit-worthiness, and not repeated.[9] Melville was far from pleased by the Finance Committee's report which called for estimates of no more than £6m. The Prime Minister suggested reducing building and repair in favour of dockyard improvements and Melville sourly noted that 'Liverpool's suggestions will not be practicable without producing consequences which he does not contemplate'. Forced to make hard choices between ships, men and infrastructure, choices that they would have preferred to avoid, the Admiralty ultimately came down in favour of continuing work on the battlefleet. The existing ships were in poor order, the most modern having been built of inferior timber and the remainder worn out by war service. To fund this work, which Byam Martin declared would create 'for the first time, a really sound and durable fleet, to the sure saving of enormous sums of money', he cut back on seamen and dockyard work. At the same time Melville warned that revenue would fall if overseas trade was not supported by warships. Byam Martin argued that estimates limited to £6m would curtail both yard improvements and the purchase of stores. Yet for 1817 the building fund was cut by one quarter and that for dockyard improvements halved. His opposition to further cuts in 1818, however, was adequate to end the cycle of 'rigid, unsparing economy'.[10] Despite apparent improvements in the economy, naval funding remained close to the figure of £6m set by the 1817 committee until 1830. In 1818 the Navy had to secure an extra £500,000, demonstrating the limits of effective administration. In 1819 the question was quickly settled.[11] The following year 1,000 men had to be cut, saving £250,000, to secure Cabinet support after a meeting involving Byam Martin, Melville, Huskisson, Arbuthnot and Lord Hill.[12]

Another round of reductions in 1821, over £500,000, provoked a bitter outburst from the King. George IV adopted his father's opinions, and recognised in the Navy a vital element of national power. Any further reductions he declared, would be 'inimical to the best interests of the country'. Liverpool's reply spoke eloquently of the Government's political weakness. Low corn prices encouraged the economising tendencies of a Parliament dominated by independent Tory landowners. The Opposition were never slow to exploit this fundamental division in Tory support. The Ministers,

> have gone to the utmost limit that could be warranted by any attention to the public safety or interest; that they have been mainly influenced ... by the consideration that the adoption of them would enable them to take up ground which they could steadily and effectually defend; and that it was their firm determination to make every effort to resist any further reduction in the numbers, or alteration in the character or description of the national force.[13]

By 1823 Melville for one was more confident, or at least more combative; he was prepared to accept petty cuts, but not serious reductions.[14] The armament crisis of 1826 generated a little more money, but new work had to be funded by shifting priorities, not generating new revenue. As Byam Martin noted, 'year after year everything is sacrificed in order to pull down the estimates'.[15]

After the deaths of Canning and Liverpool finance became a major political issue, both as one of the twin themes of Whig opposition, and as a divisive factor within the Cabinet. Wellington believed foreign policy should be trimmed to economic realities, while Canning and his disciples preferred to cover weakness with bluster. Seeking to balance the budget as a measure to meet the international crises during his premiership the Duke presided over a series of economy measures, but the Finance Committee was sufficiently impressed by Admiral Cockburn's gloomy assessment of the growth of foreign naval powers to avoid further reductions after the pattern of 1817. In 1829 Pitt's device for reassuring the financiers, the Sinking Fund for the redemption of the National Debt, was abolished. As might be expected, the political problems of the period encouraged succeeding governments to use any surplus for tax cuts, rather than the intended reductions in the National Debt. The 1830 session saw the Wellington Ministry reduced to buying off hostile motions with promises of reductions, which the Duke very properly acted upon. As a naval officer and a Tory politician Byam Martin was furious.

> We yield much too easily to a set of noisy, ignorant blockheads who make no discrimination between foolish and needless extravagance, & objects of vital importance to the interest and credit of the country: – but the thing, of all others, to me the most annoying is that they seem to forget that the safety & glory of England depends upon her naval strength, & her constant and ample state of naval preparation; & we shall perhaps (at no distant time) rue the day that such mischevious opinions prevailed. I shall, however, have the consolation to know that I am no party to such views or measures.[16]

At this stage he could not have known that his next political master would be Sir James Graham, one of the very blockheads to whom he referred. Byam Martin, the most consistent critic of reduced naval expenditure, realised the degree to which the ideal position outlined in 1815 had been undermined by the shortfall of funding, the demands of diplomacy and other pressures beyond his control; for this he blamed the politicians. While his arguments were valid, they are the common stock of all service chiefs in peace time, calling for high levels of spending to prepare for the next war. As it was, his gloom turned out to have been exaggerated. The battlefleet he created

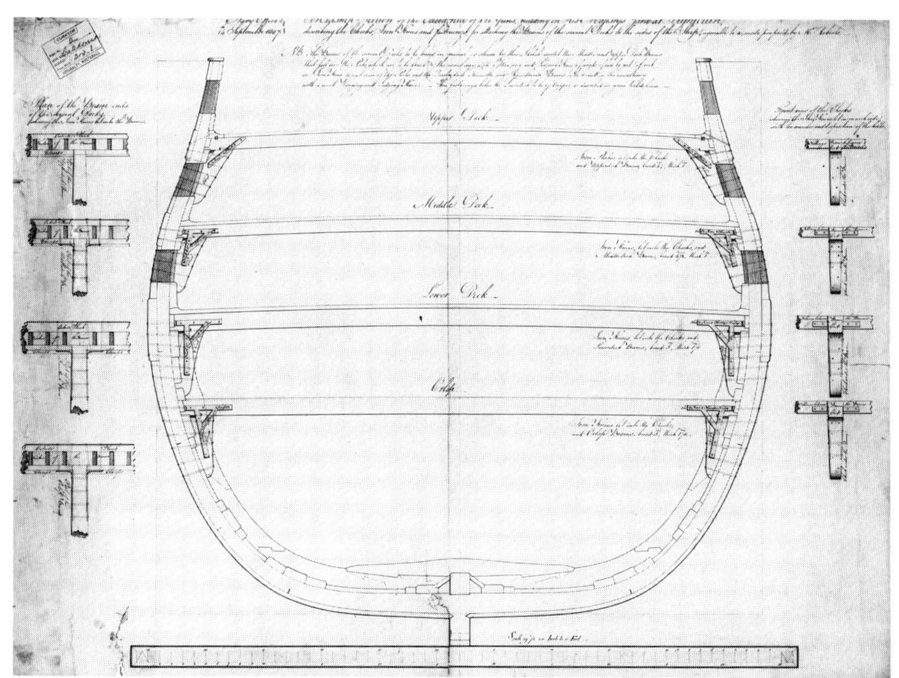

A midship section of the 120-gun Caledonia, *dated September 1807. The structural use of iron is already evident, and is credited to the Assistant Master Shipwright, Thomas Roberts, one of the Seppings's less well known contemporaries. The knees are 5in broad and 1in thick.* (NMM)

proved more enduring than he had intended, forming the basis of British strength up to 1850, and as such provided a deterrent of unrivalled economy and efficiency.

In reviewing this period Hilton argues that the loss of the Sinking Fund, although part of a long-term search for financial reserves to meet a future war, forced the governments of the day to rationalise their weaknesses with a more peaceful foreign policy.[17] Not appreciating the success of postwar naval policy Hilton exaggerated the impact of the financial squeeze on naval policy. For all Martin and Melville's gloom it should be noted that theirs was the professional and technical view. Under Palmerston's direction the deficit-financed Whig Governments of the 1830s maintained a higher profile abroad than the financially responsible Tory ministries. That was more a question of ideology than finance, for it is possible to trace clear party political views on defence from 1827 to 1850. The Tories followed the 1815 programme of building a solid foundation for any emergency, while the Canningite and later the Whig party, led by the Canningite Palmerston, used their funds to bolster deterrent forces. The clash of these two ideologies during the Peel Administration of 1841–46, with Aberdeen and Graham representing the alternatives, made the role of Cabinet and Premier of crucial interest.

The change of government in 1830 reflected the success of Whig calls for reform and financial savings. Economy was a bribe to dissident elements in the natural Tory majority returned by both unreformed and reformed parliaments in this period; it was in many ways a more important element of the Grey Ministry's programme than reform. In their campaign for reform, which came to dominate the political scene, the Whigs were forced to accept the prospect of financial deficit, which Hilton characterises as 'spineless finance'. This political expediency was the only way in which Opposition hopes for power in the late 1820s, with Wellington's willingness to carry out economies, could be pursued. Wellington's economic reforms forced the Whigs to extremes in their efforts to prove that the previous Administration had failed. It is clear that the Parliament of 1830 would not have swallowed the Reform Bill without the substantial inducement held out in the form of reduced taxes.[18]

Within the context of 'economic reform' Graham pushed through a programme of change in naval administration with the twin aims of reducing the Navy Board and saving money. His reformed Board of Admiralty had far more control over expenditure than its predecessor for the Navy Board had been a strong opponent of expedient and short-term savings. However, unable to achieve real savings he was forced to employ misleading statistics in an attempt to defend his policies. His successors, Whig and Tory, were less than charitable in their assessment of his work. Reduced funding for the Navy after 1830, unlike that of the first postwar decade, resulted in serious cuts in the battlefleet. While it is possible to employ hindsight to conclude that the post-1830 reduction in battlefleet construction was of no particular moment, that would give too much credit to the policy makers of the period. Unwilling to face the simple fact that the existing revenue could not meet the expenditure, the Whig Governments limped along as best they could. Naval funding was cut and put under increased pressure by the manpower requirements of a more active, if hardly Whig, foreign policy, and the addition of steamships to the Navy.

Whig Chancellors attempted to remedy the deficit. Althorp, for instance, proposed reviving the Income Tax in return for ending duties on imported raw materials. The Cabinet would not follow this bold programme and were no more impressed by Althorps' call for duties on the transfer of land. Typically, they feared the opposition of the very landed elite who were vital to the passage of the Reform Bill. Consequently, there were only four years of government surplus in the 1830s, while the tax concessions were too limited to help maintain support for the Government. It was hardly a surprise that the Melbourne Administration finally fell on the issue of sugar duties for it was the culmination of a financial policy that had been conducted in a piecemeal and unconvincing manner.[19] Yet the impact of Whig fiscal policy on British political culture was significant. Peel became convinced that finance was the central issue and his first Ministry cut the Naval Estimates to the lowest level simply to create the right impression with the public.[20]

In his second Ministry Peel reintroduced Income Tax, as part of a programme designed to restore sound finance but the additional funds did nothing to improve the policy-making process. Only with the Auckland reform was a thorough control exerted over naval finance. By December 1848 the First Lord

Postwar wooden warships were increasingly influenced by the new technology of the industrial age. Unicorn *carries a Downton pump, introduced in 1825. Although it is probable that this pump was not fitted until the 1870s this pattern was installed on wooden warships in the sailing era.* (Author)

The Unicorn *was fitted with an epicylic gearbox for her capstan, similar to the old three-speed hub gearbox used by bicycles, with a 3 : 1 ratio of advantage.* (Author)

could report to his Premier that the condition of the Navy was 'very satisfactory at the present time', and this allowed him to reduce the estimates back to the levels of 1845, saving £800,000 and 3,000 men.[21] The efforts of Haddington, Ellenborough and Auckland finally restored the administration of the civil branch of the Navy to a state where it was capable of long-term planning, budgeting and effective control over the spending departments.

The cost of the Navy was never a major political issue because there was a basic cross-party consensus on it. Isolated protests concerning particular issues, and politically motivated acts of spite were of little long-term significance. It has been argued that the annual round of financial horse trading in the Cabinet had minimal effect.[22] This is to ignore, however, the role of politics in British defence planning, the existence of identifiable Whig and Tory approaches to naval policy, and the value of facing hard choices. Between 1815 and 1850 little money was wasted on the Navy; the premature rush into iron and aspects of the early screw ships are the only significant examples.

The Naval Estimates as a Percentage of Gross National Expenditure

Year	*GNE (£ millions)*	*Naval Estimates (£ millions)*	*Men (1,000s)*	*Percentage*	*Contributory factors*
1814	111.1	22.5		20	war
1815	112.9	22.8		20	war
1816	99	16.8	35	16	run down war fleet
1817	71.3	10.2	22	14	run down war fleet
1818	58.7	6.6	23	11	
1819	57.6	6.6	23	11	
1820	57.5	6.4	23	11	
1821	58.4	6.4	24	11	
1822	58.4	6.3	23	11	
1823	56.3	5.2	26	9	crisis of Liverpool Administration
1824	54.3	5.6	30	9	
1825	55.5	6.2	31	11	
1826	54.1	5.8	32	11	
1827	56.1	6.5	33	12	Canning
1828	55.9	6.4	31	12	Canning
1829	53.5	5.7	32	11	
1830	53.7	5.9	31	11	
1831	51.9	5.3	29	10	Graham
1832	51.5	5.7	27	11	Graham
1833	50.6	4.9	27	9	Graham
1834	48.8	4.4	28	9	Graham
1835	48.9	4.5	26	9	Peel
1836	48.5	4.1	30	8	Minto
1837	49.9	4.2	31	8	Minto
1838	51.1 includes packets	4.8	32	10	(should be lower)
1839	51.7	4.4	34	8	Minto
1840	53.4	5.3	37	10	Syrian Crisis
1841	53.2	5.4	41	10	Pay off
1842	54.3	6.2	43	11	
1843	55.1	6.2	40	11	
1844	55.4	5.4	38	10	
1845	54.8	6.3	40	11	
1846	53.7	7.3	43	14	Invasion scare
1847	55.4	7.5	44	14	Invasion scare
1848	59.1	7.5	43	12	
1849	59.0	6.2	39	10	
1850	55.5	5.7	39	10	

Within the estimates the amounts spent on construction, repair, infrastructure and active ships was to vary from year to year.

These estimates were in no way a response to the growth of the merchant marine. In 1815, for instance, there were 21,861 sailing vessels totalling 2,447,000 tons and eight steamers totalling 1,000 tons in the British Merchant Marine. By 1850 there were 24,797 sailing vessels totalling 3,397,000 tons and 1,187 steamers totalling 168,000 tons and the average size of sailing vessels had increased from 111.9 tons to 136.9 tons. However, the increase in the merchant marine was restricted to the period after 1839 for up to that time there had been a real decline in the number of ships.[23]

Part Two

NAVAL POLICY 1815–50

1 *Creating a New Battlefleet: 1815–30*

While it has long been fashionable to look upon the aftermath of any conflict as a time of peace, allowing the victors to reduce defence expenditure and relax their efforts, this has never been the case. No sooner does one conflict end than new rivalries and tensions spring up, often out of the very peace process itself. In this respect 1814–15 was no different from 1945. Britain was confronted by a bitter and defeated France and the three northern powers – Russia, Prussia and Austria – who resented her pre-eminence. In particular, Russia had the ambitions, resources and naval strength to be a real menace to the Empire and against this background the search for a postwar policy must be viewed as a process of coming to terms with financial limits while at the same time meeting strategic demands. As late as 1845 Sir Robert Peel suggested that war itself might be preferable to the unending pressure of Anglo-French naval rivalry, thereby reflecting the constant strain of British defence planning.

Between 1815 and 1830 the Admiralty and Navy Board attempted to build a durable battlefleet of around one hundred units. To achieve this they were forced by economic constraints to sacrifice other aspects of naval policy, notably the active fleet and dockyard improvements. The measure of their success can be seen in the battlefleet of 1850, ordered and largely built by this team, with the addition of only eight capital ships dating from 1832–50. As this battlefleet served to deter France on at least two occasions, in addition to exercising a large degree of influence over Russia in 1833 and 1849, it is important to consider the programme under which it was created.

The end of the war

The First Lord of the Admiralty for almost the entire remaining life of the Navy Board was Robert Saunders Dundas, Second Viscount Melville, (1771–1851). Melville was the son and heir of Henry Dundas, the First Viscount and confidant of Pitt. He inherited the declining remnants of his father's vast Scottish political power base and as such was a vital part of any Tory Administration. His particular interests in India and the Navy reflected the work of his father in filling both services with reliable Scots nominees. Melville began to build an independent position before his father died in 1812, but shortly thereafter moved from the Board of Control to the Admiralty. He served as First Lord from 25 March 1812 to April 1827, and again between 19 September 1828 and November 1830. These two periods, lasting a total of seventeen years, made him the most experienced First Lord ever. As such he had great influence on postwar naval policy, from the selection of Seppings and Martin to a number of issues on which he demonstrated his independence of both the Navy Board and the Government. Melville has never been accorded the detailed study that his long experience in Cabinet deserves; his decision to leave the Ministry when Canning became Prime Minister has been cited against him, and his refusal to serve again after 1830 left a long period of semi-active retirement. On the first occasion his action reflected an unwillingness to serve in an all pro-Catholic Administration, while later he sought to avoid the overbearing conduct of Wellington as Prime Minister. After 1830 he retained a degree of influence through his nominees and relations, notably Sir George Clerk and his son Robert, who served as Storekeeper General until the 1860s.

The career of General Bonaparte, as his British opponents insisted upon calling him, ended in April 1814, although the Hundred Days, lasting from March to June 1815, did cause a certain amount of naval activity, most notably orders to prepare four three-deckers for service.[1] The War of 1812 lingered on across the Atlantic with a small British fleet blockading the coast of the United States and launching punitive raids between New England and New Orleans. This conflict ended with the Treaty of Ghent on 24 December 1814, although it had had little impact on naval policy even at its height.

From early 1814 the British had taken control of the various Imperial dockyards of occupied Europe, most notably Antwerp, Genoa and Venice. All three were stocked with timber, contained ships in various stages of completion and had represented a serious threat to Britain. All three were handed over to new owners who could not exploit their potential and who would look to Britain for protection from future French ambition. The ships and materials were distributed according to the value placed on them by the occupying British. The materials at Antwerp, despite the large fleet and extensive timber piles, were of little interest. One of the Surveyors of the Navy went to inspect the facilities and his report was conclusive: 'Mr Tucker is of opinion that the materials are not of a desirable quality for the British Navy'.[2] His decision may have been influenced by the short career of the *Chatham*, captured in frame at Flushing in 1809, and only five years later condemned and destined to serve out her days as a sheer hulk.

The timbers at Genoa were of far higher quality. The 74-

gun *Brilliant* was taken over and completed, at a cost of £60,000 and the timber piles were loaded aboard the new ship and brought to Chatham.[3] Venice, with the ships and materials at Malamocco on the Lido, was handed to the Austrian Government. There were three 84-gun ships, another fitting out and five building, together with frigates and smaller craft. The Austrians realised they had no use for the large ships and so offered them for sale in May 1815.[4] Although the ships at Venice were constructed of better materials than those at Antwerp they were unattractive to the postwar Navy Board because of their light scantlings. The one ship from that yard placed on the Navy List, the prize *Rivoli*, proved to be a poor specimen. Although a large Third Rate, a desirable class, the small scantlings of her frame, widespread fungal infection and hurried building made it unwise to carry out large repairs. She was thus condemned and taken to pieces in late 1818.[5] The Austrians rebuilt some of the two-deckers as large frigates, and contrived to burn much of the timber along with the incomplete ships, so ending all efforts to sell their unwanted fleet. Examination of the French dockyards revealed the extent to which Bonaparte had compromised the quality of his fleet in his attempt to outbuild the British. This only added emphasis to the need for long-term planning.

The battlefleet

During the later stages of the war, particularly after 1807, a debate had gone on in British policy making circles as to the best method of maintaining a large active battlefleet. One school believed that only large-scale new construction, most of it necessarily carried out in merchant shipyards, would meet the need. Alternatively, those around Robert Saunders Dundas, Second Lord Melville and First Lord of the Admiralty from 1812, wanted to create a major new dockyard in which to repair the existing fleet. This policy had its origins in the work of Earl St Vincent. Melville favoured replacing the Thames yards with a new arsenal at Northfleet, further down the river. At an annual cost of £250,000 he anticipated both building the new yard over a number of years, and repairing large numbers of ships. This site had been recommended for the new East Coast yard to the Commissioners of Naval Revision in 1807 by John Rennie and included in their secret, unpublished 15th Report. By 1817 over 500 acres of land had been purchased, but later Boards preferred to rebuild Sheerness and rely on steam dredgers to keep the Thames yards clear. The changing priorities of peace time resulted in the suspension of all work until the fall of the Navy Board; the land was auctioned off after 1831 and dockyard development restricted to the old sites.[6] Once the War had ended the small yard at Deal was closed and some thought given to purchasing land near Edinburgh, but nothing came of the latter and the Scots were still complaining about the absence of a yard north of the Tweed in 1856.[7]

Unicorn, *a 46-gun frigate of 1824. This ship is doubly unique being the only survivor of all the ships built after 1815 for the wooden sailing Navy. She is also largely unaltered from her completion. Never commissioned, the* Unicorn *still carries the original housing built on her after her launch to preserve her while in reserve. This structure kept the ship free of rain water, thereby playing a major part in preserving her.* (Author)

After mid-1814 the Admiralty placed no new orders with merchant shipyards. It took stock of the ships already building and carefully scrutinised the interests of the service when considering which ships were to be repaired. The 1814 Navy Board dockyard visits resulted in the order for a new 74 the *Thunderer*, later *Talavera*, which was to be built on Seppings' plan with frigate timbers at Woolwich, and the *Prince Regent* at Chatham. Otherwise, the suspension of work on several vessels building and repairing was ordered. *Russell*, *Trafalgar*, *Talavera* (later *Bellerophon*), *Britannia* and *Agincourt* were left to season in frame; *Boscawen*, *Princess Charlotte*, *London* (later *Royal Adelaide*) and *Belleisle* were in varying states of progress from collecting timber to fixing the thickstuff. At Plymouth the new *Agincourt* had been suspended under cover for 14 months, in frame with her planking alongside. The Board hoped that this would prevent the dry rot. Ships repairing were also allowed to stand over. *Canopus*, then undergoing a large repair, had been suspended for six months and was reported to be 'in a very improved and excellent state'.[8] More advanced ships, *Howe*, *St Vincent*, *Cambridge*, *Defence* and *Hercules* were launched to clear the slipways for frigates to be hauled up and repaired.[9] Only two new battleships were ordered in 1815, the teak 74-gun *Malabar* at Bombay and the 84-gun *Formidable*, a replica of *Canopus*, which was to be built with the timber from Genoa.[10] The Royal Navy was short of large two-deckers and the teak ship demonstrated the high opinion already formed of that material.

Repair policy became increasingly cost-conscious as the period progressed, given the large surfeit of tonnage over requirements. Ships that were well regarded, and of a desirable class, were permitted large repairs, but obsolete and old ships were quickly condemned. In 1814 the old three-decker *St George*, ex-*Britannia* of 1762 was reported to need a large repair lasting 16 months, and costing £70,000. The Navy Board considered that, 'in consequence of the bad qualities of the *St George* as a sea going ship, and taking into account her defective state we are of opinion she should be taken to pieces'. In the event she was renamed *Barfleur* and kept on in harbour service for another decade. However, the most significant point is that such an old ship should even have been considered for major work. The more recent *Royal George*, on the other hand, only required a small repair costing £18,000 which was permitted.[11] While relatively new ships were always repaired there had to be a point beyond which it was not economic to do so. The amount had a habit of being at least as high as the cost of a new ship, and often higher. The *Achille*, for instance, a large Third Rate of 1798 was allowed a large repair over 18 months costing in excess of £70,000, fitting testimony to a well regarded ship and a Trafalgar veteran.[12]

Making policy for the long term

With Bonaparte safely ensconced on St Helena the Admiralty could turn to the major issue requiring settlement: the future of the fleet. Up to the end of 1815 there had been little more than a commonsense approach to policy, and no attempt to impose a plan of action on the general direction of affairs. As the central role in material policy was held by the Controller of the Navy, as Head of the Navy Board, Melville decided to replace the retiring Vice Admiral Sir Thomas Boulden Thompson with an officer who had already proved his merits in every branch of the naval service, Rear Admiral Sir Thomas Byam Martin. The only obstacle to this arrangement was the concurrent wish of the Navy Board to dismiss Martin's father-in-law, Admiral Fanshawe from his post of Commissioner at Plymouth. Initially, Martin refused the high post offered, fearing it would be connected in some discreditable way with Fanshawe's case. He was also reluctant to sit in Parliament, which had always been part of the Controller's duties. However, he was persuaded to negotiate and after settling a healthy pension for himself, and excellent terms for his father-in-law, he accepted the post on 11 November 1815. This was announced to the Prince Regent later in the month, although not gazetted until February 1816. He did not enter Parliament until 1817.

Admiral of the Fleet Sir Thomas Byam Martin, 1773–1854, was born the third son of a senior naval officer, Henry Martin, who was Commissioner at Portsmouth in 1780 and Controller of the Navy 1790–94. He was created a baronet in 1791 and died in 1794. The young Martin was always destined for a naval career. He joined the Navy in 1786, aboard the *Pegasus*, which was under the command of Prince William (later William IV), and he continued under the Prince in the *Andromeda* until 1789. In 1790 he joined the *Southampton* under Captain Richard Keats and then the *Royal George* during the Spanish Armament of 1792. During this crisis Pitt liaised directly with Martin's father, the only example of such a relationship between a Prime Minister and Controller, though in his own period as Controller Martin was to try to exert similar influence. Martin rose to Commander in 1793 and made Post Captain before the year ended, demonstrating the value of well-placed relatives. After commanding the *Tisiphone*, *Modeste* and *Fisgard* he took the 74-gun *Implacable* to the Baltic in 1808 and joined Samuel Hood in taking the Russian 74 *Sewolod*, the only Russian capital ship ever taken by the Royal Navy. His conduct during the defence of Riga excited the praise of all concerned, and in late 1812 he was selected for a mission to improve co-operation between the Navy and Wellington's Army in the peninsula. This reflected the high opinion already formed of his abilities by those in power, particularly Lord Melville. A mission to inspect the French dockyard at Antwerp kept him employed until the end of the War, but by then he had been marked out for high office. After 1831 he twice refused the Mediterranean command on the grounds of his wife's ill-health. His considerable pension must also have played a part. He remained a major figure in the Navy until his death in 1854, which occurred shortly after helping to plan the Baltic campaign of that year, and considering the applicability of Lord Cochrane's poison gas plan for use at Kronstadt.[13]

It was unusual to appoint an officer already on the Flag List to the post of Controller though most rose to be flag officers while serving. This emphasised both the importance Melville attached to the position, and his anxiety to secure the services of Martin. Thompson finally moved to the honourable retirement of Treasurer at Greenwich Hospital on 24 February 1816. In the meantime, Martin had been paid as Deputy Controller, which was an unofficial temporary arrangement allowing him to take his seat at the Board from 1 December. The post itself of Deputy Controller was held by William Shield who continued in that role until 24 February 1816. The confusion simply reflects the less than rigorous administrative standards of the era; wanting to have the services of the new Controller as soon as possible, Melville put him on the Board unofficially, and paid him, until Thompson retired.

The simple wooden housing fitted to the Unicorn *at Chatham in 1826. Many wooden warships were given a similar housing, and this allowed them to spend long periods in reserve without serious decay, as they could be kept dry and ventilated.* (Author)

Postwar retrenchment

The reason for Melville's haste soon became evident. The Prime Minister, Lord Liverpool, and the Chancellor of the Exchequer, Nicholas Vansittart, were looking for an early return to peace-time estimates, selecting 1792 as the example. This provided figures for men afloat that were far too low for the increased requirements of the postwar world, and persuaded Melville that he must develop a coherent programme with which to counter financial pressures.[14] With Byam Martin available in London it can be safely assumed that Melville had the benefit of discussions with him before the Admiralty issued their first major policy statement of the postwar period, on 8 December 1815. The subject was the postwar Establishment of the fleet. As might be expected, the impact of financial pressure was evident from the opening lines. Having decided that the maximum number of seamen that could be raised in the first two years of any future war would be approximately 100,000, the Admiralty outlined the fleet that such a number could man. They then took a general view of the ships, 'with the purpose of making all the reductions of expense in time of peace, which may be consistent with an adequate preparation for the event of war'. To this end they called for a fleet of one hundred sailing ships of the line, excluding those under construction. Fourteen would be guard ships and flagships, with the rest laid up in Ordinary. Rather optimistically they expected that more than this number would be in a suitable condition to give long service and that new construction in the Royal yards would keep the fleet up to establishment.

Although this force was considered 'fully adequate to any possible necessity' the Board would not permit the sale of any ships in good condition. To reduce dockyard work and expense, floating depots of every description would be replaced by shore establishments. One hundred and sixty frigates would also be required. The Admiralty called for lists of all First to Fifth Rates fit for service, of all hulks, of ships suitable to break up and of minor vessels. Melville shared Byam Martin's assessment of the threat posed by Bonaparte's pan-European fleet and much later he expressed the conviction that the French would ultimately;

> have sent forth such powerful fleets that our Navy must eventually have been destroyed, since we could never have kept pace with him in building ships nor equipped numbers sufficient to cope with the tremendous power he could have brought against us'.[15]

Fixing the Establishment would allow the Navy Board to calculate the level of dockyard labour that would be required postwar, together with the expenditure on timber and other stores. Byam Martin had already given this subject a good deal of thought. His approach was not exactly what the Treasury would have hoped, although it clearly reflected the naval officer's perspective. In reducing dockyard expenditure he set great store by keeping up the largest possible number of shipwrights, considering these skilled men to be among the most important of all war reserves. Revising the pay structure for task and job work and reducing the working hours would cut costs, and also leave the men available 'whenever the emergency of an armament shall call for their services'. With these restrictions in place the Surveyors calculated on building and repairing eight or ten battleships and fifteen frigates every year. All ships would be able to stand over to season for six months and as this was a long-term measure it would be necessary to keep all the existing ships fit for temporary service so that the Navy would not be 'found off our guard in the event of war'. Once an adequate number of sound ships had been prepared the time for seasoning was to be increased and more care taken in selecting timbers of equal durability. The cornerstone of the long-term programme was the creation of a fleet of sound ships and though this could only be done by slow and careful methods it would ultimately prove to be a saving. The contrast was forcibly made with the decay so evident in the hastily run up ships of the earlier war. After consultations between Byam Martin and the Surveyors and the Admiralty it was decided that a labour force based on about 2,000 shipwrights should be able to create a serviceable fleet of 100 battleships and 130 Fifth Rate frigates in six years. The existing fleet comprised:

First Rates:	100–120 guns	13 three-deckers
Second Rates	98 guns	10 three-deckers
Large Third Rates	80 guns	10 two-deckers
Medium Third Rates	76 guns	1 two-decker
Small Third Rates	74 guns	78 two-deckers
Total		112 [16]

The Navy Board began to impose more rational views on repair and construction policy, reflecting Martin's influence. On first taking office he had prepared a series of notes for his own use, the first of which concerned the need to standardise all future ships on the best models. For these, in 1815 he favoured the three-decker *Caledonia* and the Third Rate *Impeteux*. He wanted to abolish the small three-decker, something with which Seppings was entirely in accord. By April 1816 he had added the *Canopus* for Second Rates, anticipating the alteration in the rating of warships that would be promulgated in November. The object of having three basic designs was to save on the duplication of stores, and allow for the easy conversion of timber in the certain knowledge of what would be required. For repairs the Board advised against continuing the programme of razeeing old 74s into spar-deck Fourth Rates. Although these ships had been successful in the War of 1812 they were all at least twenty years old and better ships could be built for the money. In addition, the Navy Board had never favoured large cruisers. The Admiralty also acted to restrict the freedom of Dockyard Commissioners, after the Sixth Rate *Cyrus* had been rebuilt under orders for a refit, by calling for all large refits to be submitted for their approval.[17]

The Treasury, reflecting Government weakness in the House of Commons, kept up the pressure for peace related savings.[18] Having established his programme, Byam Martin, however, used his expertise and semi-independent position at Somerset Place to argue for more money. Meanwhile he treated the remainder of 1816 as a trial period to determine the impact of financial restrictions on dockyard work.

The Admiralty had already decided that the postwar fleet

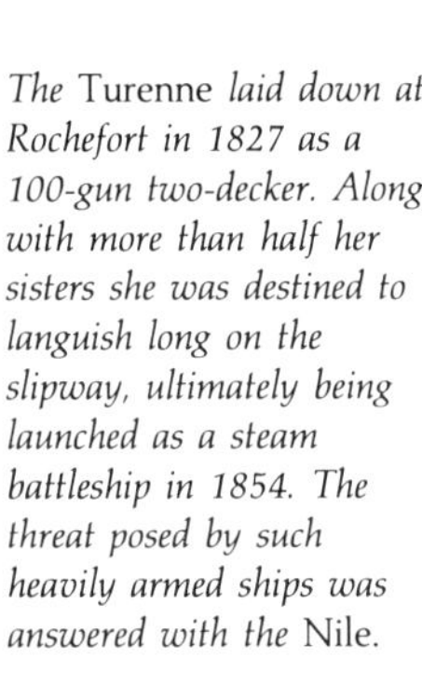

The Turenne *laid down at Rochefort in 1827 as a 100-gun two-decker. Along with more than half her sisters she was destined to languish long on the slipway, ultimately being launched as a steam battleship in 1854. The threat posed by such heavily armed ships was answered with the* Nile.

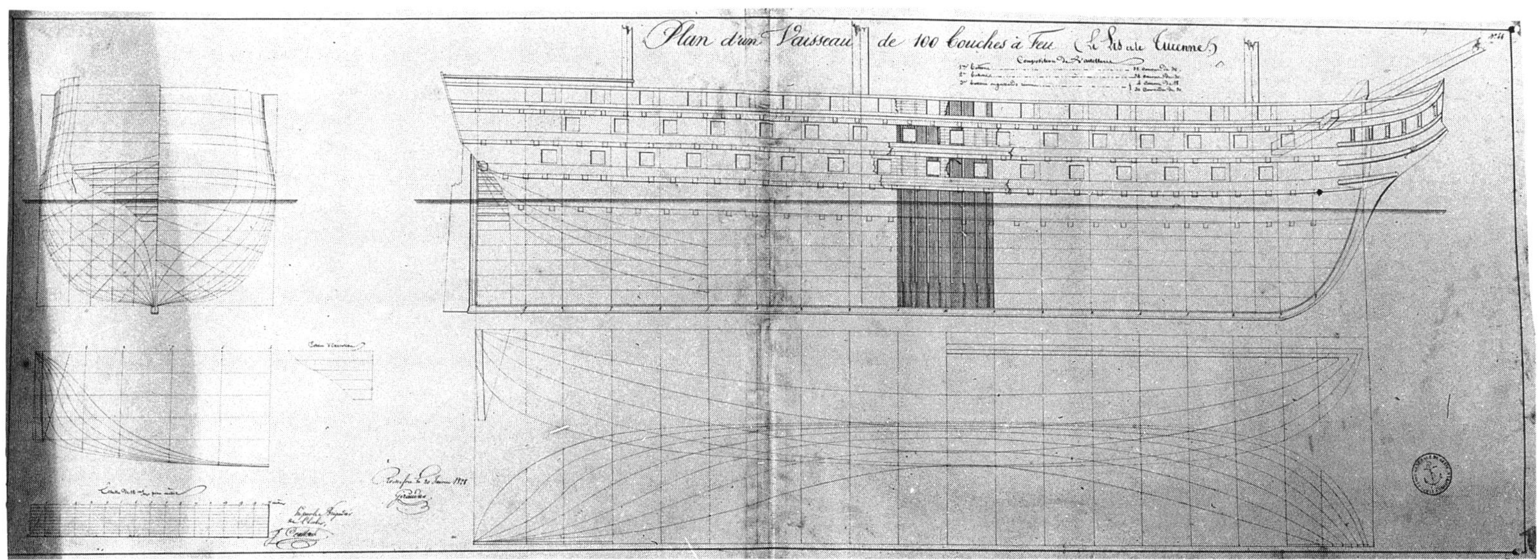

would require a heavy armament and the large three-deckers and 80-gun ships were made the most important classes. While the Navy Board was happy to build whatever was required, Byam Martin took a very narrow view of what could be achieved for he was well aware of the serious strains imposed on a ship by carrying too much weight of armament over a sustained cruise.[19] Byam Martin responded to the Admiralty by reviewing the first year of the postwar programme.

> The experience of the last year has shewn how difficult it is to calculate with any certainty upon the real condition of the fleet without a more minute examination of the ships than can be obtained while they remain afloat, and the unexpected state of decay in which many of them have been found on being opened, has exhibited in a very forcible manner the necessity of proceeding on a more extended scale in repairing Ships of the Line, building and repairing frigates and in converting materials for new ships.

Merchant-built vessels were particularly disappointing, and Byam Martin urged that the period of peace be used to avoid any need to have recourse to 'that evil' in future. Later he attributed the failure of these ships to the use of unseasoned timber and specifically discounted any suggestion of poor workmanship. Having reduced the dockyard labour force by one-quarter to save money, while still attempting to prepare ten battleships and fifteen frigates each year, Byam Martin had to report that only four ships of the line had been launched, four more repaired, with one new frigate and six more repaired.

> The whole of the line of battleships taken in hand for repair were found much more defective than could be ascertained while they remained afloat.
>
> The failure in Frigates... has been to a still greater extent. Out of 18... supposed to require only slight or middling repairs 7 have been taken to pieces and the others will require much larger repair than was at first estimated, except the *Briton*, so that a considerable proportion of the Artificers have been employed in examining ships, and in subsequently taking them to pieces.

The current state of the Navy List was far from satisfactory.

	Battleships	*Frigates*
Fit for 6 to 9 years service	24	23
Fit for 4 to 6 years service	35	17
Fit for 2 to 3 years service	20	38
In need of repair	20	12
Under repair	10	18
Ordered and building	17	11
Total	126	119

To rectify this Byam Martin wanted to work the artificers one more hour per day, at an annual cost of £500,000, while additional sawyers would cut the frames for as many three-deckers and 80-gun ships as the Admiralty desired. As the yards were short of slipways he wanted at least two more at Pembroke and suggested allowing frames to season before they were set up by immersing the timbers in salt water and storing under cover. By converting the timber and building the ships under cover he expected to create durable vessels. To emphasise the shortage of labour the Navy Board recommended that the frigate *Leda* be sold for there were not enough men available to take her to pieces and salvage any sound materials.[20]

The Admiralty hoped to get by by replacing defective ships on their list of 102 with some of the 18 on harbour service; frigates were a more urgent concern, but they wanted to resolve the difficulty while at the same time cutting back one-quarter of the labour force. Verbal communication with Byam Martin and Seppings had persuaded the Admiralty that 2,000 artificers could meet the Establishment in six years and so they looked for a wholesale dismissal of inefficient men, while offering superfluous shipwrights lower paid work as carpenters and joiners. Spare depot ships would be broken up while the shortage of frigates would have to be met by new construction and razeeing small battleships.[21] Political and economic pressures made any more extensive programme unthinkable. Later the Admiralty obtained further funds to cover the extra cost of revenue cruisers, just transferred to naval control, and transports for the Army in France. This necessitated the conversion of the frames for four 84-gun ships, one 52-gun ship and 20 Fifth Rates.[22] Melville struggled for more money, pointing out to his colleagues the extra demands on the Navy over and above those of 1792.[23] At the end of the year the list appeared adequate, but the bare figures covered many defects, as time would reveal.

Fit for service	78
In need of repair	21
Building	9
Repairing	11
Ordered, but not commenced	10
Total	129

The battlefleet

Of the ships judged fit for service after a cursory examination at least fifteen proved beyond economic repair, and only two of those listed as in need of repair ever served at sea again. Part of the problem lay in the large percentage of the fleet that was composed of old and small ships. In an effort to rectify this the least advanced of the small 74s, the *Boscawen*, was reordered as an 82-gun ship, being lengthened and broadened to take 24-pounders rather than 18s on the main deck. In the following year the last two Second Rate three-deckers, *Princess Charlotte* and *London* (later *Royal Adelaide*), were broadened to the same end. This process was to be followed at every opportunity; rebuilding, modifying and redesigning ships to enable them to carry a heavier battery. In this way Martin's fleet, although shrinking in numbers, became steadily more powerful.[24]

The Government urged the Admiralty to cut the Navy Estimates for 1818–19 from £6,450,000 to £6,000,000. When Lord Liverpool suggested cutting construction and repair, Melville sarcastically informed Byam Martin that this would have consequences the Prime Minister had not anticipated. Byam Martin kept his First Lord provided with information to support a more extensive naval programme. During this period he increased the import of foreign timber in order to drive down native prices, break the timber monopoly, and, more fundamentally, preserve the native supply for wartime. He called for more work to cover in the slipways and permit long-term construction, so that 'we shall have for the first time, a really sound and durable fleet, to the sure saving of enormous sums of money'.[25] Sadly, although a week was not a particularly long time in the more relaxed politics of the early nineteenth century, a year certainly was, and Byam Martin's 'enormous sums' would only be available in years to come. Liverpool and his colleagues were less than enthusiastic.

Anticipating further pressure to reduce expenditure Byam Martin argued that the figure of £6 million was too low, and that if the Government insisted they would have to take responsibility for prioritising the areas to be cut. Seppings suggested that the better ships should not be docked until after those in poor order, save to stop the spread of fungus. At the same time he argued that the widespread use of North American oak and fir left the war-built fleet hostage to fungal decay. Byam Martin, accompanying Seppings on his dockyard visits, reported in similar vein. Even the 120-gun *Nelson*, the largest ship built in the dockyards during the war, was seriously compromised by the indiscriminate use of mixed timber. Byam Martin proposed a new system for repairs, believing that the dockyards were excessively thorough, dismantling the ships to an unnecessary degree.[26]

When Liverpool returned to the attack he did so confident Melville and the Second Naval Lord, Admiral Cockburn, would find ways of affecting reductions. By contrast, Melville was well prepared with arguments in favour of retaining the 1817–18 figures. The war surplus stocks were now finished and the Navy Board believed that the low level of work would not keep pace with the decay of the fleet, particularly that built with inferior timber after 1807. He also noted the lack of any programme comparable to that of Pitt the Younger, Liverpool's political mentor, between 1782 and 1786. Melville remained convinced Parliament would happily vote the money. If he had to make cuts they would come in the area of seamen and dockyard improvements, not shipbuilding and repair.[27]

Melville had his own views, as he was to demonstrate on the question of armament, and was always prepared to disagree with the Navy Board. He had an opportunity to make the Navy Board play a very different tune in 1818. Benjamin Tucker, brother of Joseph Tucker, the Surveyor and an acolyte of the Whig Party, submitted a particularly hostile commentary on the wasteful and inefficient policy of the Navy Board. Tucker, St Vincent's one-time Secretary, was well informed and knew how to make his attack most effective. He was also provided with advice and support by his famous master, the most thorough of all naval reformers. The letter was sent to Cockburn at the Admiralty and it is clear that the object was political, being closely related to the Whig/Grenvillite Parliamentary attack of the period, although he allowed sibling loyalties to surface in an ill-informed attack on Seppings. Despite his connections, Tucker's details were unreliable. The 120-gun *St Vincent*, which he claimed to be in very poor order, proved to be particularly sound when inspected. Martin and Seppings were furious and sent a succession of letters to Melville and the Admiralty calling for the dismissal of Joseph

Baron Tupinier's beau ideal *for commerce destruction, the 60-gun frigate* Didon *of 1828. As with all French frigates of this rate she carries a full spar-deck battery. The stern is completely unadorned and carries the side planking right around with no galleries. Ships of this class were in part responsible for the policy of razeeing the small 74s into powerful 50-gun frigates.* (Author)

Tucker who they contended had supplied privileged information. Melville refused, claiming to believe the Surveyor's protestations of innocence. Privately, he expressed some satisfaction, believing the enquiry would keep the Navy Board on its toes.[28]

Melville lost little time exploiting the findings of the joint Admiralty/Navy Board enquiry into Tucker's allegations, which had concluded that the fleet was in far better order than had been suggested, in order to impose his views on the subordinate Board. 'My Lords feel great satisfaction at the state in which the ships have generally been found, which is so much better than they had been, by your previous reports, led to expect.' In consequence, the Admiralty was happy to bear the cost of the enquiry, and noted the need to open those ships that were housed over so as to allow the circulation of air.[29] Later in the year the Admiralty was able to order two 120-gun ships and one 84. In addition, the small three-decker *Ocean* was told off to be razeed into an 80-gun ship. The old *Prince of Wales* and *Royal George* were also considered, but both would have required a £60,000 repair and being old ships were taken to pieces. The pace at which the Navy shed unwanted ships picked up, several from the 1817 list being dismantled or, in the case of some ex-French ships, sold.[30]

In searching for acceptable reductions Byam Martin elected to close the shipyard at Deptford which saved £100,000 a year and cutting 1,000 seamen was to save a further £258,000 but even this would not meet the Government's demands.[31] These cuts came in early 1821. After reviewing foreign navies and their own resources the Board concluded, 'we are of opinion that under present circumstances it is not necessary in this country to continue the expenditure in the dockyards at its present level'. While the Admiralty had wanted to maintain the establishment at 100 battleships and 150 frigates, they now considered that it was no longer necessary to achieve those figures in such a short time as had originally been envisaged. As a result, the labour force was able to be cut by one-fifth. At the Navy Board Byam Martin responded by advising upon the cancellation of construction in India, so that timber could be worked in England in order to keep up dockyard labour. Later he also advised keeping up the hours of work. The King was sufficiently provoked by these cutbacks, of £500,000, to protest that any further projects would be 'inimical to the best interests of the country'. Liverpool responded by promising that the Cabinet's objection had been 'to take up ground which they could steadily and effectually defend; and that it was their firm determination to make every effort to resist any further reduction in the numbers, or alteration in the character of the national forces'.[32] One result of the Royal outburst was a supplementary estimate of £750,000 for building and repair, but in return wages at all the yards was to be cut back to the rates paid at Pembroke, with earnings limited to 5 shillings a day while the ban on Saturday work was to remain until the number of shipwrights had been reduced. It was clear from the 1821 Enquiry that a significant degree of overmanning had been supported by Byam Martin, in his efforts to keep up a labour force equal to wartime demands. By mid-1822 the Admiralty insisted; 'they cannot sanction a longer continuance of the existing system, the yards must be placed on a footing agreeable to the public interest'.[33]

While Earl St Vincent had always criticised the administration of the Dockyards he was steadfast in his refusal to exploit Admiralty problems for political advantage. He saw in the dockyard reductions the 'rapid ruin of the British Navy', and called instead for the reduction of administrators, adding that 'one of the projectors of the present diabolical measures ought to be gibbeted opposite the Deptford Yard, and the other opposite to Woolwich Yard, on the Isle of sad Dogs'. The old Admiral had less than a year to live, but the fire of commitment to the Navy burned in him to the end. He had fallen out with the Opposition over the question of naval reductions, and saw no reason to support the ministers on this issue. It was fortunate he did not live to see his friends in office after 1830.[34]

Between 1823 and 1825 the estimates were kept below the magic figure of £6 million set by the 1817 Committee of Public Finance, but the number of seamen borne rose steadily from 21,000 in 1821 to 29,000 in 1825. The extra manpower, made necessary by the deteriorating international situation, had to be funded by cutting back on stores and dockyard work.

The armament crisis of 1826

Only in 1826 did naval policy return to central stage. This was brought about principally by the rapid recovery of the French fleet. The large ships they were laying down, particularly the 100-gun two-deckers with a full spar deck battery following the American fashion, were too powerful and too numerous to be ignored. Jean-Louis Barrallier, a war-time Assistant Surveyor now at work in Toulon, reported that these were the only two-deckers being considered by the French.[35] The Navy Board had been up-gunning the fleet in 1825, broadening the *Impregnable* for the armament of *Princess Charlotte* and proposing to improve the 120-gun ships under order to carry new 32-pounder 47cwt guns on the main deck. They had also ordered a new 76, the *Valiant*, on the lines of the *Bulwark*. This ship did not meet the new requirements of 1826 and was never commenced.[36] In view of the French programme, Byam Martin advised broadening the 120s by 6 in to 9 in, 'where it can be done without injury to their frames'. It was also necessary that it be kept secret. In consequence, the correspondence was conducted by the Controller personally and not a trace remains in the official archive. He also advised repairing the *Caledonia*, which had only just been taken into dock for work ordered in 1815. The intervening years had increased the cost by one third to £60,000.[37] In addition, Byam Martin presented the draught of a new class of 100-gun two-decked ships, with a full spar deck battery. This feature had gone out of fashion with the Royal Navy shortly after the War of 1812, Martin in particular arguing for a reduction in the weight of the upperworks to improve durability and sailing. The new ship, the *Nile*, the first British battleship of the postwar era, was designed for a full battery of 32-pounders. He wanted to build three.[38]

With this work already in hand to meet the challenge from France, the Cabinet became alarmed by reports of the formidable armament of the USS *Ohio*, which included a lower deck battery of heavy 42-pounders. The First Lord called for all future two-deckers to be of the new *Nile*-class; 'until several of that description have been provided', or, in less ambiguous language, enough to outnumber the Americans. Byam Martin prepared a memorandum for Melville to read to his Cabinet colleagues, giving details of the broadside of the American ship and the most recent British designs.

Ohio	1792lbs
Caledonia	1568lbs
Ganges	1172lbs
with 32pdrs on the main deck	1300lbs
Ocean	1220lbs
Albion, a typical small 74	938lbs

Byam Martin rated *Caledonia*, even with an inferior broadside, as more than a match for *Ohio* because a three-decker possessed the advantage of firing down into her adversary at decisive ranges. The small 74s were to be razeed into powerful frigates, but the larger Third Rates were equal to French ships of the same class. Significantly, the new *Nile*-class 100-gun ships would be equal to *Ohio* and built to a better design but would take five years to complete, taking into account the latest views on seasoning. It was clear to Byam Martin that the *Ohio*, which was little larger than *Ganges* even if her form was better suited to a heavy armament, was seriously over-gunned and would be badly damaged by sustained cruising.

With the Cabinet interested enough to call the Controller into a session it was time to press for additional funds. Byam Martin hurried off orders to broaden all the three-deckers that were not too far advanced and to increase the scantling of the main deck beams of the 84-gun ships to carry long 32-pounders. These orders were later cancelled and replaced by more detailed structural modifications.[39] Byam Martin revealed his views on armaments with proposals to broaden the *Nelson* and *Queen Charlotte*, then under repair, to carry long 42-pounders on the lower deck. He was bitterly opposed to over-arming unmodified ships, something that had already been done to the *Asia*. When Melville approved of this plan he pressed for all 120- and 84-gun ships building to be modified and more shipwrights to be placed on them, largely by restoring those men who had been doing duty as house carpenters. Seppings and Byam Martin developed a new scheme to permit the ships building in both major classes to carry long 32-pounders on the main deck. They also promised to deliver six improved First Rates, equal to the *Ohio*, within six years.[40]

For all the seriousness with which the Government had viewed the situation it did not result in the provision of any further funds. This alarmed Byam Martin, as he could not even afford to pay off the ships in commission, given the large amount of wages due.[41] The programme of new and rebuilt ships was scheduled, and particular efforts made to keep secret the 100-gun ships and the broadening of the three-deckers. Rumours were soon abroad, for which Byam Martin blamed Chatham.

Anticipated dates of completion of new and rebuilt ships

		Anticipated launch date			*Launched*
Three-decked ships					
Royal George	120	October	1827	New	22.9.1827
Nelson	120	June	1828	Rebuilt	
Royal William	120	June	1828	N	2.4.1833
Royal Adelaide	100	July	1828	N	28.7.1828
Neptune	120	December	1828	N	22.9.1832
Trafalgar	120	November	1829	N	21.6.1841
Caledonia	120	August	1829	R	
St George	120		1830	N	27.8.1840
Waterloo	120	November	1831	N	2.4.1833
Large two-decked ships					
London	100	September	1831	N	28.9.1840
Nile	100	August	1831	N	28.6.1839
Rodney	100	two years after the *Goliath*, which was due in July 1827		N	18.6.1833

Battleships incapable of bearing such a heavy armament were stood aside. The *Hindostan* at Plymouth, for example, was suspended in favour of the *Nile*.[42] To save money Byam Martin tried to abolish the quarantine hulks at Milford, where eleven large warships provided the nearby dockyard with a constant distraction from new work.[43]

The Lord High Admiral

Following the review of design and armament policy Byam Martin provided the new Prime Minister, George Canning, and the Lord High Admiral with a detailed statement of the fleet in order to support a claim for more resources. He also explained the improved designs already underway.

The state of the fleet 12 April 1827

	First	*Second*	*Third*	*Fourth*	*Fifth*
Fit for service	7	6	44	7	46
In need of repair	4	1	11	2	6
Undergoing repair	3	–	3	1	1
Building	4	6	–	2	11
Ordered	6	2	1	3	18
In commission	3	4	10	5	19
Total	27	19	69	20	101

Battleships fit for service and in commission 57 + 17 = 74[44]

Over the next two years new orders were restricted to razeeing four more 74s and the old First Rates *Union* and *Boyne*.[45] The emphasis on dockyard work reflected the pressure on the existing slipways with the large number of major units building, in all twenty-three. When Byam Martin eventually secured a new order for a First Rate, to bring the number of 120-gun ships up to ten, it was significant that the *Royal Frederick* was to be built at Portsmouth on the slip occupied by the *Neptune*. Reference to the table above suggests why she was still on order four years later, and, indeed, she was the last ship of the line ordered by the Navy Board. The pressure for rearmed large ships had declined by 1828 for the Mediterranean emergency pitted Britain against foes less powerful than the Americans, while in the New World there was a marked reduction of tension. This encouraged Byam Martin to press for a delay of six months on the five most advanced three-deckers in order to prolong the seasoning period.[46] Under pressure to reduce the estimates he agreed to suspend weekend working, save on three-deckers and 100-gun ships.[47]

Even so, the Lord High Admiral cut the timber store from three years to two, and ordered a large programme to increase the force of Advanced Ships with a full set of masts and sails aboard and the ground tier of water tanks in place and closed in. Some were brought to an even higher state of readiness.[48]

In the prevailing economic and diplomatic climate it was hardly surprising that on his return to office Melville should solicit a new set of figures on the state of the fleet from Cockburn, by now the First Naval Lord and increasingly influential. Cockburn suggested that under the current programme there would be eighty effective ships by 1830, of which only the Navarino veterans *Albion* and *Genoa* would not be fit for service. In fact, the Admiralty had already ordered the former to be taken to pieces and the latter turned over to Harbour Service as beyond economic repair. He also suggested that the French were in a less satisfactory situation, which was certainly the case. In a period of political uncertainty and international tension Cockburn was better equipped to advise on overall policy, but Byam Martin, his senior on the Flag List, held a strong position.

During his period out of office Melville had given some thought to the structure of naval administration. From his decision to amalgamate the Admiralty and Navy Board, it would appear he had decided that the office of Controller, as filled by Byam Martin, was altogether too powerful a post in peace-time.[49]

The Board refused to sanction any increase in expenditure, forcing the cancellation of two new 52-gun ships at Plymouth. The Fourth Rate class was to be kept up by razeeing old 74s, but they did express doubts as to the ability of the existing dockyard labour force to replace any of the fleet. Increased specialisation of the yards, with Sheerness taking more maintenance work leaving building and repair to Chatham and Woolwich, was also seen as a potential saving.[50]

In early 1830 Byam Martin returned to the attack, calling for a revision of the Establishment to a total of ninety. He urged Melville to order five more First Rates, of an improved design, to take the Establishment in that class up to twenty-four units. These would be built at Chatham, Portsmouth, Plymouth and Pembroke, following the units building in 1826. One was to be the much delayed *Royal Frederick* and work was able to begin immediately, preparing the frames to allow for lengthy seasoning. These ships were to be broadened *Caledonias*, 'with an additional five feet of length which Sir Robert Seppings is of opinion will admit of a better distribution of the ports, and tend to the improvement of the ships altogether'. The lower decks would be armed with 63cwt 32-pounders.

There were now twenty-one Second Rates, of which fourteen were armed with 32-pounders on the main deck. Byam Martin argued that any ship not equal to this arming should no longer be considered a Second Rate. This reflected the considerable up-gunning of the fleet since he had argued for any two-decker incapable of bearing 24-pounders to be a Third Rate. Experience with the *Asia* was to reveal whether the large Second Rates were equal to 32-pounders.

> If these ships, (built after the *Canopus*) were more full in their after and fore body, there is no doubt they would have been far better ships, and much more equal to 32-pounders on the main deck, but unfortunately the *Calcutta* now building at Bombay is the only ship so improved.

Byam Martin also lamented that the Bombay ships had heavier teak upper works. In consequence, he argued that all

A French frigate under sail, long after the end of the sailing fleet. Photographs of large sailing ships at sea are very rare, and this one gives a good impression. (CMP)

save *Calcutta* should only carry 24-pounders for although the English ships could carry the heavier guns it would be at the expense of their durability. Any future ships were to be built to the improved design. He suggested an establishment of twenty-two large Second Rates, including three of the *Nile* class. This included the *Boyne*, then docked to be repaired and razeed at Plymouth. Any future Third Rates should be of the 24-pounder *Bulwark* class. The *Valiant* was still on order, but had made no progress.

The battlefleet in 1830

	In good order	*Ordered/building*	*Total*	*Proposed Establishment*
First	11	8	19	24
Second	12	10	22	22
Third	48	1	49	44
Total	71	19	90*	90

*less six 74s to be razeed into Fourth Rates.[51]

By September Byam Martin was anxious to begin the *Royal Frederick* and, having revised the Establishment in that class to twenty-four, found a shortfall of two Second Rates, which he proposed to remedy by razeeing the *Union* and ordering another *Calcutta*. Melville had insisted on arming all the *Canopus* derivatives with 32-pounders. However, much as Byam Martin complained of this, to Cockburn and his own brother among others, he had become aware of the more serious problem of block obsolescence. He feared that the success of Navy Board policy over the preceding 15 years had created the erroneous impression that ships built along the postwar lines would last for half a century if left in the Ordinary. With the existing workforce it would not be possible to replace the fleet before it became overage and undersize.

> A certain number *must* be built or considerably repaired year after year, and probably about five sail of the line will be constantly in hand – and if 80 ships are expected to be constantly *ready* the Establishment ought to be fixed at 90 sail.

The solutions he advanced were unremarkable. More men were to be engaged in new work and commissions extended from three to four or more years. Fitting out and the incidental repairs were a major distraction for the arsenals which explains why Pembroke could achieve superior productivity. Melville, given the political situation, was not prepared to trouble the Cabinet for more money, preferring to ignore Byam Martin's repeated warning. No new battleships were ordered and Byam Martin, with a professional warrior's contempt, blamed the politicians of all parties. They appeared, he informed Admiral Sir Pulteney Malcolm;

> to forget that the safety and glory of England depends on her naval strength and her constant and ample state of naval preparation; and we shall perhaps (at no distant time) rue the day that such mischevious opinions prevailed.

It was to be the supreme irony that the leading Opposition spokesman of defence reductions, Sir James Graham, would be the next First Lord.[52]

As a serving member of the House of Commons, Byam Martin was well aware of Graham's economic reputation, something that coloured his first memorandum to the new political head of the Navy. The object was to impress upon Graham the skill with which the Navy Board had been handling the material policy, and support a claim for further funds. After listing the ships in Ordinary he disclosed that masts and sails for fifty battleships and forty-five frigates had been prepared, although there was a shortage of cables.

> ...the care and preservation of ships in Ordinary is much beyond anything known at any former period and has been the cause of a great saving of the public money and there is scarcely any *visible* defect in the ships, but if they were taken into dock and opened it is impossible to suppose that such immense fabrics of timber can be free from partial decay and perhaps in some instances to a considerable extent and it is desirable, and has been directed, that the ships shall be taken into dock alternately to undergo an inspection and such repair as may be found necessary. The *Pitt*, for instance is now in dock and will cost in her slight refit about £4,000; but the works going on upon ships in commission, and so frequently brought forward for service is a great interruption to the necessary inspection and repairs of the ships in Ordinary.

In addition Byam Martin listed ten ships in need of repair: *Boyne, Ocean, Ramillies, Malta, Spartiate, Anson, Duncan, Cressy, Greenwich* (ex *Rodney*) and *Renown*. While Seppings believed the first four were equal to sea service in an emergency without repair, Martin wanted an early report on all; breaking up the worst would release a large amount of copper, which was in short supply. In the event only *Ocean* was ever to serve at sea again. There were also twenty-five sheer hulks, depot ships and receiving and training ships also on the list which Byam Martin considered surplus to need and which could be sold off to take the pressure off the Establishment. The two ships still on order from 1826 were little advanced; one seventh of *Royal Frederick*'s frame had been prepared, while nothing had yet been done for *Valiant*. There were still insufficient slips – a total of twenty-eight and not all of them could support a battleship – so that an early recourse to the merchant yards in the event of war would be necessary.[53]

It is hard to avoid the impression that Byam Martin had been in office too long. For all his sterling qualities he lacked the flexibility to respond to the great political changes that followed the death of Lord Liverpool, and the breakdown of international stability. His reversing of the roles of active ships and those in Ordinary, claiming that the active fleet interfered with the reserve, was particularly revealing. The Navy was no longer near the top of national priorities and in consequence it would have to accept whatever the new Ministry was prepared to provide. Byam Martin, Seppings and their colleagues had done a good job for the battlefleet was better than it had ever been in terms of numbers of ships in good order and ready for service. An emergency in 1830 would have found the fleet equal to any call. As a result the incoming Government, like their predecessors after 1826, felt safe to cut the estimates and impose a very different set of priorities on the available funds; to facilitate this process it became expedient to down-grade the material department.

For perhaps the first time in its long history the Navy Board had been an outstanding success so it is curious that it should have then been abolished for political profit in a programme conditioned by memories of 1806–7 and the views of Earl St Vincent.

2 The Abolition of the Navy Board

Sir James Graham and his politics of reform

The new First Lord entered office laden with the economic and reforming baggage of the Whig party, and his own not inconsiderable reputation in these areas. In part, this reflected the politics of recovery after twenty years in the wilderness, and in part the heritage of Earl Grey, the last Whig First Lord (in 1806) and his one-time professional advisor, Earl St Vincent. Grey had the lowest possible opinion of the Navy Board, which he passed on to Graham, who was directed to look at the three Boards, including the Victualling Board, and advised that there might well be a need for concentration. For all his arrogance, and the appearance of vaunting self-confidence, Graham was fundamentally insecure, deferring all major decisions to the Prime Minister and this left Grey in a particularly strong position to exercise decisive influence over the direction of policy.[1]

From its first days in office it was clear that the new Government was determined to continue the reductions of the previous four years and had no interest in the opinions of the Navy Board. In response to Martin's memorandum, Graham ordered that no more First Rates were to be laid down, no materials to be collected for them and no more to be doubled; no new Second Rates were to be fitted out as suggested by Seppings; there would be no more Third Rates, while Fourth Rates unequal to the razee armament were not to be considered. In effect, the new Admiralty Board suspended anything that appeared to be in the least contentious, partly to allow time to take stock, but also as the start of a campaign of concerted political attack on the Navy Board. The line of complaint soon became obvious. The Navy Board was directed to provide accounts of the real expenditure on stores over the past decade, and the uses made of any surpluses. Graham was well aware that Somerset Place treated the estimates as an overall figure within which sums could be moved between heads of expenditure without the need for any fresh sanction by Parliament or the Government. He was particularly interested in what was happening in the large programme of dockyard works, Weevil Victualling Yard at Plymouth and Woolwich, although it was necessary to tread carefully on this matter as the work had been ordered by the King when he had been Lord High Admiral. To add to the discomfiture of Martin and his colleagues they were instructed to speed up the reduction of dockyard artificers down to the figure of 6,000 set by Melville in the previous year.[2]

The object of the attack was to discredit the Navy Board, and in particular the Controller, in the eyes of the King so that a wide ranging programme of reform could be introduced. Reforming naval administration would yield two important political benefits. First, it would reinforce the commitment to change that had been central to the Whigs appeal to the radical elements; and second it would provide the financial savings needed as a bribe to the independent landowning members who were vital to the passage of the major item on the political agenda, the Bill to reform Parliamentary representation. However, Graham knew that Martin and the King were old shipmates and close friends and so he impressed on Grey the need for the most careful of manoeuvres.

Melville, the leading political figure of the previous regime, realised that the administrative reform elements were principally a continuation of the work of his Board, but he picked up hints of the dirty tricks in store for the Navy Board from the First Lord's private secretary. 'The purport of it [the conversation] was anything but creditable to the official character of Lord Grey and Sir James' [Graham].[3] By the same token the new Government believed themselves under threat from the permanent officials remaining in office. At the Admiralty Sir John Barrow was known to be a diehard Tory at heart, while the Navy Board was perceived as a seat of politically motivated opposition to economy and reform. Such tendencies were reinforced when the King informed Martin that he believed the new Government, bent on reform, would not last. In addition, he requested the Controller to meet him at least once a month to discuss naval affairs. Martin would not have been human if he did not consider that his relationship with the King placed him above politics and moreover above the control of the Admiralty.[4]

When the King jibbed at the investigation of past expenditure, particularly that connected with his period in office, Graham insisted that he was not to blame for misappropriation by his successors. Graham also deliberately and dishonestly prepared a paper to 'prove' that the major stores, which were the responsibility of the Navy Board, were in short supply. In addition, he blamed supposed insubordination by the Navy Board for the apparent weakness of the fleet in specific areas, particularly in Fourth Rates and steam vessels: but this complaint was specious and ill-founded for Fourth Rates had no place in the Royal Navy while steam warships were still inefficient and unreliable despatch boats. Yet the effect he created helped to secure his object: royal assent to a thorough reform of naval accounting methods and, ultimately, this was to lead to the overhaul of naval administration.[5]

Grey stressed to Graham that it was important for him to impose his will on the Navy Board; 'you must insist on their obeying you'. He also revealed a deep dislike of Seppings, a

The Formidable, *as a training ship at Portishead on the Bristol Channel. This ship was the first result of the Navy Board's programme to reconstruct the Navy after 1815.* (CMP)

The 120-gun St Vincent *of 1815. This ship was a major asset for the fleet throughout the period, ending her active career carrying French troops to the Baltic in 1854.* (CMP)

matter in which the King was, at least insofar as it related to round sterns and the small dimensions of British ships, largely in agreement.

> I was particularly pleased with what he says about the Surveyor of the Navy. Seppings has, I believe, done more mischief than any man ever did, in the same situation; and he requires the more watching as I am afraid that he certainly governs Sir B. Martin with respect to everything in his department. During the three years I was at Plymouth, the whole strength of the Dockyard was wasted in alterations – square sterns to round, brigs to ships – men of war to packets – putting on & then taking off again Sir H. Davy's protectors, widening, altering & doubling old, bad ships & turning out of the service many that were still serviceable etc. etc. so that not a stroke of new work was done during all that time, the Navy was left in the state in which you have found it.

Allowing for a degree of wilful blindness, this was as dishonest a record of what took place at Plymouth as it would be possible to construct. Benjamin Tucker's attacks in 1817, and the opinions of Grey's uncle, once Flag Captain to St Vincent, had coloured an already exaggerated political perception of Tory naval policy.[6]

The King defended Byam Martin stoutly, as Graham had anticipated. He made no response to Graham's opening attack on misappropriation until after he had seen Martin; 'of whose professional character, zeal, efficiency and integrity . . . H.M. has always entertained the highest opinion'. William followed Byam Martin's argument on the need for flexibility in the discharge of public duties, accepted the Navy Board view of the condition of the fleet, and warned the Government against going too far in attempting to correct 'what *may* seem [to be] abuses'. Byam Martin stressed that although he had won the argument 'every day gives me reason to be more than cautious in my official dealings, and you may well imagine the difficulty of my position'.

After a renewed assault the King argued for an annual balance sheet to show the actual expenditure, a point Graham accepted, and began to give way on the issue of Fourth Rates and steamers. He stressed the subordination of the Navy Board to the Admiralty, and the ability of the senior Board to control the Surveyor on the question of which class of ship should be built. Royal approval was given for the constructive dismissal of Surveyor Tucker and Commissioner Captain Courteney Boyle.[7] The end of this first round of attacks was to be no more than a temporary relief for the beleagured Navy Board. The independence and authority of the Navy Board was a threat to the Government's political programme, and it was to be resolved by whatever means were necessary. If those means were in conflict with long-term policy making, the needs of the moment were to take priority.

The Tory response

Melville was far from pleased by 'misrepresentations' in Graham's speeches on the Navy Estimates, but remained reluctant to come down to London and take up the issue.[8] The fact that he was particularly anxious for his youngest son Robert to continue in the Naval administration, in a post entirely at the mercy of the present Administration, clearly had a calming influence. In consequence he remained on the best of terms with Graham while bitterly attacking his policies in private.[9] Robert Dundas, younger son of Lord Melville and Deputy Controller, survived the wreck of the Navy Board, serving as Storekeeper General for another thirty years.

The impact of Graham's assault on the Navy Board ended the co-operation that had been such a successful feature of the preceding fifteen years. Melville and Byam Martin had, from their very different standpoints, combined to establish long-term policy requirements and create a fleet to match those needs. The new Administration took little heed of what had been done earlier, preferring to begin again with a quite different agenda. To some degree this reflected the clear divergence of political philosophy between the two parties, but much more it was a question of asserting control over what was perceived as a hostile body. By April 1831 the Navy Board had been ordered to refer the details of any contract for steam machinery for Admiralty supervision.[10]

In a move that revealed his political *naïveté*, Byam Martin responded to one of Graham's political assaults on the reputation of the preceding Administration by demanding, on the floor of the House, that he retract the imputation that public monies had been misappropriated. Graham argued that he had merely pointed out that the money had been applied to public works other than those for which it had been voted. As a member of the House Graham admitted he had a duty to reply, but as a member of the same Administration he declared that the First Lord had no duty to make an official reply to the Controller. Lord Althorp reported Byam Martin's public demand for an explanation and the altogether too-well prepared intervention of Sir George Clerk. After reading Althorps' report the King was moved to lament that Byam Martin 'should not have acted with more discretion upon this occasion'. William was aware that Graham's statements had been misrepresented and that they were widely believed to contain the very imputations

Byam Martin complained of, but as a subordinate officer the Controller was not responsible for any misapplication of funds.[11]

After Byam Martin's outburst Althorp, as Leader of the House, pressed him to attend and vote on the Reform Bill, knowing full well that the Controller was entirely opposed to the measure.[12] The Dissolution that month provided Graham with an opportunity to remove Byam Martin from the Commons but this was bungled leaving Byam Martin in his seat and the political objectives of the Government exposed to hostile comment. Graham invited Byam Martin to give up his seat at Plymouth, where the influence of his wife's family, the Fanshawes, had been built up over many years. The King agreed that it was not necessary for the Controller to sit in the House and Byam Martin was happy to withdraw, being at best an unwilling parliamentarian. But the Admiralty desired to put up the First Secretary, Captain George Elliot, for the constituency, and with Cockburn also standing it was decided that Martin should stand, if only to keep out Cockburn. Later, the adverse indications for Elliot during early canvassing persuaded the Admiralty to change their view and call on Byam Martin to withdraw. With his own position so far advanced Byam Martin considered this would be improper and despite the arrival of Surveyor Tucker and various Admiralty officials to support Elliot, Byam Martin and Cockburn headed the poll with 99 and 89 votes to Elliot's 61. This was a humiliation for the Government, particularly in the light of Byam Martin's outburst in the Commons the previous month. Byam Martin agreed to withdraw from Parliament at some suitable date and after another interview with the King the matter appeared to have been closed.[13]

Faced with a determined attack on their programme the Navy Board responded to the new situation in a fashion common to any professional body: they stressed the importance of the work they were engaged upon. Central to Byam Martin's conception of his duty was the maintenance of the battlefleet, and it was on this subject that he questioned the new policy coming from the Admiralty. Byam Martin held the highest regard for the power of the three-decked battleship, and the order cancelling any work on new units of this class struck him as seriously misguided. He requested guidance on the future of the *Royal Frederick*, for which one quarter of the frame had already been provided.[14] Though the ship was allowed to continue she remained the target for suspension and alteration. Seppings suggested that future three-deckers should follow the *Howe*, with additional breadth and depth for long 32-pounders on the main deck, an armament equal to that of the French.[15] Martin wanted to build five more First Rates to the design agreed in 1830, for an Establishment of twenty-four. He noted the argument in favour of steamships, but observed the need to maintain superiority in existing types while other powers were similarly equipped. He reckoned that the majority of the nineteen First Rates on the list were inferior to French and to the rumoured American ships and that an additional £30,000 per year would remove any cause for concern. Furthermore, he noted that several Second and Third Rate ships were fit for little but breaking up and that new units would have to be placed on the stocks to replace them in an emergency.[16] In response, the Board finally addressed itself to the central issue of the Establishment they wished the Navy Board to maintain.

Rate	*Number required*	*Build or repair*	*Total*	*Frames*
First	15	5	20	5
Second	15	5	20	5
Third	30	–	30	–
Fourth	30	10	40	5
Steamers	10 of 800 tons each			

This was a significantly smaller Establishment than that argued for by the preceding Admiralty. Only seventy battleships, with ten frames 'prepared so that they may be seasoned and run up in haste in the event of war', did not compare with one hundred, particularly as there was no increase in the number of large ships, merely a reduction in the number of Third Rates. In addition, Byam Martin's call for additional funds was refused though his argument for the improved *Calcutta* was accepted along with that for *Bulwark*, should any such ships be required. Fourth Rates were to be of the razee specification. However, no response was made on the question of First Rates.[17]

On the same day the Board complained that Somerset Place had not acted quickly enough in reducing dockyard artificers. At least 200 were to be dismissed each month, and there were still 2,650 shipwrights in service instead of 2,500 as ordered. Consideration was to be given to ending construction at Sheerness, which could allow the reduction of, 'a considerable number of shipwrights'.[18] Having provided the details of the Establishment the Admiralty immediately ensured that it would be difficult to achieve their figures and in addition they provided a clear warning of their intentions by ordering a new Fourth Rate design from Captain Symonds, the protégé of the Duke of Portland and Lord Vernon. Though to be armed and masted like the *Barham*, there were to be no restrictions on the dimensions of the new ship and on at least one major point

The French 120-gun ships of the First Empire. This one, the Montebello *of 1812, remained at the core of the French battlefleet until 1860. Some were only launched in the 1850s, after forty years high and dry.*

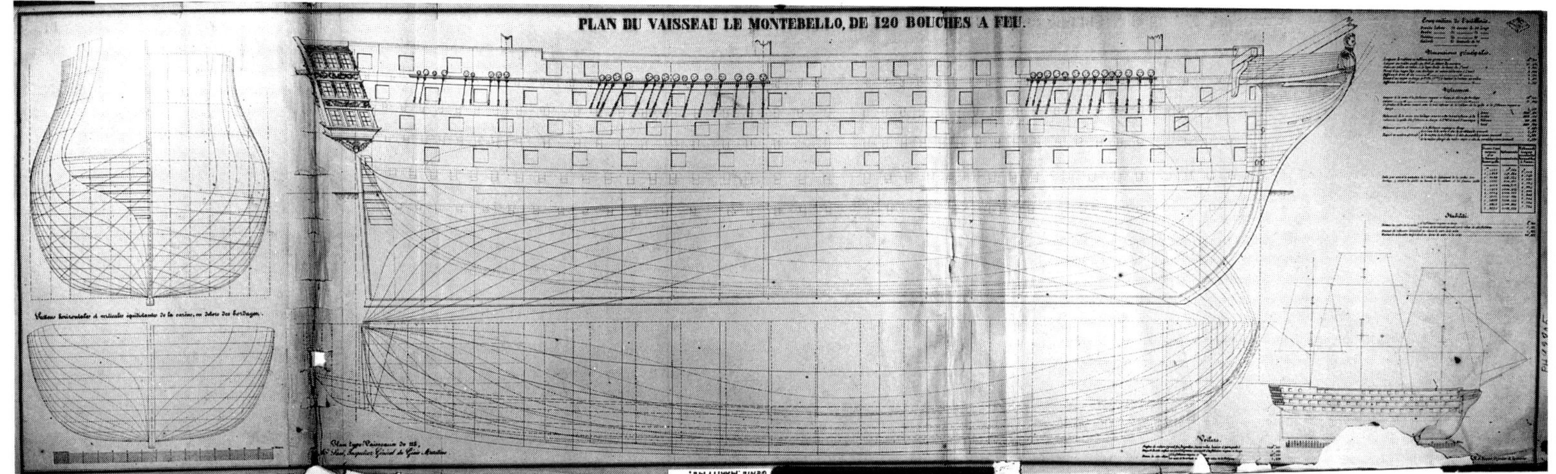

Symonds was given an entirely free hand. 'Her stern must be such as would admit of equal areas of attack and defence with those of Round Stern ships' and it was indicative of the objects of this policy that the letter was addressed to Symonds at Troon, the Duke of Portland's Scottish shipyard.[19]

Graham had been thinking of building outside the Royal Yards from the beginning of his term and ordered mobilisation designs for large corvettes and 28-gun ships in February. He continued in this vein throughout the year, ordering two brigs of Symonds's design, the *Serpent* and *Snake*, from merchant yards in October. They were, in part, a test of capacity but more significantly they were to be rushed to completion as part of the build-up to the long planned installation of Symonds as Surveyor of the Navy.[20] Graham consulted Thomas Brocklebank based at Whitehaven in Cumberland, and one of the largest shipowners and builders in the northwest, on the relative merits of naval and mercantile shipbuilding. His opinions were made clear in the opening remarks of the request.

> I am not satisfied with the present plan of building ships in H.M.'s dockyards; it is much more expensive and more tardy than in private yards. I believe the waste of materials to be greater, and the check over the work done by the artificers employed more expensive and less efficient.

The letter developed these assumptions, which were all adverse to naval shipbuilding and, more significantly, adverse to the lessons of the wartime construction programmes. Warships, which were built to very different standards from merchant ships, made far greater demands on labour and on the quality of the materials employed. In response, Brocklebank could only inform Graham of mercantile construction practices and his letter did not provide the desired ammunition to attack the Navy Board.[21]

In the interval Graham had succeeded in his major aim for 1831 for Byam Martin was summarily dismissed on 17 October, the consent of the King having been secured only two days previously. Byam Martin had been absent from the divisions on the Reform issue, a fact that did not go unnoticed both in and outside the Government, and he was reported as boasting that the Ministers would get no votes from him. On 11 October he missed the vote on Lord Ebrington's motion and was called upon to explain himself by Edward Ellice, patronage secretary to the Treasury. Byam Martin merely observed that he had left the House before the vote. Grey informed the King that Byam Martin's conduct in Parliament and the fact that Graham and Hardy, another of the King's favourites, found it impossible to conduct the business of the Admiralty with Byam Martin in office, made it essential that he be removed. Byam Martin was taken by surprise, and after the briefest of protests he gave way. His place was filled, for the remaining days of the Navy Board, by Admiral George Dundas, Second Naval Lord and the particular political confidant of Graham.[22]

The dismissal of Byam Martin

To the end of his term in office Byam Martin continued to search for order and stability in construction policy. His final submission to the Admiralty, the day before his dismissal, set out in some detail the implications of the policy statements of 10 January and 30 June. To meet the figures for First Rates it would be necessary to launch *Neptune* and *Royal William* before laying down *Royal Frederick* and one other ship. Similarly, two Second Rates would have to be launched, the *Rodney* and *Monarch*. Razeeing *Union* and *Boyne* into 76-gun ships, to be included among the Second Rates because of their heavier armament on the main deck, would leave the force two over Establishment, and limit the number of new frames to three. There were forty-four Third Rates suitable for service, leaving Byam Martin to re-open the question of repairing them or reducing some to Fourth Rates, where the greatest deficiency existed. Byam Martin wanted to increase the amount of work carried out in the yards with the Admiralty setting out the priorities.[23]

Having removed the head of the old Board Graham was determined to investigate every aspect of his empire and he launched into a programme of dockyard visits.[24] New orders were restricted, with only the razeeing of *Hercules* being ordered in the remaining months of 1831. In the event policy on razees changed before anything could be done.[25] By contrast the Admiralty prepared a new dockyard policy. Repairs were not to be carried out if they equalled the cost of a new ship, and in any calculation the value of the old ship added to the opportunity cost of the dock in which the rebuild would take place, a rather larger sum than that for a slipway, had to be considered. In addition, a repaired ship could never be the equal of a new vessel and consequently it was decided that repairs were not to exceed one-quarter, or at the most three-eighths, of the cost of a new ship and the reduction in number of excessively long repairs would free docks for smaller repairs. A review of all repair work since 1815 was to assist the Board in arriving at a more detailed programme.[26]

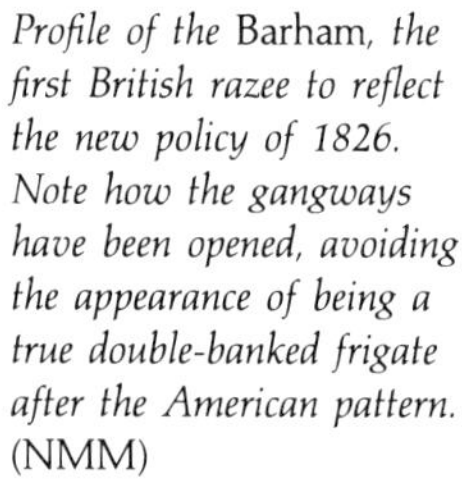

Profile of the Barham, *the first British razee to reflect the new policy of 1826. Note how the gangways have been opened, avoiding the appearance of being a true double-banked frigate after the American pattern.* (NMM)

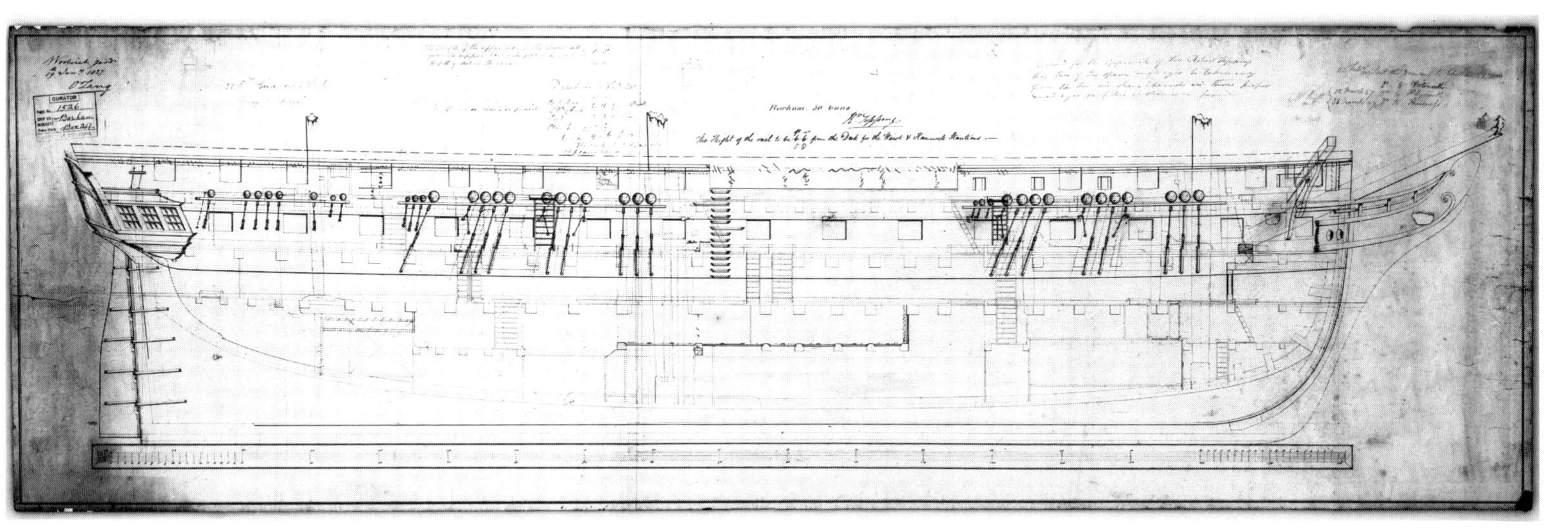

Before this programme could be acted upon, Graham had a more important task: the final abolition of the Navy Board. With George Dundas as Controller, the Board was reduced to complete subordination. Graham now proposed to replace it with a system based upon individual responsibility on Benthamite principles. Individual naval lords would each be responsible for a particular aspect of Admiralty business and would report back to the First Lord who was responsible to Parliament. The object was to gain greater political control over the major spending departments, specifically those of the Storekeeper and the Surveyor, and save money. The only change to the professional personnel was to be the retirement of Seppings in favour of Symonds. Hardy, Dundas and Barrow had all been consulted on the measure, while exchanges with the King had encouraged Graham to expect his approval. This was granted, though with reservations:

> H.M. does not enter into the political considerations connected with the question, for these must depend upon contingencies and may or may not apply to all individuals under all circumstances.[27]

Anticipating Opposition attacks, though the Tories were now short of talented speakers with naval experience following the retirement of Croker and the defeat of Clerk, Graham pressed on with work on the *Vernon*, which was to act as the public trial for the new system. Furthermore, Graham wanted to limit the members of the Board, other than the First Lord, eligible to sit in the commons, to three.[28]

After the plan had been set before Parliament on 14 February Melville admitted that he had considered a similar measure while out of office in 1827–8 and sent the draft to Graham. Melville's plan for the Admiralty was based on the system used by the Board of Ordnance, then a great favourite with the influential House of Commons Financial Committee. Graham was careful to avoid any political rancour and kept his distance from his predecessor.[29]

The Navy Board lingered on until June 1832, but with no power to influence policy. A new 84-gun ship design, called for under the programme of 30 June 1831, was delivered with a model in February 1832 but it was cleared away by the new Surveyor within a month of his taking office, along with other relics of the past.[30] By Admiralty order the *Royal Frederick* was suspended, allowing *Neptune* to remain on the ways, in favour of completing two 50-gun ships.[31]

At this stage there was little indication of the future direction of naval policy, for Graham had not committed himself to any major measures, preferring to wait on the increased power that would flow from the consolidation of the functions of the junior boards under the roof of the Admiralty. A Whig tendency to prefer new work over repairs, and an active fleet over long-term preparations were evident, but increased financial control was the one feature that could be guaranteed. In other areas the preceding eighteen months had done little to add to the fleet. Much would depend upon the Surveyor's office and in particular on the new Surveyor. Shorn of the guidance and support that a strong Controller could provide the Surveyor would have to deal directly with the Admiralty and the First Lord. The selection of the new officer would be difficult and his instructions, function and responsibilities would require careful attention. In the event political expediency overrode the larger part of such concerns, leading to a weak department, lacking the strength to conduct long-term programmes, particularly in the restricted financial climate of the middle 1830s.

Governments and naval administrations: 1815–50

	Prime Minister	*Foreign Secretary*	*Chancellor of the Exchequer*	*First Lord*	*First Naval Lord*	*First Secretary*
1815	Lord Liverpool	Viscount Castlereagh	Nicholas Vansittart	Viscount Melville	Admiral Sir Joseph Yorke	John Croker
1818 Apr					Admiral Sir Graham Moore	
1820 Mar					Admiral Sir Wm. Johnston-Hope	
1822 Sept		George Canning				
1823 Jan			Frederick Robinson			
1827 Apr	George Canning	Viscount Dudley	George Canning	Duke of Clarence (Lord High Admiral not in Cabinet)		
1827 Sept	Viscount Goderich		John Herries			
1828 Jan	Wellington	Earl Dudley	Henry Goulburn			
1828 Mar					Admiral Sir George Cockburn	
1828 June		Lord Aberdeen				
1828 Sep				Viscount Melville		
1830 Nov	Earl Grey	Lord Palmerston	Viscount Althorp	Sir J Graham	Admiral Sir T Hardy	Captain G Elliot
1834 June				Lord Auckland		
1834 Jul	Viscount Melbourne					
1834 Aug					Admiral George Dundas	
1834 Nov					Admiral Sir Charles Adam	
1834 Dec	Sir R Peel	Wellington	Sir R Peel	Earl de Grey	Admiral Sir J Beresford	George Dawson
1835 Mar	Viscount Melbourne	Lord Palmerston	Thomas Spring-Rice	Lord Auckland	Admiral Sir Charles Adam	Charles Wood
1835 Sep				Earl Minto		
1839 Aug			Sir Francis Baring			R Moore O'Ferrall
1839 Oct						John Parker
1841 Jun				Earl Haddington	Admiral Cockburn	Sidney Herbert
1841 Sep	Sir R Peel	Lord Aberdeen	Henry Goulburn			Henry Lowry-Corry
1846 Jan				Earl Ellenborough		
1846 Jul	Lord John Russell	Lord Palmerston	Sir Charles Wood	Lord Auckland	Admiral Sir C Adam	Henry Ward
1847 Jul					Admiral Sir J Dundas	
1849 Jan				Sir Francis Baring		
1849 May						John Parker

3 Policy Without the Navy Board

The Surveyor as Controller

On taking office the Surveyor was issued with a new set of instructions. He would be responsible for preparing the drawings 'of such ships as may be ordered', to report on submissions from the shipwright officers and establish the proper dimensions of the masts and yards. He was to report to the Board on any plans submitted to him, prepare scantlings, consider the purchase of the necessary timber and report on materials in use. The Surveyor was to be in overall control of the building programme, visiting the yards frequently and reporting on their administration, considering the merits of day pay and task and job. He was to report on the state of all ships in the fleet, and recommend any necessary work, keeping a progress book. All orders to be issued to the dockyards were to be placed before the Board by the First Sea Lord, who was responsible for the department. These duties differed from those laid down at the time of the 1806 Committee of Revision in two important areas. First, they imposed a policy framing requirement; second, they separated the Surveyor from the shipwright officers, upon whom he was to report, by sending all communications through the Admiralty.[1]

Shorn of the *aegis* of the Navy Board, the Surveyor's office at Somerset Place was weak and isolated from the mainstream of Admiralty policy making. The staff was reduced and given little status. John Edye, usually referred to as the Deputy Surveyor, was in fact only chief clerk, and was paid less than the Master Shipwrights, while the office staff were all on low pay grades. Furthermore, Symonds was given little guidance as to the wider scope of his department, being left to concentrate on design work, a trend reinforced by vitriolic attacks made on his competence, and the ineffective defence raised by Graham in the House. Graham clearly intended the Board to be the centre for policy decisions, and presumed that First Lords of future Boards would be equally anxious to exercise control. In the event, he provided only fitful guidance and his successors left Symonds in peace for long periods.

On a more positive note Symonds had strong views on construction policy, ideas which he lost little time putting into effect. On his recommendation the Board quickly agreed to suspend work on the *Valiant* and the 46-gun frigates building at Plymouth; returned all designs related to ships not yet started; and ordered two new Second Rates at Pembroke.[2] The new ships were initially referred to as having the scantlings of the *Canopus* class, but it was soon made clear that they were to be of an entirely new design. *Vanguard*, like *Vernon* before her, was a large ship for her armament, not only in comparison with the ships built by Seppings, but also with foreign designs. Although of the same displacement as the *Rodney*, the new ship was rated for only 78 guns, of which four were the poop-deck 18-pounders. It has never been acknowledged just how much larger Symonds's ships were than those from France and Russia but it is so and the extra size enabled him to provide both a roomy, well laid out battery deck and greater speed. The point is important because Symonds's ships fitted in perfectly with the tactical philosophy of the day which called for the pursuit and destruction of a flying enemy.

To speed up construction, 1,100 loads of seasoned timber were sent round from Plymouth, Portsmouth and Sheerness – a most unusual undertaking.[3] At Graham's direction Sir John Barrow, the Second Secretary of the Admiralty, produced a memorandum, largely for Symonds's benefit, calling for further reductions in dockyard labour in the interests of economy. Graham adopted what he believed to be an American idea, the preparation of a duplicate set of frames for any ship under construction to season in store ready for rapid completion. He called for the frame of the second ship ordered at Pembroke, the *Collingwood*, to be converted and a detailed set of accounts prepared. The same programme was applied to a pair of new First Rates to be started at Portsmouth, the *Royal Frederick*, using timber already prepared for the original ship of that name, and the duplicate frame for the *Royal Sovereign*.[4]

It was significant that Symonds secured the order for work to continue on First Rates. He was also troubled by the number of ships already ordered to have major repairs. The last years of the Tory Administration had multiplied this class of work, notably razee Fourth Rates and large repairs for First and Second Rates. Initially, Graham had been happy to prepare more Fourth Rates in this way but Symonds did not like the razee and repair policy. Convinced that older ships could never be anything but inferior specimens, he secured the cancellation of an order to razee the small 74 *Belleisle*, reordered *Union* to be taken to pieces and the materials reused in a *Vanguard*-class ship but this was never carried out.[5] Realising that *Valiant* had no place in the new fleet, Symonds had her cancelled, and after allowing the *Boscawen* to be reordered as the *Vernon*-class frigate *Indefatigable*, worked on Hardy to have her restored to the line as a new design of 70-gun ship, carrying 32-pounders throughout.[6] Symonds realised that only the largest and most well-armed ships had any place in the fleet of the future.

The Navy Board had allowed a degree of inertia to creep into construction policy by continuing with *Valiant* and *Boscawen*, ships which were only equal to 24-pounders on the main deck. Symonds saw that this made little sense and so timber collected for the first went to Pembroke for the *Vanguard*, while that of the latter was considered too large and valuable to be used in a Fourth Rate.

The acid test of Symonds's system, upon which the fate of the whole Admiralty Reform was acknowledged to rest, was the seagoing performance of the *Vernon*. By late September Graham was able to report that she had been a success, carrying more sail than one of the best Third Rates and satisfying Hardy. This was by no means as impressive as Graham suggested, although beating Seppings's last frigate, the well regarded *Castor*, five miles into the wind's eye was creditable. Grey was relieved to have some justification for the removal of Seppings and for his replacement by the first naval officer to hold the post of Surveyor.[7]

Naval policy and the new regime

In 1833, Symonds's first full year in office, the main emphasis in policy concerned economies and reductions. Graham was relieved to see an apparent end to the Portuguese Civil War, with the Constitutional Party, favoured by the British Government, successful. With the Belgian coast at last quiet he wanted to reinforce the Mediterranean Squadron and 'talk boldly to Russia'. Grey remained committed to a high profile diplomatic policy, and expressed his preference for high estimates rather than for enforcing any reductions on the Navy. In fact, the estimates for 1832–3 were underspent by half a million pounds, indicating the degree to which Graham's obsession with reduction had come to dominate policy. The following year saw attention shift to the Baltic. The King, unable to believe in the Tsar's goodwill, wanted twenty battleships in commission and Graham relied on the usual manipulation of figures to calm the Royal alarm. Even as he left the Board in June 1834, on the question of appropriating the surplus revenues of the Irish Church, Graham continued to argue that his work had been an unblemished sequence of savings and improvements. The abolition of the Navy Board, individual responsibility and the reduction of the estimates from £5.4 million to £4.4 million formed the basis for self congratulation. The final step, he argued, was the maintenance of a force of advanced ships consisting of twelve battleships and six large frigates ready for their crews, with topmasts pointed and fitted internally. These would be of 'incalculable advantage in an emergency' as France and Russia maintained larger active fleets than Britain in peace time.[8]

If he believed his own memorandum Graham was, perhaps, alone in doing so in any branch of the naval administration. Hardy had already left for the quiet retirement of Greenwich, disgusted with the programme of reductions. He was not alone. The only way to square the circle of increased commitments and political pressures for reduced estimates lay in the cutting back of long-term programmes, in particular shipbuilding, repair and dockyard development. Peel considered Graham's reductions and reforms outstanding public relations successes, for they were the one area in which he could not defend the record of the last Tory Administration. He did not feel himself equipped to explain how the Whigs could have saved £1.2 million. With no naval experts left in the Commons he called on Sir George Clerk, Junior Naval Lord under Melville, for some guidance. Clerk dismissed Graham's work as a dishonest public relations exercise, intended to deceive the unwary into believing that his Board was responsible for all the savings, when much work had been carried out, or set in motion by the Melville Board. In addition, the 1831 estimates had been framed to prove that there had been a serious shortfall in stores, in order to discredit the Navy Board, though there was no real factual basis. Other aspects of Graham's attacks, such as on dockyard development, were irrelevant. After a few days further reflection Clerk declared that the whole subject of economic reform had been over emphasised by Graham and the Whigs for political benefit.[9] However, the following year would demonstrate that Clerk's reservations would be far less significant than Graham's reforms, both with Peel and in the wider political field. It was one thing to prove the fallaciousness of political claims, quite another to reverse an opinion already formed.

The Board continued its assault on 'overmanning' by refusing permission to enter any more apprentices except in the smithy. They sought further economies by increasing dockyard specialisation. The major fleet bases at Portsmouth and Plymouth, along with Woolwich, were to remain as construction and repair facilities while Chatham would maintain only a limited repair role, leaving the majority of such work to Sheerness which would lose new construction work. Pembroke would remain 'exclusively set apart for building' and by the end of the year another new slip had been ordered, along with a pair of First Rates.[10]

The Admiralty pressed for alterations in the method of paying for labour. The convicts were reduced at Plymouth as well as infirm artificers, the able-bodied labourers being given preference for retention. In addition task and job work was abolished as being 'not only unnecessary in time of peace, but moreover liable to considerable abuse and extravagance both as to wages and materials'. Day pay was to become the norm although task and job work could be resorted to in times of emergency which was explicit recognition of the innate superiority of incentive-based pay structures. The new pay rates were arranged so as to give the dockyard men less than those in private employ because, as Graham argued, the former had greater job security. As with many other reforms of the period, day pay had been considered by the Melville Administration shortly before it left office.[11] By June 1833 the yards were sixty-one shipwrights below their establishment but the Board did not allow the vacancies to be filled as the yards were short of work.[12]

The next victims of Graham's economy drive were the various stores used by the Navy. He demanded that the accounts be modified to reflect the falling prices and ended the timber contract with the Woods and Forests Department. It became clear that the postwar fall in timber prices had reached the stage where private suppliers were charging £2 6s 2d less than the Government Department, and the Admiralty saw no reason to sponsor inefficiency in Whitehall. However, they wanted to know how much timber was sold during the following years as they regarded the Royal Forests as a war reserve.[13] Symonds was interested in the possibilities of using chestnut and more African timber and he reckoned that the three major building yards, other than Pembroke, should each carry a stock of 8,000 loads of sided seasoned oak. He ended the use of saltwater seasoning and removed the doubling applied to the *Royal George* and other First Rates in the late 1820s because he considered it both defective and damaging to the main timber of the hull. Realising that biological reactions at the joint faces of the major timbers were a prime cause of premature decay, Symonds ordered felt patches to be used in all such joints.[14]

New battleship orders for 1833 comprised the *Victoria* and *Algiers*, First Rates ordered at Pembroke, the latter as a duplicate frame; the *Vanguard*-class *Goliath* and the 70-gun *Cumberland*, both at Chatham. In 1834 *Boscawen* was finally reordered as a 70-gun ship. Symonds also began to impose his views on disposal and repair and, to save time and labour, he persuaded the Board to break up four old depot ships at Deptford by contract. He also refused to order a large repair on the 74-gun ship *Marlborough*. 'I cannot but be of opinion that it would be a waste of the public money to expend so large a sum (£48,000) a second time on this ship at the risk of her lasting only a few years.'

While the Surveyor did not want to razee good 74s, he was unwilling to spend money on bad ships. It would have been hard to argue with his logic, and the transitory Board of Lord Auckland was happy to let him have his way. Their successors were not to be so easily persuaded.[15]

Vanguard, after a prolonged debate, was listed as a Second Rate with a crew of 700. The frame of her duplicate, the *Collingwood*, was ordered to be converted larger than designed, to allow for shrinkage during storage. Edye and Symonds secured the use of copper bolts for the upperworks of future construction, while their new timbering plan was adopted for all new ships, including the duplicate First Rate at Portsmouth, the *Royal Sovereign*. Her half sister, the *Royal Frederick* was given priority throughout the latter stages of the year, a sharp reversal of previous policy on First Rates, and a move that emphasised the political importance of completing and trying Symonds's ships. It also demonstrated the influence of Symonds in favour of three-decked ships.[16]

The Establishment

The brief Administration of the Earl of Auckland saw the first attempts to undo some of the more serious errors of the Graham Board. Auckland called for a more intelligent management of the dockyards and examined the methods employed but he did not survive long enough to put his findings into effect. However, he did lay down a new Establishment for the fleet. The role of the fleet in peace time was to protect commerce and 'for demonstrations of strength, which political events may, from time to time, render necessary'. The Navy list included 141 battleships.

In commission	11
Advanced ships	11
In good repair	36
In need of repair	30
Building or repairing	15
Harbour service	38

Auckland proposed a new Establishment.

First Rates	25
Second Rates	25
Third Rates	25
Fourth Rates	25

Of these fifty would be afloat, twenty-five complete on the stocks and twenty-five frames ready for erection. The Advanced Ships, so vaunted by Graham were, it was discovered, decaying as fast as those in commission and this forced the Board to reduce them to a less complete level of preparation.

A brief Tory Administration

When Sir Robert Peel's minority Conservative Government took office in December 1834 the only priority worthy of serious consideration was political survival. Peel had already expressed his conviction on the value of naval economy, as part of an overall programme of savings, and believed that it was the one way the Whigs could be outmanoeuvred. He sent all departmental heads a straightforward statement of policy.

> I think that we should gain so much of public good will by announcing in the King's speech (if we can announce) the fact that notwithstanding all former reductions, – the estimates of the present year were lower than any preceeding estimates since 1793 – that it is most important that the head of each Department should commence, without delay, a consideration of what retrenchments can be made consistently with the true and permanent interests of the public service, in that branch of it over which he presides. If a little be done in each department the aggregate may justify such a declaration as that to which I have referred. I need not say that I would not purchase the advantage of such a declaration by any reduction that could not safely be made – at the same time, I think that if we can honestly have the advantage, it may have a very material bearing upon the stability of our Government.

Peel's colleagues accepted his priorities. The Navy even gave serious consideration to his idea of voting the estimates for six months, although Briggs, the Accountant-General, advised against. He pointed out that such a vote would force the Admiralty to recall ships from abroad, to prevent a build up of pay, break all existing long-term contracts, damage public credit and give rise to legal claims. The First Lord, Earl De Grey, consulted Wellington at the Foreign Office as to the level of force required before attempting to set the estimates. In the event the estimates were voted through in the normal manner, with one thousand less seamen than had been planned by Auckland. In this respect 1835 marks a nadir of the Navy Estimates and they were never again to be so subject to political pressures.[17]

The Minto Board

Peel's efforts for political survival came to nothing and his Administration fell in late April 1835. However, the economic situation in the country had not improved and forced his successor, Melbourne, to press the First Lord, initially Auckland, to keep to the existing estimates. Auckland was far from pleased, and with hindsight reflected: 'There never was a piece of more flagrant time-servingness than the reductions made by the Tories in 1835, and subsequent occurrences have only proved the absolute necessity of repairing their fault.'[18]

Against this background of severe reductions it was hardly possible to carry on a material programme as anything other than a series of expedient gestures. Symonds investigated estimates for the repair of the razee *Barham* at Chatham and discovered excessive thoroughness and serious over-ordering of materials. The ship was moved to Sheerness where she was repaired without being dismantled, the real cause of heavy expense. He also rejected a plan to razee the 74 *Warspite* on account of serious defects. This ship later became the centrepiece of a long running policy battle.[19]

Symonds also gave considerable attention to timber policy. He rejected Kyan's process of timber treatment on the grounds that there was no dry rot in the Navy. Careful selection of timber would be a more effective preventative. Furthermore;

> In time of peace I consider that British timber should be allowed to increase. East India and African teak and Tuscan oak is to be obtained in great quantities and at low prices at present and as there is a large stock of timber partly seasoned . . . 66,107 loads . . . I recommend Their Lordships to enforce a strict and careful selection of sound timber for the frames and essential parts of all ships building or repairing, and that in all cases it is sufficiently seasoned.

That this paper could have been written by Byam Martin 20 years previously is evidence of the unchanging nature of basic naval requirements. Despite the weakness of his Department and the lack of funds, Symonds was well aware of the need for long-term planning. Unlike Byam Martin, he lacked a power base from which to fight, and it should be observed that the political shifts of the 1830s were a far cry from the stability of the Liverpool era.[20]

The armament of the fleet was re-examined. All the older classes were given new and more powerful warrants. The small 74s which were commissioned were fitted with 40cwt bored up Bloomfield guns in lieu of the main deck 18-pounders.[21]

The return of a Whig Administration provided a new slant to naval policy. After the Treaty of Unkiar Skelessi, Palmerston, then Foreign Secretary, had convinced himself that Russia was the greatest danger to Britain.

> The great enemy of England is Russia, not from personal feeling, but from her having views and objects quite incompatible with our interests and safety and the main object of our foreign policy must be for years to come to counteract her.

He believed Russia would wait until Britain was at a disadvantage, and then force her into war. To this end the three eastern powers, Russia and her satellites Austria and Prussia, were seeking to alienate Britain and France. Only the Anglo-French understanding prevented them pressurising France and causing further trouble.[22] The King shared Palmerston's distrust of Russia, although he did not value co-operation with France. Lord Minto, the new First Lord, commissioned additional ships and by mid-1836 could boast of six battleships in the Mediterranean, three at Lisbon with eight at home and three First Rate guard ships. William was only half satisfied, calling twenty ships a 'defensive force'. When Minto tried to reduce the number in commission the King stressed the unreliability of both Russia and France.[23]

From January 1836 the Advanced Ships were ordered to be placed on a higher level of readiness.[24] Fitting out and commissioning additional ships to meet the perceived threat was a prudent measure, but the money for additional men had to be found within the existing budget. The obvious victim of such demands was the long-term programme for shipbuilding. Minto, under pressure to make the best of a small budget, accepted the argument of his brother-in-law, the First Sea Lord Admiral Sir Charles Adam, in favour of repairs rather than new construction.[25]

Symonds had his own programme of work for the reserve fleet. He had discovered that the cement filling used in the bottom of ships built or repaired postwar was causing decay. After inspecting the *Thunderer* in early 1837 he ordered an inspection of all ships in Ordinary, beginning with three ships on the ways, *Nile*, *St George* and the Fourth Rate *Worcester*.[26] He also wanted to carry out Graham's programme of replacing the sheer hulks with dockside equipment, but the Board refused to spend any money at Devonport to replace the defective *Sans Pareil*, which was to linger on for another decade. Shipbuilding and infrastructure were being sacrificed to maintain a larger active force.[27]

Pressure from the Surveyor's office

By the middle of 1837 Symonds had realised that nothing short of some profound shock would galvanise the prevaricating Minto Board into taking any decisive measures to improve the state of the fleet. In a powerful memorandum he argued that the durability of the reserve fleet was far less than had been anticipated, while the size of the active fleet had been increased significantly since 1832. More than half the convicts that had been employed in the yards had been reduced over the same period from 2,886 to 1,224 and there had been no compensating increase in labourers. Day pay had reduced the amount of work done, even if it had saved materials. To be fully efficient more shipwrights had to be taken on because, with the end of construction in India, the number of new ships coming forward had been seriously reduced, 'it being well known to Their Lordships that at the present time the work upon new Line of Battle Ships is almost entirely suspended'. As the fleet had fallen from 100 units to 88 in the past decade and dockyard labour from 11,345 men to 7,599, he urged restarting work in India, reducing the amount of minor work done in the yards (boats and trenails were available by outside contract) and adding to the artificers. In this way he believed an efficient fleet could be created in five years. In another submission the Surveyor reiterated his call for the construction of more ships. At the Board Wood, the First Secretary, contended that Symonds did not know 'the *real* state of our ships in Ordinary'. The Board was still operating on a plan set out by Auckland, to repair the best ships first, and had paid little attention to the construction of new battleships.[28]

By contrast the Board ignored Symonds' objections to razeeing the *Warspite*, which required a large repair costing £40,000. As a new ship could be built for only £6,000 more Symonds observed, 'It is always preferable to take ships to pieces than to enter into such very large repairs'. However, this approach was not accepted. The recently-retired Second Sea Lord, Admiral Sir George Elliot, brother of the First Lord, advised carrying on, though keeping a careful watch on costs.[29]

Economic problems forced the Government to maintain the pressure. The Admiralty were ordered;

> to take every step in their power to reduce the Public Expenditure in their Lordships' department, to the utmost possible extent which is practicable without detriment to H.M.'s service the voted estimates were not to be exceeded'.[30]

Three days later Minto produced a paper advocating repair rather than new construction, as a more efficient use of dockyard labour and recommending the removal of men from the large ships in favour of steamers and Sixth Rates.[31] Despite this, Symonds had achieved much of what he had intended. The Board were forced to take some action on the condition of the Ordinary after his 'alarming report', though the prospect of the having to find more money was equally alarming. Consequently, Edye was sent to inspect the various Ordinaries. His report was altogether more reassuring, as inevitably it would be. Symonds's real object had always been to increase construction,

Midship section of the Vanguard, *showing the scantling of the timber, alignment of the iron diagonals and stowage.* (NMM)

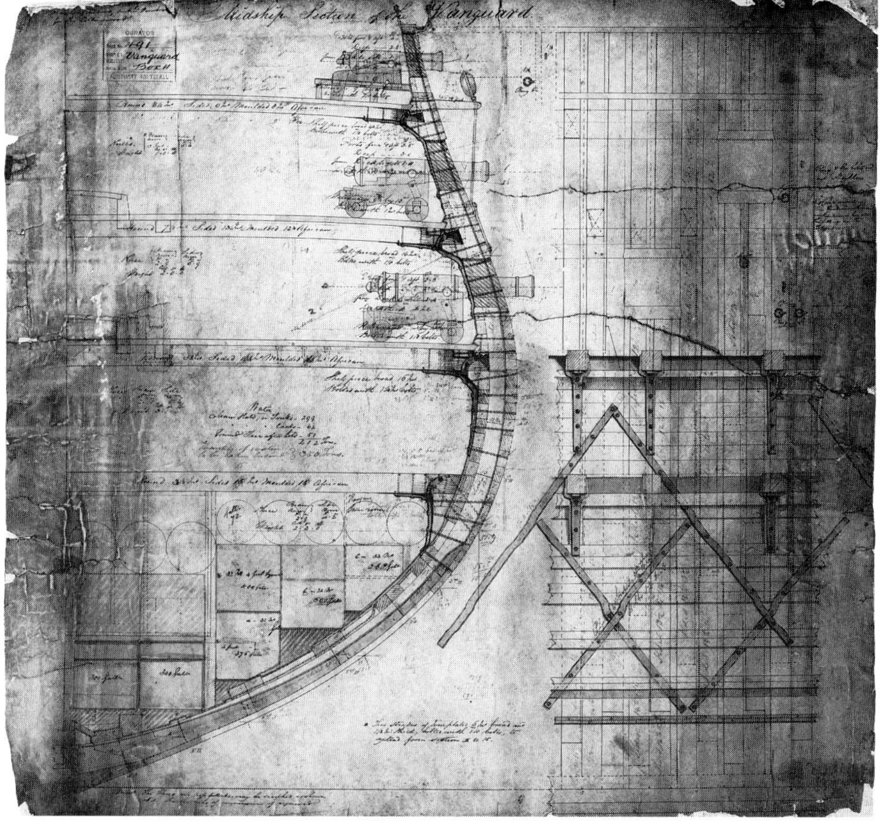

a policy that would not be helped by a healthy Ordinary and a programme of large repairs and razees. Consequently, he had exaggerated the danger. Wood called his initial report 'fallacious', but then set out a series of minor alterations in dockyard work to increase repairs, rather than shipbuilding, and took a more serious interest in India. Wood argued that repair saved money, and while he accepted some of Symonds's minor labour-saving modifications such as re-rating former shipwrights who had been acting as house carpenters and boatbuilders to provide another 600 shipwrights, the emphasis was on economy. New construction was to be concentrated in India and shipbuilding at home subjected to clear regulations on the length of time required for seasoning at the various stages of the process.[32]

Symonds had already revealed one major reason for the inability of his department to set out and support long-term programmes: there were only eight people in his office which represented a reduction of 50 per cent over the previous 18 years. The extra clerk he requested would be hard pressed to make any real impact on the sheer weight of information coming in, and the amount of correspondence required to manage the dockyards and their work. To improve morale Symonds argued that Edye should have an improved status, and the clerks a satisfactory career structure. The addition, and an overdue upgrading of the staff, had to wait another 18 months to receive Treasury assent. When the Government prepared to leave office in June 1839, before the Bedchamber Crisis, the reorganisation of the Surveyor's Office was one of the few concrete achievements they could claim.[33]

During 1838 only one more battleship, the 78-gun *Superb* was ordered, from the moulds of the *Vanguard* at Pembroke. Rather more effort and paperwork went into the long-drawn-out battle over the *Warspite*. In many ways this ship came to symbolise the point of difference between the Surveyor and his political masters. Though he was eventually forced to carry out the razee, his defeat was sealed just as a large number of new ships were ordered in response to international tension.[34] The vagaries of dockyard work resulted in rather more man days being put into these new ships than had been anticipated, though Symonds still pressed his case for new construction as being more economic than repairs.[35]

By this time the succession of reports and complaints from Symonds was beginning to have some effect on the First Lord. In August Minto had expressed himself satisfied with the state of the thirty Advanced Ships. Arguing that only Russia posed a serious threat, he dismissed the warnings of Sir Robert Inglis and Captain Sir Charles Napier as alarmist and persuaded Barrow to append a supplemental chapter to his *Life of George, Lord Anson*, published in 1839, rebutting public criticism of the Administration with considerable use of official statistics.[36] Later, Adam called for more Second Rates to be commissioned but Wood informed him that the amount of construction planned for the year amounted to only three-quarters of one Second Rate. In addition, increasing work would force a large-scale launching of existing ships, unless more money was to be spent on slips and roofs. The villain of the piece was Graham who had now joined the Tory party. After a Cabinet meeting on 15 October it was clear that, in view of the Russian threat, increased estimates would be required to add to the active fleet, but the pressing problem for Minto was now the reserve, a subject that had for long been at the bottom of successive governments' lists of priorities. By November he was expressing serious concern. It was bad enough that there were not enough men to commission the fleet in an emergency,

> But for very many years past our Navy has been dwindling away and the number of serviceable ships is reduced quite as low, if not more so, as is at all safe and prudent. A large proportion of these are old and upon their last legs, and in other respects very inferior to modern men of war. Little has been, or can be, done towards replacing them with the present establishment of our dockyards, which is nearly wholly occupied with the current demands of the service afloat, or in such repair of ships in Ordinary as is necessary to keep a powerful fleet at our disposal. We should deserve impeachment if it was to appear on the breaking out of a war that we had neglected to supply the places of our old, unserviceable ships, and that the country had a Navy only on paper, yet this must be the consequence of Graham's most improvident reduction of some establishments, which might be well enough as a temporary relief when we had too much in hand of stores – ships & everything, and could live awhile upon our surplus capital; but which it was dishonest to represent as a system of permanent retrenchment compatible with the maintenance of our Navy.
>
> I ... have had the conclusion forced upon me that we cannot allow the process of exhaustion to proceed further and that the means must be found of providing for an increase of exertions in our dockyards.

It was interesting that Graham should be blamed for the adverse long-term impact of a programme adopted by the entire Grey Cabinet, most of whom were now serving under Melbourne.[37]

The one major programme of 1838 was the re-arming of the older ships in the fleet. More old 18- and 24-pounders were bored up and by September all battleships were to carry nothing but 32- and 68-pounder guns. This posed some problems for the Ordnance but did constitute a major improvement in the fighting power of the battlefleet. In early 1838 the *Vanguard*-class were upgunned to carry eighty heavy guns, although they were not equal to the 56cwt weapons on the main deck, a curious state of affairs given the specification to which they had been ordered in 1832. In the same manner *Boscawen* and *Cumberland* were ordered to carry seventy guns, exclusive of any poop battery.[38] These measures were particularly well timed as intelligence reports revealed that the vast majority of the battleships maintained abroad were of the heavier classes so limiting the value of the remaining British Third Rates.[39]

A new programme

In response to Minto's alarm Wood prepared a memorandum on the measures already in hand to improve the strength of the fleet. He identified the lack of reliable information on the capabilities of the dockyards as a major hindrance to rectifying the problem. From 1831 to 1836 men had worked only five days a week, and a large number had been taken off shipbuilding to work on infrastructure and even house repairs. Only in late 1837 had all shipwright vacancies been filled and additional labourers taken on, while in April extra artificers had been taken on for house work. As a result, dockyard wages had risen from £300,000 to £384,000. The 1838/9 programme of works was, Wood observed, 'the first attempt at any systematic arrangement of the kind since the suppression of the Navy Board'. Repair work was given priority, although it was noted that Pembroke and Woolwich, which had no repair work, were the most efficient construction yards.

With only seventy-five battleships available afloat, of which twelve were beyond economic repair, there was a pressing

The Irresistible, *ordered in 1840 as part of the Minto Board's panic response to the state of the battlefleet. The real strength of the Navy was such that she did not take to the water until 1859, as a steamship.* (IWM)

need for more new ships, at least four every year, or three if built of teak. New vessels were all to be of the largest classes, the French having no 74s. In order to build the equivalent of four large ships per year another 350 shipwrights would be required, along with additional slips to a total of twenty-six, and 10,000 loads of Italian and English oak each year for two years. Five ships were to be laid down in 1839, each with a duplicate frame. The Board accepted the programme on 18 February.[40]

In view of the political dangers noted by Minto, the Board were anxious to put the best possible gloss on the existing fleet. To this end Symonds, albeit unwillingly, had to include the 78-gun *Achille* on the list of Second Rates. Together with the *Canopus* she required a considerable repair and, if he could not dismantle her, the Surveyor wanted orders to carry out the work over two years in order to reduce the commitment of the artificers. He was allowed two years to repair the two ships, but Wood requested a revision of Symonds's programme of works to leave out the shipwrights needed to maintain the Ordinary and concentrate more men on repairs. By the end of the year Symonds had secured a minor, but significant, concession: the last three large 74s, *Achille, Kent* and *Revenge,* were re-rated as 76-gun Third Rates.[41]

In addition to the order of February 1839, to construct ships in India, six new Second Rates were ordered in May. *Albion* and *Aboukir* at Plymouth were to be 90-gun ships, while *Mars* and *Majestic* at Chatham with *Centurion* and *Colossus* at Pembroke were to be additions to the modified *Vanguard* type. Finally, the duplicate 110-gun vessel at Pembroke, the *Algiers,* was re-ordered as a 90, although that had no effect on her construction.[42] The *Albion* was a two-decker on the same scale as the *Queen* and capable of carrying heavier metal than any foreign two-decker. This increase in combat power was required to ensure victory in battle, the one safe method of resolving the strategic dilemmas of a world empire reliant upon sea control.

During 1839 and 1840 naval policy became a major subject of discussion as the prospect of war with one of the major powers became greater. The activities of Mehemet Ali, Pasha of Egypt, in Syria and the Lebanon exposed a clear divergence of interest between Britain and France. Britain supported the Ottoman Empire as the best barrier to Russian expansion to the Mediterranean seaboard where her presence, and her fleet, would add to Britain's strategic problems, increase her level of peace-time defence expenditure and make the conduct of economic government particularly difficult. Therefore, when Mehemet Ali threatened to destroy the Ottoman Empire Britain was forced to take measures against him, measures that were bound to be unpopular in France, where the romantic link of Bonaparte and Egypt, and the more pragmatic desire to expand the North African empire, combined as reasons to support Mehemet against the Sultan. Palmerston had anticipated problems as early as June 1838, and kept a careful watch on the two Russian fleets while developing a strategy to exploit the Mediterranean Fleet against Egyptian communications. The Admiralty were less easily satisfied. Minto was alarmed by the prospect of a long war with France at a time when the danger from Russia appeared to be growing, though Palmerston was convinced Louis Phillipe would not go to war with the other four powers to support Mehemet Ali, having created a pro-Turkish alliance with Russia, Austria and Prussia.[43]

By early 1840 Minto was alarmed enough to be watching the French fleet in detail, and considering how to counter the obvious increase in French strength in the Mediterranean. He wanted to commission another four battleships to keep the balance, and doubted whether France could build up her forces much further without launching her incomplete ships. Even so there was a need to increase the estimates, for more seamen and more dockyard work, and for fitting out ships coming forward. Additional funds were secured to the amount of £600,000 to cover an additional 1,000 seamen and the dockyard work. In August fourteen large ships were brought forward:

Britannia, Monarch, London, Caledonia, Bombay, Vengeance, Clarence, Queen, Indus, Formidable, Vanguard, Howe, Achille and *Impregnable.* Five First Rates, one 90-gun ship, six Second Rates and two large Third Rates made up a powerful force. It was a war fleet envisaged by every policy maker since Byam Martin and reflected the real strength of the Royal Navy. By early 1841 the fleet in commission reached an all-time high for the period under review: twenty-six battleships in commission.

At Home: *Camperdown, Queen, Caledonia*

Fitting Out: *Monarch, Indus, Impregnable, Cornwallis*

Mediterranean: *Britannia, Howe, Princess Charlotte, Rodney, Ganges, Powerful, Thunderer, Calcutta, Vanguard, Cambridge, Bellerophon, Revenge, Implacable, Hastings, Edinburgh, Benbow.*

East Indies: *Wellesley, Melville, Blenheim*[44]

In the event the future of Syria and the Lebanon was resolved without a war. France, as Palmerston had long believed, would not fight for Mehemet Ali. The bombardment and capture of Acre on 3 November 1840 was the work of the small, undermanned peace-time fleet. Thereafter, diplomacy took over, war was avoided and British prestige in the Mediterranean basin, and elsewhere, greatly enhanced. Acre, Palmerston believed, was:

> an event of immense political importance as regards the interests of England not only in connection with the Turkish Question, but in relation to every other question which we may have to discuss with other powers. Every country that has towns within cannon shot of deep water will remember the operations of the British Fleet on the Coast of Syria in September, October and November 1840, whenever such country has any differences with us.[45]

In the aftermath of the crisis Palmerston recognised that the French would be bitter. He advised basing the estimates for 1841 on the level of the French fleet, and keeping a close eye on Morocco and Tunis where he feared France might seek some addition to her Algerian holdings. Russell warned that keeping up the existing fleet in time of peace would force the Government to raise new taxes, something a wavering, ill-supported and seemingly doomed Administration was unwilling to countenance.[46] Lord Aberdeen, Conservative Foreign Minister elect, shared Russell's view: 'this *armed peace* is a new and an intolerable state of things, which if not terminated by some means or other, must infallibly lead to mischief'.[47] Before Minto could consider any reductions he found Russell pressing him to send four or five battleships to North America where a new crisis was developing to test the mettle of the Government.[48]

On leaving office Minto put his views into order as an *aide memoire* for his successor. Clearly the experience of 1840 had produced the most profound effect. He called for an Establishment of one hundred battleships; seventy afloat, ten ready to launch, ten building and ten in frame. The fleet then comprised:

Afloat:	73	of which 31 were small 74s, and 9 of them were only fit to break up
Building:	14	
Ordered:	5	
Total:	92	

> 'looking to our extended commerce and possessions for whose security it is essential that we should not cease for a moment to be masters of the sea, and considering the amount of force we found it necessary to employ in the last war, as well as the scale upon which other navies are now maintained I am of opinion that we ought to have not less than 80 sail of the line, promptly available in the event of war.

To keep up this figure it would be necessary to build the equivalent of four Second Rates every year, in addition to any from India. More shell guns should be issued, particularly the 10in, which produced a 'devastating effect'. He also argued for an increase in the number of Naval Lords, believing that an additional Lord was essential to control the dockyards. This role was distinct from the shipbuilding and policy-making role of the First Naval Lord. He considered Graham's reforms to have been on the right principles but that they had not given the Admiralty the strength to function as a policy-making body.[49]

Minto's successors were to demonstrate that money was not the real problem, for in the absence of clear and sound policy spending more only created bigger problems.

4 *The Peel Administration 1841–46*

Sir Robert Peel

In forming his second Administration Sir Robert Peel continued the trend evident in 1834, creating a Cabinet within which he would reign supreme, the ultimate arbiter of all aspects of policy, with the support of a small inner Cabinet. The most influential member of the Government, Graham, was appointed to the key post of Home Secretary but remained a major contributor to all policy debates throughout the period, particularly those affecting the Navy. The person chosen as First Lord, Lord Haddington, was a life-long friend and a significant figure in the politics of Scotland, but not an experienced service chief. Peel intended to keep a close control on this high-spending department and appointed his protégé Sidney Herbert to the vital post of First Secretary and his friend Cockburn to that of First Naval Lord. They would be

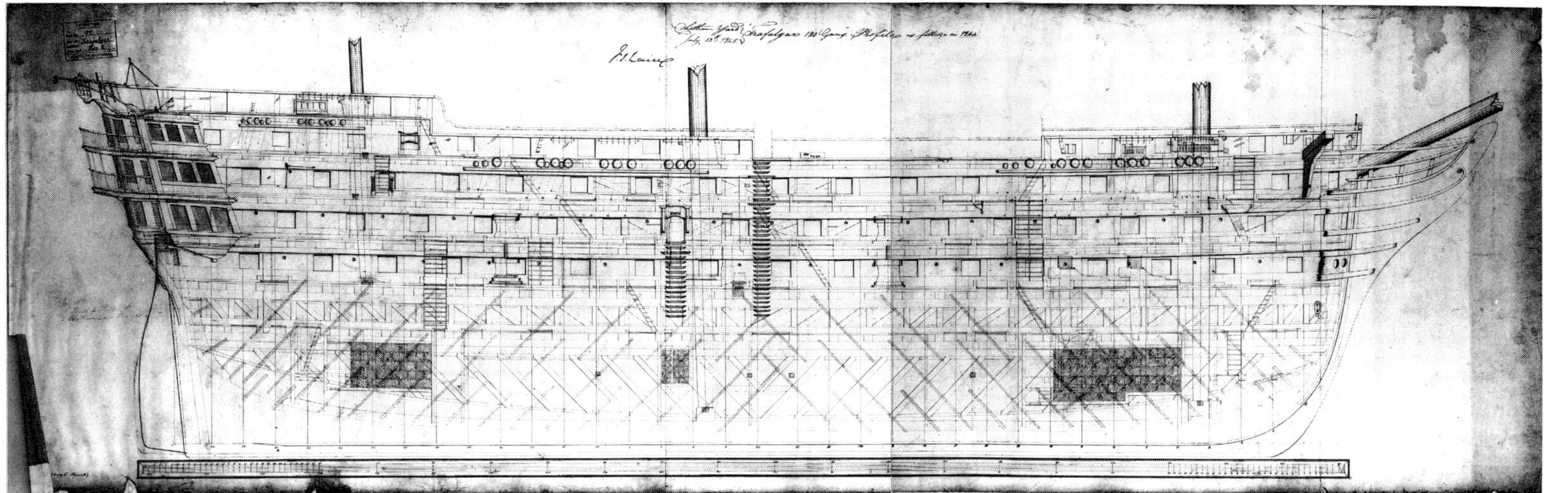

Profile of the Trafalgar *dated 1845, showing the modified stern fitted by Oliver Lang, and the additional iron diagonals. This ship, the last of the* Caledonia*-class, was a great disappointment under sail, because she trimmed too much by the stern, but she remained a strongly-built and heavily-armed First Rate equal to any possible opponent. Her last service in this configuration came with the bombardment of Sevastopol on 17 October 1854.* (NMM)

reliable guides on political and service issues; Haddington would be restricted to uncontentious aspects and to preserving the tone of the service. All major decisions would be taken by Peel. Centralising decision-making did not, of itself, guarantee any improvement in the quality of these decisions. Peel, able as he was, could hardly master all aspects of government and the major programmes of his term were, with the benefit of hindsight, technologically and strategically unsound. Peel's lasting contribution to naval policy in the period came with the re-introduction of the Income Tax in 1842 and the relative freedom this provided after 1843 resulted in more wasted effort than by any other naval administration during the century. Essentially, the economic improvement that Peel orchestrated was no sooner in place than a new series of crises with France added to the defence burden. As a result, all the usual targets were cut; slipways, stores and the battlefleet were sacrificed to new steamships and the steam arsenals at Portsmouth and Plymouth.

Naval policy

On coming to office the major problem for Peel lay in the still far from satisfactory state of relations with France and the United States. Minto had been ready to send several of the Mediterranean battleships to North America in early 1841, and it was to be some little time before the new Administration could rest easy in this area. Despite the clear lessons of 1840, France still posed the most immediate threat. Lord Aberdeen, the Foreign Secretary, was distinctly pro-Russian. Peel saw the ambitious nature of French policy in Spain, Belgium, Morocco, Tunis and later Tahiti as good reason for caution. Within the Cabinet two opposing strands of policy were evident from the outset. Aberdeen wanted to lower tension, seek a good understanding with the other major powers and avoid an excessive show of force. In the Mediterranean he called for two less battleships than the French, to salve their wounded pride and offer a gesture of support to the conservative Guizot Administration. Graham and others preferred to look for demonstrations of sincerity from France in the first instance. The Home Secretary argued that the Naval Estimates would depend upon the size of the fleet kept in commission by France and as Louis Phillippe and Guizot shared the basic aims of European conservatism he trusted they would reduce their fleet and work for good relations.[1]

Initially, Haddington adopted Aberdeen's approach, calling for a reduction of the British force in the Mediterranean to ten units, two less than the French. With three more ships coming home from Lisbon and the East Indies this would make an overall cut of six.[2] However, Peel was more interested in re-establishing British prestige in the Mediterranean, in particular at Tunis, where the French had been making large naval demonstrations. Sending the *Implacable* went a long way to recovering influence with the Bey, and warning off the French from any attempt to increase their North African holdings.[3] Peel retained his suspicion of France, placing the least favourable interpretation on every action and warning Aberdeen not to place too much trust in protestations of good faith.[4]

When the crisis came it revealed the limits of the deterrent value of the existing fleet which were part technological and part structural. However, the crisis in Anglo-French relations was not to develop until 1844 and in the interval of quiet relations there was an opportunity to reduce the active battlefleet to the lowest level for many years. Although the number of men voted was higher than had been the case in the 1830s, the majority were deployed in light units, both cruisers and survey vessels, on detached stations. In addition, the major units were, after the shock of 1840, rather better manned and this also reduced the number of units at sea. At one point there were only half the number of battleships at sea as under Minto, although the large number of razees did go some way to making up for the loss of battle power.

In the interval, the major issues of naval policy were political and technical. Disappointed at not finding any concrete, unimpeachable rationale for his attacks on Symonds, Cockburn simply turned to other sources for new designs. After ordering the *Prince of Wales*, a sister to the *Royal Frederick* at Portsmouth, the remaining heavy ships of the period were an attack on Symonds. The 120-gun *Royal Albert* was ordered from Lang, together with the steam frigate *Terrible*. Fincham was given orders for the 50-gun *Raleigh*, and for a series of screw steamers, while the final insult came when the lines were taken off the sheer hulk *Sans Pareil* in order to build a facsimile. Symonds insisted on having an opportunity to comment on the new designs before they were given Admiralty approval. The order for *Cressy* and the 50-gun *Leander* by Blake in 1843 marked an end to work on new heavy ships; the large number of ships to Symonds's designs ordered in 1840 had created a distinct shortage of slips.

The attack on Symonds continued in other directions, notably with the resumed interest in razees. The dockyards were instructed to select the best 74-gun ship in the Ordinary for a simple conversion. Though *Devonshire* was earmarked, the 120-

gun *Prince Regent* was the first ship to be subjected to this process. Symonds objected to this on the grounds that to razee all similar three-deckers would remove 240 guns from the Navy, when the higher command of the upper deck guns of a three-decker made them particularly valuable. Apart from her round stern there was no particular reason to modify *Prince Regent*, her defects being low down in the hull, not in the upper-works. Admiral Hyde Parker pressed for an order to go ahead, but the Board had second thoughts. The 104-gun *Camperdown* was also ordered to be converted, but more important work prevented the project coming to fruition.[5] In 1844 *Prince Regent* was ordered to be cut down, and the *Tremendous* was razeed. As the latter had been condemned by Symonds, this was a particularly galling decision.[6]

In early 1844 more new ships were ordered to Symonds's designs: the 110s *Royal Sovereign*, *Marlborough* and *Windsor Castle* with the 90-gun *St Jean d'Acre* and the 80-gun *Brunswick*. None were to be laid down as designed, and along with the *Algiers*, which had yet to be commenced, were re-ordered in a variety of configurations.[7] Following the 1844 Squadron of Evolution, Symonds requested permission to modify the *Queen* and suspend all 110- and 90-gun ships under order that 'are not so far advanced as to preclude the possibility of alteration', until the results of the modifications to the *Queen* were known. The only exception was the *Royal Frederick*, already effectively complete.[8] The 90-gun *Aboukir* and *Exmouth* proved too far advanced for major modifications, but the remaining ships were held over. The modifications to the *Queen* involved alterations to the magazines and gripe, an additional false keel, a new rudder post and new fore- and mainmasts at a cost of £4,330. She was prepared in time for the 1845 Experimental Cruise, where she recovered her good name.[9]

Symonds's connection with the preceeding Administration was both personal and political. He had been the pet of the Whig regimes, with the unwavering support of Minto, Wood and Parker. In return he supplied his old friends with sensitive information. In part this reflected old loyalties, in part Symonds's very real alarm at the nature of the attack being made on his ships. The situation was complicated by the arrival of Admiral Sir William Bowles as Third Naval Lord in May 1844. Although a Tory Bowles was a committed Symondite who saw no problem in communicating with Lord Minto.[10] By the middle of the year even the most committed of Symonds's patrons were preparing to shift their ground from absolute to qualified support.[11] Hitherto, the Whigs had supported Symonds because of the unfair and violent attacks made on him and his ships, although they claimed to have seen the problems at an earlier date. They also noted a certain ingratitude in his dealings with them, which was a novel way of describing his supply of confidential information. The Whigs had finally realised Symonds could not be sustained, and that as they had appointed him it would be better not to make his tenure of office into a political one, and one which would invite defeat.[12]

When Admiral Pym, a strong Tory, was appointed to replace Hyde Parker in command of the 1845 Squadron, Minto advised Symonds to consult Bowles about this appointment. Bowles approached Cockburn, and the matter finally reached Haddington, then in Scotland. Haddington was annoyed by the manner in which Minto's letter had been shown around the Board. After a soothing note from Minto Haddington lamented the lack of perfection in warship design and hoped that Symonds would be prepared to modify his ships, if necessary.[13] After such a furore it was hardly surprising that the torpid Pym should return a brief report of the superiority of *Queen* and *Albion* in heavy weather. Despite this, Bowles reported that Symonds's health was shaken and that his official career could not be much prolonged. He was confident the Surveyor would be prepared to modify his ships.[14]

The crisis in naval policy was initially the product of a growing fear that the advance of steam, both for warships and merchantmen, was affecting a profound alteration in the strategic position of Britain, shifting the balance between land and sea power. The steamships' freedom of movement ended the defensive role of the elements and reduced the period

The French 120-gun ship Valmy, *launched in 1847. This ship was the only French three-decker ordered after 1815, indicating the degree to which the French had abandoned any hopes of contesting command of the sea with the Royal Navy. She was an unsatisfactory ship of poor performance, something that was loudly trumpeted in Britain, notably by Symonds and his partisans.* (Author)

available for the mobilisation of Britain's extensive reserves. This in turn promoted a fresh look at manning and the nature of naval service. It should be emphasised that the war scare did not lead to any questioning of British superiority in sailing battleships, but rather to the position of the conventional warship in the face of the strategic opportunities provided by new technology.

Notes sur l'etat des forces navales de la France

Concern was given a particularly sharp focus with news of the French assumption of a protectorate over Tahiti in late 1843 and the publication of the Prince de Joinville's pamphlet *Notes sur l'etat des forces navales de la France* in May 1844. A vigorous and effective young officer, the 25-year-old Joinville was only demonstrating the natural impatience of youth in the face of the prevarications of Admiral de Mackau, the Minister of Marine, and urging the minority findings of the commission upon which he had been sitting. However, the rank and family connections of the young man gave rather more weight to his opinions, and they became the catalyst of a crisis that was to last for two years. The basic argument of the pamphlet was that France should turn to a steam Navy if she wished to challenge Britain. He also observed that the lessons of Syria were clear: the existing fleet was too small for a sustained war with Britain. Rather than attempt to build along the existing mixed fleet pattern, in which France remained inferior in every vital area to Britain, Joinville called for an end to the construction of sailing battleships. He argued that fleet actions were inconsistent with French strategic interests and that what was required was a reduced battlefleet to support operations against fortified harbours. This role was to be retained in French strategy throughout the latter half of the century, with increasing specialisation of warship types for that function after 1855.[15] By concentrating on paddle steam frigates for Europe and North Africa and sailing Fourth Rates for commerce destruction on the distant stations, France could avoid decisive battle and yet pose a threat so serious that Britain would have to accord her the respect she desired. In home waters commerce destruction and raids or invasions would be used to take the war to Britain. Similarities with Tirpitz's *riskoflotte* are both obvious and unsurprising for European powers with a major land frontier to guard required a 'cheap' strategy in contrast to the sea-control strategy forced on Britain. Joinville believed he could achieve his aims without increasing the naval budget. In the event, Mackau's Supplementary Naval Law of 1846 covering the following seven years mixed the Prince's plans with additional battleships, and cost the sum of 93 million francs. However, Joinville's paper, as a statement of the opinions of the French Navy, remained central to war planning into the Second Empire.

While some commentators have seen Joinville's work as 'an intelligent plan', there was nothing novel in the strategic permutations offered, merely a revision of Paixhan's work and the 1825 Tupinier Report, which attempted to put forward an alternative French strategy.[16] Joinville did not suggest how a steam Navy could break the inevitable British blockade, or defend Algeria in the face of a superior battlefleet; this last was the Achilles' heel of French naval policy throughout the period 1830–1904. Technically, Joinville's policy was rendered obsolete by the British screw fleet, in itself a response to French developments. Joinville's dream was no closer to realisation in 1854, or 1859, despite the best efforts of his co-adjutor Dupuy de Lôme.

The reaction of British observers to Joinville was conditioned more by their earlier attitude towards France rather than by anything Joinville had written. Some saw the catalogue of French naval weaknesses as a ruse, prominent among them the ageing Duke of Wellington, Minister without Portfolio and a regular contributor of papers calling for increased defence expenditure. Palmerston merely observed that it reinforced the need to keep up the Navy. Aberdeen and the Queen feared the effect on Anglo-French relations, to which they had already made considerable sacrifices. Clearly, the pamphlet focused attention on the Royal Navy, and added a certain political value to the visit of the Tsar in June who wanted the support of Britain against the Orleans regime, of which he had a marked dislike.

On 26 July news arrived that the British consul in Tahiti, Pritchard, had been arrested, and although he was soon released the effect was marked. The Government were already sufficiently alarmed to send the new 80-gun *Collingwood* as Pacific flagship, where she served to deter both France and, later, the Americans.[17] The succession of events, each in itself of minor importance, gave credence to the conspiracy theory that France was planning an invasion.

Morocco

Joinville had no sooner left the centre stage than he was thrust back into focus, this time with a fleet under his command. French relations with the Sultan of Morocco had been problematic for several years. It was well known that the Sultan provided aid to the Algerian resistance leader Abd-el-Kadr. Marshal Bugeaud was sent to command the land forces, which triumphed at Isly, and the young Prince-Admiral was given two battleships and a number of steamers to conduct a separate campaign. News of the appointment reached London on 12 June, which Aberdeen considered poor repayment for his efforts to maintain good relations; he went so far as to request that the appointment be suspended, but received the inevitable refusal. However, the French were determined to make good use of the opportunity provided by Moroccan intransigence and both commanders were urged to create the greatest effect in the least time both to discipline the Sultan and impress the rest of the world. Joinville, for example, was to make no secret of his operations from the British. Using Gibraltar as a base, the French squadron bombarded Tangier on 5 August, and later occupied the island of Mogador, which controlled important custom revenues.[18] These actions, combined with the defeat at Isly, persuaded the Sultan to accept the French interpretation of the Algerian question.

Although the crisis had been some time brewing the British Fleet was not ready. There were only nine battleships in commission, of which one was on passage out of the Mediterranean. To reinforce Sir Edward Owen's force the guardships at Cork and Plymouth *Albion* and the *Caledonia* were despatched to join *Formidable* and *Warspite* at Gibraltar. Haddington was far from certain that he would not have to send the Portsmouth and Sheerness ships, along with *St Vincent* and *Queen* as well. Haddington reviewed the existing policy, and called for more men. He had agreed to reduce the number of battleships outside home waters, including the Mediterranean, in return for permission to keep two battleships in commission in each of the major home ports to meet emergencies and form a squadron of exercise. Cut back in Cabinet he nevertheless retained 1,500 men over the Estimate; then because he had a large force in China he had to pay off the next ship to come home, Parker's flagship, the *Cornwallis*. He wanted more seamen, even if a supplementary Estimate was not possible, to man another four battleships. In addition, he made the usual comparison between the French fleet in port and the problems that would be experienced in manning the thirty Advanced Ships. Confident the House would raise no difficulties Haddington pressed for Peel's sanction.[19]

Conscious of the possible threat to Anglo-French relations, Peel sent the letter to Aberdeen in which he took a jaundiced view of the measures already planned for the summer, notably a trial squadron of brigs which he argued would use up valuable men. In addition, he argued that any measure passed in Britain would meet a swift response in France.

> I think it may be necessary to incur the risk of this, but I think the considerations involved are very grave ones, and you had better summon a cabinet after personal communication with Aberdeen.

Haddington held his ground.[20]

In need of help Peel turned to Graham and returned to the attack a fortnight later with a series of questions on manpower that were a direct reflection of the Home Secretary's views. Graham argued that complements could be reduced, allowing more ships to be fitted out, and more officers provided with sea experience without raising the Estimates. Henry Corry, political Secretary, and Haddington prepared papers to defend the higher complements adopted by the Tory Administration, but Corry in particular could not resist the opportunity to attack Graham's reductions. This provoked a bitter, arrogant refutation and the claim that complements could be safely cut to increase the active force.[21]

Graham's advice was coloured by the Whig policy that so marked the naval programmes of the 1830s, when he had made the maximum use of the money voted to support British diplomacy. Graham was the most ruthless opponent of the 'tail' services and made the maximum use of his funds for 'teeth'. The Tory Party were still more disposed to spend on long-term measures, even if that did imply weakness. Graham's contribution to this debate is perhaps the most obvious demonstration that the political parties did maintain distinct attitudes towards defence spending.

But if Peel was inclined to play down the degree of tension he did not wholeheartedly adopt the advice of Aberdeen. The Foreign Secretary was prepared to rely on French good faith, but Peel would hear none of that, reflecting sourly on their shared experience as members of the Wellington Cabinet in 1830. 'Remember the *assurances* we received about Algiers and how they have been kept'.[22] The issue of Algiers remained a standard for Peel; 'it would be very inconvenient to us to have the Algerine precedent carried further in respect to that part of the Coast of Africa'. Like Palmerston, Peel acknowledged that Algiers had been a defeat for British policy, and was prepared to fight to keep France out of Morocco and Tunis. Algiers was in the process of becoming a first-class naval base with a massive breakwater and the strategic implications were obvious; the need to make retaliatory improvements at Gibraltar and Malta was economically undesirable but inevitable. The Premier was concerned with France and linked the pamphlet, Morocco and the danger of a steam invasion. Peel had no faith in Guizot or his King, and concluded; 'the most strenuous exertions are making in every port from which England can be threatened . . . in order that they may be prepared for a naval war with England'.[23]

In this mood it is hardly surprising that Peel sanctioned the Admiralty's call to exceed the estimates. C J Bartlett argues that no efforts were made to raise extra seamen during the crisis, relying for evidence on the official Admiralty letters to the dockyard superintendents.[24] This assumption reflects a limited understanding of the nature of the nineteenth-century Navy. With an issue as politically sensitive and potentially problematic as the raising of seamen in an emergency another system was employed.

> Private & Confidential
>
> Admiralty Aug.9/44
>
> My dear Sir David,
>
> I am directed by the government to write to you in this private and confidential manner to request & authorise you to raise as fast as may be practicable all the seamen you can procure in & about Plymouth, taking them on board the Flag Ship for General Service, but it is wished that this should be done as quietly as possible, & so as to avoid as far may be in your power, drawing attention to it, and of course you will keep this strictly to yourself, letting any orders you give upon it have the appearance of coming from yourself.[25]

The advantage of this arrangement was that it could be disavowed, should it come to the attention of the French, the Opposition, or possibly even Aberdeen, who would not be pleased by any action that threatened the *entente*.

Graham's initial willingness to wait out the crisis with reduced crews did not survive the bombardment of Tangier. He urged Peel to state the British case, commission three or four battleships for the Channel and act resolutely. He believed these measures would tend to keep Guizot in power. He also expressed doubts about Aberdeen's belief that to commission one more battleship might result in France responding with a

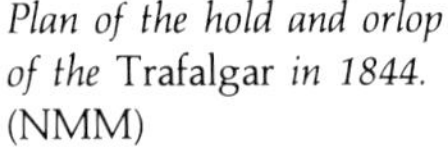

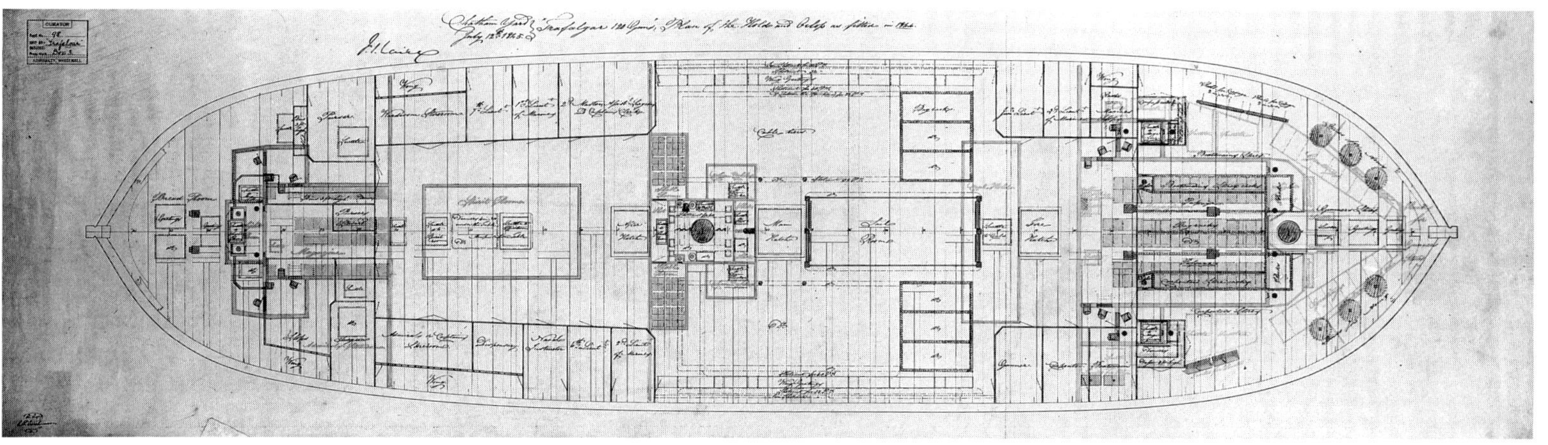

Plan of the hold and orlop of the Trafalgar *in 1844.* (NMM)

The Trafalgar, *cut down into a screw two-decker serving as the training ship* Boscawen *in 1906. There is a* Triumph-*class pre-dreadnought battleship under her bowsprit.* (IWM)

larger number. Aberdeen had argued that one ship would be just the sort of half measure and contradictory signal that a good diplomat should avoid sending. If the French were about to bring forward four ships at Toulon, as reported in the Whig press, he urged six as a minimum number; anything less would be an ineffective menace.[26] Wellington weighed in late with what Peel considered to be an excessive response and called for a local superiority on every station as the only guarantee of peace with France.[27]

Ultimately, Aberdeen's views received some justification with the Franco-Moroccan Treaty of 10 September, which did not appear to aim at the incorporation of Moorish territory, and the recall of Joinville. By late September Peel was turning his attention to the Oregon dispute, advising Aberdeen to send the *Collingwood* to the Columbia River.[28]

The Admiralty and Wellington gave their attention to the lessons to be drawn from the Moroccan crisis. Diplomacy and the deterrence of minimum force had been effective, but the threat of more resolute French action could not be dismissed. The Admiralty used the opportunity to reconsider the basic themes of post-1832 policy-making while Wellington made more extreme demands for military spending. Peel had shifted his ground during the crisis to favour a more forthright response to French activity.

Administrative reform

Although the threat posed by a French steam fleet played a large part in stimulating the discussion about naval policy within the smaller inner Cabinet, it was not the real cause of the reforms for which Peel, Haddington and Herbert strove. They believed that the whole administration of the Navy required a fundamental overhaul but they had to find a method of achieving that without annoying Graham who tended to see every new initiative as an attempt to resuscitate the Navy Board. This complicated what could otherwise have been a simple reform and delayed any serious steps until after the break-up of the great Ministry in late 1845; any real policy changes were postponed until after the return of the Whigs. In many ways the changes that had to be made were vital for the well being of the Navy, and went beyond the narrow party politics of the Graham process.

Alongside the discussions about naval administration ran a strand of technical progress best summarised under the theme of the auxiliary screw steam fleet. This is not the place for a detailed resumé of the screw propellor and its impact on the Royal Navy, but it must be emphasised how far the screw allowed the Peel Administration to rationalise their response to Joinville and the paddle steam threat. The blockships of 1845, the harbours of refuge at Dover and Alderney, and the Portsmouth steam factory provided the means to blockade Cherbourg and Brest, and to take the initiative. Technological superiority provided Britain with the best response to the challenge from France.

This general theme should not obscure the flaws in Peel's overall handling of design and construction issues. The iron frigate programme of 1844, largely pushed through on the advice of Herbert and Corry, provided the Navy with several large and outrageously expensive ships which were not fit for combat, and had never been armed as anything more than screw-driven *Terrible*'s. The money would have been better spent on new battleships, slipways and small steamers, as the succeeding Board would soon realise. The one man with the responsibility and expertise to advise on these issues, Symonds, was ignored as a part of Cockburn's assault on his position. Cockburn preferred to conduct his discussions through Edye, while ignoring the objections of both Symonds and his deputy.

The Cabinet discussion on naval policy that followed the scare of mid-1844 developed into a consideration of whether to increase defence spending, and if so, on what it should be spent. Wellington opened the discussion with a long paper on the insufficiency of the Naval Estimates. He believed that there were two problems at issue: forces on the distant stations and the defence of the Home Islands. Steam vessels were, he argued, only useful for maritime and coastal operations; naval war would still be decided by well-manned sailing battleships. However, the new challenge of steam made it essential for batteries to be built as defences for the dockyards, something that had not been necessary hitherto. In this the Duke reflected the report of the 1844 Commission on Coastal Defences, chaired by Thomas Hastings. This body had come down firmly in favour of floating batteries for the defence of the more exposed dockyards.[29]

In the interval, Herbert presented the results of the Admiralty investigation into the state of the Navy and of coastal defences as the time had come to draw up the annual estimates. The First Secretary identified six areas of concern.

1 The insufficiency of the steam force.
2 The inability of existing dockyards to maintain the steam Navy.
3 The lack of dockyard defences.
4 The lack of a reserve squadron to act as a squadron of evolution in time of peace.
5 The Flag List lacked vigorous and experienced admirals.
6 The lack of harbours of refuge.

Herbert proposed building fifteen steam vessels per annum, three being iron vessels from the merchant yards, making up for the shortage of slips and labour in the Royal yards. The cost was to be £268,000. Dockyard improvements would cost another £200,000. The only reserve squadron consisted of the three home flagships which were now fully manned. This was not an adequate response to the danger:

> a respectable force in case of emergency and in peace would be invaluable as a squadron of exercise, both to test the comparative qualities of our ships, thereby giving us safe data for building and (which is of immense importance) to instruct our officers in naval tactics, a matter very much neglected of late years, but the importance of which cannot be rated too high and has not been overlooked by our neighbours.

This would require an additional 4,000 men to man the four extra battleships and at least six steamers which would be a respectable force when linked with the flagships. The cost would be £224,000. The extra men were needed because, although there were more men afloat than there had been in 1839, 9,500 were on the West Africa, China and Pacific stations rather than at home or in the Mediterranean. The Flag List would also require serious and costly attention, totalling £51,000.[30]

Herbert's report helped Peel to respond to Wellington's letter. The Premier stressed the need to make conscious decisions on the priority of the many projects then on offer, both to avoid damage to the financial well-being of the nation that would be caused by reckless profligacy and reduce the danger of annoying the French. Looking for a little support Peel sent the Duke's papers on coastal defence to Aberdeen.[31]

Aberdeen responded with an attack on the underlying rationale of the Duke's programme, a programme that he considered to be the result of taking a narrow, purely professional view of the military situation. He believed Peel would take a political view, by implication a more balanced and sophisticated one, and realise that the French were not intent on war and invasion. He stressed 'war is not to be made against England by a *coup de main*', and if any danger should arise:

> I think we ought mainly to rely, as we have hitherto relied, on our naval superiority for our security against any serious attack. It is true, that the invention of steam as an instrument, may be expected materially to affect the results of naval warfare; and yet I cannot but imagine that the power of steam will give us great advantages as compared with any other state. Our steam force is incomparably superior to that of France; and we are annually devoting much larger sums than the French Government to the improvement of this formidable arm.

This last comment served to underline his belief that the Joinville pamphlet demonstrated just how little there was to fear from the French. He poured justifiable scorn on Wellington's claim that Naples, Sardinia and Brazil were all building steamers to join an attack on British commerce. However, Aberdeen saw that the post-1840 reductions, combined with the expansion of extra European commitments, might have been carried too far. While commerce had to be protected he did not understand why battleships had been sent to the distant stations. There were no foreign vessels of that class so that frigates would be quite adequate. In this he revealed a limited understanding of the nature of the British fleet. Old 74s were little more costly to run than large frigates, certainly more impressive, and better suited to such coastal operations as the passing of the Bogue Forts.

> I would therefore keep a fleet of eight Line of Battle Ships, including the three Guard ships, in the Channel. I would leave a Line of Battle Ship at Malta to carry the Admiral's Flag, and for the purposes of parade and ceremony. I would not at this moment remove the Line of Battle Ship from the Pacific – although two good frigates would be much more useful there. But I would recall forthwith the *Illustrious* from the West Indies, and the *Agincourt* from China where neither of them is at all required. By these means we should have ten sail of the line in commission, eight of which would be at near hand and ready for any emergency. This is not the force to create any reasonable jealousy, and I do not believe that the addition of smaller vessels, in such proportions as might fairly be required for the discharge of the duties of the service, would provoke any objection or remark.

Two months before Guizot had been at Windsor and had expressed no objection to any reasonable increase. Harbours of Refuge, Aberdeen decided, were acceptable, given their camouflage as havens for merchant shipping.[32] Apart from the obvious unsuitability of small 74s for European service, the most startling aspect of the Foreign Secretary's programme was the persistence in keeping only one battleship inside the Straits. Problems with the Oregon boundary turned the attention of the Cabinet to the Columbia River in February, and Peel responded by accepting the 4,000 increase in the number of men that Herbert had suggested. This passed a quiet House of Commons on 1 April without a division.[33]

The screw steam fleet

The next question was how to employ the additional men and money to increase national security without provoking the reaction that Aberdeen feared. Napier pressed Peel on the dangers from the French steam Navy, which he exaggerated as a force superior in numbers and quality to the Royal Navy. Napier was still looking to a paddle wheel fleet, but Cockburn, Herbert and Corry were committed to the screw steamer. Cockburn reported that the frigate *Amphion* was about to be fitted with an auxiliary screw;

> if we find this to answer more of that class of ship, and indeed our ships of the line may be so fitted at moderate expense and without inconvenience to their internal arrangements.[34]

Haddington supported Cockburn's paper and, confident in the success of the screw, followed Corry's suggestion that a separate vote be taken for screw-driven blockships which were to be converted from some of the less seaworthy 74s and then serve as temporary defences for Pembroke and Sheerness, the most exposed of the dockyards. The First Lord favoured waiting until the next estimates for the money but Peel, in a confidential letter, gave permission to spend up to £100,000 on the blockships.[35]

Initially, the eight blockships were to have been converted from unseaworthy units destined for the quarantine service. The *Saturn* was told off to be sheathed in 2in fir plank and prepared for the fitting of an engine. When work began she was found to be defective and the programme was upgraded in September to employ ships in good repair.[36] This decision involved fitting a more effective rig, in essence making the blockships into seagoing warships, rather than the jury-rigged hulks initially envisaged. Much of the credit for this has been given to Corry, and while the programme proved to be a technical success it should be recalled that the four ships ultimately converted, *Ajax*, *Blenheim*, *Edinburgh* and *Hogue*, saw active service in the Gulf of Finland, one of the areas where all subsequent British coastal defence types were expected to operate. Of the ships converted, three were dockyard-built, and all had been given a major repair in the Seppings' era. They were fitted with 450nhp machinery, two by Seaward and the other pair by Maudslay. The poop was removed and the armament reduced to 60 guns:

Gundeck	28	32pdr	56cwt
Maindeck	26	8in	53cwt
Upper deck	2	68pdr	95cwt
	4	10in	67cwt

One of Admiral Cockburn's more unusual means of attacking the Surveyor was to order the Sans Pareil. *Her form was copied from that of a French prize of the same name taken at the Glorious First of June in 1794. The ship was completed as a steam battleship.* (IWM)

This was a powerful battery, well able to deal with any vessel outside the first rank, and in coastal waters the advantages conferred by steam power should have given these vessels a decisive edge over any other ship afloat. *Ajax* and *Blenheim*, completed in September 1846, were the world's first steam-powered battleships. They played a major role in the development of the screw battlefleet of the 1850s, demonstrating the inestimable advantages of mechanical power and the possibility of keeping it within the confines of a wooden warship armed with broadside guns. Despite the added weight, the midship port was kept 6ft above the waterline by limiting the stores and water.[37]

Wellington's response to the danger was altogether less measured. Having censured his Premier for not publicly admitting to the defenceless state of the country, he urged Peel to collect an Army of 100,000 regular troops in Britain as the only secure defence against an invasion. Peel was not disposed to follow such advice, preferring to repair the weaknesses recently uncovered in as unostentatious a manner as possible. With the National Debt standing at £787 million, and the annual interest at £28 million there was a need to be careful in deciding the priorities of defence spending. Debt reduction and imperial defence were competing claims on a burgeoning revenue, and while he had given an additional £1.1 million to the Ordnance and Navy, as well as the £100,000 promised for the blockships, he could hardly do more. At heart, he did not believe the country was defenceless, for although steam had altered the basic strategic issues he was confident that Britain was better provided with steam warships, and particularly with merchant steamers to serve as a reserve force, than France. In addition, Haddington promised that the thirty Advanced Ships, fitted with water tanks, guns and lower masts could be at sea within a week, once men were aboard. These precautions gave him the confidence to wait on the French.[38]

Peel received further disheartening advice from Sir George Murray, Master General of the Ordnance, who contended that steam neutralised British naval supremacy, making it necessary to build up a central bastion in the heart of the country, and pointed to the works at Weedon, begun in 1803. Curiously enough, Graham approved of this defeatist nonsense.[39] Peel also sent Graham his response to Wellington's letter, and here the Home Secretary was on rather more certain ground. He argued that invasion out of the blue was 'beyond the range of ordinary calculation'. In consequence, 'This country will never consent to a war establishment in time of peace, *unless cause be shown*'. If Wellington did not agree then he should make his case public, something Peel was hardly willing to consider given the excitable nature of public opinion.[40]

When Cockburn called for a permanent force of steamers to be retained in the Channel, Graham supported him and urged the rapid completion of the blockships as 'quite essential' to the defence of the dockyards. Graham was relieved to hear that this would take only eight months.[41] Peel had raised the sum available for the blockships to £150,000, for five 74s and five frigates, but it quickly became obvious that only two-thirds of that figure could be spent because of the shortage of engine-building capacity, and Corry advised putting the rest into other steam warships. While Cockburn wanted to expedite one of the large ships as an experiment, Corry stressed that such caution was unnecessary, and in existing circumstances, far from wise. Peel accepted Corry's prognosis, while raising doubts about the screw, merchant steamers, the Advanced Ships and the general state of preparedness. He also advised Corry not to be deluded by the Report of the French Naval Commission on their steam marine.

> I strongly suspect, if the accounts which I see of this Report in the newspapers be correct that it is purposely intended for English readers, that it is hoped that our vigilance will be relaxed, and our jealousy abated, and that under cover of this report setting forth the inefficiency and imperfections of the steam marine of France, a large vote for the improvement of it will be proposed to the Chambers.[42]

Aberdeen was greatly alarmed by all these warlike preparations and he found no support in the Paris Embassy, from whence Lord Cowley had returned convinced the French would start a war with an invasion within six months of the death of Louis Philippe. These views had considerable influence upon Peel and Graham, rather more than those of Cowley's brother, Wellington. Peel requested him to keep a sharp eye on the French Channel ports for invasion preparations, and pointed out that more work had been done on battleships in the previous year than was normal so that the equivalent of over four units was in place rather than the normal three.[43] The Foreign Secretary now anticipated a great difference of opinon with Peel, noting that Peel and Graham had recently shifted their views and appeared to mistrust France. These were the Duke's views, for which he saw no rationale, and instead he argued that Britain already possessed a measure of superiority in all classes of warship. If his views were not supported he considered it would be best if he retired. Peel hurried to sooth his colleague. Aberdeen continued to place his trust in Guizot, but Peel could see no reason to place his faith in men who were not masters of their own house.[44] Peel was well aware of the dangers inherent in Aberdeen's policy, which he considered 'impracticable'. Graham believed his loss, 'would be fatal and irreperable', stressing the Foreign Secretary's willingness to accept reasonable precautions. He was also prepared to forgo his own views to keep Aberdeen. Even so the consensus was that precautions were necessary, and Graham had as little trust in France as Peel. The current crop of French naval preparations struck him as unnecessary, particularly the sudden increase in the number of steamers and battleships. This resembled all too closely the build up to a naval war, a war which Graham was convinced the French would launch at the first favourable moment.[45] While Aberdeen was persuaded to remain in the Cabinet Peel did have his way on defence spending. Convinced of the need, and of the unreliability of the French, he would brook no opposition. Aberdeen spent a weekend at Peel's country house in late September, agreeing to differ on the defence question and absent himself from future Cabinet discussions on the subject.[46]

While the inner Cabinet debated the level of current expenditure the Board of the Admiralty was more interested in the underlying issue of who controlled construction policy. This question had been brewing for much of the period of Peel's Administration, but was to remain unresolved until the Whigs returned.

Just as Cockburn was bringing his attack on Symonds to a conclusion the political problems of the Peel Administration forced a change at the head of the Admiralty and Haddington was replaced with the altogether more determined Ellenborough. This change, in combination with the French challenge that had placed the Navy at the centre of attention, created the right atmosphere in which to resolve the central dilemma of naval policy-making.

5 *Lord Ellenborough and the Review of Naval Policy: January–July 1846*

A new man at the helm

The political problems that surrounded the break-up of Peel's Administration and the repeal of the Corn Laws in 1846 forced a change at the head of naval administration. After losing Lord Stanley, later the Earl of Derby, from the front bench in the House of Lords Peel left office. As part of this process he committed himself to support any increases in the Naval and Military Estimates considered necessary to meet the danger from France.[1] However, struggles within the Whig party prevented Lord John Russell from taking over the Government. On resuming office Peel was acutely conscious of the need to reinforce his debating strength in the House of Lords. During the political crisis Haddington dutifully placed his office at Peel's disposal. This was both a recognition of his own role as a reliable cipher, and the act of a close friend. Peel accepted the offer, and appointed Lord Ellenborough (1790–1871), the recently returned Governor General of India, to the post of First Lord. Ellenborough refused any nominal posts in Cabinet, such as Lord Privy Seal, to which Haddington moved.[2]

Other members of the Cabinet were rather less certain of the wisdom of the appointment; that it was made at all demonstrated the extent to which Peel saw the Admiralty as being in the second rank of Cabinet posts, an office which did not provide the power base for so independent and powerful a personality to make a serious nuisance of himself. While warning that Ellenborough 'jumps always hastily to extreme conclusions', Graham admitted the need to secure his services and believed the Admiralty would, 'under proper restraint', prevent the Earl's *terribilis celeritas* from causing too much harm. Characteristically, Aberdeen feared that the new man would combine with Wellington as *duo fulmina belli* in Cabinet. That Graham knew of the appointment before Peel confirmed it, and Aberdeen only after, indicates the degree to which the Foreign Secretary was being excluded from major issues relating to naval preparations.[3] In her more open correspondence, the Queen suggested that Ellenborough, 'will be of great use' and that he 'is become very quiet, and is a very good speaker'. These would appear to have been Peel's arguments, rather than her opinions. Privately, she evidently shared Aberdeen's fear, telling Peel that the new First Lord might combine with the Duke to urge warlike preparations, 'a little too strongly'.[4]

Ellenborough, a powerful speaker, a confident and ambitious politician and conscious of his own great gifts was, after his experience in India, unwilling to play the role of a cipher. He did not share the basic objects of the Peel Administration, in particular on the issues of the Corn Laws and Tariff Reform. Even as Peel was approaching him to join the Administration he had been acting in concert with Lord Brougham to reform the Administration by detaching Peel and Graham, re-integrating the protectionists and taking the lead himself. After the break-up of the Administration he was the one Cabinet Minister to move into the Protectionist camp.[5] Along with Auckland, Ellenborough has been studied in connection with his work in relation to India, a subject that dominates the only biography to the exclusion of any appreciation of his brief but important tenure at the Admiralty.[6] However, certain basic administrative traits can be traced in Ellenborough's earlier career. He was a determined opponent of corruption, misapplied patronage and inefficiency. He did not have any time for half-measures, pursuing his policies to their logical conclusion, whatever the financial or political cost. These highly individualistic traits made him a far from ideal subordinate for a premier of Peel's stamp. The relationship began tolerably well, but by the time the Government broke up Ellenborough had become a bitter critic of Peel, and would have waited little longer before resigning. In particular he found Peel's reliance on Herbert, now Secretary at War, and Corry, his replacement as First Secretary to the Admiralty, particularly galling.[7]

Ellenborough's views on the role of the Navy were, as might be expected, imperial. He had been very conscious of the need to defend commerce back in 1828, when he had been more than willing to become First Lord under Wellington.[8] The intervening years had widened his horizons, as evidenced by his powerful interest in Indian resources and the distant stations. This element in his thinking was given particular stress when a series of ships were renamed to reflect victories and connections with India and China. He had also developed a more balanced view of the challenges to British supremacy, in particular from France and the United States. His view of the international situation in early 1846 displayed an imperial breadth of vision, and a grand strategic conception of the essential unity of the problems and potential of British power.

Although he only held office for six months, Ellenborough achieved a commendable grasp of naval issues. Despite opposition from many quarters, not least his Cabinet colleagues, he began a programme to modernise, reform and strengthen the Navy, its ships, dockyards and bases. Auckland and Baring were to build on his work.

Arriving at the Admiralty Ellenborough found the Board dominated by the veteran Cockburn.[9] Within six days of taking office he uncovered, to his disgust, a serious shortage of shipbuilding timber. While urging several Indian connections to help with a supply of teak he revealed just how ineffective he believed the Board had become under Haddington;

> I find I shall require some tact and management to make things go on quickly here in the first instance, for in practise there has been no First Lord of the Admiralty for more than four years, and as you know I am not in the habit of allowing other men to do the work for which I am responsible. As for the business so much complained of on account of its extent, it is child's play to that of a G.G. (Governor General).[10]

Strategy and policy

Among several matters of concern the danger of an American War was given the greatest attention in the early months of Ellenborough's term. He wanted to meet the danger on the Great Lakes by sending out Napier as Naval Commander, with extra seamen and materials to build war steamers at Kingston. On the Pacific station he was concerned to meet, or overmatch, the American force. He argued for a demonstration in the West Indies, sending the *Superb* and *Grampus* from home waters to

Line of battle ships in naval service 1834–46

	1834	1836	1838	1840	1842	1844	1846
Afloat	88*	75	78	77	75	78	71
Building	7	11	11	12	13	12	12
Orders	8	3	3	6	5	7	11
	103	89	92	95	93	97	94
Harbour Service	37	42	36	33	34	33	32

*of which 17 were unserviceable

join the West Indies flagship *Vindictive* off Chesapeake Bay. This action was to serve both to recover British seamen from American warships for service in Canada, and as a clear and easily read diplomatic signal.[11]

Peel was less enthusiastic and warned against trusting Napier with any command that called for discretion and the submission of all such measures for Aberdeen's opinion. He also urged the suspension of orders for demonstrations and the construction of war steamers on the Lakes in view of the pacific response he expected the Americans would make to the Queen's speech.[12] The First Lord was not shifted from his pessimistic prognosis by such temporary considerations. There were already 1,000 more men afloat than had been voted and even so he could do no more than bring the ships in service up to their war complements. He required Peel's sanction to keep up recruitment, and a vote to increase the marines. Only this, Ellenborough believed, would meet the possibility of war with France, the United States or, possibly, both.

> I cannot divest my mind of the impression that there is a great storm coming on. France and America must see, altho' people here will not, that in India we are beginning a great and dangerous war. This must affect our relations with America, and I feel satisfied that nothing can prevent a French War six months after an American war is on our hands, unless in that time we crush the American Navy.[13]

The danger anticipated was real enough and if British seapower was unequal to the challenge of closing down one war the temptation for another power to take advantage of the problem would be considerable. Peel was not impressed. Admitting the dangers of being taken by surprise he argued that the measures in hand were adequate. In addition, the increases to Naval and Ordnance Estimates for 1845–6 had been around one million pounds.

> Between increased expenditure on the one hand, and reduced taxation on the other, we are about to incur the serious evil of deficit in time of peace. We really had better have a war at once than incur many of the evils of it by making constantly increasing preparation for it.
>
> It is a very good thing no doubt to be prepared at all points – to have twice the naval force of any other country – to have every colony in a state of complete defence, well garrisoned and the fortifications in good order – to have nothing to fear in the event of hostilities all this is very desirable if you can afford it – but if you cannot, if in order to secure these advantages you must incur debt in the time of peace – you are crippling your resources (for money and credit are resources) in the event of war.

Furthermore, he did not see anything in the most recent communications from the United States to justify increased preparations. If they became necessary he would put forward a fresh demand in Parliament; but Peel made it clear he did not favour such a move.

> I for one shall sincerely regret that necessity, for I know of few evils greater in the present state of this country than a deficit in the public revenue as compared with the expenditure.[14]

The first impact of this rebuff came when the Flagship in the Pacific was to be relieved. Ellenborough wanted to send the *Rodney*, to overmatch the USS *Columbia*, but without additional recruitment he could not man so large a ship as well as those required in home waters to meet the immediate danger from France. Consequently, he was forced to send the less powerful *Collingwood*.[15]

With so clear a rebuff to his policy Ellenborough turned to the wider problems of war preparedness and administrative reform. His first thoughts concerned the actual state of the battlefleet. If Peel wanted to rely on the deterrent and war fighting power of the Navy Ellenborough wanted a clear idea of the real state of the battlefleet (see tables).

State of ships building or on order February 1846

Those already laid down are classed as building, the remaining ships are 'on order'.

	Guns	*Laid Down*	*State*
Royal Albert	120	1845	2/8
Marlborough	110	–	nothing provided
Prince of Wales	110	–	2/8 of frame provided
Royal Frederick	110	1841	5/8
Royal Sovereign	110	–	1/2 of frame
Victoria	110	1844	1/8
Windsor Castle	110	–	nothing provided
Aboukir	90	1840	3/8
Algiers	90	–	keel provided
Exmouth	90	1841	2.25/8
Hannibal	90	–	3/4 of frame
Princess Royal	90	1841	4/8
St Jean d'Acre	90	–	nothing provided
Agamemnon	80	–	1/16 of frame
Brunswick	80	–	frame provided
Colossus	80	1843	4/8
Cressy	80	–	frame provided
Irresistible	80	–	frame provided
Lion	80	1840	3/8
Meeanee	80	1842	4/8
Majestic	80	1841	2/8
Mars	80	1839	5/16
Sans Pareil	80	1845	3/16

Deptford had been ordered to put the *Hannibal* in frame in January. In addition, there were nine 50-gun frigates in various states, between awaiting the collection of materials and ready to launch; the *Raleigh* was already afloat.[16]

With this list of ships in various states of construction there was no requirement, or slip space, for any further sailing ship orders. It remained to be seen whether the existing designs for these vessels would be followed, particularly with those to which the Navy had as yet made no real commitment. There were enough battleships on the Navy List, even if a large proportion of those afloat were old and small, and the reserve and new construction included enough large, powerful units to deter the French. Ellenborough concluded that the fleet was not a major issue. His attention focused on the administration of the dockyards and the design of new vessels.

The policy-making machine

The single most important improvement effected in the conduct of naval administration in the 1840s was the overhaul of long-term construction policy. Here Auckland, and to a lesser extent Baring, made a radical break with the past based on pioneering work by Ellenborough. These reforms were vital if Britain was to maintain the naval supremacy that formed the cornerstone of her strategic policy. When he came to office Ellenborough discovered a complete lack of anything that might be dignified with the label of a policy. After the abolition of the Navy Board in 1832 there had been no effective long-term control over shipbuilding and the dockyards. These had been the major peace-time tasks of the Navy Board. From 1832 this task was given to the Surveyor when it had hitherto been the responsibility of the Controller. The attack of the Master Shipwrights and pupils of the School of Naval Architecture on Symonds's designs made the debate appear narrow and technical when the real problem was that successive Governments had allowed the careful policy of the Navy Board to be replaced by dangerously low estimates within which shipbuilding was reduced to an absolute minimum. The alarms of 1838–40 and 1844–6 forced the Admiralty to react but without a sound policy framework they could only produce panic measures. The single greatest failure followed the panic of 1844–5. In the absence of firm control from the First Lord, the Board was pressed into sanctioning a huge programme of iron steamships, screw frigates and the conversion of old battleships and frigates into harbour defence blockships. Symonds, who was not consulted, opposed these measures. Panic and ignorance of the true state of development of the screw propeller allowed the programmes to go ahead. Ellenborough was horrified by the waste and his testament for Auckland said as much though political considerations prevented him naming the guilty men.

The first problem was Symonds. Strong minded and combative Symonds struck the mild Earl of Haddington as 'a very difficult man to deal with when you venture to differ'. Furthermore, he was a committed Whig and still in contact with his political friends.[17] Haddington advised Ellenborough to adopt Cockburn's proposed Committee on Naval Construction. The First Naval Lord adopted the concept following a suggestion by Russell in the House of Commons. Cockburn wanted to alter the duties of the Surveyor from designer to overseer of design and construction. Cockburn and Haddington believed it was impossible for any one man to master all of the branches of naval architecture and engineering. However, Peel implied that Symonds's patron, Portland, was too important to be offended by any unnecessary step.[18] Graham, the Home Secretary, had been the Whig First Lord in 1832, responsible both for abolishing the Navy Board and appointing Symonds. He objected to the new Committee as a resurrection of the Navy Board. Haddington had merely assumed that as the Committee would be under direct Admiralty control Graham would be satisfied.[19] This was not the case; the Navy Board had also been under direct Admiralty control. Before he could act Haddington made way for Ellenborough.

Ellenborough found Symonds every inch as combative as had Haddington, but being made of sterner stuff dealt firmly with him. After some deliberation he appointed a Committee of Reference on Shipbuilding on 26 May 1846. Symonds was now to share responsibility for design with a group of outsiders, all of whom were bitter opponents. The final decision was to be taken up by the Board.[20] Ellenborough had intended to place Symonds on the Committee but soon realised that the debate was a political issue and could not be resolved quietly. Instead, Captain Lord John Hay was to chair the Committee in order to ensure fair play. To forestall the inevitable objections Symonds was warned that further complaints would be referred to the Board, which had already suspended work on all large ships building to his designs.[21] Far from being even-handed, Hay was an opponent of Symonds's work and predisposed to find fault. He also delighted in rank and position, without responsibility.[22] However, much of this would only become apparent after Ellenborough left office.

The dockyards

The new round of reform was to require much more serious consideration of the dockyards than had been given in 1832. Ellenborough had pointed out their weaknesses. The 1832 process had reduced the number of shipwrights without improving working practices and the dockyards remained wedded to eighteenth-century notions of patronage; they were badly manned and haphazardly administered and unless they were placed on a modern system no long-term policy could be attempted. On departing from office Ellenborough left a long memorandum setting out twelve issues, which either required immediate attention or were in the process of being decided, with the Second Secretary, Captain W A B Hamilton.

The memorandum on the dockyards, as the opening move in the process of reform, merits detailed consideration.

> 8thly. The sums expended in the dockyards seem to be so totally disproportioned to the work done that it is impossible not to apprehend that there must be a want of due supervision and control and a great defect of system.
>
> It is distressing to think how much of real permanent advantage to the Naval Service might have been derived from the judicious application to good purposes of the sums thrown away in fanciful alterations of ships, in hastily adopted novelties of construction, and in ill-considered repairs. The newly appointed Committee of Reference will, it is hoped, obviate the recurrence of some of these abuses, but to Lord Ellenborough it appeared that the best security against extravagance in the dockyards was to be found in the careful selection of the most zealous and competent officers as superintendents of dockyards, and in the principle that no office to which any responsibility is attached, should be given simply as a reward for past services, without reference to the capacity of the person to perform good future service in the particular office conferred upon him.
>
> It was therefore not merely on account of his past services, but with a view to the future service he was peculiarly

qualified to perform in that office that Lord John Hay was appointed to act as Superintendent of the dockyard at Woolwich.[23]

Lord Auckland was to adopt the main measures of this memorandum, most notably the value placed upon the proper selection of individuals as an answer to administrative problems that arose from more deep-seated failings in the structure of naval administration. It was indicative of the fundamental nature of the problem that both Symonds and his opponents could argue that much of the tonnage constructed over the past half decade had been unsuitable. While Tory members of the Board, such as Admiral Rous, considered the Symondite sailing ships the most unsuitable, Symonds pointed to the iron frigates, large numbers of screw steamers and ill-considered alternative battleship designs. While both cases had some merit only the most doctrinaire could suggest that the Surveyor was not more sinned against than sinning after 1841. In particular he, and others, pointed to a sharp reduction in the number of battleships on order.[24]

The invasion scare

However, long-term policies could not be adopted before the immediate issue of defence against invasion had been settled. In early 1846 the naval technical issue of the moment was to decide how steam power could be best used in the immediate future. Ellenborough sent out an evolutionary squadron in which steam and sailing ships were in roughly equal proportions for the first time. The squadron was intended to comprise nine battleships, two 50-gun frigates and ten to twelve steamers. The instructions given to Rear Admiral Sir William Parker, the most suitable officer on the Navy List for such exercises, were to practise every combination of sail and steam, 'principally using steamers to tow battleships, for the purposes of ascertaining in what manner the two arms can best be made to assist each other in war'. At the same time Parker was to keep station approximately 300 miles west of Cape Finisterre in case of trouble with the Americans. Parker made his report to the new Administration in the autumn, but the credit for the squadron, as with much else of value in the last years of the sailing battlefleet, goes to Ellenborough.[25]

Ellenborough left office in July 1846. In six months he had made a major effort to improve the efficiency and war-readiness of the Royal Navy. The most important elements of his work were set down in his memorandum for Lord Auckland and formed the basis of a successful attempt to make the administration of the Navy less political. In part this required a reversal of the more controversial aspects of the 1832 process, in part the introduction of more modern concepts of management into the dockyards. For all his failings as a politician Ellenborough was a first-class administrator. It was singularly fortunate for the Navy that his successor was to be a man of equal ability if very different in most other respects.

6 *The Russell Government: Naval Policy and National Defence 1846–52*

The Whig Administration that took office in mid-1846 can be seen as a major contrast with the outgoing Tory Administration. Russell was not the dominant figure in Cabinet that Peel had been. Pulled in various directions by internal faction fights Russell was more concerned with maintaining his hold on power than the detailed control of policy, something that was only too evident to the Queen, among others.[1] Furthermore, Russell's whole approach to government was reflected in his 'hands off' approach to department heads.

Initially, Russell had intended to return Minto, his father-in-law, to the Admiralty. However, a party faction fight resulted in the exclusion of Minto and his brother, Admiral Sir George Elliot, from the new Board under Auckland. The devious political manoeuvres employed to this end reflected the aversion felt by many toward Minto both as a colleague and as the father of Russell's formidable wife. Although Minto and Auckland were old friends, the events of July 1846 soured relations between the two, though they had resumed their friendship by the end of the year.[2]

Minto's brother in law Admiral Sir Charles Adam returned as First Naval Lord, but only for the first year of the Administration. The long-term consequences of excluding Minto and his clan – in favour of the more dynamic Auckland, would be the reform of naval administration. However, such laudable aims were far from the thoughts of those involved in the faction fight. George Eden, Earl of Auckland (1784–1849), has been portrayed as a somewhat colourless aristocrat of limited abilities. His one major error of judgement, the Afghan campaign of 1840, has obscured important work at the Admiralty in 1834, 1835 and 1846–8. In retrospect, Auckland was a most effective service chief, ready to argue the departmental case against more powerful ministers, notably Palmerston, and in addition he received effective support from Russell. The lacklustre image conveyed by subsequent commentators does little justice to him and contemporaries were deeply shocked by his sudden death for they were aware of the scale of the loss suffered by the Administration. Auckland had the ability to conciliate the most hot-tempered of admirals, a talent that more than made up for brief and unimpressive performances in the House of Lords, which was never an important forum for naval debate in the period covered by this book. Sir William Parker attempted to summarise his qualities:

> It is scarcely possible to estimate the loss of such a man

too highly. His sterling worth was known to yourself. To the Navy it is almost irreperable, for he administered the duties of his office with a sound judgement and impartiality that won him the golden opinions of the service, in which I do not think he created an enemy. I hope your Lordship may be fortunate in finding a successor for the Admiralty, but it will indeed be difficult to select anyone so eminently gifted for the post as poor Lord Auckland was.[3]

Russell and naval administration

Russell's administrative style was closer to the modern idea of a premier, leading the Cabinet but not dominating the entire policy-making process. The attempt to act otherwise, even in the nineteenth century, was fraught with problems as the early deaths of Pitt and Canning indicate. Even the most dynamic and effective minister could not be an over-arching expert and while many contemporaries criticised Russell for his lack of decisive leadership and clear policy it is possible to see him as a politician who was at least prepared to delegate authority to capable ministers.[4] Certainly, if judged on results, his handling of naval affairs was more successful than that of Peel. This was despite the fragmentary nature of the Whig Party, and its complete reliance on external support for its continued survival. Indeed, until his early death in 1850 their most important ally was Peel himself. Against this background any attempt to assert Peel-like authority would have been difficult even for a man with real leadership qualities. It is worthy of note that as he formed his Administration Russell was left in no doubt that he had an unlikely collection of allies. The Duke of Portland offered support to turn out Peel, through his son-in-law, J E Denison. Although a committed protectionist, Portland preferred revenge to the continuance of the conservative team. Portland had always favoured a centre party formed by the moderates from both Whig and Tory groups, to exclude both radicals and high Tories. At the same time he was funding Disraeli's purchase of Hughenden, so that the protectionist leader could make an acceptable figure in landed society.[5] Russell must have been aware of the methods by which Portland could be conciliated, and while the new Prime Minister was not going to reimpose the Corn Laws the issue over which Portland had broken with Peel, Symonds's position was still a major issue.

Although he left the final decision to Auckland, Russell did have an influence on the membership of the Board which included several of his supporters, particularly H G Ward, the First Secretary, and Admiral Sir James W D Dundas, Second and later First Naval Lord. During Auckland's term Ward's correspondence generally reflected the views of the First Lord but after Baring took over, Ward found having his chief in the same House such a burden that he pressed Russell to find him another appointment. Furthermore, with Minto still interested in naval affairs and still in contact with many senior officers, Russell had advice aplenty. When Auckland died it was Minto who suggested that Baring was the best man for the post.[6] Even so, Russell was primarily a passive contributor to the policy debate; he waited for issues to be referred for his opinion, or to become public as with the 'Indiscreet Admiral' incident of 1850–1. Where his service chief had arrived at a firm decision Russell would not override him. On the other hand he would also leave them to fight their own battles in Cabinet.

The politics of defence

The traditional approach to the defence policy of the Russell Administration (1846–1852) has been to examine the political debate on the creation of an effective militia and improved coastal fortifications. Adopting this argument as a starting point, most authors have seriously undervalued the role of the Royal Navy as the first line of defence for the British Isles.[8]

Palmerston had a large measure of independence at the Foreign Office and used that to set the tone of Britain's international relations. He had little of Aberdeen's regard for the fine feelings and honest conduct of the French Government. The Anglo-French *entente*, which Aberdeen had valued so highly, had collapsed even before the new Administration took office. After the diplomatic sharp practice of the Spanish Marriages in 1846, Palmerston determined on a policy of deterrence, using strength to avoid a situation in which the French could use an incident to leave Britain with the alternatives of going to war or accepting a humiliating climb-down. His policy had always been a simple one:

My doctrine is that we should reckon upon ourselves; pursue a policy of our own; aim at objects of our own, and act upon principles of our own; use other governments as we can, when we want them and find them willing to serve us; but never to place ourselves in the wake of any of them. Lead when and where we can; but follow never.

This might involve recourse to war, but Palmerston never doubted that Britain had the resources and ability to win. When he lamented the weakness of national defences he was regretting temporary weakness, not a long-term problem. His confidence in the strength of Britain was unequalled and it was, perhaps, hardly surprising that one of his first acts involved a little naval pressure:

it would do no harm at the Tuileries if any orders about fitting out line of battleships could be given in our dockyards, and mentioned in the newspapers, even if no active or real steps were taken to carry them into effect.[9]

While the defence of British interests was paramount, the Foreign Secretary was well aware that the liberal cause of Europe could only be maintained by Anglo-French concert in the face of determined opposition from the northern powers, very much under the leadership of the Tsar. In 1849 he was prepared to work with the French but not at the expense of British interests in Belgium and the Iberian peninsula. The French had been particularly active in the Mediterranean in 1846, and after the problems in Spain Palmerston was anxious to secure British control in Portugal. To this end Auckland

The 100-gun Queen, *last of the sailing three-deckers, and often regarded as Symond's masterpiece, in the Keyham dock in 1853.* (GA Osbon)

provided a very potent deterrent force consisting of five three-deckers and reinforcements for the squadron inside the Straits. Once there they were a threat to French communications with Algiers, the one sea lane for which the French navy might risk a battle.

The central role of the Royal Navy in the nineteenth century was to deter the threat of war with another major power. To this end naval dispositions reflected the political climate in Europe. When France and Russia were quiet there was no need to keep a large battlefleet in home waters and ships could then be sent to more distant stations, both to avoid criticism in Parliament and fulfil other duties. When the climate of Anglo-French, or Anglo-Russian, relations deteriorated a powerful force would be prepared for the Channel and the Mediterranean.

The uncertainty created in many minds by the introduction of steam has been attributed to 'defence planners'. Insofar as this is a reference to senior naval officers the comment is unjustified. Naval officers of any professional pretensions were well aware of the role of steam in any future war and saw no cause for alarm. Those who broke with the traditions of silent service, such as Sir Charles Napier, by making alarmist speeches, did so for personal or political reasons and reinforced their points with blatant exaggeration. By accepting the argument that lack of Cabinet discussion is synonymous with lack of concern it has been possible for some commentators to argue that the naval policy of the Russell Cabinet was 'not marked by any radical departures'.[10] In fact, the policy adopted by Russell's First Lords, Auckland between 1846 and 1849 and Baring from then until 1852, was radical, and while not discussed in Cabinet did require Treasury sanction. After the 20-year hiatus that followed the abolition of the Navy Board in 1832 Auckland re-established the Admiralty as a long-term policy-making body. As a result, in 1854, the Admiralty proved more efficient, less political and entirely capable of waging a major war which was in sharp contrast to the army.[11] During the Russian War Auckland's measures, and several of the men he selected, proved outstanding.

Naval policy

In reviewing the naval policy of the Russell Government it is necessary to make a distinction between short-term responses to the movement of French and Russian forces in the crises of the period, and the long-term requirement to maintain British command of the sea. In both areas the work of Lord Auckland and Sir Francis Baring met the requirements of the hour, allowing the futile militia and fortifications debates to continue behind the real security of a superior fleet. Far from 'presiding over a period of reduction in the Naval Estimates without misgivings',[12] Baring resisted Cabinet pressure for further economies by emphasising the continued danger from the French.[13]

On taking office in July 1846, Auckland received a coherent statement of the problems facing the Royal Navy, both in the short- and the long-term, from Ellenborough. Twelve areas were identified: dockyard defences, with armed dockyard workmen to man them; improved promotion for the Marine Officers; retirement for old captains; administrative improvements; securing a base in the Pacific; resolving the Borneo issue; reforming the Surveyor's Department; ending the employment of over-age captains; reconsidering policy on war steamers; securing 5,000 more seamen; and a supply of timber from India.[14] The building of dockyard defences and the raising of battalions were carried through by the Russell Government. Wellington's comment that the workmen could not be used in the open was irrelevant[15] because they were always intended to garrison the fortifications of the yard thereby relieving regular troops for service in the field. Retirement for captains was attempted as it had been throughout the preceding 15 years, but there were many old officers on the list, swelled by the wars of 1793–1815, and only mortality resolved the problem in the 1850s. It was in the field of long-term policy-making that Ellenborough's work had the greatest impact. Before any long-term policy decisions could be reached it was essential to resolve the immediate strategic issue. Could the Royal Navy be relied upon to defend the British Isles against invasion?

At no period in the nineteenth century was the Royal Navy ever so weak, or so lacking in sound views on strategy, that France or Russia could have staged an invasion. Small-scale raids were always possible but would have been as futile as the landing at Fishguard in 1798. Almost without exception those who suggested that Britain lay open to invasion had their own particular motives. For all their eminence in their own fields neither Wellington nor Sir John Burgoyne were qualified to give an opinion on the abilities of the Navy, particularly the Inspector General of Fortifications who, unsurprisingly, contended that more permanent defences were essential. Palmerston's dogged refusal to give up the militia plans of Burgoyne and Anglesey still requires explanation. One thing, however, remains certain. Whatever their real intentions, French policymakers under the Orleans monarchy, the Second Republic and the Second Empire were aware that the invasion of Britain was not a realistic possibility. The willingness of British politicians to interpret every move of the French fleet as a secret preparation for invasion served their purpose far more economically. The French fleet was normally strong enough to prevent the British ignoring it, but rarely so strong as to be a real threat. After 1852 Louis Napoleon hoped to use naval power to secure a British alliance, much as Tirpitz was to fifty years later. He produced the same effects, forcing increased British Naval Estimates and hostility.

When Auckland came to office the problem of the moment lay in deciding on the best use to be made of steam power in the immediate future. Ellenborough left a strong legacy, sending Parker's evolutionary squadron of steam and sailing ships out to the Western Approaches to practise every combination of sail and steam, principally using steamers to tow battleships.[16] Nine months later Auckland, reflecting on the results of the 1846 evolutions, set out his policy. Each large warship would be accompanied by a steam vessel capable of towing her.[17] The steamers would defend the sailing ships against other steamers, bring a fleeing enemy to action, and secure prizes.[18] The second point was vital. Alarmist views that steam would allow the French to evade a British blockade and land anywhere on the undefended coast were based on the opinion that steam was ill-suited to defence but this was far from true. In pressing for a militia Palmerston argued that the French Navy was 'on a par' with the British, would be superior in the Channel during the opening days of any war and could land 30,000 men in one night. The Navy, he contended, could not guarantee to stop them and so ships were not a complete guarantee of security:

> in the first period of war we could not put a sufficient number to sea, to have command of the sea; and even if we had what is called a decided superiority at sea we could not be secure against invasion.[19]

Wellington was more reasonable, calling for harbour defences and new bases to assist the Navy in carrying out its anti-invasion duties.[20] Initially, Auckland accepted these arguments:

> no disposition, nor possible augmentation of our naval forces could altogether secure our coasts from aggressions of a desultory, or even from those of a serious character.

Therefore he supported the call for 'large bodies of men, well trained to arms' as the only certain guarantee.[21] Palmerston even raised the shadow of Napoleon's 1805 attempt to lure the British fleet to the West Indies in order to attempt an invasion. His fears, based on a reading of Thiers' history of the Empire, were shared by Napier.[22] Despite having a senior naval officer as a brother-in-law, Rear Admiral Sir William Bowles, Third Naval Lord under Peel, Palmerston would appear to have had no idea that in three centuries of war at sea the Navy had developed a solid doctrine to cover the threat of invasion. At both the tactical and strategic levels the Royal Navy had defeated every invasion attempt since the time of Henry VIII. Reduced to the bare essentials the sailing Navy always blockaded enemy invasion shipping with a force adequate to destroy it while the battlefleet covered the enemy main strength. If either force left port they would be brought to battle and destroyed. If the enemy battlefleet and transports were encountered together the destruction of the transports was given priority. The effect of close-range broadsides on merchant vessels crowded with troops was too appalling for any sane man to risk.[23] No opponent could launch an invasion 'unless he had inflicted on our covering fleet such a defeat as would have given him command of the sea'.[24] Therefore, in the militia and fortifications debate Palmerston, Wellington and Auckland were arguing against basic principles, principles which were not affected by the changing technology of the 1840s, 1860s or the 1930s and it is clear that the French Army shared these reservations.[25]

Russell shifted his ground on the militia question which reflected internal political problems. Despite a serious shortfall in the revenue he became convinced of the need for increased defences but he was unable to decide on what was to take priority.

> It can hardly be doubted that the French have for a long time made preparations for a naval war; that such preparations can be directed against no other power than England; and that the preparations of England have been, as is usual in such cases, slackened by the security which the great victories of the end of the last war have inspired.
>
> There are three modes by which the French may injure and assail England on the breaking out of war.
>
> 1. By sending steamers to alarm our coasts and interrupt our trade as proposed by the Prince de Joinville.
> 2. By landing a force to bombard and destroy our naval and military arsenals.
> 3. By invading England with an army of 30,000 or 40,000 men, and marching at once to London.

Despite a basic faith in the Navy Russell settled on a combination of naval, militia and fortification works. This reflected a refusal to make hard choices which was, once again, for internal political reasons. Without a strong service lead, which Auckland had yet to provide, the Premier had little option. Within months the situation had changed but Palmerston continued his pressure for a militia, even if the cost forced Income Tax up from 7d to 1s in the pound.[26]

Auckland finally realised his error in January 1848. While at Windsor Castle Prince Albert asked how many steamers would be required to bring over between 10 and 30,000 infantry, up to 5,000 cavalry and ten to thirty guns. For the first time Auckland actually consulted a naval officer about the logistics of invasion, sending the query to Captain Lord John Hay, the Fourth Naval Lord. Arguing from the experience of commanding a steamer during the Spanish Carlist Wars Hay considered that a 1,000-ton steamer could carry one soldier for every ton displacement, but only 100 horses, or three guns with teams. To embark the largest force envisaged by Prince Albert would therefore require one hundred 1,000 ton steamers. Hay did not trouble to point out that the French had nowhere near this number, concentrating his argument instead on the confusion that would reign in such an unwieldy flotilla, and the inability of the steamers to defend themselves when so crowded.

> I will however venture to say that 5 steamers of the *Gorgon*'s class (1,000 ton) would effectively resist the progress of an unprotected expedition, and be the protecting force what it might, I think 20 of *Gorgon*'s class, 10 of them run at *all hazards* into the centre of the enemy's convoy would annihilate the expedition, or at least would throw it into such confusion as to materially check its advance on the coast.
>
> I will only further add that in my opinion no attempt could be made with a reasonable hope of success – to transport a force of either class across the Channel without first securing the command of the sea.[27]

Auckland was now convinced the danger of invasion, as aside from a minor raid, had never been serious. He had already assembled five suitable steamers at Portsmouth and expected to have twenty on the south coast before the year ended, in addition to those at sea with the Western Squadron.[28] The point made by Hay about the need to secure command of the sea, echoed in Corbett's summation of the experience of the sailing Navy, emphasised the long-term efforts required to maintain security. While Britain took care to maintain a superior force of naval vessels her shores could not be invaded. The question to be resolved now was in what type of warship was it essential to have a clear superiority. Hitherto, the battlefleet had been the central strength for maritime defence. Would the advance of technology alter that? This aspect of Auckland's work, the long-term policy programming, properly comes later in the chapter.

To meet the 'bolt from the blue' invasion, which Palmerston found so menacing, Auckland continually shifted his active forces to balance the French squadrons in the Channel ports and the Mediterranean. This was a common feature of nineteenth-century Admiralty business, particularly in times of crisis.

The Algiers *in service as a steamship. Although normally considered to be a Symonds design the ship was, in fact, recast by John Edye, after Symonds retired, as a 90-gun version of the* Queen, *and later lengthened for the screw.* (NMM)

The active battlefleet 1847

THE MEDITERRANEAN FLEET

Ship	*Guns*	*Supporting steamer*
Hibernia	104	*Terrible*
Albion	90	*Cyclops*
Vanguard	80	*Avenger*
Superb	80	*Gladiator*
Rodney	90	*Sidon*
Trafalgar	120	*Retribution*
Canopus	84	*Odin*
America	50	*Scourge*
Thetis	36	*Dragon*
LISBON		
Queen	110	two steamers
HOME OR CHANNEL SQUADRON		
St Vincent	120	*Centaur*
Howe	120	*Gorgon*
Britannia	120	*Sphynx*
Caledonia	120	*Stromboli*
Vengeance	84	*Geyser*
PACIFIC		
Collingwood	80 Flagship	

Auckland was equally anxious to keep the ships of the two nations apart, if only to avoid accidents.[29]

In line with Auckland's views on Third Rates, the other distant stations were occupied by razees and new 50-gun ships. The active fleet in 1847 was the most powerful peace-time mobilisation of battlefleet strength ever and the object was deterrence. Before the Russell Administration left office these ships were to be shifted around to face French forces in the Mediterranean and Channel, and Russian threats in the Baltic and the Dardanelles. In every case they proved persuasive diplomats. Baring explained the rationale to the Premier in 1850:

> The policy of the present board has been to gather its strength near home. With France powerful – and Russia, a large fleet in number and not to be despised, and the present state of affairs I am of opinion that we do not want our strength at a distance and did want it near at home...
>
> They will be moveable according to the movements of the French, but I have little doubt that our allies mean to keep their fleet at Brest, or a large portion of it.

It did not make Auckland's task any easier that the French Commander in the Mediterranean was that well-known pamphleteer de Joinville. Throughout this delicate balancing act, Auckland was permanently short of men; problems on the River Plate, in Portugal and on the coast of Ireland combined to reduce his disposable force.[30] Yet at no stage did he allow the French the fleeting luxury of even a temporary advantage in the Channel. There were always three powerful guard ships in full commission, exercised at sea and ready to join the active fleet under the dynamic Rear-Admiral Napier. In addition, the Advanced Ships – ten at Sheerness, Portsmouth and Plymouth – could be rapidly filled up with impressed men and sent to sea to counter the movements of an invasion force. From their widely separated bases at least one third of these ships could reach the central Channel whatever the wind direction, even without steam tugs. Later, Baring attempted to keep the French active fleet in the Mediterranean by reinforcing the British squadron there.

It should be emphasised that Lord John Hay's views on repelling invasion and the use of steamers were neither unique, nor even untypical; if anything Hay was a little behind the times. The senior Commanders afloat and prospective ones held advanced opinions. In the Mediterranean Admiral Parker was universally admitted to be the most experienced sea officer of the era. He had seen every stage of the development of steam power, including the introduction of the screw propellor of which he heartily approved.[31] Auckland's only major appointment, Napier, was rather more controversial. However, Napier was a pioneer of the steam warship and his paddle frigate design, the *Sidon*, was the finest vessel of her class. Along with Parker he practised towing battleships with large steamers, and in action both men would have used this new tactical combination to bring the enemy to action. Among the other senior officers, Auckland believed Lord Cochrane, now Earl of Dundonald, was the man the service looked to see placed in charge of any 'enterprise'. He understood that his predecessors back to 1835 had always intended Dundonald to have a prominent post in time of war.[32] He also valued the old Admiral's views on steam tactics, among the most advanced then available.[33] In addition, Dundonald resubmitted his poison gas plans, for the penultimate time. The target for these plans, as with so much else in the period, was Cherbourg. All three officers, and the great majority of the officer corps, would have followed Hay's outline. That none felt it necessary to set down their views, unless asked, merely indicates that they were unquestioned. The last prospective seaborne invasion, that of 1940, would have been met in exactly the same way, with the warships concentrating on the transports against all hazard. With this philosophy, adequate forces and intelligent preparation Britain had nothing to fear from a French attempt in the late 1840s; rather the French would be exposed to appalling casualties.[34] Even so, Baring believed it was essential to maintain force levels in the Channel in time of tension.[35] The strength of the Western Squadron during the Russell Administration reflected the level of danger anticipated by those in office. From a maximum of five battleships and five large steamers in 1847 Napier was soon reduced to a pair of each and sent to police the coast of Ireland in mid-1848.[36] The spare ships went to join Parker, the French having moved their active units to the Mediterranean. With the overthrow of the Orleans regime on 24 February 1848 much of the tension in Anglo-French relations disappeared, allowing Russell and Wood to press for reductions in naval spending. By 1849 there was no Western Squadron and Napier was ashore. Thereafter, annual cruises were held from Lisbon which Baring believed offered the advantage of being midway between home waters and the Mediterranean, out of sight of the British taxpayers and well suited to experiments with steam.[37]

Having established that the Royal Navy remained the first line of defence for Britain, it only remained for the Government to determine how that role could best be carried out and this only required the defending steamers to be brought into contact with invasion transports. This would require keeping watch over the principal French ports: Cherbourg, Brest, L'Orient, Rochefort, Dunkirk and Calais. At the outbreak of every war between the two nations British cruisers established a blockade of the French coast. The problem was that many outside the Navy believed that the old blockade system, the foundation of British strategy, could not be relied upon in the steam age. This was not the case, for steamers could remain at sea in any weather in which an invasion force could put to sea and their only requirement was for secure coaling facilities to keep them

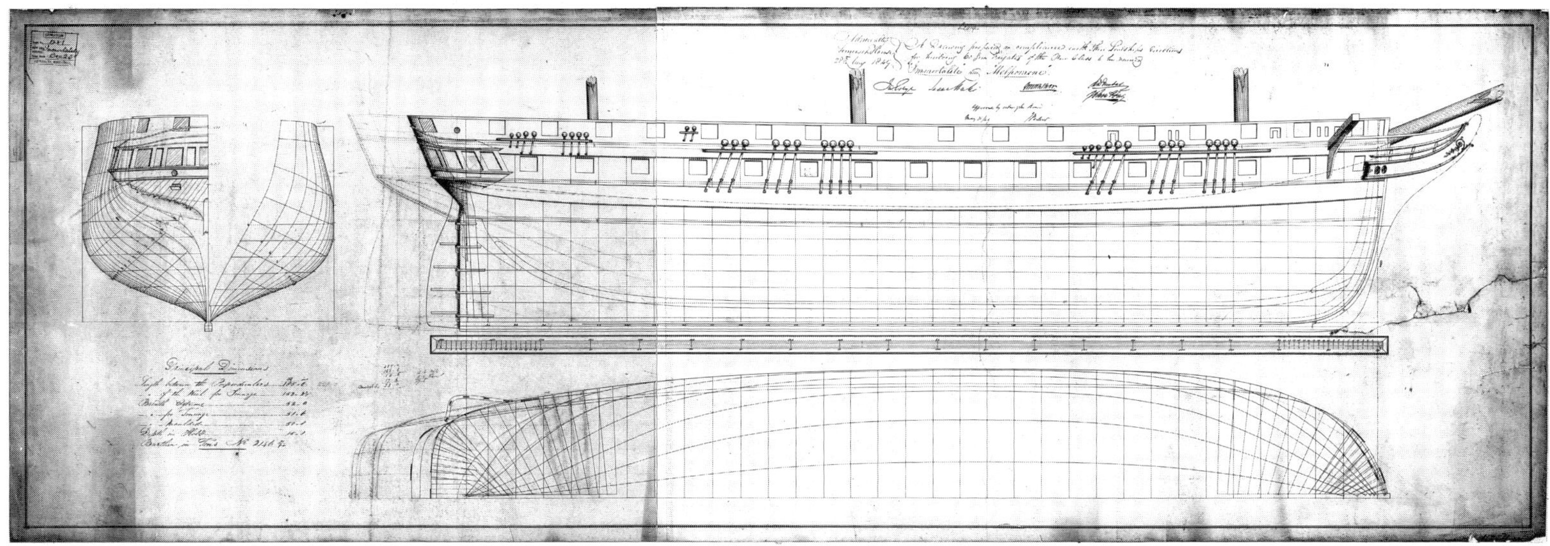

The draught adopted by the Board of Admiralty for building the 60-gun frigates Immortalite *and* Melpomene *in August 1849. Both ships were completed as 50-gun screw frigates. Although not as sharp a form as that of the* Vernon *this is still a far cry from the old hull designs, and demonstrates both John Edye's contribution to Symonds's work, and the basic soundness of the controversial surveyor and his work.* (NMM)

on station. Existing bases had been developed to support the sailing Navy but they were either too insecure for coaling or inconveniently distant from the French bases. New harbours of refuge had been ordered by the Peel Government though recent discussion of these harbours has treated them as essentially defensive.[38] This was not the intention of naval planners. Even Wellington realised that seapower was the key to the defence of Britain and he saw the harbours of refuge in the Channel Islands as the bases from which blockading steamers could cover Cherbourg and Brest. With a powerful force at Alderney, only 25 miles from Cherbourg, any invasion could be intercepted. Similar facilities as far east as Harwich and the Downs would cover Dunkirk and Calais.[39] The Chancellor of the Exchequer, Sir Charles Wood, had been First Secretary at the Admiralty between 1835 and 1839 and demonstrating something of the service view he declared Alderney 'commands Cherbourg and the entrance to the Channel'. The Harbours of Refuge,

> are in fact, under that pacific name, to be used not only for that purpose, but as deep water harbours for steamers so as to lie in war, for the purposes of guarding the Channel.

Of more significance he was prepared to fund the works.[40]

Palmerston's famous letter of December 1859 is often used to support the argument that steam blockades could be unreliable.[41] The object of this letter was to persuade a reluctant Gladstone to fund the forts now suitably named 'Palmerston's Follies'. It can be argued that Palmerston himself did not believe what he wrote. During the Russian War (1854–56), British steamers kept up a very effective blockade of the Russian Black Sea and the Baltic coast, so effective that in 1856 Palmerston himself agreed to modify the old rules of maritime warfare under the provisions of the Declaration of Paris.[42]

Naval strategy during the period 1846–52 focussed on war with France. Steam added a new dimension but it did not alter the essential basis of war planning, and nor did it give the invaders any advantage. British coastal defence had always been conducted on the coast of the enemy and with steam new possibilities were opening. The screw steam fleet would be a far more flexible and dangerous instrument than had been any wind-driven force.

In 1849 the sense of danger shifted. The new French Government had been forced to cut back on naval expenditure and while ministers maintained a watching brief, they were prepared to dispatch forces to the West Indies in the summer. By the autumn the latest crisis in Russo-Turkish relations brought Parker's Mediterranean Fleet to the entrance of the Dardanelles. Baring was concerned with the danger posed by the Russian Baltic Fleet as only four battleships were in commission at home. Advised by Minto and Russell, he began to build up the domestic reserve and kept a significant Western Squadron close by under Fanshawe Martin.[43] In the following year the French stepped up work at Cherbourg and Brest, then sent the bulk of their fleet back to the Mediterranean. Baring followed them with reinforcements for Parker, and advice that relations had now improved.[44]

Throughout his term in office Baring remained confident that any invasion could be met and destroyed at sea. In the event, the last great crisis for the sailing battlefleet involved an altogether less impressive task. Parker's fleet blockaded the harbour of Piraeus in support of the financial claims of Dom Pacifico against the Greek Government. Despite severe criticism from France and the domestic Opposition, Palmerston secured the compensation demanded and won a resounding victory in the Commons with his most famous speech. Battlefleets were the most flexible instruments of diplomacy, as both Nelson and Palmerston were well aware. With so large and powerful a fleet Britain could exert influence in almost every country, with the bare minimum of effort, and deter the most powerful of her rivals. Between 1815 and 1850 her statesmen maintained this fleet and were never afraid to use it.

The reform of naval administration

The short-term policy response to the invasion threat was not in any way remarkable. It was in the overhaul of long-term construction policy that Auckland, and to a lesser extent Baring, made a radical break with the immediate past. This break was vital if Britain was to maintain the battlefleet strength that lay at the heart of her naval supremacy and strategic policy. In this context the programme of the Haddington Board had been a disaster, as Symonds observed: 'I am sorry to say that since 1834 there is a great falling off of ships of the line which it will take many years to recover'.[45] The post-1846 programmes provided the new battleships that made up the steam fleet of the 1850s, and in that respect proved to be peculiarly timely.

In the short term the Committee of Reference was retained;

Hay became Fourth Naval Lord and kept the chair of the Committee. Auckland accepted Ellenborough's advice on the need for change at the Surveyor's Office but realised nothing could be done while Symonds remained. However, removing him was no easy matter for the shakey Russell Administration could ill afford to offend Portland, who was prepared to support a Whig Government. To avoid this Auckland used the harsh criticisms of the Committee of Reference, which he did not entirely support, to pressurise the 65-year-old Symonds to retire. The final blows were the order to take down the frame of the half-built 90-gun ship *Princess Royal* and rebuild her with a different hull form, replacing Symonds's characteristic deep 'V' with the 'U' form of the older constructions. Symonds was ordered to refer all designs to the Committee, while the Board remained free to obtain designs from any source they might select.[46] Symonds, having conveniently reached 65, the age for superannuation, retired claiming ill health. Auckland was able to smooth the retirement with a handsome pension, fulsome praise and a promise to consult him in the future.

With Symonds out of the way Auckland began to lay the foundations of an effective naval policy in which the vital element was a long-term construction programme. First, he had to remove Hay, who had become a nuisance with his outdated and potentially costly views on steam ships.[47] Even before Symonds's departure Auckland had begun to take the heat out of the development of the screw steamer. Accepting Ellenborough's advice he suspended those ships not yet laid down in October 1846 and then, on Symonds's advice, suspended the iron steamers and the conversion of the older ships.[48] These steps were entirely correct. The experimental nature of all screw steamers in 1846–47 caused repeated and expensive modifications. The frame of the small converted frigate *Amphion*, for example, had been taken down so many times that Symonds was convinced she would eventually cost more than the largest battleship.

A new Surveyor was required to control the reformed office. Hay had already demonstrated how not to act, leading Auckland to rename the Committee of Reference the Council of Science and in order to end his annoying career membership was restricted to naval architects. For sound policy he turned to one of the outstanding officers of the nineteenth century, Captain Sir Baldwin Walker. It was convenient that Walker was then in the Pacific and did not reach Britain until February 1848. This left the Surveyor's Office to be run by Edye, under close control from the Board. Walker was appointed on the 5th and in his instructions Auckland redefined the duties of the post, ending the confusion inherent in the 1832 process. The Surveyor was to be a policy maker, not a designer. He had two assistant surveyors, Edye and Isaac Watts, a pupil of the First School of Naval Architecture, for detailed design and was to refer to the Council of Science, composed of educated Master Shipwrights, when the Admiralty deemed it necessary. Walker was to liaise between the Board and the designers, using his experience as a sea officer to guide his decisions. He was to control the dockyards and the material of the Navy, much as the old Controller had. Among the objectives were the need to ensure greater economy, the avoidance of 'rash experiments' and 'ill-considered expenditure'. These arguments also helped secure Treasury sanction for a small increase in the salaries of the Surveyor's Office, partially offset by ending the posts of the Master Attendant at Chatham and the Officers of Works at Woolwich.[49] While economy had also been the object behind the 1832 reforms, it had been carried to extremes for political purposes.

The dockyards

The new round of reform required a more serious consideration of the dockyards than had been made in 1832. Essentially, the 1832 process had reduced the number of shipwrights without improving efficiency. Auckland ordered a general review of the dockyards and the Navy afloat, particularly the battleships. His intention was to establish a three-year programme to prepare fifty First and Second Rate battleships afloat.[50] One month later Walker submitted a very detailed five-year programme of construction and repair, warning that the general adoption of the screw propeller would not be long delayed. This work load could be carried out by a dockyard labour force of 3,500 shipwrights, with the other trades in proportion, and would necessitate an annual expenditure of 30,000 loads of timber (approximately 20,000 tons).[51] Auckland then ordered a Committee of Revision to report on the dockyards. This body comprised the Fourth Naval Lord, Captain Alexander Milne, the Accountant General, John Bromley and Walker under the Chairmanship of Henry Ward, the First Secretary. The report was submitted two months later, revealing both Walker's growing stature and his confidence in a workforce of 3,500 shipwrights, the value of piece work and the success of using experienced Naval Officers as Dockyard Superintendents. Auckland was not entirely convinced that so few men could meet the need, but gave way in the interests of economy.[52] The report was then published and circulated.[53] By that time Auckland was dead, after a series of strokes in the first days of 1849, but his policy was confirmed in February.[54] The work of Ellenborough and Auckland was brought to a conclusion so that the long-term policy of the Navy was placed on a sound foundation for the first time since 1832. In 1851 Berkeley had nothing but praise for the new Surveyor:

> there never was so fortunate a choice as the appointment of Sir B. Walker to the Surveyorship of the Navy. As a naval officer and thorough seaman he was known to be *A – No. 1* He has proved himself fully equal to the Post of Surveyor and although nominally I superintend the Department he leaves me nothing to do but write *approve* to his propositions and I sincerely wish – ex-officio, that he had a seat at the Board.[55]

Ellenborough, Auckland and Baring all worked to remove political influence and patronage from the dockyards. The leading Dockyard Superintendent of the 1840s, Admiral Sir William Shireff, made the ending of political influence the *sine qua non* for any efficient use of the yards. When the First Secretary of the Duke of Northumberland's brief Admiralty, Sir Augustus Stafford, made a crude attempt to use the dockyards for election advantage, the resulting outcry signalled the complete success of Auckland's policies.[56] Dockyard appointments, from the Captain Superintendent to the humblest workman, were in future to be made on professional merit.

The Committee on Naval and Military Estimates had been called to investigate the high estimates proposed for 1848. Graham, one of the more prominent members, had strong opinions on this subject. He was certain that a 5 per cent Income or War Tax would either produce war by exciting rivals, or create unrest at home.

> You know that I have always considered the Naval Expenditure most prodigal; and I am certain that great savings might even now be effected in that department without impairing the efficiency of the service.

> Look at the Coast of Africa, New Zealand, & the Rio Plata, not to mention Canada and the Cape of Good Hope, and then say whether we might not retrench somewhat of our colonial expenditure when we are called on to concentrate our force and to prepare for the defence of our homes.[57]

After Auckland's death Russell offered Graham the post of First Lord as an encouragement for the Peelites to join his Administration which they were effectively keeping in office with their support. Graham turned the offer down because Russell 'does not appear to me sufficiently impressed with the urgent necessity of large retrenchments'. He supported the selection of Baring as a man capable of stemming the tide. He was particularly scathing of the Administration's inability to act on any of the recommendations of the Committee particularly those relating to the distant stations.[58]

The Establishment

Between 1830 and 1847 economy-minded Admiralties had ordered so few battleships that the strength in that class of ship, up to the Russian War, was made up by ships ordered between 1795 and 1826. By 1846 only eight of Symonds's battleships had been launched. The total British force of battleships, over sixty afloat with another twenty in various stages of construction appeared impressive, being double the strength of France. In fact, the position was decidedly unsatisfactory, and Auckland realised that there were still twenty Third Rate 74s on the list. In place of the old figures for the Establishment of between seventy and one hundred battleships he made the bold decision of including only First and Second Rates in his figure of fifty ships afloat. By mid-1848 Auckland was forced to launch three of Symonds's 80-gun ships, *Colossus*, *Mars* and *Meeanee*, to maintain this figure. Even then he was guilty of a degree of sharp practice, for on his list were the 50-year-old large Third Rates *Kent* and *Achille* along with *Revenge* which would soon be scrapped, and *Foudroyant*, *Bellerophon*, *Indus*, *Hindostan* and *Cambridge*.[59] Alongside the fifty ships afloat Auckland also required fifteen building and the same number of duplicate frames ready for immediate erection. Walker's programme of works submitted in October 1848 provided a detailed course of action to meet these criteria by making better use of the existing dockyard labour force.

Auckland was convinced that the old Third Rates, the staple of the postwar fleet, were no longer fit to carry the prestige of the Royal Navy in European waters. This was an overdue recognition of the progress in design and armament over the past three decades. Faced with the possibility of a collision between Parker and de Joinville in the Mediterranean he observed:

> I have great doubts upon the expediency of largely employing 3rd rates. They have become unfit to cope with the ships of other nations, and their tactic and handling are not good practice for ships of the present day.

The French were already employing ships of the heaviest classes, with only a handful of upgunned 74s.[60]

To meet the challenge Auckland needed to overhaul the Establishment, excluding Third Rates, in order to produce a fleet ready to meet that of France. While many have criticised the Royal Navy for persisting with the 74s these vessels were not only excellent value on distant stations, particularly in the First China War, but their survival as effective units for so long was a credit to the dockyards. Furthermore, Auckland was quick to find a new role for the blockships. Even before their completion the First Lord was telling Russell: 'they will, I am satisfied, be powerful instruments of defence, and possibly under favourable circumstances of attack'.[61] The target of their attack was perfectly clear. While *Achille* and *Kent* were over 50 years old, several ships had seen out 40 years afloat, when the effective life of a large wooden warship was not considered to be over 30 years. Succeeding Boards of Admiralty had been living on the resources built up by Seppings and Byam Martin before 1832, a position that Auckland attempted to repair.[62]

Baring was generally content to follow the guidelines laid down by Auckland, with Walker's 5-year-plan as the basic document. Walker's influence grew, his views on general policy and the introduction of steam being developed from the experience of 1845 and further experiments at sea.[63] Walker survived six changes of Government which created the continuity of policy that had been so lacking after 1832. This was part of the new professional approach to naval administration.

The 1847–48 programme, the first over which the new Administration had any influence, demonstrated some improvement over the haphazard conduct of the Peel years. In place of the iron screw steamers and the multiplication of private designs, the new Board began to tamper with Symonds's ships in a way which reflected old prejudices. The Committee of Reference's design for the new 90-gun *Caesar* was only a revised *Rodney* while Symonds's *Princess Royal* and *Hannibal* were taken down and modified. The 80-gun *Brunswick* had her mid-section reduced and filled out; the *Windsor Castle*-class ships were lengthened to carry 120 guns; the *Algiers*, now a 90-gun ship, was initially ordered to be built on lines provided by the Chatham Committee, but commenced as a razee *Queen* modified by Edye. The one new design, Edye's *Audacious*, was a screw propellor 80-gun ship with a flush upper deck armed with ten heavy pivot guns. By the end of the year Hayes' suspended *Agamemnon* had been ordered as a sister ship. The experimental days of the propeller were over, a new order of seapower was beginning, and the mark of the Royal Navy was that Auckland's Board made the decision to enter the steam age with two new vessels in 1847. The importance of this design was obvious for the only sailing ships designed after this vessel were the *Orion*-class 80s, ordered in December 1847. It should come as no surprise to learn that not one of the battleships discussed during the preparation of the 1847–48 estimates would enter the water as a sailing vessel.

Conclusion

The reform of the civil administration of the Navy by Lord Auckland was the most important change in defence policy during the Russell Administration; more significant than any step taken in regard to the militia or the permanent defences. Throughout the Admiralty the impact of Auckland's term was to improve efficiency by introducing younger Naval Lords who were not necessarily Government supporters. Alexander Milne was the outstanding example.[64] The flaw in the new system was less obvious. Auckland's reforms depended on the personal qualities of the new appointees. While the Surveyor had a duty to provide the Board with policy guidelines, the Board had no duty to seek such guidance, or give it any attention when submitted. In short, the Board had no obligation to act as a policy-making body and the successes of 1846–49 reflected Auckland's personal contribution rather than a new administrative structure.

Part Three

THE SURVEYOR'S OFFICE

1 *Introduction*

The Surveyor's Office lay at the heart of the decision-making process that governed the design of all new warships. The Surveyor of the Navy, being responsible for the design, construction and repair of the Royal Navy's warships and the management of the Royal Dockyards, was the second most important member of the Navy Board after the Controller.

The office of Surveyor of the Navy had a continuous history going back to 1660. Until 1832 it had always been held by one or more professional shipwrights with experience of the Royal Dockyards, almost always as Master Shipwright at one of the five principal yards. As the expert constructor on the Board the incumbent had a strong position in the debate on design and construction.

During the period under review the Surveyor's Office was located in Somerset House, along with the other offices of the Navy Board. The physical separation of the Admiralty at Whitehall and the Navy Board at the other end of the Strand allowed the Controller to assume a major role in naval administration. After the abolition of the Navy Board the Surveyor was isolated from the remaining centre of decision-making, and in consequence lost much of the influence he had once held.

This section of the book is concerned to examine the office, the three major incumbents and the development of design philosophy. In many ways it forms the heart of the book, but can only be understood in the wider context provided by the detailed coverage of the policy making debates in the previous section.

The Surveyors of the Navy: 1815–1850

1813 (4 June)	Sir Henry Peake
	Joseph Tucker
	Robert Seppings
1822 (20 February)	Joseph Tucker
	Sir Robert Seppings
1831 (1 March)	Sir Robert Seppings
1832 (1 April)	Captain William Symonds
1847 (June)	resigns
1847–8	Deputy Surveyor John Edye
1848 (5 February)	Captain Sir Baldwin Walker

Naval architecture, the policy makers and ship design

It is now widely accepted that the Royal Navy was belated in adopting a scientific base for ship design.[1] The criticism relates specifically to the period after 1832 but is equally applicable to the years after 1815 and it begs the question as to why politicians and naval administrators did not employ better qualified personnel. The answer is simple. They lacked the education needed to make any accurate judgement of the merits of the competing scientific and empirical schools. This led them to adopt a simplistic and unreliable measurement of performance, the sailing trial, and stand by the results.

It is clear from the attitudes of the Navy Board, the Admiralty, Byam Martin and even Seppings himself that the scientific approach to naval design was at a discount in 1815. Naval architecture was an interesting theoretical issue but it was regarded as entirely detached from practical application. Those who built experimental ships were few in number and all were considered eccentric. Samuel Bentham and the Earl of Stanhope were the most prominent before 1815. The Navy Board's one foray into this field, the 74-gun *Plantagenet* encouraged less, rather than more experimentation.

After the winding up of the Society for the Improvement of Naval Architecture at the turn of the eighteenth century the case for a scientific education was carried by Lord Barham. The formation of the First School of Naval Architecture in 1809 was a response to the findings of Barham's Commission to revise the Civil Affairs of the Admiralty, set up in 1803. The 3rd and 8th reports of 1808 recommended the formation of a School attached to the Royal Naval College at Portsmouth. These were carried into effect by an Order in Council in 1809, courses beginning in January 1811. However, it should be stressed that, whatever might be claimed by the descendants of these early professional naval architects, the School was not seen, in the short term, as the source for improved, science-based designs. Superior Shipwright Officers were to be raised up through the School to compete for design opportunities, not to have them by right.

After 20 years of war, all policy makers were confident that the best qualities could be obtained by replicating the most successful designs, ships that were familiar to all concerned. In the period up to 1830 no-one in authority suggested that there was a need to adopt new full forms for battleships. Under pressure from well-connected yachtsmen with new ideas on naval architecture they preferred to use empirical methods, working up new forms from experimental yachts and brigs. Only in the 1840s was the Board prepared to order a new battleship based on scientific principles and even then the new constructors had to prove their merit with an experimental brig before being given this opportunity. It should come as little surprise that the science deployed was that of Frederik af Chapman who, through Professor Inman's translation, dominated the work of the First School. Unable to comprehend why the new designs by Read, Chatfield and Creuze took so long to prepare the Cockburn Board cancelled further work, largely on grounds of expense.

Before 1830 modifications were made to the form of the standard designs; for example, extra beam was added to the *Caledonia*, greater fullness to the *Canopus*, and their structure was radically improved. Even the one new design of the period, the *Nile*, was little more than a razee *Caledonia*. Seppings was quite content to tinker with favoured drafts, and in this he was justified by the results; his ships were reliable, effective and uncontroversial.

When Sir James Graham appointed Symonds to replace Seppings he did so on the advice of naval officers who had seen the new system at sea, and judged it on an entirely practical level. Returning from the trial of the *Vernon*, which he made the acid test of both Symonds's appointment and the entire 1832 reform process, Graham told the Duke of Portland, 'after what I have seen today...' it should be evident that science counted for nothing. Quite simply, the School had not been as successful in their experimental craft as Symonds. The trial was everything, and this forced the Surveyor's rivals to meet him on his home ground, the yacht race. They could make little headway attacking him for lack of science, and his retort was to lambast their lack of practical experience both at sea and in construction.

Lord Melville criticised the appointment of Symonds as an attack on science, but Barrow deflected such comments by comparing the relative success of Seppings and the more highly educated Jean Louis Barallier. Furthermore, Symonds was not the only naval officer to build warships on non-scientific lines; Admiral Hayes and Captain Elliot were both successful with brigs and frigates designed in a similar fashion.

In conclusion, the policy makers of the period were not equipped to reach informed conclusions on the value of science, and quickly became disillusioned with the cost and delay it appeared to involve. Political weight and prejudice were far stronger influences on design than science. In this respect the staff and pupils of the School were doubly unfortunate. They lacked the level of support that Symonds had acquired through his success as a yacht builder and they did not have the numbers to gain political support in return for their votes. Furthermore, their cause was too dull to evoke the kind of enthusiasm generated by one of Symonds's great yachts under a press of sail. Only Hume spoke up for them in the House; others, most notably Cockburn, merely used them to attack Symonds.

2 Sir Robert Seppings and the Advance of Naval Architecture: 1815–32

This chapter will consider the career of Sir Robert Seppings and discuss the advances in the structure of warships that he developed. His work should be seen as a vital aspect of the policy of the Admiralty Administration of Lord Melville, under whom he served for the greatest part of his career.

Sir Robert Seppings: 1767–1840

In an official career lasting 50 years Sir Robert Seppings resolved the major problems that had hitherto constrained the development of the wooden warship. His work made individual ships larger, stronger and more durable and it was a vital element in the postwar process of maintaining naval supremacy.

Born in Fakenham, Norfolk, one of seven children of a cattle dealer, Seppings spent part of his youth delivering letters. The vital break with his past came in 1781 when his father died and he was adopted by his maternal uncle, Captain John Milligen, then living in Plymouth. In 1782 Milligen secured his nephew an apprenticeship with the Master Shipwright, John Henslow, previously First Assistant Surveyor 1771–75 and a man marked out for the highest post. While Seppings is normally described as an ordinary Working Apprentice Shipwright, the speed of his rise in the service and connection with Henslow makes it altogether more likely that he was a Premium Apprentice, a situation acquired by the payment of a suitable fee. This is confirmed by his application to the Prince Regent in 1819, in which he complains of being a 'considerable expense to his friends during that apprenticeship'.[2] Whatever the limits of his education in Norfolk, particularly in mathematics, the young man was able to benefit from this opportunity. The seven-year apprenticeship ended in 1789, and within eight years Seppings had risen through the grades of shipwright, quarterman and foreman to the post of assistant to the Master Shipwright, then Joseph Tucker, with whom he was to serve as a Surveyor after 1813. By this time Henslow had moved on, becoming one of the Surveyors of the Navy in 1784, a post he held until 1806, which suggests that his apprentice deserves all the more credit for his success. Henslow supported Seppings's appointment as Master Shipwright at Chatham in 1804 during Earl St Vincent's attack on the Navy Board, but thereafter he had to rely on his own merits and connections.

This appointment was in part earned by his work on an improved method of hanging rudders, adopted by the Navy Board in 1800, and as a result of procedures he introduced for

Sir Robert Seppings (1767–1840) as Surveyor of the Navy. In 1814 Seppings explained his system as follows.'The strength of a fabric consists not so much in the quantity of the materials of which it is composed as in the dispositions, the connection and security of its general parts' and 'the strength of a ship let its construction be what it may, can never exceed that of its weakest parts'. (NMM)

docking ships. The latter was one of his major responsibilities as Assistant. In 1801 he produced a new system which replaced the labour-intensive and costly process of lifting ships up in dock on blocks, by shifting wedges which allowed 20 men to carry out the work of 500 in two-thirds of the time. The system was demonstrated in 1801 using the *Canopus*, and not in 1800 on the 112-gun *San Josef* as is normally stated. Comparison with the docking of the *Spartiate* revealed a cost of £30.11.3d instead of £253.6.9d and only one day instead of three. In 1803 the Admiralty awarded Seppings £1,000, while the Society of Arts conferred their Gold Medal. The advantages of the idea were clear, and in the middle of a long war particularly timely. By 1806 St Vincent held the highest opinion of Seppings, recommending him to the new First Lord as eminently suitable to become one of the Surveyors. In the event he would have to wait another seven years for that post.[3]

The problem of structural weakness

Seppings's most important contribution to the battlefleet lay in the field of the structure of the wooden ship. This work provided the strength for a marked increase in the length and weight of warships and merchant vessels after 1815.

Before 1800 the wooden warship was almost invariably built of transverse frames with longitudinal planking. This was, as Seppings demonstrated, very far from the ideal design to resist the strains imposed on ships of any length in a seaway. In particular, the effect produced by leaving the bow and stern unsupported, known as 'hogging', degraded the fastenings of the ship and led, eventually, to the sheer being broken. Once the fastenings had been damaged the seams would open and render the ship leaky and prone to further degradation. Modern vessels bend as a single piece, but the wooden warship could all too easily be reduced to a loosely-assembled collection of parts. Experimental vessels were built in France, Spain and Russia, but none demonstrated any worthwhile advantages. The first fully effective scheme was that devised by Gabriel Snodgrass, Chief Surveyor of the East India Company. Familiar with the problems of large ships wracked out of shape by sea service, Snodgrass developed the use of iron reinforcement, additional thick planking and transverse diagonals to retain the stiffness of the frames. Despite the opposition of the Surveyors the Snodgrass system was widely used in 1805. The famous programme of doubling and bracing, applied as an emergency measure, provided a fleet for the North Sea but it was not developed for use in new vessels.[4] The ships subjected to the Snodgrass system were the 98s *London* and *Formidable*, the 80s *Pompee* and *Caesar*, and the 74s *Thunderer, Audacious* and *Captain* all at Plymouth. At Portsmouth the 98-gun *Prince George*, the 80-gun *Gibraltar*, and the 74s *Bellona, Canada, Defiance, Ganges* and *Zealous* were similarly treated.[5]

As Master Shipwright at Chatham, one of the major building and repairing yards, Seppings was able to continue his work on the reform of the structural design. In 1800 he had repaired the 36-gun *Glenmore*, a fir-built Fifth Rate launched in 1796, using his own ideas on structural strength. This experience enabled him to propose an alternative to the Snodgrass system of doubling and internal bracing.

The ship to be repaired, the large 74-gun *Kent*, was in an advanced state of structural collapse. Nelson had sent her home after expressing doubts as to her ability to reach Britain. Seppings argued that Snodgrass's methods were inadequate and put forward his own plan which would use diagonal braces along the sides of the ship. He claimed that this would produce a stronger ship, use less timber and hold the sheer better. The success of the measure can be seen in the career of the *Kent* which was still on the list of Advanced Ships in 1850 and later used as a sheer hulk before being broken up in 1881. In 1806 the Navy Board gave permission for further work on a frigate and another 74. The large 74-gun *Warspite*, launched in 1807, was fitted with a modified diagonal frame using a considerable amount of second-hand timber. When the *Warspite* was cut down into a 50-gun ship in 1837, Admiral Sir George Elliot was not impressed with the durability of Seppings's work:

> As far as they have been able to examine she is by no means in a state of great decay, and what there is appears to me chiefly caused by the old system of placing a quantity of diagonal timber of large size, from the keel to the lower deck beams with longitudinal pieces of the same size in the angles. All the fresh water which is wasted in filling tanks, or leaks & slops into the hold is caught by these riders and the decay begins on both riders and the timbers at the upper edge of them. I believe the system is given up, if not a sight of *Warspite*'s hold would, I think be enough to knock it on the head, a more mischevious waste of timber could hardly be devised, and the expense of such masses of timber and the long copper bolts which go even through the outer plank must be very great.[6]

This is a rather harsh analysis, given the age of the ship, and although the collection of fresh water on the riders was a major weakness, it had not been identified as such in 1809.

In February 1810 Seppings proposed a full adoption of the diagonal principle, and secured permission to use it during the large repair of three old ships, the *Tremendous* in 1810 and *Ramillies* and *Albion* in 1811. The four elements of the system were: the diagonal trussed frames; filling in of the bottom and the caulking of the ceiling; continuous shelf pieces to connect the frames to the beams; and diagonal deck planking.

Filling in the frame with small pieces of oak, and then cementing over the resulting mass of timbers was an additional reinforcement for the frame. Initially, water-based cement caused decay, but the substitution of coal tar and linseed oil ensured the longevity of the ship. The resulting solid body of timber proved extremely strong in a series of groundings, notably of the frigate *Pique* and the 84-gun *Formidable*. Continuous shelf pieces had been used by French constructors for some years, but as with so much of Seppings's system the secret lay in the complete plan, and not just with the individual elements. On completion the Surveyors of the Navy inspected the *Tremendous* and claimed to find no advantage, despite a clear demonstration that she had suffered almost no deflection on being undocked. However, her officers gave her high praise, while the offices of Malta Dockyard commented on the lack of movement in her upperworks. The opposition of the Surveyors was something Seppings would have to live with for the rest of his career. His success encouraged Barrow to call a meeting of scientists on 24 November 1811 to consider Seppings's work. Thomas Young's tortuous mathematical report accepted most of the system, but was far too complex to be of any use to the Admiralty. It is of interest that within days of Barrow's meeting Napoleon had details of the discussion and invited Charles Dupin to comment.

The relationship with Barrow proved to be a fitting replacement for that with Henslow. Barrow persuaded that high-minded nobleman, Sir Charles Yorke, to order the adoption of the system, which was carried out on 29 October 1812, and publicly defended Seppings from those who suggested he had plagiarised the ideas of others from the pages of the influential *Quarterly Review*.

Seppings was elected to the Royal Society in late 1814, the first Surveyor to achieve this distinction for many years, following the publication of his pamphlet, 'On a new principle of constructing His Majesty's Ships of War'. In this paper he used the example of the five-barred gate, familiar from the Norfolk countryside of his childhood, to demonstrate the value of the diagonal, triangulating system.

Seppings was active in the affairs of the Society, taking part in the election of new members, and discussing his ideas with such luminaries as Babbage. In 1818 he was awarded a second Gold Medal for the diagonal system.[7] Yorke was also a member of the Royal Society. Seppings's membership gave him a distinction that emphasised the degree to which he had risen above the professional limits of the dockyard-raised Surveyors. While this invested his work with an added authority it was certainly not conducive to good relations with his fellow shipwright officers and it is evident that his fellow Surveyors Peake and Tucker resented their famous colleague.[8]

After experience with the rebuilt ships Seppings used his system on new vessels, the first being the 120-gun *Howe* building under his supervision at Chatham and ordered in September 1812. Seppings claimed that the final version of his diagonal system saved almost 10 per cent of the weight of a 74-gun ship, and made the vessel far stronger. The saving in timber, particularly the large pieces of oak, was an important part of the overall scheme.

Rivals and critics claimed that the new framing would waste timber, take up space in the hold, prove too expensive and spoil sailing qualities that they believed depended on the elasticity of the ship. The practical response was to modify the design until it used smaller timbers, second-hand materials for the fillings and even the frames, and allowed major elements of the frame to be constructed from more small pieces.[9]

As a means of defending himself Seppings became a master of the pamphlet war, and in this the friendship of Barrow must have been a great advantage. He wasted no opportunity to trumpet his successes, both in science and sailing, but despite the success of the *Tremendous* the Navy Board was reluctant to use the new system for anything beyond repair work. Peake and Tucker argued against the universal adoption of the Seppings system on the grounds that it had not been given an adequate trial but the Admiralty was not put off by such self-serving criticism and ordered the universal adoption of diagonal frames.[10] The first ship ordered with the new frame was the *Malabar*, a 74-gun ship to be built at Bombay.

> The Commissioner is to be informed that the interior of the ship is to be built in one respect on a new principle, by omitting the ceiling and substituting diagonal riders and straps according to a plan of Mr Seppings.[11]

This was not the end of the issue. The Board was still undecided and took the opportunity provided by the docking of the *Albion* four months later to ask for another report.[12]

The final round of practical trials of the diagonal principle involved the extremes of structural strength, and the ships used were the badly hogged old ex-Danish 74, the *Justitia*, the rebuilt *Albion* and the new *Howe*. The *Justitia* was docked at Portsmouth just prior to her demolition and when she had settled on the blocks sights, placed on the upper deck, proved her sheer had broken 2ft $3\frac{1}{4}$in. She was then equipped with a series of temporary diagonal trusses in the hold stretching up from the keelson to the gun deck beams. These were arranged slanting up toward the bow and stern, the wrong layout

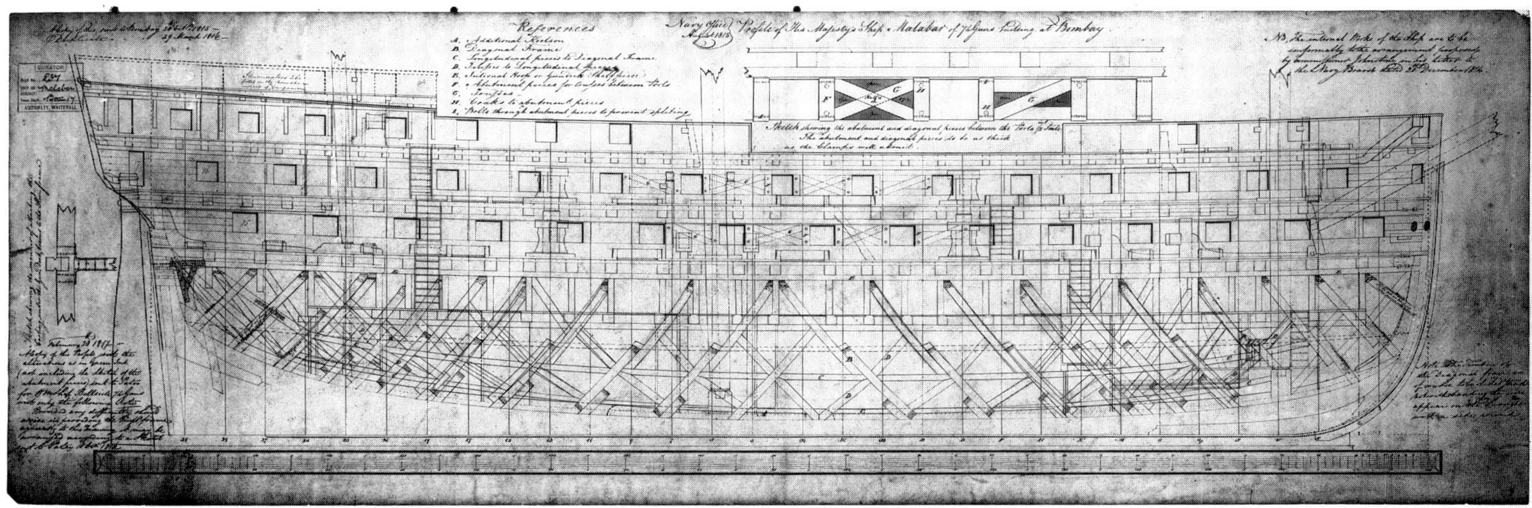

Profile of Malabar, *a Bombay-built 74-gun ship, the first to be ordered after the final defeat of Napoleon and the first to incorporate the major elements of Seppings's system. This plans shows the layout of the diagonal hull timbers and the bracing pieces employed between the gunports.* (NMM)

The stern of the Camperdown, *100 guns, serving as the coal hulk* Pitt *in the 1890s. This style of stern was in vogue until the adoption of Seppings's design. There is a defect in the negative running across the photograph.* (IWM)

Seppings's round stern, on the right, compared to the previous square form, emphasising the degree of all-round fire obtained in the new form. The glazed in quarters contain the officers' heads. (ScM)

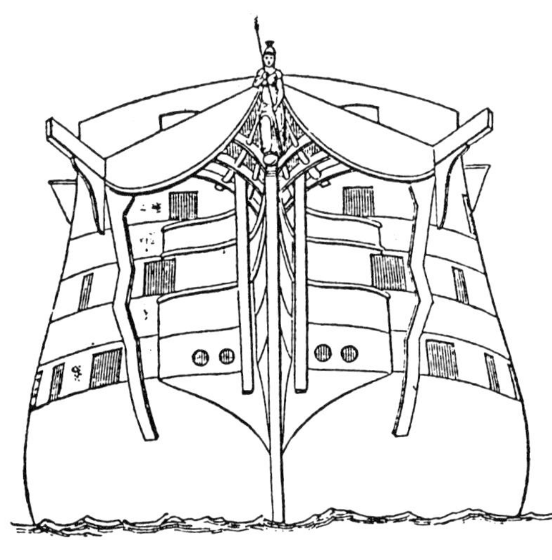

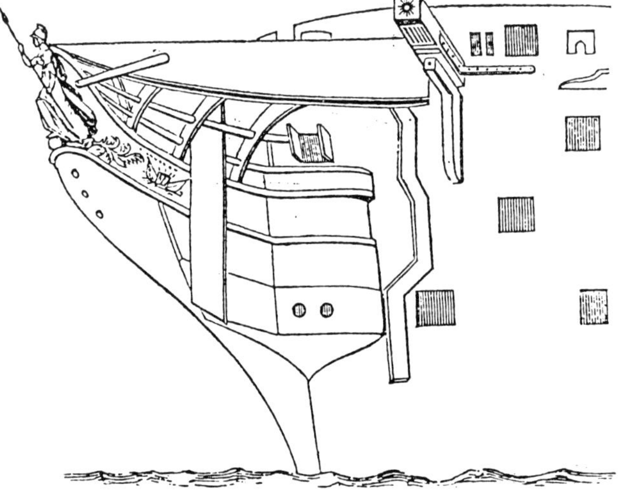

The round bow as built on the 120-gun Britannia. (Author)

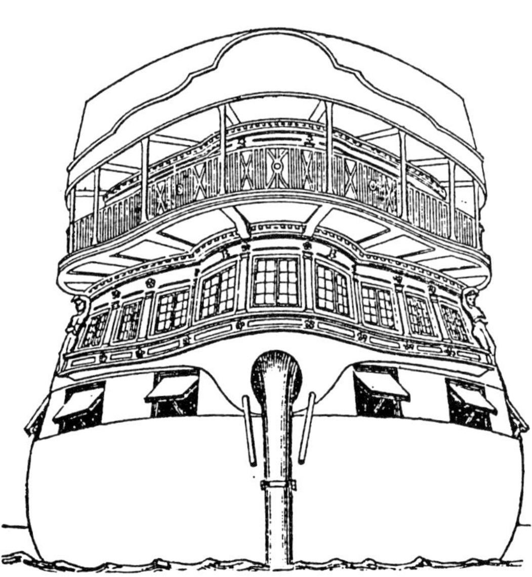

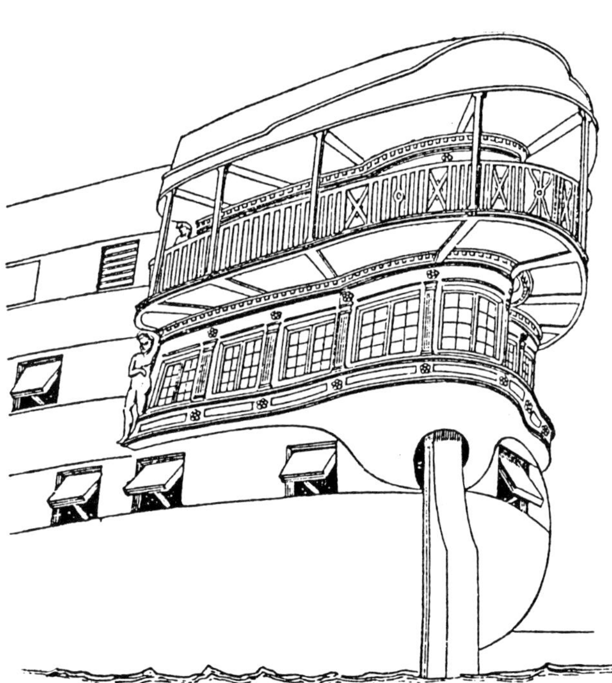

The original round stern, as fitted to Kent, *78 guns, in 1817. This form was unsatisfactory on both aesthetic and practical grounds, being hideous to behold and lacking adequate toilet facilities.* Formidable *and* Prince Regent *were similarly fitted.* (Author)

according to modern naval architects, and furthermore they were not cross-braced. In addition, the gun ports were fitted with single or double cross-braces. When floated she went up $14\frac{1}{2}$in at the mid-deck, and another $2\frac{1}{2}$in over the following 24 hours. On removing the braces she returned to within 1in of her original state. The braces in the gun ports alone were able to improve her sheer by 3in.[13]

In his pamphlet of 1817 Seppings made reference to the comparative performance of the *Howe* with her sister, the *St Vincent*; the service of the rebuilt *Albion* at Algiers; and the new diagonal deck of the *Northumberland* on the passage to St Helena, taking Bonaparte into captivity. In it he acknowledged the influence of the design of a bridge at Schaffhausen in order to refute claims of plagiarism made by other naval architects and to emphasise the degree to which he saw his work as part of the contemporary revolution in engineering. If further proof of success was required, the arrival of the Indian-built 74 *Malabar*, which had sailed from Bombay without any of her structural ironwork, was conclusive:

> although the ship was loaded with timber in the hold and on the decks up to the upper deck, and encountered four very severe gales of wind on her passage, yet their Lordships will perceive by the survey that there is but little appearance of any of her materials or fastenings having been disturbed, which we consider to be an additional proof of the strength and security of this system of shipbuilding.[14]

In 1817 Seppings abolished the use of chocks between the frame timbers which he argued were a cause of premature decay. He also reduced the length of the frame timbers and improved the fastenings. Reflecting the divisions at the Surveyor's Office, Seppings's plan was not supported by his two colleagues, which led the Admiralty to enquire why their views had not been forwarded.[15]

In 1819 Seppings put forward a plan which replaced the diagonal riders with iron straps. This time Peake took care to append a favourable opinion although Tucker claimed the strakes at the heads and heels of the timbers were unnecessary. This, the final stage of his work on the framing of warships, was confined to the frigates and smaller vessels until after 1832.[16] The plan was immediately adopted by the Admiralty.[17] The object was to save timber and increase the stowage space, both critical factors in small warships and merchant vessels.[18] The frigate *Unicorn*, afloat today at Dundee, was built on these lines at Chatham in 1826. This system was extended into the battlefleet by Edye during Symonds's reign at the Surveyor's office, his new form being less space efficient than that of Seppings.[19]

The Seppings system

It should be stressed that Seppings's work was not, as is often suggested, a series of innovations connected only by their author and subject. As a shipwright officer Seppings was familiar with all the problems affecting the wooden warship. He realised that structural strength was the most serious issue and the one from which many others flowed. The timber problem during the Revolutionary and Napoleonic wars compounded that of structural weakness. In 1810 he wrote of the continuing profligate use of large timber:

> This will appear more extraordinary when it is considered our very existence as a nation depends upon our naval superiority, and when it is further understood that a deficiency of oak timber but more particularly that of a large scantling, calls for such an application of it as will reduce its consumption and make up for the deficiency of its size.[20]

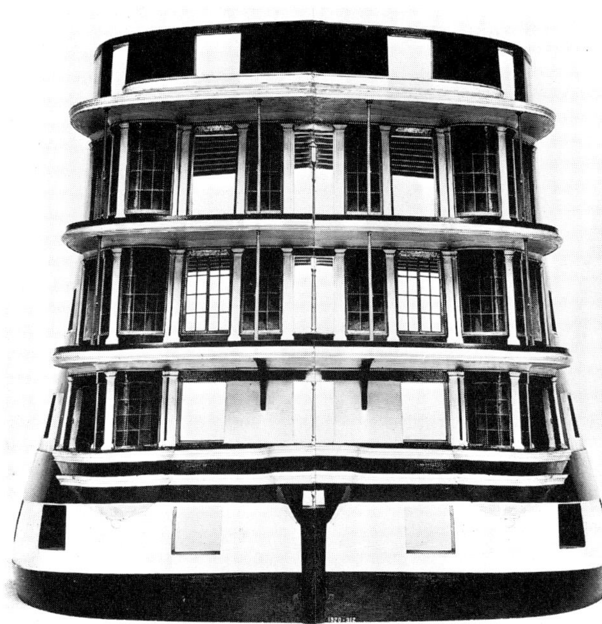

The stern of the Hibernia, *110, as rebuilt 1820–22. The similarities between this design and the contemporary domestic architecture of John Nash help to place the round stern in a wider context.* (ScM)

The saving in timber was a major aspect of Seppings's work. In 1802 he had been advocating the use of iron knees and supports to replace scarce curved timber, and as his work developed so the role of iron in hull structures played an increasingly important part. However, as the *Malabar* demonstrated, he did not carry this to the point where iron became vital to the integrity of the ship. The Admiralty dockyard visits of 1813 lead to some comment on the large amount of timber used for the frames of frigates lying in all yards. Seppings responded with a plan to build battleships with frigate timbers, avoiding the use of compass timber where possible. The resulting ship, the *Thunderer* (later renamed *Talavera*) was ordered in February 1814 and she cost £900 less than the *Black Prince* of the same rate. Both ships were built at Woolwich. As an experimental design it is hardly surprising that *Talavera* was the last battleship ordered during the Napoleonic War but because of her peculiar timber requirements she was laid down before several ships that were already on order. She proved to be a successful ship, before her untimely end, and demonstrated the degree to which the timber problem had been caused by a profilgate use of materials, rather than an actual shortage. As Seppings noted in 1819:

> The saving produced by the adoption of this proposition, although considerable, is of little moment in comparison with the inconvenience and delay before experienced for the want of the article, which in many instances could not be procured but with the greatest difficulty.

The frame of the *Talavera*, converted from Adriatic oak of enormous toughness, was a particular success.

The bow and stern

Seppings's famous modifications to the timber plan of the bow and stern were a development of his attitude toward the whole structure of the wooden ship. That they also improved the defensive strength of the ship against gunfire was secondary.

Seppings's use of iron diagonals was restricted to frigates, here seen in the hold of the 46-gun Unicorn, *still afloat at Dundee. The iron diagonals had less impact on the stowage available in the hold, and saved on timber. Edye and Symonds brought iron diagonals into the battlefleet.* (Author)

After his experience cutting down old three-deckers into two-deckers Seppings concluded that there could be no logical reason for removing the heavy main deck bow and replacing it with the normal light bow bulkhead screen. The first ship to come under Seppings's attention as Master Shipwright at Chatham to be razeed was the *Namur* in 1804. The *Victory* was refitted with the new higher bow after Trafalgar, to the approval of Hardy, and all nineteenth-century photographs of the ship show her with this feature. Seppings applied for the system to be adopted for all new ships in 1807, but had to wait until 29 May 1811 for belated recognition. Thereafter, all new warships were built with the round bow, although one of the first to be affected was the old *Ramillies*, another razee three-decker.[21]

This solution, applied to the bow, whereby the timbering of the ship followed the lines of the extremities, was then applied to the stern. In 1816 Seppings proposed a new timber plan, in which the vertical frame timbers were continued up beyond the old counter to form the basis of the entire structure. This was soon christened the 'round stern' and it was sold to the Admiralty as 'similar' to the bow adopted in 1811 with the supporting argument that it would be an improved defence against a following sea. The Admiralty accepted the idea immediately and ordered the new *Formidable* and *Prince Regent*, and the *Kent* once again undergoing a major repair, to be fitted.[22] These sterns, which were late additions, and experiments at that, were of unequalled ugliness, but Seppings soon created a pleasing if rather utilitarian upright structure that featured on all his mature designs. One easy modification, which was done solely to improve the appearance of the ship, was to increase the rake of the sternpost.[23] The improved model was adopted for the entire Navy in June 1817 and the famous Cooke etching of the *Asia* illustrates a classic Regency design, as close to the work of John Nash as a wooden warship would allow.[24]

The improved strength of the new stern was unquestioned and it completed the process begun with the *Glenmore* in 1800. The hull was now a continuous collection of united elements with a large measure of protection against raking fire. However, it did not cover the rudder head, and the original central gallery proved inadequate for the officers' heads. The design was greeted with a storm of protest on practical, cultural and aesthetic grounds. Seppings moved the officers' heads out into two new quarter galleries, which reduced the all-round fire of the stern, and provided a false counter to cover the rudder head. The idea that the Royal Navy should not show the rest of the world how to defend their sterns was very short sighted. Ships of war required all round fire from relatively well protected positions, something that became increasingly important as the steam ship replaced oared gunboats as the great threat in a dead calm. The experience of the *Asia* at Navarino demonstrated the need for more timber and less glass. The elliptical stern of Roberts and Blake, as adapted by Symonds, was no better protected, and was an inferior battery. It is clear that Seppings intended to abolish the stern galleries altogether but their retention was a response to the wishes of sea officers.[25]

Had Seppings been allowed to carry his design to the logical conclusion, producing a stern similar to that of the French battleships of the 1850s, he might have avoided much of the controversy that dogged his last decade in office, when he had to fend off the claims of Master Shipwright Thomas Roberts, Admirals Sir Charles Ekins and Sir Henry Blackwood among others to have invented, improved or modified his work. In the end Byam Martin had to step in to cool the debate. He was hardly surprised at the ill-feeling raised and in particular he suggested 'Seppings's annoyance, I apprehend has its fount in the ungenerous prejudice which has been excited against him'.[26]

The postwar policy debate

Though Seppings's structural reforms have always been considered his greatest work it must be recalled that he developed new methods of shipbuilding, designed composite masts and a new apparatus to raise masts out of ships; he improved iron mooring chains and assisted Richard Pering in his work on anchor design. In addition, he promoted the empirical study of timber decay, reformed the dockyard pay structure and developed the design of new classes of ship.

He could not have done all this without the assistance of his superiors at the Navy Board and Admiralty. Seppings's closest colleague after 1816 was Byam Martin, who admired Seppings and followed his advice on almost every question relating to ships, timber and dockyards. In 1823 Seppings sent Byam Martin copies of his many published papers on shipbuilding, which amounted to a record of his services which had raised up such opposition over the years.

> Such opposition I have lived to see gradually subside, as my plans have been submitted to the test of practice; but I never can forget how materially I have been assisted by the firm and uniform friendship of well informed persons, in which list you stand conspicuous.[27]

Seppings was appointed one of the Surveyors of the Navy, along with Tucker, on 14 June 1813, on the retirement of Sir William Rule. He was fortunate that the exigencies of war led Melville to call for an additional Surveyor. Melville would appear to have been instrumental in securing his promotion.[28] One thing is certain; Melville's views on the best method of rebuilding the Navy required the services of Seppings who had made his reputation with repair work, which Melville intended to promote at the new Northfleet Dockyard. It should be recalled that in financial terms Seppings was no better off as a Surveyor than he was as Master Shipwright at Chatham. For the next nine years he was a junior Surveyor, spending much of his time visiting the dockyards. Sir Henry Peake, his nominal superior, and Joseph Tucker, were far from happy at having so famous a colleague. When Benjamin Tucker sent his letter to Cockburn, attacking the Navy Board for forming a conspiracy against his brother and its handling of the fleet, Byam Martin was quick to respond:

> A more unfounded assertion never was made, and the whole Board can bear testimony that the conspiracy was on the part of Mr Surveyor Tucker and Sir Henry Peake, who on every occasion thwarted the proposals of Mr Seppings, whose various inventions would have been borne down by such a power of opposition, if they had not been so evidently good as to defy the efforts of those who were jealous of his professional fame; and it stands upon record, that in the circumstances which Mr B Tucker alludes to as a conspiracy, it was proved that two official reports from the Woolwich Officers, which were unfavourable to the assertions of Mr Surveyor Tucker, were concealed, and that those officers were compelled to fill up a statement to meet the ideas of Sir Henry Peake and Mr Tucker, which suborned report was delivered to the Board, and the other two withheld, facts which were collected on oath by a Committee of the Navy Board composed of Sir B Martin, Mr Legge and Mr Bowen.[29]

Seppings's friendship with Byam Martin had other uses. For example, the Controller applied to Lord Liverpool for some token of reward for his friend in 1818 and the sum hinted at was £10,000. Given the financial embarrassment of the Administration, the limited response of the Prime Minister, a one-off grant of £5,000 should not be seen as a comment on the merits of the Surveyor. Byam Martin persuaded Melville to look into the issue in 1820 and suggested that a pension of £500 per annum, with a reversion to his children would be suitable. The Admiralty and Treasury settled on £400 per annum, with a reversion to his wife.[30]

Melville had been far from pleased by Seppings's conduct during the Tucker enquiry, in particular by his decision to distribute his paper attacking Peake and Tucker for preparing false reports on the *Eolus*, which had been demolished, and the *Devonshire*, rebuilt at great cost. Although he had mastered the use of the pamphlet early in his career, Seppings was not at his best in such circumstances. After a long interview Seppings managed to clear the air with the First Lord and recovered his position sufficiently to request some reward and promotion.[31] Two months later, in March 1819, Seppings sent a long *resumé* of his service to the Prince Regent and was rewarded with the bestowing of a knighthood aboard the Royal Yacht *Royal George* on 17 August 1819.[32] In 1825 Byam Martin wrote to the East India Company to press them to treat his son John Seppings, the Surveyor to the Marine Board at Calcutta, more liberally so that he would remain in their service. While Sepping's son was a very useful officer the value of friendship was no small part of this request.[33]

Naval architecture was a major topic among officers, the Duke of Clarence included, and it reached the popular press in many forms, not least in the heated dispute between William James and Edward Brenton over the correct interpretation of the Great War at Sea. Unsurprisingly, James came out entirely in favour of Seppings, while Brenton adopted a diametrically opposed view.[34]

Much of Seppings's postwar work was concerned with the development of pre-1815 designs and the improvement of existing ships. The Tory programme of repair and slow construction involved much work to make 80-gun ships out of half built 74s and increase the weight of arming aboard both large and small three-deckers in an attempt to keep pace with the developments of the 1820s. The modifications to the *Boscawen*, *Impregnable*, razee 74s, improved *Caledonia* and *Canopus* types all made increased demands on the structural strength of the wooden warship. The one new design of the period, the *Nile*, was essentially a razee *Caledonia* initially with a full spar deck and 100 guns. She was, along with the last 84-gun design, a powerful ship built to far higher specification than foreign counterparts.

If the hull forms of Seppings's battleships were unadventurous, merely modifications of proven forms, they were certain and safe performers in all weathers. The experimental frigate *Castor* demonstrated that the Surveyor could design fast ships for a modern armament, but the lessons were only very slowly applied to the battlefleet; even the last was simply a modified *Canopus*. Seppings placed little faith in the sailing trial as a measure of the merit of any design and before the 1825 brig trials he observed that unless the dimensions, masts and other aspects of all the entries were equal it would be impossible to learn anything of the value of 'peculiar forms'. He was instrumental in placing a pupil of the School of Naval Architecture aboard each of the brigs in the 1827 trial, with instructions to note 'every change'.[35]

The only fundamental problem of Seppings's ships was their lack of capacity to meet the demands of steadily increasing armament. The inadequate dimensions of older designs were beyond his control, although it should be noted that even when offered extra tonnage by Byam Martin, Seppings preferred to reorganise the materials of an existing design.

Retirement

Seppings's position was enhanced, albeit temporarily, by the retirement of Tucker on 1 March 1831. During the financial crisis of the late 1820s Melville had considered reducing Tucker, but on discovering that the actual saving would be trifling, because Tucker qualified for a full pension, kept him on with special responsibility for all areas of timber management.

In 1829 Byam Martin, unaware of Melville's plan, proposed that the duties of the two remaining Surveyors should be separated, and he gave Seppings 'special duties of an important

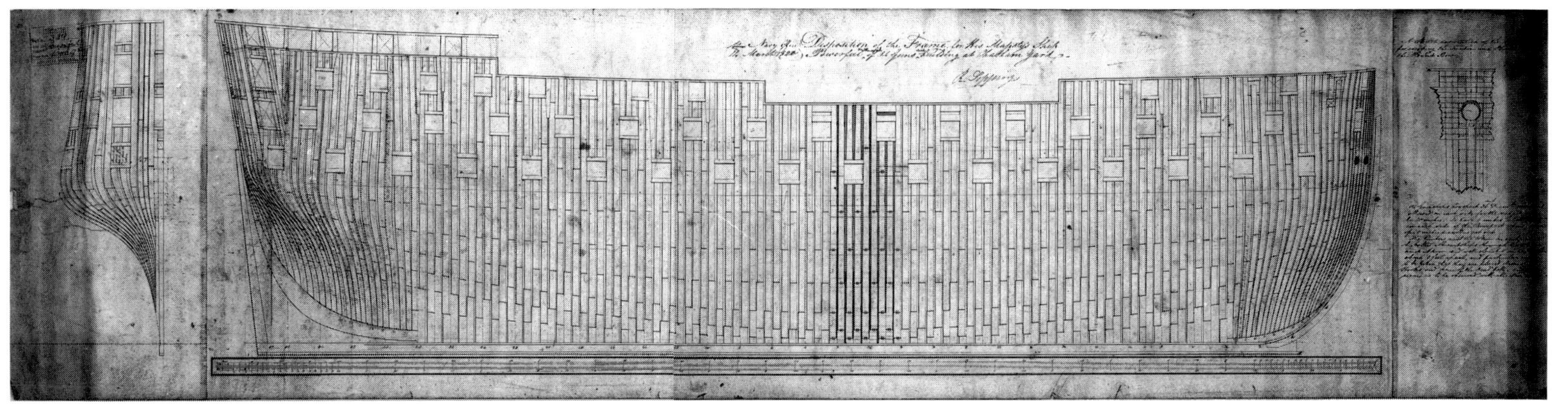

The timber plan for the Powerful, *an 84-gun ship of the* Formidable-*class. This drawing was prepared in 1820, by which time the class had been given an altogether better integrated and more pleasing round stern. Although only joint Surveyor, with Henry Peake and Joseph Tucker, it is worth noting that Seppings alone has signed the drawing.* (NMM)

nature, connected with ships'. When he realised that he could not hope to prolong both offices, Byam Martin preferred to see only one Surveyor, with a well qualified assistant.[36]

Seppings's fate was soon placed in the hands of a new Government. Earl Grey's views on naval administration made some reform of the Navy Board inevitable. At an interview with the King in February 1831 Grey secured some support for the government plan to reduce the Navy Board, and he discovered that the King was not a committed supporter of the Surveyor; in particular, he disliked the round stern. The Prime Minister believed, with some justification it should be admitted, that Seppings 'governs Sir B. Martin with respect to everything in his department'. It was hardly surprising that the First Lord's memorandum on consolidating the Navy Board of December 1831 should include the replacement of Seppings by Symonds.[37] Graham was peculiarly harsh and unjust in his criticism of Seppings's ships, because they had been a vital element in the success of the old regime.[38]

In dismissing the Surveyor the Admiralty were partly motivated by spite, for he was treated in a less generous fashion than any of his recent predecessors. He was dismissed from 31 March 1832, but only informed of this decision, which he accepted as inevitable, as late as 4 February. After the reduction of Byam Martin he lacked the political support to fight. Instead, he requested an allowance at least equal to that of Rule and Peake. In 1824 Peake's pension had been settled at £950, with a reversion of £300 for his widow.[39] Seppings's official salary had been £1,000 and he was offered a pension of £750, with a reversion of £300 to his wife. He already held the £400 pension awarded in 1820, which had a reversion. He had also received a total of £6,000 in grants. The dispute concerned the last £200 of his pension entitlement, although Graham argued it was, in fact, only a matter of £80. Considering the negative view Grey took of Seppings's work Graham soon secured his veto on any reconsideration of the pension, along with a similar response from the Treasury. Seppings continued the argument into 1833. He considered that he was being cheated of his entitlement for 15 years that properly qualified for a pension and as he was only 64 at the time of his reduction, every year was important. By ignoring his apprenticeship it

Seppings's masterpiece, the Rodney *of 92 guns, seen here on her return from service as Flagship on the China Station as late as 1870, by which time she was the last British wooden battleship in service. Although fitted with steam machinery in 1859–60 the* Rodney *remained largely unaltered.* (RNM)

was possible to pay him less. The final letter was written by his old friend Barrow who had proved far more adept at surviving the changes.[40]

Seppings did not despair of further service and kept up a correspondence with several of his old patrons and friends. His letter to Cockburn attacking the new system of design introduced by Symonds elicited a somewhat cagey reply. The ex-First Sea Lord was very unhappy with the *Vernon* whose performance confirmed Seppings's argument.

> I most sincerely congratulate you on the character your *Castor* still maintains, and have no doubts of her being an excellent ship for sea work, which is what men of war should be built for, a ship that fails you whenever you get into a heavy sea may do for a pleasure yacht, but is very unfit for frigate duties.

In addition, he spoke with great enthusiasm of the *Rodney* and Seppings's ships in general. The new designs were far from an improvement. However, he did not want to re-open the issue of naval architecture and advised Seppings to take advantage of the, 'quiet and beautiful scenery around Taunton . . . to repair all damage your constitution may have suffered during so many years of official fog'. Cockburn realised that there was no political mileage in resuscitating the issue and no purpose in encouraging Seppings along similar lines. Cockburn's letters to Graham on the performance of the *Vernon* resulted in the recasting of the bow of all Symonds's ships.[41] Seppings died at Taunton, where he had retired, on 25 September 1840.

Hardly a single aspect of the material policy of the Navy was unaffected by Seppings; his energy and innovation made him the last and greatest of all the shipwright officers raised in the dockyards. His influence on naval policy can be seen in the programmes of Byam Martin. The two men worked together to build the postwar battlefleet and their legacy was two decades of cheap security based on the battlefleet of 1815–30. It was entirely appropriate that the House of Commons Finance Committee of 1817 should have provided the most fulsome tribute to his work, for in the superior economy and durability of his ships lay the material foundations of seapower.

3 Sir William Symonds: Surveyor of the Navy

The abolition of the Navy Board and the changes that were to follow at the Surveyor's Office had a serious impact on the long-term policy programming required to maintain an adequate battlefleet. In examining Sir William Symonds's term in office it becomes clear how far the politics of his appointment, the bitterness aroused by placing him over the professional shipwrights and architects, and the character of the man hampered attempts to re-establish a sound base for decision-making. Only with the arrival of a determined First Lord, Lord Ellenborough, and later with the retirement of Symonds, would the damage of 1832 be repaired.

Appointed on 9 June 1832, the new Surveyor, Captain William Symonds, was perhaps the most controversial member of any nineteenth-century naval administration. His character, overall approach to naval issues and detailed designs marked the last period of the sailing Navy more surely than Byam Martin and Seppings had dominated the preceeding 15 years. Professional naval architects have always disparaged Symonds as an amateur: his contemporaries did so following career disappointments, their descendents from an exaggerated pride in their profession. All commentators have missed the fundamental point that Symonds was not appointed as a naval architect. He was intended to replace Byam Martin as a policy-programmer for shipbuilding and dockyard work. That he elected to enter the controversy on design reflected weak drafting and the lack of interest in the minutiae of construction displayed by the Boards of the 1830s.

After 1815 interest in naval subjects remained high. Outside the profession this was particularly evident with the growth of yachting as an aristocratic pastime. The leading yachtsmen vied for the services of the best designers. Among the most successful of these was John White, the Cowes shipbuilder. The Yacht Club, which became the Royal Yacht Squadron in 1833, was formed at Cowes, Isle of Wight, in 1815. The Squadron enjoyed a close relationship with the Navy, a point underlined after 1829 when its members were permitted to fly the white ensign. The most prominent members of this group were Lord Lauderdale, the Earl of Belfast, Lord Anglesea, Lord Yarborough, the Hon George Vernon and the Duke of Portland. These amateurs achieved a degree of influence on naval design previously denied to far more scientific groups. Clearly, policy makers preferred the sight of ships under sail to learned papers crammed with obscure (and not always correct) calculations. More particularly, those yachtsmen who possessed enough social weight to influence government policy were interested in practical matters. It was this lobby which secured the post of Surveyor of Navy for one of their nominees ahead of both the traditional dockyard-raised men and the pupils of the School of Naval Architecture after the abolition of the Navy Board. There remains something peculiarly British in this veneration of the amateur. All naval officers had opinions on ship design; some would become successful constructors, notably Admiral Hayes and George Elliot, and even those at the Admiralty Board could not resist dabbling in the subject.

> A design of an 80 gun ship was one morning placed upon the Board Room table for the inspection and approval of 'My Lords'. When Lord Auckland entered the room, Sir William Parker, kneeling on a chair with pencil in hand, was altering the lines of the bow; Admiral Dundas, in a similar position, was suggesting alterations in the stern, and marking them off; whilst the two other lords were engaged in making

Captain Sir William Symonds, 1782–1856. As Surveyor of the Navy between 1832 and 1847 Symonds made radical alterations in the design philosophy and form of British battleships. A man of great practical skill at sea and firm opinions, his term was marked by bitter controversy between the professional naval architects and the inspired amateurs. (NMM)

calculations as to an entirely new armament, and to the improvement of the rig. Lord Auckland carefully examined the surveyor's design and listened patiently to all that each naval member had to advance in support of his particular amendment. His lordship then desired me to hand him a piece of india-rubber, and after he had deliberately erased the pencil marks in question, he turned to the surveyor and dryly observed: 'I really do not feel justified in introducing so many improvements' with a strong emphasis on the words improvements – 'into a single ship'. The original design was then approved, and the First Lord and naval lords affixed their signatures.[1]

Captain Sir William Symonds, 1782–1856

Symonds was born the son of a naval captain in 1782. He was first at sea in 1794 and he was present at Lord Bridport's action of 1795 and the Spithead mutiny of 1797. Although an excellent seaman, Symonds lacked the influence and connections needed for a successful career. Only his sister's husband, a relative of Admiral Cornwallis, could provide any help and when the old Admiral died he left a legacy for Symonds. In 1819 Symonds, still only a commander, was appointed Captain of Malta Dockyard, something of a backwater where he remained until 1825. During this period he used his legacy to build an experimental yacht, the *Nancy Dawson*, launched in 1821. The success of his design, which his critics suggested had been copied from the typical 'greek brig' of the eastern Mediterranean, brought him into contact with the Hon G Vernon, later the fourth Lord Vernon, one of the more adventurous spirits among the new fraternity of noble yachtsmen and anxious to improve the sailing qualities of British warships.[2] Vernon built the *Harlequin* to Symonds's form.[3]

As a career seaman Symonds was dominated by his desire to perfect the sailing warship. From an early age he had been conditioned to treat seamanship as the bench mark of a naval officer's skill. This involved personal responsibility for the peculiarly difficult and complex propulsion system that is sail, one that required years of experience to master. This helps to explain his obsession with speed and his hostility to the advance of steam, which threatened to overturn his entire value system. As Surveyor in the early years of steam he needed to be flexible and capable of lateral thinking; he was capable of neither. On several occasions during the Napoleonic Wars he had the mortification of discovering that British ships were out-sailed by their opponents. His response was to create warships with all the qualities, and defects, of yachts, and in so doing he provided the last element in the postwar battlefleet. Unlike their predecessors, Symonds's ships had the power under sail to force a flying enemy to fight. If he achieved nothing else this should have earned him great credit.

In 1824 Symonds published a pamphlet on naval architecture and Vernon attempted to interest the Navy Board in his work. The response amounted to a form of studied indifference on the part of Byam Martin, who cannot have been impressed by an elderly Commander making ascerbic comments on the *Vengeur*-class 74s, commonly referred to as the Forty Thieves, although no-one on the current board bore any responsibility for those ships.[3] Despite this, Vernon possessed enough influence at the Admiralty, with Melville and Cockburn, to have the 18-gun corvette *Columbine* ordered in February 1825. She was built to Symonds's design at Portsmouth in 1826 for the 1827 Experimental Squadron. The following month Vernon put up a bond for £20,000 to cover the loss to the Government should she fail.[4]

In 1824 Symonds described his principles of naval architecture:

> Great breadth of beam and extraordinary sharpness are characteristic features of my system; with a careful attention to stowage, the stand of the masts, and the cut and setting of the sails.

Most contemporary yacht builders would have concurred with this basic approach.

In December 1826 Vernon's father introduced Symonds to William Cavendish-Bentinck, fourth Duke of Portland. This meeting had a decisive bearing on Symonds's career. A lifelong enthusiast for all matters connected with the Royal Navy, Portland was so taken by the form of the *Columbine* that he ordered his shipyard at Troon to build the *Clown* in 1827, and in 1829 the *Pantaloon*, to Symonds's design. Both vessels served as yachts, and as further examples of Symonds's form to set before the Admiralty.[5] After this first contact Portland became Symonds's most committed patron, pressing the Duke of Clarence to order the construction of a large frigate to Symonds's design and offering a surety of £5,000 in the event of her failing under sail. Clarence was prepared to ignore the opposition of Byam Martin for he had already decided to build four experimental frigates, and unlike his predecessors did not feel the need for financial assistance.[6]

Symonds's rise to prominence can be dated from the formation of Canning's Administration in April 1827. Portland, the Prime Minister's brother-in-law, temporarily took the office of Lord Privy Seal although he was promised office without the labour of attending Cabinet, the benefit of his rank and name being all that was required. He was quite ill-suited to office combining as he did the family inability to speak in the House with a personal reluctance to spend much time in London. Subsequent events forced him to remain in Cabinet as Minister without Portfolio and Lord President of Council under Lord Goderich, but he was never an active parliamentary politician. Portland preferred to work in the background, deploying his considerable electoral influence in support of Canning. Once in the Administration Portland's politics were those of Canning, namely Liberal Conservative. Later, he was to shift to the Tory camp on the issue of agricultural protection, where, as an agricultural improver, he remained committed to high grain prices. Before 1827 he had been considered a semi-detached Whig, largely from his opposition to the Royal Divorce in 1820.[7] Although a colleague of Clarence, he studiously refrained from direct interference in naval matters while in office.[8] Portland favoured a union between the Liberal Conservatives and Whigs in order to exclude both the high Tory and Radical factions. As such he used his local influence to support the election of Lord Howick, Earl Grey's son, in 1826. Later, he was to regret Grey's retirement from office, which he blamed on radical elements, and attempted to form a coalition government in late 1834.[9] Portland's politics, and his political weight, were central in securing Symonds's appointment as Surveyor.

Portland's career had been devoted to the recovery of the family estates and fortune which had been left burdened with debt by his father's political career. His marriage to Miss Scott, heiress of a large Scots landowner, added a healthy cash surplus, the town of Troon and large tracts of Ayrshire to his holdings. The great interests in his life were land improvement, forestry and shipbuilding. He was able to combine all three with a degree of benefit, planting over 5,000 acres of naval timber – oak, sweet chestnut and larch – on the inferior lands of his estates in Nottinghamshire, Derbyshire and Scotland. He also built a harbour and shipyard at Troon. By 1844 the estates, including a large part of West London, provided an income of £104,000 a year. Portland's family, including his son Lord George Bentinck and son-in-law John Denison, who were both MPs, gave him a considerable influence, while his proxy in the Lords, where he rarely attended in person, was to be of value in the Reform crisis.

The 1827 trials of 28-gun ships and 18-gun corvettes, under the command of Hardy, demonstrated the superiority of Symonds's ships over the designs of Captain John Hayes, the School of Naval Architecture and Seppings. The designs submitted by Symonds, Hayes and the School were unduly hampered by the Navy Board's insistence on retaining the old measurement, which with a restricted length, forced all to compromise. Hayes cut the beam of his entry, which failed, while Symonds and Inman built below the allowed length to provide more beam. Their entries, *Columbine* and *Sapphire*, would have been better ships had there been less restriction on the tonnage.[10] It should be observed that Symonds had permission to shift the masts and alter the yards of the *Columbine* during the trial.

Portland was among those who observed the trials aboard the *Clown*. Despite the criticisms levelled by various commentators Hardy knew his own mind; his report concluded:

> *Columbine*'s capacity of stowage is much inferior to *Wolf*, *Satellite* or *Acorn*; but her greater breadth of beam and lower bulwarks enable her to stand under her canvas & in general weather her sailing qualities are very superior to the whole of the squadron.[11]

With such evidence Clarence lost little time in rewarding the successful designer and commander of the *Columbine*. Symonds was rapidly promoted to Captain through a brief period of service aboard the Royal Yacht *William and Mary*, a recognised route for those in favour. All the relevant orders were signed by the Lord High Admiral and his seniority as Post Captain dated from 5 December 1827.[12]

Following a suggestion by Hardy, Clarence ordered Symonds, Hayes, Inman and Seppings to build an experimental 46-gun frigate but the order was suspended for lack of money. The design parameters indicate an attempt to break the mould in warship design.

New ship		*Standard 46-gun frigate*
Length on Gun Deck	170ft	159ft
Beam	48ft	42ft
Masted as a 74-gun ship		
Armament		
Main deck (thirty-two guns)	32 pdr 56 cwt	8 pdr long guns
Forecastle	two 12 pdr guns	same
Quarter deck	twelve 32 pdr carronades	same [13]

Portland continued to urge the construction of more vessels on Symonds's lines, but out of office Clarence could not help: 'But I must ever rejoice to find Your Grace turning your thoughts to matters connected with the naval resources of our Empire'.[14] In the interval the Duke built the 10-gun brig *Pantaloon* at Troon.[15]

Portland left office on the fall of the Goderich Administration. The Duke of Wellington had little time for him, although he was considered enough of a Tory to be nominated for the Committee of the Carlton Club. Only with the arrival of the Whigs would his influence be such that he could effect the naval policy debate.[16]

Inboard profile of Symonds's first battleship, the 78-gun Goliath *design of 1835. The iron diagonals that Symonds and Edye introduced can be seen, along with the supports added to the overhanging elliptical stern.* (NMM)

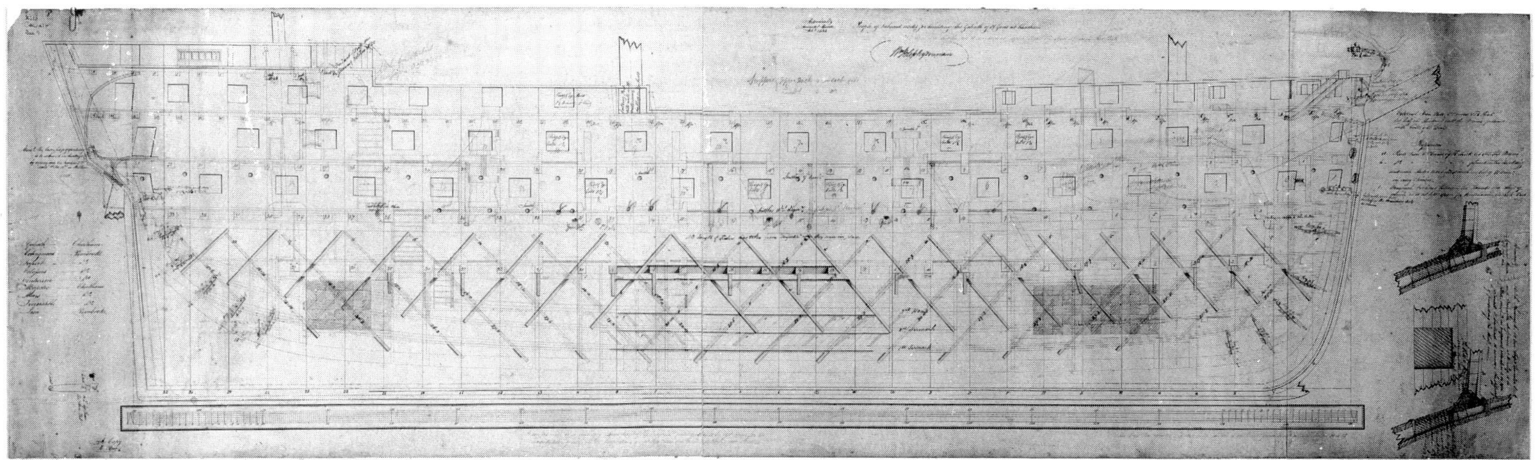

A model of the bow of the 70-gun Cumberland, *bearing a bust of Symonds's greatest supporter in Government, the Whig First Lord of the Admiralty 1830–1834 Sir James Graham, Member of Parliament for the County of Cumberland.* (ScM)

After the formation of Earl Grey's Administration in November 1830 Portland established contact with the First Lord. Graham was well known to the Bentinck family; his father had been created baronet by the Third Duke, while Graham served on the staff of Lord William Bentinck in Sicily in 1813–14.[17] Portland and Graham corresponded on several issues, but hardly a trace remains in either archive; several relevant letters published by Sharp have simply disappeared. Among Graham's papers there is a document that sheds some light on this relationship, the programme for the April 1834 Meeting at Newmarket, endorsed with the name of the Duke's most famous son, Lord George Bentinck.[18]

Graham also corresponded with other yachtsmen interested in shipbuilding, notably Vernon, Yarborough, Lauderdale and Anglesey, then Lord Lieutenant of Ireland. In their efforts to secure support in the House of Lords for the Reform Bill, Grey and Graham were quite happy to buy votes. Lord Yarborough wished to be created Vice Admiral of the Isle of Wight and this was granted, 'on account of his generous support to our measures'. In addition, the Patronage Secretary paid £4,000 for Yarborough's four pocket boroughs on the Isle.[19]

After a long discussion with Symonds in early April 1831, Portland sent a letter to Graham and received the most flattering reply. The First Lord expressed his admiration of Symonds's system and gave permission for the Duke to join the Squadron of Evolution that would assemble in June. Within days Sir John Pechell, a junior Naval Lord and Royal favourite, informed Symonds that the Board proposed that he should design a 50-gun frigate to the armament and rigging specification of the razee *Barham*. He had complete freedom to select the lines of the ship and could design his own stern and even select the yard at which she would be built. In return Portland was to attend the Lords in May and vote for the Government. The object was to impress the Opposition with the strength of the Reform party after the dissolution of the Commons in April. Attendance entailed a certain sacrifice, namely missing the launch of his brig *Pantaloon* at Troon. By August the Board were anxious to have the lines of the frigate, an anxiety which subsequent events explain.[20]

Early in July Portland and Symonds sailed down the west coast aboard *Pantaloon* and *Clown* to join the Squadron at Plymouth. There they met up with Yarborough and took a full part in the proceedings of Sir Edward Codrington's fleet. In a regular trial *Pantaloon* beat *Curacao*, the pick of the warships, three miles to windward in two and a half hours. As she passed under the stern of the flagship, Portland heard the Admiral call out 'well done Symonds'. In private, Codrington called her 'a most extraordinary sailer'. Symonds took note of *Curacao*'s captain, David Dunn, who was to be one of the first to command one of his two-decked ships.[21] Portland was anxious to prove the suitability of Symonds's design, and requested Graham to obtain from Hardy the correct loading for a warship of her class. Within ten days of joining the Squadron he believed the point had been made. 'I now consider all trials as a mere loss of time, & I have written to Sir J. Graham that since the trial of Thursday I consider my case to be proved'. However, he found the Board somewhat evasive with Graham insisting on yet more weight being carried 'in order to silence all objection'. By the end of the month *Pantaloon* was carrying 3 tons more than the brigs of the Squadron and all were satisfied.[22] On 1 October the *Pantaloon* was purchased by the Navy.[23]

In drafting his 50-gun frigate, the *Vernon*, Symonds required considerable technical assistance; even so he made a major error in the draft, describing the keel as only 136ft, rather than 144ft.[24] For the detailed structure of the ship Symonds liaised with Oliver Lang, Master Shipwright at Woolwich and favourite of Seppings. For the lines he settled on those of the ex-Spanish 80-gun ship *Gibraltar*, ex *El Phenix*, captured in 1780, which he had always considered a fine sailing ship.

	Gibraltar	*Vernon*
Length on gun deck	178ft 11¼in	176ft
Length of keel	144ft 6in	164ft 6⅞in
Beam	53ft 3¾in	52ft ¼in (extreme)
Depth in hold	22ft 4in	17ft 1in
Tonnage	2,185 tons	2,082 16/94 tons 24

The stern of the Cumberland. *The degree of rake was reduced after problems with the* Warspite *and the* Vanguard, *but the lower deck guns would still set fire to the stern if fired alongside the rudder, while any guns mounted in the upper decks would be too far aft to be supported by the hull.* (ScM)

The ship was laid down in October 1831, and hurried on to completion in six months, the only ship building in a Royal dockyard on which the men were allowed to work extra hours. This proved singularly unfortunate, as she developed a serious outbreak of dry rot, the only postwar ship so affected. Haste was forced on Graham by his decision to appoint Symonds, for *Vernon* was the only vessel likely to be available for years to come that would serve to prove the new system, and with it the entire Admiralty Reform programme.[25]

To emphasise their commitment the *Vernon* was launched by Lady Graham, and bore a bust of Lord Vernon, Symonds's patron rather than the eighteenth-century Admiral. It would appear that Vernon entered into another performance bond for this ship, of £20,000, but once Symonds became Surveyor this was allowed to lapse. As she went down the ways on 1 May 1832 the ship ran into the *Lancaster* and suffered some damage to her head, main channels and gangway. It was a rather embarrassing start and the Admiralty was far from pleased with Woolwich.[26]

Following the trial cruise of 1831 further orders for Symonds's designs were soon forthcoming; the 18-gun sloops *Serpent* and *Snake* were ordered on 13 October to be built 'with as little delay as possible', by Fletcher of Limehouse in 1832. These were the largest warships built in a merchant yard since 1815, and further proof of Graham's anxiety to have Symonds's ships at sea. The 26-gun *Vestal*, ordered on 8 December 1832, was launched at Sheerness in 1833.[27]

The final crisis of the Reform Bill came in early 1832 in the House of Lords where the Opposition had the strength to defeat the measure. The Government were desperate for support and had already demonstrated their complete lack of scruple in obtaining votes from any source. Grey had elevated a number of naval worthies into the Lords, notably Admiral Saumarez who received 20 years too late the just reward of a brilliant career. It hardly needs to be said that his solitary vote was cast in favour of reform.[28]

Portland had supported the Bill, but when the Ministers called for the large-scale creation of new peers to force the measure through he was one of many who considered this was going too far along the path of radical reform. From his rank and connections he was seen as the leader of the 'waverers', a group which persuaded the Opposition to allow the Bill to pass in order to prevent any more serious eruption upon its defeat, or the dangerous precedent of the creation of a large number of new peers.[29]

In the period leading up to the passage of the Reform Bill Portland possessed great influence, as he would in all political crises up to 1852. Given the predilection of the Grey Administration to purchase support it would appear reasonable to assume that there was a positive connection between the appointment of Symonds and the electoral influence of his patron. This is made all the more likely by the coincidence of dates. By December 1831 Graham had determined on replacing Seppings with Symonds, the only personnel change to be made under his Bill to consolidate the Navy and Victualling Boards. He claimed to have consulted Hardy, William Parker, Charles Rowley and other senior naval officers before reaching his decision, although there were other influences at work. Thirty years later he made it clear that the real object was to concentrate the functions of the Navy Board under one head.[30]

While the appointment was officially made on 9 June 1832, as part of the abolition of the Navy Board, Symonds and Portland knew of it in February.[31] The timing of this leak suggests that the object was to influence Portland's course during the Reform crisis. That does not imply that Symonds was entirely without merit, merely that his claims would not have been placed before the Government in so forceful a manner without the advocacy of Portland.

In the Commons Graham claimed that the success of the *Vernon* would be the test of the soundness of the appointment. Portland attended the 1832 cruise and watched *Vernon*, *Snake* and *Pantaloon* lead the fleet in the expected fashion, after numerous alterations to the rigging of *Vernon*.[32]

Graham still felt the need to trumpet the success of the *Vernon* in September 1832, months after the appointment of Symonds. This was a response to the concern voiced by Hardy, who was anxious to see the ship for himself and who had great influence with the King. Grey was pleased to be rid of Seppings, accepting Graham's praise of the new Surveyor, 'at all events it must have been a good thing to get rid of Seppings', while the King was happy that all the new ships had done well.[33] The following year Symonds's *Vestal* was sent out with the famous old *Endymion* for trials.[34]

Graham continued to feel pride in the appointment of Symonds and on leaving office he told Portland:

> I am gratified by the kindness of your letter, and there is no man whose praise I value more highly since, in addition to the worth of him who bestows it, it possessed the merit of very perfect sincerity.
>
> The appointment of Captain Symonds to be Surveyor of the Navy is among the Acts, on which I can look back with most satisfaction and with least hesitation as to the result. His ships will speak for themselves, and when the passing jealousies and angry feelings of the day are long forgotten, his genius will be remembered, his services appreciated and his advancement praised. . . .
>
> I shall never cease to watch with fond anxiety the progress of this great improvement so connected with our naval greatness, and I am sure I may rely on your assistance, in case of need, to secure justice for an honest man, against whom there is a disposition to make a run.[35]

Portland was to be his only lasting ally with any political weight to place behind Symonds and together they were to work to smooth the Surveyor's path in office and afterwards. For all his use of the word 'sincerity' it remains open to question how far Graham had been sincere in his actions. At best he can be accused of simply leaving Symonds the poisoned chalice of badly-drafted instructions.

Symonds's system: 1832–47

Symonds's warship designs attempted to combine the new armament of heavy long guns with improved speed and weatherly qualities. His ships were larger than those of other nations in order to outsail and outfight them and they reflected his view of the future of war at sea. Primarily, he directed policy rather than designed the hull form. He set out the design parameters for the new ships and provided the lines he believed to be most effective but he left the detailed structure to John Edye. The fragile, yacht-like balance of qualities possessed by Symonds's warships meant that they required skilled handling. They were at their best in trials under sea officers of Symonds's own stamp, like David Dunn, Anwar Lowry Corry and Thomas Symonds; in less sympathetic hands, or badly stowed or in need of new copper they did not sail as well as the old models.

There were certain important underlying characteristics common to all the Surveyor's work. Symonds's ships were much less heavily armed on a measure of guns per ton of displacement than earlier ships. This was a vital pre-requisite for improved sailing performance and in both the *Vanguard* and *Queen* classes he took this to the extreme, leaving these ships carrying fewer guns than the old designs for which they were a direct replacement. This also conditioned his attitude to older vessels. Symonds's ships had higher and wider gun decks, which allowed for the full recoil of heavy guns, and gave adequate head room for the gun crew. In addition, he attempted to reduce the amount of permanent ballast, substituting beam for iron weights as the provider of stability.

The prime consideration was speed under sail which was condemned by many as being more relevant to yacht building. Symonds knew, however, that speed in the tactical phase of a pursuit battle was vital. Nelson argued that a British ship only needed to get alongside to defeat a Frenchman, but Symonds removed the qualification, and introduced a degree of tactical finesse that could resolve the great strategic problem of the sailing era: how to bring an unwilling enemy to decisive battle.

Symonds's opposition to steam has been exaggerated, both by later commentators and by Sharp. In 1839 the Surveyor supported an application by Seaward Brothers to place a 60hp auxiliary paddle steam engine on the orlop deck of a new 80-gun ship but the Board turned it down. While steam remained an auxiliary of negligible impact on sailing qualities, particularly while it was confined to special steam ships, the Surveyor could concentrate on his real work, but the screw steam auxiliary of the mid 1840s struck him as a premature and misguided step. In as much as the steam ships of this period were only ever qualified successes his views had some justification.

The Surveyor's Office: 1832–47

After the 1832 Reform process the Surveyor's Office remained at Somerset House. Graham's plan to unite the entire civil and military strength of the Admiralty at Whitehall proved difficult to carry out, primarily on grounds of cost. Largely left to his own devices, under the nominal superintendence of Hardy, Symonds was free to run his department as he pleased. He was clearly a favourite with the First Sea Lord. However, his real freedom was severely circumscribed by lack of money and the restrictive trend of Admiralty policy. Hardy supported the design trends that the Surveyor introduced, and gave him access to the highest level of patronage, both to destroy the last designs of Seppings, and to promote his own relatives.[36]

Somerset House had practical disadvantages. The offices were located in cramped, 'low, badly lit rooms', which was hardly conducive to the particular needs of a drawing office. In 1836 they were moved into the rooms used by the Navy Pay Office, which had been relocated at Whitehall.[37] In addition, the staff of the office had shrunk over the past two decades. In 1820 there were twenty, in 1830 eleven and by 1838 only eight in the department.[38] Symonds called for at least one extra clerk. There were a series of mistakes that appear to have resulted from pressure of work, one example being the unusually low main deck of the *Albion*, approved in June 1839. It was accepted that the Office was 'too weak' to act as a long-term policy programming centre and by 1839 the Board had agreed to improve the arrangement, up-rating Edye to Chief Assistant and Draughtsman to the Surveryor, with one first-, one second- and three third-class clerks.

> The duties of Mr Edye will be to assist the Surveyor in his capacity of Draughtsman in all calculations, details etc for the construction of ships, with a general control over the office and clerks and in the absence of the Surveyor to perform all his duties.

There were no extra clerks but it was hoped that the provision of a career structure would encourage the existing staff to meet the increased workload.[39]

The final point in Edye's instructions reflected the fact that Symonds had required long periods away, in 1837 and again in 1839, on both occasions with a badly broken leg. On the second occasion he combined a visit to the spas of Germany with a cruise to St Petersburg where he was invited to view the Russian naval manoeuvres by the Tsar.[40] The Office was not subjected to any further modification until the integration of the Steam Department, and the move to Whitehall in 1855.

John Edye

Between 1832 and 1850 the structure of the battlefleet reflected the work of one man, the Chief Clerk and later Assistant Surveyor, John Edye. Edye formed the calm centre around which the great drama of the Symonds's era and the technological revolution of steam were played out. Largely ignored by contemporary and subsequent commentators, his work was the link between Seppings and Isaac Watts.

From his date of retirement it would appear that Edye was born in 1792 and he entered Plymouth Dockyard in 1803–04 as an apprentice indentured to Joseph Tucker. Two of his brothers followed naval careers; William became a Master Shipwright while Joseph retired in 1865 as Paymaster-in-Chief. As all three could trace the decisive steps in their careers to the Whig Party, it would suggst that their father was one of those in the dockyard with a vote.

From the outset, Edye specialised in drawing, working almost continuously in the Drawing Office until his apprenticeship ended in 1810. Thereafter, he served as Dockyard Draughtsman until 1814, when he moved to the new yard at Pembroke in a supervisory capacity. In 1818 he was sent out to the East Indies to report on the shipbuilding resources of the region, of which he formed a high opinion, and he then served for five years as Master Shipwright at Trincomalee and Cochin, forming a particularly low opinion of the financial probity of the East India Company. While serving at Trincomalee he lost the sight of one eye from sun-stroke. In 1823 he returned to work as a foreman at Chatham where he received much favourable comment from his superiors. Sir Henry Blackwood wrote to recommend him to Graham in 1831. In 1829 he published a detailed work on the measurement of ships. His work, with his Whig politics, secured him promotion in 1832 to Chief Clerk in the Surveyor's Office where he was to act as Symonds's technical assistant. To stress the extent to which he, rather than Symonds, was the direct replacement for Seppings, Edye was elected a Fellow of the Royal Society.

Edye's contribution to the sailing battlefleet was restricted to the details of structure and construction. He introduced a new shift of frames to save timber; improved the security of beams; and modified the waterways to allow the guns to run out properly. He applied iron fastenings to the iron riders that were introduced by him into the battlefleet, and modified the rudder head, though with less than complete success. He chain bolted the frames of later ships for improved rigidity and reorganised the buttock planking, allowing it to run directly up to the counter, thereby saving work and timber while improving strength. With steam ships, where the Surveyor had neither the time nor the inclination to act, he played a larger role. His conversion of the old 44-gun frigate *Penelope* into a paddlesteam frigate and the design of the new paddle frigate *Retribution* were only moderate successes. In view of the troubled record of all steam ship designs of the 1840s there was no discredit in this, as he was to demonstrate later. Those were early experiments that led him to becoming a very good architect. He was responsible for the programme to arm merchant steamers, set in train by the Tory Board in 1844–45 and for everyday liaison with the Steam Department.

Edye proved a loyal and diligent second for the Surveyor,

and it would appear that the two men worked closely together on all major issues, including attempts to improve his pay. Edye was paid £650 per annum, the same as a Master Shipwright, but without the valuable extra of a house. This matter was raised several times by the Surveyor, but the final resolution had to wait until the Office was reconstructed in 1848, when £150 was added to his salary.

After Symonds's retirement Edye stood in as acting Surveyor for a period of nine months. With considerable courage he gave an unqualified eulogy for the work of his one-time chief, who he credited with the introduction of larger, wide beamed ships. He hoped that the Surveyor's retirement would end 'the rancour and controversy which is so destructive to the well being, discipline and harmony of our dockyards'. In the same month he fought a major and vital policy battle with the Committee of Reference on the timber plan for all future warships. His success demonstrated the limited value of the work of the Committee, and must have played a considerable part in Lord Auckland's decision to downgrade the Committee. When reinforced by Isaac Watts in the following year he was able to give the *coup de grace* to the Committee, now reduced to the Committee of Science.

While acting for the Surveyor, Edye made his major contribution to the battlefleet. His pioneer screw-steam battleship, the *Agamemnon*, designed in 1846–47, was the model for the ships of the following decade and was unequalled by any foreign competitor. The Board publicly thanked him for this work. In addition, he designed the last sailing battleships, the *Orion* class, and a series of heavy frigates. In tandem with Isaac Watts he provided the design expertise for Captain Sir Baldwin Walker's steam battlefleet, for both the new and converted ships.

Edye retired in 1857 after 50 years service, half as assistant to the Surveyor. As he left he set out his views on the timber question, reflecting on the great increase in the durability of ships, the value of Italian oak and the superiority of teak, which he considered to be 10 to 15 years more durable than the best oak. In 1863 he was created a Civil Companion of the Order of the Bath.

Edye gave Symonds first class support. None of the ships for which he provided the structure were ever lost from weakness, and none suffered from the ravages of premature decay. Edye continued the work of Seppings, and under Walker, who acted as a true Controller, he made the design process into a liaison between technical skill and sea experience. The benefits were immense and Walker's battlefleet was as uncontroversial as that of Symonds had been controversial.[41]

The Surveyor and his rivals

The most serious criticism of Symonds's appointment came from Byam Martin, Cockburn and others in 1832, and was sustained over the entire period. In the early 1840s Byam Martin committed his thoughts to paper, calling Symonds a 'fancy builder' appointed to,

> take charge of the whole duties of the dockyards, for which (whatever may be his good judgement about the lines of a ship) he is totally incompetent. The duties of a dockyard are manifold and highly important and a man needs to be a thorough practical shipwright to detect false workmanship, otherwise he cannot usefully superintend the construction and repair of the fleet.

He favoured the claims of the pupils of the School of Naval Architecture, who wished to unite professional skill with practical achievement and thought that the administration of the civil department of the Navy would be best handled by a subordinate board, the Controller of which would sit at the Admiralty. In 1837 he dined with Minto at the Admiralty and was surprised to hear the First Lord admit to him that the existing system could not stand in wartime, and was incapable of functioning properly under any circumstances. Minto admitted the need for reform, but lacked the courage to overturn Graham's work.[42]

When professional naval architects, past and present, attack the appointment of Symonds as Surveyor of the Navy they are reflecting a fundamental misunderstanding of the reform process that Graham undertook in 1832, and of the duties he expected of the new Surveyor. Symonds was not appointed as a direct replacement for Seppings; he was in essence a permanent official responsible for the long-term material programmes of the Navy. Liaising with the First Naval Lord, he was to fill the role of the old Controller, setting out the construction and

The profile of the Boscawen *as modified, showing the new frame, with iron diagonals.* (NMM)

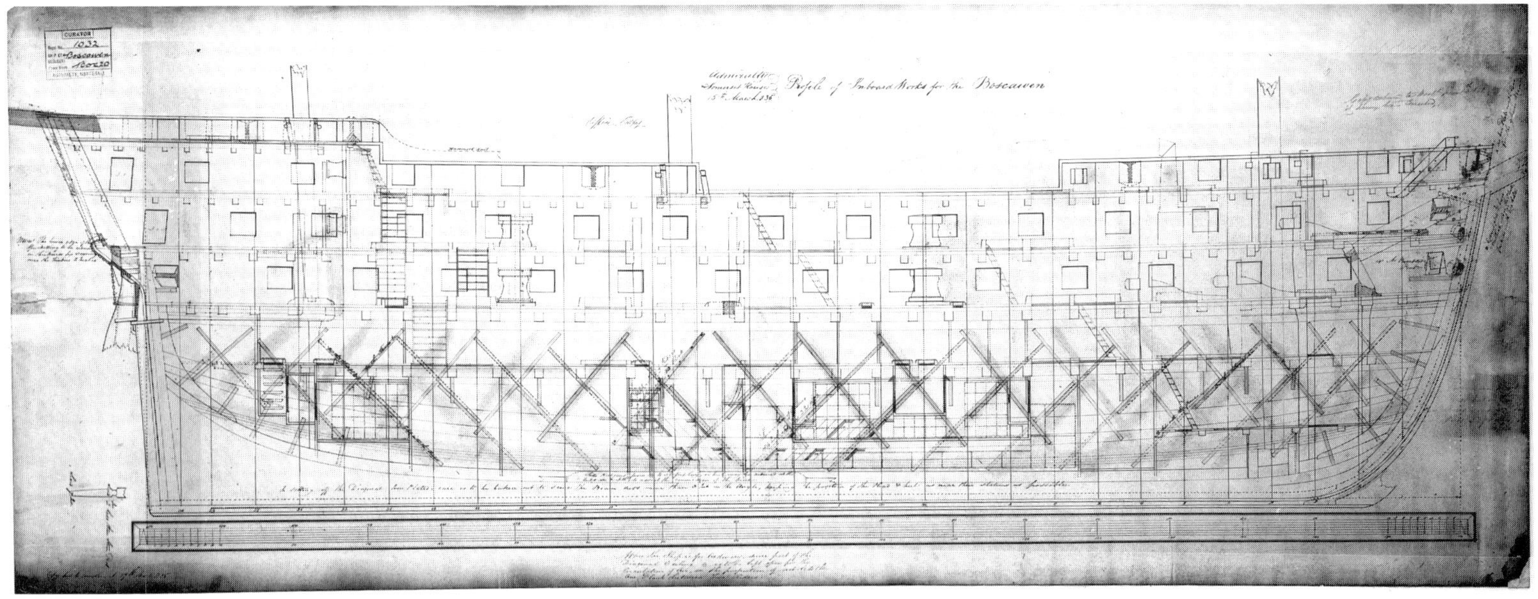

repair schedule for each year, apportioning work between yards and deciding on designs and modifications. He was not appointed to design ships, and the fact that he was an amateur designer merely served to confuse the issue. The structural and design effort was to be provided by the Chief Clerk John Edye, an experienced and well-educated shipwright officer. This was the basic thrust of Graham's speech in the House on 6 April 1832 when he claimed that no shipwright officer was competent to take up the post as redefined. The confusion of contemporary and subsequent commentators reflects the weak drafting of the original instructions as well as Symonds's powerful character and the reluctance of the Whig Boards between 1832 and 1841 to keep real control over the Surveyor who remained down at Somerset House.

The obvious failings of the Graham system effectively created a vacuum in policy making for no-one was truly responsible for the construction programme. The Surveyor could only act under the First Sea Lord, and he had many other tasks to occupy his time, and, as Sir Charles Adam admitted, this ensured that he rarely went down to Somerset House.

In the Skeleton of Instructions of 9 June 1832 the Surveyor's duties are set out under thirteen heads. It is clear from the second head that Graham intended the Surveryor to consider designs from other sources; the seventh head establishes the requirement for policy programming, and the ninth the Surveyor's central position with overall control of material. All orders were to pass through the Board.[43]

To complement the Surveyor, a Committee on Naval Improvements was to be assembled whenever the Surveyor should desire to report on proposals. It would appear that Graham intended this body to combine the Master Shipwrights and pupils of the School of Naval Architecture under the direction of the policy programmer. However, it was never called because the Surveyor was not the man to refer any issue to another body when he could reach a decision himself. Furthermore, in spite of the intent of his instructions, he had no intention of giving design opportunities to others when he could carry out the work himself.[44]

The two groups wasted no time in attacking the new Surveyor, which, in turn did nothing to improve his attitude and Symonds's decision not to make any gesture of reconciliation towards either body resulted in a bitter debate. The blame can be apportioned equally for neither party appeared to be interested in a compromise. Of the Master Shipwrights Symonds observed: 'At some yards matters went smoothly, but at others I experienced a good deal of secret opposition'. The resulting shake up removed some dead wood, the Master Shipwrights at Portsmouth and Plymouth among them, but did not placate the irreconcilable elements, in particular Oliver Lang. On the other hand, the pupils of the old School were, 'too proud of their own theories, of which they had a monopoly, to listen with deference to the suggestions of seamen of experience'.[45] That the accusations should revolve around conspiracy and lack of deference reveals much of Symonds's character. He was a difficult man, more used to the automatic obedience of the quarterdeck than the even-handed debate of departmental life.

In the following years all three parties struggled for influence and art and science were as nothing to the value of political support. Symonds lined up Portland and the Whig Party; the shipwrights secured the Tory naval fraternity; while the School were left with a most unlikely pair, Lord Melville and Joseph Hume. It can be argued that the decision of the King to knight Symonds in 1836, without receiving any request to do so from the Admiralty, 'considering the situation Captain Symonds holds, the able manner in which he fills it and the necessity of upholding him in it' marked the Surveyor's triumph over his opponents. Minto agreed that this, 'cannot fail of proving advantageous to the public service in the countenance and support it affords to that able and zealous officer'.[46]

The School of Naval Architecture

The attacks on Symonds began within a month of his appointment. On 23 June John Fincham, lately an instructor at the School, published a letter to Graham arguing for a more scientific approach to shipbuilding, particularly in the collection of data and the limited understanding of the laws of resistance. In addition, he contended that all the eminent builders of the day had failed to find 'some fixed principle' of length and breadth. This was a reasonable document and lacked the bitter personal attacks of later publications.[47]

Barrow provided Graham with a memorandum on this question. He argued that the French had separated the design and construction aspects of their shipbuilding department, and that the School of Naval Architecture, by attempting to link theory with practice, had only created mongrel ships. In addition, the primary duty of the Surveyor was to set the Establishment, the number and class of ships required for the naval service. This had never been the duty of the old Surveyor, and reflected the conflation of the posts of Controller and Surveyor, to the detriment of long-term programming.[48] The following year an anonymous pamphlet in the form of an open letter to Graham, now usually attributed to Henry Chatfield, made an altogether more serious allegation. Arguing in favour of the SNA it reprinted the 1832 House of Commons debate and concluded: 'We cannot, for an instant, suppose that Sir James Graham could have appointed a naval officer to the situation of Surveyor of the Navy for the mere purpose of patronage'.[49]

From this point the tone of the debate rapidly descended. Symonds had been supported by Captain Marryatt in his *Metropolitan Magazine* and Marryatt reviewed Chatfield's paper soon after publication. Having lambasted Seppings over the supposed spoiling of the *Caledonia* (an invention of the Whig press) Marryatt went on to accuse him of being an ignorant 'dockyard matey from Chatham'. He praised Symonds as a practical man, in contrast to the SNA pupils, who were already well provided for and of no social distinction: 'some, it appears, cannot legally make claim to any father'. Among those not accorded any father on the published list was Henry Chatfield. Marryatt concluded that 'if the major part of them were dismissed, the work of the dock-yards would go on much better than it does at this present moment'.[50] It would appear that the material for this blistering assault on the School was provided by Symonds; certainly the detailed list of the situations held by the twenty-five pupils remaining in Government service was drawn up in his office.[51]

A rather dispirited group of men from the School withdrew from the lists. When one of their number, John Henwood, submitted the draft of a First Rate, he quickly discovered how Symonds regarded any alternative views on shipbuilding. The Surveyor condemned his plan as, 'formed upon mistaken principles', while the supporting statements was at once, 'crude and visionary'.[52]

The last hope of the SNA was the support of Melville, patron of the School and a modest enthusiast for its work. In 1836 Melville corresponded with Barrow on the subject of naval design. While admitting the merits of Symonds, he argued that the abolition of the School was 'reverting to barbarous ignorance'. In addition, he supported Byam Martin's argument that Symonds was incompetent to manage the dockyards. Barrow rehearsed the Whig line: 'it appears to me that a small portion of theoretical science is sufficient for the planning of the hull of a good ship', while Symonds made no pretence at originality, 'but admits that he borrowed his ideas from an American bottom'. The success of the razees and the work of such unscientific constructors as Seppings, in contrast to the highly-trained Barrallier, and the fact that the pupils of the School had not distinguished themselves, was reason enough for the closure. The argument that Symonds was ignorant of the civil branch was accepted, but under the new system he was to work with the Storekeeper (this officer was Melville's son), and the Dockyard Superintendents. Barrow did not explain the different role of the new Surveyor for that aspect of the argument had been lost sight of years before and was only to resurface with the appointment of Walker in 1848 and the subsequent renaming of the department.[53]

Symonds was a vindictive and bitter man; having defeated the School he then began to persecute them. When they became eligible for promotion he objected that the old dockyard-raised men were superior as dockyard officers, and specifically attacked Henwood who, he argued:

> is not a practical shipwright, being a compound of mathematics, logic and stupidity. Litigious and a writer against the acts of his superiors, to which he puts his name with effrontery.

Symonds's comments were sent to Lord Minto, who took a rather more favourable view of the SNA men, and ultimately forced Symonds to follow a policy of sharing out the appointments between the old and new shipwright officers, to achieve a combination of theoretical and practical talents.[54] The issue was raised again in 1840 when the Surveyor remained implacable in his opposition to over-promoting, as he saw it, the SNA men. Minto was critical of the Surveyor's position, and urged the wisdom of giving them greater opportunities. He observed that not one of the SNA men had been promoted to the position of Assistant Master Shipwright since he took office in 1835. He realised that this was an issue of adminstrative policy outside the Surveyor's competence and he hinted that he thought the reasons were based on criteria other than professional merit. Minto was more interested in the political persuasion of the officers suitable for promotion and he noted with approval that Joseph Hoskins at Portsmouth was 'politically recommended by Mr Carter' (the Whig MP).[55]

Before the end of 1841 the School men were gathering to take a calculated revenge on the Surveyor, and on Minto. Deprived of his veto over dockyard appointments after 1841, Symonds found his enemies moving into positions of real power and with the support of the new Tory Administration the Chatham Committee of 1842 would begin an attack on his designs.

The Master Shipwrights

Having temporarily defeated the claims of the School, Symonds had to deal with the other irreconcilable element under his department: the Master Shipwrights and in particular Oliver Lang. Symonds and Lang had collaborated on the design of the *Vernon* and Symonds elected to have the ship built in Lang's yard, though his price was higher than any other.[56]

The 36-gun frigate Pique. *This ship and her class were the Surveyor's standard frigate type. He did not favour the large Fourth Rate 50-gun ship, preferring to use timber of this scantling for 70-gun two deckers.* Pique *carried a full battery of long 32-pounders, making her a much more powerful unit than the old 46-gun ships of the* Unicorn-*class.* (CMP)

Lang, then 53, was the youngest Master Shipwright by several years. He had been Seppings's First Assistant in the early 1820s and in position at Sheerness and Woolwich for nine years. He was marked out as the coming man among the shipwright officers. With some justification Lang believed that he was the natural successor to his mentor and friend Seppings and his pioneering work on the early naval steam ships reinforced his case. Symonds, however, had a rather lower estimation of his value, offering him the job of Master Shipwright at Portsmouth in October 1832. Lang's refusal suggests he preferred remaining close to Somerset House to keep an eye on the post he most coveted.[57]

The dockyard reforms of the Graham Board were not to the liking of the Master Shipwrights for they found their freedom of action severely constrained. The flexibility of task and job pay was removed and the Surveyor expected them to become cogs in his machine. A typical example of the new spirit was the apparently minor matter of Woolwich's failure to execute a design alteration in the stern of a packet brig, which caused Symonds to explode into a caustic rage. Matters were not helped by a lackadaisical response to his initial, temperate enquiry.

> Woolwich Yard
> 26 July 1833
>
> Sir,
>
> in reply to your minute of the 26th & Mr Barrow's letter of the 26th Inst, we beg to acquaint you that we are very sorry such a mistake should have occurred, it appears that the right aft part of the *Pandora* was built agreeably to the design shewn on the sheer drawing previous to the design shewn on the sketch sent on the 22nd of April, that on receipt of the sketch alluded to the Master Shipwright was absent on the death of his father in law & his assistant was sent to the Admiralty respecting the defects of the *Buffalo*, the drawing was handed by the Master Shipwrights' clerk to

the Foreman of the new work who inadvertently mislaid it in his cabin, & it was not seen by us until called for by the Surveyor's letter of the 23rd Inst.

We are, Sir

Your most obedient servants

O. Lang R. Abethell

Captain Warren. Captain-Superintendant of Woolwich Dockyard

The marginal notes contain the following draft reply.

Admiralty Order 27th July 1833

The Supt. at Woolwich is acquainted that their Lordships grieve to find that the Shw't officers are reduced to the expedient of making such frivolous excuses which are worse than the original mistake, if it was one, and if what is stated by them be correct, the effect of it is to impress on their Lordships mind that the business of Woolwich Yard in the Shw't department is very slovenly conducted.[58]

This Admiralty Order bears all the hallmarks of Symonds, calling into question the veracity and professionalism of the Master Shipwrights in language that could only excite ill-feeling. In the following month a new set of Instructions for Dockyard Officers was distributed. These Instructions were both comprehensive and centralising, further circumscribing the freedom of action of the Master Shipwrights.[59] The Master Shipwrights had generally concurred in the decision to restrict task and job pay to specific areas, but this new assault can hardly have helped the Surveyor's relations with the yards at a time when he was trying to take control of policy.

The great issues at stake between Symonds and Lang concerned the rapid decay of the *Vernon*, and the modified stern built onto the *Trafalgar* by Lang. Symonds approved the plan for the new stern, which was intended to lighten the scantling without sacrificing strength.[60] Several ships left over from the Seppings era were given modifed sterns by the Master Shipwright of the relevant yard, with the approval of the new Surveyor. However, the work on the *Trafalgar* proved to be ill-conceived and worse executed. The two issues came to a head in early 1837. Graham commiserated with the Surveyor:

I am sorry that the dry rot has appeared in the *Vernon*; but we always knew that she was built hastily, and we always feared that Lang had forced upon you ill-seasoned timber. You remember also, how anxious the Duke of Portland was, that she should not be sent to the West Indies: he anticipated the evil which has occurred. The responsibility rests in great measure with me and Sir Thomas Hardy, and I shall not shrink from it. Was *Vernon* filled in on your improved felt principle, or was the filling in that used by Seppings, under our direction applied to *Vernon*?[61]

On her arrival at Sheerness Lang was ordered down to inspect the ship; she was then docked and the Surveyor went to make up his own mind. The necessary repairs cost over £12,000 and had to be repeated 10 years later when she was found to be so defective while serving in the East Indies as to be considered unfit to sail home.[62]

The stern of *Trafalgar* came to Symonds's attention shortly after the disappointment of the *Vernon*. Symonds called on the Captain Superintendent and Lang to explain the obvious deviations from the agreed draft.[63] From this point there could be no disguising the bitterness in relations between the two men. When Symonds attacked the individualism of the Master Shipwrights it was predictable that the ship selected to illustrate his point, the Seppings-designed frigate *Amphion*, was building at Woolwich.

Explain to Sir Charles Adam how inexpedient it is that every Master Shipwright should construct upon his own plan. If that officer is exchanged or removed who is to be responsible?[64]

He even caused the Board to send a letter to Woolwich complaining of the leaks in the roof over *Trafalgar*'s slip.[65]

While the Whig Board remained Symonds made life very difficult for Lang and harrassed him at every turn, but once the Government changed Lang could take his revenge. He provided the coach that took Cockburn to the hustings in 1842, to symbolise a complete reversal of fortunes.[66]

The naval officers

Symonds was not the only naval officer to design ships for the Royal Navy in this period. Both Captain John Hayes and Admiral Sir George Elliot put forward alternative forms that offered some advantages. Hayes, promoted to Post rank in 1802, spent the first five years of his working life as a shipwright apprentice at Deptford where his great uncle was Master Shipwright. He joined the Navy in 1787 on the death of the old shipwright and he came to earn the highest praise for his skill as a seaman and his bravery in action. He suggested razeeing certain old 74s to meet the large American frigates and was appointed to the *Majestic*, one of the first, armed with long 32-pounders and 42-pounder carronades, in 1813. In

The proposed plan for razeeing the Warspite *in 1838. The stern, which is seriously overhung, has been shaded out, and is to be replaced by a more modest example of the elliptical form. The debate over whether or not to razee this ship showed up clear divisions between the Minto Board and the Surveyor, while the partial collapse of her stern created a crisis of confidence.* (NMM)

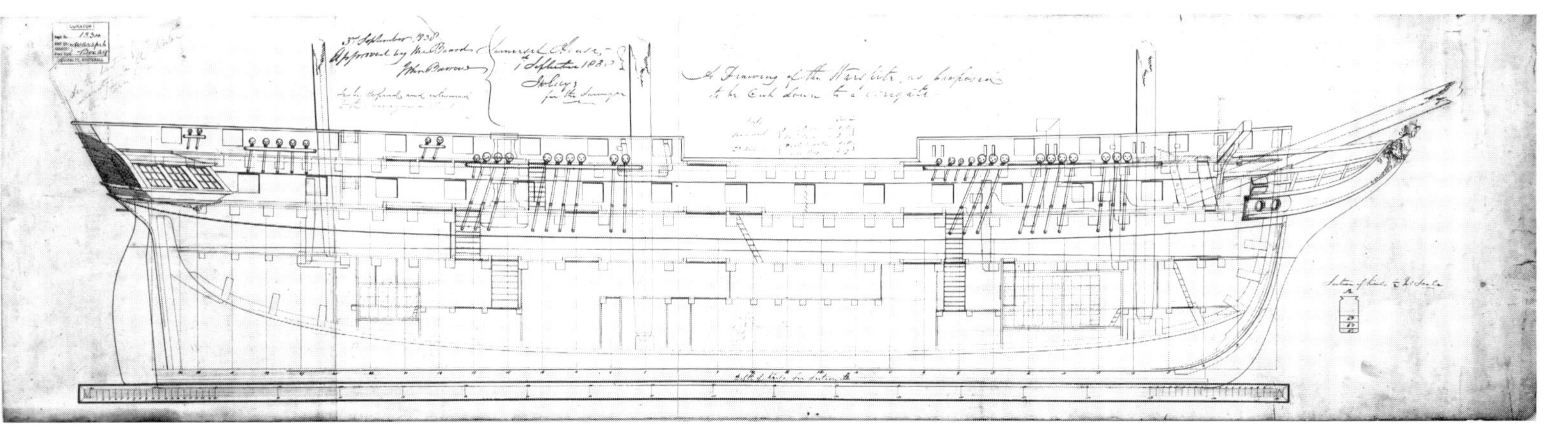

January 1815 she supported the *Endymion* at the capture of the USS *President* after a rare contest of seamanship between two officers of great skill, Henry Hope and Stephen Decatur. After the war Hayes published a pamphlet on naval architecture in which he argued that a given section could be used in every class from a cutter to a First Rate, giving each outstanding qualities. He did not, unlike Symonds, claim to have found such a section, but began to develop his ideas in a series of craft beginning with a cutter. His sloop *Sapphire* was entered in the 1827 trials.[67]

When Symonds took office Hayes was employed building the 36-gun frigate *Inconstant* at Portsmouth. She proved superior to Symonds's *Pique* and so provoked a typical response. The Surveyor drew the attention of the Senior Naval Lord to the lighter scantling of Hayes's ship. With her frames 3ft 1in apart, instead of 2ft 3in the ship was some 25 per cent lighter.[68] This detailed defence was essential with a sailor king and William was soon requesting more details of the new ship.[69]

Well aware of Symonds's views the Board had to work carefully to avoid giving offence when attempting to secure Hayes's draft for an 80-gun ship. Hayes, however, proved to be as unreasonable as the Surveyor. He had no faith in the conduct of Symonds and consequently was unwilling to entrust his design to the Admiralty. Encouragement was given to both men, the promotion of their sons to the rank of Commander being specifically linked to the success of their ships. The First Secretary to the Admiralty, Tuffnell, admitted that the minute had been carefully drawn to avoid creating jealousy.[70] After Hayes's death his son sent in the papers, including the 80-gun design, and was rewarded with promotion. With the rival no longer alive it might have been thought that Symonds might relax his efforts, but he maintained his opposition to Hayes's designs throughout his term in office.[71]

The other naval designer of the period was too well connected to become a victim of Symonds's normal tactics of all-out assault. Admiral Sir George Elliot (1784–1863) was the First Lord's brother.[72] He was appointed First Secretary to the Graham Board on the advice of the King and served under his brother between 1835 and 1837 as a junior Lord. Elliot considered Symonds's ships to be too deep, and argued that their qualities could be achieved with a significantly reduced draft, primarily by returning to a flat floor. While at the Board he took the opportunity to propose building a vessel with one-tenth less draft than the Surveyor's ship of the same class. His colleagues complied.[73] The 18-gun sloop *Modeste*, completed in 1837, proved a relatively successful ship. She met the design criteria but could not match the power of the Surveyor's ships. This vessel led the Cockburn Board to order a ship of 24 guns, the ill-fated *Eurydice*, which was completed in 1843.

Believing that Symonds's success was entirely due to the large size of his ships, Elliot observed that the length-to-beam ratio varied from ship to ship. He suggested that:

> some fixed rule would at least prevent many of the animadversions now so liberally dealt out – both on Symonds & the Board, among scientific, or would be scientific, men.
>
> I confess after giving the thing all the consideration in my power I believe Symonds' ships to have no one good quality which belongs to their peculiar shape. He builds very large ships with great power, to compete with small ships, carrying more weight, and with less power – but any body can do that, if allowed, on the ordinary lines and proportions and I believe avoid his defects. Our 18 gun brigs were 395 tons, *Rover* 568 tons, to carry the same weight!

In view of these criticisms Elliot tended to support Hayes, and adopt policies that were at variance with those preferred by the Surveyor, notably the decision to razee the *Warspite*.[74]

Symonds's thin-skinned response to any criticism, implicit or otherwise, was well known at the Board, leading to some provocative comments of a humorous intent. In late 1838 the old 'donkey' frigate *Talbot*, under Captain Henry Codrington, beat Symonds's 36-gun *Dido* 3 miles into the wind; her Captain sent some verses in celebration.

> Parker had the temerity, this morning, to show them to Symonds, having taken especial care however, to get through the morning's work previously. The Surveyor, as you may imagine, looked rather glum at the intelligence.[75]

After 1841 such comments were read out with greater frequency, and less light-hearted purpose.

4 'A Very Difficult Man to Deal With': the Decline of Symonds: 1841–47

The second half of Symonds's term at the Surveyor's Office was dominated by the political problems of a Whig nominee serving under a Tory Board of Admiralty. This period demonstrates more than the preceeding nine years the dominating influence of politics and the limited impact of the scientific debate on those who actually made the naval policy of Sir Robert Peel's Administration. The Surveyor was forced to spend a great deal of time and effort to defend his ships and his system from the attacks of various individuals and groups who, with the support of the Admiralty, sought to discredit him. If Symonds had little to show for his last six years in office the fault must be seen to lie elsewhere.

In the period 1832–41 Symonds had been the pet of the Whig Boards and the brief Peel Administration of 1834–35 had lacked the time or motivation to alter his terms of service. The return of a strong Tory Administration in September 1841 marked a major shift in the balance of power between Whitehall and Somerset House and the rivalries of the preceding decade now resurfaced. The Surveyor's opponents, having gained the ear of Tory admirals, could now look forward to some reward.

Cockburn was the dominant voice at the Board and he had given his opinion on the appointment of Symonds, as well as on the performance of the *Vernon*, long before. The signs were not good and left Symonds trying to keep up his contacts with the outgoing Board, the Whig Party in general and Portland. Minto realised what would happen:

> I think there is some danger now that the anti-Symonds prejudice at the Admiralty may become as much too strong as the pro-Symonds particularity was in our time, and that you and I may some day find ourselves defending him and his ships from being too much run down, as we had formerly to protect the public and all rivals from his jealous intolerance and power.

He expressed some sympathy when the attack began:

> Poor Symonds finds himself in a very uncomfortable position: from having been too powerful and too little controlled, he has now fallen to the other extreme, and is neither trusted, nor consulted, nor considered. Cockburn appears to have resolved to trample upon him & to give full scope to all his old antipathy. This is neither decent towards such a man in such a station as Symonds, nor consistent with the interests of the service.[1]

The Woolwich Committee

Cockburn's hostility to the new designs was soon made manifest. The alarms of the Minto Board over the absurd degree of rake employed in Symonds's early stern designs was well known. Lang had provided the carriage to take Cockburn to his election, indicating his return to favour and his reward came with an opportunity to attack Symonds's work and to design two large warships.[2] Relying on his allies among the Master Shipwrights, in particular Lang, Cockburn ordered a Committee of Master Shipwrights to assemble at Woolwich in January 1842 to consider the best means of strengthening ships of war and their powers of attack and defence. While the only ship named as displaying any signs of weakness at the stern was the *Britannia*, other ships were to be examined and the report submitted to the Surveyor for his comments. Lang was joined by Hawkes, Fincham and Atkins while Master Shipwright Blake from Portsmouth proposed an improved bow, and carrying the normal planking around the stern.[3]

The Committee called for the plans of several older ships, although for none of Symonds's construction as they could examine the work already carried out on the *Boscawen* then building at the yard. This was particularly unfortunate for Symonds as she was one of the ships built with an over-raked stern. The stern had been reconfigured in 1840 which had resulted in a weak structure that had to be reinforced with iron straps. The initial reports concerned minor structural improvements for the old frigates still on the slips at Woolwich, the *Chichester* and *Amphion*, but the Committee soon progressed to the core of their attack, in particular *Boscawen*'s stern was subjected to a damning critique. 'We are of opinion that the shift of timber is not good, and that, as they are at present disposed the stern is likely to be weak'.[4] Lang went much further, arguing that the stern should be as strong as the broadside: 'Why should the *Boscawen*, a new ship building, have her stern patched up in such a weak, disgraceful manner, there being 70 timbers already hanging unsupported without a shift, a jumble of short snaps, wedges and butts, the most ridiculous specimen of marine architecture I ever saw'.[5] The Committee observed that the lower deck guns could not be run out at the stern and proposed an entirely new structure which the Board adopted; 'their Lordships, wishing every ship to be effective, intend to order the reconstruction of this stern'. The new drawing was also to be used for the *Cumberland*, once Symonds had approved the design.[6]

Symonds protested that Lang had been responsible for changing the original stern of *Boscawen* and then used his own incompetent handiwork to attack the Surveyor. The *Cumberland*, then building at Chatham with the Surveyor's own stern, was certainly a superior design. The Board prevaricated, claiming that they did not intend to make any general alteration in the stern design of the fleet.[7] The Board ordered the stern to be modified after the new plan, which allowed eleven guns to bear across the stern, and increased the strength of the frame at the cost of filling in several windows.[8] When he received the new design Symonds resumed the offensive. The Master Shipwright's design would add weight in a ratio of 11 to 7, reduce defensive power and accommodation; cut out light and ventilation; leave the quarter galleries too narrow for guns; expose the rudder and deform the after body to the detriment of sailing qualities. He also made specific accusations against Lang, pointing to the cumbersome and heavy stern he had inflicted on the *Trafalgar*, so heavy that she now floated 5ft deeper at the stern instead of 2ft 6in as designed. There was too much timber and a false counter, which had to be removed to caulk the timbers beneath. The same fault could be seen on the *Vernon*. In the face of Symonds's attack Lang's immediate superior, the Captain Superintendent at Woolwich, supported the Master Shipwright.[9]

In response the Board offered Symonds the opportunity to make his own improvements in the stern of the *Cumberland* in order that a comparison might be made with the new design by the Woolwich Committee on the *Boscawen*. The Surveyor's design was accepted a month later.[10]

Any facade of professional debate was removed when the Board ordered a new 120-gun ship, significantly to be named the *Royal Albert*, to Lang's design of 1831. Symonds would have been less than human if he had not taken this as a direct criticism of his designs but the insult was compounded in July when Lang was ordered to design the largest paddle warship yet to be built.[11] In addition, Fincham and Blake were also rewarded for their part in the work of the Committee, although on a less generous scale, with the opportunity to design the 50-gun frigates *Raleigh* and *Leander*;[12] and when the first of these ships had been drafted, out of office, Symonds had to request that the drawings be sent for his approval.[13] The import of these public rebuffs was obvious to all and Sir Charles Adam wrote in from the West Indies:

> We have a report now (it comes from that vexatious paper the United Services Gazette to be sure) that Symonds has been dismissed & his department put under a Committee of Shipwrights & suchlike persons. God help the poor Navy under such guidance, more especially if honest Mr Lang is at the head of it, as I conclude will be the case.[14]

Symonds, however, was not without means of reply. At his request, Portland wrote to Haddington in June, receiving a promise that justice would be done to the *Albion*, then being commissioned.[15] Although the Woolwich Committee had produced evidence of weakness in the sterns of the early Symondite ships, their real work had been directed to structural details. In December 1844 the Admiralty adopted the stern designs of the Committee as the standard pattern for the future, and published their report.[16]

Oliver Lang

In the middle years of the Peel Administration Symonds came under serious attack from Lang. In response the Surveyor launched a furious assault on Lang's design for the stern of *Trafalgar*, a ship that Lang was claiming as his own design. In the event the criticisms raised by Sir Thomas Hastings of the *Excellent* resulted in a revised design being ordered from Fincham.[17]

Lang was far from pleased by this rebuff, and waited for a fresh opportunity to attack. This came when Symonds ordered the demolition of the old 74 *Tremendous* at Deptford. She was reported to be sound and Lang proposed that she be razeed into a frigate. Her good sailing qualities were the only reason given for putting so much money into a sixty-year-old ship.[18]

Symonds had been criticised for his decision to sell the old 74 *Scarborough* for £6,000 in 1836. It was thought that she was fit for service and Symonds was accused of selling her to make way for more new construction. In view of the marked preference given to repairs by the Minto Board it was ironic that Wood had to defend him.[19]

Lang promoted the plan to razee the *Tremendous* as an attack on Symonds, and as an act of piety for his late master, for the *Tremendous* had been Seppings first great rebuild. In addition, Lang was identified with the razee programme, having carried out the first postwar razee, that of the *Barham* in 1826. Renamed *Grampus* in May 1845, the ship was finally completed in early 1846 and sent to sea.

The Naval and Military Gazette, an Admiralty journal, praised 'the beautiful, powerful frigate *Grampus*', but her Captain, Henry Martin, took a different view of his new command. He realised that £15,000 had been wasted on an old ship merely to meet 'the partisan views of Woolwich Dock Yard' which the Board adopted for reasons he did not care to specify. When initially invited to put in for the command Henry Martin declined 'because I thought her a bad ship'. In essence the razee had been hurried and carried out within a firm cash limit. The result was a seriously over-masted and badly-stowed frigate fitted out with cheap materials and made all the worse by a low and badly ventilated main deck. Henry Martin eventually took her after his elder brother had to refuse it for personal reasons.[20]

Viewed as an act of spite by Lang against Symonds, the conversion was a great success, but the ship herself was a waste of time and money. The *Grampus* served only one commission, in the Pacific, where she was out of the sight of those responsible for her. She was converted to a powder hulk in 1856 and lasted until 1897, which proved that Lang was at least correct in asserting that her timbers were sound.

Lang made another attempt to secure the Post of Surveyor when Ellenborough formed the Committee of Reference in 1846. Finding himself excluded he pressed his claims as the senior Master Shipwright, Sepping's deputy, the architect of the *Grampus* and the builder of many steamers. He was moritified at having

> been so long kept from the situation I was so justly entitled to expect on the retirement of the late Sir Robert Seppings, to be again passed over for men of much less standing and experience.

He also noted how all the pupils of the old School had been sent to study under him at Somerset House to complete their education. Ellenborough was 'perfectly aware of his great merits' but would, nonetheless, not add to the Committee. In a second letter three days later Lang attacked Symonds for his supposed lack of practical knowledge, as made manifest in the untimely demolition of old ships, notably the *Scarborough*. He now suggested that he should be made a visiting Surveyor, a role in which Seppings had been a marked success. He would be happy to be one of the Surveyors.[21]

Ultimately, Lang was to be disappointed. Ellenborough did nothing to advance his ambition and nor did the returning Whig Board. In May 1847 he applied for the post of Surveyor and he was ordered to submit his draft for an 80-gun screw-

Model of Symonds's great two-decker, the Albion *of 1842. The waist area on the last sailing battleships was almost entirely filled in, creating a more convenient working area for the crew.* (ScM)

The stern of the 90-gun Albion *of 1842. Symonds's stern was an altogether simpler affair than that of Seppings, but lacked the defensive strength of the true round stern. There was simply too much glass to offer any protection to the crews of the stern battery in action.* (ScM)

steam battleship. It was not adopted, however, Edye's *James Watt* draft being preferred.[22] Despite the publication of a long pamphlet in 1848 outlining his contribution to the development of naval architecture Lang was to make no further progress.[23] His last battleship projects, a 90-gun ship on the scantlings of an 80 of 1844, and the 80-gun screw steamer drafted in 1847, were never built and Lang ended his career a bitter and disappointed man. Cockburn used Lang and others simply to attack Symonds and they mistook this for patronage to advance their cause. They were all disappointed.

The Chatham Committee

Following the report of the Woolwich Committee, three pupils of the old School of Naval Architecture, Samuel Read, Henry Chatfield and Augustin Creuze, approached the Board for an opportunity to argue their case. Their first letter was sent in the form of a protest to Cockburn, the obvious patron for Symonds's opponents, in which they complained of being neglected during the past 10 years when Lord Melville, who had taken a real interest in their work, had been out of office. Symonds had deliberately deprived them of opportunities. Characterising the Surveyor's efforts as 'mere speculation', they offered to draft designs for each class, and provide full mathematical reasoning to support their work. They argued that only a truly scientific education, combined with all the available geometric and stability calculations added to the collation of sea experience, could hope to produce superior ships. This offered a scientific avenue of attack for the First Naval Lord, which was readily grasped. Cockburn ordered them to assemble as a Committee of Naval Architecture at Chatham on 27 April 1842, only seven days after their first letter.

However, the three men soon discovered that Cockburn did not share their view of the value of the exercise. They were restricted to their own efforts and repeatedly pressed to provide quick results so they could return to their regular posts at the various dockyards. The first completed draft, that of the 36-gun frigate *Thetis*, was finally submitted in February 1843 but the Admiralty simply responded by ordering them to restrict their efforts to the 80-gun ship. Cockburn was unimpressed with their progress and rejected their requests for an interview, ordering them back to their stations on 7 October 1843. Fortunately, Henry Corry, the Junior Civil Lord, was then in the yard and took the order back to Whitehall where it was cancelled. The draft of the new 80-gun ship, built as the *Cressy*, was complete on the 16th. They were then allowed a further period to draft a 12-gun brig, the 420-ton *Espiegle*. Chatfield and Creuze requested permission to complete the full series of drafts but as these would take four months each to calculate the Board informed them that the existing designs would be tried before any further orders were placed. The Committee finally broke up in August 1844, having designed four vessels, the three built and an alternative, longer, 80-gun ship.[24]

It is clear that Cockburn was happy to support the pupils of the old School only for so long as they could be employed in his battle with Symonds. However, their interminable calculations were time-consuming and incomprehensible to the layman and consequently did not serve his purpose. As a result they were dropped before their work could be tried. Symonds showed his disgust at the entire episode by holding up the plans for the *Cressy*.[25]

The work the Committee had been able to complete was in fact largely correct, both in method and principle, but the limitations of timber construction made their efforts little more than academic. The hull form they adopted was a compromise between the flat floor of the 1820s and the sharp rise of floor employed by Symonds. *Thetis* did well, but her captain was a first class jockey. *Cressy* used too much compass timber and demonstrated no merits after conversion to steam. The lessons to be drawn from these designs would have been useful had they been drawn up in collaboration with the Surveyor's Office, but as they were used for a politically motivated assault on the Surveyor it was inevitable they would be sacrificed in favour of more effective methods of harrassing that official. As D K Brown has pointed out, the calculations which the Committee used were not the special preserve of the old School but the fact of publication marked them out as scientific.[26]

Henry Chatfield resumed the pamphlet war in 1846, in response to the pamphlet *Facts versus Fiction*, prepared in the Surveyor's Office to defend Symonds and his ships. He attempted to keep a sense of proportion, defending the work of the Chatham Committee against the latest attack, and arguing for a more scientific approach. He observed that the new pro-Symonds work was unlikely to be the work of Marryatt, as it lacked his 'wit and originality'. The bulk of the text concerned itself with a blow by blow critique of *Facts* and reinforced the School case.

When Symonds retired in 1847 Chatfield, the most bitter of the School pupils, published another critical pamphlet. While admitting that Symonds held:

> bold and comprehensive views of the enlarged dimensions, so often considered requisite for ships of war, [he] has still very arbitrary doctrinal opinions subversive of sound principles in science.

The basis of his attack lay in Symonds's modifications to *Vanguard*, *Queen* and other ships, and the 'manipulation of evidence' which was intended to make the Surveyor's ships appear cheaper to build and maintain. He also attacked the carpentry arrangements and stern framing of the Symonds/Edye regime, but there was nothing new in this, and simply reflected, yet again, Chatfield's bitterness at their failure to supplant Symonds.[27]

Cockburn and the alternative designs

Having failed to secure irrefutable evidence of Symonds's failure, either from the Master Shipwrights or the Chatham Committee, Cockburn fell back on blind prejudice. His support for the decision to build a replica of the old *Sans Pareil*, and his continuing advocacy of the razee policy, demonstrated the degree to which he had failed to understand the real impact of Symonds on naval design.

After the failure of the initial professional attack the Symonds debate became increasingly politicised. The only recourse left to Cockburn was the sailing trial, which he did not place much faith in particularly as it was the one area in which Symonds had always excelled. However, the results that came from the trials of 1844 and 1845 were sufficiently contradictory to give Cockburn his opportunity.

Portland rejoined the debate, and in a letter to Peel attacked Lang and the decision to allow him to build a new First Rate. He called for more thorough comparative sea trials for all new ships, in particular for the *Albion* and the *Collingwood* and the whole tone of the correspondence reflected the prompting of Symonds who was a regular guest at Welbeck.[28]

Peel passed on the letter to Haddington, who understood the nature of the problem.

> I understand from you that you wish'd he should be satisfied. If by satisfied you mean convinced, I have no such expectation...
>
> Symonds is everything with him, and I have no doubt that I may fairly consider his letter as Symonds'
>
> Symonds & I are very good friends – tho' he is a very difficult man to deal with when you venture to differ on opinion with him. I have no doubt he *thinks* Cockburn assumes too much dominion over him – but he would think the same of any person in Cockburn's situation who ventured with his own eyes and to judge for himself.
>
> I believe Cockburn has acted with perfect fairness towards him – I am certain he wishes to do so. Symonds ought to be properly supported – but Symonds is I think spoilt and certainly is unreasonable very often.[29]

Haddington, having waited to discuss the subject with Cockburn, wrote again to Peel, deprecating the reliability of trial results and the impact of skillful 'jockey' captains on any trials. He admitted that there was a great deal of party feeling in the Navy about Symonds's ships, but expressed himself satisfied that there was no bias at the Board.[30] Portland responded by pointing out the failings of the Captains sent to try the *Vernon* and *Pique*, both of whom had ignored Symonds's advice on the trim and sails of their vessels. He also suggested it would have been safer to try out Lang's ideas in a brig before building a first rate.[31] Haddington began to despair of this correspondence with 'the indefatigable amateur' but he realised that Peel could not afford to alienate the Duke, and that he would have to accommodate Portland's opinions and stage some large-scale sailing trials.[32] In the event Symonds and Portland would have been better advised to keep their own council. The 1844 trials gave an opportunity for a further display of Tory hostility toward the Surveyor's ships, something that could hardly be avoided when a Tory Board selected Tory officers to command them.

With his supporter Admiral Bowles in command the Squadron of Evolution should have worked to Symonds's advantage, but the Captains were less than committed to the new ships. William Fanshawe Martin, the eldest son of the last Controller, took command of the *Queen*, and ensured she finished way behind the old *St Vincent*. Symonds observed that his masterpiece was seriously out of trim, requesting William Martin to have her on an even keel to lift the buttocks out of the water.

Byam Martin gave his son some sound advice:

> the eyes of the service are on the *Queen*, with violent prejudices for and against her and her constructor and his eyes (not bad ones as a seaman) will be upon your sails to see if they are well hoisted up, and well trained, that in case the ship has not a decided superiority over the others he may, if he can, put in a salvo on that point.
>
> I have a long letter from Admiral Bowles this evening, and much regret to find Sir W. Symonds is at his elbow: it would be better if he were left to his own uninfluenced judgement.

Later the old Admiral suggested that any comments on the *Queen* be kept for private and official correspondence.[33]

In the event Symonds reacted just as Byam Martin had ancitipated and accused William Martin of over-staying the masts. Captain Henry Martin was satisfied his brother stood too high in the opinion of the service for such comments to have any adverse effect. While he expected the Surveyor might be able to improve his ships he expected him to be removed from office when Parliament reassembled.[34] Byam Martin reopened old wounds by attacking Graham and Admiral Pechell, one of the Naval Lords in 1832, for appointing the Surveyor:

> The only principle Sir W. Symonds has *maintained*, is that of excessive breadth, which to a degree was needed by our old ships, but he has carried it too far, and everything he does amounts to a tacit confession that his principle, *in extremis*, is erroneous, but he has not the candour, (it is not in the nature of the man) frankly to avow it; he will never consent to acknowledge that any notion he adopts can be wrong.[35]

In truth the performance of the ship was seriously affected by William Martin's handling of her, and with the failure of the two-deckers *Albion* and *Vanguard* this was the final straw for many of Symonds's patrons. Even Bowles admitted that the trial results, with the new ships more often being beaten by their elderly squadron mates, indicated a need to modify the new ships.[36]

Symonds's supporters in the Whig Party, particularly Minto and Sir Charles Wood, Secretary to the Admiralty 1835–39, had maintained their contacts, but their object was to gain information to use in the House. Wood felt some awkwardness in going to Somerset House for it was bound to be reported and could only harm Symonds.[37] Initially, they had been pleased to see Admiral Bowles join the Board, Sir Charles Adam observing: 'I rejoice that Symonds will have a person there who will support him as he deserves'.[38] When the 1844 trials went against the Surveyor it was clear that he would have to bend to the criticism coming in from all sides. The Whigs were no longer prepared to provide an open ended defence and Wood made the obvious point, one that had occurred to many 10 years earlier:

> It may do very well for a yacht to require as nice trimming and handling as the *Albion*, seems to do, when they are only running a race from Cowes and back, but it is a serious drawback in a two decker.

This sudden enlightenment marked the end of Symonds's term of office. The appointment had been made on party grounds, and once the Whig Party no longer cared to defend it the post would be terminated. Wood continued: 'I am afraid after giving Symonds great and full credit we must admit that there is something yet wanted beyond beam to make a good ship of war'.[39] Another member of the Minto Board, the Whig Admiral J W D Dundas, remained loyal to Symonds but only in correspondence with the Surveyor; later events were to demonstrate that he had taken the same lessons from 1844 as Wood.[40]

Symonds now turned to Minto for support, something he felt entitled to expect while he was acting as the Whig mole at Somerset House. He accused his competitors of cheating in the brig trials, particularly John Fincham, Master Shipwright at Portsmouth, who was emerging as the main professional threat. In addition he reported that Captain Lord Hardwicke had publicly accused him of building Whig ships 'which he knew by their smell'.[41]

Aware of the extent to which his reputation had suffered from vicious attacks in such Tory journals as the *Morning Herald* and *Standard*, Symonds employed all the tools of the self-publicity trade. He requested Portsmouth Yard to provide information on the launch weight of the *Royal Albert*, to highlight the problems of building such a large ship; he persuaded Portland to request that Captain Sir Baldwin Walker, one of the finest sea officers in the service and a known advocate of the Surveyors' ships, be given the command of the *Queen* which was to be modified before the 1845 cruise; he leaked official papers to the *Morning Post*, for which he was rebuked by the Board; and continued his correspondence with Minto, noting the success of his *Flying Fish* over the Chatham Committee's *Espiegle* in the latest brig trials and pressing him to have an MP call for the publication of Bowles's report. Later in the year he persuaded Edye to compile a powerful pamphlet attack on his critics.[42]

Despite these measures the attacks continued. Bowles's report was published, along with that of the Woolwich Committee, while Hume repeated his lament for the 'ill-used' pupils of the SNA, many of whom were compiling acid copy for newspapers in the dockyard towns. However, while Wood and Minto could agree that the SNA had not discovered the secrets of naval architecture, they now no longer believed that Symonds had either.[43]

Placing Walker in the *Queen* worked wonders. She beat all comers and earned the highest paise from all that cared to see. However, the Whigs were no longer impressed by such testimonials.

> there is a growing impression that good as ships are, there is need of further improvement to obviate the uneasiness & dispense with the extreme nicety of handling which seems necessary to get their qualities out of them.
>
> it would have been better for Symonds himself if he had been more prepared to improve certain defective points in his ships some time ago – but the run against him was so unfair that he required at our hands all the backing up that we could give him.[44]

Symonds was reaching the end of his strength, writing to Minto that he had been 'a victim of party since the breaking up of Sir James Graham's Administration at the Admiralty. The stream of prejudice has been a torrent against me, and I have found the dockyard current difficult to stem'. Of the present Board he considered that only Bowles understood naval architecture. 'I am well aware that whatever I have done is susceptible of great improvement and all that I ask is to be permitted to make them more perfect after fair and sufficient trials'.[45] Going to see his ships underway restored his spirits, as it always had. He noted their relative failure in light airs, but exulted in the way they 'shewed a vast superiority over everything' in a breeze.[46]

He spent September at Clipstone, one of Portland's seats, and, still in search of support, used the opportunity of a figurehead being needed for the frigate *Constance* to renew his contact with Graham, now Peel's Home Secretary, as this required a bust of Graham's daughter. In his reply the Home Secretary advised him to keep quiet and hold on, 'correcting errors where experience shows that improvements are necessary, or that mistakes have been made'.[47]

The 1845 trials were placed under the command of Rear Admiral Sir Samuel Pym. In view of the bias widely ascribed to the veteran officer Symonds consulted Minto. He was advised to consult Bowles and through him to present his fears to Cockburn. Minto attempted to keep the Surveyor quiet, and pointed out that his pamphlet *Facts versus Fiction* had not been well timed in view of the impending trials.[48] This intervention resulted in a sharp clash between Minto and his fellow Scottish peer, Haddington. Minto's letter was shown to various members of the Board by Symonds and ultimately came to the notice of the First Lord who, already aware of the relationship between the Surveyor and Minto, sent a firm protest, deprecating the idea that Pym was biased, disapproving of Minto's interference with the Board, and requesting that he write directly to Haddington himself. After Minto had excused himself Haddington enlarged on his views:

> It has ever appeared a marvellous thing to me that we should have lorded it over the world so long at sea & had more experience of ships than all the other nations of the earth combined – and yet be so far from to seek for anything approach to perfection in our vessels.
>
> I hope if Symonds' ships are convicted of having some faults that he will be induced to profit by the experience offered to him – & correct the defects. I am quite certain there will be a perfect readiness to secure to the service the benefits of his improvements.[49]

In the event, Pym's cruise proved to be something of an anti-climax. The old Admiral was hardly out of sight of land before he had made his mind up as to the superiority of the large Symondites over their rivals in strong breezes. The squadron was ranked in descending order of merit *Queen*, *Albion* and *Rodney*, *Canopus* and *Vanguard*, *Trafalgar* slow but weatherly, and *St Vincent* leewardly and crank.[50] On reflection Bowles was satisfied with Pym's cruise, but while he was confident Symonds could improve his ships he did not believe he would long remain in office: 'His health is however much shaken by anxiety and annoyance, and I am afraid his active career is almost run'.[51] The Surveyor allowed himself to indulge in a little gloating, blaming the Captains for the problems of the 80-gun ships *Vanguard* and *Superb*, and observing that William Martin was 'dreadfully disconcerted' by the failure of his new ship, the *Trafalgar*. Minto urged Symonds to consider modifying his form, arguing that the superior performance of the *Queen* over the *Albion* was a reflection of her less radical floor, particularly as a two-decker should normally beat a three-decker.[52]

Symonds's satisfaction proved to be short-lived.

The Committee of Reference

In view of the mixed results of the 1845 trials, both for brigs and battleships, Cockburn, still without a clear rationale for anything more than harrassing Symonds, elected to suspend all ships of 110 and 90 guns building to Symonds's designs. In a memorandum of 15 November he argued that the sudden improvement by the *Queen* proved that 'there is not at present any fixed or scientific principle by which the construction of our ships is to be regulated'. This was a comment that was particularly ill-timed, given the attempts of Bowles and Minto to persuade the Surveyor to modify his 'system'. While Cockburn's Board had encouraged competition, with beneficial results, he supported the suggestion made by Lord John Russell in the House, that a Scientific Board of Construction should be set up under the Admiralty to inspect all new drafts. Expressing the highest confidence in the ability of 'science' to discover some 'fixed & certain principles of construction', he did not give the Surveyor any role in these proceedings, either by name or position. In a memorandum of 1847 Cockburn argued that the Committee of Reference removed the need for a Surveyor, whether he was a designer or not.[53] The object of the exercise was to deprive the Surveyor of the function he had been allowed to assume under the new instructions of 1832: that of being the principal architect of designs to the Admiralty. In this role the Surveyor was to report on the plans of others; exercise a general supervision over the building department and attempt to provide some general principle of construction; avoid the danger of building bad ships; and save the money being spent on experiments and alterations. Haddington considered that in view of 'his abilities' Symonds should be a member of the Committee of Construction, a matter on which Cockburn had studiously avoided commenting. The other members, under a naval chairman, would be Professors Inman and Main of the Naval College and Joseph Large, Surveyor of Lloyd's although a pupil of the old School. However, he did anticipate that Symonds and 'his keen partisans' would take offence, although the potential for improvement would justify the measure. Peel concurred, having made a similar suggestion in Cabinet some months before. He recalled that Graham objected that the Admiralty should undertake the work and considered £200 per annum an over generous remuneration for the Committee members. On reflection Peel returned to the point, and urged Haddington to refer the matter to Graham without mentioning Peel's role. The Home Secretary considered that this new body would be a resuscitation of the Navy Board, which he had abolished 13 years before.[54]

In Haddington's last dealings with the Admiralty he urged the need for a Commission to investigate the dockyards, and for the early appointment of the construction Board to avoid 'the suspicion of extravagence'. As most of the extravagant measures of the past five years had come about as the result of the work of Herbert, Corry and Cockburn this was a peculiarly unjust rationale for an attack on Symonds, who had opposed the over-anxious rush into large screw steamers.[55]

The appointment of the Committee was postponed by the political problems of the Peel Administration. Haddington was replaced by Ellenborough on 13 January in order to reinforce the Ministers in the Upper House, but even the new First Lord's *terribilis celeritas* could not immediately master the multiplicity of issues facing the Board. By the end of March construction was once again a live issue. The Junior Naval Lord, Captain Henry Rous, no friend of the Surveyor, provided

The 90-gun Princess Royal, *completed as a steamship in 1854, had been subjected to a series of modifications from her original design as a unit of the* Albion*-class. The controversy surrounding this ship and her half sister, the* Hannibal, *brought on Symonds's resignation.* (IWM)

the First Lord with a *resumé* of the recent developments in Naval Architecture:

> a sudden revolution of opinion persuaded naval men – great beam, few guns & those of heavy calibre and power to stand up under canvas found universal favour – at that time the merits of a long bow were not sufficiently understood – and the only rock which proved fatal to the service was a public declaration of Sir W. Symonds that he had at last discovered the new principle and that all his ships from a three decker to a cutter should fit one class into the other like a Chinese puzzle. . . .
>
> his first frigates, *Vernon* and *Pique*, were built with a bluff bow above water and with fine lines underneath, consequently when full of water and provisions they could not rise to a heavy sea, they strained their rigging and they floated from 12 to 16 inches deeper in the water than he ever calculated, a mistake he has made in every large ship he has ever built, notwithstanding he has reduced his ballast nearly 5/6ths. . . .
>
> during the Minto administration the road to employment, to promotion was only open to officers who were ready to swear that Symonds' ships were the *ne plus ultra* of perfection – and no wonder for in those days Sir C. Adam and Sir W. Parker took upon themselves the responsibility of order . . . upwards of ten sail of the line to be built before they had ever tried the *Vanguard* in a gale of wind.
>
> With respect to Sir W. Symonds, the Navy is indebted to him for many beautiful and efficient vessels. Brigs, corvettes & 26 gun frigates – his large frigates he has latterly laid down are great improvements upon his old lines, but he has failed in all his steam vessels and in his ships of the line.

In conclusion, Rous accused the Surveyor of systematic false accounting in the dockyards in order to obscure the real cost of his ships. In searching for an Admiral to command the 1846 Squadron of Evolution he suggested Sir William Parker, or Sir Charles Napier.[56] Ellenborough responded by drawing up a minute calling for the establishment of a three-man Committee which would advise the Board, one of whom would be the Surveyor, by submitting reports and models. In future, something approximating to the modern Ships' Cover would be kept, including lines, costs, modifications and sailing reports.[57] Rous put forward a similar proposal, restricting the Surveyor to dockyard management and an advisory role on shipbuilding, but the Governor-General, not surprisingly, preferred his own draft which left the new Board responsible for the advice it tendered.[58]

In May, acting on advice from Symonds, Portland prepared a detailed case against further razees, in particular the proposal to alter the *Camperdown*, for which Ellenborough thanked him. The Surveyor was still dealing with small issues and urged the First Lord to appoint his son Thomas to the 26-gun *Spartan*, to ensure she had a fair trial against the Elliots' *Eurydice*. Thomas repaid the First Lord for his appointment by offering the commissioning vacancy for a first class volunteer to Minto, who was quick to accept. Later the young Symonds overpressed his case for a particular First Lieutenant and was severely rebuked by Ellenborough. Both father and son were soon to realise that the new man was far removed from the mild Haddington.[59]

On May 26 1848 the Committee of Reference was finally named. The members were Professor Inman and the shipwright officers Richard Abethell and John Fincham. Symonds immediately complaind that he could not work with Inman and called for a naval officer to be placed on the Committee. Ellenborough considered the objections to be personal and would not change his Board, and he warned Symonds that the matter would be raised at the Admiralty if he continued his protest; in the meantime he appointed Captain Lord John Hay as Chairman. Lang was equally displeased by the thought of Abethell, his long-time assistant at Woolwich, in the place he coveted.[60] Before any work could be carried out the Peel Administration fell. Ellenborough wrote up his views on naval administration, giving a prominent place to the Committee; however, he believed the appointment of efficient dockyard superintendents was the real answer to waste.[61]

The Hannibal, *at the end of the century, showing the modified stern of the late 1840s, some of the windows being closed in.* (NMM)

The 1846 Squadron, sent out by Ellenborough under William Parker provided the results that could have been achieved two years before had a more efficient and less partisan man than Hyde Parker been sent. While Symonds's ships were fast and weatherly, William Parker had been told that in bad weather their roll was 'so violent as to render them unable to use their guns with any precision as compared with ships of the same class of different construction'. He had no proof for this and excused the *Queen* from any criticism. Parker believed more ballast would be the answer but Symonds had been averse to this as his battleships were already too deep.[62]

The return of the Whigs

When the Peel Administration fell, in mid-1846, the Committee of Reference, a Tory device intended to attack the Whig appointed Surveyor, might have appeared to have little future. However, it survived under the new regime because of the Whig/Scottish connections of Lord John Hay and the determination of the Whigs to sacrifice Symonds. The bitter in-party fight over the Admiralty during the formation of the new Administration resulted in the exclusion of Minto and as such completed the process of dissociating the party from the man they had selected 15 years before. Symonds kept up his correspondence with Minto and Portland, but the former was out of office and the latter had little influence once the Russell Administration could be certain of the support of the Peelite faction. When the Committee began to criticise his work Symonds responded with his normal bitter tirade. Minto and Admiral Sir Charles Adam, the First Naval Lord, advised him to tone down his remarks and try to keep a sense of professional detachment. Minto admitted that Symonds had endured much, but advised him to avoid a 'false step'. Unfortunately, his only friend on the Board, Adam, was not to last long. Adam left the Board to become Governor of Greenwich Hospital in July 1847, by which time Symonds was effectively out of office.[63]

In April 1847 the final humiliation was applied. The Board ordered the Surveyor to adhere strictly to the instruction of 9 May 1846, whereby all drawings were to be referred to the Committee of Reference before any decision was taken by the Board. In addition, he was to liaise more closely with the Steam Department:

> and the Surveyor will understand that it is their Lordships' intention to call for plans and drawings for vessels of every class from such parties as they may select, if they should deem it adviseable.

Among these parties were the Chatham Committee and the Committee of Reference, while Symonds was restricted to modifying the incomplete *Albion*-class 90-gun ships, and designing an 80-gun screw steamer.[64]

The Committee of Reference provided a report that could have been anticipated. It criticised the extreme manifestations of Symonds's system and advised a more moderate length-to-beam ratio and a flatter floor. The results were similar to the views of Fredrik af Chapman, who was still the model for three men who had served at the old School of Naval Architecture. The Surveyor ordered his ships to be modified in line with the recommendations of his critics and the most offensive modifications were those made to the draft of the *Albion*'s sister ships. This time there was no-one with sufficient influence to save Symonds's system, and without his system Symonds would not remain. Though convinced that he was correct Symonds saw no reason to fight on, being 65 and in poor health. Portland tried to revive his interest with another offer to sponsor a brig. The new craft would have reproduced Symonds's *Flying Fish* with an additional 1ft of beam but Symonds did not have the stomach for another battle and as Portland was no longer a political force, it was time to stop. At this time Symonds decided to have the last word in the debate on hull form, making a provision in his will to have his views published after his death.[65]

Portland continued the argument after Symonds's retirement, but he achieved nothing. Auckland had decided to replace Symonds's system and if Symonds would not bend, as he fully expected he would not, then it was time for him to go. The First Lord treated Portland with every consideration, keeping him informed of the latest thinking on hull forms, and pointing to the success of the screw steamers, both under sail and steam.[66] These new auxiliary steam ships were the final reason for abandoning Symonds's system. The most effective hull form for a low-powered screw steamer was the exact opposite of that preferred by the Surveyor.

On the Committee of Reference it was Fincham, rather than Inman, who turned out to be the real threat to Symonds's position. His combining in argument of both theory and practice made him hard to contradict. His ambition appears to have dovetailed with that of Hay for where the Chairman looked for power without responsibility, Fincham wanted to be the next Surveyor; Cockburn rewarded the Master Shipwright for his contradiction of the Surveyor. By 1846 Fincham had quite supplanted Lang; he secured orders to design several major screw steamers, rebuild the controversial stern of the *Trafalgar* and supervise the conversion of the blockship 74s. In his book *A History of Naval Architecture*, published in 1851, Fincham attempted to portray himself with a modesty that Lang, Symonds and others had failed to demonstrate. He argued that Symonds had failed because he was technically and numerically illiterate. His criticism of Symonds's form appeared reasonable and gave his words an impartial authority that was not entirely honest. Fincham had been a competitor for the post of Surveyor, and a disappointed one at that. However, his criticism of sailing trials of the period, for their relative inaccuracy and failure to equalise the ships in every respect before the start, was well made.[67]

Fincham, for all his claims to professional skill, made a serious blunder in his work on screw steamships. Disregarding the views of Petit Smith and Brunel, he persevered with the old round stern instead of adopting the fine lines considered vital by those two engineers. As a result, his ships failed to achieve their design speed and several were even modified by Symonds who must have taken a curious pleasure in proving his skill with the screw steamers that were hateful to him.

Despite his failings Fincham was the leading light in the work of the Committee. His views conditioned its work, from the design of steam warships to the new carpentry plan proposed for the *Caesar*. However, it would appear that he was a supporter of the Tory Party and as such he could never have achieved the one prize to which he aspired under a Whig Board, even if the post had remained open to constructors.

Retirement

Symonds effectively retired in mid-1847 and concluded his official career by sending the Board an unsolicited collection of papers in defence of his ships and his system, in particular their relative cost. The First Naval Lord, Admiral Dundas, minuted 'I am not aware that the Board of Admiralty ever called for any refutation from Sir W. Symonds'.[68] After the Surveyor's departure Edye was ordered to prepare a full list of the Surveyor's minutes. Now that he was no longer a political liability Dundas was prepared to laud Symonds.

> Nothing can shew so clearly the zealous and indefatigable services of Sir W. Symonds than this schedule. I recommend that it should be printed by our own press – a few copies given to the members of the Board, and the original kept in the Record Office.

Auckland agreed, for the list would be a useful piece of evidence to deflect any protest in the House of Commons over the level of Symonds's pension. Early in 1848 a Parliamentary Return on the sailing qualities of Symonds's ships was prepared in such a manner as to be entirely favourable to the late Surveyor. The inference was clear: once the man was removed his system could be defended.[69] Although he left office in June Symonds's retirement was dated from October 1847. The pension amounted to a modest £500 per annum in addition to his half pay of £228, and this was only three quarters of that awarded to Seppings. From July John Edye had been acting for the Surveyor and was to remain Acting Surveyor until February 1848.

After the official retirement date had passed Graham told Symonds that he thought it for the best that he enjoy his retirement for he was confident that history would judge him well. He hoped to see him made Naval Aide de Camp, an honour that he was eventually to bestow when he next became First Lord.[70] In the intervening period Symonds had been created a Civil Commander of the Order of the Bath, on 1 May 1848. He was then placed on the retired list of Rear Admirals as a Captain lacking three years sea time. After his retirement Symonds spend much of his time abroad, principally for the benefit of his health, and died at sea between Malta and Marseilles on 30 March 1856. Under the terms of his will he left money to publish a valedictory biography, in the form of a defence of his system and his ships. James Sharp's book of 1858 had the singular curiosity of reviving the great debate of the 1830s and 1840s at a time when sailing ships were of historical interest. There is hardly one word about the screw propeller.

Graham, having appointed Symonds, was the perfect man to pronounce upon his contribution. On 29 April 1847 he told the House that:

> except on matters of religion he did not know that any difference of opinion had been attended with so much bitterness – so much anger – so much resentment, as the merits of Sir W. Symonds and the virtue of his ships.[71]

In 1849 he told Symonds:

> You laid the foundation of the better system. The public is indebted to you for the germ of the improvement which constitutes the real merit.[72]

In 1853 he was more reflective.

> I have encountered much obloquy on account of his appointment, yet I am satisfied that I did the state good service when I made it: for without the genius and firmness of Sir William Symonds the rapid advance in the improvements of naval architecture never would have realised.[73]

Given that this letter would be shown to Portland it is not clear if Graham was referring to the advances actually made by Symonds, which would have pleased Portland, or with a degree of irony that would be lost on his noble co-adjudicator in the cause, to the general quickening of the pace of advance occasioned by Symonds's controversial term of office.

Conclusion

Symonds built the last and largest sailing battleships. They combined great power under sail with a large, well-spaced battery and the ultimate in speed in the right conditions. They were the culmination of the postwar attempt to rationalise the experience of 1793–1815 and create a Navy capable of battlefleet sea control and, vitally, of winning the battles that would be the acid test of success. If his ships had their faults they were nonetheless far in advance of their foreign competitors. The last British sailing battleships possessed an edge in performance that made it possible to resolve the age-old tactical problem of how to bring a flying enemy to battle and force him to fight. If this was the case, it would be harsh to adjudge that the speed was purchased too dearly.

Although the Symonds form was not perfect, it did demonstrate that it was possible to build battleships of improved performance. The work of the 1846 Committee of Reference promised much, combining the new dimensions, which Symonds had secured, with a compromise form based on af Chapman. The rapid perfection of the screw propeller prevented their work from reaching the sea in its original form.

Symonds was a seaman first and foremost. His ships were built for experts, from whom they received great praise. They were not, however, seen to any advantage in the hands of less capable officers, though as part of a balanced battlefleet they could provide the key to tactical success, acting as a detached squadron. While he was almost the last amateur shipbuilder to work for the Navy, Symonds was far from the failure that professional critics have argued. Edward Reed gave it as his opinion that Graham, 'made war, not only upon professional naval architects, but upon the profession of naval architecture itself'. He believed that Symonds had been born too late, and that his work had been replaced by the scientific work of the School.[74] What Reed and all those who have followed his line have failed to appreciate is the degree to which the Symonds debate was based on political animus stemming from the abolition of the Navy Board and the politicised nature of the early nineteenth century officer corps. When Tory critics could seriously argue that the Surveyor's ships were inferior to those of France or the United States it was clear that reality had long ceased to influence their views.

In 1846 a relatively junior officer published his contribution to the debate. Commander Adolphus Slade called for a more scientific approach, citing the results of the French system as his *beau ideal*. As a result he praised the efforts of the School, and lamented their 20-year period of obscurity. He was well aware of the damage done to the concept of an impartial report by partisan divisions within the officer corps. He was sure that Symonds's form would answer for brigs and yachts, but not for battleships, particularly in northern waters. He was not convinced that speed was a virtue worth the sacrifice of stability, although the limited stowage of the Surveyor's designs was not a problem given the wide spread of British bases. His conclusion was the same as all reasonable men: that the office of Surveyor should arbitrate between designs, rather than provide them. Given the limitations of any individual he favoured a Board of Naval Construction. Slade summed up the problem, provided the rational solution and leaves historians to consider why the obvious was resisted for so long.[75]

Viewed against the changing political alignments of the period Symonds's career makes more sense. He was the one man who combined success in sailing trials with powerful patrons and a degree of good fortune in the timing of his career. The Master Shipwrights were no longer suitable for the new Surveyor's Office, while the pupils of the School were too young and lacked the stamp of success. Symonds's term of office was a significant contribution to the development of the sailing warship, and with more liberal estimates might have had an even more profound impact on the Navy.

5 *Captain Sir Baldwin Walker and the Reconstruction of the Surveyor's Office: 1848–50*

The interregnum at the Surveyor's Office

During the period between Symonds's retirement in July 1847 and the appointment of a new Surveyor in February 1848 John Edye was in charge of the Surveyor's Office. Despite his relatively weak position, being intimately connected with a discredited regime, Edye was able to deflect and defeat many of the more extreme proposals of the Committee, and find the time to defend Symonds and himself. The searing critique of his framing, as a 'cumbersome and useless expenditure of timber', was rebutted and consequently withdrawn.[1] He was equally successful in forestalling Hay's plans to install the surplus engines left over from the iron frigate programme in the *Nile, London, Powerful* and *Worcester*.[2] His own designs were either for modified versions of Symonds's ships, or in the case of the 80-gun screw steamer *Audacious/James Watt*, something entirely new that demonstrated his mastery of the screw steamship that Symonds had so despised.[3]

Sir Baldwin Walker

Walker was born in 1802, entered the Navy in 1820 and rapidly earned a reputation as the smartest sea officer of the era. As First Lieutenant of the *Vanguard* he provided Symonds with early evidence to support his form. His period as effective Commander-in-Chief of the Turkish fleet, between 1838 and 1844, combined active service on the Syrian coast, in particular at Acre and for which he was knighted, with administration and service education, including the introduction of a new tactical doctrine. Returning to the Royal Navy in 1845 he took command of the *Queen* during the 1845 Squadron of Evolution, and was then rewarded with the command of the 50-gun *Constance* on the Pacific station, where he could expect to earn several thousand pounds in freight money. He soon brought the ship up to his own high standards and maintained them throughout his period in command. Despite his own wishes he was recalled from the Pacific in late 1847 and turned over his ship which, he argued, had cost him in the region of £4,000. On arriving in Britain he refused the Surveyor's Office, but was 'pressed by many friends, and those in office'. Despite the nature of the office – 'one of, if not the most disagreeable appointments under government' – and the extra work involved as Comptroller of Steam, Walker was paid £694 – less than half the amount given to Dockyard Superintendents. He received another £300 for the house in Somerset Place he had been obliged to leave in 1848. Only in 1853 did Graham secure him a rise to £1,000 per annum, which brought his pay more in line with his responsibilities.[4]

In selecting Walker for the post of Surveyor, Lord Auckland made a clear signal that he intended to reform the post. He could see the damage that had been done by the Symonds era, not so much as a result of the ships which had been built, but in the poor relations between the various parties and the bitter feuds which had erupted. As part of his overhaul of naval administration Auckland instituted the concept of non-political appointments in the dockyards, thereby creating a system that could not function under a partisan Surveyor. Auckland wanted to use the Surveyor to arbitrate between designs and draw up long-term programmes. His original memorandum on the reconstruction of the office, drawn up on 8 May, became an official minute on 2 June, on receipt of Treasury sanction. The most interesting point of distinction between the two drafts lies in paragraph three in which Auckland stressed that the Surveyor was not to design ships before establishing his own duties. In addition, Professor Inman was originally cited as the head of the Committee of Science, but the final draft omitted his name.

SURVEYOR OF THE NAVY

RETURN to an Order of the Honourable The House of Commons,
dated 5 June 1848;—for,

COPY 'of the MINUTE of the BOARD of ADMIRALTY respecting the
Reconstruction of the Office of the SURVEYOR of the NAVY.'

SURVEYOR OF THE NAVY.

Admiralty, 2 June 1848.

The 50-gun frigate Constance, *commanded by Walker in 1846–47, seen here after her conversion to steam. The* Constance *was the second of Symonds's 50-gun frigates to be completed, and under Walker's command she proved a fine sailing ship, equal to any of her competitors, most particularly John Fincham's* Raleigh. *Her figurehead was a bust of Sir James Graham's daughter.* (CMP)

MY Lords have had under their consideration the necessity of such a reconstruction of the office of the Surveyor of the Navy, as may render it more adequate to the duties which it has to perform.

The importance of these duties it is impossible to overrate, for upon the Surveyor's Department mainly depends the proper application of the large sums voted by Parliament annually, for maintaining the naval strength of the country, and the establishment of such general principles, with regard to the building and fitting of ships, as may prevent rash experiments and wasteful expenditure in alterations and repairs, while they regulate and systematize the whole labours of the Dock-yards.

My Lords are, therefore, of opinion, that the principal duties of the Surveyor of the Navy are rather to take the general superintendence of the 'materiel' of the Navy; to prepare and submit to the Board the programme of works for the year, and to fix the Yards in which, with reference to the establishment of artificers, and stores in each, it can best be executed, than actually to prepare in detail the lines of the ships and vessels ordered to be built.

For this purpose, you will visit the Dock-yards frequently, with the sanction of the Board, and inform yourself upon all points connected with the duties of the several shipwright officers, and in what manner they are executed, and also as to the distribution of the workmen, and their division into gangs.

You will submit any alteration which may appear to you advisable, in the number of artificers and workmen in the several Dock-yards; you will report those who, from age or infirmity, are incapable of performing a proper day's work, with their ages and time of servitude.

You will examine and report to the Board what ships are worn out, and what shipbuilding stores are so deteriorated as to make it advisable to put both up to public sale, or to take the ship to pieces.

The reports of all surveys of Her Majesty's ships by the officers of the Yards will be laid before you, and you will take care that a correct account of the forwardness of all Her Majesty's ships building, and under repair, with the names and conditions of all those lying up in ordinary, be at all times kept in your office.

When projects for building ships, or other proposals having relation to any of Her Majesty's ships or vessels, are submitted to you, it will be your duty to communicate the same in writing, with your reasons for approving or objecting to such proposals.

In all professional details of matters connected with your duties, in requiring information or explanation on professional points, you will be at liberty to correspond with the officers of the Yards; but you are not to issue any orders of a general nature, or to enter upon any part of the general correspondence with the Superintendents of the Yards.

In all matters connected with the duties of your situation, you will advise with and consult the Lord of the Admiralty who shall be appointed to superintend the duties with which you are charged; and you will be prepared also, on all occasions, with regard to the selection and preparation of ships for commission, to give all the information that may be required by the First Sea Lord.

For the performance of these duties, and for the efficient conduct of your office, you will, in addition to your present Assistant, be allowed the services, as Second Assistant, of one of the most experienced and eminent of the present Master Shipwrights, from whose assistance and advice it is hoped, that in all matters of construction you will derive the greatest benefit.

My Lords have been pleased to select Mr. Isaac Watts, Master Shipwright of Sheerness Yard, to fill this situation.

It is further proposed, that a Committee shall be constituted, consisting of two or more Master Shipwrights or others, who shall, whenever called upon, be a 'Council of Science' whenever referred to for advice, either by their Lordships or yourself.

The Board will expect that all plans of new ships be laid before them by the Superintending Lord and yourself; and, if the opinion of this Council shall not have been previously taken, it will be for their Lordships to determine whether reference shall not be made to it; and you will bear in mind, that it is not only to the good construction of particular ships that in such consultations you are to look, but to the clear establishment of principles by which the building of ships is permanently to be governed.

Lastly, in the construction and repair of steam-vessels, you will consider your department as absolutely identified with that of the Comptroller of Steam Machinery; and it will be your study to establish with that officer a practice of general information and co-operation in all that regards the two departments.

My Lords are convinced, that by a strict adherence to these principles, most important reductions may be effected in the expenditure of the Navy; and in selecting you as successor to Sir William Symonds, they have, consequently, looked more to sound practical knowledge and ability as a seaman, than to your qualifications as a shipbuilder.

They wish you to bring a free and unbiassed judgment to bear upon the plans of others, and they think it necessary to give you such additional assistance at Somerset House as will enable you to undertake, personally, those duties of general regulation and supervision, to which they look for the attainment of the advantages adverted to in this communication.

In order to ensure the most searching examination of all drawings for the construction of ships, such drawings are, in future, to be prepared by the two Assistant Surveyors, and submitted by you to the Board, with your own remarks in writing, and referred by the Board to the Committee of Master Shipwrights, should any doubt be entertained as to the expediency of your recommendations.

My Lords conceive, that by this process, every precaution will be taken that past experience can suggest against ill-considered expenditure, while no useful change can long escape the notice of so many practical men, whose time and attention will be devoted to the consideration of all matters connected with Her Majesty's naval service.

The following will be the future establishment of the Surveyor's Office—

The Surveyor.

Two Assistant-surveyors, Mr John Edye and Mr. Isaac Watts; with salaries of 800 *l.* a year each, including all allowances.

One Chief Clerk.

Two Second-class Clerks; My Lords having been pleased to promote Mr. Eden to be a Second-class Clerk, in consideration of his long and faithful services.

Four Third-class Clerks; being one in addition to the present establishment.

The above increase of the establishment to take effect from the 4th of last month.

By command of their Lordships,

(signed) *H. G. Ward.*[5]

Down-grading the Committee of Reference to a Committee of Science, with or without Inman, was a mark of Auckland's confidence in Walker. The Surveyor was no longer to be subordinate to Hay, who had become a nuisance with his urging of further hasty work on screw steam conversions. In addition, the work of the Committee had little value once it had achieved the major objective, the retirement of Symonds. That Symonds, and not his system, was the target for Auckland had been demonstrated when the Board accepted Edye's defence of the Surveyor's Office from the attacks of the Committee of Reference.

Auckland's proposal was sent to the Treasury, for official sanction of the cost of the extra assistant and another third class clerk. Ward stressed that the intention was to ensure the 'proper application of the large sums voted annually by parliament for maintaining the Naval strength of the country'. By appointing Walker the Admiralty anticipated 'important reductions' through the avoidance of 'rash experiments'. The extra cost, £150 more for Edye, £800 for Watts and £250 for the clerk, was to be offset by eventually abolishing the posts of Master Attendant at Chatham, and the Officer in charge of Works at Woolwich, which would amount to a total saving of £850. The Treasury were quick to approve these measures, which were put on record and carried into effect on the following day.[6] Ten days later the Surveyor was instructed to consider the possibility of any new ships being converted to steam at a later date when drawing up designs.[7] The co-incidence of dates serves to emphasise that Walker's great contribution lay in the next decade, with the creation of the steam Navy, the gunboat flotilla of the Russian War and the first ironclads.[8] While he had almost no impact on the sailing battlefleet it should be recalled that the reforms instituted by Lord Auckland and largely directed by Walker were intended to sustain the sailing battlefleet into the 1850s.

Programming the new Navy

Once Walker was established in office Auckland pressed him to prepare a programme for a Navy of fifty First and Second Rate battleships afloat. This required the launch of three 80s, the inclusion of several marginal ships in both Rates and the

The large three-decker Britannia, *ex* Prince of Wales, *as part of the* Britannia *training establishment in the River Dart at the turn of the century. This ship had been ordered in 1843 as a* Queen-*class ship of 110 guns, before being modified by Walker into a separate class of longer 120-gun sailing ships, and then further lengthened for steam. The small 78-gun stretched Third Rate* Hindostan *emphasises the increase in size of wooden warships between 1815 and 1850.* (Author)

promotion to Advanced Ship status of the *Royal Frederick*, which was still on the stocks.

On 1 September 1848 the Board called for a detailed statement of the actual state of the Navy, with particular reference to battleships, in order to form the basis of a building programme to cover the following three years. The requirement was for fifty ships afloat, fifteen in progress and fifteen frames trimmed. Within a month Walker had drawn up a five-year plan to meet these figures. He called for the completion of fifteen new battleships, with eight in progress seven frames cut, and another fifteen to be repaired. The new designs for battleships must take into account the requirement for a finer stern run. There were also to be three new large frigates and two repairs each year resulting in a total of thirty-six frigates afloat, nine building and six frames trimmed. No smaller sailing ships were to be considered. The whole programme would require 3,500 shipwrights and 30,000 loads of timber per annum and every ship was to be apportioned a slip and a time for completion.[9]

Recognising the importance of efficient dockyards to the success of Walker's programme Auckland immediately appointed a committee of revision to investigate the conduct of the dockyards. Walker, Rear Admiral Sir Alexander Milne, the Fourth Naval Lord, and John Bromley worked under Ward to produce a report in two months. Auckland found Walker's conclusion on the number of shipwrights required almost too low, despite the pressure for reductions. However, the basic tenets concerning improved handling of materials and control over the workforce did promise well.[10]

The Board adopted Walker's five-year programme in February, by which time Baring had replaced Auckland, commended the Surveyor for the care he had taken with this task, and undertook not to send any orders to the yards that would interfere with the execution of the plan, without first consulting the Surveyor.[11]

The results were to be less clear cut than the Board had anticipated for the sudden shift to steam upset much of Walker's careful calculation, and the Russian War and the subsequent introduction of iron and armour within the decade made all talk of five-year plans meaningless. In March 1850 the Office of Comptroller of Steam was combined with that of Surveyor and there was now little doubt that an all-steam Navy would soon follow. Three steam battleships had already been commenced.[12]

With the prompting of Auckland, Walker recreated the role of a Controller, but there was one serious flaw. Auckland's reforms were as much a matter of personnel as structure and would only work while he, or another of like-mind, held the post of First Lord. While Sir Francis Baring continued Auckland's work the Tory Ministry of 1852 attempted to undo the non-partisan policy, with disastrous results for the First Secretary. In addition, Walker found that as a policy programmer the separation of his office from Whitehall was a profound handicap and this was only resolved by Graham during the Russian War.[13]

The design process

After the departure of Symonds there remained little to discuss with reference to sailing ship forms. The compromise form of Edye and others was generally accepted. The only sailing battleship drafted after Walker took office, the 80-gun *Orion*, was typical of this compromise. Although there were now two particularly able architects at Somerset House the Board was still interested in designs from the Chatham Committee, for 50- and 60-gun frigates, once they had been approved by the Council of Science.

Once appointed Walker moved to regain full control over the design process. Edye and Watts were not impressed by either the Chatham Committee ships or the report of the Council on their work. The Council thought that the Office design would float too high, that her midship section was not suitable for speed and that the guns were too close together. Edye and Watts, the Assistant Surveyors, replied by observing that the bow and stern were not heavily armed because of the fine lines fore an aft. Fincham's *Raleigh*, which the Council cited as an excellent model, was attacked for marginal stability. Walker went further in criticising the *Raleigh*, for having sailed against her in the *Constance* in 1846 he considered her deficient.[14] The views of Edye and Watts form an interesting conclusion to the Symonds era:

> The experience of late years has brought the question of the best form of ships within a comparatively narrow compass so that educated Naval Architects generally differ but little from each other in their designs.
>
> What remains at present undetermined in regard to the forms and essential elements of good ships, the application of the principle of induction to the analysis of their sailing qualities will gradually supply.
>
> In the designs referred to we have endeavoured to embody all the known essentials of a good construction and we believe that in drawing their conclusions the Council of Science have been in some measure deceived by erroneous data, which we have corrected in red ink.
>
> We consider their inferences in regard to stability and the necessary relation between the Transverse and Diametric sections to be altogether gratuitous.

The Board ordered the Council-designed ships to be built to their original drafts, and sent the members of the Council, Fincham, Abethell, Read and Large back to their posts in the various dockyards.[15]

The Council was never called again. When the Chatham Committee designs eventually arrived Edye and Watts felt sufficiently confident to attack the excessive length, widely-spaced frames and an unnecessarily full bow. The Board, however, accepted the drafts, but these were the last sailing ships designed outside the Surveyor's Office.[16]

As Surveyor Walker was more concerned with sound construction and well laid out battery decks than speed under sail. He valued the three-decked ship for its decisive impact in battle and adopted full decks of shell guns to ensure common charges and elevation. His views were to be reflected more closely in the designs of the following decade. His office was renamed that of Controller in 1859 and, in addition, he served as Graham's strategic advisor during the war against Russia.[17]

In 1861 Graham provided a fitting tribute to one of the greatest naval administrators of the nineteenth, or any, century.

> I never knew Sir Baldwin Walker till I went to the Admiralty in 1853, and I formed so high an opinion of his capacity and his judgement that I regarded him as an intimate friend, and upon all naval matters of importance during the Russian War, quite apart from the Board, but with the knowledge of the Board, I consulted him upon everything. He was in daily communication with me at all times of the day, and it is impossible for any person filling the office of First Lord to have received greater assistance than I received from him during the whole of that time.[18]

Part Four

INFLUENCES ON DESIGN

1 Fleet Tactics in the Last Years of the Sailing Battlefleet

The tactical problems in the age of sail

Much effort and ink have been applied to the subject of naval tactics in the sailing ship era. Armchair admirals, experienced officers and interested amateurs have spent their energies in pursuit of the 'explanation' for the indecisive nature of naval battles in the period before 1782.

No existing account of the Royal Navy in the nineteenth century gives adequate emphasis to the central fact that British naval forces were strategically and tactically *very* aggressive. Examples from the end of the Napoleonic Wars are legion: the Aix Roads; Exmouth's brush with the Toulon Fleet in 1813; the ascent of the Potomac by two frigates in 1814; the attacks on Baltimore, New Orleans and Mobile; the bombardment of Algiers and Acre, and the conduct of amphibious operations against Russia in 1854–56. All these incidents demonstrate a rare combination of confidence and experience that distinguished the Royal Navy from all its rivals. No other naval power matched the degree of arrogance and aggression that such men as Codrington, Hardy and Napier considered no more than their legacy. The sheer effrontery of Codrington's entrance into the Bay at Navarin, or of Napier's storming of Sidon and subsequent negotiations with Mehemet Ali in 1840 cannot be explained away as aberrations. They were the heritage of the wartime officer corps. Aggression can be seen in every aspect of naval thought after 1815, from pursuit tactics, based on the presumption that all enemy squadrons would be encountered flying, to the coastal and amphibious emphases in steamship designs of the 1830s and 1840s and the grand raid tradition in strategy which stretched back to Cadiz in 1587. The Royal Navy sought the complete defeat of its enemies, a defeat to be pressed home to the utmost extent. In consequence, the battle fixation identified with, if not understood by, Mahan was not the exaggerated obsession as perceived by Corbett, but a rational and logical response to that rare combination of skill and opportunity. Battle would drive the enemy off the sea and once located in his harbours he could then be assaulted, as far as was possible. The elimination of all enemy warships was not a pointless exercise, but the route to the most efficient exploitation of command of the sea, where command is not in doubt and the enemy had nothing more than a few light craft with which to contest the use of oceans. After Trafalgar the Royal Navy developed into a composite force. The battlefleets remained because the French bases proved invulnerable, but the larger part of the fleet spent its time harassing coastal shipping, capturing convoys and small ports and opening up the continent to British trade. The same tactics were then employed with great success against the United States in 1814. Late Victorian apologists for seapower, the Colomb brothers in particular, attempted to legitimise naval strength for a liberal empire by stressing a purely defensive employment that had no connection with the experiences of 1793–1815 or of 1854–56, or even with the plans of 1877. Seapower carried force right up to the low water mark of the enemy shore and beyond for it was capable of influencing events on land and making a major contribution to strategy.

The combination of numbers and this spirit of aggression ensured that, for British battlefleets in the last days of sail, the normal situation was that of attempting to force battle on an enemy which had ulterior strategic objectives but little inclination to test its mettle against the aggressive, battle-dominated and heavily gunned Royal Navy. This situation exposed the basic problem at the heart of British tactics. In order to bring the enemy to battle it was vital to be to windward of him, that is to be bearing down on him with the wind largely astern. However, this same wind would enable the opposing force to put their helms up and avoid action, or break off any action at the time of their choosing. The basic, and indeed the only useful, tactical formation of the period remained the sailing line of battle. Adopted by the Commonwealth Navy in the First Dutch War (1652–54), the line remained the essential formation simply because of the inability of even the most skilled fleets to co-ordinate their movements in any more complex patterns.

The only effective solution to the British dilemma was the manoeuvre developed by Earl Howe and followed by all subsequent commanders of merit: breaking the line. Many works suggest that breaking the enemy line was, of itself, a decisive tactic. This is simply not the case because it was only decisive if it enabled the enemy to be engaged. Breaking through the enemy formation and engaging him from the leeward placed him in a position from which he could not make sail to escape. The problem with this seemingly simple

Victory, *flying the Trafalgar signal and firing a salute. The heavy broadside of British battleships was the* raison d'etre *of the fleet.* (CMP)

manoeuvre was the danger to which it exposed the attacking force. Bearing down on the enemy, as at the Glorious First of June in 1794, at Camperdown on 11 October 1797, and more particularly at Trafalgar, left the leading ships almost unable to reply to the enemy broadsides. Hardy was not alone in recognising that against an enemy with adequate gunnery the cost would be too high. At Lissa, on 13 March 1811, Hoste made Dubordieu pay dearly for his temerity in exposing his bows.

The French, largely in response to the more complex objectives set for sea power in their national strategy, developed tactical thought onto a higher plane than the more pragmatic British. The works of Pere Paul Hoste, Bigot, Comte de Morogues and others argued that tactical finesse could win battles. In the event it only served to avoid defeat for actions between sailing battlefleets were only ever decided by sheer hard fighting. Following in the French tradition the over-praised Laird, Clerk of Eldin, argued for a concentration of force against a portion of the enemy fleet. As might be expected of a land-bound critic, Clerk was attempting to militarise the conduct of war at sea and to employ the precise, rigid tactics of Frederick the Great on a field where tactical errors were more easily retrieved because of the slow approach to combat. Frederick used dead ground to cover the approach of his armies, disguised his formations and employed cavalry charges to cover retreat, much as Scheer was to do later at Jutland. Admirals were left to make the best of slow moving units which revealed the battle plan to the enemy long before action had been joined.

What Frederick achieved by skill at Leuthen, Rodney was given by a shift of wind at the Saintes. Clerk's descendants later had the temerity to claim the merit for Lord Rodney breaking the Line at the Saintes in 1782, a manoeuvre as nearly involuntary as could be imagined. The concept of concentration of force, for all its allure on the printed page, was simply not possible in combat with an enemy under sail. It is often argued that Nelson's end on attack at Trafalgar was a conscious effort to engage only a part of the Franco-Spanish fleet, leaving the van squadron out of the battle. It is unlikely that Nelson believed this to be possible. His real hope was to 'bring on a pell-mell battle', a battle at close quarters where the superior training and discipline of his fleet would provide the victory. In this he was following the example of Duncan at Camperdown, an example which he had both praised and understood. Duncan, confident in the superior combat power of his fleet once closely engaged, went into action without waiting to form a line. At Trafalgar Nelson's fleet *never* outnumbered that of the enemy *in action* and, furthermore, the van squadron under Admiral Dumanoir, far from being kept out of the battle by this daring move – a move which was seen by the allied line some hours before the battle began it should be remembered – put his ships about and made to return to the battle around *Victory* and *Bucentaure*. He decided not to join the action because fresh units of Nelson's column were coming up, and the more intelligent officers, particularly Codrington in the *Orion*, aware of Dumanoir's ships, moved to shield the disabled *Victory*. Nelson's victory was complete because the enemy elected to stand and fight, and were then pinned in action by the partial breaking of their line. At Camperdown a similar tactical problem was resolved by Duncan ordering his fleet to break into the enemy formation and get to leeward without taking the time required to form any tactical unit.

It did not matter how British ships brought the enemy to action on their lee sides, only that they did. Howe's drill offered a formal response, and an ideal to emulate. It was particularly suited to exercise, and to the situation of 1794 in which there was a large, half-formed fleet of ships and officers, few of which met the exacting standards set by their admiral. Nelson, after ten years of war, could rely on a higher level of professional skill and greater motivation. The 'Nelson touch' had far more to do with morale and initiative than any magical rigid battle plan. Nelson's system can be seen as an early example of *Auftragstaktik*, the German military doctrine of 'mission oriented tactics'. Had he lived it is certain that the skill of Codrington would have excited his warmest praise. It is therefore fitting that Codrington should have been the postwar Navy's leading Fleet Admiral, not for the bloody combat at Navarin fought at anchor in a bay, but for his contribution to the debate on fleet tactics and his command of the Evolutionary Squadrons of 1831 and 1832. As late as 1846 Sir William Parker suggested that if Codrington went to sea he could achieve far more than any other officer. He was then 76 years of age.

The signal book of 1826

For the first postwar revision of the signal book, the by now official compendium of orders and evolutions that was to form the basis for tactical thought, the Admiralty adopted in 1816 Sir Home Popham's code, as used at Trafalgar. The tactical permutations were unremarkable and made no attempt to integrate the more ambitious memoranda of Nelson. While Corbett saw this as a reason to criticise the process, blaming Lord Keith for the formal system adopted, the reasons behind the revisions were quite simple.[1] Keith and his colleagues recognised that Nelson's system relied on three things that could not be depended upon in any future war: the incompetence of the enemy, the skill of the fleet and the genius of the commander. Wisely, the new signal book did not take as a model the remarkable and spectacular but satisifed itself with the sound and certain. It was to form the basis for the future and did not represent a return to the hard and fast rules that Nelson had so decisively broken. Codrington and Hardy were on the committee, assisted by Mr Lethbridge, Popham's Secretary, an able man with much valuable correspondence and material relating to the signalling system introduced on the eve of Trafalgar, and its possible development. It is important to observe that this high-powered Committee concentrated on improving the legibility of signals, adding words and removing those considered unnecessary; it did not attempt to introduce any 'Nelson' or 'Clerk of Eldin' concepts. As a basis for tactics the new book was ideal, and this was recognised ten years later when another group of officers reconsidered the process. Each book was to be fitted with a lead case, to avoid the danger of capture. Once established in the Mediterranean Codrington was anxious to have the new book in order to exercise his Squadron using the new signals.[2]

The new book was given a thorough trial when Codrington commanded the Squadron of Evolution in 1831. The Whig/progressive Admirals sent him their ideas on what was needed to improve the fleet and the results were a silent testimony in favour of the 1826 Signal Book. Hallowell contributed a masthead semaphore, which saved much wear and tear on signal flags, and Hardy an improved battle lantern. Codrington earned his reputation as a handler of fleets without equal during this cruise, not least by the frequency and urgency of his signals.[3] Having been appointed to practise in evolutions Codrington was far from impressed by the general ability of his squadron, and found some officers hard to deal with. 'I am quite surprised at the want of comprehension evinced by Hyde Parker. It is almost impossible to beat into him what Dick & Colley see at once.' Hyde Parker's ship he called 'the slug of the squadron, in all respects'.[4] William Parker's flag captain aboard the *Prince Regent*, James Whitley Deans Dundas later First Sea Lord and Commander-in-Chief in the Mediterranean and Black Sea 1852–55, had hardly been at sea since 1812 and was ill-equipped to meet the demands posed by Codrington, but could call on his Admiral for guidance.[5]

Even the most generous reading of the cruise of Codrington's squadrons in 1831 and 1832, particularly the first, would suggest that the peace-time Navy was lacking in basic skills and too concerned with what William Parker called 'foolish frippery'. These squadrons provided the perfect background against which to settle the old 'sterility of tactical thought' argument. Quite simply, the line of battle was the basic competence required before any British fleet could go to war. A signal book that expected more would be useless for the first year or eighteen months of any conflict, and if required, could be adopted by the Admiral fortunate enough to build up an *esprit de corps* and expertise equal to that which was available at the Nile or Trafalgar.

Seamanship and drill in time of peace

After 1815 British naval forces were spread out around the world in a manner that reflected the priority given to the support of diplomatic and commercial interests; new squadrons were formed and new stations occupied. In line with the pressures on Naval Estimates, the number of ships of the line in full commission was reduced so that in 1816 there were only three, and they were on separate stations. The line of battleship was now a flagship and floating embassy rather than an integral part of a fleet. The international situation up until 1830 ensured that the Mediterranean at least had more than one battleship for much of the 1820s, but these numbers were quite inadequate for serious squadron exercises, even if the Admiral resorted to the common practice of filling up his line with any smaller vessels that happened to be available. Hallowell's squadron in 1826, together with the well-intentioned if politically catastrophic mobilisation of the guard ships by the Lord High Admiral in 1828, were among the few bright spots of this period. The combination of the Tory defence policy, economic difficulties and the lack of any serious challenge at sea allowed the general professional standards of the Navy to decline during the 15 years after 1815.

The consequences of this decline were felt after 1830 when larger fleets were required. However, the line of battle, which remained the basis of all tactical thought inside the Navy, required, as it had always done, only a relatively low level of competence, and it could be easily acquired on a single cruise. This aspect of the line has never been really considered. The fleet always cruised in a linear formation, tacking and wearing in succession or together. Once they could manage a reasonably close order the ships could be classed as a fleet and, more significantly, were ready for action. Anything more was a bonus, and was never required in any sea battle under sail. The ability to resolve tactical problems during combat, notably the conduct of Nelson at Cape St Vincent and Codrington at Trafalgar, was not expected of any officer below the rank of Admiral and, moreover, was a clear breach of discipline.

However, the sheer unsuitability of naval forces for tactical finesse in the age of sail should not disguise the fact that there were two important developments in this period that heralded the new order, an order it must be stressed, that was equally content to rely on the sailing line of battle.

The training ships Implacable *and* Foudroyant (Trincomalee) *lying in Portsmouth Harbour in 1947. This shot emphasises the relative size of the standard 74 and 46 of the late war period, and the commanding effect given to the larger ship by her extra deck.* (CMP)

Speed under sail

After 1815 the peace-time Navy began to shift its priorities away from gunnery and battle drill towards seamanship and smart sail handling. It has been usual to attack naval inefficiency during this period and characterise these developments as some form of dereliction of duty which, in an unspecified way, contributed to the inferior performance of the fleet when next at war. It needs to be stressed, however, that the Royal Navy performed particularly well in the conflicts of the period and only the scratch-manned Baltic Fleet of 1854 was anything other than excellent. Furthermore, there is simply no comparison between a peace-time Army in barracks and a fleet at sea, for the officers and men of the Navy are still professional seamen, relying every day on their own skill and discipline; the spit and polish aspect of the complaint simply ignores the reality of life on board a sailing battleship in peace-time. As a ship could be navigated in almost all weathers by a small fraction of the crew and spent long periods in harbour, the men had to be found tasks that would both keep them busy, and benefit the ship. Once they were proficient at ship handling – speed and precision of work aloft were vital in all squadron exercises – they were left with long periods with little professional work. That many officers elected to fill this time with decorative refinement was harmless in itself, and by increasing the men's sense of belonging and their pride in their ship, they may well have assisted in the retention of seamen. Even this, it must be stressed, was rarely carried to excess. During the first cruise of the *Albion* in the Mediterranean her first officer spent so much money on the ship that she became known throughout the fleet as 'the gilded toyshop', and senior officers were pleased when a new captain imposed a more moderate regime.

As the period of peace lengthened sea officers turned their attention to the speed and seakeeping of their ships. At first this was largely a question of improved stowage and rig, but in the 1820s some began to think in terms of new hull forms. In this they reflected the growing interest in all matters nautical and the formation of the Royal Yacht Squadron was one indication of this trend. The quest for speed has often been regarded as a rather futile exercise, with minute gains being achieved that could have no significance in fleet actions. Such criticism ignores what was seen at the time as the reality of future war at sea. Most naval officers accepted that France remained the most serious rival, though the French were unlikely to seek combat. Therefore, the Royal Navy would have to force them to battle, and to do so an advantage in sailing performance would be crucial. In his autobiographical fragments Symonds often noted the inability of British ships and fleets to force action on unwilling French units and his hull form was an attempt to resolve this dilemma without following the French practice of building lightweight hulls. Even if it was not fully exploited, the superior speed under sail of his ships offered an opportunity for more complex tactical handling of squadrons. Their speed, combined with an ability to sail several points closer to the wind than the French, made them more flexible. In the event this school of thought was defeated in the last days of the sailing fleet by the close-quarters battle pragmatists, and Symonds's large racers were supplanted by more modest pure fighting ships. That, however, should not detract from the merit of the principle. The ability to pin the enemy, and force him either to stand and fight, or break formation in flight, was the only method available to bring on a battle. Nor was the search for speed confined to the small group which included Symonds, Hayes and Elliot. Codrington and Hardy were both well aware of the importance of speed and both men appreciated Nelson's first Trafalgar plan, which involved using the third unit of fast sailing 74s for separate tactical functions. They would also have known of Strachan's use of frigates in his defeat of Dumanoir in October 1805 off Finisterre. Later senior officers without their experience and insight, Deans Dundas among them, were content to compromise with the Tory close action school. Symonds's opponents built on one feature of his system – the superior space of the battery deck – but downgraded the search for speed, the tactical panacea that would enable British ships to make their superior gunnery tell. Comparing the performance of frigates and battleships was important, when the heavy frigate was expected to play a specific role, and all ships needed to keep up with the fastest in order to decide the combat.

The sailing trials and Squadrons of Evolution that were such a feature of this period produced the most inconclusive set of results that could be imagined, largely because of the great gulf in the ability and motivation of the officers, and the radical changes in performance that could be achieved by restowing the hold or pumping out the water tanks. Despite this they did have the singular merit of establishing ship handling as a royal road to favour and early promotion. If the Tory school could point to the surprising performance of the hitherto little regarded *St Vincent* in 1845/6 as an argument against Symonds's designs, a more reflective man than the Surveyor might have retorted that it was the measure of his success that older vessels were being driven hard to meet bench marks he had laid down. Furthermore, if the Navy possessed officers with the skill to achieve these results then the pursuit battle was a real possibility. The French Navy, for a variety of reasons, lost touch with the British during the postwar period, due mainly to excessive standardisation and poor design. Contemporary observers from the Prince de Joinville to the die-hard Tory William Martin admitted the superiority of the Royal Navy.

The other novel strand in contemporary tactics, the heavy frigate, had a longer history. Although they were intended as an attempt to match new French designs intended for cruiser warfare, the razee 74s of the late 1820s were integrated into the battle line as a fast wing for tactical purposes. However, they were both too expensive and, being configured for distant action, unsuitable for British frigate duties. Some served as flagships with the major squadrons. Symonds disliked these ships, preferring the 36-gun ship for frigate service and the two-decker 70-gun vessel for work with the fleet.

The impact of steam

If Symonds's attempt to revolutionise tactics failed – as much from the personality of the man and the politics of his appointment, as from any inherent weakness in the concept – there was another technical development during the era that did, eventually, have a profound effect on naval tactics. Symonds was attempting to provide the Royal Navy with a qualitative edge that would allow it to force battle on the enemy. An alternative to his hull form, however, lay in the provision of mechanical power. Free from dependence on the wind, a fleet could easily pin its opponents in action if they did not possess a similar power. This made the Anglo-French rivalry in the development of steam warships a vital element in the naval calculations of the period, for whichever side had the advantage in quality or numbers would derive incalculable benefits in battle.

The steam warship was only a practical proposition when its machinery was reliable, economical and safe. The first warships that offered these qualities were the new British steam battleships of the early 1850s. Even then steam ships remained purely tactical weapons for they lacked the range for sustained cruising. The first true steam capital ship was the turret ship *Dreadnought* of 1875 so, consequently, sail remained a major influence on naval warfare far longer than is usually admitted. The Anglo-French fleets of 1854 were largely sailing fleets and those of Russia entirely so. Furthermore, many steamers were reduced to sail due to mechanical failure.

The problem which had to be solved during the period under consideration was how to combine the conflicting demands of wooden sailing warship design and steam power. There were three stages in this process. The first, advanced by Captain Ryder Burton in 1817 and perfected by Sir Charles Napier in 1829–31, employed the muscle power of the crew to drive paddle wheels shipped aboard a regular sailing ship. These were simple and easily removed and seldom interfered with the sailing and fighting qualities of the ship. Napier's work with the frigate *Galatea* surprised even the most jaundiced critics, and earned the approbation of Codrington. The technology required for the man-powered wheel was simple and cheap and the only argument ever advanced against it was that it might discourage seamen from entering the service.

The second stage involved the steam-driven paddle wheel which rapidly overtook the man-powered vessel. But whether fitted to a tug or a large steam frigate, the propulsion system and inefficient engines made it a poor performer and unequal to the close combat of fleet action. Steam-driven paddle vessels were thus restricted to a subordinate role.

The third stage involved the introduction of the screw propeller and permitted an effective union of heavy sailing battleship with auxiliary steamer. In this form the wooden warship passed a final decade as the ultimate arbiter of war at sea.

As steam was introduced into the naval arena the Royal Navy went into action with mixed fleets on several occasions. The Syrian campaign of 1840, which was a classic amphibious action, made much use of paddle steamers as tugs, distant fire support vessels and dispatch boats. However, on the only occasion when they might have provided a real tactical advantage, when the fleet took up positions to bombard Acre on 3 November, there were not enough to be usefully employed. Napier was not alone in suggesting they be used to tow the heavy ships into position, but in the event the wind shifted into the right quarter and the fleet went in under sail. In China, in 1840–43, the East India Company steam fleet was altogether more important, helping the fleet to ascend the Bogue river below Canton. In this campaign steam made a vital contribution. The firepower of the British 74s was the key to success, but they had to be towed into position. Subsequently, the tactical combination of steam and sail became established and by 1846 the First Lord could speak of each battleship having its attendant steamer. In the Black Sea campaign of 1854 all the minor units were steam powered. The battlefleet had but one moment of glory, before Sevastopol on 17 October, and even then each heavy sailing ship went into battle with a steamer lashed alongside. From this point on the true steam battleship was an inevitability that had only to wait for the necessary engineering improvements.

Tactics under sail in the 1840s

Although several large fleets were assembled during the period under review there were few opportunities for tactical training. The Squadrons of Evolution proved to be little more than stern chases of the most unremarkable type, while the Mediterranean Fleet, even if large enough to be worth exercising, was invariably diverted to diplomatic duties and usually split up into individual units. The one Admiral to see prolonged sea service in the period 1840–50, Sir William Parker, was far from satisfied with what he found. His words were very similar to those both he and Codrington had employed in 1831.

> I find the ships here all desirous of being perfect in training to arms of all kinds, but I cannot help perceiving that they are in some instances declining into the old habit of not getting everything on deck as if for action, and avoiding to move things that will disturb *paintwork*, or dirty their white deck etc.[6]

During the last decade of the sailing battlefleet, tactical thought advanced but little. Officers, with the exception of Codrington made little use of their opportunities. Even Parker, considered by many the very best fleet commander of the period, deferred to Codrington when the 1847 Squadron of Evolution was under consideration. 'I shall always be ready to do my best, but he, I am confident, would do much better than I can pretend to.'[7] In 1851 Captain Milne candidly observed to Parker that,

> In our service we have no authorised work on naval tactics, it is a subject not taught, and each Captain must learn his lesson when appointed to a ship, the best way he can from the works of Paul Hoste, Steel, Gowen, Ekins etc if he has time.

The signal book was of no help as it lacked guidance on such basic issues as the distance between columns and other basic questions of naval tactical thought. Among his contemporaries only one officer had made any effort to execute the more complex signals, and even he encountered serious problems of comprehension.

> Sir C. Napier, who I must remark was the only officer I ever sailed under who attempted to put the evolutions of the signal book into execution, was obliged to have all the signals classed on a sheet of paper. This I drew up for him...I contemplated having this printed and inserted in the signal books.

Parker offered no help, merely a few additional signals.[8]

Napier's Sailing Master, George Biddlecombe advocated a complex *en echelon* approach to maximise gunpower but such schemes proved unworkable with steam in the 1860s, although in the 1840s they were quite visionary.[9] The only tactics that could be relied upon in battle during this period were the most simple; finesse could not alter the result of a battle between fleets of sailing warships.

2 *Guns and Gunnery: The Unseen Revolution*

Britain's insular position and her dependence on trade forced the Royal Navy to develop and apply a battlefleet strategy. This required the construction and maintenance of a battlefleet capable of defeating any potential enemy. Before 1815 British ships were always more heavily armed per ton than those of her major rivals, France and Spain, who had alternative requirements for naval units. The number and weight of guns dominated the whole design process, from the scantling of the deck beams to the size of the crew and between 1815 and 1850 the destructive power of the broadside of line of battleships increased by a factor of between two and three. This is all the more remarkable when it is realised that several ships were at sea throughout the period, and that the basic technology did not alter. This huge increase in fighting power was brought about by the gunnery revolution, and the Royal Navy, which entered the postwar era uncertain of its weapons, by 1850 was rightly confident that it was pre-eminent in this field, as in so many others. The frigate actions of the War of 1812 offered the possibility of exploiting superior sailing performance and long-range guns to batter a sluggish fleet configured for close range action, as the Royal Navy was, into helpless surrender. By 1850 the Royal Navy had taken the lead in sailing and gunnery. These developments were neither accidental nor isolated; the Royal Navy maintained naval mastery by creating a fleet that outnumbered, outsailed and outgunned those of its opponents.

Before 1815 the chief determining factors in selecting an armament for a new warship were tradition and structural strength. However, as the eighteenth century came to an end the old order at sea was changing. In this respect it should be noted that the line was broken by Hawke as early as 1744 at the battle of Toulon, an act that inspired the young St Vincent to reconsider the accepted tactical order. Actions dominated by the line of battle tactics laid down in the Fighting Instructions gradually gave way to break-through battles, and as a result combat ranges were reduced to pistol and half-pistol shot. At close quarters the armament of existing ships became much more effective, and the Navy finally accepted that the 42-pounder was too cumbersome and slow firing for the lower decks of First Rates, and it was replaced by the standard 32-pounder. On the upper decks close action encouraged the widespread adoption of the carronade. The famous short gun, one third the weight and less than half the barrel length of the normal cannon of the same calibre, made a major contribution to combat power at close quarters, both by the extra weight of metal it could discharge from the upper deck, and the rapidity with which it could be fired. In addition, the windage of the carronade, the space between the bore and the diameter of the ball, was reduced and this made for more efficient use of the powder charge.

The integrated revolution

The armament of British battleships during the Revolutionary and Napoleonic Wars combined the classic long guns with an upper deck battery of carronades, although this development was far from universal at the outset. The total effect was to maximise firepower at medium to close range, while retaining the potential for long range, a potential that was rarely employed by battleships. Before any major improvement could be made in the fighting power of the battlefleet it was necessary to make the individual ships larger and stronger. While Sir William Congreve's light 24-pounders allowed a degree of up-gunning to take place by substituting the heavier calibre for 18- and even 12-pounder guns on the upper decks of some ships, this was achieved at the expense of striking power at long range, and the ability to fire double-shotted broadsides at close quarters.

Naval actions against the French and Spanish were characterised by Nelson's maxim 'outmanoeuvre a Russian, but close with a Frenchman'. French fleets were unable to match the British in the rate of fire due to lack of sea training and inferior guns. As a result the gun crews became unsteady at close quarters; Sir Charles Douglas observed them running into the hold as the *Formidable* broke through at the Battle of Saintes. In this period the majority of officers who gave any particular attention to gunnery did so in terms of rate of fire. Collingwood, as Captain of the *Excellent*, was an outstanding example and the effect of her rapid broadsides at the Battle of Cape St Vincent was clear to all. The introduction of the flintlock provided for a more certain ignition of the charge and reduced the time lag between the order to fire and the actual discharge. This made British broadsides more uniform and consequently more terrible.

The conduct of Sir Edward Codrington at Trafalgar, in command of the *Orion*, can be taken as an outstanding example of battlefleet gunnery under sail. Coming into action in the centre of the column astern of Nelson, Codrington witheld his fire until within a ship's length of the French *Swiftsure*. In minutes his opponent was dismasted and forced to strike. After assisting other ships and beating off Dumanoir's van division, which threatened to enter the battle around *Victory* and *Bucentaure*, Codrington closed with *L'Intrepide* raked her astern and then demolished her with a fire that he considered, 'the best directed and best kept up I ever saw'. This was no idle observation, for Codrington had already seen two major fleet actions aboard the *Queen Charlotte*, flagship of Earl Howe and Lord Bridport. He was particularly proud of having witheld his fire until the *Orion* was within decisive range, inside one hundred yards.[1]

Trafalgar demonstrated the merits and failings of the existing system. Where Codrington and a few others made their ships truly efficient gunnery platforms, the majority were content to run in close and leave the rest to their men. Against poor opposition from harbour-bound Frenchmen and untrained Spaniards this was good enough, but in future gunnery of a higher order would be required.

Where Codrington was in a distinct minority, the most innovative gunner of the Napoleonic era, Philip Broke, was effectively unique. In command of a frigate, and expecting single ship actions, Broke laid great emphasis on hitting the target. He fitted his ships' guns with tangent sights and locks, exercised his officers and men in firing on the roll, and gave prizes for good shooting. His target was the enemy main deck. To resolve the common problem of holding the enemy in battle he mounted light guns, 9-pounders, on the poop with good arcs of fire and plentiful supplies of bar, canister and grape shot to cripple the enemy rig, dismantle her wheel and kill the helmsman. Aboard the *Shannon* he introduced blind firing and concentration of fire for use in fog, or in the fog of battle. These developments, combined with a six-year wartime commission, enabled Broke to create as perfect a fighting

The lower gun deck of the Victory, *taken in 1953. The guns are 32-pounders. They have no sights and only the most rudimentary means of concentrating fire.* (CMP)

platform as ever went to sea in the age of sail. The capture of the *Chesapeake* in 1813 was the outstanding frigate action of the age of sail. Both ships were in high order and the casualties, per minute, were greater than at Trafalgar.[2]

The importance of Broke's work lay in the gradual transmission of his ideas into the service, something that was to take another two decades. Good gunnery was to make the existing armament more effective and, when combined with the heavier postwar battery, formed a vital element in the retention of British naval supremacy. Interest in gunnery had been increased by the capture of three British frigates by the Americans. The American ships, *Constitution* and *United States*, were heavier, had larger crews and, most significantly, opposed 24-pounders to the 18-pounders of their opponents. In addition, the British ships, unlike the Americans, had little gunnery experience. However, those reverses had a salutary effect on contemporary opinion and one officer suitably impressed with the American use of heavy guns was Henry Chads, First Lieutenant of the *Java* and later Captain of *Excellent*.

Another single ship action of the War of 1812 which had important lessons for the future was the capture of the USS *Essex* by *Phoebe* on 28 February 1814 off Valparaiso. Despite the protests of her Captain, the *Essex* had been sent to sea armed with 32-pounder carronades. Captain James Hillyar of the *Phoebe* exploited this weakness to pound the American ship with long 18-pounders from outside the effective range of her battery. After two and a half hours, in which they were quite unable to force a close action, the Americans surrendered.

After the *Chesapeake* action Broke's gunnery innovations were viewed with great favour. Captain John Pechell, of the North American station Flagship *San Domingo*, adopted the Broke drill, while Henry Hotham, Captain of the Fleet, had already been converted to the new faith.[3] Pechell was to be the conduit for the transmission of Broke's legacy, along with Sir Howard Douglas who happened to be a land gunner.

As for the rest of the Navy, the position was far from good. Writing after the War, Napier made the most serious criticism of the gunnery of the Mediterranean Fleet in 1812–4.

> I served in it three years, and I don't believe there was one-fourth of the line of battle ships in that fleet that had been exercised at firing powder and shot (and without that all other exercise, even with powder, is of little use; for if not accustomed regularly to load their guns, they will know nothing of it; and if powder alone is used in exercise, one half of them will forget to put in their shot in action); and as firing with precision, they knew nothing about it. Had Lord Exmouth gone to Algiers direct from Toulon, with five ships, and without any previous preparation, the chances are, he would have been beat. I believe the squadron he took there, though fitted out in a hurry, knew more about their guns and ships that had been in commission all the war: they knew they were going to fight, and took pains to qualify themselves: the fleet in the war never expected it, and never were prepared, and the officers generally were too old to exert themselves without a stimulus. The Government also were not without their share of blame, for allowing so small a proportion of powder and shot for exercise.[4]

The Mediterranean Fleet was armed with various calibres of cannon and carronades, unchanged from the previous decade. It was still more than a match for any French squadron, as much from the legacy of victory and defeat that were the birthright of the two forces as from any inherent superiority. The idea that it had atrophied after Trafalgar does not bear scrutiny. The Royal Navy remained superior to any European competition, and its best ships were equal to anything the Americans could muster. There was a danger of postwar complacency but with Broke, Pechell and Douglas on hand, and the vital encouragement of the Duke of Clarence, it never happened.

The gunport

One aspect of wooden warship design that has too often been ignored and which is worth mentioning here is the size of the gunport. This was determined by the tactical situation for which the ship was designed. Therefore, while the heavy artillery of the 1840s could be fired at considerable elevation, this was not possible from the lower decks of battleships because they were configured for close-range action, firing at point blank. In this role the protection afforded by a narrow gunport far outweighed the potential value of long-range fire. The standard lower deck port allowed 26 degrees of training on either side.

In 1815 a review of the fleet found there was only 1in deviation in sill height in British-built ships, although understandably there was rather more difference in foreign-built prizes. This reflected a conscious effort by the Navy Board, under pressure from the Carriage Department of the Ordnance, to allow for standard gun carriages. In 1834 the Ordnance made the same request. Admiral Sir George Elliot prepared a paper setting out the details in 1836, and this was adopted by the Admiralty as the standard for the main and middle deck ports of all ships larger than Sixth Rates:

Deck to upper sill	4ft 9in
Deck to lower sill	1ft 11in
Depth of port	2ft 10in
Deck to centre of gun	3ft

Elevation and depression (degrees)	
32-pounder 56cwt	10° −6°
32 pounder 48cwt	12° −7°[5]

The question of port sizes was re-opened by Sir Thomas Hastings in 1841, when a request was put in to cut down the sills of the frigate *Portland* by 3in, to allow for increased angles of depression. Symonds reported that anything more than 1/2in would be very costly. Hastings then requested a standard port allowing 10 degrees 30 minutes elevation, and 5 degrees 30 minutes depression. Ultimately, Symonds and Hastings agreed on new parameters, permitting 10 degrees of elevation and 7 to 8 degrees of depression, with 11 degrees of elevation on the upper deck, for bombardment.

Deck to Lower Sill	1ft 11in or 2ft 3in
Depth of Port	2ft 11in or 2ft 8in
Width of Port	3ft 5in or 3ft 6in

Elevation (degrees)	
Main deck	10 to −7′7
Upper deck	11 to −7[6]

These remained the standard figures for battleships to the end of the wooden fleet, although the 68-pounders required a slight increase all round.

Arming the postwar fleet

At the end of the War the Admiralty review of policy included positive decisions to improve the armament of the battlefleet for close-range action, which included using Congreve 24-

pounders *in lieu* of long 18-pounders, and reducing the number of calibres on each ship. The first ships so affected were the ex-French 74 *Donegal* and the new 120 *Nelson*, followed by all other First Rates. From the outset it was clear that the Navy Board did not share the enthusiasm of the senior body for heavier metal. The initial warrant proposed for the *Formidable* included an upper deck battery of Congreve 24s, which the Admiralty properly insisted should be replaced by the long 24-pounders that *Canopus* had always mounted. The chase guns on the upper deck, along with the boat and poop carronades, were ordered to be of the same calibre as the main deck battery.[7]

The appointment of Byam Martin as Controller did not alter the opinion of the Navy Board. He shared the view that increasing the armament of battleships would ruin them as cruising men of war, and pull them to pieces during a winter blockade. In addition, he had little time for the Congreve, or any other long gun that could not stand double-shotting. The real answer to the problem of increasing the armament of the battlefleet lay in the work of Seppings. Stronger ships could carry additional metal without undue strain and new ships could be built to larger dimensions, allowing for more efficient use of the new battery. With the introduction of the round bow and stern the opportunity for shifting guns from the broadside into effective firing positions placed further demands on the fabric of the ship.

However, Martin did allow ships to be up-gunned for particular service. The first, and in this period the only, significant example was the Bombardment of Algiers in 1816. Of the five battleships engaged two, *Impregnable* and *Superb*, had their upper deck 12- or 18-pounders exchanged for long 18- or 24-pounders. These were only temporary alterations to make the ships more powerful, and *Impregnable* resumed her original warrant at the end of the year. *Superb*'s captain complained that the heavy garrison pattern 24-pounders were literally tearing his ship to pieces but this was hardly surprising, given the age and strenuous service of the old 74.[8]

Exmouth's plan for the Algiers operation had the advantage of having been matured while at anchor in the Bay, and aided by long contemplation. He selected five battleships as the greatest number that could profitably be engaged with the Algerian works, assisted by one 50-gun ship, four frigates and bomb vessels. The guns of the fleet were fitted with sights, new pattern carronades with chain cables, and after bitts for mooring the ship by the stern. In all Byam Martin earned Exmouth's gratitude for the assistance rendered by his department.[9]

The naval force at Algiers

Ship	*Guns*
Queen Charlotte	100
Impregnable	98
Minden	74
Albion	74
Superb	74
Leander	50
Glasgow, Severn	40
Hebrus, Graunicus	36
Seven sloops	
Four bomb vessels	
Five Dutch frigates and one corvette	

The lower deck of the Nelson, *then a two-decker of 90 guns serving as a schoolship in New South Wales. The diagonal deck was introduced by Seppings. Symonds returned to the normal layout when the new, and more powerful, 32-pounders began to cut up the diagonal planking. The guns are the last 56cwt 32-pounders, and have been fitted with sights, improved means of shifting the carriages and a simple set of concentration marks. The improvement over the* Victory *might appear to be small, but in action the effect would have been far greater.*

Gunnery exercise was conducted twice daily, and a full six broadsides were to be discharged from each ship at least twice a week. On board the flagship Lieutenant Crichton introduced sub-calibre target shooting and claimed to have increased the rate of fire, although that was almost certainly a product of increased drill. The contrast with the wartime Mediterranean Fleet, made by Napier, was entirely just. The object of the exercises was clear. Exmouth intended taking on the batteries as well as burning the Algerian fleet: this would combine a demonstration of the city's vulnerability with material damage that related directly to the offence complained of, namely, piracy and the enslavement of victims. He did not intend battering the city, merely exposing its vulnerability. Each battleship had a specific role in the attack while the frigates were to draw the fire of the remaining Algerian batteries. Exploiting the Algerian decision not to open fire as the fleet moved in, *Queen Charlotte* closed to within 80 yards of the molehead battery, to a point where only five guns could bear on her, before anchoring and awaiting the inevitable action. This position gave her the advantage of weight of metal to offset the steady platform of the land-based guns. The second flagship, Sir David Milne's *Impregnable*, was less skilfully placed having anchored within the arc of fire from the three-tiered lighthouse battery, 450 yards out. While she came close to silencing the most powerful battery at Algiers the ship was roughly handled, and the cost was heavy. Once the molehead battery had been silenced Exmouth burnt the Algerian fleet and as night fell his flotilla bombarded the town with mortars, rockets and guns. By the time *Minden* had covered the withdrawal of the other battleships the squadron had been in action almost nine hours. The Bey accepted terms the following day, which was fortunate for Exmouth as the squadron was effectively without ammunition. With 818 casualties, 128 fatal, which represented some 16 per cent of the men involved, the action was as hot as any of the age of sail.[10]

The lessons to be drawn depended on the view point of the analyst. Many contemporary naval officers considered Algiers to be a special case that did not alter the basic maxim that ships should not engage forts. In truth, it served to establish the skill, confidence, arrogance and commitment of the Royal Navy. No other fleet would have attempted or could have achieved as much, and Algiers was to stand as a warning to all hostile coastal cities, until superseded in that capacity by the attack on Acre.

After Algiers the fleet had little serious work for heavy guns. Many officers were still committed to close action, Benjamin Hallowell calling for 68-pounder carronades to be mounted at the main deck ports in the round of the bow aboard the *Tonnant*. His purpose was to avoid the interference to the service of the other guns caused by mounting a long gun at these ports and the idea took hold so that a pair of these carronades became part of the lower deck establishment of all large two-deckers, pre-dating the shell gun.

This did not prevent Byam Martin from securing the use of long guns on all two-deckers. He was prepared to tolerate light pieces on three-deckers, which were intended to maximise firepower at close quarters, but would not accept the same limits for the two-deckers. When reducing the weight of metal mounted aboard the large two-deckers Martin was careful to dispense with carronades or guns masked by the rigging.[11] The trend was away from the upper deck carronade battery towards a heavy armament of long guns, and the razee 98-gun *Ocean* was the first ship warranted for a full battery of 32-pounder guns on two decks, with carronades of the same calibre and only six 12-pounder chase guns.

The case for the carronade was not helped by the slide carriages on which they were mounted, and they remained inefficient and unreliable. When the Captain of the *Ganges* reported adversely on those aboard his ship a joint Admiralty, Navy Board and Board of Ordnance Committee investigated. Cockburn, Sir Henry Hardinge, Lt Col Burgh, Byam Martin and Seppings, reported in favour of short 68-pounder guns on regular truck carriages. When it arrived the 50cwt Miller 68-pounder was adopted, but only as a supplement to the carronades.[12]

A replica 68-pounder carronade on the forecastle of the Victory. This gun was issued to several battleships after 1815 as a lower deck bow gun, predating the 8in shell gun in the role of increased close-range firepower. The slide was soon replaced by an improved carriage designed by Hardy. (CMP)

The real problem was how to fit any significant increase in firepower into the existing fleet. Seppings's rebuilds provided additional strength, and in some cases capacity was increased by broadening. The alternative solution, designing new guns of reduced weight, was not looked upon with favour by the Controller. Faced by a new 49cwt 32-pounder Martin recommended they should be adopted, but only 'if they prove as effective for a long sustained cannonading, and carrying two shot as heavy 24 pounders'. A further problem lay in an increase of 1.5 tons weight for the guns, and almost one ton for heavier shot if these guns replaced the long 24-pounders. Martin commented:

> It would be more satisfactory if the capacity of the new ships was more decidedly calculated to master this heavier description of arming, and this may be done in some degree in the new First Rates ordered to be built.

Over-gunning ships, even the new *Bombay*, was condemned as 'very injurious to their fabric, particularly on long service'. After experience in the *Asia* Codrington had confirmed that long 32-pounders on the main deck had had an adverse effect on the ships' sea-going qualities.[13]

At Navarin the power of *Asia*'s broadsides quickly disposed of both Turkish and Egyptian flagships, forcing her to shift her berth by hauling in the stern moorings to find fresh targets. This was hardly surprising as both gun decks mounted long 32-pounders and the upper deck mounted 42-pounder carronades. With his experience of naval action Codrington can be assumed to have laid stress on gun drill. Codrington was well satisfied with the speed and precision of her fire although the carronades were disabled, the slides capsizing once the breech ropes stretched, much as they had during the French wars, and he called for the upper deck carronades to be replaced by medium 40cwt 32-pounders. With the carronades disabled he sent the crews below to man the main deck battery, which was short-handed due to her having a peace complement and large detachments on duty in tenders. This helped to keep down the number of casualties for neither of the two covered decks were penetrated by enemy fire, save at the ports. The round stern was 'an improvement, the advantages of which are incalculably great'. In return, the side of the Egyptian flagship, a double-banked frigate, was quite literally beaten in, several ports being smashed into one gaping hole. *Asia*'s two consorts, *Albion* and *Genoa*, were less powerful, being 18- and 24-pounder 74s. The opposition was lightly armed and the vessels badly built. Their gunners lacked the experience and were quite ineffective even at anchor in a sheltered bay. Once again the lessons of combat were in favour of heavy guns and full crews. By contrast, the damage caused by Ottoman fire on the upper deck and cabin battery of *Asia*, a teak-built ship with upperworks considered too heavy by Byam Martin, was ignored. The Admiral's son, Henry, badly wounded in the leg by a piece of iron stern rail, which was driven into the cabin, observed: 'had all the cabin guns been mounted and manned the slaughter would have been great'. If guns were to be mounted on the upper deck, for the high command which all naval officers valued, they required better protection than was accorded them in any ship afloat.[14] Only in the last years of the sailing ship was attention shifted to the upperworks. Captain Sir Henry Chads of *Excellent* conducted a series of trial firings against the standard fir bulwarks, and these reflected the changing tactics of steam warfare which involved the increased use of heavy guns on the upper decks of steam vessels. With the main armament of many ships mounted on the upper deck, some improvement was vital.[15]

The new ships

Byam Martin's reluctance to increase the armament of the fleet disappeared in the face of design developments abroad. The French had made a considerable effort to rebuild their fleet with 100-gun two-deckers, essentially *Canopus*-type ships, armed throughout with new 30-pounder guns. (The French *livre* was slightly heavier than the English pound, so this calibre was approximately equal to that of the British 32-pounder.) The new British 47cwt 32-pounder, and a large degree of modification to ships on order, allowed a suitable counter to be made. The design of the *Calcutta* reflected the shift to a single-calibre battery of 32-pounders, but only with the new *Nile*-class of 1826 did the Surveyor have an opportunity to combine his structural reforms with the new armament and the enlarged dimensions. Initially, a 100-gun ship, the *Nile*, was soon relieved of her American type spar-deck battery for a final warrant of 92 guns. In this form the new class were also superior to USS *Ohio*, an over-armed spar deck ship that had been packed with 42-pounders, 32-pounders and 42-pounder carronades. To counter the 42-pounder, Byam Martin equipped the *Nile* class with heavy 63cwt 32-pounders, which were superior to the standard 55cwt pattern.[16]

Rearmed as 92-gun ships, the three *Niles* were to form the heart of the battlefleet, providing the gunpower to decide any future engagement. The French, despite their large construction programme, were making but little progress with the new guns required to arm their ships and by 1828 only 380 out of a total of 4,650 required had been cast.[17]

Byam Martin equipped the poop deck of every battleship with four carronades intended for ships' boats, either 9- or 12-pounders, for use in dismantling the enemy rigging. He retained his belief in the benfits of close action, and the value of the three-decked ship. The fleet in existence at the date of the abolition of the Navy Board was far stronger than that inherited by Byam Martin; the new 120-, 92- and 84-gun ships had transformed the battlefleet and provided a nucleus of modern, heavily-armed units that were capable of retaining the command of the sea against any potential opponent.

After the Navy Board

The revolution in naval architecture that followed the abolition of the Navy Board had at its heart the desire to create ships of improved sailing performance which at the same time had a better battery deck for the guns. Symonds's greatest claim to fame lay in the sheer size of his ships, and the sharp rise in the number of tons per gun gave crews the space to work without impinging upon one another, while the width of deck allowed for the full recoil of the heaviest carriage guns. His ships carried no carronades, and the lightest gun mounted was the 25cwt 32-pounder gunnade which was used in three-deckers in an attempt to retain the rate of fire of the short weapon, without sacrificing range. The objection to the old 74-gun ships was not the number of guns they mounted but the weakness of the 18-pounders mounted on the main deck. Consequently, Symonds's 70-gun ship, which carried 32-pounders throughout, was a useful battleship because it was large enough, and sufficiently heavily built, to stand up to a heavy arming. His larger designs were equally impressive as spacious gun platforms, and by the end of the sailing Navy almost all new designs being brought forward reflected the increased dimensions introduced by Symonds.

The Committee of Reference attempted with the *Caesar* to build a modernised *Nile*, but contemporary opinion suggested they had gone too far and cramped the guns. Under Walker the Surveyor's Office gave more attention to the requirement for space on the gun decks and the spacing of main deck guns came to dominate the wooden steam battlefleet.

The gun deck of the Unicorn, *showing the use of iron knees, which reduced the obstruction and allowed an increase in effective concentration of fire.* (Author)

HMS *Excellent* and the profession of naval gunnery

In 1818 the Admiralty published the first official *Instructions for the Exercise of Great Guns*. This was an altogether unremarkable document that did little to advance the science of gunnery. After the capture of the *Chesapeake*, Broke never again served at sea. Grievously wounded by a sabre cut across the head, and later by a fall from his horse, he was forced to pass on his legacy in writing. He shared his ideas with others, notably Pechell and through him General Sir Howard Douglas. Both men published works on naval gunnery that benefited from long correspondence with Broke; and Pechell, as a Junior Lord of the Admiralty and Royal favourite, had considerable influence over the establishment of a permanent gunnery training ship, while Douglas's famous *Treatise on Naval Gunnery* provided the basic text for the remaining years of the wooden Navy. As a soldier, Douglas advocated a permanent corps of seamen gunners which was intended to remove from the captain of each ship the onus of drilling his men.

Douglas, the son of the innovative Captain Sir Charles Douglas who was largely responsible for the introduction in 1780 of the flintlock for cannon aboard warships, was alarmed at the low standard of exercise and the poor results of British sea service gunnery. After the French Wars he devoted a considerable effort to the subject, focusing on both the theory of ballistics and the practical problems of sea service. He came to the conclusion that officers should have a basic knowledge as part of their initial training, and that a seaman gunner should be induced to remain in the service. In 1818 he presented his findings to the Admiralty through Rear Admiral Sir Graham Moore, brother of the Peninsula hero. The Board were unwilling to act, but permitted the publication of the work. In the interval Douglas began his correspondence with Broke.[18]

Gunnery was not accorded the highest priority after 1815, something all too evident in the unenthusiastic response made to Douglas's treatise. One of the failings of the dual administration of the Navy, with policy and strategy in the hands of the Admiralty and material and personnel controlled from Somerset Place, was that it condemned training and doctrine to the limbo of individual officers' inclinations. This was a particular problem while the Admiralty continued to be dominated by professional men who believed that close action and no special training could still win battles. Cockburn, for all his merits, was not an advocate of modern gunnery and made no effort to act on Douglas's work, or profit by Broke's example.

The subject was finally raised at the Admiralty by the Lord High Admiral. Devoted to the best interests of the service, Clarence believed good gunnery was the paramount virtue for any officer. Captain George Elliot, then commanding the *Victory*, earned the favour of the Duke with the gun drill on his ship and his subsequent appointment as First Secretary in the Graham Administration was a belated reward. Clarence's Secretary, Captain Robert Spencer, sent out a circular calling on all ships to make a quarterly return of gunnery exercises and appointed a Committee to formulate a service doctrine. It was entirely in keeping with this anxiety for improvement that in his haste to set up the Committee Clarence should have overstepped the bounds of his Patent as Lord High Admiral by entering into an open-ended financial commitment without consulting his Council, which was led by the formidable Cockburn. For this offence he was forced to resign. Before acting, however, Clarence had consulted Broke. It was his intention to adopt the whole of Broke's system which incorporated aiming at the main deck, blindfold fire and concentration of fire. Clarence realised that too much attention had been given to smartness aloft rather than the less glamorous skill of fighting the guns. Broke made clear his preference for close quarters combat, where the British had always won their battles, but accepted that foreign developments made it essential for them to become masters of long-range fire as well. Clarence discussed using one of the Port Guard Ships as a depot for training seaman gunners, but the idea was not pressed before he left office. Even after his administration had ended the Duke retained his commitment to gunnery, pressing the subject on Napier, one of the few officers afloat who did not need to be reminded.[19]

A final stimulus for the creation of a permanent gunnery establishment was the publication of a pamphlet by Captain William Bowles in 1830, under the pen-name 'An Old Flag Officer', which drew attention to the poor condition of the Navy. In it Bowles commended Douglas's scheme to the Admiralty. The pamphlet was favourably reported on in the *Times* during May, and on 19 June 1830 the Melville Board gave orders to establish *Excellent* as an experimental gunnery ship, under the direction of the Fort Admiral. Two officers and forty gunners from the Marine Artillery were to be borne, under Commander George Smith, who had recently submitted an able, if derivative, pamphlet detailing a method of improving naval gunnery.

Cockburn had consulted Smith on the site for a gunnery training ship and on the selection of the *Excellent*, which was a happy choice given her connection with Collingwood. The ship was already 43 years old and had been razeed into a spar deck 58. Within a month Smith had her moored with her port broadside directed up Fareham Creek, Portsmouth, and a system of exercise and training based on a distillation of Broke, Douglas and Pechell in operation. At the end of September the Port Admiral, Sir Thomas Foley, was directed to place various calibres of artillery on board for testing, and *Excellent* was at work. Her arrival on the scene was already overdue, as Sir William Parker discovered when he raised his flag aboard the *Prince Regent* in 1831. His Flag Captain, J W D Dundas, had a mania for neatness that precluded drill and the exercise of the guns. As a result her crews were so ill-trained that when they did use live ammunition one gun captain forgot to stop the vent, and two of his crew were 'blown to atoms' by the premature detonation of the charge.[20]

It has been suggested that the Melville Board was little interested in the success or failure of the ship, and that only the advent of the Graham Board, with Pechell as one of the Junior Naval Lords, ensured its survival. In truth, there was not enough time for the outgoing Board to do more than make a start, but they had made the vital step. With the arrival of Pechell Smith was superseded in 1832 by another Royal favourite, Captain Thomas Hastings, and the ship placed on a permanent footing with the enlistment of seamen gunners for five and seven years for additional pay. Under Hastings the ship had a crew of two hundred, and it was entirely appropriate that the needs of naval gunnery created the first permanent body of seamen. In recognition of the permanence of the system itself, the old ship was paid off and dismantled and immediately replaced by the *Boyne*, which had herself been slated for a razee, only to be saved by Symonds. The new *Excellent* was too small for the battlefleet, but that battlefleet was made more powerful by her students.

Excellent was far more than a platform for firing guns, or even for training men in the legacy of Broke. Trials, new inventions, ranging, magazine developments, theoretical science and mechanics were all on the officers' gunnery course. The training of seamen was equally rigorous, if less technical and extended to small arms and magazine duty. The estimated cost of training of £300 per man encouraged the Admiralty to take a close interest in the progress of the establishment. To protect the system Hastings soon established a policy that no man could be considered for promotion to Gunner without a first-class seaman gunner certificate from the school.

The final triumph of the *Excellent* system was recognised by the Admiralty in 1838. The Board ordered the establishment of a uniform system of gunnery throughout the fleet, based on the drill employed aboard the training ship. Officers and men were to be trained in sufficient numbers, and a warrant for Gunner's Mates and seaman gunners was laid down for each class in the Navy.

	Gunner's Mates	*Seaman Gunners*
First Rate	4	12
Second & Third Rate	2	10
Fourth Rate	2	8
Fifth Rate	2	6
Sixth Rate	2	4
Steamers & sloops	1	3
Brigs	1	1
Cutters & schooners	1	0

To make best use of these trained men all battleships and frigates were ordered to be armed with nothing but 32-pounders and 68-pounder shell guns. Any remaining suitable 24-pounders were to be bored up, the carriages of the 68-pounders improved and both calibres, following the *Prince George* trials, to be equipped for shell firing.[21] This combination of trained personnel and increased weight of metal was a vital part of the process whereby the Royal Navy maintained its pre-eminence during the last years of the sailing Navy.

After 1839 the Captain of the *Excellent* was also Superintendent of the Royal Naval College which reflected the growing

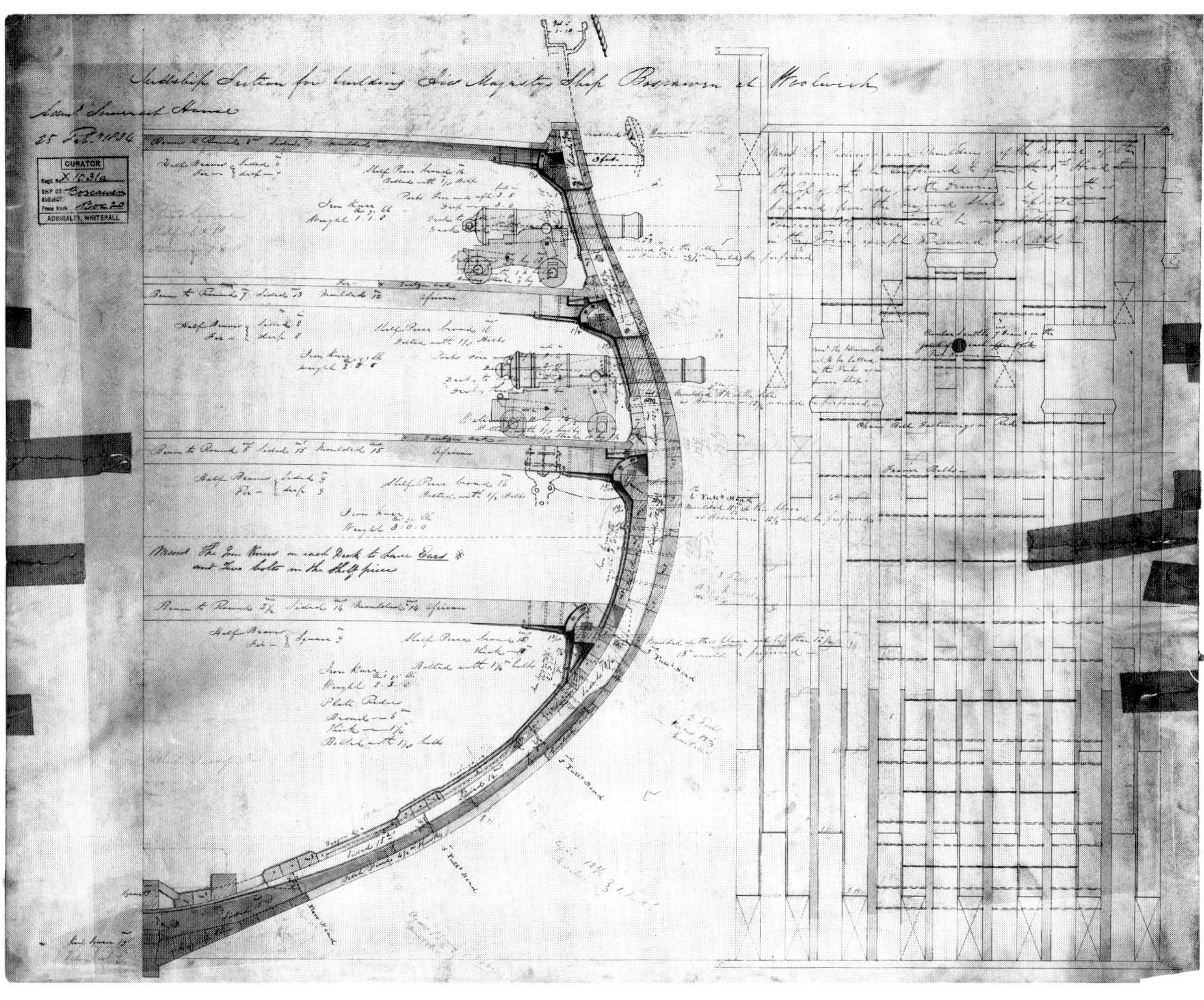

A midship section through the 70-gun Symondite Boscawen, *showing the concave scuppers and increased use of iron that were a feature of Symonds's regime. Both measures improved the run out of the gun, and allowed for greater lateral movement. Both guns are 32-pounders, the lower 56cwt and the upper of 48cwt. The deck beams are specified as African timber.* (NMM)

importance of gunnery and science in the education of the new officer corps. Plymouth was given its own training establishment in 1838, aboard the *San Josef* which was moved into the *Cambridge* in 1856.[22]

The magazine and the supply system are aspects of gunnery that have never been given due credit. During the period under review the magazine and supply arrangements were essentially unaltered from the wartime design although a good deal of *Excellent*'s time was given over to the possibility of improvement. In the late 1820s the Admiralty flirted with the midships magazine for battleships but after fitting a skeleton arrangement to the *Thunderer* it became obvious that what was adequate for frigates, or even powerful razees, could not cope with the demands of one or two more covered gun decks.[23]

Later Codrington was consulted and he came down in favour of a modified version of the existing system. In this he did not go as far as Napier, who opened up the magazine crown of the *Powerful* in order to increase the speed of supply. Napier's contemporaries considered he had exposed the ship to the danger of a shell reaching the magazine. His ideas on gun drill were equally novel for he would wander around the gun decks with a basket of wads during drill, throwing them at random to produce 'casualties'. The men hit were considered 'dead' and Napier watched to see how quickly the others could compensate. Everything was dominated by the quest for speed and precision.[24]

Many have seen the performance of the fleet at Acre as the high water mark of naval gunnery during the age of sail, but this is only partly true. The Mediterranean Fleet was largely composed of small and obsolescent ships armed with short-range guns. Had they been replaced by new 120- and 90-gun ships the results would have been even more impressive. *Excellent* gunnery made the fleet a serious threat to naval forts and arsenals and in 1845 even the alarmist Napier considered he could take Cherbourg. Another Acre captain, Houston Stewart, believed the new armament had altered the tactical situation in favour of long-range. He suggested officers should be encouraged to think of their ships as nothing more than floating batteries, something that had been an axiom with his old Captain, Lord Cochrane.

> The precision and rapidity of the fire from our great guns will, I should think, prevent much of the long protracted yard arm to yard arm work when the ships lay like hulks alongside each other and the musketry swept the upper decks, as at Trafalgar.[25]

Hasting's works earned him a knighthood in 1839, and created a tradition of excellence that shifted the parameters of naval action further outward. Accurate individual rounds were now fired out to 1,000 yards, with success against boat-sized targets. While it would still be necessary to close in for a decisive kill British warships would never be out-gunned at long-range. In addition, long-range fire gave them the opportunity to damage or cripple the flying enemy at hitherto unimagined distances. Hastings also advised the Admiralty on the offensive and defensive qualities of new ships and his report on the sterns of the *Trafalgar* and *Cumberland* was both intelligent and damning. In the first case the problem had been noted as early as 1831, but nothing had been done. The second was all the more serious as it effectively involved every stern in Symonds's battlefleet.[26]

After turning the *Excellent* over to his successor, the same Henry Chads who had surrendered the *Java* to the USS *Constitution* in 1812, Hastings was appointed to Storekeeper to the Board of Ordnance where he was able to retain his intimate connection with the development of heavy artillery.

Chads took up his post in August 1845, carrying on the practical tradition of the ship, introducing improvements in magazine stowage, shells and a seagoing drill ship, initially the steam guard ship *Edinburgh*. The system of training was still far from popular with officers who had to take mates and even unpassed midshipmen from the Naval College in order to keep up numbers. Passing the course entitled the student to count his year as two for seatime, but failure meant the time was lost. However, by the mid-1840s *Excellent* gunnery was known throughout the fleet, exciting emulation and competition, rather than derision. Ships now fired at barrels 500 yards off and rarely failed to score hits. Progressive young officers, Astley Cooper-Key being a prime example, saw the gunnery course as an opportunity for advancement and up to 1860 103 lieutenants took the trouble to become qualified in gunnery. In 1851 it had been estimated that some 2,500 seamen had qualified as gunners.[27]

Both Hastings and Chads carried out practical experiments to determine the effectiveness and accuracy of the guns employed afloat. The 1838 trials against the old *Prince George* were conducted at a range of 1,200 yards, and they demonstrated that the 32-pounder was far more powerful at such ranges than the 18-pounder for the old ship was ripped apart by heavy shot which penetrated up to 48in through her sides. The implications of this were clear: battle could be decided at much longer range than had been anticipated. The next major set of trials, in 1847, provided more information on the accuracy at the new ranges. All standard guns, solid shot and shell firing hit with 75 per cent of rounds at 1,500 yards and 45 per cent at 2,000 yards. Solid shot guns made 25 per cent hits at 2,500 and 11–12 per cent at 3,000 yards. The shell guns were less accurate, only achieving 22 per cent and 8–9 per cent respectively with hollow shot, and 25 per cent less than that with filled shells. Very long-range fire was suitable for bombardment but at 2,000 yards enough hits could be made on a ship to make it worthwhile opening fire. The most important conclusion to be drawn from these trials was that the paddle warship, with a few heavy shell guns, was not capable of taking on a battleship at long range, because solid shot guns out-performed shell guns, and as they were also more numerous the chances were all against the steamer. This had a considerable impact on the decision to fit the screw to the line of battleship, in preference to further development of the paddle wheel ship.[28]

The *Excellent* concept was adopted by all major Navies and, indeed, the French paid rather more attention to Douglas's work in the 1820s than did the British. Seagoing gunnery became a science in the last days of the sailing Navy. After 1838 ships were commissioned with a nucleus of trained gunnery ratings and warrant officers capable of drilling the crew in order to make the best use of new and more powerful guns. In this the Royal Navy was, if anything, further in advance of her rivals in 1850 than she had been in 1815.

The move towards heavier artillery

Between 1815 and 1850 the design and construction of naval artillery made little fundamental progress, yet the calibre and power of individual pieces made rapid advances. Sir Howard Douglas was the best known, and among the best informed commentators on the development of naval artillery. He identified several strands in the development of naval guns, and provided a clear programme.

Alongside his work to set up a gunnery training ship, Douglas gave close attention to the guns. While he admitted that the greatest splintering effect was produced by firing shot at the smallest velocity adequate to penetrate an enemy vessel, and noted the suitability of the carronade for such work at close quarters, Douglas was not among those who retained an unquestioning faith in the old methods. He soon concluded that the day of the carronade was over and that tactical changes rendered the close-range gun little more than a dangerous illusion of strength. Indeed, his general conclusion was that only the most powerful solid shot weapons that could be mounted should feature on the gun decks of British warships.

The decision taken in 1826 to establish all battleships with a single-calibre arming of 32-pounders of varying weights encouraged the Ordnance to bore up about 1,600 24-pounders. These guns, equally divided between Congreve and Bloomfield patterns became 41 and 50cwt 32-pounders of reduced windage (the gap between the ball and the bore of the gun). As a temporary expedient they were useful, increasing the broadside weight of metal of existing ships, without pulling them to pieces. They were not, however, a substitute for new weapons of the same dimensions, designed for the larger shot, and benefitting from the most recent trends in casting and boring. The bored up guns required greater elevation to make the range, had a more severe recoil and were quite unsafe with double shot, the standard method of increasing firepower at decisive range. By 1850 the supply of new 42cwt and Monk's 50cwt guns, which were almost the equal of the 56cwt pattern, enabled most modern vessels to carry the new pieces. While the practice of boring up was extended to a large portion of the old guns below 32-pounders, most were only suitable for small vessels or auxiliaries.

Reducing windage and allowing more of the charge to drive the shot rather than waste its effort, was a particular interest of Douglas's. He recommended this step to the Master General of the Ordnance in 1817 and lived to see it carried through in the new guns, particularly the last new gun designed for the wooden battleship, the 58cwt 32-pounder. Previously, British guns were given an excessive windage, in part a legacy from the era when guns were cast around a core and in part to permit the use of imperfect shot and to allow for the severe heating effect of sustained fire. With improved shot casting, and more careful storage windage could be safely reduced. At the same time the new guns required the full barrel length to make maximum use of the charge. His reasoning indicated the degree to which his views formed a complete system, rather than a mere collection of opinions.

> The advocates of the short gun system support their theory by quoting the deductions from the ballistics experiments, from which it appears that the superior velocity of shot discharged from long guns is reduced to an equality with the velocity of balls from short guns, after passing over certain spaces, and that the extreme ranges do not much differ; but the main principle which should govern our choice of naval guns is, to prefer those which, with equal calibre, possess the

greatest point-blank range; and the practical maxim for using them should be, to close to, or within that range, and depend upon precision and rapidity of fire. This is the most simple and the most efficacious use of artillery: it avoids all the difficulty of determining, and the uncertainty in regulating elevation, and it is therefore of the greatest importance in naval gunnery.

This was the armament philosophy to make the best use of Broke's drill. Douglas was convinced that the fleet with the longest point blank range would have a major advantage in fleet action, because of the ease with which it could keep up an accurate fire. The decision of 1838 to adopt a two-calibre battery of 32-pounders and 68-pounder shell guns in 1838 was only a partial reflection of Douglas's ideas.

Douglas has often been subjected to criticism for his views on shell guns, but in truth his opinions have a great deal to recommend them. From the time of General Henri Paixhan's trials shell guns – chambered ordnance to fire hollow shot and filled shells – were inferior in range, accuracy and rate of fire to the equivalent solid shot guns. In addition, just as the shell was a dangerous projectile, it was also a hazardous thing to have on board ship for in addition to the common accidents in the magazine and gun deck, shells might be struck by round shot and brought to explode, or if the fuse was incorrectly fitted it could explode in the gun. Either event could have serious effects on the ship, and the one recorded accident of the latter type occurred aboard the *Hogue* in 1852. The type of shell that particularly concerned Douglas was the one that used a time fuse, for if these lodged in the fabric of the ship they could explode with an appalling 'mining' effect. However, the *Excellent* trials of 1853, against the old 74 *York*, suggested that the failure rate for fuses of all types of shell was very high. Those that did function properly were of the percussion type, and they failed either to sink the ship, or set her on fire. The final test came under the guns of Sevastopol, on 17 October 1854, during the last action of the sailing battlefleet when shells damaged several ships but did not sink any. The shell was, as Douglas observed, not a decisive weapon, and Broke concurred; he disliked the shell because it was a weapon of long range and like Douglas he wanted to fight at close quarters which were, he rightly observed, Britain's 'shining point'.[29]

Hastings, on the other hand, was an early convert to the shell. Reporting on the 1843 trials he recorded that of twenty-four fired only eleven exploded, but this was compensated by 'the tremendous power of shells fired at low angles against ships'. He noted that the service prejudice against shells was subsiding.[30] His own views, however, were conditioned by a clear understanding of the problems of naval gunnery. He called for the 10in 86cwt guns placed aboard the *Thunderer* in 1834 to be replaced by 56- or 68-pounder solid shot weapons as the 10in gun was inferior in range and accuracy to the standard 32-pounder of 56cwt. Shell guns had to fit in with the existing armament; if they did not they had no place aboard battlefleet units, whatever their value as the main armament of paddle steamers.[31]

The French, from Paixhan onward thought that the shell would make a profound alteration in the balance between offence and defence in battleship design. Paixhan favoured abandoning the battleship altogether, but his countrymen could only be brought to abandon the three-decker, and that temporarily, in favour of the 90-gun ship. This, with the benefit of hindsight, would appear to have been another French attempt to move away from the three-decker, symbol of close battle and the British way, toward the more flexible two-decker.

Douglas's opposition to the shell gun was not mere conservatism. He thought that some were required, but that the trend evident in the late 1840s towards a full gun deck battery of the 65cwt 8in guns was excessive and that it reduced the real power of the fleet. The first ship to carry a full battery of shell guns, the rebuilt *Prince Regent*, required stowage for 740 shells but this reduced the space for shot lockers. However, the 65cwt

The upper deck of the 50-gun steam frigate Narcissus *in 1861. This gives a good impression of the degree to which the upper deck guns were exposed to the risk of falling rigging. In action they were also more likely to be disabled by shot penetrating the light bulwarks.* (CMP)

gun of 1838 did have the saving quality of being capable of accurate use with solid shot.

One alternative to the shell which found favour with Douglas was the red hot shot. The idea of employing incendiary missiles against the inflammable hull of warships was an old one, having been outstandingly successful during the siege of Gibraltar in 1780–82. However, the dangers of carrying a furnace on board made the system more of a hazard to the firing ship than any target. Consequently, hot shot was the preserve of land batteries. However, by 1815 British experiments encouraged the installation of a long 24-pounder and a furnace aboard four gun brigs. These were specialist coast attack craft, and no attempt was made to fit battleships to fire hot shot until they had their own furnace as part of a steam plant. Consequently, early steamers were the first to use hot shot afloat, the *Karteria* during the Greek War of Independence being the best known example.

The advantages of red hot shot were amply demonstrated by the fate of the Danish battleship *Christian VIII*, set on fire and destroyed by shells and red hot shot during the Battle of Eckernfjorde in 1848. However, firing the enlarged shot was far from safe, as was demonstrated when 32-pounders burst at Gibraltar and Malta in the early 1850s with fatal results. Using missiles was fraught with danger on board wooden ships in the heat of battle and was far from ideal. Steamers, with far fewer guns to serve, could give more attention to them, yet the results of hot shot practice, the Danish example apart, were not such as to encourage their widespread use. During the Russian War several ships were hit and set on fire by hot shot, but all were able to remove the missiles and extinguish the fire. Good discipline and the ability to withdraw from action saved several ships before Sevastopol on 17 October 1854.

In place of the shell gun Douglas argued for a battery of heavy solid shot pieces. He noted with some alarm the continued use of the 42-pounder in America and Russia and the French 36-pounder. New 42-pounders were tried aboard *Excellent* in 1843 but they required two more men to serve them and were still less easily handled, without offering any particular advantages. In the search for range and power, four of General Dundas's 112cwt 68-pounders were tried on the lower deck of *Albion*, with slide carriages, but they interfered with the other guns and were too cumbersome. Rumours that the 1838 65cwt gun was a solid shot 56-pounder caused the French to issue 50-pounders for their gun decks, but these were soon withdrawn for the same reason that heavier British weapons were not employed. The 32-pounder was an optimum size of gun and shot for rapid service on a crowded gun deck with the pre-industrial technology of the truck carriage and rope tackle.

Heavier guns were adopted by the Navy, but these were not regularly mounted aboard battleships before the steam battleship period. They were too heavy for easy handling, and the demands they placed on their crews were blamed for a short-fall in recruiting. Mr. Monk's 56-pounder of 97cwt, a piece designed for coast defence batteries, was employed aboard the paddle frigate *Terrible*. This gun, following Congreve's principles, was designed with more metal around the seat of the charge. It was capable of ranges up to 5,000 yards. Ultimately, the 95cwt 68-pounder was the preferred heavy gun. Resembling nothing so much as a slightly enlarged 32-pounder, it combined range, accuracy and a common shot size with the 65cwt shell gun. This was, however, the gun of another generation, and was to require larger ships to carry it. Even the largest of the wooden steam battleships were not equal to such an armament. Land gunners noted the improved range and accuracy of the postwar naval guns, and made good use of the weapons and men of the new Navy before Sevastopol.[32]

Broke employed horizontal fire to smash the enemy gun deck. To determine the precise moment to fire he fitted pendulums on his own battery decks, and these were adopted aboard all battleships as the period progressed, installed in the square of the hatchways. His opponent, like all American ships of the period, had similar equipment. For elevation a simple brass tangent scale was employed, with chocks to shift the gun. The French moved over to an elevating screw, but this was considered too slow and unnecessarily precise for the demands of battleship gunnery. Other aspects of Broke's work, notably concentration of fire, were less widely followed. On board *Excellent* concentration was restricted to ranges below 400 yards, and in tolerable weather. The work of more adventurous gunners, Captain Moorsom and Commander Jerningham, was moving toward a system of director-firing similar to that adopted after 1900. With this method a single officer provided the range and direction of the target to all guns and it could be used when the target was obscured from the view of the lower decks. Douglas, as might be expected, retained his faith in the ability and judgement of the seaman gunner, and deprecated moves intended to deprive him of responsibility.

With the development of the flintlock, Douglas's own 1817 double flintlock, and finally the springless tube lock as developed by Colonel Dundas from the American 'hidden' pattern of 1842, speed and reliability of fire improved. Most Navies relied on springless locks, but the Austrian spring lock did relieve the gunner of the additional task of giving the hammer its impetus. In 1845 Major Jacob, of the Bombay Artillery, conducted a series of trials with standard percussion locks and caps which had the singular merit of reducing wear in the vent. With normal ignition systems the vent became over large after approximately 250 rounds while the percussion lock had no effect on the vent after 300 rounds. Potentially, this was a major advantage, as the vent was the weakest part of a heavy naval gun.

British tactical thought continued to emphasise firing into the hull in order to disable the gun crews and, with the more powerful ordnance, sink the ship. Accuracy at long range could cripple a flying enemy, while small guns on the poop could be used to dismantle an opponent's steering gear and empty the lower mast-tops of riflemen. The small guns were a feature of all the secret armament warrants issued by Byam Martin after 1826. Advances in gunnery made in the years after 1815 promised to make any action involving the British battlefleet far more destructive than the great actions of the French Wars. Heavier shot, increased range and accuracy, shell fire, and concentration at close quarters would reduce less well served opponents to floating charnel houses in a matter of minutes. The Royal Navy of 1850 retained its faith in decisive battles because it offered the only certain security for the British Isles, the Empire and commerce. In maintaining the fleet to meet the task they were also altering the balance between land and sea power.

The attack on forts and arsenals

Before 1815 naval forces only attacked regular maritime fortresses under the most pressing circumstances. The gunnery and weight of metal fired by battleships could not compensate for the advantages of height, accuracy and defensive strength possessed by forts. By 1840 improvements in both areas were so significant that the old maxims, despite being repeated in the House of Lords by Wellington, had lost their authority. Naval forces could now take on sea forts. The attack on Acre, by a scratch force that had no specialist equipment, was a complete success. Even the generally pessimistic Napier followed a visit to Cherbourg by drawing up plans for an attack by naval forces on the most formidable of all the French bases.

Larger, more heavily armed and better manned battleships went a long way toward countering the power of forts. Steam ships made naval forces more flexible, allowing them to exploit weaknesses ashore and withdraw badly damaged ships from the fight. To supplement the battlefleet all artillerists favoured the mortar. The 13in sea service mortar out-ranged all regular guns, fired an impressive shell and, being mounted aboard specialist small craft, did not have any impact on the battlefleet. To supplement this purpose-built weapon, gun boats and rockets were available. Only after the flotilla had worn down the defences would it be necessary for the heavy ships to close in and once placed close alongside they had a good chance of silencing works already damaged. By 1852 a whole series of artillery trials at Shoeburyness were conducted to refine the design of heavy guns for sustained firing at extreme ranges. The targets were to be the French arsenals, and in particular Cherbourg. The strategic object was to destroy any threat of an invasion at its root. While it has been common for historians of the nineteenth century to argue that the Royal Navy was unable to defend the British Isles from invasion the truth is very different. No French harbour was safe from assault and no French fleet could hope to escort an invasion convoy of steam ships it did not possess across the Channel until it had obtained a working command of the sea. Visionary schemes re-using Napoleon's 1805 strategy were no more than attempts to create alarm for political or service ends.

Gun crews 1828

Guns			*Carronades*		
32pdr	63cwt	14	68pdr	36cwt	11
32pdr	55 or 49cwt	13	42pdr	22cwt	10
24pdr	47cwt	12	32pdr	17cwt	8[33]

Naval artillery in store 1839

Guns			*Carronades*		
68pdr	65cwt	66	68pdr	36cwt	18
32pdr	56cwt	1,159	42pdr	22cwt	683
	63cwt	136*	32pdr	17cwt	1,762
	48–50cwt	133	24pdr	13cwt	1,983
24pdr	50cwt	343	18pdr	10cwt	2,865
18pdr		6,000	*Mortars* (at Woolwich)		
*(lower deck guns for the *Nile*-class)			13in	101cwt	17[34]

This is the number of weapons which were in store after the fleet at sea and the Advanced Ships had been equipped, not the total stock of naval artillery. The figures indicate the revolution in naval artillery then in progress. The small number of 24-pounders, and bored up 32-pounders fits in with the peace-time deployment of small, up-gunned ships. A few shell guns were already in store, while there were enough heavy 32-pounders to fit the gun decks of forty-two battleships, but only enough upper deck guns for seventeen, which was somewhere near the number that would have been required to reinforce the active fleet and the Advanced Ships in the event of a major war. The frigates would have been seriously embarassed. The 18-pounders and small carronades were of little relevance, while the shortage of mortars reveals one serious weakness in the British position, namely the Government's reliance on industry to provide specialist equipment in wartime.[35]

The guns of the sailing battlefleet: May 1848

	Weight	*Length*	*Bore*	*Designer/date*
Solid shot				
68pdr	95cwt	10ft	8.12in	Col Dundas 1853
56pdr	98cwt	11ft	7.65in	Mr Monk 1839
32pdr	58cwt	9ft 6in	6.41in	Col Dundas 1855
32pdr	56cwt	9ft 6in	6.41in	Sir Thomas Blomefield The standard 32-pounder, throughout the period under review
32pdr	50cwt	9ft	6.41in	Initially bored up guns, but by 1850 largely new weapons to Monk's pattern: Bore 6.35in
32pdr	41cwt	8ft	6.35in	Bored up guns
32pdr	42cwt	8ft	6.35in	New Dundas gun
32pdr	25cwt	6ft	6.3in	Bored up Blomefield 18-pounder
32pdr	25cwt	6ft	6.3in	New Dundas gun
32pdr	17cwt	4ft	6.25in	Carronade
24pdr	47cwt	9ft	5.823in	Not issued for sea service in 1848, along with the smaller broadside guns dating back to the war
Shell guns				
10in	86cwt	10ft	10in	Gen Millar. For use in Steamers
68pdr	65cwt	9ft	8.05in	Gen Millar 1839
68pdr	52cwt	8ft	8.05in	Gen Millar
Mortar				
13in	101cwt	4ft 5in	13in	Sir Thomas Blomefield

(The new 32-pounder and the old 24-pounder are included for reference.)

3 *Timber: Supply and Seapower*

The single most important material resource for the maintenance of naval power in the early nineteenth century was timber. Without an adequate supply of suitable trees the existing fleet could not be repaired and the new ships, necessary to replace those that had passed beyond economic repair, could not be built. Timber was a major concern of all naval policymakers, but it was not, as is usually suggested, the case that the supply of British oak, the staple component for the hull of a battleship, was ever in any real danger of 'failing'. The Navy took careful steps to preserve and sustain its sources of timber, and over the period under review the quality and quantity of timber used in the Royal dockyards remained high. However, following the publication of Robert Albion's, *Forests and Seapower: The Timber Problem of the Royal Navy 1652–1862* (Harvard 1926), it has been usual to assert that the timber supply failed, principally during the Napoleonic Wars. Albion put forward an argument concerning the inter-relationship between shipbuilding and forestry that had little relationship to fact. Timber supply did not dominate policy-making, because the 'cutting off the supply', upon which he bases his argument, never occurred.[1] Albion's views have already been subject to revision, both in specific areas, and more generally. Morriss notes how contemporary concern with monopolistic trading companies in the USA encouraged Albion to overestimate the cohesion and power of the 'timber trust', while recent research suggests that eighteenth-century administration was more efficient, and much less corrupt, than was believed in the 1920s. If, after 1803, the Navy Board had to resort to the use of foreign and unseasoned timber, it was never without an avenue of supply. Between 1793 and 1807 the stock of timber in the dockyards fluctuated, but at the end of the period there was over one quarter more than there had been at the beginning. The problem had been occasioned by the rapid increase in the price of timber after 1800. St Vincent's reluctance to continue the relaxed regime of his predecessors caused more trouble than any problems in the forests.[2]

The main gate of the premises of Castles, the shipbreakers at Millbank in London. The building was destroyed by bombing in 1941. A large collection of material relating to the last days of the wooden warships was lost in the resulting conflagration. (CMP)

Further, as this chapter will make clear, Albion reflected a fundamental misunderstanding of forestry and timber management. When Albion talks of a failure of supply forcing the Navy to look elsewhere for timber, he confuses the basic shipbuilding material, seasoned timber, with timber. The supply of timber in England was never in any danger of failure, but the availability of seasoned timber could never meet the sudden explosion of demand that followed the outbreak of war, and the continued high level of demand during any conflict. Seasoning requires between one and two years, depending partly on the size of the timber, partly on the method employed to season it and partly on the use for which the timber is required. Similarly, it will be shown that the search for external sources of supply, a major support for Albion's argument, has a very different explanation from the one he advanced.

Oliver Rackham, the Cambridge botanist, suggests an alternative view. He argues that the long stream of alarmist comments going back to the Elizabethan period had more to do with the cost of transport than the timber supply. He calculated that nearly half of all the timber shipping, naval and merchant ever built in Britain was constructed in the period 1800 to 1860, while the area of British woodland suitable for oak was, in this period, ten times greater than would be required to grow the entire naval supply.[3]

As a example of Albion's misunderstanding there is a detailed discussion in his book of the state of Nelson's fleet in the two years before Trafalgar, and the short-term measures which were adopted to cover the lack of serviceable units. The whole discussion is dominated by the theme of the 'failure' of the native timber supply.[4] In fact, the only failure was that occasioned by the First Lord from 1801 to 1804, Earl St Vincent, who launched a zealous assault on the monopoly position of the timber suppliers, who he accused of profiteering. During the brief Peace of Amiens, St Vincent allowed timber stocks to run down while he attacked corruption, in particular targeting the Navy Board and the timber suppliers. The only effect of his action was to run down the dockyard timber piles.[5]

When war broke out his successors were forced to enter into contracts which were even less agreeable than those the old Admiral had cancelled, and permit the use of green timber in merchant-built battleships; and the use of green timber was the direct cause of the post-1805 explosion of dry rot. This was all the more unfortunate given the relatively high levels of timber available when St Vincent took office. Had he bought up the supply, laid down large stores and created a reserve of seasoned timber his zeal would have produced better rewards. Initially, his successors had no time even to build, being forced to patch up defective ships with pine and foreign oak following the innovative system proposed by Gabriel Snodgrass, the East India Company Surveyor. With hindsight the later administrations might have been better advised to continue this repair policy, if only to give time for new ships to be built with seasoned timber. Wartime construction and repairs were never the equal of those carried out in peace, for a number of reasons connected with political/operational pressure, shortages of suitable seasoned timber and the lack of time to stand over. As a result, they did not provide the additional service offered by more leisurely repairs carried out in peacetime. The famous example of the *Queen Charlotte*, somewhat unfairly considered to have been the most rotten ship ever to be built for the Navy, will be considered in more detail in the chapter on decay, but the one thing her case does *not* prove is that the native supply failed.

In his treatment of the period covered by this book Albion claims that the timber 'problem' remained:

> There was the old concern over the diminishing oak supply of England, the same complaints of negligence in the Royal Forests.

The argument that foreign supplies were essential is sustained by inaccurate analysis of the use of Italian oak, teak and Polish larch. Even the argument that the Navy Board felt a degree of repugnance at James Morrice's near monopoly is not borne out by the documents: relations between Morrice and the Controller were excellent.[6]

The most serious weakness of Albion's work is to be found in his attack on English Forestry. He completely misunderstood the nature of a forest and proposed a method of improving the timber supply that would have proved as ill-advised as the construction methods employed on the *Queen Charlotte*. Forests are complex biological entities, involving the inter-relationship of man, flora and fauna with soil, climate and geology. Forests were reserved areas where Kings or noblemen retained rights to hunt and that some of them included a large amount of woodland was accidental. The barren uplands of Dartmoor, it should be remembered, was also a forest though it had never been woodland. The concept was introduced to England by William the Conqueror and worked by imposing charges on local people for any use they made of the products of the forest. Within this system the production of timber trees was never the *raison d'etre*, or even the predominant economic return. Underwood, non-timber products such as wood, fencing, hop-poles, firewood and brush were always more valuable, even in time of war.

Modern forestry, of which Albion wrote, is the science of raising trees as a commercial crop. It is commonly associated with the large-scale plantation of areas with one or two species. This system dates back to the early Stuart period in England, and received a great deal of emphasis with the publication of John Evelyn's *Sylva*, first delivered to the Royal Society in 1664. Evelyn advocated large-scale plantations, and his book became the standard source for manuals on forest management for 150 years. As a result English timber producers were led up a blind alley.[7] When more timber was required it was to Evelyn that landowners turned. By contrast, the traditional woodland management systems, evolved over a long period, made much greater use of the natural properties of the trees. English mixed woodland was a self regenerating source of timber and wood. Coppicing for wood allowed a number of timber trees or 'standards' to assert themselves above the underwood. In this way they tended to grow with a long trunk, which made them more valuable for naval use. In a mixed woodland it was generally accepted that twelve standards could be grown to the acre as against thirty in a single species plantation producing no wood.[8] Individual hedgerow and field trees were also able to grow unhindered into the shapes required for the Navy. These last two types tended to be irregular and thus suitable for frame curves.

After the publication of *Sylva* the existing management system fell out of favour and by the end of the eighteenth century woodlands were being grubbed out and replaced by plantations. These appeared to offer two irresistible advantages. First, they carried the new rational farming methods of the age of reason into timber production; and second, they could provide all the timber required from the smallest possible acreage of land. With arable land suitable for oak timber production under heavy economic pressure during the Wars of the French Revolution and Empire, the apparent waste of land covered by woods, as against plantations, could not be supported. In truth, the destruction of native woodland was caused by wheat production, not shipbuilding or iron smelting. The point is easily made for the counties with the smallest acreage of standing woodland, such as Norfolk, were dominated by arable farming.[9]

Commentators, from disparate backgrounds, such as Nelson, Snodgrass and the Third Duke of Portland, Prime Minister 1807–09, tried to impose fixed returns on a crop that required up to 150 years to mature.[10] Fortunately, the total failure of this system did not become apparent until naval timber had ceased to be an important issue. In the Forest of Dean succeeding waves of enclosure and plantation replaced the indigenous sessile oak with the penduculate variety which did not do so well. When, after 1842, the Navy resumed taking direct supplies from the Royal Forests, they discovered the drawbacks of the new forestry. A combination of plantation, the new variety and over zealous thinning produced a uniform crop of poor, low crowned and stunted trees. After 1898 parts of the Forest were returned to mixed woodland.[11] Other woodland areas proved even less receptive with the plantation trees soon dying out. Essentially, the plantation system did not work.

Naval supply remained secure throughout the period under review. By 1833 the cost of timber from the Royal Forests was one-quarter higher than that from commercial suppliers, which led to a 15-year hiatus in direct sales to the Navy.[12] Furthermore, it should be recalled that the Navy was often outbid for prime timber by local users, even in 1810.[13]

The timber supply in Britain was reduced because of the growth of agriculture, but this did not lead to the failure in the supply of British oak for warship building, despite the large-scale demands made on native resources up to 1815, and the vast growth in naval and particularly mercantile tonnage in the first half of the nineteenth century. Instead, the Navy Board made the timber supply a priority issue as part of Byam Martin's programme to create a strategic reserve for the next major war.

Oak

The favoured native timber tree for ship construction, the oak, has numerous qualities that make it well suited to ship building. The sap wood is not suitable for any use as it is prone to decay if exposed to damp, but the heart wood is tough and resilient when dry. Modern timber ratings place British oak as durable and suitable for use in contact with the ground for between 15 and 25 years; only teak and iroko are superior. Central European oaks are less durable though easier to work. The presence of tannic acid is largely responsible for the durability of the timber, although it reacts adversely with iron. It can also benefit from the application of preservatives. Oak can be bent using steam or hot sand, and keeps its shape when fully seasoned. Less satisfactory aspects are the length of time taken for the tree to reach commercial maturity, around 120 years, and the danger of decay setting in before the crop can be harvested. In the short term oak standards made no return, but these merely forced those involved to take a long-term view, something well within the compass of the aristocratic elements of British society, and the retention of several

The training ship Worcester *lying in the Thames off Grays, Essex, in August 1948 awaiting demolition. She was much altered from her original design as a 100-gun ship of the* Queen-*class and was launched as the 86-gun steam ship* Royal Frederick *in 1859 and renamed* Frederick William *on 28 January 1860, in honour of the Crown Prince of Prussia on the day he married the Princess Royal. The screw trunk can be seen ahead of the rudder.* (CMP)

important timber producing Royal Forests. More significantly, oak will only produce good quality timber on fine, well drained loams, soils equally suited to agriculture, which helps to explain the conflict between timber and wheat.[14]

Albion characterises the English predilection for oak as 'stupid', and contends that the main ship destroyer of the Napoleonic wars, dry rot, was never mastered.[15] Both statements are quite without foundation. A native supply was always preferable to dependence on foreign sources, as Albion makes clear in his section on the role of timber in Baltic diplomacy, and oak was the equal of any other timber available in Europe or North America. Teak, although superior, was uneconomic for use in England because of the cost of carriage. Byam Martin observed that carefully built and properly seasoned oak vessels were almost as durable as teak warships. Futher mixing of timber was a major cause of decay. As the supply of oak never failed, and alternatives offered no advantages in terms of durability it is difficult to understand how using any other timber would have improved matters. Battleships built from north German oak, along with the pine and fir frigates of the Napoleonic period, were an unmitigated disaster.[16]

The source of supply

In the period under review the supply of timber can be discussed under three heads: the Royal Forests, the private contractors, and foreign supplies, the latter also normally purchased through commercial houses.

Around 90 per cent of naval timber was purchased through commercial timber merchants, and merchant shipyards relied on this source for their entire stock. Only the Royal Forests were in any way amenable to government control but as they were outside the ambit of the Navy this was of little practical value. The Royal Forests never supplied timber at less than the market price.

The supply of naval timber had been a source of concern in 1771 when a Committee of the House of Commons investigated the issue. The evidence received suggested that in future there would be problems, but they did not, at that time, make any recommendations. In the 1780s Gabriel Snodgrass urged the systematic plantation of Royal and Crown lands, to provide a certain supply in 50 years but in the interval private supplies were to be exploited. He also noted that there was a large amount of prime timber within 40 or 50 miles of water carriage, and that government intervention would preclude any possibility of shortage in future. The main body of his evidence, however, concerned improved design and construction of the ships themselves.[17] The Parliamentary Commission on Land Revenue appointed in 1783, under Sir Charles Middleton Controller of the Navy, was to examine the condition of the woods and forests of the Crown. After a thorough investigation, including another interview with Snodgrass, the report of 1792 revealed serious concern. While oak was no longer commonly used in house building, it was in increasing demand for the barges, machinery and transport facilities of the industrial revolution. (In the eighteenth century this required more timber than iron.) They estimated the annual mercantile use at 158,679 loads and that of the Navy at 50,000 loads, concluding that the chance of oak in private hands being allowed to stand over and mature to the size required by the Navy was reduced by the growing demand for smaller timber; they thus recommended the improvement of the Royal Forests to a state where they could meet the average naval demand of 50,000 loads. This would require 70,000 acres under oak. Despite some improvements following this report the Navy still continued to depend on private contractors for 90 per cent of its timber supply. Improved management allowed the Royal Forests to supply an average of 4,000 loads from an annual total requirement of 53,000 loads after 1800. The cost of this supply was both financial, and bureaucratic. The Surveyor General's Office looked for a regular annual income, which was far from compatible with waiting for trees to reach their full size, and had different views on price and treatment.[18]

By 1810 Lord Melville observed that naval timber requirements had doubled, and with another 90,000 loads being needed for mercantile vessels the increased requirement over

The Worcester *sank while at her moorings on 30 August 1948, and was finally raised in May 1953. The boat under her stern serves to indicate the scale of the last sailing battleships. Her long sojourn on the ways was seen as an experiment in durability, and she was the first ship to be classed as an Advanced Ship without being launched.* (CMP)

the 1792 figure was 141,000 loads. Melville believed that nothing had been done to improve the supply and during his brief tenure at the Admiralty he directed the Board of Naval Revision to consider the subject again. Their 14th Report of 1808 was withheld from Parliament, as it appeared to reveal a serious shortage of timber. Observing that timber did not fall into the normal category of goods in which the supply could be expanded to meet increased demand, Melville urged the improvement of all suitable Royal Forests which would represent a permanent source unaffected by the vagaries of changing patterns in land use. He also returned to a favourite panacea: the extensive use of Indian construction facilities. The Prime Minister, Spencer Perceval, ensured that some response was made, and after 1810 most Royal Forests established oak nurseries. But the only effective wartime response was to accept the dangers of green timber, and to make as efficient use as possible of what was available.[19]

It has been customary to view Snodgrass's designs as an attempt to improve shipbuilding, but the incentive lay in timber supply. When the Government considered restricting the size of East India ships he argued to the contrary that large ships were more economic to run, and that it was demand for medium-sized timber that restricted the supply for the Navy. Snodgrass put forward his famous doubling and bracing plan as an alternative to giving ships a large repair while his design modifications were aimed at reducing the consumption of timber, and improving structural strength.[20]

The Melvilles, father and son, urged an alternative policy. They favoured building a new dockyard at Northfleet to repair the existing fleet. The need for a new east coast yard was obvious enough and both General Samuel Bentham, the Inspector of Works, and Sir John Rennie, the leading engineer, were in accord. The Commissioners of Naval Revision accepted Rennie's suggestion for a yard at Northfleet in 1807 and purchased the land but nothing further was done. The cost of basins to hold 300 ships, with the associated docks and slips, would have been astronomical and the project was shelved by 1810. The Second Lord Melville continued to urge the plan calculating that it would be more cost effective to repair the existing fleet in a new dockyard, intended to have the capacity to hold 300 ships, than to build a new fleet. The Navy Board, on the other hand, preferred using new steam dredgers to enlarge the existing yards and Melville was to change his views after the War.[21]

Concern for the state of naval timber did not lead to any radical programme, and this suggests as much as anything that the problem was not as serious as the pamphleteers claimed. Melville saw in the subject an opportunity to demonstrate the soundness of his own administration and recover some weight in British politics.

When it turned to foreign sources the Navy Board, being a large and bureaucratic business organisation, preferred to deal with commercial houses rather than individuals. This, allied to the reputation of the Baltic timber traders and their role in providing masts, made that region the natural choice for supplies of oak. However, the oak provided did not meet naval requirements, for reasons that will be examined elsewhere. The dangers of dependence on continental supply were obvious before 1809, and then received added emphasis. This encouraged the use of North American oak which proved to be no better once it reached the dockyards. Other sources of supply were not available in wartime, notably the central Italian forests, which supplied the bulk of timber for French warship construction in the eighteenth century.

Albion argues that the use of fir reflected the lack of oak, but in fact the Surveyors ordered the wood in an effort to bring down the price of oak by reducing demand. This enabled them to hold the price steady, which was a considerable achievement in wartime.[22]

In conclusion, the problem of timber supply was more closely related to price than availability. St Vincent's attempt to break the timber 'combination' merely alienated the domestic market. So long as the Navy Board would pay the going price timber could be found, but after 20 years of war it is not surprising that there was little time for seasoning, particularly in the merchant yards. Improving the Royal Forests was never going to solve the problem, for the reasons outlined above, and because Crown timber was an economic resource with its own dynamic. Foreign supplies were tainted by the failure of Baltic and Canadian oak, while the superior resources of Italy and India could not be tapped in the short term. Improved internal transport, better seasoning, better design and the availability of serious alternatives reduced the demand for oak after 1815, and much of this can be attributed to the work of Byam Martin and Seppings.

Timber as a strategic reserve

The lessons of the period 1805–15 demonstrated that the cause of premature decay was, as well informed shipbuilders knew before the War, the use of unseasoned timber. As a result Byam Martin and Seppings set a priority on securing adequate reserves of good quality timber for seasoning, building up the domestic stock of trees to meet the danger of another 20-year war, and making better use of the timber provided, both in design and construction. The object was to banish the spectre of dry rot from the Navy and make new ships last as long as those of earlier generations. This promised considerable long-term savings, but although the programme was a technical success it came too late in the history of the wooden warship, for design progress became sufficiently rapid to render a ship obsolete before she needed to be repaired.

As Controller Byam Martin occupied the central role in postwar timber policy for every contract or proposal had to pass through his office. He quickly built up a detailed overview of the major timber issues, including the size and output of the Royal Forests, the consumption of timber for individual ships and the effects of postwar recession on prices.

Materials in the fabric of a 74-gun ship of 1,745 tons

Oak:	timber	739 loads	
	thickstuff	160 loads	
	plank	192 loads at 55lbs per cubic ft	1,339 tons
Fir:	timber	74 loads	
	deals	76 loads at 35lbs per cubic ft	117 tons
Elm:	timber & plank	12 loads at 60lbs per cubic ft	16 tons
Copper			46 tons
Iron			90 tons
Lead			5 tons
Loads 1,253 nett contents			1,613 tons

The proportions were the same for all wooden warships of the period.[23]

The Royal Forests: 1815–30

Forest	*County*	*Acres*	*Dockyard using the timber*
New	Hampshire	92,365	Portsmouth
Dean	Gloucestershire	22,791	Plymouth & Pembroke
Salcey & Whittlewood	Northamptonshire	1,847	Deptford & Woolwich
Wychwood	Oxfordshire	3,742	Deptford & Woolwich
Bere	Hampshire	929	Portsmouth
Alice Holt	Hampshire	16,072	Portsmouth
Hainault	Essex	3,278	Deptford & Woolwich
Sherwood	Nottinghamshire	1,487	Deptford & Woolwich
Total		142,515	

Total quantity of oak timber, felled in the Royal Forests

Year	*Loads*
1812	3,611
1813	4,130
1814	4,188
1815	2,828
1816	3,788
1817	2,420
1818	2,827
1819	2,194
1820	1,398
1821	2,023
1822	1,528
1823	1,402
1824	1,519

While the 1792 Commission expected 70,000 acres to provide a naval requirement of 50,000 loads per annum the existing forests were only capable of around 5,000, and then only for short periods.[24]

By the end of the War the Navy Board were pressing the Office of Woods and Forests to modify their felling practice, in an attempt to improve the quality of timber received and in 1814 the timber was stripped of its bark while still standing, at an additional cost of 6s 6d per load for the extra labour required. The bark of the oak was a valuable commodity in its own right, used in the tanning industry and could be sold. Byam Martin preferred timber felled during the winter in the belief that the small amount of sap in the timber in winter would help to prevent decay. However, that same lack of sap made it difficult to remove the bark. With the benefit of hindsight it is clear that proper seasoning was the real answer, although the Sixth Rate *North Star*, the frigate *Clyde* and the 84-gun *Thunderer* were largely built of winter felled timber as an experiment, with somewhat ambiguous results. Furthermore, such ideas could only be applied to the Royal Forests, which supplied such a small proportion of the total.[25]

Peace provided an opportunity to improve the stock by thinning out defective, over-age and badly shaped trees. Large quantities supplied from Alice Holt and the New Forest were so 'overgrown and defective' that they had to be sold on. In the first six years of peace 1,000 such loads were received at Woolwich, chiefly from Alice Holt, and much of this had been specially barked and winter felled, at considerable extra cost.[26]

The cost of this timber did not fall as quickly as that available on the open market. The transport costs remained high, influencing the ultimate price.

Forest	*Transport cost*	*Destination*
Dean	£4.3.3	to Plymouth
New	£2.19.4	to Portsmouth
Alice Holt	£4.2.6	to Deptford
Waltham	£3.3.8	to Deptford, barge from Hertford
Salcey & Wychwood	£3.15.8	to Deptford, barge from Oxford[27]

The contract supply

Before Byam Martin joined the Navy Board contracts had been issued for a supply roughly equal to the wartime average. In this area, as with so many others, it is clear that Seppings had a profound influence on the Controller. The Surveyor was a man of great experience in the selection, handling and use of timber, and his opinions carried real weight. In December 1816 Martin submitted a paper on the timber supply to Melville.

> The procuring of timber for the naval service without trespassing upon what is now standing in Great Britain is a subject of the highest national importance, and cannot be considered with too much attention, for if, now in a moment of general peace, we are consuming our home resources it is impossible to calculate upon the expense, inconvenience and danger we may be exposed to in the event of a general war.

He favoured securing a supply from Austrian Dalmatia, as repayment for the loan made at the time of the Second Coalition. This would reduce the estimates, provide high quality timber and attack a 'sort of monopoly which has given to a few individuals in this country a power that leaves the public much at their mercy'. But the ultimate issue was the preservation of the domestic supply as a strategic reserve for a future war.

> That the timber of this country should have some respite from the hands of the contractor cannot be disputed and it is a melancholy reflection that those persons are now under engagement with the Navy Board to produce no less than 77,500 loads of British Oak before the termination of 1818 in completion of contracts to supply 140,000 loads.

Byam Martin continued to urge this policy on Melville, and was even prepared to pay the same price for Adriatic timber as the native product. In addition, he was prepared to take the stock of seasoned timber collected at Venice by the French, and dismantle the ships on the stocks.

With the Navy using some 54,000 loads per annum Byam Martin favoured an annual supply of 50,000 of these from Austria. He believed that the prices charged by Morrice, the leading contractor, were too high at £14.14s per load. In addition there were also outstanding contracts for timber to be shipped out of Fiume, which had been interrupted by the defeat of Austria in 1809. Martin sent Mr Smith, the Assistant Secretary to the Navy Board, to the city where he recovered a debt of £8,000 and contracted for 20,000 loads, saving £2 per load.[28] In the following year Martin, responding to the call for economy, pointed out the advantages of employing foreign timber. It could be bought up to £4 per load cheaper, to build up a three-year supply, which would help to break the power of the growers. As he noted: 'the actual quantity in the country is considerable', although he hoped this would not be cut at present. By 1831 the Navy was spending more money on African timber than English oak, and half as much on Italian as English.[29]

The Conway *(ex* Nile*), shortly after running aground in the Menai Straits on 14 April 1953.* (CMP)

Postwar construction and repair policy, itself a response to the dry rot problems of the war, was conditioned by the timber supply. A new fleet would use far more timber than one largely reconstructed from existing ships.[30] Alternative sources of supply were increased as part of the peace-time policy. For instance, the forests of the Cape were considered, although Barrow thought that they had few suitable trees and poor transport. Only the extremely heavy iroko of Sierra Leone, usually referred to as African teak, was considered suitable for naval use. The timber was ideal for beams, but could not be bent.[31] Further afield the resources of Australia and New Zealand were considered. The produce of Norfolk Island was already known to be unsuitable, but Martin requested Governor McQuarrie to reserve all timber lands to the Crown and find 10–12,000 loads of mahogany or cedar per annum, to be shipped home in convict ships. This trade was not without its dangers and in 1809 the crew of the *Boyd* had been eaten by cannibals as they loaded Kauri spars for Cape Town.[32] American live oak, so celebrated by *Albion*, was held in high regard by the Controller, but he found the contractors' terms unacceptable.[33] More satisfactory arrangements were made in 1831 for 12,000 loads from the Roman States, Parma and Modena.[34] Even the Duke of Wellington became involved in naval timber procurement, through unsuccessful negotiations by the nation to buy Lord River's Estate for him, and later when Stratfield Saye was purchased. In both cases the Navy were to have purchased all the suitable timber, through Morrice, as part of the purchase price for the Estate.[35]

The Duke of Atholl urged the use of larch grown on his estates. Though his snow *Larch*, was a sound ship the timber would cost as much to deliver to the dockyards as prime oak and was for that reason only employed for the experimental 28-gun frigate *Atholl*. Other experiments with timber included her sister *Niemen* which used Polish fir, while the *Andromeda* was built of African teak.[36] Larch was eventually purchased from Italy and Poland, and only a small quantity from the estates of Atholl and Portland in Scotland. Portland's timber was used to build the steamer *Tartarus* at Pembroke, but Symonds preferred best mountain-grown timber from Italy.

	£	s.	d
Italian larch plank cost	£ 8	7s.	6d
duty	2	15	0
total	11	2	6
English oak plank cost	13	4	6

At this rate, and because it is a lighter timber, Symonds preferred larch for steam vessels.[37]

The success of Byam Martin's programme became apparent in 1822 when he was able to limit the contract for native oak to 25,000 loads per annum, and significantly gave the monopoly of supply to Morrice.[38] When the existing contracts ended in 1827 Martin was able to pause for a few months before re-

A close up of the Conway, *showing her sheer broken after only one day aground. Internally, several beams had given way and she was declared a total loss. The training ship was being towed to Birkenhead for refit when she lost one of her tow ropes in the treacherous Straits and took the ground.* (CMP)

negotiating, and even when the new arrangements were made with Morrice and Lennox for one year's supply the contractors were requested to hold over deliveries, so they could appear in the 1828 estimates. Early in 1828 the Controller told Morrice, 'it is quite uncertain when we may make any new timber contracts'.[39]

Oak timber in store 31.12.1827

	Loads
Deptford	2,722
Woolwich	7,711
Chatham	22,176
Sheerness	1,448
Portsmouth	22,127
Plymouth	33,310
Pembroke	8,376
Total	97,870

[40]

The amount of timber in store reflected the nature of a yard's workload. The three large building yards had over 20,000 loads on hand, while Pembroke, which did only new building, had less than half that amount because of the greater pace of work.

By May it was obvious that a shortfall of 12,000 loads would force the Navy Board back into the market. Annual use of oak remained around 26,000 loads, and African timber at 10,000 loads. In a repetition of his response to St Vincent's programme Morrice refused to contract for the new oak supply, which Martin considered 'entirely unwarranted'. The Lord High Admiral reduced the requirement for timber held in store from three years consumption to two, but Martin was able to order yet more timber by attributing over one year's consumption as already converted for specific uses.[41] The Lord High Admiral's action, while in accord with the views of most shiprights who believed two years to be a perfectly adequate period for seasoning, was only the first round in a sustained assault on the cost and handling of timber. Economic pressures forced the Treasury, and at their behest the Admiralty, to question the amount of timber in store and the method of receiving fresh supplies. When the Chancellor of the Exchequer found it worthwhile to ask why timber was received squared rather than in the round, Byam Martin found it necessary to defend himself. He pointed out the greater ease with which defects could be spotted and the lack of waste as justification enough.[42] But he also realised that this sudden interest in timber could be made to work to his advantage and he persuaded Melville to keep on Surveyor Tucker specifically to deal with timber and revise down the task and job pay scale for shipwrights, the two areas that offered the largest potential savings.[43] The Navy Board was now prepared to substitute African timber for oak, and even suggest the use of larch and fir to construct small vessels. Yet by 1831 there was so much rough timber in store that Byam Martin had to stop all deliveries.[44]

During this period the price of oak did fall, although not as quickly as that of other agricultural products.

Average price of timber per load in pounds sterling

		1818	*1823*
British oak	rough	8.19.6	8.10.6
	sided	13. 8.0	12.14.7
African	sided		8.13.3

[45]

Two views of the Conway *on 6 August 1956. Having become a hazard to navigation the decision was finally taken to break her up* in situ. *Although badly damaged, the ship was still in one piece and her survival is a fitting tribute to the strength of Seppings's design and the durability of her timbers.* (CMP)

As with much of Byam Martin's policy success was only evident after the abolition of the Navy Board. Prices fell so far that the protected prices of the Royal Forests could no longer be justified, ending direct sales to the Navy for fifteen years. The Surveyor's Office retained a strong interest in the amounts felled, but the Navy could not control forestry policy however highly they valued a strategic reserve of mature timber. By 1840 the Duke of Bedford's estate manager discovered that the price of timber on the Thames had fallen so low that his trees would not bear the cost of transport and, without local demand, were quite unsaleable.[46]

Timber policy without the Navy Board

After the abolition of the Navy Board responsibility for the specification of timber passed to the new Surveyor who was both professionally incompetent in such matters and appointed, under the most haphazard supervision, persons equally incapable of reaching informed conclusions. Despite this, the problems of the next decade had far more to do with short-sighted economies than any failings on the part of the Surveyor's Office. Barrow advised Graham to improve the handling of timber in the yards, principally stacking and use of the rough timber by age.[47] However, the spectre of shortages was apparent within months of Symonds taking office and 60,000 loads of seasoned oak had to be sent round from Woolwich to Pembroke for the new ships building there. A new level of timber storage was established for the yards to meet this problem. Eight thousand loads of sided timber were to be stored at Portsmouth, Devonport and Chatham, the rest to be kept rough, as sided timber only lasted five years compared to eight for rough.

In November 1835 the following timber was in store.

	English Oak	*Foreign Oak*	*African Timber*
Rough	3,326		
Sided	6,493	20,765	13,936
Converted	4,901	1,944	4,662
Total			66,107 loads.[48]

In view of the increasing demand for new steam vessels it was fortunate that these were normally constructed from larch, which was light enough to increase the flotation of the ship.[49] Larch was also introduced into the upper works of larger ships in place of fir. The *Powerful* of 1826 was one of the first ships built with any larch which was later opened and inspected. In 1842 it was still in good condition, and was less affected than oak would have been by iron bolts. Portland advised using chestnut, particularly for frames where the danger of splintering would be reduced, but nothing came of his proposal, despite the support of Symonds. Official prejudice was, on such occasions, useful for chestnut had no merit at all as a naval timber.[50]

More significantly, the postwar fall in prices on the domestic market had reached the point where it had become uneconomic to pay £5 per load plus carriage to the Office of Woods and Forests, a government department controlled by the Treasury. In future timber was to be purchased direct from the contractors, although the Admiralty still wanted to treat the Royal Forests as a war reserve of standing timber. The Treasury was glad to reduce the timber purveyors in the forests and save a little money.[51] Within four years the entire object of the relationship, which was to secure timber felled at the time and in the manner required by the Navy, had been forgotten. Byam Martin was horrified to discover that Sir Charles Adam, the First Naval Lord, was not aware of the work already carried out on construction with winter felled timber, and had had to request information on this subject from the Surveyor.[52]

The English supply remained adequate, though it did show signs of failing in the specific area of curved frame timber. This increased interest in Italian timber which was largely mountain grown and which contained a far higher proportion of curves. The use of Italian timber was growing and led to the establishment of a second purveyor in Tuscany in 1833.[53] Although Tuscany was the favoured region, rising prices and competition with the French encouraged the Admiralty to look to Sardinia where the supply was large and of equal quality to that of Tuscany though difficult to exploit. Symonds favoured the Italian timber and argued for a greater use of that source. As a part of his sustained attack on dockyard individualism Symonds insisted on the timber specified being used, unless his authority were obtained for any deviation.[54]

The sudden interest in timber reflected the marked increase in construction during 1839–40, which revealed a shortage of 5,000 loads. Symonds, although not a professional shipbuilder, had firm opinions on this subject and refused to purchase anything but the finest timber. His strict standards of inspection caused the Board some problems. By 1841 he had developed his ideas to include the delivery of all timber sided, and the use of kilns to complete the seasoning process.[55]

In January 1840 Robert Dundas, the Storekeeper General, had submitted a memorandum on the level of timber to be kept in the yards. He referred back to an order of 1828, calling for two years in store, which had been estimated at the time as 63,000 loads of rough timber. He argued that the consumption of English timber was much higher than that of Italian, and advised purchasing more on the domestic market, while deferring any new Italian contracts until after 1842. Symonds did not agree and argued that the use of Italian timber should be increased, both for more efficient conversions and to reserve the English supply to cover a possible failure in the supply of African beams and the loss of foreign resources in wartime.

The storekeeper reviewed the case.

Timber in store and on order: 1840

	English	*Italian*	*African*
In store & due	27,743	26,498	12,103
Proposed supply to end of 1842	8,000	8,000	8,000
Estimated use to the end of 1842	16,569	5,517	7,481
Leaving in store	19,174	28,981	12,622

These figures led Dundas to propose purchasing the following timber in 1840.

English	22,000 loads
African	8,000
Italian	none
English thickstuff	5,750
English plank	3,200
Dantzic plank	1,000

Symonds responded vigorously:

> This is not a fair calculation as the frames, beams etc. of at least seven line of battleships will be required to be provided between 30th Sept 1839 and 31 March 1841, in addition to smaller ships & vessels both building & repairing with an increased establishment of 800 artificers.

The Admiralty responded by ordering the increased use of Italian timber on the same day.[56]

Symonds visited the Forest of Dean in September 1840, and discovered that the forest was producing good quality straight timber suitable for thickstuff and plank. This would complement the Italian supply, if Morrice could be persuaded to reduce his prices and include less rough timber. Minto tried to reopen the timber contract with the Office of Woods and Forests, both to cut out Morrice and to take advantage of the new source for curved timber. Much of the wartime shortage had been in curved and frame timbers, but these were now in less demand as a result of postwar developments in hull form and the trend away from the extreme tumble-home of the old French style.[57] Symonds advised taking a thorough survey of the Forest of Dean and preserving it for naval shipbuilding. The Board concurred but, following Minto's approach to the Woods and Forests, noted that they could not buy directly for two years, because the existing contracts could not be cancelled. However, by 1842 the Woods and Forests were happy to assist Symonds's inspection of their property with a view to husbanding the supply for wartime.[58]

The New Forest was the first to be inspected. Symonds advised the construction of a railway to facilitate the exploitation of the entire forest, along with the usual naval measures for preserving the trees until mature. Further reports were prepared on the resources in Italy, while the Royal Botanical Gardens at Kew offered to plant trees suitable for shipbuilding. The Board agreed with Symonds on the value of the domestic supply, noting the difficulty of obtaining a regular supply of English thickstuff and plank, and pointed out 'the impolicy of exhausting what is adapted for such purposes, of the growth of this country, when foreign supplies can be obtained'. These words could have been written by Byam Martin in 1816 and demonstrate well the continuity in timber policy throughout the period under review.[59]

In 1848 the Admiralty finally resumed relations with the Office of Woods and Forests and this was on the same basis as in 1815, £5 per load plus carriage with a naval purveyor to inspect before felling. The Office of Woods proved anxious to contract for timber and specified four forests: New, Dean, Wychwood and Whittlewood. After Walker took over at the Surveyor's Office this new supply led to another experiment with winter felled timber. On the starboard side of the 60-gun frigate *Emerald* the affected timber was marked W.F.[60] This experiment was never concluded for with the sudden demise of the wooden warship it became irrelevant.

At this point it would be well to consider the details of timber usage. In 1844 the Shipwright Officers at Portsmouth reported on the deck beams of the *Princess Royal* then under construction. These should have been of African timber but this was in short supply and it led them to use beams built up with the ends made from African timber and the central parts made of larch and several pieces of mahogany. While explaining this deviation from the detailed timber specification they set out their views on the use of various woods. They regarded African timber as preferable for this use 'from its regular growth'. On the more general use of woods they reported:

> From the contact of timber of different species, in dry situations, I have never known any injurious effect. African and English and Italian oaks are, in the present day, brought to a very great extent in contact with each other, without any other interposing substance than tar and paint inasmuch as the shelf pieces, waterways and most of the inside planking are of African and the frame timbers are of English and Italian oak.

Deck beams had been built with oak ends on fir, but the new African beams, even with larch centres, were far stronger and more durable, particularly at the ends where decay always occurred. The Master Shipwright even recommended reducing the scantling of the gun deck beams from 17in to 14in in view of the additional strength of the new beams.[61]

The steady increase in the prices began to affect timber selection and the use of standard 4in Dantzic oak to plank the bottom of the hull had been discontinued. Four-inch oak plank was now required on all gun decks, leaving none for the hull which now had to be planked with pitch pine.[62]

As Auckland overhauled the administration of the civil departments of the Navy he was initially uncertain about the level of timber which needed to be held in store but, as with so much else at the end of the decade, Walker was quick to provide a detailed answer. The new Surveyor calculated on the basis of his three-year construction programme which would consume:

> 30,000 loads per annum.
> 19,000 loads of oak
> 2,590 loads of fir and elm
> 3,500 loads of oak thickstuff
> 2,600 loads oak plank
> 860 loads Dantzic oak plank
> 1,450 loads deck deals [63]

The Committee of Revision on Dockyards found the arrangements for handling timber 'generally of the most unsatisfactory character'. They made a series of recommendations to improve the inspection, storage and movement of timber. These included the use of tramways, which were to be installed at Chatham, Portsmouth and Woolwich under the 1849–50 estimates. In addition, the Master Shipwright and Timber Master at each yard were to produce a general plan.[64] These measures came into effect in time to assist the rapid increase in construction occasioned by the steam battlefleet, the Russian War and the Anglo-French naval race of 1857–60.

Between 1815 and 1850 the selection, purchase, storage and seasoning of naval timber was gradually improved to a point where dry rot came to be considered as an historical subject of limited interest. At the same time the sources of supply were expanded, with Italian and African timber being used as a substitute for the local product. Consequently, had the nation faced another 20 years of war the domestic timber supply would have performed far better than it had between 1793 and 1814. Timber was the greatest single item on the naval construction budget, and as such was treated with considerable caution. There were no major mistakes, just different approaches to the same basic issue. When the large scale use of timber for warship construction ended, the native supply was equal to far greater demands than ever before.

4 Timber Decay and Naval Policy

In the period 1802–15 dry rot, with other forms of premature timber decay, had a profound effect on naval policy. Once the existing supply of seasoned timber had been used, an inevitable result of increased construction in wartime, unseasoned timber combined with an imperfect understanding of the impact of heat, light and rain water on timber structures, caused a huge increase in decay. This forced the Navy to run harder in the construction race with France simply to maintain roughly one hundred ships of the line in service, and there was serious additional pressure on timber supply. In consequence, dry rot had become a major concern for naval policy makers by 1815, and the prevention of decay remained a priority for the remaining years of the wooden warship.

Dry rot (*merulius lacrymans*) is a fungal growth that feeds on organic matter in damp timber, both living and dead. It reproduces from microscopic spores and spreads through timber by extremely fine fungal threads (*hyphae*). From its filamentous nature dry rot can spread across non-organic materials, including brick, stone and metals. The results of infestation are catastrophic for any wooden structure. As the timber is broken down by the cellulose it becomes discoloured, loses strength and toughness; it loses up to 80 per cent of its weight; takes on a different smell; absorbs more water and loses calorific value.

Dry rot can only occur in certain conditions. It requires oxygen and moisture, but timber with less than 20 per cent moisture, or totally water-logged (hence the wet storage of timber) is not susceptible. Contact between timber and iron is often at the heart of an infection. For use in ships timber needs to be seasoned until it possesses only 15 per cent moisture, but in Britain air drying cannot reduce the moisture content to below 17 per cent. Kiln-drying the timber to 15 per cent or less involves much higher costs and so there developed a number of preventative solutions which could be applied, pumped or injected into the timber.[1]

The prime conditions for dry rot occurred in the lower reaches of a large wooden warship. Damp, warm and badly ventilated spaces, particularly where fresh water had penetrated, or leaked from the tanks or decks, could be guaranteed to produce the spores of infection. The example of the *Queen Charlotte*, which was rotten before being launched, provided a clear demonstration of how not to build a wooden warship. Laid down at Deptford in 1805, she was constructed over five years from an unholy alliance of unseasoned British and foreign timber. Her lower strakes were bolted on prematurely, allowing rainwater to collect and once afloat the spread of infection was rapid, aided by closing in the ship and installing stoves. To save the ship she was docked, her planking stripped off to reveal her frame timbers and then the whole frame was washed with chemical preparations at a total cost in excess of her original construction. However, it should be recalled that, once repaired, she was the flagship at Algiers and survived as the *Excellent* until 1892. Dry rot was a serious problem, but it could be dealt with. The experience of the *Queen Charlotte* was a constant reminder to the Navy Board and it was one that they took to heart. The unusual aspect of this case was that the ship had been built slowly in a Royal Yard, while the majority of the infamous rotten ships were the products of merchant shipyards.[2]

The almost continuous nature of the wartime construction programmes from 1793 to 1812 used up timber faster than it could be seasoned, which restricted the supply of seasoned timber to the merchant yards. War also prevented the normal handling of timber through the construction of most major ships in the Royal Yards, which had always followed a simple seasoning system. The situation was entirely outside previous experience, and could not have been anticipated. Therefore, a secure supply of *seasoned* timber formed the basis for postwar work, and was part of Byam Martin's preparations for another 20 years of conflict.

When the Admiralty made a tour of the dockyards in the autumn of 1813 several postwar policy-makers were present, notably Melville and Barrow. They were encouraged to consider the problem of dry rot simply by the virtue of the numerous examples set before them. At Portsmouth the Board observed that it was bad practice to have ordered the *Princess Charlotte* when there was no timber to build her, and to have left the *Victory* to lie in Ordinary in need of repair. At Woolwich they found the workmanship aboard the *Nelson* to be of a very high standard, although she was built from a mixture of timbers. Seppings conducted the Board around Chatham, pointing out that the *Howe*, with her hatchways on and some side planking left off, had no rot. The 74s *Eagle* and *Poictiers* were both seriously infested because the timber had not been properly seasoned though these merchant-built ships had ample evidence of good workmanship. The builders had not had the time to let the timber season. The infection was particularly bad where two pieces were scarphed together. At Plymouth thirty-six contract-built 74s were inspected and all were affected by dry rot as a result of lack of seasoning. Aboard *Mulgrave* the waterways were one continuous sheet of fungus after only two years in service. In conclusion, the Board noted that the problem was caused by rapid building, and deprecated artificial attempts at seasoning as expensive and of doubtful utility. The shortage of timber was restricted to the special large frame sections. Seppings had already responded with his plan for a 74 to be framed with frigate timbers at Woolwich (the *Talavera*, ex-*Thunderer*), and he was to meet the prevalence of decay in the chocks with a similarly imaginative measure.[3]

The issue had already been drawn to the attention of the Navy Board, in January 1812 to be precise, but their reply only arrived in June 1815. Their conclusions were unremarkable. They blamed the decay on the lack of seasoned oak and too rapid completion of construction and repairs which had happened because of the shortage of slips and docks. They suggested that an improved circulation of air would help.[4]

Postwar policy

As with so much else, matters improved rapidly when Byam Martin took office. In his first full statement of Navy Board policy Byam Martin argued for keeping up the largest number of shipwrights, as a war reserve, and using them to build and repair a sound fleet.

> I consider it the best possible policy to give every ship in the progress of building or repairing a sufficient seasoning; and not to do so is to build up a rotten Navy, which will lead to endless repairs and a ruinous expense; and there never

The Implacable, *being stripped out at Portsmouth in preparation for scuttling on 27 October 1949. The decision to scuttle the ship was brought about by the serious state of timber decay. A French group from Rochefort, where the ship was launched in 1789, wished to save her for the town as a museum, but the Admiralty argued that it would cost too much to put her into a safe condition for the journey. The figurehead and other details were removed and presented to the National Maritime Museum.* (CMP)

> was a period better calculated than the present, to bring forward a durable fleet such as may do credit to the nation, and produce the much required curtailment of expense.
>
> Whenever a sufficient number of ships have been built and repaired, the period of seasoning should be lengthened, and great care taken that all parts of a ship be formed as much as possible of timber of equal durability; and that which is known to be of a sound and lasting quality, should not be interspersed with that which experience has shewn to be of quick decay; it is this which has produced a rotten Navy, and occasioned an enormous expense.[5]

To allow time for the new ships to be built defective ships were to be fitted for temporary service. The fir frigates *Hebrus* and *Graunicus*, in action at Algiers, were so rotten that when they arrived home they had to be sold. The point is worth developing. Dry rot did not destroy ships for long before the ravages of fungal decay had eaten away the timber the structure of the vessel was so compromised that it could no longer hold together. Dry rot weakened the timber, reducing the grip of the wooden and metal fastenings in the pieces they were attempting to hold together and it had a particular predilection for joint surfaces. As the structure of the ship broke down it allowed more opportunity for decay to attack newly exposed timbers. Once this process had gone far enough vital structural elements would fail. The classic sign of a ship beyond repair was a broken back, but long before that the vessel would be a danger to her crew, particularly on the type of arduous service which British battleships carried out. It should be emphasised that this stage of decay was almost unheard of in an active British ship, although other Navies, especially the Russian, were less particular. The legend that the bottom fell out of the *Royal George* in 1782, repeated by *Albion*, is entirely without foundation. The ship was lost by incompetent deck officers.[6]

In 1815 ships in various stages of construction in the Royal Yards were allowed to stand for a degree of seasoning. Seppings conducted practical work to improve seasoning methods. He suggested sinking the ship/sloop *Eden* in the Hamoaze to determine the effect of salt water of a ship already badly affected by dry rot. With Byam Martin's support this measure was adopted and the vessel sent to the bottom for four months. The *Mersey* served as a test piece for comparison. The experiment was deemed a great success, the ship coming up free from rot, tighter and stronger. As a result the Navy Board, reflecting on the lack of suitable slips, recommended that all timber should be converted and then seasoned in salt water for a few months. Thereafter, it could be dried off in covered sheds. The new practice included the riverine yards, Deptford and Woolwich, which were supplied with salt water from Sheerness by tank vessels. The salt water tank at Deptford cost £600. All such timber was then marked S and represented part of the continuing empirical search for the perfect solution to dry rot.[7]

There were many more suggestions for seasoning timber. The most impressive came from Marc Brunel, who also advised immersion, but his relations with Seppings following the collapse of a chimney at Chatham, were poor, and the Navy Board were content to rely on their own experiments.[8] Any proposal deemed worthy of note was subjected to the acid test of being buried in a wet pit.[9]

By 1819 a variety of prophylactics were in use. Timber was payed with fish or train oil, and all points of contact between timbers painted with white lead. Chocks were no longer used. Byam Martin was confident:

> We have obtained very satisfactory proof that coal tar is the best preventative of Dry Rot, and every ship is now completely saturated with it by means of a forcing pump. The frigate lately launched at Woolwich had 1900 gallons injected, and I shall be much disappointed if she is not a sound ship thirty years hence. The coal tar is about 4d a gallon.[10]

By 1822 the system had been refined.

> In the wake of the breadroom, and for some distance forward, mineral tar has been discontinued and linseed oil & whiting substituted, and from thence forward the mineral tar is applied with slaked lime in the proportion of 2/3 of the latter and 1/3 of the former, which fixes the substance, and reduces the *smell.*[11]

By 1824 at least thirteen battleships had been injected with mineral, vegetable, linseed or train oil and whiting.[12] The space between timbers, filled up with short ends in Seppings's new system, was sealed up with cement in an effort to keep the ship dry.

In 1824 Byam Martin believed enough time had elapsed to make a provisional judgement on the success of the system. He called on the Master Shipwright to report if dry rot had appeared on any timber treated with coal tar, and if they believed the present methods would tend to produce a more durable fleet.[13] This was a timely request, as the Navy Board was under attack from a variety of sources. The Benjamin Tucker enquiry had demonstrated the soundness of the fleet, but John Burridge petitioned the House of Lords with an account of the defective state of several ships, one of which, the *Rodney*, was in an advanced state of decay. He wanted to impeach Melville, Byam Martin and Seppings, claiming they were ruining the fleet by stripping the timber standing in order to sell the bark.[14] Such nonsense did not long detain the Government. However, the new men from the School of Naval Architecture were also making suggestions contrary to the practises of the Navy Board. This was altogether more important at a time when the Admiralty were attacking the subordinate Board.[15]

The period of seasoning on the stocks was lengthened during the 1820s; and even the crisis of 1826 did not result in

Implacable *begins her final journey on 1 December 1949, passing the sponsons of the light fleet carrier* Vengeance. *Amidships it is clear that the ship is in a very poor state, although the sheer seems to be unbroken.* (CMP)

The scuttling charges explode aboard the Implacable *off Selsey Bill, 2 December 1949.* (CMP)

improper haste. The idea of seasoning the structure, as well as the timber, reflected the central theme of Seppings's work: that the ship was one solid mass of timber. Ships undergoing a large repair were also allowed to stand over for six months to a year. Among those so treated was the *Queen Charlotte*, having her second large repair in ten years. This time the work proved entirely successful.[16]

In 1829 Byam Martin pronounced an obituary for the dry rot problem. He had read yet another book on the subject with interest:

> but being satisfied that the measures now adopted in seasoning our ships are so successful as to make any more intricate mode less an object of interest I saw no reason to recommend your proposal.[17]

This might smack of complacency, a degree of which had crept into the Controller's conduct, but it was very close to the truth.

Improving seasoning was only part of the answer. It was equally important to exclude any rainwater from ships building or in Ordinary. In consequence, the slipways were given roofs, while ships in Ordinary were housed over. The expense of roofing was considerable: the large roof over No 3 slip at Plymouth costing £9,511.[18] The *Scarborough* was the first ship to be fully housed over, but after a decade it became obvious that the process of closing in the ships had been carried too far for some were beginning to deteriorate from lack of ventilation, among them the *Scarborough* herself.[19]

Under the guidance of Byam Martin and Seppings a new policy of thorough repair was adopted after 1815 to prepare the war-built fleet for lengthy service. This would save the larger part of the timber already used, and keep up a larger number of shipwrights than an all new fleet. Many of the ships were badly strained by long service at sea and contained inferior materials. The response developed by Seppings, with little help from his fellow surveyors, was to strip out each suitable ship, remove all defective timber, add a diagonal frame to improve structural strength, fit a round bow and stern and replank. Ships treated in this way were almost as durable as new constructions. Examples such as the *St Vincent, Achille, Canopus* and the razee 50-gun ships indicate the success of the programme.

Seppings's plan for ridding the fleet of dry rot involved docking the worst affected ships before those in good order, unless an infestation could be stopped without a thorough repair. When repaired ships in good order tended to be opened far further than was really required. It was better to limit work on them so that they could remain ready for war service. However, he was alarmed at the widespread wartime use of North American oak and fir: 'that experience has proved to be particularly friendly to the growth of that destructive vegetation fungus'.[20] Seppings and Byam Martin developed a less costly approach to overhauling the fleet, avoiding the need for a large repair when a ship was stripped out but it proved difficult to operate from London.[21] The Master Shipwrights preferred the most thorough investigation, and their deep-rooted aversion to anything cheap and simple took many years to overcome. When the *Nelson* was taken into dock, in the mid 1820s, the main object was to remove all 'foreign' timber. She, like others of her generation, was to remain afloat until the end of the century, while the new *Nile* was destroyed by fire after being wrecked in the Menai Straits as late as 1954.

Following Seppings's experiments with the *Eden* and other empirical research, new ships were dominated by the need for thorough seasoning and slow construction. This allowed the Navy Board and later Symonds, to regulate the period of construction. There were to be specified intervals between the various identifiable stages of the building process to allow for seasoning. Initially, these ideas were essentially pragmatic, Byam Martin extending the time allowed for completion as international tension decreased. With the shrinking fleet the process became increasing regulated under Symonds and later Walker. The new methods were largely successful, although nothing could prevent a certain degree of decay in any large wooden structure, no matter how much care was taken.

The end, under the flags of the two nations that she served. (CMP)

Instructions to Dock-Yard Officers for Building Ships of the Line, &c.

Stages of Providing.	Stages of Building.	Directions for each Stage.	General Remarks.
1st STAGE. Providing Frame.		On the receipt of drawings, specifications, &c. Frame, fillings for the openings, and particularly Dantzic deck planks, and deals are to be provided.	These materials are to be selected from the store that has been the longest in the yard.
	2d STAGE. Completing the ship in frame, $\frac{2}{8}$ths built.	When the frame is converted and such parts as may be necessary are provided sufficient to employ a proportion of Shipwrights, the frame is to be raised and taken to its scantlings, and when complete the ship is to stand to season.	It is to be understood that before this or any subsequent stage of building is commenced the ship is to be proposed in the scheme of works, and their Lordships' directions obtained to proceed with her.
3d STAGE. Providing the general large conversions.		Whilst the ship is standing to season the principal conversions are to be provided, and placed under cover near the ship; the iron knees, hooks, riders, &c. are also to be prepared, and the fractional parts which may be provided are to be reported in the Monthly Progress.	If it is not intended that the ship should be launched for service as soon as she can be completed, she is to stand in this state for two years.
	4th STAGE. Completing to $\frac{4}{8}$ths.	When the time necessary for seasoning has expired, and sufficient materials for planking are provided, the wales are to be worked, and the planking proceeded with, within and without board, which is to be screwed up with Blake's screws, with the exception of the planks that come in the wake of shelf-bolts, which alone, are to be fastened.	In order to provide for shrinkage and refaying of such planks as are screwed up, every fourth strake of outside planking is to be provided but not worked until the general fastenings require it. The screws are to be used in the line of the general fastenings, so that the holes may be filled by a bolt or treenail.
		The shelf-pieces, gun, and orlop-deck beams, and *knees* are to be proceeded with; and the deck flat is to be edged and laid upon the half beams (on battens) but hutch-hooked only. Diagonal iron riders, hooks, bands at the heads and heels of the frame timbers down to about the floor, or first heads, are to be worked.	During this 4th. stage of the work, no part of the fillings in of the openings below the floor heads, or the working of the elm planking, keel, &c, is to be performed: the materials however are to be provided in readiness for use.
5th STAGE. Providing iron work, bulkheads, &c.		Iron knees for the upper, quarter-decks, and forecastle, riders, hooks, and other iron work, and materials generally required for the ship are to be provided, as well as the bulk-heads and other conversions requisite.	If not required for service, the ship is to stand in this state for two years.
	6th STAGE. Completing to $\frac{6}{8}$ths.	On the expiration of this further period for seasoning, the planking from the wales to the top sides is to be proceeded with, the bulkheads in the hold fitted, beams secured, and the general framing of the decks laid.	Whilst in this stage the keel is not to be secured, the openings below the floor heads of the frame are not to be filled in, nor the elm garboard strakes worked or fixed.
		The ship is to be prepared for caulking with the exception of the flat of the decks, which is not to be reconciled. When this is done she is again to stand to season.	Shifts of planking are to be left open in the bottom, topsides, and decks for the purpose of ventilation
7th STAGE. Providing materials for completion of building.		Petty conversions, and any materials that may be required for the completion of the ship, are to be provided.	As before, if the ship is not wanted, she is to stand in this state for two years.
	8th STAGE. Completing to $\frac{7}{8}$ths.	The keel and kelson are to be bolted, and the filling in of the openings completed, as well as the planking, decks, channels, head, stern, quarters, cabins, bulkheads, ladders, gratings, and all the Shipwrights' and Joiners' work that may be necessary.	In this stage of progress the ring and eye Bolts to the ports, port hooks, chain bolts, and channel fastenings are not to be driven. The Ship's sides, bottom, and decks are not to be caulked or painted beyond what may be requisite to prevent injury.
9th STAGE. Providing iron work, &c, for completion for Ordinary.		The iron work that may be required for the final completion of the ship for ordinary is to be provided, as well as bulkheads and any Joiner's work necessary.	In such ships of the line, and large frigates as are intended to be kept on the stocks, no part of the caulking of the sides or decks is to be performed. The ship is to stand in this state till final orders for completing her are given; and care is to be taken to keep her well ventilated.

After the abolition of the Navy Board the Admiralty took a greater interest in timber decay. Graham favoured keeping more ships on the stocks, and duplicate frames ready for rapid construction.[22] In addition, Symonds had his own ideas on timber seasoning, and in concert with the Master Shipwrights he soon revoked many of Seppings's major measures. Tar injections were stopped and the system of filling in the frame was restricted to the area below the floor heads. Salt water seasoning was cancelled as it tended to split the timber, damage the fastenings and cause shakes in the timber. The new measures included placing felt between the timbers at all joint faces, air seasoning under cover and replacing the iron fastenings used from 2ft above the load water line with mixed metal bolts.[23] Inspecting the fleet in Ordinary resulted in further measures. Advanced Ships were found to be decaying nearly as fast as those in full commission for being too closely confined their tanks rusted and fungus soon appeared. The doubling fixed on several of the older 120-gun ships was removed, having already caused the first signs of decay.[24]

When John Kyan tried to interest the Admiralty in his prophylactic, corrosive sublimate (chloride of mercury), he found Barrow and Symonds united in opposing such measures. The process required the timber to be immersed for seven to fourteen days in a mixture of one pound of sublimate to 8 gallons of water. In view of the substance this could not be carried out in iron or copper tanks. Although Captain Hayes and four civilians were appointed to report on the substance it was evident that nothing could be expected in the short term. Experimental use in 'the most exposed parts of HM ships' would take several years to provide results. The merchant-built revenue cruiser *Linnet* was selected for the trial. Kyan complained to Peel of blind Whig prejudice at the Admiralty which demonstrated the political support required for any innovation in the period after the first Reform Act.[25] Symonds was not impressed by the process, or by Kyan. He noted the failure of the sublimate to penetrate into the timber, the length of time required for results and the condition of the Navy.

> I am not aware of the existence of any dry rot in the Navy at present, and considering the many salutary measures that have been taken to avoid it in future, I apprehend that if there is a careful attention to the use of nothing but well seasoned timber and a just selection of that which is not infected with decay for the purposes of repairs, as well as for building new ships, the Navy will be preserved far more effectively than by the use of a solution which would entail a great additional expense upon the public of time, labour and material.

He argued that oak could last for 60 years, and that in time of peace the best measure was to allow the domestic reserves to build up by relying on foreign supplies.[26] Despite this opinion the Board ordered a trial at five dockyards.[27] Two years later Kyan renewed his approach, using the whaler *Samuel Enderby*, just returned after two years at sea. This was no more successful.[28]

In 1837 decay appeared in Symonds's 'rot free' Navy. His first large ship, the *Vernon*, was seriously infested with fungus at the futtock heads. This reflected her hasty completion, and despite the initial success of fish oil injections, broke out again in the 1840s. Other vessels with signs of trouble included the 84-gun *Thunderer*, where the cement filling caused serious problems.[29] Symonds and Edye reflected on this news and then argued in favour of an increase in new construction, characterising large repairs as 'false economy'. This was a part of Symonds's attempt to overhaul policy.[30] Ultimately, he succeeded in increasing the amount of new work.

The Vernon *serving as part of the torpedo school in Portsmouth Harbour. Her survival in this role was a tribute to the ability of the Royal dockyards to eradicate even the most serious outbreaks of dry rot.* (NMM)

Although it should have been clear to all concerned that the careful methods of the Seppings era had solved the real problem nevertheless the search for a preventive went on. By 1841 Symonds was convinced that the Kyan process had failed, although it was not officially discontinued until 1847. In 1845 Sir William Burnett, Inspector General of the Medical Department of the Navy, offered an alternative process. This was a solution of chloride of zinc, forced into the timber at 150 pounds per square inch. This, it was argued, formed a compound with the vegetable juices in the timber. The owners of his process charged twelve shillings a load, which encouraged the Admiralty to buy their own apparatus. Even Portland was involved in testing the new system. Lord Auckland elected to try the process at three yards, Chatham, Portsmouth and Woolwich, until there were concrete results. Portland found Burnettised timber was less successful than that treated with Kyan's solution, and the final opinion of Walker was that it had some benefits in soft woods, but was of no use in hard wood.[31]

Despite the inconsistent approach of Seppings and later Symonds to the basic issues, the problem of timber decay had been resolved by 1830. The pre-1815 ships had been repaired, while those built subsequently were constructed with more attention to the seasoning requirements of oak, or the use of teak which required far less delicate handling. The use of foreign timbers helped to banish the spectre of dry rot, but careful seasoning and slow construction was the only effective preventive measure, anything else was only an attempt to stop an infestation already firmly established, and as such unlikely to succeed. Modern chemicals kill dry rot and others forms of decay, but the technology of the period could not make such claims. The battlefleet of 1850 was far superior to that of 1815 in durability, as the later careers of so many large units was to demonstrate.

Part five

THE SHIPS

1 The Three-Decker 1815–60: Battlefleet Strategy and Warship Design

British strategy, from the Commonwealth period, was based on command of the sea secured by the ability to defeat any rival in combat. Consequently, British designers and seamen were in the vanguard of the technical and tactical developments which increased the battle power of warships, and of fleets. The introduction of the line of battle as the standard formation is normally dated to the First Dutch War, 1652–54. This tactical system was a recognition of the central role of the heavy gun in sailing ship combat and remained unchallenged until artillery was no longer the supreme arbiter of war at sea. The line of battle and the pressure on British commanders for decisive action reinforced the tendency to build heavily-armed ships. The ultimate expression of this was the three-decked ship which offered the heaviest broadside, the strongest hull, and the best return in action for the cost of the men and guns carried. Between 1650 and 1850 Britain invested a greater percentage of her naval resources in three-decked ships than any of her rivals, and was alone in her unwavering support for battle as the decisive point of any maritime campaign.

In the seventeenth century the three-decked ship, often as a flagship, was at the centre of the battle, but limited seakeeping made it a liability in winter and few were deployed in peace time. The loss of Admiral Balchen's *Victory* off Alderney in 1744 provided a shocking warning to over-bold Admiralty Boards. Yet by the mid-eighteenth century Hawke took *Royal George* into Quiberon Bay confident that she would survive in the most difficult coastal waters. This example, followed by many, but not all, squadron and divisional commanders, gave the British fleets an important advantage in close action. The Bourbon Navies had different strategic requirements for their battlefleets and repeatedly found themselves outgunned by the British. The Spanish built a fleet of large, lightly-armed ships for oceanic escort duty. After the disaster at Cape Passaro in 1718 a number of more powerful ships were built, but before 1763 only one was a three-decker. The experience of 1761–63 encouraged the Spaniards to build another three-decker, but it required the alarming events of 1778–82 to convince them that their fleet must be configured for battle if it was to achieve decisive results. Between 1779 and 1794 Spain built ten very large three-deckers and added extra decks to a two-decker and even to a three-decker of the 1760s, the famous *Santissima Trinidad.* While they maintained a large oceanic escort force the Spanish elected to increase their battle line power, in belated recognition that that was the only way in which their strategic ambitions could be secured, in the face of British opposition.[1]

In the same period the French had built three-decked ships but never to the same extent as the British, partly from reluctance to crowd guns into ships intended for a more flexible role. After the Seven Year's War France had only two three-deckers, but the Battle of Ushant in July 1778, for all its tarnished image among British historians, produced the most profound impact upon the French. The French line had been badly mauled by the more numerous British three-deckers and this discouraged Admiral d'Orvilliers from any further close action during the Channel campaigns. In addition, three new three-deckers were ordered before the year was out. These new vessels were all launched in 1780, further evidence of the perceived need. While three-deckers gave the British a major advantage, their poor sailing qualities hampered tactical deployment, which in part helps to explain the unsatisfactory results of the campaigns that followed Ushant. When concerting efforts for the combined fleet of 1779 the French requested their allies to send as many of their 80-gun ships as possible, to increase the firepower of a line with only two very heavy ships. By 1787 the French fleet included five 110-gun ships, with two much larger 118-gun vessels, the largest in the world, the *Commerce de Marseilles* and *Etats de Bourgogne* (later *Ocean*), under construction.[2]

The Wars of 1793–1814 provided further evidence, if any were needed, of the value of three-decked ships. At the Glorious First of June 1794, and on 23 June 1795, the British flagship, *Queen Charlotte*, passed through the French line, fighting both batteries. On both occasions this had a decisive impact on the course of the battle. At the second engagement the three ships taken had all been disabled by her concentrated fire.[3]

After Trafalgar the French, who had no three-deckers in that battle, moved toward a British style battlefleet, ordering fifteen three-deckers in six years. Furthermore, these were large ships, and overgunned at that. For the first time in a century the French were creating a battlefleet to contest the command of

The Britannia, *120 guns, entering Portsmouth Harbour in the 1820s. Along with her sisters of the* Caledonia*-class, this ship represented the very essence of British strategy and naval policy in the first 15 years of peace. The firepower of the large First Rate made it the supreme arbiter of combat at sea, and the executive symbol of Britannia's supremacy.* (NMM)

the sea, rather than attempting a strategic programme to avoid decisive maritime conflict. It should be emphasised that it was the move to a true battlefleet, rather than the sheer number of new ships built after Trafalgar, that gave particular emphasis to the French challenge. At the end of the Napoleonic Empire three-deckers constituted one third of the ships building, and one sixth of the force afloat. This was a considerable shift in the balance of the French fleet, one that later French policy makers would acknowledge had only been possible because of the vast resources commanded by the Imperial sway.[4]

When the other side had neither built for, nor desired, close combat the poor sailing of the bulk of British three-deckers created tactical problems that limited success when the strategy called for battle. The majority, the Second Rate 90- and 98-gun ships, were small, over-armed and designed with little throught for speed. The fact that this type was not copied by the Bourbon fleets played no small part in the Channel campaign of 1778–82. After the battle of Ushant the French and Spanish had no desire to close with the out-numbered, sluggish British fleet; and the British, conscious of their critical position as the last line of defence against invasion, would take no risks. That the succession of senior admirals tended to caution was not the problem, for they did not have the equipment to force battle on the enemy. Indeed, there are very few examples in the eighteenth century of British fleets, with their ponderous three-deckers, forcing an unwilling enemy, encountered at sea, to fight. Even at Cape St Vincent the Spanish would have escaped with a fusillade were it not for the high morale and initiative of Nelson and other captains in the two-decked ships. Squadrons without the heavy ships were more successful in bringing the enemy to battle.

With rare exceptions the sailing of British three-deckers had not improved before the Wars of the French Revolution. Those that did sail were in demand as flagships, notably *Victory* and *Boyne*, although some preferred large two-deckers; Admiral Keith shifted into the *Foudroyant* after the destruction of *Queen Charlotte*. Later, *Caledonia* demonstrated that the ultimate in gunpower could be combined with fine sailing, and here was a ship that would stand the winter weather. After the war her class was to multiply, which solved the age-old British problem of making superior battle power tell in action. The role of battle in British strategy, and the deterrent value of the fleet, were given greater emphasis by these ships and their mobilisation was a clear signal to the French, or Russians, that Britain was not only prepared to fight, but was also preparing the materials with which to fight. If any other power wanted to challenge British naval mastery they would have to defeat the battlefleet, and combat the terrible close-range power of the three-deckers.

Byam Martin shared the high opinion of the three-decker for he valued close-range gun power and the height of the upper deck battery from the water.[5]

Furthermore, by 1823 the cost per ton of the 120-gun ship was only slightly higher than that of the 74.

Cost of warships in 1823

Guns	*Tons*	*Materials*	*Labour*	*Total*	*Cost per ton*
120	2,616	£75,200	£16,600	£91,800	£35.2
84	2,257	£55,600	£11,400	£67,000	£29.14
74	1,747	£50,500	£10,000	£60,500	£34.13
60	1,458	£31,800	£6,600	£38,400	£26.7
50	1,277	£26,000	£4,500	£30,700	£24
46	1,077	£21,000	£3,700	£24,700	£22.19 [6]

The stern galleries of the Britannia *while serving as the cadet training ship in Portsmouth Harbour in the late 1850s.* (Tenby)

These figures indicate why, for most nations, the construction of three-deckers required a positive decision. They were particularly expensive and made such great demands on infrastructure as to be incompatible with any rational naval programme other than one aimed at sea control through battle. For Britain the question did not arise for her security and empire made sea control the only suitable strategy.

As rival navies became more powerful Britain was forced to make far greater use of her strength. This was particularly noticeable after 1830 when all serious crises brought the 120- and 84-gun ships into the fleet: in 1833, 1840 and most particularly after 1846. Then the Russell Administration responded to the troubled Anglo-French relationship for economic and diplomatic reasons, by sending into the Channel the most powerful squadron ever manned in peace time, under their most dynamic admiral, a man widely regarded as too unreliable for peace-time service. Rear Admiral Sir Charles Napier's Western Squadron of 1847–49 was, as formed, the outstanding demonstration that the three-decked ship had at last come into its inheritance. His six battleships included only one two-decker, and crossed the Bay of Biscay in the teeth of a gale. The Mediterranean Fleet also contained an unusually high proportion of three-deckers, and continued to do so right up to the outbreak of the Russian War in 1854. In terms of diplomatic signalling this was very significant. After 1830 the challenge from Russia and France increased, forcing Britain to deploy an ever greater level of battle power to emphasise her position. In 1833 razee 50s were considered adequate. In 1840 the advanced First and Second Rates had been brought forward, and the guardships commissioned to reinforce a Mediterranean Squadron. The ability to mobilise so many powerful ships in late 1840, when the Atlantic timber trade was closing down for the winter, raised the stakes beyond those which the French King was prepared to entertain.

No other fleet contained such a high proportion of three-deckers. The French had five afloat, and of these only one was a postwar ship, while the Russians had three and four in their two fleets, although it is unlikely that they were all seaworthy at one time. Turkey and Egypt both built three-deckers but they were never armed on British lines, while the American *Pennsylvania* was a unique overgunned blockade breaker, rather than a fleet unit.

These costly ships, demanding the largest and costliest timber, were only useful in battle. They were, however, poor cruising ships, overcrowded and lacking in stowage, and they made huge demands on seamanship and manpower. By 1845 Napier was complaining that to build any larger would result in the rigging passing the limits of manual handling.

Policy

During the Napoleonic conflict the role of the three-decker was sustained by the challenge of France, so that by 1814 they were as important to the overall balance of the fleet as they had ever been. However, foreign construction and wartime experience did encourage a move toward larger ships. The *Caledonia* ordered in 1797 was the first full 120-gun ship, while the three *Nelson*-class ships followed in 1806. The Second Rate three-decker lost its significance as the 80-gun two-decker became more common, largely through French prizes. The last such ship, the *Trafalgar* of 1806, later *Camperdown*, was larger than the *Victory* and other 100-gun First Rates. However, a certain amount of confusion remained, and the small First Rates *Princess Charlotte* and *London*, later *Royal Adelaide*, were ordered as late as 1813. Peace allowed policy makers the time to consider the issues and advance more logical solutions. When the Admiralty ordered the *Prince Regent* in 1814 they specified a ship of the *Queen Charlotte*-class, but Seppings, at that stage the one progressive member of the Navy Board, considered this absurd. Pointing to the greater size of the *Trafalgar/Camperdown*, he called for the new ship to be reordered to the *Nelson* draught. The Admiralty accepted his logic, but preferred the highly-praised *Caledonia* which they selected to replace the *Nelson* as the established design for 120-gun ships. That they had already ordered the *Britannia* to the *Caledonia*'s draught in 1812 merely emphasises the confusion at the senior Board.[7]

The arrival of Byam Martin as Controller reinforced the influence of the Navy Board, and in particular of Seppings. Before taking his post Byam Martin had suggested that all new three-deckers should be 120-gun ships, once in office he accepted the *Caledonia* as the model for a new establishment, with 84-gun two-decked ships as the next class.[8] Byam Martin gave the postwar fleet an unparalleled degree of uniformity, although this only came at the end of his regime. On entering office he was faced by a bloated list of ships, few of which had the necessary qualities and durability. By 1817 the useful three-deckers numbered twenty-four and all were classed as First Rates and armed with at least 102 guns.

Three-decked ships in 1817

120-gun: *Howe, Nelson, St Vincent, Caledonia.*

110-gun: *Hibernia, Ville de Paris, San Josef.*

102–6-gun: *Boyne, Dreadnought, Impregnable, Ocean, Prince of Wales, Queen Charlotte, Royal George, Royal Sovereign, Union, Victory.*

IN NEED OF REPAIR

102-gun: *Neptune, Temeraire.*

BUILDING

120-gun: *Prince Regent, Britannia* (frames being raised to be left to stand over for seasoning.)

106-gun: *Trafalgar* (frame complete, standing over.)

ORDERED

106-gun *London, Princess Charlotte* (most materials for frame assembled.)[9]

There were several more ships available, but none were worth considering because of age and inferior design and so they were left for harbour service and quarantine duty. As the most recent of them, the *Prince*, was all but 30 years afloat this decision was not particularly difficult. To maintain the fleet new ships were required because many of those on the list would not last long, and over the next 15 years the older ships were broken up: *Neptune* in 1818, *Prince of Wales* and *Royal George* in 1822, the two latter after being considered for razeeing into 74s. *Ocean* was razeed in 1819; *Boyne* and *Union* were to have followed after 1827, but were never completed. *Temeraire* had been on harbour service since 1813 and others followed; *Ville de Paris* in 1824, *Royal Sovereign* in 1826,*Dreadnought* in 1827 and *San Josef* and *Victory* soon after. These ten ships were replaced by six new ones, and an order for a seventh, which was never completed in the period.

1819: *Royal George, St. George*
1822: *Neptune*
1823: *Royal William, Waterloo*
1825: *Trafalgar*
1827: *Royal Frederick*

In addition, all those ships considered adequate for postwar duty were given a thorough repair, initially to cover the ravages of extensive wartime service, and of hurried building with mixed and semi-seasoned timber. Later the opportunity was taken to increase the armament of large and small three-deckers, both old and new.[10]

In 1826 there were, counting those building, still twenty-four three-deckers on the serviceable list, and with new orders this figure reached twenty-seven in 1827. By 1829 Byam Martin was taking a more determined attitude to his force, permitting only nineteen to feature and this list was more representative of the fleet he required. All were fit for another two decades of service.

120-gun: three *Nelson*-class, ten *Caledonia*-class
110-gun: *Hibernia*
104-gun: *Prince Charlotte, Royal Adelaide, Camperdown, Queen Charlotte, Impregnable.*

Byam Martin had been at pains to emphasise the role of the three-decker, and when the new Government came into office renewed his pressure for an additional five ships which would make a force of twenty-four, of which eighteen would be of the largest class. The Whig Administration cancelled work on any new First Rates and effectively suspended the *Royal Frederick*. Byam Martin attempted to combat the Whig perception that the First Rate had been rendered obsolete by steamships by observing the number which were building in France and rumoured to have been ordered in the United States. He tried to resume work on the *Royal Frederick* and called for an establishment of twenty-four first class ships. Given his relationship with Graham, and the low regard both Grey and Graham had for Seppings, it is hardly surprising that Byam Martin was unsuccessful. This should not be seen as the Whigs moving away from the battlefleet strategy, merely a political manoeuvre in the campaign against Byam Martin.[11]

After their initial reluctance, the Graham Board, under the influence of Hardy, came over to the classic British view of three-decked ships, ordering the *Royal Sovereign* in 1833 as a duplicate frame for the modified *Royal Frederick*. The new ship took the name *Royal Frederick* when the original was renamed. Another pair of 110-gun ships were ordered, at Pembroke, as the *Victoria* and *Algiers*. At the same time the *Frederick* was given priority over all other work at Portsmouth. The ship was launched and renamed in 1839.[12] The reordering of *Algiers* as a smaller 90-gun ship in 1840 reflected the sudden accession of strength in the First Rate division afloat, which had come about as a result of the launching of the *Queen* in 1839 and the last *Caledonia*-class ships, *St George* and *Trafalgar* in 1840 and 1841. In addition it was now clear that the French were building only one new three-decker, the *Valmy*.

	Britain	*France*
Large three-decked ships	13	8
Small three-decked ships	6	0
Total	19	8 [13]

There were now three *Nelson*-class ships, nine *Caledonias*, one *Queen* and four smaller ships afloat, and two building. The Tory Board, reflecting a closer affinity with Byam Martin's plans and an awareness of the limited value of small three-deckers in the aftermath of the Syrian campaign, ordered two new ships in 1842, the *Prince of Wales* after the *Queen* at Portsmouth and the 120-gun *Royal Albert* designed by their favourite Master Shipwright, Oliver Lang at Woolwich.[14] The following year three more of the *Queen*-class were ordered, another *Royal Sovereign* and *Marlborough* at Portsmouth, and

The Camperdown *of 1820, ordered as the* Trafalgar *but renamed in 1818. The last three-decked ship ordered as a Second Rate, in 1807. Too small for front line service in the postwar fleet the* Camperdown *spent most of her life in harbour and was never modified, although she was ordered to be razeed in the 1840s, and the draught bears the evidence that she was considered for conversion into a steamship. From the design of the screw this would appear to have been quite early in the steam period, possibly in 1848.* (NMM)

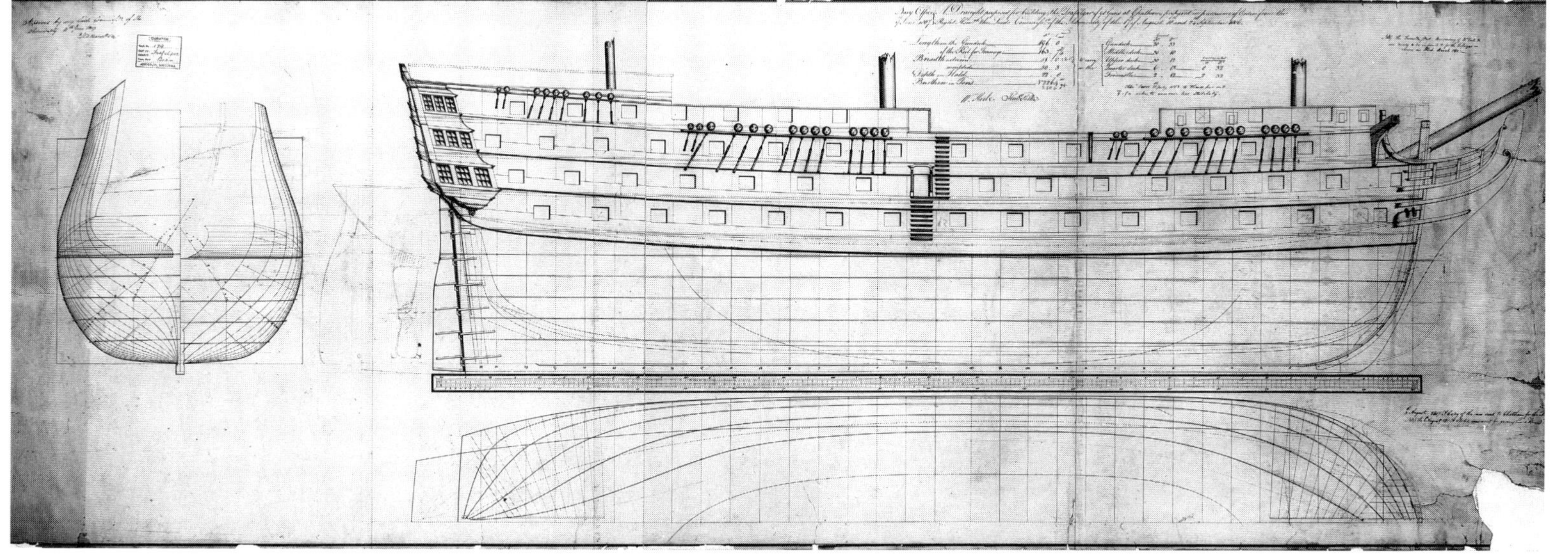

Nelson as a hulk in Australia. (Author)

Windsor Castle at Pembroke.[15] Little work was carried out on these three ships before the end of the decade. With the *Prince of Wales* they were ultimately to be modified first into a new 120-gun class, with a less radical hull form, and then into lengthened steam ships of 131 guns, with the *Windsor Castle* renamed *Duke of Wellington*. As such they, with the *Royal Albert*, which was also completed as a steamship, demonstrate the continuing dominance of the three-decked ship in British tactical thought and strategic policy even after the end of the sailing Navy.[16] All the large ships survived to the end of the sailing Navy. The first to be broken up was the *Howe*, in 1854, with *Hibernia* and *Caledonia* being reduced to harbour service in the following year. All other 120-gun ships, save the *St Vincent*, were fitted with steam between 1852 and 1860.

Improving the small three-deckers

One major problem for the Navy Board was how to make the best use of those ships built as Second Rates or as small First Rates. The 104-gun *Princess Charlotte, Royal Adelaide, Camperdown, Queen Charlotte* and *Impregnable* were an integral part of the postwar fleet, at least until 1840, and as such they had to be kept up to date. They were given Congreve 24-pounders on the middle deck in 1817 as part of the postwar rearmament. Given their limited battle strength it is hardly surprising that they were among the last battlefleet units to be so treated, but that the Royal Navy retained such obsolescent ships is, in itself, fitting testimony to the role of the three-decker in national strategy.[17] While it would have been wise to standardise as early as possible on 120- and 84-gun ships, the amount of material already assembled for the *Princess Charlotte* and *London* made it all but impossible to abandon them. In 1816–17 no-one at either board considered the hard choice of completing them as 84-gun ships, into which they could have quite easily been converted from their size, scantling and gunport spacing. The superior value of the three-decked ships made such a step unthinkable. Only later would the smaller *Ocean* be razeed. In 1818 Seppings suggested that they should be broadened to carry a heavier armament and when ultimately completed the ships were 11ft 7in longer and 1ft 5in broader than the original design.[18] The additional breadth involved a complex process of doubling: in 1849 the *Royal Adelaide* had to have the rotten fir plank stripped off, after some 22 years of harbour service.[19]

The postwar armament of the small three-deckers was standardised at 104 guns.

Gun deck	30	32pdr	56cwt
Middle deck	32	24pdr	49cwt
Main deck	32	24pdr	Congreve
Quarter deck	4	12pdr	guns
	10	32pdr	17cwt
Forecastle	2	12pdr	guns
	2	32pdr	17cwt
	104		

The smaller ships – *Victory, Boyne, Impregnable, Dreadnought* and *Union* – could only mount Congreve 24-pounders on the middle deck.[20] While under repair Seppings produced a plan to increase the breadth of the *Impregnable* by 22in 'by bringing chocks on the timbers and placing regular thickstuff and plank over them, instead of the usual method [of doubling]'. In this form she could mount the same battery as the *Princess Charlotte*. In addition, she would be 6in wider than the *Queen Charlotte* and 138 tons larger. This method could not be employed with the other small three-deckers, which were shorter and less heavily framed.[21]

After the shift to a single calibre battery in 1826 the small three-deckers were once again given a more powerful warrant.

Gun deck	26	32pdr	56cwt	2	68pdr	65cwt
Middle deck	28	32pdr	48cwt	2	68pdr	50cwt
Main deck	30	32pdr	32cwt			
Quarter deck	12	32pdr	17cwt	2	12pdr	guns
Forecastle	2	68pdr	carronades			
	104					

The 12-pounders were to be replaced by 25cwt gunnades when these became available. When *Princess Charlotte* was commissioned as Mediterranean flagship in 1837 she carried two more 68-pounders on the gun deck, 32-pounder carronades in place of the 68-pounders on the forecastle, 39cwt 32-pounders in place of the 12 pounders on the quarter deck and landed the 50cwt shell guns. She was the last of the old Second Rate three-deckers to be commissioned for active service.[22] After the *Princess Charlotte*'s service in the Syrian campaign it became clear that small three-deckers were of no use in the modern fleet. She was still armed for close-range fire; was no more powerful than a large two-decker; was a poor performer under canvas; and she inflated the apparent strength of the British fleet. She never served at sea again, while the *Adelaide* and the *Camperdown* (ex-*Trafalgar*) had never even been commissioned.

In 1844 the Board proposed razeeing the *Camperdown*. Symonds opposed the idea and secured a letter from his patron, Portland, calling for the ship to be tried with her poop removed and the upper deck reduced to carronades and no guns mounted on the quarter deck and forecastle.[23] Nothing came of the proposal for the *Prince Regent*, a *Caledonia*-class ship had been razeed in 1845–47 and had proved far too expensive to be repeated. Napier suggested that rather than razee the small three-deckers they should have their lower deck disarmed to accommodate the crew, be armed with long 32-pounders at the remaining ports, ballasted accordingly and have the poop removed. In this form they could serve as powerful 80-gun ships.[24]

In 1845 the *Hibernia* was fitted out to carry the flag of Sir William Parker in the Mediterranean. The Board had originally intended him to have the *Rodney* but Parker expressed a strong preference for a three-decker, even one armed and manned as a two-decker. In the event his ship was fully fitted.

Gun deck	24	32pdr	56cwt	4	68pdr	65cwt
Middle deck	28	32pdr	48cwt	2	68pdr	65cwt
Main deck	30	32pdr	33cwt			
Quarter deck	10	32pdr	17cwt			
Forecastle	6	32pdr	45cwt			
	104					[25]

After three years in the old ship Parker admitted that, 'though strong and fit for any service – [*Hibernia*] is slow in sailing, and inferior to the majority of three deckers'. Parker had been less than happy to find her the aftermost ship in the squadron on every trial, despite having the best crew. In addition, her armament was inferior to that of all other British three-decked ships. Faced with the prospect of another three years on station he requested the *Queen* for his new flagship.[26]

Design

The design history of the period 1815–31 is essentially about the *Caledonia*-class. One of the more significant contemporary reports on the *Caledonia* came from Admiral Lord Exmouth in 1814. He had the highest regard for his flagship:

> I have never during my service seen a ship that was so easy in all weather, sailed better, or was so governable by her helm. At this moment when six years coppered, she is scarcely equalled by any ship in the Fleet; and as far as my judgement or experience may be valued, the *Caledonia* is in my opinion, the finest ship of war in the British Navy and does infinite honour to the man who constructed her.

She was carrying 400 tons of ballast, with her midship gunport almost 5ft out of the water.[27] After the Admiralty decision of September 1814 this was the only class ordered. However, it had to reflect the considerable changes in armament that were a feature of the period. *Caledonia* had been designed for the classic battery of single-calibre decks.

Gun deck	32	32pdr	56cwt
Middle deck	34	24pdr	49cwt
Main deck	34	18pdr	guns
Quarter deck	6	12pdr	guns
	10	32pdr	17cwt
Forecastle	2	12pdr	guns
	2	32pdr	17cwt
	120		
Complement	837	men	[28]

This did not long survive the war, however. The upper deck was fitted with Congreve 24 pounders in April 1815 and those ships ordered before 1826 were to carry the armament of the early postwar period.

Gun deck	32	32pdr	56cwt
Middle deck	34	24pdr	49cwt
Main deck	34	24pdr	Congreve
Quarter deck	6	12pdr	guns
	10	32pdr	17cwt
Forecastle	2	12pdr	guns
	2	32pdr	17cwt
	120		
Complement	900	men	[29]

In late 1825 Byam Martin advised putting the new light 32-pounders on the middle deck, if they were safe for sustained fire and double shot.[30] To carry this increased arming Byam Martin and Seppings advised adding 6in to 9in to the beam of the ships still building. This was increased to 1ft, and carried into effect without any public orders. The object was for an 'increased weight of arming'.

> To increase the breadth from four feet below the seat of the water & thence upwards, one foot; to be accomplished in putting together the timbers of the frame; the curves of the frame from four feet below the seat of the water downwards, to break in gradually with the form of the ship as laid off.
>
> The gun deck is to be placed as directed in the draught, but the Orlop is to be dropped so that the height from the upper side of the beam to the gundeck plank at the middle of the beam may be 8 feet.
>
> Such part of the plank of the middle deck as is usually of Fir is to be of good Dantzic or Riga Fir, 4 inches thick.[31]

Royal George had to be doubled with fir, because the order

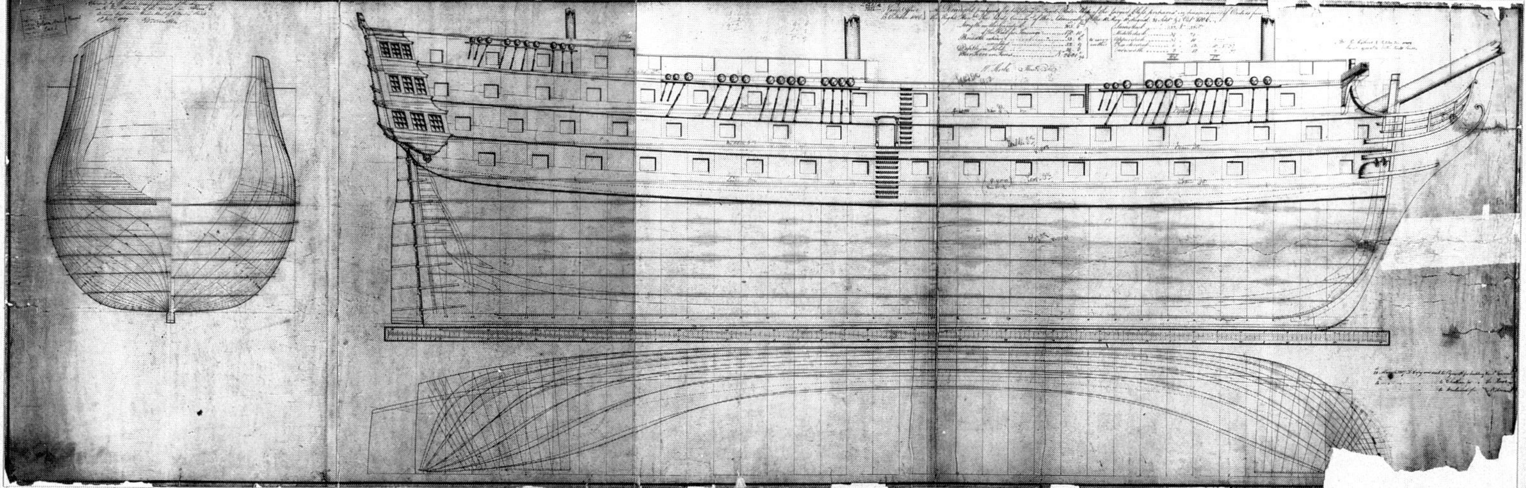

The draught of the Nelson-*class, dated 13 October 1806.*

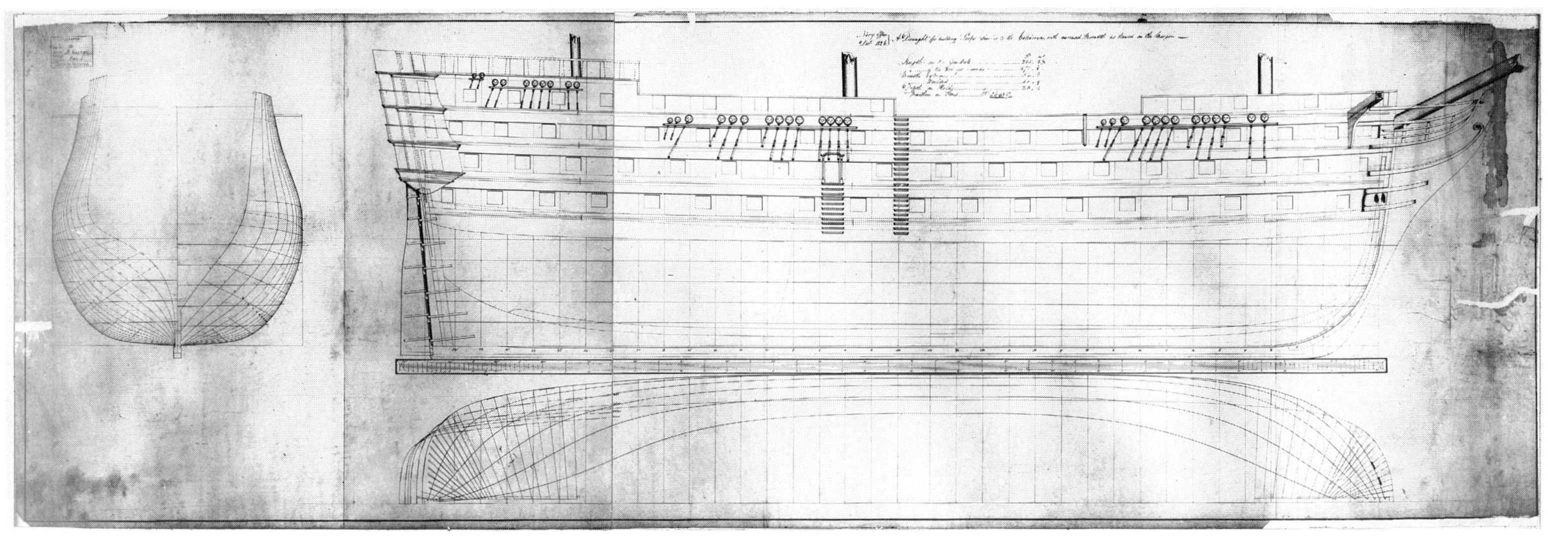

The modified Caledonia-*class draught used for the* Royal George *December 1826. The enclosed bow and round stern give this ship an altogether more modern appearance than the* Nelson. (NMM)

Inboard profile of the Neptune. *The diagonal frame and strengthened bow and stern were a vital part of the success of this class, which was rearmed with heavier guns from 1826.* (NMM)

to cease work arrived too late to allow her frame to be stretched.[32] At the same time, the ships under repair, *Caledonia, Nelson, Howe* and *Queen Charlotte,* were broadened and given the new 1826 armament of 32-pounders throughout, when suitable guns could be found. Byam Martin preferred 42-pounders, but the service was unwilling to return to the heavier guns, and the ships lacked the capacity for such a weight of armament.[33] The Lord High Admiral, an advocate of increasing the armament of all ships, ordered the *Britannia* to carry the new 32-pounder warrant, only to be informed by Byam Martin that she was incapable of bearing such a load because she had not been broadened and had only 3in plank on her middle deck when 4in plank was required for 32-pounders. This in turn provoked Seppings to suggest that in future new 120s should be built on the draught of *Nelson,* which had considerably greater capacity at the line of flotation. The Lord High Admiral did not incline to this proposal. In 1830 Byam Martin supported Seppings's call for the new ships to have an extra 5ft on the keel to improve the spacing of the guns, but nothing came of this either.[34]

After her rebuild, which provoked a good deal of controversy, *Caledonia* emerged with a lower deck battery of 63cwt 32-pounders. As such she was 16 tons overweight and her gun deck ports were far too close to the water. The additional breadth could not cope with 16 tons, as much of the increased capacity was taken up with solid timber. Byam Martin begged Cockburn to remove the guns, which had been set aside for the *Nile*-class, to no avail. Finally, Codrington had them taken out during the cruise of the 1831 Evolutionary Squadron. Her sailing improved as the weights were decreased and having changed the guns Codrington observed her to be 'the finest ship of war ever sent to sea'.[35] In the Mediterranean Admiral Hotham found the *St Vincent* answered well with the additional ballast, equalling the *Ganges,* then the fastest ship on the station, on most points of sailing.[36] In trials throughout the 1830s *Caledonia* in particular, although all the rebuilt 120-gun ships were similar, demonstrated a reluctance to carry to full weight of the new single calibre battery and the necessary ballast. She sailed much better with 300 tons less water.[37] With the old sailing ships sailing well the three-decker could become a part of the peace-time cruising Navy. This had never been the case hitherto for these ships, being a war service type, that spent most of their lives in reserve.

In 1843 the Tory Board ordered the *Prince Regent* to be razeed into a 90-gun ship, and although the Surveyor admitted that she was crank he still opposed this as a matter of policy. Symonds observed that all the old 120-gun ships were similar and that if the whole class were cut down it would entail the sacrifice of 240 guns and the powerful effect of a three-decked ship's concentration of fire. In addition, the defects of the ship, and of most others, were to be found in the bottom. However, Master Shipwright Blake from Fortsmouth had submitted plans for the *Prince Regent* and *Queen Charlotte* to be cut down, with very low estimates of the cost, and the strong endorsement of

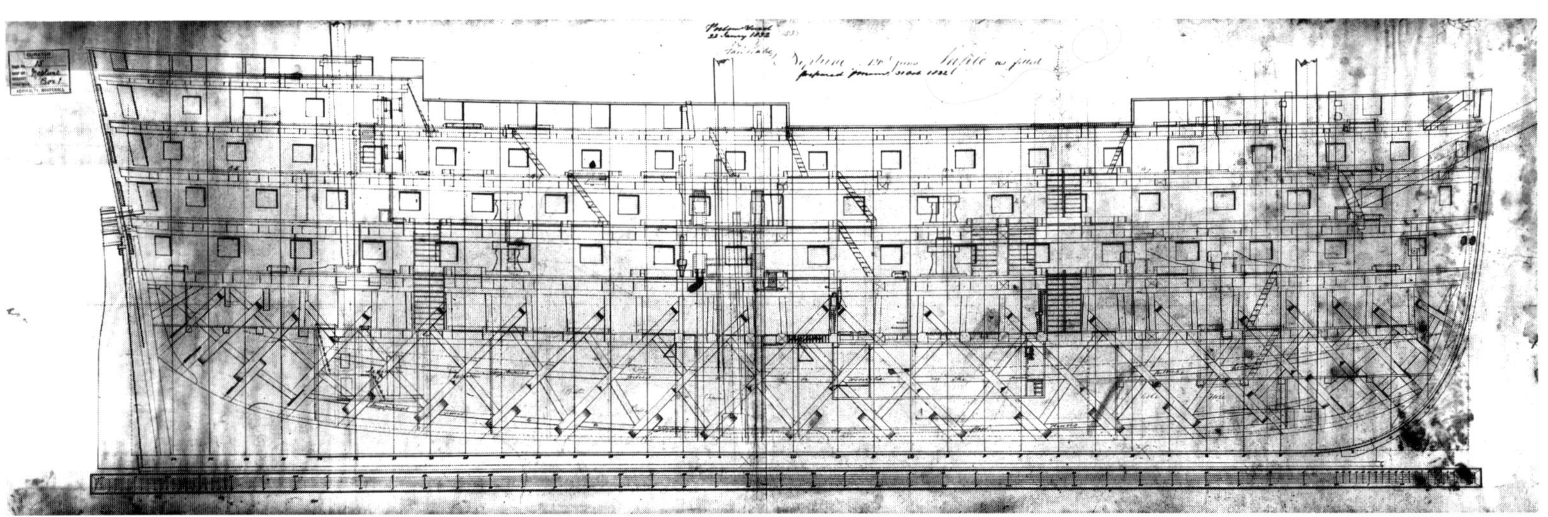

the Admiral Superintendent, Hyde Parker. The ship was initially removed from the dock while the project was considered, but the momentum for change had built up and she was finally ordered to be cut down in early 1844. As Symonds had anticipated, the process proved very costly, a total of £53,815 being expended.[38] Once completed the *Prince Regent* became, effectively, a unit of the *Nile*-class, sharing the heavy arming and smaller complement of the 90-gun ship. Remaining in active service until 1855, she was paid off to keep the *Neptune* and *St George* in commission. In time of war there was no substitute for gun power, and although the sailing ship was of limited value, the Admiralty still preferred the 120-gun ship to the 90. Improved sailing qualities were only of interest if they did not impinge upon the prime function of a battleship which was to develop the greatest concentration of firepower.

In 1850 the *St Vincent* was given a less costly, £17,528 repair that involved taking off her poop and disarming the upper works, leaving only a pair of 68-pounder 95cwt guns and this was a more effective method of modernising old ships.[39]

The *Queen*-class

The last three-decked ship to complete for the Royal Navy began her life as one of the *Caledonia*-class. In 1831 the frames of the *Royal Frederick*, of which one-seventh had been converted, were suspended in favour of work on Fourth Rate ships. After the abolition of the Navy Board they were modified and reordered as a new 110-gun ship of Symonds's form. This was a particularly complex task which had to be placed under the supervision of the Assistant Master Shipwright. From 1833 the ship had preference in the mould loft, which was pressed to prepare the frames for seasoning by April 1834. This allowed for rapid completion. When launched the ship was renamed *Queen*, being the first three-decker completed since the accession of the young sovereign.[40]

Orders for Queen-*class ships*

1832 *Queen* ex *Royal Frederick*

1833 *Royal Frederick* ex *Royal Sovereign*
Victoria (ultimately completed as the *Windsor Castle*, renamed 6.1.1855.)
Algiers (any materials ever collected for this ship became part of the *Duke of Wellington*, ex *Windsor Castle*.) In 1840 the *Algiers* was reordered as a 90-gun ship.

1842 *Prince of Wales*

1843 *Royal Sovereign*
Marlborough
Windsor Castle renamed the *Duke of Wellington* in 1852.

The last four became a separate class and the complexity of ships and names requires some attention.[41] The provisional armament of the new ship reflected her size

Gun deck	28 32pdr 55cwt	2 68pdr 60cwt
Middle deck	28 32pdr 55cwt	2 68pdr 60cwt
Upper deck	32 32pdr 49cwt	
Quarter deck	10 32pdr 40cwt	
Forecastle	2 32pdr 40cwt	2 68pdr 36cwt carronades
Roundhouse	4 18pdr 10cwt carronades	
	110	[42]

The Worcester, *ex* Frederick William, *ex* Royal Frederick, *ex* Royal Sovereign, *at anchor on the Thames sometime after World War 1. The four-masted barque* Magdalene Vinnen *lies in the background.* (CMP)

Byam Martin was not alone in criticising this warrant as too light, though not in the individual weapons but in the number of pieces. He was alarmed by reports of the *Pennsylvania*'s 140 guns, and feared that France and Russia might follow this pattern.[43] If British battleships were out-gunned by their adversaries the very heart of national strategy could be threatened.

Brought forward during the Syrian crisis, and finally commissioned for the flag of Sir Edward Owen in the Mediterranean in 1841, the *Queen* spent the remainder of the decade as one of the two centre pieces of the Symonds's debate.[44] Despite that it should be emphasised that her performance did not affect the decision to order a new 120-gun ship from Oliver Lang and it is unlikely that any real impression of her qualities had been received by the Board by March 1842.[45] During her time in the Mediterranean *Queen* earned a high reputation for her performance under canvas. In the 1844 Squadron of Evolution she was captained by William Fanshawe Martin, son of the old Controller and a committed opponent of the Symonds system. Despite the advice of his father to do justice to the ship he wasted no opportunity to criticise and make difficulties. Fellow Tories from Hyde Parker to the Earl of Hardwicke gloated at the 'failure' of the *Queen* and *Albion*. Symonds was concerned and requested permission to dock the *Queen* and make small modifications. He also moved William Martin and his crew into the *Trafalgar* so that they could experience a truly bad sailing ship.[46] This was exactly what Cockburn required: evidence of uncertainty from the Surveyor's own pen. Two days later he suspended work on all Symonds's 110- and 90-gun ships, save the *Royal Frederick*.[47] Further evidence to support this policy came from Captain Maunsell, lately returned from the Mediterranean. He claimed that *Queen*'s early reputation had been built on trials in smooth water, and in the absence of his own ship, the *Rodney*. This 'astonished' Cockburn, Gage, and Captains Dundas and Hamilton.[48] Suffice it to say Maunsell was a committed Tory, in need of employment.

In 1844 Admiral Bowles, one of Symonds's few Tory supporters came down from the Board to take command. He

A model of the 116-gun Queen, *Symonds's masterpiece and without question the ultimate sailing three-decked warship.* (ScM)

tried to give *Queen* and *Albion* a fair trial, but his actions merely clouded the issue. Similarly Symonds began to make use of 'leaks' to the Whig paper the *Morning Post*. In 1845 the ships would speak for themselves.[49]

As *Queen* fitted out for service questions were asked in the House concerning the cost of the alterations. Work on her magazine, false keel, gripes, rudder post and fore- and mainmasts came to a total of £4,330.[50] The brief cruise under Sir Samuel Pym served to demonstrate that 1844 had been an aberration. Her new Captain, Baldwin Walker, reported her to be 'the finest ship in the world', while even Cockburn had to admit that she had given a very severe lesson to her rivals. Henry Byam Martin, viewing from aboard another ship, reported that the ship 'runs away from all of us'. Lord Haddington sent the news to Parker who rejoiced that Symonds had vindicated himself in such style.[51]

Midship section of the Queen. *The gunnade carriages, designed by Hardy, on the upper deck are of particular interest.* (NMM)

Work on the *Queen*-class resumed in late 1845, with a reduced rake of the sternpost being one of the few signs of any lessons having been learnt from the trial cruises. As Parker observed:

> We will say nothing of the objection to an *overhanging stern*, Your Lordship tested the inefficiency of it at Portsmouth, but I shall venture to hope that we may not under any circumstances have occasion to use our *stern guns*![52]

In response to the repeated observations made on the small number of guns mounted in so large a ship Edye attempted to fit an extra port on the quarter of the *Royal Frederick* but the Surveyor would not alter his draught.[53] A further trial in 1846 under Parker's command only confirmed what everyone with eyes to see already knew and he observed that 'take her all in all, she [*Queen*] is the finest ship, in my opinion, that ever went to sea'.[54]

After Symonds left office three of the ships ordered by Haddington were modified by the addition of 3ft at the bow and stern to allow for 118 or 120 guns. The frame of the fourth unit, *Marlborough*, was converted to the new design in

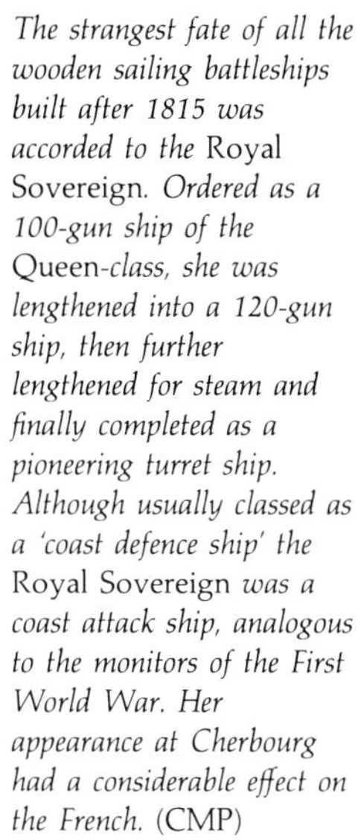
The strangest fate of all the wooden sailing battleships built after 1815 was accorded to the Royal Sovereign. *Ordered as a 100-gun ship of the* Queen*-class, she was lengthened into a 120-gun ship, then further lengthened for steam and finally completed as a pioneering turret ship. Although usually classed as a 'coast defence ship' the* Royal Sovereign *was a coast attack ship, analogous to the monitors of the First World War. Her appearance at Cherbourg had a considerable effect on the French.* (CMP)

1849. Parker had crammed another six or eight guns onto the upper deck and quarter deck of the *Queen*, but the ship was not designed for any increase in the important lower decks.

Gun deck	30	68pdr	68cwt
Middle deck	30	32pdr	56cwt
Upper deck	32	32pdr	42cwt
Quarter deck	8	32pdr	42cwt
Forecastle	16	32pdr	25cwt
	116		[55]

Royal Sovereign and *Marlborough*, the two least advanced of the new ships, were reordered in 1850 for gun deck of 68-pounders, and this was the last modification made to any British sailing three-decker.[56] *Royal Frederick* remained on the ways for almost 20 years, from 1848 being classed as an Advanced Ship, the first to be so rated before being launched.[57]

The largest sailing three-decker designed for the Royal Navy, Oliver Lang's *Royal Albert*, was never completed as a sailing ship. Given Lang's relationship with Seppings and his pride in the *Trafalgar*, the design of 1831 was little more than an expanded version of Seppings's last three-decker. Lang always claimed that the additional foot of beam had been worked into the *Trafalgar* on his own principle, and he had certainly been subjected to heavy criticism for failing to follow the draft, and for the clumsy and inefficient stern.[58]

Her size excited some comment but she survived the troubled times that followed Symonds's retirement. Finally, in early 1852 the inevitable redesign removed her from the list of the sailing Navy. Her qualities as a sailing ship can only be assessed from imperfect evidence, but as a steam ship she stood up very well under canvas and while not as fine below as her contemporaries, she would not have been disgraced in any sailing contest, and more especially not in fleet action.

With the *Queen* the three-decked ship was finally capable of resolving the age-old dilemma of weight of metal versus seaworthiness. Symonds's great ship had the mix of qualities, in part from her size, to catch a flying enemy and make any action tell. The three-decker remained central to British naval thought well into the steamship era because it was the only guarantor of supremacy. Between 1815 and 1850 nothing altered the reliance of the Royal Navy on battle, and within that context three full decks of heavy guns were an irresistible argument.

The Windsor Castle, *ex* Victoria *as the Devonport gunnery training ship* Cambridge *in the 1870s.* (CMP)

2 Canopus and the 84-Gun Ship

Once the structural problems of the large two-decked ship had been overcome by Seppings's work it became the cost-effective method of improving the battle power of the fleet. Byam Martin observed that they were one-seventh cheaper per ton than 120- and 74-gun ships, a figure which remained constant throughout the period.[1]

When the Admiralty took stock of the fleet in 1815 they were aware of a serious shortage in the most modern and powerful classes, particularly 120-gun First Rates and large two-decked ships, which had replaced the small three-decker as a more suitable tactical unit for a fleet constantly pursuing the enemy. After the War of American Independence two 80-gun ships, *Caesar* and *Foudroyant*, had been built at Plymouth. During the Napoleonic conflict two more units had been ordered, *Bellerophon*, (ex *Waterloo*, ex *Talavera*) of 1809 and the *Cambridge* of 1810. The latter was built on the lines of the captured Danish ship *Christian VII*. Neither had been launched when the War ended and so this class of ships was largely represented on the Navy List by captured enemy tonnage – *Pompee, Sans Pareil, Canopus, Tonnant, Spartiate, Malta* and *Christian VII*. In 1815 not one of these ships was in good repair, for all of them had been in service for much of the war. *Foudroyant* and *Canopus* were undergoing large repairs, while the remainder were either in need of, or beyond, similar treatment. *Malta* was reported as strong, though her sheer was breaking. Her sailing had been spoiled by alterations to the storerooms, which now prevented her from being put in trim.

Armament of Malta, *a typical 84-gun ship at the end of the War*

Gun deck	30	32pdrs
	2	68pdr carronades
Main deck	32	24pdrs
Quarter deck	16	24pdr (Congreve)
Forecastle	2	12pdrs
	2	68pdr carronades
	2	24pdr carronades
Roundhouse	5	24pdr carronades

The war-time service of the existing large two-deckers encouraged the construction of further units. Large two-deckers reinforced the battleline, filled in the spaces between the three-deckers, provided alternative strong points in the line and, as Nelson noted in 1805, were so far superior to small 74s that they could take on two enemy ships in an emergency. In addition, the superior power under canvas made them a natural element in a fleet committed to a strategy that required them to pursue a flying enemy. With these advantages in mind it was clear that the class would be reinforced before any other. When the timber pile of Bonaparte's Genoa Dockyard was examined in 1814 the Committee of Surveyors informed the Navy Board that the timber was suitable for a Third Rate of 80 guns. However, when the Navy Board came to select a design they demonstrated an astonishing lack of imagination. They selected the last British-built vessel of which they had any experience:

> The ship to be similar to the *Foudroyant*, keeping the orlop where it is, but taking six inches from the hanging of the deck to enable her to carry her guns higher out of the water amidships.[2]

Although a fine ship, *Foudroyant* was too small to carry an armament of more real power than the large class of 74s, and her lower decks were crowded by mounting an extra gun on each broadside. The Admiralty lost no time ordering that a 'facsimile' of the *Canopus* be built and registered on the Navy List as the *Formidable*. They requested the Board to provide an armament, and reminded them that when last at sea *Canopus* had borne 700 men.[3] The Navy Board still refused to assess the lessons of the war.

Gun deck	32	32pdrs
Main deck	32	24pdrs (Congreve)
Quarter deck	4	24pdrs (Congreve)
	14	32pdr carronades
Forecastle	4	24pdr carronades
Complement	700 men	

The Admiralty insisted on heavy 24-pounders on the main deck, a warrant which was well within the capability of *Canopus*. Reasons for selecting *Canopus* from the available models were not hard to find. Her last sailing report, from February 1812, credited her with a speed of 12.5 knots, an easy roll and the midship main deck port 7ft 3in out of the water with 270 tons of ballast aboard. She was noted as sailing well on all points, but particularly with the wind abeam, the common point of advantage for large French-built two-deckers. With her guns so high out of the water she had the capacity to carry heavier metal, and to use it in all weathers. The ability to use all her guns in heavy weather made the large two-decked ship attractive to a fleet that had to operate in all weathers and all seas, and was a significant point of distinction between this class and the generality of three-deckers, where the lower deck was often too close to the water for the guns to be used.[4]

The Navy Board quickly prepared the design.

> As far as the lines underwater are concerned it is a facsimile of the *Canopus*, but that we have made the following alterations in other particulars, which we submit for their Lordships' direction.
>
> The size of the ports on the several decks are altered conformably to the present practice (for the calibre of guns that it is intended she shall carry) in British ships of war – and that there may be sufficient space between those on the

The 80-gun ships

	Caesar	*Foudroyant*	*Bellerophon*	*Cambridge*
Gun deck	181ft	184ft 10in	192ft	187ft 2 1/4in
Keel, for tonnage	148ft 3 3/4in	151ft 5in	159ft 10in	154ft 10 1/2in
Breadth, extreme	51ft 3in	50ft 6in	49ft	50ft 11 1/2in
Breadth, moulded				
Depth in hold	22ft 4in	22ft 6in	21ft	21ft 7in
Tonnage	1,992	2,062	2,041	2,139

Quarter Deck to work the guns, there is one on each side less than the *Canopus*. The Gun Deck beams of the *Canopus* have a round of 10", it is proposed that those in the *Formidable* shall round only 5" – the upper deck beams of the former ship round 1'1", it is proposed that those of the latter shall round only 7 1/2". The Quarter Deck and Forecastle beams round in the *Canopus* 1'0", it is proposed that they shall have a rounding of 8 1/2". The roundhouse beams have a rounding of 8 1/2" in the *Canopus*, in the draught proposed it is 11".

The bottom of the *Canopus* is 5 1/4" thick, we propose that it shall be 4 1/2" in the *Formidable*. In order to facilitate the conversion of timber for the bow and to prevent difficulty in bringing on the plank we have made an alteration therein from the ticked to the drawn line upon the draught. We also beg to call their Lordships attention to an alteration in the mizzen channels, by carrying the dead eyes to the top of the side, also in the Transoms as it is proposed they shall be omitted except the wing transom or a wing and filling transom conformal to a plan now practised on the *Thunderer* building at Woolwich.

In proposing these deviations we have been chiefly guided by our present practice on British ships of war, and which cannot injure the ships sailing qualities but will, we believe render her more convenient as a ship of war.

The *Thunderer* (later *Talavera*) was the 74 ordered to be built to a new Seppings structural plan allowing the use of frigate timbers. The impact of all these alterations, including the flattening of the deck mentioned above, can be seen in the dimensions of the new ship (see table).

The extent to which the new ship was a facsimile of Nelson's prize can be judged from the placement of her masts. In 1829 Captain Hayes of the *Ganges*, a noted seaman, requested permission to shift the mizzen mast. He pointed out that, following the French ship, this had been placed approximately 1ft 3in forward of the position in the *Caledonia*. As the mizzen mast was stepped on the gun deck he was permitted to move it back 6ft. It has been argued that these ships were new designs using only the lines of the French model. This confuses the structural reforms of Seppings, which were applied to the whole fleet, with the hull form of the ship, for which Sane can justly claim credit.[5]

Nelson's greatest prize, the Canopus, *ex* Franklin, *at Devonport in the 1860s.* (Tenby)

At this stage the *Formidable* followed *Canopus* in having the closed, or round, bow developed by Seppings, and an open stern. The Science Museum model, long catalogued as an unknown 84-gun ship, is, in fact, the Navy Board model of *Formidable* as originally ordered in 1815. The main point of identification is the higher position of the mizzen deadeyes.[6]

Although ordered in 1815 *Formidable* could not be laid down until the timber from Genoa arrived in May 1816. The following month the Admiralty accepted Seppings's round stern, agreed to build ships to the new design and made *Formidable* one of

	Formidable	*Canopus*	*Asia* and *Bombay*
	July 1815	1815	1820
Gun deck	193ft 10in	193ft 4 1/2in	196ft 1 1/2in
Keel, for tonnage	160ft 2 5/8in	159ft 10in	161ft 11 1/2in
Breadth, extreme	51ft 5 1/4in	52ft 4in	51ft 5 1/4in
Breadth, moulded	50ft 8 1/4in	50ft 10in	50ft 8 1/2in
Depth in hold		23ft 0in	22ft 6in
Tonnage	2,269/94	2,269 46/94	2,279 24/96

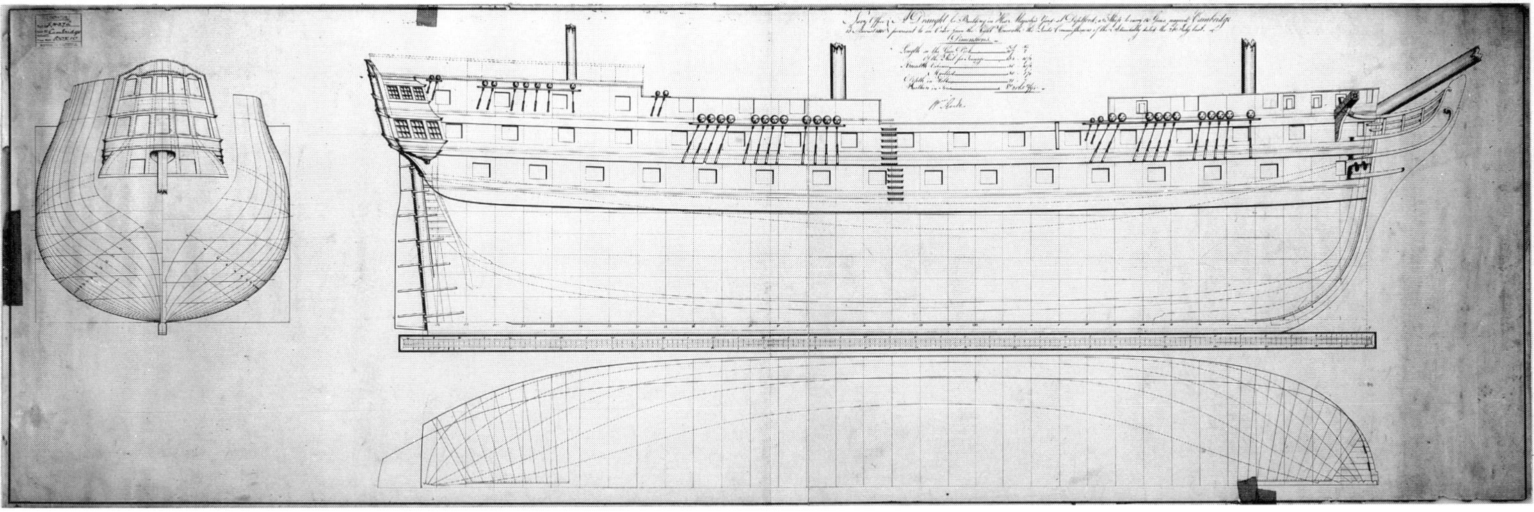

The draught of the 80-gun Cambridge, *based on the lines of the Danish prize* Christian VII *as designed, dated 1810, with enclosed bow and open stern. A successful ship, she was not of adequate dimensions for the postwar fleet.* (NMM)

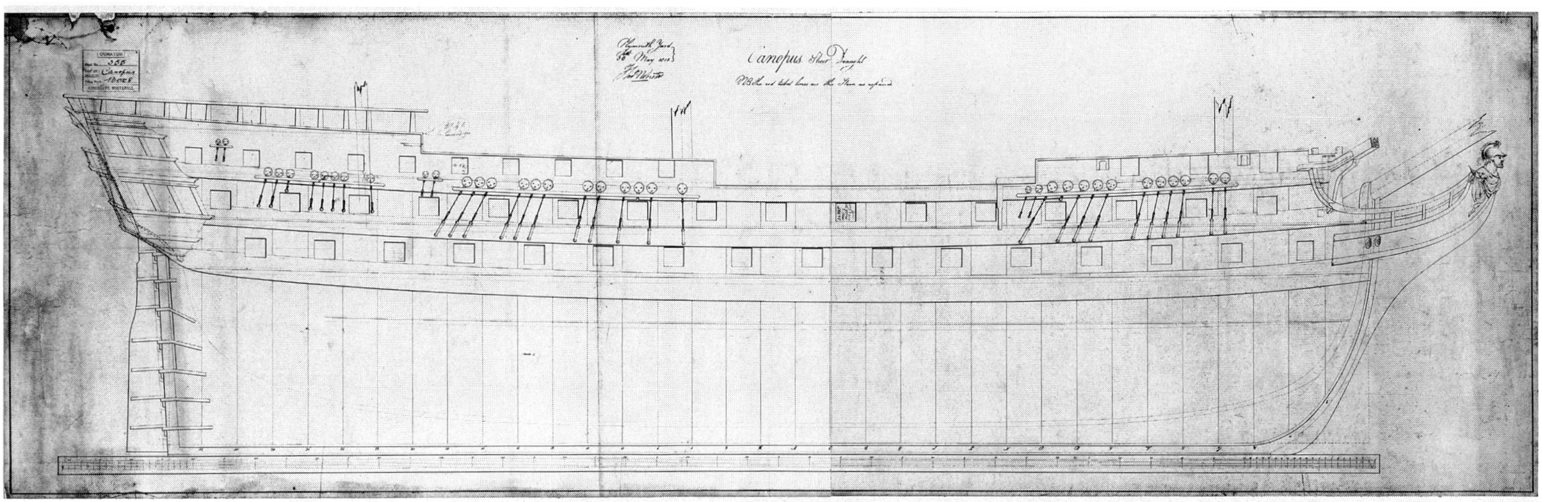

The Canopus *sheer draught dated May 1815. The dotted lines at the stern mark a repair.*

the first three to be so fitted. As a result the ship went through a long career with the most unsightly of all the round sterns in sharp contrast with the elegant raked stern of the model. Later round sterns were much improved.[7] At the same time the Admiralty decided to build another ship of the same design at Bombay, once they had been reassured that the docks were large enough. This demonstrated the importance of the large two-decker in the Admiralty's conception of the postwar fleet. The Navy Board, on the other hand, did not adopt the same scale of priorities until the end of 1815, when Byam Martin joined the Board, bringing his extensive recent experience to bear.[8]

Further orders for 84-gun ships of this class followed and formed the centre of the postwar fleet. In 1817 the Navy Board secured extra money, allowing sawyers to convert the frames of another four ships. In 1819 two more vessels were ordered from Bombay, the *Asia* and the *Bombay*, along with the *Goliath* (later *Clarence*) at Pembroke, where the oak piles contained a large quantity of suitable timber. In the following year *Powerful, Thunderer, Monarch* and *Vengeance* were added to the list, using the frames already converted. All were based on the *Canopus*, but, as indicated above, the later ships used modified dimensions, although the Surveyors reported that 'the form of the body, however, is correct for that ship'.[9]

Despite a clear requirement for more large two-decked ships, the shortage of slipways and the long-term construction methods adopted by the Navy Board prevented any further units being laid down in Britain. To emphasise this point the frame of *Monarch* was moved from Deptford in 1825 to follow the *Formidable* at Chatham. By the time further slips had been cleared more powerful ships were demanded. To make up the shortfall the Navy Board proposed razeeing some small three-deckers. As such they conformed to the policy of Byam Martin and Seppings. The first such ship, the *Ocean* of 1805, was as rebuilt perhaps the first in the Navy configured for a single-calibre battery. Where the original ship had carried 18-pounders on the middle/main deck, when rebuilt with stronger deck beams she carried two full batteries of long 32-pounders.

Proposed armament 4.2.1820

Gun deck	30	32-pounders
Main deck	32	32-pounders
Quarter deck	10	32-pounder carronades
	4	12-pounders
Forecastle	2	32-pounder carronades
	2	12-pounders
Complement	740 men	

Although the next two proposed, the old *Prince of Wales* and *Royal George*, were rejected as poor ships in need of large repair, *Union* and *Boyne* were ordered to be cut down in 1827 and 1828, though neither ship was to be completed. They would have had only 28 guns on the lower deck, and 30 on the main deck, thus conforming to the layout of a 74-gun ship. Although only able to mount a battery of 76 guns the weight of each piece meant that they would have been classed as 80-gun Second Rates.[10]

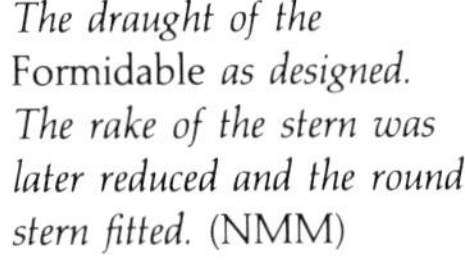

The draught of the Formidable *as designed. The rake of the stern was later reduced and the round stern fitted.* (NMM)

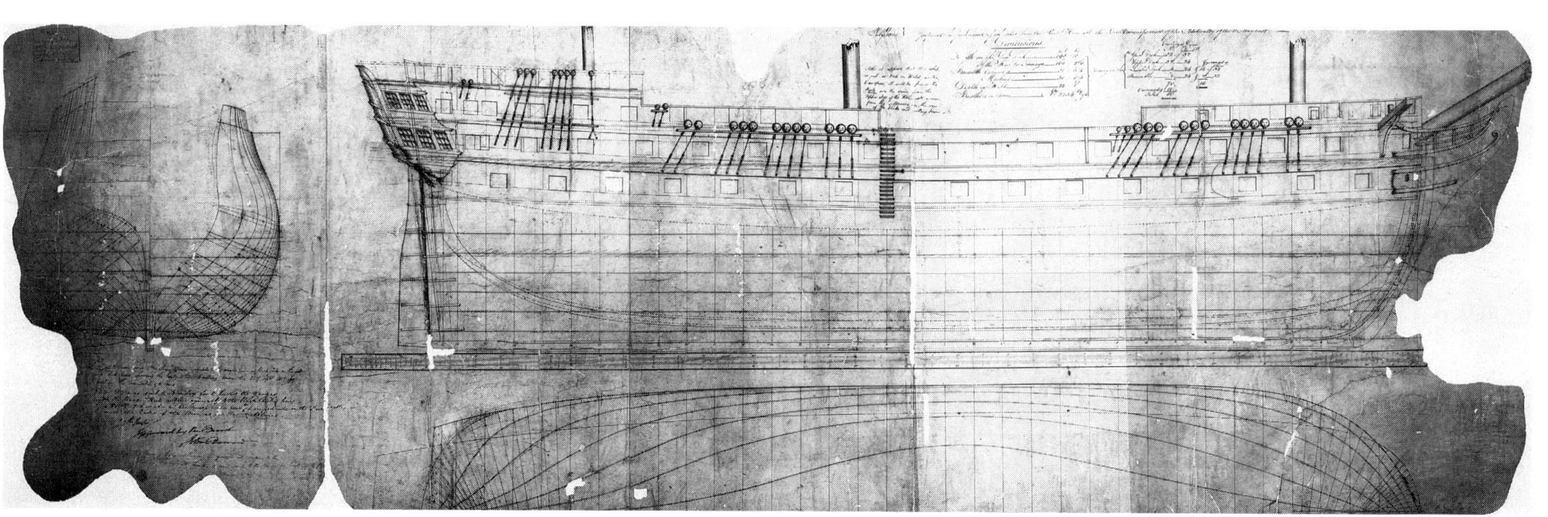

The Powerful *in 1839–40, under Captain Charles Napier. In the crisis of 1840 the* Canopus-*class were, with the* Caledonia-*class 120-gun ships, the core of the fleet that deterred the French. In addition,* Powerful *and* Thunderer *played a leading part in the Syrian campaign, including the bombardment of Acre in November.* (NMM)

The armament crisis 1825

From the early 1820s it had become clear that foreign Navies were adopting a heavier armament for all classes. In this respect the Americans and French were particularly prominent. In 1825 the upper deck beams of the 84-gun ships then under construction were increased from 3in scantling to 4in 'in case it is at any time desirable' to place heavier guns there. The Admiralty were already considering using the new 47cwt 32-pounders on the upper deck, and when they did so the following year, aboard the *Asia*, Byam Martin complained to Cockburn and sent an official letter. Having been informed that the *Asia*'s deck beams were undersize he reckoned that the additional 25 tons so high up would ruin the ship.[11]

While the Admiralty reconsidered the policy of mounting such large pieces so high up, the Navy Board reflected on the basic design:

> The second rates are built on the lines of the *Canopus* but it is proposed in future to give a greater length of floor and bearing both in the fore and after parts, as the model for future ships.

Seppings modifications provided the displacement for a heavier battery. In the event the Admiralty insited that all ships of the *Canopus* type should carry the same. The only ship to follow this new design was the *Calcutta*, ordered in April 1827.

The Canopus *after her 1839–40 repair. The mizzen deadeyes have now been moved up to the quarter deck and an enclosed bow fitted. In this form she took part in the Squadrons of Evolution in 1847 and 1848 with great success.* (NMM)

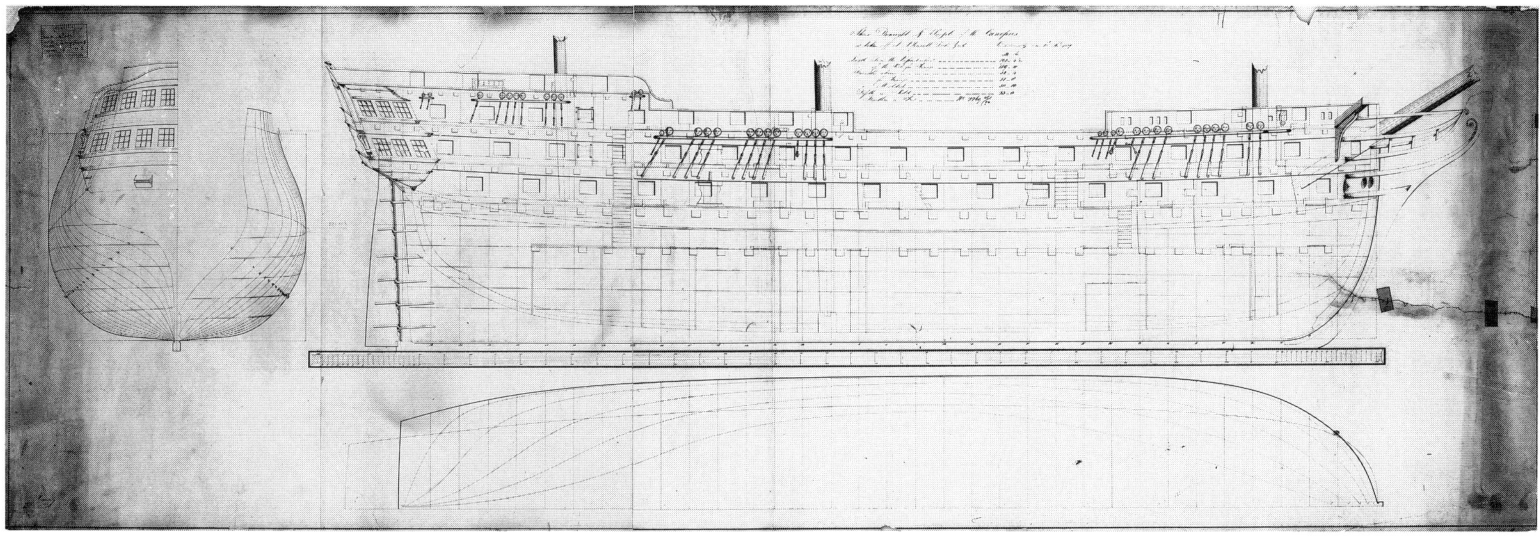

The Formidable *serving as a school ship off Portishead in the Bristol Channel. This view shows the round stern.* (Author)

Calcutta

Length	196ft 0in
Length of keel for tonnage	162ft 4 1/2in
Breadth, extreme	52ft 6in
Breadth, moulded	50ft 9in
Depth in hold	22ft 6in
Tonnage, old measurement	2,290 62/94

Bombay Proposed Armament Warrant 8.12.1828

Gun deck	28	32pdrs
	2	68pdr carronades
Main deck	32	32pdrs
Quarter deck	10	32pdr carronades
Forecastle	4	32pdr carronades
	2	12pdrs
Complement (peace)	660 men	

This heavy battery did not leave Somerset Place without a protest.

> We at the same time beg to state that we are decidedly of the opinion that increasing the weight of metal in ships is very injurious to their fabrics, and that the ill effects thereof would be apparent after any considerable length of service.[12]

The Admiralty ignored such outbursts. By the following year the success of Byam Martin's programme for the battlefleet had become clear. The Navy Board admitted that the major weakness in the fleet lay in the Sixth Rates and smaller classes. To this end a pair of new Fourth Rates were cancelled and no further battleships were even considered.[13]

When the new Board took office they demanded that the *Calcutta* design be cancelled and a new draught either larger or merely of increased breadth be substituted. In this they were adopting Byam Martin's reservations about the additional capacity provided in Seppings's design. He suggested to Graham that an extra foot of breadth would suffice for two full decks of heavy 32-pounders with 25cwt Dixon guns, later termed 'gunnades', on the quarter deck. This would also make the ships more powerful under sail and more efficient in battle. The Establishment was to include fifteen ships, with five building and five converted frames. Razeeing *Boyne* and *Union* would reduce the requirement for new frames to three. A new draught was ordered on 30 June 1831.[14]

The new design was submitted on 8 February and included a new stern to provide more protection to the rudder head in response to one of the major criticisms levelled at Seppings's designs. The frames of two Second Rate ships 'similar in scantling to the *Canopus*' were ordered at Pembroke in June, within days of the abolition of the Navy Board. But in the following month it was made clear that the *Vanguard* and *Collingwood* would be of a different class.[15]

The fate of Seppings's last design reveals much.

> Dear Sir Thomas Hardy,
>
> will you please do me the favour to send me the plans of ships which may be at the Admiralty. I believe there is one of an 80 of Sir R. Seppings', a brig of Inman, a corvette of Mr. Reid of Chatham and some others.
>
> your most faithful and obed't serv't
>
> 3 July 1832 W. Symonds
>
> July 4th. The plans described to be sent to the Surveyor of the Navy, T.M.H.[16]

The sailing qualities of the new 84-gun ships were rarely tried in the 1830s. The Indian ships were reported on during their passage home, with undersized masts. *Ganges* and *Asia* were commissioned in 1822 and 1825, and the first sailing report of the former concentrated on her strength, observing that she sailed 'very well' with other ships. Later her warrant officers reported her as having every good quality, although she was not a fast ship. *Asia* earned higher praise as, 'a fast sailing ship' in 1830.[17] In service the *Canopus* derivatives earned the highest regard for their strength and sailing qualities, and were widely considered to be the superior of their famous model and without equal in the pre-Symonds fleet.

The *Canopus/Formidable*-class, with *Cambridge* and *Bellerophon*, were a vital part of the postwar battlefleet. They were mobilised for every crisis, took part in each campaign and were still a major part of the fleet in 1854. *Ganges* was the last British sailing battleship in full commission. During 40 years service the *Canopus*-class maintained a high reputation for power under sail, durability and efficiency as gun platforms.

The Vengeance *housed over as depot at Keyham Yard, Devonport, with* Indus *outboard. The two ships lay outside the North Basin.* (IWM)

3 Stretched 74-Gun Ships

At the end of the war all 74-gun ships building or on order were of the small class, with 18-pounder guns on the upper deck. There were fourteen ships building: *Defence, Hercules, Redoubtable, Wellesley, Black Prince, Minotaur, Pitt, Wellington, Agincourt, Melville, Thunderer,* (later *Talavera*), *Belleisle, Hawke* and *Boscawen*. In addition, two duplicate frames from Bombay would be delivered aboard the *Wellesley* and *Melville*. The *Malabar*, with a duplicate frame, was ordered in 1815 and the *Genoa* and *Hastings* were purchased in 1815 and 1817, bringing the total number of new small 74-gun ships available to eighteen. As the larger part of all construction after 1804 had been in this class it was evident that no further units were required, and some thought was given to improving the armament of the ships available. Existing Third Rates that were equal to Congreve 24-pounders on the upper deck, such as the ex French *Donegal*, were rearmed. However, this was not regarded as a particularly significant improvement as long 24-pounders were rated much more highly. Some ships were launched in 1815, particularly those building in merchant yards and those nearly complete, which cleared slipways for frigate repairs. Of the others only *Boscawen* had not been set up in frame. Her timbers had not been provided.[1]

The Admiralty expressed a clear preference for the more powerful ships, requesting the Navy Board to provide information on how far they could look forward to the building of large three-deckers and 80-gun ships. To emphasise the point six days later they altered the rating of His Majesty's ships so that 80-gun two-deckers became Second Rates.[2] Henceforth, only one class of three-decker was to be built.

The Navy Board was in no particular haste to respond to this pressure. Eleven months later they determined to exploit the suspension of the wartime ships.

> It appears to us advisable that as many ships of the line on two decks of large dimensions should be provided as possible, and to propose to their Lordships that H.M. ship *Boscawen* ordered to be built at Woolwich, may be lengthened and increased in dimensions as shewn by the accompanying draught.

The 78-gun Indus *lying at Devonport as a receiving ship sometime after 1860. Built at Portsmouth using the duplicate frame sent home in the 74-gun* Melville *the* Indus *served only one commission, being too small for the modern armament and too large to take the place of the old 74s as the cheapest battleship to man. The stern is a compromise between the round and elliptical forms, and as such is neither elegant nor functional.* (NMM)

The Admiralty concurred, specifying that the breadth of the ship be taken out to 50ft. The final draught of the new ship was submitted in the following year, signed by Seppings and Tucker. The decks were straightened out, as in all postwar construction, with 6ft to 6ft 3in between them to improve habitability. The conversion was ordered on 20 November 1817 as an 82-gun ship.

Boscawen

	As *Repulse* (74 guns)	As an 82-gun ship
Length of gun deck	174ft	187ft 4 1/2in
Length of keel	143ft 2in	153ft 8in
Breadth, extreme	50ft	
Breadth, moulded	47ft 4in	49ft 9in
Depth in hold	20ft	24ft 6in
	1,709 tons	2,043 41/94 tons

The profile draught of the Boscawen, *showing details of the frame.* (NMM)

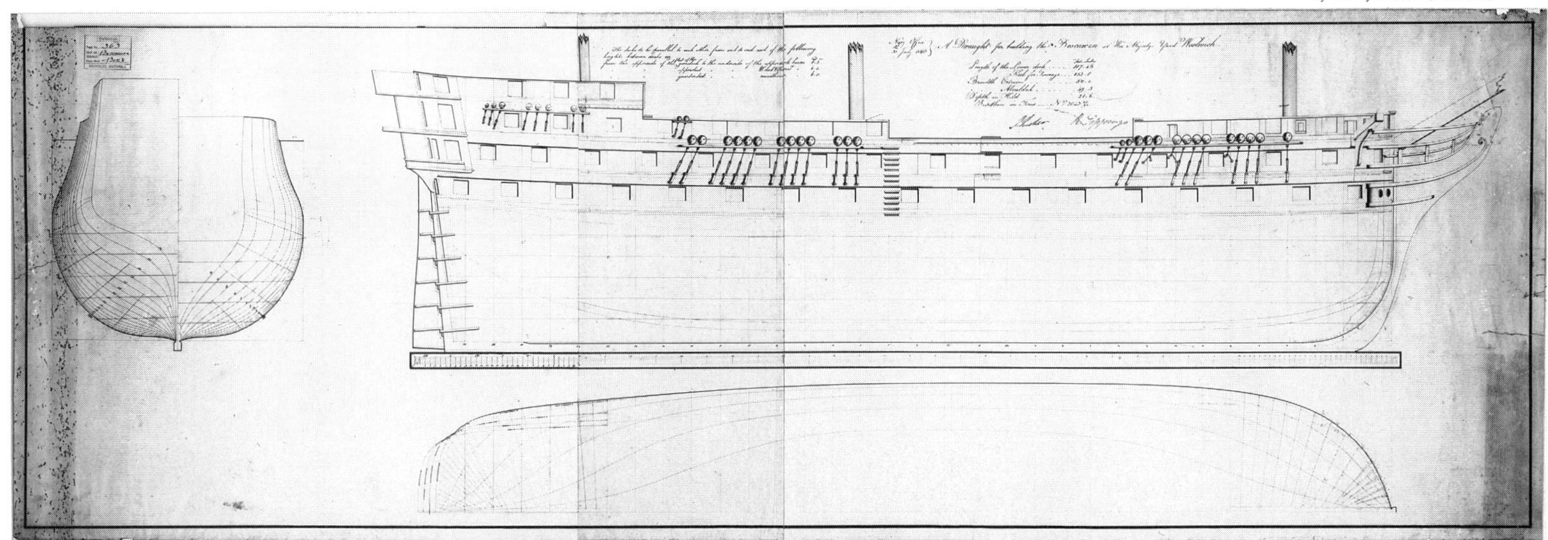

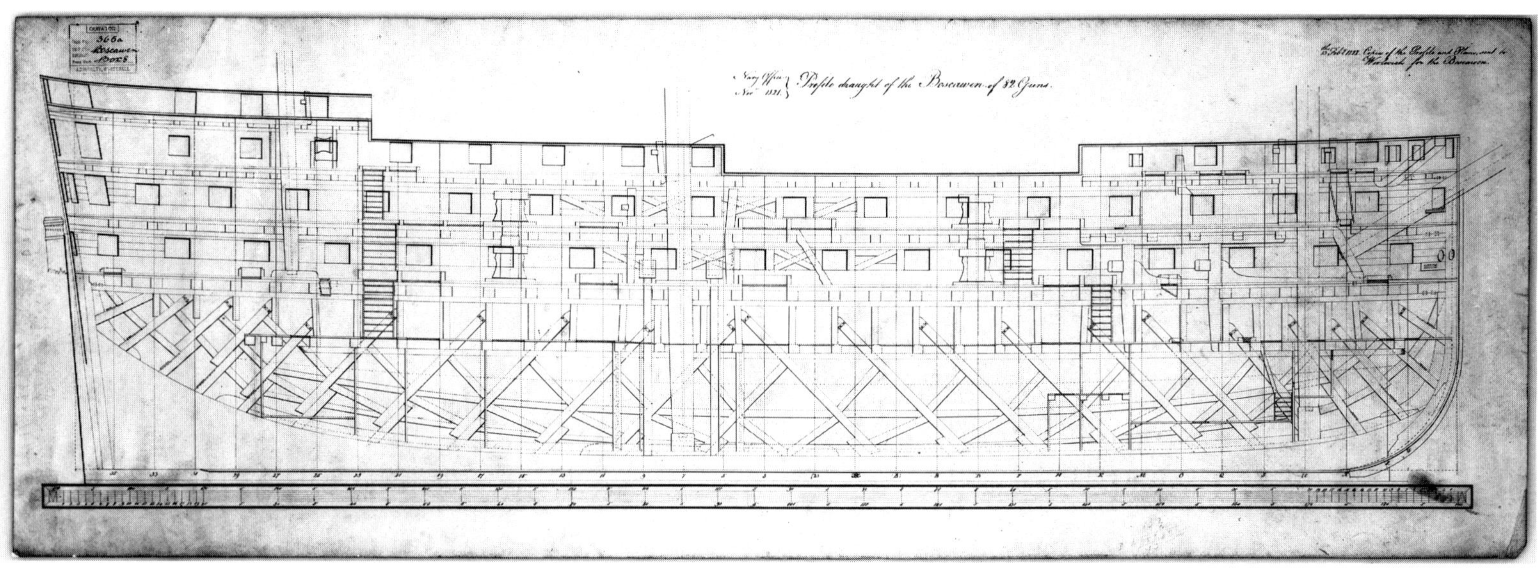

The profile draught of the Boscawen *showing details of the frame.* (NMM)

Armament warrant

Gun deck	28	32-pounders
	2	68-pounder carronades
Main deck	32	24-pounders (long)
Quarter deck	12	32-pounder carronades
	2	12-pounders
Forecastle	2	32-pounder carronades
	2	12-pounders
	82 guns	
Complement	650 men	[3]

The new ship was rated alongside the *Foudroyant, Caesar* and *Cambridge*.

The Admiralty and Navy Board had reservations about the initial rearming of the fleet. The 82-gun ships were deprived of one hard-to-use quarter deck carronade on each side and re-classed as 80-gun ships, the minimum level for Second Rates, while the Admiralty stated that no ship unable to sustain long 24-pounders on the main deck was to be rated above 74 guns in future.[4]

The duplicate frame of the *Melville* had been ordered to be set up at Portsmouth on 10 November 1817, as the *Indus*, and that of the *Malabar* follow at Plymouth on 21 September 1819 as the *Hindostan*. From the outset she was to follow the enlarged dimensions of *Boscawen*. *Indus* was reordered as an 80-gun ship in May 1820.[5] The teak *Carnatic*, an earlier duplicate frame brought home by the *Cornwallis*, was already too advanced for any conversion although she was eventually fitted with a round stern, despite Navy Board doubts.[6] No particular urgency was displayed in completing these three ships, as with several new 120- and 84-gun ships building, repairs being carried out on existing ships of the larger classes and urgent work in hand on new and repaired frigates, they were never going to be accorded any priority. In addition, the two teak vessels were reliant on timber cut to order at Bombay.

The turning point for the 74, both of the stretched or large class and the ordinary 18-pounder ships occurred in 1825. Byam Martin advised building a new 76, shorthand for a 24-pounder Third Rate, using the form of the *Bulwark*, the outstanding British large 74. In commission at the end of the American War, *Bulwark* had been an outstanding ship under canvas, and carried long 24-pounders on the main deck.[7]

The *Valiant* was ordered but no significant work had been put into collecting her timbers when, in 1831, she was cancelled.[8] This type was not in demand, and the armament crisis of 1826 merely served to emphasise this. *Boscawen* and similar ships were no more powerful than *Valiant* and were no match for the new 84s. Being of appreciably lighter scantling they could not be rearmed. After 1826 the stretched ships were placed even further down the list in the yards at Plymouth.

The draught for the Boscawen *in 1835, metamorphosed into 70-gun ship of Symonds's form.* (NMM)

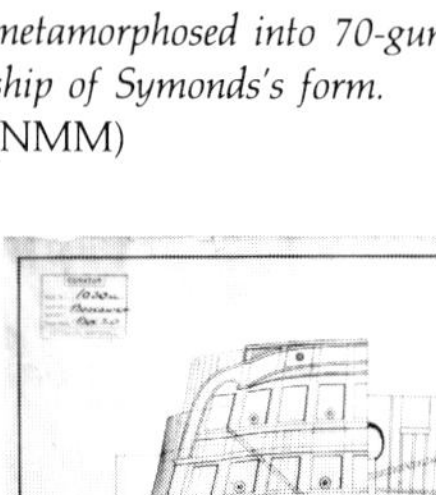

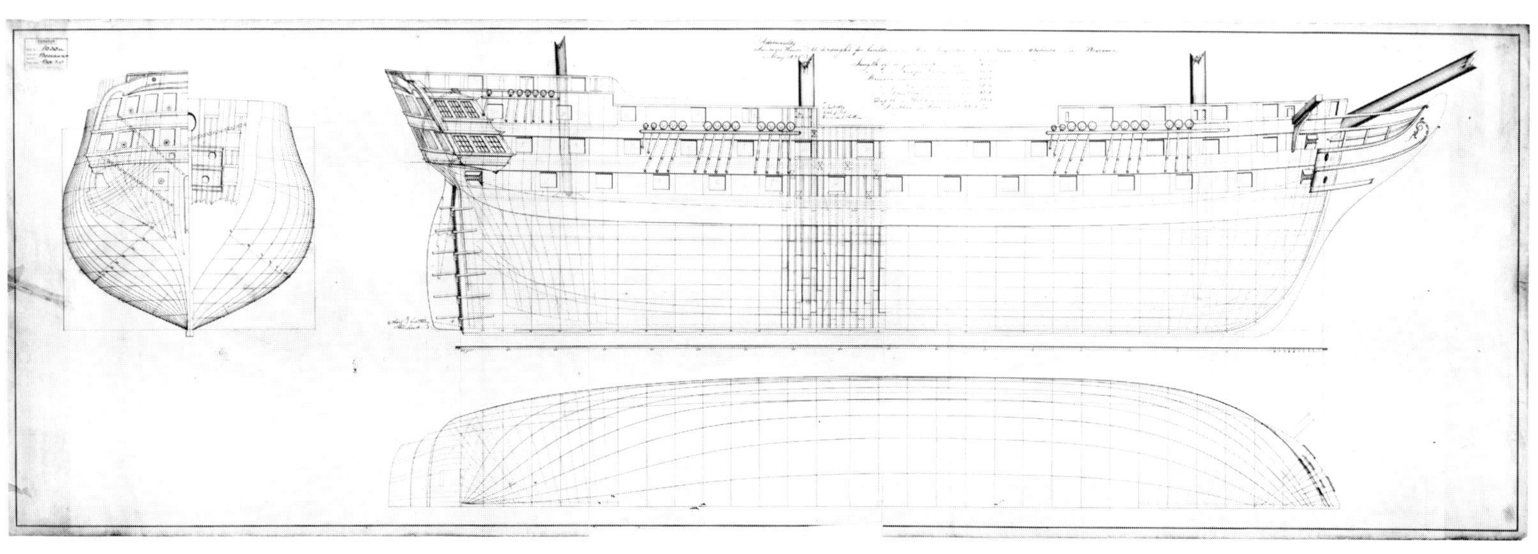

Hindostan was suspended in favour of *Nile*. By 1829 the surfeit of 80-gun ships was officially recognised.[9]

When the new Admiralty Board took office *Boscawen* was largely finished, needing only 10 months work to complete. Five months after the abolition of the Navy Board the ship was reordered as the *Indefatigable*, a 50-gun frigate using the *Vernon*'s moulds.[10] However, the new Surveyor considered this as a waste of large timber and in 1834 secured the support of the First Naval Lord, Hardy, to reorder her as a 70-gun ship to his own design, essentially identical to the *Cumberland* ordered at Chatham in 1833. Modifying the old 'U' form to the new 'V' profile posed serious problems to the Woolwich shipwrights, but the ship was at least, for the first time, accorded some degree of priority.[11]

Armament warrant for *Cumberland* and *Boscawen*. 3.12.1834

Gun deck	24	32-pounder	56cwt
	2	68-pounder	60cwt
Main deck	2	68-pounder	60cwt
	26	32-pounder	48cwt
Quarter deck	8	32-pounder	25cwt
Forecastle	2	32-pounder	25cwt
	2	32-pounder	48cwt
Roundhouse	4	18-pounder	10cwt

Hindostan suffered a more undignified fate. Although she continued, albeit slowly and at the expense of the duplicate frame teak frigate *Tigris*, she was widely rcognised as obsolescent and her timbers diverted to the *Gorgon*, a steam ship building at Pembroke. By 1835 over 500 loads of timber had been dispatched from Plymouth, and *Hindostan* was forced to make do with inferior made-up deck beams of African oak, Dantzic oak and pitch pine, despite the widely held view that mixing teak and other timbers was destructive to both.[12] *Indus* was eventually launched because her slip was badly decayed, rather than because there was any need for ships of her class and she was the only ship of her type to see active service. Commissioned in 1840, under Captain Sir James Stirling, she served three years on the Mediterranean station. Little can be said of her performance, for as one of her officers complained, the ship was handled in the most irresolute manner.[13] *Hindostan*, which never commissioned, is better known for her role as dormitory to the *Britannia* establishment in the River Dart. These ships were too small for war but too large for peace. In comparison with the 18-pounder 74s their stronger main deck was negated by the availability of bored up guns for the 18-pounder ships, which required smaller crews and used masts and yards already in store. The completion of the modern 70-gun ships, *Boscawen* and *Cumberland*, removed any last hope of employment, the new ships being far better suited to the role of peace-time station flagships.

The 70-gun Cumberland *of 1842 as a training ship in the Clyde, before her destruction by fire in 1889. The severe rake of the bow and stern are apparent.* (NMM)

4 *The Razee 50-Gun Ship and the Third Rate 74 after 1815*

Between 1815 and 1850 the Royal Navy converted, and later built, heavy frigates of a size equal to the basic 74-gun ship of the French Wars. These ships reflected changes in the British strategic position following the defeat of France and progress in the technology of warship construction. Later commentators have criticised British policy makers for not adopting the type more enthusiastically, given the large programmes of similar ships in the French and United States Navies, but the heavy frigate, the classic intermediate warship, was expensive and ill-suited to British requirements because it wasted resources better employed on the battlefleet. The divergence of opinion between those who moulded naval policy and contemporary critics, who have been too widely followed in later accounts, concerns the basis of strategic planning. Succeeding planners and policy makers at the Navy Board, the Surveyor's Office and the Admiralty adopted a sound, pragmatic view of British strategy and the related construction policy, and made a positive response to foreign challenges. Too little note has been taken of the 'official' view of British strategy in the nineteenth century which continued to be based on battlefleet superiority. Imitating foreign warship types, designed for a *guerre de course* strategy, offered no advantages.[1]

The frigate

As naval warfare evolved the design of warships became increasingly specialist. The 100-ship battle lines of the Anglo-Dutch wars of the seventeenth century were replaced by smaller more homogeneous forces of battleships. In Britain the work of Admiral Lord Anson in the period 1745–62 consolidated these developments into a coherent philosophy of ship design. The critical move was the shift from small general-purpose warships to specialist cruisers for scouting and trade protection. The new frigate class sacrificed gun power, the second covered gundeck, for speed and seaworthiness. As the century progressed the size and armament of the type increased faster than that of the battleship. In the Napoleonic Wars the standard British type, the Fifth Rate 38-gun ship carried a main deck battery of 18-pounder long guns with carronades. While their potential opponents were similarly armed, it made economic sense for Britain to persevere with this class rather than build larger ships which, from the high cost of large timber, would be more expensive in cost per ton, and consequently less numerous. In addition, the Royal Navy never had the manpower to spare for more powerful frigates. Those it had were always short handed in wartime and larger ships would only have exacerbated the problem. Furthermore, frigates should not be seen in isolation. They were, in British service, one element in a balanced fleet, which regarded sea control as its *raison d'etre*. They were not the final arbiter of the situation – that function belonged to the battlefleet – but were intended to assist the fleet and exploit the command it had secured.[2]

The heavy frigate

Although Frederik af Chapman built a class of heavy frigates for the Swedish Navy in the 1780s, the origins of the 50-gun frigate as an intermediate type in British service lie in the increasing power of French frigates during the Napoleonic Wars, and the success of the American 44s in the War of 1812. The heavy 24-pounder main deck batteries of the American ships proved far more effective than the 18-pounders in British ships. As an interim measure the British cut down four old 74s into spar deck 58-gun razees, with 32-pounders on the upper deck and 42-pounder carronades. One of these razees, the *Majestic*, persuaded Captain Decatur of the USS *President* to surrender. However, the American ship had been heavily damaged in action with the 24-pounder frigate *Endymion*, a rare example of the type built for British service in 1797. The *Saturn*-class spar deck 58s needed the extra deck to retain some hull girder strength but while far more powerful in heavy weather they displayed no marked improvement in sailing in light airs. *Majestic*, despite the best efforts of Captain John Hayes, was the last ship of her squadron to come up with the *President* although she had led the chase the previous day in a heavy sea.

The Cornwall, *a 50-gun razee frigate, serving as a training ship in the Thames. The* Cornwall *never served as a 50-gun ship and remained largely unaltered from 1830. The original Seppings frigate round stern distinguishes her from several of her erstwhile sisters.* (NMM)

At the same time, 24-pounder 50- and 60-gun frigates were ordered as the *Forth* and *Leander* classes, but these weak, rush-built fir ships were not a type to be pursued in peace time. The smaller ships were based on the *Endymion*. The captured *President* was at first ordered to be refitted as a Fifth Rate, but was broken up and replaced by a new ship built on her lines.[3]

In outlining a postwar establishment the Admiralty admitted a weakness in serviceable frigates, and although they considered there were enough Fourth Rates they asked the Navy Board to consider cutting down old 74s, ships dating back to the 1780s. The Navy Board were interested in razeeing them into spar deck frigates, starting with the *Elephant*, in 1816. These ships followed the war time conversion of the *Saturn* in their armament, having no carronades in the waist, unlike the new construction 60-gun ships. The spark deck was not armed, being a separate structure for working the ship and stowing the boats. In *Elephant* the full 60-gun battery was mounted, with guns in the waist. She was the last effective ship of the class and was considered for a rebuild as late as 1830. All were from the old *Arrogant*-class, built 1782–86, but the programme was cut short by the drying up of funds in 1817.[4] The last 60-gun razee, the *Excellent*, ordered in 1820, was not completed, ultimately becoming the first gunnery training ship. The armament proposed for the converted ship reflected current thinking on tactics and combined the heaviest battery of long guns with the most powerful carronades. No frigate-built ship in any service had the hull form and scantling to carry such a weight of metal, or to sustain combat with a vessel of this class.

Excellent 1820

Upper deck	28 32-pounder 56cwt guns
Quarter deck and forecastle	28 42-pounder carronades
	2 12-pounder long guns [5]

No admiral would leave so powerful a ship out of a fleet action, which had generally been the rule hitherto for frigates.

It was accepted that such ships represented a poor use of resources, because of their age, and that better use of funds could be made by building new ships.[6] However, this did not mean new ships of the same power. The Navy Board adopted the 24-pounder 52-gun design, based on the wartime 60s, but built only a limited number alongside numerous classic 44-gun 18-pounder Fifth Rates in the 160-ship frigate Establishment adopted in 1816. The 60-gun 24-pounder *Southampton*-class and *President* were better built than the pitch pine *Forth* and *Leander* but were otherwise unremarkable and could not, by any stretch of the imagination, be called battlefleet units. This policy was followed until 1826. The only modification being the order to end the war-time practice of mounting guns on the gangways, reducing the 24-pounder Fourth Rates to 52 guns.[7]

Guerriere, the razee as a commerce destroyer

In developing a fleet for a commerce warfare strategy the French consciously followed the American lead, adopting the heavy frigate as an ideal type. Alongside the 24-pounder frigate the French adopted the new techniques of frame design then being pioneered by Seppings in England, as reported by Baron Dupin, and even acquired the plans of the latest British heavy frigates. In 1817 the Navy was established with fifty frigates,

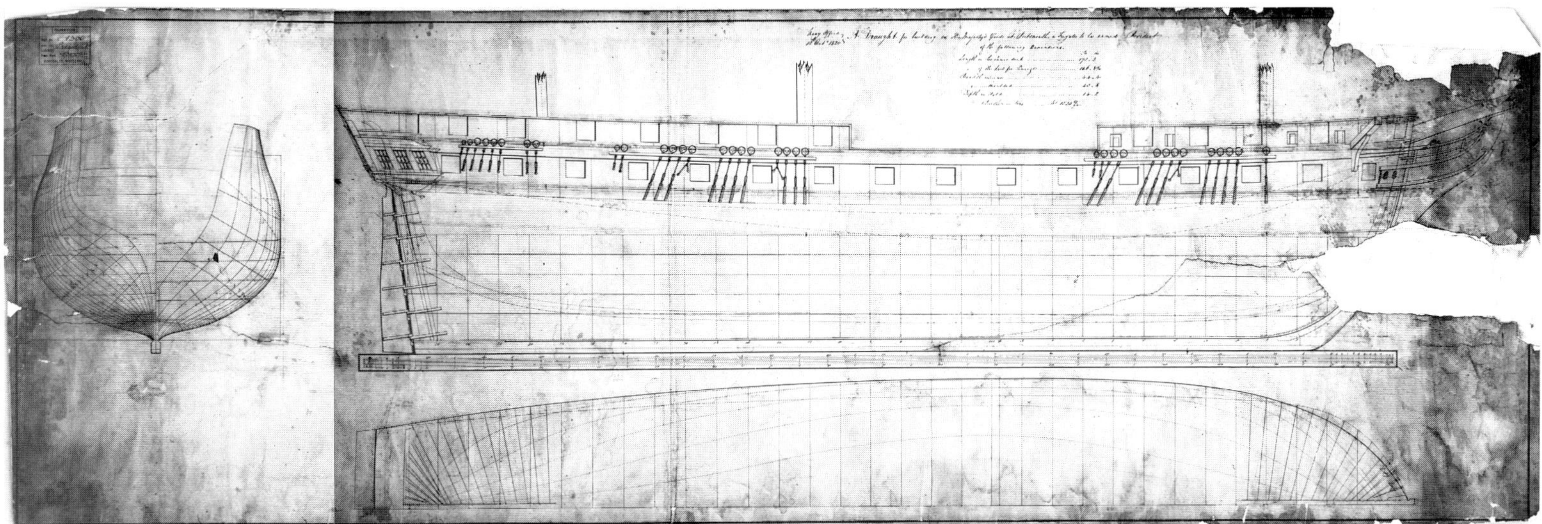

The draught used to build the replacement President, *based on the lines of the American ship taken in 1815. The ship was completed with a modified round stern reflecting the prejudices of Admiral Sir Henry Blackwood. Although a fine ship, the* President *could not carry the armament of a razee and was therefore of no particular value in the post-1826 fleet.* (NMM)

half to be the 24-pounder class, the remainder smaller 18-pounder types. The first 24-pounder ship, *Jeanne d'Arc*, was ruined by the addition of eight guns in the waist, demonstrating the limits of the design. By contrast the razee *Guerriere*, the ex 74 *Romulus*, proved an outstanding seaboat with a main deck battery of 36-pounders. As a result the new 24-pounder frigates were enlarged to carry the armament of *Guerriere* and were supplemented by a new class of 30-pounder ships with the single calibre armament recommended in the report of Baron Tupinier.[8]

The French completed four razees, although only one proved particularly durable, but they embarked on an extensive programme of 30-pounder frigates, ordering eighteen, of which eight had been launched by 1830.[9] This provided a suitable force of raiding ships for at least two squadrons, with the older types being used alongside ships of the line. The last class of 30-pounder frigates were credited with sixty guns, a figure that exercised commentators on British designs for many years. As late as 1855 Sir Howard Douglas was critical of the failure of the Royal Navy to adopt the 60-gun frigate, in contrast to the French. The only distinction lay in the fact that the French retained the armament on the waist gangways, which the Royal Navy had discontinued. This was of no moment in peace time, merely adding weight and strain to already marginal ships. The additional guns could easily be shipped if they were required, but they were difficult to serve efficiently without an addition to the crew, which was highly unlikely in war time. British postwar experience, particularly after the establishment of the *Excellent*, favoured a well spaced battery with full gun crews for rapid, accurate fire. This was of particular significance for the razees, which had a different profile of armament and seagoing performance compared with conventional battleships and frigates. Only in 1848 did the Royal Navy order 60-gun frigates, but these, like the French ships, were only overarmed 50s.

British policy makers were aware of the French challenge, receiving detailed reports from their consuls in the dockyard towns. The razee and the 30-pounder frigate were well known in Britain by the late 1820s, and this was reflected in British planning.[10] One thing is clear; British policy makers in the period before 1830 made no effort to match the French in Fourth Rates because they understood the strategic aims of French construction policy, were confident in the resources at hand, and reckoned the existing fleet contained ships suitable to meet the new threat.

In addition to the French, British planners had to consider other potential adversaries. The United States built up a significant force of heavy Fourth Rates, including one, the *Independence*, which was a razee. However, the United States had a small battlefleet and in the event of war Britain would have battleships to spare for convoy protection. There was no requirement here for Britain to follow the type.

Russia, the other significant naval power, did not build heavy frigates. Russian policy required large battlefleets in the Baltic and the Black Sea to exercise sea control against local powers, Sweden and Turkey, and assist the defence of the Russian territory against a more powerful foe, Britain. There was no programme for cruiser warfare. Poor construction methods, failure to season timber and the shortage of docks, particularly in the Black Sea, forced Russia to build more ships than Britain. The Baltic fleet retained the 74 as its basic unit until the 1850s which was partly in response to the shallow and dangerous navigation. This combination of circumstances militated against the construction of heavy Fourth Rates. The Black Sea ships were similar, but could mount up to 60 guns in view of the superior flotation and more agreeable weather. In both seas these ships were restricted to the role of small battleships by the limited nature of the theatre. Russia did create one razee, the *Alexander Nevsky*, in 1836. While her sailing was reported to be much improved the type was not copied, and the *Nevsky*, like all Russian warships, did not last long. Quite simply the landlocked Baltic and Black Sea did not place any premium on sailing performance, and the Russians tacitly admitted their limited abilities in this area by overgunning all their ships. Under Nicholas I the Russian Navy was configured for battle and transport duties. To meet the danger of an action in confined waters the Royal Navy maintained a large force of 74s right up to the end of the sailing battlefleet. The Advanced Ships of this rate were concentrated at Sheerness and Chatham, ready for the Baltic or the blockade of the Belgian ports.

Barham, the razee as a battlefleet unit

Largely as a reaction to the extensive French naval rearmament programme and influenced by individual ships of the small American fleet, there was implemented a policy to rearm the existing battlefleet of 120- and 84-gun ships with a single calibre armament of 32-pounder guns of varying lengths. Long before that, it was clear to informed observers that the small

The razee Dublin *as a hulk at Plymouth before her demolition in 1885. The stern of the ship was modified to reflect the prejudices of William IV and her first Captain, Lord James Townshend.* (NMM)

74-gun ship with 18-pounders on the main deck had no place in the modern battlefleet. This reflected concern at their weak armament rather than their size for the small ships did not possess the deck strength for heavier guns. All 74-gun ships in the postwar fleet had a 32-pounder lower deck battery. The distinction lay on the main deck. Large 74s employed 24-pounders while smaller ships could only carry 18-pounders. The smaller ships, with a broadside weight of under 1,000lbs, would require a complete rebuild to improve their armament. Those still building at the end of the War were stretched and strengthened to carry 80 guns, including a main deck battery of 24-pounders. The postwar Navy had no interest in the smaller class and none were ordered.

The 1826 policy on armament included a statement that no more repairs were to be carried out on the smaller class, as 74s.[11] In late 1825 Byam Martin made the following suggestion.

> The following ships may be cut down to Frigates and armed with 32 pounder heavy guns on the Gun Decks and light 32 pounders on the Quarter Deck and Forecastle, viz:
>
> *Barham, Ramillies, Cornwall, Vigo, Clarence and America.*
>
> The *Saturn* is cut down so as to have a spar deck without guns; the advantage of which is to shelter the guns, and the men working them from the rigging a spars coming from aloft in action, and leave the men upon the spar deck to work the ship without being interrupted by other employment; but ships so cut down will require more men; they would mount 60 32 pounder long guns and would require a complement of 520 men.
>
> Those cut down as Frigates ought to have 480 men.[12]

This policy was officially proposed in March 1826, although with some different ships which reflected the poor condition of those on Byam Martin's first list.

> We beg to submit for the consideration of the Lords' Commissioners of the Admiralty that HMS *Barham* at Woolwich, *Alfred* at Chatham, and *Dublin* at Plymouth be reduced to frigates. In doing this we propose they shall differ from the 74 gun ships hitherto cut down – viz. by giving them a stern similar to frigates, placing quarter galleries on their present gundecks (which will be their main decks) and by cutting proper scuttles in their orlop, which will serve as lower decks when frigates.
>
> We would also propose that they be armed with 32 pounder long guns on their main decks, and if they be in the service short 32 pounders, we would propose that they should be put on their quarter decks and forecastles, if not we would recommend that they should be armed there with 42 pounder carronades.[13]

The decision to razee the ships into frigates was finally taken in May 1826.[14] During the following year more *Vengeur*-class ships were added to the list, to be converted when 'the other works conveniently allow'. They included *Conquestador* at Sheerness, *Clarence, Rodney* and *Cressy* at Portsmouth and *America* at Plymouth. All five had been omitted from the list of ships in condition for service, and were 'of a class not desireable to be repaired as ships of the line'. One month earlier *Cornwall* had been detailed for conversion on account of her defective topsides.[15]

Paying off ships in need of repair for reduction to razee 50s turned obsolete vessels into powerful cruisers which could be in the battlefleet. The object was to make the best use of otherwise obsolete ships, and the valuable materials they contained, rather than create a force of Fourth Rates similar to that of the French.

Repair was a vital element in the process. All had been rush-built in war-time, and most in merchant yards where the shortage of seasoned timber had promoted early decay. A large repair also provided an opportunity to introduce Seppings's diagonal frame which was needed to preserve the girder strength of the hull, shift the lower deck beams to improve the height of the ports out of the water, and the space on the lower deck, and reinforce the hull with iron where possible. Some professional opinion suggested that the policy of rebuilding the razees was not always necessary, and that a check should be kept on the cost of these open-ended commitments. In addition, a razee and rebuild occupied one of the scarce battleships docks for a long period and could easily cost as much as a new ship.[16] Opening *Barham* tended to support those wary of such large-scale work on old ships.

> Proceeding with your directions to reduce the *Barham* to a frigate we have discovered that dry rot (not however in appearance, of recent formation, the fungi, with some

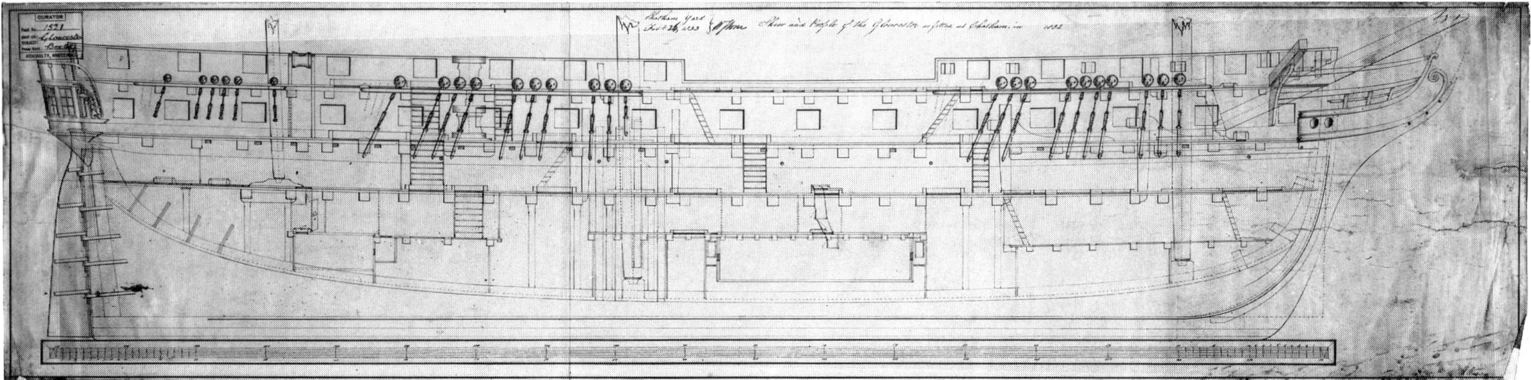

Sheer and profile of the Gloucester, *a 50-gun razee.* (NMM)

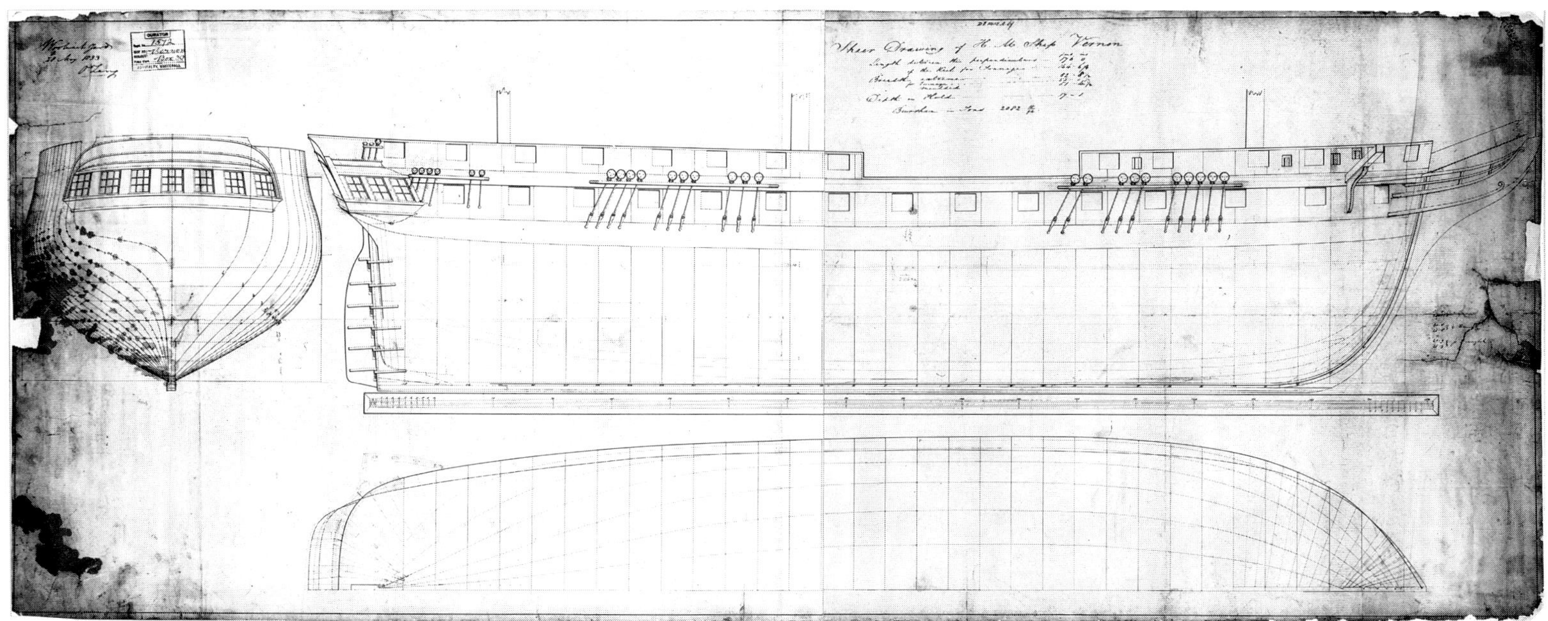

The sheer drawing of the new 50-gun ship Vernon *as built. The lines of this ship were the very antithesis of the earlier razees.* (NMM)

> exceptions being in a dead state) has made such inroads upon the timbers of the frame and inside planking, that to put the ship in a good condition it will be necessary to give her at least a large repair; but from the consideration that the orlop decks, clamps etc, were taken off and replaced, the beams taken out, separated and made good, with a considerable number of new when she was repaired in 1815, and that these parts, as well as the bottom plank, appear sound, we are induced to submit to your Honourable Board, that, instead of entering into so extensive a repair it would be more advantageous to the service to make good the defects of the ships frame in the Hold, by shifting such timbers as absolutely require it, and piecing others, that can be got at without disturbing the gun and orlop decks and their fastenings, the defects in the timbers which run up behind them being few in number and apparently unimportant as we are of opinion she may with such repair be made equal to service at sea for five to seven years.[17]

The Navy Board was reluctant to spend more time and money on this first ship than was absolutely necessary and left the razee with a square stern, despite the Admiralty order of 1817 that all large vessels built or given a large repair should have a round stern.

Despite these unforeseen problems the conversions went ahead, in line with overall policy of the postwar Navy Board, dominated by Byam Martin and Seppings. Melville called for a fleet of 100 battleships and 160 frigates, with smaller classes in proportion. Byam Martin and Seppings wanted to provide this by careful new construction with seasoned timber, but the economic problems of the Government meant that they lacked the slipways, shipwrights and timber to build an all-new fleet. Instead, they elected to repair the best elements of the existing fleet, which was far larger than the new Establishment, but largely obsolete and worn out. New ships were built after the 120-gun *Caledonia* and the 84-gun *Canopus*, while *Blake* and *Impeteux* were the models proposed for any new 74s and *Leander* for Fourth Rates. The existing fleet would gradually be taken into dock, stripped out and reported on. Where the ship merited a rebuild, and her fabric justified the expense, she would be given all the benefit of Seppings's new frame, and new bow and stern. This would prepare her for another decade or two of service. Ships too small for their rate, small three-deckers and 18-pounder 74s, were cut down.

Between 1826 and 1830 nine small 74s were ordered to be cut down; two more were proposed but never taken in hand. Most came from the *Vengeur*, or Surveyor's class, built in merchant shipyards. One ship proposed from this class, *Rodney*, was built in only 11 months and it was hardly surprising that she proved defective. The majority of the ships cut down were from the same class, and had been built in similar haste.

The Navy Board continued to order 44-gun Fifth Rates, and 52-gun 24-pounder Fourth Rates. Melville responded to the 1826 armament crisis by asking if the 52-gun 24-pounder ships on order could be increased to carry 32-pounders, as part of the general up-gunning of the fleet. He did not consider building 32-pounder 50s because he did not see any role for them that would justify new construction, as opposed to razeeing.[18] By the end of the year progress on new battleships lead Byam Martin to propose that *Cornwall, Rodney, Vigo, Clarence, America, Conquestador* and the old spar-deck 58 *Elephant* be converted into troopships when six new 120s were completed. Further razees, *Vindictive* and *Eagle*, were ordered in 1829, following recommendations by the Navy Board after they had been docked for examination.[19] As with *Barham*, opening these ships revealed more problems. It had been thought that *Vindictive* would prove a cheap rebuild, even with a new stern but once she had been thoroughly inspected the Master Shipwright at Portsmouth reported that it would be necessary to shift one fifth of the frame, and two thirds of the beams, along with almost all the other fabric of the ship. Consequently, the estimated cost rose from £16,000 to £25,000. The Duke of Clarence, during his brief administration as Lord High Admiral, requested a statement of the costs of a razee. Woolwich provided details of the *Barham*.

Timber and Materials	£19,973
Workmanship	£8,734
	£28,707
Estimate for repairing and coppering the ship as a 74	£16,580
Cost of conversion into a frigate	£12,127

Sending in their report the Navy Board informed the Duke

'that we are of opinion that a new frigate of that class may be built for about £45,000'.[20]

Whatever the reason for the Duke's interest, no ship of the razee specification was designed or ordered. The Navy Board took the classic approach to the frigate-battleship distinction: ships were either fit or not fit to lay in the line. Frigates were not to be so powerful as to blur this distinction. The Lord High Admiral's real interest was made manifest by orders to increase the armament of battleships and the order for a pair of improved Fifth Rates, *Castor* and *Ambuscade*:

Main deck	22 32-pounder 55cwt
Quarter deck and forecastle	14 18-pounder long guns

This new, heavier, armament was 'better calculated for a distant fire than the 32-pounder carronades', and therefore better suited to modern conditions. To mount this improved battery the new frigates were to be 1ft broader than the existing 44-gun Fifth Rates, although otherwise of identical form.[21] At the same time Byam Martin argued that the 24-pounder 52s should be considered Fifth Rates and those building to be altered to carry a new armament similar to *Ambuscade*.[22] This armament was altered for the *Castor* and the incomplete *Amphion* in 1831, the Navy Board proposing twelve 32-pounder 25cwt carronades and two 32-pounder 47cwt long guns on the upper deck. In an effort to retain uniformity the long guns were then replaced by another pair of carronades.[23] This was not an attempt to make frigates into potential battlefleet units, but merely to improve their power for cruising duties, responding to trends in France and America. Had Clarence intended to follow the French example of 60-gun Fourth Rates he would have ordered new ships far larger than the *Castor*. The 36-gun ships of the next decade continued this approach, being cruisers with no pretensions to a battlefleet role.

Among the critics of the postwar Admiralty, Captain Charles Napier was the most vocal and, ultimately, the most successful. He argued that the 32-pounder 50-gun ships had rendered small two-deckers, including 18-pounder 74s, obsolete. Frigates, with their crews berthed on the lower deck, were always ready for action and able to use their guns when a 74 would be forced to close her lower deck ports. In the event of war he considered that a 50-gun frigate in the Mediterranean would be the prize command. Yet such opinions did not predispose him to favour the razees. Noting the sad experiences with the razee 64s of the Revolutionary Wars, which were infamous for their rolling, and observing measures taken to improve stowage, he concluded that shifting the deck beams would increase costs and render the whole process of doubtful utility.[24] As with so much of Napier's commentary there was much sound good sense, but also a degree of blindness that deprived his criticism of real weight. Lacking war-time experience of battlefleet action he tended to underrate the value of battleships.

The end of the Navy Board

The new Board of Admiralty that took office under Sir James Graham in November 1830 dissolved the Navy Board, and with it the restrictions that had governed British ship design for two centuries. However, the economic policy of the Whig Government made reductions essential, and this dominated naval policy. When first in office Graham, with no clear ideas on warship design, favoured razees as an economical method of making modern warships out of the obsolescent 74- and 44-gun ships. Within two months of taking office he ordered the work on four razees to be expedited.[25]

A closer understanding of the political pressures for a change in policy, garnered from Earl Grey, correspondence with the Duke of Portland and the outstanding sailing of Portland's brig *Pantaloon*, designed by Symonds, convinced him that new designs, and a new designer, were needed.[26] Consequently, Graham's Board ordered only one razee, the *Gloucester*, in February 1831, 14 months before Symonds took office as Surveyor of the Navy. In addition, she had already received a large repair making the conversion relatively cheap and quick. The latter was important because Symonds soon stopped work on ships from his predecessor's regime, particularly razees. Graham had intended to carry out more razees, naming three ships, but none were completed. *Hercules*, a late dockyard-built ship was estimated to cost £17,500, nearly one third of the cost of a new 74, while the teak *Wellesley*, was noted for her poor sailing.[27] Orders were sent to razee the *Belleisle* at Pembroke, where she had been built, and use the surplus

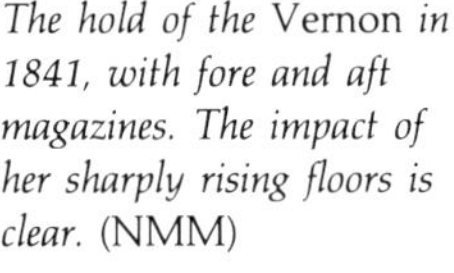

The hold of the Vernon *in 1841, with fore and aft magazines. The impact of her sharply rising floors is clear.* (NMM)

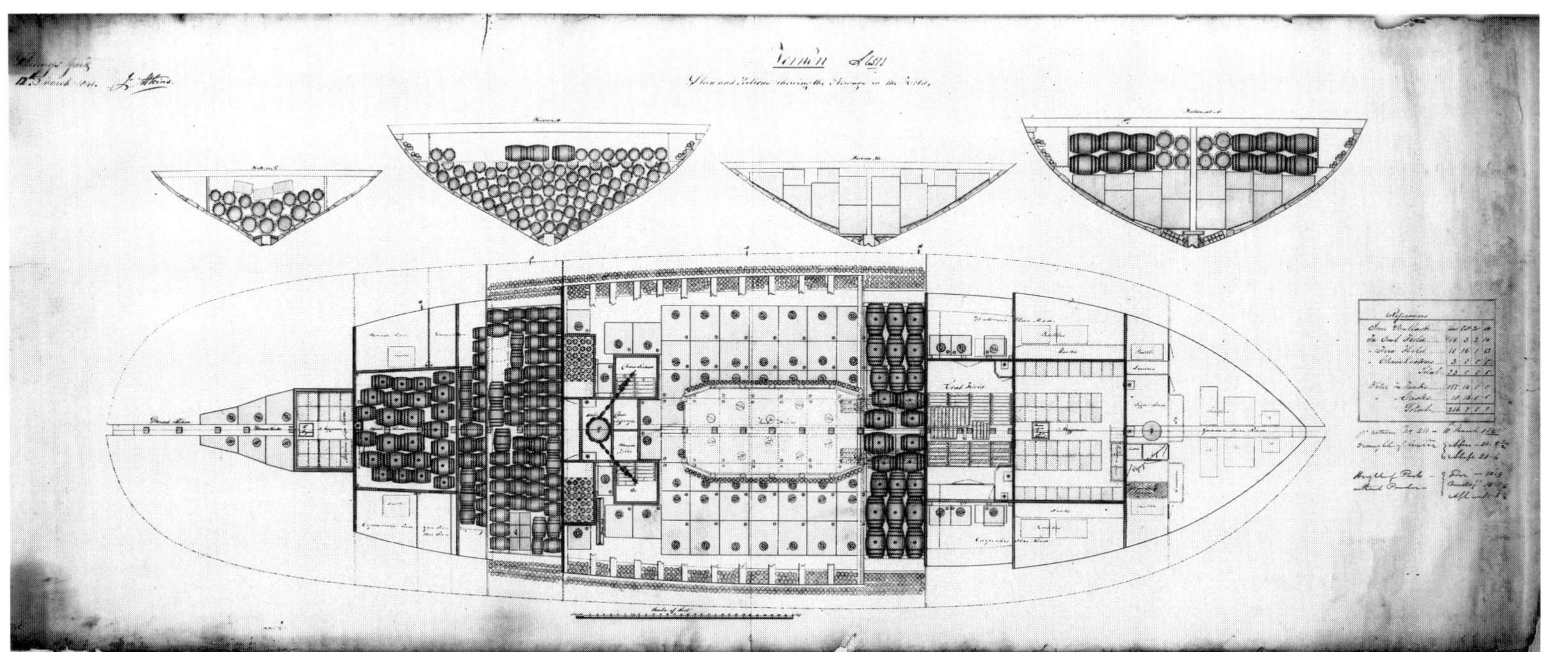

The Leander *in 1855, carrying Commissioners to the United States, hence the Stars and Stripes at the fore. She was a well built ship, but not in the same class as Symonds's* Arethusa. *Her appearance is typical of the last generation of sailing Fourth Rates.* (NMM)

materials for a pair of 16-gun brigs. Pembroke, a construction centre without the full range of skilled labour of the major dockyards, had never rebuilt a major vessel.[28] Having been navigated round to Pembroke and thoroughly examined Symonds persuaded the Admiralty to repair the ship as a 74 and so she was towed back to Plymouth and the conversion abandoned. *Belleisle* ended her days as a hospital and troopship in the Baltic campaigns of 1854–55.[29]

Graham made much of the failure of the Navy Board to keep pace with France in the construction of Fourth Rates, and this is normally cited as evidence of his support for the class which was considered to have been based on the opinions of Sir Thomas Hardy.[30] In reality, Graham used the figures as part of a calculated attack on the Navy Board. The King, William IV, could be relied upon to overreact to suggestions of naval inadequacy and that Graham and Grey were deliberately trying to win support for the dismissal of Byam Martin, a royal favourite, as the key element in securing the abolition of the Navy Board. Martin refuted Graham's attacks, pointing out that the Admiralty ban on the construction of the new Second Rates prevented any more 74s being razeed. In desperation, he proposed modifying the 44s now building to carry a heavier armament although he had little time for such modified ships, having urged Melville only to class frigates as Fourth Rates if they were equal to *Barham*'s armament.[31] The Admiralty cancelled numerous 44s and 52s that had not reached an advanced stage of construction, rejecting the Navy Board's half-hearted submission that the 44s be modified to carry 50 guns. Graham had no interest in large frigates not strong enough for the razee armament, and would not order a wasteful conversion of existing timber.[32] This was a sound policy for the scantling of expanded 44s would not have been equal to the increased weights, let alone sustained hard service. Existing frames were reordered in a more appropriate form, as modern 36-gun ships.[33]

In 1831 Graham ordered a new ship, the *Vernon*, to the *Barham* specification. She was an experimental vessel, intended to demonstrate the soundness of Symonds's hull form in a large ship after the successful trials with 16-gun brigs in 1831.[34] The ship was launched within 11 months of being ordered which represented an unprecedented rate of construction in peace time for a vessel of her size, particularly as no timber had been prepared before laying down. As a result, *Vernon* proved defective and was twice subjected to the degree of rebuilding similar to that required for the war-built 74s. This made her by far the most expensive major warship of the postwar sailing Navy. Such rapid construction was not repeated. The Admiralty acted in haste anticipating a political controversy would follow Symonds appointment and wanted to use *Vernon* to defend the appointment and the entire Admiralty reform of 1832. Graham decided to superannuate Seppings and appoint Symonds in December 1831, but only made this public in April 1832, when the Navy Board was abolished.[35] In securing estimates of the cost of *Vernon*, named after another of Symonds's patrons, the Admiralty had asked for figures which covered an unlimited period of construction, and also for rushed completion in six months. One Master Shipwright, the Whig William Edye, sent in a low estimate, but added plaintively; 'P.S. I hope you will not name me, Sir, as being the author of this estimate, lest it should prove injurious to my interests with the Navy Board.' He also observed, 'she will be a ship of immense tonnage (2,017 20/94) for a Frigate.'[36] The 50-gun heavy frigate was an ideal trials vehicle, less costly than a battleship, yet of similar size and form, and more quickly built. In the 1840s the Admiralty ordered a series of new 50s to experiment with alternative hull forms.[37]

Symonds and the razee

The lack of interest of the new Admiralty, and in particular of the new Surveyor, in intermediate types was clear. No more Fourth Rates were ordered after *Vernon*, and no more razees. Initially, the stretched 74 *Boscawen*, begun in 1812, was reordered as the 50-gun *Indefatigable*, using *Vernon*'s moulds. Symonds, with the blessing of Sir Thomas Hardy, generally credited as a supporter of the Fourth Rate, secured her reordering as a 70-gun ship of his own design.[38] Both Hardy and Symonds appreciated that the best use for the well-seasoned timbers of the long-delayed 74, and any more of the same scantling, was to build a small battleship. Symonds's first 70-gun ship, the *Cumberland*, ordered in 1833, was accorded the ultimate accolade, bearing a bust of the First Lord, the member for Cumberland, as her figurehead. The existing timbers of *Boscawen*, of the scantling of the *Vengeur*-class, were ideal for the conversion, although the detailed carpentry required to metamorphose the 'U' profile frame into the new 'V' form was complex. The result was a ship with outstanding sailing qualities, and a more powerful battery than *Vernon*, or any French or American design.[39]

The convoluted design history of the *Boscawen* established the unifying element in naval strategy and design policy in the postwar period: an appreciation of the primacy of the battlefleet as the ultimate arbiter of seapower. Symonds, like Byam Martin before him, made the distinction between line and non-line units. He understood that Britain could not afford the luxury of building Fourth Rates for commerce protection, because small- or medium-sized two-deckers were a more powerful and a more flexible investment, given the responsive needs of British strategy. He was also well aware of the political imperatives that limited naval finance. In this climate he had no hesitation in abandoning the Fourth Rate and concentrating on battle line units.

Symonds was entirely opposed to the conversion of old ships, which he considered a waste of timber and labour, an opinion which was supported by John Edye.[40] Among his first acts on taking office was to cancel the razeeing of the old three decker *Union*, then in dock at Plymouth. Although ordered to be taken to pieces and the materials employed in a new 78 of Symonds's *Vanguard*-class, the ship was quickly dismantled and her fabric simply disappeared.[41] Symonds's opinion was well known. Rear Admiral Sir Charles Paget called on him to use his influence to have the Surveyor's class 74s broken up or sold; 'The only way, and that I believe *you* don't patronise, is to make *Barhams* of the best of them.'[42]

The training ship Implacable *lying at Falmouth, displaying her original French stern.* (CMP)

Later, Symonds fought a long battle with the First Lord, Lord Minto, the two senior Naval Lords, Admiral Sir Charles Adam and Admiral Sir William Parker and the Political Secretary, Charles Wood, to prevent the conversion of *Warspite*. Ultimately, this was forced on him, which marked a return to the Navy Board policy of razeeing 74s as new two-deckers became available.[43] With the Government in constant economic difficulties the Minto Board could not resist the politically attractive alternative to new construction. Minto's memorandum on leaving office stated that no new Fourth Rates should be built, razees being prepared from the 74s that he advised should not be repaired as battleships.[44] Like Graham, Minto suggested razeeing the teak 74s once the battlefleet reached adequate numbers.[45] He had not done this while in office, because there were not enough battleships and because he had in Symonds a most persuasive opponent of such a step. Indeed, the teak 74s were a very valuable resource, and as they never required a large repair there was no reason to open them up for a rebuild. They gave excellent service in the Far East, and their volume of fire was decisive in reducing Chinese forts during the First Opium War. In addition, they remained on the list as battleships, and in a period of armed diplomacy appearances were often more important than reality.

The Duke of Portland, Symonds's long-term patron and an authority on naval architecture, shared his objections to the policy. He observed that a bad 74 might in some cases be more useful than a good 50, as was the case in all situations short of a major naval war, and that the cost of the most expensive razee, *Dublin*, (£32,000), should discourage any further razees of three- and two-decked ships. Another opinionated individual with powerful support, Captain Lord John Hay, brother of the Marquess of Tweeddale, shared both Portland's objection to razeeing and his solution of disarming the upper deck. Both observed that retaining the upper deck, or as a desperate measure, cutting off the poop, would provide protection for the gun crews of the old main deck battery. Hay observed;

> Possibly the Razee might have some trifling advantage in sailing, but certainly not enough to compensate for the difference of expence.

This was of little moment because he had first-hand experience to support the widely held belief that contemporary French warships were inferior performers under canvas.[46] Furthermore, the improvement was not universal: *Warspite* was an outstanding ship, both as a 74 and as a razee, while *Dublin* was a mediocrity in either configuration.

To save on manpower, small 74s were occasionally sent abroad with frigate complements and a battery of guns stowed in the hold. Another development of the 1830s, the extension of the uniform 32-pounder armament to the 74, increased the combat value of the old ships, even if only at close range.

The new Board that took office in October 1841 gradually shifted toward increased new construction, which was almost inevitable given the increasing age of the 74s. Yet Lord Haddington's Board considered further razees, ordering Portsmouth and Chatham to propose suitable 74s. Cockburn wanted to use the simple conversion accorded the old *Indefatigable*, Pellew's frigate, which had been a 64. This involved leaving

The Vernon *at the turn of the century. From right to left the ships are: the* Vernon, Marlborough, Warrior *and* Donegal. *The contrast between the two frigates is merely one of size.* (IWM)

the original transom and merely cutting down the battleship stern to make a quarter deck cabin.[47] *Hogue* was reported to be the best ship in the Chatham Ordinary for razeeing, and could be converted for £5,822. The incomplete teak 74 *Carnatic* at Portsmouth was also considered suitable, and would cost £15,000 for the full conversion applied to *Warspite*, or £12,000 for the limited *Indefatigable* rebuild.[48] *Devonshire* was selected from the Chatham Ordinary.[49] *Wellington* and *Benbow* were also told off for razeeing in 1845.[50] No progress was made on any of these ships. *Devonshire* was cancelled in early 1847, although still named for conversion by the 1847–48 Committee.[51] Finally, the *Grampus*, ex *Tremendous*, was converted as an attack on Symonds by Cockburn's Board, at the behest of their favourite, Oliver Lang. Having been ordered to Deptford to be broken up, she was reprieved at Lang's suggestion and sent to Woolwich.[52] Because the point of the of the process was entirely financial, severe constraints were placed on the cost of the conversion. The end result was an inferior, roughly-finished ship with poor accommodation for the crew and bad ventilation.[53]

The end of this last wave of enthusiasm for razees came when the Admiralty decided to install small engines in four 74s to adapt them into coast defence blockships. The initial plan was for mobile batteries, but rising expectations of the screw propeller encouraged the substitution of more effective ships, and, as the project progressed, increased interest in their seagoing performance. The ships finally converted, *Hogue*, *Blenheim*, *Ajax* and *Edinburgh*, had all been rebuilt after the War, making them ideal for razeeing, or for conversion to steam. All four served through the Russian War, although they were by then 40 years afloat, merchant-built and had been subjected to the heat, vibration and damp of early steam engines.[54]

The 50-gun Fourth Rate in the British service

Unlike the American and French Navies, the Royal Navy never shifted to an offensive *guerre de course* strategy. Therefore, although termed frigates, the 32-pounder 50s were seen as interchangeable with battlefleet units, and normally deployed as such. As they used the same timber and slipways as line of battle ships they were considered a bad bargain in periods of restricted new construction, notably between 1832 and the alarms of 1840, when Russia, rather than France, was the main concern. This explains why none were built, and only one converted. By contrast, the new 36-gun frigate of the *Pique*-class replaced the old 44 as an ideal ship to build alongside a battleship, using undersized timber from the larger vessel, and a smaller slipway.

New 50-gun ships were ordered after 1841 in large numbers, including one, *Constance*, reordered from a 36 for which no timber had been provided. The first new 50, *Raleigh*, ordered in late 1842, was designed by Master Shipwright John Fincham, a leading member of the old School of Naval Architecture and one of Symonds's critics, though the ship demonstrated the influence of the latter's principles.[55]

Tactical thought and the razee 50

With British strategy committed to the battlefleet, powerful units like the razee were brought into the fleet. The lesson of Sir Richard Strachan's action in November 1805, when his frigates helped to slow Dumanoir's flying ships, joined the action by doubling on the French ships and then continued the pursuit when some of the battle line dropped astern, demonstrated a degree of tactical flexibility that postwar commanders would have been anxious to adopt.[56]

Improved performance under sail was a factor in determining the final shape of the 1826 razees. The earlier spar-deck 58s had not been greatly improved by their reduction from full 74s. Removing another deck would cut the windage of the two-decker, improve her stability and enable her to retain a heavy rig. As a result, the razees retained the 74-gun ship masts and carried every extra inch of canvas that could be spread. This 'overmasting' arose from two, linked, developments in naval thought. First, the only specific role for the razee in a fleet action was to catch and hold a flying enemy and second, the peace-time Navy was obsessed with fine weather speed. The appointment of Symonds and the trials of sailing that were such a feature of the period were only the most public aspects of this misunderstood facet of naval life. This common tendency during long periods of peace for naval officers to turn their attention to the non-military aspects of their profession provided the most serious subject of debate, and a sure road to professional advancement for the best seamen. The early career of Admiral Sir Baldwin Walker, Surveyor of the Navy 1847–61, provides an oustanding example for his seamanship secured the favour of Symonds and Whig politicians. The same stress upon performance under sail was manifest in the growing number of captains who considered a Fourth Rate to be the ideal warship.

By her conversion *Barham* was transformed from a dull sailing 74 into an outstanding frigate and in the trials with *Vernon* she was generally accepted to have had the better of her purpose-built rival. Improved stowage and trim, with more practised shiphandling help to explain this. In addition, the razees, like Symonds's ships, had more displacement to carry their weights, which improved fine weather performance. At the same time older officers were less enthusiastic. Admiral Sir Henry Hotham reported *Alfred* unsafe with her rig, even in the Mediterranean, and he had her lower masts reduced at the heel in the Malta Dockyard.[57]

Razees were an economical peace-time substitute for battleships in the main fleet, for they carried a crew of 475 against at least 650 for a small 74. They were also a flexible element of the fleet and could be used to swell numbers when placating a King worried about British strength in the Mediterranean; 'the *Barham* and *Alfred*, which are equal to 74s', could just as easily be described as mere frigates when dealing with sensitive foreign powers.[58] Sending the same information to the Prime Minister, Graham was careful to say that the razees were 'almost equal to a 74'.[59] Most others were content to call them powerful ships and mention them in a separate category, as 50-gun ships somewhere between the line of battle and frigates.[60] This category did not include the 24-pounder 50s, which were never considered equal to service in the line of battle.

However, in the last resort men of experience still reckoned the loss of the extra deck a serious reduction of battle power because they were convinced future action would be decided at close range by commanding fire from the higher deck. It is worthy of note that only *Vernon* was fitted out during the war scare of 1840 for while Britain's predominant concern lay in battlefleet strength, the razee was a luxury unit, to be prepared after the modern battleships – the 120s, 92s, and the 84s – were manned, although before their 74-gun half sisters. *Eagle, Gloucester, America, Vindictive, Warspite, Cornwall* and *Conquestador* were all brought forward though not fitted.[61]

Razees were to join the battlefleet only after the First and Second Rate battleships; the 24-pounder 50s were destined for commerce protection; and the smaller frigates for fleet scouting and cruising. Several of the razees brought forward in 1840 were fitted out in 1841, in lieu of a battleship, for the distant stations and the Mediterranean, and represented an economy measure. The success of these powerful ships may have influenced the Cockburn Board to press for further razees. In 1834 Graham reckoned that the Fourth Rates were 'a class on which great reliance must be placed in a future naval war' and told Byam Martin they were vital for commerce protection.[62]

The razees used a midships magazine because they rode higher in the water than they had as 74s, leaving the forward magazine crown, which was intended to be well below the waterline, dangerously near the waterline. Lowering the crown made the magazine too small to be useful and so it was moved amidships, with occasional space in the bread room which had been the after magazine. Stowage in the razees was always cramped and in an effort at improvement those ships that needed to have their orlop deck beams shifted had them replaced with new timber of reduced scantling. In converting these ships the Navy Board attempted to keep them uniform, particularly as regards their internal arrangements, and waited on experience with *Barham* before deciding how far modifications such as the midship magazines could be taken.[63]

In line with the experience of Sir Richard Strachan's action in November 1805, the deployment patterns and gunnery developments of the postwar period, the battle role of the razee was for it to hold a flying enemy, and engage at a long range where the 32-pounder battery would be most effective. It was not to close to the decisive range, under 1,000 yards, until the battleships were engaged. Razees could then complete the destruction of damaged ships, secure prizes and, most significantly, double on units already engaged. However, they were definitely not equal to a close action with a two-decker. Naval opinion from 1815 to 1860 agreed that an extra deck, even with an inferior armament, would be decisive at close quarters, given the commanding position from which to fire down onto the decks of the enemy. In addition, the single covered gun deck meant that almost half the ship's armament, the faster firing short guns, was seriously exposed. By contrast, the covered gun and main decks of a battleship were rarely affected by gunfire. *Victory* had no fatalities on her main deck at Trafalgar.

Rather than building or converting 50-gun ships, Symonds built battleships with similar sailing qualities, for the same strategic and tactical functions. He saw the small two-decker as a true battlefleet unit, and therefore more than a match for any frigate, which could be constructed from timber of the same scantling. They were also more economical (*Vernon* cost £48,000, against only £45,000 for the *Cumberland*). His contemporaries would not have considered a combat between *Boscawen* and *Vernon* equal, therefore his two 70-gun ships should be seen, not as weak anomalies, but as commerce protection battleships. The two ships alternated as flagship on the North America and West Indies Station, where the American cruisers offered them a clear war-time role, but in 1854 both joined the main battlefleet for the Russian War. Symonds supported the old distinction between line and non-line units, favouring the 36-gun *Pique* type as the true frigate and securing the re-ordering of *Boscawen* as a 70. This was the correct interpretation of British experience, one that has been confirmed by the repeated growth of powerful cruiser types, all of which have ended up being absorbed into the line of battle. In the War of 1812 the powerful American cruisers were, after the unpleasant surprises of 1812, countered by British 74s, or by small squadrons of Fifth Rates. With commerce protection strategy based on convoys the use of small battleships or frigate squadrons was logical and in line with a battlefleet strategy. In these circumstances the 50-gun frigate made a welcome addition to the battlefleet with a specific role, or served on distant stations leading commerce protection squadrons. However, they were not of sufficient value to justify their cost because Britain did not adopt a *guerre de course* strategy.

The heavy frigate was an anomalous design, created for the role of commerce destroyer in the national strategies of the United States and France. It was adopted by the Royal Navy in a limited way, not because foreign designs appeared to possess any real advantages over the 18-pounder type for cruiser duties, but to make use of existing battleships which were no longer adequate for the battlefleet role. Even so, the razee 50s were soon integrated into the British battlefleet. The true answer to the heavy frigate was, as Symonds understood, not another ship of the same class, but a battleship. British strategists had always used battle line units to escort high value convoys through areas where powerful raiders could be anticipated. Well escorted convoys were the antidote to the type. However, the picture is complicated by the razee. The small 74 was obsolete as a battlefleet unit after 1815, although ideal for convoy protection. By razeeing these ships they became powerful and modern ships with battlefleet potential and outstanding sailing qualities. The Navy Board, a much-maligned body with sound, if unspectacular, views on warship design, was content to improve the armament of existing frigate classes, and to razee the small 74s. They were not interested in larger ships, sharing the widespread belief that a ship of *Barham* or *Vernon* type was a waste of timber and slip time which could be better devoted to a battleship. The heavy frigate remained a perennial chimera of the nineteenth century.

Time and again it failed to answer the fundamental question of how a defensive seapower could guarantee control of vital sea areas if not by battlefleet strength. The most spectacular demonstration of this folly came at the Battle of Jutland, but similar results would have been occasioned by throwing the razees into a fleet action in 1840. Once closely engaged by an enemy vessel with more protected guns they would have been quickly silenced or driven out of action. At best, such types were a useful supplement for the battlefleet, but they were no substitute for modern battleships and certainly too expensive for the frigate duties of a Navy with worldwide commitments.

During the Russian War the Black Sea Fleet included two new 50-gun frigates, *Arethusa* and *Leander*. Both were condemned to subordinate roles, carrying stores for the battlefleet and serving as station ships out of the war zone. *Arethusa* was heavily damaged bombarding Sevastopol on 17 October 1854 and went home. *Leander* stayed on as the depot/flagship in Balaklava Harbour. Having several steamers and no opposition at sea Admiral Dundas realised that these two ships were of no real value. Skilful handling during the bombardment of Odessa only demonstrated that, despite her heavy armament and outstanding sailing, *Arethusa* had no role in a British fleet. In the Baltic three heavy steam frigates were employed, acting as the van of the fleet, pushing up into the Gulf of Finland, and keeping station late into the autumn. However, it became clear that these functions could equally well be conducted by smaller screw steamers. Once again the war should have illustrated the futility of the heavy frigate but instead the French, American and Russian construction of such ships persuaded the Admiralty to follow suit, which led to the creation of a large fleet of 50-gun ships with a very limited role in British strategy. Alongside this standard type the Admiralty was lured into the cult of gigantism by the American *Merrimack*-class. The resulting *Mersey* and *Orlando*, among the largest wooden ships ever built, were structurally weak, but they provided the hull form and conception for *Warrior*, which was in essence an armoured frigate.[64]

5 *The 90-Gun Ship*

The first ships designed *ab initio* for the 1826 armament were the 90-gun *Nile*-class. Postwar pressure for larger two-decked ships did not end with the *Canopus* type 84s. By 1820 both the French and the Americans were moving toward large two-deckers armed with up to one hundred guns. In both cases the new designs reflected an alternative strategy, not an attempt to secure sea control in battle.

American experience in the War of 1812 appeared to confirm the wisdom of building for a significant degree of superiority over foreign ships of ostensibly the same rate. Their first battleships had been rated as 74s, although they were pierced for over 90 guns, and often carried 102 guns. Though of similar dimensions to the *Canopus* these ships had a particularly full form and could support a weight of arming that would have ruined European vessels, if only for a short period. The USS *Ohio* laid down in 1817 and launched in 1820 was the outstanding example. Initially armed with a full battery of 32-pounders she was later fitted with long 42-pounders on the gun deck and carronades of the same calibre on the spar deck. As such her broadside was 200 pounds heavier than that of the largest British three-deckers in 1826.[1] The weight of arming given to the *Ohio* and her sisters supports the contention that their war-time role against Britain was to break the blockade of American ports. This would allow cruisers and privateers to reach the open seas, and the return of the occasional merchant ship. That such factors came to dominate American design was a back-handed tribute to the success of the British blockade in 1812–15.

The French arrived at the heavy two-decker by a rather more circuitous route. Having moved to 60-gun 24-pounder frigates in 1819 they discovered that the standard 74, with an 18-pounder upper deck, was no longer capable of meeting the

The last survivor of the post-1815 battlefleet, the 90-gun Nile, *anchored in the Mersey in 1937 as the training ship* Conway. (CMP)

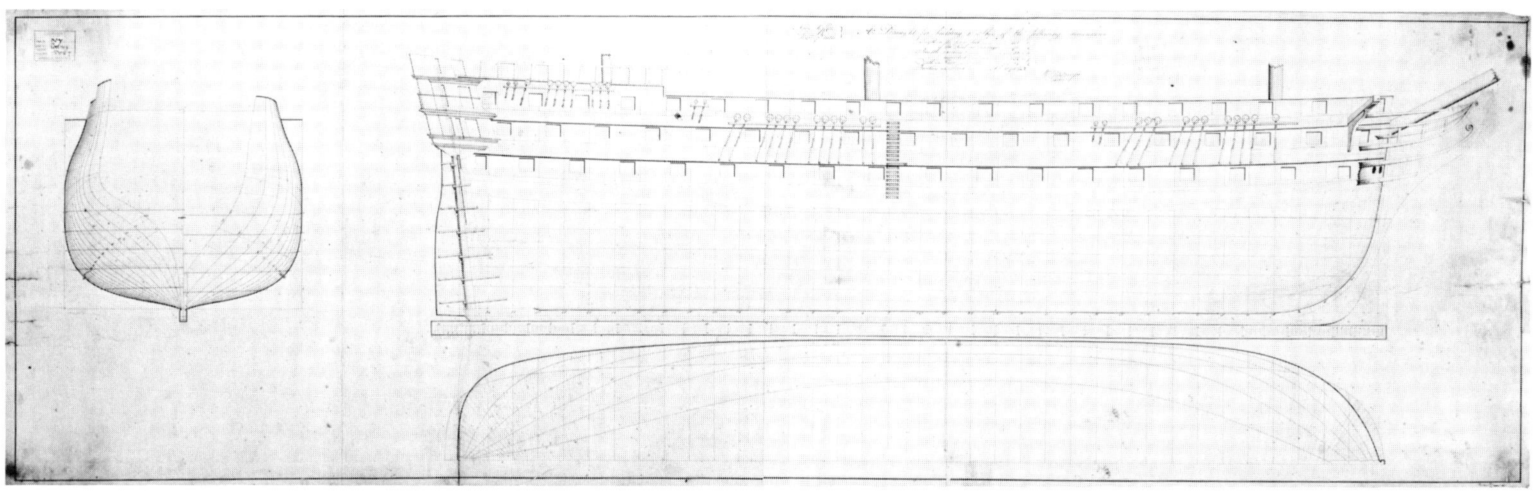

Draught of a 100-gun flush deck two-decked ship, dated November 1826. The Nile*-class were originally conceived as a response to French ships mounting 100 guns, but the views of Byam Martin ensured that they were completed with open gangways. Despite the apparent loss of firepower they were still far superior to the French ships, being larger, stronger and carrying more long guns. Seppings alone signed the draught.* (NMM)

frigate in heavy weather. Equipping the two-deckers with 24-pounders and a full spar deck of 36-pounder carronades made them into 94-gun ships, although they were only 6in broader than the old 74s. With new 30-pounder guns the full warrant of 94 guns could be carried. In 1822 the new programme introduced by Baron Tupinier replaced the 74 hull as the standard battleship with that of the 80, another design by Sane, the most famous of which was HMS *Canopus* (formerly the French *Franklin*). These ships were rated as 90s, although less strongly built than their British cousins, and this figure had an undue influence on British policy. In addition, a new 100-gun two-decker was designed by the simple expedient of razeeing the existing design for the 118-gun three-decker. The success of the razee 74 *Guerriere* as a heavy frigate persuaded the French to employ the same method for the heavy two-decker. The new class were to mount 30-pounders throughout, when enough new guns had been provided. Fifteen of the new class were laid down between 1823 and 1833 though only one was launched before 1840. The French preferred to keep their ships on the ways until required, and use up the remaining ships of the First Empire.[2]

It should be stressed that the French programme was the main spring of the British decision to build a class of heavy two-deckers. The politicians were alarmed by the heavy broadside of the *Ohio*, but Byam Martin reassured them that as a two-decker she was still inferior in combat terms to the *Caledonia*. He also stressed that the American ship was unlikely to carry such a heavy armament for long. He realised that her role was not that of a cruising man of war:

> the whole scantling of the timber is greater than in our service, and in fact everything is done with a view to the essential matter of strength in battle and not having distant colonies, or anything in the nature their warfare likely to require any perseverance at sea, they feel no inconvenience from their enormous weight of arming, but employed as the British Fleet were last war, when many ships were at sea eleven months out of the twelve, the American Ships would tear themselves to pieces – they are not calculated for a long continuous sea service.

Because of the earlier alarm at the armament of the new French ships he could take comfort in the fact that three ships of similar force, but 'constructed on a better principle' were on order. Barralier, Master Shipwright at Toulon, advised Byam Martin of the French shift to spar deck 100-gun ships. Later in the year he provided more details of the *Royal Charles* (renamed *le Jemappes* in 1830). She mounted sixty-four long 30-pounders, and thirty-six carronades.

	Royal Charles	*Nile*
Length	205ft 0 1/2in	205ft 6in
Moulded breadth	53ft 1 3/4in	52ft 9in
Depth in hold	27ft 0	23ft 2in
		2,598

[3]

After the second report the new design was sealed. The *Nile*, *London* and *Rodney* initially followed the French and American practice of mounting a full spar-deck battery of one hundred 32-pounders, exclusive of the bow and stern ports. These would have been the first flush decked British battleships and Melville was sufficiently impressed to order three, suggesting that 'several of that description' should be provided.[4] The ships were laid down in early 1827, using the two timber frame system. Although Byam Martin had made a particular effort to keep their details secret news soon leaked out, for which he blamed Chatham. Throughout the year the class had priority over all other work.

The *Nile* design, which is normally considered to have been Seppings's masterpiece, was in essence little more than a razee *Caledonia*.[5] This reflected the Surveyor's lack of ambition in the area of hull form, and his attention to architectural strength. The basic lesson of the 1826 armament scare was that most wartime designs would only retain their good qualities with a modern battery if reduced by one deck. This process exploited Seppings's improved structure and avoided any risk of the vessel failing as a sea boat when the pressing need was to begin work on several new heavy ships.

By 1827 Byam Martin was beginning to speak of them as 'capable of receiving guns on the spar deck', and clearly preferred a more conventional design deleting the twelve-gun waist battery and fitting the normal poop. This alteration was affected in 1828.[6] The Controller did not have a very high opinion of the new class, believing that the improved *Calcutta* would be a more suitable two-decker, and if ships were to be built to *Caledonia*'s scantling they should carry the extra deck for battle power. In January 1830 he called for five more three-deckers, but there were only to be the three Second Rates of the *Nile*-class already commenced. These would increase their battle power by mounting 50cwt 68-pounder shell guns on the quarter deck and forecastle. Their other distinguishing feature were the 63cwt 32-pounders on the gun deck.[7]

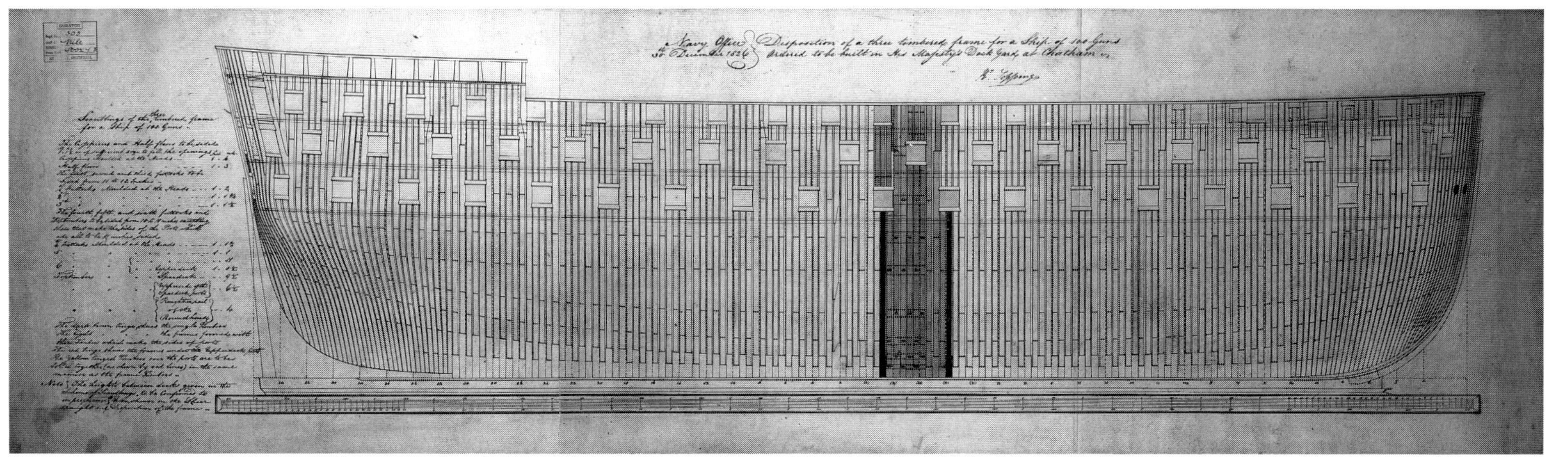

Timbering plant for the 100-gun ships, on the three timber system. Because these ships were of a novel class, the scantling had to be set out in detail on the plan. (NMM)

The Graham Board accepted the new warrant and concurred in building no more 92-gun ships.

Armament of the Nile

Gun deck	32	32pdr	63cwt
	2	68pdr	50cwt
Main deck	32	32pdr	55cwt
	2	68pdr	50cwt
Quarter deck			
& Forecastle	24	32pdr	49cwt
Poop	4	12pdr	carronades

[8]

Byam Martin expressed a preference for the new 64cwt 42-pounder in these ships, but his influence on policy had been tenuous since early 1831 and he was ignored.[9]

The only ship of this class to be in active commission before 1850 was the *Rodney*. This was largely as a result of her having been built at Pembroke, where construction periods were shorter due to the lack of repair work. Her sister, the Chatham-built *London*, served a commission with *Rodney* on the Mediterranean station in 1853–55, the two ships taking part in the bombardment of Sevastopol, but by that date they were considered old fashioned. Both *Nile* and *London* had their sterns modified by the Master Shipwright at the relevant dockyard, Roberts and Fincham respectively. The cost was around £500 and the object was to improve both the appearance and the fighting qualities.

Early reports on the *Rodney* were particularly favourable. Cockburn comforted the recently-dismissed Seppings and doubted the strength of the French 100-gun ships; 'I am persuaded the class of the *Rodney* will prove the finest and most efficient ships upon the seas.'[10] In the Mediterranean, under Captain Hyde Parker, the *Rodney* soon established herself as the most powerful ship in the squadron, carrying her midship port all but 7ft out of the water and making 11.4 knots sailing large, with deep but easy roll. When Symonds's *Vanguard* joined the fleet she was relegated to an honourable second place, well ahead of the remaining ships.[11] After minor modifications in the early 1840s, *Rodney*'s performance fell off quite considerably. Her midship magazine was moved forward, minor work carried out on the bow and stern, and the masts raked, all of which proved 'injurious to her sailing and working'. She was now a slow ship and this helps to explain why her two sisters were initially told off to be converted into heavy blockships in 1847. Lord John Hay regarded her hull form as 'objectionable'.[12] Even in 1854 *Rodney* remained a slow ship, although with the *Trafalgar* in the same squadron she was never going to be the worst offender in this area.

Seppings's 90-gun ships were the most powerful warships in the world when designed. They were the first to carry a full armament of long guns for accurate fire at ranges outside those of previous battles. With no carronades they would have out-gunned French and American ships of the same nominal rate. This was the real purpose of the Broke/Pechell/Douglas gunnery reforms: to give the Royal Navy the equipment to fight at any range. However, as with all the ships of that period they were lacking in any finesse under sail, and though *Rodney* made quite a show in heavy weather she was never again a fast ship.

The *Albion*-class

The success of the first 90-gun ship established the class and under the pressure of foreign designs further ships of this type were ordered from Symonds. In 1837 reports from the Mediterranean drew attention to the apparent danger from the large American ships. The USS *North Carolina* was credited with 100 guns, with 42- and 32-pounder long guns, heavy carronades and a war complement of 1,000 men. This was a very powerful ship, one which it would not be safe to encounter in an 80- or 84-gun Second Rate. The Russians did not enter the

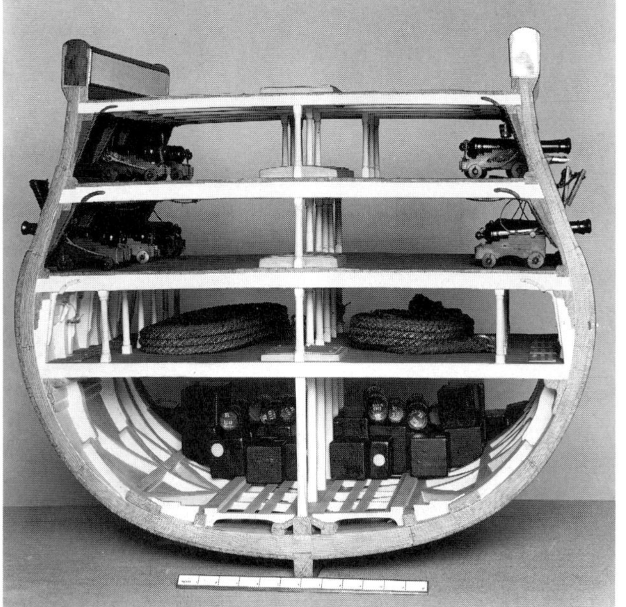

A midship model of the Rodney. *Both decks are armed with 56cwt 32-pounders. The form and framing of the ship are clear.* (ScM)

lists for their 84-gun two-deckers were already showing unmistakable signs of structural weakness. The French programme, however, gave further cause for alarm. By crediting French ships with the ability to mount all the guns they were rated for, and ignoring their limitations, Symonds persuaded the Board that Britain stood in a position of alarming inferiority, having three large Second Rates to twenty-six French. In fact, half the French ships were over-gunned *Canopus* derivatives. Britain was superior in 84-gun ships by nineteen to five, and all but one of the remaining large French two-deckers were incomplete. Sir Charles Adam consulted the Surveyor on this issue and from their deliberations came with the order for a new 90-gun design in early 1839.[13]

	Albion	*Nile*
Length	204ft	205ft 6in
Moulded breadth	60ft 1/2in	54ft 6in
Depth in hold	23ft 8in	23ft 2in
	3,100	2,598 tons

Symonds had already prepared the draught when the Board provided details of the proposed armament.

Gun deck	34	68pdr	65cwt
Main deck	32	32pdr	56cwt
Quarter deck and Forecastle	24	32pdr	40cwt
Complement	820 men		

[14]

In December 1840 this was modified, two guns were removed from the gun deck to the upper deck.

Symonds submitted the draught in June 1839. Orders for two such ships had already been placed at Devonport and they were given priority the following day. The names selected were *Albion* and *Aboukir*, in preference to *Bulwark*.[15] Further 90-gun ships were ordered in 1840: *Prince Albert* (later *Princess Royal*) from Portsmouth, *Exmouth* from Devonport, and *Hannibal* from Woolwich.[16] The stern rake on the *Aboukir* and *Exmouth* was modified following experience with that of the *Warspite*.[17] Finally the *Algiers* at Pembroke was reordered as a 90-gun ship of the *Albion*-class.[18] Under the 1841–42 programme set out by the Minto Board, the *Albion* was pushed ahead while the remaining ships being brought up to a state of 2/8th completion save the *Algiers*, which had yet to have a frame provided.[19]

With the new Board came a marked reduction in work on Symonds's designs. The *Albion* was ordered to complete by task and job while the other ships were suspended, largely from the lack of shipwrights. The *Hannibal* was moved onto a smaller slip to make way for the *Royal Albert* and then for Hayes's *Agamemnon*. In early 1843 she was taken down and stored at Woolwich. *Prince Albert* was renamed *Princess Royal*.[20]

Symonds was alarmed by the actions of the new Board and called on Portland for support. Haddington promised 'that justice should be done to her [the *Albion*] and to the surveyor of the navy in the appointment of an officer to command her'.[21] The Board had other plans for the ship which included fitting four 112cwt 68-pounders on slide and compressor carriages on the lower deck. Sir Thomas Hastings had experimented with such weapons and mounting aboard the *Excellent*, and hoped that these heavy weapons could be shifted to the bow or stern ports as desired.

Gun deck	28	32pdr	56cwt
	4	68pdr	112cwt
Main deck	26	32pdr	56cwt
	6	68pdr	65cwt
Quarter deck	2	68pdr	52cwt
	16	32pdr	42cwt
Forecastle	8	32pdr	42cwt
Complement	750 men (peace time)		

After sending Edye down to Plymouth to supervise the work in late 1843 Symonds reported 'such guns and slides are not adapted to the broadside of sailing ships'. The guns were replaced by 65cwt pieces on common truck carriages.[22] As fitting out completed it became clear that the Surveyor's office had made an error in calculating the height between decks, and that there was too little headroom. This reflected the over-stretched regime at Somerset Place but it was rectified for the remaining ships.[23]

Under the 1844–45 programme of works a new 90, the *St Jean d'Acre*, was ordered and work resumed on *Aboukir*, *Exmouth* and *Princess Royal*.[24] By the end of the year both Devonport ships had fallen behind schedule and required additional shipwrights to reach the stage of 2/8 called for by Symonds.[25]

Albion did not do well in the 1844 cruise and the Tory Officers believed her a complete failure. Consequently, in December, Cockburn secured the suspension of all work on the *Albion*-class ships.

	As suspended	*Work resumed*
Aboukir	3/8	28.2.1846 to 5/8
Exmouth	2/8	28.2.1846 to 3/8
St Jean d'Acre	Nil	
Algiers	Nil	

In contrast, Bowles argued that *Albion* was weighted down by some particularly heavy Italian oak but that she made a remarkable 13 knots and steered 'like a cutter'. While he admitted she rolled quickly he observed she was easy and very strong.[26] After the 1845 trials *Albion* had still not redeemed herself, although it is unlikely she could ever have done so in the eyes of Cockburn who claimed she had no superiority over *Rodney*, a ship which gained by being steadier in a seaway. Symonds believed the wind had not been strong enough to allow his ships to make the best of their broad-beamed form.[27]

In the last months of the Tory Administration the three most advanced of *Albion*'s sisters were restarted as they were thought to be too far advanced for any modification. The *Aboukir* was ordered to complete in 1847–48, while *Exmouth* was to reach 4/8 in 1846, and *Princess Royal* 3/8.

The incoming Whig Board ordered further trials with *Albion* in which up to 150 tons of ballast was added in an attempt to cure the 'deep and quick rolling of this ship'. Auckland was convinced that the 90-gun design would have to be modified to follow the moulds of the *Queen*.[28] Symonds responded by modifying the 90-gun design to carry 68-pounders on the lower deck with the midship port 7ft out of the water. This did not satisfy the Board, which had clearly decided to make far more radical changes. Lord Auckland lamented that the *Princess Royal* was too far advanced, but considered she would be a fine ship. *Hannibal* would be modified with 2ft less beam and a more full midship section.

	Albion	*Hannibal*
Length	204ft	208ft
Moulded breadth	60ft 1/2in	58ft
Depth in hold	23ft 8in	24ft

Aboukir and *Exmouth* were briefly suspended, but they were too far advanced to be taken down.[29] Eventually the *Princess Royal* was taken down and her midship section made less radical. This work began with the midship frames and worked toward the extremities. This saved some labour and helped to justify the complex process of removing Symonds's hull form in so large a ship.[30] The other incomplete ship, the *Hannibal*, was initially ordered to be assimilated more closely with the *Queen*, by now considered a successful ship. She then had an additional 2ft added into the bow and stern for finer waterlines and adopted the *Princess Royal* midship section. The design was sealed in July and her materials transferred to Deptford from June 1847 in order to clear Woolwich for more favoured ships. This process was not attended with any particular urgency and vital parts still remained at Woolwich in December 1848.[31]

Auckland expected that little could be done with the *Albion*, even with the large addition of ballast that Parker proposed

> We do not expect here much of good result from the addition of ballast to the *Albion*. I should nevertheless like to try the experiment of heavier guns in her. Though always a fine ship I fear that she must always be an uneasy one, and though we are obliged to finish two other ships of her class, we are forcing upon Sir William Symonds some alterations in a third which was less advanced.[32]

Despite this, *Albion* soon built a fine reputation for herself and once Symonds had left office the controversy ended. This supports the view that the debate had been inspired by factors other than the design of the ships. Parker added 70 tons of ballast and discovered the ship answered to perfection. She became even stiffer under canvas and kept her lower deck ports open long after the remainder of the fleet and sailed with great style. His second in command, the Tory Admiral Sir Lucius Curtis reported:

> aware that the anxiety of the Admiralty is very great about the *Albion*, I take leave to say as I do, satisfied that she is in every respect the finest ship in the Navy.

More significantly, the Prince de Joinville confessed that the French fleet had nothing to match her. By contrast, the *Rodney*

The London *(opposite page and below) as a depot ship in 1875, shortly before departing for Zanzibar, where she acted as depot and headquarters for the East African slavery patrol. The additional heads amidships and glazed in ports were not features of her front-line career which culminated on 17 October 1854, before the batteries of Sevastopol. Her figurehead is now in the Museum of London.* (CMP)

had been spoiled by her alterations. Auckland was very pleased and sent a copy of Parker's letter to Symonds, although he told Parker that Symonds was 'fearfully soured and I expect no expression of satisfaction from him'. This was scarcely to be wondered at.[33] Portland continued to urge measures which he believed, on the advice of Symonds who was generally at his elbow, to assist the *Albion* establish her true merits. He proposed heavier lower deck guns and Auckland humoured him though he stressed that the success of ships as different from Symonds's form as the *Canopus* proved to his satisfaction that a fuller midship section was desirable.[34] A year later the Duke was still lamenting that it was 'folly to spoil the 90-gun ships by diminishing their beam'.[35] *Aboukir* was launched on 4 April 1849, but did not commission until converted to steam. By contrast, the *Albion*, which was effectively in continuous commission until 1856, fitted out in May 1849 for another tour in the Mediterranean.

Gun deck	32	68pdr	65cwt
Main deck	34	32pdr	56cwt
Upper deck	24	32pdr	42cwt
Complement	820 men (peace time)		

[36]

With this heavier arming and more ballast she maintained her place as the finest large two-decker afloat. Throughout this commission the *Albion* and the *Ganges* were the fastest ships on the station.[37]

Like all Symonds's designs, *Albion* was a poor performer against a head sea, particularly in heavy weather, but otherwise her speed, steadiness and strength were qualities appreciated by almost all who ever sailed in her. The quick rolling which afflicted all Symonds's ships when out of trim was gradually improved by heavier weights and ballast, although it was never to be completely erased. *Albion*, more than any of Symonds's other ships, required the most careful handling if she was to produce her best results.

The new 90-gun designs of 1847

Under the 1847–48 programme new designs for 90-gun ships were considered. Some re-used names that had been allocated to *Albion*-class ships, others were entirely new. The *St Jean d'Acre* was to be built to lines provided by the Committee of Reference, along with another ship of the same design, which became the *Caesar*, at Portsmouth. This insult can hardly have improved the Surveyor's temper. A new *Algiers* was to be drawn by Read, Chatfield and Creuze, designers of the *Thetis*.[38] The *St Jean d'Acre* made no progress at Devonport and the two latter ships had a remarkably chequered design history. The first design, which the Committee took pains to stress was a modernised *Rodney*, was eventually built at Pembroke as the *Caesar*.

	Caesar	*Rodney*
Length, waterline	208ft	204.40ft
Breadth, extreme	56ft	54.40ft
Depth, forward	23.50ft	23.66ft
aft	24.50ft	24.75ft
Height of Port	7	7.40ft
Midship area	919.25sq ft	947.00sq ft
Load displacement	4247.30	4254.60 tons
Ballast	100	180 tons
Sail area	29,473sq ft	28,102sq ft
Stability at 7 per cent	3,904 tons	3,032 tons

[39]

The Albion *of 1842, Symonds's largest warship and his most controversial. Capable of astonishing speed and carrying her guns well in moderate weather the* Albion *slowed badly in a head sea and rolled badly when lightly loaded. One of the most handsome sailing warships ever built, and the envy of every other Navy the* Albion *had every quality that the* Rodney *lacked.* (NMM)

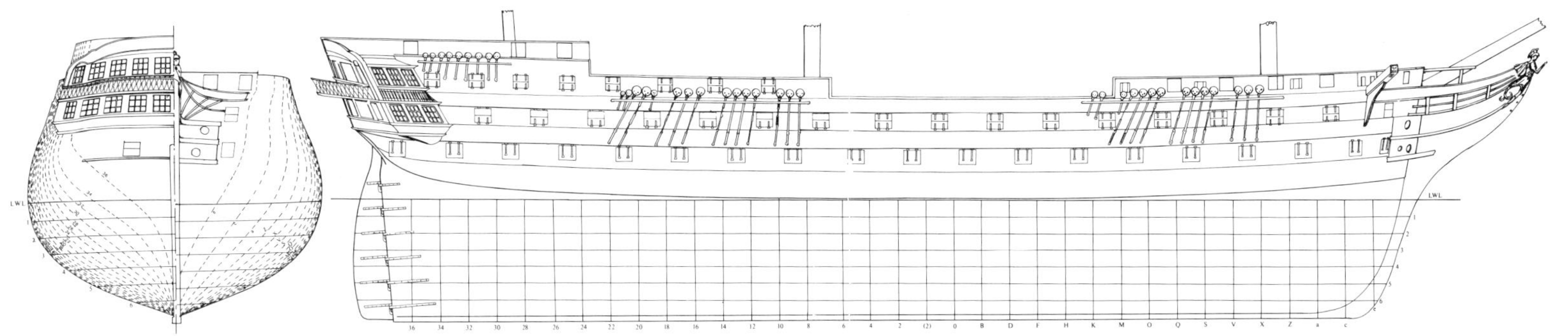

Profile of the Albion, *redrawn by Brian Lavery.*

The *Algiers*, having been reordered to the *Caesar* draught and then given the name of the ship cancelled at Portsmouth, ultimately became a stretched two-decker version of the *Queen*, and a contemporary of the *Duke of Wellington*-class three-deckers.

	Caesar	*Algiers*
Length	208ft	210ft
Moulded breadth	56ft	60ft
Depth in hold	23ft 4in	24ft 5in

A history of HMS Algiers

30.10.1833	Ordered to build at Pembroke as a First Rate.
6.12.1834	To be of 110 guns (*Queen*-class).
26.12.1840	Reordered as a 90-gun ship (*Albion*-class).
5. 3.1844	Suspended.
18.12.1844	Suspend conversion of frames.
15. 4.1847	Suspended pending the results of the trials of the 80-gun ships *Cressy* and *Agamemnon*.
25. 4.1847	Build to the lines of the constructors of the *Cressy*.
14. 6.1847	The Surveyor to report on the 90-gun design by the Committee of Reference.
24. 6.1847	This design to be the *Caesar* built at Portsmouth.
28. 6.1847	Cancel the last order and build *Algiers* to the Committee of Reference.
13. 8.1847	*Algiers* to be renamed *Caesar*.
20.10.1847	Edye asks to which draught the *Algiers* is to be built.
20.10.1847	To build 'upon the lines of the *Queen*, with an elongation not exceeding six feet'.
17. 1.1848	*Algiers* to follow *Exmouth* at Devonport. (Laid down on another slip in August 1848, as *Exmouth* was not launched until 1854.)[40]

Armament

Gun deck	32	68pdrs	65cwt
Main deck	32	32pdrs	56cwt
Upper deck	4	68pdrs	52cwt
	24	32pdrs	42cwt[41]

Caesar was commenced at Pembroke in July 1848.[42] Along with *Algiers* she made little progress before the larger sailing battlefleet units on the stocks were converted into steamships. Here the contrasts between the two designs was marked. *Caesar* was a steady performer, like her design ancestor. *Algiers*, on the other hand, was a heavy roller and a poor sea boat, although it would be unjust to blame her failings on Edye's original design.

Order dates for 90-gun ships

1826: *Nile, Rodney, London*
1839: *Albion, Aboukir*
1840: *Exmouth, Princess Royal, Hannibal* and *Algiers* reordered
1844: *St Jean d'Acre*
1845: *Prince Regent* razee
1847: *Caesar*

Of these twelve ships which were built over 21 years only 5 were launched as sailing ships. Under Walker's five-year programme of construction the fifteen new ships were divided into four three-deckers, three 90s, seven 80-gun ships and a screw steamer. Right up to the end of the sailing battlefleet the 90-gun ship was still an odd packet, neither as powerful as the three-decker nor as economic to build as an 80. Only the tactical potential of a more powerful two-decked ship capable of outsailing the three-deckers could justify the type, and as the experience of the 1840s demonstrated, the last three-deckers were quite capable of holding their own with the 90-gun ships.

The Exmouth *being broken up at Penarth in 1905 after many years as a training ship on the Thames.* (CMP)

6 *The Vanguard-Class and the 80-Gun Ship: 1832–50*

It should hardly be a surprise that the first new battleships ordered by the Whig Board after 1830 were of Symonds's design. The *Vanguard*-class were a direct replacement for Seppings's 84-gun *Canopus/Formidable*-class. They were the standard two-decked battleship class of the second postwar era, and were not exceeded in size or firepower before the end of the sailing battlefleet. However, alternative designs were ordered, raising questions about the success of Symonds's ships, even after a series of modifications.

Two new 80-gun ships, the *Vanguard* and *Collingwood*, were ordered from Pembroke Yard in June 1832, although it was another ten days before the Board made it clear that they were not of the *Formidable* type. This was most obvious by the number of guns, only 78 as designed, and even then the guns on the main deck were not the long 32-pounders, as demanded by the 1830 design specification, but 48cwt medium guns of the same calibre.[1] Following a long memorandum from Barrow, Graham elected to order the *Collingwood* as a duplicate frame, using the moulds of the *Vanguard*, to test the efficacy of an American scheme whereby duplicate frames were stored for many years. This scheme was extended to include the new 110-gun ships *Victoria* and *Algiers*.[2] There were problems with the programme. Pembroke was already feeling the effects of Graham's cuts in dockyard stores and had no timber to convert the second frame. Moving 1,800 loads from others yards provided the timber, but revealed serious shortages elsewhere, as Byam Martin had warned. Then the dockyard officers pointed out that there was no weatherproof building available to store the converted frame.[3]

The final draft was dispatched from London on 28 November 1832. The *Collingwood* frame was to be converted slightly oversize to allow for shrinkage and warping during storage. The work would occupy forty shipwrights for 11 weeks. The *Vanguard* would require sixty skilled men for 16 weeks to set up the frame and she was actually laid down in May 1833, with an anticipated launch date of August 1835. The 1833 Programme of Works included two more 78s, duplicates of the first pair. The first of these, the *Goliath*, was ordered at Chatham in October and laid down the following February.[4]

Under the existing rating system the new ships were only Third Rates but Symonds secured a re-rating, based on the full 700-man crew, to place his new ships in the Second Rate, where they belonged by right. This process was not an easy one. Years later Wood re-opened the issue with Minto: 'do you remember the difficulty we had to make the *Vanguard* a second rate? & the state Symonds was in'. The inference is that the design did not possess the displacement to carry her armament and the 1844 trials appeared to confirm this surmise.[5] It is worth noting in passing that they were the first Royal Navy vessels to be fastened with copper bolts and nails in the wales and topsides.[6]

Long before the *Vanguard* had been completed Symonds began the process of modifying her form, commencing with the buttock lines.[7] The changes would increase her ability to carry weight. Of more significance was the first Atlantic cruise of the *Vernon*, and the scathing reports of Cockburn about her motion in a seaway. Following pressure from the Admiralty, the forebody of the drawing was altered, to be followed in *Collingwood*. By this stage *Vanguard* had been launched, on schedule in August 1835, and the *Goliath* completed in frame to stand over some three months before. These two units were too far advanced for such major modification, but *Collingwood*, which followed *Vanguard* onto the slip in September, could be altered.[8] Once these modifications had been made the Board gave Symonds new directions.

> The Superintendent at Pembroke be informed that it is their Lordships intention that the frame of the *Collingwood* should stand to season; but that he direct the officers to proceed in providing the wales, clamps, diminishing stuff, shelf pieces, and beams of the Orlop, Gun and Upper decks, and all other timber materials of large scantlings for seasoning at the same time, leaving out every fourth strake, which however should be provided; that the thickstuff be only screwed up for the present, except such strakes as receive shelf bolts, which should be fastened: to provide and edge all the oak plank for the decks which may be hatch chocked to the beams where they are crossed.
>
> To cause the heavy iron work to be taken in hand, such as riders, knees, hooks and crutches, as the current works of the Yard will allow.

The same orders were issued for *Goliath*.[9]

The Chatham ship became the centrepiece in the first of many similar controversies between Symonds and the Master Shipwrights at various yards. Symonds complained that his specification and scantling had been ignored when the frame of the *Goliath* had been converted. Accordingly, he requested Admiralty authority to have a very detailed account of all work on the ship.[10]

A midship section model of the Vanguard, *Symonds's first battleship. The form and the framing are a complete contrast to the similar model of* Rodney. *The* Vanguard *was a remarkable performer under sail, but particularly sensitive to minor alterations in trim and stowage.* (ScM)

By 1837 the critics of Symonds's system were having an effect on Minto, the First Lord. Minto's brother, Admiral Sir George Elliot, the designer of the ill-fated *Eurydice*, pointed out that any ship built on such large dimensions would out-sail the constrained models of the Navy Board period. Admiral John Hayes, one of the most highly-regarded amateur naval designers, pointed out that Symonds's vessels were only carrying the same weights as the old type, but with nearly twice the power of sail.

Elliot and Hayes were negotiating for an 80-gun ship to be built to Hayes design, but Hayes would only accept if he were appointed Dockyard Superintendent at the responsible yard, because he feared Symonds's interference.[11] Minto, Elliot and Wood were agreed that the alternative design should be tried, but as they had no intention of launching any British-built battleships in the foreseeable future they suggested that the new design be built in India. Hayes refused, so instead, the Board ordered another standard ship at Pembroke, the *Superb*, in June 1838, re-using the *Collingwood* moulds.

In 1839 the Admiralty took the obvious step, ordering 'such modifications in the frame of the *Superb* as to enable her to carry 80 guns instead of 78'. An extra port on each side of the quarter deck soon made up the numbers, allowing *Goliath* and *Collingwood* to be modified.[12]

Tension in the Mediterranean in 1839, allied to the failure of efforts to secure large-scale construction in India finally persuaded the Board to place a large order for new battleships in May. The six two-deckers included two 90s and four 80s; *Mars* and *Majestic* at Chatham, *Centurion* and *Colossus* at Pembroke. *Centurion* was laid down only two months later, using one of the duplicate frames from the 1833 programme. The following year the *Irresistible* and *Lion* followed at the two yards.[13]

Further problems with the original design surfaced in 1839. The near collapse of the stern of *Warspite* forced the Board to examine the sterns of all other new ships. To their horror they discovered that the *Vanguard* and *Queen* were raked out to an equally absurd extent and some alarm was also expressed at the sterns of *Goliath* and *Collingwood*. In the event only *Vanguard* and *Goliath* were beyond salvation.[14] This may explain why *Goliath* was never commissioned, although she was the third of the class to be launched. Both her bow and stern were known to be inferior to the modified design, and as such she was not a ship that the Surveyor would select for sea service. The stern of *Collingwood* was shifted to conform with the new plan, while that of *Goliath* modified, as far as possible, to take into account the gunnery problems of the *Vanguard*.[15] The cumulative effect of these modifications was, in some ships, to leave the stern timbers badly arranged, weakly supported and held together with iron straps. A detailed investigation of the two new 70s after 1841 indicated how far strength had been sacrificed in rebuilding the stern.

In service

Vanguard was commissioned in 1837 by Captain Sir Thomas Fellowes, with the normal picked complement of officers, including Baldwin Walker as First Lieutenant and Mr Miller, one of Symonds's favourite sailing masters. The object was clear. Symonds wanted his ships to be tried by men capable of making the best of their qualities. In addition, a degree of political reliability was useful, in view of the hostile press he had received from Tory journals and officers. Out in the Mediterranean *Vanguard* soon made a name for herself as the fastest ship in the fleet, with the handiness of a frigate when beating out of Grand Harbour. Symonds made certain that Minto, Adam, Parker and Wood saw his private correspondence from the ship's officers which was full of praise for her qualities.[16] Further praise came in a more official form with Admiral Stopford's report, in which it was concluded that *Vanguard* 'had the advantage in a most decided manner' over the rest of his fleet. After three years in command Fellowes was well satisfied. She had 'great stability' was 'very easy at sea and works less than ships of her class' and had 'great advantage in all points of sailing'.[17]

Alternative designs

After coming to office in 1841 the Haddington Board was quick to move against Symonds's designs. The first four two-deckers to complete in 1842 were ordered to be placed in Ordinary after completion, a sure sign that their designer lacked the favour of the Board. The alternative of fitting for sea was costly and there was now little need for the vessels but these new ships should have been fitted as Advanced Ships. As an example *Vanguard* cost £56,983 to build, and a further £20,756 to fit for sea.[18]

In 1841 Minto finally ordered an 80-gun ship to Hayes's

The draught of the Vanguard *and* Collingwood, *dated November 1832.* Vanguard *was completed with the exaggerated rake to the stern, as was the* Goliath, *while the later ships of the class were given a more practical angle. The bow was also modified for the ships that were not too far advanced.* (NMM)

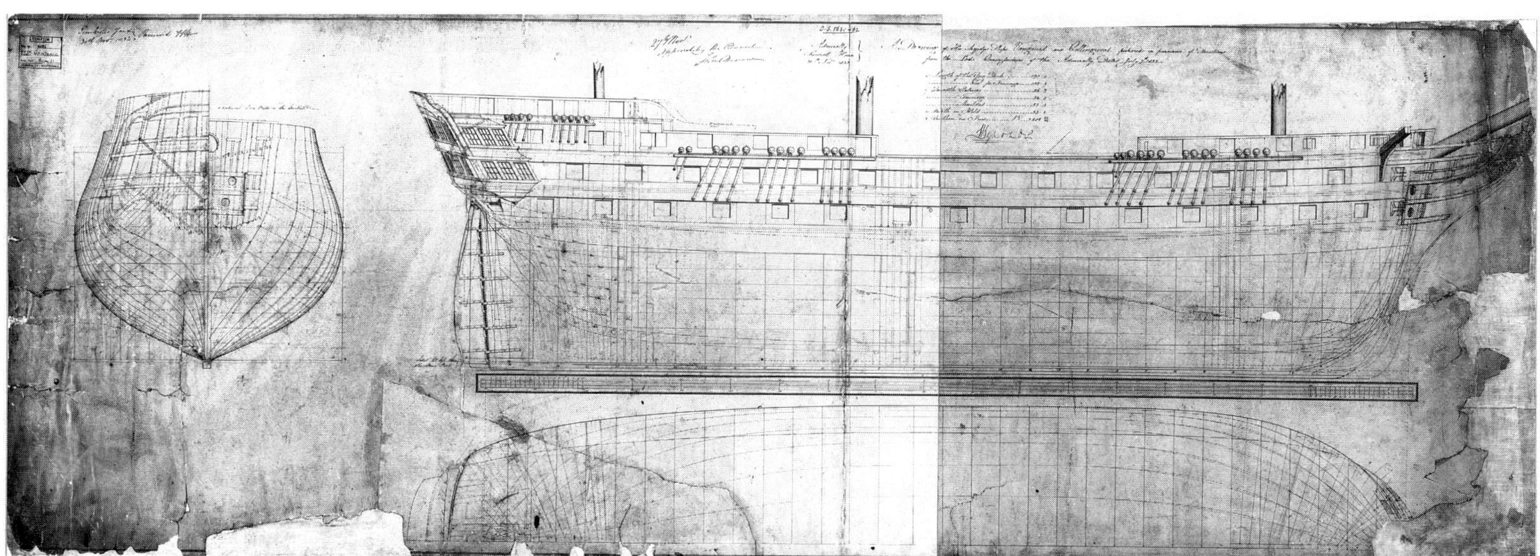

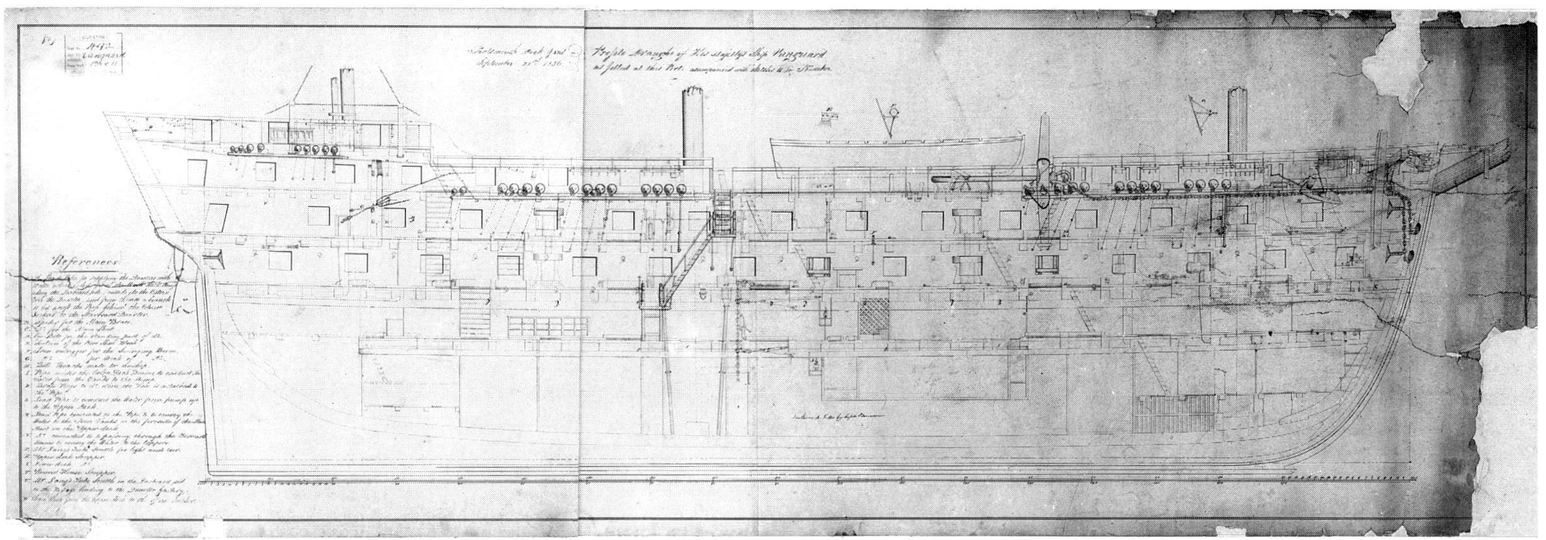

As fitted profile of Vanguard, *1836.* (NMM)

lines after the Admiral died, promoting his son as a reward for submitting the drawings. This ship limped along at Woolwich as the *Agamemnon.*[19] His successor, Haddington, was responsible for more retrograde steps allowing Cockburn to take off the lines of the old *Sans Pareil*, for many years the sheer hulk at Plymouth, in order to build a new ship to her form and dimensions. As Sir George Seymour, a Junior Naval Lord, pointed out the ship was 'broken and swayed', forcing the Surveyor's department to fall back on the original British survey of 1794, where these were in conflict with the new set.[20] Although the details of the design were revised to bring them into line with contemporary practice and the scantling of *Vanguard* adopted, the order for the *Sans Pareil* had no logic. Whatever the intention of the First Sea Lord, she can only have been seen by the Surveyor as a gross insult. The ship had been available to the Admiralty for over 40 years, and yet had never been reproduced. Her short career with the Royal Navy hardly justified such an act, particularly when the *Canopus* was so clearly the superior design.[21] *Sans Pareil* shared with her contemporary, the *Cressy*, a decidedly old-fashioned and excessive degree of tumble-home, a feature more common in French ships of the eighteenth century than in those of the Royal Navy in the 1840s. Bowles was scathing in his condemnation of such 'servile imitation'. The new ship was ordered at Chatham in 1844 after an unduly prolonged gestation. To maintain some degree of balance the *Brunswick* was ordered at Pembroke, to the Surveyor's build.[22] Symonds did nothing to aid the *Cressy*, forcing Samuel Read to write directly to Herbert in an attempt to speed up the passage of the drawings through Somerset House.[23]

After the suspension of the 110- and 90-gun ships the 80s were the only Symonds's design being built. *Colossus* and her sisters at Pembroke were the standby job for the men taken off the larger ships.[24] Further humiliations were to be heaped on the shoulders of the Surveyor. He was finally asked to comment on the two new designs in March 1847. He argued that the *Cressy* would turn out to be 100 tons overweight, and would not sail well, while the *Agamemnon* would be seven tons too heavy.[25] However, these observations were ignored, and they were, as it turned out, Symonds's last contribution to the debate. Six months later, after he had resigned, the Deputy Surveyor was given new orders:

> You are to prepare drawings for the *Brunswick* and *Sutlej*, [a 50-gun Fourth Rate] with a reduction of one foot of breadth for each, and to fill the midship section and body, to compensate for the reduction of beam, and then submit them for Their Lordship's inspection, you are to execute this without delay as the people have been removed from these vessels for the present.

The men taken off the two ships were put onto the *Victoria* and *Colossus* until the frames of two steamers were ready for further labour.[26]

Building information

	Tonnage (builder's measurement)	*Loads, Timber*	*Men to build, in one year*
Canopus	2,257	3,420	160
Vanguard	2,609	3,560	186
Cumberland	2,214	2,999	153
Sans Pareil	2,339	3,600	167

Dimensions of the post-1832 80-gun ships

	Vanguard	*Brunswick*	*Sans Pareil*	*Cressy*	*Orion*
Length, gun deck	190ft	190ft	193ft	198ft 5in	198ft
Keel	155ft 3in	154ft 4 3/4in	158ft 11 1/2in	162ft 1 3/8in	161ft 3/4in
Breadth	56ft 9in	55ft 9in	52ft 1in	55ft	55ft 9in
Depth in hold	23ft 4in	23ft 4in	22ft 8in	21ft 8 1/4in	23ft 4in
Tons	2,889	2,484	2,242	2,537	–

The significance of these figures lies in the close links between *Brunswick* and *Orion*, the latter designed by Edye and Watts. By adding length the new team achieved for the Symonds form the same results they were seeking with the 90-gun *Hannibal*, *Algiers* and the *Windsor Castle*-class. System and order were returning. *Orion* and *Hood* were ordered at Chatham in March 1848, the last new sailing battleships to be commenced for the Royal Navy. The design was finally accepted in November and drawings sent out the following month. Significantly, the scantling adopted was that of the *Mars*, a *Vanguard*-class ship building at the yard. This marked a major triumph for Edye over the Committee of Reference, which was then in decline, emphasising the role of Edye in establishing the more basic aspects of all Symonds's ships. The detailed form of the *Orion* reflected the influence of Frederik af Chapman's work on the students of the First School of Naval Architecture. The additional materials of the *Sans Pareil* reflected her excessive tumble-home and the costs of updating an old design, rather than creating a new draft to meet the requirements.[27]

The squadrons of 1845 and 1846

In the Evolutionary Squadrons of the mid-1840s the performances of the *Vanguard* and *Superb* were perhaps the most varied of all the ships tried. The second ship was included in order to test the merits of her longer bow, a response to experience with the *Vernon*. She was given another racing captain, Anwar Lowry Corry, who had jockeyed the razee *Barham* past the *Vernon* ten years earlier. The test ship for the standard two-deckers was the *Canopus*, under Fairfax Moresby, a fine seaman, but no jockey.

From the first trial in 1845 the two 80s were aftermost ships, behind such wagons as the *Rodney* and *Trafalgar*. These trials were, if anything, less useful than the others of this series for the prolonged illness of Admiral Hyde Parker precluded anything more than forming a line and testing the speed of the ships under sail.[28]

Symonds sought for some explanation for the failure of the 80-gun ships which did not contain a criticism of his system and focussed on the foul state of their copper and their being out of trim. His friends and patrons were entirely satisfied with this and also blamed the officers for faults in trim and handling. The Board, however, rejected Symonds's request to have them both re-coppered, although they did permit any measure that did not require the ship to be docked.[29] By calling on all his connections, and garnishing his letters with specimens of weed 15ft long, Symonds managed to have the Board decision reversed. Portsmouth yard put men on task and job to re-copper the *Superb* and reduce her rudder to the original size. Bowles, his one friend on the Board, argued that *Vanguard* had been badly stowed, while *Superb* was too deep and foul, and he was instrumental in having both ships re-coppered.[30] The sudden reverse in the fortunes of the two ships after re-coppering, which was almost certainly caused by re-stowing and improving the trim rather than the clean hull, was a source of confusion for Haddington. He considered their initial failure to have been 'unaccountable'. Parker provided him with qualified comfort;

> I have no doubt Sir Wm. Symonds two deckers will be found excellent ships, but susceptible of improvement in construction, as well as by stowage.[31]

The Mars *in June 1929, on her way to be demolished after serving as a Training Ship on the River Tay.* (CMP)

More revealing was the correspondence of Corry. After the refit he reported that *Superb*, 'sails remarkably fast' when in trim and that 'she has a good spread for her rigging; roomy decks, and broad gangways for working the ship'. He added, however, that,

> she will not stow her weights in the assigned places, and be in trim. Her rolling is quick, and in proportion to *Canopus*, as about 3 to 2; which in light airs, with any swell whatever, renders her very unsteady; and makes it difficult to take accurate aim with her guns. With the sea or swell on the beam or quarter, she rolls considerably, but, whether deeper than other ships, I have no means of judging. Her motion, when right before the sea or swell, is very trifling.[32]

Coming from a seaman of Corry's stamp, this was a serious criticism. However, the performance of both 80-gun ships had improved dramatically as the cruise continued. With stores consumed and trim recovered they were flyers. Captain George Willes of the *Vanguard* reported a marked improvement after recoppering and an addition to her ballast;

> such an entire change has taken place in her motion at sea, steering and working generally (although she is still deficient in her weights low down) that I can scarcely bring myself to believe she is the same ship.[33]

The Lion, *as a steam ship at Devonport shortly after her conversion in 1859.* (IWM)

Among contemporary commentators there was a marked tendency to report only those trials that supported a particular design or system. The 1845 trials merely proved that no clear cut results could be expected from well-manned and well-rigged ships, each striving to surpass the next. Consequently, each chose to write up what most suited his brief. Fincham devoted four and a half pages to the early trials of 1845, which were seen as going against Symonds, and only one page, without even the dates of the later trials, which were more favourable to *Superb* and *Vanguard*.[34] Because of his standing as a professional naval architect, Fincham has been treated as more reliable than the amateur writers. Fincham was, however, a serious rival for Symonds's position, a member of the Committee of Reference and a noted designer in his own right. His work was no more objective than that of Symonds and to treat his book of 1851 as anything more than the crowing triumph of a man over a fallen foe is unwise. Brown reminds us that the 'evils' of Symonds's form were still being taught to new entrants into the Royal Corps of Naval Constructors in the late 1940s and this demonstrates that the Corps historian has not been able to shake off this early conditioning, electing to follow Fincham's account without question. This provides a one-sided account of the trials, while missing the real weaknesses of Symonds' designs.[35]

After the last trials of 1845 Symonds was still criticising the badly-stayed and generally injured state of *Vanguard*'s masts and her poor stowage. Both ships were refitted for the 1846 Experimental Squadron, along with the *Canopus*. Repairs took men off several new ships, including *Sans Pareil*.[36] The trials under Commodore Collier in May 1846 saw *Superb* generally take the lead, but they are not covered by Fincham, who preferred to discuss the later trial when his 50-gun Fourth Rate *Raleigh* was the outstanding ship.[37] The August trials under Parker were a final attempt to restore some sanity to the process. He considered the *Vanguard* and *Canopus* to be nearly alike in performance, with the former superior in smooth water, the latter in rough. As *Superb* had recently beaten *Vanguard* the new ships could be regarded as being better overall. Parker was scathing about the modern practice, normally associated with Symonds, though he did not mention him by name, of reducing the iron ballast.[38]

Collier's trials in May had included a relatively rare occurrence: an order to exercise the stern batteries. *Vanguard* cleared for action in ten minutes, and fired two rounds from each gun. These set fire to the ship because the extreme overhang prevented the muzzles running clear. *Superb* took 15 minutes to clear, but her sashes required a full hour to remove. Collier reported that, 'I am of opinion that the stern is too open, and has too much rake for an efficient battery, and that the windows in it should be differently fitted'.[39] The failure of the prototype was acceptable, but the damning comments on the so-called improved version called into question the competence of the Surveyor's Office and it served to emphasise that the Chatham Committee really had been necessary. However, it should be observed that Moresby was excused from clearing the *Canopus* at all.

The only other new 80-gun ship to commission was the *Collingwood*, which went out to the Pacific bearing the flag of George Seymour. Her poop deck was extended forward to create the necessary accommodation.[40] By 1850 her sister, the *Centurion*, then lying in Ordinary at Devonport, was reported as 'rotten and fungoid in parts'. She was repaired to see service with a steam engine aboard. The new ships of the 1840s were all destined to enter service in a form that precludes any realistic judgement of the quality of the original sailing ship design. Symonds had been prepared to install a 60hp screw steam engine in the orlop of a *Vanguard*-class ship in 1839, only to find the Admiralty opposing such innovations.[41] Later he became less flexible. *Sans Pareil* was suspended on 2 October 1848 and prepared to receive 350hp screw steam engines. No more ships of this class were altered before 1850, but the timber collected for the *Agamemnon* metamorphosed into the first purpose-built British steam battleship.[42]

Armament

Vanguard 4.7.1832

Gun deck	26	32pdrs	56cwt
	2	68pdr carronades	
Main deck	30	32pdrs	56cwt
Quarter deck	10	32pdrs	25cwt
Forecastle	2	18pdrs	42cwt
	4	32pdrs	25cwt
Poop	4	18pdrs	10cwt

Vanguard 3.12.1834

Gun deck	26	32pdrs	55cwt
	2	68pdrs	60cwt
Main deck	26	32pdrs	48cwt
	2	68pdrs	60cwt
Quarter deck	14	32pdrs	48cwt
Forecastle	2	32pdrs	48cwt
	4	32pdrs	25cwt
Poop	4	18pdrs	10cwt

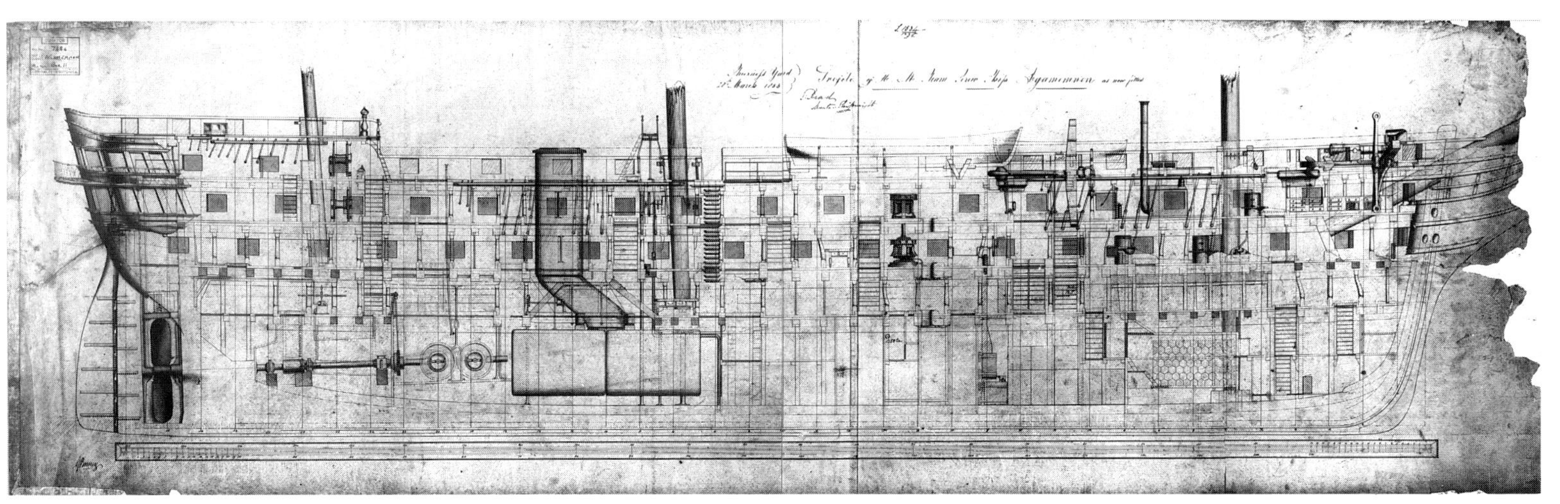

The Inboard profile of the Agamemnon, *showing the impact of the machinery.* (NMM)

Vanguard gun crews 2.6.1837

Gun deck	14	32pdrs	56cwt,	13 men	182
Main deck	15	32pdrs	50cwt,	13 men	195
Upper deck	10	32pdrs	40cwt,	11 men	100
	2	18pdrs	10cwt,	7 men	14
extra men					21
Total gun crews					702

The 84-gun ships had the same complement, but only mounted 25cwt guns on the upper deck.

Cressy 23.2.1843 & *Sans Pareil* 22.4.1843

Gun deck	20 32pdrs 56cwt
	8 68pdrs 65cwt
Main deck	24 32pdrs 50cwt
	4 68pdrs 65cwt *Cressy*, 4 extra 68pdrs
Quarter deck & Forecastle	24 32pdrs 41cwt

Collingwood 1.1.1845

Gun deck	20 32pdrs 56cwt
	8 68pdrs 65cwt
Main deck	24 32pdrs 50cwt
	4 68pdrs 65cwt
Quarter deck & Forecastle	24 32pdrs 41cwt

Construction programme: 80-gun ships 1832–50

Ship	*Built*	*Laid down*		*Launched*
Vanguard-class				
Vanguard	Pembroke	5.33		25.8.1835
Goliath	Chatham	2.34		25.7.1842
Collingwood	Pembroke	9.35		17.8.1841
Superb	Pembroke	11.38		6.9.1842
Centurion	Pembroke	7.39		2.5.1844
Mars	Chatham	12.39		1.7.1848
Lion	Pembroke	7.40		29.7.1847
Majestic	Chatham	2.41	(steam)	15.5.1853
Meeanee	Bombay	4.42		11.11.1848
Colossus	Pembroke	10.43		1.6.1848
Brunswick	Pembroke	30.8.47	(steam)	27.6.1855
Irresistible	Chatham	1.1.49	(steam)	27.10.1859
Agamemnon	Woolwich	3.42	(steam)	25.5.1852
Cressy	Chatham	4.46	(steam)	21.7.53
Sans Pareil	Devonport	1.9.45	(steam)	18.3.51
Orion-class				
Orion	Chatham	1.2.50	(steam)	6.11.1854
Hood	Chatham	13.8.49	(steam)	4.5.1859

The first steam battleship

Although the steam blockship 74s of 1844 were eventually completed as steam battleships they were always a compromise between the limited scope offered by small 40-year-old ships and the coast defence role for which they were originally intended. After the first cruise of *Blenheim* and *Ajax* the Board were satisfied that the screw would resolve many of the difficulties posed by paddle vessels. The Programme of Works for 1847–48, drawn up in April 1847, included the installation of 620 or 700nhp machinery, originally built for the iron frigates *Euphrates* and *Vulcan*, in the 80-gun *Audacious*, then on order, and the ship was to be built without a poop. On 18 November 1847 Edye was ordered to prepare the drawings for an 80-gun screw steamship of 700nhp, renamed *James Watt*. The ship was to be put in frame without delay. The armament reflected the then current state of opinion on the tactical role of steamships.

The Edgar *of 1858, a purpose-built 90-gun steam battleship, drying sails.*

Gun deck	36	68-pdr	65cwt
Upper deck	34	32-pdr	56cwt
Spar deck	2	68-pdr	95cwt
	8	10in	87cwt
Complement	850 men		

This was not a battleship, but an enlarged steam warship designed for individual action, when some of the spar-deck battery would be shifted across to the engaged side. The ship was a great success both under sail and steam, although a more conventional upper deck battery was installed long before completion.[43]

Dimensions

Length: between perpendiculars	230ft
of keel, for tonnage	194ft 7 1/4in
Breadth: extreme	55ft 3in
for tonnage	54ft 6in
Depth in hold	24ft 6in
Burthen	3,074 tons
Draught: fwd	23ft 6in
aft	24ft 6in
Height of midship port	6ft 8in

The Committee of Reference approved of the draft in 1847 although the ship was only ordered on 14 January 1850.[44] Eighteen months later Edye re-used the draft for the *Agamemnon*, at Woolwich using timber collected for the Haye's designed 80. The armament remained that of the original draft, although the engines were new 400 and later 600nhp. The ship was ordered on 20 June 1849.[45]

By 1851 the armament of the screw battleships had been assimilated to that of the sailing battleships, and they were now the precursors of an all steam fleet, rather than individual units acting with the sailing ships.

Part Six

CONSTRUCTION

1 *The Development of the Dockyards*

During the Revolutionary and Napoleonic Wars the administration of the Royal dockyards was subjected to a period of sustained reform. This resulted in improved efficiency of management, improved economy in the use of resources and greater professionalism among officials. At heart, this reflected a growing trend towards centralisation.[1]

The success of this process allowed the Admiralty to make one of the most significant changes in British construction policy: the shift to the building of all new ships in the Royal dockyards. The reasons for the desire to build in the Royal yards have already been discussed, and were primarily to do with the issues of timber decay and new construction methods. This chapter will consider the impact of this policy on the yards themselves. The buildings and other structures of the yards were generally left alone. The real object of policy was to change the size and management of the workforce, for most policy makers recognised that the exploitation of the skills of the artisans was at least as important as the structure of the yards. The real debate concerned the size of the labour force and the influence of political affiliations. By 1850 significant improvements had been made in both these areas.

Dockyards and naval bases

The three great naval bases of Portsmouth, Plymouth and Chatham each contained a dockyard though they were also arsenals for the mobilisation of the reserve fleet that was anchored close by. In 1815 Britain possessed these three major bases and four other significant dockyards at Woolwich and Deptford on the Thames, Sheerness at the mouth of the Medway and Pembroke Dock in Milford Haven. By this date Chatham was in decline because of the shallow approaches in the River Medway. It was later rescued, though only as a dockyard, by the steam dredger. The other two bases were

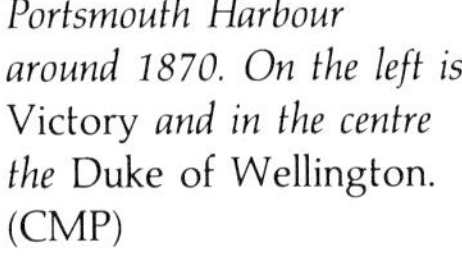

Portsmouth Harbour around 1870. On the left is Victory *and in the centre the* Duke of Wellington. (CMP)

strategically better placed for a war with France, and offered superior anchorages for active and reserve fleets. Chatham's base function was increasingly taken up by Sheerness, which also acted as such for the two Thames yards. All these three yards were threatened by the navigational difficulties of the rivers on whose banks they were sited. But for the inhospitable site and infestation of *teredo navalis*, Sheerness might have become the third great base, but the limited demands of the third reserve squadron, the North Sea Fleet, were easily met.

The three great bases had all been rebuilt during the second half of the eighteenth century, but the work at Chatham concentrated on the construction and repair facilities, while Portsmouth and Plymouth were retained as complete arsenals. As a result of this programme little needed to be done on these sites in the years up to 1850. However, both bases were given new victualling yards, while Woolwich, Portsmouth, and finally Plymouth, were equipped with steam factories. By contrast, Sheerness was rebuilt by Sir John Rennie between 1815 and 1830, finally resolving the old problems of poor facilities and weak foundations. The final yard, the construction facility at Pembroke, was built up from nothing after 1814. Overseas a new yard was built at Bermuda, to meet the danger of war with the United States, while attempts were made to develop a base at Trincomalee and to improve existing facilities at Malta. The dockyards entered the machine age at approximately the same rate as the fleet they served with the first modern metal structures being erected in the late 1840s.

The most obvious development of the period was the roofing over of all slips and many of the docks. The pace of this work was conditioned by the other demands on the estimates, and was far from complete in 1840, despite the obvious value of keeping rainwater out of ships. The real problem of the yards was that there were other areas of more pressing urgency, and repeated emergencies, both naval and political, reduced the amount of money available for yard improvements. The first mention of roofing over the slips dates from 1812, following Samuel Bentham's tour of Sweden, while the Admiralty inspection of 1817 called for the roofing over of all slips and those docks not required for ships in commission (with their masts still in place), 'to completely subdue the dry rot'. Some were of a temporary nature, but the more impressive wooden structures with copper, or occasionally slate roofs, were both expensive, up to £10,000, and difficult to erect. At Sheerness the *Royal George* was used as a building stage while under repair. The surviving wooden roof at Chatham dates from 1838, and is probably the last such to be built. In the following decade iron structures were built, with surprisingly modern corrugated iron sheeting, and in this respect the Navy was the pioneer of large-span iron roofing, well in advance of the railway industry.[2]

In the last years of the War Melville caused the Navy to buy 433 acres of land on the Thames at Northfleet, with a view to creating a new arsenal downstream from Woolwich, Deptford and Sheerness. The land was ultimately sold in 1831, long after the project had been abandoned. The opposition of the Navy Board to new yards, because of their effect on the supply of labour and timber, along with the introduction of the steam dredger which allowed the Thames and Medway to be kept navigable meant that the project never materialised. More effective was the creation of the new yard at Pembroke Dock in 1813. This involved shifting the facilities from Milford yard, which had been hired during the War, to Crown land occupied by the Board of Ordnance.[3]

In 1817 the Board of Admiralty decided that shipbuilding under cover offered major advantages, and thereafter all the major yards were equipped with large timber roofs over their slipways. This is the wooden structure covering Number 3 slipway at Chatham. It was one of the last wooden roofs erected over a large slipway, and was completed in 1838. (Author)

Construction policy

When the Admiralty made the decision to carry out all new construction in the Royal yards they were well aware of the burden that this would create, and they made an immediate attempt to reduce the workload by ordering all floating hulks to be replaced by magazines on shore. The size of the postwar Establishment, 100 battleships and 160 frigates, at least placed a limit on the amount of work required, although it was a high one.[4] The new Controller, Byam Martin, responded to the Establishment by setting out a programme to reduce expenses while at the same time keeping up the level of work and of employment. Martin argued that the shipwrights were a major war-time resource and therefore could not be summarily dismissed; he preferred, therefore, to limit earnings in order to preserve jobs. In summer the shipwrights were earning 6s 7d for a working day that lasted from 6am to 6pm with half an hour for breakfast, and one and a half hours for dinner. Cutting this to 7am to 5pm would save 1s 4d per day and over a year would equal the saving of around 8 per cent required by the Admiralty without shedding labour. With 3,854 shipwrights and 541 apprentices, the latter rated at half a man, the saving would be £85,219 per annum, or the pay of 835 shipwrights. The total saving in all trades would be £253,184. This would retain the men for an emergency and encourage them to look on the yard as their home. In addition, a few shipwright companies could be allowed to earn full pay as an inducement. If Byam Martin's programme did not work after three months men could be discharged. The Surveyors reckoned that the labour force would be equal to building and repairing eight to ten battleships and fifteen or sixteen frigates a year, allowing due time for seasoning. Surveyor Tucker wanted the men to grade themselves, to cut the pay of the least able, and stressed the need for careful seasoning.[5]

After one year Byam Martin had to report considerable disappointment. Eight battleships and six frigates had been produced, but all those opened for repair had required more work than estimated and so he urged the Admiralty to permit an additional hour per day, at a cost of £500,000 for both materials and labour. When he pointed out the numbers of new ships on order, ten battleships and eleven frigates as

An internal perspective on the roof over Number 3 slip at Chatham. The structure is similar to that used to house over the frigate Unicorn, *comprising straight timbers and iron reinforcements.* (Author)

compared with thirty-two and thirty in 1784 at the end of the American war when private yards were still in use, he drew attention to the shortage of slips in the Royal yards and the consequent pressure on seasoning timber. The Admiralty, under pressure for economies, pressed the Board to work with a maximum of 2,000 shipwrights and other trades in proportion, giving the least able the chance to work in less well paid jobs.[6] During 1817 the Admiralty relented on some issues, permitting additional sawyers to convert the frames of new ships, and the construction of four more slips at Pembroke. The former was intended to repay the Navy for taking over the maintenance of the revenue cruisers, and the transports that were bringing the Army home from France.[7] Byam Martin was anxious to press on with work at Sheerness, because the yard would be disabled as a wartime base until the new docks and basins were complete, and there was no alternative site. This gave particular colour to the ships-versus-infrastructure debates of the period.[8] Melville suggested day pay in contrast to piece work as a method of reducing expenditure, but Byam Martin objected to this on the grounds that it 'naturally occasions a dilatory, remiss discharge of duty, & consequently but a small produce of work', and warned that the yards had already been reduced by one twelfth in three years. To 'carry it further would be an act of oppression which they will retaliate when war shall again make us sensible of their consequence to the state'. He accepted any blame for the supposed failure of the system of keeping up the number of men.[9]

Number 7 covered slipway at Chatham, an all metal structure completed in 1855. The Sunderland flying boat inside gives an impression of the scale of these buildings. (Author)

In 1821, the Admiralty reduced the fleet Establishment, and lengthened the time for it to be completed. This, they argued, would allow for a reduction by a fifth of the dockyard labour force. To protect domestic labour Byam Martin persuaded Melville to end construction in India. At the same time a Committee of the Navy Board investigated the management of the yards. The Committee concluded, in line with Martin's opinions, that a degree of overmanning was necessary. The Admiralty, faced with serious pressure from the Treasury, could not agree. They had accepted this practice in the immediate aftermath of war,

> – but they cannot sanction a longer continuance of the existing system, & must now take the necessary steps for placing the several establishments of the dockyards on such a footing as is due to the Public Interest.

To this end they wanted to reduce some of the present number of shipwrights to joiners and carpenters, though they could be re-rated in an emergency. They ordered all wages reduced to those of Pembroke, which were 20 per cent down on the other yards; restricted daily earnings to 5 shillings and maintained the suspension of Saturday working until the reductions were achieved. The Board settled on a workforce of 7,000 with no Saturday working. The last saved one fifth of the total pay due.[10] Byam Martin also favoured continuing the existing organisation of the yards, although in 1822 the Admiralty forced through the shift to make the Dockyard Commissioner, a member of the Navy Board, the only person who could correspond with the Board. This increased the degree of central control and established a clear line of subordination. By December 1823 the men at Chatham were petitioning for the restoration of the 20 per cent, which was granted, but continued unrest among the disrated ex-shipwrights led the Admiralty to order that those dissatisfied should be discharged, while the earnings of the remainder were restricted to 33 shillings, plus chip money, per week. To supplement the increasingly skilled dockyard workforce Byam Martin requested the loan of 300 more convicts, for a total of 1,500, to carry out basic labouring.[11]

Dockyard labour as a war reserve

As Byam Martin had been arguing since the War, conditions in the shipbuilding industry were far from good. The depressed market for merchant ships lasted through to 1835 and was a combination of over-capacity and reduced protection as the Navigation Laws were gradually reduced. With the Navy and the East India Company making limited demands on the market there was little alternative for any men dismissed from the Royal dockyards. The builders competed among themselves by offering low prices which in turn drove down wages. This led to the formation of the Shipwrights Union in 1824. Political agitators blamed the failure of the Government to act in defence of liberal causes abroad, which would increase naval work, and for admitting foreign shipping. The repeal of the Combination Laws in 1824 gave the shipwrights the opportunity they needed to unionise their labour. They sought reduced hours, uniform prices and a fair share of the available work to preserve employment. With around 1,400 members the union soon had the funds for a prolonged strike. In February 1825 the Union took on Wigram, and subborned men discharged from the dockyards to work for the merchant shipbuilders. In the face of this alarming demonstration of the power of organised labour Home Secretary Robert Peel favoured re-introducing the Combination Laws. The shipbuilders then tried to force the Union to concede defeat, dismissing all Union men unless the Union accepted the Builders Regulations. By May the strike had begun. The Laws were not restored, but a combination of fresh legislation on ship repairs and the loan of men from the Royal yards did break the strike. This strike reinforced Byam Martin's view that the skills of the shipwrights were too valuable to be trifled with. Initially, the Board was unwilling to accede to the shipbuilders' request, but ultimately agreed to do so to avoid:

> the mischevious consequences that may arise to the public at large, and more particularly to the mercantile interests of the country by the continued misconduct of the working shipwrights.

Byam Martin was more hard-headed. Claiming a shortfall in naval work he pressed the shipbuilders to work in concert to break the strike. Within a month the strike began to crumble.[12]

After the strike Byam Martin kept a watching brief on the level of shipwright employment. The shipbuilders warned him that the number of working shipwrights was falling, and that the apparent increase in new work since 1825 merely counterbalanced the loss of repair work to the Baltic under the 1825 legislation, and included a large amount of speculative construction by the builders.[13]

Further pressure for reduction led Martin to anticipate the end of task and job pay, while the yards remained closed on Saturdays. In the event, Deptford yard was closed, saving £3,750 per annum, by reducing the officers, while the men were moved to Woolwich. This was also done to increase the

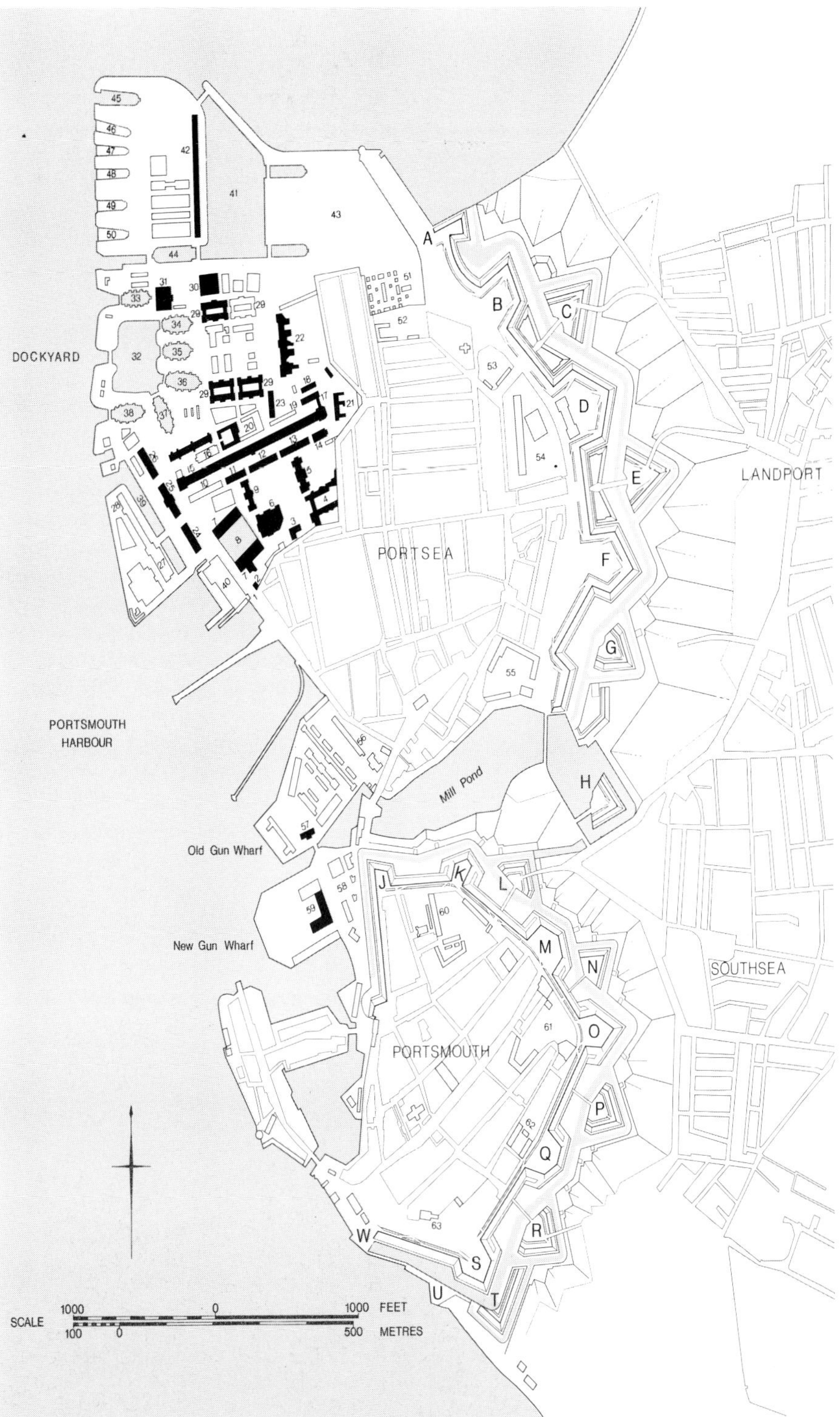

Portsmouth: Naval and Ordnance Establishment; Principal Buildings *c.* 1850
(Buildings in solid black still survive)

Portsmouth Dockyard
1. Main Gateway
2. Porter's Lodge
3. Pay Office
4. Naval Academy
5. Commissioner's House
6. No. 6 Boathouse
7. Boathouse
8. Boat Pond
9. School for Naval Architecture
10. West Sea Store
11. East Sea Store
12. West Hemphouse
13. East Hemphouse
14. St Ann's Church
15. Double Ropehouse
16. Tarring House
17. Hatchelling House
18. Hemp Store
19. Painted Canvas Shed
20. Converter's Pound
21. Short Row
22. Long Row or The Parade
23. Firefighting Water Tank
24. South Store
25. Middle Store
26. Present Use Store
27. Sail Loft
28. Rigging House
29. Workshops and Storehouses
30. Smithery
31. Block Mills
32. Ship Basin
33–38. Nos 1–6 Dry Docks
39. Camber Channel
40. Boathouse
41. Great Steam Basin
42. Ship Shop
43. New Ground: timber seasoning area
44. No. 7 Dry Dock
45. No. 8 Dry Dock
46–50. Building Slips

Portsmouth Ordnance Buildings
51. Ordnance Laboratories
52. Barrack Depot
53. Barrack Stores
54. Anglesey Barracks
55. Engineer's yard
56. Old Gunwharf: Storehouses
57. Old Gunwharf: Offices
58. New Gunwharf: Storehouses
59. New Gunwharf: Grand Storehouses
60. Colewort Barracks
61. Cambridge Barracks
62. Royal Clarence Barracks
63. Domus Dei or Garrison Chapel

Portsmouth and Portsea Defences
A Sluice
B Left Demi-Bastion
C Unicorn Ravelin
D Duke of York's Bastion
E Lion Ravelin
F Townshend's Bastion
G Right Ravelin
H Amherst Redoubt
J Beeston's Bastion
K Guy's Bastion
L Landport Ravelin
M Townmount Bastion
N East Ravelin
O East Bastion
P Montagu Ravelin
Q Pembroke Bastion
R King's Ravelin
S King's Bastion
T King's Counterguard
U Spur Redoubt
W Point Redoubt

(The Royal Commission on the Historical Monuments of England)

amount of specialisation between yards. For instance, Sheerness would fit out ships from Woolwich and Chatham, as Plymouth fitted those from Pembroke. Rennie's scheme for a Great Basin at Portsmouth was rejected by Clarence on grounds of the cost which was estimated at £913,000, and the injury to the rights of commoners over the Hard.[14]

Pressure for savings mounted as the Wellington Administration entered 1830. The Admiralty, under far greater central control than had been the case hitherto, demanded that the Navy Board achieve the long desired figure of 6,000 workmen in the yards by the following year; reduce wages to allow a good man to earn 5 shillings in ten hours and abolish chip money. This was a complete reversal of the logic of Byam Martin's work. Demonstrating a somewhat distant approach to the issues, they suggested reducing the number of labourers, increasing wages and resuming work on Saturday. This last boon was to be the reward for reductions. When the number employed in the yards fell to 7,000 the men could work on Wednesday afternoons; at 6,500 they would be permitted to work on Saturday mornings, but only at 6,000 would they be allowed to work throughout the sixth day. The final total would include 2,500 shipwrights, exclusive of apprentices. The labour force would be employed as follows:

Woolwich	500
Chatham	1,000
Sheerness	600
Portsmouth	1,800
Plymouth	1,600
Pembroke	500

Byam Martin accepted Cockburn's argument that chip money was 'monstrous', but observed that it was vital to keeping the shipwrights' goodwill. He preferred to cut wages. Later, task and job payments were extended to cover new and almost all repair work in order to reduce the number of measurers required. Melville defended the new arrangements, claiming that men in the Royal dockyards earned less than those in merchant yards because they had job security. This was certainly worth something for many Thames shipwrights were unemployed for two or three months each year.[15]

Victory lying in Number 2 Dock at Portsmouth in 1987. (Author)

When he left office in November 1830 Melville set out the reductions that had been achieved in the dockyards since 1822.

	Salaried officers	*Salary*
Navy office	15	£3,255
Home yards	468	£88,650
Foreign yards	29	£13,600
	512	£105,505

Inferior salaried officers to be reduced this year 198

Artificers and labourers in the Home yards

1822	12,043	
1830	7,220	
	4,823 at £55 each	£265,265
	Total	£370,770

A new system this year dispenses with 22 clerks in the yards and the discontinuance of chip money alone saves £30,000 a year

Victualling reductions £30,215

£430,985[16]

Economic reform

The new Board, under Graham, had a more radical agenda for the yards. Barrow's memorandum of November 1831 pointed toward greater responsibility by the leading men who would inspect the work of their team. Task and job was still considered the best system for all measurable work. The Board accepted that they would have to go back into the market for ships in the event of war and used this as an argument to reduce the numbers of battleships kept on the Navy List, taking the figure of seventy-five. To increase the efficient use of the yards, repairs were to be limited to a quarter or at most three-eighths, of the cost of a new ship, and large repairs would be reduced by increased attention to small repairs. The paper ended by calling for a more detailed examination of the value of all repairs carried out since 1815. Graham also consulted his constituent, the shipbuilder and owner Thomas Brocklebank of Whitehaven, on the distinctions between merchant and warship building. While Graham wanted to find evidence for reducing the yards, Brocklebank reckoned that the cost of a warship would exceed that of a first-class merchant vessel by around 10 shillings a ton.

By 1832 Graham had made several decisions. He believed the yards were badly run and uneconomic and that there were more workmen than necessary; also that there was too little supervision and little chance of promotion. He wanted to make a considerable reduction in men and end task and job pay as 'contrary to every sound principle of political economy'. As the fleet was far too large it was decided that any ship requiring a repair beyond half the cost of a new ship should be disposed of, and a battlefleet of sixty taken as the standard, which would require four new ships a year if the figure of 15 years was accepted as the average life of a ship. He did not believe any future war would last even a fifth of the time occupied by the previous one, which would allow the peace estimates to be reduced. This in turn would reduce the number of artificers to a mere 4,500. Byam Martin's argument about the fall in the number of shipwrights was rebutted by pointing out that there were 13,000 men working at that trade in the United Kingdom.[17]

The results of these decisions were quick to follow. Men were discharged in large numbers. Hitherto, the yards had operated under the charitable fiction that men would be kept at work until they qualified for a pension, which was only granted for 20 years service, and as a result many halt, lame and blind men were to be found in the yards, even after 15 years of peace. Among those paid off in 1833 were men who had lost a leg or an arm, had been reduced to imbecility by falls from the building stages or into the docks, or who were suffering from incurable diseases. The reductions fell particularly hard on the older shipwrights.[18] Opinion on these measures was divided. Many saw it as a long overdue reform, but those with a political interest in the welfare of the dockyard voters took a very different view. Admiral Codrington was far from being impressed:

> The Admiralty go on reducing the dockyards, and thereby exciting great discontent proportional to the severity of the distress it occasions, and to the people thus thrown with their families on the parishes! The pensions of the navy are equally illiberal.[19]

Symonds favoured task and job pay for new work and skilled labour, but the Board had long ago decided to end this practice. Finally, in July 1833 task and job was abolished as 'not only unnecessary in time of peace, but was moreover liable to considerable abuse and extravagence both as to wages and materials'. The yards were already 61 men under the 6,000 Establishment, but the Admiralty saw no need to fill up the vacancies.[20]

The drive for centralisation had been hastened by the abolition of the Navy Board, and it was now reaching the limits of practical management. With Symonds at the Surveyor's Office the independence of the yards was reduced. Specialisation was also pressed. Sheerness, for example, would cease construction work and send the Timber Converter to Pembroke, which Graham believed would become the principal building yard of the Navy. This also affected Woolwich, which was responsible for the ironwork of the remaining yards.[21]

When Graham left office his memorandum emphasised the degree to which the Admiralty reforms of the past four years had given the Board control over the administration of the dockyards. The recent abolition of task and job was reckoned to save £100,000 per annum while, with a species of wild optimism common among reformers, it was claimed that the same work was being done with less materials used. The Surveyor had a very different perspective. Reflecting on the changes over the past 20 years, he observed that in 1816 Devonport had had 3,704 workmen working six days a week, while in 1834 there were only 1,672 men, and they were on a five-day week. He pointed to the alarming state of the Ordinary, called for the resumption of Saturday working and the end of large repairs for obsolescent ships.[22]

The impact of economies

In 1834 Auckland made a fresh investigation of the yards and called for more systematic work. He divided the artificers into three classes in line with the 1803 Inquiry with 6d per day differential. At the levels then set the second-class men were earning as much as those in merchant shipyards.[23] The policy debate of the late 1830s, between Symonds and the Minto Board, concerned the best use to be made of the existing yard

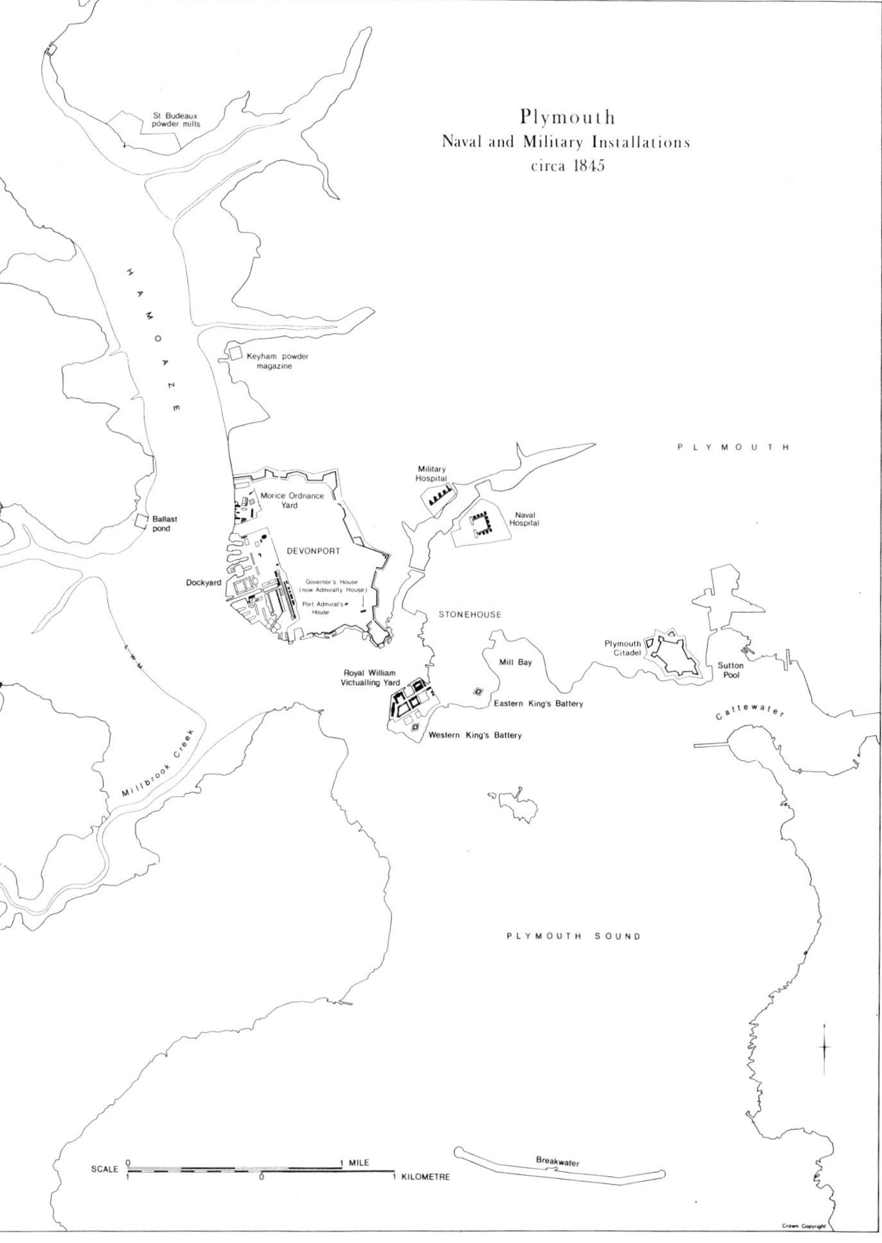

Plymouth area: naval and military installations c 1845

(The Royal Commission on the Historical Monuments of England)

capacity. The Surveyor favoured new construction but his masters wanted to keep up the fleet by repairing the Ordinary. Symonds gradually secured a resumption of work on Saturday and by late 1837 his message was beginning to have an effect on the Board. However, with only 6,090 workmen, 1,224 convicts and 285 hired labourers the yards were not capable of meeting the demands placed on them by either large-scale repairs or increased new construction. Symonds wanted to break up more hulks and build new slipways but the Board could not find the money. Shipwrights were moved from work on the infrastructure to increase the number building ships. In 1838 Symonds reported on the strength in the shipwright department.

There were 2,557 listed
2,562 on the books
83 sick
784 not working on ships
1,005 working on repairs
which left 690 for new work

continued.

This force was equal to constructing in one year:

7 steamers
6/8 of a battleship
2/8 of a Fourth Rate
4/8 of a Fifth Rate
4/8 of a Sixth Rate
4/8 of a sloop
5 3/4 brigs

Symonds called for the construction of four battleships per annum, with five to be laid down in 1839. There were twenty-six suitable slips, but if four were kept for steamers, and one or two for large frigates, there was only adequate capacity for construction and left for seasoning ships, he called for more slips. Day pay, he concluded, by removing incentive, reduced the amount of work done.[24]

Minto was finally persuaded to act by Symonds's alarming figures. He blamed Graham for a situation that had been allowed to persist for four years after Sir James left office, despite repeated warnings from the Surveyor. Wood at least was sanguine:

I do not entertain the least apprehension of difficulties in

Devonport Naval and Ordnance Buildings *c.* 1850 *(Buildings in solid black still survive)* (The Royal Commission on the Historical Monuments of England)

Dockyard
1. Main Gateway
2. Master Warden's House
3. Stables
4. Chapel
5. Reservoir
6. Pay Office
7. Team Stables
8. Painters' Shed
9. Painters' Workshop
10. Guardhouse
11. Officers' Terrace
12. Officers' Stables
13. Master Ropemaker's Offices
14. White Yarn Houses
15. Tarring House
16. Black Yarn House
17. Hemp Houses
18. Spinning House
19. Laying House
20. Topping House
21. Boathouse
22. Office
23. Plank Store with Mast Locks underneath
24. Mould Loft
25. Masthouses
26. Saw Pits
27. Cabin
28. Hemp and Pitch House
29. Guardhouse
30. Plumbers' Shop
31. Smithery
32. Bricklayers' Yard
33. House Carpenters' Workshop
34. Shipwrights' Sheds
35. Dry docks' pump
36. Joiners' Workshop
37. Sheds
38. Main Offices
39. Cabin
40. Timber Yard
41. Rigging House
42. Sail Loft
43. Quadrangle Storehouses
44. Offices
45. Cabin
46. Cabin
47. Carpenters' Workshop
48. Stores
49. Stores
50. Steaming Kilns
51. Offices
52. The original 1692 Offices
53. South Channel
54. Dry Docks
55. Building Slips
56. 1692 West Dock
57. Inner Mast Pond
58. Outer Mast Pond
59. Graving Slip
60. Former Commissioner's Garden
61. Gazebo
62. Boat Pond
63. Master Ropemaker's House

Morice Ordnance Yard
64. Main Gate
65. Magazine
66. Gun Carriage Store
67. Storehouse and Blacksmith's Shop
68. Former Artillery Hospital and Nurses' Quarters, now Stores
69. Officer's Terrace
70. Storehouse
71. Storehouse
72. Guardhouse
73. Storehouse
74. Gun Searchers' Store
75. Storehouse
76. Storehouse
77. Gun Carriage Store/Wheelwrights' Shop and Furbisher's Shop

Royal William Victualling Yard
78. Guardhouse
79. Officers' Houses
80. Slaughterhouse
81. Bakery
82. Open storage area
83. Melville Square Storehouse
84. Cooperage
85. Brewery
86. Clarence Wharf Storehouses
87. Military Hospital
88. Naval Hospital

A North Demi-Bastion
B Marlborough Bastion
C Granby Bastion
D Frederick Gateway
E Frederick Bastion
F George's Bastion
G Marlborough Square
H Granby Square
J Frederick Square
K Ligonier Square
L Cumberland Square
M George's Square
N Port Admiral's House
P Mont Wise
Q Laboratory

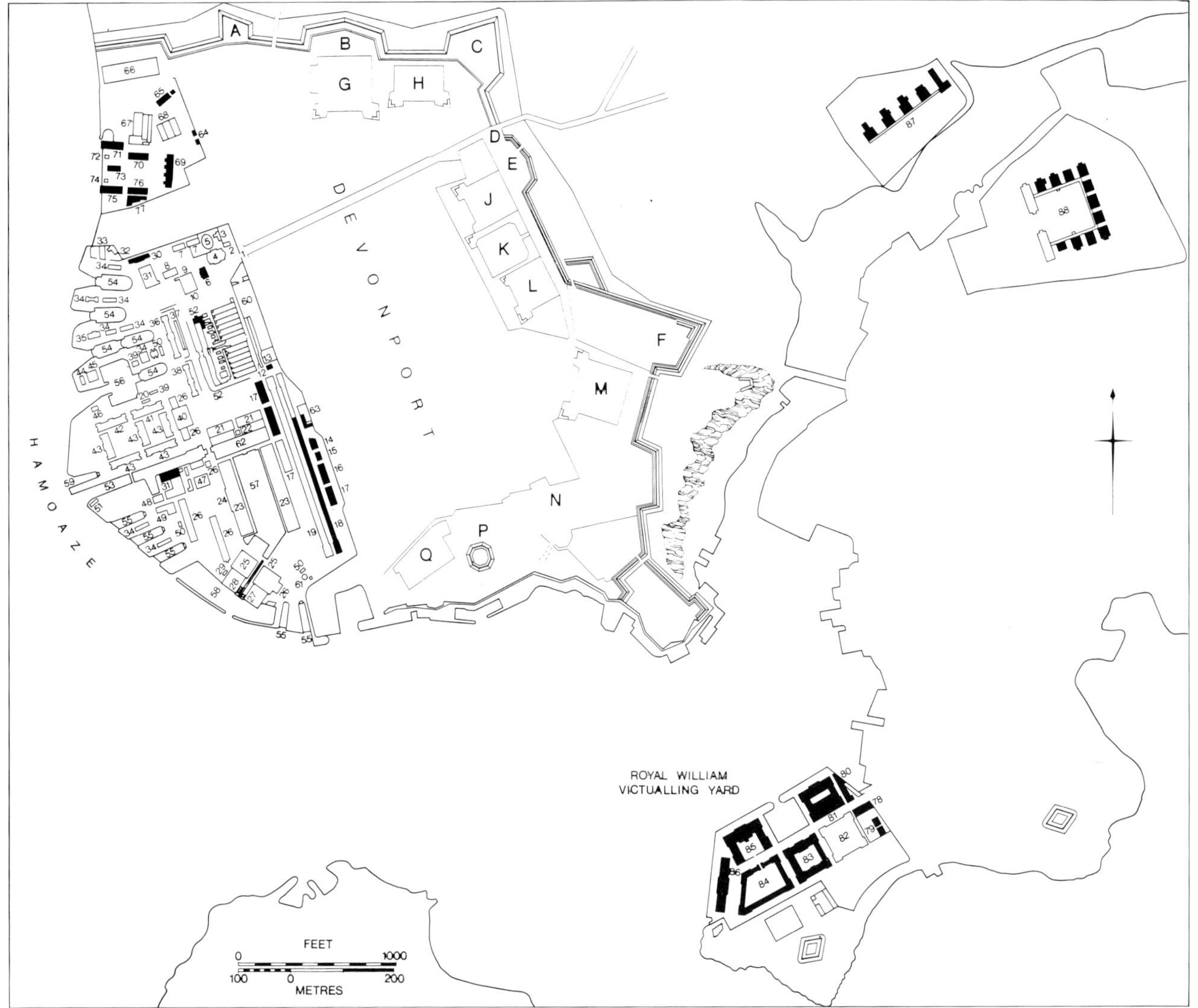

> the House of Commons as to anything we may think it right to propose; in general the guardians of the public purse have of late been more extravagent than ourselves, but undoubtedly Rice (The Chancellor) will object. I confess, however that I do not think we should be justified with what we now see of our means, in repeating again the expence of last year, and postponing what we thought right, on account of his difficulties. . .
>
> But if we increase our building, we must unless we are prepared to launch largely, expend money in No. 11 for *roofs* and *slips*. We postponed last year one roof and two slips for want of money, and if we are to make that good we ought in fairness to have three slips and two roofs this year.[25]

Accepting the need to build three battleships a year, and repair two more the Board permitted the yards to recruit extra labour, for a total of 7,000 shipwrights. This involved a total of 779 new men which included:

480 shipwrights
40 caulkers
95 smiths
95 sawyers
60 labourers

The extra cost was £52,000 for wages and materials. Despite this concession the Board was still anxious to save money by patching up the existing fleet. In June 1839 Wood resigned on a separate issue. His policy had been to build up the infrastructure and stores ready to increase construction and he blamed Graham for a situation that it had been in his power to influence since 1835. Symonds argued that only a significant increase in the number of shipwrights would allow the yards to build and repair at the agreed levels. This applied in almost every area, but specifically in the smithy departments. Ironwork for new ships was late, while the two Indian-built 84s that had yet to be commissioned were still without their ironwork.[26]

The panic orders of 1839 and 1840 ensured that when Minto left office the lists were filled with phantom ships, which allowed him to claim: 'we have greatly increased the building in our yards'. In addition, he admitted that the Establishment had to be brought back to eighty by new and repair work, which required extra slips. To control the yards Minto wanted an additional Naval Lord, not in Parliament, specifically for the task.[27]

In 1841 the yards were beginning to fill with new work. The block launchings of 1839–40 had cleared many slips, allowing the 1841–42 programme to take on a degree of novelty that had been missing during the 1830s. However, the *Trafalgar*, *Boscawen*, *Hindostan* and *Amphion* were all long-term residents of their particular slipways.

Sheerness *c.* 1815 and *c.* 1830 *(Buildings in solid black still survive)* (The Royal Commission on the Historical Monuments of England)

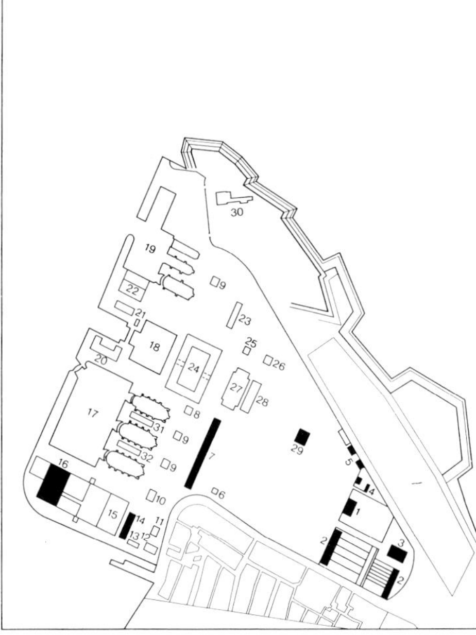

1. Commissioner's House and Office
2. Officers' accommodation
3. Chapel
4. Commissioner's Coach House and Stable
5. Dockyard Entrance
6. Tap House
7. Saw Pits, Plank Store and Mould Loft
8. Shipwrights' Store Cabin
9. Suppling Boiler
10. Top and Capstan House
11. Store Cabin
12. Poor House
13. Bricklayers' Yard
14. Steam Engine House
15. Mast and Boathouse
16. Working Masthouse
17. Great Basin
18. Small Basin
19. Boat Basin
20. Victualling Storehouse
21. Officers' Offices
22. Working Boathouse
23. Saw Pits
24. Quadrangle Storehouse
25. Pitch House
26. Caulkers' Cabin
27. Smiths' Shop
28. Iron and Coal Store
29. Military Guardhouse and Pay Office
30. Admiral's House
31. Working Sheds
32. Working Sheds
33. Garrison Barracks
34. Dockyard Workmen's Lodgings
35. Storehouses
36. Sail Loft and Rigging House
37. Rope Ground
38. Sheds
39. Mast Pond
40. Reed House
41. Mould Loft
42. New Pier

Programme of works for 1841–42: distribution of shipwrights

Ship	*Guns or steam vessel*	*State in 1841*	*Work for 1842*	*No of men to be employed*
WOOLWICH				
New Ships				
Trafalgar	120	complete launch		
Hannibal	90	frame not quite provided, advance to 2/8		38
Boscawen	70	advance from 4/8 by 2/8		32
Amphion	40	advance from 4/8 to 1/8		10
Siren	brig	complete launch		
Heroine	brig	complete launch		
Devastation	Steam	complete launch		
Duplicate	Steam	by 8/8 & launch		60
as *Cyclops*	Steam	by 2/8 & duplicate frame		18
Total men building ships				158
Repairs & casual				112
Houses & conversions				76
Sick				9
Total dockyard force				355
CHATHAM				
New Ships				
Irresistible	80	provide frame		
Goliath	80	advance by 5/8 to launch		51
Majestic	80	advance by 3/8 put in frame		34
Cumberland	70	advance from 5/16 to 7/16		40
Growler	Steam	advance from 4/8 to launch		36
duplicate	Steam	advance by 8/8 to launch		60
duplicate	Steam	put in frame		
				221
Repair				
Gloucester	50			37
Latona	44			8
Eurotas	44			5
Tortoise	storeship			15
Ships in Ordinary.				12
				77
Casual ships commissioning and brought forward				89
Mast house				40
Boat house				20
Capstan house				6
Conversion, single stationed men				36
				102
Absent & sick				11
				500
SHEERNESS				
New Ships				
Spy	Brig	to launch		
Duplicate	Steam *Styx*-class	8/8		60
Repair				
Achille	76			5
Conquestador	50			11
Cornwall	50			10
Amazon	44			8
Leonidas	44			8
Casual, ships commissioning and brought forward				181
Houses and conversions				82
Absent & sick				25
				380

Ship	*Guns or steam vessel*	*State in 1841*	*Work for 1842*	*No of men to be employed*
PORTSMOUTH				
New Ships				
Prince Albert	90	from 1/32 to 2/8 (9in frame)		38
Frolic	brig	advance by 2/8		1 & 8 boys
Caisson		3/16		1 & 13 boys
Royal Frederick	110	by 2/8 (in frame if timber ready)		46
1st class	Steam	as *Cyclops* by 4/8		36
2nd class	Steam	as *Driver* by 8/8		60
& duplicate frames for both the above st v				206
Repairs				
Prince Regent	120	30		
Imaum	74	30		
Dublin	50	20		
Warspite	50	15		
Ordinary, Defects of		25		
				120
Casual, ships commissioning and brought forward				249
Houses and Conversions				188
Absent & sick				17
				780
PLYMOUTH				
New Ships				
Albion	90	advance from 2/8 to 5/8		95
Exmouth	90	advance from 3/4 of frame to 2/8		38
Hindostan	80	advance from 6/8 by 2/8 to launch		34
Spartan	36	advance from 4/8 to 8/8 to launch		26
Philomel	brig	advance from 6/8 to 8/8 to launch		4 & 12 boys
				209
Repair				
Canopus	84	56		
America	50	10		
Melampus	44	7		
Fisgard	44	7		
Ordinary, defects of		20		
				100
Casual, ships commissioning and brought forward				254
Houses and Conversions				167
Absent & sick				17
				750
PEMBROKE				
New ships				
Collingwood	80	from 4/8 to 8/8 to launch		68
Superb	80	from 2/8 by 2/8		34
Centurion	80	from 2/8 by 2/8		34
Cambrian	36	from 6/8 by 2/8 to launch		20
Geyser	steam	15/16 by 1/16 to launch		8
2nd class	steam	as *Vixen* 8/8		60
1st class	steam	as *Cyclops* 4/8		60
& duplicate frames for the last two st v				
Repair				
Casual, ships commissioning and brought forward				4
Houses and Conversions				38
Absent & sick				8
				310 [28]

With clear and understood targets, and with the addition of almost 1,000 men, there was now a possibility that the yards could keep up with the workload though the sudden advance of steam forced a reconsideration within three years. Short of steam ships, slips and shipwrights, the First Secretary, Sidney Herbert, advised going into the merchant yards for iron steamships. This, he argued, would allow the Royal yards to build twelve wooden steamers a year, while three iron vessels were obtained outside. This, rather than any particular enthusiasm for iron, was responsible for the premature ordering of iron ships.[29]

Politics and patronage

The last major obstacle to the efficient use of the yards lay in the political affiliations of the workmen. The dockyard towns had always been represented in Parliament, and many of the senior men in the yards had the vote before 1832. Inevitably, a degree of political patronage surrounded appointments and promotion. Despite their long period out of office and the swinging cuts in the yards made under Graham, the Whigs were very successful in building support. Codrington, as the MP for Devonport, had a large following in the yard which he used to shout down and even stone his opponents. However, when he became Admiral Commander-in-Chief at Portsmouth he found the boot very much on the other foot, calling on Lord Haddington for a first class Captain Superintendent to administer the yard and control the 'idleness and insolence of many of the people employed in it'.[30] The removal of political influence from the yards was to be the last major reform of the sailing Navy. Until it had been carried through the workmen would continue to look for outside help, or ascribe their lack of success to the malign influence of politics.

Symonds's view of the situation reflected the frustrations of his office in the face of entrenched loyalties and outmoded concepts of public duty. His claims of disinterested use of patronage are hard to swallow, but he was far from the worst offender in this area.

Admiralty.

As I hear frequent complaints from the Superintendents, and the principal officers of the Dockyards, of the insubordination and other hurtful effects arising out of the present system of appointing and advancing Dockyard officers, and workmen; and am credibly informed that committees composed of persons perfectly unconnected with the Dockyards, exist in the towns at the principal seaports, for the sole purpose of selecting individuals possessed of the greatest borough, or political interest, whereby many unqualified persons are admitted, and others advanced, without regard to merit or ability, and contrary to the recommendation of the professional officers, which I consider is both prejudicial to Her Majesty's Service, and injurious to the discipline of the Dockyard; I fearlessly venture to call their Lordships' attention to this crying evil.

From the date of my appointment in June, 1832, until September, 1841, all appointments, advancements, and removals were referred to me, as provided for in the General Instructions; but have been omitted since that period. It was then my duty, as it was my greatest satisfaction, to find out from the officers the most exemplary and deserving men; and

Chatham Naval and Ordnance Buildings *c.* 1830 *(Buildings in solid black still survive)* (The Royal Commission on the Historical Monuments of England)

1. Main Gate
2. Dockyard Wall of 1718
3. Wall towers
4. Commissioner's hayfield
5. Lead and Paint Mill
6. Hemp House
7. White Yarn Store
8. Tarring House
9. Black Yarn Store
10. Hatchelling House
11. Ropery
12. Fitting Rigging House and Storehouse
13. No. 3 Storehouse
14. Anchor Wharf
15. Dockyard Chapel
16. Officers' Stables
17. Sail Loft
18. Commissioner's House
19. Commissioner's Office
20. Officers' Terrace
21. Main Offices
22. Present Use Store
23. Dock Pumping Station
24. Smithery
25. House Carpenters' Shop
26. Timber Seasoning Sheds
27. Masthouses
28. Masthouses and Mould Loft
29. Sawmills
30. South Mast Pond
31. North Mast Pond
32. Boat Store
33. Guardhouse
34. No. 3 Slip
35. No. 4 Slip
36. No. 5 Slip
37. No. 6 Slip
38. No. 7 Slip
39. Area of land reclaimed 1835–50

A Ordnance Basin and St Mary's Battery
B Left Demi-Bastion
C Right Demi-Bastion
D Long Branch
E Duke of Cumberland's Bastion
F Ravelin
G Prince Frederick's Bastion
H Townshend Redoubt
K Prince Henry's Bastion
L Prince Edward's Bastion
M King's Bastion
P Couvre Porte
R Prince of Wales Bastion
S Spur Battery
T Prince William Henry's Bastion
U Amherst Redoubt
W Belvedere Battery
X Upper Cornwallis Battery
Y Lower Cornwallis Battery
Z Old Works

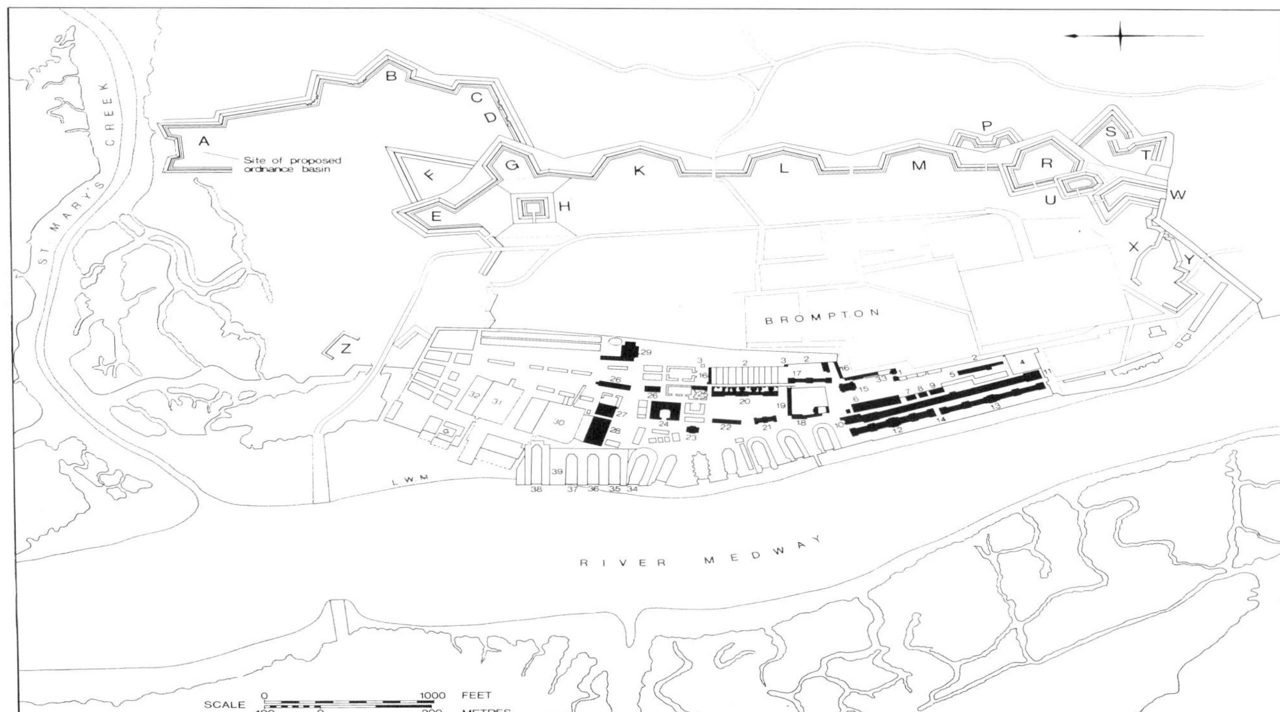

> without fear of contradiction, I declare, that *merit* from service, good conduct, and ability, were my sole guides in recommending the appointments, in the course of between nine and ten years. The greatest boon to the service would certainly be the disfranchisement of persons in the Dockyard, similar to the Customs, Excise, and the Post Office; and in the meantime I recommend that the most able and deserving people should in future be selected by the principal executive officers, who must be necessarily acquainted with their merits; and the nominations be transmitted to the Board for selection.
>
> W. SYMONDS

Haddington noted the increased costs of the dockyards, which he ascribed to the development of steam, and suggested to his successor that some enquiry should be made into the management of the yards which was affected by the abuse of patronage. Ellenborough soon prepared a minute, calling for much closer control of the yards by the Board. Ultimately, he decided that only first class Superintendents could achieve the necessary degree of control.[31]

Lord Auckland and the beginnings of modern management

Auckland followed up the lead given by Lord Ellenborough's memorandum, which had identified political abuses as the major area of concern, and secured a report from the experienced superintendent Rear Admiral William Shireff. Shireff had been five years at Deptford and then Chatham before moving on as Admiral Superintendent at Portsmouth. He considered that until the influence of politics was entirely removed from the yards nothing more could be expected of the men. The Dockyard Police were the first problem. Many were nominated by local MPs, and did not meet the Metropolitan Police standards on height. Shireff urged that no-one from within 20 miles of the yard be entered in this capacity. The workmen were also taught to look to their votes, rather than their abilities, to secure their careers. He wanted a clear test of ability to be made on all promotion gained on merit:

> to break up that equality which so generally exists among the workmen and those immediately above them ... owing to which it is very rare that an officer will complain of a man for being idle, or for working badly'.

Reform was the only answer, because no private builder could afford to build or repair 'in the same costly manner as in these public establishments'. For example overmanning at Chatham allowed the shipwrights to waste their time carrying timber to and from the kilns, and to make little use of modern machinery. At a higher level he found the Master Shipwrights used far too much material, and of too high a specification, in building their own designs. In conclusion, he suggested that if all else failed officers should be dismissed for attempting to influence the politics of the men, or that the men should be disenfranchised, as had been the case with the Customs and Excise.[32]

Shireff's report resulted in a new Dockyard Circular. Henry Ward warned Russell of this momentous change:

> I am equally convinced that there is no cure for the evils ... but an improved feeling among the men. They are now what we have made them; and if you could see one tithe of the proofs, with which my drawers are filled, of the wild expectations excited by a change of government, – the unreasonable demands, and insolent remonstrances that precede and follow every appointment, – & the firm conviction entertained by all that service has nothing to do with promotion, but that some 'sinister' influence has been at work, you would see at once, how impossible it is for the public to receive a fair return for the enormous amounts of wages paid, until the men are taught to believe that they have something to gain by doing their duty, and nothing to hope from the interference of political friends.[33]

As part of Auckland's reform of civil administration the yards were to be removed from the political sphere by a combination of Admiralty Order and improved superintendence. Having appointed Walker to administer the Surveyor's Department, Auckland then turned the attention of the Surveyor, the Accountant, the Fourth Naval Lord and the Political Secretary to the dockyards. Their report of December 1848 marked the beginning of a new system. The report made twenty-nine distinct recommendations, ranging from the duties of the Superintendent to the nature of the muster system. The object was to give greater control over the men, and more efficient handling of stores. Walker argued that these changes would allow for a reduction of 12,498 to 9,911 men by the middle of the following year, with, at the same time, the introduction of a detailed programme of works. Superannuation and the hope of an increase in merchant building would prevent the burden of the cuts falling too heavily on the working classes. Walker estimated that the eighty-ship Establishment called for by Auckland would require a workforce based on 3,500 shipwrights. Of these 1,000 would build new ships, 1,600 carry out repairs and 580 make masts and boats.[34] Walker's five-year plan involved the following new work:

Sir Baldwin Walker's five-year construction programme: 1849–1854.

Dockyard	1849	1850	1851	1852	1853	1854
Deptford			90-gun ship 1851/52			
Woolwich	80-gun ship in 1849/50			120-gun ship 1852/53		
Chatham	*Orion* & *Hood* 1849/50			90- and 80-gun ships 1852/53		
Portsmouth			120-gun ship 1851/52			
					120-gun ship 1853/54	
Plymouth	*St Jean d'Acre* 1850/51					
			80-gun ship 1851/52			
Pembroke	*James Watt* 1849/50					
			80-gun ship 1851/52		120- and 80-gun ships 1853/54	

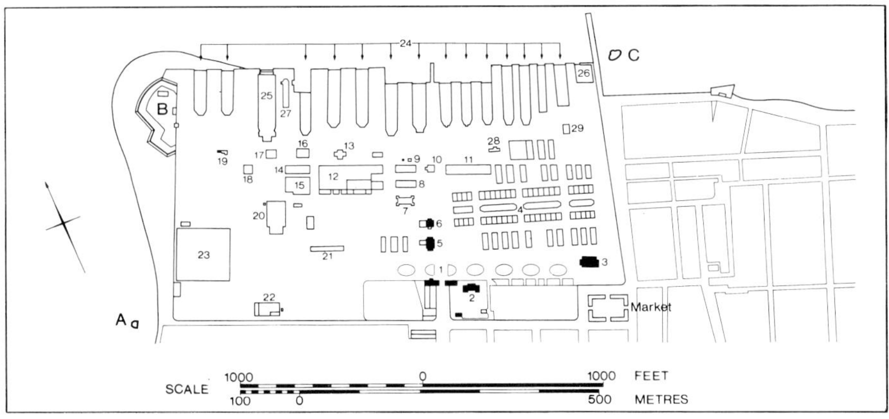

Pembroke Dockyard c. 1850

(Buildings in solid black still survive)

1. Main Gate
2. Officers' houses
3. Chapel
4. Timber seasoning sheds
5. Admiral Superintendent's house
6. Offices
7. Fire Engine House and Schoolroom
8. Storehouse
9. Storehouse
10. Offices
11. Mould Loft and Joiners' shop
12. Smitheries
13. Steam Kiln
14. Foundry
15. Coal Yard
16. Oakum Store
17. Pitch House
18. Guardhouse
19. Steam Kiln
20. Sawmills and Workshops
21. Saw Pits
22. Workshops
23. Timber Pond
24. Building Slips
25. Dry Dock
26. Boat Slip
27. Saw Mills and Dock Pump
28. Steam Kiln
29. Boathouse

A Gun Tower
B Pater Battery
C Gun Tower

(The Royal Commission on the Historical Monuments of England)

The Admiralty was entirely satisfied with the programme and promised not to interfere without specific consultation. The workforce to carry out this programme was approved by Order in Council in 1850:

Deptford	581	Portsmouth	2,351
Woolwich	998	Plymouth	2,158
Chatham	1,607	Pembroke	880
Sheerness	1,046	Total	9,621 men

This would be 'sufficient for the wants of the service, unless some unforseen emergency should arise'. In 1852 Walker reported that the reduced labour force was equal to the work load.[35] Alongside these new programmes Baring carried on the work of Auckland in imposing a political qualification on all dockyard officers. Each new man was offered his appointment on the specific condition that he did not interfere in local politics. The clumsy attempts of the Northumberland Administration to resuscitate the dockyards as electioneering machines in 1852 was defeated by Walker's obstinacy and the fall of the Administration. That did not stop Disraeli attempting both to remove Walker and alter the balance of power in the yards. He considered the Whig party had captured the patronage of the yards, and then kicked away the machinery by which the Tories might have recovered their support.[36]

Slips and docks and area within the wall: 1830

	Slips	*Docks*	*Acres*
Deptford	5	2	31 (closed 1832–44)
Woolwich	7	2	50
Chatham	6	5	76
Sheerness	1	4	54
Portsmouth	5	7	85
Plymouth	5	4	77
Pembroke	4	1	65
	(10 slips by 1850)		
	28	23	

Repairs

A very large repair	equal to the cost of a new ship
A large repair	9/10 of the cost of a new ship
A middling to large repair	3/4
A middling repair	5/8
A small to middling repair	3/8
A small repair	1/5
A very small repair	1/8

Repairs were classified according to their cost relative to a new ship of the same size.
With new work materials and labour were in the ratio of 5 to 1
With repairs materials and labour were in the ratio of 3 to 1

Workmen: 1814–1835, (on first day of the year)

	Dockyard & Ropery	*Shipwright*	*Apprentices*
1814	15,634	3,714	
1822	11,601	3,555	
1823	8,951	3,197	411
1824	8,673	3,339	263
1825	8,576	3,324	230
1826	8,573	3,097	364
1827	8,571	3,057	406
1830	7,716	2,852	404
1834	5,885	2,515	34
1835	6,165	2,455	110

Workmen at the individual yards September 1835

	Shipwrights	*Apprentices*	*Workmen*
Woolwich	285	15	685
Chatham	394	24	1,045
Sheerness	262	17	715
Portsmouth	634	28	1,594
Plymouth	631	27	1,640
Pembroke	223	13	484
Total	2,429	124	6,163

Average earnings

	Shipwrights	*Labourers*
War	6s 7d	3s 3d
April 1825	5s 0$\frac{1}{4}$d	3s 1$\frac{1}{4}$d
April 1827	5s 0$\frac{1}{4}$d	3s 0$\frac{3}{4}$d
December 1821	3s 11$\frac{3}{4}$d	2s 4$\frac{1}{2}$d
December 1827	4s 10$\frac{1}{2}$d	3s 1d

Caulkers earned slightly more than shipwrights, smiths 1s less. The differential between the two December figures can be explained by reference to the heightened level of international tension in the latter year.

Breaking up a ship. The 64-gun Diadem

Plymouth Yard

Labour: seventy shipwrights, three apprentices & convicts	£395.12s
Serviceable Materials, timber copper, lead & pumps	£444.17. 5d
Materials sold	£2,616. 9. 5d
Total	£3,061. 6.10d

Many timbers were re-used, in less vital areas; some went into slipways, others were used to build storehouses and jetties, harbour craft and mud barges.

Sources: Martin Memoranda Add 41,403/4.
Wood Memoranda Add 49,571.

Docks and slips May 1848, and class of ship able to be built or repaired

	Docks	*Ships*	*Slips*	*Ships*
Deptford	2	1 frigate	5	1 1st Rate, 3 frigates, 1 sloop
Woolwich	3	1 1st Rate	7	3 1st Rates, 1 3rd Rate, 1 sloop, 2 (unserviceable)
Chatham	4	2 1st Rates, 2 frigates	7	6 1st Rate, 1 16-gun ship
Sheerness	5	3 1st Rates, 1 frigate, 1 sloop	1	1 5th Rate
Portsmouth	8	2 1st Rates, (2 bldg), 1 2nd Rate, 3 3rd Rates	5	1 1st Rate, 1 2nd Rate, 1 5th Rate, 2 steam sloops
Devonport	4	2 1st Rates, 2 2nd Rates	6	3 2nd Rates, 1 4th Rate, 1 6th Rate, 1 graving slip
Pembroke	1	1st Rate	14	6 1st Rates, 4 2nd Rates, 1 26-gun ship, 2 brigs, 1 boat, last 3 incomplete
	27		45	

Current and projected slip use: May 1848

Ship no	*Ship*	*No of guns or steam vessel*	*State of vessel*	*Ship to follow*	*No of guns or steam vessel*	*Roof status*
DEPTFORD						
1.	*Phaeton*	50	6/8	*Hannibal*	90	
2.	vacant			*Cracker*	steam	
3.	*Wasp*	steam				
4.	*Leopard*	steam frigate				
5.	*Archer*	steam				all roofed
WOOLWICH						
1.	*Royal Albert*	120	4/8			
2.	*Basilisk*	steam		*Hornet*	steam	
3.	vacant			timber shed		
4.	vacant			*Brisk*	steam	
5.	vacant			for repair		
6.	vacant			for repair		
7.	*Nankin*	50	4/8			1,2, & 4 roofed
SHEERNESS						
1.	*Diamond*	steam	6/8	*Miranda*	steam	Roofed
PORTSMOUTH						
1.	*Princess Royal*	90	2/8	*Marlborough*	120	
2.	*Royal Frederick*	110	7/8	*Royal Sovereign*	120	
3.	*Prince of Wales*	110				
4.	*Argus* st v			*Resolute* st v		
5.	*Furious* st f					3 have roofs
DEVONPORT						
1.	*Niobe*	28	2/8	*Liffey*	50	
2.	*Indefatigable*	50	7/8	*Phoebe*	50	
3.	*Aboukir*	90	8/8	*Algiers*	90	
4.	*Exmouth*	90	5/8	*James Watt*	80 steam	
5.	*Sans Pareil*	80	2/8	*St Jean d'Acre*	90	all roofed
PEMBROKE						
1.	vacant					not roofed
2.	vacant					not roofed
3.	*Brunswick*	80	2/8			Zinc roof
4.	*Victoria*	110	3/8			
5.	*Arethusa*	50	6/8	*Windsor Castle*	110	
6.	*Colossus*	80	8/8	*Caesar*	90	
7.	*Sutlej*	50	1/8			Iron roof
8.	*Octavia*	50	2/8			Iron roof
9.	*Desperate*	steam	5/8			Iron roof
10.	*Magicienne*	steam	4/8	*Valorous*	steam	
11.	*Buzzard*	steam	3/8			
12.	vacant			*Barracouta*	steam	
13.	vacant			*Liberty*	brig	

Source P.P. 1847–8 pp. 917–9

2 *Empire and Seapower: the Exploitation of Indian Resources*

Between 1805 and 1855 Britain made use of Indian resources, particularly the timber reserves and shipbuilding facilities of Bombay and the Malabar coast, to reinforce the efforts of the home country. This resulted in the construction of major warships in India, together with a similar number built in England with Indian timber. These ships were not intended to operate from Indian harbours, and were never fitted out for service in India, but formed part of the imperial battlefleet operating from home ports, in the Mediterranean and even on the coast of China. Although India remained outside the Empire at this period it was more fully integrated into the imperial defence structure than it was to be in any subsequent period.

British Government policy towards Indian resources can be divided into two periods: first, the years up to 1815, when naval resources were valued beyond price; second, the postwar period, when growing pressure for economy led to the abandonment of ship construction in India, although materials were still sent home, on no less than three occasions. Attempts to create a complete naval arsenal in the Indian Ocean foundered on the opposition of the East India Company, the shortage of skilled labour, the cost of transporting raw materials to the theatre and, perhaps most fundamentally, on the reluctance of the administrators in London to create a major base that would not be under their direct control. Consequently, the import of Indian timber proved the most enduring policy, for domestic political reasons. Existing accounts of the Indian shipbuilding effort are unreliable and later commentators have perpetuated their errors and added further confusion.[1]

Teak and forest policy

Teak has long been recognised as the finest shipbuilding timber. The modern classification considers it very durable, of the highest grade of timber and unusually resistant to marine borers such as the dread *teredo navalis*. Its disadvantages are that it is only suitable for moderate bends, and possesses a severe blunting effect on tools.[2] It requires only the most brief period of seasoning and the natural oils, in sharp contrast to the tannic acid of oak sap, act as a preservative of ferrous metals. Indian shipbuilders had always fastened their vessels with iron spikes and had no experience of boring and fitting trenails on the European pattern. The ability to deliver fully seasoned ships in little more than a year from the laying of the keel was a major attraction of the Bombay yard. In addition, these ships could be used in hot climates when new, something that was considered unwise for European oak-built ships, and they proved more resistant to the climate of the Indian and China seas.

Before 1800 Britain had no interest in, and almost no access to, this Indian and Burmese product. Unlike Spain, her own

The pride of the Bombay yard, Asia, *an 84-gun derivative of the* Canopus *launched in 1824. As the Flagship of Sir Edward Codrington she played a major part in the destruction of the Turco-Egyptian fleet at Navarin in 1827, and survived into the twentieth century.* (NMM)

timber resources had held up to the demands of war.[3] Only after 1802 did the failure of British timber policy, brought about in particular by Earl St Vincent's ill-timed attack on the timber suppliers' monopoly, shift attention to India. The second war against Tippu Sultan, ruler of Mysore, in 1799 placed almost the whole west coast of India from Bombay to the extreme south in British hands and this area, in particular the Malabar hills, produced the finest teak. The quality of this timber had long been recognised by the Arab traders of the Persian Gulf who purchased cargoes already sawn into planks. British recognition of the value of the teak forests came when the East India Company embargoed the export of teak to the Arabs in an attempt to coerce the Quasimi traders.[4] By 1813 it was admitted that these efforts had failed, but by then the Company had other reasons to concern itself with timber.[5]

The Company had been building ships at Bombay for many years before 1800 using British designs, Indian labour and materials. With the increasing cost of constructing large Indiamen on the Thames in the traditional Blackwall yards – both timber and labour costs rocketed during the Revolutionary Wars – first-class Indiamen were built at Bombay, beginning with the *Scaleby Castle* of 1798.[6] With increasing tempo, and the ever larger ships being built at Bombay, there arose concern for the timber supply. Tippu Sultan had established teak as a 'Royal' tree which belonged to the Sultan, a regulation the Company continued. In 1800 the felling of trees over 21in in girth was prohibited.[7]

The origins of naval construction at Bombay

The apparent failure of native oak in Britain to supply the needs of the Royal Navy had become a source of concern by 1802. This forced the Admiralty to permit paying increased prices, and reducing contract specification. Furthermore, in that year the Admiralty accepted the Navy Board's proposal that the size of East India Company ships building on the Thames be limited. The First Lord, St Vincent, threatened to limit the Company to 800-ton ships, in place of the normal 1,200 tons. At the same time he expressed a desire for the Company to build one ship of the line and one frigate at Bombay on an annual basis. These, he concluded, would be of great importance to the support of the naval strength of the Empire.[8]

An order for a 74 and a frigate were sent out in 1803 and the Company was to build the ships at Bombay, under the supervision of Naval Constructors. In return, they were to be paid for the hire of the dock while the ship was being built, their costs and 20 per cent on top. The Navy was to provide a large quantity of the tools, including axes and adzes, ropes and blocks for hoisting up the frames, along with iron bolts, nails and weights.[9] This arrangement, entered into in time of war, proved to be a charter for the less scrupulous members of the company to exploit naval funds. The inspiration for this policy came from Henry Dundas, First Viscount Melville, in 1801, shortly after St Vincent took office.[10] When Pitt replaced Addington as Prime Minister in 1804 Dundas took over as First Lord of the Admiralty. He continued the initiative, alongside hurried efforts to increase construction in Britain. Dundas was a great enthusiast for developing the resources of India *in situ*, rather than exploiting them in Britain, for one of his objects was to increase the area under British control.[11]

This policy was well known in political circles, and not particularly popular. Thomas Grenville, First Lord 1806–7, preferred to use Indian timber in British dockyards because of the costs of setting up facilities in India, particularly the new works on Prince of Wales Island on the coast of Mysore, which many considered to be politically motivated.[12] Dundas's wide network of Hiberno-Indian connections, built up through his long tenure at the Indian Administration as President of the Board of Control, provided him with useful reports on the resources of the region and kept him informed of the progress of work. The most important of these connections was the Governor-General, Lord Wellesley. Dundas claimed to have been studying the possibilities of shipbuilding in India for the past 20 years, and discussing the subject with Sir Charles Middleton, one-time Controller of the Navy and later, as Lord Barham, First Lord. He was impressed by the teak-built ships already seen in Britain, and while his nephew just back from Bombay had been far from sanguine as to the supply of timber, the shortages in Britain made it essential to act. He hoped to build 64s at Bombay, 44s at Cochin, with Rangoon, Pegu and Prince of Wales Island providing the 74s. The forests at Pegu were reckoned to be inexhaustible. The letter to Wellesley was sent with Sir Edward Pellew who proved a powerful advocate.[13]

The Bombay-built 74-gun Wellesley *of 1815 serving as the training ship* Cornwall. *Although normally cited as a member of the* Black Prince*-class this ship was actually built to the lines of the previous Bombay 74, the* Cornwallis, *as her plans were lost when the USS* Constitution *destroyed the* Java *in 1812.* (CMP)

Under pressure from the Government, the Court of Directors ordered a survey of the timber resources in India. The Bombay Government's initial inspection of the major forests caused a sharp downward revision of the earlier estimates. Malabar teak was no longer seen as an inexhaustible resource and the Government at Bombay took action in November 1806, resuming Tippu's claim to the trees and appointing Captain Watson of the Bombay Police as Conservator of Forests. While his powers were wide-ranging, they were also ill-defined, and ultimately counter-productive. They were renounced in 1823, a dangerous backward step which prevented any attempt at a long term forestry policy.[14] Though the impact of any forestry policy would not have had time to have any impact on the remaining years of the wooden battlefleet, this was not known at the time. Furthermore, the supply of large curved timber was already a major problem for Bombay and remained one for the rest of the period.

Although out of office after 1805, Dundas kept his finger on the pulse of Indian policy. The Governor of Bombay, Jonathan Duncan, one of his Scots nominees, kept him informed on the progress of the New Docks, and the 74 that was being built in them as they were completed. In 1808 he estimated the timber supply as equal to two 74s a year, with one or two frigates. This proved over optimistic in many respects. Problems with the bed rock delayed the dock, and while a magnificent construction it had been built as a double dock, one inside the other, and the inner dock was entirely dependent on progress in the outer. When the cost overrun threatened to reach 50 per cent Duncan, nervous that he might be held responsible, claimed that Pellew had overpersuaded him of the importance of the docks for naval service.[15] This may explain why Duncan proved so ruthless in squeezing the Navy for every rupee of dock hire.

The shipyard set up on Prince of Wales Island collapsed before the first 74 could be launched, from lack of resources and manpower, and this forced the Navy to concentrate its efforts at Bombay where the Company could provide the infrastructure.[16] There was a concerted effort to build a naval arsenal in Ceylon, at Trincomalee, to avoid the dangers of becoming completely dependent on the Company. Relations between the Sea Officers, the Naval Commissioners and the Bombay administration remained poor throughout the war period, and coloured the decision to move to Trincomalee, which was fated to fail for want of any postwar commitment.[17]

In Britain the Board of Control saw the latest series of forest reports as indicating 'a permanent and valuable supply of large ship timber', which they wanted to exploit to repay the cost of the surveys and rather more significantly of the new docks. To this end they hoped to build two 74s per year.[18] Negotiations with the Admiralty indicated that both parties were anxious to contract for a second 74, although Barrow, Second Secretary to the Admiralty, accused the Company of throwing up 'insuperable obstacles ... as they do at all times and to all proposals whenever they can'.[19]

The Navy Board Commissioner at Bombay, George Dundas, was able to report good progress on the first 74, the *Minden*, although construction of the dock in which she was building was interfering, as was the shortage of structural ironwork. However, the delay had been exploited to prepare almost all the timber for the next ship, the *Cornwallis*. The latest forest reports, particularly on the Forest of Ernaud, the principle source of shipbuilding timber, were mixed and replanting up to 7,000 trees a year was recommended, acknowledging that only two years supply remained.[20]

Within a year of this first account of progress Dundas was reporting problems with Governor Duncan, who was intent on a little sharp practice, if nothing worse, at the Admiralty's expense. Not only was he charging the Navy for the use of a dock in which a merchant ship was being built, but he was deliberately delaying work on the timbers for *Cornwallis*. Dundas was convinced that the object was to ensure that more work had to be done after the keel was laid, from which point dock hire was chargeable, 'by which means the ship will be so many months longer in docks, and he will receive so many more thousands of rupees for these additional months'. Furthermore, Duncan refused point blank to provide any information on the cost of timber, having his assistant secretary respond to Dundas's enquiries with a mean, obstructive and legalistic letter that simply ignored the request. Unsurprisingly, Dundas advocated direct negotiations with the Board of Control in London in order to deprive Duncan of the power which he held over the Navy Board's local representative.[21]

To a certain extent the delay can be traced to the lack of rain in the monsoon season of 1812 which left the rivers in the forests too dry for floating down large quantities of timber. This prompted the Commissioner at Madras, Peter Puget, to press for the Navy to enter into timber contracts with local merchants, as he considered the Company charged 'an exhorbitant price'. Commissioner Johnstone at Bombay noted that it was at least 20 per cent above cost.[22]

While the war continued, the Admiralty was happy to re-order ships as soon as the dock was vacant. The capture of the *Java*, along with plans, by the USS *Constitution* on 29 December 1812, deprived the dockyard of several new designs which were to be built in the following year. Most significantly, the new 74 *Wellesley* was to have been built as a replica of *Black Prince*, but with no plans to hand the Commissioner elected to re-use the moulds prepared for the *Cornwallis*. When *Wellesley*'s ironwork arrived it did not fit and, unwilling to trust the alterations to the local blacksmiths, Johnstone elected to hold it over for the next 74, the *Melville*. The duplicate frame sent home in *Wellesley* to be erected in England was prepared to the plans of the *Melville*. At such a distance the Surveyors of the Navy were obliged to accept the local decision to re-use the *Cornwallis* draft.[23]

Postwar policy

The end of the War allowed the Admiralty and Navy Board to take stock of the arrangements for building in India. By this stage the Surveyors of the Navy were sufficiently impressed with teak ships and the advantages of building new, useable tonnage in such a short time that they recommended procuring as many teak ships as possible. The first postwar order was for

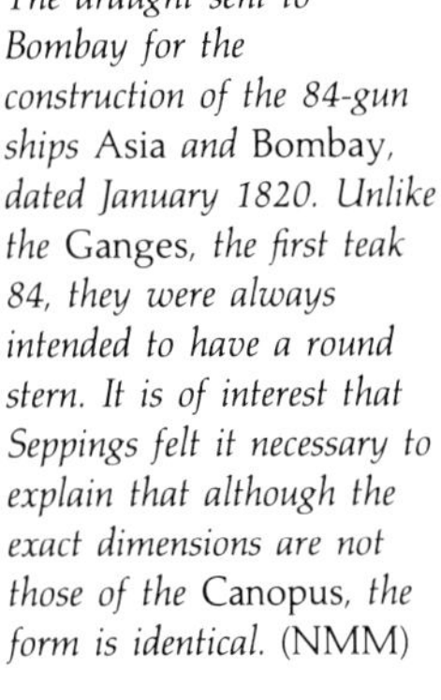

The draught sent to Bombay for the construction of the 84-gun ships Asia *and* Bombay, *dated January 1820. Unlike the* Ganges, *the first teak 84, they were always intended to have a round stern. It is of interest that Seppings felt it necessary to explain that although the exact dimensions are not those of the* Canopus, *the form is identical.* (NMM)

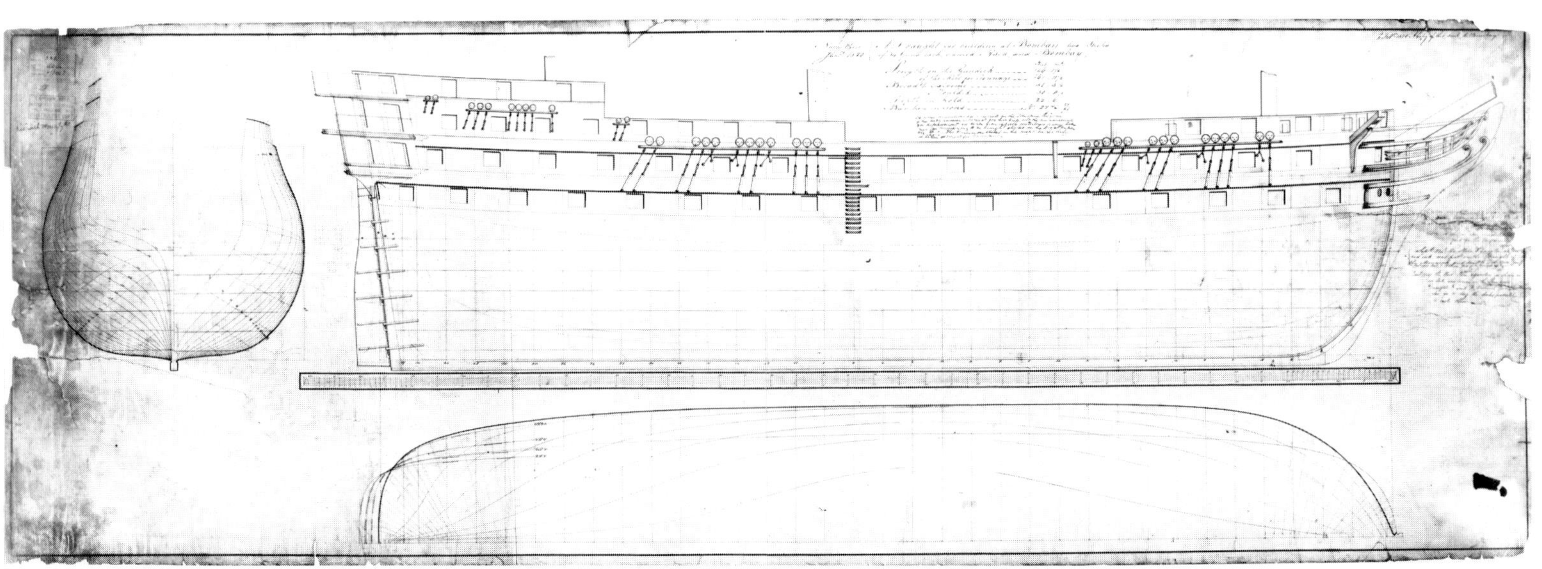

the *Malabar* to be constructed after the *Melville* had been launched and that she should bring home two duplicate frames. The new ship was also to be the first to incorporate Seppings's diagonal structure.[24] *Malabar* was the last 74 ordered by the Admiralty, only two months before the 84-gun *Formidable*. The decision to carry on building at Bombay after the War reflected the poor condition of the existing fleet, the high opinion already formed of the Indian ships, in particular their immediate availability for foreign stations, and the value of the duplicate teak frame.

A more considered approach to postwar policy required time for the officials of both the Navy and the Company in London and Bombay to consult. During this era an exchange of correspondence between London and Bombay required at least a year. On hearing of the first abdication of Bonaparte, Commissioner Johnstone suggested mooring some new ships at Bombay, as a reserve. He also argued that more materials should be sent out, notably the masts, as local supplies were inadequate and expensive. He sustained the attack on the Company, which he accused of taking no steps to ascertain the actual resources of the forests or to secure the supply. Plank was still plentiful, but curved timber from the north was hard to come by. In addition, charges for dock hire (2,000 rupees a month), labour and timber were all excessive. Dock hire raised the cost per ton of the Indian ships from £31.10s per ton to £34 and this price did not include the cost of sending them home.[25] The Admiralty had been subjected to a powerful campaign against Indian-built teak ships by the ship builders of the Thames. All manner of arguments had been used, from poor sailing to excessive splinters. None were real, although Dundas's son, the Second Viscount Melville, then First Lord of the Admiralty, did require some convincing, despite inheriting his father's interest in matters Indian.[26]

At the same time alternative sources of supply, both for timber and ships, were advocated with varying degrees of vigour. The capture of Java in 1812 gave Britain access to more teak forests. William Domett, Master Shipwright at Plymouth, urged Melville, who he knew to be 'favourably disposed to the wise measure of building ships in India', to press the Dutch to allow the exploitation of these forests when the island was returned to them. He believed the forests were inexhaustible. The timber was highly regarded and considered to be equal to the best Malabar teak, but imports to the Indian market did dry up after the return of the Dutch; the Court at the Hague left their colonial forests idle allowing colonial shipbuilding in Java, promoted by the British, to wither while Dutch warships continued to be built at home of inferior Baltic timber.[27]

Calcutta

A more thorough approach to the problem was made by the shipbuilding interest at Calcutta. Realising that the profit margin on large warships was superior to ordinary commercial construction, a group of merchants and builders took shares in building a 74-gun ship at Kyd's Dock, Kidderpore, downstream of Calcutta. The Anglo-Indian James Kyd had been arguing the case for Calcutta for some years, with little success, and this speculative measure was his last throw. The *Hastings* was built as an 18-pounder 74 on Seppings's diagonal system. Given the object of the exercise it is not surprising that she was fastened with copper, rather than iron, and included the best materials. The final cost, £108,938 ready for sea, was way above the value of such a unit, and on her arrival on the Thames the shareholders received a mere £34 per ton, the price of the last Bombay 74, with £4,000 for the masts. A total of £70,000 was placed in the estimates for 1819 to buy the ship. The builders claimed the ship had been built as a 'patriotic measure' in war time, but the underlying motive must have been commercial. The Navy received a ship of a class effectively obsolete, and the good citizens of Calcutta made a loss. The Navy Board had serious reservations about teak from anywhere other than the Malabar coast, with good reason. The Calcutta builders blamed prejudice for this attitude, but in truth they had failed to provide ships of the finest workmanship. In addition, the use of saul, sisso, Burma and Java teak did not help. The Navy had accepted Malabar timber, but it was expecting a great deal for them to take further, unproven, new species on trust. Melville, in particular, had reservations about the saul. In addition, the new ship was of the wrong class. However, it is worthy of note that she proved to be a strong and particularly well built ship, which is hardly surprising given the object of her financiers and builders. *Hastings* required a further 2,730 man days to complete for service. Converted into a steam blockship in 1855 she survived as a coal hulk until 1885.

Later efforts to interest the Admiralty in Calcutta were given a particular emphasis by the collapse of merchant shipbuilding

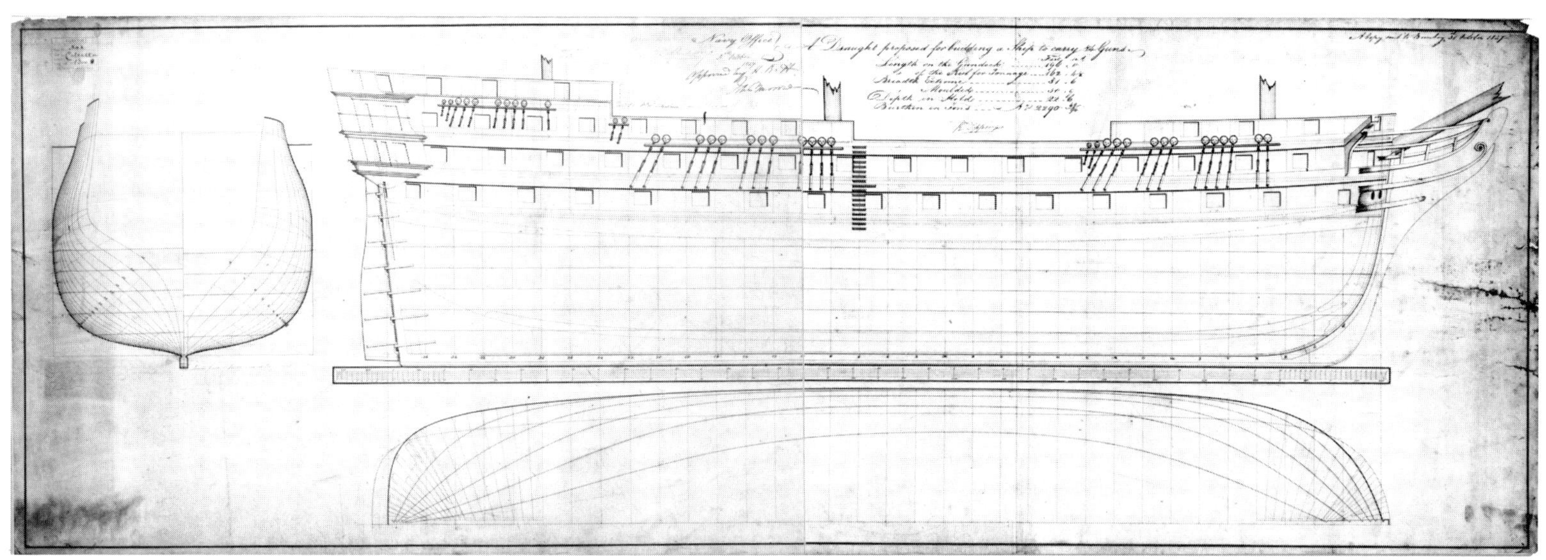

The draught sent to Bombay for the Calcutta *in October 1827. This ship was an intermediate design, coming between the* Asia *and Seppings's final 84-gun ship of 1831, which carried a full complement of long 32-pounders.* Calcutta *was more strongly built than her predecessors and could sustain a heavier arming. The price was a noticeable filling out of her waterlines.* (NMM)

The last remains of Ganges, *being broken up at Plymouth in 1929. The sheer size of the diagonal riders helps to explain why these ships proved so strong, and why the Malabar forests proved incapable of supplying the duplicate frames that the Navy had so valued. Unlike their English-built sisters, the teak 84s were fastened with iron spikes, taking advantage of the preservative qualities of teak oil.* (RNM)

in the area after 1817. However, Calcutta lacked a native timber supply of the quality required by the Royal Navy and so naval interest in the Bay of Bengal as a shipbuilding area quickly moved into Tenasserim and Malacca.[28]

The *Ganges*-class

The failure of these alternatives returned naval attention to Bombay. In 1815 the Navy Board warned the Admiralty that the Company was intending to use the middle dock for a 1,300-ton merchant ship, and the Company was also demanding from the Navy Board that the new Master Shipwright, Joseph Seaton, should have no authority in the dockyard independent of the Governor.[29] Despite this, the Admiralty clearly intended to continue work at Bombay as an integral part of their postwar programme. The Navy Board was requested by the Admiralty to enquire if the docks would take a ship of the *Canopus*-class. Within days an affirmative response was followed by an order for a facsimile to be built.[30] *Ganges*, as the new ship was named, was to be the first of four 84-gun Second Rates (under the revised rating system) built at Bombay. At the same time the yard also produced 46-gun frigates. As these were the two classes identified as standing in need of further units by the Navy Board it is clear that teak ships were seen as the only way to build new tonnage that could be brought into service quickly. It was no accident the *Asia* was the first of the new *Canopus* type ships to see action; it was simply that none of her British sisters had been completed by 1827.

Ganges *as a training ship.*

The Navy Board prepared figures to support a long-term re-appraisal of the Indian policy. They estimated that Indian ships cost £34 per ton, against £32 19s 4d for home-built ships, with a substantial premium cost to bring home the Bombay vessels. Against this could be set the valuable duplicate frame and some 500 loads of timber at £10 to £15 per load, as well as the admitted superior durability of teak. They favoured Commissioner Johnstone's plan to lay down moorings at Bombay for two battleships and suggested breaking up old frigates locally to rig and crew new construction.[31]

Far from happy with the financial arrangements of the existing contract of 1810 Byam Martin attempted to follow the old plan of building smaller ships somewhere outside the control of the Company, Cochin in this case. Battleships would have to be built at Bombay and orders for *Asia* and *Bombay* were urged by the Navy Board in 1819 as *Ganges* was almost complete and no other work was in hand. Melville, as the son of Dundas, was more enthusiastic about construction in India, instructing the retiring station Admiral to provide his successor with 'the most minute information as to our shipbuilding system at Bombay and Cochin at both of which places we are anxious to push it as far as their respective means will allow'. He had less enthusiasm for the offer to build at Calcutta, being uncertain of the merits of the saul timber. Only a month later Byam Martin gave up any hope of building at Cochin. Although some small vessels were provided the project proved once again that far more investment was needed to make any real breakthrough in the face of the Company's monopoly, and Byam Martin was already contemplating bringing home the timber in order to build in Britain, as an economy measure in the overall naval policy package.[32]

At Bombay the native Master Builder was finding it hard to secure timber for the duplicate frame of the *Malabar*, while at the same time building one ship and collecting the timber for the next. This was a particular problem with rising and first floors. He recommended ending the practice after the frame in the *Melville* was sent while further studies were made. The Governor rejected this plea, demanding further action to secure timber.[33] *Malabar* carried home one frame, rather than the pair called for by the Admiralty.

Construction in India halted

In 1819 the Board of Control ordered another forest survey and, anxious to make the most of their expensive dock, urged the Governor to lower his hire charges to entice the Imaum of Muscat to place an order. Within days the Admiralty placed the first of two battleship orders that year, with two more frigates.[34] In the event the failure of the frame timber supply led to the cancellation of Indian building. The Governor of Bombay warned that providing a duplicate frame for *Ganges* would delay the *Asia* by 12 months. When the Admiralty announced that the Company was unable to carry out this part of their contract the Navy Board pointed out that in view of the lack of shipwright work in Britain bringing the timber home was 'more consistent than building the ships at Bombay by the natives of India'. The duplicate frame had been one of the chief inducements to continue the contract, and if the

Company could not be pressed to keep their bargain it was felt that it would be better to cancel the contract and secure a supply of large timber. Six months later the Admiralty accepted Byam Martin's advice to end construction at Bombay as part of the package of reductions forced on them by the Government.[35]

The Admiralty called on the Board of Control not to delay the *Ganges* by waiting on a duplicate frame, but to load her with as much timber as could be secured. In addition, they were to begin the *Asia* at once, but suspend the next 84, the *Bombay*, in favour of further 46-gun frigates, of which duplicate frames could be built. *Ganges* came home with over 600 pieces of timber as well as the crew of *Liverpool*, which had been sold to the Imaum of Muscat. Delays in completing this first 84 were blamed by the Governor on rising prices and shortage of timber but Admiral Blackwood took a very different view which was based on the low opinion, long held by naval officers serving in the area, of the honesty and integrity of the Company's servants. He noted that men had been taken to work on merchant ships, while the Navy Board pointed out that far from increasing demands on timber or labour the new round stern reduced the amount needed of both by omitting the transom and counter. However, the Board would not support Blackwood's call for the time of completion to be stipulated, and for the Company to bear the risk of fire, 'when it is recollected that the company undertakes the concern without any charge in the way of profit or commission'.[36] Accepting that timber prices had risen by 50 per cent the Board took action by reducing the high exchange rate between the Bengal sicca rupee from 2/6d to 2/1d, and excluding all interest on transactions with India. This did not stop *Asia* costing £34/9/3d per ton, significantly more than *Ganges* at £32/13/8d. The redundant Royal yard at Bombay was hired out to the Company at 1,000 rupees per month.[37]

Construction resumed and abandoned again

In 1825, only four years after the cessation of construction the arrangement was reopened. The Navy Board secured the same terms, with the important distinction that dock hire was only to be chargeable when at least fifty men were at work on the ship. Having closed down one source of difficulty the new work soon revealed another. Master Shipwright John Pollexfen sent home an order for 1,500 tons of metal fittings, 200 panes of glass, paint, tar, oakum, dockyard machinery and tools, and even twenty paint brushes. For all that the Company had a major dockyard at Bombay they were still entirely dependent upon the home base for stores, a fact that would be emphasised in succeeding decades by the steam engine.[38]

The *Bombay*, which had been suspended while the contract was in abeyance, was further delayed by the Imaum's battleship *Liverpool*, which would later become HMS *Imaum*. Pollexfen used the time to trim frames, saving dock hire, and trying to contract directly for timber. The Company had returned the forests to their native owners but remained unwilling to let the Navy contract directly for timber. Governor Mounstuart Elphinstone claimed that Pollexfen, by advertising for timber, would create native combinations which in turn would drive up prices and prevent any construction. The Master Shipwright admitted the sense of Elphinstone's comment when he despatched the *Bombay* loaded with specific pieces cut for the *Hindostan* and *Tigris* building at Devonport from Bombay frames, rather than the duplicate frames so often credited to the 84-gun ships.[39]

The Indian ships and their duplicate frames

More duplicate frames have been claimed than were actually provided. The historian of the Bombay Yard, A R Wadia, understandably exaggerates the number provided after 1815, and his figures have been largely adopted by subsequent authors. In view of the value ascribed by the Navy Board to these frames it is necessary to reconsider the evidence.

Year	*Ship launched*	*no of guns*	*Wadia*	*Actual*
1810	*Minden*	74	----	----
1813	*Cornwallis*	74	frame sent	*Carnatic* 1817.[1]
1815	*Wellesley*	74	----	----
1817	*Melville*	74	*Carnatic*	*Indus* 1817.[2]
1818	*Malabar*	74	----	*Hindostan* 1819.[3]
1821	*Ganges*	84	*Indus*	no frame.[4]
1824	*Asia*	84	*Vengeance*	no frame.[5]
1828	*Bombay*	84	*Hindostan*	no frame.[6]
1831	*Calcutta*	84	*Clarence*	no frame.[7]
1848	*Meeanee*	80		

Wadia's claim is supported by the final settlement of the native builders' claims after the end of construction at Bombay, which specifically names *Hindostan* as the duplicate of *Bombay*, and gives duplicates to all the postwar ships save *Calcutta*.[8] However, the purpose of the document was to establish the payment to be made to the master builder. Consequently, the figures have been inflated to allow an extra £50 for each of these fictitious frames. This would cover the loss of future earnings, and the value of the large quantity of heavy frame timber that each ship did bring home. The key to the duplicate frame system lies in the names accorded to the ships. Those built at home from a duplicate frame always carried Indian names. The three 74s actually brought home in frame were all given such names.

1. Admiralty Order 13.7.1815 to build at Portsmouth ADM 106/2267
2. Admiralty Order 10.11.1817 to build at Portsmouth /2274
3. Admiralty Order 21.1.1819 to build at Plymouth /2278
4. Admiralty to Board of Control 22.2.1821 ADM 106/131
5. *Vengeance* was laid down in 1819 and launched 6 months after *Asia*, long before the *Asia* could have arrived in Britain.
6. This ship brought specific frame timbers for the conversion of *Hindostan* into an 80, and for the frigate *Tigris*.
7. *Clarence* was laid down in 1824 and launched in 1827.
8. Admiralty to Board of Control 5.5.1832 ADM 106/2296.

No duplicate frames came home with the four 84-gun ships, although all were heavily laden with large timber and teak plank. In contrast to the 74s there were no orders to set up any such frame in a British dockyard, while the order dates of the British 84s do not coincide with the arrival of the Indian ships. The Navy Board secured permission to order ships as the dock became vacant, sending the draft for *Calcutta*, an improved 84, with the frigate *Manilla*.[40] However, the arrangement was still far from satisfactory, and Pollexfen's reports must have had some influence on the decision to end construction for a second time in 1828. Byam Martin submitted a detailed memorandum to the Duke of Clarence:

> I beg to submit to Your Royal Highness a statement of the expense of building a ship of 84 guns in the East Indies and in England, by which YRH will observe that the cost of such a ship built at Bombay may fairly be stated as £18,000 more than one built at home.
>
> Each ship built at Bombay usually brings to England a

duplicate frame to be set up in this country, the value of which may be taken at £10,000 and having some doubt whether the statement from Bombay of the expense of building the ship on which my comparison is founded might have included any part of the charge for such a duplicate frame, I directed that the subject should be minutely examined – and, to prevent the possibility of doubt I desired Mr. Seaton the Master Shipwright at Sheerness, who for many years was the Superintendant of Building at Bombay, to come to town for the purpose of examining the accounts – and he admits the accuracy of the statement, and that the charges are independent of the duplicate frame.

I have confined the contrast to the actual expense of building at Bombay and at home, of course adding to the former the necessary expense incurred on the ship's arrival in England for iron knees which cannot be so well completed in India: but I do not include the expense of navigating the ship from India to England. It may be proper to remark to YRH that building in India was discontinued in 1822 and renewed in 1825 and I take the liberty of submitting whether the great and evident difference in expense may not be considered a sufficient reason for again discontinuing that practice. I am aware that arguments are used to shew that Teak built ships possess advantages as to durability, and it has even been asserted that the material is almost imperishable, but the inclosed report of the defects in the *Seringapatam* shews that that is not the case; – and I might also quote the *Minden* which was built in 1818 and in 1823 had cost more than £42,000 for repairs necessary in consequence of decay; and I am confident that Teak built ships cannot be proved to be so superior to those of oak, carefully built and seasoned as they now are, – as to compensate for so great a difference in the original cost.

To the foregoing considerations of economy I would beg further to add that important one of justice and policy which should induce us to secure all practicable employment in this country for the shipwrights at home, rather than have a considerable portion of our shipbuilding executed out of the country, by persons who have not so strong a claim to consideration; – particularly when the confinement of all the building we require to our yards at home, while it affords provision for our people, would at the same time embrace the important point of keeping up to the highest allowable extent the useful body of shipwrights.

Under these circumstances, I would venture to submit to YRH the expediency of discontinuing the practice of building ships at Bombay.

Comparative costs of building an 84-gun ship in England and India

	In England Average of *Formidable* and *Powerful*	In India *Asia*
Materials	£53,610	£56,602
Workmanship	11,420	13,619
		8,140*
Dockhire	----	4,917
Total	65,102	83,278
Cost per Ton	28/8/9	36/7/7

*for placing iron knees, building cabins, storerooms etc. in England.[41]

It is difficult to avoid the conclusion that the Controller had been worked on by the Thames builders, with whom he had been thrown into intimate contact by the 1825 shipwrights' strike. They were largely the same firms that had sponsored the extensive campaign against Indian-built teak shipping in the last years of the War, and with the collapse of their order books and the poor labour relations it is unlikely they would have missed an opportunity to exploit the easily raised fears of Byam Martin for his war-time reserves of capacity and labour. Once this policy had been adopted by the Admiralty, the Navy Board, in view of the latest and far from encouraging, news from Bombay, decided that the two new ships, *Calcutta* and *Manilla*, could not have been commenced. Therefore, they directed the Master Shipwright to return the stores sent out for those ships and close the Royal dockyard, which was never more than a depot and office.[42] This order was to create a good deal of confusion, and inflate the final costs of the *Calcutta*. In January Pollexfen had been unhappy with the work rate of the dockyard, noting sardonically that the Master Builder was putting up a merchant ship 'with a celerity that I should be happy to see equalled in H.M. ships'. But by March he could report that *Calcutta*'s keel had been laid, that 110 men were at work trimming the frames, and that this had been accompanied with the sale of certain sloops for high prices to local opium traders, so that their crews could bring the *Bombay* home. The next major report was written in another hand. John Pollexfen died during a serious outbreak of fever on 24 September 1828 leaving his brother George, the Storekeeper, as the sole representative of the Navy Board at the dockyard.[43]

The order to close the dockyard arrived in early December. The Storekeeper, lacking the authority to continue work, consulted the Superintendent of the Bombay Marine, Captain Sir Charles Malcolm, in April 1829 and requested that he apply to the Station Commander. Malcolm reported that the native Master Builder was perfectly competent to complete the ship, being the equal of any Master Shipwright in England, while one-third of the timber was already set up and the whole ship laid off in the mould loft.[44] Malcolm was rather more candid with the Chairman of the Board of Control, Hugh Lindsay. As a resident at Bombay, and a member of a family with important Indian connections, he had a thorough understanding of the issues. He was able to put his finger onto the major weaknesses, both of shipbuilding at Bombay and the relationship between the servants of the Company and those of the Navy Board.

> As for Bombay Yard, I view it with dismay. In a space of not above --- which contains four large docks, is crowded all the timber for building 3 large ships – repairing at least two more, repairing and building boats for the Marine, Navy and Merchantmen – with Bunder Boats, Masts making etc. etc. a bad smithy with still worse smiths, for all our fine work is sent to the Gun Carriage manufactory. Not at present a store house in the yard, not a place to build one so that our own men of war who come into dock are obliged to bundle all our stores and provisions of every kind into lock up boats as they are called. The only remedy is to get back our stores and yard from the Navy who never use them and should war come give them what accommodation can be spared, or let them build somewhere else. Without more room I fear we shall be unable to bring that disorder to order, which I am sure for many reasons would be attended with a very great saving.[45]

Malcolm noted the skill, and inferior manners, of Master Builder Norojee and while he praised Pollexfen to Byam Martin as an 'honest and zealous officer', he had clearly lacked both the management skills and equable temper to work with the native builder. Until a suitable person could be sent, however, he believed the younger Pollexfen equal to supervising the yard. On receiving the order that appeared to cancel work on the *Calcutta*, Malcolm requested instructions from Admiral Gage, the Naval station commander, but he, far from happy with his lot, would only refer home for further instructions.

The Navy Board ordered the Foreman shipwright at Trincomalee, Thomas Craven, to Bombay, but George Pollexfen was reluctant to hand over the stores to him without more authority. However, *Calcutta* restarted on 17 September 1829, having been suspended on 3 December the previous year. The Navy Board admitted responsibility for the misunderstanding and advised the Admiralty to pay dock hire for the time the ship had been suspended.[46] Thereafter, *Calcutta* proceeded more smoothly, floating out on 14 March 1831 and being brought home with the rigging and crew of the frigate *Success*. One third of her well-stowed hold was taken up by specific timbers cut for teak ships building in Britain. All the Indian battleships were fitted with a raft port in the starboard buttock to facilitate loading and several orlop beams were omitted from the later 84s to increase the space. The yard finally closed on 6 August 1831.[47]

Teak in use at home

Malabar teak retained the high opinions of all shipbuilders. The timbers of the frigate *Tigris* were diverted to complete the stretched 74 *Hindostan*, and then over 500 loads of beams, diagonal riders and plank were shipped out of Plymouth yard to build the large steam frigate *Gorgon* at Pembroke. There was no spare slip at Plymouth and the teak was believed to be deteriorating.[48] However, the option of constructing new ships in Britain using teak was never financially feasible. With the price of native, Italian and African timber falling, the cost of shipping timber from India was far above the added value of the ships built of such material. In addition, the Navy continued to believe it was 'destructive to mix woods of a different description with it'.[49]

Bombay ships and Indian teak forced themselves back into view with the arrival of the Imaum's Bombay-built 74-gun teak battleship *Liverpool* laden with teak at Portsmouth. The King graciously accepted this unusual addition to his fleet, named her *Imaum* in honour of her original owner, and presented a yacht in return. In 1841 she provided evidence that all was not well at Bombay. The shipwright officers reported that *Imaum* was 'wretchedly ill built of the worst materials'. She was reserved for Harbour Service and ended her days as a depot ship at Jamaica. Captain Cogan of the Bombay Marine, having navigated the ship home, was also attempting to interest the Admiralty in reviving construction at Bombay.[50]

With the return of Admiral Maitland from the Indian Ocean in August 1837 Minto and his Board obtained more useful information. The Admiral believed that India could once again build two battleships at a time and Edye added a frigate in order to use up the undersized timber. The object was to build ships for current use in India, leaving those in Britain on the slip as a reserve.[51] Reflecting the disappointment of previous

The Asia *late in her career, with a row of scuttles for the orlop deck. The improved stern was more pleasing to the eye, and allowed the guns to be used, but it was still a poor substitute for the hull timbers of the broadside in action, as the Battle of Navarin demonstrated.* (IWM)

contracts much reliance was placed on the practical experience of Edye, the most senior constructor to have been in India. The Admiralty required full costs of the *Bombay* and *Calcutta*, including all necessary work to complete them on arrival in England. In fact, both ships were still without their structural ironwork and no steps had been taken to provide the moulds. Edye advised simplifying and tightening up the contract. He suggested that the contract should leave everything to the East India Company, with only the final price to be paid for the complete ship. Additional materials – iron, copper, pitch etc – were to be provided by the Navy and landed free of charge at Bombay; and the rate of exchange between the pound sterling and the rupee should be fixed in advance. The duplicate frame was to be recorded in great detail, and two thirds of the price paid, thereby allowing the dockyard timber inspectors to report on it before the whole amount was settled. He hoped that two 80-gun ships and six frigates could be built in three years, using Cochin for the small ships.[52]

The driving force behind renewed interest in Bombay was the alarming report on the state of the battlefleet submitted by Symonds in 1837. He had urged the construction of six new ships in India. The Company proved less enthusiastic, and after initial negotiations Wood had to report that it was not possible to build there, only to bring home timber. At the same time Symonds noted the superior longevity and serviceability of teak ships, giving *Ganges* nine years without repair, rather than three. Wood urged the Storekeeper to contract for teak.[53]

The Admiralty had been interested in two 80-gun ships and two 26-gun frigates, with duplicate frames for the battleships, as suggested by Cogan. The key issues were the availability of timber and the ability of the docks to handle the increased breadth of the Symondite *Vanguard*-class; if they could not slips could be constructed. The Court of Directors reported the failure of their efforts and blamed the adverse reports of the timber supply. To counter the more obvious difficulties, Charles Malcolm, still Superintendent of the Indian Navy, recommended the establishment of an agent in the Malabar district to contract for large timber.[54]

The last battleship from Bombay

Initial disappointment was not allowed to kill off the project, particularly as it soon became clear that the chance of securing an economic supply of timber from India was all but zero. 'I think we must make it a *sine qua non* with the new Governor of Bombay that he build us some ships. We can make nothing of getting teak thro' the merchants'.[55]

India had become the cornerstone of the revived shipbuilding effort of a thoroughly alarmed Board. Wood considered it,

> most adviseable to incur in conjunction with the East India Company, even a considerable expense to provide the means of procuring teak ships. It is not intended that any Government establishment should be formed, but that two or three shipwright officers, trustworthy and intelligent, should be sent from home with detailed drawings and plans to overlook the work performed by the native artificers as formerly.

The level of construction to be undertaken in Britain would be dependant upon the success of the Indian efforts. The Board readily concurred.[56] Once again the difficult relationship between the British Government, the East India Company and the Bombay presidency had precluded the only effective method of exploiting the resources of India: namely, the creation of a fully integrated Royal Navy dockyard at Bombay. In February 1839 a contract was exchanged with the Company to build two 80-gun ships, and Maitland (in concert with the Governor), returning to India, was to decide whether to build in dock or on new slips. A shipwright officer and foreman from Chatham, John Allen, was to be sent out to superintend preparations. Symonds meanwhile prepared a list of the necessary tools and stores.[57] Finally, Maitland elected to build two new slips outside the ramparts of the fortress.[58]

The Government of Bombay was soon under pressure from London to provide more timber. In addition, the Governor General, Lord Auckland, made it clear that the Navy would only be interested while there was timber to build large warships.[59] Edye arranged to send out one of the teak 74s as a store ship. He still urged caution in dealing with the Company, and in particular with its servants at Bombay. His original plan, to pay for completed ships, had been rejected in favour of an improved version of the old arrangement, but he still urged the sense of the more certain arrangement. Disappointment followed almost immediately upon Allen's arrival at Bombay when he discovered that the slipways would require another 30 months to complete, and, what was far worse:

> I fear that the prospects of obtaining timber of proper dimensions and in sufficient quantities to build ships for H.M.'s service is still more unfavourable and that the time commencement will be protracted to a very distant, but uncertain period'.[60]

The Board were becoming discouraged, and following a sequence of letters from Cogan, the original projector of the plan, elected to suspend any further activity.[61]

It must be noted that the Board had other matters to consider at the time and that the delay was only temporary. In addition, Allen was already ill when he made his report. Minto, however, retained his faith in the prospect. He recommended that further efforts be made to exploit the forests of Tenasserim, with the aid of John Seppings, son of the late Surveyor and Marine Surveyor to the Bengal presidency. Indian battleships, he considered, would be a bonus in addition to the four Second Rates he advised building in Britain every year. Furthermore, he wanted to razee the teak 74s, once enough large two-deckers had been provided.[62]

Allen's replacement, Frederick Laire, quickly discovered that whatever the Government at Bombay might do to advance the slips and timber supply, the timber contractors would be certain to combine and drive up prices. Parker, for so long on Minto's Board but now Commander in Chief in China, advised starting only one battleship, because of the timber combination. The Company responded by advising that more use be made of Moulmein timber from Burma. The Board were not interested. In 1842 the Marine Board did, not before time, begin a small plantation in the Malabar country. Only in 1846 did the Admiralty finally contract for Moulmein teak, with Cockerell of Calcutta.[63]

The Company considered widening the dock gates to 62ft, and lengthening them to take the latest steamships and Symondite sailing models, but the cost, around 80,000 rupees, ensured that nothing was done. Fear of combinations led the Board to suspend any work on the frigates, although the moulds of the *Madras* had already been laid off. Work finally commenced on the new ship at the end of 1843. When Parker returned from the Opium War to find that the timber supply had improved, he decided to commence work on the frigates

The Bombay *undergoing conversion to steam at Chatham in 1860. This conversion was a fitting tribute to the superiority of her teak timbers; the* Powerful *had been stripped for conversion, but proved to be defective.* (NMM)

as well as the battleship. In 1844 Laire went home to be Master Shipwright at Pembroke and was replaced by George Turner. Repair work on Royal Navy ships, in particular on *Fox* in 1846, delayed work on *Madras* and the frigate *Malacca*.[64]

In 1846 more serious problems came to light on the new ships. Faulty work in driving the bolts into the lower hull led to one leading man being dismissed and seventeen others being mulcted 10 days pay. Shortage of men persuaded the Bombay Government to suspend slip hire on the frigates *Goshawk* and *Zebra*, if not the 1,000 rupees a month being levied for the two-decker.[65] In addition, the Master Builder and his assistant were often called away to work on Company vessels, leaving 'no check on the indolent propensities of the native workmen'.

A perceptible shift in emphasis followed the accession to office of the Earl of Ellenborough. Ellenborough, recently returned from four years as Governor General of India, could be expected to make some changes. The first were to the names of the three ships building at Bombay. *Madras* became *Meeanee*, in honour of the victory of his favourite General, Sir Charles Napier, over the Sikhs. *Goshawk* became *Nerbudda*, and *Zebra* the *Jumna*. This change came too late for the figurehead of the battleship, which for the rest of her career portrayed a native of Madras, rather than Napier.[66] Ellenborough shared the imperial vision of the two Melvilles and wanted to integrate the Indian empire into a wider structure. With his breadth of local experience Ellenborough had fixed ideas on the best method of using Indian resources. He did not support shipbuilding at Bombay, preferring to bring home Moulmein timber. Haddington had purchased a mere 1,218 loads in 1845, averaging one ton per load at £14.10s per load and this had been hardly enough to keep the existing teak fleet in repair. Despite contradictory messages on local prices and supplies Ellenborough urged the policy of keeping up teak supplies in his resignation memorandum, having contracted for a supply from Calcutta.[67]

Following Ellenborough's departure the urgency went out of teak policy and his successor, Auckland, sent the old 74 *Hercules* out with stores, and brought home a cargo of teak, but it was already clear that building at Bombay would prove to be no happier an experience in the 1840s. *Meeanee* was infested with white ants, one of the few natural threats to teak, and was consequently hurried to completion. At the same time the Bombay yard was querying the powers of the Admiralty officials, and the dock hire due. From 1848 it was evident that no more ships would be built at Bombay for the Royal Navy.[68]

Arrangements were made to pay off the *Melampus* to provide a crew for the *Meeanee* 18 months before she was launched. The dockyard injected her with 937 gallons of a poisonous oil, to destroy the infestation. The launch, on 11 November 1849 was, unsurprisingly, the last of a British sailing battleship. In announcing the end of the contract the East India Company were quick to place the blame squarely on Bombay dockyard, the Admiralty having been informed that the cost of the ships would be up to 50 per cent above that of British-built vessels.[69]

The failure of the Bombay dockyards

The reasons for the ending of the contract were not hard to find. A 1,200-ton steamship had already been ordered at Moulmein, and as the *Malacca* she would demonstrate that teak ships could be obtained without the problems attendant upon the Bombay yard.[70] Bombay had managed to work an astonishing amount more timber into *Meeanee* than had been used in *Calcutta*, despite their relative similarity in size. In addition, far more had been paid for labour than would have been expected. The average cost of the four Seppings 84-gun ships built in India had been £86,457 while *Meeanee* cost £101,846. The Company admitted to overcharging for timber to the extent of £9,382 but blamed the remaining over-run on the cost of slips and new moulds. The Admiralty was more forthright, finding the difference in labour charges almost unbelievable. At home labour on an 80-gun ship cost £8,178, whereas Bombay spent £18,665 which represented an excess of £10,487. In essence timber was overvalued by some 25 per cent and labour by 33 per cent. On the positive side, *Meeanee* had been fitted with her ironwork at Bombay, and 'the workmanship was, moreover, much more elaborately executed'. The new Surveyor adopted the advice Edye had tendered 10 years before that if any further work was to be given to Bombay it must be on a fixed price contract.[71]

The Company soon discovered that the cost over-run was not confined to large warships. The buoy vessel *Grappler*, built for the Bengal Government, turned out 30 per cent over estimate. 'We can hardly be surprised that H.M.G. should hesitate to continue the building of ships for the Royal Navy at Bombay when such gross mismanagement appears to pervade the arrangements of your dockyard'. That the final accounts for the last three Bombay ships should only be sent in six years after the last had been completed was no more than an admission of failure by the Dockyard managers.[72]

The idea of reopening work at Bombay was considered once more, early in 1855 during the crisis of the Russian War, a time when cost was once more a secondary issue to supply. Even so, this and the well-known inefficiency of the dockyard ensured that nothing came of the initiative. This was fortunate, as the tortured career of the last major Indian warship, the *Dalhousie*, would demonstrate.[73]

It is clear that the practice of building at Bombay made sense while everything worked in its favour: namely, the wartime shortage of ships, the availability of enough timber to permit at least one duplicate frame to be sent with each ship, a buoyant domestic shipbuilding industry and a relatively high level of naval estimates. When those elements began to falter British policy-makers gradually lost faith, although for differing reasons. Teak remained a major attraction and was the only reason for re-opening the relationship in 1827 and 1841. However, teak was, once the problems of seasoned oak construction were solved, never a great enough attraction to make up for the poor returns made by Bombay.

Conclusion

Between 1815 and 1850 the British battlefleet was modernised and improved to meet the challenge from foreign rivals, particularly France, Russia and the United States. This process reflected the increased weight of artillery which needed to be carried; the improved understanding of ship structures and timber seasoning; and a knowledge of the management of human resources acquired during and after the Napoleonic Wars.

The basic question to be addressed in concluding this study is a simple one. How successful were the policy makers, naval architects and dockyard managers? The answer is equally simple. The British battlefleet sustained the one world empire of the period, deterred her rivals and defeated those minor powers who dared to presume, from Algiers to China. In addition, this was achieved on low estimates and with only a modest active fleet. The real power of the last sailing battlefleet was only apparent to those who saw the long lines of Advanced and Reserve Ships lying at Portsmouth, Plymouth and Sheerness. Those ships, not the small peace-time squadrons, as Canning so eloquently stated, were the key to British power. When this fleet was mobilised, in response to the Syrian Crisis of 1840, the result was clear: France backed away from a conflict she could not win. This incident was fitting tribute to the strength of the Royal Navy and basic soundness of postwar policy.

The ships of the new battlefleet were the strongest wooden battleships ever built and those that were repaired were brought up to the modern standard. The first postwar generation, the *Canopus* and *Caledonia* derivatives, were solid and effective ships of sterling quality. The controversial broad-beamed ships built by Sir William Symonds added the speed that would allow them to force a flying enemy to stand and fight, resolving the age-old tactical dilemma of the sailing navy. Furthermore, Symonds's ships were larger and more efficient gun platforms than anything built abroad; the astonishment of the Prince de Joinville at the size of the 90-gun *Albion* was genuine. British design philosophy was sound and was based on the primacy of battle in securing command of the sea. While these ideas were not given clear expression until Mahan's seminal book appeared in 1890, British statesmen and Admirals were well aware that national and imperial defence could only be secured by superior strength at sea. This was reflected in the percentage of three-decked ships in the British fleet, which was more than double that of any other major navy, and the number that were mobilised in 1840 and 1846–49 to meet the possibility of war.

The sailing battlefleet remained central to British imperial power until it was superseded by the steam battlefleet of the 1850s. Until battleships were fitted with their own steam power, in the shape of the screw propeller, the sailing battleship was the ultimate arbiter of war at sea. The popular idea that steam made sailing ships obsolete overnight is based on a telescoping of invention and successful application, a process which in fact occupied the entire lifetime of the last sailing battlefleet. It is no coincidence that the first successful steam battleship, *Le Napoleon*, should have been launched in 1850, for only then was it possible to create an effective balance of qualities that included a steam plant. In the same year the Surveyor's Office was amalgamated with that of Controller of Steam. The age of the steam Navy had arrived.

APPENDIX

Building programme: launch and order dates

Launched	*Ordered*
1815 Seven	Two
120 *St Vincent, Howe*	
80 *Cambridge*	*Formidable*
74 *Defence, Hercules, Redoubtable, Wellesley*	*Malabar*
1816 Four	One
74 *Black Prince, Minotaur, Pitt, Wellington*	*Ganges*
1817 Two	Seven
74 *Agincourt, Melville*	*Monarch, Powerful, Thunderer, Vengeance, Carnatic, Indus, Boscawen*
1818 Three	
80 *Bellerophon*	
74 *Malabar, Talavera*	
1819	Seven
74 *Belleisle*	*Asia, Royal George, Clarence, Neptune, St George, Hindostan, Hastings* (purchased)
1820 Three	
120 *Britannia*	
106 *Camperdown*	
74 *Hawke*	
1821 One	
84 *Ganges*	
1822 None	
1832 Two	Two
120 *Prince Regent*	*Royal William, Waterloo*
74 *Carnatic*	
1824 Two	
84 *Asia, Vengenace*	
1825 One	Two
84 *Formidable*	*Bombay, Trafalgar*
1826 One	Two
84 *Powerful*	*Rodney, Nile, London*
1827 One	One
84 *Clarence*	*Calcutta*
1828 Two	
104 *Royal Adelaide*	
84 *Bombay*	
1829 None	
1830 None	
1831 Two	
84 *Calcutta, Thunderer*	
1832 Two	Six
120 *Neptune*	*Vanguard, Collingwood, Royal Frederick, Royal Sovereign, Victoria, Algiers* (110)
84 *Monarch*	
1833 Three	Two
120 *Royal William, Waterloo*	*Goliath, Cumberland*
92 *Rodney*	
1834 None	
1835 One	
80 *Vanguard*	
1836 None	One
	Imaum (gift)
1837 None	
1838 None	One
	Superb
1839 Three	Six
110 *Queen*	*Albion, Aboukir, Mars, Majestic, Centurion, Colossus*
92 *Nile*	
80 *Indus*	
1840 Two	Six
120 *St George*	*Lion, Irresistible, Hannibal, Exmouth, Prince Albert, Algiers* (90)
92 *London*	
1841 Three	One
120 *Trafalgar*	*Meeanee*
80 *Collingwood, Hindostan*	
1842 Four	One
90 *Albion*	*Royal Albert, Prince of Wales*
80 *Goliath, Superb*	
70 *Cumberland*	
1843 None	Three
	Cressy, Sans Pareil, Agamemnon
1844 Two	Five
80 *Centurion*	*Brunswick, St Jean d'Acre, Royal Sovereign, Marlborough, Windsor Castle*
70 *Boscawen*	
1845 None	
1846 None	
1847 One	Two
80 *Lion*	*Audacious (James Watt) Caesar*
1848 Four	Two
90 *Aboukir*	*Orion, Hood*
80 *Colossus, Mars, Meeanee*	
1849 None	One
	Agamemnon
Total 58	63

BIBLIOGRAPHY

The existing secondary literature on the post-1815 battlefleet reflects a general lack of interest in this period on the part of naval historians. Little work has been done on the large body of papers that have survived from the Surveyor's Office, and none on the relevant collections of senior officers and prominent politicians. As a result, many accounts of the Royal Navy in the first half of the nineteenth century have nothing new to add, while historians working in other areas have been prepared to accept the most inadequate work as a basis for comment on the role and efficiency of the Royal Navy. The one major work on this period, C J Bartlett's *Great Britain and Sea Power: 1815–1853* has little on the ships and makes no attempt to link the design process with British strategic requirements. However, it is a valuable introduction to the policy making of the period and remains required reading. Brian Lavery's *The Ship of the Line* introduces the period, but does not carry the design history of the British sailing battleships into the 1840s, leaving several ships off the end of an otherwise exhaustive listing. My own *Battleships in Transition: The Creation of the Steam Battlefleet* dealt with the 1850s when many of the post-1815 ships were converted into screw steamers. Elsewhere, D K Brown has provided an invaluable assessment of the technical developments of the period in *Before the Ironclad,* but his approach to the controversial regime of Sir William Symonds at the Surveyor's Office is open to a more overtly political approach. The work of Peter Goodwin, James Lees and further books by Brian Lavery have covered the structure, masting and fitting of British warships in detail. This work does not require duplication.

This book has concentrated on the political, economic, tactical and strategic areas, and in so doing attempts to understand the design process by reference to external factors. Some of my conclusions are diametерically opposite to those adopted by those who have researched the subject from a different angle. This reflects the wealth of new material that has been uncovered, the importance of party politics in defence decision making, and the value of the good work that has already been produced by others.

Some of the material from the MS collections has either not been used before, or has not been used in any published work. The most important is the naval and strategic correspondence of successive First Lords of the Admiralty, from Melville, through Graham to Auckland and Baring. The Prime Ministers of the period left significant collections of papers, and naval officers also provide a rich legacy. These help to fill out the Admiralty collections and the drafts preserved at the National Maritime Museum.

Among secondary sources, the late Victorian biographies of senior officers offer a rich haul of published correspondence. However, recent work from scholars in other fields has had a major impact on this study; that of Oliver Rackham on forestry, Boyd Hilton on economic policy and John Brewer on the development of the modern state all require a special mention.

Primary sources

Public Papers held at the Public Record Office, Kew.

Admiralty Papers: ADM

1. Secretary's In letters
2. Secretary's Out letters
3. Special Minutes
7. Special Papers
12. Digest
50. Admiral's Journals
83. Surveyor of the Navy
84. Steam Department
87. Surveyor's Department
91. Material Department Out letters
92. Surveyor's Submission Book
95. Sailing Reports
106. Navy Board Correspondence
135. Progress Book
180. Progress Book
222. Surveyor's Submission Book 1832–39

Treasury Papers

T25/6 Department of Woods and Forests
National Maritime Museum
ADM A/ Navy Board Papers
Admiralty Draughts
The India Record Office: Papers of the Maritime Department, and the Bombay Presidency

Private Papers

THE ROYAL ARCHIVE: Windsor Castle
Royal Correspondence
Lord Melbourne

THE BRITISH LIBRARY: Manuscripts division
Lord Aberdeen, William Huskisson, Sir Robert Peel, Lord Liverpool, Lord Palmerston, Lord Melville, the three Admirals Martin, Admiral Sir Charles Napier, Sir Charles Wood.

THE PUBLIC RECORD OFFICE
Lord Ellenborough, Lord John Russell, Sir Charles Napier.

THE INDIA OFFICE
Sir Charles Wood.

THE NATIONAL MARITIME MUSEUM
Sir Edward and Sir Henry Codrington, Admiral Sir J W D Dundas, Lord Melville, Sir Alexander Milne, Lord Minto, Sir Charles Napier, Sir William Parker, Sir Robert Seppings, Sir Thomas Foley, Sir Charles Yorke, Sir Baldwin Walker.

SCOTTISH RECORD OFFICE
Sir George Clerk, Admiral Sir R S Dundas, the First and Second Lord Melville.

THE NATIONAL LIBRARY OF SCOTLAND
Lord Minto

THE UNIVERSITY LIBRARY, NOTTINGHAM
The Fourth Duke of Portland, the Fifth Duke of Newcastle.

BEDFORD COUNTY RECORD OFFICE
Earl de Grey
Bedford Estate Papers

THE BORTHWICK INSTITUTE, YORK
Sir Charles Wood

THE UNIVERSITY LIBRARY, CAMBRIDGE
The Graham papers, on microfilm.

THE UNIVERSITY LIBRARY, SOUTHAMPTON
Lord Palmerston, Duke of Wellington.

THE UNIVERSITY LIBRARY, DURHAM
Earl Grey

Published Documents

Parliamentary Papers: Great Britain
1847–8, Vol xxi

Hansard's Parliamentary Debates, Third Series

Collections

Arbuthnot, Charles *The Correspondence of Charles Arbuthnot,* ed A Aspinall, London 1941
Baring, *Journals and Correspondence of Francis Thornhill Baring, afterwards Lord Northbrook,* London 1905, 2 vols
Bathurst, Earl *Report on the Manuscripts of the Earl Bathurst,* Historical Manuscripts Commission, London 1923
Canning, George *The Formation of Canning's Ministry,* ed A Aspinall
Castlereagh, Viscount *Memoirs and Correspondece,* ed Marquess of Londonderry, London 1848–53, 12 vols
Croker, John *Correspondence and Diaries,* ed Jennings, L J, London 1884
George IV *Correspondence* ed A Aspinall
Greville, *Memoirs,* ed Strachey and Fulford, London 1938, 8 vols
Palmerston *The Palmerston – Sullivan Correspondence 1804–1863* ed K Bourne, London 1979

Russell *The Later Correspondence of Lord John Russell, 1840–1878,* ed G P Gooch, London 1925, 2 vols
Victoria *The Letters of Queen Victoria 1837–1861* ed Benson and Esher, London 1907, 3 vols
Wellington, Duke of *Dispatches, Correspondence and Memoranda: 1819–1832* ed 2nd Duke of Wellington, London 1867–80, 8 vols
Wellington, Duke of *Political Correspondence 1833–34 & 1834–35* ed Brooke & Gandy, London 1975 & 1987

Publications of the Navy Records Society
Bonner-Smith, D *The Letters of Earl St. Vincent* London 1933–35, 2 vols
Bromley, J S *The Manning of the Royal Navy,* London 1974
Corbett, J S *Fighting Instructions 1530–1816,* London 1905
Corbett, J S *Signals and Instructions 1776–1794,* London 1909
Hamilton, C I Selections from the Phinn Committee of Inquiry, 1855 in *The Naval Miscellany,* vol V, ed N A M Rodger, London 1985
Hamilton, Adm Sir R V *Letters and Papers of Sir T Byam Martin,* London 1899, 1900, 1903, 3 vols

The Navy List, 1823–50

Newspapers
The Times
The Metropolitan Magazine
The United Services Journal

Secondary sources

Books
Albion, R G *Forests and Seapower,* Harvard, 1925
Anderson, R G *Naval Wars in the Baltic in the Sailing Ship Epoch, 1522–1850,* London 1910
Anderson, R G *Naval Wars in the Levant 1559–1853,* Liverpool 1952
Anglesey, Marquess *One Leg, The Life of the First Marquess of Anglesey,* London 1961
Banbury, P *Shipbuilders of the Thames and Medway,* Newton Abbot 1971
Barrow, John *Life of George, Lord Anson,* London 1839
Barrow, Sir John *An Autobiographical Memoir,* London 1847
Bartlett, C J *Great Britain and Seapower, 1815–1853,* Oxford 1963
Baxter, J P *The Introduction of the Ironclad Warship,* Cambridge Mass 1933
Beamish, R *Memoir of the Life of Sir Marc Isambard Brunel,* London 1862
Bentham, M S *Life of General Sir Samuel Bentham,* London 1862
Biddlecombe, G *Naval Tactics and Sailing Trials,* London 1850
Biddulph, Lady *Charles Philip Yorke: Fourth Earl of Hardwicke, Vice-Admiral R.N. A Memoir,* London 1910
Bindoff, S T *The Scheldt Question to 1839,* London 1945
Black, J & Woodfine, P *The British Navy and the use of Naval Power in the Eighteenth Century,* Leicester 1988
Blake, R *Disraeli,* London 1966
Bourchier, Lady *Memoir of the Life Admiral Sir Edward Codrington.* 2 vols, London 1873
Bourchier, Lady *Selections from the Correspondence of Sir Henry Codrington,* London 1880
Bourne, J M *Patronage and Society in Nineteenth Century England,* London 1986
Bourne, K *Britain and the Balance of Power in North America 1815–1908,* London 1967
— and Watt, D C *Studies in International History,* London 1967
— *The Foreign Policy of Victorian England 1830–1902,* Oxford 1970
— *Palmerston: the early years,* London 1982
Bowles, Admiral Sir W *Pamphlets on Naval Subjects,* London 1854
Brereton, Major General W *The British Fleet in the Black Sea under the command of Vice Admiral Sir J W D Dundas,* London 1856
Brewer, J *The Sinews of Power,* London 1989
Briggs, Sir J *Naval Administrations, 1827–1892,* London 1897
Brighton, Rev J G *A Memoir of Admiral Sir P B V Broke,* London 1865
Brown, D K *Before the Ironclad: development of ship design, propulsion and armament in the Royal Navy, 1815–60,* London 1990
Bullen, R *Palmerston, Guizot and the collapse of the Entente Cordiale,* London 1974
Burridge, J *The Naval Dry Rot,* London 1824
Burrows, M *Memoirs of Admiral Sir H D Chads,* Portsea 1867
— *Autobiography,* ed S M Burrows, London 1908
Burton, Capt J Ryder *On the Concentration of the Material, the Manual and Physical Force in Her Majestys' Vessels of War,* London 1847
Busk, H *The Navies of the World,* London 1859
Chamberlain, M E *Lord Aberdeen,* London 1982
Chappelle, H I *A History of the American Sailing Navy,* New York 1949
Chatfield, H *An Apology for English Shipbuilders,* London 1833 (pub anon)
— *The present shipbuilding controversy, or which is the misrepresented party?,* London 1846, (pub anon)
Chevalier, E *Histoire de la Marine Francais,* 5 vols, Paris 1905
Clausewitz, K *On War,* ed Brodie, Howard and Paret, Princeton 1982
Clowes, W L, ed *The Royal Navy, vol 6,* London 1903
Coad, J *The Royal Dockyards, 1690–1850,* London 1989
Colledge, J J *Ships of the Royal Navy,* London 1987
Collinge, J M *Navy Board Officials: 1660–1832,* London 1978
Colomb, Admiral P H *Naval Warfare,* London 1891
— *Memoirs of Sir Astley Cooper-Key,* London 1898
Conacher, J E *The Aberdeen Coalition 1852–1855,* Cambridge 1968
— *The Peelites and the Party System, 1846–1852,* Newton Abbot 1972
Cookson, J E *Lord Liverpool's Administration 1815–1822,* Edinburgh 1975
Corbett, J S *Some Principles of Maritime Strategy,* London 1911
Crauford, *The Russian Fleet in the Baltic in 1836,* London 1837
Crowhurst, P *The Defence of British Trade: 1689–1815,* Folkstone 1977
Davis, C *The Age of Grey and Peel,* Oxford 1929
Day, Admiral Sir A *The Admiralty Hydrographic Service,* London 1967
Dear, I *The Royal Yacht Squadron; 1815–1985,* London 1985
Douglas, General Sir H *A Treatise on Naval Gunnery,* London 1861, sixth edition
— *Naval Warfare under Steam,* London 1857
Dull, J R *The French Navy and American Independence,* Princeton 1975
Eardley-Wilmot, Captain S *The Life of Vice-Admiral Lord Lyons,* London 1898
Edlin, H L *British Woodland Trees,* London 1944
Edye, J *Facts versus Fiction, or Sir Wm. Symonds Principles of Naval Architecture vindicated,* London 1845 (pub anon)
Egerton, F *Admiral Sir Geoffrey Phipps Hornby,* London 1896
Ekins, Adm Sir C *Naval Battles,* London 1824
Ekins, Adm Sir C *A Reply to the letter of Sir Robert Seppings,* London 1824
Elers-Napier, General G *The Life and Correspondence of Admiral Sir Charles Napier,* London 1862
Emmerson, G S *John Scott-Russell,* London 1977
Erickson, A B *The Public Career of Sir James Graham,* Oxford 1952
Evelyn, J *Sylva,* London 1825 edn
Fanshawe, A *Admiral Sir Edward Gennys Fanshawe,* London 1904
Farmer, Dr R H *Handbook of Hardwoods,* London 1972, second edition
— *Timber* in *Materials and Technology,* ed De Bussy, London 1973
— *Handbook of Softwoods,* London 1977, second edition
Fay, C R *Huskisson and his Age,* London 1951
Fincham, J *A letter to the Right Hon. Sir James Graham,* Portsmouth 1832
Fincham, J *A Treatise on Masting Ships and Mast Making,* London 1854
Fincham, J *A History of Naval Architecture,* London 1851
Friendly, A *Beaufort of the Admiralty,* London 1977
Furber, H *Henry Dundas, First Viscount Melville,* Oxford 1931
Gash, N *Politics in the Age of Peel,* London 1953
— *Mr Secretary Peel,* London 1961
— *Sir Robert Peel,* London 1972
— *Lord Liverpool,* London 1984
Giffard, Admiral Sir G *Reminiscences of a Naval Officer,* Exeter 1892
Glover, R *Britain and Bay: Defence against Bonaparte 1803–1814,* London 1973
Goodwin, P *The Construction and Fitting of the Sailing Man of War: 1650–1850,* London 1987
Gorshkov, Admiral S *The Seapower of the State,* Oxford 1979
Gosset, W P *The Lost Ships of the Royal Navy, 1793–1900,* London 1986
Gough, B M *The Royal Navy and the Northwest Coast of North America: 1810–1914,* Vancouver 1971
Graham, G S *The Politics of Naval Supremacy,* Cambridge 1965
— *Great Britain and the Indian Ocean: 1810–1850,* Oxford 1967
— *The China Station,* Oxford 1978
Gray, D *Spencer Perceval,* Manchester 1963
Hamilton, Admiral Sir R V *Naval Administration,* London 1897
Harbron, J *Trafalgar and the Spanish Navy,* London 1988
Hart, C R *Royal Forest: A History of Dean's Woods as Producers of Timber,* Oxford 1966
Heath, Admiral L G *Letters from the Black Sea,* London 1897
Hilton, B *Corn, Cash, Commerce: The Economic policies of the Tory Governments 1815–1830,* Oxford 1977
Hinde, T *Forests of Britain,* London 1985
Hinde, W *George Canning,* London 1973
Hoseason, Commander J C *The Steam Navy,* London 1853

Hoskins, H L *British Routes to India,* London 1928
Imlah, A H *Economic elements in the Pax Britannica,* London 1958
— *Lord Ellenborough,* London 1939
Ingram, E, ed *Two Views of British India* London 1969
James, W *The Naval History of Great Britain,* London 1902, 6 vols
Jane, F T *The Imperial Russian Navy,* London 1904
— *Heresies of Seapower* London 1907
Jenkins E H *A History of the French Navy,* London 1974
Joinville, Prince *Vieux Souveniers,* Paris 1894
— *The Naval Forces of France compared to those of England,* London 1844
Kennedy, P *The Rise and Fall of British Naval Mastery,* London 1976
Keppel, Admiral Sir H *A Sailor's Life under Four Sovereigns,* London 1899, 3 vols
King-Hall, L *Sea Saga,* London 1935
Kitson-Clark, G *Peel and the Conservative Party,* London 1929
Lambert, A D *Battleships in Transition: The Creation of the Steam Battlefleet 1815–1860,* London 1984
— *Warrior: Restoring the World's First Ironclad,* London 1987
— *The Crimean, War: British Grand Strategy against Russia 1853–1856,* Manchester 1990
Lang, O, *Improvements in Naval Architecture,* London 1848
Laughton, J K *Memoirs of the Life and Correspondence of Henry Reeve,* London 1898, 2 vols
Lavery B *The Ship of the Line,* London 1983–84, 2vols.
— *The Arming and Fitting of English Ships of War: 1660–1815,* London 1987
Lewis, M *A Social History of the Navy 1793–1815,* London 1960
— *The Navy in Transition, 1814– 1865,* London 1965
Lloyd, C *Mr Barrow of the Admiralty,* London 1970
Lloyd, C and Coulter *Medicine and the Navy, 1200–1900,.* Edinburgh 1963, vol 4
Low, C R *A History of the Indian Navy,* London 1877
Mahan, Capt A T *The Influence of Seapower Upon History,* London 1890
— *Naval Strategy,* London 1911
Manning, Capt T D & Walker, Cdr C F *British Warship Names,* London 1959
Melville, Viscount *A Letter to Right Hon Spencer Perceval on the subject of Naval Timber,* London 1810
Mends, B S *The Life of Admiral Sir William Mends,* London 1899
Moresby, Admiral J *Two Admirals,* London 1913
Morriss, R *The Royal Dockyards during the Revolutionary and Napoleonic Wars,* Leicester 1983
Mitchell, A *The Whigs in Opposition: 1815–1830,* Oxford 1967
Mitchell, D *A History of Russian and Soviet Seapower,* London 1974
Mitchell, P *British Historical Statistics,* Cambridge 1988
Napier, Admiral Sir C *The Navy,* London 1851
Otway, A *Autobiography and Journals of Admiral Lord Clarence Paget,* London 1896
O'Byrne, W *Naval Biographical Dictionary,* London 1849, 2 vols
Padfield, P *Broke and the Shannon,* London 1965
Parker, C S *Life and Letters of Sir James Graham, 1792–1861,* London 1907, 2 vols
Parkinson, C N *Viscount Exmouth,* London 1934
Parry, A *The Admirals Fremantle,* London 1971
Partridge, M S *Military Planning for the Defence of the United Kingdom, 1814–1870,* London 1989
Pasley, L *Life of Sir T S Pasley,* London 1900
Penrose, Admiral Sir C *Remarks on the Conduct of the Naval Administration of Great Britain since 1815,* London 1830 (pub anon)
Phillimore, A *Life of Admiral Sir William Parker,* London 1876–80, 3 vols
Phipps, J *Papers on Shipbuilding In India,* Calcutta 1840
Pool, B *Navy Board Contracts: 1660–1832,* London 1966
Preston, A and Major, J *Send a gunboat,* London 1967
Prest, J M *Lord John Russell,* London 1972
Prothero, I *Artisans and Politics in early nineteenth century London,* Folkstone 1979
Pugh, P *The Cost of Seapower,* London 1986
Rackham, O *Trees and Woodland in the British Landscape,* London 1976
— *The History of the Countryside,* London 1986
— *The Last Forest,* London 1989
Rasor, E L *Reform in the Royal Navy; A Social history of the Lower Deck 1850–1880,* Hamden Ct 1976
Read, E J *On the Modifications which the ships of the Royal Navy have undergone in the Present Century,* London 1859
Richmond, Admiral Sir H *National Policy and Naval Strength,* London 1928
— *Statesmen and Seapower,* Oxford 1946
Rodger, N A M *The Admiralty,* Lavenham 1979
Rolt, L T C *Isambard Kingdom Brunel,* London 1957
Roseveare, H *The Treasury: 1660–1870,* London 1973
Roskill, S W *H.M.S. Warspite,* London 1957
Ross, Sir, J *Memoirs of Lord de Saumarez,* London 1838, 2 vols
Sainty, J C *Admiralty Officials: 1660–1870,* London 1975
Schurman, D M *The Education of a Navy,* London 1965
— *Sir Julian Stafford Corbett, 1856–1922,* London 1981
Semmel, B *Liberalism and Naval Strategy,* London 1986
Seppings, R *On a New Principle of Constructing H.M. Ships of War,* London 1814
— *Apparatus for Raising Masts out of their Steps,* London 1816
— *On the great strength given to Ships of War by the addition of Diagonal Braces,* London 1818
— *On a new Principle of Constructing Merchant Ships,* London 1820
Seton-Watson, H *The Russian Empire, 1801–1917,* Oxford 1967
Sharp, J A *Memoirs of Rear Admiral Sir William Symonds,* London 1858
Slade, Com A *A Few Words on Naval Construction and Naval Promotion,* London 1846
Snodgrass, G *A letter to the Right Hon. Henry Dundas on the mode of Improving the Navy,* London 1796
Southey, R *Life of Lord Nelson,* London 1833
Southgate, D *The Most English Minister: The Policies and Politics of Palmerston,* London 1966
Stanmore, Lord *Life of Sidney Herbert,* London 1906, 2 vols
Stebbings, E P *The Forests of India,* London 1922, 1 vol
Strachan, H *Wellington's Legacy: The Reform of the British Army, 1830–1854,* Manchester 1984
— *From Waterloo to Balaklava,* Cambridge 1985
Sulivan, H N *Life and Letters of Admiral Sir B J Sulivan,* London 1896
Sumida, J *In Defence of Naval Supremacy: Financial Limitation, Technological Innovation, and British Naval Policy, 1889–1914,* London 1989
Sumner, B H *A Survey of Russian History,* London 1947
Taylor, A J P *The Struggle for Mastery in Europe, 1848–1918,* Oxford 1954
Temperley H M W *The Foreign Policy of Canning 1822–7,* London 1925
— *England and the Near East: The Crimea,* London 1936
Trevelyan, G *Lord Grey of the Reform Bill,* London 1929
Tucker, J S *Memoirs of the Right Hon. Earl St. Vincent,* London 1855, 2 vols
Tunstall, W C B *Naval Warfare in the Age of Sail,* ed Tracy, N, London 1990
Tupinier, M *Observations sur les Dimensions des Vaissaux et des fregates dans la Marine Francais,* Paris 1822
Uden, G *The Fighting Temeraire,* Oxford 1961
Van Crefeld, M *Supplying War,* London 1977
Wadia, R A *The Bombay Dockyard and the Wadia Master Builders,* Bombay 1955
Ward, J T *Sir James Graham,* London 1967
Warner, O *Captain Marryat,* London 1953
Webster, Sir C *The Foreign Policy of Castlereagh 1812–22,* London 1931–34, 2 vols
— *The Foreign Policy of Palmerston,* London 1951, 2 vols
Wells, Capt J *Whaley: the Story of HMS Excellent,* Portsmouth 1980
Williams, H N *The Life and Letters of Admiral Sir Charles Napier,* London 1917
Winton, J *Hurrah for the Life of a Sailor!,* London 1977
Woodhouse, C M *The Battle of Navarino,* London 1965
Ziegler, P *King William IV,* London 1971

Articles

Brown, D K 'Shells at Sevastopol', *Warship,* April 1979
Glover, R 'The French Fleet, 1807–1814; Britain's problem and Madison's opportunity', *Historical Journal* 1967
Hamilton, C I 'Sir James Graham, the Baltic Campaign and War Planning at the Admiralty in 1854', *The Historical Journal,* 1976
Hamilton, C I 'Naval hagiography and the Victorian Hero', *The Historical Journal,* 1980
— The Royal Navy, la Royale and the Militarisation of Naval Warfare, 1840–1870. *Journal of Strategic Studies,* 1983
— The Diplomacy and Naval Effects of the Prince de Joinville's Note Sur l'Etat des Forces Navales de la France of 1844. *The Historical Journal,* 1989
Lloyd, C 'Dundonald's Crimean war plans', *MM* vol 32
Packard, J J 'Sir Robert Seppings and the Timber Problem', *MM* vol 44
Ranft, B 'Restraints on war at sea before 1945', in *Restraints on War,* ed M Howard
Roberts, S 'Combatant Ships of the French Navy after 1814', *The Belgian Shiplover,* 1975
Taylor, A H 'Admiral the Hon. Sir George Elliot', *MM* vol 35
Taylor, R I 'Manning the Royal Navy: the reform of the recruiting system, 1852–1862', *MM* 1959, 1960, vols 44, 45

Unpublished Dissertations

Hamilton, C I 'The Royal Navy, Seapower, and the Screw Ship of the Line; 1845–1860', Cambridge 1973
Lambert, A D 'Great Britain, the Baltic and the Russian War; 1854–1856', London 1983
McMillan, D F 'The Development of British Naval Gunnery; 1815–1853', London 1967
Roberts, S S 'The Introduction of Steam Technology into the French Navy; 1818–1852', Chicago 1976

NOTES

Abbreviations used in the Notes

Add. British Library Additional Manuscripts. This large group covers the correspondence of Admiral Sir Thomas, Sir William and Henry Martin, Admiral Sir Charles Napier, Lord Aberdeen, Lord Liverpool, Lord Palmerston, Lord Melville, Sir Robert Peel and Sir Charles Wood.
ADM. Admiralty Papers, Public Record Office, Kew.
Althorp. Spencer Family Mss. Now at the British Library.
BGY. Papers of Sir Robert Seppings, NMM.
Briggs. *Naval Administrations.* London 1892, Sir T Briggs.
Bourchier. *Memoir of the Life of Admiral Sir Edward Codrington*, ed Lady Bourchier, 2 vols, London 1873.
CAS. *Memoirs and Correspondence of Viscount Castlereagh.* ed Lord Londonderry, 12 vols, London 1848–53.
COD. Papers of Admiral Sir Edward Codrington, NMM.
De Grey. Papers of Earl De Grey, Bedford Record Office.
ELL. Papers of Lord Minto, NMM.
E Marine Board Correspondence, East India Company Records, India Record Office, London.
F Marine Board Correspondence, East India Company Records, India Record Office, London.
GC. Private Papers of Lord Palmerston, Southampton University Library.
GD. Papers of Lord Melville and Sir George Clerk, Scottish Record Office.
Gr. Papers of Sir James Graham. Microfilm at Cambridge University Library.
HLW. Papers of Admiral Sir Benjamin Hallowell, NMM.
HMC. Publication of the Historical Manuscripts Commission.
MEL. Papers of Lord Melville, NMM.
MELB. Papers of Lord Melbourne, Royal Archive.
MLN. Papers of Admiral Sir David and Sir Alexander Milne, NMM.
MM. *Mariner's Mirror.*
MRF. Papers of Sir George Cockburn, microfilm at the NMM.
NeC. Papers of the Fifth Duke of Newcastle, Nottingham University Library.
NLS. Papers of Lord Minto, National Library of Scotland.
NMM. Collection held at the National Maritime Museum, London.
NRS. Publication of the Navy Records Society.
PAR. Papers of Admiral Sir William Parker, NMM.
Phillimore. *Life of Admiral Sir William Parker*, Phillimore, A, London 1876–78, 3 vols.
P P Parliamentary Papers. In this case the published evidence and reports of a series of enquiries into naval finance and administration.
PRO Private Papers of Lord Ellenborough and Lord John Russell, held at the Public Record Office, Kew.
PwH. Private Papers of the Fourth Duke of Portland, Nottingham University Library.
QVL. *The Letters of Queen Victoria 1837 to 1861*, ed A C Benson and Lord Esher, London 1908, 3 vols.
R A. Royal Archive Windsor Castle.
SPB. Miscellaneous Papers on Shipbuilding, NMM.
T. Treasury Papers, Public Record Office, Kew.
WD. *The Dispatches of the Duke of Wellington*, ed Col J Gurwood, London 1834–1847, 13 vols.
WND. *Dispatches, Correspondence and Memoranda of the Duke of Wellington*, ed Wellington, London 1867–1880, 8 vols.
Wood. Papers of Sir Charles Wood, Borthwick Institute, York.
WWL. Papers of Admiral Sir Baldwin Walker, photocopies held at NMM.
YOR. Papers of Sir Charles Yorke, NMM.

Part One: THE FOUNDATIONS OF SEAPOWER

1 Strategy

1. There has been a considerable debate on the strategic requirements of British security. Several historians have argued that the Army had an equally important role, but this is not borne out by the nature and disposition of the Army in the period under review. At no time between 1815 and 1850 was there ever an adequate force in Britain to repel a serious invasion, or to act on the Continent.
2. *On War*, Book One, Chapter One, clause 24, p87.
3. Castlereagh to Aberdeen 13.11.1813 & Castlereagh to Earl Clancarty 1.2.1814; CAS, 3rd Ser, vol 1, pp73–5, 223–24.
4. Webster, Sir C *The Foreign Policy of Castlereagh*, London 1931, vol I, p194.
5. Lord Clancarty to Lord Bathurst 29.3.1814; CAS, IX, p365–66.
6. Liverpool to Castlereagh 16.4.1814, Webster, I. pp536–37 & 269;
   Byam Martin to Castlereagh 30.5.1814, Add 41,389.
7. Castlereagh to Clancarty 16.5.1814, CAS, IX, p374, Webster, I, p267.
   Bindoff, S T *The Scheldt Question to 1839*, London 1945, pp138–55.
8. Webster, I, pp285–86.
9. Wellington to Castlereagh 2.7.1815, WD, VIII, p187.
   Wellington to Viscount Beresford 6.9.1828, WND, V, pp29–30.
10. Glover, R 'The French Fleet, 1807–1814; Britain's problem and Madison's opportunity'. *Journal of Modern History*, 1967, pp233–52.
11. *Voyage dans la Grande-Bretagne, enterpris relativement au Services Publics de la Guerre, de Marine, des Ponts et Chauses, an Commerce et a Industrie depuis 1816*, 2 vols, Paris pp1825–26.
12. *The Cambridge History of the British Empire* section written by Brian Tunstall, Cambridge 1940, Vol II, pp826–40. French, D *The British Way in Warfare: 1688–2000*, London 1990, pp124–5.
13. Castlereagh to Liverpool 24.12.1814, Add 38,566, ff31–35.

14. Castlereagh to Liverpool 20.10.1818, quoted in Webster, II, p152.
15. Bartlett, C *Great Britain and Seapower: 1815–1853*, Oxford 1963, p23.
Webster, II, pp280–81, 362.
Temperley, H *The Foreign Policy of Canning: 1822–1827*, London 1925, pp320–21.
16. Sign put up in the windows of the Admiralty upon the declaration of peace in 1814, Add 45,045, f142.
17. For an example of this philsophy see: Lambert, A D *The Royal Navy and the Introduction of the Screw propeller, 1837–1847* in 'Innovation in Shipping and Trade' ed Stephen Fisher, Exeter 1989, pp61–88.
18. Black & Woodfine (eds) *The British Navy and the Use of Naval Power in the Eighteenth Century*, Leicester, 1988, p17.
19. Clancarty to Castlereagh 14.12.1813, CAS IX, pp97–102.
20. Temperley, pp119–20.
21. French O, *The British Way in Warfare*, London 1990, makes this error, pp130–31.
22. Lambert, A D *The Crimean War: British Grand Strategy against Russia 1853–1856*, Manchester 1990, Ch1.
23. Bourne, K *Palmerston, the Early Years 1784–1841*, London 1982, pp576–620.
Mitchell, D W *A History of Russian and Soviet Seapower*, London 1974, p138.
24. Graham, G S *Great Britain and the Indian Ocean: 1810–1850*, Oxford 1967.
25. Mahan, Capt A T *The Influence of Seapower Upon History 1660–1793*, London 1890. For a criticism of Mahan see: Kennedy P M *The Rise and Fall of British Naval Mastery*, London 1976. However, Kennedy in his turn is open to significant reservations. His reliance on Halford Mackinder's 'Heartland' thesis merely replaces Mahan's subjective slant on history with half-baked geostrategic arguments that had more to do with Russophobia than strategy. Writing in 1990 it seems particularly inappropriate to suggest that the 'Heartland' can overcome the maritime preponderance.
26. Symcox, G *The Crisis of French Seapower: 1688–1697*, The Hague 1974.
Pritchard, J *Louis XV's Navy 1748–1762. A Study of Organisation and Administration*, Kingston & Montreal 1987.
Dull, J R *The French Navy and American Independence 1774–1787*, Princeton 1975.
Crowhurst, P *The Defence of British Trade: 1689–1815*, London 1977.
27. Bonaparte to Minister of Marine Decres 17.9.1810, in Glover, R *Britain at Bay, Defence against Bonaparte, 1803–1814*, London 1973, pp182–93.
28. Baugh, Daniel A, 'Why did Britain lose command of the sea during the war for America?' in Black & Woodfine, pp149–70.
29. Roberts, Stephen S *The Introduction of Steam Technology in the French Navy 1818–1852*, Unpub PhD thesis, Univ of Chicago 1976, pp1–40, 442.
Tupinier, M *Observations sur les dimensions des vaisseaux et des Fregates dans la Marine Francais*, Paris 1822. For a discussion of the invasion question see Ch.II for the period 1846–50, when the issues involved were given the most thorough examination.
30. Partridge, M S *Military Planning for the Defence of the United Kingdom 1814–1870*, Westport, Conn 1989.
31. Hamilton, C I 'The Royal Navy, *la Royale*, and the Militarisation of Naval Warfare: 1840–1870', *Journal of Strategic Studies*, 1986, p208.
32. Lambert, *Crimean War*, pp35–36, 82–107, 280–88.
33. Chappelle, H I *A History of the American Sailing Navy*, New York 1949.
Symonds, Craig L *Navalists and Anti-Navalists: The Naval Policy debate in the United States, 1785–1827*, Newark, Del 1980.
34. Schroeder, John H *Shaping a Maritime Empire: The Commercial and Diplomatic role of the American Navy, 1829–1861*, Westport, Conn 1985.
35. Bourne, K *Great Britain and the Balance of Power in North America, 1815–1908*, London 1967.
Hagan, K (ed) *In Peace and War*, Westport, Conn 1984, pp46–106.
36. Craufurd, H W *The Russian Fleet in the Baltic in 1836*, London 1837.
37. Ranft, B Mcl *Technical Change and British Naval Policy: 1860–1939*, London 1977.

2 Economics

1. Brewer, J *The Sinews of Power*, London 1989, provides a thorough study of the creation of the military/economic power of the British state after 1688.
Sumida, J T *In Defence of Naval Supremacy*, London 1989.
2. Pritchard and Dull both emphasise the weakness of French naval finance.
3. Mitchell, A *The Whigs in Opposition: 1815–1830*, Oxford 1967, pp98, 104, 107, 121, 140–5, 165, 172–73, 223–24.
4. Liverpool to Castlereagh 11.8.1815, CAS, X pp476–77.
5. Cookson, J E *Lord Liverpool's Administration 1815–1822*. Edinburgh 1975, pp31–2.
6. Mitchell, pp95–97; Croker, Vol I, pp80–85.
7. Hilton, B *Corn, Cash, Commerce*, Oxford 1977, p233.
Cookson, p118.
8. P P, 1817, iv, pp203–5, 169.
9. Byam Martin memo 24.1 & 2.2.1817, Add 41,400, ff13–14.
Memo by John T Briggs, Accountant General of the Navy 13.3.1835, Add 40,416, fl13.
10. Cookson, pp120–23.
Liverpool to Melville 24.6.1818 & Melville to Byam Martin 30.6.1818, Add 41,400, f54.
Melville to Liverpool 28.7.1818, Add 38,272, ff334–42.
11. Cookson, pp145–47, 173.
12. Byam Martin memo 8.5.1820, Add 41,400, f66.
13. Cookson, pp341–43.
George IV to Liverpol 27.7.1821 & Liverpool to George IV 31.7.1821, Aspinall, A (ed) *The Letters of George IV: 1812–1830*, Cambridge 1938, vol 1, pp451–52.
14. Melville to Canning 5.8.1823, Add 38,296, ff56–59.
15. Byam Martin memo 29.12.1826, Add 41,400, f73.
16. Byam Martin to Admiral Malcolm 1.6.1830, Add 41,398, f156.
17. Hilton, pp240–56.
18. Hilton, p306, quotation p267.
Mitchell, pp223–24.
19. Davis, C *The Age of Grey and Peel*, Oxford 1929, pp 274–76.
20. Peel to Wellington 5.1.1835, Add 43,061, ff163–64.
21. Auckland to Russell 20.11 & 17.12.1848, PRO 30/22/7D.
22. Partridge, 1990, p12.
23. Mitchell, P *British Historical Statistics*, Cambridge 1988.
Bartlett, pp339–40.

Part Two: NAVAL POLICY 1815–50

1 Creating a New Battlefleet: 1815–30

1. Admiralty to Navy Board 21.3.1815, order to delay paying off the Fleet due to problems in France, ADM 1/3459.
Admiralty to Navy Board 30.3.1815, order to prepare *Royal Sovereign*, *San Josef*, *Ville de Paris* and *Queen Charlotte* for service at sea. ADM 1/3459.
2. Navy Board to Admiralty 11.8.1814, ADM 106/2264.
3. Navy Board to Admiralty 16.7.1814, ADM 106/2264.
Admiralty to Navy Board 11 & 23.3.1815, ADM A/3106.
4. Foreign Office to Admiralty 27.1. & 24.5.1815, ADM 1/4232.
5. Navy Board to Admiralty 18.3.1816, ADM 2/1617. Also 10.12.1818, ADM 106/2276.
6. Melville to Liverpool 7.3.1813, GD 51/2/473/3.
Morris, R *The Royal Dockyards during the Revolutionary and Napoleonic Wars*, Leicester 1983, pp53–5, 205.
7. Admiralty to Navy Board 3 & 7.1.1815, ADM A/3104.
8. Navy Board to Admiralty 4.10.1814, ADM 7/593.
Memo by Byam Martin late 1815, Add 41,406, ff33, 42, 62.
Navy Board to Admiralty 7.12.1816, GD 51/2/888.
9. Admiralty to Navy Board 28.1.1815, ADM A/3104.
10. Admiralty to Navy Board 7.3. & 1.5.1815, ADM A/3106 & 8.
11. Navy Board to Admiralty 25.8.1814, ADM 106/2264.

12. Navy Board to Admiralty 15.9.1815, ADM 106/2268.
13. Byam Martin to Melville 10 & 11.11.1815, GD 51/2/83, 1–2.
Melville to Prince Regent 27.11.1815 & 7.2.1816, GD 51/1/214, ff26–28.
Collinge, J M *Navy Board Officials; 1660–1832*, London 1978, p20.
The Letters of Sir T.B. Martin: vol. III ed Admiral Sir R V Hamilton, Navy Records Society, London 1901, pxi.
14. Memo by Lord Liverpool and Vansittart 12.9.1815, GD 51/2/555.
15. Admiralty to Navy Board, ADM 83/1, f218.
Reeve H (ed) *The Greville Memoirs*, London 1815, vol. 1.
16. Byam Martin memo on reducing dockyard expenses 2.1816, GD 51/2/984.
Admiralty to Navy Board 19.2.1816, ADM 106/71.
17. Byam Martin memo undated, late 1815, Add 41,406, f33.
Byam Martin memo 4.1816, Add 41,394, ff5–8.
Navy Board to Admiralty 5.4.1816, ADM 106/2269.
Admiralty to Navy Board 10.9.1816, ADM 2/1618, f98.
18. Treasury to Admiralty 5.3.1816, ADM 1/4298.
19. Admiralty to Navy Board 3.12.1816, ADM 106/2274.
20. Navy Board to Admiralty 16.1. & 18.2.1817, ADM 106/2272.
Byam Martin memo on improving dockyard management 24.12.1821, ADM 1/3462.
21. Admiralty to Navy Board 21.2.1817, ADM 83/2.
22. Admiralty to Navy Board 10.7.17, ADM 106/75.
23. Melville to Lord Bathurst, Secretary of State for War and the Colonies, 11.8.1817, Bathurst Mss, HMC.
24. Navy Board to Admiralty 5.11.1817, ADM 106/2274.
Navy Board to Admiralty 31.7.1818, ADM 106/2275; also Admiralty to Navy Board 1.8.1818, ADM 83/2.
List of the Navy 26.11.1817, MEL/102.
25. Liverpool to Melville 24.6.1818; Melville to Byam Martin 30.6.1818; Byam Martin memo undated; Add 41,400, f54.
26. Byam Martin to Melville 8.7.1818, GD 51/2/587.
Seppings to Melville 14.7.1818, GD 51/2/558.
Byam Martin to Melville 6.8.1818, Add 41,400, f59.
27. Liverpool to Lord Sidmouth 6.8.1818, Add 38,273, ff14–20.
Melville to Liverpool 28.8.1818, Add 38,272, ff334–42.
28. Melville to Liverpool 28.8.1818, GD 51/2/437/9.
Navy Board to Admiralty 20.1.1819, Add 41,402. This whole volume consists of materials relating to the Tucker enquiry.
Thomas Grenville to St Vincent 19.7.1818, Tucker J S *Memoirs of the Right Hon. Earl of St. Vincent*, London 1855, 2 vols, II p421.
29. Admiralty to Navy Board 13.3.1819, ADM 83/2.
30. Admiralty to Navy Board 27.5., 2.9., & 2.10.1819, 6.11.1820, 12.12.1821, ADM 106/2282. Also 21.11.1822, ADM 106/2277-8, 2280, 2282 & 2284.
31. Byam Martin to Melville 23.12.1819, Add 41,395, ff56–59.
Byam Martin memo 8.5.1820, Add 41,400, f66.
32. Admiralty to Navy Board, secret, 1.1.1821 & Navy Board to Admiralty 7.1.1821, ADM 106/30.
Byam Martin memo of reductions 5.7.1821, Add 41,395, f84.
Byam Martin memo on improving the management of the dockyards 24.12.1821, ADM 1/3462.
King to Liverpool 27.7.1821 & reply 31.7.1821, *Letters of George the Fourth*, (ed) Aspinall, A, vol II, pp451–52.
33. Admiralty order of 6.8.1821 & Admiralty to Navy Board 20.6.1822, ADM 1/3462.
34. St Vincent to Ben Tucker 11.9.1822, Tucker, vol II, pp425–26.
35. Intelligence Report on the *Royal Charles* building at L'Orient 1826, ADM 1/3464.
Byam Martin to Melville 23.8.1826, GD 51/2/1014/2.
36. Navy Board to Admiralty 17.1. & 6.6.1825, ADM 106/2289.
Byam Martin memo 14.12.1825, Add 41,396.
37. Byam Martin to Melville 16.3.1826, Add 41,396, ff109–116.
Navy Board to Admiralty 22.2.1815, ADM 106/2266.
Navy Board to Admiralty 30.6.1826, ADM 106/2290.
38. Byam Martin to Melville 31.5.1826, Add 41,396, f116.
Seppings to Melville 7.6.1826, GD 51/2/700.
Byam Martin Memoranda late 1815, Add 41,405, f42.
39. Melville to Byam Martin 22.7.1826, Add 41,396, f133.
Byam Martin memo for Melville to read before the Cabinet 25.7.1826, Add 41,396, f128.
Byam Martin to the Dockyard Commissioners 25.7. & 1.8.1826, *ibid.*
40. Byam Martin to Melville 1.8.1826, Add 41,396, f132.
Byam Martin to Melville 21.8.1826, GD 51/2/1014/2.
Byam Martin to Cockburn 19.10.1826, Add 41,367.
Byam Martin to Melville 31.10.1826, Add 41,396, f152.
41. Byam Martin memo 29.12.1826, Add 41,400, f73.
42. Byam Martin to Commissioner Cunningham (Chatham) 31.1.1827, Add 41,397, f9.
Byam Martin to Commissioner Shiel (Plymouth) 17.3.1827, *ibid*, f11. Byam Martin memo 23.3.1827, *ibid*, f17.
43. Byam Martin to Huskisson 8.6.1827, Add 41,397, f29.
44. Byam Martin memo for Canning and Clarence 12.4.1827, Add 41,397, f32.
Byam Martin to the Lord High Admiral 9.5.1827, *ibid*, f22.
45. Admiralty to Navy Board 19 & 23.3. & 27.4.1827, ADM 106/2292. Also 2 & 9.7.1828. The two three-deckers were never completed.
46. Admiralty to Navy Board 24.101.1827, ADM 106/2292.
47. Byam Martin to dockyards 26.6.1827, Add 41,397, f37.
Admiralty to Navy Board 29.6.1827, ADM 106/2292.
48. Admiralty to Navy Board 7.11.1828, ADM 106/2293.
Byam Martin to Commissioners 26.3.1828, Add 41,400, f75.
49. Cockburn to Melville 28.10.1828, GD 51/2/792.
Admiralty to Navy Board 28.2. & 9.9.1828, ADM 106/2293.
50. Admiralty to Navy Board 20.2.1829, ADM 106/2294.
Byam Martin to Melville 25.1.1829, GD 51/2/1017.
51. Byam Martin to Melville late January 1830, Add 41,397, f120.
52. Byam Martin to Melville 18.9.1830, Add 41,397, f40.
Byam Martin to Sir Henry Martin 1830, Add 41,397, f202.
Byam Martin to Cockburn 6.8.1830, Add 41,397, f176.
Byam Martin to Melville late 1830, Add 41,368, ff265–70.
Byam Martin to Admiral Malcolm 1.6.1830, Add 41,398.
53. Byam Martin memo delivered to Graham when he came into office. November/December 1830, Add 41,405, ff6–12.

2 The Abolition of the Navy Board

1. Parker, C S *The Life and Letters of Sir James Graham: 1792–1861*, London 1907, 2 vols.
Erickson, A B *The Public Career of Sir James Graham*, Oxford 1952.
Ward, J T *Sir James Graham*, London 1967. All three are weak on the political dynamics of the 1832 reform of naval administration, and even less satisfactory in dealing with the wider issues of naval policy.
Graham, evidence before the Select Committee on Naval Administration 30.4.1861, P P, V, pp102–04.
2. Admiralty to Navy Board 10.1.1831, ADM 1/3743.
Admiralty to Navy Board 17 & 25.1.1831, ADM 3/223.
Graham to Grey 24 & 28.1.1831, Gr B26.
3. Graham to Grey 24.1.1831, Gr B26.
Melville to Sir George Clerk, NLS GD 18/3335.
4. Graham to Grey 18.1.1831, Gr B26.
Byam Martin memo of conversation with the King 18.11.1830, Add 41,368.
5. Graham to Grey 28.1. & 2 & 4.2.1831, Gr B26.
Graham to the King 2.1831, Gr B55.
6. Grey to Graham 11.1. & 4.2.1831, Gr B54.
7. King to Graham 30.1.3 & 10.2.1831, Gr B54. It is significant that the King took the trouble to reply to these letters in person, rather than leaving his Secretary, Sir Herbert Taylor, to communicate with the ministers, as was normal.
Taylor to Byam Martin 9.2.1831, Add 41,368, f11.
Byam Martin to Taylor 10.2.1831, *ibid*, f13.
8. Melville to Clerk 2 & 4.3.1831, NLS GD 18/3335.
9. Melville to Graham 30.3.1832, Gr B26.
10. Admiralty to Navy Board 19.4.1831, ADM 3/223.
11. Graham to Martin 5.3.1831, Add 41,368, f16.
Althorp to the King 26.3.1831, Althorp, H6.
King to Lord Althorp 27.3.1831, Althorp H8.
12. Althorp to Byam Martin 7.4.1831, Add 41,368, f20.
13. Byam Martin correspondence with Graham, Elliot,

Taylor and the King 22.4. to 12.5.1831, Add 41,368, ff25–96.
Taylor to Graham 27.4.1831, Gr B54.
14. Navy Board to Admiralty 17.2.1831, ADM 106/2296.
15. Seppings to Byam Martin 12.4.1831, Add 41,395, f104.
16. Byam Martin to Graham 16.6.1831, Add 41,399, f64. Also ADM 106/223.
17. Admiralty to Navy Board 30.6.1831, ADM 3/233.
18. Admiralty to Navy Board 30.6.1831, ADM 3/223.
19. Admiralty to Symonds 20.5.1831, ADM 3/223.
20. Byam Martin to Seppings (confidential) 17.2. 1831, Add 41,399, f34.
Admiralty to Navy Board 13.10.1831, ADM 3/224.
21. Graham to Brocklebank 14.10.1831, Gr B49.
Brocklebank to Graham 12.11.1831, ADM 1/3480.
22. Graham to Grey 28.7.1831, Gr B26.
Kriegel, A D (ed) *The Holland House Diaries: 1831–1840*, London 1977, p77.
Ellice to Byam Martin & reply 12.10.1831, Add 41,368, f118.
Grey to Graham 15.10.1831, Gr B56.
Graham to Byam Martin 17.10.1831, Gr B26.
Graham to Grey 21.10.1832, *ibid.*
23. Navy Board to Admiralty 14.10.1831, ADM 106/233.
24. Graham to Lord Robert Grosvenor 23.11.1831, Gr B50.
25. Navy Board to Admiralty 1.11.1831, ADM 106/2296A.
26. Memo on dockyards by Sir John Barrow 22.11.1831, ADM 1/3475.
27. Graham draft memo on the consolidation of the Navy and Victualling Boards 6.12.1831, Gr B27.
Graham to Grey 7.12.1831, Gr B27.
Taylor to Graham 11.12.1831, Gr B55.
King to Graham 18.12.1831, Gr B55.
28. Admiralty to Navy Board 17.1.1832, ADM 3/225.
Graham to the King 9.2.1831, Gr B27.
29. Melville to Graham 30.3.1831 & Graham to Melville 11.4.1831, Gr B27.
30. Navy Board to Admiralty 8.2.1832, ADM 106/2297.
Surveyor to Admiralty 3.7.1832, ADM 222/1.
31. Admiralty to Navy Board 28.3.1832, ADM 3/226.
Navy Board to Admiralty 30.4.1832, ADM 106/2297.

3 Policy Without the Navy Board

1. The Duty of the Surveyor of the Navy 1806, ADM 87/1.
Skeleton of instructions to the several heads of departments; Surveyor of the Navy, ADM 1/3477.
2. Admiralty to Surveyor 16. & 26.6.1832, ADM 83/4.
Symonds to Hardy 3.7.1832, ADM 222/1.
3. Surveyor to Admiralty 7.7.1832, ADM 222/1.
4. Barrow memo on dockyard administration 27.8.1832, ADM 1/3477.
Graham minute 21.10.1832, ADM 1/3478.
Admiralty to Surveyor 22.11.1832, ADM 83/4.
5. Surveyor to Admiralty 15.9.1832, ADM 222/1.
Admiralty to Surveyor 20.9.1832, ADM 83/4.
Admiralty to Surveyor 23.11. & 3.12.1832, ADM 83/4.
6. Surveyor to Admiralty 31.10.1832, ADM 92/5.
Surveyor to Admiralty 28.11.1832, ADM 222/1.
Admiralty to Surveyor 29.11.1832, ADM 83/4.
Admiralty to Surveyor 3.3.1834, ADM 83/9.
7. Graham to Taylor 27.8. & 6.9.1832, Gr B55.
Graham to Grey 20.9.1832 & Grey to Graham 10.9.1832, Gr B28.
8. Graham to Grey 2.8.1833, Gr B28.
Grey to Graham 21.10.1833, Gr B56.
Treasury to Admiralty 31.1.1834, ADM 1/4309.
The King to Graham 13.3. and Graham to the King 15.3.1834, Gr B57.
Graham memo on leaving office 14.6.1834, ADM 1/3483.
9. Admiral Bowles, evidence before the 1848 Committee on Naval Estimates, P P, 1847–48.
Peel to Clerk 4.4.1833, GD 18/3340.
Clerk to Peel 8 & 10.4.1833, Add 40,403, ff219–25.
10. Admiralty to Surveyor 11.1.1833, ADM 83/4.
Surveyor to Admiralty 1.5.1833, ADM 222/2.
Graham to the Earl of Cawdor 6.10.1833, Gr B49.
Admiralty to Surveyor 1.10.1833, ADM 92/6.
11. Surveyor to Admiralty 3.6.1833, ADM 222/2.
Admiralty Standing Order 24.6.1833, ADM 1/3480.
Admiralty to Surveyor 8.7.1833, ADM 83/4.
Admiralty to Treasury 8.3.1835, ADFM 1/3485.
12. Admiralty to Surveyor 28.6.1833, ADM 222/2.
13. Admiralty to Surveyor and Storekeeper 18.1834, ADM 83/9.
Admiralty to Woods & Forests 18.6.1833, ADM 1/3480.
14. Surveyor to Admiralty 18 & 30.1.1833, ADM 92/5.
Admiralty to Surveyor 30 & 31.1. & 21.3.1833, ADM 83/4.
Surveyor to Admiralty 2.3.1833, ADM 222/2.
Admiralty to Surveyor 2 & 3.10.1833, ADM 83/8.
15. Admiralty to Surveyor 1 & 7.10.1833, ADM 92/6. Admiralty to Surveyor 21 & 30.4.1834, ADM 83/9. Surveyor to Admiralty 12.11.1834, ADM 222/5.
16. Admiralty to Surveyor 25.2.1833, ADM 83/7.
Surveyor to Admiralty 12.3.1833, ADM 222/2.
Admiralty to Surveyor 1.10. & 26.12.1833, ADM 92/6.
Admiralty to Surveyor 14.9.1833, ADM 83/8.
17. Peel to Wellington 5.1.1835, Add 43,061, ff163–64.
Herries to Peel 7.1.1835, Add 40,409, f192.
De Grey to Wellington 2.1.1835 De Grey, Mss L/30/53/1.
Memorandum by J T Briggs 12.3.1835, Add 40,417, f1–13.
18. Treasury to Admiralty 11.5.1835, ADM 1/4309.
Auckland to Minto 24.7.1836, NLS 11,793, f79.
19. Surveyor to Admiralty 27.2. & 7.8.1835, ADM 222/6 & 7.
20. Surveyor to Admiralty 12.11.1835, ADM 222/7.
21. Surveyor to Admiralty 13.1.1835, ADM 92/6.
Admiralty to Ordnance 13.4.1836, ADM 1/3489.
22. Palmerston to Melbourne 24.9.1835 & 1.3.1836, R A, 859/11 5 & 35.
23. Taylor to Minto 8.1.1836, ELL 211a.
Minto to Cockburn 11.3.1836, ELL 262.
Minto to the King 27.6. & 1 & 17.9.1836. Also Taylor to Minto 28.6 & 18.9.1836, ELL 211a.
24. Admiralty to Dockyards 8.1.1836, ADM 1/3488.
25. Adam to Minto 28.9.1836, ELL 228.
26 Surveyor to Admiralty 18.3.1837, ADM 222/10.
Surveyor to Admiralty 2.6.1837, ADM 1/5581.
Admiralty to Surveyor 7.6.1837, ADM 83/15.
27. Surveyor to Admiralty 6.6.1837, ADM 222/10 and marginal note.
28. Surveyor to Admiralty 13.6.1837, ADM 222/11.
Surveyor to Admiralty 14.7.1837, ADM 92/8.
Wood to Minto 20.7.1837, ELL 224.
29. Surveyor to Admiralty 13 & 16.6.1837, ADM 222/11.
Elliot to Minto 26.12.1837, ELL 219.
30. Treasury to Admiralty 25.7.1837, ADM 1/4311.
31. Minto memo 28.7.1837, ADM 3/264/4.
32. Wood memo February 1838, ADM 3/264/4.
33. Surveyor to Admiralty 25.1.1838, ADM 222/12.
Surveyor to Admiralty 27.4.1839, ADM 222/14.
Treasury to Admiralty 11.6.1839, ADM 1/4313.
Memo on leaving office June 1839, Add 49,572, f141.
34. Admiralty to Surveyor 30.4, 25.5 & 22.6.1838, ADM 83/17.
Surveyor to Admiralty 20.9.1838, ADM 92/8.
35. Admiralty Minute 14.11.1838, ADM 1/3497.
Surveyor to Admiralty 21.11.1838, ADM 92/8.
36. Lloyd, C *Barrow of the Admiralty*, London 1970, pp178–79.
37 Adam to Minto 8.9.1838, ELL 228.
Wood to Minto 18.10 & 8.11.1838, ELL 224.
Minto to Melbourne 26.8 & 15.11.1838, R A, 859 9/24 & 28.
38. Admiralty to Ordnance 1.2, 24.9 & 24.12.1838, ADM 1/3494. Captain Hastings, HMS *Excellent* to Admiralty 22.12.1838, ADM 83/17.
Admiralty to Surveyor 1 & 15.1.1838, ADM 83/17.
Surveyor to Admiralty 10 & 17.1839, ADM 92/8.
39. Admiralty to Ordnance 30.12.1838, ADM 1/3497.
40. Wood memo on shipbuilding and dockyard work 11.1838, ADM 3264/5.
41. Surveyor to Admiralty 18.1.1839 & minute of 4.2.1839, ADM 92/8.
Wood to Symonds 19.2.1839, ADM 83/19.
Admiralty to Surveyor 17.7.1839, ADM 83/19.
42. Admiralty to Admiral Maitland 18.2.1839, ADM 1/3498.
Surveyor to Admiralty 11.5 & 13.6.1839, ADM 222/14.
Admiralty to Surveyor 20.5 & 21.6.1839, ADM 83/19.
Admiralty to Surveyor 26.12.1840, ADM 83/22.
43. For the diplomatic ramifications of the crisis see: Bourne, K *Palmerston*, London 1982; Temperley, H *England and the Near East: The Crimea*, London 1936, Webster, Sir C *The Foreign Policy of Palmerston*, London 1951, 2 vols.
Bartlett, pp127–47 also covers the crisis.
44. Ships in commission 7.5.1841, NLS 12,052, f94.
45. Palmerston to Sir Charles Adam 29.11.1840, ELL 228.
46. Palmerston to Melbourne 12 & 23.12.1840, MELB, 859/6/13/15 & 17.
Russell to Minto 14.12.1840, NLS 12,126, f62.
47. Aberdeen to Peel 15.1.1841, Add 40,312, f302.

48. Russell to Minto 16.2.1841, NLS 12, 126, f86.
49. Minto memo 8.9.1841 ELL 239 & ADM 3/265.

4 The Peel Adminstration 1841–46

1. Graham to Peel 1.8.1841, Add 40,446, f9.
2. Haddington to Peel late 1841, Add 40,456, f44.
3. Peel to Aberdeen 13.10.1841, Add 43,061, f287.
4. Peel to Aberdeen 16.11.1842, Add 40,453.
5. Admiralty to Surveyor 1.2.1843, ADM 83/28.
   Admiralty to Surveyor 4.4.1843, ADM 83/28.
   Admiralty to Surveyor 7 & 10.9.1843, ADM 83/33.
   Admiralty to Surveyor, 3, 8 & 11.11.1843, ADM 83/30.
6. Admiralty to Surveyor 16.3 & 7.5.1844, ADM 83/31, f2.
7. Admiralty to Surveyor 20.3.1844, ADM 83/31.
8. Admiralty to Surveyor 7, 9 & 18.12.1844, ADM 83/33.
9. Admiralty to Surveyor 19.2 & 24.4.1845, ADM 83/34.
10. Bowles to Minto 23.1.1845, ELL 237.
11. Wood to Minto 11.6.1845, *ibid.*
12. Wood to Minto 16.6.1845, *ibid.*
13. Symonds to Minto 23.9.1845. Also Haddington to Minto 25 & 30.9.1845, ELL 237.
14. Bowles to Minto 18.10.1845, ELL 237.
15. Ropp, T *The Development of a Modern Navy*, Annapolis 1988.
16. Bartlett, pp158–60.
    Hamilton, C I 'The Diplomatic and Naval effects of the Prince de Joinville's Note sur l'etat des forces navales de la France of 1844', *Historical Journal* 1989, pp675–87. Provides a valuable review of the 1844 crisis and the strategic plans.
17. Admiralty to Surveyor 30.3.1844, ADM 83/31.
18. Hamilton, pp677–78.
19. Haddington to Peel 11.7.1844, Add 40,457, f170.
20. Peel to Haddington (secret) 12.7.1844. Haddington to Peel 12.7.1844, Add 40,457, ff174, 176.
21. Graham to Peel 21.7 & 22.8.1844, Add 40,450, ff81–83; 40, 457, f249.
22. Peel to Aberdeen 2.7.1844, Add 40,454, f180.
23. Peel to Aberdeen 11 & 12.8.1844, Add 40,454, f202–06.
24. Bartlett, p163.
25. Cockburn to Admiral Sir David Milne 9.8.1844, MLN 36/6.
26. Graham to Peel 18, 22 & 23.8.1844, Add 40,450, ff101–15.
27. Wellington to Peel 23.8.1844, Add 40,460, f260.
28. Peel to Aberdeen 28.9.1844, Add 40,454, f270.
29. Wellington to Peel 29.11.1844, Add 40,460, f297.
30. Memo enclosed in Herbert to Peel 16.12.1844, Add 40,556, ff8–12.
31. Peel to Wellington 26.12.1844, Add 40,460, f322.
    Peel to Aberdeen 29.12.1844, Add 40,454, f366.
32. Aberdeen to Peel 31.12.1844, Add 40,454, f368.
33. Peel to Aberdeen 23.2.1845, Add 40,454, f413.
    Peel to the Queen 1.4.1845, Add 40,440.
34. Napier to Peel 5.6.1845, Add 40,568.
    Cockburn memo 9.6.1845, ADM 3/265 & part in Add 40,456.
35. Haddington to Peel 18.6 & reply 25.6.1845, Add 40,456, ff76, 92.
36. Admiralty to Surveyor 20.7, 30.8 & 2.9.1845, ADM 83/35, f6.
37. Brown, D K *Before the Ironclad*, London 1990, pp122–24.
    Lambert, A D *Battleships in Transition*, London 1986, pp19–24, 139.
38. Wellington to Peel 7.8 & reply 9.8.1845, Add 40,461, ff154–60.
    Haddington to Peel 9.8.1845, Add 40,456, f157.
39. Murray to Peel 9.8 & Graham to Peel 1845, Add 40,451, ff148–58.
40. Graham to Peel 10.8.1845, Add 40,451, f160.
41. Graham to Peel 18.8 & 6.9.1845, *ibid*, ff199, 251.
    Cockburn to Peel 16.8.1845, Add 40,572, f250.
42. Corry to Peel 18.8 & secret reply 5.9.1845, Add 40,572, ff269–73.
43. Peel to Aberdeen 1, 11 & 18.9.1845, Add 40,455, ff128,153–57.
44. Aberdeen to Peel 18.9 & Peel to Aberdeen 20.9 & 16.10.1845, Add 40,455, ff159, 163, 220.
45. Peel to Graham 21.9 & Graham to Peel 22.9 & 22.10.1845, Add 40,451, ff292, 297, 420.
46. Chamberlain, M E *Lord Aberdeen*, London 1983, p374.

5 Lord Ellenborough and the Review of Naval Policy: January–July 1846

1. Peel to the Queen 8.12.1845, Add 40,440, f374.
2. Peel to Haddington 25.12.1845, Add 40,458, ff252–55.
   Peel to Ellenborough 27.12.1845, Add 40,473, f25.
3. Graham to Peel 26.12.1845, Add 40,452, f75.
   Aberdeen to Peel 29.12.1845, Add 40,455, f192.
4. The Queen to King Leopold of the Belgians, *QVL*, ii, p70.
   The Queen to Peel 27.12.1845, Add 40,440, f453.
5. Memo by Prince Albert 28.6.1846, *QVL*, ii, pp80–82.
   Conacher, J B *The Peelites and the Party System: 1846–1852*, Newton Abbot 1972, pp13–14, 16, 180.
6. Imlah, A H *Lord Ellenborough*, London 1939.
7. *ibid*, pp195–97, 232–34.
8. Colchester, Lord (ed) *A Political Diary 1828–1830: Lord Ellenborough*, London 1881, 2 vols, vol 2 pp31–32, 207, 216–17.
9. Ellenborough to Peel 20.3.1846, PRO 30/12/4/5/, f105.
10. Ellenborough to Captain Durand 19.1.1846, PRO 30/12/34/1.
11. Ellenborough to Peel 18.1 & 2 & 7.2.1846, Add 40,473, ff37, 44, 48, 50.
12. Peel to Ellenborough 18.1 & 8.2.1846, Add 40,473, ff38, 53.
13. Ellenborough to Peel 5 & 8.3.1846, *ibid*, f76, 86.
14. Peel to Ellenborough (secret) 17.3.1846, *ibid*, f120.
15. Ellenborough to Peel 5 & 6.4.1846, PRO 30/12/4/1, f173, 181.
16. The State of the Navy 2.1846, PRO 30/12/5/1.
    Admiralty to Surveyor 28.1.1846, ADM 83/37.
17. Haddington to Peel 4.1844, BL Add 40,542, ff205–06.
    Wood to Minto 20.1.1843 & 15.2.1845. Also Symonds to Minto 7.1.1845, ELL 237.
18. Memo by Cockburn 15.11.1845, & Haddington in support undated, Add 40,458, f241–48.
19. Haddington to Peel 27 & 29.12.1845, Add 40,458, ff265–71.
20. Ellenborough minute on the building and repairing and altering of ships 5.4.1846, PRO 30/12/34/1.
21. Ellenborough to Symonds 31.5. & 3.6.1846, PRO 30/12/34/1.
    Admiralty Special Minutes 1845–46, ADM 3/265.
22. Ellenborough to Hay 6.5.1846 & Hay to Ellenborough 4.6.1846, PRO 30/12/34/1.
23. Ellenborough to Hamilton 6.7.1846, PRO 30/12/34/12.
24. Rous to Ellenborough 8.4.1846, ADM 3/265.
    Symonds to Minto 10.10.1847, NLS 12,068, f119.
    Napier to Russell undated 1849, *The Navy* pp188–92.
25. Ellenborough to Peel 17.3.1846, PRO 30/12/4/1, f105.
    Ellenborough to Parker 27.3.1846, PRO 30/12/4/1, f347.
    Ellenborough to the Queen 14.4.1846, PRO 30/12/4/11, ff29–33.
    Admiral Sir W Parker to Ellenborough 5.10.1846, PRO 30/12/6/7, ff25–40.

6 The Russell Government: Naval Policy and National Defence 1846–52

1. The Queen to King Leopold of Belgium 14.7.1846, *QVL*, II pp88–89.
2. Minto memo and correspondence of the formation of the Board of Admiralty June–July 1846, NLS 12,068.
3. Bartlett, p260.
   Greville, C G *Journal of the Reign of Queen Victoria 1837–1852*, London 1885, vol III, pp254–56.
   Parker to Lord John Russell 13.1.1849, Phillimore, III, p458.
4. Gash, N *Reaction and Reconstruction in English Politics 1832–1852*, Oxford 1965, p197.
   Several are quoted in: Bullen, R *Palmerston, Guizot and the collapse of the Entente Cordiale*, London 1974, pp60–61.
5. Denison to Russell 23.6.1846 including Portland to Denison 11.6.1846, PRO 30/22/5A, ff275–79.
   Turberville, A S *'A History of Welbeck Abbey and its Owners'*, London 1939, p345.
6. Auckland to Russell 29.6.1846, PRO 30/22/5A.
   Ward to Russell 23.3.1849, PRO 30/22/7F, ff57–60.
   Minto to Russell 7.1.1849, PRO 30/22/7E, f131.
7. Partridge, M S 'The Russell Cabinet and National Defence, 1846–1852', *History*, Vol 72, June 1987, pp231–50.
8. Partridge, p231.
9. Palmerston to Beauvale 21.3.1838 & to Russell 27.9.1846, quoted in Bullen pp54–56.
10. Partridge, p234.
11. The performance of the Royal Navy during the Russian War (1854–56) stands in need of reassessment. Far from reflecting the weaknesses so clearly pointed up ashore, the Navy was the most professional and the most successful armed service of the war. Partridge's statement at p250 concerning the Navy in the war is both inaccurate and misleading. Naval re-equipment was far from complete in 1854, because the steam battlefleet had only been accepted, and funded, from October 1852, during the Duke of Northumberland's period at the Admiralty. Napier's Baltic fleet included seven sailing battleships, because there were not enough steamers available. Far from not

daring to approach Kronstadt, the baltic fleet spent most of 1855 in sight of the great Russian arsenal, planning its destruction. By 1856 the fleet was both equipped and ready for the attack and this had a major influence on Russia's decision to accept peace. At Sevastopol the fleet went into action solely to assist the army, and against the express advice of the Admiral Commander in Chief. Its only function was to act as a diversion. The popular impression referred to was not current among the politicians and naval officers who decided British naval policy in 1856.

12. Partridge, p234.
13. Baring to Russell 2.12.1849, PRO 30/22/8b, f291–94.
14. Ellenborough to Captain Hamilton 6.7.1846, PRO 30/12/34/12.
15. Partridge, p238.
16. Ellenborough to the Queen 14.4.1846, PRO 30/12/4/11, ff29–33.
Sir W Parker to Ellenborough 5.10.1846, PRO 30/12/6/7, ff25–40.
17. Auckland to Russell 20.3.1847, PRO 30/22/6B, ff275–77.
18. Auckland to Russell 21.3.1848, PRO 30/22/7B, ff136–37.
19. Palmerston memo 12.1846, PRO 30/22/5F, ff11–28.
Palmerston to Wood 24.12.1846, GC/WO? 186/1–4.
20. Duke of Wellington memo 8.2.1847, PRO 30/22/6B, ff41–45.
21. Auckland to Russell 2.4.1847, PRO 30/22/6C, f9.
22. Palmerston memo 18.4.1847, PRO 30/22/6C, ff13–14.
Palmerston memo 31.12.1847, PRO 30/22/6H, ff 274–79.
23. Corbett, J S *Some Principles of Maritime Strategy*, London 1911, pp235–63, quote from p260. Corbett was the most reflective and well informed of the many commentators on strategy at the turn of the century. His work was based upon an unrivalled understanding of the sailing Navy, and some appreciation of Clausewitz.
24. *Ibid*, p260.
25. Hamilton, C I 'The Royal Navy, *la Royale*, and the Militarisation of Naval Warfare, 1840–1870', *Journal of Strategic Studies*, 1983, p198.
26. Russell memo of January 1848, Bartlett p190–91.
27. Hay to Auckland 16.1.1848, PRO 30/22/7A, ff143–46.
28. Auckland to Russell 17.1.1848, PRO 30/22/7A, ff139–41.
29. Auckland to Russell 28.9 & 10.10.1846, PRO 30/22/5C, f351. Also 5D f145.
30. Auckland to Russell 2.4.1847, PRO 30/22/6C, f9.
31. Parker to Ellenborough 5.10.1846, PRO 30/12/6/7, ff25–40.
32. Auckland to Russell 5.5.1847, PRO 30/22/6c, ff9–13.
33. Auckland to Russell 21.3.1848, PRO 30/22/7B, ff136–37.
34. Baring to Russell 11.12.1851, PRO 30/22/9Ji, ff121–24.
35. Baring to Russell 31.1.1852, PRO 30/22/10Ai, f1.
36. Auckland to Earl Clarendon (Viceroy of Ireland) 22.7.1848, PRO 30/22/7C, ff263–68.
Auckland to Russell 30.8.1846, PRO 30/22/7C, ff415–18.
37. Baring to Russell 14.10.1850, PRO 30/22/8F, ff57–64.
Baring to Russell 19.9.1851, PRO 30/22/9F, ff73–76.
38. Partridge, M S 'A Supplement to the Naval defences of Great Britain; Harbours of Refuge, 1814–1870' M M 1986 vol 72, pp17–24.
39. Duke of Wellington memo 8.2.1847, PRO 30/22/6B, f41.
40. Wood memo 21.3.1847, PRO 30/22/6B, ff279–82.
41. Partridge, M M p17.
42. Palmerston to Clarendon 8, 10 & 12.4.1856, Add 48,580, ff70–80.
43. Baring to Russell 21.10.1849, PRO 30/22/8B.
44. Baring to Russell 5.1850, 8, 9, 14 & 19.10.1850, 30/22/8D, E & F.
45. Symonds to Minto 10.10.1847, NLS 12,607.
46. Admiralty Board minute 25.4.1847, ADM 1/5581.
47. Lambert, *Battleships*, pp21–28.
48. Admiralty to Surveyor 6.10.1846, ADM 83/40.
49. Admiralty to Surveyor 13.1.1848, ADM 83/48.
Admiralty to Treasury 8.5.1848, ADM 1/5990.
Instructions to the Surveyor 2.6.1848, WWL.10.
50. Admiralty to Surveyor 1.9.1848, ADM 83/52.
Partridge, *History*, at p237 misunderstands this letter.
51. Surveyor to Admiralty 2.10.1848, ADM 83/52.
52. Auckland to Ward 16.12.1848, ADM 1/5991.
53. Admiralty Order 25.1.1849, ADM 83/54.
54. Admiralty to Surveyor 5.2.1849, ADM 83/55.
55. Berkeley to Baring 5.12.1851, ADM 1/5999.
56. Gash, N *Politics in the Age of Peel*, London 1953, pp330–31, 449.
Walker Papers relating to the Stafford Inquiry, WWL 2.
57. Graham to Peel 17.1.1848, Add 40,452.
58. Graham to Peel 12, 16 & 21.1.1849, Add 40,452.
59. Admiralty to Surveyor 10.6.1848, ADM 83/50.
60. Auckland to Minto 1.10.1846, NLS 11,793, f154.
61. Auckland to Russell 8.10.1846, PRO 30/22/5D, f97.
62. Auckland to Minto 1.10.1846, NLS 11,793.
63. Baring to Russell undated, early 1852, PRO 30/22/10Ai, ff1–16.
64. Auckland to Russell 5.12.1847, PRO 30/22/6H, ff92–95. That hardly a word relating to the reform of the civil administration and long-term policy remains in the Russell papers should not be allowed to obscure the importance of the change.

Part Three: THE SURVEYOR'S OFFICE

2 Sir Robert Seppings and the Advance of Naval Architecture: 1815–32

1. Brown, *Ironclad*, pp15–24.
2. Seppings to the Prince Regent in Council 1.3.1819, BGY/S/6/3.
3. Seppings Mss, BGY/S/6.
Earl St Vincent to the Hon C Grey (First Lord) February 1806 in *The Naval Miscellany* Vol IV, ed Lloyd, C, London, Navy Records Society 1952, p473.
4. Nepean to Hamond 4.2.1805 & Admiralty to Navy Board 7.2.1805, GD51/2/338.
5. Surveyors to Navy Board July 1806, ADM 87/1.
6. Admiral Elliot to Lord Minto 26.12.1837, ELL 221.
7. Taylor Combe to Seppings 11.11.1814, BGY/S/6 1/2.
Seppings to Babbage 23.6.1820, Add 37,182. Also 23.3.1825, Add 37,183.
Seppings to the Prince Regent 1.3.1819, BGY/S/6/3.
8. Seppings to Yorke 25.8.1813 & 11.5.1824, YOR/16a.
9. Lavery, B *The Ship of the Line*, London 1983, vol I, pp141–42.
10. Navy Board to Admiralty 27.10.1814, ADM 106/2265.
Admiralty to Navy Board 18.2.1815, ADM 83/1.
11. Admiralty to Navy Board 7.3.1815, ADM A/3106.
12. Navy Board to Admiralty 27.10.1814, ADM 106/2265.
Admiralty to Navy Board 15.2.1815, ADM A/3105.
Navy Board to Admiralty 27.6.1815, ADM 106/2267.
13. Simon Goodrich notebooks 10.2.1817, Science Museum Box. 5. Goodrich was the Dockyard Engineer at Portsmouth. His figures have been used because they differ from those of Seppings, if only to a limited extent, and he sketched the arrangements in use.
Seppings, R 'On the great strength given to ships of war by the application of diagonal braces', *Philosophical Transactions*, Vol. 54, 1817.
Navy Board to Admiralty 19.2.1817, ADM 106/2272.
14. Navy Board to Admiralty 8.11.1819, ADM 106/2278.
15. Navy Board to Admiralty 6, 9 & 1.12.1817, ADM 106/2274. Carried into effect by Admiralty Order 4.2.1818.
16. Navy Board to Admiralty 22.1.1819, ADM 106/2277.
17. Admiralty to Navy Board 23.1.1819, ADM 83/2.
18. Admiralty to Navy Board 4.2.1818, ADM 83/3.
19. Seppings, R *A new principle of constructing Merchant ships*, London 1820.
20. Seppings to Admiralty 5.12.1810, ADM 7/709.
21. Seppings to the Prince Regent 1.3.1819, BGY/S/6/3.
22. Navy Board to Admiralty 14 & 22.6.1816, ADM 106/2270.
23. Navy Board to Admiralty 3.10.1816, ADM 106/2271.
24. Navy Board to Admiralty 11.6.1817, ADM 106/2273.

25. Navy Board to Admiralty 6.7.1830, ADM 106/2295.
26. Ekins, Sir C *Naval Battles*, London 1824, pp406 & Appendix I.
Ekins, Sir C *A reply to the letter of S R S Knt. F.R.S. Surveyor of the Navy on the Round Bows and Circular Sterns*, London 1824.
An Old Sea Officer, *A Short Letter... Round or Circular Sterns*, Portsea 1822.
Byam Martin to Admiral Blackwood 7.5.1829, Add 41,398.
27. Seppings to Byam Martin 1.1.1823, dedication on volume of Papers in NMM collection, ref 629.12.011.21.
28. Melville to the Prince Regent 27.5.1813, GD51/1/214.
29. Martin Report on the Tucker Enquiry 19.10.1818, Add 41,402.
30. Byam Martin to Liverpool 1818, Add 38,368.
Melville to Liverpool 8.5.1820, Add 38,284.
Treasury to Admiralty 29.11.1820, ADM 1/4299.
31. Extracts on the correspondence of Peake and Tucker; endorsed by Melville 24.12.1818 & Seppings to Melville 15.1.1819, GD51/2/595–6.
32. Seppings to the Prince Regent 1.3.1819, BGY/S/6/3.
33. Byam Martin to Majoribanks 23.7.1825 Add 41,396.
34. James, W *A Naval History of Great Britain*, London 1902, Vol VI, p417.
35. Brown, *Ironclad*, pp32–33.
Navy Board to Admiralty 2.3.1825 & 3.1.1827, ADM 106/2289/2292.
36. Navy Board to Admiralty 30.1.1829, ADM 1/3469.
Byam Martin to Melville 25.5.1829, Add 41,398.
37. Grey to Graham 4.2.1831, Gr B54.
Graham, memo 6.12.1831, Gr B27.
38. Graham to Marquess of Angelsey 18.2.1832, Gr B49.
39. Seppings to Graham 6.2.1832, Gr B52.
Admiralty to Navy Board 7.12.1824, ADM 1/3463.
40. Treasury to Admiralty 6, 7 & 3.8.1832, ADM 1/4307.
Graham to Grey 28.10 & 18.11.1832, Gr B27.
Admiralty to Seppings 16.3.1833, BGY/S/5/2.
41. Cockburn to Seppings 21.12.1833 & Cockburn to Graham 1.3, 27.3 & 5.11.1833, MRF/D/8.

3 Sir William Symonds: Surveyor of the Navy

1. Briggs, p82. Parker was only on Auckland's Board from 13–26 July 1846. The one 80-gun design to pass across the Board Room table in that period was the *Brunswick*.
2. Sharp, James A *Memoirs of the Life and Services of Rear Admiral Sir William Symonds*, London 1858. This remains the basic text for any appreciation of Symonds's life and career; but it is a vindictive and one-sided eulogy written under the terms of Symonds's will from papers no longer extant. It is not entirely reliable on the contentious aspects of his career, and makes little reference to such important contemporary issues as the screw propeller.
Dear, Ian, *The Royal Yacht Squadron: 1815–1985*, London 1985, p41.
3. Byam Martin to the Hon G Vernon 29.11.1824, Add 41,396, f19.
4. Order for *Columbine* 22.2.1825 & other experimental vessels. ADM 1/3464.
ADM 180/10, *Vernon* entry.
5. Portland to Symonds 12.4.1831, Sharp pp84–86.
Turberville, A S *A History of Welbeck Abbey and its Owners*, London 1939, Vol II, pp322–97. Provides the only detailed *resume* of Portland's life.
6. Portland to Croker 5 & 16.9.1827, Add 52,467, ff147–49.
Captain Lord Robert Spencer (Private Secretary to Clarence) to Portland 19.9.1827, PwH 1092.
7. Aspinall, A (ed) *The Formation of Canning's Ministry*, Camden Society London 1937, pp155–56, 189–91, 197, 256.
Rosselli, J *Lord William Bentinck: The Making of a Liberal Imperialist: 1774–1839*, London 1974, p73.
8. Portland to Codrington 4.3.1828, Bourchier, Vol II, pp217–18. Portland wrote to congratulate Codrington on Navarin, but only after leaving office, as he would not break the Cabinet consensus to express his own opinion.
9. Portland to Earl Grey 6.2 & 25.6.1826: 25.7.1834: Portland to Lord Howick 26.11.1834, Grey Mss Durham Univ.
10. Penrose, Admiral Sir C *Remarks on the conduct of the Naval Administration of Great Britain since 1815*, London 1830, pp15–18.
11. Navy Board to Admiralty 25.4.1827, ADM 106/2292.
Hardy: enclosed in Portland to Duchess 8.9.1827, PwH 1029. That a copy of his report should have been given to Portland on the spot indicates the general acceptance of 'amateur' interest by intelligent officers.
For an alternative view of these trials, reflecting the Naval Architects view see: Brown, p34 where *Acorn* and *Satellite* are given the lead.
12. Admiralty Order 25.10, 15.11, & 4.12.1827, ADM 1/3466.
13. Byam Martin memo 31.10. & Byam Martin to Nolloth (MsW Portsmouth) 24.11. Also Herries to Byam Martin 22.11.1827, Add 41,397, ff89–93.
Sharp, p75.
Penrose, p22.
14. Clarence to Portland 13.7.1828, PwH 1171.
15. Account: Troon Shipyard 30.11.1829, PwH 2088.
16. Aspinall, A (ed) *The Correspondence of Charles Arbuthnot*, London 1941, Camden Society, p149.
17. Ward, pp5, 12, 13, 53: Rosselli, pp58–61, 114, 174.
18. Graham to Grey 4.11.1832, Gr B27.
Graham to Portland 14.6.1834, Gr B28.
Newmarket Programme April 1834, Gr B51.
19. Graham to Grey 5.5.1831, Gr B26. Also Admiralty Minute 7.5.1831, ADM 3/222.
Butler, J R M *The Passing of the Great Reform Bill*, London 1914, p221.
20. Portland to Duchess of Portland 2.4.1831, PwH 1040.
Portland to Symonds 12.4.1831; Pechell to Symonds 20.4.1831, *Sharp* pp84–6.
Admiralty to Symonds, draught 20.5.1831, ADM 3/222.
Brock, M *The Great Reform Act*, London 1973, p231.
21. Portland to Duchess 6, 10, 13, 14, 16, 17.7.1831, PwH 1044–50.
Codrington to Lady Codrington 19 & 28.7.1831, Bourchier, Vol II, pp479–80.
22. Portland to Duchess 22 & 25.8.1831, PwH 1053–4.
23. ADM 1/3475 & 3/224, 1.10.1831.
24. Woolwich to Navy Board 28.4.1832, ADM 106/1806.
NMM draught 1572/30.
25. Admiralty Minute 13.10.1831 & 17.1.1832, ADM 3/224 & /225.
26. Sharp, p135.
Admiralty Progress Book *Vernon*, ADM 180/10 S10305-56.
Admiralty Minute to Navy Board 2.5.1832, ADM 3/224.
Woolwich to Navy Board 2.5.1832, ADM 106/1806.
Surveyor to Admiralty 15.12.1832, ADM 222/1.
27. Admiralty Minutes 13.10 & 8.12.1831, ADM 3/224.
28. Grey to Graham 8.9.1831, B54.
Ross, Sir J *Life of Lord Saumarez*, London 1840.
29. Brock, pp270–72.
30. Graham memo 6.12.1831, Gr MSS B27.
Graham in the House 16.3.1835, Sharp, p166.
Graham evidence 3.5.1861, P P, 1861 vol V, p131.
31. Symonds to Portland 17.2.1832 & Portland to Symonds 21.2.1832. Sharp, p134.
32. Sharp p148.
Portland to Duchess 7 to 29.8.1832, PwH 1056–66.
33. Graham to Grey 2.9 & Grey to Graham 10.9.1832, Gr B27.
Graham to the King 11.8 & King to Graham 8.9.1832, Gr B55.
34. Graham to Stanley 18.9.1833, Gr B28.
35. Graham to Portland 14.6.1834, Gr B28.
36. Barrow memo to Graham 11.9.1832, ADM 1/3478.
Symonds to Hardy 3.11.1832, ADM 222/1.
Lady Hardy to Symonds 21.9.1839, ELL 225, calling on him to help in finding a place for Sir Thomas's servant.
37. Admiralty to Treasury 25.11.1836, ADM 1/3490.
38. Surveyor to Admiralty 25.1.1838, ADM 222/12.
39. Wood memo on the Board leaving office during the Bedchamber crisis 6.1839, Add 49,572.
Treasury to Admiralty 11.6.1839, ADM 1/4313.
Admiralty to Surveyor 28.6.1839, ADM 83/19.
40. Tuffnell to Minto 1.8.1837, ELL 232.
Surveyor to Admiralty 11.5 & 25.7.1839, ADM 222/14.
41. Edye, J *Calculations on the Equipment and Displacement of Ships of War*, London 1829.
Papers in the case of John Edye 21.7.1847, ADM 1/5563.
A paper on the subject of the dockyards and the construction of ships given to the Earl of Auckland in October 1847, by Mr John Edye, when acting Surveyor of the Navy.
Lambert, *Battleships*, for this aspect of Edye's career. Remarks on the subject of naval shipbuilding timber etc, by John Edye September 1857, to Sir Charles Wood. SPB/3.
42. Byam Martin, *Remarks on Naval Administration*, Byam Martin, Vol III, pp369–95.
43. Duties of the Surveyor of the Navy 9.6.1832, ADM 1/3477.

44. Minute on the Committee on Naval Improvements 29.6.1832, ADM 83/4.
45. Sharp, pp91,102.
46. Taylor to Minto 12.6 & Minto to Taylor 13.6.1836, ELL 211a.
47. Fincham, J SNA *To the Right Honourable Sir James Graham, Bart F.R.S. First Lord of the Admiralty: 23.6.1832*. The copy in the NMM library belonged to John Edye, his annotations are sharply critical of the SNA and its failures.
48. Barrow to Graham 27.8.1832, ADM 1/3477.
49. Anon (H Chatfield) *An Apology for English Shipbuilders; showing that it is not necessary that the country should look to the navy for Naval Architects*, London 1833. The copy in the NMM library belonged to John Edye, and bears his annotations.
50. Captain F Marryatt, 'School of Naval Architecture', *Metropolitan Magazine*, November 1833, pp225–32.
51. Surveyor's Minute 20.2.1833, ADM 222/2.
52. Surveyor to Admiralty 3.11.1835, ADM 222/7.
53. Melville to Barrow 21.5.1836 & Barrow to Melville 29.5.1836, ADM 1/3489.
54. Tufnell to Minto 6.9.1837, ELL 232.
Symonds to Parker 8.9.1837, ELL 246.
Adam to Minto 19.9.1837, ELL 228.
55. Edye to Melgund (Minto's son and PS) 19.1.1840. Also Symonds minute of 20.1.1841 with Minto's marginalia ELL 246.
56. Estimates for building the *Vernon* 24.3.1832, ADM 1/3476.
57. Shipwright Officers 4.10.1832, ADM 1/3478.
Surveyor to Admiralty 11.2.1835, Services of the Master Shipwrights, ADM 222/6.
58. Admiralty to Surveyor 27.7.1833, ADM 83/7.
59. Printed Instructions for Dockyard Officers 18.7.1833, ADM 1/3480.
60. Woolwich to Surveyor 8.1.1834, ADM 87/3.
61. Graham to Symonds 8.1.1837, Sharp, p193.
62. Admiralty order 27.3 & 3.4.1837, ADM 83/15. ADM 180/10 *Vernon* Progress Book.
63. Surveyor to Admiralty 28.3 & 26.4.1837, ADM 222/9.
64. Surveyor to Admiralty 19.4.1838, ADM 83/17.
65. Surveyor to Admiralty 2.2.1839, ADM 222/15.
66. Sharp, p291.
67. Marshall, *Naval Biography*, pp673–83.
68 Symonds to Adam 12.2.1836, ADM 1/3490.
Surveyor to Admiralty 19.5.1836, ADM 222/8.
69. Minto to the King 12.9.1836, ELL 211b.
70. Parker to Minto 19 to 23.9 & 11.10.1837, ELL 225.
Admiral Elliot to Minto 2.10.1837, ELL 219.
Tuffnell to Minto 16.10.1837, ELL 233.
71. Admiralty Minute 20.9.1839, ADM 3/248.
Surveyor to Admiralty 18.8.1841, ADM 83/24.
72. Taylor, A H 'Admiral the Honourable Sir George Elliot', M M, XXXV pp316–32.
73. Elliot to Admiralty 6.8.1836, ADM, 1/3490.
74. Elliot to Minto 2 & 23.10.1837, ELL/219. Also 26.12.1837, ELL 221.
75. Tuffnell to Minto 22.9.1838, ELL/233.

4 'A Very Difficult Man to Deal With' The Decline of Symonds 1841–47

1. Minto to Parker 13.11.1841 & 6.3.1842, PAR/154/A.
2. Sharp, p291.
3. Admiralty to Surveyor 23.12.1841, ADM 87/24, encl Blake to Admiralty 21.12.1841.
4. Master Shipwrights to Admiralty 15.1.1842, ADM 83/25.
5. Lang to Captain Superintendent Collier 1.2.1842, *ibid.*
6. Admiralty to Symonds 7.2.1842, ADM 83/25.
7. Surveyor to Admiralty 4.3.1842 & Board marginalia of 5.3.1842, ADM 1/5522.
8. Admiralty to Surveyor 31.3.1842, ADM 83/25.
9. Surveyor to Admiralty 5 & 8.4.1842, ADM 1/5522.
10. Admiralty to Surveyor 11.4 & 14.5.1842, ADM 83/26.
11. Admiralty to Surveyor 26.3 & 22.7.1842, ADM 83/25 & /26.
12. Admiralty to Surveyor 8.7.1843, ADM 83/28.
13. Admiralty to Surveyor 30.5.1842, ADM 83/26.
14. Adam to Minto 21.6.1842, ELL 229.
15. Haddington to Portland 30.6.1842, PwH 31.
16. Admiralty to Surveyor 10.12.1844, ADM 83/34.
17. Admiralty to Surveyor 7.11.1842 & 26.5 & 26.11.1843, ADM 83/27/29/30.
18. Captain Superintendent at Deptford to Herbert 26.4.1844.
Admiralty to Surveyor 17.5.1844, ADM 83/32.
19. Hansard 7.4.1837, pp907–10. Speeches by G F Young, Wood & Hume.
20. Byam Martin Journal, Add 41,472 & note of 11.45, Add 41,465, ff232–40.
21. Lang to Ellenborough 9.6 & Lang to Henry Law (E's Private Secretary) 12.6.1846, PRO 30/12/34/2.
22. Lang to Admiralty 16.7.1847, ADM 12/512.
Admiralty to Woolwich 6.6.1849, ADM 12/512.
23. Lang, Oliver *Improvements in Naval Architecture*, London 1848, p28.
24. Committee of Naval Architecture 16.4.1842–August 1844, ADM 7/577.
25. Read, Chatfield and Creuze to Herbert 25.11.1844, ADM 83/33.
26. Brown, pp41–42.
27. A naval architect, *The Present Shipbuilding Controversy; or which is the misrepresented party*, 1846.
Anon, *Review of the course pursued by the Shipbuilding Department of the Admiralty between the years 1832 and 1847*, Plymouth 1847. Normally attributed to Chatfield, who was Assistant Master Shipwright at Devonport, becoming Master Shipwright at Deptford in 1853.
28. Portland to Peel 12. & 13.4.1844, Add 40,452.
29. Haddington to Peel undated, *ibid.*
30. Haddington to Peel 20.4.1844, Add 40,457.
31. Portland to Peel 29.4.1844, Add 40,457.
32. Haddington to Peel 1.5.1844, Add 40,457.
33. Symonds to W F Martin 3.10.1844 & T B Martin to W F Martin 22.10.1844 & T B Martin to W F Martin 3.12.1844, Add 41,490.
34. W F Martin to Hyde Parker 12.12.1844 & H B Martin to W F Martin 5.12.1844, *ibid.*
35. T B Martin to W F Martin 12.1844, *ibid.*
36. Bowles to Minto 26.12.1844, NLS 12,067.
37. Minto to Wood 18.1.1843, ELL 248.
Wood to Minto 20.1.1843, ELL 237.
38. Adam to Minto 2.7.1843, ELL 229.
39. Wood to Minto 30.11.1844, NLS 12,067.
40. Dundas to Symonds 10.12.1844, Sharp, p321.
41. Symonds to Minto 14.12.1844 & 7.1.1845, NLS 12,067 & ELL 237.
42. Portsmouth Yard to Surveyor 17.2.1845, ADM 87/15.
Herbert to Portland 22.2 & Haddington to Portland 19.2.1845, PwH 32 & 810.
Admiralty to Surveyor 4.3.1845, ADM 83/34.
Symonds to Minto 25.3.1845 & 17.6.1845, ELL 237.
43. Wood to Minto 9.4.1845, ELL 237.
44. Wood to Minto 11 & 13.6.1845, enclosing Walker to Symonds 4.6.1845, ELL 237.
45. Symonds to Wood 13.6.1845, ELL 237.
46. Symonds to Minto 22.7.1845, ELL 237.
Symonds to Portland 16.7.1845, PwH 1105.
47. Graham to Symonds 25.9.1845, Sharp p340.
48. Symonds to Minto 23.9.1845, ELL 237.
Minto to Symonds 24.9.1845, Sharp, pp342–3.
49. Haddington to Minto 25 & 30.9.1845, ELL 237.
50. Bowles to Minto 13.10.1845, enclosing Pym to Admiralty 10.10.1845, ELL 237.
51. Bowles to Minto 18.10.1845, *ibid.*
52. Symonds to Minto 19.10.1845, ELL 237.
Minto to Symonds 24.10.1845, Sharp, p344.
53. Cockburn minute calling for a Construction Board 15.11.1845. The first half of this paper is in ADM 3/265, the second in Add 40,458, ff241–45.
Cockburn memo on the Admiralty, MRF/D/11.
54. Haddington memo for Ellenborough, Add 40,458, ff246–48.
Haddington to Peel 26.12 & Peel to Haddington 27 & 29.12.1845, *ibid.*
55. Haddington to Peel 1.1.1846, *ibid.*
56. Rous to Ellenborough 25.3.1846, PRO 30/12/34/9.
57. Ellenborough minute on the building, repairing and altering of ships 5.4.1846, PRO 30/12/34/4.
58. Rous to Ellenborough 8.4 & Ellenborough to Rous 12.4.1846, PRO 30/12/34/9.
59. Symonds to Ellenborough 11 & 14.5.1846, PRO 30/12/34/1 & 13 T M C Symonds to Minto 20.5.1846, NLS 12,068.
T M C Symonds to Ellenborough & reply 21 & 22.6.1846, PRO 30/12/34/13.
60. Symonds to Ellenborough 31.5 & 3.6 & reply 1 & 3.6.1846. Also Ellenborough to Hay, PRO 30/12/34/1.
Admiralty to Surveyor 22.6.1846, ADM 83/39.
61. Memo for Lord Auckland 6.7.1846, PRO 30/12/34/12.
62. Parker to Ellenborough 5.10.1846, PRO 30/12/34/6/7.
63. Minto to Symonds 12.12.1846 & Symonds to Minto 17.12.1846, NLS 12,068.
64. Admiralty minute by H G Ward 25.4.1847, ADM 1/5581.
65. Portland to Auckland 4.5.1847, Auckland to Symonds 9.5.1846, Symonds to Auckland 11.5.1846, Portland to Symonds 14 & 20.5 & 30.6.1847, Sharp, pp360–64.
66. Auckland to Portland 31.12.1847 & 20.7–10.9.1848, PwH 607–13.
67. Fincham, J *A History of Naval Architecture*, London 1851.
John Fincham 1785–1859 Master Shipwright at Portsmouth until he retired in 1852.
68. Surveyor to Admiralty 3.6.1847, ADM 1/5581.
69. Schedule of Minutes by Symonds 20.8.1847, ADM 1/5581.
House of Commons Order 15.2.1848, Report 8.5.1848, ADM 1/5592.
70. Graham to Symonds 26.11.1847, Sharp, p374.
The Queen to Graham 11.7.1853, Gr B114.
Graham to the Duke of Newcastle 26.10.1853,

Newcastle NeC f12,537a.
71. Hansard 29.4.1847.
72. Graham to Symonds 5.7.1849, Sharp, pp383–84.
73. Graham to the Duke of Newcastle 26.10.1853, Newcastle NeC f12,537a.
74. Reed, E *On the Modifications which the ships of the Royal Navy had undergone in the present century*, London 1859, pp7–9.
75. Slade, Commander A *A few words on naval construction and naval promotion*, London 1846. This pamphlet would appear to have been published before the announcement of the Committee of Reference. The section on naval architecture is only 24 pages long.

5 Captain Baldwin Walker and the Reconstruction of the Surveyor's Office: 1848–50

1. Committee of Reference to Admiralty 5.11.1847, ADM 87/18.
Admiralty to Surveyor 6.11.1847, ADM 83/46.
2. Admiralty to Surveyor 3.12.1847 & 5 & 13.1.1848, ADM 83/47–8.
3. Admiralty to Surveyor 16.12.1847, ADM 83/5565.
4. Walker to Captain Pelham 8.11.1851, WWL/11. Walker to Graham 19.1.1853 & Treasury to Admiralty 28.1.1853, ADM 1/5619.
This measure was made necessary by the pressure on the office accommodation. Walker to Admiralty 14.6.1848 & Admiralty to Walker 23.6.1848 WWL/1. Walker refused the initial Treasury offer of £200, which was less than that offered to other residents, before moving to Westbourne Terrace.
5. Auckland memo 8.5.1848, ADM 1/5990.
6. Ward to Trevelyan 8.5.1848, ADM 1/5990.
Treasury to Admiralty 1.6.1848, ADM 1/5592.
7. Admiralty to Surveyor 12.6.1848, ADM 12/497.
8. Lambert, *Battleships* gives a full review of Walker's later career.
9. Admiralty to Surveyor 1.9 & Surveyor to Admiralty 2.10.1848, ADM 83/52.
10. Report of the Committee of Revision on Dockyards 14.12.1848, appointed 3.10.1848, Auckland minute 16.12.1848, ADM 1/5591.
11. Admiralty to Surveyor 5.2.1849, ADM 83/54.
12. Admiralty to Surveyor 6.3.1850, ADM 83/60.
13. Walker to Northumberland 1.3.1852, WWL/2.
Graham 30.4.1861. Evidence to the Enquiry into Naval Administration P P, 1861, Vol v, p104–5.
14. Council of Science to Admiralty 28.7.1848, enclosed in below.
15. Edye & Watts to the Surveyor 1.8.1848 & Admiralty to Surveyor 9.8.1848, ADM 83/51.
16. Admiralty to Surveyor 29 & 31.1.1849, ADM 83/54.
17. Lambert, *Battleships*.
Lambert, *Crimean War*.
18. Graham 30.4.1861, P P, 1861, p105.

Part Four: INFLUENCES ON DESIGN

1 Fleet Tactics in the Last Years of the Sailing Battlefleet

1. Corbett, Sir J S, *Fighting Instructions 1530–1816*, London 1905, p336.
2. Codrington to Admiral Sir B Hallowell-Carew 17.9.1827, HLW/6, f2.
3. Codrington to Admiralty 6.8.1831, COD 17/1, f133.
4. Codrington to Lady Codrington 19 & 28.7.1831, COD 21/3.
5. Phillimore, vol II, pp18–29.
6. Parker to Captain H D Chads (*Excellent*) 19.3.1846, Phillimore III, p44.
7. Parker to Sir C Adam 12.8.1846, Phillimore III, p72.
8. Milne to Parker 4.10.1851 & Parker to Milne 21.1.1852, MLN 150/1.
9. Biddlecombe, G *Naval Tactics and Sailing Trials*, London 1850.

2 Guns and Gunnery: The Unseen Revolution

See generally:
Douglas, Sir H *A treatise on Naval Gunnery*, London 1855 (reprinted 1982). While Douglas remains controversial in some areas the good sense and encyclopaedic nature of his book makes it the essential reference for the guns and gunnery of the last sailing battlefleet.
Macmillan, D F *The Development of British Naval Gunnery, 1815–1853*, Unpublished PhD thesis, London 1967, contains some new material and serves to update Douglas.
1. Bourchier I pp60–61.
2. Padfield, P *Broke and the Shannon*, London 1968, pp1–30.
3. *ibid*, pp196–97, 205–06.
4. A post captain to Lord Melville 1.1.1816, in Napier, Sir C *The Navy: its past and present state*, London 1851, pp1–6.
5. Admiralty to Navy Board 11.3 & 7, 11., 13.4 & 8, 15.5.1815, ADM/A 3107–8.
Ordnance to Admiralty 27.2.1815, ADM 1/4022.
6. Admiralty to Surveyor 15.5.1834, ADM 83/9. Also 23.11.1836, ADM 1/3490.
Surveyor to Admiralty 27.4.1836, ADM 222/6.
7. Surveyor to Admiralty 27.4 & 10.8.1841, ADM 83/23 & /24.
8. Navy Board to Surveyor 2.7 & 28.11.1816, ADM 83/1 & /2.
9. Exmouth to Martin 21.7.1816, NRS Martin III, pp69–70.
10. Northcote Parkinson, C *Viscount Exmouth*, London 1934, pp435–69.
11. Admiralty to Navy Board 26.6.1817, ADM 106/2273. Also 12.4.1819, ADM 106/2277. Warrant for a 78-gun ship (*Revenge*) 25.1.1820, ADM 196/2279. Warrant for *Implacable*.
12. Admiralty to Ordnance 8.8 & 24.9.1823, ADM 1/3462.
Ordnance to Admiralty 20.9.1826, ADM 1/4025.
13. Byam Martin memo 14.12.1825, Add 41,396, ff87–89.
Navy Board to Admiralty 8.12.1828, ADM 106/2293.
Codrington to Clarence 21.10.1827, Bourchier Vol II, pp83–85.
14. Bourchier, Vol II, pp83–88.
15. Chads to Admiral C-in-C Portsmouth 25.10.1848, ADM 83/53.
16. Martin to Graham 16.6.1831, Add 41,399, f164.
17. Cockburn to Wellington 12.4.1828, WND IV pp361–69.
18. Padfield, pp203–10.
Fullom, S W *The Life of General Sir Howard Douglas*, London 1853, pp226–38.
19. Taylor, A H 'Admiral The Hon. George Elliot', M M xxxv, pp327–28. Spencer to Broke 11.1.1828, Padfield, p213.
Brighton, Rev J G *A Memoir of Admiral Sir P.B.V. Broke*, London 1865, pp350–53.
Byam Martin, papers on Guard Ships 7.1827, Add 41,397, ff35.
Clarence to Napier 5.3.1829, Noel-Williams, H N *Sir Charles Napier*, London 1918, p66.
20. Bartlett, pp40–41.
Fullom, pp305–07.
Wells, Capt J *Whaley: The Story of HMS Excellent*, Portsmouth 1980, pp3–6, 201–05.
Admiralty to Sir T Foley 29.9.1830, ADM 1/3472.
Phillimore Vol II, pp18, 34.
21. Admiralty to Ordnance 24.5 & 24.9.1838, ADM 1/3495 & 3496.
22. Wells, pp9–15.
23. Admiralty to Navy Board 28.1.1831, ADM 1/3473.
24. Elers-Napier, Vol I, pp370–71.
25. Houston Stewart to Minto 8.4.1843, NLS 12,607.
26 Navy Board to Admiralty 11.5.1831, ADM 106/2296.
Hastings to Minto 31.10.1842, ELL 237.
27. Colomb, Admiral P H *Memoirs of Sir Astley Cooper Key*, London 1898, pp59, 62, 85.
Moresby, Admiral Sir J *Two Admirals*, London 1909, pp89–91. Wells, pp17–21.
28. Brown, D K 'Attack and Defence I' *Warship 18*, pp136–38.
Brown, D K *Before the Ironclad*, London 1990, p64.
Experiments on Board HMS Excellent, Portsea 1850.
29. Padfield, p216.
30. Hastings to Minto 30.12.1843, NLS 12,607.
31. Admiralty to Surveyor 3.1.1834 regarding two 10in Miller guns to be fitted on the lower deck, ADM 83/9.
Hastings to Admiralty 18.4.1841, ADM 87/12.
32. Strachan, H *From Waterloo to Balaclava: Tactics, Technology and the British Army, 1815–1854*, Cambridge 1985, pp126–35.
33. Navy Board to Admiralty 20.7.1828, ADM 1/3468.
34. Ordnance to Admiralty undated 1839; ADM 1/4035.
35. Lambert, *Crimean War*, pp281–95.

3 Timber: Supply and Seapower

1. Albion, p20 & Ch III.
2. Morriss, Roger, *The Royal Dockyards during the Revolutionary and Napoleonic Wars*, Leicester 1983, pp78–84.
3. Rackham, O *Trees and Woodland in the British Landscape*, London 1977, pp99–102.
4. Albion, pp316–45.
5. Morriss, p78.
6. Albion, pp399, 400–1, 403.
   Martin to Morriss undated 1822, Add 41,395, f151.
7. Rackham, pp95–96.
8. Hart, C E *Royal Forest: A History of Dean's Woods as producers of Timber*, Oxford 1966, p73.
   Rackham, O *The Last Forest: the Story of Hatfield Forest*, London 1989, p7.
9. Rackham, 1977, p102.
10. Hart, p207.
11. Hart, p2, 289.
12. Hart, p216.
13. Rackham, 1977, p102. The example is from Suffolk.
14. Edlin, H L *British Woodland Trees*, London 1949 (3rd Ed), pp35–40.
    Farmer, R H (ed) *Handbook of Hardwoods*, London 1972 (2nd Ed) pp46–48.
15. Albion, pp10, 11.
16. Byam Martin to the Lord High Admiral 19.4.1828, Add 41,397, f121.
17. Snodgrass, G 'Letters on the Mode of Improving the Navy' *The Naval Chronicle*, London 1801, Volume V, pp227–30.
18. Morriss, p80.
19. Melville, Lord, *A letter from Lord Viscount Melville to the Right Hon. Spencer Perceval on the subject of Naval Timber*, London 1810.
    Morriss, p84.
20. Snodgrass, *The Naval Chronicle*, Vol V, pp148–53.
21. Melville, Lord, *A letter from Lord Viscount Melville to the Right Hon. Spencer Perceval relative to establishment of a Naval Arsenal at Northfleet*, London 1810.
    Advantages of a Dockyard at Northfleet, on a partial completion of the plan proposed, John Barrow 1812 or 1813, GD51/2/975.
    Morriss, pp52–55, 205.
    Melville to Liverpool 7.3.1813, GD51/2/437/3.
22. Committee of Surveyors to Navy Board 10 & 21.12.1813, ADM 92/1.
23. Byam Martin memo, Add 41,403, ff15–30.
24. Byam Martin memo, Add 41,403, ff15–30.
25. Woods & Forests to Treasury 10.4.1813, 2.2.1814, T 25/6. This series details all Treasury authorisations to fell timber and indicates that the New Forest and Forest of Dean were still providing significant quantities of naval timber. (Where the number of loads and the number of trees are equal, or the first figure is higher, then the timber is at least of the right size.)
    Navy Board to Admiralty 26.9.1826, complaining of a lack of timber for *Thunderer* and *Clyde* ordered to be built of winter felled timber, ADM 106/2291.
26. Woolwich to Navy Board 14.2, 28.5.1824, ADM 106/1796.
    Woolwich to Navy Board 26.10.1825, ADM 106/1797.
27. ADM 87/1.
28. Byam Martin memo 7.12.1816 & 30.1.1817, Byam Martin to Commissioners of the Navy 26.9.1817, Add 41,394, ff66–7, 79, 131.
    Byam Martin to Lord Castlereagh 6.8.1817, Add 41,400, f22.
    Byam Martin to Melville 29.10.1817, *ibid*, ff41–43.
    Byam Martin memo on cost of stores for 1831, Add 41,368, f251.
29. Packhard, J J 'Sir Robert Seppings and the Timber Problem', M M Vol 64, pp45–56.
    Byam Martin to Melville 8.7.1818, GD 51/2/587.
30. Melville to Liverpool 28.8.1818, GD 51/2/437/9.
31. Byam Martin to Sir Jahleel Brenton 3.1.1818, Add 41,394, f141.
    Byam Martin to R W Hay 14.12.1830, Add 41,398, f217.
32. Byam Martin to McQuarrie 30.7.1819, Add 41,394, f195–8.
    Albion, p364.
33. Byam Martin to Melville 12.3.1821, Add 41,398, f69.
34. Navy Board to Admiralty 19.10.1821, ADM 106/2282.
35. Byam Martin to Wellington 7.1.1819, Add 41,394, ff186–93.
36. Byam Martin to Melville 9.5.1817, Add 41,395, ff27–28.
    Atholl to Melville 25.3.1820, GD 51/2/613.
    Byam Martin to Melville 9.5.1820, *ibid*, 613/2.
    Navy Board to Admiralty 17.3.1823, ADM 106/2285.
37. Navy Board to Admiralty 17.4.1823, ADM 106/2285.
    Surveyor to Admiralty 10.10.1833 & 23.12.1837, ADM 92/6.
38. Byam Martin to Morrice 1822, Add 41,395, f151.
39. Papers for 1827 Estimates, Add 41,396, f197.
    Byam Martin to Lennox and Morrice 2.6.1827, Add 41,397, f27.
    Byam Martin to Morrice 12.1.1828, *ibid*, f104.
40. Byam Martin memo undated, Add 41,403, ff15–30.
41. Navy Board to Admiralty 8 & 15.5, 11.7.1828, ADM 106/2293.
    Byam Martin to Morrice 5.7.1828, Add 41,397, f131.
42. Nolloth (MsW at Portsmouth) to Seppings 27.1.1829, Add 41,398, f7, reporting an enquiry by Sir George Clerk.
    Byam Martin to Goulburn (Chancellor) 13.5.1830, Add 41,398, f152.
43. Byam Martin to Melville 25.5.1829, Add 41,398, f35.
44. Navy Board to Admiralty 18.10.1830, ADM 106/2295.
    Byam Martin to Morrice 3.6.1831, Add 41,399, f56.
45. Byam Martin memo undated, Add 41,403, ff15–30.
46. Russell Estate Papers R3/2592, 3032, 3239, 4183, 4188 cover period 1835–40. Bedfordshire Record Office.
47. Barrow to Graham, 27.8.1832, ADM 1/3477.
48. Admiralty to Surveyor 26.12.1832, ADM 83/4.
    Admiralty to Surveyor 11.9.1833, ADM 1/3481.
    Surveyor to Admiralty 12.11.1835, ADM 222/7.
49. Surveyor to Admiralty 13.9.1832, ADM 92/6.
50. Treasury to Admiralty 29.1.1833, ADM 1/4308.
    Portland to Admiralty 6.2.1833, ADM 92/5.
    Portland to Symonds 13.2.1833, ADM 92/5.
    Surveyor to Admiralty 15.10.1842, ADM 87/12.
51. Admiralty to Treasury 18.6.1832, ADM 1/3480.
    Treasury to Admiralty 21.3.1834, ADM 1/4309.
52. Adam to Byam Martin 16.11.1836 & memo, Add 41,369, f69.
53. Surveyor to Admiralty 14.3.1833, ADM 222/23.
54. Surveyor to Admiralty 26.5.1837, 24.1, 13 & 14.4.1840, 6.1840, ADM 92/8, 91/9, 87/16.
    Surveyor to Dockyards 3.7.1835, ADM 83/12.
    See Appendix for Symonds's reports on timber.
55. Parker to Minto 5.1.1841, ELL 224.
    Symonds minutes of 20.4 & 24.6.1841, ADM 1/5581.
56. Memo on the timber supply by the Storekeeper-General 24.1.1840, with marginal notes by the Surveyor, ADM 91/9.
    Admiralty Order 24.1.1840, ADM 92/9.
57. Symonds Report 29.9.1840, ADM 92/9 & Sharp pp256–59.
    Minto to Lord Duncannon (Woods & Forests) 15.10.1840, ELL 268.
58. Surveyor to Admiralty 29.12.1840, ADM 92/9.
    Admiralty to Surveyor 29.3.1841, ADM 83/23.
    Admiralty to Surveyor 28.9.1842, ADM 83/27.
59. W J Hooker to Surveyor 22.5.1843, ADM 87/13.
    Admiralty to Surveyor 23.2.1843, ADM 83/50.
60. Admiralty to Surveyor 16.11 & 11.12.1848 & 29.1.1849, ADM 83/53 /54.
61. Portsmouth Officers to Admiral Superintendent 31.8.1844, ADM 87/14.
62. Auckland to Russell 27.3.1848, PRO 30/22/7B.
    Surveyor to Admiralty 2.10.1848, ADM 83/53.
63. Surveyor to Admiralty 19.10.1848, ADM 83/53.
64. Report of the Committee of Revision 14.12.1848, ADM 1/5991.
    General Orders and Board Minutes on Dockyards 25.1.1849, MLN 155/2.

4 Timber: Decay and Naval Policy

1. Farmer, Dr R H Wood in *Materials and Technology*, London 1973, vol VI, pp62–65, 109–21.
2. Albion, pp394–96.
   Findlay W F K *Dry Rot and other Timber Troubles*, London 1956, pp224–28.
3. Admiralty visits to Dockyards 21.9 to 7.10.1813, ADM 7/593, ff28–102.
4. Navy Board to Admiralty 28.6.1815, ADM 106.
5. Byam Martin memo for Melville 2.1816, GD 51/2/984.
6. Albion, p12.
7. Navy Board to Admiralty 9.10.1816, ADM 106/2272. Also 16.1 & 25.2.1817, 106/2272.
   Admiralty to Navy Board 10.7.1817, ADM 83/2.
   Navy Board to Admiralty 24.8.1817, ADM 106/2274.
8. Navy Board to Admiralty 15.1.1817, ADM 1067/2272.
   Beamish, R *Memoirs of Sir Marc Brunel*, London 1862, p309–11.
9. Navy Board to Admiralty 4.3.1817, ADM 106/2272.
10. Navy Board to Admiralty 1.1.1819, ADM 106/2277.
    Byam Martin to Sir Jahleel Brenton 20.9.1819, Add 41,395, ff1–4.
11. Navy Board to Admiralty 8.2.1822, ADM 106/2284.
12. Surveyor to Navy Board 12.4.1824, ADM 87/2.
13. Byam Martin to Dockyard Commissioners

26.2.1824, Add 41,396, f3.
14. Treasury to Admiralty 29.4.1825, ADM 1/4302.
15. Navy Board to Admiralty 19.7.1828, ADM 106/2293.
16. Byam Martin to Clarence 4.3.1828, Add 41,397, f112.
17. Byam Martin to George 27.3.1829, Add 41,398, f24.
18. Byam Martin memo of a visit to Sheerness and Chatham 24.11.1817, Add 41,397, f136.
Byam Martin memo 8.7.1818, GD 51/2/587.
19. Byam Martin to Graham 18.4.1831, Add 41,399, f53.
20. Seppings to Melville 14.7.1818, GD 51/2/558.
21. Byam Martin to Melville 6.8.1818, Add 41,400, f59.
22. Barrow to Graham 27.8.1832, ADM 1/3477.
23. Symonds to Admiralty 22.6.1832, ADM 22/1 28.8.1832, ADM 83/5, 30.1, 20.2, 9.3, 28.12.1833, ADM 92/5, ADM 95/11 & ADM 222/3.
24. Surveyor to Admiralty 30.1833, ADM 92/5.
Auckland memo 6.1834, ELL 239.
25. Admiralty to Maitland 24.11.1834, ADM 1/3484.
Admiralty to Hayes 11. & 29.4.1835, ADM 1/3485.
Kyan to Peel 2.5.1835, Add 40,420, f227.
26. Surveyor to Admiralty 12.11.1835, ADM 222/7.
27. Admiralty to Surveyor 1.12.1835, ADM 1/3487.
28. Admiralty to Surveyor 6.3.1837, ADM 83/14.
29. Admiralty to Surveyor 18.3 & 3.4.1837, ADM 83/14.
30. Surveyor to Admiralty 21.11.1837, ADM 222/10.
31. Admiralty to Surveyor 1.6 & 20.9.1848, ADM 83/50 & 52.
Auckland to Ward 16.12.1848, ADM 1/5991.
Burnett to Minto 7.1851, NLS 12,608.
Surveyor to Admiralty 16.11.1853, ADM 1/5619.

Part Five: THE SHIPS

1 The Three-Decker 1815–60: Battleship Strategy and Warship Design

1. Harbron, J *Trafalgar and the Spanish Navy*, London 1988.
2. Dull, J R *The French Navy and American Independence*, Princeton 1975, pp135, 138, 146, 337, 378.
3. Admiral Sir E Codrington to the Admiralty 20.11.1842. Part of a report on magazines and firepower. Codrington had been an officer aboard the flagship at both battles. COD/20/4 NMM.
4. Glover, R 'The French Fleet, 1807–1814'; 'Britain's Problem'; and Madison's Opportunity', *Journal of Modern History*, 1967, vol 39, pp232–52. It does not consider this aspect of post-1805 French policy.
5. Byam Martin to Sir Henry Martin 1830, Add 49,372, f202.
6. Byam Martin memo 1823, Add 41,403, f39.
7. Navy Board to Admiralty 31.8 & 1 & 9.9.1814, ADM 105/2264, f425.
8. Byam Martin memo pre-1816, & April 1816, Add 41,406 & 41,394, ff5–8.
9. Melville memo on the state of the Navy 26.11.1817, MEL/102. Curiously, this paper did not include the *Impregnable* which was to be part of the postwar fleet for the next 50 years.
Memo on ships building in the Royal Yards 7.12.1816, GD 51/888.
10. Byam Martin to Melville (secret) 6.8.1818, Add 41,400. Order to repair the *Nelson*, removing all foreign timber.
In 1824 £8,000 was spent on the *Howe* to remove American timber 'liable to early decay', ADM 180/10.
11. Byam Martin to Melville 18.9.1830, Add 41,397, f40.
Byam Martin memo delivered to Sir J Graham 1830, Add 41,405.
Admiralty to Navy Board 10.1.1831, ADM 1/3473.
Byam Martin to Graham 16.6.1831, Add 41,399, f64.
Admiralty to Navy Board 30.6.1831, ADM 106/233.
Admiralty to Navy Board 14.10.1831, *ibid.*
12. Byam Martin memo 18.11.1830, Add 41,405, f9.
Admiralty minute 28.3.1832, ADM 3/225.
Admiralty to Surveyor 22.10.1832, ADM 83/4.
Surveyor to Admiralty 1.10 & 26.12.1833, ADM 92/6.
Surveyor to dockyards 1.10.1833, ADM 83/8.
Surveyor to Portsmouth 26.12.1833, ADM 92/6.
Admiralty to Surveyor 13.4.1839, ADM 83/4.
13. Report on the state of the Navy 11.1838, ADM 3/264.
14. Admiralty to Surveyor 18 & 26.3.1842, ADM 83/26.
15. Admiralty to Surveyor 20.3.1844, ADM 83/31.
16. Lambert *Battleships*, pp36–37, 127–28.
17. Navy Board to Admiralty 26.6.1817, ADM 106/2273.
18. Surveyor to Navy Board 1.8.1818, ADM 83/2.
19. Surveyor to Admiralty 11.7.1849, ADM 87/26.
20. Armament Warrant for *Princess Charlotte* 1.10.1824, ADM 106/2288.
21. Navy Board to Admiralty 17.1.1825, ADM 106/2289. In contrast to *Princess Charlotte* she would mount six 12-pounders and eight 32-pounder carronades on her quarter deck.
Progress Book, ADM 180/10. The cost of this rebuild was £46,021.
22. Armament Warrant for small three-deckers 6.3.1834, ADM 83/8.
Warrant as modified for *Princess Charlotte* in 1837, ADM 83/15.
23. Admiralty to Surveyor 7.9.1844, ADM 83/33.
24. Napier to Ward 9.4.1847, ADM 83/42.
25. Armament Warrant for *Hibernia* 12.3.1845, ADM 83/34.
Parker to Auckland 28.2.1845, Phillimore, Vol III, p2.
26. Parker to Admiral Sir J W D Dundas 4.11.1848, Phillimore, Vol III, p422.
27. Pellew to Navy Board 23.2.1814, ADM 95/47.
Report on *Caledonia* 5.9.1814, ADM 95/48.
28. Armament Warrant for *Prince Regent* 9.9.1814, ADM 106/2294. Six smaller pieces on the poop were never counted in the rating.
29. Order for *St George* 2.6.1819, ADM 83/2. The additional complement were required to handle the heavier guns.
30. Byam Martin memo 14.12.1825, Add 41,396, ff87–89.
31. Byam Martin to Melville 16.3.1826, Add 41,396, f109.
Byam Martin to Commissioner Cunningham (confidential) 21.8.1826, *ibid*, ff140–42.
Byam Martin marginal notes on Seppings submission of 12.4.1831, Add 41,396, f104.
32. Byam Martin to Seppings 1.9.1826, Add 41,396, f144–45.
33. Byam Martin to Melville 1.8.1826, GD 51/1012/5.
34. Navy Board to Admiralty 27.6.1828, ADM 106/2293.
Admiralty to Navy Board 1.7.1828, ADM 106/212.
Navy Board to Admiralty 13.7.1828, ADM 106/2293.
Seppings to Byam Martin 12.4.1831, Add 41,396, f104.
35. Byam Martin to Cockburn 6.8.1830, Add 41,397, f176.
Codrington to Admiralty 6.8 & 20.9.1831, COD 17/1.
Codrington to Graham 2.10.1831, Gr B27.
36. Hotham to Byam Martin 27.8.1831, ADM 95/51.
37. Sailing Report on *Caledonia* 1.1.1836, ADM 95/54.
38. Admiralty to Surveyor 3.11.1843; Symonds minute of 7.11.1843. Also Admiralty Order 13.11.1843, ADM 83/30.
Admiralty to Surveyor 16.3.1844, ADM 83/31.
Progress Book, ADM 180/10.
39. ADM 180/10.
Admiralty to Surveyor 28.5.1850, ADM 83/62.
40. Admiralty to Surveyor to rename the ship 12.4.1839, ADM 83/19.
Admiralty to Surveyor 26.11.1838, ADM 83/18.
41. Admiralty to Surveyor 22.10.1832, ADM 83/4.
Surveyor to Admiralty 1.10 & 26.12.1833, ADM 92/6.
Admiralty to Surveyor 26.12.1840, ADM 83/4.
42. Armament of the *Royal Frederick* 3.12.1834, ADM 83/15.
43. Byam Martin to Sir William Parker 6.4.1840, Letters & Papers of Sir T Byam, Vol III, p154.
44. Admiralty Orders 26.8.1840, ADM 83/22: 30.9.1841, ADM 83/24.
45. Admiralty Order 26.3.1842, ADM 83/26.
46. Byam Martin to W F Martin 22.10.1844, Add 41,490, f59.
Hyde Parker to W F Martin 8.12.1844, *ibid*, f65.
Admiralty to Surveyor 7.12.1844, ADM 83/33.
47. Admiralty to Surveyor 9.12.1844, ADM 3/265.

48. Henry Byam Martin to W F Martin 24.2.1845, Add 41,399, f83.
49. Bowles to Minto 23.1.1845, ELL 237.
Admiralty to Surveyor 4.3.1845, ADM 83/34.
50. Admiralty to Surveyor 31.3 & 24.4.1845, ADM 83/34.
51. Walker to Symonds 15.10.1845, Sharp, p240.
Cockburn memo 15, 11.1845, ADM 3/265.
H B Martin to Byam Martin 25.8.1845, Add 41,465, ff201–04.
Haddington to Parker 7.11 & Parker to Haddington 28.11.1845, Phillimore, Vol III, pp20–21.
52. Parker to Minto 10.11.1849, NLS 068.
53. Admiralty to Surveyor 20.3.1846, ADM 83/38.
Surveyor to Admiralty 22.10.1846, ADM 87/15.
54. Parker to Haddington 26.11.1846, Phillimore, Vol III, p96.
55. Armament of *Queen* 22.5.1849, ADM 83/56.
Admiralty Order 21.12.1847, ADM 1/5581.
Admiralty to Surveyor 25 & 29.6.1848 & 27.7.1848, ADM 83/50/1.
Admiralty to Surveyor 8.6.1849, ADM 83/56.
56. Surveyor to Admiralty 28.3.1850, ADM 87/30.
57. Admiralty to Surveyor 26.6.1848, ADM 83/50.
58. Lang, O *Improvements in Naval Architecture*, London 1848, pp20, 26.

2 *Canopus* and the 84-Gun Ship

1. Wood official memo, Add 49,571, ff49–50.
2. Committee of Surveyors to the Navy Board 28.4.1815, ADM 92/1.
Navy Board to Admiralty 4.5.1815, ADM 106/2267.
3. Admiralty to Navy Board 8.5.1815, ADM A/3108.
4. Navy Board to Admiralty 13.5.1815, ADM 106/2267.
Admiralty to Navy Board 15.5.1815, ADM A/3108.
Sailing report on *Canopus* 11.2.1812, ADM 95/44.
5. Navy Board to Admiralty 27.7.1815, ADM 106/2267.
Navy Board to Admiralty 11 & 19.9.1829, ADM 106/2294.
Brown, D K *Before the Ironclad*, London 1990, p3.
6. Admiralty Draught July 1815, NMM 459/8.
7. Navy Board to Admiralty 16.5; 4, 14, 22.6.1816, ADM 106/2269 & 70.
8. Navy Board to Admiralty 4 & 14.6.1816, ADM 106/2270.
Admiralty to Navy Board 5.6.1816, ADM 83/1.
9. Admiralty to Navy Board 10.7.1817; 28.4.1819; 2.6.1819; 1.7.1820, ADM 83/2.
Navy Board to Admiralty 27.5.1819, ADM 106/2277.
Admiralty Draught, NMM 332, of *Asia* and *Bombay*.
10. Navy Board to Admiralty 2.10.1819; 4.2.1820; 6.11.20; 12.12.1821; 19.2.1825; 27.4.1827; 9.7 & 7.8.1828, ADM 106/2278, 2279, 2282, 2292 & 2293.
Admiralty to Navy Board 4.10.1819 & 5.2.1820, ADM 83/2.
11. Navy Board to Admiralty 6.6.1825 & 19.10.1826, ADM 106/2289, 2291.
Byam Martin to Cockburn 19.10.1826, Add 41,367, f247.
12. Navy Board to Admiralty 8.12.1828, ADM 106/2293.
Admiralty Draught of *Calcutta* 3.10.1827, NMM.
13. Navy Board to Admiralty 20.2.1829, ADM 106/2294.
14. Admiralty to Navy Board 10.1.1831, ADM 1/3743.
Byam Martin to Graham 16.6.1831, & Navy Board to Admiralty 30.6.1831, ADM 106/233.
15. Navy Board to Admiralty 8.2.1832, ADM 106/2297.
Admiralty to Surveyor 26.6.1832, ADM 83/4.
Admiralty Order no.536 7.7.1832, ADM 92/5.
16. Symonds to Sir Thomas Hardy 3.7.1832, ADM 222/1.
17. Sailing Reports for 1824, 1829 and 1830, ADM 95/50 & 51.

3 Stretched 74-Gun Ships

1. Admiralty to Navy Board 11 & 21.3.1815, ADM A/3106.
Navy Board List of ships in progress 7.12.1816, GD 51/2/888.
2. Admiralty to Navy Board 3.12.1816. Also Admiralty to Navy Board 9.12.1816, ADM 83/2.
3. Navy Board to Admiralty 5 & 22.11.1817, ADM 106/2274.
Admiralty to Navy Board 20.11.1817, ADM 83/2.
Admiralty Draught of *Boscawen*, NMM 363/8.
4. Navy Board to Admiralty 12.4.1819, ADM 106/2277.
Admiralty to Navy Board 1.1.1820, ADM 83/2.
5. Navy Board to Admiralty 10.11.1817, ADM 106/2276.
Admiralty to Navy Board 21.9.1819, ADM 106/2278.
Navy Board to Admiralty 16.5.1820, ADM 106/2279.
6. Navy Board to Admiralty 24.1.1818, ADM 106/2275.
7. Sailing Report, *Bulwark* 25.8.1815, ADM 95/48.
8. Navy Board to Admiralty 6.6.1825, ADM 106/2289.
9. Byam Martin to Commissioner Shiel (Plymouth) 17.3.1827, Add 41,397, f11.
Navy Board to Admiralty 20.2.1829, ADM 106/2294.
10. Navy Board to Admiralty 21.5.1831, ADM 87/2.
Admiralty to Surveyor 29.11.1832, ADM 83/4.
11. Admiralty to Surveyor 7.10.1833, ADM 92/6.
Surveyor to Admiralty 18.7.1834, ADM 222/5.
Admiralty 3.3.1834, ADM 83/8.
Surveyor to Admiralty 8.7.1834, ADM 92/6.
12. Surveyor to Admiralty 30.7.1833; 16.10.1834, ADM 92/5, 92/6.
Admiralty to Surveyor 31.10.1835, ADM 83/12.
Surveyor to Admiralty 16.11.1835, ADM 92/7.
13. King-Hall, L *Sea Saga*, London 1935, pp130–38.

4 The Razee 50-Gun Ship and the Third Rate 74 after 1815

1. Bartlett, C J *Great Britain and Seapower; 1815–1853*, Oxford 1963. The standard work on this period.
Tunstall, B *The Realities of Naval History*, London 1936, p121 & Corbett, Sir J *Some Principles of Maritime Strategy*, Annapolis 1988 (new ed) pp111–13.
2. Admiralty to Navy Board 19.8.1815, ADM 83/1, f143.
3. Admiralty to Navy Board 21.2.1817, ADM 83/2, f55.
Navy Board to Admiralty 28.3.1817, ADM 106/2272, f436. Also 21.8.1817, ADM 106/274, f91.
4. Navy Board to Admiralty 5.5.1820, & 18.5.1820, ADM 106/2279, 379, 410.
5. Navy Board to Admiralty 5.4.1816, ADM 106/2269, f438.
6. Admiralty to Navy Board 25.5.1818, ADM 83/2, f195.
7. Navy Board to Admiralty 6.5.1823, ADM 106/2285, f224.
8. Roberts, S S *The Introduction of Steam Technology into the French Navy; 1818–1852*, Unpublished PhD thesis, University of Chicago 1976, pp16–34.
Tupinier, M *Observations sur les dimensions des Vaisseaux et des Frigates dans la Marine Francaise*, Paris 1822. The French were not alone in razeeing their wartime two-deckers; both the Austrians and the Dutch cut down ex-French ships obtained at Venice and Antwerp. It would appear that the ships required a thorough overhaul, and the opportunity was taken to reduce their crews, as neither power was over blessed with seamen.
9. Roberts, S S 'List of the French Sailing Navy', *The Belgian Shiplover*, April 1975.
10. Cockburn to Wellington 12.4.1828 and enclosures, *Wellington Letters & Dispatches*, London 1867–80, vol IV, pp361–67.
10A Chappelle, H I *The History of the American Sailing Navy*, New York 1947.
10B Foreign Office to Admiralty 11.3.1836, ADM 1/4262.
11. Byam Martin to Clarence 9.5.1827, Add 41,397, f22.
12. Byam Martin to Melville 25.10.1825, Add 41,396, f78–79.
13. Navy Board to Admiralty 9.3.1826, ADM 106/2290, f110.
14. Byam Martin to Melville 31.5.1826, Add 41,396, f116.
15. Navy Board to Admiralty 19.3 & 23.2.1827, ADM 106/2292, f140,102.
16. Nolloth, Master Shipwright at Portsmouth to Byam Martin 27.12.1830, f203.
17. Woolwich Yard Officers to the Navy Board 1.5.1826, ADM 106/1800, f203.
18. Melville to Byam Martin 21.7.1826, Add 41,396, f133.
19. Byam Martin to Melville 16.12.1826, Add 41,396, f163.
Portsmouth Yard Officers to the Navy Board 1.8.1829, ADM 106/1908.
Surveyor's minutes 6.8.1829 for *Vindictive*, 14.4.1830, and 6.5.1830 for *Eagle*, ADM 92/2.
20. Woolwich Yard officers to the Navy Board 12.1.1827; Navy Board minute to the Lord High Admiral, ADM 106/1802, f210.
21. Navy Board to Admiralty 8.5.1828, ADM 106/2293, f194.
22. Byam Martin memo to Melville 12.1.1830, Add 41,397, f113.
23. Navy Board to Admiralty 7.3 & 16.4.1832, ADM 106/2297, ff72, 124.
24. Napier to the Lord High Admiral 13.2.1828, & Napier to the Editor of the *Hampshire Telegraph*

15.4.1828, Add 40,037, ff39, 45.
25. Portland to Symonds 12.4.1831, Sharp, pp84–86.
26. Surveyor's minutes 19.1.1831 re *Vindictive, Eagle, America* and *Conquestador*, ADM 92/3.
27. Sir Herbert Taylor (Private Secretary to King William IV) to Graham 14.10.31, Gr Ms 55.
Navy Board to Admiralty 1.11.1831, ADM 106/2296.
28. Surveyor to Admiralty 15.9.1832, ADM 222/1.
29. Admiralty to Surveyor 20.9, 29.10 & 3.12.32, ADM 83/4.
30. Graham to the King February 1831.
Bartlett, pp32–34.
Briggs, J *Naval Administrations 1827–92*, London 1897, pp23–26. In this case, as in several others, Briggs is entirely inaccurate.
31. Byam Martin to Graham 21.1.1831, Add 41,368, f239.
Byam Martin to Melville, Add 41,368, ff265–70.
32. Sharp, pp86–87.
33. Graham memo on the consolidation of the Navy Board 6.12.1831, Gr MS 27.
34. Estimates for building *Vernon* 24.3.1832, ADM 1/3476.
35. See Appendix 10 for full details.
36. Admiralty to Surveyor 28.11.1832, ADM 222/1.
37. Admiralty to Navy Board 10.1.1831, in Graham's hand, ADM 1/3743.
38. Admiralty to Surveyor 12.9.1833, ADM 83/12, f3144.
39. Sulivan, H N *The Life and Letters of Admiral Sir B J Sulivan*, London 1896, p132. Sulivan speaks of her as one of the fastest sailing ships in the Baltic Fleet of 1854, a credit to Symonds.
40. Admiralty to Surveyor 16.6.1832 & 3.12.1832, ADM 83/4.
41. Symonds's views on rebuilding *Achille* and *Canopus* provide the most complete statement of his policy. Surveyor to Admiralty 18.1.1839, ADM 222/14, f57.
See also Appendix notes on *Warspite*.
42. Sharp, p443. Paget to Symonds, undated 1836.
43. Lord Minto to Rear Admiral Sir William Parker 27.8.1843, PAR 154/A.
44. Minto memo on leaving Office 6.9.1841, ELL 239.
45. Portland to The Earl of Ellenborough 15.5.1846, Ellenborough MSS PRO 30/12/34/2.
Captain Lord John Hay to the Marquis of Tweedale 1.1.1839, ELL 240.
46. Admiralty to Surveyor 1.2.1843, ADM 83/28, f5501.
47. Chatham and Portsmouth Dockyard Officers to the Surveyor 14.2.1843, ADM 87/13, f5493.
48. Admiralty to Surveyor 4.4.1843, ADM 82/28, f5942.
49. Admiralty to Surveyor 16.8.1845, ADM 83/35, f4885.
50. Admiralty to Surveyor 10.3.1847, ADM 83/42, f363.
51. Admiralty to Surveyor 28.2.1844, ADM 83/31, f498. Also 17.5.1844, ADM 83/32, f1206.
52. Her only Captain, Henry Byam Martin, left a detailed account of the origins and conversion of this ship, Add 41,472.
53. Brown, D K 'The First Steam Battleships', M M, vol 63, 1977.
54. Admiralty to Surveyor 14.9.1842, ADM 83/27. Also Sharp, p357.
55. Corbett, J S *The Campaign of Trafalgar*, London 1910, pp440–49.
56 Hotham to Graham 4.12.1831, Gr MS 54.
Navy Board to Admiralty 28.2.1832, ADM 106/2297, p60.
57. Graham to Grey 2.10.1833, Gr MS 28.
58. Graham to the King 30.3.1833, Gr MS 56.
59. Earl De Grey to Wellington 2.1.1835, De Grey MSS L30/62/1; Bedford Record Office.
60. Admiralty to Surveyor 31.10.1840, to fit *Vernon*, ADM 83/20.
61. Admiralty to Surveyor 25.11.1840, ADM 83/20.
62. Graham to Cockburn 24.1.1834, Gr MS 53.
Graham to Byam Martin 22.1.1831, Add 41,399, f10.
63. Byam Martin to Oliver Lang 8.10.1830, Add 41,397, f192.
Navy Board to Admiralty 8.7.1831, ADM 106/2296, f343.
64. Lambert, *Battleships*, pp55–60, 114.
Lambert, *Warrior, The World's First Ironclad*, London 1987, pp22–23.

5 The 90-Gun Ship

1. Chappelle, H I *The American Sailing Navy*, New York 1947, pp313–18, 334, 372.
2. Roberts, Stephen S *The Introduction of Steam Technology into the French Navy: 1818–1852*, Unpublished PhD thesis, Chicago University, 1976, pp23–36. Roberts, Stephen S 'Combatant Ships of the French Sail Navy after 1814', *The Belgian Shiplover*, vol 4, 1975, pp241–48.
3. Byam Martin memo for Melville to read at the Cabinet 25.7.1826, Add 41,128, f128.
Byam Martin to Melville 23.8.1826, GD 51/1014/2. Also Cockburn Report 1.11.1826.
4. Seppings to Melville 7.6.1826, GD 51/700.
Byam Martin to Melville 31.5.1826, Add 41,396, f116.
Melville to Byam Martin 22.7.1826, *ibid*, f133.
Seppings design 17.11.1826, NMM Collection of Admiralty Draught drawings.
5. Byam Martin to Commissioner Cunningham 2 & 31.1.1827, Add 41,397, ff2, 9.
6. Byam Martin to Plymouth 17.3 & 26.6.1827, Add 41.397, ff11, 37.
7. Brown, *Before the Ironclad*, p32.
8. Byam Martin to Clarence 9.5.1827, Add 41,397, f22.
9. Byam Martin to Melville 1.1830, Add 41,397, f120.
Byam Martin to Cockburn 6.8.1830, *ibid*, f176.
10. Admiralty Order 18.1.1831, Add 41,368, f257.
11. Byam Martin to Graham 16.6.1831, Add 41,399, f64.
12. Cockburn to Seppings 21.12.1833, MRF/D/8.
13. Sailing report 1.1.1836, ADM 95/36.
Stopford to Admiralty 27.8.1838, ADM 83/18.
14. Parker to Admiralty 8.10.1847, ADM 83/45.
Surveyor to Admiralty 1.3.1849, ADM 87/25.
Evidence of Hay before the Committee on Naval and Military Estimates 6.4.1848, P P, 1847/8, Vol xxi, pp2064–88.
15. Wood memo on the state of the Navy 11.1838, ADM 3/264.
Sir Charles Adam to Minto 8.9.1838, ELL 228.
16. Admiralty Order 28.3.1839, ADM 83/19.
17. Surveyor to Admiralty 13.6.1839, ADM 222/14 Also Admiralty to Surveyor 14.6.1839. Also Admiralty to Surveyor 20.5 & 21.6.1839, ADM 83/19.
18. Admiralty to Surveyor 27.3 & 14.5.1840, ADM 83/21.
19. Surveyor to Admiralty 23.9.1840, ADM 87/10.
20. Surveyor to Admiralty 26.12.1840, ADM 83/22.
21. 1841/2 Programme of Works, ELL 248.
22. Surveyor to Admiralty 26.3 & 2.4.1842 & 1 & 24.2.1843, ADM 83/26 & 28.
23. Haddington to Portland 30.6.1842, PwH 401.
24. Hastings to Minto 6.10.1842, ELL 237.
Surveyor to Admiralty 25.10.1842 & 30.10 & 3.11.1843, ADM 83/27, 29 & 30.
25. Wood to Minto 22.10.1843, NLS 12,607.
Surveyor to Portsmouth 23.11.1843, ADM 87/13.
26. Programme 5.3.1844, ADM 83/31.
27. Surveyor to Admiralty 16.9.1844, ADM 83/33.
28. Cockburn memo 9.12.1844, ADM 3/265.
Bowles to Minto 23.1.1845, ELL 237.
29. Cockburn memo 15.11.1845, ADM 3/265.
Symonds to Portland 16.7.1845, PwH 1105.
30. Admiralty to Surveyor 28.12.1846, ADM 83/38.
Auckland to Parker 5.1.1847, PAR 157/A.
31. Programme for 1847/8 approved, with modifications by the Board 26.4.1847, ADM 1/5581.
32. Surveyor to Adiralty 16.6.1847, ADM 83/44.
33. Surveyor to Admiralty 16 & 19.1.1847, ADM 83/44.
Surveyor to Woolwich 3.12.1848, ADM 87/18.
NMM Draught dated 30.7.1847, signed by John Edye.
34. Auckland to Parker 4.4.1847, PAR 157/A.
35. Parker to Admiralty 8.10.1847, enclosed Curtis to Parker 5.9.1847, ADM 83/45.
Auckland to Parker 12.10.1847, PAR 157/A.
36. Auckland to Parker 4.12.1847, PAR 157/A.
Auckland to Portland 31.12.1847, PwH 607.
37. Portland to Auckland 7.9.1848, PwH 612.
38. Surveyor to Admiralty 4.4 & 22.5.1849, ADM 83/56.
39. Parry, A *The Admirals Freemantle*, London 1971, pp173–75.
40. Programme 1847/8 as modified by the Board April 1847, ADM 1/5581.
Admiralty to Surveyor 24, 28.6.1847. Also Committee of Reference to Admiralty 11.6.1847, ADM 83/44.
41. Design of *Caesar*, submitted by The Committee of Reference, signed by Inman, Fincham & S Read 24.6.1847, ADM 83/44.
42. Surveyor to Admiralty 23.3.1848, ADM 83/49.

6 The *Vanguard*-Class and the 80-Gun Ship

1. Admiralty to Surveyor 26.6.1832, ADM 83/4.
Admiralty Order 7.7.1832, ADM 92/5.
2. Graham minute 21.10.1832, ADM 1/3478.
Admiralty to Surveyor 22.10.1832, ADM 83/4.
3. Surveyor to Admiralty 30.10.1832, ADM 92/5.
Surveyor to Admiralty 28.11.1832, ADM 222/1.
4. Admiralty to Surveyor 28.11.1832 & 25.2.1833, ADM 83/4.
Surveyor to Admiralty 2.2.1833, ADM 92/5.
Surveyor to Admiralty 24.6 & 7.10.1833, ADM 222/2.
5. Surveyor to Admiralty 12.3.1833, ADM 222/2.
Wood to Minto 27 & 30.11.1844, NLS 12,607.
6. Admiralty to Surveyor 23.1.1834, ADM 83/9.

7. Portsmouth to Surveyor 1.11.1833 & Chatham to Surveyor 11.10.1834, ADM 87/3.
8. Surveyor to Admiralty 11.12.1835, ADM 92/7. Surveyor to Admiralty 1.5.1835, ADM 92/7.
9. Admiralty to Symonds 16.3.1836, ADM 92/7. Surveyor to Admiralty 10.5.1836, ADM 222/8.
10. Surveyor to Admiralty 1.7.1835 & 18.1.1837, ADM 92/5 & 7.
11. George Elliot to Minto 2.10.1837, ELL 219.
12. Admiralty to Surveyor 1.1.1839, ADM 83/9. Surveyor to Admiralty 10.1.1839, 92/8.
13. Surveyor to Admiralty 11.5.1839, ADM 222/14. Admiralty to Surveyor 20.5.1839, 14.5.1840, ADM 83/19 & 21.
14. Wood to Minto 14 & 20.10.1839, ELL 224.
15. Admiralty to Surveyor 13.4 & 5.5.1840, ADM 83/21.
16. W F Martin memo book 1845, Add 41,457, ff2–50. Adam to Minto 16.10.1839, ELL 228.
17. Stopford to Admiralty 27.8.1838, ADM 83/18. Fellowes to Admiral Sir E Codrington C-in-C Portsmouth 29.3.1840, ADM 87/10.
18. Admiralty to Surveyor 11.4.1842, ADM 83/26.
19. Admiralty to Surveyor 26.7.1841, ADM 83/24.
20. Admiralty to Surveyor 21.9.1843, ADM 83/27. Seymour to Surveyor 30.9.1842 & Plymouth Officers to Surveyor 19.11.1842, ADM 87/12.
21. Admiralty to Surveyor 24.2, 25.5 & 3.8.1843, ADM 83/28 & 9.
22. Admiralty Programme 1844/5, ADM 83/31. Ellenborough minute on shipbuilding 5.4.1846, ADM 3/265.
23. Admiralty to Surveyor 12.8 & 2.12.1844, ADM 83/32 & 33. Read to Herbert 25.11.1844, *ibid*, /33.
24. Surveyor's submission 19.3.1847, ADM 1/5581.
25. Admiralty to Surveyor 28.9. & 2.10.1847, ADM 83/45.
26. Surveyor to Admiralty 18.12.1848, ADM 87/22.
27. Admiralty to Surveyor 14.10.1848, ADM 83/52 & note by Edye . Creuze, A *Treatise on Shipbuilding*, London 1851, reprinted from the 7th ed of the *Encyclopaedia Britannica*.
28. Henry Byam Martin to Thomas Byam Martin 25.8.1845, Add 41,465, ff201–04.
29. Symonds to Portland 16.7.1845, PwH 1105. Minto and Graham to Symonds 17 & 25.9.1845, Sharp, pp340–41. Admiralty to Surveyor 22.9.1845, ADM 83/36.
30. Symonds to Minto 23.9.1845, ELL 237. Admiralty to Surveyor 29.9.1845, ADM 83/36. Bowles to Minto 29.9.1845, ELL 237.
31. Haddington to Parker 7.11.1845 & Parker to Haddington 28.11.1845, Phillimore Vol III, pp20–22.
32. Corry to Sir Charles Ogle 18.12.1845, Sharp, p302.
33. Willes to Admiralty 17.11.1845, Fincham, *History of Naval Architecture 1857*, p238.
34. Fincham, pp234–39.
35. Brown, *Before the Ironclad*, p38.
36. Surveyor to Admiralty 17.1.1846, ADM 87/16. Admiralty to Surveyor 24 & 29.1.1846, ADM 83/37.
37. Fincham, p239–40; Sharp, p347.
38. Parker to Adam 23.8.1846, Phillimore, Vol III, p77.
39. Collier to Admiralty 29.5.1846, ADM 1/559.
40. Admiralty to Surveyor 20.3.1844, ADM 83/31. Alison, Kay H (ed) *HMS Collingwood 1844–1848; (Pacific Station)*, Edinburgh 1986, has a diary of her service.
41. Surveyor's submission 30.10.1839 & Surveyor to Messrs Seaward & Co 9.12.1839, ADM 91/9.
42. Admiralty to Surveyor 2.10.1848, ADM 83/52. Lambert, *Battleships*, for the further history of these ships as steamers.
43. Edye to Admiralty 16.12.1847, ADM 1/5665. Sent to Committee of Reference 21.12.1847.
44. Lord John Hay to Admiralty 8.3.1850, ADM 83/57.
45. Admiralty to Surveyor 3.7.1849, ADM 83/57.

Part Six: CONSTRUCTION

1 The Development of the Dockyards

1. Morriss, R *The Royal Dockyards during the Revolutionary and Napoleonic Wars*, Leicester 1983. An outstanding study of this period.
2. Coad, J *The Royal Dockyards 1690–1850: Architecture and Engineering Works of the Sailing Navy*, London 1989. Provides a complete account of the construction and modification of the yards, covering in detail the docks, slips, roofs, buildings and other structures that made up the yards.
3. Melville to Liverpool 19.11.1812, Add 38,250.
4. Admiralty to Navy Board 8.12.1815, ADM 83/1. Admiralty to Navy Board 19.2.1816, ADM 106/71.
5. Byam Martin memo 2.1816, GD 51/2/984.
6. Navy Board to Admiralty 16.1.1817, ADM 106/2272. Admiralty to Navy Board 21.2.1817, ADM 83/2.
7. Admiralty to Navy Board 10.7.1817, ADM 106/88.
8. Byam Martin to Rennie 18.1.1817, Add 41,394.
9. Byam Martin to Commissioner Barlow 5.6.1818, Add 41,400.
10. Admiralty to Navy Board 1.1.1821, secret reply 9.1, adopted 19.1.1821, ADM 106/30. Navy Board to Admiralty 18.10.1821, reply 20.6.1822, ADM 1/3462.
11. Navy Board to Admiralty 24.12.1821, ADM 1/3462. Byam Martin to Melville 1825, Add 41,396.
12. Prothero, I *Artisans and Politics in early nineteenth century London: John Gast and His Times*, London 1979, pp163–71. Navy Board to Admiralty 15.9.1825, ADM 106/2289. Admiralty to Navy Board (secret) 26 & 28.9.1825, ADM 1/1693. Byam Martin to Fearnall 27.9.1825, Add 41,396. Byam Martin to Melville 25.10.1825, *ibid*.
13. Byam Martin to Fearnall 11 & 20.6; replies 13 & 23.6.1828, Add 41,398.
14. Admiralty Inspection of Portsmouth 12.7.1828, ADM 7/665. Dockyard memo 13.7.1828, GD 51/2/1017. Byam Martin to Morrice 2.6.1827, Add 41,397. Navy Board to Admiralty 29.6.1827 & reply same date, ADM 106/2292 & 1/3471.
15. Admiralty to Navy Board 9 & 14.1 & 1.3.1830, ADM 1/3471. Byam Martin memo 12.1.1830, Add 41,398. Melville to Byam Martin 24.9.1830, GD 51/1018/7.
16. Reductions in the dockyards, and in consequence thereof in the Navy Office since 1822, GD 51/722/1.
17. Barrow memo 22.11.1831 & Barrow to Graham 27.8.1832, ADM 1/3475 & 7. Graham to Brocklebank 14.10 & reply 12.11.1831, Gr B49 & ADM 1/3480.
18. Details of men discharged 12.1.1833, ADM 222/2 & 3. Surveyor to Admiralty 3.6.1833, ADM 222/2.
19. Codrington to Lady Codrington 7.4.1833, Bourchier, Vol II, p496–97.
20. Surveyor to Admiralty 28.6.1833, ADM 222/2. Admiralty Order 18.7.1833, ADM 83/7.
21. Admiralty to Surveyor 11.1.1833 & 16.12.1833, ADM 222/2 & 83/8.
22. Barrow memo 14.6.1834, ADM 1/3483. Surveyor to Admiralty 10.7 & 8.10.1834, ADM 222/3.
23. Auckland memo on dockyards, ELL 239. Admiralty Order 15.11.1834, ADM 1/3484. Admiralty to Surveyor 21.7.1835, ADM 1/3486.
24. Memoranda on the state of the Navy, ADM 3/264/4.
25. Minto to Melbourne 5.11.1838, MELB 859/9/28. Wood to Minto 8.11.1838, ELL 224.
26. Admiralty to Surveyor 17.12.1838, ADM 83/21. Wood to Symonds 2.1839, ADM 83/19. Wood memo 6.1839, Add 49,572. Surveyor's submission 8.1.1840, ADM 92/9. Admiralty to Surveyor 17.1.1840, ADM 83/23.
27. Minto memo 6.9.1841, ELL 239.
28. Programme of works for 1841–2, ELL 249.
29. Herbert memo on the steam Navy 16.12.1844, Add 40,556.
30. Codrington to Haddington 20.4.1842, COD 20/2. Sharp, p403.
31. Haddington to Peel 1.1846, Add 40,458. Ellenborough to Peel 5.4.1846, Add 40,473. Ellenborough minute for Lord Auckland 6.7.1846, PRO 30/12/34.
32. Shireff to Ward 3.10.1846, Shireff MSS NMM SHI/6.
33. Ward to Russell 27.2.1847, PRO 30/22/6B.
34. Surveyor to Admiralty 2.10.1848, ADM 83/52. Report of the Committee of Revision on Dockyards 14.12.1848, ADM 1/5991.

35. Admiralty to Surveyor 5.2.1849, ADM 83/54. Order in Council 19.6.1850, ADM 83/59. Baring memo 1.1852, PRO 30/22/10 Ai.
36. Bourne, J M *Patronage and Society in Nineteenth-century England*, London 1986, pp172–73.

2 Empire and Seapower: The Exploitation of Indian Resources

1. Wadia, R A *The Bombay Dockyard and the Wadia Master Builders*, Bombay 1955. Family loyalty precludes Wadia from dealing with the collapse of dockyard administration after the death of Jamsetjee Jehubhuoy, the greatest of the Parsee Master Builders, in 1821. Low, C R *A History of the Indian Navy*, London, 1877, 2 vols. Low, as an embittered ex-Indian Navy Officer, exaggerates the Indian contribution, and, like Wadia, overlooks many of the failings on the dockyard.
2. Farmer, R H *The Handbook of Hardwoods*, London 1972, (2nd ed) pp201–03.
3. Harbron, J D *Trafalgar and the Spanish Navy*, London 1988.
4. Quasimi, Sultan M *The Myth of Arab Piracy in the Gulf*, London 1986, pp11, 158, 185.
5. Board of Control to the Governor of Bombay 18.12.1812, F/4/429 10.507. India Record Office.
6. Lubbock, B in *The Trade Winds* (ed) C N Parkinson, London 1948, p89.
7. Stebbings, E P *The Forests of India*, London 1922, vol 1, p63.
8. Navy Board to Admiralty 5.5.1802, ADM 106/2229 quoted in Morriss, *Royal Dockyards* p82.
9. Earl St Vincent to the deputy Chairman of the East India Company 31.3.1802 & 17.4.1802 in *The Letters of Lord St Vincent 1801– 04*, (ed) D B Smith, London Navy Records Society 1921 & 1926, vol 11, pp238 & 241–43.
10. East India Company to Navy Board 3.4.1805 enclosing Deptford Dockyard to Navy Board 22.1.1805, ADM 87/1. St Vincent to Dundas 14.7.1801, *ibid*, vol I, p301.
11. Furber, H *Henry Dundas*, London 1931, pp126–41.
12. Benjamin Tucker to Thomas Grenville 16.9.1807, Add 41,857, f44. Thomas Grenville to Lord Grenville 11.10.1811, HMC *Papers of the Hon J Fortescue at Dropmore*, vol X, pp176.
13. Dundas to Wellesley 4.7.1804, Add 37,275, ff260–387.
14. Stebbings, pp63–65.
15. Duncan to Dundas 14.10.1808 & 16.4.1809, GD 51/3/158 1 & 2.
16. Albion, pp366–69.
17. Graham, G S *Great Britain and the Indian Ocean: 1810–1850*, Oxford 1967, pp305–28. The yard was closed down in 1821, still incomplete.
18. Board of Control to Bombay 27.6.1810 & 18.12.1812, F 4/429.
19. Barrow to Sir C Yorke, First Lord of the Admiralty 23.10.1811, Add 45,045, ff37–39. Admiralty to Sir Wm Ramsay (Chairman of the East India Company) 9.11.1811, MEL/103, NMM.
20. George Dundas to Navy Board 26.1.1810, received 20.7.1810, ADM 106/2008.
21. Dundas to Navy Board 14.3.1811 & 9.8.1811 received 27.4.1812, ADM 106/2009.
22. Puget to Navy Board 14.10.1813, received 13.6.1814. Also Johnstone to Navy Board 10.5.1813, received 7.6.1814, ADM 106/2010.
23. Johnstone to Navy Board 26.9.1813, received 24.5.1814; 15.12.1813 & 13.6.1814, received 14.12.1814, with marginal comments by the Committee of the Surveyors of the Navy, ADM 106/2011 & 2012. Governor of Bombay to Board of Control 16.4.1814, IRO F 4/429. The re-use of the first design is not noted in any source on British warships.
24. Committee of the Surveyors of the Navy Minute 4.7.1815, ADM 92/1. Admiralty to Navy Board 7.3.1815, ADM A/3106. Board of Control to Governor Bombay 5.5.1815, F 4/429, 13, 761.
25. Johnstone to Navy Board 2.1.15 received 20.1.1816; 24.4.1815 received 14.11.1815; 20.5.1815: 26.1.1816 received 15.8.1816, ADM 106/2012-3.
26. Joseph Cotton (Trinity House) to Melville 17.10.1816, GD 51/2/570 1 & 2 quoted from Money, W T *Observations on Shipbuilding at Bombay*, he set out to disprove the claim that teak produced more splinters than oak.
27. Domett to Melville 9.5.1814, GD 51/2/519. Phipps, J *Papers relative to Shipbuilding in India*, Calcutta 1840, pp39, 185–87.
28. Navy Board to Admiralty 27.2.1819, ADM 106/2277 198. Melville to Admiral King 1.1.1820, GD 51/2/609. Phipps ppxiii–xvii, 7, 41.
29. Navy Board to Admiralty 4 & 6.5.1815, ADM 106/2267 413 & 429.
30. Admiralty to Navy Board 1.6.1816, ADM 106/75. Navy Board to Admiralty 4.6.1816, ADM 106/2270. Admiralty to Navy Board 5.6.1816, ADM 83/1 261. Board of Control to Bombay 3.7.1816, E/4/1034.
31. Navy Board to Admiralty 4.10.1816, 16 & 28.11.1816, ADM 106/2271 16, 264 & 338.
32. Byam Martin to Admiral Sir R King, C-in-C India, 4.6.1818, Add 41,394, f170. Navy Board to Admiralty 23.1.1819, ADM 106/2271 260. Byam Martin to John Edye Master Shipwright at Cochin 1.2.1820, Add 41,395, f20. Melville to Admiral King 1.1.1820, GD 51/2/609.
33. Bombay to Board of Control 27.3.1817, F 4/13, 761.
34. Board of control to Bombay 18.5 & 30.6.1819, E 4/1038.
35. Admiralty to Navy Board 5.1.1821 & Navy Board to Admiralty 7.1.1821; endorsed on the 19th the Navy Board was informed that the Admiralty preferred to build in Britain, ADM 106/30. Byam Martin memo on reductions 5.7.1821, Add 41,39 5, f84.
36. Admiralty to Board of Control 22.2.1821, ADM 106/131. Board of Control to Governor at Bombay 28.2.1821, E 4/415–23. Master Shipwright at Bombay to Navy Board 29.4, 30.4 & 6.5.1822, ADM 106/2017. Navy Board to Admiralty 14.2.1822, ADM 106/2283 123.
37. Navy Board to Admiralty 21.3.1823, ADM 106/2285 157. Master Shipwright to Navy Board 20.1 & 1.5.1824, ADM 106/132.
38. Navy Board to Admiralty 4.4.1825, ADM 106/2289 152. Board of Control to Marine & Forest Dept 4.5.1825, E 4/1045. Pollexfen to Navy Board 13.11.1825, ADM 106/132.
39. Pollexfen to Navy Board 28.1.1826, received 1.8.1826; 17.3.1826, received 25.6.1827, ADM 106/132. 106/2292 179. Byam Martin to Pollexfen 6.10.1827, Add 41,397, f84.
41. Byam Martin to the Duke of Clarence 4.3.1828, Add 41,397, f121. These figures are somewhat unreliable, given the origins of the *Formidable*'s timber.
42. Navy Board to Pollexfen 5 & 21.6.1828, ADM 106/2292.
43. Pollexfen to Navy Board 24.1, 1.5 & 28.9.1828, ADM 106/2292.
44. George Pollexfen to Navy Board 24.4.1829, ADM 106/2292.
45. Malcolm to Hugh Lindsay 21.9.1828; Malcolm to Byam Martin 24.9.1828; Malcolm to Rear Admiral Gage 5.1.1829 & Malcolm to Sir John Malcolm probably September 1829, Malcolm MSS 3 NMM.
46. Navy Board to Admiralty 8.12.1828, 23.3 & 13.6.1829, 10.11.1830, ADM 106/2292, 3 & 5. Pollexfen to Navy Board 18.9.1829, *ibid*, 30.
47 Admiralty to Navy Board 4.10.1830 enclosing Craven to Admiral Sir E Owen 29.3.1830 & Navy Board to Seaton 32.1.1822, ADM 1/3472. Craven to Navy Board 14.1 & 5.8.1831, ADM 106/30. Navy Board to Admiralty 6.10 & 10.11.1830 & 17.1.1831, ADM 106/2293 & 5.
48. Admiralty to Surveyor 31.8.1832, ADM 83/4. Admiralty to Surveyor 9.2.1835, ADM 83/11. Admiralty to Surveyor 10.12.1835, ADM 92/7.
49. Admiralty to Surveyor 16.10.1834, ADM 92/6.
50. India Board to Admiralty 3.3.1836, ADM 1/4262. Lord Minto to Sir Herbert Taylor 6.3.1836, ELL 211b. Cogan to Superintendent of the Indian Navy 26.12.1834, E 4/1062. Minto memorandum 6.9.1841, ELL 24. Admiralty to Surveyor 2.7.1841, ADM 83/24.
51. Admiral Sir Charles Adam to Minto 9.8.1837, ELL 226. Admiral Sir William Parker to Minto 29.8.1837, ELL 225. Parker to Minto 14.10.1837, ELL 225. Minto to Admiral John Hayes 21.10.1837, ELL 254.
52. Edye, remarks for Sir Charles Adam 24.2.1838, ADM 1/3494.
53. Wood memo on shipbuilding 2.1838, ADM 3/264. Wood Minute to Storekeeper 16.6.1838, ADM 1/3495.
54. Marine Department to Bombay Dockyard 14.3.1838, E4/10612. Marine Department to Bombay Dockyard

16.6.1838, E4/1063.
Report by Malcolm 5.1838, Stebbins, p78.
55. Wood to Minto 8.11.1838, ELL/224.
56. Wood Memo 2.1839, endorsed by the Board 18.2.1839, ADM 3/264/5.
57. Symonds to Admiralty 1.3.1839, ADM 222/14.
Admiralty to Admiral Sir F W Maitland 18.2.1839, ADM 1/3498. Wood memo 6.1839, Add 49,572.
58. Bombay to Court of Directors 7.8.1839, E4/1064.
59. Court of Directors to Bombay 9.3.1840, E4/1067.
60. Edye to Sir Charles Adam 20.7.1840, ADM 1/3494.
Allen to Surveyor 29.9.1840, ADM 87/10.
61. Admiralty to Surveyor 28.10.1840, ADM 92/9.
Admiralty to Surveyor 3.11.1840, ADM 83/22.
62. Minto memo on leaving office 6.9.1841, ELL 24.
63. Laire to Symonds 15 & 19.7.1841, ADM 87/10.
Admiralty to Surveyor 14.10 & 17.2.1841, ADM 83/24.
64. Marine Board to Bombay 28.9.1842, E4/1071.
Admiralty to Surveyor 11.4.1842, ADM 83/26.
Laire to Symonds 5.5.1843, ADM 87/13.
Admiralty to Surveyor 6.2 & 23.4.1844, ADM 83/31.
Turner to Symonds 26.8.1844 & 27.6.1846, ADM 87/14 & 16.
65. Turner to Symonds 30.4.1845 & 4.2.1846, ADM 87/15 & 16.
66. Ellenborough to Corry 17.1.1846, PRO 30/12/34/9.
67. Ellenborough to Sir H Maddock & Lord Ripon (President of the Board of Control) 19.1.1846; Maddock to Ellenborough 21.3.1846; Captain Durand to Ellenborough 22.3.1846, PRO 30/12/34/9.
Ellenborough memorandum on the purchase of teak in 1845, 22.6.1846, PRO 30/12/5/1.
Turner to Symonds 27.6.1846, ADM 87/16.
Ellenborough memo for Lord Auckland 6.7.1846, PRO 30/12/34/12.
68. Admiralty to Surveyor 1.11.1847, ADM 83/46.
Court of Directors to Bombay 3.11.1847, E4/1085.
Admiralty to Surveyor 8.12.1847, ADM 83/47.
Bombay to Court of Directors 24.2.1847, E4/1082.
69. Admiralty to Surveyor 4.3.1848, ADM 83/49.
Turner to Symonds 31.10 & 13.11.1849, ADM 87/24.
Marine Board to Bombay Dockyard 4.4.1848, E4/1086.
70. Admiralty to Surveyor 5.1.1848, ADM 83/48.
71. Surveyor to Admiralty 8.9.1850 enclosing Watts to Surveyor 20.6.1850, ADM 83/62.
Surveyor to Admiralty 18.11.1850, ADM 83/62.
72. Court of Directors to Bombay 8.1.1851, E4/1092.
Marine Board to Bombay 4.6.1856, E4/1104.
73. Graham to Wood 22.1.1855, Wood MSS A4/70.
Lambert, *Dalhousie, last flagship of the Indian Navy*, unpublished Mss.

Index

Ships listed are of British nationality unless otherwise indicated by the following: Am–American (USA); Da–Danish; Fr–French; Ru–Russian; Sp–Spanish; Sw–Sweden; Ve–Venetian.

Ranks given are the highest recorded in the text. The people concerned may sometimes be found under a lower rank.

Page references in italic denote illustrations or captions.